A Concordance to the Poems of

SAMUEL JOHNSON

THE CORNELL CONCORDANCES

S. M. Parrish, *General Editor*

Supervisory Committee

M. H. Abrams
Donald D. Eddy
Ephim Fogel
Alain Seznec

POEMS OF MATTHEW ARNOLD, *edited by S. M. Parrish*
POEMS OF W. B. YEATS, *edited by S. M. Parrish*
POEMS OF EMILY DICKINSON, *edited by S. P. Rosenbaum*
WRITINGS OF WILLIAM BLAKE, *edited by David V. Erdman*
BYRON'S *DON JUAN, edited by C. W. Hagelman, Jr., and R. J. Barnes*
THÉÂTRE ET POÉSIES DE JEAN RACINE, *edited by Bryant C. Freeman*
BEOWULF, *edited by J. B. Bessinger, Jr.*
PLAYS OF W. B. YEATS, *edited by Eric Domville*
POEMS OF JONATHAN SWIFT, *edited by Michael Shinagel*
POEMS OF SAMUEL JOHNSON, *edited by Helen Naugle*
PLAYS OF WILLIAM CONGREVE, *edited by David Mann*

A Concordance to the Poems of

SAMUEL JOHNSON

Edited by

HELEN HARROLD NAUGLE

In collaboration with

PETER B. SHERRY

Cornell University Press

ITHACA AND LONDON

First published 1973 by Cornell University Press.
Published in the United Kingdom by Cornell University Press Ltd.,
2–4 Brook Street, London W1Y 1AA

International Standard Book Number 0-8014-0769-9
Library of Congress Catalog Card Number 72-13383

Printed in the United States of America by Vail-Ballou Press, Inc.

Library of Congress Cataloging in Publication Data
(For library cataloging purposes only.)

Naugle, Helen Harrold.
    A concordance to the poems of Samuel Johnson.

    (The Cornell concordances)
    1. Johnson, Samuel, 1709–1784—Concordances.
I. Title.   II. Series.
PR3532.N3   1973   821'.6   72-13383
ISBN 0-8014-0769-9

To my family
Helen Weddle Harrold
Jefferson B. Naugle
Helen Elizabeth Naugle Deibler
Elizabeth Ann Deibler

CONTENTS

Preface   ix

Abbreviated Titles: English Poems
(together with French and Greek)   xvii

Abbreviated Titles: Latin Poems   xxv

Concordance to Poems in English   1

Frequencies   409

Concordance to Poems in Latin   427

Frequencies   451

Concordance to Poems of Doubtful Attribution   561

Frequencies   577

PREFACE

I am not yet so lost in lexicography, as to forget that words are the daughters of earth, and that things are the sons of heaven. Language is only the instrument of science, and words are but the signs of ideas: I wish, however, that the instrument might be less apt to decay, and that signs might be permanent, like the things they denote.

—Samuel Johnson
"Preface" to *A Dictionary of the English Language*, London, 1755

Johnson the lexicographer was naturally interested in words, but hardly more than Johnson the critic, or Johnson the poet. And Johnson the poet, whose vocabulary is arrayed in this concordance, is probably closer to the essential Johnson than are any others of his multiple identities. "Johnson's most characteristic utterance, and the turbulent imagination and impulsive temperament of the man," Bertrand H. Bronson has pointed out, "belonged to a poet. . . . In the deepest sense of the word—in his imaginative apprehension of the quality and texture of experience, in his dynamic attitude to life and its values, in his need of the shaping expression of his perceptions—he was a poet, a maker." [1]

One is not really surprised, then, to find among Johnson's most frequently used words LOVE (95 occurrences) and LIFE (80)—normal concerns of poetry—and such abstractions as SOUL (73), HEAV'N (61), FATE (60), POW'RE (57), and VIRTUE (55). But Johnson uses also many ordinary, even physical, terms, like FAIR (67), HAND (51), EYES (49), BREAST (48), and HEART (38). Equally interesting are some of the key words of eighteenth-century Neoclassicism. The word NATURE, for example, which Johnson defines in the general, Neoclassical sense in his *Dictionary* as "the state or operation of the material word," or "the constitution of an animated body," appears in his poetry thirty-four times. Not once, however, does NATURE mean for Johnson the Romantic charm of natural scenery. Other pervasive Neoclassical words duly appear with decent though not excessive frequency: HONOUR (15), WIT (14), and ART (14).

[1] "Johnson Agonistes," in *Samuel Johnson: A Collection of Critical Essays,* ed. Donald J. Greene (Englewood Cliffs, New Jersey: Prentice-Hall, 1965), p. 45.

A look at his most frequently used words belies the accuracy of Goldsmith's gentle jibe that if Johnson "were to write a fable of little fishes he would make them speak like great whales." Indeed, it might be argued that Johnson the poet uses contemporary, familiar language, "the real language of men," as faithfully as Wordsworth does. Of his twenty-five most frequently used nouns, only three are polysyllabic, and all but seven are of Anglo-Saxon origin. Throughout the higher frequencies in the concordance, one looks in vain for those " 'tall, opaque words' taken from 'the first row of the rubric' " that Hazlitt, extolling the familiar style, assailed Johnson for using.

A concordance may be valuable, moreover, in showing not only what a poet chooses to utter but also what he does not choose to utter. Though Johnson's poetic vocabulary abounds in everyday words, it contains no "low" and "vulgar" words or profanity. Nor does he use what he termed "Miltonic uncouth, unnatural jargon." Nevertheless, he does not altogether eschew a "poetic" vocabulary. He uses DARKLING as did Shakespeare, Milton, and Dryden, and in the way later to be employed so effectively by Keats and Arnold. And he occasionally uses words in their archaic sense, such as UNBALLAST and EXTATICK. Curiously enough, Johnson uses REPRESS (3) or REPRESS'D (2) with the Freudian connotation rather than in the older meaning of "to suppress lawless persons."

A concordance of Johnson's poetry should be useful in charting the course of the English language, particularly the poetic vocabulary of the eighteenth century, and in supplementing the history of poetic taste. It may well be that the road from Twickenham to Grasmere goes by way of the Old Cheshire Cheese. Certainly, the concordance furnishes significant clues to the nature of the Johnsonian temper, sensibility, and intellect.

Basic Text and Format

The choice of text for this concordance involved a compromise. The scholarly Clarendon Press edition of the poems of Samuel Johnson has not been truly superseded; hence, by permission of The Clarendon Press, Oxford, *The Poems of Samuel Johnson*, edited by David Nichol Smith and Edward L. McAdam (Oxford, 1941), is here used as the definitive edition. But, with the permission of Yale University Press, *Poems*, edited by McAdam with George Milne (1964) in the *Yale Edition of the Works of Samuel Johnson*, Vol. VI, supplements the basic text. That is, both poems and variant readings in the Yale edition that do not appear in the Clarendon edition are indexed. The editions are designated by "O" for Oxford and "Y" for Yale with pagination to the volume cited. Variants in the Yale edition to poems which appear in the Oxford edition are indicated by the letter "V" before the line number. Yale citings without the "V" are poems in the Yale edition.

On the concordance page, the index word is followed by the lines in

which it appears; then for each line the source ("O" or "Y"), the page number, the abbreviated title, "V" if variant, and the line number (or "T" for a title being indexed). The lines are listed in the order in which they fall in the basic text. Variants follow the line they supplement. A line is repeated if the index word occurs in it more than once. Lines too long to fit the space allowed for the entry end with dots, signifying ellipsis, and the second part of the line begins with dots. All titles, subtitles, and their variants, except those added by the editors of the basic text and those in the Yale edition, are indexed. Minor parts of long titles have been omitted, with ellipses indicating places of omission.

For the title abbreviations, long titles have been reduced to fourteen spaces. No very consistent principle has been followed: occasionally the opening words are used, but more often a catch title of key words seems likely to identify the poem more readily. On pp. xvii–xxx may be found the lists of abbreviated titles with corresponding complete titles and their locations.

In alphabetizing, the computer program followed one principle which the user must keep in mind: hyphen and apostrophe fall ahead of the alphabet. The following sequences of words will illustrate the principle: ALL, ALL-CONSCIOUS, ALL-PITYING, ALL-SUBDUING, ALLA, AM, AM'ROUS, AMARILLIS', AMAZ'D; DEW-DROPS, DEWDROPS, DEWS, DIFF'RENT, DIFFERENT. Words that begin with an apostrophe have been moved to their appropriate position. Thus 'MIDST appears just ahead of AMIDST, 'ROUND ahead of AROUND, and the like; the ampersand is indexed just following AND. A hyphenated word is treated like a single word, and the second part appears in the alphabetical listing with a cross reference (e.g., SPEARS see BULRUSH-SPEARS). Blanks have been filled in when the letters completing them are known or can be conjectured with fair accuracy.

No attempt has been made to consolidate variant spellings, but the rarer ones have been cross-referenced from conventional spellings (when conventional spelling appears) unless the variant happens to fall adjacent to the conventional spelling. Since the users of this concordance are likely to be familiar with eighteenth-century English spellings, cross references are not generally provided for such well-known practices as (1) the apostrophe in place of a vowel (EV'RY), (2) ou for o (FAVOURITE), (3) ie for y (FLIE), (4) y for i (OYL), (5) u for w (AUKWARD), (6) u for o or oo (CHUSE), (7) ea for ee (CHEAR), (8) eat for ete (COMPLEAT), (9) t for d (CONTEMN), and (10) ck for c (MUSICK).

Variants

Variant readings shown in the apparatus to both the Oxford and the Yale texts are fully indexed. Where a Yale reading supersedes the earlier Oxford reading, it is also shown, with a "V" reference. No variants are

cited, however, for minor differences in spelling and hyphenation, changes from plural to singular or vice versa, capitalization or punctuation, including possessives, italics, accents, and apostrophization; or for shifts in word order. Nor are variants cited for the renumbering or moving about of identical lines that are relatively close together in the text, unless each line in which these inconsequential variants appear contains major variants (in such cases all variants of any kind are noted). When two variants appear for the same line, they are frequently telescoped into one variant reference for that line. Not indexed, of course, are obvious printers' errors identified as such in the Yale or Clarendon texts; nor are variants in speaker identifications, stage directions, dates, and all such other unpoetical matter bearing no line numbers.

The Three Concordances

In an attempt to make this volume more readily useful, I have divided Johnson's poetic corpus into three separate concordances: Poems in English, Poems in Latin, and Poems of Doubtful Attribution. Frequency tables appear at the end of each of these concordances. The words in each of Johnson's vocabularies (including words not indexed) are there arranged in descending order of frequency; under each frequency the arrangement is alphabetical, and here as in the concordance proper, hyphen and apostrophe precede the alphabet.

A few anomalies in the separation of these vocabularies will soon be apparent. For reasons of economy and convenience, Johnson's French poem and his Greek, transliterated letter for letter according to the equivalents listed in *Webster's New International Dictionary*, 3d ed., are indexed in the English concordance. In it also are found Latin words that appear within English poems. Conversely, a few English words appear in the Latin concordance; these are from English titles and subtitles to Latin poems.

Concordance to Poems in English

The order of line references to Johnson's English vocabulary shows his most important works first: *London, The Vanity of Human Wishes,* and the four prologues. The minor poems follow, arranged chronologically, by date of composition generally, but occasionally by date of publication, and *Irene* concludes this main body of poems.

Change of speakers within one line in *Irene* is indicated by indenting the second speaker's part in a separate full entry. Verse lines in "The First Draft of *Irene*" are indexed, but in the prose only those lines are included that appear to be originals for the later poetical text. The prose translation in "Translation of Greek Epigrams" (p. 113) is not indexed. The italicized lines in "Translations from Boethius de Consolatione Philosophiae" (p. 143) are not indexed because they were composed by Mrs. Thrale (p. 144). The

"[Version in *Thraliana* and *Anecdotes*]" (p. 155), of "Epitaph on Hogarth" (p. 153), is treated as a variant with only variants from the manuscript copy (p. 154) indexed. The two versions in different languages (in Latin and translated into English) of "Venus in Armour" ("Epigramma" and "Englished," p. 384) and (in Greek and translated into Latin) of "On a Riddle by Eliza" ("Eis to tes Elisses peri ton Oneiron Ainigma," and "In Elizae Aenigma," p. 103) are each indexed because they appear as two distinct compositions. Similarly, the two versions, "(First Version)" (p. 65) and "(Final Version)" (p. 66) of "Translation of *Horace*. Book I. Ode xxii," are indexed separately because the number of changes in the final version is significant. But "Translations of French Verses on Skating" I and II, are handled as though II were a variant of I, in accordance with Mrs. Piozzi's testimony (p. 202).

There exists a further problem with *Irene, The Vanity of Human Wishes, London,* and "Translations from Boethius de Consolatione Philosophiae": the established edition does not contain certain lines appearing in some of the drafts. In these cases, letters are appended serially to the line number of the established edition. For example, 0 290 V 40A indicates a line following line 40 in an earlier edition but not in the definitive edition. A 40B reference following the 40A indicates a second line in the original that is omitted in the final form, and so on.

Since the inclusion of all of Johnson's poetical vocabulary would have doubled the size of the volume, some English words have been declared "nonsignificant" and appear in the concordance only with their frequencies, not their contexts. The list of these nonsignificant words follows; it might be observed that some variant forms of some of the omitted words have been kept (TH' and FRO').

Nonsignificant words

A, AN, AND, ARE, AT, BUT, BY, FOR, FROM, HE, HER, HERE,
HERS, HIM, HIS, IN, IS, NO, NOT, NOW, OF, ON, OR, OUR,
OURS, THAT, THE, THIS, TO, WAS, WHAT, WHEN, WHERE, WITH

Concordance to Poems in Latin

A separate Latin concordance is provided which indexes all of Johnson's Latin poems except "7.553 Damascius" (p. 212), which is identical to "Translation of Greek Epigrams" (p. 113). (However, the variants to the "Translation of Greek Epigrams" that occur in "7.553 Damascius" are indexed in this section.) Latin poems of doubtful attribution are also included. The poems are arranged chronologically.

Something should be said of Johnson's Latin poetic vocabulary. Its bulk (3,895 individual words) is perhaps less impressive than at first appears, considering that Johnson composed as readily in Latin as in English and

that his Latin verse spans his entire lifetime. But to express his deepest personal feelings he more often wrote in Latin, sometimes using words not appropriate to the objective tone he maintained in his English poems. At the same time, in Latin, Johnson the moralist never wholly yields to Johnson the man. As in his English poems, words of high moral seriousness tend to abound: VITAE (19), VITA (17), PATER (14), DEUS (11), HOMINUM (11), and AMOR (10) are among the words of highest frequency. Moreover, as in the works of his Latin models, the high-frequency words reveal the sententious philosopher with a classical concern for the passage of time and the life of the intellect: DIES (10), HORA (8), and LUX (7); MENTE (9), MENTEM (7), and OPUS (9).

Concordance to Poems of Doubtful Attribution

The concordance to poems of doubtful attribution follows the same principles as the other two concordances. Poems in English and Greek, classed by the editors as "Poems of Doubtful Authorship," are included with three exceptions: (1) "Verses wrote on a Window of an Inn at Calais" (Clarendon, p. 394) is not indexed because the editors of the Clarendon edition express strong doubt of Johnson's authorship, and the editors of the Yale edition frankly state that "the poem cannot be Johnson's" (Yale, p. 392). (2) Yale's "Translations of Mottoes and Quotations in the *Adventurer*" (p. 371) is not indexed because, as the editors admit, the question of authorship is very doubtful, the quality is below Johnson's level, and several translations seem to be recollections of known translations. (3) Finally, Yale's "Lord Hervey's Epitaph on Queen Caroline" is not indexed, again because the evidence of Johnson's authorship is inconclusive (see Yale, p. 362).

The Computer Program

The basic program used to produce this concordance was provided by James A. Painter (International Business Machines Corporation, San Jose, California), and the general features of the program are set forth in the Programmer's Preface to *A Concordance to the Poems of W. B. Yeats*, edited by S. M. Parrish (Ithaca, 1963). The program was originally written for an IBM 704 computer but later was revised to operate on the IBM 360 using PL-1 programming language to take advantage of a number of improvements now available with this equipment. It was decided also to rewrite a considerable portion of the program to achieve a general program that could be run on other IBM 360 computers. A drastic reduction in the core memory requirement and in the central processor time used by the program was achieved by using revised sorts. Several other changes increased the overall efficiency of the program. Because this work contains a number of variant words and lines, the program has been modified so that

*Concordance to Poems
in English*

ABSOLUTE

	PAGE	TITLE	LINE
And sways thy Breast with absolute Dominion, ...	O 266	Irene	18

ABSORB'D

| Absorb'd in Thought; then starting from his Trance, . . | O 311 | Irene | 6 |
| Absorb'd by thought, then waking from his dream . . . | Y 187 | Irene | V 6 |

ABSURDITY

| With ev'ry wild absurdity comply, ... | O 16 | London | 138 |

ACCENT

| And if one varied Accent prove thy Falshood, ... | O 332 | Irene | 14 |

ACCENTS

| And tender Accents quiver'd on my Lips, ... | O 282 | Irene | 67 |

ACCEPT

| O, hear my Pray'rs! accept, all-pitying heaven, . . . | O 328 | Irene | 52 |

ACCIDENT

| Here malice, rapine, accident, conspire, ... | O 9 | London | 13 |
| Mistake shall blast, or Accident destroy; . . . . . | O 335 | Irene | 13 |

ACCIDENTAL

| Some accidental Gust of Opposition . . . . | O 269 | Irene | 6 |
| O'erthrow such weak, such accidental Virtue, . . . | O 301 | Irene | 83 |

ACCIDENTS

| Think on the various Accidents of War; . . . . . . | O 252 | Irene | 87 |
| What trivial Accidents determine Fate! . . . . . . | O 367 | Irene | V 23 |

ACCLAMATIONS

| Rocks send their acclamations to the skie . . . . | Y 7 | Virgil Daphnis | 40 |

ACCOMPLICE

| And thou, the curs'd Accomplice of her Treason, . . | O 331 | Irene | 5 |

ACCORDED   SEE WELL-ACCORDED

ACCUMULATED

| Th' accumulated Wealth of toiling Ages. . . . . . | O 249 | Irene | 19 |

ACCUS'D

| Accus'd the Gods and curs'd each luckless star. . . . | Y 6 | Virgil Daphnis | 6 |

ACCUSATION

| Whate'er thy Accusation, ... | O 323 | Irene | 11 |

ACCUSER

| There dauntless Truth shall blast the vile Accuser, . . | O 326 | Irene | 42 |

ACCUSTOM'D

| At length rekindled his accustom'd Fury, ... | O 259 | Irene | 110 |
| Than Amurath, accustom'd to Command, ... | O 264 | Irene | 21 |

ACHILLES

| How great Achilles godlike Hector slew? . . . . . . | Y 22 | Tr Add. Battle | 11 |

ACHILLES'

| My father fell by fierce Achilles' hand . . . . . . | Y 18 | Tr. Iliad Bk 6 | 28 |

ACQUAINT

| With his own form acquaint the forward fool, ... | O 81 | Lady Birthday | 15 |

ACQUAINTED

| My soul not oft acquainted with remorse . . . . . . | Y 159 | Irene | V 8 |

ACQUIR'D

| Acquir'd by wounds, and battles bravely fought! . . | O 74 | Tr. Iliad Bk 6 | 7 |

ACQUIT

| Nor justice can acquit, nor mercy spare . . . . . . | Y 210 | Irene | V 25B |

ACRES

| What are acres? What are houses? . . . . | O 196 | Song Congratu. | 23 |

ACROSS

| Their wings extend themselves across the land. . . . . | Y 24 | Tr Add. Battle | 79 |

ACT

Each act betrays the fever of renown	Y 97	Vanity Wishes	V 137
In ev'ry act refulgent virtue glow'd.	O 118	Epitaph Hanmer	16
Records each Act, each Thought of sov'reign Man, . . .	O 276	Irene	21
Let one just Act conclude the hateful Day.	O 333	Irene	50

ACTION

And one base action sully all my fame, ...	O 74	Tr. Iliad Bk 6	6
Is ripe for Action, and demands the Sword.	O 256	Irene	37
And of To-morrow's Action fix the Scene.	O 283	Irene	18
To-morrow's Action? Can that hoary Wisdom	O 283	Irene	19
To wait remote from Action, and from Honour, ...	O 305	Irene	22
--And loiter'd with his troop remote from Action . .	O 376	Irene	V 15
Thy Look, thy Speech, thy Action, all is Wildness-- . .	O 323	Irene	5

ACTIONS

Surveys your actions with a careless glance	Y 146	Irene	V 22
And then leaves your actions the busy trifler	O 355	Irene	V 12
unregarded			

ACTIVE

Nor there confin'd his active Soul;	O 79	Feast St Simon	43
Age call'd at length his active mind to rest, ...	O 118	Epitaph Hanmer	35
How active light, and thoughtful shade, ...	O 121	To Miss Playin	27
Our warlike Prophet loves an active Faith, ...	O 264	Irene	25
Our warlike Prophet loves an active zeal	Y 131	Irene	V 25
To mark the noblest Minds, with active Heat	O 293	Irene	112
To mark the noblest Minds. With active fire	O 369	Irene	V 3
What sleepy Charms benumb these active Heroes, . . .	O 325	Irene	14

ACTS

Nor whilst she Simons acts persues	O 80	Feast St Simon	49
Great George's acts let tuneful Cibber sing;	O 114	On C. Cibber	3
And his more glorious acts eclipse his father's fame. .	Y 20	Tr. Iliad Bk 6	104

ADAMANT

| A frame of adamant, a soul of fire, ... | O 40 | Vanity Wishes | 193 |
| bend tyrant adamant--melt harlot . . . . | Y 181 | Irene | V 56 |

ADAMANTINE

| Does adamantine Faith invest his Heart? . . . . . . | O 255 | Irene | 21 |

ADD

| Much could I add,--but see the boat at hand, ... | O 22 | London | 254 |

4

ABANDON
    Who hear thee speak, and not abandon Reason?   . . . .   O 281 Irene   43
ABANDON'D
    Forsake a Wretch abandon'd to Despair, ...   O 320 Irene   14
ABASH
    Lead us to Danger, and abash their Victors?   . . . .   O 284 Irene   43
ABDALLA
    Then rouzing know the fiery Chief Abdalla, ...   O 254 Irene   125
    Behold our future Sultaness, Abdalla;--   . . . . .   O 267 Irene   1
    Conduct these Queens, Abdalla, to the Palace: . . .   O 269 Irene   40
    All this we know already from Abdalla.   . . . . .   O 270 Irene   6
    Is this the fierce Conspirator Abdalla?   . . . . .   O 279 Irene   1
    Who merits most, Demetrius or Abdalla.   . . . . .   O 284 Irene   45
    When Cali mounts the Throne Abdalla dies, ...   O 288 Irene   13
    Abdalla--   . . . .   O 299 Irene   34
        Can Abdalla then dissemble, ...   O 299 Irene   34
    And hot Abdalla hates the happy Lover.   . . . . .   O 300 Irene   75
    And utters Fate, unmindful of Abdalla.   . . . . .   O 306 Irene   3
    Abdalla, Cali, go--proclaim my Purpose.   . . . . .   O 309 Irene   43
    With him Abdalla we beheld--   . . . .   O 311 Irene   8
        Abdalla!   . . . .   O 311 Irene   8
    Abdalla--   . . . .   O 315 Irene   9
    Abdalla, while we waited near the Palace,--   . . . .   O 316 Irene   25
    What Cry? The Stratagem? Did then Abdalla?--   . . .   O 317 Irene   30
    What cry? what stratagem? had then Abdalla--   . . .   Y 194 Irene   V   30
    Stood torpid in Suspence; but soon Abdalla   . . . .   O 317 Irene   37
    Thy Life, too mean a Prey to lure Abdalla.   . . . .   O 319 Irene   27
    Abdalla fails, now Fortune all is mine.   . . . . .   O 319 Irene   1
    Abdalla fails now is my slave   . . . .   Y 198 Irene   V   1
    All is not lost, Abdalla, see the Queen, ...   O 326 Irene   1
    Perhaps her pois'nous Tongue might blast Abdalla.   . .   O 327 Irene   19
    Abdalla, bid thy troubled Breast be calm;   . . . .   O 329 Irene   2
    But let no thoughtless Hint involve Abdalla.   . . . .   O 329 Irene   15
    I heard, and soften'd, till Abdalla brought   . . . .   O 334 Irene   61
    Abdalla brought her Doom! Abdalla brought it!   . . .   O 334 Irene   63
    Abdalla brought her Doom! Abdalla brought it!   . . .   O 334 Irene   63
    Abdalla brought her Doom!   . . . .   O 334 Irene   66
        Abdalla brought it, ...   O 334 Irene   66
ABDALLA'S
    And wait Abdalla's unsuspected Visits: . . . . .   O 260 Irene   145
    Yet can Ambition in Abdalla's Breast   . . . . . .   O 280 Irene   25
    Far more I dread Abdalla's fiery Folly, ...   O 287 Irene   7
    Abdalla's Rage and Cali's Stratagems.   . . . . . .   O 301 Irene   94
    Dar'st thou thus dally with Abdalla's Passion?   . . .   O 307 Irene   8
    Steal from Abdalla's Eye the Sign to smile.   . . . .   O 318 Irene   5
ABDALLAH
    Then rouzing know the firy Chief Abdallah, ...   O 254 Irene   V   125
    Attend these queens, Abdallah, to the (palace)   . . .   Y 137 Irene   V   40
ABDICATED
    And snatch'd the Reins of abdicated Pow'r   . . . .   O 256 Irene   45
ABHORD
    By crimes abhord, and treasons not her own   . . . .   Y 217 Irene   V   10A
ABHORS
    Oh! how my soul abhors so mean a thought.   . . . .   O 74 Tr. Iliad Bk 6   8
ABJECT
    From generous piety, or abject fear?   . . . . . .   Y 189 Irene   V   1B
ABODES
    Yet shall I see the blest abodes, ...   O 70 Hor.II Ode XX   6
    Withdraw their cars and seek the blesst abodes.   . .   Y   6 Virgil Daphnis   21
ABOUND
    For still where wishes most abound   . . . .   O 144 Tr Boeth. II.2   11
ABOUT
    While wretched we about the world must roam, ...   O 64 Virgil Past.I   3
    about his private neglects the publick   . . . . . .   Y 113 Irene   V   27
    Throws his fond Arms about Aspasia's Neck, ...   O 286 Irene   4
    Confus'd about the streets I roam   . . . .   Y 11 Tr Hor Epode 9   33
    About to rush into the field of fate   . . . . . .   Y 18 Tr. Iliad Bk 6   4
ABOVE
    Among the Saints above.   . . . .   O 79 Feast St Simon   24
    Shall aid our Happiness above.   . . . .   O 100 Ode Friendship   28
    Shall aid y<ou>r Happiness above.   . . . .   O 100 Ode Friendship   V   28
    With sport above and death below;   . . . .   O 203 Tr. on Skating   2
    How will the bright Aspasia shine above her!   . . .   O 261 Irene   23
    Bear him aloft above the wond'ring Clouds, ...   O 274 Irene   62
    Flash out at once, with Strength above Resistance.   . .   O 282 Irene   60
    Demetrius towrd--Above the Female pleasures   . . .   O 371 Irene   V   2
    Sure 'tis the happy Hour ordain'd above, ...   O 321 Irene   35
    That reign'st supreme among the pow'rs above,   . . .   Y 20 Tr. Iliad Bk 6   100
    Above their heads th' embattled squadrons hung   . . .   Y 25 Tr Add. Battle   94
    Hurling vast mounts against the realms above   . . . .   Y 26 Tr Add. Battle   138
ABSENCE
    If e'er thy Youth has known the Pangs of Absence,   . .   O 285 Irene   3
    O say, bright Being, in this Age of Absence, ...   O 295 Irene   21
    Aspasia's Absence will inflame Suspicion;   . . . . .   O 296 Irene   5
    The Greeks disorder'd by their Leader's Absence,   . .   O 304 Irene   10
ABSENT
    Why rove I now, when absent from my Fair, ...   O 263 Irene   19
        When thou art absent   . . . .   O 265 Irene   11

Abbreviation	*Title*	*Page*
Tr. Gk. 11.167	Translations from the Greek Anthology 11.167 Pollianus	223
Tr. Gk. 11.176	Translations from the Greek Anthology 11.176 Lucillius	223
Tr. Gk. 11.186	Translations from the Greek Anthology 11.186 Nicarchus	223
Tr. Gk. 11.213	Translations from the Greek Anthology 11.213 Leonidas	223
Tr. Gk. 11.391	Translations from the Greek Anthology 11.391 Lucillius	224
Tr. Gk. 11.430	Translations from the Greek Anthology 11.430 Lucianus	224
Tr. Gk. 11.432	Translations from the Greek Anthology 11.432 Lucianus	224
Tr. Gk. 16.168	Translations from the Greek Anthology 16.168 Anonymous	225
Tr. Gk. 16.209	Translations from the Greek Anthology 16.209 Anonymous	225
Tr. Gk. 16.326	Translations from the Greek Anthology 16.326 Anonymous	225
Tr. Gk. 16.331	Translations from the Greek Anthology 16.331 Agathias	225
Tr. Gk. 16.364	Translations from the Greek Anthology 16.364 Leontius	225
Tr Gk Epigrams	Translation of Greek Epigrams	113
Tr. Greek	Translations from the Greek Anthology Unidentified	226
Tr. Greek 5.67	Translations from the Greek Anthology 5.67 Capito	209
Tr. Greek 5.74	Translations from the Greek Anthology 5.74 (or 73) Rufinus	209
Tr. Greek 6.1	Translations from the Greek Anthology 6.1 Plato	209
Tr Greek 7.128	Translations from the Greek Anthology 7.128 Anonymous	209
Tr Greek 7.136	Translations from the Greek Anthology 7.136 Antipater	210
Tr Greek 7.151	Translations from the Greek Anthology 7.151 Anonymous	210
Tr Greek 7.239	Translations from the Greek Anthology 7.239 Parmenio	210
Tr Greek 7.265	Translations from the Greek Anthology 7.265 Plato	210
Tr Greek 7.282	Translations from the Greek Anthology 7.282 Theodoridas	210
Tr Greek 7.284	Translations from the Greek Anthology 7.284 Asclepiades	210
Tr Greek 7.318	Translations from the Greek Anthology 7.318 Callimachus	211

Abbreviation	Title	Page
Tr Greek 7.319	Translations from the Greek Anthology 7.319 Anonymous	211
Tr Greek 7.350	Translations from the Greek Anthology 7.350 Anonymous	211
Tr Greek 7.459	Translations from the Greek Anthology 7.459 Callimachus	211
Tr Greek 7.461	Translations from the Greek Anthology 7.461 Meleager	211
Tr Greek 7.471	Translations from the Greek Anthology 7.471 Callimachus	211
Tr Greek 7.538	Translations from the Greek Anthology 7.538 Anyte	212
Tr Greek 7.553	Translations from the Greek Anthology 7.553 Damascius	212
Tr Greek 7.560	Translations from the Greek Anthology 7.560 Paulus Silentiarius	212
Tr Greek 7.590	Translations from the Greek Anthology 7.590 Julianus Aegyptius	212
Tr Greek 7.669	Translations from the Greek Anthology 7.669 Plato	212
Tr Greek 7.676	Translations from the Greek Anthology 7.676 Anonymous	212
Tr Greek 8.137	Translations from the Greek Anthology 8.137 Anonymous	213
Tr Greek 9.13	Translations from the Greek Anthology 9.13 Plato Junior	213
Tr Greek 9.18	Translations from the Greek Anthology 9.18 Germanicus Caesar	213
Tr Greek 9.29	Translations from the Greek Anthology 9.29 Antiphilus	213
Tr Greek 9.39	Translations from the Greek Anthology 9.39 Musicius	213
Tr Greek 9.44	Translations from the Greek Anthology 9.44 Plato	213
Tr Greek 9.48	Translations from the Greek Anthology 9.48 Anonymous	214
Tr Greek 9.50	Translations from the Greek Anthology 9.50 Mimnermus	214
Tr Greek 9.54	Translations from the Greek Anthology 9.54 Menecrates	214
Tr Greek 9.55	Translations from the Greek Anthology 9.55 Lucillius, or Menecrates	214
Tr Greek 9.65	Translations from the Greek Anthology 9.65 Anonymous	214
Tr Greek 9.66	Translations from the Greek Anthology 9.66 Antipater Sidonius	214
Tr Greek 9.74	Translations from the Greek Anthology 9.74 Anonymous	215
Tr Greek 9.110	Translations from the Greek Anthology 9.110 Alpheus	215

Abbreviation	Title	Page
Tr Greek 9.112	Translations from the Greek Anthology 9.112 Antipater Thessalonicensis	215
Tr Greek 9.133	Translations from the Greek Anthology 9.133 Anonymous	215
Tr Greek 9.138	Translations from the Greek Anthology 9.138 Anonymous	215
Tr Greek 9.148	Translations from the Greek Anthology 9.148 Anonymous	216
Tr Greek 9.160	Translations from the Greek Anthology 9.160 Anonymous	216
Tr Greek 9.163	Translations from the Greek Anthology 9.163 Anonymous	216
Tr Greek 9.250	Translations from the Greek Anthology 9.250 Onestes	216
Tr Greek 9.288	Translations from the Greek Anthology 9.288 Geminus	216
Tr Greek 9.304	Translations from the Greek Anthology 9.304 Parmenio	217
Tr Greek 9.359	Translations from the Greek Anthology 9.359 Posidippus, or Plato Comicus	217
Tr Greek 9.360	Translations from the Greek Anthology 9.360 Metrodorus	217
Tr Greek 9.375	Translations from the Greek Anthology 9.375 Anonymous	217
Tr Greek 9.394	Translations from the Greek Anthology 9.394 Pallades	218
Tr Greek 9.444	Translations from the Greek Anthology 9.444 Eratosthenes Scholasticus	218
Tr Greek 9.523	Translations from the Greek Anthology 9.523 Anonymous	218
Tr Greek 9.530	Translations from the Greek Anthology 9.530 Anonymous	218
Tr Greek 9.573	Translations from the Greek Anthology 9.573 Ammianus	218
Tr Greek 9.577	Translations from the Greek Anthology 9.577 Ptolemaeus	219
Tr Greek 9.647	Translations from the Greek Anthology 9.647 Pompeius	219
Tr Greek 9.648	Translations from the Greek Anthology 9.648 Macedonius	219
Tr Greek 9.654	Translations from the Greek Anthology 9.654 Julianus Aegyptius	219
Tr Greek 9.702	Translations from the Greek Anthology 9.702 Anonymous	219
Tr Greek 10.26	Translations from the Greek Anthology 10.26 Lucianus	219
Tr Greek 10.27	Translations from the Greek Anthology 10.27 Lucianus	220
Tr Greek 10.28	Translations from the Greek Anthology 10.28 Lucianus	220

Abbreviation	Title	Page
Tr Greek 10.30	Translations from the Greek Anthology 10.30 Anonymous	220
Tr Greek 10.31	Translations from the Greek Anthology 10.31 Lucianus	220
Tr Greek 10.58	Translations from the Greek Anthology 10.58 Palladas	220
Tr Greek 10.60	Translations from the Greek Anthology 10.60 Palladas	220
Tr Greek 10.72	Translations from the Greek Anthology 10.72 Palladas	221
Tr Greek 10.74	Translations from the Greek Anthology 10.74 Paulus Silentiarius	221
Tr Greek 10.84	Translations from the Greek Anthology 10.84 Palladas	221
Tr Greek 10.93	Translations from the Greek Anthology 10.93 Palladas	221
Tr Greek 10.98	Translations from the Greek Anthology 10.98 Palladas	221
Tr Greek 10.108	Translations from the Greek Anthology 10.108 Anonymous	221
Tr Greek 11.50	Translations from the Greek Anthology 11.50 Automedon	222
Tr Greek 11.53	Translations from the Greek Anthology 11.53 Anonymous	223
Tr Greek 13.3	Translations from the Greek Anthology 13.3 Theocritus	224
Tr Greek 16.1	Translations from the Greek Anthology 16 (Appendix Planudea). 1 Damacetus	224
Tr Greek 16.16	Translations from the Greek Anthology 16.16 Anonymous	224
Tr Greek 16.87	Translations from the Greek Anthology 16.87 Julianus Aegyptius	225
Tr Medea III	Translations from the Medea of Euripedes III	193
Tr of Crashaw	Translation of Verses by Crashaw	393
Tr Pope Grotto	Translation of Pope's Verses on His Grotto	115
Tr. Simonides	Translations from the Greek Anthology Simonides: Thucydides, vi. 59	226
* Waltoni Piscat	Waltoni Piscator perfectus	181

ABBREVIATED TITLES

Latin Poems

Page references are to the Oxford edition, unless "Yale" precedes the page number. An asterisk marks titles thought to be assigned by Johnson. Latin poems on pages 383–394 in the Oxford edition, and on pages 361–389 of the Yale edition, are poems of doubtful attribution, but are indexed in the Concordance to Latin Poems.

Abbreviation	Title		Page
A Meditation	A Meditation		208
A Meditation	A Meditation		227
° Ad Lauram Epig	Ad Lauram parituram Epigramma		115
° Ad R Savage	Ad Ricardum Savage, Arm. Humani Generis Amatorem.		102
° Ad TL MD	Ad T.L. M.D.		186
° Ad Urbanum	Ad Urbanum		101
° Adjecere bonae	Adjecere bonae Etc.		85
Aurora Musis	Aurora est Musis Amica	Yale	28
° Cantico Solom	Ex Cantico Solomonis		384
Christ Sinner	Christ to the Sinner		203
Christianus	Christianus Perfectus		205
° Collari Caprae	Versus Collari Caprae Domini Banks inscribendi		156
Death Mother	On the Death of his Mother	Yale	387
° Elizae Aenigma	In Elizae Aenigma		103
Epigram III	Epigrams III		229
Epigram IV	Epigrams IV		229
° Epigramma	Venus in Armour: Epigramma		384
° Epilogus	Epilogus		188
° Geographia Met	Geographia Metrica		229
° Gnothi Seauton	Gnothi Seauton		159
° In Birchium	In Birchium		386
° In Theatro	In Theatro: March 8, 1771		153
° Insula Kenneth	Insula Sancti Kennethi		169
° Jactura Tempor	Jactura Temporis [Epigram II]		228
° Jejunium Cibus	Jejunium et Cibus [Epigram I]		228
° Lady Defence	To a Lady who spoke in Defence of Liberty		105
Losing Speech	Prayer on Losing the Power of Speech		204
° Mea nec Falern	Mea nec Falernae Etc.		85
° Medico Aeger S	Nugae anapaesticae in lecto lusae. Medico Aeger S.		198

xxv

Abbreviation	Title	Page
° Messiah	Messia	88
° Oda Isle Skye	Oda	166
° Oda to Thrale	Oda	167
On Lord Anson	On Lord Anson	142
On Mrs Thrale	On Mrs. Thrale	197
On the Gin-Act	On the Gin-Act	383
° Post-Genitis	Post-Genitis	109
Prayer	Prayer	232
Prayer on Xmas	Prayer on Christmas Day, 1779	193
Prayers I	Prayers I	206
Prayers II	Prayers II	206
Prayers III	Prayers III	206
Prayers IV	Prayers IV	207
Prayers V	Prayers V	207
Prayers VI	Prayers VI	207
Prayers VII	Prayers VII	207
Recover Eyes	On recovering the Use of his Eyes	164
° Rivum a Stoana	In Rivum a Mola Stoana Lichfeldiae diffluentem	228
° Septem Aetates	Septem Aetates	226
° Spes	Spes	204
Summ Lawrence	A Summons to Dr. Lawrence	197
° Syl Urb Thes	In Locupletissimum ornatissimumque Syl. Urb. Thesaurum.	383
° The Warehouse	The Logical Warehouse: Occasioned by an Auctioneer's having the Groundfloor of the Oratory in Lincoln's-Inn-Fields	385
° To Dr Lawrence	Verses addressed to Dr. Lawrence, composed by Dr. Johnson, as he lay confined with an inflamed Eye.	162
To Eliz Carter	To Elizabeth Carter	103
Tr Ash Wed	Translation of the Collect for Ash Wednesday	197
Tr Busy Fly	Translation of 'Busy, Curious, Thirsty Fly'	170
Tr Cleanthes	[Translations from the Greek Anthology] Cleanthes: Epictetus, *Enchiridion*, ad fin.	226
Tr Doncast Epi	Translation of Robin of Doncaster's Epitaph	164
Tr Dryden Milt	Translation of Dryden's Epigram on Milton	86
Tr Epi Madoc	Translation of a Welch Epitaph on Prince Madoc	386
Tr. Gk. 10.113	Translations from the Greek Anthology 10.113 Anonymous	222
Tr. Gk. 10.119	Translations from the Greek Anthology 10.119 Anonymous	222
Tr. Gk. 10.123	Translations from the Greek Anthology 10.123 Aesopus	222
Tr. Gk. 10.124	Translations from the Greek Anthology 10.124 Glyco	222
Tr. Gk. 11.118	Translations from the Greek Anthology 11.118 Callicter	223
Tr. Gk. 11.145	Translations from the Greek Anthology 11.145 Anonymous	223

the frequency count of nonvariant words is not inflated by lines that contain one or more variant words. Other features were added to aid the editor in the tedious job of proofreading.

The revised program has been documented and is available either in the form of a PL-1 program deck or an object deck to any researcher desiring to use it. A tape of the original card images of the text has been deposited in the Price Gilbert Memorial Library at the Georgia Institute of Technology.

Acknowledgments

With sincere gratitude I express appreciation to many friends and acquaintances for help in making this concordance become a reality. And indeed without the love, encouragement, and endurance of my family, this work could not have been done at all.

I especially thank Professor Stephen Parrish, General Editor of the Cornell Concordances, who has overseen and directed this endeavor. James A. Painter has been most generous in sharing his computer program and in offering assistance in adapting it to this work. Dean William H. Eberhardt and Professor David B. Comer III, colleagues at the Georgia Institute of Technology, afforded invaluable assistance. Professor Ralph Spillman has given me helpful advice, and Margrit Rub and Barbara Scoggins, of the Georgia Tech English staff, generous help. My thanks are due also to two distinguished scholars of eighteenth-century literature, Professors James L. Clifford and Donald J. Greene.

Adequate appreciation can scarcely be expressed to my collaborator, Peter Sherry, for his tireless effort, his enthusiasm, and his expertise. Also indispensable in the computer work on this volume have been Rand H. Childs and Spotswood D. Stoddard, who worked long and faithfully, adding significant innovations to the program, and Robert L. Nitschke and Thomas L. Sasser, who key-punched with remarkable accuracy. Recognition, too, is due the University of Georgia Computer Center for the use of its IBM 360/65 Computer and the Rich Electronic Computing Center of the Georgia Institute of Technology for the use of its COPE terminal from which all the indexing runs were made.

For financial support I wish to acknowledge the aid of the Georgia Tech Foundation, Inc.

HELEN NAUGLE

ABBREVIATED TITLES

English Poems (together with French and Greek)

Page references are to the Oxford edition, unless "Yale" precedes the page number. An asterisk marks titles thought to be assigned by Johnson. Poems on pages 383–394 in the Oxford edition, and on pages 361–389 of the Yale edition, are poems of doubtful attribution; the English and Greek poems on these pages are indexed in the Concordance to Poems of Doubtful Attribution.

Abbreviation	Title	Page
° A Song	A Song	388
° An Evening Ode	An Evening Ode: To Stella	390
° An Ode	An Ode	124
° Anacreon Ode 9	Anacreon, Ode IX	185
Burlesque Vega	Burlesque of Lines by Lope de Vega	182
° Charade!	Charade!	179
° Death Dr Levet	On the Death of Dr. Robert Levet	200
° Eis Birchion	Eis Birchion	108
° Eis Elisses	Eis to tes Elisses peri ton Oneiron Ainigma	103
° Eliza plucking	To Eliza plucking Laurel in Mr Pope's Gardens	106
Englished	Venus in Armour: Englished	384
° Epi Dist Moth	Epilogue [to 'The Distressed Mother'] intended to have been spoken by a Lady who was to personate the Ghost of Hermione	83
Epi Goldsmith	Epitaph on Goldsmith	171
Epigram More	Epigram on Sir Thomas More, Erasmus, and Micyllus	393
° Epilogue	Epilogue	188
° Epit Phillips	An Epitaph on Claudy Phillips, a Musician	113
Epita Hogarth	Epitaph on Hogarth	153
° Epitaph Hanmer	A Translation of the Latin Epitaph On Sir Thomas Hanmer Written By Doctor Freind	117
Extemp Elegy	An Extempore Elegy	Yale 300
Fanny Burney	A Song for Fanny Burney	Yale 299
° Feast St Simon	Upon the Feast of St Simon & St Jude	78
° Festina Lente	Festina Lentè	77
French Distich	French Distichs	172
° Hickman Spinet	To Miss Hickman playing on the Spinet	96
° Hor Epode II	[Translation of] Horace. Epode the 2d.	71

Abbreviation	Title	Page
* Hor I Ode xxii	Translation of Horace [Odes], Book I. Ode xxii.	65
Hor II Ode IX	Translation of Horace Odes, Book II. ix	67
* Hor II Ode 14	[Translation of] Horace [Odes], Book 2d. Ode 14	68
* Hor II Ode XX	[Translation of] Horace [Odes], Book 2d. Ode 20th	70
In Baretti Bk.	Verses in Baretti's Commonplace Book	142
* Irene	Irene: A Tragedy. As it is Acted at the Theatre Royal in Drury-Lane	245
Irene Epilogue	Epilogue	247
Irene Prologue	Prologue	246
* Lady Birthday	To a Young Lady on her Birth-day	80
* Lady F Assizes	To Lady F [irebra] ce at Bury Assizes	107
Lady Leaving	An Ode on a Lady Leaving her Place of Abode; Almost Impromptu	Yale 38
* London	London: A Poem In Imitation of the Third Satire of Juvenal.	7
* Natural Beauty	The Natural Beauty To Stella	389
* Ode Friendship	An Ode on Friendship	99
On a Daffodill	On a Daffodill: The First Flower the Author Had Seen that Year	Yale 3
On C Cibber	On Colley Cibber	114
* On Lord Lovat	On Lord Lovat's Execution	387
On Marlborough	On the Duke of Marlborough	172
On Thrale Hat	On Hearing Miss Thrale Deliberate About Her Hat	194
Par Hermit I	Parodies of the Hermit of Warkworth I	157
Par Hermit II	Parodies of the Hermit of Warkworth II	157
Par Hermit III	Parodies of the Hermit of Warkworth III	158
Parody of Pope	Parody of Pope	Yale 309
Parody Warton	Parody of Thomas Warton	180
* Pro Drury-Lane	Prologue Spoken by Mr. Garrick, At the Opening of the Theatre in Drury-Lane 1747	51
* Pro Good Nat'd	Prologue to 'The Good Natur'd Man'	59
* Pro Word Wise	Prologue to 'A Word to the Wise'	61
* Prologue Comus	A New Prologue Spoken by Mr Garrick, Thursday, April 5, 1750. At The Representation of Comus, for the Benefit of Mrs Elizabeth Foster, Milton's Grand-Daughter, and only surviving Decendant.	56
Prologue Lethe	Prologue to Garrick's Lethe	Yale 67
* Psalmus 117	Psalmus 117	155
Ridicul Warton	Lines Written in Ridicule of Thomas Warton's Poems	179
Seeing Montagu	On Seeing a Portrait of Mrs. Montagu	189
* Song Congratu	A Short Song of Congratulation	196
* Sprig of Myrtl	On a Lady's presenting a Sprig of Myrtle to a Gentleman	95
* Stella Mourn	Stella in Mourning	122

Abbreviation	Title	Page
° The Ant	The Ant: From Proverbs, chap. vi. ver. 6	151
° The Happy Life	The Happy Life	392
Thrale 35 Year	To Mrs. Thrale, on Her Completing Her Thirty-fifth Year	177
° To A Fuscus	[Translation of Horace, Odes, Book I, xxii.] To Aristius Fuscus	66
° To Lyce, Lady	To Lyce, an elderly Lady	126
° To Miss Playin	To Miss —— On her playing upon the Harpsicord in a Room hung with some Flower-Pieces of her own Painting	120
° To Miss Purse	To Miss —— On her giving the Author a Gold and Silk net-work Purse of her own weaving	119
° To Posterity	To Posterity	110
Tr Add Battle	Translation of Addison's 'Battle of the Cranes and Pygmies'	75
Tr Benserade	Translation of Lines by Benserade	183
Tr Boet III.12	Translations from Boethius de Consolatione Philosophiae Book III. Metre 12	147
Tr Boeth II.2	Translations from Boethius de Consolatione Philosophiae Book II. Metre 2	144
Tr Boeth II.4	Translations from Boethius de Consolatione Philosophiae Book II. Metre 4	144
Tr Boeth III.1	Translations from Boethius de Consolatione Philosophiae Book III. Metre 1	145
Tr Boeth III.3	Translations from Boethius de Consolatione Philosophiae Book III. Metre 3	145
Tr Boeth III.4	Translations from Boethius de Consolatione Philosophiae Book III. Metre 4	146
Tr Boeth III.5	Translations from Boethius de Consolatione Philosophiae Book III. Metre 5	146
Tr Boeth III.6	Translations from Boethius de Consolatione Philosophiae Book III. Metre 6	146
Tr Dist Modena	Translation of a Distich on the Duke of Modena	176
Tr Easy Phrase	Translation of Lines in Baretti's 'Easy Phraseology'	174
Tr Epitaph Dog	Translation of an Epitaph on a Dog	173
Tr Fr Pantomim	Translation of Verses from a French Pantomime	173
Tr Hor Epode XI	Translation of Horace Epode XI	Yale 10
Tr Horace IV.7	Translation of Horace Odes, Book IV.vii	231
° Tr Iliad Bk 6	Translation of part of the Dialogue between Hector and Andromache; from the Sixth Book of Homer's Iliad	74
Tr Medea I	Translations from the Medea of Euripides I	190
Tr Medea II	Translations from the Medea of Euripides II	191
Tr Metastas II	Translations from Metastasio II	176
Tr Metastasi I	Translations from Metastasio I	176
Tr on Skating	Translations of French Verses on Skating	202
Tr. Rambler 6	Translations of Mottoes and Quotations in 'The Rambler' Numb. 6. Saturday, April 7, 1750	129

Abbreviation	Title	Page
Tr. Rambler 7	Translations of Mottoes and Quotations in 'The Rambler' Numb. 7. Tuesday, April 10, 1750	129
Tr. Rambler 8	Translations of Mottoes and Quotations in 'The Rambler' Numb. 8. Saturday, April 14, 1750	130
Tr. Rambler 10	Translations of Mottoes and Quotations in 'The Rambler' Numb. 10. Saturday, April 21, 1750	130
Tr. Rambler 12	Translations of Mottoes and Quotations in 'The Rambler' Numb. 12. Saturday, April 28, 1750	130
Tr. Rambler 17	Translations of Mottoes and Quotations in 'The Rambler' Numb. 17. Tuesday, May 15, 1750	131
Tr. Rambler 21	Translations of Mottoes and Quotations in 'The Rambler' Numb. 21. Tuesday, May 29, 1750	131
Tr. Rambler 32	Translations of Mottoes and Quotations in 'The Rambler' Numb. 32. Saturday, July 7, 1750	131
Tr. Rambler 33	Translations of Mottoes and Quotations in 'The Rambler' Numb. 33. Tuesday, July 10, 1750	131
Tr. Rambler 39	Translations of Mottoes and Quotations in 'The Rambler' Numb. 39. Tuesday, July 31, 1750	131
Tr. Rambler 45	Translations of Mottoes and Quotations in 'The Rambler' Numb. 45. Tuesday, August 21, 1750	131
Tr. Rambler 46	Translations of Mottoes and Quotations in 'The Rambler' Numb. 46. Saturday, August 25, 1750	132
Tr. Rambler 48	Translations of Mottoes and Quotations in 'The Rambler' Numb. 48. Saturday, September 1, 1750	132
Tr. Rambler 54	Translations of Mottoes and Quotations in 'The Rambler' Numb. 54. Saturday, September 22, 1750	132
Tr. Rambler 65	Translations of Mottoes and Quotations in 'The Rambler' Numb. 65. Tuesday, October 30, 1750	132
Tr. Rambler 67	Translations of Mottoes and Quotations in 'The Rambler' Numb. 67. Tuesday, November 6, 1750	133
Tr. Rambler 71	Translations of Mottoes and Quotations in 'The Rambler' Numb. 71. Tuesday, November 20, 1750	133
Tr. Rambler 81	Translations of Mottoes and Quotations in 'The Rambler' Numb. 81. Tuesday, December 25, 1750	133
Tr. Rambler 82	Translations of Mottoes and Quotations in 'The Rambler' Numb. 82. Saturday, December 29, 1750	133
Tr. Rambler 83	Translations of Mottoes and Quotations in 'The Rambler' Numb. 83. Tuesday, January 1, 1751	133
Tr. Rambler 85	Translations of Mottoes and Quotations in 'The Rambler' Numb. 85. Tuesday, January 8, 1751	133

Abbreviation	Title	Page
Tr. Rambler 89	Translations of Mottoes and Quotations in 'The Rambler' Numb. 89. Tuesday, January 22, 1751	134
Tr. Rambler 90	Translations of Mottoes and Quotations in 'The Rambler' Numb. 90. Saturday, January 26, 1751	134
Tr. Rambler 93	Translations of Mottoes and Quotations in 'The Rambler' Numb. 93. Tuesday, February 5, 1751	134
Tr. Rambler 96	Translations of Mottoes and Quotations in 'The Rambler' Numb. 96. Saturday, February 16, 1751	134
Tr Rambler 104	Translations of Mottoes and Quotations in 'The Rambler' Numb. 104. Saturday, March 16, 1751	134
Tr Rambler 105	Translations of Mottoes and Quotations in 'The Rambler' Numb. 105. Tuesday, March 19, 1751	134
Tr Rambler 106	Translations of Mottoes and Quotations in 'The Rambler' Numb. 106. Saturday, March 23, 1751	135
Tr Rambler 111	Translations of Mottoes and Quotations in 'The Rambler' Numb. 111. Tuesday, April 9, 1751	135
Tr Rambler 117	Translations of Mottoes and Quotations in 'The Rambler' Numb. 117. Tuesday, April 30, 1751	135
Tr Rambler 122	Translations of Mottoes and Quotations in 'The Rambler' Numb. 122. Saturday, May 18, 1751	135
Tr Rambler 127	Translations of Mottoes and Quotations in 'The Rambler' Numb. 127. Tuesday, June 4, 1751	135
Tr Rambler 128	Translations of Mottoes and Quotations in 'The Rambler' Numb. 128. Saturday, June 8, 1751	136
Tr Rambler 129	Translations of Mottoes and Quotations in 'The Rambler' Numb. 129. Tuesday, June 11, 1751	136
Tr Rambler 132	Translations of Mottoes and Quotations in 'The Rambler' Numb. 132. Saturday, June 22, 1751	136
Tr Rambler 135	Translations of Mottoes and Quotations in 'The Rambler' Numb. 135. Tuesday, July 2, 1751	137
Tr Rambler 138	Translations of Mottoes and Quotations in 'The Rambler' Numb. 138. Saturday, July 13, 1751	137
Tr Rambler 139	Translations of Mottoes and Quotations in 'The Rambler' Numb. 139. Tuesday, July 16, 1751	137
Tr Rambler 140	Translations of Mottoes and Quotations in 'The Rambler' Numb. 140. Saturday, July 20, 1751	137
Tr Rambler 141	Translations of Mottoes and Quotations in 'The Rambler' Numb. 141. Tuesday, July 23, 1751	137
Tr Rambler 143	Translations of Mottoes and Quotations in 'The Rambler' Numb. 143. Tuesday, July 30, 1751	137
Tr Rambler 153	Translations of Mottoes and Quotations in 'The Rambler' Numb. 153. Tuesday, September 3, 1751	138

Abbreviation	*Title*	*Page*
Tr Rambler 156	Translations of Mottoes and Quotations in 'The Rambler' Numb. 156. Saturday, September 14, 1751	138
Tr Rambler 160	Translations of Mottoes and Quotations in 'The Rambler' Numb. 160. Saturday, September 28, 1751	138
Tr Rambler 161	Translations of Mottoes and Quotations in 'The Rambler' Numb. 161. Tuesday, October 1, 1751	138
Tr Rambler 164	Translations of Mottoes and Quotations in 'The Rambler' Numb. 164. Saturday, October 12, 1751	138
Tr Rambler 168	Translations of Mottoes and Quotations in 'The Rambler' Numb. 168. Saturday, October 26, 1751	139
Tr Rambler 169	Translations of Mottoes and Quotations in 'The Rambler' Numb. 169. Tuesday, October 29, 1751	139
Tr Rambler 170	Translations of Mottoes and Quotations in 'The Rambler' Numb. 170. Saturday, November 2, 1751	139
Tr Rambler 171	Translations of Mottoes and Quotations in 'The Rambler' Numb. 171. Tuesday, November 5, 1751	139
Tr Rambler 173	Translations of Mottoes and Quotations in 'The Rambler' Numb. 173. Tuesday, November 12, 1751	139
Tr Rambler 176	Translations of Mottoes and Quotations in 'The Rambler' Numb. 176. Saturday, November 23, 1751	140
Tr Rambler 178	Translations of Mottoes and Quotations in 'The Rambler' Numb. 178. Saturday, November 30, 1751	140
Tr Rambler 180	Translations of Mottoes and Quotations in 'The Rambler' Numb. 180. Saturday, December 7, 1751	140
Tr Rambler 182	Translations of Mottoes and Quotations in 'The Rambler' Numb. 182. Saturday, December 14, 1751	140
Tr Rambler 183	Translations of Mottoes and Quotations in 'The Rambler' Numb. 183. Tuesday, December 17, 1751	140
Tr Rambler 188	Translations of Mottoes and Quotations in 'The Rambler' Numb. 188. Saturday, January 4, 1752	140
Tr Rambler 199	Translations of Mottoes and Quotations in 'The Rambler' Numb. 199. Tuesday, February 11, 1752	141
Tr Rambler 208	Translations of Mottoes and Quotations in 'The

Abbreviation	Title	Page
	Rambler' Numb. 208. Saturday, March 14, 1752	141
Tr Rio Verde	Translations of the Beginning of 'Rio Verde'	159
° Vanity Wealth	The Vanity of Wealth An Ode To a Friend	391
° Vanity Wishes	The Vanity of Human Wishes. The Tenth Satire of Juvenal, Imitated by Samuel Johnson.	29
Virgil Daphnis	The Hymns to Daphnis from the Fifth Pastoral of Virgil	Yale 6
Virgil Past I	Translation of Virgil Pastoral I	64
° Winter's Walk	The Winter's Walk	123
° Young Author	The Young Author	81

```
ADD          (CONTINUED)                                        PAGE     TITLE                LINE
      And add new lustre to the Grecian name.   . . . . . .     Y 117  Irene              V 109B
      And add new Roses to the faded Cheek. . . . . . . .       O 278  Irene                 66
      And add new Terrors to the Face of Death.   . . . . .     O 330  Irene                  8
ADDED
      Her statue would have breath'd an added grace,  . . . .   O 189  Seeing Montagu         4
ADDER
      Like a fell Adder swelling in a Brake,   . . . . . .      O 275  Irene                 77
ADDRESS
      With more address a lover's note convey,  . . . . . .     O  13  London                77
      He scorns the meek Address, the suppliant Strain,  . . .  O 246  Irene Prologue        31
      His bland Address, and Sorcery of Tongue;   . . . . .     O 273  Irene                 40
      How did Aspasia welcome your Address? . . . . . . . .     O 282  Irene                 61
ADDRESS'D
      Ode on Friendship address'd To the Lady--------  . . .    O  99  Ode Friendship      V  T
ADDREST
      In fervent prayer addrest the deities:   . . . . . .      Y  20  Tr. Iliad Bk 6        98
ADDS
      Adds Shame to Grief, and Infamy to Ruin. . . . . . .      O 250  Irene                 25
ADJOINING
      Remote from Tumult, in th' adjoining Palace,   . . . .    O 263  Irene                  1
ADMIR'D
      For arts like these preferr'd, admir'd, caress'd,  . . .  O  17  London               152
      I once admir'd, I'd then despise: . . . . . . . . .       O  73  Hor. Epode II       V 60
      So late admir'd and prais'd, alas! in vain!  . . . . .    Y   4  On a Daffodill        24
ADMIRATION
      My admiration only I exprest,  . . . . . . . . . . .      O  64  Virgil Past.I         13
      Confounded, aw'd, and lost in Admiration,   . . . . .     O 282  Irene                 64
ADMIRER
      Each youth admires, though each admirer dies;   . . . .   O  83  Epi Dist Moth.         6
ADMIRES
      Admires their wond'rous talents for the stage: . . . .    O  16  London               133
      Each youth admires, though each admirer dies;   . . . .   O  83  Epi Dist Moth.         6
      Beneath his feet admires each shining star,  . . . . .    Y   7  Virgil Daphnis        34
ADMISSION
      Admission ne'er had sought, or could not find. . . . .    O 192  Tr. Medea II          12
      Asks at the Gate Admission to Aspasia,   . . . . . .      O 294  Irene                  2
      The Breast where Guilt like this has found   . . . . .    O 349  Irene               V 23
         admission
ADMIT
      Thanks for this kind Relief--with Speed admit him.   . .  O 294  Irene                  5
      Will not admit a Lover's long Farewell,  . . . . . .      O 297  Irene                 13
ADMITTANCE
      Intreats admittance to the fair Aspasia  . . . . . .      O 367  Irene               V 20
ADOR'D
      Fair Justice then, without constraint ador'd,   . . . .   O  22  London               250
ADORATION
      Such heav'nly Beauty form'd for Adoration,   . . . . .    O 269  Irene                 41
ADORE
      Exalt each trifle, ev'ry vice adore,   . . . . . . .      O  17  London               148
      Praise evry trifle, ev'ry vice adore,    . . . . . .      Y  55  London              V 148
      So shall you guiltless reign, and all mankind adore. . .  O  84  Epi Dist Moth.        47
      Adore the Beauty but despise th' Apostate.   . . . . .    O 350  Irene               V 26
ADORING
      Th' adoring youth, and envious fair,   . . . . . . .      O 122  Stella Mourn.         13
      Of prostrate princes and adoring nations   . . . . .     Y 131  Irene               V 31
      Th' adoring Soldiers would revenge their Idol.  . . . .   O 273  Irene                 42
ADORN
      To point a moral, or adorn a tale. . . . . . . . . .      O  41  Vanity Wishes        222
      Adorn Philander's head, or grace his tomb.   . . . . .    O  95  Sprig of Myrtl        14
      Adorn a Throne, and dignify Dominion.    . . . . . .      O 276  Irene                 10
      As vines the elms, as grapes adorn the vine,   . . . .    Y   6  Virgil Daphnis        17
ADORN'D
      Thy form more lovely, more adorn'd thy mind;   . . . .    O  80  Lady Birthday          4
      Adorn'd in Roman time the brightest days,  . . . . .      O 189  Seeing Montagu         2
ADORNS
      Adorns my Palace with its brightest Virgins;   . . . .    O 263  Irene                 15
ADULATION
      Or tune thine Ear to soothing Adulation, . . . . . . .    O 289  Irene                  4
      Or tune your ear to soothing Adulation.  . . . . . .      O 366  Irene               V 20
ADVANCE
      Advance, and perish in the frantic Boast.   . . . . .     O 318  Irene                  7
ADVANCES
      Claim leads to claim, and pow'r advances pow'r;   . . .   O  34  Vanity Wishes        106
ADVENT'ROUS
      Direct O Goddess, my advent'rous song;   . . . . . .      Y  22  Tr Add. Battle         3
ADVERSE
      Into the adverse Scale, nor shakes the Balance.   . . .   O 260  Irene                140
ADVICE
      Swell not thy Soul beyond Advice or Friendship,   . . .   O 289  Irene                  2
AEGYPTIANS
      Then scorn those flowers to which the Aegyptians bow'd, . Y   4  On a Daffodill        15
AENEAS'
      How Turnus by Aeneas' sword expir'd?   . . . . . . .      Y  22  Tr Add. Battle        12
AERIAL
      This habitant th' aerial regions boast.  . . . . . .      O 138  Tr Rambler 161         1
      To guide thy Passage shall th' aerial Spirits   . . . .   O 322  Irene                  7
AFAR
      Afar they mark the flambeau's bright approach,  . . . .   O  21  London               234
      Mark from afar the flambeau's bright approach,  . . . .   Y  59  London              V 234
      Safe in his pow'r, whose eyes discern afar   . . . . .    O  47  Vanity Wishes        353
```

5

```
AFAR          (CONTINUED)                                    PAGE    TITLE              LINE
    With bright effulgence  The travell<er> afar    . . . .  Y 131 Irene            V  36
    Still stretch in vain their longing Arms afar;  . . . .  O 292 Irene               91
    I mark'd her wily Messenger afar,  . . . . . . .         O 327 Irene               24
    The fearless Pygmies view them from afar . . . . . .     Y  25 Tr Add. Battle       96
AFFAIRS
    For trifling sports I quitted grave affairs.    . . . .  O 130 Tr. Rambler 10        1
    if human miseries or affairs yet claim your  . . . . .   Y 181 Irene            V  54
        regard
AFFECTATION
    Till Affectation, rip'ning to Belief,  . . . . . . .     O 266 Irene               31
AFFECTED
    In vain affected Raptures flush the Cheek,  . . . . .    O 315 Irene               29
        borro<wd or a>ffected <gayety>  . . . . . . .        Y 185 Irene            V   3
AFFECTING
    Reflect that Life and Death, affecting Sounds,  . . . .  O 290 Irene               26
AFFECTION
    Such Ecstacy of Love! such pure Affection,  . . . . .    O 295 Irene               15
AFFECTION'S
    Yet still he fills affection's eye,  . . . . . . .       O 201 Death Dr Levet        9
AFFECTS
    Ev'n from the Birth affects supreme Command,  . . . .    O 280 Irene               19
AFFLICT
    Or storms afflict the ruffled main.  . . . . . . .       O  67 Hor. II Ode IX        4
AFFLICTED
    And bids afflicted worth retire to peace.  . . . . .     O  45 Vanity Wishes       310
    Shall I not wish to chear afflicted Kings,  . . . . .    O 291 Irene               67
    With every curse of angry heav'n afflicted beneath  . . O 357 Irene            V  15
        each
AFFLICTIVE
    Fate wings with ev'ry wish th' afflictive dart,  . . .   O  31 Vanity Wishes       15
AFFLUENCE
    To Want give Affluence? and to Slav'ry Freedom?  . . .   O 277 Irene               46
AFFORD
    And, while thy grounds a cheap repast afford,  . . . .   O  20 London             218
    And, while thy beds a cheap repast afford,  . . . . .    O  20 London           V 218
    All times their scenes of pompous woes afford,  . . . . O  41 Vanity Wishes       223
    Cali, methinks yon waving Trees afford  . . . . . .      O 268 Irene               36
AFFORDS
    Kind Heav'n affords thee, and inviting Mercy  . . . .    O 321 Irene               41
AFFRIGHT
    Shrieks of Affright, and Wailings of Distress.  . . . .  O 251 Irene               72
    Astonish'd nations view with wild affright  . . . . .    Y  24 Tr Add. Battle       74
AFFRIGHTED
    But hark! th' affrighted crowd's tumultuous cries  . .   O  18 London             182
    The Bear enrag'd th' affrighted Moon shall dread;  . . . O 111 To Posterity         17
    And shook the (affrighted) world lab'ring earth licentious  Y 115 Irene         V 49A
        conquest
    Affrighted at Impiety like thine,  . . . . . . .         O 289 Irene               19
    The child starts back affrighted at the blaze  . . . .   Y  20 Tr. Iliad Bk 6       92
    Affrighted views; and looking o'er the plain  . . . .    Y  23 Tr Add. Battle       32
AFRAID
    Still fierce to threaten, still afraid to fight;  . . .  O 110 To Posterity         10
    All the World afraid but thee,  . . . . . . . .          O 145 Tr Boeth. II.4        20
AFRESH
    Now bleeds the war afresh, the Crane from high  . . . .  Y  26 Tr Add. Battle      130
AFRIC'S
    Or torrid Afric's faithless Sands,  . . . . . . .        O  66 To A. Fuscus          6
    And Afric's torrid Sands in search of Cali.  . .. . . .  O 274 Irene               60
AFRICK'S
    Or horrid Africk's faithless sands;  . . . . . . .       O  65 Hor I Ode xxii         6
    Or torrid Africk's faithless sands;  . . . . . . .       O  65 Hor I Ode xxii     V   6
AFRICS
    And Africs torrid shores in search of Cali  . . . . .    Y 143 Irene            V  60
AFTER
    And panting Time toil'd after him in vain:  . . . . .    O  51 Pro Drury-Lane        6
    After your death, the lavish heir  . . . . . . .         O  69 Hor.II Ode 14        25
    So the young author panting after fame,  . . . . . .     O  82 Young Author      V  11
    How Nation after Nation falls before him.  . . . . .     O 268 Irene               27
    How nation after nation falls before me  . . . . . .     Y 136 Irene            V  27
AGAIN
    If dreams yet flatter, once again attend,  . . . . .     O  38 Vanity Wishes      163
    If hope yet flatter, once again attend,  . . . . . .     Y  99 Vanity Wishes    V 163
    Next Month he sets it out again.  . . . . . . .          O  73 Hor. Epode II        79
    "Tempts me to be wild again:  . . . . . . . .            O 185 Anacreon Ode 9       22
    The fields, and woods, again, are green,  . . . . .      O 231 Tr Horace IV.7    V   2
    The rivers know their banks again,  . . . . . . .        O 231 Tr Horace IV.7         4
    And Winter chils the World again.  . . . . . . .         O 232 Tr Horace IV.7        12
    Nor found again the bright Temptation fail?  . . . . .   O 259 Irene              125
    Again should golden Splendour grace her Cities,  . . .   O 290 Irene               53
    Again her prostrate Palaces should rise,  . . . . .      O 291 Irene               54
    Again her Temples sound with holy Musick:  . . . . .     O 291 Irene               55
    Aspasia! do I once again behold thee?  . . . . . .       O 294 Irene                2
    Soon may we meet again, secure and free,  . . . . .      O 303 Irene               23
    We started at the Sound, again enquir'd,  . . . . .      O 325 Irene               25
    Again his .thund'ring Voice return'd, Irene.  . . . .    O 325 Irene               26
    To tast again the sweets of liberty.  . . . . . . .      Y  19 Tr. Iliad Bk 6       41
AGAINST    SEE GAINST
    Against your fame with fondness hate combines,  . . . .  O  46 Vanity Wishes      331
    Or arm his Breast against the Force of Love?  . . . .    O 261 Irene                8
    Against returning Guilt.  . . . . . . . . .              O 265 Irene               11
```

AGAINST   (CONTINUED)   PAGE   TITLE   LINE
  And arm the Persian Heretick against thee; . . . . .   O 274 Irene   55
  Or set The Persian Heretic in arms against Me . . . . O 348 Irene   V 17
  Against his King, and cry, Remember Justice?   O 286 Irene   12
  Reclines against the Shore: Our Grecian Troop . . . . O 304 Irene   3
  Against the Head which Innocence secures, ... O 322 Irene   1
  Against th' omnipotence of gold . . . . Y 11 Tr Hor Epode 9   22
  Against th' invading birds their native land: . . . . Y 23 Tr Add. Battle 37
  Hurling vast mounts against the realms above . Y 26 Tr Add. Battle 138
AGE
  But all whom hunger spares, with age decay: . . . O   9 London   12
  In pleasing dreams the blissful age renew, ... O 10 London   25
  And lull to servitude a thoughtless age. . . . O 12 London   60
  Besides, with justice, this discerning age . . . . O 16 London   132
  Blest age! but ah! how diff'rent from our own! . . . O 22 London   253
  Blest age! but ha! how diff'rent from our own! . . . O 22 London   V 253
  With age, with cares, with maladies oppress'd, ... O 35 Vanity Wishes 117
  From age to age in everlasting debt; . . . . . O 39 Vanity Wishes 188
  From age to age in everlasting debt; . . . . O 39 Vanity Wishes 188
  Bless with an age exempt from scorn or crime; . . . O 44 Vanity Wishes 292
  An age that melts with unperceiv'd decay, ... O 44 Vanity Wishes 293
  An age that melts in unperceiv'd decay, . . . O 44 Vanity Wishes V 293
  Such age there is, and who shall wish its end? . . . O 44 Vanity Wishes 298
  Such age there is, and who could wish its end? . . . O 44 Vanity Wishes V 298
  Such age the is, and who could wish its end? . . . Y 105 Vanity Wishes V 298
  They pleas'd their Age, and did not aim to mend. . . . O 52 Pro Drury-Lane 22
  Bid scenic Virtue form the rising Age, ... O 53 Pro Drury-Lane 61
  Her Youth laborious, and her blameless Age: . . . O 58 Prologue Comus 30
  Nor did King Priam's hoary age . . . . . O 68 Hor. II Ode IX 15
  Yet Hecuba's, nor Priam's hoary age, . . . O 74 Tr. Iliad Bk 6 15
  Illustrious age! how bright thy glories shone, . . . O 118 Epitaph Hanmer 21
  Age call'd at length his active mind to rest, . . . O 118 Epitaph Hanmer 35
  Lead a long and peaceful Age, ... O 145 Tr Boeth. II.4 21
  One and Twenty 1810: Improviso on a young heir's coming O 196 Song Congratu. V T
    of age.
  But cautious Age suspects the flatt'ring Form, . . . O 255 Irene   18
  Why should Cali rebel--unexpensive age . . . . Y 120 Irene   V 40
  These tedious Narratives of frozen Age . . . . O 259 Irene   113
  That Maxim publish'd in an impious Age, . . . O 291 Irene   60
  O say, bright Being, in this Age of Absence, . . . O 295 Irene   21
AGES
  And rising Ages hasten to be just. . . . . . . O 57 Prologue Comus 14
  "Secure of praise from ages yet unborn." . . . . . O 82 Young Author V 18
  Th' accumulated Wealth of toiling Ages. . . . . O 249 Irene   19
    to the hiss of future ages . . . . . Y 113 Irene   V 22
  Through hissing Ages, a proverbial Coward, . . . O 305 Irene   28
  In former ages while upheld by fate . . . . - Y 23 Tr Add. Battle 26
AGGRAVATE
  And dreaded losses aggravate his pains; . . . . O 44 Vanity Wishes 286
  Which aggravate a fault with feign'd excuses, . . . O 176 Tr Metastas II   8
AGGREGATED
  Shrinks from this heap of aggregated crime . . . . Y 159 Irene   V   9
AGHAST
  Aghast you start, and scarce with aking sight . . . O 18 London   186
AGONIES
  In his last Agonies the gasping Coward, ... O 272 Irene   14
  Whence all the Bliss and Agonies of Love? . . . O 277 Irene   42
AGONIZING
  With gloomy State and agonizing Pomp. . . . O 294 Irene   135
  These chilling doubts, and agonizing horrours? . . . Y 189 Irene   V 1A
AGONY
  Horror and Agony are in that Sound! . . . . . O 328 Irene   32
AGREE
  Mark, when the diff'rent notes agree . . . . . O 121 To Miss Playin 29
AH
  Ah! what avails it, that, from slav'ry far, ... O 15 London   117
  Blest age! but ah! how diff'rent from our own! . . . O 22 London   253
  Ah! let not Censure term our Fate our Choice, . . . O 53 Pro Drury-Lane 51
  Ah! never to return! . . . . . O 80 Feast St Simon 48
  Ah! think not, in the dang'rous hour, ... O 121 To Miss Playin   7
  Ah! think not, in the dang'rous Bower, ... O 121 To Miss Playin V 7
  Ah! how shall envy sooth her pain? . . . . O 122 Stella Mourn.   12
  Ah, little needs the Minstrel's pow'r . . . . O 191 Tr. Medea I   17
  Ah! cease, Irene, cease those flowing Sorrows, . . . O 276 Irene   3
  Ah! let me rather seek the Convent's Cell; . . . O 292 Irene   93
  And ah! behold the shriveling blossoms die, . . . Y   4 On a Daffodill 23
  But, ah! before arise that hapless day . . . . Y 18 Tr. Iliad Bk 6 24
  "Ah! let not tears down that fair count'nance rowl, . . Y 21 Tr. Iliad Bk 6 113
AID
  Then shall thy friend, nor thou refuse his aid, . . . O 23 London   260
  All aid the farce, and all thy mirth maintain, . . . O 33 Vanity Wishes 67
  Implore his aid, in his decisions rest, ... O 48 Vanity Wishes 355
  And Virtue call'd Oblivion to her Aid. . . . . O 52 Pro Drury-Lane 28
  Shall aid our Happiness above. . . . . . O 100 Ode Friendship 28
  Shall aid y<our>r Happiness above. . . . . O 100 Ode Friendship V 28
  Thus early wise, th' endanger'd realm to aid, . . . O 117 Epitaph Hanmer   9
  In greater scenes each other aid; . . . . . O 121 To Miss Playin 28
  When fainting nature call'd for aid, ... O 201 Death Dr Levet 13
  His useful aid was ever nigh . . . . . . O 201 Death Dr Levet V 18
  Did unresisted Lightning aid their Cannon, . . . O 251 Irene   54
  Call to your Aid your Courage, and your Wisdom; . . . O 252 Irene   85

```
AID            (CONTINUED)                                    PAGE    TITLE          LINE
    Let fierce resentment aid... . . . . . . . . . .       Y 133 Irene             V   9
        your feeble fainting virtue . . . . . . . .
    Let fierce resentment aid your feeble. . . . . .       Y 133 Irene             V   9
        fainting virtue
    With counterfeited Fears the Aid of Man; . . . . .     O 266 Irene                28
    His groaning Country claims Leontius' Aid; . . . . .   O 270 Irene                17
    Call to your Aid with boundless Promises . . . . .     O 287 Irene                10
    Should Heav'n yet unappeas'd refuse its Aid, . . . .   O 301 Irene                97
AIDED
    And aided wine with dulcet-streaming sound. . . . . .  O 192 Tr. Medea II          8
AIDS
    Grief aids disease, remember'd folly stings, . . .     O  35 Vanity Wishes       119
    The Lover's Int'rest aids the Patriot's Claim. . . .   O 305 Irene                46
AIM
    They pleas'd their Age, and did not aim to mend. . .   O  52 Pro Drury-Lane       22
    I thought, forgive my Fair, the noblest Aim, . . .     O 278 Irene                61
AIMS
    Insidious Malice aims her Darts in vain; . . . . . .   O 322 Irene                 2
AINIGMA
    Eis to tes Elisses peri ton Oneiron Ainigma . . . . . O 103 Eis Elisses           T
AIR
    To breathe in distant fields a purer air, . . . . .   O   9 London                6
    Their air, their dress, their policticks import; . .  O  15 London              110
    I drew the breath of life in English air; . . . .     O  15 London              118
    He gropes his breeches with a monarch's air. . . . .  O  17 London              151
    With brisker air the silken courtiers gaze, . . . .   O  17 London              164
    And hang aloft suspended in the air. . . . . . .      O  76 Tr Add. Battle        7
    Nor sprightly Folly wantons in his Air, . . . . .     O 255 Irene                15
    Dissolve in Air, and vanish into Nothing. . . . . .   O 265 Irene                 8
    Thy awful air, thy dignity of virtue. . . . . .       Y 134 Irene             V  34
    horrid joy--his air now fearful now resolv'd. . . .   Y 145 Irene             V  82
    That Air resistless and enchanting Blush, . . . . .   O 277 Irene                27
    Dispers'd in Air or mingled with the Dust. . . . . .  O 298 Irene                24
    His Air disorder'd, and his Gait unequal, . . . . .   O 311 Irene                 3
    horrid joy--gloomy resolution--his air now fearful now Y 187 Irene             V   7
        resolv'd.
    Resumes th' imperious Air of haughty Virtue. . . .    O 314 Irene                15
    That bears the Fate of Empires in her Air, . . . .    O 317 Irene                 2
    Her piercing Cries yet fill the loaded Air, . . . .   O 329 Irene                 8
    Nor feel the inclemencies of wintry air; . . . . .    Y   3 On a Daffodill        6
    And scarce the lab'ring air sustains the throng . .   Y  25 Tr Add. Battle       95
    In his fell claws, then into th' air he springs. . .  Y  26 Tr Add. Battle      126
    Its useless force the weapon spends in air. . . . . . Y  26 Tr Add. Battle      135
AIRS
    Tea, scandal, ivory teeth, and languid airs; . . .    O  84 Epi Dist Moth.       19
AIRY
    Shuns fancied ills, or chases airy good; . . . . . .  O  31 Vanity Wishes        10
    Shun the Mountain's airy Brow, . . . . . . . . .      O 145 Tr Boeth. II.4        7
    The airy Flights of unexperienced Virtue . . . . .    O 347 Irene             V  20
    Can brave Leontius call for airy Wonders, . . . . .   O 250 Irene                42
    Important Hazard! What's that airy Bubble . . . . .   O 260 Irene               137
    How the new Monarch, swell'd with airy Rule, . . .    O 306 Irene                 1
AKING
    Aghast you start, and scarce with aking sight . . .   O  18 London              186
ALARM
    Must no dislike alarm, no wishes rise, . . . . . .    O  47 Vanity Wishes       347
    Enquirer cease alarm, no wishes rise, . . . . . . .   Y 108 Vanity Wishes     V 347
    In Sophia's Temple!--What Alarm!--Proceed. . . . . .  O 258 Irene                97
ALARMS
    The rustling brake alarms, and quiv'ring shade, . .   O  32 Vanity Wishes        42
    Tir'd with vain joys, and false alarms, . . . . . .   O 124 Winter's Walk        17
    And when blest Peace has silenc'd War's Alarms, . .   O 247 Irene Epilogue       23
    That Vessel, if observ'd, alarms the Court, . . . .   O 258 Irene                83
    Each lin'gring Hour alarms me for Aspasia. . . . . .  O 270 Irene                20
ALAS
    No sounds alas would touch th' impervious ear, . . .  O  43 Vanity Wishes       269
    Alas! 'tis hard for beauty to be just. . . . . . .    O  81 Lady Birthday        12
    Yet hear, alas! this mournful truth, . . . . . .      O 159 Par Hermit III        9
    --How chang'd alas!--Now ghastly Desolation . . . .   O 251 Irene                66
        Alas! delusive Dream! . . . . . . .              O 267 Irene                45
    Freedom and Love? Alas! I'm all Confusion, . . . .    O 295 Irene                11
    How soon, alas! will Int'rest, Fear, or Envy, . . .   O 301 Irene                82
    Alas! they come, commanded by the Sultan, . . . .     O 325 Irene                 8
    'Tis ours, alas! to punish, not to judge, . . . . .   O 326 Irene                33
    So late admir'd and prais'd, alas! in vain! . . . .   Y   4 On a Daffodill       24
ALASS
    Alass, dear Friend, the fleeting years . . . . . .    O  68 Hor.II Ode 14         1
    I want alass thy steadiness of Soul . . . . .        O 366 Irene             V  29
    But now alass! the fatall hour drew nigh . . . . .    Y  24 Tr Add. Battle       62
ALBANIAN
        yet the fierce Albanian lyon . . . . . . . . .   Y 130 Irene             V  13-
ALCOVE
    But shun, rash youth, the gay alcove, . . . . . . .   O 121 To Miss Playin        9
ALE
    With weekly libels and septennial ale, . . . . . .    O  34 Vanity Wishes        97
ALETHEIE
    Eiden Aletheie proen chairoysa graphonta . . . . . .  O 108 Eis Birchion         1
ALFRED'S
    A single jail, in Alfred's golden reign, . . . . . .  O  22 London              248
```

	PAGE	TITLE		LINE
ALIKE				
Distrest alike, the statesman and the wit,	O 59	Pro Good Nat'd		9
Inflames alike with raging fires.	O 99	Ode Friendship		8
Torments alike with equal Fire.	O 99	Ode Friendship	V	8
Alike o'er all his lightnings fly;	O 100	Ode Friendship		10
And Love and Hate alike implore	O 122	Stella Mourn.		15
Wild hope, vain fear, alike remov'd,	O 125	An Ode		26
What soon is perfect, soon alike is past;	O 142	In Baretti Bk.		9
Alike my Death or thine is gain to thee,	O 319	Irene		32
Alike must fall the poet and his theme.	Y 4	On a Daffodill		28
Shall sink alike into the gloomy grave.	Y 21	Tr. Iliad Bk 6		120
ALIVE				
I scorn the multitude, alive and dead.	O 141	Tr Rambler 208		4
Oft in Danger yet alive	O 178	Thrale 35 Year		1
ALL				
But all whom hunger spares, with age decay:	O 9	London		12
All Marlb'rough hoarded, or all Villiers spent,	O 14	London		86
All Marlb'rough hoarded, or all Villiers spent,	O 14	London		86
All that at home no more can beg or steal,	O 15	London		107
All sciences a fasting Monsieur knows,	O 15	London		115
Watch the weak hour, and ransack all the heart;	O 17	London		155
All crimes are safe, but hated poverty.	O 17	London		159
Of all the griefs that harrass the distress'd,	O 17	London		166
But here more slow, where all are slaves to gold,	O 18	London		178
And leave your little All to flames a prey;	O 18	London		189
While all neglect, and most insult your woes.	O 19	London		193
Now bless'd with all the baubles of the great,	O 19	London		206
On all thy hours security shall smile,	O 20	London		222
And all the busy scenes of crouded life;	Y 92	Vanity Wishes	V 4
All aid the farce, and all thy mirth maintain,	O 33	Vanity Wishes		67
All aid the farce, and all thy mirth maintain,	O 33	Vanity Wishes		67
All fird with hope, and panting to be great;	Y 95	Vanity Wishes	V 74
Through all his veins the fever of renown	O 36	Vanity Wishes		137
"And all be mine beneath the polar sky."	O 40	Vanity Wishes		204
"And all is mine beneath the polar sky."	O 40	Vanity Wishes	V 204
All times their scenes of pompous woes afford,	O 41	Vanity Wishes		223
And all the sons of ravage croud the war;	O 43	Vanity Wishes		250
With all the sons of ravage croud the war;	O 43	Vanity Wishes	V 250
And shuts up all the passages of joy:	O 43	Vanity Wishes		260
Tost in one common storm with all the great;	O 59	Pro Good Nat'd		8
Must hear all taunts, and hear without reply.	O 59	Pro Good Nat'd		14
For that blest year when all that vote may rail;	O 60	Pro Good Nat'd		18
Till that glad night when all that hate may hiss.	O 60	Pro Good Nat'd		20
The man whom fate has laid, where all must lye.	O 61	Pro Word Wise		6
By all, like him, must praise and blame be found;	O 62	Pro Word Wise		19
Two tender kids, the hopes of all the flock.	O 64	Virgil Past.I		20
To whom all nations tribute bring	O 68	Hor. II Ode IX		20
We all must view the Stygian flood	O 69	Hor.II Ode 14		17
That post, and all the rest, shall be my care;	O 74	Tr. Iliad Bk 6		3
And one base action sully all my fame,	O 74	Tr. Iliad Bk 6		6
Parent of ills! and source of all our woe!	O 77	Festina Lente		10
Thro' all the spacious ball;	O 79	Feast St Simon		27
All pains, all cares, may favouring heav'n remove,	O 81	Lady Birthday		5
All pains, all cares, may favouring heav'n remove,	O 81	Lady Birthday		5
All but the sweet solicitudes of love!	O 81	Lady Birthday		6
This thought once form'd, all counsel comes too late,	O 82	Young Author		19
Where sable night in all her horrour reigns;	O 83	Epi Dist Moth.		11
And pois'nous vapours, black'ning all the sky,	O 84	Epi Dist Moth.		33
Inflicting all those ills which once they knew;	O 84	Epi Dist Moth.		37
Their foul deformities by all descry'd,	O 84	Epi Dist Moth.		40
So shall you guiltless reign, and all mankind adore.	O 84	Epi Dist Moth.		47
To all the lower world deny'd;	O 99	Ode Friendship		4
Alike o'er all his lightnings fly;	O 100	Ode Friendship		10
Are all transporting, all divine.	O 100	Ode Friendship		24
Are all transporting, all divine.	O 100	Ode Friendship		24
Gives all the harmony of life;	O 121	To Miss Playin		32
In all the pomp of heav'n;	O 126	To Lyce, Lady		4
Engross not all the beams on high,	O 126	To Lyce, Lady		5
And all the pens of Cupid's wing	O 127	To Lyce, Lady		19
And all her bards express,	O 127	To Lyce, Lady		22
But now 'tis hatred all.----	O 131	Tr. Rambler 45		3
All is my own, my honour and my shame.	O 132	Tr. Rambler 46		2
All useless science is an empty beast.	O 133	Tr. Rambler 83		1
And own all glories of the mine outdone,	O 141	Tr Rambler 199		6
Its charms are fled and all its powers destroyed.	O 142	In Baretti Bk.		8
Not all the gifts of Fate combin'd	O 144	Tr Boeth. II.2		7
But swallowing all the mighty Store,	O 144	Tr Boeth. II.2		9
All the World afraid but thee,	O 145	Tr Boeth. II.4		20
Must bid his Passions all obey;	O 146	Tr Boeth III.5		2
All Men throughout the peopled Earth	O 146	Tr Boeth III.6		1
All from one Source derive their Birth	O 146	Tr Boeth III.6		3
All her Charms to thee belong;	O 150	Tr Boet III.12		42
Open to all, true only to thyself,	O 176	Tr Metastas II		6
And all who wisely wish to wive,	O 178	Thrale 35 Year	V 17
All is strange, yet nothing new;	O 179	Ridicul Warton		2
Endless Labour all along,	O 179	Ridicul Warton		3
Liquid fragrance all the way:	O 185	Anacreon Ode 9		4
"Grac'd with all that charms the heart,	O 185	Anacreon Ode 9		9
"This is all;--be quick and go,	O 186	Anacreon Ode 9		41
"More than all thou canst not know;	O 186	Anacreon Ode 9		42
And Murder, all blood-bolter'd, schemes the wound.	O 192	Tr. Medea II		16

Great Sir John, are all your own.	O 196	Song Congratu.	4
All the Names that banish Care, ...	O 196	Song Congratu. V	10
All that prey on vice and folly	O 196	Song Congratu.	13
And all that prey in vice or folly	O 196	Song Congratu. V	13
All else is empty Sound, and idle Show.	O 246	Irene Prologue	14
Shou'd partial Cat-calls all his Hopes confound,	O 246	Irene Prologue	23
But how the Devil should he please us all!	O 247	Irene Epilogue	8
My Pride's to have that little all my own.	O 247	Irene Epilogue	10
These all are Trifles, to what we can give. . . .	O 247	Irene Epilogue	20
And all the Maladies of sinking States.	O 250	Irene	39
That froze our Veins, and wither'd all our Powers.	O 251	Irene	57
All Thought on her is Madness:	O 252	Irene	79
With all the Diffidence of long Experience, ...	O 254	Irene	130
Now summon all thy Soul, illustrious Christian! . . .	O 254	Irene	1
Unhappy Lot of all that shine in Courts;	O 256	Irene	50
Sure all unite to hold her League of Rule	O 257	Irene	62
A blooming monarch--in all the bloom of honour...	Y 122	Irene V	67
Fills all th' astonish'd Empire with Confusion, . . .	O 257	Irene	77
Gain'd all his Heart; at length his eager Love . .	O 259	Irene	123
Aspasia's thine, and all thy Life is Rapture--	O 260	Irene	142
Death rises to my View, with all his Terrors;	O 265	Irene	12
Not all like thee can brave the Shocks of Fate, . . .	O 266	Irene	34
And all Aspasia but her Beauty's Man.	O 266	Irene	37
Toils all its languages to flatter me.	Y 136	Irene V	29
Blasts all the Beauties of his new Creation, ...	O 269	Irene	7
In all the sweet Oblivion of Delight, ...	O 269	Irene	13
In all the sweet forgetfulness of Love	O 367	Irene V	26
In all the sweet forgetfulness of Love	Y 138	Irene V	13
In all the Popperies of meeting Lovers;	O 269	Irene	14
All this we know already from Abdalla.	O 270	Irene	6
All there is Hope, and Gaiety, and Courage, ...	O 271	Irene	26
I share, by secret Instinct, all his Joys, ...	O 272	Irene	10
Were all our Favours lavish'd on a Villain?	O 272	Irene	12
Conceal'd from all but him! All! all conspire	O 273	Irene	20
Conceal'd from all but him! All! all conspire	O 273	Irene	20
Conceal'd from all but him! All! all conspire	O 273	Irene	20
With all the allurements of persuasive	Y 142	Irene V	38
wealth--gold			
And all the giddy rage of desperation	Y 142	Irene V	39
With all the Speed of Terror and of Guilt.	O 275	Irene	86
With all the graceful Pride of Greatness heighten'd, . .	O 276	Irene	8
Why all this Glare of splendid Eloquence, ...	O 276	Irene	11
Vain Raptures all--For your inferiour Natures	O 276	Irene	15
Cast off all idle terrours of hereafter	Y 146	Irene V	19
Whence all those Hopes and Fears Despair and	O 355	Irene V	18
Rapture			
Whence all the Bliss and Agonies of Love?	O 277	Irene	42
Whence all the pleasures, and the pains of love. . . .	Y 148	Irene V	42
Exhausted all her nobler Gifts on you;	O 278	Irene	54
That all her Faculties receive his Chains?	O 281	Irene	39
That loses all because she hazards nothing:	O 281	Irene	45
With all the Heroe's dull Security, ...	O 283	Irene	9
With all the Licence of Authority, ...	O 283	Irene	16
This Night with all her conscious Stars be witness, . .	O 284	Irene	44
I displaid--before her all the gay luscious scene... . .	Y 158	Irene V	8
And all the proud magnificence of empire	Y 158	Irene V	9
Sooth her with all the Pleasures of Command, ...	O 287	Irene	17
Treat her With all the confidence of artless love . . .	Y 159	Irene V	17
Than all the Wisdom of the grave Divan.	O 287	Irene	8
And all the sweet varieties of nature	Y 165	Irene V	79
Thy dazzled Soul with all its boasted Greatness, . . .	O 292	Irene	99
In easy State presides o'er all their Motions, ...	O 293	Irene	122
Freedom and Love? Alas! I'm all Confusion, ...	O 295	Irene	11
But all give way to Rapture and Demetrius.	O 295	Irene	20
Fill all thy ardent Breast with Greece and Virtue, . . .•. .	O 298	Irene	8
All fading toys, and transitory glories	Y 177	Irene V	110
All the Western kingdoms	Y 177	Irene V	115
Guide all thy Steps, calm ev'ry stormy Thought, . . .	O 303	Irene	21
And granted all his wishes	Y 179	Irene V	31
All ye, whose Blood tyrannick Rage effus'd, ...	O 306	Irene	53
O Happiness! sure thou art all Aspasia's.	O 310	Irene	14
Reserv'd to be the Pangs of tedious Death.	O 312	Irene	25
Doom'd me to die with all the Turkish Captains. . . .	O 313	Irene	16
See how the Moon through all th' unclouded Sky . . .	O 313	Irene	1
And all within is Darkness and Confusion;	O 315	Irene	32
Then all is past he cried--and darted from us; . . .	O 317	Irene	32
Abdalla fails, now Fortune all is mine.	O 319	Irene	1
And bless'd with all the joy that Guilt	O 365	Irene V	11
allows			
Fill all the starry Lamps with double Blaze;	O 322	Irene	8
Fill all the Starry Lamps with Fav'ring Sky	O 364	Irene V	27
<Radiance>.			
Th' applauding Sky shall pour forth all its Beams . . .	O 322	Irene	9
And all the terrors of the dreadful main	Y 201	Irene V	10C
Thy Look, thy Speech, thy Action, all is Wildness-- . .	O 323	Irene	5
All is not lost, Abdalla, see the Queen, ...	O 326	Irene	1
The Plot all Cali's, the Detection thine.	O 329	Irene	4
Dwell on my Ear, and sadden all my Soul;	O 329	Irene	9
And all Irene now is breathless Clay.	O 330	Irene	4
Remorse and Anguish seize on all my Breast;	O 333	Irene	45

```
ALL        (CONTINUED)                              PAGE   TITLE            LINE
     And all the withering woods confess their woe   . . . .   Y   6  Virgil Daphnis        4
     O'er all the warbling founts a cooling shade.   . . . . .  Y   7  Virgil Daphnis       27
     That all the fair their favours sold;   . . . . .      Y  11  Tr Hor Epode 9       20
     Pledge of their love and source of all their joy  . . .   Y  18  Tr. Iliad Bk 6       10
     All stemm'd in one sad day the Stygian tyde.   . . . .    Y  18  Tr. Iliad Bk 6       35
     A father, brother, husband, all in thee.   . . . . . .    Y  19  Tr. Iliad Bk 6       45
     Within the town assemble all thy powers   . . . . .      Y  19  Tr. Iliad Bk 6       50
     Guarded from all but winged enemies   . . . . . .        Y  23  Tr Add. Battle       25
     When all conspiring leave Maeon's lake   . . . .         Y  24  Tr Add. Battle       66
     All her life was naught but guilt,   . . . . . . .       Y 300  Extemp. Elegy        11
     Mock'd our impatient steps, for all was fairy ground.  . Y 310  Parody of Pope        4
ALL-CONSCIOUS
     So fix'd the Justice of all-conscious Heav'n.   . . . .   O 335  Irene                11
ALL-PITYING
     O, hear my Pray'rs! accept, all-pitying Heaven,   . . .   O 328  Irene                52
ALL-SUBDUING
     This all-subduing hand, this gen'ral terror   . . . . .   Y 136  Irene          V    32
ALLA
     Alla tod eis Thnetous Kupris epempseu onar   . . . . .    O 103  Eis Elisses           4
ALLIANCE
     For what are pompous Titles, proud Alliance,   . . . .    O 267  Irene                 8
ALLMIGHTY
     "Immortal Gods! and thou allmighty Jove   . . . . . .     Y  20  Tr. Iliad Bk 6       99
ALLON
     Sou pote grapsomenon Birchion allon echois.   . . . . .   O 108  Eis Birchion          4
ALLOTS
     Whatever course of Life great Jove allots,   . . . . .    O  77  Festina Lente         1
ALLOW
     And him who cannot hurt, allow to please;   . . . . .     O  62  Pro Word Wise        12
     Allow no Pause for Art or for Contrivance;   . . . . .    O 275  Irene                88
ALLOW'D
     Where Woman's not allow'd to speak her Mind;   . . . .    O 247  Irene Epilogue       12
ALLOWS
     And bless'd with all the joy that Guilt   . . . . . .     O 365  Irene          V    11
           allows
ALLUR'D
     With pleasing sound allur'd the rural throng.   . . . .   Y   6  Virgil Daphnis        8
ALLUREMENTS
     With all the allurements of persuasive   . . . . . . .    Y 142  Irene          V    38
           wealth--gold
ALLURING
     Alluring Grandeur courts her to his Arms,   . . . . .     O 261  Irene                15
     I drew to my party with (alluring) promises artfull  . .  Y 158  Irene          V    11
ALLY'D
     By kings protected, and to kings ally'd?   . . . . . .    O  36  Vanity Wishes       132
ALMIGHTY'S
     And mortals trace th' Almighty's path in v<ain>   . . .   Y 217  Irene          V    14
ALOFT
     While Crowds aloft the laureat Bust behold,   . . . . .   O  58  Prologue Comus       23
     While Crowds aloft the laureat Bust behold,   . . . . .   O  58  Prologue Comus  V    23
     And hang aloft suspended in the air.   . . . . . .       O  76  Tr Add. Battle        7
     Bear him aloft above the wond'ring Clouds,   . . . . .    O 274  Irene                62
     Then flies aloft; th' astonish'd warriours feel   . . .   Y  26  Tr Add. Battle      132
ALONE
     His smile alone security bestows:   . . . . . . .        O  34  Vanity Wishes       104
     To you alone this happy state remains.   . . . . . .     O  64  Virgil Past.I        16
     Alone the Cypress shall attend.   . . . . . . .          O  69  Hor.II Ode 14        24
     'tis thine alone to calm the pious breast   . . . . .     O 130  Tr. Rambler 7         5
     On names now found alone on books and tombs.   . . . .    O 134  Tr. Rambler 93        2
     Love alone to Love is Law:   . . . . . .                 O 150  Tr Boet III.12       48
     For us alone, they Honour's Paths pursue:   . . . . .     O 247  Irene Epilogue       16
     Alone, with am'rous Haste to seek his Love.   . . . . .   O 262  Irene                29
     Learn, that the present Hour alone is Man's.   . . . .    O 283  Irene                33
     Derives its Value from its Use alone;   . . . . .        O 290  Irene                29
     'Tis Love combin'd with Guilt alone, that melts   . . .   O 303  Irene                16
     This Night alone is ours--Our mighty Foe,   . . . . .     O 303  Irene                25
     The Doom of Guilt alone, nor dare to seize   . . . . .    O 316  Irene                14
     Henceforth shall live for me; for me alone   . . . . .    O 317  Irene                 3
     Alone preserv'd the town from Grecian fire.   . . . . .   Y  18  Tr. Iliad Bk 6       14
     My mother who alone escap'd the grave   . . . . .        Y  19  Tr. Iliad Bk 6       38
     His arm alone rais'd bulwarks of the dead.   . . . . .    Y  25  Tr Add. Battle      121
ALONG
     Along the marble floor shall flow.   . . . . . . .       O  69  Hor.II Ode 14        28
     Where Riv'lets gently purl along   . . . . . .           O  72  Hor. Epode II        31
     I walk'd along the Strand,   . . . . . . .               O 158  Par. Hermit II  V     2
     Moor and Christian, roll along.   . . . . . . .          O 159  Tr. Rio Verde         4
     Endless Labour all along,   . . . . . . . .              O 179  Ridicul Warton        3
     Extends its Lines along the sandy Beach,   . . . . .      O 304  Irene                 4
     I feel new Spirit shoot along my Nerves,   . . . . .      O 306  Irene                49
     And Death exulting stalk'd along the land.   . . . . .    Y  23  Tr Add. Battle       53
ALPHIUS
     Thus did the Us'rer Alphius praise,   . . . . . . .       O  73  Hor. Epode II        73
ALREADY
     Or boasts a happier Soil, already thine?   . . . . .      O 265  Irene                36
     Or boasts a happier glebe, is Yours already,   . . . .    O 366  Irene          V    13
     All this we know already from Abdalla.   . . . . .       O 270  Irene                 6
     Already shakes his bloody Sabre o'er thee.   . . . . .    O 327  Irene                10
     Already brandishes his Sabre o'er You   . . . . . .       O 368  Irene          V    18
ALTAR
     Oft on his altar shall my firstlings lie,   . . . . .     O  64  Virgil Past.I         9
```

ALTAR (CONTINUED)
PAGE   TITLE   LINE
   On cruel Pluto's Altar dye, ... O 69 Hor.II Ode 14   6
ALTARS
   Usurp our Temples, and profane our Altars. . . . . O 251 Irene   69
   Implor'd the Eternal Pow'r, at Sophia's altars . . . . Y 163 Irene   V 49
   Here have I rais'd four sacred altars, two . . . . . Y   7 Virgil Daphnis   43
ALTERNATE
   Alternate rest and labour long endure. . . . . . O 131 Tr. Rambler 33   1
   May ye th' alternate blessings share . . . . . . O 189 Epilogue   V 5
   My Bosom harrass'd with alternate Passions, ... O 299 Irene   54
ALWAYS
   And Slaves, the Maxim tells, are always Foes. . . . O 46 Vanity Wishes V330B
   Vice always found a sympathetick Friend; . . . . . O 52 Pro Drury-Lane   21
   Clouds do not always veil the skies, ... O 67 Hor. II Ode IX   1
   Nor do the billows always rise, ... O 67 Hor. II Ode IX   3
   Do the chain'd waters always freeze; . . . . . . O 67 Hor. II Ode IX   6
   Not always furious Boreas roars, ... O 67 Hor. II Ode IX   7
   Disaster always waits an early wit. . . . . . . O 135 Tr Rambler 111   1
   Always young and always pretty, ... O 175 Tr Easy Phrase   2
   Always young and always pretty, ... O 175 Tr Easy Phrase   2
   Always pretty, always young, ... O 175 Tr Easy Phrase   3
   Always pretty, always young, ... O 175 Tr Easy Phrase   3
   Always young and always pretty; . . . . O 175 Tr Easy Phrase   5
   Always young and always pretty; . . . . O 175 Tr Easy Phrase   5
   Should she, for Proselytes are always zealous, ... O 262 Irene   24
   Not always do the fairest Flow'rs diffuse . . . . . O 277 Irene   31
AM
   I am Cassander, come down from the Sky, ... O 173 Tr Fr Pantomim   1
   That I am Cassander come down from the Sky. . . . . O 173 Tr Fr Pantomim   3
   I am not yet a Queen, or an Apostate. . . . . . . O 289 Irene   22
   When I am gone remember, O! remember, ... O 294 Irene   7
   How am I chang'd! How lately did Irene . . . . . O 322 Irene   13
AM'ROUS
   And chang'd th' endearing Smile and am'rous Whisper . . O 259 Irene   111
   Alone, with am'rous Haste to seek his Love. . . . . O 262 Irene   29
   My tongue with am'rous eloquence displaid . . . . . Y 158 Irene   V 7
   No longer lost in am'rous Solitude, ... O 303 Irene   26
   Shall dart their am'rous Glances at the Fair, ... O 304 Irene   35
AMARILLIS'
   And the wood rings with Amarillis' name. . . . . . O 64 Virgil Past.I   6
AMAZ'D
   I stand amaz'd, and ask, if yet I clasp thee. . . . O 296 Irene   37
   Breathless, amaz'd, and on the guarded Beach . . . . O 335 Irene   8
AMAZEMENT
   Thus meaner Spirits with Amazement mark . . . . . O 293 Irene   117
   Thus meaner Spirits with amazement see . . . . . O 369 Irene   V 11
   Amazement seiz'd us, and the hoary Bassa . . . . . O 317 Irene   36
   O name not Death! Distraction and Amazement, ... O 328 Irene   31
AMAZING
   Oerthrow the obelisks amazing height . . . . . . Y 177 Irene   V 108
AMAZON
   Why then did not this warlike Amazon . . . . . . O 290 Irene   40
AMBIGUOUS
   Ambiguous emblem of uncertain fate! . . . . . O 95 Sprig of Myrtl   2
   Ambiguous emblem of my future fate! . . . . . . O 95 Sprig of Myrtl V 2
   There in soft Hints in ambiguous Phrase, ... O 254 Irene   129
AMBITION
   Fear and Ambition, urge her to Compliance; . . . . O 261 Irene   13
   And kind Ambition points the Way to Greatness. . . . O 280 Irene   14
   Yet can Ambition in Abdalla's Breast . . . . . O 280 Irene   25
   Ambition is the Stamp impress'd by Heav'n . . . . . O 293 Irene   111
   For I know ambition seduc'd her . . . . Y 186 Irene   V 3
   Ambition only gave her to my Arms, ... O 310 Irene   7
   Ambition was her Crime, but meaner Folly . . . . . O 310 Irene   9
   Disease shall chase the Phantoms of Ambition, ... O 322 Irene   60
   Or Flights of Pow'r, or Projects of Ambition. . . . O 327 Irene   21
AMBITION'S
   Will he not melt before Ambition's Fire? . . . . . O 255 Irene   23
   Must then Ambition's Votaries infringe . . . . . O 280 Irene   15
   Untouch'd by fierce Ambition's raging Fires. . . . . O 293 Irene   110
AMBITIOUS
   Ambitious catches at his tow'ring Name: . . . . . O 57 Prologue Comus   20
   Ambitious Fury fir'd the Grecian King: . . . . . O 97 Hickman Spinet   10
   Ambitious only now to please the Fair, ... O 97 Hickman Spinet   18
   This fir'd the youthful King's ambitious Breast, . . . O 256 Irene   47
   Ambitious to prevent the fatal summons . . . . Y 136 Irene   V 27A
   No more I boast th' ambitious Name of Friend, ... O 289 Irene   10
   Ambitious Cali dreads the Statesman's Arts, ... O 300 Irene   74
AMBROSIAL
   And scents ambrosial breathe in every gale: . . . . O 84 Epi Dist Moth.   17
AMBUSH
   Their ambush here relentless ruffians lay, ... O 9 London   15
   The secret ambush of a specious pray'r. . . . . . O 48 Vanity Wishes   354
   Beset the treacherous Way with fatal Ambush; . . . . O 300 Irene   72
AMBUSH'D
   Shall spring to seize thee like an ambush'd foe. . . . O 152 The Ant   16
AMIABLE
   Thus bright in Tears, thus amiable in Ruin, ... O 276 Irene   7
AMID
   Amid the storms of war, with curious eyes . . . . . O 130 Tr. Rambler 8   1

12

```
                                                      PAGE   TITLE           LINE
'MIDST
     How should I joy, 'midst the fierce Shock of Nations,    .   O 309 Irene           40
AMIDST
     Amidst the gen'ral massacre of gold;  . . . . . .   Y  92 Vanity Wishes    V  22
     Amidst the toils of this returning year, . . . . .   O  59 Pro Good Nat'd   V  4A
     Amidst the drousy charms of dull delight,  . . . .   O 152 The Ant              13
     Where amidst the roarings of the Northern  . . . .   Y 121 Irene            V  56
       main
     Swoln with Success, secure amidst his native Rocks   .   O 352 Irene          V  28
     And though built on feeble columns--Its lofty turrets   .   Y 131 Irene       V  35
       blaze amidst
     Amidst the Tortures of the burning Steel,  . . . .   O 272 Irene               15
     Amidst the Camp to howl his Life away. . . . . .   O 273 Irene               37
     Amidst the Blaze of Jewels and of Gold,  . . . . .   O 276 Irene                9
     Now lost amidst the gloom of disappointment . . . .   Y 148 Irene            V 43B
     Hast thou grown old amidst the Croud of Courts,  . . .   O 281 Irene             32
     Amidst the Splendor of encircling Beauty,  . . . .   O 288 Irene                1
     Amidst the Glare of Courts, the Shouts of Armies,  . . .   O 293 Irene           131
     Amidst his gloomy Guards and fiery Vassals . . . .   O 372 Irene            V  19
     O'erwhelm'd and lost amidst the publick Ruins  . . .   O 302 Irene              107
     Amidst her kind Solicitudes for me!  . . . . . .   O 332 Irene               21
AMIENS
     A Amiens  . . . . . . . . . . . .   O 172 French Distich       7
AMITY
     Bear lives in amity with bear.  . . . . . . . .   O 138 Tr Rambler 160      2
AMONG
     Among the quivering branches sighs;  . . . . . .   O  66 Hor I Ode xxii     18
     Among the quivering Branches sighs,  . . . . . .   O  67 To A. Fuscus        18
     Among the Saints above. . . . . . . . . . .   O  79 Feast St Simon      24
     descend in a proverb among thy enemies . . . . .   Y 113 Irene            V  21
     Where now thou shin'st among thy Fellow-saints,  . . .   O 253 Irene            100
     What Passions reign among thy Crew, Leontius?  . . .   O 270 Irene               21
     But sink among thy Slaves without a Murmur.  . . . .   O 289 Irene               11
     Mix in the War, and shine among the Heroes?  . . . .   O 290 Irene               41
     Among their flocks the blooming heroes fell  . . . .   Y  18 Tr. Iliad Bk 6     36
     That reign'st supreme among the pow'rs above,  . . .   Y  20 Tr. Iliad Bk 6    100
AMONGST
     While Love, unknown amongst the blest,  . . . . .   O  99 Ode Friendship   V   5
AMOROUS
     Here at your ease you sing your amorous flame, . . .   O  64 Virgil Past.I        5
AMPLE
     The Man who pants for ample Sway  . . . . . . .   O 146 Tr Boeth III.5       1
AMURATH
     Great Amurath, at my Request, forsook  . . . . .   O 256 Irene               43
     Than Amurath--  . . . . . . . . . . .   O 264 Irene               20
          Still full of Amurath!  . . . . . . .   O 264 Irene               20
     Than Amurath, accustom'd to Command,  . . . . . .   O 264 Irene               21
AMURATH'S
     Calmly he heard, till Amurath's Resumption  . . . .   O 270 Irene               10
AMUSEMENT
     Some vain Amusement of a vacant Soul!  . . . . . .   O 280 Irene                8
AN
          52                                                OMITTED WORD
ANACREON
     Anacreon, Ode IX . . . . . . . . . .   O 185 Anacreon Ode 9       T
     "Now Anacreon rules my flight:  . . . . . . .   O 185 Anacreon Ode 9      14
ANACREON'S
     "Soft Anacreon's vows I bear,  . . . . . . .   O 185 Anacreon Ode 9       7
     "As it leaves Anacreon's lip,  . . . . . . .   O 185 Anacreon Ode 9      32
ANCESTORS
     Nought from my birth or ancestors I claim;  . . . .   O 132 Tr. Rambler 46      1
ANCIENT
     Who keeps the rigid rules of ancient honour;  . . .   O 176 Tr Metastas II      2
     That keeps the rigid rules of ancient honour;  . . .   O 176 Tr Metastas II  V   2
     The rites deriv'd from ancient days  . . . . .   O 190 Tr. Medea I          1
     Her ancient Empire o'er the yielding Heart;  . . . .   O 302 Irene              121
     Call forth her ancient Heroes to the Field,  . . . .   O 309 Irene               39
     Call forth her ancient Scipios to the field  . . . .   Y 185 Irene            V  39
     In pompous numbers ancient heroes rise;  . . . . .   Y  22 Tr Add. Battle       8
AND
          1524                                               OMITTED WORD
&
     Upon the feast of St Simon & St Jude  . . . . .   O  78 Feast St Simon      T
     I discover by this state & retinue . . . . . .   Y 160 Irene            V   8
     Vain pride & wealth . . . . . . . . .   Y 177 Irene            V 110
     she courted fate & scornd a crown  . . . . . .   Y 191 Irene            V  16
ANDROMACHE
     Hector and Andromache;  . . . . . .   O  74 Tr.Iliad Bk 6       T
     He met Andromache his beauteous wife  . . . . .   Y  18 Tr. Iliad Bk 6      5
     Mournfull Andromache the silence broke,  . . . .   Y  18 Tr. Iliad Bk 6     17
     Andromache looks back with weeping eyes,  . . . .   Y  21 Tr. Iliad Bk 6    127
ANEW
     And live her guiltless Moments o'er anew!  . . . .   O 323 Irene               16
ANGEL
     And what protecting angel led thee hither  . . . .   Y 170 Irene            V  33
     Thou kind Assistant of my better Angel,  . . . .   O 298 Irene               10
     And steal thy Life away. Death's horrid Angel  . . .   O 327 Irene                9
     And steal your life away.  Death's horrid Angel  . .   O 368 Irene            V  17
ANGELIC
     Angelic Greatness is Angelic Virtue.  . . . . .   O 293 Irene              130
     Angelic Greatness is Angelic Virtue.  . . . . .   O 293 Irene              130

                                    13
```

ANGELICK

		PAGE	TITLE	LINE
Angelick choirs have sung.		O 80	Feast St Simon	60

ANGELS

To Men and Angels only giv'n,		O 99	Ode Friendship	3
To W<ortley> and to Angels given		O 99	Ode Friendship	V 3
Till angels wake thee with a note like thine.		O 113	Epit. Phillips	6
Did interposing Angels guard her from him?		O 259	Irene	116
And wearied angels rest upon their stars spheres		Y 128	Irene	V 4B
And anxious Angels wait the mighty Birth;		O 313	Irene	4

ANGER

Then, swift as thought, by headlong anger driv'n		O 76	Tr Add. Battle	10
Art thou too fall'n? ere anger could subside		O 132	Tr. Rambler 54	1
But say, great Bassa, why the Sultan's Anger,		O 257	Irene	65
Who knows if Mahomet's awaking Anger		O 284	Irene	38
Did savage Anger, and licentious Conquest		O 296	Irene	30
Perhaps in vain the Sultan's Anger spar'd me,		O 298	Irene	32
While unavailing Anger crouds thy Tongue		O 327	Irene	6
And wish'd my rising anger could remove		Y 11	Tr Hor Epode 9	23

ANGRY

And hopes from angry heav'n another fire.		O 19	London	209
In angry numbers warn'st succeeding times;		O 23	London	259
Th' offended burgess hoards his angry tale,		O 60	Pro Good Nat'd	17
With every curse of angry heav'n afflicted beneath each		O 357	Irene	V 15
Till angry Heav'n shall mark them out for Ruin,		O 309	Irene	36
An angry Murmur, a rebellious Frown,		O 312	Irene	19
An angry look had sunk him into Hell		O 376	Irene	V 23
An angry look had sunk him into Hell		Y 188	Irene	V 20

ANGUISH

And steals to death from anguish and from shame.		O 43	Vanity Wishes	254
And baffled Spite, with hopeless Anguish dumb,		O 57	Prologue Comus	17
Where hopeless anguish pour'd his groan,		O 201	Death Dr Levet	19
Where hopeless anguish pour'd the groan,		O 201	Death Dr Levet	V 19
When hopeless anguish pours her groan,		O 201	Death Dr Levet	V 19
Learn here what Anguish racks the guilty Breast,		O 246	Irene Prologue	11
And Anguish gnashes on the fatal Wheel.		O 266	Irene	16
Thou fountain of existence I pour the		Y 189	Irene	V 1
anguish of my soul before Thee.		Y 189	Irene	V 1
When Fear and Anguish labour in the Breast,		O 315	Irene	31
Remember, Peace and Anguish are before thee,		O 321	Irene	37
Unutterable Anguish:		O 328	Irene	49
Remorse and Anguish seize on all my Breast;		O 333	Irene	45
And with fell rage and secret anguish burn.		Y 24	Tr Add. Battle	65

ANIMATE

Thy satire point, and animate thy page.		O 23	London	263
My soul could animate a larger frame		Y 132	Irene	V 41A
Such slight Defeats but animate the Brave		O 270	Irene	7

ANIMATED

| Whose snowy breasts, whose animated eyes, | | O 83 | Epi Dist Moth. | 5 |

ANIMATES

| Swells the fair Breast or animates the Glance, | | O 262 | Irene | 14 |

ANN

| When Hanmer fill'd the chair, and Ann the throne. | | O 118 | Epitaph Hanmer | 22 |

ANNOUNC'D

| Announc'd the dinner to the regions round, | | O 192 | Tr. Medea II | 6 |

ANNUAL

| Nor annual tax was rais'e by annual wars. | | Y 94 | Vanity Wishes | V 60B |
| Nor annual tax was rais'e by annual wars. | | Y 94 | Vanity Wishes | V 60B |

ANNUALL

| The farmer annuall honours pays | | O 73 | Hor. Epode II | 64 |

ANOTHER

And hopes from angry heav'n another fire.		O 19	London	209
To rig another convoy for the k<in>g.		O 22	London	247
And there I met another man		O 158	Par. Hermit II	3
I there did meet another man		O 158	Par. Hermit II	V 3
Another dish of tea.		O 158	Par Hermit III	4
Another Plund'rer brought the bright Irene;		O 259	Irene	118
And yet another Voice, forgive me Greece,		O 270	Irene	18
Nor give him Leisure for another Crime.		O 271	Irene	32
Another Hour in dull Deliberation.		O 271	Irene	34
But thou, too old to bear another Cheat,		O 283	Irene	32
But soon thou shalt repent: another Moment		O 319	Irene	33
But take another to my arms.		Y 11	Tr Hor Epode 9	28

ANOTHER'S

And view each object with another's eye;		O 16	London	139
Warn'd by another's fate, vain youth, be wise,		O 82	Young Author	23
And only build upon another's ruin.		O 176	Tr Metastas II	13
Not one takes warning, by another's end.		Y 67	Prologue Lethe	6

ANSWER'D

| She ceas'd; then godlike Hector answer'd kind,-- | | O 74 | Tr. Iliad Bk 6 | 1 |

ANT

The Ant		O 151	The Ant	T
"Go to the Ant thou Sluggard".		O 151	The Ant	V T
Turn on the prudent Ant, thy heedful eyes,		O 151	The Ant	1

ANTIENT

| But forc'd at length her antient Reign to quit, | | O 52 | Pro Drury-Lane | 35 |
| Far from their antient fields and humble cots. | | O 64 | Virgil Past.I | 18 |

ANTILOCHUS

| Mourn'd not Antilochus so long; | | O 68 | Hor. II Ode IX | 14 |

ANTIQUE

| Trickt in Antique Ruff and Bonnet, | | O 179 | Ridicul Warton | 7 |

```
                                                        PAGE     TITLE              LINE
ANXIETIES
     Th' Anxieties of Love. . . . . . . . . . . .     O 300 Irene                   55
ANXIETY
     With temp'rate zeal, and wise anxiety;    . . . . O 118 Epitaph Hanmer         30
ANXIOUS
     Remark each anxious toil, each eager strife,  . . . O  30 Vanity Wishes         3
     Explore each restless toil, each anxious strife,  . . . Y  92 Vanity Wishes    V  3
     He turns, with anxious heart and cripled hands,  . . . O  44 Vanity Wishes    287
     The teeming mother, anxious for her race,  . . . . . O  45 Vanity Wishes      319
     Our anxious Bard, without complaint, may share . . . O  59 Pro Good Nat'd      5
     In vain with anxious breasts we fear    . . . . . O  69 Hor.II Ode 14          15
     And ease the throbbings of an anxious heart;  . . . O  95 Sprig of Myrtl       12
     And cure the throbbing of an anxious heart;  . . . O  95 Sprig of Myrtl     V  12
     When pale, and anxious for their Years to come,  . . O 287 Irene                4
     And anxious Angels wait the mighty Birth;  . . . . O 313 Irene                  4
     Those anxious fears that fan'd the flame of Love.  . Y  11 Tr Hor Epode 9      24
     Whene'er the lab'ring bird with anxious care  . . . Y  23 Tr Add. Battle       44
     Without a boding fear, or anxious sigh,  . . . . . Y  67 Prologue Lethe        3
ANY
     If wrought by any hand but thine,  . . . . . . . O 119 To Miss Purse          4
     If there be any Land, as Fame reports,  . . . . . O 256 Irene                 55
     Lies as dead as any nail! . . . . . . . . . .    Y 300 Extemp. Elegy          2
APART
     To mix with nobler Cares, I'll set apart  . . . . . O 368 Irene             V  27
APARTMENTS
     And Business from the Day. In her Apartments  . . . O 260 Irene              131
APHROSI
     Aphrosi me semnen, Xeine, podessi patei  . . . . . O 171 Epi. Goldsmith       2
APOSTACY
     And dwells on the guilt of apostacy   . . . . . . Y 186 Irene              V  11
     He knows how near Apostacy to Treason--  . . . . . O 324 Irene                 21
APOSTATE
     How shall I scorn the beautiful Apostate!  . . . . O 261 Irene                 22
     The future Miseries that wait th' Apostate;  . . . . O 266 Irene                20
     I am not yet a Queen, or an Apostate. . . . . . . O 289 Irene                  22
     Will not th' Apostate feel the Pangs of Guilt,  . . . O 294 Irene             132
     And idolize th' Apostate I contemn.  . . . . . . . O 310 Irene                 11
     Adore the Beauty but despise th' Apostate.  . . . . O 350 Irene             V  26
     Yet she--fair--so shone first apostate   . . . . . Y 211 Irene              V  10
     Play'd on her Cheek--So shone the first Apostate--  . . O 330 Irene              11
     And in the traytress bad th' apostate bleed . . . . Y 217 Irene             V  12
APOSTLES
     Th' Apostles round the world were sent,  . . . . . O  79 Feast St Simon       25
APPEAL
     But will not Britain hear the last appeal,  . . . . O  34 Vanity Wishes        91
     He seiz'd her melting in the fond Appeal,  . . . . O 334 Irene                 70
APPEAR
     If want of skill, or want of care appear,  . . . . O  62 Pro Word Wise        17
     And thou impearl'd with dew appear more gay.  . . . Y   3 On a Daffodill       12
     Quickly the Cranes appear before their eyes;  . . . Y  25 Tr Add. Battle       92
APPEAR'D
     The moderator firmly mild appear'd,  . . . . . . . O 118 Epitaph Hanmer       25
APPEAS'D
     Soon as with gold appeas'd, he set her free . . . . Y  19 Tr. Iliad Bk 6       40
APPEASE
     Let one great payment every claim appease,  . . . . O  62 Pro Word Wise       11
APPETITE
     So much my Appetite would please   . . . . . . . O  73 Hor. Epode II        60
     Their Rage, and pall'd their Appetite of Murder;  . . O 249 Irene                8
APPLAUD
     Can Balbo's eloquence applaud, and swear . . . . . O  17 London              150
     Applaud her Charms, and court her to be Great. . . . O 287 Irene                18
APPLAUDING
     To shine the Goddess of applauding Nations,  . . . O 278 Irene                 68
     Th' applauding Sky shall pour forth all its Beams  . . O 322 Irene                9
APPLAUSE
     To force Applause no modern Arts are try'd. . . . . O 246 Irene Prologue       22
APPLES
     Or when with golden Apples crown'd   . . . . . . . O  72 Hor. Epode II        23
APPLY'D
     But ne'er the Flute or Lyre apply'd   . . . . . . . O 190 Tr. Medea I           7
APPOINTED
     Th' appointed Vessel to yon' shaded Bay,  . . . . . O 284 Irene                 51
     Our Bark unseen has reach'd th' appointed Bay,  . . . O 304 Irene                 1
     The Place appointed for his Master's Death. . . . . O 326 Irene                 30
APPRENTICE
     This night our wit, the pert apprentice cries,  . . . O  60 Pro Good Nat'd      23
APPROACH
     Afar they mark the flambeau's bright approach,  . . . O  21 London             234
     Mark from afar the flambeau's bright approach,  . . . Y  59 London            V 234
     Approach, ye minstrels, try the soothing strain,  . . O  43 Vanity Wishes      267
     By regular Approach essay'd the Heart;  . . . . . O  51 Pro Drury-Lane       12
     By regular Approach assail'd the Heart;  . . . . . O  51 Pro Drury-Lane     V  12
     To good that mocks approach. . . . . . . . . . . O 133 Tr. Rambler 67        3
     The near approach a bed may shew   . . . . . . . O 184 Tr. Benserade         3
     Each Pleasure brightens at its near Approach,  . . . O 261 Irene                 20
     Approach the    and crowd    . . . . . . . . . . Y 131 Irene              V 32B
     At her Approach each ruder Gust of Thought  . . . . O 275 Irene                 91
     But see, the lofty Maid at our Approach,  . . . . . O 314 Irene                 14
     Some furious soldier would approach that bore . . . Y  23 Tr Add. Battle       46
```

	PAGE	TITLE		LINE

APPROACH'D
A furious wolf approach'd and fled. . . . . O 65 Hor I Ode xxii V 12
A furious Wolf approach'd, and fled. . . . . O 66 To A. Fuscus 12
Tho' the Hind approach'd to hear . . . . O 148 Tr Boet III.12 7
Soon as the chief approach'd the Scaean Gate . . . . Y 18 Tr. Iliad Bk 6 3

APPROACHING
Sustain th' approaching fire's tremendous light; . . . O 18 London 187
And view with cheerful eyes approaching death. . . . . O 74 Tr. Iliad Bk 6 10
Rage with disdain, and hope th' approaching war; . . . O 75 Tr Add. Battle 1
A doubtful Glimpse of our approaching Friends; . . . . . O 268 Irene 37
And heard in my first approaching . . . . Y 144 Irene V 79
Give me, before th' approaching Hour of Fate, ... O 285 Irene 5
Justice demands--But see th' approaching Sultan. . . . O 286 Irene 15
Pourd Storms of fire upon th' approaching Foe . . . . O 364 Irene V 1
Th' approaching Sultan forc'd me from the Palace; . . . O 299 Irene 47
My Soul expands to meet approaching Freedom. . . . . O 306 Irene 50
Hail beautious earnest of approaching spring! . . . . Y 3 On a Daffodill 2

APPROBATION
Cold Approbation gave the ling'ring Bays, ... O 51 Pro Drury-Lane 13

APPROV'D
Then old in honours, and approv'd in faith, ... Y 131 Irene V 32

APPROVE
Approve it only--'tis too late to praise. . . . . . O 62 Pro Word Wise 16

APPROVING   SEE SELF-APPROVING
Approving Justice smiles upon your Cause, ... O 297 Irene 2

APULIA'S
Apulia's spacious wilds with gore; . . . . O 66 Hor I Ode xxii 14
Apulia's spacious Wilds with Gore; . . . . O 67 To A. Fuscus 14

ARABIA'S
Arabia's roving Troops, the Sons of Swiftness, ... O 274 Irene 54

ARBITER
Think how the sov'reign Arbiter of Kingdoms . . . . . O 300 Irene 56

ARBITRARY
Such are the Woes when arbitrary Pow'r, ... O 256 Irene 53

ARCH
Beneath the Covert of this verdant Arch . . . . . . O 275 Irene 78
The pompous theatre the tow'ring arch . . . . Y 177 Irene V 109

ARCHANGEL
While some Archangel nearer to Perfection, ... O 293 Irene 121
While some Archangel of superiour Nature . . . . . . O 369 Irene V 13

ARCHITECT
And whelms the swelling Architect beneath it. . . . . O 269 Irene 9

ARDENT
With ardent Haste, each Candidate of Fame . . . . . O 57 Prologue Comus 19
With ardent love of virtue fir'd, ... O 79 Feast St Simon 38
Warm with an ardent lover's fondest pray'r. . . . . . O 80 Lady Birthday 2
Fill all thy ardent Breast with Greece and Virtue, . . O 298 Irene 8
Ardent of fame, yet fearless of disgrace. . . . . . Y 67 Prologue Lethe 2

ARDOUR
With virtue's sacred ardour glows, ... O 65 Hor I Ode xxii 2
With Virtue's sacred Ardour glows, ... O 66 To A. Fuscus 2
Could Rome with generous ardour fire, ... O 188 Epilogue V 2
The Warrior's Ardour, and the Patriot's Zeal; . . . . O 255 Irene 4
This Regal Confidence, this pious Ardour, ... O 264 Irene 33
Had our first Asian Foes but known this Ardour, . . . O 284 Irene 40
No more shall glow with Friendship's hallow'd Ardour: . O 289 Irene 16
Is this your ardour for your masters safety . . . . . Y 207 Irene V 14

ARDOURS
Oh, must their ardours cease to glow . . . . O 100 Ode Friendship 25
Nor shall thine ardours cease to glow . . . . O 100 Ode Friendship V 25
No more shall feel Religion's hallow'd ardours . . . . O 349 Irene V 24

ARE
66

ARES   OMITTED WORD
Toios Ares Brotoloigos eni ptolemoisi memene, ... O 172 On Marlborough 1

ARGIVE
Then shall some Argive loud insulting cry, ... O 74 Tr. Iliad Bk 6 25

ARGO'S
Who hath not heard of Argo's valiant crew? . . . . . Y 22 Tr Add. Battle 10

ARGUE
Or argue with the Slave that sav'd Demetrius. . . . . O 330 Irene 23

ARISE
Once more, Democritus, arise on earth, ... O 32 Vanity Wishes 49
New forms arise, and diff'rent views engage, ... O 45 Vanity Wishes 307
Loud roar the billows, high the waves arise, ... O 82 Young Author V 8
Thou see'st one pleasing form arise, ... O 121 To Miss Playin 26
But, ah! before arise that hapless day . . . . . . Y 18 Tr. Iliad Bk 6 24
From Isther's flood unnumber'd flocks arise . . . . . Y 24 Tr Add. Battle 69

ARISTIUS
To Aristius Fuscus . . . . O 66 To A. Fuscus T

ARM
Or arm his Breast against the Force of Love? . . . . O 261 Irene 8
And arm the Persian Heretick against thee; . . . . . O 274 Irene 55
Unnerv'd with shrieks the soldier's vig'rous arm . . . Y 163 Irene V 48
I felt the Force of his tempestuous Arm, ... O 307 Irene 19
His arm alone rais'd bulwarks of the dead. . . . . . Y 25 Tr Add. Battle 121

ARM'D
There, with your Soldiers arm'd, and Sails expanded, . O 284 Irene 53

ARMENIAN
Nor, Valgius, on th' Armenian shores . . . . O 67 Hor. II Ode IX 5
By Daphnis' skill th' Armenian tigers broke . . . . . Y 6 Virgil Daphnis 13

ARMIES

	PAGE	TITLE	LINE
And what their Armies lost, their Cringes gain?	O 16	London	V 122
Conducts their Armies and asserts their Cause.	O 251	Irene	51
Which Armies guard, and Citadels inclose?	O 258	Irene	91
Amidst the Glare of Courts, the Shouts of Armies,	O 293	Irene	131
See Cali, Dread of Kings, and Pride of Armies,	O 311	Irene	16
Fiercely contending two vast armies stood	Y 23	Tr Add. Battle	56

ARMS

	PAGE	TITLE	LINE
And flattery subdues when arms are vain?	O 16	London	122
And flattery prevails when arms are vain.	O 16	London	V 122
The queen, the beauty, sets the world in arms;	O 42	Vanity Wishes	246
Her Grandsire leaves her in Britannia's Arms,	O 58	Prologue Comus	34
Swords, arms and wings are scatter'd o'er the plain	O 76	Tr Add. Battle	18
Their foes attacks, and wield their arms with pain.	O 76	Tr Add. Battle	27
But move their numrous arms to Musicks sound,	O 77	Tr Add. Battle	51
Form'd to delight, they use no foreign arms,	O 84	Epi Dist Moth.	22
And found a Thousand Worlds in Stella's Arms.	O 97	Hickman Spinet	20
Snatch me, my Stella, to thy arms,	O 124	Winter's Walk	19
Receives his full Reward in Beauty's Arms.	O 247	Irene Epilogue	24
Their Arms prevail'd, though Cali was our Friend.	O 253	Irene	119
Alluring Grandeur courts her to his Arms,	O 261	Irene	15
Receive th' impatient Sultan to thy Arms;	O 267	Irene	10
Or set The Persian Heretic in arms against Me	O 348	Irene	V 17
Still to the Lover's long-expecting Arms,	O 283	Irene	30
The present Hour with open Arms invites;	O 284	Irene	34
Throws his fond Arms about Aspasia's Neck,	O 286	Irene	4
Our only Arms are Innocence and Meekness.	O 290	Irene	45
Her only arms are innocence and meekness	Y 162	Irene	V 45
Still stretch in vain their longing Arms afar;	O 292	Irene	91
Concur'd to give me to Aspasia's Arms,	O 296	Irene	36
With noisy Falshoods forc'd me from your Arms,	O 299	Irene	39
Soon shalt thou scorn, in Safety's Arms repos'd,	O 301	Irene	93
Science and Arms find every where a Country.	O 352	Irene	V 32
Spread wide their kind Arms to Science and to Beauty.	O 353	Irene	V 5
Aspasia left her sighing in his Arms,	O 303	Irene	29
Nor wish for Houries in Irene's Arms.	O 308	Irene	10
Ambition only gave her to my Arms,	O 310	Irene	7
Aspasia now within her Lover's Arms,	O 325	Irene	17
Clasp'd in her Arms, or slumb'ring on her Breast,	O 331	Irene	19
But take another to my arms.	Y 11	Tr Hor Epode 9	28
Lyciscus whose soft arms excell	Y 12	Tr Hor Epode 9	37
The chief, this spoke, into the mother's arms	Y 20	Tr. Iliad Bk 6	107
Soon forth in arms had some bold soldier stood,	Y 23	Tr Add. Battle	40

ARMY

	PAGE	TITLE	LINE
The liv'ried army, and the menial lord.	O 35	Vanity Wishes	116
The liv'ried army, or the menial lord.	Y 96	Vanity Wishes	V 116

AROMATIC

	PAGE	TITLE	LINE
And India join her aromatic shade	Y 150	Irene	V 85

AROSE

	PAGE	TITLE	LINE
Arose to Heav'n, and pierc'd my bleeding Breast,	O 251	Irene	74
From hence the seeds of discord first arose	Y 23	Tr Add. Battle	50

'ROUND

	PAGE	TITLE	LINE
May throngs of beautious virgins 'round thee crowd,	Y 3	On a Daffodill	13

AROUND   SEE 'ROUND, ROUND

	PAGE	TITLE	LINE
Tho' confiscation's vulters clang around.	O 32	Vanity Wishes	V 36
Tho' confiscation's bloodhounds yelp around.	Y 93	Vanity Wishes	V 36
Around his tomb let Art and Genius weep,	O 39	Vanity Wishes	173
Around in beauteous order stand.	O 73	Hor. Epode II	72
Of Fields with dead bestrew'd around,	O 78	Feast St Simon	1
Around them pleasures wait, and joys for ever new.	O 84	Epi Dist Moth.	27
Then melt, ye fair, while crouds around you sigh,	O 84	Epi Dist Moth.	42
Around the fav'rites of the sky.	O 100	Ode Friendship	12
And pleasure propagates around	O 121	To Miss Playin	5
Her baleful eyes where Sorrow rolls around;	O 192	Tr. Medea II	14
I bad a hundred Virgins wait around her,	O 287	Irene	16
Why, when Destruction rag'd around our Walls,	O 290	Irene	38
Around these fatal Walls, the Tide of War	O 312	Irene	8
Guilt and Despair! pale Spectres, grin around me,	O 328	Irene	50
And planted elms around his monument	Y 18	Tr. Iliad Bk 6	33
I'll sing the chiefs dispensing fate around.	Y 22	Tr Add. Battle	19
Here with dead mice the marsh was strew'd around;	Y 24	Tr Add. Battle	58

ARRAS

	PAGE	TITLE	LINE
Arras	O 172	French Distich	5

ARRAY

	PAGE	TITLE	LINE
Teach me to range my troopes in just array	Y 22	Tr Add. Battle	5

ARRAY'D

	PAGE	TITLE	LINE
Array'd in purer Light, look down on me:	O 253	Irene	101
New from the Maker's Hand, and fair array'd	O 314	Irene	4
New from the Maker's Hand, and far array'd	O 314	Irene	V 4

ARRIVE

	PAGE	TITLE	LINE
Long may better Years arrive,	O 178	Thrale 35 Year	3
Oft may better Years arrive,	O 178	Thrale 35 Year	V 3

ARROGANCE

	PAGE	TITLE	LINE
Nor, letter'd arrogance, deny	O 201	Death Dr Levet	11
How Heav'n in Scorn of human Arrogance,	O 269	Irene	1
Conceal the Gem; let female Arrogance	O 277	Irene	33
Assume the boastful Arrogance of Man.	O 277	Irene	50
Till in the midst of Arrogance and Fondness,	O 299	Irene	46

```
ARROWS                                                    PAGE    TITLE           LINE
    At busy hearts in vain love's arrows fly;     . . . . .   O 133  Tr. Rambler 85      1
    Or fix'd the pointed arrows in their hearts.  . . . .    Y  23  Tr Add. Battle     43
ART
    Others with softer smiles, and subtler art,   . . . . .   O  13  London             75
    Well may they venture on the mimick's art,    . . . . .   O  16  London            134
    Explore your secrets with insidious art,      . . . . .   O  17  London            154
    Each gift of nature, and each grace of art,   . . . . .   O  31  Vanity Wishes      16
    Each gift of nature, and each charm of art,   . . . . .   Y  92  Vanity Wishes   V  16
    Around his tomb let Art and Genius weep,      . . . . .   O  39  Vanity Wishes     173
    Who frown with vanity, who smile with art,    . . . . .   O  46  Vanity Wishes     327
    His studious Patience, and laborious Art,     . . . . .   O  51  Pro Drury-Lane     11
    Nor wish'd for Johnson's Art, or Shakespear's Flame;  . .  O  52  Pro Drury-Lane     18
    Art thou forgotten by the Muse,   . . . . . . . .         O  80  Feast St Simon     50
    May powerful nature join with grateful art,   . . . . .   O  81  Lady Birthday       7
    May powerful nature join with graceful art,   . . . . .   Y  36  Lady Birthday   V   7
    His learning, join'd with each endearing art, . . . . .   O 117  Epitaph Hanmer      7
    Thy hand that knows the subtler art,  . . . . . .         O 120  To Miss Purse       5
    And forming, with unerring art,   . . . . . . . .         O 121  To Miss Playin     17
    Thy musick teach the nobler art  . . . . . . . . .        O 121  To Miss Playin     35
    Bright wisdom teach me Curio's art,   . . . . . .         O 126  An Ode             38
    Art thou too fall'n? ere anger could subside  . . . . .   O 132  Tr. Rambler 54      1
    The Hand of Art here torpid lies  . . . . . . . .         O 154  Epita. Hogarth      1
    Grown old in courts, thou art not surely one  . . . . .   O 176  Tr Metastas II      1
    "Blushing nature, smiling art.   . . . . . . . .          O 185  Anacreon Ode 9     10
    The power of art without the show.  . . . . . . .         O 201  Death Dr Levet     16
        When thou art absent  . . . . . . . .                 O 265  Irene              11
    Soon would his Art or Valour set us free,     . . . . .   O 267  Irene              43
    How blest art thou, still jocund and serene,  . . . . .   O 271  Irene               6
    Allow no Pause for Art or for Contrivance;    . . . . .   O 275  Irene              88
    Whoe'er thou art, or whatsoe'er thy Message,  . . . . .   O 294  Irene               4
    (The) pride of Roman (power), and Grecian     . . . . .   Y 177  Irene           V 111
        art
    Labour'd monuments of art.  . . . . . . . . .             Y 177  Irene           V111G
    If thou art more than the gay Dream of Fancy, . . . .     O 310  Irene              12
    O Happiness! sure thou art all Aspasia's.     . . . . .   O 310  Irene              14
    Forbear--But thou art sunk beneath Reproach;  . . . . .   O 315  Irene              28
    What more could Force attempt, or Art contrive?  . . .    O 317  Irene              35
    Frame your Report with circumspective Art,    . . . . .   O 329  Irene              13
ARTFUL
    Obsequious, artful, voluble and gay,  . . . . . . .       O  15  London            111
    While artful shades thy downy couch enclose,  . . . .     O 151  The Ant            11
    Let artful Flatt'ry now, to lull Suspicion,   . . . . .   O 267  Irene               2
    Your artful Suit, your Monarch's fierce Denial,  . . .    O 270  Irene               3
    Detested Cali too, with artful Wonder,   . . . . .        O 273  Irene              27
    Some artful Wile of counterfeited Love!   . . . . .       O 331  Irene               3
ARTFULL
    With artfull hand the teeming vines,  . . . . . . .       O  71  Hor. Epode II      18
    I drew to my party with (alluring) promises artfull  . .  Y 158  Irene           V  11
ARTHRITIC
    Arthritic tyranny consigns,   . . . . . . . . . .         O 125  An Ode             10
ARTIFICIAL
    With artificial Smiles, and seeming Friendship.  . . .    O 271  Irene              38
ARTISTS
        by artists for thee.  . . . . . . . . . .             O 350  Irene           V  25
ARTLESS
    Only ev'ry bush there artless music sings     . . . .     Y  58  London          V 220
    Intriguing Wits! his artless Plot forgive;    . . . . .   O 246  Irene Prologue     19
    Treat her with all the confidence of artless love  . . .  Y 159  Irene           V  17
ARTS
    These arts in vain our rugged natives try,    . . . . .   O  16  London            129
    For arts like these prefer'd, admir'd, caress'd,  . . .   O  17  London            152
    The slighted Arts Futurity shall trust,   . . . . .       O  57  Prologue Comus     13
    The studied arts of Luxury:   . . . . . . . . .           O  73  Hor. Epode II      56
    The various arts of Luxury:   . . . . . . . . .           O  73  Hor. Epode II   V  56
    Then, when dark arts obscur'd each fierce debate,  . .    O 118  Epitaph Hanmer     23
    Thou know'st those arts which blast with envious praise,  O 176  Tr Metastas II      7
    To force Applause no modern Arts are try'd.   . . . . .   O 246  Irene Prologue     22
    That sweep away religion arts and freedom     . . . .     Y 117  Irene           V109D
    Teach me the Grecian arts of soft persuasion  . . . .     O 349  Irene           V  27
    I dread his Arts of seeming Innocence,    . . . . .       O 273  Irene              39
    These Arts I try'd, and to inflame her more,  . . . .     O 287  Irene              14
    Ambitious Cali dreads the Statesman's Arts,   . . . .     O 300  Irene              74
    The mighty Tuscan courts the banish'd Arts    . . . .     O 302  Irene             116
    Where Florence gives the banish'd arts protection  . . .  O 351  Irene           V   3
    They cultivate at ease the gentler arts in quiet  . . .   Y 177  Irene           V 117
    The Politician's Arts, and Heroe's Flame.     . . . .     O 307  Irene              27
AS
    Spurn'd as a beggar, dreaded as a spy,    . . . . .       O  14  London             81
    Spurn'd as a beggar, dreaded as a spy,    . . . . .       O  14  London             81
    Spurn'd as a begger, dreaded as a spy,    . . . . .       O  14  London          V  81
    Spurn'd as a begger, dreaded as a spy,    . . . . .       O  14  London          V  81
    And as their patron hints the cold or heat,   . . . .     O  16  London            142
    Flush'd as they are with folly, youth and wine,  . . .    O  21  London            232
    Flush'd as they are with youth confused with wine,  . .   Y  59  London          V 232
    As treach'rous phantoms in the mist delude,   . . . .     O  31  Vanity Wishes       9
    The dangers gather as the treasures rise.     . . . . .   O  31  Vanity Wishes      28
    The gen'ral fav'rite as the gen'ral friend:   . . . . .   O  44  Vanity Wishes     297
    The common fav'rite as the gen'ral friend:    . . . . .   Y 105  Vanity Wishes   V 297
    New sorrow rises as the day returns,  . . . . . . .       O  45  Vanity Wishes     301
    Themselves they studied, as they felt, they writ,  . . .  O  52  Pro Drury-Lane     19
```

AS   (CONTINUED)

		PAGE	TITLE		LINE
Then crush'd by Rules, and weaken'd as refin'd,		O 52	Pro Drury-Lane		29
As Tyrants doom their Tools of Guilt to die;		O 53	Pro Drury-Lane		56
As mongrels bay the lion in a cage.		O 60	Pro Good Nat'd		16
As children fret the lion in a cage.		O 60	Pro Good Nat'd	V	16
By plumes is viel'd; see! quick as thought		O 70	Hor. II Ode XX		11
Blest as th' immortal Gods is he		O 71	Hor. Epode II		1
Such as the Sun-burnt Sabines were,		O 72	Hor. Epode II		49
As herbs of which the forrests nigh		O 73	Hor. Epode II		61
As herbs of which the fields nigh		O 73	Hor. Epode II	V	61
As the sad thought of your impending fate:		O 74	Tr. Iliad Bk 6		20
Then, swift as thought, by headlong anger driv'n		O 76	Tr Add. Battle		10
Dispersing blessings as they went,		O 79	Feast St Simon		26
Soon must this bough, as you shall fix his doom,		O 95	Sprig of Myrtl		13
Soon shall this sprig, as you shall fix its doom,		O 95	Sprig of Myrtl	V	13
Thy pleasures, permanent as great,		O 100	Ode Friendship		23
Thy pleasures, lasting, as they're great,		O 100	Ode Friendship	V	23
Thy pleasures, charms as great,		Y 71	Ode Friendship	V	23
As learn'd Eliza, sister of the Muse,		O 106	Eliza plucking		1
Loud as the Billows bursting on the Ground.		O 110	To Posterity		6
The nymph fictitious, as the flow'r;		O 121	To Miss Playin		8
Delighting, as the youth draws nigh,		O 121	To Miss Playin		15
Proclaim'd her, not so fair as fine.		O 122	Stella Mourn.		4
As virtue rises in distress,		O 122	Stella Mourn.		10
But as your sister of the sky,		O 126	To Lyce, Lady		7
My Lyce makes as good a sky,		O 127	To Lyce, Lady		23
As not to grant me this, can Milton find?		O 137	Tr Rambler 140		2
Frail as the leaves that quiver on the sprays,		O 138	Tr Rambler 161		1
Though countless as the Grains of Sand		O 144	Tr Boeth. II.2		1
Though countless as the lamps of night		O 144	Tr Boeth. II.2		3
Rivers rested as they ran,		O 148	Tr Boet III.12	V	10
As with my hat upon my head		O 158	Par. Hermit II	V	1
As I can gulp it down.		O 159	Par Hermit III		12
Scatt'ring, as thy pinions play,		O 185	Anacreon Ode 9		3
"Blissful bondage such as mine?		O 185	Anacreon Ode 9		24
"As it leaves Anacreon's lip,		O 185	Anacreon Ode 9		32
"Or from wine as courage springs,		O 186	Anacreon Ode 9		37
Such strains as, mingled with the lyre,		O 188	Epilogue		1
Wild as wind, and light as feather		O 196	Song Congratu.		7
Wild as wind, and light as feather		O 196	Song Congratu.		7
Let it wander as it will;		O 196	Song Congratu.		18
As on we toil from day to day,		O 200	Death Dr Levet		2
Such had I trusted once as soon as seen,		O 255	Irene		17
Such had I trusted once as soon as seen,		O 255	Irene		17
If there be any Land, as Fame reports,		O 256	Irene		55
Unbroken as the sacred Chain of Nature,		O 257	Irene		63
Fierce as he was, he dreaded to destroy		O 257	Irene		68
Soon as the Sultan's unexpected Fate		O 257	Irene		76
Unshaken be thy Throne as Earth's firm Base,		O 262	Irene		2
As those that bless the Mansions of the Good.		O 262	Irene		12
Long have as oblig'd by vow		Y 130	Irene	V	9
Then Visions horrid as a Murd'rer's Dreams		O 266	Irene		13
Horrid as a murd'rers dreams, madman's laughter		Y 133	Irene	V	13
Born to command, as thou to charm Mankind,		O 268	Irene		23
Observe, bright Maid, as his resistless Voice		O 268	Irene		25
Behold, my fair, as my resistless hand		Y 136	Irene	V	25
Just as I mark'd them, they forsook the Shore,		O 269	Irene		38
As blasted by my Presence, they withdrew		O 275	Irene		85
Mean as we are, this Tyrant of the World		O 277	Irene		39
As when a Deluge overspreads the Plains,		O 280	Irene		22
When ev'n as Love was breaking off from Wonder,		O 282	Irene		66
Soon as the Veil of Evening clouds the Sky,		O 284	Irene		49
With Raptures such as fire the Pagan Crouds,		O 286	Irene		3
Virtue is uncha unvarying as its Authour		O 348	Irene	V	23
Virtue is fixd unvarying as its Author		O 348	Irene	V	23
And as my thoughts at intervals of Prayer		O 349	Irene	V	9
Curst as the Tyrant of th' infernal Realms,		O 294	Irene		134
Commission'd, as he says, by Cali Bassa.		O 294	Irene		3
As glittring dewdrops quiver to the sun		Y 173	Irene	V	19
Far as Futurity's untravell'd Waste		O 300	Irene		68
Count not these Hours as Parts of vulgar Time,		O 302	Irene		5
Pure as the Thoughts of infant Innocence?		O 304	Irene		15
Fidelity so firm, so pure, as this		O 308	Irene		17
Close, as we might unseen, we watch'd his Steps;		O 311	Irene		2
Just as it reach'd my Lips, a sudden Cry		O 316	Irene		27
Bids Beauty, such as thine, prepare to die.		O 324	Irene		3
Just as the Rack forc'd out his struggling Soul,		O 330	Irene		13
As vines the elms, as grapes adorn the vine,		Y 6	Virgil Daphnis		17
As vines the elms, as grapes adorn the vine,		Y 6	Virgil Daphnis		17
As corn the fields, as bulls the herds of kine,		Y 6	Virgil Daphnis		18
As corn the fields, as bulls the herds of kine,		Y 6	Virgil Daphnis		18
Soon as the chief approach'd the Scaean Gate		Y 18	Tr. Iliad Bk 6		3
Her tears in show'rs descending as she spoke.		Y 18	Tr. Iliad Bk 6		18
Soon as with gold appeas'd, he set her free		Y 19	Tr. Iliad Bk 6		40
Soon as their young began to draw their breath		Y 24	Tr Add. Battle		86
As when great Briareus with matchless might		Y 26	Tr Add. Battle		137
Lies as dead as any nail!		Y 300	Extemp. Elegy		2
Lies as dead as any nail!		Y 300	Extemp. Elegy		2
She was once as cherry plump		Y 300	Extemp. Elegy		5
Red her cheek as Cath'rine pear,		Y 300	Extemp. Elegy		6
And as quiet as a lamb.		Y 301	Extemp. Elegy		20

```
AS              (CONTINUED)                                    PAGE    TITLE          LINE
     And as quiet as a lamb.  . . . . . . . . . . .      Y 301 Extemp. Elegy      20
ASCEND
     Inspir'd by us, they Glory's Heights ascend;   . . . .  O 247 Irene Epilogue    17
ASCENDING
     Their fumes ascending to the Skie;  . . . . . . .  O  69 Hor.II Ode 14       8
     Ascending to the skies he shone  . . . . . . . . .  O  79 Feast St Simon     22
ASEM
     And dash'd the Might of Asem from the Ramparts.   . . .  O 312 Irene          12
ASHAM'D
     Studious to please, yet not asham'd to fail.  . . . .  O 246 Irene Prologue    30
ASHES
     Pause at this tomb where Hanmer's ashes lie;   . . .  O 117 Epitaph Hanmer     2
     Pause on this tomb where Hanmer's ashes lie;   . . .  O 117 Epitaph Hanmer  V  2
     Is naught but Ashes and a Shade.  . . . . . . .  O 232 Tr Horace IV.7     16
ASIA
     Such bribes the rapid Greek o'er Asia whirl'd,  . . .  O  39 Vanity Wishes    179
     For you fair Asia spreads her wealthy plains.  . . . .  Y 132 Irene         V 41C
     There will his boundless Wealth, the Spoil of Asia,  . .  O 274 Irene          50
ASIA'S
            Cn Asia's Coast,  . . . . . . . . . . . .  O 257 Irene               74
     When Asia's Nations own me for their Lord,   . . . .  O 306 Irene             5
ASIAN
     Had our first Asian Foes but known this Ardour,   . . .  O 284 Irene          40
ASIDE
     Nor e'er from virtue's path was lur'd aside,   . . . .  O 118 Epitaph Hanmer    31
     Nor e'er from virtue's paths was turn'd aside,  . . .  O 118 Epitaph Hanmer  V 31
     Yet, lay the sonnet for an hour aside,  . . . . .  O 142 In Baretti Bk.     7
     To mix with nobler Cares, I'll throw aside   . . . .  O 275 Irene             70
     And lay the tow'ring Sultaness aside,  . . . . . .  O 289 Irene              8
ASK
     And ask no questions but the price of votes;   . . . .  O  34 Vanity Wishes    96
     And ask the latest fashion of the heart,   . . . . .  O  46 Vanity Wishes   328
     And Indias rajas ask their doom from thee   . . . .  Y 131 Irene         V 32
     What I can grant, you cannot ask in vain--   . . . .  O 285 Irene             14
     And ask, what guilty Pow'r's rebellious Hand   . . .  O 293 Irene            119
     I stand amaz'd, and ask, if yet I clasp thee.  . . . .  O 296 Irene           37
     I ask no Witness, but attesting Conscience,   . . . .  O 305 Irene            34
     Ask to whose Sword the Greeks will trust their Cause,  .  O 305 Irene         39
     Ask of thy Heart; attend the Voice of Conscience--  . .  O 323 Irene           7
ASK'D
     We ask'd, with tim'rous Tongue, th' Offender's Name,  . .  O 325 Irene        23
ASKS
     Asks at the Gate Admission to Aspasia,   . . . . . .  O 294 Irene             2
ASLEEP
     "Drop asleep upon his lyre.  . . . . . . . . . .  O 186 Anacreon Ode 9     40
ASPASIA
     Ladies introduces the mention of Aspasia.   . . . .  O 351 Irene         V 12
     I felt his Pains, and trembled for Aspasia.  . . . .  O 251 Irene            75
     Aspasia! spare that lov'd, that mournful Name:   . . .  O 252 Irene           76
     My reasoning Pow'rs--Dear, hapless, lost Aspasia!  . . .  O 252 Irene         78
     While thus we mourn the Fortune of Aspasia,   . . . .  O 253 Irene           107
     If Happiness can be without Aspasia.  . . . . . .  O 253 Irene            110
            Aspasia.  . . . . . . . . . . . . . .  O 259 Irene              103
     Aspasia calls me, let me fly to save her.   . . . . .  O 259 Irene           107
     What hazards would I shun to clasp for Greece and for  .  Y 125 Irene      V 133
         Aspasia
     When weigh'd with Greece, with Virtue, with Aspasia?  . .  O 260 Irene        138
     Whats Life when weighed with Greece or Aspasia?  . . .  O 371 Irene       V 24
     How will the bright Aspasia shine above her!   . . . .  O 261 Irene           23
     There let Aspasia, since my Fair entreats it,   . . . .  O 263 Irene           3
     Aspasia, yet pursue the sacred Theme;  . . . . . .  O 265 Irene             1
     To make Aspasia and Irene name each other.   . . . .  Y 133 Irene         V 10
     And all Aspasia but her Beauty's Man.  . . . . . .  O 266 Irene            37
     Whose Soul, perhaps, yet mindful of Aspasia,   . . . .  O 267 Irene           39
     Had not my ready thought remov'd Aspasia   . . . .  O 367 Irene         V 24
     Each lin'gring Hour alarms me for Aspasia.   . . . .  O 270 Irene            20
     Aspasia! who can look upon thy Beauties?   . . . . .  O 281 Irene            42
     How did Aspasia welcome your Address?  . . . . . .  O 282 Irene            61
     Once to behold the Charms of bright Aspasia,   . . . .  O 285 Irene            6
     Asks at the Gate Admission to Aspasia,   . . . . . .  O 294 Irene             2
     Intreats admittance to the fair Aspasia   . . . . .  O 367 Irene         V 20
     Aspasia! do I once again behold thee?  . . . . . .  O 294 Irene             2
     He envies none the Converse of Aspasia.   . . . . .  O 296 Irene             4
     'Tis Greece, 'tis Freedom calls Aspasia hence,   . . .  O 297 Irene            9
     Aspasia should not fear a second Insult.   . . . . .  O 299 Irene            42
     Shall guard Aspasia from triumphant Lust.   . . . .  O 301 Irene            89
     Aspasia left her sighing in his Arms,  . . . . . .  O 303 Irene            29
     Nor hope, nor wish, nor live but for Aspasia.  . . . .  O 307 Irene            14
     I love her still, but shall esteem Aspasia:  . . . . .  Y 186 Irene         V  5
     Aspasia stands--  . . . . . . . . . . . . .  O 314 Irene              11
     For. which Aspasia scorn'd the Turkish Crown?   . . .  O 314 Irene            17
     Broke out in Perfidy--Oh curs'd Aspasia,   . . . . .  O 316 Irene            10
     Forbear, Demetrius, 'tis Aspasia calls thee;   . . . .  O 318 Irene            8
     Thy Love, Aspasia, calls; restrain thy Sword;   . . .  O 318 Irene            9
     Aspasia now within her Lover's Arms  . . . . . .  O 325 Irene            17
ASPASIA'S
     Aspasia's thine, and all thy Life is Rapture--   . . .  O 260 Irene           142
     Still at Aspasia's Voice a sudden Rapture   . . . .  O 265 Irene             4
     Throws his fond Arms about Aspasia's Neck,   . . . .  O 286 Irene             4
     Esteem Aspasia's Breast, the noblest Kingdom.  . . . .  O 289 Irene            14
```

20

ASPASIA'S (CONTINUED)	PAGE	TITLE	LINE
And boast no title but Aspasia's friend	Y 161	Irene	V 14
Behold the Hero with Aspasia's Eyes?	O 296	Irene	31
Concur'd to give me to Aspasia's Arms, ...	O 296	Irene	36
Aspasia's Absence will inflame Suspicion;	O 296	Irene	5
Nor Wealth, nor Titles, make Aspasia's Bliss.	O 302	Irene	106
Aspasia's Lovers know but one Desire, ...	O 307	Irene	13
O Happiness! sure thou art all Aspasia's.	O 310	Irene	14
Hang Sit these black clouds upon Aspasia's brow? . . .	Y 191	Irene	V 15

ASPECT
| Of aspect stern for in his face he wears . . . . . . | Y 24 | Tr Add. Battle | 82 |

ASPIR'D
| Yet Bards like these aspir'd to lasting Praise, . . | O 52 | Pro Drury-Lane | 23 |

ASPIRATIONS
| If aspirations to the skies aspires, ... | Y 108 | Vanity Wishes | V 358 |

ASPIRE
Orgilio sees the golden pile aspire, ...	O 19	London	208
Sejano sees the golden pile aspire, ...	Y 58	London	V 208
While I to nobler themes aspire, ...	O 78	Feast St Simon	7
At length aspire to Mantuan praise.	O 139	Tr Rambler 169	2

ASPIRES
| And strong devotion to the skies aspires, ... | O 48 | Vanity Wishes | 358 |
| If aspirations to the skies aspires, ... | Y 108 | Vanity Wishes | V 358 |

ASPIRING
| Soon th' aspiring Fabric falls, ... | O 145 | Tr Boeth. II.4 | 9 |

ASSAIL
| There mark what ills the scholar's life assail, . . . | O 38 | Vanity Wishes | 159 |

ASSAIL'D
| By regular Approach assail'd the Heart; . . . . . . | O 51 | Pro Drury-Lane | V 12 |
| In vain, when Turkey's troops assail'd our Walls, . . . | O 253 | Irene | 117 |

ASSAILS
Yet still one gen'ral cry the skies assails, ...	O 32	Vanity Wishes	45
Yet still the gen'ral cry the skies assails, ...	O 32	Vanity Wishes	V 45
Assails the skies load the tainted gales;	Y 93	Vanity Wishes	V 46

ASSASSIN
| Can then th' Assassin lift his treach'rous Hand . . . | O 286 | Irene | 11 |

ASSASSIN'S
| What gave great Villiers to th' assassin's knife, . . . | O 35 | Vanity Wishes | 129 |

ASSASSINATION
| And my blood freezes at Assassination . . . . | O 353 | Irene | V 23 |

ASSAY'D
| And thrice to mount the battlements assay'd . . . . | Y 19 | Tr. Iliad Bk 6 | 57 |

ASSEMBLE
| Within the town assemble all thy powers . . . . . . | Y 19 | Tr. Iliad Bk 6 | 50 |

ASSEMBLED
| Before th' assembled Troops proclaim his Crimes; . . . | O 273 | Irene | 35 |

ASSEMBLING
| Assembling nations croud thy port. . . . . | Y 136 | Irene | V 27 |

ASSERTING
| And Nature's Rights entreat th' asserting Sword. . . . | O 297 | Irene | 3 |

ASSERTS
| Conducts their Armies and asserts their Cause. . . . . | O 251 | Irene | 51 |

ASSIGN'D
| Now Daedalus, behold, by fate assign'd, ... | O 136 | Tr Rambler 129 | 1 |
| These Hours assign'd to Pleasure and Irene. . . . . . | O 272 | Irene | 15 |

ASSIST
So shall Timidity assist thy Reason, ...	O 266	Irene	21
To assist the Grecians	Y 166	Irene	V 106
Then strike secure, and Heav'n assist the Blow. . . .	O 298	Irene	9
The fav'ring Winds assist the great Design, ...	O 304	Irene	6
Assist her Efforts with thy strong Persuasion;	O 321	Irene	34

ASSISTANT
| Thou kind Assistant of my better Angel, ... | O 298 | Irene | 10 |

ASSIZES
| To Lady F<irebra>ce at Bury Assizes . . . . . . | O 107 | Lady F Assizes | T |

ASSOCIATE
| Declar'd the chief Associate of his Guilt. . . . . . | O 331 | Irene | 11 |

ASSOCIATES
| Detests thy false Associates black Designs, ... | O 300 | Irene | 57 |

ASSUASIVE
| In pleasing Visions, and assuasive Dreams; . . . . . | O 253 | Irene | 102 |

ASSUME
| Assume the boastful Arrogance of Man. . . . . | O 277 | Irene | 50 |

ASSWAGE
| While t' asswage the Pangs of Love . . . . | O 149 | Tr Boet III.12 | 15 |

ASSYRIA
| So by their great decree Assyria fell . . . . | O 76 | Tr Add. Battle | 37 |

ASTONISH'D
Tantalus astonish'd stood	O 149	Tr Boet III.12	37
Fills all th' astonish'd Empire with Confusion, . . .	O 257	Irene	77
Astonish'd nations view with wild affright	* Y 24	Tr Add. Battle	74
And first a sound invades th' astonish'd ear.	Y 25	Tr Add. Battle	91
Then flies aloft; th' astonish'd warriours feel . . .	Y 26	Tr Add. Battle	132

ASTRAY
| Now led astray by hopes fallacious glimm'rings . . . . | Y 148 | Irene | V 43A |

ASTYANAX
| But call'd Astyanax because his sire . . . . | Y 18 | Tr. Iliad Bk 6 | 13 |
| From the fair nurse Astyanax demands. . . . . | Y 20 | Tr. Iliad Bk 6 | 91 |

AT
156   OMITTED WORD

```
ATHEIST                                              PAGE    TITLE             LINE
     And here a female atheist talks you dead.  . . . . .   0    9 London          18
ATHIRST
     Athirst for wealth, and burning to be great;  . . .   0   33 Vanity Wishes    74
ATLAS
     Where Atlas was believ'd to bear  . . . . . . . .     0   79 Feast St Simon   31
ATOM
     A floating Atom, Dust that falls unheeded  . . . .    0  260 Irene           139
ATOMS
     Leave to the schools their atoms and their void.  . . 0  140 Tr Rambler 180    2
     and the first gust shake<s> it into atom<s>  . . . . Y  132 Irene        V   39
ATRIDAE
     Th' atridae there and Tydeus' mighty son,  . . . . . Y   19 Tr. Iliad Bk 6    54
ATTACK
     Attack my gentle lines.  . . . . . . . . . .         0  127 To Lyce, Lady     20
ATTACKS
     Their foes attacks, and wield their arms with pain. . . 0 76 Tr Add. Battle   27
ATTAIN
     Dream not of Pow'r thou never can'st attain:  . . . . 0 291 Irene            69
ATTEMPT
     No cries attempt the mercies of the skies?  . . . . . 0  47 Vanity Wishes   348
     How can a single Hand attempt a Life  . . . . . . .   0  258 Irene            90
         But yet th' Attempt  . . . . . . . . .           0  260 Irene           132
     Lest unacquainted with our bold Attempt,  . . . . .   0  285 Irene            12
     Yet shall the Conscience of the great Attempt  . . . 0  301 Irene            99
     What could Force attempt, or Art contrive?  . . . .   0  317 Irene            35
     What more could force attempt or thought contrive . . Y 194 Irene        V   35
     I first attempt in never-dying lays  . . . . . . .    Y   22 Tr Add. Battle   16
ATTEND
     On ev'ry stage the foes of peace attend,  . . . . .   0   33 Vanity Wishes    77
     If dreams yet flatter, once again attend,  . . . . .  0   38 Vanity Wishes   163
     If hope yet flatter, once again attend,  . . . . . .  Y   99 Vanity Wishes V 163
     Nor lute nor lyre his feeble pow'rs attend,  . . . .  0   43 Vanity Wishes   271
     Attend this Prelude of perpetual Praise!  . . . . . . 0   57 Prologue Comus    6
     Alone the Cypress shall attend.  . . . . . . . .      0   69 Hor.II Ode 14     24
     His various worth, through varied life attend,  . . . 0  117 Epitaph Hanmer    3
     Once more on wisdom's voice attend.  . . . . . .      0  125 An Ode           24
     Attend these queens, Abdallah, to the (palace)  . . . Y 137 Irene         V  40
     Or Persecution drank, attend our Call;  . . . . . .   0  306 Irene            54
     May Penitence attend thy mournful Bed,  . . . . . .   0  322 Irene            61
     Ask of thy Heart; attend the Voice of Conscience-- . . 0 323 Irene            7
     Attend my prayers propitious, hear my vow,  . . . . . Y   7 Virgil Daphnis   42
ATTENDANT
     Attendant Flatt'ry counts his myriads o'er,  . . . .  0   42 Vanity Wishes   229
ATTENDING
     Shall throw th' attending Janizaries round thee.  . . 0 319 Irene            34
     The nurse attending bore a lovely boy  . . . . . . .  Y   18 Tr. Iliad Bk 6    9
ATTENDS
     Attends to waft us to Repose and Safety.  . . . . .   0  258 Irene            82
     My Soul attends thy Voice, and banish'd Virtue  . . . 0 320 Irene            32
ATTENTION
     Attention rouses from the dream of Love  . . . . .    0  369 Irene        V  21
     Attention rise, survey the fair Creation,  . . . . .  0  313 Irene             6
ATTENTIVE
     Attentive truth and nature to descry,  . . . . . .    0   33 Vanity Wishes    63
     And attentive to the sound  . . . . . . . . .        0  148 Tr Boet III.12    9
     Here clos'd in Death th' attentive Eyes  . . . . .    0  155 Epita. Hogarth V  3
     Shall plume her Charms, and, with attentive Watch, . . 0 318 Irene            4
     Shall play the glance, and with attentive watch  . . . Y 195 Irene        V  4
ATTESTING
     I ask no Witness, but attesting Conscience,  . . . .  0  305 Irene            34
ATTORNEY
     And here the fell attorney prowls for prey;  . . . .  0    9 London           16
ATTRACTED
     Her mournful Charms attracted his Regards,  . . . .   0  259 Irene           121
ATTRACTIVE
     That Smile resistless and attractive Grace  . . . .   0  355 Irene        V  16
     Th' attractive Softness, and th' indearing Smile, . . 0 277 Irene            51
ATTRACTS
     By secret charms our native land attracts.  . . . .   0  135 Tr Rambler 122    1
AU
     Au Mouton  . . . . . . . . . . . . . . .             0  172 French Distich    9
AUCTIONS
     And smoak'd in kitchens, or in auctions sold,  . . .  0   34 Vanity Wishes    85
AUGHT
     Where aught of bright, or fair, the piece displays, . . 0 62 Pro Word Wise    15
     Did aught but Luxury relax our Nerves  . . . . . .    0  347 Irene        V   5
     Nor left us aught but Flattery and State.  . . . . .  0  291 Irene            73
AUGUSTAN
     Shames the mean Pensions of Augustan Times;  . . . .  0   57 Prologue Comus    4
AUGUSTUS
     Augustus still survives in Maro's strain,  . . . .    0  114 On C. Cibber      1
AUGUSTUS'
     Augustus' numerous trophies sing;  . . . . . . . .   0   68 Hor. II Ode IX   18
AUKWARD
     And gain a kick for aukward flattery.  . . . . . . .  0   16 London       V 131
AUSPICIOUS
     And beauty smile auspicious in each face;  . . . . .  0   84 Epi Dist Moth.   45
AUSTER
     When loud Auster shakes her Walls,  . . . . . . . .   0  145 Tr Boeth. II.4   10
```

22

```
                                                             PAGE    TITLE            LINE
AUSTRIA
     Short sway! fair Austria spreads her mournful charms,    .    O  42 Vanity Wishes    245
     Short sway! for Austria spreads her mournful charms, .  .    Y 103 Vanity Wishes  V 245
AUTHOR
     The Young Author . . . . . . . . . . .                        O  81 Young Author      T
     So the young author panting for a name,   . . . . . .        O  82 Young Author      11
     So the young author panting after fame,    . . . . .         O  82 Young Author   V 11
     To Miss <Carpenter> On her giving the Author    . . . .      O 119 To Miss Purse      T
     Virtue is fixd unvarying as its Author    . . . . . .        O 348 Irene           V 23
AUTHOR'S
     To wit, reviving from its author's dust,  . . . . . .        O  61 Pro Word Wise      7
     On the Author's receiving a Sprig of Myrtle . . . . .        O  95 Sprig of Myrtl  V  T
AUTHORITY
     With all the Licence of Authority,  . . . . . . . .          O 283 Irene             16
AUTHOUR
     Virtue is uncha unvarying as its Authour   . . . . . .       O 348 Irene           V 23
AUTOU
     Kupridi, med autou skeptra memele theo.   . . . . . .        O 103 Eis Elisses        2
AUTUMN
     Autumn o'erlooks the smiling Ground    . . . . . . .         O  72 Hor. Epode II     24
AUTUMN'S
     Then Summer sinks in Autumn's reign,   . . . . . . .         O 231 Tr Horace IV.7    11
AUTUMNAL
     The fruit autumnal, and the vernal flow'r,    . . . .        O  43 Vanity Wishes    262
AV'RICE
     If Sorrow pine or Av'rice crave,   . . . . . . .             O 146 Tr Boeth III.5     9
     Lamenting Av'rice now too late discovers  . . . . . .        O 250 Irene             26
AVAILS
     Ah! what avails it, that, from slav'ry far, . . . . .        O  15 London           117
        But what avails . . . . . . . . . . . .                   O 254 Irene            137
AVARICE
     But unextinguish'd Avarice still remains,    . . . . .       O  44 Vanity Wishes    285
     Ye Sons of Avarice! a Moment spare:    . . . . . .           O 246 Irene Prologue     4
     When Avarice corrupts th' emasculated Nation--or  . . .      O 347 Irene           V 25
     For ever mourn their Avarice or Factions?    . . . . .       O 305 Irene             44
AVARICIOUS
     Nor lures the search of avaricious eyes,   . . . . . .       O 141 Tr Rambler 199     2
     Glory, the Bribe of avaricious Virtue!    . . . . . .        O 305 Irene             32
AVENGING
     Nor farther tempt the avenging rage of Heaven  . . . .       Y 168 Irene           V 134
AVERSION
     My Vows, 'tis true, she hears with less Aversion,  . . .     O 287 Irene              7
AW'D
     See when the vulgar 'scape, despis'd or aw'd,  . . . .       O  39 Vanity Wishes    167
     Aw'd into Love, our conquer'd hearts obey,    . . . .        O  96 Hickman Spinet     4
     Confounded, aw'd, and lost in Admiration,  . . . . .         O 282 Irene             64
     Aw'd by the Rigour of the Sultan's Justice,   . . . .        O 288 Irene              8
     Aw'd by the Croud, and by their Slaves restrain'd?  . .      O 312 Irene             22
AWAIT
     But few there are whom hours like these await, . . . .       O  45 Vanity Wishes    311
     And bids us thus disguis'd await him here.    . . . .        O 253 Irene            115
     Await our coming, equally prepar'd . . . . . . .             O 284 Irene             54
AWAITS
     "Freedom my return awaits,    . . . . . . . . .              O 185 Anacreon Ode 9    20
AWAKE
     Awake, Demetrius, from this dismal Dream,  . . . . .         O 252 Irene             83
     Sounds in my sleeping Ear, "Awake Demetrius,   . . . .       O 254 Irene            122
     "Awake, and follow me to better Fortunes;"    . . . .        O 254 Irene            123
     Awake each Faculty that sleeps within thee,   . . . .        O 254 Irene              2
     Renew our Sorrows, and awake our Fears.  . . . . . .         O 268 Irene             35
AWAKEN'D
     Like one awaken'd from a pleasing dream,   . . . . . .       Y   4 On a Daffodill    26
AWAKING
     At length awaking, with contemptuous frown,   . . . .        O  10 London            33
     Who knows if Mahomet's awaking Anger   . . . . . .           O 284 Irene             38
AWARD
     Now let us wait the last Award of Heav'n,  . . . . .         O 302 Irene            113
AWAY
     There none are swept by sudden fate away,  . . . . .         O   9 London            11
     Explain their country's dear-bought rights away,  . .        O  11 London            53
     Or bribe a virgin's innocence away.   . . . . . .            O  13 London            78
     Sense, freedom, piety, refin'd away,   . . . . . .           O  15 London           105
     Walks the wild heath, and sings his toil away. . . . .       O  32 Vanity Wishes     38
     With unexpected legions bursts away,   . . . . . .           O  42 Vanity Wishes    243
     With unexpected legions pow'rs away,   . . . . . .           Y 103 Vanity Wishes  V 243
     And glides in modest Innocence away;   . . . . . .           O  44 Vanity Wishes    294
     Still drops some joy from with'ring life away; . . . .       O  45 Vanity Wishes    306
     Will quickly drive away his woe,   . . . . . . .             O  69 Hor.II Ode 14     26
     Or prunes the barren boughs away;  . . . . . . .             O  71 Hor. Epode II     19
     And unrelenting sport ten thousand lives away; . . . .       O  83 Epi Dist Moth.     9
     "Fate! snatch away the bright disguise,    . . . . .         O 122 Stella Mourn.      5
     In quest of wealth who throw their lives away.  . . . .      O 132 Tr. Rambler 48     2
     Yet timely provident, she hastes away    . . . . .           O 151 The Ant            5
     Be Vice and Dulness far away . . . . . . . .                 O 154 Epita. Hogarth     7
     Phrase that Time has flung away,   . . . . . . .             O 179 Ridicul Warton     5
     Our social comforts drop away.  . . . . . . . .              O 200 Death Dr Levet     4
     Thus lightly skim, and haste away. . . . . . . .             O 203 Tr. on Skating  V  4
     That sweep away religion arts and freedom  . . . . .         Y 117 Irene          V109D
     Far from his Troops, he toys his Hours away.   . . . .       O 258 Irene             93
     Amidst the Camp to howl his Life away.    . . . . .          O 273 Irene             37
     And varied Life steal unperceiv'd away.  . . . . . .         O 279 Irene             91
```

```
AWAY          (CONTINUED)                                         PAGE    TITLE              LINE
     Reason commands to cast the less away;        .   .   .   .   .   .    O 290  Irene                33
     There wear the tedious Hours of Life away,    .   .   .   .   .   .    O 292  Irene                85
     And sweeps th' exulting Conqueror away:       .   .   .   .   .   .    O 298  Irene                31
     What Hand, when Death has snatch'd away Demetrius,    .   .          O 301  Irene                88
     Constrains a sullen Smile, and shoots away.   .   .   .   .   .   .    O 311  Irene                 7
     Cali disarm'd was born away to Death;   .   .   .   .   .   .   .    O 317  Irene                40
     Behold thy boasted Honours snatch'd away.     .   .   .   .   .   .    O 317  Irene                43
     And drag away thy Life in Scorn and Safety,   .   .   .   .   .    O 319  Irene                26
     And Heav'n forbids to lavish Life away,    .   .   .   .   .   .    O 321  Irene                49
     And steal thy Life away. Death's horrid Angel   .   .   .   .    O 327  Irene                 9
     And steal your life away.  Death's horrid Angel    .   .   .    O 368  Irene            V  17
     With Hector's life away my pleasures fly.    .   .   .   .   .    Y  18  Tr. Iliad Bk 6       27
AWE
     While growing hopes scarce awe the gath'ring sneer,    .   .    O  44  Vanity Wishes       277
     Not Rome itself that held the world in awe    .   .   .   .   .    O  76  Tr Add. Battle       39
     But what Laws can Lovers awe?    .   .   .   .   .   .   .   .    O 150  Tr Boet III.12       47
AWEFUL
     At once is lost the pride of aweful state,    .   .   .   .   .    O  35  Vanity Wishes       113
     Now drops at once the pride of aweful state,    .   .   .   .    O  35  Vanity Wishes    V 113
AWFUL
     With pity soften every awful grace,    .   .   .   .   .   .   .    O  84  Epi Dist Moth.       44
     Think on the mighty Pow'r of awful Virtue;    .   .   .   .   .    O 252  Irene                88
     Thy awful air, thy dignity of virtue.   .   .   .   .   .   .   .    Y 134  Irene            V  34
     While Heav'n's high Minister, whose awful Volume    .   .    O 276  Irene                20
AWFULL
     While Heaven's high Minister whose unerring awfull    .   .    O 355  Irene            V   9
          volume
AWHILE
     And pause awhile from letters, to be wise;    .   .   .   .   .    O  38  Vanity Wishes       158
     And pause awhile from Learning to be wise;    .   .   .   .   .    O  38  Vanity Wishes    V 158
     Suspend awhile the Privilege of Pow'r    .   .   .   .   .   .    O 289  Irene                 5
     Suspend awhile the privilege of powr (and Beauty)    .   .    O 366  Irene            V  21
     My Spirits fail, awhile support me, Vengeance--    .   .   .    O 334  Irene                72
     He turn'd awhile the fortune of the day    .   .   .   .   .   .    Y  25  Tr Add. Battle      123
AWKWARD
     And get a kick for awkward flattery.    .   .   .   .   .   .   .    O  16  London              131
BABES
     Surveys his smiling babes, the sons of    .   .   .   .   .   .    Y 122  Irene            V  60
          freedom,
     <And> plants for his prattling babes the future shade    .    Y 122  Irene            V  62
BACCHUS
     Thou shalt with Bacchus equal honours share   .   .   .   .   .    Y   7  Virgil Daphnis       51
BACCHUS'
     And trod to Bacchus' praise the mystick ground.    .   .   .    Y   6  Virgil Daphnis       16
BACK
     And call Britannia's glories back to view;    .   .   .   .   .    O  10  London               26
     The Stage but echoes back the publick Voice.   .   .   .   .    O  53  Pro Drury-Lane       52
     Looks back on what She left behind,    .   .   .   .   .   .   .    O 150  Tr Boet III.12       57
     Threw back the glitt'ring Bribe.    .   .   .   .   .   .   .   .    O 258  Irene               102
     Stoop from thy Flight, trace back th' entangled Thought,    O 293  Irene               127
     Holds out her Hand to lead thee back to Truth.    .   .   .   .    O 321  Irene                42
     Shrinks back from the hated task, for thy destruction;    .    Y 204  Irene            V  21
     Back through the city trod his former way.    .   .   .   .   .    Y  17  Tr. Iliad Bk 6        2
     The child starts back affrighted at the blaze    .   .   .   .    Y  20  Tr. Iliad Bk 6       92
     Andromache looks back with weeping eyes,    .   .   .   .   .    Y  21  Tr. Iliad Bk 6      127
BACKS
     Part turn their Backs, part seiz'd with wild surprise    .    O  76  Tr Add. Battle       28
BACKWARD
     Times gloomy backward with judicious eyes;    .   .   .   .   .    O 192  Tr. Medea II          2
BACKWARDS
     Turn'd backwards by the powerful Breath of Heav'n.    .   .    O 322  Irene                 3
BACON'S
     And Bacon's mansion trembles o'er his head.    .   .   .   .   .    O  37  Vanity Wishes       140
BAD
     And bad the feast, and song, and bowl,    .   .   .   .   .   .    O 190  Tr. Medea I           5
     In Passion lost, he bad the conqu'ring Fair    .   .   .   .   .    O 258  Irene                99
     And bad imperial splendour glare (blaze) before her    .   .    Y 158  Irene            V  10
     I bad a hundred Virgins wait around her,    .   .   .   .   .   .    O 287  Irene                16
     Urg'd us to Speed, and bad us banish Pity,    .   .   .   .   .    O 332  Irene                30
     And in the traytress bad th' apostate bleed    .   .   .   .   .    Y 217  Irene            V  12
BADE
     And bade his new Confederates seize the Traitors.    .   .   .    O 317  Irene                39
BAFFLED
     The baffled prince in honour's flatt'ring bloom    .   .   .    O  43  Vanity Wishes       251
     And baffled Spite, with hopeless Anguish dumb,    .   .   .   .    O  57  Prologue Comus       17
     To some retreat the baffled writer flies,    .   .   .   .   .    O  82  Young Author         26
BALANCE
     Into the adverse Scale, nor shakes the Balance.    .   .   .    O 260  Irene               140
BALBO'S
     Can Balbo's eloquence applaud, and swear    .   .   .   .   .   .    O  17  London              150
BALBOS
     Who dwell on Balbos courtly mien--    .   .   .   .   .   .   .   .    Y  55  London           V 150
BALEFUL
     Her baleful eyes where Sorrow rolls around;    .   .   .   .   .    O 192  Tr. Medea II         14
     And scatter Discord from their baleful Beams.    .   .   .   .    O 271  Irene                 5
BALL
     Thou to a scene of bloodshed turn'st the Ball,    .   .   .   .    O  77  Festina Lente        11
     Thro' all the spacious ball;    .   .   .   .   .   .   .   .   .   .    O  79  Feast St Simon       27
BALLANCE
     Sustain'd the Ballance, but resign'd the Sword;    .   .   .    O  22  London           V 251
```

```
BALLS   SEE EYE-BALLS                                   PAGE    TITLE              LINE
BALM
    Why, when the Balm of Sleep descends on Man,     . . . . .   O 277 Irene               43
    On weary Mortals sheds the balm of rest   . . . . . . .      O 356 Irene           V  10
BALMY
    And hope the balmy blessings of repose:   . . . . . .        O  21 London             237
    And, murm'ring, balmy Sleep prolong,   . . . . . . . .       O  72 Hor. Epode II       32
    The balmy kiss, for which poor Thyrsis dies;   . . . .       O  84 Epi Dist Moth.      21
    And balmy spirits thro' thy foliage play,   . . . . . .      Y   3 On a Daffodill      10
    May balmy spirits thro thy foliage play,   . . . . . .       Y   3 On a Daffodill  V  10
BAND
    With well-feign'd gratitude the pension'd band   . . . .     O  19 London             200
    Propose your schemes, ye Senatorian band,   . . . . .        O  21 London             244
    His chearfull Slaves, a num'rous band,   . . . . . .         O  73 Hor. Epode II       71
    Selected by my Care, a hardy Band,   . . . . . . . .         O 254 Irene              136
    Such was the Will of Heav'n--A Band of Greeks   . . . .      O 335 Irene                5
BANDS
    The vanquish'd hero leaves his broken bands,   . . . . .     O  41 Vanity Wishes      211
BANE
    Our bane and physic the same earth bestows,   . . . . .      O 131 Tr. Rambler 21       1
BANEFUL
    Lest baneful discord crush our infant Scheme,   . . . .      O 299 Irene               52
BANEFULL
    The banefull weeds spring up, and choak the grain.   . .     Y   7 Virgil Daphnis      23
BANISH
    All the Names that banish Care,   . . . . . . . . .          O 196 Song Congratu.   V  10
    To banish Doubt, and brand him for a Villain.   . . . .      O 273 Irene               21
    Urg'd us to Speed, and bad us banish Pity,   . . . . .       O 332 Irene               30
BANISH'D
    Far hence are banish'd vapours, spleen, and tears,   . .     O  84 Epi Dist Moth.      18
    For her, Repose is banish'd from the Night   . . . . .       O 260 Irene              130
    The mighty Tuscan courts the banish'd Arts   . . . . .       O 302 Irene              116
    Where Florence gives the banish'd arts protection   . . .    O 351 Irene           V   3
    My Soul attends thy Voice, and banish'd Virtue   . . . .     O 320 Irene               32
    And banish'd sorrow flies the joyous plains;   . . . . .     Y   7 Virgil Daphnis      37
BANK
    Some pleasing bank where verdant osiers play,   . . . . .    O  11 London              45
    On some green bank supinely Laid,   . . . . . . . .          O  72 Hor. Epode II       30
BANKS
    On Thames's banks, in silent thought we stood,   . . . .     O  10 London              21
    For the fair banks of Severn or of Trent;   . . . . .        O  19 London             211
    The wisest justice on the banks of Trent?   . . . . .        O  35 Vanity Wishes      124
    The richest Landlord on the banks of Trent?   . . . . .      O  35 Vanity Wishes    V 124
    The wealthiest landlord on the banks of Trent?   . . . .     Y  97 Vanity Wishes    V 124
    On Isis banks he waves, from noise withdrawn   . . . .       Y  98 Vanity Wishes    V138A
    The rivers know their banks again,   . . . . . . . .         O 231 Tr Horace IV.7       4
    And warm Cayster's flowing banks forsake   . . . . . .       Y  24 Tr Add. Battle      67
    And Strymon's hollow banks resounded with their groans. .    Y  24 Tr Add. Battle      89
BANNERS
    Dominion hovers o'er their conquering banners   . . . .      Y 115 Irene            V 49D
    Bribe to his Cause and list beneath his Banners   . . .      O 274 Irene               53
    Rush to the War, display thy dreadful Banners,   . . . .     O 333 Irene               40
BANQUET
    Pollutes his banquet and insults his guest;   . . . . .      O 130 Tr. Rambler 12       2
BAR
    The midnight murd'rer bursts the faithless bar;   . . .      O  21 London             239
    The strength of a Bar, and the sweetness of Nard.   . . .    O 179 Charade!             4
    And bar the Passes of Irene's Mind   . . . . . . . .         O 265 Irene               10
BAR'D
    And bar'd my Bosom to the Ruffian's Dagger.   . . . . .      O 331 Irene               20
BARB'ROUS
    In gay hostility, and barb'rous pride,   . . . . . .         O  42 Vanity Wishes      225
    When Learning's Triumph o'er her barb'rous Foes   . . .      O  51 Pro Drury-Lane       1
    They, pleas'd, thro' barb'rous nations roam   . . . . .      O  79 Feast St Simon      29
    Whilst you deride their pangs in barb'rous play,   . . .     O  83 Epi Dist Moth.       7
    The dreadful Dissonance of barb'rous Triumph,   . . . .      O 251 Irene               71
    Whence is this Rage? what barb'rous Tongue has wrong'd  .    O 325 Irene               27
      me?
    I feel, I see the Ruffian's barb'rous Rage.   . . . . .      O 334 Irene               69
BARBARIAN
    I saw without a sigh the fierce barbarian   . . . . .        Y 176 Irene            V 106
BARBARIANS
    Though fierce Barbarians threatend death   . . . . .         O  79 Feast St Simon      40
BARBAROUS
    His liquid wealth o'er barbarous lands.   . . . . . .        O  65 Hor I Ode xxii       8
    His liquid Wealth thro' barbarous Lands.   . . . . . .       O  66 To A. Fuscus         8
    The dreadfull dissonance of barbarous triumph   . . . .      Y 169 Irene            V  11
BARD
    From Bard, to Bard, the frigid Caution crept,   . . . .      O  52 Pro Drury-Lane      31
    From Bard, to Bard, the frigid Caution crept,   . . . .      O  52 Pro Drury-Lane      31
    Our anxious Bard, without complaint, may share   . . .       O  59 Pro Good Nat'd       5
    Our little Bard, without complaint, may share   . . . .      O  59 Pro Good Nat'd   V   5
    The bard may supplicate, but cannot bribe.   . . . . .       O  60 Pro Good Nat'd      26
    Some zealous bard to wake the sleeping lyre.   . . . .       O 107 Lady F Assizes       4
    "On the bard her Dove bestow'd.   . . . . . . . .            O 185 Anacreon Ode 9      12
    Our daring Bard with Spirit unconfin'd,   . . . . . .        O 246 Irene Prologue       7
    Not the Maeonian Bard in lofty strain   . . . . . .          Y  23 Tr Add. Battle      54
    The bard obdurate sees his brother die.   . . . . . .        Y  67 Prologue Lethe       4
    Oft has our bard in this disastrous year,   . . . . .        Y  67 Prologue Lethe       7
BARD'S
    At length our mighty Bard's victorious Lays   . . . . .      O  57 Prologue Comus      15
```

25

```
                                                          PAGE     TITLE            LINE
BARDS
     Yet Bards like these aspir'd to lasting Praise,    .  .  .  . O  52 Pro Drury-Lane      23
     And all her bards express,   .  .  .  .  .  .  .  .  .       O 127 To Lyce, Lady        22
BARK
     Our Bark unseen has reach'd th' appointed Bay,    .  .  .  . O 304 Irene                 1
     Bound o'er the sparkling Waves. Go, happy Bark,    .  .  .   O 322 Irene                 5
     Dance o'er the Sparkling Waves--Go happy Bark    .  .  .  .  O 364 Irene             V  30
     Go Happy Bark, thy sacred Freight secures thee    .  .  .    O 364 Irene             V  24
BARREN
     His fall was destin'd to a barren strand,    .  .  .  .  .   O  41 Vanity Wishes       219
     Or prunes the barren boughs away;   .  .  .  .  .  .  .  .   O  71 Hor. Epode II         19
     And drove the swarthy troops to their own barren sands. .   O  78 Festina Lente         20
     Infest the barren Lands.   .  .  .  .  .  .  .  .  .  .      O  79 Feast St Simon        42
BARRICADES
     And Winter barricades the realms of Frost;    .  .  .  .  .  O  41 Vanity Wishes       208
BARS
     Unconquer'd bars on earth and sea withstand;    .  .  .  .   O 136 Tr Rambler 129        3
     Did we not see the bars of nature broken?    .  .  .  .  .   Y 115 Irene             V  49F
     Till interposing darkness bars the prospect.    .  .  .  .   Y 155 Irene             V  25
     Close like th' eternal Bars of Death upon thee,    .  .  .   O 292 Irene                80
     Close like th' eternal Bars of Death upon You    .  .  .  .  O 357 Irene             V  10
BASE
     And one base action sully all my fame,    .  .  .  .  .  .   O  74 Tr. Iliad Bk 6        6
     Unshaken be thy Throne as Earth's firm Base,    .  .  .  .   O 262 Irene                 2
     Live till the tott'ring Earth forsakes its    .  .  .  .  .  O 347 Irene             V  29
          Base
     His Fav'rite faithless, and his Mistress base.    .  .  .  . O 310 Irene                 6
     Some ill designing Statesman's base Intrigue!    .  .  .  .  O 326 Irene                36
BASENESS
     Resign their Charge to Baseness and to Ruin.    .  .  .  .   O 289 Irene                20
BASIS
     And on its basis would have been enroll'd,    .  .  .  .  .  O 190 Seeing Montagu        5
BASSA
         From Cali Bassa .  .  .  .  .  .  .  .               O 253 Irene               111
     Or hear himself, for see the Bassa comes.    .  .  .  .  .   O 254 Irene               141
     But say, great Bassa, why the Sultan's Anger,    .  .  .  .  O 257 Irene                65
     They put the riches of Cali Bassa on board.    .  .  .  .    Y 123 Irene             V  81
     Rise Cali Bassa counsellor of Kings    .  .  .  .  .         O 351 Irene             V  24
     Th' insidious Bassa fir'd by Disappointment--    .  .  .  .  O 273 Irene                32
     Twice since the Morning rose I saw the Bassa,    .  .  .  .  O 275 Irene                76
     Now pause, great Bassa, from the Thoughts of Blood,    .  .  O 285 Irene                 1
     Commission'd, as he says, by Cali Bassa.    .  .  .  .  .  . O 294 Irene                 3
     The Bassa, reeking with his Master's Murder,    .  .  .  .   O 300 Irene                80
     Caraza speak--have ye remark'd the Bassa?    .  .  .  .  .   O 311 Irene                 1
     Amazement seiz'd us, and the hoary Bassa    .  .  .  .  .    O 317 Irene                36
     The Greek, Demetrius! whom th' expiring Bassa    .  .  .  .  O 331 Irene                10
BASSA'S
     Whate'er their Scheme the Bassa's Death defeats it,    .  .  O 312 Irene                 4
BASSAS
     But still yet my Soul detests the Bassas    .  .  .  .  .  . O 353 Irene             V  22
          treason
BATT'RIES
     Lay pointed at our Batt'ries yet unform'd,    .  .  .  .  .  O 273 Irene                25
BATTALIONS
     Your thin battalions and your empty tents    .  .  .  .  .   Y 120 Irene             V  29A
     Feather'd battalions, squadrons on the wing    .  .  .  .    Y  22 Tr Add. Battle         1
BATTERS
     The rival batters, and the lover mines.    .  .  .  .  .  .  O  46 Vanity Wishes       332
BATTLE
     Their foes the shock sustain in Battle skill'd,    .  .  .   O  76 Tr Add. Battle        12
     Sure some kind Sabre in the Heat of Battle,    .  .  .  .    O 252 Irene                93
     Then, Cali, shall the Toils of Battle cease,    .  .  .      O 265 Irene                44
     For you shall plough the main, and fight the battle    .  .  Y 146 Irene             V  23B
     Why fled this haughty Heroine from the Battle?    .  .  .  . O 290 Irene                39
     Behold I quit her to the Chance of Battle.    .  .  .  .  .  O 319 Irene                29
     Nor from the battle look for his return.    .  .  .  .  .  . Y  21 Tr. Iliad Bk 6       131
     Where'er the battle rages bends his course.    .  .  .  .  . Y  25 Tr Add. Battle       119
BATTLEMENTS
     And thrice to mount the battlements assay'd    .  .  .  .  . Y  19 Tr. Iliad Bk 6        57
BATTLES
     Acquir'd by wounds, and battles bravely fought!    .  .  .   O  74 Tr. Iliad Bk 6         7
BATTRIES
     Our Mines discover'd, and, our Battries ruind    .  .  .  .  O 368 Irene             V   2
BAUBLES
     Now bless'd with all the baubles of the great,    .  .  .   O  19 London               206
BAVARIA'S
     From Persia's tyrant to Bavaria's lord.    .  .  .  .  .  .  O  41 Vanity Wishes       224
BAVARIAN
     The bold Bavarian, in a  luckless hour,    .  .  .  .  .  .  O  42 Vanity Wishes       241
BAY
     As mongrels bay the lion in a cage.    .  .  .  .  .  .  .   O  60 Pro Good Nat'd        16
     Th' appointed Vessel to yon' shaded Bay,    .  .  .  .  .    O 284 Irene                51
     Our Bark unseen has reach'd th' appointed Bay,    .  .  .  . O 304 Irene                 1
     This Bay has prov'd my ,fondness for the Sultan;    .  .  .  O 324 Irene                19
BAYS
     Cold Approbation gave the ling'ring Bays,    .  .  .  .  .   O  51 Pro Drury-Lane        13
BE
     Lest ropes be wanting in the tempting spring,    .  .  .  .  O  22 London               246
     And ropes be wanting in the tempting spring,    .  .  .  .   Y  60 London             V 246
     Athirst for wealth, and burning to be great;    .  .  .  .   O  33 Vanity Wishes        74
     All fir'd with hope, and panting to be great;    .  .  .  .  Y  95 Vanity Wishes      V  74
```

		PAGE	TITLE	LINE
Shall Wolsey's wealth, with Wolsey's end be thine?		O 35	Vanity Wishes	122
And pause awhile from letters, to be wise;		O 38	Vanity Wishes	158
And pause awhile from Learning to be wise;		O 38	Vanity Wishes	V 158
"And all be mine beneath the polar sky."		O 40	Vanity Wishes	204
Whom Pleasure keeps too busy to be wise,		O 46	Vanity Wishes	324
And rising Ages hasten to be just.		O 57	Prologue Comus	14
But confident of praise, if praise be due,		O 60	Pro Good Nat'd	29
Be kind, ye judges, or at least be just:		O 61	Pro Word Wise	8
Be kind, ye judges, or at least be just:		O 61	Pro Word Wise	8
By all, like him, must praise and blame be found;		O 62	Pro Word Wise	19
That post, and all the rest, shall be my care;		O 74	Tr. Iliad Bk 6	3
Observe your steps; be carefull to command		O 77	Festina Lente	3
My fair, be mindful of the mighty trust,		O 81	Lady Birthday	11
Alas! 'tis hard for beauty to be just.		O 81	Lady Birthday	12
No more let coquets to themselves be blind,		O 81	Lady Birthday	18
Warn'd by another's fate, vain youth, be wise,		O 82	Young Author	23
Glad to be hid, and proud to be forgot.		O 82	Young Author	30
Glad to be hid, and proud to be forgot.		O 82	Young Author	30
The heart, once caught, should ne'er be freed?		O 120	To Miss Purse	12
Let pain deserv'd without complaint be borne.		O 131	Tr. Rambler 32	1
Hear, and be just.		O 133	Tr. Rambler 81	1
On swelling mortals to be proud no more.		O 135	Tr Rambler 106	2
Place may be chang'd; but who can change his mind?		O 137	Tr Rambler 135	1
Let ev'ry piece be simple and be one.		O 137	Tr Rambler 139	1
Let ev'ry piece be simple and be one.		O 137	Tr Rambler 139	1
On life, on morals, be thy thoughts employ'd;		O 140	Tr Rambler 180	1
Be gone ye blockheads, Heraclitus cries,		O 141	Tr Rambler 208	1
By wit, by knowledge, studious to read,		O 141	Tr Rambler 208	3
Must bid each wild Desire be still,		O 146	Tr Boeth III.5	3
Observe her labours, Sluggard, and be wise.		O 151	The Ant	2
Be Vice and Dulness far away		O 154	Epita. Hogarth	7
Endless Labour to be wrong;		O 179	Ridicul Warton	4
"Tempts me to be wild again:		O 185	Anacreon Ode 9	22
"This is all;--be quick and go,		O 186	Anacreon Ode 9	41
Soon those nine lives would be past.		O 194	On Thrale Hat	4
Be this at least his Praise; be this his Pride;		O 246	Irene Prologue	21
Be this at least his Praise; be this his Pride;		O 246	Irene Prologue	21
Ye Fops be silent! and ye Wits be just!		O 246	Irene Prologue	34
Ye Fops be silent! and ye Wits be just!		O 246	Irene Prologue	34
My Swain is little--true--but be it known,		O 247	Irene Epilogue	9
Men will be ever to their Errors blind,		O 247	Irene Epilogue	11
That Wealth, too pleasing to be lost for Freedom!		O 250	Irene	21
Ere yet the Foe found Leisure to be cruel,		O 252	Irene	94
If Happiness can be without Aspasia.		O 253	Irene	110
If there be any Land, as Fame reports,		O 256	Irene	55
Renounce her Faith, and be the Queen of Turkey;		O 258	Irene	100
It must, it must be She; her Name?		O 258	Irene	103
At least this Day be calm--If we succeed,		O 260	Irene	141
Soon will th' unequal Contest be decided,		O 261	Irene	18
Unshaken be thy Throne as Earth's firm Base,		O 262	Irene	18
but if your influence be too wide--your dissipated rays		Y 132	Irene	V 41
Each Day and shall be made happy with new entertainments		O 350	Irene	V 24
And new forms of pleasure shall be invented		O 350	Irene	V 25
Or only struggles to be more enslav'd?		O 281	Irene	41
Now be some Moments Master of thyself,		O 282	Irene	70
Hence! or be calm--To disagree is Ruin.		O 282	Irene	72
This Night with all her conscious Stars be witness,		O 284	Irene	44
Let Prudence, ere the Suit be farther urg'd,		O 285	Irene	8
Long be the Sultan bless'd with happy Love!		O 286	Irene	1
Applaud her Charms, and court her to be Great.		O 287	Irene	18
Deep in my Breast be treasur'd this Resolve.		O 288	Irene	12
Be virtuous Ends pursued by virtuous Means,		O 291	Irene	58
to be guilty, though penitent . . .		Y 165	Irene	V 81
Love be my Wealth, and my Distinction Virtue.		O 302	Irene	111
Can brave Leontius be the Slave of Glory?		O 305	Irene	30
Be but my Country free, be thine the Praise;		O 305	Irene	33
Be but my Country free, be thine the Praise;		O 305	Irene	33
Return, Demetrius, and be free for ever.		O 306	Irene	60
Far be such black Ingratitude from Cali,		O 306	Irene	4
Wealth, and Command, and Grandeur shall be thine		O 306	Irene	6
Henceforth for ever happy be this Day,		O 308	Irene	1
Will she that's false to Heavn, to me be faithfull		Y 186	Irene	V 4
Be fruitless Grief		O 316	Irene	13
Haste, seize them, guards, be quick--my thoughtless hast		Y 198	Irene	V 34
While I protract their Stay. Be swift and faithful.		O 319	Irene	4
Be thine, that Wealth can give, or Guilt receive.		O 322	Irene	58
Henceforth be wise, nor hope a second Pardon.		O 323	Irene	3
Far be the Thought--But hear my Protestation.		O 326	Irene	32
Far be the horrid thought--but hear my protestation		Y 205	Irene	V 32
Recall th' extorted Doom.--It must be so,		O 326	Irene	40
Enrob'd in Death--Dispatch her and be great.		O 326	Irene	3
O let me be but heard, nor fear from me		O 327	Irene	20
Short be thy Pains.		O 328	Irene	49
Be charg'd upon my Soul. O, Mercy! Mercy!		O 329	Irene	55
Abdalla, bid thy troubled Breast be calm;		O 329	Irene	2
And wish'd--Be still thy Fate to wish in vain.		O 334	Irene	60
Be just ye Slaves, and, to be just, be cruel,		O 334	Irene	73
Be just ye Slaves, and, to be just, be cruel,		O 334	Irene	73
Be just ye Slaves, and, to be just, be cruel,		O 334	Irene	73
Be thou the favorite of the indulgent sky,		Y 3	On a Daffodill	5

		PAGE	TITLE		LINE
BE	(CONTINUED)				
May the morn's earliest tears on thee be shed,		Y 3	On a Daffodill		11
On his dead body let a tomb be plac'd		Y 7	Virgil Daphnis		28
And be the stone with this inscription grac'd:		Y 7	Virgil Daphnis		29
Think shouldst thou fall how wretched shall we be,		Y 19	Tr. Iliad Bk 6		48
There let the web and distaff be your care.		Y 21	Tr. Iliad Bk 6		122
And he'll be hang'd to-morrow.		Y 300	Fanny Burney		5
BEACH					
Extends its Lines along the sandy Beach,		O 304	Irene		4
Breathless, amaz'd, and on the guarded Beach		O 335	Irene		8
BEACONS					
From hill to hill the beacons rousing blaze		O 43	Vanity Wishes		247
BEAKS					
The Cranes with beaks and claws provoke the fight.		O 75	Tr Add. Battle		3
Whilst beaks and swords engage in bloody fray		Y 22	Tr Add. Battle		6
Which whet their beaks, for flight their wings prepare,		Y 24	Tr Add. Battle		70
BEAM					
Thy lambent glories only beam		O 100	Ode Friendship		11
Thy milder glories only beam		Y 71	Ode Friendship	V	11
That spread their Colours to the genial Beam,		O 298	Irene		20
Confirm your Troops; and when the Moon's fair Beam		O 306	Irene		58
BEAMS					
Engross not all the beams on high,		O 126	To Lyce, Lady		5
With mouldring cement and with beams disjointed		Y 114	Irene	V	45
Live till the Sun forgets to dart his Beams,		O 262	Irene		3
And scatter Discord from their baleful Beams.		O 271	Irene		5
Now but reflects those Beams that flow'd from thee.		O 298	Irene		15
Or glare on Cali with malignant Beams.		O 304	Irene		36
Shall shed his Beams upon the bridal Bed,		O 309	Irene		24
Th' applauding Sky shall pour forth all its Beams		O 322	Irene		9
BEAMY					
And plac'd the beamy terror on the ground		Y 20	Tr. Iliad Bk 6		96
BEAR					
I cannot bear a French metropolis.		O 15	London		98
And bear oppression's insolence no more.		O 18	London		175
Where Atlas was believ'd to bear		O 79	Feast St Simon		31
The Bear enrag'd th' affrighted Moon shall dread;		O 111	To Posterity		17
Bear lives in amity with bear.		O 138	Tr Rambler 160		2
Bear lives in amity with bear.		O 138	Tr Rambler 160		2
The lust of wealth can never bear delay.		O 140	Tr Rambler 182		1
"Soft Anacreon's vows I bear,		O 185	Anacreon Ode 9		7
Besides, he has fifty Wives; and who can bear		O 247	Irene Epilogue		5
Could bear his Son upon the Turkish Throne.		O 264	Irene		22
And bear us far from Servitude and Crimes.		O 267	Irene		44
Bear him aloft above the wond'ring Clouds,		O 274	Irene		62
But thou, too old to bear another Cheat,		O 283	Irene		32
Relax'd with Fear, refuse to bear me forward.		O 320	Irene		12
Bear off with eager Haste th' unfinish'd Sentence,		O 333	Irene		53
BEARS					
There ev'ry breeze bears health upon its wings;		O 20	London		221
And bears me to the peaceful shades,		O 125	An Ode		15
Bears toilsome Days, and wakes long tedious Nights:		O 247	Irene Epilogue		22
That bears the Fate of Empires in her Air,		O 317	Irene		2
BEAST					
No beast more dreadful ever stain'd		O 66	Hor I Ode xxii	V	13
No Beast more dreadful ever stain'd		O 67	To A. Fuscus		13
No Beast more fierce Numidia's Land,		O 67	To A. Fuscus		15
BEASTS					
Beasts of each kind their fellows spare;		O 138	Tr Rambler 160		1
BEAT					
Ye Nymphs, whose Bosoms beat at Milton's Name,		O 57	Prologue Comus		2
When ev'ry Wave shall beat a Turkish Shore,		O 265	Irene		43
Till every Wave shall beat a Turkish Shore.		O 354	Irene	V	26
BEATING					
Lull'd by the beating winds and dashing show'rs!		O 135	Tr Rambler 117		2
Pensive and listning to the beating Surge.		O 254	Irene		128
BEATS					
Where Tigris beats his sounding shore		O 80	Feast St Simon		52
My Heart still beats responsive to the Sultan's;		O 272	Irene		9
Beats not the female Breast with gen'rous Passions,		O 278	Irene		57
BEAU					
Behold the warrior dwindled to a beau;		O 15	London		104
BEAUTEOUS SEE BEAUTIOUS					
Her heav'nly voice, and beauteous face.		O 66	Hor I Ode xxii		24
Around in beauteous order stand.		O 73	Hor. Epode II		72
Tears, at my name, shall drown those beauteous eyes,		O 75	Tr. Iliad Bk 6		27
For such thy beauteous mind, and lovely face,		O 107	Lady F Assizes		5
At sight of sparkling bowls or beauteous dames,		O 142	In Baretti Bk.		1
And brought his beauteous Plunder to the Sultan.		O 258	Irene		96
Unless the beauteous Fabrick was design'd		O 277	Irene		28
Now beauteous Daphnis cloath'd with heav'nly light,		Y 7	Virgil Daphnis		32
But the next blooming virgin's beauteous face		Y 12	Tr Hor Epode 9		41
He met Andromache his beauteous wife		Y 18	Tr. Iliad Bk 6		5
BEAUTIES					
At length must Suffolk's beauties shine in vain,		O 107	Lady F Assizes		1
The beauties of the gay brocade,		O 122	Stella Mourn.		2
And spare him, Beauties! tho' his Lovers live.		O 246	Irene Prologue		20
Forgetful of Command, with captive Beauties,		O 258	Irene		92
And dwell upon the Beauties of Irene.		O 262	Irene		10
O may her Beauties last unchang'd by Time,		O 262	Irene		11
Blasts all the Beauties of his new Creation,		O 269	Irene		7

28

		PAGE	TITLE	LINE

BEAUTIES   (CONTINUED)

How will the matchless Beauties of Irene, ... O 276 Irene 6
Aspasia! who can look upon thy Beauties? . . . . . O 281 Irene 42
Recline upon my Breast thy sinking Beauties: . . . . O 295 Irene 8
Unlike the trifling Race of vulgar Beauties, ... O 298 Irene 18
Deform the beauties of the breathing statue (marble hero Y 177 Irene V111A
And melt her treach'rous Beauties into Ruin. . . . . O 315 Irene 37
And melt the treach'rous Beauties into Ruin. . . . . O 315 Irene V 37
Beauties insulted by a slave-- . . . . Y 202 Irene V 1
Heard her last Cries, and fann'd her dying Beauties, . . O 333 Irene 47

BEAUTIFUL

How shall I scorn the beautiful Apostate! . . . . . O 261 Irene 22

BEAUTIOUS

Hail beauteous earnest of approaching spring! . . . . Y 3 On a Daffodill 2
May throngs of beauteous virgins 'round thee crowd, . . Y 3 On a Daffodill 13

BEAUTY

Should Beauty blunt on fops her fatal dart, ... O 37 Vanity Wishes 151
The queen, the beauty, sets the world in arms; . . . . O 42 Vanity Wishes 246
Yet Vane could tell what ills from beauty spring; . . . O 45 Vanity Wishes 321
Now beauty falls betray'd, despis'd, distress'd, . . . O 47 Vanity Wishes 341
Here beauty falls betray'd, despis'd, distress'd, . . . O 47 Vanity Wishes V 341
Alas! 'tis hard for beauty to be just. . . . . . O 81 Lady Birthday 12
And every beauty withers at the blast: . . . . . O 84 Epi Dist Moth. 35
And beauty smile auspicious in each face; . . . . . O 84 Epi Dist Moth. 45
Where Beauty lavishes her pow'rs . . . . O 120 To Miss Playin 3
Tho' rapture sings, and beauty shines. . . . . . O 125 An Ode 12
Oft when the Cries of violated Beauty . . . . . . O 251 Irene 73
Of equal Beauty, but of softer Mien, ... O 259 Irene 119
Why should the Sultan shun the Joys of Beauty, . . . O 261 Irene 7
Each Realm where Beauty turns the graceful Shape, . . . O 262 Irene 13
And sought An easier conquest in my softer beauty . . . Y 134 Irene V 35
Diffuse Irene's Beauty though the World. . . . . . O 268 Irene 14
Such heav'nly Beauty form'd for Adoration, ... O 269 Irene 41
Such Beauty must not shine to vulgar Eyes. . . . . O 269 Irene 43
Irene rise, thou daughter of perfection--or . . . . Y 145 Irene V 1
   beauty
Amidst the Splendor of encircling Beauty, ... O 288 Irene 1
Suspend awhile the privilege of powr (and Beauty) . . . O 366 Irene V 21
Those forms of men that play before a . . . . . . Y 173 Irene V 18
   beauty
Spread wide their kind Arms to Science and to Beauty. . . O 353 Irene V 5
Now, Tyrant, with Satiety of Beauty, ... O 304 Irene 33
That fatal Beauty plighted to Demetrius . . . . . O 307 Irene 15
Adore the Beauty but despise th' Apostate. . . . . O 350 Irene V 26
Bids Beauty, such as thine, prepare to die. . . . . O 324 Irene 3
Some cruel Stratagem of jealous Beauty! . . . . . O 326 Irene 37
Deem us not deaf to Woe, nor blind to Beauty, ... O 327 Irene 29
Such Beauty, Sweetness, Love, were cheaply bought, . . O 332 Irene 35
Behold the Model of consummate Beauty, ... O 334 Irene 3

BEAUTY'S

Here beauty's drops her pomp, despis'd, distress'd . . Y 107 Vanity Wishes V 341
Receives his full Reward in Beauty's Arms. . . . . O 247 Irene Epilogue 24
And all Aspasia but her Beauty's Man. . . . . . . O 266 Irene 37

BECALM

Must dull Suspence becalm still the stagnant mind? . . Y 107 Vanity Wishes V 344

BECALMS

Nor dull Serenity becalms his Eyes. . . . . . . O 255 Irene 16

BECAME

There I became, nor blush to make it known, ... O 312 Irene 13
There she soon became a jilt, ... Y 300 Extemp. Elegy 9

BECAUSE

That loses all because she hazards nothing: . . . . O 281 Irene 45
Because I love: . . . . O 281 Irene 48
Because my slighted Passion burns in vain! . . . . O 281 Irene 49
But call'd Astyanax because his sire . . . . . . Y 18 Tr. Iliad Bk 6 13

BECOME

And bid Success become the Test of Truth; . . . . O 291 Irene 64

BED

That concord smile on the connubial bed; . . . . . O 131 Tr. Rambler 45 2
In bed we laugh, in bed we cry, ... O 184 Tr. Benserade 1
In bed we laugh, in bed we cry, ... O 184 Tr. Benserade 1
And born in bed, in bed we die; . . . . O 184 Tr. Benserade 2
And born in bed, in bed we die; . . . . O 184 Tr. Benserade 2
The near approach a bed may shew . . . . O 184 Tr. Benserade 3
Rise from the happy Bed; and future Queens . . . . O 268 Irene 13
Shall shed his Beams upon the bridal Bed, ... O 309 Irene 24
May Penitence attend thy mournful Bed, ... O 322 Irene 61

BEDECK'D

Truth in platonic ornaments bedeck'd, ... O 134 Tr. Rambler 96 1

BEDROP'D

With Purple varied and bedrop'd with Gold, ... O 277 Irene 35

BEDS

And, while thy beds a cheap repast afford, ... O 20 London V 218
On beds of never-fading flow'rs, ... O 120 To Miss Playin 4
Unhappy! whom to beds of pain . . . . O 125 An Ode 9

BEECHEN

Play on your pipe beneath this beechen shade; . . . . O 64 Virgil Past.I 2

BEEN

Had we not been perverse and careless grown, ... O 64 Virgil Past.I 21
Epilogue intended to have been spoken by a Lady . . . O 83 Epi Dist Moth. T
And on its basis would have been enroll'd, ... O 190 Seeing Montagu 5

		PAGE	TITLE	LINE
BEEN	(CONTINUED)			
This were enough, if Cali had been Mahomet	. . . . .	Y 132	Irene	V 41D
Half were too much had Mahomet been Cali.	. . . . .	Y 132	Irene	V 41E
BEER				
--Come, my lad, and drink some beer.	. . . .	O 181	Parody Warton	8
BEES				
Or drains the Labour of the Bees,	. . . .	O 71	Hor. Epode II	21
While bees shall feed on thyme, and birds shall haunt the grove		Y 7	Virgil Daphnis	50
BEFIT				
Might well befit the solitary Student,	. . . . . .	O 281	Irene	36
BEFORE				
And raise his treasures higher than before.	. . . . . .	O 19	London	205
And sign your will before you sup from home.	. . . . .	O 21	London	225
And make will before you sup from home.	. . . . . .	Y 59	London	V 225
And senates heard before they judg'd a cause;	. . . .	O 33	Vanity Wishes	60
Before that day, by some brave hero's hand,	. . . . .	O 75	Tr. Iliad Bk 6	29
And shades of Pygmies swim before their eye.	. . . . .	O 77	Tr Add. Battle	48
His tortur'd Sons shall die before his Face,	. . . . .	O 111	To Posterity	23
Find here that calm thou gav'st so oft before;	. . . . .	O 113	Epit. Phillips	4
Why boast their Birth before his Eyes,	. . . . . .	O 147	Tr Boeth III.6	17
To sink the fatal precipice before him,	. . . . .	O 176	Tr Metastas II	4
To sink the fatal precipice before them,	. . . . .	O 176	Tr Metastas II	V 4
Before such Foes of more than human Force;	. . . . .	O 250	Irene	49
And teror and confusion stalk before them	. . . . .	Y 115	Irene	V 49E
Will he not melt before Ambition's Fire?	. . . . .	O 255	Irene	23
Long have I wish'd, before our Prophet's Tomb,	. . . .	O 263	Irene	9
Stern Torture shakes his bloody Scourge before me,	. . .	O 266	Irene	15
How Nation after Nation falls before him.	. . . . .	O 268	Irene	27
How nation after nation falls before me	. . . . . .	Y 136	Irene	V 27
Before th' assembled Troops proclaim his Crimes;	. . .	O 273	Irene	35
Should we before the Troops proclaim his Crimes	. . . .	O 273	Irene	38
Security shall spread her Shield before them,	. . . . .	O 279	Irene	82
Give me, before th' approaching Hour of Fate,	. . . . .	O 285	Irene	5
I displaid--before her all the gay luscious scene...	. .	Y 158	Irene	V 8
And bad imperial splendour glare (blaze) before her	. .	Y 158	Irene	V 10
The Present, Past, and Future swim before me,	. . . . .	O 295	Irene	13
Those forms of men that play before a	. . . .	Y 173	Irene	V 18
beauty				
And saw my scatter'd Squadrons fly before him.	. . . . .	O 307	Irene	20
When next we meet before we storm the Palace,	. . . . .	O 308	Irene	28
The houries of our Prophet blush before her	. . . . .	Y 184	Irene	V 10
anguish of my soul before Thee.	. . . . . .	Y 189	Irene	V 1
faded before her	. . . . . .	Y 191	Irene	V 14
Remember, Peace and Anguish are before thee,	. . . . .	O 321	Irene	37
While she yet beg'd to plead her Cause before thee.	. .	O 334	Irene	67
But, ah! before arise that hapless day	. . . .	Y 18	Tr. Iliad Bk 6	24
Or how before Nassau the Gallick troops retir'd?	. . .	Y 22	Tr Add. Battle	13
Quickly the Cranes appear before their eyes;	. . . .	Y 25	Tr Add. Battle	92
Before his face the frighted Cranes gave way.	. . . .	Y 25	Tr Add. Battle	122
BEG				
All that at home no more can beg or steal,	. . . . .	O 15	London	107
This Hour I'll beg, with unsuspecting Face,	. . . .	O 258	Irene	86
But who can hear thee beg without compliance	. . . .	Y 205	Irene	V 33
BEG'D				
While she yet beg'd to plead her Cause before thee.	. .	O 334	Irene	67
BEGAN				
In life's first bloom his publick toils began,	. . . .	O 117	Epitaph Hanmer	11
Soon as their young began to draw their breath	. . .	Y 24	Tr Add. Battle	86
BEGAN'ST				
Thou, who began'st a man, wilt end a boy.	. . . . .	O 135	Tr Rambler 127	2
BEGG'D				
Says swelling Crispin, begg'd a cobbler's vote.	. . .	O 60	Pro Good Nat'd	22
BEGGAR				
Spurn'd as a beggar, dreaded as a spy,	. . . . . .	O 14	London	81
BEGGAR'D				
Refund the plunder of the beggar'd land.	. . . . . .	O 19	London	201
BEGGER				
Spurn'd as a begger, dreaded as a spy,	. . . . .	O 14	London	V 81
BEGGER'D				
Refund the plunder of the begger'd land.	. . . . .	O 19	London	V 201
BEGIN				
Must begin by Thirty five:	. . . .	O 178	Thrale 35 Year	16
BEGINNING				
From one sublime Beginning spring;	. . . .	O 146	Tr Boeth III.6	2
BEGINS				
The march begins in military state,	. . . . . .	O 40	Vanity Wishes	205
Now say, where virtue stops and vice begins?	. . . .	O 139	Tr Rambler 173	1
And so here begins my tale.	. . . .	Y 300	Extemp. Elegy	4
BEGS				
Begs for each birth the fortune of a face:	. . . .	O 45	Vanity Wishes	320
There begs of heav'n a less distinguish'd lot;	. . . .	O 82	Young Author	29
BEGUILE				
Slaves that with serious impudence beguile,	. . . . .	O 17	London	146
BEHELD				
Beheld with love, with veneration heard.	. . . . . .	O 118	Epitaph Hanmer	26
With false Security beheld Invasion.	. . . . . .	O 250	Irene	30
Beheld without Concern, expiring Greece,	. . . . . .	O 250	Irene	34
With him Abdalla we beheld--	. . . . . .	O 311	Irene	8
Beheld the tragic heroes taught to fear.	. . . . . .	Y 67	Prologue Lethe	8

		PAGE	TITLE	LINE
BEHIND				
Delude the most; few pry behind the scene.	. . . . .	O 139	Tr Rambler 168	2
Leaves the Load of Earth behind.	. . . .	O 147	Tr Boet III.12	4
Looks back on what She left behind,	. . . . . .	O 150	Tr Boet III.12	57
Has left the slaves behind, nay then there's danger.	. . .	Y 198	Irene V	34
Leave Slav'ry, Guilt, and Infamy behind.	. . . . .	O 320	Irene	31
Oft from behind they wounded them with darts	. . . .	Y 23	Tr Add. Battle	42
BEHNS				
New Behns, new Durfeys, yet remain in Store.	. . . .	O 53	Pro Drury-Lane	42
BEHOLD				
Behold her cross triumphant on the main,	. . . . . .	O 10	London	27
Behold rebellious virtue quite o'erthrown,	. . . .	O 13	London	63
Behold our fame, our wealth, our lives your own.	. . .	O 13	London	64
Behold the warrior dwindled to a beau;	. . . . . .	O 15	London	104
Behold surrounding kings their pow'r combine,	. . . .	O 40	Vanity Wishes	199
Behold this Theatre, and grieve no more.	. . . . .	O 57	Prologue Comus	10
While Crowds aloft the laureat Bust behold,	. . . .	O 58	Prologue Comus	23
While Crowds aloft the laureat Dust behold,	. . . .	O 58	Prologue Comus V	23
I should behold with scornful eye	. . . . .	O 73	Hor. Epode II	55
Behold the wife of Hector, guard of Troy!	. . . .	O 74	Tr. Iliad Bk 6	26
Behold my fair, where-e'er we rove,	. . . . .	O 123	Winter's Walk	1
Unhappy man! behold thy doom,	. . . . . .	O 124	Winter's Walk	14
Now Daedalus, behold, by fate assign'd,	. . . . .	O 136	Tr Rambler 129	1
The fields, and woods, behold, are green,	. . . .	O 231	Tr Horace IV.7	2
Behold the Monsters gaze with savage Rapture,	. . . .	O 252	Irene	81
Behold how Lust and Rapine struggle round her.	. . .	O 252	Irene	82
Behold our future Sultaness, Abdalla;--	. . . .	O 267	Irene	1
Behold, my fair, as my resistless hand	. . . . .	Y 136	Irene V	25
Behold contending nations vie for bondage	. . . .	Y 136	Irene V	26
Once to behold the Charms of bright Aspasia,	. . .	O 285	Irene	6
Aspasia! do I once again behold thee?	. . . . . .	O 294	Irene	2
Behold the Hero with Aspasia's Eyes?	. . . . .	O 296	Irene	31
Behold him here, in Love, in War successful,	. . . .	O 310	Irene	4
Behold him wretched in his double Triumph;	. . . .	O 310	Irene	5
Behold, within th' embow'ring Grove	. . . . .	O 314	Irene	10
Behold thy boasted Honours snatch'd away.	. . . .	O 317	Irene	43
Once more I dare thy Sword, behold the Prize,	. . .	O 319	Irene	28
Behold I quit her to the Chance of Battle.	. . . .	O 319	Irene	29
Behold a Boaster's Worth. Now snatch, my Fair,	. . .	O 320	Irene	7
Behold the Model of consummate Beauty,	. . . .	O 334	Irene	3
Behold Irene--o'erthrown	. . . . . .	Y 217	Irene V	10
And ah! behold the shriveling blossoms die,	. . . .	Y 4	On a Daffodill	23
BEHOLDS				
How pleas'd beholds his Oxen bow	. . . .	O 73	Hor. Epode II	69
Beholds a long posterity of freemen	. . . . .	Y 122	Irene V	61
Beholds the fainting Garrison retire,	. . . . .	O 298	Irene	28
BEING				
Or wand'ring in the Wilds of future Being,	. . . .	O 255	Irene	6
Expands the boundless scenes of future being	. . .	Y 133	Irene V	8
Are only varied Modes of endless Being;	. . . .	O 290	Irene	27
Deny'd Debard each privilege of human nature being	. .	Y 165	Irene V	81
O say, bright Being, in this Age of Absence,	. . .	O 295	Irene	21
But being counsell'd to go home	. . . . . .	Y 11	Tr Hor Epode 9	31
BEINGS				
Those holy Beings, whose superiour Care	. . . .	O 289	Irene	17
Those holy Beings whose unseen Direction	. . . .	O 346	Irene V	5
En<v>ies the meanest minister of Heav'n of celestial beings.	. .	Y 168	Irene	V135A
BELESSI				
Kai Bion, eipen, otan ripses Thanatio Belessi,	. . .	O 108	Eis Birchion	3
BELIEF				
Till Affectation, rip'ning to Belief,	. . . . .	O 266	Irene	31
BELIEV'D				
Where Atlas was believ'd to bear	. . . . . .	O 79	Feast St Simon	31
BELINDA'S				
So shall Belinda's charms improve mankind.	. . . .	O 81	Lady Birthday	19
BELONG				
All her Charms to thee belong;	. . . . .	O 150	Tr Boet III.12	42
BELONGS				
To men belongs the dreadfull work of war."	. . . .	Y 21	Tr. Iliad Bk 6	123
BELOV'D				
From his belov'd retirement draw,	. . . . . .	O 71	Hor. Epode II	14
BELOW				
With louder ruin to the gulphs below?	. . . . .	O 35	Vanity Wishes	128
Those pageant Honours which he scorn'd below:	. . .	O 57	Prologue Comus	22
Or move the haughty King below,	. . . . .	O 69	Hor.II Ode 14	10
Now in the realms below the Pygmie shades	. . . .	O 76	Tr Add. Battle	41
What rais'd our Virtues here below,	. . . . .	O 100	Ode Friendship	27
What rais'd your Virtue here below,	. . . . .	O 100	Ode Friendship V	27
And soaring mocks the broken frame below.	. . . .	O 131	Tr. Rambler 17	1
Shun the Sea-sapp'd Sand below;	. . . . .	O 145	Tr Boeth. II.4	8
Say what is happiness below?	. . . . . .	O 146	Tr Boeth III.4	8
Rushes on the Realms below.	. . . . . .	O 149	Tr Boet III.12	18
With sport above and death below;	. . . . .	O 203	Tr. on Skating	2
BEND				
Will he not bend beneath a Tyrant's Frown?	. . . .	O 255	Irene	22
bend tyrant adamant--melt harlot	. . . . .	Y 181	Irene V	56
Perhaps I will not bend to plead my cause	. . . .	Y 210	Irene V	22
BENDING				
And weaves her bending boughs in pleasing glooms;	. . .	O 84	Epi Dist Moth.	15

```
BENDS                                                   PAGE    TITLE            LINE
    Or bends with violent force the trees.  .  .  .  .  .   O  67  Hor. II Ode IX      8
    Where'er the battle rages bends his course.  .  .  .  .  Y  25  Tr Add. Battle    119
BENEATH
    Low skulks the hind beneath the rage of pow'r,  .  .  .  O  32  Vanity Wishes      33
    Why but to sink beneath misfortune's blow,  .  .  .  .  O  35  Vanity Wishes     127
    "And all be mine beneath the polar sky."  .  .  .  .  .  O  40  Vanity Wishes     204
    "And all is mine beneath the polar sky."  .  .  .  .  .  O  40  Vanity Wishes   V 204
    Play on your pipe beneath this beechen shade;  .  .  .  O  64  Virgil Past.I        2
    Place me beneath the burning line,  .  .  .  .  .  .  .  O  66  Hor I Ode xxii     21
    Place me beneath the burning Zone,  .  .  .  .  .  .  .  O  67  To A. Fuscus       21
    And where beneath th' inclement Skie  .  .  .  .  .  .  O  70  Hor.II Ode XX      15
    Beneath some spreading Ilex Shade  .  .  .  .  .  .  .  O  72  Hor. Epode II      29
    Beneath some venerable Shade  .  .  .  .  .  .  .  .  .  O  72  Hor. Epode II   V  29
    Beneath Hyperia's waters shall you sweat,  .  .  .  .  O  74  Tr. Iliad Bk 6     23
    Beneath Pygmean steel what numbers dye!  .  .  .  .  .  O  75  Tr Add. Battle      5
    But where the Realms beneath the Pole  .  .  .  .  .  .  O  79  Feast St Simon     44
    Whene'er this Stone, now hid beneath the Lake,  .  .  .  O 110  To Posterity        1
    From beneath the cumbrous Weight;  .  .  .  .  .  .  .  O 145  Tr Boeth. II.4     12
    For tho' beneath thy haughty Brow  .  .  .  .  .  .  .  O 146  Tr Boeth III.5      5
    When some neglected Fabrick nods beneath  .  .  .  .  .  O 250  Irene              44
    Sink not beneath imaginary Sorrows:  .  .  .  .  .  .  O 252  Irene              84
    Will he not bend beneath a Tyrant's Frown?  .  .  .  .  O 255  Irene              22
    Each Land that smiles beneath benigner Skies  .  .  .  O 366  Irene           V  12
    And whelms the swelling Architect beneath it.  .  .  .  O 269  Irene               9
    Beneath the Load of Business, and of Years.  .  .  .  .  O 271  Irene               7
    Bribe to his Cause and list beneath his Banners  .  .  O 274  Irene              53
    Beneath the Covert of this verdant Arch  .  .  .  .  .  O 275  Irene              78
    Unbounded Wealth shall flow beneath thy feet  .  .  .  O 350  Irene           V  23
    Beneath each Curse of unrelenting Heav'n,  .  .  .  .  O 292  Irene              86
    With every curse of angry heav'n afflicted beneath  .  O 357  Irene           V  15
      each
    And thought the petty Dross beneath a Sigh.  .  .  .  .  O 302  Irene             109
    Forbear--But thou art sunk beneath Reproach;  .  .  .  O 315  Irene              28
    Beneath his feet admires each shining star,  .  .  .  .  Y   7  Virgil Daphnis     34
    May I lye cold beneath a load of clay.  .  .  .  .  .  Y  18  Tr. Iliad Bk 6     25
BENEFICENT
    For when was Pow'r beneficent in vain?  .  .  .  .  .  O 313  Irene              23
    For Non Who was e'er beneficent in vain?  .  .  .  .  O 377  Irene           V   4
BENEVOLENCE
    Heroic worth, benevolence divine:  .  .  .  .  .  .  .  O  34  Vanity Wishes      88
    Whose peaceful day Benevolence endears,  .  .  .  .  .  O  44  Vanity Wishes     295
    The lambent Flames of mild Benevolence,  .  .  .  .  .  O 293  Irene             109
BENIGNER
    Each Land that smiles beneath benigner Skies  .  .  .  O 366  Irene           V  12
BENUMB
    What sleepy Charms benumb these active Heroes,  .  .  .  O 325  Irene              14
BESET
    Beset the treacherous Way with fatal Ambush;  .  .  .  O 300  Irene              72
BESIDE
    In private Conference; beside him stood  .  .  .  .  .  O 275  Irene              79
BESIDES
    Besides, with justice, this discerning age  .  .  .  .  O  16  London            132
    Besides, he has fifty Wives; and who can bear  .  .  .  O 247  Irene Epilogue      5
BESIEG'D
    Ill-fated Race! So oft besieg'd in vain,  .  .  .  .  .  O 250  Irene              29
BESIEGERS
    Oft when the fierce Besiegers eager Host  .  .  .  .  .  O 298  Irene              27
BEST
    Secure whate'er he gives, he gives the best.  .  .  .  O  48  Vanity Wishes     356
    And hope with humble confidence the best  .  .  .  .  .  Y 108  Vanity Wishes   V 356
    At best, a fleeting gleam, or empty sound.  .  .  .  .  O  62  Pro Word Wise      20
    Then best enjoy'd, when most improv'd.  .  .  .  .  .  O 125  An Ode             28
    When best enjoy'd, when most improv'd.  .  .  .  .  .  O 125  An Ode          V  28
BESTOW
    A transient calm the happy scenes bestow,  .  .  .  .  O  10  London             31
    He sees, and pitying sees, vain Wealth bestow  .  .  .  O  57  Prologue Comus     21
    If such on Earth can Bliss bestow,  .  .  .  .  .  .  .  O 146  Tr Boeth III.4      7
BESTOW'D
    New pow'rs are claim'd, new pow'rs are still bestow'd,  .  O  42  Vanity Wishes     233
    Those blessings, friend, a deity bestow'd,  .  .  .  .  O  64  Virgil Past.I       7
    "On the bard her Dove bestow'd.  .  .  .  .  .  .  .  .  O 185  Anacreon Ode 9     12
BESTOWS
    Wit, brav'ry, worth, his lavish tongue bestows;  .  .  .  O  16  London            126
    His smile alone security bestows:  .  .  .  .  .  .  .  O  34  Vanity Wishes     104
    Nor deem, when learning her last prize bestows,  .  .  .  O  38  Vanity Wishes     165
    Nor deem, when learning her lost prize bestows,  .  .  .  O  38  Vanity Wishes   V 165
    Nor think though learning her last prize bestows,  .  .  Y  99  Vanity Wishes   V 165
    Our bane and physic the same earth bestows,  .  .  .  .  O 131  Tr. Rambler 21      1
    "Now my better lot bestows  .  .  .  .  .  .  .  .  .  .  O 185  Anacreon Ode 9     29
    When Heav'n bestows the Privilege to bless,  .  .  .  .  O 313  Irene              21
BESTREW'D
    Of Fields with dead bestrew'd around,  .  .  .  .  .  .  O  78  Feast St Simon      1
BESTROW
    Ye swains! bestrow the ground with leaves and spread  .  Y   7  Virgil Daphnis     26
BETIMES
    Betimes the greedy Thrush to kill  .  .  .  .  .  .  .  O  72  Hor. Epode II      41
BETRAY
    Commence your lords, and govern or betray.  .  .  .  .  O  17  London            157
    Where Hate sits musing to betray,  .  .  .  .  .  .  .  O 191  Tr. Medea I        11
    Betray my King to Negligence of Danger.  .  .  .  .  .  O 275  Irene              73
```

```
BETRAY              (CONTINUED)                      PAGE    TITLE           LINE
  Or but one Moment's Pause betray Confusion,  . . . . .   O 332 Irene           15
BETRAY'D
  Where wav'ring man, betray'd by vent'rous pride,   . . .  O  31 Vanity Wishes      7
  Now beauty falls betray'd, despis'd, distress'd,   . . .  O  47 Vanity Wishes    341
  Here beauty falls betray'd, despis'd, distress'd,  . . .  O  47 Vanity Wishes  V 341
  Till Shame regain'd the Post that Sense betray'd,  . . .  O  52 Pro Drury-Lane    27
  His kind Intelligence betray'd their Measures;  . . . .   O 253 Irene           118
  Betray'd some Traytor lurking near my Bosom.   . . . .    O 273 Irene            23
  Betray'd the wild Emotions of his Mind.  . . . . . .      O 311 Irene             4
  Betray'd by Falshood, or by Crouds o'erborn?   . . . .    O 315 Irene             7
  Whose Fear, or Rage, or Treachery betray'd us. . . . .    O 316 Irene            17
  Why did you stay? deserted and betray'd?   . . . . .      O 317 Irene            34
  Perhaps my Zeal too fierce betray'd my Prudence;   . . .  O 330 Irene            20
BETRAYS
  Each act betrays the fever of renown  . . . . . . .       Y  97 Vanity Wishes  V 137
  Your careless Love betrays your Country's Cause.  . . .   O 297 Irene            10
BETTER
  Or like a gibbet better than a wheel;   . . . . . . .     O  15 London          108
  To better features yields the frame of gold;   . . . .    O  34 Vanity Wishes     86
  Long may better Years arrive,   . . . . . . . .           O 178 Thrale 35 Year     3
  Oft may better Years arrive,  . . . . . . . .             O 178 Thrale 35 Year   V 3
  Better Years than Thirty five;  . . . . . . . .           O 178 Thrale 35 Year     4
  "Now my better lot bestows  . . . . . . . . .             O 185 Anacreon Ode 9    29
  The better use of notes, or sweet or shrill,   . . . .    O 192 Tr. Medea II       9
  "Awake, and follow me to better Fortunes;"   . . . .      O 254 Irene            123
  Thou kind Assistant of my better Angel,  . . . . . .      O 298 Irene            10
BETTYS
  Call the Bettys, Kates, and Jennys  . . . . . . . .       O 196 Song Congratu.     9
BETWEEN
  Translation of part of the Dialogue between  . . . . .    O  74 Tr. Iliad Bk 6     T
  And share the Pleasures of the World  . . . . . .         O 348 Irene           V 20
    between Us
BEUTEOUS
  --The beuteous Fiend The shining mischief   . . . . .     O 375 Irene           V 12
BEWAIL'D
  The nymphs bewail'd poor Daphnis' hapless death   . . .   Y   6 Virgil Daphnis     1
  The nymphs bewail'd his fall with loud lament   . . . .   Y  18 Tr. Iliad Bk 6    32
BEWARE
  Beware of Mustapha, beware of Treason.   . . . . . .      O 273 Irene            29
  Beware of Mustapha, beware of Treason.   . . . . . .      O 273 Irene            29
  But yet, great Emperor, beware of Treason;   . . . . .    O 273 Irene            31
BEWILDER'D
  Propitious Guide of my bewilder'd Soul,  . . . . . .      O 298 Irene            11
BEWILDERD
  To man bewilderd in this maze of sorrows   . . . . .      Y 148 Irene           V 43
BEYOND
  'Tis yours to crown Desert--beyond the Grave!  . . . .    O  58 Prologue Comus    38
  Beyond the Power of Constancy and Courage;   . . . .      O 251 Irene            53
  Th' eternal Snows that freeze beyond Meotis,   . . . .    O 274 Irene            59
  The eternal Snows that shine beyond Maeotis  . . . .      O 360 Irene           V  2
  Swell not thy Soul beyond Advice or Friendship,  . . .    O 289 Irene             2
  Swell not your Soul beyond reproof or Counsel  . . . .    O 366 Irene           V 18
  But should I sin beyond the Hope of Mercy,   . . . . .    O 289 Irene            23
  Beyond my warmest Hope, or wildest Wishes,   . . . .      O 296 Irene            35
  Beyond the Mists of Care thy Pinion tow'rs.  . . . . .    O 313 Irene             8
  Thrown beyond the verge of providence  . . . . . .        Y 199 Irene           V 16
  Beyond the Fear of ling'ring Punishment,   . . . . . .    O 325 Irene            16
BID
  And bid him go to hell, to hell he goes.   . . . . . .    O  15 London          116
  'Tis yours this Night to bid the Reign commence  . . .    O  53 Pro Drury-Lane    57
  Bid scenic Virtue form the rising Age,   . . . . . .      O  53 Pro Drury-Lane    61
  We bid propitious Heav'n prolong your reign,   . . . .    O  96 Hickman Spinet     7
  Must bid his Passions all obey;  . . . . . . . .          O 146 Tr Boeth III.5     2
  Must bid each wild Desire be still,   . . . . . .         O 146 Tr Boeth III.5     3
  Bid your teizing doubts depart;  . . . . . . . .          O 176 Tr Metastasi I     2
  Bid the slaves of thrift farewell.   . . . . . . .        O 196 Song Congratu.     8
  Bid the Sons of thrift farewell.   . . . . . . .          O 196 Song Congratu.   V 8
  Bid them come, and take their fill.  . . . . . . .        O 196 Song Congratu.    20
  A Winged Messenger, or bid the Grave   . . . . . .        O 365 Irene           V 21
  To bid the prostrate Captive rise and live,  . . . . .    O 278 Irene            70
  Bid Pleasure bloom and Cities reascend.  . . . . .        O 372 Irene           V 10
  To Bid wasted Regions flourish at her smile  . . . . .    O 372 Irene           V  8
  And bid Success become the Test of Truth;  . . . . .      O 291 Irene            64
  Or bid soft Science polish Britain's Heroes:   . . . .    O 293 Irene           106
  Or bid fair Science polish Britains Heroes   . . . .      O 348 Irene           V 22
  Prudence and Friendship bid me force her from you.  . .   O 296 Irene             7
  Then--O my Fair, I cannot bid thee goe;  . . . . .        O 297 Irene            15
  Then--O my Fair, I cannot bid thee go;   . . . . . .      O 297 Irene           V 15
  When Heav'n shall bid the swelling Billows rage,   . .    O 300 Irene            60
  And bid thy visionary Throne farewell.   . . . . .        O 307 Irene            11
  Or bid her great Camilli  . . . . . . . . .               Y 185 Irene           V 39
  And bid the master Genius rule the World.  . . . . .      O 309 Irene            42
  Shall the whirle, and bid the Rock subside   . . . .      O 365 Irene           V  4
  Abdalla, bid thy troubled Breast be calm;  . . . . .      O 329 Irene             2
BIDS
  When injur'd Thales bids the town farewell,  . . . . .    O   8 London             2
  And bids afflicted worth retire to peace.  . . . . .      O  45 Vanity Wishes    310
  He bids the Sword destroy, the Flame devour.   . . . .    O  97 Hickman Spinet    14
  He bids no Trumpet quell the fatal Sound.  . . . . .      O 246 Irene Prologue    24
  And bids us thus disguis'd await him here.   . . . . .    O 253 Irene           115
```

	PAGE	TITLE	LINE
BIDS (CONTINUED)			
But bids you rove the Paths of Bliss, secure	O 276	Irene	18
And Duty bids me chuse a distant Walk,	O 288	Irene	13
Bids Beauty, such as thine, prepare to die.	O 324	Irene	3
On dangers which your safety bids you shun,	Y 18	Tr. Iliad Bk 6	20
BIER			
Now kindred Merit fills the sable bier,	O 45	Vanity Wishes	303
Now kindred Merit fills the mournful bier,	Y 106	Vanity Wishes	V 303
BIGOT			
What doating bigot to his faults so blind,	O 137	Tr Rambler 140	1
BIGOTRY			
Then Bigotry might send her Slaves to War,	O 291	Irene	63
BILLOWS			
Through purple billows and a floating host.	O 42	Vanity Wishes	240
Nor do the billows always rise,	O 67	Hor. II Ode IX	3
Loud roars the tempest, high the billows rise,	O 82	Young Author	8
Loud roar the billows, high the waves arise,	O 82	Young Author	V 8
Loud as the Billows bursting on the Ground.	O 110	To Posterity	6
When Heav'n shall bid the swelling Billows rage,	O 300	Irene	60
BIND			
Whom neither Vows could fix, nor Favours bind?	O 330	Irene	2
BINDS			
Nor binds the neck, nor sparkles in the hair,	O 141	Tr Rambler 199	3
BION			
Kai Bion, eipen, otan ripses Thanatio Belessi,	O 108	Eis Birchion	3
BIOUS			
Eroon te Bious Birchion, ede Sophon,	O 108	Eis Birchion	2
BIRCHION			
Eis Birchion	O 108	Eis Birchion	T
Eroon te Bious Birchion, ede Sophon,	O 108	Eis Birchion	2
Sou pote grapsomenon Birchion allon echois.	O 108	Eis Birchion	4
BIRD			
Whene'er the lab'ring bird with anxious care	Y 23	Tr Add. Battle	44
Till thither an huge bird the tumult drew	Y 25	Tr Add. Battle	124
BIRDS			
While bees shall feed on thyme, and birds shall haunt the grove	Y 7	Virgil Daphnis	50
Against th' invading birds their native land:	Y 23	Tr Add. Battle	37
Hence men and birds promiscuous press'd the sand	Y 23	Tr Add. Battle	52
Thick clouds of hostile birds obscure the skies.	Y 25	Tr Add. Battle	93
The birds elude the stroke with cautious care;	Y 26	Tr Add. Battle	134
BIRTH			
Struck with the seat that gave Eliza birth,	O 10	London	23
Begs for each birth the fortune of a face:	O 45	Vanity Wishes	320
Nought from my birth or ancestors I claim;	O 132	Tr. Rambler 46	1
All from one Source derive their Birth	O 146	Tr Boeth III.6	3
Why boast their Birth before his Eyes,	O 147	Tr Boeth III.6	17
Or Eloquence, or splendid birth,	O 232	Tr Horace IV.7	23
And gives a thousand fatal Questions Birth;	O 258	Irene	84
Ev'n from the Birth affects supreme Command,	O 280	Irene	19
Demand a Voice, and struggle into Birth;	O 295	Irene	18
And strangled Freedom perish in the Birth.	O 299	Irene	53
And anxious Angels wait the mighty Birth;	O 313	Irene	4
Which gave a thousand pleasures birth.	Y 39	Lady Leaving	8
BIRTH-DAY			
To a Young Lady on her Birth-day	O 80	Lady Birthday	T
BIT			
Nor my brave brothers, that have bit the ground,	O 74	Tr. Iliad Bk 6	17
Our little dog has bit his tail	Y 300	Fanny Burney	4
BITTER			
Sure the most bitter is a scornful jest;	O 17	London	167
The bitter pangs of slighted love?	O 72	Hor. Epode II	46
BLACK			
To vote a patriot black, a courtier white;	O 11	London	52
Dispelling the black horrors of the Night,	O 77	Tr Add. Battle	46
Detests thy false Associates black Designs,	O 300	Irene	57
Far be such black Ingratitude from Cali,	O 306	Irene	4
In that black Day when slaughter'd Thousands fell	O 312	Irene	7
Hang Sit these black clouds upon Aspasia's brow?	Y 191	Irene	V 15
In vain, from heaven's black concave, like a cloud,	Y 23	Tr Add. Battle	20
Black her eye with many a blow,	Y 301	Extemp. Elegy	17
BLACK'NING			
And pois'nous vapours, black'ning all the sky,	O 84	Epi Dist Moth.	33
BLADE			
When the bonny Blade carouses,	O 196	Song Congratu.	21
Whilst the bonny Blade carouses,	O 196	Song Congratu.	V 21
BLAME			
His foes derision, and his subjects blame,	O 43	Vanity Wishes	253
By all, like him, must praise and blame be found;	O 62	Pro Word Wise	19
That leave the blame of rigour to the prince,	O 176	Tr Metastas II	10
Not Pow'r I blame, but Pow'r obtain'd by Crime,	O 293	Irene	129
BLAMELESS			
Her Youth laborious, and her blameless Age:	O 58	Prologue Comus	30
BLAND			
And Sloth's bland Opiates shed their fumes in vain,	O 37	Vanity Wishes	V 150
Gay with the smile of bland equality;	O 130	Tr. Rambler 12	6
His bland Address, and Sorcery of Tongue;	O 273	Irene	40
BLAST			
And every beauty withers at the blast:	O 84	Epi Dist Moth.	35
Thou know'st those arts which blast with envious praise,	O 176	Tr Metastas II	7

34

		PAGE	TITLE	LINE

BLAST   (CONTINUED)

Chill my Resolves, and blast my blooming Virtue: . . . O 266 Irene 14
Though Disappointment blast our general Scheme, . . . O 317 Irene 44
There dauntless Truth shall blast the vile Accuser, . . O 326 Irene 42
Perhaps her pois'nous Tongue might blast Abdalla. . . . O 327 Irene 19
Mistake shall blast, or Accident destroy; . . . . . O 335 Irene 13

BLASTED

Where blasted patriots never shrunk to peers . . . . Y 94 Vanity Wishes V 60A
Our trees were blasted by the thunder stroke, ... O 65 Virgil Past.I 23
As blasted by my Presence, they withdrew . . . . . . O 275 Irene 85
And blasted Kingdoms flourish at thy Smile? . . . . . O 278 Irene 72
Whome'er the Hope, still blasted, still renew'd, . . . O 310 Irene 1

BLASTS

By sudden blasts, or slow decline, ... O 200 Death Dr Levet 3
Rough Winter's blasts to Spring give way, ... O 231 Tr Horace IV.7 9
Blasts all the Beauties of his new Creation, ... O 269 Irene 7
May no rude blasts thy sacred bloom destroy; . . . . Y 3 On a Daffodill 7

BLAZE

From hill to hill the beacons rousing blaze . . . . . O 43 Vanity Wishes 247
I walk'd superior, through the Blaze of Charms, . . . O 263 Irene 17
Through half his Course reflects the blaze of . . . . O 353 Irene V 2
   War
And though built on feeble columns--Its lofty turrets Y 131 Irene V 35
   blaze amidst
Amidst the Blaze of Jewels and of Gold, ... O 276 Irene 9
And bad imperial splendour glare (blaze) before her . . Y 158 Irene V 10
Shrinks at th' oerpowring blaze of regal State . . . . O 368 Irene V 30
Stoops from the Blaze like a degenerate Eagle, ... O 292 Irene 101
Stoops at the Blaze like a degenerate Eagle . . . . . O 368 Irene V 31
Fill all the starry Lamps with double Blaze; . . . . O 322 Irene 8
The child starts back affrighted at the blaze . . . . Y 20 Tr. Iliad Bk 6 92

BLAZES

The festal blazes, the triumphal show, ... O 39 Vanity Wishes 175

BLED

That day what legions by his faulchion bled! . . . . Y 25 Tr Add. Battle 120

BLEED

That Priam's house, and Priam's self shall bleed: . . . O 74 Tr. Iliad Bk 6 12
And in the traytress bad th' apostate bleed . . . . . Y 217 Irene V 12

BLEEDING

Arose to Heav'n, and pierc'd my bleeding Breast, . . . O 251 Irene 74
And fill the bleed<in>g world with desolation . . . . O 352 Irene V 5
Prowls like a lyon oer the wealthy Spoils of bleeding . O 352 Irene V 29
   Turkey.
Prowls o'er the wealthy Spoils of bleeding Turkey? . . O 264 Irene 15
Fierce persecution wears the bleeding world with . . . Y 164 Irene V 66
   fraud
Our bleeding Bosoms plead Irene's Cause. . . . . . . O 328 Irene 39

BLEEDS

Now bleeds the war afresh, the Crane from high . . . . Y 26 Tr Add. Battle 130

BLESS

And bless thine evening walk and morning toil. . . . . O 20 London 223
And bless the evening walk and morning toil. . . . . . O 20 London V 223
And bless thy evening walk and morning toil. . . . . . O 20 London V 223
Bless with an age exempt from scorn or crime; . . . . O 44 Vanity Wishes 292
Yet then shall calm reflection bless the night, . . . O 62 Pro Word Wise 21
But bless the Northern shoars, ... O 79 Feast St Simon 36
Bless with a smile, or with a frown destroy; . . · . . O 83 Epi Dist Moth. 2
We bless the Tyrant, and we hug the Chain. . . . . . O 96 Hickman Spinet 8
Ye glitt'ring Train! whom Lace and Velvet bless, . . . O 246 Irene Prologue 1
Surpriz'd I start, and bless the happy Dream; . . . . O 254 Irene 124
As those that bless the Mansions of the Good. . . . . O 262 Irene 12
O seize the Power to bless--Irene's Nod . . . . . . O 278 Irene 75
When Heav'n bestows the Privilege to bless, ... O 313 Irene 21
Shall bless our Wand'rings, and propitiate Heav'n. . . O 320 Irene 19
And bless me with continu'd day. . . . . Y 39 Lady Leaving 12

BLESS'D

Now bless'd with all the baubles of the great, ... O 19 London 206
Which lately bless'd my gentle Government, ... O 257 Irene 75
Long be the Sultan bless'd with happy Love! . . . . . O 286 Irene 1
The matchless Fair has bless'd me with Compliance; . . O 308 Irene 3
And bless'd with all the joy that Guilt . . . . . . O 365 Irene V 11
   allows

BLESSING

For blessing, raise the supplicating voice, ... Y 108 Vanity Wishes V 351
Sure, not unconscious of the mighty Blessing, ... O 256 Irene 59
Charm'd with the Thought of blessing human Kind, . . . O 278 Irene 73
Reflect that Life, like ev'ry other Blessing, ... O 290 Irene 28

BLESSINGS

And hope the balmy blessings of repose: . . . . . . O 21 London 237
Those blessings, friend, a deity bestow'd, ... O 64 Virgil Past.I 7
Dispersing blessings as they went, ... O 79 Feast St Simon 26
"While I these transitory blessings scorn, ... O 82 Young Author 47
"While I those transitory blessings scorn, ... O 82 Young Author V 17
The blessings of a golden Show'r, ... O 144 Tr Boeth. II.2 6
To snatch the blessings of the plenteous day; . . . . O 151 The Ant 6
May ye the varied blessings share . . . . O 189 Epilogue 5
May ye th' alternate blessings share . . . . O 189 Epilogue V 5
Enjoy the prayers and blessings of the needy, ... Y 130 Irene V 12C

BLESST

Withdraw their cars and seek the blesst abodes. . . . Y 6 Virgil Daphnis 21

35

BLEST
    Blest age! but ah! how diff'rent from our own! . . . .   O 22 London   253
    Blest age! but ha! how diff'rent from our own! . . . .   O 22 London   V 253
    For that blest year when all that vote may rail; . . .   O 60 Pro Good Nat'd   18
    Yet shall I see the blest abodes, ...   O 70 Hor.II Ode XX   6
    Blest as th' immortal Gods is he . . . .   O 71 Hor. Epode II   1
    While Love, a stranger to the blest, ...   O 99 Ode Friendship   5
    While Love, unknown amongst the blest, ...   O 99 Ode Friendship V 5
    And when blest Peace has silenc'd War's Alarms, . . .   O 247 Irene Epilogue   23
    How blest art thou, still jocund and serene, ...   O 271 Irene   6
    To make thee blest each Region shall combine . . . .   O 351 Irene   V 26
    Let my blest Eyes for ever gaze-- . . . . . .   O 294 Irene   4
    Blest Prince, for whom indulgent Heav'n ordains . . .   O 308 Irene   6
    <Ho>w blest our state could every bosom . . . . .   Y 184 Irene   V 16
BLIND
    No more let coquets to themselves be blind, ...   O 81 Lady Birthday   18
    Impelled by passion, and with folly blind. . . . . .   O 134 Tr Rambler 105   2
    What doating bigot to his faults so blind, ...   O 137 Tr Rambler 140   1
    Men will be ever to their Errors blind, ...   O 247 Irene Epilogue   11
    Deem us not deaf to Woe, nor blind to Beauty, . . .   O 327 Irene   29
    Ye blind officious Ministers of Folly, ...   O 332 Irene   23
BLINDLY
    Thus blindly pray'd the fretful fair, ...   O 122 Stella Mourn.   7
    He who blindly trusts, will find . . . .   O 176 Tr Metastasi I   3
BLISS
    With ev'ry bliss that man can gain. . . . .   O 136 Tr Rambler 128   6
    If such on Earth can Bliss bestow, ...   O 146 Tr Boeth III.4   7
    When grasping Bliss th' unsteady mind . . . .   O 150 Tr Boet III.12   56
    Where is bliss? and which the way? . . . . .   O 181 Parody Warton   4
    What is bliss? and which the way? . . . . .   O 181 Parody Warton   V 4
    Of human bliss to human woe. . .   O 184 Tr. Benserade   4
    But bids you rove the Paths of Bliss, secure . . .   O 276 Irene   18
    Whence all the Bliss and Agonies of Love? . . .   O 277 Irene   42
    Sooth the delighted Soul with empty Bliss? . . .   O 277 Irene   45
    There shall we find the yet untasted Bliss . . .   O 292 Irene   88
    Nor Wealth, nor Titles, make Aspasia's Bliss. . .   O 302 Irene   106
    Suspend thy Passage to the Seats of Bliss, . . .   O 308 Irene   9
    Is this the boasted Bliss of conscious Virtue? . . .   O 314 Irene   19
BLISSFUL
    In pleasing dreams the blissful age renew, ...   O 10 London   25
    Some pompous palace, or some blissful bow'r, ...   O 18 London   185
    In blissful dreams he digs the golden mine, ...   O 82 Young Author   V 6C
    Expell'd and exil'd from the blissful seats, . . .   O 84 Epi Dist Moth.   29
    When souls to blissful climes remove? . . . . .   O 100 Ode Friendship   26
    "Blissful bondage such as mine? . . . .   O 185 Anacreon Ode 9   24
    Empire and Love shall share the blissful Day, . . .   O 279 Irene   90
BLOCK
    And fatal Learning leads him to the block: . . . .   O 39 Vanity Wishes   172
BLOCKADE
    Lay siege to life and press the dire blockade; . . .   O 44 Vanity Wishes   284
BLOCKHEAD'S
    Than when a blockhead's insult points the dart. . . .   O 18 London   169
BLOCKHEADS
    But hear his death, ye blockheads, hear and sleep. . .   O 39 Vanity Wishes   174
    But hear his death, ye blockheads, hear and weep. . .   O 39 Vanity Wishes   V 174
    Be gone ye blockheads, Heraclitus cries, . . .   O 141 Tr Rambler 208   1
BLOOD
    And stain with blood the Danube or the Rhine; . . . .   O 39 Vanity Wishes   182
    Their blood the consecrated stones shall dye: . . . .   O 64 Virgil Past.I   10
    Whose blood shall quench some Grecian's thirsty rage, . .   O 74 Tr. Iliad Bk 6   16
    The plain contested flows with mingled blood. . . .   O 76 Tr Add. Battle   21
    Secure, and triumph'd oft' in hostile blood. . . .   O 76 Tr Add. Battle   34
    No more the glutted Sabre thirsts for Blood, . . .   O 249 Irene   9
    or chill our blood but Fear . . . . . .   O 347 Irene   V 4
    With Christian blood, let Leontares dye. . . . .   Y 129 Irene   V 26
    Sure, chill'd with sixty winter Camps, thy Blood . . .   O 263 Irene   5
    Ransom of Kings, the purchass of your blood . . .   O 351 Irene   V 14
    And hungry Slaughter scents Imperial Blood? . . . .   O 279 Irene   5
    Now pause, great Bassa, from the Thoughts of Blood, . .   O 285 Irene   1
    Why does the Blood forsake thy lovely Cheek? . . .   O 295 Irene   5
    And my blood freezes at Assassination . . . .   O 353 Irene   V 32
    All ye, whose Blood tyrannick Rage effus'd, ...   O 306 Irene   53
    But my blood freezes and weak nature shudders . . .   Y 189 Irene   V 1G
    My trembling nerves--sink at the dreadful scenes of blood   Y 189 Irene   V 1H
        and death
    I go, lest Vengeance urge my Hand to Blood, ...   O 324 Irene   23
    To Blood, too mean to stain a Soldier's Sabre. . . .   O 324 Irene   24
    Those Hounds of Blood, that catch the Hint to kill, . .   O 333 Irene   52
    And stain'd with blood Pelides' vengefull steel. . .   Y 18 Tr. Iliad Bk 6   37
    Fresh foes descending glut their swords with blood. . .   Y 23 Tr Add. Battle   21
    Soon had the wrathfull faulchion drank his blood. . .   Y 23 Tr Add. Battle   41
    And dy'd their bulrush-spears in mutual blood. . . .   Y 24 Tr Add. Battle   57
    The feather'd race and thirsted for their blood: . .   Y 24 Tr Add. Battle   85
BLOOD-BOLTER'D
    And Murder, all blood-bolter'd, schemes the wound. . .   O 192 Tr. Medea II   16
BLOODHOUNDS
    Tho' confiscation's bloodhounds yelp around. . . .   Y 93 Vanity Wishes   V 36
BLOODSHED
    Thou to a scene of bloodshed turn'st the Ball, . . .   O 77 Festina Lente   11
BLOODY
    And cruel Danaus' bloody Brood . . . .   O 69 Hor.II Ode 14   19

```
BLOODY        (CONTINUED)                              PAGE   TITLE          LINE
   May I lie slain, and spurn the bloody sand!   . . . . .   O  75 Tr. Iliad Bk 6     30
   And grasps the bloody sand involv'd in death.   . . .     O  76 Tr Add. Battle     17
   Stern Torture shakes his bloody Scourge before me,        O 266 Irene             15
   And fix the fierce Usurper's bloody Title.   . . . . .     O 291 Irene             62
   Already shakes his bloody Sabre o'er thee.   . . . . .     O 327 Irene             10
   Rush not impetuous to the bloody fray   . . . . . . .      Y  19 Tr. Iliad Bk 6     46
   Whilst beaks and swords engage in bloody fray   . . .     Y  22 Tr Add. Battle      6
BLOOM
   The baffled prince in honour's flatt'ring bloom   . . .   O  43 Vanity Wishes    251
   Henceforth th' inviolable Bloom invade,   . . . . . .     O 111 To Posterity      21
   In life's first bloom its publick toils began,   . . .    O 117 Epitaph Hanmer    11
   A blooming monarch--in all the bloom of honour...   . .   Y 122 Irene          V  67
   Let Pleasure bloom and Cities reascend.   . . . . . .     O 372 Irene          V  10
   Bid Pleasure bloom and Cities reascend.   . . . . . .     O 372 Irene          V  10
   May no rude blasts thy sacred bloom destroy;   . . . .    Y   3 On a Daffodill      7
   Ev'n in the bloom of life depriv'd of breath.   . . . .   Y   6 Virgil Daphnis      2
BLOOMING
   Ye blooming train, who give despair or joy,   . . . .     O  83 Epi Dist Moth.  · 1
   A blooming monarch--in all the bloom of honour...   . .   Y 122 Irene          V  67
   Chill my Resolves, and blast my blooming Virtue:   . .    O 266 Irene             14
   Permits the blooming maid secure and thoughtless   . .    Y 146 Irene          V  18
   But the next blooming virgin's beauteous face   . . .     Y  12 Tr Hor Epode 9     41
   Among their flocks the blooming heroes fell   . . . . .   Y  18 Tr. Iliad Bk 6     36
BLOOMS
   For kind, for tender nymphs the myrtle blooms,   . . .    O  84 Epi Dist Moth.   14
   And near the noisome nettle blooms the rose.   . . . .    O 131 Tr. Rambler 21      2
BLOSSOMS
   And ah! behold the shriveling blossoms die,   . . . .     Y   4 On a Daffodill     23
BLOW
   Why but to sink beneath misfortune's blow,   . . . . .    O  35 Vanity Wishes    127
   Defer an hour the fatal blow.   . . . . . . . .           O  69 Hor.II Ode 14     12
   And hov'ring death prepar'd the blow,   . . . . .         O 201 Death Dr Levet    14
   Then strike secure, and Heav'n assist the Blow.   . .     O 298 Irene              9
   'Tis well--A single Blow compleats our Wishes:   . . .    O 304 Irene              8
   Thus shall he live to strike th' important Blow,   . .    O 308 Irene             32
   Black her eye with many a blow,   . . . . . . . . .       Y 301 Extemp. Elegy     17
BLOWN   SEE FULL-BLOWN,NEW-BLOWN
   In full blown pow'r see mighty Wolsey stand,   . . .      Y  96 Vanity Wishes   V  99
   In full blown state, see Wolsey stand,   . . . . . .      Y  96 Vanity Wishes   V  99
BLOWS
   Wouldst thou when fierce Eurus blows   . . . . . . .      O 144 Tr Boeth. II.4      3
BLUNT
   Should Beauty blunt on fops her fatal dart,   . . . . .   O  37 Vanity Wishes    151
BLUSH
   Who start at theft, and blush at perjury?   . . . . .     O  13 London             68
   And lye without a blush, without a smile;   . . . . .     O  17 London            147
   Yet Reason blush on War's unequal game,   . . . . . .     Y 100 Vanity Wishes  V 185
   That Air resistless and enchanting Blush,   . . . . .     O 277 Irene             27
   A sigh, a blush inform'd him You consented   . . . . .    O 366 Irene          V  28
   The houries of our Prophet blush before her   . . . .     Y 184 Irene          V  10
   There I became, nor blush to make it known,   . . . .     O 312 Irene             13
BLUSH'D
   Her gifts despis'd, corruption blush'd and fled,   . .    O 118 Epitaph Hanmer    33
BLUSHES
   No conscious blushes there their cheeks inflame,   . .    O  84 Epi Dist Moth.   24
   She sighs, she blushes, but she still denies.   . . .     O 287 Irene              8
BLUSHING
   Hide, blushing Glory, hide Pultowa's day:   . . . . .     O  41 Vanity Wishes    210
   Plucking the blushing Grape and Pear,   . . . . . .       O  72 Hor. Epode II     26
   "Blushing nature, smiling art.   . . . . . . . . .        O 185 Anacreon Ode 9    10
   Smiling Consent she sat, and blushing Love.   . . . .     O 303 Irene             32
BLUSTRING
   Go, blustring Slave.--He has not heard of Murza.   . .    O 324 Irene             25
BLYTHE
   Summon'd the singer blythe, and harper gay,   . . . .     O 192 Tr. Medea II       7
BOAR
   The grizly foaming Boar surrounds   . . . . . . . .       O  72 Hor. Epode II     39
   The foaming Boar he then with op'ning hounds   . . . .    O  72 Hor. Epode II  V  39
BOARD
   The regal palace, the luxurious board,   . . . . . .      O  35 Vanity Wishes    115
   The pompous palace, the luxurious board,   . . . . . .    Y  96 Vanity Wishes  V 115
   With unbought dainties load the board;   . . . . . .      O  73 Hor. Epode II     54
   We round thy board the cheerful menials see,   . . . .    O 130 Tr. Rambler 12      5
   The board with varied plenty crown'd   . . . . . . .      O 191 Tr. Medea I       19
   They put the riches of Cali Bassa on board.   . . . .     Y 123 Irene          V  81
BOARS
   While boars the rocks, while fish the rivers love,   . .  Y   7 Virgil Daphnis     49
BOAST
   All useless science is an empty boast.   . . . . . .      O 133 Tr. Rambler 83      1
   This habitant th' aerial regions boast.   . . . . . .     O 138 Tr Rambler 161      1
   Why boast their Birth before his Eyes,   . . . . . .      O 147 Tr Boeth III.6     17
   For howe'er we boast and strive,   . . . . . . . .        O 178 Thrale 35 Year     13
   Not you, Torquatus, boast of Rome,   . . . . . . . .      O 232 Tr Horace IV.7     21
   The Empire's Darling, and the Soldier's Boast;   . . .    O 257 Irene             69
   the reward of conquest boast of nature   . . . . . .      Y 137 Irene          V  42
   No more I boast th' ambitious Name of Friend,   . . .     O 289 Irene             10
   And boast no title but Aspasia's friend   . . . . . .     Y 161 Irene          V  14
   And Persecution boast the Call of Heav'n.   . . . . .     O 291 Irene             66
   What can'st thou boast superiour to Demetrius?   . . .    O 305 Irene             38
   Advance, and perish in the frantic Boast.   . . . . .     O 318 Irene              7
```

```
BOAST          (CONTINUED)                                      PAGE    TITLE           LINE
     Shall then the Savage live, to boast his Insult;    . . .  O 318 Irene              12
     And Cowardice to dread the Boast of Folly. . . . . .      O 318 Irene              22
BOASTED
     We oft (notwithstanding this boasted superiour genius  .   Y 148 Irene          V  49
     Thy dazzled Soul with all its boasted Greatness,          O 292 Irene              99
     O could her fabled Saints, and boasted Prayers . . . .    O 309 Irene              38
     O could her boasted saints, and powerfull prayers . . .   Y 185 Irene          V  38
     Is this the boasted Bliss of conscious Virtue? . . . .    O 314 Irene              19
     Behold thy boasted Honours snatch'd away.  . . . . . .    O 317 Irene              43
BOASTER
     Had stretch'd the fiery Boaster in the Grave.  . . . .    O 312 Irene              20
BOASTER'S
     Behold a Boaster's Worth.  Now snatch, my Fair,  . . .    O 320 Irene               7
BOASTFUL
     Assume the boastful Arrogance of Man. . . . . . . .       O 277 Irene              50
     Not idly flutters on a boastful Tongue,  . . . . . .      O 290 Irene              37
BOASTS
     Whate'er the swarthy Lybian boasts,  . . . .  . . .       O  73 Hor. Epode II   V  57
     Or boasts a happier Soil, already thine? . . . . . .      O 265 Irene              36
     Or boasts a happier glebe, is Yours already,  . . . .     O 366 Irene          V  13
     Tis cowardise to fear the boasts of folly  . . . . .      Y 197 Irene          V  22
     Who matchless strength and bulk gygantick boasts, . . .   Y  24 Tr Add. Battle     81
BOAT
     Much could I add,--but see the boat at hand,  . . . .     O  22 London             254
BODIES
     Scatters their breathless bodies o'er the plain. . . .    O  76 Tr Add. Battle     32
     Small bones and mangled bodies scatter'd there . . . .    Y  23 Tr Add. Battle     31
BODING
     Without a boding fear, or anxious sigh,  . . . . . .      Y  67 Prologue Lethe      3
BODLEY'S
     O'er Bodley's dome his future labours spread,  . . . .    O  37 Vanity Wishes      139
BODY
     On his dead body let a tomb be plac'd . . . . . . .       Y   7 Virgil Daphnis     28
BOILING
     The Surface of the boiling Deep,  . . . . . . . .         O  71 Hor. Epode II      12
     Persue thy course through boiling eddies,  . . . . .      Y 201 Irene          V 10A
BOIST'ROUS
     He sees no boist'rous Tempests sweep  . . . . . . .       O  71 Hor. Epode II      11
BOLD
     Rules the bold hand, or prompts the suppliant voice; . .  O  31 Vanity Wishes       12
     But scarce observ'd, the knowing and the bold  . . .     O  31 Vanity Wishes       21
     The bold Bavarian, in a  luckless hour,  . . . . .        O  42 Vanity Wishes      241
     From bold invaders clear'd th' Italian lands  . . . .     O  78 Festina Lente       19
     Shows his bold Front, the Harbinger of Ruin,  . . . .     O 250 Irene               41
     Lest unacquainted with our bold Attempt, . . . . . .      O 285 Irene               12
     Bold Slave, I know them both--I know them Traytors. . .   O 324 Irene               16
     Soon forth in arms had some bold soldier stood,  . . .    Y  23 Tr Add. Battle      40
BOLT
     And snatch the flaming Bolt with hasty Hand.  . . . .     O 314 Irene               25
BOLTER'D     SEE BLOOD-BOLTER'D
BOLTS
     Should heaven's just bolts Orgilio's wealth confound, .   O  19 London             194
     And Bolts and rocks encounter in the Skie,  . . . . .     O  76 Tr Add. Battle      23
BON
     Rien de Bon.  . . . . . . . . . . /. . .                  O 172 French Distich      10
BONDAGE
     "Blissful bondage such as mine? . . . . . . . .           O 185 Anacreon Ode 9      24
     Behold contending nations vie for bondage  . . . . .      Y 136 Irene          V  26
     Vye for my submission, sollicite bondage. . . . . .       Y 136 Irene          V 27C
BONDS
     His bonds of debt, and mortgages of lands;  . . . . .     O  44 Vanity Wishes      288
     The Laws of Kindness, break the Bonds of Nature? . . .    O 280 Irene               16
BCNES
     Small bones and mangled bodies scatter'd there . . . .    Y  23 Tr Add. Battle      31
BONNET
     Trickt in Antique Ruff and Bonnet,  . . . . . . .         O 179 Ridicul Warton       7
BCNNY
     And leaves the bonny Traytor in the Tow'r,  . . . . .     O  32 Vanity Wishes    V  34
     When the bonny Blade carouses,  . . . . . . . . .         O 196 Song Congratu.      21
     Whilst the bonny Blade carouses,  . . . . . . . .         O 196 Song Congratu.   V  21
BOOK
     Translation of Horace. Book I. Ode xxii. . . . . . .      O  65 Hor I Ode xxii       T
     Horace. Book 2d. Ode 14  . . . . . . . . .               O  68 Hor.II Ode 14        T
     Horace Book 2d. Ode 20th  . . . . . . . . .              O  70 Hor.II Ode XX        T
          from the Sixth Book of Homer's Iliad . . . . .       O  74 Tr. Iliad Bk 6      T
BOOKS
     On names now found alone on books and tombs.  . . . .     O 134 Tr. Rambler 93       2
BOON
     Friendship! peculiar boon of heav'n,  . . . . . . .       O  99 Ode Friendship       1
BORE
     Dire nurse of raging lions, bore.  . . . . . . . .        O  66 Hor I Ode xxii       16
     The lyon's thirsty parent, bore.  . . . . . . . .         O  66 Hor I Ode xxii   V  16
     The lion's thirsty Parent, bore.  . . . . . . . .         O  67 To A. Fuscus        16
     Bore me victorious onward, where Demetrius . . . . .      O 312 Irene                9
     Endur'd the stinging lash, and tamely bore the yoke. .    Y   6 Virgil Daphnis      14
     The nurse attending bore a lovely boy . . . . . . .       Y  18 Tr. Iliad Bk 6       9
     Some furious soldier would approach that bore  . . . .    Y  23 Tr Add. Battle      46
BOREAS
     Not always furious Boreas roars,  . . . . . . . .         O  67 Hor. II Ode IX       7
```

BORN
                       PAGE TITLE   LINE

	PAGE	TITLE		LINE
The supple Gaul was born a parasite:	O 16	London		124
And feed with change of new born fools th' eternal jest:	Y 94	Vanity Wishes	V	52
A Mortal born he met the general Doom,	O 51	Pro Drury-Lane		15
And born in bed, in bed we die;	O 184	Tr. Benserade		2
Who thinks us Women born to dress and sing	O 247	Irene Epilogue		2
Born to command, as thou to charm Mankind,	O 268	Irene		23
Born down with Years, still doat upon To-morrow?	O 283	Irene		20
Born to compleat the Ruin of her Country;	O 316	Irene		11
Cali disarm'd was born away to Death;	O 317	Irene		40

BORNE

	PAGE	TITLE		LINE
Let pain deserv'd without complaint be borne.	O 131	Tr. Rambler 32		1
Borne on the Surface of the smiling Deep,	O 301	Irene		92

BOROUGH

	PAGE	TITLE		LINE
When one a borough courts, and one the pit.	O 59	Pro Good Nat'd		10

BOROUGHS

	PAGE	TITLE		LINE
The price of boroughs and of souls restore,	O 19	London		204

BORROW'D

	PAGE	TITLE		LINE
To pluck a titled Poet's borrow'd wing;	O 13	London		70
Who play from morn to night a borrow'd part;	O 16	London		135

BORROWD

	PAGE	TITLE		LINE
borro<wd or a>ffected <gayety>	Y 185	Irene	V	3

BOSOM

	PAGE	TITLE		LINE
Can in my bosom half that grief create,	O 74	Tr. Iliad Bk 6		19
And that fair bosom heave with rising sighs!	O 75	Tr. Iliad Bk 6		28
Unbounded prospects in his bosom roll,	O 82	Young Author	V	6A
Vex ev'ry eye, and every bosom tear;	O 84	Epi Dist Moth.		39
Smite thy bosom, sage, and tell,	O 181	Parody Warton		3
Strike thy bosom, sage, and tell,	O 181	Parody Warton	V	3
And reign without a Rival in his Bosom.	O 373	Irene	V	29
And ease my loaded Soul upon her Bosom?	O 263	Irene		22
That clouds thy Brow and labours in thy Bosom	O 369	Irene	V	19
Betray'd some Traytor lurking near my Bosom.	O 273	Irene		23
Two Men unknown, the Partners of his Bosom;	O 275	Irene		80
And Gales of softer Passion fan my Bosom.	O 275	Irene		93
And softer passion steals upon my Bosom	O 367	Irene	V	14
Seize the kind Fair, and press her to thy Bosom.	O 284	Irene		35
That raises tumults in the female bosom seditions (mutinies	Y 158	Irene	V	12
And lodge the fate of kingdoms in her bosom.	Y 159	Irene	V	18
My Bosom feels, enkindled from the Sky,	O 293	Irene		108
My Bosom harrass'd with alternate Passions,	O 299	Irene		54
Each Turkish Bosom burns for thy Destruction,	O 300	Irene		73
And still thy Bosom with the Voice of Peace.	O 303	Irene		22
Have I for this preserv'd my guiltless Bosom,	O 304	Irene		14
<Ho>w blest our state could every bosom	Y 184	Irene	V	16
Wet the dim eye or swell the throbbing bosom?	Y 191	Irene	V	19A
Irene's Chamber! From my faithful Bosom	O 326	Irene		31
Irene's chamber from Irene's guiltless bosom	Y 205	Irene	V	31
Does not thy Bosom, for I know thee tender,	O 329	Irene		5
And bar'd my Bosom to the Ruffian's Dagger.	O 331	Irene		20
My bosom glows with fiercer fire;	Y 10	Tr Hor Epode 9		2
And in his nurse's bosom hides his face.	Y 20	Tr. Iliad Bk 6		94

BOSOMS

	PAGE	TITLE		LINE
Ye Nymphs, whose Bosoms beat at Milton's Name,	O 57	Prologue Comus		2
On selfish bosoms only prey.	O 100	Ode Friendship		16
Trumpet or lyre--to their harsh bosoms chill,	O 192	Tr. Medea II		11
Disclos'd some Traytor lurking near our Bosoms	O 368	Irene	V	3
Our bleeding Bosoms plead Irene's Cause.	O 328	Irene		39

BOTH

	PAGE	TITLE		LINE
Disabled both to combat, or to fly,	O 59	Pro Good Nat'd		13
Uncheck'd on both, loud rabbles vent their rage,	O 59	Pro Good Nat'd		15
Uncheck'd on both, caprice may vent its rage,	O 59	Pro Good Nat'd	V	15
Both your religion and your country are concern'd	Y 181	Irene	V	52
Bold Slave, I know them both--I know them Traytors.	O 324	Irene		16
Till purse and carcase both were low.	Y 300	Extemp. Elegy		12

BOTTOM

	PAGE	TITLE		LINE
When once unto the bottom I	O 159	Par Hermit III		7

BOUGH

	PAGE	TITLE		LINE
Soon must this bough, as you shall fix his doom,	O 95	Sprig of Myrtl		13
Sweeps o'er the Grove, forsake the lab'ring Bough,	O 298	Irene		23

BOUGHS

	PAGE	TITLE		LINE
Or prunes the barren boughs away;	O 71	Hor. Epode II		19
And weaves her bending boughs in pleasing glooms;	O 84	Epi Dist Moth.		15
Had not the Breeze untwin'd the meeting Boughs,	O 269	Irene		10

BOUGHT SEE DEAR-BOUGHT

	PAGE	TITLE		LINE
Was this the Maid whose Love I bought with Empire!	O 330	Irene		9
Such Beauty, Sweetness, Love, were cheaply bought,	O 332	Irene		35

BOUND

	PAGE	TITLE		LINE
Nor dare to pass th' insuperable Bound.	O 292	Irene		92
Bound o'er the sparkling Waves. Go, happy Bark,	O 322	Irene		5

BOUNDED

	PAGE	TITLE		LINE
Existence saw him spurn her bounded Reign,	O 51	Pro Drury-Lane		5

BOUNDLESS

	PAGE	TITLE		LINE
No secret island in the boundless main?	O 18	London		172
His vast Designs, his Plans of boundless Pow'r.	O 265	Irene		41
His vast designs, and plans of boundless Empire.	O 356	Irene	V	29
Expands the boundless scenes of future being	Y 133	Irene	V	8
There will his boundless Wealth, the Spoil of Asia,	O 274	Irene		50

	PAGE	TITLE	LINE

BOUNDLESS   (CONTINUED)
There (or might) shall his boundless Wealth the . . . O 351 Irene V 13
Call to your Aid with boundless Promises . . . . . . O 287 Irene 10

BOUNDS
Heroes, proceed! what bounds your pride shall hold? . . O 13 London 61
To ev'ry empire bounds the Gods ordain . . . . . O 76 Tr Add. Battle 35
O'er the Bounds of Thirtyfive: . . . . O 178 Thrale 35 Year 8

BOUNTEOUS
In vain their gifts the bounteous seasons pour, . . . O 43 Vanity Wishes 261
Profuse of Wealth, or bounteous of Success, ... O 313 Irene 20
And bounteous Heaven repay the mighty Mercy . . . . . O 328 Irene 46
And may bounteous Heav'n repay the mercy on Your . . . O 344 Irene V 27
    Heads

BOUNTIES
Heap'd by your Father's ill-plac'd Bounties on him, . . O 274 Irene 51
Heap'd by my Fathers illplac'd Bounties on Him . . . . O 351 Irene V 13
Profusely pour'd her Bounties upon Woman? . . . . . O 276 Irene 25

BOUNTY
Thro' him the rays of regal bounty shine, ... O 34 Vanity Wishes 102
And mirth was bounty with a humbler name. . . . . . O 62 Pro Word Wise 24

BOW
How pleas'd beholds his Oxen bow . . . . O 73 Hor. Epode II 69
He sees the wearied Oxen bow . . . . O 73 Hor. Epode II V 69
Warm India's supple Sons should bow, ... O 146 Tr Boeth III.5 6
Bow down and own thyself a Slave. . . . . O 146 Tr Boeth III.5 10

BOW-STRING
May spare the fatal Bow-string till To-morrow? . . . . O 284 Irene 39

BOW'D
Then scorn those flowers to which the Aegyptians bow'd, . Y 4 On a Daffodill 15

BOW'R
Some pompous palace, or some blissful bow'r, ... O 18 London 185
Teach me, thou venerable bow'r, ... O 125 An Ode 29

BOW'RS
Direct thy rivulets, and twine thy bow'rs; . . . . . O 20 London 217
Direct the rivulets, and plan the bow'rs; . . . . . Y 58 London V 217
To deck these Bow'rs each Region shall combine, . . . O 279 Irene 88

BOWER
Ah! think not, in the dang'rous Bower, ... O 121 To Miss Playin V 7

BOWERS   SEE BOW'RS, BOWRS
No fragrant bowers, no delightful glades, ... O 83 Epi Dist Moth. 12
And in those Bowers of Innocence and . . . . . . O 349 Irene V 7
    Quiet

BOWING
Through bowing Slaves, I range the private Rooms, . . . O 283 Irene 17

BOWL
And crown the bowl with new-prest wine . . . . . O 72 Hor. Epode II 52
"Now the generous bowl I sip . . . . O 185 Anacreon Ode 9 31
And bad the feast, and song, and bowl, ... O 190 Tr. Medea I 5
The Bowl shall circle to confirm our League, ... O 308 Irene 29
With ill-tim'd Mirth propos'd the Bowl of Love. . . . O 316 Irene 26

BOWLS
At sight of sparkling bowls or beauteous dames, . . . O 142 In Baretti Bk. 1
Two bowls with oyl and milk I'll yearly crown, ... Y 7 Virgil Daphnis 45
Then when repeated bowls unlock'd the heart . . . . . Y 11 Tr Hor Epode 9 17

BOWRS
Still dost thou linger in these fatal bowrs . . . . . Y 196 Irene V 18A

BOWS
Nor needs the guard of Moorish bows: . . . . O 65 Hor I Ode xxii 4
Nor needs the Guard of Moorish Bows. . . . . O 66 To A. Fuscus 4

BOX
Here Hunt may box, or Mahomet may dance. . . . . . . O 53 Pro Drury-Lane 46

BOY
Thou, who began'st a man, wilt end a boy. . . . . . O 135 Tr Rambler 127 2
Or boy, whose snowy neck the flowing ringlets grace. . . Y 12 Tr Hor Epode 9 42
The nurse attending bore a lovely boy . . . . Y 18 Tr. Iliad Bk 6 9
Propitious hear my prayers, protect the boy, ... Y 20 Tr. Iliad Bk 6 101

BOYS
The sport of boys, and scandall of the town. . . . . Y 11 Tr Hor Epode 9 12

BRAIN
Do gay Delusions, wand'ring o'er the Brain, ... O 277 Irene 44
And gay delusions wandring o'er the brain . . . . . O 356 Irene V 11

BRAKE
The rustling brake alarms, and quiv'ring shade, . . . O 32 Vanity Wishes 42
Like a fell Adder swelling in a Brake, ... O 275 Irene 77

BRAKES
Now each parterre with thorny brakes is fill'd . . . . Y 7 Virgil Daphnis 24

BRAMBLE
The loiterer finds a bramble for a flow'r. . . . . . O 133 Tr. Rambler 71 2

BRAMBLES
Who sleeps on brambles till he kills his man; . . . . O 21 London 227

BRANCHES
Among the quivering branches sighs; . . . . O 66 Hor I Ode xxii 18
Among the quivering Branches sighs, ... O 67 To A. Fuscus 18
He drew his scymetar and lop'd the branches. . . . . Y 187 Irene V 7

BRAND
How would the Trojans brand great Hector's name! . . . O 74 Tr. Iliad Bk 6 5
To banish Doubt, and brand him for a Villain. . . . . O 273 Irene 21

BRANDISHES
Already brandishes his Sabre o'er You . . . . O 368 Irene V 18

BRASS
Of light reflected from the polish'd brass . . . . . Y 20 Tr. Iliad Bk 6 93

	PAGE	TITLE	LINE
BRAV'RY			
Wit, brav'ry, worth, his lavish tongue bestows; . . .	O 16	London	126
BRAVE			
With force resistless o'er the brave prevail.	O 39	Vanity Wishes	178
Fears of the brave, and follies of the wise?	O 45	Vanity Wishes	316
Yours is the Charge, ye Fair, ye Wise, ye Brave! . . .	O 58	Prologue Comus	37
Nor my brave brothers, that have bit the ground, . . .	O 74	Tr. Iliad Bk 6	17
Before that day, by some brave hero's hand, ...	O 75	Tr. Iliad Bk 6	29
Directress of the brave and just, ...	O 100	Ode Friendship	13
For not the brave, or wise, or great, ...	O 136	Tr Rambler 128	1
Can brave Leontius call for airy Wonders, ...	O 250	Irene	42
Not all like thee can brave the Shocks of Fate, . . .	O 266	Irene	34
Such slight Defeats but animate the Brave	O 270	Irene	7
Can brave Leontius be the Slave of Glory?	O 305	Irene	30
Intimidates the Brave, degrades the Great.	O 311	Irene	15
But brave Demetrius scorn'd the mean Revenge, . . .	O 313	Irene	17
By that dire sword my sev'n brave brothers dy'd; . . .	Y 18	Tr. Iliad Bk 6	34
Then rises the brave leader of their hosts	Y 24	Tr Add. Battle	80
BRAVELY			
Acquir'd by wounds, and battles bravely fought! . . .	O 74	Tr. Iliad Bk 6	7
BRAVEST			
Mann'd with the bravest of our fellow Captives, . . .	O 254	Irene	135
The bravest of the Greeks the wall invade.	Y 19	Tr. Iliad Bk 6	53
The bravest hero and the fearfull'st slave	Y 21	Tr. Iliad Bk 6	119
BREACH			
Stem'd in the Breach the Deluge of Destruction, . . .	O 295	Irene	28
BREAD			
"From his fingers snatch his bread, ...	O 185	Anacreon Ode 9	34
BREAK			
The Horse shall trample, or the Plough shall break, . .	O 110	To Posterity	2
The groaning Greeks break up their golden Caverns . .	O 249	Irene	17
Break through the Politician's tedious Forms, . . .	O 259	Irene	106
Shall break the Fetters of the groaning Christian; . .	O 278	Irene	76
The Laws of Kindness, break the Bonds of Nature? . .	O 280	Irene	16
Would break the sacred laws of peace and	O 352	Irene	V 3
order			
BREAKING			
When ev'n as Love was breaking off from Wonder, . . .	O 282	Irene	66
BREAST			
Tho' grief and fondness in my breast rebel, ...	O 8	London	1
They first invade your table, then your breast; . . .	O 17	London	153
And leaves, unseen, a dagger in your breast. . . .	O 21	London	241
And plants, unseen, a dagger in your breast. . . .	O 21	London	V 241
Quick fires his breast the fever of renown	Y 97	Vanity Wishes	V 137
An envious Breast with certain Mischief glows, . . .	O 46	Vanity Wishes	V330A
An rivals breast with certain mischief glows . . .	Y 107	Vanity Wishes	V330A
When strong devotion fills thy glowing Breast, . . .	O 48	Vanity Wishes	V 358
And unresisted Passion storm'd the Breast.	O 51	Pro Drury-Lane	8
(No spark of envy harbours in my breast)	O 64	Virgil Past.I	14
Fix'd in his canker'd breast remain:	O 73	Hor. Epode II	78
The human and the savage breast	O 99	Ode Friendship	7
Grief swell thine Eyes, and Terror chill thy Breast. . .	O 110	To Posterity	4
I feel thy pow'r usurp my breast.	O 123	Winter's Walk	8
And nature, on her naked breast, ...	O 124	An Ode	3
'tis thine alone to calm the pious breast	O 130	Tr. Rambler 7	5
Rag'd within the Master's Breast	O 148	Tr Boet III.12	14
Learn here what Anguish racks the guilty Breast, . . .	O 246	Irene Prologue	11
Arose to Heav'n, and pierc'd my bleeding Breast, . . .	O 251	Irene	74
This fir'd the youthful King's ambitious Breast, . . .	O 256	Irene	47
Or arm his Breast against the Force of Love? . . .	O 261	Irene	8
Those pow'rful Tyrants of the Female Breast	O 261	Irene	12
Swells the fair Breast or animates the Glance, . . .	O 262	Irene	14
And sways thy Breast with absolute Dominion, . . .	O 266	Irene	18
Unactive (unkindled) in the breast--rouse it . . .	Y 133	Irene	V 19
Beats not the female Breast with gen'rous Passions, . .	O 278	Irene	57
Swells in the Breast, and with resistless Force, . .	O 280	Irene	20
Yet can Ambition in Abdalla's Breast	O 280	Irene	25
She mark'd my sparkling Eyes, and heaving Breast, . .	O 282	Irene	68
Dwells on her Lips, and sighs upon her Breast; . . .	O 286	Irene	5
That raises Tumults in the female Breast, ...	O 287	Irene	12
Deep in my Breast be treasur'd this Resolve, . . .	O 288	Irene	12
I'll open my breast--clasp thee--forget	Y 161	Irene	V 13
greatness--			
Esteem Aspasia's Breast, the noblest Kingdom.	O 289	Irene	14
Recline upon my Breast thy sinking Beauties. . . .	O 295	Irene	8
Fill all thy ardent Breast with Greece and Virtue, . .	O 298	Irene	8
How Guilt once harbour'd in the conscious Breast, . .	O 311	Irene	14
When Guilt like this once harbours in the Breast . .	O 346	Irene	V 4
The Breast where Guilt like this has found	O 349	Irene	V 23
admission			
When Fear and Anguish labour in the Breast, ...	O 315	Irene	31
The Breast where Virtue guards the Throne of Peace. . .	O 316	Irene	15
The breast where truth supports the throne of peace. . .	Y 193	Irene	V 15
Watch each unquiet Flutter of the Breast, ...	O 320	Irene	24
Irradiate and obscure my Breast by Turns:	O 321	Irene	45
He struck his tortur'd Breast, and roar'd, Irene! . .	O 325	Irene	24
Abdalla, bid thy troubled Breast be calm;	O 329	Irene	2
Clasp'd in her Arms, or slumb'ring on her Breast, . .	O 331	Irene	19
Remorse and Anguish seize on all my Breast;	O 333	Irene	45
Invades my soul, and rages in my breast.	Y 11	Tr Hor Epode 9	6
Sighs issued from my heaving breast;	Y 11	Tr Hor Epode 9	14

41

BREAST	(CONTINUED)	PAGE	TITLE	LINE

BREAST   (CONTINUED)   PAGE   TITLE   LINE
    From Hector's breast each gloomy trouble flies . . . .   Y 18 Tr. Iliad Bk 6   15
    And Grecian spears shall quiver in your breast. . . . . Y 18 Tr. Iliad Bk 6   23
    Tumultuous passions strugle in her breast . . . . .   Y 21 Tr. Iliad Bk 6   109
BREASTS
    In vain with anxious breasts we fear . . . .   O 69 Hor.II Ode 14   15
    With breasts resolv'd, they follow'd still . . . . .   O 79 Feast St Simon   16
    Whose snowy breasts, whose animated eyes, ...   O 83 Epi Dist Moth.   5
BREATH
    I drew the breath of life in English air; . . . . .   O 15 London   118
    Impeachment stops the speaker's pow'rful breath, . . .   O 31 Vanity Wishes   19
    You could not gain a Moments breath, ...   O 69 Hor.II Ode 14   9
    Long since I learn'd to slight this fleeting breath, . . O 74 Tr. Iliad Bk 6   9
    There a stout warriour fainting gasps for breath . . .   O 76 Tr Add. Battle   16
    And scarce can breath th' infected sky, ...   O 79 Feast St Simon   35
    And Serpents with their poys'nous breath . . . . . .   O 79 Feast St Simon   41
    And sparkling quiver to the Breath of May; . . . . .   O 298 Irene   21
    Turn'd backwards by the powerful Breath of Heav'n. . .   O 322 Irene   3
    His Breath prolong'd but to detect her Treason, . . .   O 331 Irene   15
    Ev'n in the bloom of life depriv'd of breath. . . . .   Y   6 Virgil Daphnis   2
    Soon as their young began to draw their breath . . . .   Y 24 Tr Add. Battle   86
    Hot her breath with many a dram, ...   Y 301 Extemp. Elegy   18
BREATHE
    Her statue would have breath'd an added grace, ...   O 189 Seeing Montagu   4
BREATHE
    To breathe in distant fields a purer air, ...   O   9 London   6
    Breathe forth thy fervours for a soul . . . . . .   Y 108 Vanity Wishes V 359
    And scents ambrosial breathe in every gale: . . . . .   O 84 Epi Dist Moth.   17
    Here ev'ry Fragrance breathe of ev'ry Spring: . . . .   O 279 Irene   87
BREATHING
    Th' inestimable Privilege of Breathing! . . . . . .   O 260 Irene   136
    Deform the beauties of the breathing statue (marble hero Y 177 Irene   V111A
BREATHLESS
    Breathless at length they leave th' unfinish'd war . .   O 76 Tr Add. Battle   6
    Scatters their breathless bodies o'er the plain. . . .   O 76 Tr Add. Battle   32
    Till breathless Fury rested from Destruction . . . .   O 249 Irene   5
    And all Irene now is breathless Clay. . . . . . .   O 330 Irene   4
    Breathless, amaz'd, and on the guarded Beach . . . .   O 335 Irene   8
BREECHES
    He gropes his breeches with a monarch's air. . . . .   O 17 London   151
BREEZE
    There ev'ry breeze bears health upon its wings; . . .   O 20 London   221
    While the breeze whispers and the streamers play. . . . O 82 Young Author   6
    Sooner the Breeze shall catch the flying Sounds, . . .   O 255 Irene   28
    We learn to shudder at the rustling Breeze, ...   O 266 Irene   29
    Had not the Breeze untwin'd the meeting Boughs, . . .   O 269 Irene   10
    Fenc'd from the sun and shelterd from the breeze. . . . Y 163 Irene   V 43
    Fenc'd from the summer breeze, and vernal . . . . .   Y 163 Irene   V 43
        show'r.
BRIAREUS
    As when great Briareus with matchless might . . . . .   Y 26 Tr Add. Battle   137
BRIB'D
    And guests are brib'd to hear; . . . .   Y 104 Vanity Wishes V 278
BRIBE
    Or bribe a virgin's innocence away. . . . .   O 13 London   78
    Turn from the glitt'ring bribe thy scornful eye, . . .   O 14 London   87
    And scarce a legacy can bribe to hear; . . . . . .   O 44 Vanity Wishes   278
    The bard may supplicate, but cannot bribe. . . . . .   O 60 Pro Good Nat'd   26
    Threw back the glitt'ring Bribe. . . . .   O 258 Irene   102
    Bribe to his Cause and list beneath his Banners . . .   O 274 Irene   53
    Glory, the Bribe of avaricious Virtue! . . . . . .   O 305 Irene   32
BRIBES
    Where won by bribes, by flatteries implor'd, ...   O 18 London   180
    No bribes were paid, no special juries known, ...   Y 61 London   V 252
    Such bribes the rapid Greek o'er Asia whirl'd, ...   O 39 Vanity Wishes   179
    Nor bribes your Eyes to prejudice your Heads. . . . .   O 246 Irene Prologue   28
BRIDAL
    Shall shed his Beams upon the bridal Bed, ...   O 309 Irene   24
BRIDE
    Conquring Poet take thy Bride! . . . .   O 150 Tr Boet III.12   40
    Fondly view'd his following Bride, ...   O 150 Tr Boet III.12   51
    To-morrow brings the visionary Bride. . . . . . .   O 283 Irene   31
BRIDGNORTH
    at Bridgnorth, Salop; who died very poor . . . .   O 113 Epit. Phillips   V T
BRIGHT
    Afar they mark the flambeau's bright approach, ...   O 21 London   234
    Mark from afar the flambeau's bright approach, ...   O 59 London   V 234
    That hung the bright Palladium of the place, ...   O 33 Vanity Wishes   84
    Where aught of bright, or fair, the piece displays, . . O 62 Pro Word Wise   15
    Bright Stella, form'd for universal Reign, ...   O 96 Hickman Spinet   1
    With bright, but oft destructive gleam, ...   O 100 Ode Friendship   9
    With bright, but oft destructive gloom, ...   O 100 Ode Friendship V 9
    Thou seem'st at once, bright nymph, a Muse and Grace. . O 107 Lady F Assizes   6
    Illustrious age! how bright thy glories shone, ...   O 118 Epitaph Hanmer   21
    "Fate! snatch away the bright disguise, ...   O 122 Stella Mourn.   5
    Bright wisdom teach me Curio's art, ...   O 126 An Ode   38
    His frame was firm, his powers were bright, ...   O 202 Death Dr Levet   31
    From those bright Regions of eternal Day, ...   O 253 Irene   99
    Her grateful Sons shine bright with ev'ry Virtue; . . . O 256 Irene   60
    Another Plund'rer brought the bright Irene; . . . . .   O 259 Irene   118
    Nor found again the bright Temptation fail? . . . . .   O 259 Irene   125

BRIGHT	(CONTINUED)		PAGE	TITLE	LINE	
How will the bright Aspasia shine above her!	. . . .	O	261	Irene	23	
With bright effulgence The travell<er> afar	. . . .	Y	131	Irene	V 36	
Observe, bright Maid, as his resistless Voice	. . . .	O	268	Irene	25	
Thus bright in Tears, thus amiable in Ruin,	. . . .	O	276	Irene	7	
Too high, bright Maid, thou rat'st exterior Grace;	. .	O	277	Irene	30	
Once to behold the Charms of bright Aspasia,	. . . .	O	285	Irene	6	
Make haste, bright Maid, to rule the willing World;	. .	O	288	Irene	7	
O say, bright Being, in this Age of Absence,	. . . .	O	295	Irene	21	
My Soul first kindled by thy bright Example,	. . . .	O	298	Irene	13	
Thou shin'st, bright Maid, superior to Distress;	. .	O	298	Irene	17	
In the bright Colours of primaeval Spring;	. . . . .	O	314	Irene	5	
We come, bright Virgin, tho' relenting Nature	. . .	O	325	Irene	20	
See! Sol's bright chariot seeks the western main,	. . .	Y	4	On a Daffodill	22	
BRIGHTEN'D						
But brighten'd by the sable dress,	. . . .	O	122	Stella Mourn.	9	
BRIGHTENS						
Each Pleasure brightens at its near Approach,	. . . .	O	261	Irene	20	
BRIGHTEST						
Should Reason guide thee with her brightest ray,	. . .	O	37	Vanity Wishes	145	
Adorn'd in Roman time the brightest days,	. . . .	O	189	Seeing Montagu	2	
Adorns my Palace with its brightest Virgins;	. . . .	O	263	Irene	15	
BRIGHTNESS						
Diffuse a Brightness on our future Days;	. . . . .	O	301	Irene	100	
BRING						
Nor light nor darkness bring his pain relief,	. . . .	O	32	Vanity Wishes	43	
To whom all nations tribute bring.	. . . . . .	O	68	Hor. II Ode IX	20	
And bring her former Sentence new confirm'd.	. . . .	O	327	Irene	27	
I bring a tardy Message from Irene.	. . . . . .	O	331	Irene	2	
And of a fruitful year fair omens bring.	. . . . .	Y	3	On a Daffodill	4	
And of a faithful year fair omens bring.	. . . . .	Y	3	On a Daffodill	V 4	
BRINGS						
To-morrow brings the visionary Bride.	. . . . . .	O	283	Irene	31	
BRINK						
And panted on the brink of violation	. . . . . .	Y	124	Irene	V 112	
BRISKER						
With brisker air the silken courtiers gaze,	. . . .	O	17	London	164	
BRITAIN						
But will not Britain hear the last appeal,	. . . .	O	34	Vanity Wishes	91	
That never Britain can in vain excel;	. . . . . .	O	57	Prologue Comus	V 12	
Ye Sons of Britain, deign to hear,	. . . . . .	O	188	Epilogue	V 3	
BRITAIN'S						
Who scarce forbear, tho' Britain's Court he sing,	. . .	O	13	London	69	
On Britain's fond credulity they prey.	. . . . .	O	15	London	112	
How wouldst thou shake at Britain's modish tribe,	. . .	O	33	Vanity Wishes	61	
Evn low built towns they Britain's modish tribe,	. . .	Y	94	Vanity Wishes	V 61	
And visits Britain's hardy Sons	. . . .	O	80	Feast St Simon	47	
Or bid soft Science polish Britain's Heroes:	. . . .	O	293	Irene	106	
BRITAINS						
Or bid fair Science polish Britains Heroes	. . . .	O	348	Irene	V 22	
BRITANNIA'S						
And call Britannia's glories back to view;	. . . .	O	10	London	26	
Her Grandsire leaves her in Britannia's Arms,	. . . .	O	58	Prologue Comus	34	
BRITISH						
Nor hope the British lineaments to trace,	. . . .	O	15	London	101	
BRITON						
Give to St. David one true Briton more.	. . . . .	O	9	London	8	
Where once the harrass'd Briton found repose,	. . . .	O	11	London	47	
That never Briton can in vain excel;	. . . . . .	O	57	Prologue Comus	12	
BRITON'S						
Was early taught a Briton's right to prize,	. . . .	O	15	London	119	
BRITONS						
For such in distant lands the Britons shine,	. . . .	O	39	Vanity Wishes	181	
For these in distant lands the Britons shine,	. . . .	Y	100	Vanity Wishes	V 181	
BROCADE						
The beauties of the gay brocade,	. . . .	O	122	Stella Mourn.	2	
BROIL						
Provokes a broil, and stabs you for a jest.	. . . .	O	21	London	229	
BROKE						
Death broke at once the vital chain,	. . . . . .	O	202	Death Dr Levet	35	
And broke the meditated Lines of War.	. . . . .	O	273	Irene	26	
Broke out in Perfidy--Oh curs'd Aspasia,	. . . . .	O	316	Irene	10	
By Daphnis' skill th' Armenian tigers broke	. . . .	Y	6	Virgil Daphnis	13	
Mournfull Andromache the silence broke,	. . . . .	Y	18	Tr. Iliad Bk 6	17	
BROKEN						
The vanquish'd hero leaves his broken bands,	. . . .	O	41	Vanity Wishes	211	
And soaring mocks the broken frame below.	. . . .	O	131	Tr. Rambler 17	1	
Did we not see the bars of nature broken?	. . . .	Y	115	Irene	V 49F	
Then in short Sighs forsook his broken Frame.	. . .	O	331	Irene	16	
BROOD						
And cruel Danaus' bloody Brood	. . . .	O	69	Hor.II Ode 14	19	
Scream in the nests and brood their young in peace.	. .	Y	23	Tr Add. Battle	35	
BROODS						
Melancholly broods or pours her influence oer the	. . .	Y	165	Irene	V 82	
BROTHER						
And quit the Names of Brother, Friend, and Father?	. .	O	280	Irene	17	
A father, brother, husband, all in thee.	. . . .	Y	19	Tr. Iliad Bk 6	45	
The bard obdurate sees his brother die.	. . . . .	Y	67	Prologue Lethe	4	
BROTHERS						
Nor my brave brothers, that have bit the ground,	. . .	O	74	Tr. Iliad Bk 6	17	
By that dire sword my sev'n brave brothers dy'd;	. . .	Y	18	Tr. Iliad Bk 6	34	

43

                                                          PAGE   TITLE   LINE
BROTHERS'
    Who has not read the Theban brothers' hate? . . . . .   Y 22 Tr Add. Battle   14
BROTOLOIGOS
    Toios Ares Brotoloigos eni ptolemoisi memene, ... O 172 On Marlborough   1
BROUGHT
    And brought his beauteous Plunder to the Sultan. . . . O 258 Irene   96
    Another Plund'rer brought the bright Irene; . . . . .   O 259 Irene   118
    I heard, and soften'd, till Abdalla brought . . . . .   O 334 Irene   61
    Abdalla brought her Doom! Abdalla brought it! . . . .   O 334 Irene   63
    Abdalla brought her Doom! Abdalla brought it! . . . .   O 334 Irene   63
    Abdalla brought her Doom! . . . .   O 334 Irene   66
        Abdalla brought it, ...   O 334 Irene   66
    The victor hither brought, a royall slave. . . . . .   Y 19 Tr. Iliad Bk 6   39
BROW
    Shun the Mountain's airy Brow, ...   O 145 Tr Boeth. II.4   7
    For tho' beneath thy haughty Brow . . . .   O 146 Tr Boeth III.5   5
    I see the Gloom that low'rs upon thy Brow, ...   O 271 Irene   1
    That clouds thy Brow and labours in thy Bosom . . .   O 369 Irene   V   19
    Wealh in her hand, and olive on her brow. . . . .   O 374 Irene   V   32
    Did regal Diadems invest my Brow, ...   O 289 Irene   12
    He wears of late Resentment on his Brow, ...   O 311 Irene   9
    Hang Sit these black clouds upon Aspasia's brow? . . . Y 191 Irene   V   15
    Then on his brow the mighty soldier plac'd . . . .   Y 21 Tr. Iliad Bk 6   124
BROWS
    Her brows a cloudy show, ...   O 127 To Lyce, Lady   10
    But let us try to clear our clouded Brows, ...   O 329 Irene   10
BRYAN'S
    So long renown'd in B<rya>n's deathless strain? . . .   O 107 Lady F Assizes   2
BUBBLE
    Important Hazard! What's that airy Bubble . . . . .   O 260 Irene   137
BUBBLES
    And chase the new-blown Bubbles of the Day. . . . . .   O 53 Pro Drury-Lane   50
BUDA
    And Buda fall, and proud Vienna tremble, ...   O 309 Irene   27
BUDS
    Whose early buds unusual glories wear, ...   Y   3 On a Daffodill   3
BUILD
    And only build upon another's ruin. . . . .   O 176 Tr Metastas II   13
    Build caravanseral . . . .   Y 130 Irene   V 12B
BUILDING
    Who to the ground the shatter'd building flung . . .   Y 23 Tr Add. Battle   48
BUILDS
    See! while he builds, the gaudy vassals come, ...   O 19 London   202
BUILT
    Evn low built towns they Britain's modish tribe . . . Y '94 Vanity Wishes V 61
    To offer up my vows in the temple built by the Father of O 348 Irene   V   1
        Mankind
    And though built on feeble columns--Its lofty turrets . Y 131 Irene   V 35
        blaze amidst
    If built on settled Thought, this Constancy . . . .   O 290 Irene   36
    Nor built on Faith, nor fortify'd by Conscience? . . . O 301 Irene   84
BULK
    Who matchless strength and bulk gygantick boasts, . . . Y 24 Tr Add. Battle   81
BULLOCKS
    <Or> sees from far his Bullocks play . . . .   O 71 Hor. Epode II   20
BULLS
    As corn the fields, as bulls the herds of kine, . . .   Y   6 Virgil Daphnis   18
BULRUSH-SPEARS
    And dy'd their bulrush-spears in mutual blood. . . . . Y 24 Tr Add. Battle   57
BULWARKS
    His arm alone rais'd bulwarks of the dead. . . . . .   Y 25 Tr Add. Battle   121
BURDEN
    Divide the burden of his care, ...   O 72 Hor. Epode II   50
BURGESS
    Th' offended burgess hoards his angry tale, ...   O 60 Pro Good Nat'd   17
BURIED
    To buried merit raise the tardy bust. . . . .   O 38 Vanity Wishes   162
    Immur'd, and buried in perpetual Sloth, ...   O 292 Irene   81
BURN
    Ye patriot Crouds, who burn for England's Fame, . . .   O 57 Prologue Comus   1
    Should costly Loads of incense burn, ...   O 69 Hor.II Ode 14   7
    They clap their wings, and with new fury burn; . . . . O 76 Tr Add. Battle   9
    By thee wholl citys burn, wholl nations fall! . . . .   O 77 Festina Lente   12
    but if your influence be too wide--your dissipated rays Y 132 Irene   V 41
        will burn no more . . . .   Y 132 Irene   V 41
    And this is my Reward--to burn, to languish, ...   O 285 Irene   1
    No more I burn for Fame or for Dominion; . . . . .   O 333 Irene   43
    And with fell rage and secret anguish burn. . . . . .   Y 24 Tr Add. Battle   65
BURN'D
    His force of genius burn'd in early youth, ...   O 117 Epitaph Hanmer   5
BURNING
    Athirst for wealth, and burning to be great; . . . . . O 33 Vanity Wishes   74
    Place me beneath the burning line, ...   O 66 Hor I Ode xxii   21
    Place me beneath the burning Zone, ...   O 67 To A. Fuscus   21
    Burning in vain, delays the Stroke of Death? . . . .   O 257 Irene   66
    Amidst the Tortures of the burning Steel, ...   O 272 Irene   15
    Till burning Death shoots through their wither'd Limbs? . O 282 Irene   6
    And burning daemons tremble at her torments . . . .   Y 168 Irene   V135D
BURNS
    Resistless burns the fever of renown . . . .   O 36 Vanity Wishes V 137
    Burns from the strong contagion of the gown; . . . .   O 36 Vanity Wishes   138

44

```
BURNS            (CONTINUED)                              PAGE    TITLE          LINE
    Where Lybia's swarthy offspring burns,       . . . . . .   O  70 Hor.II Ode XX      14
    Because my slighted Passion burns in vain!   . . . . .     O 281 Irene             49
    Each Turkish Bosom burns for thy Destruction,  . . . .     O 300 Irene             73
    The hungry Janizary burns for Plunder,       . . . . . .   O 309 Irene             21
    The raging Sultan burns till our Return,     . . . . . .   O 327 Irene             11
    And disappointed Vengeance burns in vain;    . . . . .     O 330 Irene              6
BURNT     SEE SUN-BURNT
    And burnt him decent on a funerall pile.     . . . . . .   Y  18 Tr. Iliad Bk 6     31
BURST
    Like subterraneous tempests with dire eruption burst their  Y 115 Irene        V  49
        caverns
    From ev'ry Palace burst a mingled Clamour,   . . . . .     O 251 Irene             70
    When from his Lips the fatal Name burst out, . . . .       O 270 Irene             12
BURSTING
    Loud as the Billows bursting on the Ground.  . . . . .     O 110 To Posterity       6
    Fierce through the bursting Caverns rend their Way?  . .   O 281 Irene             53
    Nor bursting through the ranks in wild distraction  . .    Y 163 Irene        V  47
BURSTS
    The midnight murd'rer bursts the faithless bar;  . . .     O  21 London           239
    With unexpected legions bursts away,         . . . . . .   O  42 Vanity Wishes    243
BURTHEN
    Hypocrisy which I ha<ve> worn is a burthen:  . . . . .     Y 185 Irene         V   2
    Had form'd her nest and plac'd her burthen there,  . .     Y  23 Tr Add. Battle    45
BURTHEN'D
    To tire the burthen'd rack and gorge destruction  . . .    Y 196 Irene         V 18C
BURY
    To Lady F<irebra>ce at Bury Assizes          . . . . . .   O 107 Lady F Assizes     T
BUS'NESS
    Who lives from toilsome bus'ness free,       . . . . . .   O  71 Hor. Epode II      2
    In bus'ness dext'rous, weighty in debate,    . . . . .     O 118 Epitaph Hanmer    13
BUSH
    There ev'ry bush with nature's musick rings, . . . . .     O  20 London           220
    Only ev'ry bush there artless music sings    . . . . . .   Y  58 London       V 220
BUSIED
    When every Man busied   . . . . . . . . .                  O 347 Irene         V  21
BUSINESS
    Is it business? is it love?   . . . . . . . .              O 185 Anacreon Ode 9     5
    From grov'ling Business and superfluous Care, . . . .      O 246 Irene Prologue     3
    And Business from the Day. In her Apartments . . . . .     O 260 Irene            131
    Beneath the Load of Business, and of Years.  . . . . .     O 271 Irene              7
    By hateful Business hurried from her Sight,  . . . . .     O 287 Irene             15
BUST
    To buried merit raise the tardy bust.        . . . . . .   O  38 Vanity Wishes    162
    While Crowds aloft the laureat Bust behold,  . . . . .     O  58 Prologue Comus    23
BUSTLING
    This bustling season's epidemic care;        . . . . . .   O  59 Pro Good Nat'd     6
    The bustling season's epidemic care.         . . . . . .   O  59 Pro Good Nat'd V   6
BUSY
    And watch the busy scenes of crouded life;   . . . . .     O  30 Vanity Wishes      4
    And all the busy scenes of crouded life;     . . . . . .   Y  92 Vanity Wishes  V   4
    Whom Pleasure keeps too busy to be wise,     . . . . .     O  46 Vanity Wishes    324
    The busy candidates for power and fame,      . . . . .     O  59 Pro Good Nat'd    11
    At busy hearts in vain love's arrows fly;    . . . . .     O 133 Tr. Rambler 85     1
    The busy day, the peaceful night,   . . . . . . .         O 202 Death Dr Levet    29
    The busy day, the cheerful night,   . . . . . . . .       O 202 Death Dr Levet V  29
    And then leaves your actions the busy trifler  . . . .    O 355 Irene         V  12
        unregarded
    Fly from the busy Pleasures of her Sex,      . . . . . .   O 322 Irene             14
BUT
            195                                               OMITTED WORD
BUY
    Let such raise palaces, and manors buy,      . . . . . .   O  12 London            57
    Nor sell for gold, what gold could never buy,  . . . .    O  14 London            88
BUYS
    Wealth heap'd on wealth, nor truth nor safety buys,  . .   O  31 Vanity Wishes     27
    Who buys without discretion, buys to sell.   . . . .      O 133 Tr. Rambler 82     1
    Who buys without discretion, buys to sell.   . . . . .    O 133 Tr. Rambler 82     1
BY
            206                                               OMITTED WORD
BYSTANDER
    To tell each Bystander, what none can deny,  . . . . .     O 173 Tr Fr Pantomim     2
CADMUS
    Nor Cadmus, scap'd the shafts of pain,       . . . . . .   O 136 Tr Rambler 128     4
CAESAR
    Let Caesar spread his conquests far,         . . . . . .   O 137 Tr Rambler 143     1
CAESAR'S
    Like Caesar's pilot, dignified by fate,      . . . . . .   O  59 Pro Good Nat'd     7
CAGE
    As mongrels bay the lion in a cage.          . . . . . .   O  60 Pro Good Nat'd    16
    As children fret the lion in a cage.         . . . . . .   O  60 Pro Good Nat'd V  16
    And in this earthly cage confin'd;           . . . . . .   O 147 Tr Boeth III.6 V  10
CALAIS
    A Calais    . . . . . . . . . .                           O 172 French Distich     1
CALI
    From Cali Bassa    . . . . . . . . .                      O 253 Irene            111
    Their Arms prevail'd, though Cali was our Friend.  . . .  O 253 Irene            119
    And led me to the Shore where Cali stood,    . . . . .    O 254 Irene            127
    So small a Force? or why should Cali fly?    . . . . .    O 254 Irene            138
    Why should Cali rebel--unexpensive age       . . . . .    Y 120 Irene         V  40
    He murmurs Vengeance at the Name of Cali,    . . . . .    O 256 Irene             48
```

CALI   (CONTINUED)   PAGE   TITLE   LINE

      They put the riches of Cali Bassa on board. . . . . .   Y 123 Irene   V 81
      Why stor'd for Flight? and why prepar'd by Cali?   . . .   O 258 Irene   85
      Rise Cali Bassa counsellor of Kings . . . . . .   O 351 Irene   V 24
      But, Cali, let Irene share thy Prayers; . . . . . .   O 262 Irene   5
      This were enough, if Cali had been Mahomet   . . . .   Y 132 Irene   V 41D
      Half were too much had Mahomet been Cali. . . . . .   Y 132 Irene   V 41E
      Then, Cali, shall the Toils of Battle cease, ...   O 265 Irene   44
      Cali, methinks yon waving Trees afford   . . . . .   O 268 Irene   36
      Despotick Rage pursues the Life of Cali.   . . . .   O 270 Irene   16
      Can Cali dare the Stroke of heav'nly Justice, ...   O 272 Irene   3
      Are these the Counsels? This the Faith of Cali?   . . . .   O 272 Irene   11
      Detested Cali too, with artful Wonder, ...   O 273 Irene   27
      Cali, this Day with hypocritick Zeal, ...   O 273 Irene   43
      And Afric's torrid Sands in search of Cali. . . . . .   O 274 Irene   60
      And Africs torrid shores in search of Cali   . . . .   Y 143 Irene   V 60
      Rouse, Cali, shall the Sons of conquer'd Greece   . . .   O 284 Irene   42
      Justice demands the forfeit Life of Cali; . . . . .   O 286 Irene   13
      When Cali mounts the Throne Abdalla dies, ...   O 288 Irene   13
      Commission'd, as he says, by Cali Bassa.   . . . . .   O 294 Irene   3
      Ambitious Cali dreads the Statesman's Arts, ...   O 300 Irene   74
      To-morrow's Dawn shall see the mighty Cali   . . . . .   O 303 Irene   11
      Or glare on Cali with malignant Beams.   . . . . .   O 304 Irene   36
      Is not the Fate of Greece and Cali thine? . . . . .   O 304 Irene   19
      Far be such black Ingratitude from Cali, ...   O 306 Irene   4
      Forbear--.i know the long try'd Faith of Cali.   . . .   O 308 Irene   11
      Abdalla, Cali, go--proclaim my Purpose. . . . . .   O 309 Irene   43
      Still Cali lives, and must he live To-morrow?   . . . .   O 310 Irene   1
      See Cali, Dread of Kings, and Pride of Armies, ...   O 311 Irene   16
      Nor at the Call of Cali deign'd to turn.   . . . . .   O 317 Irene   33
      Cali disarm'd was born away to Death; . . . . .   O 317 Irene   40
      Know'st thou not Cali? know'st thou not Demetrius?   . . .   O 324 Irene   15
      Expiring Cali nam'd Irene's Chamber, ...   O 326 Irene   29
      Irene's Chamber! Did not roaring Cali, ...   O 330 Irene   12
      The Wretch, whose Guilt declar'd by tortur'd Cali,   . .   O 334 Irene   64
      The wretch whose crimes declar'd by tortur'd Cali   . . .   Y 215 Irene   V 69A
CALI'S
      Or how can Cali's Flight restore our Country?   . . . .   O 254 Irene   139
      Join'd Cali's Hand to mine, and falt'ring cry'd,   . . .   O 272 Irene   8
      With venerable Cali's faithful Counsels?   . . . . .   O 272 Irene   10
      Can Cali's Voice . . . .   O 288 Irene   9
      Abdalla's Rage and Cali's Stratagems. . . . . . .   O 301 Irene   94
      Now joins thy People's, and thy Cali's Prayers,   . . .   O 308 Irene   8
      The Plot all Cali's, the Detection thine. . . . . .   O 329 Irene   4
CALL
      And call Britannia's glories back to view;   . . . . .   O 10 London   26
      Delusive Fortune hears th' incessant call, ...   O 33 Vanity Wishes   75
      They call them Fairies; these now free from care   . . .   O 77 Tr Add. Battle   49
      Rapacity would call for more; . . . .   O 144 Tr Boeth. II.2   10
      Call the Bettys, Kates, and Jennys   . . . . . .   O 196 Song Congratu.   9
      Call the Jocky, call the Pander, ...   O 196 Song Congratu. V 19
      Call the Jocky, call the Pander, ...   O 196 Song Congratu. V 19
      Can brave Leontius call for airy Wonders, ...   O 250 Irene   42
      Call to your Aid your Courage, and your Wisdom;   . . .   O 252 Irene   85
      Consult in private, call me when your Scheme   . . . .   O 256 Irene   36
      I go to wait thy Call; this kind Consent   . . . . .   O 285 Irene   15
      Call to your Aid with boundless Promises . . . . .   O 287 Irene   10
      Detain me here. But Nations call upon me, ...   O 288 Irene   12
      And Persecution boast the Call of Heav'n. . . . . .   O 291 Irene   66
      Call me to civilize the Russian Wilds, ...   O 292 Irene   105
      Or Persecution drank, attend our Call;   . . . . .   O 306 Irene   54
      Call forth her ancient Heroes to the Field, ...   O 309 Irene   39
      Call forth her ancient Scipios to the field   . . . .   Y 185 Irene   V 39
      Call them--but let them not prolong their Tale,   . . .   O 310 Irene   8
      Nor at the Call of Cali deign'd to turn.   . . . . .   O 317 Irene   33
      Yet much remains to hope. I shall not call   . . . . .   O 317 Irene   45
      The Pow'r of Turkey waits upon my Call. . . . . .   O 319 Irene   24
      The pow'r of Turkey rises at my Call, ...   Y 197 Irene   V 24
      Well mayst thou call thy Master to the Combat,   . . .   O 319 Irene   30
      In vain I listen to th' inviting Call . . . . . .   O 320 Irene   10
      Fly, Slaves, and call the Sultan to my Rescue.   . . .   O 322 Irene   56
      Then call it not our Cruelty, nor Crime, ...   O 327 Irene   28
      Quick at my Call shall execute your Charge; . . . . .   O 328 Irene   43
      O seize me, Madness--Did she call on me!   . . . . .   O 334 Irene   68
CALL'D
      And Virtue call'd Oblivion to her Aid.   . . . . .   O 52 Pro Drury-Lane   28
      His country call'd him from the studious shade;   . . .   O 117 Epitaph Hanmer   10
      Age call'd at length his active mind to rest,   . . .   O 118 Epitaph Hanmer   35
      Till nature call'd him to the gen'ral doom, ...   O 118 Epitaph Hanmer   43
      Insulting chance ne'er call'd with louder voice,   . . .   O 135 Tr Rambler 106   1
      Nor call'd them to the gloomy cells . . . . . .   O 191 Tr. Medea I   9
      When fainting nature call'd for aid, ...   O 201 Death Dr Levet   13
      My Father call'd me to his Couch of Death, ...   O 272 Irene   7
      Not call'd to try the Cause, we hear the Sentence,   . .   O 326 Irene   34
      And stopp'd the heav'nly Voice that call'd on me.   . . .   O 334 Irene   71
      Which murder'd Innocence that call'd on me. . . . . .   O 334 Irene   76
      By Hector call'd Scamandrius from the god . . . . .   Y 18 Tr. Iliad Bk 6   11
      But call'd Astyanax because his sire   . . . . . .   Y 18 Tr. Iliad Bk 6   13
CALL'DST
      Say, how thou call'dst in Tears upon Demetrius!   . . .   O 295 Irene   26

46

```
                                                       PAGE    TITLE          LINE
CALLS   SEE CAT-CALLS
     The tide retiring, calls me from the land:     .  .  .  .  .  O  22 London            255
     With distant voice neglected Virtue calls,     .  .  .  .  .  O  46 Vanity Wishes     333
     Diana calls to life in vain, .  .  .  .  .  .  .  .  .  .  .  O 232 Tr Horace IV.7     26
     Aspasia calls me, let me fly to save her.      .  .  .  .  .  O 259 Irene            107
     Religion calls her from the wish'd Embrace,    .  .  .  .  .  O 261 Irene             16
     'Tis Greece, 'tis Freedom calls Aspasia hence,   .  .  .  .  O 297 Irene              9
     Forbear, Demetrius, 'tis Aspasia calls thee;   .  .  .  .  .  O 318 Irene              8
     Thy Love, Aspasia, calls; restrain thy Sword;    .  .  .  .  O 318 Irene              9
     Forgive, my Fair, 'tis Life, 'tis Nature calls.  .  .  .  .  O 318 Irene             19
     Who calls for Pardon from a Wretch condemn'd?   .  .  .  .   O 323 Irene              4
     Unhappy Fair! Compassion calls upon me  .  .  .  .  .  .  .  O 327 Irene              4
CALM
     A transient calm the happy scenes bestow,      .  .  .  .  .  O  10 London            31
     Yet then shall calm reflection bless the night,  .  .  .  .  O  62 Pro Word Wise      21
     The floods of rage, and calm thy rufled soul.  .  .  .  .  .  O  77 Festina Lente      8
     Find here that calm thou gav'st so oft before;   .  .  .  .  O 113 Epit. Phillips      4
     Calm conscience then his former life survey'd,   .  .  .  .  O 118 Epitaph Hanmer     41
     'tis thine alone to calm the pious breast      .  .  .  .  .  O 130 Tr. Rambler 7      5
     Daring, tho' calm; and vigorous, tho' resign'd.  .  .  .  .  O 246 Irene Prologue     10
     At least this Day be calm--If we succeed,      .  .  .  .  .  O 260 Irene            141
     Too calm I listen to the flatt'ring Sounds.    .  .  .  .  .  O 278 Irene             74
     Hence! or be calm--To disagree is Ruin.  .  .  .  .  .  .  .  O 282 Irene             72
     With silent Sorrows, and with calm Devotion.   .  .  .  .  .  O 290 Irene             50
     Calm of my Cares, and Guardian of my Virtue.   .  .  .  .  .  O 298 Irene             12
     Guide all thy Steps, calm ev'ry stormy Thought,  .  .  .  .  O 303 Irene             21
     This Calm, these Joys, dear Innocence! are thine,  .  .  .    O 313 Irene              9
     This elemental Joy, this gen'ral Calm,  .  .  .  .  .  .  .   O 314 Irene              8
     Abdalla, bid thy troubled Breast be calm;      .  .  .  .  .  O 329 Irene              2
     Restrain your sorrows, calm your troubled soul.  .  .  .     Y  21 Tr. Iliad Bk 6    114
CALMER
     Yet still my calmer thoughts his choice commend,  .  .  .    O   8 London             3
              Your calmer Though  .  .  .  .  .  .  .  .  .  .  .  O 321 Irene             53
CALMLY
     Calmly rest in safe Repose?  .  .  .  .  .  .  .  .  .  .  .  O 144 Tr Boeth. II.4     4
     Calmly he heard, till Amurath's Resumption     .  .  .  .  .  O 270 Irene             10
CALMS
     With these celestial wisdom calms the mind,    .  .  .  .  .  O  48 Vanity Wishes     367
     Enough--resistless Reason calms my Soul--      .  .  .  .  .  O 297 Irene              1
CAMBRIA'S
     And, fix'd on Cambria's solitary shore,  .  .  .  .  .  .  .  O   9 London             7
CAMBRIAN
     Still foe to vice, forsake his Cambrian shade;   .  .  .  .   O  23 London           261
     Still foe to vice, exert his Cambrian shade;   .  .  .  .   Y  61 London         V 262
CAME
     Then Johnson came, instructed from the School,   .  .  .  .   O  51 Pro Drury-Lane     9
     I came obedient to thy friendly Summons,  .  .  .  .  .  .    O 253 Irene            105
     I came to heighten Tortures by Reproach,  .  .  .  .  .  .    O 330 Irene              7
     But there came a country 'squire  .  .  .  .  .  .  .  .     Y 301 Extemp. Elegy      13
CAMILLI
     Or bid her great Camilli  .  .  .  .  .  .  .  .  .  .  .    Y 185 Irene          V  39
CAMP
     To quit the Tumults of the noisy Camp,  .  .  .  .  .  .  .   O 264 Irene             11
     They croud my camp with voluntary tribute      .  .  .  .   Y 136 Irene          V 27B
     Amidst the Camp to howl his Life away.  .  .  .  .  .  .  .   O 273 Irene             37
     The shudd'ring Camp shall murmur out Demetrius.  .  .  .  .   O 305 Irene             42
CAMPS
     Sure, chill'd with sixty winter Camps, thy Blood  .  .  .    O 263 Irene              5
     Thou Thou chilld by sixty winter camps canst gaze  .  .    Y 129 Irene          V   5
          on
     Rolls half his Floods unheard through shouting Camps?   .    O 264 Irene             18
     Pours half his Floods unheard through shouting camps  .  .   O 353 Irene          V  32
CAN   SEE CAN'ST, CANST
     Here let those reign, whom pensions can incite  .  .  .  .    O  11 London            51
     A Statesman's logick unconvinc'd can hear,     .  .  .  .  .  O  13 London            71
     Can sap the principles, or taint the heart;    .  .  .  .  .  O  13 London            76
     All that at home no more can beg or steal,     .  .  .  .  .  O  15 London           107
     No gainful trade their industry can 'scape,    .  .  .  .  .  O  15 London           113
     Can surly virtue hope to fix a friend?  .  .  .  .  .  .  .   O  16 London           145
     Can Balbo's eloquence applaud, and swear  .  .  .  .  .  .    O  17 London           150
     For where can starving merit find a home?      .  .  .  .  .  O  18 London           191
     Scarce can our fields, such crowds at Tyburn die,  .  .  .    O  21 London           242
     This pow'r has praise, that virtue scarce can warm,  .  .    O  39 Vanity Wishes     183
     Such pow'r has praise, that virtue scarce can charm,  .     Y 100 Vanity Wishes  V 183
     And scarce a legacy can bribe to hear;  .  .  .  .  .  .  .   O  44 Vanity Wishes     278
     For love, which scarce collective man can fill;  .  .  .  .   O  48 Vanity Wishes     361
     For love, whose grasp Creation collective man can  .  .  .  Y 108 Vanity Wishes  V 361
          fill;
     But who the coming Changes can presage,  .  .  .  .  .  .    O  52 Pro Drury-Lane    39
     Perhaps, for who can guess th' Effects of Chance?  .  .  .    O  53 Pro Drury-Lane    45
     That never Briton can in vain excel;  .  .  .  .  .  .  .    O  57 Prologue Comus    12
     That never Britain can in vain excel;  .  .  .  .  .  .  .   O  57 Prologue Comus  V 12
     The great, 'tis true, can charm th' electing tribe;  .  .    O  60 Pro Good Nat'd    25
     No setting Sol can ease your cares,  .  .  .  .  .  .  .  .   O  67 Hor. II Ode IX    11
     Can more delicious food supply.  .  .  .  .  .  .  .  .  .   O  73 Hor. Epode II   V 62
     Can in my bosom half that grief create,  .  .  .  .  .  .    O  74 Tr. Iliad Bk 6    19
     And scarce can breath th' infected sky,  .  .  .  .  .  .    O  79 Feast St Simon    35
     For those who feel no guilt can know no shame;   .  .  .  .   O  84 Epi Dist Moth.    25
     Nor can I hope thy silken chain  .  .  .  .  .  .  .  .  .   O 120 To Miss Purse      9
     And can with thunder roar.  .  .  .  .  .  .  .  .  .  .  .  O 127 To Lyce, Lady     16
     With ev'ry bliss that man can gain.  .  .  .  .  .  .  .  .   O 136 Tr Rambler 128     6
```

	PAGE	TITLE	LINE
Place may be chang'd; but who can change his mind?	O 137	Tr Rambler 135	1
As not to grant me this, can Milton find?	O 137	Tr Rambler 140	2
The lust of wealth can never bear delay.	O 140	Tr Rambler 182	1
I too can feel the rapture, fierce and strong;	O 142	In Baretti Bk.	3
I too can pour the extemporary song:	O 142	In Baretti Bk.	4
No wealth his life from weary care can save,	O 146	Tr Boeth III.3	5
No care his wealth can carry to the grave.	O 146	Tr Boeth III.3	6
If such on Earth can Bliss bestow,	O 146	Tr Boeth III.4	7
But what Laws can Lovers awe?	O 150	Tr Boet III.12	47
As I can gulp it down.	O 159	Par Hermit III	12
To tell each Bystander, what none can deny,	O 173	Tr Fr Pantomim	2
"Can a prudent Dove decline	O 185	Anacreon Ode 9	23
Can yield no room to Music's soothing pow'r.	O 193	Tr. Medea II	20
You can hang or drown at last.	O 197	Song Congratu.	28
Nor can the might of Theseus rend	O 232	Tr Horace IV.7	27
Let him persuade me to it--if he can:	O 247	Irene Epilogue	4
Besides, he has fifty Wives; and who can bear	O 247	Irene Epilogue	5
These all are Trifles, to what we can give.	O 247	Irene Epilogue	20
Can brave Leontius call for airy Wonders,	O 250	Irene	42
If Happiness can be without Aspasia.	O 253	Irene	110
Can he restore the State he could not save?	O 253	Irene	116
Or how can Cali's Flight restore our Country?	O 254	Irene	139
But can thy Friend sustain the glorious Cause,	O 255	Irene	8
What can reverse thy Doom?	O 257	Irene	73
How can a single Hand attempt a Life	O 258	Irene	90
Not all like thee can brave the Shocks of Fate,	O 266	Irene	34
Can Mahomet's imperial Hand descend	O 268	Irene	15
To clasp a Slave? or, can a Soul like mine,	O 268	Irene	16
Can Cali dare the Stroke of heav'nly Justice,	O 272	Irene	3
Wherever Guilt can fly, Revenge can follow.	O 274	Irene	65
Wherever Guilt can fly, Revenge can follow.	O 274	Irene	65
Him I can crush at leisure.	O 367	Irene	V 30
Yet can Ambition in Abdalla's Breast	O 280	Irene	25
Aspasia! who can look upon thy Beauties?	O 281	Irene	42
To-morrow's Action? Can that hoary Wisdom	O 283	Irene	19
What I can grant, you cannot ask in vain--	O 285	Irene	14
Can then th' Assassin lift his treach'rous Hand	O 286	Irene	11
Can Cali's Voice	O 288	Irene	9
What Worth can merit? or what Faith reward?	O 295	Irene	16
Can Abdalla then dissemble,	O 299	Irene	34
Nor fear the Fair and Learn'd can want Protection.	O 302	Irene	115
Can brave Leontius be the Slave of Glory?	O 305	Irene	30
You may provoke but never can convince	Y 197	Irene	V 31
Be thine, that Wealth can give, or Guilt receive.	O 322	Irene	58
But who can hear thee beg without compliance	Y 205	Irene	V 33
That Vengeance can invent, or Pow'r inflict.	O 326	Irene	45
To meet that Fate we can delay no longer.	O 328	Irene	41
Nor justice can acquit, nor mercy spare	Y 210	Irene	V 25B
Inflict whatever Treason can deserve,	O 334	Irene	75
Whate'er perfidious villany can suffer	Y 216	Irene	V 75

CAN'ST

Dream not of Pow'r thou never can'st attain:	O 291	Irene	69
But how can'st thou support the Woes of Exile?	O 301	Irene	102
Can'st thou forget hereditary Splendours,	O 301	Irene	103
What can'st thou boast superiour to Demetrius?	O 305	Irene	38

CAN'T

I can't prevent, and will not share.	O 126	An Ode	36

CANCELL

Could cancell their irrevocable Law.	O 76	Tr Add. Battle	40

CANDIDATE

With ardent Haste, each Candidate of Fame	O 57	Prologue Comus	19

CANDIDATES

The busy candidates for power and fame,	O 59	Pro Good Nat'd	11

CANDOUR

Trusts without fear, to candour, and to you.	O 60	Pro Good Nat'd	V 30
Were Pope once void of wonted candour found,	O 106	Eliza plucking	7

CANKER'D

Fix'd in his canker'd breast remain:	O 73	Hor. Epode II	78

CANNIBAL

Wouldst thou subdue th' obdurate Cannibal	O 267	Irene	4

CANNON

Did unresisted Lightning aid their Cannon,	O 251	Irene	54
Oft have I rag'd, when their wide-wasting Cannon	O 273	Irene	24
Direct the loaded Cannon, grasp the Sword	O 364	Irene	V 40
Direct the loaded cannon, grasp the sword	Y 162	Irene	V 41

CANNOT

I cannot bear a French metropolis.	O 15	London	98
The bard may supplicate, but cannot bribe.	O 60	Pro Good Nat'd	26
And him who cannot hurt, allow to please;	O 62	Pro Word Wise	12
Forbear to hiss--the Poet cannot hear.	O 62	Pro Word Wise	18
What I can grant, you cannot ask in vain--	O 285	Irene	14
We cannot obviate, for we cannot guess.	O 287	Irene	11
We cannot obviate, for we cannot guess.	O 287	Irene	11
She cannot, must not, shall not linger here,	O 296	Irene	6
Then--O my Fair, I cannot bid thee goe;	O 297	Irene	15
Then--O my Fair, I cannot bid thee go;	O 297	Irene	V 15
Then shall you feel what Language cannot utter,	O 326	Irene	43
The Prayer I cannot grant--I dare not hear.	O 328	Irene	48
My spirits fail, I cannot name his death	Y 216	Irene	V 72

```
                                                    PAGE    TITLE        LINE
CANONIZE
    To canonize the Slaves of Superstition,  . . . . . .  O 309 Irene          34
CANOPY
    The golden canopy, the glitt'ring plate,  . . . . . . O  35 Vanity Wishes  114
CANST    SEE CAN'ST
    Thou canst not make the tea so fast   . . . . . . .   O 159 Par Hermit III  11
    "More than all thou canst not know;   . . . . . . .   O 186 Anacreon Ode 9  42
    Thou Thou chilld by sixty winter camps canst gaze . . Y 129 Irene        V  5
      on
CANT
    To cant, at last, of Reason to a Lover?   . . . . . . O 281 Irene          34
CANVASS
    Search every state, and canvass ev'ry pray'r.  . . . .O  33 Vanity Wishes  72
CAPITULATE
    And one capitulate, and one resign;   . . . . . . .   O  40 Vanity Wishes  200
    See one capitulate, and one resign;   . . . . . . .   Y 101 Vanity Wishes V 200
CAPRICE
    Thou who couldst laugh where want enchain'd caprice, . . O  32 Vanity Wishes  53
    With ev'ry Meteor of Caprice must play,  . . . . . .  O  53 Pro Drury-Lane  49
    Uncheck'd on both, caprice may vent its rage,  . . . .O  59 Pro Good Nat'd V 15
    Vain man runs headlong, to caprice resign'd;  . . . . O 134 Tr Rambler 105  1
CAPRICIOUS
    Not less capricious than a reigning fair,  . . . . . .O  95 Sprig of Myrtl  5
    Not less capricious than the reigning fair,  . . . . .O  95 Sprig of Myrtl V  5
    Capricious Man! to Good and Ill inconstant,  . . . . .O 300 Irene          76
CAPTAINS
    Two faithful Captains, Hasan and Caraza, . . . . . .  O 310 Irene           5
    Doom'd me to die with all the Turkish Captains.  . . .O 313 Irene          16
CAPTIVATE
    No Snares to captivate the Judgment spreads;  . . . . O 246 Irene Prologue  27
CAPTIVATED
    Hold in her Chains the captivated Sultan?  . . . . . .O 261 Irene           2
CAPTIVE
    Till captive Science yields her last retreat;  . . . .O  37 Vanity Wishes  144
    The ravish'd standard, and the captive foe,  . . . . .O  39 Vanity Wishes  176
    New chains to hold the captive heart. . . . . . . .   O 121 To Miss Playin  18
    New Tortures for the captive heart.   . . . . . . .   O 121 To Miss Playin V 18
    Forgetful of Command, with captive Beauties,  . . . . O 258 Irene          92
    To bid the prostrate Captive rise and live,  . . . . .O 278 Irene          70
    The Captive of his Sword. The coward Greeks,  . . . . O 312 Irene          14
    Then ling'ring with his captive Mistress here.  . . . O 331 Irene           9
CAPTIVE'S
    Concur to press a hapless Captive's Ruin?  . . . . . .O 288 Irene          10
    Concur to press a helpless Captive's Ruin? . . . . . .O 288 Irene        V 10
CAPTIVES
    Mann'd with the bravest of our fellow Captives,  . . .O 254 Irene          135
    Ye Christian Captives, follow me to Freedom:  . . . . O 321 Irene          51
CARAVANSERAL
    Build caravanseral  . . . . . . . . . . .            Y 130 Irene        V 12B
CARAZA
    Two faithful Captains, Hasan and Caraza, . . . . . .  O 310 Irene           5
    Caraza speak--have ye remark'd the Bassa?  . . . . .  O 311 Irene           1
CARCASE
    Till purse and carcase both were low.  . . . . . . .  Y 300 Extemp. Elegy  12
CARE
    Few know the toiling statesman's fear or care, . . . .O  32 Vanity Wishes  47
    What care, what rules your heedless charms shall save, . O  46 Vanity Wishes  329
    What care, youre charms from wretchedness shall save . .Y 107 Vanity Wishes V 329
    This bustling season's epidemic care;  . . . . . . .  O  59 Pro Good Nat'd  6
    The bustling season's epidemic care.  . . . . . . .   O  59 Pro Good Nat'd V  6
    If want of skill, or want of care appear,  . . . . .  O  62 Pro Word Wise  17
    The wine you kept with so much care,  . . . . . . .   O  69 Hor.II Ode 14  27
    Divide the burden of his care,  . . . . . . . . .     O  72 Hor. Epode II  50
    That post, and all the rest, shall be my care; . . . .O  74 Tr. Iliad Bk 6  3
    They call them Fairies; these now free from care . . .O  77 Tr Add. Battle  49
    Those sovereign charms with strictest care employ; . .O  81 Lady Birthday  13
    Now grants, and now rejects the Lover's Care  . . . . O  95 Sprig of Myrtl V  6
    Resign the heart to spleen and care,  . . . . . . .   O 123 Winter's Walk  10
    No social care the gracious lord disdains;  . . . . . O 130 Tr. Rambler 12  7
    No wealth his life from weary care can save,  . . . . O 146 Tr Boeth III.3  5
    No care his wealth can carry to the grave. . . . . . .O 146 Tr Boeth III.3  6
    "Void of care, and free from dread  . . . . . . .    O 185 Anacreon Ode 9  33
    To dens of guilt and shades of care  . . . . . . . .  O 191 Tr. Medea I    13
    Ev'ry name that laughs at Care,  . . . . . . . .     O 196 Song Congratu. 10
    All the Names that banish Care,  . . . . . . . .     O 196 Song Congratu. V 10
    His useful care was ever nigh,  . . . . . . . . .     O 201 Death Dr Levet 18
    From grov'ling Business and superfluous Care,  . . . .O 246 Irene Prologue  3
    O Providence! extend thy Care to me,  . . . . . . .   O 252 Irene          90
    Selected by my Care, a hardy Band,  . . . . . . .    O 254 Irene          136
    Thy Care shall guard this Treasure of my Soul; . . . .O 263 Irene           2
    Molest these private Walks, or Care invade  . . . . . O 272 Irene          14
    Trusts to my Care his Mistress and his Life,  . . . . O 283 Irene          10
    Nor taint with Care the Privacies of Love. . . . . . .O 288 Irene          14
    Those holy Beings, whose superiour Care  . . . . . .  O 289 Irene          17
    Beyond the Mists of Care thy Pinion tow'rs.  . . . . .O 313 Irene           8
    Here let me tend her with officious Care,  . . . . . .O 320 Irene          23
    There let the web and distaff be your care.  . . . . .Y  21 Tr. Iliad Bk 6 122
    Whene'er the lab'ring bird with anxious care  . . . . Y  23 Tr Add. Battle  44
    The birds elude the stroke with cautious care;  . . . Y  26 Tr Add. Battle 134
CAREFULL
    Observe your steps; be carefull to command . . . . . .O  77 Festina Lente   3
```

CARELESS

	PAGE	TITLE	LINE
Now, Tityrus, you, supine and careless laid, ...	O 64	Virgil Past.I	1
Had we not been perverse and careless grown, ...	O 64	Virgil Past.I	21
Me singing, careless and unarm'd, ...	O 65	Hor I Ode xxii	11
Me singing, careless and unarm'd, ...	O 66	To A. Fuscus	11
How sweet in sleep to pass the careless hours, ...	O 135	Tr Rambler 117	1
Swift, let us rush upon the careless Tyrant, ...	O 271	Irene	31
Of total Death and careless of Hereafter;	O 276	Irene	19
Secure of total death, and careless of hereafter or gay .	Y 146	Irene	V 20
Surveys your triflings with a careless glance	O 355	Irene	V 11
Surveys your actions with a careless glance	Y 146	Irene	V 22
Directs the Planets with a careless Nod, ...	O 293	Irene	123
Your careless Love betrays your Country's Cause. . . .	O 297	Irene	10

CARES

With age, with cares, with maladies oppress'd, ...	O 35	Vanity Wishes	117
No setting Sol can ease your cares, ...	O 67	Hor. II Ode IX	11
All pains, all cares, may favouring heav'n remove, . .	O 81	Lady Birthday	5
With honour sated, and with cares opprest;	O 118	Epitaph Hanmer	36
The Warrior's Labours, and the Monarch's Cares. . . .	O 261	Irene	10
Desires more pure, and other Cares than Love.	O 263	Irene	8
Soars unencumber'd with our idle Cares, ...	O 266	Irene	36
To mix with nobler Cares, I'll throw aside	O 275	Irene	70
To mix with nobler Cares, I'll set apart	O 368	Irene	V 27
Important Cares detain'd me from your Counsels. . . .	O 279	Irene	6
While vulgar Souls compassionate their Cares, ...	O 293	Irene	115
Calm of my Cares, and Guardian of my Virtue.	O 298	Irene	12
Whence rise these restless cares? these strong emotions?	Y 189	Irene	V 1
When did Content sigh out her Cares in secret?	O 314	Irene	20
No feasts could e'er my cares dispell;	Y 11	Tr Hor Epode 9	13

CARESS

Mark whom the great caress, who frown on me!	O 14	London	92

CARESS'D

For arts like these preferr'd, admir'd, caress'd, . . .	O 17	London	152

CARESSES

From false caresses, causeless strife, ...	O 125	An Ode	25
With coy Caresses and with pleasing Wiles	O 260	Irene	128

CARNAGE

And weary Murther slumbers o'er the Carnage	O 350	Irene	V 9

CAROUSES

When the bonny Blade carouses, ...	O 196	Song Congratu.	21
Whilst the bonny Blade carouses, ...	O 196	Song Congratu.	V 21

CARPATHIAN

No fish from the Carpathian coast	O 73	Hor. Epode II	57

CARPENTER

To Miss <Carpenter> On her giving the Author	O 119	To Miss Purse	T
To Miss <Carpenter> On her playing	O 120	To Miss Playing	T

CARRY

No care his wealth can carry to the grave.	O 146	Tr Boeth III.3	6

CARS

On flying Cars new Sorcerers may ride.	O 53	Pro Drury-Lane	44
Withdraw their cars and seek the blesst abodes. . . .	Y 6	Virgil Daphnis	21

CASE

And in this earthly Case confin'd;	O 147	Tr Boeth III.6	10

CASSANDER

I am Cassander, come down from the Sky, ...	O 173	Tr Fr Pantomim	1
That I am Cassander come down from the Sky.	O 173	Tr Fr Pantomim	3

CAST

"This is Minerva, cast in Virtue's mould."	O 190	Seeing Montagu	6
Cast off all idle terrours of hereafter	Y 146	Irene	V 19
Reason commands to cast the less away;	O 290	Irene	33

CASUAL

No regal Pageant deck'd with casual Honours, ...	O 268	Irene	19
Glory, the casual Gift of thoughtless Crouds!	O 305	Irene	31

CAT

Hadst thou nine lives like a cat, ...	O 194	On Thrale Hat	3

CAT-CALLS

Shou'd partial Cat-calls all his Hopes confound, . . .	O 246	Irene Prologue	23

CATCALL'S

And heard th' ill omen'd catcall's direful cry. . . .	Y 67	Prologue Lethe	10

CATCH

To weave those nets that catch the heart.	O 120	To Miss Purse	6
Thy nets may catch, but not confine, ...	O 120	To Miss Purse	8
Delights to catch the gales of life.	O 124	An Ode	4
Sooner the Breeze shall catch the flying Sounds, . . .	O 255	Irene	28
Those Hounds of Blood, that catch the Hint to kill, . .	O 333	Irene	52

CATCHES

Ambitious catches at his tow'ring Name:	O 57	Prologue Comus	20

CATES

When cates luxuriant pile the spacious dish, ...	O 193	Tr. Medea II	17

CATH'RINE

Red her cheek as Cath'rine pear, ...	Y 300	Extemp. Elegy	6

CATO'S

Gaurus pretends to Cato's fame;	O 138	Tr Rambler 164	1
And proves, by Cato's vice, his claim.	O 138	Tr Rambler 164	2

CATTLE

How pleas'd he sees his Cattle come, ...	O 73	Hor. Epode II	67
Joyfull he sees his Cattle come, ...	O 73	Hor. Epode II	V 67
The sympathising cattle hung their heads	Y 6	Virgil Daphnis	9
The harmless wolves no more our cattle fear, ...	Y 7	Virgil Daphnis	38

CAUCUSUS

O'er icy Caucusus he treads, ...	O 66	To A. Fuscus	5

```
                                                           PAGE    TITLE          LINE
CAUGHT
    Caught from the strong contagion of the gown;  . . . .   O  36 Vanity Wishes   V 138
    The heart, once caught, should ne'er be freed? . . . .   O 120 To Miss Purse     12
    Who caught the chief, ev'n in his soldiers' view  . . .  Y  25 Tr Add. Battle   125
CAUS'D
    To share the Miseries herself has caus'd.  . . . . .     O 320 Irene             15
CAUSE
    In virtue's cause once more exert his rage, . . . . . .  O  23 London           262
    In virtue's cause once more forsake his rage,  . . . .   O  23 London         V 262
    And senates heard before they judg'd a cause;  . . . .   O  33 Vanity Wishes     60
    Their Cause was gen'ral, their Supports were strong, . . O  52 Pro Drury-Lane    25
    Conducts his Armies and asserts their Cause. . . . . .   O 251 Irene             51
    But can thy Friend sustain the glorious Cause, . . . .   O 255 Irene              8
    The Cause of Liberty, the Cause of Nations? . . . . .    O 255 Irene              9
    The Cause of Liberty, the Cause of Nations? . . . . .    O 255 Irene              9
    Bribe to his Cause and list beneath his Banners  . . .   O 274 Irene             53
    The Cause that shrinks from Reason's powerful Voice. . . O 293 Irene            126
    Your careless Love betrays your Country's Cause. . . .   O 297 Irene             10
    Nor think thy Cause neglected while I gaze, . . . . .    O 297 Irene             20
    Approving Justice smiles upon your Cause, . . . . . .    O 297 Irene              2
    Did not the Cause of Greece restrain my Sword, . . . .   O 299 Irene             41
    Nor mingled Guilt pollute the sacred Cause!  . . . . .   O 300 Irene             64
    Tell me the Cause, that while thy Name, Demetrius, . .   O 305 Irene             25
    Ask to whose Sword the Greeks will trust their Cause, .  O 305 Irene             39
    Not call'd to try the Cause, we hear the Sentence, . .   O 326 Irene             34
    Our Bleeding Bosoms plead Irene's Cause. . . . . . . .   O 328 Irene             39
    Perhaps I will not stoop to plead my Cause; . . . . .    O 330 Irene             22
    Perhaps I will not bend to plead my cause  . . . . . .   Y 210 Irene           V 22
    While she yet beg'd to plead her Cause before thee. . .  O 334 Irene             67
CAUSELESS
    Whose joys are causeless, or whose griefs are vain. . .  O  33 Vanity Wishes     68
    In groundless hope, and causeless fear, . . . . . . .    O 124 Winter's Walk     13
    From false caresses, causeless strife,  . . . . . . .    O 125 An Ode            25
CAUSES
    To thee I told the causes of my smart,  . . . . . . .    Y  11 Tr Hor Epode 9    18
CAUTION
    From Bard, to Bard, the frigid Caution crept, . . . .    O  52 Pro Drury-Lane    31
    Think--but excuse a Woman's needless Caution, . . . .    O 298 Irene              5
    What need of Caution to report the Fate . . . . . .      O 329 Irene             16
CAUTION'D
    By Solon caution'd to regard his end, . . . . . . .      O  45 Vanity Wishes    314
CAUTIOUS
    But cautious Fabius from impending fate . . . . . . .    O  78 Festina Lente     17
    But cautious Age suspects the flatt'ring Form, . . . .   O 255 Irene             18
    With cautious Secrecy, Leontius steer . . . . . . . .    O 284 Irene             50
    With cautious Vigilance, at my Command, . . . . . .      O 310 Irene              4
    The birds elude the stroke with cautious care; . . . .  Y  26 Tr Add. Battle   134
CAVERNS
    In misery's darkest caverns known, . . . . . . . . .     O 201 Death Dr Levet    17
    The groaning Greeks break up their golden Caverns . . .  O 249 Irene             17
    Like subterraneous tempests with dire eruption burst their
        caverns                                              Y 115 Irene           V 49
    And (terror) horrour shudders in their gloomy caverns .  Y 136 Irene           V 31A
    And wish their gloomy Caverns more obscure. . . . . .    O 268 Irene             32
    Fierce through the bursting Caverns rend their Way? . .  O 281 Irene             53
CAYSTER'S
    And warm Cayster's flowing banks forsake  . . . . . .    Y  24 Tr Add. Battle    67
CEAS'D
    Till conquest unresisted ceas'd to please, . . . . .     O  34 Vanity Wishes    107
    She ceas'd; then godlike Hector answer'd kind,-- . . .   O  74 Tr. Iliad Bk 6     1
    Suspended faction ceas'd from rage and strife, . . .     O 118 Epitaph Hanmer    17
CEASE
    Enquirer cease alarm, no wishes rise, . . . . . . . .    Y 108 Vanity Wishes   V 347
    Enquirer, cease, petitions yet remain, . . . . . . .     O  47 Vanity Wishes    349
    Restrain your tears and cease your cries, . . . . . .    O  70 Hor.II Ode XX     21
    Oh, must their ardours cease to glow  . . . . . . . .    O 100 Ode Friendship    25
    Oh may this Flame neer cease to glow . . . . . . . .     O 100 Ode Friendship  V 25
    Nor shall thine ardours cease to glow  . . . . . . .     O 100 Ode Friendship  V 25
    O! Shall thy flames then cease to glow . . . . . . .     O 100 Ode Friendship  V 25
    Cease, lovely thief! my tender limbs to wound, . . . .   O 106 Eliza plucking     5
    Cease, cease thy Censures, for the Sultan comes . . .    O 262 Irene             28
    Cease, cease thy Censures, for the Sultan comes . . .    O 262 Irene             28
    Then, Cali, shall the Toils of Battle cease, . . . .     O 265 Irene             44
    Ah! cease, Irene, cease those flowing Sorrows, . . . .   O 276 Irene              3
    Ah! cease, Irene, cease those flowing Sorrows, . . . .   O 276 Irene              3
    Remember Mahomet, and cease thy Labour. . . . . . .      O 310 Irene              3
    Cease this wild Roar of savage Exultation; . . . . .     O 318 Irene              6
CEASES
    When the confusion of new conquests ceases  . . . . .    Y 164 Irene           V 76
CEDAR
    With cedar vaulted and inlayd with gold . . . . . .      Y 177 Irene           V111F
CELEBRATE
    Nations shall celebrate my Name . . . . . . . . .        O  70 Hor.II Ode XX     19
    Haste Go Mustapha go to celebrate the day  . . . . .     Y 129 Irene           V 25
CELEBRATED
    An Epitaph upon the celebrated Claudy Philips, . . . .   O 113 Epit. Phillips   V  T
CELESTIAl
    With these celestial wisdom calms the mind, . . . . .    O  48 Vanity Wishes    367
    Celestial pow'rs! that piety regard, . . . . . . . .     O 141 Tr Rambler 208     1
        Celestial Goodness! . . . . . . . . .                O 258 Irene            102
    Celestial fair--maid--new wonders fix me thine, . . .    Y 149 Irene           V 59
```

CELESTIAL   (CONTINUED)   PAGE   TITLE   LINE
        En<v>ies the meanest minister of Heav'n of celestial . .   Y 168 Irene   V135A
        beings.
CELL
        Some secret cell, ye pow'rs, indulgent give. . . . . .   O 11 London   49
        Should tempting Novelty thy cell refrain, ...   O 37 Vanity Wishes 149
        While tutelary Nations guard her Cell. . . . . . .   O 58 Prologue Comus 36
        Hermit hoar, in solemn cell, ...   O 181 Parody Warton   1
        Ah! let me rather seek the Convent's Cell; . . . . .   O 292 Irene   93
        Chearful I follow to the rural Cell, ...   O 302 Irene   110
CELLS
        Nor call'd them to the gloomy cells . . . . . .   O 191 Tr. Medea I   9
CEMENT
        With mouldring cement and with beams disjointed . . .   Y 114 Irene   V 45
CENSURE
        By numbers here from shame or censure free, ...   O 17 London   158
        For those who durst not censure, scarce cou'd praise. . . O 51 Pro Drury-Lane 14
        Ah! let not Censure term our Fate our Choice, ...   O 53 Pro Drury-Lane 51
        Teach mimick censure her own faults to find, ...   O 81 Lady Birthday   17
CENSURES
        Cease, cease thy Censures, for the Sultan comes . . .   O 262 Irene   28
CENTER
        Now haste to mingle in one common Center, ...   O 287 Irene   4
CENTRAL
        And columns leaning from their central firmness . . .   Y 114 Irene   V 45A
CENTURIES
        Yields to Renown the Centuries to come. . . . . . .   O 57 Prologue Comus 18
CERTAIN
        Great Xerxes comes to seize the certain prey, ...   O 42 Vanity Wishes 227
        An envious Breast with certain Mischief glows, ...   O 46 Vanity Wishes V330A
        An rivals breast with certain mischief glows . . . .   Y 107 Vanity Wishes V330A
CESAREAN
        Tries the dread summits of Cesarean pow'r, ...   O 42 Vanity Wishes 242
CHAIN
        If the gull'd conqueror receives the chain, ...   O 16 London   121
        We bless the Tyrant, and we hug the Chain. . . . . .   O 96 Hickman Spinet   8
        Nor can I hope thy silken chain . . . .   O 120 To Miss Purse   9
        Death broke at once the vital chain, ...   O 202 Death Dr Levet 35
        Unbroken as the sacred Chain of Nature, ...   O 257 Irene   63
CHAIN'D
        Do the chain'd waters always freeze; . . . .   O 67 Hor. II Ode IX   6
CHAINS
        New chains to hold the captive heart. . . . .   O 121 To Miss Playin 18
        The chains of hell that hold his friend. . . . . . .   O 232 Tr Horace IV.7 28
        Hold in her Chains the captivated Sultan? . . . . .   O 261 Irene   2
        Go, seize him, load him with reproachful Chains; . . .   O 273 Irene   34
        That all her Faculties receive his Chains? . . . . .   O 281 Irene   39
        Still languish in our Chains, and dream of Freedom, . .   O 282 Irene   4
CHAIR
        When Hanmer fill'd the chair, and Ann the throne. . . .   O 118 Epitaph Hanmer 22
CHAIROYSA
        Eiden Aletheie proen chairoysa graphonta . . . . . .   O 108 Eis Birchion   1
CHAMBER
        "Round his chamber dance and play, ...   O 186 Anacreon Ode 9 36
        Expiring Cali nam'd Irene's Chamber, ...   O 326 Irene   29
        Irene's Chamber! From my faithful Bosom . . . . . .   O 326 Irene   31
        Irene's chamber frcm Irene's guiltless bosom . . . .   Y 205 Irene   V 31
        Irene's Chamber! Did not roaring Cali, ...   O 330 Irene   12
        Name for the Scene of Death Irene's Chamber? . . . .   O 330 Irene   14
        Said not the Villain in Irene's Chamber . . . . . .   O 375 Irene   V 13
        Decr'eed to perish in Irene's Chamber! . . . . . .   O 331 Irene   17
CHANCE
        But did not Chance at length her error mend? . . . .   O 41 Vanity Wishes 215
        Perhaps, for who can guess th' Effects of Chance? . . .   O 53 Pro Drury-Lane 45
        Insulting chance ne'er call'd with louder voice, . . .   O 135 Tr Rambler 106   1
        Commits to trivial Chance the Fate of Nations! . . . .   O 269 Irene   2
        Commits to trivial chance the Work of Fate! . . . . .   O 374 Irene   V 11
        Nor will I trust th' uncertain Chance of Combat; . . .   O 307 Irene   21
        Behold I quit her to the Chance of Battle. . . . . .   O 319 Irene   29
CHANCES
        Such strange Events, such unexpected Chances, ...   O 296 Irene   34
CHANG'D
        Place may be chang'd; but who can change his mind? . .   O 137 Tr Rambler 135   1
        --How chang'd alas!--Now ghastly Desolation . . . .   O 251 Irene   66
        And chang'd th' endearing Smile and am'rous Whisper . .   O 259 Irene   111
        How am I chang'd! How lately did Irene . . . . . .   O 322 Irene   13
CHANGE
        Or change the rocks of Scotland for the Strand? . . .   O   9 London   10
        And feed with change of new born fools th' eternal . .   Y 94 Vanity Wishes V 52
        jest:
        Where change of fav'rites made no change of laws, . . .   O 33 Vanity Wishes   59
        Where change of fav'rites made no change of laws, . . .   O 33 Vanity Wishes   59
        Each Change of many-colour'd Life he drew, ...   O 51 Pro Drury-Lane   3
        See! how the mighty Change is wrought; . . . . . .   O 70 Hor.II Ode XX   9
        Kings change their Laws, and Kingdoms change their . .   O 110 To Posterity   16
        Kings.
        Kings change their Laws, and Kingdoms change their . .   O 110 To Posterity   16
        Kings.
        Place may be chang'd; but who can change his mind? . .   O 137 Tr Rambler 135   1
        Think on the sudden Change of human Scenes; . . . . .   O 252 Irene   86
        The sparkling ornaments, the glittring dress (the change   Y 164 Irene   V 71

		PAGE	TITLE	LINE

CHANGE   (CONTINUED)
    of dress
      Each piercing Torture, every Change of Pain, ... O 326 Irene 44
      Thus I t' effect this mighty change design'd . . . . Y 11 Tr Hor Epode 9 29
CHANGEFUL
      Still changing with the changeful year, ... O 124 Winter's Walk 15
CHANGES
      But who the coming Changes can presage, ... O 52 Pro Drury-Lane 39
CHANGING
      Still changing with the changeful year, ... O 124 Winter's Walk 15
      The changing year renews the plain, ... O 231 Tr Horace IV.7 3
      The changing year's successive plan . . . . O 231 Tr Horace IV.7 7
CHANNELS
      When a river is drain'd by too many channels the stream is Y 132 Irene V 41B
    dry.
CHARACTERS
      And know'st the Characters of Vice and Virtue, ... O 255 Irene 12
CHARADE
      Charade! . . . . O 179 Charade! T
CHARG'D
      Be charg'd upon my Soul. O, Mercy! Mercy! . . . . . O 329 Irene 55
CHARGE
      Yours is the Charge, ye Fair, ye Wise, ye Brave! . . . O 58 Prologue Comus 37
      I grant the charge; forgive the fault confess'd. . . . O 139 Tr Rambler 170 1
      "Weighty charge consign'd to me: . . . . O 185 Anacreon Ode 9 16
      A Galley mann'd with Greeks, thy charge, Leontius, . . O 258 Irene 81
      And your new Charge, that dear, that heavn'ly Maid.-- . O 270 Irene 5
      Resign their Charge to Baseness and to Ruin. . . . . O 289 Irene 20
      And quit their Charge to Horror and to Ruin. . . . . O 346 Irene V 8
      Superiour Man possess'd the Charge of Rule, ... O 291 Irene 71
      The weighty Charge of Royalty confer; . . . . . . O 292 Irene 104
      Return with speed, Leontius, to your Charge; . . . . O 304 Irene 9
      Perhaps her Malice might transfer the Charge, ... O 327 Irene 18
      Quick at my Call shall execute your Charge; . . . . . O 328 Irene 43
CHARGES
      Who charges Guilt on me? . . . . O 323 Irene 6
      Who charges Guilt, ... O 323 Irene 6
      Who charges Guilt! lay by this proud Resentment . . . O 323 Irene 8
CHARIOT
      See! Sol's bright chariot seeks the western main, . . Y 4 On a Daffodill 22
CHARIOTS
      And seat him in the Pleiad's golden Chariots, ... O 274 Irene 63
CHARIS
      Oisi memele phusis, metron charis, erga palaion, . . . O 171 Epi. Goldsmith 3
CHARLES
      How just his hopes let Swedish Charles decide; . . . . O 40 Vanity Wishes 192
      The Wits of Charles found easier Ways to Fame, ... O 52 Pro Drury-Lane 17
CHARM
      Each gift of nature, and each charm of art, ... Y 92 Vanity Wishes V 16
      Such pow'r has praise, that virtue scarce can charm, . Y 100 Vanity Wishes V 183
      Till fame supplies the universal charm. . . . . . O 39 Vanity Wishes 184
      The great, 'tis true, can charm th' electing tribe; . . O 60 Pro Good Nat'd 25
      Each charm of modulated sound, ... O 121 To Miss Playin 6
      Dress'd in each Charm of gay Magnificence, ... O 261 Irene 14
      Born to command, as thou to charm Mankind, ... O 268 Irene 23
      These Days of Love and Pleasure charm not thee; . . . O 271 Irene 2
      Will it not charm a Mind like thine exalted, ... O 278 Irene 67
      If Pleasure charm thee, view this soft Retreat; . . . O 279 Irene 85
      And unaccustom'd warblings charm the grove (pleasing . Y 150 Irene V 86
        disson<ance>
      This lucky Stratagem shall charm the Sultan, ... O 319 Irene 5
      This night he hopes to shew that farce may charm, . . Y 67 Prologue Lethe 13
CHARM'D
      For while by Chloe's image charm'd, ... O 65 Hor I Ode xxii 9
      For while in Sabine Forests, charm'd . . . . . . O 66 To A. Fuscus 9
      Charm'd with the scene the smiling ocean yields, . . . O 81 Young Author 3
      Charm'd ev'ry ear, and gain'd on ev'ry heart. . . . . O 117 Epitaph Hanmer 8
      Where first great nature charm'd my sight, ... O 125 An Ode 19
      Charm'd with the Thought of blessing human Kind, . . . O 278 Irene 73
CHARMS
      Peace courts his hand, but spreads her charms in vain; . O 40 Vanity Wishes 201
      Short sway! fair Austria spreads her mournful charms, . O 42 Vanity Wishes 245
      Short sway! for Austria spreads her mournful charms, . Y 103 Vanity Wishes V 245
      What care, what rules your heedless charms shall save, . O 46 Vanity Wishes 329
      What care, youre charms from wretchedness shall save . Y 107 Vanity Wishes V 329
      To chase the Charms of Sound, the Pomp of Show, . . . O 53 Pro Drury-Lane 59
      Thus grac'd with humble Virtue's native Charms . . . . O 58 Prologue Comus 33
      I'll sing of Chloe's charms divine, ... O 66 Hor I Ode xxii 23
      Those sovereign charms with strictest care employ; . . O 81 Lady Birthday 13
      So shall Belinda's charms improve mankind. . . . . . O 81 Lady Birthday 19
      Nor torturing whalebones pinch them into charms; . . . O 84 Epi Dist Moth. 23
      Unfaded still their former charms they shew, ... O 84 Epi Dist Moth. 26
      Resign'd his Thirst of Empire to her Charms, ... O 97 Hickman Spinet 19
      Thy pleasures, charms as great, ... Y 71 Ode Friendship V 23
      Thy charms at least, fair F<irebrac>e, might inspire . O 107 Lady F Assizes 3
      Though gold and silk their charms unite, ... O 119 To Miss Purse 1
      When charms thus press on ev'ry sense, ... O 121 To Miss Playin 11
      By secret charms our native land attracts. . . . . . O 135 Tr Rambler 122 1
      Its charms are fled and all its powers destroyed. . . O 142 In Baretti Bk. 8
      All her Charms to thee belong; . . . . O 150 Tr Boet III.12 42
      Amidst the drousy charms of dull delight, ... O 152 The Ant 13

CHARMS (CONTINUED)

	PAGE	TITLE		LINE
"Grac'd with all that charms the heart,	O 185	Anacreon Ode 9		9
A Virgin shining with distinguish'd Charms,	O 258	Irene		95
Her mournful Charms attracted his Regards,	O 259	Irene		121
I walk'd superior, through the Blaze of Charms,	O 263	Irene		17
heav'nly charms without emotion	Y 129	Irene	V	6
At Sight of female Charms will glow no more.	O 263	Irene		6
Well may those Eyes that view these heav'nly Charms,	O 267	Irene		6
Whence then those Charms thy Tongue has deign'd to flatter,	O 277	Irene		26
Why then Those charms your tongue has deign'd to flatter	O 355	Irene	V	15
And smiling, conscious of her Charms, withdrew.	O 282	Irene		69
And various charms displays to various eyes	Y 155	Irene	V	27
The various charms displays to various eyes	O 374	Irene	V	28
The present hour invites with genuine charms	O 375	Irene	V	7
Once to behold the Charms of bright Aspasia,	O 285	Irene		6
Applaud her Charms, and court her to be Great.	O 287	Irene		18
Fix'd and intent on his Irene's Charms,	O 296	Irene		3
Lest unrewarded Mercy lose its Charms.	O 313	Irene		19
Shall plume her Charms, and, with attentive Watch,	O 318	Irene		4
What sleepy Charms benumb these active Heroes,	O 325	Irene		14
Could not her Charms repress your Zeal for Murder?	O 332	Irene		24
Nor trust our Passions with her fatal Charms.	O 332	Irene		31
And view thy charms with no malignant eyes:	Y 3	On a Daffodill		14
Since from Inachia's charms set free	Y 11	Tr Hor Epode 9		9
And quit Inachia's venal charms	Y 11	Tr Hor Epode 9		26
And quite Inachia's venal charms	Y 11	Tr Hor Epode 9	V	26
Returns his child; she views his infant charms,	Y 20	Tr. Iliad Bk 6		108

CHASE

And chase the new-blown Bubbles of the Day.	O 53	Pro Drury-Lane		50
To chase the Charms of Sound, the Pomp of Show,	O 53	Pro Drury-Lane		59
And chase discountenanc'd virtue from the throne:	O 176	Tr Metastas II	V	9
With Converse chase the melancholy Moments.	O 263	Irene		4
Disease shall chase the Phantoms of Ambition,	O 322	Irene		60

CHASES

Shuns fancied ills, or chases airy good;	O 31	Vanity Wishes		10
Year chases year, decay pursues decay,	O 45	Vanity Wishes		305
Year chases year, with unremitted flight,	O 152	The Ant		14

CHASING

If chasing past Events with vain Pursuit,	O 255	Irene		5

CHAST

A frugal, chast, industrious, Wife,	O 72	Hor. Epode II		48

CHATTER'D

"I have chatter'd like a pye."	O 186	Anacreon Ode 9		44

CHEAP

Wants ev'n the cheap reward of empty praise;	O 10	London		36
And, while thy grounds a cheap repast afford,	O 20	London		218
And, while thy beds a cheap repast afford,	O 20	London	V	218
And scorns the lazy Hermit's cheap Devotion;	O 264	Irene		28

CHEAPLY

And Virtue cheaply sav'd with loss of Life.	O 290	Irene		35
Is then your Sov'reign's Life so cheaply rated,	O 327	Irene		14
Such Beauty, Sweetness, Love, were cheaply bought,	O 332	Irene		35

CHEAR

And chear the clouded mind with light divine.	O 130	Tr. Rambler 7		4
And chear the weary Passenger with Musick.	O 277	Irene		38
And chear the weary passenger with warblings	O 355	Irene	V	21
Shall I not wish to chear afflicted Kings,	O 291	Irene		67

CHEAR'D

Chear'd the rough road, we wish'd the rough road long,	Y 310	Parody of Pope		2

CHEARFUL

With chearful wisdom and instructive mirth,	O 32	Vanity Wishes		50
The chearful sage, when solemn dictates fail,	O 132	Tr. Rambler 65		1
And sigh for chearful Poverty in vain;	O 292	Irene		84
Chearful I follow to the rural Cell,	O 302	Irene		110
And tell the horrid Tale with chearful Face;	O 329	Irene		11

CHEARFULL

His chearfull Slaves, a num'rous band,	O 73	Hor. Epode II		71
That day, that mournfull day, no chearfull song	Y 6	Virgil Daphnis		7

CHEARLESS

And chearless treads the desolated stage,	Y 106	Vanity Wishes	V	308
Does chearless Diffidence oppress their Hearts?	O 270	Irene		22

CHEAT

Only teaches how to cheat.	O 176	Tr Metastasi I		6
But thou, too old to bear another Cheat,	O 283	Irene		32

CHEATED

The cheated nation's happy fav'rites, see!	O 14	London		91

CHEATS

In pleasing Dreams he cheats the Day	O 72	Hor. Epode II		35
Which Cheats interpret, and which Fools regard?	O 250	Irene		43

CHECK

What check restrain your thirst of pow'r and gold?	O 13	London		62
There shall he waste thy Frontiers, check thy Conquests,	O 274	Irene		56
To check this Torrent of imperious Rage,	O 327	Irene		5

CHECKS

Supicion checks the rising transport	Y 186	Irene	V	2

CHEEK

Flush in my cheek, and wander in my Veins	O 349	Irene	V	26
And add new Roses to the faded Cheek.	O 278	Irene		66
My Zeal marks Gladness dawning on thy Cheek,	O 286	Irene		2

		PAGE	TITLE		LINE
CHEEK	(CONTINUED)				
Why does the Blood forsake thy lovely Cheek?		O 295	Irene		5
In vain affected Raptures flush the Cheek, ...		O 315	Irene		29
At once a Thousand Passions fir'd his Cheek:		O 317	Irene		31
To see the Cloud forsake her kindling Cheek, ...		O 320	Irene		26
That fires thy Cheek, and elevates thy Mien, ...		O 323	Irene		9
Play'd on her Cheek--So shone the first Apostate-- . .		O 330	Irene		11
Red her cheek as Cath'rine pear, ...		Y 300	Extemp. Elegy		6
CHEEKS					
In whose fair cheeks destructive Cupids wait, . . .		O 83	Epi Dist Moth.		3
No conscious blushes there their cheeks inflame, . . .		O 84	Epi Dist Moth.		24
Flush in my cheeks, and sally in veins		Y 189	Irene	V	1E
I then (my cheeks still glow with shame) was grown .		Y 11	Tr Hor Epode 9		11
CHEER SEE CHEAR					
To cheer despair, or soften pride, ...		O 190	Tr. Medea I		8
CHEERFUL SEE CHEARFUL					
And view with cheerful eyes approaching death.		O 74	Tr. Iliad Bk 6		10
We round thy board the cheerful menials see, ...		O 130	Tr. Rambler 12		5
The busy day, the cheerful night, ...		O 202	Death Dr Levet	V	29
CHEERS					
Whose night congratulating Conscience cheers;		O 44	Vanity Wishes		296
CHER					
Tout est cher.		O 172	French Distich		4
CHERRY					
She was once as cherry plump		Y 300	Extemp. Elegy		5
CHIEF					
This is the chief felicity of life, ...		O 131	Tr. Rambler 45		1
The Chief, whose Wisdom guides the Turkish Counsels. . .		O 253	Irene		112
Then rouzing know the fiery Chief Abdalla, ...		O 254	Irene		125
Then rouzing know the firy Chief Abdallah, ...		O 254	Irene	V	125
That long to hail thee Chief.		O 254	Irene		137
That fiery Chief, renown'd for gen'rous Freedom, . . .		O 299	Irene		35
That firy Chief, renown'd for gen'rous Freedom, . . .		O 299	Irene	V	35
Ere guilty Fear depress'd the hoary Chief, ...		O 312	Irene		18
Declar'd the chief Associate of his Guilt.		O 331	Irene		11
Soon as the chief approach'd the Scaean Gate		Y 18	Tr. Iliad Bk 6		3
The parents smil'd, the chief his helm unbound		Y 20	Tr. Iliad Bk 6		95
The chief, this spoke, into the mother's arms		Y 20	Tr. Iliad Bk 6		107
Who caught the chief, ev'n in his soldiers' view . . .		Y 25	Tr Add. Battle		125
CHIEFS					
Chiefs confus'd in mutual slaughter, ...		O 159	Tr. Rio Verde		3
Have I for this defy'd the Chiefs of Turkey, ...		O 304	Irene		16
League with our Chiefs, and propagate Sedition? . .		O 312	Irene		3
I'll sing the chiefs dispensing fate around.		Y 22	Tr Add. Battle		19
CHILD					
A sister sickens, or a child offends.		Y 105	Vanity Wishes	V	302
The nurse took up the squealing child, ...		O 157	Par. Hermit I		3
But still the child squeal'd on.		O 157	Par. Hermit I		4
But yet the child squeal'd on.		O 157	Par. Hermit I	V	4
Gladness, fair child, of innocence and freedom. . . .		Y 165	Irene	V	81
The child starts back affrighted at the blaze . . .		Y 20	Tr. Iliad Bk 6		92
Returns his child; she views his infant charms, . . .		Y 20	Tr. Iliad Bk 6		108
CHILDREN					
As' children fret the lion in a cage.		O 60	Pro Good Nat'd	V	16
CHILDREN'S					
Must Greece, still wretched by her Children's Folly, . .		O 305	Irene		43
CHILL					
Grief swell thine Eyes, and Terror chill thy Breast. . .		O 110	To Posterity		4
Trumpet or lyre--to their harsh bosoms chill, ...		O 192	Tr. Medea II		11
No summons mock'd by chill delay, ...		O 201	Death Dr Levet		21
No summons shock'd by chill delay, ...		O 201	Death Dr Levet	V	21
or chill our blood but Fear		O 347	Irene	V	4
Chill my Resolves, and blast my blooming Virtue: . .		O 266	Irene		14
The chill inhabitant repines, ...		Y 38	Lady Leaving		3
CHILL'D					
Sure, chill'd with sixty winter Camps, thy Blood . . .		O 263	Irene		5
CHILLD					
Thou Thou chilld by sixty winter camps canst gaze . . on		Y 129	Irene	V	5
CHILLING					
These chilling doubts, and agonizing horrours?		Y 189	Irene	V	1A
CHILLS					
Now, Traytor, feel the Fear that chills my Hand. . . .		O 318	Irene		20
CHILNESS					
Why shoots this Chilness through thy shaking Nerves? . .		O 295	Irene		6
CHILS					
And Winter chils the World again.		O 232	Tr Horace IV.7		12
CHIMAERA					
And publick Spirit deemd a wild Chimaera		O 347	Irene	V	19
CHIMERAS					
And Folly, frighted at her own Chimeras, ...		O 266	Irene		32
CHINA					
Survey mankind, from China to Peru;		O 30	Vanity Wishes		2
O'erlook mankind, from China to Peru;		Y 91	Vanity Wishes	V	2
CHLOE'S					
For while by Chloe's image charm'd, ...		O 65	Hor I Ode xxii		9
I'll sing of Chloe's charms divine, ...		O 66	Hor I Ode xxii		23
CHOAK					
The banefull weeds spring up, and choak the grain. . .		Y 7	Virgil Daphnis		23
CHOICE					
Yet still my calmer thoughts his choice commend, . . .		O 8	London		3

CHOICE   (CONTINUED)   PAGE   TITLE   LINE
    How rarely reason guides the stubborn choice, ...   O 31 Vanity Wishes   11
    How rarely reason guides the hasty choice, ...   Y 92 Vanity Wishes   V 11
    But leave to heav'n the measure and the choice, ...   O 47 Vanity Wishes   352
    Ah! let not Censure term our Fate our Choice, ...   O 53 Pro Drury-Lane   51
    Resistless merit fix'd the Senate's choice, ...   O 118 Epitaph Hanmer   19
    His Choice our sacred Seats disgrac'd, ...   O 146 Tr Boeth III.4   5
    Prescribes her duties, or directs her choice, ...   O 151 The Ant   4
    And Nature justifies our Monarch's Choice.   . . . . . .   O 288 Irene   3
    Yet should my Soul, still faithful to her Choice,   . .   O 289 Irene   13
    Why has thy Choice then pointed out Leontius, ...   O 305 Irene   20
    Now make thy Choice, while yet the Pow'r of Choice   . .   O 321 Irene   40
    Now make thy Choice, while yet the Pow'r of Choice   . .   O 321 Irene   40
CHOIRS
    Angelick choirs have sung.   . . . .   O 80 Feast St Simon   60
CHOSEN
    The Queen requested that a chosen Troop . . . .   O 331 Irene   7
    A chosen Troop--to intercept--Demetrius--   . . . . .   O 331 Irene   12
CHRIST
    When Christ had conquer'd Hell and fate . . . .   O 79 Feast St Simon   19
CHRISTIAN
    Moor and Christian, roll along. . . . .   O 159 Tr. Rio Verde   4
    Now summon all thy Soul, illustrious Christian! . . .   O 254 Irene   1
    With Christian blood, let Leontares dye.   . . . . .   Y 129 Irene   V 26
    Shall break the Fetters of the groaning Christian;   .   O 278 Irene   76
    Ye Christian Captives, follow me to Freedom: . . .   O 321 Irene   51
CHRISTIAN'S
    The Christian's tenderness? or womans weakness   . . .   Y 189 Irene   V 1C
CHURCH
    To him the church, the realm, their pow'rs consign, . .   O 34 Vanity Wishes   101
    To him the church, the state, their pow're resign,   . .   Y 96 Vanity Wishes   V 101
    To whom the church each rolling year   . . . .   O 78 Feast St Simon   11
CHUSE
    Was but to chuse the Graces of the Day; . . . .   O 278 Irene   63
    And Duty bids me chuse a distant Walk, ...   O 288 Irene   13
CIBBER
    Great George's acts let tuneful Cibber sing;   . . .   O 114 On C. Cibber   3
CILICIA
    Whose sire Eetion in Cilicia reign'd   . . . .   Y 18 Tr. Iliad Bk 6   7
CIRCLE
    The Bowl shall circle to confirm our League,   . . .   O 308 Irene   29
CIRCLES
    In everlasting Circles run, ...   O 68 Hor.II Ode 14   2
CIRCLING
    When nought but mine the circling Sun shall . . . . .   O 357 Irene   V 29
        see
CIRCULATING
    Or trace his Form on circulating Gold, ...   O 58 Prologue Comus   24
    A happy Land, where circulating Pow'r   . . . .   O 256 Irene   57
CIRCUMSPECTIVE
    Frame your Report with circumspective Art, ...   O 329 Irene   13
CITADELS
    Which Armies guard, and Citadels inclose?   . . . . .   O 258 Irene   91
CITIES
    And Cities smoaking on the ground   . . . .   O 78 Feast St Simon   2
    To see new Cities tow'r at thy Command, ...   O 278 Irene   71
    Let Pleasure bloom and Cities reascend. . . . . ·. . .   O 372 Irene   V 10
    Bid Pleasure bloom and Cities reascend. . . . .   O 372 Irene   V 10
    Again should golden Splendour grace her Cities, . . .   O 290 Irene   53
CITY
    Thy' wealth O city ill-gotten ill-preserv'd . . . . .   Y 113 Irene   V 20
        shall
    Quitting my close Retreat, I range the City, ...   O 251 Irene   60
    The holy city with converted millions--or nations. . .   Y 131 Irene   V 32C
    Not then with raving Cries I fill'd the City,   . . .   O 290 Irene   46
    (Yet) not with idle cries I fill'd the city . . . . .   Y 163 Irene   V 46
    Back through the city trod his former way.   . . . . .   Y 17 Tr. Iliad Bk 6   2
CITYS
    By thee wholl citys burn, wholl nations fall!   . . .   O 77 Festina Lente   12
CIVIL
    When unsuccessful Wars, and civil Factions, ...   O 256 Irene   41
CIVILITY
    To spread Civility through Russian snows . . . . . .   O 348 Irene   V 21
    To spread Civility through Russia's Forests . . . . .   O 348 Irene   V 21
CIVILIZE
    Call me to civilize the Russian Wilds, ...   O 292 Irene   105
CLADES
    <H>oc fonte derivat<a> clades--In patriam populumque . .   O 347 Irene   V 22
        fluxit.
CLAIM
    Claim leads to claim, and pow'r advances pow'r; . . .   O 34 Vanity Wishes   106
    Claim leads to claim, and pow'r advances pow'r; . . .   O 34 Vanity Wishes   106
    Nor claim the triumph of a letter'd heart;   . . . . .   O 37 Vanity Wishes   152
    Let one great payment every claim appease, ...   O 62 Pro Word Wise   11
    Nought from my birth or ancestors I claim;   . . . . .   O 132 Tr. Rambler 46   1
    More safely truth to urge her claim presumes,   . . .   O 134 Tr. Rambler 93   1
    And proves, by Cato's vice, his claim.   . . . .   O 138 Tr Rambler 164   2
    Claim my divided Soul. This Wretch unworthy . . . . .   O 275 Irene   69
    Claim but the second Place: there mighty Love   . . .   O 280 Irene   26
    What Claim hast thou to plead?   . . . .   O 286 Irene   8
        The Claim of Pow'r, ...   O 286 Irene   8

CLAIM	(CONTINUED)	PAGE	TITLE		LINE
	Th' unquestion'd Claim of Conquerors, and Kings!	O 286	Irene		9
	The Lover's Int'rest aids the Patriot's Claim.	O 305	Irene		46
	if human miseries or affairs yet claim your regard	Y 181	Irene	V	54
	Leave but this Maid, resign a hopeless Claim,	O 319	Irene		25
	Quit but this maid, resign a hopeless claim	Y 197	Irene	V	25
	Your hasty Zeal defrauds the Claim of Justice,	O 330	Irene		5
CLAIM'D					
	New pow'rs are claim'd, new pow'rs are still bestow'd,	O 42	Vanity Wishes		233
CLAIMS					
	Now lacerated Friendship claims a tear.	O 45	Vanity Wishes		304
	Yet softer Claims the melting Heart engage,	O 58	Prologue Comus		29
	His groaning Country claims Leontius' Aid;	O 270	Irene		17
	The petty Claims of Empire and of Honour;	O 307	Irene		23
CLAM'ROUS					
	When, summon'd by the Sultan's clam'rous Fury,	O 325	Irene		22
CLAMOUR					
	From ev'ry Palace burst a mingled Clamour,	O 251	Irene		70
CLANDESTINE					
	And vent our Suff'rings in clandestine Groans?	O 249	Irene		4
CLANG					
	Tho' confiscation's vulturs clang around.	O 32	Vanity Wishes	V	36
CLAP					
	They sing, they dance, clean shoes, or cure a clap;	O 15	London		114
	They clap their wings, and with new fury burn;	O 76	Tr Add. Battle		9
	The joyfull Cranes triumphant clap their wings:	Y 26	Tr Add. Battle		127
CLASH					
	Of slaughter'd Infidels, and Clash of Swords!	O 305	Irene		24
CLASP					
	What hazards would I shun to clasp for Greece and for Aspasia	Y 125	Irene	V	133
	Still restless, till I clasp the lovely Maid,	O 263	Irene		21
	To clasp a Slave? or, can a Soul like mine,	O 268	Irene		16
	I'll open my breast--clasp thee--forget greatness--	Y 161	Irene	V	13
	I stand amaz'd, and ask, if yet I clasp thee.	O 296	Irene		37
CLASP'D					
	Clasp'd in her Arms, or slumb'ring on her Breast,	O 331	Irene		19
CLAUDE					
	Epitaph on Claude Phillips, an Itinerant Musician	O 113	Epit. Phillips	V	T
CLAUDIUS					
	On Claudius Phillips, an excellent Musician	O 113	Epit. Phillips	V	T
CLAUDY					
	An Epitaph on Claudy Phillips, a Musician	O 113	Epit. Phillips		T
	An Epitaph upon the celebrated Claudy Philips,	O 113	Epit. Phillips	V	T
CLAWS					
	The Cranes with beaks and claws provoke the fight.	O 75	Tr Add. Battle		3
	Sharpen their claws, and meditate the war.	Y 24	Tr Add. Battle		71
	The prints of claws and honourable scars.	Y 24	Tr Add. Battle		83
	In his fell claws, then into th' air he springs.	Y 26	Tr Add. Battle		126
CLAY					
	Left by the Hand of Heav'n on human Clay.	O 255	Irene		13
	And all Irene now is breathless Clay.	O 330	Irene		4
	May I lye cold beneath a load of clay.	Y 18	Tr. Iliad Bk 6		25
CLEAN					
	They sing, they dance, clean shoes, or cure a clap;	O 15	London		114
CLEAR					
	Down whose current clear and strong,	O 159	Tr. Rio Verde		2
	But let us try to clear our clouded Brows,	O 329	Irene		10
CLEAR'D					
	From bold invaders clear'd th' Italian lands	O 78	Festina Lente		19
CLEMENCY					
	Her Sons malicious Clemency shall spare,	O 309	Irene		32
CLEORA					
	If mix'd with these, divine Cleora smile,	Y 4	On a Daffodill		17
	Cleora thus regretted flies,	Y 39	Lady Leaving		5
	O would Cleora thus return,	Y 39	Lady Leaving		11
CLEORA'S					
	Cleora's smiles a genial warmth dispense;	Y 4	On a Daffodill		18
	Cleora's self, fair flower, shall fade like thee,	Y 4	On a Daffodill		27
CLIFF					
	Tho' Scythia's icy cliff he treads,	Y 74	Hor I Ode xxii	V	5
CLIFFS					
	Though Scythia's icy cliffs he treads,	O 65	Hor I Ode xxii		5
	Thro' Scythia's icy cliffs he treads,	Y 74	Hor I Ode xxii	V	5
	Down cliffs the roaring Torrent pours	O 72	Hor. Epode II		38
	Nor down steep cliffs precipitately move	O 77	Festina Lente		5
	Now, wand'ring o'er the cliffs the traveller	Y 23	Tr Add. Battle		30
CLIMBS					
	When Pride, by guilt, to greatness climbs,	O 126	An Ode		33
CLIME					
	A clime deny'd to human race;	O 66	Hor I Ode xxii		22
	A Clime deny'd to human Race;	O 67	To A. Fuscus		22
CLIMES					
	To distant realms and climes unknown,	O 70	Hor.II Ode XX		18
	When souls to blissful climes remove?	O 100	Ode Friendship		26
	till you to happier climes remove?	O 100	Ode Friendship	V	26
	Tho' Northern Climes confess thy Sway,	O 146	Tr Boeth III.5		7
CLOAK					
	The sober trader at a tatter'd cloak,	O 17	London		162

CLOATH'D
Now beauteous Daphnis cloath'd with heav'nly light, . . Y 7 Virgil Daphnis 32
CLODIO'S
And strive in vain to laugh at Clodio's jest. . . . . O 13 London V 74
CLOISTER'S
The Cloister's Ease, resum'd the tott'ring Throne, . . O 256 Irene 44
CLOS'D
Here death has clos'd the curious eyes . . . . . O 154 Epita. Hogarth 3
Here clos'd in Death th' attentive Eyes . . . . . O 155 Epita. Hogarth V 3
CLOSE
In vain, these dangers past, your doors you close, . . O 21 London 236
With close Malevolence, or public Rage; . . . . . O 57 Prologue Comus 8
Quitting my close Retreat, I range the City, . . . O 251 Irene 60
Close like th' eternal Bars of Death upon thee, . . O 292 Irene 80
Close like th' eternal Bars of Death upon You . . . O 357 Irene V 10
Close, as we might unseen, we watch'd his Steps; . . O 311 Irene 2
CLOSELY
Observe him closely with a Statesman's Eye, ... O 255 Irene 10
Would shake his wily Head, and closely whisper, . . O 273 Irene 28
The steely troops embodied closely stand . . . Y 24 Tr Add. Battle 78
CLOSEST
And saw him skulking in the closest Walks: . . . . O 327 Irene 25
CLOSING
And fixed disease on Harley's closing life? . . . . O 36 Vanity Wishes 130
CLOUD
Will cloud my Triumphs, and pollute the Day. . . . O 310 Irene 3
Will damp my joys, and cloud the happy days . . . . O 370 Irene 23
To see the Cloud forsake her kindling Cheek, . . . O 320 Irene 26
In vain, from heaven's black concave, like a cloud, . . Y 23 Tr Add. Battle 20
CLOUDED
O'erspread with snares the clouded maze of fate, . . . O 31 Vanity Wishes 6
And chear the clouded mind with light divine. . . . O 130 Tr. Rambler 7 4
But let us try to clear our clouded Brows, ... O 329 Irene 10
CLOUDS
Where clouds condens'd for ever veil . . . . . O 66 Hor I Ode xxii 19
Where Clouds, condens'd, for ever veil . . . . . O 67 To A. Fuscus 19
Clouds do not always veil the skies, ... O 67 Hor. II Ode IX 1
I pierce the Clouds a tunefull Swan. . . . . . . O 70 Hor.II Ode XX 12
In clouds of Ign'rance mourn, ... O 79 Feast St Simon 45
Joys insincere! thick clouds invade the skies, . . . O 82 Young Author 7
The Clouds, a Signal of impending Show'rs, . . . O 250 Irene 32
That clouds thy Brow and labours in thy Bosom . . . O 369 Irene V 19
Bear him aloft above the wond'ring Clouds, ... O 274 Irene 62
Perhaps the Clouds of dark Conspiracy . . . . . O 275 Irene 74
Like thirsty Sailors gazing on the Clouds, ... O 282 Irene 5
Soon as the Veil of Evening clouds the Sky, . . . O 284 Irene 49
Hang Sit these black clouds upon Aspasia's brow? . . Y 191 Irene V 15
The Gleams of Reason, and the Clouds of Passion, . . O 321 Irene 44
Thick clouds of hostile birds obscure the skies. . . Y 25 Tr Add. Battle 93
The northern shores to clouds and frost . . . . Y 38 Lady Leaving 2
CLOUDY
Her brows a cloudy show, ... O 127 To Lyce, Lady 10
Their cloudy Summits, and the Sons of Fierceness, . . O 268 Irene 29
No cloudy Doubts, or languishing Delays; . . . . . O 271 Irene 27
CLOY
Nor deign the festive dome to cloy . . . . O 191 Tr. Medea I 15
COACH
And shun the shining train, and golden coach. . . . O 21 London 235
COARSELY
"Slightly shelter'd, coarsely fed? . . . . O 185 Anacreon Ode 9 28
Obscurely wise, and coarsely kind; . . . . O 201 Death Dr Levet 10
COAST
Stern Famine guards the solitary coast, ... O 41 Vanity Wishes 207
Th' incumber'd oar scarce leaves the dreaded coast . . O 42 Vanity Wishes 239
No fish from the Carpathian coast . . . . . . O 73 Hor. Epode II 57
On Asia's Coast, ... O 257 Irene 74
To live obscure upon a foreign Coast, ... O 301 Irene 104
Then seize fair Italy's delightful Coast, ... O 309 Irene 30
COASTS
Whate'er from India spicy coasts . . . . O 73 Hor. Epode II V 58
COAT
This day the powder'd curls and golden coat, . . . O 60 Pro Good Nat'd 21
COBBLER'S
Says swelling Crispin, begg'd a cobbler's vote. . . O 60 Pro Good Nat'd 22
COFFERS
Or views his coffers with suspicious eyes, ... O 44 Vanity Wishes 289
COIN
Spread out by me, the roving coin, ... O 120 To Miss Purse 7
Spread for their prey, the roving coin . . . . . O 120 To Miss Purse V 7
COLD
And as their patron hints the cold or heat, ... O 16 London 142
He comes, not want and cold his course delay;-- . . O 41 Vanity Wishes 209
He comes, nor want nor cold his course delay;------ . . O 41 Vanity Wishes V 209
Cold Approbation gave the ling'ring Bays, ... O 51 Pro Drury-Lane 13
No cold gradations of decay, ... O 202 Death Dr Levet 34
May I lye cold beneath a load of clay. . . . . . Y 18 Tr. Iliad Bk 6 25
COLLECT
Collect a tax, or farm a lottery, ... O 12 London 58
Collect a tax, or form a lottery, ... O 12 London V 58
COLLECTED
His money he collected strait, ... O 73 Hor. Epode II 75

```
                                                          PAGE    TITLE           LINE
COLLECTIVE
    For love, which scarce collective man can fill;   . . .   O  48 Vanity Wishes     361
    For love, whose grasp Creation collective man can . . .   Y 108 Vanity Wishes   V 361
       fill;
COLLEGE
    When first the college rolls receive his name, . . . .   O  36 Vanity Wishes     135
COLOUR'D   SEE MANY-COLOUR'D
COLOURS
    Dispose the Colours of the flowing Robe, . . . . . .     O 278 Irene             65
    That spread their Colours to the genial Beam, . . . .    O 298 Irene             20
    In the bright Colours of primaeval Spring; . . . . .     O 314 Irene              5
    In warring colours shew the warring throng; . . . . .    Y  22 Tr Add. Battle     4
COLUMNS
    And columns leaning from their central firmness . . .    Y 114 Irene           V 45A
    And though built on feeble columns--Its lofty turrets .  Y 131 Irene           V 35
       blaze amidst
COMBAT
    Disabled both to combat, or to fly, . . . . . . . .      O  59 Pro Good Nat'd    13
    For Courage droops unequal to the Combat, . . . . . .    O 252 Irene             91
    Nor will I trust th' uncertain Chance of Combat; . . .   O 307 Irene             21
    Well mayst thou call thy Master to the Combat, . . . .   O 319 Irene             30
COMBIN'D
    Not all the gifts of Fate combin'd . . . . . . . .       O 144 Tr Boeth. II.2     7
    Of Grandeur and Tranquillity combin'd. . . . . . . .     O 292 Irene             89
    'Tis Love combin'd with Guilt alone, that melts . . .    O 303 Irene             16
COMBINE
    Behold surrounding kings their pow'r combine, . . . .    O  40 Vanity Wishes    199
    In vain surrounding kings their pow'rs combine, . . .    Y 101 Vanity Wishes   V 199
    The rites that taught us to combine . . . . . . . .      O 190 Tr. Medea I        3
    To deck these Bow'rs each Region shall combine, . . .    O 279 Irene             88
    To make thee blest each Region shall combine . . . .     O 351 Irene           V 26
COMBINES
    Against your fame with fondness hate combines, . . . .   O  46 Vanity Wishes    331
COME
    See! while he builds, the gaudy vassals come, . . . .    O  19 London           202
    From every part, the gaudy vassals come, . . . . . .     Y  57 London         V 202
    Yields to Renown the Centuries to come. . . . . . .      O  57 Prologue Comus     18
    How pleas'd he sees his Cattle come, . . . . . . . .     O  73 Hor. Epode II      67
    Joyfull he sees his Cattle come, . . . . . . . . .       O  73 Hor. Epode II    V 67
    The day will come, in which proud Troy shall yield, . .  O  74 Tr. Iliad Bk 6     13
    I am Cassander, come down from the Sky, . . . . . .      O 173 Tr Fr Pantomim      1
    That I am Cassander come down from the Sky. . . . . .    O 173 Tr Fr Pantomim      3
    Comets! come every day--and stay a year. . . . . .       O 177 Tr Dist Modena      2
    We are come to Thirtyfive; . . . . . . . . . .          O 178 Thrale 35 Year      2
    --Come, my lad, and drink some beer. . . . . . . .       O 181 Parody Warton       8
    Bid them come, and take their fill. . . . . . . .        O 196 Song Congratu.     20
    Come my lads and take your fill. . . . . . . . .         O 196 Song Congratu.   V 20
    I come from empty Noise, and tasteless Pomp, . . . .     O 262 Irene              7
    When pale, and anxious for their Years to come, . . .    O 287 Irene              4
    Come haste, and live--Thy Innocence and Truth . . . .    O 320 Irene             18
    Come let us seek new Pleasures in the Palace, . . . .    O 323 Irene             17
    Alas! they come, commanded by the Sultan, . . . . .      O 325 Irene              8
    We come, bright Virgin, tho' relenting Nature . . . .    O 325 Irene             20
    My death is now decreed my death will come. . . . .      Y  21 Tr. Iliad Bk 6    118
COMES
    He comes, not want and cold his course delay;-- . . .    O  41 Vanity Wishes    209
    He ccmes, nor want nor cold his course delay;------ . .  O  41 Vanity Wishes  V 209
    Great Xerxes comes to seize the certain prey, . . . .    O  42 Vanity Wishes    227
    This thought once form'd, all counsel comes too late, .  O  82 Young Author      19
    The fickle crowd with fortune comes and goes; . . . .    O 138 Tr Rambler 153     1
    Or hear himself, for see the Bassa comes. . . . . .      O 254 Irene            141
    See! Mustapha, the Tyrant's Minion, comes; . . . . .     O 260 Irene            143
    Cease, cease thy Censures, for the Sultan comes . . .    O 262 Irene             28
    But when an earthquake comes weak and unsupported . . .  Y 131 Irene          V 36B
    Comes Mustapha.--Your Turkish Robes conceal you-- . . .  O 271 Irene             36
    The Sultan comes, impatient for his Love; . . . . .      O 272 Irene             12
    Do thou resolve: For see, Irene comes! . . . . . .       O 275 Irene             90
    --But see Irene comes . . . . . . . . . . . .           O 367 Irene            V 11
    He comes, perhaps, to separate us forever; . . . . .     O 294 Irene              6
    New joy comes rushing on me and o'erwhelms . . . . .     Y 169 Irene            V 12
    The Sultan comes, still gloomy, still enrag'd. . . . .   O 330 Irene             26
COMET'S
    Prescribes the dreadfull comet's flaming path . . . .    Y 167 Irene           V 124
COMETS
    Comets! come every day--and stay a year. . . . . . .     O 177 Tr Dist Modena      2
COMFORT
    Each passing day some comfort sorrow finds. . . . . .    Y 105 Vanity Wishes   V 301
COMFORTS
    Our social comforts drop away. . . . . . . . . .        O 200 Death Dr Levet      4
COMING
    But who the coming Changes can presage, . . . . . .      O  52 Pro Drury-Lane     39
    Foretold the coming evil by their dismal croak. . . .    O  65 Virgil Past.I      25
    If at your coming princes disappear, . . . . . . .       O 177 Tr Dist Modena      1
    One and Twenty 1810: Improviso on a young heir's coming  O 196 Song Congratu.   V T
       of age.
    Await our coming, equally prepar'd . . . . . . . .       O 284 Irene             54
COMMAND
    Let hist'ry tell where rival kings command, . . . . .    O  31 Vanity Wishes     29
    Historians tell where rival kings command, . . . . .     Y  93 Vanity Wishes   V 29
    Observe your steps; be carefull to command . . . . .     O  77 Festina Lente      3
    The Myrtle (ensign of supreme command . . . . . . .      O  95 Sprig of Myrtl     3
```

COMMAND   (CONTINUED)   PAGE   TITLE   LINE
  That roll at Eurus loud command;   . . . .   O 144 Tr Boeth. II.2   2
  Only this Command obey, ...   O 150 Tr Boet III.12   43
  No stern command, no monitory voice   . . .   O 151 The Ant   3
  Urg'd by th' imperious Soldier's fierce Command,   . . .   O 249 Irene   16
  By his Command, equipp'd for speedy Flight, ...   O 254 Irene   133
  Forgetful of Command, with captive Beauties, . . .   O 258 Irene   92
  Invest Leontius with his new Command;   . . .   O 260 Irene   144
  Than Amurath, accustom'd to Command,   . . .   O 264 Irene   21
  Born to command, as thou to charm Mankind,   . . .   O 268 Irene   23
  To see new Cities tow'r at thy Command,   . . .   O 278 Irene   71
  Smile on my Wishes, and command the Globe.   . . .   O 279 Irene   81
  Ev'n from the Birth affects supreme Command, . . .   O 280 Irene   19
  At my Command yon' Iron Gates unfold;   . . .   O 283 Irene   14
  At my Command the Sentinels retire;   . . .   O 283 Irene   15
  Sooth her with all the Pleasures of Command, . . .   O 287 Irene   17
  Grasp at Command, and tow'r in quest of Empire; . .   O 293 Irene   114
  Wealth, and Command, and Grandeur shall be thine   . .   O 306 Irene   6
  With cautious Vigilance, at my Command,   . . .   O 310 Irene   4
  Has taught my Slave the Language of Command! . . .   O 323 Irene   2
COMMANDED
  Alas! they come, commanded by the Sultan, ...   O 325 Irene   8
COMMANDS
  Reason commands to cast the less away;   . . . .   O 290 Irene   33
  What hadst thou lost by slighting those Commands? . .   O 332 Irene   32
COMMENC'D
  At once commenc'd the Senator and Man.   . . . . . .   O 117 Epitaph Hammer   12
COMMENCE
  Commence your lords, and govern or betray.   . . . .   O 17 London   157
  'Tis yours this Night to bid the Reign commence   . . .   O 53 Pro Drury-Lane   57
COMMEND
  Yet still my calmer thoughts his choice commend, . . .   O   8 London   3
COMMERCE
  The guard of commerce, and the dread of Spain,   . . .   O 10 London   28
  Where Commerce lavish'd unexhausted Plenty, ...   O 251 Irene   64
COMMISSION
  Some fiery fop, with new commission vain, ...   O 21 London   226
  So some fiery fop, with new commission vain, ...   Y 59 London   V 226
  Perhaps my Warmth exceeded my Commission;   . . . .   O 330 Irene   21
COMMISSION'D
  Commission'd, as he says, by Cali Bassa.   . . . . .   O 294 Irene   3
COMMITS
  Commits to trivial Chance the Fate of Nations!   . . . .   O 269 Irene   2
  Commits to trivial chance the Work of Fate!   . . . .   O 374 Irene   V 11
COMMON
  The common shore of Paris and of Rome;   . . . .   O 14 London   94
  The common sewer of Paris and of Rome;   . . . .   O 14 London   V 94
  The common fav'rite as the gen'ral friend: . . . .   Y 105 Vanity Wishes V 297
  Tost in one common storm with all the great; . . . .   O 59 Pro Good Nat'd   8
  Henceforth shall form one common pray'r, ...   O 122 Stella Mourn.   14
  Where common Laws restrain the Prince and Subject, . .   O 256 Irene   56
  Where King and People own one common Law   . . . .   O 352 Irene   V 16
  one common Interest, mutual duties   . . . . . .   O 352 Irene   V 17
  Now haste to mingle in one common Center, ...   O 287 Irene   4
COMMUNION
  To court Communion with the Skies, ...   O 150 Tr Boet III.12   54
COMPANION
  Companion of our Flight, illustrious Exile, ...   O 320 Irene   30
COMPASSION
  What e'er our Crimes, our Woes demand Compassion. . .   O 251 Irene   58
  The Ministers of Wrath forget Compassion.   . . . .   O 314 Irene   24
  Unhappy Fair! Compassion calls upon me   . . . . .   O 327 Irene   4
COMPASSIONATE
  While vulgar Souls compassionate their Cares,   . . .   O 293 Irene   115
COMPETENCE
  Secure with Peace, with Competence, to dwell,   . . .   O 58 Prologue Comus   35
COMPETITORS
  How, when competitors like these contend, ...   O 16 London   144
COMPLAIN
  In Myrtle shades despairing ghosts complain; . . . .   O 95 Sprig of Myrtl   8
  Nor shall the passive Coward once complain.   . . . .   O 111 To Posterity   26
  Unjustly mortals triumph and complain   . . . . . .   Y 217 Irene   V 14
COMPLAIN'D
  To thee I then with tears complain'd   . . . .   Y 11 Tr Hor Epode 9   19
COMPLAINT
  Our anxious Bard, without complaint, may share   . . .   O 59 Pro Good Nat'd   5
  Our little Bard, without complaint, may share   . . .   O 59 Pro Good Nat'd V   5
  Let pain deserv'd without complaint be borne.   . . .   O 131 Tr. Rambler 32   1
COMPLAINTS
  In soft Complaints, and idle Protestations.   . . . . .   O 269 Irene   16
COMPLEAT
  If to compleat this heav'nly Life   . . . .   O 72 Hor. Epode II   47
  E'er yet had happiness compleat;   . . . .   O 136 Tr Rambler 128   2
  Born to compleat the Ruin of her Country;   . . . .   O 316 Irene   11
COMPLEATS
  Thy Soul compleats the Triumphs of thy Face. . . . .   O 278 Irene   60
  'Tis well--A single Blow compleats our Wishes: . . .   O 304 Irene   8
COMPLETES
  Completes the Gift of Freedom and of Life.   . . . . .   O 285 Irene   16
COMPLIANCE
  For forc'd Compliance, or for zealous Virtue,   . . .   O 256 Irene   51

```
COMPLIANCE        (CONTINUED)                                    PAGE     TITLE              LINE
     Fear and Ambition, urge her to Compliance;   . . . . .     O 261 Irene                 13
     The matchless Fair has bless'd me with Compliance;   . .   O 308 Irene                   3
     But who can hear thee beg without compliance  . . . .     Y 205 Irene             V    33
COMPLY
     With ev'ry wild absurdity comply,   . . . . . . . .       O  16 London                138
COMPOSE
     The swelling passions to compose,   . . . . . . . .       O 126 An Ode                 39
COMPOSURE
     And stern Composure of despairing Heroes;   . . . . .     O 275 Irene                 83
COMPREHENSIVE
     Do not we share the comprehensive Thought,   . . . .      O 278 Irene                 55
     Do not we share the comprehensive thought,   . . . .      Y 149 Irene             V    57
COMPULSION
     Let kind Compulsion terminate the Contest.   . . . .      O 321 Irene                 50
COMUS
          At The Representation of Comus,...                   O  56 Prologue Comus          T
CONCAVE
     In vain, from heaven's black concave, like a cloud,   . . Y  23 Tr Add. Battle         20
CONCEAL
     Comes Mustapha.--Your Turkish Robes conceal you--   . .   O 271 Irene                 36
     Conceal the Gem; let female Arrogance . . . . . . .       O 277 Irene                 33
     The pains I labour'd to conceal  . . . . . . . .          Y  11 Tr Hor Epode 9        15
CONCEAL'D
     Conceal'd from all but him! All! all conspire   . . . .   O 273 Irene                 20
     And heard within the Thicket that conceal'd us,   . . .   O 311 Irene                 12
     Shall then the Greeks, unpunish'd and conceal'd,   . . .  O 312 Irene                  1
     Lies in the Womb of Providence conceal'd,   . . . .       O 313 Irene                  3
CONCEALS
     Conceals the moral council in a tale.  . . . . . .        O 132 Tr. Rambler 65         2
     And, though refus'd, conceals it from the Sultan.  . . .  O 258 Irene                 89
CONCEIT
     Toil crush'd conceit, and man was of a piece;   . . . .   O  32 Vanity Wishes         54
CONCEIV'D
     Sure this is Love which heretofore I conceiv'd  . . . .   O 349 Irene             V    28
CONCERN
     Beheld without Concern, expiring Greece,   . . . . . .    O 250 Irene                 34
CONCERN'D
     Both your religion and your country are   . . . . . .     Y 181 Irene             V    52
          concern'd
CONCLUDE
     Let one just Act conclude the hateful Day.   . . . . .    O 333 Irene                 50
CONCORD
     That concord smile on the connubial bed;   . . . . . .    O 131 Tr. Rambler 45         2
CONCUR
     Concur to press a hapless Captive's Ruin?   . . . . . .   O 288 Irene                 10
     Concur to press a helpless Captive's Ruin?   . . . . .    O 288 Irene             V    10
CONCUR'D
     Concur'd to give me to Aspasia's Arms,   . . . . . .      O 296 Irene                 36
CONDEMN'D
     Condemn'd a needy supplicant to wait,   . . . . . .       O  41 Vanity Wishes        213
     Let Wit, condemn'd the feeble War to wage   . . . . .     O  57 Prologue Comus         7
     Condemn'd to everduring pains.   . . . . . . . .          O  69 Hor.II Ode 14         20
     Condemn'd to hope's delusive mine,   . . . . . . .        O 200 Death Dr Levet         1
     The Coward, and the Fool, condemn'd to lose   . . . .     O 283 Irene                 22
     Who calls for Pardon from a Wretch condemn'd?   . . . .   O 323 Irene                  4
     Of her the Sultan's Voice condemn'd to die?   . . . .     O 329 Irene                 17
CONDEMNS     SEE CONTEMNS
     Nor dare to spare the Life his Frown condemns.   . . . .  O 325 Irene                 10
CONDENS'D
     Where clouds condens'd for ever veil   . . . . . .        O  66 Hor I Ode xxii        19
     Where Clouds, condens'd, for ever veil   . . . . . .      O  67 To A. Fuscus          19
CONDENSING
     Like the dread Stillness of condensing Storms.   . . . .  O 270 Irene                 14
CONDITION
     And yet such is the condition of human   . . . . . .      Y 186 Irene             V     2
          happiness
CONDUCT
     Thy pictures shall thy conduct frame,   . . . . . . .     O 121 To Miss Playin        33
     His Conduct Human Kind debased:   . . . . . . . .         O 146 Tr Boeth III.4         6
     Conduct these Queens, Abdalla, to the Palace:   . . . .   O 269 Irene                 40
     Conduct her hither, let no rude Intrusion   . . . . .     O 272 Irene                 13
     Conduct her hither, see that no intrusion   . . . . .     O 368 Irene             V    24
     Thanks for this kind relief. Conduct him hither   . . .   O 370 Irene             V    15
     And wait your Summons to report his Conduct.   . . . .    O 310 Irene                  7
CONDUCTS
     Conducts their Armies and asserts their Cause.   . . . .  O 251 Irene                 51
     Conducts the Sun, and regulates the Spheres.   . . . .    O 293 Irene                124
CONFEDERATES
     And bade his new Confederates seize the Traitors.   . . . O 317 Irene                 39
CONFER
     The weighty Charge of Royalty confer;   . . . . . . .     O 292 Irene                104
CONFERENCE
     In private Conference; beside him stood   . . . . . .     O 275 Irene                 79
CONFESS
     O then, when conquer'd crouds confess thy sway,   . . .   O  81 Lady Birthday          9
     Tho' Northern Climes confess thy Sway,   . . . . .        O 146 Tr Boeth III.5         7
     Confess your Crime, or lead me to the Sultan,   . . . .   O 326 Irene                 41
     And all the withering woods confess their woe   . . . .   Y   6 Virgil Daphnis         4
CONFESS'D
     This mournful truth is ev'ry where confess'd,   . . . .   O  18 London                176
```

61

CONFESS'D   (CONTINUED)   PAGE   TITLE   LINE
   I grant the charge; forgive the fault confess'd.   . . .   O 139 Tr Rambler 170   1
   My silence and my groans confess'd.   . . . . . .   Y 11 Tr Hor Epode 9   16
CONFEST
   Stern winter, is thy force confest, ...   O 123 Winter's Walk   6
   Stern winter, in thy force confest, ...   O 123 Winter's Walk   V   6
   Confest?--   O 272 Irene   13
     Confest by dying Menodorus.   . . . . . .   O 272 Irene   13
   Confest--confest by dying Leontares   . . . . . .   O 356 Irene   31
   Confest--confest by dying Leontares   . . . . . .   O 356 Irene   V 31
   And joy and sorrow stand by turns confest.   . . . .   Y 21 Tr. Iliad Bk 6   110
CONFIDENCE
   And lend a lye the confidence of truth.   . . . . .   O 12 London   56
   Then soon your ill-plac'd confidence repay, ...   O 17 London   156
   And hope with humble confidence the best   . . . . .   Y 108 Vanity Wishes V 356
   With silent confidence and holy rest: . . . . . .   O 130 Tr. Rambler 7   6
   This Regal Confidence, this pious Ardour, ...   O 264 Irene   33
   Treat her With all the confidence of artless love   . . .   Y 159 Irene   V 17
   Is this th' unshaken Confidence in Heav'n?   . . . .   O 314 Irene   18
   Secure his Confidence, and fix his Love.   . . . . .   O 319 Irene   6
CONFIDENT
   But confident of praise, if praise be due, ...   O 60 Pro Good Nat'd   29
   Sunk in his Pleasures, confident and gay, ...   O 283 Irene   8
CONFIDING
   Whatever Crane confiding in his might   . . . . . .   Y 23 Tr Add. Battle   38
CONFIN'D
   Nor there confin'd his active Soul;   . . . . . .   O 79 Feast St Simon   43
   He pants for room, in one poor World confin'd.   . .   O 97 Hickman Spinet   12
   And in this earthly Case confin'd;   . . . .   O 147 Tr Boeth III.6   10
   And in this earthly cage confin'd;   . . . .   O 147 Tr Boeth III.6   V 10
CONFINE
   Their prudent insults to the poor confine;   . . . .   O 21 London   233
   Thy nets may catch, but not confine, ...   O 120 To Miss Purse   8
   Thy nets may snare, but not confine, ...   O 120 To Miss Purse   V   8
CONFIRM
   And, to confirm my Thought, at sight of me,   . . .   O 275 Irene   84
   Confirm your Troops; and when the Moon's fair Beam   . .   O 306 Irene   58
   The Bowl shall circle to confirm our League,   . . .   O 308 Irene   29
CONFIRM'D
   And Pantomime, and Song, confirm'd her Sway.   . . .   O 52 Pro Drury-Lane   38
   But now confirm'd, and swelling with his Conquests,   . .   O 257 Irene   70
   My Doom confirm'd establishes my Purpose.   . . . .   O 270 Irene   9
   And bring her former Sentence new confirm'd.   . . .   O 327 Irene   27
CONFISCATION'S
   Tho' confiscation's vulturs hover round.   . . . . .   O 32 Vanity Wishes   36
   Tho' confiscation's vulturs clang around.   . . . .   O 32 Vanity Wishes   V 36
   Tho' confiscation's bloodhounds yelp around.   . . .   Y 93 Vanity Wishes   V 36
CONFLICTS
   Forbear this Triumph--still new Conflicts wait us,   . .   O 298 Irene   25
CONFOUND
   Should heaven's just bolts Orgilio's wealth confound,   . .   O 19 London   194
   Shou'd partial Cat-calls all his Hopes confound,   . . .   O 246 Irene Prologue   23
CONFOUNDED
   Confounded, aw'd, and lost in Admiration, ...   O 282 Irene   64
CONFUS'D
   Chiefs confus'd in mutual slaughter, ...   O 159 Tr. Rio Verde   3
   Confus'd about the streets I roam   . . . .   Y 11 Tr Hor Epode 9   33
CONFUSED
   Flush'd as they are with youth confused with wine,   . .   Y 59 Irene   V 232
CONFUSION
   That when confusion o'er the country reigns,   . . .   O 64 Virgil Past.I   15
   And teror and confusion stalk before them   . . . .   Y 115 Irene   V 49E
   Fills all th' astonish'd Empire with Confusion,   . . .   O 257 Irene   77
   When the confusion of new conquests ceases   . . . .   Y 164 Irene   V 76
   Freedom and Love? Alas! I'm all Confusion, ...   O 295 Irene   11
   On ev'ry Side Confusion, Rage and Death, ...   O 300 Irene   70
   And all within is Darkness and Confusion;   . . . .   O 315 Irene   32
   Or but one Moment's Pause betray Confusion, ...   O 332 Irene   15
CONGRATULATING
   Whose night congratulating Conscience cheers;   . . . .   O 44 Vanity Wishes   296
CONGRATULATION
   A Short Song of Congratulation   . . . .   O 196 Song Congratu.   T
CONGRATULATIONS
   That fawning Villain's forc'd Congratulations   . . . .   O 310 Irene   2
   That hoary Villain's forc'd congratulations   . . . . .   O 370 Irene   V 22
CONJECTURE
   The dull conjecture fawning niece and pamper'd guest,   .   Y 104 Vanity Wishes V 276
CONJECTURE'S
   Lies open to Conjecture's dubious Ken, ...   O 300 Irene   69
CONJOINS
   But oft conjoins in woman's softer mould/frame   . . . .   Y 149 Irene   V 55
CONNUBIAL
   That concord smile on the connubial bed;   . . . . . .   O 131 Tr. Rambler 45   2
CONQU'RING
   In Passion lost, he bad the conqu'ring Fair   . . . .   O 258 Irene   99
   And hail unanimous their conqu'ring God.   . . . . .   O 287 Irene   6
CONQUER
   I rouse to War, and conquer for Irene.   . . . . . .   O 309 Irene   25
   Such Ills are sent for Souls like thine to conquer.   . .   O 332 Irene   38
CONQUER'D
   When Christ had conquer'd Hell and fate   . . . . . .   O 79 Feast St Simon   19

```
CONQUER'D        (CONTINUED)                                PAGE    TITLE          LINE
    O then, when conquer'd crouds confess thy sway,    . . .  O  81 Lady Birthday        9
    Aw'd into Love, our conquer'd hearts obey,    . . . . .   O  96 Hickman Spinet       4
    Rouse, Cali, shall the Sons of conquer'd Greece    . . .  O 284 Irene               42
    The victor Cranes the conquer'd realms possess,    . . .  Y  23 Tr Add. Battle      34
CONQUERING    SEE CONQURING
    Dominion hovers o'er their conquering banners    . . . .  Y 115 Irene           V 49D
CONQUEROR
    If the gull'd conqueror receives the chain,    . . . . . .  O  16 London            121
    And sweeps th' exulting Conqueror away:    . . . . . .    O 298 Irene               31
CONQUERORS
    But now our Turkish Conquerors have quench'd    . . . .   O 249 Irene                7
    Th' unquestion'd Claim of Conquerors, and Kings!    . . . O 286 Irene                9
CONQUEROUR
    At length the Conquerour has spent his    . . . . . .    O 350 Irene           V   8
      rage--
    And forget (or lose) the conquerour in the    . . . . .  Y 123 Irene           V 100
      lover
CCNQUEST
    Till conquest unresisted ceas'd to please,    . . . . .  O  34 Vanity Wishes      107
    The Lust of Gold succeeds the Rage of Conquest,    . . .  O 249 Irene               13
    And shook the (affrighted) world lab'ring earth licentious  Y 115 Irene         V 49A
      conquest
    Empire and conquest hover or . . . . . . . . .           Y 115 Irene           V 49C
    Elate with Conquest, in his native Mountains,    . . . .  O 264 Irene               14
    And sought An easier conquest in my softer beauty    . . . Y 134 Irene           V  35
    The Pride of Monarchs, the Reward of Conquest;    . . . .  O 269 Irene               42
    the reward of conquest boast of nature    . . . . .      Y 137 Irene           V  42
    The full-blown pride of conquest and of empire    . . . .  Y 149 Irene           V  58
    Did you proclaim this unexpected Conquest?    . . . .    O 282 Irene               62
    The Refuse of our Swords, the Dross of Conquest,    . . .  O 286 Irene                3
    Freed from the Tumults of unsettled Conquest,    . . . .  O 291 Irene               77
    When eer the tumult of unestablish'd Conquest    . . . .  O 357 Irene           V   6
    Did savage Anger, and licentious Conquest    . . . . .   O 296 Irene               30
    Secure of Happiness from Flight or Conquest,    . . . .   O 302 Irene              114
    And perish ere he tastes the Joys of Conquest.    . . . . O 308 Irene               33
    Success and Conquest now are empty Sounds,    . . . . .  O 333 Irene               44
    Pleas'd with the conquest, he forebore the spoil    . . . Y  18 Tr. Iliad Bk 6      30
CONQUESTS
    Let Caesar spread his conquests far,    . . . . . .      O 137 Tr Rambler 143        1
    But now confirm'd, and swelling with his Conquests,    . .  O 257 Irene               70
    There shall he waste thy Frontiers, check thy Conquests,  O 274 Irene               56
    When the confusion of new conquests ceases    . . . . .  Y 164 Irene           V  76
CONQURING
    Conquring Poet take thy Bride!    . . . . . . . .        O 150 Tr Boet III.12       40
CCNSCIENCE
    Unsullied fame, and conscience ever gay.    . . . .      O  14 London               90
    Whose night congratulating Conscience cheers;    . . . .  O  44 Vanity Wishes      296
    Calm conscience then his former life survey'd,    . . . .  O 118 Epitaph Hanmer      41
    And for one Man--one Wife's enough in Conscience.    . . . O 247 Irene Epilogue      14
    Nor built on Faith, nor fortify'd by Conscience?    . . .  O 301 Irene               84
    Yet shall the Conscience of the great Attempt    . . . .  O 301 Irene               99
    I ask no Witness, but attesting Conscience,    . . . . .  O 305 Irene               34
    Ask of thy Heart; attend the Voice of Conscience--    . .  O 323 Irene                7
CONSCIOUS    SEE ALL-CONSCIOUS
    The man, my friend, whose conscious heart    . . . . .   O  65 Hor I Ode xxii        1
    The Man, my Friend, whose conscious Heart    . . . . .   O  66 To A. Fuscus         1
    No conscious blushes there their cheeks inflame,    . . .  O  84 Epi Dist Moth.      24
    Her conscious hand his laurel leaves invite.    . . . .   O 106 Eliza plucking       4
    And tell the Secrets of their conscious Walks;    . . . .  O 255 Irene               27
    To tell the Secrets of their conscious Shades    . . . .  O 373 Irene           V  20
    Think on th' insulting Scorn, the conscious Pangs,    . .  O 266 Irene               19
    And smiling, conscious of her Charms, withdrew.    . . .  O 282 Irene               69
    This Night with all her conscious Stars be witness,    . .  O 284 Irene               44
    Then pleas'd, and conscious of Superiour    . . . . .    O 369 Irene           V   6
      Greatness
    How Guilt once harbour'd in the conscious Breast,    . . . O 311 Irene               14
    Till conscious of th' incircling Deity,    . . . . . .   O 313 Irene                7
    Is this the boasted Bliss of conscious Virtue?    . . . .  O 314 Irene               19
    Does conscious Virtue shake the fainting knee?    . . . .  O 373 Irene           V   8
CONSECRATE
    Could just intention consecrate the Guilt    . . . . .   O 360 Irene           V  35
CONSECRATED
    We kneel, and kiss the consecrated earth;    . . . . .   O  10 London               24
    Their blood the consecrated stones shall dye:    . . . .  O  64 Virgil Past.I       10
    And pour them on the consecrated stone;    . . . . . .   Y   7 Virgil Daphnis      46
CONSENT
    I go to wait thy Call; this kind Consent    . . . . .    O 285 Irene               15
    Smiling Consent she sat, and blushing Love.    . . . . .  O 303 Irene               32
CONSENTED
    A sigh, a blush inform'd him You consented    . . . . .   O 366 Irene           V  28
CONSIGN
    To him the church, the realm, their pow'rs consign,    . .  O  34 Vanity Wishes      101
CONSIGN'D
    Consign'd by Venus to Melissa's hand)    . . . . . . .   O  95 Sprig of Myrtl       4
    "Weighty charge consign'd to me:    . . . . . .         O 185 Anacreon Ode 9      16
CONSIGNS
    Arthritic tyranny consigns,    . . . . . . . . .        O 125 An Ode               10
CONSISTENT
    Consistent still, though not the same,    . . . . .     O 121 To Miss Playin       34
```

CONSORT PAGE TITLE LINE
   For his lovely Consort gone, ... O 148 Tr Boet III.12 6
   For his lovely Consort gone, ... O 148 Tr Boet III.12 V 8
CONSPIRACY
   Perhaps the Clouds of dark Conspiracy . . . . O 275 Irene 74
   Is then conspiracy so slight a crime . . . . Y 207 Irene V 14
CONSPIRATOR
   Is this the fierce Conspirator Abdalla? . . . . . . O 279 Irene 1
CONSPIRE
   Here malice, rapine, accident, conspire, ... O   9 London 13
   Conceal'd from all but him! All! all conspire . . . . O 273 Irene 20
   Prudence and Love conspire in this Request, ... O 285 Irene 11
CONSPIRING
   When all conspiring leave Maeon's lake . . . . . . Y 24 Tr Add. Battle 66
CONSTANCY
   Beyond the Power of Constancy and Courage; . . . . . O 251 Irene 53
   If built on settled Thought, this Constancy . . . . O 290 Irene 36
   If fix'd on settled thought this Constancy . . . . . O 364 Irene V 8
CONSTELLATION
   --Till every constellation shines for me . . . . . Y 132 Irene V 45
CONSTELLATIONS
   Too slow these gentle Constellations roll, ... O 271 Irene 3
CONSTRAIN'D
   That thus constrain'd we speed the Stroke of Death. . . O 327 Irene 30
CONSTRAINS
   Constrains a sullen Smile, and shoots away. . . . . . O 311 Irene 7
CONSTRAINT
   Fair Justice then, without constraint ador'd, ... O 22 London 250
CONSULT
   Consult in private, call me when your Scheme . . . . O 256 Irene 36
CONSUMMATE
   Behold the Model of consummate Beauty, ... O 334 Irene 3
CONTAGION
   Burns from the strong contagion of the gown; . . . . O 36 Vanity Wishes 138
   Caught from the strong contagion of the gown; . . . . O 36 Vanity Wishes V 138
   Spreads from the strong contagion of the gown; . . . . O 36 Vanity Wishes V 138
CONTAIN
   Could half the nation's criminals contain; . . . . . O 22 London 249
CONTAINS
   While Thales waits the wherry that contains . . . . . O   9 London 19
CONTEMN
   Heav'n will contemn the mercenary Fervour, ... O 262 Irene 26
   And idolize th' Apostate I contemn. . . . . . . O 310 Irene 11
CONTEMNS
   Contemns at length the treachrous toys, ... O 145 Tr Boeth III.1 11
   --The gen'rous mind contemns . . . . Y 177 Irene V 109
CONTEMPLATIVE
   Surveys with new contemplative delight . . . . . . O 106 Eliza plucking 2
CONTEMPT
   Tir'd with contempt, she quits the slipp'ry reign, . . O 46 Vanity Wishes 335
CONTEMPTUOUS
   At length awaking, with contemptuous frown, ... O 10 London 33
   Looks down, contemptuous, from his fancy'd Height, . . O 306 Irene 2
   And when, contemptuous of imperial Pow'r, ... O 322 Irene 59
CONTEND
   How, when competitors like these contend, ... O 16 London 144
CONTENDING
   Reject the Daughters of contending Kings; . . . . . O 267 Irene 7
   Behold contending nations vie for bondage . . . . . Y 136 Irene V 26
   Fiercely contending two vast armies stood . . . . . Y 23 Tr Add. Battle 56
CONTENT
   Could'st thou resign the park and play content, . . . O 19 London 210
   Could thou resign the park and court content, ... Y 58 London V 210
   Or liv'st thou now, with safer pride content, ... O 35 Vanity Wishes 123
   Or states mens now, with safer pride content, ... Y 97 Vanity Wishes V 123
   From meaner minds, tho' smaller fines content, ... O 39 Vanity Wishes 169
   Content to live the Roman's slave, ... O 68 Hor. II Ode IX 23
   For none are rich without content. . . . . O 144 Tr Boeth. II.2 14
   Content with Science, Innocence and Love? . . . . . O 301 Irene 105
   When did Content sigh out her Cares in secret? . . . . O 314 Irene 20
   Content with Freedom, and precarious Greatness. . . . O 321 Irene 39
CONTENTICUS
   Him no contentious suits in law . . . . O 71 Hor. Epode II 13
CONTENTMENT
   When did contentment with struggling sorrow . . . . . Y 191 Irene V 20
     throb?
CONTEST
   Soon will th' unequal Contest be decided, ... O 261 Irene 18
   Let kind Compulsion terminate the Contest. . . . . . O 321 Irene 50
CONTESTED
   The plain contested flows with mingled blood. . . . . O 76 Tr Add. Battle 21
CONTINU'D   SEE LONG-CONTINU'D
   And bless me with continu'd day. . . . . Y 39 Lady Leaving 12
CONTRACTED
   Whome no contracted debts molest . . . . O 71 Hor. Epode II 7
CONTRARIETY
   In friendly contrariety, ... O 121 To Miss Playin 30
CONTRIVANCE
   Allow no Pause for Art or for Contrivance; . . . . . O 275 Irene 88
CONTRIVE
   Could Philosophers contrive . . . . O 178 Thrale 35 Year 5

		PAGE	TITLE	LINE
CONTRIVE	(CONTINUED)			
Contrive perhaps, the Ruin of our Empire, ...		O 312	Irene	2
What more could Force attempt, or Art contrive? . .		O 317	Irene	35
What more could force attempt or thought contrive . . .		Y 194	Irene	V 35
Contrive new Racks, imbitter every Pang, ...		O 334	Irene	74
CONTROUL				
Let Reason with superiour force controul		O 77	Festina Lente	7
CONTROULING				
Degrading nobles and controuling kings;		O 34	Vanity Wishes	94
CONVENT'S				
Ah! let me rather seek the Convent's Cell;		O 292	Irene	93
CONVENTS				
Seek out some peacefull Convents holy Shade		O 348	Irene	V 24
CONVERSE				
My whole, is a Man in whose converse is shar'd, . . .		O 179	Charade!	3
With Converse chase the melancholy Moments.		O 263	Irene	4
The social gayety the improving converse		Y 165	Irene	V 81
He envies none the Converse of Aspasia.		O 296	Irene	4
CONVERTED				
The holy city with converted millions--or nations. . .		Y 131	Irene	V 32C
And wishes Irene were converted by some		Y 186	Irene	V 11
doctor				
CONVEY				
With more address a lover's note convey, ...		O 13	London	77
Wreaths which at last the dear-bought right convey . .		O 40	Vanity Wishes	189
Great souls whose the dear-bought right convey		Y 100	Vanity Wishes	V 189
Convey him to the Prison's inmost Depths, ...		O 312	Irene	24
CONVEY'D				
O say, what guardian Pow'r convey'd thee hither. . .		O 296	Irene	33
CONVICTION				
And fame pursu'd him, where conviction led.		O 118	Epitaph Hanmer	34
Stay--in this dubious Twilight of Conviction, ...		O 321	Irene	43
CONVINC'D				
By Reason not convinc'd, nor won by Love.		O 310	Irene	8
CONVINCE				
You may provoke but never can convince		Y 197	Irene	V 31
CONVIVIAL				
To speed the light convivial hour;		O 191	Tr. Medea I	18
CONVOY				
To rig another convoy for the k<in>g.		O 22	London	247
CONVULSION				
the world recovering from its convulsion		Y 164	Irene	V 77
COOL				
With cool submission joins the labouring train, . . .		O 59	Pro Good Nat'd	3
Cool meditation's quiet seat, ...		O 125	An Ode	30
COOLING				
O'er all the warbling founts a cooling shade. . . .		Y 7	Virgil Daphnis	27
COQUETS				
No more let coquets to themselves be blind, ...		O 81	Lady Birthday	18
CORN				
As corn the fields, as bulls the herds of kine, . . .		Y 6	Virgil Daphnis	18
CORPOREAL				
With mental and corporeal strife, ...		O 124	Winter's Walk	18
CORRESPONDENCE				
His correspondence with our Foes of Greece!		O 273	Irene	18
CORRUPT				
Must dull Suspence corrupt the stagnant mind?		O 47	Vanity Wishes	344
CORRUPTED				
Sucks in the dregs of each corrupted state.		O 14	London	96
CORRUPTION				
Her gifts despis'd, corruption blush'd and fled, . . .		O 118	Epitaph Hanmer	33
The last Corruption of degenerate Man!		O 249	Irene	15
Vain expence the parent of necessity the parent of . .		O 347	Irene	V 26
corruption				
CORRUPTS				
When Avarice corrupts th' emasculated Nation--or . . .		O 347	Irene	V 25
COST				
Nor wish'd to glitter at his country's cost;		O 118	Epitaph Hanmer	28
COSTLY				
Should costly Loads of incense burn, ...		O 69	Hor.II Ode 14	7
... the gay luscious scene of costly pleasure, ...		Y 158	Irene	V 8
COTS				
Far from their antient fields and humble cots. . . .		O 64	Virgil Past.I	18
Whether you sit on thrones, or dwell in cots, ...		O 77	Festina Lente	2
COTTAGE				
Untouch'd his cottage, and his slumbers sound, ...		O 32	Vanity Wishes	35
secure his cottage, and his slumbers sound, ...		Y 93	Vanity Wishes	V 35
There shalt thou view from far the quiet Cottage, . .		O 292	Irene	83
--O Demetrius O for a cottage in those happy regions		Y 177	Irene	V 108
COTTAGES				
For humble cottages and rural sports.		O 137	Tr Rambler 138	2
COU'D				
For those who durst not censure, scarce cou'd praise. .		O 51	Pro Drury-Lane	14
COUCH				
While artful shades thy downy couch enclose, ...		O 151	The Ant	11
My Father call'd me to his Couch of Death, ...		O 272	Irene	7
COULD SEE COU'D				
Nor sell for gold, what gold could never buy, ...		O 14	London	88
Could thou resign the park and court content, ...		Y 58	London	V 210
Could half the nation's criminals contain;		O 22	London	249
Much could I add,--but see the boat at hand, ...		O 22	London	254

COULD   (CONTINUED)   PAGE   TITLE   LINE

		PAGE	TITLE	LINE
And scarce a sycophant could feed on pride;	. . . . .	Y 94	Vanity Wishes	V 56
Such age there is, and who could wish its end?	. . . .	O 44	Vanity Wishes	V 298
Such age the is, and who could wish its end?	. . .	Y 105	Vanity Wishes	V 298
Yet Vane could tell what ills from beauty spring;	. . .	O 45	Vanity Wishes	321
Perhaps if Skill could distant Times explore,	. . . .	O 53	Pro Drury-Lane	41
You could not gain a Moments breath,	. . . . . .	O 69	Hor.II Ode 14	9
Could cancell their irrevocable Law.	. . . . . .	O 76	Tr Add. Battle	40
Phillips! whose touch harmonious could remove	. .	O 113	Epit. Phillips	1
Could Stella, sprightly, fair and young,	. . . . .	O 121	To Miss Playin	21
Art thou too fall'n? ere anger could subside	. . .	O 132	Tr. Rambler 54	1
Could Philosophers contrive	. . . .	O 178	Thrale 35 Year	5
Could Rome with future greatness fire,	. . . .	O 188	Epilogue	2
Could Rome with generous ardour fire,	. . . .	O 188	Epilogue	V 2
Admission ne'er had sought, or could not find.	. . . .	O 192	Tr. Medea II	12
Can he restore the State he could not save?	. . . . .	O 253	Irene	116
Could bear his Son upon the Turkish Throne.	. . . .	O 264	Irene	22
For those who could not please by nobler Service.--	. .	O 264	Irene	24
My scul could animate a larger frame	. . . . . .	Y 132	Irene	V 41A
O! could the Grave restore the pious Hero,	. . . .	O 267	Irene	42
Could Omens fright the Resolute and Wise,	. . . .	O 269	Irene	1
Ere I could range them on the crowded Deck,	. . . .	O 271	Irene	28
I gaz'd, I trembled; but I could not speak:	. . . . .	O 282	Irene	65
Could just intention consecrate the Guilt	. . . . .	O 360	Irene	V 35
Oh could thy Hand unaided free thy Country,	. . . .	O 300	Irene	63
O! could the Eyes of Kings, like those of Heav'n,	. . .	O 308	Irene	12
<Ho>w blest our state could every bosom	. . . .	Y 184	Irene	V 16
O could her fabled Saints, and boasted Prayers	. . .	O 309	Irene	38
O could her boasted saints, and powerfull prayers	. .	Y 185	Irene	V 38
What more could Force attempt, or Art contrive?	. .	O 317	Irene	35
What more could force attempt or thought contrive	. .	Y 194	Irene	V 35
Could we reverse the Sentence of the Sultan,	. .	O 328	Irene	38
Whom neither Vows could fix, nor Favours bind?	. .	O 330	Irene	2
Could not her Charms repress your Zeal for Murder?	. .	O 332	Irene	24
Could not her Prayers, her Innocence, her Tears,	. .	O 332	Irene	25
No feasts could e'er my cares dispell;	. . . .	Y 11	Tr Hor Epode 9	13
No wit nor honesty could stand	. . . .	Y 11	Tr Hor Epode 9	21
And wish'd my rising anger could remove	. . . . .	Y 11	Tr Hor Epode 9	23
COULD'ST				
Could'st thou resign the park and play content,	. . .	O 19	London	210
COULDST				
Thou who couldst laugh where want enchain'd caprice,	. .	O 32	Vanity Wishes	53
Nor couldst thou more support a Life of Sloth	. . . .	O 264	Irene	19
COUNCIL				
Conceals the moral council in a tale.	. . . .	O 132	Tr. Rambler 65	2
COUNCILS				
now hover oer us and direct our councils	. . . . . .	Y 181	Irene	V 51
COUNSEL				
This thought once form'd, all counsel comes too late,	.	O 82	Young Author	19
Scorn their counsel and their pother,	. . . .	O 197	Song Congratu.	27
Swell not your Soul beyond reproof or Counsel	. . . .	O 366	Irene	V 18
COUNSELL'D				
But being counsell'd to go home	. . . .	Y 11	Tr Hor Epode 9	31
COUNSELLOR				
Rise Cali Bassa counsellor of Kings	. . . .	O 351	Irene	V 24
The Grecian Counsellor.	. . . .	O 263	Irene	25
COUNSELLS				
Nor counsells nor reproach expell	. . . .	Y 12	Tr Hor Epode 9	39
COUNSELS				
And hop'd to share thy Counsels, not thy Sorrows:	. .	O 253	Irene	106
The Chief, whose Wisdom guides the Turkish Counsels.	. .	O 253	Irene	112
To stronger Efforts, and maturer Counsels.	. . .	O 270	Irene	8
But see, where destin'd to protract our Counsels,	. . .	O 271	Irene	35
With venerable Cali's faithful Counsels?	. . .	O 272	Irene	10
Are these the Counsels? This the Faith of Cali?	. . .	O 272	Irene	11
And dark Perplexity distracts my Counsels.	. . .	O 275	Irene	89
Important Cares detain'd me from your Counsels.	. . .	O 279	Irene	6
Vers'd in the secret Counsels of the Sky.	. . . . .	O 314	Irene	27
COUNT				
Count not these Hours as Parts of vulgar Time,	. . . .	O 302	Irene	5
COUNT'NANCE				
"Ah! let not tears down that fair count'nance rowl,	. .	Y 21	Tr. Iliad Bk 6	113
COUNTED				
Till counted myriads sooth his pride no more;	. . . .	O 42	Vanity Wishes	230
COUNTERFEITED				
To pour at will the counterfeited tear,	. . . . . .	O 16	London	141
With counterfeited Fears the Aid of Man;	. . . . .	O 266	Irene	28
Some artful Wile of counterfeited Love!	. . . . . .	O 331	Irene	3
COUNTLESS				
Though countless as the Grains of Sand	. . . . .	O 144	Tr Boeth. II.2	1
Though countless as the lamps of night	. . . . .	O 144	Tr Boeth. II.2	3
COUNTRY				
That when confusion o'er the country reigns,	. . . .	O 64	Virgil Past.I	15
Then, O my Country! shalt thou groan distrest,	. . . .	O 110	To Posterity	3
His country call'd him from the studious shade;	. . .	O 117	Epitaph Hanmer	10
And wander o'er the Ruins of our Country	. . .	O 351	Irene	V 1
To raise our prostrate country from its ruins.	. . . .	Y 117	Irene	V109A
Or how can Cali's Flight restore our Country?	. . .	O 254	Irene	139
What has the Wretch that has surviv'd his Country,	. .	O 260	Irene	134
His groaning Country claims Leontius' Aid;	. . . .	O 270	Irene	17
Implor'd th' eternal Power to shield my Country,	. . .	O 290	Irene	49

COUNTRY   (CONTINUED)   PAGE   TITLE   LINE
    To shield my Lover, and preserve my Country.   . . . . .   O 364 Irene   V   4
    Oh could thy Hand unaided free thy Country, ...   O 300 Irene   63
    Deface Erase the glories of my native . . . .   Y 177 Irene   V 107
        country
    Science and Arms find every where a   . . . .   O 352 Irene   V 32
        Country.
    Be but my Country free, be thine the Praise;   . . . .   O 305 Irene   33
    Both your religion and your country are   . . . . . .   Y 181 Irene   V 52
        concern'd
    While yet the future Fortune of my Country   . . . . .   O 313 Irene   2
    Born to compleat the Ruin of her Country;   . . . . .   O 316 Irene   11
    But there came a country 'squire   . . . .   Y 301 Extemp. Elegy   13
COUNTRY'S
    Explain their country's dear-bought rights away,   . .   O 11 London   53
    Nor wish'd to glitter at his country's cost;   . . . .   O 118 Epitaph Hanmer   28
    That Wealth, too sacred for their Country's Use!   . .   O 250 Irene   20
    And snatch'd her timely from her Country's Fate.   . .   O 252 Irene   98
    Your careless Love betrays your Country's Cause.   . .   O 297 Irene   10
    Nor will his Country's Groans reproach Demetrius. .   O 301 Irene   101
    My Pride shall ne'er protract my Country's Woes;   . .   O 306 Irene   47
COUNTS
    Attendant Flatt'ry counts his myriads o'er, ...   O 42 Vanity Wishes   229
    Unlocks his gold, and counts it till he dies.   . . . .   O 44 Vanity Wishes   290
    Counts death kind Nature's signal of retreat: . . . .   O 48 Vanity Wishes   364
    Who knows if Jove who counts our Score   . . . . . .   Y 232 Tr Horace IV.7   17
    With horrour counts the number of the slain.   . . . .   Y 23 Tr Add. Battle   33
COURAGE
    With fatal heat impetuous courage glows, ... O 31 Vanity Wishes   17
    "Or from wine as courage springs, ...   O 186 Anacreon Ode 9   37
    Beyond the Power of Constancy and Courage;   . . . . . . O 251 Irene   53
    Call to your Aid your Courage, and your Wisdom;   . . .   O 252 Irene   85
    For Courage droops unequal to the Combat, ...   O 252 Irene   91
    With Monuments of Death proclaim his Courage;   . . . .   O 255 Irene   31
    To heav'n and earth the courage of Leontius   . . . . .   Y 120 Irene   V 31B
    Too well I know him, his immod'rate Courage, ...   O 267 Irene   46
    All there is Hope, and Gaiety, and Courage, ...   O 271 Irene   26
    Inform me rather, how thy happy Courage   . . . . .   O 295 Irene   27
    New Force, new Courage, from each Glance I gain,   . . . O 297 Irene   21
    Nor rush on useless Wounds with idle Courage.   . . . .   O 318 Irene   10
COURIER
    Lovely courier of the sky, ...   O 185 Anacreon Ode 9   1
COURSE
    He comes, not want and cold his course delay;--   . . .   O 41 Vanity Wishes   209
    He comes, nor want nor cold his course delay;------ .   O 41 Vanity Wishes V 209
    Whatever course of Life great Jove allots, ...   O 77 Festina Lente   1
    Through half his Course reflects the blaze of   . . . .   O 353 Irene   V   2
        War
    Persue thy course through boiling eddies, ...   Y 201 Irene   V 10A
    That mark'd my Course, suspicious of my Purpose,   . .   O 335 Irene   6
    Where'er the battle rages bends his course.   . . . . .   Y 25 Tr Add. Battle 119
COURSES
    And weary Planets loiter in their Courses.   . . . . .   O 262 Irene   4
COURT
    Who scarce forbear, tho' Britain's Court he sing,   . .   O 13 London   69
    Hiss'd from the stage, or hooted from the court,   . .   O 15 London   109
    Could thou resign the park and court content,   . . .   Y 58 London   V 210
    To court Communion with the Skies, ...   O 150 Tr Boet III.12   54
    That Vessel, if observ'd, alarms the Court, ...   O 258 Irene   83
    Instructed from our infant Years to court   . . . . .   O 266 Irene   27
    To State and Pow'r I court thee, not to Ruin: . . .   O 279 Irene   80
    Applaud her Charms, and court her to be Great.   . . .   O 287 Irene   18
    We court thy Gentleness.   . . . .   O 288 Irene   9
    To fix his Court, and regulate his Pleasures, ...   O 291 Irene   78
    To form his Court and regulate his pleasures   . . . .   Y 164 Irene   V 78
    Yet think a Moment, ere you court Destruction,   . . .   O 301 Irene   87
    To court the sword and tempt the glutted rack   . . .   Y 196 Irene   V 18D
COURTED
    "Venus, courted with an ode, ...   O 185 Anacreon Ode 9   11
    "Venus, courted by an ode, ...   O 185 Anacreon Ode 9 V 11
    she courted fate & scornd a crown   . . . .   Y 191 Irene   V 16
COURTIER
    To vote a patriot black, a courtier white;   . . . . .   O 11 London   52
    The Vet'ran Courtier half reveal'd his Project.   . . .   O 254 Irene   132
COURTIER'S
    The Courtier's Policy, the Sage's Firmness, ...   O 255 Irene   3
COURTIERS
    With brisker air the silken courtiers gaze, ...   O 17 London   164
COURTING
    Still courting his embrace and still eluding   . . . .   Y 155 Irene   V 35
COURTLY
    Who dwell on Balbos courtly mien--   . . . .   Y 55 London   V 150
COURTS
    What but their wish indulg'd in courts to shine,   . . . O 36 Vanity Wishes   133
    Peace courts his hand, but spreads her charms in vain; . O 40 Vanity Wishes   201
    Peace courts his hand, her fondness he disdains   . . .   Y 101 Vanity Wishes V 201
    When one a borough courts, and one the pit.   . . . . .   O 59 Pro Good Nat'd   10
    Whom smiling nature courts in vain, ...   O 125 An Ode   11
    With me retire and leave the pomp of courts   . . . .   O 137 Tr Rambler 138   1
    And soft solicitation courts repose, ...   O 151 The Ant   12
    Grown old in courts, thou art not surely one   . . . .   O 176 Tr Metastas II   1

COURTS   (CONTINUED)   PAGE   TITLE   LINE

    Unhappy Lot of all that shine in Courts; . . . . O 256 Irene   50
    Alluring Grandeur courts her to his Arms, ... O 261 Irene   15
    Courts thee to shake on a dependent Throne; . . . . . O 268 Irene   22
    Hast thou grown old amidst the Croud of Courts, . . . O 281 Irene   32
    Amidst the Glare of Courts, the Shouts of Armies, . . O 293 Irene   131
    The mighty Tuscan courts the banish'd Arts . . . . .   O 302 Irene   116
    How rarely would they meet in crouded Courts, ... O 308 Irene   16
COURTSHIP
    With warmer Courtship press the yielding Fair, ... O 287 Irene   9
COVERT
    Beneath the Covert of this verdant Arch . . . . . .   O 275 Irene   78
COWARD
    Nor shall the passive Coward once complain. . . . . .   O 111 To Posterity   26
    In his last Agonies the gasping Coward, ...   O 272 Irene   14
    The Coward, and the Fool, condemn'd to lose . . . .   O 283 Irene   22
    Through hissing Ages, a proverbial Coward, ...   O 305 Irene   28
    The Captive of his Sword. The coward Greeks, ...   O 312 Irene   14
COWARDICE
    Habitual Cowardice usurps the Soul. . . . .   O 266 Irene   33
    Distrust is Cowardice, and Prudence Folly. . . . . .   O 301 Irene   86
    The soften'd Soul to Cowardice and Sloth; . . . . .   O 303 Irene   17
    And Cowardice to dread the Boast of Folly. . . . . .   O 318 Irene   22
COWARDISE
    Tis cowardise to fear the boasts of folly . . . . .   Y 197 Irene   V 22
COXCOMBS
    The (coxcombs) whisper and the fopling's song . . . . Y 128 Irene   V 17
COY
    With coy Caresses and with pleasing Wiles . . . . .   O 260 Irene   128
CRACKLING
    On crackling ice, o'er gulphs profound, ...   O 203 Tr. on Skating V   1
CRAFTY
    The Watchful slumber, and the Crafty trust. . . . . .   O 283 Irene   13
CRANE
    For fear retards their flight, the cruell Crane . . . O 76 Tr Add. Battle   31
    Whatever Crane confiding in his might . . . . . .   Y 23 Tr Add. Battle   38
    Now bleeds the war afresh, the Crane from high . . .   Y 26 Tr Add. Battle 130
CRANES
    The screaming Cranes and fearfull Hares. . . . . . .   O 72 Hor. Epode II   44
    The Cranes with beaks and claws provoke the fight. . . O 75 Tr Add. Battle   3
    And giv'n to mirth, the Cranes no longer fear, . . .   O 77 Tr Add. Battle   50
    The victor Cranes the conquer'd realms possess, . . . Y 23 Tr Add. Battle   34
    The injur'd Cranes their murther'd offspring mourn . . Y 24 Tr Add. Battle   64
    This forc'd the Cranes to utter dolefull moans, . . . Y 24 Tr Add. Battle   88
    Quickly the Cranes appear before their eyes; . . . .   Y 25 Tr Add. Battle   92
    Before his face the frighted Cranes gave way. . . . .   Y 25 Tr Add. Battle 122
    The joyfull Cranes triumphant clap their wings: . . . Y 26 Tr Add. Battle 127
CRAVE
    If Sorrow pine or Av'rice crave, ...   O 146 Tr Boeth III.5   9
CREAM
    With cream and sugar soften'd well, ...   O 158 Par Hermit III   3
    With cream and sugar temper'd well, ...   O 158 Par Hermit III V 3
CREATE
    Can in my bosom half that grief create, ...   O 74 Tr. Iliad Bk 6   19
    What hopes, what terrors does thy gift create, . . .   O 95 Sprig of Myrtl   1
    What Fears, what terrors does this gift create, . . . O 95 Sprig of Myrtl V 1
    The Weakness we lament, our selves create, ...   O 266 Irene   26
CREATED
    Whose voice created, and whose wisdom guides, ... O 129 Tr. Rambler 7   2
CREATION
    For love, whose grasp Creation collective man can . .   Y 108 Vanity Wishes V 361
      fill;
    Blasts all the Beauties of his new Creation, ...   O 269 Irene   7
    Attention rise, survey the fair Creation, ...   O 313 Irene   6
CREATURE
    Who holds no human Creature mean; . . . .   O 147 Tr Boeth III.6   18
CREDIT
    Or if old womens tales may credit gain, ...   O 77 Tr Add. Battle   44
    Soon might her Tears engage a Lover's Credit; . . . . O 327 Irene   17
CREDITORS
    No griping Creditors infesst. . . . .   O 71 Hor. Epode II   8
CREDITS
    And only credits what Experience tells. . . . . . .   O 255 Irene   19
CREDULITY
    On Britain's fond credulity they prey. . . . . . .   O 15 London   112
CREEK
    Deep in a winding Creek a Galley lies, ...   O 254 Irene   134
CREPT
    From Bard, to Bard, the frigid Caution crept, ... O 52 Pro Drury-Lane   31
    There frogs crept croaking o'er the swampy ground. . . Y 24 Tr Add. Battle   59
CRESCENT
    Of stern Sebalias the triumphant Crescent, ...   O 312 Irene   11
CREW
    What Passions reign among thy Crew, Leontius? . . . . O 270 Irene   21
    Who hath not heard of Argo's valiant crew? . . . . .   Y 22 Tr Add. Battle   10
CRIED
    Till at length stern Pluto cried, ...   O 149 Tr Boet III.12   39
    Then all is past he cried--and darted from us; . . .   O 317 Irene   32
CRIES
    Since worth, he cries, in these degen'rate days, . . . O 10 London   35
    But hark! th' affrighted crowd's tumultuous cries . . . O 18 London   182

CRIES	(CONTINUED)	PAGE	TITLE	LINE
"Think nothing gain'd, he cries, till nought remain,		O 40	Vanity Wishes	202
No cries attempt the mercies of the skies?		O 47	Vanity Wishes	348
No cries invoke the mercies of the skies?		O 47	Vanity Wishes	V 348
This night our wit, the pert apprentice cries,		O 60	Pro Good Nat'd	23
Restrain your tears and cease your cries,		O 70	Hor.II Ode XX	21
No trumpets sound, no Soldiers cries,		O 71	Hor. Epode II	9
That, fav'ring, listen to his cries.		O 72	Hor. Epode II	28
That grant his Prayers, and hear his cries.		O 72	Hor. Epode II	V 28
Utter sad groans and lamentable cries.		O 76	Tr Add. Battle	29
"Toil on, dull croud, in extacy, he cries,		O 82	Young Author	15
Be gone ye blockheads, Heraclitus cries,		O 141	Tr Rambler 208	1
If the man who turnips cries,		O 183	Burlesque Vega	1
Oft when the Cries of violated Beauty		O 251	Irene	73
Has heard unhurt the cries of slaughterd thousands		Y 126	Irene	V 145
The loudest Cries of Nature urge us forward;		O 270	Irene	15
Not then with raving Cries I fill'd the City,		O 290	Irene	46
(Yet) not with idle cries I fill'd the city		Y 163	Irene	V 46
An idle List'ner to the distant Cries		O 305	Irene	23
But Cries and Tears are vain, prepare with Patience		O 328	Irene	40
Her piercing Cries yet fill the loaded Air,		O 329	Irene	8
Heard her last Cries, and fann'd her dying Beauties,		O 333	Irene	47
With dolefull cries their living lord they mourn		Y 21	Tr. Iliad Bk 6	130

CRIME
Bless with an age exempt from scorn or crime;		O 44	Vanity Wishes	292
Nor give him Leisure for another Crime.		O 271	Irene	32
Shrinks from this heap of aggregated crime		Y 159	Irene	V 9
The Soul once tainted with so foul a Crime,		O 289	Irene	15
On me, should Providence, without a Crime,		O 292	Irene	103
Not Pow'r I blame, but Pow'r obtain'd by Crime,		O 293	Irene	129
Ambition was her Crime, but meaner Folly		O 310	Irene	9
Confess your Crime, or lead me to the Sultan,		O 326	Irene	41
Is then conspiracy so slight a crime		Y 207	Irene	V 14
Then call it not our Cruelty, nor Crime,		O 327	Irene	28

CRIMES
When publick crimes inflame the wrath of heav'n:		O 13	London	66
Who shares Orgilio's crimes, his fortune shares.		O 14	London	84
All crimes are safe, but hated poverty.		O 17	London	159
And tir'd like me with follies and with crimes,		O 23	London	258
And crouds with crimes the records of mankind;		O 31	Vanity Wishes	24
Here let me learn to shun the crimes		O 126	An Ode	35
What e'er our Crimes, our Woes demand Compassion.		O 251	Irene	58
And bear us far from Servitude and Crimes.		O 267	Irene	44
Before th' assembled Troops proclaim his Crimes;		O 273	Irene	35
Should we before the Troops proclaim his Crimes		O 273	Irene	38
Justice demands that I reveal your Crimes;		O 286	Irene	14
To form new Legends, sanctify new Crimes,		O 309	Irene	33
While I not yet familiar to my Crimes,		O 322	Irene	11
What Fraud misleads him? or what Crimes incense?		O 325	Irene	28
Nor let the Crimes of this detested Day		O 329	Irene	54
Irene's crimes, forget not her repentance.		Y 209	Irene	V 55
Inflame her Crimes, exalt your own Obedience,		O 329	Irene	14
The wretch whose crimes declar'd by tortur'd Cali		Y 215	Irene	V 69A
So sure the Fall of Greatness rais'd on Crimes,		O 335	Irene	10
By crimes abhord, and treasons not her own		Y 217	Irene	V 10A

CRIMINALS
| Could half the nation's criminals contain; | | O 22 | London | 249 |

CRINGES
| And what their Armies lost, their Cringes | | O 16 | London | V 122 |
| gain? | | | | |

CRIPLED
| He turns, with anxious heart and cripled hands, | | O 44 | Vanity Wishes | 287 |

CRISPIN
| Says swelling Crispin, begg'd a cobbler's vote. | | O 60 | Pro Good Nat'd | 22 |

CRITICK
| Deaf to the critick, sullen to the friend, | | Y 67 | Prologue Lethe | 5 |

CRITICK'S
| And weakly hopes to 'scape the critick's rage. | | Y 67 | Prologue Lethe | 12 |

CRITICKS
| Where no sour criticks damn, nor sneers molest, | | O 82 | Young Author | 27 |
| Where no sour criticks snarl, no sneers molest, | | O 82 | Young Author | V 27 |

CROAK
| Foretold the coming evil by their dismal croak. | | O 65 | Virgil Past.I | 25 |

CROAKING
| There frogs crept croaking o'er the swampy ground. | | Y 24 | Tr Add. Battle | 59 |

CROATIAN
| The fierce Croatian, and the wild Hussar, | | O 43 | Vanity Wishes | 249 |

CROP
| Insatiate pluck the Fruit, and crop the Flow'r: | | O 110 | To Posterity | 12 |

CROP'D
| Nor crop'd the tastfull herb, nor trac'd the verdant meads | | Y 6 | Virgil Daphnis | 10 |

CROPS
| She crops the harvest, and she stores the grain. | | O 151 | The Ant | V 8 |

CROSS
| Behold her cross triumphant on the main, | | O 10 | London | 27 |
| To cross the Tow'rings of an equal Soul, | | O 309 | Irene | 41 |

CROSS'D
| Our Schemes for ever cross'd, our Mines discover'd, | | O 273 | Irene | 22 |

CROUD
| Unnumber'd suppliants croud Preferment's gate, | | O 33 | Vanity Wishes | 73 |
| And all the sons of ravage croud the war; | | O 43 | Vanity Wishes | 250 |

CROUD	(CONTINUED)	PAGE	TITLE	LINE
With all the sons of ravage croud the war;		O 43	Vanity Wishes	V 250
But everlasting dictates croud his tongue,		O 43	Vanity Wishes	273
In croud at once, where none the pass defend,		O 46	Vanity Wishes	337
"Toil on, dull croud, in extacy, he cries,		O 82	Young Author	15
And croud the fattend fields, the ghosts that wander		Y 120	Irene	V 31
Assembling nations croud thy port.		Y 136	Irene	V 27
They croud my camp with voluntary tribute		Y 136	Irene	V 27B
Hast thou grown old amidst the Croud of Courts,		O 281	Irene	32
Aw'd by the Croud, and by their Slaves restrain'd?		O 312	Irene	22

CROUDED
And watch the busy scenes of crouded life;		O 30	Vanity Wishes	4
And all the busy scenes of crouded life;		Y 92	Vanity Wishes	V 4
And Fate lies crouded in a narrow Space.		O 287	Irene	5
How rarely would they meet in crouded Courts,		O 308	Irene	16

CROUDS
And crouds with crimes the records of mankind;		O 31	Vanity Wishes	24
Ye patriot Crouds, who burn for England's Fame,		O 57	Prologue Comus	1
O then, when conquer'd crouds confess thy sway,		O 81	Lady Birthday	9
Then melt, ye fair, while crouds around you sigh,		O 84	Epi Dist Moth.	42
From Crouds that hide a Monarch from himself,		O 262	Irene	8
From Solitude to Crouds, from Crouds to Solitude,		O 263	Irene	20
From Solitude to Crouds, from Crouds to Solitude,		O 263	Irene	20
With Raptures such as fire the Pagan Crouds,		O 286	Irene	3
Glory, the casual Gift of thoughtless Crouds!		O 305	Irene	31
Betray'd by Falshood, or by Crouds o'erborn?		O 315	Irene	7
While unavailing Anger crouds thy Tongue		O 327	Irene	6
While unavailing passion crouds your tongue		O 368	Irene	V 14
And with laborious crouds the plains were fill'd.		Y 23	Tr Add. Battle	29

CROWD
And crowd with sudden wealth the rising dome;		O 19	London	203
In crowd at once, where none the fort defend,		Y 107	Vanity Wishes	V 337
The fickle crowd with fortune comes and goes;		O 138	Tr Rambler 153	1
Round him crowd the listing Woods,		O 148	Tr Boet III.12	V 11
Approach the and crowd		Y 131	Irene	V 32B
May throngs of beautious virgins 'round thee crowd,		Y 3	On a Daffodill	13

CROWD'S
| But hark! th' affrighted crowd's tumultuous cries | | O 18 | London | 182 |

CROWDED
| Ere I could range them on the crowded Deck, | | O 271 | Irene | 28 |

CROWDS
Scarce can our fields, such crowds at Tyburn die,		O 21	London	242
Well may we fear, such crowds at Tyburn die,		Y 60	London	V 242
While Crowds aloft the laureat Bust behold,		O 58	Prologue Comus	23
While Crowds aloft the laureat Dust behold,		O 58	Prologue Comus	V 23
And crowds of godlike Romans sunk to hell.		O 77	Festina Lente	16
He stop unmindfull of observing crowds		Y 187	Irene	V 5

CROWN
'Tis yours to crown Desert--beyond the Grave!		O 58	Prologue Comus	38
And crown the bowl with new-prest wine		O 72	Hor. Epode II	52
To her transferr'd the Offer of a Crown.		O 259	Irene	124
she courted fate & scorn'd a crown		Y 191	Irene	V 16
For which Aspasia scorn'd the Turkish Crown?		O 314	Irene	17
Two bowls with oyl and milk I'll yearly crown,		Y 7	Virgil Daphnis	45

CROWN'D
| Or when with golden Apples crown'd | | O 72 | Hor. Epode II | 23 |
| The board with varied plenty crown'd | | O 191 | Tr. Medea I | 19 |

CROWNS
| The Myrtle crowns the happy lovers heads, | | O 95 | Sprig of Myrtl | 9 |
| Immortal Crowns and Fulness of Enjoyment? | | O 276 | Irene | 14 |

CROWS
| And left-hand crows, from an old hollow oak, | | O 65 | Virgil Past.I | 24 |

CRUEL
Cruel with guilt, and daring with despair,		O 21	London	238
On cruel Pluto's Altar dye,		O 69	Hor.II Ode 14	6
And cruel Danaus' bloody Brood		O 69	Hor.II Ode 14	19
More false, more cruel than the seas and wind.		O 82	Young Author	14
More false, more cruel than the seas or wind.		O 82	Young Author	V 14
But cruel virgins meet severer fates;		O 84	Epi Dist Moth.	28
Ere yet the Foe found Leisure to be cruel,		O 252	Irene	94
The cruel Doom of hapless Menodorus--		O 270	Irene	4
Some cruel Stratagem of jealous Beauty!		O 326	Irene	37
Be just ye Slaves, and, to be Slaves, be cruel,		O 334	Irene	73
But now their cruel enemies draw near		Y 24	Tr Add. Battle	90

CRUELL
| For fear retards their flight, the cruell Crane | | O 76 | Tr Add. Battle | 31 |

CRUELTY
And weary Cruelty remits her Tortures.		O 249	Irene	10
Then call it not our Cruelty, nor Crime,		O 327	Irene	28
Ye Slaves of Cruelty, ye Tools of Rage,		O 332	Irene	22
In which the Pygmie wept his cruelty.		Y 24	Tr Add. Battle	63

CRUSH
Does envy seize thee? crush th' upbraiding joy,		O 32	Vanity Wishes	39
For idle Hours, and crush him at my Leisure.		O 275	Irene	71
Him I can crush at leisure.		O 367	Irene	V 30
Lest baneful discord crush our infant Scheme,		O 299	Irene	52

CRUSH'D
Toil crush'd conceit, and man was of a piece;		O 32	Vanity Wishes	54
Then crush'd by Rules, and weaken'd as refin'd,		O 52	Pro Drury-Lane	29
And crush'd the yet unanimated young.		Y 23	Tr Add. Battle	49

		PAGE	TITLE		LINE
CRY					
	Yet still one gen'ral cry the skies assails, ...	O	32	Vanity Wishes	45
	Yet still one gen'ral cry the skies assails, ...	O	32	Vanity Wishes	V 45
	Then shall some Argive loud insulting cry, ...	O	74	Tr. Iliad Bk 6	25
	Cry not when his father dies, ...	O	183	Burlesque Vega	2
	In bed we laugh, in bed we cry, ...	O	184	Tr. Benserade	1
	Against his King, and cry, Remember Justice?	O	286	Irene	12
	Just as it reach'd my Lips, a sudden Cry	O	316	Irene	27
	What Cry? The Stratagem? Did then Abdalla?--	O	317	Irene	30
	What cry? what stratagem? had then Abdalla-- . .	Y	194	Irene	V 30
	And heard th' ill omen'd catcall's direful cry.	Y	67	Prologue Lethe	10
CRY'D					
	(Cry'd Daphne whisp'ring from the yielding tree;) . .	O	106	Eliza plucking	6
	Join'd Cali's Hand to mine, and falt'ring cry'd, . .	O	272	Irene	8
CULTIVATE					
	They cultivate at ease the gentler arts in quiet . . .	Y	177	Irene	V 117
CUMBROUS					
	From beneath the cumbrous Weight;	O	145	Tr Boeth. II.4	12
CUP					
	Shall long detain the cup, ...	O	159	Par Hermit III	6
CUPID					
	No pug, nor favourite Cupid there enjoys	O	84	Epi Dist Moth.	20
CUPID'S					
	And all the pens of Cupid's wing	O	127	To Lyce, Lady	19
CUPIDS					
	In whose fair cheeks destructive Cupids wait, ...	O	83	Epi Dist Moth.	3
CURE					
	They sing, they dance, clean shoes, or cure a clap; . .	O	15	London	114
	And cure the throbbing of an anxious heart;	O	95	Sprig of Myrtl	V 12
	To yield to remedies is half the cure.	O	140	Tr Rambler 178	1
	When desp'rate Ills demand a speedy Cure, ...	O	301	Irene	85
CURIO'S					
	Bright wisdom teach me Curio's art, ...	O	126	An Ode	38
CURIOUS					
	Thou, who survey'st these walls with curious eye, . . .	O	117	Epitaph Hanmer	1
	To make thy curious web delight, ...	O	119	To Miss Purse	2
	To make the curious web delight, ...	O	119	To Miss Purse	V 2
	Amid the storms of war, with curious eyes	O	130	Tr. Rambler 8	1
	Here death has clos'd the curious eyes	O	154	Epita. Hogarth	3
CURLING					
	They to the dome where smoke with curling play . . .	O	192	Tr. Medea II	5
CURLS					
	This day the powder'd curls and golden coat, ...	O	60	Pro Good Nat'd	21
CURRENT					
	Swim darkling down the Current of his fate?	O	47	Vanity Wishes	V 346
	Down whose current clear and strong, ...	O	159	Tr. Rio Verde	2
CURS'D					
	In those curs'd walls, devote to vice and gain, ...	O	10	London	37
	And Sedley curs'd the form that pleas'd a king.	O	46	Vanity Wishes	322
	Despis'd and curs'd, Leontius must descend	O	305	Irene	27
	Broke out in Perfidy--Oh curs'd Aspasia, ...	O	316	Irene	10
	And thou, the curs'd Accomplice of her Treason, . . .	O	331	Irene	5
	Accus'd the Gods and curs'd each luckless star. . . .	Y	6	Virgil Daphnis	6
CURSE					
	Beneath each Curse of unrelenting Heav'n, ...	O	292	Irene	86
	With every curse of angry heav'n afflicted beneath . .	O	357	Irene	V 15
	each					
CURSES					
	Curses the dull Delays of ling'ring Mercy, ...	O	327	Irene	12
CURST					
	Curst as the Tyrant of th' infernal Realms, ...	O	294	Irene	134
CUT					
	And cut with joy the wond'ring Skies.	O	70	Hor.II Ode XX	4
CUTS					
	That silent cuts the dreary plains, ...	O	69	Hor.II Ode 14	18
CYNTHIA					
	When pale-fac'd Cynthia sheds her silver light	O	77	Tr Add. Battle	45
CYPRESS					
	Alone the Cypress shall attend.	O	69	Hor.II Ode 14	24
DAEDALUS					
	Now Daedalus, behold, by fate assign'd, ...	O	136	Tr Rambler 129	1
DAEMONS					
	And burning daemons tremble at her torments	Y	168	Irene	V135D
DAGGER					
	And leaves, unseen, a dagger in your breast.	O	21	London	241
	And plants, unseen, a dagger in your breast.	O	21	London	V 241
	Guide the Sons dagger to the Fathers heart	O	352	Irene	V 4
	And bar'd my Bosom to the Ruffian's Dagger.	O	331	Irene	20
DAGGERS					
	Meet unexpected Daggers in his Way, ...	O	274	Irene	48
	Imperfect sounds of Greece--and love--and	Y	144	Irene	V 80
	daggers					
	Daggers and love? What love but fair	Y	144	Irene	V 81
	Irene?					
DAILY					
	Thank Heav'n in daily hymns for my our deliverance . .	Y	166	Irene	V 93
DAINTIES					
	Despise the dainties of a venal lord:	O	20	London	219
	With unbought dainties load the board;	O	73	Hor. Epode II	54
DALLY					
	Dar'st thou thus dally with Abdalla's Passion?	O	307	Irene	8

		PAGE	TITLE	LINE
DAME				
	When some proud Grecian dame shall tasks impose,	O 74	Tr. Iliad Bk 6	21
	I pleas'd my Master, and I pleas'd my Dame.	O 174	Tr Epitaph Dog	2
DAMES				
	At sight of sparkling bowls or beauteous dames,	O 142	In Baretti Bk.	1
DAMN				
	Where no sour criticks damn, nor sneers molest,	O 82	Young Author	27
DAMNATION				
	And stun me with the Yellings of Damnation!	O 328	Irene	51
DAMP				
	Will damp my joys, and cloud the happy days	O 370	Irene	V 23
DANAUS'				
	And cruel Danaus' bloody Brood	O 69	Hor.II Ode 14	19
DANC'D				
	Round him danc'd the listning Woods,	O 148	Tr Boet III.12	11
DANCE				
	They sing, they dance, clean shoes, or cure a clap;	O 15	London	114
	By day the frolick, and the dance by night,	O 46	Vanity Wishes	326
	Here Hunt may box, or Mahomet may dance.	O 53	Pro Drury-Lane	46
	"Round his chamber dance and play,	O 186	Anacreon Ode 9	36
	The mazy dance together trace.	O 231	Tr Horace IV.7	6
	Dance o'er the Sparkling Waves--Go happy Bark	O 364	Irene	V 30
DANCES				
	Jocund he dances o'er the wat'ry way,	O 82	Young Author	5
	Then dances jocund o'er the watery way,	O 82	Young Author	V 5
DANCING				
	Though dancing mountains witness'd Orpheus near;	O 43	Vanity Wishes	270
DANG'ROUS				
	Ah! think not, in the dang'rous hour,	O 121	To Miss Playin	7
	Ah! think not, in the dang'rous Bower,	O 121	To Miss Playin	V 7
DANGER				
	Yet hope not life from grief or danger free,	O 37	Vanity Wishes	155
	Yet dream not life from grief or danger free,	Y 99	Vanity Wishes	V 155
	Mingles Danger with Delight;	O 145	Tr Boeth. II.4	14
	Oft in Danger yet alive	O 178	Thrale 35 Year	1
	And every Danger shocks with double Horror.	O 261	Irene	21
	Betray my King to Negligence of Danger.	O 275	Irene	73
	Lead us to Danger, and abash their Victors?	O 284	Irene	43
	Impartial weigh the Pleasure with the Danger.	O 285	Irene	9
	No more should Danger fright, or Want distress	O 291	Irene	56
	Gaze at their Height and tremble at their Danger:	O 293	Irene	116
	Dispatch; th' encreasing Danger	O 297	Irene	12
	Will not the Patriot share the Traytor's Danger?	O 300	Irene	62
	Let Prudence obviate an impending Danger.	O 309	Irene	19
	'Tis Madness to provoke superfluous Danger,	O 318	Irene	21
	Has left the slaves behind, nay then there's danger.	Y 198	Irene	V 34
	But since none knows the Danger of a Moment,	O 321	Irene	48
	We are in danger by this pause	Y 206	Irene	V 11
DANGEROUS				
	Mark'd out by dangerous parts he meets the shock,	O 39	Vanity Wishes	171
	Yet dares to venture on the dangerous stage,	Y 67	Prologue Lethe	11
DANGERS				
	In vain, these dangers past, your doors you close,	O 21	London	236
	The dangers gather as the treasures rise.	O 31	Vanity Wishes	28
	No dangers fright him, and no labours tire;	O 40	Vanity Wishes	194
	Yet in that narrow Space what Dangers rise?--	O 287	Irene	6
	What Fears, what Griefs, what Dangers hast thou known?	O 295	Irene	22
	Foes unforeseen, and Dangers unsuspected.	O 298	Irene	26
	Resolve to share our Dangers and our Toils,	O 320	Irene	29
	On dangers which your safety bids you shun,	Y 18	Tr. Iliad Bk 6	20
	Nor tempt the dangers of this deathfull day	Y 19	Tr. Iliad Bk 6	47
DANUBE				
	And stain with blood the Danube or the Rhine;	O 39	Vanity Wishes	182
	Pour forth their Legions, and the roaring Danube	O 264	Irene	17
	Pour forth the Legions and the Wondring Danube	O 353	Irene	V 1
DAPHNE				
	(Cry'd Daphne whisp'ring from the yielding tree;)	O 106	Eliza plucking	6
DAPHNIS				
	Daphnis with ivy wreath'd the jav'lins round	Y 6	Virgil Daphnis	15
	Now beauteous Daphnis cloath'd with heav'nly light,	Y 7	Virgil Daphnis	32
	Libations he shall pour to Daphnis praise.	Y 7	Virgil Daphnis	V 52
DAPHNIS'				
	The nymphs bewail'd poor Daphnis' hapless death	Y 6	Virgil Daphnis	1
	By Daphnis' skill th' Armenian tigers broke	Y 6	Virgil Daphnis	13
DAR'D				
	Dar'd have provok'd a foe to single fight,	Y 23	Tr Add. Battle	39
DAR'ST				
	Dar'st thou thus dally with Abdalla's Passion?	O 307	Irene	8
DARE SEE DURST				
	And dare to slumber o'er the Gazetteer:	O 13	London	72
	Or dare to murmur in the flow'ry Glade;	O 111	To Posterity	22
	Can Cali dare the Stroke of heav'nly Justice,	O 272	Irene	3
	Nor dare to pass th' insuperable Bound.	O 292	Irene	92
	The Doom of Guilt alone, nor dare to seize	O 316	Irene	14
	Once more I dare thy Sword, behold the Prize,	O 319	Irene	28
	Nor dare henceforth to shock Irene's Walks.	O 325	Irene	7
	Nor dare to spare the Life his Frown condemns.	O 325	Irene	10
	The Prayer I cannot grant--I dare not hear.	O 328	Irene	48
DARES				
	None dares with impious steel the grove to rend,	O 139	Tr Rambler 168	1
	In Reason, Nature, Truth he dares to trust:	O 246	Irene Prologue	33

	PAGE	TITLE	LINE
DARES (CONTINUED)			
Dares join Leontius' Name with Fear or Falsehood? . . .	O 304	Irene	13
Yet dares to venture on the dangerous stage, ...	Y 67	Prologue Lethe	11
DARING			
Cruel with guilt, and daring with despair, ...	O 21	London	238
The daring Greeks deride the martial show, ...	O 42	Vanity Wishes	235
Might Truth intrude with daring flight, ...	O 121	To Miss Playin	20
Forgive, great Jove, the daring enterprize.	O 136	Tr Rambler 129	6
Our daring Bard with Spirit unconfin'd, ...	O 246	Irene Prologue	7
Daring, tho' calm; and vigorous, tho' resign'd. . . .	O 246	Irene Prologue	10
Trembling to grant, nor daring to refuse, ...	O 260	Irene	126
With vain (fruitless) labour of the daring flight . . .	Y 127	Irene	V 3
For daring Truth, and Turbulence of Honour?	O 299	Irene	37
When daring Vice insults eternal Justice, ...	O 314	Irene	23
But soon though shalt lament thy daring folly	Y 198	Irene	V 33
DARK			
Then, when dark arts obscur'd each fierce debate, . . .	O 118	Epitaph Hanmer	23
Dark is the sun, and loathsome is the day.	O 139	Tr Rambler 171	1
Obscure, unpriz'd, and dark, the magnet lies, . . .	O 141	Tr Rambler 199	1
Start at the Light, and tremble in the Dark;	O 266	Irene	30
In the dark Precincts of the gaping Grave, ...	O 272	Irene	4
Perhaps the Clouds of dark Conspiracy	O 275	Irene	74
And dark Perplexity distracts my Counsels.	O 275	Irene	89
They see the Sun surmount the dark Eclipse, ...	O 287	Irene	5
Search to the dark Recesses of the Soul, ...	O 308	Irene	13
In these dark Moments of suspended Fate, ...	O 313	Irene	1
I guess'd her dark Designs, and warn'd the Sultan, . .	O 327	Irene	26
The dark horizon ravish'd from their sight. . . .	Y 24	Tr Add. Battle	75
DARKEN'D			
A sudden Mist o'ercasts my darken'd Soul, ...	O 295	Irene	12
DARKEST			
In misery's darkest caverns known, ...	O 201	Death Dr Levet	17
DARKLING			
Roll darkling down the torrent of his fate?	O 47	Vanity Wishes	346
Swim darkling down the Current of his fate?	O 47	Vanity Wishes	V 346
On darkling man in pure effulgence shine, ...	O 130	Tr. Rambler 7	3
DARKNESS			
Nor light nor darkness bring his pain relief, ...	O 32	Vanity Wishes	43
Her teeth the night with darkness dyes, ...	O 127	To Lyce, Lady	13
Each Night protected by the friendly Darkness, . . .	O 251	Irene	59
Till interposing darkness bars the prospect.	Y 155	Irene	V 25
To Silence and to Rest. The Hours of Darkness, . . .	O 302	Irene	2
And all within is Darkness and Confusion;	O 315	Irene	32
Dispells the darkness with his golden ray	Y 23	Tr Add. Battle	23
In half a year of darkness lost.	Y 38	Lady Leaving	4
DARKSOM			
Where the wild fig trees join their darksom shade . . .	Y 19	Tr. Iliad Bk 6	52
DARKSOME			
O guide me through life's darksome way, ...	O 100	Ode Friendship	14
O guide us through life's darksome way, ...	O 100	Ode Friendship	V 14
DARKVISAG'D			
Where the darkvisag'd Natives fry, ...	O 79	Feast St Simon	34
DARLING			
This, only this, provokes the darling muse.	O 17	London	V 161
How nations sink, by darling schemes oppress'd, . . .	O 31	Vanity Wishes	13
How families sink, by darling schemes oppress'd, . . .	Y 92	Vanity Wishes	V 13
The Empire's Darling, and the Soldier's Boast; . . .	O 257	Irene	69
Now shalt thou shine the Darling of the Sultan, . . .	O 329	Irene	3
DART			
Than when a blockhead's insult points the dart. . . .	O 18	London	169
Fate wings with ev'ry wish th' afflictive dart, . . .	O 31	Vanity Wishes	15
Dart the quick taunt, and edge the piercing gibe? . .	O 33	Vanity Wishes	62
Should Beauty blunt on fops her fatal dart, ...	O 37	Vanity Wishes	151
Nor taints with death the envenom'd dart, ...	O 65	Hor I Ode xxii	3
Nor taints with Death th' envenom'd Dart, ...	O 66	To A. Fuscus	3
By thee Orestes plung'd his vengefull dart	O 77	Festina Lente	13
Live till the Sun forgets to dart his Beams, ...	O 262	Irene	3
Shall dart their am'rous Glances at the Fair, . . .	O 304	Irene	35
When erring Fury throws the random dart	O 345	Irene	V 28
Weak Man with erring Rage may throw the Dart, . . .	O 335	Irene	14
Provok'd Diana with a vengefull dart	Y 19	Tr. Iliad Bk 6	42
DARTED			
Then all is past he cried--and darted from us; . . .	O 317	Irene	32
DARTS			
Insidious Malice aims her Darts in vain;	O 322	Irene	2
Oft from behind they wounded them with darts . . .	Y 23	Tr Add. Battle	42
Temper their swords and point their missive darts. . .	Y 24	Tr Add. Battle	77
DASH			
Urg'd me to dash it to the Ground untouch'd, ...	O 316	Irene	28
DASH'D			
And dash'd the Might of Asem from the Ramparts. . . .	O 312	Irene	12
DASHING			
Lull'd by the beating winds and dashing show'rs! . . .	O 135	Tr Rambler 117	2
Dashing Waves and shatter'd Shoars, ...	O 145	Tr Boeth. II.4	18
DAUBER			
And hiss the dauber ruin dawb the wall.	Y 95	Vanity Wishes	V 90
DAUGHTER			
A sister sickens, or a daughter mourns.	O 45	Vanity Wishes	302
Wilt thou descend, fair Daughter of Perfection, . . .	O 276	Irene	1
Irene rise, thou daughter of perfection--or	Y 145	Irene	V 1
beauty			

73

```
                                                      PAGE   TITLE          LINE
DAUGHTER'S
     The daughter's petulance, the son's expence,  . . . .  O  44 Vanity Wishes    280
DAUGHTERS
     Reject the Daughters of contending Kings;  . . . . .   O 267 Irene              7
DAUNTLESS
     There dauntless Truth shall blast the vile Accuser,  . .  O 326 Irene          42
DAVID
     Give to St. David one true Briton more.  . . . . . .   O   9 London             8
DAWB
     And why should odious ruin dawb the wall.  . . . . .   Y  95 Vanity Wishes  V  90
     And hiss the dauber ruin dawb the wall.  . . . . . .   Y  95 Vanity Wishes  V  90
DAWN
     To-morrow's Dawn shall see the Turkish King  . . . . .  O 303 Irene             9
     To-morrow's Dawn shall see the mighty Cali  . . . . .   O 303 Irene            11
     And hail the rosy Dawn of rising Health.  . . . . . .   O 320 Irene            27
DAWNING
     My Zeal marks Gladness dawning on thy Cheek,  . . . . .  O 286 Irene            2
DAY    SEE BIRTH-DAY
     And plead for pirates in the face of day;  . . . . .   O  11 London            54
     The peaceful slumber, self-approving day,  . . . . .   O  14 London            89
     Illustrious Edward! from the realms of day,  . . . . .  O  15 London           99
     And pour on misty Doubt resistless day;  . . . . . .   O  37 Vanity Wishes    146
     Hide, blushing Glory, hide Pultowa's day:  . . . . .   O  41 Vanity Wishes    210
     Whose peaceful day Benevolence endears,  . . . . . .   O  44 Vanity Wishes    295
     New sorrow rises as the day returns,  . . . . . . .    O  45 Vanity Wishes    301
     Each passing day some comfort sorrow finds.  . . . . .  Y 105 Vanity Wishes  V 301
     By day the frolick, and the dance by night,  . . . .   O  46 Vanity Wishes    326
     Exulting Folly hail'd the joyful Day,  . . . . . . .   O  52 Pro Drury-Lane    37
     And chase the new-blown Bubbles of the Day.  . . . . .  O  53 Pro Drury-Lane    50
     This day the powder'd curls and golden coat,  . . . .  O  60 Pro Good Nat'd    21
     In pleasing Dreams he cheats the Day  . . . . . . .    O  72 Hor. Epode II     35
     The day will come, in which proud Troy shall yield,  . .  O  74 Tr. Iliad Bk 6  13
     Before that day, by some brave hero's hand,  . . . .   O  75 Tr. Iliad Bk 6    29
     May this returning day for ever find  . . . . . . .    O  80 Lady Birthday      3
     Dark is the sun, and loathsome is the day.  . . . . .  O 139 Tr Rambler 171     1
     To snatch the blessings of the plenteous day;  . . . .  O 151 The Ant           6
     Comets! come every day--and stay a year.  . . . . . .  O 177 Tr Dist Modena     2
     As on we toil from day to day,  . . . . . . . .       O 200 Death Dr Levet     2
     As on we toil from day to day,  . . . . . . . .       O 200 Death Dr Levet     2
     The modest wants of ev'ry day  . . . . . . . .        O 201 Death Dr Levet    23
     The toil of ev'ry day supplied.  . . . . . . . .      O 201 Death Dr Levet    24
     The busy day, the peaceful night,  . . . . . . .      O 202 Death Dr Levet    29
     The busy day, the cheerful night,  . . . . . . .      O 202 Death Dr Levet  V 29
     From those bright Regions of eternal Day,  . . . . .   O 253 Irene             99
     And Business from the Day. In her Apartments  . . . .  O 260 Irene            131
     At least this Day be calm--If we succeed,  . . . . .   O 260 Irene            141
     Haste Go Mustapha go to celebrate the day  . . . . .   Y 129 Irene          V  25
     Cali, this Day with hypocritick Zeal,  . . . . . . .   O 273 Irene             43
     Was but to chuse the Graces of the Day;  . . . . . .   O 278 Irene             63
     Each Day and shall be made happy with new entertainments  O 350 Irene       V  24
     Empire and Love shall share the blissful Day,  . . . .  O 279 Irene           90
     Yet, on a Day like this, when Expectation  . . . . .   O 280 Irene             30
     Not till this Day thou saw'st this fatal Fair;  . . .  O 281 Irene             54
     Strange! that this gen'ral Fraud from Day to Day  . .   O 283 Irene            26
     Strange! that this gen'ral Fraud from Day to Day  . .   O 283 Irene            26
     Henceforth for ever happy be this Day,  . . . . . .    O 308 Irene             1
     Will cloud my Triumphs, and pollute the Day.  . . . .  O 310 Irene             3
     In that black Day when slaughter'd Thousands fell  . .  O 312 Irene            7
     The Day disast'rous that secures our Flight;  . . . .  O 317 Irene            46
     The day disastrous, that secures my honor  . . . . .   Y 195 Irene          V  46
     Review this Day.  . . . . . . . . . .                 O 323 Irene             11
     Nor let the Crimes of this detested Day  . . . . . .   O 329 Irene             54
     Let one just Act conclude the hateful Day.  . . . . .  O 333 Irene            50
     That day, that mournfull day, no chearfull song  . . .  Y   6 Virgil Daphnis    7
     That day, that mournfull day, no chearfull song  . . .  Y   6 Virgil Daphnis    7
     But, ah! before arise that hapless day  . . . . . .   Y  18 Tr. Iliad Bk 6    24
     All stemm'd in one sad day the Stygian tyde.  . . . .  Y  18 Tr. Iliad Bk 6    35
     Nor tempt the dangers of this deathfull day  . . . .   Y  19 Tr. Iliad Bk 6    47
     And paint the horrors of the dreadfull day.  . . . .   Y  22 Tr Add. Battle     7
     That day what legions by his faulchion bled!  . . . .  Y  25 Tr Add. Battle   120
     He turn'd awhile the fortune of the day  . . . . . .   Y  25 Tr Add. Battle   123
     And bless me with continu'd day.  . . . . . . . .     Y  39 Lady Leaving      12
DAY'S
     Of two day's long  . . . . . . . . . . .             Y 300 Fanny Burney       2
DAYS   SEE DOG-DAYS
     Since worth, he cries, in these degen'rate days,  . . .  O  10 London          35
     Enlarge my life with multitude of days,  . . . . . .  O  43 Vanity Wishes    255
     And proudly hop'd to pimp in future Days.  . . . . .   O  52 Pro Drury-Lane    24
     Immortal Patrons of succeeding Days,  . . . . . . .    O  57 Prologue Comus     5
     Then to the Gods, on solemn days,  . . . . . . .      O  73 Hor. Epode II     63
     Adorn'd in Roman time the brightest days,  . . . . .   O 189 Seeing Montagu     2
     The rites deriv'd from ancient days  . . . . . . .    O 190 Tr. Medea I        1
     Bears toilsome Days, and wakes long tedious Nights:  . .  O 247 Irene Epilogue  22
     For what is Length of Days without Irene?  . . . . .   O 262 Irene             6
     The Pride and Terror of succeeding Days,  . . . . . .  O 268 Irene            12
     These Days of Love and Pleasure charm not thee;  . . .  O 271 Irene            2
     Diffuse a Brightness on our future Days;  . . . . . .  O 301 Irene            100
     Will damp my joys, and cloud the happy days  . . . .   O 370 Irene          V 23
DAZZLED
     Thy dazzled Soul with all its boasted Greatness,  . . .  O 292 Irene          99
```

		PAGE	TITLE	LINE

DE
Trop de frais. . . . . O 172 French Distich 2
Rien de Bon. . . . . O 172 French Distich 10
Oude lithos, oude Sideron--nostro sequitur de Vulnere . O 347 Irene V 23
   sanguis.

DEAD
And here a female atheist talks you dead. . . . . . O 9 London 18
For English vengeance wars not with the dead. . . . O 61 Pro Word Wise 4
For Mystes dead you ever mourn; . . . . O 67 Hor. II Ode IX 10
Of Fields with dead bestrew'd around, ... O 78 Feast St Simon 1
I scorn the multitude, alive and dead. . . . . . O 141 Tr Rambler 208 4
Or wake the Dead to warn us of its Fall? . . . . O 250 Irene 47
Pour forth her Dead to warn us of its fall? . . . O 365 Irene V 22
Who? the dead Irene? . . . . O 332 Irene 17
On his dead body let a tomb be plac'd . . . . . Y 7 Virgil Daphnis 28
Here with dead mice the marsh was strew'd around; . . Y 24 Tr Add. Battle 58
His arm alone rais'd bulwarks of the dead. . . . . Y 25 Tr Add. Battle 121
Lies as dead as any nail! . . . . Y 300 Extemp. Elegy 2

DEAF
Deem us not deaf to Woe, nor blind to Beauty, . . . O 327 Irene 29
Deaf to the critick, sullen to the friend, ... Y 67 Prologue Lethe 5

DEAR
Alass, dear Friend, the fleeting years . . . . . O 68 Hor.II Ode 14 1
Who to their Lord were ever dear, ... O 78 Feast St Simon 10
I Therefore pray thee, Renny dear, ... O 158 Par Hermit III 1
I pray thee, gentle Renny dear, ... O 158 Par Hermit III V 1
Dear hapless Maid--tempestuous Grief o'erbears . . . O 252 Irene 77
Dear helpless Maid--tempestuous Grief o'erbears . . . O 252 Irene V 77
My reasoning Pow'rs--Dear, hapless, lost Aspasia! . . O 252 Irene 78
And your new Charge, that dear, that heavn'ly Maid.-- . O 270 Irene 5
But while Demetrius, dear lamented Name! . . . . . O 290 Irene 47
Yet let me watch her dear departing Steps, ... O 297 Irene 17
This Calm, these Joys, dear Innocence! are thine, . . O 313 Irene 9
Devolve, dear Maid, thy Sorrows on the Wretch, . . . O 316 Irene 16
Those Groves, whose Shades embow'r'd the dear Irene, . O 333 Irene 46

DEAR-BOUGHT
Explain their country's dear-bought rights away, . . O 11 London 53
Wreaths which at last the dear-bought right convey . . O 40 Vanity Wishes 189
Great souls whose the dear-bought right convey . . . Y 100 Vanity Wishes V 189

DEARER
Far dearer than his own or father's life . . . . . Y 18 Tr. Iliad Bk 6 6

DEAREST
And fruitfull fields, my dearest Friend, ... O 69 Hor.II Ode 14 22
But dearest Hector while thou liv'st I see . . . . Y 19 Tr. Iliad Bk 6 44

DEATH
Prepare for death, if here at night you roam, . . . O 21 London 224
And restless fire precipitates on death. . . . . . O 31 Vanity Wishes 20
And restless enterprize impells to death. . . . . Y 92 Vanity Wishes V 20
But hear his death, ye blockheads, hear and sleep. . O 39 Vanity Wishes 174
But hear his death, ye blockheads, hear and weep. . . O 39 Vanity Wishes V 174
And steals to death from anguish and from shame. . . O 43 Vanity Wishes 254
Counts death kind Nature's signal of retreat: . . . O 48 Vanity Wishes 364
Thinks death kind Nature's signal of retreat: . . . O 48 Vanity Wishes V 364
Nor taints with death the envenom'd dart, ... O 65 Hor I Ode xxii 3
Nor taints with Death th' envenom'd Dart, ... O 66 To A. Fuscus 3
Nor would inexorable Death . . . . O 69 Hor.II Ode 14 11
After your death, the lavish heir . . . . O 69 Hor.II Ode 14 25
And view with cheerful eyes approaching death. . . . O 74 Tr. Iliad Bk 6 10
And grasps the bloody sand involv'd in death. . . . O 76 Tr Add. Battle 17
Impending death they strive to 'scape in vain . . . O 76 Tr Add. Battle 30
Hurry'd to death by thee, Flaminius fell, ... O 77 Festina Lente 15
Though fierce Barbarians threatend death . . . . . O 79 Feast St Simon 40
Here death has clos'd the curious eyes . . . . . O 154 Epita. Hogarth 3
Here clos'd in Death th' attentive Eyes . . . . . O 155 Epita. Hogarth V 3
On the Death of Dr. Robert Levet . . . . O 200 Death Dr Levet T
And hov'ring death prepar'd the blow, ... O 201 Death Dr Levet 14
Death broke at once the vital chain, ... O 202 Death Dr Levet 35
With sport above and death below; . . . . O 203 Tr. on Skating 2
With Monuments of Death proclaim his Courage; . . . O 255 Irene 31
Burning in vain, delays the Stroke of Death? . . . O 257 Irene 66
   The Tyrant's Death. . . . . O 257 Irene 73
To Threats of Torture, Death and Violation. . . . . O 259 Irene 112
Then 'tis decreed. (then death or empire.) . . . . Y 130 Irene V 20
Death rises to my View, with all his Terrors; . . . O 265 Irene 12
Too strong for Love, have hurried him on Death. . . O 267 Irene 48
My Father call'd me to his Couch of Death, ... O 272 Irene 7
Of total Death and careless of Hereafter; . . . . O 276 Irene 19
Secure of total death, and careless of hereafter or gay . Y 146 Irene V 20
Till burning Death shoots through their wither'd Limbs? . O 282 Irene 6
And laughs and wantons in the Jaws of Death. . . . O 283 Irene 11
Till interposing Death destroys the Prospect! . . . O 283 Irene 25
Till interposing Death denys the prospect. . . . . O 374 Irene V 26
The Dread of instant Death restrains my Tongue? . . O 289 Irene 25
Reflect that Life and Death, affecting Sounds, . . . O 290 Irene 26
Close like th' eternal Bars of Death upon thee, . . O 292 Irene 80
Close like th' eternal Bars of Death upon You . . . O 357 Irene V 10
And pass'd uninjur'd through the Walks of Death? . . O 296 Irene 29
Nor end my Terrors with the Sultan's Death; . . . . O 300 Irene 67
On ev'ry Side Confusion, Rage and Death, ... O 300 Irene 70
What Hand, when Death has snatch'd away Demetrius, . . O 301 Irene 88
Propitious Hours to Stratagem and Death, ... O 302 Irene 3

DEATH   (CONTINUED)   PAGE   TITLE   LINE
    Wake from thy Dream of Pow'r to Death and Tortures, . .   O 307 Irene   10
    Reserv'd to all the Pangs of tedious Death. . . . . .   O 312 Irene   25
    Whate'er their Scheme the Bassa's Death defeats it, . .   O 312 Irene   4
    My trembling nerves--sink at the dreadful scenes of blood Y 189 Irene   V 1H
        and death
    Cali disarm'd was born away to Death; . . . . . .   O 317 Irene   40
    Still dost thou flutter in the Jaws of Death? . . . .   O 318 Irene   17
    Alike my Death or thine is gain to thee, ...   O 319 Irene   32
    Your Robe of Mourning, and your Dogs of Death. . . .   O 325 Irene   5
    The Place appointed for his Master's Death. . . . . .   O 326 Irene   30
    Ordain'd the mournful Messengers of Death. . . . . .   O 326 Irene   35
    Enrob'd in Death--Dispatch her and be great. . . . .   O 326 Irene   3
    That thus constrain'd we speed the Stroke of Death. . .   O 327 Irene   30
    O name not Death! Distraction and Amazement, ...   O 328 Irene   31
    With peaceful Death, and Happiness eternal. . . . . .   O 328 Irene   47
    Safe in her Death, and in Demetrius' Flight, ...   O 329 Irene   1
    And add new Terrors to the Face of Death. . . . . .   O 330 Irene   8
    Name for the Scene of Death Irene's Chamber? . . . .   O 330 Irene   14
    Doom'd to her Death unpity'd and unheard, ...   O 332 Irene   20
    My spirits fail, I cannot name his death . . . . . .   Y 216 Irene   V 72
    The nymphs bewail'd poor Daphnis' hapless death . . .   Y   6 Virgil Daphnis   1
    My death is now decreed my death will come. . . . . .   Y 21 Tr. Iliad Bk 6   118
    My death is now decreed my death will come. . . . . .   Y 21 Tr. Iliad Bk 6   118
    Death in his look, and hands imbru'd in gore . . . .   Y 23 Tr Add. Battle   47
    And Death exulting stalk'd along the land. . . . . .   Y 23 Tr Add. Battle   53
    He tore them down and trampled them to death. . . . .   Y 24 Tr Add. Battle   87
DEATH'S
    And steal thy Life away. Death's horrid Angel . . . .   O 327 Irene   9
    And steal your life away. Death's horrid Angel . . .   O 368 Irene   V 17
DEATHFULL
    Nor tempt the dangers of this deathfull day . . . . .   Y 19 Tr. Iliad Bk 6   47
DEATHLESS
    So long renown'd in B<rya>n's deathless strain? . .   O 107 Lady F Assizes   2
DEBARD
    Deny'd Debard each privilege of human nature being . .   Y 165 Irene   V 81
DEBASED
    His Conduct Human Kind debased: . . . .   O 146 Tr Boeth III.4   6
DEBATE
    Where ne'er was known the form of mock debate, . . .   O 33 Vanity Wishes   57
    Where ne'er was heard the form of mock debate, ...   Y 94 Vanity Wishes   V 57
    While ladies interpose, and slaves debate. . . . . .   O 41 Vanity Wishes   214
    In bus'ness dext'rous, weighty in debate, ...   O 118 Epitaph Hanmer   13
    Then, when dark arts obscur'd each fierce debate, . . .   O 118 Epitaph Hanmer   23
DEBAUCH'D
    Ere masquerades debauch'd, excise oppress'd, ...   O 10 London   29
DEBT
    From age to age in everlasting debt; . . . .   O 39 Vanity Wishes   188
    Their grandsires glories debt; . . . .   Y 100 Vanity Wishes   V 188
    His bonds of debt, and mortgages of lands; . . . . .   O 44 Vanity Wishes   288
DEBTS
    Whome no contracted debts molest . . . .   O 71 Hor. Epode II   7
DECAY
    But all whom hunger spares, with age decay: . . . .   O   9 London   12
    To rust on medals, or on stones decay, ...   O 40 Vanity Wishes   190
    An age that melts with unperceiv'd decay, ...   O 44 Vanity Wishes   293
    An age that melts in unperceiv'd decay, ...   O 44 Vanity Wishes   V 293
    Year chases year, decay pursues decay, ...   O 45 Vanity Wishes   305
    Year chases year, decay pursues decay, ...   O 45 Vanity Wishes   305
    And Want hung threat'ning o'er her slow Decay. . . .   O 58 Prologue Comus   26
    No cold gradations of decay, ...   O 202 Death Dr Levet   34
DECAYS
    Like them man flourishes, like them decays. . . . . .   O 138 Tr Rambler 161   2
DECEIT
    He who still expects deceit, ...   O 176 Tr Metastasi I   5
DECEITFUL
    Deceitful Hope, and vain Desire, ...   O 121 To Miss Playin   13
    Thus on deceitful Etna's flow'ry Side, ...   O 315 Irene   33
DECEIVE
    Deceive--And make us happy by deceiving . . . . . .   Y 148 Irene   V 50
DECEIVING
    Deceive--And make us happy by deceiving . . . . . .   Y 148 Irene   V 50
DECEMBER
    To shake in dog-days, in December sweat. . . . . . .   O 16 London   143
    Thrice has December stripp'd the tree . . . .   Y 11 Tr Hor Epode 9   7
DECENT
    And burnt him decent on a funerall pile. . . . . . .   Y 18 Tr. Iliad Bk 6   31
DECIDE
    How just his hopes let Swedish Charles decide; . . . .   O 40 Vanity Wishes   192
    Soon may the final Stroke decide our Fate, ...   O 299 Irene   51
    The Rights of Princes let the Sword decide, ...   O 307 Irene   22
DECIDED
    Soon will th' unequal Contest be decided, ...   O 261 Irene   18
DECISIONS
    Implore his aid, in his decisions rest, ...   O 48 Vanity Wishes   355
DECK
    Perennial roses deck each purple vale, ...   O 84 Epi Dist Moth.   16
    Ere I could range them on the crowded Deck, ...   O 271 Irene   28
    To deck these Bow'rs each Region shall combine, . . .   O 279 Irene   88
DECK'D
    No regal Pageant deck'd with casual Honours, ...   O 268 Irene   19

	PAGE	TITLE	LINE

DECKS
    Nor dignifies the great, nor decks the fair.   . . . . .   O 141 Tr Rambler 199   4
    That decks the fair, or dignifies the great.   . . . . .   O 141 Tr Rambler 199   8
DECLAMATICN
    Till Declamation roar'd, while Passion slept.   O 52 Pro Drury-Lane   32
    Till Declamation soar'd, whilst Passion slept.   . . . . .   O 52 Pro Drury-Lane   V 32
DECLAR'D
    Declar'd the chief Associate of his Guilt.   . . . . .   O 331 Irene   11
    The Wretch, whose Guilt declar'd by tortur'd Cali,   . . .   O 334 Irene   64
    The wretch whose crimes declar'd by tortur'd Cali   . . .   Y 215 Irene   V 69A
DECLARE
    How just that scorn ere yet thy voice declare, ...   O 33 Vanity Wishes   71
    Declare thy Message, and expect thy Doom.   O 331 Irene   6
DECLIN'D
    For Years the Pow'r of Tragedy declin'd;   . . . .   O 52 Pro Drury-Lane   30
DECLINE
    The nymphs, who found their pow'r decline, ...   O 122 Stella Mourn.   3
    "Can a prudent Dove decline   . . . .   O 185 Anacreon Ode 9   23
    By sudden blasts, or slow decline, ...   O 200 Death Dr Levet   3
DECLINES
    Life declines from Thirtyfive;   . . . .   O 178 Thrale 35 Year   14
DECLINING
    Secure he tramples my declining Fame, ...   O 257 Irene   71
    Secure he tramples my declining Frame, ...   O 257 Irene   V 71
DECORATICNS
    The Wondring Sky shall shine with Decorations   . . . .   O 364 Irene   V 28
DECOY
    Some soft Decoy to lure me to Destruction!   . . . . .   O 331 Irene   4
DECREE
    So by their great decree Assyria fell   . . . .   O 76 Tr Add. Battle   37
DECREED
    The inexorable sisters have decreed   . . . . .   O 74 Tr. Iliad Bk 6   11
    Why, Sylvia, was it then decreed, ...   O 120 To Miss Purse   11
    Why, Stella, was it then decreed, ...   O 120 To Miss Purse   V 11
    Then 'tis decreed. (then death or empire.)   . . .   Y 130 Irene   V 20
    Well,--'tis decreed--This Night shall fix our Fate.   .   O 284 Irene   48
    Decreed to perish in Irene's Chamber!   . . . . . .   O 331 Irene   17
    Eternal justice thus her doom decreed   . . . .   O 345 Irene   V 32
    well th' Eternal Mind thus her doom decreed   . . . .   O 345 Irene   V 34
    My death is now decreed my death will come.   . . . . .   Y 21 Tr. Iliad Bk 6   118
DECRY
    Then prompt no more the Follies you decry, ...   O 53 Pro Drury-Lane   55
DEDICATOR
    To growing wealth the dedicator flies, ...   O 33 Vanity Wishes   82
DEDOKEN
    Tei Kallous dunamei ti telos; Zeus panta dedoken   . . .   O 103 Eis Elisses   1
DEED
    Records each deed each thought of sovereign Man   . . .   O 355 Irene   V 10
    Nor think th' Intention sanctifies the Deed: . . . .   O 291 Irene   59
    When future histories record the deed.   . . . . .   Y 180 Irene   V 27
DEEM
    Nor deem, when learning her last prize bestows,   . . .   O 38 Vanity Wishes   165
    Nor deem, when learning her lost prize bestows,   . . .   O 38 Vanity Wishes   V 165
    Which heav'n may hear, nor deem religion vain.   . . . .   O 47 Vanity Wishes   350
    Shall deem our hoar progenitors unwise.   . . . . . .   O 192 Tr. Medea II   4
    Deem us not deaf to Woe, nor blind to Beauty, ...   O 327 Irene   29
DEEMD
    And publick Spirit deemd a wild Chimaera   . . . . .   O 347 Irene   V 19
DEEP
    Fate never wounds more deep the gen'rous heart,   . . .   O 18 London   168
    The Surface of the boiling Deep, ...   O 71 Hor. Epode II   12
    And vows to trust the faithless deep no more.   . . . .   O 82 Young Author   10
    High to soar and deep to dive   . . . .   O 178 Thrale 35 Year   9
    Deep in a winding Creek a Galley lies, ...   O 254 Irene   134
    Form'd by this Garden jutting on the Deep;   . . . . .   O 284 Irene   52
    Deep in my Breast be treasur'd this Resolve, ...   O 288 Irene   12
    Borne on the Surface of the smiling Deep, ...   O 301 Irene   92
    Sport in our Sails, and murmur o'er the Deep.   . . . .   O 304 Irene   7
DEEP'D
    Held high the steady scale, but deep'd the sword;   . . .   O 22 London   251
DEEPEST
    And share the deepest Secrets of my Soul, ...   O 256 Irene   39
DEER
    No toils shall intercept the nimble deer.   . . . . .   Y 7 Virgil Daphnis   39
DEFACE
    Deface Erase the glories of my native   . . . .   Y 177 Irene   V 107
         country
DEFAME
    Perhaps yourselves the Villains that defame me,   . . .   O 326 Irene   38
DEFEATED
    Our schemes defeated and our mines discoverd   . . .   Y 141 Irene   V 22
    Say, by what Fraud, what Force were you defeated?   . . .   O 315 Irene   6
    Smiles at the Threat'nings of defeated Rage.   . . . .   O 325 Irene   19
DEFEATS
    Such slight Defeats but animate the Brave   . . . . .   O 270 Irene   7
    Whate'er their Scheme the Bassa's Death defeats it,   . .   O 312 Irene   4
DEFENCE
    What thought of flight, or of defence?   . . . . . .   O 121 To Miss Playin   12
    For speedy Flight, or obstinate Defence.   . . . . . .   O 284 Irene   55
DEFENCELESS
    And sees defenceless realms receive his sway;   . . . .   O 42 Vanity Wishes   244

DEFEND
                                                                       PAGE   TITLE   LINE

In croud at once, where none the pass defend, ... O 46 Vanity Wishes 337
In crowd at once, where none the fort defend, ... Y 107 Vanity Wishes V 337
DEFENSELESS
And pushes feeble (thrusts defenseless) virtue from her . Y 158 Irene V 13
    throne
DEFER
Defer an hour the fatal blow. . . . . O 69 Hor.II Ode 14 12
DEFORM
Deform the beauties of the breathing statue (marble hero Y 177 Irene V111A
DEFORM'D
At length deform'd with many a grisly wound . . . . . O 76 Tr Add. Battle 24
And thrice deform'd the verdant year . . . . Y 11 Tr Hor Epode 9 8
DEFORMITIES
Their foul deformities by all descry'd, ... O 84 Epi Dist Moth. 40
DEFRAUDS
Your hasty Zeal defrauds the Claim of Justice, ... O 330 Irene 5
DEFY'D
And safe in poverty defy'd his foes; . . . . O 11 London 48
Have I for this defy'd the Chiefs of Turkey, ... O 304 Irene 16
DEGEN'RATE
Since worth, he cries, in these degen'rate days, . . . O 10 London 35
DEGENERATE
The last Corruption of degenerate Man! . . . . . . O 249 Irene 15
Stoops from the Blaze like a degenerate Eagle, ... O 292 Irene 101
Stoops at the Blaze like a degenerate Eagle . . . . . O 368 Irene V 31
DEGRADES
Intimidates the Brave, degrades the Great. . . . . . O 311 Irene 15
DEGRADING
Degrading nobles and controuling kings; . . . . . . O 34 Vanity Wishes 94
DEGREES
Spread by Degrees, and dread th' oppressing Stream; . . O 282 Irene 58
DEIGN
Deign on the passing world to turn thine eyes, ... O 38 Vanity Wishes 157
Yet still did Virtue deign the Stage to tread, ... O 52 Pro Drury-Lane 33
Ye Sons of England, deign to hear, ... O 188 Epilogue 3
Ye Sons of Britain, deign to hear, ... O 188 Epilogue V 3
Nor deign the festive dome to cloy . . . . O 191 Tr. Medea I 15
DEIGN'D
Whence then those Charms thy Tongue has deign'd to . . O 277 Irene 26
    flatter,
Why then Those charms your tongue has deign'd to . . . O 355 Irene V 15
    flatter
Nor at the Call of Cali deign'd to turn. . . . . . . O 317 Irene 33
DEITIES
Gratefull, rewards the Deities, ... O 72 Hor. Epode II 27
Rewards the fav'ring Deities, ... O 72 Hor. Epode II V 27
Which prostrate Memphis own'd her deities. . . . . . Y 4 On a Daffodill 16
In fervent prayer addrest the deities: . . . . . . Y 20 Tr. Iliad Bk 6 98
DEITY
Those blessings, friend, a deity bestow'd, ... O 64 Virgil Past.I 7
Till conscious of th' incircling Deity, ... O 313 Irene 7
And woods and mountains hail the deity. . . . . . . Y 7 Virgil Daphnis 41
DELAY
He comes, not want and cold his course delay;-- . . . O 41 Vanity Wishes 209
He comes, nor want nor cold his course delay;------ . . O 41 Vanity Wishes V 209
The lust of wealth can never bear delay. . . . . . . O 140 Tr Rambler 182 1
No summons mock'd by chill delay, ... O 201 Death Dr Levet 21
No summons shock'd by chill delay, ... O 201 Death Dr Levet V 21
She feeds his Hopes, and sooths him to Delay. . . . . O 260 Irene 129
Willing to delay you here they give you on earth the . . Y 184 Irene V 10
To meet that Fate we can delay no longer. . . . . . O 328 Irene 41
DELAYS
Burning in vain, delays the Stroke of Death? . . . . O 257 Irene 66
No cloudy Doubts, or languishing Delays; . . . . . . O 271 Irene 27
Reproach not, Greece, a Lover's fond Delays, ... O 297 Irene 19
Curses the dull Delays of ling'ring Mercy, ... O 327 Irene 12
DELIBERATION
Another Hour in dull Deliberation. . . . . O 271 Irene 34
DELICIOUS
Can more delicious food supply. . . . . O 73 Hor. Epode II V 62
DELIGHT
Should no false Kindness lure to loose delight, . . . O 37 Vanity Wishes 147
When liberal pity dignify'd delight; . . . . O 62 Pro Word Wise 22
Form'd to delight, they use no foreign arms, ... O 84 Epi Dist Moth. 22
The noble mind's delight and pride, ... O 99 Ode Friendship 2
Surveys with new contemplative delight . . . . O 106 Eliza plucking 2
To make thy curious web delight, ... O 119 To Miss Purse 2
To make the curious web delight, ... O 119 To Miss Purse V 2
But on these regions of delight, ... O 121 To Miss Playin 19
But on those regions of delight, ... O 121 To Miss Playin V 19
Mingles Danger with Delight; . . . . O 145 Tr Boeth. II.4 14
Amidst the drousy charms of dull delight, ... O 152 The Ant 13
In all the sweet Oblivion of Delight, ... O 269 Irene 13
Form'd to delight, and happy by delighting, ... O 276 Irene 16
No more I sing, no more delight . . . . Y 11 Tr Hor Epode 9 3
That mirth may mend, and innocence delight. . . . . . Y 67 Prologue Lethe 16
DELIGHTED
No more delighted with destructive War, ... O 97 Hickman Spinet 17
Delighted still to please mankind, or mend, ... O 118 Epitaph Hanmer 39
Sooth the delighted Soul with empty Bliss? . . . . . O 277 Irene 45

78

```
                                                    PAGE    TITLE           LINE
DELIGHTFUL
     No fragrant bowers, no delightful glades,    . . . . .  O  83 Epi Dist Moth.   12
     Then seize fair Italy's delightful Coast,    . . . . .  O 309 Irene           30
     Securely sleeps, and, in delightful Dreams,  . . . . .  O 325 Irene           18
DELIGHTING
     Delighting, as the youth draws nigh,  . . . . . . . .   O 121 To Miss Playin   15
     Form'd to delight, and happy by delighting,  . . . .   O 276 Irene           16
DELIGHTS
     Delights to catch the gales of life.  . . . . . . . .   O 124 An Ode           4
DELIVER'D
     Is Greece deliver'd? is the Tyrant fall'n?   . . . . .  O 315 Irene            3
DELIVERANCE
     Deliverance is at Hand; for Turkey's Tyrant  . . . . .  O 283 Irene            7
     Thank Heav'n in daily hymns for my our deliverance  . . Y 166 Irene         V 93
     Snare'd with thy fears, and senseless of deliverance  . Y 196 Irene         V 18
DELUDE
     As treach'rous phantoms in the mist delude,  . . . . . O  31 Vanity Wishes     9
     Delude the most; few pry behind the scene.   . . . . . O 139 Tr Rambler 168    2
DELUGE
     Lost in the deluge of impetuous war  . . . . . .  . . . Y 136 Irene         V 25
     As when a Deluge overspreads the Plains, . . . . .  . . O 280 Irene           22
     Stem'd in the Breach the Deluge of Destruction, . .  . O 295 Irene           28
DELUSIONS
     Do gay Delusions, wand'ring o'er the Brain,  . . . . .  O 277 Irene           44
     And gay delusions wandring o'er the brain  . . . . .  . O 356 Irene         V 11
DELUSIVE
     Delusive Fortune hears th' incessant call,   . . . . .  O  33 Vanity Wishes   75
     Delusive hope still points to distant good,  . . . . .  O 133 Tr. Rambler 67   2
     Condemn'd to hope's delusive mine,  . . . . . . . .   . O 200 Death Dr Levet   1
     In pleasing Visions, and delusive Dreams;    . . . . .  O 253 Irene        V 102
          Alas! delusive Dream!   . . . . . . . . . . . .   O 267 Irene           45
DEMAND
     What e'er our Crimes, our Woes demand Compassion. . . . O 251 Irene           58
     These Years, unconquer'd Mahomet, demand . . . . . .  . O 263 Irene            7
     Demand a Voice, and struggle into Birth; . . . . . . .  O 295 Irene           18
     When desp'rate Ills demand a speedy Cure,  . . . . . .  O 301 Irene           85
     Demand whose Force yon Turkish Heroes dread, . . . . .  O 305 Irene           41
     Has serv'd his Prince so well, demand our Silence?  . . O 329 Irene           19
DEMANDS
     Is ripe for Action, and demands the Sword.   . . . . .  O 256 Irene           37
     Justice demands the forfeit Life of Cali;  . . . . . .  O 286 Irene           13
     Justice demands that I reveal your Crimes;    . . . . . O 286 Irene           14
     Justice demands--But see th' approaching Sultan.  . . . O 286 Irene           15
     From the fair nurse Astyanax demands. . . . . . . . .   Y  20 Tr. Iliad Bk 6   91
DEMEANOUR
     His Mien is lofty, his Demeanour great,  . . . . . . .  O 255 Irene           14
DEMETRIUS
     And is it thus Demetrius meets his Friend,   . . . . .  O 249 Irene            1
     Awake, Demetrius, from this dismal Dream,    . . . . .  O 252 Irene           83
     Enough of unavailing Tears, Demetrius,   . . . . . . .  O 253 Irene          104
     Sounds in my sleeping Ear, "Awake Demetrius,  . . . . . O 254 Irene          122
     Demetrius will not lead me to Dishonour.   . . . . . .  O 256 Irene           35
     Haste to the safe retreat, from whence Demetrius  . . . Y 126 Irene        V 144
     Each generous Sentiment is thine, Demetrius, . . . . .  O 267 Irene           38
     The pow'rful Voice of Love inflames Demetrius,  . . . . O 270 Irene           19
     Nor let Demetrius know thee for a Rival.   . . . . . .  O 282 Irene           71
     Who merits most, Demetrius or Abdalla.   . . . . . . .  O 284 Irene           45
     But while Demetrius, dear lamented Name!  . . . . . .   O 290 Irene           47
          Demetrius!   . . . . . . . . . . . . . . .  . .   O 294 Irene            4
     But all give way to Rapture and Demetrius.   . . . . .  O 295 Irene           20
     Say, how thou call'dst in Tears upon Demetrius!  . . .  O 295 Irene           26
     What Hand, when Death has snatch'd away Demetrius,  . . O 295 Irene           88
     Nor will his Country's Groans reproach Demetrius. . . . O 301 Irene          101
     --O Demetrius  O for a scene in those happy regions  .  Y 177 Irene        V 108
     Tell me the Cause, that while thy Name, Demetrius,  . . O 305 Irene           25
     What can'st thou boast superiour to Demetrius?  . . . . O 305 Irene           38
     The shudd'ring Camp shall murmur out Demetrius. . . . . O 305 Irene           42
     Demetrius justly pleads a double Title,  . . . . . . .  O 305 Irene           45
     Return, Demetrius, and be free for ever.   . . . . . .  O 306 Irene           60
     That fatal Beauty plighted to Demetrius  . . . . . . .  O 307 Irene           15
     Bore me victorious onward, where Demetrius   . . . . .  Y 188 Irene         V 10
     Demetrius the soul of Greece  . . . . . . . . . . .     O 312 Irene            9
     But brave Demetrius scorn'd the mean Revenge, . . . . . O 313 Irene           17
     Demetrius towrd--Above the Female pleasures  . . . . .  O 371 Irene          V 2
     Forbear, Demetrius, 'tis Aspasia calls thee;  . . . . . O 318 Irene            8
     Tell how Demetrius shun'd his single Hand, . . . . . .  O 318 Irene           13
     Depart, Demetrius, lest my Fate involve thee, . . . . . O 320 Irene           13
     Know'st thou not Cali? know'st thou not Demetrius?  . . O 324 Irene           15
     Or argue with the Slave that sav'd Demetrius.   . . . . O 330 Irene           23
     Or reason with the slave thats saved Demetrius  . . . . Y 210 Irene         V 23
     Might intercept the Traitor Greek, Demetrius,  . . . .  O 331 Irene            8
     The Greek, Demetrius! whom th' expiring Bassa  . . . .  O 331 Irene           10
     A chosen Troop--to intercept--Demetrius--    . . . . .  O 331 Irene           12
     Detain'd me till Demetrius set me free.  . . . . . . .  O 335 Irene            9
DEMETRIUS'
     Then shall these Juices taint Demetrius' Draught,  . . . O 308 Irene          30
     Safe in her Death, and in Demetrius' Flight, . . . . .  O 329 Irene            1
DEMOCRITUS
     Once more, Democritus, arise on earth,   . . . . . . .  O  32 Vanity Wishes   49
DENIAL
     Your artful Suit, your Monarch's fierce Denial,  . . .  O 270 Irene            3
```

79

		PAGE	TITLE	LINE
DENIES				
Denies my Lyce shines,	. . . .	O 127	To Lyce, Lady	18
And weak Philosophy denies her Succours.	. . . .	O 252	Irene	92
She sighs, she blushes, but she still denies.	. . . .	O 287	Irene	8
DENS				
To dens of guilt and shades of care	. . . .	O 191	Tr. Medea I	13
DENY				
To tell each Bystander, what none can deny,	. . . . .	O 173	Tr Fr Pantomim	2
Nor, letter'd arrogance, deny	. . . .	O 201	Death Dr Levet	11
Nor, letter'd ignorance, deny	. . . .	O 201	Death Dr Levet	V 11
Nor to deny.	. . . .	O 307	Irene	16
DENY'D				
A clime deny'd to human race;	. . . .	O 66	Hor I Ode xxii	22
A Clime deny'd to human Race;	. . . .	O 67	To A. Fuscus	22
To all the lower world deny'd;	. . . .	O 99	Ode Friendship	4
Deny'd Debard each privilege of human nature being	. .	Y 165	Irene	V 81
Not granted--nor deny'd--a softend glance	. . . . .	Y 179	Irene	V 32
Deny'd the Government of Servia's Province.	. . . . .	O 311	Irene	10
DENYS				
Till interposing Death denys the prospect.	. . . . .	O 374	Irene	V 26
DEPART				
Nor from the pleasing groves depart,	. . . .	O 125	An Ode	18
Bid your teizing doubts depart;	. . . .	O 176	Tr Metastasi I	2
If no wild Draught depart from Reason's Rules,	. . . .	O 246	Irene Prologue	17
Depart, Demetrius, lest my Fate involve thee,	. . . .	O 320	Irene	13
DEPARTING				
Yet let me watch her dear departing Steps,	. . . . .	O 297	Irene	17
When the departing sun resigns	. . . .	Y 38	Lady Leaving	1
DEPARTURE				
Hung on your Neck, and hinder'd your Departure.	. . .	O 280	Irene	10
DEPENDENT				
With servile grief dependent nobles sigh	. . . . . .	Y 57	London	V 198
In Pow'r dependent, in Success deprest.	. . . . . .	O 246	Irene Prologue	12
Courts thee to shake on a dependent Throne;	. . . . .	O 268	Irene	22
DEPRESS				
Depress their Spirits, and retard their Speed?	. . . .	O 325	Irene	15
DEPRESS'D				
Slow Rises Worth, By Poverty Depress'd:	. . . .	O 18	London	177
Ere guilty Fear depress'd the hoary Chief,	. . . . . .	O 312	Irene	18
DEPREST				
In Pow'r dependent, in Success deprest.	. . . . . .	O 246	Irene Prologue	12
DEPRIV'D				
Ev'n in the bloom of life depriv'd of breath.	. . . . .	Y 6	Virgil Daphnis	2
DEPTHS				
Convey him to the Prison's inmost Depths,	. . . . .	O 312	Irene	24
DERIDE				
The daring Greeks deride the martial show,	. . . . .	O 42	Vanity Wishes	235
Whilst you deride their pangs in barb'rous play,	. . . .	O 83	Epi Dist Moth.	7
And deride their utmost Rage.	. . . .	O 145	Tr Boeth. II.4	22
DERISION				
His foes derision, and his subjects blame,	. . . . .	O 43	Vanity Wishes	253
DERIV'D				
The rites deriv'd from ancient days	. . . .	O 190	Tr. Medea I	1
DERIVATA				
<H>oc fonte derivat<a> clades--In patriam populumque fluxit.	. .	O 347	Irene	V 22
DERIVE				
All from one Source derive their Birth	. . . . . .	O 146	Tr Boeth III.6	3
DERIVES				
The Sultan from himself derives his Greatness.	. . . .	O 268	Irene	24
Derives its Value from its Use alone;	. . . .	O 290	Irene	29
DERVISE				
Th' unpractis'd Dervise, or sequester'd Faquir.	. . .	O 281	Irene	37
DESART				
No peaceful desart yet unclaim'd by Spain?	. . . . .	O 18	London	173
DESARTS				
When did Felicity repine in Desarts?	. . . .	O 314	Irene	21
Or gay felicity retire to desarts?	. . . .	Y 191	Irene	V 21
DESCEND				
From Lydia's monarch should the search descend,	. . .	O 45	Vanity Wishes	313
Though from no Princes I descend,	. . . .	O 70	Hor.II Ode XX	5
Descend, impetuous, from the vault of Heav'n.	. . . .	O 76	Tr Add. Battle	11
On fools and villains ne'er descend;	. . . .	O 100	Ode Friendship	18
From wealth and grandeur easy to descend,	. . . . .	O 130	Tr. Rambler 12	3
Lest on himself the destin'd stroke descend.	. . . . .	O 139	Tr Rambler 168	2
See Levet to the grave descend;	. . . .	O 201	Death Dr Levet	6
descend in a proverb among thy enemies	. . . . . .	Y 113	Irene	V 21
Can Mahomet's imperial Hand descend	. . . . . .	O 268	Irene	15
Wilt thou descend, fair Daughter of Perfection,	. . .	O 276	Irene	1
Will yet Irenes haughty Soul descend	. . . . . .	O 372	Irene	V 6
Descend to range these Mansions of Misfortune,	. . .	O 292	Irene	95
Descend from Heavn, to range the distant World	. . .	O 349	Irene	V 10
Despis'd and curs'd, Leontius must descend	. . . . .	O 305	Irene	27
Descend, to sweeten Labours once your own.	. . . .	O 306	Irene	56
DESCENDING				
Spreads her mild Radiance, and descending Dews	. . .	O 313	Irene	2
Her tears in show'rs descending as she spoke.	. . . .	Y 18	Tr. Iliad Bk 6	18
Fresh foes descending glut their swords with blood.	. .	Y 23	Tr Add. Battle	21
Forcefull descending strikes his enemy,	. . . . . .	Y 26	Tr Add. Battle	131
DESCENDS				
From every room descends the painted face,	. . . . .	O 33	Vanity Wishes	83

		PAGE	TITLE	LINE
DESCENDS	**(CONTINUED)**			
From every wall descends the painted face,	. . . . .	Y 95	Vanity Wishes	V 83
Superiour man descends which	. . . . .	Y 147	Irene	V 39
Why, when the Balm of Sleep descends on Man,	. . . .	O 277	Irene	43
DESCRY				
Attentive truth and nature to descry,	. . . .	O 33	Vanity Wishes	63
DESCRY'D				
Their foul deformities by all descry'd,	. . . . .	O 84	Epi Dist Moth.	40
DESERT				
'Tis yours to crown Desert--beyond the Grave!	. . . .	O 58	Prologue Comus	38
Desert her own original.	. . . .	O 129	Tr. Rambler 6	2
DESERTED				
Some hireling senator's deserted seat;	. . . . . .	O 20	London	213
Why did you stay? deserted and betray'd?	. . . . .	O 317	Irene	34
DESERTS				
Deserts her nobler Origin.	. . . .	O 147	Tr Boeth III.6	20
DESERV'D				
Let pain deserv'd without complaint be borne.	. . . .	O 131	Tr. Rambler 32	1
DESERVE				
Inflict whatever Treason can deserve,	. . . . . .	O 334	Irene	75
DESIGN				
The fav'ring Winds assist the great Design,	. . . . .	O 304	Irene	6
The Life, which only this Design supported,	. . . . .	O 316	Irene	22
DESIGN'D				
Unless the beauteous Fabrick was design'd	. . . .	O 277	Irene	28
Thus I t' effect this mighty change design'd	. . . .	Y 11	Tr Hor Epode 9	29
DESIGNING				
Some ill designing Statesman's base Intrigue!	. . . .	O 326	Irene	36
DESIGNS				
My Wrongs, my Fears, my Motives, my Designs:--	. . . .	O 256	Irene	40
His vast Designs, his Plans of boundless Pow'r.	. . .	O 265	Irene	41
His vast designs, and plans of boundless Empire.	. .	O 356	Irene	V 29
Detests thy false Associates black Designs,	. . . . .	O 300	Irene	57
Disperse our Hopes, and frustrate our Designs,	. . .	O 301	Irene	98
I guess'd her dark Designs, and warn'd the Sultan,	. .	O 327	Irene	26
DESIRE				
Then say how hope and fear, desire and hate,	. . . .	O 31	Vanity Wishes	5
Then say how fierce desire and raging hate,	. . . . .	Y 92	Vanity Wishes	V 5
Then say how hot desire and raging hate,	. . . . .	Y 92	Vanity Wishes	V 5
Parent of Rage and hot desire,	. . . . .	O 99	Ode Friendship	V 6
Deceitful Hope, and vain Desire,	. . . . . .	O 121	To Miss Playin	13
Enliv'ning hope, and fond desire,	. . . . . .	O 123	Winter's Walk	9
Must bid each wild Desire be still,	. . . . . .	O 146	Tr Boeth III.5	3
And Peace propitious smile on fond Desire;	. . . .	O 302	Irene	119
Aspasia's Lovers know but one Desire,	. . . . .	O 307	Irene	13
A girl's, inflames me with desire;	. . . . .	Y 12	Tr Hor Epode 9	38
DESIRES				
But still desires of sordid gain	. . . . .	O 73	Hor. Epode II	77
Parent of thousand wild desires,	. . . . . .	O 99	Ode Friendship	6
Desires more pure, and other Cares than Love.	. . . .	O 263	Irene	8
DESOLATED				
And chearless treads the desolated stage,	. . . . .	Y 106	Vanity Wishes	V 308
Despotic o'er the desolated Plain,	. . . . .	O 111	To Posterity	20
DESOLATION				
--How chang'd alas!--Now ghastly Desolation	. . . .	O 251	Irene	66
And in the (paths) of war and desolation	. . . . .	Y 150	Irene	V 71
And fill the bleed<in>g world with desolation	. . .	O 352	Irene	V 5
DESP'RATE				
When desp'rate Ills demand a speedy Cure,	. . . . .	O 301	Irene	85
DESPAIR				
Cruel with guilt, and daring with despair,	. . . . .	O 21	London	238
Ye blooming train, who give despair or joy,	. . . . .	O 83	Epi Dist Moth.	1
Vexation, Fury, Jealousy, Despair,	. . . . .	O 84	Epi Dist Moth.	38
And rapture saddens to despair.	. . . .	O 123	Winter's Walk	12
To cheer despair, or soften pride,	. . . . . .	O 190	Tr. Medea I	8
Whence flow the Hopes and Fears, Despair and Rapture,	.	O 277	Irene	41
Whence all those Hopes and Fears Despair and Rapture	. . . .	O 355	Irene	V 18
Despair, and Slav'ry, Solitude, and Guilt.	. . . . .	O 292	Irene	87
Forsake a Wretch abandon'd to Despair,	. . . . .	O 320	Irene	14
Guilt and Despair! pale Spectres, grin around me,	. . .	O 328	Irene	50
One Hour had sav'd me from Despair and Madness.	. . .	O 332	Irene	28
While his sad mother frantick with despair	. . . . .	Y 6	Virgil Daphnis	5
DESPAIRING				
In Myrtle shades despairing ghosts complain;	. . . .	O 95	Sprig of Myrtl	8
And stern Composure of despairing Heroes;	. . . .	O 275	Irene	83
DESPATCH				
Must watchfull providence despatch from Heav'n	. . . .	Y 114	Irene	V 46
DESPERATION				
And all the giddy rage of desperation	. . . . . .	Y 142	Irene	V 39
DESPIS'D				
See when the vulgar 'scape, despis'd or aw'd,	. . . .	O 39	Vanity Wishes	167
Now beauty falls betray'd, despis'd, distress'd,	. . .	O 47	Vanity Wishes	341
Here beauty falls betray'd, despis'd, distress'd,	. . .	O 47	Vanity Wishes	V 341
Here beauty's drops her pomp, despis'd, distress'd	. .	Y 107	Vanity Wishes	V 341
Her gifts despis'd, corruption blush'd and fled,	. . .	O 118	Epitaph Hanmer	33
Despis'd and curs'd, Leontius must descend	. . . .	O 305	Irene	27
DESPISE				
Despise a fool in half his pension dress'd,	. . . . .	O 13	London	73
Despise the dainties of a venal lord:	. . . . . .	O 20	London	219
I once admir'd, I'd then despise:	. . . .	O 73	Hor. Epode II	V 60

		PAGE	TITLE	LINE

DESPISE   (CONTINUED)
- Adore the Beauty but despise th' Apostate.   O 350 Irene   V 26

DESPOTIC
- Despotic o'er the desolated Plain,   O 111 To Posterity   20

DESPOTICK
- And yield, reluctant, to despotick Sway.   O 96 Hickman Spinet   5
- Despotick Rage pursues the Life of Cali;   O 270 Irene   16
- There shall despotick Eloquence resume   O 302 Irene   120

DESTIN'D
- His fall was destin'd to a barren strand,   O 41 Vanity Wishes   219
- Lest on himself the destin'd stroke descend.   O 139 Tr Rambler 168   2
- But see, where destin'd to protract our Counsels,   O 271 Irene   35
- So weak is Man, when destin'd to Destruction,   O 283 Irene   12

DESTROY
- Increase his riches and his peace destroy;   O 32 Vanity Wishes   40
- Time hovers o'er, impatient to destroy,   O 43 Vanity Wishes   259
- Bless with a smile, or with a frown destroy;   O 83 Epi Dist Moth.   2
- He bids the Sword destroy, the Flame devour.   O 97 Hickman Spinet   14
- Succeeding years thy early fame destroy;   O 135 Tr Rambler 127   1
- Fierce as he was, he dreaded to destroy   O 257 Irene   68
- Would loose the wild Enthusiast to destroy,   O 291 Irene   61
- Yet when your Hand is lifted to destroy,   O 298 Irene   4
- While I destroy th' Oppressor of Mankind?   O 305 Irene   37
- Mistake shall blast, or Accident destroy;   O 335 Irene   13
- May no rude blasts thy sacred bloom destroy;   Y 3 On a Daffodill   7

DESTROY'D
- Destroy'd the fairest Workmanship of Heav'n!   O 332 Irene   19
- Whose direfull rage destroy'd my native land.   Y 18 Tr. Iliad Bk 6   29

DESTROYED
- Its charms are fled and all its powers destroyed.   O 142 In Baretti Bk.   8

DESTROYS
- Till interposing Death destroys the Prospect!   O 283 Irene   25

DESTRUCTION
- Till breathless Fury rested from Destruction   O 249 Irene   5
- <t>o stop this raging torrent of destruction   Y 117 Irene   V109C
- So weak is Man, when destin'd to Destruction,   O 283 Irene   12
- Why, when Destruction rag'd around our Walls,   O 290 Irene   38
- Stem'd in the Breach the Deluge of Destruction,   O 295 Irene   28
- Destruction flashes from th' insidious Mine,   O 298 Irene   30
- Each Turkish Bosom burns for thy Destruction,   O 300 Irene   73
- Yet think a Moment, ere you court Destruction,   O 301 Irene   87
- Fly, fly, my Love, Destruction rushes on us,   O 315 Irene   1
- Destruction is at Hand.   O 347 Irene   V 21
- To tire the burthen'd rack and gorge destruction   Y 196 Irene   V 18C
- Shrinks at the hated Task, for thy Destruction;   O 325 Irene   21
- Shrinks back from the hated task, for thy destruction;   Y 204 Irene   V 21
- The tongue that forges mandates for destruction   Y 210 Irene   V 25A
- Some soft Decoy to lure me to Destruction!   O 331 Irene   4
- Her final Doom, and hurried her Destruction.   O 334 Irene   62

DESTRUCTIVE
- In whose fair cheeks destructive Cupids wait,   O 83 Epi Dist Moth.   3
- No more delighted with destructive War,   O 97 Hickman Spinet   17
- With bright, but oft destructive gleam,   O 100 Ode Friendship   9
- With bright, but oft destructive gloom,   O 100 Ode Friendship   V 9
- Drives on the Tempest of destructive War,   O 268 Irene   26
- And stream destructive through his freezing Veins: O 308 Irene   31

DETAIN
- Shall long detain the cup,   O 159 Par Hermit III   6
- Detain me here. But Nations call upon me,   O 288 Irene   12

DETAIN'D
- Important Cares detain'd me from your Counsels.   O 279 Irene   6
- Detain'd me till Demetrius set me free.   O 335 Irene   9

DETECT
- His Breath prolong'd but to detect her Treason,   O 331 Irene   15

DETECTED
- That oft' had practis'd Fraud, and oft' detected,   O 254 Irene   131
- That thus you parly with detected Treason?   O 327 Irene   15

DETECTION
- The Plot all Cali's, the Detection thine.   O 329 Irene   4

DETERMINE
- What trivial Accidents determine Fate!   O 367 Irene   V 23

DETESTATION
- And detestation rids th' indignant wall.   O 34 Vanity Wishes   90

DETESTED
- Detested Cali too, with artful Wonder,   O 273 Irene   27
- Fly the Detested mansions of Impiety   O 346 Irene   V 7
- Detested residence of lust and tyranny   Y 165 Irene   V 79
- Nor let the Crimes of this detested Day   O 329 Irene   54

DETESTS
- Detests thy false Associates black Designs,   O 300 Irene   57
- But still yet my Soul detests the Bassas treason   O 353 Irene   V 22

DEVIL
- But how the Devil should he please us all!   O 247 Irene Epilogue   8

DEVOLVE
- Devolve, dear Maid, thy Sorrows on the Wretch,   O 316 Irene   16

DEVOTE
- In those curs'd walls, devote to vice and gain,   O 10 London   37
- Just Phoebus would devote his plant to thee.   O 106 Eliza plucking   8

DEVOTION
- And strong devotion to the skies aspires,   O 48 Vanity Wishes   358

```
                                                        PAGE   TITLE           LINE
DEVOTION        (CONTINUED)
    When strong devotion fills thy glowing Breast,  . . . .  O  48 Vanity Wishes   V 358
    And scorns the lazy Hermit's cheap Devotion;    . . . .  O 264 Irene            28
    I rais'd his Thoughts to more sublime Devotion. . . . .  O 274 Irene            46
    With silent Sorrows, and with calm Devotion.    . . . .  O 290 Irene            50
    With supplicating tears and pure Devotion       . . . .  O 364 Irene          V  2
    With mad Devotion idolizes Honour.  . . . . . . . . .    O 300 Irene            79
DEVOUR
    He bids the Sword destroy, the Flame devour.             O  97 Hickman Spinet   14
    The teeming Year's whole Product shall devour,  . . . .  O 110 To Posterity     11
DEVOURING
    Insidious sands, shallows rough rocks and whirling  . .  Y 201 Irene           V 10B
        devouring gulphs
DEW
    And thou impearl'd with dew appear more gay.    . . . .  Y   3 On a Daffodill   12
DEW-DROPS
    Those glitt'ring Dew-drops of a vernal Morn,             O 298 Irene            19
DEWDROPS
    As glittring dewdrops quiver to the sun  . . . . . .     Y 173 Irene           V 19
DEWS
    That pours the dews upon the thristy vales  . . . . . .  Y 168 Irene           V135C
    Spreads her mild Radiance, and descending Dews          O 313 Irene             2
DEXT'ROUS
    In bus'ness dext'rous, weighty in debate,   . . . . .    O 118 Epitaph Hanmer   13
    That dext'rous Message frees me from Suspicion.  . . .   O 324 Irene            26
DIADEMS
    Did regal Diadems invest my Brow,  . . . . . . . .       O 289 Irene            12
DIALOGUE
    Translation of part of the Dialogue between . . . . .    O  74 Tr. Iliad Bk 6    T
DIANA
    Diana calls to life in vain,  . . . . . . . . . .        O 232 Tr Horace IV.7   26
    Provok'd Diana with a vengefull dart  . . . . . . . .    Y  19 Tr. Iliad Bk 6   42
DICTATES
    But everlasting dictates croud his tongue,  . . . . .    O  43 Vanity Wishes   273
    The chearful sage, when solemn dictates fail,   . . . .  O 132 Tr. Rambler 65    1
DID
    For why did Wolsey near the steeps of fate,  . . . . .   O  35 Vanity Wishes   125
    For why did Wolsey by the Steps of fate,  . . . . .      O  35 Vanity Wishes  V 125
    But did not Chance at length her error mend?  . . . .    O  41 Vanity Wishes   215
    Did no subverted empire mark his end?  . . . . . .       O  41 Vanity Wishes   216
    Did rival monarchs give the fatal wound?  . . . . .      O  41 Vanity Wishes   217
    They pleas'd their Age, and did not aim to mend.  . . .  O  52 Pro Drury-Lane   22
    Yet still did Virtue deign the Stage to tread,  . . . .  O  52 Pro Drury-Lane   33
    Nor did King Priam's hoary age  . . . . . . . . .        O  68 Hor. II Ode IX   15
    Thus did the Us'rer Alphius praise,  . . . . . . .       O  73 Hor. Epode II    73
    I there did meet another man  . . . . . . . . .          O 158 Par. Hermit II  V  3
    Did we not see the bars of nature broken?  . . . . .     Y 115 Irene           V 49F
    Did not our sails receive the wondring winds  . . . .    Y 115 Irene           V 49G
    Did unresisted Lightning aid their Cannon,   . . . . .   O 251 Irene            54
    Did Did Lightnings flash?  . . . . . . . . . .           O 347 Irene          V  2
    Did Did Lightnings flash?  . . . . . . . . . .           O 347 Irene          V  2
    Did roaring Whirlwinds sweep us from the Ramparts:       O 251 Irene            55
    Did Earthquakes shake our walls?  . . . . . . . .        O 347 Irene          V  3
    Did aught but Luxury relax our Nerves . . . . . .        O 347 Irene          V  5
    Did Mahomet reproach or praise her Virtue?  . . . . .    O 259 Irene           108
    Say, did a Voice from Heav'n restrain the Tyrant?   . .  O 259 Irene           115
    Did interposing Angels guard her from him?  . . . . .    O 259 Irene           116
    Why then did Natures vain Munificence . . . . . .        O 355 Irene          V 13
    Did ever Passion make so swift a Progress?  . . . . .    O 281 Irene            55
    How did Aspasia welcome your Address?  . . . . . . .     O 282 Irene            61
    Did you proclaim this unexpected Conquest?  . . . . .    O 282 Irene            62
    Did regal Diadems invest my Brow,  . . . . . . . .       O 289 Irene            12
    Why then did not this warlike Amazon  . . . . . .        O 290 Irene            40
    O! did Irene shine the Queen of Turkey,  . . . . . .     O 290 Irene            51
    Did savage Anger, and licentious Conquest   . . . . .    O 296 Irene            30
    Did not the Cause of Greece restrain my Sword,  . . .    O 299 Irene            41
    When did Content sigh out her Cares in secret?  . . .    O 314 Irene            20
    When did contentment with struggling sorrow . . . .      Y 191 Irene          V 20
        throb?
    When did Felicity repine in Desarts?  . . . . .          O 314 Irene            21
    What Cry? The Stratagem? Did then Abdalla?--    . . . .  O 317 Irene            30
    Why did you stay? deserted and betray'd?  . . . . .      O 317 Irene            34
    How am I chang'd! How lately did Irene  . . . . .        O 322 Irene            13
    Irene's Chamber! Did not roaring Cali,  . . . . . .      O 330 Irene            12
    O seize me, Madness--Did she call on me!  . . . . .      O 334 Irene            68
    To his own house her did lug.  . . . . . . . . .         Y 301 Extemp. Elegy    16
DID'ST
    Hear! shall I hear thee! did'st thou hear Irene?   . .   O 333 Irene            56
DIE     SEE DYE
    Live unregarded, unlamented die.                         O  14 London           82
    Scarce can our fields, such crowds at Tyburn die,        O  21 London          242
    Well may we fear, such crowds at Tyburn die,    . . . .  Y  60 London         V 242
    As Tyrants doom their Tools of Guilt to die;    . . . .  O  53 Pro Drury-Lane   56
    His tortur'd Sons shall die before his Face,    . . . .  O 111 To Posterity     23
    And born in bed, in bed we die;  . . . . . . .           O 184 Tr. Benserade     2
    And lonely want retir'd to die.  . . . . . . .           O 201 Death Dr Levet   20
        Go see him die;  . . . . . . . . . .                 O 263 Irene            25
    And in some distant Land obscurely die.   . . . . .      O 274 Irene            49
    Force her! profane her with a Touch, and die.   . . . .  O 296 Irene             8
        No! let us die together.  . . . . . . . .            O 297 Irene            11
    Doom'd me to die with all the Turkish Captains.  . . .   O 313 Irene            16
```

DIE	(CONTINUED)		PAGE	TITLE		LINE
Bids Beauty, such as thine, prepare to die.			O 324	Irene		3
Of her the Sultan's Voice condemn'd to die?			O 329	Irene		17
And ah! behold the shriveling blossoms die,			Y 4	On a Daffodill		23
The bard obdurate sees his brother die.			Y 67	Prologue Lethe		4

DIED   SEE DY'D

... Musician, who died very poor			O 113	Epit. Phillips	V	T
... at Bridgnorth, Salop; who died very poor			O 113	Epit. Phillips	V	T
And love return, has great Erasmus died?			O 132	Tr. Rambler 54		2
Viewing lost and losing died.			O 150	Tr Boet III.12		52
Viewing lost and loving died.			O 150	Tr Boet III.12	V	52

DIES   SEE DYES

Unlocks his gold, and counts it till he dies.			O 44	Vanity Wishes		290
Lies at my feet, I hiss him, and he dies.			O 60	Pro Good Nat'd		24
Each youth admires, though each admirer dies;			O 83	Epi Dist Moth.		6
The balmy kiss, for which poor Thyrsis dies;			O 84	Epi Dist Moth.		21
Cry not when his father dies,			O 183	Burlesque Vega		2
When Cali mounts the Throne Abdalla dies,			O 288	Irene		13

DIFF'RENT

Blest age! but ah! how diff'rent from our own!			O 22	London		253
Blest age! but ha! how diff'rent from our own!			O 22	London	V	253
New forms arise, and diff'rent views engage,			O 45	Vanity Wishes		307
she sees whom diff'rent views engage,			Y 106	Vanity Wishes	V	307
Mark, when the diff'rent notes agree			O 121	To Miss Playin		29

DIFFERENT

| Our distant Int'rests, and our different Passions | | | O 287 | Irene | | 3 |

DIFFICULTY

| Nor Praise relax, nor Difficulty fright; | | | O 37 | Vanity Wishes | | 148 |

DIFFIDENCE

Strain out with fault'ring diffidence a lye,			O 16	London		130
With all the Diffidence of long Experience,			O 254	Irene		130
Does chearless Diffidence oppress their Hearts?			O 270	Irene		22

DIFFUSE

Diffuse the tuneful lenitives of pain:			O 43	Vanity Wishes		268
Diffuse the soothin lenitives of pain:			Y 104	Vanity Wishes	V	268
And Truth diffuse her Radiance from the Stage.			O 53	Pro Drury-Lane		62
Diffuse Irene's Beauty though the World.			O 268	Irene		14
Not always do the fairest Flow'rs diffuse			O 277	Irene		31
Diffuse a Brightness on our future Days;			O 301	Irene		100

DIGNIFIED

| Like Caesar's pilot, dignified by fate, | | | O 59 | Pro Good Nat'd | | 7 |

DIGNIFIES

| Nor dignifies the great, nor decks the fair. | | | O 141 | Tr Rambler 199 | | 4 |
| That decks the fair, or dignifies the great. | | | O 141 | Tr Rambler 199 | | 8 |

DIGNIFY

| Adorn a Throne, and dignify Dominion. | | | O 276 | Irene | | 10 |

DIGNIFY'D

| When liberal pity dignify'd delight; | | | O 62 | Pro Word Wise | | 22 |
| And virtue's sorrow dignify'd his tomb. | | | O 118 | Epitaph Hanmer | | 44 |

DIGNITY

In full-blown dignity, see Wolsey stand,			O 34	Vanity Wishes		99
Thy awful air, thy dignity of virtue.			Y 134	Irene		99
Nor thus usurp the Dignity of Virtue.			O 323	Irene	V	34

DIGS

| In blissful dreams he digs the golden mine, | | | O 82 | Young Author | V | 6C |

DILATORY

| Thou sluggish Idler, dilatory Slave? | | | O 334 | Irene | | 2 |

DILIGENCE

| Is this the restless Diligence of Treason? | | | O 279 | Irene | | 2 |
| No Pray'r recals, no Diligence redeems; | | | O 303 | Irene | | 8 |

DIM

| Dim, scorn'd and impotent, his torches lie. | | | O 133 | Tr. Rambler 85 | | 2 |
| Wet the dim eye or swell the throbbing bosom? | | | Y 191 | Irene | V | 19A |

DIN

| In vain we shun the Din of war, | | | O 69 | Hor.II Ode 14 | | 13 |
| Where unaffrighted by the din of war | | | Y 177 | Irene | V | 116 |

DINNER

| Announc'd the dinner to the regions round, | | | O 192 | Tr. Medea II | | 6 |

DIOS

| Ek Dios estin onar, Theios pot egrapsen Homeros, | | | O 103 | Eis Elisses | | 3 |
| Ommasi lampra Dios Kupris oista pherei. | | | O 103 | Eis Elisses | | 6 |

DIRE

Now fears in dire vicissitude invade,			O 32	Vanity Wishes		41
New fears in dire vicissitude invade,			O 32	Vanity Wishes	V	41
Lay siege to life and press the dire blockade;			O 44	Vanity Wishes		284
This dire event by omens was foreshown;			O 64	Virgil Past.I		22
Dire nurse of raging lions, bore.			O 66	Hor I Ode xxii		16
Imbibes with dire docility the wrong.			O 136	Tr Rambler 132		2
Like subterraneous tempests with dire eruption burst their caverns			Y 115	Irene	V	49
Has Treason's dire Infection reach'd my Palace?			O 272	Irene		2
Soon shall the dire Seraglio's horrid Gates			O 291	Irene		7,9
Soon shall the dire Seraglio's dreadful Gates			O 357	Irene	V	9
By that dire sword my sev'n brave brothers dy'd;			Y 18	Tr. Iliad Bk 6		34

DIRECT

Direct thy rivulets, and twine thy bow'rs;			O 20	London		217
Direct the rivulets, and plan the bow'rs;			Y 58	London	V	217
Direct the loaded Cannon, grasp the Sword			O 364	Irene	V	14
Direct the loaded cannon, grasp the sword			Y 162	Irene	V	41
now hover oer us and direct our councils			Y 181	Irene	V	51
Direct O Goddess, my advent'rous song;			Y 22	Tr Add. Battle		3

```
                                                              PAGE    TITLE        LINE
DIRECTION
    Those holy Beings whose unseen Direction  . . . . . .     O 346 Irene          V   5
DIRECTRESS
    Directress of the brave and just,  . . . . . .            O 100 Ode Friendship    13
    Reason! the hoary Dotard's dull Directress, . . . . .     O 281 Irene             44
DIRECTS
    Prescribes her duties, or directs her choice, . . . .     O 151 The Ant            4
    Directs the Planets with a careless Nod, . . . . . .      O 293 Irene            123
DIREFUL
    And heard th' ill omen'd catcall's direful cry.  . . .    Y  67 Prologue Lethe    10
DIREFULL
    Whose direfull rage destroy'd my native land.  . . .      Y  18 Tr. Iliad Bk 6     29
DIRT
    Only dirt, or wet or dry. . . . . . . . .                 O 196 Song Congratu.     24
DISABLED
    Disabled both to combat, or to fly,  . . . . . .          O  59 Pro Good Nat'd     13
DISAGREE
    Hence! or be calm--To disagree is Ruin.  . . . . .        O 282 Irene             72
DISAPPEAR
    If at your coming princes disappear,  . . . . . .         O 177 Tr Dist Modena     1
DISAPPOINTED
    And disappointed Vengeance burns in vain;  . . . . .      O 330 Irene              6
DISAPPOINTMENT
    Th' insidious Bassa fir'd by Disappointment--            O 273 Irene             32
    Now lost amidst the gloom of disappointment . . . .       Y 148 Irene          V 43B
    Though Disappointment blast our general Scheme,  . . .    O 317 Irene             44
DISAPPOINTMENTS
    Well might we fear impending Disappointments.  . . .      O 269 Irene              2
DISARM'D
    Disarm'd his Rage, and in repeated Visits . . . . .       O 259 Irene            122
    Cali disarm'd was born away to Death; . . . . . .         O 317 Irene             40
DISARRAY
    Uncouth Words in Disarray:  . . . . . . .                 O 179 Ridicul Warton     6
DISAST'ROUS
    The Day disast'rous that secures our Flight; . . . .      O 317 Irene             46
DISASTER
    Disaster always waits an early wit.  . . . . . .          O 135 Tr Rambler 111     1
DISASTROUS
    Oft' shall I dwell on our disastrous Friendship, . . .    O 292 Irene             96
    Oft shall I swell on our disastrous Friendship . . .      O 349 Irene          V 11
    The day disastrous, that secures my honor  . . . .        Y 195 Irene          V 46
    Oft has our bard in this disastrous year, . . . . .       Y  67 Prologue Lethe     7
DISCERN
    Safe in his pow'r, whose eyes discern afar . . . . .      O  47 Vanity Wishes    353
DISCERNING
    Besides, with justice, this discerning age . . . .        O  16 London           132
DISCLOS'D
    And through the parted Shade disclos'd the Greeks,  . .   O 269 Irene             11
    Disclos'd some Traytor lurking near our Bosoms . . . .    O 368 Irene          V  3
DISCLOSE
    In vain your mournful narrative disclose,  . . . . .      O  19 London           192
DISCORD
    Then o'er the World shall Discord stretch her Wings, . .  O 110 To Posterity      15
    Still discord hovers o'er divided thrones. . . . . .      O 140 Tr Rambler 183     2
    And scatter Discord from their baleful Beams.  . . . .    O 271 Irene              5
    Lest baneful discord crush our infant Scheme,  . . . .    O 299 Irene             52
    From hence the seeds of discord first arose  . . . . .    Y  23 Tr Add. Battle    50
DISCOUNTENANC'D
    And drive discountenanc'd virtue from the throne:  . .    O 176 Tr Metastas II     9
    And chase discountenanc'd virtue from the throne:  . .    O 176 Tr Metastas II  V  9
DISCOVER
    I discover by this state & retinue . . . . . . .          Y 160 Irene          V  8
    A private Station may discover more; . . . . . .          O 316 Irene             18
DISCOVER'D
    Our Schemes for ever cross'd, our Mines discover'd,  . .  O 273 Irene             22
    Our Mines discover'd, and, our Battries ruind  . . . .    O 368 Irene          V  2
DISCOVERD
    Our schemes defeated and our mines discoverd . . . .      Y 141 Irene          V 22
DISCOVERS
    Lamenting Av'rice now too late discovers . . . . .        O 250 Irene             26
DISCRETION
    Who buys without discretion, buys to sell. . . . . .      O 133 Tr. Rambler 82     1
DISDAIN
    Rage with disdain, and hope th' approaching war; . . .    O  75 Tr Add. Battle     1
    Nor let disdain sit low'ring in your eye;  . . . .        O  84 Epi Dist Moth.    43
DISDAIN'D
    No petty gain disdain'd by pride,  . . . . . . .          O 201 Death Dr Levet    22
DISDAINS
    Peace courts his hand, her fondness he disdains  . . .    Y 101 Vanity Wishes  V 201
    No social care the gracious lord disdains; . . . .        O 130 Tr. Rambler 12     7
    The Faith of Mustapha disdains Suspicion;  . . . .        O 273 Irene             30
DISEASE
    Grief aids disease, remember'd folly stings, . . . .      O  35 Vanity Wishes    119
    And fixed disease on Harley's closing life?  . . . .      O  36 Vanity Wishes    130
    Should no Disease thy torpid veins invade, . . . . .      O  37 Vanity Wishes    153
    Nor should disease thy torpid veins invade,  . . . .      Y  99 Vanity Wishes  V 153
    Yet, tho' my limbs disease invades,  . . . . . .          O 125 An Ode            13
    Disease shall chase the Phantoms of Ambition,  . . . .    O 322 Irene             60
DISEASES
    That wafts diseases from the sleeping infant.  . . . .    Y 168 Irene           V135B
```

```
                                                              PAGE    TITLE              LINE
DISENCUMBER'D
    And seize my Sword with disencumber'd Hand.  .  .  .  .  .  O 316 Irene                 29
DISENTANGLED
    When the mind disentangled from the senses  .  .  .  .  .  Y 133 Irene              V   6
DISGRACD
    His Choice our sacred Seats disgracd,  .  .  .  .  .  .  .  O 146 Tr Boeth III.4         5
DISGRACE
    Where honesty and sense are no disgrace;  .  .  .  .  .  .  O  11 London                44
    Ardent of fame, yet fearless of disgrace.  .  .  .  .  .  Y  67 Prologue Lethe        2
DISGUIS'D
    And bids us thus disguis'd await him here.  .  .  .  .  .  O 253 Irene                115
    By Smiles, and Oaths, and Praises ill disguis'd.  .  .  .  O 308 Irene                 15
DISGUISE
    "Fate! snatch away the bright disguise,  .  .  .  .  .  .  O 122 Stella Mourn.          5
    Where mischief lurks in gay disguise,  .  .  .  .  .  .  .  O 203 Tr. on Skating        3
    Hid in the mean Disguise of Turkish Robes,  .  .  .  .  .  O 249 Irene                  2
DISGUISES
    These Groans were fatal, these Disguises vain:  .  .  .  .  O 249 Irene                  6
DISH
    Another dish of tea.  .  .  .  .  .  .  .  .  .  .  .  .  .  O 158 Par Hermit III        4
    When cates luxuriant pile the spacious dish,  .  .  .  .  O 193 Tr. Medea II           17
DISHONOUR
    Demetrius will not lead me to Dishonour;  .  .  .  .  .  .  O 256 Irene                 35
DISJOIN'D
    Tranquillity and Guilt, disjoin'd by Heav'n,  .  .  .  .  O 292 Irene                  90
DISJOINTED
    With mouldring cement and with beams disjointed  .  .  .  Y 114 Irene              V  45
DISLIKE
    Must no dislike alarm, no wishes rise,  .  .  .  .  .  .  O  47 Vanity Wishes         347
DISMAL
    Swift o'er the land the dismal rumour flies,  .  .  .  .  O  19 London               196
    Foretold the coming evil by their dismal croak.  .  .  .  O  65 Virgil Past.I         25
    To dismal realms, and regions void of peace,  .  .  .  .  O  84 Epi Dist Moth.        30
    Awake, Demetrius, from this dismal Dream,  .  .  .  .  .  O 252 Irene                 83
DISMAY'D
    May droop dismay'd, or kindle into Madness.  .  .  .  .  .  O 304 Irene                 11
DISMISS
    Their schemes of spite the poet's foes dismiss,  .  .  .  O  60 Pro Good Nat'd        19
    Dismiss the pleasing Phantoms for an Hour.  .  .  .  .  .  O 246 Irene Prologue        6
    Wilt thou dismiss the Savage from the Toils  .  .  .  .  .  O 275 Irene                 66
    If Dismiss this glittring train these sudden  .  .  .  .  O 366 Irene              V  17
        Splendors
    To hear the Voice of Truth; dismiss thy Train,  .  .  .  .  O 289 Irene                  6
    To hear the voice of truth, dismiss your train  .  .  .  .  O 366 Irene              V  22
    Dismiss these needless Fears--a Troop of Greeks  .  .  .  O 301 Irene                 90
DISMISS'D
    Their souls dismiss'd through many a ghastly wound,  .  .  O  74 Tr. Iliad Bk 6        18
    Dismiss'd her to the Sky.  .  .  .  .  .  .  .  .  .  .  .  O 252 Irene                 95
DISORDER
    Disorder sits upon thy Face--retire.  .  .  .  .  .  .  .  O 286 Irene                 17
DISORDER'D
    The Greeks disorder'd by their Leader's Absence,  .  .  .  O 304 Irene                 10
    His Air disorder'd, and his Gait unequal,  .  .  .  .  .  O 311 Irene                  3
DISPATCH
    Must Heaven dispatch the Messengers of Light,  .  .  .  .  O 250 Irene                 46
    Distract my Soul, dispatch thy ling'ring Tale;  .  .  .  .  O 259 Irene                114
        Dispatch; th' encreasing Danger  .  .  .  .  .  .  .  O 297 Irene                 12
    Dispatch his Guards to stop the flying Traytors,  .  .  .  O 319 Irene                  3
    Enrob'd in Death--Dispatch her and be great.  .  .  .  .  O 326 Irene                  3
    Dispatch, ye ling'ring Slaves, or nimbler Hands  .  .  .  O 328 Irene                 42
    Dispatch, and learn a fitter Time for Pity.  .  .  .  .  .  O 328 Irene                 44
DISPELL
    No feasts could e'er my cares dispell;  .  .  .  .  .  .  Y  11 Tr Hor Epode 9        13
DISPELLING
    Dispelling the black horrors of the Night,  .  .  .  .  .  O  77 Tr Add. Battle        46
DISPELLS
    Dispells the darkness with his golden ray  .  .  .  .  .  Y  23 Tr Add. Battle        23
DISPENSE
    Cleora's smiles a genial warmth dispense;  .  .  .  .  .  Y   4 On a Daffodill        18
DISPENSING
    I'll sing the chiefs dispensing fate around.  .  .  .  .  Y  22 Tr Add. Battle        19
DISPERS'D
    Dispers'd in Air or mingled with the Dust.  .  .  .  .  .  O 298 Irene                 24
DISPERSE
    Disperse Rebellion through the Eastern World;  .  .  .  .  O 274 Irene                 52
    Disperse our Hopes, and frustrate our Designs,  .  .  .  .  O 301 Irene                 98
DISPERSING
    Dispersing blessings as they went,  .  .  .  .  .  .  .  .  O  79 Feast St Simon       26
DISPLAID
    My tongue with am'rous eloquence displaid  .  .  .  .  .  Y 158 Irene              V   7
    I displaid--before her all the gay luscious scene...  .  .  Y 158 Irene              V   8
DISPLAY
    Her silver locks display the moon,  .  .  .  .  .  .  .  .  O 127 To Lyce, Lady         9
    Rush to the War, display thy dreadful Banners,  .  .  .  .  O 333 Irene                 40
DISPLAY'D
    When, lately, Stella's form display'd  .  .  .  .  .  .  .  O 122 Stella Mourn.         1
    His vig'rous remedy display'd  .  .  .  .  .  .  .  .  .  .  O 201 Death Dr Levet       15
DISPLAYS
    Where aught of bright, or fair, the piece displays,  .  .  O  62 Pro Word Wise         15
    Had this fair figure which this frame displays,  .  .  .  O 189 Seeing Montagu         1
    And various charms displays to various eyes  .  .  .  .  .  Y 155 Irene              V  27
```

```
                                                         PAGE    TITLE          LINE
DISPLAYS         (CONTINUED)
     The various charms displays to various eyes  . . . . .  O 374 Irene         V  28
DISPLEASURE
     --When of late The storm of Heav'ns displeasure thundred  Y 136 Irene       V  27
        on you.
DISPOSE
     Dispose the Colours of the flowing Robe,  . . . . . .    O 278 Irene           65
DISPOSSEST
     Venus, the sacred Sisters dispossest,  . . . . . . .     Y  11 Tr Hor Epode 9   5
DISSEMBLE
     Can Abdalla then dissemble,  . . . . . . . . .           O 299 Irene           34
DISSIPATED
     Of dissipated wealth the small remains,  . . . . . .     O   9 London          20
     but if your influence be too wide--your dissipated rays  Y 132 Irene        V  41
     Here recollect thy dissipated Pow'rs.--  . . . . . .     O 287 Irene            2
DISSOLV'D
     The snow dissolv'd no more is seen,  . . . . . . .       O 231 Tr Horace IV.7    1
DISSOLVE
     Dissolve thy vigour, and enchain thy powers?  . . . .    O 151 The Ant         10
     Dissolve in Air, and vanish into Nothing.  . . . . .     O 265 Irene            8
DISSOLVING
     Or flow dissolving in a Woman's Tears?  . . . . . .      O 255 Irene           25
DISSONANCE
     The dreadful Dissonance of barb'rous Triumph,  . . .     O 251 Irene           71
     The dreadfull dissonance of barbarous triumph  . . . .   Y 169 Irene        V  11
     And unaccustom'd warblings charm the grove  (pleasing .  Y 150 Irene        V  86
        disson<ance>
DISTAFF
     There let the web and distaff be your care.  . . . . .   Y  21 Tr. Iliad Bk 6  122
DISTANCE
     Prospects obscur'd by Distance faintly strike.  . . . .  O 261 Irene           19
DISTANT
     To breathe in distant fields a purer air,  . . . . .    O   9 London           6
     For such in distant lands the Britons shine,  . . . .    O  39 Vanity Wishes  181
     For these in distant lands the Britons shine,  . . . .   Y 100 Vanity Wishes V 181
     And shews his miseries in distant lands; . . . . . .     O  41 Vanity Wishes  212
     And hides his miseries in distant lands; . . . . . .     Y 102 Vanity Wishes V 212
     With distant voice neglected Virtue calls,  . . . . .    O  46 Vanity Wishes  333
     Perhaps if Skill could distant Times explore,  . . . .   O  53 Pro Drury-Lane  41
     To distant realms and climes unknown,  . . . . . .       O  70 Hor.II Ode XX    18
     The mountain shepherd hears the distant noise.  . . .    O 132 Tr. Rambler 65    3
     Delusive hope still points to distant good,  . . . . .   O 133 Tr. Rambler 67    3
     Yet strangers in some distant world proclaim  . . . .    Y 120 Irene         V 31A
     Paints future Joys, and points to distant Glories.  . .  O 261 Irene           17
     At his dread Name the distant Mountains shake  . . .     O 268 Irene           28
     At my dread name the distant mountains shake  . . . .    Y 136 Irene        V  28
     And in some distant Land obscurely die.  . . . . . .     O 274 Irene           49
     Our distant Int'rests, and our different Passions  . .   O 287 Irene            3
     And Duty bids me chuse a distant Walk,  . . . . .        O 288 Irene           13
     Descend from Heavn, to range the distant World  . . .    O 349 Irene        V  10
     An idle List'ner to the distant Cries  . . . . . .       O 305 Irene           23
     I see the distant vessel  . . . . . . . . . .            Y 201 Irene        V  10
     Let distant regions echo with his name  . . . . . .      Y  20 Tr. Iliad Bk 6  103
DISTENDED
     Their dugs with milk distended, home!  . . . . . . .     O  73 Hor. Epode II    68
DISTINCTION
     Love be my Wealth, and my Distinction Virtue.  . . .     O 302 Irene          111
DISTINCTIONS
     The poor distinctions of a flying moment  . . . . .      Y 177 Irene         V110A
DISTINGUISH'D
     This Night, distinguish'd by your Smile, shall tell,  .  O  57 Prologue Comus   11
     There begs of heav'n a less distinguish'd lot; . . . .   O  82 Young Author     29
     In its wild ravages distinguish'd thee  . . . . . . .    Y 115 Irene        V 49B
     A Virgin shining with distinguish'd Charms,  . . . . .    O 258 Irene           95
     Shine thou distinguish'd by superior Merit.  . . . .     O 264 Irene           29
DISTORTED
     The form distorted justifies the fall,  . . . . . .      O  34 Vanity Wishes   89
     But find the form distorted by the fall  . . . . . .     Y  95 Vanity Wishes V  89
DISTORTS
     For gold the hireling judge distorts the laws; . . . .   O  31 Vanity Wishes   26
DISTRACT
     Distract my Soul, dispatch thy ling'ring Tale; . . . .   O 259 Irene          114
DISTRACTED
     A thousand Thoughts imperfect and distracted,  . . . .   O 295 Irene           17
DISTRACTION
     Nor bursting through the ranks in wild distraction  . .  Y 163 Irene        V  47
     O name not Death! Distraction and Amazement,  . . . .    O 328 Irene           31
     Hew down, ye Guards, those Vassals of Distraction,  . .  O 333 Irene           51
DISTRACTS
     And dark Perplexity distracts my Counsels.  . . . . .    O 275 Irene           89
DISTRESS
     Since hope but sooths to double my distress,  . . . .    O  10 London          39
     As virtue rises in distress,  . . . . . . . . .          O 122 Stella Mourn.   10
     Shrieks of Affright, and Wailings of Distress. . . . .   O 251 Irene           72
     No more should Danger fright, or Want distress  . . .    O 291 Irene           56
     Thou shin'st, bright Maid, superior to Distress; . . .   O 298 Irene           17
DISTRESS'D
     Of all the griefs that harrass the distress'd, . . . .   O  17 London         166
     Now beauty falls betray'd, despis'd, distress'd,  . . .  O  47 Vanity Wishes  341
     Here beauty falls betray'd, despis'd, distress'd,  . .   O  47 Vanity Wishes V 341
     Here beauty's drops her pomp, despis'd, distress'd  . .  Y 107 Vanity Wishes V 341
```

DISTRESS'D   (CONTINUED)   PAGE   TITLE   LINE
    Why roars the Lioness distress'd by Hunger? . . . . .   O 281 Irene   50
DISTREST
    Distrest alike, the statesman and the wit, ...   O 59 Pro Good Nat'd   9
    Then, O my Country! shalt thou groan distrest, . . .   O 110 To Posterity   3
    Rest here distrest by poverty no more, ...   O 113 Epit. Phillips   3
DISTRIBUTE
    And with unerring shafts distribute fate; . . . . .   O 83 Epi Dist Moth.   4
DISTRUST
    Distrust th' eternal Fortresses of Nature, ...   O 268 Irene   31
    Distrust is Cowardice, and Prudence Folly. . . . . .   O 301 Irene   86
    Still, still Distrust sits heavy on my Heart. . . . .   O 301 Irene   95
    Let no distrust the gen'rous Hand restrain . . . . .   O 377 Irene   V   3
DIVAN
    Than all the Wisdom of the grave Divan. . . . . . .   O 287 Irene   8
DIVE
    High to soar and deep to dive . . . .   O 178 Thrale 35 Year   9
DIVIDE
    Divide the burden of his care, ...   O 72 Hor. Epode II   50
    While Heav'n and Mahomet divide her Fears, ...   O 260 Irene   127
DIVIDED
    Still discord hovers o'er divided thrones. . . . . .   O 140 Tr Rambler 183   2
    Claim my divided Soul. This Wretch unworthy . . . .   O 275 Irene   69
DIVINE
    From ev'ry tongue flows harmony divine. . . . . . .   O 16 London   129
    Heroic worth, benevolence divine: . . . .   O 34 Vanity Wishes   88
    I'll sing of Chloe's charms divine, ...   O 66 Hor I Ode xxii   23
    Are all transporting, all divine. . . . . . .   O 100 Ode Friendship   24
    And chear the clouded mind with light divine. . . . .   O 130 Tr. Rambler 7   4
    Essence Divine with Matter join'd. . . . .   O 147 Tr Boeth III.6   12
    If mix'd with these, divine Cleora smile, ...   Y   4 On a Daffodill   17
DO
    Clouds do not always veil the skies, ...   O 67 Hor. II Ode IX   1
    Nor do the billows always rise, ...   O 67 Hor. II Ode IX   3
    Do the chain'd waters always freeze; . . . .   O 67 Hor. II Ode IX   6
    Thrice happy Saints--where do I rove? . . . . . .   O 80 Feast St Simon   55
    Do they with Pain repress the struggling Shout, . . .   O 270 Irene   24
    Do thou resolve: For see, Irene comes! . . . . . .   O 275 Irene   90
    Not always do the fairest Flow'rs diffuse . . . . .   O 277 Irene   31
    Do gay Delusions, wand'ring o'er the Brain, ...   O 277 Irene   44
    Do we not share the comprehensive Thought, ...   O 278 Irene   55
    Do not we share the comprehensive thought, ...   Y 149 Irene   V   57
    Forbear--O do not urge me to my Ruin! . . . . . .   O 278 Irene   79
    Aspasia! do I once again behold thee? . . . . . .   O 294 Irene   2
       Do thou repay the Gift, ...   O 313 Irene   18
DOAT
    Born down with Years, still doat upon To-morrow? . . . O 283 Irene   20
    Marks for His own still doat upon to Morrow . . . .   O 374 Irene   V   21
    Dooms me to loath at once, and doat on Falshood, . . . O 310 Irene   10
DOATING
    What doating bigot to his faults so blind, ...   O 137 Tr Rambler 140   1
DOCILITY
    Imbibes with dire docility the wrong. . . . .   O 136 Tr Rambler 132   2
DOCTOR
       Written By Doctor Freind . . . .   O 117 Epitaph Hanmer   T
    And wishes Irene were converted by some . . . . . .   Y 186 Irene   V   11
       doctor
DOES
    Does envy seize thee? crush th' upbraiding joy, . . .   O 32 Vanity Wishes   39
    And makes the happiness she does not find. . . . . .   O 48 Vanity Wishes   368
    What hopes, what terrors does thy gift create, . . .   O 95 Sprig of Myrtl   1
    What Fears, what terrors does this gift create, . . .   O 95 Sprig of Myrtl   V   1
    Does adamantine Faith invest his Heart? . . . . .   O 255 Irene   21
    By what Enchantment does this lovely Greek . . . . .   O 261 Irene   1
    Does chearless Diffidence oppress their Hearts? . . .   O 270 Irene   22
    To morrow strike--Does then that experienc'd . . . .   Y 154 Irene   V   19
       wisdom
    Why does the Blood forsake thy lovely Cheek? . . . .   O 295 Irene   5
    Why does thy Soul retire into herself? . . . . .   O 295 Irene   7
    Does conscious Virtue shake the fainting knee? . . .   O 373 Irene   V   8
    Does not thy Bosom, for I know thee tender, ...   O 329 Irene   5
DOG
    Our little dog has bit his tail . . . .   Y 300 Fanny Burney   4
DOG-DAYS
    To shake in dog-days, in December sweat. . . . . . .   O 16 London   143
DOGS
    Hate dogs their flight, and insult mocks their end. . . O 33 Vanity Wishes   78
    Your Robe of Mourning, and your Dogs of Death. . . . . O 325 Irene   5
DOLEFULL
    With dolefull cries their living lord they mourn . . . Y 21 Tr. Iliad Bk 6   130
    This forc'd the Cranes to utter dolefull moans, . . .   Y 24 Tr Add. Battle   88
DOMAIN
    O'er love, o'er fear, extends his wide domain, ... O 40 Vanity Wishes   195
    O'er love, o'er Force, extends his wide domain, . . .   O 40 Vanity Wishes   V   195
    When ev'ry Storm in my Domain shall roar, ...   O 265 Irene   42
    Till ev'ry Storm in my Domain shall roar, ...   O 354 Irene   V   25
DOME
    And crowd with sudden wealth the rising dome; . . . .   O 19 London   203
    O'er Bodley's dome his future labours spread, ...   O 37 Vanity Wishes   139
    In every dome, in every sacred place, ...   O 189 Seeing Montagu   3
    Nor deign the festive dome to cloy . . . .   O 191 Tr. Medea I   15

DOME	(CONTINUED)	PAGE	TITLE	LINE
They to the dome where smoke with curling play		O 192	Tr. Medea II	5

DOMES
With silent Pangs I view the tow'ring Domes, ...   O 251 Irene   62
DOMESTIC
Hers the mild Merits of domestic Life, ...   O 58 Prologue Comus   31
DOMESTICK
To rural grandeur, and domestick worth; . . . . . .   O 118 Epitaph Hanmer   38
Some petty Passion! some domestick Trifle! . . . . .   O 280 Irene   7
DOMINICN
No faith of partnership dominion owns;   . . . . . .   O 140 Tr Rambler 183   1
Dominion hovers o'er their conquering banners . . . .   Y 115 Irene   V 49D
And sways thy Breast with absolute Dominion, ...   O 266 Irene   18
Adorn a Throne, and dignify Dominion. . . . .   O 276 Irene   10
The subject World, familiar to Dominion. . . . . . .   O 369 Irene   V 10
No more I burn for Fame or for Dominion; . . . . . .   O 333 Irene   43
Yet ere I quit the Scepter of Dominion, ...   O 333 Irene   49
DOMINICNS
When the revolving seasons shall only visit my dominions   Y 132 Irene   V 44
DONE
While I foretell thy Fate; that Office done,-- . . . .   O 289 Irene   9
DOOM
Sign her foes doom, or guard her fav'rites zeal?   . . .   O 34 Vanity Wishes   92
Sign her foes' doom, or guard her patriots zeal;   . . .   Y 95 Vanity Wishes   V 92
Nor think the doom of man revers'd for thee: . . . .   O 38 Vanity Wishes   156
Of hasty greatness finds the fatal doom, ...   O 43 Vanity Wishes   252
Of hasty greatness finds the hasty doom, ...   Y 103 Vanity Wishes   V 252
A Mortal born he met the general Doom, ...   O 51 Pro Drury-Lane   15
As Tyrants doom their Tools of Guilt to die;   . . . .   O 53 Pro Drury-Lane   56
Soon must this bough, as you shall fix his doom,   . . .   O 95 Sprig of Myrtl   13
Soon shall this sprig, as you shall fix its doom, . . .   O 95 Sprig of Myrtl   V 13
Till nature call'd him to the gen'ral doom, ...   O 118 Epitaph Hanmer   43
Unhappy man! behold thy doom, ...   O 124 Winter's Walk   14
When Minos once has fix'd your doom, ...   O 232 Tr Horace IV.7   22
What can reverse thy Doom? . . . .   O 257 Irene   73
Enquires the final Doom of Menodorus, ...   O 263 Irene   24
And Indias rajas ask their doom from thee . . . . .   Y 131 Irene   V 32
The cruel Doom of hapless Menodorus-- . . . . . .   O 270 Irene   4
My Docm confirm'd establishes my Purpose. . . . . .   O 270 Irene   9
The Doom of Guilt alone, nor dare to seize   . . . .   O 316 Irene   14
Recall th' extorted Doom.--It must be so, ...   O 326 Irene   40
Declare thy Message, and expect thy Doom. . . . . .   O 331 Irene   6
Her final Doom, and hurried her Destruction.   . . . .   O 334 Irene   62
Abdalla brought her Doom! Abdalla brought it! . . . .   O 334 Irene   63
Abdalla brought her Doom! . . . .   O 334 Irene   66
Eternal justice thus her doom decreed . . . . . .   O 345 Irene   V 32
well th' Eternal Mind thus her doom decreed . . . .   O 345 Irene   34
But if by their irrevocable doom   . . . . . .   Y 21 Tr. Iliad Bk 6   117
DOOM'D
Unblest, still doom'd to wed with misery. . . . .   O 131 Tr. Rambler 39   1
Immured for ever--and for ever doom'd . . . . . .   O 357 Irene   V 11
Doom'd me to die with all the Turkish Captains. . . .   O 313 Irene   16
Doom'd to her Death unpity'd and unheard, ...   O 332 Irene   20
DOOMS
And dooms my rash Fidelity to Ruin. . . . . . .   O 256 Irene   49
Frowns unrestrain'd, and dooms me with his Eyes.   . . .   O 257 Irene   72
Dooms me to loath at once, and doat on Falshood,   . . .   O 310 Irene   10
DOOR
Love ends with hope, the sinking statesman's door . . .   O 33 Vanity Wishes   79
And stop'd unwilling at her door. . . . .   Y 11 Tr Hor Epode 9   34
DOORS
In vain, these dangers past, your doors you close,   . .   O 21 London   236
DOST
Whence or whither dost thou fly?   . . . .   O 185 Anacreon Ode 9   2
Whence and whither dost thou fly? . . . .   O 185 Anacreon Ode 9   V   2
Still dost thou flutter in the Jaws of Death? . . . .   O 318 Irene   17
Still dost thou linger in these fatal bowrs . . . .   Y 196 Irene   V 18A
DOTAGE
From Marlb'rough's eyes the streams of dotage flow, . .   O 45 Vanity Wishes   317
Forgive the frozen Narratives of Dotage . . . . .   O 366 Irene   V 16
Hence with the frozen Narratives of Dotage   . . . .   O 366 Irene   V 16
DOTARD
With listless eyes the dotard views the store,   . . .   O 43 Vanity Wishes   263
DOTARD'S
Reason! the hoary Dotard's dull Directress, ...   O 281 Irene   44
DOTH
Where doth extatick fury move   . . . .   O 80 Feast St Simon   56
DOUBLE
Since hope but sooths to double my distress, ...   O 10 London   39
And every Danger shocks with double Horror. . . . .   O 261 Irene   21
Demetrius justly pleads a double Title, ...   O 305 Irene   45
Behold him wretched in his double Triumph;   . . . .   O 310 Irene   5
Fill all the starry Lamps with double Blaze;   . . . .   O 322 Irene   8
DOUBLE-FORM'D
A Poet double-form'd I rise, ...   O 70 Hor.II Ode XX   2
DOUBT
And pour on misty Doubt resistless day; . . . . .   O 37 Vanity Wishes   146
To banish Doubt, and brand him for a Villain. . . . .   O 273 Irene   21
Let no weak Doubt the gen'rous Hand restrain, ...   O 313 Irene   22
Frozen with doubt, and maz'd in stupefaction   . . . .   Y 196 Irene   V 18B

```
                                                          PAGE    TITLE           LINE
DOUBTFUL
     Whose quick Impatience seiz'd my doubtful Hand,  . . .  O 254  Irene            126
     A doubtful Glimpse of our approaching Friends; . . . .  O 268  Irene             37
DOUBTFULL
     And victory hangs doubtfull o'er the field. . . . . .   O  76  Tr Add. Battle    13
DOUBTS
     Bid your teizing doubts depart; . . . . . . . . .       O 176  Tr Metastasi I     2
     No cloudy Doubts, or languishing Delays; . . . . . .    O 271  Irene             27
     These chilling doubts, and agonizing horrours? . . . .  Y 189  Irene          V  1A
DOVE
     Tell me, tell me, gentle Dove. . . . . . . . . .        O 185  Anacreon Ode 9     6
     "On the bard her Dove bestow'd. . . . . . . . . .       O 185  Anacreon Ode 9    12
     "Can a prudent Dove decline . . . . . . . . . .         O 185  Anacreon Ode 9    23
DOWN
     Roll darkling down the torrent of his fate? . . . . .   O  47  Vanity Wishes    346
     Swim darkling down the Current of his fate? . . . . .   O  47  Vanity Wishes  V 346
     Down cliffs the roaring Torrent pours . . . . . . .     O  72  Hor. Epode II     38
     Nor down steep cliffs precipitately move . . . . .      O  77  Festina Lente      5
     Down the steep hill the roaring torrent pours; . . .    O 132  Tr. Rambler 65     2
     Bow down and own thyself a Slave. . . . . . . . .       O 146  Tr Boeth III.5    10
     Fell down upon the stone; . . . . . . . . . .           O 157  Par. Hermit I      2
     Fell down upon a stone; . . . . . . . . . .             O 157  Par. Hermit I  V  2
     As I can gulp it down. . . . . . . . . . . .            O 159  Par Hermit III    12
     Down whose current clear and strong, . . . . . . .      O 159  Tr. Rio Verde      2
     I am Cassander, come down from the Sky, . . . . .       O 173  Tr Fr Pantomim  · 1
     That I am Cassander come down from the Sky. . . . .     O 173  Tr Fr Pantomim     3
     Array'd in purer Light, look down on me: . . . . .      O 253  Irene            101
     Thence should my Fury drag him down to Tortures; . .    O 274  Irene             64
     Born down with Years, still doat upon To-morrow? . .    O 283  Irene             20
     Looks down, contemptuous, from his fancy'd Height, .    O 306  Irene              2
     Hew down, ye Guards, those Vassals of Distraction, .    O 333  Irene             51
     "Ah! let not tears down that fair count'nance rowl,     Y  21  Tr. Iliad Bk 6   113
     He tore them down and trampled them to death. . . .     Y  24  Tr Add. Battle    87
DOWNY
     While artful shades thy downy couch enclose, . . .      O 151  The Ant           11
     Pleasure shall spread her downy Pinions o'er thee  . .  O 350  Irene          V 21
     And Love infold thee with his downy Wings. . . . .      O 279  Irene             83
     And pleasure shall shade thee with her downy . . .      Y 150  Irene          V 83
         pinions
DR
     Dr. Johnson upon Friendship . . . . . . . . . .         O  99  Ode Friendship  V  T
     On the Death of Dr. Robert Levet . . . . . . . .        O 200  Death Dr Levet     T
DRAG
     Thence should my Fury drag him down to Tortures; . .    O 274  Irene             64
     And drag away thy Life in Scorn and Safety, . . . .     O 319  Irene             26
DRAIN
     And, yet more strange! his Veins a Horse shall drain,   O 111  To Posterity      25
DRAIN'D
     When a river is drain'd by too many channels the stream is  Y 132  Irene      V 41B
         dry.
DRAINS
     Or drains the Labour of the Bees, . . . . . . . .       O  71  Hor. Epode II     21
DRAM
     Hot her breath with many a dram, . . . . . . . .        Y 301  Extemp. Elegy     18
DRAMA'S
     The Drama's Laws the Drama's Patrons give, . . . .      O  53  Pro Drury-Lane    53
     The Drama's Laws the Drama's Patrons give, . . . .      O  53  Pro Drury-Lane    53
DRANK
     Have drank the liquor up. . . . . . . . . . .           O 159  Par Hermit III     8
     Or Persecution mark, attend our Call; . . . . .         O 306  Irene             54
     Soon had the wrathfull faulchion drank his blood. . .   Y  23  Tr Add. Battle    41
DRAUGHT
     If no wild Draught depart from Reason's Rules, . . .    O 246  Irene Prologue    17
     Quaff the full draught of each terrestrial joy . . .    Y 146  Irene          V 20
     Then shall these Juices taint Demetrius' Draught, . .   O 308  Irene             30
DRAUGHTS
     Thou that hast long perus'd the Draughts of Nature, .   O 255  Irene             11
DRAW
     From his belov'd retirement draw, . . . . . . .         O  71  Hor. Epode II     14
     And faintly draw th' inverted Plow. . . . . . .         O  73  Hor. Epode II     70
     And draw new Virtue from her heav'nly Tongue. . . .     O 285  Irene              7
     Shall Monarchs fear to draw the Sword of Justice, . .   O 312  Irene             21
     Soon as their young began to draw their breath . . .    Y  24  Tr Add. Battle    86
     But now their cruel enemies draw near . . . . . .       Y  24  Tr Add. Battle    90
DRAWN    SEE LONG-DRAWN
DRAWS
     For gold his sword the hireling ruffian draws, . . .    O  31  Vanity Wishes     25
     Delighting, as the youth draws nigh, . . . . . .        O 121  To Miss Playin    15
DREAD
     The guard of commerce, and the dread of Spain, . . .    O  10  London            28
     Tries the dread summits of Cesarean pow'r, . . . .      O  42  Vanity Wishes    242
     From zeal or malice now no more we dread, . . . .       O  61  Pro Word Wise      3
     The Bear enrag'd th' affrighted Moon shall dread; . .   O 111  To Posterity      17
     "Void of care, and free from dread . . . . . . .        O 185  Anacreon Ode 9    33
     At his dread Name the distant Mountains shake . . .     O 268  Irene             28
     At my dread name the distant mountains shake . . .      Y 136  Irene          V 28
     Like the dread Stillness of condensing Storms. . . .    O 270  Irene             14
     I dread his Arts of seeming Innocence, . . . . . .      O 273  Irene             39
     Pants for the dread Event--But let us reason-- . . .    O 280  Irene             31
     Spread by Degrees, and dread th' oppressing Stream;  .  O 282  Irene             58
     Far more I dread Abdalla's fiery Folly, . . . . .       O 287  Irene              7
```

```
                                                              PAGE    TITLE            LINE
DREAD              (CONTINUED)
    The Dread of instant Death restrains my Tongue?    . . .   O 289 Irene               25
    Demand whose Force yon Turkish Heroes dread,       . . . . O 305 Irene               41
    See Cali, Dread of Kings, and Pride of Armies,     . . .   O 311 Irene               16
    And Cowardice to dread the Boast of Folly.    . . . . .    O 318 Irene               22
DREADED
    Spurn'd as a beggar, dreaded as a spy,        . . . . .    O  14 London              81
    Spurn'd as a begger, dreaded as a spy,        . . . . .    O  14 London            V  81
    Th' incumber'd oar scarce leaves the dreaded coast   . .   O  42 Vanity Wishes      239
    And dreaded losses aggravate his pains;     . . . . . .    O  44 Vanity Wishes      286
    Fierce as he was, he dreaded to destroy       . . . .      O 257 Irene               68
    Shake at my dreaded name and the frighted world   . .     Y 136 Irene             V  28
DREADFUL
    No beast more dreadful ever stain'd     . . . . . .        O  66 Hor I Ode xxii    V  13
    No Beast more dreadful ever stain'd     . . . . . .        O  67 To A. Fuscus        13
    The dreadful Dissonance of barb'rous Triumph,   . . . .    O 251 Irene               71
    Forbear this lavish Pomp of dreadful Praise,    . . . .    O 268 Irene               33
    Still fond of Life, groan'd out the dreadful Secret,  . .  O 272 Irene               16
    Soon shall the dire Seraglio's dreadful Gates   . . . .    O 357 Irene             V   9
    My trembling nerves--sink at the dreadful scenes of blood  Y 189 Irene             V  1H
        and death
    And all the terrors of the dreadful main    . . . . . .   Y 201 Irene             V 10C
    Suspend the dreadful Sentence for an Hour?    . . . . .    O 332 Irene               26
    Rush to the War, display thy dreadful Banners,  . . . .    O 333 Irene               40
DREADFULL
    Thus wak'd to rage by Musick's dreadfull Pow'r,    . . ,   O  97 Hickman Spinet      13
    Treason so near us?  at the dreadfull name of   . . . .    O 369 Irene             V  20
        Treason
    Still fond of Life reveald the dreadfull secret,  . . .    O 356 Irene             V  33
    Prescribes the dreadfull comet's flaming path   . . . .    Y 167 Irene             V 124
    The dreadfull dissonance of barbarous triumph   . . . .    Y 169 Irene             V  11
    Thrice to the wall their dreadfull hosts have led  . . .   Y  19 Tr. Iliad Bk 6      56
    To men belongs the dreadfull work of war."    . . . . .   Y  21 Tr. Iliad Bk 6     123
    And paint the horrors of the dreadfull day.   . . . . .   Y  22 Tr Add. Battle       7
    Such was the horrour of the dreadfull fight   . . . . .   Y  26 Tr Add. Battle     136
DREADS
    Where gloom-enamour'd Mischief dreads the Sun,  . . . .    O 192 Tr. Medea II        15
    Ambitious Cali dreads the Statesman's Arts,   . . . . .    O 300 Irene               74
DREAM
    Wakes from his dream, and labours for a joke;   . . . . .  O  17 London             163
    Rais'd from some pleasing dream of wealth and pow'r,  . .  O  18 London             184
    Yet dream not life from grief or danger free,   . . . . .  Y  99 Vanity Wishes     V 155
    The Dream of idle Maids and wanton Poets  . . . . . .      O 350 Irene             V   1
    Awake, Demetrius, from this dismal Dream,     . . . . .    O 252 Irene               83
    Surpriz'd I start, and bless the happy Dream;   . . . .    O 254 Irene              124
    Nor dream of peace, think of rest   . . . . . . .         Y 130 Irene             V  13
    Then dream of Prayer, and Pilgrimage, and Peace.   . .     O 265 Irene               45
    Then dream of (prayer), or (vows) and pilgrimage and  .   Y 132 Irene             V  45
        peace,
        Alas! delusive Dream!    . . . . . . . .              O 267 Irene               45
    Attention rouses from the dream of Love   . . . . .        O 369 Irene             V  21
    A fancy'd Treasure, and a waking Dream.   . . . . .        O 277 Irene               48
    Still languish in our Chains, and dream of Freedom,  . .   O 282 Irene                4
    Dream not of Pow'r thou never can'st attain:    . . . .    O 291 Irene               69
    Wake from thy Dream of Pow'r to Death and Tortures,  . .   O 307 Irene               10
    And War o'erwhelm them in their Dream of Vice.   . . .     O 309 Irene               37
    If thou art more than the gay Dream of Fancy,   . . . .    O 310 Irene               12
    Absorb'd by thought, then waking from his dream   . .      Y 187 Irene             V   6
        What Dream of sudden Power    . . . . . . .           O 323 Irene                1
    Like one awaken'd from a pleasing dream,    . . . . . .    Y   4 On a Daffodill      26
DREAMS
    In pleasing dreams the blissful age renew,    . . . . .    O  10 London              25
    If dreams yet flatter, once again attend,     . . . . .    O  38 Vanity Wishes      163
    No fav'ring Muse her morning Dreams inspire;    . . . .    O  58 Prologue Comus      28
    In pleasing Dreams he cheats the Day    . . . . . .        O  72 Hor. Epode II       35
    In blissful dreams he digs the golden mine,   . . . . .    O  82 Young Author      V  6C
    These dreams were Settle's once and Ogilby's.   . . .      O  82 Young Author        24
    Those dreams were Settle's once and Ogilby's.   . . .      O  82 Young Author      V  24
    In pleasing Visions, and assuasive Dreams;    . . . . .    O 253 Irene              102
    In pleasing Visions, and delusive Dreams;     . . . . .    O 253 Irene            V 102
    Then Visions horrid as a Murd'rer's Dreams    . . . . .    O 266 Irene               13
    Horrid as a murd'rers dreams, madman's laughter   . .     Y 133 Irene             V  13
    Securely sleeps, and, in delightful Dreams,   . . . . .    O 325 Irene               18
DREARY
    To tread the dreary paths without a guide,    . . . . .    O  31 Vanity Wishes        8
    That silent cuts the dreary plains,     . . . . . .        O  69 Hor.II Ode 14       18
    What dreary prospects round us rise,    . . . . . .        O 123 Winter's Walk        2
DREGS
    Sucks in the dregs of each corrupted state.   . . . . .    O  14 London              96
    By Treason levell'd with the Dregs of Men.    . . . .      O 311 Irene               17
DRESS
    Their air, their dress, their politicks import;   . . .    O  15 London             110
    But brighten'd by the sable dress,      . . . . . .        O 122 Stella Mourn.        9
    Suspend the soft Sollicitudes of Dress;     . . . . .      O 246 Irene Prologue       2
    Who thinks us Women born to dress and sing    . . . . .    O 247 Irene Epilogue       2
    The sparkling ornaments, the glittring dress (the change   Y 164 Irene             V  71
        of dress
    The sparkling ornaments, the glittring dress (the change   Y 164 Irene             V  71
        of dress
DRESS'D
    Despise a fool in half his pension dress'd,   . . . . .    O  13 London              73
```

DRESS'D (CONTINUED)	PAGE	TITLE	LINE
See motley life in modern trappings dress'd, ...	O 32	Vanity Wishes	51
Dress'd in each Charm of gay Magnificence, ...	O 261	Irene	14
DRESSD			
The weary Soldier--Still sees to Morrow	O 374	Irene	V 30
dressd in			
DREST			
Who shine, by lavish lovers drest, ...	O 126	To Lyce, Lady	3
Still sees To-morrow drest in Robes of Triumph; . . .	O 283	Irene	29
DREW			
I drew the breath of life in English air;	O 15	London	118
Each Change of many-colour'd Life he drew, ...	O 51	Pro Drury-Lane	3
From her high Seats he drew the Soul, ...	O 147	Tr Boeth III.6	9
Who drew th' essential Form of Grace:	O 155	Epita. Hogarth	V 2
I drew to my party with (alluring) promises artfull . .	Y 158	Irene	V 11
He drew his scymetar and lop'd the branches. . . .	Y 187	Irene	V 7
But now alass! the fatall hour drew nigh	Y 24	Tr Add. Battle	62
Till thither an huge bird the tumult drew	Y 25	Tr Add. Battle	124
DRINK			
That drink the Phasis or the Rhone.	O 70	Hor.II Ode XX	20
--Core, my lad, and drink some beer.	O 181	Parody Warton	8
and drink the holy waters the fountain of	Y 130	Irene	V 11
remission			
DRIV'LER			
And Swift expires a driv'ler and a show.	O 45	Vanity Wishes	318
DRIV'N			
Driv'n hither by inclement skies	O 73	Hor. Epode II	V 59
Then, swift as thought, by headlong anger driv'n . . .	O 76	Tr Add. Battle	10
By vice or passion driv'n	O 345	Irene	V 26
DRIVE			
Here I, though faint myself, must drive my goats, . .	O 64	Virgil Past.I	17
Will quickly drive away his woe, ...	O 69	Hor.II Ode 14	26
Drive the soft Slumbers from his eyes, ...	O 71	Hor. Epode II	10
Drive the soft Slumbers for his eyes.	O 71	Hor. Epode II	V 10
And drive discountenanc'd virtue from the throne: . .	O 176	Tr Metastas II	9
Time his Hours should never drive	O 178	Thrale 35 Year	7
Drive Int'rest, Love, and Vengeance from thy Thoughts, .	O 298	Irene	7
DRIVES			
Drives on the Tempest of destructive War, ...	O 268	Irene	26
D<r>ives to (holds o'er) the south or west the	Y 136	Irene	V 26
storm			
DROOP			
Droop at your tears and soften at your smile . . .	Y 145	Irene	V 4
May droop dismay'd, or kindle into Madness.	O 304	Irene	11
DROOPING			
There prune thy walks, support thy drooping flow'rs, . .	O 20	London	216
There prune thy shades, support the drooping flow'rs, .	Y 58	London	V 216
DROOPS			
For Courage droops unequal to the Combat, ...	O 252	Irene	91
DROP			
"Drop asleep upon his lyre.	O 186	Anacreon Ode 9	40
Our social comforts drop away.	O 200	Death Dr Levet	4
and drop sometimes a tear for lost Irene	O 349	Irene	V 1
DROPP'D			
Held high the steady scale, but dropp'd the sword; . .	O 22	London	V 251
With soften'd Voice she dropp'd the faint Refusal, . .	O 303	Irene	31
DROPS SEE DEW-DROPS			
Now drops at once the pride of aweful state, ...	O 35	Vanity Wishes	V 113
Still drops some joy from with'ring life away; . . .	O 45	Vanity Wishes	306
Here beauty's drops her pomp, despis'd, distress'd . .	Y 107	Vanity Wishes	V 341
DROSS			
The Refuse of our Swords, the Dross of Conquest, . .	O 286	Irene	3
And thought the petty Dross beneath a Sigh.	O 302	Irene	109
DROUSY			
Amidst the drousy charms of dull delight, ...	O 152	The Ant	13
DROVE			
And drove the swarthy troops to their own barren sands. .	O 78	Festina Lente	20
DROWN			
Tears, at my name, shall drown those beauteous eyes, . .	O 75	Tr. Iliad Bk 6	27
You can hang or drown at last.	O 197	Song Congratu.	28
Then we with wine will drown our troubles, laid . . .	Y 7	Virgil Daphnis	47
DROWN'D			
But you are ever drown'd in tears, ...	O 67	Hor. II Ode IX	9
DROWSY			
He rolls no Thunders o'er the drowsy Pit.	O 246	Irene Prologue	26
DRUNKARD			
Some frolick drunkard, reeling from a feast, . . .	O 21	London	228
Some gamesome drunkard, reeling from a feast, . . .	Y 59	London	V 228
DRURY-LANE			
... The Theatre In Drury-lane 1747.	O 50	Pro Drury-Lane	T
DRY			
Only dirt, or wet or dry.	O 196	Song Congratu.	24
When a river is drain'd by too many channels the stream is	Y 132	Irene	V 41B
dry.			
DUBIOUS			
And dubious title shakes the madded land, ...	O 31	Vanity Wishes	30
From dubious titles shakes the madded land, ...	Y 93	Vanity Wishes	V 30
A petty fortress, and a dubious hand;	O 41	Vanity Wishes	220
Lies open to Conjecture's dubious Ken, ...	O 300	Irene	69
Stay--in this dubious Twilight of Conviction, . . .	O 321	Irene	43

		PAGE	TITLE	LINE

DUE
But confident of praise, if praise be due, ... — O 60 Pro Good Nat'd 29
In vain proud Man usurps what's Woman's Due; . . . . — O 247 Irene Epilogue 15
And learn the Rev'rence due to Turkey's Queen. . . . . — O 322 Irene 55
When to the nymphs the swain due homage pays . . . . — Y 7 Virgil Daphnis V 51

DUGS
Their dugs with milk distended, home! . . . . — O 73 Hor. Epode II 68

DULCET-STREAMING
And aided wine with dulcet-streaming sound. . . . . . — O 192 Tr. Medea II 8

DULL
The dull conjecture fawning niece and pamper'd guest, . — Y 104 Vanity Wishes V 276
Must dull Suspence corrupt the stagnant mind? . . . — O 47 Vanity Wishes 344
Must dull Suspence becalm still the stagnant mind? . . — Y 107 Vanity Wishes V 344
"Toil on, dull croud, in extacy, he cries, ... — O 82 Young Author 15
Amidst the drousy charms of dull delight, ... — O 152 The Ant 13
Nor dull Serenity becalms his Eyes. . . . . — O 255 Irene 16
Mocks the dull Vows of Solitude and Penance, ... — O 264 Irene 27
Preach thy dull Politics to vulgar Kings, ... — O 265 Irene 39
Another Hour in dull Deliberation. . . . . — O 271 Irene 34
Reason! the hoary Dotard's dull Directress, ... — O 281 Irene 44
With all the Heroe's dull Security, ... — O 283 Irene 9
Go, languish on in dull Obscurity; . . . . — O 292 Irene 98
Curses the dull Delays of ling'ring Mercy, ... — O 327 Irene 12

DULNESS
Be Vice and Dulness far away . . . . — O 154 Epita. Hogarth 7

DULY
Sing duly hymns to Heaven . . . . — Y 166 Irene V 94

DUMB
And baffled Spite, with hopeless Anguish dumb, ... — O 57 Prologue Comus 17

DUN
Oh! send them to the sullen mansions dun, ... — O 192 Tr. Medea II 13

DUNAMEI
Tei Kallous dunamei ti telos; Zeus panta dedoken . . . — O 103 Eis Elisses 1

DUNGEON'S
Hide me with Murd'rers in the Dungeon's Gloom, ... — O 328 Irene 34

DUNGEONS
For less than rent the dungeons of the Strand; . . . . — O 20 London 215
For less than hires the dungeons of the Strand; . . . — Y 58 London V 215

DURFEYS
New Behns, new Durfeys, yet remain in Store. . . . . — O 53 Pro Drury-Lane 42

DURST
For those who durst not censure, scarce cou'd praise. . — O 51 Pro Drury-Lane 14

DUSKY
But search the wonders of the dusky stone, ... — O 141 Tr Rambler 199 5

DUST
While Crowds aloft the laureat Dust behold, ... — O 58 Prologue Comus V 23
To wit, reviving from its author's dust, ... — O 61 Pro Word Wise 7
Great Hogarth's honour'd Dust is here. . . . . . . — O 154 Epita. Hogarth 8
A floating Atom, Dust that falls unheeded . . . . . — O 260 Irene 139
Dispers'd in Air or mingled with the Dust. . . . . . — O 298 Irene 24
And tread the living picture in the dust . . . . . . — Y 177 Irene V111B
Stretch'd in the Dust, or tow'ring on his Throne; . . . — O 303 Irene 10

DUTIES
Prescribes her duties, or directs her choice, ... — O 151 The Ant 4
one common Interest, mutual duties . . . . — O 352 Irene V 17

DUTY
Forgive, great Sultan, that intrusive Duty . . . . . — O 263 Irene 23
And Duty bids me chuse a distant Walk, ... — O 288 Irene 13
Or why should he, whose Violence of Duty . . . . . . — O 329 Irene 18
Why should the man whose violence of duty . . . . . . — Y 210 Irene V 18

DWELL
Who dwell on Balbos courtly mien-- . . . . — Y 55 London V 150
Secure with Peace, with Competence, to dwell, ... — O 58 Prologue Comus 35
Whether you sit on thrones, or dwell in cots, ... — O 77 Festina Lente 2
Where gloom-enamour'd Mischief loves to dwell, ... — O 192 Tr. Medea II V 15
And dwell upon the Beauties of Irene. . . . . . . — O 262 Irene 10
Oft' shall I dwell on our disastrous Friendship, . . . — O 292 Irene 96
Dwell on my Ear, and sadden all my Soul; . . . . . . — O 329 Irene 9

DWELLS
Dwells on her Lips, and sighs upon her Breast; . . . . — O 286 Irene 5
And dwells on the guilt of apostacy . . . . — Y 186 Irene V 11

DWINDLED
Behold the warrior dwindled to a beau; . . . . . . — O 15 London 104

DY'D
Where wealth unlov'd without a mourner dy'd, ... — O 33 Vanity Wishes 55
Perhaps, where Lear has rav'd, and Hamlet dy'd, . . . — O 53 Pro Drury-Lane 43
By that dire sword my sev'n brave brothers dy'd; . . . — Y 18 Tr. Iliad Bk 6 34
And dy'd their bulrush-spears in mutual blood. . . . . — Y 24 Tr Add. Battle 57

DYE
Their blood the consecrated stones shall dye: . . . . — O 64 Virgil Past.I 10
On cruel Pluto's Altar dye, ... — O 69 Hor.II Ode 14 6
Beneath Pygmean steel what numbers dye! . . . . . . — O 75 Tr Add. Battle 5
With Christian blood, let Leontares dye. . . . . . . — Y 129 Irene V 26
To linger is to dye . . . . — Y 199 Irene V 17

DYES
Mark, when from thousand mingled dyes . . . . — O 121 To Miss Playin 25
Her teeth the night with darkness dyes, ... — O 127 To Lyce, Lady 13

DYING   SEE NEVER-DYING
Confest by dying Menodorus. . . . . — O 272 Irene 13
Confest--confest by dying Leontares . . . . — O 356 Irene V 31
A weeping Wife perhaps, or dying Friend, ... — O 280 Irene 9

```
      Heard her last Cries, and fann'd her dying Beauties, . .    O 333 Irene              47
E'ER    SEE WHERE-E'ER
      None e'er more fierce Numidia's land, . . . . . . .     O  66 Hor I Ode xxii    V  15
      Where e'er they fly their lovers ghosts pursue,  . . .     O  84 Epi Dist Moth.       36
      Nor e'er from virtue's path was lur'd aside, . . . . .     O 118 Epitaph Hanmer       31
      Nor e'er from virtue's paths was turn'd aside, . . . .     O 118 Epitaph Hanmer   V  31
      E'er yet had happiness compleat; . . . . . . . . .     O 136 Tr Rambler 128       2
      What e'er our Crimes, our Woes demand Compassion. . . .     O 251 Irene              58
      If e'er thy Youth has known the Pangs of Absence, . . .     O 285 Irene               3
      Will e'er an happier Hour revisit Greece? . . . . . .     O 301 Irene              96
      For Non Who was e'er beneficent in vain? . . . . . .     O 377 Irene              V   4
      No feasts could e'er my cares dispell; . . . . . . .     Y  11 Tr Hor Epode 9      13
E'RE
      None e're rejects hyperbolies of praise. . . . . . .     O 134 Tr Rambler 104       1
EACH
      Sucks in the dregs of each corrupted state. . . . . .     O  14 London              96
      And view each object with another's eye; . . . . . .     O  16 London             139
      Exalt each trifle, ev'ry vice adore, . . . . . . .     O  17 London             148
      Remark each anxious toil, each eager strife, . . . . .     O  30 Vanity Wishes        3
      Remark each anxious toil, each eager strife, . . . . .     O  30 Vanity Wishes        3
      Explore each restless toil, each anxious strife, . . .     Y  92 Vanity Wishes    V   3
      Explore each restless toil, each anxious strife, . . .     Y  92 Vanity Wishes    V   3
      Each gift of nature, and each grace of art, . . . . .     O  31 Vanity Wishes       16
      Each gift of nature, and each grace of art, . . . . .     O  31 Vanity Wishes       16
      Each gift of nature, and each charm of art, . . . . .     Y  92 Vanity Wishes    V  16
      Each gift of nature, and each charm of art, . . . . .     Y  92 Vanity Wishes    V  16
      And pierce each scene with philosophic eye. . . . . .     O  33 Vanity Wishes       64
      Each act betrays the fever of renown . . . . . . .     Y  97 Vanity Wishes    V 137
      Unnumber'd maladies each Joint invade, . . . . . .     O  44 Vanity Wishes    V 283
      Each passing day some comfort sorrow finds. . . . . .     Y 105 Vanity Wishes    V 301
      Begs for each birth the fortune of a face: . . . . .     O  45 Vanity Wishes      320
      Each nymph your rival, and each youth your slave? . . .     O  46 Vanity Wishes      330
      Each nymph your rival, and each youth your slave? . . .     O  46 Vanity Wishes      330
      Each Change of many-colour'd Life he drew, . . . . .     O  51 Pro Drury-Lane       3
      With ardent Haste, each Candidate of Fame . . . . .     O  57 Prologue Comus       19
      Should Hecatombs each rising Morn . . . . . . .     O  69 Hor.II Ode 14        5
      Whilst each Musician of the Grove . . . . . . . .     O  72 Hor.        Epode II   33
      To whom the church each rolling year . . . . . . .     O  78 Feast St Simon       11
      To point each glance, and force it to the heart! . . .     O  81 Lady Birthday        8
      Each youth admires, though each admirer dies, . . . .     O  83 Epi Dist Moth.       6
      Each youth admires, though each admirer dies; . . . .     O  83 Epi Dist Moth.       6
      Perennial roses deck each purple vale, . . . . . .     O  84 Epi Dist Moth.      16
      And beauty smile auspicious in each face; . . . . .     O  84 Epi Dist Moth.      45
      His learning, join'd with each endearing art, . . . .     O 117 Epitaph Hanmer       7
      Then, when dark arts obscur'd each fierce debate, . . .     O 118 Epitaph Hanmer      23
      Each charm of modulated sound, . . . . . . . . .     O 121 To Miss Playin       6
      In greater scenes each other aid; . . . . . . . .     O 121 To Miss Playin      28
      Beasts of each kind their fellows spare; . . . . . .     O 138 Tr Rambler 160       1
      Each grace of form, each ornament of state, . . . . .     O 141 Tr Rambler 199       7
      Each grace of form, each ornament of state, . . . . .     O 141 Tr Rambler 199       7
      Must bid each wild Desire be still, . . . . . . .     O 146 Tr Boeth III.5       3
      To tell each Bystander, what none can deny, . . . .     O 173 Tr Fr Pantomim       2
      Each Night protected by the friendly Darkness, . . . .     O 251 Irene              59
      Awake each Faculty that sleeps within thee, . . . . .     O 254 Irene               2
      Flows through each Member of th' embodied State, . . .     O 256 Irene              58
      Dress'd in each Charm of gay Magnificence, . . . . .     O 261 Irene              14
      Each Pleasure brightens at its near Approach, . . . .     O 261 Irene              20
      Each Realm where Beauty turns the graceful Shape, . . .     O 262 Irene              13
      Is not each Realm that smiles with kinder Suns, . . .     O 265 Irene              35
      Each Land that smiles beneath beniger Skies . . . .     Y 366 Irene              V  12
      To make Aspasia and Irene name each other. . . . .     Y 133 Irene              V  10
      Each weakness sooth and flatter ev'ry folly. . . . .     Y 134 Irene              V  27
      Each generous Sentiment is thine, Demetrius, . . . .     O 267 Irene              38
      Each lin'gring Hour alarms me for Aspasia. . . . . .     O 270 Irene              20
      At her Approach each ruder Gust of Thought . . . . .     O 275 Irene              91
      Quaff the full draught of each terrestrial joy . . . .     Y 146 Irene              V  20
      Records each Act, each Thought of sov'reign Man, . . .     O 276 Irene              21
      Records each Act, each Thought of sov'reign Man, . . .     O 276 Irene              21
      Records each deed each thought of sovereign Man . . .     O 355 Irene              V  10
      Records each deed each thought of sovereign Man . . .     O 355 Irene              V  10
      Each Day and shall be made happy with new entertainments     O 350 Irene              V  24
      To deck these Bow'rs each Region shall combine, . . .     O 279 Irene              88
      To make thee blest each Region shall combine . . . .     O 351 Irene              V  26
      O'erbears each gentler Motion of the Mind. . . . . .     O 280 Irene              21
      Each rebel Wish, each traitor Inclination . . . . .     O 287 Irene              11
      Each rebel Wish, each traitor Inclination . . . . .     O 287 Irene              11
      every traytor inclination each traytor passion . . .     Y 158 Irene              V  11
      Deny'd Debard each privilege of human nature being . .     Y 165 Irene              V  81
      Beneath each Curse of unrelenting Heav'n, . . . . .     O 292 Irene              86
      With every curse of angry heav'n afflicted beneath  . .     O 357 Irene              V  15
        each
      New Force, new Courage, from each Glance I gain, . . .     O 297 Irene              21
      Each Turkish Bosom burns for thy Destruction, . . . .     O 300 Irene              73
      Submissive and prepar'd for each Event, . . . . . .     O 302 Irene             112
      <E>ach hero fir'd piety or freedom . . . . . . .     Y 181 Irene              V  51
      Watch each unquiet Flutter of the Breast, . . . . .     O 320 Irene              24
      Each piercing Torture, every Change of Pain, . . . .     O 326 Irene              44
      Accus'd the Gods and curs'd each luckless star. . . .     Y   6 Virgil Daphnis       6
      Now each parterre with thorny brakes is fill'd . . . .     Y   7 Virgil Daphnis      24
      Beneath his feet admires each shining star, . . . . .     Y   7 Virgil Daphnis      34
```

```
EACH          (CONTINUED)                                    PAGE    TITLE           LINE
     From Hector's breast each gloomy trouble flies  . . . .  Y  18 Tr. Iliad Bk 6     15
EAGER
     With eager thirst, by folly or by fate,  . . . . . .     O  14 London            95
     Remark each anxious toil, each eager strife,    . . . .  O  30 Vanity Wishes      3
     Thither with eager hast he runs . . . . . . . . .        O  80 Feast St Simon    46
     Orpheus turn'd his eager Sight,  . . . . . . . .         O 150 Tr Boet III.12    50
     Gain'd all his Heart; at length his eager Love  . . . .  O 259 Irene            123
     And listen eager to the rising Wind? . . . . . . .       O 270 Irene             25
     When eager Vengeance shows a naked Foe,  . . . . . .     O 280 Irene             13
     Oft when the fierce Besiegers eager Host . . . . . .     O 298 Irene             27
     Bear off with eager Haste th' unfinish'd Sentence,  . .  O 333 Irene             53
EAGLE
     Stoops from the Blaze like a degenerate Eagle, . . . . . O 292 Irene            101
     Stoops at the Blaze like a degenerate Eagle  . . . . .   V 368 Irene             31
EAR
     No sounds alas would touch th' impervious ear, . . . .   O  43 Vanity Wishes    269
     The notes unfelt would strike th' impervious ear,  . .   Y 104 Vanity Wishes  V 269
     Charm'd ev'ry ear, and gain'd on ev'ry heart. . . . .    O 117 Epitaph Hanmer     8
     Sounds in my sleeping Ear, "Awake Demetrius,   . . . .   O 254 Irene            122
     Glide through Irene to the Sultan's Ear. . . . . . .     O 267 Irene              3
     And kindly grant an Ear to gentler Sounds:  . . . . .    O 285 Irene              2
     In my weak Ear th' intoxicating Sounds. . . . . . .      O 288 Irene              6
     Or tune thine Ear to soothing Adulation. . . . . . .     O 289 Irene              4
     Or tune your ear to soothing Adulation.  . . . . . .     O 366 Irene           V 20
     Dwell on my Ear, and sadden all my Soul; . . . . . .     O 329 Irene              9
     And first a sound invades th' astonish'd ear.  . . . .   Y  25 Tr Add. Battle    91
EARLIEST
     May the morn's earliest tears on thee be shed, . . . .   Y   3 On a Daffodill    11
EARLY
     Was early taught a Briton's right to prize, . . . . .    O  15 London           119
     His force of genius burn'd in early youth, . . . . . .   O 117 Epitaph Hanmer     5
     Thus early wise, th' endanger'd realm to aid, . . . .    O 117 Epitaph Hanmer     9
     Disaster always waits an early wit. . . . . . . .        O 135 Tr Rambler 111     1
     Succeeding years thy early fame destroy; . . . . . .     O 135 Tr Rambler 127     1
     Whose early buds unusual glories wear, . . . . . . .     Y   3 On a Daffodill     3
EARNEST
     Hail beautious earnest of approaching spring!  . . . .   Y   3 On a Daffodill     2
EARTH
     We kneel, and kiss the consecrated earth;  . . . . .     O  10 London            24
     Once more, Democritus, arise on earth,   . . . . . .     O  32 Vanity Wishes     49
     Our bane and physic the same earth bestows,  . . . . .   O 131 Tr. Rambler 21     1
     Unconquer'd bars on earth and sea withstand; . . . . .   O 136 Tr Rambler 129     3
     If such on Earth can Bliss bestow,  . . . . . . .        O 146 Tr Boeth III.4     7
     All Men throughout the peopled Earth . . . . . . .       O 146 Tr Boeth III.6     1
     Leaves the Load of Earth behind. . . . . . . . .         O 147 Tr Boet III.12     4
     Or Virtue shall replace on earth.  . . . . . . .         O 232 Tr Horace IV.7    24
     Or Virtue shall restore to earth.  . . . . . . .         O 232 Tr Horace IV.7  V 24
     And shook the (affrighted) world lab'ring earth licentious
          conquest                                            Y 115 Irene          V 49A
     To waft our gallies o'er the trembling earth? . . . .    Y 115 Irene          V 49H
     To heav'n and earth the courage of Leontius  . . . . .   Y 120 Irene          V 31B
     Live till the tott'ring Earth forsakes its . . . . .     O 347 Irene           V 29
          Base
     Willing to delay you here they give you on earth the . . Y 184 Irene           V 10
     Torn from the mourning Earth by thy Neglect.  . . . . .  O 334 Irene              4
     "Whose fame from earth resounded to the skies."  . . .   Y   7 Virgil Daphnis    31
EARTH'S
     Unshaken be thy Throne as Earth's firm Base,  . . . .    O 262 Irene              2
EARTHLY
     And in this earthly Case confin'd; . . . . . . . .       O 147 Tr Boeth III.6    10
     And in this earthly cage confin'd; . . . . . . . .       O 147 Tr Boeth III.6  V 10
EARTHQUAKE
     But when an earthquake comes weak and unsupported  . . . Y 131 Irene          V 36B
EARTHQUAKES
     Did Earthquakes shake our walls? . . . . . . . .         O 347 Irene           V  3
EASE
     But lost in thoughtless ease, and empty show,  . . . .   O  15 London           103
     But sunk in thoughtless ease, and empty show,  . . . .   Y  53 London         V 103
     The young enthusiast quits his ease for fame;  . . . .   O  36 Vanity Wishes    136
     Here at your ease you sing your amorous flame, . . . .   O  64 Virgil Past.I      5
     And me to tune at ease th' unequal reeds. . . . . .      O  64 Virgil Past.I     12
     No setting Sol can ease your cares,  . . . . . . .       O  67 Hor. II Ode IX    11
     With transports kindled, rural ease, . . . . . . .       O  73 Hor. Epode II     74
     To ease their pains exert your milder power, . . . . .   O  84 Epi Dist Moth.    46
     And ease the throbbings of an anxious heart; . . . .     O  95 Sprig of Myrtl    12
     To letter'd ease retir'd, and honest mirth, . . . .      O 118 Epitaph Hanmer    37
     Greatness with ease, and gay severity. . . . . . .       O 137 Tr Rambler 141     1
     Would ease the hunger of the mind, . . . . . . .         O 144 Tr Boeth. II.2     8
     The Cloister's Ease, resum'd the tott'ring Throne, . .   O 256 Irene             44
     And ease my loaded Soul upon her Bosom?  . . . . .       O 263 Irene             22
     They cultivate at ease the gentler arts in quiet . . .   Y 177 Irene          V 117
EASIER
     The Wits of Charles found easier Ways to Fame, . . . .   O  52 Pro Drury-Lane    17
     And sought An easier conquest in my softer beauty  . . . Y 134 Irene           V 35
EASTERN
     By Eastern Tempests hither tost, . . . . . . . .         O  73 Hor. Epode II     58
     I swear this Eastern Pageantry is Nonsense, . . . .      O 247 Irene Epilogue    13
     Disperse Rebellion through the Eastern World;  . . . .   O 274 Irene             52
EASY
     From wealth and grandeur easy to descend, . . . . .      O 130 Tr. Rambler 12     3
```

		PAGE	TITLE	LINE

EASY   (CONTINUED)
My Policy shall raise an easy Throne;   . . . .   O 257 Irene   78
In easy State presides o'er all their Motions, ...   O 293 Irene   122
ECHO
My Name shall echo through the shouting Field;   . . . .   O 305 Irene   40
Let distant regions echo with his name   . . . . . .   Y 20 Tr. Iliad Bk 6   103
ECHOES
The Stage but echoes back the publick Voice.   . . .   O 53 Pro Drury-Lane   52
For wisdom ever echoes nature's voice.   . . . . . .   O 138 Tr Rambler 156   1
ECHOING
And spread their echoing grief from shore to shore.   . . .   Y   6 Virgil Daphnis   12
ECHOIS
Sou pote grapsomenon Birchion allon echois.   . . . . .   O 108 Eis Birchion   4
ECLIPSE
They see the Sun surmount the dark Eclipse, ...   O 287 Irene   5
And his more glorious acts eclipse his father's fame.   .   Y 20 Tr. Iliad Bk 6   104
ECSTACY
Such Ecstacy of Love! such pure Affection, ...   O 295 Irene   15
EDDIES
Persue thy course through boiling eddies, ...   Y 201 Irene   V 10A
EDE
Eroon te Bious Birchion, ede Sophon, ...   O 108 Eis Birchion   2
EDGE
Dart the quick taunt, and edge the piercing gibe?   . . .   O 33 Vanity Wishes   62
And unexhausted laughter, and edge the piercing gibe   . .   Y 94 Vanity Wishes   V 62
EDWARD
Illustrious Edward! from the realms of day, ...   O 15 London   99
EER
When eer the tumult of unestablish'd Conquest   . . . .   O 357 Irene   V 6
EETION
Whose sire Eetion in Cilicia reign'd   . . . .   Y 18 Tr. Iliad Bk 6   7
EFFECT
Thus I t' effect this mighty change design'd   . . . .   Y 11 Tr Hor Epode 9   29
EFFECTS
Perhaps, for who can guess th' Effects of Chance?   . . .   O 53 Pro Drury-Lane   45
EFFORT
The strongest Effort of a female Soul, ...   O 278 Irene   62
Nor think that Effort lost which rescues thee.   . . . .   O 317 Irene   47
EFFORTS
To stronger Efforts, and maturer Counsels.   . . . . .   O 270 Irene   8
Assist her Efforts with thy strong Persuasion;   . . . .   O 321 Irene   34
EFFULGENCE
On darkling man in pure effulgence shine, ...   O 130 Tr. Rambler 7   3
With bright effulgence The travell<er> afar   . . . .   Y 131 Irene   V 36
EFFUS'D
All ye, whose Blood tyrannick Rage effus'd, ...   O 306 Irene   53
EFFUSE
And Sloth effuse her opiate fumes in vain;   . . . . .   O 37 Vanity Wishes   150
EGRAPSEN
Ek Dios estin onar, Theios pot egrapsen Homeros,   . . .   O 103 Eis Elisses   3
EGYPT'S
But left, like Egypt's Kings, a lasting Tomb.   . . . .   O 51 Pro Drury-Lane   16
EIDEN
Eiden Aletheie proen chairoysa graphonta   . . . . . .   O 108 Eis Birchion   1
EIGHTIETH
Tho' now his eightieth year was nigh.   . . . .   O 202 Death Dr Levet   32
EIPEN
Kai Bion, eipen, otan ripses Thanatio Belessi, ...   O 108 Eis Birchion   3
EIS
Eis to tes Elisses peri ton Oneiron Ainigma   . . . . .   O 103 Eis Elisses   T
Alla tod eis Thnetous Kupris epempseu onar   . . . . .   O 103 Eis Elisses   4
Eis Birchion   . . . .   O 108 Eis Birchion   T
EISORAAS
Ton taphon eisoraas ton Olibarioio, Konien   . . . . .   O 171 Epi. Goldsmith   1
Ton taphon eisoraas ton Oleiberioio, konien   . . . . .   O 171 Epi. Goldsmith   V 1
Ton taphon eisoraas ton Olibaroio, konien   . . . . .   O 171 Epi. Goldsmith   V 1
EITHER
And show'rs from either flow.   . . . .   O 127 To Lyce, Lady   12
And rain from either flow.   . . . .   Y 86 To Lyce, Lady   V 12
I mark'd them well, and trac'd in either Face   . . . .   O 275 Irene   81
EK
Ek Dios estin onar, Theios pot egrapsen Homeros,   . . .   O 103 Eis Elisses   3
EKPERSE
Zeus mounos phlogoenti poleis ekperse kerauno, ...   O 103 Eis Elisses   5
ELATE
Elate with Conquest, in his native Mountains, ...   O 264 Irene   14
Elate with Hope, and panting for a Foe.   . . . . . .   O 304 Irene   5
ELDERLY
To Lyce, an elderly Lady   . . . .   O 126 To Lyce, Lady   T
ELECTING
The great, 'tis true, can charm th' electing tribe;   . .   O 60 Pro Good Nat'd   25
ELEGANCE
Greatness of mind with elegance of form.   . . . . . .   Y 149 Irene   V 56
ELEGANT
There might'st thou find some elegant retreat, ...   O 20 London   212
The might you find some elegant retreat, ...   Y 58 London   V 212
ELEGIES
I without fun'ral elegies   . . . .   O 70 Hor.II Ode XX   23
ELEGY
Ode and Elegy and Sonnet.   . . . .   O 179 Ridicul Warton   8

		PAGE	TITLE	LINE
ELEMENTAL				
This elemental Joy, this gen'ral Calm,	. . . . . .	O 314	Irene	8
ELEMENTS				
That links the jarring Elements in Peace.	. . . . .	O 257	Irene	64
ELEVATE				
That sooth the sense, and elevate the thought	. . . .	Y 165	Irene	V 80
ELEVATES				
That fires thy Cheek, and elevates thy Mien,	. . . .	O 323	Irene	9
ELISSES				
Eis to tes Elisses peri ton Oneiron Ainigma	. . . .	O 103	Eis Elisses	T
ELIZA				
Struck with the seat that gave Eliza birth,	. . . . . .	O 10	London	23
To Eliza plucking Laurel in Mr Pope's Gardens	. . . .	O 106	Eliza plucking	T
As learn'd Eliza, sister of the Muse,	. . . . . .	O 106	Eliza plucking	1
ELIZA'S				
And Spenser's verse prolongs Eliza's reign;	. . . . . .	O 114	On C. Cibber	2
ELMS				
As vines the elms, as grapes adorn the vine,	. . . .	Y 6	Virgil Daphnis	17
And planted elms around his monument	. . . .	Y 18	Tr. Iliad Bk 6	33
ELOCUTION				
With fatal sweetness elocution flows,	. . . .	O 31	Vanity Wishes	18
ELOQUENCE				
Can Balbo's eloquence applaud, and swear	. . . . .	O 17	London	150
To hear his eloquence, and praise his life.	. . . . .	O 118	Epitaph Hanmer	18
Or Eloquence, or splendid birth,	. . . . .	O 232	Tr Horace IV.7	23
Exhaust the Stores of pious Eloquence,	. . . . .	O 265	Irene	2
Why all this Glare of splendid Eloquence,	. . . . .	O 276	Irene	11
My tongue with am'rous eloquence displaid	. . . . .	Y 158	Irene	V 7
There shall despotick Eloquence resume	. . . . .	O 302	Irene	120
Go then, and with united Eloquence	. . . . . .	O 306	Irene	57
ELSE				
All else is empty Sound, and idle Show.	. . . . . .	O 246	Irene Prologue	14
ELUDE				
And though at length subdued, elude thy Vengeance.	. .	O 274	Irene	57
Elude my Vengeance? no--My Troops shall range	. . .	O 274	Irene	58
The birds elude the stroke with cautious care;	. . .	Y 26	Tr Add. Battle	134
ELUDED				
A feeble Government, eluded Laws,	. . . .	O 250	Irene	37
ELUDING				
Still courting his embrace and still eluding	. . . .	Y 155	Irene	V 35
ELYSIAN				
And wander sportive o'er th' Elysian plain:	. . . . .	O 77	Tr Add. Battle	43
EMASCULATED				
When Avarice corrupts th' emasculated Nation--or	. .	O 347	Irene	V 25
EMBARK'D				
Embark'd with Treason on the Seas of Fate,	. . . . .	O 300	Irene	59
EMBATTLED				
With half mankind embattled at his side,	. . . . . .	O 42	Vanity Wishes	226
With half mankind embattled on his side,	. . . . . .	Y 102	Vanity Wishes	V 226
Had rang'd embattled Nations at our Gates:	. . . . .	O 250	Irene	23
Above their heads th' embattled squadrons hung	. . . .	Y 25	Tr Add. Battle	94
EMBLEM				
Ambiguous emblem of uncertain fate!	. . . . . .	O 95	Sprig of Myrtl	2
Ambiguous emblem of my future fate!	. . . . . .	O 95	Sprig of Myrtl	V 2
With grief this emblem of mankind I see,	. . .	Y 4	On a Daffodill	25
EMBODIED				
Flows through each Member of th' embodied State,	. . .	O 256	Irene	58
The steely troops embodied closely stand	. . . . . .	Y 24	Tr Add. Battle	78
EMBOW'RING				
Behold, within th' embow'ring Grove	. . . . .	O 314	Irene	10
EMBOWER'D				
Those Groves, whose Shades embower'd the dear Irene,	. .	O 333	Irene	46
EMBRACE				
Practis'd their master's notions to embrace,	. . . .	O 16	London	136
While he lies melting in a lewd Embrace;	. . . . . .	O 111	To Posterity	24
Will he not soften in a Friend's Embrace?	. . . . .	O 255	Irene	24
Religion calls her from the wish'd Embrace,	. . . . .	O 261	Irene	16
Still courting his embrace and still eluding	. . . .	Y 155	Irene	V 35
EMBRACES				
In Sighs and Tears, in Transports and Embraces,	. . .	O 269	Irene	15
In sighs and tears, and transports and embraces,	. . .	O 367	Irene	V 27
EMBROIL'D				
Embroil'd the Turkish State--our Sultan's Father	. . .	O 256	Irene	42
EMERGING				
Just emerging into Light,	. . . .	O 150	Tr Boet III.12	49
EMINENCE				
The glitt'ring eminence exempt from foes;	. . . . .	O 38	Vanity Wishes	166
The glitt'ring eminence exempt from woes;	. . . . .	O 38	Vanity Wishes	V 166
EMITTED				
The subtler Flames emitted from the Sky,	. . . . . .	O 282	Irene	59
EMOTION				
heav'nly charms without emotion	. . . .	Y 129	Irene	V 6
EMOTIONS				
Yet unacquainted with these soft Emotions	. . . .	O 263	Irene	16
The strong Emotions of my troubled Soul	. . . . .	O 275	Irene	87
Betray'd the wild Emotions of his Mind.	. . . . . .	O 311	Irene	4
Whence rise these restless cares? these strong emotions?		Y 189	Irene	V 1
EMPEROR				
But yet, great Emperor, beware of Treason;	. . . . .	O 273	Irene	31
EMPIRE				
Did no subverted empire mark his end?	. . . .	O 41	Vanity Wishes	216

EMPIRE   (CONTINUED)   PAGE   TITLE   LINE
  To ev'ry empire bounds the Gods ordain . . . . . .   O 76 Tr Add. Battle   35
  Resign'd his Thirst of Empire to her Charms, ... O 97 Hickman Spinet   19
  Well might the Weakness of our Empire sink . . . . .   O 250 Irene   48
  Empire and conquest hover or . . . .   Y 115 Irene   V 49C
  Fills all th' astonish'd Empire with Confusion, . . . O 257 Irene   77
  Then 'tis decreed. (then death or empire.) . . . .   Y 130 Irene   V 20
  Extended Empire, like expanded Gold, ...   O 265 Irene   37
  His vast designs, and plans of boundless Empire. . . . O 356 Irene   V 29
  Empire or Wealth, to Excellence like thine? . . . . . O 267 Irene   9
  Suspend his Sentence--Empire and Irene . . . . . .   O 275 Irene   68
  --Love and empire . . . .   Y 144 Irene   V 68
  And turn thy Thoughts henceforth to Love and Empire. . O 276 Irene   5
  The Thirst of Empire, and the Love of Glory? . . . . O 278 Irene   58
  The thirst of empire and the love of virtue? . . . . Y 149 Irene   V 58
  The full-blown pride of conquest and of empire . . . Y 149 Irene   V 58
  Empire and Love shall share the blissful Day, . . .   O 279 Irene   90
  And all the proud magnificence of empire . . . . .   Y 158 Irene   V 9
  Grasp at Command, and tow'r in quest of Empire; . . . O 293 Irene   114
  Her ancient Empire o'er the yielding Heart; . . . .   O 302 Irene   121
  Will now remount the slighted Seat of Empire, . . .   O 303 Irene   27
  The petty Claims of Empire and of Honour; . . . . .   O 307 Irene   23
  At once the Joys of Paradise and Empire, ...   O 308 Irene   7
  Contrive perhaps, the Ruin of our Empire, ...   O 312 Irene   2
  Joys ill exchang'd for Gold, and Pride, and Empire. . . O 313 Irene   10
  Strives to regain her Empire of the Mind: . . . . .   O 320 Irene   33
  Was this the Maid whose Love I bought with Empire! . . O 330 Irene   9
EMPIRE'S
  The Empire's Darling, and the Soldier's Boast; . . . . O 257 Irene   69
EMPIRES
  That bears the Fate of Empires in her Air, ... O 317 Irene   2
EMPLOY
  Those sovereign charms with strictest care employ; . . O 81 Lady Birthday   13
EMPLOY'D
  On life, on morals, be thy thoughts employ'd; . . . . O 140 Tr Rambler 180   1
  The single talent well employ'd. . . . .   O 201 Death Dr Levet   28
  His single talent well employ'd. . . . .   O 201 Death Dr Levet V 28
EMPLOYS
  <He> sets his nets, employs his skill. . . . . . .   O 72 Hor. Epode II   42
EMPTY
  Wants ev'n the cheap reward of empty praise; . . . .   O 10 London   36
  But lost in thoughtless ease, and empty show, ... O 15 London   103
  But sunk in thoughtless ease, and empty show, ... Y 53 London   V 103
  To thee were solemn toys or empty shew, ...   O 33 Vanity Wishes   65
  At best, a fleeting gleam, or empty sound. . . . .   O 62 Pro Word Wise   20
  At last, a fleeting gleam, or empty sound. . . . .   O 62 Pro Word Wise V 20
  All useless science is an empty boast. . . . . . .   O 133 Tr. Rambler 83   1
  All else is empty Sound, and idle Show. . . . . . .   O 246 Irene Prologue   14
  Your thin battalions and your empty tents . . . . .   Y 120 Irene   V 29A
  I come from empty Noise, and tasteless Pomp, ... O 262 Irene   7
  The glitt'ring Vanities of empty Greatness, ... O 265 Irene   6
  Sooth the delighted Soul with empty Bliss? . . . . . O 277 Irene   45
  With empty threats, and fruitless Exclamation, . . . O 368 Irene   V 15
  Success and Conquest now are empty Sounds, ... O 333 Irene   44
EMULATION
  To noble Thought and gen'rous Emulation, ... O 298 Irene   14
ENAMOUR'D   SEE GLOOM-ENAMOUR'D
  Perhaps, enamour'd of resembling Virtue, ... O 252 Irene   96
ENCHAIN
  Dissolve thy vigour, and enchain thy powers? . . . . O 151 The Ant   10
  Unnerve thy vigour, and enchain thy pow'rs; . . . . . O 151 The Ant   V 10
ENCHAIN'D
  Thou who couldst laugh where want enchain'd caprice, . . O 32 Vanity Wishes   53
ENCHAINS
  The waves he lashes, and enchains the wind; . . . . . O 42 Vanity Wishes   232
ENCHANTING
  That Air resistless and enchanting Blush, ...   O 277 Irene   27
ENCHANTMENT
  By what Enchantment does this lovely Greek . . . . . O 261 Irene   1
ENCIRCLING   SEE INCIRCLING
  Amidst the Splendor of encircling Beauty, ...   O 288 Irene   1
ENCLOSE
  While artful shades thy downy couch enclose, ... O 151 The Ant   11
ENCOUNTER
  And Bolts and rocks encounter in the Skie, ... O 76 Tr Add. Battle   23
ENCREAS'D
  So much our splendour was encreas'd by thine. . . . . Y   6 Virgil Daphnis   19
ENCREASING
  Dispatch; th' encreasing Danger . . . .   O 297 Irene   12
ENCUMBER'D
  Where hast thou linger'd while th' encumber'd Hours . . O 279 Irene   3
END
  Hate dogs their flight, and insult mocks their end. . . O 33 Vanity Wishes   78
  Shall Wolsey's wealth, with Wolsey's end be thine? . . O 35 Vanity Wishes 122
  Hear Lydiat's life, and Galileo's end. . . . . . .   O 38 Vanity Wishes 164
  Did no subverted empire mark his end? . . . .   O 41 Vanity Wishes 216
  Such age there is, and who shall wish its end? . . . . O 44 Vanity Wishes 298
  Such age there is, and who could wish its end? . . . . O 44 Vanity Wishes V 298
  Such age the is, and who could wish its end? . . . . Y 105 Vanity Wishes V 298
  By Solon caution'd to regard his end, ...   O 45 Vanity Wishes 314
  And learn his virtues, while thou mourn'st his end. . . O 117 Epitaph Hanmer   4

```
END            (CONTINUED)                          PAGE    TITLE              LINE
     Path, motive, guide, original, and end.  . . . . . .   O 130  Tr. Rambler 7          8
     Thou, who began'st a man, wilt end a boy.    . . . .   O 135  Tr Rambler 127         2
     Woman the Source, the Object, and the End.   . . . .   O 247  Irene Epilogue        18
     Not for itself but for a nobler End   . .  . . . .     O 290  Irene                 30
     Th' Eternal gave it, and that End is Virtue. . . . .   O 290  Irene                 31
     Nor end my Terrors with the Sultan's Death;  . . . .   O 300  Irene                 67
     Not one takes warning, by another's end. . . . . .     Y  67  Prologue Lethe         6
ENDANGER'D
     Thus early wise, th' endanger'd realm to aid,  . . .   O 117  Epitaph Hanmer         9
ENDEAR'D
     And recollected toils endear'd the shade;   . . . .    O 118  Epitaph Hanmer        42
ENDEARING    SEE INDEARING
     His learning, join'd with each endearing art,  . . .   O 117  Epitaph Hanmer         7
     And chang'd th' endearing Smile and am'rous Whisper . .  O 259  Irene              111
     There had she lull'd me with endearing Falshoods, . . .  O 331  Irene               18
ENDEARMENTS
     In soft Endearments, and in gentle Murmurs, . . . .    O 303  Irene                 14
ENDEARS
     For what but social guilt the friend endears?  . . .   O  14  London                83
     Whose peaceful day Benevolence endears,  . . . . .     O  44  Vanity Wishes        295
ENDEAV'RING
     He grasp'd her hand endeav'ring kind relief. . . .     Y  21  Tr. Iliad Bk 6       112
ENDED
     Ended her wretched life and pierc'd her heart. . . .   Y  19  Tr. Iliad Bk 6        43
ENDLESS
     And fir'd with pleasing hope of endless fame, . . .    O  82  Young Author          12
     Polish'd with endless toil, my lays   . . . . . .      O 139  Tr Rambler 169         1
     Endless Labour all along, . . . . . . . . . .          O 179  Ridicul Warton         3
     Endless Labour to be wrong;  . . . . . . . . .         O 179  Ridicul Warton         4
     Are only varied Modes of endless Being;  . . . . .     O 290  Irene                 27
ENDS
     Love ends with hope, the sinking statesman's door . . .  O  33  Vanity Wishes       79
     Be virtuous Ends pursued by virtuous Means, . . . .    O 291  Irene                 58
ENDUR'D
     Endur'd the stinging lash, and tamely bore the yoke. . .  Y   6  Virgil Daphnis     14
ENDURE
     Alternate rest and labour long endure.   . . . . .     O 131  Tr. Rambler 33         1
ENEMIES
     descend in a proverb among thy enemies . . . . . .     Y 113  Irene            V    21
     Guarded from all but winged enemies  . . . . . . .     Y  23  Tr Add. Battle        25
     But now their cruel enemies draw near  . . . . . .     Y  24  Tr Add. Battle        90
ENEMY
     Forcefull descending strikes his enemy,  . . . . .     Y  26  Tr Add. Battle       131
ENGAGE
     New forms arise, and diff'rent views engage, . . .     O  45  Vanity Wishes        307
     she sees whom diff'rent views engage,  . . . . . .     Y 106  Vanity Wishes    V  307
     Yet softer Claims the melting Heart engage,  . . .     O  58  Prologue Comus        29
     Soon might her Tears engage a Lover's Credit;  . . .   O 327  Irene                 17
     Whilst beaks and swords engage in bloody fray  . . .   Y  22  Tr Add. Battle         6
ENGLAND
     Ye Sons of England, deign to hear, . . . . . . .       O 188  Epilogue               3
ENGLAND'S
     Ye patriot Crouds, who burn for England's Fame, . .    O  57  Prologue Comus         1
ENGLISH
     Or English honour grew a standing jest.  . . . . .     O  10  London                30
     I drew the breath of life in English air;  . . . .     O  15  London               118
     For English vengeance wars not with the dead. . . .    O  61  Pro Word Wise          4
ENGROSS
     Engross not all the beams on high, . . . . . . .       O 126  To Lyce, Lady          5
     Virtue and Liberty engross his Soul, . . . . . .       O 255  Irene                 32
ENI
     Toios Ares Brotoloigos eni ptolemoisi memene, . . .    O 172  On Marlborough         1
ENJOY
     Enjoy the prayers and blessings of the needy, . . .    Y 130  Irene            V  12C
     Name and enjoy thy Wish-- . . . . . . . . . .          O 307  Irene                 12
ENJOY'D
     Then best enjoy'd, when most improv'd. . . . .         O 125  An Ode                28
     When best enjoy'd, when most improv'd. . . . . .       O 125  An Ode           V    28
ENJOYMENT
     Immortal Crowns and Fulness of Enjoyment?  . . . .     O 276  Irene                 14
ENJOYS
     No pug, nor favourite Cupid there enjoys . . . . .     O  84  Epi Dist Moth.        20
     And real Happiness enjoys. . . . . . . . . .           O 145  Tr Boeth III.1        12
     Yet Greece enjoys no Gleam of transient Hope, . . .    O 249  Irene                 11
ENKINDLED
     Gross Fires, enkindled by a mortal Hand, . . . . .     O 282  Irene                 57
     My Bosom feels, enkindled from the Sky,  . . . . .     O 293  Irene                108
ENLARG'D
     Thy Soul by Nature great, enlarg'd by Knowledge, . .   O 266  Irene                 35
ENLARGE
     .Enlarge my life with multitude of days, . . . . .     O  43  Vanity Wishes        255
ENLIV'NING
     Enliv'ning hope, and fond desire,  . . . . . . .       O 123  Winter's Walk          9
ENLIVENING
     Th' enlivening Wit, the penetrating Reason? . . . .    O 278  Irene                 56
ENNOBLED
     Ennobled, yet unchang'd, if Nature shine:  . . . .     O 246  Irene Prologue        16
ENORMOUS
     On weak foundations raise th' enormous weight? . . .   O  35  Vanity Wishes        126
     Th' enormous Gyants smoke upon the Ground. . . . .     O  76  Tr Add. Battle        25
```

		PAGE	TITLE	LINE
ENOUGH				
And for one Man--one Wife's enough in Conscience.	. . .	O 247	Irene Epilogue	14
Enough of unavailing Tears, Demetrius,	. . . . .	O 253	Irene	104
This were enough, if Cali had been Mahomet	. . . .	Y 132	Irene	V 41D
Is 't not enough, he lives by our Indulgence,	. . . .	O 286	Irene	6
Enough--resistless Reason calms my Soul--	. . . .	O 297	Irene	1
ENQUIR'D				
We started at the Sound, again enquir'd,	. . . . . .	O 325	Irene	25
ENQUIRER				
Enquirer cease alarm, no wishes rise,	. . . .	Y 108	Vanity Wishes	V 347
Enquirer, cease, petitions yet remain,	. . . . . .	O 47	Vanity Wishes	349
ENQUIRES				
Enquires the final Doom of Menodorus,	. . . . . .	O 263	Irene	24
ENRAG'D				
The Bear enrag'd th' affrighted Moon shall dread;	. . .	O 111	To Posterity	17
Enrag'd by Wrongs, exulting with Success,	. . . .	O 313	Irene	15
The Sultan comes, still gloomy, still enrag'd.	. . . .	O 330	Irene	26
ENROB'D				
Enrob'd in Death--Dispatch her and be great.	. . . .	O 326	Irene	3
ENROLL'D				
And on its basis would have been enroll'd,	. . . . .	O 190	Seeing Montagu	5
ENSIGN				
The Myrtle (ensign of supreme command	. . . . . .	O 95	Sprig of Myrtl	3
ENSLAV'D				
Save him whose Soul enslav'd to Vice	. . . . . .	O 147	Tr Boeth III.6	19
Or only struggles to be more enslav'd?	. . . . . .	O 281	Irene	41
ENSNARES				
With secret springs oft ensnares	. . . .	O 72	Hor. Epode II	43
ENTANGLED				
Stoop from thy Flight, trace back th' entangled Thought,		O 293	Irene	127
ENTERPRISING				
The noble flame of enterprising Virtue	. . . . . .	O 371	Irene	V 28
ENTERPRIZE				
And restless enterprize impells to death.	. . . .	Y 92	Vanity Wishes	V 20
Forgive, great Jove, the daring enterprize.	. . . . .	O 136	Tr Rambler 129	6
ENTERPRIZING				
The holy Flame of enterprizing Virtue,	. . . . . .	O 264	Irene	26
ENTERTAINMENTS				
Each Day and shall be made happy with new entertainments		O 350	Irene	V 24
ENTHUSIAST				
The young enthusiast quits his ease for fame;	. . . .	O 36	Vanity Wishes	136
Would loose the wild Enthusiast to destroy,	. . . . .	O 291	Irene	61
ENTRAILS				
Insatiate on her wasted Entrails prey,	. . . . . .	O 315	Irene	36
ENTRANCE				
'Tis yours to grant, or to refuse him entrance	. . .	Y 168	Irene	V 3
ENTREAT				
And Nature's Rights entreat th' asserting Sword.	. . .	O 297	Irene	3
ENTREATS SEE INTREATS				
There let Aspasia, since my Fair entreats it,	. . . .	O 263	Irene	3
ENVENOM'D				
Nor taints with death the envenom'd dart,	. . . . .	O 65	Hor I Ode xxii	3
Nor taints with Death th' envenom'd Dart,	. . . . .	O 66	To A. Fuscus	3
ENVIES				
En<v>ies the meanest minister of Heav'n of celestial	. .	Y 168	Irene	V135A
beings.				
He envies none the Converse of Aspasia.	. . . . . .	O 296	Irene	4
ENVIOUS				
An envious Breast with certain Mischief glows,	. . . .	O 46	Vanity Wishes	V330A
From th' envious world with scorn I spring,	. . . . .	O 70	Hor.II Ode XX	3
Th' adoring youth, and envious fair,	. . . .	O 122	Stella Mourn.	13
Thou know'st those arts which blast with envious praise,	.	O 176	Tr Metastas II	7
Pensive, and envious of Irene's Greatness,	. . . . .	O 314	Irene	12
ENVY				
Does envy seize thee? crush th' upbraiding joy,	. . .	O 32	Vanity Wishes	39
Toil, envy, want, the patron, and the jail.	. . . . .	O 38	Vanity Wishes	160
Toil, envy, want, the Garret, and the jail.	. . . . .	O 38	Vanity Wishes	V 160
(No spark of envy harbours in my breast)	. . . . .	O 64	Virgil Past.I	14
Ah! how shall envy sooth her pain?	. . . .	O 122	Stella Mourn.	12
Pregnant with Stores, that India's Mines might envy,	. .	O 249	Irene	18
And ev'n our Prophet's Gardens envy thine:	. . . . .	O 279	Irene	89
And Gennah's happy <to> Gardens envy thine.	. . . .	O 351	Irene	V 27
And envy the slave that toils whose labour procures her	.	Y 165	Irene	V 81
sleep				
How soon, alas! will Int'rest, Fear, or Envy,	. . . .	O 301	Irene	82
And taint the sweets of Paradise with envy	. . . .	Y 184	Irene	V 9
EPEMPSEU				
Alla tod eis Thnetous Kupris epempseu onar	. . . . .	O 103	Eis Elisses	4
EPIDEMIC				
This bustling season's epidemic care;	. . . . . .	O 59	Pro Good Nat'd	6
The bustling season's epidemic care.	. . . . . .	O 59	Pro Good Nat'd	V 6
EPILOGUE				
Prologue And Epilogue	. . . .	O 50	Pro Drury-Lane	T
Epilogue intended to have been spoken by a Lady	. . .	O 83	Epi Dist Moth.	T
Epilogue	. . . .	O 188	Epilogue	T
EPIROT				
the fierce Epirot	. . . .	Y 130	Irene	V 13
EPIRUS				
Was it for this, that sick'ning in Epirus,	. . . . .	O 272	Irene	6
EPITAPH				
An Epitaph on Claudy Phillips, a Musician	. . . . .	O 113	Epit. Phillips	T

```
                                                        PAGE     TITLE              LINE
EPITAPH        (CONTINUED)
    An Epitaph upon the celebrated Claudy Philips,  . . . .   O 113 Epit. Phillips   V  T
    Epitaph on Claude Phillips, an Itinerant Musician  . . .  O 113 Epit. Phillips   V  T
    A Translation Of The Latin Epitaph On Sir Thomas  . . .   O 117 Epitaph Hanmer      T
      Hanmer
EPODE
    Horace. Epode the 2d.  . . . . . . . . . . . .           O  71 Hor. Epode II        T
EQUAL
    Torments alike with equal Fire. . . . . . . . .          O  99 Ode Friendship   V  8
    Of equal Beauty, but of softer Mien,  . . . . .          O 259 Irene             119
    With equal zeal persue the task of war  . . . .          Y 131 Irene            V 30
    Reason with Reason fights on equal Terms,  . . .         O 287 Irene               9
    Too much to fear or trust, is equal Weakness.  . .       O 300 Irene              77
    To cross the Tow'rings of an equal Soul,  . . . .        O 309 Irene              41
    Thou shalt with Bacchus equal honours share  . . .       Y   7 Virgil Daphnis     51
EQUALITY
    Gay with the smile of bland equality;  . . . . . .       O 130 Tr. Rambler 12      6
EQUALLY
    Await our coming, equally prepar'd . . . . . . .         O 284 Irene              54
EQUIPP'D
    By his Command, equipp'd for speedy Flight,  . . .       O 254 Irene             133
ERASE
    Deface Erase the glories of my native  . . . . . .       Y 177 Irene            V 107
      country
ERASMUS
    And love return, has great Erasmus died?  . . . .        O 132 Tr. Rambler 54      2
ERE
    Ere masquerades debauch'd, excise oppress'd,  . . . .    O  10 London             29
    To shake with laughter ere the jest they hear,  . . .   O  16 London            140
    How just that scorn ere yet thy voice declare,  . . .   O  33 Vanity Wishes      71
    Art thou too fall'n? ere anger could subside  . . . .   O 132 Tr. Rambler 54      1
    Ere yet the Foe found Leisure to be cruel,  . . . .     O 252 Irene              94
    Ere I could range them on the crowded Deck,  . . . .    O 271 Irene              28
    Who knows, ere this important Morrow rise,  . . . .     O 284 Irene              36
    Let Prudence, ere the Suit be farther urg'd,  . . . .   O 285 Irene               8
    Yet think a Moment, ere you court Destruction,  . . .   O 301 Irene              87
    And perish ere he tastes the Joys of Conquest.  . . .   O 308 Irene              33
    Yet ere we give our loosen'd Thoughts to Rapture,  . .  O 309 Irene              18
    To still their Murmurs, ere the twentieth Sun  . . .    O 309 Irene              23
    Ere guilty Fear depress'd the hoary Chief,  . . . .     O 312 Irene              18
    Ere he return with Thousands at his Side.  . . . .      O 320 Irene               9
    Now haste to murder, ere returning Thought  . . . .     O 326 Irene              39
    Yet ere I quit the Scepter of Dominion,  . . . . .      O 333 Irene              49
ERGA
    Oisi memele phusis, metron charis, erga palaion,  . . . O 171 Epi. Goldsmith      3
EROON
    Eroon te Bious Birchion, ede Sophon,  . . . . . . .      O 108 Eis Birchion        2
EROTI
    Kai toios Paphien plexen eroti Thean. . . . . . . .      O 172 On Marlborough      2
ERR
    Err shall they not, who resolute explore  . . . . .      O 192 Tr. Medea II        1
ERRING
    Guides erring Mortals to the Paths of Virtue,  . . . .   O 289 Irene              18
    When erring Fury throws the random dart  . . . . . .     O 345 Irene            V 28
    Weak Man with erring Rage may throw the Dart,  . . .     O 335 Irene              14
ERROR
    But did not Chance at length her error mend?  . . . .    O  41 Vanity Wishes     215
    Now Superstition, Ignorance and Error,  . . . . .        O 251 Irene              68
    One Hour had freed me from the fatal Error,  . . . .     O 332 Irene              27
ERRORS
    Men will be ever to their Errors blind,  . . . . . .     O 247 Irene Epilogue     11
ERST
    Which erst in Frost and Freedom lay,  . . . . . . .      O 146 Tr Boeth III.5      8
ERUPTION
    Like subterraneous tempests with dire eruption burst their  Y 115 Irene         V 49
      caverns
ESCAP'D    SEE SCAP'D
    Myself escap'd, or favour'd or neglected.  . . . . .     O 317 Irene              41
    My mother who alone escap'd the grave  . . . . . .       Y  19 Tr. Iliad Bk 6     38
'SCAPE
    No gainful trade their industry can 'scape,  . . . .     O  15 London            113
    See when the vulgar 'scape, despis'd or aw'd,  . . . .   O  39 Vanity Wishes     167
    Impending death they strive to 'scape in vain  . . .     O  76 Tr Add. Battle     30
    And weakly hopes to 'scape the critick's rage.  . . . .  Y  67 Prologue Lethe     12
ESCAPE    SEE 'SCAPE
    From his Escape learn thou the Pow'r of Virtue,  . . .   O 330 Irene              24
'SQUIRE
    But there came a country 'squire  . . . . . . . .        Y 301 Extemp. Elegy      13
ESSAY'D
    By regular Approach essay'd the Heart;  . . . . . .      O  51 Pro Drury-Lane     12
ESSENCE
    Essence Divine with Matter join'd. . . . . . . . .       O 147 Tr Boeth III.6     12
ESSENTIAL
    That traced th' essential form of Grace,  . . . . .      O 154 Epita. Hogarth      2
    That wav'd th' essential form of Grace,  . . . . .       O 154 Epita. Hogarth   V  2
    Who drew th' essential Form of Grace;  . . . . . .       O 155 Epita. Hogarth   V  2
EST
    Tout est cher.  . . . . . . . . . . . . . .              O 172 French Distich      4
ESTABLISHES
    My Doom confirm'd establishes my Purpose.  . . . . .     O 270 Irene               9
```

```
                                                          PAGE    TITLE          LINE
ESTEEM
    Esteem Aspasia's Breast, the noblest Kingdom.  . . . .  O 289  Irene            14
    I love her still, but shall esteem Aspasia: . . . . .   Y 186  Irene         V  5
ESTIN
    Ek Dios estin onar, Theios pot egrapsen Homeros,  . . . O 103  Eis Elisses       3
ETC
    From Horace.  Integer Vitae, etc. . . . . . . . .       O  65  Hor I Ode xxii V  T
ETERNAL
    And feed with varied fools th' eternal jest:  . . . .   O  32  Vanity Wishes    52
    And feed with change of new born fools th' eternal . .  Y  94  Vanity Wishes V 52
        jest:
    And sure th' Eternal Master found  . . . . . . .        O 201  Death Dr Levet   27
    And Jollity maintain'd eternal Revels.--  . . . . . .   O 251  Irene            65
    From those bright Regions of eternal Day,  . . . . .    O 253  Irene            99
    Distrust th' eternal Fortresses of Nature,  . . . . .   O 268  Irene            31
    Th' eternal Snows that freeze beyond Meotis,  . . . .   O 274  Irene            59
    The eternal Snows that shine beyond Maeotis . . . . .   O 360  Irene         V  2
    Th' Eternal gave it, and that End is Virtue.  . . . .   O 290  Irene            31
    Implor'd th' eternal Power to shield my Country,  . . . O 290  Irene            49
    Implor'd the Eternal Pow'r, at Sophia's altars . . . .  Y 163  Irene         V 49
    Close like th' eternal Bars of Death upon thee,  . . .  O 292  Irene            80
    Close like th' eternal Bars of Death upon You  . . . .  O 357  Irene         V 10
    Rolls with eternal Toil the pond'rous Orbs; . . . . .   O 293  Irene           120
    When daring Vice insults eternal Justice,  . . . . .    O 314  Irene            23
    Let us not struggle with th' eternal Will,  . . . . .   O 320  Irene            16
    With peaceful Death, and Happiness eternal.  . . . .    O 328  Irene            47
    Eternal justice thus her doom decreed  . . . . . .      O 345  Irene         V 32
    well th' Eternal Mind thus her doom decreed  . . . .    O 345  Irene         V 34
ETNA'S
    Thus on deceitful Etna's flow'ry Side,  . . . . . .     O 315  Irene            33
EUNUCHS
    With warbling eunuchs fill a licens'd stage,  . . . .   O  12  London           59
    With warbling eunuchs fill our silenc'd stage,  . . .   O  12  London        V 59
EUROPE
    The Turkish Pow'rs from Europe shall retreat,  . . . .  O 257  Irene            79
EURUS
    That roll at Eurus loud command; . . . . . . . .        O 144  Tr Boeth. II.2    2
    Wouldst thou when fierce Eurus blows . . . . . . .      O 144  Tr Boeth. II.4    3
EV'N   SEE EVN
    Wants ev'n the cheap reward of empty praise; . . . .    O  10  London           36
    Yet ev'n these heroes, mischievously gay,  . . . . .    O  21  London          230
    Yet ev'n those heroes, mischievously gay,  . . . . .    Y  59  London        V 230
    Yet ev'n on this her load Misfortune flings,  . . . .   O  44  Vanity Wishes   299
    When ev'n proud wealth and prouder wit obey,  . . . .   O  81  Lady Birthday    10
    And ev'n our Prophet's Gardens envy thine:  . . . . .   O 279  Irene            89
    Ev'n from the Birth affects supreme Command,  . . . .   O 280  Irene            19
    When ev'n as Love was breaking off from Wonder,  . . .  O 282  Irene            66
    Perhaps ev'n now the Lovers unpursu'd . . . . . . .     O 322  Irene             4
    Ev'n in the bloom of life depriv'd of breath.  . . . .  Y   6  Virgil Daphnis    2
    Who caught the chief, ev'n in his soldiers' view . . .  Y  25  Tr Add. Battle  125
EV'RY
    And ev'ry moment leaves my little less;  . . . . . .    O  10  London           40
    In ev'ry face a thousand graces shine,  . . . . . .     O  16  London          127
    From ev'ry tongue flows harmony divine.  . . . . . .    O  16  London          128
    With ev'ry wild absurdity comply,  . . . . . . .        O  16  London          138
    Exalt each trifle, ev'ry vice adore,  . . . . . .       O  17  London          148
    Praise evry trifle, ev'ry vice adore,  . . . . . .      Y  55  London        V 148
    This mournful truth is ev'ry where confess'd,  . . . .  O  18  London          176
    There ev'ry bush with nature's music rings,  . . . .    O  20  London          220
    Only ev'ry bush there artless music sings  . . . . .    Y  58  London        V 220
    There ev'ry breeze bears health upon its wings; . . .   O  20  London          221
    Fate wings with ev'ry wish th' afflictive dart,  . . .  O  31  Vanity Wishes    15
    Renew'd at ev'ry glance on humankind;  . . . . . .      O  33  Vanity Wishes    70
    Search every state, and canvass ev'ry pray'r. . . . .   O  33  Vanity Wishes    72
    On ev'ry stage the foes of peace attend, . . . . . .    O  33  Vanity Wishes    77
    For now no more we trace in ev'ry line . . . . . .      O  34  Vanity Wishes    87
    With ev'ry Meteor of Caprice must play,  . . . . .      O  53  Pro Drury-Lane   49
    On ev'ry side rise mountains of the slain,  . . . . .   O  76  Tr Add. Battle   19
    To ev'ry empire bounds the Gods ordain  . . . . . .     O  76  Tr Add. Battle   35
    The weight of ev'ry rolling sphere,  . . . . . . .      O  79  Feast St Simon   32
    Vex ev'ry eye, and every bosom tear; . . . . . . .      O  84  Epi Dist Moth.   39
    Charm'd ev'ry ear, and gain'd on ev'ry heart. . . . .   O 117  Epitaph Hanmer    8
    Charm'd ev'ry ear, and gain'd on ev'ry heart. . . . .   O 117  Epitaph Hanmer    8
    In ev'ry speech persuasive wisdom flow'd,  . . . . .    O 118  Epitaph Hanmer   15
    In ev'ry act refulgent virtue glow'd.  . . . . . .      O 118  Epitaph Hanmer   16
    When charms thus press on ev'ry sense,  . . . . . .     O 121  To Miss Playin   11
    With ev'ry bliss that man can gain. . . . . . . .       O 136  Tr Rambler 128    6
    Let ev'ry piece be simple and be one.  . . . . . .      O 137  Tr Rambler 139    1
    Ev'ry name that laughs at Care, . . . . . . . .         O 196  Song Congratu.   10
    Of ev'ry friendless name the friend.  . . . . . .       O 201  Death Dr Levet    8
    The modest wants of ev'ry day  . . . . . . . .          O 201  Death Dr Levet   23
    The toil of ev'ry day supplied. . . . . . . . .         O 201  Death Dr Levet   24
    From ev'ry Palace burst a mingled Clamour,  . . . . .   O 251  Irene            70
    Her grateful Sons shine bright with ev'ry Virtue; . . . O 256  Irene            60
    And mingles unperceiv'd with ev'ry Thought.  . . . . .  O 261  Irene             6
    And ev'ry Suppliant lift his Eyes to Mecca.  . . . . .  O 264  Irene            32
    When ev'ry Storm in my Domain shall roar,  . . . . .    O 265  Irene            42
    Till ev'ry Storm in my Domain shall roar,  . . . . .    O 354  Irene         V 25
    When ev'ry Wave shall beat a Turkish Shore,  . . . . .  O 265  Irene            43
    Each weakness sooth and flatter ev'ry folly.  . . . .   Y 134  Irene         V 27
    Here ev'ry Warbler of the Sky shall sing; . . . . .     O 279  Irene            86
```

EV'RY	(CONTINUED)		PAGE	TITLE		LINE
Here ev'ry Fragrance breathe of ev'ry Spring:			O 279	Irene		87
Here ev'ry Fragrance breathe of ev'ry Spring:			O 279	Irene		87
Reflect that Life, like ev'ry other Blessing,			O 290	Irene		28
Purge well thy Mind from ev'ry private Passion,			O 298	Irene		6
On ev'ry Side Confusion, Rage and Death,			O 300	Irene		70
Guide all thy Steps, calm ev'ry stormy Thought,			O 303	Irene		21
Farewell, unhappy Maid, may ev'ry Joy			O 322	Irene		57
New verdure ev'ry fading leaf shall fill,			Y 4	On a Daffodill		19
Pleasure in ev'ry nymph and shepherd reigns,			Y 7	Virgil Daphnis		36
While Hector lives I tast of ev'ry joy			Y 18	Tr. Iliad Bk 6		26
EVAPORATE						
They mount, they shine, evaporate, and fall.			O 33	Vanity Wishes		76
EVENING						
And bless thine evening walk and morning toil.			O 20	London		223
And bless the evening walk and morning toil.			O 20	London	V	223
And bless thy evening walk and morning toil.			O 20	London	V	223
Wearing out life's evening gray;			O 181	Parody Warton		2
Soon as the Veil of Evening clouds the Sky,			O 284	Irene		49
EVENT						
This dire event by omens was foreshown;			O 64	Virgil Past.I		22
Pants for the dread Event--But let us reason--			O 280	Irene		31
Submissive and prepar'd for each Event,			O 302	Irene		112
EVENTS						
If chasing past Events with vain Pursuit,			O 255	Irene		5
Such strange Events, such unexpected Chances,			O 296	Irene		34
EVER SEE E'ER, E'RE, HOWE'ER						
Unsullied fame, and conscience ever gay.			O 14	London		90
No beast more dreadful ever stain'd			O 66	Hor I Ode xxii	V	13
Where clouds condens'd for ever veil			O 66	Hor I Ode xxii		19
No Beast more dreadful ever stain'd			O 67	To A. Fuscus		13
Where Clouds, condens'd, for ever veil			O 67	To A. Fuscus		19
But you are ever drown'd in tears,			O 67	Hor. II Ode IX		9
For Mystes dead you ever mourn;			O 67	Hor. II Ode IX		10
They roll, and ever will roll on.			O 68	Hor.II Ode 14		4
The hardy Scythian ever mourns.			O 70	Hor.II Ode XX		16
Shall live for ever in my verse.			O 70	Hor.II Ode XX		24
Who to their Lord were ever dear,			O 78	Feast St Simon		10
May this returning day for ever find			O 80	Lady Birthday		3
Around them pleasures wait, and joys for ever new.			O 84	Epi Dist Moth.		27
Where furies ever howl, and serpents hiss.			O 84	Epi Dist Moth.		31
For ever flutter o'er her lyre,			O 121	To Miss Playin		14
For wisdom ever echoes nature's voice.			O 138	Tr Rambler 156		1
That slowly grows, which must for ever last.			O 142	In Baretti Bk.		10
He that ever hopes to thrive			O 178	Thrale 35 Year		15
His useful care was ever nigh,			O 201	Death Dr Levet		18
His useful aid was ever nigh			O 201	Death Dr Levet	V	18
His ready help was ever nigh,			O 201	Death Dr Levet	V	18
Men will be ever to their Errors blind,			O 247	Irene Epilogue		11
Our Schemes for ever cross'd, our Mines discover'd,			O 273	Irene		22
The Rocks of Life, for ever flies the Port.			O 281	Irene		47
Did ever Passion make so swift a Progress?			O 281	Irene		55
A little longer, and she's thine for ever.			O 285	Irene		10
Immured for ever--and for ever doom'd			O 357	Irene	V	11
Immured for ever--and for ever doom'd			O 357	Irene	V	11
Let my blest Eyes for ever gaze--			O 294	Irene		4
For ever mourn their Avarice or Factions?			O 305	Irene		44
Return, Demetrius, and be free for ever.			O 306	Irene		60
Henceforth for ever happy be this Day,			O 308	Irene		1
Shall hide me from the tasteless World for ever.			O 333	Irene		48
EVERDURING						
Condemn'd to everduring pains.			O 69	Hor.II Ode 14		20
EVERLASTING						
From age to age in everlasting debt;			O 39	Vanity Wishes		188
But everlasting dictates croud his tongue,			O 43	Vanity Wishes		273
In everlasting Circles run,			O 68	Hor.II Ode 14		2
EVERY SEE EV'RY, EVRY						
From every part, the gaudy vassals come,			Y 57	London	V	202
Search every state, and canvass ev'ry pray'r.			O 33	Vanity Wishes		72
From every room descends the painted face,			O 33	Vanity Wishes		83
From every wall descends the painted face,			Y 95	Vanity Wishes	V	83
Let one great payment every claim appease,			O 62	Pro Word Wise		11
And scents ambrosial breathe in every gale:			O 84	Epi Dist Moth.		17
And every beauty withers at the blast:			O 84	Epi Dist Moth.		35
Vex ev'ry eye, and every bosom tear;			O 84	Epi Dist Moth.		39
With pity soften every awful grace,			O 84	Epi Dist Moth.		44
Faith from every generous mind:			O 176	Tr Metastasi I		4
And of his every gift usurp the merit;			O 176	Tr Metastas II		11
And yet of every gift usurp the merit;			O 176	Tr Metastas II	V	11
Comets! come every day--and stay a year.			O 177	Tr Dist Modena		2
In every dome, in every sacred place,			O 189	Seeing Montagu		3
In every dome, in every sacred place,			O 189	Seeing Montagu		3
When every Man busied			O 347	Irene	V	21
And every Danger shocks with double Horror.			O 261	Irene		21
Till every Nation reverence the Koran,			O 264	Irene		31
Till every Nation reverence our Prophet			O 354	Irene	V	17
Till every Wave shall beat a Turkish Shore.			O 354	Irene	V	26
--Till every constellation shines for me			Y 132	Irene	V	45
Since Fear predominates in every Thought,			O 266	Irene		17
They sympathise with us in every fear			Y 134	Irene	V	26
And every language toils to flatter me.			Y 136	Irene	V	32B

103

```
EVERY          (CONTINUED)                              PAGE    TITLE            LINE
     And every Voice was Liberty and Greece.  . . . . . .   O 271  Irene              30
     every traytor inclination each traytor passion  . . . .   Y 158  Irene          V  11
     With every curse of angry heav'n afflicted beneath  . .   O 357  Irene          V  15
        each
     Science and Arms find every where a  . . . . . .   O 352  Irene              V  32
        Country.
     Let every Tongue resound Irene's Praise,  . . . . .   O 308  Irene               4
     <Ho>w blest our state could every bosom  . . . . . .   Y 184  Irene          V  16
     I w<ould> have every smile g<enu>ine to<morrow no>  . .   Y 185  Irene          V   3
     Each piercing Torture, every Change of Pain,  . . . .   O 326  Irene              44
     Contrive new Racks, imbitter every Pang,  . . . . . .   O 334  Irene              74
EVIL
     Foretold the coming evil by their dismal croak.  . . .   O  65  Virgil Past.I      25
EVN
     Evn low built towns they Britain's modish tribe  . .   Y  94  Vanity Wishes    V  61
EVRY
     Praise evry trifle, ev'ry vice adore,  . . . . . . .   Y  55  London           V 148
     Woods to evry Sigh replying,  . . . . . . . . . .   O 148  Tr Boet III.12   V   6
EXALT
     Exalt each trifle, ev'ry vice adore,  . . . . . . .   O  17  London             148
     Or sprightly Hope exalt their kindling Spirits?  . . .   O 270  Irene              23
     Exalt my soul, and swell it into raptures.  . . . .   Y 189  Irene          V  1F
     Inflame her Crimes, exalt your own Obedience,  . . . .   O 329  Irene              14
EXALTED
     Will it not charm a Mind like thine exalted,  . . . .   O 278  Irene              67
EXALTS
     Exalts my Soul, and fortifies my Heart.  . . . . . .   O 265  Irene               5
EXAMPLE
     My Soul first kindled by thy bright Example,  . . . .   O 298  Irene              13
EXASP'RATED
     The Pygmies thus exasp'rated their foes.  . . . . . .   Y  23  Tr Add. Battle     51
EXCEEDED
     Perhaps my Warmth exceeded my Commission;  . . . . .   O 330  Irene              21
EXCEEDING
     Now she lies exceeding low,  . . . . . . . . . .   Y 301  Extemp. Elegy      19
EXCEL
     That never Briton can in vain excel;  . . . . . . .   O  57  Prologue Comus     12
     That never Britain can in vain excel;  . . . . . . .   O  57  Prologue Comus   V  12
EXCELL
     Lyciscus whose soft arms excell  . . . . . . . . .   Y  12  Tr Hor Epode 9     37
EXCELLENCE
     Empire or Wealth, to Excellence like thine?  . . . .   O 267  Irene               9
     Forgive, fair Excellence, th' unwilling Tongue,  . . .   O 324  Irene               1
EXCELLENT
     On Claudius Phillips, an excellent Musician  . . . .   O 113  Epit. Phillips   V   T
EXCESS
     We mark'd him storming in Excess of Fury,  . . . . .   O 311  Irene              11
EXCESSIVE
     Th' impetuous Sallies of excessive Virtue,  . . . . .   O 267  Irene              47
EXCHANG'D
     Joys ill exchang'd for Gold, and Pride, and Empire.  . .   O 313  Irene              10
EXCHANGES
     Exchanges solid Strength for feeble Splendor.  . . . .   O 265  Irene              38
EXCISE
     Ere masquerades debauch'd, excise oppress'd,  . . . .   O  10  London             29
EXCLAMATION
     With idle Threats and fruitless Exclamation,  . . . .   O 327  Irene               7
     With empty threats, and fruitless Exclamation  . . . .   O 368  Irene          V  15
EXCURSIVE
     There shall soft Leisure wing th' excursive Soul,  . . .   O 302  Irene             118
EXCUSE
     Think--but excuse a Woman's needless Caution,  . . . .   O 298  Irene               5
EXCUSES
     Which aggravate a fault with feign'd excuses,  . . . .   O 176  Tr Metastas II      8
EXECUTE
     Quick at my Call shall execute your Charge;  . . . .   O 328  Irene              43
EXECUTIONER
     Is but the executioner of Heavn--or Instrument  . . .   O 345  Irene          V  27
EXEMPT
     The glitt'ring eminence exempt from foes;  . . . . .   O  38  Vanity Wishes     166
     The glitt'ring eminence exempt from woes;  . . . . .   O  38  Vanity Wishes    V 166
     Bless with an age exempt from scorn or crime;  . . . .   O  44  Vanity Wishes     292
EXERT
     In virtue's cause once more exert his rage,  . . . . .   O  23  London             262
     Still foe to vice, exert his Cambrian shade;  . . . .   Y  61  London           V 262
     To ease their pains exert your milder power,  . . . .   O  84  Epi Dist Moth.     46
EXHAUST
     Exhaust the well of Zemzem.  . . . . . . . . . .   Y 131  Irene          V 32D
     Exhaust the Stores of pious Eloquence,  . . . . . .   O 265  Irene               2
EXHAUSTED
     Lest scarce the exhausted should rope supply.  . . . .   Y  60  London           V 243
     And starves exhausted regions in his way;  . . . . .   O  42  Vanity Wishes     228
     Exhausted Worlds, and then imagin'd new:  . . . . . .   O  51  Pro Drury-Lane      4
     Exhausted all her nobler Gifts on you;  . . . . . .   O 278  Irene              54
EXIGENCE
     The pressing Exigence forbids Relation.  . . . . . .   O 315  Irene               8
EXIL'D
     What murder'd Wentworth, and what exil'd Hyde,  . . . .   O  36  Vanity Wishes     131
     Expell'd and exil'd from the blissful seats,  . . . .   O  84  Epi Dist Moth.     29
```

		PAGE	TITLE	LINE

EXILE
But how can'st thou support the Woes of Exile? . . . . O 301 Irene 102
Companion of our Flight, illustrious Exile, ... O 320 Irene 30
EXILES
Exiles, the proverb says, subsist on hope. . . . . . O 133 Tr. Rambler 67 1
EXISTENCE
Existence saw him spurn her bounded Reign, ... O 51 Pro Drury-Lane 5
Thou fountain of existence I pour the . . . . Y 189 Irene V 1
EXPANDED
Extended Empire, like expanded Gold, ... O 265 Irene 37
There, with your Soldiers arm'd, and Sails expanded, . . O 284 Irene 53
Th' expanded hand of lib'ral Heav'n . . . . Y 199 Irene V 16
EXPANDS
Expands the boundless scenes of future being . . . . Y 133 Irene V 8
My Soul expands to meet approaching Freedom. . . . . O 306 Irene 50
EXPECT
Well known, long try'd, expect us on the Shore. . . . O 301 Irene 91
Declare thy Message, and expect thy Doom. . . . . . O 331 Irene 6
EXPECTATION
Yet, on a Day like this, when Expectation . . . . . O 280 Irene 30
EXPECTED   SEE LONG-EXPECTED
EXPECTING   SEE LONG-EXPECTING
EXPECTS
He who still expects deceit, ... O 176 Tr Metastasi I 5
The Rack expects us, and the Sword pursues. . . . . . O 315 Irene 2
EXPELL
Nor counsells nor reproach expell . . . . Y 12 Tr Hor Epode 9 39
EXPELL'D
Expell'd and exil'd from the blissful seats, ... O 84 Epi Dist Moth. 29
EXPENCE
The daughter's petulance, the son's expence, ... O 44 Vanity Wishes 280
The ruinous insolence, the son's expence, ... Y 104 Vanity Wishes V 280
Vain expence the parent of necessity the parent of . . O 347 Irene V 26
  corruption
EXPERIENC'D
The wise experienc'd Grecian sage . . . . O 68 Hor. II Ode IX 13
To morrow strike--Does then that experienc'd . . . . Y 154 Irene V 19
  wisdom
EXPERIENCE
With all the Diffidence of long Experience, ... O 254 Irene 130
And only credits what Experience tells. . . . . . . O 255 Irene 19
EXPIR'D
How Turnus by Aeneas' sword expir'd? . . . . Y 22 Tr Add. Battle 12
EXPIRES
And Swift expires a driv'ler and a show. . . . . . . O 45 Vanity Wishes 318
EXPIRING
Beheld without Concern, expiring Greece, ... O 250 Irene 34
Expiring Cali nam'd Irene's Chamber, ... O 326 Irene 29
The Greek, Demetrius! whom th' expiring Bassa . . . . O 331 Irene 10
EXPLAIN
Explain their country's dear-bought rights away, . . . O 11 London 53
EXPLORE
Explore your secrets with insidious art, ... O 17 London 154
Quick let us rise, the happy seats explore, ... O 18 London 174
Explore each restless toil, each anxious strife, . . . Y 92 Vanity Wishes V 3
Perhaps if Skill could distant Times explore, ... O 53 Pro Drury-Lane 41
Err shall they not, who resolute explore . . . . . . O 192 Tr. Medea II 1
EXPOS'D
Then to the inclement skies expos'd I sat . . . . . Y 11 Tr Hor Epode 9 35
EXPRESS
And all her bards express, ... O 127 To Lyce, Lady 22
EXPRESSES
My second, expresses a Syrian perfume; . . . . . . O 179 Charade! 2
EXPREST
My admiration only I exprest, ... O 64 Virgil Past.I 13
EXTACY
"Toil on, dull croud, in extacy, he cries, ... O 82 Young Author 15
EXTATICK
Where doth extatick fury move . . . . O 80 Feast St Simon 56
EXTEMPORARY
I too can pour the extemporary song: . . . . O 142 In Baretti Bk. 4
EXTEND
"O'er his face extend my wings; . . . . O 186 Anacreon Ode 9 38
And o'er the globe extend your reign, ... O 189 Epilogue 7
O Providence! extend thy Care to me, ... O 252 Irene 90
Where Hypoplacus' lofty shades extend. . . . . . . Y 18 Tr. Iliad Bk 6 8
Their wings extend themselves across the land. . . . . Y 24 Tr Add. Battle 79
EXTENDED
Extended Empire, like expanded Gold, ... O 265 Irene 37
Hector, this speaking, with extended hands . . . . . Y 20 Tr. Iliad Bk 6 90
EXTENDS
O'er love, o'er fear, extends his wide domain, ... O 40 Vanity Wishes 195
O'er love, o'er Force, extends his wide domain, . . . O 40 Vanity Wishes V 195
Since Stella still extends her reign, ... O 122 Stella Mourn. 11
Extends his mighty Schemes of Wealth and Pow'r, . . . O 269 Irene 4
Extends its Lines along the sandy Beach, ... O 304 Irene 4
EXTENSIVE
Let observation with extensive view, ... O 30 Vanity Wishes 1
EXTERIOR
Too high, bright Maid, thou rat'st exterior Grace; . . O 277 Irene 30

EXTORTED

    Recall th' extorted Doom.--It must be so, ...   O 326 Irene   40

EXULTATICN

    Cease this wild Roar of savage Exultation; . . . . .   O 318 Irene   6

EXULTING

    Exulting Folly hail'd the joyful Day, ...   O 52 Pro Drury-Lane   37

    And sweeps th' exulting Conqueror away: . . . .   O 298 Irene   31

    Enrag'd by Wrongs, exulting with Success, ...   O 313 Irene   15

    And Death exulting stalk'd along the land. . . . . .   Y 23 Tr Add. Battle   53

EXULTS

    When haughty Guilt exults with impious Joy, ...   O 335 Irene   12

EYE

    Turn from the glitt'ring bribe thy scornful eye, . . .   O 14 London   87

    And view each object with another's eye; . . . . . .   O 16 London   139

    And swell with tears the prostituted eye . . . . .   Y 57 London   V 199

    And pierce each scene with philosophic eye. . . . . .   O 33 Vanity Wishes   64

    Where-e'er he turns he meets a stranger's eye, . . .   O 35 Vanity Wishes   111

    And nations on his eye suspended wait; . . . . . .   O 40 Vanity Wishes   206

    A generous foe regards, with pitying eye, ...   O 61 Pro Word Wise   5

    I should behold with scornfull eye . . . .   O 73 Hor. Epode II   55

    And shades of Pygmies swim before their eye. . . .   O 77 Tr Add. Battle   48

    Vex ev'ry eye, and every bosom tear; . . . .   O 84 Epi Dist Moth.   39

    Nor let disdain sit low'ring in your eye; . . . . .   O 84 Epi Dist Moth.   43

    Thou, who survey'st these walls with curious eye, . .   O 117 Epitaph Hanmer   1

    Strict, on the right he fix'd his steadfast eye, . .   O 118 Epitaph Hanmer   29

    To point the glances of her eye, ...   O 121 To Miss Playin   16

    Yet spite of fair Zelinda's eye, ...   O 127 To Lyce, Lady   21

    Yet still he fills affection's eye, ...   O 201 Death Dr Levet   9

    Observe him closely with a Statesman's Eye, ...   O 255 Irene   10

    Fear in her Eye, Submission on her Tongue, ...   O 259 Irene   120

    Wet the dim eye or swell the throbbing bosom? . . .   Y 191 Irene   V 19A

    Unfading Verdure glads the roving Eye, ...   O 315 Irene   34

    Steal from Abdalla's Eye the Sign to smile. . . . .   O 318 Irene   5

    Black her eye with many a blow, ...   Y 301 Extemp. Elegy   17

EYE-BALLS

    That struggling pants, and rowls her eye-balls round. .   O 76 Tr Add. Battle   15

EYES

    Indignant Thales eyes the neighb'ring town. . . . . .   O 10 London   34

    Deign on the passing world to turn thine eyes, . . .   O 38 Vanity Wishes   157

    With listless eyes the dotard views the store, . . .   O 43 Vanity Wishes   263

    Or views his coffers with suspicious eyes, ...   O 44 Vanity Wishes   289

    From Marlb'rough's eyes the streams of dotage flow, .   O 45 Vanity Wishes   317

    Ye nymphs of rosy lips and radiant eyes, ...   O 46 Vanity Wishes   323

    Safe in his pow'r, whose eyes discern afar . . . .   O 47 Vanity Wishes   353

    Drive the soft Slumbers from his eyes, ...   O 71 Hor. Epode II   10

    Drive the soft Slumbers for his eyes. . . . . . .   O 71 Hor. Epode II   V 10

    And view with cheerful eyes approaching death. . . .   O 74 Tr. Iliad Bk 6   10

    Tears, at my name, shall drown those beauteous eyes, .   O 75 Tr. Iliad Bk 6   27

    Whose snowy breasts, whose animated eyes, ...   O 83 Epi Dist Moth.   5

    When in your Eyes resistless Lightnings play, . . .   O 96 Hickman Spinet   3

    Grief swell thine Eyes, and Terror chill thy Breast. .   O 110 To Posterity   4

    "And let the goddess trust her eyes." . . . .   O 122 Stella Mourn.   6

    Striped rainbows round her eyes are seen, ...   O 127 To Lyce, Lady   11

    Amid the storms of war, with curious eyes . . . . .   O 130 Tr. Rambler 8   1

    Nor lures the search of avaricious eyes, ...   O 141 Tr Rambler 199   2

    Why boast their Birth before his Eyes, ...   O 147 Tr Boeth III.6   17

    Happy he whose Eyes have view'd . . . .   O 147 Tr Boet III.12   1

    Turn on the prudent Ant, thy heedful eyes, ...   O 151 The Ant   1

    Here death has clos'd the curious eyes . . . . .   O 154 Epita. Hogarth   3

    Here clos'd in Death th' attentive Eyes . . . . .   O 155 Epita. Hogarth   V 3

    Times gloomy backward with judicious eyes; . . . .   O 192 Tr. Medea II   2

    Her baleful eyes where Sorrow rolls around; . . . .   O 192 Tr. Medea II   14

    Nor bribes your Eyes to prejudice your Heads. . . .   O 246 Irene Prologue   28

    Nor dull Serenity becalms his Eyes. . . . .   O 255 Irene   16

    Frowns unrestrain'd, and dooms me with his Eyes. . .   O 257 Irene   72

    And ev'ry Suppliant lift his Eyes to Mecca. . . . .   O 264 Irene   32

    Well may those Eyes that view these heav'nly Charms, .   O 267 Irene   6

    Such Beauty must not shine to vulgar Eyes. . . . .   O 269 Irene   43

    To tune the Tongue, to teach the Eyes to roll, . .   O 278 Irene   64

    Or pay with speaking Eyes a Lover's Homage? . . . .   O 282 Irene   63

    She mark'd my sparkling Eyes, and heaving Breast, . .   O 282 Irene   68

    To gaze with longing Eyes upon To-morrow, ...   O 283 Irene   24

    And various charms displays to various eyes . . . .   Y 155 Irene   V 27

    The various charms displays to various eyes . . . .   Y 374 Irene   V 28

    Nor think my eyes oerflow with Female . . . . . .   O 357 Irene   V 17

        Weakness

    Let this blest Eyes for ever gaze-- . . . .   O 294 Irene   4

    Behold the Hero with Aspasia's Eyes? . . . .   O 296 Irene   31

    I stole unheeded from their ravish'd Eyes, ...   O 299 Irene   49

    Now feast thine Eyes, thine Eyes that ne'er hereafter   O 304 Irene   34

    Now feast thine Eyes, thine Eyes that ne'er hereafter   O 304 Irene   34

    O! could the Eyes of Kings, like those of Heav'n, . .   O 308 Irene   12

    Sudden he stops, and inward turns his Eyes, ...   O 311 Irene   5

    And view thy charms with no malignant eyes: . . . .   Y   3 On a Daffodill   14

    And secret pleasures sparkled in his eyes. . . . .   Y 18 Tr. Iliad Bk 6   16

    Andromache looks back with weeping eyes, ...   Y 21 Tr. Iliad Bk 6   127

    Quickly the Cranes appear before their eyes; . . .   Y 25 Tr Add. Battle   92

    While the sad Pygmies mourn with weeping eyes . . .   Y 26 Tr Add. Battle   128

    Withdraws the influence of those eyes, ...   Y 39 Lady Leaving   7

FABIUS

    But cautious Fabius from impending fate . . . . . .   O 78 Festina Lente   17

		PAGE	TITLE	LINE

FABLED
O could her fabled Saints, and boasted Prayers . . . . O 309 Irene 38
FABRIC
Soon th' aspiring Fabric falls, ... O 145 Tr Boeth. II.4 9
FABRICK
When some neglected Fabrick nods beneath . . . . . O 250 Irene 44
O'erturns the Fabrick of presumptuous Reason, ... O 269 Irene 8
Unless the beauteous Fabrick was design'd . . . . . O 277 Irene 28
FAC'D SEE PALE-FAC'D
FACE
And plead for pirates in the face of day; . . . . . O 11 London 54
In ev'ry face a thousand graces shine, ... O 16 London 127
Repeat his maxims, and reflect his face: . . . . . O 16 London 137
From every room descends the painted face, ... O 33 Vanity Wishes 83
From every wall descends the painted face, ... Y 95 Vanity Wishes V 83
Begs for each birth the fortune of a face: . . . . O 45 Vanity Wishes 320
Her heav'nly voice, and beauteous face. . . . . . . O 66 Hor I Ode xxii 24
With livid hue the fairest face o'ercast, ... O 84 Epi Dist Moth. 34
And beauty smile auspicious in each face; . . . . . O 84 Epi Dist Moth. 45
For such thy beauteous mind, and lovely face, . . . O 107 Lady F Assizes 5
His tortur'd Sons shall die before his Face, ... O 111 To Posterity 23
That saw the manners in the Face. . . . . O 154 Epita. Hogarth 4
"O'er his face extend my wings; . . . . O 186 Anacreon Ode 9 38
This Hour I'll beg, with unsuspecting Face, ... O 258 Irene 86
I mark'd them well, and trac'd in either Face . . . O 275 Irene 81
Thy Soul compleats the Triumphs of thy Face. . . . O 278 Irene 60
Disorder sits upon thy Face--retire. . . . . O 286 Irene 17
And tell the horrid Tale with chearful Face; . . . O 329 Irene 11
And add new Terrors to the Face of Death. . . . . . O 330 Irene 8
And see my mistress' face no more . . . . Y 11 Tr Hor Epode 9 32
But the next blooming virgin's beauteous face . . . Y 12 Tr Hor Epode 9 41
And in his nurse's bosom hides his face. . . . . . Y 20 Tr. Iliad Bk 6 94
Of aspect stern for in his face he wears . . . . . Y 24 Tr Add. Battle 82
Before his face the frighted Cranes gave way. . . . Y 25 Tr Add. Battle 122
FACTION
Suspended faction ceas'd from rage and strife, . . . O 118 Epitaph Hanmer 17
FACTIONS
Or raging factions rush to war, ... O 126 An Ode 34
When unsuccessful Wars, and civil Factions, ... O 256 Irene 41
For ever mourn their Avarice or Factions? . . . . . O 305 Irene 44
FACTIOUS
A factious Populace, luxurious Nobles, ... O 250 Irene 38
FACULTIES
That all her Faculties receive his Chains? . . . . O 281 Irene 39
FACULTY
Awake each Faculty that sleeps within thee, ... Q 254 Irene 2
FADE
Fade <glide> from the sight, and Vanish into . . . O 358 Irene V 11
  nothing.
Cleora's self, fair flower, shall fade like thee, . . . Y 4 On a Daffodill 27
FADED
And add new Roses to the faded Cheek. . . . . . . O 278 Irene 66
faded before her . . . . Y 191 Irene V 14
FADES
Soon fades the rose; once past the fragrant hour, . . O 133 Tr. Rambler 71 1
FADING SEE NEVER-FADING
Nor grace with fading flours my Herse, ... O 70 Hor.II Ode XX 22
All fading toys, and transitory glories . . . . . . Y 177 Irene V 110
New verdure ev'ry fading leaf shall fill, ... Y 4 On a Daffodill 19
FAIL
The chearful sage, when solemn dictates fail, . . . O 132 Tr. Rambler 65 1
Studious to please, yet ashem'd to fail. . . . . . O 246 Irene Prologue 30
Nor found again the bright Temptation fail? . . . . O 259 Irene 125
My Spirits fail, awhile support me, Vengeance-- . . . O 334 Irene 72
My spirits fail, I cannot name his death . . . . . Y 216 Irene V 72
FAIL'D
Were now well lost, in hearing how you fail'd. . . . O 316 Irene 23
FAILS
Abdalla fails, now Fortune all is mine. . . . . . O 319 Irene 1
Abdalla fails now is my slave . . . . Y 198 Irene V 1
FAINT
Less heard and less, the faint remonstrance falls; . . O 46 Vanity Wishes 334
Here I, though faint myself, must drive my goats, . . O 64 Virgil Past.I 17
O'erpower'd and faint the Pygmies scarce sustain . . O 76 Tr Add. Battle 26
With soften'd Voice she dropp'd the faint Refusal, . . O 303 Irene 31
FAINTING
And, fainting, scarce support the liquid weight: . . . O 74 Tr Iliad Bk 6 24
There a stout warriour fainting gasps for breath . . O 76 Tr Add. Battle 16
When fainting nature call'd for aid, ... O 201 Death Dr Levet 13
  your feeble fainting virtue . . . . Y 133 Irene V 9
He 's gone--Here rest, my Soul, thy fainting Wing, . . O 287 Irene 1
My fainting Soul with Violence of transport. . . . . O 371 Irene V 15
Beholds the fainting Garrison retire, ... O 298 Irene 28
Does conscious Virtue shake the fainting knee? . . . O 373 Irene V 8
FAINTLY
And faintly draw th' inverted Plow. . . . . O 73 Hor. Epode II 70
Prospects obscur'd by Distance faintly strike. . . . O 261 Irene 19
FAINTS
She faints and quits her hold. . . . . O 150 Tr Boet III.12 58
FAIR
For the fair banks of Severn or of Trent; . . . . . O 19 London 211

```
FAIR              (CONTINUED)                          PAGE   TITLE         LINE
    Fair Justice then, without constraint ador'd,  . . . .  O  22 London         250
    Short sway! fair Austria spreads her mournful charms,  .  O  42 Vanity Wishes  245
    Yours is the Charge, ye Fair, ye Wise, ye Brave!    .    O  58 Prologue Comus   37
    Where aught of bright, or fair, the piece displays,  . .  O  62 Pro Word Wise   15
    And that fair bosom heave with rising sighs!     . . . .  O  75 Tr. Iliad Bk 6   28
    This tributary verse receive, my fair,  . . . . . .     O  80 Lady Birthday     1
    My fair, be mindful of the mighty trust,  . . . . . .    O  81 Lady Birthday    11
    In whose fair cheeks destructive Cupids wait,  . . . .   O  83 Epi Dist Moth.    3
    For you, ye fair, I quit the gloomy plains,   . . . . .  O  83 Epi Dist Moth.   10
    Then melt, ye fair, while crouds around you sigh,  . . .  O  84 Epi Dist Moth.   42
    Not less capricious than a reigning fair,  . . . . .    O  95 Sprig of Myrtl     5
    Not less capricious than the reigning fair,  . . . . .   O  95 Sprig of Myrtl  V  5
    Ambitious only now to please the Fair,  . . . . . .     O  97 Hickman Spinet   18
    Thy charms at least, fair F<irebrac>e, might inspire  .  O 107 Lady F Assizes    3
    Could Stella, sprightly, fair and young,  . . . . . .   O 121 To Miss Playin   21
    Wou'd Stella, sprightly, fair and young,  . . . . . .   O 121 To Miss Playin  V 21
    Proclaim'd her, not so fair as fine.  . . . . . . . .   O 122 Stella Mourn.     4
    Thus blindly pray'd the fretful fair,  . . . . . . .    O 122 Stella Mourn.     7
    Th' adoring youth, and envious fair,  . . . . . . . .   O 122 Stella Mourn.    13
    Behold my fair, where-e'er we rove,  . . . . . . . .    O 123 Winter's Walk     1
    Yet spite of fair Zelinda's eye,  . . . . . . . . . .   O 127 To Lyce, Lady    21
    Nor dignifies the great, nor decks the fair.   . . . .   O 141 Tr Rambler 199    4
    That decks the fair, or dignifies the great.   . . . .   O 141 Tr Rambler 199    8
    Fair plenty, gracious Queen, shou'd pour . . . . . .    O 144 Tr Boeth."II.2    5
    "Vows to Myrtale the fair;  . . . . . . . . . . . .     O 185 Anacreon Ode 9    8
    Had this fair figure which this frame displays,  . . .   O 189 Seeing Montagu    1
    In Passion lost, he bad the conqu'ring Fair . . . . .   O 258 Irene            99
    Swells the fair Breast or animates the Glance,  . . .   O 262 Irene            14
    Why rove I now, when absent from my Fair,  . . . . .    O 263 Irene            19
    There let Aspasia, since my Fair entreats it,  . . . .  O 263 Irene             3
    While fair Hungaria's unexhausted Vallies  . . . . .    O 264 Irene            16
    While fair yet Hungaria's inexhausted Vallies  . . . .  O 352 Irene         V  33
    For you fair Asia spreads her wealthy plains.   . . .   Y 132 Irene         V 41C
    Behold, my fair, as my resistless hand . . . . . .     Y 136 Irene         V  25
    Daggers and love?  What love but fair . . . . . .      Y 144 Irene         V  81
    Irene?
    Wilt thou descend, fair Daughter of Perfection,  . . .  O 276 Irene             1
    Celestial fair--maid--new wonders fix me thine,  . . .  Y 149 Irene         V  59
    I thought, forgive my Fair, the noblest Aim,   . . . .  O 278 Irene            61
    For thee, my fair, shall India's spices . . . . . .    Y 150 Irene         V  81
    ripen
    Not till this Day thou saw'st this fatal Fair;  . . . .  O 281 Irene            54
    Seize the kind Fair, and press her to thy Bosom.  . .   O 284 Irene             35
    With warmer Courtship press the yielding Fair,  . . .   O 287 Irene             9
    Reserve this Homage for some other Fair,  . . . . . .   O 288 Irene             4
    Gladness, fair child, of innocence and freedom.  . . .  Y 165 Irene         V  81
    Or bid fair Science polish Britains Heroes  . . . . .   O 348 Irene         V  22
    Intreats admittance to the fair Aspasia  . . . . . .    O 367 Irene         V  20
    Then--O my Fair, I cannot bid thee goe;  . . . . . .    O 297 Irene            15
    Then--O my Fair, I cannot bid thee go;  . . . . . .     O 297 Irene         V  15
    Nor fear the Fair and Learn'd can want Protection.  . .  O 302 Irene           115
    Retire, my Fair, that Pow'r that smiles on Goodness  .  O 303 Irene            20
    Shall dart their am'rous Glances at the Fair,  . . .    O 304 Irene            35
    Confirm your Troops; and when the Moon's fair Beam  . .  O 306 Irene            58
    The matchless Fair has bless'd me with Compliance;  . .  O 308 Irene             3
    Then seize fair Italy's delightful Coast,   . . . . .   O 309 Irene            30
    Attention rise, survey the fair Creation,  . . . . .    O 313 Irene             6
    New from the Maker's Hand, and fair array'd . . . . .   O 314 Irene             4
    Forgive, my Fair, 'tis Life, 'tis Nature calls.  . . .  O 318 Irene            19
    Forgive my fair what fame what nature prompts . . . .   Y 197 Irene         V  19
    Behold a Boaster's Worth.  Now snatch, my Fair,  . . .  O 320 Irene             7
    Fair Falshood stay.  . . . . . . . . . . . . .         O 323 Irene             1
    Forgive, fair Excellence, th' unwilling Tongue,  . . .  O 324 Irene             1
    Unhappy Fair! Compassion calls upon me . . . . . .     O 327 Irene             4
    Where 's this fair Trait'ress? Where 's this smiling  . .  O 330 Irene            1
    Mischief?
    True, she was fair; the Smile of Innocence  . . . . .   O 330 Irene            10
    Yet she--fair--so shone first apostate  . . . . . .    Y 211 Irene         V  10
    And of a fruitful year fair omens bring.  . . . . . .   Y   3 On a Daffodill    4
    And of a faithful year fair omens bring.  . . . . . .   Y   3 On a Daffodill  V  4
    Cleora's self, fair flower, shall fade like thee,  . .   Y   4 On a Daffodill   27
    I first foresook the scornful fair.  . . . . . . .     Y  11 Tr Hor Epode 9   10
    That all the fair their favours sold;  . . . . . . .    Y  11 Tr Hor Epode 9   20
    From the fair nurse Astyanax demands.  . . . . . . .    Y  20 Tr. Iliad Bk 6   91
    "Ah! let not tears down that fair count'nance rowl,  .  Y  21 Tr. Iliad Bk 6  113
    Fair source of wit, and love, and mirth,  . . . . .    Y  39 Lady Leaving      6
FAIRER
    A Habitation for a fairer Soul?  . . . . . . . . . .   O 277 Irene            29
    "Here fairer than his flock the shepherd lyes  . . . .  Y   7 Virgil Daphnis   30
FAIREST
    With livid hue the fairest face o'ercast,   . . . . .   O  84 Epi Dist Moth.   34
    Not always do the fairest Flow'rs diffuse  . . . . .    O 277 Irene            31
    Destroy'd the fairest Workmanship of Heav'n!  . . . .   O 332 Irene            19
FAIRIES
    They call them Fairies; these now free from care  . .   O  77 Tr Add. Battle   49
FAIRY
    Mock'd our impatient steps, for all was fairy ground.  .  Y 310 Parody of Pope   4
FAITH
    And his last sighs reproach the faith of kings.  . . .  O  35 Vanity Wishes   120
    And his last words reproach the faith of kings.  . . .  Y  96 Vanity Wishes  V 120
```

		PAGE	TITLE	LINE
FAITH	(CONTINUED)			
For faith, that panting for a happier seat,		O 48	Vanity Wishes	363
Their faith, or force them to forsake		O 79	Feast St Simon	14
No faith of partnership dominion owns;		O 140	Tr Rambler 183	1
Faith from every generous mind:		O 176	Tr Metastasi I	4
Does adamantine Faith invest his Heart?		O 255	Irene	21
Renounce her Faith, and be the Queen of Turkey;		O 258	Irene	100
But will she yet receive the Faith of Mecca?		O 261	Irene	11
Our warlike Prophet loves an active Faith,		O 264	Irene	25
Then old in honours, and approv'd in faith,		Y 131	Irene	V 32
Are these the Counsels? This the Faith of Cali?		O 272	Irene	11
The Faith of Mustapha disdains Suspicion;		O 273	Irene	30
What Worth can merit? or what Faith reward?		O 295	Irene	16
Nor built on Faith, nor fortify'd by Conscience?		O 301	Irene	84
Forbear--.i know the long try'd Faith of Cali.		O 308	Irene	11
FAITHFUL				
The patient Suff'rer, and the faithful Wife.		O 58	Prologue Comus	32
Shewn in the faithful glass of ridicule;		O 81	Lady Birthday	16
With venerable Cali's faithful Counsels?		O 272	Irene	10
Yet should my Soul, still faithful to her Choice,		O 289	Irene	13
Two faithful Captains, Hasan and Caraza,		O 310	Irene	5
While I protract their Stay. Be swift and faithful.		O 319	Irene	4
Irene's Chamber! From my faithful Bosom		O 326	Irene	31
And of a faithful year fair omens bring.		Y 3	On a Daffodill	V 4
FAITHFULL				
Will she that's false to Heavn, to me be faithfull		Y 186	Irene	V 4
FAITHLESS				
The midnight murd'rer bursts the faithless bar;		O 21	London	239
Or horrid Africk's faithless sands;		O 65	Hor I Ode xxii	6
Or torrid Africk's faithless sands;		O 65	Hor I Ode xxii	V 6
Or torrid Afric's faithless Sands,		O 66	To A. Fuscus	6
And vows to trust the faithless deep no more.		O 82	Young Author	10
When Genoa's faithless Sons forsook the Ramparts		O 351	Irene	V 5
Too fierce, too faithless for Neglect or Trust.		O 288	Irene	14
His Fav'rite faithless, and his Mistress base.		O 310	Irene	6
FALL				
Fall in the gen'ral massacre of gold;		O 31	Vanity Wishes	22
They mount, they shine, evaporate, and fall.		O 33	Vanity Wishes	76
The form distorted justifies the fall,		O 34	Vanity Wishes	89
But find the form distorted by the fall		Y 95	Vanity Wishes	V 89
His fall was destin'd to a barren strand,		O 41	Vanity Wishes	219
By thee wholl cities burn, wholl nations fall!		O 77	Festina Lente	12
To raise them from their fall.		O 79	Feast St Simon	30
But, lest I fall by subtler foes,		O 126	An Ode	37
And then lament his fall with seeming friendship:		O 176	Tr Metastas II	5
And then lament their fall with seeming friendship:		O 176	Tr Metastas II	V 5
Or wake the Dead to warn us of its Fall?		O 250	Irene	47
Pour forth her Dead to warn us of its fall?		O 365	Irene	V 22
And there must fall.		O 260	Irene	132
And should he fall unheard, by sudden Justice,		O 273	Irene	41
An Let fall sometimes a tear for lost Irene		O 349	Irene	V 1
And Buda fall, and proud Vienna tremble,		O 309	Irene	27
So sure the Fall of Greatness rais'd on Crimes,		O 335	Irene	10
Alike must fall the poet and his theme.		Y 4	On a Daffodill	28
Now, at thy fall incens'd, the rural Gods		Y 6	Virgil Daphnis	20
Soon shall you fall by num'rous hosts opprest		Y 18	Tr. Iliad Bk 6	22
The nymphs bewail'd his fall with loud lament		Y 18	Tr. Iliad Bk 6	32
Think shouldst thou fall how wretched shall we be,		Y 19	Tr. Iliad Bk 6	48
FALL'N				
Art thou too fall'n? ere anger could subside		O 132	Tr. Rambler 54	1
Is Greece deliver'd? is the Tyrant fall'n?		O 315	Irene	3
FALLACIOUS				
Now led astray by hopes fallacious glimm'rings		Y 148	Irene	V 43A
FALLACY				
And set the glitt'ring Fallacy to view.		O 293	Irene	128
FALLING				
Here falling houses thunder on your head,		O 9	London	17
Or weep some falling King.		O 78	Feast St Simon	6
FALLS				
Less heard and less, the faint remonstrance falls;		O 46	Vanity Wishes	334
Now beauty falls betray'd, despis'd, distress'd,		O 47	Vanity Wishes	341
Here beauty falls betray'd, despis'd, distress'd,		O 47	Vanity Wishes	V 341
Soon th' aspiring Fabric falls,		O 145	Tr Boeth. II.4	9
A floating Atom, Dust that falls unheeded		O 260	Irene	139
How Nation after Nation falls before him.		O 268	Irene	27
How nation after nation falls before me		Y 136	Irene	V 27
FALSE				
Should no false Kindness lure to loose delight,		O 37	Vanity Wishes	147
More false, more cruel than the seas and wind.		O 82	Young Author	14
More false, more cruel than the seas or wind.		O 82	Young Author	V 14
Tir'd with vain joys, and false alarms,		O 124	Winter's Walk	17
From false caresses, causeless strife,		O 125	An Ode	25
With false Security beheld Invasion.		O 250	Irene	30
To rough--Too false too fierce to trust or to neglect		O 374	Irene	V 1
Soon shouldst thou see, how false thy weak Reproach.		O 293	Irene	107
Soon wouldst thou see, how false thy weak Reproach.		O 293	Irene	V 107
Detests thy false Associates black Designs,		O 300	Irene	57
Will she that's false to Heavn, to me be faithfull		Y 186	Irene	V 4
FALSEHOOD				
Dares join Leontius' Name with Fear or Falsehood?		O 304	Irene	13

```
FALSHOOD                                              PAGE     TITLE            LINE
     Dooms me to loath at once, and doat on Falshood,    .  .  .   O 310 Irene              10
     Betray'd by Falshood, or by Crouds o'erborn?     .  .  .  .   O 315 Irene               7
     Fair Falshood stay.  .  .  .  .  .  .  .  .  .    .  .  .  .   O 323 Irene               1
     And if one varied Accent prove thy Falshood,     .  .  .  .   O 332 Irene              14
FALSHOODS
     With noisy Falshoods forc'd me from your Arms,   .  .  .  .   O 299 Irene              39
     There had she lull'd me with endearing Falshoods,  .  .  .    O 331 Irene              18
FALT'RING
     Join'd Cali's Hand to mine, and falt'ring cry'd,   .  .  .    O 272 Irene               8
FAM'D
     Or where the fam'd Hydaspes spreads   .  .  .  .  .  .  .     O  65 Hor I Ode xxii       7
     Or where the fam'd Hydaspes spreads   .  .  .  .  .  .  .     O  66 To A. Fuscus         7
FAME
     Behold our fame, our wealth, our lives your own.   .  .  .    O  13 London             64
     Unsullied fame, and conscience ever gay.  .  .  .  .  .  .    O  14 London             90
     The young enthusiast quits his ease for fame;    .  .  .  .   O  36 Vanity Wishes     136
     Till fame supplies the universal charm.  .  .  .  .  .  .     O  39 Vanity Wishes     184
     On what foundation stands the warrior's hope?    .  .  .  .   Y 101 Vanity Wishes   V 191
     Against your fame with fondness hate combines,   .  .  .  .   O  46 Vanity Wishes     331
     The Wits of Charles found easier Ways to Fame,   .  .  .  .   O  52 Pro Drury-Lane     17
     Ye patriot Crouds, who burn for England's Fame,  .  .  .  .   O  57 Prologue Comus      1
     With ardent Haste, each Candidate of Fame    .  .  .  .  .    O  57 Prologue Comus     19
     The busy candidates for power and fame,  .  .  .  .  .  .     O  59 Pro Good Nat'd     11
     My Works shall propagate my fame,    .  .  .  .  .  .  .  .   O  70 Hor.II Ode XX      17
     And one base action sully all my fame,   .  .  .  .  .  .     O  74 Tr. Iliad Bk 6      6
     So the young author panting after fame,   .  .  .  .  .  .    O  82 Young Author     V 11
     And fir'd with pleasing hope of endless fame,    .  .  .  .   O  82 Young Author       12
     And fame pursu'd him, where conviction led.  .  .  .  .  .    O 118 Epitaph Hanmer     34
     Succeeding years thy early fame destroy;  .  .  .  .  .  .    O 135 Tr Rambler 127      1
     Gaurus pretends to Cato's fame;   .  .  .  .  .  .  .  .  .   O 138 Tr Rambler 164      1
     Vot'ries of Fame and Worshippers of Pow'r!   .  .  .  .  .    O 246 Irene Prologue      5
     If there be any Land, as Fame reports,   .  .  .  .  .  .     O 256 Irene              55
     Secure he tramples my declining Fame,    .  .  .  .  .  .     O 257 Irene              71
     Forgive my fair what fame what nature prompts    .  .  .  .   Y 197 Irene            V 19
     No more I burn for Fame or for Dominion;  .  .  .  .  .  .    O 333 Irene              43
     "Whose fame from earth resounded to the skies."  .  .  .  .   Y   7 Virgil Daphnis     31
     And his more glorious acts eclipse his father's fame.  .  .   Y  20 Tr. Iliad Bk 6    104
     Their growing fame re'echoes to the skies.   .  .  .  .  .    Y  22 Tr Add. Battle      9
     Ardent of fame, yet fearless of disgrace.    .  .  .  .  .    Y  67 Prologue Lethe      2
FAMILIAR
     The subject World, familiar to Dominion.  .  .  .  .  .  .    O 369 Irene            V 10
     While I not yet familiar to my Crimes,   .  .  .  .  .  .     O 322 Irene              11
FAMILIES
     How families sink, by darling schemes oppress'd,   .  .  .    Y  92 Vanity Wishes   V 13
FAMINE
     Stern Famine guards the solitary coast,   .  .  .  .  .  .    O  41 Vanity Wishes     207
FAN
     And Gales cf softer Passion fan my Bosom.    .  .  .  .  .    O 275 Irene              93
FAN'D
     Those anxious fears that fan'd the flame of Love.  .  .  .    Y  11 Tr Hor Epode 9     24
FANCIED
     Shuns fancied ills, or chases airy good;  .  .  .  .  .  .    O  31 Vanity Wishes      10
FANCY
     To please his Fancy,--see no other Man--  .  .  .  .  .  .    O 247 Irene Epilogue      3
     If thou art more than the gay Dream of Fancy,    .  .  .  .   O 310 Irene              12
FANCY'D
     A fancy'd Treasure, and a waking Dream.   .  .  .  .  .  .    O 277 Irene              48
     Upbraid me not with fancy'd Wickedness,   .  .  .  .  .  .    O 289 Irene              21
     Looks down, contemptuous, from his fancy'd Height,   .  .     O 306 Irene               2
FANN'D
     Heard her last Cries, and fann'd her dying Beauties,   .  .   O 333 Irene              47
FANS
     And fans the slumb'ring Spark of heav'nly Fire.  .  .  .  .   O 303 Irene              19
FAQUIR
     Th' unpractis'd Dervise, or sequester'd Faquir.  .  .  .  .   O 281 Irene              37
FAR
     Resolved at length, from vice and London far,    .  .  .  .   O   9 London              5
     Who now resolves, from vice and London far,  .  .  .  .  .    O   9 London            V 5
     Ah! what avails it, that, from slav'ry far,  .  .  .  .  .    O  15 London            117
     Far from their antient fields and humble cots.   .  .  .  .   O  64 Virgil Past.I      18
     Too far in Sabine woods I stray'd;   .  .  .  .  .  .  .  .   O  65 Hor I Ode xxii     10
     By Lalage, too far I stray'd,     .  .  .  .  .  .  .  .  .   O  66 To A. Fuscus       10
     <Or> sees from far his Bullocks play  .  .  .  .  .  .  .     O  71 Hor. Epode II      20
     Far from their happy native home  .  .  .  .  .  .  .  .  .   O  79 Feast St Simon     28
     Far hence are banish'd vapours, spleen, and tears,   .  .     O  84 Epi Dist Moth.     18
     Let Caesar spread his conquests far,  .  .  .  .  .  .  .     O 137 Tr Rambler 143      1
     Be Vice and Dulness far away  .  .  .  .  .  .  .  .  .  .    O 154 Epita. Hogarth      7
     Far from his Troops, he toys his Hours away.     .  .  .  .   O 258 Irene              93
     And bear us far from Servitude and Crimes.   .  .  .  .  .    O 267 Irene              44
     Far more I dread Abdalla's fiery Folly,   .  .  .  .  .  .    O 287 Irene               7
     There shalt thou view from far the quiet Cottage,  .  .  .    O 292 Irene              83
     Far as Futurity's untravell'd Waste   .  .  .  .  .  .  .     O 300 Irene              68
     Far be such black Ingratitude from Cali,  .  .  .  .  .  .    O 306 Irene               4
     New from the Maker's Hand, and far array'd   .  .  .  .  .    O 314 Irene            V  4
     Far be the Thought--But hear my Protestation.    .  .  .  .   O 326 Irene              32
     Far be the horrid thought--but hear my protestation  .  .     Y 205 Irene            V 32
     Far dearer than his cwn or father's life  .  .  .  .  .  .    Y  18 Tr. Iliad Bk 6      6
FARCE
     All aid the farce, and all thy mirth maintain,   .  .  .  .   O  33 Vanity Wishes      67
     This night he hopes to shew that farce may charm,  .  .  .    Y  67 Prologue Lethe     13
```

```
                                                          PAGE    TITLE            LINE
FAREWELL
    When injur'd Thales bids the town farewell, . . . . .   O   8 London             2
    Farewell!--When youth, and health, and fortune spent,  .  O  23 London          256
    Bid the slaves of thrift farewell. . . . . . . . .     O 196 Song Congratu.      8
    Bid the Sons of thrift farewell. . . . . . . . .       O 196 Song Congratu.  V   8
    Will not admit a Lover's long Farewell, . . . . . .     O 297 Irene             13
    And bid thy visionary Throne farewell. . . . . . .      O 307 Irene             11
    Farewell, unhappy Maid, may ev'ry Joy . . . . . .       O 322 Irene             57
FARM
    Collect a tax, or farm a lottery, . . . . . . . .       O  12 London            58
FARMER
    The farmer annuall honours pays . . . . . . . . .       O  73 Hor. Epode II     64
FARTHER
    Let Prudence, ere the Suit be farther urg'd, . . . .    O 285 Irene              8
    Nor farther tempt the avenging rage of Heaven . . . .   Y 168 Irene         V 134
FASHION
    And ask the latest fashion of the heart, . . . . . .    O  46 Vanity Wishes    328
FAST
    Thou canst not make the tea so fast . . . . . . .       O 159 Par Hermit III    11
FASTING
    All sciences a fasting Monsieur knows, . . . . . .      O  15 London           115
    fasting, pennan<ce> and works of goodness . . . . .     O 348 Irene         V  15
FATAL
    With fatal heat impetuous courage glows, . . . . . .    O  31 Vanity Wishes     17
    With fatal sweetness elocution flows, . . . . . .       O  31 Vanity Wishes     18
    Should Beauty blunt on fops her fatal dart, . . . .     O  37 Vanity Wishes    151
    And fatal Learning leads him to the block: . . . . .    O  39 Vanity Wishes    172
    Did rival monarchs give the fatal wound? . . . . .      O  41 Vanity Wishes    217
    Of hasty greatness finds the fatal doom, . . . . . .    O  43 Vanity Wishes    252
    Defer an hour the fatal blow. . . . . . . . .          O  69 Hor.II Ode 14     12
    To sink the fatal precipice before him, . . . . . .     O 176 Tr Metastas II     4
    To sink the fatal precipice before them, . . . . .      O 176 Tr Metastas II  V  4
    He bids no Trumpet quell the fatal Sound. . . . . .     O 246 Irene Prologue    24
    These Groans were fatal, these Disguises vain: . . .    O 249 Irene              6
    And gives a thousand fatal Questions Birth; . . . .     O 258 Irene             84
    And Anguish gnashes on the fatal Wheel. . . . . .       O 266 Irene             16
    Ambitious to prevent the fatal summons . . . . . .      Y 136 Irene         V 27A
    Some fatal gust of sudden Opposition . . . . . .        O 374 Irene         V  15
    When from his Lips the fatal Name burst out, . . . .    O 270 Irene             12
    Held forth this fatal Scroll, then sunk to nothing. . . O 272 Irene             17
    Held out this fatal roll--then sunk to Nothing. . . .   O 357 Irene         V   1
    Not till this Day thou saw'st this fatal Fair; . . . .  O 281 Irene             54
    That fatal Mistress of the Young, the Lazy, . . . .     O 283 Irene             21
    May spare the fatal Bow-string till To-morrow? . . .    O 284 Irene             39
    Beset the treacherous Way with fatal Ambush; . . . .    O 300 Irene             72
    That fatal Beauty plighted to Demetrius . . . . .       O 307 Irene             15
    Around these fatal Walls, the Tide of War . . . . .     O 312 Irene              8
    Still dost thou linger in these fatal bowrs . . . . .   Y 196 Irene         V 18A
    And thinks his fatal Mandates ill obey'd. . . . . .     O 327 Irene             13
    One Hour had freed me from the fatal Error, . . . .     O 332 Irene             27
    Nor trust our Passions with her fatal Charms. . . . .   O 332 Irene             31
FATALL
    But now alass! the fatall hour drew nigh . . . . .      Y  24 Tr Add. Battle    62
FATE
    There none are swept by sudden fate away, . . . . .     O   9 London            11
    With eager thirst, by folly or by fate, . . . . .       O  14 London            95
    Fate never wounds more deep the gen'rous heart, . . .   O  18 London           168
    How virtue wars with persecuting fate; . . . . .        O  19 London           199
    O'erspread with snares the clouded maze of fate, . .    O  31 Vanity Wishes      6
    Fate wings with ev'ry wish th' afflictive dart, . . .   O  31 Vanity Wishes     15
    For why did Wolsey near the steeps of fate, . . . .     O  35 Vanity Wishes    125
    For why did Wolsey by the Steps of fate, . . . . .      Y  98 Vanity Wishes  V 125
    Yet should thy fate indulge the gen'rous heat, . . .    O  45 Vanity Wishes  V 143
    Who set unclouded in the gulphs of fate. . . . . .      O  45 Vanity Wishes    312
    Roll darkling down the torrent of his fate? . . . .     O  47 Vanity Wishes    346
    Swim darkling down the Current of his fate? . . . .     O  47 Vanity Wishes  V 346
    Ah! let not Censure term our Fate our Choice, . . .     O  53 Pro Drury-Lane    51
    Like Caesar's pilot, dignified by fate, . . . . .       O  59 Pro Good Nat'd     7
    The man whom fate has laid, where all must lye. . . .   O  61 Pro Word Wise      6
    As the sad thought of your impending fate: . . . .      O  74 Tr. Iliad Bk 6    20
    But cautious Fabius from impending fate . . . . .       O  78 Festina Lente     17
    When Christ had conquer'd Hell and fate . . . . .       O  79 Feast St Simon    19
    He plies the press, and hurries on his fate; . . . .    O  82 Young Author      20
    He flies to press, and hurries on his fate; . . . .     O  82 Young Author   V  20
    Warn'd by another's fate, vain youth, be wise, . . .    O  82 Young Author      23
    And with unerring shafts distribute fate; . . . . .     O  83 Epi Dist Moth.     4
    Ambiguous emblem of uncertain fate! . . . . . .        O  95 Sprig of Myrtl     2
    Ambiguous emblem of my future fate! . . . . . .        O  95 Sprig of Myrtl  V   2
    "Fate! snatch away the bright disguise, . . . . .       O 122 Stella Mourn.      5
    And fate malicious heard the pray'r. . . . . . .        O 122 Stella Mourn.      8
    Now Daedalus, behold, by fate assign'd, . . . . .       O 136 Tr Rambler 129     1
    Not all the gifts of Fate combin'd . . . . . . .        O 144 Tr Boeth. II.2     7
    And not one Prodigy foretold our Fate. . . . . .        O 250 Irene             35
    And snatch'd her timely from her Country's Fate. . .    O 252 Irene             98
    Soon as the Sultan's unexpected Fate . . . . . .        O 257 Irene             76
    O lead me quickly to the Scene of Fate; . . . . .       O 259 Irene            105
    Just in the Moment of impending Fate, . . . . .         O 259 Irene            117
    Not all like thee can brave the Shocks of Fate, . . .   O 266 Irene             34
    Commits to trivial Chance the Fate of Nations! . . .    O 269 Irene              2
    What trivial Accidents determine Fate! . . . . .        O 367 Irene         V  23
    Commits to trivial chance the Work of Fate! . . . .     O 374 Irene         V  11
```

111

FATE   (CONTINUED)

	PAGE	TITLE	LINE
Fly lab'ring with the Fate of future Nations,	O 279	Irene	4
That Hoary Head, that Head which hungry fate	O 374	Irene	V 20
Well,--'tis decreed--This Night shall fix our Fate.	O 284	Irene	48
Give me, before th' approaching Hour of Fate,	O 285	Irene	5
And lodge the fate of kingdoms in her bosom.	Y 159	Irene	V 18
And Fate lies crouded in a narrow Space.	O 287	Irene	5
While I foretell thy Fate; that Office done,--	O 289	Irene	9
If Fate pursues me, let it find me here.	O 297	Irene	18
If Fate persues me, let it find me here	O 297	Irene	V 18
To find a meaner Fate from treach'rous Friendship--	O 299	Irene	33
Soon may the final Stroke decide our Fate,	O 299	Irene	51
Embark'd with Treason on the Seas of Fate,	O 300	Irene	59
Is not the Fate of Greece and Cali thine?	O 304	Irene	19
And utters Fate, unmindful of Abdalla.	O 306	Irene	3
In these dark Moments of suspended Fate,	O 313	Irene	1
she courted fate & scorn'd a crown	Y 191	Irene	V 16
That bears the Fate of Empires in her Air,	O 317	Irene	2
Infatuate Loiterer, has Fate, in vain,	O 318	Irene	15
Luckless slave Ilfated loiterer has fate in vain	Y 196	Irene	V 15
Depart, Demetrius, lest my Fate involve thee,	O 320	Irene	13
To meet that Fate we can delay no longer.	O 328	Irene	41
Melt at Irene's Fate, and share her Woes?	O 329	Irene	7
What need of Caution to report the Fate	O 329	Irene	16
Forgive, great Sultan! that by Fate prevented,	O 331	Irene	1
And wish'd--Be still thy Fate to wish in vain.	O 334	Irene	60
Touch'd with thy fate Numidia's lyons roar	Y 6	Virgil Daphnis	11
About to rush into the field of fate	Y 18	Tr. Iliad Bk 6	4
And the sad fate of Pygmie realms I sing.	Y 22	Tr Add. Battle	2
And wept unhappy Pompey's hapless fate?	Y 22	Tr Add. Battle	15
I'll sing the chiefs dispensing fate around.	Y 22	Tr Add. Battle	19
In former ages while upheld by fate	Y 23	Tr Add. Battle	26

FATED   SEE ILL-FATED

FATES

	PAGE	TITLE	LINE
But cruel virgins meet severer fates;	O 84	Epi Dist Moth.	28
Your sighs are spent in vain; if fates withstand	Y 21	Tr. Iliad Bk 6	115

FATHER

	PAGE	TITLE	LINE
A guide, a father, and a friend;	O 125	An Ode	22
Cry not when his father dies,	O 183	Burlesque Vega	2
Have a turnip than his father.	O 183	Burlesque Vega	4
Have a turnip than a father.	O 183	Burlesque Vega	V 4
Embroil'd the Turkish State--our Sultan's Father	O 256	Irene	42
To offer up my vows in the temple built by the Father of Mankind	O 348	Irene	V 1
My Father call'd me to his Couch of Death,	O 272	Irene	7
And quit the Names of Brother, Friend, and Father?	O 280	Irene	17
My father fell by fierce Achilles' hand	Y 18	Tr. Iliad Bk 6	28
A father, brother, husband, all in thee.	Y 19	Tr. Iliad Bk 6	45

FATHER'S

	PAGE	TITLE	LINE
Young, and unsettled in his Father's Kingdoms,	O 257	Irene	67
Heap'd by your Father's ill-plac'd Bounties on him,	O 274	Irene	51
Far dearer than his own or father's life	Y 18	Tr. Iliad Bk 6	48
And his more glorious acts eclipse his father's fame.	Y 20	Tr. Iliad Bk 6	104

FATHERS

	PAGE	TITLE	LINE
Heap'd by my Fathers illplac'd Bounties on Him	O 351	Irene	V 13
Guide the Sons dagger to the Fathers heart	O 352	Irene	V 4

FATIGUE

	PAGE	TITLE	LINE
Till soft Fatigue invite us to repose.	O 323	Irene	18

FATTEN

	PAGE	TITLE	LINE
Rob without Fear, and fatten without Toil.	O 110	To Posterity	14

FATTEND

	PAGE	TITLE	LINE
And croud the fattend fields, the ghosts that wander	Y 120	Irene	V 31

FAULCHION

	PAGE	TITLE	LINE
Soon had the wrathfull faulchion drank his blood.	Y 23	Tr Add. Battle	41
That day what legions by his faulchion bled!	Y 25	Tr Add. Battle	120

FAULT

	PAGE	TITLE	LINE
I grant the charge; forgive the fault confess'd.	O 139	Tr Rambler 170	1
Which aggravate a fault with feign'd excuses,	O 176	Tr Metastas II	8

FAULT'RING

	PAGE	TITLE	LINE
Strain out with fault'ring diffidence a lye,	O 16	London	130

FAULTS

	PAGE	TITLE	LINE
Teach mimick censure her own faults to find,	O 81	Lady Birthday	17
What doating bigot to his faults so blind,	O 137	Tr Rambler 140	1

FAUSTUS

	PAGE	TITLE	LINE
She saw great Faustus lay the Ghost of Wit:	O 52	Pro Drury-Lane	36

FAV'RING

	PAGE	TITLE	LINE
No fav'ring Muse her morning Dreams inspire;	O 58	Prologue Comus	28
Rewards the fav'ring Deities,	O 72	Hor. Epode II	V 27
That, fav'ring, listen to his cries.	O 72	Hor. Epode II	28
The fav'ring Winds assist the great Design,	O 304	Irene	6
Fill all the Starry Lamps with Fav'ring Sky <Radiance>.	O 364	Irene	V 27

FAV'RITE

	PAGE	TITLE	LINE
The gen'ral fav'rite as the gen'ral friend:	O 44	Vanity Wishes	297
The common fav'rite as the gen'ral friend:	Y 105	Vanity Wishes	V 297
His Fav'rite faithless, and his Mistress base.	O 310	Irene	6

FAV'RITES

	PAGE	TITLE	LINE
The cheated nation's happy fav'rites, see!	O 14	London	91
Where change of fav'rites made no change of laws,	O 33	Vanity Wishes	59
Sign her foes doom, or guard her fav'rites zeal?	O 34	Vanity Wishes	92
Around the fav'rites of the sky.	O 100	Ode Friendship	12

```
FAV'RITES        (CONTINUED)                              PAGE    TITLE           LINE
    He tires his Fav'rites with Irene's Praise, . . . . .   O 261 Irene              3
FAVORITE
    Be thou the favorite of the indulgent sky,  . . . . .   Y   3 On a Daffodill      5
FAVOUR'D
    Though favour'd by the pow'rs on high,   . . . . .      O 136 Tr Rambler 128      5
    Myself escap'd, or favour'd or neglected.   . . . . .   O 317 Irene             41
FAVOURING
    All pains, all cares, may favouring heav'n remove,  . . O  81 Lady Birthday       5
FAVOURITE
    No pug, nor favourite Cupid there enjoys . . . . . .    O  84 Epi Dist Moth.     20
FAVOURS
    The groom retails the favours of his lord. . . . . .    O  18 London            181
    Oft favours, oft rejects a lover's pray'r: . . . . .    O  95 Sprig of Myrtl      6
    Oft favours, oft rejects the poet's pray'r: . . . . .   O  95 Sprig of Myrtl  V   6
    Were all our Favours lavish'd on a Villain? . . . . .   O 272 Irene             12
    Whom neither Vows could fix, nor Favours bind? . . . .  O 330 Irene              2
    That all the fair their favours sold; . . . . . .      Y  11 Tr Hor Epode 9     20
FAWNING
    Perplex the fawning niece and pamper'd guest, . . . .   O  44 Vanity Wishes     276
    The dull conjecture fawning niece and pamper'd guest, . Y 104 Vanity Wishes  V 276
    That fawning Villain's forc'd Congratulations . . . .   O 310 Irene              2
FEAR
    Well may we fear, such crowds at Tyburn die, . . . .    Y  60 London          V 242
    Then say how hope and fear, desire and hate, . . . .    O  31 Vanity Wishes       5
    Few know the toiling statesman's fear or care, . . . .  O  32 Vanity Wishes      47
    O'er love, o'er fear, extends his wide domain, . . . .  O  40 Vanity Wishes     195
    Where then shall Hope and Fear their objects find? . .  O  47 Vanity Wishes     343
    When senators and nobles learn to fear; . . . . . .    O  59 Pro Good Nat'd  V  4B
    Trusts without fear, to merit, and to you. . . . . .    O  60 Pro Good Nat'd     30
    Trusts without fear, to candour, and to you. . . . .    O  60 Pro Good Nat'd  V  30
    In vain with anxious breasts we fear . . . . . . .     O  69 Hor.II Ode 14      15
    For fear retards their flight, the cruell Crane . . .   O  76 Tr Add. Battle     31
    And giv'n to mirth, the Cranes no longer fear, . . . .  O  77 Tr Add. Battle     50
    Sick'ning with fear he longs to view the shore, . . .   O  82 Young Author        9
    Rob without Fear, and fatten without Toil. . . . . .    O 110 To Posterity       14
    In groundless hope, and causeless fear, . . . . . .    O 124 Winter's Walk      13
    Wild hope, vain fear, alike remov'd, . . . . . . .     O 125 An Ode             26
    Nor fear that I, my gentle maid, . . . . . . . . .     O 159 Par Hermit III      5
    Why should they fear?--That Power that kindly spreads   O 250 Irene             31
    or chill our blood but Fear . . . . . . . . . .       O 347 Irene           V   4
    And leave no Place for Perfidy or Fear. . . . . . .    O 255 Irene             33
    Fear in her Eye, Submission on her Tongue, . . . . .   O 259 Irene            120
    Fear and Ambition, urge her to Compliance; . . . . .   O 261 Irene             13
    Since Fear predominates in every Thought, . . . . .   O 266 Irene             17
    They sympathise with us in every fear . . . . . . .    Y 134 Irene           V  26
    Well might we fear impending Disappointments. . . . .   O 269 Irene              2
    But Fear, or Mutiny may taint the Greeks? . . . . .   O 284 Irene             37
    Aspasia should not fear a second Insult. . . . . . .    O 299 Irene             42
    Perhaps the Phantoms of a Woman's Fear, . . . . . .    O 300 Irene             71
    Too much to fear or trust, is equal Weakness. . . . .   O 300 Irene             77
    How soon, alas! will Int'rest, Fear, or Envy, . . . .   O 301 Irene             82
    Nor fear the Fair and Learn'd can want Protection. . .  O 302 Irene            115
    Which squander'd by Neglect, or Fear, or Folly, . . .   O 302 Irene              7
    Dares join Leontius' Name with Fear or Falsehood? . .   O 304 Irene             13
    Ere guilty Fear depress'd the hoary Chief, . . . . .   O 312 Irene             18
    Shall Monarchs fear to draw the Sword of Justice, . .   O 312 Irene             21
    From generous piety, or abject fear? . . . . . . .     Y 189 Irene           V  1B
    When Fear and Anguish labour in the Breast, . . . . .   O 315 Irene             31
    Whose Fear, or Rage, or Treachery betray'd us. . . . .  O 316 Irene             17
    Now, Traytor, feel the Fear that chills my Hand. . . .  O 318 Irene             20
    Tis cowardise to fear the boasts of folly . . . . .   Y 197 Irene           V  22
    Relax'd with Fear, refuse to bear me forward. . . . .   O 320 Irene             12
    Beyond the Fear of ling'ring Punishment, . . . . . .   O 325 Irene             16
    See the last Witness of thy Guilt and Fear . . . . .   O 326 Irene              2
    O let me be but heard, nor fear from me . . . . . .    O 327 Irene             20
    The harmless wolves no more our cattle fear, . . . .   Y   7 Virgil Daphnis     38
    Without a boding fear, or anxious sigh, . . . . . .    Y  67 Prologue Lethe      3
    Beheld the tragic heroes taught to fear. . . . . . .    Y  67 Prologue Lethe      8
FEARFUL
    horrid joy--his air now fearful now resolv'd. . . . .   Y 145 Irene           V  82
    horrid joy--gloomy resolution--his air now fearful now  Y 187 Irene           V   7
        resolv'd.
FEARFULL
    The screaming Cranes and fearfull Hares. . . . . .    O  72 Hor. Epode II      44
FEARFULL'ST
    The bravest hero and the fearfull'st slave . . . . .   Y  21 Tr. Iliad Bk 6    119
FEARLESS
    This fierce Virago, fearless and unshaken . . . . .   O 364 Irene           V  13
    This fierce virago, fearless and unshaken . . . . .   Y 162 Irene           V  40
    Play'd fearless in th' inviolated Shades. . . . . .    O 314 Irene              7
    The fearless Pygmies view them from afar . . . . .    Y  25 Tr Add. Battle     96
    Ardent of fame, yet fearless of disgrace. . . . . .    Y  67 Prologue Lethe      2
FEARS
    Now fears in dire vicissitude invade, . . . . . . .    O  32 Vanity Wishes     41
    New fears in dire vicissitude invade, . . . . . . .    O  32 Vanity Wishes  V  41
    Fears of the brave, and follies of the wise? . . . .   O  45 Vanity Wishes    316
    Have hopes, and fears, and wishes, just the same; . .   O  59 Pro Good Nat'd     12
    What Fears, what terrors does this gift create, . . .   O  95 Sprig of Myrtl V   1
    My Wrongs, my Fears, my Motives, my Designs:-- . . .   O 256 Irene             40
    While Heav'n and Mahomet divide her Fears, . . . . .   O 260 Irene            127
```

FEARS   (CONTINUED)   PAGE   TITLE   LINE

```
FEARS        (CONTINUED)                                 PAGE    TITLE              LINE
   The Hopes and Fears, the Joys and Pains of Life,  . . .  O 265  Irene                7
   Let nobler Hopes and juster Fears succeed,              O 265  Irene                9
   Forgive those Fears that shake the tender Frame?   . . .  O 266  Irene               25
   With counterfeited Fears the Aid of Man.               O 266  Irene               28
   Renew our Sorrows, and awake our Fears.  . . . . . .    O 268  Irene               35
   Whence flow the Hopes and Fears, Despair and Rapture,  . O 277  Irene               41
   Whence all those Hopes and Fears Despair and  . . . .  O 355  Irene          V    18
      Rapture
   Has fix'd his Hopes, Inquietudes, and Fears,           O 280  Irene               27
   What Fears, what Griefs, what Dangers hast thou known?  . O 295  Irene               22
   Now hopes, now fears--                                 O 299  Irene               55
   Dismiss these needless Fears--a Troop of Greeks  . . .  O 301  Irene               90
   Snar'd with thy Fears, and maz'd in Stupefaction.  . .  O 318  Irene               18
   Snare'd with thy fears, and senseless of deliverance   Y 196  Irene          V    18
   Those anxious fears that fan'd the flame of Love. . . . Y  11  Tr Hor Epode 9      24
FEARST
   Who fearst lest I should gain, or thou  . . . . . .    Y 198  Irene          V    32
FEAST
   Some frolick drunkard, reeling from a feast,     . . .  O  21  London             228
   Some gamesome drunkard, reeling from a feast,     . .   Y  59  London         V  228
   Upon the feast of St Simon & St Jude  . . . . . . .    O  78  Feast St Simon      T
   "And when feast and frolic tire,  . . . . . . . .      O 186  Anacreon Ode 9      39
   And bad the feast, and song, and bowl,  . . . . . .    O 190  Tr. Medea I          5
   Now feast thine Eyes, thine Eyes that ne'er hereafter  . O 304  Irene               34
FEASTS
   Or feasts on Kids the Wolves had kill'd  . . . . . .   O  73  Hor. Epode II       65
   No feasts could e'er my cares dispell;  . . . . . .    Y  11  Tr Hor Epode 9      13
FEATHER
   Wild as wind, and light as feather  . . . . . . . .    O 196  Song Congratu.       7
FEATHER'D
   Observe the feather'd Wand'rers of the Sky,  . . . . . O 277  Irene               34
   Feather'd battalions, squadrons on the wing  . . . .   Y  22  Tr Add. Battle       1
   The feather'd race and thirsted for their blood:  . .  Y  24  Tr Add. Battle      85
FEATHERS
   Thick from their wounded wings the feathers fly,  . .  O  75  Tr Add. Battle       4
FEATURES
   To better features yields the frame of gold;  . . . . O  34  Vanity Wishes       86
FED
   And scarce a sycophant was fed by pride;  . . . . . .  O  33  Vanity Wishes       56
   "Slightly shelter'd, coarsely fed?  . . . . . . . .    O 185  Anacreon Ode 9      28
FEEBLE
   Nor lute nor lyre his feeble pow'rs attend,  . . . .   O  43  Vanity Wishes      271
   Let Wit, condemn'd the feeble War to wage  . . . . .   O  57  Prologue Comus       7
   A feeble Government, eluded Laws,  . . . . . . . .     O 250  Irene               37
   And though built on feeble columns--Its lofty turrets  . Y 131  Irene          V    35
      blaze amidst
   Exchanges solid Strength for feeble Splendor.  . . . . O 265  Irene               38
   your feeble fainting virtue . . . . . . . . .         Y 133  Irene          V     9
   And wove the feeble Texture of her Nerves,  . . . . .  O 266  Irene               24
   No feeble Tyrant of a petty State  . . . . . . . .     O 268  Irene               21
   And pushes feeble (thrusts defenseless) virtue from her . Y 158  Irene          V    13
      throne
   Press not her Flight, while yet her feeble Nerves  . . O 320  Irene               20
FEED
   And feed with varied fools th' eternal jest:  . . . .  O  32  Vanity Wishes       52
   And feed with change of new born fools th' eternal  . . Y  94  Vanity Wishes  V    52
      jest:
   And scarce a sycophant could feed on pride;  . . . .   Y  94  Vanity Wishes  V    56
   While bees shall feed on thyme, and birds shall haunt the  Y   7  Virgil Daphnis      50
      grove
FEEDS
   She feeds his Hopes, and sooths him to Delay.  . . . . O 260  Irene              129
FEEL
   For those who feel no guilt can know no shame;  . . .  O  84  Epi Dist Moth.      25
   I feel thy pow'r usurp my breast.  . . . . . . . .     O 123  Winter's Walk        8
   I too can feel the rapture, fierce and strong;  . . .  O 142  In Baretti Bk.       3
   And feel no happiness and one misfortune.  . . . . .   Y 121  Irene          V    57
   And feel no Sorrow while my Sov'reign smiles.  . . . . O 272  Irene               11
   Shall feel the Vengeance of an injur'd King.  . . . .  O 273  Irene               33
   Will not th' Apostate feel the Pangs of Guilt,  . . .  O 294  Irene              132
   To feel no more the Pangs of Separation.  . . . . . .  O 303  Irene               24
   I feel new Spirit shoot along my Nerves,  . . . . . .  O 306  Irene               49
   Then shall Venetia feel the Turkish Pow'r,  . . . . .  O 309  Irene               28
   No more shall feel Religion's hallow'd ardours;  . . . O 349  Irene          V    24
   Now, Traytor, feel the Fear that chills my Hand.  . .  O 318  Irene               20
   And joy to feel the vital Warmth return,  . . . . . .  O 320  Irene               25
   Then shall you feel what Language cannot utter,  . . . O 326  Irene               43
   I feel, I see the Ruffian's barb'rous Rage.  . . . . . O 334  Irene               69
   Nor feel the inclemencies of wintry air;  . . . . . .  Y   3  On a Daffodill       6
   Then flies aloft; th' astonish'd warriours feel  . . . Y  26  Tr Add. Battle     132
FEELS
   He feels no want of ill-persuading gold;  . . . . . .  O  60  Pro Good Nat'd      28
   He feels th' unfading wreath surround his head;  . . . O  82  Young Author        22
   And feels the unfading wreath surround his head;  . .  O  82  Young Author   V    22
   My Bosom feels, enkindled from the Sky,  . . . . . .   O 293  Irene              108
FEET
   Lies at my feet, I hiss him, and he dies.  . . . . . . O  60  Pro Good Nat'd      24
   Implores our Smiles, and trembles at our Feet:  . . .  O 277  Irene               40
   Unbounded Wealth shall flow beneath thy feet  . . . .  O 350  Irene          V    23
   Beneath his feet admires each shining star,  . . . . . Y   7  Virgil Daphnis      34
```

FEIGN'D   SEE WELL-FEIGN'D
   Which aggravate a fault with feign'd excuses, ...   O 176 Tr Metastas II   8
FELICITY
   Or gay felicity retire to desarts? . . . .   Y 191 Irene   V 21
FELICITY
   This is the chief felicity of life, ...   O 131 Tr. Rambler 45   1
   When did Felicity repine in Desarts? . . . .   O 314 Irene   21
FELL
   And here the fell attorney prowls for prey; . . . . .   O   9 London   16
   Thus fell the Pygmie state, which long had stood . . .   O 76 Tr Add. Battle   33
   So by their great decree Assyria fell . . . . .   O 76 Tr Add. Battle   37
   Hurry'd to death by thee, Flaminius fell, ...   O 77 Festina Lente   15
   Fell down upon the stone; . . . .   O 157 Par. Hermit I   2
   Fell down upon a stone; . . . .   O 157 Par. Hermit I   V 2
   Like a fell Adder swelling in a Brake, ...   O 275 Irene   77
   In that black Day when slaughter'd Thousands fell . .   O 312 Irene   7
   My father fell by fierce Achilles' hand . . . . .   Y 18 Tr. Iliad Bk 6   28
   Among their flocks the blooming heroes fell . . .   Y 18 Tr. Iliad Bk 6   36
   And with fell rage and secret anguish burn. . . . . .   Y 24 Tr Add. Battle   65
   In his fell claws, then into th' air he springs. . .   Y 26 Tr Add. Battle   126
FELLOW
   Mann'd with the bravest of our fellow Captives, . . .   O 254 Irene   135
FELLOW-SAINTS
   Where now thou shin'st among thy Fellow-saints, . . .   O 253 Irene   100
FELLOW'S
   'Tis true, the Fellow's handsome, strait and tall; . .   O 247 Irene Epilogue   7
FELLOWS
   Beasts of each kind their fellows spare; . . . . . .   O 138 Tr Rambler 160   1
FELT
   Themselves they studied, as they felt, they writ, . . .   O 52 Pro Drury-Lane   19
   And Persia felt the force of Grecian steel; . . . . .   O 76 Tr Add. Battle   38
   Soon had the Monarch felt a nobler fire, ...   O 97 Hickman Spinet   16
   Nor made a pause, nor felt a void; . . . . .   O 201 Death Dr Levet   V 26
   I felt thy Pains, and trembled for Aspasia. . . . .   O 251 Irene   75
   Or felt th' Impatience of obstructed Love, ...   O 285 Irene   4
   I felt the Force of his tempestuous Arm, ...   O 307 Irene   19
FEMALE
   And here a female atheist talks you dead. . . . .   O   9 London   18
   Those pow'rful Tyrants of the Female Breast . . . .   O 261 Irene   12
   At Sight of female Charms will glow no more. . . . .   O 263 Irene   6
   Conceal the Gem; let female Arrogance . . . . . .   O 277 Irene   33
   Beats not the female Breast with gen'rous Passions, . .   O 278 Irene   57
   The strongest Effort of a female Soul, ...   O 278 Irene   62
   Unprofitable, peaceful, female Virtues! . . . . . .   O 280 Irene   12
   That raises tumults in the female bosom seditions . .   Y 158 Irene   V 12
     (mutinies
   That raises Tumults in the female Breast, ...   O 287 Irene   12
   Nor think my eyes oerflow with Female . . . . . .   O 357 Irene   V 17
     Weakness
   Demetrius towrd--Above the Female pleasures . . .   O 371 Irene   V 2
FEN
   Sung such a war when in a miry fen . . . . . .   Y 23 Tr Add. Battle   55
   To Mareotis' fen the rumour flies . . . .   Y 24 Tr Add. Battle   68
FENC'D
   Fenc'd from the sun and shelterd from the breeze. . . .   Y 163 Irene   V 43
   Fenc'd from the summer breeze, and vernal . . . .   Y 163 Irene   V 43
     show'r.
FERVENT
   In fervent prayer addrest the deities: . . . . . .   Y 20 Tr. Iliad Bk 6   98
FERVOUR
   Heav'n will contemn the mercenary Fervour, ...   O 262 Irene   26
   Restrain the Fervour of impetuous Youth . . . . .   O 272 Irene   9
FERVOURS
   Pour forth thy fervours for a healthful mind, ...   O 48 Vanity Wishes   359
   Breathe forth thy fervours for a soul . . . . . .   Y 108 Vanity Wishes   V 359
FESTAL
   The festal blazes, the triumphal show, ...   O 39 Vanity Wishes   175
FESTINA
   Festina Lente . . . .   O 77 Festina Lente   T
FESTIVE
   Nor deign the festive dome to cloy . . . .   O 191 Tr. Medea I   15
   And purple nectar glads the festive hour, ...   O 193 Tr. Medea II   18
FETTERS
   Shall break the Fetters of the groaning Christian; . .   O 278 Irene   76
FEVER
   Through all his veins the fever of renown . . . .   O 36 Vanity Wishes   137
   Resistless burns the fever of renown . . . . .   O 36 Vanity Wishes   V 137
   Each act betrays the fever of renown . . . .   Y 97 Vanity Wishes   V 137
   Quick fires his breast the fever of renown . . .   Y 97 Vanity Wishes   V 137
FEW
   Few know the toiling statesman's fear or care, ...   O 32 Vanity Wishes   47
   But few there are whom hours like these await, . . .   O 45 Vanity Wishes   311
   Delude the most; few pry behind the scene. . . . .   O 139 Tr Rambler 168   2
FI'RY
   Unhurt by Phoebus fi'ry ray. . . . .   O 72 Hor. Epode II   36
FICKLE
   The fickle crowd with fortune comes and goes; . . . .   O 138 Tr Rambler 153   1
FICTITIOUS
   The nymph fictitious, as the flow'r; . . . . . .   O 121 To Miss Playin   8
FIDELITY
   And dooms my rash Fidelity to Ruin. . . . . . .   O 256 Irene   49

		PAGE	TITLE	LINE

FIDELITY (CONTINUED)
Fidelity so firm, so pure, as mine! . . . . O 308 Irene 17

FIELD
War sounds the trump, he rushes to the field; . . . . . O 40 Vanity Wishes 198
And frighted, left upon the field, ... O 73 Hor. Epode II 66
And spread its smoking ruins o'er the field. . . . . . O 74 Tr. Iliad Bk 6 14
And victory hangs doubtfull o'er the field. . . . . O 76 Tr Add. Battle 13
My Name shall echo through the shouting Field; . . . . O 305 Irene 40
Call forth her ancient Heroes to the Field, ... O 309 Irene 39
Call forth her ancient Scipios to the field . . . . . Y 185 Irene V 39
About to rush into the field of fate . . . . Y 18 Tr. Iliad Bk 6 4

FIELDS
To breathe in distant fields a purer air, ... O   9 London 6
Scarce can our fields, such crowds at Tyburn die, . . . O 21 London 242
And leave our pleasing fields and native home, . . . O 64 Virgil Past.I 4
Far from their antient fields and humble cots. . . . . O 64 Virgil Past.I 18
And scarce forsakes his native fields. . . . . . O 68 Hor.II Ode 14 24
And fruitfull fields, my dearest Friend, ... O 69 Hor.II Ode 14 22
As herbs of which the fields nigh . . . . O 73 Hor. Epode II V 61
Of Fields with dead bestrew'd around, ... O 78 Feast St Simon 1
He scorns the flow'ry vales and verdant fields; . . . O 81 Young Author 4
He scorns the verdant meads and flow'ry fields; . . . O 81 Young Author V 4
Then thro' thy Fields shall scarlet Reptiles stray, . . O 110 To Posterity 7
"Over hills and fields to roam, ... O 185 Anacreon Ode 9 25
The fields, and woods, behold, are green, ... O 231 Tr Horace IV.7 2
The fields, and woods, again, are green, ... O 231 Tr Horace IV.7 2
And croud the fattend fields, the ghosts that wander . . Y 120 Irene V 31
As corn the fields, as bulls the herds of kine, . . . Y   6 Virgil Daphnis 18
The fruitfull fields th' industrious people till'd, . . Y 23 Tr Add. Battle 28

FIEND
--The beuteous Fiend The shining mischief . . . . . O 375 Irene V 12

FIERCE
Then say how fierce desire and raging hate, ... Y 92 Vanity Wishes V 5
The fierce Croatian, and the wild Hussar, ... O 43 Vanity Wishes 249
None e'er more fierce Numidia's land, ... O 66 Hor I Ode xxii V 15
No Beast more fierce Numidia's Land, ... O 67 To A. Fuscus 15
Though fierce Barbarians threaten'd death . . . . . O 79 Feast St Simon 40
Still fierce to threaten, still afraid to fight; . . . O 110 To Posterity 10
Then, when dark arts obscur'd each fierce debate, . . . O 118 Epitaph Hanmer 23
I too can feel the rapture, fierce and strong; . . . . O 142 In Baretti Bk. 3
Wouldst thou when fierce Eurus blows . . . . . . O 144 Tr Boeth. II.4 3
Urg'd by th' imperious Soldier's fierce Command, . . . O 249 Irene 16
Fierce as he was, he dreaded to destroy . . . . . . O 257 Irene 68
    yet the fierce Albanian lyon . . . . Y 130 Irene V 13
Let fierce resentment aid . . . . Y 133 Irene V 9
Your artful Suit, your Monarch's fierce Denial, . . . O 270 Irene 3
Should the fierce North upon his frozen Wings . . . . O 274 Irene 61
Is this the fierce Conspirator Abdalla? . . . . . . O 279 Irene 1
Fierce through the bursting Caverns rend their Way? . . O 281 Irene 53
Too fierce, too faithless for Neglect or Trust. . . . O 288 Irene 14
To rough--Too false too fierce to trust or to neglect . O 374 Irene V 1
This fierce Virago, fearless and unshaken . . . . . O 364 Irene V 13
This fierce virago, fearless and unshaken . . . . . Y 162 Irene V 40
Pour'd Storms of Fire upon our fierce Invaders, . . . O 290 Irene 48
And fix the fierce Usurper's bloody Title. . . . . O 291 Irene 62
Fierce persecution wears the bleeding world with . . . Y 164 Irene V 66
    fraud
Untouch'd by fierce Ambition's raging Fires. . . . . O 293 Irene 110
Oft when the fierce Besiegers eager Host . . . . . . O 298 Irene 27
I saw without a sigh the fierce barbarian . . . . . Y 176 Irene V 106
How should I joy, 'midst the fierce Shock of Nations, . O 309 Irene 40
Perhaps my Zeal too fierce betray'd my Prudence; . . . O 330 Irene 20
Your fierce Impatience forc'd us from your Presence, . . O 332 Irene 29
My father fell by fierce Achilles' hand . . . . . . Y 18 Tr. Iliad Bk 6 28

FIERCELY
Fiercely contending two vast armies stood . . . . . Y 23 Tr Add. Battle 56

FIERCENESS
The Sultan's majesty the warriours fierceness . . . . Y 123 Irene V 98
Their cloudy Summits, and the Sons of Fierceness, . . . O 268 Irene 29
Their snowy summits, and the sons of fierceness . . . Y 136 Irene V 29

FIERCER
None fiercer Juba's thirsty land, ... O 66 Hor I Ode xxii 15
My bosom glows with fiercer fire; . . . . Y 10 Tr Hor Epode 9 2

FIERY   SEE FIRY
Some fiery fop, with new commission vain, ... O 21 London 226
So some fiery fop, with new commission vain, ... Y 59 London V 226
Then with no throbbing fiery pain, ... O 202 Death Dr Levet 33
Then with no throbs of fiery pain, ... O 202 Death Dr Levet V 33
Then rouzing know the fiery Chief Abdalla, ... O 254 Irene 125
Far more I dread Abdalla's fiery Folly, ... O 287 Irene 7
Amidst his gloomy Guards and fiery Vassals . . . . . O 372 Irene V 19
That fiery Chief, renown'd for gen'rous Freedom, . . . O 299 Irene 35
Had stretch'd the fiery Boaster in the Grave. . . . . O 312 Irene 20

FIFTIETH
To have the fiftieth Part her paultry Share? . . . . O 247 Irene Epilogue 6

FIFTY
Besides, he has fifty Wives; and who can bear . . . . O 247 Irene Epilogue 5

FIG
Where the wild fig trees join their darksom shade . . . Y 19 Tr. Iliad Bk 6 52

FIGHT
The Cranes with beaks and claws provoke the fight. . . O 75 Tr Add. Battle 3

```
                                                     PAGE   TITLE            LINE
FIGHT          (CONTINUED)
     Still fierce to threaten, still afraid to fight;  . . .   O 110 To Posterity      10
     For you shall plough the main, and fight the battle . .   Y 146 Irene          V 23B
     Swifter than lightning to the fight he flies. . . . .     Y  21 Tr. Iliad Bk 6    126
     Dar'd have provok'd a foe to single fight, . . . . .      Y  23 Tr Add. Battle     39
     Such was the horrour of the dreadfull fight . . . . .     Y  26 Tr Add. Battle    136
FIGHTS
     For us the Statesman labours, Hero fights,  . . . . .     O 247 Irene Epilogue     21
     Reason with Reason fights on equal Terms,  . . . . .      O 287 Irene              9
FIGURE
     Had this fair figure which this frame displays,  . . .    O 189 Seeing Montagu     1
FILL
     With warbling eunuchs fill a licens'd stage, . . . .      O  12 London            59
     With warbling eunuchs fill our silenc'd stage, . . . .    O  12 London          V 59
     For love, which scarce collective man can fill;  . . .    O  48 Vanity Wishes    361
     For love, whose grasp Creation collective man can . .     Y 108 Vanity Wishes  V 361
        fill;
     Fill the loud Voice of universal Praise, . . . . .        O  57 Prologue Comus    16
     Bid them come, and take their fill.  . . . . .            O 196 Song Congratu.    20
     Come my lads and take your fill. . . . . .                O 196 Song Congratu.  V 20
     Should fill the World with Wretches undetected. . . .     O 283 Irene             27
     And fill the bleed<in>g world with desolation  . . .      O 352 Irene           V  5
     Fill all thy ardent Breast with Greece and Virtue, . .    O 298 Irene              8
     And fill the World with Follies and Impostures, . . .     O 309 Irene             35
     Fill all the starry Lamps with double Blaze; . . . .      O 322 Irene              8
     Fill all the Starry Lamps with Fav'ring Sky  . . . .      O 364 Irene           V 27
       <Radiance>.
     Her piercing Cries yet fill the loaded Air,  . . . .      O 329 Irene              8
     New verdure ev'ry fading leaf shall fill, . . . . .       Y   4 On a Daffodill     19
FILL'D
     Such was the scorn that fill'd the sage's mind,  . . .    O  33 Vanity Wishes     69
     When Hanmer fill'd the chair, and Ann the throne. . . .   O 118 Epitaph Hanmer    22
     Not then with raving Cries I fill'd the City, . . . .     O 290 Irene             46
     (Yet) not with idle cries I fill'd the city . . . .       Y 163 Irene           V 46
     Now each parterre with thorny brakes is fill'd . . .      Y   7 Virgil Daphnis    24
     And with laborious crouds the plains were fill'd. . .     Y  23 Tr Add. Battle    29
FILLS
     Now kindred Merit fills the sable bier,  . . . . .        O  45 Vanity Wishes    303
     Now kindred Merit fills the mournful bier, . . . .        Y 106 Vanity Wishes  V 303
     When strong devotion fills thy glowing Breast, . . .      O  48 Vanity Wishes  V 358
     Yet still he fills affection's eye,  . . . . .            O 201 Death Dr Levet     9
     Fills all th' astonish'd Empire with Confusion, . . .     O 257 Irene             77
FINAL
     Enquires the final Doom of Menodorus, . . . . .           O 263 Irene             24
     Soon may the final Stroke decide our Fate, . . . .        O 299 Irene             51
     Her final Doom, and hurried her Destruction. . . .        O 334 Irene             62
FIND
     Grant me, kind heaven, to find some happier place, . .    O  11 London            43
     For where can starving merit find a home?  . . . .        O  18 London           191
     There might'st thou find some elegant retreat, . . .      O  20 London           212
     The might you find some elegant retreat, . . . .          Y  58 London         V 212
     But find the form distorted by the fall  . . . .         Y  95 Vanity Wishes   V 89
     Where then shall Hope and Fear their objects find? . .    O  47 Vanity Wishes    343
     And makes the happiness she does not find. . . . .        O  48 Vanity Wishes    368
     May this returning day for ever find . . . . .            O  80 Lady Birthday      3
     Teach mimick censure her own faults to find, . . . .      O  81 Lady Birthday     17
     Find here that calm thou gav'st so oft before; . . .      O 113 Epit. Phillips     4
     As not to grant me this, can Milton find?  . . . .        O 137 Tr Rambler 140     2
     He who blindly trusts, will find . . . . .                O 176 Tr Metastasi I     3
     Admission ne'er had sought, or could not find. . . .      O 192 Tr. Medea II      12
     Sooner these trembling Leaves shall find a Voice, . .     O 255 Irene             26
     Sooner the trembling Leaves shall find a Voice, . . .     O 373 Irene           V 19
     Well pleas'd to find thy Precepts not forgotten. . . .    O 267 Irene             41
     There shall we find the yet untasted Bliss . . . .        O 292 Irene             88
     If Fate pursues me, let it find me here. . . . .          O 297 Irene             18
     If Fate persues me, let it find me here  . . . .          O 297 Irene           V 18
     And find our Passions not infus'd in vain. . . . .        O 297 Irene             22
     To find a meaner Fate from treach'rous Friendship-- . .   O 299 Irene             33
     Science and Arms find every where a . . . .              O 352 Irene           V 32
        Country.
     Oft would they find Ingratitude and Treason, . . . .      O 308 Irene             14
FINDS
     Of hasty greatness finds the fatal doom, . . . .          O  43 Vanity Wishes    252
     Of hasty greatness finds the hasty doom, . . . .          Y 103 Vanity Wishes  V 252
     Each passing day some comfort sorrow finds.  . . . .      Y 105 Vanity Wishes  V 301
     But finds you sad at his return.  . . . . .               O  67 Hor. II Ode IX    12
     The loiterer finds a bramble for a flow'r. . . . .        O 133 Tr. Rambler 71     2
     Wealth still finds followers, and misfortunes foes. . .   O 138 Tr Rambler 153     2
FINE
     Proclaim'd her, not so fair as fine. . . . . .            O 122 Stella Mourn.      4
FINES
     From meaner minds, tho' smaller fines content, . . . .    O  39 Vanity Wishes    169
FINGERS
     "From his fingers snatch his bread,  . . . . .            O 185 Anacreon Ode 9    34
FIR'D
     With ardent love of virtue fir'd,  . . . . .             O  79 Feast St Simon    38
     And fir'd with pleasing hope of endless fame, . . . .     O  82 Young Author      12
     Ambitious Fury fir'd the Grecian King: . . . .           O  97 Hickman Spinet    10
     This fir'd the youthful King's ambitious Breast, . . .    O 256 Irene             47
     Th' insidious Bassa fir'd by Disappointment-- . . . .     O 273 Irene             32
     <E>ach hero fir'd piety or freedom  . . . . .             Y 181 Irene           V 51
```

FIR'D   (CONTINUED)

		PAGE	TITLE	LINE
At once a Thousand Passions fir'd his Cheek:	. . . .	O 317	Irene	31
Or their own souls with hopes of vict'ry fir'd."	. . .	Y 19	Tr. Iliad Bk 6	59

FIRD

| All fird with hope, and panting to be great; | . . . . | Y 95 | Vanity Wishes | V 74 |

FIRE

And now a rabble rages, now a fire;	. . . . . .	O 9	London	14
And hopes from angry heav'n another fire.	. . . . .	O 19	London	209
And restless fire precipitates on death.	. . . . . .	O 31	Vanity Wishes	20
A frame of adamant, a soul of fire,	. . . . . .	O 40	Vanity Wishes	193
What tho' she shine with no Miltonian Fire,	. . . .	O 58	Prologue Comus	27
And heap the fire, and milk the Kine	. . . . . .	O 72	Hor. Epode II	51
Soon had the Monarch felt a nobler fire,	. . . . .	O 97	Hickman Spinet	16
Torments alike with equal Fire.	. . . .	O 99	Ode Friendship	V 8
The Patriot's fire yet sparkled in the friend.	. . .	O 118	Epitaph Hanmer	40
Scarce frighted love maintains his fire,	. . . . .	O 123	Winter's Walk	11
Scarce frighted love maintains her fire,	. . . . .	O 123	Winter's Walk	V 11
Could Rome with future greatness fire,	. . . . . .	O 188	Epilogue	2
Could Rome with generous ardour fire,	. . . . . .	O 188	Epilogue	V 2
Will he not melt before Ambition's Fire?	. . . . .	O 255	Irene	23
If yet one spark of Heav'nly fire remain	. . . . .	Y 133	Irene	V 18
Rose to his Thought, and set his Soul on Fire:	. . .	O 270	Irene	11
With Raptures such as fire the Pagan Crouds,	. . . .	O 286	Irene	3
Pour'd Storms of Fire upon our fierce Invaders,	. . .	O 290	Irene	48
Pourd Storms of fire upon th' approaching Foe	. . .	O 364	Irene	V 1
To mark the noblest Minds. With active fire	. . . .	O 369	Irene	V 3
And fans the slumb'ring Spark of heav'nly Fire.	. . .	O 303	Irene	19
If winter by the fire, if summer in the shade.	. . .	Y 7	Virgil Daphnis	48
My bosom glows with fiercer fire;	. . . . . .	Y 10	Tr Hor Epode 9	2
The raging of the kindled fire	. . . . . .	Y 12	Tr Hor Epode 9	40
Alone preserv'd the town from Grecian fire.	. . . .	Y 18	Tr. Iliad Bk 6	14

FIRE'S

| Sustain th' approaching fire's tremendous light; | . . . | O 18 | London | 187 |

FIREBRACE

| To Lady F<irebra>ce at Bury Assizes | | O 107 | Lady F Assizes | T |
| Thy charms at least, fair F<irebrac>e, might inspire | . | O 107 | Lady F Assizes | 3 |

FIRED

| When pleasure fired her torch at Virtue's flame, | . . . | O 62 | Pro Word Wise | 23 |

FIRES

Quick fires his breast the fever of renown	. . . .	Y 97	Vanity Wishes	V 137
Fresh praise is try'd till madness fires his mind,	. .	O 42	Vanity Wishes	231
New praise is try'd till madness fires his mind,	. .	Y 102	Vanity Wishes	V 231
Yet when the sense of sacred presence fires,	. . . .	O 48	Vanity Wishes	357
Inflames alike with raging fires.	. . . . . .	O 99	Ode Friendship	8
Inflame with unrelented fires.	. . . . . .	Y 71	Ode Friendship	V 8
Why shakes the Ground, when subterraneous Fires	. . .	O 281	Irene	52
Gross Fires, enkindled by a mortal Hand,	. . . .	O 282	Irene	57
Untouch'd by fierce Ambition's raging Fires.	. . .	O 293	Irene	110
That fires thy Cheek, and elevates thy Mien,	. . .	O 323	Irene	9

FIRM

Firm and low thy Mansion found;	. . . . . .	O 145	Tr Boeth. II.4	16
His frame was firm, his powers were bright,	. . . .	O 202	Death Dr Levet	31
Unshaken be thy Throne as Earth's firm Base,	. . .	O 262	Irene	2
Fidelity so firm, so pure, as mine!	. . . .	O 308	Irene	17

FIRMLY

| The moderator firmly mild appear'd, | . . . . . . | O 118 | Epitaph Hanmer | 25 |

FIRMNESS

| And columns leaning from their central firmness | . . . | Y 114 | Irene | V 45A |
| The Courtier's Policy, the Sage's Firmness, | . . . . | O 255 | Irene | 3 |

FIRST

They first invade your table, then your breast;	. . .	O 17	London	153
When first the college rolls receive his name,	. . .	O 36	Vanity Wishes	135
First rear'd the Stage, immortal Shakespear rose;	. .	O 51	Pro Drury-Lane	2
Like the first race in Saturns reign	. . . .	O 71	Hor. Epode II	3
When first the peasant, long inclin'd to roam,	. . .	O 81	Young Author	1
In life's first bloom his publick toils began,	. . .	O 117	Epitaph Hanmer	11
Where first great nature charm'd my sight,	. . . .	O 125	An Ode	19
Where wisdom first inform'd my heart.	. . . .	O 125	An Ode	20
My first, shuts out Thieves from your house or your Room		O 179	Charade!	1
and the first gust shake<s> it into atom<s>	. . .	Y 132	Irene	V 39
And heard in my first approaching	. . . .	Y 144	Irene	V 79
Had our first Asian Foes but known this Ardour,	. . .	O 284	Irene	40
When social Laws first harmonis'd the World,	. . .	O 291	Irene	70
My Soul first kindled by thy bright Example,	. . .	O 298	Irene	13
Yet she--fair--so shone first apostate	. . .	Y 211	Irene	V 10
Play'd on her Cheek--So shone the first Apostate--	.	O 330	Irene	11
Hail lovely flower, first honour of the year!	. . .	Y 3	On a Daffodill	1
I first foresook the scornful fair.	. . . . .	Y 11	Tr Hor Epode 9	10
I first attempt in never-dying lays	. . . .	Y 22	Tr Add. Battle	16
From hence the seeds of discord first arose	. . .	Y 23	Tr Add. Battle	50
And first a sound invades th' astonish'd ear.	. . .	Y 25	Tr Add. Battle	91

FIRSTLINGS

| Oft on his altar shall my firstlings lie, | . . . . | O 64 | Virgil Past.I | 9 |

FIRY

| Then rouzing know the firy Chief Abdallah, | . . . . | O 254 | Irene | V 125 |
| That firy Chief, renown'd for gen'rous Freedom, | . . . | O 299 | Irene | V 35 |

FISH

| No fish from the Carpathian coast | . . . . . . | O 73 | Hor. Epode II | 57 |
| While boars the rocks, while fish the rivers love, | . . | Y 7 | Virgil Daphnis | 49 |

FIT

| And fit her for the joys of paradise:-- | . . . . . | Y 130 | Irene | V 11 |

FITTER
Dispatch, and learn a fitter Time for Pity. . . . . . O 328 Irene 44

FIVE
Better Years than Thirty five; . . . . . . O 178 Thrale 35 Year 4
Trifle nct at Thirty five: . . . . O 178 Thrale 35 Year 12
Must begin by Thirty five: . . . . . O 178 Thrale 35 Year 16

FIX
Can surly virtue hope to fix a friend? . . . O 16 London 145
Soon must this bough, as you shall fix his doom, . O 95 Sprig of Myrtl 13
Soon shall this sprig, as you shall fix its doom, . O 95 Sprig of Myrtl V 13
Fix not where the tempting Height . . . O 145 Tr Boeth. II.4 13
Illustrious Maid, new Wonders fix me thine, . . O 278 Irene 59
Celestial fair--maid--new wonders fix me thine, . Y 149 Irene V 59
And of To-morrow's Action fix the Scene. . . O 283 Irene 18
Well,--'tis decreed--This Night shall fix our Fate. . O 284 Irene 48
And fix the fierce Usurper's bloody Title. . . . O 291 Irene 62
To fix his Court, and regulate his Pleasures, . . O 291 Irene 78
Here will I fix the limits of transgression . . . Y 168 Irene V 133
To fix your Standard in Imperial Rome. . . . O 309 Irene 31
Secure his Confidence, and fix his Love. . . . . O 319 Irene 6
Whom neither Vows could fix, nor Favours bind? . . O 330 Irene 2

FIX'D
And, fix'd on Cambria's solitary shore, ... O 9 London 7
Fix'd in his canker'd breast remain: . . . . . O 73 Hor. Epode II 78
The limits fix'd they strive to pass in vain; . . O 76 Tr Add. Battle 36
Resistless merit fix'd the Senate's choice, . . . O 118 Epitaph Hanmer 19
Strict, on the right he fix'd his steadfast eye, . O 118 Epitaph Hanmer 29
When Minos once has fix'd your doom, ... O 232 Tr Horace IV.7 22
Has fix'd his Hopes, Inquietudes, and Fears, . . O 280 Irene 27
If fix'd on settled thought this Constancy . . O 364 Irene V 8
Fix'd and intent on his Irene's Charms, ... O 296 Irene 3
So fix'd the Justice of all-conscious Heav'n. . . O 335 Irene 11
Or fix'd the pointed arrows in their hearts. . . . Y 23 Tr Add. Battle 43

FIXD
Virtue is fixd unvarying as its Author . . . . . O 348 Irene V 23

FIXED
And fixed disease on Harley's closing life? . . . . O 36 Vanity Wishes 130

FLAGGING
To press the weary minutes flagging wings: . . . . O 44 Vanity Wishes 300
And time hangs his flagging wings . . . . . . Y 128 Irene V 4

FLAGITIOUS
Oh! rather scornful of flagitious Greatness, . . . O 320 Irene 28

FLAMBEAU'S
Afar they mark the flambeau's bright approach, . . O 21 London 234
Mark from afar the flambeau's bright approach, . . Y 59 London V 234

FLAME
Nor wish'd for Johnson's Art, or Shakespear's Flame; . O 52 Pro Drury-Lane 18
When pleasure fired her torch at Virtue's flame, . . O 62 Pro Word Wise 23
Here at your ease you sing your amorous flame, . . O 64 Virgil Past.I 5
My Flame for Lalage I'll own; . . . . O 67 To A. Fuscus 23
He bids the Sword destroy, the Flame devour. . . . O 97 Hickman Spinet 14
Oh may this Flame neer cease to glow . . . . . O 100 Ode Friendship V 25
The holy Flame of enterprizing Virtue . . . . . O 264 Irene 26
The noble flame of enterprising Virtue . . . . . O 371 Irene V 28
The Politician's Arts, and Heroe's Flame. . . . O 307 Irene 27
Those anxious fears that fan'd the flame of Love. . Y 11 Tr Hor Epode 9 24

FLAMES
And leave your little All to flames a prey; . . . O 18 London 189
O! Shall thy flames then cease to glow . . . . O 100 Ode Friendship V 25
The subtler Flames emitted from the Sky, ... O 282 Irene 59
The lambent Flames of mild Benevolence, ... O 293 Irene 109
While secret Flames, with unextinguish'd Rage, . . O 315 Irene 35
And spread their Flames resistless o'er the World? . O 325 Irene 13

FLAMING
And spread his flaming palace on the ground, . . O 19 London 195
Prescribes the dreadfull comet's flaming path . . Y 167 Irene V 124
Than ruind palaces or flaming temples . . . . Y 177 Irene V111D
Intrepid in the flaming Front of War? . . . . . O 304 Irene 17
And snatch the flaming Bolt with hasty Hand. . . O 314 Irene 25

FLAMINIUS
Hurry'd to death by thee, Flaminius fell, ... O 77 Festina Lente 15

FLASH
Did Did Lightnings flash? . . . . O 347 Irene V 2
Flash out at once, with Strength above Resistance. . O 282 Irene 60

FLASHES
Destruction flashes from th' insidious Mine, . . . O 298 Irene 30

FLATT'RING
The baffled prince in honour's flatt'ring bloom . . O 43 Vanity Wishes 251
Whose gen'rous Zeal, unbought by flatt'ring Rhimes, . O 57 Prologue Comus 3
By flatt'ring poets giv'n; . . . . O 126 To Lyce, Lady 2
But cautious Age suspects the flatt'ring Form, . . O 255 Irene 18
Too calm I listen to the flatt'ring Sounds. . . . O 278 Irene 74
The traveller persues the flatt'ring wandring . . Y 155 Irene V 34
splendor

FLATT'RY
Attendant Flatt'ry counts his myriads o'er, . . . O 42 Vanity Wishes 229
By Int'rest, Prudence; and by Flatt'ry, Pride. . . O 47 Vanity Wishes 340
To Int'rest, Prudence; and to Flatt'ry, Pride. . . O 47 Vanity Wishes V 340
Let artful Flatt'ry now, to lull Suspicion, . . . O 267 Irene 2

FLATTER
If dreams yet flatter, once again attend, ... O 38 Vanity Wishes 163

119

FLATTER   (CONTINUED)   PAGE   TITLE   LINE

Entry	PAGE	TITLE	LINE
If hope yet flatter, once again attend,	Y 99	Vanity Wishes	V 163
No maid to flatter, and no paint to hide.	O 84	Epi Dist Moth.	41
And I but flatter less.	O 127	To Lyce, Lady	24
Each weakness sooth and flatter ev'ry folly.	Y 134	Irene	V 27
Toils all its languages to flatter me.	Y 136	Irene	V 29
And every language toils to flatter me.	Y 136	Irene	V 32B
Whence then those Charms thy Tongue has deign'd to flatter,	O 277	Irene	26
Why then Those charms your tongue has deign'd to flatter	O 355	Irene	V 15

FLATTER'D

Entry	PAGE	TITLE	LINE
He sigh'd, He rag'd, he threatend and he flatter'd	O 364	Irene	V 20
Say, how the Tyrant threaten'd, flatter'd, sigh'd,	O 295	Irene	23
Say, how he threaten'd, flatter'd, sigh'd in vain!	O 295	Irene	24

FLATTERD

Entry	PAGE	TITLE	LINE
But flatterd threatend, sigh'd and rag'd in vain	Y 170	Irene	V 24

FLATTERER

Entry	PAGE	TITLE	LINE
And hugs a flatterer for a friend.	O 100	Ode Friendship	20
Who hugs a flatterer for a friend.	O 100	Ode Friendship	V 20

FLATTERIES

Entry	PAGE	TITLE	LINE
Where won by bribes, by flatteries implor'd,	O 18	London	180

FLATTERY

Entry	PAGE	TITLE	LINE
And flattery subdues when arms are vain?	O 16	London	122
And flattery prevails when arms are vain.	O 16	London	V 122
And get a kick for awkward flattery.	O 16	London	131
And gain a kick for aukward flattery.	O 16	London	V 131
And gold and flattery--thoughtless mirth--hurry	Y 164	Irene	V 72
Nor left us aught but Flattery and State.	O 291	Irene	73

FLED

Entry	PAGE	TITLE	LINE
Philosophy remain'd, though Nature fled.	O 52	Pro Drury-Lane	34
A grizly wolf surprised, and fled.	O 65	Hor I Ode xxii	12
A furious wolf approach'd and fled.	O 65	Hor I Ode xxii	V 12
A furious Wolf approach'd, and fled.	O 66	To A. Fuscus	12
Her gifts despis'd, corruption blush'd and fled,	O 118	Epitaph Hanmer	33
Its charms are fled and all its powers destroyed.	O 142	In Baretti Bk.	8
Why fled this haughty Heroine from the Battle?	O 290	Irene	39

FLEECE

Entry	PAGE	TITLE	LINE
Or sheers the Lambkins snowy fleece.	O 71	Hor. Epode II	22

FLEET

Entry	PAGE	TITLE	LINE
With hemp the gallows and the fleet supply.	O 21	London	243

FLEETING

Entry	PAGE	TITLE	LINE
At best, a fleeting gleam, or empty sound.	O 62	Pro Word Wise	20
At last, a fleeting gleam, or empty sound.	O 62	Pro Word Wise	V 20
Alass, dear Friend, the fleeting years	O 68	Hor.II Ode 14	1
Long since I learn'd to slight this fleeting breath,	O 74	Tr. Iliad Bk 6	9

FLIE

Entry	PAGE	TITLE	LINE
Swifter than Icarus Ill flie	O 70	Hor.II Ode XX	13
<?storms huge> Promontories flie	O 76	Tr Add. Battle	22
In rat'ling storms huge promontories flie	Y 26	Tr Add. Battle	V 140

FLIES

Entry	PAGE	TITLE	LINE
Swift o'er the land the dismal rumour flies,	O 19	London	196
To growing wealth the dedicator flies,	O 33	Vanity Wishes	82
He flies to press, and hurries on his fate;	O 82	Young Author	V 20
To some retreat the baffled writer flies,	O 82	Young Author	26
O'er ice the rapid skaiter flies,	O 203	Tr. on Skating	1
The Rocks of Life, for ever flies the Port.	O 281	Irene	47
And flies for Shelter to the Shades of Life.	O 292	Irene	102
The. Laws unread, and flies to his Irene.	O 296	Irene	2
And banish'd sorrow flies the joyous plains;	Y 7	Virgil Daphnis	37
From Hector's breast each gloomy trouble flies	Y 18	Tr. Iliad Bk 6	15
Swifter than lightning to the fight he flies.	Y 21	Tr. Iliad Bk 6	126
To Mareotis' fen the rumour flies	Y 24	Tr Add. Battle	68
Then flies aloft; th' astonish'd warriours feel	Y 26	Tr Add. Battle	132
Cleora thus regretted flies,	Y 39	Lady Leaving	5

FLIGHT

Entry	PAGE	TITLE	LINE
Hate dogs their flight, and insult mocks their end.	O 33	Vanity Wishes	78
A single skiff to speed his flight remains:	O 42	Vanity Wishes	238
For fear retards their flight, the cruell Crane	O 76	Tr Add. Battle	31
What thought of flight, or of defence?	O 121	To Miss Playin	12
Might Truth intrude with daring flight,	O 121	To Miss Playin	20
Here stop, my soul, thy rapid flight,	O 125	An Ode	17
Year chases year, with unremitted flight,	O 152	The Ant	14
"Now Anacreon rules my flight	O 185	Anacreon Ode 9	14
By his Command, equipp'd for speedy Flight,	O 254	Irene	133
Or how can Cali's Flight restore our Country?	O 254	Irene	139
Why stor'd for Flight? and why prepar'd by Cali?	O 258	Irene	85
With vain (fruitless) labour of the daring flight	Y 127	Irene	V 3
For speedy Flight, or obstinate Defence.	O 284	Irene	55
Surprize o'erwhelm her, and retard our Flight.	O 285	Irene	13
Stoop from thy Flight, trace back th' entangled Thought,	O 293	Irene	127
Secure of Happiness from Flight or Conquest,	O 302	Irene	114
Plays on the quiv'ring Waves, to guide our Flight,	O 306	Irene	59
The Day disast'rous that secures our Flight;	O 317	Irene	46
Fly, Wretch, while yet my Pity grants thee Flight;	O 319	Irene	23
Press not her Flight, while yet her feeble Nerves	O 320	Irene	20
Companion of our Flight, illustrious Exile,	O 320	Irene	30
Safe in her Death, and in Demetrius' Flight,	O 329	Irene	1
Which whet their beaks, for flight their wings prepare,	Y 24	Tr Add. Battle	70

		PAGE	TITLE	LINE

FLIGHTS
    The airy Flights of unexperienced Virtue . . . . .   O 347 Irene   V 20
    Or Flights of Pow'r, or Projects of Ambition. . . . .   O 327 Irene   21
FLINGS
    Yet ev'n on this her load Misfortune flings, ...   O 44 Vanity Wishes   299
FLOATING
    Through purple billows and a floating host. . . . . .   O 42 Vanity Wishes   240
    A floating Atom, Dust that falls unheeded . . . . .   O 260 Irene   139
FLOCK
    Two tender kids, the hopes of all the flock. . . .   O 64 Virgil Past.I   20
    "Here fairer than his flock the shepherd lyes   . . .   Y 7 Virgil Daphnis   30
FLOCKS
    He gave my flocks to graze the flowery meads,   . . .   O 64 Virgil Past.I   11
    Among their flocks the blooming heroes fell   . . .   Y 18 Tr. Iliad Bk 6   36
    From Isther's flood unnumber'd flocks arise . . . . .   Y 24 Tr Add. Battle   69
FLOOD
    Where Greenwich smiles upon the silver flood: . . . .   O 10 London   22
    We all must view the Stygian flood . . . . .   O 69 Hor.II Ode 14   17
    Whose mortal wounds pour forth a purple flood, . . .   O 76 Tr Add. Battle   20
    Scorning now th' o'erflowing Flood, ...   O 149 Tr Boet III.12   38
    Perhaps the flood of time now rolls towards us . . .   Y 117 Irene   V 108
    That laves proud Ilion with his rapid flood, ...   Y 18 Tr. Iliad Bk 6   12
    From Isther's flood unnumber'd flocks arise . . . . .   Y 24 Tr Add. Battle   69
FLOODS
    When floods of Nectar stain'd the main, ...   O 71 Hor. Epode II   4
    The floods of rage, and calm thy rufled soul. . . . .   O 77 Festina Lente   8
    Silent Wonder stopt the Floods; . . . . . .   O 148 Tr Boet III.12   12
    Rolls half his Floods unheard through shouting Camps?   O 264 Irene   18
    Pours half his Floods unheard through shouting camps   O 353 Irene   V 32
    Shed floods of tears, and sympathiz'd in pain. . . .   Y 21 Tr. Iliad Bk 6   129
FLOOR
    Along the marble floor shall flow. . . . .   O 69 Hor.II Ode 14   28
FLORENCE
    Where Florence gives the banish'd arts protection . . .   O 351 Irene   V 3
FLOURISH
    And blasted Kingdoms flourish at thy Smile? . . . .   O 278 Irene   72
    To Bid wasted Regions flourish at her smile   . . .   O 372 Irene   V 8
    And thou shalt flourish by her influence. . . . . .   Y 4 On a Daffodill   20
FLOURISH'D
    Securely flourish'd the Pygmiean state, ...   Y 23 Tr Add. Battle   27
FLOURISHES
    Like them man flourishes, like them decays. . . . .   O 138 Tr Rambler 161   2
FLOURS
    Nor grace with fading flours my Herse, ...   O 70 Hor.II Ode XX   22
FLOW
    From Marlb'rough's eyes the streams of dotage flow, .   O 45 Vanity Wishes   317
    Along the marble floor shall flow. . . . .   O 69 Hor.II Ode 14   28
    Rashness! thou spring from whence misfortunes flow! .   O 77 Festina Lente   9
    And show'rs from either flow. . . . .   O 127 To Lyce, Lady   12
    And rain from either flow. . . . .   Y 86 To Lyce, Lady   V 12
    Learn here that Peace from Innocence must flow;   .   O 246 Irene Prologue   13
    Or flow dissolving in a Woman's Tears? . . . .   O 255 Irene   25
    Whence flow the Hopes and Fears, Despair and Rapture,   O 277 Irene   41
    For thee shall Forests rise and Rivers flow . . . .   O 350 Irene   V 22
    Unbounded Wealth shall flow beneath thy feet   . . .   O 350 Irene   V 23
    The limpid streams with ruefull murmurs flow   . .   Y 6 Virgil Daphnis   3
FLOW'D
    In ev'ry speech persuasive wisdom flow'd, ...   O 118 Epitaph Hanmer   15
    Now but reflects those Beams that flow'd from thee. . .   O 298 Irene   15
FLOW'R
    The fruit autumnal, and the vernal flow'r,   . . .   O 43 Vanity Wishes   262
    Insatiate pluck the Fruit, and crop the Flow'r: . . .   O 110 To Posterity   12
    The nymph fictitious, as the flow'r; . . . . .   O 121 To Miss Playin   8
    The loiterer finds a bramble for a flow'r. . . . .   O 133 Tr. Rambler 71   2
FLOW'RS
    There prune thy walks, support thy drooping flow'rs, .   O 20 London   216
    There prune thy shades, support the drooping flow'rs, .   Y 58 London   V 216
    To pluck the flow'rs of pleasure or of pride. . . . .   O 118 Epitaph Hanmer   32
    On beds of never-fading flow'rs, ...   O 120 To Miss Playin   4
    Instruction with her flow'rs might spring, ...   O 121 To Miss Playin   23
    Not always do the fairest Flow'rs diffuse   . . . .   O 277 Irene   31
    Revive the languid Flow'rs; thus Nature shone   . . .   O 314 Irene   3
FLOW'RY
    Mix'd with old Heroes trace the flow'ry meads,   . . .   O 76 Tr Add. Battle   42
    He scorns the flow'ry vales and verdant fields; . . .   O 81 Young Author   4
    He scorns the verdant meads and flow'ry fields; . . .   O 81 Young Author   V 4
    Or dare to murmur in the flow'ry Glade; . . . . .   O 111 To Posterity   22
    O'er treacherous pleasure's flow'ry ground   . . . .   O 203 Tr. on Skating   V 3
    Thus on deceitful Etna's flow'ry Side, ...   O 315 Irene   33
FLOWER
    Hail lovely flower, first honour of the year! . . . .   Y 3 On a Daffodill   1
    Cleora's self, fair flower, shall fade like thee, . . .   Y 4 On a Daffodill   27
FLOWER-PIECES
    ... Room hung with some Flower-pieces . . . . . .   O 120 To Miss Playing   T
FLOWERS   SEE FLOURS, FLOW'RS
    Then scorn those flowers to which the Aegyptians bow'd, .   Y 4 On a Daffodill   15
FLOWERY
    He gave my flocks to graze the flowery meads,   . . .   O 64 Virgil Past.I   11
    Through shades of peace and flowery labyrinths . . . .   Y 146 Irene   V 21
FLOWING
    Ah! cease, Irene, cease those flowing Sorrows, ...   O 276 Irene   3

```
FLOWING        (CONTINUED)                                PAGE    TITLE           LINE
    Dispose the Colours of the flowing Robe, . . . . . .  O 278  Irene             65
    Or boy, whose snowy neck the flowing ringlets grace.  Y  12  Tr Hor Epode 9    42
    And warm Cayster's flowing banks forsake . . . . .    Y  24  Tr Add. Battle    67
FLOWN
    Ling'ring year at last is flown,  . . . . . . . .     O 196  Song Congratu.     2
    Years at length are flown, . . . . . . . . . .        O 196  Song Congratu.  V  2
FLOWS
    From ev'ry tongue flows harmony divine. . . . . .     O  16  London           128
    With fatal sweetness elocution flows, . . . . .       O  31  Vanity Wishes     18
    Turn'd by his nod the stream of honour flows, . .     O  34  Vanity Wishes    103
    The plain contested flows with mingled blood. . .     O  76  Tr Add. Battle    21
    Thy gentle flows of guiltless joys . . . . . .        O 100  Ode Friendship    17
    Flows through each Member of th' embodied State, . .  O 256  Irene             58
FLUNG
    Phrase that Time has flung away, . . . . . .          O 179  Ridicul Warton     5
    Who to the ground the shatter'd building flung . . .  Y  23  Tr Add. Battle    48
FLUSH
    Flush in my cheek, and wander in my Veins  . . . .    O 349  Irene          V  26
    Flush in my cheeks, and sally in veins . . . . .      Y 189  Irene          V  1E
    In vain affected Raptures flush the Cheek, . . . .    O 315  Irene             29
FLUSH'D
    Flush'd as they are with folly, youth and wine, . . . O  21  London           232
    Flush'd as they are with youth confused with wine, .  Y  59  London         V 232
FLUTE
    But ne'er the Flute or Lyre apply'd . . . . . .       O 190  Tr. Medea I        7
FLUTTER
    For ever flutter o'er her lyre, . . . . . .           O 121  To Miss Playin    14
    Ordain'd, like you, to flutter and to shine, . . .    O 277  Irene             37
    Still dost thou flutter in the Jaws of Death? . . .   O 318  Irene             17
    Watch each unquiet Flutter of the Breast, . . . .     O 320  Irene             24
FLUTTERS
    Not idly flutters on a boastful Tongue, . . . . .     O 290  Irene             37
FLUXIT
    <H>oc fonte derivat<a> clades--In patriam populumque  O 347  Irene          V  22
        fluxit.
FLY   SEE FLIE
    You fly for refuge to the wilds of Kent: . . . .      Y  61  London         V 257
    His suppliants scorn him, and his followers fly; . .  O  35  Vanity Wishes    112
    "On Moscow's walls till Gothic standards fly, . .     O  40  Vanity Wishes    203
    Disabled both to combat, or to fly, . . . . .         O  59  Pro Good Nat'd    13
    Thick from their wounded wings the feathers fly, . .  O  75  Tr Add. Battle     4
    Where e'er they fly their lovers ghosts pursue, . .   O  84  Epi Dist Moth.    36
    Alike o'er all his lightnings fly; . . . . . .        O 100  Ode Friendship    10
    At busy hearts in vain love's arrows fly; . . . .     O 133  Tr. Rambler 85     1
    Whence or whither dost thou fly? . . . . .            O 185  Anacreon Ode 9     2
    Whence and whither dost thou fly? . . . . . .         O 185  Anacreon Ode 9  V  2
    Joy to see their quarry fly, . . . . . . .            O 196  Song Congratu.    14
    So small a Force? or why should Cali fly? . . . .     O 254  Irene            138
    Aspasia calls me, let me fly to save her. . . .       O 259  Irene            107
    Wherever Guilt can fly, Revenge can follow. . . . .   O 274  Irene             65
    Fly lab'ring with the Fate of future Nations, . . .   O 279  Irene              4
    And saw my scatter'd Squadrons fly before him. . .    O 346  Irene          V  7
    Fly, fly, my Love, Destruction rushes on us, . . .    O 307  Irene             20
    Fly, fly, my Love, Destruction rushes on us,  . .     O 315  Irene              1
        It now remains to fly! . . . . .                  O 315  Irene              1
    Fly, Wretch, while yet my Pity grants thee Flight; .  O 318  Irene             11
    Fly, Slaves, and call the Sultan to my Rescue. . . .  O 319  Irene             23
    Fly from the busy Pleasures of her Sex, . . . .       O 322  Irene             56
    But while I sing, the nimble moments fly, . . . .     O 322  Irene             14
    With Hector's life away my pleasures fly. . . .       Y   4  On a Daffodill    21
    Oft has he seen the poignant orange fly, . . . . .    Y  18  Tr. Iliad Bk 6    27
FLY'ST                                                    Y  67  Prologue Lethe     9
    Thou fly'st for refuge to the wilds of Kent; . . .    O  23  London           257
FLYING
    On flying Cars new Sorcerers may ride. . . . . .      O  53  Pro Drury-Lane    44
    Sooner the Breeze shall catch the flying Sounds, . .  O 255  Irene             28
    The poor distinctions of a flying moment . . . .      Y 177  Irene          V110A
    Dispatch his Guards to stop the flying Traytors, . .  O 319  Irene              3
FOAM
    Why foam the swelling Waves when Tempests rise? . .   O 281  Irene             51
FOAMING
    The grizly fcaming Boar surrounds . . . . . . .       O  72  Hor. Epode II     39
    The foaming Boar he then with op'ning hounds . . .    O  72  Hor. Epode II  V  39
    Wouldst thou see the foaming Main, . . . . . .        O 144  Tr Boeth. II.4     5
    And where yon Trees wave o'er the foaming Surge . .   O 304  Irene              2
FOE
    Still foe to vice, forsake his Cambrian shade; . . .  O  23  London           261
    Still foe to vice, exert his Cambrian shade;  . . .   Y  61  London         V 262
    The ravish'd standard, and the captive foe, . . . .   O  39  Vanity Wishes    176
    And heap their vallies with the gaudy foe; . . . .    O  42  Vanity Wishes    236
    A generous foe regards, with pitying eye, . . . .     O  61  Pro Word Wise      5
    Shall spring to seize thee like an ambush'd foe. . .  O 152  The Ant           16
    Well skill'd to sooth a foe with looks of kindness, . O 176  Tr Metastas II     3
    Ere yet the Foe found Leisure to be cruel, . . . .    O 252  Irene             94
    When eager Vengeance shows a naked Foe, . . . .       O 280  Irene             13
    Pourd Storms of fire upon th' approaching Foe . . .   O 364  Irene          V  1
    This Night alone is ours--Our mighty Foe, . . . .     O 303  Irene             25
    Elate with Hope, and panting for a Foe. . . . .       O 304  Irene              5
    Dar'd have provok'd a foe to single fight, . . . .    Y  23  Tr Add. Battle    39
```

	PAGE	TITLE	LINE

FOES

And safe in poverty defy'd his foes;	O 11	London	48
On ev'ry stage the foes of peace attend,	O 33	Vanity Wishes	77
Sign her foes doom, or guard her fav'rites zeal?	O 34	Vanity Wishes	92
The glitt'ring eminence exempt from foes;	O 38	Vanity Wishes	166
His foes derision, and his subjects blame,	O 43	Vanity Wishes	253
And Slaves, the Maxim tells, are always Foes.	O 46	Vanity Wishes	V330B
When Learning's Triumph o'er her barb'rous Foes	O 51	Pro Drury-Lane	1
Their schemes of spite the poet's foes dismiss,	O 60	Pro Good Nat'd	19
Their foes the shock sustain in Battle skill'd,	O 76	Tr Add. Battle	12
Their foes attacks, and wield their arms with pain.	O 76	Tr Add. Battle	27
But, lest I fall by subtler foes,	O 126	An Ode	37
Wealth still finds followers, and misfortunes foes.	O 138	Tr Rambler 153	2
Before such Foes of more than human Force,	O 250	Irene	49
Scorn'd by his Subjects, trampled by his Foes;	O 268	Irene	20
His correspondence with our Foes of Greece!	O 273	Irene	18
Had our first Asian Foes but known this Ardour,	O 284	Irene	40
Foes unforeseen, and Dangers unsuspected.	O 298	Irene	26
What Ties to Slaves? what Gratitude to Foes?	O 312	Irene	6
Fresh foes descending glut their swords with blood.	Y 23	Tr Add. Battle	21
The Pygmies thus exasp'rated their foes.	Y 23	Tr Add. Battle	51

FOES'

Sign her foes' doom, or guard her patriots zeal,	Y 95	Vanity Wishes	V 92

FOLIAGE

And balmy spirits thro' thy foliage play,	Y 3	On a Daffodill	10
May balmy spirits thro thy foliage play,	Y 3	On a Daffodill	V 10

FOLLIES

And tir'd like me with follies and with crimes,	O 23	London	259
Fears of the brave, and follies of the wise?	O 45	Vanity Wishes	316
The wise man's follies,	Y 106	Vanity Wishes	V 316
Then prompt no more the Follies you decry,	O 53	Pro Drury-Lane	55
Not yet inspire the Follies of a Queen,	O 289	Irene	3
And fill the World with Follies and Impostures,	O 309	Irene	35

FOLLOW

"Awake, and follow me to better Fortunes;"	O 254	Irene	123
Wherever Guilt can fly, Revenge can follow.	O 274	Irene	65
Chearful I follow to the rural Cell,	O 302	Irene	110
Ye Christian Captives, follow me to Freedom:	O 321	Irene	51

FOLLOW'D

With breasts resolv'd, they follow'd still	O 79	Feast St Simon	16

FOLLOWERS

His suppliants scorn him, and his followers fly;	O 35	Vanity Wishes	112
Wealth still finds followers, and misfortunes foes.	O 138	Tr Rambler 153	2

FOLLOWING

Hares forgot the following hound,	O 148	Tr Boet III.12	10
Fondly view'd his following Bride,	O 150	Tr Boet III.12	51
Till want, now following fraudulent and slow,	O 152	The Ant	15

FOLLY

With eager thirst, by folly or by fate,	O 14	London	95
Flush'd as they are with folly, youth and wine,	O 21	London	232
Grief aids disease, remember'd folly stings,	O 35	Vanity Wishes	119
Exulting Folly hail'd the joyful Day,	O 52	Pro Drury-Lane	37
Impelled by passion, and with folly blind.	O 134	Tr Rambler 105	2
All that prey on vice and folly	O 196	Song Congratu.	13
And all that prey in vice or folly	O 196	Song Congratu.	V 13
Nor sprightly Folly wantons in his Air,	O 255	Irene	15
Each weakness sooth and flatter ev'ry folly.	Y 134	Irene	V 27
And Folly, frighted at her own Chimeras,	O 266	Irene	32
Such ill-tim'd Gravity, such serious Folly,	O 281	Irene	35
Once more reflect, suppress this infant Folly.	O 281	Irene	56
Far more I dread Abdalla's fiery Folly,	O 287	Irene	7
Distrust is Cowardice, and Prudence Folly.	O 301	Irene	86
Which squander'd by Neglect, or Fear, or Folly,	O 302	Irene	7
Must Greece, still wretched by her Children's Folly,	O 305	Irene	43
Ambition was her Crime, but meaner Folly	O 310	Irene	9
And Cowardice to dread the Boast of Folly.	O 318	Irene	22
Tis cowardise to fear the boasts of folly	Y 197	Irene	V 22
You perish (for) by your folly not your zeal,	Y 198	Irene	V 32
But soon though shalt lament thy daring folly	Y 198	Irene	V 33
Ye blind officious Ministers of Folly,	O 332	Irene	23

FOND

On Britain's fond credulity they prey.	O 15	London	112
Enliv'ning hope, and fond desire,	O 123	Winter's Walk	9
Still fond of Life, groan'd out the dreadful Secret,	O 272	Irene	16
Still fond of Life reveald the dreadfull secret,	O 356	Irene	V 33
Throws his fond Arms about Aspasia's Neck,	O 286	Irene	4
Reproach not, Greece, a Lover's fond Delays,	O 297	Irene	19
And Peace propitious smile on fond Desire;	O 302	Irene	119
He seiz'd her melting in the fond Appeal,	O 334	Irene	70

FONDEST

Warm with an ardent lover's fondest pray'r.	O 80	Lady Birthday	2

FONDLY

Fondly view'd his following Bride,	O 150	Tr Boet III.12	51

FONDNESS

Tho' grief and fondness in my breast rebel,	O 8	London	1
Peace courts his hand, her fondness he disdains	Y 101	Vanity Wishes	V 201
Against your fame with fondness hate combines,	O 46	Vanity Wishes	331
When fondness melts me, or when wine inflames,	O 142	In Baretti Bk.	2
To me my Lover's Fondness will restore,	O 291	Irene	74
Till in the midst of Arrogance and Fondness,	O 299	Irene	46
This Bay has prov'd my ,fondness for the Sultan;	O 324	Irene	19

FONTE

                                                                         PAGE   TITLE   LINE

    <H>oc fonte derivat<a> clades--In patriam populumque . .   O 347 Irene   V 22
       fluxit.

FOOD
    Can more delicious food supply. . . . .   O 73 Hor. Epode II V 62
FOOL
    Despise a fool in half his pension dress'd, ...   O 13 London   73
    With his own form acquaint the forward fool, ...   O 81 Lady Birthday   15
    The Coward, and the Fool, condemn'd to lose . . . . .   O 283 Irene   22
FOOL'S
    When vengeance listens to the fool's request. . . . .   O 31 Vanity Wishes   14
FOOLS
    And feed with varied fools th' eternal jest: . . . .   O 32 Vanity Wishes   52
    And feed with change of new born fools th' eternal . .   Y 94 Vanity Wishes V 52
       jest:
    On fools and villains ne'er descend: . . . .   O 100 Ode Friendship   18
    Nor Gods his Heroes, nor his Lovers Fools: . . . . .   O 246 Irene Prologue 18
    Which Cheats interpret, and which Fools regard? . . .   O 250 Irene   43
    The Tale of Women, and the Scorn of Fools? . . . . .   O 305 Irene   29
FOP
    Some fiery fop, with new commission vain, ...   O 21 London   226
    So some fiery fop, with new commission vain, ...   Y 59 London   V 226
FOPLING'S
    The (coxcombs) whisper and the fopling's song . . . .   Y 128 Irene   V 17
FOPPERIES
    In all the Fopperies of meeting Lovers; . . . . . .   O 269 Irene   14
FOPS
    Should Beauty blunt on fops her fatal dart, ...   O 37 Vanity Wishes   151
    Ye Fops be silent! and ye Wits be just! . . . . . .   O 246 Irene Prologue 34
FOR
       265
FORBEAR   OMITTED WORD
    Who scarce forbear, tho' Britain's Court he sing, . . .   O 13 London   69
    Forbear to hiss--the Poet cannot hear. . . . . . .   O 62 Pro Word Wise   18
         Forbear to speak of Hazards, ...   O 260 Irene   133
    Forbear this lavish Pomp of dreadful Praise; . . . .   O 268 Irene   33
    Forbear--O do not urge me to my Ruin! . . . . . .   O 278 Irene   79
    Young Man, forbear--The Heat of Youth, no more-- . . .   O 284 Irene   47
    Forbear--.i know the long try'd Faith of Cali. . . .   O 298 Irene   25
    Forbear thy Threats, proud Prophetess of Ill, ...   O 308 Irene   11
    Forbear--But thou art sunk beneath Reproach; . . . .   O 314 Irene   26
    Forbear, Demetrius, 'tis Aspasia calls thee; . . . .   O 315 Irene   28
         Forbear this Rudeness, ...   O 318 Irene   8
FORBEARS   O 322 Irene   54
    Forbears the long-continu'd strife, ...   O 124 An Ode   2
FORBIDS
    The pressing Exigence forbids Relation. . . . . . .   O 315 Irene   8
    And Heav'n forbids to lavish Life away, ...   O 321 Irene   49
FORC'D
    But forc'd at length her antient Reign to quit, . . .   O 52 Pro Drury-Lane 35
    He ne'er with forc'd Submission waits . . . .   O 71 Hor. Epode II   15
    And forc'd his soul the nearest way. . . . .   O 202 Death Dr Levet V 36
    For forc'd Compliance, or for zealous Virtue, ...   O 256 Irene   51
    With noisy Falshoods forc'd me from your Arms, . . .   O 299 Irene   39
    Th' approaching Sultan forc'd me from the Palace; . .   O 299 Irene   47
    That fawning Villain's forc'd Congratulations . . . .   O 310 Irene   2
    That hoary Villain's forc'd congratulations . . . .   O 370 Irene   V 22
    The Tongue, that, forc'd by strong Necessity, ...   O 324 Irene   2
    Just as the Rack forc'd out his struggling Soul, . . .   O 330 Irene   13
    Your fierce Impatience forc'd us from your Presence, . .   O 332 Irene   29
    This forc'd the Cranes to utter dolefull moans, . . .   Y 24 Tr Add. Battle   88
FORCE
    With force resistless o'er the brave prevail. . . . .   O 39 Vanity Wishes   178
    O'er love, o'er Force, extends his wide domain, . . .   O 40 Vanity Wishes V 195
    The guardians yield, by force superior ply'd; . . . .   O 47 Vanity Wishes   339
    The guardians yield, with force resistless ply'd; . . .   Y 107 Vanity Wishes V 339
    Or bends with violent force the trees. . . . . . .   O 67 Hor. II Ode IX   8
    And Persia felt the force of Grecian steel; . . . . .   O 76 Tr Add. Battle   38
    Let Reason with superiour force controul . . . . . .   O 77 Festina Lente   7
    Their faith, or force them to forsake . . . . . .   O 79 Feast St Simon 14
    To point each glance, and force it to the heart! . . .   O 81 Lady Birthday   8
    His force of genius burn'd in early youth, ...   O 117 Epitaph Hanmer   5
    Stern winter, is thy force confest, ...   O 123 Winter's Walk   6
    Stern winter, in thy force confest, ...   O 123 Winter's Walk V 6
    To force Applause no modern Arts are try'd. . . . . .   O 246 Irene Prologue 22
    Before such Foes of more than human Force; . . . . .   O 250 Irene   49
    So small a Force? or why should Cali fly? . . . . .   O 254 Irene   138
    Or arm his Breast against the Force of Love? . . . .   O 261 Irene   8
    Swells in the Breast, and with resistless Force, . . .   O 280 Irene   20
    Prudence and Friendship bid me force her from you. . .   O 296 Irene   7
    Force her! profane her with a Touch, and die. . . . .   O 296 Irene   8
    New Force, new Courage, from each Glance I gain, . . .   O 297 Irene   21
    Demand whose Force yon Turkish Heroes dread, ...   O 305 Irene   41
    I felt the Force of his tempestuous Arm, ...   O 307 Irene   19
    Say, by what Fraud, what Force were you defeated? . . .   O 315 Irene   6
    What more could Force attempt, or Art contrive? . . .   O 317 Irene   35
    What more could force attempt or thought contrive . .   Y 194 Irene   V 35
    Return'd with Force that made Resistance vain, . . .   O 317 Irene   38
    The valiant Prince with unresisted force . . . . .   Y 25 Tr Add. Battle 118
    Its useless force the weapon spends in air. . . . . .   Y 26 Tr Add. Battle 135

		PAGE	TITLE		LINE

FORCEFULL
Forcefull descending strikes his enemy, ... Y 26 Tr Add. Battle 131

FOREBORE
Pleas'd with the conquest, he forebore the spoil . . . Y 18 Tr. Iliad Bk 6 30

FOREIGN
Form'd to delight, they use no foreign arms, ... O 84 Epi Dist Moth. 22
To live obscure upon a foreign Coast, ... O 301 Irene 104

FORESHOWN
This dire event by omens was foreshown; . . . . . . O 64 Virgil Past.I 22

FORESOOK
I first foresook the scornfull fair. . . . . Y 11 Tr Hor Epode 9 10

FORESTS   SEE FORRESTS
For while in Sabine Forests, charm'd . . . . . . O 66 To A. Fuscus 9
Listning forests learnt the Strain, ... O 148 Tr Boet III.12 V 9
For thee shall Forests rise and Rivers flow . . . . O 350 Irene V 22
To spread Civility through Russia's Forests . . . . O 348 Irene V 21

FORETELL
While I foretell thy Fate; that Office done,-- . . . . O 289 Irene 9

FORETOLD
Foretold the coming evil by their dismal croak. . . . O 65 Virgil Past.I 25
And not one Prodigy foretold our Fate. . . . . . . O 250 Irene 35
A thousand horrid Prodigies foretold it. . . . . . . O 250 Irene 36

FOREVER
He comes, perhaps, to separate us forever; . . . . . O 294 Irene 6

FORFEIT
Justice demands the forfeit Life of Cali; . . . . . O 286 Irene 13

FORGES
The tongue that forges mandates for destruction . . . Y 210 Irene V 25A

FORGET
And forget (or lose) the conquerour in the . . . . . Y 123 Irene V 100
   lover
I'll open my breast--clasp thee--forget . . . . . . Y 161 Irene V 13
   greatness--
Can'st thou forget hereditary Splendours, ... O 301 Irene 103
The Ministers of Wrath forget Compassion, ... O 314 Irene 24
Irene's crimes, forget not her repentance. . . . . . Y 209 Irene V 55

FORGETFUL
Forgetful of Command, with captive Beauties, ... O 258 Irene 92

FORGETFULL
Forgetfull of your wife, forgetfull of your son? . . . Y 18 Tr. Iliad Bk 6 21
Forgetfull of your wife, forgetfull of your son? . . . Y 18 Tr. Iliad Bk 6 21

FORGETFULNESS
In all the sweet forgetfulness of Love . . . . . . O 367 Irene V 26
In all the sweet forgetfulness of love . . . . . . Y 138 Irene V 13

FORGETS
Live till the Sun forgets to dart his Beams, ... O 262 Irene 3
The weary Sun forgets his Revolutions . . . . O 347 Irene V 30

FORGIVE
Forgive my transports on a theme like this, ... O 15 London 97
Forgive, great Jove, the daring enterprize. . . . . . O 136 Tr Rambler 129 6
I grant the charge; forgive the fault confess'd. . . . O 139 Tr Rambler 170 1
Intriguing Wits! his artless Plot forgive; . . . . . O 246 Irene Prologue 19
   Forgive an old Man's Weakness, ... O 256 Irene 38
Forgive the frozen Narratives of Dotage . . . . . . O 366 Irene V 16
Forgive, great Sultan, that intrusive Duty . . . . . O 263 Irene 23
Forgive those Fears that shake the tender Frame? . . . O 266 Irene 25
And yet another Voice, forgive me Greece, ... O 270 Irene 18
I thought, forgive my Fair, the noblest Aim, ... O 278 Irene 61
Forgive, my Fair, 'tis Life, 'tis Nature calls. . . . O 318 Irene 19
Forgive my fair what fame what nature prompts . . . . Y 197 Irene V 19
Forgive, fair Excellence, th' unwilling Tongue, . . . O 324 Irene 1
Forgive, great Sultan! that by Fate prevented, . . . O 331 Irene 1

FORGOT
Glad to be hid, and proud to be forgot. . . . . . . O 82 Young Author 30
Wisdom at proper times is well forgot. . . . . O 134 Tr. Rambler 89 1
Hares forgot the following hound, ... O 148 Tr Boet III.12 10
But Greece is still forgot. . . . . O 257 Irene 74

FORGOTTEN
Art thou forgotten by the Muse, ... O 80 Feast St Simon 50
Well pleas'd to find thy Precepts not forgotten. . . . O 267 Irene 41

FORM
Collect a tax, or form a lottery, ... O 12 London V 58
Where ne'er was known the form of mock debate, . . . O 33 Vanity Wishes 57
Where ne'er was heard the form of mock debate, . . . Y 94 Vanity Wishes V 57
The form distorted justifies the fall, ... O 34 Vanity Wishes 89
But find the form distorted by the fall . . . . . . Y 95 Vanity Wishes V 89
And Sedley curs'd the form that pleas'd a king. . . . O 46 Vanity Wishes 322
Bid scenic Virtue form the rising Age, ... O 53 Pro Drury-Lane 61
Or trace his Form on circulating Gold, ... O 58 Prologue Comus 24
Thy form more lovely, more adorn'd thy mind; . . . . O 80 Lady Birthday 4
With his own form acquaint the forward fool, ... O 81 Lady Birthday 15
Thou see'st one pleasing form arise, ... O 121 To Miss Playin 26
When, lately, Stella's form display'd . . . . O 122 Stella Mourn. 1
Henceforth shall form one common pray'r, ... O 122 Stella Mourn. 14
Each grace of form, each ornament of state, ... O 141 Tr Rambler 199 7
That traced th' essential form of Grace, ... O 154 Epita. Hogarth 2
That wav'd th' essential form of Grace, ... O 154 Epita. Hogarth V 2
Who drew th' essential Form of Grace; . . . . O 155 Epita. Hogarth V 2
But cautious Age suspects the flatt'ring Form, . . . O 255 Irene 18
Greatness of mind with elegance of form. . . . . . . Y 149 Irene V 56
To form his Court and regulate his pleasures . . . . Y 164 Irene V 78

125

```
FORM              (CONTINUED)                          PAGE     TITLE           LINE
    To form new Legends, sanctify new Crimes,  . . . . .   O 309  Irene            33
FORM'D    SEE DOUBLE-FORM'D
    This thought once form'd, all counsel comes too late,  .   O  82  Young Author     19
    Form'd to delight, they use no foreign arms,   . . . .   O  84  Epi Dist Moth.   22
    Bright Stella, form'd for universal Reign,   . . . . .   O  96  Hickman Spinet    1
    For Nature form'd the Poet for the King. . . . . . .   O 114  On C. Cibber      4
    Will not that Pow'r that form'd the Heart of Woman,  . .   O 266  Irene            23
    Unus'd to Power, and form'd for humbler Scenes,  . . .   O 268  Irene            17
    Such heav'nly Beauty form'd for Adoration,   . . . . .   O 269  Irene            41
    Form'd to delight, and happy by delighting,  . . . . .   O 276  Irene            16
    Form'd by this Garden jutting on the Deep;   . . . . .   O 284  Irene            52
    Had form'd her nest and plac'd her burthen there,  . . .   Y  23  Tr Add. Battle   45
FORMER
    And mortgag'd states their former wreaths regret,  . . .   Y 100  Vanity Wishes   V 187
    Unfaded still their former charms they shew,   . . . .   O  84  Epi Dist Moth.   26
    Calm conscience then his former life survey'd,   . . . .   O 118  Epitaph Hanmer   41
    And bring her former Sentence new confirm'd. . . . . .   O 327  Irene            27
    Back through the city trod his former way. . . . . .   Y  17  Tr. Iliad Bk 6    2
    In former ages while upheld by fate  . . . . . . .   Y  23  Tr Add. Battle   26
FORMING
    And forming, with unerring art, . . . . . . . . .   O 121  To Miss Playin    17
FORMS
    New forms arise, and diff'rent views engage,   . . . .   O  45  Vanity Wishes   307
    Break through the Politician's tedious Forms,  . . . .   O 259  Irene           106
    And new forms of pleasure shall be invented  . . . . .   O 350  Irene           V 25
    The wily sorc'ress wears a thousand forms,   . . . . .   Y 155  Irene           V 26
    Those forms of men that play before a  . . . . . . .   Y 173  Irene           V 18
        beauty
FORRESTS
    As herbs of which the forrests nigh  . . . . . . .   O  73  Hor. Epode II    61
    The painted meads and Forrests nigh  . . . . . . .   O  73  Hor. Epode II  V 61
FORSAKE
    Still foe to vice, forsake his Cambrian shade;   . . . .   O  23  London          261
    In virtue's cause once more forsake his rage,  . . . .   O  23  London          V 262
    But shall I, then, forsake the unfinish'd war? . . . .   O  74  Tr. Iliad Bk 6    4
    Their faith, or force them to forsake  . . . . . . .   O  79  Feast St Simon   14
    Why does the Blood forsake thy lovely Cheek? . . . . .   O 295  Irene             5
    Sweeps o'er the Grove, forsake the lab'ring Bough, . . .   O 298  Irene            23
    Forsake a Wretch abandon'd to Despair,   . . . . . .   O 320  Irene            14
    To see the Cloud forsake her kindling Cheek,   . . . .   O 320  Irene            26
    And warm Cayster's flowing banks forsake   . . . . . .   Y  24  Tr Add. Battle   67
FORSAKES
    And scarce forsakes his native fields.   . . . . . .   O  68  Hor. II Ode IX   24
    Forsakes his rural seats and peaceful home,  . . . . .   O  81  Young Author      2
    Forsakes his rural sports and peaceful home,   . . . .   O  81  Young Author    V 2
    Live till the tott'ring Earth forsakes its   . . . . .   O 347  Irene           V 29
        Base
FORSOOK
    When Genoa's faithless Sons forsook the Ramparts   . . .   O 351  Irene           V 5
    Great Amurath, at my Request, forsook  . . . . . . .   O 256  Irene            43
    Just as I mark'd them, they forsook the Shore, . . . .   O 269  Irene            38
    Then in short Sighs forsook his broken Frame.  . . . .   O 331  Irene            16
FORT
    In crowd at once, where none the fort defend,  . . . .   Y 107  Vanity Wishes   V 337
FORTH
    Pour forth thy fervours for a healthful mind,  . . . .   O  48  Vanity Wishes   359
    Breathe forth thy fervours for a soul  . . . . . . .   Y 108  Vanity Wishes   V 359
    Whose mortal wounds pour forth a purple flood, . . . .   O  76  Tr Add. Battle   20
    Pour forth her Dead to warn us of its fall?  . . . . .   O 365  Irene           V 22
    Pour forth their Legions, and the roaring Danube   . . .   O 264  Irene            17
    Pour forth the Legions and the Wondring Danube . . . .   O 353  Irene           V 1
    Held forth this fatal Scroll, then sunk to nothing. . .   O 272  Irene            17
    Call forth her ancient Heroes to the Field,  . . . . .   O 309  Irene            39
    Call forth her ancient Scipios to the field  . . . . .   Y 185  Irene           V 39
    Th' applauding Sky shall pour forth all its Beams  . . .   O 322  Irene             9
    Soon forth in arms had some bold soldier stood,  . . .   Y  23  Tr Add. Battle   40
FORTIFIE
    And man the walls and fortifie the tow'rs.   . . . . .   Y  19  Tr. Iliad Bk 6   51
FORTIFIES
    Exalts my Soul, and fortifies my Heart.  . . . . . .   O 265  Irene             5
FORTIFY'D
    Nor built on Faith, nor fortify'd by Conscience?   . . .   O 301  Irene            84
FORTITUDE
    Made passive Fortitude the Praise of Woman:  . . . . .   O 290  Irene            44
FORTRESS
    A petty fortress, and a dubious hand;  . . . . . . .   O  41  Vanity Wishes   220
    A nameless fortress, and a nameless hand;  . . . . . .   Y 102  Vanity Wishes   V 220
FORTRESSES
    Distrust th' eternal Fortresses of Nature,   . . . . .   O 268  Irene            31
FORTUNE
    Who shares Orgilio's crimes, his fortune shares. . . .   O  14  London           84
    Farewell!--When youth, and health, and fortune spent,  .   O  23  London          256
    Delusive Fortune hears th' incessant call,   . . . . .   O  33  Vanity Wishes    75
    Law in his voice, and fortune in his hand:   . . . . .   O  34  Vanity Wishes   100
    Begs for each birth the fortune of a face:   . . . . .   O  45  Vanity Wishes   320
    Hard is his lot, that here by Fortune plac'd,  . . . .   O  53  Pro Drury-Lane   47
    The fickle crowd with fortune comes and goes;  . . . .   O 138  Tr Rambler 153    1
    While thus we mourn the Fortune of Aspasia,  . . . . .   O 253  Irene           107
    While yet the future Fortune of my Country   . . . . .   O 313  Irene             2
    Abdalla fails, now Fortune all is mine.  . . . . . .   O 319  Irene             1
```

```
FORTUNE          (CONTINUED)                            PAGE    TITLE             LINE
     Nor hope his Fortune while thou want'st his Worth.  .  .  .   O 330 Irene              25
     He turn'd awhile the fortune of the day  .  .  .  .  .  .    Y  25 Tr Add. Battle     123
FORTUNE'S
     Out of Fortune's Pow'r retreat?  .  .  .  .  .  .  .  .  .   O 144 Tr Boeth. II.4       2
     "Fortune's guest, without a home,  .  .  .  .  .  .  .  .    O 185 Anacreon Ode 9      26
FORTUNES
     "Awake, and follow me to better Fortunes;"  .  .  .  .  .   O 254 Irene             123
FORWARD
     With his own form acquaint the forward fool,  .  .  .  .     O  81 Lady Birthday       15
     The loudest Cries of Nature urge us forward;  .  .  .  .     O 270 Irene               15
     Relax'd with Fear, refuse to bear me forward.  .  .  .  .    O 320 Irene               12
FOUGHT
     Acquir'd by wounds, and battles bravely fought!  .  .  .    O  74 Tr. Iliad Bk 6       7
FOUL
     Their foul deformities by all descry'd,  .  .  .  .  .  .    O  84 Epi Dist Moth.      40
     The Soul once tainted with so foul a Crime,  .  .  .  .  .   O 289 Irene               15
FOUND    SEE NEW-FOUND
     Where once the harrass'd Briton found repose,  .  .  .  .    O  11 London              47
     The Wits of Charles found easier Ways to Fame,  .  .  .  .   O  52 Pro Drury-Lane      17
     Vice always found a sympathetick Friend;  .  .  .  .  .  .   O  52 Pro Drury-Lane      21
     By all, like him, must praise and blame be found;  .  .  .   O  62 Pro Word Wise       19
     And found a Thousand Worlds in Stella's Arms.  .  .  .  .    O  97 Hickman Spinet      20
     Were Pope once void of wonted candour found,  .  .  .  .     O 106 Eliza plucking       7
     The nymphs, who found their pow'r decline,  .  .  .  .  .    O 122 Stella Mourn.        3
     On names now found alone on books and tombs.  .  .  .  .     O 134 Tr. Rambler 93       2
     Unquench'd the thirst of gain is found;  .  .  .  .  .  .    O 144 Tr Boeth. II.2      12
     Firm and low thy Mansion found;  .  .  .  .  .  .  .  .  .   O 145 Tr Boeth. II.4      16
     And sure th' Eternal Master found  .  .  .  .  .  .  .  .    O 201 Death Dr Levet      27
     Ere yet the Foe found Leisure to be cruel,  .  .  .  .  .    O 252 Irene               94
     Nor found again the bright Temptation fail?  .  .  .  .  .   O 259 Irene             125
     The Breast where Guilt like this has found  .  .  .  .  .    O 349 Irene          V   23
        admission
FOUNDATION
     On what foundation stands the warrior's pride,  .  .  .  .   O  40 Vanity Wishes      191
     On what foundation stands the warrior's fame?  .  .  .  .    Y 101 Vanity Wishes   V  191
FOUNDATIONS
     On weak foundations raise th' enormous weight?  .  .  .  .   O  35 Vanity Wishes      126
FOUNT
     The transparent Fount of Good;  .  .  .  .  .  .  .  .  .    O 147 Tr Boet III.12       2
FOUNTAIN
     and drink the holy waters the fountain of  .  .  .  .  .     Y 130 Irene          V   11
        remission
     Thou fountain of existence I pour the  .  .  .  .  .  .  .   Y 189 Irene          V    1
FOUNTS
     O'er all the warbling founts a cooling shade.  .  .  .  .    Y   7 Virgil Daphnis      27
FOUR
     Here have I rais'd four sacred altars, two  .  .  .  .  .    Y   7 Virgil Daphnis      43
FOWL
     Here lies a fowl transfix'd with many a wound  .  .  .  .    O  76 Tr Add. Battle      14
FOWLS
     Nor Lybian fowls, nor Snipes of Greece,  .  .  .  .  .  .    O  73 Hor. Epode II       59
FRAGRANCE
     Liquid fragrance all the way:  .  .  .  .  .  .  .  .  .  .   O 185 Anacreon Ode 9       4
     Here ev'ry Fragrance breathe of ev'ry Spring:  .  .  .  .    O 279 Irene               87
FRAGRANT
     No fragrant bowers, no delightful glades,  .  .  .  .  .     O  83 Epi Dist Moth.      12
     Soon fades the rose; once past the fragrant hour,  .  .  .   O 133 Tr. Rambler 71       1
FRAIL
     Frail as the leaves that quiver on the sprays,  .  .  .  .   O 138 Tr Rambler 161       1
FRAILTY
     And Wisdom into Virtue turn thy Frailty.  .  .  .  .  .  .   O 266 Irene               22
FRAIS
     Trop de frais.  .  .  .  .  .  .  .  .  .  .  .  .  .  .  .   O 172 French Distich       2
FRAME
     To better features yields the frame of gold;  .  .  .  .    O  34 Vanity Wishes       86
     A frame of adamant, a soul of fire,  .  .  .  .  .  .  .     O  40 Vanity Wishes      193
     Thy pictures shall thy conduct frame,  .  .  .  .  .  .  .   O 121 To Miss Playin      33
     And soaring mocks the broken frame below.  .  .  .  .  .     O 131 Tr. Rambler 17       1
     Had this fair figure which this frame displays,  .  .  .     O 189 Seeing Montagu       1
     His frame was firm, his powers were bright,  .  .  .  .  .   O 202 Death Dr Levet      31
     Secure he tramples my declining Frame,  .  .  .  .  .  .     Y 132 Irene          V   71
     My soul could animate a larger frame  .  .  .  .  .  .  .    Y 132 Irene          V  41A
     Forgive those Fears that shake the tender Frame?  .  .  .    O 266 Irene               25
     But oft conjoins in woman's softer mould/frame  .  .  .  .   Y 149 Irene          V   55
     Frame your Report with circumspective Art,  .  .  .  .  .    O 329 Irene               13
     Then in short Sighs forsook his broken Frame.  .  .  .  .    O 331 Irene               16
FRANCE
     Of France the mimick, and of Spain the prey.  .  .  .  .     O  15 London             106
FRANTIC
     Advance, and perish in the frantic Boast.  .  .  .  .  .     O 318 Irene                7
FRANTICK
     While his sad mother frantick with despair  .  .  .  .  .    Y   6 Virgil Daphnis       5
FRAUD
     That oft' had practis'd Fraud, and oft' detected,  .  .  .   O 254 Irene             131
     Strange! that this gen'ral Fraud from Day to Day  .  .  .    O 283 Irene               26
     Fierce persecution wears the bleeding world with  .  .  .    Y 164 Irene          V   66
        fraud
     When Purity, while Fraud was yet unknown,  .  .  .  .  .     O 314 Irene                6
     Say, by what Fraud, what Force were you defeated?  .  .  .   O 315 Irene                6
     What Fraud misleads him? or what Crimes incense?  .  .  .    O 325 Irene               28
```

		PAGE	TITLE		LINE

FRAUDFUL
    The fraudful Moments ply their silent Wings, ... O 327 Irene 8
FRAUDS
    When mutual frauds perplex'd the maze of State, . . . O 118 Epitaph Hanmer 24
FRAUDULENT
    Till want, now following fraudulent and slow, ... O 152 The Ant 15
    Or meanly fraudulent, or madly gay, ... O 316 Irene 24
FRAUGHT
    Now roll full fraught with Thunder o'er your Head. . . O 275 Irene 75
FRAY
    Rush not impetuous to the bloody fray . . . . . . Y 19 Tr. Iliad Bk 6 46
    Whilst beaks and swords engage in bloody fray . . . . Y 22 Tr Add. Battle 6
FREE
    By numbers here from shame or censure free, ... O 17 London 158
    Yet hope not life from grief or danger free, ... O 37 Vanity Wishes 155
    Yet dream not life from grief or danger free, ... Y 99 Vanity Wishes V 155
    Who lives from toilsome bus'ness free, ... O 71 Hor. Epode II 2
    They call them Fairies; these now free from care . . . O 77 Tr Add. Battle 49
    "Void of care, and free from dread . . . . O 185 Anacreon Ode 9 33
    Free to mortgage or to sell, ... O 196 Song Congratu. 6
    Soon would his Art or Valour set us free, ... O 267 Irene 43
    Oh could thy Hand unaided free thy Country, ... O 300 Irene 63
    Soon may we meet again, secure and free, ... O 303 Irene 23
    Be but my Country free, be thine the Praise; . . . . O 305 Irene 33
    Return, Demetrius, and be free for ever. . . . . . O 306 Irene 60
    Unclasp'd his Iron Gripe to set thee free? . . . . . O 318 Irene 16
    Detain'd me till Demetrius set me free. . . . . . . O 335 Irene 9
    Since from Inachia's charms set free . . . . Y 11 Tr Hor Epode 9 9
    Then would I free from torments live . . . . Y 11 Tr Hor Epode 9 25
    Soon as with gold appeas'd, he set her free . . . . . Y 19 Tr. Iliad Bk 6 40
FREE'D
    And free'd his soul the nearest way. . . . . O 202 Death Dr Levet 36
FREED
    The heart, once caught, should ne'er be freed? . . . . O 120 To Miss Purse 12
    Freed from the harsh severities of virtue . . . . . Y 146 Irene V 23
    Freed from the Tumults of unsettled Conquest, ... O 291 Irene 77
    One Hour had freed me from the fatal Error, ... O 332 Irene 27
FREEDOM
    Sense, freedom, piety, refin'd away, ... O 15 London 105
    The harmless Freedom, and the private Friend. . . . . O 46 Vanity Wishes 338
    Which erst in Frost and Freedom lay, ... O 146 Tr Boeth III.5 8
    "Freedom my return awaits, ... O 185 Anacreon Ode 9 20
    That Wealth, too pleasing to be lost for Freedom! . . . O 250 Irene 21
    That sweep away religion arts and freedom . . . . . Y 117 Irene V109D
    Projects at once our Freedom and his own; . . . . . O 253 Irene 114
    Surveys his smiling babes, the sons of . . . ⚓ . . Y 122 Irene V 60
      freedom,
    Remember Freedom, Glory, Greece, and Love. . . . . . O 260 Irene 146
    To Want give Affluence? and to Slav'ry Freedom? . . . O 277 Irene 46
    Give Wealth to Poverty to Slavery Freedom . . . . . O 356 Irene V 13
    Still languish in our Chains, and dream of Freedom, . . O 282 Irene 4
    Completes the Gift of Freedom and of Life. . . . . . O 285 Irene 16
    Gladness, fair child, of innocence and freedom. . . . Y 165 Irene V 81
    Revive--Revive to Freedom and to Love. . . . . . . O 295 Irene 9
    Freedom and Love? Alas! I'm all Confusion, ... O 295 Irene 11
    'Tis Greece, 'tis Freedom calls Aspasia hence, . . ' . O 297 Irene 9
    That fiery Chief, renown'd for gen'rous Freedom, . . . O 299 Irene 35
    That firy Chief, renown'd for gen'rous Freedom, . . . O 299 Irene V 35
    And strangled Freedom perish in the Birth. . . . . . O 299 Irene 53
    My Soul expands to meet approaching Freedom. . . . . O 306 Irene 50
    <E>ach hero fir'd piety or freedom . . . . Y 181 Irene V 51
    Of Freedom and of Love: My trembling Joints . . . . . O 320 Irene 11
    Content with Freedom, and precarious Greatness. . . . O 321 Irene 39
    Ye Christian Captives, follow me to Freedom: . . . . O 321 Irene 51
FREEDOM'S
    Through Freedom's sons no more remonstrance rings, . . O 34 Vanity Wishes 93
FREEMEN
    Beholds a long posterity of freemen . . . . Y 122 Irene V 61
FREES
    That dext'rous Message frees me from Suspicion. . . . O 324 Irene 26
FREEZE
    Do the chain'd waters always freeze; . . . . O 67 Hor. II Ode IX 6
    Th' eternal Snows that freeze beyond Meotis, ... O 274 Irene 59
FREEZES
    And my blood freezes at Assassination . . . . O 353 Irene V 23
    But my blood freezes and weak nature shudders . . . . Y 189 Irene V 1G
FREEZING
    And stream destructive through his freezing Veins: . . O 308 Irene 31
FREIGHT
    Thy sacred Freight shall still the raging Main. . . . O 322 Irene 6
    The sacred Freight shall still the raging Main. . . . O 322 Irene V 6
    Go Happy Bark, thy sacred Freight secures thee . . . . O 364 Irene V 24
    Thy sacred freight of innocence and truth . . . . . Y 201 Irene V 10D
FREIND
    Written By Doctor Freind . . . . O 117 Epitaph Hanmer T
FRENCH
    I cannot bear a French metropolis. . . . . O 15 London 98
FRESH
    Fresh praise is try'd till madness fires his mind, . . O 42 Vanity Wishes 231
    Fresh foes descending glut their swords with blood. . . Y 23 Tr Add. Battle 21

		PAGE	TITLE	LINE

FRET
As children fret the lion in a cage. . . . . O 60 Pro Good Nat'd V 16

FRETFUL
Thus blindly pray'd the fretful fair, ... O 122 Stella Mourn. 7

FRIEND
I praise the hermit, but regret the friend, . . . O 8 London 4
But what, my friend, what hope remains for me, ... O 13 London 67
For what but social guilt the friend endears? . . . . O 14 London 83
Can surly virtue hope to fix a friend? . . . . . O 16 London 145
Then shall thy friend, nor thou refuse his aid, . . . O 23 London 260
Nor sweeter musick of a virtuous friend, ... O 43 Vanity Wishes 272
The gen'ral fav'rite as the gen'ral friend: . . . O 44 Vanity Wishes 297
The common fav'rite as the gen'ral friend: . . . . . Y 105 Vanity Wishes V 297
The harmless Freedom, and the private Friend. . . O 46 Vanity Wishes 338
Vice always found a sympathetick Friend; . . . . . . O 52 Pro Drury-Lane 21
Those blessings, friend, a deity bestow'd, ... O 64 Virgil Past.I 7
The man, my friend, whose conscious heart . . . . O 65 Hor I Ode xxii 1
The Man, my Friend, whose conscious Heart . . . . O 66 To A. Fuscus 1
Alass, dear Friend, the fleeting years . . . . . . O 68 Hor.II Ode 14 1
And fruitfull fields, my dearest Friend, ... O 69 Hor.II Ode 14 22
Yet, great Maecenas, shall your friend . . . . O 70 Hor.II Ode XX 7
And hugs a flatterer for a friend. . . . . O 100 Ode Friendship 20
Who hugs a flatterer for a friend. . . . . O 100 Ode Friendship V 20
The Patriot's fire yet sparkled in the friend. . . . O 118 Epitaph Hanmer 40
A guide, a father, and a friend; . . . . O 125 An Ode 22
Thou joy'st to lose the master in the friend: . . . . O 130 Tr. Rambler 12 4
Should the guardian friend or mother . . . . O 197 Song Congratu. V 25
Of ev'ry friendless name the friend. . . . . . . O 201 Death Dr Levet 8
What with your friend you nobly share . . . . . . O 232 Tr Horace IV.7 19
The chains of hell that hold his friend. . . . . . . O 232 Tr Horace IV.7 28
And is it thus Demetrius meets his Friend, ... O 249 Irene 1
And yet, my Friend, what Miracles were wrought . . . O 251 Irene 52
Their Arms prevail'd, though Cali was our Friend. . . O 253 Irene 119
But can thy Friend sustain the glorious Cause, ... O 255 Irene 8
A weeping Wife perhaps, or dying Friend, ... O 280 Irene 9
And quit the Names of Brother, Friend, and Father? . . O 280 Irene 17
No more I boast th' ambitious Name of Friend, ... O 289 Irene 10
And boast no title but Aspasia's friend . . . . Y 161 Irene V 14
This open Friend, this undesigning Hero, ... O 299 Irene 38
Succeed, my Friend, unenvied by Leontius. . . . O 306 Irene 48
Deaf to the critick, sullen to the friend, ... Y 67 Prologue Lethe 5

FRIEND'S
Will he not soften in a Friend's Embrace? . . . . . O 255 Irene 24

FRIENDLESS
Of ev'ry friendless name the friend. . . . . O 201 Death Dr Levet 8

FRIENDLY
In friendly contrariety, ... O 121 To Miss Playin 30
Each Night protected by the friendly Darkness, ... O 251 Irene 59
I came obedient to thy friendly Summons, ... O 253 Irene 105

FRIENDS
His Friends, his Liberty, to hazard? . . . . O 260 Irene 135
A doubtful Glimpse of our approaching Friends; . . . . O 268 Irene 37
But the sight of friends soul sinking into vice (a soul . Y 177 Irene V111C
Took her from her friends and sire, ... Y 301 Extemp. Elegy 15

FRIENDSHIP
Now lacerated Friendship claims a tear. . . . . . . O 45 Vanity Wishes 304
An Ode on Friendship . . . . O 99 Ode Friendship T
Ode on Friendship address'd To the Lady——— . . . O 99 Ode Friendship V T
Dr. Johnson upon Friendship . . . . O 99 Ode Friendship V T
Friendship! peculiar boon of heav'n, ... O 99 Ode Friendship 1
Friendship! peculiar Gift of heav'n, ... O 99 Ode Friendship V 1
And then lament his fall with seeming friendship: . . O 176 Tr Metastas II 5
And then lament their fall with seeming friendship: . . O 176 Tr Metastas II V 5
To prove the Sweets of Privacy and Friendship, . . . O 262 Irene 9
To tender Friendship, praise him to his Mistress. . . O 267 Irene 5
With artificial Smiles, and seeming Friendship. . . . O 271 Irene 38
Swell not thy Soul beyond Advice or Friendship, . . . O 289 Irene 2
Oft' shall I dwell on our disastrous Friendship, . . . O 292 Irene 96
Oft shall I swell on our disastrous Friendship . . . O 349 Irene V 11
Prudence and Friendship bid me force her from you. . . O 296 Irene 7
To find a meaner Fate from treach'rous Friendship— . . O 299 Irene 33
Perhaps may start at violated Friendship. . . . . . O 300 Irene 81
Henceforward hope no more my slighted Friendship, . . O 307 Irene 9

FRIENDSHIP'S
No more shall glow with Friendship's hallow'd Ardour: . O 289 Irene 16

FRIGHT
Nor Praise relax, nor Difficulty fright; . . . . . . O 37 Vanity Wishes 148
No dangers fright him, and no labours tire; . . . . O 40 Vanity Wishes 194
Their hungry Swarms the peaceful Vale shall fright . . O 110 To Posterity 9
Could Omens fright the Resolute and Wise, ... O 269 Irene 1
The voice of war no more shall fright . . . . . . Y 150 Irene V 82
Irene
No more should Danger fright, or Want distress . . . . O 291 Irene 56

FRIGHTED
And frighted, left upon the field, ... O 73 Hor. Epode II 66
Scarce frighted love maintains his fire, ... O 123 Winter's Walk 11
Scarce frighted love maintains her fire, ... O 123 Winter's Walk V 11
And Folly, frighted at her own Chimeras, ... O 266 Irene 32
Shake at my dreaded name and the frighted world . . . Y 136 Irene V 28
Before his face the frighted Cranes gave way. . . . . Y 25 Tr Add. Battle 122

		PAGE	TITLE	LINE
FRIGID				
From Bard, to Bard, the frigid Caution crept, ...		O 52	Pro Drury-Lane	31
FROGS				
There frogs crept croaking o'er the swampy ground. . .		Y 24	Tr Add. Battle	59
FROLIC				
"And when feast and frolic tire,		O 186	Anacreon Ode 9	39
FROLICK				
Some frolick drunkard, reeling from a feast, ...		O 21	London	228
By day the frolick, and the dance by night, ...		O 46	Vanity Wishes	326
FRO'				
Rambling often to and fro'		Y 300	Extemp. Elegy	10
FROM				
275			OMITTED WORD	
FRONT				
Shows his bold Front, the Harbinger of Ruin, ...		O 250	Irene	41
Intrepid in the flaming Front of War?		O 304	Irene	17
FRONTIERS				
There shall he waste thy Frontiers, check thy Conquests,		O 274	Irene	56
FROST				
And Winter barricades the realms of Frost;		O 41	Vanity Wishes	208
Which erst in Frost and Freedom lay, ...		O 146	Tr Boeth III.5	8
The northern shores to clouds and frost		Y 38	Lady Leaving	2
Revolving springs their frost repay.		Y 39	Lady Leaving	10
FROWN				
At length awaking, with contemptuous frown, ...		O 10	London	33
Mark whom the great caress, who frown on me!		O 14	London	92
Who frown with vanity, who smile with art, ...		O 46	Vanity Wishes	327
Bless with a smile, or with a frown destroy;		O 83	Epi Dist Moth.	2
Nor hear it with a frown;--		O 159	Par Hermit III	10
Will he not bend beneath a Tyrant's Frown?		O 255	Irene	22
Thou long'st for Stars that frown on human Kind, . .		O 271	Irene	4
An angry Murmur, a rebellious Frown, ...		O 312	Irene	19
Nor dare to spare the Life his Frown condemns. . . .		O 325	Irene	10
FROWNING				
With horrid gloom the frowning skies:		O 66	Hor I Ode xxii	20
With horrid Gloom the frowning Skies:		O 67	To A. Fuscus	20
The hoary ground, the frowning skies.		O 123	Winter's Walk	4
FROWNS				
At length his sov'reign frowns--the train of state . .		O 34	Vanity Wishes	109
Yet Reason frowns on War's unequal game, ...		O 39	Vanity Wishes	185
Frowns unrestrain'd, and dooms me with his Eyes. . .		O 257	Irene	72
And frowns on Perjury, Revenge and Murder.		O 300	Irene	58
FROZE				
That froze our Veins, and wither'd all our Powers. . .		O 251	Irene	57
FROZEN				
These tedious Narratives of frozen Age		O 259	Irene	113
Forgive the frozen Narratives of Dotage		O 366	Irene	V 16
Hence with the frozen Narratives of Dotage		O 366	Irene	V 16
Should the fierce North upon his frozen Wings		O 274	Irene	61
Frozen with doubt, and maz'd in stupefaction		Y 196	Irene	V 18B
FRUGAL				
A frugal, chast, industrious, Wife, ...		O 72	Hor. Epode II	48
Nor has impartial Nature's frugal Hand		O 277	Irene	53
FRUIT				
The fruit autumnal, and the vernal flow'r, ...		O 43	Vanity Wishes	262
Insatiate pluck the Fruit, and crop the Flow'r: . . .		O 110	To Posterity	12
FRUITFUL				
When fruitful summer loads the teeming plain, ...		O 151	The Ant	7
And of a fruitful year fair omens bring.		Y 3	On a Daffodill	4
FRUITFULL				
And stretch thy prospects o'er your fruitfull land, . .		Y 58	London	V 214
And fruitfull fields, my dearest Friend, ...		O 69	Hor.II Ode 14	22
The fruitfull fields th' industrious people till'd, . .		Y 23	Tr Add. Battle	28
FRUITLESS				
Let Study, worn with Virtue's fruitless Lore, ...		O 57	Prologue Comus	9
With vain (fruitless) labour of the daring flight . . .		Y 127	Irene	V 3
Be fruitless Grief		O 316	Irene	13
With idle Threats and fruitless Exclamation, ...		O 327	Irene	7
With empty threats, and fruitless Exclamation		O 368	Irene	V 15
FRUITS				
When rip'ning fruits perfume the year, ...		O 72	Hor. Epode II	25
FRUSTRATE				
Disperse our Hopes, and frustrate our Designs, ...		O 301	Irene	98
FRY				
Where the darkvisag'd Natives fry, ...		O 79	Feast St Simon	34
FULL				
Their wish is full to riot and to rail.		O 34	Vanity Wishes	98
In full blown pow'r see mighty Wolsey stand, ...		Y 96	Vanity Wishes	V 99
In full blown state, see Wolsey stand, ...		Y 96	Vanity Wishes	V 99
Pockets full, and Spirits high, ...		O 196	Song Congratu.	22
Receives his full Reward in Beauty's Arms.		O 247	Irene Epilogue	24
Still full of Amurath!		O 264	Irene	20
Now roll full fraught with Thunder o'er your Head. . .		O 275	Irene	75
Quaff the full draught of each terrestrial joy		Y 146	Irene	V 20
FULL-BLOWN				
In full-blown dignity, see Wolsey stand, ...		O 34	Vanity Wishes	99
The full-blown pride of conquest and of empire		Y 149	Irene	V 58
FULNESS				
Immortal Crowns and Fulness of Enjoyment?		O 276	Irene	14
FUMES				
And Sloth effuse her opiate fumes in vain;		O 37	Vanity Wishes	150

		PAGE	TITLE	LINE
FUMES	(CONTINUED)			
And Sloth's bland Opiates shed their fumes in vain;		O 37	Vanity Wishes	V 150
Their fumes ascending to the Skie;		O 69	Hor.II Ode 14	8
FUN'RAL				
I without fun'ral elegies		O 70	Hor.II Ode XX	23
FUNERALL				
And burnt him decent on a funerall pile.		Y 18	Tr. Iliad Bk 6	31
FURIES				
Where furies ever howl, and serpents hiss.		O 84	Epi Dist Moth.	31
FURIOUS				
A furious wolf approach'd and fled.		O 65	Hor I Ode xxii	V 12
A furious Wolf approach'd, and fled.		O 66	To A. Fuscus	12
Not always furious Boreas roars,		O 67	Hor. II Ode IX	7
To Robbers furious, and to Lovers tame,		O 174	Tr Epitaph Dog	1
Some furious soldier would approach that bore		Y 23	Tr Add. Battle	46
The wound, and, furious, wave the shining steel.		Y 26	Tr Add. Battle	133
FURY				
They clap their wings, and with new fury burn;		O 76	Tr Add. Battle	9
Where doth extatick fury move		O 80	Feast St Simon	56
Vexation, Fury, Jealousy, Despair,		O 84	Epi Dist Moth.	38
Ambitious Fury fir'd the Grecian King:		O 97	Hickman Spinet	10
Till breathless Fury rested from Destruction		O 249	Irene	5
At length rekindled his accustom'd Fury,		O 259	Irene	110
Thence should my Fury drag him down to Tortures;		O 274	Irene	64
We mark'd him storming in Excess of Fury,		O 311	Irene	11
When, summon'd by the Sultan's clam'rous Fury,		O 325	Irene	22
When erring Fury throws the random dart		O 345	Irene	V 28
FUSCUS				
To Aristius Fuscus		O 66	To A. Fuscus	T
FUTURE				
O'er Bodley's dome his future labours spread,		O 37	Vanity Wishes	139
And proudly hop'd to pimp in future Days.		O 52	Pro Drury-Lane	24
And mark the future Periods of the Stage?--		O 53	Pro Drury-Lane	40
And future millions lift his rising soul;		O 82	Young Author	V 6B
Ambiguous emblem of my future fate!		O 95	Sprig of Myrtl	V 2
Could Rome with future greatness fire,		O 188	Epilogue	2
to the hiss of future ages		Y 113	Irene	V 22
Or wand'ring in the Wilds of future Being,		O 255	Irene	6
<And> plants for his prattling babes the future shade		Y 122	Irene	V 62
Paints future Joys, and points to distant Glories.		O 261	Irene	17
Thou know'st not yet thy Master's future Greatness,		O 265	Irene	40
Expands the boundless scenes of future being		Y 133	Irene	V 8
The future Miseries that wait th' Apostate;		O 266	Irene	20
Behold our future Sultaness, Abdalla;--		O 267	Irene	1
Rise from the happy Bed; and future Queens		O 268	Irene	13
Heav'n has reserv'd no future Paradise,		O 276	Irene	17
Fly lab'ring with the Fate of future Nations,		O 279	Irene	4
The Present, Past, and Future swim before me,		O 295	Irene	13
Diffuse a Brightness on our future Days;		O 301	Irene	100
When future histories record the deed.		Y 180	Irene	V 27
While yet the future Fortune of my Country		O 313	Irene	2
FUTURITY				
The slighted Arts Futurity shall trust,		O 57	Prologue Comus	13
FUTURITY'S				
Far as Futurity's untravell'd Waste		O 300	Irene	68
GAIETIES				
Ill suits with Guilt the Gaieties of Triumph;		O 314	Irene	22
GAIETY				
All there is Hope, and Gaiety, and Courage,		O 271	Irene	26
GAIN				
In those curs'd walls, devote to vice and gain,		O 10	London	37
And what their Armies lost, their Cringes gain?		O 16	London	V 122
And gain a kick for aukward flattery.		O 16	London	V 131
And gain and grandeur load the tainted gales;		O 32	Vanity Wishes	46
And gain and greatness load the tainted gales;		Y 93	Vanity Wishes	V 46
These goods he grants, who grants the pow'r to gain;		O 48	Vanity Wishes	366
You could not gain a Moments breath,		O 69	Hor.II Ode 14	9
But still desires of sordid gain		O 73	Hor. Epode II	77
Or if old womens tales may credit gain,		O 77	Tr Add. Battle	44
Too well You know to keep the Slaves You gain.		O 96	Hickman Spinet	2
With ev'ry bliss that man can gain.		O 136	Tr Rambler 128	6
Unquench'd the thirst of gain is found;		O 144	Tr Boeth. II.2	12
Till the Realms of Light you gain.		O 150	Tr Boet III.12	46
Would you hope to gain my heart,		O 176	Tr Metastasi I	1
No petty gain disdain'd by pride,		O 201	Death Dr Levet	22
New Force, new Courage, from each Glance I gain,		O 297	Irene	21
Alike my Death or thine is gain to thee,		O 319	Irene	32
Who fearst lest I should gain, or thou		Y 198	Irene	V 32
Should she prevail to gain the Sultan's Presence,		O 327	Irene	16
GAIN'D-				
"Think nothing gain'd, he cries, till nought remain,		O 40	Vanity Wishes	202
Charm'd ev'ry ear, and gain'd on ev'ry heart.		O 117	Epitaph Hanmer	8
Gain'd all his Heart; at length his eager Love		O 259	Irene	123
GAINFUL				
No gainful trade their industry can 'scape,		O 15	London	113
This task perform'd, he sought no gainful post,		O 118	Epitaph Hanmer	27
GAINS				
Th' insulted sea with humbler thoughts he gains,		O 42	Vanity Wishes	237
Love prompts to love, and rev'rence rev'rence gains.		O 130	Tr. Rambler 12	8

	PAGE	TITLE	LINE
GAINST			
And gainst the pow'r of Venus steel'd my mind.	Y 11	Tr Hor Epode 9	30
GAIT			
His Air disorder'd, and his Gait unequal,	O 311	Irene	3
GALE			
Place me where no soft summer gale	O 66	Hor I Ode xxii	17
Place me where no soft Summer Gale	O 67	To A. Fuscus	17
And scents ambrosial breathe in every gale:	O 84	Epi Dist Moth.	17
GALES			
And gain and grandeur load the tainted gales;	O 32	Vanity Wishes	46
Assails the skies load the tainted gales;	Y 93	Vanity Wishes	V 46
And gain and greatness load the tainted gales;	Y 93	Vanity Wishes	V 46
Delights to catch the gales of life.	O 124	An Ode	4
And Gales of softer Passion fan my Bosom.	O 275	Irene	93
GALILEO'S			
Hear Lydiat's life, and Galileo's end.	O 38	Vanity Wishes	164
GALLANT			
O spare the gallant Greek, in him we lose	O 307	Irene	26
GALLEY			
Deep in a winding Creek a Galley lies,	O 254	Irene	134
A Galley mann'd with Greeks, thy charge, Leontius,	O 258	Irene	81
A Galley waits us, and the Winds invite.	O 321	Irene	52
GALLICK			
Or how before Nassau the Gallick troops retir'd?	Y 22	Tr Add. Battle	13
GALLIES			
To waft our gallies o'er the trembling earth?	Y 115	Irene	V 49H
GALLOWS			
With hemp the gallows and the fleet supply.	O 21	London	243
GAME			
Yet Reason frowns on War's unequal game,	O 39	Vanity Wishes	185
Yet Reason blush on War's unequal game,	Y 100	Vanity Wishes	V 185
GAMESOME			
Some gamesome drunkard, reeling from a feast,	Y 59	London	V 228
GAMESTER			
Here the Gamester light and jolly	O 196	Song Congratu.	15
There the Gamester light and jolly	O 196	Song Congratu.	V 15
GAPING			
Th' insidious rival and the gaping heir.	O 32	Vanity Wishes	48
In the dark Precincts of the gaping Grave,	O 272	Irene	4
GARDEN			
And turn'd their hasty Steps towards the Garden.	O 269	Irene	39
Form'd by this Garden jutting on the Deep;	O 284	Irene	52
GARDENS			
To Eliza plucking Laurel in Mr Pope's Gardens	O 106	Eliza plucking	T
And ev'n our Prophet's Gardens envy thine:	O 279	Irene	89
And Gennah's happy <to> Gardens envy thine.	O 351	Irene	V 27
GARRET			
Toil, envy, want, the Garret, and the jail.	O 38	Vanity Wishes	V 160
GARRICK			
A New Prologue Spoken By Mr Garrick, ...	O 56	Prologue Comus	T
GARRISON			
Beholds the fainting Garrison retire,	O 298	Irene	28
GASPING			
In his last Agonies the gasping Coward,	O 272	Irene	14
GASPS			
There a stout warriour fainting gasps for breath	O 76	Tr Add. Battle	16
GATE			
Unnumber'd suppliants croud Preferment's gate,	O 33	Vanity Wishes	73
Asks at the Gate Admission to Aspasia,	O 294	Irene	2
And sigh'd and wept at her relentless gate.	Y 11	Tr Hor Epode 9	36
Soon as the chief approach'd the Scaean Gate	Y 18	Tr. Iliad Bk 6	3
GATES			
Obsequious, at his Patrons gates;	O 71	Hor. Epode II	16
"Smiling at my master's gates,	O 185	Anacreon Ode 9	19
Had rang'd embattled Nations at our Gates:	O 250	Irene	23
At my Command yon' Iron Gates unfold;	O 283	Irene	14
Soon shall the dire Seraglio's horrid Gates	O 291	Irene	79
Soon shall the dire Seraglio's dreadful Gates	O 357	Irene	V 9
GATH'RING			
While growing hopes scarce awe the gath'ring sneer,	O 44	Vanity Wishes	277
GATHER			
The dangers gather as the treasures rise.	O 31	Vanity Wishes	28
GAUDY			
See! while he builds, the gaudy vassals come,	O 19	London	202
From every part, the gaudy vassals come,	Y 57	London	V 202
And heap their vallies with the gaudy foe;	O 42	Vanity Wishes	236
GAUL			
The supple Gaul was born a parasite:	O 16	London	124
GAURUS			
Gaurus pretends to Cato's fame;	O 138	Tr Rambler 164	1
GAV'ST			
Find here that calm thou gav'st so oft before;	O 113	Epit. Phillips	4
GAVE			
Struck with the seat that gave Eliza birth,	O 10	London	23
What gave great Villiers to th' assassin's knife,	O 35	Vanity Wishes	129
Cold Approbation gave the ling'ring Bays,	O 51	Pro Drury-Lane	13
He gave my flocks to graze the flowery meads,	O 64	Virgil Past.I	11
Th' Eternal gave it, and that End is Virtue.	O 290	Irene	31
Ambition only gave her to my Arms,	O 310	Irene	7
And gave me Life--	O 313	Irene	18
Before his face the frighted Cranes gave way.	Y 25	Tr Add. Battle	122

		PAGE	TITLE	LINE
GAVE	(CONTINUED)			
	Which gave a thousand pleasures birth. • • • • • •	Y 39	Lady Leaving	8
GAY				
	Some peaceful vale with nature's paintings gay; • • •	O 11	London	46
	Unsullied fame, and conscience ever gay. • • • • • •	O 14	London	90
	Obsequious, artful, voluble and gay, • • • • • •	O 15	London	111
	Yet ev'n these heroes, mischievously gay, • • • • •	O 21	London	230
	Yet ev'n those heroes, mischievously gay, • • • • •	Y 59	London	V 230
	The needy traveller, serene and gay, • • • • • •	O 32	Vanity Wishes	37
	The needy traveller, secure and gay, • • • • • •	Y 93	Vanity Wishes	V 37
	In gay hostility, and barb'rous pride, • • • • •	O 42	Vanity Wishes	225
	But shun, rash youth, the gay alcove, • • • • • •	O 121	To Miss Playin	9
	The beauties of the gay brocade, • • • • • • •	O 122	Stella Mourn.	2
	Gay with the smile of bland equality; • • • • •	O 130	Tr. Rambler 12	6
	Greatness with ease, and gay severity. • • • • •	O 137	Tr Rambler 141	1
	"Then with luscious plenty gay • • • • • • •	O 186	Anacreon Ode 9	35
	Summon'd the singer blythe, and harper gay, • • •	O 192	Tr. Medea II	7
	Where mischief lurks in gay disguise, • • • • •	O 203	Tr. on Skating	3
	Dress'd in each Charm of gay Magnificence, • • • •	O 261	Irene	14
	Secure of total death, and careless of hereafter or gay •	Y 146	Irene	V 20
	Do gay Delusions, wand'ring o'er the Brain, • • • •	O 277	Irene	44
	And gay delusions wandring o'er the brain • • • •	O 356	Irene	V 11
	Sunk in his Pleasures, confident and gay, • • • • •	O 283	Irene	8
	I displaid—before her all the gay luscious scene... •	Y 158	Irene	V 8
	If thou art more than the gay Dream of Fancy, • • •	O 310	Irene	12
	Or gay felecity retire to desarts? • • • • • •	Y 191	Irene	V 21
	Or meanly fraudulent, or madly gay, • • • • •	O 316	Irene	24
	And thou impearl'd with dew appear more gay. • • • •	Y 3	On a Daffodill	12
GAYETY				
	The social gayety the improving converse • • • • •	Y 165	Irene	V 81
	borro<wd or a>ffected <gayety> • • • • •	Y 185	Irene	V 3
GAZ'D				
	The Sultan gaz'd, he wonder'd and he lov'd; • • • •	O 258	Irene	98
	I gaz'd, I trembled; but I could not speak: • • • •	O 282	Irene	65
	Then while he gaz'd upon his yielding Mistress, • • •	O 299	Irene	48
GAZE				
	With brisker air the silken courtiers gaze, • • • • •	O 17	London	164
	Behold the Monsters gaze with savage Rapture, • • • •	O 252	Irene	81
	Thou Thou chilld by sixty winter camps canst gaze on • • •	Y 129	Irene	V 5
	To gaze with longing Eyes upon To-morrow, • • • • •	O 283	Irene	24
	Gaze at their Height and tremble at their Danger: • • •	O 293	Irene	116
	Let my blest Eyes for ever gaze-- • • • • • •	O 294	Irene	4
	Nor think thy Cause neglected while I gaze, • • • •	O 297	Irene	20
GAZETTE'S				
	The senate's thanks, the gazette's pompous tale, • • •	O 39	Vanity Wishes	177
GAZETTEER				
	And dare to slumber o'er the Gazetteer; • • • • •	O 13	London	72
GAZING				
	Like thirsty Sailors gazing on the Clouds, • • • • •	O 282	Irene	5
GEM				
	Conceal the Gem; let female Arrogance • • • • • •	O 277	Irene	33
GEN'RAL				
	London! the needy villain's gen'ral home, • • • • •	O 14	London	93
	Fall in the gen'ral massacre of gold; • • • • • •	O 31	Vanity Wishes	22
	Amidst the gen'ral massacre of gold; • • • • • •	Y 92	Vanity Wishes	V 22
	Yet still one gen'ral cry the skies assails, • • • •	O 32	Vanity Wishes	45
	Yet still the gen'ral cry the skies assails, • • • •	O 32	Vanity Wishes	V 45
	The gen'ral fav'rite as the gen'ral friend: • • • •	O 44	Vanity Wishes	297
	The gen'ral fav'rite as the gen'ral friend: • • • •	O 44	Vanity Wishes	297
	The common fav'rite as the gen'ral friend: • • • •	Y 105	Vanity Wishes	V 297
	Their Cause was gen'ral, their Supports were strong, • •	O 52	Pro Drury-Lane	25
	Till nature call'd him to the gen'ral doom, • • •	O 118	Epitaph Hanmer	43
	This all-subduing hand, this gen'ral terror • • • •	Y 136	Irene	V 32
	Mix undistinguish'd with the gen'ral Roar. • • • •	O 280	Irene	24
	Strange! that this gen'ral Fraud from Day to Day • •	O 283	Irene	26
	And thus protected in the gen'ral Ruin, • • • • •	O 296	Irene	32
	This elemental Joy, this gen'ral Calm, • • • • •	O 314	Irene	8
GEN'ROUS				
	Fate never wounds more deep the gen'rous heart, • • •	O 18	London	168
	Yet should thy soul indulge the gen'rous heat, • • •	O 37	Vanity Wishes	143
	Yet should thy fate indulge the gen'rous heat, • • • •	Y 98	Vanity Wishes	V 143
	Whose gen'rous Zeal, unbought by flatt'ring Rhimes, • •	O 57	Prologue Comus	3
	Simon by gen'rous Zeal inspir'd, • • • • • •	O 79	Feast St Simon	37
	The gen'rous scorn of venal pow'r, • • • • • •	O 125	An Ode	31
	To You whose gen'rous Wishes rise • • • • • •	O 150	Tr Boet III.12	53
	Beats not the female Breast with gen'rous Passions, • •	O 278	Irene	57
	To noble Thought and gen'rous Emulation, • • • •	O 298	Irene	14
	That fiery Chief, renown'd for gen'rous Freedom, • • •	O 299	Irene	35
	That firy Chief, renown'd for gen'rous Freedom, • • •	O 299	Irene	V 35
	--The gen'rous mind contemns • • • • • • •	Y 177	Irene	V 109
	Let no weak Doubt the gen'rous Hand restrain, • • •	O 313	Irene	22
	Let no distrust the gen'rous Hand restrain • • • •	O 377	Irene	V 3
	"Why gen'rous warriour will you rashly run • • • •	Y 18	Tr. Iliad Bk 6	19
GENERAL				
	A Mortal born he met the general Doom, • • • • •	O 51	Pro Drury-Lane	15
	Surveys the general toil of human kind; • • • •	O 59	Pro Good Nat'd	2
	And spread the general Transport through Mankind. • • •	O 308	Irene	5
	Though Disappointment blast our general Scheme, • • •	O 317	Irene	44
GENERALLY				
	Maxims like these, if generally persued • • • • • •	O 352	Irene	V 2

GENEROUS

	PAGE	TITLE	LINE
A generous foe regards, with pitying eye,	O 61	Pro Word Wise	5
Nor give the generous pain, the worthless joy:	O 81	Lady Birthday	14
Faith from every generous mind:	O 176	Tr Metastasi I	4
"Now the generous bowl I sip	O 185	Anacreon Ode 9	31
Could Rome with generous ardour fire,	O 188	Epilogue	V 2
Each generous Sentiment is thine, Demetrius,	O 267	Irene	38
Nor has impartial Natures generous hand	O 356	Irene	V 20
From generous piety, or abject fear?	Y 189	Irene	V 18

GENIAL

That spread their Colours to the genial Beam,	O 298	Irene	20
Cleora's smiles a genial warmth dispense;	Y 4	On a Daffodill	18

GENIUS

Around his tomb let Art and Genius weep,	O 39	Vanity Wishes	173
His force of genius burn'd in early youth,	O 117	Epitaph Hanmer	5
If Genius warm thee, Reader, stay,	O 154	Epita. Hogarth	5
We oft (notwithstanding this boasted superiour genius	Y 148	Irene	V 49
And bid the master Genius rule the World.	O 309	Irene	42

GENNAH'S

And Gennah's happy <to> Gardens envy thine.	O 351	Irene	V 27

GENOA'S

When Genoa's faithless Sons forsook the Ramparts	O 351	Irene	V 5

GENTLE

Had Stella's gentle touches mov'd the Lyre,	O 97	Hickman Spinet	15
Thy gentle flows of guiltless joys	O 100	Ode Friendship	17
Attack my gentle lines.	O 127	To Lyce, Lady	20
I pray thee, gentle Renny dear,	O 158	Par Hermit III	V 1
Nor fear that I, my gentle maid,	O 159	Par Hermit III	5
Tell me, tell me, gentle Dove.	O 185	Anacreon Ode 9	6
With gentle Hand restrain'd the Streams of Life,	O 252	Irene	97
Which lately bless'd my gentle Government,	O 257	Irene	75
Too slow these gentle Constellations roll,	O 271	Irene	3
In soft Endearments, and in gentle Murmurs,	O 303	Irene	14

GENTLEMAN

... to a Gentleman	O 95	Sprig of Myrtl	T
Verses, written at the request of a Gentleman	O 95	Sprig of Myrtl	V T

GENTLENESS

We court thy Gentleness.	O 288	Irene	9

GENTLER

O'erbears each gentler Motion of the Mind.	O 280	Irene	21
And kindly grant an Ear to gentler Sounds:	O 285	Irene	2
They cultivate at ease the gentler arts in quiet	Y 177	Irene	V 117
Will teach a gentler Term.	O 321	Irene	54

GENTLY

Where Riv'lets gently purl along	O 72	Hor. Epode II	31
May storms howl gently o'er and learn to spare.	Y 3	On a Daffodill	8
May lambent zephyrs gently wave thy head,	Y 3	On a Daffodill	9

GENUINE

The present hour invites with genuine charms	O 375	Irene	V 7
I w<ould> have every smile g<enu>ine to<morrow no>	Y 185	Irene	V 3

GEORGE'S

Great George's acts let tuneful Cibber sing;	O 114	On C. Cibber	3

GET

And get a kick for awkward flattery.	O 16	London	131

GHASTLY

Their souls dismiss'd through many a ghastly wound,	O 74	Tr. Iliad Bk 6	18
--How chang'd alas!--Now ghastly Desolation	O 251	Irene	66

GHOST

She saw great Faustus lay the Ghost of Wit:	O 52	Pro Drury-Lane	36
who was to personate the Ghost of Hermione	O 83	Epi Dist Moth.	T

GHOSTS

The Shepherds oft' see little ghosts glide by	O 77	Tr Add. Battle	47
Receive th' unhappy ghosts of scornful maids.	O 83	Epi Dist Moth.	13
Where e'er they fly their lovers ghosts pursue,	O 84	Epi Dist Moth.	36
In Myrtle shades despairing ghosts complain;	O 95	Sprig of Myrtl	8
And croud the fattend fields, the ghosts that wander	Y 120	Irene	V 31
Ye venerable ghosts of noble patriots	Y 181	Irene	V 53

GIANT

Tore unresisted from the Giant Hand	O 312	Irene	10

GIBBET

Or like a gibbet better than a wheel;	O 15	London	108

GIBE

Dart the quick taunt, and edge the piercing gibe?	O 33	Vanity Wishes	62
And unexhausted laughter, and edge the piercing gibe	Y 94	Vanity Wishes	V 62

GIDDY

From giddy Mahomet's unskilful Hand.	O 256	Irene	46
And all the giddy rage of desperation	Y 142	Irene	V 39

GIFT

Each gift of nature, and each grace of art,	O 31	Vanity Wishes	16
Each gift of nature, and each charm of art,	Y 92	Vanity Wishes	V 16
What hopes, what terrors does thy gift create,	O 95	Sprig of Myrtl	1
What Fears, what terrors does this gift create,	O 95	Sprig of Myrtl	V 1
O! then the meaning of thy gift impart,	O 95	Sprig of Myrtl	11
Friendship! peculiar Gift of heav'n,	O 99	Ode Friendship	V 1
And of his every gift usurp the merit;	O 176	Tr Metastas II	11
And yet of every gift usurp the merit;	O 176	Tr Metastas II	V 11
Completes the Gift of Freedom and of Life.	O 285	Irene	16
Glory, the casual Gift of thoughtless Crouds!	O 305	Irene	31
Do thou repay the Gift,	O 313	Irene	18

GIFTS

In vain their gifts the bounteous seasons pour,	O 43	Vanity Wishes	261

GIFTS   (CONTINUED)

	PAGE	TITLE		LINE
Her gifts despis'd, corruption blush'd and fled,	O 118	Epitaph Hanmer		33
Not all the gifts of Fate combin'd	O 144	Tr Boeth. II.2		7
In vain the shining Gifts are sent,	O 144	Tr Boeth. II.2		13
Exhausted all her nobler Gifts on you;	O 278	Irene		54

GILD

Which gild a lover's lays,	O 126	To Lyce, Lady		6

GIRL'S

A girl's, inflames me with desire;	Y 12	Tr Hor Epode 9		38

GIV'N

To such, a groaning nation's spoils are giv'n,	O 13	London		65
To such, the Plunder of a Land is giv'n,	O 13	London	V	65
And giv'n to mirth, the Cranes no longer fear,	O 77	Tr Add. Battle		50
To Men and Angels only giv'n,	O 99	Ode Friendship		3
By flatt'ring poets giv'n;	O 126	To Lyce, Lady		2

GIVE

Give to St. David one true Briton more.	O 9	London		8
Some secret cell, ye pow'rs, indulgent give.	O 11	London		49
Did rival monarchs give the fatal wound?	O 41	Vanity Wishes		217
The Drama's Laws the Drama's Patrons give,	O 53	Pro Drury-Lane		53
Nor give the generous pain, the worthless joy:	O 81	Lady Birthday		14
Ye blooming train, who give despair or joy,	O 83	Epi Dist Moth.		1
That thou wilt give to me,	O 158	Par Hermit III		2
Rough Winter's blasts to Spring give way,	O 231	Tr Horace IV.7		9
These all are Trifles, to what we can give.	O 247	Irene Epilogue		20
And give the weary passenger refreshment.	Y 130	Irene	V	12D
Nor give him Leisure for another Crime.	O 271	Irene		32
To hear my Vows and give Mankind a Queen?	O 276	Irene		2
To hear my suit and give a Queen to Turkey?	O 372	Irene	V	7
To Want give Affluence? and to Slav'ry Freedom?	O 277	Irene		46
Give Wealth to Poverty to Slavery Freedom	O 356	Irene	V	13
And give the Tortures of Suspense a Period?	O 282	Irene		2
Give me, before th' approaching Hour of Fate,	O 285	Irene		5
When eer the tumult of unestablish'd Conquest	O 357	Irene	V	6
shall give the Tyrant leisure--	O 357	Irene	V	7
And give the short remnant of my life to prayer,	O 348	Irene	V	14
They give the nations laws, and view serene	Y 167	Irene	V	117
But all give way to Rapture and Demetrius.	O 295	Irene		20
Concur'd to give me to Aspasia's Arms,	O 296	Irene		36
Heav'n makes not mine to give.	O 307	Irene		16
Willing to delay you here they give you on earth the	Y 184	Irene	V	10
Yet ere we give our loosen'd Thoughts to Rapture,	O 309	Irene		18
Proceed, and give a loose to Love and Treason.	O 316	Irene		20
Be thine, that Wealth can give, or Guilt receive.	O 322	Irene		58

GIVEN

to whom a Lady had given a Sprig of Myrtle	O 95	Sprig of Myrtl	V	T
To W<ortley> and to Angels given	O 99	Ode Friendship	V	3

GIVES

Secure whate'er he gives, he gives the best.	O 48	Vanity Wishes		356
Secure whate'er he gives, he gives the best.	O 48	Vanity Wishes		356
Gives all the harmony of life;	O 121	To Miss Playin		32
Nature gives at Thirtyfive;	O 178	Thrale 35 Year		10
And gives a thousand fatal Questions Birth;	O 258	Irene		84
Indulgent nature gives some transient pleasures	Y 148	Irene	V	43C
That Reason gives her Scepter to his Hand,	O 281	Irene		40
Where Florence gives the banish'd arts protection	O 351	Irene	V	3

GIVING

To Miss <Carpenter> On her giving the Author	O 119	To Miss Purse		T

GLAD

Till that glad night when all that hate may hiss.	O 60	Pro Good Nat'd		20
Glad to be hid, and proud to be forgot.	O 82	Young Author		30
That glad us with vicarious light;	O 144	Tr Boeth. II.2		4

GLADE

Or dare to murmur in the flow'ry Glade;	O 111	To Posterity		22

GLADES

No fragrant bowers, no delightful glades,	O 83	Epi Dist Moth.		12
Pope's hallow'd glades, and never tiring views,	O 106	Eliza plucking		3

GLADNESS

My Zeal marks Gladness dawning on thy Cheek,	O 286	Irene		2
Those gloomy walks where Gladness never smiles	Y 165	Irene	V	81
Gladness, fair child, of innocence and freedom.	Y 165	Irene	V	81

GLADS

And purple nectar glads the festive hour,	O 193	Tr. Medea II		18
Unfading Verdure glads the roving Eye,	O 315	Irene		34

GLANCE

Renew'd at ev'ry glance on humankind;	O 33	Vanity Wishes		70
Mark the keen glance, and watch the sign to hate.	O 34	Vanity Wishes		110
To point each glance, and force it to the heart!	O 81	Lady Birthday		8
Swells the fair Breast or animates the Glance,	O 262	Irene		14
Surveys your Plays with inattentive Glance,	O 276	Irene		22
Surveys your triflings with a careless glance	O 355	Irene	V	11
Surveys your actions with a careless glance	Y 146	Irene	V	22
And pow'rful Glance, 'tis granted, are our own;	O 277	Irene		52
New Force, new Courage, from each Glance I gain,	O 297	Irene		21
Not granted--nor deny'd--a softend glance	Y 179	Irene	V	32
Shall play the glance, and with attentive watch	Y 195	Irene	V	4

GLANCES

To point the glances of her eye,	O 121	To Miss Playin		16
Shall dart their am'rous Glances at the Fair,	O 304	Irene		35

```
                                                       PAGE    TITLE            LINE
GLARE
   Why all this Glare of splendid Eloquence,    . . . . . .   O 276  Irene            11
   And bad imperial splendour glare (blaze) before her  . .   Y 158  Irene        V  10
   Amidst the Glare of Courts, the Shouts of Armies,  . . .   O 293  Irene           131
   Or glare on Cali with malignant Beams.  . . . . . .        O 304  Irene            36
GLASS
   Shewn in the faithful glass of ridicule;  . . . . . .      O  81  Lady Birthday     16
GLASSY
   Glassy water, glassy water,  . . . . . . . . . . .         O 159  Tr. Rio Verde      1
   Glassy water, glassy water,  . . . . . . . . . . .         O 159  Tr. Rio Verde      1
GLEAM
   At best, a fleeting gleam, or empty sound.  . . . . .      O  62  Pro Word Wise     20
   At last, a fleeting gleam, or empty sound.  . . . . .      O  62  Pro Word Wise  V  20
   With bright, but oft destructive gleam,  . . . . . .       O 100  Ode Friendship     9
   Yet Greece enjoys no Gleam of transient Hope,  . . .       O 249  Irene             11
GLEAMS
   Shrinks at th' o'erpow'ring Gleams of regal State,  . .    O 292  Irene            100
   The Gleams of Reason, and the Clouds of Passion,  . .      O 321  Irene             44
GLEAN
   When statutes glean the refuse of the sword,  . . . .      O  31  Vanity Wishes     31
GLEANS
   She gleans the harvest, and she stores the grain.  . .     O 151  The Ant            8
GLEBE
   Or boasts a happier glebe, is Yours already,  . . . .      O 366  Irene          V  13
GLIDE
   The Shepherds oft' see little ghosts glide by  . . . .     O  77  Tr Add. Battle    47
   With nimble glide the skaiters play;  . . . . . .          O 203  Tr. on Skating V   2
   Fade <glide> from the sight, and Vanish into  . . . .      O 358  Irene          V  11
      nothing.
   Glide through Irene to the Sultan's Ear.  . . . . . .      O 267  Irene              3
GLIDED
   Unfelt, uncounted, glided by;  . . . . . . . . .           O 202  Death Dr Levet    30
GLIDES
   And glides in modest Innocence away;  . . . . . . .        O  44  Vanity Wishes    294
GLIMM'RINGS
   Now led astray by hopes fallacious glimm'rings  . . .      Y 148  Irene          V 43A
GLIMPSE
   A doubtful Glimpse of our approaching Friends;  . . .      O 268  Irene             37
GLITT'RING
   Turn from the glitt'ring bribe thy scornful eye,  . . .    O  14  London            87
   The golden canopy, the glitt'ring plate,  . . . . .        O  35  Vanity Wishes    114
   The glitt'ring eminence exempt from foes;  . . . . .       O  38  Vanity Wishes    166
   The glitt'ring eminence exempt from woes;  . . . . .       O  38  Vanity Wishes  V 166
   The glitt'ring vagrants shall restrain;  . . . . . .       O 120  To Miss Purse     10
   Ye glitt'ring Train! whom Lace and Velvet bless,  . .      O 246  Irene Prologue     1
   Threw back the glitt'ring Bribe.  . . . . . . .            O 258  Irene            102
   The glitt'ring Vanities of empty Greatness,  . . . .       O 265  Irene              6
   And set the glitt'ring Fallacy to view.  . . . . .         O 293  Irene            128
   Those glitt'ring Dew-drops of a vernal Morn,  . . . .      O 298  Irene             19
   Unmov'd I saw the glitt'ring Trifles perish,  . . . .      O 302  Irene            108
GLITTER
   Nor wish'd to glitter at his country's cost;  . . . .      O 118  Epitaph Hanmer    28
   The tinsel glitter, and the specious mein,  . . . . .      O 139  Tr Rambler 168     1
GLITTERING
   And then leaves the glittering reptile, reasoning  . . .   Y 146  Irene          V  23
      insect
   Urge me not on to glittering Guilt, nor pour  . . . .      O 288  Irene              5
GLITTRING
   If yet these glittring Robes these sudden Splendors  . .   O 366  Irene          V  17
   If Dismiss this glittring train these sudden  . . . .      O 366  Irene          V  17
      Splendors
   The sparkling ornaments, the glittring dress (the change   Y 164  Irene          V  71
      of dress
   As glittring dewdrops quiver to the sun  . . . . . .       Y 173  Irene          V  19
GLOBE
   And o'er the globe extend your reign,  . . . . . . .       O 189  Epilogue           7
   Smile on my Wishes, and command the Globe.  . . . .        O 279  Irene             81
   With half the grov'ling Slaves that load the Globe.  . .   O 332  Irene             36
GLOOM
   With horrid gloom the frowning skies:  . . . . . . .       O  66  Hor I Ode xxii    20
   With horrid Gloom the frowning Skies:  . . . . . . .       O  67  To A. Fuscus      20
   With bright, but oft destructive gloom,  . . . . . .       O 100  Ode Friendship V   9
   The slave of sunshine and of gloom.  . . . . . . .         O 124  Winter's Walk     16
   I see the Gloom that low'rs upon thy Brow,  . . . . .      O 271  Irene              1
   Now lost amidst the gloom of disappointment  . . . .       Y 148  Irene          V 43B
      stagnant soul.  The gloom of idleness.
   Hide me with Murd'rers in the Dungeon's Gloom,  . . . .    Y 165  Irene          V  82
GLOOM-ENAMOUR'D                                               O 328  Irene             34
   Where gloom-enamour'd Mischief dreads the Sun,  . . . .    O 192  Tr. Medea II      15
   Where gloom-enamour'd Mischief loves to dwell,  . . . .    O 192  Tr. Medea II   V  15
GLOOMS
   And weaves her bending boughs in pleasing glooms;  . . .   O  84  Epi Dist Moth.    15
GLOOMY
   For you, ye fair, I quit the gloomy plains,  . . . . .     O  83  Epi Dist Moth.    10
   Nor call'd them to the gloomy cells  . . . . . . .         O 191  Tr. Medea I        9
   Times gloomy backward with judicious eyes;  . . . . .      O 192  Tr. Medea II       2
   And (terror) horrour shudders in their gloomy caverns      Y 136  Irene          V 31A
   And wish their gloomy Caverns more obscure.  . . . .       O 268  Irene             32
   The gloomy Resolution, horrid Greatness,  . . . . .        O 275  Irene             82
   Those gloomy walks where Gladness never smiles  . . . .    Y 165  Irene             81
   That gloomy Slumber of the stagnant Soul;  . . . . .       O 292  Irene          V  82
```

```
GLOOMY        (CONTINUED)                          PAGE   TITLE            LINE
    To wander pensive in those gloomy walks  . . . . .   Y 165  Irene         V  85
    With gloomy State and agonizing Pomp. . . . . . . .   O 294  Irene            135
    Amidst his gloomy Guards and fiery Vassals  . . . .   O 372  Irene         V  19
    horrid joy--gloomy resolution--his air now fearful now  .  Y 187  Irene    V   7
        resolv'd.
    The Sultan comes, still gloomy, still enrag'd. . . . .   O 330  Irene           26
    From Hector's breast each gloomy trouble flies  . . .   Y  18  Tr. Iliad Bk 6   15
    Shall sink alike into the gloomy grave. . . . . . .   Y  21  Tr. Iliad Bk 6  120
GLORIES
    And call Britannia's glories back to view;  . . . .   O  10  London           26
    Their grandsires glories debt; . . . . . . . . .   Y 100  Vanity Wishes  V 188
    Thy lambent glories only beam  . . . . . . . . .   O 100  Ode Friendship    11
    Thy milder glories only beam . . . . . . . . . .   Y  71  Ode Friendship V  11
    Illustrious age! how bright thy glories shone,  . . .   O 118  Epitaph Hanmer   21
    And own all glories of the mine outdone,  . . . . .   O 141  Tr Rambler 199    6
    Paints future Joys, and points to distant Glories. . .   O 261  Irene           17
    Surveys the glories of the splendid pile  . . . . .   Y 131  Irene         V 36A
    Deface Erase the glories of my native  . . . . . .   Y 177  Irene         V 107
        country
    All fading toys, and transitory glories  . . . . .   Y 177  Irene         V 110
    Whose early buds unusual glories wear,  . . . . . .   Y   3  On a Daffodill     3
GLORIOUS
    But can thy Friend sustain the glorious Cause, . . . .   O 255  Irene            8
    And his more glorious acts eclipse his father's fame. .   Y  20  Tr. Iliad Bk 6  104
GLORY
    Hide, blushing Glory, hide Pultowa's day: . . . . .   O  41  Vanity Wishes    210
    Tho' Wealth, and Pow'r, and Glory they receive, . . .   O 247  Irene Epilogue   19
    Remember Freedom, Glory, Greece, and Love. . . . . .   O 260  Irene           146
    Think on Revenge and Glory Greece and Love  . . . .   O 361  Irene         V   5
    The Thirst of Empire, and the Love of Glory?  . . . .   O 278  Irene           58
    Shall soar triumphant on the Wings of Glory,  . . . .   O 305  Irene           26
    Can brave Leontius be the Slave of Glory?  . . . . .   O 305  Irene           30
    Glory, the casual Gift of thoughtless Crouds! . . . .   O 305  Irene           31
    Glory, the Bribe of avaricious Virtue!  . . . . . .   O 305  Irene           32
GLORY'S
    Inspir'd by us, they Glory's Heights ascend; . . . .   O 247  Irene Epilogue   17
GLOSSY
    They prune the Wing, and spread the glossy Plumes, . .   O 277  Irene           36
    They prune the wing and spread the glossy tail . . .   O 355  Irene         V  23
GLOW
    Oh, must their ardours cease to glow  . . . . . . .   O 100  Ode Friendship   25
    Oh may this Flame neer cease to glow  . . . . . . .   O 100  Ode Friendship V  25
    Nor shall thine ardours cease to glow  . . . . . .   O 100  Ode Friendship V  25
    O! Shall thy flames then cease to glow  . . . . . .   O 100  Ode Friendship V  25
    At Sight of female Charms will glow no more.  . . . .   O 263  Irene            6
    No more shall glow with Friendship's hallow'd Ardour: .   O 289  Irene           16
    I then (my cheeks still glow with shame) was grown . .   Y  11  Tr Hor Epode 9   11
GLOW'D
    In ev'ry act refulgent virtue glow'd. . . . . . . .   O 118  Epitaph Hanmer    16
GLOWING
    When strong devotion fills thy glowing Breast, . . . .   O  48  Vanity Wishes  V 358
    His glowing Wishes, and his jealous Pangs. . . . . .   O 280  Irene            28
GLOWS
    With fatal heat impetuous courage glows, . . . . . .   O  31  Vanity Wishes    17
    An envious Breast with certain Mischief glows, . . . .   O  46  Vanity Wishes  V330A
    An rivals breast with certain mischief glows  . . . .   Y 107  Vanity Wishes  V330A
    With virtue's sacred ardour glows, . . . . . . . .   O  65  Hor I Ode xxii    2
    With Virtue's sacred Ardour glows, . . . . . . . .   O  66  To A. Fuscus      2
    My bosom glows with fiercer fire;  . . . . . . . .   Y  10  Tr Hor Epode 9    2
GLUT
    Fresh foes descending glut their swords with blood. . .   Y  23  Tr Add. Battle   21
GLUTTED
    No more the glutted Sabre thirsts for Blood,  . . . .   O 249  Irene            9
    To court the sword and tempt the glutted rack . . . .   Y 196  Irene         V 18D
GLUTTON
    Shall glutton on the industrious Peasants Spoil, . . .   O 110  To Posterity     13
GNASHES
    And Anguish gnashes on the fatal Wheel.  . . . . . .   O 266  Irene            16
GO    SEE GOE
    And bid him go to hell, to hell he goes. . . . . . .   O  15  London           116
    "Go to the Ant thou Sluggard".  . . . . . . . . .   O 151  The Ant       V   T
    "This is all;--be quick and go,  . . . . . . . . .   O 186  Anacreon Ode 9    41
    Thus lightly touch and quickly go. . . . . . . . .   O 203  Tr. on Skating     4
        Go see him die;  . . . . . . . . . . . . .   O 263  Irene            25
    Haste Go Mustapha go to celebrate the day  . . . .   Y 129  Irene         V  25
    Haste Go Mustapha go to celebrate the day  . . . .   Y 129  Irene         V  25
    Go, seize him, load him with reproachful Chains; . . .   O 273  Irene            34
    Now let him go, pursu'd by silent Wrath, . . . . . .   O 274  Irene            47
    I go to wait thy Call; this kind Consent  . . . . .   O 285  Irene            15
    Go, languish on in dull Obscurity; . . . . . . . .   O 292  Irene            98
    Then--O my Fair, I cannot bid thee go; . . . . . . .   O 297  Irene         V  15
    Go then, and with united Eloquence . . . . . . . .   O 306  Irene            57
    Abdalla, Cali, go--proclaim my Purpose.  . . . . . .   O 309  Irene            43
    Bound o'er the sparkling Waves.  Go, happy Bark, . . .   O 322  Irene            5
    Dance o'er the Sparkling Waves--Go happy Bark . . . .   O 364  Irene         V  30
    Go Happy Bark, thy sacred Freight secures thee . . . .   O 364  Irene         V  24
    I go, lest Vengeance urge my Hand to Blood, . . . . .   O 324  Irene            23
    Go, blustring Slave.--He has not heard of Murza. . . .   O 324  Irene            25
    But being counsell'd to go home  . . . . . . . . .   Y  11  Tr Hor Epode 9   31
```

```
                                                             PAGE    TITLE              LINE
GOATS
     Here I, though faint myself, must drive my goats,  . . .   O  64  Virgil Past.I         17
GOD
     Till rude resistance lops the spreading god;      . . . .  O  42  Vanity Wishes       234
     For I shall never think him less than God;        . . . . . O  64  Virgil Past.I         8
     Their master and their God.    . . . . . . . . .          O  79  Feast St Simon       18
     From thee, great God, we spring, to thee we tend,  . . .  O 130  Tr. Rambler 7         7
     And hail unanimous their conqu'ring God.    . . . . . .   O 287  Irene                 6
     By Hector call'd Scamandrius from the god    . . . . .    Y  18  Tr. Iliad Bk 6       11
GODDESS
     "And let the goddess trust her eyes."    . . . . . . .    O 122  Stella Mourn.         6
     To shine the Graces of applauding Nations,   . . . . .    O 278  Irene                68
     Direct O Goddess, my advent'rous song;    . . . . . .     Y  22  Tr Add. Battle        3
GODLIKE
     She ceas'd; then godlike Hector answer'd kind,--   . . .  O  74  Tr. Iliad Bk 6        1
     And crowds of godlike Romans sunk to hell.    . . . . .   O  77  Festina Lente        16
     Idomeneus, the godlike Telamon    . . . . . . . . . .     Y  19  Tr. Iliad Bk 6       55
     How great Achilles godlike Hector slew?    . . . . . .    Y  22  Tr Add. Battle       11
     Their godlike hero strugling in the skies.    . . . . .   Y  26  Tr Add. Battle      129
GODS
     Quaff Nectar with th' immortal Gods.    . . . . . . .     O  70  Hor.II Ode XX         8
     Blest as th' immortal Gods is he    . . . . . . . . .     O  71  Hor. Epode II         1
     Then to the Gods, on solemn days,    . . . . . . . .      O  73  Hor. Epode II        63
     To ev'ry empire bounds the Gods ordain    . . . . . .     O  76  Tr Add. Battle       35
     Nor Gods his Heroes, nor his Lovers Fools:    . . . . .   O 246  Irene Prologue       18
     Accus'd the Gods and curs'd each luckless star.   . . .   Y   6  Virgil Daphnis       16
     Now, at thy fall incens'd, the rural Gods    . . . . .    Y   6  Virgil Daphnis       20
     Thyrsis while sings shall the gods    . . . . . . . .     Y   7  Virgil Daphnis     V 49
     "Immortal Gods! and thou allmighty Jove    . . . . . .    Y  20  Tr. Iliad Bk 6       99
GOE
     Then--O my Fair, I cannot bid thee goe;    . . . . . .    O 297  Irene                15
GOES
     And bid him go to hell, to hell he goes.    . . . . .     O  15  London              116
     Still to his int'rest true, where'er he goes,   . . . .   O  16  London              125
     The fickle crowd with fortune comes and goes;   . . . .   O 138  Tr Rambler 153        1
GOLD
     What check restrain your thirst of pow'r and gold?   . .  O  13  London               62
     Nor sell for gold, what gold could never buy,   . . . .   O  14  London               88
     Nor sell for gold, what gold could never buy,   . . . .   O  14  London               88
     But here more slow, where all are slaves to gold,  . . .  O  18  London              178
     Fall in the gen'ral massacre of gold;    . . . . . . .    O  31  Vanity Wishes        22
     Amidst the gen'ral massacre of gold;    . . . . . . .     Y  92  Vanity Wishes      V 22
     For gold his sword the hireling ruffian draws,   . . . .  O  31  Vanity Wishes        25
     For gold the hireling judge distorts the laws;   . . . .  O  31  Vanity Wishes        26
     To better features yields the frame of gold;   . . . .    O  34  Vanity Wishes        86
     Unlocks his gold, and counts it till he dies.   . . . .   O  44  Vanity Wishes       290
     Or trace his Form o'er circulating Gold,    . . . . .     O  58  Prologue Comus       24
     He feels no want of ill-persuading gold;    . . . . .     O  60  Pro Good Nat'd       28
     ... a Gold and Silk net-work Purse of her own weaving     O 119  To Miss Purse         T
     Though gold and silk their charms unite,    . . . . .     O 119  To Miss Purse         1
     The Lust of Gold succeeds the Rage of Conquest,  . . .    O 249  Irene                13
     The Lust of Gold, unfeeling and remorseless!   . . . .    O 249  Irene                14
     Extended Empire, like expanded Gold,    . . . . . . :     O 265  Irene                37
     With all the allurements of persuasive   . . . . . .      Y 142  Irene              V 38
          wealth--gold
     Amidst the Blaze of Jewels and of Gold,    . . . . . .    O 276  Irene                 9
     With Purple varied and bedrop'd with Gold,    . . . . .   O 277  Irene                35
     And gold and flattery--thoughtless mirth--hurry   . . .   Y 164  Irene              V 72
     With cedar vaulted and inlayd with gold    . . . . . .    Y 177  Irene             V111F
     Joys ill exchang'd for Gold, and Pride, and Empire.  . .  O 313  Irene                10
     Against th' omnipotence of gold    . . . . . . . . .      Y  11  Tr Hor Epode 9       22
     Soon as with gold appeas'd, he set her free   . . . . .   Y  19  Tr. Iliad Bk 6       40
GOLDEN
     Orgilio sees the golden pile aspire,    . . . . . . .     O  19  London              208
     Sejano sees the golden pile aspire,    . . . . . . .      Y  58  London            V 208
     And shun the shining train, and golden coach.   . . . .   O  21  London              235
     A single jail, in Alfred's golden reign,    . . . . .     O  22  London              248
     The golden canopy, the glitt'ring plate,    . . . . .     O  35  Vanity Wishes       114
     This day the powder'd curls and golden coat,   . . . .    O  60  Pro Good Nat'd       21
     Or when with golden Apples crown'd    . . . . . . . .     O  72  Hor. Epode II        23
     In blissful dreams he digs the golden mine,   . . . . .   O  82  Young Author       V 6C
     The blessings of a golden Show'r,    . . . . . . . .      O 144  Tr Boeth. II.2        6
     The groaning Greeks break up their golden Caverns  . .    O 249  Irene                17
     And seat him in the Pleiad's golden Chariots,   . . . .   O 274  Irene                63
     Again should golden Splendour grace her Cities,  . . .    O 290  Irene                53
     Dispells the darkness with his golden ray    . . . . .    Y  23  Tr Add. Battle       23
GONE
     Be gone ye blockheads, Heraclitus cries,    . . . . .     O 141  Tr Rambler 208        1
     For his lovely Consort gone,    . . . . . . . . . .       O 148  Tr Boet III.12        6
     For his lovely Consort gone,    . . . . . . . . . .       O 148  Tr Boet III.12     V 8
     He 's gone--Here rest, my Soul, thy fainting Wing,   . .  O 287  Irene                 1
     When I am gone remember, O! remember,    . . . . . .      O 294  Irene                 7
GOOD
     Shuns fancied ills, or chases airy good;    . . . . .     O  31  Vanity Wishes        10
     Still raise for good the supplicating voice,   . . . .    O  47  Vanity Wishes       351
     Prologue to "The Good Natur'd Man"    . . . . . . . .     O  59  Pro Good Nat'd        T
     My Lyce makes as good a sky,    . . . . . . . . . .       O 127  To Lyce, Lady        23
     Delusive hope still points to distant good,   . . . .     O 133  Tr. Rambler 67        2
     To good that mocks approach.    . . . . . . . . . .       O 133  Tr. Rambler 67        3
     The transparent Fount of Good;    . . . . . . . . .       O 147  Tr Boet III.12        2
     Think on that Providence that guards the Good.   . . .    O 252  Irene                89
```

138

		PAGE	TITLE	LINE
GOOD	(CONTINUED)			
As those that bless the Mansions of the Good.		O 262	Irene	12
When inconsistent with a greater Good, ...		O 290	Irene	32
Capricious Man! to Good and Ill inconstant, ...		O 300	Irene	76
GOODNESS				
Celestial Goodness!		O 258	Irene	102
Struck with the Wonder of a Statesman's Goodness, . . .		O 274	Irene	45
fasting, pennan<ce> and works of goodness		O 348	Irene	V 15
Retire, my Fair, that Pow'r that smiles on Goodness . .		O 303	Irene	20
GOODS				
These goods for man the laws of heav'n ordain, ...		O 48	Vanity Wishes	365
These goods he grants, who grants the pow'r to gain; . .		O 48	Vanity Wishes	366
GORE				
Apulia's spacious wilds with gore;		O 66	Hor I Ode xxii	14
Apulia's spacious Wilds with Gore;		O 67	To A. Fuscus	14
The haughty Persian in thy gore		O 80	Feast St Simon	53
Death in his look, and hands imbru'd in gore		Y 23	Tr Add. Battle	47
GORGE				
To tire the burthen'd rack and gorge destruction . . .		Y 196	Irene	V 18C
GOTHIC				
"On Moscow's walls till Gothic standards fly, ...		O 40	Vanity Wishes	203
GOTTEN SEE ILL-GOTTEN				
GOVERN				
Commence your lords, and govern or betray.		O 17	London	157
GOVERNMENT				
A feeble Government, eluded Laws, ...		O 250	Irene	37
Which lately bless'd my gentle Government, ...		O 257	Irene	75
Deny'd the Government of Servia's Province.		O 311	Irene	10
GOVERNOUR				
You are like the sun the governour of the world . . .		Y 132	Irene	V 40
GOWN				
Burns from the strong contagion of the gown;		O 36	Vanity Wishes	138
Caught from the strong contagion of the gown;		O 36	Vanity Wishes	V 138
Spreads from the strong contagion of the gown;		O 36	Vanity Wishes	V 138
Wear the gown, and wear the hat, ...		O 194	On Thrale Hat	1
GRAC'D				
Thus grac'd with humble Virtue's native Charms		O 58	Prologue Comus	33
"Grac'd with all that charms the heart, ...		O 185	Anacreon Ode 9	9
And be the stone with this inscription grac'd:		Y 7	Virgil Daphnis	29
His shining helm with nodding horse hair grac'd. . . .		Y 21	Tr. Iliad Bk 6	125
GRACE				
The rustick grandeur, or the surly grace, ...		O 15	London	102
The rustick grandeur, and the manly grace, ...		Y 53	London	V 102
Each gift of nature, and each grace of art, ...		O 31	Vanity Wishes	16
Her voice and Smiles my Song shall grace.		O 67	To A. Fuscus	24
Nor grace with fading flours my Herse, ...		O 70	Hor.II Ode XX	22
Those Saints my numbers grace		O 78	Feast St Simon	9
With pity soften every awful grace, ...		O 84	Epi Dist Moth.	44
Adorn Philander's head, or grace his tomb.		O 95	Sprig of Myrtl	14
Thou seem'st at once, bright nymph, a Muse and Grace. .		O 107	Lady F Assizes	6
Each grace of form, each ornament of state, ...		O 141	Tr Rambler 199	7
That traced th' essential form of Grace, ...		O 154	Epita. Hogarth	7
That wav'd th' essential form of Grace, ...		O 154	Epita. Hogarth	V 2
Who drew th' essential Form of Grace;		O 155	Epita. Hogarth	V 2
Her statue would have breath'd an added grace, ...		O 189	Seeing Montagu	4
The spritely Nymph and naked Grace		O 231	Tr Horace IV.7	5
That Smile resistless and attractive Grace		O 355	Irene	V 16
Too high, bright Maid, thou rat'st exterior Grace; . .		O 277	Irene	30
Again should golden Splendour grace her Cities, . . .		O 290	Irene	53
To grace the Triumph of victorious Virtue;		O 322	Irene	10
Or boy, whose snowy neck the flowing ringlets grace. . .		Y 12	Tr Hor Epode 9	42
GRACEFUL				
May powerful nature join with graceful art, ...		Y 36	Lady Birthday	V 7
Each Realm where Beauty turns the graceful Shape, . . .		O 262	Irene	13
With all the graceful Pride of Greatness heighten'd, . .		O 276	Irene	8
GRACES				
In ev'ry face a thousand graces shine, ...		O 16	London	127
Was but to chuse the Graces of the Day;		O 278	Irene	63
GRACIOUS				
No social care the gracious lord disdains;		O 130	Tr. Rambler 12	7
Fair plenty, gracious Queen, shou'd pour		O 144	Tr Boeth. II.2	5
Receive her, and protect her, gracious Heav'n!		O 297	Irene	16
GRADATIONS				
No cold gradations of decay, ...		O 202	Death Dr Levet	34
GRAIN				
She gleans the harvest, and she stores the grain. . . .		O 151	The Ant	8
She crops the harvest, and she stores the grain. . . .		O 151	The Ant	V 8
The banefull weeds spring up, and choak the grain. . .		Y 7	Virgil Daphnis	23
GRAINS				
Though countless as the Grains of Sand		O 144	Tr Boeth. II.2	1
GRANDEUR				
The rustick grandeur, or the surly grace, ...		O 15	London	102
The rustick grandeur, and the manly grace, ...		Y 53	London	V 102
And gain and grandeur load the tainted gales;		O 32	Vanity Wishes	46
To rural grandeur, and domestick worth;		O 118	Epitaph Hanmer	38
The silent grandeur of retreat.		O 125	An Ode	32
From wealth and grandeur easy to descend, ...		O 130	Tr. Rambler 12	3
Alluring Grandeur courts her to his Arms, ...		O 261	Irene	15
Of Grandeur and Tranquillity combin'd.		O 292	Irene	89
From splendid wretchedness and guilty scepters (grandeur)		Y 166	Irene	V 93
Wealth, and Command, and Grandeur shall be thine . . .		O 306	Irene	6

139

	PAGE	TITLE	LINE
GRANDSIRE			
Her Grandsire leaves her in Britannia's Arms, ...	O 58	Prologue Comus	34
GRANDSIRE'S			
Lavish of your Grandsire's guineas, ...	O 196	Song Congratu.	11
Lavish of thy Grandsire's guineas, ...	O 196	Song Congratu.	V 11
GRANDSIRES			
And mortgag'd states their grandsires wreaths regret, .	O 39	Vanity Wishes	187
Their grandsires glories debt;	Y 100	Vanity Wishes	V 188
GRANDSON			
Nor Peleus, grandson of the sky, ...	O 136	Tr Rambler 128	3
GRANT			
Grant me, kind heaven, to find some happier place, . .	O 11	London	43
But grant, the virtues of a temp'rate prime	O 44	Vanity Wishes	291
That grant his Prayers, and hear his cries.	O 72	Hor. Epode II	V 28
As not to grant me this, can Milton find?	O 137	Tr Rambler 140	2
I grant the charge; forgive the fault confess'd. . . .	O 139	Tr Rambler 170	1
"But the liberal grant in vain	O 185	Anacreon Ode 9	21
Trembling to grant, nor daring to refuse, ...	O 260	Irene	126
And kindly grant an Ear to gentler Sounds:	O 285	Irene	2
What I can grant, you cannot ask in vain--	O 285	Irene	14
'Tis yours to grant, or to refuse him entrance	Y 168	Irene	V 3
O grant thy sacred Influence, pow'rful Virtue!	O 313	Irene	5
Grant me one Hour, O grant me but a Moment, ...	O 328	Irene	45
Grant me one Hour, O grant me but a Moment, ...	O 328	Irene	45
The Prayer I cannot grant--I dare not hear.	O 328	Irene	48
Grant him like me to guard the walls of Troy.	Y 20	Tr. Iliad Bk 6	102
GRANTED			
That Wealth, which granted to their weeping Prince, . .	O 250	Irene	22
Which granted, hides my Purpose from the World, . . .	O 258	Irene	88
And pow'rful Glance, 'tis granted, are our own; . . .	O 277	Irene	52
And granted all his wishes	Y 179	Irene	V 31
Not granted--nor deny'd--a softend glance	Y 179	Irene	V 32
GRANTS			
These goods he grants, who grants the pow'r to gain; . .	O 48	Vanity Wishes	366
These goods he grants, who grants the pow'r to gain; . .	O 48	Vanity Wishes	366
Now grants, and now rejects the Lover's Care	O 95	Sprig of Myrtl	V 6
Fly, Wretch, while yet my Pity grants thee Flight; . .	O 319	Irene	23
GRAPE			
Plucking the blushing Grape and Pear, ...	O 72	Hor. Epode II	26
GRAPES			
As vines the elms, as grapes adorn the vine, ...	Y 6	Virgil Daphnis	17
GRAPHONTA			
Eiden Aletheie proen chairoysa graphonta	O 108	Eis Birchion	1
GRAPSCMENON			
Sou pote grapsomenon Birchion allon echois.	O 108	Eis Birchion	4
GRASP			
For love, whose grasp Creation collective man can . . .	Y 108	Vanity Wishes	V 361
fill;			
Direct the loaded Cannon, grasp the Sword	O 364	Irene	V 14
Direct the loaded cannon, grasp the sword	Y 162	Irene	V 41
Grasp at Command, and tow'r in quest of Empire; . . .	O 293	Irene	114
GRASP'D			
He grasp'd her hand endeav'ring kind relief.	Y 21	Tr. Iliad Bk 6	112
GRASPING			
When grasping Bliss th' unsteady mind	O 150	Tr Boet III.12	56
GRASPS			
And grasps the bloody sand involv'd in death.	O 76	Tr Add. Battle	17
GRATEFUL			
May powerful nature join with grateful art, ...	O 81	Lady Birthday	7
Her grateful Sons shine bright with ev'ry Virtue; . . .	O 256	Irene	60
What well known Voice pronounc'd the grateful Sounds . .	O 295	Irene	10
GRATEFULL			
Gratefull, rewards the Deities, ...	O 72	Hor. Epode II	27
GRATITUDE			
With well-feign'd gratitude the pension'd band	O 19	London	200
What Ties to Slaves? what Gratitude to Foes?	O 312	Irene	6
GRATITUDE'S			
And Gratitude's strong Ties restrain my Tongue. . . .	O 312	Irene	5
GRAVE			
Perversely grave, or postively wrong.	O 43	Vanity Wishes	274
Perversely grave, and positively wrong.	Y 104	Vanity Wishes	V 274
'Tis yours to crown Desert--beyond the Grave!	O 58	Prologue Comus	38
For trifling sports I quitted grave affairs.	O 130	Tr. Rambler 10	1
No care his wealth can carry to the grave.	O 146	Tr Boeth III.3	6
There the Lender grave and sly.	O 196	Song Congratu.	16
See Levet to the grave descend;	O 201	Death Dr Levet	6
A Winged Messenger, or bid the Grave	O 365	Irene	V 21
And sink into the silent Grave in Peace.	O 264	Irene	12
O! could the Grave restore the pious Hero, ...	O 267	Irene	42
In the dark Precincts of the gaping Grave, ...	O 272	Irene	4
Than all the Wisdom of the grave Divan.	O 287	Irene	8
Rouse from the grave the rivals of Pharsalia	Y 185	Irene	V 39
Had stretch'd the fiery Boaster in the Grave.	O 312	Irene	20
My mother who alone escap'd the grave	Y 19	Tr. Iliad Bk 6	38
Shall sink alike into the gloomy grave.	Y 21	Tr. Iliad Bk 6	120
GRAVE'S			
Th' oblivious grave's inviolable shade.	O 62	Pro Word Wise	10
GRAVES			
Th' unhappy lovers graves the Myrtle spreads;	O 95	Sprig of Myrtl	10
GRAVITY			
Such ill-tim'd Gravity, such serious Folly, ...	O 281	Irene	35

		PAGE	TITLE	LINE
GRAY				
Wearing out life's evening gray;	· · · · · · ·	O 181	Parody Warton	2
GRAZE				
He gave my flocks to graze the flowery meads,	· · · ·	O 64	Virgil Past.I	11
GREAT				
Mark whom the great caress, who frown on me!	· · · ·	O 14	London	92
Now bless'd with all the baubles of the great,	· · · ·	O 19	London	206
Athirst for wealth, and burning to be great;	· · · ·	O 33	Vanity Wishes	74
All fir'd with hope, and panting to be great;	· · · ·	Y 95	Vanity Wishes	V 74
What gave great Villiers to th' assassin's knife,	· · · ·	O 35	Vanity Wishes	129
And pow'r too great to keep, or to resign?	· · · · ·	O 36	Vanity Wishes	134
Great souls whose the dear-bought right convey	· · · ·	Y 100	Vanity Wishes	V 189
Great Xerxes comes to seize the certain prey,	· · · ·	O 42	Vanity Wishes	227
She saw great Faustus lay the Ghost of Wit:	· · · · ·	O 52	Pro Drury-Lane	36
Tost in one common storm with all the great;	· · · · ·	O 59	Pro Good Nat'd	8
The great, 'tis true, can charm th' electing tribe;	· · · ·	O 60	Pro Good Nat'd	25
Let one great payment every claim appease,	· · · · ·	O 62	Pro Word Wise	11
Yet, great Maecenas, shall your friend	· · · · · ·	O 70	Hor.II Ode XX	7
How would the Trojans brand great Hector's name!	· · ·	O 74	Tr. Iliad Bk 6	5
So by their great decree Assyria fell	· · · · ·	O 76	Tr Add. Battle	37
Whatever course of Life great Jove allots,	· · · · ·	O 77	Festina Lente	1
Thy pleasures, permanent as great,	· · · · · · ·	O 100	Ode Friendship	23
Thy pleasures, lasting, as they're great,	· · · · ·	O 100	Ode Friendship	V 23
Thy pleasures, charms as great,	· · · · · · · ·	Y 71	Ode Friendship	V 23
Great George's acts let tuneful Cibber sing;	· · · ·	O 114	On C. Cibber	3
Where first great nature charm'd my sight,	· · · · ·	O 125	An Ode	19
Once more great nature's work review,	· · · · ·	O 125	An Ode	23
Once more great nature's works renew	· · · · ·	O 125	An Ode	V 23
From thee, great God, we spring, to thee we tend,	· · ·	O 130	Tr. Rambler 7	7
And love return, has great Erasmus died?	· · · · ·	O 132	Tr. Rambler 54	2
For not the brave, or wise, or great,	· · · · · ·	O 136	Tr Rambler 128	1
Forgive, great Jove, the daring enterprize.	· · · ·	O 136	Tr Rambler 129	6
How small to others, but how great to me.	· · · · ·	O 138	Tr Rambler 161	1
Nor dignifies the great, nor decks the fair.	· · · ·	O 141	Tr Rambler 199	4
That decks the fair, or dignifies the great.	· · · ·	O 141	Tr Rambler 199	8
Great Hogarth's honour'd Dust is here.	· · · · ·	O 154	Epita. Hogarth	8
Great Sir John, are all your own.	· · · · · · ·	O 196	Song Congratu.	4
Great Sir John, are now your own.	· · · · · · ·	O 196	Song Congratu.	V 4
His Mien is lofty, his Demeanour great,	· · · · ·	O 255	Irene	14
Great Amurath, at my Request, forsook	· · · · ·	O 256	Irene	43
But say, great Bassa, why the Sultan's Anger,	· · · ·	O 257	Irene	65
Forgive, great Sultan, that intrusive Duty	· · · · ·	O 263	Irene	23
Thy Soul by Nature great, enlarg'd by Knowledge,	· · ·	O 266	Irene	35
But yet, great Emperor, beware of Treason;	· · · ·	O 273	Irene	31
Now pause, great Bassa, from the Thoughts of Blood,	· ·	O 285	Irene	1
Applaud her Charms, and court her to be Great.	· · ·	O 287	Irene	18
That none are great, or happy, but the Virtuous.	· · ·	O 294	Irene	8
Yet shall the Conscience of the great Attempt	· · · ·	O 301	Irene	99
But virtuous Passion prompts the great Resolve,	· · ·	O 303	Irene	18
The fav'ring Winds assist the great Design,	· · · ·	O 304	Irene	6
Or bid her great Camilli	· · · · · · · · ·	Y 185	Irene	V 39
Intimidates the Brave, degrades the Great.	· · · ·	O 311	Irene	15
Enrob'd in Death--Dispatch her and be great.	· · · ·	O 326	Irene	3
Forgive, great Sultan! that by Fate prevented,	· · ·	O 331	Irene	1
Great is thy Woe! but think, illustrious Sultan,	· · ·	O 332	Irene	37
Then hear, great Mahomet, the Voice of Truth.	· · ·	O 333	Irene	55
To great Latona's son, and two to you;	· · · · ·	Y 7	Virgil Daphnis	44
How great Achilles godlike Hector slew?	· · · · ·	Y 22	Tr Add. Battle	11
As when great Briareus with matchless might	· · · ·	Y 26	Tr Add. Battle	137
GREATER				
In greater scenes each other aid;	· · · · · · ·	O 121	To Miss Playin	28
When inconsistent with a greater Good,	· · · · ·	O 290	Irene	32
the Particulam) strikes me with greater horror	· ·	Y 176	Irene	V111C
GREATNESS				
And gain and greatness load the tainted gales;	· · ·	Y 93	Vanity Wishes	V 46
Of hasty greatness finds the fatal doom,	· · · · ·	O 43	Vanity Wishes	252
Of hasty greatness finds the hasty doom,	· · · · ·	Y 103	Vanity Wishes	V 252
When Pride, by guilt, to greatness climbs,	· · · ·	O 126	An Ode	33
Greatness with ease, and gay severity.	· · · · ·	O 137	Tr Rambler 141	1
Could Rome with future greatness fire,	· · · · ·	O 188	Epilogue	2
Which Love of Greatness, not of Truth, inflames.	· · ·	O 262	Irene	27
Thou know'st not yet thy Master's future Greatness,	·	O 265	Irene	40
The glitt'ring Vanities of empty Greatness,	· · · ·	O 265	Irene	6
Support the splendid Miseries of Greatness?	· · · ·	O 268	Irene	18
The Sultan from himself derives his Greatness.	· · ·	O 268	Irene	24
And tow'rs and triumphs in ideal Greatness;	· · · ·	O 269	Irene	5
Let not th' unbounded Greatness of his Mind	· · · ·	O 275	Irene	72
The gloomy Resolution, horrid Greatness,	· · · · ·	O 275	Irene	82
With all the graceful Pride of Greatness heighten'd,	·	O 276	Irene	8
Greatness of mind with elegance of form.	· · · ·	Y 149	Irene	V 56
If Greatness please thee, mount th' imperial Seat;	· ·	O 279	Irene	84
And kind Ambition points the Way to Greatness.	· · ·	O 280	Irene	14
I'll open my breast--clasp thee--forget	· · · · ·	Y 161	Irene	V 13
greatness--				
Thy dazzled Soul with all its boasted Greatness,	· ·	O 292	Irene	99
Then pleas'd, and conscious of Superiour	· · · · ·	O 369	Irene	V 6
Greatness				
Angelic Greatness is Angelic Virtue.	· · · · · ·	O 293	Irene	130
With native Lustre and unborrow'd Greatness,	· · ·	O 298	Irene	16
Pensive, and envious of Irene's Greatness,	· · · ·	O 314	Irene	12
Oh! rather scornful of flagitious Greatness,	· · ·	O 320	Irene	28

```
GREATNESS    (CONTINUED)                                           PAGE      TITLE           LINE
     Content with Freedom, and precarious Greatness.   .  .  .   O 321  Irene              39
     So sure the Fall of Greatness rais'd on Crimes,   .  .  .   O 335  Irene              10
GRECIAN
     The wise experienc'd Grecian sage                            O  68  Hor. II Ode IX     13
     When some proud Grecian dame shall tasks impose,   .  .  .   O  74  Tr. Iliad Bk 6     21
     And Persia felt the force of Grecian steel;  .  .  .  .  .   O  76  Tr Add. Battle     38
     Ambitious Fury fir'd the Grecian King:   .  .  .  .  .  .    O  97  Hickman Spinet     10
     And add new lustre to the Grecian name.  .  .  .  .  .  .    Y 117  Irene            V109B
     Teach me the Grecian arts of soft persuasion                O 349  Irene            V  27
     The Grecian Counsellor.  .  .  .  .  .  .  .  .  .  .  .     O 263  Irene              25
     (The) pride of Roman (power), and Grecian   .  .  .  .  .    Y 177  Irene            V 111
        art
     Reclines against the Shore: Our Grecian Troop   .  .  .  .   O 304  Irene               3
     Alone preserv'd the town from Grecian fire.  .  .  .  .  .   Y  18  Tr. Iliad Bk 6     14
     And Grecian spears shall quiver in your breast.   .  .  .    Y  18  Tr. Iliad Bk 6     23
GRECIAN'S
     Whose blood shall quench some Grecian's thirsty rage,   .    O  74  Tr. Iliad Bk 6     16
GRECIANS
     To assist the Grecians  .  .  .  .  .  .  .  .  .  .  .  .   Y 166  Irene            V 106
GREECE
     Nor Lybian fowls, nor Snipes of Greece,   .  .  .  .  .  .   O  73  Hor. Epode II      59
     Yet Greece enjoys no Gleam of transient Hope,   .  .  .  .   O 249  Irene              11
     Reproach not Misery.--The Sons of Greece,   .  .  .  .  .    O 250  Irene              28
     Beheld without Concern, expiring Greece,  .  .  .  .  .  .   O 250  Irene              34
     But Greece is still forgot.  .  .  .  .  .  .  .  .  .  .    O 257  Irene              74
     And harrass Greece no more with wasteful War.  .  .  .  .    O 257  Irene              80
     What hazards would I shun to clasp for Greece and for       Y 125  Irene            V 133
        Aspasia
     When weigh'd with Greece, with Virtue, with Aspasia?  .  .   O 260  Irene             138
     Whats Life when weighed with Greece or Aspasia?   .  .  .    O 371  Irene            V  24
     Remember Freedom, Glory, Greece, and Love.  .  .  .  .  .    O 260  Irene             146
     Think on Revenge and Glory Greece and Love   .  .  .  .  .   O 361  Irene            V   5
     And yet another Voice, forgive me Greece,   .  .  .  .  .    O 270  Irene              18
     And every Voice was Liberty and Greece.   .  .  .  .  .  .   O 271  Irene              30
     His correspondence with our Foes of Greece!  .  .  .  .  .   O 273  Irene              18
     Imperfect sounds of Greece--and love--and   .  .  .  .  .    Y 144  Irene            V  80
        daggers
     Greece, in her lovely Patroness secure,   .  .  .  .  .  .   O 278  Irene              77
     Rouse, Cali, shall the Sons of conquer'd Greece   .  .  .    O 284  Irene              42
     No more should Greece lament those Prayers rejected.  .  .   O 290  Irene              52
     'Tis Greece, 'tis Freedom calls Aspasia hence,  .  .  .  .   O 297  Irene               9
     Reproach not, Greece, a Lover's fond Delays,   .  .  .  .    O 297  Irene              19
     Fill all thy ardent Breast with Greece and Virtue,   .  .    O 298  Irene               8
     Did not the Cause of Greece restrain my Sword,  .  .  .  .   O 299  Irene              41
     Will e'er an happier Hour revisit Greece?   .  .  .  .  .    O 301  Irene              96
     Is not the Fate of Greece and Cali thine?   .  .  .  .  .    O 304  Irene              19
     Must Greece, still wretched by her Children's Folly,  .  .   O 305  Irene              43
     Demetrius the soul of Greece  .  .  .  .  .  .  .  .  .  .   Y 188  Irene            V  10
     The thoughts of happy love, and rescu'd Greece  .  .  .  .   Y 189  Irene            V  1D
     Is Greece deliver'd? is the Tyrant fall'n?   .  .  .  .  .   O 315  Irene               3
     Greece is no more, the prosp'rous Tyrant lives,  .  .  .     O 315  Irene               4
     Hide me, oh hide me from upbraiding Greece,   .  .  .  . .   O 316  Irene              12
     O Greece! renown'd for Science and for Wealth,   .  .  .  .  O 317  Irene              42
GREEDY
     Betimes the greedy Thrush to kill   .  .  .  .  .  .  .  .   O  72  Hor. Epode II      41
GREEK
     Such bribes the rapid Greek o'er Asia whirl'd,  .  .  .  .   O  39  Vanity Wishes     179
     By what Enchantment does this lovely Greek   .  .  .  .  .   O 261  Irene               1
     To rave unheeded, while the happy Greek,  .  .  .  .  .  .   O 285  Irene               2
     O spare the gallant Greek, in him we lose   .  .  .  .  .    O 307  Irene              26
     Might intercept the Traitor Greek, Demetrius,   .  .  .  .   O 331  Irene               8
     The Greek, Demetrius! whom th' expiring Bassa   .  .  .  .   O 331  Irene              10
GREEKS
     The daring Greeks deride the martial show,   .  .  .  .  .   O  42  Vanity Wishes     235
     The groaning Greeks break up their golden Caverns   .  .  .  O 249  Irene              17
     A Galley mann'd with Greeks, thy charge, Leontius,   .  .    O 258  Irene              81
     His martial Rhet'rick taught the Greeks Resistance;   .  .   O 263  Irene              26
     And through the parted Shade disclos'd the Greeks,   .  .    O 269  Irene              11
     But Fear, or Mutiny may taint the Greeks?  .  .  .  .  .  .  O 284  Irene              37
     Dismiss these needless Fears--a Troop of Greeks  .  .  .  .  O 301  Irene              90
     The Greeks disorder'd by their Leader's Absence,  .  .  .    O 304  Irene              10
     Ask to whose Sword the Greeks will trust their Cause,  .  .  O 305  Irene              39
     Shall then the Greeks, unpunish'd and conceal'd,   .  .  .   O 312  Irene               1
     The Captive of his Sword. The coward Greeks,   .  .  .  .    O 312  Irene              14
     Such was the Will of Heav'n--A Band of Greeks   .  .  .  .   O 335  Irene               5
     The bravest of the Greeks the wall invade.  .  .  .  .  .    Y  19  Tr. Iliad Bk 6     53
GREEN
     On some green bank supinely Laid,   .  .  .  .  .  .  .  .   O  72  Hor. Epode II      30
     The fields, and woods, behold, are green,   .  .  .  .  .    O 231  Tr Horace IV.7      2
     The fields, and woods, again, are green,  .  .  .  .  .  .   O 231  Tr Horace IV.7   V  2
GREENWICH
     Where Greenwich smiles upon the silver flood:   .  .  .  .   O  10  London             22
GREW
     Or English honour grew a standing jest.   .  .  .  .  .  .   O  10  London             30
     He left the name, at which the world grew pale,   .  .  .    O  41  Vanity Wishes     221
GRIEF
     Tho' grief and fondness in my breast rebel,   .  .  .  .  .  O   8  London              1
     With servile grief dependent nobles sigh  .  .  .  .  .  .   Y  57  London           V 198
     Grief aids disease, remember'd folly stings,   .  .  .  .    O  35  Vanity Wishes     119
     Yet hope not life from grief or danger free,   .  .  .  .    O  37  Vanity Wishes     155

                                142
```

			PAGE	TITLE	LINE
GRIEF	(CONTINUED)				
Yet dream not life from grief or danger free,	. . . .	Y	99	Vanity Wishes	V 155
Can in my bosom half that grief create,	. . . . .	O	74	Tr. Iliad Bk 6	19
Grief swell thine Eyes, and Terror chill thy Breast.	. .	O	110	To Posterity	4
Grief and Madness unrepress'd		O	148	Tr Boet III.12	13
Adds Shame to Grief, and Infamy to Ruin.	. . . .	O	250	Irene	25
Dear hapless Maid--tempestuous Grief o'erbears	. . . .	O	252	Irene	77
Dear helpless Maid--tempestuous Grief o'erbears	. . .	O	252	Irene	V 77
Be fruitless Grief	. . . .	O	316	Irene	13
A little Life for Grief, and for Repentance.	. . .	O	327	Irene	23
A little life from grief and for repentance.	. . .	Y	207	Irene	V 23
Shake off this Weight of unavailing Grief,	. . . .	O	333	Irene	39
My Rage and Grief had hid from my Remembrance.	. . .	O	334	Irene	65
My rage and grief had had from my remembrance	. . .	Y	215	Irene	V 69B
With grief this emblem of mankind I see,	. . .	Y	4	On a Daffodill	25
And spread their echoing grief from shore to shore.	. .	Y	6	Virgil Daphnis	12
This Hector saw; his soul was touch'd with grief.	. . .	Y	21	Tr. Iliad Bk 6	111
GRIEFS					
Of all the griefs that harrass the distress'd,	. . . .	O	17	London	166
Whose joys are causeless, or whose griefs are vain.	. .	O	33	Vanity Wishes	68
What Fears, what Griefs, what Dangers hast thou known?	.	O	295	Irene	22
GRIEVE					
Behold this Theatre, and grieve no more.	. . . . . .	O	57	Prologue Comus	10
GRIN					
Guilt and Despair! pale Spectres, grin around me,	. . .	O	328	Irene	50
GRIPE					
Unclasp'd his Iron Gripe to set thee free?	. . . .	O	318	Irene	16
Let Slav'ry harrass, and let Hunger gripe.	. . . . .	O	328	Irene	37
GRIPING					
No griping Creditors infesst.	. . . .	O	71	Hor. Epode II	8
GRISLY					
At length deform'd with many a grisly wound	. . . . .	O	76	Tr Add. Battle	24
GRIZLY					
A grizly wolf surprised, and fled.	. . . .	O	65	Hor I Ode xxii	12
The grizly foaming Boar surrounds	. . . .	O	72	Hor. Epode II	39
GROAN					
Then, O my Country! shalt thou groan distrest,	. . . .	O	110	To Posterity	3
Hebrus heard her Poet groan,	. . . . .	O	148	Tr Boet III.12	V 7
Where hopeless anguish pour'd his groan,	. . . . .	O	201	Death Dr Levet	19
Where hopeless anguish pour'd the groan,	. . . . .	O	201	Death Dr Levet	V 19
When hopeless anguish pours her groan,	. . . .	O	201	Death Dr Levet	V 19
GROAN'D					
Still fond of Life, groan'd out the dreadful Secret,	. .	O	272	Irene	16
GROANING					
To such, a groaning nation's spoils are giv'n,	. . . .	O	13	London	65
The groaning Greeks break up their golden Caverns	. . .	O	249	Irene	17
His groaning Country claims Leontius' Aid;	. . . . .	O	270	Irene	17
Shall break the Fetters of the groaning Christian;	. .	O	278	Irene	76
GROANS					
Utter sad groans and lamentable cries.	. . . .	O	76	Tr Add. Battle	29
And vent our Suff'rings in clandestine Groans?	. . . .	O	249	Irene	4
These Groans were fatal, these Disguises vain:	. . . .	O	249	Irene	6
Nor will his Country's Groans reproach Demetrius.	. . .	O	301	Irene	101
My silence and my groans confes'd.	. . . .	Y	11	Tr Hor Epode 9	16
And Strymon's hollow banks resounded with their groans.	.	Y	24	Tr Add. Battle	89
GROOM					
The groom retails the favours of his lord.	. . . . .	O	18	London	181
GROPES					
He gropes his breeches with a monarch's air.	. . . .	O	17	London	151
GROSS					
Gross Fires, enkindled by a mortal Hand,	. . . . . .	O	282	Irene	57
GROUND					
And spread his flaming palace on the ground,	. . . .	O	19	London	195
Or hostile millions press him to the ground?	. . . .	O	41	Vanity Wishes	218
Autumn o'erlooks the smiling Ground	. . . . .	O	72	Hor. Epode II	24
Nor my brave brothers, that have bit the ground,	. . .	O	74	Tr. Iliad Bk 6	17
Th' enormous Gyants smoke upon the Ground.	. . . .	O	76	Tr Add. Battle	25
And tread in mystick rings the mossie ground.	. . .	O	77	Tr Add. Battle	52
And Cities smoaking on the ground	. . . . .	O	78	Feast St Simon	2
Loud as the Billows bursting on the Ground.	. . . .	O	110	To Posterity	6
The hoary ground, the frowning skies.	. . . . . .	O	123	Winter's Walk	4
Safe upon the rocky Ground,	. . . . . .	O	145	Tr Boeth. II.4	15
O'er treacherous pleasure's flow'ry ground	. . . .	O	203	Tr. on Skating	V 3
Why shakes the Ground, when subterraneous Fires	. . .	O	281	Irene	52
Urg'd me to dash it to the Ground untouch'd,	. . . .	O	316	Irene	28
And trod to Bacchus' praise the mystick ground.	. . .	Y	6	Virgil Daphnis	16
Ye swains! bestrow the ground with leaves and spread	. .	Y	7	Virgil Daphnis	26
And plac'd the beamy terror on the ground	. . . . .	Y	20	Tr. Iliad Bk 6	96
Who to the ground the shatter'd building flung	. . .	Y	23	Tr Add. Battle	48
There frogs crept croaking o'er the swampy ground.	. .	Y	24	Tr Add. Battle	59
Mock'd our impatient steps, for all was fairy ground.	.	Y	310	Parody of Pope	4
GROUNDLESS					
In groundless hope, and causeless fear,	. . . . .	O	124	Winter's Walk	13
GROUNDS					
And, while thy grounds a cheap repast afford,	. . . .	O	20	London	218
GROV'LING					
From grov'ling Business and superfluous Care,	. . . .	O	246	Irene Prologue	3
With half the grov'ling Slaves that load the Globe.	. .	O	332	Irene	36
GROVE					
Whilst each Musician of the Grove	. . . .	O	72	Hor. Epode II	33
The naked hills, the leafless grove,	. . . . . .	O	123	Winter's Walk	3

GROVE   (CONTINUED)   PAGE   TITLE   LINE
   None dares with impious steel the grove to rend, . . .   O 139 Tr Rambler 168   1
   And unaccustom'd warblings charm the grove (pleasing .   Y 150 Irene   V 86
     disson⟨ance⟩
   Sweeps o'er the Grove, forsake the lab'ring Bough,   . .   O 298 Irene   23
   And sought this happy Grove in quest of Thee. . . . .   O 299 Irene   50
     Behold, within th' embow'ring Grove . . . .   O 314 Irene   10
   While bees shall feed on thyme, and birds shall haunt the   Y   7 Virgil Daphnis   50
     grove
GROVES
   Your shady Groves, your pleasing wife, ...   O 69 Hor.II Ode 14   21
   In Myrtle groves oft sings the happy swain, ...   O 95 Sprig of Myrtl   7
   Love warbles in the vocal groves, ...   O 125 An Ode   7
   Nor from the pleasing groves depart, ...   O 125 An Ode   18
   Those Groves, whose Shades embower'd the dear Irene, . .   O 333 Irene   46
GROWING
   For growing names the weekly scribbler lies, ...   O 33 Vanity Wishes   81
   To growing wealth the dedicator flies, ...   O 33 Vanity Wishes   82
   To growing names the weekly scribbler lies, ...   Y 95 Vanity Wishes   V 82
   While growing hopes scarce awe the gath'ring sneer, . .   O 44 Vanity Wishes   277
   Their growing fame re'echoes to the skies.   . . . . .   Y 22 Tr Add. Battle   9
GROWLS
   And growls in private o'er his idle Sabre.   . . . . .   O 309 Irene   22
GROWN
   Had we not been perverse and careless grown,   . . .   O 64 Virgil Past.I   21
   Grown old in courts, thou art not surely one   . . .   O 176 Tr Metastas II   1
   Hast thou grown old amidst the Croud of Courts,   . .   O 281 Irene   32
   I then (my cheeks still glow with shame) was grown   . .   Y 11 Tr Hor Epode 9   11
GROWS
   That slowly grows, which must for ever last.   . . . .   O 142 In Baretti Bk.   10
GUARD
   The guard of commerce, and the dread of Spain, ...   O 10 London   28
   Sign her foes doom, or guard her fav'rites zeal?   . . .   O 34 Vanity Wishes   92
   Sign her foes' doom, or guard her patriots zeal,   . . .   Y 95 Vanity Wishes   V 92
   And virtue guard thee to the throne of Truth!   . . .   O 37 Vanity Wishes   142
   While tutelary Nations guard her Cell.   . . . . . .   O 58 Prologue Comus   36
   Nor needs the guard of Moorish bows: . . . .   O 65 Hor I Ode xxii   4
   Nor needs the Guard of Moorish Bows.   . . . .   O 66 To A. Fuscus   4
   Behold the wife of Hector, guard of Troy!   . . . . .   O 74 Tr. Iliad Bk 6   26
   Which Armies guard, and Citadels inclose?   . . . . .   O 258 Irene   91
   Did interposing Angels guard her from him?   . . . . .   O 259 Irene   116
   Thy Care shall guard this Treasure of my Soul;   . . .   O 263 Irene   2
   Shall guard Aspasia from triumphant Lust.   . . . . .   O 301 Irene   89
   Grant him like me to guard the walls of Troy.   . . . .   Y 20 Tr. Iliad Bk 6   102
GUARDED
   Breathless, amaz'd, and on the guarded Beach   . . . .   O 335 Irene   8
   Guarded from all but winged enemies   . . . .   Y 23 Tr Add. Battle   25
GUARDIAN
   If the Guardian or the Mother   . . . .   O 197 Song Congratu.   25
   Should the guardian friend or mother   . . . .   O 197 Song Congratu.   V 25
   O say, what guardian Pow'r convey'd thee hither.   . . .   O 296 Irene   33
   Calm of my Cares, and Guardian of my Virtue.   . . . .   O 298 Irene   12
GUARDIANS
   The guardians yield, by force superior ply'd;   . . . .   O 47 Vanity Wishes   339
   The guardians yield, with force resistless ply'd;   . . .   Y 107 Vanity Wishes   V 339
GUARDS
   Stern Famine guards the solitary coast, ...   O 41 Vanity Wishes   207
   Think on that Providence that guards the Good.   . . . .   O 252 Irene   89
   Amidst his gloomy Guards and fiery Vassals   . . . . .   O 372 Irene   V 19
   The Breast where Virtue guards the Throne of Peace.   . .   O 316 Irene   15
   Haste, seize them, guards, be quick--my thoughtless hast   Y 198 Irene   V 34
   Dispatch his Guards to stop the flying Traytors,   . . .   O 319 Irene   3
   Hew down, ye Guards, those Vassals of Distraction,   . .   O 333 Irene   51
GUESS
   Perhaps, for who can guess th' Effects of Chance?   . . .   O 53 Pro Drury-Lane   45
   We cannot obviate, for we cannot guess.   . . . . . .   O 287 Irene   11
GUESS'D
   I guess'd her dark Designs, and warn'd the Sultan,   . .   O 327 Irene   26
GUEST
   Perplex the fawning niece and pamper'd guest, ...   O 44 Vanity Wishes   276
   The dull conjecture fawning niece and pamper'd guest,   .   Y 104 Vanity Wishes   V 276
   Pollutes his banquet and insults his guest;   . . . . .   O 130 Tr. Rambler 12   2
   "Fortune's guest, without a home, ...   O 185 Anacreon Ode 9   26
   The guest, without a want, without a wish, ...   O 193 Tr. Medea II   19
GUESTS
   And guests are brib'd to hear;   . . . .   Y 104 Vanity Wishes   V 278
   The watchful guests still hint the last offence,   . . .   O 44 Vanity Wishes   279
   The treachrous guests still hint the last offence,   . .   Y 104 Vanity Wishes   V 279
GUIDE
   To tread the dreary paths without a guide, ...   O 31 Vanity Wishes   8
   Should Reason guide thee with her brightest ray,   . . .   O 37 Vanity Wishes   145
   Your passions; guide the reins with steady hand,   . . .   O 77 Festina Lente   4
   O guide me through life's darksome way, ...   O 100 Ode Friendship   14
   O guide us through life's darksome way, ...   O 100 Ode Friendship   V 14
   A guide, a father, and a friend;   . . . .   O 125 An Ode   22
   Path, motive, guide, original, and end.   . . . . . .   O 130 Tr. Rambler 7   8
   Guide the Sons dagger to the Fathers heart   . . . . .   O 352 Irene   V 4
   Propitious Guide of my bewilder'd Soul, ...   O 298 Irene   11
   Guide all thy Steps, calm ev'ry stormy Thought,   . . .   O 303 Irene   21
   Plays on the quiv'ring Waves, to guide our Flight,   . .   O 306 Irene   59
   o'er the tide--providence our guide--   . . . .   Y 199 Irene   V 16A

		PAGE	TITLE	LINE
GUIDE	(CONTINUED)			
To guide thy Passage shall th' aerial Spirits	. . . .	O 322	Irene	7
To Guide thy passage shall th' Starry Spirits	. . . .	O 364	Irene	V 26
But Heav'n shall guide it to the guilty Heart.	. . . .	O 335	Irene	15
GUIDES				
How rarely reason guides the stubborn choice,	. . . .	O 31	Vanity Wishes	11
How rarely reason guides the hasty choice,	. . . . .	Y 92	Vanity Wishes	V 11
Whose voice created, and whose wisdom guides,	. . . .	O 129	Tr. Rambler 7	2
The Chief, whose Wisdom guides the Turkish Counsels.	. .	O 253	Irene	112
Guides erring Mortals to the Paths of Virtue,	. . . .	O 289	Irene	18
Guides through the Maze of Life the Steps of Man	. . . .	O 346	Irene	V 6
GUILT				
For what but social guilt the friend endears?	. . . .	O 14	London	83
Cruel with guilt, and daring with despair,	. . . . .	O 21	London	238
As Tyrants doom their Tools of Guilt to die;	. . . .	O 53	Pro Drury-Lane	56
For those who feel no guilt can know no shame;	. . . .	O 84	Epi Dist Moth.	25
When Pride, by guilt, to greatness climbs,	. . . .	O 126	An Ode	33
To dens of guilt and shades of care	. . . . . .	O 191	Tr. Medea I	13
Against returning Guilt.	. . . .	O 265	Irene	11
Wherever Guilt can fly, Revenge can follow.	. . . .	O 274	Irene	65
With all the Speed of Terror and of Guilt.	. . . .	O 275	Irene	86
Urge me not on to glittering Guilt, nor pour	. . . .	O 288	Irene	5
Could just intention consecrate the Guilt	. . . .	O 360	Irene	V 35
Despair, and Slav'ry, Solitude, and Guilt.	. . . .	O 292	Irene	87
Tranquillity and Guilt, disjoin'd by Heav'n,	. . . .	O 292	Irene	90
Will not th' Apostate feel the Pangs of Guilt,	. . . .	O 294	Irene	132
Nor mingled Guilt pollute the sacred Cause!	. . . . .	O 300	Irene	64
'Tis Love combin'd with Guilt alone, that melts	. . .	O 303	Irene	16
And dwells on the guilt of apostacy	. . . . .	Y 186	Irene	V 11
How Guilt once harbour'd in the conscious Breast,	. . .	O 311	Irene	14
When Guilt like this once harbours in the Breast	. . .	O 346	Irene	V 4
The Breast where Guilt like this has found admission	. .	O 349	Irene	V 23
Ill suits with Guilt the Gaieties of Triumph;	. . . .	O 314	Irene	22
The Doom of Guilt alone, nor dare to seize	. . . . .	O 316	Irene	14
Leave Slav'ry, Guilt, and Infamy behind.	. . . . .	O 320	Irene	31
Be thine, that Wealth can give, or Guilt receive.	. . .	O 322	Irene	58
And bless'd with all the joy that Guilt allows	. . . .	O 365	Irene	V 11
Who charges Guilt on me?	. . . .	O 323	Irene	6
Who charges Guilt,	. . . .	O 323	Irene	6
Who charges Guilt! lay by this proud Resentment	. . .	O 323	Irene	8
See the last Witness of thy Guilt and Fear	. . . .	O 326	Irene	2
Guilt and Despair! pale Spectres, grin around me,	. . .	O 328	Irene	50
Declar'd the chief Associate of his Guilt.	. . . .	O 331	Irene	11
The Wretch, whose Guilt declar'd by tortur'd Cali,	. .	O 334	Irene	64
When haughty Guilt exults with impious Joy,	. . . . .	O 335	Irene	12
All her life was naught but guilt,	. . . .	Y 300	Extemp. Elegy	11
GUILTLESS				
So shall you guiltless reign, and all mankind adore.	. .	O 84	Epi Dist Moth.	47
Thy gentle flows of guiltless joys	. . . .	O 100	Ode Friendship	17
Have I for this preserv'd my guiltless Bosom,	. . . .	O 304	Irene	14
And live her guiltless Moments o'er anew!	. . . . .	O 323	Irene	16
Irene's chamber from Irene's guiltless bosom	. . . .	Y 205	Irene	V 31
Was she then guiltless! Has my thoughtless Rage	. . .	O 332	Irene	18
GUILTY				
The pangs of guilty pow'r, and hapless love,	. . . .	O 113	Epit. Phillips	2
The pangs of guilty pow'r, or hapless love,	. . . . .	O 113	Epit. Phillips	V 2
Learn here what Anguish racks the guilty Breast,	. . .	O 246	Irene Prologue	11
To paint the Pageantries of guilty State?	. . . . .	O 276	Irene	12
to be guilty, though penitent .	. . . .	Y 165	Irene	V 81
From splendid wretchedness and guilty scepters (grandeur)		Y 166	Irene	V 93
And ask, what guilty Pow'r's rebellious Hand	. . . .	O 293	Irene	119
Ere guilty Fear depress'd the hoary Chief,	. . . . .	O 312	Irene	18
But Heav'n shall guide it to the guilty Heart.	. . . .	O 335	Irene	15
Heav'n turns its point upon the guilty Heart	. . . .	O 345	Irene	V 29
GUINEAS				
Lavish of your Grandsire's guineas,	. . . .	O 196	Song Congratu.	11
Lavish of thy Grandsire's guineas,	. . . .	O 196	Song Congratu.	V 11
GULL'D				
If the gull'd conqueror receives the chain,	. . . . .	O 16	London	121
GULP				
As I can gulp it down.	. . . .	O 159	Par Hermit III	12
GULPHS				
With louder ruin to the gulphs below?	. . . . .	O 35	Vanity Wishes	128
Who set unclouded in the gulphs of fate.	. . . . .	O 45	Vanity Wishes	312
On crackling ice, o'er gulphs profound,	. . . . .	O 203	Tr. on Skating	V 1
Insidious sands, shallows rough rocks and whirling devouring gulphs	. .	Y 201	Irene	V 10B
GUST				
and the first gust shake<s> it into atom<s>	. . . . .	Y 132	Irene	V 39
Some accidental Gust of Opposition	. . . . . .	O 269	Irene	6
Some fatal gust of sudden Opposition	. . . . . .	O 374	Irene	V 15
At her Approach each ruder Gust of Thought	. . . .	O 275	Irene	91
GYANTS				
Th' enormous Gyants smoke upon the Ground.	. . . .	O 76	Tr Add. Battle	25
GYGANTICK				
Who matchless strength and bulk gygantick boasts,	. . .	Y 24	Tr Add. Battle	81
HA				
Blest age! but ha! how diff'rent from our own!	. . . .	O 22	London	V 253

HABITANT
    This habitant th' aerial regions boast. . . . . . .

HABITATION
    A Habitation for a fairer Soul? . . . .

HABITUAL
    Habitual Cowardice usurps the Soul. . . . . . .

HAD
    Had we not been perverse and careless grown, ...
    Or feasts on Kids the Wolves had kill'd . . . .
    Thus fell the Pygmie state, which long had stood . . .
    When Christ had conquer'd Hell and fate . . . . .
      to whom a Lady had given a Sprig of Myrtle . . .
    Had Stella's gentle touches mov'd the Lyre, ...
    Soon had the Monarch felt a nobler fire, ...
    E'er yet had happiness compleat; . . . . . .
    'Tis a proof that he had rather . . . .
    'Tis a sign that he had rather . . . .
    Had this fair figure which this frame displays, ...
    Admission ne'er had sought, or could not find. . . . .
    Had rang'd embattled Nations at our Gates: . . . . .
    When the tenth Sun had set upon our Sorrows, ...
    That oft' had practis'd Fraud, and oft' detected, . . .
    Such had I trusted once as soon as seen, ...
    Had they prevail'd, I ne'er had known Irene. . . . .
    Had they prevail'd, I ne'er had known Irene. . . . .
    This were enough, if Cali had been Mahomet . . . . .
    Half were too much had Mahomet been Cali. . . . .
    Had not the Breeze untwin'd the meeting Boughs, . . .
    Had not my ready thought remov'd Aspasia . . . . .
    Th' important Hour had pass'd unheeded by, ...
    Had our first Asian Foes but known this Ardour, . . .
    We still had wander'd on Tartarian Hills. . . . . .
    Had stretch'd the fiery Boaster in the Grave. . . . .
    An angry look had sunk him into Hell . . . . .
    An angry look had sunk him into Hell . . . . .
    What cry? what stratagem? had then Abdalla-- . . .
    There had she lull'd me with endearing Falshoods, . . .
    One Hour had freed me from the fatal Error, ...
    One Hour had sav'd me from Despair and Madness. . . .
    Well if a Thousand Lives like thine had perish'd; . . .
    Thou mightst have liv'd, nor had I lost Irene . . . .
    My Rage and Grief had hid from my Remembrance. . . . .
    My rage and grief had had from my remembrance . . . .
    My rage and grief had had from my remembrance . . . .
    Soon forth in arms had some bold soldier stood, . . .
    Soon had the wrathfull faulchion drank his blood. . . .
    Had form'd her nest and plac'd her burthen there, . . .

HAD'ST
    Had'st thou heard a Moment, ...

HADST
    Hadst thou nine lives like a cat, ...
    What hadst thou lost by slighting those Commands? . . .
    Thou might'st have liv'd, for thou hadst spar'd Irene. .

HAIL
    That long to hail thee Chief. . . . . . .
    Hail, Terror of the Monarchs of the World, ...
    Hail illustrious Sultan . . . .
    And hail unanimous their conqu'ring God. . . . . .
    And hail the rosy Dawn of rising Health. . . . . .
    Hail lovely flower, first honour of the year! . . . .
    Hail beautious earnest of approaching spring! . . . .
    And woods and mountains hail the deity. . . . . .

HAIL'D
    Exulting Folly hail'd the joyful Day, ...
    Who hail'd him Speaker, with united voice. . . . . .

HAIR
    Nor binds the neck, nor sparkles in the hair, ...
    His shining helm with nodding horse hair grac'd. . . .

HALF
    Despise a fool in half his pension dress'd, ...
    Could half the nation's criminals contain; . . . . .
    With half mankind embattled at his side, ...
    With half mankind embattled on his side, ...
    And social sorrow loses half its pain: . . . . . .
    Can in my bosom half that grief create, ...
    To yield to remedies is half the cure. . . . . . .
    The Vet'ran Courtier half reveal'd his Project. . . . .
    Rolls half his Floods unheard through shouting Camps?
    Through half his Course reflects the blaze of . . . .
      War
    Pours half his Floods unheard through shouting camps . .
    Half were too much had Mahomet been Cali. . . . . .
    With half the grov'ling Slaves that load the Globe. . .
    In half a year of darkness lost. . . . .

HALLOW'D
    Pope's hallow'd glades, and never tiring views, . . .
    No more shall glow with Friendship's hallow'd Ardour: .
    No more shall feel Religion's hallow'd ardours' . . .

HAMLET
    Perhaps, where Lear has rav'd, and Hamlet dy'd, . . .

		PAGE	TITLE		LINE
		O 138	Tr Rambler 161		1
		O 277	Irene		29
		O 266	Irene		33
		O 64	Virgil Past.I		21
		O 73	Hor. Epode II		65
		O 76	Tr Add. Battle		33
		O 79	Feast St Simon		19
		O 95	Sprig of Myrtl	V	T
		O 97	Hickman Spinet		15
		O 97	Hickman Spinet		16
		O 136	Tr Rambler 128		2
		O 183	Burlesque Vega		3
		O 183	Burlesque Vega	V	3
		O 189	Seeing Montagu		1
		O 192	Tr. Medea II		12
		O 250	Irene		23
		O 254	Irene		120
		O 254	Irene		131
		O 255	Irene		17
		O 263	Irene		27
		O 263	Irene		27
		Y 132	Irene	V	41D
		Y 132	Irene	V	41E
		O 269	Irene		10
		O 367	Irene	V	24
		O 269	Irene		12
		O 284	Irene		40
		O 284	Irene		41
		O 312	Irene		20
		O 376	Irene	V	23
		Y 188	Irene	V	20
		Y 194	Irene	V	30
		O 331	Irene		18
		O 332	Irene		27
		O 332	Irene		28
		O 332	Irene		34
		Y 214	Irene	V	58
		O 334	Irene		65
		Y 215	Irene	V	69B
		Y 215	Irene	V	69B
		Y 23	Tr Add. Battle		40
		Y 23	Tr Add. Battle		41
		Y 23	Tr Add. Battle		45
		O 333	Irene		57
		O 194	On Thrale Hat		3
		O 332	Irene		32
		O 333	Irene		58
		O 254	Irene		137
		O 262	Irene		1
		O 351	Irene	V	23
		O 287	Irene		6
		O 320	Irene		27
		Y 3	On a Daffodill		1
		Y 3	On a Daffodill		2
		Y 7	Virgil Daphnis		41
		O 52	Pro Drury-Lane		37
		O 118	Epitaph Hanmer		20
		O 141	Tr Rambler 199		3
		Y 21	Tr. Iliad Bk 6		125
		O 13	London		73
		O 22	London		249
		O 42	Vanity Wishes		226
		Y 102	Vanity Wishes	V	226
		O 59	Pro Good Nat'd		4
		O 74	Tr. Iliad Bk 6		19
		O 140	Tr Rambler 178		1
		O 254	Irene		132
		O 264	Irene		18
		O 353	Irene	V	2
		O 353	Irene	V	32
		Y 132	Irene	V	41E
		O 332	Irene		36
		Y 38	Lady Leaving		4
		O 106	Eliza plucking		3
		O 289	Irene		16
		O 349	Irene	V	24
		O 53	Pro Drury-Lane		43

				PAGE	TITLE	LINE
HAND SEE LEFT-HAND						
Much could I add,--but see the boat at hand,	. . .		O	22	London	254
Rules the bold hand, or prompts the suppliant voice;	. .		O	31	Vanity Wishes	12
Law in his voice, and fortune in his hand:	. . . . .		O	34	Vanity Wishes	100
Peace courts his hand, but spreads her charms in vain;	.		O	40	Vanity Wishes	201
Peace courts his hand, her fondness he disdains	. . .		Y	101	Vanity Wishes	V 201
A petty fortress, and a dubious hand;	. . . .		O	41	Vanity Wishes	220
A nameless fortress, and a nameless hand;	. . . . . .		Y	102	Vanity Wishes	V 220
Manuring with laborious hand	. . . .		O	71	Hor. Epode II	5
With artfull hand the teeming vines,	. . . . .		O	71	Hor. Epode II	18
Before that day, by some brave hero's hand,	. . . . .		O	75	Tr. Iliad Bk 6	29
Your passions; guide the reins with steady hand,	. .		O	77	Festina Lente	4
Consign'd by Venus to Melissa's hand)	. . . .		O	95	Sprig of Myrtl	4
Her conscious hand his laurel leaves invite.	. . .		O	106	Eliza plucking	4
If wrought by any hand but thine,	. . . .		O	119	To Miss Purse	4
Thy hand that knows the subtler art,	. . . . . .		O	120	To Miss Purse	5
The Hand of Art here torpid lies	. . . .		O	154	Epita. Hogarth	1
The hand of him here torpid lies	. . . .		O	155	Epita. Hogarth	V 1
Who's hat was in his hand.	. . . .		O	158	Par. Hermit II	4
With his hat in his hand.	. . . .		O	158	Par. Hermit II	V 4
With gentle Hand restrain'd the Streams of Life,	. . .		O	252	Irene	97
Whose quick Impatience seiz'd my doubtful Hand,	. . .		O	254	Irene	126
Left by the Hand of Heav'n on human Clay.	. . . .		O	255	Irene	13
From giddy Mahomet's unskilful Hand.	. . . . .		O	256	Irene	46
How can a single Hand attempt a Life	. . . . .		O	258	Irene	90
Can Mahomet's imperial Hand descend	. . . . . .		O	268	Irene	15
Behold, my fair, as my resistless hand	. . . .		Y	136	Irene	V 25
This all-subduing hand, this gen'ral terror	. . .		Y	136	Irene	V 32
Join'd Cali's Hand to mine, and falt'ring cry'd,	. . .		O	272	Irene	8
His Hand! His Seal! The Secrets of my Soul	. . .		O	273	Irene	19
Nor has impartial Nature's frugal Hand	. . . . . .		O	277	Irene	53
Nor has impartial Natures generous hand	. . . . .		O	356	Irene	V 20
That Reason gives her Scepter to his Hand,	. . . .		O	281	Irene	40
Gross Fires, enkindled by a mortal Hand,	. . . . .		O	282	Irene	57
Deliverance is at Hand; for Turkey's Tyrant	. . . .		O	283	Irene	7
Wealh in her hand, and olive on her brow.	. . .		O	374	Irene	V 32
Can then th' Assassin lift his treach'rous Hand	. . .		O	286	Irene	11
Heav'n, when its Hand pour'd Softness on our Limbs	. .		O	290	Irene	42
He Heav'n, when its hand pourd softness on our limbs	.		Y	162	Irene	V 42
And ask, what guilty Pow'r's rebellious Hand	. . .		O	293	Irene	119
Say, how the Hand of Violence was rais'd,	. . . . .		O	295	Irene	25
Yet when your Hand is lifted to destroy,	. . . . .		O	298	Irene	4
Oh could thy Hand unaided free thy Country,	. . . .		O	300	Irene	63
What Hand, when Death has snatch'd away Demetrius,	.		O	301	Irene	88
Tore unresisted from the Giant Hand	. . . . .		O	312	Irene	10
Tore, unresisted, from the mighty hand	. . . . .		Y	188	Irene	V 10
Let no weak Doubt the gen'rous Hand restrain,	. . .		O	313	Irene	22
Let no distrust the gen'rous Hand restrain	. . . . .		O	377	Irene	V 3
New from the Maker's Hand, and fair array'd	. . . .		O	314	Irene	4
New from the Maker's Hand, and far array'd	. . . .		O	314	Irene	V 4
And snatch the flaming Bolt with hasty Hand.	. . .		O	314	Irene	25
Destruction is at Hand.	. . . .		O	347	Irene	V 21
And seize my Sword with disencumber'd Hand.	. . . .		O	316	Irene	29
Tell how Demetrius shun'd his single Hand,	. . . .		O	318	Irene	13
Now, Traytor, feel the Fear that chills my Hand.	. .		O	318	Irene	20
Th' expanded hand of lib'ral Heav'n	. . . .		Y	199	Irene	V 16
Holds out her Hand to lead thee back to Truth.	. . .		O	321	Irene	42
I go, lest Vengeance urge my Hand to Blood,	. . . .		O	324	Irene	23
My father fell by fierce Achilles' hand	. . . . .		Y	18	Tr. Iliad Bk 6	28
He grasp'd her hand endeav'ring kind relief.	. . .		Y	21	Tr. Iliad Bk 6	112
Hector shall perish by no warriour's hand.	. . . . .		Y	21	Tr. Iliad Bk 6	116
HANDLE						
To handle the melodious lyre.	. . . .		Y	11	Tr Hor Epode 9	4
HANDS						
He turns, with anxious heart and cripled hands,	. . .		O	44	Vanity Wishes	287
Dispatch, ye ling'ring Slaves, or nimbler Hands	. . .		O	328	Irene	42
Hector, this speaking, with extended hands	. . . .		Y	20	Tr. Iliad Bk 6	90
Death in his look, and hands imbru'd in gore	. . .		Y	23	Tr Add. Battle	47
HANDSOME						
'Tis true, the Fellow's handsome, strait and tall;	. .		O	247	Irene Epilogue	7
HANG						
And hang aloft suspended in the air.	. . . .		O	76	Tr Add. Battle	7
You can hang or drown at last.	. . . .		O	197	Song Congratu.	28
Hang Sit these black clouds upon Aspasia's brow?	. . .		Y	191	Irene	V 15
HANG'D						
And he'll be hang'd to-morrow.	. . . .		Y	300	Fanny Burney	5
HANGING						
To press the weary minutes hanging wings:	. . . .		Y	105	Vanity Wishes	V 300
HANGS						
And victory hangs doubtfull o'er the field.	. . . .		O	76	Tr Add. Battle	13
Imagination hangs her weary wings	. . . . . .		Y	127	Irene	V 2
And time hangs his flagging wings	. . . . . .		Y	128	Irene	V 4
HANMER						
A Translation Of The Latin Epitaph On Sir Thomas	. . .		O	117	Epitaph Hanmer	T
Hanmer						
When Hanmer fill'd the chair, and Ann the throne.	. . .		O	118	Epitaph Hanmer	22
HANMER'S						
Pause at this tomb where Hanmer's ashes lie;	. . . .		O	117	Epitaph Hanmer	2
Pause on this tomb where Hanmer's ashes lie;	. . . .		O	117	Epitaph Hanmer	V 2
HAPLESS						
The pangs of guilty pow'r, and hapless love,	. . . .		O	113	Epit. Phillips	2

HAPLESS   (CONTINUED)

	PAGE	TITLE	LINE	
The pangs of guilty pow'r, or hapless love,	O 113	Epit. Phillips	V	2
Dear hapless Maid--tempestuous Grief o'erbears	O 252	Irene		77
My reasoning Pow'rs--Dear, hapless, lost Aspasia!	O 252	Irene		78
The cruel Doom of hapless Menodorus--	O 270	Irene		4
Concur to press a hapless Captive's Ruin?	O 288	Irene		10
The nymphs bewail'd poor Daphnis' hapless death	Y 6	Virgil Daphnis		1
But, ah! before arise that hapless day	Y 18	Tr. Iliad Bk 6		24
And wept unhappy Pompey's hapless fate?	Y 22	Tr Add. Battle		15

HAPPIER

Grant me, kind heaven, to find some happier place,	O 11	London		43
For faith, that panting for a happier seat,	O 48	Vanity Wishes		363
For hope, that panting for a happier seat,	Y 108	Vanity Wishes	V	363
till you to happier climes remove?	O 100	Ode Friendship	V	26
Or boasts a happier Soil, already thine?	O 265	Irene		36
Or boasts a happier glebe, is Yours already,	O 366	Irene	V	13
Will e'er an happier Hour revisit Greece?	O 301	Irene		96

HAPPINESS

And makes the happiness she does not find.	O 48	Vanity Wishes		368
Intrusts his happiness to human kind,	O 82	Young Author		13
Shall aid our Happiness above.	O 100	Ode Friendship		28
Shall aid y<ou>r Happiness above.	O 100	Ode Friendship	V	28
E'er yet had happiness compleat;	O 136	Tr Rambler 128		2
And real Happiness enjoys.	O 145	Tr Boeth III.1		12
Say what is happiness below?	O 146	Tr Boeth III.4		8
But hope, yet hope, to Happiness and Honour;	O 253	Irene		109
If Happiness can be without Aspasia.	O 253	Irene		110
And feel one happiness and one misfortune.	Y 121	Irene	V	57
To scatter Happiness and Plenty round thee,	O 278	Irene		69
And plan the Happiness of mourning Millions?	O 291	Irene		68
'Tis she--My Hope, my Happiness, my Love!	O 294	Irene		1
Secure of Happiness from Flight or Conquest,	O 302	Irene		114
Of Happiness, lures on from Toil to Toil,	O 310	Irene		2
And yet such is the condition of human happiness	Y 186	Irene	V	2
O Happiness! sure thou art all Aspasia's.	O 310	Irene		14
With peaceful Death, and Happiness eternal.	O 328	Irene		47

HAPPY

A transient calm the happy scenes bestow,	O 10	London		31
The cheated nation's happy fav'rites, see!	O 14	London		91
Quick let us rise, the happy seats explore,	O 18	London		174
To you alone this happy state remains.	O 64	Virgil Past.I		16
Far from their happy native home	O 79	Feast St Simon		28
Thrice happy Saints--where do I rove?	O 80	Feast St Simon		55
In Myrtle groves oft sings the happy swain,	O 95	Sprig of Myrtl		7
In Myrtle shades oft sings the happy swain,	O 95	Sprig of Myrtl	V	7
The Myrtle crowns the happy lovers heads,	O 95	Sprig of Myrtl		9
Happy he whose Eyes have view'd	O 147	Tr Boet III.12		1
Happy whose unfetter'd Mind	O 147	Tr Boet III.12		2
Surpriz'd I start, and bless the happy Dream;	O 254	Irene		124
A happy Land, where circulating Pow'r	O 256	Irene		57
Rise from the happy Bed; and future Queens	O 268	Irene		13
Form'd to delight, and happy by delighting,	O 276	Irene		16
Deceive--And make us happy by deceiving	Y 148	Irene	V	50
Each Day and shall be made happy with new entertainments	O 350	Irene	V	24
And Gennah's happy <to> Gardens envy thine.	O 351	Irene	V	27
To rave unheeded, while the happy Greek,	O 285	Irene		2
Long be the Sultan bless'd with happy Love!	O 286	Irene		1
That none are great, or happy, but the Virtuous.	O 294	Irene		8
Inform me rather, how thy happy Courage	O 295	Irene		27
And sought this happy Grove in quest of Thee.	O 299	Irene		50
And hot Abdalla hates the happy Lover.	O 300	Irene		75
--O Demetrius O for a cottage in those happy regions	Y 177	Irene	V	108
Henceforth for ever happy be this Day,	O 308	Irene		1
Will damp my joys, and cloud the happy days	O 370	Irene	V	23
The thoughts of happy love, and rescu'd Greece	Y 189	Irene	V	1D
The happy Moment, hasten to the Shore,	O 320	Irene		8
Sure 'tis the happy Hour ordain'd above,	O 321	Irene		35
Bound o'er the sparkling Waves. Go, happy Bark,	O 322	Irene		5
Dance o'er the Sparkling Waves--Go happy Bark	O 364	Irene	V	30
Go Happy Bark, thy sacred Freight secures thee	O 364	Irene	V	24
Not long the happy Russians mourn;	Y 39	Lady Leaving		9

HARBINGER

| Vice the harbinger of ruin. | Y 114 | Irene | V | 39 |
| Shows his bold Front, the Harbinger of Ruin, | O 250 | Irene | | 41 |

HARBOUR'D

| How Guilt once harbour'd in the conscious Breast, | O 311 | Irene | | 14 |

HARBOURS

| (No spark of envy harbours in my breast) | O 64 | Virgil Past.I | | 14 |
| When Guilt like this once harbours in the Breast | O 346 | Irene | V | 4 |

HARD

Hard is his lot, that here by Fortune plac'd,	O 53	Pro Drury-Lane		47
Alas! 'tis hard for beauty to be just.	O 81	Lady Birthday		12
"Think not yet my service hard,	O 185	Anacreon Ode 9		17
Hard was the Strife of Justice and of Love;	O 324	Irene		13

HARDY

The hardy Scythian ever mourns.	O 70	Hor.II Ode XX		16
And visits Britain's hardy Sons	O 80	Feast St Simon		47
Selected by my Care, a hardy Band,	O 254	Irene		136

HARES

| The screaming Cranes and fearfull Hares. | O 72 | Hor. Epode II | | 44 |

```
HARES             (CONTINUED)                              PAGE    TITLE          LINE
     Hares forgot the following hound,  . . . . . . . .   O 148 Tr Boet III.12     10
HARK
     But hark! th' affrighted crowd's tumultuous cries . . .   O  18 London        182
HARLEY'S
     And fixed disease on Harley's closing life? . . . . .    O  36 Vanity Wishes  130
HARLOT
     bend tyrant adamant--melt harlot . . . . . . . . .   Y 181 Irene           V  56
HARMLESS
     The harmless Freedom, and the private Friend. . . . .    O  46 Vanity Wishes  338
     By harmless merriment, or useful sense. . . . . . .     O  62 Pro Word Wise    14
     The harmless wolves no more our cattle fear,  . . . .   Y   7 Virgil Daphnis   38
HARMONIOUS
     Phillips! whose touch harmonious could remove . . . .   O 113 Epit. Phillips    1
     And sees the motions of th' harmonious sphere; . . . .  Y   7 Virgil Daphnis   35
HARMONIS'D
     When social Laws first harmonis'd the World,  . . . .   O 291 Irene            70
HARMONY
     From ev'ry tongue flows harmony divine. . . . . . .     O  16 London         128
     Gives all the harmony of life;  . . . . . . . . .   O 121 To Miss Playin     32
HARPER
     Summon'd the singer blythe, and harper gay, . . . . .   O 192 Tr. Medea II      7
HARPSICORD
     To Miss <Carpenter> On her playing upon the Harpsicord  .   O 120 To Miss Playin    T
HARRASS
     Of all the griefs that harrass the distress'd, . . . .  O  17 London         166
     And harrass Greece no more with wasteful War. . . . .   O 257 Irene            80
     Let Slav'ry harrass, and let Hunger gripe. . . . . .    O 328 Irene            37
HARRASS'D
     Where once the harrass'd Briton found repose, . . . .   O  11 London          47
     My Bosom harrass'd with alternate Passions, . . . . .   O 299 Irene            54
HARSH
     Trumpet or lyre--to their harsh bosoms chill, . . . .   O 192 Tr. Medea II     11
     Freed from the harsh severities of virtue . . . . .     Y 146 Irene          V  23
HARVEST
     She gleans the harvest, and she stores the grain. . .   O 151 The Ant           8
     She crops the harvest, and she stores the grain. . .    O 151 The Ant        V   8
     And not a harvest ripen but for me . . . . . . . .  Y 132 Irene          V  42
HAS
     Let----live here, for----has learn'd to live. . . . .   O  11 London          50
     Has heaven reserv'd, in pity to the poor, . . . . .     O  18 London         170
     This pow'r has praise, that virtue scarce can warm,     O  39 Vanity Wishes  183
     Such pow'r has praise, that virtue scarce can charm,    Y 100 Vanity Wishes  V 183
     Perhaps, where Lear has rav'd, and Hamlet dy'd, .       O  53 Pro Drury-Lane   43
     The man whom fate has laid, where all must lye. .       O  61 Pro Word Wise     6
     And love return, has great Erasmus died? . . . . .      O 132 Tr. Rambler 54    2
     Here death has clos'd the curious eyes  . . . . .       O 154 Epita. Hogarth    3
     Phrase that Time has flung away,  . . . . . . . .   O 179 Ridicul Warton     5
     When Minos once has fix'd your doom, . . . . . . .      O 232 Tr Horace IV.7   22
     Besides, he has fifty Wives; and who can bear . .       O 247 Irene Epilogue    5
     And when blest Peace has silenc'd War's Alarms, . .     O 247 Irene Epilogue   23
     At length the Conquerour has spent his  . . . . .       O 350 Irene          V   8
          rage--
     Has Silence press'd her Seal upon his Lips? . . . .     O 255 Irene            20
     What has the Wretch that has surviv'd his Country,  . . O 260 Irene           134
     What has the Wretch that has surviv'd his Country, . .  O 260 Irene           134
     Has heard unhurt the cries of slaughterd thousands  . . Y 126 Irene          V 145
     Has Treason's dire Infection reach'd my Palace? . .     O 272 Irene             2
     Heav'n has reserv'd no future Paradise, . . . . . .     O 276 Irene            17
     Why then has Nature's vain Munificence  . . . . .       O 276 Irene            24
     Whence then those Charms thy Tongue has deign'd to  . . O 277 Irene            26
          flatter,
     Why then Those charms your tongue has deign'd to  . . . O 355 Irene          V  15
          flatter
     Nor has impartial Nature's frugal Hand  . . . . .       O 277 Irene            53
     Nor has impartial Natures generous hand . . . . .       O 356 Irene          V  20
     Has fix'd his Hopes, Inquietudes, and Fears, . . . .    O 280 Irene            27
     If e'er thy Youth has known the Pangs of Absence, . .   O 285 Irene             3
     Whate'er Man's Pride has ravish'd from our Sex. . .     O 291 Irene            75
     What Hand, when Death has snatch'd away Demetrius, . .  O 301 Irene            88
     But the sight of friends soul sinking into vice (a soul .  Y 177 Irene        V111C
          that has
     Our Bark unseen has reach'd th' appointed Bay, . . . .  O 304 Irene             1
     Why has thy Choice then pointed out Leontius, . .       O 305 Irene            20
     The matchless Fair has bless'd me with Compliance;  . . O 308 Irene             3
     The Breast where Guilt like this has found  . . . . .   O 349 Irene          V  23
          admission
     Infatuate Loiterer, has Fate, in vain, . . . . . .      O 318 Irene            15
     Luckless slave Ilfated loiterer has fate in vain . . .  Y 196 Irene          V  15
     Has left the slaves behind, nay then there's danger. .  Y 198 Irene          V  34
     To share the Miseries herself has caus'd. . . . . .     O 320 Irene            15
     Has taught my Slave the Language of Command! . . . .    O 323 Irene             2
     But now 'tis o'er, and Justice has prevail'd. . . .     O 324 Irene            14
     This Bay has prov'd my ,fondness for the Sultan; . . .  O 324 Irene            19
     Go, blustring Slave.--He has not heard of Murza. .      O 324 Irene            25
     Whence is this Rage? what barb'rous Tongue has wrong'd .  O 325 Irene           27
          me?
     Has serv'd his Prince so well, demand our Silence?  . . O 329 Irene            19
     Was she then guiltless! Has my thoughtless Rage . . .   O 332 Irene            18
     Thrice has December stripp'd the tree . . . . . . .  Y  11 Tr Hor Epode 9     7
     Who has not read the Theban brothers' hate? . . . . .   Y  22 Tr Add. Battle   14
```

HAS   (CONTINUED)   PAGE   TITLE   LINE
     Oft has our bard in this disastrous year, ...   Y 67 Prologue Lethe   7
     Oft has he seen the poignant orange fly, ... Y 67 Prologue Lethe   9
     Our little dog has bit his tail . . . .   Y 300 Fanny Burney   4
HASAN
     Two faithful Captains, Hasan and Caraza, ... O 310 Irene   5
HAST
     Thither with eager hast he runs . . . .   O 80 Feast St Simon   46
     Thou that hast long perus'd the Draughts of Nature,   . . O 255 Irene   11
     Where hast thou linger'd while th' encumber'd Hours . .   O 279 Irene   3
     Hast thou grown old amidst the Croud of Courts,   . .   O 281 Irene   32
     What Claim hast thou to plead? . . . .   O 286 Irene   8
     What Fears, what Griefs, what Dangers hast thou known?   O 295 Irene   22
     Hast thou not search'd my Soul's profoundest Thoughts? .   O 304 Irene   18
     And try the Hazard that hast Nought to stake;   . . . .   O 319 Irene   31
     Haste, seize them, guards, be quick--my thoughtless hast   Y 198 Irene   V 34
HASTE
     With ardent Haste, each Candidate of Fame   . . . . .   O 57 Prologue Comus   19
     Thus lightly skim, and haste away.   . . . . .   O 203 Tr. on Skating   V 4
     Haste to the safe retreat, from whence Demetrius   . .   Y 126 Irene   V 144
     Alone, with am'rous Haste to seek his Love.   . . . . .   O 262 Irene   29
     Haste Go Mustapha go to celebrate the day   . . . .   Y 129 Irene   V 25
     Now haste to mingle in one common Center, ...   O 287 Irene   4
     Make haste, bright Maid, to rule the willing World; . .   O 288 Irene   7
     Haste, seize them, guards, be quick--my thoughtless hast   Y 198 Irene   V 34
     Haste, Murza, to the Palace, let the Sultan   . . . . .   O 319 Irene   2
     Come haste, and live--Thy Innocence and Truth . . . .   O 320 Irene   18
     Now haste to murder, ere returning Thought   . . . .   O 326 Irene   39
     Bear off with eager Haste th' unfinish'd Sentence,   . .   O 333 Irene   53
HASTEN
     And rising Ages hasten to be just. . . . .   O 57 Prologue Comus   14
     The happy Moment, hasten to the Shore, ...   O 320 Irene   8
HASTES
     Yet timely provident, she hastes away   . . . . . . O 151 The Ant   5
HASTY
     How rarely reason guides the hasty choice, ...   Y 92 Vanity Wishes   V 11
     Of hasty greatness finds the fatal doom, ...   O 43 Vanity Wishes   252
     Of hasty greatness finds the hasty doom, ...   Y 103 Vanity Wishes   V 252
     Of hasty greatness finds the hasty doom, ...   Y 103 Vanity Wishes   V 252
     And turn'd their hasty Steps towards the Garden.   . .   O 269 Irene   39
     It parts you now--The hasty Sultan sign'd   . . . . .   O 296 Irene   1
     And snatch the flaming Bolt with hasty Hand.   . . . .   O 314 Irene   25
     Your hasty Zeal defrauds the Claim of Justice, ...   O 330 Irene   5
HAT
     I put my hat upon my head . . . .   O 158 Par. Hermit II   1
     As with my hat upon my head   . . . .   O 158 Par. Hermit II   V 1
     Who's hat was in his hand.   . . . .   O 158 Par. Hermit II   4
     With his hat in his hand.   . . . .   O 158 Par. Hermit II   V 4
     Wear the gown, and wear the hat, ...   O 194 On Thrale Hat   1
HATE
     Then say how hope and fear, desire and hate, ...   O 31 Vanity Wishes   5
     Then say how fierce desire and raging hate, ...   Y 92 Vanity Wishes   V 5
     Then say how hot desire and raging hate, ...   Y 92 Vanity Wishes   V 5
     Hate dogs their flight, and insult mocks their end. . .   O 33 Vanity Wishes   78
     Mark the keen glance, and watch the sign to hate. . . .   O 34 Vanity Wishes   110
     Against your fame with fondness hate combines, ...   O 46 Vanity Wishes   331
     Till that glad night when all that hate may hiss.   . .   O 60 Pro Good Nat'd   20
     And Love and Hate alike implore . . . .   O 122 Stella Mourn.   15
     Where Hate sits musing to betray, ...   O 191 Tr. Medea I   11
     For Zeal unguarded, undissembled Hate, ...   O 299 Irene   36
     Who has not read the Theban brothers' hate? . . . . . .   Y 22 Tr Add. Battle   14
HATED
     All crimes are safe, but hated poverty.   . . . . .   O 17 London   159
     A surer Passage to his hated Heart.   . . . . .   O 307 Irene   25
             Hated Name! his jealous Rage   . . . . .   O 316 Irene   9
     Shrinks at the hated Task, for thy Destruction; . . .   O 325 Irene   21
     Shrinks back from the hated task, for thy destruction; .   Y 204 Irene   V 21
HATEFUL
     By hateful Business hurried from her Sight, ...   O 287 Irene   15
     Let one just Act conclude the hateful Day.   . . . . .   O 333 Irene   50
HATES
     And hot Abdalla hates the happy Lover.   . . . . .   O 300 Irene   75
HATH
     Who hath not heard of Argo's valiant crew? . . . . . .   Y 22 Tr Add. Battle   10
HATRED
     Urg'd headlong on by hatred or by love: . . . . .   O 77 Festina Lente   6
     But now 'tis hatred all.---- . . . .   O 131 Tr. Rambler 45   3
HAUGHTY
     Or move the haughty King below, ...   O 69 Hor.II Ode 14   10
     The haughty Persian in thy gore   . . . .   O 80 Feast St Simon   53
     For tho' beneath thy haughty Brow . . . .   O 146 Tr Boeth III.5   5
     Marry a Turk! a haughty, Tyrant King, ...   O 247 Irene Epilogue   1
     What! think of Peace while haughty Scanderbeg . . . .   O 264 Irene   13
     Will yet Irenes haughty Soul descend . . . . . .   O 372 Irene   V 6
     Why fled this haughty Heroine from the Battle? . . . .   O 290 Irene   39
     Resumes th' imperious Air of haughty Virtue.   . . . .   O 314 Irene   15
     At length the Prize is mine--The haughty Maid . . . .   O 317 Irene   1
     When haughty Guilt exults with impious Joy, ...   O 335 Irene   12
HAUNT
     Nor Melancholy's phantoms haunt thy shade;   . . . . .   O 37 Vanity Wishes   154
     Nor Melancholy's spectres haunt thy shade;   . . . . .   Y 99 Vanity Wishes   V 154

		PAGE	TITLE	LINE
HAUNT	(CONTINUED)			
While bees shall feed on thyme, and birds shall haunt the grove		Y 7	Virgil Daphnis	50
HAVE				
Have hopes, and fears, and wishes, just the same; . . .		O 59	Pro Good Nat'd	12
The inexorable sisters have decreed		O 74	Tr. Iliad Bk 6	11
Nor my brave brothers, that have bit the ground, . . .		O 74	Tr. Iliad Bk 6	17
Angelick choirs have sung.		O 80	Feast St Simon	60
Epilogue intended to have been spoken by a Lady		O 83	Epi Dist Moth.	T
Happy he whose Eyes have view'd		O 147	Tr Boet III.12	1
Have drank the liquor up.		O 159	Par Hermit III	8
Have a turnip than his father.		O 183	Burlesque Vega	4
Have a turnip than a father.		O 183	Burlesque Vega	V 4
"I have chatter'd like a pye."		O 186	Anacreon Ode 9	44
Her statue would have breath'd an added grace,		O 189	Seeing Montagu	4
And on its basis would have been enroll'd, ...		O 190	Seeing Montagu	5
To have the fiftieth Part her paultry Share?		O 247	Irene Epilogue	6
My Pride's to have that little all my own.		O 247	Irene Epilogue	10
But now our Turkish Conquerors have quench'd		O 249	Irene	7
Long have I wish'd, before our Prophet's Tomb, ...		O 263	Irene	9
Long have as oblig'd by vow		Y 130	Irene	V 9
Too strong for Love, have hurried him on Death. . . .		O 267	Irene	48
Oft have I rag'd, when their wide-wasting Cannon . . .		O 273	Irene	24
Have I for this preserv'd my guiltless Bosom, ...		O 304	Irene	14
Have I for this defy'd the Chiefs of Turkey, ...		O 304	Irene	16
I w<ould> have every smile g<enu>ine to<morrow no>		Y 185	Irene	V 3
Hypocrisy which I ha<ve> worn is a burthen:		Y 185	Irene	V 2
Caraza speak--have ye remark'd the Bassa?		O 311	Irene	1
Thou might'st have liv'd, for thou hadst spar'd Irene. .		O 333	Irene	58
Thou mightst have liv'd, nor had I lost Irene		Y 214	Irene	V 58
Here have I rais'd four sacred altars, two		Y 7	Virgil Daphnis	43
Thrice to the wall their dreadfull hosts have led . . .		Y 19	Tr. Iliad Bk 6	56
Dar'd have provok'd a foe to single fight, ...		Y 23	Tr Add. Battle	39
HAZARD				
His Friends, his Liberty, to hazard?		O 260	Irene	135
Important Hazard! What's that airy Bubble		O 260	Irene	137
And try the Hazard that hast Nought to stake;		O 319	Irene	31
HAZARDOUS				
Is hazardous.		O 260	Irene	133
Is hazardous but--Talk no more of Hazards		O 365	Irene	V 23
HAZARDS				
Forbear to speak of Hazards, ...		O 260	Irene	133
Is hazardous but--Talk no more of Hazards		O 365	Irene	V 23
What hazards would I shun to clasp for Greece and for Aspasia	.	Y 125	Irene	V 133
That loses all because she hazards nothing:		O 281	Irene	45
HE			OMITTED WORD	
154				
HE'LL				
And he'll be hang'd to-morrow.		Y 300	Fanny Burney	5
HEAD				
Here falling houses thunder on your head, ...		O 9	London	17
And Bacon's mansion trembles o'er his head.		O 37	Vanity Wishes	140
He feels th' unfading wreath surround his head; . . .		O 82	Young Author	22
And feels the unfading wreath surround his head; . . .		O 82	Young Author	V 22
Adorn Philander's head, or grace his tomb.		O 95	Sprig of Myrtl	14
I put my hat upon my head		O 158	Par. Hermit II	1
As with my hat upon my head		O 158	Par. Hermit II	V 1
"Under leaves to hide one's head,		O 185	Anacreon Ode 9	27
<In> Triumphant at the head of thy new votaries . . .		Y 131	Irene	V 32A
Would shake his wily Head, and closely whisper, . . .		O 273	Irene	28
Now roll full fraught with Thunder o'er your Head. . .		O 275	Irene	75
That Hoary Head, that Head which hungry fate		O 374	Irene	V 20
That Hoary Head, that Head which hungry fate		O 374	Irene	V 20
Wilt thou then head the Troop upon the Shore, ...		O 305	Irene	36
Against the Head which Innocence secures, ...		O 322	Irene	1
May lambent zephyrs gently wave thy head, ...		Y 3	On a Daffodill	9
HEADLONG				
Then, swift as thought, by headlong anger driv'n . . .		O 76	Tr Add. Battle	10
Urg'd headlong on by hatred or by love:		O 77	Festina Lente	6
Vain man runs headlong, to caprice resign'd;		O 134	Tr Rambler 105	1
Shook headlong from his throne imperial Jove.		Y 26	Tr Add. Battle	139
HEADS				
The Myrtle crowns the happy lovers heads, ...		O 95	Sprig of Myrtl	9
Nor bribes your Eyes to prejudice your Heads.		O 246	Irene Prologue	28
And may bounteous Heav'n repay the mercy on Your Heads	. .	O 344	Irene	V 27
The sympathising cattle hung their heads		Y 6	Virgil Daphnis	9
Above their heads th' embattled squadrons hung . . .		Y 25	Tr Add. Battle	94
HEADY				
Improve his heady rage with treach'rous skill, . . .		O 44	Vanity Wishes	281
HEALTH				
There ev'ry breeze bears health upon its wings; . . .		O 20	London	221
Farewell!--When youth, and health, and fortune spent, .		O 23	London	256
In health, in sickness, thus the suppliant prays; . .		O 43	Vanity Wishes	256
And hail the rosy Dawn of rising Health.		O 320	Irene	27
HEALTHFUL				
Pour forth thy fervours for a healthful mind, ...		O 48	Vanity Wishes	359
For healthful indigence in vain they pray, ...		O 132	Tr. Rambler 48	1
HEAP				
And heap their vallies with the gaudy foe;		O 42	Vanity Wishes	236

		PAGE	TITLE		LINE

HEAP (CONTINUED)

And heap the fire, and milk the Kine	O	72	Hor. Epode II		51
Shrinks from this heap of aggregated crime	Y	159	Irene	V	9
Let me but live, heap Woes on Woes upon me, ...	O	328	Irene		33

HEAP'D

Wealth heap'd on wealth, nor truth nor safety buys, . .	O	31	Vanity Wishes		27
Heap'd by your Father's ill-plac'd Bounties on him, . .	O	274	Irene		51
Heap'd by my Fathers illplac'd Bounties on Him	O	351	Irene	V	13

HEAR

A Statesman's logick unconvinc'd can hear, ...	O	13	London		71
To shake with laughter ere the jest they hear, ...	O	16	London		140
But will not Britain hear the last appeal, ...	O	34	Vanity Wishes		91
Hear Lydiat's life, and Galileo's end.	O	38	Vanity Wishes		164
But hear his death, ye blockheads, hear and sleep. . .	O	39	Vanity Wishes		174
But hear his death, ye blockheads, hear and sleep. . .	O	39	Vanity Wishes		174
But hear his death, ye blockheads, hear and weep. . .	O	39	Vanity Wishes	V	174
But hear his death, ye blockheads, hear and weep. . .	O	39	Vanity Wishes	V	174
And scarce a legacy can bribe to hear;	O	44	Vanity Wishes		278
And guests are brib'd to hear;	Y	104	Vanity Wishes	V	278
Which heavn may hear	Y	108	Vanity Wishes	V	348
Which heav'n may hear, nor deem religion vain.	O	47	Vanity Wishes		350
Must hear all taunts, and hear without reply.	O	59	Pro Good Nat'd		14
Must hear all taunts, and hear without reply.	O	59	Pro Good Nat'd		14
Forbear to hiss--the Poet cannot hear.	O	62	Pro Word Wise		18
That grant his Prayers, and hear his cries.	O	72	Hor. Epode II	V	28
Unpitying see them weep, and hear them pray, ...	O	83	Epi Dist Moth.		8
To hear his eloquence, and praise his life.	O	118	Epitaph Hanmer		18
One moment hear the moral song, ...	O	121	To Miss Playin		22
Hear, and be just.	O	133	Tr. Rambler 81		1
Tho' the Hind approach'd to hear	O	148	Tr Boet III.12		7
Yet hear, alas! this mournful truth, ...	O	159	Par Hermit III		9
Yet hear, at last, this mournful truth, ...	O	159	Par Hermit III	V	9
Nor hear it with a frown;--	O	159	Par Hermit III		10
Ye Sons of England, deign to hear, ...	O	188	Epilogue		3
Ye Sons of Britain, deign to hear, ...	O	188	Epilogue	V	3
Or hear himself, for see the Bassa comes.	O	254	Irene		141
To hear my Vows and give Mankind a Queen?	O	276	Irene		2
To hear my suit and give a Queen to Turkey?	O	372	Irene	V	7
Who hear thee speak, and not abandon Reason?	O	281	Irene		43
To hear the Voice of Truth; dismiss thy Train, ...	O	289	Irene		6
To hear the voice of truth, dismiss your train	O	366	Irene	V	22
To tell, or hear, were Waste of Life.	O	316	Irene		21
Far be the Thought--But hear my Protestation.	O	326	Irene		32
Far be the horrid thought--but hear my protestation . .	Y	205	Irene	V	32
But who can hear thee beg without compliance	Y	205	Irene	V	33
Not call'd to try the Cause, we hear the Sentence, . .	O	326	Irene		34
The Prayer I cannot grant--I dare not hear.	O	328	Irene		48
O, hear my Pray'rs! accept, all-pitying Heaven, . . .	O	328	Irene		52
Then hear, great Mahomet, the Voice of Truth.	O	333	Irene		55
Hear! shall I hear thee! did'st thou hear Irene? . . .	O	333	Irene		56
Hear! shall I hear thee! did'st thou hear Irene? . . .	O	333	Irene		56
Hear! shall I hear thee! did'st thou hear Irene? . . .	O	333	Irene		56
Hear but a Moment.	O	333	Irene		57
Attend my prayers propitious, hear my vow, ...	Y	7	Virgil Daphnis		42
The swains shall pay their vows, and thou shalt hear their prayer.	Y	7	Virgil Daphnis		52
Propitious hear my prayers, protect the boy, ...	Y	20	Tr. Iliad Bk 6		101

HEARD

Where ne'er was heard the form of mock debate, . . .	Y	94	Vanity Wishes	V	57
And senates heard before they judg'd a cause;	O	33	Vanity Wishes		60
Less heard and less, the faint remonstrance falls; . .	O	46	Vanity Wishes		334
Beheld with love, with veneration heard.	O	118	Epitaph Hanmer		26
And fate malicious heard the pray'r.	O	122	Stella Mourn.		8
Hebrus heard her Poet groan, ...	O	148	Tr Boet III.12	V	7
Has heard unhurt the cries of slaughterd thousands . .	Y	126	Irene	V	145
Calmly he heard, till Amurath's Resumption	O	270	Irene		10
And heard in my first approaching	Y	144	Irene	V	79
And heard within the Thicket that conceal'd us, . . .	O	311	Irene		12
Go, blustring Slave.--He has not heard of Murza. . . .	O	324	Irene		25
O let me be but heard, nor fear from me	O	327	Irene		20
Heard her last Cries, and fann'd her dying Beauties, . .	O	333	Irene		47
Had'st thou heard a Moment, ...	O	333	Irene		57
I heard her, pitied her, and wish'd to save her. . . .	O	333	Irene		59
I heard, and soften'd, till Abdalla brought	O	334	Irene		61
Hector, this heard without a moment's stay, ...	Y	17	Tr. Iliad Bk 6		1
Who hath not heard of Argo's valiant crew?	Y	22	Tr Add. Battle		10
And heard th' ill omen'd catcall's direful cry. . . .	Y	67	Prologue Lethe		10

HEARING

| Were now well lost, in hearing how you fail'd. . . . . | O | 316 | Irene | | 23 |

HEARS

Delusive Fortune hears th' incessant call, ...	O	33	Vanity Wishes		75
The mountain shepherd hears the distant noise.	O	132	Tr. Rambler 65		3
My Vows, 'tis true, she hears with less Aversion, . . .	O	287	Irene		7

HEART

Can sap the principles, or taint the heart;	O	13	London		76
Watch the weak hour, and ransack all the heart; . . .	O	17	London		155
Fate never wounds more deep the gen'rous heart, . . .	O	18	London		168
Nor claim the triumph of a letter'd heart;	O	37	Vanity Wishes		152
He turns, with anxious heart and cripled hands, . . .	O	44	Vanity Wishes		287
And ask the latest fashion of the heart, ...	O	46	Vanity Wishes		328
By regular Approach essay'd the Heart;	O	51	Pro Drury-Lane		12

HEART	(CONTINUED)	PAGE	TITLE	LINE
By regular Approach assail'd the Heart;		O 51	Pro Drury-Lane	V 12
Yet softer Claims the melting Heart engage,		O 58	Prologue Comus	29
The man, my friend, whose conscious heart		O 65	Hor I Ode xxii	1
The Man, my Friend, whose conscious Heart		O 66	To A. Fuscus	1
Into his supplicating mothers heart.		O 77	Festina Lente	14
To point each glance, and force it to the heart!		O 81	Lady Birthday	8
And ease the throbbings of an anxious heart;		O 95	Sprig of Myrtl	12
And cure the throbbing of an anxious heart;		O 95	Sprig of Myrtl	V 12
Charm'd ev'ry ear, and gain'd on ev'ry heart.		O 117	Epitaph Hanmer	8
To weave those nets that catch the heart.		O 120	To Miss Purse	6
The heart, once caught, should ne'er be freed?		O 120	To Miss Purse	12
New chains to hold the captive heart.		O 121	To Miss Playin	18
New Tortures for the captive heart.		O 121	To Miss Playin	V 18
To tune the regulated heart.		O 121	To Miss Playin	36
Resign the heart to spleen and care,		O 123	Winter's Walk	10
Where wisdom first inform'd my heart.		O 125	An Ode	20
And quell the rebels of the heart.		O 126	An Ode	40
Would you hope to gain my heart,		O 176	Tr Metastasi I	1
"Grac'd with all that charms the heart,		O 185	Anacreon Ode 9	9
Does adamantine Faith invest his Heart?		O 255	Irene	21
Gain'd all his Heart; at length his eager Love		O 259	Irene	123
Exalts my Soul, and fortifies my Heart.		O 265	Irene	5
Will not that Pow'r that form'd the Heart of Woman,		O 266	Irene	23
My Heart still beats responsive to the Sultan's;		O 272	Irene	9
That melt a Heart, impregnable till now,		O 276	Irene	4
Guide the Sons dagger to the Fathers heart		O 352	Irene	V 4
Still, still Distrust sits heavy on my Heart.		O 301	Irene	95
Her ancient Empire o'er the yielding Heart;		O 302	Irene	121
A surer Passage to his hated Heart.		O 307	Irene	25
Ask of thy Heart; attend the Voice of Conscience--		O 323	Irene	7
But Heav'n shall guide it to the guilty Heart.		O 335	Irene	15
Heav'n turns its point upon the guilty Heart		O 345	Irene	V 29
Then when repeated bowls unlock'd the heart		Y 11	Tr Hor Epode 9	17
Ended her wretched life and pierc'd her heart.		Y 19	Tr. Iliad Bk 6	43
May then his mother's heart with joys o'erflow		Y 20	Tr. Iliad Bk 6	105
HEARTS				
Aw'd into Love, our conquer'd hearts obey,		O 96	Hickman Spinet	4
At busy hearts in vain love's arrows fly;		O 133	Tr. Rambler 85	1
Does chearless Diffidence oppress their Hearts?		O 270	Irene	22
Or fix'd the pointed arrows in their hearts.		Y 23	Tr Add. Battle	43
Meantime the Pygmies with undaunted hearts		Y 24	Tr Add. Battle	76
HEAT				
And as their patron hints the cold or heat,		O 16	London	142
With fatal heat impetuous courage glows,		O 31	Vanity Wishes	17
Yet should thy soul indulge the gen'rous heat,		O 37	Vanity Wishes	143
Yet should thy fate indulge the gen'rous heat,		Y 98	Vanity Wishes	V 143
Sure some kind Sabre in the Heat of Battle,		O 252	Irene	93
Young Man, forbear--The Heat of Youth, no more--		O 284	Irene	47
To mark the noblest Minds, with active Heat		O 293	Irene	112
HEATH				
Walks the wild heath, and sings his toil away.		O 32	Vanity Wishes	38
HEAV'N				
When publick crimes inflame the wrath of heav'n:		O 13	London	66
And hopes from angry heav'n another fire.		O 19	London	209
Which heav'n may hear, nor deem religion vain.		O 47	Vanity Wishes	350
But leave to heav'n the measure and the choice,		O 47	Vanity Wishes	352
These goods for man the laws of heav'n ordain,		O 48	Vanity Wishes	365
Descend, impetuous, from the vault of Heav'n.		O 76	Tr Add. Battle	11
All pains, all cares, may favouring heav'n remove,		O 81	Lady Birthday	5
There begs of heav'n a less distinguish'd lot;		O 82	Young Author	29
We bid propitious Heav'n prolong your reign,		O 96	Hickman Spinet	7
Friendship! peculiar boon of heav'n,		O 99	Ode Friendship	1
Friendship! peculiar Gift of heav'n,		O 99	Ode Friendship	V 1
In all the pomp of heav'n;		O 126	To Lyce, Lady	4
Now he sighs to heav'n, and now		O 149	Tr Boet III.12	17
Learn here how Heav'n supports the virtuous Mind,		O 246	Irene Prologue	9
Must watchfull providence despatch from Heav'n		Y 114	Irene	V 46
Some Pow'r invisible, from Heav'n or Hell,		O 251	Irene	50
Arose to Heav'n, and pierc'd my bleeding Breast,		O 251	Irene	74
A signal hour marked out by pitying Heav'n		Y 117	Irene	V 109
Left by the Hand of Heav'n on human Clay.		O 255	Irene	13
To heav'n and earth the courage of Leontius		Y 120	Irene	V 31B
Say, did a Voice from Heav'n restrain the Tyrant?		O 259	Irene	115
While Heav'n and Mahomet divide her Fears,		O 260	Irene	127
Heav'n will contemn the mercenary Fervour,		O 262	Irene	26
How Heav'n in Scorn of human Arrogance,		O 269	Irene	1
Must I for these renounce the Hope of Heav'n,		O 276	Irene	13
Heav'n has reserv'd no future Paradise,		O 276	Irene	17
Heav'n, when its Hand pour'd Softness on our Limbs		O 290	Irene	42
He Heav'n, when its hand pourd softness on our limbs		Y 162	Irene	V 42
And Persecution boast the Call of Heav'n.		O 291	Irene	66
Beneath each Curse of unrelenting Heav'n,		O 292	Irene	86
With every curse of angry heav'n afflicted beneath each		O 357	Irene	V 15
Tranquillity and Guilt, disjoin'd by Heav'n,		O 292	Irene	90
Thank Heav'n in daily hymns for my our deliverance		Y 166	Irene	V 93
Ambition is the Stamp impress'd by Heav'n		O 293	Irene	111
En<v>ies the meanest minister of Heav'n of celestial beings.		Y 168	Irene	V135A
Sure Heav'n, for Wonders are not wrought in vain,		O 296	Irene	38

HEAV'N   (CONTINUED)   PAGE   TITLE   LINE
    Receive her, and protect her, gracious Heav'n!   . . . .   O 297 Irene   16
    Then strike secure, and Heav'n assist the Blow.   . . .   O 298 Irene   9
    When Heav'n shall bid the swelling Billows rage, . . .   O 300 Irene   60
    Permitted oft, though not inspir'd by Heav'n, ... O 300 Irene   65
    Sometimes the Wretch unaw'd by Heav'n or Hell, ... O 300 Irene   78
    Should Heav'n yet unappeas'd refuse its Aid, ... O 301 Irene   97
    Now let us wait the last Award of Heav'n, ... O 302 Irene   113
    Think them a sacred Treasure lent by Heav'n,   . . .   O 302 Irene   6
    Heav'n makes not mine to give. . . . .   O 307 Irene   16
    Blest Prince, for whom indulgent Heav'n ordains   . . .   O 308 Irene   6
    O! could the Eyes of Kings, like those of Heav'n, . . .   O 308 Irene   12
    Till angry Heav'n shall mark them out for Ruin,   . . .   O 309 Irene   36
    When Heav'n bestows the Privilege to bless, ... O 313 Irene   21
    Is sure the Smile of unoffended Heav'n. . . . .   O 314 Irene   9
    Is this th' unshaken Confidence in Heav'n? . . . . . .   O 314 Irene   18
    Reserv'd, for other Lands, the Scourge of Heav'n. . . . . O 315 Irene   5
    Th' expanded hand of lib'ral Heav'n . . . .   Y 199 Irene   V 16
    Shall bless our Wand'rings, and propitiate Heav'n. . .   O 320 Irene   19
    And Honour and Reproach, and Heav'n and Hell. . . . .   O 321 Irene   38
    Kind Heav'n affords thee, and inviting Mercy   . . . .   O 321 Irene   41
    And Heav'n forbids to lavish Life away, ...   O 321 Irene   49
    And wing thy latest Pray'r to pitying Heav'n. . . . .   O 322 Irene   62
    Turn'd backwards by the powerful Breath of Heav'n. . .   O 322 Irene   3
    And may bounteous Heav'n repay the mercy on Your . . .   O 344 Irene   V 27
      Heads
    Destroy'd the fairest Workmanship of Heav'n!   . . . .   O 332 Irene   19
    Such was the Will of Heav'n--A Band of Greeks   . . . .   O 335 Irene   5
    So fix'd the Justice of all-conscious Heav'n.   . . . .   O 335 Irene   11
    But Heav'n shall guide it to the guilty Heart. . . . . . O 335 Irene   15
    Heav'n turns its point upon the guilty Heart.   . . . .   O 345 Irene   V 29
    Whether urg'd on by seers from heav'n inspir'd . . . .   Y 19 Tr. Iliad Bk 6   58
HEAV'N'S
    While Heav'n's high Minister, whose awful Volume . . .   O 276 Irene   20
HEAV'NLY
    Her heav'nly voice, and beauteous face. . . . . . .   O 66 Hor I Ode xxii   24
    If to compleat this heav'nly Life . . . .   O 72 Hor. Epode II   47
    Obsequious to his heav'nly will . . . .   O 79 Feast St Simon   17
      heav'nly charms without emotion   . . . .   Y 129 Irene   9
    If yet one spark of Heav'nly fire remain   . . . . .   Y 133 Irene   V 18
    Well may those Eyes that view these heav'nly Charms, . . O 267 Irene   6
    Such heav'nly Beauty form'd for Adoration, ...   O 269 Irene   41
    Can Cali dare the Stroke of heav'nly Justice,   . . .   O 272 Irene   3
    And draw new Virtue from her heav'nly Tongue.   . . . .   O 285 Irene   7
    And fans the slumb'ring Spark of heav'nly Fire.   . . .   O 303 Irene   19
    And stopp'd the heav'nly Voice that call'd on me. . . . O 334 Irene   71
    Now beauteous Daphnis cloath'd with heav'nly light, . . Y   7 Virgil Daphnis   32
HEAV'NS
    --When of late The storm of Heav'ns displeasure thundred Y 136 Irene   V 27
      on you.
HEAVE
    And that fair bosom heave with rising sighs!   . . . .   O 75 Tr. Iliad Bk 6   28
HEAVEN   SEE HEAV'N, HEAVN
    Grant me, kind heaven, to find some happier place,   . . O 11 London   43
    Has heaven reserv'd, in pity to the poor, ...   O 18 London   170
    Must Heaven dispatch the Messengers of Light, ...   O 250 Irene   46
    Sing duly hymns to Heaven . . . .   Y 166 Irene   V 94
    Nor farther tempt the avenging rage of Heaven   . . . .   Y 168 Irene   V 134
    And bounteous Heaven repay the mighty Mercy . . . . .   O 328 Irene   46
    O, hear my Pray'rs! accept, all-pitying Heaven,   . . .   O 328 Irene   52
HEAVEN'S
    Should heaven's just bolts Orgilio's wealth confound, . O 19 London   194
    While Heaven's high Minister whose unerring awfull   . . O 355 Irene   V   9
      volume
    In vain, from heaven's black concave, like a cloud, . . Y 23 Tr Add. Battle   20
HEAVING
    She mark'd my sparkling Eyes, and heaving Breast,   . . . O 282 Irene   68
    Sighs issued from my heaving breast;   . . . .   Y 11 Tr Hor Epode 9   14
HEAVN
    Which heavn may hear . . . .   Y 108 Vanity Wishes V 348
    Descend from Heavn, to range the distant World   . . .   O 349 Irene   V 10
    Will she that's false to Heavn, to me be faithfull   . . Y 186 Irene   V   4
    Is but the executioner of Heavn--or Instrument   . . .   O 345 Irene   V 27
HEAVN'LY
    And your new Charge, that dear, that heavn'ly Maid.--   . O 270 Irene   5
HEAVY
    Still, still Distrust sits heavy on my Heart.   . . . .   O 301 Irene   95
HEBRUS
    Hebrus heard her Poet groan, ... ,   O 148 Tr Boet III.12 V 7
HECATOMBS
    Should Hecatombs each rising Morn   . . . .   O 69 Hor.II Ode 14   5
HECTOR
    Hector and Andromache;   . . . .   O 74 Tr.Iliad Bk 6   T
    She ceas'd; then godlike Hector answer'd kind,--   . .   O 74 Tr. Iliad Bk 6   1
    Behold the wife of Hector, guard of Troy!   . . . . .   O 74 Tr. Iliad Bk 6   26
    Hector, this heard without a moment's stay, ...   Y 17 Tr. Iliad Bk 6   1
    By Hector call'd Scamandrius from the god   . . . . .   Y 18 Tr. Iliad Bk 6   11
    While Hector lives I tast of ev'ry joy   . . . . . .   Y 18 Tr. Iliad Bk 6   26
    But dearest Hector while thou liv'st I see   . . . . .   Y 19 Tr. Iliad Bk 6   44
    Hector, this speaking, with extended hands   . . . . .   Y 20 Tr. Iliad Bk 6   90
    This Hector saw; his soul was touch'd with grief. . . . Y 21 Tr. Iliad Bk 6   111

		PAGE	TITLE	LINE
HECTOR	(CONTINUED)			
Hector shall perish by no warriour's hand.		Y 21	Tr. Iliad Bk 6	116
How great Achilles godlike Hector slew?		Y 22	Tr Add. Battle	11
HECTOR'S				
How would the Trojans brand great Hector's name! . . .		O 74	Tr. Iliad Bk 6	5
From Hector's breast each gloomy trouble flies . . .		Y 18	Tr. Iliad Bk 6	15
With Hector's life away my pleasures fly.		Y 18	Tr. Iliad Bk 6	27
HECUBA'S				
Yet Hecuba's, nor Priam's hoary age, ...		O 74	Tr. Iliad Bk 6	15
HEEDFUL				
Turn on the prudent Ant, thy heedful eyes, ...		O 151	The Ant	1
HEEDLESS				
What care, what rules your heedless charms shall save, .		O 46	Vanity Wishes	329
HEIGHT				
Not long they stood, when stooping from their height . .		O 75	Tr Add. Battle	2
Fix not where the tempting Height		O 145	Tr Boeth. II.4	13
Gaze at their Height and tremble at their Danger: . . .		O 293	Irene	116
Oerthrow the obelisks amazing height		Y 177	Irene	V 108
Looks down, contemptuous, from his fancy'd Height, . .		O 306	Irene	2
HEIGHTEN				
I came to heighten Tortures by Reproach, ...		O 330	Irene	7
HEIGHTEN'D				
With all the graceful Pride of Greatness heighten'd, . .		O 276	Irene	8
HEIGHTS				
Still to new heights his restless wishes tow'r, . . .		O 34	Vanity Wishes	105
Inspir'd by us, they Glory's Heights ascend;		O 247	Irene Epilogue	17
HEIR				
Th' insidious rival and the gaping heir.		O 32	Vanity Wishes	48
After your death, the lavish heir		O 69	Hor.II Ode 14	25
Show the Spirit of an heir.		O 196	Song Congratu.	12
At least you rescue from your heir.		O 232	Tr Horace IV.7	20
HEIR'S				
One and Twenty 1810: Improviso on a young heir's coming .		O 196	Song Congratu.	V T
of age.				
HELAS				
Helas!		O 172	French Distich	6
HELD				
Held high the steady scale, but deep'd the sword; . . .		O 22	London	251
Held high the steady scale, but sheath'd the sword; . .		O 22	London	V 251
Held high the steady scale, but dropp'd the sword; . .		O 22	London	V 251
Not Rome itself that held the world in awe		O 76	Tr Add. Battle	39
Held forth this fatal Scroll, then sunk to nothing. . .		O 272	Irene	17
Held out this fatal roll--then sunk to Nothing. . . .		O 357	Irene	V 1
HELL				
And bid him go to hell, to hell he goes.		O 15	London	116
And bid him go to hell, to hell he goes.		O 15	London	116
And crowds of godlike Romans sunk to hell.		O 77	Festina Lente	16
When Christ had conquer'd Hell and fate		O 79	Feast St Simon	19
The chains of hell that hold his friend.		O 232	Tr Horace IV.7	28
Some Pow'r invisible, from Heav'n or Hell, ...		O 251	Irene	50
Sometimes the Wretch unaw'd by Heav'n or Hell, ...		O 300	Irene	78
An angry look had sunk him into Hell		O 376	Irene	V 23
An angry look had sunk him into Hell		Y 188	Irene	V 20
And Honour and Reproach, and Heav'n and Hell.		O 321	Irene	38
HELM				
The parents smil'd, the chief his helm unbound		Y 20	Tr. Iliad Bk 6	95
His shining helm with nodding horse hair grac'd. . . .		Y 21	Tr. Iliad Bk 6	125
HELP				
His ready help was ever nigh, ...		O 201	Death Dr Levet	V 18
HELPLESS				
Must helpless man, in ignorance sedate, ...		O 47	Vanity Wishes	345
Dear helpless Maid--tempestuous Grief o'erbears . . .		O 252	Irene	V 77
Yet let me think--I see the helpless Maid, ...		O 252	Irene	80
Concur to press a helpless Captive's Ruin?		O 288	Irene	V 10
A widow I, an helpless orphan he.		Y 19	Tr. Iliad Bk 6	49
HEMP				
With hemp the gallows and the fleet supply.		O 21	London	243
HENCE				
Far hence are banish'd vapours, spleen, and tears, . .		O 84	Epi Dist Moth.	18
Hence with the frozen Narratives of Dotage		O 366	Irene	V 16
Hence from her sable wings returning night		Y 148	Irene	V 43E
Hence! or be calm--To disagree is Ruin.		O 282	Irene	72
'Tis Greece, 'tis Freedom calls Aspasia hence, ...		O 297	Irene	9
What wild Mistake is this? Take hence with speed . . .		O 325	Irene	4
Hence to the palace and your maids repair;		Y 21	Tr. Iliad Bk 6	121
From hence the seeds of discord first arose		Y 23	Tr Add. Battle	50
Hence men and birds promiscuous press'd the sand . . .		Y 23	Tr Add. Battle	52
HENCEFORTH				
Henceforth th' inviolable Bloom invade, ...		O 111	To Posterity	21
Henceforth shall form one common pray'r, ...		O 122	Stella Mourn.	14
And turn thy Thoughts henceforth to Love and Empire. . .		O 276	Irene	5
Henceforth for ever happy be this Day, ...		O 308	Irene	1
Henceforth shall live for me; for me alone		O 317	Irene	3
Henceforth be wise, nor hope a second Pardon. . . .		O 323	Irene	3
Nor dare henceforth to shock Irene's Walks.		O 325	Irene	7
HENCEFORWARD				
Henceforward hope no more my slighted Friendship, . . .		O 307	Irene	9
HENRY'S				
And lisp the tale of Henry's victories;		O 15	London	120
HER				

```
HERACLITUS                                                      PAGE   TITLE              LINE
     Be gone ye blockheads, Heraclitus cries,  . . . . . .  O 141  Tr Rambler 208         1
HERB
     Nor crop'd the tastfull herb, nor trac'd the verdant meads  Y   6  Virgil Daphnis       10
HERBS
     As herbs of which the forrests nigh  . . . . . . . .  O  73  Hor. Epode II          61
     As herbs of which the fields nigh  . . . . . . . . .  O  73  Hor. Epode II      V  61
HERDS
     As corn the fields, as bulls the herds of kine,  . . .  Y   6  Virgil Daphnis       18
HERE
          55
HERE'S                                                             OMITTED WORD
     Here's a woman of the town,  . . . . . . . . . .  Y 300  Extemp. Elegy          1
HEREAFTER
     Of total Death and careless of Hereafter;  . . . . .  O 276  Irene                 19
     Cast off all idle terrours of hereafter  . . . . . .  Y 146  Irene              V  19
     Secure of total death, and careless of hereafter or gay .  Y 146  Irene          V  20
     Now feast thine Eyes, thine Eyes that ne'er hereafter  .  O 304  Irene              34
HEREDITARY
     His own hereditary Land,  . . . . . . . . . . .  O  71  Hor. Epode II           6
     Can'st thou forget hereditary Splendours,  . . . . .  O 301  Irene                103
HERETIC
     Or set The Persian Heretic in arms against Me  . . . .  O 348  Irene              V  17
HERETICK
     And arm the Persian Heretick against thee;  . . . . .  O 274  Irene                 55
HERETOFORE
     Sure this is Love which heretofore I conceiv'd  . . . .  O 349  Irene              V  28
HERMIONE
     who was to personate the Ghost of Hermione  . . . . .  O  83  Epi Dist Moth.        T
HERMIT
     I praise the hermit, but regret the friend,  . . . . .  O   8  London                4
     Hermit hoar, in solemn cell,  . . . . . . . . . .  O 181  Parody Warton          1
HERMIT'S
     And scorns the lazy Hermit's cheap Devotion;  . . . .  O 264  Irene                 28
HERO
     The vanquish'd hero leaves his broken bands,  . . . .  O  41  Vanity Wishes        211
     For us the Statesman labours, Hero fights,  . . . . .  O 247  Irene Epilogue        21
     O! could the Grave restore the pious Hero,  . . . . .  O 267  Irene                 42
     Behold the Hero with Aspasia's Eyes?  . . . . . . .  O 296  Irene                 31
     This open Friend, this undesigning Hero,  . . . . . .  O 299  Irene                 38
     Deform the beauties of the breathing statue (marble hero  Y 177  Irene              V111A
     Nor lose in Love the Patriot and the Hero.  . . . . .  O 303  Irene                 15
     <E>ach hero fir'd piety or freedom  . . . . . . . .  Y 181  Irene              V  51
     The bravest hero and the fearfull'st slave  . . . . .  Y  21  Tr. Iliad Bk 6       119
     Their godlike hero strugling in the skies.  . . . . .  Y  26  Tr Add. Battle       129
HERO'S
     Before that day, by some brave hero's hand,  . . . . .  O  75  Tr. Iliad Bk 6        29
HEROE'S
     With some victorious Heroe's praise  . . . . . . .  O  78  Feast St Simon         5
     With all the Heroe's dull Security,  . . . . . . .  O 283  Irene                  9
     The Politician's Arts, and Heroe's Flame.  . . . . .  O 307  Irene                 27
HEROES
     Heroes, proceed! what bounds your pride shall hold?  . .  O  13  London                61
     The land of heroes and of saints survey;  . . . . . .  O  15  London               100
     Yet ev'n these heroes, mischievously gay,  . . . . .  O  21  London               230
     Yet ev'n those heroes, mischievously gay,  . . . . .  Y  59  London             V 230
     Mix'd with old Heroes trace the flow'ry meads,  . . . .  O  76  Tr Add. Battle       42
     Nor Gods his Heroes, nor his Lovers Fools:  . . . . .  O 246  Irene Prologue        18
     And stern Composure of despairing Heroes;  . . . . .  O 275  Irene                 83
     Mix in the War, and shine among the Heroes?  . . . . .  O 290  Irene                 41
     Or bid soft Science polish Britain's Heroes:  . . . . .  O 293  Irene                106
     Or bid fair Science polish Britains Heroes  . . . . .  O 348  Irene              V  22
     Demand whose Force yon Turkish Heroes dread,  . . . . .  O 305  Irene                 41
     Call forth her ancient Heroes to the Field,  . . . . .  O 309  Irene                 39
     What sleepy Charms benumb these active Heroes,  . . . .  O 325  Irene                 14
     Among their flocks the blooming heroes fell  . . . . .  Y  18  Tr. Iliad Bk 6        36
     In pompous numbers ancient heroes rise;  . . . . . .  Y  22  Tr Add. Battle         8
     Beheld the tragic heroes taught to fear.  . . . . . .  Y  67  Prologue Lethe         8
HEROES'
     To propagate the Pygmie heroes' praise.  . . . . . .  Y  22  Tr Add. Battle        17
HEROIC
     Heroic worth, benevolence divine:  . . . . . . . .  O  34  Vanity Wishes         88
HEROINE
     Why fled this haughty Heroine from the Battle?  . . . .  O 290  Irene                 39
HERS                                                               OMITTED WORD
HERSE
     Nor grace with fading flours my Herse,  . . . . . .  O  70  Hor.II Ode XX         22
HERSELF
     Why does thy Soul retire into herself?  . . . . . .  O 295  Irene                  7
     To share the Miseries herself has caus'd.  . . . . .  O 320  Irene                 15
HERVEY'S
     And strive in vain to laugh at H<erve>y's jest.  . . .  O  13  London                74
HETTY
     Long may live my lovely Hetty!  . . . . . . . . .  O 175  Tr Easy Phrase         1
     Live my lovely Hetty long!  . . . . . . . . . .  O 175  Tr Easy Phrase         4
     Long may live my lovely Hetty!  . . . . . . . . .  O 175  Tr Easy Phrase         6
HEW
     Hew down, ye Guards, those Vassals of Distraction,  . .  O 333  Irene                 51
HIBERNIA'S
     For who would leave, unbrib'd, Hibernia's land,  . . .  O   9  London                9
```

```
HICKMAN                                            PAGE    TITLE              LINE
     To Miss Hickman playing on the Spinet  . . . . . . .   O  96  Hickman Spinet      T
HID
     Glad to be hid, and proud to be forgot.  . . . . . .   O  82  Young Author        30
     Whene'er this Stone, now hid beneath the Lake,  . . .  O 110  To Posterity         1
     Hid in the mean Disguise of Turkish Robes,  . . . . .  O 249  Irene                2
     My Rage and Grief had hid from my Remembrance. . . . . O 334  Irene               65
HIDE
     Hide, blushing Glory, hide Pultowa's day:   . . . . .  O  41  Vanity Wishes      210
     Hide, blushing Glory, hide Pultowa's day:   . . . . .  O  41  Vanity Wishes      210
     No maid to flatter, and no paint to hide.   . . . . .  O  84  Epi Dist Moth.      41
     And hide me from the sight of life.  . . . . . . . .   O 124  Winter's Walk    V  20
     That hide in seeming zeal a wicked purpose, . . . . .  O 176  Tr Metastas II      12
     "Under leaves to hide one's head,  . . . . . . . .    O 185  Anacreon Ode 9      27
     From Crouds that hide a Monarch from himself, . . . .  O 262  Irene                8
     Well may'st thou hide in Labyrinths of Sound  . . . . O 293  Irene              125
     Hide me, oh hide me from upbraiding Greece, . . . . .  O 316  Irene               12
     Hide me, oh hide me from upbraiding Greece, . . . . .  O 316  Irene               12
     Oh, hide me from myself!  . . . . . . . . . . . . .   O 316  Irene               13
     Hide me with Murd'rers in the Dungeon's Gloom,  . . . O 328  Irene               34
     Shall hide me from the tasteless World for ever.  . . O 333  Irene               48
HIDES
     One shews the plunder, and one hides the thief.  . . . O  32  Vanity Wishes       44
     And hides his miseries in distant lands; . . . . . .  Y 102  Vanity Wishes    V 212
     Hides from himself his state, and shuns to know, . . . O  43  Vanity Wishes      257
     Which granted, hides my Purpose from the World,  . . . O 258  Irene               88
     And in his nurse's bosom hides his face.   . . . . .  Y  20  Tr. Iliad Bk 6      94
HIGH
     Held high the steady scale, but deep'd the sword; . . O  22  London             251
     Held high the steady scale, but sheath'd the sword;  . O  22  London           V 251
     Held high the steady scale, but dropp'd the sword;  . O  22  London           V 251
     That hung on high Palladium of the place, . . . . .  Y  95  Vanity Wishes    V  84
     Loud roars the tempest, high the billows rise, . . .  O  82  Young Author         8
     Loud roar the billows, high the waves arise, . . . .  O  82  Young Author     V   8
     Engross not all the beams on high, . . . . . . . .   O 126  To Lyce, Lady        5
     Though favour'd by the pow'rs on high, . . . . . . .  O 136  Tr Rambler 128       5
     From her high Seats he drew the Soul, . . . . . . .   O 147  Tr Boeth III.6       9
     High to soar and deep to dive  . . . . . . . . . .   O 178  Thrale 35 Year       9
     Pockets full, and Spirits high, . . . . . . . . . .  O 196  Song Congratu.      22
     While Heav'n's high Minister, whose awful Volume  . . O 276  Irene               20
     While Heaven's high Minister whose unerring awfull     O 355  Irene            V   9
       volume
     Too high, bright Maid, thou rat'st exterior Grace; . . O 277  Irene               30
     Now bleeds the war afresh, the Crane from high . . . . Y  26  Tr Add. Battle     130
     She was once of high renown,--  . . . . . . . . . .  Y 300  Extemp. Elegy        3
HIGHER
     And raise his treasures higher than before. . . . . . O  19  London             205
HIGHEST
     He, tir'd of Slav'ry, tho' the highest Slave,  . . .  O 253  Irene              113
HILL
     From hill to hill the beacons rousing blaze . . . . . O  43  Vanity Wishes      247
     From hill to hill the beacons rousing blaze . . . . . O  43  Vanity Wishes      247
     Down the steep hill the roaring torrent pours; . . . . O 132  Tr. Rambler 65       2
HILLS
     The naked hills, the leafless grove, . . . . . . . .  O 123  Winter's Walk        3
     "Over hills and fields to roam, . . . . . . . . . .  O 185  Anacreon Ode 9      25
     We still had wander'd on Tartarian Hills. . . . . . . O 284  Irene               41
HIM
          74                                                    OMITTED WORD
HIMSELF
     Hides from himself his state, and shuns to know,  . . O  43  Vanity Wishes      257
     Lest on himself the destin'd stroke descend. . . . .  O 139  Tr Rambler 168       2
     Or hear himself, for see the Bassa comes.  . . . . .  O 254  Irene              141
     From Crouds that hide a Monarch from himself, . . . .  O 262  Irene                8
     The Sultan from himself derives his Greatness. . . . . O 268  Irene               24
HIND
     Low skulks the hind beneath the rage of pow'r, . . .  O  32  Vanity Wishes       33
     Tho' the Hind approach'd to hear  . . . . . . . .    O 148  Tr Boeth III.12      7
     In vain the lab'ring hind manures the plain, . . . .  Y   6  Virgil Daphnis      22
HINDER'D
     Hung on your Neck, and hinder'd your Departure. . . . O 280  Irene               10
HINT
     The watchful guests still hint the last offence, . . . O  44  Vanity Wishes      279
     The treachrous guests still hint the last offence,  . . Y 104  Vanity Wishes    V 279
     But let no thoughtless Hint involve Abdalla.  . . . .  O 329  Irene               15
     Those Hounds of Blood, that catch the Hint to kill, . . O 333  Irene               52
     Tho' no lewd hint the mantling virgin warm. . . . . . Y  67  Prologue Lethe      14
HINTS
     And as their patron hints the cold or heat, . . . . . O  16  London             142
     There in soft Hints and in ambiguous Phrase, . . . .  O 254  Irene              129
HIPPOLYTUS
     Hippolytus unjustly slain . . . . . . . . . . . . .  O 232  Tr Horace IV.7      25
HIRELING
     Some hireling senator's deserted seat;  . . . . . .  O  20  London             213
     For gold his sword the hireling ruffian draws, . . .  O  31  Vanity Wishes       25
     For gold the hireling judge distorts the laws; . . .  O  31  Vanity Wishes       26·
HIRES
     For less than hires the dungeons of the Strand;  . . . Y  58  London           V 215
HIS
          454                                                   OMITTED WORD
```

HISS
                                                              PAGE   TITLE   LINE

	PAGE	TITLE	LINE
HISS			
And hiss the dauber ruin dawb the wall.	Y 95	Vanity Wishes	V 90
Till that glad night when all that hate may hiss.	O 60	Pro Good Nat'd	20
Lies at my feet, I hiss him, and he dies.	O 60	Pro Good Nat'd	24
Forbear to hiss--the Poet cannot hear.	O 62	Pro Word Wise	18
Where furies ever howl, and serpents hiss.	O 84	Epi Dist Moth.	31
to the hiss of future ages	Y 113	Irene	V 22
HISS'D			
Hiss'd from the stage, or hooted from the court,	O 15	London	109
HISSES			
The pamphlet spreads, incessant hisses rise,	O 82	Young Author	25
HISSING			
And hissing Infamy proclaims the rest.	O 47	Vanity Wishes	342
Through hissing Ages, a proverbial Coward,	O 305	Irene	28
HIST'RY			
Let hist'ry tell where rival kings command,	O 31	Vanity Wishes	29
HISTORIANS			
Historians tell where rival kings command,	Y 93	Vanity Wishes	V 29
HISTORIES			
When future histories record the deed.	Y 180	Irene	V 27
HISTORIKON			
Klaiete poieten, historikon, phusikon.	O 171	Epi. Goldsmith	4
HITHER			
By Eastern Tempests hither tost,	O 73	Hor. Epode II	58
Driv'n hither by inclement skies	O 73	Hor. Epode II	V 59
Conduct her hither, let no rude Intrusion	O 272	Irene	13
Conduct her hither, see that no intrusion	O 368	Irene	V 24
Thanks for this kind relief. Conduct him hither	O 370	Irene	V 15
O say, what guardian Pow'r convey'd thee hither.	O 296	Irene	33
And what protecting angel led thee hither	Y 170	Irene	V 33
The victor hither brought, a royall slave.	Y 19	Tr. Iliad Bk 6	39
HIVE			
Ladies--stock and tend your Hive,	O 178	Thrale 35 Year	11
HOAR			
Hermit hoar, in solemn cell,	O 181	Parody Warton	1
Shall deem our hoar progenitors unwise.	O 192	Tr. Medea II	4
HOARDED			
All Marlb'rough hoarded, or all Villiers spent,	O 14	London	86
HOARDS			
Th' offended burgess hoards his angry tale,	O 60	Pro Good Nat'd	17
HOARY			
Nor did King Priam's hoary age	O 68	Hor. II Ode IX	15
Yet Hecuba's, nor Priam's hoary age,	O 74	Tr. Iliad Bk 6	15
The hoary ground, the frowning skies.	O 123	Winter's Walk	4
When the hoary sage reply'd--	O 181	Parody Warton	V 7
Reason! the hoary Dotard's dull Directress,	O 281	Irene	44
To-morrow's Action? Can that hoary Wisdom	O 283	Irene	19
That Hoary Head, that Head which hungry fate	O 374	Irene	V 20
That hoary Villain's forc'd congratulations	O 370	Irene	V 22
Ere guilty Fear depress'd the hoary Chief,	O 312	Irene	18
Amazement seiz'd us, and the hoary Bassa	O 317	Irene	36
HOC			
<H>oc fonte derivat<a> clades--In patriam populumque fluxit.	O 347	Irene	V 22
HOGARTH'S			
Great Hogarth's honour'd Dust is here.	O 154	Epita. Hogarth	8
HOLD			
Heroes, proceed! what bounds your pride shall hold?	O 13	London	61
New chains to hold the captive heart.	O 121	To Miss Playin	18
She faints and quits her hold.	O 150	Tr Boet III.12	58
The chains of hell that hold his friend.	O 232	Tr Horace IV.7	28
And lawless Passion, hold the Sword of Justice.	O 256	Irene	54
Sure all unite to hold her League of Rule	O 257	Irene	62
Hold in her Chains the captivated Sultan?	O 261	Irene	2
HOLDS			
Who holds no human Creature mean;	O 147	Tr Boeth III.6	18
D<r>ives to (holds o'er) the south or west the storm	Y 136	Irene	V 26
Holds out her Hand to lead thee back to Truth.	O 321	Irene	42
HOLLOW			
And left-hand crows, from an old hollow oak,	O 65	Virgil Past.I	24
And Strymon's hollow banks resounded with their groans.	Y 24	Tr Add. Battle	89
HOLY			
With silent confidence and holy rest:	O 130	Tr. Rambler 7	6
and drink the holy waters the fountain of remission	Y 130	Irene	V 11
And at the holy place pour out my prayers	Y 130	Irene	V 12
The holy Flame of enterprizing Virtue,	O 264	Irene	26
The holy city with converted millions--or nations.	Y 131	Irene	V 32C
Those holy Beings, whose superiour Care	O 289	Irene	17
Those holy Beings whose unseen Direction	O 346	Irene	V 5
Again her Temples sound with holy Musick:	O 291	Irene	55
Seek out some peacefull Convents holy Shade	O 348	Irene	V 24
Ye holy shades of--martyrs	Y 181	Irene	V 52
HOMAGE			
Or pay with speaking Eyes a Lover's Homage?	O 282	Irene	63
Reserve this Homage for some other Fair,	O 288	Irene	4
When to the nymphs the swain due homage pays	Y 7	Virgil Daphnis	V 51
HOME			
London! the needy villain's gen'ral home,	O 14	London	93
All that at home no more can beg or steal,	O 15	London	107

HOME   (CONTINUED)
    For where can starving merit find a home? . . . . .   O 18 London   191
    And sign your will before you sup from home. . . . . O 21 London   225
    And make will before you sup from home. . . . . . .   Y 59 London   V 225
    And leave our pleasing fields and native home, . . . O 64 Virgil Past.I   4
    Their dugs with milk distended, home! . . . .   O 73 Hor. Epode II   68
    Far from their happy native home . . . .   O 79 Feast St Simon   28
    Forsakes his rural seats and peaceful home, ... O 81 Young Author   2
    Forsakes his rural sports and peaceful home, ... O 81 Young Author   V 2
    "Fortune's guest, without a home, ...   O 185 Anacreon Ode 9   26
    A single Thought now rove, recall it home. . . . . . O 255 Irene   7
    But being counsell'd to go home . . . .   Y 11 Tr Hor Epode 9   31
HOMER'S
    from the Sixth Book of Homer's Iliad . . . . . .   O 74 Tr. Iliad Bk 6   T
HOMEROS
    Ek Dios estin onar, Theios pot egrapsen Homeros, . . . O 103 Eis Elisses   3
HONEST
    To letter'd ease retir'd, and honest mirth, ... O 118 Epitaph Hanmer   37
HONESTY
    Where honesty and sense are no disgrace; . . . . . . O 11 London   44
    No wit nor honesty could stand . . . .   Y 11 Tr Hor Epode 9   21
HONOR
    The day disastrous, that secures my honor . . . . .   Y 195 Irene   V 46
HONOUR
    Or English honour grew a standing jest. . . . . . .   O 10 London   30
    Turn'd by his nod the stream of honour flows, ... O 34 Vanity Wishes   103
    With honour sated, and with cares opprest; . . . . . O 118 Epitaph Hanmer   36
    All is my own, my honour and my shame. . . . . . .   O 132 Tr. Rambler 46   2
    The more I honour thee, the less I love. . . . . . . O 140 Tr Rambler 188   1
    Who keeps the rigid rules of ancient honour; . . . . O 176 Tr Metastas II   2
    That keeps the rigid rules of ancient honour; . . . . O 176 Tr Metastas II   V 2
    But hope, yet hope, to Happiness and Honour; . . . . O 253 Irene   109
    A blooming monarch--in all the bloom of honour... . . Y 122 Irene   V 67
    Then let me once, in honour of our Sex, ...   O 277 Irene   49
    For daring Truth, and Turbulence of Honour? . . . . . O 299 Irene   37
    With mad Devotion idolizes Honour. . . . .   O 300 Irene   79
    To wait remote from Action, and from Honour, ... O 305 Irene   22
    The petty Claims of Empire and of Honour: . . . . . . O 307 Irene   23
    And Honour and Reproach, and Heav'n and Hell. . . . . O 321 Irene   38
    Hail lovely flower, first honour of the year! . . . . Y   3 On a Daffodill   1
HONOUR'D
    Great Hogarth's honour'd Dust is here. . . . . . .   O 154 Epita. Hogarth   8
HONOUR'S
    The baffled prince in honour's flatt'ring bloom . . . O 43 Vanity Wishes   251
    For us alone, they Honour's Paths pursue: . . . . .   O 247 Irene Epilogue   16
HONOURABLE
    The prints of claws and honourable scars. . . . . .   Y 24 Tr Add. Battle   83
HONOURS
    Those pageant Honours which he scorn'd below: . . . . O 57 Prologue Comus   22
    The farmer annuall honours pays . . . .   O 73 Hor. Epode II   64
    Her solemn honours pays. . . . .   O 78 Feast St Simon   12
    And the long honours of a lasting name . . . . . .   O 82 Young Author   V 12
    Then old in honours, and approv'd in faith, ... Y 131 Irene   V 32
    No regal Pageant deck'd with casual Honours, ... O 268 Irene   19
    If yet this shining Pomp, these sudden Honours, . . . O 289 Irene   1
    His Wealth, his Rank, his Honours he recounted, . . . O 299 Irene   45
    Behold thy boasted Honours snatch'd away. . . . . .   O 317 Irene   43
    Thou shalt with Bacchus equal honours share . . . . . Y   7 Virgil Daphnis   51
HOOTED
    Hiss'd from the stage, or hooted from the court, . . . O 15 London   109
    Or right, or wrong, once hooted from the stage; . . . O 61 Pro Word Wise   2
HOOTING
    Let Shame and hooting Infamy pursue me, ...   O 328 Irene   36
HOP'D
    And proudly hop'd to pimp in future Days. . . . . .   O 52 Pro Drury-Lane   24
    And hop'd to share thy Counsels, not thy Sorrows: . . O 253 Irene   106
HOPE
    Since hope sooths to double my distress, ... O 10 London   39
    But what, my friend, what hope remains for me, . . . O 13 London   67
    Nor hope the British lineaments to trace, ...   O 15 London   101
    Can surly virtue hope to fix a friend? . . . . . .   O 16 London   145
    And hope the balmy blessings of repose: . . . . . . O 21 London   237
    Then say how hope and fear, desire and hate, ... O 31 Vanity Wishes   5
    All fir'd with hope, and panting to be great; . . . . Y 95 Vanity Wishes   V 74
    Love ends with hope, the sinking statesman's door . . O 33 Vanity Wishes   79
    Yet hope not life from grief or danger free, ... O 37 Vanity Wishes   155
    If hope yet flatter, once again attend, ...   Y 99 Vanity Wishes   V 163
    Spreads wide the hope of plunder and of praise; . . . O 43 Vanity Wishes   248
    Where then shall Hope and Fear their objects find? . . O 47 Vanity Wishes   343
    And hope with humble confidence the best . . . . . .   Y 108 Vanity Wishes   V 356
    For hope, that panting for a happier seat, ... Y 108 Vanity Wishes   V 363
    Rage with disdain, and hope th' approaching war; . . . O 75 Tr Add. Battle   1
    And fir'd with pleasing hope of endless fame, ... O 82 Young Author   12
    Nor can I hope thy silken chain . . . .   O 120 To Miss Purse   9
    Deceitful Hope, and vain Desire, ...   O 121 To Miss Playin   13
    Enliv'ning hope, and fond desire, ...   O 123 Winter's Walk   9
    In groundless hope, and causeless fear, ...   O 124 Winter's Walk   13
    Wild hope, vain fear, alike remov'd, ...   O 125 An Ode   26
    Exiles, the proverb says, subsist on hope. . . . . . O 133 Tr. Rambler 67   1
    Delusive hope still points to distant good, ... O 133 Tr. Rambler 67   2
    Would you hope to gain my heart, ...   O 176 Tr Metastasi I   1

HOPE   (CONTINUED)   PAGE   TITLE   LINE
     Yet Greece enjoys no Gleam of transient Hope, ...   O 249 Irene   11
     But hope, yet hope, to Happiness and Honour;   . . . .   O 253 Irene   109
     But hope, yet hope, to Happiness and Honour;   . . . .   O 253 Irene   109
     But whence this new sprung Hope?   . . . .   O 253 Irene   111
     Or sprightly Hope exalt their kindling Spirits?   . . .   O 270 Irene   23
     All there is Hope, and Gaiety, and Courage, ...   O 271 Irene   26
     Must I for these renounce the Hope of Heav'n, ...   O 276 Irene   13
     Still must we linger in uncertain Hope?   . . . . . .   O 282 Irene   3
     But should I sin beyond the Hope of Mercy, ...   O 289 Irene   23
     'Tis she--My Hope, my Happiness, my Love!   . . . . .   O 294 Irene   1
     Beyond my warmest Hope, or wildest Wishes, ...   O 296 Irene   35
     Elate with Hope, and panting for a Foe. . . . . . .   O 304 Irene   5
     Henceforward hope no more my slighted Friendship, . . .   O 307 Irene   9
     Nor hope, nor wish, nor live but for Aspasia. . . . . .   O 307 Irene   14
     Whome'er the Hope, still blasted, still renew'd, . . .   O 310 Irene   1
     Yet much remains to hope. I shall not call . . . . .   O 317 Irene   45
     Henceforth be wise, nor hope a second Pardon. . . . .   O 323 Irene   3
          That Hope is past; . . . .   O 324 Irene   12
     Nor hope his Fortune while thou want'st his Worth. . .   O 330 Irene   25
     Hope not thy threats shall stay . . . .   Y 210 Irene   V 25
HOPE'S
     Condemn'd to hope's delusive mine, ...   O 200 Death Dr Levet   1
HOPELESS
     And baffled Spite, with hopeless Anguish dumb, ...   O 57 Prologue Comus   17
     Where hopeless anguish pour'd his groan, ...   O 201 Death Dr Levet   19
     Where hopeless anguish pour'd the groan, ...   O 201 Death Dr Levet   V 19
     When hopeless anguish pours her groan, ...   O 201 Death Dr Levet   V 19
     Leave but this Maid, resign a hopeless Claim, ...   O 319 Irene   25
     Quit but this maid, resign a hopeless claim . . . . .   Y 197 Irene   V 25
HOPES
     And hopes from angry heav'n another fire. . . . . .   O 19 London   209
     How just his hopes let Swedish Charles decide; . . . .   O 40 Vanity Wishes   192
     While growing hopes scarce awe the gath'ring sneer, . .   O 44 Vanity Wishes   277
     Have hopes, and fears, and wishes, just the same; . . .   O 59 Pro Good Nat'd   12
     Two tender kids, the hopes of all the flock. . . . .   O 64 Virgil Past.I   20
     What hopes, what terrors does thy gift create, ...   O 95 Sprig of Myrtl   1
     He that ever hopes to thrive . . . .   O 178 Thrale 35 Year   15
     Shou'd partial Cat-calls all his Hopes confound, . . .   O 246 Irene Prologue   23
     What Hopes, what Terrors rush upon my Soul! . . . . .   O 259 Irene   104
     She feeds his Hopes, and sooths him to Delay. . . . .   O 260 Irene   129
     The Hopes and Fears, the Joys and Pains of Life, . . .   O 265 Irene   7
     Let nobler Hopes and juster Fears succeed, ...   O 265 Irene   9
     Whence flow the Hopes and Fears, Despair and Rapture, .   O 277 Irene   41
     Whence all those Hopes and Fears Despair and . . . .   O 355 Irene   V 18
          Rapture
     Now led astray by hopes fallacious glimm'rings . . . .   Y 148 Irene   V 43A
     Has fix'd his Hopes, Inquietudes, and Fears, ...   O 280 Irene   27
     Now hopes, now fears-- . . . .   O 299 Irene   55
     Disperse our Hopes, and frustrate our Designs, ...   O 301 Irene   98
     My Hopes, my Wishes, terminate in Life, ...   O 327 Irene   22
     Or their own souls with hopes of vict'ry fir'd." . . .   Y 19 Tr. Iliad Bk 6   59
     And weakly hopes to 'scape the critick's rage. . . . .   Y 67 Prologue Lethe   12
     This night he hopes to shew that farce may charm, . . .   Y 67 Prologue Lethe   13
HORACE
     Translation of Horace. Book I. Ode xxii. . . . . . .   O 65 Hor I Ode xxii   T
     From Horace. Integer Vitae, etc. . . . .   O 65 Hor I Ode xxii   V T
     Horace. Book 2d. Ode 14 . . . .   O 68 Hor.II Ode 14   T
     Horace Book 2d. Ode 20th . . . .   O 70 Hor.II Ode XX   T
     Horace. Epode the 2d. . . . .   O 71 Hor. Epode II   T
HORIZON
     The dark horizon ravish'd from their sight. . . . . .   Y 24 Tr Add. Battle   75
HORRID
     Or horrid Africk's faithless sands; . . . .   O 65 Hor I Ode xxii   6
     With horrid gloom the frowning skies: . . . . . .   O 66 Hor I Ode xxii   20
     With horrid Gloom the frowning Skies: . . . . . .   O 67 To A. Fuscus   20
     Still wider spreads thy horrid reign, ...   O 123 Winter's Walk   7
     A thousand horrid Prodigies foretold it. . . . . . .   O 250 Irene   36
     Then Visions horrid as a Murd'rer's Dreams . . . .   O 266 Irene   13
     Horrid as a murd'rers dreams, madman's laughter . . .   Y 133 Irene   V 13
     The horrid Images of War and Slaughter . . . . .   O 268 Irene   34
     The gloomy Resolution, horrid Greatness, ...   O 275 Irene   82
     horrid joy--his air now fearful now resolv'd. . . . .   Y 145 Irene   V 82
     Soon shall the dire Seraglio's horrid Gates . . . .   O 291 Irene   79
     The horrid pomp of ostentatious woe . . . .   Y 168 Irene   V 135
     horrid joy--gloomy resolution--his air now fearful now .   Y 187 Irene   V 7
          resolv'd.
     Far be the horrid thought--but hear my protestation . .   Y 205 Irene   V 32
     And steal thy Life away. Death's horrid Angel . . . .   O 327 Irene   9
     And steal your life away. Death's horrid Angel . . .   O 368 Irene   V 17
     And tell the horrid Tale with chearful Face; . . . .   O 329 Irene   11
HORROR
     And every Danger shocks with double Horror. . . . .   O 261 Irene   21
     Now, Mustapha, pursue thy Tale of Horror. . . . . .   O 272 Irene   1
     And quit their Charge to Horror and to Ruin. . . . .   O 346 Irene   V 8
          the Particulam) strikes me with greater horror . .   Y 176 Irene   V111C
     Horror and Agony are in that Sound! . . . .   O 328 Irene   32
HORRORS
     Swift from pursuing horrors take your way, ...   O 18 London   188
     Dispelling the black horrors of the Night, ...   O 77 Tr Add. Battle   46
     And paint the horrors of the dreadfull day. . . . . .   Y 22 Tr Add. Battle   7

                                                          PAGE   TITLE   LINE
HORROUR
    Where sable night in all her horrour reigns;   . . . .   O 83 Epi Dist Moth.   11
    And (terror) horrour shudders in their gloomy caverns   Y 136 Irene   V 31A
    With horrour counts the number of the slain.   . . . .   Y 23 Tr Add. Battle   33
    Such was the horrour of the dreadfull fight . . . . .   Y 26 Tr Add. Battle   136
HORROURS
    These chilling doubts, and agonizing horrours?   . . . . Y 189 Irene   V 1A
HORSE
    The Horse shall trample, or the Plough shall break,   . . O 110 To Posterity   2
    And, yet more strange! his Veins a Horse shall drain, . . O 111 To Posterity   25
    His shining helm with nodding horse hair grac'd.   . . .   Y 21 Tr. Iliad Bk 6 125
HOSPITABLE
    To kind Italia's hospitable Shades;   . . . .   O 302 Irene   117
HOST
    Through purple billows and a floating host,   . .   O 42 Vanity Wishes   240
    Oft when the fierce Besiegers eager Host . . . . . .   O 298 Irene   27
HOSTILE
    Or hostile millions press him to the ground?   . . .   O 41 Vanity Wishes   218
    Secure, and triumph'd oft' in hostile blood.   . . . .   O 76 Tr Add. Battle   34
    Thick clouds of hostile birds obscure the skies.   . .   Y 25 Tr Add. Battle   93
HOSTILITIES
    For no renew'd hostilities invade . . . .   O 61 Pro Word Wise   V 9
HOSTILITY
    In gay hostility, and barb'rous pride, ...   O 42 Vanity Wishes   225
HOSTS
    Soon shall you fall by num'rous hosts opprest   . . . .   Y 18 Tr. Iliad Bk 6   22
    Thrice to the wall their dreadfull hosts have led   . .   Y 19 Tr. Iliad Bk 6   56
    Then rises the brave leader of their hosts   . . . .   Y 24 Tr Add. Battle   80
HOT
    Then say how hot desire and raging hate, ...   Y 92 Vanity Wishes V 5
    Parent of Rage and hot desire, ...   O 99 Ode Friendship V 6
    And hot Abdalla hates the happy Lover.   . . . . . .   O 300 Irene   75
    Hot her breath with many a dram, ...   Y 301 Extemp. Elegy   18
HOUND
    Hares forgot the following hound, ...   O 148 Tr Boet III.12   10
HOUNDS
    The foaming Boar he then with op'ning hounds   . . . .   O 72 Hor. Epode II   V 39
    With twisted toils, and op'ning hounds;   . . . . . .   O 72 Hor. Epode II   40
    Those Hounds of Blood, that catch the Hint to kill, . .   O 333 Irene   52
HOUR
    Watch the weak hour, and ransack all the heart;   . . .   O 17 London   155
    Invades the sacred hour of silent rest, ...   O 21 London   240
    The bold Bavarian, in a luckless hour, ...   O 42 Vanity Wishes   241
    Defer an hour the fatal blow.   . . . .   O 69 Hor.II Ode 14   12
    Ah! think not, in the dang'rous hour, ...   O 121 To Miss Playin   7
    Soon fades the rose; once past the fragrant hour,   . .   O 133 Tr. Rambler 71   1
    Yet, lay the sonnet for an hour aside, ...   O 142 In Baretti Bk.   7
    To speed the light convivial hour;   . . . .   O 191 Tr. Medea I   19
    And purple nectar glads the festive hour, ...   O 193 Tr. Medea II   18
    Dismiss the pleasing Phantoms for an Hour.   . . . .   O 246 Irene Prologue   6
    A signal hour marked out by pitying Heav'n   . . . .   Y 117 Irene   V 109
    At Midnight's private Hour a Voice unknown   . . . .   O 254 Irene   121
    Reserve these Questions for a safer Hour, ...   O 254 Irene   140
    This Hour I'll beg, with unsuspecting Face, ...   O 258 Irene   86
    Th' important Hour had pass'd unheeded by, ...   O 269 Irene   12
    Each lin'gring Hour alarms me for Aspasia.   . . . .   O 270 Irene   20
    Another Hour in dull Deliberation, ...   O 271 Irene   34
    Learn, that the present Hour alone is Man's.   . . . .   O 283 Irene   33
    The present Hour with open Arms invites;   . . . . .   O 284 Irene   34
    The present hour invites with genuine charms   . . . .   O 375 Irene   V 7
    Give me, before th' approaching Hour of Fate,   . . .   O 285 Irene   5
    Will e'er an happier Hour revisit Greece?   . . . . .   O 301 Irene   96
    Sure 'tis the happy Hour ordain'd above, ...   O 321 Irene   35
    Grant me one Hour, O grant me but a Moment, ...   O 328 Irene   45
    Suspend the dreadful Sentence for an Hour?   . . . .   O 332 Irene   26
    One Hour had freed me from the fatal Error, ...   O 332 Irene   27
    One Hour had sav'd me from Despair and Madness.   . .   O 332 Irene   28
    But now alass! the fatall hour drew nigh . . . . .   Y 24 Tr Add. Battle   62
HOURIES
    Nor wish for Houries in Irene's Arms. . . . .   O 308 Irene   10
    The houries of our Prophet blush before her . . . .   Y 184 Irene   V 10
HOURS
    On all thy hours security shall smile, ...   O 20 London   222
    But few there are whom hours like these await,   . . .   O 45 Vanity Wishes   311
    How sweet in sleep to pass the careless hours,   . . .   O 135 Tr Rambler 117   1
    How long shall sloth usurp thy useless hours,   . . .   O 151 The Ant   9
    Time his Hours should never drive   . . . .   O 178 Thrale 35 Year   7
    Far from his Troops, he toys his Hours away.   . . . .   O 258 Irene   93
    These Hours assign'd to Pleasure and Irene.   . . . .   O 272 Irene   15
    For idle Hours, and crush him at my Leisure.   . . . .   O 275 Irene   71
    Where hast thou linger'd while th' encumber'd Hours . . O 279 Irene   3
    There wear the tedious Hours of Life away, ...   O 292 Irene   85
    To languish out the tedious hours of life   . . . .   O 357 Irene   V 14
    To Silence and to Rest. The Hours of Darkness,   . .   O 302 Irene   2
    Propitious Hours to Stratagem and Death, ...   O 302 Irene   3
    Count not these Hours as Parts of vulgar Time,   . . .   O 302 Irene   5
HOUSE
    That Priam's house, and Priam's self shall bleed: . . . O 74 Tr. Iliad Bk 6   12
    My first, shuts out Thieves from your house or your Room O 179 Charade!   1
    To his own house her did lug. . . . .   Y 301 Extemp. Elegy   16

```
                                                           PAGE    TITLE           LINE
HOUSES
    Here falling houses thunder on your head,    . . . . .  O   9  London             17
    What are acres? What are houses?   . . . . . . . .      O 196  Song Congratu.     23
HOV'RING
    And hov'ring death prepar'd the blow, . . . . . . .     O 201  Death Dr Levet     14
HOVER
    Tho' confiscation's vulturs hover round. . . . . . .    O  32  Vanity Wishes      36
    Empire and conquest hover or . . . . . . . . .          Y 115  Irene          V 49C
    Now hover o'er us with propitious Wings, . . . . . .    O 306  Irene              51
    now hover oer us and direct our councils . . . . . .    Y 181  Irene          V  51
HOVERS
    Time hovers o'er, impatient to destroy, . . . . . .     O  43  Vanity Wishes     259
    Still discord hovers o'er divided thrones. . . . . .    O 140  Tr Rambler 183      2
    Dominion hovers o'er their conquering banners  . . . .  Y 115  Irene          V 49D
    Now hovers o'er this melancholy Shade,  . . . . . .     O 267  Irene              40
HOW
    How, when competitors like these contend,  . . . . .    O  16  London            144
    How virtue wars with persecuting fate; . . . . . .      O  19  London            199
    Blest age! but ah! how diff'rent from our own! . . .    O  22  London            253
    Blest age! but ha! how diff'rent from our own! . . .    O  22  London         V 253
    Then say how hope and fear, desire and hate,  . . . .   O  31  Vanity Wishes       5
    Then say how fierce desire and raging hate, . . . . .   Y  92  Vanity Wishes  V   5
    Then say how hot desire and raging hate, . . . . . .    Y  92  Vanity Wishes  V   5
    How rarely reason guides the stubborn choice, . . . .   O  31  Vanity Wishes      11
    How rarely reason guides the hasty choice, . . . . .    Y  92  Vanity Wishes  V  11
    How nations sink, by darling schemes oppress'd, . . .   O  31  Vanity Wishes      13
    How families sink, by darling schemes oppress'd, . . .  Y  92  Vanity Wishes  V  13
    How much more safe the vassal than the lord;  . . . .   O  31  Vanity Wishes      32
    How wouldst thou shake at Britain's modish tribe, . .   O  33  Vanity Wishes      61
    How just that scorn ere yet thy voice declare, . . .    O  33  Vanity Wishes      71
    How just his hopes let Swedish Charles decide; . . .    O  40  Vanity Wishes     192
    See! how the mighty Change is wrought! . . . . . .      O  70  Hor.II Ode XX       9
    See! how whate'er remain'd of Man . . . . . . . .       O  70  Hor.II Ode XX      10
    How pleas'd he sees his Cattle come, . . . . . . .      O  73  Hor. Epode II      67
    How pleas'd beholds his Oxen bow  . . . . . . . .       O  73  Hor. Epode II      69
    How would the Trojans brand great Hector's name! . .    O  74  Tr. Iliad Bk 6      5
    Oh! how my soul abhors so mean a thought. . . . . .     O  74  Tr. Iliad Bk 6      8
    Illustrious age! how bright thy glories shone, . . .    O 118  Epitaph Hanmer     21
    How active light, and thoughtful shade, . . . . . .     O 121  To Miss Playin     27
    How passion's well-accorded strife . . . . . . . .      O 121  To Miss Playin     31
    Ah! how shall envy sooth her pain? . . . . . . . .      O 122  Stella Mourn.      12
    How sweet in sleep to pass the careless hours, . . .    O 135  Tr Rambler 117      1
    How small to others, but how great to me. . . . . .     O 138  Tr Rambler 161      1
    How small to others, but how great to me. . . . . .     O 138  Tr Rambler 161      1
    How long shall sloth usurp thy useless hours, . . . .   O 151  The Ant             9
    Only teaches how to cheat. . . . . . . . . . .          O 176  Tr Metastasi I      6
    Learn here how Heav'n supports the virtuous Mind,  . .  O 246  Irene Prologue      9
    But how the Devil should he please us all! . . . . .    O 247  Irene Epilogue      8
    --How chang'd alas!--Now ghastly Desolation  . . . .    O 251  Irene              66
    Behold how Lust and Rapine struggle round her. . . .    O 252  Irene              82
    O! sooth my Soul, and teach me how to lose thee. . .    O 253  Irene             103
    Or how can Cali's Flight restore our Country? . . . .   O 254  Irene             139
    How can a single Hand attempt a Life . . . . . .        O 258  Irene              90
    How shall I scorn the beautiful Aspasia! . . . . .      O 261  Irene              22
    How will the bright Aspasia shine above her! . . . .    O 261  Irene              23
    How Nation after Nation falls before him. . . . . .     O 268  Irene              27
    How nation after nation falls before me  . . . . . .    Y 136  Irene          V  27
    How Heav'n in Scorn of human Arrogance, . . . . . .     O 269  Irene               1
    How blest art thou, still jocund and serene, . . . .    O 271  Irene               6
    How will the matchless Beauties of Irene, . . . . .     O 276  Irene               6
    How did Aspasia welcome your Address? . . . . . .       O 282  Irene              61
    Soon shouldst thou see, how false thy weak Reproach. .  O 293  Irene             107
    Soon wouldst thou see, how false thy weak Reproach. .   O 293  Irene          V 107
    Say, how the Tyrant threaten'd, flatter'd, sigh'd, . .  O 295  Irene              23
    Say, how he threaten'd, flatter'd, sigh'd in vain! . .  O 295  Irene              24
    Say, how the Hand of Violence was rais'd, . . . . .     O 295  Irene              25
    Say, how thou call'dst in Tears upon Demetrius! . . .   O 295  Irene              26
    Inform me rather, how thy happy Courage . . . . .       O 295  Irene              27
    Think how the sov'reign Arbiter of Kingdoms . . . .     O 300  Irene              56
    How soon, alas! will Int'rest, Fear, or Envy? . . . .   O 301  Irene              82
    But how can'st thou support the Woes of Exile? . . .    O 301  Irene             102
    How the new Monarch, swell'd with airy Rule, . . . .    O 306  Irene               1
    How rarely would they meet in crouded Courts, . . . .   O 308  Irene              16
    <Ho>w blest our state could every bosom  . . . . . .    Y 184  Irene          V  16
    How should I joy, 'midst the fierce Shock of Nations,   O 309  Irene              40
    How Guilt once harbour'd in the conscious Breast, . .   O 311  Irene              14
    See how the Moon through all th' unclouded Sky . . .    O 313  Irene               1
    Were now well lost, in hearing how you fail'd. . . .    O 316  Irene              23
    Tell how Demetrius shun'd his single Hand, . . . . .    O 318  Irene              13
    How am I chang'd! How lately did Irene  . . . . . .     O 322  Irene              13
    How am I chang'd! How lately did Irene  . . . . . .     O 322  Irene              13
    He knows how near Apostacy to Treason-- . . . . .       O 324  Irene              21
    Think shouldst thou fall how wretched shall we be,  . . Y  19  Tr. Iliad Bk 6     48
    How great Achilles godlike Hector slew? . . . . .       Y  22  Tr Add. Battle     11
    How Turnus by Aeneas' sword expir'd? . . . . . .        Y  22  Tr Add. Battle     12
    Or how before Nassau the Gallick troops retir'd? . . .  Y  22  Tr Add. Battle     13
HOWE'ER
    For howe'er we boast and strive, . . . . . . . .        O 178  Thrale 35 Year     13
HOWL
    Where furies ever howl, and serpents hiss. . . . . .    O  84  Epi Dist Moth.     31
    Amidst the Camp to howl his Life away. . . . . . .      O 273  Irene              37
```

```
HOWL        (CONTINUED)                                   PAGE   TITLE          LINE
    May storms howl gently o'er and learn to spare.  . . .  Y   3 On a Daffodill     8
HUE
    With livid hue the fairest face o'ercast,   . . . . .  O  84 Epi Dist Moth.     34
HUG
    We bless the Tyrant, and we hug the Chain.  . . . . .  O  96 Hickman Spinet      8
HUGE
    <?storms huge> Promontories flie  . . . . . . .       O  76 Tr Add. Battle     22
    In rat'ling storms huge promontories flie   . . . . .  Y  26 Tr Add. Battle  V 140
    Till thither an huge bird the tumult drew   . . . . .  Y  25 Tr Add. Battle    124
HUGS
    And hugs a flatterer for a friend. . . . . . . . .    O 100 Ode Friendship     20
    Who hugs a flatterer for a friend. . . . . . . . .    O 100 Ode Friendship  V  20
HUMAN
    The Vanity of Human Wishes. ...                       O  29 Vanity Wishes       T
    Surveys the general toil of human kind;  . . . . . .  O  59 Pro Good Nat'd      2
    A clime deny'd to human race;  . . . . . . . . .      O  66 Hor I Ode xxii     22
    A Clime deny'd to human Race;  . . . . . . . . .      O  67 To A. Fuscus       22
    Intrusts his happiness to human kind,  . . . . . .    O  82 Young Author       13
    The human and the savage breast  . . . . . . . .     O  99 Ode Friendship      7
    His Conduct Human Kind debased:  . . . . . . . .     O 146 Tr Boeth III.4      6
    Who holds no human Creature mean;  . . . . . . .     O 147 Tr Boeth III.6     18
    Of human bliss to human woe. . . . . . . . . .       O 184 Tr. Benserade       4
    Of human bliss to human woe. . . . . . . . . .       O 184 Tr. Benserade       4
    Before such Foes of more than human Force;  . . . .  O 250 Irene              49
    Think on the sudden Change of human Scenes;  . . . .  O 252 Irene              86
    Left by the Hand of Heav'n on human Clay.  . . . .   O 255 Irene              13
    How Heav'n in Scorn of human Arrogance,  . . . . .   O 269 Irene               1
    Thou long'st for Stars that frown on human Kind,  . .  O 271 Irene               4
    Charm'd with the Thought of blessing human Kind,  . .  O 278 Irene              73
    And turn'd th' instructive Page of Human Life,  . .   O 281 Irene              33
    Deny'd Debard each privilege of human nature being    Y 165 Irene           V  81
    if human miseries or affairs yet claim your  . . . .  Y 181 Irene           V  54
      regard
    And yet such is the condition of human   . . . . .    Y 186 Irene           V   2
      happiness
HUMANKIND
    Renew'd at ev'ry glance on humankind;  . . . . . . .  O  33 Vanity Wishes      70
HUMBLE
    Speak thou, whose thoughts at humble peace repine,  .  O  35 Vanity Wishes     121
    And hope with humble confidence the best  . . . . .   Y 108 Vanity Wishes   V 356
    Thus grac'd with humble Virtue's native Charms  . . .  O  58 Prologue Comus     33
    Far from their antient fields and humble cots.  . . .  O  64 Virgil Past.I      18
    Rest undisturb'd within this humble shrine,  . . . .  O 113 Epit. Phillips   V   5
    Where ----'s humble turrets rise,  . . . . . . . .    O 125 An Ode             16
    For humble cottages and rural sports.  . . . . . .    O 137 Tr Rambler 138      2
HUMBLER
    Th' insulted sea with humbler thoughts he gains,  . .  O  42 Vanity Wishes     237
    And mirth was bounty with a humbler name.  . . . . .  O  62 Pro Word Wise      24
    Niphates rolls an humbler wave,  . . . . . . . .     O  68 Hor. II Ode IX     21
    Unus'd to Power, and form'd for humbler Scenes,  . .  O 268 Irene              17
HUMOUR
    That useful truth with humour may unite,  . . . . .   Y  67 Prologue Lethe     15
HUNDRED
    At once a hundred Voices thunder'd round me,  . . . .  O 271 Irene              29
    I had a hundred Virgins wait around her,  . . . . .   O 287 Irene              16
HUNG
    That hung the bright Palladium of the place,  . . . .  O  33 Vanity Wishes      84
    That hung on high Palladium of the place,  . . . . .  Y  95 Vanity Wishes   V  84
    And Want hung threat'ning o'er her slow Decay.  . . .  O  58 Prologue Comus     26
    ... in a Room hung with some Flower-pieces  . . . . .  O 120 To Miss Playing     T
    Hung on your Neck, and hinder'd your Departure.  . .  O 280 Irene              10
    The sympathising cattle hung their heads  . . . . .   Y   6 Virgil Daphnis      9
    Above their heads th' embattled squadrons hung  . . .  Y  25 Tr Add. Battle     94
HUNGARIA'S
    While fair Hungaria's unexhausted Vallies  . . . .   O 264 Irene              16
    While fair yet Hungaria's inexhausted Vallies  . . .  O 352 Irene           V  33
HUNGER
    But all whom hunger spares, with age decay:  . . . .  O   9 London             12
    Would ease the hunger of the mind,  . . . . . . .    O 144 Tr Boeth. II.2      8
    Why roars the Lioness distress'd by Hunger?  . . . .  O 281 Irene              50
    Let Slav'ry harrass, and let Hunger gripe.  . . . .   O 328 Irene              37
HUNGRY
    Their hungry Swarms the peaceful Vale shall fright  .  O 110 To Posterity        9
    And hungry Slaughter scents Imperial Blood?  . . . .  O 279 Irene               5
    That Hoary Head, that Head which hungry fate  . . . .  O 374 Irene           V  20
    The hungry Janizary burns for Plunder,  . . . . . .  O 309 Irene              21
HUNT
    Here Hunt may box, or Mahomet may dance.  . . . . .   O  53 Pro Drury-Lane     46
    Only to hunt him round the ravag'd World?  . . . .   O 275 Irene              67
HURLING
    Hurling vast mounts against the realms above  . . . .  Y  26 Tr Add. Battle    138
HURRIED
    Too strong for Love, have hurried him on Death.  . .  O 267 Irene              48
    By hateful Business hurried from her Sight,  . . . .  O 287 Irene              15
    Her final Doom, and hurried her Destruction.  . . . .  O 334 Irene              62
HURRIES
    He plies the press, and hurries on his fate;  . . . .  O  82 Young Author       20
    He flies to press, and hurries on his fate;  . . . .  O  82 Young Author    V  20
HURRY
    And gold and flattery--thoughtless mirth--hurry  . .  Y 164 Irene           V  72
```

		PAGE	TITLE	LINE
HURRY'D				
Hurry'd to death by thee, Flaminius fell,	. . . . .	O 77	Festina Lente	15
HURT				
And him who cannot hurt, allow to please;	. . . . .	O 62	Pro Word Wise	12
HUSBAND				
A father, brother, husband, all in thee.	. . . . . .	Y 19	Tr. Iliad Bk 6	45
HUSSAR				
The fierce Croatian, and the wild Hussar,	. . . .	O 43	Vanity Wishes	249
HYDASPES				
Or where the fam'd Hydaspes spreads	. . . .	O 65	Hor I Ode xxii	7
Or where the fam'd Hydaspes spreads	. . . .	O 66	To A. Fuscus	7
HYDE				
What murder'd Wentworth, and what exil'd Hyde,	. . . .	O 36	Vanity Wishes	131
HYMNS				
Thank Heav'n in daily hymns for my our deliverance	. .	Y 166	Irene	V 93
Sing duly hymns to Heaven	. .	Y 166	Irene	V 94
HYPERBOLIES				
None e're rejects hyperbolies of praise.	. . . . . .	O 134	Tr Rambler 104	1
HYPERIA'S				
Beneath Hyperia's waters shall you sweat,	. . . . .	O 74	Tr. Iliad Bk 6	23
HYPOCRISY				
Hypocrisy which I ha<ve> worn is a burthen:	. . . . .	Y 185	Irene	V 2
HYPOCRITICK				
Cali, this Day with hypocritick Zeal,	. . . .	O 273	Irene	43
HYPOPLACUS'				
Where Hypoplacus' lofty shades extend.	. . . . . .	Y 18	Tr. Iliad Bk 6	8
I				
I praise the hermit, but regret the friend,	. . . .	O 8	London	4
Well may they rise, while I, whose rustick tongue	. . .	O 14	London	79
I cannot bear a French metropolis.	. . . .	O 15	London	98
I drew the breath of life in English air;	. . . . .	O 15	London	118
Much could I add,--but see the boat at hand,	. . . .	O 22	London	254
Lies at my feet, I hiss him, and he dies.	. . . . .	O 60	Pro Good Nat'd	24
For I shall never think him less than God;	. . . . .	O 64	Virgil Past.I	8
My admiration only I exprest,	. . . .	O 64	Virgil Past.I	13
Here I, though faint myself, must drive my goats,	. . .	O 64	Virgil Past.I	17
This scarce I lead, who left on yonder rock	. . . .	O 64	Virgil Past.I	19
Translation of Horace. Book I. Ode xxii.	. . . . .	O 65	Hor I Ode xxii	T
Too far in Sabine woods I stray'd;	. . . .	O 65	Hor I Ode xxii	10
By Lalage, too far I stray'd,	. . . .	O 66	To A. Fuscus	10
A Poet double-form'd I rise,	. . . . .	O 70	Hor.II Ode XX	2
From th' envious world with scorn I spring,	. . . . .	O 70	Hor.II Ode XX	3
Though from no Princes I descend,	. . . .	O 70	Hor.II Ode XX	5
Yet shall I see the blest abodes,	. . . .	O 70	Hor.II Ode XX	6
I pierce the Clouds a tunefull Swan.	. . . .	O 70	Hor.II Ode XX	12
I without fun'ral elegies	. . . .	O 70	Hor.II Ode XX	23
I should behold with scornfull eye	. . . .	O 73	Hor. Epode II	55
I once admir'd, I'd then despise:	. . . . . .	O 73	Hor. Epode II	V 60
But shall I, then, forsake the unfinish'd war?	. . . .	O 74	Tr. Iliad Bk 6	4
Long since I learn'd to slight this fleeting breath,	. . .	O 74	Tr. Iliad Bk 6	9
May I lie slain, and spurn the bloody sand!	. . . . .	O 75	Tr. Iliad Bk 6	30
While I to nobler themes aspire,	. . . . . .	O 78	Feast St Simon	7
Thrice happy Saints--where do I rove?	. . . . .	O 80	Feast St Simon	55
"While I these transitory blessings scorn,	. . . . .	O 82	Young Author	17
"While I those transitory blessings scorn,	. . . . .	O 82	Young Author	V 17
For you, ye fair, I quit the gloomy plains,	. . . . .	O 83	Epi Dist Moth.	10
Nor can I hope thy silken chain	. . . .	O 120	To Miss Purse	9
I feel thy pow'r usurp my breast.	. . . . .	O 123	Winter's Walk	8
I can't prevent, and will not share.	. . . . .	O 126	An Ode	36
But some Zelinda while I sing	. . . .	O 126	An Ode	37
But, lest I fall by subtler foes,	. . . . . .	O 127	To Lyce, Lady	17
And I but flatter less.	. . . .	O 127	To Lyce, Lady	24
I trace the planets and survey the skies.	. . . . .	O 130	Tr. Rambler 8	2
For trifling sports I quitted grave affairs.	. . . . .	O 130	Tr. Rambler 10	1
Nought from my birth or ancestors I claim;	. . . . .	O 132	Tr. Rambler 46	1
I grant the charge; forgive the fault confess'd.	. . . .	O 139	Tr Rambler 170	1
The more I honour thee, the less I love.	. . . . .	O 140	Tr Rambler 188	1
The more I honour thee, the less I love.	. . . . .	O 140	Tr Rambler 188	1
I scorn the multitude, alive and dead.	. . . . .	O 141	Tr Rambler 208	4
I too can feel the rapture, fierce and strong;	. . . .	O 142	In Baretti Bk.	3
I too can pour the extemporary song:	. . . . .	O 142	In Baretti Bk.	4
I put my hat upon my head	. . . .	O 158	Par. Hermit II	1
I walk'd along the Strand,	. . . .	O 158	Par. Hermit II	V 2
And there I met another man	. . . .	O 158	Par. Hermit II	3
I there did meet another man	. . . .	O 158	Par. Hermit II	V 3
I Therefore pray thee, Renny dear,	. . . . . .	O 158	Par Hermit III	1
I pray thee, gentle Renny dear,	. . . . . .	O 158	Par Hermit III	V 1
Nor fear that I, my gentle maid,	. . . . . .	O 159	Par Hermit III	5
When once unto the bottom I	. . . .	O 159	Par Hermit III	7
As I can gulp it down.	. . . .	O 159	Par Hermit III	12
I am Cassander, come down from the Sky,	. . . .	O 173	Tr Fr Pantomim	1
That I am Cassander come down from the Sky.	. . .	O 173	Tr Fr Pantomim	3
I pleas'd my Master, and I pleas'd my Dame.	. . . .	O 174	Tr Epitaph Dog	2
I pleas'd my Master, and I pleas'd my Dame.	. . . .	O 174	Tr Epitaph Dog	2
Wheresoe'er I turn my View,	. . . .	O 179	Ridicul Warton	1
Thus I spoke; and speaking sigh'd;	. . . . . .	O 181	Parody Warton	5
"Soft Anacreon's vows I bear,	. . . .	O 185	Anacreon Ode 9	7
"Now the generous bowl I sip	. . . .	O 185	Anacreon Ode 9	31
"I have chatter'd like a pye."	. . . . . .	O 186	Anacreon Ode 9	44
I swear this Eastern Pageantry is Nonsense,	. . . .	O 247	Irene Epilogue	13
Quitting my close Retreat, I range the City,	. . . .	O 251	Irene	60

I

	PAGE	TITLE	LINE
(CONTINUED)			
With silent Pangs I view the tow'ring Domes,	O 251	Irene	62
I felt thy Pains, and trembled for Aspasia.	O 251	Irene	75
Yet let me think--I see the helpless Maid,	O 252	Irene	80
I came obedient to thy friendly Summons,	O 253	Irene	105
To what I know not!	O 253	Irene	108
Surpriz'd I start, and bless the happy Dream;	O 254	Irene	124
Such had I trusted once as soon as seen,	O 255	Irene	17
I scorn a Trust unwillingly repos'd;	O 256	Irene	34
What hazards would I shun to clasp for Greece and for Aspasia	Y 125	Irene	V 133
How shall I scorn the beautiful Apostate!	O 261	Irene	22
I come from empty Noise, and tasteless Pomp,	O 262	Irene	7
I walk'd superior, through the Blaze of Charms,	O 263	Irene	17
Sure this is Love which heretofore I conceiv'd	O 349	Irene	V 28
Why rove I now, when absent from my Fair,	O 263	Irene	19
Still restless, till I clasp the lovely Maid,	O 263	Irene	21
Had they prevail'd, I ne'er had known Irene.	O 263	Irene	27
Long have I wish'd, before our Prophet's Tomb,	O 263	Irene	9
I want alass thy steadiness of Soul	O 366	Irene	V 29
Too well I know him, his immod'rate Courage,	O 267	Irene	46
Just as I mark'd them, they forsook the Shore,	O 269	Irene	38
Ere I could range them on the crowded Deck,	O 271	Irene	28
Retire with Speed, while I prepare to meet him	O 271	Irene	37
I see the Gloom that low'rs upon thy Brow,	O 271	Irene	1
I share, by secret Instinct, all his Joys,	O 272	Irene	10
Oft have I rag'd, when their wide-wasting Cannon	O 273	Irene	24
I dread his Arts of seeming Innocence,	O 273	Irene	39
I rais'd his Thoughts to more sublime Devotion.	O 274	Irene	46
Him I can crush at leisure.	O 367	Irene	V 30
Twice since the Morning rose I saw the Bassa,	O 275	Irene	76
I mark'd them well, and trac'd in either Face	O 275	Irene	81
Must I for these renounce the Hope of Heav'n,	O 276	Irene	13
I thought, forgive my Fair, the noblest Aim,	O 278	Irene	61
Too calm I listen to the flatt'ring Sounds.	O 278	Irene	74
To State and Pow'r I court thee, not to Ruin:	O 279	Irene	80
Because I love:	O 281	Irene	48
I gaz'd, I trembled; but I could not speak:	O 282	Irene	65
I gaz'd, I trembled; but I could not speak:	O 282	Irene	65
I gaz'd, I trembled; but I could not speak:	O 282	Irene	65
Through bowing Slaves, I range the private Rooms,	O 283	Irene	17
Who merits most!--I knew not we were Rivals.	O 284	Irene	46
What I can grant, you cannot ask in vain--	O 285	Irene	14
I go to wait thy Call; this kind Consent	O 285	Irene	15
Justice demands that I reveal your Crimes;	O 286	Irene	14
I displaid--before her all the gay luscious scene...	Y 158	Irene	V 8
I drew to my party with (alluring) promises artfull	Y 158	Irene	V 11
These Arts I try'd, and to inflame her more,	O 287	Irene	14
I bad a hundred Virgins wait around her,	O 287	Irene	16
Far more I dread Abdalla's fiery Folly,	O 287	Irene	7
I discover by this state & retinue	Y 160	Irene	V 8
While I foretell thy Fate; that Office done,--	O 289	Irene	9
No more I boast th' ambitious Name of Friend,	O 289	Irene	10
I am not yet a Queen, or an Apostate.	O 289	Irene	22
But should I sin beyond the Hope of Mercy,	O 289	Irene	23
Not then with raving Cries I fill'd the City,	O 290	Irene	46
(Yet) not with idle cries I fill'd the city	Y 163	Irene	V 46
Shall I not wish to chear afflicted Kings,	O 291	Irene	67
Oft' shall I dwell on our disastrous Friendship,	O 292	Irene	96
Oft shall I swell on our disastrous Friendship	O 349	Irene	V 11
Not Pow'r I blame, but Pow'r obtain'd by Crime,	O 293	Irene	129
Nor think to say here will I stop	Y 168	Irene	V 132
Here will I fix the limits of transgression	Y 168	Irene	V 133
When I am gone remember, O! remember,	O 294	Irene	7
Aspasia! do I once again behold thee?	O 294	Irene	2
I stand amaz'd, and ask, if yet I clasp thee.	O 296	Irene	37
I stand amaz'd, and ask, if yet I clasp thee.	O 296	Irene	37
Then--O my Fair, I cannot bid thee goe;	O 297	Irene	15
Then--O my Fair, I cannot bid thee go;	O 297	Irene	V 15
Nor think thy Cause neglected while I gaze,	O 297	Irene	20
New Force, new Courage, from each Glance I gain,	O 297	Irene	21
I stole unheeded from their ravish'd Eyes,	O 299	Irene	49
I saw without a sigh the fierce barbarian	Y 176	Irene	V 106
Unmov'd I saw the glitt'ring Trifles perish,	O 302	Irene	108
Chearful I follow to the rural Cell,	O 302	Irene	110
Have I for this preserv'd my guiltless Bosom,	O 304	Irene	14
Have I for this defy'd the Chiefs of Turkey,	O 304	Irene	16
I ask no Witness, but attesting Conscience,	O 305	Irene	34
While I destroy th' Oppressor of Mankind?	O 305	Irene	37
I feel new Spirit shoot along my Nerves,	O 306	Irene	49
I need not name it;	O 307	Irene	12
Too well I know him, since on Thracia's Plains	O 307	Irene	18
I felt the Force of his tempestuous Arm,	O 307	Irene	19
Nor will I trust th' uncertain Chance of Combat;	O 307	Irene	21
Forbear--.i know the long try'd Faith of Cali.	O 308	Irene	11
I rouse to War, and conquer for Irene.	O 309	Irene	25
How should I joy, 'midst the fierce Shock of Nations,	O 309	Irene	40
Hypocrisy which I ha<ve> worn is a burthen:	Y 185	Irene	V 2
I w<ould> have every smile g<enu>ine to<morrow no>	Y 185	Irene	V 3
For I know ambition seduc'd her	Y 186	Irene	V 4
I love her still, but shall esteem Aspasia:	Y 186	Irene	V 5

I   (CONTINUED)

	PAGE	TITLE		LINE
And idolize th' Apostate I contemn.	O 310	Irene		11
There I became, nor blush to make it known,	O 312	Irene		13
Thou fountain of existence I pour the	Y 189	Irene	V	1
Yet much remains to hope. I shall not call	O 317	Irene		45
Once more I dare thy Sword, behold the Prize,	O 319	Irene		28
Behold I quit her to the Chance of Battle.	O 319	Irene		29
Who fearst lest I should gain, or thou	Y 198	Irene	V	32
lose or I possess her	Y 198	Irene	V	32
While I protract their Stay. Be swift and faithful.	O 319	Irene		4
In vain I listen to th' inviting Call	O 320	Irene		10
In vain I listen to the inviting voice	Y 198	Irene	V	10
I see the distant vessel	Y 201	Irene		10
While I not yet familiar to my Crimes,	O 322	Irene		11
How am I chang'd! How lately did Irene	O 322	Irene		13
Bold Slave, I know them both--I know them Traytors.	O 324	Irene		16
Bold Slave, I know them both--I know them Traytors.	O 324	Irene		16
But 'tis not mine to judge--I scorn and leave thee.	O 324	Irene		22
I go, lest Vengeance urge my Hand to Blood,	O 324	Irene		23
I mark'd her wily Messenger afar,	O 327	Irene		24
I guess'd her dark Designs, and warn'd the Sultan,	O 327	Irene		26
The Prayer I cannot grant--I dare not hear.	O 328	Irene		48
The Prayer I cannot grant--I dare not hear.	O 328	Irene		48
Does not thy Bosom, for I know thee tender,	O 329	Irene		5
Perhaps I will not stoop to plead my Cause;	O 330	Irene		22
Perhaps I will not bend to plead my cause	Y 210	Irene	V	22
I came to heighten Tortures by Reproach,	O 330	Irene		7
Was this the Maid whose Love I bought with Empire!	O 330	Irene		9
I bring a tardy Message from Irene.	O 331	Irene		2
Robb'd of the Maid, with whom I wish'd to triumph,	O 333	Irene		42
No more I burn for Fame or for Dominion;	O 333	Irene		43
Yet ere I quit the Scepter of Dominion,	O 333	Irene		49
Hear! shall I hear thee! did'st thou hear Irene?	O 333	Irene		56
Thou mightst have liv'd, nor had I lost Irene	Y 214	Irene	V	58
I heard her, pitied her, and wish'd to save her.	O 333	Irene		59
I heard, and soften'd, till Abdalla brought	O 334	Irene		61
I feel, I see the Ruffian's barb'rous Rage.	O 334	Irene		69
I feel, I see the Ruffian's barb'rous Rage.	O 334	Irene		69
My spirits fail, I cannot name his death	Y 216	Irene	V	72
But while I sing, the nimble moments fly,	Y 4	On a Daffodill		21
With grief this emblem of mankind I see,	Y 4	On a Daffodill		25
Here have I rais'd four sacred altars, two	Y 7	Virgil Daphnis		43
Pettius no more I verses write;	Y 10	Tr Hor Epode 9		1
No more I sing, no more delight	Y 11	Tr Hor Epode 9		3
I first foresook the scornfull fair.	Y 11	Tr Hor Epode 9		10
I then (my cheeks still glow with shame) was grown	Y 11	Tr Hor Epode 9		11
The pains I labour'd to conceal	Y 11	Tr Hor Epode 9		15
To thee I told the causes of my smart,	Y 11	Tr Hor Epode 9		18
To thee I then with tears complain'd	Y 11	Tr Hor Epode 9		19
Then would I free from torments live	Y 11	Tr Hor Epode 9		25
Thus I t' effect this mighty change design'd	Y 11	Tr Hor Epode 9		29
Confus'd about the streets I roam	Y 11	Tr Hor Epode 9		33
Then to the inclement skies expos'd I sat	Y 11	Tr Hor Epode 9		35
May I lye cold beneath a load of clay.	Y 18	Tr. Iliad Bk 6		25
While Hector lives I tast of ev'ry joy	Y 18	Tr. Iliad Bk 6		26
But dearest Hector while thou liv'st I see	Y 19	Tr. Iliad Bk 6		44
A widow I, an helpless orphan he.	Y 19	Tr. Iliad Bk 6		49
And the sad fate of Pygmie realms I sing.	Y 22	Tr Add. Battle		2
I first attempt in never-dying lays	Y 22	Tr Add. Battle		16

I'D

	PAGE	TITLE		LINE
I once admir'd, I'd then despise:	O 73	Hor. Epode II	V	60

I'LL

	PAGE	TITLE		LINE
I'll sing of Chloe's charms divine,	O 66	Hor I Ode xxii		23
My Flame for Lalage I'll own;	O 67	To A. Fuscus		23
This Hour I'll beg, with unsuspecting Face,	O 258	Irene		86
To mix with nobler Cares, I'll throw aside	O 275	Irene		70
To mix with nobler Cares, I'll set apart	O 368	Irene	V	27
I'll open my breast--clasp thee--forget greatness--	Y 161	Irene	V	13
Two bowls with oyl and milk I'll yearly crown,	Y 7	Virgil Daphnis		45
I'll sing the chiefs dispensing fate around.	Y 22	Tr Add. Battle		19

I'M

	PAGE	TITLE		LINE
Freedom and Love? Alas! I'm all Confusion,	O 295	Irene		11

ICARUS

	PAGE	TITLE		LINE
Swifter than Icarus Ill flie	O 70	Hor.II Ode XX		13

ICE

	PAGE	TITLE		LINE
O'er ice the rapid skaiter flies,	O 203	Tr. on Skating		1
On crackling ice, o'er gulphs profound,	O 203	Tr. on Skating	V	1

ICY

	PAGE	TITLE		LINE
Though Scythia's icy cliffs he treads,	O 65	Hor I Ode xxii		5
Tho' Scythia's icy cliff he treads,	Y 74	Hor I Ode xxii	V	5
Thro' Scythia's icy cliffs he treads,	Y 74	Hor I Ode xxii	V	5
O'er icy Caucusus he treads,	O 66	To A. Fuscus		5

IDEAL

	PAGE	TITLE		LINE
And tow'rs and triumphs in ideal Greatness;	O 269	Irene		5

IDLE

	PAGE	TITLE		LINE
All else is empty Sound, and idle Show.	O 246	Irene Prologue		14
The Dream of idle Maids and wanton Poets	O 350	Irene	V	1
Soars unencumber'd with our idle Cares,	O 266	Irene		36
In soft Complaints, and idle Protestations.	O 269	Irene		16
Then let us now resolve, nor idle waste	O 271	Irene	V	33

```
IDLE            (CONTINUED)                              PAGE    TITLE           LINE
     For idle Hours, and crush him at my Leisure.    . . . .  O 275  Irene              71
     Cast off all idle terrours of hereafter    . . . . . .  Y 146  Irene         V    19
     (Yet) not with idle cries I fill'd the city  . . . . .  Y 163  Irene         V    46
     An idle List'ner to the distant Cries  . . . . .        O 305  Irene              23
     And growls in private o'er his idle Sabre.  . . . . .   O 309  Irene              22
     Nor rush on useless Wounds with idle Courage.  . . . .  O 318  Irene              10
     With idle Threats and fruitless Exclamation,  . . . .   O 327  Irene               7
IDLENESS
     stagnant soul.  The gloom of idleness.   . . . . . .    Y 165  Irene         V    82
IDLER
     Thou sluggish Idler, dilatory Slave?  . . . . . . .     O 334  Irene               2
IDLY
     Then let us now resolve, nor idly waste  . . . . . .    O 271  Irene              33
     Not idly flutters on a boastful Tongue,  . . . . . .    O 290  Irene              37
IDOL
     Th' adoring Soldiers would revenge their Idol.  . . .   O 273  Irene              42
IDOLIZE
     And idolize th' Apostate I contemn.  . . . . . . .      O 310  Irene              11
IDOLIZES
     With mad Devotion idolizes Honour.  . . . . . . . .     O 300  Irene              79
IDOMENEUS
     Idomeneus, the godlike Telamon  . . . . . . . . .       Y  19  Tr. Iliad Bk 6     55
IF
     If the gull'd conqueror receives the chain,  . . . . .  O  16  London            121
     Prepare for death, if here at night you roam,  . . . .  O  21  London            224
     Here life is ventur'd if the streets you roam  . . . .  Y  59  London        V  224
     If dreams yet flatter, once again attend,  . . . . . .  O  38  Vanity Wishes     163
     If hope yet flatter, once again attend,  . . . . . . .  Y  99  Vanity Wishes  V  163
     If aspirations to the skies aspires,  . . . . . . .     Y 108  Vanity Wishes  V  358
     Perhaps if Skill could distant Times explore,  . . . .  O  53  Pro Drury-Lane     41
     But confident of praise, if praise be due,  . . . . .   O  60  Pro Good Nat'd     29
     If want of skill, or want of care appear,  . . . . . .  O  62  Pro Word Wise      17
     If to compleat this heav'nly Life  . . . . . . .        O  72  Hor. Epode II      47
     Or if old womens tales may credit gain,  . . . . . .    O  77  Tr Add. Battle     44
     If wrought by any hand but thine,  . . . . . . . .      O 119  To Miss Purse       4
     If such on Earth can Bliss bestow,  . . . . . . . .     O 146  Tr Boeth III.4      7
     If Sorrow pine or Av'rice crave,  . . . . . . . .       O 146  Tr Boeth III.5      9
     If Genius warm thee, Reader, stay,  . . . . . . .       O 154  Epita. Hogarth      5
     If Merit touch thee, shed a tear,  . . . . . . . .      O 154  Epita. Hogarth      6
     If at your coming princes disappear,  . . . . . . .     O 177  Tr Dist Modena      1
     If the man who turnips cries,  . . . . . . . . .        O 183  Burlesque Vega      1
     Let it wander if it will;  . . . . . . . . . .          O 196  Song Congratu. V   18
     If the Guardian or the Mother  . . . . . . . .          O 197  Song Congratu.     25
     Who knows if Jove who counts our Score  . . . . .       O 232  Tr Horace IV.7     17
     If Truths like these with pleasing Language join;  . .  O 246  Irene Prologue     15
     Ennobled, yet unchang'd, if Nature shine:  . . . . .    O 246  Irene Prologue     16
     If no wild Draught depart from Reason's Rules,  . . .   O 246  Irene Prologue     17
     Let him persuade me to it--if he can:  . . . . . .      O 247  Irene Epilogue      4
     If Happiness can be without Aspasia.  . . . . . . .     O 253  Irene             110
     If chasing past Events with vain Pursuit,  . . . . .    O 255  Irene               5
     If there be any Land, as Fame reports,  . . . . . .     O 256  Irene              55
     That Vessel, if observ'd, alarms the Court,  . . . .    O 258  Irene              83
     At least this Day be calm--If we succeed,  . . . . .    O 260  Irene             141
     but if your influence be too wide--your dissipated rays . Y 132  Irene         V   41
        will burn no more
     This were enough, if Cali had been Mahomet  . . . .    Y 132  Irene         V   41D
     If yet one spark of Heav'nly fire remain  . . . . .     Y 133  Irene         V    18
     If Greatness please thee, mount th' imperial Seat;  .   O 279  Irene              84
     If Pleasure charm thee, view this soft Retreat;  . .    O 279  Irene              85
     Who knows if Mahomet's awaking Anger  . . . . .         O 284  Irene              38
     If e'er thy Youth has known the Pangs of Absence,  . .  O 285  Irene               3
     If yet this shining Pomp, these sudden Honours,  . . .  O 289  Irene               1
     If yet these glittring Robes these sudden Splendors  .  O 366  Irene         V    17
     If Dismiss this glittring train these sudden  . . . .   O 366  Irene         V    17
        Splendors
     If when Religion prompts me to refuse,  . . . . .       O 289  Irene              24
     If built on settled Thought, this Constancy  . . . .    O 290  Irene              36
     If fix'd on settled thought this Constancy  . . . .     O 364  Irene         V    8
     Maxims like these, if generally persued  . . . . .      O 352  Irene         V    2
     Maxims like these, if once reduc'd to practice  . . .   O 352  Irene         V    2
     I stand amaz'd, and ask, if yet I clasp thee.  . . .    O 296  Irene              37
     If we must part--  . . . . . . . . . . .                O 297  Irene              11
     If we must part--  . . . . . . . . . . .                O 297  Irene              12
     If Fate pursues me, let it find me here.  . . . . .     O 297  Irene              18
     If Fate persues me, let it find me here  . . . . .      O 297  Irene         V    18
     if human miseries or affairs yet claim your  . . . . .  Y 181  Irene         V    54
        regard
     If thou art more than the gay Dream of Fancy,  . . . .  O 310  Irene              12
     And if one varied Accent prove thy Falshood,  . . . .   O 332  Irene              14
     Well if a Thousand Lives like thine had perish'd;  . .  O 332  Irene              34
     If mix'd with these, divine Cleora smile,  . . . . .    Y   4  On a Daffodill     17
     If winter by the fire, if summer in the shade.  . . .   Y   7  Virgil Daphnis     48
     If winter by the fire, if summer in the shade.  . . .   Y   7  Virgil Daphnis     48
     Your sighs are spent in vain; if fates withstand  . .   Y  21  Tr. Iliad Bk 6    115
     But if by their irrevocable doom  . . . . . . . .       Y  21  Tr. Iliad Bk 6    117
IGN'RANCE
     In clouds of Ign'rance mourn,  . . . . . . . .          O  79  Feast St Simon     45
IGNORANCE
     Must helpless man, in ignorance sedate,  . . . . . .    O  47  Vanity Wishes     345
     Nor, letter'd ignorance, deny  . . . . . . . . .        O 201  Death Dr Levet  V  11


                                    167
```

```
IGNORANCE          (CONTINUED)                          PAGE    TITLE            LINE
    Now Superstition, Ignorance and Error,    . . . . . .    O 251 Irene                68
    And wake from Ignorance the Western World.   . . . . .   O 302 Irene               123
ILEX
    Beneath some spreading Ilex Shade   . . . . . . . .      O  72 Hor. Epode II         29
ILFATED
    Luckless slave Ilfated loiterer has fate in vain   . . .  Y 196 Irene          V  15
ILIAD
         from the Sixth Book of Homer's Iliad  . . . . . .    O  74 Tr. Iliad Bk 6       T
ILION
    That laves proud Ilion with his rapid flood,   . . . .    Y  18 Tr. Iliad Bk 6      12
ILL
    For patience sov'reign o'er transmuted ill;  . . . . .    O  48 Vanity Wishes      362
    Swifter than Icarus Ill flie  . . . . . . . . . .         O  70 Hor.II Ode XX        13
    Capricious Man! to Good and Ill inconstant,   . . . .     O 300 Irene                76
    By Smiles, and Oaths, and Praises ill disguis'd.  . . .   O 308 Irene                15
    Joys ill exchang'd for Gold, and Pride, and Empire.  . .  O 313 Irene                10
    Ill suits with Guilt the Gaieties of Triumph;  . . . .    O 314 Irene                22
    Forbear thy Threats, proud Prophetess of Ill,  . . . .    O 314 Irene                26
    Some ill designing Statesman's base Intrigue!  . . . .    O 326 Irene                36
    And thinks his fatal Mandates ill obey'd.  . . . . .      O 327 Irene                13
    And heard th' ill omen'd catcall's direful cry.   . . .   Y  67 Prologue Lethe       10
ILL-FATED    SEE ILFATED
    Ill-fated Race! So oft besieg'd in vain,   . . . . . .    O 250 Irene                29
ILL-GOTTEN
    Thy wealth O city ill-gotten ill-preserv'd   . . . . .    Y 113 Irene           V  20
       shall
ILL-PERSUADING
    He feels no want of ill-persuading gold;   . . . . . .    O  60 Pro Good Nat'd       28
ILL-PLAC'D
    Then soon your ill-plac'd confidence repay,  . . . . .    O  17 London              156
    Heap'd by your Father's ill-plac'd Bounties on him,  . .  O 274 Irene                51
ILL-PRESERV'D
    Thy wealth O city ill-gotten ill-preserv'd   . . . . .    Y 113 Irene           V  20
       shall
ILL-TIM'D
    Such ill-tim'd Gravity, such serious Folly,  . . . . .    O 281 Irene                35
    With ill-tim'd Mirth propos'd the Bowl of Love.  . . . .  O 316 Irene                26
ILLPLAC'D
    Heap'd by my Fathers illplac'd Bounties on Him   . . . .  O 351 Irene           V  13
ILLS
    Shuns fancied ills, or chases airy good;   . . . . . .    O  31 Vanity Wishes        10
    There mark what ills the scholar's life assail,  . . . .  O  38 Vanity Wishes       159
    Yet Vane could tell what ills from beauty spring;  . . .  O  45 Vanity Wishes       321
    Parent of ills! and source of all our woe!   . . . . .    O  77 Festina Lente        10
    Inflicting all those ills which once they knew;  . . . .  O  84 Epi Dist Moth.       37
    And screen me from the ills of life.  . . . . . . . .     O 124 Winter's Walk        20
    When desp'rate Ills demand a speedy Cure,   . . . . . .   O 301 Irene                85
    Such Ills are sent for Souls like thine to conquer.  . .  O 332 Irene                38
ILLUSTRIOUS
    Illustrious Edward! from the realms of day,  . . . . .    O  15 London               99
    Are these thy views? proceed, illustrious youth,  . . .   O  37 Vanity Wishes       141
    Illustrious age! how bright thy glories shone,   . . . .  O 118 Epitaph Hanmer       21
    Now summon all thy Soul, illustrious Christian!  . . . .  O 254 Irene                 1
    Hail illustrious Sultan   . . . . . . . . . . . .         O 351 Irene           V  23
    Illustrious Maid, new Wonders fix me thine,  . . . . .    O 278 Irene                59
    Unfit to share this Night's illustrious Toils?  . .. . .  O 305 Irene                21
    Companion of our Flight, illustrious Exile,  . . . . .    O 320 Irene                30
    Great is thy Woe! but think, illustrious Sultan,  . . .   O 332 Irene                37
IMAGE
    For while by Chloe's image charm'd,   . . . . . . . .     O  65 Hor I Ode xxii        9
IMAGES
    The horrid Images of War and Slaughter   . . . . . . .    O 268 Irene                34
IMAGIN'D
    Exhausted Worlds, and then imagin'd new:   . . . . . .    O  51 Pro Drury-Lane        4
    Swiftly he sees the imagin'd laurels spread,   . . . . .  O  82 Young Author         21
IMAGINARY
    In sober state th' imaginary lawn   . . . . . . . .       Y  98 Vanity Wishes   V138B
    Sink not beneath imaginary Sorrows:   . . . . . . . .     O 252 Irene                84
    Still labours with imaginary Woe;   . . . . . . . .       O 320 Irene                22
IMAGINATION
    Her wings Imagination tries,  . . . . . . . . . . .       O 125 An Ode               14
    Imagination hangs her weary wings  . . . . . . . . .      Y 127 Irene           V   2
IMBIBES
    Imbibes with dire docility the wrong.  . . . . . . . .    O 136 Tr Rambler 132        2
IMBITTER
    Contrive new Racks, imbitter every Pang,   . . . . . .    O 334 Irene                74
IMBRU'D
    His wrathfull sword imbru'd.  . . . . . . . . . . .       O  80 Feast St Simon       54
    Death in his look, and hands imbru'd in gore   . . . .    Y  23 Tr Add. Battle       47
IMITATED
    In scenes of imitated Spring,  . . . . . . . . . .        O 120 To Miss Playin        2
IMMERSE
    Nor showers immerse the verdant plain;   . . . . . .      O  67 Hor. II Ode IX        2
IMMOD'RATE
    Too well I know him, his immod'rate Courage,   . . . .    O 267 Irene                46
IMMORTAL
    First rear'd the Stage, immortal Shakespear rose;  . . .  O  51 Pro Drury-Lane        2
    Immortal Patrons of succeeding Days,   . . . . . . .      O  57 Prologue Comus        5
    Quaff Nectar with th' immortal Gods.   . . . . . . .      O  70 Hor.II Ode XX         8
    Blest as th' immortal Gods is he   . . . . . . . .        O  71 Hor. Epode II         1
```

```
                                                    PAGE   TITLE            LINE
IMMORTAL          (CONTINUED)
    Those names which in immortal strains  . . . . .  O  80 Feast St Simon    59
    Immortal Crowns and Fulness of Enjoyment?  . . . . O 276 Irene            14
    "Immortal Gods! and thou allmighty Jove  . . . .  Y  20 Tr. Iliad Bk 6    99
IMMUR'D
    Immur'd, and buried in perpetual Sloth,  . . . . . O 292 Irene            81
IMMURED
    Immured for ever--and for ever doom'd . . . . . . O 357 Irene         V  11
IMPAIRS
    Improves it's lustre, but impairs its  . . . . . . O 366 Irene         V   4
        Strength.
IMPART
    O! then the meaning of thy gift impart,  . . . . . O  95 Sprig of Myrtl   11
IMPARTIAL
    Nor has impartial Nature's frugal Hand   . . . . . O 277 Irene            53
    Nor has impartial Natures generous hand  . . . . . O 356 Irene         V  20
    Impartial weigh the Pleasure with the Danger. . . . O 285 Irene           9
IMPATIENCE
    Whose quick Impatience seiz'd my doubtful Hand,  . . O 254 Irene         126
    Or felt th' Impatience of obstructed Love,  . . . . O 285 Irene           4
    Your fierce Impatience forc'd us from your Presence, . . O 332 Irene      29
IMPATIENT
    Time hovers o'er, impatient to destroy,  . . . . . O  43 Vanity Wishes   259
    Receive th' impatient Sultan to thy Arms;  . . . . O 267 Irene           10
    The Sultan comes, impatient for his Love;  . . . . O 272 Irene           12
    Mock'd our impatient steps, for all was fairy ground. . Y 310 Parody of Pope  4
IMPEACHMENT
    Impeachment stops the speaker's pow'rful breath,  . . . O  31 Vanity Wishes  19
IMPEARL'D
    And thou impearl'd with dew appear more gay. . . . . Y   3 On a Daffodill  12
IMPELLED
    Impelled by passion, and with folly blind. . . . . O 134.Tr Rambler 105   2
IMPELLS
    And restless enterprize impells to death. . . . . . Y  92 Vanity Wishes  V  20
IMPENDING
    As the sad thought of your impending fate:  . . . . O  74 Tr. Iliad Bk 6   20
    Impending death they strive to 'scape in vain  . . . O  76 Tr Add. Battle  30
    But cautious Fabius from impending fate  . . . . . O  78 Festina Lente    17
    The Clouds, a Signal of impending Show'rs,  . . . . O 250 Irene           32
    Just in the Moment of impending Fate,  . . . . . . O 259 Irene          117
    Well might we fear impending Disappointments.  . . . O 269 Irene           2
    Let Prudence obviate an impending Danger.  . . . . . O 309 Irene          19
IMPERFECT
    A sudden Pause th' imperfect Sense suspended,  . . . O 270 Irene          13
    Imperfect sounds of Greece--and love--and  . . . . Y 144 Irene         V  80
        daggers
    A thousand Thoughts imperfect and distracted,  . . . O 295 Irene          17
IMPERIAL
    Can Mahomet's imperial Hand descend  . . . . . . . O 268 Irene           15
    If Greatness please thee, mount th' imperial Seat;  . . O 279 Irene        84
    And hungry Slaughter scents Imperial Blood? . . . . O 279 Irene           5
    And bad imperial splendour glare (blaze) before her  . Y 158 Irene      V  10
    To fix your Standard in Imperial Rome.  . . . . . . O 309 Irene          31
    And when, contemptuous of imperial Pow'r,  . . . . O 322 Irene           59
    Shook headlong from his throne imperial Jove. . . . Y  26 Tr Add. Battle 139
IMPERIOUS
    Urg'd by th' imperious Soldier's fierce Command,  . . O 249 Irene          16
    Resumes th' imperious Air of haughty Virtue.  . . . O 314 Irene          15
    To check this Torrent of imperious Rage,  . . . . . O 327 Irene           5
IMPERVIOUS
    No sounds alas would touch th' impervious ear,  . . . O  43 Vanity Wishes  269
    The notes unfelt would strike th' impervious ear,  . . Y 104 Vanity Wishes V 269
IMPETUOUS
    With fatal heat impetuous courage glows,  . . . . . O  31 Vanity Wishes   17
    Descend, impetuous, from the vault of Heav'n.  . . . O  76 Tr Add. Battle  11
    Th' impetuous Sallies of excessive Virtue,  . . . . O 267 Irene           47
    Lost in the deluge of impetuous war  . . . . . . . Y 136 Irene         V  25
    Restrain the Fervour of impetuous Youth  . . . . . O 272 Irene            9
    Rush not impetuous to the bloody fray . . . . . . . Y  19 Tr. Iliad Bk 6   46
IMPIETY
    Affrighted at Impiety like thine,  . . . . . . . . O 289 Irene            19
    Fly the Detested mansions of Impiety  . . . . . . . O 346 Irene         V   7
IMPIOUS
    None dares with impious steel the grove to rend,  . . . O 139 Tr Rambler 168  1
    That Maxim publish'd in an impious Age,  . . . . . O 291 Irene            60
    Successful Treasons punish impious Kings. . . . . . O 300 Irene           66
    When haughty Guilt exults with impious Joy,  . . . . O 335 Irene          12
IMPLACABLE
    With rage implacable he still persue'd  . . . . . . Y  24 Tr Add. Battle   84
IMPLOR'D
    Where won by bribes, by flatteries implor'd,  . . . . O  18 London        180
    Implor'd my Leave to visit Mecca's Temple;  . . . . O 273 Irene           44
    Implor'd th' eternal Power to shield my Country,  . . . O 290 Irene        49
    Implor'd the Eternal Pow'r, at Sophia's altars . . . . Y 163 Irene      V  49
IMPLORE
    Implore his aid, in his decisions rest,  . . . . . O  48 Vanity Wishes   355
    And Love and Hate alike implore . . . . . . . . . O 122 Stella Mourn.    15
IMPLORES
    Implores our Smiles, and trembles at our Feet:  . . . O 277 Irene          40
IMPORT
    Their air, their dress, their politicks import;  . . . O  15 London       110
```

IMPORTANT
```
    Important Hazard! What's that airy Bubble      . . . . .  O 260 Irene              137
    Th' important Hour had pass'd unheeded by,     . . . . .  O 269 Irene               12
    Important Cares detain'd me from your Counsels.  . .  .   O 279 Irene                6
    Who knows, ere this important Morrow rise,     . . . . .  O 284 Irene               36
    Then waste no longer these important Moments   . . . .    O 303 Irene               13
    Thus shall he live to strike th' important Blow,  . . .   O 308 Irene               32
```
IMPOSE
```
    When some proud Grecian dame shall tasks impose,  . . .  O  74 Tr. Iliad Bk 6       21
```
IMPOSTURES
```
    And fill the World with Follies and Impostures,   . . .  O 309 Irene               35
```
IMPOTENT
```
    Dim, scorn'd and impotent, his torches lie.  . . . . . .  O 133 Tr. Rambler 85       2
```
IMPREGNABLE
```
    That melt a Heart, impregnable till now,  . . . . . . .   O 276 Irene                4
```
IMPRESS'D
```
    His pow'rful Strokes presiding Truth impress'd,  . . . .  O  51 Pro Drury-Lane       7
    Ambition is the Stamp impress'd by Heav'n  . . . . . .    O 293 Irene              111
```
IMPROV'D
```
    Then best enjoy'd, when most improv'd.  . . . . . .       O 125 An Ode              28
    When best enjoy'd, when most improv'd.  . . . . . . .     O 125 An Ode          V   28
```
IMPROVE
```
    Improve his heady rage with treach'rous skill,  . . . .   O  44 Vanity Wishes      281
    So shall Belinda's charms improve mankind.  . . . . .     O  81 Lady Birthday       19
```
IMPROVES
```
    Improves it's lustre, but impairs its  . . . . . . .      O 366 Irene           V    4
         Strength.
```
IMPROVING
```
    The social gayety the improving converse  . . . . . .    Y 165 Irene           V   81
```
IMPROVISO
```
    One and Twenty 1810: Improviso on a young heir's coming . O 196 Song Congratu.  V    T
         of age.
```
IMPUDENCE
```
    Slaves that with serious impudence beguile,  . . . . .    O  17 London             146
```
IN
     501   OMITTED WORD
INACHIA'S
```
    Since from Inachia's charms set free  . . . . . . . .     Y  11 Tr Hor Epode 9       9
    And quit Inachia's venal charms . . . . . . . . . .       Y  11 Tr Hor Epode 9      26
    And quite Inachia's venal charms  . . . . . . . . .       Y  11 Tr Hor Epode 9  V   26
```
INATTENTIVE
```
    Surveys your Plays with inattentive Glance,  . . . . .    O 276 Irene               22
```
INAUSPICIOUS
```
    Quick from my Sight you inauspicious Monsters,  . . . .   O 325 Irene                6
```
INCENS'D
```
    Now, at thy fall incens'd, the rural Gods  . . . . .      Y   6 Virgil Daphnis      20
```
INCENSE
```
    Should costly Loads of incense burn,  . . . . . .  . .    O  69 Hor.II Ode 14        7
    What Fraud misleads him? or what Crimes incense?  . . .   O 325 Irene               28
```
INCESSANT
```
    Delusive Fortune hears th' incessant call,  . . . . .     O  33 Vanity Wishes       75
    The pamphlet spreads, incessant hisses rise,  . . . .    O  82 Young Author        25
    While with incessant Thought laborious Man  . . . . .     O 269 Irene                3
```
INCIRCLING
```
    Till conscious of th' incircling Deity,  . . . . . .      O 313 Irene                7
```
INCITE
```
    Here let those reign, whom pensions can incite  . . . .   O  11 London              51
```
INCLEMENCIES
```
    Nor feel the inclemencies of wintry air;  . . . . . .     Y   3 On a Daffodill       6
```
INCLEMENT
```
    And where beneath th' inclement Skie  . . . . . . .       O  70 Hor.II Ode XX       15
    Driv'n hither by inclement skies  . . . . . . . .         O  73 Hor. Epode II   V   59
    Then to the inclement skies expos'd I sat  . . . . .      Y  11 Tr Hor Epode 9      35
```
INCLIN'D
```
    When first the peasant, long inclin'd to roam,  . . . .   O  81 Young Author         1
```
INCLINATION
```
    Each rebel Wish, each traitor Inclination  . . . . .      O 287 Irene               11
    every traytor inclination each traytor passion  . . . .   Y 158 Irene           V   11
```
INCLOSE
```
    Which Armies guard, and Citadels inclose?  . . . . .      O 258 Irene               91
```
INCONSISTENT
```
    When inconsistent with a greater Good,  . . . . . .       O 290 Irene               32
```
INCONSTANT
```
    Capricious Man! to Good and Ill inconstant,  . . . . .    O 300 Irene               76
```
INCREAS'D   SEE ENCREAS'D
```
    But when increas'd by Winter shours  . . . . . . .        O  72 Hor. Epode II       37
```
INCREASE
```
    Increase his riches and his peace destroy;  . . . . .     O  32 Vanity Wishes       40
```
INCUMBER'D
```
    Th' incumber'd oar scarce leaves the dreaded coast  . .   O  42 Vanity Wishes      239
```
INCUMBRANCES
```
    Shake off th' Incumbrances of State a moment,  . . . .    O 289 Irene                7
```
INCUMBRED
```
    And lags superfluous on th' incumbred stage,  . . . . .   Y 106 Vanity Wishes   V  308
```
INDEARING
```
    Th' attractive Softness, and th' indearing Smile,  . . .  O 277 Irene               51
```
INDEED
```
    Love is indeed the Privilege of Youth;  . . . . . .       O 280 Irene               29
```
INDIA
```
    Whate'er from India spicy coasts  . . . . . . .           O  73 Hor. Epode II   V   58
    And India join her aromatic shade  . . . . . . . .        Y 150 Irene           V   85
```

		PAGE	TITLE	LINE
INDIA'S				
Warm India's supple Sons should bow, ...		O 146	Tr Boeth III.5	6
Pregnant with Stores, that India's Mines might envy, . .		O 249	Irene	18
For thee, my fair, shall India's spices . . . . . . ripen		Y 150	Irene	V 81
INDIAS				
And Indias rajas ask their doom from thee		Y 131	Irene	V 32
INDIGENCE				
For healthful indigence in vain they pray, ...		O 132	Tr. Rambler 48	1
INDIGNANT				
Indignant Thales eyes the neighb'ring town.		O 10	London	34
And detestation rids th' indignant wall.		O 34	Vanity Wishes	90
INDIGNATION				
The pious Maid, with modest Indignation, ...		O 258	Irene	101
INDULG'D				
What but their wish indulg'd in courts to shine, . . .		O 36	Vanity Wishes	133
INDULGE				
Yet should thy soul indulge the gen'rous heat, ...		O 37	Vanity Wishes	143
Yet should thy fate indulge the gen'rous heat, ...		Y 98	Vanity Wishes	V 143
INDULGENCE				
Is 't not enough, he lives by our Indulgence, ...		O 286	Irene	6
INDULGENT				
Some secret cell, ye pow'rs, indulgent give.		O 11	London	49
Indulgent nature gives some transient pleasures . . .		Y 148	Irene	V 43C
Blest Prince, for whom indulgent Heav'n ordains . . .		O 308	Irene	6
Be thou the favorite of the indulgent sky, ...		Y 3	On a Daffodill	5
INDUSTRIOUS				
A frugal, chast, industrious, Wife, ...		O 72	Hor. Epode II	48
Shall glutton on the industrious Peasants Spoil, . . .		O 110	To Posterity	13
The fruitfull fields th' industrious people till'd, .		Y 23	Tr Add. Battle	28
INDUSTRY				
No gainful trade their industry can 'scape, ...		O 15	London	113
INESTIMABLE				
Th' inestimable Privilege of Breathing!		O 260	Irene	136
INEXHAUSTED				
While fair yet Hungaria's inexhausted Vallies		O 352	Irene	V 33
INEXORABLE				
Nor would inexorable Death		O 69	Hor.II Ode 14	11
The inexorable sisters have decreed		O 74	Tr. Iliad Bk 6	11
INFAMY				
And hissing Infamy proclaims the rest.		O 47	Vanity Wishes	342
And shout Infamy proclaims the rest.		Y 107	Vanity Wishes	V 342
Adds Shame to Grief, and Infamy to Ruin.		O 250	Irene	25
Leave Slav'ry, Guilt, and Infamy behind.		O 320	Irene	31
Let Shame and hooting Infamy pursue me, ...		O 328	Irene	36
INFANT				
The tender infant, meek and mild, ...		O 157	Par. Hermit I	1
Instructed from our infant Years to court		O 266	Irene	27
Once more reflect, suppress this infant Folly. . . .		O 281	Irene	56
That wafts diseases from the sleeping infant.		Y 168	Irene	V135B
Lest baneful discord crush our infant Scheme, ...		O 299	Irene	52
Pure as the Thoughts of infant Innocence?		O 304	Irene	15
Returns his child; she views his infant charms, . . .		Y 20	Tr. Iliad Bk 6	108
INFATUATE				
Infatuate Loiterer, has Fate, in vain, ...		O 318	Irene	15
INFECTED				
And scarce can breath th' infected sky, ...		O 79	Feast St Simon	35
INFECTION				
Has Treason's dire Infection reach'd my Palace? . . .		O 272	Irene	2
INFERIOUR				
Vain Raptures all--For your inferiour Natures		O 276	Irene	15
INFERNAL				
Curst as the Tyrant of th' infernal Realms, ...		O 294	Irene	134
INFESST				
No griping Creditors infesst.		O 71	Hor. Epode II	8
INFEST				
Infest the barren Lands.		O 79	Feast St Simon	42
INFIDELS				
Of slaughter'd Infidels, and Clash of Swords!		O 305	Irene	24
INFLAME				
When publick crimes inflame the wrath of heav'n: . . .		O 13	London	66
No conscious blushes there their cheeks inflame, . . .		O 84	Epi Dist Moth.	24
Inflame with unrelented fires.		Y 71	Ode Friendship	V 8
These Arts I try'd, and to inflame her more, ...		O 287	Irene	14
Aspasia's Absence will inflame Suspicion;		O 296	Irene	5
Inflame her Crimes, exalt your own Obedience, ...		O 329	Irene	14
INFLAMES				
Inflames alike with raging fires.		O 99	Ode Friendship	8
When fondness melts me, or when wine inflames, ...		O 142	In Baretti Bk.	2
Which Love of Greatness, not of Truth, inflames. . . .		O 262	Irene	27
The pow'rful Voice of Love inflames Demetrius, ...		O 270	Irene	19
A girl's, inflames me with desire;		Y 12	Tr Hor Epode 9	38
INFLICT				
That Vengeance can invent, or Pow'r inflict.		O 326	Irene	45
Inflict whatever Treason can deserve, ...		O 334	Irene	75
INFLICTING				
Inflicting all those ills which once they knew; . . .		O 84	Epi Dist Moth.	37
INFLUENCE				
but if your influence be too wide--your dissipated rays . will burn no more		Y 132	Irene	V 41
shall influence whole nations		Y 150	Irene	V 76

INFLUENCE   (CONTINUED)   PAGE   TITLE   LINE
   Melancholly broods or pours her influence oer the . . . .   Y 165 Irene   V 82
   O grant thy sacred Influence, pow'rful Virtue! . . . . .   O 313 Irene   5
   And thou shalt flourish by her influence. . . . . . .   Y   4 On a Daffodill   20
   Withdraws the influence of those eyes, ...   Y 39 Lady Leaving   7
INFOLD
   And Love infold thee with his downy Wings. . . . . .   O 279 Irene   83
INFORC'D
   Inforc'd we love, unheeding recollect. . . . . . .   O 134 Tr. Rambler 96   2
INFORM
   Inform me rather, how thy happy Courage . . . . . .   O 295 Irene   27
INFORM'D
   Where wisdom first inform'd my heart. . . . . . .   O 125 An Ode   20
   Inform'd they mount the Precipice of Pow'r, ...   O 293 Irene   113
   A sigh, a blush inform'd him You consented . . . . .   O 366 Irene   V 28
INFRINGE
   Must then Ambition's Votaries infringe . . . . . .   O 280 Irene   15
INFUS'D
   And find our Passions not infus'd in vain. . . . . .   O 297 Irene   22
INGRATITUDE
   Far be such black Ingratitude from Cali, ...   O 306 Irene   4
   Oft would they find Ingratitude and Treason, ...   O 308 Irene   14
INHABITANT
   The chill inhabitant repines, ...   Y 38 Lady Leaving   3
INJUR'D
   When injur'd Thales bids the town farewell, ...   O   8 London   2
   Shall feel the Vengeance of an injur'd King. . . . .   O 273 Irene   33
   Then Let me once to right our injur'd Sex . . . . .   O 356 Irene   V 16
   The injur'd Cranes their murther'd offspring mourn . .   Y 24 Tr Add. Battle   64
INLAYD
   With cedar vaulted and inlayd with gold . . . . . .   Y 177 Irene   V111F
INMOST
   Convey him to the Prison's inmost Depths, ...   O 312 Irene   24
INNOCENCE
   Or bribe a virgin's innocence away. . . . .   O 13 London   78
   And glides in modest Innocence away; . . . .   O 44 Vanity Wishes   294
   Learn here that Peace frcm Innocence must flow; . . .   O 246 Irene Prologue   13
   I dread his Arts of seeming Innocence, ...   O 273 Irene   39
   Our only Arms are Innocence and Meekness. . . . . .   O 290 Irene   45
   Her only arms are innocence and meekness . . . . .   Y 162 Irene   V 45
   Gladness, fair child, of innocence and freedom. . . .   Y 165 Irene   V 81
   And in those Bowers of Innocence and . . . . . .   O 349 Irene   V 7
      Quiet
   And wish too late for Innocence and Peace? . . . . .   O 294 Irene   133
   Content with Science, Innocence and Love? . . . . .   O 301 Irene   105
   Pure as the Thoughts of infant Innocence? . . . . .   O 304 Irene   15
   This Calm, these Joys, dear Innocence! are thine, . .   O 313 Irene   9
   Come haste, and live--Thy Innocence and Truth . . .   O 320 Irene   18
   Against the Head which Innocence secures, ...   O 322 Irene   1
   Thy sacred freight of innocence and truth . . . . .   Y 201 Irene   V 10D
   True, she was fair; the Smile of Innocence . . . . .   O 330 Irene   10
   Could not her Prayers, her Innocence, her Tears, . .   O 332 Irene   25
   Which murder'd Innocence that call'd on me. . . . .   O 334 Irene   76
   That mirth may mend, and innocence delight. . . . .   Y 67 Prologue Lethe   16
INNOCENT
   Officious, innocent, sincere, ...   O 201 Death Dr Levet   7
INNOVATION
   Untainted with the Lust of Innovation, ...   O 257 Irene   61
INQUIETUDES
   Has· fix'd his Hopes, Inquietudes, and Fears, ...   O 280 Irene   27
INSATIATE
   Insatiate pluck the Fruit, and crop the Flow'r: . . .   O 110 To Posterity   12
   Insatiate on her wasted Entrails prey, ...   O 315 Irene   36
INSCRIPTION
   And be the stone with this inscription grac'd: . . . .   Y   7 Virgil Daphnis   29
INSECT
   And then leaves the glittering reptile, reasoning . . .   Y 146 Irene   V 23
      insect
INSIDIOUS
   Explore your secrets with insidious art, ...   O 17 London   154
   Th' insidious rival and the gaping heir. . . . . . .   O 32 Vanity Wishes   48
   Th' insidious Bassa fir'd by Disappointment-- . . . .   O 273 Irene   32
   Destruction flashes from th' insidious Mine, ...   O 298 Irene   30
   Insidious Malice aims her Darts in vain; . . . . . .   O 322 Irene   2
   Insidious sands, shallows rough rocks and whirling . .   Y 201 Irene   V 10B
      devouring gulphs
INSINCERE
   Joys insincere! thick clouds invade the skies, ...   O 82 Young Author   7
INSOLENCE
   And bear oppression's insolence no more. . . . . . .   O 18 London   175
   The ruinous insolence, the son's expence, ...   Y 104 Vanity Wishes   V 280
   Her lofty mien, and insolence of virtue--my . . . . .   Y 191 Irene   V 14
      state
   ----By taunt and insolence . . . .   Y 197 Irene   V 30
INSPIR'D
   Simon by gen'rous Zeal inspir'd, ...   O 79 Feast St Simon   37
   Inspir'd by us, they Glory's Heights ascend; . . . .   O 247 Irene Epilogue   17
   His Pride and Love by Turns inspir'd his Tongue, . .   O 299 Irene   43
   Permitted oft, though not inspir'd by Heav'n, ...   O 300 Irene   65
   Whether urg'd on by seers from heav'n inspir'd . . . .   Y 19 Tr. Iliad Bk 6   58

		PAGE	TITLE	LINE
INSPIRE				
No fav'ring Muse her morning Dreams inspire;	. . . .	O 58	Prologue Comus	28
Thy charms at least, fair P<irebrac>e, might inspire	. .	O 107	Lady F Assizes	3
Not yet inspire the Follies of a Queen,	. . . . .	O 289	Irene	3
Not yet inspire th' omniscience of a queen	. . . . .	O 366	Irene	V 19
INSTANT				
The Dread of instant Death restrains my Tongue?	. . .	O 289	Irene	25
INSTINCT				
I share, by secret Instinct, all his Joys,	. . . . .	O 272	Irene	10
INSTRUCTED				
Then Johnson came, instructed from the School,	. . . .	O 51	Pro Drury-Lane	9
Instructed from our infant Years to court	. . . . .	O 266	Irene	27
INSTRUCTION				
Instruction with her flow'rs might spring,	. . . . . .	O 121	To Miss Playin	23
INSTRUCTIVE				
With chearful wisdcm and instructive mirth,	. . . . .	O 32	Vanity Wishes	50
And turn'd th' instructive Page of Human Life,	. . . .	O 281	Irene	33
INSTRUMENT				
Is but the executioner of Heavn--or Instrument	. . . .	O 345	Irene	V 27
INSULT				
Than when a blockhead's insult points the dart.	. . . .	O 18	London	169
While all neglect, and most insult your woes.	. . . .	O 19	London	193
Hate dogs their flight, and insult mocks their end.	. .	O 33	Vanity Wishes	78
Aspasia should not fear a second Insult.	. . . . .	O 299	Irene	42
Shall then the Savage live, to boast his Insult;	. . .	O 318	Irene	12
INSULTED				
Th' insulted sea with humbler thoughts he gains,	. . .	O 42	Vanity Wishes	237
Beauties insulted by a slave--	. . . .	Y 202	Irene	V 1
INSULTING				
Then shall some Argive loud insulting cry,	. . . . .	O 74	Tr. Iliad Bk 6	25
Insulting chance ne'er call'd with louder voice,	. . .	O 135	Tr Rambler 106	1
Think on th' insulting Scorn, the conscious Pangs,	. .	O 266	Irene	19
INSULTS				
Their prudent insults to the poor confine;	. . . . .	O 21	London	233
Pollutes his banquet and insults his guest;	. . . . .	O 130	Tr. Rambler 12	2
When daring Vice insults eternal Justice,	. . . . .	O 314	Irene	23
INSUPERABLE				
Nor dare to pass th' insuperable Bound.	. . . . . .	O 292	Irene	92
INT'REST				
Still to his int'rest true, where'er he goes,	. . . .	O 16	London	125
By Int'rest, Prudence; and by Flatt'ry, Pride.	. . . .	O 47	Vanity Wishes	340
To Int'rest, Prudence; and to Flatt'ry, Pride.	. . . .	O 47	Vanity Wishes	V 340
Drive Int'rest, Love, and Vengeance from thy Thoughts,	. .	O 298	Irene	7
How soon, alas! will Int'rest, Fear, or Envy,	. . . .	O 301	Irene	82
The Lover's Int'rest aids the Patriot's Claim.	. . . .	O 305	Irene	46
INT'RESTS				
Our distant Int'rests, and our different Passions	. . .	O 287	Irene	3
INTEGER				
From Horace. Integer Vitae, etc.	. . . .	O 65	Hor I Ode xxii	V T
INTELLIGENCE				
His kind Intelligence betray'd their Measures;	. . . .	O 253	Irene	118
INTENDED				
Epilogue intended to have been spoken by a Lady	. . .	O 83	Epi Dist Moth.	T
INTENT				
Fix'd and intent on his Irene's Charms,	. . . . . .	O 296	Irene	3
INTENTION				
Nor think th' Intention sanctifies the Deed:	. . . .	O 291	Irene	59
Could just intention consecrate the Guilt	. . . . .	O 360	Irene	V 35
INTERCEPT				
Might intercept the Traitor Greek, Demetrius,	. . . .	O 331	Irene	8
A chosen Troop--to intercept--Demetrius--	. . . . .	O 331	Irene	12
No toils shall intercept the nimble deer.	. . . . .	Y 7	Virgil Daphnis	39
INTERCOURSE				
The long-drawn Intercourse of Sighs and Kisses.	. . .	O 297	Irene	14
INTEREST				
one common Interest, mutual duties	. . . .	O 352	Irene	V 17
INTERMIX'D				
And intermix'd my Praises with his own;	. . . . . .	O 299	Irene	44
INTERPOSE				
While ladies interpose, and slaves debate.	. . . . .	O 41	Vanity Wishes	214
INTERPOSING				
Did interposing Angels guard her from him?	. . . . .	O 259	Irene	116
Till interposing Death destroys the Prospect!	. . . .	O 283	Irene	25
Till interposing Death denys the prospect.	. . . . .	O 374	Irene	V 26
Till interposing darkness bars the prospect.	. . . . .	Y 155	Irene	V 25
INTERPRET				
Which Cheats interpret, and which Fools regard?	. . .	O 250	Irene	43
INTERVAL				
No soothing Interval of peaceful Sorrow;	. . . . . .	O 249	Irene	12
There when my Thoughts, at interval of Pray'r,	. . . .	O 292	Irene	94
INTERVALS				
And as my thoughts at intervals of Prayer	. . . . .	O 349	Irene	V 9
INTIMIDATES				
Intimidates the Brave, degrades the Great.	. . . . .	O 311	Irene	15
INTO				
Into his supplicating mothers heart.	. . . .	O 77	Festina Lente	14
Nor torturing whalebones pinch them into charms;	. . .	O 84	Epi Dist Moth.	23
Aw'd into Love, our conquer'd hearts obey,	. . . . .	O 96	Hickman Spinet	4
Work'd into sudden rage by wintry show'rs,	. . . . .	O 132	Tr. Rambler 65	1
Just emerging into Light,	. . . .	O 150	Tr Boet III.12	49
And walk'd into the Strand,	. . . .	O 158	Par. Hermit II	2

	PAGE	TITLE	LINE
Sinks into milkness and softens to submission.	Y 123	Irene	V 99
Into the adverse Scale, nor shakes the Balance. . . .	O 260	Irene	140
And sink into the silent Grave in Peace.	O 264	Irene	12
and the first gust shake<s> it into atom<s> . . .	Y 132	Irene	V 39
Dissolve in Air, and vanish into Nothing.	O 265	Irene	8
Fade <glide> from the sight, and Vanish into nothing.	O 358	Irene	V 11
And Wisdom into Virtue turn thy Frailty. . . .	O 266	Irene	22
Sinks into sighs like the sighing of a Tempest spent . .	O 367	Irene	V 13
Unfit for Toil, and polish'd into Weakness, ...	O 290	Irene	43
Why does thy Soul retire into herself?	O 295	Irene	7
Demand a Voice, and struggle into Birth;	O 295	Irene	18
But the sight of friends soul sinking into vice (a soul	Y 177	Irene	V111C
May droop dismay'd, or kindle into Madness.	O 304	Irene	11
An angry look had sunk him into Hell	O 376	Irene	V 23
An angry look had sunk him into Hell	Y 188	Irene	V 20
Exalt my soul, and swell it into raptures.	Y 189	Irene	V 1F
And melt her treach'rous Beauties into Ruin.	O 315	Irene	37
And melt the treach'rous Beauties into Ruin. . . .	O 315	Irene	V 37
About to rush into the field of fate	Y 18	Tr. Iliad Bk 6	4
The chief, this spoke, into the mother's arms	Y 20	Tr. Iliad Bk 6	107
Shall sink alike into the gloomy grave.	Y 21	Tr. Iliad Bk 6	120
Or lift themselves into the wonted skies.	Y 24	Tr Add. Battle	61
In his fell claws, then into th' air he springs. . . .	Y 26	Tr Add. Battle	126

INTOXICATING

| In my weak Ear th' intoxicating Sounds. . . . . . | O 288 | Irene | 6 |

INTREATS

| Intreats admittance to the fair Aspasia . . . . . | O 367 | Irene | V 20 |

INTREPID

| Intrepid in the flaming Front of War? . . . . | O 304 | Irene | 17 |

INTRIGUE

| Intrigue was Plot, Obscenity was Wit. . . . . | O 52 | Pro Drury-Lane | 20 |
| Some ill designing Statesman's base Intrigue! . . . . | O 326 | Irene | 36 |

INTRIGUING

| Intriguing Wits! his artless Plot forgive; . . . . . | O 246 | Irene Prologue | 19 |

INTRODUCES

| Ladies introduces the mention of Aspasia. . . . . | O 351 | Irene | V 12 |

INTRUDE

| Might Truth intrude with daring flight, ... | O 121 | To Miss Playin | 20 |

INTRUSION

| Conduct her hither, let no rude Intrusion . . . . . | O 272 | Irene | 13 |
| Conduct her hither, see that no intrusion . . . . . | O 368 | Irene | V 24 |

INTRUSIVE

| Forgive, great Sultan, that intrusive Duty . . . . . | O 263 | Irene | 23 |

INTRUSTS

| Intrusts his happiness to human kind, ... | O 82 | Young Author | 13 |

INVADE

They first invade your table, then your breast; . . .	O 17	London	153
Now fears in dire vicissitude invade, ...	O 32	Vanity Wishes	41
New fears in dire vicissitude invade, ...	O 32	Vanity Wishes	V 41
Should no Disease thy torpid veins invade, ...	O 37	Vanity Wishes	153
Nor should disease thy torpid veins invade, ...	Y 99	Vanity Wishes	V 153
Unnumber'd maladies his joints invade, ...	O 44	Vanity Wishes	283
Unnumber'd maladies each Joint invade, ...	O 44	Vanity Wishes	V 283
Let no resentful petulance invade	O 61	Pro Word Wise	9
For no renew'd hostilities invade	O 61	Pro Word Wise	V 9
Let no revengeful petulance invade	O 61	Pro Word Wise	V 9
Joys insincere! thick clouds invade the skies, ...	O 82	Young Author	7
Henceforth th' inviolable Bloom invade, ...	O 111	To Posterity	21
Molest these private Walks, or Care invade	O 272	Irene	14
The bravest of the Greeks the wall invade.	Y 19	Tr. Iliad Bk 6	53

INVADERS

| From bold invaders clear'd th' Italian lands . . . . | O 78 | Festina Lente | 19 |
| Pour'd Storms of Fire upon our fierce Invaders, . . . | O 290 | Irene | 48 |

INVADES

Invades the sacred hour of silent rest, ...	O 21	London	240
Yet, tho' my limbs disease invades, ...	O 125	An Ode	13
Know'st thou not yet, when Love invades the Soul, . . .	O 281	Irene	38
Invades my soul, and rages in my breast.	Y 11	Tr Hor Epode 9	6
And first a sound invades th' astonish'd ear. . . .	Y 25	Tr Add. Battle	91

INVADING

| Against th' invading birds their native land: . . . . | Y 23 | Tr Add. Battle | 37 |

INVASION

| With false Security beheld Invasion. . . . . | O 250 | Irene | 30 |

INVENT

| To please in Method, and invent by Rule; . . . . . | O 51 | Pro Drury-Lane | 10 |
| That Vengeance can invent, or Pow'r inflict. . . . . | O 326 | Irene | 45 |

INVENTED

| And new forms of pleasure shall be invented . . . . | O 350 | Irene | V 25 |

INVERTED

| And faintly draw th' inverted Plow. . . . . . . | O 73 | Hor. Epode II | 70 |

INVEST

Ye nymphs whom starry rays invest, ...	O 126	To Lyce, Lady	1
Does adamantine Faith invest his Heart?	O 255	Irene	21
Invest Leontius with his new Command;	O 260	Irene	144
Did regal Diadems invest my Brow, ...	O 289	Irene	12

INVIOLABLE

| Th' oblivious grave's inviolable shade. . . . . . | O 62 | Pro Word Wise | 10 |
| Henceforth th' inviolable Bloom invade, ... | O 111 | To Posterity | 21 |

	PAGE	TITLE	LINE
INVIOLATED			
Play'd fearless in th' inviolated Shades.	O 314	Irene	7
INVISIBLE			
Some Pow'r invisible, from Heav'n or Hell, ...	O 251	Irene	50
INVITE			
Whom Joys with soft varieties invite, ...	O 46	Vanity Wishes	325
Whom Joys in soft vicissitudes invite, ...	Y 107	Vanity Wishes	V 325
Her conscious hand his laurel leaves invite. . . .	O 106	Eliza plucking	4
A Galley waits us, and the Winds invite.	O 321	Irene	52
Till soft Fatigue invite us to repose.	O 323	Irene	18
INVITES			
The present Hour with open Arms invites;	O 284	Irene	34
The present hour invites with genuine charms . . .	O 375	Irene	V 7
INVITING			
In vain I listen to th' inviting Call	O 320	Irene	10
In vain I listen to the inviting voice	Y 198	Irene	V 10
Kind Heav'n affords thee, and inviting Mercy . . .	O 321	Irene	41
INVOKE			
No cries invoke the mercies of the skies?	O 47	Vanity Wishes	V 348
INVOLV'D			
And grasps the bloody sand involv'd in death. . .	O 76	Tr Add. Battle	17
INVOLVE			
Depart, Demetrius, lest my Fate involve thee, . . .	O 320	Irene	13
But let no thoughtless Hint involve Abdalla. . . .	O 329	Irene	15
INWARD			
Sudden he stops, and inward turns his Eyes, ...	O 311	Irene	5
IRENE			
Irene: A Tragedy.	O 245	Irene	T
Another Plund'rer brought the bright Irene;	O 259	Irene	118
And seeks the Shades to muse upon Irene;	O 261	Irene	4
Irene steals unheeded from his Tongue, ...	O 261	Irene	5
But, Cali, let Irene share thy Prayers;	O 262	Irene	5
For what is Length of Days without Irene?	O 262	Irene	6
And dwell upon the Beauties of Irene.	O 262	Irene	10
Had they prevail'd, I ne'er had known Irene. . . .	O 263	Irene	27
To make Aspasia and Irene name each other.	Y 133	Irene	V 10
Glide through Irene to the Sultan's Ear.	O 267	Irene	3
These Hours assign'd to Pleasure and Irene.	O 272	Irene	15
Suspend his Sentence--Empire and Irene	O 275	Irene	68
Daggers and love? What love but fair	Y 144	Irene	V 81
Irene?			
Do thou resolve: For see, Irene comes!	O 275	Irene	90
--But see Irene comes	O 367	Irene	V 11
Irene rise, thou daughter of perfection--or	Y 145	Irene	V 1
beauty			
Ah! cease, Irene, cease those flowing Sorrows, . . .	O 276	Irene	3
How will the matchless Beauties of Irene, ...	O 276	Irene	6
The voice of war no more shall fright	Y 150	Irene	V 82
Irene			
O! did Irene shine the Queen of Turkey, ...	O 290	Irene	51
And shed the pitying Tear for lost Irene.	O 292	Irene	97
An Let fall sometimes a tear for lost Irene	O 349	Irene	V 1
and drop sometimes a tear for lost Irene	O 349	Irene	V 1
The laws unread, and flies to his Irene.	O 296	Irene	2
And show Irene to the shouting People:	O 303	Irene	28
Sacred to Love, to Pleasure, and Irene:	O 308	Irene	2
I rouse to War, and conquer for Irene.	O 309	Irene	25
And wishes Irene were converted by some	Y 186	Irene	V 11
doctor			
How am I chang'd! How lately did Irene	O 322	Irene	13
Their Treason throws no Stain upon Irene.	O 324	Irene	18
He struck his tortur'd Breast, and roar'd, Irene: .	O 325	Irene	24
Again his thund'ring Voice return'd, Irene.	O 325	Irene	26
And all Irene now is breathless Clay.	O 330	Irene	4
I bring a tardy Message from Irene.	O 331	Irene	2
Who? the dead Irene?	O 332	Irene	17
Thy life perhaps--Were but Irene spar'd, ...	O 332	Irene	33
Those Groves, whose Shades embower'd the dear Irene, . .	O 333	Irene	46
Hear! shall I hear thee! did'st thou hear Irene? . .	O 333	Irene	56
Thou might'st have liv'd, for thou hadst spar'd Irene. .	O 333	Irene	58
Thou mightst have liv'd, nor had I lost Irene . . .	Y 214	Irene	V 58
Behold Irene--o'erthrown	Y 217	Irene	V 10
IRENE'S			
He tires his Fav'rites with Irene's Praise, ...	O 261	Irene	3
And bar the Passes of Irene's Mind	O 265	Irene	10
Diffuse Irene's Beauty though the World.	O 268	Irene	14
O seize the Power to bless--Irene's Nod	O 278	Irene	75
Purity of prayer--Irene's smile	Y 150	Irene	V 75
Fix'd and intent on his Irene's Charms, ...	O 296	Irene	3
Let every Tongue resound Irene's Praise, ...	O 308	Irene	4
Nor wish for Houries in Irene's Arms.	O 308	Irene	10
Pensive, and envious of Irene's Greatness.	O 314	Irene	12
Then let me rid them of Irene's Presence:	O 316	Irene	19
He knew Irene's Truth.	O 324	Irene	20
Nor dare henceforth to shock Irene's Walks. . . .	O 325	Irene	7
Expiring Cali nam'd Irene's Chamber, ...	O 326	Irene	29
Irene's Chamber! From my faithful Bosom	O 326	Irene	31
Irene's chamber from Irene's guiltless bosom . . .	Y 205	Irene	V 31
Irene's chamber from Irene's guiltless bosom . . .	Y 205	Irene	V 31
Our bleeding Bosoms plead Irene's Cause.	O 328	Irene	39
Irene's crimes, forget not her repentance.	Y 209	Irene	V 55

IRENE'S   (CONTINUED)   PAGE   TITLE   LINE
    Melt at Irene's Fate, and share her Woes? . . . . O 329 Irene   7
    Irene's Chamber! Did not roaring Cali, ... O 330 Irene   12
    Name for the Scene of Death Irene's Chamber? . . . . O 330 Irene   14
    Said not the Villain in Irene's Chamber . . . . . . O 375 Irene   V   13
    Decreed to perish in Irene's Chamber! . . . . O 331 Irene   17
IRENES
    Will yet Irenes haughty Soul descend . . . . O 372 Irene   V   6
IRON
    At my Command yon' Iron Gates unfold; . . . . O 283 Irene   14
    Unclasp'd his Iron Gripe to set thee free? . . . . . O 318 Irene   16
IRRADIATE
    Irradiate and obscure my Breast by Turns: . . . . . O 321 Irene   45
IRREPARABLE
    Nor languish o'er irreparable Ruins; . . . . O 320 Irene   17
IRREVOCABLE
    Could cancell their irrevocable Law. . . . . O 76 Tr Add. Battle   40
    But if by their irrevocable doom . . . . Y 21 Tr. Iliad Bk 6   117
'S
    He 's gone--Here rest, my Soul, thy fainting Wing, . . O 287 Irene   1
    Where 's this fair Trait'ress? Where 's this smiling . . O 330 Irene   1
      Mischief?
    Where 's this fair Trait'ress? Where 's this smiling . . O 330 Irene   1
      Mischief?
IS
     119
IS   OMITTED WORD
ISIS
    On Isis banks he waves, from noise withdrawn . . . . Y 98 Vanity Wishes   V138A
ISLAND
    No secret island in the boundless main? . . . . . . O 18 London   172
ISSUED
    Sighs issued from my heaving breast; . . . . Y 11 Tr Hor Epode 9   14
ISTHER'S
    From Isther's flood unnumber'd flocks arise . . . . Y 24 Tr Add. Battle   69
'T
    Is 't not enough, he lives by our Indulgence, ... O 286 Irene   6
'TIS
    'Tis yours this Night to bid the Reign commence . . . O 53 Pro Drury-Lane   57
    'Tis yours to crown Desert--beyond the Grave! . . . O 58 Prologue Comus   38
    The great, 'tis true, can charm th' electing tribe; . . O 60 Pro Good Nat'd   25
    Approve it only--'tis too late to praise. . . . . . O 62 Pro Word Wise   16
    Alas! 'tis hard for beauty to be just. . . . . . . O 81 Lady Birthday   12
    'tis thine alone to calm the pious breast . . . . . O 130 Tr. Rambler 7   5
    But now 'tis hatred all.---- . . . . O 131 Tr. Rambler 45   3
    'Tis a proof that he had rather . . . . O 183 Burlesque Vega   3
    'Tis a sign that he had rather . . . . O 183 Burlesque Vega V   3
    'Tis true, the Fellow's handsome, strait and tall; . . O 247 Irene Epilogue   7
    Then 'tis decreed. (then death or empire.) . . . . Y 130 Irene   V   20
    And pow'rful Glance, 'tis granted, are our own; . . . O 277 Irene   52
    Well,--'tis decreed--This Night shall fix our Fate. . . O 284 Irene   48
    My Vows, 'tis true, she hears with less Aversion, . . O 287 Irene   7
    'Tis yours to grant, or to refuse him entrance . . . Y 168 Irene   V   3
    'Tis she--My Hope, my Happiness, my Love! . . . . O 294 Irene   1
    'Tis Greece, 'tis Freedom calls Aspasia hence, . . . O 297 Irene   9
    'Tis Greece, 'tis Freedom calls Aspasia hence, . . . O 297 Irene   9
    'Tis Love combin'd with Guilt alone, that melts . . . O 303 Irene   16
    'Tis well--A single Blow compleats our Wishes: . . . O 304 Irene   8
    Forbear, Demetrius, 'tis Aspasia calls thee; . . . . O 318 Irene   8
    Forgive, my Fair, 'tis Life, 'tis Nature calls. . . . O 318 Irene   19
    Forgive, my Fair, 'tis Life, 'tis Nature calls. . . . O 318 Irene   19
    'Tis Madness to provoke superfluous Danger, ... O 318 Irene   21
    Sure 'tis the happy Hour ordain'd above, ... O 321 Irene   35
    But now 'tis o'er, and Justice has prevail'd. . . . O 324 Irene   14
    But 'tis not mine to judge--I scorn and leave thee. . O 324 Irene   22
    'Tis ours, alas! to punish, not to judge, ... O 326 Irene   33
'TWAS
    'Twas Vice that shcok our Nerves, 'twas Vice, Leontius . O 251 Irene   56
    'Twas Vice that shook our Nerves, 'twas Vice, Leontius . O 251 Irene   56
IT
    Ah! what avails it, that, from slav'ry far, ... O 15 London   117
    Unlocks his gold, and counts it till he dies. . . . . O 44 Vanity Wishes   290
    Approve it only--'tis too late to praise. . . . . . O 62 Pro Word Wise   16
    Next Month he sets it out again. . . . . O 73 Hor. Epode II   79
    To point each glance, and force it to the heart! . . . O 81 Lady Birthday   8
    Why, Sylvia, was it then decreed, ... O 120 To Miss Purse   11
    Why, Stella, was it then decreed, ... O 120 To Miss Purse V   11
    Nor hear it with a frown;-- . . . . O 159 Par Hermit III   10
    As I can gulp it down. . . . . O 159 Par Hermit III   12
    Is it business? is it love? . . . . O 185 Anacreon Ode 9   5
    Is it business? is it love? . . . . O 185 Anacreon Ode 9   5
    "As it leaves Anacreon's lip, ... O 185 Anacreon Ode 9   32
    Let it wander as it will; . . . . O 196 Song Congratu.   18
    Let it wander as it will; . . . . O 196 Song Congratu.   18
    Let it wander if it will; . . . . O 196 Song Congratu.   18
    Let it wander if it will; . . . . O 196 Song Congratu. V 18
    Let it wander if it will; . . . . O 196 Song Congratu. V 18
    With Merit needless, and without it vain. . . . . . O 246 Irene Prologue   32
    Let him persuade me to it--if he can: . . . . O 247 Irene Epilogue   4
    My Swain is little--true--but be it known, ... O 247 Irene Epilogue   9
    And is it thus Demetrius meets his Friend, ... O 249 Irene   1
    A thousand horrid Prodigies foretold it. . . . . . O 250 Irene   36
    A single Thought now rove, recall it home. . . . . . O 255 Irene   7

		PAGE	TITLE	LINE
IT	(CONTINUED)			
And, though refus'd, conceals it from the Sultan.		O 258	Irene	89
It must, it must be She; her Name?		O 258	Irene	103
It must, it must be She; her Name?		O 258	Irene	103
There let Aspasia, since my Fair entreats it,		O 263	Irene	3
It spreads the wide plain an unregarded ruin.		Y 131	Irene	V 36C
and the first gust shake<s> it into atom<s>		Y 132	Irene	V 39
Unactive (unkindled) in the breast—rouse it		Y 133	Irene	V 19
And whelms the swelling Architect beneath it.		O 269	Irene	9
Was it for this, that sick'ning in Epirus,		O 272	Irene	6
Will it not charm a Mind like thine exalted,		O 278	Irene	67
Th' Eternal gave it, and that End is Virtue.		O 290	Irene	31
It parts you now—The hasty Sultan sign'd		O 296	Irene	1
If Fate pursues me, let it find me here.		O 297	Irene	18
If Fate persues me, let it find me here		O 297	Irene	V 18
I need not name it;		O 307	Irene	12
Whate'er their Scheme the Bassa's Death defeats it,		O 312	Irene	4
There I became, nor blush to make it known,		O 312	Irene	13
Exalt my soul, and swell it into raptures.		Y 189	Irene	V 1F
Just as it reach'd my Lips, a sudden Cry		O 316	Irene	27
Urg'd me to dash it to the Ground untouch'd,		O 316	Irene	28
It now remains to fly!		O 318	Irene	11
The Sultan knows it,		O 324	Irene	20
Recall th' extorted Doom.—It must be so,		O 326	Irene	40
Then call it not our Cruelty, nor Crime,		O 327	Irene	28
Abdalla brought her Doom! Abdalla brought it!		O 334	Irene	63
Abdalla brought it,		O 334	Irene	66
But Heav'n shall guide it to the guilty Heart.		O 335	Irene	15
IT'S				
Improves it's lustre, but impairs its Strength.		O 366	Irene	V 4
ITALIA'S				
To kind Italia's hospitable Shades;		O 302	Irene	117
ITALIAN				
From bold invaders clear'd th' Italian lands		O 78	Festina Lente	19
ITALY'S				
Then seize fair Italy's delightful Coast,		O 309	Irene	30
ITINERANT				
Epitaph on Claude Phillips, an Itinerant Musician		O 113	Epit. Phillips	V T
ITS				
There ev'ry breeze bears health upon its wings;		O 20	London	221
Such age there is, and who shall wish its end?		O 44	Vanity Wishes	298
Such age there is, and who could wish its end?		O 44	Vanity Wishes	V 298
Such age the is, and who could wish its end?		Y 105	Vanity Wishes	V 298
And social sorrow loses half its pain:		O 59	Pro Good Nat'd	4
Uncheck'd on both, caprice may vent its rage,		O 59	Pro Good Nat'd	V 15
To wit, reviving from its author's dust,		O 61	Pro Word Wise	7
And spread its smoking ruins o'er the field.		O 74	Tr. Iliad Bk 6	14
Soon shall this sprig, as you shall fix its doom,		O 95	Sprig of Myrtl	V 13
Its charms are fled and all its powers destroyed.		O 142	In Baretti Bk.	8
Its charms are fled and all its powers destroyed.		O 142	In Baretti Bk.	8
And on its basis would have been 'enroll'd,		O 190	Seeing Montagu	5
Or wake the Dead to warn us of its Fall?		O 250	Irene	47
Pour forth her Dead to warn us of its fall?		O 365	Irene	V 22
In its wild ravages distinguish'd thee		Y 115	Irene	V 49B
To raise our prostrate country from its ruins.		Y 117	Irene	V109A
Each Pleasure brightens at its near Approach,		O 261	Irene	20
Live till the tott'ring Earth forsakes its Base		O 347	Irene	V 29
Adorns my Palace with its brightest Virgins;		O 263	Irene	15
And though built on feeble columns—Its lofty turrets blaze amidst the sky		Y 131	Irene	V 35
Improves it's lustre, but impairs its Strength.		O 366	Irene	V 4
Toils all its languages to flatter me.		Y 136	Irene	V 29
Derives its Value from its Use alone;		O 290	Irene	29
Derives its Value from its Use alone;		O 290	Irene	29
Heav'n, when its Hand pour'd Softness on our Limbs		O 290	Irene	42
He Heav'n, when its hand pourd softness on our limbs		Y 162	Irene	V 42
Virtue is uncha unvarying as its Authour		O 348	Irene	V 23
Virtue is fixd unvarying as its Author		O 348	Irene	V 23
the world recovering from its convulsion		Y 164	Irene	V 77
Thy dazzled Soul with all its boasted Greatness,		O 292	Irene	99
Should Heav'n yet unappeas'd refuse its Aid,		O 301	Irene	97
Extends its Lines along the sandy Beach,		O 304	Irene	4
Lest unrewarded Mercy lose its Charms.		O 313	Irene	19
Th' applauding Sky shall pour forth all its Beams		O 322	Irene	9
Heav'n turns its point upon the guilty Heart		O 345	Irene	V 29
Its useless force the weapon spends in air.		Y 26	Tr Add. Battle	135
ITSELF				
Not Rome itself that held the world in awe		O 76	Tr Add. Battle	39
Not for itself but for a nobler End		O 290	Irene	30
IVORY				
Tea, scandal, ivory teeth, and languid airs;		O 84	Epi Dist Moth.	19
IVY				
Daphnis with ivy wreath'd the jav'lins round		Y 6	Virgil Daphnis	15
JAIL				
A single jail, in Alfred's golden reign,		O 22	London	248
Toil, envy, want, the patron, and the jail.		O 38	Vanity Wishes	160
Toil, envy, want, the Garret, and the jail.		O 38	Vanity Wishes	V 160

177

```
JANIZARIES
    Shall throw th' attending Janizaries round thee.  . . .   O 319  Irene          34
JANIZARY                                                PAGE   TITLE          LINE
    The hungry Janizary burns for Plunder,  . . . . . .   O 309  Irene          21
JARRING
    That links the jarring Elements in Peace.  . . . . .   O 257  Irene          64
    Unites the jarring voices of mankind  . . . . . . .   Y 136  Irene        V 32A
JAV'LINS
    Daphnis with ivy wreath'd the jav'lins round  . . .   Y   6  Virgil Daphnis  15
JAWS
    And laughs and wantons in the Jaws of Death.  . . .   O 283  Irene          11
    Still dost thou flutter in the Jaws of Death?  . . .   O 318  Irene          17
JEALOUS
    His glowing Wishes, and his jealous Pangs.  . . . .   O 280  Irene          28
       Hated Name! his jealous Rage  . . . . .   O 316  Irene           9
    Some cruel Stratagem of jealous Beauty!  . . . . .   O 326  Irene          37
JEALOUSY
    Vexation, Fury, Jealousy, Despair,  . . . . . . .   O  84  Epi Dist Moth.  38
    Revenge and subtle Jealousy shall teach  . . . . .   O 307  Irene          24
JENNYS
    Call the Bettys, Kates, and Jennys  . . . . . . .   O 196  Song Congratu.   9
JEST
    Or English honour grew a standing jest.  . . . . .   O  10  London         30
    And strive in vain to laugh at H<erve>y's jest.  . .   O  13  London         74
    And strive in vain to laugh at Clodio's jest.  . . .   O  13  London       V 74
    To shake with laughter ere the jest they hear,  . . .   O  16  London        140
    Sure the most bitter is a scornful jest;  . . . . .   O  17  London        167
    Provokes a broil, and stabs you for a jest.  . . . .   O  21  London        229
    And feed with varied fools th' eternal jest:  . . .   O  32  Vanity Wishes  52
    And feed with change of new born fools th' eternal    Y  94  Vanity Wishes V 52
       jest,
    The still returning tale, and ling'ring jest,  . . .   O  44  Vanity Wishes 275
    Still rise the long tale, and ling'ring jest,  . . .   Y 104  Vanity Wishes V 275
    Safe from the keen lampoon and stinging jest;  . . .   O  82  Young Author   28
    Safe from the tart lampoon and stinging jest;  . . .   O  82  Young Author V 28
    Unlike the ribald, whose licentious jest  . . . . .   O 130  Tr. Rambler 12  1
    a proverb and a jest  . . . . . . . . . .   Y 113  Irene        V 22
JEWELS
    Amidst the Blaze of Jewels and of Gold,  . . . . . .   O 276  Irene           9
JILT
    There she soon became a jilt,  . . . . . . . .   Y 300  Extemp. Elegy    9
JOCKY
    See the Jocky, see the Pander,  . . . . . . . .   O 196  Song Congratu.  19
    Call the Jocky, call the Pander,  . . . . . . .   O 196  Song Congratu. V 19
JOCUND
    Jocund he dances o'er the wat'ry way,  . . . . . .   O  82  Young Author    5
    Then dances jocund o'er the watery way,  . . . . .   O  82  Young Author  V  5
    How blest art thou, still jocund and serene,  . . .   O 271  Irene           6
JOHN
    Great Sir John, are all your own.  . . . . . . .   O 196  Song Congratu.   4
    Great Sir John, are now your own.  . . . . . . .   O 196  Song Congratu. V  4
    Wealth, Sir John, was made to wander,  . . . . . .   O 196  Song Congratu.  17
JOHNSON
    Then Johnson came, instructed from the School,  . . .   O  51  Pro Drury-Lane  9
    Dr. Johnson upon Friendship  . . . . . . . . .   O  99  Ode Friendship V  T
JOHNSON'S
    Nor wish'd for Johnson's Art, or Shakespear's Flame;  . .   O  52  Pro Drury-Lane  18
JOIN
    May powerful nature join with grateful art,  . . . .   O  81  Lady Birthday   7
    May powerful nature join with graceful art,  . . . .   Y  36  Lady Birthday V  7
    And sister souls together join,  . . . . . . . .   O 100  Ode Friendship  22
    And sister minds together join,  . . . . . . . .   Y  71  Ode Friendship V 22
    If Truths like these with pleasing Language join;  . .   O 246  Irene Prologue  15
    And India join her aromatic shade  . . . . . . .   Y 150  Irene        V 85
    Dares join Leontius' Name with Fear or Falsehood?  . .   O 304  Irene          13
    Where the wild fig trees join their darksom shade  . .   Y  19  Tr. Iliad Bk 6  52
JOIN'D
    His learning, join'd with each endearing art,  . . .   O 117  Epitaph Hanmer   7
    Essence Divine with Matter join'd.  . . . . . . .   O 147  Tr Boeth III.6  12
    Join'd Cali's Hand to mine, and falt'ring cry'd,  . .   O 272  Irene           8
JOINS
    With cool submission joins the labouring train,  . . .   O  59  Pro Good Nat'd   3
    That joins us thus, will never part us more.  . . .   O 296  Irene          39
    Now joins thy People's, and thy Cali's Prayers,  . . .   O 308  Irene           8
JOINT
    Unnumber'd maladies each Joint invade,  . . . . . .   O  44  Vanity Wishes V 283
JOINTS
    Unnumber'd maladies his joints invade,  . . . . . .   O  44  Vanity Wishes 283
    Of Freedom and of Love: My trembling Joints  . . . .   O 320  Irene          11
JOKE
    Wakes from his dream, and labours for a joke;  . . .   O  17  London        163
JOLLITY
    And Jollity maintain'd eternal Revels.--  . . . . .   O 251  Irene          65
JOLLY
    Here the Gamester light and jolly  . . . . . . .   O 196  Song Congratu.  15
    There the Gamester light and jolly  . . . . . . .   O 196  Song Congratu. V 15
JOVE
    Whatever course of Life great Jove allots,  . . . .   O  77  Festina Lente    1
    Forgive, great Jove, the daring enterprize.  . . . .   O 136  Tr Rambler 129   6
    Who knows if Jove who counts our Score  . . . . . .   O 232  Tr Horace IV.7  17
    "Immortal Gods! and thou allmighty Jove  . . . . .   Y  20  Tr. Iliad Bk 6  99
```

```
JOVE              (CONTINUED)                        PAGE    TITLE              LINE
     Shook headlong from his throne imperial Jove.  . . . .  Y  26  Tr Add. Battle     139
JOY
     Does envy seize thee? crush th' upbraiding joy,   . . .  O  32  Vanity Wishes       39
     And shuts up all the passages of joy:  . . . . . . .  O  43  Vanity Wishes      260
     Still drops some joy from with'ring life away;  . . . .  O  45  Vanity Wishes      306
     And cut with joy the wond'ring Skies. . . . . . . .  O  70  Hor.II Ode XX        4
     Nor give the generous pain, the worthless joy:    . . .  O  81  Lady Birthday       14
     Ye blooming train, who give despair or joy,  . . . . .  O  83  Epi Dist Moth.       1
     With superfluities of joy.  . . . . . . . . .  O 191  Tr. Medea I         16
     Joy to see their quarry fly,  . . . . . . . . .  O 196  Song Congratu.      14
     horrid joy--his air now fearful now resolv'd.    . . .  Y 145  Irene             V  82
     Quaff the full draught of each terrestrial joy   . . .  Y 146  Irene             V  20
     New joy comes rushing on me and o'erwhelms   . . . .  Y 169  Irene             V  12
     Lost in a wild Perplexity of Joy.   . . . . . . .  O 295  Irene               14
     Sanguinary joy--Slaves now watch her nod  . . . . .  Y 184  Irene             V   9
     How should I joy, 'midst the fierce Shock of Nations,  .  O 309  Irene               40
     horrid joy--gloomy resolution--his air now fearful now  .  O 187  Irene             V   7
          resolv'd.
     This elemental Joy, this gen'ral Calm,   . . . . .  O 314  Irene                8
     And joy to feel the vital Warmth return,   . . . . .  O 320  Irene               25
     Farewell, unhappy Maid, may ev'ry Joy  . . . . . .  O 322  Irene               57
     And bless'd with all the joy that Guilt   . . . . .  O 365  Irene             V  11
          allows
     A Stranger to th' Oppressor's savage Joy,   . . . . .  O 329  Irene                6
     When haughty Guilt exults with impious Joy,   . . . .  O 335  Irene               12
     Pledge of their love and source of all their joy  . . .  Y  18  Tr. Iliad Bk 6      10
     While Hector lives I tast of ev'ry joy   . . . . .  Y  18  Tr. Iliad Bk 6      26
     And joy and sorrow stand by turns confest.   . . . .  Y  21  Tr. Iliad Bk 6     110
JOY'ST
     Thou joy'st to lose the master in the friend:  . . . .  O 130  Tr. Rambler 12       4
JOYFUL
     Exulting Folly hail'd the joyful Day,  . . . . . . .  O  52  Pro Drury-Lane      37
     And rushes joyful to the naked Wall,   . . . . . .  O 298  Irene               29
JOYFULL
     Joyfull he sees his Cattle come,   . . . . . . . .  O  73  Hor. Epode II     V  67
     The universal smile of joyfull nature  . . . . . . .  Y 190  Irene             V   9
     The joyfull Cranes triumphant clap their wings:   . . .  Y  26  Tr Add. Battle     127
JOYLESS
     Now pall the tasteless meats, and joyless wines,   . . .  O  43  Vanity Wishes      265
     "Joyless task without reward:  . . . . . . . .  O 185  Anacreon Ode 9      18
JOYOUS
     And banish'd sorrow flies the joyous plains;   . . . .  Y   7  Virgil Daphnis      37
JOYS
     Whose joys are causeless, or whose griefs are vain.  . .  O  33  Vanity Wishes       68
     No joys to him pacific scepters yield,   . . . . .  O  40  Vanity Wishes      197
     Whom Joys with soft varieties invite,  . . . . . .  O  46  Vanity Wishes      325
     Whom Joys in soft vicissitudes invite,   . . . . .  Y 107  Vanity Wishes     V 325
     Joys insincere! thick clouds invade the skies,   . . .  O  82  Young Author         7
     Around them pleasures wait, and joys for ever new.   . .  O  84  Epi Dist Moth.      27
     Thy gentle flows of guiltless joys   . . . . . .  O 100  Ode Friendship      17
     Tir'd with vain joys, and false alarms,   . . . . .  O 124  Winter's Walk       17
     The joys of music and of wine,   . . . . . . .  O 190  Tr. Medea I          4
     Why should the Sultan shun the Joys of Beauty,   . . .  O 261  Irene                7
     Paints future Joys, and points to distant Glories.   . .  O 261  Irene               17
     And fit her for the joys of paradise:--  . . . . .  Y 130  Irene             V  11
     The Hopes and Fears, the Joys and Pains of Life,   . . .  O 265  Irene                7
     I share, by secret Instinct, all his Joys,   . . . .  O 272  Irene               10
     Such are Love's Joys, the Lenitives of Life,   . . . .  O 277  Irene               47
     And perish ere he tastes the Joys of Conquest.   . . .  O 308  Irene               33
     At once the Joys of Paradise and Empire,   . . . . .  O 308  Irene                7
     Will damp my joys, and cloud the happy days  . . . .  O 370  Irene             V  23
     This Calm, these Joys, dear Innocence! are thine,  . . .  O 313  Irene                9
     Joys ill exchang'd for Gold, and Pride, and Empire.  . .  O 313  Irene               10
     Are these th' unceasing Joys, th' unmingled Pleasures  .  O 314  Irene               16
     May then his mother's heart with joys o'erflow   . . .  Y  20  Tr. Iliad Bk 6     105
JUBA'S
     None fiercer Juba's thirsty land,  . . . . . . . .  O  66  Hor I Ode xxii      15
JUDE
     Upon the feast of St Simon & St Jude   . . . . . .  O  78  Feast St Simon       T
     Most venerable Jude!   . . . . . . . . . .  O  80  Feast St Simon      51
JUDG'D
     And senates heard before they judg'd a cause;    . . .  O  33  Vanity Wishes       60
     Yet judg'd by those, whose voices ne'er were sold,   . .  O  60  Pro Good Nat'd      27
JUDGE
     For gold the hireling judge distorts the laws;   . . .  O  31  Vanity Wishes       26
     The Sultan is my Judge. . . . . . . . .  O 323  Irene               12
     But 'tis not mine to judge--I scorn and leave thee.  . .  O 324  Irene               22
     'Tis ours, alas! to punish, not to judge,   . . . .  O 326  Irene               33
JUDGES
     Be kind, ye judges, or at least be just:  . . . . .  O  61  Pro Word Wise        8
JUDGMENT
     Your taste in snuff, your judgment in a whore;   . . .  O  17  London             149
     His taste in snuff, his judgment in a whore;   . . . .  Y  55  London            V 149
     No Snares to captivate the Judgment spreads;   . . . .  O 246  Irene Prologue      27
JUDICIOUS
     Times gloomy backward with judicious eyes;   . . . .  O 192  Tr. Medea II         2
JUICES
     Then shall these Juices taint Demetrius' Draught,  . . .  O 308  Irene               30
JURIES
     No spies were paid, no special juries known,   . . . .  O  22  London             252
```

		PAGE	TITLE	LINE
JURIES	**(CONTINUED)**			
No bribes were paid, no special juries known, ...		Y 61	London	V 252
JUST				
Should heaven's just bolts Orgilio's wealth confound, .		O 19	London	194
How just that scorn ere yet thy voice declare, ...		O 33	Vanity Wishes	71
See nations slowly wise, and meanly just, ...		O 38	Vanity Wishes	161
How just his hopes let Swedish Charles decide;		O 40	Vanity Wishes	192
And rising Ages hasten to be just. . . .		O 57	Prologue Comus	14
Have hopes, and fears, and wishes, just the same; . . .		O 59	Pro Good Nat'd	12
Be kind, ye judges, or at least be just:		O 61	Pro Word Wise	8
Alas! 'tis hard for beauty to be just. . . .		O 81	Lady Birthday	12
Directress of the brave and just, ...		O 100	Ode Friendship	13
Just Phoebus would devote his plant to thee. . . .		O 106	Eliza plucking	8
Hear, and be just.		O 133	Tr. Rambler 81	1
Just emerging into Light, ...		O 150	Tr Boet III.12	49
Ye Fops be silent! and ye Wits be just!		O 246	Irene Prologue	34
Just in the Moment of impending Fate, ...		O 259	Irene	117
Just as I mark'd them, they forsook the Shore, ...		O 269	Irene	38
Could just intention consecrate the Guilt		O 360	Irene	V 35
Just as it reach'd my Lips, a sudden Cry		O 316	Irene	27
Just as the Rack forc'd out his struggling Soul, ...		O 330	Irene	13
Let one just Act conclude the hateful Day.		O 333	Irene	50
Be just ye Slaves, and, to be just, be cruel, ...		O 334	Irene	73
Be just ye Slaves, and, to be just, be cruel, ...		O 334	Irene	73
Teach me to range my troopes in just array		Y 22	Tr Add. Battle	5
JUSTER				
Let nobler Hopes and juster Fears succeed, ...		O 265	Irene	9
JUSTICE				
Besides, with justice, this discerning age		O 16	London	132
Fair Justice then, without constraint ador'd, ...		O 22	London	250
The wisest justice on the banks of Trent?		O 35	Vanity Wishes	124
When publick Villainy, too strong for Justice, ...		O 250	Irene	40
And lawless Passion, hold the Sword of Justice.		O 256	Irene	54
Can Cali dare the Stroke of heav'nly Justice, ...		O 272	Irene	3
And should he fall unheard, by sudden Justice, ...		O 273	Irene	41
Yet in the Use of Pow'r remember Justice.		O 286	Irene	10
Against his King, and cry, Remember Justice?		O 286	Irene	12
Justice demands the forfeit Life of Cali;		O 286	Irene	13
Justice demands that I reveal your Crimes;		O 286	Irene	14
Justice demands--But see th' approaching Sultan. . . .		O 286	Irene	15
Oppose my Wishes, and--Remember Justice.		O 286	Irene	16
Aw'd by the Rigour of the Sultan's Justice, ...		O 288	Irene	8
The Scale of Justice, and the Sword of Pow'r, ...		O 291	Irene	72
Approving Justice smiles upon your Cause, ...		O 297	Irene	2
Shall Monarchs fear to draw the Sword of Justice, . . .		O 312	Irene	21
When daring Vice insults eternal Justice, ...		O 314	Irene	23
Hard was the Strife of Justice and of Love;		O 324	Irene	13
But now 'tis o'er, and Justice has prevail'd.		O 324	Irene	14
Th' unpitying Ministers of Turkish Justice, ...		O 325	Irene	9
Nor justice can acquit, nor mercy spare		Y 210	Irene	V 25B
Your hasty Zeal defrauds the Claim of Justice, ...		O 330	Irene	5
So fix'd the Justice of all-conscious Heav'n.		O 335	Irene	11
Eternal justice thus her doom decreed		O 345	Irene	V 32
JUSTIFIES				
The form distorted justifies the fall, ...		O 34	Vanity Wishes	89
And Nature justifies our Monarch's Choice.		O 288	Irene	3
JUSTLY				
Demetrius justly pleads a double Title, ...		O 305	Irene	45
JUTTING				
Form'd by this Garden jutting on the Deep;		O 284	Irene	52
KAI				
Kai Bion, eipen, otan ripses Thanatio Belessi, ...		O 108	Eis Birchion	3
Kai toios Paphien plexen eroti Thean.		O 172	On Marlborough	2
KALLOUS				
Tei Kallous dunamei ti telos; Zeus panta dedoken . . .		O 103	Eis Elisses	1
KATES				
Call the Bettys, Kates, and Jennys		O 196	Song Congratu.	9
KEEN				
Mark the keen glance, and watch the sign to hate. . . .		O 34	Vanity Wishes	110
Safe from the keen lampoon and stinging jest;		O 82	Young Author	28
KEEP				
And pow'r too great to keep, or to resign?		O 36	Vanity Wishes	134
Too well You know to keep the Slaves You gain.		O 96	Hickman Spinet	2
KEEPS				
Whom Pleasure keeps too busy to be wise, ...		O 46	Vanity Wishes	324
Who keeps the rigid rules of ancient honour;		O 176	Tr Metastas II	2
That keeps the rigid rules of ancient honour;		O 176	Tr Metastas II	V 2
KEN				
Lies open to Conjecture's dubious Ken, ...		O 300	Irene	69
KENT				
Thou fly'st for refuge to the wilds of Kent;		O 23	London	257
You fly for refuge to the wilds of Kent:		Y 61	London	V 257
KEPT				
The wine you kept with so much care		O 69	Hor.II Ode 14	27
KERAUNO				
Zeus mounos phlogoenti poleis ekperse kerauno, ...		O 103	Eis Elisses	5
KICK				
And get a kick for awkward flattery.		O 16	London	131
And gain a kick for aukward flattery.		O 16	London	V 131
KIDS				
Two tender kids, the hopes of all the flock.		O 64	Virgil Past.I	20

	PAGE	TITLE	LINE
KIDS (CONTINUED)			
Or feasts on Kids the Wolves had kill'd	O 73	Hor. Epode II	65
KILL			
Betimes the greedy Thrush to kill	O 72	Hor. Epode II	41
Those Hounds of Blood, that catch the Hint to kill, . .	O 333	Irene	52
KILL'D			
Or feasts on Kids the Wolves had kill'd	O 73	Hor. Epode II	65
KILLS			
Who sleeps on brambles till he kills his man;	O 21	London	227
KIND			
Grant me, kind heaven, to find some happier place, . .	O 11	London	43
Counts death kind Nature's signal of retreat:	O 48	Vanity Wishes	364
Thinks death kind Nature's signal of retreat: . . .	O 48	Vanity Wishes	V 364
Surveys the general toil of human kind;	O 59	Pro Good Nat'd	2
Be kind, ye judges, or at least be just:	O 61	Pro Word Wise	8
She ceas'd; then godlike Hector answer'd kind,-- . .	O 74	Tr. Iliad Bk 6	1
Intrusts his happiness to human kind, ...	O 82	Young Author	13
For kind, for tender nymphs the myrtle blooms, . . .	O 84	Epi Dist Moth.	14
Beasts of each kind their fellows spare;	O 138	Tr Rambler 160	1
His Conduct Human Kind debased:	O 146	Tr Boeth III.4	6
Obscurely wise, and coarsely kind;	O 201	Death Dr Levet	10
Sure some kind Sabre in the Heat of Battle, ...	O 252	Irene	93
His kind Intelligence betray'd their Measures; . . .	O 253	Irene	118
Thou long'st for Stars that frown on human Kind, . . .	O 271	Irene	4
Charm'd with the Thought of blessing human Kind, . . .	O 278	Irene	73
And kind Ambition points the Way to Greatness. . . .	O 280	Irene	14
Seize the kind Fair, and press her to thy Bosom. . .	O 284	Irene	35
I go to wait thy Call; this kind Consent	O 285	Irene	15
Thanks for this kind Relief--with Speed admit him. .	O 294	Irene	5
Thanks for this kind relief. Conduct him hither . .	O 370	Irene	V 15
Thou kind Assistant of my better Angel, ...	O 298	Irene	10
Spread wide their kind Arms to Science and to Beauty. .	O 353	Irene	V 5
To kind Italia's hospitable Shades;	O 302	Irene	117
Kind Heav'n affords thee, and inviting Mercy	O 321	Irene	41
Let kind Compulsion terminate the Contest.	O 321	Irene	50
Amidst her kind Solicitudes for me!	O 332	Irene	21
He grasp'd her hand endeav'ring kind relief.	Y 21	Tr. Iliad Bk 6	112
KINDER			
Is not each Realm that smiles with kinder Suns, . . .	O 265	Irene	35
KINDLE			
May droop dismay'd, or kindle into Madness.	O 304	Irene	11
KINDLED			
With transports kindled, rural ease, ...	O 73	Hor. Epode II	74
My Soul first kindled by thy bright Example, . . .	O 298	Irene	13
The raging of the kindled fire	Y 12	Tr Hor Epode 9	40
KINDLING			
Or sprightly Hope exalt their kindling Spirits? . . .	O 270	Irene	23
To see the Cloud forsake her kindling Cheek, ...	O 320	Irene	26
KINDLY			
Why should they fear?--That Power that kindly spreads .	O 250	Irene	31
And kindly grant an Ear to gentler Sounds:	O 285	Irene	2
KINDNESS			
Should no false Kindness lure to loose delight, . . .	O 37	Vanity Wishes	147
Well skill'd to sooth a foe with looks of kindness, . .	O 176	Tr Metastas II	3
The Laws of Kindness, break the Bonds of Nature? . .	O 280	Irene	16
KINDOMS			
Spoil of <kindoms> Nations	O 351	Irene	V 13
KINDRED			
Now kindred Merit fills the sable bier, ...	O 45	Vanity Wishes	303
Now kindred Merit fills the mournful bier, ...	Y 106	Vanity Wishes	V 303
When Virtues kindred Virtues meet, ...	O 100	Ode Friendship	21
KINE			
And heap the fire, and milk the Kine	O 72	Hor. Epode II	51
As corn the fields, as bulls the herds of kine, . . .	Y 6	Virgil Daphnis	18
KING			
To rig another convoy for the k<in>g.	O 22	London	247
And Sedley curs'd the form that pleas'd a king. . . .	O 46	Vanity Wishes	322
Nor did King Priam's hoary age	O 68	Hor. II Ode IX	15
Or move the haughty King below, ...	O 69	Hor.II Ode 14	10
Or weep some falling King.	O 78	Feast St Simon	6
Ambitious Fury fir'd the Grecian King:	O 97	Hickman Spinet	10
For Nature form'd the Poet for the King.	O 114	On C. Cibber	4
The same their Parent and their King.	O 146	Tr Boeth III.6	4
Marry a Turk! a haughty, Tyrant King, ...	O 247	Irene Epilogue	1
Where King and People own one common Law	O 352	Irene	V 16
Shall feel the Vengeance of an injur'd King.	O 273	Irene	33
Betray my King to Negligence of Danger.	O 275	Irene	73
Against his King, and cry, Remember Justice?	O 286	Irene	12
To-morrow's Dawn shall see the Turkish King	O 303	Irene	9
KING'S			
This fir'd the youthful King's ambitious Breast, . . .	O 256	Irene	47
KINGDOM			
Now, o'er the rural kingdom roves	O 125	An Ode	5
Esteem Aspasia's Breast, the noblest Kingdom. . . .	O 289	Irene	14
KINGDOMS SEE KINDOMS			
Kings change their Laws, and Kingdoms change their . .	O 110	To Posterity	16
Kings.			
Young, and unsettled in his Father's Kingdoms, . . .	O 257	Irene	67
And blasted Kingdoms flourish at thy Smile?	O 278	Irene	72
And lodge the fate of kingdoms in her bosom.	Y 159	Irene	V 18
Think how the sov'reign Arbiter of Kingdoms	O 300	Irene	56

```
KINGDOMS        (CONTINUED)                              PAGE    TITLE           LINE
    All the Western kingdoms  . . . . . . . . . . .      Y 177  Irene         V 115
    That pour with sudden Violence on Kingdoms, .   . . .  O 325  Irene           12
    Shuns Pluto's kingdoms and the realms of night;   . . .  Y   7  Virgil Daphnis  33
KINGS
    Let hist'ry tell where rival kings command, . . . . .  O  31  Vanity Wishes    29
    Historians tell where rival kings command,  . . . . .  Y  93  Vanity Wishes  V 29
    Degrading nobles and controuling kings;   . . . . .   O  34  Vanity Wishes    94
    And his last sighs reproach the faith of kings.  . . .  O  35  Vanity Wishes   120
    And his last words reproach the faith of kings.  . . .  Y  96  Vanity Wishes  V 120
    By kings protected, and to kings ally'd?  . . . . . .  O  36  Vanity Wishes   132
    By kings protected, and to kings ally'd?  . . . . . .  O  36  Vanity Wishes   132
    Behold surrounding kings their pow'r combine, . . . .  O  40  Vanity Wishes   199
    In vain surrounding kings their pow'rs combine,  . . .  Y 101  Vanity Wishes  V 199
    But left, like Egypt's Kings, a lasting Tomb.   . . .  O  51  Pro Drury-Lane   16
    Kings change their Laws, and Kingdoms change their     O 110  To Posterity     16
        Kings.
    Kings change their Laws, and Kingdoms change their . .  O 110  To Posterity     16
        Kings.
    Rise Cali Bassa counsellor of Kings  . . . . . . .    O 351  Irene         V  24
    Preach thy dull Politics to vulgar Kings,  . . . . .  O 265  Irene           39
    Reject the Daughters of contending Kings;  . . . . .  O 267  Irene            7
    Ransom of Kings, the purchass of your blood  . . . .  O 351  Irene         V  14
    Th' unquestion'd Claim of Conquerors, and Kings!  . .  O 286  Irene            9
    Shall I not wish to chear afflicted Kings,  . . . . .  O 291  Irene           67
    Successful Treasons punish impious Kings.  . . . . .  O 300  Irene           66
    O! could the Eyes of Kings, like those of Heav'n, . .  O 308  Irene           12
    See Cali, Dread of Kings, and Pride of Armies, . . .  O 311  Irene           16
KISS
    We kneel, and kiss the consecrated earth;  . . . . .  O  10  London          24
    The balmy kiss, for which poor Thyrsis dies;  . . . .  O  84  Epi Dist Moth.  21
    And weeping, kiss the venerable Ruins:  . . . . . .   O 251  Irene           61
KISSES
    The long-drawn Intercourse of Sighs and Kisses.  . .  O 297  Irene           14
KIST
    Then kist his son and raising to the skies  . . . . .  Y  20  Tr. Iliad Bk 6  97
KITCHENS
    And smoak'd in kitchens, or in auctions sold,  . . .  O  34  Vanity Wishes    85
KLAIETE
    Klaiete poieten, historikon, phusikon.  . . . . . .   O 171  Epi. Goldsmith   4
KNEE
    Does conscious Virtue shake the fainting knee?  . . .  O 373  Irene         V  8
KNEEL
    We kneel, and kiss the consecrated earth;  . . . . .  O  10  London          24
KNEW
    Ne'er knew to puzzle right, or varnish wrong,  . . .  O  14  London          80
    Inflicting all those ills which once they knew;  . . .  O  84  Epi Dist Moth.  37
    Who merits most!--I knew not we were Rivals.  . . . .  O 284  Irene           46
    He knew Irene's Truth.  . . . . . . . . . . . . . .   O 324  Irene           20
KNIFE
    What gave great Villiers to th' assassin's knife,  . .  O  35  Vanity Wishes   129
KNOW
    Few know the toiling statesman's fear or care,  . . .  O  32  Vanity Wishes    47
    Hides from himself his state, and shuns to know,  . .  O  43  Vanity Wishes   257
    For those who feel no guilt can know no shame;  . . .  O  84  Epi Dist Moth.  25
    Too well You know to keep the Slaves You gain.  . . .  O  96  Hickman Spinet   2
    "More than all thou canst not know;  . . . . . . . .   O 186  Anacreon Ode 9  42
    The rivers know their banks again,  . . . . . . . .   O 231  Tr Horace IV.7   4
        To what I know not!  . . . . . . . . . .          O 253  Irene          108
    Then rouzing know the fiery Chief Abdalla,  . . . . .  O 254  Irene          125
    Then rouzing know the firy Chief Abdallah,  . . . . .  O 254  Irene         V 125
    Too well I know him, his immod'rate Courage,  . . . .  O 267  Irene           46
    All this we know already from Abdalla.  . . . . . .   O 270  Irene            6
    Nor let Demetrius know thee for a Rival.  . . . . . .  O 282  Irene           71
    Aspasia's Lovers know but one Desire,  . . . . . . .  O 307  Irene           13
    Too well I know him, since on Thracia's Plains  . . .  O 307  Irene           18
    Forbear--.i know the long try'd Faith of Cali.  . . .  O 308  Irene           11
    For I know ambition seduc'd her  . . . . . . . . . .  Y 186  Irene         V  3
    Bold Slave, I know them both--I know them Traytors.  .  O 324  Irene           16
    Bold Slave, I know them both--I know them Traytors.  .  O 324  Irene           16
    Does not thy Bosom, for I know thee tender,  . . . .  O 329  Irene            5
    And may she ne'er returning sorrows know."  . . . . .  Y  20  Tr. Iliad Bk 6  106
KNOW'ST
    Thou know'st those arts which blast with envious praise, O 176  Tr Metastas II   7
    And know'st the Characters of Vice and Virtue, . . . .  O 255  Irene           12
    Thou know'st not yet thy Master's future Greatness,  .  O 265  Irene           40
    Know'st thou not yet, when Love invades the Soul,  . .  O 281  Irene           38
    Obtain her and possess, thou know'st thy Rival.  . . .  O 307  Irene           17
    Know'st thou not Cali? know'st thou not Demetrius?  . .  O 324  Irene           15
    Know'st thou not Cali? know'st thou not Demetrius?  . .  O 324  Irene           15
    Perfidious!--yes--too well thou know'st them Traytors.  O 324  Irene           17
KNOWING
    But scarce observ'd, the knowing and the bold  . . .  O  31  Vanity Wishes    21
KNOWLEDGE
    With thirst of knowledge, and with love of truth;  . .  O 117  Epitaph Hanmer   6
    By wit, by knowledge, studious to be read,  . . . . .  O 141  Tr Rambler 208   3
    Thy Soul by Nature great, enlarg'd by Knowledge,  . .  O 266  Irene           35
KNOWN
    No spies were paid, no special juries known,  . . . .  O  22  London          252
    No bribes were paid, no special juries known,  . . . .  Y  61  London        V 252
    Where ne'er was known the form of mock debate,  . . .  O  33  Vanity Wishes    57
```

```
KNOWN              (CONTINUED)                      PAGE    TITLE          LINE
    In misery's darkest caverns known, . . . . . . . .  O 201 Death Dr Levet      17
    My Swain is little--true--but be it known, . . . . . O 247 Irene Epilogue      9
    Had they prevail'd, I ne'er had known Irene. . . . . O 263 Irene              27
    Had our first Asian Foes but known this Ardour, . . . O 284 Irene             40
    If e'er thy Youth has known the Pangs of Absence, . . O 285 Irene              3
    What well known Voice pronounc'd the grateful Sounds . O 295 Irene            10
    What Fears, what Griefs, what Dangers hast thou known? O 295 Irene            22
    Well known, long try'd, expect us on the Shore.  . . . O 301 Irene            91
    There I became, nor blush to make it known, . . . . . O 312 Irene            13
KNOWS
    All sciences a fasting Monsieur knows, . . . . . .  O  15 London             115
    Thy hand that knows the subtler art, . . . . . . .  O 120 To Miss Purse       5
    Who knows if Jove who counts our Score . . . . . .  O 232 Tr Horace IV.7      17
    Who knows, ere this important Morrow rise, . . . .  O 284 Irene              36
    Who knows if Mahomet's awaking Anger . . . . . . .  O 284 Irene              38
    But since none knows the Danger of a Moment,  . . .  O 321 Irene             48
        The Sultan knows it, . . . . . . . . . .       O 324 Irene             20
    He knows how near Apostacy to Treason--  . . . . .  O 324 Irene             21
KONIEN
    Ton taphon eisoraas ton Olibarioio, Konien . . . .  O 171 Epi. Goldsmith      1
    Ton taphon eisoraas ton Oleiberioio, konien  . . .  O 171 Epi. Goldsmith  V   1
    Ton taphon eisoraas ton Olibarioio, konien . . . .  O 171 Epi. Goldsmith  V   1
KORAN
    Till every Nation reverence the Koran, . . . . . .  O 264 Irene              31
KUPRIDI
    Kupridi, med autou skeptra memele theo. . . . . . .  O 103 Eis Elisses        2
KUPRIS
    Alla tod eis Thnetous Kupris epempseu onar . . . .  O 103 Eis Elisses        4
    Ommasi lampra Dios Kupris oista pherei. . . . . . .  O 103 Eis Elisses        6
LAB'RING
    Unbounded Projects lab'ring in his Mind, . . . . .  O  97 Hickman Spinet     11
    And shook the (affrighted) world lab'ring earth licentious  Y 115 Irene   V 49A
        conquest
    Fly lab'ring with the Fate of future Nations, . . .  O 279 Irene              4
    The Soldier lab'ring through a Winter's March, . . .  O 283 Irene             28
    Sweeps o'er the Grove, forsake the lab'ring Bough, . O 298 Irene             23
    In vain the lab'ring hind manures the plain,  . . .  Y   6 Virgil Daphnis     22
    Whene'er the lab'ring bird with anxious care  . . .  Y  23 Tr Add. Battle     44
    And scarce the lab'ring air sustains the throng  . .  Y  25 Tr Add. Battle     95
LABORIOUS
    His studious Patience, and laborious Art, . . . . .  O  51 Pro Drury-Lane     11
    Her Youth laborious, and her blameless Age: . . . .  O  58 Prologue Comus     30
    Manuring with laborious hand . . . . . . . . . .    O  71 Hor. Epode II       5
    While with incessant Thought laborious Man  . . . .  O 269 Irene              3
    And with laborious crouds the plains were fill'd. . .  Y  23 Tr Add. Battle    29
LABOUR
    Or drains the Labour of the Bees, . . . . . . . .   O  71 Hor. Epode II      21
    Alternate rest and labour long endure. . . . . . .  O 131 Tr. Rambler 33      1
    Endless Labour all along, . . . . . . . . . . .     O 179 Ridicul Warton      3
    Endless Labour to be wrong; . . . . . . . . . . .   O 179 Ridicul Warton      4
    With vain (fruitless) labour of the daring flight . .  Y 127 Irene          V   3
    And envy the slave that toils whose labour procures her  Y 165 Irene       V  81
        sleep
    Remember Mahomet, and cease thy Labour. . . . . . .  O 310 Irene              3
    When Fear and Anguish labour in the Breast, . . . .  O 315 Irene             31
LABOUR'D
    Thrice ten long years he labour'd for the State; . .  O 118 Epitaph Hanmer    14
    The pains I labour'd to conceal . . . . . . . . .   Y  11 Tr Hor Epode 9      15
LABOURD
    Labourd monuments of art. . . . . . . . . . . .    Y 177 Irene            V111G
LABOURING
    With cool submission joins the labouring train, . .  O  59 Pro Good Nat'd      3
LABOURS
    Wakes from his dream, and labours for a joke; . . .  O  17 London            163
    O'er Bodley's dome his future labours spread,  . . .  O  37 Vanity Wishes     139
    No dangers fright him, and no labours tire; . . . .  O  40 Vanity Wishes     194
    And leave my labours to the learn'd and wise, . . .  O 141 Tr Rambler 208      2
    From you my labours wait their last reward. . . . .  O 141 Tr Rambler 208      2
    Observe her labours, Sluggard, and be wise. . . . .  O 151 The Ant            2
    For us the Statesman labours, Hero fights, . . . .  O 247 Irene Epilogue     21
    The Warrior's Labours, and the Monarch's Cares. . . .  O 261 Irene            10
    That clouds thy Brow and labours in thy Bosom . . .  O 369 Irene            V  19
    Descend, to sweeten Labours once your own. . . . .  O 306 Irene             56
    Still labours with imaginary Woe; . . . . . . . .   O 320 Irene             22
LABYRINTHS
    Through shades of peace and flowery labyrinths . . .  Y 146 Irene           V  21
    Well may'st thou hide in Labyrinths of Sound  . . .  O 293 Irene            125
    Pursue him through his Labyrinths of Treason, . . .  O 310 Irene              6
LACE
    Ye glitt'ring Train! whom Lace and Velvet bless, . .  O 246 Irene Prologue     1
LACERATED
    Now lacerated Friendship claims a tear. . . . . . .  O  45 Vanity Wishes     304
LAD
    --Come, my lad, and drink some beer. . . . . . . .  O 181 Parody Warton      8
    Wealth, my lad, was made to wander, . . . . . . .   O 196 Song Congratu.  V  17
LADIES
    While ladies interpose, and slaves debate. . . . .  O  41 Vanity Wishes     214
    Ladies--stock and tend your Hive, . . . . . . . .   O 178 Thrale 35 Year     11
    Ladies introduces the mention of Aspasia. . . . . .  O 351 Irene           V  12
```

		PAGE	TITLE	LINE

LADS
Come my lads and take your fill. . . . . O 196 Song Congratu. V 20
LADY
To a Young Lady on her Birth-day . . . . O 80 Lady Birthday T
Epilogue intended to have been spoken by a Lady . . O 83 Epi Dist Moth. T
from a young Lady . . . . O 95 Sprig of Myrtl V T
to whom a Lady had given a Sprig of Myrtle . . O 95 Sprig of Myrtl V T
Ode on Friendship address'd To the Lady-------- . . O 99 Ode Friendship V T
To Lady F<irebra>ce at Bury Assizes . . . . . . O 107 Lady F Assizes T
To Lyce, an elderly Lady . . . . O 126 To Lyce, Lady T
LADY'S
On a Lady's presenting a Sprig of Myrtle . . . . . . O 95 Sprig of Myrtl T
LAGS
Superfluous lags the vet'ran on the stage, ... O 45 Vanity Wishes 308
And lags superfluous on th' incumbred stage, . . . Y 106 Vanity Wishes V 308
LAID
The man whom fate has laid, where all must lye. . . . O 61 Pro Word Wise 6
Now, Tityrus, you, supine and careless laid, . . . O 64 Virgil Past.I 1
On some green bank supinely Laid, ... O 72 Hor. Epode II 30
Where Priam and his sons are laid, ... O 232 Tr Horace IV.7 15
Then we with wine will drown our troubles, laid . . . Y 7 Virgil Daphnis 47
LAKE
Whene'er this Stone, now hid beneath the Lake, ... O 110 To Posterity 1
The wand'ring Rivulet, and silver Lake, ... O 280 Irene 23
When all conspiring leave Maeon's lake . . . . . . Y 24 Tr Add. Battle 66
LALAGE
By Lalage, too far I stray'd, ... O 66 To A. Fuscus 10
My Flame for Lalage I'll own; . . . . O 67 To A. Fuscus 23
LAMB
And as quiet as a lamb. . . . . Y 301 Extemp. Elegy 20
LAMBENT
Thy lambent glories only beam . . . . O 100 Ode Friendship 11
The lambent Flames of mild Benevolence, ... O 293 Irene 109
May lambent zephyrs gently wave thy head, ... Y 3 On a Daffodill 9
LAMBKINS
Or sheers the Lambkins snowy fleece. . . . . O 71 Hor. Epode II 22
LAMENT
So much lament his slaughter'd son. . . . . . . O 68 Hor. II Ode IX 16
And then lament his fall with seeming friendship: . . O 176 Tr Metastas II 5
And then lament their fall with seeming friendship: . . O 176 Tr Metastas II V 5
The Weakness we lament, our selves create, . . . O 266 Irene 26
No more should Greece lament those Prayers rejected. . . O 290 Irene 52
But soon though shalt lament thy daring folly . . . . Y 198 Irene V 33
The nymphs bewail'd his fall with loud lament . . . Y 18 Tr. Iliad Bk 6 32
LAMENTABLE
Utter sad groans and lamentable cries. . . . . . . O 76 Tr Add. Battle 29
LAMENTED
But while Demetrius, dear lamented Name! . . . . . . O 290 Irene 47
LAMENTING
Lamenting warbles out his love, ... O 72 Hor. Epode II 34
Lamenting Av'rice now too late discovers . . . . . O 250 Irene 26
LAMPOON
Safe from the keen lampoon and stinging jest; . . . . O 82 Young Author 28
Safe from the tart lampoon and stinging jest; . . . . O 82 Young Author V 28
LAMPRA
Ommasi lampra Dios Kupris oista pherei. . . . . . . O 103 Eis Elisses 6
LAMPS
Though countless as the lamps of night . . . . . . O 144 Tr Boeth. II.2 3
Fill all the starry Lamps with double Blaze; . . . . O 322 Irene 8
Fill all the Starry Lamps with Fav'ring Sky . . . . . O 364 Irene V 27
' <Radiance>.
LAND
For who would leave, unbrib'd, Hibernia's land, . . . O 9 London 9
To such, the Plunder of a Land is giv'n, ... O 13 London V 65
The land of heroes and of saints survey; . . . . . . O 15 London 100
Swift o'er the land the dismal rumour flies, ... O 19 London 196
Refund the plunder of the beggar'd land. . . . . . O 19 London 201
Refund the plunder of the begger'd land. . . . . . O 19 London V 201
And stretch thy prospects o'er the smiling land, . . . O 20 London 214
And stretch thy prospects o'er your fruitfull land, . . Y 58 London V 214
Whose Ways and Means support the sinking land; . . . . O 21 London 245
Whose Ways and Means support a sinking land; . . . . Y 60 London V 245
The tide retiring, calls me from the land: . . . . . O 22 London 255
And dubious title shakes the madded land, ... O 31 Vanity Wishes 30
From dubious titles shakes the madded land, ... Y 93 Vanity Wishes V 30
None fiercer Juba's thirsty land, ... O 66 Hor I Ode xxii 15
None e'er more fierce Numidia's land, ... O 66 Hor I Ode xxii V 15
No Beast more fierce Numidia's Land, ... O 67 To A. Fuscus 15
His own hereditary Land, ... O 71 Hor. Epode II 6
By secret charms our native land attracts. . . . . . O 135 Tr Rambler 122 1
Thine, Minos, is the main, and thine the land. . . . . O 136 Tr Rambler 129 4
If there be any Land, as Fame reports, ... O 256 Irene 55
A happy Land, where circulating Pow'r . . . . . O 256 Irene 57
Each Land that smiles beneath benigner Skies . . . . O 366 Irene V 12
And in some distant Land obscurely die. . . . . . . O 274 Irene 49
Whose direfull rage destroy'd my native land. . . . . Y 18 Tr. Iliad Bk 6 29
Against th' invading birds their native land: . . . . Y 23 Tr Add. Battle 37
And Death exulting stalk'd along the land. . . . . . Y 23 Tr Add. Battle 53
Their wings extend themselves across the land. . . . . Y 24 Tr Add. Battle 79
LANDLORD
The richest Landlord on the banks of Trent? . . . . . O 35 Vanity Wishes V 124

		PAGE	TITLE	LINE
LANDLORD	(CONTINUED)			
	The wealthiest landlord on the banks of Trent?	Y 97	Vanity Wishes	V 124
LANDS				
	For such in distant lands the Britons shine, ...	O 39	Vanity Wishes	181
	For these in distant lands the Britons shine, ...	Y 100	Vanity Wishes	V 181
	And shews his miseries in distant lands;	O 41	Vanity Wishes	212
	And hides his miseries in distant lands;	Y 102	Vanity Wishes	V 212
	His bonds of debt, and mortgages of lands;	O 44	Vanity Wishes	288
	His liquid wealth o'er barbarous lands.	O 65	Hor I Ode xxii	8
	His liquid Wealth thro' barbarous Lands.	O 66	To A. Fuscus	8
	From bold invaders clear'd th' Italian lands	O 78	Festina Lente	19
	Infest the barren Lands.	O 79	Feast St Simon	42
	Reserv'd, for other Lands, the Scourge of Heav'n. . .	O 315	Irene	5
LANE	**SEE DRURY-LANE**			
LANGUAGE				
	If Truths like these with pleasing Language join; . . .	O 246	Irene Prologue	15
	And every language toils to flatter me.	Y 136	Irene	V 32B
	Has taught my Slave the Language of Command!	O 323	Irene	2
	Then shall you feel what Language cannot utter, . . .	O 326	Irene	43
LANGUAGES				
	Toils all its languages to flatter me.	Y 136	Irene	V 29
LANGUID				
	Tea, scandal, ivory teeth, and languid airs;	O 84	Epi Dist Moth.	19
	Revive the languid Flow'rs; thus Nature shone . . .	O 314	Irene	3
LANGUISH				
	Still languish in our Chains, and dream of Freedom, . .	O 282	Irene	4
	And this is my Reward--to burn, to languish, ...	O 285	Irene	1
	To languish out the tedious hours of life	O 357	Irene	V 14
	Go, languish on in dull Obscurity;	O 292	Irene	98
	Nor languish o'er irreparable Ruins;	O 320	Irene	17
LANGUISHING				
	No cloudy Doubts, or languishing Delays;	O 271	Irene	27
LARGER				
	My soul could animate a larger frame	Y 132	Irene	V 41A
LASCIVIOUS				
	That range lascivious through the lonesome	Y 7	Virgil Daphnis	V 50
	roads			
LASH				
	Endur'd the stinging lash, and tamely bore the yoke. . .	Y 6	Virgil Daphnis	14
LASHES				
	The waves he lashes, and enchains the wind;	O 42	Vanity Wishes	232
LAST				
	But will not Britain hear the last appeal, ...	O 34	Vanity Wishes	91
	And his last sighs reproach the faith of kings. . .	O 35	Vanity Wishes	120
	And his last words reproach the faith of kings. . .	Y 96	Vanity Wishes	V 120
	Till captive Science yields her last retreat;	O 37	Vanity Wishes	144
	Nor deem, when learning her last prize bestows, . .	O 38	Vanity Wishes	165
	Nor think though learning her last prize bestows, . .	Y 99	Vanity Wishes	V 165
	Wreaths which at last the dear-bought right convey . .	O 40	Vanity Wishes	189
	The watchful guests still hint the last offence. . .	O 44	Vanity Wishes	279
	The treachrous guests still hint the last offence, . .	Y 104	Vanity Wishes	V 279
	Till pitying Nature signs the last release, ...	O 45	Vanity Wishes	309
	In life's last scene what prodigies surprise, . . .	O 45	Vanity Wishes	315
	At last, a fleeting gleam, or empty sound.	O 62	Pro Word Wise	V 20
	From you my labours wait their last reward.	O 141	Tr Rambler 208	2
	That slowly grows, which must for ever last. . . .	O 142	In Baretti Bk.	10
	Yet hear, at last, this mournful truth, ...	O 159	Par Hermit III	V 9
	Snatch thy pleasures while they last;	O 194	On Thrale Hat	2
	Snatch your pleasures while they last;	O 194	On Thrale Hat	V 2
	Ling'ring year at last is flown, ...	O 196	Song Congratu.	2
	You can hang or drown at last.	O 197	Song Congratu.	28
	The last Corruption of degenerate Man!	O 249	Irene	15
	O may her Beauties last unchang'd by Time, ...	O 262	Irene	11
	In his last Agonies the gasping Coward, ...	O 272	Irene	14
	To cant, at last, of Reason to a Lover?	O 281	Irene	34
	Now let us wait the last Award of Heav'n, ...	O 302	Irene	113
	Pursue the last Remains of ling'ring Light.	O 302	Irene	4
	See the last Witness of thy Guilt and Fear	O 326	Irene	2
	These Tears, these Pangs, these last Remains of Life, .	O 329	Irene	53
	Heard her last Cries, and fann'd her dying Beauties, . .	O 333	Irene	47
LASTING				
	But left, like Egypt's Kings, a lasting Tomb. . . .	O 51	Pro Drury-Lane	16
	Yet Bards like these aspir'd to lasting Praise, . . .	O 52	Pro Drury-Lane	23
	And the long honours of a lasting name	O 82	Young Author	V 12
	Thy pleasures, lasting, as they're great, ...	O 100	Ode Friendship	V 23
LATE				
	Approve it only--'tis too late to praise.	O 62	Pro Word Wise	16
	This thought once form'd, all counsel comes too late, .	O 82	Young Author	19
	Lamenting Av'rice now too late discovers	O 250	Irene	26
	--When of late The storm of Heav'ns displeasure thundred	Y 136	Irene	V 27
	on you.			
	And wish too late for Innocence and Peace?	O 294	Irene	133
	He wears of late Resentment on his Brow, ...	O 311	Irene	9
	So late admir'd and prais'd, alas! in vain!	Y 4	On a Daffodill	24
	Where late the lilies mix'd with violets smil'd. . . .	Y 7	Virgil Daphnis	25
LATELY				
	When, lately, Stella's form display'd	O 122	Stella Mourn.	1
	Which lately bless'd my gentle Government, ...	O 257	Irene	75
	How am I chang'd! How lately did Irene	O 322	Irene	13
LATEST				
	And ask the latest fashion of the heart, ...	O 46	Vanity Wishes	328

```
LATEST          (CONTINUED)                                    PAGE    TITLE            LINE
     And wing thy latest Pray'r to pitying Heav'n.  . . . . .  O 322 Irene              62
LATIAN
     Preserv'd the reliques of the Latian state  . . . . . .  O  78 Festina Lente       18
LATIN
     A Translation Of The Latin Epitaph On Sir Thomas  . . .  O 117 Epitaph Hanmer       T
        Hanmer
LATONA'S
     To great Latona's son, and two to you;  . . . . . .      Y   7 Virgil Daphnis      44
LAUD
     Rebellion's vengeful talons seize on Laud.  . . . . . .  O  39 Vanity Wishes      168
LAUGH
     And strive in vain to laugh at H<erve>y's jest.  . . .   O  13 London              74
     And strive in vain to laugh at Clodio's jest.  . . . .   O  13 London           V  74
     Thou who couldst laugh where want enchain'd caprice,  .  O  32 Vanity Wishes       53
     In bed we laugh, in bed we cry,  . . . . . . . . .       O 184 Tr. Benserade        1
LAUGHING
     Soft Pleasure with her laughing train,  . . . . . .      O 125 An Ode               6
LAUGHS
     Ev'ry name that laughs at Care,  . . . . . . . . .       O 196 Song Congratu.      10
     And laughs and wantons in the Jaws of Death.  . . . .    O 283 Irene               11
LAUGHTER
     To shake with laughter ere the jest they hear,  . . . . O  16 London             140
     And unexhausted laughter, and edge the piercing gibe  .  Y  94 Vanity Wishes    V  62
     Horrid as a murd'rers dreams, madman's laughter  . . .   Y 133 Irene            V  13
LAUREAT
     The laureat tribe in servile verse relate,  . . . . .    O  19 London             198
     The laureat tribe in venal verse relate,  . . . . . .    O  19 London           V 198
     While Crowds aloft the laureat Bust behold,  . . . . .   O  58 Prologue Comus      23
     While Crowds aloft the laureat Dust behold,  . . . . .   O  58 Prologue Comus   V  23
LAUREL
     To Eliza plucking Laurel in Mr Pope's Gardens  . . . .   O 106 Eliza plucking       T
     Her conscious hand his laurel leaves invite.  . . . .    O 106 Eliza plucking       4
LAURELS
     Swiftly he sees the imagin'd laurels spread,  . . . .    O  82 Young Author        21
LAVES
     That laves proud Ilion with his rapid flood,  . . . .    Y  18 Tr. Iliad Bk 6      12
LAVISH
     Wit, brav'ry, worth, his lavish tongue bestows;  . . .   O  16 London             126
     After your death, the lavish heir  . . . . . . . .       O  69 Hor.II Ode 14       25
     Who shine, by lavish lovers drest,  . . . . . . . .      O 126 To Lyce, Lady        3
     Lavish of your Grandsire's guineas,  . . . . . . .       O 196 Song Congratu.      11
     Lavish of thy Grandsire's guineas,  . . . . . . . .      O 196 Song Congratu.   V  11
     Forbear this lavish Pomp of dreadful Praise;  . . . .    O 268 Irene               33
     And Heav'n forbids to lavish Life away,  . . . . . .     O 321 Irene               49
LAVISH'D
     Where Commerce lavish'd unexhausted Plenty,  . . . . .   O 251 Irene               64
     Were all our Favours lavish'd on a Villain?  . . . . .   O 272 Irene               12
LAVISHES
     Where Beauty lavishes her pow'rs  . . . . . . . .        O 120 To Miss Playin       3
LAW
     This, only this, the rigid law pursues,  . . . . . .     O  17 London             160
     This, only this, the rigid law persues,  . . . . . .     O  17 London           V 160
     Law in his voice, and fortune in his hand:  . . . . .    O  34 Vanity Wishes      100
     Him no contentious suits in law  . . . . . . . . .       O  71 Hor. Epode II       13
     Could cancell their irrevocable Law.  . . . . . . .      O  76 Tr Add. Battle      40
     Love alone to Love is Law:  . . . . . . . .              O 150 Tr Boet III.12      48
     Where King and People own one common Law  . . . . .      O 352 Irene            V  16
     With pious Warmth receive our Prophet's Law----  . . .   O 262 Irene               25
LAWGIVER
     This Pilgrimage our Lawgiver ordain'd--  . . . . . .     O 264 Irene               23
LAWLESS
     And lawless Passion, hold the Sword of Justice.  . . .   O 256 Irene               54
LAWN
     In sober state th' imaginary lawn  . . . . . . . .       Y  98 Vanity Wishes    V138B
LAWS
     For gold the hireling judge distorts the laws;  . . . .  O  31 Vanity Wishes       26
     Where change of fav'rites made no change of laws,  . . . O  33 Vanity Wishes       59
     These goods for man the laws of heav'n ordain,  . . . .  O  48 Vanity Wishes      365
     The Drama's Laws the Drama's Patrons give,  . . . . .    O  53 Pro Drury-Lane      53
     Kings change their Laws, and Kingdoms change their  . .  O 110 To Posterity        16
        Kings.
     But what Laws can Lovers awe?  . . . . . . . . .         O 150 Tr Boet III.12      47
     A feeble Government, eluded Laws,  . . . . . . . .       O 250 Irene               37
     Where common Laws restrain the Prince and Subject,  . .  O 256 Irene               56
     The Laws of Kindness, break the Bonds of Nature?  . . .  O 280 Irene               16
     Would break the sacred laws of peace and  . . . . .      O 352 Irene            V   3
        order
     When social Laws first harmonis'd the World,  . . . .    O 291 Irene               70
     They give the nations laws, and view serene  . . . . .   Y 167 Irene            V 117
     The Laws unread, and flies to his Irene.  . . . . . .    O 296 Irene                2
LAY
     Their ambush here relentless ruffians lay,  . . . . .    O   9 London              15
     Lay siege to life and press the dire blockade;  . . . .  O  44 Vanity Wishes      284
     She saw great Faustus lay the Ghost of Wit:  . . . . .   O  52 Pro Drury-Lane      36
     Unknown, unheeded, long his Offspring lay,  . . . . .    O  58 Prologue Comus      25
     Yet, lay the sonnet for an hour aside,  . . . . . .      O 142 In Baretti Bk.       7
     Which erst in Frost and Freedom lay,  . . . . . . .      O 146 Tr Boeth III.5       8
     Lay pointed at our Batt'ries yet unform'd,  . . . . .    O 273 Irene               25
     And lay the tow'ring Sultaness aside,  . . . . . . .     O 289 Irene                8
     Who charges Guilt! lay by this proud Resentment  . . .   O 323 Irene                8
```

```
                                            PAGE    TITLE              LINE
LAYS
    At length our mighty Bard's victorious Lays  . . . . .    O  57  Prologue Comus     15
    Let them prolong their turgid lays . . . . . . . .       O  78  Feast St Simon      4
    Which gild a lover's lays,  . . . . . . . .             O 126  To Lyce, Lady       6
    Polish'd with endless toil, my lays  . . . . . .       O 139  Tr Rambler 169      1
    I first attempt in never-dying lays  . . . . . .       Y  22  Tr Add. Battle     16
LAZY
    And scorns the lazy Hermit's cheap Devotion;    . . . .  O 264  Irene              28
    That fatal Mistress of the Young, the Lazy,  . . . . .  O 283  Irene              21
LEAD
    This scarce I lead, who left on yonder rock  . . . . .  O  64  Virgil Past.I      19
    Lead a long and peaceful Age,  . . . . . . . .         O 145  Tr Boeth. II.4     21
    Demetrius will not lead me to Dishonour;  . . . . . .  O 256  Irene              35
    O lead me quickly to the Scene of Fate;  . . . . . .   O 259  Irene             105
    Lead us to Danger, and abash their Victors?  . . . .   O 284  Irene              43
    Holds out her Hand to lead thee back to Truth.  . . .  O 321  Irene              42
    Confess your Crime, or lead me to the Sultan,  . . .   O 326  Irene              41
    And lead thy Troops victorious round the World.  . .   O 333  Irene              41
LEADER
    Then rises the brave leader of their hosts  . . . . .  Y  24  Tr Add. Battle     80
LEADER'S
    The Greeks disorder'd by their Leader's Absence,  . . . O 304  Irene              10
LEADS
    Claim leads to claim, and pow'r advances pow'r;  . . . O  34  Vanity Wishes     106
    And fatal Learning leads him to the block:  . . . . .  O  39  Vanity Wishes     172
LEAF
    New verdure ev'ry fading leaf shall fill,  . . . . .   Y   4  On a Daffodill     19
LEAFLESS
    The naked hills, the leafless grove,  . . . . . . .    O 123  Winter's Walk       3
LEAGUE
    Sure all unite to hold her League of Rule  . . . . .   O 257  Irene              62
    The Bowl shall circle to confirm our League,  . . . .  O 308  Irene              29
    League with our Chiefs, and propagate Sedition?  . . . O 312  Irene               3
LEANING
    And columns leaning from their central firmness  . . . Y 114  Irene           V 45A
LEAR
    Perhaps, where Lear has rav'd, and Hamlet dy'd,  . . . O  53  Pro Drury-Lane     43
LEARN
    When senators and nobles learn to fear;  . . . . . .   O  59  Pro Good Nat'd    V 4B
    And learn his virtues, while thou mourn'st his end.  . O 117  Epitaph Hanmer      4
    Here let me learn the use of life,  . . . . . . . .    O 125  An Ode             27
    Here let me learn to shun the crimes  . . . . . . .    O 126  An Ode             35
    Learn here how Heav'n supports the virtuous Mind,  . . O 246  Irene Prologue      9
    Learn here what Anguish racks the guilty Breast,  . .  O 246  Irene Prologue     11
    Learn here that Peace from Innocence must flow;  . .   O 246  Irene Prologue     13
    We learn to shudder at the rustling Breeze,  . . . .   O 266  Irene              29
    Learn, that the present Hour alone is Man's.  . . . .  O 283  Irene              33
    And learn the Rev'rence due to Turkey's Queen.  . . .  O 322  Irene              55
    Dispatch, and learn a fitter Time for Pity.  . . . .   O 328  Irene              44
    From his Escape learn thou the Pow'r of Virtue,  . .   O 330  Irene              24
    May storms howl gently o'er and learn to spare.  . .   Y   3  On a Daffodill      8
LEARN'D
    Let----live here, for----has learn'd to live.  . . .   O  11  London             50
    Long since I learn'd to slight this fleeting breath,  .O  74  Tr. Iliad Bk 6      9
    As learn'd Eliza, sister of the Muse,  . . . . . . .   O 106  Eliza plucking      1
    And leave my labours to the learn'd and wise,  . . .   O 141  Tr Rambler 208      2
    Nor fear the Fair and Learn'd can want Protection.  .  O 302  Irene             115
LEARNING
    And pause awhile from Learning to be wise;  . . . . .  O  38  Vanity Wishes    V 158
    Nor deem, when learning her last prize bestows,  . .   O  38  Vanity Wishes     165
    Nor deem, when learning her lost prize bestows,  . .   O  38  Vanity Wishes   V 165
    Nor think though learning her last prize bestows,  .   Y  99  Vanity Wishes   V 165
    And fatal Learning leads him to the block:  . . . . .  O  39  Vanity Wishes     172
    His learning, join'd with each endearing art,  . . .   O 117  Epitaph Hanmer      7
LEARNING'S
    When Learning's Triumph o'er her barb'rous Foes  . .   O  51  Pro Drury-Lane      1
LEARNT
    Listing forests learnt the Strain,  . . . . . . .     O 148  Tr Boet III.12    V  9
LEAST
    Be kind, ye judges, or at least be just:  . . . . .   O  61  Pro Word Wise       8
    Thy charms at least, fair F<irebrac>e, might inspire  .O 107  Lady F Assizes      3
    At least you rescue from your heir.  . . . . . . .    O 232  Tr Horace IV.7     20
    Be this at least his Praise; be this his Pride;  . .   O 246  Irene Prologue     21
    At least this Day be calm--If we succeed,  . . . . .   O 260  Irene             141
LEAVE
    For who would leave, unbrib'd, Hibernia's land,  . .   O   9  London              9
    And leave your little All to flames a prey;  . . . .   O  18  London            189
    But leave to heav'n the measure and the choice,  . .   O  47  Vanity Wishes     352
    And leave our pleasing fields and native home,  . . . O  64  Virgil Past.I       4
    Leave off, at length, these woman's sighs,  . . . . . O  68  Hor. II Ode IX     17
    You'll leave together with your life,  . . . . . . .  O  69  Hor.II Ode 14      23
    Breathless at length they leave th' unfinish'd war  . O  76  Tr Add. Battle      6
    With me retire and leave the pomp of courts  . . . .  O 137  Tr Rambler 138      1
    Leave to the schools their atoms and their void.  . . O 140  Tr Rambler 180      2
    And leave my labours to the learn'd and wise,  . . .  O 141  Tr Rambler 208      2
    That leave the blame of rigour to the prince,  . . .  O 176  Tr Metastas II     10
    And leave no Place for Perfidy or Fear.  . . . . . .  O 255  Irene              33
    Leave to perform my Pilgrimage to Mecca;  . . . . .   O 258  Irene              87
    Then leave him stretch'd upon the ling'ring Rack,  .  O 273  Irene              36
    Implor'd my Leave to visit Mecca's Temple;  . . . .   O 273  Irene              44
    Leave but this Maid, resign a hopeless Claim,  . . .  O 319  Irene              25
```

	PAGE	TITLE	LINE
LEAVE (CONTINUED)			
Leave Slav'ry, Guilt, and Infamy behind.	O 320	Irene	31
But 'tis not mine to judge--I scorn and leave thee. . .	O 324	Irene	22
When all conspiring leave Maeon's lake	Y 24	Tr Add. Battle	66
LEAVES			
And ev'ry moment leaves my little less;	O 10	London	40
And leaves, unseen, a dagger in your breast. . . .	O 21	London	241
And leaves the wealthy traytor in the Tow'r, ...	O 32	Vanity Wishes	34
And leaves the bonny Traytor in the Tow'r, ...	O 32	Vanity Wishes	V 34
The vanquish'd hero leaves his broken bands, ...	O 41	Vanity Wishes	211
Th' incumber'd oar scarce leaves the dreaded coast . .	O 42	Vanity Wishes	239
Her Grandsire leaves her in Britannia's Arms, ...	O 58	Prologue Comus	34
Her conscious hand his laurel leaves invite. . . .	O 106	Eliza plucking	4
Frail as the leaves that quiver on the sprays, . . .	O 138	Tr Rambler 161	1
Leaves the Load of Earth behind.	O 147	Tr Boet III.12	4
"Under leaves to hide one's head, ...	O 185	Anacreon Ode 9	27
"As it leaves Anacreon's lip, ...	O 185	Anacreon Ode 9	32
Sooner these trembling Leaves shall find a Voice, . .	O 255	Irene	26
Sooner the trembling Leaves shall find a Voice, . . .	O 373	Irene	V 19
And leaves the lovely Trifler unregarded	O 276	Irene	23
And then leaves the glittering reptile, reasoning . . . insect	Y 146	Irene	V 23
And then leaves your actions the busy trifler . . . . unregarded	O 355	Irene	V 12
Ye swains! bestrow the ground with leaves and spread . .	Y 7	Virgil Daphnis	26
LED			
And fame pursu'd him, where conviction led.	O 118	Epitaph Hanmer	34
And led me to the Shore where Cali stood, ...	O 254	Irene	127
Now led astray by hopes fallacious glimm'rings . . .	Y 148	Irene	V 43A
And what protecting angel led thee hither	Y 170	Irene	V 33
Thrice to the wall their dreadfull hosts have led . .	Y 19	Tr. Iliad Bk 6	56
LEFT			
And rights submitted, left him none to seize.	O 34	Vanity Wishes	108
He left the name, at which the world grew pale, . . .	O 41	Vanity Wishes	221
But left, like Egypt's Kings, a lasting Tomb.	O 51	Pro Drury-Lane	16
This scarce I lead, who left on yonder rock	O 64	Virgil Past.I	19
And frighted, left upon the field, ...	O 73	Hor. Epode II	66
Looks back on what She left behind, ...	O 150	Tr Boet III.12	57
Nor made a pause, nor left a void;	O 201	Death Dr Levet	26
Left by the Hand of Heav'n on human Clay.	O 255	Irene	13
Prais'd without Rapture, left without Regret.	O 263	Irene	18
Nor left us aught but Flattery and State.	O 291	Irene	73
Aspasia left her sighing in his Arms, ...	O 303	Irene	29
Has left the slaves behind, nay then there's danger. . .	Y 198	Irene	V 34
LEFT-HAND			
And left-hand crows, from an old hollow oak, ...	O 65	Virgil Past.I	24
LEGACY			
And scarce a legacy can bribe to hear;	O 44	Vanity Wishes	278
LEGENDS			
To form new Legends, sanctify new Crimes, ...	O 309	Irene	33
LEGIONS			
With unexpected legions bursts away, ...	O 42	Vanity Wishes	243
With unexpected legions pow'rs away, ...	Y 103	Vanity Wishes	V 243
Pour forth their Legions, and the roaring Danube . . .	O 264	Irene	17
Pour forth the Legions and the Wondring Danube	O 353	Irene	V 1
That day what legions by his faulchion bled!	Y 25	Tr Add. Battle	120
LEISURE			
Ere yet the Foe found Leisure to be cruel, ...	O 252	Irene	94
Nor give him Leisure for another Crime.	O 271	Irene	32
For idle Hours, and crush him at my Leisure.	O 275	Irene	71
Him I can crush at leisure.	O 367	Irene	V 30
the Tyrant leisure --	O 357	Irene	V 7
There shall soft Leisure wing th' excursive Soul, . . .	O 302	Irene	118
LEND			
And lend a lye the confidence of truth.	O 12	London	56
LENDER			
There the Lender grave and sly.	O 196	Song Congratu.	16
LENGTH			
Resolved at length, from vice and London far, ...	O 9	London	5
At length awaking, with contemptuous frown, ...	O 10	London	33
At length his sov'reign frowns--the train of state . .	O 34	Vanity Wishes	109
But did not Chance at length her error mend?	O 41	Vanity Wishes	215
But forc'd at length her antient Reign to quit, . . .	O 52	Pro Drury-Lane	35
At length our mighty Bard's victorious Lays	O 57	Prologue Comus	15
Leave off, at length, these woman's sighs;	O 68	Hor. II Ode IX	17
At length the undaunted Scythian yields, ...	O 68	Hor. II Ode IX	22
Breathless at length they leave th' unfinish'd war . .	O 76	Tr Add. Battle	6
At length deform'd with many a grisly wound	O 76	Tr Add. Battle	24
At length must Suffolk's beauties shine in vain, . . .	O 107	Lady F Assizes	1
Age call'd at length his active mind to rest, ...	O 118	Epitaph Hanmer	35
At length aspire to Mantuan praise.	O 139	Tr Rambler 169	2
Contemns at length the treachrous toys, ...	O 145	Tr Boet III.1	11
Till at length stern Pluto cried, ...	O 149	Tr Boet III.12	39
Years at length are flown, ...	O 196	Song Congratu.	V 2
At length the Conqueror has spent his . . . . . . rage--	O 350	Irene	V 8
At length rekindled his accustom'd Fury, ...	O 259	Irene	110
Gain'd all his Heart; at length his eager Love . . .	O 259	Irene	123
For what is Length of Days without Irene?	O 262	Irene	6
And though at length subdued, elude thy Vengeance. . .	O 274	Irene	57
At length th' unwilling Sun resigns the World	O 302	Irene	1

188

```
LENGTH          (CONTINUED)                        PAGE    TITLE           LINE
   At length the Prize is mine--The haughty Maid  .  .  .  .   O 317 Irene             1
LENITIVES
   Diffuse the tuneful lenitives of pain:     .  .  .  .  .  .   O  43 Vanity Wishes    268
   And yield the tuneful lenitives of pain:   .  .  .  .  .  .   O  43 Vanity Wishes  V 268
   Diffuse the soothin lenitives of pain:     .  .  .  .  .  .   Y 104 Vanity Wishes  V 268
   Such are Love's Joys, the Lenitives of Life,  .  .  .  .   O 277 Irene            47
LENT
   Think them a sacred Treasure lent by Heav'n,  .  .  .  .   O 302 Irene             6
LENTE
   Festina Lente  .  .  .  .  .  .  .  .  .  .  .  .  .  .   O  77 Festina Lente      T
LEONTARES
   With Christian blood, let Leontares dye.   .  .  .  .  .   Y 129 Irene          V  26
   Confest--confest by dying Leontares   .  .  .  .  .  .   O 356 Irene          V  31
LEONTIUS
   Can brave Leontius call for airy Wonders,  .  .  .  .   O 250 Irene            42
   'Twas Vice that shook our Nerves, 'twas Vice, Leontius  .   O 251 Irene            56
   To heav'n and earth the courage of Leontius  .  .  .   Y 120 Irene          V 31B
   Leontius stay.  .  .  .  .  .  .  .  .  .  .  .  .  .   O 256 Irene            38
   A Galley mann'd with Greeks, thy charge, Leontius,  .   O 258 Irene            81
   Invest Leontius with his new Command;   .  .  .  .   O 260 Irene           144
   What Passions reign among thy Crew, Leontius?  .  .  .   O 270 Irene            21
   With cautious Secrecy, Leontius steer  .  .  .  .  .   O 284 Irene            50
   Return with speed, Leontius, to your Charge;  .  .  .   O 304 Irene             9
   Why has thy Choice then pointed out Leontius,  .  .  .   O 305 Irene            20
   Despis'd and curs'd, Leontius must descend  .  .  .  .   O 305 Irene            27
   Can brave Leontius be the Slave of Glory?  .  .  .  .   O 305 Irene            30
   Succeed, my Friend, unenvied by Leontius.  .  .  .  .   O 306 Irene            48
LEONTIUS'
   His groaning Country claims Leontius' Aid;  .  .  .  .   O 270 Irene            17
   Dares join Leontius' Name with Fear or Falsehood?  .  .  .   O 304 Irene            13
LESS
   And ev'ry moment leaves my little less;  .  .  .  .  .   O  10 London           40
   For less than rent the dungeons of the Strand;  .  .  .   O  20 London          215
   For less than hires the dungeons of the Strand;  .  .  .   Y  58 London        V 215
   Less heard and less, the faint remonstrance falls;  .  .  .   O  46 Vanity Wishes    334
   Less heard and less, the faint remonstrance falls;  .  .  .   O  46 Vanity Wishes    334
   For I shall never think him less than God;  .  .  .  .   O  64 Virgil Past.I     8
   There begs of heav'n a less distinguish'd lot;  .  .  .   O  82 Young Author     29
   Not less capricious than a reigning fair,  .  .  .  .   O  95 Sprig of Myrtl     5
   Not less capricious than the reigning fair,  .  .  .  .   O  95 Sprig of Myrtl   V  5
   And I but flatter less.   .  .  .  .  .  .  .  .  .   O 127 To Lyce, Lady    24
   Less pleas'd to triumph than to spare.   .  .  .  .  .   O 137 Tr Rambler 143    2
   The more I honour·thee, the less I love.   .  .  .  .   O 140 Tr Rambler 188    1
   Nor think our wishes less sincere.   .  .  .  .  .  .   O 188 Epilogue          4
   My Vows, 'tis true, she hears with less Aversion,  .  .  .   O 287 Irene             7
   Reason commands to cast the less away;   .  .  .  .  .   O 290 Irene            33
LEST
   Lest scarce the exhausted should rope supply.  .  .  .  .   Y  60 London        V 243
   Lest ropes be wanting in the tempting spring,  .  .  .   O  22 London          246
   But, lest I fall by subtler foes,   .  .  .  .  .  .  .   O 126 An Ode           37
   Lest on himself the destin'd stroke descend.  .  .  .   O 139 Tr Rambler 168    2
   Lest unacquainted with our bold Attempt,  .  .  .  .   O 285 Irene            12
   Lest baneful discord crush our 'infant Scheme,  .  .  .   O 299 Irene            52
   Lest unrewarded Mercy lose its Charms.   .  .  .  .  .   O 313 Irene            19
   Who fearst lest I should gain, or thou  .  .  .  .  .   Y 198 Irene          V  32
   Depart, Demetrius, lest my Fate involve thee,  .  .  .   O 320 Irene            13
   I go, lest Vengeance urge my Hand to Blood,  .  .  .  .   O 324 Irene            23
   And speed the Stroke lest Mercy should o'ertake them.  .   O 333 Irene            54
LET
   Let----live here, for----has learn'd to live.  .  .  .  .   O  11 London           50
   Here let those reign, whom pensions can incite  .  .  .   O  11 London           51
   Let such raise palaces, and manors buy,  .  .  .  .  .   O  12 London           57
   Quick let us rise, the happy seats explore,  .  .  .  .   O  18 London          174
   Let observation with extensive view,  .  .  .  .  .   O  30 Vanity Wishes      1
   Let hist'ry tell where rival kings command,  .  .  .  .   O  31 Vanity Wishes     29
   Around his tomb let Art and Genius weep,  .  .  .  .   O  39 Vanity Wishes    173
   How just his hopes let Swedish Charles decide;  .  .  .  .   O  40 Vanity Wishes    192
   Ah! let not Censure term our Fate our Choice,  .  .  .   O  53 Pro Drury-Lane    51
   Let Wit, condemn'd the feeble War to wage  .  .  .  .   O  57 Prologue Comus     7
   Let Study, worn with Virtue's fruitless Lore,  .  .  .   O  57 Prologue Comus     9
   Let no resentful petulance invade  .  .  .  .  .  .   O  61 Pro Word Wise      9
   Let no revengeful petulance invade  .  .  .  .  .  .   O  61 Pro Word Wise    V  9
   Let one great payment every claim appease,  .  .  .  .   O  62 Pro Word Wise     11
   Let Reason with superiour force controul  .  .  .  .   O  77 Festina Lente      7
   Let vulgar Poets sing,  .  .  .  .  .  .  .  .  .  .   O  78 Feast St Simon     3
   Let them prolong their turgid lays  .  .  .  .  .  .   O  78 Feast St Simon     4
   No more let coquets to themselves be blind,  .  .  .  .   O  81 Lady Birthday     18
   Nor let disdain sit low'ring in your eye;  .  .  .  .   O  84 Epi Dist Moth.    43
   And let the tortures of mistrust  .  .  .  .  .  .  .   O 100 Ode Friendship    15
   Great George's acts let tuneful Cibber sing;  .  .  .  .   O 114 On C. Cibber      3
   "And let the goddess trust her eyes."  .  .  .  .  .   O 122 Stella Mourn.      6
   Here let me thro' the vales pursue  .  .  .  .  .  .   O 125 An Ode           21
   Here let me learn the use of life,  .  .  .  .  .  .   O 125 An Ode           27
   Here let me learn to shun the crimes  .  .  .  .  .   O 126 An Ode           35
   Let Lyce share the praise.  .  .  .  .  .  .  .  .  .   O 126 To Lyce, Lady     8
   Let pain deserv'd without complaint be borne.  .  .  .   O 131 Tr. Rambler 32    1
   The skies are open--let us try the skies:  .  .  .  .   O 136 Tr Rambler 129    5
   Let ev'ry piece be simple and be one.  .  .  .  .  .   O 137 Tr Rambler 139    1
   Let Caesar spread his conquests far,  .  .  .  .  .   O 137 Tr Rambler 143    1
   "Let me now my pinions ply,  .  .  .  .  .  .  .  .  .   O 186 Anacreon Ode 9    43
```

LET   (CONTINUED)   PAGE   TITLE   LINE

Entry	PAGE	TITLE		LINE
Let it wander as it will;	O 196	Song Congratu.		18
Let it wander if it will;	O 196	Song Congratu.	V	18
Let him persuade me to it--if he can:	O 247	Irene Epilogue		4
Yet let me think--I see the helpless Maid,	O 252	Irene		80
Aspasia calls me, let me fly to save her.	O 259	Irene		107
But, Cali, let Irene share thy Prayers;	O 262	Irene		5
With Christian blood, let Leontares dye.	Y 129	Irene	V	26
There let Aspasia, since my Fair entreats it,	O 263	Irene		3
Let Prudence moderate, though not suppress.	O 264	Irene		34
Let nobler Hopes and juster Fears succeed,	O 265	Irene		9
Let fierce resentment aid	Y 133	Irene	V	9
Let artful Flatt'ry now, to lull Suspicion,	O 267	Irene		2
Swift, let us rush upon the careless Tyrant,	O 271	Irene		31
Then let us now resolve, nor idly waste	O 271	Irene		33
Then let us now resolve, nor idle waste	O 271	Irene	V	33
Conduct her hither, let no rude Intrusion	O 272	Irene		13
Now let him go, pursu'd by silent Wrath,	O 274	Irene		47
Let not th' unbounded Greatness of his Mind	O 275	Irene		72
Conceal the Gem; let female Arrogance	O 277	Irene		33
Then let me once, in honour of our Sex,	O 277	Irene		49
Then Let me once to right our injur'd Sex	O 356	Irene	V	16
Let Pleasure bloom and Cities reascend.	O 372	Irene	V	10
Pants for the dread Event--But let us reason--	O 280	Irene		31
Nor let Demetrius know thee for a Rival.	O 282	Irene		71
Let Prudence, ere the Suit be farther urg'd,	O 285	Irene		8
Ah! let me rather seek the Convent's Cell;	O 292	Irene		93
An Let fall sometimes a tear for lost Irene	O 349	Irene	V	1
Let my blest Eyes for ever gaze--	O 294	Irene		4
No! let us die together.	O 297	Irene		11
Yet let me watch her dear departing Steps,	O 297	Irene		17
If Fate pursues me, let it find me here.	O 297	Irene		18
If Fate persues me, let it find me here	O 297	Irene	V	18
Now let us wait the last Award of Heav'n,	O 302	Irene		113
The Rights of Princes let the Sword decide,	O 307	Irene		22
Let every Tongue resound Irene's Praise,	O 308	Irene		4
Let Prudence obviate an impending Danger.	O 309	Irene		19
Call them--but let them not prolong their Tale,	O 310	Irene		8
Let no weak Doubt the gen'rous Hand restrain,	O 313	Irene		22
Let no distrust the gen'rous Hand restrain	O 377	Irene	V	3
Then let them rid them of Irene's Presence:	O 316	Irene		19
Haste, Murza, to the Palace, let the Sultan	O 319	Irene		2
Let us not struggle with th' eternal Will,	O 320	Irene		16
Here let me tend her with officious Care,	O 320	Irene		23
Let kind Compulsion terminate the Contest.	O 321	Irene		50
Come let us seek new Pleasures in the Palace,	O 323	Irene		17
O let me be but heard, nor fear from me	O 327	Irene		20
Let me but live, heap Woes on Woes upon me,	O 328	Irene		33
Let Shame and hooting Infamy pursue me,	O 328	Irene		36
Let Slav'ry harrass, and let Hunger gripe.	O 328	Irene		37
Let Slav'ry harrass, and let Hunger gripe.	O 328	Irene		37
Nor let the Crimes of this detested Day	O 329	Irene		54
But let us try to clear our clouded Brows,	O 329	Irene		10
But let no thoughtless Hint involve Abdalla.	O 329	Irene		15
Let one just Act conclude the hateful Day.	O 333	Irene		50
On his dead body let a tomb be plac'd	Y 7	Virgil Daphnis		28
Let distant regions echo with his name	Y 20	Tr. Iliad Bk 6		103
"Ah! let not tears down that fair count'nance rowl,	Y 21	Tr. Iliad Bk 6		113
There let the web and distaff be your care.	Y 21	Tr. Iliad Bk 6		122

LETTER'D

Entry	PAGE	TITLE		LINE
Nor claim the triumph of a letter'd heart;	O 37	Vanity Wishes		152
To letter'd ease retir'd, and honest mirth,	O 118	Epitaph Hanmer		37
Nor, letter'd arrogance, deny	O 201	Death Dr Levet		11
Nor, letter'd ignorance, deny	O 201	Death Dr Levet	V	11

LETTERS

Entry	PAGE	TITLE		LINE
And pause awhile from letters, to be wise;	O 38	Vanity Wishes		158
"His the letters which you see,	O 185	Anacreon Ode 9		15
"His the letters that you see,	O 185	Anacreon Ode 9	V	15

LEVELL'D

Entry	PAGE	TITLE		LINE
By Treason levell'd with the Dregs of Men.	O 311	Irene		17

LEVET

Entry	PAGE	TITLE		LINE
On the Death of Dr. Robert Levet	O 200	Death Dr Levet		T
See Levet to the grave descend;	O 201	Death Dr Levet		6

LEWD

Entry	PAGE	TITLE		LINE
While he lies melting in a lewd Embrace;	O 111	To Posterity		24
Tho' no lewd hint the mantling virgin warm.	Y 67	Prologue Lethe		14

LIB'RAL

Entry	PAGE	TITLE		LINE
Th' expanded hand of lib'ral Heav'n	Y 199	Irene	V	16

LIBATIONS

Entry	PAGE	TITLE		LINE
Libations he shall pour to Daphnis praise.	Y 7	Virgil Daphnis	V	52

LIBELS

Entry	PAGE	TITLE		LINE
With weekly libels and septennial ale,	O 34	Vanity Wishes		97

LIBERAL   SEE LIB'RAL

Entry	PAGE	TITLE		LINE
When liberal pity dignify'd delight;	O 62	Pro Word Wise		22
"But the liberal grant in vain	O 185	Anacreon Ode 9		21

LIBERTY

Entry	PAGE	TITLE		LINE
The Cause of Liberty, the Cause of Nations?	O 255	Irene		9
Virtue and Liberty engross his Soul,	O 255	Irene		32
His Friends, his Liberty, to hazard?	O 260	Irene		135
And every Voice was Liberty and Greece.	O 271	Irene		30
To tast again the sweets of liberty.	Y 19	Tr. Iliad Bk 6		41

```
                                                        PAGE    TITLE          LINE
LICENCE
     With all the Licence of Authority,  . . . . . . .  O 283  Irene             16
LICENS'D
     With warbling eunuchs fill a licens'd stage,  . . . .  O  12  London         59
LICENTIOUS
     Unlike the ribald, whose licentious jest . . . . . .  O 130  Tr. Rambler 12   1
     And shook the (affrighted) world lab'ring earth licentious  Y 115  Irene   V 49A
        conquest
     Did savage Anger, and licentious Conquest  . . . . .  O 296  Irene           30
LIE   SEE LYE
     Oft on his altar shall my firstlings lie,  . . . . .  O  64  Virgil Past.I    9
     May I lie slain, and spurn the bloody sand!  . . . .  O  75  Tr. Iliad Bk 6  30
     Pause at this tomb where Hanmer's ashes lie;  . . . .  O 117  Epitaph Hanmer   2
     Pause on this tomb where Hanmer's ashes lie;  . . . .  O 117  Epitaph Hanmer V 2
     Dim, scorn'd and impotent, his torches lie. . . . . .  O 133  Tr. Rambler 85   2
LIES
     For growing names the weekly scribbler lies, . . . .  O  33  Vanity Wishes   81
     To growing names the weekly scribbler lies, . . . . .  Y  95  Vanity Wishes V 82
     Lies at my feet, I hiss him, and he flies. . . . . .  O  60  Pro Good Nat'd  24
     Here lies a fowl transfix'd with many a wound  . . .  O  76  Tr Add. Battle  14
     While he lies melting in a lewd Embrace;  . . . . . .  O 111  To Posterity    24
     Obscure, unpriz'd, and dark, the magnet lies,  . . .  O 141  Tr Rambler 199   1
     The Hand of Art here torpid lies  . . . . . . . . . .  O 154  Epita. Hogarth   1
     The hand of him here torpid lies  . . . . . . . . . .  O 155  Epita. Hogarth V 1
     But wretched Man, when once he lies  . . . . . . . .  O 232  Tr Horace IV.7  14
     Deep in a winding Creek a Galley lies, . . . . . . .  O 254  Irene          134
     And Fate lies crouded in a narrow Space. . . . . . .  O 287  Irene            5
     Lies open to Conjecture's dubious Ken, . . . . . . .  O 300  Irene           69
     Lies in the Womb of Providence conceal'd,  . . . . .  O 313  Irene            3
     Lies as dead as any nail! . . . . . . . . . . . . . .  Y 300  Extemp. Elegy    2
     Now she lies exceeding low,  . . . . . . . . . . . .  Y 301  Extemp. Elegy   19
LIFE
     And life still vig'rous revels in my veins;  . . . .  O  10  London          42
     I drew the breath of life in English air;  . . . . .  O  15  London         118
     Here life is ventur'd if the streets you roam  . . .  Y  59  London       V 224
     And watch the busy scenes of crouded life; . . . . .  O  30  Vanity Wishes    4
     And all the busy scenes of crouded life; . . . . . .  Y  92  Vanity Wishes  V 4
     See motley life in modern trappings dress'd, . . . .  O  32  Vanity Wishes   51
     And fixed disease on Harley's closing life? . . . . .  O  36  Vanity Wishes  130
     Yet hope not life from grief or danger free, . . . .  O  37  Vanity Wishes  155
     Yet dream not life from grief or danger free,  . . .  Y  99  Vanity Wishes V 155
     There mark what ills the scholar's life assail,  . .  O  38  Vanity Wishes  159
     Hear Lydiat's life, and Galileo's end. . . . . . . .  O  38  Vanity Wishes  164
     Enlarge my life with multitude of days,  . . . . . .  O  43  Vanity Wishes  255
     That life protracted is protracted woe. . . . . . . .  O  43  Vanity Wishes  258
     Lay siege to life and press the dire blockade; . . .  O  44  Vanity Wishes  284
     Still drops some joy with with'ring time away; . . .  O  45  Vanity Wishes  306
     Each Change of many-colour'd Life he drew, . . . . .  O  51  Pro Drury-Lane   3
     Hers the mild Merits of domestic Life,  . . . . . . .  O  58  Prologue Comus  31
     Prest by the load of life, the weary mind  . . . . .  O  59  Pro Good Nat'd   1
     You'll leave together with your life, . . . . . . . .  O  69  Hor.II Ode 14   23
     If to compleat this heav'nly Life  . . . . . . . . .  O  72  Hor. Epode II   47
     Whatever course of Life great Jove allots, . . . . .  O  77  Festina Lente    1
     His various worth, through varied life attend, . . .  O 117  Epitaph Hanmer   3
     To hear his eloquence, and praise his life. . . . . .  O 118  Epitaph Hanmer  18
     Calm conscience then his former life survey'd, . . .  O 118  Epitaph Hanmer  41
     Gives all the harmony of life; . . . . . . . . . . .  O 121  To Miss Playin  32
     And screen me from the ills of life. . . . . . . . .  O 124  Winter's Walk   20
     And hide me from the sight of life.  . . . . . . . .  O 124  Winter's Walk  V 20
     Delights to catch the gales of life. . . . . . . . .  O 124  An Ode           4
     Here let me learn the use of life, . . . . . . . . .  O 125  An Ode          27
     This is the chief felicity of life,  . . . . . . . .  O 131  Tr. Rambler 45   1
     On life, on morals, be thy thoughts employ'd;  . . .  O 140  Tr Rambler 180   1
     No wealth his life from weary care can save, . . . .  O 146  Tr Boeth III.3   5
     Life to stop at Thirtyfive,  . . . . . . . . . . . .  O 178  Thrale 35 Year   6
     Life declines from Thirtyfive; . . . . . . . . . . .  O 178  Thrale 35 Year  14
     Diana calls to life in vain, . . . . . . . . . . . .  O 232  Tr Horace IV.7  26
     With gentle Hand restrain'd the Streams of Life, . .  O 252  Irene           97
     How can a single Hand attempt a Life . . . . . . . .  O 258  Irene           90
     Life. . . . . . . . . . . . . . . . . . . . . . . . .  O 260  Irene          135
     Whats Life when weighed with Greece or Aspasia?  . .  O 371  Irene        V  24
     Aspasia's thine, and all thy Life is Rapture-- . . .  O 260  Irene          142
     for the long Life and prosperity of my sovereign . .  Y 130  Irene        V 12A
     Nor couldst thou more support a Life of Sloth  . . .  O 264  Irene           19
     The Hopes and Fears, the Joys and Pains of Life, . .  O 265  Irene            7
     Despotick Rage pursues the Life of Cali; . . . . . .  O 270  Irene           16
     Still fond of Life, groan'd out the dreadful Secret, . .  O 272  Irene       16
     Still fond of Life reveal'd the dreadfull secret, . .  O 356  Irene        V 33
     Amidst the Camp to howl his Life away.  . . . . . . .  O 273  Irene           37
     Such are Love's Joys, the Lenitives of Life, . . . .  O 277  Irene           47
     And varied Life steal unperceiv'd away.  . . . . . .  O 279  Irene           91
     And turn'd th' instructive Page of Human Life, . . .  O 281  Irene           33
     The Rocks of Life, for ever flies the Port. . . . . .  O 281  Irene           47
     Trusts to my Care his Mistress and his Life, . . . .  O 283  Irene           10
     An useless Life in waiting for To-morrow,  . . . . .  O 283  Irene           23
     Completes the Gift of Freedom and of Life. . . . . .  O 285  Irene           16
     Justice demands the forfeit Life of Cali;  . . . . .  O 286  Irene           13
     Guides through the Maze of Life the Steps  . . . . .  O 346  Irene        V  6
        of Man
     Reflect that Life and Death, affecting Sounds, . . .  O 290  Irene           26
     Reflect that Life, like ev'ry other Blessing,  . . .  O 290  Irene           28
```

LIFE	(CONTINUED)		PAGE	TITLE		LINE
Thus Life, with loss of Wealth, is well preserv'd,	. .		O 290	Irene		34
And Virtue cheaply sav'd with loss of Life.	. . . . .		O 290	Irene		35
There wear the tedious Hours of Life away,	. . .		O 292	Irene		85
To languish out the tedious hours of life	. . . .		O 357	Irene	V	14
And give the short remnant of my life to	. . . . .		O 348	Irene	V	14
prayer,						
And flies for Shelter to the Shades of Life.	. . . .		O 292	Irene		102
And gave me Life--	. . . . . .		O 313	Irene		18
To tell, or hear, were Waste of Life.	. . . . .		O 316	Irene		21
The Life, which only this Design supported,	. . . .		O 316	Irene		22
And stole his Life and Mistress from his Sabre?	. .		O 318	Irene		14
Forgive, my Fair, 'tis Life, 'tis Nature calls.	. .		O 318	Irene		19
And drag away thy Life in Scorn and Safety,	. . . .		O 319	Irene		26
And test thy life in scorn and safety	. . . . . .		Y 197	Irene	V	26
Thy Life, too mean a Prey to lure Abdalla.	. . . .		O 319	Irene		27
Refuse their Office, and uncertain Life	. . . . .		O 320	Irene		21
And Heav'n forbids to lavish Life away,	. . . . .		O 321	Irene		49
Nor dare to spare the Life his Frown condemns.	. .		O 325	Irene		10
And steal thy Life away. Death's horrid Angel	. . .		O 327	Irene		9
And steal your life away. Death's horrid Angel	. .		O 368	Irene	V	17
Is then your Sov'reign's Life so cheaply rated,	. .		O 327	Irene		14
My Hopes, my Wishes, terminate in Life,	. . . . .		O 327	Irene		22
A little Life for Grief, and for Repentance.	. .		O 327	Irene		23
A little life from grief and for repentance.	. . .		Y 207	Irene	V	23
These Tears, these Pangs, these last Remains of Life,	.		O 329	Irene		53
Thy Life perhaps--Were but Irene spar'd,	. . . . . .		O 332	Irene		33
Ev'n in the bloom of life depriv'd of breath.	. . . .		Y 6	Virgil Daphnis		2
Far dearer than his own or father's life	. . . . . .		Y 18	Tr. Iliad Bk 6		6
With Hector's life away my pleasures fly.	. . . . .		Y 18	Tr. Iliad Bk 6		27
Ended her wretched life and pierc'd her heart.	. . .		Y 19	Tr. Iliad Bk 6		43
All her life was naught but guilt,	. . . .		Y 300	Extemp. Elegy		11
LIFE'S						
In life's last scene what prodigies surprise,	. . . .		O 45	Vanity Wishes		315
O guide me through life's darksome way,	. . . .		O 100	Ode Friendship		14
O guide us through life's darksome way,	. . . .		O 100	Ode Friendship	V	14
In life's first bloom his publick toils began,	. .		O 117	Epitaph Hanmer		11
Wearing out life's evening gray;	. . . . . .		O 181	Parody Warton		2
LIFT						
And future millions lift his rising soul;	. . . .		O 82	Young Author	V	6B
And ev'ry Suppliant lift his Eyes to Mecca.	. . . .		O 264	Irene		32
Can then th' Assassin lift his treach'rous Hand	. . .		O 286	Irene		11
Or lift themselves into the wonted skies.	. . . . .		Y 24	Tr Add. Battle		61
LIFTED						
Yet when your Hand is lifted to destroy,	. . . . . .		O 298	Irene		4
LIGHT						
Sustain th' approaching fire's tremendous light;	. .		O 18	London		187
Nor light nor darkness bring his pain relief,	. . .		O 32	Vanity Wishes		43
When pale-fac'd Cynthia sheds her silver light	. . .		O 77	Tr Add. Battle		45
How active light, and thoughtful shade,	. . . . .		O 121	To Miss Playin		27
And chear the clouded mind with light divine.	. . .		O 130	Tr. Rambler 7		4
That glad us with vicarious light;	. . . .		O 144	Tr Boeth. II.2		4
Till the Realms of Light you gain.	. . . .		O 150	Tr Boet III.12		46
Just emerging into Light,	. . . .		O 150	Tr Boet III.12		49
To speed the light convivial hour;	. . . .		O 191	Tr. Medea I		18
Wild as wind, and light as feather	. . . .		O 196	Song Congratu.		7
Here the Gamester light and jolly	. . . . . .		O 196	Song Congratu.		15
There the Gamester light and jolly	. . . .		O 196	Song Congratu.	V	15
Must Heaven dispatch the Messengers of Light,	. . .		O 250	Irene		46
Array'd in purer Light, look down on me:	. . . . .		O 253	Irene		101
Start at the Light, and tremble in the Dark;	. . .		O 266	Irene		30
Pursue the last Remains of ling'ring Light.	. . . .		O 302	Irene		4
Will spread resistless Light upon my Soul.	. . . .		O 321	Irene		47
Now beauteous Daphnis cloath'd with heav'nly light,	. .		Y 1	Virgil Daphnis		32
Of light reflected from the polish'd brass	. . . .		Y 20	Tr. Iliad Bk 6		93
LIGHTLY						
Thus lightly touch and quickly go.	. . . .		O 203	Tr. on Skating		4
Thus lightly skim, and haste away.	. . . .		O 203	Tr. on Skating	V	4
LIGHTNING						
Her tongue like nimble lightning plies,	. . . . . .		O 127	To Lyce, Lady		15
Did unresisted Lightning aid their Cannon,	. . .		O 251	Irene		54
Swifter than lightning to the fight he flies.	. . .		Y 21	Tr. Iliad Bk 6		126
LIGHTNINGS						
When in your Eyes resistless Lightnings play,	. . .		O 96	Hickman Spinet		3
Alike o'er all his lightnings fly;	. . . . . .		O 100	Ode Friendship		10
Did Did Lightnings flash?	. . . .		O 347	Irene	V	2
And point vindictive Lightnings at Rebellion,	. . .		O 300	Irene		61
LIKE						
Forgive my transports on a theme like this,	. . . .		O 15	London		97
Or like a gibbet better than a wheel;	. . . . .		O 15	London		108
How, when competitors like these contend,	. . . .		O 16	London		144
For arts like these preferr'd, admir'd, caress'd,	. .		O 17	London		152
And tir'd like me with follies and with crimes,	. .		O 23	London		258
But few there are whom hours like these await,	. .		O 45	Vanity Wishes		311
But left, like Egypt's Kings, a lasting Tomb.	. . .		O 51	Pro Drury-Lane		16
Yet Bards like these aspir'd to lasting Praise,	. .		O 52	Pro Drury-Lane		23
Like Caesar's pilot, dignified by fate,	. . . . .		O 59	Pro Good Nat'd		7
By all, like him, must praise and blame be found;	. .		O 62	Pro Word Wise		19
Like the first race in Saturns reign	. . . . . .		O 71	Hor. Epode II		3
Till angels wake thee with a note like thine.	. . .		O 113	Epit. Phillips		6
Her tongue like nimble lightning plies,	. . . . . .		O 127	To Lyce, Lady		15

```
LIKE         (CONTINUED)                                  PAGE    TITLE           LINE
     Like them man flourishes, like them decays. . . . . .  O 138 Tr Rambler 161        2
     Like them man flourishes, like them decays.           O 138 Tr Rambler 161        2
     Shall spring to seize thee like an ambush'd foe. . . .  O 152 The Ant             16
     "I have chatter'd like a pye." . . . . . . . . . .  O 186 Anacreon Ode 9       44
     Hadst thou nine lives like a cat,                     O 194 On Thrale Hat         3
     If Truths like these with pleasing Language join; . . . O 246 Irene Prologue      15
     Like subterraneous tempests with dire eruption burst their Y 115 Irene        V  49
        caverns
     Prowls like a lyon oer the wealthy Spoils of bleeding  .  O 352 Irene          V  29
        Turkey.
     Extended Empire, like expanded Gold,  . . . . . . .  O 265 Irene               37
     You are like the sun the governour of the world      Y 132 Irene           V  40
     Not all like thee can brave the Shocks of Fate,   . . .  O 266 Irene             34
     Empire or Wealth, to Excellence like thine? . . . . .  O 267 Irene              9
     To clasp a Slave? or, can a Soul like mine,      . . .  O 268 Irene             16
     Like the dread Stillness of condensing Storms. . . . .  O 270 Irene             14
     Like a fell Adder swelling in a Brake,  . . . . . .  O 275 Irene               77
     Sinks like the sighing of a Tempest spent,  . . . . .  O 275 Irene             92
     Sinks into sighs like the sighing of a Tempest spent  .  O 367 Irene          V  13
     Ordain'd, like you, to flutter and to shine,  . . . .  O 277 Irene             37
     Will it not charm a Mind like thine exalted,  . . . .  O 278 Irene             67
     Yet, on a Day like this, when Expectation  . . . . .  O 280 Irene             30
     Like thirsty Sailors gazing on the Clouds,  . . . . .  O 282 Irene              5
     Affrighted at Impiety like thine,  . . . . . . . .  O 289 Irene               19
     Reflect that Life, like ev'ry other Blessing,  . . . .  O 290 Irene             28
     Maxims like these, if generally persued  . . . . . .  O 352 Irene          V   2
     Maxims like these, if once reduc'd to practice  . . . .  O 352 Irene          V   2
     Close like th' eternal Bars of Death upon thee,  . . .  O 292 Irene             80
     Close like th' eternal Bars of Death upon You  . . . .  O 357 Irene          V  10
     Stoops from the Blaze like a degenerate Eagle  . . . .  O 292 Irene            101
     Stoops at the Blaze like a degenerate Eagle . . . . .  O 368 Irene          V  31
     O! could the Eyes of Kings, like those of Heav'n,  . . .  O 308 Irene             12
     When Guilt like this once harbours in the Breast  . . .  O 346 Irene          V   4
     The Breast where Guilt like this has found  . . . . .  O 349 Irene          V  23
        admission
     Well if a Thousand Lives like thine had perish'd;  . . .  O 332 Irene             34
     Such Ills are sent for Souls like thine to conquer.  . .  O 332 Irene             38
     Like one awaken'd from a pleasing dream, . . . . . .  Y   4 On a Daffodill       26
     Cleora's self, fair flower, shall fade like thee,  . . .  Y   4 On a Daffodill       27
     Grant him me to guard the walls of Troy.  . . . . . .  Y  20 Tr. Iliad Bk 6      102
     In vain, from heaven's black concave, like a cloud,  . .  Y  23 Tr Add. Battle      20
LILIES
     The Lilies o'er the Vales triumphant spread;  . . . .  O 111 To Posterity        18
     Where late the lilies mix'd with violets smil'd.  . . .  Y   7 Virgil Daphnis      25
LIMBS
     Cease, lovely thief! my tender limbs to wound,  . . . .  O 106 Eliza plucking       5
     Yet, tho' my limbs disease invades,  . . . . . . .  O 125 An Ode               13
     Till burning Death shoots through their wither'd Limbs?  .  O 282 Irene              6
     Heav'n, when its Hand pour'd Softness on our Limbs  . . .  O 290 Irene             42
     He Heav'n, when its hand pourd softness on our limbs  . .  Y 162 Irene          V  42
     Those trembling Limbs--Speak out, thou shiv'ring  . . .  O 332 Irene             16
        Traitor.
LIMITS
     The limits fix'd they strive to pass in vain;  . . . .  O  76 Tr Add. Battle      36
     Here will I fix the limits of transgression . . . . .  Y 168 Irene          V 133
LIMPID
     The limpid streams with ruefull murmurs flow  . . . .  Y   6 Virgil Daphnis       3
LIN'GRING
     Each lin'gring Hour alarms me for Aspasia.  . . . . .  O 270 Irene               20
LINE
     For now no more we trace in ev'ry line  . . . . . .  O  34 Vanity Wishes        87
     Place me beneath the burning line,  . . . . . . .  O  66 Hor I Ode xxii       21
LINEAMENTS
     Nor hope the British lineaments to trace,  . . . . .  O  15 London              101
LINES
     Attack my gentle lines.  . . . . . . . . . . .  O 127 To Lyce, Lady        20
     And broke the meditated Lines of War. . . . . . . .  O 273 Irene               26
     Extends its Lines along the sandy Beach,  . . . . . .  O 304 Irene              4
LING'RING    SEE LIN'GRING, LINGRING
     The still returning tale, and ling'ring jest,  . . . .  O  44 Vanity Wishes       275
     Still rise the long tale, and ling'ring jest,  . . . .  Y 104 Vanity Wishes    V 275
     Cold Approbation gave the ling'ring Bays,  . . . . .  O  51 Pro Drury-Lane       13
     Ling'ring year at last is flown,  . . . . . . . .  O 196 Song Congratu.        2
     Distract my Soul, dispatch thy ling'ring Tale;  . . . .  O 259 Irene              114
     Then leave him stretch'd upon the ling'ring Rack, . . .  O 273 Irene               36
     Pursue the last Remains of ling'ring Light.  . . . . .  O 302 Irene              4
     Beyond the Fear of ling'ring Punishment,  . . . . . .  O 325 Irene               16
     Curses the dull Delays of ling'ring Mercy,  . . . . .  O 327 Irene               12
     Dispatch, ye ling'ring Slaves, or nimbler Hands  . . . .  O 328 Irene               42
     Then ling'ring with his captive Mistress here.  . . . .  O 331 Irene               9
LINGER
     Still must we linger in uncertain Hope?  . . . . . .  O 282 Irene                3
     She cannot, must not, shall not linger here,  . . . .  O 296 Irene                6
     Still dost thou linger in these fatal bowrs  . . . . .  Y 196 Irene          V 18A
     To linger is to dye . . . . . . . . . . . . .  Y 199 Irene          V  17
LINGER'D
     Where hast thou linger'd while th' encumber'd Hours  . .  O 279 Irene                3
LINGRING
     Loads the lingring minutes weary wings:  . . . . . .  Y 105 Vanity Wishes    V 300
```

193

		PAGE	TITLE	LINE
LINKS				
That links the jarring Elements in Peace.		O 257	Irene	64
LINNET				
To warn the wand'ring Linnet to the Shade, ...		O 250	Irene	33
LION SEE LYON				
As mongrels bay the lion in a cage.		O 60	Pro Good Nat'd	16
As children fret the lion in a cage.		O 60	Pro Good Nat'd	V 16
LION'S				
The Lion's thirsty Parent, bore.		O 67	To A. Fuscus	16
LIONESS				
Why roars the Lioness distress'd by Hunger?		O 281	Irene	50
LIONS				
Dire nurse of raging lions, bore.		O 66	Hor I Ode xxii	16
LIP				
"As it leaves Anacreon's lip, ...		O 185	Anacreon Ode 9	32
LIPS				
Ye nymphs of rosy lips and radiant eyes, ...		O 46	Vanity Wishes	323
Has Silence press'd her Seal upon his Lips?		O 255	Irene	20
When from his Lips the fatal Name burst out, ...		O 270	Irene	12
And tender Accents quiver'd on my Lips, ...		O 282	Irene	67
Dwells on her Lips, and sighs upon her Breast;		O 286	Irene	5
Just as it reach'd my Lips, a sudden Cry		O 316	Irene	27
LIQUID				
His liquid wealth o'er barbarous lands.		O 65	Hor I Ode xxii	8
His liquid Wealth thro' barbarous Lands.		O 66	To A. Fuscus	8
And, fainting, scarce support the liquid weight: . . .		O 74	Tr. Iliad Bk 6	24
Liquid fragrance all the way:		O 185	Anacreon Ode 9	4
LIQUOR				
Have drank the liquor up.		O 159	Par Hermit III	8
LISP				
And lisp the tale of Henry's victories;		O 15	London	120
LIST				
Bribe to his Cause and list beneath his Banners . . .		O 274	Irene	53
LIST'NER				
An idle List'ner to the distant Cries		O 305	Irene	23
LIST'NING				
And list'ning to the pleasing Tale of Pow'r, ...		O 303	Irene	30
LISTEN				
That, fav'ring, listen to his cries.		O 72	Hor. Epode II	28
And listen eager to the rising Wind?		O 270	Irene	25
Too calm I listen to the flatt'ring Sounds.		O 278	Irene	74
In vain I listen to th' inviting Call		O 320	Irene	10
In vain I listen to the inviting voice		Y 198	Irene	V 10
LISTENS				
When vengeance listens to the fool's request.		O 31	Vanity Wishes	14
LISTLESS				
With listless eyes the dotard views the store, ...		O 43	Vanity Wishes	263
LISTNING				
Listning forests learnt the Strain, ...		O 148	Tr Boet III.12	V 9
Round him danc'd the listning Woods, ...		O 148	Tr Boet III.12	11
Round him crowd the listning Woods, ...		O 148	Tr Boet III.12	V 11
Pensive and listning to the beating Surge.		O 254	Irene	128
LITHOS				
Oude lithos, oude Sideron--nostro sequitur de Vulnere .		O 347	Irene	V 23
sanguis.				
LITTLE				
And ev'ry moment leaves my little less;		O 10	London	40
And leave your little All to flames a prey;		O 18	London	189
Our little Bard, without complaint, may share		O 59	Pro Good Nat'd	V 5
The Shepherds oft' see little ghosts glide by		O 77	Tr Add. Battle	47
Ah, little needs the Minstrel's pow'r		O 191	Tr. Medea I	17
My Swain is little--true--but be it known, ...		O 247	Irene Epilogue	9
My Pride's to have that little all my own.		O 247	Irene Epilogue	10
A little longer, and she's thine for ever.		O 285	Irene	10
A little Life for Grief, and for Repentance.		O 327	Irene	23
A little life from grief and for repentance.		Y 207	Irene	V 23
Our little dog has bit his tail		Y 300	Fanny Burney	4
LIV'D				
Thou might'st have liv'd, for thou hadst spar'd Irene. .		O 333	Irene	58
Thou mightst have liv'd, nor had I lost Irene		Y 214	Irene	V 58
LIV'RIED				
The liv'ried army, and the menial lord.		O 35	Vanity Wishes	116
The liv'ried army, or the menial lord.		Y 96	Vanity Wishes	V 116
LIV'ST				
Or liv'st thou now, with safer pride content, ...		O 35	Vanity Wishes	123
But dearest Hector while thou liv'st I see		Y 19	Tr. Iliad Bk 6	44
LIVE				
Let----live here, for----has learn'd to live.		O 11	London	50
Let----live here, for----has learn'd to live.		O 11	London	50
Live unregarded, unlamented die.		O 14	London	82
For we that live to please, must please to live. . . .		O 53	Pro Drury-Lane	54
For we that live to please, must please to live. . . .		O 53	Pro Drury-Lane	54
Content to live the Roman's slave, ...		O 68	Hor. II Ode IX	23
Shall live for ever in my verse.		O 70	Hor.II Ode XX	24
Long may live my lovely Hetty!		O 175	Tr Easy Phrase	1
Live my lovely Hetty long!		O 175	Tr Easy Phrase	4
Long may live my lovely Hetty!		O 175	Tr Easy Phrase	6
And spare him, Beauties! tho' his Lovers live.		O 246	Irene Prologue	20
Live till the tott'ring Earth forsakes its		O 347	Irene	V 29
Base				
Live till the Sun forgets to dart his Beams, ...		O 262	Irene	3

```
LIVE          (CONTINUED)                              PAGE    TITLE            LINE
     He yet may live. . . . . . . . . . . . . . . .    O 267  Irene               45
     To bid the prostrate Captive rise and live,  . .  O 278  Irene               70
     But he must live to make his Masters wretched? .  O 286  Irene                7
     To live obscure upon a foreign Coast, . . . . .   O 301  Irene              104
     Nor hope, nor wish, nor live but for Aspasia. . . O 307  Irene               14
     Thus shall he live to strike th' important Blow,  O 308  Irene               32
     Still Cali lives, and must he live To-morrow? . . O 310  Irene                1
     Henceforth shall live for me; for me alone . . .  O 317  Irene                3
     Shall then the Savage live, to boast his Insult;  O 318  Irene               12
     Come haste, and live--Thy Innocence and Truth . . O 320  Irene               18
     And live her guiltless Moments o'er anew! . . .   O 323  Irene               16
     Let me but live, heap Woes on Woes upon me, . . . O 328  Irene               33
     Then would I free from torments live . . . . . .  Y  11  Tr Hor Epode 9      25

LIVES
     Behold our fame, our wealth, our lives your own.  O  13  London              64
     Who lives from toilsome bus'ness free, . . . .    O  71  Hor. Epode II        2
     And unrelenting sport ten thousand lives away;    O  83  Epi Dist Moth.       9
     In quest of wealth who throw their lives away. .  O 132  Tr. Rambler 48       2
     Bear lives in amity with bear. . . . . . . . . .  O 138  Tr Rambler 160       2
     Hadst thou nine lives like a cat, . . . . . . .   O 194  On Thrale Hat        3
     Soon those nine lives would be past. . . . . . .  O 194  On Thrale Hat        4
     He lives---- . . . . . . . . . . . . . . . . .    O 260  Irene              132
     Is 't not enough, he lives by our Indulgence, .   O 286  Irene                6
     Still Cali lives, and must he live To-morrow? .   O 310  Irene                1
     Greece is no more, the prosp'rous Tyrant lives,   O 315  Irene                4
     Well if a Thousand Lives like thine had perish'd; O 332  Irene               34
     While Hector lives I tast of ev'ry joy . . . . .  Y  18  Tr. Iliad Bk 6      26

LIVID
     With livid hue the fairest face o'ercast, . . .   O  84  Epi Dist Moth.      34

LIVING
     And tread the living picture in the dust . . . .  Y 177  Irene             V111B
     With dolefull cries their living lord they mourn  Y  21  Tr. Iliad Bk 6     130

LOAD
     And gain and grandeur load the tainted gales; .   O  32  Vanity Wishes       46
     Assails the skies load the tainted gales, . . .   Y  93  Vanity Wishes     V  46
     And gain and greatness load the tainted gales; .  Y  93  Vanity Wishes     V  46
     Yet ev'n on this her load Misfortune flings, . .  O  44  Vanity Wishes      299
     Prest by the load of life, the weary mind . . .   O  59  Pro Good Nat'd       1
     With unbought dainties load the board; . . . .    O  73  Hor. Epode II       54
     Leaves the Load of Earth behind. . . . . . . .    O 147  Tr Boet III.12       4
     Beneath the Load of Business, and of Years. . .   O 271  Irene                7
     And load with Perjuries his parting Soul? . . .   O 272  Irene                5
     Go, seize him, load him with reproachful Chains;  O 273  Irene               34
     With half the grov'ling Slaves that load the Globe. O 332 Irene              36
     May I lye cold beneath a load of clay. . . . . .  Y  18  Tr. Iliad Bk 6      25

LOADED
     And ease my loaded Soul upon her Bosom? . . . .   O 263  Irene               22
     Direct the loaded Cannon, grasp the Sword . . .   O 364  Irene             V  14
     Direct the loaded cannon, grasp the sword . . .   Y 162  Irene             V  41
     Her piercing Cries yet fill the loaded Air, . .   O 329  Irene                8

LOADS
     Loads the lingring minutes weary wings: . . . .   Y 105  Vanity Wishes     V 300
     Should costly Loads of incense burn, . . . . .    O  69  Hor.II Ode 14        7
     When fruitful summer loads the teeming plain, .   O 151  The Ant              7

LOATH
     Dooms me to loath at once, and doat on Falshood,  O 310  Irene               10

LOATHSOME
     Dark is the sun, and loathsome is the day. . . .  O 139  Tr Rambler 171       1

LOCKS
     Her silver locks display the moon, . . . . . . .  O 127  To Lyce, Lady        9

LODGE
     And lodge the fate of kingdoms in her bosom. . .  Y 159  Irene             V  18

LOFTY
     But round the lofty Popular twines . . . . . . .  O  71  Hor. Epode II       17
     His Mien is lofty, his Demeanour great, . . . .   O 255  Irene               14
     And though built on feeble columns--Its lofty turrets Y 131 Irene          V  35
         blaze amidst
     But see,the lofty Maid at our Approach, . . . .   O 314  Irene               14
     Her lofty mien, and insolence of virtue--my . .   Y 191  Irene             V  14
         state
     Where Hypoplacus' lofty shades extend. . . . .    Y  18  Tr. Iliad Bk 6       8
     Not the Maeonian Bard in lofty strain . . . . .   Y  23  Tr Add. Battle      54

LOGICK
     A Statesman's logick unconvinc'd can hear, . . .  O  13  London              71

LOITER
     And weary Planets loiter in their Courses. . . .  O 262  Irene                4

LOITER'D
     --And loiter'd with his troop remote from Action  O 376  Irene             V  15

LOITERER
     The loiterer finds a bramble for a flow'r. . . .  O 133  Tr. Rambler 71       2
     Infatuate Loiterer, has Fate, in vain, . . . .    O 318  Irene               15
     Luckless slave Ilfated loiterer has fate in vain  Y 196  Irene             V  15

LONDON
     London: A Poem ...                                O   7  London               T
     Resolved at length, from vice and London far, .   O   9  London               5
     Who now resolves, from vice and London far, . .   O   9  London            V  5
     London! the needy villain's gen'ral home, . . .   O  14  London              93

LONELY
     And lonely want retir'd to die. . . . . . . . .   O 201  Death Dr Levet      20
```

```
                                                                    PAGE    TITLE              LINE
LONESOME
        That range lascivious through the lonesome  . . . . .    Y   7  Virgil Daphnis     V  50
            roads
LONG
        Still rise the long tale, and ling'ring jest,    . . .   Y 104  Vanity Wishes      V 275
        Their Slaves were willing, and their Reign was long;  . . O  52  Pro Drury-Lane        26
        Unknown, unheeded, long his Offspring lay,  . . . . .   O  58  Prologue Comus        25
        Mourn'd not Antilochus so long;  . . . . . . . . .      O  68  Hor. II Ode IX        14
        Long since I learn'd to slight this fleeting breath,  . . O  74  Tr. Iliad Bk 6         9
        Not long they stood, when stooping from their height  . . O  75  Tr Add. Battle        2
        Thus fell the Pygmie state, which long had stood  . . .  O  76  Tr Add. Battle        33
        When first the peasant, long inclin'd to roam,  . . . .  O  81  Young Author          1
        And the long honours of a lasting name  . . . . . .     O  82  Young Author       V  12
        So long renown'd in B<rya>n's deathless strain?  . . .   O 107  Lady F Assizes        2
        Thrice ten long years he labour'd for the State;  . . .  O 118  Epitaph Hanmer        14
        Alternate rest and labour long endure.  . . . . . .     O 131  Tr. Rambler 33        1
        Lead a long and peaceful Age,  . . . . . . . .          O 145  Tr Boeth. II.4        21
        And thus the Mind tormented long  . . . . . . .         O 145  Tr Boeth III.1         9
        How long shall sloth usurp thy useless hours,  . . . .  O 151  The Ant               9
        Shall long detain the cup,  . . . . . . . . . .         O 159  Par Hermit III        6
        Long may live my lovely Hetty!  . . . . . . . .         O 175  Tr Easy Phrase        1
        Live my lovely Hetty long!  . . . . . . . . . .         O 175  Tr Easy Phrase        4
        Long may live my lovely Hetty!  . . . . . . . .         O 175  Tr Easy Phrase        6
        Long may better Years arrive,  . . . . . . . .          O 178  Thrale 35 Year        3
        Bears toilsome Days, and wakes long tedious Nights:  . .  O 247  Irene Epilogue       22
        With all the Diffidence of long Experience,  . . . .    O 254  Irene               130
        That long to hail thee Chief.  . . . . . . . .          O 254  Irene               137
        Thou that hast long perus'd the Draughts of Nature,  . .  O 255  Irene                11
        Beholds a long posterity of freemen  . . . . . .        Y 122  Irene              V  61
        Long have I wish'd, before our Prophet's Tomb,  . . .    O 263  Irene                9
        Long have as oblig'd by vow  . . . . . . . . .          Y 130  Irene              V   9
        for the long life and prosperity of my sovereign  . . .  Y 130  Irene              V 12A
        And may a long Posterity of Monarchs,  . . . . . .      O 267  Irene                11
        Long be the Sultan bless'd with happy Love!  . . . . .   O 286  Irene                1
        Long would my Zeal for Mahomet and Thee  . . . . .      O 288  Irene                11
        Will not admit a Lover's long Farewell,  . . . . .      O 297  Irene                13
        Well known, long try'd, expect us on the Shore.  . . .   O 301  Irene                91
        Forbear--.i know thy try'd Faith of Cali.  . . . .      O 308  Irene                11
        Not so while long th' undaunted race maintain'd  . . .   Y  23  Tr Add. Battle       36
        Not long the happy Russians mourn;  . . . . . . .       Y  39  Lady Leaving          9
        Of two day's long  . . . . . . . . . . .               Y 300  Fanny Burney          2
        Chear'd the rough road, we wish'd the rough road long,  . Y 310  Parody of Pope       2
LONG-CONTINU'D
        Forbears the long-continu'd strife,  . . . . . . .      O 124  An Ode               2
LONG-DRAWN
        The long-drawn Intercourse of Sighs and Kisses.  . . .   O 297  Irene                14
LONG-EXPECTED
        Long-expected one and twenty  . . . . . . . .          O 196  Song Congratu.        1
LONG-EXPECTING
        Still to the Lover's long-expecting Arms,  . . . . .    O 283  Irene                30
LONG'ST
        Thou long'st for Stars that frown on human Kind,  . . .  O 271  Irene                4
LONGER
        And giv'n to mirth, the Cranes no longer fear,  . . . .  O  77  Tr Add. Battle       50
        A little longer, and she's thine for ever.  . . . . .   O 285  Irene                10
        Then waste no longer these important Moments  . . . .   O 303  Irene                13
        No longer lost in am'rous Solitude,  . . . . . .        O 303  Irene                26
        To meet that Fate we can delay no longer.  . . . . .    O 328  Irene                41
LONGING
        To gaze with longing Eyes upon To-morrow,  . . . . .    O 283  Irene                24
        Still stretch in vain their longing Arms afar;  . . . .  O 292  Irene                91
LONGS
        Sick'ning with fear he longs to view the shore,  . . .   O  82  Young Author          9
LOOK
        Look not on her by the way;  . . . . . . . . .         O 150  Tr Boet III.12       44
        Must look on Thrale at Thirtyfive.  . . . . . . .       O 178  Thrale 35 Year       18
        Array'd in purer Light, look down on me:  . . . . .     O 253  Irene               101
        Aspasia! who can look upon thy Beauties?  . . . . .     O 281  Irene                42
        An angry look had sunk him into Hell  . . . . . .       O 376  Irene              V  23
        An angry look had sunk him into Hell  . . . . . .       Y 188  Irene              V  20
        Thy Look, thy Speech, thy Action, all is Wildness--  . .  O 323  Irene                 5
        Nor from the battle look for his return.  . . . . .     Y  21  Tr. Iliad Bk 6      131
        Death in his look, and hands imbru'd in gore  . . . .   Y  23  Tr Add. Battle       47
LOOKING
        Affrighted views; and looking o'er the plain  . . . .   Y  23  Tr Add. Battle       32
LOOKS
        Where looks are merchandise, and smiles are sold;  . . .  O  18  London              179
        Looks back on what She left behind,  . . . . . .        O 150  Tr Boet III.12       57
        Well skill'd to sooth a foe with looks of kindness,  . .  O 176  Tr Metastas II        3
        Looks down, contemptuous, from his fancy'd Height,  . .   O 306  Irene                2
        Andromache looks back with weeping eyes.  . . . . .     Y  21  Tr. Iliad Bk 6      127
LOOSE
        Should no false Kindness lure to loose delight,  . . .   O  37  Vanity Wishes       147
        Would loose the wild Enthusiast to destroy,  . . . .    O 291  Irene                61
        Proceed, and give a loose to Love and Treason.  . . . .  O 316  Irene                20
LOOSEN'D
        Loosen'd from the Minor's tether,  . . . . . . .        O 196  Song Congratu.        5
        Yet ere we give our loosen'd Thoughts to Rapture,  . . .  O 309  Irene                18
LOP'D
        He drew his scymetar and lop'd the branches.  . . . .   Y 187  Irene              V   7
```

```
                                          PAGE    TITLE              LINE
LOPS
    Till rude resistance lops the spreading god;    .    .    .    .    O  42 Vanity Wishes      234
LORD
    The groom retails the favours of his lord.    .    .    .    .    O  18 London            181
    Despise the dainties of a venal lord:    .    .    .    .    .    .    O  20 London            219
    How much more safe the vassal than the lord;    .    .    .    .    O  31 Vanity Wishes       32
    The liv'ried army, and the menial lord.    .    .    .    .    .    O  35 Vanity Wishes      116
    The liv'ried army, or the menial lord.    .    .    .    .    .    .    Y  96 Vanity Wishes    V 116
    Unconquer'd lord of pleasure and of pain;    .    .    .    .    .    O  40 Vanity Wishes      196
    From Persia's tyrant to Bavaria's lord.    .    .    .    .    .    O  41 Vanity Wishes      224
    And waiting for her weary lord    .    .    .    .    .    .    .    O  73 Hor. Epode II       53
    Who to their Lord were ever dear,    .    .    .    .    .    .    O  78 Feast St Simon      10
    No social care the gracious lord disdains;    .    .    .    .    O 130 Tr. Rambler 12       7
    The sport of Tyranny, or Lord of Nations.    .    .    .    .    O 303 Irene              12
    When Asia's Nations own me for their Lord,    .    .    .    .    O 306 Irene               5
    With dolefull cries their living lord they mourn    .    .    .    Y  21 Tr. Iliad Bk 6     130
LORDS
    Commence your lords, and govern or betray.    .    .    .    .    .    O  17 London            157
    Lords of the street, and terrors of the way;    .    .    .    .    O  21 London            231
LORE
    Let Study, worn with Virtue's fruitless Lore,    .    .    .    .    O  57 Prologue Comus      9
LOSE
    Thou joy'st to lose the master in the friend:    .    .    .    .    O 130 Tr. Rambler 12       4
    O! sooth my Soul, and teach me how to lose thee.    .    .    .    O 253 Irene             103
    And forget (or lose) the conquerour in the    .    .    .    .    Y 123 Irene            V 100
        lover
    The Coward, and the Fool, condemn'd to lose    .    .    .    .    O 283 Irene              22
    Nor lose in Love the Patriot and the Hero.    .    .    .    .    O 303 Irene              15
    O spare the gallant Greek, in him we lose    .    .    .    .    O 307 Irene              26
    Lest unrewarded Mercy lose its Charms.    .    .    .    .    .    O 313 Irene              19
    lose or I possess her    .    .    .    .    .    .    .    .    .    Y 198 Irene            V  32
LOSES
    And social sorrow loses half its pain:    .    .    .    .    .    O  59 Pro Good Nat'd       4
    That loses all because she hazards nothing:    .    .    .    .    O 281 Irene              45
LOSING
    Viewing lost and losing died.    .    .    .    .    .    .    .    O 150 Tr Boet III.12      52
LOSS
    Thus Life, with loss of Wealth, is well preserv'd,    .    .    O 290 Irene              34
    And Virtue cheaply sav'd with loss of Life.    .    .    .    .    O 290 Irene              35
LOSSES
    And dreaded losses aggravate his pains;    .    .    .    .    .    O  44 Vanity Wishes      286
    Her losses soon the Moon supplies,    .    .    .    .    .    .    O 232 Tr Horace IV.7      13
LOST
    But lost in thoughtless ease, and empty show,    .    .    .    .    O  15 London            103
    And what their Armies lost, their Cringes    .    .    .    .    .    O  16 London           V 122
        gain?
    At once is lost the pride of aweful state,    .    .    .    .    O  35 Vanity Wishes      113
    Nor deem, when learning her lost prize bestows,    .    .    .    O  38 Vanity Wishes     V 165
    But their lost strength and vigour soon return,    .    .    .    O  76 Tr Add. Battle       8
    Viewing lost and losing died.    .    .    .    .    .    .    .    O 150 Tr Boet III.12      52
    Viewing lost and loving died.    .    .    .    .    .    .    .    O 150 Tr Boet III.12    V  52
    That Wealth, too pleasing to be lost for Freedom!    .    .    .    O 250 Irene              21
    My reasoning Pow'rs--Dear, hapless, lost Aspasia!    .    .    .    O 252 Irene              78
    In Passion lost, he bad the conqu'ring Fair    .    .    .    .    O 258 Irene              99
    Lost in the deluge of impetuous war    .    .    .    .    .    Y 136 Irene            V  25
    Now lost amidst the gloom of disappointment    .    .    .    .    Y 148 Irene            V 43B
    Confounded, aw'd, and lost in Admiration,    .    .    .    .    O 282 Irene              64
    And shed the pitying Tear for lost Irene.    .    .    .    .    O 292 Irene              97
    An Let fall sometimes a tear for lost Irene    .    .    .    .    O 349 Irene            V   1
    and drop sometimes a tear for lost Irene    .    .    .    .    O 349 Irene            V   1
    Lost in a wild Perplexity of Joy.    .    .    .    .    .    .    O 295 Irene              14
    O'erwhelm'd and lost amidst the publick Ruins    .    .    .    .    O 302 Irene             107
    No longer lost in am'rous Solitude,    .    .    .    .    .    .    O 303 Irene              26
    Were now well lost, in hearing how you fail'd.    .    .    .    O 316 Irene              23
    Nor think that Effort lost which rescues thee.    .    .    .    O 317 Irene              47
    All is not lost, Abdalla, see the Queen,    .    .    .    .    O 326 Irene               1
    What hadst thou lost by slighting those Commands?    .    .    .    O 332 Irene              32
    Thou mightst have liv'd, nor had I lost Irene    .    .    .    .    Y 214 Irene            V  58
    In half a year of darkness lost.    .    .    .    .    .    .    Y  38 Lady Leaving        4
LOT
    Hard is his lot, that here by Fortune plac'd,    .    .    .    .    O  53 Pro Drury-Lane      47
    There begs of heav'n a less distinguish'd lot;    .    .    .    O  82 Young Author        29
    "Now my better lot bestows    .    .    .    .    .    .    .    O 185 Anacreon Ode 9      29
    Unhappy Lot of all that shine in Courts;    .    .    .    .    .    O 256 Irene              50
LOTTERY
    Collect a tax, or farm a lottery,    .    .    .    .    .    .    O  12 London              58
    Collect a tax, or form a lottery,    .    .    .    .    .    .    O  12 London           V  58
LOUD
    Fill the loud Voice of universal Praise,    .    .    .    .    .    O  57 Prologue Comus      16
    Uncheck'd on both, loud rabbles vent their rage,    .    .    .    O  59 Pro Good Nat'd      15
    Then shall some Argive loud insulting cry,    .    .    .    .    O  74 Tr. Iliad Bk 6      25
    Loud roars the tempest, high the billows rise,    .    .    .    O  82 Young Author        8
    Loud roar the billows, high the waves arise,    .    .    .    O  82 Young Author     V   8
    Loud as the Billows bursting on the Ground.    .    .    .    .    O 110 To Posterity         6
    That roll at Eurus loud command;    .    .    .    .    .    .    O 144 Tr Boeth. II.2       2
    When loud Auster shakes her Walls,    .    .    .    .    .    .    O 145 Tr Boeth. II.4      10
    The nymphs bewail'd his fall with loud lament    .    .    .    Y  18 Tr. Iliad Bk 6      32
LOUDER
    With louder ruin to the gulphs below?    .    .    .    .    .    O  35 Vanity Wishes      128
    Insulting chance ne'er call'd with louder voice,    .    .    .    O 135 Tr Rambler 106      1
```

LOUDEST
    There, mid Tempests loudest roars, ...   O 145 Tr Boeth. II.4   17
    The loudest Cries of Nature urge us forward; . . . .   O 270 Irene   15
LOV'D
    Aspasia! spare that lov'd, that mournful Name: O 252 Irene   76
    The Sultan gaz'd, he wonder'd and he lov'd; . . . .   O 258 Irene   98
LOVE
    Love ends with hope, the sinking statesman's door . .   O 33 Vanity Wishes   79
    O'er love, o'er fear, extends his wide domain, ...   O 40 Vanity Wishes   195
    O'er love, o'er Force, extends his wide domain, . . .   O 40 Vanity Wishes V 195
    For love, which scarce collective man can fill; . . .   O 48 Vanity Wishes   361
    For love, whose grasp Creation collective man can . . .   Y 108 Vanity Wishes V 361
      fill;
    Lamenting warbles out his love, ...   O 72 Hor. Epode II   34
    The bitter pangs of slighted love? . . . .   O 72 Hor. Epode II   46
    Urg'd headlong on by hatred or by love: . . . . .   O 77 Festina Lente   6
    O prodigy of Love! . . . .   O 79 Feast St Simon   21
    With ardent love of virtue fir'd, ...   O 79 Feast St Simon   38
    All but the sweet solicitudes of love! . . . . .   O 81 Lady Birthday   6
    Aw'd into Love, our conquer'd hearts obey, ...   O 96 Hickman Spinet   4
    While Love, a stranger to the blest, ...   O 99 Ode Friendship   5
    While Love, unknown amongst the blest, ...   O 99 Ode Friendship V 5
    The pangs of guilty pow'r, and hapless love, ...   O 113 Epit. Phillips   2
    The pangs of guilty pow'r, or hapless love, ...   O 113 Epit. Phillips V 2
    With thirst of knowledge, and with love of truth; . .   O 117 Epitaph Hanmer   6
    Beheld with love, with veneration heard. . . . . .   O 118 Epitaph Hanmer   26
    Nor tempt the snares of wily love. . . . .   O 121 To Miss Playin   10
    And Love and Hate alike implore . . . .   O 122 Stella Mourn.   15
    Scarce frighted love maintains his fire, ...   O 123 Winter's Walk   11
    Scarce frighted love maintains her fire, ...   O 123 Winter's Walk V 11
    Love warbles in the vocal groves, ...   O 125 An Ode   7
    Love prompts to love, and rev'rence rev'rence gains. . .   O 130 Tr. Rambler 12   8
    Love prompts to love, and rev'rence rev'rence gains. . .   O 130 Tr. Rambler 12   8
    And love return, has great Erasmus died? . . . . . .   O 132 Tr. Rambler 54   2
    Inforc'd we love, unheeding recollect. . . . . . .   O 134 Tr. Rambler 96   2
    The more I honour thee, the less I love. . . . . . .   O 140 Tr Rambler 188   1
    While t' asswage the Pangs of Love . . . .   O 149 Tr Boet III.12   15
    Love alone to Love is Law: . . . .   O 150 Tr Boet III.12   48
    Love alone to Love is Law: . . . .   O 150 Tr Boet III.12   48
    Is it business? is it love? . . . .   O 185 Anacreon Ode 9   5
    Gain'd all his Heart; at length his eager Love . . . .   O 259 Irene   123
    Remember Freedom, Glory, Greece, and Love. . . . . .   O 260 Irene   146
    Think on Revenge and Glory Greece and Love . . . . .   O 361 Irene V 5
    Or arm his Breast against the Force of Love? . . . . .   O 261 Irene   8
    Love, that with sweet Vicissitude relieves . . . . .   O 261 Irene   9
    Which Love of Greatness, not of Truth, inflames. . .   O 262 Irene   27
    Alone, with am'rous Haste to seek his Love. . . . . .   O 262 Irene   29
    Sure this is Love which heretofore I conceiv'd . . . .   O 349 Irene V 28
    Desires more pure, and other Cares than Love. . . . .   O 263 Irene   8
    Too strong for Love, have hurried him on Death. . . .   O 267 Irene   48
    In all the sweet forgetfulness of Love . . . . . .   O 367 Irene V 26
    In all the sweet forgetfulness of love . . . . . .   Y 138 Irene V 13
    The pow'rful Voice of Love inflames Demetrius, ...   O 270 Irene   19
    These Days of Love and Pleasure charm not thee; . . .   O 271 Irene   2
    The Sultan comes, impatient for his Love; . . . . .   O 272 Irene   12
    Attention rouses from the dream of Love . . . . . .   O 369 Irene V 21
    --Love and empire . . . .   Y 144 Irene V 6
    Imperfect sounds of Greece--and love--and . . . . .   Y 144 Irene V 80
      daggers
    Daggers and love? What love but fair . . . .   Y 144 Irene V 81
      Irene?
    Daggers and love? What love but fair . . . .   Y 144 Irene V 81
      Irene?
    And turn thy Thoughts henceforth to Love and Empire. . .   O 276 Irene   5
    Whence all the Bliss and Agonies of Love? . . . . .   O 277 Irene   42
    Whence all the pleasures, and the pains of love. . . .   Y 148 Irene V 42
    The Thirst of Empire, and the Love of Glory? . . . .   O 278 Irene   58
    The thirst of empire and the love of virtue? . . . .   Y 149 Irene V 58
    And Love infold thee with his downy Wings. . . . . .   O 279 Irene   83
    Empire and Love shall share the blissful Day, ...   O 279 Irene   90
    Claim but the second Place: there mighty Love . . . .   O 280 Irene   26
    Love is indeed the Privilege of Youth; . . . . .   O 280 Irene   29
    Know'st thou not yet, when Love invades the Soul, . . .   O 281 Irene   38
    Because I love: . . . .   O 281 Irene   48
    When ev'n as Love was breaking off from Wonder, . . .   O 282 Irene   66
    Or felt th' Impatience of obstructed Love, ...   O 285 Irene   4
    Prudence and Love conspire in this Request, ...   O 285 Irene   11
    Long be the Sultan bless'd with happy Love! . . . . .   O 286 Irene   1
    The Love of Pow'r, of Pleasure, and of Show. . . . .   O 287 Irene   13
    Treat her With all the confidence of artless love . . .   Y 159 Irene V 17
    Nor taint with Care the Privacies of Love. . . . . .   O 288 Irene   14
    'Tis she--My Hope, my Happiness, my Love! . . . . .   O 294 Irene   1
    Revive--Revive to Freedom and to Love. . . . . . .   O 295 Irene   9
    Freedom and Love? Alas! I'm all Confusion, ...   O 295 Irene   11
    Such Ecstacy of Love! such pure Affection, ...   O 295 Irene   15
    Your careless Love betrays your Country's Cause. . . .   O 297 Irene   10
    Drive Int'rest, Love, and Vengeance from thy Thoughts, .   O 298 Irene   7
    To shock my Virtue with a Tale of Love. . . . . . .   O 299 Irene   40
    His Pride and Love by Turns inspir'd his Tongue, . . .   O 299 Irene   43
    Th' Anxieties of Love. . . . .   O 300 Irene   55
    Content with Science, Innocence and Love? . . . . .   O 301 Irene   105

LOVE   (CONTINUED)   PAGE   TITLE   LINE
    Love be my Wealth, and my Distinction Virtue. . . . . .   O 302 Irene   111
    Nor lose in Love the Patriot and the Hero. . . . . .   O 303 Irene   15
    'Tis Love combin'd with Guilt alone, that melts . . .   O 303 Irene   16
    Smiling Consent she sat, and blushing Love. . . .   O 303 Irene   32
    Sacred to Love, to Pleasure, and Irene: . . . . . .   O 308 Irene   2
    Behold him here, in Love, in War successful,   O 310 Irene   4
    I love her still, but shall esteem Aspasia: . . . . .   Y 186 Irene   V   5
    By Reason not convinc'd, nor won by Love.   O 310 Irene   8
    The thoughts of happy love, and rescu'd Greece . . . .   Y 189 Irene   V 1D
    Fly, fly, my Love, Destruction rushes on us, ...   O 315 Irene   1
    Proceed, and give a loose to Love and Treason. . .   O 316 Irene   20
    With ill-tim'd Mirth propos'd the Bowl of Love.   O 316 Irene   26
    Thy Love, Aspasia, calls; restrain thy Sword; . . .   O 318 Irene   9
    Secure his Confidence, and fix his Love. . . . . .   O 319 Irene   6
    Of Freedom and of Love: My trembling Joints . . .   O 320 Irene   11
    Hard was the Strife of Justice and of Love; . . . .   O 324 Irene   13
    Was this the Maid whose Love I bought with Empire!   O 330 Irene   9
    Some artful Wile of counterfeited Love! . . .   O 331 Irene   3
    Such Beauty, Sweetness, Love, were cheaply bought,   O 332 Irene   35
    While boars the rocks, while fish the rivers love,   Y   7 Virgil Daphnis   49
    Those anxious fears that fan'd the flame of Love. . . .   Y 11 Tr Hor Epode 9   24
    Pledge of their love and source of all their joy   Y 18 Tr. Iliad Bk 6   10
    Fair source of wit, and love, and mirth, ...   Y 39 Lady Leaving   6
LOVE'S
    At busy hearts in vain love's arrows fly; . . . . .   O 133 Tr. Rambler 85   1
    Such are Love's Joys, the Lenitives of Life, ...   O 277 Irene   47
LOVELY
    Thy form more lovely, more adorn'd thy mind; . . . .   O 80 Lady Birthday   4
    Cease, lovely thief! my tender limbs to wound, . . .   O 106 Eliza plucking   5
    For such thy beauteous mind, and lovely face, . . .   O 107 Lady F Assizes   5
    For his lovely Consort gone, ...   O 148 Tr Boet III.12   6
    For his lovely Consort gone, ...   O 148 Tr Boet III.12   V   8
    Long may live my lovely Hetty! . . . .   O 175 Tr Easy Phrase   1
    Live my lovely Hetty long! . . . .   O 175 Tr Easy Phrase   4
    Long may live my lovely Hetty! . . . .   O 175 Tr Easy Phrase   6
    Lovely courier of the sky, ...   O 185 Anacreon Ode 9   1
    By what Enchantment does this lovely Greek . . . .   O 261 Irene   1
    Still restless, till I clasp the lovely Maid, ...   O 263 Irene   21
    And leaves the lovely Trifler unregarded . . . .   O 276 Irene   23
    Greece, in her lovely Patroness secure, ...   O 278 Irene   77
    Why does the Blood forsake thy lovely Cheek? . . .   O 295 Irene   5
    Hail lovely flower, first honour of the year! . . . .   Y   3 On a Daffodill   1
    The nurse attending bore a lovely boy . . . . . .   Y 18 Tr. Iliad Bk 6   9
LOVER
    The rival batters, and the lover mines. . . . . .   O 46 Vanity Wishes   332
    And forget (or lose) the conquerour in the . . . .   Y 123 Irene   V 100
      lover
    To cant, at last, of Reason to a Lover? . . . . .   O 281 Irene   34
    The Merchant sees her with wealh, the lover with his . . O 374 Irene   29
      Mistress
    To shield my Lover, and preserve my Country. . . . .   O 364 Irene   V   4
    And hot Abdalla hates the happy Lover. . . . . .   O 300 Irene   75
LOVER'S
    With more address a lover's note convey, ...   O 13 London   77
    Warm with an ardent lover's fondest pray'r. . . . .   O 80 Lady Birthday   2
    Oft favours, oft rejects a lover's pray'r: . . . . .   O 95 Sprig of Myrtl   6
    Now grants, and now rejects the Lover's Care . . . .   O 95 Sprig of Myrtl V   6
    Which gild a lover's lays, ...   O 126 To Lyce, Lady   6
    Or pay with speaking Eyes a Lover's Homage? . . . .   O 282 Irene   63
    Still to the Lover's long-expecting Arms, ...   O 283 Irene   30
    To me my Lover's Fondness will restore, ...   O 291 Irene   74
    Will not admit a Lover's long Farewell, ...   O 297 Irene   13
    Reproach not, Greece, a Lover's fond Delays, ...   O 297 Irene   19
    The Lover's Int'rest aids the Patriot's Claim. . . . .   O 305 Irene   46
    Nor press too much upon a Lover's Patience. . . . .   O 310 Irene   9
    Aspasia now within her Lover's Arms . . . . . .   O 325 Irene   17
    Soon might her Tears engage a Lover's Credit; . . . .   O 327 Irene   17
LOVERS
    Where e'er they fly their lovers ghosts pursue, ...   O 84 Epi Dist Moth.   36
    The Myrtle crowns the happy lovers heads, ...   O 95 Sprig of Myrtl   9
    Th' unhappy lovers graves the Myrtle spreads; . . . .   O 95 Sprig of Myrtl   10
    Who shine, by lavish lovers drest, ...   O 126 To Lyce, Lady   3
    But what Laws can Lovers awe? . . . .   O 150 Tr Boet III.12   47
    To Robbers furious, and to Lovers tame: . . . . .   O 174 Tr Epitaph Dog   1
    Nor Gods his Heroes, nor his Lovers Fools: . . . .   O 246 Irene Prologue   18
    And spare him, Beauties! tho' his Lovers live. . . . .   O 246 Irene Prologue   20
    In all the Fopperies of meeting Lovers; . . . . . .   O 269 Irene   14
    Aspasia's Lovers know but one Desire, ...   O 307 Irene   13
    Perhaps ev'n now the Lovers unpursu'd . . . . . .   O 322 Irene   4
LOVES
    Where gloom-enamour'd Mischief loves to dwell, ...   O 192 Tr. Medea II   V 15
    Our warlike Prophet loves an active Faith, ...   O 264 Irene   25
    Our warlike Prophet loves an active zeal . . . .   Y 131 Irene   V 25
LOVING
    Viewing lost and loving died. . . . .   O 150 Tr Boet III.12   V 52
LOW
    Low skulks the hind beneath the rage of pow'r, ...   O 32 Vanity Wishes   33
    Evn low built towns they Britain's modish tribe   Y 94 Vanity Wishes V   61
    Firm and low thy Mansion found; . . . .   O 145 Tr Boeth. II.4   16
    In a low vale by rocks that pierce the skies . . . .   Y 23 Tr Add. Battle   24

LOW   (CONTINUED)   PAGE   TITLE   LINE
        Till purse and carcase both were low. . . . .   Y 300 Extemp. Elegy   12
        Now she lies exceeding low, ...   Y 301 Extemp. Elegy   19
LOW'RING
        Nor let disdain sit low'ring in your eye; . . . . .   O 84 Epi Dist Moth.   43
LOW'RS
        I see the Gloom that low'rs upon thy Brow, ...   O 271 Irene   1
LOWER
        To all the lower world deny'd; . . . .   O 99 Ode Friendship   4
LUCKLESS
        The bold Bavarian, in a luckless hour, ...   O 42 Vanity Wishes   241
        Luckless slave Ilfated loiterer has fate in vain   . . . Y 196 Irene   V 15
        Accus'd the Gods and curs'd each luckless star.   . . .   Y   6 Virgil Daphnis   6
LUCKY
        This lucky Stratagem shall charm the Sultan, ...   O 319 Irene   5
LUG
        To his own house her did lug. . . . .   Y 301 Extemp. Elegy   16
LULL
        And for a moment lull the sense of woe. . . . . . .   O 10 London   32
        And lull to servitude a thoughtless age. . . . . . .   O 12 London   60
        Let artful Flatt'ry now, to lull Suspicion, ...   O 267 Irene   2
LULL'D
        Lull'd by the beating winds and dashing show'rs!   . . . O 135 Tr Rambler 117   2
        There had she lull'd me with endearing Falshoods, . . . O 331 Irene   18
LUR'D
        Nor e'er from virtue's path was lur'd aside, ...   O 118 Epitaph Hanmer   31
LURE
        Should no false Kindness lure to loose delight,   . . .   O 37 Vanity Wishes   147
        But thus reserv'd to lure the Wolves of Turkey, . . .   O 250 Irene   24
        Thy Life, too mean a Prey to lure Abdalla. . . . . .   O 319 Irene   27
        Some soft Decoy to lure me to Destruction! . . . . .   O 331 Irene   4
LURES
        Nor lures the search of avaricious eyes, ...   O 141 Tr Rambler 199   2
        Of Happiness, lures on from Toil to Toil, ...   O 310 Irene   2
LURK
        With servile Secrecy to lurk in Shades, ...   O 249 Irene   3
LURKING
        Treason so near us? lurking in our Palace . . . . .   O 369 Irene   V 20
        Betray'd some Traytor lurking near my Bosom. . . . .   O 273 Irene   23
        Disclos'd some Traytor lurking near our Bosoms . . . .   O 368 Irene   V   3
LURKS
        Where mischief lurks in gay disguise, ...   O 203 Tr. on Skating   3
LUSCIOUS
        "Then with luscious plenty gay . . . .   O 186 Anacreon Ode 9   35
        I displaid--before her all the gay luscious scene... . . Y 158 Irene   V   8
LUST
        The lust of wealth can never bear delay. . . . . . .   O 140 Tr Rambler 182   1
        The Lust of Gold succeeds the Rage of Conquest, . . .   O 249 Irene   13
        The Lust of Gold, unfeeling and remorseless! . . . .   O 249 Irene   14
        Behold how Lust and Rapine struggle round her. . . . .   O 252 Irene   82
        Untainted with the Lust of Innovation, ...   O 257 Irene   61
        Detested residence of lust and tyranny . . . . . .   Y 165 Irene   V 79
        To range those walks of tyranny and lust . . . . . .   Y 165 Irene   V 85
        Shall guard Aspasia from triumphant Lust. . . . . .   O 301 Irene   89
LUSTRE
        And add new lustre to the Grecian name. . . . . . .   Y 117 Irene   V109B
        Improves it's lustre, but impairs its . . . .   O 366 Irene   V   4
                Strength.
        With native Lustre and unborrow'd Greatness, ...   O 298 Irene   16
LUTE
        Nor lute nor lyre his feeble pow'rs attend, ...   O 43 Vanity Wishes   271
LUXURIANT
        When cates luxuriant pile the spacious dish, ...   O 193 Tr. Medea II   17
LUXURIES
        May spare the luxuries of sound. . . . .   O 191 Tr. Medea I   20
LUXURIOUS
        The regal palace, the luxurious board, ...   O 35 Vanity Wishes   115
        The pompous palace, the luxurious board, ...   Y 96 Vanity Wishes V 115
        A factious Populace, luxurious Nobles, ...   O 250 Irene   38
LUXURY
        And Luxury with sighs her slave resigns. . . . . . .   O 43 Vanity Wishes   266
        The studied arts of Luxury: . . . .   O 73 Hor. Epode II   56
        The various arts of Luxury: . . . .   O 73 Hor. Epode II V 56
        Did aught but Luxury relax our Nerves . . . . . .   O 347 Irene   V   5
LYBIA'S
        Where Lybia's swarthy offspring burns, ...   O 70 Hor.II Ode XX   14
LYBIAN
        Whate'er the swarthy Lybian boasts, ...   O 73 Hor. Epode II V 57
        Nor Lybian fowls, nor Snipes of Greece, ...   O 73 Hor. Epode II   59
        There trod the Lybian sands, ...   O 79 Feast St Simon   39
LYCE
        To Lyce, an elderly Lady . . . .   O 126 To Lyce, Lady   T
        Let Lyce share the praise. . . . .   O 126 To Lyce, Lady   8
        Denies my Lyce shines, ...   O 127 To Lyce, Lady   18
        My Lyce makes as good a sky, ...   O 127 To Lyce, Lady   23
LYCISCUS
        Lyciscus whose soft arms excell . . . .   Y 12 Tr Hor Epode 9   37
LYDIA'S
        From Lydia's monarch should the search descend,   . . .   O 45 Vanity Wishes   313
LYDIAT'S
        Hear Lydiat's life, and Galileo's end. . . . . . .   O 38 Vanity Wishes   164

	PAGE	TITLE	LINE	

LYE
And lend a lye the confidence of truth. . . . . O 12 London 56
Strain out with fault'ring diffidence a lye, ... O 16 London 130
And lye without a blush, without a smile; . . . . . O 17 London 147
The man whom fate has laid, where all must lye. . . . O 61 Pro Word Wise 6
May I lye cold beneath a load of clay. . . . . . . Y 18 Tr. Iliad Bk 6 25

LYES
"Here fairer than his flock the shepherd lyes . . . . Y 7 Virgil Daphnis 30

LYON
Nor shall the Lyon, wont of old to reign . . . . . O 111 To Posterity 19
yet the fierce Albanian lyon . . . . Y 130 Irene V 13
Prowls like a lyon oer the wealthy Spoils of bleeding . O 352 Irene V 29
Turkey.

LYON'S
The lyon's thirsty parent, bore. . . . . O 66 Hor I Ode xxii V 16

LYONESS
Where the Lyoness stood near, ... O 148 Tr Boet III.12 8

LYONS
Touch'd with thy fate Numidia's lyons roar . . . . . Y 6 Virgil Daphnis 11

LYRE
Nor lute nor lyre his feeble pow'rs attend, ... O 43 Vanity Wishes 271
To nobler subjects tune my lyre; . . . . O 78 Feast St Simon 8
Had Stella's gentle touches mov'd the Lyre, ... O 97 Hickman Spinet 15
Some zealous bard to wake the sleeping lyre. . . . . O 107 Lady F Assizes 4
For ever flutter o'er her lyre, ... O 121 To Miss Playin 14
"Drop asleep upon his lyre. . . . . O 186 Anacreon Ode 9 40
Such strains as, mingled with the lyre, ... O 188 Epilogue 1
But ne'er the Flute or Lyre apply'd . . . . O 190 Tr. Medea I 7
Trumpet or lyre--to their harsh bosoms chill, ... O 192 Tr. Medea II 11
To handle the melodious lyre. . . . . Y 11 Tr Hor Epode 9 4

MAD
With mad Devotion idolizes Honour. . . . . O 300 Irene 79

MADDED
And dubious title shakes the madded land, ... O 31 Vanity Wishes 30
From dubious titles shakes the madded land, ... Y 93 Vanity Wishes V 30

MADE SEE NEW-MADE
Where change of fav'rites made no change of laws, . . . O 33 Vanity Wishes 59
Tho' when Orpheus made his Moan . . . . O 148 Tr Boet III.12 5
Wealth, Sir John, was made to wander, ... O 196 Song Congratu. 17
Wealth, my lad, was made to wander, ... O 196 Song Congratu. V 17
Nor made a pause, nor left a void; . . . . O 201 Death Dr Levet 26
Nor made a pause, nor felt a void; . . . . O 201 Death Dr Levet V 26
Each Day and shall be made happy with new entertainments O 350 Irene V 24
Made passive Fortitude the Praise of Woman: . . . . O 290 Irene 44
Return'd with Force that made Resistance vain, ... O 317 Irene 38
Till she made the neighbours stare. . . . . Y 300 Extemp. Elegy 8

MADLY
Or meanly fraudulent, or madly gay, ... O 316 Irene 24

MADMAN'S
Horrid as a murd'rers dreams, madman's laughter . . . Y 133 Irene V 13
The raging Madman's unconnected Schemes . . . . . O 287 Irene 10

MADNESS
Fresh praise is try'd till madness fires his mind, . . O 42 Vanity Wishes 231
New praise is try'd till madness fires his mind, . . . Y 102 Vanity Wishes V 231
Grief and Madness unrepress'd . . . . O 148 Tr Boet III.12 13
All Thought on her is Madness . . . . O 252 Irene 79
May droop dismay'd, or kindle into Madness. . . . . O 304 Irene 11
'Tis Madness to provoke superfluous Danger, ... O 318 Irene 21
One Hour had sav'd me from Despair and Madness. . . . O 332 Irene 28
O seize me, Madness--Did she call on me! . . . . . O 334 Irene 68
Prodigious madness of the writing race! . . . . . . Y 67 Prologue Lethe 1

MAECENAS
Yet, great Maecenas, shall your friend . . . . . . O 70 Hor.II Ode XX 7

MAEON'S
When all conspiring leave Maeon's lake . . . . . . Y 24 Tr Add. Battle 66

MAEONIAN
Not the Maeonian Bard in lofty strain . . . . Y 23 Tr Add. Battle 54

MAEOTIS
The eternal Snows that shine beyond Maeotis . . . . . O 360 Irene V 2

MAGNET
Obscure, unpriz'd, and dark, the magnet lies, ... O 141 Tr Rambler 199 1

MAGNIFICENCE
Dress'd in each Charm of gay Magnificence, ... O 261 Irene 14
And all the proud magnificence of empire . . . . . . Y 158 Irene V 9

MAHOMET
Here Hunt may box, or Mahomet may dance. . . . . . O 53 Pro Drury-Lane 46
Did Mahomet reproach or praise her Virtue? . . . . . O 259 Irene 108
While Heav'n and Mahomet divide her Fears, ... O 260 Irene 127
These Years, unconquer'd Mahomet, demand . . . . . O 263 Irene 7
This were enough, if Cali had been Mahomet . . . . . Y 132 Irene V 41D
Half were too much had Mahomet been Cali. . . . . . Y 132 Irene V 41E
Long would my Zeal for Mahomet and Thee . . . . . . O 288 Irene 11
Remember Mahomet, and cease thy Labour. . . . . . . O 310 Irene 3
Then hear, great Mahomet, the Voice of Truth. . . . . O 333 Irene 55

MAHOMET'S
From giddy Mahomet's unskilful Hand. . . . . O 256 Irene 46
Can Mahomet's imperial Hand descend . . . . O 268 Irene 15
Who knows if Mahomet's awaking Anger . . . . O 284 Irene 38

MAID
No maid to flatter, and no paint to hide. . . . . . O 84 Epi Dist Moth. 41
Nor fear that I, my gentle maid, ... O 159 Par Hermit III 5

```
     Dear hapless Maid--tempestuous Grief o'erbears  . . . .    O 252 Irene              77
     Dear helpless Maid--tempestuous Grief o'erbears . . .      O 252 Irene          V   77
     Yet let me think--I see the helpless Maid,  . . . . .      O 252 Irene              80
     The pious Maid, with modest Indignation, . . . . . .       O 258 Irene             101
     Still restless, till I clasp the lovely Maid,  . . . .     O 263 Irene              21
     Observe, bright Maid, as his resistless Voice  . . . .     O 268 Irene              25
     And your new Charge, that dear, that heavn'ly Maid.--  .   O 270 Irene               5
     Permits the blooming maid secure and thoughtless   . . .  Y 146 Irene          V   18
     Too high, bright Maid, thou rat'st exterior Grace;  . .    O 277 Irene              30
     Illustrious Maid, new Wonders fix me thine, . . . . .      O 278 Irene              59
     Celestial fair--maid--new wonders fix me thine,  . . .     Y 149 Irene          V   59
     Make haste, bright Maid, to rule the willing World;  . .   O 288 Irene               7
     Thou shin'st, bright Maid, superior to Distress;  . . .    O 298 Irene              17
     But see,the lofty Maid at our Approach, . . . . . .        O 314 Irene              14
     Devolve, dear Maid, thy Sorrows on the Wretch,  . . . .    O 316 Irene              16
     At length the Prize is mine--The haughty Maid   . . .      O 317 Irene               1
     Leave but this Maid, resign a hopeless Claim,  . . . .     O 319 Irene              25
     Quit but this maid, resign a hopeless claim  . . . . .     Y 197 Irene          V   25
     Farewell, unhappy Maid, may ev'ry Joy . . . . . . .        O 322 Irene              57
     Was this the Maid whose Love I bought with Empire!  . .    O 330 Irene               9
     Robb'd of the Maid, with whom I wish'd to triumph,  . .    O 333 Irene              42
MAIDS
     Receive th' unhappy ghosts of scornful maids.  . . . .     O  83 Epi Dist Moth.      13
     The Dream of idle Maids and wanton Poets  . . . . . .      O 350 Irene          V    1
     Hence to the palace and your maids repair;  . . . . .      Y  21 Tr. Iliad Bk 6    121
MAIN
     Behold her cross triumphant on the main,  . . . . . .      O  10 London             27
     No secret island in the boundless main? . . . . . . .      O  18 London            172
     Or storms afflict the ruffled main.  . . . . . . .         O  67 Hor. II Ode IX      4
     And terrours of the Stormy Main,  . . . . . . . . .        O  69 Hor.II Ode 14      14
     When floods of Nectar stain'd the main,  . . . . . .       O  71 Hor. Epode II       4
     Thine, Minos, is the main, and thine the land.  . . .      O 136 Tr Rambler 129      4
     Wouldst thou see the foaming Main,  . . . . . . . .        O 144 Tr Boeth. II.4      5
     Unbounded Masters of the main.  . . . . . . . . .          O 189 Epilogue            8
     Unbounded Rulers of the main.   . . . . . . . . .          O 189 Epilogue       V    8
     Where amidst the roarings of the Northern   . . . . .      Y 121 Irene          V   56
       main
     For you shall plough the main, and fight the battle  . .   Y 146 Irene          V  23B
     Thy sacred Freight shall still the raging Main.  . . .     Y 322 Irene               6
     The sacred Freight shall still the raging Main.  . . .     O 322 Irene          V    6
     And all the terrors of the dreadful main . . . . .         Y 201 Irene          V  10C
     See! Sol's bright chariot seeks the western main, . . .    Y   4 On a Daffodill     22
MAINTAIN
     All aid the farce, and all thy mirth maintain,  . . . .    O  33 Vanity Wishes      67
MAINTAIN'D
     And Jollity maintain'd eternal Revels.--   . . . . . .     O 251 Irene              65
     Not so while long th' undaunted race maintain'd  . . .     Y  23 Tr Add. Battle     36
MAINTAINS
     Scarce frighted love maintains his fire,  . . . . . .      O 123 Winter's Walk      11
     Scarce frighted love maintains her fire, . . . . . . .     O 123 Winter's Walk  V   11
MAJESTICK
     A turkish Stranger of majestick Mien, . . . . . . .        O 294 Irene               1
MAJESTY
     The Sultan's majesty the warriours rage  . . . . .         Y 123 Irene          V   98
     The Sultan's majesty the warriours fierceness  . . .       Y 123 Irene          V   98
     Superiour Majesty proclaims the Queen,  . . . . . . .      O 288 Irene               2
     Superiour Majesty proclaims thee Queen,  . . . . . . .     O 288 Irene          V    2
MAKE
     And make will before you sup from home.  . . . . . .       Y  59 London          V  225
     And mould his passions till they make his will.  . . .     O  44 Vanity Wishes     282
     To make thy curious web delight,  . . . . . . . .          O 119 To Miss Purse       2
     To make the curious web delight,  . . . . . . . .          O 119 To Miss Purse   V   2
     Thou canst not make the tea so fast  . . . . . . .         O 159 Par Hermit III     11
     To make Aspasia and Irene name each other.  . . . . .      Y 133 Irene          V   10
     Deceive--And make us happy by deceiving  . . . . . .       Y 148 Irene          V   50
     To make thee blest each Region shall combine  . . . .      O 351 Irene          V   26
     Did ever Passion make so swift a Progress?  . . . . .      O 281 Irene              55
     But he must live to make his Masters wretched?  . . . .    O 286 Irene               7
     Make haste, bright Maid, to rule the willing World;  . .   O 288 Irene               7
     Nor Wealth, nor Titles, make Aspasia's Bliss.  . . . .     O 302 Irene             106
     There I became, nor blush to make it known, . . . . .      O 312 Irene              13
     Now make thy Choice, while yet the Pow'r of Choice  . .    O 321 Irene              40
MAKER'S
     New from the Maker's Hand, and fair array'd  . . . . .     O 314 Irene               4
     New from the Maker's Hand, and far array'd . . . . .       O 314 Irene          V    4
MAKES
     And makes the happiness she does not find. . . . . .       O  48 Vanity Wishes     368
     My Lyce makes as good a sky,  . . . . . . . . . .          O 127 To Lyce, Lady      23
     Heav'n makes not mine to give.  . . . . . . . . .          O 307 Irene              16
MALADIES
     With age, with cares, with maladies oppress'd,  . . . .    O  35 Vanity Wishes     117
     Unnumber'd maladies his joints invade,  . . . . . .        O  44 Vanity Wishes     283
     Unnumber'd maladies each Joint invade,  . . . . . .        O  44 Vanity Wishes  V  283
     And all the Maladies of sinking States.  . . . . . .       O 250 Irene              39
MALEVOLENCE
     With close Malevolence, or public Rage;  . . . . . .       O  57 Prologue Comus      8
MALICE
     Here malice, rapine, accident, conspire, . . . . . . .     O   9 London             13
     From zeal or malice now no more we dread,  . . . . . .     O  61 Pro Word Wise       3
     Insidious Malice aims her Darts in vain;  . . . . . .      O 322 Irene               2
```

```
MALICE          (CONTINUED)                         PAGE    TITLE          LINE
    Perhaps her Malice might transfer the Charge,  .  .  .  .  .   O 327 Irene               18
MALICIOUS
    And fate malicious heard the pray'r.  .  .  .  .  .  .        O 122 Stella Mourn.         8
    Her Sons malicious Clemency shall spare,  .  .  .  .  .  .    O 309 Irene                32
MALIGNANT
    Or glare on Cali with malignant Beams.  .  .  .  .  .         O 304 Irene                36
    And view thy charms with no malignant eyes:  .  .  .  .  .    Y   3 On a Daffodill       14
MAN
    Who sleeps on brambles till he kills his man;  .  .  .  .     O  21 London              227
    Where wav'ring man, betray'd by vent'rous pride,  .  .  .     O  31 Vanity Wishes         7
    Toil crush'd conceit, and man was of a piece;  .  .  .  .     O  32 Vanity Wishes        54
    Nor think the doom of man revers'd for thee:  .  .  .  .      O  38 Vanity Wishes       156
    Must helpless man, in ignorance sedate,  .  .  .  .  .  .     O  47 Vanity Wishes       345
    For love, which scarce collective man can fill;  .  .  .      O  48 Vanity Wishes       361
    For love, whose grasp Creation collective man can  .  .  .    Y 108 Vanity Wishes    V 361
        fill;
    These goods for man the laws of heav'n ordain,  .  .  .  .    O  48 Vanity Wishes       365
    Prologue to "The Good Natur'd Man"  .  .  .  .  .  .          O  59 Pro Good Nat'd        T
    The man whom fate has laid, where all must lye.  .  .  .      O  61 Pro Word Wise         6
    The man, my friend, whose conscious heart  .  .  .  .  .      O  65 Hor I Ode xxii        1
    The Man, my Friend, whose conscious Heart  .  .  .  .  .      O  66 To A. Fuscus          1
    See! how whate'er remain'd of Man  .  .  .  .  .  .  .        O  70 Hor.II Ode XX        10
    At once commenc'd the Senator and Man.  .  .  .  .  .         O 117 Epitaph Hanmer       12
    Unhappy man! behold thy doom,  .  .  .  .  .  .  .            O 124 Winter's Walk        14
    On darkling man in pure effulgence shine,  .  .  .  .  .      O 130 Tr. Rambler 7         3
    Vain man runs headlong, to caprice resign'd;  .  .  .  .      O 134 Tr Rambler 105        1
    Thou, who began'st a man, wilt end a boy.  .  .  .  .  .      O 135 Tr Rambler 127        2
    With ev'ry bliss that man can gain.  .  .  .  .  .  .         O 136 Tr Rambler 128        6
    Like them man flourishes, like them decays.  .  .  .  .  .    O 138 Tr Rambler 161        2
    The Man who pants for ample Sway  .  .  .  .  .  .  .         O 146 Tr Boeth III.5        1
    And there I met another man  .  .  .  .  .  .  .              O 158 Par. Hermit II        3
    I there did meet another man  .  .  .  .  .  .  .             O 158 Par. Hermit II   V   3
    My whole, is a Man in whose converse is shar'd,  .  .  .      O 179 Charade!              3
    If the man who turnips cries,  .  .  .  .  .  .  .            O 183 Burlesque Vega        1
    Proclaims mortality to Man.  .  .  .  .  .  .  .  .           O 231 Tr Horace IV.7        8
    But wretched Man, when once he lies  .  .  .  .  .  .         O 232 Tr Horace IV.7       14
    To please his Fancy,--see no other Man--  .  .  .  .  .       O 247 Irene Epilogue        3
    And for one Man--one Wife's enough in Conscience.  .  .  .    O 247 Irene Epilogue       14
    In vain proud Man usurps what's Woman's Due;  .  .  .  .      O 247 Irene Epilogue       15
    The last Corruption of degenerate Man!  .  .  .  .  .         O 249 Irene                15
    When every Man busied  .  .  .  .  .  .  .  .  .             O 347 Irene             V  21
    With counterfeited Fears the Aid of Man;  .  .  .  .  .       O 266 Irene                28
    And all Aspasia but her Beauty's Man.  .  .  .  .  .  .       O 266 Irene                37
    While with incessant Thought laborious Man  .  .  .  .        O 269 Irene                 3
    Records each Act, each Thought of sov'reign Man,  .  .  .     O 276 Irene                21
    Records each deed each thought of sovereign Man  .  .  .      O 355 Irene             V  10
    Superior man descends which  .  .  .  .  .  .  .             Y 147 Irene             V  39
    Why, when the Balm of Sleep descends on Man,  .  .  .  .      O 277 Irene                43
    To man bewilderd in this maze of sorrows  .  .  .  .  .       Y 148 Irene             V  43
    Assume the boastful Arrogance of Man.  .  .  .  .  .  .       O 277 Irene                50
    So weak is Man, when destin'd to Destruction,  .  .  .  .     O 283 Irene                12
    Young Man, forbear--The Heat of Youth, no more--  .  .  .     O 284 Irene                47
    Guides through the Maze of Life the Steps  .  .  .  .  .      O 346 Irene             V   6
        of Man
    Superiour Man possess'd the Charge of Rule,  .  .  .  .       O 291 Irene                71
    Capricious Man! to Good and Ill inconstant,  .  .  .  .       O 300 Irene                76
    Why should the man whose violence of duty  .  .  .  .  .      Y 210 Irene             V  18
    Weak Man with erring Rage may throw the Dart,  .  .  .  .     O 335 Irene                14
    And man the walls and fortifie the tow'rs.  .  .  .  .  .     Y  19 Tr. Iliad Bk 6       51
MAN'S
    The wise man's follies,  .  .  .  .  .  .  .  .              Y 106 Vanity Wishes    V 316
        Forgive an old Man's Weakness,  .  .  .  .  .  .  .       O 256 Irene                38
    Learn, that the present Hour alone is Man's.  .  .  .  .      O 283 Irene                33
    Whate'er Man's Pride has ravish'd from our Sex.  .  .  .      O 291 Irene                75
MANDATES
    And thinks his fatal Mandates ill obey'd.  .  .  .  .  .      O 327 Irene                13
    The tongue that forges mandates for destruction  .  .  .      Y 210 Irene             V 25A
MANGLED
    Small bones and mangled bodies scatter'd there  .  .  .  .    Y  23 Tr Add. Battle       31
MANKIND
    Survey mankind, from China to Peru;  .  .  .  .  .  .         O  30 Vanity Wishes         2
    O'erlook mankind, from China to Peru;  .  .  .  .  .  .       Y  91 Vanity Wishes    V   2
    And crouds with crimes the records of mankind;  .  .  .       O  31 Vanity Wishes        24
    With half mankind embattled at his side,  .  .  .  .  .       O  42 Vanity Wishes       226
    With half mankind embattled on his side,  .  .  .  .  .       Y 102 Vanity Wishes    V 226
    So shall Belinda's charms improve mankind.  .  .  .  .  .     O  81 Lady Birthday        19
    So shall you guiltless reign, and all mankind adore.  .  .    O  84 Epi Dist Moth.       47
    Delighted still to please mankind, or mend,  .  .  .  .  .    O 118 Epitaph Hanmer       39
    Spreads wide the mighty Moral for Mankind.  .  .  .  .        O 246 Irene Prologue        8
    Spreads wide the mighty Moral of Mankind.  .  .  .  .  .      O 246 Irene Prologue   V   8
    To offer up my vows in the temple built by the Father of     O 348 Irene             V   1
        Mankind
    Born to command, as thou to charm Mankind,  .  .  .  .  .     O 268 Irene                23
    Unites the jarring voices of mankind  .  .  .  .  .  .        Y 136 Irene             V 32A
    To hear my Vows and give Mankind a Queen?  .  .  .  .  .      O 276 Irene                 2
    While I destroy th' Oppressor of Mankind?  .  .  .  .  .      O 305 Irene                37
    And spread the general Transport through Mankind.  .  .  .    O 308 Irene                 5
    With grief this emblem of mankind I see,  .  .  .  .  .  .    Y   4 On a Daffodill       25
MANLY
    The rustick grai eur, and the manly grace,  .  .  .  .  .     Y  53 London           V 102
```

MANN'D

	PAGE	TITLE	LINE
Mann'd with the bravest of our fellow Captives,	O 254	Irene	135
A Galley mann'd with Greeks, thy charge, Leontius,	O 258	Irene	81

MANNERS

That saw the manners in the Face.	O 154	Epita. Hogarth	4

MANORS

Let such raise palaces, and manors buy,	O 12	London	57

MANSION

And Bacon's mansion trembles o'er his head.	O 37	Vanity Wishes	140
Firm and low thy Mansion found;	O 145	Tr Boeth. II.4	16

MANSIONS

Oh! send them to the sullen mansions dun,	O 192	Tr. Medea II	13
As those that bless the Mansions of the Good.	O 262	Irene	12
Fly the Detested mansions of Impiety	O 346	Irene	V 7
Descend to range these Mansions of Misfortune,	O 292	Irene	95
And from the Mansions of perpetual Peace	O 306	Irene	55

MANTLING

Tho' no lewd hint the mantling virgin warm.	Y 67	Prologue Lethe	14

MANTUAN

At length aspire to Mantuan praise.	O 139	Tr Rambler 169	2

MANURES

In vain the lab'ring hind manures the plain,	Y 6	Virgil Daphnis	22

MANURING

Manuring with laborious hand	O 71	Hor. Epode II	5

MANY

Their souls dismiss'd through many a ghastly wound,	O 74	Tr. Iliad Bk-6	18
Here lies a fowl transfix'd with many a wound	O 76	Tr Add. Battle	14
At length deform'd with many a grisly wound	O 76	Tr Add. Battle	24
Well tried through many a varying year,	O 201	Death Dr Levet	5
When a river is drain'd by too many channels the stream is dry.	Y 132	Irene	V 41B
Black her eye with many a blow,	Y 301	Extemp. Elegy	17
Hot her breath with many a dram,	Y 301	Extemp. Elegy	18
While many a merry tale, and many a song,	Y 310	Parody of Pope	1
While many a merry tale, and many a song,	Y 310	Parody of Pope	1

MANY-COLOUR'D

Each Change of many-colour'd Life he drew,	O 51	Pro Drury-Lane	3

MARBLE

The polish'd marble, and the shining plate,	O 19	London	207
Along the marble floor shall flow.	O 69	Hor.II Ode 14	28
Deform the beauties of the breathing statue (marble hero	Y 177	Irene	V111A

MARCH

The march begins in military state,	O 40	Vanity Wishes	205
The Soldier lab'ring through a Winter's March,	O 283	Irene	28

MAREOTIS'

To Mareotis' fen the rumour flies	Y 24	Tr Add. Battle	68

MARK

Mark whom the great caress, who frown on me!	O 14	London	92
Afar they mark the flambeau's bright approach,	O 21	London	234
Mark from afar the flambeau's bright approach,	Y 59	London	V 234
Mark the keen glance, and watch the sign to hate.	O 34	Vanity Wishes	110
There mark what ills the scholar's life assail,	O 38	Vanity Wishes	159
Did no subverted empire mark his end?	O 41	Vanity Wishes	216
And mark the future Periods of the Stage?--	O 53	Pro Drury-Lane	40
Mark, when from thousand mingled dyes	O 110	To Posterity	8
Mark, when the diff'rent notes agree	O 121	To Miss Playin	25
To mark the noblest Minds, with active Heat	O 121	To Miss Playin	29
To mark the noblest Minds. With active fire	O 293	Irene	112
Thus meaner Spirits with Amazement mark	O 369	Irene	V 3
Till angry Heav'n shall mark them out for Ruin,	O 293	Irene	117
	O 309	Irene	36

MARK'D

Mark'd out by dangerous parts he meets the shock,	O 39	Vanity Wishes	171
Just as I mark'd them, they forsook the Shore,	O 269	Irene	38
I mark'd them well, and trac'd in either Face	O 275	Irene	81
She mark'd my sparkling Eyes, and heaving Breast,	O 282	Irene	68
We mark'd him storming in Excess of Fury,	O 311	Irene	11
I mark'd her wily Messenger afar,	O 327	Irene	24
That mark'd my Course, suspicious of my Purpose,	O 335	Irene	6

MARKED

A signal hour marked out by pitying Heav'n	Y 117	Irene	V 109

MARKS

Marks for His own still doat upon to Morrow	O 374	Irene	V 21
My Zeal marks Gladness dawning on thy Cheek,	O 286	Irene	2

MARLB'ROUGH

All Marlb'rough hoarded, or all Villiers spent,	O 14	London	86

MARLB'ROUGH'S

From Marlb'rough's eyes the streams of dotage flow,	O 45	Vanity Wishes	317

MARO'S

Augustus still survives in Maro's strain,	O 114	On C. Cibber	1

MARRY

Marry a Turk! a haughty, Tyrant King,	O 247	Irene Epilogue	1

MARSH

Here with dead mice the marsh was strew'd around;	Y 24	Tr Add. Battle	58

MARTIAL

The daring Greeks deride the martial show,	O 42	Vanity Wishes	235
His martial Rhet'rick taught the Greeks Resistance;	O 263	Irene	26

MARTYR

Some virgin Martyr,	O 252	Irene	95

MARTYRS

Ye sacred Shades of Patriots and of Martyrs;	O 306	Irene	52

```
MARTYRS          (CONTINUED)                         PAGE    TITLE          LINE
     Ye holy shades of--martyrs  . . . . . . . .     Y 181 Irene           V 52
MASQUERADES
     Ere masquerades debauch'd, excise oppress'd,  . . . .   O  10 London          29
MASSACRE
     Fall in the gen'ral massacre of gold;  . . . . . . .    O  31 Vanity Wishes   22
     Amidst the gen'ral massacre of gold;  . . . . . . .     Y  92 Vanity Wishes  V 22
     Unpitying Massacre might waste the World,  . . . . .    O 291 Irene           65
MASTER
     Their master and their God.  . . . . . . . . .         O  79 Feast St Simon   18
     Thou joy'st to lose the master in the friend:  . . . . O 130 Tr. Rambler 12    4
     I pleas'd my Master, and I pleas'd my Dame.  . . . . . O 174 Tr Epitaph Dog    2
     And sure th' Eternal Master found  . . . . . . .       O 201 Death Dr Levet   27
     Now be some Moments Master of thyself,  . . . . .      O 282 Irene            70
     And bid the master Genius rule the World.  . . . .     O 309 Irene            42
     Well mayst thou call thy Master to the Combat,  . . .  O 319 Irene            30
MASTER'S
     Practis'd their master's notions to embrace,  . . . .  O  16 London         136
     Rag'd within the Master's Breast  . . . . . . .        O 148 Tr Boet III.12   14
     "Vested with a master's right  . . . . . . .           O 185 Anacreon Ode 9   13
     "Smiling at my master's gates,  . . . . . . .          O 185 Anacreon Ode 9   19
     Thou know'st not yet thy Master's future Greatness,  . O 265 Irene            40
     The Bassa, reeking with his Master's Murder,  . . .    O 300 Irene            80
     The Place appointed for his Master's Death.  . . . .   O 326 Irene            30
MASTERS
     Unbounded Masters of the main.  . . . . . . .          O 189 Epilogue          8
     But he must live to make his Masters wretched?  . . .  O 286 Irene             7
     Is this your ardour for your masters safety  . . . .   Y 207 Irene           V 14
MATCHLESS
     How will the matchless Beauties of Irene,  . . . . .   O 276 Irene             6
     The matchless Fair has bless'd me with Compliance;  .  O 308 Irene             3
     Who matchless strength and bulk gygantick boasts,  .   Y  24 Tr Add. Battle   81
     As when great Briareus with matchless might  . . . .   Y  26 Tr Add. Battle  137
MATTER
     Essence Divine with Matter join'd.  . . . . . . .      O 147 Tr Boeth III.6   12
MATURER
     To stronger Efforts, and maturer Counsels.  . . . . .  O 270 Irene             8
MAXIM
     And Slaves, the Maxim tells, are always Foes.  . . .   O  46 Vanity Wishes  V330B
     That Maxim publish'd in an impious Age,  . . . . .     O 291 Irene            60
MAXIMS
     Repeat his maxims, and reflect his face;  . . . . .    O  16 London         137
     Maxims like these, if generally persued  . . . . .     O 352 Irene           V  2
     Maxims like these, if once reduc'd to practice  . . .  O 352 Irene           V  2
MAY
     Well may they rise, while I, whose rustick tongue  . . O  14 London          79
     Well may they venture on the mimick's art,  . . . .    O  16 London         134
     Well may we fear, such crowds at Tyburn die,  . . .    Y  60 London         V 242
     Which heavn may hear  . . . . . . . . .               Y 108 Vanity Wishes  V 348
     Which heav'n may hear, nor deem religion vain.  . . .  O  47 Vanity Wishes  350
     On flying Cars new Sorcerers may ride.  . . . . .      O  53 Pro Drury-Lane   44
     Here Hunt may box, or Mahomet may dance.  . . . .      O  53 Pro Drury-Lane   46
     Here Hunt may box, or Mahomet may dance.  . . . . .    O  53 Pro Drury-Lane   46
     Our anxious Bard, without complaint, may share  . . .  O  59 Pro Good Nat'd    5
     Our little Bard, without complaint, may share  . . .   O  59 Pro Good Nat'd  V  5
     Uncheck'd on both, caprice may vent its rage,  . . .   O  59 Pro Good Nat'd  V 15
     For that blest year when all that vote may rail;  . .  O  60 Pro Good Nat'd   18
     Till that glad night when all that hate may hiss.  . . O  60 Pro Good Nat'd   20
     The bard may supplicate, but cannot bribe.  . . . .    O  60 Pro Good Nat'd   26
     May I lie slain, and spurn the bloody sand!  . . .     O  75 Tr. Iliad Bk 6   30
     Or if old womens tales may credit gain,  . . . . .     O  77 Tr. Add. Battle  44
     May this returning day for ever find  . . . . .        O  80 Lady Birthday     3
     All pains, all cares, may favouring heav'n remove,  .  O  81 Lady Birthday     5
     May powerful nature join with grateful art,  . . . .   O  81 Lady Birthday     7
     May powerful nature join with graceful art,  . . . .   Y  36 Lady Birthday   V  7
     Oh may this Flame neer cease to glow  . . . . . .      O 100 Ode Friendship  V 25
     Thy nets may catch, but not confine,  . . . . .        O 120 To Miss Purse     8
     Thy nets may snare, but not confine,  . . . . . .      O 120 To Miss Purse   V  8
     Place may be chang'd; but who can change his mind?  .  O 137 Tr Rambler 135    1
     Long may live my lovely Hetty!  . . . . . . . .        O 175 Tr Easy Phrase    1
     Long may live my lovely Hetty!  . . . . . . .          O 175 Tr Easy Phrase    6
     Long may better Years arrive,  . . . . . . . .         O 178 Thrale 35 Year    3
     Oft may better Years arrive,  . . . . . . . .          O 178 Thrale 35 Year  V  3
     The near approach a bed may shew  . . . . . .          O 184 Tr. Benserade     3
     May ye the varied blessings share  . . . . . . .       O 189 Epilogue          5
     May ye th' alternate blessings share  . . . . . .      O 189 Epilogue        V  5
     May spare the luxuries of sound.  . . . . . . .        O 191 Tr. Medea I      20
     O may her Beauties last unchang'd by Time,  . . . .    O 262 Irene            11
     He yet may live.  . . . . . . . . . . .               O 267 Irene            45
     Well may those Eyes that view these heav'nly Charms,  .O 267 Irene             6
     And may a long Posterity of Monarchs,  . . . . .       O 267 Irene            11
     But Fear, or Mutiny may taint the Greeks?  . . . .     O 284 Irene            37
     May spare the fatal Bow-string till To-morrow?  . . .  .O 284 Irene           39
     And sparkling quiver to the Breath of May;  . . . .    O 298 Irene            21
     Soon may the final Stroke decide our Fate,  . . . .    O 299 Irene            51
     Perhaps may start at violated Friendship.  . . . .     O 300 Irene            81
     Soon may we meet again, secure and free,  . . . .      O 303 Irene            23
     May droop dismay'd, or kindle into Madness.  . . . .   O 304 Irene            11
     A private Station may discover more;  . . . . .        O 316 Irene            18
     You may provoke but never can convince  . . . . .      Y 197 Irene           V 31
     Farewell, unhappy Maid, may ev'ry Joy  . . . . . .     O 322 Irene            57
```

			PAGE	TITLE		LINE

MAY   (CONTINUED)

May Penitence attend thy mournful Bed, ...   O 322 Irene   61
And may bounteous Heav'n repay the mercy on Your . . . O 344 Irene   V 27
    Heads
Weak Man with erring Rage may throw the Dart, ...   O 335 Irene   14
May no rude blasts thy sacred bloom destroy; . . . . .   Y   3 On a Daffodill   7
May storms howl gently o'er and learn to spare. . . . .   Y   3 On a Daffodill   8
May lambent zephyrs gently wave thy head, ...   Y   3 On a Daffodill   9
May balmy spirits thro thy foliage play, ...   Y   3 On a Daffodill   V 10
May the morn's earliest tears on thee be shed, ...   Y   3 On a Daffodill   11
May throngs of beautious virgins 'round thee crowd, . .   Y   3 On a Daffodill   13
May I lye cold beneath a load of clay. . . . . . .   Y 18 Tr. Iliad Bk 6   25
May then his mother's heart with joys o'erflow . . . .   Y 20 Tr. Iliad Bk 6 105
And may she ne'er returning sorrows know." . . . . .   Y 20 Tr. Iliad Bk 6 106
This night he hopes to shew that farce may charm, . . .   Y 67 Prologue Lethe   13
That useful truth with humour may unite, ...   Y 67 Prologue Lethe   15
That mirth may mend, and innocence delight. . . . . .   Y 67 Prologue Lethe   16
MAY'ST
Well may'st thou hide in Labyrinths of Sound . . . .   O 293 Irene   125
MAYOR'S
Or seen a new-made mayor's unwieldy state; . . . . .   O 33 Vanity Wishes   58
Or seen the new-made mayor's unwieldy state; . . . .   Y 94 Vanity Wishes   V 58
MAYST
Well mayst thou call thy Master to the Combat, ...   O 319 Irene   30
MAZ'D
Snar'd with thy Fears, and maz'd in Stupefaction. . . .   O 318 Irene   18
Frozen with doubt, and maz'd in stupefaction. . . . .   Y 196 Irene   V 18B
MAZE
O'erspread with snares the clouded maze of fate, . . .   O 31 Vanity Wishes   6
When mutual frauds perplex'd the maze of State, . . .   O 118 Epitaph Hanmer   24
To man bewilderd in this maze of sorrows . . . . . .   Y 148 Irene   V 43
Guides through the Maze of Life the Steps . . . . .   O 346 Irene   V 6
    of Man
MAZY
The mazy dance together trace. . . . .   O 231 Tr Horace IV.7   6
ME
Grant me, kind heaven, to find some happier place, . . .   O 11 London   43
But what, my friend, what hope remains for me, ...   O 13 London   67
Mark whom the great caress, who frown on me! . . . .   O 14 London   92
The tide retiring, calls me from the land: . . . . .   O 22 London   255
And tir'd like me with follies and with crimes, ...   O 23 London   258
And me to tune at ease th' unequal reeds. . . . . .   O 64 Virgil Past.I   12
Me singing, careless and unarm'd, ...   O 65 Hor I Ode xxii   11
Place me where no soft summer gale . . . .   O 66 Hor I Ode xxii   17
Place me beneath the burning line, ...   O 66 Hor I Ode xxii   21
Me singing, careless and unarm'd, ...   O 66 To A. Fuscus   11
Place me where no soft Summer Gale . . . .   O 67 To A. Fuscus   17
Place me beneath the burning Zone, ...   O 67 To A. Fuscus   21
O guide me through life's darksome way, ...   O 100 Ode Friendship   14
Spread out by me, the roving coin, ...   O 120 To Miss Purse   7
Snatch me, my Stella, to thy arms, ...   O 124 Winter's Walk   19
And screen me from the ills of life. . . . .   O 124 Winter's Walk   20
And hide me from the sight of life. . . . .   O 124 Winter's Walk   V 20
And bears me to the peaceful shades, ...   O 125 An Ode   15
Here let me thro' the vales pursue . . . .   O 125 An Ode   21
Here let me learn the use of life, ...   O 125 An Ode   27
Teach me, thou venerable bow'r, ...   O 125 An Ode   29
Here let me learn to shun the crimes . . . .   O 126 An Ode   35
Bright wisdom teach me Curio's art, ...   O 126 An Ode   38
With me retire and leave the pomp of courts . . . . .   O 137 Tr Rambler 138   1
As not to grant me this, can Milton find? . . . . . .   O 137 Tr Rambler 140   2
How small to others, but how great to me. . . . . .   O 138 Tr Rambler 161   1
On me you turn the nose.----- . . . .   O 140 Tr Rambler 176   1
When fondness melts me, or when wine inflames, ...   O 142 In Baretti Bk.   2
That thou wilt give to me, ...   O 158 Par Hermit III   2
Aphrosi me semnen, Xeine, podessi patei . . . . . .   O 171 Epi. Goldsmith   2
Tell me, tell me, gentle Dove. . . . .   O 185 Anacreon Ode 9   6
Tell me, tell me, gentle Dove. . . . .   O 185 Anacreon Ode 9   6
"Weighty charge consign'd to me: . . . .   O 185 Anacreon Ode 9   16
"Tempts me to be wild again: . . . .   O 185 Anacreon Ode 9   22
"Let me now my pinions ply, ...   O 186 Anacreon Ode 9   43
Let him persuade me to it--if he can: . . . .   O 247 Irene Epilogue   4
Yet let me think--I see the helpless Maid, ...   O 252 Irene   80
O Providence! extend thy Care to me, ...   O 252 Irene   90
Array'd in purer Light, look down on me: . . . . . .   O 253 Irene   101
O! sooth my Soul, and teach me how to lose thee. . . .   O 253 Irene   103
"Awake, and follow me to better Fortunes;" . . . . .   O 254 Irene   123
And led me to the Shore where Cali stood, ...   O 254 Irene   127
Demetrius will not lead me to Dishonour; . . . . . .   O 256 Irene   35
Consult in private, call me when your Scheme . . . . .   O 256 Irene   36
Frowns unrestrain'd, and dooms me with his Eyes. . . .   O 257 Irene   72
O lead me quickly to the Scene of Fate; . . . . . .   O 259 Irene   105
Aspasia calls me, let me fly to save her. . . . . . .   O 259 Irene   107
Aspasia calls me, let me fly to save her. . . . . . .   O 259 Irene   107
Teach me the Grecian arts of soft persuasion . . . . .   O 349 Irene   V 27
And not a harvest ripen but for me . . . .   Y 132 Irene   V 42
--Till every constellation shines for me . . . . . .   Y 132 Irene   V 45
And teach me to repell the Sultan's Passion. . . . . .   O 265 Irene   3
Stern Torture shakes his bloody Scourge before me, . . .   O 266 Irene   15
How nation after nation falls before me . . . . . .   Y 136 Irene   V 27
Toils all its languages to flatter me. . . . . . .   Y 136 Irene   V 29

ME   (CONTINUED)   PAGE   TITLE   LINE

	PAGE	TITLE	LINE
And every language toils to flatter me.	Y 136 Irene		V 32B
And yet another Voice, forgive me Greece,	O 270 Irene		18
Each lin'gring Hour alarms me for Aspasia.	O 270 Irene		20
At once a hundred Voices thunder'd round me,	O 271 Irene		29
My Father call'd me to his Couch of Death,	O 272 Irene		7
Or set The Persian Heretic in arms against Me	O 348 Irene		V 17
And, to confirm my Thought, at sight of me,	O 275 Irene		84
Then let me once, in honour of our Sex,	O 277 Irene		49
Then Let me once to right our injur'd Sex	O 356 Irene		V 16
Illustrious Maid, new Wonders fix me thine,	O 278 Irene		59
Celestial fair--maid--new wonders fix me thine,	Y 149 Irene		V 59
Forbear--O do not urge me to my Ruin!	O 278 Irene		79
Important Cares detain'd me from your Counsels.	O 279 Irene		6
Give me, before th' approaching Hour of Fate,	O 285 Irene		5
Urge me not on to glittering Guilt, nor pour	O 288 Irene		5
Detain me here. But Nations call upon me,	O 288 Irene		12
Detain me here. But Nations call upon me,	O 288 Irene		12
And Duty bids me chuse a distant Walk,	O 288 Irene		13
Upbraid me not with fancy'd Wickedness,	O 289 Irene		21
If when Religion prompts me to refuse,	O 289 Irene		24
To me my Lover's Fondness will restore,	O 291 Irene		74
Ah! let me rather seek the Convent's Cell;	O 292 Irene		93
On me, should Providence, without a Crime,	O 292 Irene		103
Call me to civilize the Russian Wilds,	O 292 Irene		105
New joy comes rushing on me and o'erwhelms	Y 169 Irene		V 12
The Present, Past, and Future swim before me,	O 295 Irene		13
Inform me rather, how thy happy Courage	O 295 Irene		27
Concur'd to give me to Aspasia's Arms,	O 296 Irene		36
Prudence and Friendship bid me force her from you.	O 296 Irene		7
Yet let me watch her dear departing Steps,	O 297 Irene		17
If Fate pursues me, let it find me here.	O 297 Irene		18
If Fate pursues me, let it find me here.	O 297 Irene		18
If Fate persues me, let it find me here	O 297 Irene		V 18
If Fate persues me, let it find me here	O 297 Irene		V 18
Perhaps in vain the Sultan's Anger spar'd me,	O 298 Irene		32
With noisy Falshoods forc'd me from your Arms,	O 299 Irene		39
Th' approaching Sultan forc'd me from the Palace;	O 299 Irene		47
the Particulam) strikes me with greater horror	Y 176 Irene		V111C
Tell me the Cause, that while thy Name, Demetrius,	O 305 Irene		25
When Asia's Nations own me for their Lord,	O 306 Irene		5
Is this the Recompence reserv'd for me?	O 307 Irene		7
The matchless Fair has bless'd me with Compliance;	O 308 Irene		3
Will she that's false to Heavn, to me be faithfull	Y 186 Irene		V 4
Dooms me to loath at once, and doat on Falshood,	O 310 Irene		10
Bore me victorious onward, where Demetrius	O 312 Irene		9
Doom'd me to die with all the Turkish Captains.	O 313 Irene		16
And gave me Life--	O 313 Irene		18
Hide me, oh hide me from upbraiding Greece,	O 316 Irene		12
Hide me, oh hide me from upbraiding Greece,	O 316 Irene		12
Oh, hide me from myself!	O 316 Irene		13
Then let me rid them of Irene's Presence:	O 316 Irene		19
Urg'd me to dash it to the Ground untouch'd,	O 316 Irene		28
Henceforth shall live for me; for me alone	O 317 Irene		3
Henceforth shall live for me; for me alone	O 317 Irene		3
Relax'd with Fear, refuse to bear me forward.	O 320 Irene		12
Here let me tend her with officious Care,	O 320 Irene		23
Ye Christian Captives, follow me to Freedom:	O 321 Irene		51
Who charges Guilt on me?	O 323 Irene		6
That dext'rous Message frees me from Suspicion.	O 324 Irene		26
Whence is this Rage? what barb'rous Tongue has wrong'd me?	O 325 Irene		27
Perhaps yourselves the Villains that defame me,	O 326 Irene		38
Confess your Crime, or lead me to the Sultan,	O 326 Irene		41
Unhappy Fair! Compassion calls upon me	O 327 Irene		4
O let me be but heard, nor fear from me	O 327 Irene		20
O let me be but heard, nor fear from me	O 327 Irene		20
Let me but live, heap Woes upon me,	O 328 Irene		33
Let me but live, heap Woes on Woes upon me,	O 328 Irene		33
Hide me with Murd'rers in the Dungeon's Gloom,	O 328 Irene		34
Send me to wander on some pathless Shore,	O 328 Irene		35
Let Shame and hooting Infamy pursue me,	O 328 Irene		36
Grant me one Hour, O grant me but a Moment,	O 328 Irene		45
Grant me one Hour, O grant me but a Moment,	O 328 Irene		45
Guilt and Despair! pale Spectres, grin around me,	O 328 Irene		50
And stun me with the Yellings of Damnation!	O 328 Irene		51
There had she lull'd me with endearing Falshoods,	O 331 Irene		18
Some soft Decoy to lure me to Destruction!	O 331 Irene		4
Amidst her kind Solicitudes for me!	O 332 Irene		21
One Hour had freed me from the fatal Error,	O 332 Irene		27
One Hour had sav'd me from Despair and Madness.	O 332 Irene		28
Shall hide me from the tasteless World for ever.	O 333 Irene		48
O seize me, Madness--Did she call on me!	O 334 Irene		68
O seize me, Madness--Did she call on me!	O 334 Irene		68
And stopp'd the heav'nly Voice that call'd on me.	O 334 Irene		71
My Spirits fail, awhile support me, Vengeance--	O 334 Irene		72
Which murder'd Innocence that call'd on me.	O 334 Irene		76
Rush'd out and seiz'd me, thoughtless and unarm'd,	O 335 Irene		7
Detain'd me till Demetrius set me free.	O 335 Irene		9
Detain'd me till Demetrius set me free.	O 335 Irene		9
A girl's, inflames me with desire;	Y 12 Tr Hor Epode 9		38

ME (CONTINUED)

		PAGE	TITLE	LINE
Grant him like me to guard the walls of Troy.	. . . .	Y 20	Tr. Iliad Bk 6	102
Teach me to range my troopes in just array	. . . .	Y 22	Tr Add. Battle	5
And bless me with continu'd day.	. . . . .	Y 39	Lady Leaving	12
She shall sing me a song,	. . . . .	Y 300	Fanny Burney	1

MEADS

He gave my flocks to graze the flowery meads,	. . . .	O 64	Virgil Past.I	11
The painted meads and Forrests nigh	. . . .	O 73	Hor. Epode II	V 61
Mix'd with old Heroes trace the flow'ry meads,	. . .	O 76	Tr Add. Battle	42
He scorns the verdant meads and flow'ry fields;	. . .	O 81	Young Author	V 4
Nor crop'd the tastfull herb, nor trac'd the verdant meads		Y 6	Virgil Daphnis	10

MEAN

Shames the mean Pensions of Augustan Times;	. . . .	O 57	Prologue Comus	4
Oh! how my soul abhors so mean a thought.	. . . .	O 74	Tr. Iliad Bk 6	8
Who holds no human Creature mean;	. . .	O 147	Tr Boeth III.6	18
Hid in the mean Disguise of Turkish Robes,	. . .	O 249	Irene	2
Mean as we are, this Tyrant of the World	. . . .	O 277	Irene	39
But brave Demetrius scorn'd the mean Revenge,	. . .	O 313	Irene	17
Thy Life, too mean a Prey to lure Abdalla.	. . .	O 319	Irene	27
To Blood, too mean to stain a Soldier's Sabre.	. . .	O 324	Irene	24

MEANER

From meaner minds, tho' smaller fines content,	. . . .	O 39	Vanity Wishes	169
Thus meaner Spirits with Amazement mark	. . . .	O 293	Irene	117
Thus meaner Spirits with amazement see	. . . .	O 369	Irene	V 11
To find a meaner Fate from treach'rous Friendship--	. .	O 299	Irene	33
Ambition was her Crime, but meaner Folly	. . . . .	O 310	Irene	9

MEANEST

| En<v>ies the meanest minister of Heav'n of celestial | . . | Y 168 | Irene | V135A |
| beings. | | | | |

MEANING

| O! then the meaning of thy gift impart, | . . . . . | O 95 | Sprig of Myrtl | 11 |
| More than a pleasing Sound without a Meaning, | . . . . | O 310 | Irene | 13 |

MEANLY

| See nations slowly wise, and meanly just, | . . . . . | O 38 | Vanity Wishes | 161 |
| Or meanly fraudulent, or madly gay, | . . . . . . | O 316 | Irene | 24 |

MEANS

Whose Ways and Means support the sinking land;	. . . .	O 21	London	245
Whose Ways and Means support a sinking land;	. . . .	Y 60	London	V 245
Be virtuous Ends pursued by virtuous Means,	. . . .	O 291	Irene	58

MEANTIME

| Meantime the Pygmies with undaunted hearts | . . . . | Y 24 | Tr Add. Battle | 76 |

MEASURE

| But leave to heav'n the measure and the choice, | . . . | O 47 | Vanity Wishes | 352 |

MEASURES

| His kind Intelligence betray'd their Measures; | . . . | O 253 | Irene | 118 |

MEATS

| Now pall the tasteless meats, and joyless wines, | . . . | O 43 | Vanity Wishes | 265 |

MECCA

Leave to perform my Pilgrimage to Mecca;	. . . . .	O 258	Irene	87
But will she yet receive the Faith of Mecca?	. . .	O 261	Irene	11
And ev'ry Suppliant lift his Eyes to Mecca.	. . . .	O 264	Irene	32

MECCA'S

| Implor'd my Leave to visit Mecca's Temple; | . . . . . | O 273 | Irene | 44 |

MED

| Kupridi, med autou skeptra memele theo. | . . . . . . | O 103 | Eis Elisses | 2 |

MEDALS

| To rust on medals, or on stones decay, | . . . . . . | O 40 | Vanity Wishes | 190 |

MEDITATE

| Sharpen their claws, and meditate the war. | . . . . . | Y 24 | Tr Add. Battle | 71 |

MEDITATED

| And broke the meditated Lines of War. | . . . . . . | O 273 | Irene | 26 |

MEDITATES

| And Murder meditates his prey. | . . . . | O 191 | Tr. Medea I | 12 |

MEDITATION'S

| Cool meditation's quiet seat, | . . . . | O 125 | An Ode | 30 |

MEDITATICNS

| Steal unperceiv'd upon her Meditations-- | . . . . . | O 314 | Irene | 13 |

MEEK

| The tender infant, meek and mild, | . . . . | O 157 | Par. Hermit I | 1 |
| He scorns the meek Address, the suppliant Strain, | . . . | O 246 | Irene Prologue | 31 |

MEEKNESS

| Our only Arms are Innocence and Meekness. | . . . . . | O 290 | Irene | 45 |
| Her only arms are innocence and meekness | . . . . . | Y 162 | Irene | V 45 |

MEET

But cruel virgins meet severer fates;	. . . . .	O 84	Epi Dist Moth.	28
When Virtues kindred Virtues meet,	. . . . .	O 100	Ode Friendship	21
I there did meet another man	. . . . . .	O 158	Par. Hermit II	V 3
Retire with Speed, while I prepare to meet him	. . .	O 271	Irene	37
Meet unexpected Daggers in his Way,	. . . .	O 274	Irene	48
Soon may we meet again, secure and free,	. . . .	O 303	Irene	23
My Soul expands to meet approaching Freedom.	. . . .	O 306	Irene	50
When next we meet before we storm the Palace,	. . .	O 308	Irene	28
How rarely would they meet in crouded Courts,	. . .	O 308	Irene	16
To meet that Fate we can delay no longer.	. . . . .	O 328	Irene	41

MEETING

| Had not the Breeze untwin'd the meeting Boughs, | . . . | O 269 | Irene | 10 |
| In all the Fopperies of meeting Lovers; | . . . . . | O 269 | Irene | 14 |

MEETS

Where-e'er he turns he meets a stranger's eye,	. . .	O 35	Vanity Wishes	111
Mark'd out by dangerous parts he meets the shock,	. . .	O 39	Vanity Wishes	171
And is it thus Demetrius meets his Friend,	. . . . .	O 249	Irene	1

```
MEIN                                                    PAGE    TITLE              LINE
    The tinsel glitter, and the specious mein,   . . . . .   O 139 Tr Rambler 168      1
MELANCHOLLY
    Melancholly broods or pours her influence oer the  . . .  Y 165 Irene          V  82
MELANCHOLY
    With Converse chase the melancholy Moments.  . . . . .   O 263 Irene              4
    Now hovers o'er this melancholy Shade,   . . . . . .     O 267 Irene             40
        With melanchcly Mien, . . . . . . . . . . .         O 314 Irene             11
MELANCHOLY'S
    Nor Melancholy's phantoms haunt thy shade;   . . . . .   O  37 Vanity Wishes     154
    Nor Melancholy's spectres haunt thy shade;   . . . . .   Y  99 Vanity Wishes  V 154
MELISSA'S
    Consign'd by Venus to Melissa's hand)  . . . . . . .     O  95 Sprig of Myrtl      4
MELODIOUS
    To handle the melodious lyre.  . . . . . . . . .        Y  11 Tr Hor Epode 9      4
MELODY
    Ye sons of Melody repair,  . . . . . . . . . . .        O 191 Tr. Medea I        14
MELT
    Then melt, ye fair, while crouds around you sigh,  . . .  O  84 Epi Dist Moth.    42
    Will he not melt before Ambition's Fire?  . . . . .     O 255 Irene             23
    That melt a Heart, impregnable till now,  . . . . .     O 276 Irene              4
    bend tyrant adamant--melt harlot . . . . . . . .       Y 181 Irene           V  56
    And melt her treach'rous Beauties into Ruin.  . . . .   O 315 Irene             37
    And melt the treach'rous Beauties into Ruin.  . . . .   O 315 Irene           V  37
    Melt at Irene's Fate, and share her Woes?  . . . . .    O 329 Irene              7
MELTING
    Yet softer Claims the melting Heart engage,  . . . . .   O  58 Prologue Comus    29
    While he lies melting in a lewd Embrace;  . . . . . .    O 111 To Posterity      24
    He seiz'd her melting in the fond Appeal,  . . . . .    O 334 Irene             70
MELTS
    An age that melts with unperceiv'd decay,  . . . . .    O  44 Vanity Wishes    293
    An age that melts in unperceiv'd decay,  . . . . . .    O  44 Vanity Wishes  V 293
    When fondness melts me, or when wine inflames,  . . .   O 142 In Baretti Bk.     2
    'Tis Love combin'd with Guilt alone, that melts  . . .  O 303 Irene             16
MEMBER
    Flows through each Member of th' embodied State,  . . .  O 256 Irene             58
MEMELE
    Kupridi, med autou skeptra memele theo.  . . . . . .    O 103 Eis Elisses         2
    Oisi memele phusis, metron charis, erga palaion,  . . .  O 171 Epi. Goldsmith    3
MEMENE
    Toios Ares Brotoloigos eni ptolemoisi memene,  . . . .   O 172 On Marlborough     1
MEMPHIS
    Which prcstrate Memphis own'd her deities.  . . . . .   Y   4 On a Daffodill     16
MEN
    To Men and Angels only giv'n,  . . . . . . . . .       O  99 Ode Friendship      3
    All Men throughout the peopled Earth . . . . . . .     O 146 Tr Boeth III.6      1
    Men will be ever to their Errors blind,  . . . . . .    O 247 Irene Epilogue    11
    Two Men unknown, the Partners of his Bosom;  . . . .   O 275 Irene             80
    Those forms of men that play before a . . . . . . .    Y 173 Irene           V  18
        beauty
    By Treason levell'd with the Dregs of Men.  . . . . .   O 311 Irene             17
    To men belongs the dreadfull work of war."  . . . .    Y  21 Tr. Iliad Bk 6    123
    Hence men and birds promiscuous press'd the sand  . .   Y  23 Tr Add. Battle    52
MEND
    But did not Chance at length her error mend?  . . . .   O  41 Vanity Wishes    215
    They pleas'd their Age, and did not aim to mend.  . . .  O  52 Pro Drury-Lane    22
    Delighted still to please mankind, or mend,  . . . .    O 118 Epitaph Hanmer    39
    That mirth may mend, and innocence delight.  . . . .   Y  67 Prologue Lethe    16
MENIAL
    The liv'ried army, and the menial lord.  . . . . . .    O  35 Vanity Wishes    116
    The liv'ried army, or the menial lord.  . . . . . .     Y  96 Vanity Wishes  V 116
    Then sought the palace where the menial train  . . .   Y  21 Tr. Iliad Bk 6    128
MENIALS
    We round thy board the cheerful menials see,  . . . .   O 130 Tr. Rambler 12      5
MENODORUS
    Enquires the final Doom of Menodorus,  . . . . . . .    O 263 Irene             24
    The cruel Doom of hapless Menodorus--  . . . . . . .    O 270 Irene              4
        Confest by dying Menodorus.  . . . . . . . .       O 272 Irene             13
MENS
    Or states mens now, with safer pride content,  . . . .  Y  97 Vanity Wishes  V 123
MENTAL
    With mental and corporeal strife,  . . . . . . . .     O 124 Winter's Walk     18
MENTION
    Ladies introduces the mention of Aspasia.  . . . . .   O 351 Irene           V  12
MEOTIS
    Th' eternal Snows that freeze beyond Meotis,  . . . .   O 274 Irene             59
MERCENARY
    Heav'n will contemn the mercenary Fervour,  . . . . .   O 262 Irene             26
MERCHANDISE
    Where looks are merchandise, and smiles are sold;  . .  O  18 London           179
MERCHANT
    The Merchant sees her with wealh, the lover with his . .  O 374 Irene         V  29
        Mistress
MERCIES
    No cries attempt the mercies of the skies?  . . . . .   O  47 Vanity Wishes    348
    No cries invoke the mercies of the skies?  . . . . .    O  47 Vanity Wishes  V 348
MERCY
    But should I sin beyond the Hope of Mercy,  . . . . .   O 289 Irene             23
    Lest unrewarded Mercy lose its Charms.  . . . . . .     O 313 Irene             19
    Kind Heav'n affords thee, and inviting Mercy  . . . .   O 321 Irene             41
    Curses the dull Delays of ling'ring Mercy,  . . . . .   O 327 Irene             12
```

MERCY	(CONTINUED)		PAGE	TITLE	LINE
And bounteous Heaven repay the mighty Mercy	. . . . .		O 328	Irene	46
And may bounteous Heav'n repay the mercy on Your Heads			O 344	Irene	V 27
Be charg'd upon my Soul. O, Mercy! Mercy!	. . . . .		O 329	Irene	55
Be charg'd upon my Soul. O, Mercy! Mercy!			O 329	Irene	55
Nor justice can acquit, nor mercy spare	. . . .		Y 210	Irene	V 25B
And speed the Stroke lest Mercy should o'ertake them.	.		O 333	Irene	54
MERIT					
For where can starving merit find a home?	. . . . .		O 18	London	191
To buried merit raise the tardy bust.			O 38	Vanity Wishes	162
Now kindred Merit fills the sable bier,	. . . . .		O 45	Vanity Wishes	303
Now kindred Merit fills the mournful bier,			Y 106	Vanity Wishes	V 303
Trusts without fear, to merit, and to you.	. . . .		O 60	Pro Good Nat'd	30
Resistless merit fix'd the Senate's choice,	. . . .		O 118	Epitaph Hanmer	19
If Merit touch thee, shed a tear, ...			O 154	Epita. Hogarth	6
And of his every gift usurp the merit;	. . . . .		O 176	Tr Metastas II	11
And yet of every gift usurp the merit;			O 176	Tr Metastas II	V 11
Thy praise to merit unrefin'd.			O 201	Death Dr Levet	12
With Merit needless, and without it vain.	. . . .		O 246	Irene Prologue	32
Shine thou distinguish'd by superior Merit,	. . . .		O 264	Irene	29
What Worth can merit? or what Faith reward?	. . . .		O 295	Irene	16
MERITS					
Hers the mild Merits of domestic Life,	. . . . .		O 58	Prologue Comus	31
Who merits most, Demetrius or Abdalla.	. . . . .		O 284	Irene	45
Who merits most!--I knew not we were Rivals.	. . .		O 284	Irene	46
MERRIMENT					
By harmless merriment, or useful sense.	. . . . .		O 62	Pro Word Wise	14
MERRY					
While many a merry tale, and many a song,	. . . .		Y 310	Parody of Pope	1
MESSAGE					
Whoe'er thou art, or whatsoe'er thy Message,	. . .		O 294	Irene	4
That dext'rous Message frees me from Suspicion.	. .		O 324	Irene	26
I bring a tardy Message from Irene.	. . . . .		O 331	Irene	2
Declare thy Message, and expect thy Doom.	. . . .		O 331	Irene	6
The Queen requested--Wretch, repeat the Message;	. . .		O 331	Irene	13
The Queen requested--Wretch, repeat thy Message;	. . .		O 331	Irene	V 13
MESSENGER					
A Winged Messenger, or bid the Grave	. . . . . .		O 365	Irene	V 21
I mark'd her wily Messenger afar,	. . . . . .		O 327	Irene	24
MESSENGERS					
Must Heaven dispatch the Messengers of Light,	. . .		O 250	Irene	46
Ordain'd the mournful Messengers of Death.	. . . .		O 326	Irene	35
MET					
A Mortal born he met the general Doom,	. . . . .		O 51	Pro Drury-Lane	15
And there I met another man	. . . . . .		O 158	Par. Hermit II	3
He met Andromache his beauteous wife	. . . . .		Y 18	Tr. Iliad Bk 6	5
METEOR					
With ev'ry Meteor of Caprice must play,	. . . . .		O 53	Pro Drury-Lane	49
METHINKS					
Cali, methinks yon waving Trees afford	. . . . .		O 268	Irene	36
METHOD					
To please in Method, and invent by Rule;	. . . . .		O 51	Pro Drury-Lane	10
METRON					
Oisi memele phusis, metron charis, erga palaion,	. . .		O 171	Epi. Goldsmith	3
METROPOLIS					
I cannot bear a French metropolis.			O 15	London	98
MICE					
Here with dead mice the marsh was strew'd around;	. . .		Y 24	Tr Add. Battle	58
MID					
There, mid Tempests loudest roars, ...			O 145	Tr Boeth. II.4	17
MIDNIGHT					
The midnight murd'rer bursts the faithless bar;	. . .		O 21	London	239
MIDNIGHT'S					
At Midnight's private Hour a Voice unknown	. . . .		O 254	Irene	121
MIDST					
Till in the midst of Arrogance and Fondness,	. . . .		O 299	Irene	46
MIEN					
Who dwell on Balbos courtly mien--			Y 55	London	V 150
His Mien is lofty, his Demeanour great,	. . . . .		O 255	Irene	14
Of equal Beauty, but of softer Mien,	. . . . .		O 259	Irene	119
A turkish Stranger of majestick Mien,	. . . . .		O 294	Irene	1
With melancholy Mien, ...			O 314	Irene	11
Her lofty mien, and insolence of virtue--my state	. . . .		Y 191	Irene	V 14
That fires thy Cheek, and elevates thy Mien,	. . . .		O 323	Irene	9
MIGHT					
The might you find some elegant retreat,	. . . . .		Y 58	London	V 212
Thy charms at least, fair F<irebrac>e, might inspire	. .		O 107	Lady F Assizes	3
Might Truth intrude with daring flight,	. . . . .		O 121	To Miss Playin	20
Instruction with her flow'rs might spring,	. . . .		O 121	To Miss Playin	23
Nor can the might of Theseus rend	. . . . .		O 232	Tr Horace IV.7	27
Pregnant with Stores, that India's Mines might envy,	. .		O 249	Irene	18
Well might the Weakness of our Empire sink	. . . .		O 250	Irene	48
Well might we fear impending Disappointments.	. . .		O 269	Irene	2
There (or might) shall his boundless Wealth the	. . .		O 351	Irene	V 13
Might well befit the solitary Student,	. . . . .		O 281	Irene	36
Then Bigotry might send her Slaves to War,	. . . .		O 291	Irene	63
Unpitying Massacre might waste the World,	. . . .		O 291	Irene	65
Close, as we might unseen, we watch'd his Steps;	. . .		O 311	Irene	2
And dash'd the Might of Asem from the Ramparts.	. . .		O 312	Irene	12

		PAGE	TITLE	LINE
MIGHT	(CONTINUED)			
And push'd the Might of Moluc from the Ramparts. . . .		O 363	Irene	V 15
Soon might her Tears engage a Lover's Credit;		O 327	Irene	17
Perhaps her Malice might transfer the Charge, ...		O 327	Irene	18
Perhaps her pois'nous Tongue might blast Abdalla. . . .		O 327	Irene	19
Might intercept the Traitor Greek, Demetrius, ...		O 331	Irene	8
Whatever Crane confiding in his might		Y 23	Tr Add. Battle	38
As when great Briareus with matchless might		Y 26	Tr Add. Battle	137
MIGHT'ST				
There might'st thou find some elegant retreat, ...		O 20	London	212
Thou might'st have liv'd, for thou hadst spar'd Irene. .		O 333	Irene	58
MIGHTST				
Thou mightst have liv'd, nor had I lost Irene		Y 214	Irene	V 58
MIGHTY				
In full blown pow'r see mighty Wolsey stand, ...		Y 96	Vanity Wishes	V 99
At length our mighty Bard's victorious Lays		O 57	Prologue Comus	15
See! how the mighty Change is wrought!		O 70	Hor.II Ode XX	9
My fair, be mindful of the mighty trust, ...		O 81	Lady Birthday	11
A task proportion'd to thy mighty mind!		O 136	Tr Rambler 129	2
But swallowing all the mighty Store, ...		O 144	Tr Boeth. II.2	9
Spreads wide the mighty Moral for Mankind.		O 246	Irene Prologue	8
Spreads wide the mighty Moral of Mankind.		O 246	Irene Prologue	V 8
Think on the mighty Pow'r of awful Virtue;		O 252	Irene	88
Sure, not unconscious of the mighty Blessing, ...		O 256	Irene	59
Extends his mighty Schemes of Wealth and Pow'r, . . .		O 269	Irene	4
Claim but the second Place: there mighty Love		O 280	Irene	26
The mighty Tuscan courts the banish'd Arts		O 302	Irene	116
To-morrow's Dawn shall see the mighty Cali		O 303	Irene	11
This Night alone is ours--Our mighty Foe, ...		O 303	Irene	25
Tore, unresisted, from the mighty hand		Y 188	Irene	V 10
And anxious Angels wait the mighty Birth;		O 313	Irene	4
And bounteous Heaven repay the mighty Mercy		O 328	Irene	46
Thine Orders, mighty Sultan! are perform'd, ...		O 330	Irene	3
Thus I t' effect this mighty change design'd		Y 11	Tr Hor Epode 9	29
Th' atridae there and Tydeus' mighty son, ...		Y 19	Tr. Iliad Bk 6	54
Then on his brow the mighty soldier plac'd		Y 21	Tr. Iliad Bk 6	124
MILD				
Hers the mild Merits of domestic Life, ...		O 58	Prologue Comus	31
The moderator firmly mild appear'd, ...		O 118	Epitaph Hanmer	25
The tender infant, meek and mild, ...		O 157	Par. Hermit I	1
The lambent Flames of mild Benevolence, ...		O 293	Irene	109
Spreads her mild Radiance, and descending Dews		O 313	Irene	2
MILDER				
To ease their pains exert your milder power, ...		O 84	Epi Dist Moth.	46
Thy milder glories only beam		Y 71	Ode Friendship	V 11
MILITARY				
The march begins in military state, ...		O 40	Vanity Wishes	205
MILK				
And heap the fire, and milk the Kine		O 72	Hor. Epode II	51
Their dugs with milk distended, home!		O 73	Hor. Epode II	68
Two bowls with oyl and milk I'll yearly crown, ...		Y 7	Virgil Daphnis	45
MILKNESS				
Sinks into milkness and softens to submission.		Y 123	Irene	V 99
MILLIONS				
Or hostile millions press him to the ground?		O 41	Vanity Wishes	218
And future millions lift his rising soul;		O 82	Young Author	V 6B
The holy city with converted millions--or nations. . .		Y 131	Irene	V 32C
And plan the Happiness of mourning Millions?		O 291	Irene	68
MILTON				
As not to grant me this, can Milton find?		O 137	Tr Rambler 140	2
MILTON'S				
Ye Nymphs, whose Bosoms beat at Milton's Name, ...		O 57	Prologue Comus	2
MILTONIAN				
What tho' she shine with no Miltonian Fire, ...		O 58	Prologue Comus	27
MIMICK				
Of France the mimick, and of Spain the prey.		O 15	London	106
Mimick your tears, and ridicule your woes;		O 74	Tr. Iliad Bk 6	22
Teach mimick censure her own faults to find, ...		O 81	Lady Birthday	17
MIMICK'S				
Well may they venture on the mimick's art, ...		O 16	London	134
MIND				
Such was the scorn that fill'd the sage's mind, . . .		O 33	Vanity Wishes	69
Fresh praise is try'd till madness fires his mind, . .		O 42	Vanity Wishes	231
New praise is try'd till madness fires his mind, . . .		Y 102	Vanity Wishes	V 231
Must dull Suspence corrupt the stagnant mind?		O 47	Vanity Wishes	344
Must dull Suspence becalm still the stagnant mind? . .		Y 107	Vanity Wishes	V 344
Pour forth thy fervours for a healthful mind, ...		O 48	Vanity Wishes	359
With these celestial wisdom calms the mind, ...		O 48	Vanity Wishes	367
Prest by the load of life, the weary mind		O 59	Pro Good Nat'd	1
Thy form more lovely, more adorn'd thy mind;		O 80	Lady Birthday	4
Unbounded Projects lab'ring in his Mind, ...		O 97	Hickman Spinet	11
For such thy beauteous mind, and lovely face, ...		O 107	Lady F Assizes	5
Age call'd at length his active mind to rest, ...		O 118	Epitaph Hanmer	35
And chear the clouded mind with light divine.		O 130	Tr. Rambler 7	4
A task proportion'd to thy mighty mind!		O 136	Tr Rambler 129	2
The mind of mortals, in perverseness strong, ...		O 136	Tr Rambler 132	1
Place may be chang'd; but who can change his mind? . .		O 137	Tr Rambler 135	1
Would ease the hunger of the mind, ...		O 144	Tr Boeth. II.2	8
And thus the Mind tormented long		O 145	Tr Boeth III.1	9
Happy whose unfetterd Mind		O 147	Tr Boet III.12	3
When grasping Bliss th' unsteady mind		O 150	Tr Boet III.12	56

MIND   (CONTINUED)

	PAGE	TITLE	LINE
Faith from every generous mind:	O 176	Tr Metastasi I	4
Learn here how Heav'n supports the virtuous Mind, ...	O 246	Irene Prologue	9
Where Woman's not allow'd to speak her Mind;	O 247	Irene Epilogue	12
When the mind disentangled from the senses	Y 133	Irene	V 6
And bar the Passes of Irene's Mind	O 265	Irene	10
Let not th' unbounded Greatness of his Mind	O 275	Irene	72
Greatness of mind with elegance of form.	Y 149	Irene	V 56
Will it not charm a Mind like thine exalted, ...	O 278	Irene	67
O'erbears each gentler Motion of the Mind.	O 280	Irene	21
Purge well thy Mind from ev'ry private Passion, . . .	O 298	Irene	6
--The gen'rous mind contemns	Y 177	Irene	V 109
Betray'd the wild Emotions of his Mind.	O 311	Irene	4
Strives to regain her Empire of the Mind:	O 320	Irene	33
well th' Eternal Mind thus her doom decreed	O 345	Irene	V 34
And gainst the pow'r of Venus steel'd my mind.	Y 11	Tr Hor Epode 9	30

MIND'S

The noble mind's delight and pride, ...	O 99	Ode Friendship	2

MINDFUL

My fair, be mindful of the mighty trust, ...	O 81	Lady Birthday	11
Whose Soul, perhaps, yet mindful of Aspasia, ...	O 267	Irene	39

MINDS

From meaner minds, tho' smaller fines content, ...	O 39	Vanity Wishes	169
And sister minds together join, ...	Y 71	Ode Friendship	V 22
To mark the noblest Minds, with active Heat	O 293	Irene	112
To mark the noblest Minds. With active fire	O 369	Irene	V 3

MINE

"And all be mine beneath the polar sky."	O 40	Vanity Wishes	204
"And all is mine beneath the polar sky."	O 40	Vanity Wishes	V 204
Mine unharmonious verse profanes	O 80	Feast St Simon	58
In blissful dreams he digs the golden mine, ...	O 82	Young Author	V 6C
And own all glories of the mine outdone, ...	O 141	Tr Rambler 199	6
"Blissful bondage such as mine?	O 185	Anacreon Ode 9	24
Condemn'd to hope's delusive mine, ...	O 200	Death Dr Levet	1
When nought but mine the circling Sun shall	O 357	Irene	V 29
see			
To clasp a Slave? or, can a Soul like mine, ...	O 268	Irene	16
Join'd Cali's Hand to mine, and falt'ring cry'd, . . .	O 272	Irene	8
Destruction flashes from th' insidious Mine, ...	O 298	Irene	30
Heav'n makes not mine to give.	O 307	Irene	16
Fidelity so firm, so pure, as mine!	O 308	Irene	17
At length the Prize is mine--The haughty Maid	O 317	Irene	1
Abdalla fails, now Fortune all is mine.	O 319	Irene	1
But 'tis not mine to judge--I scorn and leave thee. . .	O 324	Irene	22

MINERVA

"This is Minerva, cast in Virtue's mould."	O 190	Seeing Montagu	6

MINES

The rival batters, and the lover mines.	O 46	Vanity Wishes	332
Pregnant with Stores, that India's Mines might envy, . .	O 249	Irene	18
Our schemes defeated and our mines discoverd	Y 141	Irene	V 22
Our Schemes for ever cross'd, our Mines discover'd, . .	O 273	Irene	22
Our Mines discover'd, and, our Battries ruind	O 368	Irene	V 2

MINGLE

Now haste to mingle in one common Center, ...	O 287	Irene	4
Then mingle with your slaves without a murmur	Y 161	Irene	V 11

MINGLED

The plain contested flows with mingled blood.	O 76	Tr Add. Battle	21
Mark, when from thousand mingled dyes	O 121	To Miss Playin	25
Such strains as, mingled with the lyre, ...	O 188	Epilogue	1
From ev'ry Palace burst a mingled Clamour, ...	O 251	Irene	70
Dispers'd in Air or mingled with the Dust.	O 298	Irene	24
Nor mingled Guilt pollute the sacred Cause!	O 300	Irene	64

MINGLES

Mingles Danger with Delight;	O 145	Tr Boeth. II.4	14
And mingles unperceiv'd with ev'ry Thought.	O 261	Irene	6

MINION

See! Mustapha, the Tyrant's Minion, comes;	O 260	Irene	143

MINISTER

While Heav'n's high Minister, whose awful Volume . . .	O 276	Irene	20
While Heaven's high Minister whose unerring awfull . .	O 355	Irene	V 9
volume			
En<v>ies the meanest minister of Heav'n of celestial . .	Y 168	Irene	V135A
beings.			

MINISTERS

The Ministers of Wrath forget Compassion, ...	O 314	Irene	24
Th' unpitying Ministers of Turkish Justice, ...	O 325	Irene	9
Ye blind officious Ministers of Folly, ...	O 332	Irene	23

MINOR'S

Loosen'd from the Minor's tether, ...	O 196	Song Congratu.	5

MINOS

Thine, Minos, is the main, and thine the land.	O 136	Tr Rambler 129	4
When Minos once has fix'd your doom, ...	O 232	Tr Horace IV.7	22

MINSTREL'S

Ah, little needs the Minstrel's pow'r	O 191	Tr. Medea I	17

MINSTRELS

Approach, ye minstrels, try the soothing strain, . . .	O 43	Vanity Wishes	267

MINUTES

To press the weary minutes flagging wings:	O 44	Vanity Wishes	300
Loads the lingring minutes weary wings:	Y 105	Vanity Wishes	V 300
To press the weary minutes hanging wings:	Y 105	Vanity Wishes	V 300

			PAGE	TITLE	LINE
MIRACLES					
And yet, my Friend, what Miracles were wrought	. . . .		O 251	Irene	52
MIRTH					
With chearful wisdom and instructive mirth,	. . . . .		O 32	Vanity Wishes	50
All aid the farce, and all thy mirth maintain,	. . . .		O 33	Vanity Wishes	67
For useful Mirth, and salutary Woe;	. . . . .		O 53	Pro Drury-Lane	60
And mirth was bounty with a humbler name.	. . . . .		O 62	Pro Word Wise	24
And giv'n to mirth, the Cranes no longer fear,	. . . .		O 77	Tr Add. Battle	50
To letter'd ease retir'd, and honest mirth,	. . . . .		O 118	Epitaph Hanmer	37
And gold and flattery--thoughtless mirth--hurry	. . .		Y 164	Irene	V 72
With ill-tim'd Mirth propos'd the Bowl of Love.	. . .		O 316	Irene	26
Fair source of wit, and love, and mirth,	. . . . . .		Y 39	Lady Leaving	6
That mirth may mend, and innocence delight.	. . . . .		Y 67	Prologue Lethe	16
MIRY					
Sung such a war when in a miry fen	. . . .		Y 23	Tr Add. Battle	55
MISCHIEF					
An envious Breast with certain Mischief glows,	. . . .		O 46	Vanity Wishes	V330A
An rivals breast with certain mischief glows	. . . .		Y 107	Vanity Wishes	V330A
Where gloom-enamour'd Mischief dreads the Sun,	. . . .		O 192	Tr. Medea II	15
Where gloom-enamour'd Mischief loves to dwell,	. . . .		O 192	Tr. Medea II	V 15
Where mischief lurks in gay disguise,	. . . .		O 203	Tr. on Skating	3
Where 's this fair Trait'ress? Where 's this smiling	. .		O 330	Irene	1
Mischief?					
--The beuteous Fiend The shining mischief	. . . . .		O 375	Irene	V 12
MISCHIEVOUSLY					
Yet ev'n these heroes, mischievously gay,	. . . . .		O 21	London	230
Yet ev'n those heroes, mischievously gay,	. . . . .		Y 59	London	V 230
MISERIES					
And shews his miseries in distant lands;	. . . . . .		O 41	Vanity Wishes	212
And hides his miseries in distant lands;	. . . . . .		Y 102	Vanity Wishes	V 212
The future Miseries that wait th' Apostate;	. . . . .		O 266	Irene	20
Support the splendid Miseries of Greatness?	. . . .		O 268	Irene	18
if human miseries or affairs yet claim your	. . . . .		Y 181	Irene	V 54
regard					
To share the Miseries herself has caus'd.	. . . . .		O 320	Irene	15
MISERY					
Unblest, still doom'd to wed with misery.	. . . . .		O 131	Tr. Rambler 39	1
Reproach not Misery.--The Sons of Greece,	. . . . .		O 250	Irene	28
MISERY'S					
In misery's darkest caverns known,	. . . - . . .		O 201	Death Dr Levet	17
MISFORTUNE					
Yet ev'n on this her load Misfortune flings,	. . . .		O 44	Vanity Wishes	299
And feel one happiness and one misfortune.	. . . . .		Y 121	Irene	V 57
The swellings of misfortune--	. . . . .		Y 164	Irene	V 76
Descend to range these Mansions of Misfortune,	. . . .		O 292	Irene	95
Still, still the same--unclouded by Misfortune!	. . .		O 294	Irene	3
MISFORTUNE'S					
Why but to sink beneath misfortune's blow,	. . . . .		O 35	Vanity Wishes	127
MISFORTUNES					
Rashness! thou spring from whence misfortunes flow!	. .		O 77	Festina Lente	9
Wealth still finds followers, and misfortunes foes.	. .		O 138	Tr Rambler 153	2
MISLEADS					
What Fraud misleads him? or what Crimes incense?	. . .		O 325	Irene	28
MISS					
To Miss Hickman playing on the Spinet	. . . . . .		O 96	Hickman Spinet	T
To Miss <Carpenter> On her giving the Author	. . .		O 119	To Miss Purse	T
To Miss <Carpenter> On her playing upon the Harpsicord	.		O 120	To Miss Playin	T
MISSIVE					
Temper their swords and point their missive darts.	. .		Y 24	Tr Add. Battle	77
MIST					
As treach'rous phantoms in the mist delude,	. . . . .		O 31	Vanity Wishes	9
A sudden Mist o'ercasts my darken'd Soul,	. . . . .		O 295	Irene	12
MISTAKE					
What wild Mistake is this? Take hence with speed	. . .		O 325	Irene	4
Mistake shall blast, or Accident destroy;	. . . .		O 335	Irene	13
MISTRESS					
To tender Friendship, praise him to his Mistress.	. . .		O 267	Irene	5
Trusts to my Care his Mistress and his Life,	. . . .		O 283	Irene	10
That fatal Mistress of the Young, the Lazy,	. . . .		O 283	Irene	21
The Merchant sees her with wealh, the lover with his	. .		O 374	Irene	V 29
Mistress					
Then while he gaz'd upon his yielding Mistress,	. . .		O 299	Irene	48
His Fav'rite faithless, and his Mistress base.	. . . .		O 310	Irene	6
And stole his Life and Mistress from his Sabre?	. . .		O 318	Irene	14
Then ling'ring with his captive Mistress here.	. . . .		O 331	Irene	9
MISTRESS'					
And see my mistress' face no more	. . . .		Y 11	Tr Hor Epode 9	32
MISTRUST					
And let the tortures of mistrust	. . . .		O 100	Ode Friendship	15
MISTS					
Beyond the Mists of Care thy Pinion tow'rs.	. . . . .		O 313	Irene	8
MISTY					
And pour on misty Doubt resistless day;	. . . . . .		O 37	Vanity Wishes	146
MIX					
To mix with nobler Cares, I'll throw aside	. . . . .		O 275	Irene	70
To mix with nobler Cares, I'll set apart	. . . . .		O 368	Irene	V 27
Mix undistinguish'd with the gen'ral Roar.	. . . .		O 280	Irene	24
Mix in the War, and shine among the Heroes?	. . . .		O 290	Irene	41
MIX'D					
Mix'd with old Heroes trace the flow'ry meads,	. . . .		O 76	Tr Add. Battle	42
If mix'd with these, divine Cleora smile,	. . . . .		Y 4	On a Daffodill	17

MIX'D	(CONTINUED)	PAGE	TITLE	LINE
	Where late the lilies mix'd with violets smil'd. . . .	Y 7	Virgil Daphnis	25
MOAN				
	Tho' when Orpheus made his Moan	O 148	Tr Boet III.12	5
MOANS				
	This forc'd the Cranes to utter dolefull moans, . . .	Y 24	Tr Add. Battle	88
MOCK				
	Where ne'er was known the form of mock debate, ...	O 33	Vanity Wishes	57
	Where ne'er was heard the form of mock debate, ...	Y 94	Vanity Wishes	V 57
MOCK'D				
	No summons mock'd by chill delay, ...	O 201	Death Dr Levet	21
	Mock'd our impatient steps, for all was fairy ground. .	Y 310	Parody of Pope	4
MOCKS				
	Hate dogs their flight, and insult mocks their end. . .	O 33	Vanity Wishes	78
	And soaring mocks the broken frame below.	O 131	Tr. Rambler 17	1
	To good that mocks approach.	O 133	Tr. Rambler 67	3
	Mocks the dull Vows of Solitude and Penance, ...	O 264	Irene	27
MODEL				
	Behold the Model of consummate Beauty, ...	O 334	Irene	3
MODERATE				
	Let Prudence moderate, though not suppress.	O 264	Irene	34
MODERATOR				
	The moderator firmly mild appear'd, ...	O 118	Epitaph Hanmer	25
MODERN				
	See motley life in modern trappings dress'd, ...	O 32	Vanity Wishes	51
	To force Applause no modern Arts are try'd.	O 246	Irene Prologue	22
MODES				
	Are only varied Modes of endless Being;	O 290	Irene	27
MODEST				
	And glides in modest Innocence away;	O 44	Vanity Wishes	294
	The modest wants of ev'ry day	O 201	Death Dr Levet	23
	The pious Maid, with modest Indignation, ...	O 258	Irene	101
MODISH				
	How wouldst thou shake at Britain's modish tribe, . . .	O 33	Vanity Wishes	61
	Evn low built towns they Britain's modish tribe . . .	Y 94	Vanity Wishes	V 61
MODULATED				
	Each charm of modulated sound, ...	O 121	To Miss Playin	6
	By quiv'ring string, or modulated wind;	O 192	Tr. Medea II	10
MOLEST				
	Whome no contracted debts molest	O 71	Hor. Epode II	7
	Where no sour criticks damn, nor sneers molest, . . .	O 82	Young Author	27
	Where no sour criticks snarl, no sneers molest, . . .	O 82	Young Author	V 27
	Molest these private Walks, or Care invade	O 272	Irene	14
MOLUC				
	And push'd the Might of Moluc from the Ramparts. . . .	O 363	Irene	V 15
MOMENT				
	And for a moment lull the sense of woe.	O 10	London	32
	And ev'ry moment leaves my little less;	O 10	London	40
	One moment hear the moral song, ...	O 121	To Miss Playin	22
	But though the numbers for a moment please, ...	O 142	In Baretti Bk.	5
	Ye Sons of Avarice! a Moment spare:	O 246	Irene Prologue	4
	Just in the Moment of impending Fate, ...	O 259	Irene	117
	Shake off th' Incumbrances of State a moment, ...	O 289	Irene	7
	Yet think a Moment, ere you court Destruction, ...	O 301	Irene	87
	The poor distinctions of a flying moment	Y 177	Irene	V110A
	But soon thou shalt repent: another Moment	O 319	Irene	33
	The happy Moment, hasten to the Shore, ...	O 320	Irene	8
	Stay but a Moment, and prevailing Truth	O 321	Irene	46
	But since none knows the Danger of a Moment, ...	O 321	Irene	48
	Grant me one Hour, O grant me but a Moment, ...	O 328	Irene	45
	Hear but a Moment.	O 333	Irene	57
	Had'st thou heard a Moment, ...	O 333	Irene	57
MOMENT'S				
	Or but one Moment's Pause betray Confusion, ...	O 332	Irene	15
	Hector, this heard without a moment's stay, ...	Y 17	Tr. Iliad Bk 6	1
MOMENTS				
	You could not gain a Moments breath, ...	O 69	Hor.II Ode 14	9
	With Converse chase the melancholy Moments.	O 263	Irene	4
	Now be some Moments Master of thyself, ...	O 282	Irene	70
	Then waste no longer these important Moments	O 303	Irene	13
	In these dark Moments of suspended Fate, ...	O 313	Irene	1
	And live her guiltless Moments o'er anew!	O 323	Irene	16
	The fraudful Moments ply their silent Wings, ...	O 327	Irene	8
	The treacherous moments ply their silent wings	Y 206	Irene	V 8
	But while I sing, the nimble moments fly, ...	Y 4	On a Daffodill	21
MONARCH				
	From Lydia's monarch should the search descend, . . .	O 45	Vanity Wishes	313
	Soon had the Monarch felt a nobler fire, ...	O 97	Hickman Spinet	16
	In vain for thee the monarch sighs, ...	O 100	Ode Friendship	19
	Still odious to the Monarch, or the People.	O 256	Irene	52
	A blooming monarch--in all the bloom of honour... . .	Y 122	Irene	V 67
	From Crouds that hide a Monarch from himself, ...	O 262	Irene	8
	How the new Monarch, swell'd with airy Rule, ...	O 306	Irene	1
MONARCH'S				
	He gropes his breeches with a monarch's air.	O 17	London	151
	The Warrior's Labours, and the Monarch's Cares. . . .	O 261	Irene	10
	Your artful Suit, your Monarch's fierce Denial, . . .	O 270	Irene	3
	And Nature justifies our Monarch's Choice.	O 288	Irene	3
MONARCHS				
	Did rival monarchs give the fatal wound?	O 41	Vanity Wishes	217
	Hail, Terror of the Monarchs of the World, ...	O 262	Irene	1

		PAGE	TITLE	LINE
MONARCHS	(CONTINUED)			
And may a long Posterity of Monarchs, ...		O 267	Irene	11
The Pride of Monarchs, the Reward of Conquest;		O 269	Irene	42
Shall Monarchs fear to draw the Sword of Justice, . . .		O 312	Irene	21
MONASTIC				
He seeks the refuge of monastic rest.		O 35	Vanity Wishes	118
MONEY				
His money he collected strait, ...		O 73	Hor. Epode II	75
MONGRELS				
As mongrels bay the lion in a cage.		O 60	Pro Good Nat'd	16
MONITORY				
No stern command, no monitory voice		O 151	The Ant	3
MONSIEUR				
All sciences a fasting Monsieur knows, ...		O 15	London	115
MONSTERS				
Behold the Monsters gaze with savage Rapture, ...		O 252	Irene	81
Quick from my Sight you inauspicious Monsters, ...		O 325	Irene	6
MONTH				
Next Month he sets it out again.		O 73	Hor. Epode II	79
MONUMENT				
And planted elms around his monument		Y 18	Tr. Iliad Bk 6	33
MONUMENTS				
With Monuments of Death proclaim his Courage;		O 255	Irene	31
Labour'd monuments of art.		Y 177	Irene	V111G
MOON				
The Bear enrag'd th' affrighted Moon shall dread; . . .		O 111	To Posterity	17
Her silver locks display the moon, ...		O 127	To Lyce, Lady	9
Her losses soon the Moon supplies, ...		O 232	Tr Horace IV.7	13
See how the Moon through all th' unclouded Sky		O 313	Irene	1
MOON'S				
Confirm your Troops; and when the Moon's fair Beam . .		O 306	Irene	58
MOOR				
Moor and Christian, roll along.		O 159	Tr. Rio Verde	4
MOORISH				
Nor needs the guard of Moorish bows:		O 65	Hor I Ode xxii	4
Nor needs the Guard of Moorish Bows.		O 66	To A. Fuscus	4
MORAL				
To point a moral, or adorn a tale.		O 41	Vanity Wishes	222
One moment hear the moral song, ...		O 121	To Miss Playin	22
Conceals the moral council in a tale.		O 132	Tr. Rambler 65	2
Spreads wide the mighty Moral for Mankind.		O 246	Irene Prologue	8
Spreads wide the mighty Moral of Mankind.		O 246	Irene Prologue	V 8
MORALS				
On life, on morals, be thy thoughts employ'd;		O 140	Tr Rambler 180	1
MORE				
Give to St. David one true Briton more.		O 9	London	8
With more address a lover's note convey, ...		O 13	London	77
All that at home no more can beg or steal, ...		O 15	London	107
Fate never wounds more deep the gen'rous heart, . . .		O 18	London	168
And bear oppression's insolence no more.		O 18	London	175
But here more slow, where all are slaves to gold, . . .		O 18	London	178
In virtue's cause once more exert his rage, ...		O 23	London	262
In virtue's cause once more forsake his rage, ...		O 23	London	V 262
How much more safe the vassal than the lord;		O 31	Vanity Wishes	32
Once more, Democritus, arise on earth, ...		O 32	Vanity Wishes	49
Pours in the morning worshiper no more;		O 33	Vanity Wishes	80
Shews pour the morning worshiper no more;		Y 95	Vanity Wishes	V 80
For now no more we trace in ev'ry line		O 34	Vanity Wishes	87
Through Freedom's sons no more remonstrance rings, . .		O 34	Vanity Wishes	93
Till counted myriads sooth his pride no more;		O 42	Vanity Wishes	230
He views, and wonders that they please no more; . . .		O 43	Vanity Wishes	264
He views, and wonders why they please no more; . . .		Y 104	Vanity Wishes	V 264
Then prompt no more the Follies you decry, ...		O 53	Pro Drury-Lane	55
Behold this Theatre, and grieve no more.		O 57	Prologue Comus	10
From zeal or malice now no more we dread, ...		O 61	Pro Word Wise	3
No savage more portentous stain'd		O 66	Hor I Ode xxii	13
No beast more dreadful ever stain'd		O 66	Hor I Ode xxii	V 13
None e'er more fierce Numidia's land, ...		O 66	Hor I Ode xxii	V 15
No Beast more dreadful ever stain'd		O 67	To A. Fuscus	13
No Beast more fierce Numidia's Land, ...		O 67	To A. Fuscus	15
Can more delicious food supply.		O 73	Hor. Epode II	V 62
Thy form more lovely, more adorn'd thy mind; . . .		O 80	Lady Birthday	4
Thy form more lovely, more adorn'd thy mind; . . .		O 80	Lady Birthday	4
No more let coquets to themselves be blind, ...		O 81	Lady Birthday	18
And vows to trust the faithless deep no more.		O 82	Young Author	10
More false, more cruel than the seas and wind.		O 82	Young Author	14
More false, more cruel than the seas and wind.		O 82	Young Author	14
More false, more cruel than the seas or wind.		O 82	Young Author	V 14
More false, more cruel than the seas or wind.		O 82	Young Author	V 14
No more delighted with destructive War, ...		O 97	Hickman Spinet	17
And, yet more strange! his Veins a Horse shall drain, .		O 111	To Posterity	25
Rest here distrest by poverty no more, ...		O 113	Epit. Phillips	3
Rest here oppress'd by poverty no more, ...		O 113	Epit. Phillips	V 3
The skies, that Stella mourn no more.		O 122	Stella Mourn.	16
Once more great nature's work review, ...		O 125	An Ode	23
Once more great nature's works renew		O 125	An Ode	V 23
Once more on wisdom's voice attend.		O 125	An Ode	24
More safely truth to urge her claim presumes, ...		O 134	Tr. Rambler 93	1
On swelling mortals to be proud no more.		O 135	Tr Rambler 106	2
The more I honour thee, the less I love.		O 140	Tr Rambler 188	1
Rapacity would call for more;		O 144	Tr Boeth. II.2	10

		PAGE	TITLE	LINE
"More than all thou canst not know;	. . . . .	O 186	Anacreon Ode 9	42
The snow dissolv'd no more is seen,	. . . . .	O 231	Tr Horace IV.7	1
Will toss us in a morning more?	. . . . . .	O 232	Tr Horace IV.7	18
Will rouse us in a morning more?	. . . . . .	O 232	Tr Horace IV.7	V 18
No more the glutted Sabre thirsts for Blood,	. . .	O 249	Irene	9
Before such Foes of more than human Force;	. . .	O 250	Irene	49
And harrass Greece no more with wasteful War.	. .	O 257	Irene	80
Is hazardous but--Talk no more of Hazards	. . . .	O 365	Irene	V 23
At Sight of female Charms will glow no more.	. . .	O 263	Irene	6
Desires more pure, and other Cares than Love.	. . .	O 263	Irene	8
Nor couldst thou more support a Life of Sloth	. . .	O 264	Irene	19
will burn no more	. . . .	Y 132	Irene	V 41
And wish their gloomy Caverns more obscure.	. . . .	O 268	Irene	32
I rais'd his Thoughts to more sublime Devotion.	. .	O 274	Irene	46
Shall mourn no more her plunder'd Palaces.	. . . .	O 278	Irene	78
The voice of war no more shall fright	. . . . .	Y 150	Irene	V 82
Irene				
Or only struggles to be more enslav'd?	. . . , . .	O 281	Irene	41
Once more reflect, suppress this infant Folly.	. . .	O 281	Irene	56
Young Man, forbear--The Heat of Youth, no more--	. . .	O 284	Irene	47
These Arts I try'd, and to inflame her more,	. . . .	O 287	Irene	14
Far more I dread Abdalla's fiery Folly,	. . . . .	O 287	Irene	7
No more I boast th' ambitious Name of Friend,	. . .	O 289	Irene	10
No more shall glow with Friendship's hallow'd Ardour:	.	O 289	Irene	16
No more should Greece lament those Prayers rejected.	. .	O 290	Irene	52
No more should Danger fright, or Want distress	. . . .	O 291	Irene	56
That joins us thus, will never part us more.	. . . .	O 296	Irene	39
To feel no more the Pangs of Separation.	. . . . .	O 303	Irene	24
Henceforward hope no more my slighted Friendship,	. . .	O 307	Irene	9
If thou art more than the gay Dream of Fancy,	. . . .	O 310	Irene	12
More than a pleasing Sound without a Meaning,	. . . .	O 310	Irene	13
No more shall feel Religion's hallow'd ardours	. . . .	O 349	Irene	V 24
Greece is no more, the prosp'rous Tyrant lives,	. . .	O 315	Irene	4
A private Station may discover more;	. . . . .	O 316	Irene	18
What more could Force attempt, or Art contrive?	. . .	O 317	Irene	35
What more could force attempt or thought contrive	. .	Y 194	Irene	V 35
Once more I dare thy Sword, behold the Prize,	. . . .	O 319	Irene	28
When vanquish'd Vice shall tyrannize no more.	. . . .	O 321	Irene	36
No more I burn for Fame or for Dominion;	. . . . .	O 333	Irene	43
And thou impearl'd with dew appear more gay.	. . . .	Y 3	On a Daffodill	12
The harmless wolves no more our cattle fear,	. . . .	Y 7	Virgil Daphnis	38
Pettius no more I verses write;	. . . .	Y 10	Tr Hor Epode 9	1
No more I sing, no more delight	. . . .	Y 11	Tr Hor Epode 9	3
No more I sing, no more delight	. . . .	Y 11	Tr Hor Epode 9	3
And see my mistress' face no more	. . . .	Y 11	Tr Hor Epode 9	32
And his more glorious acts eclipse his father's fame.	.	Y 20	Tr. Iliad Bk 6	104
MORN				
Who play from morn to night a borrow'd part;	. . . .	O 16	London	135
Should Hecatombs each rising Morn	. . . . . .	O 69	Hor.II Ode 14	5
Those glitt'ring Dew-drops of a vernal Morn,	. . . .	O 298	Irene	19
MORN'S				
May the morn's earliest tears on thee be shed,	. . . .	Y 3	On a Daffodill	11
MORNING				
And bless thine evening walk and morning toil.	. . . .	O 20	London	223
And bless the evening walk and morning toil.	. . . . .	O 20	London	V 223
And bless thy evening walk and morning toil.	. . . .	O 20	London	V 223
Pours in the morning worshiper no more;	. . . . .	O 33	Vanity Wishes	80
Shews pour the morning worshiper no more;	. . . . .	Y 95	Vanity Wishes	V 80
No fav'ring Muse her morning Dreams inspire;	. . . .	O 58	Prologue Comus	28
Will toss us in a morning more?	. . . .	O 232	Tr Horace IV.7	18
Will rouse us in a morning more?	. . . .	O 232	Tr Horace IV.7	V 18
Twice since the Morning rose I saw the Bassa,	. . . .	O 275	Irene	76
MORROW SEE TO-MORROW				
To morrow strike--Does then that experienc'd	. . . .	Y 154	Irene	V 19
wisdom				
Marks for His own still doat upon to Morrow	. . . .	O 374	Irene	V 21
The weary Soldier--Still sees to Morrow	. . . . .	O 374	Irene	V 30
Who knows, ere this important Morrow rise,	. . . . .	O 284	Irene	36
MORROW'S SEE TO-MORROW'S				
MORTAL				
A Mortal born he met the general Doom,	. . . . . .	O 51	Pro Drury-Lane	15
Whose mortal wounds pour forth a purple flood,	. . . .	O 76	Tr Add. Battle	20
Gross Fires, enkindled by a mortal Hand,	. . . . . .	O 282	Irene	57
MORTALITY				
Proclaims mortality to Man.	. . . .	O 231	Tr Horace IV.7	8
MORTALS				
On swelling mortals to be proud no more.	. . . . .	O 135	Tr Rambler 106	2
The mind of mortals, in perverseness strong,	. . . .	O 136	Tr Rambler 132	1
On weary Mortals sheds the balm of rest	. . . . .	O 356	Irene	V 10
Guides erring Mortals to the Paths of Virtue,	. . . .	O 289	Irene	18
And mortals trace th' Almighty's path in v<ain>	. . .	Y 217	Irene	V 14
Unjustly mortals triumph and complain	. . . . . .	Y 217	Irene	V 14
MORTGAG'D				
And mortgag'd states their grandsires wreaths regret,	.	O 39	Vanity Wishes	187
And mortgag'd states their former wreaths regret,	. . .	Y 100	Vanity Wishes	V 187
MORTGAGE				
Free to mortgage or to sell,	. . . .	O 196	Song Congratu.	6
MORTGAGES				
His bonds of debt, and mortgages of lands;	. . . . .	O 44	Vanity Wishes	288

```
                                                          PAGE    TITLE              LINE
MOSCOW'S
    "On Moscow's walls till Gothic standards fly,   . . . .   O  40 Vanity Wishes     203
MOSSIE
    And tread in mystick rings the mossie ground.   . . . .   O  77 Tr Add. Battle     52
MOST
    Sure the most bitter is a scornful jest;   . . . . . . .  O  17 London            167
    While all neglect, and most insult your woes.   . . . .   O  19 London            193
    Most venerable Jude!   . . . . . . . . . .                O  80 Feast St Simon     51
    Then best enjoy'd, when most improv'd.   . . . . . .      O 125 An Ode             28
    When best enjoy'd, when most improv'd.   . . . . . .      O 125 An Ode        V   28
    Delude the most; few pry behind the scene.   . . . . .    O 139 Tr Rambler 168      2
    For still where wishes most abound   . . . . . . . .      O 144 Tr Boeth. II.2     11
    Who merits most, Demetrius or Abdalla.   . . . . . .      O 284 Irene              45
    Who merits most!--I knew not we were Rivals.   . . . .    O 284 Irene              46
MOTHER
    The teeming mother, anxious for her race,   . . . . .     O  45 Vanity Wishes     319
    If the Guardian or the Mother   . . . . . . . .           O 197 Song Congratu.     25
    Should the guardian friend or mother   . . . . . . .      O 197 Song Congratu. V   25
    While his sad mother frantick with despair   . . . .      Y   6 Virgil Daphnis      5
    My mother who alone escap'd the grave   . . . . .         Y  19 Tr. Iliad Bk 6     38
MOTHER'S
    May then his mother's heart with joys o'erflow   . .      Y  20 Tr. Iliad Bk 6    105
    The chief, this spoke, into the mother's arms   . . . .   Y  20 Tr. Iliad Bk 6    107
MOTHERS
    Into his supplicating mothers heart.   . . . . . . .      O  77 Festina Lente      14
MOTION
    O'erbears each gentler Motion of the Mind.   . . . .      O 280 Irene              21
MOTIONS
    In easy State presides o'er all their Motions,   . . .    O 293 Irene             122
    And sees the motions of th' harmonious sphere;   . . .    Y   7 Virgil Daphnis     35
MOTIVE
    Path, motive, guide, original, and end.   . . . . . .     O 130 Tr. Rambler 7       8
MOTIVES
    My Wrongs, my Fears, my Motives, my Designs:--   . . .    O 256 Irene              40
MOTLEY
    See motley life in modern trappings dress'd,   . . . .    O  32 Vanity Wishes      51
MOULD
    And mould his passions till they make his will.   . . .   O  44 Vanity Wishes     282
    "This is Minerva, cast in Virtue's mould."   . . . .      O 190 Seeing Montagu      6
    But oft conjoins in woman's softer mould/frame   . . . .  Y 149 Irene         V   55
MOULDRING
    With mouldring cement and with beams disjointed   . . .   Y 114 Irene         V   45
MOUNOS
    Zeus mounos phlogoenti poleis ekperse kerauno,   . . . .  O 103 Eis Elisses         5
MOUNT
    They mount, they shine, evaporate, and fall.   . . .      O  33 Vanity Wishes      76
    If Greatness please thee, mount th' imperial Seat;   . .  O 279 Irene              84
    Inform'd they mount the Precipice of Pow'r,   . . . .     O 293 Irene             113
    And thrice to mount the battlements assay'd   . . . . .   Y  19 Tr. Iliad Bk 6     57
MOUNTAIN
    The mountain shepherd hears the distant noise.   . . . .  O 132 Tr. Rambler 65      3
MOUNTAIN'S
    Shun the Mountain's airy Brow,   . . . . . . . . .        O 145 Tr Boeth. II.4      7
MOUNTAINS
    Though dancing mountains witness'd Orpheus near;   . . .  O  43 Vanity Wishes     270
    On ev'ry side rise mountains of the slain,   . . . .      O  76 Tr Add. Battle     19
    Elate with Conquest, in his native Mountains,   . . . .   O 264 Irene              14
    At his dread Name the distant Mountains shake   . . . .   O 268 Irene              28
    At my dread name the distant mountains shake   . . . .    Y 136 Irene         V   28
    And woods and mountains hail the deity.   . . . . . . .   Y   7 Virgil Daphnis     41
MOUNTS
    When Cali mounts the Throne Abdalla dies,   . . . . .     O 288 Irene              13
    Hurling vast mounts against the realms above   . . . .    Y  26 Tr Add. Battle    138
MOURN
    For Mystes dead you ever mourn;   . . . . . . . . .       O  67 Hor. II Ode IX      10
    In clouds of Ign'rance mourn,   . . . . . . . . .         O  79 Feast St Simon     45
    The skies, that Stella mourn no more.   . . . . . .       O 122 Stella Mourn.      16
    While thus we mourn the Fortune of Aspasia,   . . . .     O 253 Irene             107
    Shall mourn no more her plunder'd Palaces.   . . . .      O 278 Irene              78
    For ever mourn their Avarice or Factions?   . . . . .     O 305 Irene              44
    Then shall the Rhodian mourn his sinking Tow'rs,   . . .  O 309 Irene              26
    With dolefull cries their living lord they mourn   . . .  Y  21 Tr. Iliad Bk 6    130
    The injur'd Cranes their murther'd offspring mourn   . .  Y  24 Tr Add. Battle     64
    While the sad Pygmies mourn with weeping eyes   . . .     Y  26 Tr Add. Battle    128
    Not long the happy Russians mourn;   . . . . . . . .      Y  39 Lady Leaving        9
MOURN'D
    Mourn'd not Antilochus so long;   . . . . . . . .         O  68 Hor. II Ode IX     14
MOURN'ST
    And learn his virtues, while thou mourn'st his end.   . . O 117 Epitaph Hanmer      4
MOURNER
    Where wealth unlov'd without a mourner dy'd,   . . . .    O  33 Vanity Wishes      55
MOURNFUL
    This mournful truth is ev'ry where confess'd,   . . . .   O  18 London            176
    In vain your mournful narrative disclose,   . . . . .     O  19 London            192
    Short sway! fair Austria spreads her mournful charms,  .  O  42 Vanity Wishes     245
    Short sway! for Austria spreads her mournful charms,  . . Y 103 Vanity Wishes V  245
    Now kindred Merit fills the mournful bier,   . . . . .    Y 106 Vanity Wishes V  303
    Yet hear, alas! this mournful truth,   . . . . .          O 159 Par Hermit III      9
    Yet hear, at last, this mournful truth,   . . . . .       O 159 Par Hermit III  V   9
    Aspasia! spare that lov'd, that mournful Name:   . . . .  O 252 Irene              76
    Her mournful Charms attracted his Regards,   . . . . .    O 259 Irene             121
```

217

MOURNFUL   (CONTINUED)   PAGE   TITLE   LINE
    May Penitence attend thy mournful Bed, ...   O 322 Irene   61
    Ordain'd the mournful Messengers of Death. . . . . . O 326 Irene   35
MOURNFULL
    That day, that mournfull day, no chearfull song   . . .   Y   6 Virgil Daphnis   7
    Mournfull Andromache the silence broke, ...   Y 18 Tr. Iliad Bk 6   17
MOURNING
    Stella in Mourning . . . .   O 122 Stella Mourn.   T
    And plan the Happiness of mourning Millions?   . . . . O 291 Irene   68
    Your Robe of Mourning, and your Dogs of Death.   . . . . O 325 Irene   5
    Torn from the mourning Earth by thy Neglect.   . . . .   O 334 Irene   4
MOURNINGS
    And publick mournings pacify the skies; . . . . . .   O 19 London   197
MOURNS
    A sister sickens, or a daughter mourns. . . . . . .   O 45 Vanity Wishes   302
    The hardy Scythian ever mourns. . . . .   O 70 Hor.II Ode XX   16
MOUTON
    Au Mouton . . . . . .   O 172 French Distich   9
MOV'D
    Had Stella's gentle touches mov'd the Lyre, ... O 97 Hickman Spinet   15
MOVE
    Or move the haughty King below, ...   O 69 Hor.II Ode 14   10
    But move their numrous arms to Musicks sound, ... O 77 Tr Add. Battle   51
    Nor down steep cliffs precipitately move   . . . . . . O 77 Festina Lente   5
    Where doth extatick fury move   . . . . . .   O 80 Feast St Simon   56
MOVING
    O thou whose pow'r o'er moving worlds presides,   . . . O 129 Tr. Rambler 7   1
MR
    A New Prologue Spoken By Mr Garrick, ...   O 56 Prologue Comus   T
    To Eliza plucking Laurel in Mr Pope's Gardens   . . .   O 106 Eliza plucking   T
MUCH
    Much could I add,--but see the boat at hand, ...   O 22 London   254
    How much more safe the vassal than the lord;   . . . .   O 31 Vanity Wishes   32
    So much lament his slaughter'd son. . . . . . .   O 68 Hor. II Ode IX   16
    The wine you kept with so much care . . . . . .   O 69 Hor.II Ode 14   27
    So much my Appetite would please   . . . .   O 73 Hor. Epode II   60
    Half were too much had Mahomet been Cali. . . . . .   Y 132 Irene   V 41B
    Too much to fear or trust, is equal Weakness.   . . . . O 300 Irene   77
    Nor press too much upon a Lover's Patience. . . . .   O 310 Irene   9
    Yet much remains to hope. I shall not call . . . .   O 317 Irene   45
    So much our splendour was encreas'd by thine.   . . . . Y   6 Virgil Daphnis   19
MULTITUDE
    Enlarge my life with multitude of days, ... O 43 Vanity Wishes   255
    I scorn the multitude, alive and dead.   . . . . .   O 141 Tr Rambler 208   4
MULTITUDES
    Your slaughter'd Multitudes that swell the Shore, . . . O 255 Irene   30
MUNIFICENCE
    Why then has Nature's vain Munificence   . . . . . . O 276 Irene   24
    Why then did Natures vain Munificence . . . .   O 355 Irene   V 13
MURD'RER
    The midnight murd'rer bursts the faithless bar;   . . . O 21 London   239
MURD'RER'S
    Then Visions horrid as a Murd'rer's Dreams   . . . . . O 266 Irene   13
MURD'RERS
    Horrid as a murd'rers dreams, madman's laughter   . . . Y 133 Irene   V 13
    Hide me with Murd'rers in the Dungeon's Gloom, ...   O 328 Irene   34
MURDER   SEE MURTHER
    And Murder meditates his prey. . . . . .   O 191 Tr. Medea I   12
    And Murder, all blood-bolter'd, schemes the wound. . .   O 192 Tr. Medea II   16
    Their Rage, and pall'd their Appetite of Murder;   . . . O 249 Irene   8
    And frowns on Perjury, Revenge and Murder. . . . .   O 300 Irene   58
    The Bassa, reeking with his Master's Murder, ...   O 300 Irene   80
    Now haste to murder, ere returning Thought   . . . .   O 326 Irene   39
    Could not her Charms repress your Zeal for Murder?   . .   O 332 Irene   24
MURDER'D   SEE MURTHER'D
    What murder'd Wentworth, and what exil'd Hyde,   . . .   O 36 Vanity Wishes   131
    Which murder'd Innocence that call'd on me. . . . . . O 334 Irene   76
MURM'RING
    And, murm'ring, balmy Sleep prolong, ...   O 72 Hor. Epode II   32
MURMUR
    Or dare to murmur in the flow'ry Glade; . . . . . . O 111 To Posterity   22
    But sink among thy Slaves without a Murmur. . . . . .   O 289 Irene   11
    Then mingle with your slaves without a murmur   . . . . Y 161 Irene   V 11
    Sport in our Sails, and murmur o'er the Deep.   . . . . O 304 Irene   7
    The shudd'ring Camp shall murmur out Demetrius. . . .   O 305 Irene   42
    An angry Murmur, a rebellious Frown. . . . .   O 312 Irene   19
MURMURS
    He murmurs Vengeance at the Name of Cali, ...   O 256 Irene   48
    In soft Endearments, and in gentle Murmurs, ... O 303 Irene   14
    To still their Murmurs, ere the twentieth Sun   . . . . O 309 Irene   23
    The limpid streams with ruefull murmurs flow   . . . .   Y   6 Virgil Daphnis   3
MURTHER
    And weary Murther slumbers o'er the Carnage . . . . . O 350 Irene   V   9
MURTHER'D
    The injur'd Cranes their murther'd offspring mourn . .   Y 24 Tr Add. Battle   64
MURZA
    Haste, Murza, to the Palace, let the Sultan   . . . .   O 319 Irene   2
    Go, blustring Slave.--He has not heard of Murza.   . . . O 324 Irene   25
MUSE
    This, only this, provokes the snarling muse.   . . . . O 17 London   161
    This, only this, provokes the darling muse. . . . . . O 17 London   V 161

		PAGE	TITLE	LINE
MUSE	(CONTINUED)			
No fav'ring Muse her morning Dreams inspire;		O 58	Prologue Comus	28
Art thou forgotten by the Muse,		O 80	Feast St Simon	50
As learn'd Eliza, sister of the Muse,		O 106	Eliza plucking	1
Thou seem'st at once, bright nymph, a Muse and Grace.		O 107	Lady F Assizes	6
And seeks the Shades to muse upon Irene;		O 261	Irene	4
MUSIC				
Only ev'ry bush there artless music sings		Y 58	London	V 220
Verse and Music vainly strove;		O 149	Tr Boet III.12	16
The joys of music and of wine,		O 190	Tr. Medea I	4
MUSIC'S				
Can yield to room to Music's soothing pow'r.		O 193	Tr. Medea II	20
MUSICIAN				
Whilst each Musician of the Grove		O 72	Hor. Epode II	33
An Epitaph on Claudy Phillips, a Musician		O 113	Epit. Phillips	T
Musician, who died very poor		O 113	Epit. Phillips	V T
On Claudius Phillips, an excellent Musician		O 113	Epit. Phillips	V T
Epitaph on Claude Phillips, an Itinerant Musician		O 113	Epit. Phillips	V T
MUSICK				
There ev'ry bush with nature's musick rings,		O 20	London	220
Nor sweeter musick of a virtuous friend,		O 43	Vanity Wishes	272
But when your Musick sooths the raging pain,		O 96	Hickman Spinet	6
Thy musick teach the nobler art		O 121	To Miss Playin	35
Though musick thrills, or sudden sallies seize,		O 142	In Baretti Bk.	6
And chear the weary Passenger with Musick.		O 277	Irene	38
Again her Temples sound with holy Musick:		O 291	Irene	55
MUSICK'S				
Thus wak'd to rage by Musick's dreadfull Pow'r,		O 97	Hickman Spinet	13
MUSICKS				
But move their numrous arms to Musicks sound,		O 77	Tr Add. Battle	51
MUSING				
Where Hate sits musing to betray,		O 191	Tr. Medea I	11
MUST				
Must dull Suspence corrupt the stagnant mind?		O 47	Vanity Wishes	344
Must dull Suspence becalm still the stagnant mind?		Y 107	Vanity Wishes	V 344
Must helpless man, in ignorance sedate,		O 47	Vanity Wishes	345
Must no dislike alarm, no wishes rise,		O 47	Vanity Wishes	347
Must watch the wild Vicissitudes of Taste;		O 53	Pro Drury-Lane	48
With ev'ry Meteor of Caprice must play,		O 53	Pro Drury-Lane	49
For we that live to please, must please to live.		O 53	Pro Drury-Lane	54
Must hear all taunts, and hear without reply.		O 59	Pro Good Nat'd	14
The man whom fate has laid, where all must lye.		O 61	Pro Word Wise	6
By all, like him, must praise and blame be found;		O 62	Pro Word Wise	19
While wretched we about the world must roam,		O 64	Virgil Past.I	3
Here I, though faint myself, must drive my goats,		O 64	Virgil Past.I	17
We all must view the Stygian flood		O 69	Hor.II Ode 14	17
Soon must this bough, as you shall fix his doom,		O 95	Sprig of Myrtl	13
Oh, must their ardours cease to glow		O 100	Ode Friendship	25
At length must Suffolk's beauties shine in vain,		O 107	Lady F Assizes	1
That slowly grows, which must for ever last.		O 142	In Baretti Bk.	10
Must bid his Passions all obey;		O 146	Tr Boeth III.5	2
Must bid each wild Desire be still,		O 146	Tr Boeth III.5	3
Must begin by Thirty five:		O 178	Thrale 35 Year	16
Must look on Thrale at Thirtyfive.		O 178	Thrale 35 Year	18
Learn here that Peace from Innocence must flow;		O 246	Irene Prologue	13
Must Heaven dispatch the Messengers of Light,		O 250	Irene	46
Must watchfull providence despatch from Heav'n		Y 114	Irene	V 46
It must, it must be She; her Name?		O 258	Irene	103
It must, it must be She; her Name?		O 258	Irene	103
And there must fall.		O 260	Irene	132
Such Beauty must not shine to vulgar Eyes.		O 269	Irene	43
Must I for these renounce the Hope of Heav'n,		O 276	Irene	13
Must then Ambition's Votaries infringe		O 280	Irene	15
Still must we linger in uncertain Hope?		O 282	Irene	3
But he must live to make his Masters wretched?		O 286	Irene	7
She cannot, must not, shall not linger here,		O 296	Irene	6
If we must part--		O 297	Irene	11
If we must part--		O 297	Irene	12
Despis'd and curs'd, Leontius must descend		O 305	Irene	27
Must Greece, still wretched by her Children's Folly,		O 305	Irene	43
Still Cali lives, and must he live To-morrow?		O 310	Irene	1
Recall th' extorted Doom.--It must be so,		O 326	Irene	40
Alike must fall the poet and his theme.		Y 4	On a Daffodill	28
MUSTAPHA				
See! Mustapha, the Tyrant's Minion, comes;		O 260	Irene	143
Haste Go Mustapha go to celebrate the day		Y 129	Irene	V 25
Comes Mustapha.--Your Turkish Robes conceal you--		O 271	Irene	36
Now, Mustapha, pursue thy Tale of Horror.		O 272	Irene	1
Now Mustapha reveal this Tale of treason		O 369	Irene	V 18
Beware of Mustapha, beware of Treason.		O 273	Irene	29
The Faith of Mustapha disdains Suspicion;		O 273	Irene	30
MUTINIES				
That raises tumults in the female bosom seditions		Y 158	Irene	V 12
(mutinies				
MUTINY				
But Fear, or Mutiny may taint the Greeks?		O 284	Irene	37
MUTUAL				
When mutual frauds perplex'd the maze of State,		O 118	Epitaph Hanmer	24
Chiefs confus'd in mutual slaughter,		O 159	Tr. Rio Verde	3
one common Interest, mutual duties		O 352	Irene	V 17
And dy'd their bulrush-spears in mutual blood.		Y 24	Tr Add. Battle	57

219

	PAGE	TITLE	LINE
Tho' grief and fondness in my breast rebel,	O 8	London	1
Yet still my calmer thoughts his choice commend,	O 8	London	3
Since hope but sooths to double my distress,	O 10	London	39
And ev'ry moment leaves my little less;	O 10	London	40
While yet my steady steps no staff sustains,	O 10	London	41
While yet my steddy steps no staff sustains,	O 10	London	V 41
And life still vig'rous revels in my veins;	O 10	London	42
But what, my friend, what hope remains for me,	O 13	London	67
Forgive my transports on a theme like this,	O 15	London	97
Enlarge my life with multitude of days,	O 43	Vanity Wishes	255
Lies at my feet, I hiss him, and he dies.	O 60	Pro Good Nat'd	24
Oft on his altar shall my firstlings lie,	O 64	Virgil Past.I	9
He gave my flocks to graze the flowery meads,	O 64	Virgil Past.I	11
My admiration only I exprest,	O 64	Virgil Past.I	13
(No spark of envy harbours in my breast)	O 64	Virgil Past.I	14
Here I, though faint myself, must drive my goats,	O 64	Virgil Past.I	17
The man, my friend, whose conscious heart	O 65	Hor I Ode xxii	1
The Man, my Friend, whose conscious Heart	O 66	To A. Fuscus	1
My Flame for Lalage I'll own;	O 67	To A. Fuscus	23
Her voice and Smiles my Song shall grace.	O 67	To A. Fuscus	24
And fruitfull fields, my dearest Friend,	O 69	Hor.II Ode 14	22
My Works shall propagate my fame,	O 70	Hor.II Ode XX	17
My Works shall propagate my fame,	O 70	Hor.II Ode XX	17
Nations shall celebrate my Name	O 70	Hor.II Ode XX	19
Nor grace with fading flours my Herse,	O 70	Hor.II Ode XX	22
Shall live for ever in my verse.	O 70	Hor.II Ode XX	24
So much my Appetite would please	O 73	Hor. Epode II	60
That post, and all the rest, shall be my care;	O 74	Tr. Iliad Bk 6	3
And one base action sully all my fame,	O 74	Tr. Iliad Bk 6	6
Oh! how my soul abhors so mean a thought.	O 74	Tr. Iliad Bk 6	8
Nor my brave brothers, that have bit the ground,	O 74	Tr. Iliad Bk 6	17
Can in my bosom half that grief create,	O 74	Tr. Iliad Bk 6	19
Tears, at my name, shall drown those beauteous eyes,	O 75	Tr. Iliad Bk 6	27
To nobler subjects tune my lyre;	O 78	Feast St Simon	8
Those Saints my numbers grace	O 78	Feast St Simon	9
My rude unpolish'd song;	O 80	Feast St Simon	57
This tributary verse receive, my fair,	O 80	Lady Birthday	1
My fair, be mindful of the mighty trust,	O 81	Lady Birthday	11
Ambiguous emblem of my future fate!	O 95	Sprig of Myrtl	V 2
Cease, lovely thief! my tender limbs to wound,	O 106	Eliza plucking	5
Then, O my Country! shalt thou groan distrest,	O 110	To Posterity	3
Behold my fair, where-e'er we rove,	O 123	Winter's Walk	1
I feel thy pow'r usurp my breast.	O 123	Winter's Walk	8
Snatch me, my Stella, to thy arms,	O 124	Winter's Walk	19
Yet, tho' my limbs disease invades,	O 125	An Ode	13
Here stop, my soul, thy rapid flight,	O 125	An Ode	17
Where first great nature charm'd my sight,	O 125	An Ode	19
Where wisdom first inform'd my heart.	O 125	An Ode	20
Denies my Lyce shines,	O 127	To Lyce, Lady	18
Attack my gentle lines.	O 127	To Lyce, Lady	20
My Lyce makes as good a sky,	O 127	To Lyce, Lady	23
Nought from my birth or ancestors I claim;	O 132	Tr. Rambler 46	1
All is my own, my honour and my shame.	O 132	Tr. Rambler 46	2
All is my own, my honour and my shame.	O 132	Tr. Rambler 46	2
All is my own, my honour and my shame.	O 132	Tr. Rambler 46	2
Polish'd with endless toil, my lays	O 139	Tr Rambler 169	1
And leave my labours to the learn'd and wise,	O 141	Tr Rambler 208	2
From my labours wait their last reward.	O 141	Tr Rambler 208	2
I put my hat upon my head	O 158	Par. Hermit II	1
I put my hat upon my head	O 158	Par. Hermit II	1
As with my hat upon my head	O 158	Par. Hermit II	V 1
As with my hat upon my head	O 158	Par. Hermit II	V 1
Nor fear that I, my gentle maid,	O 159	Par Hermit III	5
I pleas'd my Master, and I pleas'd my Dame.	O 174	Tr Epitaph Dog	2
I pleas'd my Master, and I pleas'd my Dame.	O 174	Tr Epitaph Dog	2
Long may live my lovely Hetty!	O 175	Tr Easy Phrase	1
Live my lovely Hetty long!	O 175	Tr Easy Phrase	4
Long may live my lovely Hetty!	O 175	Tr Easy Phrase	6
Would you hope to gain my heart,	O 176	Tr Metastasi I	1
My first, shuts out Thieves from your house or your Room	O 179	Charade!	1
My second, expresses a Syrian perfume;	O 179	Charade!	2
My whole, is a Man in whose converse is shar'd,	O 179	Charade!	3
Wheresoe'er I turn my View,	O 179	Ridicul Warton	1
--Come, my lad, and drink some beer.	O 181	Parody Warton	8
"Now Anacreon rules my flight:	O 185	Anacreon Ode 9	14
"Think not yet my service hard,	O 185	Anacreon Ode 9	17
"Smiling at my master's gates,	O 185	Anacreon Ode 9	19
"Freedom my return awaits,	O 185	Anacreon Ode 9	20
"Now my better lot bestows	O 185	Anacreon Ode 9	29
"O'er his face extend my wings;	O 186	Anacreon Ode 9	38
"Let me now my pinions ply,	O 186	Anacreon Ode 9	43
Wealth, my lad, was made to wander,	O 196	Song Congratu.	V 17
Come my lads and take your fill.	O 196	Song Congratu.	V 20
My Swain is little--true--but be it known,	O 247	Irene Epilogue	9
My Pride's to have that little all my own.	O 247	Irene Epilogue	10
My Pride's to have that little all my own.	O 247	Irene Epilogue	10
And yet, my Friend, what Miracles were wrought	O 251	Irene	52
Quitting my close Retreat, I range the City,	O 251	Irene	60
Arose to Heav'n, and pierc'd my bleeding Breast,	O 251	Irene	74
My reasoning Pow'rs--Dear, hapless, lost Aspasia!	O 252	Irene	78

MY

              (CONTINUED)   PAGE   TITLE   LINE

Text	Page	Title	Line
O! sooth my Soul, and teach me how to lose thee.	O 253	Irene	103
Sounds in my sleeping Ear, "Awake Demetrius,	O 254	Irene	122
Whose quick Impatience seiz'd my doubtful Hand,	O 254	Irene	126
Selected by my Care, a hardy Band,	O 254	Irene	136
And share the deepest Secrets of my Soul,	O 256	Irene	39
My Wrongs, my Fears, my Motives, my Designs:--	O 256	Irene	40
My Wrongs, my Fears, my Motives, my Designs:--	O 256	Irene	40
My Wrongs, my Fears, my Motives, my Designs:--	O 256	Irene	40
My Wrongs, my Fears, my Motives, my Designs:--	O 256	Irene	40
Great Amurath, at my Request, forsook	O 256	Irene	43
And dooms my rash Fidelity to Ruin.	O 256	Irene	49
Secure he tramples my declining Fame,	O 257	Irene	71
Secure he tramples my declining Frame,	V 257	Irene	V 71
Which lately bless'd my gentle Government,	O 257	Irene	75
My Policy shall raise an easy Throne;	O 257	Irene	78
Leave to perform my Pilgrimage to Mecca;	O 258	Irene	87
Which granted, hides my Purpose from the World,	O 258	Irene	88
What Hopes, what Terrors rush upon my Soul!	O 259	Irene	104
Distract my Soul, dispatch thy ling'ring Tale;	O 259	Irene	114
To offer up my vows in the temple built by the Father of Mankind	O 348	Irene	V 1
Adorns my Palace with its brightest Virgins;	O 263	Irene	15
Flush in my cheek, and wander in my Veins	O 349	Irene	V 26
Flush in my cheek, and wander in my Veins	O 349	Irene	V 26
Why rove I now, when absent from my Fair,	O 263	Irene	19
And ease my loaded Soul upon her Bosom?	O 263	Irene	22
Thy Care shall guard this Treasure of my Soul;	O 263	Irene	2
There let Aspasia, since my Fair entreats it,	O 263	Irene	3
To pour my Prayers for thy successful Reign,	O 264	Irene	10
And at the holy place pour out my prayers	Y 130	Irene	V 12
for the long life and prosperity of my sovereign	Y 130	Irene	V 12A
My soul could animate a larger frame	Y 132	Irene	V 41A
When ev'ry Storm in my Domain shall roar,	O 265	Irene	42
Till ev'ry Storm in my Domain shall roar,	O 354	Irene	V 25
When the revolving seasons shall only visit my dominions	Y 132	Irene	V 44
Exalts my Soul, and fortifies my Heart.	O 265	Irene	5
Exalts my Soul, and fortifies my Heart.	O 265	Irene	5
Death rises to my View, with all his Terrors;	O 265	Irene	12
Chill my Resolves, and blast my blooming Virtue:	O 266	Irene	14
Chill my Resolves, and blast my blooming Virtue.	O 266	Irene	14
And sought An easier conquest in my softer beauty	Y 134	Irene	V 35
Behold, my fair, as my resistless hand	Y 136	Irene	V 25
Behold, my fair, as my resistless hand	Y 136	Irene	V 25
They croud my camp with voluntary tribute	Y 136	Irene	V 27B
Vye for my submission, sollicite bondage.	Y 136	Irene	V 27C
At my dread name the distant mountains shake	Y 136	Irene	V 28
Shake at my dreaded name and the frighted world	Y 136	Irene	V 28
Had not my ready thought remov'd Aspasia	O 367	Irene	V 24
My Doom confirm'd establishes my Purpose.	O 270	Irene	9
My Doom confirm'd establishes my Purpose.	O 270	Irene	9
My Heart still beats responsive to the Sultan's;	O 272	Irene	9
And feel no Sorrow while my Sov'reign smiles.	O 272	Irene	11
Has Treason's dire Infection reach'd my Palace?	O 272	Irene	2
My Father call'd me to his Couch of Death,	O 272	Irene	7
His Hand! His Seal! The Secrets of my Soul	O 273	Irene	19
Betray'd some Traytor lurking near my Bosom.	O 273	Irene	23
Implor'd my Leave to visit Mecca's Temple;	O 273	Irene	44
Heap'd by my Fathers illplac'd Bounties on Him	O 351	Irene	V 13
Elude my Vengeance? no--My Troops shall range	O 274	Irene	58
Elude my Vengeance? no--My Troops shall range	O 274	Irene	58
Thence should my Fury drag him down to Tortures;	O 274	Irene	64
Claim my divided Soul. This Wretch unworthy	O 275	Irene	69
For idle Hours, and crush him at my Leisure.	O 275	Irene	71
Betray my King to Negligence of Danger.	O 275	Irene	73
And heard in my first approaching	Y 144	Irene	V 79
And, to confirm my Thought, at sight of me,	O 275	Irene	84
As blasted by my Presence, they withdrew	O 275	Irene	85
The strong Emotions of my troubled Soul	O 275	Irene	87
And dark Perplexity distracts my Counsels.	O 275	Irene	89
And Gales of softer Passion fan my Bosom.	O 275	Irene	93
And softer passion steals upon my Bosom	O 367	Irene	V 14
To hear my Vows and give Mankind a Queen?	O 276	Irene	2
To hear my suit and give a Queen to Turkey?	O 372	Irene	V 7
I thought, forgive my Fair, the noblest Aim,	O 278	Irene	61
Forbear--O do not urge my Ruin!	O 278	Irene	79
Smile on my Wishes, and command the Globe.	O 279	Irene	81
For thee, my fair, shall India's spices	Y 150	Irene	V 81
Because my slighted Passion burns in vain!	O 281	Irene	49
And tender Accents quiver'd on my Lips,	O 282	Irene	67
She mark'd my sparkling Eyes, and heaving Breast,	O 282	Irene	68
Trusts to my Care his Mistress and his Life,	O 283	Irene	10
At my Command yon' Iron Gates unfold;	O 283	Irene	14
At my Command the Sentinels retire;	O 283	Irene	15
And this is my Reward--to burn, to languish,	O 285	Irene	1
Oppose my Wishes, and--Remember Justice.	O 286	Irene	16
My Zeal marks Gladness dawning on thy Cheek,	O 286	Irene	2
My Vows, 'tis true, she hears with less Aversion,	O 287	Irene	7
My tongue with am'rous eloquence displaid	Y 158	Irene	V 7
I drew to my party with (alluring) promises artfull	Y 158	Irene	V 11
He 's gone--Here rest, my Soul, thy fainting Wing,	O 287	Irene	1

MY   (CONTINUED)   PAGE   TITLE   LINE

Phrase	PAGE	TITLE	LINE
My soul not oft acquainted with remorse	Y 159	Irene	V 8
Deep in my Breast be treasur'd this Resolve,	O 288	Irene	12
In my weak Ear th' intoxicating Sounds.	O 288	Irene	6
Long would my Zeal for Mahomet and Thee	O 288	Irene	11
Did regal Diadems invest my Brow,	O 289	Irene	12
Yet should my Soul, still faithful to her Choice,	O 289	Irene	13
I'll open my breast--clasp thee--forget	Y 161	Irene	V 13
The Dread of instant Death restrains my Tongue?	O 289	Irene	25
Nor think my eyes oerflow with Female Weakness	O 357	Irene	V 17
Implor'd th' eternal Power to shield my Country,	O 290	Irene	49
To shield my Lover, and preserve my Country.	O 364	Irene	V 4
To shield my Lover, and preserve my Country.	O 364	Irene	V 4
To me my Lover's Fondness will restore,	O 291	Irene	74
And give the short remnant of my life to prayer,	O 348	Irene	V 14
Thank Heav'n in daily hymns for my our deliverance	Y 166	Irene	V 93
There when my Thoughts, at interval of Pray'r,	O 292	Irene	94
And as my thoughts at intervals of Prayer	O 349	Irene	V 9
My Bosom feels, enkindled from the Sky,	O 293	Irene	108
'Tis she--My Hope, my Happiness, my Love!	O 294	Irene	1
'Tis she--My Hope, my Happiness, my Love!	O 294	Irene	1
'Tis she--My Hope, my Happiness, my Love!	O 294	Irene	1
Let my blest Eyes for ever gaze--	O 294	Irene	4
Recline upon my Breast thy sinking Beauties:	O 295	Irene	8
A sudden Mist o'ercasts my darken'd Soul,	O 295	Irene	12
My fainting Soul with Violence of transport.	O 371	Irene	V 15
A thousand Questions press upon my Tongue,	O 295	Irene	19
Beyond my warmest Hope, or wildest Wishes,	O 296	Irene	35
Then--O my Fair, I cannot bid thee goe;	O 297	Irene	15
Then--O my Fair, I cannot bid thee go;	O 297	Irene	V 15
Enough--resistless Reason calms my Soul--	O 297	Irene	1
Thou kind Assistant of my better Angel,	O 298	Irene	10
Propitious Guide of my bewilder'd Soul,	O 298	Irene	11
Calm of my Cares, and Guardian of my Virtue.	O 298	Irene	12
Calm of my Cares, and Guardian of my Virtue.	O 298	Irene	12
My Soul first kindled by thy bright Example,	O 298	Irene	13
To shock my Virtue with a Tale of Love.	O 299	Irene	40
Did not the Cause of Greece restrain my Sword,	O 299	Irene	41
And intermix'd my Praises with his own;	O 299	Irene	44
My Bosom harrass'd with alternate Passions,	O 299	Irene	54
But still yet my Soul detests the Bassas	O 353	Irene	V 22
And my blood freezes at Assassination	O 353	Irene	V 23
Nor end my Terrors with the Sultan's Death;	O 300	Irene	67
Still, still Distrust sits heavy on my Heart.	O 301	Irene	95
Deface Erase the glories of my native country	Y 177	Irene	V 107
Love be my Wealth, and my Distinction Virtue.	O 302	Irene	111
Love be my Wealth, and my Distinction Virtue.	O 302	Irene	111
Retire, my Fair, that Pow'r that smiles on Goodness	O 303	Irene	20
Have I for this preserv'd my guiltless Bosom,	O 304	Irene	14
Hast thou not search'd my Soul's profoundest Thoughts?	O 304	Irene	18
Be but my Country free, be thine the Praise;	O 305	Irene	33
My Name shall echo through the shouting Field;	O 305	Irene	40
My Pride shall ne'er protract my Country's Woes;	O 306	Irene	47
My Pride shall ne'er protract my Country's Woes;	O 306	Irene	47
Succeed, my Friend, unenvied by Leontius.	O 306	Irene	48
I feel new Spirit shoot along my Nerves,	O 306	Irene	49
My Soul expands to meet approaching Freedom.	O 306	Irene	50
Henceforward hope no more my slighted Friendship,	O 307	Irene	9
And saw my scatter'd Squadrons fly before him.	O 307	Irene	20
Abdalla, Cali, go--proclaim my Purpose.	O 309	Irene	43
Will cloud my Triumphs, and pollute the Day.	O 310	Irene	3
With cautious Vigilance, at my Command,	O 310	Irene	4
Will damp my joys, and cloud the happy days	O 370	Irene	V 23
Ambition only gave her to my Arms,	O 310	Irene	7
And Gratitude's strong Ties restrain my Tongue.	O 312	Irene	5
anguish of my soul before Thee.	Y 189	Irene	V 1
Flush in my cheeks, and sally in veins	Y 189	Irene	V 1E
Exalt my soul, and swell it into raptures.	Y 189	Irene	V 1F
But my blood freezes and weak nature shudders	Y 189	Irene	V 1G
My trembling nerves--sink at the dreadful scenes of blood	Y 189	Irene	V 1H
While yet the future Fortune of my Country	O 313	Irene	2
Her lofty mien, and insolence of virtue--my state	Y 191	Irene	V 14
Fly, fly, my Love, Destruction rushes on us,	O 315	Irene	1
Just as it reach'd my Lips, a sudden Cry	O 316	Irene	27
And seize my Sword with disencumber'd Hand.	O 316	Irene	29
The day disastrous, that secures my honor	Y 195	Irene	V 46
Forgive, my Fair, 'tis Life, 'tis Nature calls.	O 318	Irene	19
Forgive my fair what fame what nature prompts	Y 197	Irene	V 19
Now, Traytor, feel the Fear that chills my Hand.	O 318	Irene	20
Fly, Wretch, while yet my Pity grants thee Flight;	O 319	Irene	23
The Pow'r of Turkey waits upon my Call.	O 319	Irene	24
The pow'r of Turkey rises at my call	Y 197	Irene	V 24
Alike my Death or thine is gain to thee,	O 319	Irene	32
Haste, seize them, guards, be quick--my thoughtless hast	Y 198	Irene	V 34
Abdalla fails now is my slave	Y 198	Irene	V 1
Behold a Boaster's Worth. Now snatch, my Fair,	O 320	Irene	7
Of Freedom and of Love: My trembling Joints	O 320	Irene	11

MY   (CONTINUED)   PAGE   TITLE   LINE
     Depart, Demetrius, lest my Fate involve thee, ...   O 320 Irene   13
     My Soul attends thy Voice, and banish'd Virtue   . . . .   O 320 Irene   32
     Irradiate and obscure my Breast by Turns: . . . .   O 321 Irene   45
     Will spread resistless Light upon my Soul.   . . . .   O 321 Irene   47
     Fly, Slaves, and call the Sultan to my Rescue.   . . . .   O 322 Irene   56
     While I not yet familiar to my Crimes, ...   O 322 Irene   11
     Has taught my Slave the Language of Command!   . . . .   O 323 Irene   2
     The Sultan is my Judge.   . . . .   O 323 Irene   12
     This Bay has prov'd my ,fondness for the Sultan;   . . . .   O 324 Irene   19
     I go, lest Vengeance urge my Hand to Blood, ...   O 324 Irene   23
     Quick from my Sight you inauspicious Monsters, ...   O 325 Irene   5
     Irene's Chamber! From my faithful Bosom   . . . .   O 326 Irene   31
     Far be the Thought--But hear my Protestation.   . . . .   O 326 Irene   32
     Far be the horrid thought--but hear my protestation . . .   Y 205 Irene   V 32
     My Hopes, my Wishes, terminate in Life, ...   O 327 Irene   22
     My Hopes, my Wishes, terminate in Life, ...   O 327 Irene   22
     Quick at my Call shall execute your Charge;   . . . .   O 328 Irene   43
     O, hear my Pray'rs! accept, all-pitying Heaven, ...   O 328 Irene   52
     Be charg'd upon my Soul. O, Mercy! Mercy!   . . . .   O 329 Irene   55
     Dwell on my Ear, and sadden all my Soul;   . . . .   O 329 Irene   9
     Dwell on my Ear, and sadden all my Soul;   . . . .   O 329 Irene   9
     Perhaps my Zeal too fierce betray'd my Prudence;   . . . .   O 330 Irene   20
     Perhaps my Zeal too fierce betray'd my Prudence;   . . . .   O 330 Irene   20
     Perhaps my Warmth exceeded my Commission;   . . . .   O 330 Irene   21
     Perhaps my Warmth exceeded my Commission, ...   O 330 Irene   21
     Perhaps I will not stoop to plead my Cause;   . . . .   O 330 Irene   22
     Perhaps I will not bend to plead my cause   . . . .   Y 210 Irene   V 22
     And bar'd my Bosom to the Ruffian's Dagger.   . . . .   O 331 Irene   20
     Was she then guiltless! Has my thoughtless Rage   . . . .   O 332 Irene   18
     Remorse and Anguish seize on all my Breast;   . . . .   O 333 Irene   45
     My Rage and Grief had hid from my Remembrance.   . . . .   O 334 Irene   65
     My Rage and Grief had hid from my Remembrance.   . . . .   O 334 Irene   65
     My rage and.grief had had from my remembrance   . . . .   Y 215 Irene   V 69B
     My rage and grief had had from my remembrance   . . . .   Y 215 Irene   V 69B
     My Spirits fail, awhile support me, Vengeance--   . . . .   O 334 Irene   72
     My spirits fail, I cannot name his death   . . . .   Y 216 Irene   V 72
     That mark'd my Course, suspicious of my Purpose, ...   O 335 Irene   6
     That mark'd my Course, suspicious of my Purpose, ...   O 335 Irene   6
     Attend my prayers propitious, hear my vow, ...   Y   7 Virgil Daphnis 42
     Attend my prayers propitious, hear my vow, ...   Y   7 Virgil Daphnis 42
     My bosom glows with fiercer fire;   . . . .   Y 10 Tr Hor Epode 9   2
     Invades my soul, and rages in my breast.   . . . .   Y 11 Tr Hor Epode 9   6
     Invades my soul, and rages in my breast.   . . . .   Y 11 Tr Hor Epode 9   6
     I then (my cheeks still glow with shame) was grown . . . .   Y 11 Tr Hor Epode 9 11
     No feasts could e'er my cares dispell;   . . . .   Y 11 Tr Hor Epode 9 13
     Sighs issued from my heaving breast;   . . . .   Y 11 Tr Hor Epode 9 14
     My silence and my groans confess'd.   . . . .   Y 11 Tr Hor Epode 9 16
     My silence and my groans confess'd.   . . . .   Y 11 Tr Hor Epode 9 16
     To thee I told the causes of my smart, ...   Y 11 Tr Hor Epode 9 18
     And wish'd my rising anger could remove   . . . .   Y 11 Tr Hor Epode 9 23
     But take another to my arms.   . . . .   Y 11 Tr Hor Epode 9 28
     And gainst the pow'r of Venus steel'd my mind.   . . . .   Y 11 Tr Hor Epode 9 30
     And see my mistress' face no more   . . . .   Y 11 Tr Hor Epode 9 32
     With Hector's life away my pleasures fly.   . . . .   Y 18 Tr. Iliad Bk 6 27
     My father fell by fierce Achilles' hand   . . . .   Y 18 Tr. Iliad Bk 6 28
     Whose direfull rage destroy'd my native land.   . . . .   Y 18 Tr. Iliad Bk 6 29
     By that dire sword my sev'n brave brothers dy'd;   . . . .   Y 18 Tr. Iliad Bk 6 34
     My mother who alone escap'd the grave   . . . .   Y 19 Tr. Iliad Bk 6 38
     Propitious hear my prayers, protect the boy, ...   Y 20 Tr. Iliad Bk 6 101
     My death is now decreed my death will come.   . . . .   Y 21 Tr. Iliad Bk 6 118
     My death is now decreed my death will come.   . . . .   Y 21 Tr. Iliad Bk 6 118
     Direct O Goddess, my advent'rous song;   . . . .   Y 22 Tr Add. Battle   3
     Teach me to range my troopes in just array   . . . .   Y 22 Tr Add. Battle   5
     While in my verse the shrilling trumpets sound, ...   Y 22 Tr Add. Battle 18
     And so here begins my tale.   . . . .   Y 300 Extemp. Elegy   4
MYRIADS
     Attendant Flatt'ry counts his myriads o'er, ...   O 42 Vanity Wishes 229
     Till counted myriads sooth his pride no more;   . . . .   O 42 Vanity Wishes 230
MYRTALE
     "Vows to Myrtale the fair;   . . . .   O 185 Anacreon Ode 9   8
MYRTLE
     For kind, for tender nymphs the myrtle blooms, ...   O 84 Epi Dist Moth. 14
     On a Lady's presenting a Sprig of Myrtle   . . . .   O 95 Sprig of Myrtl   T
     On the Author's receiving a Sprig of Myrtle   . . . .   O 95 Sprig of Myrtl V T
     ... to whom a Lady had given a Sprig of Myrtle   . . . .   O 95 Sprig of Myrtl V T
     The Myrtle (ensign of supreme command   . . . .   O 95 Sprig of Myrtl   3
     In Myrtle groves oft sings the happy swain, ...   O 95 Sprig of Myrtl   7
     In Myrtle shades oft sings the happy swain, ...   O 95 Sprig of Myrtl V 7
     In Myrtle shades despairing ghosts complain;   . . . .   O 95 Sprig of Myrtl   8
     The Myrtle crowns the happy lovers heads, ...   O 95 Sprig of Myrtl   9
     Th' unhappy lovers graves the Myrtle spreads;   . . . .   O 95 Sprig of Myrtl 10
MYSELF
     Here I, though faint myself, must drive my goats, . . .   O 64 Virgil Past.I   17
     Oh, hide me from myself!   . . . .   O 316 Irene   13
     Myself escap'd, or favour'd or neglected.   . . . .   O 317 Irene   41
     Recoil from Thought, and shudder at myself.   . . . .   O 322 Irene   12
MYSTES
     For Mystes dead you ever mourn;   . . . .   O 67 Hor. II Ode IX 10
MYSTICK
     And tread in mystick rings the mossie ground.   . . . .   O 77 Tr Add. Battle 52

MYSTICK   (CONTINUED)   PAGE   TITLE   LINE
  And trod to Bacchus' praise the mystick ground. . . .   Y   6 Virgil Daphnis   16
N'A
  On n'a rien. . . . .   O 172 French Distich   8
NAIL
  Lies as dead as any nail! . . . .   Y 300 Extemp. Elegy   2
NAKED
  The naked hills, the leafless grove, ...   O 123 Winter's Walk   3
  And nature, on her naked breast, ...   O 124 An Ode   3
  The spritely Nymph and naked Grace . . . .   O 231 Tr Horace IV.7   5
  When eager Vengeance shows a naked Foe, ...   O 280 Irene   13
  And rushes joyful to the naked Wall, ...   O 298 Irene   29
NAM'D
  Expiring Cali nam'd Irene's Chamber, ...   O 326 Irene   29
NAME
  When first the college rolls receive his name, ...   O 36 Vanity Wishes   135
  Where wasted nations raise a single name, ...   O 39 Vanity Wishes   186
  He left the name, at which the world grew pale, . . .   O 41 Vanity Wishes   221
  Ye Nymphs, whose Bosoms beat at Milton's Name, . . .   O 57 Prologue Comus   2
  Ambitious catches at his tow'ring Name: . . . . . .   O 57 Prologue Comus   20
  And mirth was bounty with a humbler name. . . . . .   O 62 Pro Word Wise   24
  And the wood rings with Amarillis' name. . . . . . .   O 64 Virgil Past.I   6
  Nations shall celebrate my Name . . . .   O 70 Hor.II Ode XX   19
  How would the Trojans brand great Hector's name! . . .   O 74 Tr. Iliad Bk 6   5
  Tears, at my name, shall drown those beauteous eyes, . .   O 75 Tr. Iliad Bk 6   27
  So the young author panting for a name, ...   O 82 Young Author   11
  And the long honours of a lasting name . . . .   O 82 Young Author   V 12
  Ev'ry name that laughs at Care, ...   O 196 Song Congratu.   10
  Of ev'ry friendless name the friend. . . . .   O 201 Death Dr Levet   8
  Aspasia! spare that lov'd, that mournful Name: . . . .   O 252 Irene   76
  And add new lustre to the Grecian name. . . . . . .   Y 117 Irene   V109B
  He murmurs Vengeance at the Name of Cali, ...   O 256 Irene   48
  It must, it must be She; her Name? . . . .   O 258 Irene   103
  To make Aspasia and Irene name each other. . . . . .   Y 133 Irene   V 10
  At his dread Name the distant Mountains shake . . . .   O 268 Irene   28
  At my dread name the distant mountains shake . . . .   Y 136 Irene   V 28
  Shake at my dreaded name and the frighted world . . .   Y 136 Irene   V 28
  When from his Lips the fatal Name burst out, ...   O 270 Irene   12
  Treason so near us? at the dreadfull name of . . . .   O 369 Irene   V 20
    Treason
  No more I boast th' ambitious Name of Friend, ...   O 289 Irene   10
  But while Demetrius, dear lamented Name! . . . . .   O 290 Irene   47
  Dares join Leontius' Name with Fear or Falsehood? . . .   O 304 Irene   13
  Tell me the Cause, that while thy Name, Demetrius? . . .   O 305 Irene   25
  My Name shall echo through the shouting Field; . . . .   O 305 Irene   40
  Name and enjoy thy Wish-- . . . .   O 307 Irene   12
    I need not name it; . . . .   O 307 Irene   12
    Hated Name! his jealous Rage . . . .   O 316 Irene   9
  We ask'd, with tim'rous Tongue, th' Offender's Name, . .   O 325 Irene   23
  O name not Death! Distraction and Amazement, ...   O 328 Irene   31
  Name for the Scene of Death Irene's Chamber? . . . .   O 330 Irene   14
  My spirits fail, I cannot name his death . . . . . .   Y 216 Irene   V 72
  Let distant regions echo with his name . . . .   Y 20 Tr. Iliad Bk 6   103
NAMELESS
  A nameless fortress, and a nameless hand; . . . . .   Y 102 Vanity Wishes   V 220
  A nameless fortress, and a nameless hand; . . . . .   Y 102 Vanity Wishes   V 220
NAMES
  For growing names the weekly scribbler lies, ...   O 33 Vanity Wishes   81
  To growing names the weekly scribbler lies, ...   O 95 Vanity Wishes   V 82
  Those names which in immortal strains . . . . . .   O 80 Feast St Simon   59
  On names now found alone on books and tombs. . . . .   O 134 Tr. Rambler 93   2
  All the Names that banish Care, ...   O 196 Song Congratu.   V 10
  And quit the Names of Brother, Friend, and Father? . .   O 280 Irene   17
NARD
  The strength of a Bar, and the sweetness of Nard. . . .   O 179 Charade!   4
NARRATIVE
  In vain your mournful narrative disclose, ...   O 19 London   192
NARRATIVES
  These tedious Narratives of frozen Age . . . . . .   O 259 Irene   113
  Forgive the frozen Narratives of Dotage . . . . . .   O 366 Irene   V 16
  Hence with the frozen Narratives of Dotage . . . . .   O 366 Irene   V 16
NARROW
  His virtues walk'd their narrow round, ...   O 201 Death Dr Levet   25
  And Fate lies crouded in a narrow Space. . . . . .   O 287 Irene   5
  Yet in that narrow Space what Dangers rise?-- . . . .   O 287 Irene   6
NASSAU
  Or how before Nassau the Gallick troops retir'd? . . .   Y 22 Tr Add. Battle   13
NATION
  When Avarice corrupts th' emasculated Nation--or . . .   O 347 Irene   V 25
  Till every Nation reverence the Koran, ...   O 264 Irene   31
  Till every Nation reverence our Prophet . . . . . .   O 354 Irene   V 17
  How Nation after Nation falls before him. . . . . .   O 268 Irene   27
  How Nation after Nation falls before him. . . . . .   O 268 Irene   27
  How nation after nation falls before me . . . . . .   Y 136 Irene   V 27
  How nation after nation falls before me . . . . . .   Y 136 Irene   V 27
  A slaughter'd nation, or a shatter'd world. . . . . .   Y 177 Irene   V111E
NATION'S
  To such, a groaning nation's spoils are giv'n, ...   O 13 London   65
  The cheated nation's happy fav'rites, see! . . . . .   O 14 London   91
  Could half the nation's criminals contain; . . . . .   O 22 London   249

NATIONS
		PAGE	TITLE	LINE
How nations sink, by darling schemes oppress'd,	· · ·	O 31	Vanity Wishes	13
See nations slowly wise, and meanly just,	· · · · ·	O 38	Vanity Wishes	161
Where wasted nations raise a single name,	· · · ·	O 39	Vanity Wishes	186
And nations on his eye suspended wait;	· · · · ·	O 40	Vanity Wishes	206
While tutelary Nations guard her Cell.	· · · · · ·	O 58	Prologue Comus	36
To whom all nations tribute bring.	· · · · · · ·	O 68	Hor. II Ode IX	20
Nations shall celebrate my Name	· · · · · ·	O 70	Hor.II Ode XX	19
By thee wholl citys burn, wholl nations fall!	· · · ·	O 77	Festina Lente	12
They, pleas'd, thro' barb'rous nations roam	· · · · ·	O 79	Feast St Simon	29
"Secure of praise from nations yet unborn."	· · · · ·	O 82	Young Author	18
Had rang'd embattled Nations at our Gates:	· · · · ·	O 250	Irene	23
The Cause of Liberty, the Cause of Nations?	· · · · ·	O 255	Irene	9
Of prostrate princes and adoring nations	· · · · ·	Y 131	Irene	V 31
The holy city with converted millions--or nations.	· ·	Y 131	Irene	V 32C
Behold contending nations vie for bondage	· · · ·	Y 136	Irene	V 26
Assembling nations croud thy port.	· · · · · ·	Y 136	Irene	V 27
Commits to trivial Chance the Fate of Nations!	· · ·	O 269	Irene	2
Spoil of <kindoms> Nations	· · · ·	O 351	Irene	V 13
To shine the Goddess of applauding Nations,	· · · · ·	O 278	Irene	68
shall influence whole nations	· · · · ·	Y 150	Irene	V 76
Fly lab'ring with the Fate of future Nations,	· · · ·	O 279	Irene	4
Detain me here. But Nations call upon me,	· · · · ·	O 288	Irene	12
They give the nations laws, and view serene	· · · ·	Y 167	Irene	V 117
The sport of Tyranny, or Lord of Nations.	· · · · ·	O 303	Irene	12
When Asia's Nations own me for their Lord,	· · · · ·	O 306	Irene	5
How should I joy, 'midst the fierce Shock of Nations,	· ·	O 309	Irene	40
Astonish'd nations view with wild affright	· · · · ·	Y 24	Tr Add. Battle	74

NATIVE
		PAGE	TITLE	LINE
Thus grac'd with humble Virtue's native Charms	· · · ·	O 58	Prologue Comus	33
And leave our pleasing fields and native home,	· · · ·	O 64	Virgil Past.I	4
And scarce forsakes his native fields.	· · · · ·	O 68	Hor. II Ode IX	24
Far from their happy native home	· · · · ·	O 79	Feast St Simon	28
By secret charms our native land attracts.	· · · · ·	O 135	Tr Rambler 122	1
Swoln with Success, secure amidst his native Rocks	· ·	O 352	Irene	V 28
Elate with Conquest, in his native Mountains,	· · · ·	O 264	Irene	14
With native Lustre and unborrow'd Greatness,	· · · ·	O 298	Irene	16
Deface Erase the glories of my native	· · · · ·	Y 177	Irene	V 107
country				
Whose direfull rage destroy'd my native land.	· · · · ·	Y 18	Tr. Iliad Bk 6	29
Against th' invading birds their native land:	· · · · ·	Y 23	Tr Add. Battle	37

NATIVES
		PAGE	TITLE	LINE
These arts in vain our rugged natives try,	· · · · ·	O 16	London	129
Where the darkvisag'd Natives fry,	· · · · · ·	O 79	Feast St Simon	34

NATUR'D
		PAGE	TITLE	LINE
Prologue to "The Good Natur'd Man"	· · · · ·	O 59	Pro Good Nat'd	T

NATURE
		PAGE	TITLE	LINE
Each gift of nature, and each grace of art,	· · · · ·	O 31	Vanity Wishes	16
Each gift of nature, and each charm of art,	· · · · ·	Y 92	Vanity Wishes	V 16
Attentive truth and nature to descry,	· · · · · ·	O 33	Vanity Wishes	63
Till pitying Nature signs the last release,	· · · · ·	O 45	Vanity Wishes	309
Philosophy remain'd, though Nature fled.	· · · · ·	O 52	Pro Drury-Lane	34
Of rescu'd Nature, and reviving Sense;	· · · · ·	O 53	Pro Drury-Lane	58
May powerful nature join with grateful art,	· · · · ·	O 81	Lady Birthday	7
May powerful nature join with graceful art,	· · · · ·	Y 36	Lady Birthday	V 7
For Nature form'd the Poet for the King.	· · · · ·	O 114	On C. Cibber	4
Till nature call'd him to the gen'ral doom,	· · · · ·	O 118	Epitaph Hanmer	43
And nature, on her naked breast,	· · · · · ·	O 124	An Ode	3
Whom smiling nature courts in vain,	· · · · · ·	O 125	An Ode	11
Where first great nature charm'd my sight,	· · · · ·	O 125	An Ode	19
Nature gives at Thirtyfive;	· · · · · · ·	O 178	Thrale 35 Year	10
"Blushing nature, smiling art.	· · · · · · ·	O 185	Anacreon Ode 9	10
When fainting nature call'd for aid,	· · · · · ·	O 201	Death Dr Levet	13
Ennobled, yet unchang'd, if Nature shine:	· · · · ·	O 246	Irene Prologue	16
In Reason, Nature, Truth he dares to trust:	· · · · ·	O 246	Irene Prologue	33
Did we not see the bars of nature broken?	· · · · ·	Y 115	Irene	V 49F
Thou that hast long perus'd the Draughts of Nature,	· ·	O 255	Irene	11
Unbroken as the sacred Chain of Nature,	· · · · ·	O 257	Irene	63
Thy Soul by Nature great, enlarg'd by Knowledge,	· · ·	O 266	Irene	35
Distrust th' eternal Fortresses of Nature,	· · · · ·	O 268	Irene	31
the reward of conquest boast of nature	· · · · ·	Y 137	Irene	V 42
The loudest Cries of Nature urge us forward;	· · · ·	O 270	Irene	15
Indulgent nature gives some transient pleasures	· · ·	Y 148	Irene	V 43C
The Laws of Kindness, break the Bonds of Nature?	· · ·	O 280	Irene	16
And Nature justifies our Monarch's Choice.	· · · · ·	O 288	Irene	3
And all the sweet varieties of nature	· · · · ·	Y 165	Irene	V 79
Deny'd Debard each privilege of human nature being	· ·	Y 165	Irene	V 81
While some Archangel of superiour Nature	· · · · ·	O 369	Irene	V 13
But my blood freezes and weak nature shudders	· · · ·	Y 189	Irene	V 1G
Revive the languid Flow'rs; thus Nature shone	· · · ·	O 314	Irene	3
The universal smile of joyfull nature	· · · · ·	Y 190	Irene	V 9
Forgive, my Fair, 'tis Life, 'tis Nature calls.	· · · ·	O 318	Irene	19
Forgive my fair what fame nature prompts	· · · · ·	Y 197	Irene	V 19
We come, bright Virgin, tho' relenting Nature	· · · ·	O 325	Irene	20

NATURE'S
		PAGE	TITLE	LINE
Some peaceful vale with nature's paintings gay;	· · ·	O 11	London	46
There ev'ry bush with nature's musick rings,	· · · · ·	O 20	London	220
Counts death kind Nature's signal of retreat:	· · · · ·	O 48	Vanity Wishes	364
Thinks death kind Nature's signal of retreat:	· · · · ·	O 48	Vanity Wishes	V 364
Once more great nature's work review,	· · · · · ·	O 125	An Ode	23
Once more great nature's works renew	· · · · · ·	O 125	An Ode	V 23

225

```
NATURE'S        (CONTINUED)                                    PAGE    TITLE              LINE
      For wisdom ever echoes nature's voice.    . . . . . .   O 138 Tr Rambler 156          1
      Why then has Nature's vain Munificence    . . . . . .   O 276 Irene                  24
      Nor has impartial Nature's frugal Hand    . . . . . .   O 277 Irene                  53
      And Nature's Rights entreat th' asserting Sword.  . . . O 297 Irene                   3
NATURES
      Vain Raptures all--For your inferiour Natures  . . . .  O 276 Irene                  15
      Why then did Natures vain Munificence . . . . . . . .   O 355 Irene            V     13
      Nor has impartial Natures generous hand . . . . . .    O 356 Irene            V     20
NAUGHT
      Is naught but Ashes and a Shade.  . . . . . . . .      O 232 Tr Horace IV.7        16
      All her life was naught but guilt, . . . . . . . .     Y 300 Extemp. Elegy         11
NAY
      Has left the slaves behind, nay then there's danger. . Y 198 Irene            V     34
NE'ER
      Ne'er knew to puzzle right, or varnish wrong, . . . .  O  14 London                  80
      Where ne'er was known the form of mock debate, . . . . O  33 Vanity Wishes           57
      Where ne'er was heard the form of mock debate, . . . . Y  94 Vanity Wishes     V     57
      Yet judg'd by those, whose voices ne'er were sold, . . O  60 Pro Good Nat'd          27
      He ne'er with forc'd Submission waits . . . . . . . .  O  71 Hor. Epode II           15
      On fools and villains ne'er descend; . . . . . . .     O 100 Ode Friendship         18
      The heart, once caught, should ne'er be freed? . . . . O 120 To Miss Purse          12
      Insulting chance ne'er call'd with louder voice, . . . O 135 Tr Rambler 106          1
      But ne'er the Flute or Lyre apply'd  . . . . . . .     O 190 Tr. Medea I             7
      Admission ne'er had sought, or could not find. . . .   O 192 Tr. Medea II           12
      Had they prevail'd, I ne'er had known Irene. . . . .   O 263 Irene                  27
      Now feast thine Eyes, thine Eyes that ne'er hereafter  O 304 Irene                  34
      My Pride shall ne'er protract my Country's Woes; . . . O 306 Irene                  47
      And may she ne'er returning sorrows know." . . . . .   Y  20 Tr. Iliad Bk 6        106
NEAR
      For why did Wolsey near the steeps of fate, . . . . .  O  35 Vanity Wishes         125
      Though dancing mountains witness'd Orpheus near; . . . O  43 Vanity Wishes         270
      And near the noisome nettle blooms the rose. . . . .   O 131 Tr. Rambler 21          2
      Where the Lyoness stood near,  . . . . . . . . .       O 148 Tr Boet III.12          8
      The near approach a bed may shew  . . . . . . . .      O 184 Tr. Benserade           3
      Each Pleasure brightens at its near Approach, . . . .  O 261 Irene                  20
      Treason so near us? at the dreadfull name of  . . . .  O 369 Irene            V     20
         Treason
      Treason so near us?  lurking in our Palace  . . . . .  O 369 Irene            V     20
      Betray'd some Traytor lurking near my Bosom. . . . .   O 273 Irene                  23
      Disclos'd some Traytor lurking near our Bosoms . . . . O 368 Irene            V      3
      Abdalla, while we waited near the Palace,  . . . . .   O 316 Irene                  25
      He knows how near Apostacy to Treason-- . . . . . .    O 324 Irene                  21
      But now their cruel enemies draw near . . . . . . .    Y  24 Tr Add. Battle         90
NEARER
      While some Archangel nearer to Perfection, . . . . .   O 293 Irene                 121
NEAREST
      And free'd his soul the nearest way. . . . . . . .     O 202 Death Dr Levet         36
      And forc'd his soul the nearest way. . . . . . . .     O 202 Death Dr Levet   V     36
NECESSITY
      Vain expence the parent of necessity the parent of  . O 347 Irene            V     26
         corruption
      The Tongue, that, forc'd by strong Necessity, . . . .  O 324 Irene                   2
NECK
      Nor binds the neck, nor sparkles in the hair, . . . .  O 141 Tr Rambler 199          3
      Hung on your Neck, and hinder'd your Departure. . . .  O 280 Irene                  10
      Throws his fond Arms about Aspasia's Neck, . . . . .   O 286 Irene                   4
      Or boy, whose snowy neck the flowing ringlets grace. . Y  12 Tr Hor Epode 9         42
NECTAR
      Quaff Nectar with th' immortal Gods.  . . . . . . .    O  70 Hor.II Ode XX           8
      When floods of Nectar stain'd the main, . . . . . .    O  71 Hor. Epode II           4
      And purple nectar glads the festive hour, . . . . .    O 193 Tr. Medea II           18
NEED
      I need not name it;  . . . . . . . .                   O 307 Irene                  12
      What need of Caution to report the Fate . . . . . .    O 329 Irene                  16
NEEDLESS
      With Merit needless, and without it vain. . . . . .    O 246 Irene Prologue         32
      Think--but excuse a Woman's needless Caution, . . . .  O 298 Irene                   5
      Dismiss these needless Fears--a Troop of Greeks . . .  O 301 Irene                  90
NEEDS
      Nor needs the guard of Moorish bows: . . . . . . .     O  65 Hor I Ode xxii          4
      Nor needs the Guard of Moorish Bows. . . . . . . .     O  66 To A. Fuscus            4
      Ah, little needs the Minstrel's pow'r . . . . . . .    O 191 Tr. Medea I            17
NEEDY
      London! the needy villain's gen'ral home, . . . . .    O  14 London                  93
      The needy traveller, serene and gay, . . . . . . .     O  32 Vanity Wishes          37
      The needy traveller, secure and gay, . . . . . . .     Y  93 Vanity Wishes    V     37
      Condemn'd a needy suppliant to wait, . . . . . . .     O  41 Vanity Wishes         213
      Enjoy the prayers and blessings of the needy, . . . .  Y 130 Vanity Wishes    V    12C
NEER
      Oh may this Flame neer cease to glow  . . . . . . .    O 100 Ode Friendship   V     25
NEGLECT
      While all neglect, and most insult your woes. . . . .  O  19 London                 193
      Too fierce, too faithless for Neglect or Trust. . . .  O 288 Irene                  14
      To rough--Too false too fierce to trust or to neglect  O 374 Irene            V      1
      Which squander'd by Neglect, or Fear, or Folly, . . .  O 302 Irene                   7
      Torn from the mourning Earth by thy Neglect. . . . .   O 334 Irene                   4
NEGLECTED
      With distant voice neglected Virtue calls, . . . . .   O  46 Vanity Wishes         333
      Her own neglected, in the publick Safety. . . . . .    O 250 Irene                  27
      When some neglected Fabrick nods beneath . . . . . .   O 250 Irene                  44
```

```
                                                            PAGE    TITLE           LINE
NEGLECTED         (CONTINUED)
     Nor think thy Cause neglected while I gaze,  . . . . .   O 297 Irene              20
     Myself escap'd, or favour'd or neglected.   . . . . .   O 317 Irene              41
NEGLECTS
     about his private neglects the publick      . . . . .   Y 113 Irene          V   27
NEGLIGENCE
     Betray my King to Negligence of Danger.     . . . . . . O 275 Irene              73
NEIGHB'RING
     Indignant Thales eyes the neighb'ring town. . . . . .   O  10 London             34
NEIGHBOURS
     Till she made the neighbours stare.   . . . . . . .     Y 300 Extemp. Elegy       8
NEITHER
     Whom neither Vows could fix, nor Favours bind? . . . .  O 330 Irene               2
NERVES
     'Twas Vice that shook our Nerves, 'twas Vice, Leontius .  O 251 Irene             56
     Did aught but Luxury relax our Nerves . . . . . . .    O 347 Irene           V    5
     And wove the feeble Texture of her Nerves,            O 266 Irene                24
     Why shoots this Chilness through thy shaking Nerves? . . O 295 Irene              6
     I feel new Spirit shoot along my Nerves,  . . . . . .  O 306 Irene               49
     My trembling nerves--sink at the dreadful scenes of blood Y 189 Irene        V   1H
        and death
     Press not her Flight, while yet her feeble Nerves  . . . O 320 Irene             20
NEST
     Had form'd her nest and plac'd her burthen there, . . . Y  23 Tr Add. Battle     45
NESTS
     Scream in the nests and brood their young in peace. . . Y  23 Tr Add. Battle     35
NET-WORK
     ... a Gold and Silk net-work Purse of her own weaving  . O 119 To Miss Purse      T
NETS
     <He> sets his nets, employs his skill.   . . . . . . .  O  72 Hor. Epode II       42
     To weave those nets that catch the heart.  . . . . . .  O 120 To Miss Purse        6
     Thy nets may catch, but not confine,  . . . . . . .    O 120 To Miss Purse        8
     Thy nets may snare, but not confine,  . . . . . . .    O 120 To Miss Purse    V   8
NETTLE
     And near the noisome nettle blooms the rose.  . . . .   O 131 Tr. Rambler 21       2
NEVER     SEE NE'ER, NEER
     Nor sell for gold, what gold could never buy,  . . . .  O  14 London              88
     Fate never wounds more deep the gen'rous heart,  . . .  O  18 London             168
     Where blasted patriots never shrunk to peers  . . . .  Y  94 Vanity Wishes   V 60A
     That never Briton can in vain excel;  . . . . . . .    O  57 Prologue Comus       12
     That never Britain can in vain excel;  . . . . . . .   O  57 Prologue Comus   V   12
     For I shall never think him less than God;  . . . .    O  64 Virgil Past.I         8
     Ah! never to return!    . . . . . . . . .             O  80 Feast St Simon        48
     Pope's hallow'd glades, and never tiring views,  . . .  O 106 Eliza plucking       3
     The lust of wealth can never bear delay.  . . . . . .  O 140 Tr Rambler 182        1
     Time his Hours should never drive  . . . . . . .      O 178 Thrale 35 Year         7
     Dream not of Pow'r thou never can'st attain:  . . . .  O 291 Irene                69
     Those gloomy walks where Gladness never smiles  . . .  Y 165 Irene            V  81
     That joins us thus, will never part us more.  . . . .  O 296 Irene                39
     You may provoke but never can convince  . . . . . .   Y 197 Irene            V  31
NEVER-DYING
     I first attempt in never-dying lays   . . . . . . .    Y  22 Tr Add. Battle       16
NEVER-FADING
     On beds of never-fading flow'rs,   . . . . . . . .     O 120 To Miss Playin        4
NEW
     Some fiery fop, with new commission vain,  . . . . .   O  21 London             226
     So some fiery fop, with new commission vain,  . . . .  Y  59 London             226
     New fears in dire vicissitude invade,  . . . . . . .  O  32 Vanity Wishes   V  41
     And feed with change of new born fools th' eternal  . . Y  94 Vanity Wishes   V  52
        jest:
     Still to new heights his restless wishes tow'r,  . . . . O  34 Vanity Wishes     105
     New praise is try'd till madness fires his mind,  . .  Y 102 Vanity Wishes   V 231
     New pow'rs are claim'd, new pow'rs are still bestow'd, . O  42 Vanity Wishes     233
     New pow'rs are claim'd, new pow'rs are still bestow'd, . O  42 Vanity Wishes     233
     New sorrow rises as the day returns,   . . . . . . .   O  45 Vanity Wishes     301
     New forms arise, and diff'rent views engage,  . . . .  O  45 Vanity Wishes     307
     Exhausted Worlds, and then imagin'd new:  . . . . . .  O  51 Pro Drury-Lane       4
     New Behns, new Durfeys, yet remain in Store.   . . . .  O  53 Pro Drury-Lane      42
     New Behns, new Durfeys, yet remain in Store.   . . . .  O  53 Pro Drury-Lane      42
     On flying Cars new Sorcerers may ride.  . . . . . .   O  53 Pro Drury-Lane      44
     A New Prologue Spoken By Mr Garrick, . . .            O  56 Prologue Comus       T
     They clap their wings, and with new fury burn;  . . .  O  76 Tr Add. Battle       9
     Around them pleasures wait, and joys for ever new.  . . O  84 Epi Dist Moth.      27
     Surveys with new contemplative delight.  . . . . . .  O 106 Eliza plucking       2
     New chains to hold the captive heart.  . . . . . . .  O 121 To Miss Playin      18
     New Tortures for the captive heart.   . . . . . . .    O 121 To Miss Playin  V  18
     All is strange, yet nothing new;   . . . . . . . .     O 179 Ridicul Warton       2
     And add new lustre to the Grecian name.  . . . . . .  Y 117 Irene           V109B
     But whence this new sprung Hope?   . . . . . . . .     O 253 Irene              111
     Invest Leontius with his new Command;  . . . . . . .  O 260 Irene              144
     <In> Triumphant at the head of thy new votaries  . .   Y 131 Irene           V 32A
     Blasts all the Beauties of his new Creation,  . . . .  O 269 Irene                7
     And your new Charge, that dear, that heavn'ly Maid.--   O 270 Irene                5
     Illustrious Maid, new Wonders fix me thine,  . . . .   O 278 Irene               59
     Celestial fair--maid--new wonders fix me thine,  . .   Y 149 Irene           V  59
     And add new Roses to the faded Cheek.  . . . . . . .  O 278 Irene               66
     To see new Cities tow'r at thy Command,  . . . . . .  O 278 Irene               71
     Each Day and shall be made happy with new entertainments O 350 Irene          V  24
     And new forms of pleasure shall be invented  . . . .   O 350 Irene           V  25
     And draw new Virtue from her heav'nly Tongue.  . . .   O 285 Irene                7
     When the confusion of new conquests ceases  . . . .   Y 164 Irene           V  76
```

NEW	(CONTINUED)		PAGE	TITLE		LINE
New joy comes rushing on me and o'erwhelms	. . . . .		Y 169	Irene	V	12
New Force, new Courage, from each Glance I gain,	. . . .		O 297	Irene		21
New Force, new Courage, from each Glance I gain,	. . . .		O 297	Irene		21
Forbear this Triumph--still new Conflicts wait us,	. .		O 298	Irene		25
I feel new Spirit shoot along my Nerves,	. . . . . .		O 306	Irene		49
How the new Monarch, swell'd with airy Rule,	. . . .		O 306	Irene		1
To form new Legends, sanctify new Crimes,	. . . . .		O 309	Irene		33
To form new Legends, sanctify new Crimes,	. . . . .		O 309	Irene		33
New from the Maker's Hand, and fair array'd	. . .		O 314	Irene		4
New from the Maker's Hand, and far array'd	. . .		O 314	Irene	V	4
And bade his new Confederates seize the Traitors.	. . .		O 317	Irene		39
Come let us seek new Pleasures in the Palace,	. . .		O 323	Irene		17
And bring her former Sentence new confirm'd.	. . . . .		O 327	Irene		27
And add new Terrors to the Face of Death.	. . . . . .		O 330	Irene		8
Contrive new Racks, imbitter every Pang,	. . . . . .		O 334	Irene		74
New verdure ev'ry fading leaf shall fill,	. . . . .		Y 4	On a Daffodill		19
NEW-BLOWN						
And chase the new-blown Bubbles of the Day.	. . . . . .		O 53	Pro Drury-Lane		50
NEW-FOUND						
And raptur'd sees the new-found ruby shine.	. . . . . .		O 82	Young Author	V	6D
NEW-MADE						
Or seen a new-made mayor's unwieldy state;	. . . . .		O 33	Vanity Wishes		58
Or seen the new-made mayor's unwieldy state;	. . . .		Y 94	Vanity Wishes	V	58
NEW-PREST						
And crown the bowl with new-prest wine	. . . . . .		O 72	Hor. Epode II		52
NEXT						
Next Month he sets it out again.	. . . .		O 73	Hor. Epode II		79
When next we meet before we storm the Palace,	. . .		O 308	Irene		28
But the next blooming virgin's beauteous face			Y 12	Tr Hor Epode 9		41
NIECE						
Perplex the fawning niece and pamper'd guest,	. . . .		O 44	Vanity Wishes		276
The dull conjecture fawning niece and pamper'd guest,	.		Y 104	Vanity Wishes	V	276
NIGH						
As herbs of which the forrests nigh	. . . .		O 73	Hor. Epode II		61
The painted meads and Forrests nigh	. . . .		O 73	Hor. Epode II	V	61
As herbs of which the fields nigh	. . . .		O 73	Hor. Epode II	V	61
Delighting, as the youth draws nigh,	. . . .		O 121	To Miss Playin		15
His useful care was ever nigh	. . . .		O 201	Death Dr Levet		18
His useful aid was ever nigh	. . . .		O 201	Death Dr Levet	V	18
His ready help was ever nigh,	. . . .		O 201	Death Dr Levet	V	18
Tho' now his eightieth year was nigh.	. . . . . .		O 202	Death Dr Levet		32
But now alass! the fatall hour drew nigh	. . . . . .		Y 24	Tr Add. Battle		62
NIGHT						
Who play from morn to night a borrow'd part;	. . .		O 16	London		135
Prepare for death, if here at night you roam,	. . .		O 21	London		224
Whose night congratulating Conscience cheers;	. . .		O 44	Vanity Wishes		296
By day the frolick, and the dance by night,	. . . . .		O 46	Vanity Wishes		326
'Tis yours this Night to bid the Reign commence			O 53	Pro Drury-Lane		57
This Night, distinguish'd by your Smile, shall tell,	.		O 57	Prologue Comus		11
Till that glad night when all that hate may hiss.	.		O 60	Pro Good Nat'd		20
This night our wit, the pert apprentice cries,	. . .		O 60	Pro Good Nat'd		23
This night presents a play, which publick taste	.		O 61	Pro Word Wise		1
Yet then shall calm reflection bless the night,	. .		O 62	Pro Word Wise		21
Dispelling the black horrors of the Night,	. . . . .		O 77	Tr Add. Battle		46
Where sable night in all her horrour reigns;	. . .		O 83	Epi Dist Moth.		11
Her teeth the night with darkness dyes,	. . . . . .		O 127	To Lyce, Lady		13
Though countless as the lamps of night	. . . . . .		O 144	Tr Boeth. II.2		3
The busy day, the peaceful night,	. . . .		O 202	Death Dr Levet		29
The busy day, the cheerful night,	. . . .		O 202	Death Dr Levet	V	29
Each Night protected by the friendly Darkness,	. . .		O 251	Irene		59
For her, Repose is banish'd from the Night	. . . .		O 260	Irene		130
Hence from her sable wings returning night	. . . .		Y 148	Irene	V	43E
This Night with all her conscious Stars be witness,	.		O 284	Irene		44
Well,--'tis decreed--This Night shall fix our Fate.	.		O 284	Irene		48
This Night alone is ours--Our mighty Foe.	. . . .		O 303	Irene		25
Seize him this Night, and through the private Passage			O 312	Irene		23
Shuns Pluto's kingdoms and the realms of night;	. . .		Y 7	Virgil Daphnis		33
This night he hopes to shew that farce may charm,	. .		Y 67	Prologue Lethe		13
NIGHT'S						
Unfit to share this Night's illustrious Toils?	. . . .		O 305	Irene		21
NIGHTS						
Bears toilsome Days, and wakes long tedious Nights:			O 247	Irene Epilogue		22
NILUS						
Where sev'nmouth'd Nilus roars,	. . . .		O 79	Feast St Simon		33
NIMBLE						
Her tongue like nimble lightning plies,	. . . . .		O 127	To Lyce, Lady		15
With nimble glide the skaiters play;	. . . . .		O 203	Tr. on Skating	V	2
But while I sing, the nimble moments fly,	. . . .		Y 4	On a Daffodill		21
No toils shall intercept the nimble deer.	. . . .		Y 7	Virgil Daphnis		39
NIMBLER						
Dispatch, ye ling'ring Slaves, or nimbler Hands	. . .		O 328	Irene		42
NINE						
Hadst thou nine lives like a cat,	. . . .		O 194	On Thrale Hat		3
Soon those nine lives would be past.	. . . . . .		O 194	On Thrale Hat		4
NIPHATES						
Niphates rolls an humbler wave,	. . . .		O 68	Hor. II Ode IX		21
NO	160			OMITTED WORD		
NOBLE						
The noble mind's delight and pride,	. . . .		O 99	Ode Friendship		2

		PAGE	TITLE	LINE
NOBLE	(CONTINUED)			
	The noble flame of enterprising Virtue	O 371	Irene	V 28
	To noble Thought and gen'rous Emulation, ...	O 298	Irene	14
	Ye venerable ghosts of noble patriots	Y 181	Irene	V 53
NOBLER				
	While I to nobler themes aspire, ...	O 78	Feast St Simon	7
	To nobler subjects tune my lyre;	O 78	Feast St Simon	8
	Soon had the Monarch felt a nobler fire, ...	O 97	Hickman Spinet	16
	Thy musick teach the nobler art	O 121	To Miss Playin	35
	Deserts her nobler Origin.	O 147	Tr Boeth III.6	20
	For those who could not please by nobler Service.--	O 264	Irene	24
	Let nobler Hopes and juster Fears succeed, ...	O 265	Irene	9
	To mix with nobler Cares, I'll throw aside	O 275	Irene	70
	To mix with nobler Cares, I'll set apart	O 368	Irene	V 27
	Exhausted all her nobler Gifts on you;	O 278	Irene	54
	Not for itself but for a nobler End	O 290	Irene	30
NOBLES				
	With servile grief dependent nobles sigh	Y 57	London	V 198
	Degrading nobles and controuling kings;	O 34	Vanity Wishes	94
	When senators and nobles learn to fear;	O 59	Pro Good Nat'd	V 4B
	A factious Populace, luxurious Nobles, ...	O 250	Irene	38
NOBLEST				
	I thought, forgive my Fair, the noblest Aim, ...	O 278	Irene	61
	Esteem Aspasia's Breast, the noblest Kingdom. . . .	O 289	Irene	14
	To mark the noblest Minds, with active Heat	O 293	Irene	112
	To mark the noblest Minds. With active fire	O 369	Irene	V 3
NOBLY				
	What with your friend you nobly share	O 232	Tr Horace IV.7	19
NOD				
	Turn'd by his nod the stream of honour flows, . . .	O 34	Vanity Wishes	103
	O seize the Power to bless--Irene's Nod	O 278	Irene	75
	Directs the Planets with a careless Nod, ...	O 293	Irene	123
	Sanguinary joy--Slaves now watch her nod	Y 184	Irene	V 9
NODDING				
	His shining helm with nodding horse hair grac'd. . . .	Y 21	Tr. Iliad Bk 6	125
NODS				
	When some neglected Fabrick nods beneath	O 250	Irene	44
NOISE				
	On Isis banks he waves, from noise withdrawn	Y 98	Vanity Wishes	V138A
	The mountain shepherd hears the distant noise. . . .	O 132	Tr. Rambler 65	3
	I come from empty Noise, and tasteless Pomp, ...	O 262	Irene	7
NOISOME				
	And near the noisome nettle blooms the rose. . . .	O 131	Tr. Rambler 21	2
NOISY				
	To quit the Tumults of the noisy Camp, ...	O 264	Irene	11
	With noisy Falshoods forc'd me from your Arms, . . .	O 299	Irene	39
NON				
	For Non Who was e'er beneficent in vain?	O 377	Irene	V 4
NONE				
	There none are swept by sudden fate away, ...	O 9	London	11
	And rights submitted, left him none to seize. . . .	O 34	Vanity Wishes	108
	In croud at once, where none the pass defend, . . .	O 46	Vanity Wishes	337
	In crowd at once, where none the fort defend, . . .	Y 107	Vanity Wishes	V 337
	None fiercer Juba's thirsty land, ...	O 66	Hor I Ode xxii	15
	None e'er more fierce Numidia's land, ...	O 66	Hor I Ode xxii	V 15
	None e're rejects hyperbolies of praise.	O 134	Tr Rambler 104	1
	None dares with impious steel the grove to rend, . .	O 139	Tr Rambler 168	1
	For none are rich without content.	O 144	Tr Boeth. II.2	14
	To tell each Bystander, what none can deny, ...	O 173	Tr Fr Pantomim	2
	That none are great, or happy, but the Virtuous. . . .	O 294	Irene	8
	He envies none the Converse of Aspasia.	O 296	Irene	4
	But since none knows the Danger of a Moment, ...	O 321	Irene	48
NONSENSE				
	Scorn their Nonsense scorn their pother, ...	O 197	Song Congratu.	V 27
	I swear this Eastern Pageantry is Nonsense, ...	O 247	Irene Epilogue	13
NOR				
	Nor sell for gold, what gold could never buy, . . .	O 14	London	88
	Nor hope the British lineaments to trace, ...	O 15	London	101
	Then shall thy friend, nor thou refuse his aid, . . .	O 23	London	260
	Wealth heap'd on wealth, nor truth nor safety buys, .	O 31	Vanity Wishes	27
	Wealth heap'd on wealth, nor truth nor safety buys, .	O 31	Vanity Wishes	27
	Nor light nor darkness bring his pain relief, . . .	O 32	Vanity Wishes	43
	Nor light nor darkness bring his pain relief, . . .	O 32	Vanity Wishes	43
	Nor annual tax was rais'e by annual wars. . . .	Y 94	Vanity Wishes	V 60B
	Nor Praise relax, nor Difficulty fright;	O 37	Vanity Wishes	148
	Nor Praise relax, nor Difficulty fright;	O 37	Vanity Wishes	148
	Nor claim the triumph of a letter'd heart;	O 37	Vanity Wishes	152
	Nor should disease thy torpid veins invade, ...	Y 99	Vanity Wishes	V 153
	Nor Melancholy's phantoms haunt thy shade;	O 37	Vanity Wishes	154
	Nor Melancholy's spectres haunt thy shade;	Y 99	Vanity Wishes	V 154
	Nor think the doom of man revers'd for thee:	O 38	Vanity Wishes	156
	Nor deem, when learning her last prize bestows, . . .	O 38	Vanity Wishes	165
	Nor deem, when learning her lost prize bestows, . . .	O 38	Vanity Wishes	V 165
	Nor think though learning her last prize bestows, . .	Y 99	Vanity Wishes	V 165
	He comes, nor want nor cold his course delay;------	O 41	Vanity Wishes	V 209
	He comes, nor want nor cold his course delay;------	O 41	Vanity Wishes	V 209
	Nor lute nor lyre his feeble pow'rs attend, ...	O 43	Vanity Wishes	271
	Nor lute nor lyre his feeble pow'rs attend, ...	O 43	Vanity Wishes	271
	Nor sweeter musick of a virtuous friend, ...	O 43	Vanity Wishes	272
	Which heav'n may hear, nor deem religion vain. . . .	O 47	Vanity Wishes	350
	Nor wish'd for Johnson's Art, or Shakespear's Flame; .	O 52	Pro Drury-Lane	18

		PAGE	TITLE	LINE
Nor taints with death the envenom'd dart,		O 65	Hor I Ode xxii	3
Nor needs the guard of Moorish bows:		O 65	Hor I Ode xxii	4
Nor taints with Death th' envenom'd Dart,		O 66	To A. Fuscus	3
Nor needs the Guard of Moorish Bows.		O 66	To A. Fuscus	4
Nor showers immerse the verdant plain;		O 67	Hor. II Ode IX	2
Nor do the billows always rise,		O 67	Hor. II Ode IX	3
Nor, Valgius, on th' Armenian shores		O 67	Hor. II Ode IX	5
Nor did King Priam's hoary age		O 68	Hor. II Ode IX	15
Nor would inexorable Death		O 69	Hor.II Ode 14	11
Nor grace with fading flours my Herse,		O 70	Hor.II Ode XX	22
Nor Lybian fowls, nor Snipes of Greece,		O 73	Hor. Epode II	59
Nor Lybian fowls, nor Snipes of Greece,		O 73	Hor. Epode II	59
Yet Hecuba's, nor Priam's hoary age,		O 74	Tr. Iliad Bk 6	15
Nor my brave brothers, that have bit the ground,		O 74	Tr. Iliad Bk 6	17
Nor down steep cliffs precipitately move		O 77	Festina Lente	5
Nor there confin'd his active Soul;		O 79	Feast St Simon	43
Nor whilst she Simons acts persues		O 80	Feast St Simon	49
Nor give the generous pain, the worthless joy:		O 81	Lady Birthday	14
Where no sour criticks damn, nor sneers molest,		O 82	Young Author	27
No pug, nor favourite Cupid there enjoys		O 84	Epi Dist Moth.	20
Nor torturing whalebones pinch them into charms;		O 84	Epi Dist Moth.	23
Nor let disdain sit low'ring in your eye;		O 84	Epi Dist Moth.	43
Nor shall thine ardours cease to glow		O 100	Ode Friendship	V 25
Nor shall the Lyon, wont of old to reign		O 111	To Posterity	19
Nor shall the passive Coward once complain.		O 111	To Posterity	26
Nor wish'd to glitter at his country's cost;		O 118	Epitaph Hanmer	28
Nor e'er from virtue's path was lur'd aside,		O 118	Epitaph Hanmer	31
Nor e'er from virtue's paths was turn'd aside,		O 118	Epitaph Hanmer	V 31
Nor can I hope thy silken chain		O 120	To Miss Purse	9
Nor tempt the snares of wily love.		O 121	To Miss Playin	10
Nor only through the wasted plain,		O 123	Winter's Walk	5
Nor only thought the wasted plain,		O 123	Winter's Walk	V 5
Nor from the pleasing groves depart,		O 125	An Ode	18
Nor Peleus, grandson of the sky,		O 136	Tr Rambler 128	3
Nor Cadmus, scap'd the shafts of pain,		O 136	Tr Rambler 128	4
Nor lures the search of avaricious eyes,		O 141	Tr Rambler 199	2
Nor binds the neck, nor sparkles in the hair,		O 141	Tr Rambler 199	3
Nor binds the neck, nor sparkles in the hair,		O 141	Tr Rambler 199	3
Nor dignifies the great, nor decks the fair.		O 141	Tr Rambler 199	4
Nor dignifies the great, nor decks the fair.		O 141	Tr Rambler 199	4
Nor yoke his Reason with his Will:		O 146	Tr Boeth III.5	4
Nor fear that I, my gentle maid,		O 159	Par Hermit III	5
Nor hear it with a frown;--		O 159	Par Hermit III	10
Nor think our wishes less sincere.		O 188	Epilogue	4
Nor call'd them to the gloomy cells		O 191	Tr. Medea I	9
Nor deign the festive dome to cloy		O 191	Tr. Medea I	15
Nor, letter'd arrogance, deny		O 201	Death Dr Levet	11
Nor, letter'd ignorance, deny		O 201	Death Dr Levet	V 11
Nor made a pause, nor left a void;		O 201	Death Dr Levet	26
Nor made a pause, nor left a void;		O 201	Death Dr Levet	26
Nor made a pause, nor felt a void;		O 201	Death Dr Levet	V 26
Nor made a pause, nor felt a void;		O 201	Death Dr Levet	V 26
Nor can the might of Theseus rend		O 232	Tr Horace IV.7	27
Nor Gods his Heroes, nor his Lovers Fools:		O 246	Irene Prologue	18
Nor Gods his Heroes, nor his Lovers Fools:		O 246	Irene Prologue	18
Nor bribes your Eyes to prejudice your Heads.		O 246	Irene Prologue	28
Nor sprightly Folly wantons in his Air,		O 255	Irene	15
Nor dull Serenity becalms his Eyes.		O 255	Irene	16
Nor found again the bright Temptation fail?		O 259	Irene	125
Trembling to grant, nor daring to refuse,		O 260	Irene	126
Into the adverse Scale, nor shakes the Balance.		O 260	Irene	140
Nor dream of peace, think of rest		Y 130	Irene	V 13
Nor couldst thou more support a Life of Sloth		O 264	Irene	19
Nor give him Leisure for another Crime.		O 271	Irene	32
Then let us now resolve, nor idly waste		O 271	Irene	33
Then let us now resolve, nor idle waste		O 271	Irene	V 33
The richest Odours, nor the speckled Shells		O 277	Irene	32
Nor has impartial Nature's frugal Hand		O 277	Irene	53
Nor has impartial Natures generous hand		O 356	Irene	V 20
Nor let Demetrius know thee for a Rival.		O 282	Irene	71
Urge me not on to glittering Guilt, nor pour		O 288	Irene	5
Nor taint with Care the Privacies of Love.		O 288	Irene	14
Nor think my eyes oerflow with Female		O 357	Irene	V 17
Weakness				
Nor bursting through the ranks in wild distraction		Y 163	Irene	V 47
Nor think th' Intention sanctifies the Deed:		O 291	Irene	59
Nor left us aught but Flattery and State.		O 291	Irene	73
Nor dare to pass th' insuperable Bound.		O 292	Irene	92
Nor think to say here will I stop		Y 168	Irene	V 132
Nor farther tempt the avenging rage of Heaven		Y 168	Irene	V 134
Nor think thy Cause neglected while I gaze,		O 297	Irene	20
Nor mingled Guilt pollute the sacred Cause!		O 300	Irene	64
Nor end my Terrors with the Sultan's Death;		O 300	Irene	67
Nor built on Faith, nor fortify'd by Conscience?		O 301	Irene	84
Nor built on Faith, nor fortify'd by Conscience?		O 301	Irene	84
Nor will his Country's Groans reproach Demetrius.		O 301	Irene	101
Nor Wealth, nor Titles, make Aspasia's Bliss.		O 301	Irene	106
Nor Wealth, nor Titles, make Aspasia's Bliss.		O 302	Irene	106
Nor fear the Fair and Learn'd can want Protection.		O 302	Irene	115
Nor lose in Love the Patriot and the Hero.		O 303	Irene	15

		PAGE	TITLE	LINE
NOR	(CONTINUED)			
Not granted--nor deny'd--a softend glance	. . . . .	Y 179	Irene	V 32
Nor hope, nor wish, nor live but for Aspasia.	. . . .	O 307	Irene	14
Nor hope, nor wish, nor live but for Aspasia.	. . . .	O 307	Irene	14
Nor hope, nor wish, nor live but for Aspasia.	. . . .	O 307	Irene	14
Nor to deny.	. . . . .	O 307	Irene	16
Nor will I trust th' uncertain Chance of Combat;	. . . .	O 307	Irene	21
Nor wish for Houries in Irene's Arms.	. . . . .	O 308	Irene	10
Nor press too much upon a Lover's Patience.	. . . .	O 310	Irene	9
By Reason not convinc'd, nor won by Love.	. . . .	O 310	Irene	8
There I became, nor blush to make it known,	. . . .	O 312	Irene	13
The Doom of Guilt alone, nor dare to seize	. . . .	O 316	Irene	14
Nor at the Call of Cali deign'd to turn.	. . . .	O 317	Irene	33
Nor think that Effort lost which rescues thee.	. . .	O 317	Irene	47
Nor rush on useless Wounds with idle Courage.	. . .	O 318	Irene	10
Nor languish o'er irreparable Ruins;	. . . . .	O 320	Irene	17
Henceforth be wise, nor hope a second Pardon.	. . .	O 323	Irene	3
Nor thus usurp the Dignity of Virtue.	. . . . .	O 323	Irene	10
Nor dare henceforth to shock Irene's Walks.	. . . .	O 325	Irene	7
Nor dare to spare the Life his Frown condemns.	. . .	O 325	Irene	10
O let me be but heard, nor fear from me	. . . . .	O 327	Irene	20
Then call it not our Cruelty, nor Crime,	. . . . .	O 327	Irene	28
Deem us not deaf to Woe, nor blind to Beauty,	. . .	O 327	Irene	29
Nor let the Crimes of this detested Day	. . . .	O 329	Irene	54
Nor hope his Fortune while thou want'st his Worth.	. . .	O 330	Irene	25
Nor justice can acquit, nor mercy spare	. . . .	Y 210	Irene	V 25B
Nor justice can acquit, nor mercy spare	. . . .	Y 210	Irene	V 25B
Whom neither Vows could fix, nor Favours bind?	. . .	O 330	Irene	2
Nor trust our Passions with their fatal Charms.	. . .	O 332	Irene	31
Thou mightst have liv'd, nor had I lost Irene	. . .	Y 214	Irene	V 58
Nor feel the inclemencies of wintry air;	. . . .	Y 3	On a Daffodill	6
Nor crop'd the tastfull herb, nor trac'd the verdant meads		Y 6	Virgil Daphnis	10
Nor crop'd the tastfull herb, nor trac'd the verdant meads		Y 6	Virgil Daphnis	10
No wit nor honesty could stand	. . . . . .	Y 11	Tr Hor Epode 9	21
Nor with too powerfull rivals strive	. . . . .	Y 11	Tr Hor Epode 9	27
Nor counsells nor reproach expell	. . . . .	Y 12	Tr Hor Epode 9	39
Nor counsells nor reproach expell	. . . . .	Y 12	Tr Hor Epode 9	39
Nor tempt the dangers of this deathfull day	. . . .	Y 19	Tr. Iliad Bk 6	47
Nor from the battle look for his return.	. . . .	Y 21	Tr. Iliad Bk 6	131
NORTH				
Should the fierce North upon his frozen Wings	. . . .	O 274	Irene	61
NORTHERN				
He sees no Northern Tempests sweep	. . . . . .	O 71	Hor. Epode II	V 11
But bless the Northern shoars,	. . . . . .	O 79	Feast St Simon	36
Tho' Northern Climes confess thy Sway,	. . . . .	O 146	Tr Boeth III.5	7
Where amidst the roarings of the Northern main	. . . .	Y 121	Irene	V 56
The northern shores to clouds and frost	. . . .	Y 38	Lady Leaving	2
NOSE				
On me you turn the nose.----	. . . . . .	O 140	Tr Rambler 176	1
Toss'd her nose, and shook her rump,	. . . . .	Y 300	Extemp. Elegy	7
NOSTRO				
Oude lithos, oude Sideron--nostro sequitur de Vulnere sanguis.	.	O 347	Irene	V 23
NOT			OMITTED WORD	
153				
NOTE				
With more address a lover's note convey,	. . . . .	O 13	London	77
Till angels wake thee with a note like thine.	. . . .	O 113	Epit. Phillips	6
NOTES				
The notes unfelt would strike th' impervious ear,	. . .	Y 104	Vanity Wishes	V 269
Mark, when the diff'rent notes agree	. . . . .	O 121	To Miss Playin	29
The better use of notes, or sweet or shrill,	. . . .	O 192	Tr. Medea II	9
NOTHING				
"Think nothing gain'd, he cries, till nought remain,	. .	O 40	Vanity Wishes	202
All is strange, yet nothing new;	. . . . . .	O 179	Ridicul Warton	2
Dissolve in Air, and vanish into Nothing.	. . . .	O 265	Irene	8
Fade <glide> from the sight, and Vanish into nothing.	. .	O 358	Irene	V 11
Held forth this fatal Scroll, then sunk to nothing.	. .	O 272	Irene	17
Held out this fatal roll--then sunk to Nothing.	. .	O 357	Irene	V 1
That loses all because she hazards nothing:	. . . .	O 281	Irene	45
NOTIONS				
Practis'd their master's notions to embrace,	. . . .	O 16	London	136
NOTWITHSTANDING				
We oft (notwithstanding this boasted superiour genius	.	Y 148	Irene	V 49
NOUGHT				
"Think nothing gain'd, he cries, till nought remain,	. .	O 40	Vanity Wishes	202
Nought from my birth or ancestors I claim;	. . . .	O 132	Tr. Rambler 46	1
When nought but mine the circling Sun shall see	. . .	O 357	Irene	V 29
And try the Hazard that hast Nought to stake;	. . .	O 319	Irene	31
NOVELTY				
Should tempting Novelty thy cell refrain,	. . . .	O 37	Vanity Wishes	149
NOW			OMITTED WORD	
103				
NUM'ROUS				
His chearfull Slaves, a num'rous band,	. . . . .	O 73	Hor. Epode II	71
Soon shall you fall by num'rous hosts opprest	. . .	Y 18	Tr. Iliad Bk 6	22
NUMBER				
With horrour counts the number of the slain.	. . . .	Y 23	Tr Add. Battle	33

NUMBERS

		PAGE	TITLE	LINE
By numbers here from shame or censure free,		O 17	London	158
In angry numbers warn'st succeeding times;		O 23	London	259
Beneath Pygmean steel what numbers dye!		O 75	Tr Add. Battle	5
Those Saints my numbers grace		O 78	Feast St Simon	9
But though the numbers for a moment please,		O 142	In Baretti Bk.	5
In pompous numbers ancient heroes rise;		Y 22	Tr Add. Battle	8

NUMEROUS   SEE NUM'ROUS, NUMROUS

NUMIDIA'S

Augustus' numerous trophies sing;		O 68	Hor. II Ode IX	18
None e'er more fierce Numidia's land,		O 66	Hor I Ode xxii	V 15
No Beast more fierce Numidia's Land,		O 67	To A. Fuscus	15
Touch'd with thy fate Numidia's lyons roar		Y 6	Virgil Daphnis	11

NUMROUS

| But move their numrous arms to Musicks sound, | | O 77 | Tr Add. Battle | 51 |

NURSE

Dire nurse of raging lions, bore.		O 66	Hor I Ode xxii	16
The nurse took up the squealing child,		O 157	Par. Hermit I	3
The nurse attending bore a lovely boy		Y 18	Tr. Iliad Bk 6	9
From the fair nurse Astyanax demands.		Y 20	Tr. Iliad Bk 6	91

NURSE'S

| And in his nurse's bosom hides his face. | | Y 20 | Tr. Iliad Bk 6 | 94 |

NYMPH

Each nymph your rival, and each youth your slave?		O 46	Vanity Wishes	330
Thou seem'st at once, bright nymph, a Muse and Grace.		O 107	Lady F Assizes	6
The nymph fictitious, as the flow'r;		O 121	To Miss Playin	8
The spritely Nymph and naked Grace		O 231	Tr Horace IV.7	5
Pleasure in ev'ry nymph and shepherd reigns,		Y 7	Virgil Daphnis	36

NYMPHS

Ye nymphs of rosy lips and radiant eyes,		O 46	Vanity Wishes	323
Ye Nymphs, whose Bosoms beat at Milton's Name,		O 57	Prologue Comus	2
For kind, for tender nymphs the myrtle blooms,		O 84	Epi Dist Moth.	14
The nymphs, who found their pow'r decline,		O 122	Stella Mourn.	3
Ye nymphs whom starry rays invest,		O 126	To Lyce, Lady	1
The nymphs bewail'd poor Daphnis' hapless death		Y 6	Virgil Daphnis	1
When to the nymphs the swain due homage pays		Y 7	Virgil Daphnis	V 51
The nymphs bewail'd his fall with loud lament		Y 18	Tr. Iliad Bk 6	32

O

O prodigy of Love!		O 79	Feast St Simon	21
O then, when conquer'd crouds confess thy sway,		O 81	Lady Birthday	9
O! then the meaning of thy gift impart,		O 95	Sprig of Myrtl	11
O guide me through life's darksome way,		O 100	Ode Friendship	14
O guide us through life's darksome way,		O 100	Ode Friendship	V 14
O! Shall thy flames then cease to glow		O 100	Ode Friendship	V 25
Then, O my Country! shalt thou groan distrest,		O 110	To Posterity	3
O thou whose pow'r o'er moving worlds presides,		O 129	Tr. Rambler 7	1
Thy wealth O city ill-gotten ill-preserv'd shall		Y 113	Irene	V 20
O Providence! extend thy Care to me,		O 252	Irene	90
O! sooth my Soul, and teach me how to lose thee.		O 253	Irene	103
O lead me quickly to the Scene of Fate;		O 259	Irene	105
O may her Beauties last unchang'd by Time,		O 262	Irene	11
O! could the Grave restore the pious Hero,		O 267	Irene	42
O seize the Power to bless--Irene's Nod		O 278	Irene	75
Forbear--O do not urge me to my Ruin!		O 278	Irene	79
O! did Irene shine the Queen of Turkey,		O 290	Irene	51
When I am gone remember, O! remember,		O 294	Irene	7
O say, bright Being, in this Age of Absence,		O 295	Irene	21
O say, what guardian Pow'r convey'd thee hither.		O 296	Irene	33
Then--O my Fair, I cannot bid thee goe;		O 297	Irene	15
Then--O my Fair, I cannot bid thee go;		O 297	Irene	V 15
--O Demetrius O for a cottage in those happy regions		Y 177	Irene	V 108
--O Demetrius O for a cottage in those happy regions		Y 177	Irene	V 108
O spare the gallant Greek, in him we lose		O 307	Irene	26
O! could the Eyes of Kings, like those of Heav'n,		O 308	Irene	12
O could her fabled Saints, and boasted Prayers		O 309	Irene	38
O could her boasted saints, and powerfull prayers		Y 185	Irene	V 38
O Happiness! sure thou art all Aspasia's.		O 310	Irene	14
O grant thy sacred Influence, pow'rful Virtue!		O 313	Irene	5
O Greece! renown'd for Science and for Wealth,		O 317	Irene	42
O let me be but heard, nor fear from me		O 327	Irene	20
O name not Death! Distraction and Amazement,		O 328	Irene	31
Grant me one Hour, O grant me but a Moment,		O 328	Irene	45
O, hear my Pray'rs! accept, all-pitying Heaven,		O 328	Irene	52
Be charg'd upon my Soul. O, Mercy! Mercy!		O 329	Irene	55
O seize me, Madness--Did she call on me!		O 334	Irene	68
Direct O Goddess, my advent'rous song;		Y 22	Tr Add. Battle	3
O would Cleora thus return,		Y 39	Lady Leaving	11

O'ER

And dare to slumber o'er the Gazetteer;		O 13	London	72
Swift o'er the land the dismal rumour flies,		O 19	London	196
And stretch thy prospects o'er the smiling land,		O 20	London	214
And stretch thy prospects o'er your fruitfull land,		Y 58	London	V 214
O'er Bodley's dome his future labours spread,		O 37	Vanity Wishes	139
And Bacon's mansion trembles o'er his head.		O 37	Vanity Wishes	140
With force resistless o'er the brave prevail.		O 39	Vanity Wishes	178
Such bribes the rapid Greek o'er Asia whirl'd,		O 39	Vanity Wishes	179
O'er love, o'er fear, extends his wide domain,		O 40	Vanity Wishes	195
O'er love, o'er fear, extends his wide domain,		O 40	Vanity Wishes	195
O'er love, o'er Force, extends his wide domain,		O 40	Vanity Wishes	V 195
O'er love, o'er Force, extends his wide domain,		O 40	Vanity Wishes	V 195

232

O'ER   (CONTINUED)

		PAGE	TITLE	LINE
Attendant Platt'ry counts his myriads o'er,		O 42	Vanity Wishes	229
Time hovers o'er, impatient to destroy,		O 43	Vanity Wishes	259
For patience sov'reign o'er transmuted ill;		O 48	Vanity Wishes	362
When Learning's Triumph o'er her barb'rous Foes		O 51	Pro Drury-Lane	1
And Want hung threat'ning o'er her slow Decay.		O 58	Prologue Comus	26
That when confusion o'er the country reigns,		O 64	Virgil Past.I	15
His liquid wealth o'er barbarous lands.		O 65	Hor I Ode xxii	8
O'er icy Caucusus he treads,		O 66	To A. Fuscus	5
And spread its smoking ruins o'er the field.		O 74	Tr. Iliad Bk 6	14
And victory hangs doubtfull o'er the field.		O 76	Tr Add. Battle	13
Swords, arms and wings are scatter'd o'er the plain		O 76	Tr Add. Battle	18
Scatters their breathless bodies o'er the plain.		O 76	Tr Add. Battle	32
And wander sportive o'er th' Elysian plain:		O 77	Tr Add. Battle	43
Jocund he dances o'er the wat'ry way,		O 82	Young Author	5
Then dances jocund o'er the watery way,	V	O 82	Young Author	5
O'er the sad plains perpetual tempests sigh;		O 84	Epi Dist Moth.	32
Alike o'er all his lightnings fly;		O 100	Ode Friendship	10
Then o'er the World shall Discord stretch her Wings,		O 110	To Posterity	15
The Lilies o'er the Vales triumphant spread;		O 111	To Posterity	18
Despotic o'er the desolated Plain,		O 111	To Posterity	20
For ever flutter o'er her lyre,		O 121	To Miss Playin	14
Now, o'er the rural kingdom roves		O 125	An Ode	5
She's starr'd with pimples o'er,		O 127	To Lyce, Lady	14
O thou whose pow'r o'er moving worlds presides,		O 129	Tr. Rambler 7	1
Still discord hovers o'er divided thrones.		O 140	Tr Rambler 183	2
O'er the Bounds of Thirtyfive:		O 178	Thrale 35 Year	8
"O'er his face extend my wings;		O 186	Anacreon Ode 9	38
And o'er the globe extend your reign,		O 189	Epilogue	7
O'er ice the rapid skaiter flies,		O 203	Tr. on Skating	1
On crackling ice, o'er gulphs profound,	V	O 203	Tr. on Skating	1
O'er treacherous pleasure's flow'ry ground	V	O 203	Tr. on Skating	3
He rolls no Thunders o'er the drowsy Pit.		O 246	Irene Prologue	26
And weary Murther slumbers o'er the Carnage	V	O 350	Irene	9
Dominion hovers o'er their conquering banners	V	Y 115	Irene	49D
To waft our gallies o'er the trembling earth?	V	Y 115	Irene	49H
And wander o'er the Ruins of our Country	V	O 351	Irene	1
Prowls o'er the wealthy Spoils of bleeding Turkey?		O 264	Irene	15
Now hovers o'er this melancholy Shade,		O 267	Irene	40
D<r>ives to (holds o'er) the south or west the storm	V	Y 136	Irene	26
Now roll full fraught with Thunder o'er your Head.		O 275	Irene	75
Do gay Delusions, wand'ring o'er the Brain,		O 277	Irene	44
And gay delusions wandring o'er the brain	V	O 356	Irene	11
Pleasure shall spread her downy Pinions o'er thee	V	O 350	Irene	21
In easy State presides o'er all their Motions,		O 293	Irene	122
Sweeps o'er the Grove, forsake the lab'ring Bough,		O 298	Irene	23
Her ancient Empire o'er the yielding Heart;		O 302	Irene	121
And where yon Trees wave o'er the foaming Surge		O 304	Irene	2
Sport in our Sails, and murmur o'er the Deep.		O 304	Irene	7
Now hover o'er us with propitious Wings,		O 306	Irene	51
And growls in private o'er his idle Sabre.		O 309	Irene	22
o'er the tide--providence our guide--	V	Y 199	Irene	16A
Nor languish o'er irreparable Ruins;		O 320	Irene	17
Bound o'er the sparkling Waves. Go, happy Bark,		O 322	Irene	5
Dance o'er the Sparkling Waves--Go happy Bark	V	O 364	Irene	30
And live her guiltless Moments o'er anew!		O 323	Irene	16
But now 'tis o'er, and Justice has prevail'd.		O 324	Irene	14
And spread their Flames resistless o'er the World?		O 325	Irene	13
Already shakes his bloody Sabre o'er thee.		O 327	Irene	10
Already brandishes his Sabre o'er You	V	O 368	Irene	18
May storms howl gently o'er and learn to spare.		Y 3	On a Daffodill	8
O'er all the warbling founts a cooling shade.		Y 7	Virgil Daphnis	27
Now, wand'ring o'er the cliffs the traveller		Y 23	Tr Add. Battle	30
Affrighted views; and looking o'er the plain		Y 23	Tr Add. Battle	32
There frogs crept croaking o'er the swampy ground.		Y 24	Tr Add. Battle	59
These when o'er winter's sway, prevail'd the spring		Y 24	Tr Add. Battle	72

O'ERBEARS

Dear hapless Maid--tempestuous Grief o'erbears		O 252	Irene	77
Dear helpless Maid--tempestuous Grief o'erbears	V	O 252	Irene	77
O'erbears each gentler Motion of the Mind.		O 280	Irene	21

O'ERBORN

Betray'd by Falshood, or by Crouds o'erborn?		O 315	Irene	7

O'ERCAST

With livid hue the fairest face o'ercast,		O 84	Epi Dist Moth.	34

O'ERCASTS

A sudden Mist o'ercasts my darken'd Soul,		O 295	Irene	12

O'ERFILL

O'erfill the saturated soul;		O 190	Tr. Medea I	6

O'FLOW   SEE OERFLOW

May then his mother's heart with joys o'erflow		Y 20	Tr. Iliad Bk 6	105

O'ERFLOWING

Scorning now th' o'erflowing Flood,		O 149	Tr Boet III.12	38

O'ERLOOK

O'erlook mankind, from China to Peru;		Y 91	Vanity Wishes	V 2

O'ERLOOKS

Autumn o'erlooks the smiling Ground		O 72	Hor. Epode II	24

O'ERPOW'RING

Shrinks at th' o'erpow'ring Gleams of regal State,		O 292	Irene	100

O'ERPOWER'D

O'erpower'd and faint the Pygmies scarce sustain		O 76	Tr Add. Battle	26

```
O'ERSPREAD                                               PAGE    TITLE              LINE
     O'erspread with snares the clouded maze of fate,  .  .  .    O  31 Vanity Wishes        6
O'ERTAKE
     And speed the Stroke lest Mercy should o'ertake them.  .     O 333 Irene               54
O'ERTHROW
     O'erthrow such weak, such accidental Virtue,   .  .  .  .    O 301 Irene               83
O'ERTHROWN
     Behold rebellious virtue quite o'erthrown,  .  .  .  .  .    O  13 London             63
     Behold Irene--o'erthrown  .  .  .  .  .  .  .  .  .  .  .    Y 217 Irene          V  10
O'ERTURNS
     O'erturns the Fabrick of presumptuous Reason,  .  .  .  .    O 269 Irene                8
O'ERWHELM
     Surprize o'erwhelm her, and retard our Flight.  .  .  .  .   O 285 Irene               13
     And War o'erwhelm them in their Dream of Vice.  .  .  .  .   O 309 Irene               37
O'ERWHELM'D
     O'erwhelm'd and lost amidst the publick Ruins  .  .  .  .    O 302 Irene              107
O'ERWHELMS
     New joy comes rushing on me and o'erwhelms  .  .  .  .  .    Y 169 Irene          V  12
OAK
     And left-hand crows, from an old hollow oak,  .  .  .  .     O  65 Virgil Past.I       24
OAR
     Th' incumber'd oar scarce leaves the dreaded coast  .  .     O  42 Vanity Wishes      239
OATHS
     By Smiles, and Oaths, and Praises ill disguis'd.  .  .  .    O 308 Irene               15
OBDURATE
     Wouldst thou subdue th' obdurate Cannibal  .  .  .  .  .     O 267 Irene                4
     The bard obdurate sees his brother die.  .  .  .  .  .  .    Y  67 Prologue Lethe       4
OBEDIENCE
     Inflame her Crimes, exalt your own Obedience,  .  .  .  .    O 329 Irene               14
OBEDIENT
     Obedient passions, and a will resign'd;  .  .  .  .  .  .    O  48 Vanity Wishes      360
     I came obedient to thy friendly Summons,  .  .  .  .  .  .   O 253 Irene              105
OBELISKS
     Oerthrow the obelisks amazing height  .  .  .  .  .  .  .    Y 177 Irene          V 108
OBEY
     When ev'n proud wealth and prouder wit obey,  .  .  .  .     O  81 Lady Birthday       10
     Aw'd into Love, our conquer'd hearts obey,  .  .  .  .  .    O  96 Hickman Spinet       4
     Must bid his Passions all obey;  .  .  .  .  .  .  .  .  .   O 146 Tr Boeth III.5        2
     Only this Command obey,  .  .  .  .  .  .  .  .  .  .  .  .  O 150 Tr Boet III.12       43
OBEY'D
     And thinks his fatal Mandates ill obey'd.  .  .  .  .  .     O 327 Irene               13
OBJECT
     And view each object with another's eye;  .  .  .  .  .  .   O  16 London             139
     Woman the Source, the Object, and the End.  .  .  .  .  .    O 247 Irene Epilogue      18
OBJECTS
     Where then shall Hope and Fear their objects find?  .  .     O  47 Vanity Wishes      343
OBLIG'D
     Long have as oblig'd by vow  .  .  .  .  .  .  .  .  .  .    Y 130 Irene          V   9
OBLIVION
     And Virtue call'd Oblivion to her Aid.  .  .  .  .  .  .     O  52 Pro Drury-Lane      28
     In all the sweet Oblivion of Delight,  .  .  .  .  .  .  .   O 269 Irene               13
OBLIVIOUS
     Th' oblivious grave's inviolable shade.  .  .  .  .  .  .    O  62 Pro Word Wise       10
OBSCENITY
     Intrigue was Plot, Obscenity was Wit.  .  .  .  .  .  .  .   O  52 Pro Drury-Lane      20
OBSCUR'D
     Then, when dark arts obscur'd each fierce debate,  .  .  .   O 118 Epitaph Hanmer      23
     Prospects obscur'd by Distance faintly strike.  .  .  .  .   O 261 Irene               19
OBSCURE
     Obscure, unpriz'd, and dark, the magnet lies,  .  .  .  .    O 141 Tr Rambler 199       1
     And wish their gloomy Caverns more obscure.  .  .  .  .  .   O 268 Irene               32
     To live obscure upon a foreign Coast,  .  .  .  .  .  .  .   O 301 Irene              104
     Irradiate and obscure my Breast by Turns:  .  .  .  .  .     O 321 Irene               45
     Thick clouds of hostile birds obscure the skies.  .  .  .    Y  25 Tr Add. Battle      93
OBSCURELY
     Obscurely wise, and coarsely kind;  .  .  .  .  .  .  .  .   O 201 Death Dr Levet      10
     And in some distant Land obscurely die.  .  .  .  .  .  .    O 274 Irene               49
OBSCURITY
     Go, languish on in dull Obscurity;  .  .  .  .  .  .  .  .   O 292 Irene               98
OBSEQUIOUS
     Obsequious, artful, voluble and gay,  .  .  .  .  .  .  .    O  15 London             111
     Obsequious, at his Patrons gates;  .  .  .  .  .  .  .  .    O  71 Hor. Epode II       16
     Obsequious to his heav'nly will  .  .  .  .  .  .  .  .  .   O  79 Feast St Simon      17
OBSERV'D
     But scarce observ'd, the knowing and the bold  .  .  .  .    O  31 Vanity Wishes       21
     That Vessel, if observ'd, alarms the Court,  .  .  .  .  .   O 258 Irene               83
OBSERVATION
     Let observation with extensive view,  .  .  .  .  .  .  .    O  30 Vanity Wishes        1
OBSERVE
     Observe your steps; be carefull to command  .  .  .  .  .    O  77 Festina Lente        3
     Observe her labours, Sluggard, and be wise.  .  .  .  .  .   O 151 The Ant              2
     Observe him closely with a Statesman's Eye,  .  .  .  .  .   O 255 Irene               10
     Observe, bright Maid, as his resistless Voice  .  .  .  .    O 268 Irene               25
     Observe the feather'd Wand'rers of the Sky,  .  .  .  .  .   O 277 Irene               34
OBSERVING
     He stop unmindfull of observing crowds  .  .  .  .  .  .     Y 187 Irene          V   5
OBSTINATE
     For speedy Flight, or obstinate Defence.  .  .  .  .  .  .   O 284 Irene               55
OBSTRUCTED
     Or felt th' Impatience of obstructed Love,  .  .  .  .  .    O 285 Irene                4.
```

		PAGE	TITLE		LINE
OBTAIN					
Obtain her and possess, thou know'st thy Rival. . . .		O 307	Irene		17
OBTAIN'D					
Not Pow'r I blame, but Pow'r obtain'd by Crime, . . .		O 293	Irene		129
OBVIATE					
We cannot obviate, for we cannot guess.		O 287	Irene		11
Let Prudence obviate an impending Danger.		O 309	Irene		19
OCCASION					
When will Occasion smile upon our Wishes, ...		O 282	Irene		1
OCEAN					
Charm'd with the scene the smiling ocean yields, . .		O 81	Young Author		3
Pleas'd with the scene the smiling ocean yields, . .		O 81	Young Author	V	3
ODE					
Translation of Horace. Book I. Ode xxii.		O 65	Hor I Ode xxii		T
Horace. Book 2d. Ode 14		O 68	Hor.II Ode 14		T
Horace Book 2d. Ode 20th		O 70	Hor.II Ode XX		T
An Ode on Friendship		O 99	Ode Friendship		T
Ode on Friendship address'd To the Lady--------		O 99	Ode Friendship	V	T
An Ode		O 124	An Ode		T
An Ode		O 124	An Ode	V	T
Spring. An Ode.		O 179	Ridicul Warton		8
Ode and Elegy and Sonnet.		O 185	Anacreon Ode 9		T
Anacreon, Ode IX		O 185	Anacreon Ode 9		11
"Venus, courted with an ode, ...		O 185	Anacreon Ode 9		11
"Venus, courted by an ode, ...		O 185	Anacreon Ode 9	V	11
ODIOUS					
And why should odious ruin dawb the wall.		Y 95	Vanity Wishes	V	90
Still odious to the Monarch, or the People.		O 256	Irene		52
ODOURS					
The richest Odours, nor the speckled Shells		O 277	Irene		32
OER					
Prowls like a lyon oer the wealthy Spoils of bleeding .		O 352	Irene	V	29
Turkey.					
Oer whom the seasons varied unperceiv'd		Y 163	Irene	V	43
Melancholly broods or pours her influence oer the . . .		Y 165	Irene	V	82
now hover oer us and direct our councils		Y 181	Irene	V	51
OERFLOW					
Nor think my eyes oerflow with Female		O 357	Irene	V	17
Weakness					
OERPOWRING					
Shrinks at th' oerpowring blaze of regal State		O 368	Irene	V	30
OERTHROW					
Oerthrow the obelisks amazing height		Y 177	Irene	V	108
OF					
1087			OMITTED WORD		
OFF					
Leave off, at length, these woman's sighs, ...		O 68	Hor. II Ode IX		17
Cast off all idle terrours of hereafter		Y 146	Irene	V	19
When ev'n as Love was breaking off from Wonder, . . .		O 282	Irene		66
Shake off th' Incumbrances of State a moment, ...		O 289	Irene		7
Shake off this Weight of unavailing Grief, ...		O 333	Irene		39
Bear off with eager Haste th' unfinish'd Sentence, . .		O 333	Irene		53
OFFENCE					
The watchful guests still hint the last offence, . .		O 44	Vanity Wishes		279
The treachrous guests still hint the last offence, . .		Y 104	Vanity Wishes	V	279
To please by scenes unconscious of offence, ...		O 62	Pro Word Wise		13
OFFENDED					
Th' offended burgess hoards his angry tale, ...		O 60	Pro Good Nat'd		17
OFFENDER'S					
We ask'd, with tim'rous Tongue, th' Offender's Name, . .		O 325	Irene		23
OFFENDS					
A sister sickens, or a child offends.		Y 105	Vanity Wishes	V	302
OFFER					
To her transferr'd the Offer of a Crown.		O 259	Irene		124
To offer up my vows in the temple built by the Father of		O 348	Irene	V	1
Mankind					
OFFERS					
His Offers oft repeated, still refus'd, ...		O 259	Irene		109
OFFICE					
While I foretell thy Fate; that Office done,-- . . .		O 289	Irene		9
Refuse their Office, and uncertain Life		O 320	Irene		21
OFFICIOUS					
Officious, innocent, sincere, ...		O 201	Death Dr Levet		7
Here let me tend her with officious Care, ...		O 320	Irene		23
Ye blind officious Ministers of Folly, ...		O 332	Irene		23
OFFSPRING					
Unknown, unheeded, long his Offspring lay, ...		O 58	Prologue Comus		25
Where Lybia's swarthy offspring burns, ...		O 70	Hor.II Ode XX		14
The injur'd Cranes their murther'd offspring mourn . .		Y 24	Tr Add. Battle		64
OFT					
Oft on his altar shall my firstlings lie, ...		O 64	Virgil Past.I		9
With secret springs oft ensnares		O 72	Hor. Epode II		43
Oft favours, oft rejects a lover's pray'r:		O 95	Sprig of Myrtl		6
Oft favours, oft rejects a lover's pray'r:		O 95	Sprig of Myrtl		6
Oft favours, oft rejects the poet's pray'r:		O 95	Sprig of Myrtl	V	6
Oft favours, oft rejects the poet's pray'r:		O 95	Sprig of Myrtl	V	6
In Myrtle groves oft sings the happy swain, ...		O 95	Sprig of Myrtl		7
In Myrtle shades oft sings the happy swain, ...		O 95	Sprig of Myrtl	V	7
With bright, but oft destructive gleam, ...		O 100	Ode Friendship		9
With bright, but oft destructive gloom, ...		O 100	Ode Friendship	V	9
Find here that calm thou gav'st so oft before;		O 113	Epit. Phillips		4
Oft in Danger yet alive		O 178	Thrale 35 Year		1

OFT (CONTINUED)

	PAGE	TITLE	LINE
Oft may better Years arrive, ...	O 178	Thrale 35 Year	V 3
Ill-fated Race! So oft besieg'd in vain, ...	O 250	Irene	29
Oft when the Cries of violated Beauty	O 251	Irene	73
His Offers oft repeated, still refus'd, ...	O 259	Irene	109
Oft have I rag'd, when their wide-wasting Cannon . .	O 273	Irene	24
We oft (notwithstanding this boasted superiour genius	Y 148	Irene	V 49
But oft conjoins in woman's softer mould/frame . . .	Y 149	Irene	V 55
My soul not oft acquainted with remorse	Y 159	Irene	V 8
Oft shall I swell on our disastrous Friendship . . .	O 349	Irene	V 11
Oft when the fierce Besiegers eager Host	O 298	Irene	27
Permitted oft, though not inspir'd by Heav'n, . .	O 300	Irene	65
Oft would they find Ingratitude and Treason, . . .	O 308	Irene	14
Oft from behind they wounded them with darts . . .	Y 23	Tr Add. Battle	42
Oft has our bard in this disastrous year, . . .	Y 67	Prologue Lethe	7
Oft has he seen the poignant orange fly, ...	Y 67	Prologue Lethe	9

OFT'

Secure, and triumph'd oft' in hostile blood. . . .	O 76	Tr Add. Battle	34
The Shepherds oft' see little ghosts glide by . .	O 77	Tr Add. Battle	47
That oft' had practis'd Fraud, and oft' detected, . . .	O 254	Irene	131
That oft' had practis'd Fraud, and oft' detected, . . .	O 254	Irene	131
Oft' shall I dwell on our disastrous Friendship, . . .	O 292	Irene	96

OFTEN

Rambling often to and fro'	Y 300	Extemp. Elegy	10

OGILBY'S

These dreams were Settle's once and Ogilby's. . . .	O 82	Young Author	24
Those dreams were Settle's once and Ogilby's. . . .	O 82	Young Author	V 24

OH

Oh! how my soul abhors so mean a thought.	O 74	Tr. Iliad Bk 6	8
Oh, must their ardours cease to glow	O 100	Ode Friendship	25
Oh may this Flame neer cease to glow	O 100	Ode Friendship	V 25
Oh! send them to the sullen mansions dun, . . .	O 192	Tr. Medea II	13
Oh could thy Hand unaided free thy Country, . . .	O 300	Irene	63
Broke out in Perfidy--Oh curs'd Aspasia, ...	O 316	Irene	10
Hide me, oh hide me from upbraiding Greece, . . .	O 316	Irene	12
Oh, hide me from myself!	O 316	Irene	13
Oh! rather scornful of flagitious Greatness, . . .	O 320	Irene	28

OISI

Oisi memele phusis, metron charis, erga palaion, . . .	O 171	Epi. Goldsmith	3

OISTA

Ommasi lampra Dios Kupris oista pherei.	O 103	Eis Elisses	6

OLD

And left-hand crows, from an old hollow oak, . .	O 65	Virgil Past.I	24
Mix'd with old Heroes trace the flow'ry meads, . . .	O 76	Tr Add. Battle	42
Or if old womens tales may credit gain, ...	O 77	Tr Add. Battle	44
When old Timotheus struck the vocal String, . . .	O 97	Hickman Spinet	9
Nor shall the Lyon, wont of old to reign . . .	O 111	To Posterity	19
Grown old in courts, thou art not surely one . .	O 176	Tr Metastas II	1
Forgive an old Man's Weakness, ...	O 256	Irene	38
Then old in honours, and approv'd in faith, . . .	Y 131	Irene	V 32
Hast thou grown old amidst the Croud of Courts, . . .	O 281	Irene	32
But thou, too old to bear another Cheat, ...	O 283	Irene	32

OLEIBERICIO

Ton taphon eisoraas ton Oleiberioio, konien . .	O 171	Epi. Goldsmith	V 1

OLIBARIOIO

Ton taphon eisoraas ton Olibarioio, Konien	O 171	Epi. Goldsmith	1

OLIBAROIC

Ton taphon eisoraas ton Olibaroio, konien	O 171	Epi. Goldsmith	V 1

OLIVE

Wealh in her hand, and olive on her brow. . . .	O 374	Irene	V 32

OMEN'D

And heard th' ill omen'd catcall's direful cry. . . .	Y 67	Prologue Lethe	10

OMENS

This dire event by omens was foreshown;	O 64	Virgil Past.I	22
Could Omens fright the Resolute and Wise, ...	O 269	Irene	1
And of a fruitful year fair omens bring.	Y 3	On a Daffodill	4
And of a faithful year fair omens bring.	Y 3	On a Daffodill	V 4

OMER

St. Omer	O 172	French Distich	3

OMMASI

Ommasi lampra Dios Kupris oista pherei.	O 103	Eis Elisses	6

OMNIPOTENCE

Against th' omnipotence of gold	Y 11	Tr Hor Epode 9	22

OMNISCIENCE

Not yet inspire th' omniscience of a queen	O 366	Irene	V 19

ON 222

OMITTED WORD

ONAR

Ek Dios estin onar, Theios pot egrapsen Homeros, . . .	O 103	Eis Elisses	3
Alla tod eis Thnetous Kupris epempseu onar	O 103	Eis Elisses	4

ONCE

Where once the harrass'd Briton found repose, . .	O 11	London	47
In virtue's cause once more exert his rage, . . .	O 23	London	262
In virtue's cause once more forsake his rage, . . .	O 23	London	V 262
Once more, Democritus, arise on earth, ...	O 32	Vanity Wishes	49
At once is lost the pride of aweful state, . . .	O 35	Vanity Wishes	113
Now drops at once the pride of aweful state, . . .	O 35	Vanity Wishes	V 113
If dreams yet flatter, once again attend, ...	O 38	Vanity Wishes	163
If hope yet flatter, once again attend, ...	Y 99	Vanity Wishes	V 163
In croud at once, where none the pass defend, . . .	O 46	Vanity Wishes	337
In crowd at once, where none the fort defend, . . .	Y 107	Vanity Wishes	V 337

```
ONCE              (CONTINUED)                              PAGE    TITLE         LINE
    Or right, or wrong, once hooted from the stage;     .   .   .   O  61 Pro Word Wise      2
    I once admir'd, I'd then despise:    .   .           .   O  73 Hor. Epode II    V 60
    This thought once form'd, all counsel comes too late,   .   O  82 Young Author     19
    These dreams were Settle's once and Ogilby's.   .   .   .   O  82 Young Author     24
    Those dreams were Settle's once and Ogilby's.   .   .   .   O  82 Young Author   V 24
    Inflicting all those ills which once they knew;     .   .   O  84 Epi Dist Moth.   37
    Were Pope once void of wonted candour found,    .   .   .   O 106 Eliza plucking    7
    Thou seem'st at once, bright nymph, a Muse and Grace.   .   O 107 Lady F Assizes    6
    Nor shall the passive Coward once complain.     .   .   .   O 111 To Posterity     26
    At once commenc'd the Senator and Man.  .   .   .   .   .   O 117 Epitaph Hanmer   12
    The heart, once caught, should ne'er be freed?  .   .   .   O 120 To Miss Purse    12
    Once more great nature's work review,   .   .   .   .   .   O 125 An Ode           23
    Once more great nature's works renew    .   .   .   .   .   O 125 An Ode         V 23
    Once more on wisdom's voice attend.     .   .   .   .   .   O 125 An Ode           24
    Soon fades the rose; once past the fragrant hour,   .   .   O 133 Tr. Rambler 71    1
    When once unto the bottom I     .   .   .   .   .   .   .   O 159 Par Hermit III    7
    Death broke at once the vital chain,    .   .   .   .   .   O 202 Death Dr Levet   35
    But wretched Man, when once he lies  .   .   .   .   .   .   O 232 Tr Horace IV.7   14
    When Minos once has fix'd your doom,    .   .   .   .   .   O 232 Tr Horace IV.7   22
    Projects at once our Freedom and his own;   .   .   .   .   O 253 Irene           114
    Such had I trusted once as soon as seen,    .   .   .   .   O 255 Irene            17
    At once a hundred Voices thunder'd round me,    .   .   .   O 271 Irene            29
    Then let me once, in honour of our Sex,     .   .   .   .   O 277 Irene            49
    Then Let me once to right our injur'd Sex   .   .   .   .   O 356 Irene          V 16
    Once more reflect, suppress this infant Folly.  .   .   .   O 281 Irene            56
    Flash out at once, with Strength above Resistance.  .   .   O 282 Irene            60
    Once to behold the Charms of bright Aspasia,    .   .   .   O 285 Irene             6
    The Soul once tainted with so foul a Crime,     .   .   .   O 289 Irene            15
    Maxims like these, if once reduc'd to practice  .   .   .   O 352 Irene          V  2
    Aspasia! do I once again behold thee?   .   .   .   .   .   O 294 Irene             2
    Descend, to sweeten Labours once your own.  .   .   .   .   O 306 Irene            56
    At once the Joys of Paradise and Empire,    .   .   .   .   O 308 Irene             7
    Dooms me to loath at once, and doat on Falshood,    .   .   O 310 Irene            10
    How Guilt once harbour'd in the conscious Breast,   .   .   O 311 Irene            14
    When Guilt like this once harbours in the Breast    .   .   O 346 Irene          V  4
    At once a Thousand Passions fir'd his Cheek:    .   .   .   O 317 Irene            31
    Once more I dare thy Sword, behold the Prize,   .   .   .   O 319 Irene            28
    She was once of high renown,--  .   .   .   .   .   .   .   Y 300 Extemp. Elegy     3
    She was once as cherry plump .   .   .   .   .   .   .   .   Y 300 Extemp. Elegy     5

ONE
    Give to St. David one true Briton more. .   .   .   .   .   O   9 London            8
    One shews the plunder, and one hides the thief. .   .   .   O  32 Vanity Wishes    44
    One shews the plunder, and one hides the thief. .   .   .   O  32 Vanity Wishes    44
    Yet still can gen'ral cry the skies assails,    .   .   .   O  32 Vanity Wishes    45
    And one capitulate, and one resign;     .   .   .   .   .   O  40 Vanity Wishes   200
    And one capitulate, and one resign;     .   .   .   .   .   O  40 Vanity Wishes   200
    See one capitulate, and one resign;     .   .   .   .   .   Y 101 Vanity Wishes V 200
    See one capitulate, and one resign;     .   .   .   .   .   Y 101 Vanity Wishes V 200
    Tost in one common storm with all the great;    .   .   .   O  59 Pro Good Nat'd    8
    When one a borough courts, and one the pit. .   .   .   .   O  59 Pro Good Nat'd   10
    When one a borough courts, and one the pit. .   .   .   .   O  59 Pro Good Nat'd   10
    Let one great payment every claim appease,  .   .   .   .   O  62 Pro Word Wise    11
    And one base action sully all my fame,  .   .   .   .   .   O  74 Tr. Iliad Bk 6    6
    He pants for room, in one poor World confin'd.  .   .   .   O  97 Hickman Spinet   12
    One moment hear the moral song, .   .   .   .   .   .   .   O 121 To Miss Playin   22
    Thou see'st one pleasing form arise,    .   .   .   .   .   O 121 To Miss Playin   26
    Henceforth shall form one common pray'r,    .   .   .   .   O 122 Stella Mourn.    14
    Let ev'ry piece be simple and be one.   .   .   .   .   .   O 137 Tr Rambler 139    1
    From one sublime Beginning spring;  .   .   .   .   .   .   O 146 Tr Boeth III.6    2
    All from one Source derive their Birth  .   .   .   .   .   O 146 Tr Boeth III.6    3
    Grown old in courts, thou art not surely one    .   .   .   O 176 Tr Metastas II    1
    One and Twenty 1810: Improviso on a young heir's coming .   O 196 Song Congratu. V  T
       of age.
    Long-expected one and twenty    .   .   .   .   .   .   .   O 196 Song Congratu.    1
    And for one Man--one Wife's enough in Conscience.   .   .   O 247 Irene Epilogue   14
    And for one Man--one Wife's enough in Conscience.   .   .   O 247 Irene Epilogue   14
    And not one Prodigy foretold our Fate.  .   .   .   .   .   O 250 Irene            35
    Where King and People own one common Law    .   .   .   .   O 352 Irene          V 16
    one common Interest, mutual duties  .   .   .   .   .   .   O 352 Irene          V 17
    And feel one happiness and one misfortune.  .   .   .   .   Y 121 Irene          V 57
    And feel one happiness and one misfortune.  .   .   .   .   Y 121 Irene          V 57
    If yet one spark of Heav'nly fire remain    .   .   .   .   Y 133 Irene          V 18
    Now haste to mingle in one common Center,   .   .   .   .   O 287 Irene             4
    Aspasia's Lovers know but one Desire,   .   .   .   .   .   O 307 Irene            13
    Grant me one Hour, O grant me but a Moment,     .   .   .   O 328 Irene            45
    And if one varied Accent prove thy Falshood,    .   .   .   O 332 Irene            14
    Or but one Moment's Pause betray Confusion,     .   .   .   O 332 Irene            15
    One Hour had freed me from the fatal Error,     .   .   .   O 332 Irene            27
    One Hour had sav'd me from Despair and Madness. .   .   .   O 332 Irene            28
    Let one just Act conclude the hateful Day.  .   .   .   .   O 333 Irene            50
    Like one awaken'd from a pleasing dream,    .   .   .   .   Y   4 On a Daffodill   26
    All stemm'd in one sad day the Stygian tyde.    .   .   .   Y  18 Tr. Iliad Bk 6   35
    Not one takes warning, by another's end.    .   .   .   .   Y  67 Prologue Lethe    6
ONE'S
    "Under leaves to hide one's head,   .   .   .   .   .   .   O 185 Anacreon Ode 9   27
ONEIRON
    Eis to tes Elisses peri ton Oneiron Ainigma     .   .   .   O 103 Eis Elisses       T
ONLY
    This, only this, the rigid law pursues,     .   .   .   .   O  17 London          160
    This, only this, the rigid law persues,     .   .   .   .   O  17 London        V 160
```

ONLY   (CONTINUED)   PAGE   TITLE   LINE
      This, only this, provokes the snarling muse. . . . . .   O 17 London   161
      This, only this, provokes the darling muse. . . . . . . O 17 London   V 161
      Only ev'ry bush there artless music sings . . . . Y 58 London   V 220
      Approve it only--'tis too late to praise. . . . . O 62 Pro Word Wise   16
      My admiration only I exprest, ... O 64 Virgil Past.I   13
      Ambitious only now to please the Fair, ...   O 97 Hickman Spinet   18
      To Men and Angels only giv'n, ...   O 99 Ode Friendship   3
      Thy lambent glories only beam . . . .   O 100 Ode Friendship   11
      Thy milder glories only beam . . . .   Y 71 Ode Friendship   V 11
      On selfish bosoms only prey. . . . .   O 100 Ode Friendship   16
      Nor only through the wasted plain, ...   O 123 Winter's Walk   5
      Nor only thought the wasted plain, ...   O 123 Winter's Walk   V 5
      Only this Command obey. . . . .   O 150 Tr Boet III.12   43
      Only teaches how to cheat. . . . .   O 176 Tr Metastasi I   6
      Open to all, true only to thyself, ...   O 176 Tr Metastas II   6
      And only build upon another's ruin. . . . .   O 176 Tr Metastas II   13
      Only dirt, or wet or dry. . . . .   O 196 Song Congratu.   24
      And only credits what Experience tells. . . . . . .   O 255 Irene   19
      When the revolving seasons shall only visit my dominions Y 132 Irene   V 44
      Only to hunt him round the ravag'd World? . . . . . .   O 275 Irene   67
      Or only struggles to be more enslav'd? . . . . . .   O 281 Irene   41
      Are his varied Modes of endless Being; . . . .   O 290 Irene   27
      Our only Arms are Innocence and Meekness. . . . . . .   O 290 Irene   45
      Her only arms are innocence and meekness . . . . . .   Y 162 Irene   V 45
      Ambition only gave her to my Arms, ...   O 310 Irene   7
      The Life, which only this Design supported, ...   O 316 Irene   22
ONWARD
      Bore me victorious onward, where Demetrius . . . . . .   O 312 Irene   9
OP'NING
      The foaming Boar he then with op'ning hounds . . . .   O 72 Hor. Epode II   V 39
      With twisted toils, and op'ning hounds; . . . . . .   O 72 Hor. Epode II   40
OPEN
      The skies are open--let us try the skies: . . . . .   O 136 Tr Rambler 129   5
      Open to all, true only to thyself, ...   O 176 Tr Metastas II   6
      The present Hour with open Arms invites; . . . . . .   O 284 Irene   34
      I'll open my breast--clasp thee--forget . . . . . .   Y 161 Irene   V 13
         greatness--
      This open Friend, this undesigning Hero, ...   O 299 Irene   38
      Lies open to Conjecture's dubious Ken, ...   O 300 Irene   69
OPENING
      Spoken At The Opening Of The Theatre . . . .   O 50 Pro Drury-lane   T
OPIATE
      And Sloth effuse her opiate fumes in vain; . . . . .   O 37 Vanity Wishes   150
OPIATES
      And Sloth's bland Opiates shed their fumes in . . . .   O 37 Vanity Wishes   V 150
         vain;
OPPOSE
      Oppose my Wishes, and--Remember Justice. . . . . . .   O 286 Irene   16
OPPOSITION
      Some accidental Gust of Opposition . . . .   O 269 Irene   6
      Some fatal gust of sudden Opposition . . . .   O 374 Irene   V 15
OPPRESS
      Does chearless Diffidence oppress their Hearts? . . .   O 270 Irene   22
OPPRESS'D
      Ere masquerades debauch'd, excise oppress'd, ...   O 10 London   29
      How nations sink, by darling schemes oppress'd, . . .   O 31 Vanity Wishes   13
      How families sink, by darling schemes oppress'd, . . . Y 92 Vanity Wishes   V 13
      With age, with cares, with maladies oppress'd, . . .   O 35 Vanity Wishes   117
      Rest here oppress'd by poverty no more, ...   O 113 Epit. Phillips   V 3
OPPRESSING
      Spread by Degrees, and dread th' oppressing Stream; . . O 282 Irene   58
OPPRESSION'S
      And bear oppression's insolence no more. . . . . . .   O 18 London   175
OPPRESSOR
      While I destroy th' Oppressor of Mankind? . . . . .   O 305 Irene   37
OPPRESSOR'S
      A Stranger to th' Oppressor's savage Joy, ...   O 329 Irene   6
OPPREST
      With honour sated, and with cares opprest; . . . . .   O 118 Epitaph Hanmer   36
      Soon shall you fall by num'rous hosts opprest . . . .   Y 18 Tr. Iliad Bk 6   22
OR   247   OMITTED WORD
ORANGE
      Oft has he seen the poignant orange fly, ...   Y 67 Prologue Lethe   9
ORBS
      Rolls with eternal Toil the pond'rous Orbs; . . . . .   O 293 Irene   120
ORDAIN
      These goods for man the laws of heav'n ordain, . . .   O 48 Vanity Wishes   365
      To ev'ry empire bounds the Gods ordain . . . . . .   O 76 Tr Add. Battle   35
ORDAIN'D
      This Pilgrimage our Lawgiver ordain'd-- . . . . . .   O 264 Irene   23
      Ordain'd, like you, to flutter and to shine, ...   O 277 Irene   37
      Sure 'tis the happy Hour ordain'd above, ...   O 321 Irene   35
      Ordain'd the mournful Messengers of Death. . . . . .   O 326 Irene   35
ORDAINS
      Blest Prince, for whom indulgent Heav'n ordains . . .   O 308 Irene   6
ORDER
      Around in beauteous order stand. . . . .   O 73 Hor. Epode II   72
      Would break the sacred laws of peace and . . . . . .   O 352 Irene   V 3
         order

```
                                                        PAGE    TITLE              LINE
ORDERS
     Thine Orders, mighty Sultan! are perform'd,  . . . . .   O 330 Irene              3
ORESTES
     By thee Orestes plung'd his vengefull dart   . . . . .   O  77 Festina Lente      13
ORGILIO
     Orgilio sees the golden pile aspire,  . . . . . . .      O  19 London            208
ORGILIO'S
     Who shares Orgilio's crimes, his fortune shares.  . . .  O  14 London             84
     Should heaven's just bolts Orgilio's wealth confound,  . O  19 London            194
ORIGIN
     Deserts her nobler Origin.  . . . . . . . . . . .        O 147 Tr Boeth III.6      20
ORIGINAL
     Desert her own original.  . . . . . . . . . .            O 129 Tr. Rambler 6        2
     Path, motive, guide, original, and end.  . . . . . .     O 130 Tr. Rambler 7        8
ORNAMENT
     Each grace of form, each ornament of state,  . . . . .   O 141 Tr Rambler 199       7
ORNAMENTS
     Truth in platonic ornaments bedeck'd,  . . . . . . .     O 134 Tr. Rambler 96       1
     The sparkling ornaments, the glittring dress (the change Y 164 Irene            V  71
          of dress
ORPHAN
     A widow I, an helpless orphan he.  . . . . . . . .       Y  19 Tr. Iliad Bk 6      49
ORPHANS
     The smiling Widows, and protected Orphans.  . . . . .    O 291 Irene              57
ORPHEUS
     Though dancing mountains witness'd Orpheus near;  . . .  O  43 Vanity Wishes      270
     Tho' when Orpheus made his Moan . . . . . . . . .        O 148 Tr Boet III.12       5
     Tho' when Orpheus sweetly sighing  . . . . . . . .       O 148 Tr Boet III.12    V   5
     Orpheus turn'd his eager Sight,  . . . . . . . . .       O 150 Tr Boet III.12      50
OSIERS
     Some pleasing bank where verdant osiers play,  . . . .   O  11 London             45
OSTENTATIOUS
     The horrid pomp of ostentatious woe  . . . . . . .       Y 168 Irene            V 135
OTAN
     Kai Bion, eipen, otan ripses Thanatio Belessi,  . . . .  O 108 Eis Birchion         3
OTHER
     In greater scenes each other aid;  . . . . . . .         O 121 To Miss Playin     28
     To please his Fancy,--see no other Man--  . . . . .      O 247 Irene Epilogue      3
     Desires more pure, and other Cares than Love.  . . . .   O 263 Irene               8
     To make Aspasia and Irene name each other.  . . . . .    Y 133 Irene            V  10
     Reserve this Homage for some other Fair,  . . . . .      O 288 Irene               4
     Reflect that Life, like ev'ry other Blessing,  . . . .   O 290 Irene              28
     Reserv'd, for other Lands, the Scourge of Heav'n. . . .  O 315 Irene               5
OTHERS
     Others with softer smiles, and subtler art,  . . . . .   O  13 London             75
     How small to others, but how great to me.  . . . . .     O 138 Tr Rambler 161       1
OUDE
     Oude lithos, oude Sideron--nostro sequitur de Vulnere .  O 347 Irene            V  23
          sanguis.
     Oude lithos, oude Sideron--nostro sequitur de Vulnere .  O 347 Irene            V  23
          sanguis.
OUR
          151                                                 OMITTED WORD
OURS
          2                                                   OMITTED WORD
OUT
     Strain out with fault'ring diffidence a lye,  . . . .    O  16 London            130
     Mark'd out by dangerous parts he meets the shock,  . . . O  39 Vanity Wishes     171
     Lamenting warbles out his love,  . . . . . . . . .       O  72 Hor. Epode II      34
     Next Month he sets it out again.  . . . . . . . .        O  73 Hor. Epode II      79
     Spread out by me, the roving coin,  . . . . . . .        O 120 To Miss Purse       7
     Out of Fortune's Pow'r retreat?  . . . . . . . . .       O 144 Tr Boeth. II.4      2
     My first, shuts out Thieves from your house or your Room O 179 Charade!            1
     Wearing out life's evening gray;  . . . . . . . .        O 181 Parody Warton       2
     A signal hour marked out by pitying Heav'n  . . . . .    Y 117 Irene            V 109
     And at the holy place pour out my prayers  . . . . .     Y 130 Irene            V  12
     When from his Lips the fatal Name burst out,  . . . .    O 270 Irene              12
     Still fond of Life, groan'd out the dreadful Secret,  .  O 272 Irene              16
     Held out this fatal roll--then sunk to Nothing.  . .     O 357 Irene            V   1
     Flash out at once, with Strength above Resistance.  .    O 282 Irene              60
     To languish out the tedious hours of life  . . . . .     O 357 Irene            V  14
     Seek out some peacefull Convents holy Shade . . . . .    O 348 Irene            V  24
     Why has thy Choice then pointed out Leontius,  . . . .   O 305 Irene              20
     The shudd'ring Camp shall murmur out Demetrius.  . .     O 305 Irene              42
     Till angry Heav'n shall mark them out for Ruin,  . . .   O 309 Irene              36
     When did Content sigh out her Cares in secret?  . .      O 314 Irene              20
     Broke out in Perfidy--Oh curs'd Aspasia,  . . . . .      O 316 Irene              10
     Holds out her Hand to lead thee back to Truth.  . .      O 321 Irene              42
     Just as the Rack forc'd out his struggling Soul,  . . .  O 330 Irene              13
     Those trembling Limbs--Speak out, thou shiv'ring  . .    O 332 Irene              16
          Traitor.
     Rush'd out and seiz'd me, thoughtless and unarm'd,  . .  O 335 Irene               7
OUTDONE
     And own all glories of the mine outdone,  . . . . .      O 141 Tr Rambler 199       6
OVER    SEE O'ER, OER
     "Over hills and fields to roam,  . . . . . . . . .       O 185 Anacreon Ode 9      25
OVERSPREADS
     As when a Deluge overspreads the Plains,  . . . . . .    O 280 Irene              22
OWN
     Behold our fame, our wealth, our lives your own.  . . .  O  13 London             64
     Blest age! but ah! how diff'rent from our own!  . . .    O  22 London            253
```

239

OWN   (CONTINUED)

		PAGE	TITLE	LINE
Blest age! but ha! how diff'rent from our own!	. . . .	O 22	London	V 253
My Flame for Lalage I'll own;	. . . .	O 67	To A. Fuscus	23
His own hereditary Land,	. . . .	O 71	Hor. Epode II	6
And drove the swarthy troops to their own barren sands.	.	O 78	Festina Lente	20
With his own form acquaint the forward fool,	. . . .	O 81	Lady Birthday	15
Teach mimick censure her own faults to find,	. . . .	O 81	Lady Birthday	17
... a Gold and Silk net-work Purse of her own weaving	.	O 119	To Miss Purse	T
... of her own Painting	. . . .	O 120	To Miss Playing	T
Desert her own original.	. . . .	O 129	Tr. Rambler 6	2
All is my own, my honour and my shame.	. . . . . .	O 132	Tr. Rambler 46	2
And own all glories of the mine outdone,	. . . . . .	O 141	Tr Rambler 199	6
Bow down and own thyself a Slave.	. . . .	O 146	Tr Boeth III.5	10
Great Sir John, are all your own.	. . . .	O 196	Song Congratu.	4
Great Sir John, are now your own.	. . . .	O 196	Song Congratu.	V 4
My Pride's to have that little all my own.	. . . . .	O 247	Irene Epilogue	10
Her own neglected, in the publick Safety.	. . . . .	O 250	Irene	27
Projects at once our Freedom and his own;	. . . . .	O 253	Irene	114
Where King and People own one common Law	. . . .	O 352	Irene	V 16
And Folly, frighted at her own Chimeras,	. . . . .	O 266	Irene	32
And pow'rful Glance, 'tis granted, are our own;	. . . .	O 277	Irene	52
Marks for His own still doat upon to Morrow	. . . .	O 374	Irene	V 21
And intermix'd my Praises with his own;	. . . . .	O 299	Irene	44
Descend, to sweeten Labours once your own.	. . . .	O 306	Irene	56
When Asia's Nations own me for their Lord,	. . . .	O 306	Irene	5
Inflame her Crimes, exalt your own Obedience,	. . . .	O 329	Irene	14
By crimes abhord, and treasons not her own	. . . .	Y 217	Irene	V 10A
Far dearer than his own or father's life	. . . .	Y 18	Tr. Iliad Bk 6	6
Or their own souls with hopes of vict'ry fir'd."	. . .	Y 19	Tr. Iliad Bk 6	59
To his own house her did lug.	. . . . .	Y 301	Extemp. Elegy	16

OWN'D

| Which prostrate Memphis own'd her deities. | . . . . . . | Y 4 | On a Daffodill | 16 |

OWNS

| No faith of partnership dominion owns; | . . . . . . | O 140 | Tr Rambler 183 | 1 |

OXEN

| How pleas'd beholds his Oxen bow | . . . . | O 73 | Hor. Epode II | 69 |
| He sees the wearied Oxen bow | . . . . | O 73 | Hor. Epode II | V 69 |

OYL

| Two bowls with oyl and milk I'll yearly crown, | . . . . | Y 7 | Virgil Daphnis | 45 |

PACIFIC

| No joys to him pacific scepters yield, | . . . . | O 40 | Vanity Wishes | 197 |

PACIFY

| And publick mournings pacify the skies; | . . . . . . | O 19 | London | 197 |

PAGAN

| With Raptures such as fire the Pagan Crouds, | . . . . | O 286 | Irene | 3 |

PAGE

| Thy satire point, and animate thy page. | . . . . | O 23 | London | 263 |
| And turn'd th' instructive Page of Human Life, | . . . . | O 281 | Irene | 33 |

PAGEANT

| Those pageant Honours which he scorn'd below: | . . . . | O 57 | Prologue Comus | 22 |
| No regal Pageant deck'd with casual Honours, | . . . . | O 268 | Irene | 19 |

PAGEANTRIES

| To paint the Pageantries of guilty State? | . . . . . | O 276 | Irene | 12 |

PAGEANTRY

| I swear this Eastern Pageantry is Nonsense, | . . . . . | O 247 | Irene Epilogue | 13 |

PAID

| No spies were paid, no special juries known, | . . . . | O 22 | London | 252 |
| No bribes were paid, no special juries known, | . . . . | Y 61 | London | V 252 |

PAIN

Nor light nor darkness bring his pain relief,	. . . .	O 32	Vanity Wishes	43
Unconquer'd lord of pleasure and of pain;	. . . . .	O 40	Vanity Wishes	196
Diffuse the tuneful lenitives of pain:	. . . . . .	O 43	Vanity Wishes	268
And yield the tuneful lenitives of pain:	. . . . . .	O 43	Vanity Wishes	V 268
Diffuse the soothin lenitives of pain:	. . . . . .	Y 104	Vanity Wishes	V 268
And social sorrow loses half its pain:	. . . . . .	O 59	Pro Good Nat'd	4
Their foes attacks, and wield their arms with pain.	. .	O 76	Tr Add. Battle	27
Nor give the generous pain, the worthless joy:	. . . .	O 81	Lady Birthday	14
But when your Musick sooths the raging pain,	. . . .	O 96	Hickman Spinet	6
Ah! how shall envy sooth her pain?	. . . .	O 122	Stella Mourn.	12
Unhappy! whom to beds of pain	. . . .	O 125	An Ode	9
Let pain deserv'd without complaint be borne.	. . . .	O 131	Tr. Rambler 32	1
Nor Cadmus, scap'd the shafts of pain,	. . . . .	O 136	Tr Rambler 128	4
Then with no throbbing fiery pain,	. . . . . .	O 202	Death Dr Levet	33
Then with no throbs of fiery pain,	. . . .	O 202	Death Dr Levet	V 33
Do they with Pain repress the struggling Shout,	. . . .	O 270	Irene	24
Each piercing Torture, every Change of Pain,	. . . .	O 326	Irene	44
Shed floods of tears, and sympathiz'd in pain.	. . . .	Y 21	Tr. Iliad Bk 6	129

PAINS

And dreaded losses aggravate his pains;	. . . . .	O 44	Vanity Wishes	286
Condemn'd to everduring pains.	. . . .	O 69	Hor.II Ode 14	20
All pains, all cares, may favouring heav'n remove,	. .	O 81	Lady Birthday	₅5
To ease their pains exert your milder power,	. . . .	O 84	Epi Dist Moth.	46
I felt thy Pains, and trembled for Aspasia.	. . . .	O 251	Irene	75
The Hopes and Fears, the Joys and Pains of Life,	. . .	O 265	Irene	7
Whence all the pleasures, and the pains of love.	. . .	Y 148	Irene	V 42
Short be thy Pains.	. . . .	O 328	Irene	49
The Pains I labour'd to conceal	. . . .	Y 11	Tr Hor Epode 9	15

PAINT

No maid to flatter, and no paint to hide.	. . . . .	O 84	Epi Dist Moth.	41
To paint the Pageantries of guilty State?	. . . . .	O 276	Irene	12
And paint the horrors of the dreadfull day.	. . . .	Y 22	Tr Add. Battle	7

```
                                                    PAGE    TITLE          LINE
PAINTED
    From every room descends the painted face,      O  33 Vanity Wishes        83
    From every wall descends the painted face,      Y  95 Vanity Wishes    V   83
    The painted meads and Forrests nigh             O  73 Hor. Epode II    V   61
PAINTING
    ... of her own Painting                         O 120 To Miss Playing      T
PAINTINGS
    Some peaceful vale with nature's paintings gay; O  11 London               46
PAINTS
    And vegetation paints the plain.                O 125 An Ode                8
    Paints future Joys, and points to distant Glories.  O 261 Irene            17
PALACE
    Some pompous palace, or some blissful bow'r,    O  18 London              185
    And spread his flaming palace on the ground,    O  19 London              195
    The regal palace, the luxurious board,          O  35 Vanity Wishes       115
    The pompous palace, the luxurious board,        Y  96 Vanity Wishes   V  115
    The plunder'd palace or sequester'd rent;       O  39 Vanity Wishes       170
    From ev'ry Palace burst a mingled Clamour,      O 251 Irene                70
    Adorns my Palace with its brightest Virgins;    O 263 Irene                15
    Remote from Tumult, in th' adjoining Palace,    O 263 Irene                 1
    Conduct these Queens, Abdalla, to the Palace:   O 269 Irene                40
    Attend these queens, Abdallah, to the (palace)  Y 137 Irene            V   40
    Has Treason's dire Infection reach'd my Palace? O 272 Irene                 2
    Treason so near us?  lurking in our Palace      O 369 Irene            V   20
    Th' approaching Sultan forc'd me from the Palace;  O 299 Irene            47
    When next we meet before we storm the Palace,   O 308 Irene                28
    Abdalla, while we waited near the Palace,       O 316 Irene                25
    Haste, Murza, to the Palace, let the Sultan     O 319 Irene                 2
    Come let us seek new Pleasures in the Palace,   O 323 Irene                17
    Hence to the palace and your maids repair;      Y  21 Tr. Iliad Bk 6      121
    Then sought the palace where the menial train   Y  21 Tr. Iliad Bk 6      128
PALACES
    Let such raise palaces, and manors buy,         O  12 London               57
    Shall mourn no more her plunder'd Palaces.      O 278 Irene                78
    Again her prostrate Palaces should rise,        O 291 Irene                54
    Than ruind palaces or flaming temples           Y 177 Irene            V111D
PALAION
    Oisi memele phusis, metron charis, erga palaion,  O 171 Epi. Goldsmith     3
PALE
    He left the name, at which the world grew pale, O  41 Vanity Wishes       221
    When pale, and anxious for their Years to come, O 287 Irene                 4
    Guilt and Despair! pale Spectres, grin around me,  O 328 Irene            50
PALE-FAC'D
    When pale-fac'd Cynthia sheds her silver light  O  77 Tr Add. Battle       45
PALL
    Now pall the tasteless meats, and joyless wines,  O  43 Vanity Wishes     265
PALL'D
    Their Rage, and pall'd their Appetite of Murder;  O 249 Irene              8
PALLADIUM
    That hung the bright Palladium of the place,    O  33 Vanity Wishes        84
    That hung on high Palladium of the place,       Y  95 Vanity Wishes    V   84
PAMPER'D
    Perplex the fawning niece and pamper'd guest,   O  44 Vanity Wishes       276
    The dull conjecture fawning niece and pamper'd guest,  Y 104 Vanity Wishes V 276
PAMPHLET
    The pamphlet spreads, incessant hisses rise,    O  82 Young Author         25
PANDER
    See the Jocky, see the Pander,                  O 196 Song Congratu.       19
    Call the Jocky, call the Pander,                O 196 Song Congratu.   V   19
PANG
    Contrive new Racks, imbitter every Pang,        O 334 Irene                74
PANGS
    The bitter pangs of slighted love?              O  72 Hor. Epode II        46
    Whilst you deride their pangs in barb'rous play,  O  83 Epi Dist Moth.      7
    The pangs of guilty pow'r, and hapless love,    O 113 Epit. Phillips        2
    The pangs of guilty pow'r, or hapless love,     O 113 Epit. Phillips    V   2
    While t' asswage the Pangs of Love              O 149 Tr Boet III.12       15
    With silent Pangs I view the tow'ring Domes,    O 251 Irene                62
    Think on th' insulting Scorn, the conscious Pangs,  O 266 Irene            19
    His glowing Wishes, and his jealous Pangs.      O 280 Irene                28
    If e'er thy Youth has known the Pangs of Absence,  O 285 Irene             3
    Will not th' Apostate feel the Pangs of Guilt,  O 294 Irene               132
    To feel no more the Pangs of Separation.        O 303 Irene                24
    Reserv'd to all the Pangs of tedious Death.     O 312 Irene                25
    These Tears, these Pangs, these last Remains of Life,  O 329 Irene         53
PANTA
    Tei Kallous dunamei ti telos; Zeus panta dedoken  O 103 Eis Elisses        1
PANTED
    And panted on the brink of violation            Y 124 Irene            V  112
PANTING
    All fird with hope, and panting to be great;    Y  95 Vanity Wishes    V   74
    For faith, that panting for a happier seat,     O  48 Vanity Wishes       363
    For hope, that panting for a happier seat,      Y 108 Vanity Wishes    V  363
    And panting Time toil'd after him in vain:      O  51 Pro Drury-Lane        6
    So the young author panting for a name,         O  82 Young Author         11
    So the young author panting after fame,         O  82 Young Author     V   11
    Elate with Hope, and panting for a Foe.         O 304 Irene                 5
PANTOMIME
    And Pantomime, and Song, confirm'd her Sway.    O  52 Pro Drury-Lane       38
PANTS
    That struggling pants, and rowls her eye-balls round.  O  76 Tr Add. Battle  15

                            241
```

PANTS   (CONTINUED)

	PAGE	TITLE	LINE
He pants for room, in one poor World confin'd.	O 97	Hickman Spinet	12
The Man who pants for ample Sway	O 146	Tr Boeth III.5	1
Pants for the dread Event--But let us reason--	O 280	Irene	31

PAPHIEN

Kai toios Paphien plexen eroti Thean.	O 172	On Marlborough	2

PARADISE

And fit her for the joys of paradise:--	Y 130	Irene	V 11
Heav'n has reserv'd no future Paradise,	O 276	Irene	17
At once the Joys of Paradise and Empire,	O 308	Irene	7
And taint the sweets of Paradise with envy	Y 184	Irene	V 9
pleasures of Paradise	Y 184	Irene	V 10

PARAPHRASE

Or rather a Paraphrase.	O 117	Epitaph Hanmer	V T

PARASITE

The supple Gaul was born a parasite:	O 16	London	124

PARDON

Henceforth be wise, nor hope a second Pardon	O 323	Irene	3
Who calls for Pardon from a Wretch condemn'd?	O 323	Irene	4

PARENT

The lyon's thirsty parent, bore.	O 66	Hor I Ode xxii	V 16
The Lion's thirsty Parent, bore.	O 67	To A. Fuscus	16
Parent of ills! and source of all our woe!	O 77	Festina Lente	10
Parent of thousand wild desires,	O 99	Ode Friendship	6
Parent of Rage and hot desire,	O 99	Ode Friendship	V 6
The same their Parent and their King.	O 146	Tr Boeth III.6	4
Vain expence the parent of necessity the parent of corruption	O 347	Irene	V 26
Vain expence the parent of necessity the parent of corruption	O 347	Irene	V 26
Tainted by Sloth, the Parent of Sedition,	O 309	Irene	20

PARENTS

The parents smil'd, the chief his helm unbound	Y 20	Tr. Iliad Bk 6	95

PARIS

The common shore of Paris and of Rome;	O 14	London	94
The common sewer of Paris and of Rome;	O 14	London	V 94

PARK

Could'st thou resign the park and play content,	O 19	London	210
Could thou resign the park and court content,	Y 58	London	V 210

PARLY

That thus you parly with detected Treason?	O 327	Irene	15

PART

Who play from morn to night a borrow'd part;	O 16	London	135
From every part, the gaudy vassals come,	Y 57	London	V 202
Translation of part of the Dialogue between	O 74	Tr. Iliad Bk 6	T
Part turn their Backs, part seiz'd with wild surprise	O 76	Tr Add. Battle	28
Part turn their Backs, part seiz'd with wild surprise	O 76	Tr Add. Battle	28
To have the fiftieth Part her paultry Share?	O 247	Irene Epilogue	6
That joins us thus, will never part us more.	O 296	Irene	39
If we must part--	O 297	Irene	11
If we must part--	O 297	Irene	12

PARTED

And through the parted Shade disclos'd the Greeks,	O 269	Irene	11

PARTERRE

Now each parterre with thorny brakes is fill'd	Y 7	Virgil Daphnis	24

PARTIAL

Shou'd partial Cat-calls all his Hopes confound,	O 246	Irene Prologue	23

PARTICULAM

the Particulam) strikes me with greater horror	Y 176	Irene	V111C

PARTING

And load with Perjuries his parting Soul?	O 272	Irene	5

PARTNERS

Two Men unknown, the Partners of his Bosom;	O 275	Irene	80

PARTNERSHIP

No faith of partnership dominion owns;	O 140	Tr Rambler 183	1

PARTS

Mark'd out by dangerous parts he meets the shock,	O 39	Vanity Wishes	171
It parts you now--The hasty Sultan sign'd	O 296	Irene	1
Count not these Hours as Parts of vulgar Time,	O 302	Irene	5

PARTY

I drew to my party with (alluring) promises artfull	Y 158	Irene	V 11

PASS

In croud at once, where none the pass defend,	O 46	Vanity Wishes	337
The limits fix'd they strive to pass in vain;	O 76	Tr Add. Battle	36
How sweet in sleep to pass the careless hours,	O 135	Tr Rambler 117	1
Nor dare to pass th' insuperable Bound.	O 292	Irene	92

PASS'D

Th' important Hour had pass'd unheeded by,	O 269	Irene	12
And pass'd uninjur'd through the Walks of Death?	O 296	Irene	29

PASSAGE

A surer Passage to his hated Heart.	O 307	Irene	25
Suspend thy Passage to the Seats of Bliss,	O 308	Irene	9
Seize him this Night, and through the private Passage	O 312	Irene	23
To guide thy Passage shall th' aerial Spirits	O 322	Irene	7
To Guide thy passage shall th' Starry Spirits	O 364	Irene	V 26

PASSAGES

And shuts up all the passages of joy:	O 43	Vanity Wishes	260

PASSENGER

And give the weary passenger refreshment.	Y 130	Irene	V 12D
And chear the weary Passenger with Musick.	O 277	Irene	38
And chear the weary passenger with warblings	O 355	Irene	V 21

		PAGE	TITLE		LINE
PASSES					
	And bar the Passes of Irene's Mind	O 265	Irene		10
PASSING					
	Deign on the passing world to turn thine eyes, ...	O 38	Vanity Wishes		157
	Each passing day some comfort sorrow finds.	Y 105	Vanity Wishes	V	301
PASSION					
	And unresisted Passion storm'd the Breast.	O 51	Pro Drury-Lane		8
	Till Declamation roar'd, while Passion slept.	O 52	Pro Drury-Lane		32
	Till Declamation soar'd, whilst Passion slept. . . .	O 52	Pro Drury-Lane	V	32
	Impell'd by passion, and with folly blind.	O 134	Tr Rambler 105		2
	And lawless Passion, hold the Sword of Justice. . . .	O 256	Irene		54
	In Passion lost, he bad the conqu'ring Fair	O 258	Irene		99
	And teach me to repell the Sultan's Passion.	O 265	Irene		3
	And Gales of softer Passion fan my Bosom.	O 275	Irene		93
	And softer passion steals upon my Bosom	O 367	Irene	V	14
	Some petty Passion! some domestick Trifle!	O 280	Irene		7
	This sov'reign Passion, scornful of Restraint, ...	O 280	Irene		18
	Because my slighted Passion burns in vain!	O 281	Irene		49
	Did ever Passion make so swift a Progress?	O 281	Irene		55
	every traytor inclination each traytor passion	Y 158	Irene	V	11
	Purge well thy Mind from ev'ry private Passion, . . .	O 298	Irene		6
	But virtuous Passion prompts the great Resolve, . . .	O 303	Irene		18
	Dar'st thou thus dally with Abdalla's Passion?	O 307	Irene		8
	The Gleams of Reason, and the Clouds of Passion, . . .	O 321	Irene		44
	While unavailing passion crouds your tongue	O 368	Irene	V	14
	By vice or passion driv'n	O 345	Irene	V	26
PASSION'S					
	How passion's well-accorded strife	O 121	To Miss Playin		31
PASSIONS					
	And mould his passions till they make his will. . . .	O 44	Vanity Wishes		282
	Obedient passions, and a will resign'd;	O 48	Vanity Wishes		360
	Your passions; guide the reins with steady hand, . . .	O 77	Festina Lente		4
	The swelling passions to compose, ...	O 126	An Ode		39
	Must bid his Passions all obey;	O 146	Tr Boeth III.5		2
	What Passions reign among thy Crew, Leontius? . . .	O 270	Irene		21
	Beats not the female Breast with gen'rous Passions, . .	O 278	Irene		57
	Our distant Int'rests, and our different Passions . . .	O 287	Irene		3
	And find our Passions not infus'd in vain.	O 297	Irene		22
	My Bosom harrass'd with alternate Passions, ...	O 299	Irene		54
	At once a Thousand Passions fir'd his Cheek:	O 317	Irene		31
	Nor trust our Passions with her fatal Charms. . . .	O 332	Irene		31
	Tumultuous passions strugle in her breast	Y 21	Tr. Iliad Bk 6		109
PASSIVE					
	Nor shall the passive Coward once complain.	O 111	To Posterity		26
	Made passive Fortitude the Praise of Woman.	O 290	Irene		44
PAST					
	In vain, these dangers past, your doors you close, . .	O 21	London		236
	Soon fades the rose; once past the fragrant hour, . .	O 133	Tr. Rambler 71		1
	What soon is perfect, soon alike is past;	O 142	In Baretti Bk.		9
	Soon those nine lives would be past.	O 194	On Thrale Hat		4
	If chasing past Events with vain Pursuit, ...	O 255	Irene		5
	The Present, Past, and Future swim before me, . . .	O 295	Irene		13
	Then all is past he cried--and darted from us; . . .	O 317	Irene		32
	That Hope is past;	O 324	Irene		12
PATEI					
	Aphrosi me semnen, Xeine, podessi patei	O 171	Epi. Goldsmith		2
PATH					
	Nor e'er from virtue's path was lur'd aside, ...	O 118	Epitaph Hanmer		31
	Path, motive, guide, original, and end.	O 130	Tr. Rambler 7		8
	Prescribes the dreadfull comet's flaming path . . .	Y 167	Irene	V	124
	And mortals trace th' Almighty's path in v<ain> . . .	Y 217	Irene	V	14
PATHLESS					
	No pathless waste, or undiscover'd shore;	O 18	London		171
	Send me to wander on some pathless Shore, ...	O 328	Irene		35
PATHS					
	To tread the dreary paths without a guide, ...	O 31	Vanity Wishes		8
	Nor e'er from virtue's paths was turn'd aside, ...	O 118	Epitaph Hanmer	V	31
	For us alone, they Honour's Paths pursue;	O 247	Irene Epilogue		16
	But bids you rove the Paths of Bliss, secure	O 276	Irene		18
	And in the (paths) of war and desolation	Y 150	Irene	V	71
	Guides erring Mortals to the Paths of Virtue, . . .	O 289	Irene		18
	And trace the paths of providence in vain.	Y 217	Irene	V	15
PATIENCE					
	For patience sov'reign o'er transmuted ill;	O 48	Vanity Wishes		362
	His studious Patience, and laborious Art, ...	O 51	Pro Drury-Lane		11
	Nor press too much upon a Lover's Patience.	O 310	Irene		9
	But Cries and Tears are vain, prepare with Patience . .	O 328	Irene		40
PATIENT					
	The patient Suff'rer, and the faithful Wife.	O 58	Prologue Comus		32
PATRIAM					
	<H>oc fonte derivat<a> clades--In patriam populumque . .	O 347	Irene	V	22
	fluxit.				
PATRIOT					
	To vote a patriot black, a courtier white;	O 11	London		52
	Our supple tribes repress their patriot throats, . . .	O 34	Vanity Wishes		95
	Ye patriot Crouds, who burn for England's Fame, . . .	O 57	Prologue Comus		1
	Will not the Patriot share the Traytor's Danger? . . .	O 300	Irene		62
	Nor lose in Love the Patriot and the Hero.	O 303	Irene		15
PATRIOT'S					
	The Patriot's fire yet sparkled in the friend.	O 118	Epitaph Hanmer		40
	The Warrior's Ardour, and the Patriot's Zeal;	O 255	Irene		4

	PAGE	TITLE	LINE
PATRIOT'S (CONTINUED)			
The Lover's Int'rest aids the Patriot's Claim.	O 305	Irene	46
PATRIOTS			
Where blasted patriots never shrunk to peers	Y 94	Vanity Wishes	V 60A
Sign her foes' doom, or guard her patriots zeal,	Y 95	Vanity Wishes	V 92
Ye sacred Shades of Patriots and of Martyrs;	O 306	Irene	52
Ye venerable ghosts of noble patriots	Y 181	Irene	V 53
PATRON			
And as their patron hints the cold or heat, ...	O 16	London	142
Toil, envy, want, the patron, and the jail.	O 38	Vanity Wishes	160
PATRONESS			
Greece, in her lovely Patroness secure, ...	O 278	Irene	77
PATRONS			
The Drama's Laws the Drama's Patrons give, ...	O 53	Pro Drury-Lane	53
Immortal Patrons of succeeding Days, ...	O 57	Prologue Comus	5
Obsequious, at his Patrons gates;	O 71	Hor. Epode II	16
PAULTRY			
To have the fiftieth Part her paultry Share? . . .	O 247	Irene Epilogue	6
PAUSE			
And pause awhile from letters, to be wise;	O 38	Vanity Wishes	158
And pause awhile from Learning to be wise;	O 38	Vanity Wishes	V 158
Pause at this tomb where Hanmer's ashes lie;	O 117	Epitaph Hanmer	2
Pause on this tomb where Hanmer's ashes lie;	O 117	Epitaph Hanmer	V 2
Nor made a pause, nor left a void;	O 201	Death Dr Levet	26
Nor made a pause, nor felt a void;	O 201	Death Dr Levet	V 26
A sudden Pause th' imperfect Sense suspended, . . .	O 270	Irene	13
Allow no Pause for Art or for Contrivance;	O 275	Irene	88
Now pause, great Bassa, from the Thoughts of Blood, .	O 285	Irene	1
we are in danger by this pause	Y 206	Irene	V 11
Or but one Moment's Pause betray Confusion, ...	O 332	Irene	15
PAY			
Or pay with speaking Eyes a Lover's Homage?	O 282	Irene	63
The swains shall pay their vows, and thou shalt hear their prayer.	Y 7	Virgil Daphnis	52
PAYMENT			
Let one great payment every claim appease, ...	O 62	Pro Word Wise	11
PAYS			
The farmer annuall honours pays	O 73	Hor. Epode II	64
Her solemn honours pays.	O 78	Feast St Simon	12
When to the nymphs the swain due homage pays . . .	Y 7	Virgil Daphnis	V 51
PEACE			
Increase his riches and his peace destroy;	O 32	Vanity Wishes	40
On ev'ry stage the foes of peace attend, ...	O 33	Vanity Wishes	77
Speak thou, whose thoughts at humble peace repine, .	O 35	Vanity Wishes	121
Peace courts his hand, but spreads her charms in vain; .	O 40	Vanity Wishes	201
Peace courts his hand, her fondness he disdains .	Y 101	Vanity Wishes	V 201
And bids afflicted worth retire to peace. . . .	O 45	Vanity Wishes	310
Secure with Peace, with Competence, to dwell, . . .	O 58	Prologue Comus	35
To dismal realms, and regions void of peace, . . .	O 84	Epi Dist Moth.	30
Of plenteous peace, and prosp'rous war;	O 189	Epilogue	2
Learn here that Peace from Innocence must flow; . .	O 246	Irene Prologue	13
And when blest Peace has silenc'd War's Alarms, . .	O 247	Irene Epilogue	23
That links the jarring Elements in Peace.	O 257	Irene	64
And sink into the silent Grave in Peace.	O 264	Irene	12
What! think of Peace while haughty Scanderbeg . . .	O 264	Irene	13
Nor dream of peace, think of rest	Y 130	Irene	V 13
Then dream of Prayer, and Pilgrimage, and Peace. . .	O 265	Irene	45
Then dream of (prayer), or (vows) and pilgrimage and peace,	Y 132	Irene	V 45
Through shades of peace and flowery labyrinths	Y 146	Irene	V 21
Would break the sacred laws of peace and order . . .	O 352	Irene	V 3
And wish too late for Innocence and Peace?	O 294	Irene	133
And Peace propitious smile on fond Desire;	O 302	Irene	119
And still thy Bosom with the Voice of Peace. . . .	O 303	Irene	22
And from the Mansions of perpetual Peace	O 306	Irene	55
The Breast where Virtue guards the Throne of Peace. .	O 316	Irene	15
The breast where truth supports the throne of peace. .	Y 193	Irene	V 15
Remember, Peace and Anguish are before thee, . . .	O 321	Irene	37
Scream in the nests and brood their young in peace. .	Y 23	Tr Add. Battle	35
PEACEFUL			
Some peaceful vale with nature's paintings gay; . .	O 11	London	46
The peaceful slumber, self-approving day, ...	O 14	London	89
No peaceful desart yet unclaim'd by Spain?	O 18	London	173
Whose peaceful day Benevolence endears, ...	O 44	Vanity Wishes	295
Forsakes his rural seats and peaceful home, ...	O 81	Young Author	2
Forsakes his rural sports and peaceful home, ...	O 81	Young Author	V 2
Their hungry Swarms the peaceful Vale shall fright .	O 110	To Posterity	9
Sleep undisturb'd within this peaceful shrine, . . .	O 113	Epit. Phillips	5
And bears me to the peaceful shades, ...	O 125	An Ode	15
Lead a long and peaceful Age, ...	O 145	Tr Boeth. II.4	21
The busy day, the peaceful night, ...	O 202	Death Dr Levet	29
No soothing Interval of peaceful Sorrow;	O 249	Irene	12
Unprofitable, peaceful, female Virtues!	O 280	Irene	12
With peaceful Death, and Happiness eternal. . . .	O 328	Irene	47
PEACEFULL			
Seek out some peacefull Convents holy Shade	O 348	Irene	V 24
PEAR			
Plucking the blushing Grape and Pear, ...	O 72	Hor. Epode II	26
Red her cheek as Cath'rine pear, ...	Y 300	Extemp. Elegy	6

		PAGE	TITLE		LINE
PEASANT					
When first the peasant, long inclin'd to roam,		O 81	Young Author		1
PEASANTS					
Shall glutton on the industrious Peasants Spoil,		O 110	To Posterity		13
PECULIAR					
Friendship! peculiar boon of heav'n,		O 99	Ode Friendship		1
Friendship! peculiar Gift of heav'n,		O 99	Ode Friendship	V	1
PEERS					
Where blasted patriots never shrunk to peers		Y 94	Vanity Wishes	V	60A
PELEUS					
Nor Peleus, grandson of the sky,		O 136	Tr Rambler 128		3
PELIDES'					
And stain'd with blood Pelides' vengefull steel.		Y 18	Tr. Iliad Bk 6		37
PENANCE					
Mocks the dull Vows of Solitude and Penance,		O 264	Irene		27
PENETRATING					
Th' enlivening Wit, the penetrating Reason?		O 278	Irene		56
The Sparkling Wit the penetrating Reason		O 356	Irene	V	23
PENITENCE					
May Penitence attend thy mournful Bed,		O 322	Irene		61
PENITENT					
to be guilty, though penitent		Y 165	Irene	V	81
PENNANCE					
fasting, pennan\<ce\> and works of goodness		O 348	Irene	V	15
PENS					
And all the pens of Cupid's wing		O 127	To Lyce, Lady		19
PENSION					
Despise a fool in half his pension dress'd,		O 13	London		73
PENSION'D					
With well-feign'd gratitude the pension'd band		O 19	London		200
PENSIONS					
Here let those reign, whom pensions can incite		O 11	London		51
Shames the mean Pensions of Augustan Times;		O 57	Prologue Comus		4
PENSIVE					
Pensive and listning to the beating Surge.		O 254	Irene		128
To wander pensive in those gloomy walks		Y 165	Irene	V	85
Pensive, and envious of Irene's Greatness.		O 314	Irene		12
PEOPLE					
Still odious to the Monarch, or the People.		O 256	Irene		52
Where King and People own one common Law		O 352	Irene	V	16
And show Irene to the shouting People:		O 303	Irene		28
The fruitfull fields th' industrious people till'd,		Y 23	Tr Add. Battle		28
PEOPLE'S					
Now joins thy People's, and thy Cali's Prayers,		O 308	Irene		8
PEOPLED					
All Men throughout the peopled Earth		O 146	Tr Boeth III.6		1
PERENNIAL					
Perennial roses deck each purple vale,		O 84	Epi Dist Moth.		16
PERFECT					
What soon is perfect, soon alike is past;		O 142	In Baretti Bk.		9
PERFECTION					
Wilt thou descend, fair Daughter of Perfection,		O 276	Irene		1
Irene rise, thou daughter of perfection--or beauty		Y 145	Irene	V	1
While some Archangel nearer to Perfection,		O 293	Irene		121
PERFIDIOUS					
Perfidious!--yes--too well thou know'st them Traytors.		O 324	Irene		17
Whate'er perfidious villany can suffer		Y 216	Irene	V	75
PERFIDY					
And leave no Place for Perfidy or Fear.		O 255	Irene		33
Broke out in Perfidy--Oh curs'd Aspasia,		O 316	Irene		10
PERFORM					
Leave to perform my Pilgrimage to Mecca;		O 258	Irene		87
PERFORM'D					
This task perform'd, he sought no gainful post,		O 118	Epitaph Hanmer		27
Thine Orders, mighty Sultan! are perform'd,		O 330	Irene		3
PERFUME					
When rip'ning fruits perfume the year,		O 72	Hor. Epode II		25
My second, expresses a Syrian perfume;		O 179	Charade!		2
PERHAPS					
Perhaps if Skill could distant Times explore,		O 53	Pro Drury-Lane		41
Perhaps, where Lear has rav'd, and Hamlet dy'd,		O 53	Pro Drury-Lane		43
Perhaps, for who can guess th' Effects of Chance?		O 53	Pro Drury-Lane		45
Perhaps, enamour'd of resembling Virtue,		O 252	Irene		96
Perhaps the flood of time now rolls towards us		Y 117	Irene	V	108
Whose Soul, perhaps, yet mindful of Aspasia,		O 267	Irene		39
Perhaps the Clouds of dark Conspiracy		O 275	Irene		74
A weeping Wife perhaps, or dying Friend,		O 280	Irene		9
He comes, perhaps, to separate us forever;		O 294	Irene		6
Perhaps in vain the Sultan's Anger spar'd me,		O 298	Irene		32
Perhaps the Phantoms of a Woman's Fear,		O 300	Irene		71
Perhaps may start at violated Friendship.		O 300	Irene		81
Contrive perhaps, the Ruin of our Empire,		O 312	Irene		2
Perhaps ev'n now the Lovers unpursu'd		O 322	Irene		4
Perhaps yourselves the Villains that defame me,		O 326	Irene		38
Perhaps her Malice might transfer the Charge,		O 327	Irene		18
Perhaps her pois'nous Tongue might blast Abdalla.		O 327	Irene		19
Perhaps my Zeal too fierce betray'd my Prudence;		O 330	Irene		20
Perhaps my Warmth exceeded my Commission;		O 330	Irene		21
Perhaps I will not stoop to plead my Cause;		O 330	Irene		22
Perhaps I will not bend to plead my cause		Y 210	Irene	V	22

PERHAPS   (CONTINUED)   PAGE   TITLE   LINE
        Thy Life perhaps--Were but Irene spar'd, ...   O 332 Irene   33
PERI
        Eis to tes Elisses peri ton Oneiron Ainigma   . . . . O 103 Eis Elisses   T
PERIOD
        And give the Tortures of Suspence a Period? . . . . . O 282 Irene   2
PERIODS
        And mark the future Periods of the Stage?-- . . . . . O 53 Pro Drury-Lane   40
PERISH
        And strangled Freedom perish in the Birth. . . . . .   O 299 Irene   53
        Unmov'd I saw the glitt'ring Trifles perish, ... O 302 Irene   108
        And perish ere he tastes the Joys of Conquest. . . . . O 308 Irene   33
        Advance, and perish in the frantic Boast. . . . . .   O 318 Irene   7
        You perish (for) by your folly not your zeal. . . . . Y 198 Irene   V 32
        Decreed to perish in Irene's Chamber! . . . .   O 331 Irene   17
        Hector shall perish by no warriour's hand. . . . . .   Y 21 Tr. Iliad Bk 6   116
PERISH'D
        Well if a Thousand Lives like thine had perish'd; . . . O 332 Irene   34
PERISHABLE
        "For wealth or title, perishable prize; . . . . . .   O 82 Young Author   16
PERJURIES
        And load with Perjuries his parting Soul? . . . . .   O 272 Irene   5
PERJURY
        Who start at theft, and blush at perjury? . . . . .   O 13 London   68
        And frowns on Perjury, Revenge and Murder. . . . . .   O 300 Irene   58
PERMANENT
        Thy pleasures, permanent as great, ...   O 100 Ode Friendship   23
PERMITS
        Permits the blooming maid secure and thoughtless . . . Y 146 Irene   V 18
PERMITTED
        Permitted oft, though not inspir'd by Heav'n, ... O 300 Irene   65
PERPETUAL
        Attend this Prelude of perpetual Praise! . . . . . .   O 57 Prologue Comus   6
        O'er the sad plains perpetual tempests sigh; . . . .   O 84 Epi Dist Moth.   32
        Immur'd, and buried in perpetual Sloth, ...   O 292 Irene   81
        And from the Mansions of perpetual Peace . . . . . .   O 306 Irene   55
PERPLEX
        Perplex the fawning niece and pamper'd guest, ... O 44 Vanity Wishes   276
PERPLEX'D
        When mutual frauds perplex'd the maze of State, . . . O 118 Epitaph Hanmer   24
PERPLEXITY
        And dark Perplexity distracts my Counsels. . . . . .   O 275 Irene   89
        Lost in a wild Perplexity of Joy. . . . .   O 295 Irene   14
PERSECUTING
        How virtue wars with persecuting fate; . . . . . .   O 19 London   199
PERSECUTION
        And Persecution boast the Call of Heav'n. . . . . .   O 291 Irene   66
        Fierce persecution wears the bleeding world with . . . Y 164 Irene   V 66
            fraud
        Or Persecution drank, attend our Call; . . . . . .   O 306 Irene   54
PERSIA
        And Persia felt the force of Grecian steel; . . . . . O 76 Tr Add. Battle   38
PERSIA'S
        From Persia's tyrant to Bavaria's lord. . . . . . .   O 41 Vanity Wishes   224
PERSIAN
        The haughty Persian in thy gore . . . .   O 80 Feast St Simon   53
        And arm the Persian Heretick against thee; . . . . .   O 274 Irene   55
        Or set The Persian Heretic in arms against Me . . . . O 348 Irene   V 17
PERSONATE
        who was to personate the Ghost of Hermione . . . . .   O 83 Epi Dist Moth.   T
PERSUADE
        Let him persuade me to it--if he can: . . . .   O 247 Irene Epilogue   4
PERSUADING   SEE ILL-PERSUADING
PERSUASION
        Teach me the Grecian arts of soft persuasion . . . .   O 349 Irene   V 27
        Assist her Efforts with thy strong Persuasion; . . .   O 321 Irene   34
PERSUASIVE
        In ev'ry speech persuasive wisdom flow'd, ...   O 118 Epitaph Hanmer   15
        With all the allurements of persuasive . . . . . .   Y 142 Irene   V 38
            wealth--gold
PERSUE
        With equal zeal persue the task of war . . . . . .   Y 131 Irene   V 30
        Persue thy course through boiling eddies, ...   Y 201 Irene   V 10A
PERSUE'D
        With rage implacable he still persue'd . . . . . .   Y 24 Tr Add. Battle   84
PERSUED
        Maxims like these, if generally persued . . . . . .   O 352 Irene   V   2
PERSUES
        This, only this, the rigid law persues, ...   O 17 London   V 160
        Nor whilst she Simons acts persues . . . .   O 80 Feast St Simon   49
        The traveller persues the flatt'ring wandring . . . . Y 155 Irene   V 34
            splendor
        If Fate persues me, let it find me here . . . . . .   O 297 Irene   V 18
PERT
        This night our wit, the pert apprentice cries, ... O 60 Pro Good Nat'd   23
PERU
        Survey mankind, from China to Peru; . . . .   O 30 Vanity Wishes   2
        O'erlook mankind, from China to Peru; . . . .   Y 91 Vanity Wishes   V 2
PERUS'D
        Thou that hast long perus'd the Draughts of Nature, . . O 255 Irene   11

		PAGE	TITLE	LINE
PERVERSE				
Had we not been perverse and careless grown,	• • • •	O 64	Virgil Past.I	21
PERVERSELY				
Perversely grave, or postively wrong.	• • • • • • •	O 43	Vanity Wishes	274
Perversely grave, and positively wrong.	• • • • • • •	Y 104	Vanity Wishes	V 274
PERVERSENESS				
The mind of mortals, in perverseness strong,	• • • •	O 136	Tr Rambler 132	1
PEST				
Wide-wasting pest! that rages unconfin'd,	• • • • •	O 31	Vanity Wishes	23
PETITIONS				
Enquirer, cease, petitions yet remain,	• • • • • •	O 47	Vanity Wishes	349
PETTIUS				
Pettius no more I verses write;	• • • • • • • • •	Y 10	Tr Hor Epode 9	1
PETTY				
A petty fortress, and a dubious hand;	• • • • • • •	O 41	Vanity Wishes	220
No petty gain disdain'd by pride,	• • • • • • •	O 201	Death Dr Levet	22
No feeble Tyrant of a petty State	• • • • • • •	O 268	Irene	21
Some petty Passion! some domestick Trifle!	• • • •	O 280	Irene	7
And thought the petty Dross beneath a Sigh.	• • • • • •	O 302	Irene	109
The petty Claims of Empire and of Honour!	• • • • •	O 307	Irene	23
PETULANCE				
The daughter's petulance, the son's expence,	• • • •	O 44	Vanity Wishes	280
Let no resentful petulance invade	• • • •	O 61	Pro Word Wise	9
Let no revengeful petulance invade	• • • •	O 61	Pro Word Wise	V 9
PHANTOMS				
As treach'rous phantoms in the mist delude,	• • • •	O 31	Vanity Wishes	9
Nor Melancholy's phantoms haunt thy shade;	• • • • •	O 37	Vanity Wishes	154
Dismiss the pleasing Phantoms for an Hour.	• • • • • •	O 246	Irene Prologue	6
Perhaps the Phantoms of a Woman's Fear,	• • • • • •	O 300	Irene	71
Disease shall chase the Phantoms of Ambition,	• • • •	O 322	Irene	60
PHARSALIA				
Rouse from the grave the rivals of Pharsalia	• • • •	Y 185	Irene	V 39
PHASIS				
That drink the Phasis or the Rhone.	• • • • • •	O 70	Hor.II Ode XX	20
PHEREI				
Ommasi lampra Dios Kupris oista pherei.	• • • • •	O 103	Eis Elisses	6
PHILANDER'S				
Adorn Philander's head, or grace his tomb.	• • • • •	O 95	Sprig of Myrtl	14
PHILIPS				
An Epitaph upon the celebrated Claudy Philips,	• • • •	O 113	Epit. Phillips	V T
PHILLIPS				
An Epitaph on Claudy Phillips, a Musician	• • • • •	O 113	Epit. Phillips	T
On Claudius Phillips, an excellent Musician	• • • •	O 113	Epit. Phillips	V T
Epitaph on Claude Phillips, an Itinerant Musician	• • •	O 113	Epit. Phillips	V T
Phillips! whose touch harmonious could remove	• • •	O 113	Epit. Phillips	1
PHILOSOPHERS				
Could Philosophers contrive	• • • • • • • • • •	O 178	Thrale 35 Year	5
PHILOSOPHIC				
And pierce each scene with philosophic eye.	• • • • •	O 33	Vanity Wishes	64
PHILOSOPHY				
Philosophy remain'd, though Nature fled.	• • • • • •	O 52	Pro Drury-Lane	34
And weak Philosophy denies her Succours.	• • • • • •	O 252	Irene	92
PHLOGOENTI				
Zeus mounos phlogoenti poleis ekperse kerauno,	• • • •	O 103	Eis Elisses	5
PHOEBUS				
Unhurt by Phoebus fi'ry ray.	• • • • • • • • •	O 72	Hor. Epode II	36
Just Phoebus would devote his plant to thee.	• • • •	O 106	Eliza plucking	8
Where radiant Phoebus rising from the sea	• • • • •	Y 23	Tr Add. Battle	22
PHRASE				
Phrase that Time has flung away,	• • • • • • •	O 179	Ridicul Warton	5
There in soft Hints and in ambiguous Phrase,	• • • •	O 254	Irene	129
PHUSIKON				
Klaiete poieten, historikon, phusikon.	• • • • • •	O 171	Epi. Goldsmith	4
PHUSIS				
Oisi memele phusis, metron charis, erga palaion,	• • • •	O 171	Epi. Goldsmith	3
PHYSIC				
Our bane and physic the same earth bestows,	• • • • •	O 131	Tr. Rambler 21	1
PICTURE				
And tread the living picture in the dust	• • • • • •	Y 177	Irene	V111B
PICTURES				
Thy pictures shall thy conduct frame,	• • • • • • •	O 121	To Miss Playin	33
PIECE				
Toil crush'd conceit, and man was of a piece;	• • • •	O 32	Vanity Wishes	54
Where aught of bright, or fair, the piece displays,	• •	O 62	Pro Word Wise	15
Let ev'ry piece be simple and be one.	• • • • • •	O 137	Tr Rambler 139	1
PIECES SEE FLOWER-PIECES				
PIERC'D				
Arose to Heav'n, and pierc'd my bleeding Breast,	• • •	O 251	Irene	74
Ended her wretched life and pierc'd her heart.	• • • •	Y 19	Tr. Iliad Bk 6	43
PIERCE				
And pierce each scene with philosophic eye.	• • • • •	O 33	Vanity Wishes	64
I pierce the Clouds a tunefull Swan.	• • • • • •	O 70	Hor.II Ode XX	12
In a low vale by rocks that pierce the skies	• • • •	Y 23	Tr Add. Battle	24
PIERCING				
Dart the quick taunt, and edge the piercing gibe?	• • •	O 33	Vanity Wishes	62
And unexhausted laughter, and edge the piercing gibe	• •	Y 94	Vanity Wishes	V 62
Each piercing Torture, every Change of Pain,	• • • •	O 326	Irene	44
Her piercing Cries yet fill the loaded Air,	• • • • •	O 329	Irene	8
PIETY				
Sense, freedom, piety, refin'd away,	• • • • • • •	O 15	London	105
Celestial pow'rs! that piety regard,	• • • • • • • •	O 141	Tr Rambler 208	1

247

PIETY   (CONTINUED)   PAGE   TITLE   LINE
    <E>ach hero fir'd piety or freedom . . . .   Y 181 Irene   V 51
    From generous piety, or abject fear? . . . .   Y 189 Irene   V 1B
PILE
    Orgilio sees the golden pile aspire, ...   O 19 London   208
    Sejano sees the golden pile aspire, ...   Y 58 London   V 208
    When cates luxuriant pile the spacious dish, . . .   O 193 Tr. Medea II   17
    Surveys the glories of the splendid pile . . . . .   Y 131 Irene   V 36A
    And burnt him decent on a funerall pile. . . . . .   Y 18 Tr. Iliad Bk 6   31
PILGRIMAGE
    Leave to perform my Pilgrimage to Mecca; . . . . .   O 258 Irene   87
    This Pilgrimage our Lawgiver ordain'd-- . . . . .   O 264 Irene   23
    Then dream of Prayer, and Pilgrimage, and Peace. .   O 265 Irene   45
    Then dream of (prayer), or (vows) and pilgrimage and . Y 132 Irene   V 45
        peace,
PILOT
    Like Caesar's pilot, dignified by fate, ...   O 59 Pro Good Nat'd   7
    Reason! the tim'rous Pilot, that to shun . . . . .   O 281 Irene   46
PIMP
    And proudly hop'd to pimp in future Days. . . . .   O 52 Pro Drury-Lane   24
PIMPLES
    She's starr'd with pimples o'er, ...   O 127 To Lyce, Lady   14
PINCH
    Nor torturing whalebones pinch them into charms; . . O 84 Epi Dist Moth.   23
PINE
    If Sorrow pine or Av'rice crave, ...   O 146 Tr Boeth III.5   9
PINION
    Beyond the Mists of Care thy Pinion tow'rs. . . . .   O 313 Irene   8
PINIONS
    Scatt'ring, as thy pinions play, ...   O 185 Anacreon Ode 9   3
    "Let me now my pinions ply, ...   O 186 Anacreon Ode 9   43
    Pleasure shall spread her downy Pinions o'er thee .   O 350 Irene   V 21
    And pleasure shall shade thee with her downy . . .   Y 150 Irene   V 83
        pinions
PIOUS
    'tis thine alone to calm the pious breast . . . .   O 130 Tr. Rambler 7   5
    The pious Maid, with modest Indignation, ...   O 258 Irene   101
    With pious Warmth receive our Prophet's Law---- . .   O 262 Irene   25
    This Regal Confidence, this pious Ardour, ...   O 264 Irene   33
    Exhaust the Stores of pious Eloquence, ...   O 265 Irene   2
    O! could the Grave restore the pious Hero, ...   O 267 Irene   42
PIPE
    Play on your pipe beneath this beechen shade; . . .   O 64 Virgil Past.I   2
PIRATES
    And plead for pirates in the face of day; . . . .   O 11 London   54
PIT
    When one a borough courts, and one the pit. . . . .   O 59 Pro Good Nat'd   10
    He rolls no Thunders o'er the drowsy Pit. . . . .   O 246 Irene Prologue   26
PITIED
    I heard her, pitied her, and wish'd to save her. . . O 333 Irene   59
PITY
    Has heaven reserv'd, in pity to the poor, ...   O 18 London   170
    When liberal pity dignify'd delight; . . . . . .   O 62 Pro Word Wise   22
    With pity soften every awful grace, ...   O 84 Epi Dist Moth.   44
    Fly, Wretch, while yet my Pity grants thee Flight; .   O 319 Irene   23
    Dispatch, and learn a fitter Time for Pity. . . .   O 328 Irene   44
    Urg'd us to Speed, and bad us banish Pity, . . .   O 332 Irene   30
PITYING   SEE ALL-PITYING
    Till pitying Nature signs the last release, ...   O 45 Vanity Wishes   309
    He sees, and pitying sees, vain Wealth bestow . . .   O 57 Prologue Comus   21
    A generous foe regards, with pitying eye, ...   O 61 Pro Word Wise   5
    A signal hour marked out by pitying Heav'n . . . .   Y 117 Irene   V 109
    And shed the pitying Tear for lost Irene. . . . .   O 292 Irene   97
    And wing thy latest Pray'r to pitying Heav'n. . .   O 322 Irene   62
PLAC'D   SEE ILL-PLAC'D
    Hard is his lot, that here by Fortune plac'd, . . .   O 53 Pro Drury-Lane   47
    On his dead body let a tomb be plac'd . . . . .   Y   7 Virgil Daphnis   28
    And plac'd the beamy terror on the ground . . . .   Y 20 Tr. Iliad Bk 6   96
    Then on his brow the mighty soldier plac'd . . . .   Y 21 Tr. Iliad Bk 6   124
    Had form'd her nest and plac'd her burthen there, . . Y 23 Tr Add. Battle   45
PLACE
    Grant me, kind heaven, to find some happier place, . O 11 London   43
    That hung the bright Palladium of the place, . . .   O 33 Vanity Wishes   84
    That hung on high Palladium of the place, ...   Y 95 Vanity Wishes   V 84
    Place me where no soft summer gale . . . .   O 66 Hor I Ode xxii   17
    Place me beneath the burning line, ...   O 66 Hor I Ode xxii   21
    Place me where no soft Summer Gale . . . .   O 67 To A. Fuscus   17
    Place me beneath the burning Zone, ...   O 67 To A. Fuscus   21
    Place may be chang'd; but who can change his mind? . O 137 Tr Rambler 135   1
    In every dome, in every sacred place, ...   O 189 Seeing Montagu   3
    And leave no Place for Perfidy or Fear. . . . . .   O 255 Irene   33
    And at the holy place pour out my prayers . . . .   Y 130 Irene   V 12
    Claim but the second Place: there mighty Love . .   O 280 Irene   26
    The Place appointed for his Master's Death. . . . .   O 326 Irene   30
PLAGUES
    What Plagues, what Tortures, are in Store for thee, . O 334 Irene   1
PLAIN
    Nor showers immerse the verdant plain; . . . . .   O 67 Hor. II Ode IX   2
    Swords, arms and wings are scatter'd o'er the plain . O 76 Tr Add. Battle   18
    The plain contested flows with mingled blood. . . .   O 76 Tr Add. Battle   21
    Scatters their breathless bodies o'er the plain. . . O 76 Tr Add. Battle   32

248

```
PLAIN        (CONTINUED)                                    PAGE    TITLE           LINE
    And wander sportive o'er th' Elysian plain:    . . . . . .  O  77 Tr Add. Battle     43
    Despotic o'er the desolated Plain,    . . . . . . . .       O 111 To Posterity       20
    Nor only through the wasted plain,    . . . . . .           O 123 Winter's Walk        5
    Nor only thought the wasted plain,    . . . . . .           O 123 Winter's Walk     V  5
    And vegetation paints the plain.    . . . . . . . .         O 125 An Ode               8
    And vegetation plants the plain.    . . . . . . . .         O 125 An Ode            V  8
    When fruitful summer loads the teeming plain,   . . . .     O 151 The Ant              7
    The changing year renews the plain,    . . . . . .          O 231 Tr Horace IV.7       3
    It spreads the wide plain an unregarded ruin.    . . .      Y 131 Irene          V 36C
    In vain the lab'ring hind manures the plain,    . . . .     Y   6 Virgil Daphnis      22
    Affrighted views; and looking o'er the plain    . . . .     Y  23 Tr Add. Battle      32
PLAINS
    That silent cuts the dreary plains,    . . . . . .          O  69 Hor.II Ode 14       18
    For you, ye fair, I quit the gloomy plains,    . . . . .    O  83 Epi Dist Moth.      10
    O'er the sad plains perpetual tempests sigh;    . . . .     O  84 Epi Dist Moth.      32
    For you fair Asia spreads her wealthy plains.    . . . .    Y 132 Irene          V 41C
    As when a Deluge overspreads the Plains,    . . . . .       O 280 Irene               22
    Too well I know him, since on Thracia's Plains    . . .     O 307 Irene               18
    And banish'd sorrow flies the joyous plains;    . . . .     Y   7 Virgil Daphnis      37
    And with laborious crouds the plains were fill'd.   . . .   Y  23 Tr Add. Battle      29
PLAN
    Direct the rivulets, and plan the bow'rs;    . . . . .      Y  58 London         V 217
    The changing year's successive plan    . . . . . .          O 231 Tr Horace IV.7       7
    And plan the Happiness of mourning Millions?    . . . .     O 291 Irene               68
PLANETS
    I trace the planets and survey the skies.    . . . . .      O 130 Tr. Rambler 8        2
    And weary Planets loiter in their Courses.    . . . . .     O 262 Irene                4
    Directs the Planets with a careless Nod,    . . . . .       O 293 Irene              123
PLANS
    His vast Designs, his Plans of boundless Pow'r.    . . .    O 265 Irene               41
    His vast designs, and plans of boundless Empire.    . . .   O 356 Irene          V  29
PLANT
    Just Phoebus would devote his plant to thee.    . . . .     O 106 Eliza plucking       8
PLANTED
    And planted elms around his monument    . . . . . . .       Y  18 Tr. Iliad Bk 6      33
PLANTS
    And plants, unseen, a dagger in your breast.    . . . .     O  21 London         V 241
    And vegetation plants the plain.    . . . . . . .           O 125 An Ode          V  8
    <And> plants for his prattling babes the future shade       Y 122 Irene          V  62
PLATE
    The polish'd marble, and the shining plate,    . . . . .    O  19 London              207
    The golden canopy, the glitt'ring plate,    . . . . . .     O  35 Vanity Wishes       114
PLATONIC
    Truth in platonic ornaments bedeck'd,    . . . . . .        O 134 Tr. Rambler 96       1
PLAY
    Some pleasing bank where verdant osiers play,    . . .      O  11 London              45
    Who play from morn to night a borrow'd part;    . . . .     O  16 London              135
    Could'st thou resign the park and play content,    . . .    O  19 London              210
    With ev'ry Meteor of Caprice must play,    . . . . .        O  53 Pro Drury-Lane       49
    This night presents a play, which publick rage,    . . .    O  61 Pro Word Wise        1
    Play on your pipe beneath this beechen shade;    . . .      O  64 Virgil Past.I        2
    <Or> sees from far his Bullocks play    . . . . . .         O  71 Hor. Epode II       20
    While the breeze whispers and the streamers play.   . .     O  82 Young Author         6
    Whilst you deride their pangs in barb'rous play,    . .     O  83 Epi Dist Moth.       7
    When in your Eyes resistless Lightnings play,    . . .      O  96 Hickman Spinet       3
    Scatt'ring, as thy pinions play,    . . . . . .             O 185 Anacreon Ode 9       3
    "Round his chamber dance and play,    . . . . . .           O 186 Anacreon Ode 9      36
    They to the dome where smoke with curling play    . .       O 192 Tr. Medea II         5
    With nimble glide the skaiters play;    . . . . . .         O 203 Tr. on Skating  V  2
    Those forms of men that play before a    . . . . . .        Y 173 Irene          V  18
        beauty
    Shall play the glance, and with attentive watch    . .      Y 195 Irene          V   4
    And balmy spirits thro' thy foliage play,    . . . . .      Y   3 On a Daffodill      10
    May balmy spirits thro thy foliage play,    . . . . . .     Y   3 On a Daffodill  V  10
PLAY'D
    Play'd fearless in th' inviolated Shades.    . . . . .      O 314 Irene                7
    Play'd on her Cheek--So shone the first Apostate--    . .   O 330 Irene               11
PLAYING
    To Miss Hickman playing on the Spinet    . . . . . . .      O  96 Hickman Spinet       T
    To Miss <Carpenter> On her playing upon the Harpsicord  .   O 120 To Miss Playin       T
PLAYS
    Surveys your Plays with inattentive Glance,    . . . .      O 276 Irene               22
    Plays on the quiv'ring Waves, to guide our Flight,   . .    O 306 Irene               59
PLEAD
    And plead for pirates in the face of day;    . . . . .      O  11 London              54
    What Claim hast thou to plead?    . . . . . . . .           O 286 Irene                8
    Our bleeding Bosoms plead Irene's Cause.    . . . . .       O 328 Irene               39
    Perhaps I will not stoop to plead my Cause;    . . . .      O 330 Irene               22
    Perhaps I will not bend to plead my cause    . . . .        Y 210 Irene          V  22
    While she yet beg'd to plead her Cause before thee.   .     O 334 Irene               67
PLEADS
    Demetrius justly pleads a double Title,    . . . . . .      O 305 Irene               45
PLEAS'D
    And Sedley curs'd the form that pleas'd a king.    . . .    O  46 Vanity Wishes       322
    They pleas'd their Age, and did not aim to mend.    . .     O  52 Pro Drury-Lane       22
    How pleas'd he sees his Cattle come,    . . . . . .         O  73 Hor. Epode II       67
    How pleas'd beholds his Oxen bow    . . . . . . .           O  73 Hor. Epode II       69
    They, pleas'd, thro' barb'rous nations roam    . . . .      O  79 Feast St Simon      29
    Pleas'd with the scene the smiling ocean yields,    . .     O  81 Young Author    V   3
    Less pleas'd to triumph than to spare.    . . . . . .       O 137 Tr Rambler 143       2
```

PLEAS'D   (CONTINUED)

	PAGE	TITLE	LINE
I pleas'd my Master, and I pleas'd my Dame.	O 174	Tr Epitaph Dog	2
I pleas'd my Master, and I pleas'd my Dame.	O 174	Tr Epitaph Dog	2
Well pleas'd to find thy Precepts not forgotten. . . .	O 267	Irene	41
Then pleas'd, and conscious of Superiour	O 369	Irene	V 6
Greatness			
Well pleas'd to search the Treasures of Remembrance, . .	O 323	Irene	15
Pleas'd with the conquest, he forebore the spoil . . .	Y 18	Tr. Iliad Bk 6	30

PLEASE

	PAGE	TITLE	LINE
Studious to please, and ready to submit, ...	O 16	London	123
Till conquest unresisted ceas'd to please, ...	O 34	Vanity Wishes	107
He views, and wonders that they please no more; . . .	O 43	Vanity Wishes	264
He views, and wonders why they please no more; . . .	Y 104	Vanity Wishes	V 264
To please in Method, and invent by Rule;	O 51	Pro Drury-Lane	10
For we that live to please, must please to live. . .	O 53	Pro Drury-Lane	54
For we that live to please, must please to live. . .	O 53	Pro Drury-Lane	54
And him who cannot hurt, allow to please;	O 62	Pro Word Wise	12
To please by scenes unconscious of offence, ...	O 62	Pro Word Wise	13
So much my Appetite would please	O 73	Hor. Epode II	60
Ambitious only now to please the Fair, ...	O 97	Hickman Spinet	18
Delighted still to please mankind, or mend, ...	O 118	Epitaph Hanmer	39
But though the numbers for a moment please, ...	O 142	In Baretti Bk.	5
Studious to please, yet not asham'd to fail. . . .	O 246	Irene Prologue	30
To please his Fancy,--see no other Man--	O 247	Irene Epilogue	3
But how the Devil should he please us all!	O 247	Irene Epilogue	8
For those who could not please by nobler Service.-- .	O 264	Irene	24
If Greatness please thee, mount th' imperial Seat; .	O 279	Irene	84

PLEASING

	PAGE	TITLE	LINE
In pleasing dreams the blissful age renew, ...	O 10	London	25
Some pleasing bank where verdant osiers play, . . .	O 11	London	45
Rais'd from some pleasing dream of wealth and pow'r, .	O 18	London	184
And leave our pleasing fields and native home, . . .	O 64	Virgil Past.I	4
Your shady Groves, your pleasing wife, ...	O 69	Hor.II Ode 14	21
In pleasing Dreams he cheats the Day	O 72	Hor. Epode II	35
And fir'd with pleasing hope of endless fame, . . .	O 82	Young Author	12
And weaves her bending boughs in pleasing glooms; . .	O 84	Epi Dist Moth.	15
Thou see'st one pleasing form arise, ...	O 121	To Miss Playin	26
Nor from the pleasing groves depart, ...	O 125	An Ode	18
Dismiss the pleasing Phantoms for an Hour.	O 246	Irene Prologue	6
If Truths like these with pleasing Language join; . .	O 246	Irene Prologue	15
That Wealth, too pleasing to be lost for Freedom! . .	O 250	Irene	21
In pleasing Visions, and assuasive Dreams;	O 253	Irene	102
In pleasing Visions, and delusive Dreams;	O 253	Irene	V 102
With coy Caresses and with pleasing Wiles	O 260	Irene	128
And unaccustom'd warblings charm the grove (pleasing .	Y 150	Irene	V 86
disson<ance>			
And list'ning to the pleasing Tale of Pow'r, . . .	O 303	Irene	30
More than a pleasing Sound without a Meaning, . . .	O 310	Irene	13
Like one awaken'd from a pleasing dream, ...	Y 4	On a Daffodill	26
With pleasing sound allur'd the rural throng. . . .	Y 6	Virgil Daphnis	8

PLEASURE

	PAGE	TITLE	LINE
The robes of pleasure and the veils of woe:	O 33	Vanity Wishes	66
Unconquer'd lord of pleasure and of pain;	O 40	Vanity Wishes	196
Whom Pleasure keeps too busy to be wise, ...	O 46	Vanity Wishes	324
When pleasure fired her torch at Virtue's flame, . .	O 62	Pro Word Wise	23
To pluck the flow'rs of pleasure or of pride. . . .	O 118	Epitaph Hanmer	32
And pleasure propagates around	O 121	To Miss Playin	5
Soft Pleasure with her laughing train, ...	O 125	An Ode	6
Pomp and Pleasure, Pride and Plenty	O 196	Song Congratu.	3
Each Pleasure brightens at its near Approach, . . .	O 261	Irene	20
These Days of Love and Pleasure charm not thee; . .	O 271	Irene	2
These Hours assign'd to Pleasure and Irene.	O 272	Irene	15
pleasure	Y 146	Irene	V 21
Let Pleasure bloom and Cities reascend.	O 372	Irene	V 10
Bid Pleasure bloom and Cities reascend.	O 372	Irene	V 10
Pleasure shall spread her downy Pinions o'er thee . .	O 350	Irene	V 21
And pleasure shall shade thee with her downy . . .	Y 150	Irene	V 83
pinions			
If Pleasure charm thee, view this soft Retreat; . .	O 279	Irene	85
And new forms of pleasure shall be invented	O 350	Irene	V 25
Impartial weigh the Pleasure with the Danger. . . .	O 285	Irene	9
pleasure, ...	Y 158	Irene	V 8
The Love of Pow'r, of Pleasure, and of Show. . . .	O 287	Irene	13
Sacred to Love, to Pleasure, and Irene:	O 308	Irene	2
And Songs of Pleasure warble from the Tongue, . . .	O 315	Irene	30
Pleasure in ev'ry nymph and shepherd reigns, . . .	Y 7	Virgil Daphnis	36

PLEASURE'S

	PAGE	TITLE	LINE
O'er treacherous pleasure's flow'ry ground	O 203	Tr. on Skating	V 3

PLEASURES

	PAGE	TITLE	LINE
Would not these pleasures soon remove	O 72	Hor. Epode II	45
Such Pleasures quickly would remove	O 72	Hor. Epode II	V 45
Around them pleasures wait, and joys for ever new. .	O 84	Epi Dist Moth.	27
Thy pleasures, permanent as great, ...	O 100	Ode Friendship	23
Thy pleasures, lasting, as they're great, ...	O 100	Ode Friendship	V 23
Thy pleasures, charms as great, ...	Y 71	Ode Friendship	V 23
Snatch thy pleasures while they last;	O 194	On Thrale Hat	2
Snatch your pleasures while they last;	O 194	On Thrale Hat	V 2
Whence all the pleasures, and the pains of love. . .	Y 148	Irene	V 42
Indulgent nature gives some transient pleasures . .	Y 148	Irene	V 43C
And share the Pleasures of the World	O 348	Irene	V 20
between Us			

PLEASURES (CONTINUED)	PAGE	TITLE	LINE
Sunk in his Pleasures, confident and gay,	O 283	Irene	8
Sooth her with all the Pleasures of Command,	O 287	Irene	17
To fix his Court, and regulate his Pleasures,	O 291	Irene	78
To form his Court and regulate his pleasures	Y 164	Irene	V 78
pleasures of Paradise	Y 184	Irene	V 10
Demetrius towrd--Above the Female pleasures	O 371	Irene	V 2
Are these th' unceasing Joys, th' unmingled Pleasures	O 314	Irene	16
Fly from the busy Pleasures of her Sex,	O 322	Irene	14
Come let us seek new Pleasures in the Palace,	O 323	Irene	17
And secret pleasures sparkled in his eyes.	Y 18	Tr. Iliad Bk 6	16
With Hector's life away my pleasures fly.	Y 18	Tr. Iliad Bk 6	27
Which gave a thousand pleasures birth.	Y 39	Lady Leaving	8
PLEDGE			
Pledge of their love and source of all their joy	Y 18	Tr. Iliad Bk 6	10
PLEIAD'S			
And seat him in the Pleiad's golden Chariots,	O 274	Irene	63
PLENTEOUS			
To snatch the blessings of the plenteous day;	O 151	The Ant	6
Of plenteous peace, and prosp'rous war;	O 189	Epilogue	6
PLENTY			
Fair plenty, gracious Queen, shou'd pour	O 144	Tr Boeth. II.2	5
"Then with luscious plenty gay	O 186	Anacreon Ode 9	35
The board with varied plenty crown'd	O 191	Tr. Medea I	19
Pomp and Pleasure, Pride and Plenty	O 196	Song Congratu.	3
Where Commerce lavish'd unexhausted Plenty,	O 251	Irene	64
To scatter Happiness and Plenty round thee,	O 278	Irene	69
PLEXEN			
Kai toios Paphien plexen eroti Thean.	O 172	On Marlborough	2
PLIES			
He plies the press, and hurries on his fate;	O 82	Young Author	20
Her tongue like nimble lightning plies,	O 127	To Lyce, Lady	15
PLIGHTED			
That fatal Beauty plighted to Demetrius	O 307	Irene	15
PLOT			
Intrigue was Plot, Obscenity was Wit.	O 52	Pro Drury-Lane	20
Intriguing Wits! his artless Plot forgive;	O 246	Irene Prologue	19
The Plot all Cali's, the Detection thine.	O 329	Irene	4
PLOUGH			
The Horse shall trample, or the Plough shall break,	O 110	To Posterity	2
For you shall plough the main, and fight the battle	Y 146	Irene	V 23B
PLOW			
And faintly draw th' inverted Plow.	O 73	Hor. Epode II	70
PLUCK			
To pluck a titled Poet's borrow'd wing;	O 13	London	70
Insatiate pluck the Fruit, and crop the Flow'r:	O 110	To Posterity	12
To pluck the flow'rs of pleasure or of pride.	O 118	Epitaph Hanmer	32
PLUCKING			
Plucking the blushing Grape and Pear,	O 72	Hor. Epode II	26
To Eliza plucking Laurel in Mr Pope's Gardens	O 106	Eliza plucking	T
PLUMAGE			
(His various plumage sporting in the wind)	O 74	Tr. Iliad Bk 6	2
PLUME			
Shall plume her Charms, and, with attentive Watch,	O 318	Irene	4
PLUMES			
By plumes is viel'd; see! quick as thought	O 70	Hor.II Ode XX	11
They prune the Wing, and spread the glossy Plumes,	O 277	Irene	36
PLUMP			
She was once as cherry plump	Y 300	Extemp. Elegy	5
PLUND'RER			
Another Plund'rer brought the bright Irene;	O 259	Irene	118
PLUNDER			
To such, the Plunder of a Land is giv'n,	O 13	London	V 65
Refund the plunder of the beggar'd land.	O 19	London	201
Refund the plunder of the begger'd land.	O 19	London	V 201
One shews the plunder, and one hides the thief.	O 32	Vanity Wishes	44
Spreads wide the hope of plunder and of praise;	O 43	Vanity Wishes	248
And brought his beauteous Plunder to the Sultan.	O 258	Irene	96
The hungry Janizary burns for Plunder,	O 309	Irene	21
PLUNDER'D			
The plunder'd palace or sequester'd rent;	O 39	Vanity Wishes	170
Shall mourn no more her plunder'd Palaces.	O 278	Irene	78
PLUNG'D			
By thee Orestes plung'd his vengefull dart	O 77	Festina Lente	13
PLUTO			
Till at length stern Pluto cried,	O 149	Tr Boet III.12	39
PLUTO'S			
On cruel Pluto's Altar dye,	O 69	Hor.II Ode 14	6
Shuns Pluto's kingdoms and the realms of night;	Y 7	Virgil Daphnis	33
PLY			
"Let me now my pinions ply,	O 186	Anacreon Ode 9	43
The fraudful Moments ply their silent Wings,	O 327	Irene	8
The treacherous moments ply their silent wings	Y 206	Irene	V 8
PLY'D			
The guardians yield, by force superior ply'd;	O 47	Vanity Wishes	339
The guardians yield, with force resistless ply'd;	Y 107	Vanity Wishes	V 339
POCKETS			
Pockets full, and Spirits high,	O 196	Song Congratu.	22
PODESSI			
Aphrosi me semnen, Xeine, podessi patei	O 171	Epi. Goldsmith	2

```
POEM                                                      PAGE    TITLE         LINE
     London: A Poem  . . .  . . . . . . . . . . .  .   O    7 London              T
POET
     Forbear to hiss--the Poet cannot hear.  . . . . .  O   62 Pro Word Wise     18
     A Poet double-form'd I rise,  . . . . . . .  .   O   70 Hor.II Ode XX      2
     For Nature form'd the Poet for the King.  . . .    O  114 On C. Cibber
     Hebrus heard her Poet groan,  . . . . . . .  .    O  148 Tr Boet III.12   V  7
     Conjuring Poet take thy Bride!  . . . . . .  .    O  150 Tr Boet III.12     40
     Alike must fall the poet and his theme.  . . . .  Y    4 On a Daffodill     28
POET'S
     To pluck a titled Poet's borrow'd wing;  . . .    O   13 London            70
     Their schemes of spite the poet's foes dismiss,  .  O   60 Pro Good Nat'd  19
     Oft favours, oft rejects the poet's pray'r:  . . .  O   95 Sprig of Myrtl  V  6
POETRY
     There Poetry shall tune her sacred Voice,  . . .   O  302 Irene            122
POETS
     Let vulgar Poets sing,  . . . . . . . . .  .   O   78 Feast St Simon      3
     By flatt'ring poets giv'n;  . . . . . . . .  .    O  126 To Lyce, Lady      2
     The Dream of idle Maids and wanton Poets  . . .    O  350 Irene            V  1
POIETEN
     Klaiete poieten, historikon, phusikon.  . . . . .  O  171 Epi. Goldsmith    4
POIGNANT
     Oft has he seen the poignant orange fly,  . . .    Y   67 Prologue Lethe    9
POINT
     Thy satire point, and animate thy page.  . . . .  O   23 London           263
     To point a moral, or adorn a tale.  . . . . . .   O   41 Vanity Wishes    222
     To point each glance, and force it to the heart!  .  O   81 Lady Birthday   8
     To point the glances of her eye,  . . . . . .  .   O  121 To Miss Playin   16
     And point vindictive Lightnings at Rebellion,  . .  O  300 Irene          61
     Heav'n turns its point upon the guilty Heart  . .  O  345 Irene           V 29
     Temper their swords and point their missive darts.  .  Y   24 Tr Add. Battle  77
POINTED
     Lay pointed at our Batt'ries yet unform'd,  . . .  O  273 Irene            25
     Why has thy Choice then pointed out Leontius,  . .  O  305 Irene           20
     Or fix'd the pointed arrows in their hearts.  . . .  Y   23 Tr Add. Battle  43
POINTS
     Than when a blockhead's insult points the dart.  .  O   18 London         169
     Delusive hope still points to distant good,  . . .  O  133 Tr. Rambler 67   2
     Paints future Joys, and points to distant Glories.  .  O  261 Irene         17
     And kind Ambition points the Way to Greatness.  . .  O  280 Irene          14
POIS'NOUS   SEE POYS'NOUS
     And pois'nous vapours, black'ning all the sky,  . .  O   84 Epi Dist Moth.  33
     Suspected still?--What Villain's pois'nous Tongue  .  O  304 Irene          12
     Perhaps her pois'nous Tongue might blast Abdalla.  .  O  327 Irene          19
POISON'D
     With slavish tenets taint our poison'd youth,  . .  O   12 London          55
POLAR
     "And all be mine beneath the polar sky."  . . . .  O   40 Vanity Wishes   204
     "And all is mine beneath the polar sky."  . . . .  O   40 Vanity Wishes  V 204
POLE
     But where the Realms beneath the Pole  . . . . .  O   79 Feast St Simon   44
POLEIS
     Zeus mounos phlogoenti poleis ekperse kerauno,  . .  O  103 Eis Elisses     5
POLICY
     The Courtier's Policy, the Sage's Firmness,  . . .  O  255 Irene            3
     My Policy shall raise an easy Throne;  . . . . .  O  257 Irene            78
POLISH
     Or bid soft Science polish Britain's Heroes:  . . .  O  293 Irene         106
     Or bid fair Science polish Britains Heroes  . . .  O  348 Irene           V 22
POLISH'D
     The polish'd marble, and the shining plate,  . . .  O   19 London         207
     Polish'd with endless toil, my lays  . . . . .  .  O  139 Tr Rambler 169   1
     Unfit for Toil, and polish'd into Weakness,  . . .  O  290 Irene           43
     Of light reflected from the polish'd brass  . . .  Y   20 Tr. Iliad Bk 6  93
POLITICIAN'S
     Break through the Politician's tedious Forms,  . .  O  259 Irene          106
     The Politician's Arts, and Heroe's Flame.  . . . .  O  307 Irene           27
POLITICKS
     Their air, their dress, their politicks import;  . .  O   15 London        110
POLITICS
     Preach thy dull Politics to vulgar Kings,  . . . .  O  265 Irene           39
POLLUTE
     Nor mingled Guilt pollute the sacred Cause!  . . .  O  300 Irene           64
     Will cloud my Triumphs, and pollute the Day.  . . .  O  310 Irene           3
POLLUTES
     Pollutes his banquet and insults his guest;  . . .  O  130 Tr. Rambler 12   2
POLLUTION
     And Rapine and Pollution mark their Way.  . . . .  O  110 To Posterity     8
POMP
     Here beauty's drops her pomp, despis'd, distress'd  . .  Y  107 Vanity Wishes  V 341
     To chase the Charms of Sound, the Pomp of Show,  . .  O   53 Pro Drury-Lane  59
     In all the pomp of heav'n;  . . . . . . . .  .   O  126 To Lyce, Lady      4
     With me retire and leave the pomp of courts  . . .  O  137 Tr Rambler 138   1
     Pomp and Pleasure, Pride and Plenty  . . . . .  .  O  196 Song Congratu.   3
     I come from empty Noise, and tasteless Pomp,  . . .  O  262 Irene            7
     Forbear this lavish Pomp of dreadful Praise;  . . .  O  268 Irene           33
     If yet this shining Pomp, these sudden Honours,  . .  O  289 Irene            1
     With gloomy State and agonizing Pomp.  . . . . .  O  294 Irene           135
     The horrid pomp of ostentatious woe  . . . . .  .  Y  168 Irene          V 135
POMPEY'S
     And wept unhappy Pompey's hapless fate?  . . . . .  Y   22 Tr Add. Battle  15
```

```
                                                         PAGE    TITLE              LINE
POMPOUS
     Some pompous palace, or some blissful bow'r,    . . . .   O  18 London              185
     The pompous palace, the luxurious board,        . . . .   Y  96 Vanity Wishes     V 115
     The senate's thanks, the gazette's pompous tale, . . .    O  39 Vanity Wishes       177
     All times their scenes of pompous woes afford,  . . . .   O  41 Vanity Wishes       223
     For what are pompous Titles, proud Alliance,    . . . .   O 267 Irene                 8
     The pompous theatre the tow'ring arch . . . . . .        Y 177 Irene             V 109
     In pompous numbers ancient heroes rise;   . . . . . .    Y  22 Tr Add. Battle        8
POND'ROUS
     Rolls with eternal Toil the pond'rous Orbs;  . . . . .   O 293 Irene               120
POOR
     Has heaven reserv'd, in pity to the poor,    . . . . .   O  18 London              170
     Their prudent insults to the poor confine;   . . . . .   O  21 London              233
     The balmy kiss, for which poor Thyrsis dies;    . . .     O  84 Epi Dist Moth.       21
     He pants for room, in one poor World confin'd. . . . .   O  97 Hickman Spinet       12
       Musician, who died very poor  . . . . . . .            O 113 Epit. Phillips      V T
       at Bridgnorth, Salop; who died very poor      . . .    O 113 Epit. Phillips      V T
     The poor distinctions of a flying moment . . . . . .     Y 177 Irene             V110A
     The nymphs bewail'd poor Daphnis' hapless death  . . .   Y   6 Virgil Daphnis        1
POPE
     Were Pope once void of wonted candour found,    . . .    O 106 Eliza plucking        7
POPE'S
     To Eliza plucking Laurel in Mr Pope's Gardens   . . .    O 106 Eliza plucking        T
     Pope's hallow'd glades, and never tiring views,  . . .   O 106 Eliza plucking        3
POPULACE
     A factious Populace, luxurious Nobles,   . . . . . .     O 250 Irene                38
POPULAR
     But round the lofty Popular twines . . . . . . . .       O  71 Hor. Epode II        17
POPULUMQUE
     <H>oc fonte derivat<a> clades--In patriam populumque .   O 347 Irene             V  22
       fluxit.
PORT
     Assembling nations croud thy port. . . . . . . . .       Y 136 Irene             V  27
     The Rocks of Life, for ever flies the Port.  . . . .     O 281 Irene                47
PORTENTOUS
     No savage more portentous stain'd . . . . . . . .        O  66 Hor I Ode xxii       13
POSITIVELY
     Perversely grave, and positively wrong.  . . . . . .     Y 104 Vanity Wishes     V 274
POSSESS
     Obtain her and possess, thou know'st thy Rival.  . . .   O 307 Irene                17
     lose or I possess her  . . . . . . . . . .               Y 198 Irene             V  32
     The victor Cranes the conquer'd realms possess,  . .     Y  23 Tr Add. Battle       34
POSSESS'D
     Superiour Man possess'd the Charge of Rule,  . . . .     O 291 Irene                71
POST
     Till Shame regain'd the Post that Sense betray'd, . . .  O  52 Pro Drury-Lane       27
     That post, and all the rest, shall be my care;  . . . .  O  74 Tr. Iliad Bk 6        3
     This task perform'd, he sought no gainful post,  . . .   O 118 Epitaph Hanmer       27
POSTERITY
     To Posterity . . . . . . . . . . . . .                   O 110 To Posterity          T
     Beholds a long posterity of freemen   . . . . . .        Y 122 Irene             V  61
     And may a long Posterity of Monarchs,  . . . . . .       O 267 Irene                11
POSTIVELY
     Perversely grave, or postively wrong. . . . . . . .      O  43 Vanity Wishes        274
POT
     Ek Dios estin onar, Theios pot egrapsen Homeros,  . . .  O 103 Eis Elisses           3
POTE
     Sou pote grapsomenon Birchion allon echois. . . . . .    O 108 Eis Birchion          4
POTHER
     Scorn their counsel and their pother, . . . . . . .      O 197 Song Congratu.       27
     Scorn their Nonsense scorn their pother, . . . . . .     O 197 Song Congratu.     V  27
POUR
     To pour at will the counterfeited tear,  . . . . . .     O  16 London              141
     Shews pour the morning worshiper no more;    . . . .     Y  95 Vanity Wishes     V  80
     And pour on misty Doubt resistless day;  . . . . .       O  37 Vanity Wishes       146
     In vain their gifts the bounteous seasons pour,  . . .   O  43 Vanity Wishes       261
     Pour forth thy fervours for a healthful mind,    . .     O  48 Vanity Wishes       359
     Whose mortal wounds pour forth a purple flood,   . . .   O  76 Tr Add. Battle       20
     I too can pour the extemporary song: . . . . . .         O 142 In Baretti Bk.        4
     Fair plenty, gracious Queen, shou'd pour . . . . .       O 144 Tr Boeth. II.2        5
     Pour forth her Dead to warn us of its fall?  . . . .     O 365 Irene             V  22
     To pour my Prayers for thy successful Reign,     . . .   O 264 Irene                10
     And at the holy place pour out my prayers    . . . .     Y 130 Irene             V  12
     Pour forth their Legions, and the roaring Danube . . .   O 264 Irene                17
     Pour forth the Legions and the Wondring Danube   . . .   O 353 Irene             V   1
     Urge me not on to glittering Guilt, nor pour . . . .     O 288 Irene                 5
     Thou fountain of existence I pour the  . . . . . .       Y 189 Irene             V   1
     Th' applauding Sky shall pour forth all its Beams  . .   O 322 Irene                 9
     That pour with sudden Violence on Kingdoms,  . . . .     O 325 Irene                12
     And pour them on the consecrated stone; . . . . . .      Y   7 Virgil Daphnis       46
     Libations he shall pour to Daphnis praise.   . . . . .   Y   7 Virgil Daphnis    V  52
POUR'D
     Where hopeless anguish pour'd his groan, . . . . .       O 201 Death Dr Levet       19
     Where hopeless anguish pour'd the groan, . . . . . .     O 201 Death Dr Levet    V  19
     Profusely pour'd her Bounties upon Woman?    . . . .     O 276 Irene                25
     Heav'n, when its Hand pour'd Softness on our Limbs  . .  O 290 Irene                42
     Pour'd Storms of Fire upon our fierce Invaders,  . . .   O 290 Irene                48
POURD
     He Heav'n, when its hand pourd softness on our limbs . . Y 162 Irene             V  42
     Pourd Storms of fire upon th' approaching Foe . . . .    O 364 Irene             V   1
```

POURS

		PAGE	TITLE	LINE
Pours in the morning worshiper no more;		O 33	Vanity Wishes	80
Down cliffs the roaring Torrent pours		O 72	Hor. Epode II	38
Down the steep hill the roaring torrent pours;		O 132	Tr. Rambler 65	2
When hopeless anguish pours her groan, ...		O 201	Death Dr Levet	V 19
Pours half his Floods unheard through shouting camps . .		O 353	Irene	V 32
Melancholly broods or pours her influence oer the . .		Y 165	Irene	V 82
That pours the dews upon the thristy vales		Y 168	Irene	V135C

POVERTY

And safe in poverty defy'd his foes;		O 11	London	48
All crimes are safe, but hated poverty.		O 17	London	159
Slow Rises Worth, By Poverty Depress'd:		O 18	London	177
Rest here distrest by poverty no more, ...		O 113	Epit. Phillips	3
Rest here oppress'd by poverty no more, ...		O 113	Epit. Phillips	V 3
Give Wealth to Poverty to Slavery Freedom		O 356	Irene	V 13
And sigh for chearful Poverty in vain;		O 292	Irene	84

POW'R

What check restrain your thirst of pow'r and gold? . .		O 13	London	62
Rais'd from some pleasing dream of wealth and pow'r, . .		O 18	London	184
Low skulks the hind beneath the rage of pow'r, ...		O 32	Vanity Wishes	33
In full blown pow'r see mighty Wolsey stand, ...		Y 96	Vanity Wishes	V 99
Claim leads to claim, and pow'r advances pow'r; . .		O 34	Vanity Wishes	106
Claim leads to claim, and pow'r advances pow'r; . .		O 34	Vanity Wishes	106
And pow'r too great to keep, or to resign?		O 36	Vanity Wishes	134
This pow'r has praise, that virtue scarce can warm, . .		O 39	Vanity Wishes	183
Such pow'r has praise, that virtue scarce can charm, . .		Y 100	Vanity Wishes	V 183
Behold surrounding kings their pow'r combine, ...		O 40	Vanity Wishes	199
Tries the dread summits of Cesarean pow'r, ...		O 42	Vanity Wishes	242
Safe in his pow'r, whose eyes discern afar		O 47	Vanity Wishes	353
These goods he grants, who grants the pow'r to gain; . .		O 48	Vanity Wishes	366
For Years the Pow'r of Tragedy declin'd;		O 52	Pro Drury-Lane	30
Thus wak'd to rage by Musick's dreadfull Pow'r, . .		O 97	Hickman Spinet	13
The pangs of guilty pow'r, and hapless love, ...		O 113	Epit. Phillips	2
The pangs of guilty pow'r, or hapless love, ...		O 113	Epit. Phillips	V 2
The nymphs, who found their pow'r decline, ...		O 122	Stella Mourn.	3
I feel thy pow'r usurp my breast.		O 123	An Ode	8
The gen'rous scorn of venal pow'r, ...		O 125	Winter's Walk	31
O thou whose pow'r o'er moving worlds presides, . . .		O 129	Tr. Rambler 7	1
Out of Fortune's Pow'r retreat?		O 144	Tr Boeth. II.4	2
Ah, little needs the Minstrel's pow'r		O 191	Tr. Medea I	17
Can yield no room to Music's soothing pow'r.		O 193	Tr. Medea II	20
Vot'ries of Fame and Worshippers of Pow'r!		O 246	Irene Prologue	5
In Pow'r dependent, in Success deprest.		O 246	Irene Prologue	12
Tho' Wealth, and Pow'r, and Glory they receive, . .		O 247	Irene Epilogue	19
Some Pow'r invisible, from Heav'n or Hell, ...		O 251	Irene	50
Think on the mighty Pow'r of awful Virtue;		O 252	Irene	88
And snatch'd the Reins of abdicated Pow'r		O 256	Irene	45
Such are the Woes when arbitrary Pow'r, ...		O 256	Irene	53
A happy Land, where circulating Pow'r		O 256	Irene	57
His vast Designs, his Plans of boundless Pow'r. . .		O 265	Irene	41
Will not that Pow'r that form'd the Heart of Woman, . .		O 266	Irene	23
Extends his mighty Schemes of Wealth and Pow'r, . .		O 269	Irene	4
To State and Pow'r I court thee, not to Ruin: . .		O 279	Irene	80
The Claim of Pow'r, ...		O 286	Irene	8
Yet in the Use of Pow'r remember Justice. . . .		O 286	Irene	10
The Love of Pow'r, of Pleasure, and of Show. . .		O 287	Irene	13
Suspend awhile the Privilege of Pow'r		O 289	Irene	5
Implor'd the Eternal Pow'r, at Sophia's altars		Y 163	Irene	V 49
Dream not of Pow'r thou never can'st attain:		O 291	Irene	69
The Scale of Justice, and the Sword of Pow'r, ...		O 291	Irene	72
Inform'd they mount the Precipice of Pow'r, ...		O 293	Irene	113
Not Pow'r I blame, but Pow'r obtain'd by Crime, . . .		O 293	Irene	129
Not Pow'r I blame, but Pow'r obtain'd by Crime, . . .		O 293	Irene	129
O say, what guardian Pow'r convey'd thee hither. . .		O 296	Irene	33
Retire, my Fair, that Pow'r that smiles on Goodness . .		O 303	Irene	20
And list'ning to the pleasing Tale of Pow'r, ...		O 303	Irene	30
Wake from thy Dream of Pow'r to Death and Tortures, . .		O 307	Irene	10
Then shall Venetia feel the Turkish Pow'r, ...		O 309	Irene	28
For when was Pow'r beneficent in vain?		O 313	Irene	23
The pow'r of Turkey waits upon my Call.		O 319	Irene	24
The pow'r of Turkey rises at my call		Y 197	Irene	V 24
Now make thy Choice, while yet the Pow'r of Choice . .		O 321	Irene	40
And when, contemptuous of imperial Pow'r, ...		O 322	Irene	59
That Vengeance can invent, or Pow'r inflict.		O 326	Irene	45
Or Flights of Pow'r, or Projects of Ambition.		O 327	Irene	21
From his Escape learn thou the Pow'r of Virtue, . .		O 330	Irene	24
And gainst the pow'r of Venus steel'd my mind.		Y 11	Tr Hor Epode 9	30

POW'R'S

| And ask, what guilty Pow'r's rebellious Hand . . . | | O 293 | Irene | 119 |

POW'RE

| To him the church, the state, their pow're resign, . . | | Y 96 | Vanity Wishes | V 101 |

POW'RFUL

Impeachment stops the speaker's pow'rful breath, . .		O 31	Vanity Wishes	19
His pow'rful Strokes presiding Truth impress'd, . .		O 51	Pro Drury-Lane	7
Those pow'rful Tyrants of the Female Breast		O 261	Irene	12
The pow'rful Voice of Love inflames Demetrius, ...		O 270	Irene	19
And pow'rful Glance, 'tis granted, are our own; . .		O 277	Irene	52
O grant thy sacred Influence, pow'rful Virtue!		O 313	Irene	5

POW'RS

| Some secret cell, ye pow'rs, indulgent give. . . . | | O 11 | London | 49 |
| To him the church, the realm, their pow'rs consign, . . | | O 34 | Vanity Wishes | 101 |

POW'RS	(CONTINUED)	PAGE	TITLE	LINE
In vain surrounding kings their pow'rs combine,		Y 101	Vanity Wishes	V 199
New pow'rs are claim'd, new pow'rs are still bestow'd,		O 42	Vanity Wishes	233
New pow'rs are claim'd, new pow'rs are still bestow'd,		O 42	Vanity Wishes	233
With unexpected legions pow'rs away,		Y 103	Vanity Wishes	V 243
Nor lute nor lyre his feeble pow'rs attend,		O 43	Vanity Wishes	271
Where Beauty lavishes her pow'rs		O 120	To Miss Playin	3
Though favour'd by the pow'rs on high,		O 136	Tr Rambler 128	5
Celestial pow'rs! that piety regard,		O 141	Tr Rambler 208	1
Unnerve thy vigour, and enchain thy pow'rs;		O 151	The Ant	V 10
My reasoning Pow'rs--Dear, hapless, lost Aspasia!		O 252	Irene	78
The Turkish Pow'rs from Europe shall retreat,		O 257	Irene	79
Here recollect thy dissipated Pow'rs.--		O 287	Irene	2
That reign'st supreme among the pow'rs above,		Y 20	Tr. Iliad Bk 6	100
POWDER'D				
This day the powder'd curls and golden coat,		O 60	Pro Good Nat'd	21
POWER SEE POW'R, POW'RE, POWR				
The busy candidates for power and fame,		O 59	Pro Good Nat'd	11
To ease their pains exert your milder power,		O 84	Epi Dist Moth.	46
The power of art without the show.		O 201	Death Dr Levet	16
Why should they fear?--That Power that kindly spreads		O 250	Irene	31
Beyond the Power of Constancy and Courage;		O 251	Irene	53
Unus'd to Power, and form'd for humbler Scenes,		O 268	Irene	17
O seize the Power to bless--Irene's Nod		O 278	Irene	75
Implor'd th' eternal Power to shield my Country,		O 290	Irene	49
(The) pride of Roman (power), and Grecian art		Y 177	Irene	V 111
What Dream of sudden Power		O 323	Irene	1
POWERFUL				
May powerful nature join with grateful art,		O 81	Lady Birthday	7
May powerful nature join with graceful art,		Y 36	Lady Birthday	V 7
Purchasd by thy powerful Song,		O 150	Tr Boet III.12	41
Purchasd by the powerful Song,		O 150	Tr Boet III.12	V 41
The Cause that shrinks from Reason's powerful Voice.		O 293	Irene	126
Turn'd backwards by the powerful Breath of Heav'n.		O 322	Irene	3
POWERFULL				
O could her boasted saints, and powerfull prayers		Y 185	Irene	V 38
Nor with too powerfull rivals strive		Y 11	Tr Hor Epode 9	27
POWERS				
Its charms are fled and all its powers destroyed.		O 142	In Baretti Bk.	8
Dissolve thy vigour, and enchain thy powers?		O 151	The Ant	10
His frame was firm, his powers were bright,		O 202	Death Dr Levet	31
That froze our Veins, and wither'd all our Powers.		O 251	Irene	57
Within the town assemble all thy powers		Y 19	Tr. Iliad Bk 6	50
POWR				
Suspend awhile the privilege of powr (and Beauty)		O 366	Irene	V 21
POYS'NOUS				
And Serpents with their poys'nous breath		O 79	Feast St Simon	41
PRACTICE				
Maxims like these, if once reduc'd to practice		O 352	Irene	V 2
PRACTICES				
And scanning right the practices of yore,		O 192	Tr. Medea II	3
PRACTIS'D				
Practis'd their master's notions to embrace,		O 16	London	136
That oft' had practis'd Fraud, and oft' detected,		O 254	Irene	131
PRAIS'D				
Prais'd without Rapture, left without Regret.		O 263	Irene	18
So late admir'd and prais'd, alas! in vain!		Y 4	On a Daffodill	24
PRAISE				
I praise the hermit, but regret the friend,		O 8	London	4
Wants ev'n the cheap reward of empty praise;		O 10	London	36
Praise evry trifle, ev'ry vice adore,		Y 55	London	V 148
Nor Praise relax, nor Difficulty fright;		O 37	Vanity Wishes	148
This pow'r has praise, that virtue scarce can warm,		O 39	Vanity Wishes	183
Such pow'r has praise, that virtue scarce can charm,		Y 100	Vanity Wishes	V 183
Fresh praise is try'd till madness fires his mind,		O 42	Vanity Wishes	231
New praise is try'd till madness fires his mind,		Y 102	Vanity Wishes	V 231
Spreads wide the hope of plunder and of praise;		O 43	Vanity Wishes	248
For those who durst not censure, scarce cou'd praise.		O 51	Pro Drury-Lane	14
Yet Bards like these aspir'd to lasting Praise,		O 52	Pro Drury-Lane	23
Attend this Prelude of perpetual Praise!		O 57	Prologue Comus	6
Fill the loud Voice of universal Praise,		O 57	Prologue Comus	16
But confident of praise, if praise be due,		O 60	Pro Good Nat'd	29
But confident of praise, if praise be due,		O 60	Pro Good Nat'd	29
Approve it only--'tis too late to praise.		O 62	Pro Word Wise	16
By all, like him, must praise and blame be found;		O 62	Pro Word Wise	19
Thus did the Us'rer Alphius praise,		O 73	Hor. Epode II	73
With some victorious Heroe's praise		O 78	Feast St Simon	5
"Secure of praise from nations yet unborn."		O 82	Young Author	18
"Secure of praise from ages yet unborn."		O 82	Young Author	V 18
To hear his eloquence, and praise his life.		O 118	Epitaph Hanmer	18
Let Lyce share the praise.		O 126	To Lyce, Lady	8
None e're rejects hyperbolies of praise.		O 134	Tr Rambler 104	1
At length aspire to Mantuan praise.		O 139	Tr Rambler 169	2
Thou know'st those arts which blast with envious praise,		O 176	Tr Metastas II	7
With thoughtless reverence we praise,		O 190	Tr. Medea I	2
Thy praise to merit unrefin'd.		O 201	Death Dr Levet	12
Be this at least his Praise; be this his Pride;		O 246	Irene Prologue	21
Did Mahomet reproach or praise her Virtue?		O 259	Irene	108
He tires his Fav'rites with Irene's Praise,		O 261	Irene	3
To tender Friendship, praise him to his Mistress.		O 267	Irene	5

PRAISE   (CONTINUED)   PAGE   TITLE   LINE
   Forbear this lavish Pomp of dreadful Praise; . . . .   O 268 Irene   33
   Made passive Fortitude the Praise of Woman: . . . . .   O 290 Irene   44
   Be but my Country free, be thine the Praise; . . . .   O 305 Irene   33
   Let every Tongue resound Irene's Praise, ...   O 308 Irene   4
   And trod to Bacchus' praise the mystick ground. . . .   Y   6 Virgil Daphnis   16
   Libations he shall pour to Daphnis praise. . . . .   Y   7 Virgil Daphnis V 52
   To propagate the Pygmie heroes' praise. . . . . . .   Y 22 Tr Add. Battle   17
PRAISES
   And intermix'd my Praises with his own; . . . . .   O 299 Irene   44
   By Smiles, and Oaths, and Praises ill disguis'd. . . . O 308 Irene   15
PRATTLING
   <And> plants for his prattling babes the future shade . Y 122 Irene   V 62
PRAY
   Unpitying see them weep, and hear them pray, ...   O 83 Epi Dist Moth.   8
   For healthful indigence in vain they pray, ...   O 132 Par Rambler 48   1
   I Therefore pray thee, Renny dear, ...   O 158 Par Hermit III   1
   I pray thee, gentle Renny dear, ...   O 158 Par Hermit III V   1
PRAY'D
   Thus blindly pray'd the fretful fair, ...   O 122 Stella Mourn.   7
PRAY'R
   Search every state, and canvass ev'ry pray'r. . . . .   O 33 Vanity Wishes   72
   The secret ambush of a specious pray'r. . . . . .   O 48 Vanity Wishes   354
   Warm with an ardent lover's fondest pray'r. . . . .   O 80 Lady Birthday   2
   Oft favours, oft rejects a lover's pray'r: . . . . .   O 95 Sprig of Myrtl   6
   Oft favours, oft rejects the poet's pray'r: . . . . .   O 95 Sprig of Myrtl V   6
   And fate malicious heard the pray'r. . . . . . .   O 122 Stella Mourn.   8
   Henceforth shall form one common pray'r, ...   O 122 Stella Mourn.   14
   There when my Thoughts, at interval of Pray'r, ...   O 292 Irene   94
   No Pray'r recals, no Diligence redeems; . . . . .   O 303 Irene   8
   And wing thy latest Pray'r to pitying Heav'n. . . . .   O 322 Irene   62
PRAY'RS
   O, hear my Pray'rs! accept, all-pitying Heaven, . . .   O 328 Irene   52
PRAYER
   Sacred to Prayer, and wander thro' the Streets; . . .   O 251 Irene   63
   Then dream of Prayer, and Pilgrimage, and Peace. . . . O 265 Irene   45
   Then dream of (prayer), or (vows) and pilgrimage and . . Y 132 Irene   V 45
     peace,
   Purity of prayer--Irene's smile . . . .   Y 150 Irene   V 75
   And give the short remnant of my life to . . . . . .   O 348 Irene   V 14
     prayer,
   And as my thoughts at intervals of Prayer . . . . .   O 349 Irene   V   9
   The Prayer I cannot grant--I dare not hear. . . . . .   O 328 Irene   48
   The swains shall pay their vows, and thou shalt hear their Y   7 Virgil Daphnis   52
     prayer.
   In fervent prayer addrest the deities: . . . . . .   Y 20 Tr. Iliad Bk 6   98
PRAYERS
   In vain you spend your vows and prayers, ...   O 68 Hor.II Ode 14   3
   That grant his Prayers, and hear his cries. . . . . .   O 72 Hor. Epode II   V 28
   But, Cali, let Irene share thy Prayers; . . . . .   O 262 Irene   5
   To pour my Prayers for thy successful Reign, ...   O 264 Irene   10
   And at the holy place pour out my prayers . . . . .   Y 130 Irene   V 12
   Enjoy the prayers and blessings of the needy, ...   Y 130 Irene   V 12C
   No more should Greece lament those Prayers rejected. . . O 290 Irene   52
   Now joins thy People's, and thy Cali's Prayers, . . .   O 308 Irene   8
   O could her fabled Saints, and boasted Prayers . . . .   O 309 Irene   38
   O could her boasted saints, and powerfull prayers . . . Y 185 Irene   V 38
   Could not her Prayers, her Innocence, her Tears, . . .   O 332 Irene   25
   Attend my prayers propitious, hear my vow, ...   Y   7 Virgil Daphnis   42
   Propitious hear my prayers, protect the boy, ...   Y 20 Tr. Iliad Bk 6   101
PRAYS
   In health, in sickness, thus the suppliant prays; . . . O 43 Vanity Wishes   256
PREACH
   Preach thy dull Politics to vulgar Kings, ...   O 265 Irene   39
PRECARIOUS
   Content with Freedom, and precarious Greatness. . . .   O 321 Irene   39
PRECEPTS
   Well pleas'd to find thy Precepts not forgotten. . . .   O 267 Irene   41
PRECINCTS
   In the dark Precincts of the gaping Grave, ...   O 272 Irene   4
PRECIPICE
   To sink the fatal precipice before him, ...   O 176 Tr Metastas II   4
   To sink the fatal precipice before them, ...   O 176 Tr Metastas II V   4
   Inform'd they mount the Precipice of Pow'r, ...   O 293 Irene   113
PRECIPITATELY
   Nor down steep cliffs precipitately move . . . . . .   O 77 Festina Lente   5
PRECIPITATES
   And restless fire precipitates on death. . . . . . .   O 31 Vanity Wishes   20
PREDOMINATES
   Since Fear predominates in every Thought, ...   O 266 Irene   17
PREFERMENT'S
   Unnumber'd suppliants croud Preferment's gate, ...   O 33 Vanity Wishes   73
PREFERR'D
   For arts like these preferr'd, admir'd, caress'd, . . . O 17 London   152
PREGNANT
   Pregnant with Stores, that India's Mines might envy, . . O 249 Irene   18
PREJUDICE
   Nor bribes your Eyes to prejudice your Heads. . . . .   O 246 Irene Prologue   28
PRELUDE
   Attend this Prelude of perpetual Praise! . . . . . .   O 57 Prologue Comus   6

	PAGE	TITLE	LINE
PREPAR'D			
And hov'ring death prepar'd the blow,	O 201	Death Dr Levet	14
Why stor'd for Flight? and why prepar'd by Cali?	O 258	Irene	85
Await our coming, equally prepar'd	O 284	Irene	54
Submissive and prepar'd for each Event,	O 302	Irene	112
PREPARE			
Prepare for death, if here at night you roam,	O 21	London	224
Retire with Speed, while I prepare to meet him	O 271	Irene	37
Bids Beauty, such as thine, prepare to die.	O 324	Irene	3
But Cries and Tears are vain, prepare with Patience	O 328	Irene	40
Which whet their beaks, for flight their wings prepare,	Y 24	Tr Add. Battle	70
PRESAGE			
But who the coming Changes can presage,	O 52	Pro Drury-Lane	39
PRESCRIBES			
Prescribes her duties, or directs her choice,	O 151	The Ant	4
Prescribes the dreadfull comet's flaming path	Y 167	Irene	V 124
PRESENCE			
Yet when the sense of sacred presence fires,	O 48	Vanity Wishes	357
Yet with the sense of sacred presence prest,	O 48	Vanity Wishes	V 357
As blasted by my Presence, they withdrew	O 275	Irene	85
Then let me rid them of Irene's Presence:	O 316	Irene	19
Should she prevail to gain the Sultan's Presence,	O 327	Irene	16
Your fierce Impatience forc'd us from your Presence,	O 332	Irene	29
PRESENT			
But thou, should tempting villainy present	O 14	London	85
Learn, that the present Hour alone is Man's.	O 283	Irene	33
The present Hour with open Arms invites;	O 284	Irene	34
The present hour invites with genuine charms	O 375	Irene	V 7
The Present, Past, and Future swim before me,	O 295	Irene	13
PRESENTING			
On a Lady's presenting a Sprig of Myrtle	O 95	Sprig of Myrtl	T
PRESENTS			
This night presents a play, which publick rage,	O 61	Pro Word Wise	1
PRESERV'D SEE ILL-PRESERV'D			
Preserv'd the reliques of the Latian state	O 78	Festina Lente	18
Thus Life, with loss of Wealth, is well preserv'd,	O 290	Irene	34
Have I for this preserv'd my guiltless Bosom,	O 304	Irene	14
Alone preserv'd the town from Grecian fire.	Y 18	Tr. Iliad Bk 6	14
PRESERVE			
To shield my Lover, and preserve my Country.	O 364	Irene	V 4
PRESIDES			
O thou whose pow'r o'er moving worlds presides,	O 129	Tr. Rambler 7	1
In easy State presides o'er all their Motions,	O 293	Irene	122
PRESIDING			
His pow'rful Strokes presiding Truth impress'd,	O 51	Pro Drury-Lane	7
PRESS			
Or hostile millions press him to the ground?	O 41	Vanity Wishes	218
Lay siege to life and press the dire blockade;	O 44	Vanity Wishes	284
To press the weary minutes flagging wings:	O 44	Vanity Wishes	300
To press the weary minutes hanging wings:	Y 105	Vanity Wishes	V 300
He plies the press, and hurries on his fate;	O 82	Young Author	20
He flies to press, and hurries on his fate;	O 82	Young Author	V 20
When charms thus press on ev'ry sense,	O 121	To Miss Playin	11
Seize the kind Fair, and press her to thy Bosom.	O 284	Irene	35
With warmer Courtship press the yielding Fair,	O 287	Irene	9
Concur to press a hapless Captive's Ruin?	O 288	Irene	10
Concur to press a helpless Captive's Ruin?	O 288	Irene	V 10
A thousand Questions press upon my Tongue,	O 295	Irene	19
Nor press too much upon a Lover's Patience.	O 310	Irene	9
Press not her Flight, while yet her feeble Nerves	O 320	Irene	20
PRESS'D			
Has Silence press'd her Seal upon his Lips?	O 255	Irene	20
Hence men and birds promiscuous press'd the sand	Y 23	Tr Add. Battle	52
PRESSING			
The pressing Exigence forbids Relation.	O 315	Irene	8
PREST SEE NEW-PREST			
Yet with the sense of sacred presence prest,	O 48	Vanity Wishes	V 357
Prest by the load of life, the weary mind	O 59	Pro Good Nat'd	1
PRESUMES			
More safely truth to urge her claim presumes,	O 134	Tr. Rambler 93	1
PRESUMPTUOUS			
O'erturns the Fabrick of presumptuous Reason,	O 269	Irene	8
PRETENDS			
Gaurus pretends to Cato's fame;	O 138	Tr Rambler 164	1
PRETTY			
Always young and always pretty,	O 175	Tr Easy Phrase	2
Always pretty, always young,	O 175	Tr Easy Phrase	3
Always young and always pretty;	O 175	Tr Easy Phrase	5
PREVAIL			
With force resistless o'er the brave prevail.	O 39	Vanity Wishes	178
Should she prevail to gain the Sultan's Presence,	O 327	Irene	16
PREVAIL'D			
Their Arms prevail'd, though Cali was our Friend.	O 253	Irene	119
Had they prevail'd, I ne'er had known Irene.	O 263	Irene	27
But now 'tis o'er, and Justice has prevail'd.	O 324	Irene	14
These when o'er winter's sway, prevail'd the spring	Y 24	Tr Add. Battle	72
PREVAILING			
Stay but a Moment, and prevailing Truth	O 321	Irene	46
PREVAILS			
And flattery prevails when arms are vain.	O 16	London	V 122

PREVENT
                                                           PAGE   TITLE   LINE

		PAGE	TITLE	LINE
PREVENT				
	I can't prevent, and will not share.	O 126	An Ode	36
	Ambitious to prevent the fatal summons	Y 136	Irene	V 27A
PREVENTED				
	Forgive, great Sultan! that by Fate prevented,	O 331	Irene	1
PREY				
	And here the fell attorney prowls for prey;	O 9	London	16
	Of France the mimick, and of Spain the prey.	O 15	London	106
	On Britain's fond credulity they prey.	O 15	London	112
	And leave your little All to flames a prey;	O 18	London	189
	Great Xerxes comes to seize the certain prey,	O 42	Vanity Wishes	227
	On selfish bosoms only prey.	O 100	Ode Friendship	16
	Spread for their prey, the roving coin	O 120	To Miss Purse	V 7
	And Murder meditates his prey.	O 191	Tr. Medea I	12
	All that prey on vice and folly	O 196	Song Congratu.	13
	And all that prey in vice or folly	O 196	Song Congratu.	V 13
	Insatiate on her wasted Entrails prey,	O 315	Irene	36
	Thy Life, too mean a Prey to lure Abdalla.	O 319	Irene	27
PRIAM				
	Where Priam and his sons are laid,	O 232	Tr Horace IV.7	15
PRIAM'S				
	Nor did King Priam's hoary age	O 68	Hor. II Ode IX	15
	That Priam's house, and Priam's self shall bleed:	O 74	Tr. Iliad Bk 6	12
	That Priam's house, and Priam's self shall bleed:	O 74	Tr. Iliad Bk 6	12
	Yet Hecuba's, nor Priam's hoary age,	O 74	Tr. Iliad Bk 6	15
PRICE				
	The price of boroughs and of souls restore,	O 19	London	204
	And ask no questions but the price of votes;	O 34	Vanity Wishes	96
PRIDE				
	Heroes, proceed! what bounds your pride shall hold?	O 13	London	61
	Where wav'ring man, betray'd by vent'rous pride,	O 31	Vanity Wishes	7
	And scarce a sycophant was fed by pride;	O 33	Vanity Wishes	56
	And scarce a sycophant could feed on pride;	Y 94	Vanity Wishes	V 56
	At once is lost the pride of aweful state,	O 35	Vanity Wishes	113
	Now drops at once the pride of aweful state,	O 35	Vanity Wishes	V 113
	Or liv'st thou now, with safer pride content,	O 35	Vanity Wishes	123
	Or states mens now, with safer pride content,	Y 97	Vanity Wishes	V 123
	On what foundation stands the warrior's pride,	O 40	Vanity Wishes	191
	In gay hostility, and barb'rous pride,	O 42	Vanity Wishes	225
	Till counted myriads sooth his pride no more;	O 42	Vanity Wishes	230
	And Pride and Prudence take her seat in vain.	O 46	Vanity Wishes	336
	By Int'rest, Prudence; and by Flatt'ry, Pride.	O 47	Vanity Wishes	340
	To Int'rest, Prudence; and to Flatt'ry, Pride.	O 47	Vanity Wishes	V 340
	The noble mind's delight and pride,	O 99	Ode Friendship	2
	To pluck the flow'rs of pleasure or of pride.	O 118	Epitaph Hanmer	32
	When Pride, by guilt, to greatness climbs,	O 126	An Ode	33
	To cheer despair, or soften pride,	O 190	Tr. Medea I	8
	Pomp and Pleasure, Pride and Plenty	O 196	Song Congratu.	3
	No petty gain disdain'd by pride,	O 201	Death Dr Levet	22
	Be this at least his Praise; be this his Pride;	O 246	Irene Prologue	21
	The Pride and Terror of succeeding Days,	O 268	Irene	12
	The Pride of Monarchs, the Reward of Conquest;	O 269	Irene	42
	With all the graceful Pride of Greatness heighten'd,	O 276	Irene	8
	The full-blown pride of conquest and of empire	Y 149	Irene	V 58
	Whate'er Man's Pride has ravish'd from our Sex.	O 291	Irene	75
	His Pride and Love by Turns inspir'd his Tongue,	O 299	Irene	43
	Vain pride & wealth	Y 177	Irene	V 110
	(The) pride of Roman (power), and Grecian art	Y 177	Irene	V 111
	My Pride shall ne'er protract my Country's Woes;	O 306	Irene	47
	See Cali, Dread of Kings, and Pride of Armies,	O 311	Irene	16
	Joys ill exchang'd for Gold, and Pride, and Empire.	O 313	Irene	10
PRIDE'S				
	My Pride's to have that little all my own.	O 247	Irene Epilogue	10
PRIMAEVAL				
	In the bright Colours of primaeval Spring;	O 314	Irene	5
PRIME				
	But grant, the virtues of a temp'rate prime	O 44	Vanity Wishes	291
PRINCE				
	The baffled prince in honour's flatt'ring bloom	O 43	Vanity Wishes	251
	That leave the blame of rigour to the prince,	O 176	Tr Metastas II	10
	That Wealth, which granted to their weeping Prince,	O 250	Irene	22
	Where common Laws restrain the Prince and Subject,	O 256	Irene	56
	Blest Prince, for whom indulgent Heav'n ordains	O 308	Irene	6
	Has serv'd his Prince so well, demand our Silence?	O 329	Irene	19
	The valiant Prince with unresisted force	Y 25	Tr Add. Battle	118
PRINCE'S				
	Repeat that prince's victories,	O 68	Hor. II Ode IX	19
PRINCES				
	Though from no Princes I descend,	O 70	Hor.II Ode XX	5
	If at your coming princes disappear,	O 177	Tr Dist Modena	1
	Of prostrate princes and adoring nations	Y 131	Irene	V 31
	The Rights of Princes let the Sword decide,	O 307	Irene	22
PRINCIPLES				
	Can sap the principles, or taint the heart;	O 13	London	76
PRINTS				
	The prints of claws and honourable scars.	Y 24	Tr Add. Battle	83
PRISON'S				
	Convey him to the Prison's inmost Depths,	O 312	Irene	24
PRIVACIES				
	Nor taint with Care the Privacies of Love.	O 288	Irene	14

		PAGE	TITLE	LINE
PRIVACY				
To prove the Sweets of Privacy and Friendship, ...		O 262	Irene	9
PRIVATE				
The harmless Freedom, and the private Friend. . . .		O 46	Vanity Wishes	338
about his private neglects the publick		Y 113	Irene	V 27
At Midnight's private Hour a Voice unknown		O 254	Irene	121
Consult in private, call me when your Scheme		O 256	Irene	36
Molest these private Walks, or Care invade		O 272	Irene	14
In private Conference; beside him stood		O 275	Irene	79
Through bowing Slaves, I range the private Rooms, . . .		O 283	Irene	17
Purge well thy Mind from ev'ry private Passion, . . .		O 298	Irene	6
And growls in private o'er his idle Sabre.		O 309	Irene	22
Seize him this Night, and through the private Passage		O 312	Irene	23
A private Station may discover more;		O 316	Irene	18
PRIVILEGE				
Th' inestimable Privilege of Breathing!		O 260	Irene	136
Love is indeed the Privilege of Youth, ...		O 280	Irene	29
Suspend awhile the Privilege of Pow'r		O 289	Irene	5
Suspend awhile the privilege of powr (and Beauty) . . .		O 366	Irene	V 21
Deny'd Debard each privilege of human nature being		Y 165	Irene	V 81
When Heav'n bestows the Privilege to bless, ...		O 313	Irene	21
PRIZE				
Was early taught a Briton's right to prize, ...		O 15	London	119
Nor deem, when learning her last prize bestows, . . .		O 38	Vanity Wishes	165
Nor deem, when learning her lost prize bestows, . . .		O 38	Vanity Wishes	V 165
Nor think though learning her last prize bestows, . . .		Y 99	Vanity Wishes	V 165
"For wealth or title, perishable prize;		O 82	Young Author	16
At length the Prize is mine--The haughty Maid		O 317	Irene	1
Once more I dare thy Sword, behold the Prize, ...		O 319	Irene	28
PROCEED				
Heroes, proceed! what bounds your pride shall hold? . .		O 13	London	61
Are these thy views? proceed, illustrious youth, . . .		O 37	Vanity Wishes	141
In Sophia's Temple!--What Alarm!--Proceed.		O 258	Irene	97
Proceed, and give a loose to Love and Treason. . . .		O 316	Irene	20
PROCLAIM				
With Monuments of Death proclaim his Courage;		O 255	Irene	31
Yet strangers in some distant world proclaim . . .		Y 120	Irene	V 31A
Before th' assembled Troops proclaim his Crimes; . . .		O 273	Irene	35
Should we before the Troops proclaim his Crimes . . .		O 273	Irene	38
Did you proclaim this unexpected Conquest?		O 282	Irene	62
Abdalla, Cali, go--proclaim my Purpose.		O 309	Irene	43
PROCLAIM'D				
Proclaim'd her, not so fair as fine.		O 122	Stella Mourn.	4
PROCLAIMS				
And hissing Infamy proclaims the rest.		O 47	Vanity Wishes	342
And shout Infamy proclaims the rest.		Y 107	Vanity Wishes	V 342
Proclaims mortality to Man.		O 231	Tr Horace IV.7	8
Superiour Majesty proclaims the Queen, ...		O 288	Irene	2
Superiour Majesty proclaims thee Queen, ...		O 288	Irene	V 2
PROCURES				
And envy the slave that toils whose labour procures her . sleep		Y 165	Irene	V 81
PRODIGIES				
In life's last scene what prodigies surprise, ...		O 45	Vanity Wishes	315
A thousand horrid Prodigies foretold it.		O 250	Irene	36
PRODIGIOUS				
Prodigious madness of the writing race!		Y 67	Prologue Lethe	1
PRODIGY				
O prodigy of Love!		O 79	Feast St Simon	21
And not one Prodigy foretold our Fate.		O 250	Irene	35
PRODUC'D				
To wondring Worlds produc'd the whole, ...		O 147	Tr Boeth III.6	11
PRODUCT				
The teeming Year's whole Product shall devour, ...		O 110	To Posterity	11
PROEN				
Eiden Aletheie proen chairoysa graphonta		O 108	Eis Birchion	1
PROFANE				
Usurp our Temples, and profane our Altars.		O 251	Irene	69
Force her! profane her with a Touch, and die.		O 296	Irene	8
PROFANES				
Mine unharmonious verse profanes		O 80	Feast St Simon	58
PROFOUND				
On crackling ice, o'er gulphs profound, ...		O 203	Tr. on Skating	V 1
PROFOUNDEST				
Hast thou not search'd my Soul's profoundest Thoughts? .		O 304	Irene	18
PROFUSE				
Profuse of Wealth, or bounteous of Success, ...		O 313	Irene	20
PROFUSELY				
Profusely pour'd her Bounties upon Woman?		O 276	Irene	25
PROGENITORS				
Shall deem our hoar progenitors unwise.		O 192	Tr. Medea II	4
PROGRESS				
Did ever Passion make so swift a Progress?		O 281	Irene	55
PROJECT				
The Vet'ran Courtier half reveal'd his Project. . . .		O 254	Irene	132
PROJECTS				
Unbounded Projects lab'ring in his Mind, ...		O 97	Hickman Spinet	11
Projects at once our Freedom and his own;		O 253	Irene	114
Or Flights of Pow'r, or Projects of Ambition.		O 327	Irene	21
PROLOGUE				
Prologue And Epilogue, ...		O 50	Pro Drury-Lane	T

PROLOGUE   (CONTINUED)   PAGE   TITLE   LINE
    A New Prologue Spoken By Mr Garrick, ... O 56 Prologue Comus   T
    Prologue to "The Good Natur'd Man" . . . .   O 59 Pro Good Nat'd   T
    Prologue to "A Word to the Wise" . . . .   O 61 Pro Word Wise   T
PROLONG
    And, murm'ring, balmy Sleep prolong, ... O 72 Hor. Epode II   32
    Let them prolong their turgid lays . . . .   O 78 Feast St Simon   4
    We bid propitious Heav'n prolong your reign, ... O 96 Hickman Spinet   7
    Call them--but let them not prolong their Tale, . . . O 310 Irene   8
PROLONG'D
    His Breath prolong'd but to detect her Treason, . . . O 331 Irene   15
PROLONGS
    And Spenser's verse prolongs Eliza's reign; . . . . . O 114 On C. Cibber   2
PROMISCUOUS
    Hence men and birds promiscuous press'd the sand . . . Y 23 Tr Add. Battle   52
PROMISES
    Call to your Aid with boundless Promises . . . . . . O 287 Irene   10
    I drew to my party with (alluring) promises artfull . . Y 158 Irene   V 11
PROMONTORIES
    <?storms huge> Promontories flie . . . .   O 76 Tr Add. Battle   22
    In rat'ling storms huge promontories flie . . . . . Y 26 Tr Add. Battle   V 140
PROMPT
    Then prompt no more the Follies you decry, ... O 53 Pro Drury-Lane   55
    When soft Security shall prompt the Sultan, ... O 291 Irene   76
    And soft Security shall prompt the Sultan . . . . .   O 364 Irene   V 6
PROMPTS
    Rules the bold hand, or prompts the suppliant voice; . . O 31 Vanity Wishes   12
    Love prompts to love, and rev'rence rev'rence gains. . . O 130 Tr. Rambler 12   8
    If when Religion prompts me to refuse, ... O 289 Irene   24
    But virtuous Passion prompts the great Resolve, . . . O 303 Irene   18
    Forgive my fair what fame what nature prompts . . . . Y 197 Irene   V 19
PRONOUNC'D
    What well known Voice pronounc'd the grateful Sounds . . O 295 Irene   10
PROOF
    'Tis a proof that he had rather . . . .   O 183 Burlesque Vega   3
PROPAGATE
    My Works shall propagate my fame, ...   O 70 Hor.II Ode XX   17
    League with our Chiefs, and propagate Sedition? . . . O 312 Irene   3
    To propagate the Pygmie heroes' praise. . . . . . . Y 22 Tr Add. Battle   17
PROPAGATES
    And pleasure propagates around . . . .   O 121 To Miss Playin   5
PROPER
    Wisdom at proper times is well forgot. . . . . . .   O 134 Tr. Rambler 89   1
PROPHET
    Our warlike Prophet loves an active Faith, ... O 264 Irene   25
    Our warlike Prophet loves an active zeal . . . . .   Y 131 Irene   V 25
    Till every Nation reverence our Prophet . . . . . . O 354 Irene   V 17
    The houries of our Prophet blush before her . . . .   Y 184 Irene   V 10
PROPHET'S
    With pious Warmth receive our Prophet's Law---- . . . O 262 Irene   25
    Long have I wish'd, before our Prophet's Tomb, . . . O 263 Irene   9
    And ev'n our Prophet's Gardens envy thine: . . . . . O 279 Irene   89
PROPHETESS
    Forbear thy Threats, proud Prophetess of Ill, ... O 314 Irene   26
PROPITIATE
    Shall bless our Wand'rings, and propitiate Heav'n. . . O 320 Irene   19
PROPITIOUS
    We bid propitious Heav'n prolong your reign, ... O 96 Hickman Spinet   7
    Propitious Guide of my bewilder'd Soul, ... O 298 Irene   11
    And Peace propitious smile on fond Desire; . . . . . O 302 Irene   119
    Propitious Hours to Stratagem and Death, ... O 302 Irene   3
    Now hover o'er us with propitious Wings, ... O 306 Irene   51
    Attend my prayers propitious, hear my vow, ... Y   7 Virgil Daphnis   42
    Propitious hear my prayers, protect the boy, ... Y 20 Tr. Iliad Bk 6   101
PROPORTION'D
    A task proportion'd to thy mighty mind! . . . . . .   O 136 Tr Rambler 129   2
PROPORTIOND
    And Strength proportiond to the task of Ruling . . . . O 369 Irene   V 7
PROPOS'D
    With ill-tim'd Mirth propos'd the Bowl of Love. . . . O 316 Irene   26
PROPOSE
    Propose your schemes, ye Senatorian band, ...   O 21 London   244
PROSELYTES
    Should she, for Proselytes are always zealous, ... O 262 Irene   24
PROSP'ROUS
    Of plenteous peace, and prosp'rous war; . . . . . . O 189 Epilogue   6
    Greece is no more, the prosp'rous Tyrant lives, . . . O 315 Irene   4
PROSPECT
    Till interposing Death destroys the Prospect! . . . . O 283 Irene   25
    Till interposing Death denys the prospect. . . . . . O 374 Irene   V 26
    Till interposing darkness bars the prospect. . . . . Y 155 Irene   V 25
PROSPECTS
    And stretch thy prospects o'er the smiling land, . . . O 20 London   214
    And stretch thy prospects o'er your fruitfull land, . . Y 58 London   V 214
    Unbounded prospects in his bosom roll, ...   O 82 Young Author   V 6A
    What dreary prospects round us rise, ...   O 123 Winter's Walk
    Prospects obscur'd by Distance faintly strike. . . . O 261 Irene   19
PROSPERITY
    for the long life and prosperity of my sovereign . . . Y 130 Irene   V 12A
PROSTITUTED
    And swell with tears the prostituted eye . . . . . . Y 57 London   V 199

		PAGE	TITLE	LINE
PROSTRATE				
To raise our prostrate country from its ruins.		Y 117	Irene	V109A
Of prostrate princes and adoring nations		Y 131	Irene	V 31
To bid the prostrate Captive rise and live, ...		O 278	Irene	70
Again her prostrate Palaces should rise, ...		O 291	Irene	54
Which prostrate Memphis own'd her deities.		Y 4	On a Daffodill	16
PROTECT				
Receive her, and protect her, gracious Heav'n! . . .		O 297	Irene	16
Propitious hear my prayers, protect the boy, ...		Y 20	Tr. Iliad Bk 6	101
PROTECTED				
By kings protected, and to kings ally'd?		O 36	Vanity Wishes	132
Each Night protected by the friendly Darkness, ...		O 251	Irene	59
The smiling Widows, and protected Orphans.		O 291	Irene	57
And thus protected in the gen'ral Ruin, ...		O 296	Irene	32
PROTECTING				
And what protecting angel led thee hither		Y 170	Irene	V 33
PROTECTION				
Nor fear the Fair and Learn'd can want Protection. . .		O 302	Irene	115
Where Florence gives the banish'd arts protection . .		O 351	Irene	V 3
PROTESTATION				
Far be the Thought--But hear my Protestation. . . .		O 326	Irene	32
Far be the horrid thought--but hear my protestation . .		Y 205	Irene	V 32
PROTESTATIONS				
In soft Complaints, and idle Protestations.		O 269	Irene	16
PROTRACT				
But see, where destin'd to protract our Counsels, . .		O 271	Irene	35
My Pride shall ne'er protract my Country's Woes; . .		O 306	Irene	47
While I protract their Stay. Be swift and faithful. . .		O 319	Irene	4
PROTRACTED				
That life protracted is protracted woe.		O 43	Vanity Wishes	258
That life protracted is protracted woe.		O 43	Vanity Wishes	258
PROUD				
The day will come, in which proud Troy shall yield, .		O 74	Tr. Iliad Bk 6	13
When some proud Grecian dame shall tasks impose, . .		O 74	Tr. Iliad Bk 6	21
In vain proud tyrants strove to shake		O 79	Feast St Simon	13
When ev'n proud wealth and prouder wit obey, ...		O 81	Lady Birthday	10
Glad to be hid, and proud to be forgot.		O 82	Young Author	30
On swelling mortals to be proud no more.		O 135	Tr Rambler 106	2
In vain proud Man usurps what's Woman's Due;		O 247	Irene Epilogue	15
For what are pompous Titles, proud Alliance, ...		O 267	Irene	8
And all the proud magnificence of empire		Y 158	Irene	V 9
And Buda fall, and proud Vienna tremble, ...		O 309	Irene	27
Forbear thy Threats, proud Prophetess of Ill, ...		O 314	Irene	26
Who charges Guilt! lay by this proud Resentment . .		O 323	Irene	8
That laves proud Ilion with his rapid flood, ...		Y 18	Tr. Iliad Bk 6	12
PROUDER				
When ev'n proud wealth and prouder wit obey, ...		O 81	Lady Birthday	10
PROUDLY				
And proudly hop'd to pimp in future Days.		O 52	Pro Drury-Lane	24
PROV'D				
This Bay has prov'd my ,fondness for the Sultan; . . .		O 324	Irene	19
PROVE				
To prove the Sweets of Privacy and Friendship, ...		O 262	Irene	9
And if one varied Accent prove thy Falshood, ...		O 332	Irene	14
PROVERB				
Exiles, the proverb says, subsist on hope.		O 133	Tr. Rambler 67	1
descend in a proverb among thy enemies		Y 113	Irene	V 21
a proverb and a jest		Y 113	Irene	V 22
PROVERBIAL				
Through hissing Ages, a proverbial Coward, ...		O 305	Irene	28
PROVES				
And proves, by Cato's vice, his claim.		O 138	Tr Rambler 164	2
PROVIDENCE				
Must watchfull providence despatch from Heav'n . . .		Y 114	Irene	V 46
Think on that Providence that guards the Good.		O 252	Irene	89
O Providence! extend thy Care to me, ...		O 252	Irene	90
On me, should Providence, without a Crime, ...		O 292	Irene	103
Lies in the Womb of Providence conceal'd, ...		O 313	Irene	16
Thrown beyond the verge of providence		Y 199	Irene	V 16
o'er the tide--providence our guide--		Y 199	Irene	V 16A
And trace the paths of providence in vain.		Y 217	Irene	V 15
PROVIDENT				
Yet timely provident, she hastes away		O 151	The Ant	5
PROVINCE				
Deny'd the Government of Servia's Province.		O 311	Irene	10
PROVOK'D				
Provok'd Diana with a vengefull dart		Y 19	Tr. Iliad Bk 6	42
Dar'd have provok'd a foe to single fight, ...		Y 23	Tr Add. Battle	39
PROVOKE				
The Cranes with beaks and claws provoke the fight. . .		O 75	Tr Add. Battle	3
'Tis Madness to provoke superfluous Danger, ...		O 318	Irene	21
You may provoke but never can convince		Y 197	Irene	V 31
PROVOKES				
This, only this, provokes the snarling muse.		O 17	London	161
This, only this, provokes the darling muse.		O 17	London	V 161
Provokes a broil, and stabs you for a jest.		O 21	London	229
PROWLS				
And here the fell attorney prowls for prey;		O 9	London	16
Prowls like a lyon oer the wealthy Spoils of bleeding .		O 352	Irene	V 29
Turkey.				
Prowls o'er the wealthy Spoils of bleeding Turkey? . .		O 264	Irene	15

PRUDENCE
                                                   PAGE   TITLE   LINE

	PAGE	TITLE		LINE
PRUDENCE				
And Pride and Prudence take her seat in vain.	O 46	Vanity Wishes		336
By Int'rest, Prudence; and by Flatt'ry, Pride.	O 47	Vanity Wishes		340
To Int'rest, Prudence; and to Flatt'ry, Pride.	O 47	Vanity Wishes	V	340
Let Prudence moderate, though not suppress.	O 264	Irene		34
Let Prudence, ere the Suit be farther urg'd,	O 285	Irene		8
Prudence and Love conspire in this Request,	O 285	Irene		11
Prudence and Friendship bid me force her from you.	O 296	Irene		7
Distrust is Cowardice, and Prudence Folly.	O 301	Irene		86
Let Prudence obviate an impending Danger.	O 309	Irene		19
Perhaps my Zeal too fierce betray'd my Prudence;	O 330	Irene		20
PRUDENT				
Their prudent insults to the poor confine;	O 21	London		233
Turn on the prudent Ant, thy heedful eyes,	O 151	The Ant		1
"Can a prudent Dove decline	O 185	Anacreon Ode 9		23
PRUNE				
There prune thy walks, support thy drooping flow'rs,	O 20	London		216
There prune thy shades, support the drooping flow'rs,	Y 58	London	V	216
They prune the Wing, and spread the glossy Plumes,	O 277	Irene		36
They prune the wing and spread the glossy tail	O 355	Irene	V	23
PRUNES				
Or prunes the barren boughs away;	O 71	Hor. Epode II		19
PRY				
Delude the most; few pry behind the scene.	O 139	Tr Rambler 168		2
PTOLEMOISI				
Toios Ares Brotoloigos eni ptolemoisi memene,	O 172	On Marlborough		1
PUBLIC				
With close Malevolence, or public Rage;	O 57	Prologue Comus		8
PUBLICK				
When publick crimes inflame the wrath of heav'n:	O 13	London		66
And publick mournings pacify the skies;	O 19	London		197
The Stage but echoes back the publick Voice.	O 53	Pro Drury-Lane		52
This night presents a play, which publick rage,	O 61	Pro Word Wise		1
In life's first bloom his publick toils began,	O 117	Epitaph Hanmer		11
Her own neglected, in the publick Safety.	O 250	Irene		27
about his private neglects the publick	Y 113	Irene	V	27
And publick Spirit deemd a wild Chimaera	O 347	Irene	V	19
When publick Villainy, too strong for Justice,	O 250	Irene		40
O'erwhelm'd and lost amidst the publick Ruins	O 302	Irene		107
PUBLISH'D				
That Maxim publish'd in an impious Age,	O 291	Irene		60
PUG				
No pug, nor favourite Cupid there enjoys	O 84	Epi Dist Moth.		20
He was a seducing pug!	Y 301	Extemp. Elegy		14
PULTOWA'S				
Hide, blushing Glory, hide Pultowa's day:	O 41	Vanity Wishes		210
PUNISH				
Successful Treasons punish impious Kings.	O 300	Irene		66
'Tis ours, alas! to punish, not to judge,	O 326	Irene		33
PUNISHMENT				
Beyond the Fear of ling'ring Punishment,	O 325	Irene		16
PURCHASD				
Purchasd by thy powerful Song,	O 150	Tr Boet III.12		41
Purchasd by the powerful Song,	O 150	Tr Boet III.12	V	41
PURCHASE				
Resolv'd to purchase a retreat.	O 73	Hor. Epode II		76
PURCHASS				
Ransom of Kings, the purchass of your blood	O 351	Irene	V	14
PURE				
On darkling man in pure effulgence shine,	O 130	Tr. Rambler 7		3
Desires more pure, and other Cares than Love.	O 263	Irene		8
With supplicating tears and pure Devotion	O 364	Irene	V	2
Such Ecstacy of Love! such pure Affection,	O 295	Irene		15
Pure as the Thoughts of infant Innocence?	O 304	Irene		15
Fidelity so firm, so pure, as mine!	O 308	Irene		17
PURER				
To breathe in distant fields a purer air,	O 9	London		6
Array'd in purer Light, look down on me:	O 253	Irene		101
PURGE				
Purge well thy Mind from ev'ry private Passion,	O 298	Irene		6
PURITY				
Purity of prayer--Irene's smile	Y 150	Irene	V	75
When Purity, while Fraud was yet unknown,	O 314	Irene		6
PURL				
Where Riv'lets gently purl along	O 72	Hor. Epode II		31
PURPLE				
Through purple billows and a floating host.	O 42	Vanity Wishes		240
Whose mortal wounds pour forth a purple flood,	O 76	Tr Add. Battle		20
Perennial roses deck each purple vale,	O 84	Epi Dist Moth.		16
And purple nectar glads the festive hour,	O 193	Tr. Medea II		18
With Purple varied and bedrop'd with Gold,	O 277	Irene		35
PURPOSE				
That hide in seeming zeal a wicked purpose,	O 176	Tr Metastas II		12
Which granted, hides my Purpose from the World,	O 258	Irene		88
My Doom confirm'd establishes my Purpose.	O 270	Irene		9
Abdalla, Cali, go--proclaim my Purpose.	O 309	Irene		43
That mark'd my Course, suspicious of my Purpose,	O 335	Irene		6
PURSE				
... a Gold and Silk net-work Purse of her own weaving	O 119	To Miss Purse		T
Till purse and carcase both were low.	Y 300	Extemp. Elegy		12

	PAGE TITLE	LINE
PURSU'D		
And fame pursu'd him, where conviction led.	O 118 Epitaph Hanmer	34
Now let him go, pursu'd by silent Wrath, ...	O 274 Irene	47
PURSUE		
Where e'er they fly their lovers ghosts pursue, . . .	O 84 Epi Dist Moth.	36
Here let me thro' the vales pursue	O 125 An Ode	21
For us alone, they Honour's Paths pursue:	O 247 Irene Epilogue	16
With wonted Zeal pursue the Task of War;	O 264 Irene	30
Aspasia, yet pursue the sacred Theme;	O 265 Irene	1
Now, Mustapha, pursue thy Tale of Horror.	O 272 Irene	1
Pursue the last Remains of ling'ring Light. . . .	O 302 Irene	4
Pursue him through his Labyrinths of Treason, ...	O 310 Irene	6
Let Shame and hooting Infamy pursue me, ...	O 328 Irene	36
PURSUED		
Be virtuous Ends pursued by virtuous Means, ...	O 291 Irene	58
PURSUES		
This, only this, the rigid law pursues, ...	O 17 London	160
Year chases year, decay pursues decay, ...	O 45 Vanity Wishes	305
Despotick Rage pursues the Life of Cali;	O 270 Irene	16
If Fate pursues me, let it find me here.	O 297 Irene	18
The Rack expects us, and the Sword pursues.	O 315 Irene	2
PURSUING		
Swift from pursuing horrors take your way, ...	O 18 London	188
PURSUIT		
If chasing past Events with vain Pursuit, ...	O 255 Irene	5
PUSH'D		
And push'd the Might of Moluc from the Ramparts. . . .	O 363 Irene	V 15
PUSHES		
And pushes feeble (thrusts defenseless) virtue from her throne	Y 158 Irene	V 13
PUT		
I put my hat upon my head	O 158 Par. Hermit II	1
They put the riches of Cali Bassa on board.	Y 123 Irene	V 81
PUZZLE		
Ne'er knew to puzzle right, or varnish wrong, . . .	O 14 London	80
PYE		
"I have chatter'd like a pye."	O 186 Anacreon Ode 9	44
PYGMEAN		
Beneath Pygmean steel what numbers dye!	O 75 Tr Add. Battle	5
PYGMIE		
Thus fell the Pygmie state, which long had stood . . .	O 76 Tr Add. Battle	33
Now in the realms below the Pygmie shades	O 76 Tr Add. Battle	41
And the sad fate of Pygmie realms I sing.	Y 22 Tr Add. Battle	2
To propagate the Pygmie heroes' praise.	Y 22 Tr Add. Battle	17
In which the Pygmie wept his cruelty.	Y 24 Tr Add. Battle	63
PYGMIEAN		
Securely flourish'd the Pygmiean state, ...	Y 23 Tr Add. Battle	27
PYGMIES		
O'erpower'd and faint the Pygmies scarce sustain . .	O 76 Tr Add. Battle	26
And shades of Pygmies swim before their eye. . . .	O 77 Tr Add. Battle	48
The Pygmies thus exasp'rated their foes.	Y 23 Tr Add. Battle	51
Meantime the Pygmies with undaunted hearts	Y 24 Tr Add. Battle	76
The fearless Pygmies view them from afar	Y 25 Tr Add. Battle	96
While the sad Pygmies mourn with weeping eyes . . .	Y 26 Tr Add. Battle	128
QUAFF		
Quaff Nectar with th' immortal Gods.	O 70 Hor.II Ode XX	8
Quaff the full draught of each terrestrial joy . . .	Y 146 Irene	V 1
QUARRY		
Joy to see their quarry fly, ...	O 196 Song Congratu.	14
QUEEN		
The queen, the beauty, sets the world in arms; . . .	O 42 Vanity Wishes	246
Fair plenty, gracious Queen, shou'd pour	O 144 Tr Boeth. II.2	5
Renounce her Faith, and be the Queen of Turkey; . .	O 258 Irene	100
To hear my Vows and give Mankind a Queen?	O 276 Irene	2
To hear my suit and give a Queen to Turkey? . . .	O 372 Irene	V 7
Superiour Majesty proclaims the Queen, ...	O 288 Irene	2
Superiour Majesty proclaims thee Queen, ...	O 288 Irene	V 2
Not yet inspire the Follies of a Queen, ...	O 289 Irene	3
Not yet inspire th' omniscience of a queen	O 366 Irene	V 19
I am not yet a Queen, or an Apostate.	O 289 Irene	22
O! did Irene shine the Queen of Turkey, ...	O 290 Irene	51
And subject Seas roar round their Queen in vain. . . .	O 309 Irene	29
And learn the Rev'rence due to Turkey's Queen. . . .	O 322 Irene	55
All is not lost, Abdalla, see the Queen, ...	O 326 Irene	1
The Queen requested that a chosen Troop	O 331 Irene	7
The Queen requested--Wretch, repeat the Message; . .	O 331 Irene	13
The Queen requested--Wretch, repeat thy Message; . .	O 331 Irene	V 13
The Queen requested--	O 332 Irene	17
QUEENS		
Rise from the happy Bed; and future Queens	O 268 Irene	13
Conduct these Queens, Abdalla, to the Palace: . . .	O 269 Irene	40
Attend these queens, Abdallah, to the (palace) . . .	Y 137 Irene	V 40
QUELL		
And quell the rebels of the heart.	O 126 An Ode	40
He bids no Trumpet quell the fatal Sound.	O 246 Irene Prologue	24
QUENCH		
Whose blood shall quench some Grecian's thirsty rage, .	O 74 Tr. Iliad Bk 6	16
QUENCH'D		
But now our Turkish Conquerors have quench'd . . .	O 249 Irene	7
QUEST		
In quest of wealth who throw their lives away.	O 132 Tr. Rambler 48	2

263

```
QUEST          (CONTINUED)                                   PAGE   TITLE          LINE
     Grasp at Command, and tow'r in quest of Empire;    . . .   O 293  Irene           114
     And sought this happy Grove in quest of Thee.      . . . . O 299  Irene            50
QUESTIONS
     And ask no questions but the price of votes;       . . .   O  34  Vanity Wishes    96
     Reserve these Questions for a safer Hour,          . . . . O 254  Irene           140
     And gives a thousand fatal Questions Birth;        . . . . O 258  Irene            84
     A thousand Questions press upon my Tongue,         . . . . O 295  Irene            19
QUICK
     Quick let us rise, the happy seats explore,        . . . . O  18  London          174
     Dart the quick taunt, and edge the piercing gibe?  . . . . O  33  Vanity Wishes    62
     Quick fires his breast the fever of renown         . . . . Y  97  Vanity Wishes  V 137
     By plumes is viel'd; see! quick as thought         . . .   O  70  Hor.II Ode XX    11
     "This is all;--be quick and go,   . . . . . . . .         O 186  Anacreon Ode 9   41
     Whose quick Impatience seiz'd my doubtful Hand,    . . .   O 254  Irene           126
     Haste, seize them, guards, be quick--my thoughtless hast   Y 198  Irene          V  34
     Quick from my Sight you inauspicious Monsters,     . . . . O 325  Irene             6
     Quick at my Call shall execute your Charge;        . . . . O 328  Irene            43
QUICKLY
     Will quickly drive away his woe,                   . . . . O  69  Hor.II Ode 14    26
     Such Pleasures quickly would remove   . . . . . .         O  72  Hor. Epode II   V 45
     Thus lightly touch and quickly go.                 . . . . O 203  Tr. on Skating    4
     O lead me quickly to the Scene of Fate;   . . . . .       O 259  Irene           105
     Quickly the Cranes appear before their eyes;       . . . . Y  25  Tr Add. Battle   92
QUIET
     Cool meditation's quiet seat,                      . . . . O 125  An Ode           30
     There shalt thou view from far the quiet Cottage,  . . .   O 292  Irene            83
     And in those Bowers of Innocence and   . . . . . .        O 349  Irene          V  7
          Quiet
     They cultivate at ease the gentler arts in quiet   . . .   Y 177  Irene          V 117
     And as quiet as a lamb.                            . . . . Y 301  Extemp. Elegy    20
QUIT
     But forc'd at length her antient Reign to quit,    . . . . O  52  Pro Drury-Lane   35
     For you, ye fair, I quit the gloomy plains,        . . . . O  83  Epi Dist Moth.   10
     To quit the Tumults of the noisy Camp,   . . . . .       O 264  Irene            11
     And quit the Names of Brother, Friend, and Father? . . . . O 280  Irene            17
     And quit their Charge to Horror and to Ruin.       . . . . O 346  Irene          V  8
     Quit but this maid, resign a hopeless claim   . . . .     Y 197  Irene          V 25
     Behold I quit her to the Chance of Battle.         . . . . O 319  Irene            29
     Yet ere I quit the Scepter of Dominion,   . . . . .       O 333  Irene            49
     And quit Inachia's venal charms                    . . . . Y  11  Tr Hor Epode 9   26
QUITE
     Behold rebellious virtue quite o'erthrown,         . . . . O  13  London           63
     And quite Inachia's venal charms   . . . . . . .         Y  11  Tr Hor Epode 9 V 26
QUITS
     The young enthusiast quits his ease for fame;      . . . . O  36  Vanity Wishes   136
     Tir'd with contempt, she quits the slipp'ry reign, . . .   O  46  Vanity Wishes   335
     She faints and quits her hold.                     . . . . O 150  Tr Boet III.12   58
QUITTED
     For trifling sports I quitted grave affairs.       . . .   O 130  Tr. Rambler 10    1
QUITTING
     Quitting my close Retreat, I range the City,       . . .   O 251  Irene            60
QUIV'RING
     The rustling brake alarms, and quiv'ring shade,    . . .   O  32  Vanity Wishes    42
     By quiv'ring string, or modulated wind;   . . . .         O 192  Tr. Medea II     10
     Plays on the quiv'ring Waves, to guide our Flight, . . .   O 306  Irene            59
QUIVER
     Frail as the leaves that quiver on the sprays,     . . . . O 138  Tr Rambler 161    1
     As glittering dewdrops quiver to the sun   . . . .        Y 173  Irene          V 19
     And sparkling quiver to the Breath of May;         . . . . O 298  Irene            21
     And Grecian spears shall quiver in your breast.    . . .   Y  18  Tr. Iliad Bk 6   23
QUIVER'D
     And tender Accents quiver'd on my Lips,   . . . . .       O 282  Irene            67
QUIVERING
     Among the quivering branches sighs;        . . . . . .    O  66  Hor I Ode xxii   18
     Among the quivering Branches sighs,        . . . . . .    O  67  To A. Fuscus     18
RABBLE
     And now a rabble rages, now a fire;        . . . . . .    O   9  London           14
RABBLES
     Uncheck'd on both, loud rabbles vent their rage,   . . .   O  59  Pro Good Nat'd   15
RACE
     The teeming mother, anxious for her race,          . . . . O  45  Vanity Wishes   319
     A clime deny'd to human race;   . . . . . . . . .        O  66  Hor I Ode xxii   22
     A Clime deny'd to human Race;   . . . . . . . . .        O  67  To A. Fuscus     22
     Like the first race in Saturns reign   . . . . . .       O  71  Hor. Epode II     3
     Ill-fated Race! So oft besieg'd in vain,   . . . . .     O 250  Irene            29
     Unlike the trifling Race of vulgar Beauties,       . . . . O 298  Irene            18
     Not so while long th' undaunted race maintain'd    . . .   Y  23  Tr Add. Battle   36
     The feather'd race and thirsted for their blood:   . . .   Y  24  Tr Add. Battle   85
     Prodigious madness of the writing race!    . . . . . .    Y  67  Prologue Lethe    1
RACK
     Then leave him stretch'd upon the ling'ring Rack,  . . .   O 273  Irene            36
     The Rack expects us, and the Sword pursues.        . . . . O 315  Irene             2
     To tire the burthen'd rack and gorge destruction   . . .   Y 196  Irene          V 18C
     To court the sword and tempt the glutted rack  . . . .   Y 196  Irene          V 18D
     Just as the Rack forc'd out his struggling Soul,   . . .   O 330  Irene            13
RACKS
     Learn here what Anguish racks the guilty Breast,   . . .   O 246  Irene Prologue   11
     Contrive new Racks, imbitter every Pang,   . . . . . .   O 334  Irene            74
RADIANCE
     And Truth diffuse her Radiance from the Stage.     . . . . O  53  Pro Drury-Lane   62
```

		PAGE	TITLE	LINE

RADIANCE   (CONTINUED)
    Spreads her mild Radiance, and descending Dews . . . .   O 313   Irene   2
    Fill all the Starry Lamps with Fav'ring Sky . . . . .   O 364   Irene   V   27
      <Radiance>.

RADIANT
    Ye nymphs of rosy lips and radiant eyes, ...   O 46   Vanity Wishes   323
    Where radiant Phoebus rising from the sea   . . . . .   Y 23   Tr Add. Battle   22

RAG'D
    Rag'd within the Master's Breast   . . . . . .   O 148   Tr Boet III.12   14
    He sigh'd, He rag'd, he threatend and he . . . . . .   O 364   Irene   V   20
      flatter'd
    Oft have I rag'd, when their wide-wasting Cannon   . .   O 273   Irene   24
    Why, when Destruction rag'd around our Walls,   . . .   O 290   Irene   38
    But flatterd threatend, sigh'd and rag'd in vain   . . .   Y 170   Irene   V   24

RAGE
    In virtue's cause once more exert his rage, ...   O 23   London   262
    In virtue's cause once more forsake his rage,   . . .   O 23   London   V 262
    Low skulks the hind beneath the rage of pow'r, ...   O 32   Vanity Wishes   33
    Improve his heady rage with treach'rous skill,   . . .   O 44   Vanity Wishes   281
    With close Malevolence, or public Rage;   . . . . . .   O 57   Prologue Comus   8
    Uncheck'd on both, loud rabbles vent their rage, . . .   O 59   Pro Good Nat'd   15
    Uncheck'd on both, caprice may vent its rage,   . . .   O 59   Pro Good Nat'd   V 15
    This night presents a play, which publick rage, . . .   O 61   Pro Word Wise   1
    Whose blood shall quench some Grecian's thirsty rage, .   O 74   Tr. Iliad Bk 6   16
    Rage with disdain, and hope th' approaching war;   . .   O 75   Tr Add. Battle   1
    The floods of rage, and calm thy rufled soul.   . . .   O 77   Festina Lente   8
    Thus wak'd to rage by Musick's dreadfull Pow'r, . . .   O 97   Hickman Spinet   13
    Parent of Rage and hot desire, ...   O 99   Ode Friendship   V   6
    Suspended faction ceas'd from rage and strife,   . . .   O 118   Epitaph Hanmer   17
    Work'd into sudden rage by wintry show'rs, ...   O 132   Tr. Rambler 65   1
    And deride their utmost Rage.   . . . .   O 145   Tr Boeth. II.4   22
    Their Rage, and pall'd their Appetite of Murder;   . .   O 249   Irene   8
    At length the Conquerour has spent his   . . . . .   O 350   Irene   V   8
      rage--
    The Lust of Gold succeeds the Rage of Conquest,   . .   O 249   Irene   13
    The Sultan's majesty the warriours rage   . . . . .   Y 123   Irene   V 98
    Disarm'd his Rage, and in repeated Visits   . . . . .   O 259   Irene   122
    Despotick Rage pursues the Life of Cali; . . . . . .   O 270   Irene   16
    And all the giddy rage of desperation   . . . . . .   Y 142   Irene   V 39
    Nor farther tempt the avenging rage of Heaven   . . .   Y 168   Irene   V 134
    When Heav'n shall bid the swelling Billows rage, . . .   O 300   Irene   60
    On ev'ry Side Confusion, Rage and Death, ...   O 300   Irene   70
    Abdalla's Rage and Cali's Stratagems.   . . . . . .   O 301   Irene   94
    All ye, whose Blood tyrannick Rage effus'd, ...   O 306   Irene   53
    An undistinguish'd Sound of threat'ning Rage.   . . .   O 311   Irene   13
    While secret Flames, with unextinguish'd Rage,   . . .   O 315   Irene   35
      Hated Name! his jealous Rage   . . . . . .   O 316   Irene   9
    Whose Fear, or Rage, or Treachery betray'd us.   . . .   O 316   Irene   17
    Smiles at the Threat'nings of defeated Rage.   . . .   O 325   Irene   19
    Whence is this Rage? what barb'rous Tongue has wrong'd .   O 325   Irene   27
      me?
    To check this Torrent of imperious Rage, ...   O 327   Irene   5
    Was she then guiltless! Has my thoughtless Rage   . .   O 332   Irene   18
    Ye Slaves of Cruelty, ye Tools of Rage, ...   O 332   Irene   22
    My Rage and Grief had hid from my Remembrance.   . . .   O 334   Irene   65
    I feel, I see the Ruffian's barb'rous Rage.   . . . .   O 334   Irene   66
    My rage and grief had had from my remembrance   . . .   Y 215   Irene   V 69B
    Weak Man with erring Rage may throw the Dart,   . . .   O 335   Irene   14
    Whose direfull rage destroy'd my native land.   . . .   Y 18   Tr. Iliad Bk 6   29
    And with fell rage and secret anguish burn.   . . . .   Y 24   Tr Add. Battle   65
    With rage implacable he still persue'd   . . . . . .   Y 24   Tr Add. Battle   84
    And weakly hopes to 'scape the critick's rage.   . . .   Y 67   Prologue Lethe   12

RAGES
    And now a rabble rages, now a fire;   . . . . . .   O   9   London   14
    Wide-wasting pest! that rages unconfin'd, ...   O 31   Vanity Wishes   23
    The stormy Sultan rages at our sway.   . . . . . .   O 329   Irene   12
    Invades my soul, and rages in my breast.   . . . . .   Y 11   Tr Hor Epode 9   6
    Where'er the battle rages bends his course.   . . . .   Y 25   Tr Add. Battle   119

RAGING
    Then say how fierce desire and raging hate, ...   Y 92   Vanity Wishes   V   5
    Then say how hot desire and raging hate, ...   Y 92   Vanity Wishes   V   5
    Dire nurse of raging lions, bore.   . . . . .   O 66   Hor I Ode xxii   16
    But when your Musick sooths the raging pain,   . . .   O 96   Hickman Spinet   6
    Inflames alike with raging fires.   . . . . . .   O 99   Ode Friendship   8
    Or raging factions rush to war, ...   O 126   An Ode   34
    <t>o stop this raging torrent of destruction . . . . .   Y 117   Irene   V109C
    The raging Madman's unconnected Schemes   . . . . .   O 287   Irene   10
    Untouch'd by fierce Ambition's raging Fires.   . . .   O 293   Irene   110
    Thy sacred Freight shall still the raging Main.   . .   O 322   Irene   6
    The sacred Freight shall still the raging Main.   . .   O 322   Irene   V   6
    The raging Sultan burns till our Return, ...   O 327   Irene   11
    The raging of the kindled fire   . . . .   Y 12   Tr Hor Epode 9   40

RAIL
    Their wish is full to riot and to rail.   . . . . .   O 34   Vanity Wishes   98
    For that blest year when all that vote may rail; . . .   O 60   Pro Good Nat'd   18
    Unmov'd tho' Witlings sneer and Rivals rail;   . . .   O 246   Irene Prologue   29

RAIN
    And rain from either flow.   . . . .   Y 86   To Lyce, Lady   V 12

RAINBOWS
    Striped rainbows round her eyes are seen, ...   O 127   To Lyce, Lady   11

```
                                                              PAGE    TITLE              LINE
RAIS'D
     Rais'd from some pleasing dream of wealth and pow'r,  . .   O  18 London             184
     And rais'd us from our wretched state,      . . . . . . .   O  79 Feast St Simon      20
     What rais'd our Virtues here below,      . . . . . . .      O 100 Ode Friendship      27
     What rais'd your Virtue here below,      . . . . . . .      O 100 Ode Friendship    V 27
     I rais'd his Thoughts to more sublime Devotion.   . . .     O 274 Irene               46
     Say, how the Hand of Violence was rais'd,    . . . . .      O 295 Irene               25
     So sure the Fall of Greatness rais'd on Crimes,   . . .     O 335 Irene               10
     Here have I rais'd four sacred altars, two    . . . . .     Y   7 Virgil Daphnis      43
     His arm alone rais'd bulwarks of the dead.   . . . . . .    Y  25 Tr Add. Battle     121
RAIS'E
     Nor annual tax was rais'e by annual wars.    . . . . .      Y  94 Vanity Wishes     V 60B
RAISE
     Let such raise palaces, and manors buy,   . . . . . . .     O  12 London             57
     And raise his treasures higher than before.  . . . . .      O  19 London            205
     On weak foundations raise th' enormous weight?   . . . .    O  35 Vanity Wishes      126
     To buried merit raise the tardy bust.    . . . . . . .      O  38 Vanity Wishes      162
     Where wasted nations raise a single name,    . . . . .      O  39 Vanity Wishes      186
     Still raise for good the supplicating voice,   . . . . .    O  47 Vanity Wishes      351
     For blessing, raise the supplicating voice,   . . . . .     Y 108 Vanity Wishes    V 351
     To raise them from their fall.   . . . . . . . . .          O  79 Feast St Simon      30
     To raise our prostrate country from its ruins.   . . .      Y 117 Irene             V109A
     My Policy shall raise an easy Throne;    . . . . . . .      O 257 Irene               78
RAISES
     That raises tumults in the female bosom seditions  . . .    Y 158 Irene             V  12
        (mutinies
     That raises Tumults in the female Breast,    . . . . .      O 287 Irene               12
RAISING
     Then kist his son and raising to the skies   . . . . .      Y  20 Tr. Iliad Bk 6      97
RAJAS
     And Indias rajas ask their doom from thee    . . . . .      Y 131 Irene             V 32
RAMBLING
     Rambling often to and fro'   . . . . . . . . . .            Y 300 Extemp. Elegy       10
RAMPARTS
     Did roaring Whirlwinds sweep us from the Ramparts:   . .    O 251 Irene               55
     When Genoa's faithless Sons forsook the Ramparts   . . .    O 351 Irene             V  5
     And dash'd the Might of Asem from the Ramparts.   . . .     O 312 Irene               12
     And push'd the Might of Moluc from the Ramparts.  . . .     O 363 Irene             V 15
RAN
     Rivers rested as they ran,   . . . . . . . . . .            O 148 Tr Boet III.12     V 10
RANDOM
     When erring Fury throws the random dart   . . . . . .       O 345 Irene             V 28
RANG'D
     Had rang'd embattled Nations at our Gates:   . . . . .      O 250 Irene               23
RANGE
     Quitting my close Retreat, I range the City,   . . . .      O 251 Irene               60
     That range unciviliz'd from Rock to Rock,    . . . . .      O 268 Irene               30
     Ere I could range them on the crowded Deck,   . . . .       O 271 Irene               28
     Elude my Vengeance? no--My Troops shall range  . . . .      O 274 Irene               58
     Through bowing Slaves, I range the private Rooms,  . . .    O 283 Irene               17
     To range those walks of tyranny and lust   . . . . .       Y 165 Irene             V 85
     Descend to range these Mansions of Misfortune,   . . .     O 292 Irene               95
     Descend from Heavn, to range the distant World   . . .     O 349 Irene             V 10
     That range lascivious through the lonesome   . . . . .      Y   7 Virgil Daphnis    V 50
        roads
     Teach me to range my troopes in just array   . . . . .     Y  22 Tr Add. Battle      5
RANK
     His Wealth, his Rank, his Honours he recounted,   . . .     O 299 Irene               45
RANKS
     Nor bursting through the ranks in wild distraction  . .     Y 163 Irene             V 47
RANSACK
     Watch the weak hour, and ransack all the heart;   . . .     O  17 London            155
RANSOM
     Ransom of Kings, the purchass of your blood  . . . . .      O 351 Irene             V 14
RAPACITY
     Rapacity would call for more;   . . . . . . . . .           O 144 Tr Boeth. II.2      10
RAPID
     Such bribes the rapid Greek o'er Asia whirl'd,   . . .      O  39 Vanity Wishes      179
     Here stop, my soul, thy rapid flight,    . . . . . . .      O 125 An Ode              17
     O'er ice the rapid skaiter flies,   . . . . . . . .         O 203 Tr. on Skating       1
     Are these the rapid Thunderbolts of War,    . . . . .       O 325 Irene               11
     That laves proud Ilion with his rapid flood,   . . . .      Y  18 Tr. Iliad Bk 6      12
RAPINE
     Here malice, rapine, accident, conspire,    . . . . .       O   9 London             13
     And Rapine and Pollution mark their Way.    . . . . .       O 110 To Posterity         8
     Behold how Lust and Rapine struggle round her.   . . .      O 252 Irene               82
RAPTUR'D
     And raptur'd sees the new-found ruby shine.   . . . . .     O  82 Young Author      V  6D
RAPTURE
     And rapture saddens to despair.   . . . . . . . .           O 123 Winter's Walk       12
     Tho' rapture sings, and beauty shines.   . . . . . .        O 125 An Ode              12
     I too can feel the rapture, fierce and strong;   . . .      O 142 In Baretti Bk.       3
     Behold the Monsters gaze with savage Rapture,   . . .       O 252 Irene               81
     Aspasia's thine, and all thy Life is Rapture--   . . .      O 260 Irene              142
     Prais'd without Rapture, left without Regret.   . . .       O 263 Irene               18
     Still at Aspasia's Voice a sudden Rapture    . . . . .      O 265 Irene                4
     Whence flow the Hopes and Fears, Despair and Rapture,  .    O 277 Irene               41
     Whence all those Hopes and Fears Despair and   . . . .      O 355 Irene             V 18
        Rapture
     But all give way to Rapture and Demetrius.   . . . . .      O 295 Irene               20
     Yet ere we give our loosen'd Thoughts to Rapture,  . . .    O 309 Irene               18
```

```
                                                     PAGE    TITLE              LINE
RAPTURES
    Vain Raptures all--For your inferiour Natures  . . . .  O 276 Irene              15
    With Raptures such as fire the Pagan Crouds,   . . . .  O 286 Irene               3
    Exalt my soul, and swell it into raptures.     . . . .  Y 189 Irene           V  1F
    In vain affected Raptures flush the Cheek,     . . . .  O 315 Irene              29
RARELY
    How rarely reason guides the stubborn choice,  . . . .  O  31 Vanity Wishes      11
    How rarely reason guides the hasty choice,     . . . .  Y  92 Vanity Wishes   V  11
    How rarely would they meet in crouded Courts,  . . . .  O 308 Irene              16
RASH
    But shun, rash youth, the gay alcove,          . . . . . . .  O 121 To Miss Playin    9
    And dooms my rash Fidelity to Ruin.            . . . . . . .  O 256 Irene             49
RASHLY
    "Why gen'rous warriour will you rashly run     . . . .  Y  18 Tr. Iliad Bk 6      19
RASHNESS
    Rashness! thou spring from whence misfortunes flow!  . .  O  77 Festina Lente       9
RAT'LING
    In rat'ling storms huge promontories flie      . . . .  Y  26 Tr Add. Battle   V 140
RAT'ST
    Too high, bright Maid, thou rat'st exterior Grace;  . .  O 277 Irene              30
RATED
    Is then your Sov'reign's Life so cheaply rated,  . . .  O 327 Irene              14
RATHER
    Or rather a Paraphrase.                        . . . . . . .  O 117 Epitaph Hanmer  V   T
    'Tis a proof that he had rather                . . . . . . .  O 183 Burlesque Vega  V   3
    'Tis a sign that he had rather                 . . . . . . .  O 183 Burlesque Vega  V   3
    Ah! let me rather seek the Convent's Cell;     . . . .  O 292 Irene              93
    Inform me rather, how thy happy Courage        . . . .  O 295 Irene              27
    Oh! rather scornful of flagitious Greatness,   . . . .  O 320 Irene              28
RAV'D
    Perhaps, where Lear has rav'd, and Hamlet dy'd,  . . .  O  53 Pro Drury-Lane      43
RAVAG'D
    Only to hunt him round the ravag'd World?      . . . .  O 275 Irene              67
RAVAGE
    And all the sons of ravage croud the war;      . . . . .  O  43 Vanity Wishes     250
    With all the sons of ravage croud the war;     . . . . .  O  43 Vanity Wishes  V 250
RAVAGES
    In its wild ravages distinguish'd thee         . . . . .  Y 115 Irene           V 49B
RAVE
    Tossing rave but rave in vain?                 . . . . . . .  O 144 Tr Boeth. II.4     6
    Tossing rave but rave in vain?                 . . . . . . .  O 144 Tr Boeth. II.4     6
    To rave unheeded, while the happy Greek,       . . . . .  O 285 Irene               2
RAVING
    Not then with raving Cries I fill'd the City,  . . . .  O 290 Irene              46
RAVISH'D
    The ravish'd standard, and the captive foe,    . . . . .  O  39 Vanity Wishes     176
    Whate'er Man's Pride has ravish'd from our Sex.  . . .  O 291 Irene              75
    I stole unheeded from their ravish'd Eyes,     . . . . .  O 299 Irene              49
    The dark horizon ravish'd from their sight.    . . . . .  Y  24 Tr Add. Battle     75
RAY
    Should Reason guide thee with her brightest ray,  . . .  O  37 Vanity Wishes     145
    Unhurt by Phoebus fi'ry ray.                   . . . . .  O  72 Hor. Epode II      36
    Spring yield<s> to Summer<'s> sovereign ray,   . . . . .  O 231 Tr Horace IV.7     10
    Dispells the darkness with his golden ray      . . . . .  Y  23 Tr Add. Battle     23
RAYS
    Thro' him the rays of regal bounty shine,      . . . . .  O  34 Vanity Wishes     102
    Ye nymphs whom starry rays invest,             . . . . . . .  O 126 To Lyce, Lady      1
    but if your influence be too wide--your dissipated rays  .  Y 132 Irene           V  41
RE'ECHOES
    Their growing fame re'echoes to the skies.     . . . . .  Y  22 Tr Add. Battle      9
REACH'D
    Has Treason's dire Infection reach'd my Palace?  . . .  O 272 Irene               2
    Our Bark unseen has reach'd th' appointed Bay, . . . .  O 304 Irene               1
    Just as it reach'd my Lips, a sudden Cry       . . . . . .  O 316 Irene              27
READ
    By wit, by knowledge, studious to be read,     . . . .  O 141 Tr Rambler 208      3
    Who has not read the Theban brothers' hate?    . . . . .  Y  22 Tr Add. Battle     14
READER
    If Genius warm thee, Reader, stay,             . . . . . . .  O 154 Epita. Hogarth      5
READY
    Studious to please, and ready to submit,       . . . . . .  O  16 London            123
    His ready help was ever nigh,                  . . . . . . .  O 201 Death Dr Levet  V  18
    Had not my ready thought remov'd Aspasia       . . . . .  O 367 Irene           V  24
REAL
    And real Happiness enjoys.                     . . . . . . .  O 145 Tr Boeth III.1     12
REALM
    To him the church, the realm, their pow'rs consign,  . .  O  34 Vanity Wishes     101
    Thus early wise, th' endanger'd realm to aid,  . . . .  O 117 Epitaph Hanmer       9
    Each Realm where Beauty turns the graceful Shape,  . . .  O 262 Irene              13
    Is not each Realm that smiles with kinder Suns,  . . .  O 265 Irene              35
REALMS
    Illustrious Edward! from the realms of day,    . . . . .  O  15 London             99
    And Winter barricades the realms of Frost;     . . . . .  O  41 Vanity Wishes     208
    And sees defenceless realms receive his sway;  . . . .  O  42 Vanity Wishes     244
    To distant realms and climes unknown,          . . . . .  O  70 Hor.II Ode XX      18
    Now in the realms below the Pygmie shades      . . . . .  O  76 Tr Add. Battle     41
    But where the Realms beneath the Pole          . . . . . . .  O  79 Feast St Simon     44
    To dismal realms, and regions void of peace,   . . . . .  O  84 Epi Dist Moth.     30
    Rushes on the Realms below.                    . . . . . . .  O 149 Tr Boet III.12     18
    Till the Realms of Light you gain.             . . . . . . .  O 150 Tr Boet III.12     46
    Curst as the Tyrant of th' infernal Realms,    . . . . .  O 294 Irene             134

                                    267
```

REALMS   (CONTINUED)   PAGE   TITLE   LINE
    Shuns Pluto's kingdoms and the realms of night;   . . .   Y   7 Virgil Daphnis   33
    And the sad fate of Pygmie realms I sing.   . . . . .   Y 22 Tr Add. Battle   2
    The victor Cranes the conquer'd realms possess,   . . . Y 23 Tr Add. Battle   34
    Hurling vast mounts against the realms above   . . . .   Y 26 Tr Add. Battle   138
REAR'D
    First rear'd the Stage, immortal Shakespear rose;   . . .   O 51 Pro Drury-Lane   2
REASCEND
    Let Pleasure bloom and Cities reascend.   . . . . . .   O 372 Irene   V 10
    Bid Pleasure bloom and Cities reascend.   . . . . . .   O 372 Irene   V 10
REASON
    How rarely reason guides the stubborn choice, ...   O 31 Vanity Wishes   11
    How rarely reason guides the hasty choice, ...   Y 92 Vanity Wishes   V 11
    Should Reason guide thee with her brightest ray,   . . .   O 37 Vanity Wishes   145
    Yet Reason frowns on War's unequal game, ...   O 39 Vanity Wishes   185
    Yet Reason blush on War's unequal game, ...   Y 100 Vanity Wishes   V 185
    Let Reason with superiour force controul   . . . . . .   O 77 Festina Lente   7
    Nor yoke his Reason with his Will: . . . .   O 146 Tr Boeth III.5   4
    In Reason, Nature, Truth he dares to trust: . . . . .   O 246 Irene Prologue   33
    So shall Timidity assist thy Reason, ...   O 266 Irene   21
    O'erturns the Fabrick of presumptuous Reason, ...   O 269 Irene   8
    Th' enlivening Wit, the penetrating Reason?   . . . . .   O 278 Irene   56
    The Sparkling Wit the penetrating Reason   . . . . . .   O 356 Irene   V 23
    Pants for the dread Event--But let us reason--   . . . .   O 280 Irene   31
    To cant, at last, of Reason to a Lover?   . . . . . .   O 281 Irene   34
    That Reason gives her Scepter to his Hand, ...   O 281 Irene   40
    Who hear thee speak, and not abandon Reason?   . . . .   O 281 Irene   43
    Reason! the hoary Dotard's dull Directress, ...   O 281 Irene   44
    Reason! the tim'rous Pilot, that to shun   . . . . . .   O 281 Irene   46
    Reason with Reason fights on equal Terms, ...   O 287 Irene   9
    Reason with Reason fights on equal Terms, ...   O 287 Irene   9
    Reason commands to cast the less away;   . . . . . .   O 290 Irene   33
    Enough--resistless Reason calms my Soul--   . . . . .   O 297 Irene   1
    By Reason not convinc'd, nor won by Love.   . . . . .   O 310 Irene   8
    The Gleams of Reason, and the Clouds of Passion,   . . .   O 321 Irene   44
    Or reason with the slave thats saved Demetrius   . . .   Y 210 Irene   V 23
REASON'S
    If no wild Draught depart from Reason's Rules, ...   O 246 Irene Prologue   17
    The Cause that shrinks from Reason's powerful Voice. . .   O 293 Irene   126
REASONING
    My reasoning Pow'rs--Dear, hapless, lost Aspasia!   . . .   O 252 Irene   78
    And then leaves the glittering reptile, reasoning   . . .   Y 146 Irene   V 23
       insect
REBEL
    Tho' grief and fondness in my breast rebel, ...   O   8 London   1
    Why should Cali rebel--unexpensive age   . . . . . .   Y 120 Irene   V 40
    Each rebel Wish, each traitor Inclination   . . . . .   O 287 Irene   11
REBELLION
    Disperse Rebellion through the Eastern World;   . . . .   O 274 Irene   52
    And point vindictive Lightnings at Rebellion, ...   O 300 Irene   61
REBELLION'S
    Rebellion's vengeful talons seize on Laud.   . . . . .   O 39 Vanity Wishes   168
REBELLIOUS
    Behold rebellious virtue quite o'erthrown, ...   O 13 London   63
    And ask, what guilty Pow'r's rebellious Hand   . . . .   O 293 Irene   119
    An angry Murmur, a rebellious Frown, ...   O 312 Irene   19
REBELS
    And quell the rebels of the heart.   . . . .   O 126 An Ode   40
RECALL
    A single Thought now rove, recall it home.   . . . . .   O 255 Irene   7
    Recall th' extorted Doom.--It must be so, ...   O 326 Irene   40
RECALS
    No Pray'r recals, no Diligence redeems;   . . . . . .   O 303 Irene   8
RECEIVE
    When first the college rolls receive his name, ...   O 36 Vanity Wishes   135
    And sees defenceless realms receive his sway;   . . . .   O 42 Vanity Wishes   244
    This tributary verse receive, my fair, ...   O 80 Lady Birthday   1
    Receive th' unhappy ghosts of scornful maids.   . . . .   O 83 Epi Dist Moth.   13
    Tho' Wealth, and Pow'r, and Glory they receive, ...   O 247 Irene Epilogue   19
    Did not our sails receive the wondring winds   . . . .   Y 115 Irene   V 49G
    But will she yet receive the Faith of Mecca?   . . . .   O 261 Irene   11
    With pious Warmth receive our Prophet's Law----   . . .   O 262 Irene   25
    Receive th' impatient Sultan to thy Arms;   . . . . .   O 267 Irene   10
    That all her Faculties receive his Chains?   . . . . .   O 281 Irene   39
    Receive her, and protect her, gracious Heav'n!   . . . .   O 297 Irene   16
    Be thine, that Wealth can give, or Guilt receive.   . . .   O 322 Irene   58
RECEIVES
    If the gull'd conqueror receives the chain, ...   O 16 London   121
    Receives his full Reward in Beauty's Arms.   . . . . .   O 247 Irene Epilogue   24
RECEIVING
    On the Author's receiving a Sprig of Myrtle   . . . . .   O 95 Sprig of Myrtl   V   T
RECESSES
    Search to the dark Recesses of the Soul, ...   O 308 Irene   13
RECLINE
    Recline upon my Breast thy sinking Beauties: . . . .   O 295 Irene   8
RECLINES
    Reclines against the Shore: Our Grecian Troop   . . . .   O 304 Irene   3
RECOIL
    Recoil from Thought, and shudder at myself.   . . . . .   O 322 Irene   12
RECOLLECT
    Inforc'd we love, unheeding recollect.   . . . . . .   O 134 Tr. Rambler 96   2

```
                                         PAGE     TITLE              LINE
RECOLLECT        (CONTINUED)
     Here recollect thy dissipated Pow'rs.--  . . . . . .   O 287  Irene               2
RECOLLECTED
     And recollected toils endear'd the shade;  . . . . .   O 118  Epitaph Hanmer     42
RECOMPENCE
     Is this the Recompence reserv'd for me?  . . . . . .   O 307  Irene               7
RECORD
     When future histories record the deed.   . . . . . .   Y 180  Irene           V  27
RECORDS
     And crouds with crimes the records of mankind;  . . .  O  31  Vanity Wishes      24
     Records each Act, each Thought of sov'reign Man,  . .  O 276  Irene              21
     Records each deed each thought of sovereign Man   . .  O 355  Irene           V  10
     No Records, but the Records of the Sky.  . . . . . .   O 305  Irene              35
     No Records, but the Records of the Sky.   . . . . .    O 305  Irene              35
RECOUNTED
     His Wealth, his Rank, his Honours he recounted,  . . . O 299  Irene              45
RECOVERING
     the world recovering from its convulsion  . . . . . .  Y 164  Irene           V  77
RED
     Red her cheek as Cath'rine pear,   . . . . . . . .     Y 300  Extemp. Elegy       6
REDEEMS
     No Pray'r recals, no Diligence redeems;   . . . . . .  O 303  Irene               8
REDUC'D
     Maxims like these, if once reduc'd to practice  . . .  O 352  Irene           V   2
REEDS
     And me to tune at ease th' unequal reeds.   . . . . .  O  64  Virgil Past.I      12
REEKING
     The Bassa, reeking with his Master's Murder,   . . . . O 300  Irene              80
REELING
     Some frolick drunkard, reeling from a feast,   . . . . O  21  London            228
     Some gamesome drunkard, reeling from a feast,  . . . . Y  59  London          V 228
REFIN'D
     Sense, freedom, piety, refin'd away,   . . . . .       O  15  London            105
     Then crush'd by Rules, and weaken'd as refin'd,  . . . O  52  Pro Drury-Lane     29
REFLECT
     Repeat his maxims, and reflect his face;  . . . . . .  O  16  London            137
     Once more reflect, suppress this infant Folly.  . . .  O 281  Irene              56
     Reflect that Life and Death, affecting Sounds,  . . .  O 290  Irene              26
     Reflect that Life, like ev'ry other Blessing,  . . .   O 290  Irene              28
REFLECTED
     Of light reflected from the polish'd brass   . . . .   Y  20  Tr. Iliad Bk 6     93
REFLECTION
     Yet then shall calm reflection bless the night,  . . . O  62  Pro Word Wise      21
REFLECTS
     Through half his Course reflects the blaze of  . . . . O 353  Irene           V   2
        War
     Now but reflects those Beams that flow'd from thee.  . O 298  Irene              15
REFRAIN
     Should tempting Novelty thy cell refrain,   . . . . .  O  37  Vanity Wishes     149
     Tho' reluctant still refrain,  . . . . . . . .         O 150  Tr Boet III.12     45
REFRESHMENT
     And give the weary passenger refreshment.   . . . . .  Y 130  Irene           V 12D
REFUGE
     Thou fly'st for refuge to the wilds of Kent;   . . . . O  23  London            257
     You fly for refuge to the wilds of Kent:  . . . . .    Y  61  London          V 257
     He seeks the refuge of monastic rest.  . . . . . .     O  35  Vanity Wishes     118
REFULGENT
     Refulgent on his starry throne  . . . . . . . .        O  79  Feast St Simon     23
     In ev'ry act refulgent virtue glow'd.  . . . . . .     O 118  Epitaph Hanmer     16
REFUND
     Refund the plunder of the beggar'd land.  . . . . .    O  19  London            201
     Refund the plunder of the begger'd land.  . . . . .    O  19  London          V 201
REFUS'D
     And, though refus'd, conceals it from the Sultan.  . . O 258  Irene              89
     His Offers oft repeated, still refus'd,   . . . . . .  O 259  Irene             109
REFUSAL
     With soften'd Voice she dropp'd the faint Refusal,  .  O 303  Irene              31
REFUSE
     Then shall thy friend, nor thou refuse his aid,  . . . O  23  London            260
     When statutes glean the refuse of the sword,   . . .  O  31  Vanity Wishes      31
     Trembling to grant, nor daring to refuse,   . . . .   O 260  Irene             126
     The Refuse of our Swords, the Dross of Conquest,  . .  O 286  Irene               3
     If when Religion prompts me to refuse,  . . . . . .    O 289  Irene              24
     'Tis yours to grant, or to refuse him entrance  . . .  Y 168  Irene           V   3
     Should Heav'n yet unappeas'd refuse its Aid,   . . .   O 301  Irene              97
     Relax'd with Fear, refuse to bear me forward.  . . .   O 320  Irene              12
     Refuse their Office, and uncertain Life  . . . . . .   O 320  Irene              21
REGAIN
     Strives to regain her Empire of the Mind:   . . . . .  O 320  Irene              33
REGAIN'D
     Till Shame regain'd the Post that Sense betray'd,  . . O  52  Pro Drury-Lane     27
REGAL
     Thro' him the rays of regal bounty shine,   . . . . .  O  34  Vanity Wishes     102
     The regal palace, the luxurious board,  . . . . . .    O  35  Vanity Wishes     115
     This Regal Confidence, this pious Ardour,   . . . . .  O 264  Irene              33
     No regal Pageant deck'd with casual Honours,   . . .   O 268  Irene              19
     Did regal Diadems invest my Brow,   . . . . . . .      O 289  Irene              12
     Shrinks at th' o'erpow'ring Gleams of regal State,  .  O 292  Irene             100
     Shrinks at th' oerpowring blaze of regal State  . . .  O 368  Irene           V  30
REGARD
     By Solon caution'd to regard his end,   . . . . . . .  O  45  Vanity Wishes     314
```

REGARD	(CONTINUED)		PAGE	TITLE	LINE
Celestial pow'rs! that piety regard, ...			O 141	Tr Rambler 208	1
Which Cheats interpret, and which Fools regard? . . .			O 250	Irene	43
if human miseries or affairs yet claim your			Y 181	Irene	V 54
regard					

REGARDS
| A generous foe regards, with pitying eye, ... | | | O 61 | Pro Word Wise | 5 |
| Her mournful Charms attracted his Regards, ... | | | O 259 | Irene | 121 |

REGION
| To deck these Bow'rs each Region shall combine, . . . | | | O 279 | Irene | 88 |
| To make thee blest each Region shall combine . . . . | | | O 351 | Irene | V 26 |

REGIONS
And starves exhausted regions in his way;			O 42	Vanity Wishes	228
To dismal realms, and regions void of peace, ...			O 84	Epi Dist Moth.	30
But on these regions of delight, ...			O 121	To Miss Playin	19
But on those regions of delight, ...			O 121	To Miss Playin	V 19
This habitant th' aerial regions boast.			O 138	Tr Rambler 161	1
Announc'd the dinner to the regions round, ...			O 192	Tr. Medea II	6
From those bright Regions of eternal Day, ...			O 253	Irene	99
To Bid wasted Regions flourish at her smile			O 372	Irene	V 8
--O Demetrius O for a cottage in those happy regions .			Y 177	Irene	V 108
Let distant regions echo with his name			Y 20	Tr. Iliad Bk 6	103

REGRET
I praise the hermit, but regret the friend, ...			O 8	London	4
And mortgag'd states their grandsires wreaths regret, .			O 39	Vanity Wishes	187
And mortgag'd states their former wreaths regret, . . .			Y 100	Vanity Wishes	V 187
Prais'd without Rapture, left without Regret.			O 263	Irene	18

REGRETTED
| Cleora thus regretted flies, ... | | | Y 39 | Lady Leaving | 5 |

REGULAR
| By regular Approach essay'd the Heart; . . . . . . | | | O 51 | Pro Drury-Lane | 12 |
| By regular Approach assail'd the Heart; . . . . . . | | | O 51 | Pro Drury-Lane | V 12 |

REGULATE
| To fix his Court, and regulate his Pleasures, ... | | | O 291 | Irene | 78 |
| To form his Court and regulate his pleasures . . . . | | | Y 164 | Irene | V 78 |

REGULATED
| To tune the regulated heart. . . . . | | | O 121 | To Miss Playin | 36 |

REGULATES
| Conducts the Sun, and regulates the Spheres. . . . . | | | O 293 | Irene | 124 |
| Rolls on the Sun, and Regulates the Spheres. . . . . | | | O 369 | Irene | V 17 |

REIGN
Here let those reign, whom pensions can incite . . .			O 11	London	51
A single jail, in Alfred's golden reign, ...			O 22	London	248
Tir'd with contempt, she quits the slipp'ry reign, . .			O 46	Vanity Wishes	335
Existence saw him spurn her bounded Reign, ...			O 51	Pro Drury-Lane	5
Their Slaves were willing, and their Reign was long; . .			O 52	Pro Drury-Lane	26
But forc'd at length her antient Reign to quit, . . .			O 52	Pro Drury-Lane	35
'Tis yours this Night to bid the Reign commence . . .			O 53	Pro Drury-Lane	57
Unwholesome Sirius' sultry reign;			O 69	Hor.II Ode 14	16
Like the first race in Saturns reign			O 71	Hor. Epode II	3
So shall you guiltless reign, and all mankind adore. . .			O 84	Epi Dist Moth.	47
Bright Stella, form'd for universal Reign, ...			O 96	Hickman Spinet	1
We bid propitious Heav'n prolong your reign, ...			O 96	Hickman Spinet	7
Nor shall the Lyon, wont of old to reign			O 111	To Posterity	19
And Spenser's verse prolongs Eliza's reign;			O 114	On C. Cibber	2
Since Stella still extends her reign, ...			O 122	Stella Mourn.	11
Still wider spreads thy horrid reign, ...			O 123	Winter's Walk	7
And o'er the globe extend your reign, ...			O 189	Epilogue	7
Then Summer sinks in Autumn's reign, ...			O 231	Tr Horace IV.7	11
And reign without a Rival in his Bosom.			O 373	Irene	V 29
To pour my Prayers for thy successful Reign, ...			O 264	Irene	10
What Passions reign among thy Crew, Leontius?			O 270	Irene	21

REIGN'D
| Whose sire Eetion in Cilicia reign'd . . . . | | | Y 18 | Tr. Iliad Bk 6 | 7 |

REIGN'ST
| That reign'st supreme among the pow'rs above, ... | | | Y 20 | Tr. Iliad Bk 6 | 100 |

REIGNING
| Not less capricious than a reigning fair, ... | | | O 95 | Sprig of Myrtl | 5 |
| Not less capricious than the reigning fair, ... | | | O 95 | Sprig of Myrtl | V 5 |

REIGNS
That when confusion o'er the country reigns, ...			O 64	Virgil Past.I	15
Where sable night in all her horrour reigns;			O 83	Epi Dist Moth.	11
Pleasure in ev'ry nymph and shepherd reigns, ...			Y 7	Virgil Daphnis	36

REINS
| Your passions; guide the reins with steady hand, . . . | | | O 77 | Festina Lente | 4 |
| And snatch'd the Reins of abdicated Pow'r . . . . . | | | O 256 | Irene | 45 |

REJECT
| Reject the Daughters of contending Kings; . . . . . | | | O 267 | Irene | 7 |

REJECTED
| No more should Greece lament those Prayers rejected. . . | | | O 290 | Irene | 52 |

REJECTS
Oft favours, oft rejects a lover's pray'r:			O 95	Sprig of Myrtl	6
Oft favours, oft rejects the poet's pray'r:			O 95	Sprig of Myrtl	V 6
Now grants, and now rejects the Lover's Care			O 95	Sprig of Myrtl	V 6
None e're rejects hyperbolies of praise.			O 134	Tr Rambler 104	1

REKINDLED
| At length rekindled his accustom'd Fury, ... | | | O 259 | Irene | 110 |

RELATE
| The laureat tribe in servile verse relate, ... | | | O 19 | London | 198 |
| The laureat tribe in venal verse relate, ... | | | O 19 | London | V 198 |

	PAGE	TITLE	LINE
RELATION			
The pressing Exigence forbids Relation.	O 315	Irene	8
RELAX			
Nor Praise relax, nor Difficulty fright;	O 37	Vanity Wishes	148
Did aught but Luxury relax our Nerves	O 347	Irene	V 5
RELAX'D			
Relax'd with Fear, refuse to bear me forward. . . .	O 320	Irene	12
RELEASE			
Till pitying Nature signs the last release, ...	O 45	Vanity Wishes	309
RELENTING			
We come, bright Virgin, tho' relenting Nature	O 325	Irene	20
RELENTLESS			
Their ambush here relentless ruffians lay, ...	O 9	London	15
And sigh'd and wept at her relentless gate.	Y 11	Tr Hor Epode 9	36
RELIEF			
Nor light nor darkness bring his pain relief, ...	O 32	Vanity Wishes	43
Thanks for this kind Relief--with Speed admit him. . .	O 294	Irene	5
Thanks for this kind relief. Conduct him hither . . .	O 370	Irene	V 15
He grasp'd her hand endeav'ring kind relief. . . .	Y 21	Tr. Iliad Bk 6	112
RELIEVE			
Shou'd welcome Sleep relieve the weary Wit, ...	O 246	Irene Prologue	25
RELIEVES			
Love, that with sweet Vicissitude relieves	O 261	Irene	9
RELIGION			
Which heav'n may hear, nor deem religion vain.	O 47	Vanity Wishes	350
That sweep away religion arts and freedom	Y 117	Irene	V109D
Religion calls her from the wish'd Embrace, ...	O 261	Irene	16
If when Religion prompts me to refuse, ...	O 289	Irene	24
Both your religion and your country are	Y 181	Irene	V 52
concern'd			
RELIGION'S			
No more shall feel Religion's hallow'd ardours	O 349	Irene	V 24
RELIQUES			
Preserv'd the reliques of the Latian state	O 78	Festina Lente	18
RELUCTANT			
And yield, reluctant, to despotick Sway.	O 96	Hickman Spinet	5
Tho' reluctant still refrain, ...	O 150	Tr Boet III.12	45
REMAIN			
"Think nothing gain'd, he cries, till nought remain, . .	O 40	Vanity Wishes	202
Enquirer, cease, petitions yet remain, ...	O 47	Vanity Wishes	349
New Behns, new Durfeys, yet remain in Store.	O 53	Pro Drury-Lane	42
Fix'd in his canker'd breast remain:	O 73	Hor. Epode II	78
If yet one spark of Heav'nly fire remain	Y 133	Irene	V 18
REMAIN'D			
Philosophy remain'd, though Nature fled.	O 52	Pro Drury-Lane	34
See! how whate'er remain'd of Man	O 70	Hor.II Ode XX	10
REMAINS			
Of dissipated wealth the small remains, ...	O 9	London	20
But what, my friend, what hope remains for me, ...	O 13	London	67
A single skiff to speed his flight remains;	O 42	Vanity Wishes	238
But unextinguish'd Avarice still remains, ...	O 44	Vanity Wishes	285
To you alone this happy state remains.	O 64	Virgil Past.I	16
Pursue the last Remains of ling'ring Light.	O 302	Irene	4
Yet much remains to hope. I shall not call	O 317	Irene	45
What now remains?	O 318	Irene	11
It now remains to fly!	O 318	Irene	11
These Tears, these Pangs, these last Remains of Life, .	O 329	Irene	53
REMARK			
Remark each anxious toil, each eager strife, ...	O 30	Vanity Wishes	3
REMARK'D			
Caraza speak--have ye remark'd the Bassa?	O 311	Irene	1
REMEDIES			
To yield to remedies is half the cure.	O 140	Tr Rambler 178	1
REMEDY			
His vig'rous remedy display'd	O 201	Death Dr Levet	15
REMEMBER			
Remember Freedom, Glory, Greece, and Love.	O 260	Irene	146
Yet in the Use of Pow'r remember Justice.	O 286	Irene	10
Against his King, and cry, Remember Justice?	O 286	Irene	12
Oppose my Wishes, and--Remember Justice.	O 286	Irene	16
When I am gone remember, O! remember, ...	O 294	Irene	7
When I am gone remember, O! remember, ...	O 294	Irene	7
Remember Mahomet, and cease thy Labour.	O 310	Irene	3
Remember, Peace and Anguish are before thee, ...	O 321	Irene	37
REMEMBER'D			
Grief aids disease, remember'd folly stings, ...	O 35	Vanity Wishes	119
REMEMBRANCE			
Well pleas'd to search the Treasures of Remembrance, . .	O 323	Irene	15
My Rage and Grief had hid from my Remembrance. . . .	O 334	Irene	65
My rage and grief had had from my remembrance	Y 215	Irene	V 69B
REMISSION			
and drink the holy waters the fountain of	Y 130	Irene	V 11
remission			
REMITS			
And weary Cruelty remits her Tortures.	O 249	Irene	10
REMNANT			
And give the short remnant of my life to	O 348	Irene	V 14
prayer,			
REMONSTRANCE			
Through Freedom's sons no more remonstrance rings, . .	O 34	Vanity Wishes	93
Less heard and less, the faint remonstrance falls; . .	O 46	Vanity Wishes	334

```
REMORSE                                                        PAGE    TITLE              LINE
    My soul not oft acquainted with remorse   . . . . . .      Y 159 Irene            V   8
    Remorse and Anguish seize on all my Breast;   . . . . .    O 333 Irene               45
REMORSELESS
    The Lust of Gold, unfeeling and remorseless!   . . . .     O 249 Irene               14
REMOTE
    Remote from Tumult, in th' adjoining Palace,               O 263 Irene                1
    To wait remote from Action, and from Honour,               O 305 Irene               22
    --And loiter'd with his troop remote from Action   . . .   O 376 Irene            V  15
REMOUNT
    Will now remount the slighted Seat of Empire,   . . . .    O 303 Irene               27
REMOV'D
    Wild hope, vain fear, alike remov'd,   . . . . . . . .     O 125 An Ode              26
    Had not my ready thought remov'd Aspasia   . . . . . .     O 367 Irene            V  24
REMOVE
    Would not these pleasures soon remove   . . . . . . . .    O  72 Hor. Epode II       45
    Such Pleasures quickly would remove   . . . . . . . .      O  72 Hor. Epode II    V  45
    All pains, all cares, may favouring heav'n remove,         O  81 Lady Birthday        5
    When souls to blissful climes remove?   . . . . . . .      O 100 Ode Friendship      26
    till you to happier climes remove?   . . . . . . . .       O 100 Ode Friendship   V  26
    Phillips! whose touch harmonious could remove   . . .      O 113 Epit. Phillips       1
    And wish'd my rising anger could remove   . . . . . .      Y  11 Tr Hor Epode 9       23
REND
    None dares with impious steel the grove to rend,   . . .   O 139 Tr Rambler 168       1
    Nor can the might of Theseus rend   . . . . . . . .        O 232 Tr Horace IV.7       27
    Fierce through the bursting Caverns rend their Way?   . .  O 281 Irene               53
RENEW
    In pleasing dreams the blissful age renew,   . . . . .     O  10 London              25
    Once more great nature's works renew   . . . . . . . .     O 125 An Ode           V  23
    Renew our Sorrows, and awake our Fears.   . . . . . .      O 268 Irene               35
RENEW'D
    Renew'd at ev'ry glance on humankind;   . . . . . . .      O  33 Vanity Wishes       70
    For no renew'd hostilities invade   . . . . . . . . .      O  61 Pro Word Wise    V   9
    Whome'er the Hope, still blasted, still renew'd,   . . .   O 310 Irene                1
RENEWS
    The changing year renews the plain,   . . . . . . .        O 231 Tr Horace IV.7        3
RENNY
    I Therefore pray thee, Renny dear,   . . . . . . . .       O 158 Par Hermit III       1
    I pray thee, gentle Renny dear,   . . . . . . . . .        O 158 Par Hermit III    V   1
RENOUNCE
    Renounce her Faith, and be the Queen of Turkey;   . . .    O 258 Irene              100
    Must I for these renounce the Hope of Heav'n,   . . . .    O 276 Irene               13
RENOWN
    Through all his veins the fever of renown   . . . . .      O  36 Vanity Wishes      137
    Resistless burns the fever of renown   . . . . . . .       O  36 Vanity Wishes   V 137
    Each act betrays the fever of renown   . . . . . . .       Y  97 Vanity Wishes   V 137
    Quick fires his breast the fever of renown   . . . . .     Y  97 Vanity Wishes   V 137
    Yields to Renown the Centuries to come.   . . . . . .      O  57 Prologue Comus      18
    She was once of high renown,--   . . . . . . . . .         Y 300 Extemp. Elegy        3
RENOWN'D
    So long renown'd in B<rya>n's deathless strain?   . . .    O 107 Lady F Assizes       2
    That fiery Chief, renown'd for gen'rous Freedom,   . .     O 299 Irene               35
    That firy Chief, renown'd for gen'rous Freedom,   . . .    O 299 Irene            V  35
    O Greece! renown'd for Science and for Wealth,   . . .     O 317 Irene               42
RENT
    For less than rent the dungeons of the Strand;   . . .     O  20 London             215
    The plunder'd palace or sequester'd rent;   . . . . .      O  39 Vanity Wishes      170
REPAIR
    Ye sons of Melody repair,   . . . . . . . . . .            O 191 Tr. Medea I          14
    Hence to the palace and your maids repair;   . . . . .     Y  21 Tr. Iliad Bk 6      121
REPAST
    And, while thy grounds a cheap repast afford,   . . . .    O  20 London             218
    And, while thy beds a cheap repast afford,   . . . . .     O  20 London           V 218
    "Sweet repast, and soft repose;   . . . . . . . . .        O 185 Anacreon Ode 9       30
REPAY
    Then soon your ill-plac'd confidence repay,   . . . . .    O  17 London             156
        Do thou repay the Gift,   . . . . . . . . . .          O 313 Irene               18
    And bounteous Heaven repay the mighty Mercy   . . . .      O 328 Irene               46
    And may bounteous Heav'n repay the mercy on Your           O 344 Irene            V  27
        Heads
    Revolving springs their frost repay.   . . . . . . . .     Y  39 Lady Leaving        10
REPEAT
    Repeat his maxims, and reflect his face;   . . . . . .     O  16 London             137
    Repeat that prince's victories,   . . . . . . . . .        O  68 Hor. II Ode IX       19
    The Queen requested--Wretch, repeat the Message;   . . .   O 331 Irene               13
    The Queen requested--Wretch, repeat thy Message;   . . .   O 331 Irene            V  13
REPEATED
    His Offers oft repeated, still refus'd,   . . . . . .      O 259 Irene              109
    Disarm'd his Rage, and in repeated Visits   . . . . .      O 259 Irene              122
    Then when repeated bowls unlock'd the heart   . . . .      Y  11 Tr Hor Epode 9       17
REPELL
    And teach me to repell the Sultan's Passion.   . . . .     O 265 Irene                3
REPENT
    But soon thou shalt repent: another Moment   . . . .       O 319 Irene               33
REPENTANCE
    A little Life for Grief, and for Repentance.   . . . .     O 327 Irene               23
    A little life from grief and for repentance.   . . . .     Y 207 Irene            V  23
    Irene's crimes, forget not her repentance.   . . . . .     Y 209 Irene            V  55
REPINE
    Speak thou, whose thoughts at humble peace repine,   . .   O  35 Vanity Wishes      121
    When did Felicity repine in Desarts?   . . . . . . .       O 314 Irene               21
```

272

```
                                                         PAGE    TITLE              LINE
REPINES
    Where Want repines, and Vengeance swells,   . . . . . .   O 191 Tr. Medea I       10
    The chill inhabitant repines,   . . . . . . . . .         Y  38 Lady Leaving       3
REPLACE
    Or Virtue shall replace on earth.   . . . . . . .         O 232 Tr Horace IV.7    24
REPLY
    Must hear all taunts, and hear without reply.   . . . .   O  59 Pro Good Nat'd    14
REPLY'D
    When the smiling sage reply'd--   . . . . . . . .         O 181 Parody Warton      7
    When the hoary sage reply'd--   . . . . . . . .           O 181 Parody Warton   V  7
REPLYING
    Woods to evry Sigh replying,   . . . . . . . . .          O 148 Tr Boet III.12  V  6
REPORT
    And wait your Summons to report his Conduct.   . . . .    O 310 Irene             7
    Frame your Report with circumspective Art,   . . . .      O 329 Irene            13
    What need of Caution to report the Fate   . . . .         O 329 Irene            16
REPORTS
    If there be any Land, as Fame reports,   . . . . . .      O 256 Irene            55
REPOS'D
    I scorn a Trust unwillingly repos'd;   . . . . . .        O 256 Irene            34
    Soon shalt thou scorn, in Safety's Arms repos'd,   . . .  O 301 Irene            93
REPOSE
    Where once the harrass'd Briton found repose,   . . .     O  11 London           47
    And hope the balmy blessings of repose:   . . . . .       O  21 London          237
    Calmly rest in safe Repose?   . . . . . . . .             O 144 Tr Boeth. II.4    4
    And soft solicitation courts repose,   . . . . .          O 151 The Ant          12
    "Sweet repast, and soft repose;   . . . . . . .           O 185 Anacreon Ode 9   30
    Attends to waft us to Repose and Safety.   . . . . .      O 258 Irene            82
    For her, Repose is banish'd from the Night   . . . .      O 260 Irene           130
    Till soft Fatigue invite us to repose.   . . . . .        O 323 Irene            18
REPRESENTATION
    At The Representation of Comus,...   . . . . . .          O  56 Prologue Comus    T
REPRESS
    Our supple tribes repress their patriot throats,   . . .  O  34 Vanity Wishes    95
    Do they with Pain repress the struggling Shout,   . . .   O 270 Irene            24
    Could not her Charms repress your Zeal for Murder?   . .  O 332 Irene            24
REPRESS'D
    Stern winter now, by spring repress'd,   . . . . .        O 124 An Ode            1
    --Scarce repress'd the starting tear;--   . . . . .       O 181 Parody Warton     6
REPROACH
    And his last sighs reproach the faith of kings.   . . .   O  35 Vanity Wishes   120
    And his last words reproach the faith of kings.   . . .   Y  96 Vanity Wishes  V 120
    Reproach not Misery.--The Sons of Greece,   . . . .       O 250 Irene            28
    Did Mahomet reproach or praise her Virtue?   . . . .      O 259 Irene           108
    Soon shouldst thou see, how false thy weak Reproach.   .  O 293 Irene           107
    Soon wouldst thou see, how false thy weak Reproach.   .   O 293 Irene         V 107
    Reproach not, Greece, a Lover's fond Delays,   . . .      O 297 Irene            19
    Nor will his Country's Groans reproach Demetrius.   . .   O 301 Irene           101
    Forbear--But thou art sunk beneath Reproach;   . . .      O 315 Irene            28
    And Honour and Reproach, and Heav'n and Hell.   . . .     O 321 Irene            38
    I came to heighten Tortures by Reproach,   . . . .        O 330 Irene             7
    Nor counsells nor reproach expell   . . . . . .           Y  12 Tr Hor Epode 9   39
REPROACHFUL
    Go, seize him, load him with reproachful Chains;   . . .  O 273 Irene            34
REPROOF
    Swell not your Soul beyond reproof or Counsel   . . . .   O 366 Irene          V  18
REPTILE
    And then leaves the glittering reptile, reasoning   . .   Y 146 Irene          V  23
      insect
REPTILES
    Then thro' thy Fields shall scarlet Reptiles stray,   . . O 110 To Posterity      7
REQUEST
    When vengeance listens to the fool's request.   . . . .   O  31 Vanity Wishes    14
    Verses, written at the request of a Gentleman   . . . .   O  95 Sprig of Myrtl  V  T
    Great Amurath, at my Request, forsook   . . . . .         O 256 Irene            43
    Prudence and Love conspire in this Request,   . . . . .   O 285 Irene            11
REQUESTED
    The Queen requested that a chosen Troop   . . . . .       O 331 Irene             7
    The Queen requested--Wretch, repeat the Message;   . . .  O 331 Irene            13
    The Queen requested--Wretch, repeat thy Message;   . . .  O 331 Irene         V  13
    The Queen requested--   . . . . . . . . .                 O 332 Irene            17
RESCU'D
    Of rescu'd Nature, and reviving Sense;   . . . . . .      O  53 Pro Drury-Lane   58
    The thoughts of happy love, and rescu'd Greece   . . . .  Y 189 Irene          V  1D
RESCUE
    At least you rescue from your heir.   . . . . . . .       O 232 Tr Horace IV.7   20
    Fly, Slaves, and call the Sultan to my Rescue.   . . . .  O 322 Irene            56
RESCUES
    Nor think that Effort lost which rescues thee.   . . . .  O 317 Irene            47
RESEMBLING
    Perhaps, enamour'd of resembling Virtue,   . . . . . .    O 252 Irene            96
RESENTFUL
    Let no resentful petulance invade   . . . . . . .         O  61 Pro Word Wise     9
RESENTMENT
    Let fierce resentment aid   . . . . . . . .               Y 133 Irene          V   9
    He wears of late Resentment on his Brow,   . . . . .      O 311 Irene             9
    Who charges Guilt! lay by this proud Resentment   . . .   O 323 Irene             8
RESERV'D
    Has heaven reserv'd, in pity to the poor,   . . . . .     O  18 London          170
    But thus reserv'd to lure the Wolves of Turkey,   . . .   O 250 Irene            24
    To what are we reserv'd?   . . . . . . . . .              O 253 Irene           108
```

RESERV'D	(CONTINUED)	PAGE	TITLE	LINE
Heav'n has reserv'd no future Paradise, ...		O 276	Irene	17
Is this the Recompence reserv'd for me?		O 307	Irene	7
Reserv'd to all the Pangs of tedious Death. . . .		O 312	Irene	25
Reserv'd, for other Lands, the Scourge of Heav'n. . . .		O 315	Irene	5

RESERVE

| Reserve these Questions for a safer Hour, ... | | O 254 | Irene | 140 |
| Reserve this Homage for some other Fair, ... | | O 288 | Irene | 4 |

RESIDENCE

| Detested residence of lust and tyranny . . . . . . | | Y 165 | Irene | V 79 |

RESIGN

Could'st thou resign the park and play content, . . .		O 19	London	210
Could thou resign the park and court content, . . .		Y 58	London	V 210
To him the church, the state, their pow're resign, . .		Y 96	Vanity Wishes	V 101
And pow'r too great to keep, or to resign?		O 36	Vanity Wishes	134
And one capitulate, and one resign;		O 40	Vanity Wishes	200
See one capitulate, and one resign;		Y 101	Vanity Wishes	V 200
Resign the heart to spleen and care, ...		O 123	Winter's Walk	10
Resign their Charge to Baseness and to Ruin. . .		O 289	Irene	20
Leave but this Maid, resign a hopeless Claim, . . .		O 319	Irene	25
Quit but this maid, resign a hopeless claim		Y 197	Irene	V 25

RESIGN'D

Sustain'd the Ballance, but resign'd the Sword; . . .		O 22	London	V 251
Obedient passions, and a will resign'd;		O 48	Vanity Wishes	360
Resign'd his Thirst of Empire to her Charms, ...		O 97	Hickman Spinet	19
Vain man runs headlong, to caprice resign'd;		O 134	Tr Rambler 105	1
Daring, tho' calm; and vigorous, tho' resign'd. . . .		O 246	Irene Prologue	10

RESIGNS

And Luxury with sighs her slave resigns.		O 43	Vanity Wishes	266
At length th' unwilling Sun resigns the World		O 302	Irene	1
When the departing sun resigns		Y 38	Lady Leaving	1

RESISTANCE

Till rude resistance lops the spreading god;		O 42	Vanity Wishes	234
His martial Rhet'rick taught the Greeks Resistance; . .		O 263	Irene	26
Flash out at once, with Strength above Resistance. . .		O 282	Irene	60
Return'd with Force that made Resistance vain, ...		O 317	Irene	38

RESISTLESS

Resistless burns the fever of renown		O 36	Vanity Wishes	V 137
And pour on misty Doubt resistless day;		O 37	Vanity Wishes	146
With force resistless o'er the brave prevail.		O 39	Vanity Wishes	178
The guardians yield, with force resistless ply'd; . .		Y 107	Vanity Wishes	V 339
When in your Eyes resistless Lightnings play, ...		O 96	Hickman Spinet	3
Resistless merit fix'd the Senate's choice, ...		O 118	Epitaph Hanmer	19
Observe, bright Maid, as his resistless Voice		O 268	Irene	25
Behold, my fair, as my resistless hand		Y 136	Irene	V 25
That Air resistless and enchanting Blush, ...		O 277	Irene	27
That Smile resistless and attractive Grace		O 355	Irene	V 16
Swells in the Breast, and with resistless Force, . . .		O 280	Irene	20
Enough--resistless Reason calms my Soul--		O 297	Irene	1
Will spread resistless Light upon my Soul.		O 321	Irene	47
And spread their Flames resistless o'er the World? . .		O 325	Irene	13

RESOLUTE

| Err shall they not, who resolute explore . . . . . . | | O 192 | Tr. Medea II | 1 |
| Could Omens fright the Resolute and Wise, ... | | O 269 | Irene | 1 |

RESOLUTION

The gloomy Resolution, horrid Greatness, ...		O 275	Irene	82
horrid joy--gloomy resolution--his air now fearful now .		Y 187	Irene	V 7
resolv'd.				

RESOLV'D

Resolv'd to purchase a retreat.		O 73	Hor. Epode II	76
With breasts resolv'd, they follow'd still		O 79	Feast St Simon	16
horrid joy--his air now fearful now resolv'd. . . .		Y 145	Irene	V 82
horrid joy--gloomy resolution--his air now fearful now .		Y 187	Irene	V 7
resolv'd.				

RESOLVE

Then let us now resolve, nor idly waste		O 271	Irene	33
Then let us now resolve, nor idle waste		O 271	Irene	V 33
Do thou resolve: For see, Irene comes!		O 275	Irene	90
Deep in my Breast be treasur'd this Resolve, ...		O 288	Irene	12
But virtuous Passion prompts the great Resolve, . . .		O 303	Irene	18
Resolve to share our Dangers and our Toils, ...		O 320	Irene	29

RESOLVED

| Resolved at length, from vice and London far, ... | | O 9 | London | 5 |

RESOLVES

| Who now resolves, from vice and London far, ... | | O 9 | London | V 5 |
| Chill my Resolves, and blast my blooming Virtue: . . . | | O 266 | Irene | 14 |

RESOUND

| Let every Tongue resound Irene's Praise, ... | | O 308 | Irene | 4 |

RESOUNDED

| "Whose fame from earth resounded to the skies." . . . | | Y 7 | Virgil Daphnis | 31 |
| And Strymon's hollow banks resounded with their groans. . | | Y 24 | Tr Add. Battle | 89 |

RESPONSIVE

| My Heart still beats responsive to the Sultan's; . . . | | O 272 | Irene | 9 |

REST

Invades the sacred hour of silent rest, ...		O 21	London	240
He seeks the refuge of monastic rest.		O 35	Vanity Wishes	118
And hissing Infamy proclaims the rest.		O 47	Vanity Wishes	342
And shout Infamy proclaims the rest.		Y 107	Vanity Wishes	V 342
Implore his aid, in his decisions rest, ...		O 48	Vanity Wishes	355
That post, and all the rest, shall be my care;		O 74	Tr. Iliad Bk 6	3
Rest here distrest by poverty no more, ...		O 113	Epit. Phillips	3

```
REST            (CONTINUED)                        PAGE    TITLE          LINE
     Rest here oppress'd by poverty no more,  . . . . . .   O 113 Epit. Phillips    V   3
     Rest undisturb'd within this humble shrine,  . . . . .  O 113 Epit. Phillips    V   5
     Age call'd at length his active mind to rest,  . . . .  O 118 Epitaph Hanmer       35
     With silent confidence and holy rest:  . . . . . . .    O 130 Tr. Rambler 7        6
     Alternate rest and labour long endure.  . . . . . . .   O 131 Tr. Rambler 33       1
     Calmly rest in safe Repose?  . . . . . . .             O 144 Tr Boeth. II.4       4
     And wearied angels rest upon their stars spheres  . .   Y 128 Irene           V  4B
     Nor dream of peace, think of rest  . . . . . . .       Y 130 Irene           V  13
     On weary Mortals sheds the balm of rest  . . . . . .    O 356 Irene           V  10
     He 's gone--Here rest, my Soul, thy fainting Wing, . .  O 287 Irene               1
     To Silence and to Rest. The Hours of Darkness,  . . .   O 302 Irene               2
RESTED
     Rivers rested as they ran,  . . . . . . . . .           O 148 Tr Boet III.12   V  10
     Till breathless Fury rested from Destruction  . . . .   O 249 Irene               5
RESTLESS
     Explore each restless toil, each anxious strife,  . .   Y  92 Vanity Wishes    V   3
     And restless fire precipitates on death.  . . . .      O  31 Vanity Wishes       20
     And restless enterprize impells to death.  . . . .     Y  92 Vanity Wishes    V  20
     Still to new heights his restless wishes tow'r,  . . .  O  34 Vanity Wishes      105
     Still restless, till I clasp the lovely Maid,  . . . .  O 263 Irene              21
     Is this the restless Diligence of Treason?  . . . .    O 279 Irene               2
     Whence rise these restless cares? these strong emotions? Y 189 Irene           V   1
RESTORE
     The price of boroughs and of souls restore,  . . . . .  O  19 London             204
     Or Virtue shall restore to earth.  . . . . .          O 232 Tr Horace IV.7    V 116
     Can he restore the State he could not save?  . . . . .  O 253 Irene             116
     Or how can Cali's Flight restore our Country?  . . . .  O 254 Irene             139
     O! could the Grave restore the pious Hero,  . . . . .   O 267 Irene              42
     To me my Lover's Fondness will restore,  . . . . . .    O 291 Irene              74
RESTRAIN
     What check restrain your thirst of pow'r and gold?  . .  O  13 London             62
     Restrain your tears and cease your cries,  . . . . .    O  70 Hor.II Ode XX       21
     The glitt'ring vagrants shall restrain;  . . . . .     O 120 To Miss Purse       10
     Where common Laws restrain the Prince and Subject, . .  O 256 Irene              56
     Say, did a Voice from Heav'n restrain the Tyrant?  . .  O 259 Irene             115
     Restrain the Fervour of impetuous Youth  . . . . .     O 272 Irene               9
     Did not the Cause of Greece restrain my Sword,  . . .   O 299 Irene              41
     And Gratitude's strong Ties restrain my Tongue.  . . .  O 312 Irene               5
     Let no weak Doubt the gen'rous Hand restrain,  . . . .  O 313 Irene              22
     Let no distrust the gen'rous Hand restrain  . . . . .   O 377 Irene           V   3
     Thy Love, Aspasia, calls; restrain thy Sword;  . . . .  O 318 Irene               9
     Restrain your sorrows, calm your troubled soul.  . . .  Y  21 Tr. Iliad Bk 6     114
RESTRAIN'D
     With gentle Hand restrain'd the Streams of Life,  . . . O 252 Irene              97
     Aw'd by the Croud, and by their Slaves restrain'd?  . . O 312 Irene              22
RESTRAINS
     The Dread of instant Death restrains my Tongue?  . . .  O 289 Irene              25
RESTRAINT
     This sov'reign Passion, scornful of Restraint,  . . . . O 280 Irene              18
RESUM'D
     The Cloister's Ease, resum'd the tott'ring Throne,  . . O 256 Irene              44
RESUME
     There shall despotick Eloquence resume  . . . . . .    O 302 Irene             120
RESUMES
     Resumes th' imperious Air of haughty Virtue.  . . . .   O 314 Irene              15
RESUMPTION
     Calmly he heard, till Amurath's Resumption  . . . . .   O 270 Irene              10
RETAILS
     The groom retails the favours of his lord.  . . . . .   O  18 London             181
RETARD
     Surprize o'erwhelm her, and retard our Flight.  . . . . O 285 Irene              13
     Depress their Spirits, and retard their Speed?  . . . . O 325 Irene              15
RETARDS
     For fear retards their flight, the cruell Crane  . . .  O  76 Tr Add. Battle      31
RETINUE
     I discover by this state & retinue  . . . . . . . .    Y 160 Irene           V   8
RETIR'D
     To letter'd ease retir'd, and honest mirth,  . . . . .  O 118 Epitaph Hanmer      37
     And lonely want retir'd to die.  . . . . . . . .       O 201 Death Dr Levet      20
     Or how before Nassau the Gallick troops retir'd?  . . . Y  22 Tr Add. Battle      13
RETIRE
     And bids afflicted worth retire to peace.  . . . . .    O  45 Vanity Wishes      310
     With me retire and leave the pomp of courts  . . . . .  O 137 Tr Rambler 138      1
     Retire with Speed, while I prepare to meet him  . . . . O 271 Irene              37
     At my Command the Sentinels retire;  . . . . . . .     O 283 Irene              15
     Disorder sits upon thy Face--retire.  . . . . . .      O 286 Irene              17
     Why does thy Soul retire into herself?  . . . . . .    O 295 Irene               7
     Beholds the fainting Garrison retire,  . . . . . . .    O 298 Irene              28
     Retire, my Fair, that Pow'r that smiles on Goodness  .  O 303 Irene              20
     Or gay felecity retire to desarts?  . . . . . . .      Y 191 Irene           V  21
RETIREMENT
     From his belov'd retirement draw,  . . . . . . .       O  71 Hor. Epode II       14
RETIRING
     The tide retiring, calls me from the land:  . . . . .   O  22 London             255
RETREAT
     There might'st thou find some elegant retreat,  . . . . O  20 London             212
     The might you find some elegant retreat,  . . . . .    Y  58 London           V 212
     Till captive Science yields her last retreat;  . . . .  O  37 Vanity Wishes      144
     Counts death kind Nature's signal of retreat:  . . . .  O  48 Vanity Wishes      364
     Thinks death kind Nature's signal of retreat:  . . . .  O  48 Vanity Wishes    V 364
```

```
RETREAT          (CONTINUED)                                 PAGE    TITLE              LINE
    Resolv'd to purchase a retreat. . . . . . . . .    O  73 Hor. Epode II       76
    To some retreat the baffled writer flies,  . . . .  O  82 Young Author        26
    The silent grandeur of retreat. . . . . . . . .    O 125 An Ode              32
    Out of Fortune's Pow'r retreat? . . . . . . . . .  O 144 Tr Boeth. II.4       2
    Soon the treachrous Sands retreat, . . . . . . .   O 145 Tr Boeth. II.4      11
    Quitting my close Retreat, I range the City, . . .  O 251 Irene               60
    The Turkish Pow'rs from Europe shall retreat, . . .  O 257 Irene               79
    Haste to the safe retreat, from whence Demetrius . . .  Y 126 Irene            V 144
    If Pleasure charm thee, view this soft Retreat; . . .  O 279 Irene               85
RETURN
    But finds you sad his return. . . . . . . . . . .  O  67 Hor. II Ode IX       12
    But their lost strength and vigour soon return, . . .  O  76 Tr Add. Battle       8
    Ah! never to return! . . . . . . . . . . . .      O  80 Feast St Simon       48
    And love return, has great Erasmus died? . . . . .  O 132 Tr. Rambler 54       2
    "Freedom my return awaits, . . . . . . . . . .     O 185 Anacreon Ode 9      20
    Return with speed, Leontius, to your Charge; . . .  O 304 Irene                9
    Return, Demetrius, and be free for ever. . . . . .  O 306 Irene               60
    Ere he return with Thousands at his Side. . . . .  O 320 Irene                9
    And joy to feel the vital Warmth return, . . . . .  O 320 Irene               25
    The raging Sultan burns till our Return, . . . . .  O 327 Irene               11
    Nor from the battle look for his return. . . . . .  Y  21 Tr. Iliad Bk 6      131
    O would Cleora thus return, . . . . . . . . . .    Y  39 Lady Leaving         11
RETURN'D
    Return'd with Force that made Resistance vain, . . .  O 317 Irene               38
    Again his thund'ring Voice return'd, Irene. . . . .  O 325 Irene               26
RETURNING
    The still returning tale, and ling'ring jest, . . .  O  44 Vanity Wishes      275
    Amidst the toils of this returning year, . . . . .  O  59 Pro Good Nat'd     V  4A
    May this returning day for ever find . . . . . . .  O  80 Lady Birthday        3
    Against returning Guilt. . . . . . . . . . . .     O 265 Irene               11
    Hence from her sable wings returning night . . . .  Y 148 Irene             V 43E
    Now haste to murder, ere returning Thought . . . .  O 326 Irene               39
    And may she ne'er returning sorrows know." . . . .  Y  20 Tr. Iliad Bk 6     106
    The rough road then, returning in a round, . . . .  Y 310 Parody of Pope       3
RETURNS
    New sorrow rises as the day returns, . . . . . . .  O  45 Vanity Wishes      301
    Returns his child; she views his infant charms, . . .  Y  20 Tr. Iliad Bk 6     108
REV'RENCE
    Love prompts to love, and rev'rence rev'rence gains.  O 130 Tr. Rambler 12       8
    Love prompts to love, and rev'rence rev'rence gains. .  O 130 Tr. Rambler 12       8
    And learn the Rev'rence due to Turkey's Queen. . . .  O 322 Irene               55
REVEAL
    Now Mustapha reveal this Tale of treason . . . . .  O 369 Irene             V  18
    Justice demands that I reveal your Crimes; . . . .  O 286 Irene               14
REVEAL'D
    The Vet'ran Courtier half reveal'd his Project. . .  O 254 Irene              132
REVEALD
    Still fond of Life reveald the dreadfull secret, . . .  O 356 Irene             V  33
REVELS
    And life still vig'rous revels in my veins; . . . .  O  10 London              42
    And Jollity maintain'd eternal Revels.-- . . . . .  O 251 Irene               65
REVENGE
    Think on Revenge and Glory Greece and Love . . . .  O 361 Irene             V   5
    Th' adoring Soldiers would revenge their Idol. . . .  O 273 Irene               42
    Wherever Guilt can fly, Revenge can follow. . . . .  O 274 Irene               65
    And frowns on Perjury, Revenge and Murder. . . . .  O 300 Irene               58
    Revenge and subtle Jealousy shall teach . . . . .  O 307 Irene               24
    But brave Demetrius scorn'd the mean Revenge, . . .  O 313 Irene               17
    ... of Revenge . . . . . . . . . . . . . . .       O 371 Irene             V   2
REVENGEFUL
    Let no revengeful petulance invade . . . . . . . .  O  61 Pro Word Wise      V   9
REVERENCE
    With thoughtless reverence we praise, . . . . . .  O 190 Tr. Medea I          2
    Till every Nation reverence the Koran, . . . . . .  O 264 Irene               31
    Till every Nation reverence our Prophet . . . . .  O 354 Irene             V  17
REVERS'D
    Nor think the doom of man revers'd for thee: . . .  O  38 Vanity Wishes      156
REVERSE
    What can reverse thy Doom? . . . . . . . . . . .    O 257 Irene               73
    Could we reverse the Sentence of the Sultan, . . .  O 328 Irene               38
REVIEW
    Once more great nature's work review, . . . . . .  O 125 An Ode              23
    Review this Day. . . . . . . . . . . . . . .       O 323 Irene               11
REVISIT
    Will e'er an happier Hour revisit Greece? . . . .  O 301 Irene               96
REVIVE
    Revive--Revive to Freedom and to Love. . . . . . .  O 295 Irene                9
    Revive--Revive to Freedom and to Love. . . . . . .  O 295 Irene                9
    Revive the languid Flow'rs; thus Nature shone . . .  O 314 Irene                3
REVIVING
    Of rescu'd Nature, and reviving Sense; . . . . . .  O  53 Pro Drury-Lane      58
    To wit, reviving from its author's dust, . . . . .  O  61 Pro Word Wise        7
REVOLUTICNS
    The weary Sun forgets his Revolutions . . . . . .  O 347 Irene             V  30
REVOLVING
    When the revolving seasons shall only visit my dominions  Y 132 Irene         V  44
    The varying Seasons, and revolving Skies, . . . .  O 293 Irene              118
    Revolving springs their frost repay. . . . . . . .  Y  39 Lady Leaving        10
REWARD
    Wants ev'n the cheap reward of empty praise; . . .  O  10 London              36
```

		PAGE	TITLE	LINE
REWARD	(CONTINUED)			
	From you my labours wait their last reward.	O 141	Tr Rambler 208	2
	"Joyless task without reward:	O 185	Anacreon Ode 9	18
	Receives his full Reward in Beauty's Arms.	O 247	Irene Epilogue	24
	The Pride of Monarchs, the Reward of Conquest; . . .	O 269	Irene	42
	the reward of conquest boast of nature	Y 137	Irene	V 42
	Reward his toils, and he shall toil for you	Y 146	Irene	V 23A
	And this is my Reward--to burn, to languish, ...	O 285	Irene	1
	What Worth can merit? or what Faith reward?	O 295	Irene	16
REWARDS				
	Gratefull, rewards the Deities, ...	O 72	Hor. Epode II	27
	Rewards the fav'ring Deities, ...	O 72	Hor. Epode II	V 27
RHET'RICK				
	His martial Rhet'rick taught the Greeks Resistance; . .	O 263	Irene	26
RHIMES				
	Whose gen'rous Zeal, unbought by flatt'ring Rhimes, . .	O 57	Prologue Comus	3
RHINE				
	And stain with blood the Danube or the Rhine;	O 39	Vanity Wishes	182
RHODIAN				
	Then shall the Rhodian mourn his sinking Tow'rs, . . .	O 309	Irene	26
RHONE				
	That drink the Phasis or the Rhone.	O 70	Hor.II Ode XX	20
RIBALD				
	Unlike the ribald, whose licentious jest	O 130	Tr. Rambler 12	1
RICH				
	For none are rich without content.	O 144	Tr Boeth. II.2	14
RICHES				
	Increase his riches and his peace destroy;	O 32	Vanity Wishes	40
	They put the riches of Cali Bassa on board.	Y 123	Irene	V 81
RICHEST				
	The richest Landlord on the banks of Trent?	O 35	Vanity Wishes	V 124
	The richest Odours, nor the speckled Shells	O 277	Irene	32
RID				
	Then let me rid them of Irene's Presence:	O 316	Irene	19
RIDE				
	On flying Cars new Sorcerers may ride.	O 53	Pro Drury-Lane	44
RIDICULE				
	Mimick your tears, and ridicule your woes;	O 74	Tr. Iliad Bk 6	22
	Shewn in the faithful glass of ridicule;	O 81	Lady Birthday	16
RIDS				
	And detestation rids th' indignant wall.	O 34	Vanity Wishes	90
RIEN				
	On n'a rien.	O 172	French Distich	8
	Rien de Bon.	O 172	French Distich	10
RIG				
	To rig another convoy for the k<in>g.	O 22	London	247
RIGHT				
	Ne'er knew to puzzle right, or varnish wrong, ...	O 14	London	80
	Was early taught a Briton's right to prize, ...	O 15	London	119
	Wreaths which at last the dear-bought right convey . .	O 40	Vanity Wishes	189
	Great souls whose the dear-bought right convey . . .	Y 100	Vanity Wishes	V 189
	Or right, or wrong, once hooted from the stage; . . .	O 61	Pro Word Wise	2
	Strict, on the right he fix'd his steadfast eye, . . .	O 118	Epitaph Hanmer	29
	"Vested with a master's right	O 185	Anacreon Ode 9	13
	And scanning right the practices of yore, ...	O 192	Tr. Medea II	3
	Then Let me once to right our injur'd Sex	O 356	Irene	V 16
RIGHTS				
	Explain their country's dear-bought rights away, . . .	O 11	London	53
	And rights submitted, left him none to seize.	O 34	Vanity Wishes	108
	And Nature's Rights entreat th' asserting Sword. . . .	O 297	Irene	3
	The Rights of Princes let the Sword decide, ...	O 307	Irene	22
RIGID				
	This, only this, the rigid law pursues, ...	O 17	London	160
	This, only this, the rigid law persues, ...	O 17	London	V 160
	Who keeps the rigid rules of ancient honour;	O 176	Tr Metastas II	2
	That keeps the rigid rules of ancient honour;	O 176	Tr Metastas II	V 2
RIGOUR				
	That leave the blame of rigour to the prince, ...	O 176	Tr Metastas II	10
	Aw'd by the Rigour of the Sultan's Justice, ...	O 288	Irene	8
RINGLETS				
	Or boy, whose snowy neck the flowing ringlets grace. .	Y 12	Tr Hor Epode 9	42
RINGS				
	There ev'ry bush with nature's musick rings, ...	O 20	London	220
	Through Freedom's sons no more remonstrance rings, . .	O 34	Vanity Wishes	93
	And the wood rings with Amarillis' name.	O 64	Virgil Past.I	6
	And tread in mystick rings the mossie ground.	O 77	Tr Add. Battle	52
RIOT				
	Their wish is full to riot and to rail.	O 34	Vanity Wishes	98
RIP'NING				
	When rip'ning fruits perfume the year, ...	O 72	Hor. Epode II	25
	Till Affectation, rip'ning to Belief, ...	O 266	Irene	31
RIPE				
	Is ripe for Action, and demands the Sword.	O 256	Irene	37
RIPEN				
	And not a harvest ripen but for me	Y 132	Irene	V 42
	For thee, my fair, shall India's spices . . . . . ripen	Y 150	Irene	V 81
RIPSES				
	Kai Bion, eipen, otan ripses Thanatio Belessi, ...	O 108	Eis Birchion	3
RISE				
	Well may they rise, while I, whose rustick tongue . . .	O 14	London	79

RISE   (CONTINUED)

	PAGE	TITLE	LINE
Quick let us rise, the happy seats explore,	O 18	London	174
The dangers gather as the treasures rise.	O 31	Vanity Wishes	28
Still rise the long tale, and ling'ring jest,	Y 104	Vanity Wishes	V 275
Must no dislike alarm, no wishes rise,	O 47	Vanity Wishes	347
Enquirer cease alarm, no wishes rise,	Y 108	Vanity Wishes	V 347
Nor do the billows always rise,	O 67	Hor. II Ode IX	3
A Poet double-form'd I rise,	O 70	Hor.II Ode XX	2
On ev'ry side rise mountains of the slain,	O 76	Tr Add. Battle	19
Loud roars the tempest, high the billows rise,	O 82	Young Author	8
The pamphlet spreads, incessant hisses rise,	O 82	Young Author	25
What dreary prospects round us rise,	O 123	Winter's Walk	2
Where ----'s humble turrets rise,	O 125	An Ode	16
To You whose gen'rous Wishes rise	O 150	Tr Boet III.12	53
Rise Cali Bassa counsellor of Kings	O 351	Irene	V 24
Rise from the happy Bed; and future Queens	O 268	Irene	13
Irene rise, thou daughter of perfection--or	Y 145	Irene	V 1
To bid the prostrate Captive rise and live,	O 278	Irene	70
For thee shall Forests rise and Rivers flow	O 350	Irene	V 22
Why foam the swelling Waves when Tempests rise?	O 281	Irene	51
Who knows, ere this important Morrow rise,	O 284	Irene	36
Yet in that narrow Space what Dangers rise?--	O 287	Irene	6
Again her prostrate Palaces should rise,	O 291	Irene	54
Whence rise these restless cares? these strong emotions?	Y 189	Irene	V 1
Attention rise, survey the fair Creation,	O 313	Irene	6
In pompous numbers ancient heroes rise;	Y 22	Tr Add. Battle	8
Wounded and spent, in vain they strive to rise	Y 24	Tr Add. Battle	60
Together rise and shoot upon the wing.	Y 24	Tr Add. Battle	73

RISES

Slow Rises Worth, By Poverty Depress'd:	O 18	London	177
New sorrow rises as the day returns,	O 45	Vanity Wishes	301
As virtue rises in distress,	O 122	Stella Mourn.	10
Death rises to my View, with all his Terrors;	O 265	Irene	12
The pow'r of Turkey rises at my call	Y 197	Irene	V 24
Then rises the brave leader of their hosts	Y 24	Tr Add. Battle	80

RISING

And crowd with sudden wealth the rising dome;	O 19	London	203
Bid scenic Virtue form the rising Age,	O 53	Pro Drury-Lane	61
And rising Ages hasten to be just.	O 57	Prologue Comus	14
Should Hecatombs each rising Morn	O 69	Hor.II Ode 14	5
And that fair bosom heave with rising sighs!	O 75	Tr. Iliad Bk 6	28
And future millions lift his rising soul;	O 82	Young Author	V 6B
And listen eager to the rising Wind?	O 270	Irene	25
Supicion checks the rising transport	Y 186	Irene	V 2
And hail the rosy Dawn of rising Health.	O 320	Irene	27
And wish'd my rising anger could remove	Y 11	Tr Hor Epode 9	23
Where radiant Phoebus rising from the sea	Y 23	Tr Add. Battle	22

RITES

The rites deriv'd from ancient days	O 190	Tr. Medea I	1
The rites that taught us to combine	O 190	Tr. Medea I	3

RIV'LETS

Where Riv'lets gently purl along	O 72	Hor. Epode II	31

RIVAL

Let hist'ry tell where rival kings command,	O 31	Vanity Wishes	29
Historians tell where rival kings command,	Y 93	Vanity Wishes	V 29
Th' insidious rival and the gaping heir.	O 32	Vanity Wishes	48
Did rival monarchs give the fatal wound?	O 41	Vanity Wishes	217
Each nymph your rival, and each youth your slave?	O 46	Vanity Wishes	330
The rival batters, and the lover mines.	O 46	Vanity Wishes	332
And reign without a Rival in his Bosom.	O 373	Irene	V 29
Nor let Demetrius know thee for a Rival.	O 282	Irene	71
Obtain her and possess, thou know'st thy Rival.	O 307	Irene	17

RIVALS

An rivals breast with certain mischief glows	Y 107	Vanity Wishes	V330A
Unmov'd tho' Witlings sneer and Rivals rail;	O 246	Irene Prologue	29
Who merits most!--I knew not we were Rivals.	O 284	Irene	46
Rouse from the grave the rivals of Pharsalia	Y 185	Irene	V 39
Nor with too powerfull rivals strive	Y 11	Tr Hor Epode 9	27

RIVER

When a river is drain'd by too many channels the stream is dry.	Y 132	Irene	V 41B

RIVERS

Rivers rested as they ran,	O 148	Tr Boet III.12	V 10
The rivers know their banks again,	O 231	Tr Horace IV.7	4
For thee shall Forests rise and Rivers flow	O 350	Irene	V 22
While boars the rocks, while fish the rivers love,	Y 7	Virgil Daphnis	49

RIVULET

The wand'ring Rivulet, and silver Lake,	O 280	Irene	23

RIVULETS

Direct thy rivulets, and twine thy bow'rs;	O 20	London	217
Direct the rivulets, and plan the bow'rs;	Y 58	London	V 217

ROAD

Chear'd the rough road, we wish'd the rough road long,	Y 310	Parody of Pope	2
Chear'd the rough road, we wish'd the rough road long,	Y 310	Parody of Pope	2
The rough road then, returning in a round,	Y 310	Parody of Pope	3

ROADS

That range lascivious through the lonesome roads	Y 7	Virgil Daphnis	V 50

ROAM

Then thro' the world a wretched vagrant roam,	O 18	London	190
Prepare for death, if here at night you roam,	O 21	London	224

		PAGE	TITLE	LINE

ROAM   (CONTINUED)
Here life is ventur'd if the streets you roam	. . . .	Y	59	London	V 224
While wretched we about the world must roam,	. . . .	O	64	Virgil Past.I	3
They, pleas'd, thro' barb'rous nations roam,	. . . .	O	79	Feast St Simon	29
When first the peasant, long inclin'd to roam,	. . . .	O	81	Young Author	1
"Over hills and fields to roam,	. . . . . .	O	185	Anacreon Ode 9	25
Confus'd about the streets I roam	. . . . .	Y	11	Tr Hor Epode 9	33

ROAR
Loud roar the billows, high the waves arise,	. . . .	O	82	Young Author	V 8
And can with thunder roar.	. . . .	O	127	To Lyce, Lady	16
When ev'ry Storm in my Domain shall roar,	. . . .	O	265	Irene	42
Till ev'ry Storm in my Domain shall roar,	. . . .	O	354	Irene	V 25
Mix undistinguish'd with the gen'ral Roar.	. . . .	O	280	Irene	24
And subject Seas roar round their Queen in vain.	. . .	O	309	Irene	29
Cease this wild Roar of savage Exultation;	. . . .	O	318	Irene	6
Touch'd with thy fate Numidia's lyons roar	. . .	Y	6	Virgil Daphnis	11

ROAR'D
| Till Declamation roar'd, while Passion slept. | . . . . | O | 52 | Pro Drury-Lane | 32 |
| He struck his tortur'd Breast, and roar'd, Irene: | . . . | O | 325 | Irene | 24 |

ROARING
Down cliffs the roaring Torrent pours	. . . . . .	O	72	Hor. Epode II	38
Down the steep hill the roaring torrent pours;	. . . .	O	132	Tr. Rambler 65	2
Did roaring Whirlwinds sweep us from the Ramparts:	. . .	O	251	Irene	55
Pour forth their Legions, and the roaring Danube	. . .	O	264	Irene	17
Irene's Chamber! Did not roaring Cali,	. . . . .	O	330	Irene	12

ROARINGS
| Where amidst the roarings of the Northern | . . . . | Y | 121 | Irene | V 56 |
| main | | | | | |

ROARS
Not always furious Boreas roars,	. . . . . .	O	67	Hor. II Ode IX	7
Where sev'nmouth'd Nilus roars,	. . . . .	O	79	Feast St Simon	33
Loud roars the tempest, high the billows rise,	. . .	O	82	Young Author	8
There, mid Tempests loudest roars,	. . . . .	O	145	Tr Boeth. II.4	17
Why roars the Lioness distress'd by Hunger?	. . . . .	O	281	Irene	50

ROB
| Rob without Fear, and fatten without Toil. | . . . . . . | O | 110 | To Posterity | 14 |

ROBB'D
| Robb'd of the Maid, with whom I wish'd to triumph, | . . | O | 333 | Irene | 42 |

ROBBERS
| To Robbers furious, and to Lovers tame, | . . . . . . | O | 174 | Tr Epitaph Dog | 1 |

ROBE
| Dispose the Colours of the flowing Robe, | . . . . . . | O | 278 | Irene | 65 |
| Your Robe of Mourning, and your Dogs of Death. | . . . . | O | 325 | Irene | 5 |

ROBERT
| On the Death of Dr. Robert Levet | . . . . . . | O | 200 | Death Dr Levet | T |

ROBES
The robes of pleasure and the veils of woe:	. . . .	O	33	Vanity Wishes	66
Hid in the mean Disguise of Turkish Robes,	. . . .	O	249	Irene	2
Comes Mustapha.--Your Turkish Robes conceal you--	. .	O	271	Irene	36
robes of triumph.	. . . .	O	374	Irene	V 31
Still sees To-morrow drest in Robes of Triumph;	. . .	O	283	Irene	29
If yet these glittring Robes these sudden Splendors	. .	O	366	Irene	V 17

ROCK
This scarce I lead, who left on yonder rock	. . . .	O	64	Virgil Past.I	19
That range unciviliz'd from Rock to Rock,	. . . .	O	268	Irene	30
That range unciviliz'd from Rock to Rock,	. . . .	O	268	Irene	30
Shall the whirle, and bid the Rock subside	. . . .	O	365	Irene	V 4

ROCKS
Or change the rocks of Scotland for the Strand?	. . .	O	9	London	10
And Bolts and rocks encounter in the Skie,	. . .	O	76	Tr Add. Battle	23
Swoln with Success, secure amidst his native Rocks	. .	O	352	Irene	V 28
The Rocks of Life, for ever flies the Port.	. . .	O	281	Irene	47
Insidious sands, shallows rough rocks and whirling	. .	Y	201	Irene	V 10B
devouring gulphs					
Rocks send their acclamations to the skie	. . . .	Y	7	Virgil Daphnis	40
While boars the rocks, while fish the rivers love,	. .	Y	7	Virgil Daphnis	49
In a low vale by rocks that pierce the skies	. .	Y	23	Tr Add. Battle	24

ROCKY
| Safe upon the rocky Ground, | . . . . | O | 145 | Tr Boeth. II.4 | 15 |

ROLL   SEE ROWL
Roll thro' the streets, and thunder to the skies;	. . .	O	18	London	183
Roll darkling down the torrent of his fate?	. . . .	O	47	Vanity Wishes	346
They roll, and ever will roll on.	. . . . .	O	68	Hor.II Ode 14	4
They roll, and ever will roll on.	. . . . .	O	68	Hor.II Ode 14	4
Unbounded prospects in his bosom roll,	. . . .	O	82	Young Author	V 6A
That roll at Eurus loud command;	. . .	O	144	Tr Boeth. II.2	2
Moor and Christian, roll along.	. . .	O	159	Tr. Rio Verde	4
Too slow these gentle Constellations roll,	. . .	O	271	Irene	3
Held out this fatal roll--then sunk to Nothing.	. .	O	357	Irene	V 1
Now roll full fraught with Thunder o'er your Head.	. .	O	275	Irene	75
To tune the Tongue, to teach the Eyes to roll,	. . .	O	278	Irene	64

ROLLING
| To whom the church each rolling year | . . . . . | O | 78 | Feast St Simon | 11 |
| The weight of ev'ry rolling sphere. | . . . | O | 79 | Feast St Simon | 32 |

ROLLS   SEE ROWLS
When first the college rolls receive his name,	. . . .	O	36	Vanity Wishes	135
Niphates rolls an humbler wave,	. . . . . .	O	68	Hor. II Ode IX	21
Her baleful eyes where Sorrow rolls around;	. . .	O	192	Tr. Medea II	14
He rolls no Thunders o'er the drowsy Pit.	. . . .	O	246	Irene Prologue	26
Perhaps the flood of time now rolls towards us	. . .	Y	117	Irene	V 108
Rolls half his Floods unheard through shouting Camps?	.	O	264	Irene	18

279

ROLLS   (CONTINUED)   PAGE   TITLE   LINE
    Rolls with eternal Toil the pond'rous Orbs; . . . . . .   O 293 Irene   120
    Rolls on the Sun, and Regulates the Spheres. . . .   O 369 Irene   V 17
ROMAN
    Adorn'd in Roman time the brightest days, ...   O 189 Seeing Montagu   2
    (The) pride of Roman (power), and Grecian . . . .   Y 177 Irene   V 111
     art
ROMAN'S
    Content to live the Roman's slave, ...   O 68 Hor. II Ode IX   23
ROMANS
    For such the steady Romans shook the world; . . . . .   O 39 Vanity Wishes   180
    For these these steady Romans shook the world; . . . .   Y 100 Vanity Wishes   V 180
    And crowds of godlike Romans sunk to hell. . . . . .   O 77 Festina Lente   15
ROME
    The common shore of Paris and of Rome; . . . . . .   O 14 London   94
    The common sewer of Paris and of Rome; . . . . . .   O 14 London   V 94
    Not Rome itself that held the world in awe . . . .   O 76 Tr Add. Battle   39
    Could Rome with future greatness fire, ...   O 188 Epilogue   2
    Could Rome with generous ardour fire, ...   O 188 Epilogue   V   2
    Not you, Torquatus, boast of Rome, ...   O 232 Tr Horace IV.7   21
    To fix your Standard in Imperial Rome. . . . . . .   O 309 Irene   31
ROOM
    From every room descends the painted face, ...   O 33 Vanity Wishes   83
    He pants for room, in one poor World confin'd. . . .   O 97 Hickman Spinet   12
    ... in a Room hung with some Flower-pieces . . . . .   O 120 To Miss Playing   T
    My first, shuts out Thieves from your house or your Room O 179 Charade!   1
    Can yield no room to Music's soothing pow'r. . . . .   O 193 Tr. Medea II   20
ROOMS
    Through bowing Slaves, I range the private Rooms, . . . O 283 Irene   17
ROPE
    Lest scarce the exhausted should rope supply. . . . .   Y 60 London   V 243
ROPES
    Lest ropes be wanting in the tempting spring, ...   O 22 London   246
    And ropes be wanting in the tempting spring, ...   Y 60 London   V 246
ROSE
    First rear'd the Stage, immortal Shakespear rose; . . . O 51 Pro Drury-Lane   2
    And near the noisome nettle blooms the rose. . . . .   O 131 Tr. Rambler 21   2
    Soon fades the rose; once past the fragrant hour, . . . O 133 Tr. Rambler 71   1
    Rose to his Thought, and set his Soul on Fire: . . . .   O 270 Irene   11
    Twice since the Morning rose I saw the Bassa, ...   O 275 Irene   76
ROSES
    Perennial roses deck each purple vale, ...   O 84 Epi Dist Moth.   16
    And scatters roses in the thorny way . . . .   Y 148 Irene   V 43D
    And add new Roses to the faded Cheek. . . . . . .   O 278 Irene   66
ROSY
    Ye nymphs of rosy lips and radiant eyes, ...   O 46 Vanity Wishes   323
    And hail the rosy Dawn of rising Health. . . . . . .   O 320 Irene   27
ROUGH
    Rough Winter's blasts to Spring give way, ...   O 231 Tr Horace IV.7   9
    To rough--Too false too fierce to trust or to neglect   O 374 Irene   V   1
    Insidious sands, shallows rough rocks and whirling . . Y 201 Irene   V 10B
     devouring gulphs
    Chear'd the rough road, we wish'd the rough road long,   Y 310 Parody of Pope   2
    Chear'd the rough road, we wish'd the rough road long, . Y 310 Parody of Pope   2
    The rough road then, returning in a round, ...   Y 310 Parody of Pope   3
ROUND
    Tho' confiscation's vulturs hover round. . . . . . .   O 32 Vanity Wishes   36
    But round the lofty Popular twines . . . .   O 71 Hor. Epode II   17
    That struggling pants, and rowls her eye-balls round. . O 76 Tr Add. Battle   15
    Th' Apostles round the world were sent, ...   O 79 Feast St Simon   25
    What dreary prospects round us rise, ...   O 123 Winter's Walk   2
    Striped rainbows round her eyes are seen, ...   O 127 To Lyce, Lady   11
    We round thy board the cheerful menials see, ...   O 130 Tr. Rambler 12   5
    Round him danc'd the listning woods, ...   O 148 Tr Boet III.12   11
    Round him crowd the listning Woods, ...   O 148 Tr Boet III.12 V 11
    "Round his chamber dance and play, ...   O 186 Anacreon Ode 9   36
    Announc'd the dinner to the regions round, ...   O 192 Tr. Medea II   6
    His virtues walk'd their narrow round, ...   O 201 Death Dr Levet   25
    Behold how Lust and Rapine struggle round her. . . . .   O 252 Irene   82
    At once a hundred Voices thunder'd round me, ...   O 271 Irene   29
    Only to hunt him round the ravag'd World? . . . . .   O 275 Irene   67
    To scatter Happiness and Plenty round thee, ...   O 278 Irene   69
    And subject Seas roar round their Queen in vain. . . .   O 309 Irene   29
    Shall throw th' attending Janizaries round thee. . . .   O 319 Irene   34
    And lead thy Troops victorious round the World. . . .   O 333 Irene   41
    Daphnis with ivy wreath'd the jav'lins round . . . .   Y   6 Virgil Daphnis   15
    The rough road then, returning in a round, ...   Y 310 Parody of Pope   3
ROUSE
    Will rouse us in a morning more? . . . .   O 232 Tr Horace IV.7 V 18
    Unactive (unkindled) in the breast--rouse it . . . .   Y 133 Irene   V 19
    Rouse, Cali, shall the Sons of conquer'd Greece . . .   O 284 Irene   42
    I rouse to War, and conquer for Irene. . . . . .   O 309 Irene   25
    Rouse from the grave the rivals of Pharsalia . . . .   Y 185 Irene   V 39
ROUSES
    Attention rouses from the dream of Love . . . . .   O 369 Irene   V 21
ROUSING
    From hill to hill the beacons rousing blaze . . . . .   O 43 Vanity Wishes   247
ROUZING
    Then rouzing know the fiery Chief Abdalla, ...   O 254 Irene   125
    Then rouzing know the firy Chief Abdallah, ...   O 254 Irene   V 125

	PAGE	TITLE	LINE

ROVE
   Thrice happy Saints--where do I rove? . . . . O 80 Feast St Simon 55
   Behold my fair, where-e'er we rove, ... O 123 Winter's Walk 1
   A single Thought now rove, recall it home. . . . . O 255 Irene 7
   Why rove I now, when absent from my Fair, ... O 263 Irene 19
   But bids you rove the Paths of Bliss, secure . . . O 276 Irene 18
   --And rove . . . . Y 146 Irene V 20

ROVES
   Now, o'er the rural kingdom roves . . . . O 125 An Ode 5

ROVING
   Spread out by me, the roving coin, ... O 120 To Miss Purse 7
   Spread for their prey, the roving coin . . . . O 120 To Miss Purse V 7
   A roving Soldier seiz'd in Sophia's Temple . . . . O 258 Irene 94
   Arabia's roving Troops, the Sons of Swiftness, ... O 274 Irene 54
   Unfading Verdure glads the roving Eye, ... O 315 Irene 34

ROWL
   "Ah! let not tears down that fair count'nance rowl, . . Y 21 Tr. Iliad Bk 6 113

ROWLS
   That struggling pants, and rowls her eye-balls round. . O 76 Tr Add. Battle 15

ROYALL
   The victor hither brought, a royall slave. . . . . Y 19 Tr. Iliad Bk 6 39

ROYALTY
   The weighty Charge of Royalty confer; . . . . O 292 Irene 104

RUBY
   And raptur'd sees the new-found ruby shine. . . . . . O 82 Young Author V 6D

RUDE
   Till rude resistance lops the spreading god; . . . . O 42 Vanity Wishes 234
   My rude unpolish'd song; . . . . O 80 Feast St Simon 57
   Conduct her hither, let no rude Intrusion . . . . O 272 Irene 13
   May no rude blasts thy sacred bloom destroy; . . . Y 3 On a Daffodill 7

RUDENESS
   Forbear this Rudeness, ... O 322 Irene 54

RUDER
   At her Approach each ruder Gust of Thought . . . . . O 275 Irene 91

RUEFULL
   The limpid streams with ruefull murmurs flow . . . Y 6 Virgil Daphnis 3

RUFF
   Trickt in Antique Ruff and Bonnet, ... O 179 Ridicul Warton 7

RUFFIAN
   For gold his sword the hireling ruffian draws, . . . O 31 Vanity Wishes 25

RUFFIAN'S
   And bar'd my Bosom to the Ruffian's Dagger. . . . . . O 331 Irene 20
   I feel, I see the Ruffian's barb'rous Rage. . . . . . O 334 Irene 69

RUFFIANS
   Their ambush here relentless ruffians lay, ... O 9 London 15

RUFFLED
   Or storms afflict the ruffled main. . . . . O 67 Hor. II Ode IX 4

RUFLED
   The floods of rage, and calm thy rufled soul. . . . . O 77 Festina Lente 8

RUGGED
   These arts in vain our rugged natives try, ... O 16 London 129

RUIN
   And why should odious ruin dawb the wall. . . . . Y 95 Vanity Wishes V 90
   And hiss the dauber ruin dawb the wall. . . . . . Y 95 Vanity Wishes V 90
   With louder ruin to the gulphs below? . . . . . . O 35 Vanity Wishes 128
   And only build upon another's ruin. . . . . . . O 176 Tr Metastas II 13
   Adds Shame to Grief, and Infamy to Ruin. . . . . O 250 Irene 25
   Vice the harbinger of ruin. . . . . . . Y 114 Irene V 39
   Shows his bold Front, the Harbinger of Ruin, . . . O 250 Irene 41
   And dooms my rash Fidelity to Ruin. . . . . . O 256 Irene 49
   It spreads the wide plain an unregarded ruin. . . . Y 131 Irene V 36C
   Thus bright in Tears, thus amiable in Ruin, ... O 276 Irene 7
   Forbear--O do not urge me to my Ruin! . . . . . O 278 Irene 79
   To State and Pow'r I court thee, not to Ruin: . . . . O 279 Irene 80
   Hence! or be calm--To disagree is Ruin. . . . . . O 282 Irene 72
   Concur to press a hapless Captive's Ruin? . . . . O 288 Irene 10
   Concur to press a helpless Captive's Ruin? . . . . O 288 Irene V 10
   Resign their Charge to Baseness and to Ruin. . . . O 289 Irene 20
   And quit their Charge to Horror and to Ruin. . . . . O 346 Irene V 8
   And thus protected in the gen'ral Ruin, ... O 296 Irene 32
   Till angry Heav'n shall mark them out for Ruin, . . . O 309 Irene 36
   Contrive perhaps, the Ruin of our Empire, ... O 312 Irene 2
   And melt her treach'rous Beauties into Ruin. . . . O 315 Irene 37
   And melt the treach'rous Beauties into Ruin. . . . O 315 Irene V 37
   Born to compleat the Ruin of her Country; . . . . O 316 Irene 11

RUIN'D
   In triumph sits upon the ruin'd Spires . . . . . O 351 Irene V 6

RUIND
   Our Mines discover'd, and, our Battries ruind . . . . O 368 Irene V 2
   Than ruind palaces or flaming temples . . . . . . Y 177 Irene V111D

RUINOUS
   The ruinous insolence, the son's expence, ... Y 104 Vanity Wishes V 280

RUINS
   And spread its smoking ruins o'er the field. . . . . O 74 Tr. Iliad Bk 6 14
   And weeping, kiss the venerable Ruins: . . . . . O 251 Irene 61
   And wander o'er the Ruins of our Country . . . . . O 351 Irene V 1
   To raise our prostrate country from its ruins. . . . Y 117 Irene V109A
   O'erwhelm'd and lost amidst the publick Ruins . . . O 302 Irene 107
   Nor languish o'er irreparable Ruins; . . . . . . O 320 Irene 17

RULE
   To please in Method, and invent by Rule; . . . . . . O 51 Pro Drury-Lane 10

```
RULE        (CONTINUED)                                  PAGE    TITLE              LINE
     Sure all unite to hold her League of Rule  . . .   O 257  Irene               62
     Make haste, bright Maid, to rule the willing World;  . .  O 288  Irene          7
     Superiour Man possess'd the Charge of Rule,  . . . . .  O 291  Irene           71
     How the new Monarch, swell'd with airy Rule,  . . . .   O 306  Irene            1
     And bid the master Genius rule the World.  . . . . .    O 309  Irene           42
RULERS
     Unbounded Rulers of the main.  . . . . . . . . .        O 189  Epilogue        V  8
RULES
     Rules the bold hand, or prompts the suppliant voice; . .  O  31  Vanity Wishes   12
     What care, what rules your heedless charms shall save,  .  O  46  Vanity Wishes  329
     Then crush'd by Rules, and weaken'd as refin'd,  . .    O  52  Pro Drury-Lane   29
     Who keeps the rigid rules of ancient honour;  . . . .   O 176  Tr Metastas II    2
     That keeps the rigid rules of ancient honour;  . . .    O 176  Tr Metastas II  V  2
     "Now Anacreon rules my flight:  . . . . . . . .         O 185  Anacreon Ode 9   14
     If no wild Draught depart from Reason's Rules,  . . .   O 246  Irene Prologue   17
RULING
     And Strength proportiond to the task of Ruling  . . .   O 369  Irene           V  7
RUMOUR
     Swift o'er the land the dismal rumour flies,  . . . .   O  19  London          196
     To Mareotis' fen the rumour flies  . . . . . . .        Y  24  Tr Add. Battle   68
RUMP
     Toss'd her nose, and shook her rump,  . . . . . .       Y 300  Extemp. Elegy     7
RUN
     In everlasting Circles run,  . . . . . . . . .          O  68  Hor.II Ode 14     2
     "Why gen'rous warriour will you rashly run  . . . .     Y  18  Tr. Iliad Bk 6   19
RUNS
     Thither with eager hast he runs  . . . . . . . .        O  80  Feast St Simon   46
     Vain man runs headlong, to caprice resign'd;  . . . .   O 134  Tr Rambler 105    1
RURAL
     With transports kindled, rural ease,  . . . . . .       O  73  Hor. Epode II    74
     Forsakes his rural seats and peaceful home,  . . . .    O  81  Young Author      2
     Forsakes his rural sports and peaceful home,  . . . .   O  81  Young Author    V  2
     To rural grandeur, and domestick worth;  . . . . .     O 118  Epitaph Hanmer   38
     Now, o'er the rural kingdom roves  . . . . . . .        O 125  An Ode            5
     For humble cottages and rural sports.  . . . . .        O 137  Tr Rambler 138    2
     Chearful I follow to the rural Cell,  . . . . . .       O 302  Irene           110
     With pleasing sound allur'd the rural throng.  . . .    Y   6  Virgil Daphnis    8
     Now, at thy fall incens'd, the rural Gods  . . . .      Y   6  Virgil Daphnis   20
RUSH
     Or raging factions rush to war,  . . . . . . . .        O 126  An Ode           34
     What Hopes, what Terrors rush upon my Soul!  . . . .    O 259  Irene           104
     Swift, let us rush upon the careless Tyrant,  . . . .   O 271  Irene            31
     Nor rush on useless Wounds with idle Courage.  . . .    O 318  Irene            10
     Rush to the War, display thy dreadful Banners,  . . .   O 333  Irene            40
     About to rush into the field of fate  . . . . . .       Y  18  Tr. Iliad Bk 6    4
     Rush not impetuous to the bloody fray  . . . . .        Y  19  Tr. Iliad Bk 6   46
RUSH'D
     Rush'd out and seiz'd me, thoughtless and unarm'd,  . .  O 335  Irene            7
RUSHES
     War sounds the trump, he rushes to the field;  . . .   O  40  Vanity Wishes   198
     Rushes on the Realms below.  . . . . . . . . .          O 149  Tr Boet III.12   18
     And rushes joyful to the naked Wall,  . . . . . .       O 298  Irene            29
     Fly, fly, my Love, Destruction rushes on us,  . . . .   O 315  Irene             1
RUSHING
     New joy comes rushing on me and o'erwhelms  . . . .     Y 169  Irene           V 12
RUSSIA'S
     To spread Civility through Russia's Forests  . . . .    O 348  Irene           V 21
RUSSIAN
     Call me to civilize the Russian Wilds,  . . . . .       O 292  Irene           105
     To spread Civility through Russian snows  . . . . .     O 348  Irene           V 21
RUSSIANS
     Not long the happy Russians mourn;  . . . . . . .       Y  39  Lady Leaving      9
RUST
     To rust on medals, or on stones decay,  . . . . .       O  40  Vanity Wishes   190
RUSTICK
     Well may they rise, while I, whose rustick tongue  . . .  O  14  London         79
     The rustick grandeur, or the surly grace,  . . . .      O  15  London          102
     The rustick grandeur, and the manly grace,  . . . .     Y  53  London          V 102
RUSTLING
     The rustling brake alarms, and quiv'ring shade,  . . .  O  32  Vanity Wishes    42
     We learn to shudder at the rustling Breeze,  . . . .    O 266  Irene            29
SABINE
     Too far in Sabine woods I stray'd;  . . . . . . .       O  65  Hor I Ode xxii   10
     For while in Sabine Forests, charm'd  . . . . . .       O  66  To A. Fuscus      9
SABINES
     Such as the Sun-burnt Sabines were,  . . . . . .        O  72  Hor. Epode II    49
SABLE
     Now kindred Merit fills the sable bier,  . . . . .      O  45  Vanity Wishes   303
     Where sable night in all her horrour reigns;  . . . .   O  83  Epi Dist Moth.   11
     But brighten'd by the sable dress,  . . . . . .         O 122  Stella Mourn.     9
     Hence from her sable wings returning night  . . . .     Y 148  Irene           V 43E
SABRE
     No more the glutted Sabre thirsts for Blood,  . . . .   O 249  Irene             9
     Sure some kind Sabre in the Heat of Battle,  . . . .    O 252  Irene            93
     And growls in private o'er his idle Sabre.  . . . .     O 309  Irene            22
     And stole his Life and Mistress from his Sabre?  . . .  O 318  Irene            14
     To Blood, too mean to stain a Soldier's Sabre.  . . .   O 324  Irene            24
     Already shakes his bloody Sabre o'er thee.  . . . .     O 327  Irene            10
     Already brandishes his Sabre o'er You  . . . . . .      O 368  Irene           V 18
```

SACRED

	PAGE	TITLE	LINE
Invades the sacred hour of silent rest, ...	O 21	London	240
Yet when the sense of sacred presence fires, . . .	O 48	Vanity Wishes	357
Yet with the sense of sacred presence prest, . . .	O 48	Vanity Wishes V	357
With virtue's sacred ardour glows, ...	O 65	Hor I Ode xxii	2
With Virtue's sacred Ardour glows, ...	O 66	To A. Fuscus	2
His Choice our sacred Seats disgrac'd, . . .	O 146	Tr Boeth III.4	5
In every dome, in every sacred place, ...	O 189	Seeing Montagu	3
That Wealth, too sacred for their Country's Use! . . .	O 250	Irene	20
Sacred to Prayer, and wander thro' the Streets; . . .	O 251	Irene	63
Unbroken as the sacred Chain of Nature, ...	O 257	Irene	63
Aspasia, yet pursue the sacred Theme;	O 265	Irene	1
Would break the sacred laws of peace and . . . . . order	O 352	Irene V	3
Nor mingled Guilt pollute the sacred Cause!	O 300	Irene	64
There Poetry shall tune her sacred Voice, ...	O 302	Irene	122
Think them a sacred Treasure lent by Heav'n, . . .	O 302	Irene	6
Ye sacred Shades of Patriots and of Martyrs; . . .	O 306	Irene	52
Sacred to Love, to Pleasure, and Irene:	O 308	Irene	2
O grant thy sacred Influence, pow'rful Virtue! . . .	O 313	Irene	5
Thy sacred Freight shall still the raging Main. . . .	O 322	Irene	6
The sacred Freight shall still the raging Main. . . .	O 322	Irene V	6
Go Happy Bark, thy sacred Freight secures thee . . .	O 364	Irene V	24
Thy sacred freight of innocence and truth	Y 201	Irene V	10D
May no rude blasts thy sacred bloom destroy; . . .	Y 3	On a Daffodill	7
Here have I rais'd four sacred altars, two	Y 7	Virgil Daphnis	43
Venus, the sacred Sisters dispossest, ...	Y 11	Tr Hor Epode 9	5

SAD

But finds you sad at his return.	O 67	Hor. II Ode IX	12
As the sad thought of your impending fate:	O 74	Tr. Iliad Bk 6	20
Utter sad groans and lamentable cries.	O 76	Tr Add. Battle	29
O'er the sad plains perpetual tempests sigh; . . .	O 84	Epi Dist Moth.	32
While his sad mother frantick with despair	Y 6	Virgil Daphnis	5
All stemm'd in one sad day the Stygian tyde. . . .	Y 18	Tr. Iliad Bk 6	35
And the sad fate of Pygmie realms I sing. . . .	Y 22	Tr Add. Battle	2
While the sad Pygmies mourn with weeping eyes . . .	Y 26	Tr Add. Battle	128

SADDEN

Dwell on my Ear, and sadden all my Soul;	O 329	Irene	9

SADDENS

And rapture saddens to despair.	O 123	Winter's Walk	12

SAFE

And safe in poverty defy'd his foes;	O 11	London	48
All crimes are safe, but hated poverty.	O 17	London	159
How much more safe the vassal than the lord; . . .	O 31	Vanity Wishes	32
Safe in his pow'r, whose eyes discern afar . . .	O 47	Vanity Wishes	353
Safe from the keen lampoon and stinging jest; . . .	O 82	Young Author	28
Safe from the tart lampoon and stinging jest; . . .	O 82	Young Author V	28
Calmly rest in safe Repose?	O 144	Tr Boeth. II.4	4
Safe upon the rocky Ground, ...	O 145	Tr Boeth. II.4	15
Haste to the safe retreat, from whence Demetrius . . .	Y 126	Irene V	144
Safe in her Death, and in Demetrius' Flight, ...	O 329	Irene	1

SAFELY

More safely truth to urge her claim presumes, . . .	O 134	Tr. Rambler 93	1

SAFER

Or liv'st thou now, with safer pride content, . . .	O 35	Vanity Wishes	123
Or states mens now, with safer pride content, . . .	Y 97	Vanity Wishes V	123
Reserve these Questions for a safer Hour, ...	O 254	Irene	140

SAFETY

Wealth heap'd on wealth, nor truth nor safety buys, . .	O 31	Vanity Wishes	27
Her own neglected, in the publick Safety.	O 250	Irene	27
Attends to waft us to Repose and Safety.	O 258	Irene	82
And drag away thy Life in Scorn and Safety, ...	O 319	Irene	26
And test thy life in scorn and safety . . .	Y 197	Irene V	26
Is this your ardour for your masters safety	Y 207	Irene V	14
On dangers which your safety bids you shun, ...	Y 18	Tr. Iliad Bk 6	20

SAFETY'S

Soon shalt thou scorn, in Safety's Arms repos'd, . . .	O 301	Irene	93

SAGE

The wise experienc'd Grecian sage	O 68	Hor. II Ode IX	13
The chearful sage, when solemn dictates fail, . . .	O 132	Tr. Rambler 65	1
Smite thy bosom, sage, and tell, ...	O 181	Parody Warton	3
Strike thy bosom, sage, and tell, ...	O 181	Parody Warton V	3
When the smiling sage reply'd--	O 181	Parody Warton	7
When the hoary sage reply'd--	O 181	Parody Warton V	7

SAGE'S

Such was the scorn that fill'd the sage's mind, . . .	O 33	Vanity Wishes	69
The Courtier's Policy, the Sage's Firmness, ...	O 255	Irene	3

SAID

Said not the Villain in Irene's Chamber	O 375	Irene V	13

SAILORS

Like thirsty Sailors gazing on the Clouds, ...	O 282	Irene	5

SAILS

Did not our sails receive the wondring winds	Y 115	Irene V	49G
There, with your Soldiers arm'd, and Sails expanded, . .	O 284	Irene	53
Sport in our Sails, and murmur o'er the Deep.	O 304	Irene	7

SAINT   SEE ST

SAINTS   SEE FELLOW-SAINTS

The land of heroes and of saints survey;	O 15	London	100
Those Saints my numbers grace	O 78	Feast St Simon	9
Among the Saints above.	O 79	Feast St Simon	24
Thrice happy Saints--where do I rove?	O 80	Feast St Simon	55

```
SAINTS        (CONTINUED)                                   PAGE    TITLE              LINE
    O could her fabled Saints, and boasted Prayers  . . . .   O 309  Irene                38
    O could her boasted saints, and powerfull prayers  . . .  Y 185  Irene            V  38
SALLIES
    Though musick thrills, or sudden sallies seize,    . . .   O 142  In Baretti Bk.        6
    Th' impetuous Sallies of excessive Virtue,  . . . . .     O 267  Irene                47
SALLY
    Flush in my cheeks, and sally in veins  . . . . . .       Y 189  Irene            V  1E
SALOP
        at Bridgnorth, Salop; who died very poor   . . . .    O 113  Epit. Phillips   V   T
SALUTARY
    For useful Mirth, and salutary Woe;  . . . . . . .        O  53  Pro Drury-Lane       60
SAME
    Have hopes, and fears, and wishes, just the same;  . . .  O  59  Pro Good Nat'd       12
    Consistent still, though not the same,  . . . . . .       O 121  To Miss Playin       34
    Our bane and physic the same earth bestows,  . . . .      O 131  Tr. Rambler 21        1
    The same their Parent and their King.    . . . . . .      O 146  Tr Boeth III.6        4
    Still, still the same--unclouded by Misfortune!   . . .   O 294  Irene                 3
SANCTIFIES
    Nor think th' Intention sanctifies the Deed:   . . . .    O 291  Irene                59
SANCTIFY
    To form new Legends, sanctify new Crimes,  . . . . .      O 309  Irene                33
SAND
    May I lie slain, and spurn the bloody sand!   . . . .     O  75  Tr. Iliad Bk 6       30
    And grasps the bloody sand involv'd in death.   . . . .   O  76  Tr Add. Battle       17
    Though countless as the Grains of Sand   . . . . . .      O 144  Tr Boeth. II.2        1
    Shun the Sea-sapp'd Sand below;   . . . . . . . .         O 145  Tr Boeth. II.4        8
    Hence men and birds promiscuous press'd the sand  . . .   Y  23  Tr Add. Battle       52
SANDS
    Or horrid Africk's faithless sands;   . . . . . . .       O  65  Hor I Ode xxii        6
    Or torrid Africk's faithless sands;   . . . . . . .       O  65  Hor I Ode xxii   V   6
    Or torrid Afric's faithless Sands,  . . . . . . . .       O  66  To A. Fuscus          6
    And drove the swarthy troops to their own barren sands. . O  78  Festina Lente        20
    There trod the Lybian sands,   . . . . . . . . .          O  79  Feast St Simon       39
    Soon the treachrous Sands retreat,   . . . . . . .        O 145  Tr Boeth. II.4       11
    And Afric's torrid Sands in search of Cali.   . . . .     O 274  Irene                60
    Insidious sands, shallows rough rocks and whirling  . .   Y 201  Irene            V 10B
        devouring gulphs
SANDY
    Extends its Lines along the sandy Beach,  . . . . . .     O 304  Irene                 4
SANGUINARY
    Sanguinary joy--Slaves now watch her nod  . . . . . .     Y 184  Irene            V   9
SANGUIS
    Oude lithos, oude Sideron--nostro sequitur de Vulnere  .  O 347  Irene            V  23
        sanguis.
SAP
    Can sap the principles, or taint the heart;  . . . . .    O  13  London               76
SAPP'D     SEE SEA-SAPP'D
SAT
    Smiling Consent she sat, and blushing Love.   . . . .     O 303  Irene                32
    Then to the inclement skies expos'd I sat   . . . .       Y  11  Tr Hor Epode 9       35
SATED
    With honour sated, and with cares opprest;  . . . . .     O 118  Epitaph Hanmer       36
SATIETY
    Now, Tyrant, with Satiety of Beauty,  . . . . . . .       O 304  Irene                33
SATIRE
    In useful satire warn succeeding times;   . . . . .       Y  61  London           V 259
    Thy satire point, and animate thy page.   . . . . .       O  23  London              263
SATURATED
    O'erfill the saturated soul;  . . . . . . . . . .         O 190  Tr. Medea I           6
SATURNS
    Like the first race in Saturns reign  . . . . . . .       O  71  Hor. Epode II         3
SAV'D
    And Virtue cheaply sav'd with loss of Life.   . . . .     O 290  Irene                35
    Or argue with the Slave that sav'd Demetrius.   . . .     O 330  Irene                23
    One Hour had sav'd me from Despair and Madness.   . . .   O 332  Irene                28
SAVAGE
    No savage more portentous stain'd   . . . . . . .         O  66  Hor I Ode xxii       13
    The human and the savage breast   . . . . . . .           O  99  Ode Friendship        7
    Behold the Monsters gaze with savage Rapture,   . .       O 252  Irene                81
    Wilt thou dismiss the Savage from the Toils  . . . .      O 275  Irene                66
    Did savage Anger, and licentious Conquest  . . . .        O 296  Irene                30
    Cease this wild Roar of savage Exultation;  . . . .       O 318  Irene                 6
    Shall then the Savage live, to boast his Insult;  . . .   O 318  Irene                12
    A Stranger to th' Oppressor's savage Joy,  . . . . .      O 329  Irene                 6
SAVE
    What care, what rules your heedless charms shall save,  . O  46  Vanity Wishes       329
    What care, youre charms from wretchedness shall save . .  Y 107  Vanity Wishes    V 329
    No wealth his life from weary care can save,  . . . .     O 146  Tr Boeth III.3        5
    Save him whose Soul enslav'd to Vice  . . . . . . .       O 147  Tr Boeth III.6       19
    Can he restore the State he could not save?   . . . .     O 253  Irene               116
    Aspasia calls me, let me fly to save her.   . . . .       O 259  Irene               107
    I heard her, pitied her, and wish'd to save her.   . .    O 333  Irene                59
SAVED
    Or reason with the slave thats saved Demetrius  . . .     Y 210  Irene            V  23
SAVIOUR
    The Steps their Saviour trod;  . . . . . . . . .          O  79  Feast St Simon       15
SAW
    Existence saw him spurn her bounded Reign,  . . . .       O  51  Pro Drury-Lane        5
    She saw great Faustus lay the Ghost of Wit:   . . . .     O  52  Pro Drury-Lane       36
    That saw the manners in the Face.   . . . . . . .         O 154  Epita. Hogarth        4
```

```
SAW           (CONTINUED)                        PAGE   TITLE            LINE
    Twice since the Morning rose I saw the Bassa,   . . . .  O 275 Irene            76
    I saw without a sigh the fierce barbarian    . . . . .  Y 176 Irene          V 106
    Unmov'd I saw the glitt'ring Trifles perish, . . . . .  O 302 Irene           108
    And saw my scatter'd Squadrons fly before him. . . . .  O 307 Irene            20
    And saw him skulking in the closest Walks:   . . . . .  O 327 Irene            25
    This Hector saw; his soul was touch'd with grief. . . . Y  21 Tr. Iliad Bk 6  111
SAW'ST
    Not till this Day thou saw'st this fatal Fair; . . . .  O 281 Irene            54
SAY
    Then say how hope and fear, desire and hate, . . . . .  O  31 Vanity Wishes     5
    Then say how fierce desire and raging hate,  . . . . .  Y  92 Vanity Wishes   V 5
    Then say how hot desire and raging hate,     . . . . .  Y  92 Vanity Wishes   V 5
    Now say, where virtue stops and vice begins? . . . . .  O 139 Tr Rambler 173    1
    Say what is happiness below? . . . . . . . . .          O 146 Tr Boeth III.4    8
    But say, great Bassa, why the Sultan's Anger, . . . .   O 257 Irene            65
    Say, did a Voice from Heav'n restrain the Tyrant? . . . O 259 Irene           115
    Nor think to say here will I stop  . . . . . .         Y 168 Irene          V 132
    O say, bright Being, in this Age of Absence, . . . . .  O 295 Irene            21
    Say, how the Tyrant threaten'd, flatter'd, sigh'd, . .  O 295 Irene            23
    Say, how he threaten'd, flatter'd, sigh'd in vain! . .  O 295 Irene            24
    Say, how the Hand of Violence was rais'd,  . . . . .    O 295 Irene            25
    Say, how thou call'dst in Tears upon Demetrius! . . .   O 295 Irene            26
    O say, what guardian Pow'r convey'd thee hither. . . .  O 296 Irene            33
    Say, by what Fraud, what Force were you defeated? . . . O 315 Irene             6
SAYS
    Says swelling Crispin, begg'd a cobbler's vote. . . .   O  60 Pro Good Nat'd    22
    Exiles, the proverb says, subsist on hope. . . . . .    O 133 Tr. Rambler 67     1
    Commission'd, as he says, by Cali Bassa. . . . . . .    O 294 Irene              3
SCAEAN
    Soon as the chief approach'd the Scaean Gate  . . . .   Y  18 Tr. Iliad Bk 6     3
SCALE
    Held high the steady scale, but deep'd the sword; . . . O  22 London           251
    Held high the steady scale, but sheath'd the sword; . . O  22 London         V 251
    Held high the steady scale, but dropp'd the sword; . .  O  22 London         V 251
    Into the adverse Scale, nor shakes the Balance. . . .   O 260 Irene            140
    The Scale of Justice, and the Sword of Pow'r, . . . .   O 291 Irene             72
SCAMANDRIUS
    By Hector call'd Scamandrius from the god  . . . . .    Y  18 Tr. Iliad Bk 6    11
SCANDAL
    Tea, scandal, ivory teeth, and languid airs; . . . .    O  84 Epi Dist Moth.    19
SCANDALL
    The sport of boys, and scandall of the town. . . . .    Y  11 Tr Hor Epode 9    12
SCANDERBEG
    What! think of Peace while haughty Scanderbeg . . . .   O 264 Irene             13
SCANNING
    And scanning right the practices of yore,  . . . . .    O 192 Tr. Medea II        3
SCAP'D
    Nor Cadmus, scap'd the shafts of pain,  . . . . . .     O 136 Tr Rambler 128      4
SCARCE
    Who scarce forbear, tho' Britain's Court he sing, . .   O  13 London             69
    Aghast you start, and scarce with aking sight . . . .   O  18 London            186
    Scarce can our fields, such crowds at Tyburn die, . .   O  21 London            242
    Lest scarce the exhausted should rope supply.  . . .    Y  60 London          V 243
    But scarce observ'd, the knowing and the bold . . . .   O  31 Vanity Wishes     21
    And scarce a sycophant was fed by pride; . . . . . .    O  33 Vanity Wishes     56
    And scarce a sycophant could feed on pride; . . . . .   Y  94 Vanity Wishes   V 56
    This pow'r has praise, that virtue scarce can warm, .   O  39 Vanity Wishes    183
    Such pow'r has praise, that virtue scarce can charm, .  Y 100 Vanity Wishes  V 183
    Th' incumber'd oar scarce leaves the dreaded coast .    O  42 Vanity Wishes    239
    While growing hopes scarce awe the gath'ring sneer, .   O  44 Vanity Wishes    277
    And scarce a legacy can bribe to hear; . . . . . .      O  44 Vanity Wishes    278
    For love, which scarce collective man can fill; . . .   O  48 Vanity Wishes    361
    For those who durst not censure, scarce cou'd praise.   O  51 Pro Drury-Lane    14
    This scarce I lead, who left on yonder rock . . . .     O  64 Virgil Past.I     19
    And scarce forsakes his native fields. . . . . . .      O  68 Hor. II Ode IX    24
    And, fainting, scarce support the liquid weight: . .    O  74 Tr. Iliad Bk 6    24
    O'erpower'd and faint the Pygmies scarce sustain . .    O  76 Tr Add. Battle    26
    And scarce can breath th' infected sky,  . . . . .      O  79 Feast St Simon    35
    Scarce frighted love maintains his fire, . . . . .      O 123 Winter's Walk     11
    Scarce frighted love maintains her fire, . . . . .      O 123 Winter's Walk   V 11
    --Scarce repress'd the starting tear;-- . . . . . .     O 181 Parody Warton      6
    And scarce the lab'ring air sustains the throng . .     Y  25 Tr Add. Battle    95
SCARLET
    Then thro' thy Fields shall scarlet Reptiles stray, .   O 110 To Posterity       7
SCARS
    The prints of claws and honourable scars. . . . . .     Y  24 Tr Add. Battle    83
SCATT'RING
    Scatt'ring, as thy pinions play,  . . . . . . .         O 185 Anacreon Ode 9     3
SCATTER
    And scatter Discord from their baleful Beams. . . . .   O 271 Irene              5
    To scatter Happiness and Plenty round thee, . . . . .   O 278 Irene             69
SCATTER'D
    Swords, arms and wings are scatter'd o'er the plain . . O  76 Tr Add. Battle    18
    And saw my scatter'd Squadrons fly before him. . . . .  O 307 Irene             20
    Small bones and mangled bodies scatter'd there . . .    Y  23 Tr Add. Battle    31
SCATTERS
    Scatters their breathless bodies o'er the plain. . . .  O  76 Tr Add. Battle    32
    And scatters roses in the thorny way  . . . . . . .     Y 148 Irene          V 43D
SCENE
    And pierce each scene with philosophic eye. . . . . .   O  33 Vanity Wishes     64
```

```
SCENE          (CONTINUED)                              PAGE    TITLE               LINE
     In life's last scene what prodigies surprise,  . . . .    O  45 Vanity Wishes       315
     Thou to a scene of bloodshed turn'st the Ball,  . . . .   O  77 Festina Lente        11
     Charm'd with the scene the smiling ocean yields.  . . .   O  81 Young Author          3
     Pleas'd with the scene the smiling ocean yields,  . . .   O  81 Young Author     V    3
     Delude the most; few pry behind the scene.   . . . . .    O 139 Tr Rambler 168        2
     O lead me quickly to the Scene of Fate;  . . . . . .      O 259 Irene               105
     And cf To-morrow's Action fix the Scene.  . . . . . .     O 283 Irene                18
     I displaid--before her all the gay luscious scene...  .   Y 158 Irene            V    8
     Name for the Scene of Death Irene's Chamber?  . . . .     O 330 Irene                14
SCENES
     A transient calm the happy scenes bestow,  . . . . .      O  10 London               31
     And watch the busy scenes of crouded life;  . . . . .     O  30 Vanity Wishes         4
     And all the busy scenes of crouded life;  . . . . . .     Y  92 Vanity Wishes    V    4
     All times their scenes of pompous woes afford,  . . . .   O  41 Vanity Wishes       223
     To please by scenes unconscious of offence,  . . . . .    O  62 Pro Word Wise        13
     In scenes of imitated Spring,  . . . . . . . . .          O 120 To Miss Playin        2
     In greater scenes each other aid;  . . . . . . . .        O 121 To Miss Playin       28
     Think on the sudden Change of human Scenes;  . . . . .    O 252 Irene                86
     Expands the boundless scenes of future being  . . . .     Y 133 Irene            V    8
     Unus'd to Power, and form'd for humbler Scenes,  . . .    O 268 Irene                17
     My trembling nerves--sink at the dreadful scenes of blood Y 189 Irene            V   1H
          and death
SCENIC
     Bid scenic Virtue form the rising Age,  . . . . . .       O  53 Pro Drury-Lane       61
SCENTS
     And scents ambrosial breathe in every gale:  . . . . .    O  84 Epi Dist Moth.       17
     And hungry Slaughter scents Imperial Blood?  . . . . .    O 279 Irene                 5
SCEPTER
     That Reason gives her Scepter to his Hand,  . . . . .     O 281 Irene                40
     Yet ere I quit the Scepter of Dominion,  . . . . . .      O 333 Irene                49
SCEPTERS
     No joys to him pacific scepters yield,  . . . . . . .     O  40 Vanity Wishes       197
     From splendid wretchedness and guilty scepters (grandeur) Y 166 Irene            V   93
SCHEME
     Consult in private, call me when your Scheme  . . . .     O 256 Irene                36
     Lest baneful discord crush our infant Scheme,  . . . .    O 299 Irene                52
     Whate'er their Scheme the Bassa's Death defeats it,  . .  O 312 Irene                 4
     Though Disappointment blast our general Scheme,  . . .    O 317 Irene                44
SCHEMES
     Propose your schemes, ye Senatorian band,  . . . . .      O  21 London              244
     How nations sink, by darling schemes oppress'd,  . . .    O  31 Vanity Wishes        13
     How families sink, by darling schemes oppress'd,  . . .   Y  92 Vanity Wishes    V   13
     Their schemes of spite the poet's foes dismiss,  . . .    O  60 Pro Good Nat'd       19
     And Murder, all blood-bolter'd, schemes the wound.  . .   O 192 Tr. Medea II         16
     Extends his mighty Schemes of Wealth and Pow'r,  . . .    O 269 Irene                 4
     Our schemes defeated and our mines discoverd  . . . .     Y 141 Irene            V   22
     Our Schemes for ever cross'd, our Mines discover'd,  . .  O 273 Irene                22
     The raging Madman's unconnected Schemes  . . . . . .      O 287 Irene                10
SCHOLAR'S
     There mark what ills the scholar's life assail,  . . .    O  38 Vanity Wishes       159
SCHOOL
     Then Johnson came, instructed from the School,  . . . .   O  51 Pro Drury-Lane        9
SCHOOLS
     Leave to the schools their atoms and their void.  . . .   O 140 Tr Rambler 180        2
SCIENCE
     Since unrewarded science toils in vain;  . . . . . .      O  10 London               38
     Till captive Science yields her last retreat;  . . . .    O  37 Vanity Wishes       144
     All useless science is an empty boast.  . . . . . .       O 133 Tr. Rambler 83        1
     Or bid soft Science polish Britain's Heroes:  . . . .     O 293 Irene               106
     Or bid fair Science polish Britains Heroes  . . . . .     O 348 Irene            V   22
     Content with Science, Innocence, and Love?  . . . . .     O 301 Irene               105
     Science and Arms find every where a  . . . . . .          O 352 Irene            V   32
          Country.
     Spread wide their kind Arms to Science and to Beauty.  .  O 353 Irene            V    5
     O Greece! renown'd for Science and for Wealth,  . . . .   O 317 Irene                42
SCIENCES
     All sciences a fasting Monsieur knows,  . . . . . . .     O  15 London              115
SCIPIOS
     Call forth her ancient Scipios to the field  . . . . .    Y 185 Irene            V   39
SCORE
     Who knows if Jove who counts our Score  . . . . . .       O 232 Tr Horace IV.7       17
SCORN
     Such was the scorn that fill'd the sage's mind,  . . .    O  33 Vanity Wishes        69
     How just that scorn ere yet thy voice declare,  . . . .   O  33 Vanity Wishes        71
     His suppliants scorn him, and his followers fly;  . . .   O  35 Vanity Wishes       112
     Bless with an age exempt from scorn or crime;  . . . .    O  44 Vanity Wishes       292
     From th' envious world with scorn I spring,  . . . . .    O  70 Hor.II Ode XX         3
     "While I these transitory blessings scorn,  . . . . .     O  82 Young Author         17
     "While I those transitory blessings scorn,  . . . . .     O  82 Young Author     V   17
     The gen'rous scorn of venal pow'r,  . . . . . . .         O 125 An Ode               31
     I scorn the multitude, alive and dead.  . . . . . .       O 141 Tr Rambler 208        4
     Scorn their counsel and their pother,  . . . . . .        O 197 Song Congratu.       27
     Scorn their Nonsense scorn their pother,  . . . . . .     O 197 Song Congratu.   V   27
     Scorn their Nonsense scorn their pother,  . . . . . .     O 197 Song Congratu.   V   27
     I scorn a Trust unwillingly repos'd;  . . . . . . .       O 256 Irene                34
     How shall I scorn the beautiful Apostate!  . . . . . .    O 261 Irene                22
     Think on th' insulting Scorn, the conscious Pangs,  . .   O 266 Irene                19
     How Heav'n in Scorn of human Arrogance,  . . . . . .      O 269 Irene                 1
     Soon shalt thou scorn, in Safety's Arms repos'd,  . . .   O 301 Irene                93
     The Tale of Women, and the Scorn of Fools?  . . . . .     O 305 Irene                29


                                   286
```

		PAGE	TITLE		LINE
SCORN	(CONTINUED)				
And drag away thy Life in Scorn and Safety,		O 319	Irene		26
And test thy life in scorn and safety		Y 197	Irene	V	26
But 'tis not mine to judge--I scorn and leave thee.		O 324	Irene		22
Then scorn those flowers to which the Aegyptians bow'd,		Y 4	On a Daffodill		15
SCORN'D					
Those pageant Honours which he scorn'd below:		O 57	Prologue Comus		22
Dim, scorn'd and impotent, his torches lie.		O 133	Tr. Rambler 85		2
Scorn'd by his Subjects, trampled by his Foes;		O 268	Irene		20
But brave Demetrius scorn'd the mean Revenge,		O 313	Irene		17
For which Aspasia scorn'd the Turkish Crown?		O 314	Irene		17
SCORND					
she courted fate & scornd a crown		Y 191	Irene	V	16
SCORNFUL					
Turn from the glitt'ring bribe thy scornful eye,		O 14	London		87
Sure the most bitter is a scornful jest;		O 17	London		167
Receive th' unhappy ghosts of scornful maids.		O 83	Epi Dist Moth.		13
This sov'reign Passion, scornful of Restraint,		O 280	Irene		18
Oh! rather scornful of flagitious Greatness,		O 320	Irene		28
SCORNFULL					
I should behold with scornfull eye		O 73	Hor. Epode II		55
I first foresook the scornfull fair.		Y 11	Tr Hor Epode 9		10
SCORNING					
Scorning now th' o'erflowing Flood,		O 149	Tr Boet III:12		38
SCORNS					
He scorns the flow'ry vales and verdant fields;		O 81	Young Author		4
He scorns the verdant meads and flow'ry fields;		O 81	Young Author	V	4
He scorns the meek Address, the suppliant Strain,		O 246	Irene Prologue		31
And scorns the lazy Hermit's cheap Devotion;		O 264	Irene		28
SCOTLAND					
Or change the rocks of Scotland for the Strand?		O 9	London		10
SCOURGE					
Stern Torture shakes his bloody Scourge before me,		O 266	Irene		15
Reserv'd, for other Lands, the Scourge of Heav'n.		O 315	Irene		5
SCREAM					
Scream in the nests and brood their young in peace.		Y 23	Tr Add. Battle		35
SCREAMING					
The screaming Cranes and fearfull Hares.		O 72	Hor. Epode II		44
SCREEN					
And screen me from the ills of life.		O 124	Winter's Walk		20
SCRIBBLER					
For growing names the weekly scribbler lies,		O 33	Vanity Wishes		81
To growing names the weekly scribbler lies,		Y 95	Vanity Wishes	V	82
SCROLL					
Held forth this fatal Scroll, then sunk to nothing.		O 272	Irene		17
SCYMETAR					
He drew his scymetar and lop'd the branches.		Y 187	Irene	V	7
SCYTHIA'S					
Though Scythia's icy cliffs he treads,		O 65	Hor I Ode xxii		5
Tho' Scythia's icy cliff he treads,		Y 74	Hor I Ode xxii	V	5
Thro' Scythia's icy cliffs he treads,		Y 74	Hor I Ode xxii	V	5
SCYTHIAN					
At length the undaunted Scythian yields,		O 68	Hor. II Ode IX		22
The hardy Scythian ever mourns.		O 70	Hor.II Ode XX		16
SEA					
Th' insulted sea with humbler thoughts he gains,		O 42	Vanity Wishes		237
Unconquer'd bars on earth and sea withstand;		O 136	Tr Rambler 129		3
Where radiant Phoebus rising from the sea		Y 23	Tr Add. Battle		22
SEA-SAPP'D					
Shun the Sea-sapp'd Sand below;		O 145	Tr Boeth. II.4		8
SEAL					
Has Silence press'd her Seal upon his Lips?		O 255	Irene		20
His Hand! His Seal! The Secrets of my Soul		O 273	Irene		19
SEARCH					
Search every state, and canvass ev'ry pray'r.		O 33	Vanity Wishes		72
From Lydia's monarch should the search descend,		O 45	Vanity Wishes		313
Nor lures the search of avaricious eyes,		O 141	Tr Rambler 199		2
But search the wonders of the dusky stone,		O 141	Tr Rambler 199		5
And Afric's torrid Sands in search of Cali.		O 274	Irene		60
And Africs torrid shores in search of Cali		Y 143	Irene	V	60
Search to the dark Recesses of the Soul,		O 308	Irene		13
Well pleas'd to search the Treasures of Remembrance,		O 323	Irene		15
SEARCH'D					
Hast thou not search'd my Soul's profoundest Thoughts?		O 304	Irene		18
SEAS					
More false, more cruel than the seas and wind.		O 82	Young Author		14
More false, more cruel than the seas or wind.		O 82	Young Author	V	14
Embark'd with Treason on the Seas of Fate,		O 300	Irene		59
And subject Seas roar round their Queen in vain.		O 309	Irene		29
SEASON'S					
This bustling season's epidemic care;		O 59	Pro Good Nat'd		6
The bustling season's epidemic care.		O 59	Pro Good Nat'd	V	6
SEASONS					
In vain their gifts the bounteous seasons pour,		O 43	Vanity Wishes		261
When the revolving seasons shall only visit my dominions		Y 132	Irene	V	44
Oer whom the seasons varied unperceiv'd		Y 163	Irene	V	43
The varying Seasons, and revolving Skies,		O 293	Irene		118
SEAT					
Struck with the seat that gave Eliza birth,		O 10	London		23
Some hireling senator's deserted seat;		O 20	London		213
And Pride and Prudence take her seat in vain.		O 46	Vanity Wishes		336

```
SEAT          (CONTINUED)                              PAGE    TITLE          LINE
    For faith, that panting for a happier seat,  . . . . .   O  48 Vanity Wishes    363
    For hope, that panting for a happier seat,   . . . . .   Y 108 Vanity Wishes  V 363
    Cool meditation's quiet seat,    . . . . . . . . .       O 125 An Ode            30
    Wouldst thou to some stedfast Seat,  . . . . . . .       O 144 Tr Boeth. II.4     1
    And seat him in the Pleiad's golden Chariots,  . . . .   O 274 Irene             63
    If Greatness please thee, mount th' imperial Seat;  . . O 279 Irene             84
    Will now remount the slighted Seat of Empire,  . . . .  O 303 Irene             27
SEATS
    Quick let us rise, the happy seats explore,  . . . . .  O  18 London           174
    Forsakes his rural seats and peaceful home,  . . . . .  O  81 Young Author       2
    Expell'd and exil'd from the blissful seats,  . . . . . O  84 Epi Dist Moth.    29
    His Choice our sacred Seats disgracd,  . . . . . . .    O 146 Tr Boeth III.4     5
    From her high Seats he drew the Soul,  . . . . . .      O 147 Tr Boeth III.6     9
    Suspend thy Passage to the Seats of Bliss,  . . . . .   O 308 Irene              9
SEBALIAS
    Of stern Sebalias the triumphant Crescent,  . . . . .   O 312 Irene             11
SECOND
    My second, expresses a Syrian perfume;  . . . . . .     O 179 Charade!           2
    Claim but the second Place: there mighty Love  . . . .  O 280 Irene             26
    Aspasia should not fear a second Insult.  . . . . . .   O 299 Irene             42
    Henceforth be wise, nor hope a second Pardon.  . . . .  O 323 Irene              3
SECRECY
    With servile Secrecy to lurk in Shades,  . . . . . .    O 249 Irene              3
    With cautious Secrecy, Leontius steer  . . . . . . .    O 284 Irene             50
SECRET
    Some secret cell, ye pow'rs, indulgent give.  . . . .   O  11 London            49
    No secret island in the boundless main?  . . . . . .    O  18 London           172
    The secret ambush of a specious pray'r.  . . . . . .    O  48 Vanity Wishes    354
    With secret springs oft ensnares  . . . . . . . .       O  72 Hor. Epode II     43
    By secret charms our native land attracts.  . . . .     O 135 Tr Rambler 122     1
    I share, by secret Instinct, all his Joys,  . . . . .   O 272 Irene             10
    Still fond of Life, groan'd out the dreadful Secret,  . O 272 Irene             16
    Still fond of Life reveald the dreadfull secret,  . .   O 356 Irene           V 33
    When did Content sigh out her Cares in secret?  . . .   O 314 Irene             20
    Vers'd in the secret Counsels of the Sky.  . . . . .    O 314 Irene             27
    While secret Flames, with unextinguish'd Rage,  . . .   O 315 Irene             35
    And secret pleasures sparkled in his eyes.  . . . . .   Y  18 Tr. Iliad Bk 6    16
    And with fell rage and secret anguish burn.  . . . .    Y  24 Tr Add. Battle    65
SECRETS
    Explore your secrets with insidious art,  . . . . .     O  17 London           154
    And tell the Secrets of their conscious Walks;  . . .   O 255 Irene             27
    To tell the Secrets of their conscious Shades  . . . .  O 373 Irene           V 20
    And share the deepest Secrets of my Soul,  . . . . .    O 256 Irene             39
    His Hand! His Seal! The Secrets of my Soul  . . . .     O 273 Irene             19
SECURE
    secure his cottage, and his slumbers sound,  . . . . .  Y  93 Vanity Wishes   V 35
    The needy traveller, secure and gay,  . . . . . . .     Y  93 Vanity Wishes   V 37
    Secure whate'er he gives, he gives the best.  . . . .   O  48 Vanity Wishes    356
    Secure with Peace, with Competence, to dwell,  . . . .  O  58 Prologue Comus    35
    Secure, and triumph'd oft' in hostile blood.  . . . .   O  76 Tr Add. Battle    34
    "Secure of praise from nations yet unborn."  . . . . .  O  82 Young Author      18
    "Secure of praise from ages yet unborn."  . . . . . .   O  82 Young Author    V 18
    Secure he tramples my declining Fame,  . . . . . .      O 257 Irene             71
    Secure he tramples my declining Frame,  . . . . . .     O 257 Irene           V 71
    Swoln with Success, secure amidst his native Rocks  . . O 352 Irene           V 28
    But bids you rove the Paths of Bliss, secure  . . . .   O 276 Irene             18
    Permits the blooming maid secure and thoughtless  . . . Y 146 Irene           V 18
    Secure of total death, and careless of hereafter or gay . Y 146 Irene         V 20
    Greece, in her lovely Patroness secure,  . . . . . .    O 278 Irene             77
    Then strike secure, and Heav'n assist the Blow.  . . .  O 298 Irene              9
    Secure of Happiness from Flight or Conquest,  . . . .   O 302 Irene            114
    Soon may we meet again, secure and free,  . . . . . .   O 303 Irene             23
    Secure his Confidence, and fix his Love.  . . . . . .   O 319 Irene              6
SECURELY
    Securely sleeps, and, in delightful Dreams,  . . . . .  O 325 Irene             18
    Securely flourish'd the Pygmiean state,  . . . . . .    Y  23 Tr Add. Battle    27
SECURES
    The Day disast'rous that secures our Flight;  . . . .   O 317 Irene             46
    The day disastrous, that secures my honor  . . . . .    Y 195 Irene           V 46
    Against the Head which Innocence secures,  . . . . .    O 322 Irene              1
    Go Happy Bark, thy sacred Freight secures thee  . . . . O 364 Irene           V 24
SECURITY
    On all thy hours security shall smile,  . . . . . .     O  20 London           222
    His smile alone security bestows:  . . . . . . . .      O  34 Vanity Wishes    104
    With false Security beheld Invasion.  . . . . . . .     O 250 Irene             30
    Security shall spread her Shield before thee,  . . . .  O 279 Irene             82
    With all the Heroe's dull Security,  . . . . . . .      O 283 Irene              9
    When soft Security shall prompt the Sultan,  . . . . .  O 291 Irene             76
    And soft Security shall prompt the Sultan  . . . . .    O 364 Irene           V  6
SEDATE
    Must helpless man, in ignorance sedate,  . . . . . .    O  47 Vanity Wishes    345
SEDITION
    Tainted by Sloth, the Parent of Sedition,  . . . . .    O 309 Irene             20
    League with our Chiefs, and propagate Sedition?  . . .  O 312 Irene              3
SEDITIONS
    That raises tumults in the female bosom seditions  . .  Y 158 Irene           V 12
        (mutinies
SEDLEY
    And Sedley curs'd the form that pleas'd a king.  . . .  O  46 Vanity Wishes    322
```

		PAGE	TITLE	LINE
SEDUC'D				
For I know ambition seduc'd her		Y 186	Irene	V 3
SEDUCING				
He was a seducing pug!		Y 301	Extemp. Elegy	14
SEE				
The cheated nation's happy fav'rites, see!		O 14	London	91
See! while he builds, the gaudy vassals come, ...		O 19	London	202
Much could I add,--but see the boat at hand,		O 22	London	254
See motley life in modern trappings dress'd, ...		O 32	Vanity Wishes	51
In full-blown dignity, see Wolsey stand, ...		O 34	Vanity Wishes	99
In full blown pow'r see mighty Wolsey stand,		Y 96	Vanity Wishes	V 99
In full blown state, see Wolsey stand, ...		Y 96	Vanity Wishes	V 99
See nations slowly wise, and meanly just,		O 38	Vanity Wishes	161
See when the vulgar 'scape, despis'd or aw'd, . . .		O 39	Vanity Wishes	167
See one capitulate, and one resign;		Y 101	Vanity Wishes	V 200
Yet shall I see the blest abodes, ...		O 70	Hor.II Ode XX	6
See! how the mighty Change is wrought!		O 70	Hor.II Ode XX	9
See! how whate'er remain'd of Man		O 70	Hor.II Ode XX	10
By plumes is viel'd; see! quick as thought		O 70	Hor.II Ode XX	11
The Shepherds oft' see little ghosts glide by		O 77	Tr Add. Battle	47
Unpitying see them weep, and hear them pray, . . .		O 83	Epi Dist Moth.	8
We round thy board the cheerful menials see, . . .		O 130	Tr. Rambler 12	5
Wouldst thou see the foaming Main, ...		O 144	Tr Boeth. II.4	5
Thou shalt sit and smile to see		O 145	Tr Boeth. II.4	19
"His the letters which you see, ...		O 185	Anacreon Ode 9	15
"His the letters that you see, ...		O 185	Anacreon Ode 9	V 15
Joy to see their quarry fly, ...		O 196	Song Congratu.	14
See the Jocky, see the Pander, ...		O 196	Song Congratu.	19
See the Jocky, see the Pander, ...		O 196	Song Congratu.	19
See Levet to the grave descend;		O 201	Death Dr Levet	6
To please his Fancy,--see no other Man--		O 247	Irene Epilogue	3
Did we not see the bars of nature broken?		Y 115	Irene	V 49F
Yet let me think--I see the helpless Maid, . . .		O 252	Irene	80
Or hear himself, for see the Bassa comes.		O 254	Irene	141
See! Mustapha, the Tyrant's Minion, comes; . . .		O 260	Irene	143
Go see him die;		O 263	Irene	25
When nought but mine the circling Sun shall		O 357	Irene	V 29
see				
But see, where destin'd to protract our Counsels, . . .		O 271	Irene	35
I see the Gloom that low'rs upon thy Brow, ...		O 271	Irene	1
Conduct her hither, see that no intrusion		O 368	Irene	V 24
Do thou resolve: For see, Irene comes!		O 275	Irene	90
--But see Irene comes		O 367	Irene	V 11
To see new Cities tow'r at thy Command, ...		O 278	Irene	71
Justice demands--But see th' approaching Sultan. . .		O 286	Irene	15
They see the Sun surmount the dark Eclipse, . . .		O 287	Irene	5
Soon shouldst thou see, how false thy weak Reproach. . .		O 293	Irene	107
Soon wouldst thou see, how false thy weak Reproach. . .		O 293	Irene	V 107
Thus meaner Spirits with amazement see		O 369	Irene	V 11
To-morrow's Dawn shall see the Turkish King . . .		O 303	Irene	9
To-morrow's Dawn shall see the mighty Cali . . .		O 303	Irene	11
See Cali, Dread of Kings, and Pride of Armies, . . .		O 311	Irene	16
See how the Moon through all th' unclouded Sky . . .		O 313	Irene	1
But see, the lofty Maid at our Approach.		O 314	Irene	14
To see the Cloud forsake her kindling Cheek, . . .		O 320	Irene	26
I see the distant vessel		Y 201	Irene	V 10
All is not lost, Abdalla, see the Queen, ...		O 326	Irene	1
See the last Witness of thy Guilt and Fear . . .		O 326	Irene	2
I feel, I see the Ruffian's barb'rous Rage. . . .		O 334	Irene	69
See! Sol's bright chariot seeks the western main, . .		Y 4	On a Daffodill	22
With grief this emblem of mankind I see, ...		Y 4	On a Daffodill	25
And see my mistress' face no more		Y 11	Tr Hor Epode 9	32
But dearest Hector while thou liv'st I see . . .		Y 19	Tr. Iliad Bk 6	44
SEE'ST				
Thou see'st one pleasing form arise, ...		O 121	To Miss Playin	26
SEEDS				
From hence the seeds of discord first arose		Y 23	Tr Add. Battle	50
SEEK				
Alone, with am'rous Haste to seek his Love. . . .		O 262	Irene	29
Ah! let me rather seek the Convent's Cell; . . .		O 292	Irene	93
Seek out some peacefull Convents holy Shade . . .		O 348	Irene	V 24
Come let us seek new Pleasures in the Palace, . . .		O 323	Irene	17
Withdraw their cars and seek the blesst abodes. . . .		Y 6	Virgil Daphnis	21
SEEKS				
He seeks the refuge of monastic rest.		O 35	Vanity Wishes	118
And seeks the Shades to muse upon Irene;		O 261	Irene	4
See! Sol's bright chariot seeks the western main, . .		Y 4	On a Daffodill	22
SEEM'ST				
Thou seem'st at once, bright nymph, a Muse and Grace. .		O 107	Lady F Assizes	6
SEEMING				
And then lament his fall with seeming friendship: . . .		O 176	Tr Metastas II	5
And then lament their fall with seeming friendship: . .		O 176	Tr Metastas II	V 5
That hide in seeming zeal a wicked purpose, ...		O 176	Tr Metastas II	12
With artificial Smiles, and seeming Friendship. . . .		O 271	Irene	38
I dread his Arts of seeming Innocence, ...		O 273	Irene	39
SEEN				
Or seen a new-made mayor's unwieldy state;		O 33	Vanity Wishes	58
Or seen the new-made mayor's unwieldy state; . . .		Y 94	Vanity Wishes	V 58
Striped rainbows round her eyes are seen, ...		O 127	To Lyce, Lady	11
The snow dissolv'd no more is seen, ...		O 231	Tr Horace IV.7	1
Such had I trusted once as soon as seen, ...		O 255	Irene	17

```
SEEN          (CONTINUED)                                     PAGE   TITLE              LINE
     Oft has he seen the poignant orange fly,  . . . . . .   Y  67 Prologue Lethe        9
SEERS
     Whether urg'd on by seers from heav'n inspir'd  . . . . Y  19 Tr. Iliad Bk 6       58
SEES
     Orgilio sees the golden pile aspire,  . . . . . . . .   O  19 London             208
     Sejano sees the golden pile aspire,  . . . . . . . .    Y  58 London           V 208
     And sees defenceless realms receive his sway;  . . . . O  42 Vanity Wishes       244
     she sees whom diff'rent views engage,  . . . . . . .   Y 106 Vanity Wishes     V 307
     He sees, and pitying sees, vain Wealth bestow  . . .   O  57 Prologue Comus       21
     He sees, and pitying sees, vain Wealth bestow  . . .   O  57 Prologue Comus       21
     He sees no boist'rous Tempests sweep  . . . . . . . .  O  71 Hor. Epode II        11
     He sees no Northern Tempests sweep  . . . . . . . . .  O  71 Hor. Epode II      V 11
     <Or> sees from far his Bullocks play  . . . . . . . .  O  71 Hor. Epode II        20
     How pleas'd he sees his Cattle come,  . . . . . . . .  O  73 Hor. Epode II        67
     Joyfull he sees his Cattle come,  . . . . . . . . . .  O  73 Hor. Epode II      V 67
     He sees the wearied Oxen bow  . . . . . . . . . . . .  O  73 Hor. Epode II      V 69
     And raptur'd sees the new-found ruby shine. . . . . . O  82 Young Author       V 6D
     Swiftly he sees the imagin'd laurels spread,  . . . . O  82 Young Author         21
     The Merchant sees her with wealh, the lover with his  . . O 374 Irene          V 29
          Mistress
     The weary Soldier--Still sees to Morrow  . . . . . . .  O 374 Irene            V 30
     Still sees To-morrow drest in Robes of Triumph;  . . . O 283 Irene               29
     And sees the motions of th' harmonious sphere; . . . . Y   7 Virgil Daphnis      35
     The bard obdurate sees his brother die.  . . . . . . . Y  67 Prologue Lethe       4
SEIZ'D
     Part turn their Backs, part seiz'd with wild surprise  . O  76 Tr Add. Battle     28
     Whose quick Impatience seiz'd my doubtful Hand,  . . . O 254 Irene              126
     A roving Soldier seiz'd in Sophia's Temple  . . . . . O 258 Irene               94
     Amazement seiz'd us, and the hoary Bassa  . . . . . . O 317 Irene               36
     He seiz'd her melting in the fond Appeal,  . . . . . . O 334 Irene               70
     Rush'd out and seiz'd me, thoughtless and unarm'd,  . . O 335 Irene               7
SEIZE
     Does envy seize thee? crush th' upbraiding joy,  . . . O  32 Vanity Wishes       39
     And rights submitted, left him none to seize.  . . . . O  34 Vanity Wishes      108
     Rebellion's vengeful talons seize on Laud.  . . . . . O  39 Vanity Wishes      168
     Great Xerxes comes to seize the certain prey,  . . . . O  42 Vanity Wishes      227
     Though musick thrills, or sudden sallies seize,  . . . O 142 In Baretti Bk.      6
     Shall spring to seize thee like an ambush'd foe.  . . O 152 The Ant             16
     Go, seize him, load him with reproachful Chains;  . . O 273 Irene               34
     O seize the Power to bless--Irene's Nod  . . . . . . . O 278 Irene               75
     Seize the kind Fair, and press her to thy Bosom.  . . O 284 Irene               35
     Then seize fair Italy's delightful Coast,  . . . . . . O 309 Irene               30
     Seize him this Night, and through the private Passage  . O 312 Irene              23
     The Doom of Guilt alone, nor dare to seize  . . . . . O 316 Irene               14
     And seize my Sword with disencumber'd Hand.  . . . . . O 316 Irene               29
     And bade his new Confederates seize the Traitors.  . . O 317 Irene               39
     Haste, seize them, guards, be quick--my thoughtless hast Y 198 Irene          V 34
     Remorse and Anguish seize on all my Breast;  . . . . . O 333 Irene               45
     O seize me, Madness--Did she call on me!  . . . . . .  O 334 Irene               68
SEJANO
     Sejano sees the golden pile aspire,  . . . . . . . .    Y  58 London           V 208
SELECTED
     Selected by my Care, a hardy Band,  . . . . . . . . .  O 254 Irene              136
SELF
     That Priam's house, and Priam's self shall bleed:  . . . O  74 Tr. Iliad Bk 6     12
     Cleora's self, fair flower, shall fade like thee,  . . Y   4 On a Daffodill      27
SELF-APPROVING
     The peaceful slumber, self-approving day,  . . . . . . O  14 London              89
SELFISH
     On selfish bosoms only prey.  . . . . . . . . . . . .  O 100 Ode Friendship      16
SELL
     Nor sell for gold, what gold could never buy,  . . . . O  14 London              88
     Who buys without discretion, buys to sell.  . . . . . O 133 Tr. Rambler 82       1
     Free to mortgage or to sell,  . . . . . . . . . . . .  O 196 Song Congratu.       6
SELVES
     The Weakness we lament, our selves create,  . . . . . O 266 Irene               26
SEMNEN
     Aphrosi me semnen, Xeine, podessi patei  . . . . . . . O 171 Epi. Goldsmith       2
SENATE'S
     The senate's thanks, the gazette's pompous tale,  . . . O  39 Vanity Wishes     177
     Resistless merit fix'd the Senate's choice,  . . . . . O 118 Epitaph Hanmer      19
SENATES
     And senates heard before they judg'd a cause;  . . . . O  33 Vanity Wishes      60
SENATOR
     At once commenc'd the Senator and Man.  . . . . . . . O 117 Epitaph Hanmer      12
SENATOR'S
     Some hireling senator's deserted seat;  . . . . . . . O  20 London             213
SENATORIAN
     Propose your schemes, ye Senatorian band,  . . . . . . O  21 London            244
SENATORS
     When senators and nobles learn to fear;  . . . . . . . O  59 Pro Good Nat'd    V 4B
     Oh! send them to the sullen mansions dun,  . . . . . . O 192 Tr. Medea II        13
     Then Bigotry might send her Slaves to War,  . . . . . O 291 Irene               63
     Send me to wander on some pathless Shore,  . . . . . . O 328 Irene               35
     Rocks send their acclamations to the skie  . . . . . . Y   7 Virgil Daphnis      40
SENSE
     And for a moment lull the sense of woe.  . . . . . . . O  10 London              32
     Where honesty and sense are no disgrace.  . . . . . . O  11 London              44
     Sense, freedom, piety, refin'd away,  . . . . . . . .  O  15 London             105
```

```
SENSE          (CONTINUED)                          PAGE    TITLE          LINE
    Yet when the sense of sacred presence fires,   .  .  .  .  .   O  48 Vanity Wishes     357
    Yet with the sense of sacred presence prest,   .  .  .  .  .   O  48 Vanity Wishes   V 357
    Till Shame regain'd the Post that Sense betray'd,  .  .  .     O  52 Pro Drury-Lane      27
    Of rescu'd Nature, and reviving Sense;   .  .  .  .  .         O  53 Pro Drury-Lane      58
    By harmless merriment, or useful sense.  .  .  .  .  .  .      O  62 Pro Word Wise       14
    When charms thus press on ev'ry sense,   .  .  .  .  .  .      O 121 To Miss Playin      11
    A sudden Pause th' imperfect Sense suspended,  .  .  .         O 270 Irene               13
    That sooth the sense, and elevate the thought  .  .  .  .      Y 165 Irene            V  80
SENSELESS
    Snare'd with thy fears, and senseless of deliverance  .  .     Y 196 Irene            V  18
SENSES
    When the mind disentangled from the senses  .  .  .  .  .      Y 133 Irene            V   6
SENT
    Th' Apostles round the world were sent,  .  .  .  .  .  .      O  79 Feast St Simon      25
    In vain the shining Gifts are sent,  .  .  .  .  .  .  .       O 144 Tr Boeth. II.2      13
    Such Ills are sent for Souls like thine to conquer.  .  .      O 332 Irene               38
SENTENCE
    Suspend his Sentence--Empire and Irene   .  .  .  .  .         O 275 Irene               68
    Not call'd to try the Cause, we hear the Sentence,  .  .       O 326 Irene               34
    And bring her former Sentence new confirm'd.   .  .  .  .      O 327 Irene               27
    Could we reverse the Sentence of the Sultan,   .  .  .  .      O 328 Irene               38
    Suspend the dreadful Sentence for an Hour?   .  .  .  .  .     O 332 Irene               26
    Bear off with eager Haste th' unfinish'd Sentence,  .  .       O 333 Irene               53
SENTIMENT
    Each generous Sentiment is thine, Demetrius,   .  .  .  .      O 267 Irene               38
SENTINELS
    At my Command the Sentinels retire;  .  .  .  .  .  .  .       O 283 Irene               15
SEPARATE
    He comes, perhaps, to separate us forever;   .  .  .  .  .     O 294 Irene                6
SEPARATION
    To feel no more the Pangs of Separation.  .  .  .  .  .  .     O 303 Irene               24
SEPTENNIAL
    With weekly libels and septennial ale,   .  .  .  .  .  .      O  34 Vanity Wishes       97
SEQUESTER'D
    The plunder'd palace or sequester'd rent;  .  .  .  .  .       O  39 Vanity Wishes      170
    Th' unpractis'd Dervise, or sequester'd Faquir.  .  .  .  .    O 281 Irene               37
SEQUITUR
    Oude lithos, oude Sideron--nostro sequitur de Vulnere  .      O 347 Irene            V  23
        sanguis.
SERAGLIO'S
    Soon shall the dire Seraglio's horrid Gates  .  .  .  .  .     O 291 Irene               79
    Soon shall the dire Seraglio's dreadful Gates  .  .  .  .      O 357 Irene            V   9
SERENE
    The needy traveller, serene and gay,  .  .  .  .  .  .  .      O  32 Vanity Wishes       37
    How blest art thou, still jocund and serene,  .  .  .  .       O 271 Irene                6
    They give the nations laws, and view serene  .  .  .  .  .     Y 167 Irene            V 117
SERENITY
    Nor dull Serenity becalms his Eyes.  .  .  .  .  .  .  .       O 255 Irene               16
SERIOUS
    Slaves that with serious impudence beguile,  .  .  .  .  .     O  17 London             146
    Such ill-tim'd Gravity, such serious Folly,  .  .  .  .  .     O 281 Irene               35
SERPENTS
    And Serpents with their poys'nous breath  .  .  .  .  .  .     O  79 Feast St Simon      41
    Where furies ever howl, and serpents hiss.   .  .  .  .  .     O  84 Epi Dist Moth.      31
SERV'D
    Has serv'd his Prince so well, demand our Silence?  .  .       O 329 Irene               19
SERVIA'S
    Deny'd the Government of Servia's Province.   .  .  .  .  .     O 311 Irene               10
SERVICE
    "Think not yet my service hard,  .  .  .  .  .  .  .  .        O 185 Anacreon Ode 9      17
    For those who could not please by nobler Service.--  .  .      O 264 Irene               24
SERVILE
    The laureat tribe in servile verse relate,   .  .  .  .  .     O  19 London             198
    With servile grief dependent nobles sigh  .  .  .  .  .  .     Y  57 London           V 198
    With servile Secrecy to lurk in Shades,  .  .  .  .  .  .      O 249 Irene                3
SERVITUDE
    And lull to servitude a thoughtless age.  .  .  .  .  .  .     O  12 London             60
    And bear us far from Servitude and Crimes.   .  .  .  .  .     O 267 Irene               44
SET
    Who set unclouded in the gulphs of fate.  .  .  .  .  .  .     O  45 Vanity Wishes      312
    When the tenth Sun had set upon our Sorrows,   .  .  .  .      O 254 Irene              120
    Soon would his Art or Valour set us free,  .  .  .  .  .       O 267 Irene               43
    Rose to his Thought, and set his Soul on Fire:   .  .  .  .    O 270 Irene               11
    Or set The Persian Heretic in arms against Me  .  .  .  .      O 348 Irene            V  17
    To mix with nobler Cares, I'll set apart   .  .  .  .  .  .    O 368 Irene            V  27
    And set the glitt'ring Fallacy to view.  .  .  .  .  .  .      O 293 Irene              128
    Unclasp'd his Iron Gripe to set thee free?   .  .  .  .  .     O 318 Irene               16
    Detain'd me till Demetrius set me free.  .  .  .  .  .  .      O 335 Irene                9
    Since from Inachia's charms set free  .  .  .  .  .  .  .      Y  11 Tr Hor Epode 9       9
    Soon as with gold appeas'd, he set her free  .  .  .  .  .     Y  19 Tr. Iliad Bk 6      40
SETS
    The queen, the beauty, sets the world in arms;   .  .  .  .    O  42 Vanity Wishes      246
    <He> sets his nets, employs his skill.   .  .  .  .  .  .      O  72 Hor. Epode II       42
    Next Month he sets it out again.  .  .  .  .  .  .  .  .       O  73 Hor. Epode II       79
SETTING
    No setting Sol can ease your cares,  .  .  .  .  .  .  .       O  67 Hor. II Ode IX      11
SETTLE'S
    These dreams were Settle's once and Ogilby's.  .  .  .  .      O  82 Young Author        24
    Those dreams were Settle's once and Ogilby's.  .  .  .  .      O  82 Young Author     V  24
```

```
SETTLED                                                  PAGE    TITLE            LINE
     If built on settled Thought, this Constancy  . . . . .  O 290  Irene              36
     If fix'd on settled thought this Constancy   . . . . .  O 364  Irene          V   8
SEV'N
     By that dire sword my sev'n brave brothers dy'd;  . . .  Y  18  Tr. Iliad Bk 6     34
SEV'NMOUTH'D
     Where sev'nmouth'd Nilus roars,  . . . . . . . . . .     O  79  Feast St Simon     33
SEVERER
     But cruel virgins meet severer fates;  . . . . . . . .   O  84  Epi Dist Moth.     28
SEVERITIES
     Freed from the harsh severities of virtue  . . . . .     Y 146  Irene          V  23
SEVERITY
     Greatness with ease, and gay severity.  . . . . . .      O 137  Tr Rambler 141      1
SEVERN
     For the fair banks of Severn or of Trent;  . . . . .     O  19  London            211
SEWER
     The common sewer of Paris and of Rome;  . . . . . .      O  14  London         V  94
SEX
     Then let me once, in honour of our Sex,  . . . . . .     O 277  Irene              49
     Then Let me once to right our injur'd Sex  . . . . .     O 356  Irene          V  16
     Whate'er Man's Pride has ravish'd from our Sex.  . . .   O 291  Irene              75
     Fly from the busy Pleasures of her Sex,  . . . . . .     O 322  Irene              14
SHADE
     Still foe to vice, forsake his Cambrian shade;  . . .    O  23  London            261
     Still foe to vice, exert his Cambrian shade;  . . . .    Y  61  London         V 262
     The rustling brake alarms, and quiv'ring shade,  . . .   O  32  Vanity Wishes      42
     Nor Melancholy's phantoms haunt thy shade;  . . . . .    O  37  Vanity Wishes     154
     Nor Melancholy's spectres haunt thy shade;  . . . . .    Y  99  Vanity Wishes  V 154
     Th' oblivious grave's inviolable shade.  . . . . . .     O  62  Pro Word Wise      10
     Play on your pipe beneath this beechen shade;  . . . .   O  64  Virgil Past.I       2
     Beneath some spreading Ilex Shade  . . . . . . . . .     O  72  Hor. Epode II      29
     Beneath some venerable Shade  . . . . . . . . . . .      O  72  Hor. Epode II  V  29
     His country call'd him from the studious shade;  . . .   O 117  Epitaph Hanmer     10
     And recollected toils endear'd the shade;  . . . . .     O 118  Epitaph Hanmer     42
     How active light, and thoughtful shade,  . . . . . .     O 121  To Miss Playin     27
     Is naught but Ashes and a Shade.  . . . . . . . . .      O 232  Tr Horace IV.7     16
     To warn the wand'ring Linnet to the Shade,  . . . . .    O 250  Irene              33
     <And> plants for his prattling babes the future shade   Y 122  Irene          V  62
     Now hovers o'er this melancholy Shade,  . . . . . .      O 267  Irene              40
     And through the parted Shade disclos'd the Greeks,  . .  O 269  Irene              11
     And pleasure shall shade thee with her downy  . . . .   Y 150  Irene          V  83
        pinions
     And India join her aromatic shade  . . . . . . . . .    Y 150  Irene          V  85
     Seek out some peacefull Convents holy Shade  . . . . .   O 348  Irene          V  24
     O'er all the warbling founts a cooling shade.  . . . .   Y   7  Virgil Daphnis     27
     If winter by the fire, if summer in the shade.  . . .    Y   7  Virgil Daphnis     48
     Where the wild fig trees join their darksom shade  . .   Y  19  Tr. Iliad Bk 6     52
SHADED
     Th' appointed Vessel to yon' shaded Bay,  . . . . . .    O 284  Irene              51
SHADES
     There prune thy shades, support the drooping flow'rs,   Y  58  London         V 216
     Now in the realms below the Pygmie shades  . . . . . .   O  76  Tr Add. Battle     41
     And shades of Pygmies swim before their eye.  . . . .    O  77  Tr Add. Battle     48
     In Myrtle shades oft sings the happy swain,  . . . . .   O  95  Sprig of Myrtl V   7
     In Myrtle shades despairing ghosts complain;  . . . .    O  95  Sprig of Myrtl      8
     And bears me to the peaceful shades,  . . . . . . . .    O 125  An Ode             15
     While artful shades thy downy couch enclose,  . . . .    O 151  The Ant            11
     To dens of guilt and shades of care  . . . . . . . .     O 191  Tr. Medea I        13
     With servile Secrecy to lurk in Shades,  . . . . . .     O 249  Irene               3
     To tell the Secrets of their conscious Shades  . . . .   O 373  Irene          V  20
     And seeks the Shades to muse upon Irene;  . . . . . .    O 261  Irene               4
     Through shades of peace and flowery labyrinths  . . .    Y 146  Irene          V  21
     And flies for Shelter to the Shades of Life.  . . . .    O 292  Irene             102
     To kind Italia's hospitable Shades;  . . . . . . . .     O 302  Irene             117
     Ye sacred Shades of Patriots and of Martyrs;  . . . .    O 306  Irene              52
     Ye holy shades of--martyrs  . . . . . . . . . . . .      Y 181  Irene          V  52
     Play'd fearless in th' inviolated Shades.  . . . . .     O 314  Irene               7
     Those Groves, whose Shades embower'd the dear Irene;    O 333  Irene              46
     Where Hypoplacus' lofty shades extend.  . . . . . .      Y  18  Tr. Iliad Bk 6      8
SHADY
     Your shady Groves, your pleasing wife,  . . . . . .      O  69  Hor.II Ode 14      21
SHAFTS
     And with unerring shafts distribute fate;  . . . . .     O  83  Epi Dist Moth.      4
     Nor Cadmus, scap'd the shafts of pain,  . . . . . .      O 136  Tr Rambler 128      4
SHAKE
     To shake with laughter ere the jest they hear;  . . .   O  16  London            140
     To shake in dog-days, in December sweat.  . . . . .      O  16  London            143
     How wouldst thou shake at Britain's modish tribe,  . .   O  33  Vanity Wishes      61
     In vain proud tyrants strove to shake  . . . . . . .     O  79  Feast St Simon     13
     Did Earthquakes shake our walls?  . . . . . . . . .      O 347  Irene          V   3
     Forgive those Fears that shake the tender Frame?  . .    O 266  Irene              25
     Courts thee to shake on a dependent Throne;  . . . .     O 268  Irene              22
     At his dread Name the distant Mountains shake  . . . .   O 268  Irene              28
     At my dread name the distant mountains shake  . . . .    Y 136  Irene          V  28
     Shake at my dreaded name and the frighted world  . . .   Y 136  Irene          V  28
     Would shake his wily Head, and closely whisper,  . . .   O 273  Irene              28
     Shake off th' Incumbrances of State a moment,  . . . .   O 289  Irene               7
     Does conscious Virtue shake the fainting knee?  . . .    O 373  Irene          V   8
     Shake off this Weight of unavailing Grief,  . . . . .    O 333  Irene              39
SHAKES
     And dubious title shakes the madded land,  . . . . .     O  31  Vanity Wishes      30
```

```
                                                      PAGE    TITLE            LINE
SHAKES          (CONTINUED)
     From dubious titles shakes the madded land,  . . . . .   Y  93 Vanity Wishes    V  30
     When loud Auster shakes her Walls, . . . . . . .         O 145 Tr Boeth. II.4      10
     Into the adverse Scale, nor shakes the Balance.          O 260 Irene              140
     and the first gust shake<s> it into atom<s>  .           Y 132 Irene            V  39
     Stern Torture shakes his bloody Scourge before me,       O 266 Irene               15
     Why shakes the Ground, when subterraneous Fires  . . .   O 281 Irene               52
     Already shakes his bloody Sabre o'er thee. . . . . .     O 327 Irene               10
SHAKESPEAR
     First rear'd the Stage, immortal Shakespear rose; . . .  O  51 Pro Drury-Lane       2
SHAKESPEAR'S
     Nor wish'd for Johnson's Art, or Shakespear's Flame; . . O  52 Pro Drury-Lane      18
SHAKING
     Why shoots this Chilness through thy shaking Nerves? . .  O 295 Irene                6
SHALL
     Heroes, proceed! what bounds your pride shall hold? . .  O  13 London              61
     On all thy hours security shall smile, . . . . . .       O  20 London             222
     Then shall thy friend, nor thou refuse his aid,  . . .   O  23 London             260
     Shall Wolsey's wealth, with Wolsey's end be thine? .     O  35 Vanity Wishes      122
     Such age there is, and who shall wish its end? . . .     O  44 Vanity Wishes      298
     What care, what rules your heedless charms shall save,   O  46 Vanity Wishes      329
     What care, youre charms from wretchedness shall save     Y 107 Vanity Wishes    V 329
     Where then shall Hope and Fear their objects find?  .    O  47 Vanity Wishes      343
     This Night, distinguish'd by your Smile, shall tell,  .  O  57 Prologue Comus      11
     The slighted Arts Futurity shall trust, . . . . .        O  57 Prologue Comus      13
     Yet then shall calm reflection bless the night,  . . .   O  62 Pro Word Wise       21
     For I shall never think him less than God;  . . . . .    O  64 Virgil Past.I        8
     Oft on his altar shall my firstlings lie,  . . . . .     O  64 Virgil Past.I        9
     Their blood the consecrated stones shall dye:  . . .     O  64 Virgil Past.I       10
     Her voice and Smiles my Song shall grace. . . . . .      O  67 To A. Fuscus        24
     Alone the Cypress shall attend. . . . . . . . .          O  69 Hor.II Ode 14       24
     Along the marble floor shall flow.  . . . . . .          O  69 Hor.II Ode 14       28
     Yet shall I see the blest abodes, . . . . . . .          O  70 Hor.II Ode XX        6
     Yet, great Maecenas, shall your friend  . . . . .        O  70 Hor.II Ode XX        7
     My Works shall propagate my fame, . . . . . . .          O  70 Hor.II Ode XX       17
     Nations shall celebrate my Name . . . . . . . .          O  70 Hor.II Ode XX       19
     Shall live for ever in my verse. . . . . . . .           O  70 Hor.II Ode XX       24
     That post, and all the rest, shall be my care;  . .      O  74 Tr. Iliad Bk 6       3
     But shall I, then, forsake the unfinish'd war? . . .     O  74 Tr. Iliad Bk 6       4
     That Priam's house, and Priam's self shall bleed:  . .   O  74 Tr. Iliad Bk 6      12
     The day will come, in which proud Troy shall yield,  .   O  74 Tr. Iliad Bk 6      13
     Whose blood shall quench some Grecian's thirsty rage,    O  74 Tr. Iliad Bk 6      16
     When some proud Grecian dame shall tasks impose,  . .    O  74 Tr. Iliad Bk 6      21
     Beneath Hyperia's waters shall you sweat, . . . .        O  74 Tr. Iliad Bk 6      23
     Then shall some Argive loud insulting cry, . . . .       O  74 Tr. Iliad Bk 6      25
     Tears, at my name, shall drown those beauteous eyes,     O  75 Tr. Iliad Bk 6      27
     So shall Belinda's charms improve mankind. . . . .       O  81 Lady Birthday       19
     So shall you guiltless reign, and all mankind adore.     O  84 Epi Dist Moth.      47
     Soon must this bough, as you shall fix his doom,  . .    O  95 Sprig of Myrtl      13
     Soon shall this sprig, as you shall fix its doom,  .     O  95 Sprig of Myrtl    V 13
     Soon shall this sprig, as you shall fix its doom,  .     O  95 Sprig of Myrtl    V 13
     Nor shall thine ardours cease to glow  . . . . .         O 100 Ode Friendship    V 25
     O! Shall thy flames then cease to glow  . . . . .        O 100 Ode Friendship    V 25
     Shall aid our Happiness above. . . . . . . .             O 100 Ode Friendship      28
     Shall aid y<ou>r Happiness above. . . . . . .            O 100 Ode Friendship    V 28
     The Horse shall trample, or the Plough shall break,      O 110 To Posterity         2
     The Horse shall trample, or the Plough shall break,      O 110 To Posterity         2
     Thy Streets with Violence of Woe shall sound, . . .      O 110 To Posterity         5
     Then thro' thy Fields shall scarlet Reptiles stray,      O 110 To Posterity         7
     Their hungry Swarms the peaceful Vale shall fright       O 110 To Posterity         9
     The teeming Year's whole Product shall devour, . . .     O 110 To Posterity        11
     Shall glutton on the industrious Peasants Spoil, . .     O 110 To Posterity        13
     Then o'er the World shall Discord stretch her Wings,     O 110 To Posterity        15
     The Bear enrag'd th' affrighted Moon shall dread;  .     O 111 To Posterity        17
     Nor shall the Lyon, wont of old to reign . . . .         O 111 To Posterity        19
     His tortur'd Sons shall die before his Face,  . . .      O 111 To Posterity        23
     And, yet more strange! his Veins a Horse shall drain,    O 111 To Posterity        25
     Nor shall the passive Coward once complain. . . . .      O 111 To Posterity        26
     The glitt'ring vagrants shall restrain; . . . . .        O 120 To Miss Purse       10
     Thy pictures shall thy conduct frame, . . . . .          O 121 To Miss Playin      33
     Ah! how shall envy sooth her pain? . . . . . .           O 122 Stella Mourn.       12
     Henceforth shall form one common pray'r,  . . . .        O 122 Stella Mourn.       14
     How long shall sloth usurp thy useless hours,  . . .     O 151 The Ant              9
     Shall spring to seize thee like an ambush'd foe.  .      O 152 The Ant             16
     Shall long detain the cup,  . . . . . . . .              O 159 Par Hermit III       6
     Err shall they not, who resolute explore  . . . .        O 192 Tr. Medea II         1
     Shall deem our hoar progenitors unwise. . . . .          O 192 Tr. Medea II         4
     Or Virtue shall replace on earth. . . . . . .            O 232 Tr Horace IV.7      24
     Or Virtue shall restore to earth.  . . . . . .           O 232 Tr Horace IV.7    V 24
     Thy wealth O city ill-gotten ill-preserv'd . . . .       Y 113 Irene             V 20
       shall
     Sooner these trembling Leaves shall find a Voice,  . . . O 255 Irene               26
     Sooner the trembling Leaves shall find a Voice,  . . .   O 373 Irene             V 19
     Sooner the Breeze shall catch the flying Sounds, . . .   O 255 Irene               28
     My Policy shall raise an easy Throne; . . . . .          O 257 Irene               78
     The Turkish Pow'rs from Europe shall retreat, . . . .    O 257 Irene               79
     How shall I scorn the beautiful Apostate! . . . .        O 261 Irene               22
     Thy Care shall guard this Treasure of my Soul; . . . .   O 263 Irene                2
     When ev'ry Storm in my Domain shall roar,  . . . .       O 265 Irene               42
     Till ev'ry Storm in my Domain shall roar,  . . . . .     O 354 Irene             V 25
     When nought but mine the circling Sun shall  . . . .     O 357 Irene             V 29
```

293

SHALL	(CONTINUED)	PAGE	TITLE	LINE
see				
When ev'ry Wave shall beat a Turkish Shore, ...	O 265	Irene	43
Till every Wave shall beat a Turkish Shore.	O 354	Irene	V 26
Then, Cali, shall the Toils of Battle cease, ...	O 265	Irene	44
When the revolving seasons shall only visit my dominions	Y 132	Irene	V 44
So shall Timidity assist thy Reason, ...	O 266	Irene	21
Shall feel the Vengeance of an injur'd King.	O 273	Irene	33
There (or might) shall his boundless Wealth the . . .	O 351	Irene	V 13
Spoil of				
There shall he waste thy Frontiers, check thy Conquests,	O 274	Irene	56
Elude my Vengeance? no--My Troops shall range	O 274	Irene	58
Reward his toils, and he shall toil for you	Y 146	Irene	V 23A
For you shall plough the main, and fight the battle . .	Y 146	Irene	V 23B
Shall break the Fetters of the groaning Christian; . .	O 278	Irene	76
shall influence whole nations	Y 150	Irene	V 76
Shall mourn no more her plunder'd Palaces.	O 278	Irene	78
For thee, my fair, shall India's spices	Y 150	Irene	V 81
ripen				
Security shall spread her Shield before thee, ...	O 279	Irene	82
Pleasure shall spread her downy Pinions o'er thee . . .	O 350	Irene	V 21
The voice of war no more shall fright	Y 150	Irene	V 82
Irene				
For thee shall Forests rise and Rivers flow	O 350	Irene	V 22
And pleasure shall shade thee with her downy	Y 150	Irene	V 83
pinions				
Unbounded Wealth shall flow beneath thy feet	O 350	Irene	V 23
Each Day and shall be made happy with new entertainments	O 350	Irene	V 24
Here ev'ry Warbler of the Sky shall sing;	O 279	Irene	86
And new forms of pleasure shall be invented	O 350	Irene	V 25
To deck these Bow'rs each Region shall combine, . . .	O 279	Irene	88
To make thee blest each Region shall combine	O 351	Irene	V 26
Empire and Love shall share the blissful Day, ...	O 279	Irene	90
Rouse, Cali, shall the Sons of conquer'd Greece . . .	O 284	Irene	42
Well,--'tis decreed--This Night shall fix our Fate. . .	O 284	Irene	48
No more shall glow with Friendship's hallow'd Ardour: .	O 289	Irene	16
Shall I not wish to chear afflicted Kings, ...	O 291	Irene	67
When soft Security shall prompt the Sultan, ...	O 291	Irene	76
And soft Security shall prompt the Sultan	O 364	Irene	V 6
shall give the Tyrant leisure--			
Soon shall the dire Seraglio's horrid Gates	O 357	Irene	V 7
Soon shall the dire Seraglio's dreadful Gates	O 291	Irene	79
There shall we find the yet untasted Bliss	O 357	Irene	V 9
Oft' shall I dwell on our disastrous Friendship, . . .	O 292	Irene	88
Oft shall I swell on our disastrous Friendship . . .	O 292	Irene	96
She cannot, must not, shall not linger here, ...	O 349	Irene	V 11
When Heav'n shall bid the swelling Billows rage, . . .	O 296	Irene	6
Shall guard Aspasia from triumphant Lust.	O 300	Irene	60
Yet shall the Conscience of the great Attempt	O 301	Irene	89
There shall soft Leisure wing th' excursive Soul, . . .	O 301	Irene	99
There shall despotick Eloquence resume	O 302	Irene	118
There Poetry shall tune her sacred Voice, ...	O 302	Irene	120
To-morrow's Dawn shall see the Turkish King	O 302	Irene	122
To-morrow's Dawn shall see the mighty Cali	O 303	Irene	9
Shall dart their am'rous Glances at the Fair, ...	O 303	Irene	11
Shall soar triumphant on the Wings of Glory, ...	O 304	Irene	35
My Name shall echo through the shouting Field;	O 305	Irene	26
The shudd'ring Camp shall murmur out Demetrius. . . .	O 305	Irene	40
My Pride shall ne'er protract my Country's Woes; . . .	O 305	Irene	42
Wealth, and Command, and Grandeur shall be thine . . .	O 306	Irene	47
Revenge and subtle Jealousy shall teach	O 306	Irene	6
The Bowl shall circle to confirm our League, ...	O 307	Irene	24
Then shall these Juices taint Demetrius' Draught, . . .	O 308	Irene	29
Thus shall he live to strike th' important Blow, . . .	O 308	Irene	30
Shall shed his Beams upon the bridal Bed, ...	O 308	Irene	32
Then shall the Rhodian mourn his sinking Tow'rs, . . .	O 309	Irene	24
Then shall Venetia feel the Turkish Pow'r, ...	O 309	Irene	26
Her Sons malicious Clemency shall spare, ...	O 309	Irene	28
Till angry Heav'n shall mark them out for Ruin, . . .	O 309	Irene	32
I love her still, but shall esteem Aspasia:	O 309	Irene	36
No more shall feel Religion's hallow'd ardours	Y 186	Irene	V 5
Shall Monarchs fear to draw the Sword of Justice, . . .	O 349	Irene	V 24
Shall then the Greeks, unpunish'd and conceal'd, . . .	O 312	Irene	21
Yet much remains to hope. I shall not call	O 312	Irene	1
Henceforth shall live for me; for me alone	O 317	Irene	45
Shall plume her Charms, and, with attentive Watch . . .	O 317	Irene	3
Shall play the glance, and with attentive watch . . .	O 318	Irene	4
Shall then the Savage live, to boast his Insult; . . .	Y 195	Irene	V 4
Shall throw th' attending Janizaries round thee. . . .	O 318	Irene	12
This lucky Stratagem shall charm the Sultan, ...	O 319	Irene	34
Shall bless our Wand'rings, and propitiate Heav'n. . .	O 319	Irene	5
When vanquish'd Vice shall tyrannize no more.	O 320	Irene	19
Disease shall chase the Phantoms of Ambition, ...	O 321	Irene	36
Thy sacred Freight shall still the raging Main. . . .	O 322	Irene	60
The sacred Freight shall still the raging Main. . . .	O 322	Irene	6
Shall the whirle, and bid the Rock subside	O 322	Irene	6
To guide thy Passage shall th' aerial Spirits	O 365	Irene	V 4
To Guide thy passage shall th' Starry Spirits	O 322	Irene	7
Th' applauding Sky shall pour forth all its Beams . .	O 26	Irene	V 26
The Wondring Sky shall shine with Decorations	O 322	Irene	9
There dauntless Truth shall blast the vile Accuser, . .	O 364	Irene	V 28
	O 326	Irene	42

		PAGE	TITLE	LINE
SHALL	(CONTINUED)			
Then shall you feel what Language cannot utter, . . .		O 326	Irene	43
Quick at my Call shall execute your Charge;		O 328	Irene	43
Hope not thy threats shall stay		Y 210	Irene	V 25
Shall hide me from the tasteless World for ever. . . .		O 333	Irene	48
Hear! shall I hear thee! did'st thou hear Irene? . . .		O 333	Irene	56
Mistake shall blast, or Accident destroy;		O 335	Irene	13
But Heav'n shall guide it to the guilty Heart. . . .		O 335	Irene	15
New verdure ev'ry fading leaf shall fill, ...		Y 4	On a Daffodill	19
Cleora's self, fair flower, shall fade like thee, . . .		Y 4	On a Daffodill	27
No toils shall intercept the nimble deer.		Y 7	Virgil Daphnis	39
Thyrsis while sings shall the gods		Y 7	Virgil Daphnis	V 49
While bees shall feed on thyme, and birds shall haunt the grove		Y 7	Virgil Daphnis	50
While bees shall feed on thyme, and birds shall haunt the grove		Y 7	Virgil Daphnis	50
The swains shall pay their vows, and thou shalt hear their prayer.		Y 7	Virgil Daphnis	52
Libations he shall pour to Daphnis praise.		Y 7	Virgil Daphnis	V 52
Soon shall you fall by num'rous hosts opprest		Y 18	Tr. Iliad Bk 6	22
And Grecian spears shall quiver in your breast. . . .		Y 18	Tr. Iliad Bk 6	23
Think shouldst thou fall how wretched shall we be, . .		Y 19	Tr. Iliad Bk 6	48
Hector shall perish by no warriour's hand.		Y 21	Tr. Iliad Bk 6	116
Shall sink alike into the gloomy grave.		Y 21	Tr. Iliad Bk 6	120
She shall sing me a song, ...		Y 300	Fanny Burney	1
SHALLOWS				
Insidious sands, shallows rough rocks and whirling devouring gulphs		Y 201	Irene	V 10B
SHALT				
Then, O my Country! shalt thou groan distrest, ...		O 110	To Posterity	3
Thou shalt sit and smile to see		O 145	Tr Boeth. II.4	19
There shalt thou view from far the quiet Cottage, . . .		O 292	Irene	83
Soon shalt thou scorn, in Safety's Arms repos'd, . . .		O 301	Irene	93
But soon thou shalt repent: another Moment		O 319	Irene	33
But soon though shalt lament thy daring folly		Y 198	Irene	V 33
Now shalt thou shine the Darling of the Sultan, . . .		O 329	Irene	3
And thou shalt flourish by her influence.		Y 4	On a Daffodill	20
Thou shalt with Bacchus equal honours share		Y 7	Virgil Daphnis	51
The swains shall pay their vows, and thou shalt hear their prayer.		Y 7	Virgil Daphnis	52
SHAME				
By numbers here from shame or censure free, ...		O 17	London	158
And steals to death from anguish and from shame. . . .		O 43	Vanity Wishes	254
Till Shame regain'd the Post that Sense betray'd, . . .		O 52	Pro Drury-Lane	27
For those who feel no guilt can know no shame;		O 84	Epi Dist Moth.	25
All is my own, my honour and my shame.		O 132	Tr. Rambler 46	2
Adds Shame to Grief, and Infamy to Ruin.		O 250	Irene	25
Let Shame and hooting Infamy pursue me, ...		O 328	Irene	36
I then (my cheeks still glow with shame) was grown . .		Y 11	Tr Hor Epode 9	11
SHAMES				
Shames the mean Pensions of Augustan Times;		O 57	Prologue Comus	4
SHAPE				
Each Realm where Beauty turns the graceful Shape, . . .		O 262	Irene	13
SHAR'D				
My whole, is a Man in whose converse is shar'd, . . .		O 179	Charade!	3
SHARE				
Our anxious Bard, without complaint, may share		O 59	Pro Good Nat'd	5
Our little Bard, without complaint, may share		O 59	Pro Good Nat'd	V 5
I can't prevent, and will not share.		O 126	An Ode	36
Let Lyce share the praise.		O 126	To Lyce, Lady	8
May ye the varied blessings share		O 189	Epilogue	5
May ye th' alternate blessings share		O 189	Epilogue	V 5
What with your friend you nobly share		O 232	Tr Horace IV.7	19
To have the fiftieth Part her paultry Share?		O 247	Irene Epilogue	6
And hop'd to share thy Counsels, not thy Sorrows: . . .		O 253	Irene	106
And share the deepest Secrets of my Soul, ...		O 256	Irene	39
But, Cali, let Irene share thy Prayers;		O 262	Irene	5
I share, by secret Instinct, all his Joys, ...		O 272	Irene	10
Do we not share the comprehensive Thought, ...		O 278	Irene	55
Do not we share the comprehensive thought, ...		Y 149	Irene	V 57
Empire and Love shall share the blissful Day, ...		O 279	Irene	90
And share the Pleasures of the World		O 348	Irene	V 20
Will not the Patriot share the Traytor's Danger? . . .		O 300	Irene	62
Unfit to share this Night's illustrious Toils?		O 305	Irene	21
To share the Miseries herself has caus'd.		O 320	Irene	15
Resolve to share our Dangers and our Toils, ...		O 320	Irene	29
Melt at Irene's Fate, and share her Woes?		O 329	Irene	7
Thou shalt with Bacchus equal honours share		Y 7	Virgil Daphnis	51
SHARES				
Who shares Orgilio's crimes, his fortune shares. . . .		O 14	London	84
Who shares Orgilio's crimes, his fortune shares. . . .		O 14	London	84
SHARPEN				
Sharpen their claws, and meditate the war.		Y 24	Tr Add. Battle	71
SHATTER'D				
Dashing Waves and shatter'd Shoars, ...		O 145	Tr Boeth. II.4	18
In Triumph sits upon our shatter'd Spires, ...		O 251	Irene	67
A slaughter'd nation, or a shatter'd world.		Y 177	Irene	V111E
Who to the ground the shatter'd building flung		Y 23	Tr Add. Battle	48
SHE				
she sees whom diff'rent views engage, ...		Y 106	Vanity Wishes	V 307
Tir'd with contempt, she quits the slipp'ry reign, . .		O 46	Vanity Wishes	335

295

SHE	(CONTINUED)	PAGE	TITLE	LINE
	And makes the happiness she does not find.	O 48	Vanity Wishes	368
	She saw great Faustus lay the Ghost of Wit:	O 52	Pro Drury-Lane	36
	What tho' she shine with no Miltonian Fire, ...	O 58	Prologue Comus	27
	She ceas'd; then godlike Hector answer'd kind,-- . . .	O 74	Tr. Iliad Bk 6	1
	Nor whilst she Simons acts persues	O 80	Feast St Simon	49
	Looks back on what She left behind, ...	O 150	Tr Boet III.12	57
	She faints and quits her hold.	O 150	Tr Boet III.12	58
	Yet timely provident, she hastes away	O 151	The Ant	5
	She gleans the harvest, and she stores the grain. . .	O 151	The Ant	8
	She gleans the harvest, and she stores the grain. . .	O 151	The Ant	8
	She crops the harvest, and she stores the grain. . .	O 151	The Ant	V 8
	She crops the harvest, and she stores the grain. . .	O 151	The Ant	V 8
	It must, it must be She; her Name?	O 258	Irene	103
	She feeds his Hopes, and sooths him to Delay.	O 260	Irene	129
	But will she yet receive the Faith of Mecca?	O 261	Irene	11
	Should she, for Proselytes are always zealous, . . .	O 262	Irene	24
	That loses all because she hazards nothing.	O 281	Irene	45
	She mark'd my sparkling Eyes, and heaving Breast, . .	O 282	Irene	68
	My Vows, 'tis true, she hears with less Aversion, . .	O 287	Irene	7
	She sighs, she blushes, but she still denies. . . .	O 287	Irene	8
	She sighs, she blushes, but she still denies. . . .	O 287	Irene	8
	She sighs, she blushes, but she still denies. . . .	O 287	Irene	8
	'Tis she--My Hope, my Happiness, my Love!	O 294	Irene	1
	She cannot, must not, shall not linger here, ...	O 296	Irene	6
	With soften'd Voice she dropp'd the faint Refusal, .	O 303	Irene	31
	Smiling Consent she sat, and blushing Love.	O 303	Irene	32
	Will she that's false to Heavn, to me be faithfull .	Y 186	Irene	V 4
	she courted fate & scornd a crown	Y 191	Irene	V 16
	Should she prevail to gain the Sultan's Presence, . .	O 327	Irene	16
	True, she was fair; the Smile of Innocence	O 330	Irene	10
	Yet she--fair--so shone first apostate	Y 211	Irene	V 10
	There had she lull'd me with endearing Falshoods, . .	O 331	Irene	18
	Was she guiltless! Has my thoughtless Rage	O 332	Irene	18
	While she yet beg'd to plead her Cause before thee. .	O 334	Irene	67
	O seize me, Madness--Did she call on me!	O 334	Irene	68
	Her tears in show'rs descending as she spoke. . . .	Y 18	Tr. Iliad Bk 6	18
	And may she ne'er returning sorrows know."	Y 20	Tr. Iliad Bk 6	106
	Returns his child; she views his infant charms, . .	Y 20	Tr. Iliad Bk 6	108
	She shall sing me a song, ...	Y 300	Fanny Burney	1
	She was once of high renown,--	Y 300	Extemp. Elegy	3
	She was once as cherry plump	Y 300	Extemp. Elegy	5
	Till she made the neighbours stare.	Y 300	Extemp. Elegy	8
	There she soon became a jilt, ...	Y 300	Extemp. Elegy	9
	Now she lies exceeding low, ...	Y 301	Extemp. Elegy	19
SHE'S				
	She's starr'd with pimples o'er, ...	O 127	To Lyce, Lady	14
	A little longer, and she's thine for ever.	O 285	Irene	10
SHEATH'D				
	Held high the steady scale, but sheath'd the sword; . .	O 22	London	V 251
SHED				
	And Sloth's bland Opiates shed their fumes in . . . . vain;	O 37	Vanity Wishes	V 150
	If Merit touch thee, shed a tear, ...	O 154	Epita. Hogarth	6
	And shed the pitying Tear for lost Irene.	O 292	Irene	97
	Shall shed his Beams upon the bridal Bed, ...	O 309	Irene	24
	May the morn's earliest tears on thee be shed, . . .	Y 3	On a Daffodill	11
	Shed floods of tears, and sympathiz'd in pain. . . .	Y 21	Tr. Iliad Bk 6	129
SHEDS				
	When pale-fac'd Cynthia sheds her silver light . . .	O 77	Tr Add. Battle	45
	On weary Mortals sheds the balm of rest	O 356	Irene	V 10
SHEERS				
	Or sheers the Lambkins snowy fleece.	O 71	Hor. Epode II	22
SHELLS				
	The richest Odours, nor the speckled Shells	O 277	Irene	32
SHELTER				
	And flies for Shelter to the Shades of Life.	O 292	Irene	102
SHELTER'D				
	"Slightly shelter'd, coarsely fed?	O 185	Anacreon Ode 9	28
SHELTERD				
	Fenc'd from the sun and shelterd from the breeze. . .	Y 163	Irene	V 43
SHEPHERD				
	The mountain shepherd hears the distant noise. . . .	O 132	Tr. Rambler 65	3
	"Here fairer than his flock the shepherd lyes . . .	Y 7	Virgil Daphnis	30
	Pleasure in ev'ry nymph and shepherd reigns, . . .	Y 7	Virgil Daphnis	36
SHEPHERDS				
	The Shepherds oft' see little ghosts glide by . . .	O 77	Tr Add. Battle	47
SHEW				
	To thee were solemn toys or empty shew, ...	O 33	Vanity Wishes	65
	Unfaded still their former charms they shew, . . .	O 84	Epi Dist Moth.	26
	The near approach a bed may shew	O 184	Tr. Benserade	3
	In warring colours shew the warring throng;	Y 22	Tr Add. Battle	4
	This night he hopes to shew that farce may charm, . .	Y 67	Prologue Lethe	13
SHEWN				
	Shewn in the faithful glass of ridicule;	O 81	Lady Birthday	16
SHEWS				
	One shews the plunder, and one hides the thief. . . .	O 32	Vanity Wishes	44
	Shews pour the morning worshiper no more;	Y 95	Vanity Wishes	V 80
	And shews his miseries in distant lands;	O 41	Vanity Wishes	212
SHIELD				
	Security shall spread her Shield before thee, ...	O 279	Irene	82

		PAGE	TITLE	LINE
SHIELD	**(CONTINUED)**			
Implor'd th' eternal Power to shield my Country,	. . .	O 290	Irene	49
To shield my Lover, and preserve my Country.	. . . .	O 364	Irene	V 4
SHIN'ST				
Where now thou shin'st among thy Fellow-saints,	. . .	O 253	Irene	100
Thou shin'st, bright Maid, superior to Distress;	. . .	O 298	Irene	17
SHINE				
In ev'ry face a thousand graces shine,	. . . . . .	O 16	London	127
They mount, they shine, evaporate, and fall.	. . . .	O 33	Vanity Wishes	76
Thro' him the rays of regal bounty shine,	. . . .	O 34	Vanity Wishes	102
What but their wish indulg'd in courts to shine,	. .	O 36	Vanity Wishes	133
For such in distant lands the Britons shine,	. . . .	O 39	Vanity Wishes	181
For these in distant lands the Britons shine,	. . . .	Y 100	Vanity Wishes	V 181
What tho' she shine with no Miltonian Fire,	. . . . .	O 58	Prologue Comus	27
And raptur'd sees the new-found ruby shine.	. . . .	O 82	Young Author	V 6D
At length must Suffolk's beauties shine in vain,	. .	O 107	Lady F Assizes	1
In vain the vary'd work would shine,	. . . .	O 119	To Miss Purse	3
Who shine, by lavish lovers drest,	. . . .	O 126	To Lyce, Lady	3
On darkling man in pure effulgence shine,	. . . . .	O 130	Tr. Rambler 7	3
Ennobled, yet unchang'd, if Nature shine:	. . . . .	O 246	Irene Prologue	16
Unhappy Lot of all that shine in Courts;	. . . . .	O 256	Irene	50
Her grateful Sons shine bright with ev'ry Virtue;	. .	O 256	Irene	60
How will the bright Aspasia shine above her!	. . . .	O 261	Irene	23
Shine thou distinguish'd by superior Merit,	. . . .	O 264	Irene	29
Such Beauty must not shine to vulgar Eyes.	. . . .	O 269	Irene	43
The eternal Snows that shine beyond Maeotis	. . . . .	O 360	Irene	V 2
Ordain'd, like you, to flutter and to shine,	. . . .	O 277	Irene	37
To shine the Goddess of applauding Nations,	. . . .	O 278	Irene	68
Mix in the War, and shine among the Heroes?	. . . .	O 290	Irene	41
O! did Irene shine the Queen of Turkey,	. . . . .	O 290	Irene	51
The Wond'ring Sky shall shine with Decorations	. . .	O 364	Irene	V 28
Now shalt thou shine the Darling of the Sultan,	. .	O 329	Irene	3
SHINES				
Tho' rapture sings, and beauty shines.	. . . . . .	O 125	An Ode	12
Denies my Lyce shines,	. . . .	O 127	To Lyce, Lady	18
--Till every constellation shines for me	. . . . .	Y 132	Irene	V 45
SHINING				
The polish'd marble, and the shining plate,	. . . .	O 19	London	207
And shun the shining train, and golden coach.	. . .	O 21	London	235
In vain the shining Gifts are sent,	. . . .	O 144	Tr Boeth. II.2	13
A Virgin shining with distinguish'd Charms,	. . . .	O 258	Irene	95
If yet this shining Pomp, these sudden Honours,	. .	O 289	Irene	1
--The beauteous Fiend The shining mischief	. . . . .	O 375	Irene	V 12
Beneath his feet admires each shining star,	. . . .	Y 7	Virgil Daphnis	34
His shining helm with nodding horse hair grac'd.	. .	Y 21	Tr. Iliad Bk 6	125
The wound, and, furious, wave the shining steel.	. .	Y 26	Tr Add. Battle	133
SHIV'RING				
Those trembling Limbs--Speak out, thou shiv'ring Traitor.	. . .	O 332	Irene	16
SHOARS				
But bless the Northern shoars,	. . . .	O 79	Feast St Simon	36
Dashing Waves and shatter'd Shoars,	. . . .	O 145	Tr Boeth. II.4	18
SHOCK				
Mark'd out by dangerous parts he meets the shock,	. .	O 39	Vanity Wishes	171
Their foes the shock sustain in Battle skill'd,	. .	O 76	Tr Add. Battle	12
And shock the Tyrant with a Tale of Treason.	. . . .	O 255	Irene	29
To shock my Virtue with a Tale of Love.	. . . . .	O 299	Irene	40
How should I joy, 'midst the fierce Shock of Nations,	.	O 309	Irene	40
Nor dare henceforth to shock Irene's Walks.	. . . .	O 325	Irene	7
SHOCK'D				
No summons shock'd by chill delay,	. . . .	O 201	Death Dr Levet	V 21
SHOCKS				
And every Danger shocks with double Horror,	. . . .	O 261	Irene	21
Not all like thee can brave the Shocks of Fate,	. .	O 266	Irene	34
SHOES				
They sing, they dance, clean shoes, or cure a clap;	. .	O 15	London	114
SHONE				
Ascending to the skies he shone	. . . .	O 79	Feast St Simon	22
Illustrious age! how bright thy glories shone,	. . .	O 118	Epitaph Hanmer	21
Revive the languid Flow'rs; thus Nature shone	. . .	O 314	Irene	3
Yet she--fair--so shone first apostate	. . . . .	Y 211	Irene	V 10
Play'd on her Cheek--So shone the first Apostate--	. .	O 330	Irene	11
SHOOK				
For such the steady Romans shook the world;	. . . . .	O 39	Vanity Wishes	180
For these steady Romans shook the world;	. . . . .	Y 100	Vanity Wishes	V 180
And shook the (affrighted) world lab'ring earth licentious conquest	. .	Y 115	Irene	V 49A
'Twas Vice that shook our Nerves, 'twas Vice, Leontius	.	O 251	Irene	56
Shook headlong from his throne imperial Jove.	. . . .	Y 26	Tr Add. Battle	139
Toss'd her nose, and shook her rump,	. . . .	Y 300	Extemp. Elegy	7
SHOOT				
I feel new Spirit shoot along my Nerves,	. . . . .	O 306	Irene	49
Together rise and shoot upon the wing.	. . . . .	Y 24	Tr Add. Battle	73
SHOOTS				
Till burning Death shoots through their wither'd Limbs?	.	O 282	Irene	6
Why shoots this Chilness through thy shaking Nerves?	. .	O 295	Irene	6
Constrains a sullen Smile, and shoots away.	. . . .	O 311	Irene	7
SHORE				
And, fix'd on Cambria's solitary shore,	. . . . .	O 9	London	7
The common shore of Paris and of Rome;	. . . . .	O 14	London	94
No pathless waste, or undiscover'd shore;	. . . . .	O 18	London	171

```
SHORE          (CONTINUED)                          PAGE   TITLE          LINE
     Where Tigris beats his sounding shore . . . . . . .   O  80 Feast St Simon    52
     Sick'ning with fear he longs to view the shore,  . . .   O  82 Young Author     9
     And led me to the Shore where Cali stood,   . . . . .   O 254 Irene           127
     Your slaughter'd Multitudes that swell the Shore, . . .   O 255 Irene            30
     When ev'ry Wave shall beat a Turkish Shore,  . . . . .   O 265 Irene            43
     Till every Wave shall beat a Turkish Shore.  . . . . .   O 354 Irene         V  26
     Just as I mark'd them, they forsook the Shore,  . . . .   O 269 Irene            38
     Well known, long try'd, expect us on the Shore.  . . .   O 301 Irene            91
     Reclines against the Shore: Our Grecian Troop   . . . .   O 304 Irene            24
     Wilt thou then head the Troop upon the Shore,  . . . .   O 305 Irene            36
     The happy Moment, hasten to the Shore,   . . . . . . .   O 320 Irene             8
     Send me to wander on some pathless Shore,   . . . . .   O 328 Irene            35
     And spread their echoing grief from shore to shore.  . .   Y   6 Virgil Daphnis   12
     And spread their echoing grief from shore to shore.  . .   Y   6 Virgil Daphnis   12
SHORES   SEE SHOARS
     Nor, Valgius, on th' Armenian shores  . . . . . . . .   O  67 Hor. II Ode IX    5
     And Africs torrid shores in search of Cali  . . . . .   Y 143 Irene         V  60
     The northern shores to clouds and frost  . . . . . .   Y  38 Lady Leaving      2
SHORT
     Short sway! fair Austria spreads her mournful charms,  .   O  42 Vanity Wishes    245
     Short sway! for Austria spreads her mournful charms,  . .   Y 103 Vanity Wishes  V 245
     A Short Song of Congratulation  . . . . . . . . . .   O 196 Song Congratu.     T
     And give the short remnant of my life to  . . . . . .   O 348 Irene         V  14
        prayer,
     Short be thy Pains.   . . . . . . . . . . . . . . .   O 328 Irene            49
     Then in short Sighs forsook his broken Frame.  . . . .   O 331 Irene            16
SHOU'D
     Fair plenty, gracious Queen, shou'd pour  . . . . . .   O 144 Tr Boeth. II.2    5
     Shou'd partial Cat-calls all his Hopes confound,  . . .   O 246 Irene Prologue   23
     Shou'd welcome Sleep relieve the weary Wit,  . . . . .   O 246 Irene Prologue   25
SHOULD
     But thou, should tempting villainy present  . . . . .   O  14 London           85
     Should heaven's just bolts Orgilio's wealth confound,  . .   O  19 London          194
     Lest scarce the exhausted should rope supply.  . . . .   Y  60 London        V 243
     And why should odious ruin dawb the wall.  . . . . . .   Y  95 Vanity Wishes  V  90
     Yet should thy soul indulge the gen'rous heat,  . . . .   O  37 Vanity Wishes    143
     Yet should thy fate indulge the gen'rous heat,  . . . .   Y  98 Vanity Wishes  V 143
     Should Reason guide thee with her brightest ray,  . . .   O  37 Vanity Wishes    145
     Should no false Kindness lure to loose delight,  . . .   O  37 Vanity Wishes    147
     Should tempting Novelty thy cell refrain,  . . . . . .   O  37 Vanity Wishes    149
     Should Beauty blunt on fops her fatal dart,  . . . . .   O  37 Vanity Wishes    151
     Should no Disease thy torpid veins invade,  . . . . .   O  37 Vanity Wishes    153
     Nor should disease thy torpid veins invade,  . . . . .   Y  99 Vanity Wishes  V 153
     From Lydia's monarch should the search descend,  . . .   O  45 Vanity Wishes    313
     Should Hecatombs each rising Morn  . . . . . . . . .   O  69 Hor.II Ode 14     5
     Should costly Loads of incense burn,  . . . . . . . .   O  69 Hor.II Ode 14     7
     I should behold with scornfull eye  . . . . . . . . .   O  73 Hor. Epode II    55
     The heart, once caught, should ne'er be freed?  . . . .   O 120 To Miss Purse    12
     Warm India's supple Sons should bow,  . . . . . . . .   O 146 Tr Boeth III.5    6
     Time his Hours should never drive  . . . . . . . . .   O 178 Thrale 35 Year    7
     Should the guardian friend or mother  . . . . . . . .   O 197 Song Congratu.  V  25
     But how the Devil should he please us all!  . . . . .   O 247 Irene Epilogue    8
     Why should they fear?--That Power that kindly spreads  .   O 250 Irene            31
     So small a Force? or why should Cali fly?  . . . . . .   O 254 Irene           138
     Why should Cali rebel--unexpensive age  . . . . . . .   Y 120 Irene         V  40
     Why should the Sultan shun the Joys of Beauty,  . . . .   O 261 Irene             7
     Should she, for Proselytes are always zealous,  . . . .   O 262 Irene            24
     Should we before the Troops proclaim his Crimes  . . .   O 273 Irene            38
     And should he fall unheard, by sudden Justice,  . . . .   O 273 Irene            41
     Should the fierce North upon his frozen Wings  . . . .   O 274 Irene            61
     Thence should my Fury drag him down to Tortures;  . . .   O 274 Irene            64
     Should fill the World with Wretches undetected.  . . .   O 283 Irene            27
     Yet should my Soul, still faithful to her Choice,  . .   O 289 Irene            13
     But should I sin beyond the Hope of Mercy,  . . . . .   O 289 Irene            23
     No more should Greece lament those Prayers rejected.  . .   O 290 Irene            52
     Again should golden Splendour grace her Cities,  . . .   O 290 Irene            53
     Again her prostrate Palaces should rise,  . . . . . .   O 291 Irene            54
     No more should Danger fright, or Want distress  . . . .   O 291 Irene            56
     On me, should Providence, without a Crime,  . . . . .   O 292 Irene           103
     Aspasia should not fear a second Insult.  . . . . . .   O 299 Irene            42
     Should Heav'n yet unappeas'd refuse its Aid,  . . . . .   O 301 Irene            97
     How should I joy, 'midst the fierce Shock of Nations,  .   O 309 Irene            40
     Who fearst lest I should gain, or thou  . . . . . . .   Y 198 Irene         V  32
        shouldst lose or I possess her
     Should she prevail to gain the Sultan's Presence,  . .   O 327 Irene            16
     Or why should he, whose Violence of Duty  . . . . . .   O 329 Irene            18
     Why should the man whose violence of duty  . . . . . .   Y 210 Irene         V  18
     And speed the Stroke lest Mercy should o'ertake them.  .   O 333 Irene            54
SHOULDST
     Soon shouldst thou see, how false thy weak Reproach.  . .   O 293 Irene           107
     Who fearst lest I should gain, or thou  . . . . . . .   Y 198 Irene         V  32
        shouldst lose or I possess her
     Think shouldst thou fall how wretched shall we be,  . .   Y  19 Tr. Iliad Bk 6    48
SHOURS
     But when increas'd by Winter shours  . . . . . . . .   O  72 Hor. Epode II    37
SHOUT
     And shout Infamy proclaims the rest.  . . . . . . . .   Y 107 Vanity Wishes  V 342
     Do they with Pain repress the struggling Shout,  . . .   O 270 Irene            24
SHOUTING
     Rolls half his Floods unheard through shouting Camps?  .   O 264 Irene            18
```

			PAGE	TITLE		LINE	
SHOUTING	(CONTINUED)						
Pours half his Floods unheard through shouting camps	. . .		O	353	Irene	V	32
And show Irene to the shouting People:			O	303	Irene		28
My Name shall echo through the shouting Field;	. . . .		O	305	Irene		40
SHOUTS							
Amidst the Glare of Courts, the Shouts of Armies,	. . .		O	293	Irene		131
SHOW SEE SHEW							
But lost in thoughtless ease, and empty show,	. . . .		O	15	London		103
But sunk in thoughtless ease, and empty show,	. . . .		Y	53	London	V	103
The festal blazes, the triumphal show,	. . . . . .		O	39	Vanity Wishes		175
The daring Greeks deride the martial show,	. . . . .		O	42	Vanity Wishes		235
And Swift expires a driv'ler of a show.	. . . . .		O	45	Vanity Wishes		318
To chase the Charms of Sound, the Pomp of Show,	. . . .		O	53	Pro Drury-Lane		59
Her brows a cloudy show,	. . . .		O	127	To Lyce, Lady		10
Show the Spirit of an heir.	. . . .		O	196	Song Congratu.		12
The power of art without the show.	. . . . . .		O	201	Death Dr Levet		16
All else is empty Sound, and idle Show.	. . . . .		O	246	Irene Prologue		14
The Love of Pow'r, of Pleasure, and of Show.	. . . .		O	287	Irene		13
And show Irene to the shouting People:	. . . . . .		O	303	Irene		28
SHOW'R							
The blessings of a golden Show'r,	. . . .		O	144	Tr Boeth. II.2		6
Fenc'd from the summer breeze, and vernal	. . . .		Y	163	Irene	V	43
show'r.							
SHOW'RS							
And show'rs from either flow.	. . . .		O	127	To Lyce, Lady		12
Work'd into sudden rage by wintry show'rs,	. . . .		O	132	Tr. Rambler 65		1
Lull'd by the beating winds and dashing show'rs!	. . .		O	135	Tr Rambler 117		2
The Clouds, a Signal of impending Show'rs,	. . . . .		O	250	Irene		32
Her tears in show'rs descending as she spoke.	. . . .		Y	18	Tr. Iliad Bk 6		18
SHOWERS SEE SHOURS							
Nor showers immerse the verdant plain;	. . . . . .		O	67	Hor. II Ode IX		2
SHOWS SEE SHEWS							
Shows his bold Front, the Harbinger of Ruin,	. . . .		O	250	Irene		41
When eager Vengeance shows a naked Foe,	. . . . .		O	280	Irene		13
SHRIEKS							
Shrieks of Affright, and Wailings of Distress.	. . . .		O	251	Irene		72
Unnerv'd with shrieks the soldier's vig'rous arm	. . .		Y	163	Irene	V	48
SHRILL							
The better use of notes, or sweet or shrill,	. . . .		O	192	Tr. Medea II		9
SHRILLING							
While in my verse the shrilling trumpets sound,	. . .		Y	22	Tr Add. Battle		18
SHRINE							
Sleep undisturb'd within this peaceful shrine,	. . . .		O	113	Epit. Phillips		5
Rest undisturb'd within this humble shrine,	. . . . .		O	113	Epit. Phillips	V	5
SHRINKS							
Shrinks from this heap of aggregated crime	. . . . .		Y	159	Irene	V	9
Shrinks at th' o'erpow'ring Gleams of regal State,	. .		O	292	Irene		100
Shrinks at th' oerpowring blaze of regal State	. . . .		O	368	Irene	V	30
The Cause that shrinks from Reason's powerful Voice.	. .		O	293	Irene		126
Shrinks at the hated Task, for thy Destruction;	.		O	325	Irene		21
Shrinks back from the hated task, for thy destruction;	.		Y	204	Irene	V	21
SHRIVELING							
And ah! behold the shriveling blossoms die,	. . . . .		Y	4	On a Daffodill		23
SHRUNK							
Where blasted patriots never shrunk to peers	. . . .		Y	94	Vanity Wishes	V	60A
SHUDD'RING							
The shudd'ring Camp shall murmur out Demetrius.	. . .		O	305	Irene		42
SHUDDER							
We learn to shudder at the rustling Breeze,	. . . . .		O	266	Irene		29
Recoil from Thought, and shudder at myself.	. . . . .		O	322	Irene		12
SHUDDERS							
And (terror) horrour shudders in their gloomy caverns	.		Y	136	Irene	V	31A
But my blood freezes and weak nature shudders	. . . .		Y	189	Irene	V	1G
SHUN							
And shun the shining train, and golden coach.	. . . .		O	21	London		235
In vain we shun the Din of war,	. . . .		O	69	Hor.II Ode 14		13
But shun, rash youth, the gay alcove,	. . . . . .		O	121	To Miss Playin		9
Here let me learn to shun the crimes	. . . . . .		O	126	An Ode		35
Shun the Mountain's airy Brow,	. . . .		O	145	Tr Boeth. II.4		7
Shun the Sea-sapp'd Sand below;	. . . .		O	145	Tr Boeth. II.4		8
What hazards would I shun to clasp for Greece and for			Y	125	Irene	V	133
Aspasia							
Why should the Sultan shun the Joys of Beauty,	. . . .		O	261	Irene		7
Reason! the tim'rous Pilot, that to shun	. . . . . .		O	281	Irene		46
On dangers which your safety bids you shun,	. . . . .		Y	18	Tr. Iliad Bk 6		20
SHUN'D							
Tell how Demetrius shun'd his single Hand,	. . . . .		O	318	Irene		13
SHUNS							
Shuns fancied ills, or chases airy good;	. . . .		O	31	Vanity Wishes		10
Hides from himself his state, and shuns to know,	. . .		O	43	Vanity Wishes		257
Shuns Pluto's kingdoms and the realms of night;	. . .		Y	7	Virgil Daphnis		33
SHUTS							
And shuts up all the passages of joy:	. . . .		O	43	Vanity Wishes		260
My first, shuts out Thieves from your house or your Room			O	179	Charade!		1
SICK'NING							
Sick'ning with fear he longs to view the shore,	. . .		O	82	Young Author		9
Was it for this, that sick'ning in Epirus,	. . . . .		O	272	Irene		6
SICKENS							
A sister sickens, or a daughter mourns.	. . . . . .		O	45	Vanity Wishes		302
A sister sickens, or a child offends.	. . . .		Y	105	Vanity Wishes	V	302

SICKNESS
    In health, in sickness, thus the suppliant prays; . . .   PAGE   TITLE   LINE

		PAGE	TITLE	LINE

SICKNESS
   In health, in sickness, thus the suppliant prays; . . .   O 43 Vanity Wishes 256
SIDE
   With half mankind embattled at his side, ...   O 42 Vanity Wishes 226
   With half mankind embattled on his side, ...   Y 102 Vanity Wishes V 226
   On ev'ry side rise mountains of the slain, ...   O 76 Tr Add. Battle 19
   On ev'ry Side Confusion, Rage and Death, ...   O 300 Irene 70
   Thus on deceitful Etna's flow'ry Side, ...   O 315 Irene 33
   Ere he return with Thousands at his Side. . . . . .   O 320 Irene 9
SIDERON
   Oude lithos, oude Sideron--nostro sequitur de Vulnere .   O 347 Irene V 23
    sanguis.
SIEGE
   Lay siege to life and press the dire blockade; . . . .   O 44 Vanity Wishes 284
SIGH
   With servile grief dependent nobles sigh . . . . . .   Y 57 London V 198
   O'er the sad plains perpetual tempest sigh . . . .   O 84 Epi Dist Moth. 32
   Then melt, ye fair, while crouds around you sigh, . .   O 84 Epi Dist Moth. 42
   Woods to evry Sigh replying, ...   O 148 Tr Boet III.12 V 6
   And sigh for chearful Poverty in vain; . . . . . .   O 292 Irene 84
   I saw without a sigh the fierce barbarian . . . . .   Y 176 Irene V 106
   And thought the petty Dross beneath a Sigh. . . . .   O 302 Irene 109
   A sigh, a blush inform'd him You consented . . . . .   O 366 Irene V 28
   When did Content sigh out her Cares in secret? . . .   O 314 Irene 20
   Without a boding fear, or anxious sigh, ...   Y 67 Prologue Lethe 3
SIGH'D
   Thus I spoke; and speaking sigh'd; . . . .   O 181 Parody Warton 5
   He sigh'd, He rag'd, he threatend and he . . . . .   O 364 Irene V 20
    flatter'd
   Say, how the Tyrant threaten'd, flatter'd, sigh'd, . .   O 295 Irene 23
   Say, how he threaten'd, flatter'd, sigh'd in vain! . .   O 295 Irene 24
   But flatterd threatend, sigh'd and rag'd in vain . . .   Y 170 Irene V 24
   And sigh'd and wept at her relentless gate. . . . . .   Y 11 Tr Hor Epode 9 36
SIGHING
   Tho' when Orpheus sweetly sighing . . . .   O 148 Tr Boet III.12 V 5
   Sinks like the sighing of a Tempest spent, ...   O 275 Irene 92
   Sinks into sighs like the sighing of a Tempest spent . .   O 367 Irene V 13
   Aspasia left her sighing in his Arms, ...   O 303 Irene 29
SIGHS
   And his last sighs reproach the faith of kings. . .   O 35 Vanity Wishes 120
   And Luxury with sighs her slave resigns. . . . .   O 43 Vanity Wishes 266
   Among the quivering branches sighs; . . . . . .   O 66 Hor I Ode xxii 18
   Among the quivering Branches sighs, ...   O 67 To A. Fuscus 18
   Leave off, at length, these woman's sighs, ...   O 68 Hor. II Ode IX 17
   And that fair bosom heave with rising sighs! . . .   O 75 Tr. Iliad Bk 6 28
   In vain for thee the monarch sighs, ...   O 100 Ode Friendship 19
   In vain for thee the tyrant sighs, ...   O 100 Ode Friendship V 19
   Now he sighs to heav'n, and now . . . .   O 149 Tr Boet III.12 17
   In Sighs and Tears, in Transports and Embraces, . .   O 269 Irene 15
   In sighs and tears, and transports and embraces, . .   O 367 Irene V 27
   Sinks into sighs like the sighing of a Tempest spent . .   O 367 Irene V 13
   Dwells on her Lips, and sighs upon her Breast; . . .   O 286 Irene 5
   She sighs, she blushes, but she still denies. . . .   O 287 Irene 8
   The long-drawn Intercourse of Sighs and Kisses. . .   O 297 Irene 14
   Then in short Sighs forsook his broken Frame. . . .   O 331 Irene 16
   Sighs issued from my heaving breast; . . . . . .   Y 11 Tr Hor Epode 9 14
   Your sighs are spent in vain; if fates withstand . .   Y 21 Tr. Iliad Bk 6 115
SIGHT
   Aghast you start, and scarce with aking sight . . . .   O 18 London 186
   And hide me from the sight of life. . . . . . .   O 124 Winter's Walk V 20
   Where first great nature charm'd my sight, ...   O 125 An Ode 19
   At sight of sparkling bowls or beauteous dames, . . .   O 142 In Baretti Bk. 1
   Orpheus turn'd his eager Sight, ...   O 150 Tr Boet III.12 50
   At Sight of female Charms will glow no more. . . .   O 263 Irene 6
   Fade <glide> from the sight, and Vanish into . . . .   O 358 Irene V 11
    nothing.
   And, to confirm my Thought, at sight of me, ...   O 275 Irene 84
   By hateful Business hurried from her Sight, ...   O 287 Irene 15
   But the sight of friends soul sinking into vice (a soul .   Y 177 Irene V111C
   Quick from my Sight you inauspicious Monsters, ...   O 325 Irene 6
   The dark horizon ravish'd from their sight. . . . . .   Y 24 Tr Add. Battle 75
SIGN
   And sign your will before you sup from home. . . .   O 21 London 225
   Sign her foes doom, or guard her fav'rites zeal? . . .   O 34 Vanity Wishes 92
   Sign her foes' doom, or guard her patriots zeal, . . .   Y 95 Vanity Wishes V 92
   Mark the keen glance, and watch the sign to hate. . . .   O 34 Vanity Wishes 110
   'Tis a sign that he had rather . . . .   O 183 Burlesque Vega V 3
   Steal from Abdalla's Eye the Sign to smile. . . . . .   O 318 Irene 5
SIGN'D
   It parts you now--The hasty Sultan sign'd . . . .   O 296 Irene 1
SIGNAL
   Counts death kind Nature's signal of retreat: . . . .   O 48 Vanity Wishes 364
   Thinks death kind Nature's signal of retreat: . . . .   O 48 Vanity Wishes V 364
   The Clouds, a Signal of impending Show'rs, ...   O 250 Irene 32
   A signal hour marked out by pitying Heav'n . . . .   Y 117 Irene V 109
SIGNS
   Till pitying Nature signs the last release, ...   O 45 Vanity Wishes 309
SILENC'D
   With warbling eunuchs fill our silenc'd stage, ...   O 12 London V 59
   And when blest Peace has silenc'd War's Alarms, . . .   O 247 Irene Epilogue 23

	PAGE	TITLE	LINE
SILENCE			
Has Silence press'd her Seal upon his Lips?	O 255	Irene	20
To Silence and to Rest. The Hours of Darkness, . .	O 302	Irene	2
Has serv'd his Prince so well, demand our Silence? . .	O 329	Irene	19
My silence and my groans confess'd.	Y 11	Tr Hor Epode 9	16
Mournfull Andromache the silence broke, ...	Y 18	Tr. Iliad Bk 6	17
SILENT			
On Thames's banks, in silent thought we stood, ...	O 10	London	21
Invades the sacred hour of silent rest, ...	O 21	London	240
That silent cuts the dreary plains, ...	O 69	Hor.II Ode 14	18
The silent grandeur of retreat.	O 125	An Ode	32
With silent confidence and holy rest:	O 130	Tr. Rambler 7	6
Silent Wonder stopt the Floods;	O 148	Tr Boet III.12	12
Ye Fops be silent! and ye Wits be just!	O 246	Irene Prologue	34
With silent Pangs I view the tow'ring Domes, ...	O 251	Irene	62
And sink into the silent Grave in Peace.	O 264	Irene	12
Now let him go, pursu'd by silent Wrath, ...	O 274	Irene	47
With silent Sorrows, and with calm Devotion. . . .	O 290	Irene	50
The fraudful Moments ply their silent Wings, . . .	O 327	Irene	8
The treacherous moments ply their silent wings	Y 206	Irene	V 8
SILK			
... a Gold and Silk net-work Purse of her own weaving .	O 119	To Miss Purse	T
Though gold and silk their charms unite, ...	O 119	To Miss Purse	1
SILKEN			
With brisker air the silken courtiers gaze, ...	O 17	London	164
Nor can I hope thy silken chain	O 120	To Miss Purse	9
SILVER			
Where Greenwich smiles upon the silver flood:	O 10	London	22
When pale-fac'd Cynthia sheds her silver light	O 77	Tr Add. Battle	45
Her silver locks display the moon, ...	O 127	To Lyce, Lady	9
The wand'ring Rivulet, and silver Lake, ...	O 280	Irene	23
SIMON			
Upon the feast of St Simon & St Jude	O 78	Feast St Simon	T
Simon by gen'rous Zeal inspir'd, ...	O 79	Feast St Simon	37
SIMONS			
Nor whilst she Simons acts persues	O 80	Feast St Simon	49
SIMPLE			
Let ev'ry piece be simple and be one.	O 137	Tr Rambler 139	1
SIN			
But should I sin beyond the Hope of Mercy, ...	O 289	Irene	23
SINCE			
Since worth, he cries, in these degen'rate days, . . .	O 10	London	35
Since unrewarded science toils in vain;	O 10	London	38
Since hope but sooths to double my distress, . . .	O 10	London	39
Long since I learn'd to slight this fleeting breath, . .	O 74	Tr. Iliad Bk 6	9
Since Stella still extends her reign, ...	O 122	Stella Mourn.	11
There let Aspasia, since my Fair entreats it, . . .	O 263	Irene	3
Since Fear predominates in every Thought, ...	O 266	Irene	17
Twice since the Morning rose I saw the Bassa, ...	O 275	Irene	76
Too well I know him, since on Thracia's Plains, . . .	O 307	Irene	18
But since none knows the Danger of a Moment, ...	O 321	Irene	48
Since from Inachia's charms set free	Y 11	Tr Hor Epode 9	9
SINCERE			
Nor think our wishes less sincere.	O 188	Epilogue	4
Officious, innocent, sincere.	O 201	Death Dr Levet	7
SING			
Who scarce forbear, tho' Britain's Court he sing, . . .	O 13	London	69
They sing, they dance, clean shoes, or cure a clap; . .	O 15	London	114
Here at your ease you sing your amorous flame, . . .	O 64	Virgil Past.I	5
I'll sing of Chloe's charms divine, ...	O 66	Hor I Ode xxii	23
Augustus' numerous trophies sing;	O 68	Hor. II Ode IX	18
Let vulgar Poets sing, ...	O 78	Feast St Simon	3
Great George's acts let tuneful Cibber sing;	O 114	On C. Cibber	3
But some Zelinda while I sing	O 127	To Lyce, Lady	17
Who thinks us Women born to dress and sing	O 247	Irene Epilogue	2
Here ev'ry Warbler of the Sky shall sing;	O 279	Irene	86
Sing duly hymns to Heaven	Y 166	Irene	V 94
But while I sing, the nimble moments fly, ...	Y 4	On a Daffodill	21
No more I sing, no more delight	Y 11	Tr Hor Epode 9	3
And the sad fate of Pygmie realms I sing.	Y 22	Tr Add. Battle	2
I'll sing the chiefs dispensing fate around.	Y 22	Tr Add. Battle	19
She shall sing me a song, ...	Y 300	Fanny Burney	1
SINGER			
Summon'd the singer blythe, and harper gay, ...	O 192	Tr. Medea II	7
SINGING			
Me singing, careless and unarm'd, ...	O 65	Hor I Ode xxii	11
Me singing, careless and unarm'd, ...	O 66	To A. Fuscus	11
SINGLE			
A single jail, in Alfred's golden reign, ...	O 22	London	248
Where wasted nations raise a single name, ...	O 39	Vanity Wishes	186
A single skiff to speed his flight remains;	O 42	Vanity Wishes	238
The single talent well employ'd.	O 201	Death Dr Levet	28
His single talent well employ'd.	O 201	Death Dr Levet	V 28
A single Thought now rove, recall it home.	O 255	Irene	7
How can a single Hand attempt a Life	O 258	Irene	90
'Tis well--A single Blow compleats our Wishes: . . .	O 304	Irene	8
Tell how Demetrius shun'd his single Hand, ...	O 318	Irene	13
Dar'd have provok'd a foe to single fight, ...	Y 23	Tr Add. Battle	39
SINGS			
Only ev'ry bush there artless music sings	Y 58	London	V 220
Walks the wild heath, and sings his toil away.	O 32	Vanity Wishes	38

301

SINGS   (CONTINUED)   PAGE   TITLE   LINE
    In Myrtle groves oft sings the happy swain, ...   O 95 Sprig of Myrtl   7
    In Myrtle shades oft sings the happy swain, ...   O 95 Sprig of Myrtl   V   7
    Tho' rapture sings, and beauty shines. . . . . .   O 125 An Ode   12
    Thyrsis while sings shall the gods . . . .   Y   7 Virgil Daphnis   V 49
SINK
    How nations sink, by darling schemes oppress'd, . . .   O 31 Vanity Wishes   13
    How families sink, by darling schemes oppress'd, . . . Y 92 Vanity Wishes   V 13
    Why but to sink beneath misfortune's blow, ...   O 35 Vanity Wishes   127
    To sink the fatal precipice before him, ...   O 176 Tr Metastas II   4
    To sink the fatal precipice before them, ...   O 176 Tr Metastas II   V   4
    Well might the Weakness of our Empire sink . . . .   O 250 Irene   48
    Sink not beneath imaginary Sorrows: . . . . . .   O 252 Irene   84
    And sink into the silent Grave in Peace. . . . . .   O 264 Irene   12
    But sink among thy Slaves without a Murmur. . . .   O 289 Irene   11
    My trembling nerves--sink at the dreadful scenes of blood Y 189 Irene   V 1H
    Shall sink alike into the gloomy grave. . . . . .   Y 21 Tr. Iliad Bk 6   120
SINKING
    Whose Ways and Means support the sinking land; . . .   O 21 London   245
    Whose Ways and Means support a sinking land; . . .   Y 60 London   V 245
    Love ends with hope, the sinking statesman's door .   O 33 Vanity Wishes   79
    And all the Maladies of sinking States. . . . .   O 250 Irene   39
    Recline upon my Breast thy sinking Beauties: . . .   O 295 Irene   8
    But the sight of friends soul sinking into vice (a soul Y 177 Irene   V111C
    Then shall the Rhodian mourn his sinking Tow'rs, . .   O 309 Irene   26
SINKS
    Then Summer sinks in Autumn's reign, ...   O 231 Tr Horace IV.7   11
    Sinks into milkness and softens to submission. . . .   Y 123 Irene   V 99
    Sinks like the sighing of a Tempest spent, ...   O 275 Irene   92
    Sinks into sighs like the sighing of a Tempest spent . . O 367 Irene   V 13
SIP
    "Now the generous bowl I sip . . . .   O 185 Anacreon Ode 9   31
SIR
    A Translation Of The Latin Epitaph On Sir Thomas . . . O 117 Epitaph Hanmer   T
        Hanmer
    Great Sir John, are all your own. . . . . . .   O 196 Song Congratu.   4
    Great Sir John, are now your own. . . . . . .   O 196 Song Congratu.   V   4
    Wealth, Sir John, was made to wander, ...   O 196 Song Congratu.   17
SIRE
    Whose sire Eetion in Cilicia reign'd . . . . .   Y 18 Tr. Iliad Bk 6   7
    But call'd Astyanax because his sire . . . . . .   Y 18 Tr. Iliad Bk 6   13
    Took her from her friends and sire, ...   Y 301 Extemp. Elegy   15
SIRIUS'
    Unwholesome Sirius' sultry reign; . . . .   O 69 Hor.II Ode 14   16
SISTER
    A sister sickens, or a daughter mourns. . . . .   O 45 Vanity Wishes   302
    A sister sickens, or a child offends. . . . .   Y 105 Vanity Wishes   V 302
    And sister souls together join, ...   O 100 Ode Friendship   22
    And sister minds together join, ...   Y 71 Ode Friendship   V 22
    As learn'd Eliza, sister of the Muse, ...   O 106 Eliza plucking   1
    But as your sister of the sky, ...   O 126 To Lyce, Lady   7
SISTERS
    The inexorable sisters have decreed . . . . . .   O 74 Tr. Iliad Bk 6   11
    Venus, the sacred Sisters dispossest, ...   Y 11 Tr Hor Epode 9   5
SIT
    Whether you sit on thrones, or dwell in cots, . . .   O 77 Festina Lente   2
    Nor let disdain sit low'ring in your eye; . . . .   O 84 Epi Dist Moth.   43
    Thou shalt sit and smile to see . . . .   O 145 Tr Boeth. II.4   19
    Hang Sit these black clouds upon Aspasia's brow? . . . Y 191 Irene   V 15
SITS
    Where Hate sits musing to betray, ...   O 191 Tr. Medea I   11
    In Triumph sits upon our shatter'd Spires, ...   O 251 Irene   67
    In triumph sits upon the ruin'd Spires . . . . .   O 351 Irene   V   6
    Disorder sits upon thy Face--retire. . . . . .   O 286 Irene   17
    Still, still Distrust sits heavy on my Heart. . . . . O 301 Irene   95
SIXTH
        from the Sixth Book of Homer's Iliad . . . . .   O 74 Tr. Iliad Bk 6   T
SIXTY
    Sure, chill'd with sixty winter Camps, thy Blood . . . O 263 Irene   5
    Thou Thou chilld by sixty winter camps canst gaze . . Y 129 Irene   V   5
SKAITER
    O'er ice the rapid skaiter flies, ...   O 203 Tr. on Skating   1
SKAITERS
    With nimble glide the skaiters play; . . . . . .   O 203 Tr. on Skating   V   2
SKEPTRA
    Kupridi, med autou skeptra memele theo. . . . . .   O 103 Eis Elisses   2
SKIE
    Their fumes ascending to the Skie; . . . . . .   O 69 Hor.II Ode 14   8
    And where beneath th' inclement Skie . . . . .   O 70 Hor.II Ode XX   15
    And Bolts and rocks encounter in the Skie, ...   O 76 Tr Add. Battle   23
    Rocks send their acclamations to the skie . . . .   Y   7 Virgil Daphnis   40
SKIES
    Roll thro' the streets, and thunder to the skies; . . O 18 London   183
    And publick mournings pacify the skies; . . . . .   O 19 London   197
    Yet still one gen'ral cry the skies assails, ...   O 32 Vanity Wishes   45
    Yet still the gen'ral cry the skies assails, ...   O 32 Vanity Wishes   V 45
    Assails the skies load the tainted gales; . . . .   Y 93 Vanity Wishes   V 46
    No cries attempt the mercies of the skies? . . . .   O 47 Vanity Wishes   348
    No cries invoke the mercies of the skies? . . . .   O 47 Vanity Wishes   V 348
    And strong devotion to the skies aspires, ...   O 48 Vanity Wishes   358
    If aspirations to the skies aspires, ...   Y 108 Vanity Wishes   V 358

302

```
                                                   PAGE      TITLE              LINE
SKIES        (CONTINUED)
   With horrid gloom the frowning skies:      . . . . .  .  O  66 Hor I Ode xxii      20
   With horrid Gloom the frowning Skies:      . . . . .  .  O  67 To A. Fuscus        20
   Clouds do not always veil the skies,       . . . . .  .  O  67 Hor. II Ode IX       1
   And cut with joy the wond'ring Skies.      . . . . . .  .  O  70 Hor.II Ode XX       4
   Driv'n hither by inclement skies           . . . . . .     O  73 Hor. Epode II    V 59
   Ascending to the skies he shone            . . . . . .  .  O  79 Feast St Simon     22
   Joys insincere! thick clouds invade the skies,  . . .  .  O  82 Young Author         7
   The skies, that Stella mourn no more.      . . . . .  .  O 122 Stella Mourn.        16
   The hoary ground, the frowning skies.      . . . . .  .  O 123 Winter's Walk         4
   I trace the planets and survey the skies.  . . . . .  .  O 130 Tr. Rambler 8         2
   The skies are open--let us try the skies:  . . . . .  .  O 136 Tr Rambler 129        5
   The skies are open--let us try the skies:  . . . . .  .  O 136 Tr Rambler 129        5
   To court Communion with the Skies,         . . . .  .     O 150 Tr Boet III.12      54
   Each Land that smiles beneath benigner Skies   . . .  .  O 366 Irene             V 12
   The varying Seasons, and revolving Skies,  . . . . . .     O 293 Irene              118
   "Whose fame from earth resounded to the skies."  . . .    Y   7 Virgil Daphnis      31
   Then to the inclement skies expos'd I sat  . . . . . .  .  Y  11 Tr Hor Epode 9      35
   Then kist his son and raising to the skies  . . . . .  .  Y  20 Tr. Iliad Bk 6      97
   Their growing fame re'echoes to the skies. . . . . . .  .  Y  22 Tr Add. Battle       9
   In a low vale by rocks that pierce the skies  . . . .  .  Y  23 Tr Add. Battle      24
   Or lift themselves into the wonted skies.  . . . . .  .  Y  24 Tr Add. Battle      61
   Thick clouds of hostile birds obscure the skies.  . . .  Y  25 Tr Add. Battle      93
   Their godlike hero strugling in the skies. . . . . .  .  Y  26 Tr Add. Battle     129
SKIFF
   A single skiff to speed his flight remains;  . . . . .    O  42 Vanity Wishes      238
SKILL
   Improve his heady rage with treach'rous skill,  . . . .  O  44 Vanity Wishes      281
   Perhaps if Skill could distant Times explore,  . . . .   O  53 Pro Drury-Lane      41
   If want of skill, or want of care appear,  . . . .  .     O  62 Pro Word Wise       17
   <He> sets his nets, employs his skill.     . . . . .  .  O  72 Hor. Epode II       42
   By Daphnis' skill th' Armenian tigers broke  . . . . .    Y   6 Virgil Daphnis      13
SKILL'D
   Their foes the shock sustain in Battle skill'd,  . . .  .  O  76 Tr Add. Battle     12
   Well skill'd to sooth a foe with looks of kindness,  . .  O 176 Tr Metastas II       3
SKIM
   Thus lightly skim, and haste away.  . . . . . . . .      O 203 Tr. on Skating    V  4
SKULKING
   And saw him skulking in the closest Walks:  . . . . .    O 327 Irene               25
SKULKS
   Low skulks the hind beneath the rage of pow'r,  . . .  .  O  32 Vanity Wishes      33
SKY     SEE SKIE
   "And all be mine beneath the polar sky."   . . . . . .    O  40 Vanity Wishes     204
   "And all is mine beneath the polar sky."   . . . . .  .  O  40 Vanity Wishes   V 204
   And scarce can breath th' infected sky,    . . . . .  .  O  79 Feast St Simon      35
   And pois'nous vapours, black'ning all the sky,  . . .  .  O  84 Epi Dist Moth.      33
   Around the fav'rites of the sky.           . . . . .  .  O 100 Ode Friendship      12
   But as your sister of the sky,             . . . . . .  .  O 126 To Lyce, Lady        7
   My Lyce makes as good a sky,               . . . . .  .  O 127 To Lyce, Lady       23
   Nor Peleus, grandson of the sky,           . . . . .  .  O 136 Tr Rambler 128       3
   I am Cassander, come down from the Sky,    . . . . .  .  O 173 Tr Fr Pantomim       1
   That I am Cassander come down from the Sky.  . . . .  .  O 173 Tr Fr Pantomim       3
   Lovely courier of the sky,                 . . . . .  .  O 185 Anacreon Ode 9       1
   Dismiss'd her to the Sky.  . . . . . . .  .  .  .  .  .  O 252 Irene               95
        blaze amidst the sky                  . . . . . .     Y 131 Irene            V 35
   Observe the feather'd Wand'rers of the Sky,  . . . .  .  O 277 Irene               34
   Here ev'ry Warbler of the Sky shall sing;  . . . . . .  .  O 279 Irene               86
   The subtler Flames emitted from the Sky,   . . . . . .  .  O 282 Irene               59
   Soon as the Veil of Evening clouds the Sky,  . . . .  .  O 284 Irene               49
   My Bosom feels, enkindled from the Sky,    . . . . .  .  O 293 Irene              108
   No Records, but the Records of the Sky.    . . . . .  .  O 305 Irene               35
   See how the Moon through all th' unclouded Sky  . . .  .  O 313 Irene                1
   Vers'd in the secret Counsels of the Sky.  . . . . .  .  O 314 Irene               27
   Fill all the Starry Lamps with Fav'ring Sky  . . . .  .  O 364 Irene            V 27
   Th' applauding Sky shall pour forth all its Beams  . .  .  O 322 Irene                9
   The Wondring Sky shall shine with Decorations  . . .  .  O 364 Irene            V 28
   Be thou the favorite of the indulgent sky,  . . . . .  .  Y   3 On a Daffodill       5
SLAIN
   May I lie slain, and spurn the bloody sand!  . . . .  .  O  75 Tr. Iliad Bk 6      30
   On ev'ry side rise mountains of the slain,  . . . . .  .  O  76 Tr Add. Battle      19
   Hippolytus unjustly slain  . . . . . . . . . . . .  .  O 232 Tr Horace IV.7      25
   With horrour counts the number of the slain.  . . . .  .  Y  23 Tr Add. Battle      33
SLAUGHTER
   Chiefs confus'd in mutual slaughter,       . . . . . .  .  O 159 Tr. Rio Verde        3
   The horrid Images of War and Slaughter     . . . . . .     O 268 Irene               34
   And hungry Slaughter scents Imperial Blood?  . . . .  .  O 279 Irene                5
SLAUGHTER'D
   So much lament his slaughter'd son.        . . . . . .  .  O  68 Hor. II Ode IX      16
   Your slaughter'd Multitudes that swell the Shore,  . .  .  O 255 Irene               30
   A slaughter'd nation, or a shatter'd world.  . . . .  .  Y 177 Irene             V111E
   Of slaughter'd Infidels, and Clash of Swords!  . . . .    O 305 Irene               24
   In that black Day when slaughter'd Thousands fell  . .  .  O 312 Irene                7
SLAUGHTERD
   Has heard unhurt the cries of slaughterd thousands  . .   Y 126 Irene            V 145
SLAV'RY
   Ah! what avails it, that, from slav'ry far,  . . . .  .  O  15 London             117
   He, tir'd cf Slav'ry, tho' the highest Slave,  . . . .    O 253 Irene              113
   To Want give Affluence? and to Slav'ry Freedom?  . . .    O 277 Irene               46
   Despair, and Slav'ry, Solitude, and Guilt.  . . . . .  .  O 292 Irene               87
   Leave Slav'ry, Guilt, and Infamy behind.   . . . . .  .  O 320 Irene               31
   Let Slav'ry harrass, and let Hunger gripe. . . . . .  .  O 328 Irene               37
```

```
                                                            PAGE    TITLE              LINE
SLAVE
      And Luxury with sighs her slave resigns.          O  43  Vanity Wishes       266
      Each nymph your rival, and each youth your slave? O  46  Vanity Wishes       330
      Content to live the Roman's slave,                O  68  Hor. II Ode IX       23
      The slave of sunshine and of glocm.               O 124  Winter's Walk        16
      Bow down and own thyself a Slave.                 O 146  Tr Boeth III.5       10
      He, tir'd cf Slav'ry, tho' the highest Slave,     O 253  Irene               113
      To clasp a Slave? or, can a Soul like mine,       O 268  Irene                16
      And envy the slave that toils whose labour procures her
        sleep                                           Y 165  Irene           V    81
      Can brave Leontius be the Slave of Glory?         O 305  Irene                30
      Luckless slave Ilfated loiterer has fate in vain  Y 196  Irene           V    15
      Abdalla fails now is my slave                     Y 198  Irene           V     1
      Beauties insulted by a slave--                    Y 202  Irene           V     1
      Has taught my Slave the Language of Command!      O 323  Irene                 2
      Bold Slave, I know them both--I know them Traytors. O 324  Irene               16
      Go, blustring Slave.--He has not heard of Murza.  O 324  Irene                25
      Or argue with the Slave that sav'd Demetrius.     O 330  Irene                23
      Or reason with the slave thats saved Demetrius    Y 210  Irene           V    23
      Thou sluggish Idler, dilatory Slave?              O 334  Irene                 2
      The victor hither brought, a royall slave.        Y  19  Tr. Iliad Bk 6       39
      The bravest hero and the fearfull'st slave        Y  21  Tr. Iliad Bk 6      119
SLAVERY
      Give Wealth to Poverty to Slavery Freedom         O 356  Irene           V    13
SLAVES
      Slaves that with serious impudence beguile.       O  17  London              146
      But here more slow, where all are slaves to gold, O  18  London              178
      While ladies interpose, and slaves debate.        O  41  Vanity Wishes       214
      And Slaves, the Maxim tells, are always Foes.     O  46  Vanity Wishes     V330B
      Their Slaves were willing, and their Reign was long; O  52  Pro Drury-Lane    26
      His chearfull Slaves, a num'rous band,            O  73  Hor. Epode II        71
      Too well You know to keep the Slaves You gain.    O  96  Hickman Spinet        2
      Bid the slaves of thrift farewell.                O 196  Song Congratu.        8
      Through bowing Slaves, I range the private Rooms, O 283  Irene                17
      But sink among thy Slaves without a Murmur.       O 289  Irene                11
      Then mingle with your slaves without a murmur     Y 161  Irene           V    11
      Then Bigotry might send her Slaves to War,        O 291  Irene                63
      Sanguinary joy--Slaves now watch her nod          Y 184  Irene           V     9
      To canonize the Slaves of Superstition,           O 309  Irene                34
      Aw'd by the Croud, and by their Slaves restrain'd? O 312  Irene                22
      What Ties to Slaves? what Gratitude to Foes?      O 312  Irene                 6
      Has left the slaves behind, nay then there's danger. Y 198  Irene          V    34
      Fly, Slaves, and call the Sultan to my Rescue.    O 322  Irene                56
      Dispatch, ye ling'ring Slaves, or nimbler Hands   O 328  Irene                42
      Ye Slaves of Cruelty, ye Tools of Rage,           O 332  Irene                22
      With half the grov'ling Slaves that load the Globe. O 332  Irene               36
      Be just ye Slaves, and, to be just, be cruel,     O 334  Irene                73
SLAVISH
      With slavish tenets taint our poison'd youth,     O  12  London               55
SLEEP
      But hear his death, ye blockheads, hear and sleep. O  39  Vanity Wishes       174
      And, murm'ring, balmy Sleep prolong,              O  72  Hor. Epode II        32
      Sleep undisturb'd within this peaceful shrine,    O 113  Epit. Phillips        5
      How sweet in sleep to pass the careless hours,    O 135  Tr Rambler 117        1
      Shou'd welcome Sleep relieve the weary Wit,       O 246  Irene Prologue       25
      Why, when the Balm of Sleep descends on Man,      O 277  Irene                43
      And envy the slave that toils whose labour procures her
        sleep                                           Y 165  Irene           V    81
SLEEPING
      Some zealous bard to wake the sleeping lyre.      O 107  Lady F Assizes        4
      Sounds in my sleeping Ear, "Awake Demetrius,      O 254  Irene               122
      That wafts diseases from the sleeping infant.     Y 168  Irene             V135B
SLEEPS
      Who sleeps on brambles till he kills his man;     O  21  London              227
      Awake each Faculty that sleeps within thee,       O 254  Irene                 2
      Securely sleeps, and, in delightful Dreams,       O 325  Irene                18
SLEEPY
      What sleepy Charms benumb these active Heroes,    O 325  Irene                14
SLENDER
      What toil in slender things!                      O 134  Tr. Rambler 90        1
SLEPT
      Till Declamation roar'd, while Passion slept.     O  52  Pro Drury-Lane       32
      Till Declamation soar'd, whilst Passion slept.    O  52  Pro Drury-Lane   V   32
SLEW
      How great Achilles godlike Hector slew?           Y  22  Tr Add. Battle       11
SLIGHT
      Long since I learn'd to slight this fleeting breath, O  74  Tr. Iliad Bk 6      9
      Such slight Defeats but animate the Brave         O 270  Irene                 7
      Is then conspiracy so slight a crime              Y 207  Irene           V    14
SLIGHTED
      The slighted Arts Futurity shall trust,           O  57  Prologue Comus       13
      The bitter pangs of slighted love?                O  72  Hor. Epode II        46
      Because my slighted Passion burns in vain!        O 281  Irene                49
      Will now remount the slighted Seat of Empire,     O 303  Irene                27
      Henceforward hope no more my slighted Friendship, O 307  Irene                 9
SLIGHTING
      What hadst thou lost by slighting those Commands? O 332  Irene                32
SLIGHTLY
      "Slightly shelter'd, coarsely fed?                O 185  Anacreon Ode 9       28
SLIPP'RY
      Tir'd with contempt, she quits the slipp'ry reign, O  46  Vanity Wishes      335
```

	PAGE	TITLE	LINE
SLOTH			
And Sloth effuse her opiate fumes in vain;	O 37	Vanity Wishes	150
How long shall sloth usurp thy useless hours,	O 151	The Ant	9
Nor couldst thou more support a Life of Sloth	O 264	Irene	19
Immur'd, and buried in perpetual Sloth,	O 292	Irene	81
The soften'd Soul to Cowardice and Sloth;	O 303	Irene	17
Tainted by Sloth, the Parent of Sedition,	O 309	Irene	20
SLOTH'S			
And Sloth's bland Opiates shed their fumes in vain;	O 37	Vanity Wishes	V 150
SLOW			
Slow Rises Worth, By Poverty Depress'd:	O 18	London	177
But here more slow, where all are slaves to gold,	O 18	London	178
And Want hung threat'ning o'er her slow Decay.	O 58	Prologue Comus	26
Till want, now following fraudulent and slow,	O 152	The Ant	15
By sudden blasts, or slow decline,	O 200	Death Dr Levet	3
Too slow these gentle Constellations roll,	O 271	Irene	3
SLOWLY			
See nations slowly wise, and meanly just,	O 38	Vanity Wishes	161
That slowly grows, which must for ever last.	O 142	In Baretti Bk.	10
SLUGGARD			
"Go to the Ant thou Sluggard".	O 151	The Ant	V T
Observe her labours, Sluggard, and be wise.	O 151	The Ant	2
SLUGGISH			
Thou sluggish Idler, dilatory Slave?	O 334	Irene	2
SLUMB'RING			
And fans the slumb'ring Spark of heav'nly Fire.	O 303	Irene	19
Clasp'd in her Arms, or slumb'ring on her Breast,	O 331	Irene	19
SLUMBER			
And dare to slumber o'er the Gazetteer;	O 13	London	72
The peaceful slumber, self-approving day,	O 14	London	89
The Watchful slumber, and the Crafty trust.	O 283	Irene	13
That gloomy Slumber of the stagnant Soul;	O 292	Irene	82
SLUMBERS			
Untouch'd his cottage, and his slumbers sound,	O 32	Vanity Wishes	35
secure his cottage, and his slumbers sound,	Y 93	Vanity Wishes	V 35
Drive the soft Slumbers from his eyes,	O 71	Hor. Epode II	10
Drive the soft Slumbers for his eyes.	O 71	Hor. Epode II	V 10
And weary Murther slumbers o'er the Carnage	O 350	Irene	V 9
SLY			
There the Lender grave and sly.	O 196	Song Congratu.	16
SMALL			
Of dissipated wealth the small remains,	O 9	London	20
How small to others, but how great to me.	O 138	Tr Rambler 161	1
So small a Force? or why should Cali fly?	O 254	Irene	138
Small bones and mangled bodies scatter'd there	Y 23	Tr Add. Battle	31
SMALLER			
From meaner minds, tho' smaller fines content,	O 39	Vanity Wishes	169
SMART			
To thee I told the causes of my smart,	Y 11	Tr Hor Epode 9	18
SMIL'D			
Where late the lilies mix'd with violets smil'd.	Y 7	Virgil Daphnis	25
The parents smil'd, the chief his helm unbound	Y 20	Tr. Iliad Bk 6	95
SMILE			
And lye without a blush, without a smile;	O 17	London	147
On all thy hours security shall smile,	O 20	London	222
His smile alone security bestows:	O 34	Vanity Wishes	104
Who frown with vanity, who smile with art,	O 46	Vanity Wishes	327
This Night, distinguish'd by your Smile, shall tell,	O 57	Prologue Comus	11
Bless with a smile, or with a frown destroy;	O 83	Epi Dist Moth.	2
And beauty smile auspicious in each face;	O 84	Epi Dist Moth.	45
Gay with the smile of bland equality;	O 130	Tr. Rambler 12	6
That concord smile on the connubial bed;	O 131	Tr. Rambler 45	2
Thou shalt eat and smile to see	O 145	Tr Boeth. II.4	19
And chang'd th' endearing Smile and am'rous Whisper	O 259	Irene	111
Droop at your tears and soften at your smile	Y 145	Irene	V 4
That Smile resistless and attractive Grace	O 355	Irene	16
Th' attractive Softness, and th' indearing Smile,	O 277	Irene	51
And blasted Kingdoms flourish at thy Smile?	O 278	Irene	72
To Bid wasted Regions flourish at her smile	O 372	Irene	V 8
Purity of prayer--Irene's smile .	Y 150	Irene	V 75
Smile on my Wishes, and command the Globe.	O 279	Irene	81
When will Occasion smile upon our Wishes,	O 282	Irene	1
And Peace propitious smile on fond Desire;	O 302	Irene	119
I w<ould> have every smile g<enu>ine to<morrow no>	Y 185	Irene	V 3
Constrains a sullen Smile, and shoots away.	O 311	Irene	7
Is sure the Smile of unoffended Heav'n.	O 314	Irene	9
The universal smile of joyfull nature	Y 190	Irene	V 9
Steal from Abdalla's Eye the Sign to smile.	O 318	Irene	5
True, she was fair; the Smile of Innocence	O 330	Irene	10
If mix'd with these, divine Cleora smile,	Y 4	On a Daffodill	17
SMILES			
Where Greenwich smiles upon the silver flood:	O 10	London	22
Others with softer smiles, and subtler art,	O 13	London	75
Where looks are merchandise, and smiles are sold;	O 18	London	179
Her voice and Smiles my Song shall grace.	O 67	To A. Fuscus	24
Is not each Realm that smiles with kinder Suns,	O 265	Irene	35
Each Land that smiles beneath benigner Skies	O 366	Irene	V 12
With artificial Smiles, and seeming Friendship.	O 271	Irene	38
And feel no Sorrow while my Sov'reign smiles.	O 272	Irene	11
Implores our Smiles, and trembles at our Feet:	O 277	Irene	40

SMILES   (CONTINUED)

	PAGE	TITLE	LINE
Those gloomy walks where Gladness never smiles	Y 165	Irene	V 81
Approving Justice smiles upon your Cause,	O 297	Irene	2
Retire, my Fair, that Pow'r that smiles on Goodness . .	O 303	Irene	20
By Smiles, and Oaths, and Praises ill disguis'd. . .	O 308	Irene	15
Smiles at the Threat'nings of defeated Rage.	O 325	Irene	19
Cleora's smiles a genial warmth dispense;	Y 4	On a Daffodill	18

SMILING

	PAGE	TITLE	LINE
And stretch thy prospects o'er the smiling land, .ˆ. .	O 20	London	214
Autumn o'erlooks the smiling Ground	O 72	Hor. Epode II	24
Charm'd with the scene the smiling ocean yields, . . .	O 81	Young Author	3
Pleas'd with the scene the smiling ocean yields, . . .	O 81	Young Author	V 3
Whom smiling nature courts in vain, ...	O 125	An Ode	11
When the smiling sage reply'd--	O 181	Parody Warton	7
"Blushing nature, smiling art.	O 185	Anacreon Ode 9	10
"Smiling at my master's gates, ...	O 185	Anacreon Ode 9	19
Surveys his smiling babes, the sons of freedom,	Y 122	Irene	V 60
And smiling, conscious of her Charms, withdrew. . . .	O 282	Irene	69
The smiling Widows, and protected Orphans.	O 291	Irene	57
Borne on the Surface of the smiling Deep, ...	O 301	Irene	92
Smiling Consent she sat, and blushing Love.	O 303	Irene	32
Where 's this fair Trait'ress? Where 's this smiling . . Mischief?	O 330	Irene	1

SMITE

	PAGE	TITLE	LINE
Smite thy bosom, sage, and tell, ...	O 181	Parody Warton	3

SMOAK'D

	PAGE	TITLE	LINE
And smoak'd in kitchens, or in auctions sold, ...	O 34	Vanity Wishes	85

SMOAKING

	PAGE	TITLE	LINE
And Cities smoaking on the ground	O 78	Feast St Simon	2

SMOKE

	PAGE	TITLE	LINE
Th' enormous Gyants smoke upon the Ground.	O 76	Tr Add. Battle	25
They to the dome where smoke with curling play	O 192	Tr. Medea II	5

SMOKING   SEE SMOAKING

	PAGE	TITLE	LINE
And spread its smoking ruins o'er the field.	O 74	Tr. Iliad Bk 6	14

SNAR'D

	PAGE	TITLE	LINE
Snar'd with thy Fears, and maz'd in Stupefaction. . .	O 318	Irene	18

SNARE

	PAGE	TITLE	LINE
Thy nets may snare, but not confine, ...	O 120	To Miss Purse	V 8

SNARE'D

	PAGE	TITLE	LINE
Snare'd with thy fears, and senseless of deliverance . .	Y 196	Irene	V 18

SNARES

	PAGE	TITLE	LINE
O'erspread with snares the clouded maze of fate, . . .	O 31	Vanity Wishes	6
Nor tempt the snares of wily love.	O 121	To Miss Playin	10
No Snares to captivate the Judgment spreads;	O 246	Irene Prologue	27

SNARL

	PAGE	TITLE	LINE
Where no sour criticks snarl, no sneers molest, . . .	O 82	Young Author	V 27

SNARLING

	PAGE	TITLE	LINE
This, only this, provokes the snarling muse.	O 17	London	161

SNATCH

	PAGE	TITLE	LINE
"Fate! snatch away the bright disguise, ...	O 122	Stella Mourn.	5
Snatch me, my Stella, to thy arms, ...	O 124	Winter's Walk	19
To snatch the blessings of the plenteous day;	O 151	The Ant	6
"From his fingers snatch his bread, ...	O 185	Anacreon Ode 9	34
Snatch thy pleasures while they last;	O 194	On Thrale Hat	2
Snatch your pleasures while they last;	O 194	On Thrale Hat	V 2
And snatch the flaming Bolt with hasty Hand.	O 314	Irene	25
Behold a Boaster's Worth. Now snatch, my Fair, . . .	O 320	Irene	7

SNATCH'D

	PAGE	TITLE	LINE
And snatch'd her timely from her Country's Fate. . . .	O 252	Irene	98
And snatch'd the Reins of abdicated Pow'r	O 256	Irene	45
What Hand, when Death has snatch'd away Demetrius, . .	O 301	Irene	88
Behold thy boasted Honours snatch'd away.	O 317	Irene	43

SNEER

	PAGE	TITLE	LINE
While growing hopes scarce awe the gath'ring sneer, . .	O 44	Vanity Wishes	277
Unmov'd tho' Witlings sneer and Rivals rail;	O 246	Irene Prologue	29

SNEERS

	PAGE	TITLE	LINE
Where no sour criticks damn, nor sneers molest, . . .	O 82	Young Author	27
Where no sour criticks snarl, no sneers molest, . . .	O 82	Young Author	V 27

SNIPES

	PAGE	TITLE	LINE
Nor Lybian fowls, nor Snipes of Greece, ...	O 73	Hor. Epode II	59

SNOW

	PAGE	TITLE	LINE
The snow dissolv'd no more is seen, ...	O 231	Tr Horace IV.7	1

SNOWS

	PAGE	TITLE	LINE
Th' eternal Snows that freeze beyond Meotis, ...	O 274	Irene	59
The eternal Snows that shine beyond Maeotis	O 360	Irene	V 2
To spread Civility through Russian snows	O 348	Irene	V 21

SNOWY

	PAGE	TITLE	LINE
Or sheers the Lambkins snowy fleece.	O 71	Hor. Epode II	22
Whose snowy breasts, whose animated eyes, ...	O 83	Epi Dist Moth.	5
Their snowy summits, and the sons of fierceness . . .	Y 136	Irene	V 29
Or boy, whose snowy neck the flowing ringlets grace. . .	Y 12	Tr Hor Epode 9	42

SNUFF

	PAGE	TITLE	LINE
Your taste in snuff, your judgment in a whore; . . .	O 17	London	149
His taste in snuff, his judgment in a whore.	Y 55	London	V 149

SO

	PAGE	TITLE	LINE
So some fiery fop, with new commission vain, ...	Y 59	London	V 226
Mourn'd not Antilochus so long;	O 68	Hor. II Ode IX	14
So much lament his slaughter'd son.	O 68	Hor. II Ode IX	16
The wine you kept with so much care	O 69	Hor.II Ode 14	27
So much my Appetite would please	O 73	Hor. Epode II	60

SO   (CONTINUED)   PAGE   TITLE   LINE

Oh! how my soul abhors so mean a thought.   . . . . .   O 74 Tr. Iliad Bk 6   8
So by their great decree Assyria fell . . . .   O 76 Tr Add. Battle   37
So shall Belinda's charms improve mankind.   O 81 Lady Birthday   19
So the young author panting for a name, ...   O 82 Young Author   11
So the young author panting after fame,   O 82 Young Author   V 11
So shall you guiltless reign, and all mankind adore. . .   O 84 Epi Dist Moth.   47
So long renown'd in B<rya>n's deathless strain?   O 107 Lady F Assizes   2
Find here that calm thou gav'st so oft before; . . . .   O 113 Epit. Phillips   4
Proclaim'd her, not so fair as fine. . . . .   O 122 Stella Mourn.   4
What doating bigot to his faults so blind,   O 137 Tr Rambler 140   1
Thou canst not make the tea so fast . . . .   O 159 Par Hermit III   11
Ill-fated Race! So oft besieg'd in vain, ...   O 250 Irene   29
So small a Force? or why should Cali fly?   O 254 Irene   138
So shall Timidity assist thy Reason, ...   O 266 Irene   21
Treason so near us? at the dreadfull name of . . . .   O 369 Irene   V 20
   Treason
Treason so near us? lurking in our Palace   O 369 Irene   V 20
Did ever Passion make so swift a Progress? . . . . .   O 281 Irene   55
So weak is Man, when destin'd to Destruction, ...   O 283 Irene   12
The Soul once tainted with so foul a Crime, ...   O 289 Irene   15
Fidelity so firm, so pure, as mine! . . . . . .   O 308 Irene   17
Fidelity so firm, so pure, as mine!   O 308 Irene   17
Recall th' extorted Doom.--It must be so, ...   O 326 Irene   40
Is then your Sov'reign's Life so cheaply rated,   O 327 Irene   14
Is then conspiracy so slight a crime . . . . . .   Y 207 Irene   V 14
Has serv'd his Prince so well, demand our Silence? . .   O 329 Irene   19
Yet she--fair--so shone first apostate . . . . . .   Y 211 Irene   V 10
Play'd on her Cheek--So shone the first Apostate-- . .   O 330 Irene   11
So sure the Fall of Greatness rais'd on Crimes, . . .   O 335 Irene   10
So fix'd the Justice of all-conscious Heav'n. . . . .   O 335 Irene   11
So late admir'd and prais'd, alas! in vain! . . . . .   Y   4 On a Daffodill   24
So much our splendour was encreas'd by thine. . . . .   Y   6 Virgil Daphnis   19
Not so while long th' undaunted race maintain'd   Y 23 Tr Add. Battle   36
And so here begins my tale. . . . .   Y 300 Extemp. Elegy   4
SOAR
High to soar and deep to dive . . . .   O 178 Thrale 35 Year   9
Shall soar triumphant on the Wings of Glory, ...   O 305 Irene   26
SOAR'D
Till Declamation soar'd, whilst Passion slept. . . . .   O 52 Pro Drury-Lane   V 32
SOARING
And soaring mocks the broken frame below. . . . . .   O 131 Tr. Rambler 17   1
SOARS
Soars unencumber'd with our idle Cares, ...   O 266 Irene   36
SOBER
The sober trader at a tatter'd cloak, ...   O 17 London   162
In sober state th' imaginary lawn . . . .   Y 98 Vanity Wishes   V138B
SOCIAL
For what but social guilt the friend endears? . . . .   O 14 London   83
And social sorrow loses half its pain: . . . . . .   O 59 Pro Good Nat'd   4
No social care the gracious lord disdains; . . . . .   O 130 Tr. Rambler 12   7
Our social comforts drop away. . . . .   O 200 Death Dr Levet   4
When social Laws first harmonis'd the World, ...   O 291 Irene   70
The social gayety the improving converse . . . . .   Y 165 Irene   V 81
SOFT
Whom Joys with soft varieties invite, ...   O 46 Vanity Wishes   325
Whom Joys in soft vicissitudes invite, ...   Y 107 Vanity Wishes   V 325
Place me where no soft summer gale . . . .   O 66 Hor I Ode xxii   17
Place me where no soft Summer Gale . . . .   O 67 To A. Fuscus   17
Drive the soft Slumbers from his eyes, ...   O 71 Hor. Epode II   10
Drive the soft Slumbers for his eyes. . . . . . .   O 71 Hor. Epode II   V 10
Soft Pleasure with her laughing train, ...   O 125 An Ode   6
And soft solicitation courts repose. . . . . . .   O 151 The Ant   12
"Soft Anacreon's vows I bear, ...   O 185 Anacreon Ode 9   7
"Sweet repast, and soft repose; . . . .   O 185 Anacreon Ode 9   30
Suspend the soft Scllicitudes of Dress; . . . . . .   O 246 Irene Prologue   2
There in soft Hints and in ambiguous Phrase, ...   O 254 Irene   129
Yet unacquainted with these soft Emotions . . . . .   O 263 Irene   16
Teach me the Grecian arts of soft persuasion . . . .   O 349 Irene   V 27
In soft Complaints, and idle Protestations. . . . .   O 269 Irene   16
If Pleasure charm thee, view this soft Retreat; . . .   O 279 Irene   85
When soft Security shall prompt the Sultan . . . .   O 291 Irene   76
And soft Security shall prompt the Sultan . . . . .   O 364 Irene   V   6
Or bid soft Science polish Britain's Heroes: . . . .   O 293 Irene   106
There shall soft Leisure wing th' excursive Soul, . .   O 302 Irene   118
In soft Endearments, and in gentle Murmurs, ...   O 303 Irene   14
Till soft Fatigue invite us to repose. . . . . . .   O 323 Irene   18
Some soft Decoy to lure me to Destruction! . . . . .   O 331 Irene   4
Lyciscus whose soft arms excell . . . .   Y 12 Tr Hor Epode 9   37
SOFTEN
With pity soften every awful grace, ...   O 84 Epi Dist Moth.   44
To cheer despair, or soften pride, ...   O 190 Tr. Medea I   8
Will he not soften in a Friend's Embrace? . . . . .   O 255 Irene   24
Droop at your tears and soften at your smile . . . .   Y 145 Irene   V   4
SOFTEN'D
With cream and sugar soften'd well, ...   O 158 Par Hermit III   3
The soften'd Soul to Cowardice and Sloth; . . . . .   O 303 Irene   17
With soften'd Voice she dropp'd the faint Refusal, . .   O 303 Irene   31
I heard, and soften'd, till Abdalla brought . . . .   O 334 Irene   61
SOFTEND
Not granted--nor deny'd--a softend glance . . . . .   Y 179 Irene   V 32

307

	PAGE	TITLE	LINE
SOFTENS			
Sinks into milkness and softens to submission.	Y 123	Irene	V 99
SOFTER			
Others with softer smiles, and subtler art, ...	O 13	London	75
Yet softer Claims the melting Heart engage, ...	O 58	Prologue Comus	29
Of equal Beauty, but of softer Mien, ...	O 259	Irene	119
And sought An easier conquest in my softer beauty . . .	Y 134	Irene	V 35
And Gales cf softer Passion fan my Bosom.	O 275	Irene	93
And softer passion steals upon my Bosom	O 367	Irene	V 14
But oft conjoins in woman's softer mould/frame	Y 149	Irene	V 55
SOFTNESS			
Th' attractive Softness, and th' indearing Smile, . . .	O 277	Irene	51
Is this a Time for Softness or for Sorrow?	O 280	Irene	11
Heav'n, when its Hand pour'd Softness on our Limbs . .	O 290	Irene	42
He Heav'n, when its hand pourd softness on our limbs . .	Y 162	Irene	V 42
SOIL			
Or boasts a happier Soil, already thine?	O 265	Irene	36
SOL			
No setting Sol can ease your cares, ...	O 67	Hor. II Ode IX	11
SOL'S			
See! Sol's bright chariot seeks the western main, . . .	Y 4	On a Daffodill	22
SOLD			
Where looks are merchandise, and smiles are sold; . . .	O 18	London	179
And smoak'd in kitchens, or in auctions sold, . .	O 34	Vanity Wishes	85
Yet judg'd by those, whose voices ne'er were sold, . .	O 60	Pro Good Nat'd	27
That all the fair their favours sold;	Y 11	Tr Hor Epode 9	20
SOLDIER			
A roving Soldier seiz'd in Sophia's Temple	O 258	Irene	94
The Soldier lab'ring through a Winter's March, ...	O 283	Irene	28
The weary Soldier--Still sees to Morrow	O 374	Irene	V 30
Then on his brow the mighty soldier plac'd	Y 21	Tr. Iliad Bk 6	124
Soon forth in arms had some bold soldier stood, ...	Y 23	Tr Add. Battle	40
Some furious soldier would approach that bore	Y 23	Tr Add. Battle	46
SOLDIER'S			
Urg'd by th' imperious Soldier's fierce Command, . . .	O 249	Irene	16
The Empire's Darling, and the Soldier's Boast;	O 257	Irene	69
Unnerv'd with shrieks the soldier's vig'rous arm . . .	Y 163	Irene	V 48
To Blood, too mean to stain a Soldier's Sabre.	O 324	Irene	24
SOLDIERS			
No trumpets sound, no Soldiers cries, ...	O 71	Hor. Epode II	9
Th' adoring Soldiers would revenge their Idol. . . .	O 273	Irene	42
There, with your Soldiers arm'd, and Sails expanded, . .	O 284	Irene	53
SOLDIERS'			
Who caught the chief, ev'n in his soldiers' view . . .	Y 25	Tr Add. Battle	125
SOLEMN			
To thee were solemn toys or empty shew, ...	O 33	Vanity Wishes	65
Then to the Gods, on solemn days, ...	O 73	Hor. Epode II	63
Her solemn honours pays.	O 78	Feast St Simon	12
The chearful sage, when solemn dictates fail, ...	O 132	Tr. Rambler 65	1
Hermit hoar, in solemn cell, ...	O 181	Parody Warton	1
SOLICITATION			
And soft solicitation courts repose, ...	O 151	The Ant	12
SOLICITUDES			
All but the sweet solicitudes of love!	O 81	Lady Birthday	6
Amidst her kind Solicitudes for me!	O 332	Irene	21
SOLID			
Exchanges solid Strength for feeble Splendor.	O 265	Irene	38
SOLITARY			
And, fix'd on Cambria's solitary shore, ...	O 9	London	7
Stern Famine guards the solitary coast, ...	O 41	Vanity Wishes	207
Might well befit the solitary Student, ...	O 281	Irene	36
SOLITUDE			
From Solitude to Crouds, from Crouds to Solitude, . . .	O 263	Irene	20
From Solitude to Crouds, from Crouds to Solitude, . . .	O 263	Irene	20
Mocks the dull Vows of Solitude and Penance, ...	O 264	Irene	27
Despair, and Slav'ry, Solitude, and Guilt.	O 292	Irene	87
No longer lost in am'rous Solitude, ...	O 303	Irene	26
SOLLICITE			
Vye for my submission, sollicite bondage.	Y 136	Irene	V 27C
SOLLICITUDES			
Suspend the soft Sollicitudes of Dress;	O 246	Irene Prologue	2
SOLON			
By Solon caution'd to regard his end, ...	O 45	Vanity Wishes	314
SOME			
Grant me, kind heaven, to find some happier place, . .	O 11	London	43
Some pleasing bank where verdant osiers play, ...	O 11	London	45
Some peaceful vale with nature's paintings gay;	O 11	London	46
Some secret cell, ye pow'rs, indulgent give.	O 11	London	49
Rais'd from some pleasing dream of wealth and pow'r, . .	O 18	London	184
Some pompous palace, or some blissful bow'r, ...	O 18	London	185
Some pompous palace, or some blissful bow'r, ...	O 18	London	185
There might'st thou find some elegant retreat, ...	O 20	London	212
The might you find some elegant retreat, ...	Y 58	London	V 212
Some hireling senator's deserted seat;	O 20	London	213
Some fiery fop, with new commission vain, ...	O 21	London	226
So some fiery fop, with new commission vain, ...	Y 59	London	V 226
Some frolick drunkard, reeling from a feast, ...	O 21	London	228
Some gamesome drunkard, reeling from a feast, ...	Y 59	London	V 228
Each passing day some comfort sorrow finds.	Y 105	Vanity Wishes	V 301
Still drops some joy from with'ring life away;	O 45	Vanity Wishes	306
Beneath some spreading Ilex Shade	O 72	Hor. Epode II	29

SOME   (CONTINUED)   PAGE   TITLE   LINE

Beneath some venerable Shade	O	72	Hor. Epode II	V	29
On some green bank supinely Laid,	O	72	Hor. Epode II		30
Whose blood shall quench some Grecian's thirsty rage,	O	74	Tr. Iliad Bk 6		16
When some proud Grecian dame shall tasks impose,	O	74	Tr. Iliad Bk 6		21
Then shall some Argive loud insulting cry,	O	74	Tr. Iliad Bk 6		25
Before that day, by some brave hero's hand,	O	75	Tr. Iliad Bk 6		29
With some victorious Heroe's praise	O	78	Feast St Simon		5
Or weep some falling King.	O	78	Feast St Simon		6
To some retreat the baffled writer flies,	O	82	Young Author		26
Some zealous bard to wake the sleeping lyre.	O	107	Lady F Assizes		4
... in a Room hung with some Flower-pieces	O	120	To Miss Playing		T
But some Zelinda while I sing	O	127	To Lyce, Lady		17
Wouldst thou to some stedfast Seat,	O	144	Tr Boeth. II.4		1
--Come, my lad, and drink some beer.	O	181	Parody Warton		8
When some neglected Fabrick nods beneath	O	250	Irene		44
Some Pow'r invisible, from Heav'n or Hell,	O	251	Irene		50
Sure some kind Sabre in the Heat of Battle,	O	252	Irene		93
Some virgin Martyr,	O	252	Irene		95
Yet strangers in some distant world proclaim	Y	120	Irene	V	31A
Some accidental Gust of Opposition	O	269	Irene		6
Some fatal gust of sudden Opposition	O	374	Irene	V	15
Sure by some wond'rous Sympathy of Souls,	O	272	Irene		8
Betray'd some Traytor lurking near our Bosom.	O	273	Irene		23
Disclos'd some Traytor lurking near our Bosoms	O	368	Irene	V	3
And in some distant Land obscurely die.	O	274	Irene		49
Indulgent nature gives some transient pleasures	Y	148	Irene	V	43C
Some petty Passion! some domestick Trifle!	O	280	Irene		7
Some petty Passion! some domestick Trifle!	O	280	Irene		7
Some vain Amusement of a vacant Soul!	O	280	Irene		8
Now be some Moments Master of thyself,	O	282	Irene		70
Reserve this Homage for some other Fair,	O	288	Irene		4
Seek out some peacefull Convents holy Shade	O	348	Irene	V	24
While some Archangel nearer to Perfection,	O	293	Irene		121
While some Archangel of superiour Nature	O	369	Irene	V	13
And wishes Irene were converted by some doctor	Y	186	Irene	V	11
Some ill designing Statesman's base Intrigue!	O	326	Irene		36
Some cruel Stratagem of jealous Beauty!	O	326	Irene		37
Send me to wander on some pathless Shore,	O	328	Irene		35
Some artful Wile of counterfeited Love!	O	331	Irene		3
Some soft Decoy to lure me to Destruction!	O	331	Irene		4
Soon forth in arms some bold soldier stood,	Y	23	Tr Add. Battle		40
Some furious soldier would approach that bore	Y	23	Tr Add. Battle		46

SOMETIMES

An Let fall sometimes a tear for lost Irene	O	349	Irene	V	1
and drop sometimes a tear for lost Irene	O	349	Irene	V	1
Sometimes the Wretch unaw'd by Heav'n or Hell,	O	300	Irene		78

SON

So much lament his slaughter'd son.	O	68	Hor. II Ode IX		16
Could bear his Son upon the Turkish Throne.	O	264	Irene		22
To great Latona's son, and two to you;	Y	7	Virgil Daphnis		44
Forgetfull of your wife, forgetfull of your son?	Y	18	Tr. Iliad Bk 6		21
Th' atridae there and Tydeus' mighty son,	Y	19	Tr. Iliad Bk 6		54
Then kist his son and raising to the skies	Y	20	Tr. Iliad Bk 6		97

SON'S

| The daughter's petulance, the son's expence, | O | 44 | Vanity Wishes | | 280 |
| The ruinous insolence, the son's expence, | Y | 104 | Vanity Wishes | V | 280 |

SONG

And Pantomime, and Song, confirm'd her Sway.	O	52	Pro Drury-Lane		38
Her voice and Smiles my Song shall grace.	O	67	To A. Fuscus		24
My rude unpolish'd song;	O	80	Feast St Simon		57
One moment hear the moral song,	O	121	To Miss Playin		22
I too can pour the extemporary song:	O	142	In Baretti Bk.		4
Purchas'd by thy powerful Song,	O	150	Tr Boet III.12		41
Purchas'd by the powerful Song,	O	150	Tr Boet III.12	V	41
And bad the feast, and song, and bowl,	O	190	Tr. Medea I		5
A Short Song of Congratulation	O	196	Song Congratu.		T
The (coxcombs) whisper and the fopling's song	Y	128	Irene	V	17
That day, that mournfull day, no chearfull song	Y	6	Virgil Daphnis		7
Direct O Goddess, my advent'rous song;	Y	22	Tr Add. Battle		3
She shall sing me a song,	Y	300	Fanny Burney		1
While many a merry tale, and many a song,	Y	310	Parody of Pope		1

SONGS

| And Songs of Pleasure warble from the Tongue, | O | 315 | Irene | | 30 |

SONNET

| Yet, lay the sonnet for an hour aside, | O | 142 | In Baretti Bk. | | 7 |
| Ode and Elegy and Sonnet. | O | 179 | Ridicul Warton | | 8 |

SONOROUS

| But when the Tempest with sonorous Wing | O | 298 | Irene | | 22 |

SONS

Through Freedom's sons no more remonstrance rings,	O	34	Vanity Wishes		93
And all the sons of ravage croud the war;	O	43	Vanity Wishes		250
With all the sons of ravage croud the war;	O	43	Vanity Wishes	V	250
And visits Britain's hardy Sons	O	80	Feast St Simon		47
His tortur'd Sons shall die before his Face,	O	111	To Posterity		23
Warm India's supple Sons should bow,	O	146	Tr Boeth III.5		6
Ye Sons of England, deign to hear,	O	188	Epilogue		3
Ye Sons of Britain, deign to hear,	O	188	Epilogue	V	3
Ye sons of Melody repair,	O	191	Tr. Medea I		14
Bid the Sons of thrift farewell.	O	196	Song Congratu.	V	8

SONS   (CONTINUED)   PAGE   TITLE   LINE
    Where Priam and his sons are laid, ...   O 232 Tr Horace IV.7   15
    Ye Sons of Avarice! a Moment spare: . . . . . .   O 246 Irene Prologue   4
    Reproach not Misery.--The Sons of Greece, ...   O 250 Irene   28
    When Genoa's faithless Sons forsook the Ramparts . . . O 351 Irene   V   5
    Her grateful Sons shine bright with ev'ry Virtue; . . . O 256 Irene   V   60
    Surveys his smiling babes, the sons of   Y 122 Irene   V   60
      freedom,
    Their cloudy Summits, and the Sons of Fierceness, . . . O 268 Irene   29
    Their snowy summits, and the sons of fierceness . . . Y 136 Irene   V   29
    Arabia's roving Troops, the Sons of Swiftness, ... O 274 Irene   54
    Rouse, Cali, shall the Sons of conquer'd Greece . . . O 284 Irene   42
    Guide the Sons dagger to the Fathers heart . . . . . . O 352 Irene   V   4
    Her Sons malicious Clemency shall spare, ...   O 309 Irene   32
SOON
    Then soon your ill-plac'd confidence repay, ... O 17 London   156
    Would not these pleasures soon remove . . . .   O 72 Hor. Epode II   45
    But their lost strength and vigour soon return, . . . O 76 Tr Add. Battle   8
    Soon must this bough, as you shall fix his doom, . . O 95 Sprig of Myrtl   13
    Soon shall this sprig, as you shall fix its doom, . . O 95 Sprig of Myrtl   V   13
    Soon had the Monarch felt a nobler fire, ... O 97 Hickman Spinet   16
    Soon fades the rose; once past the fragrant hour, . . O 133 Tr. Rambler 71   1
    What soon is perfect, soon alike is past; . . . . . O 142 In Baretti Bk.   9
    What soon is perfect, soon alike is past; . . . . . O 142 In Baretti Bk.   9
    Soon th' aspiring Fabric falls, ...   O 145 Tr Boeth. II.4   9
    Soon the treachrous Sands retreat, ...   O 145 Tr Boeth. II.4   11
    Soon those nine lives would be past. . . . .   O 194 On Thrale Hat   4
    Her losses soon the Moon supplies, ...   O 232 Tr Horace IV.7   13
    Such had I trusted once as soon as seen, ... O 255 Irene   17
    Soon as the Sultan's unexpected Fate . . . .   O 257 Irene   76
    Soon will th' unequal Contest be decided, ... O 261 Irene   18
    Soon would his Art or Valour set us free, ... O 267 Irene   43
    Soon as the Veil of Evening clouds the Sky, ... O 284 Irene   49
    Soon shall the dire Seraglio's horrid Gates . . . . . O 291 Irene   79
    Soon shall the dire Seraglio's dreadful Gates . . . . O 357 Irene   V   9
    Soon shouldst thou see, how false thy weak Reproach. . O 293 Irene   107
    Soon wouldst thou see, how false thy weak Reproach. . . O 293 Irene   V   107
    Soon may the final Stroke decide our Fate, ... O 299 Irene   51
    How soon, alas! will Int'rest, Fear, or Envy, ... O 301 Irene   82
    Soon shalt thou scorn, in Safety's Arms repos'd, . . O 301 Irene   93
    Soon may we meet again, secure and free, ... O 303 Irene   23
    Stood torpid in Suspence; but soon Abdalla . . . . . O 317 Irene   37
    But soon thou shalt repent: another Moment . . . . . O 319 Irene   33
    But soon though shalt lament thy daring folly . . . . Y 198 Irene   V   33
    Soon might her Tears engage a Lover's Credit; . . . . O 327 Irene   17
    Soon as the chief approach'd the Scaean Gate . . . . Y 18 Tr. Iliad Bk 6   3
    Soon shall you fall by num'rous hosts opprest . . . . Y 18 Tr. Iliad Bk 6   22
    Soon as with gold appeas'd, he set her free . . . . Y 19 Tr. Iliad Bk 6   40
    Soon forth in arms had some bold soldier stood, . . . Y 23 Tr Add. Battle   40
    Soon had the wrathfull faulchion drank his blood. . . Y 23 Tr Add. Battle   41
    Soon as their young began to draw their breath . . . Y 24 Tr Add. Battle   86
    There she soon became a jilt, ...   Y 300 Extemp. Elegy   9
SOONER
    Sooner these trembling Leaves shall find a Voice, . . . O 255 Irene   26
    Sooner the trembling Leaves shall find a Voice, . . . O 373 Irene   V   19
    Sooner the Breeze shall catch the flying Sounds, . . . O 255 Irene   28
SOOTH
    Till counted myriads sooth his pride no more; . . . . O 42 Vanity Wishes   230
    Ah! how shall envy sooth her pain? . . . .   O 122 Stella Mourn.   12
    Well skill'd to sooth a foe with looks of kindness, . . O 176 Tr Metastas II   3
    O! sooth my Soul, and teach me how to lose thee. . . . O 253 Irene   103
    Each weakness sooth and flatter ev'ry folly. . . . . Y 134 Irene   V   27
    Sooth the delighted Soul with empty Bliss? . . . . . O 277 Irene   45
    Sooth her with all the Pleasures of Command, ... O 287 Irene   17
    That sooth the sense, and elevate the thought . . . . Y 165 Irene   V   80
SOOTHIN
    Diffuse the soothin lenitives of pain: . . . . . .   Y 104 Vanity Wishes   V   268
SOOTHING
    Approach, ye minstrels, try the soothing strain, . . . O 43 Vanity Wishes   267
    Can yield no room to Music's soothing pow'r. . . . . O 193 Tr. Medea II   20
    No soothing Interval of peaceful Sorrow; . . . . . . O 249 Irene   12
    Or tune thine Ear to soothing Adulation, ... O 289 Irene   4
    Or tune your ear to soothing Adulation. . . . . . .   O 366 Irene   V   20
SOOTHS
    Since hope but sooths to double my distress, ... O 10 London   39
    But when your Musick sooths the raging pain, ... O 96 Hickman Spinet   6
    She feeds his Hopes, and sooths him to Delay. . . . . O 260 Irene   129
SOPHIA'S
    A roving Soldier seiz'd in Sophia's Temple . . . . . O 258 Irene   94
    In Sophia's Temple!--What Alarm!--Proceed. . . . . . O 258 Irene   97
    Implor'd the Eternal Pow'r, at Sophia's altars . . . . Y 163 Irene   V   49
SOPHON
    Eroon te Bious Birchion, ede Sophon, ...   O 108 Eis Birchion   2
SORC'RESS
    The wily sorc'ress wears a thousand forms, ... Y 155 Irene   V   26
SORCERERS
    On flying Cars new Sorcerers may ride. . . . . . .   O 53 Pro Drury-Lane   44
SORCERY
    His bland Address, and Sorcery of Tongue; . . . . .   O 273 Irene   40
SORDID
    But still desires of sordid gain . . . .   O 73 Hor. Epode II   77

```
                                                        PAGE    TITLE             LINE
SORROW
     New sorrow rises as the day returns,      . . . . . .  O  45 Vanity Wishes        301
     Each passing day some comfort sorrow finds.  . . . .  Y 105 Vanity Wishes      V 301
     And social sorrow loses half its pain:    . . . . .   O  59 Pro Good Nat'd         4
     And virtue's sorrow dignify'd his tomb.   . . . . .   O 118 Epitaph Hanmer        44
     If Sorrow pine or Av'rice crave,  . . . .             O 146 Tr Boeth III.5         9
     Her baleful eyes where Sorrow rolls around;  . . .    O 192 Tr. Medea II          14
     No soothing Interval of peaceful Sorrow;  . . . . .   O 249 Irene                 12
     And feel no Sorrow while my Sov'reign smiles.  . . .  O 272 Irene                 11
     Is this a Time for Softness or for Sorrow?  . . . .   O 280 Irene                 11
     When did contentment with struggling sorrow  . . .   Y 191 Irene              V  20
     And banish'd sorrow flies the joyous plains;  . . .   Y   7 Virgil Daphnis        37
     And joy and sorrow stand by turns confest.  . . . .   Y  21 Tr. Iliad Bk 6       110
SORROWS
     Sink not beneath imaginary Sorrows:  . . . . .        O 252 Irene                 84
     And hop'd to share thy Counsels, not thy Sorrows:  . . O 253 Irene               106
     When the tenth Sun had set upon our Sorrows,  . . .   O 254 Irene                120
     Renew our Sorrows, and awake our Fears.  . . . . .    O 268 Irene                 35
     Ah! cease, Irene, cease those flowing Sorrows,  . . . O 276 Irene                  3
     To man bewilderd in this maze of sorrows  . . . . .   Y 148 Irene              V  43
     With silent Sorrows, and with calm Devotion.  . . .   O 290 Irene                 50
     Devolve, dear Maid, thy Sorrows on the Wretch,  . . . O 316 Irene                 16
     And may she ne'er returning sorrows know."  . . . .   Y  20 Tr. Iliad Bk 6       106
     Restrain your sorrows, calm your troubled soul.  . . . Y  21 Tr. Iliad Bk 6      114
SOU
     Sou pote grapsomenon Birchion allon echois.  . . . .  O 108 Eis Birchion          4
SOUGHT
     This task perform'd, he sought no gainful post,  . . . O 118 Epitaph Hanmer       27
     Admission ne'er had sought, or could not find.  . . . O 192 Tr. Medea II         12
     And sought An easier conquest in my softer beauty  . . Y 134 Irene             V  35
     And sought this happy Grove in quest of Thee.  . . .  O 299 Irene                 50
     Then sought the palace where the menial train  . . .  Y  21 Tr. Iliad Bk 6       128
SOUL
     Yet should thy soul indulge the gen'rous heat,  . . . O  37 Vanity Wishes       143
     A frame of adamant, a soul of fire,  . . . . . . .    O  40 Vanity Wishes       193
     Breathe forth thy fervours for a soul  . . . . . .    Y 108 Vanity Wishes     V 359
     Oh! how my soul abhors so mean a thought.  . . . .    O  74 Tr. Iliad Bk 6        8
     The floods of rage, and calm thy rufled soul.  . . .  O  77 Festina Lente         8
     Nor there confin'd his active Soul;  . . . . . .      O  79 Feast St Simon        43
     And future millions lift his rising soul;  . . . . .  O  82 Young Author      V  6B
     Here stop, my soul, thy rapid flight,  . . . . . .    O 125 An Ode                17
     Unless the soul, to vice a thrall,  . . . . . . .     O 129 Tr. Rambler 6          1
     From her high Seats he drew the Soul,  . . . . . .    O 147 Tr Boeth III.6         9
     Save him whose Soul enslav'd to Vice  . . . . . .     O 147 Tr Boeth III.6        19
     O'erfill the saturated soul;  . . . . . . . . .       O 190 Tr. Medea I            6
     And free'd his soul the nearest way.  . . . . . .     O 202 Death Dr Levet        36
     And forc'd his soul the nearest way.  . . . . .       O 202 Death Dr Levet     V  36
     O! sooth my Soul, and teach me how to lose thee.  . . O 253 Irene                103
     Now summon all thy Soul, illustrious Christian!  . . . O 254 Irene                1
     Virtue and Liberty engross his Soul,  . . . . . .     O 255 Irene                 32
     And share the deepest Secrets of my Soul,  . . . .    O 256 Irene                 39
     What Hopes, what Terrors rush upon my Soul!  . . .    O 259 Irene                104
     Distract my Soul, dispatch thy ling'ring Tale;  . . . O 259 Irene                114
     And ease my loaded Soul upon her Bosom?  . . . . .    O 263 Irene                 22
     Thy Care shall guard this Treasure of my Soul;  . . . O 263 Irene                  2
     My soul could animate a larger frame  . . . . . .     Y 132 Irene             V 41A
     Exalts my Soul, and fortifies my Heart.  . . . . .    O 265 Irene                  5
     Habitual Cowardice usurps the Soul.  . . . . . .      O 266 Irene                 33
     I want alass thy steadiness of Soul  . . . . . .      O 366 Irene             V  29
     Thy Soul by Nature great, enlarg'd by Knowledge,  . . O 266 Irene                 35
     Whose Soul, perhaps, yet mindful of Aspasia,  . . .   O 267 Irene                 39
     To clasp a Slave? or, can a Soul like mine,  . . .    O 268 Irene                 16
     Rose to his Thought, and set his Soul on Fire:  . . . O 270 Irene                 11
     And load with Perjuries his parting Soul?  . . . .    O 272 Irene                  5
     His Hand! His Seal! The Secrets of my Soul  . . . .   O 273 Irene                 19
     Claim my divided Soul. This Wretch unworthy  . . .    O 275 Irene                 69
     The strong Emotions of my troubled Soul  . . . . .    O 275 Irene                 87
     Will yet Irenes haughty Soul descend  . . . . . .     O 372 Irene             V   6
     A Habitation for a fairer Soul?  . . . . . . .        O 277 Irene                 29
     Sooth the delighted Soul with empty Bliss?  . . . .   O 277 Irene                 45
     Thy Soul compleats the Triumphs of thy Face.  . . .   O 278 Irene                 60
     The strongest Effort of a female Soul,  . . . . .     O 278 Irene                 62
     Some vain Amusement of a vacant Soul!  . . . . .      O 280 Irene                  8
     Know'st thou not yet, when Love invades the Soul,  . . O 281 Irene                38
     He 's gone--Here rest, my Soul, thy fainting Wing,  . O 287 Irene                  1
     My soul not oft acquainted with remorse  . . . . .    Y 159 Irene             V   8
     Swell not thy Soul beyond Advice or Friendship,  . . . O 289 Irene                 2
     Swell not your Soul beyond reproof or Counsel  . . .  O 366 Irene             V  18
     Yet should my Soul, still faithful to her Choice,  . . O 289 Irene                13
     The Soul once tainted with so foul a Crime,  . . . .  O 289 Irene                 15
     That gloomy Slumber of the stagnant Soul;  . . . .    O 292 Irene                 82
     stagnant soul.  The gloom of idleness.  . . . . .     Y 165 Irene             V  82
     Thy dazzled Soul with all its boasted Greatness,  . . O 292 Irene                 99
     Why does thy Soul retire into herself?  . . . . .     O 295 Irene                  7
     A sudden Mist o'ercasts my darken'd Soul,  . . . .    O 295 Irene                 12
     My fainting Soul with Violence of transport.  . . .   O 371 Irene             V  15
     Enough--resistless Reason calms my Soul--  . . . .    O 297 Irene                  1
     Propitious Guide of my bewilder'd Soul,  . . . . .    O 298 Irene                 11
     My Soul first kindled by thy bright Example,  . . .   O 298 Irene                 13
     But still yet my Soul detests the Bassas  . . . . .   O 353 Irene             V  22
          treason
```

SOUL	(CONTINUED)		PAGE	TITLE	LINE

SOUL   (CONTINUED)   PAGE   TITLE   LINE

```
     But the sight of friends soul sinking into vice (a soul  .   Y 177  Irene         V111C
     But the sight of friends soul sinking into vice (a soul  .   Y 177  Irene         V111C
     There shall soft Leisure wing th' excursive Soul,  . . .    O 302  Irene         118
     The soften'd Soul to Cowardice and Sloth;  . . . . .       O 303  Irene         17
     My Soul expands to meet approaching Freedom.  . . . .      O 306  Irene         50
     Search to the dark Recesses of the Soul, . . . . . .      O 308  Irene         13
     To cross the Tow'rings of an equal Soul, . . . . . .      O 309  Irene         41
     Demetrius the soul of Greece  . . . . . . . . .           Y 188  Irene       V 10
         anguish of my soul before Thee.  . . . . . . .        Y 189  Irene       V  1
     Exalt my soul, and swell it into raptures.  . . . . .     Y 189  Irene       V 1F
     My Soul attends thy Voice, and banish'd Virtue  . . . .   O 320  Irene         32
     Will spread resistless Light upon my Soul.  . . . . .     O 321  Irene         47
     Be charg'd upon my Soul. O, Mercy! Mercy!  . . . . .      O 329  Irene         55
     Dwell on my Ear, and sadden all my Soul;  . . . . . .     O 329  Irene          9
     Just as the Rack forc'd out his struggling Soul,  . . .   O 330  Irene         13
     Invades my soul, and rages in my breast.  . . . . .       Y  11  Tr Hor Epode 9  6
     This Hector saw; his soul was touch'd with grief.  . .    Y  21  Tr. Iliad Bk 6  111
     Restrain your sorrows, calm your troubled soul.  . . .    Y  21  Tr. Iliad Bk 6  114
SOUL'S
     Hast thou not search'd my Soul's profoundest Thoughts?  .  O 304  Irene         18
SOULS
     The price of boroughs and of souls restore, . . . . .    O  19  London        204
     Great souls whose the dear-bought right convey . .       Y 100  Vanity Wishes  V 189
     Their souls dismiss'd through many a ghastly wound,  . .   O  74  Tr. Iliad Bk 6  18
     And sister souls together join, . . . . . . . . .         O 100  Ode Friendship 22
     When souls to blissful climes remove?  . . . . . . .      O 100  Ode Friendship 26
     Sure by some wond'rous Sympathy of Souls, . . . . .       O 272  Irene          8
     While vulgar Souls compassionate their Cares, . . . .     O 293  Irene        115
     Such Ills are sent for Souls like thine to conquer.  . .   O 332  Irene         38
     Or their own souls with hopes of vict'ry fir'd."  . . .   Y  19  Tr. Iliad Bk 6  59
SOUND
     Untouch'd his cottage, and his slumbers sound, . . . .    O  32  Vanity Wishes  35
     secure his cottage, and his slumbers sound, . . . . .     Y  93  Vanity Wishes  V 35
     To chase the Charms of Sound, the Pomp of Show, . . . .   O  53  Pro Drury-Lane  59
     At best, a fleeting gleam, or empty sound.  . . . . .     O  62  Pro Word Wise  20
     At last, a fleeting gleam, or empty sound.  . . . . .     O  62  Pro Word Wise  V 20
     No trumpets sound, no Soldiers cries, . . . . . . .       O  71  Hor. Epode II   9
     But move their numrous arms to Musicks sound, . . . .     O  77  Tr Add. Battle  51
     Thy Streets with Violence of Woe shall sound, . . . .     O 110  To Posterity    5
     Each charm of modulated sound,  . . . . . . . . .         O 121  To Miss Playin  6
     And attentive to the sound  . . . . . . . . . .           O 148  Tr Boet III.12  9
     May spare the luxuries of sound.  . . . . . . . . .       O 191  Tr. Medea I    20
     And aided wine with dulcet-streaming sound. . . . . .     O 192  Tr. Medea II    8
     All else is empty Sound, and idle Show. . . . . . .       O 246  Irene Prologue  14
     He bids no Trumpet quell the fatal Sound.  . . . . .      O 246  Irene Prologue  24
     Again her Temples sound with holy Musick: . . . . .       O 291  Irene          55
     Well may'st thou hide in Labyrinths of Sound  . . . .     O 293  Irene         125
     More than a pleasing Sound without a Meaning, . . . .     O 310  Irene          13
     An undistinguish'd Sound of threat'ning Rage. . . . .     O 311  Irene          13
     We started at the Sound, again enquir'd, . . . . . .      O 325  Irene          25
     Horror and Agony are in that Sound! . . . . . . .         O 328  Irene          32
     With pleasing sound allur'd the rural throng. . . . .     Y   6  Virgil Daphnis  8
     While in my verse the shrilling trumpets sound, . . . .   Y  22  Tr Add. Battle  18
     And first a sound invades th' astonish'd ear. . . . .     Y  25  Tr Add. Battle  91
SOUNDING
     Where Tigris beats his sounding shore . . . . . . .       O  80  Feast St Simon  52
SOUNDS
     War sounds the trump, he rushes to the field; . . . .     O  40  Vanity Wishes 198
     No sounds alas would touch th' impervious ear, . . . .    O  43  Vanity Wishes 269
     Sounds in my sleeping Ear, "Awake Demetrius, . . . .      O 254  Irene         122
     Sooner the Breeze shall catch the flying Sounds, . . .    O 255  Irene          28
     Imperfect sounds of Greece--and love--and  . . . .       Y 144  Irene       V  80
         daggers
     Too calm I listen to the flatt'ring Sounds. . . . . .     O 278  Irene          74
     And kindly grant an Ear to gentler Sounds:  . . . . .     O 285  Irene           2
     In my weak Ear th' intoxicating Sounds. . . . . . .      O 288  Irene           6
     Reflect that Life and Death, affecting Sounds, . . . .    O 290  Irene          26
     What well known Voice pronounc'd the grateful Sounds  . .  O 295  Irene          10
     Success and Conquest now are empty Sounds, . . . . .     O 333  Irene          44
SOUR
     Where no sour criticks damn, nor sneers molest, . . .     O  82  Young Author   27
     Where no sour criticks snarl, no sneers molest, . . .     O  82  Young Author   V 27
SOURCE
     Parent of ills! and source of all our woe! . . . . .      O  77  Festina Lente  10
     All from one Source derive their Birth  . . . . . .       O 146  Tr Boeth III.6  3
     Woman the Source, the Object, and the End.  . . . . .     O 247  Irene Epilogue  18
     Pledge of their love and source of all their joy  . . .   Y  18  Tr. Iliad Bk 6  10
     Fair source of wit, and love, and mirth, . . . . . .      Y  39  Lady Leaving    6
SOUTH
     D<r>ives to (holds o'er) the south or west the . . . .    Y 136  Irene       V  26
         storm
SOV'REIGN
     At length his sov'reign frowns--the train of state  . .   O  34  Vanity Wishes 109
     For patience sov'reign o'er transmuted ill; . . . . .     O  48  Vanity Wishes 362
     And feel no Sorrow while my Sov'reign smiles.  . . . .    O 272  Irene          11
     Records each Act, each Thought of sov'reign Man, . . .    O 276  Irene          21
     This sov'reign Passion, scornful of Restraint,  . . . .   O 280  Irene          18
     Think how the sov'reign Arbiter of Kingdoms . . . . .     O 300  Irene          56
SOV'REIGN'S
     Is then your Sov'reign's Life so cheaply rated, . . .     O 327  Irene          14
```

SOVEREIGN
    Those sovereign charms with strictest care employ;   . .   O 81 Lady Birthday   13
    Spring yield<s> to Summer<'s> sovereign ray,   . . .   O 231 Tr Horace IV.7   10
    for the long life and prosperity of my sovereign   . .   Y 130 Irene   V 12A
    Records each deed each thought of sovereign Man   . .   O 355 Irene   V 10
SPACE
    And Fate lies crouded in a narrow Space. . . . . . .   O 287 Irene   5
    Yet in that narrow Space what Dangers rise?--   . . . .   O 287 Irene   6
SPACIOUS
    Apulia's spacious wilds with gore; . . . .   O 66 Hor I Ode xxii   14
    Apulia's spacious Wilds with Gore; . . . .   O 67 To A. Fuscus   14
    Thro' all the spacious ball; . . . .   O 79 Feast St Simon   27
    When cates luxuriant pile the spacious dish,   . . .   O 193 Tr. Medea II   17
SPAIN
    The guard of commerce, and the dread of Spain, ...   O 10 London   28
    Of France the mimick, and of Spain the prey.   . . . .   O 15 London   106
    No peaceful desart yet unclaim'd by Spain? . . . . .   O 18 London   173
SPAR'D
    Perhaps in vain the Sultan's Anger spar'd me, ...   O 298 Irene   32
    Thy Life perhaps--Were but Irene spar'd, ...   O 332 Irene   33
    Thou might'st have liv'd, for thou hadst spar'd Irene. .   O 333 Irene   58
SPARE
    Less pleas'd to triumph than to spare.   . . . . .   O 137 Tr Rambler 143   2
    Beasts of each kind their fellows spare; . . . . . .   O 138 Tr Rambler 160   1
    May spare the luxuries of sound. . . . .   O 191 Tr. Medea I   20
    Ye Sons of Avarice! a Moment spare: . . . . .   O 246 Irene Prologue   4
    And spare him, Beauties! tho' his Lovers live. . . .   O 246 Irene Prologue 20
    Aspasia! spare that lov'd, that mournful Name: . . . .   O 252 Irene   76
    May spare the fatal Bow-string till To-morrow? . . . .   O 284 Irene   39
    O spare the gallant Greek, in him we lose   . . . .   O 307 Irene   26
    Her Sons malicious Clemency shall spare, ...   O 309 Irene   32
    Nor dare to spare the Life his Frown condemns. . . . .   O 325 Irene   10
    Nor justice can acquit, nor mercy spare   . . . . .   Y 210 Irene   V 25B
    May storms howl gently o'er and learn to spare.   . .   Y 3 On a Daffodill   8
SPARES
    But all whom hunger spares, with age decay: . . . .   O 9 London   12
SPARK
    (No spark of envy harbours in my breast) . . . . .   O 64 Virgil Past.I   14
    If yet one spark of Heav'nly fire remain . . . . .   Y 133 Irene   V 18
    And fans the slumb'ring Spark of heav'nly Fire. . . .   O 303 Irene   19
SPARKLED
    The Patriot's fire yet sparkled in the friend. . . . .   O 118 Epitaph Hanmer   40
    And secret pleasures sparkled in his eyes. . . . . .   Y 18 Tr. Iliad Bk 6   16
SPARKLES
    Nor binds the neck, nor sparkles in the hair, ...   O 141 Tr Rambler 199   3
SPARKLING
    At sight of sparkling bowls or beauteous dames, . . .   O 142 In Baretti Bk.   1
    The Sparkling Wit the penetrating Reason . . . . .   O 356 Irene   V 23
    She mark'd my sparkling Eyes, and heaving Breast, . . .   O 282 Irene   68
    The sparkling ornaments, the glittring dress (the change   Y 164 Irene   V 71
        of dress
    And sparkling quiver to the Breath of May; . . . .   O 298 Irene   21
    Bound o'er the sparkling Waves, Go, happy Bark,   . . .   O 322 Irene   5
    Dance o'er the Sparkling Waves--Go happy Bark . . . .   O 364 Irene   V 30
SPARROW
    The woodcock and the sparrow; . . . .   Y 300 Fanny Burney   3
SPEAK
    Speak thou, whose thoughts at humble peace repine,   . .   O 35 Vanity Wishes   121
    Where Woman's not allow'd to speak her Mind;   . . . .   O 247 Irene Epilogue   12
        Forbear to speak of Hazards, ...   O 260 Irene   133
    Who hear thee speak, and not abandon Reason? . . . .   O 281 Irene   43
    I gaz'd, I trembled; but I could not speak: . . . . .   O 282 Irene   65
    Caraza speak--have ye remark'd the Bassa?   . . . .   O 311 Irene   1
    Those trembling Limbs--Speak out, thou shiv'ring   . .   O 332 Irene   16
        Traitor.
SPEAKER
    Who hail'd him Speaker, with united voice. . . . . .   O 118 Epitaph Hanmer   20
SPEAKER'S
    Impeachment stops the speaker's pow'rful breath, . . .   O 31 Vanity Wishes   19
SPEAKING
    Thus I spoke; and speaking sigh'd; . . . .   O 181 Parody Warton   5
    Or pay with speaking Eyes a Lover's Homage? . . . .   O 282 Irene   63
    Hector, this speaking, with extended hands . . . .   Y 20 Tr. Iliad Bk 6   90
SPEARS   SEE BULRUSH-SPEARS
    And Grecian spears shall quiver in your breast.   . . .   Y 18 Tr. Iliad Bk 6   23
SPECIAL
    No spies were paid, no special juries known, ...   O 22 London   252
    No bribes were paid, no special juries known, ...   Y 61 London   V 252
SPECIOUS
    The secret ambush of a specious pray'r. . . . . . .   O 48 Vanity Wishes 354
    The tinsel glitter, and the specious mein, ...   O 139 Tr Rambler 168   1
SPECKLED
    The richest Odours, nor the speckled Shells . . . . .   O 277 Irene   32
SPECTRES
    Nor Melancholy's spectres haunt thy shade;   . . . .   Y 99 Vanity Wishes V 154
    Guilt and Despair! pale Spectres, grin around me, . . .   O 328 Irene   50
SPEECH
    In ev'ry speech persuasive wisdom flow'd, ...   O 118 Epitaph Hanmer   15
    Thy Look, thy Speech, thy Action, all is Wildness--   . .   O 323 Irene   5
SPEED
    A single skiff to speed his flight remains; . . . . .   O 42 Vanity Wishes 238

SPEED   (CONTINUED)   PAGE   TITLE   LINE
    To speed the light convivial hour; . . . .   O 191 Tr. Medea I   18
    Retire with Speed, while I prepare to meet him . . . .   O 271 Irene   37
    With all the Speed of Terror and of Guilt. . . . . .   O 275 Irene   86
    Thanks for this kind Relief--with Speed admit him. . .   O 294 Irene   5
    Return with speed, Leontius, to your Charge; . . . . .   O 304 Irene   9
    What wild Mistake is this? Take hence with speed . . .   O 325 Irene   4
    Depress their Spirits, and retard their Speed? . . . .   O 325 Irene   15
    That thus constrain'd we speed the Stroke of Death. . . O 327 Irene   30
    Urg'd us to Speed, and bad us banish Pity, ...   O 332 Irene   30
    And speed the Stroke lest Mercy should o'ertake them. . O 333 Irene   54
SPEEDY
    By his Command, equipp'd for speedy Flight, ...   O 254 Irene   133
    For speedy Flight, or obstinate Defence. . . . . .   O 284 Irene   55
    When desp'rate Ills demand a speedy Cure, ...   O 301 Irene   85
SPEND
    In vain you spend your vows and prayers, ...   O 68 Hor.II Ode 14   3
SPENDS
    Its useless force the weapon spends in air. . . . . .   Y 26 Tr Add. Battle   135
SPENSER'S
    And Spenser's verse prolongs Eliza's reign; . . . . .   O 114 On C. Cibber   2
SPENT
    All Marlb'rough hoarded, or all Villiers spent, . . .   O 14 London   86
    Farewell!--When youth, and health, and fortune spent, . O 23 London   256
    At length the Conquerour has spent his . . . . . .   O 350 Irene   V   8
        rage--
    Sinks like the sighing of a Tempest spent, ...   O 275 Irene   92
    Sinks into sighs like the sighing of a Tempest spent . . O 367 Irene   V 13
    Your sighs are spent in vain; if fates withstand . . .   Y 21 Tr. Iliad Bk 6   115
    Wounded and spent, in vain they strive to rise . . . .   Y 24 Tr Add. Battle   60
SPHERE
    The weight of ev'ry rolling sphere, ...   O 79 Feast St Simon   32
    And sees the motions of th' harmonious sphere; . . . .   Y   7 Virgil Daphnis   35
SPHERES
    And wearied angels rest upon their stars spheres . . .   Y 128 Irene   V 4B
    Conducts the Sun, and regulates the Spheres. . . . .   O 293 Irene   124
    Rolls on the Sun, and Regulates the Spheres. . . . .   O 369 Irene   V 17
SPICES
    For thee, my fair, shall India's spices . . . . . .   Y 150 Irene   V 81
        ripen
SPICY
    Whate'er from India spicy coasts . . . .   O 73 Hor. Epode II   V 58
SPIES
    No spies were paid, no special juries known, ...   O 22 London   252
SPINET
    To Miss Hickman playing on the Spinet . . . .   O 96 Hickman Spinet   T
SPIRES
    In Triumph sits upon our shatter'd Spires, ...   O 251 Irene   67
    In triumph sits upon the ruin'd Spires . . . . . .   O 351 Irene   V   6
SPIRIT
    Show the Spirit of an heir. . . . .   O 196 Song Congratu.   12
    Our daring Bard with Spirit unconfin'd, ...   O 246 Irene Prologue   7
    And publick Spirit deemd a wild Chimaera . . . . .   O 347 Irene   V 19
    I feel new Spirit shoot along my Nerves, ...   O 306 Irene   49
SPIRITS
    Pockets full, and Spirits high, ...   O 196 Song Congratu.   22
    Or sprightly Hope exalt their kindling Spirits? . . .   O 270 Irene   23
    Thus meaner Spirits with Amazement mark . . . . .   O 293 Irene   117
    Thus meaner Spirits with amazement see . . . . . .   O 369 Irene   V 11
    To guide thy Passage shall th' aerial Spirits . . . .   O 322 Irene   7
    To Guide thy passage shall th' Starry Spirits . . . .   O 364 Irene   V 26
    Depress their Spirits, and retard their Speed? . . . .   O 325 Irene   15
    My Spirits fail, awhile support me, Vengeance-- . . .   O 334 Irene   72
    My spirits fail, I cannot name his death . . . . . .   Y 216 Irene   V 72
    And balmy spirits thro' thy foliage play, ...   Y   3 On a Daffodill   10
    May balmy spirits thro thy foliage play, ...   Y   3 On a Daffodill   V 10
SPITE
    And baffled Spite, with hopeless Anguish dumb, . . .   O 57 Prologue Comus   17
    Their schemes of spite the poet's foes dismiss, . . .   O 60 Pro Good Nat'd   19
    Yet spite of fair Zelinda's eye, ...   O 127 To Lyce, Lady   21
SPLEEN
    Far hence are banish'd vapours, spleen, and tears, . .   O 84 Epi Dist Moth.   18
    Resign the heart to spleen and care, ...   O 123 Winter's Walk   10
SPLENDID
    Or Eloquence, or splendid birth, ...   O 232 Tr Horace IV.7   23
    Surveys the glories of the splendid pile . . . . . .   Y 131 Irene   V 36A
    Support the splendid Miseries of Greatness? . . . . .   O 268 Irene   18
    Why all this Glare of splendid Eloquence, ...   O 276 Irene   11
    From splendid wretchedness and guilty scepters (grandeur) Y 166 Irene   V 93
SPLENDOR
    Exchanges solid Strength for feeble Splendor. . . . .   O 265 Irene   38
    The traveller persues the flatt'ring wandring . . . .   Y 155 Irene   V 34
        splendor
    Amidst the Splendor of encircling Beauty, ...   O 288 Irene   1
SPLENDORS
    If yet these glittring Robes these sudden Splendors . . O 366 Irene   V 17
    If Dismiss this glittring train these sudden . . . .   O 366 Irene   V 17
        Splendors
SPLENDOUR
    And bad imperial splendour glare (blaze) before her . . Y 158 Irene   V 10
    Again should golden Splendour grace her Cities, . . .   O 290 Irene   53

314

```
                                                             PAGE    TITLE           LINE
SPLENDOUR       (CONTINUED)
     So much our splendour was encreas'd by thine.  . . . .  Y   6 Virgil Daphnis      19
SPLENDOURS
     Can'st thou forget hereditary Splendours,  . . . . .   O 301 Irene              103
SPOIL
     Shall glutton on the industrious Peasants Spoil,  . . . O 110 To Posterity        13
     There will his boundless Wealth, the Spoil of Asia,  .. O 274 Irene               50
     There (or might) shall his boundless Wealth the  . . . O 351 Irene             V 13
        Spoil of <kindoms> Nations  . . . . . . . . .       O 351 Irene             V 13
     Pleas'd with the conquest, he forebore the spoil  . .  Y  18 Tr. Iliad Bk 6      30
SPOILS
     To such, a groaning nation's spoils are giv'n,  . . . . O  13 London             65
     Tell the spoils of wilful waste,  . . . . . . .        O 197 Song Congratu.   V 26
     Prowls like a lyon oer the wealthy Spoils of bleeding . O 352 Irene            V 29
        Turkey.
     Prowls o'er the wealthy Spoils of bleeding Turkey?  . . O 264 Irene               15
SPOKE
     Thus I spoke; and speaking sigh'd;  . . . . . . . .     O 181 Parody Warton        5
     Her tears in show'rs descending as she spoke.  . . . .  Y  18 Tr. Iliad Bk 6      18
     The chief, this spoke, into the mother's arms  . . .    Y  20 Tr. Iliad Bk 6     107
SPOKEN
        Spoken At The Opening Of The Theatre  . . . . . .    O  50 Pro Drury-lane       T
     A New Prologue Spoken By Mr Garrick, . . . . . . .      O  56 Prologue Comus       T
     Epilogue intended to have been spoken by a Lady  . . .  O  83 Epi Dist Moth.       T
SPORT
     And unrelenting sport ten thousand lives away;  . . . . O  83 Epi Dist Moth.       9
     With sport above and death below;  . . . . . . .       O 203 Tr. on Skating       2
     The sport of Tyranny, or Lord of Nations.  . . . . .   O 303 Irene                12
     Sport in our Sails, and murmur o'er the Deep.  . . . .  O 304 Irene                7
     The sport of boys, and scandall of the town.  . . . .   Y  11 Tr Hor Epode 9      12
SPORTING
     (His various plumage sporting in the wind)  . . . . .   O  74 Tr. Iliad Bk 6       2
SPORTIVE
     And wander sportive o'er th' Elysian plain:  . . . . .  O  77 Tr Add. Battle      43
SPORTS
     Forsakes his rural sports and peaceful home,  . . . .   O  81 Young Author      V  2
     For trifling sports I quitted grave affairs.  . . . .   O 130 Tr. Rambler 10       1
     For humble cottages and rural sports.  . . . . . .     O 137 Tr Rambler 138       2
SPRAYS
     Frail as the leaves that quiver on the sprays,  . . . . O 138 Tr Rambler 161       1
SPREAD
     And spread his flaming palace on the ground,  . . . .   O  19 London             195
     O'er Bodley's dome his future labours spread,  . . . .  O  37 Vanity Wishes      139
     And spread its smoking ruins o'er the field.  . . . .   O  74 Tr. Iliad Bk 6      14
     Swiftly he sees the imagin'd laurels spread,  . . . .   O  82 Young Author        21
     The Lilies o'er the Vales triumphant spread;  . . . .   O 111 To Posterity        18
     Spread out by me, the roving coin,  . . . . . .        O 120 To Miss Purse         7
     Spread for their prey, the roving coin  . . . . . .    O 120 To Miss Purse     V  7
     Let Caesar spread his conquests far,  . . . . . .      O 137 Tr Rambler 143        1
     They prune the Wing, and spread the glossy Plumes,  .   O 277 Irene                36
     They prune the wing and spread the glossy tail  . . .  O 355 Irene             V 23
     Security shall spread her Shield before thee,  . . . .  O 279 Irene                82
     Pleasure shall spread her downy Pinions o'er thee  . .  O 350 Irene             V 21
     Spread by Degrees, and dread th' oppressing Stream;  .  O 282 Irene                58
     To spread Civility through Russian snows .  . . . . .   O 348 Irene             V 21
     To spread Civility through Russia's Forests  . . . .    O 348 Irene             V 21
     That spread their Colours to the genial Beam,  . . . .  O 298 Irene                20
     Spread wide their kind Arms to Science and to Beauty. . O 353 Irene             V  5
     And spread the general Transport through Mankind.  . .  O 308 Irene                 5
     Will spread resistless Light upon my Soul.  . . . . .   O 321 Irene                47
     And spread their Flames resistless o'er the World?  . . O 325 Irene                13
     And spread their echoing grief from shore to shore.  .  Y   6 Virgil Daphnis      12
     Ye swains! bestrow the ground with leaves and spread .  Y   7 Virgil Daphnis      26
SPREADING
     Till rude resistance lops the spreading god;  . . . .   O  42 Vanity Wishes      234
     Beneath some spreading Ilex Shade  . . . . . . .       O  72 Hor. Epode II        29
SPREADS
     Spreads from the strong contagion of the gown;  . . .  O  36 Vanity Wishes    V 138
     Peace courts his hand, but spreads her charms in vain;. O  40 Vanity Wishes      201
     Short sway! fair Austria spreads her mournful charms,.  O  42 Vanity Wishes      245
     Short sway! for Austria spreads her mournful charms, .  Y 103 Vanity Wishes    V 245
     Spreads wide the hope of plunder and of praise;  . . .  O  43 Vanity Wishes      248
     Or where the fam'd Hydaspes spreads  . . . . . . .     O  65 Hor I Ode xxii        7
     Or where the fam'd Hydaspes spreads  . . . . . . .     O  66 To A. Fuscus         7
     The pamphlet spreads, incessant hisses rise,  . . . .  O  82 Young Author        25
     Th' unhappy lovers graves the Myrtle spreads;  . . . . O  95 Sprig of Myrtl      10
     Still wider spreads thy horrid reign,  . . . . . .     O 123 Winter's Walk        7
     Spreads wide the mighty Moral for Mankind.  . . . . .   O 246 Irene Prologue       8
     Spreads wide the mighty Moral of Mankind.  . . . . .    O 246 Irene Prologue    V  8
     No Snares to captivate the Judgment spreads;  . . . .   O 246 Irene Prologue      27
     Why should they fear?--That Power that kindly spreads . O 250 Irene                31
     It spreads the wide plain an unregarded ruin.  . . . .  Y 131 Irene             V 36C
     For you fair Asia spreads her wealthy plains.  . . . .  Y 132 Irene             V 41C
     Spreads her mild Radiance, and descending Dews  . . .   O 313 Irene                 2
SPRIG
     On a Lady's presenting a Sprig of Myrtle  . . . . . .   O  95 Sprig of Myrtl       T
     On the Author's receiving a Sprig of Myrtle  . . . . .  O  95 Sprig of Myrtl    V  T
        to whom a Lady had given a Sprig of Myrtle  . . . .  O  95 Sprig of Myrtl    V  T
     Soon shall this sprig, as you shall fix its doom,  . .  O  95 Sprig of Myrtl    V 13
SPRIGHTLY
     Could Stella, sprightly, fair and young,  . . . . . .   O 121 To Miss Playin      21
```

315

```
SPRIGHTLY     (CONTINUED)                              PAGE   TITLE            LINE
    Wou'd Stella, sprightly, fair and young,  . . . . . .  O 121  To Miss Playin   V 21
    Nor sprightly Folly wantons in his Air,   . . . . . .  O 255  Irene               15
    Or sprightly Hope exalt their kindling Spirits?  . . . O 270  Irene               23
SPRING
    Lest ropes be wanting in the tempting spring,  . . . . O  22  London             246
    And ropes be wanting in the tempting spring,   . . . . Y  60  London           V 246
    Yet Vane could tell what ills from beauty spring;  . . O  45  Vanity Wishes      321
    From th' envious world with scorn I spring,  . . . . . O  70  Hor.II Ode XX        3
    Rashness! thou spring from whence misfortunes flow!  . O  77  Festina Lente        9
    In scenes of imitated Spring,   . . . . . . .  O 120  To Miss Playin       2
    Instruction with her flow'rs might spring,   . . . . . O 121  To Miss Playin      23
    Spring. An Ode.   . . . . . . . . . . .  O 124  An Ode           V  T
    Stern winter now, by spring repress'd,   . . . . . . . O 124  An Ode               1
    From thee, great God, we spring, to thee we tend,  . . O 130  Tr. Rambler 7        7
    From one sublime Beginning spring;   . . . . . . . .  O 146  Tr Boeth III.6       2
    Shall spring to seize thee like an ambush'd foe.  . .  O 152  The Ant             16
    Rough Winter's blasts to Spring give way,   . . . . .  O 231  Tr Horace IV.7       9
    Spring yield<s> to Summer<'s> sovereign ray,  . . . .  O 231  Tr Horace IV.7      10
    Here ev'ry Fragrance breathe of ev'ry Spring:  . . . . O 279  Irene               87
    In the bright Colours of primaeval Spring;   . . . . . O 314  Irene                5
    Hail beautious earnest of approaching spring!  . . . . Y   3  On a Daffodill       2
    The banefull weeds spring up, and choak the grain.  .  Y   7  Virgil Daphnis      23
    These when o'er winter's sway, prevail'd the spring  . Y  24  Tr Add. Battle      72
SPRINGS
    With secret springs oft ensnares   . . . . . . . .  O  72  Hor. Epode II       43
    "Or from wine as courage springs,   . . . . . . . .  O 186  Anacreon Ode 9      37
    In his fell claws, then into th' air he springs.  . .  Y  26  Tr Add. Battle     126
    Revolving springs their frost repay.  . . . . . . .  Y  39  Lady Leaving        10
SPRITELY
    The spritely Nymph and naked Grace   . . . . . . . .  O 231  Tr Horace IV.7       5
SPRUNG
    But whence this new sprung Hope?  . . . . . . . .  O 253  Irene              111
SPURN
    Existence saw him spurn her bounded Reign,   . . . . . O  51  Pro Drury-Lane       5
    May I lie slain, and spurn the bloody sand!  . . . . . O  75  Tr. Iliad Bk 6      30
SPURN'D
    Spurn'd as a beggar, dreaded as a spy,   . . . . . . . O  14  London              81
    Spurn'd as a begger, dreaded as a spy,   . . . . . . . O  14  London           V  81
SPY
    Spurn'd as a beggar, dreaded as a spy,   . . . . . . . O  14  London              81
    Spurn'd as a begger, dreaded as a spy,   . . . . . . . O  14  London           V  81
SQUADRONS
    And saw my scatter'd Squadrons fly before him.  . . .  O 307  Irene               20
    Feather'd battalions, squadrons on the wing  . . . . . Y  22  Tr Add. Battle       1
    Above their heads th' embattled squadrons hung  . . .  Y  25  Tr Add. Battle      94
SQUANDER'D
    Which squander'd by Neglect, or Fear, or Folly,  . . . O 302  Irene                7
SQUEAL'D
    But still the child squeal'd on.   . . . . . . . .  O 157  Par. Hermit I        4
    But yet the child squeal'd on.  . . . . . . . .  O 157  Par. Hermit I    V   4
SQUEALING
    The nurse took up the squealing child,   . . . . . . . O 157  Par. Hermit I        3
ST
    Give to St. David one true Briton more.  . . . . . .  O   9  London               8
    Upon the feast of St Simon & St Jude   . . . . . . .  O  78  Feast St Simon       T
    Upon the feast of St Simon & St Jude   . . . . . . .  O  78  Feast St Simon       T
    St. Omer   . . . . . . . . . . . . .  O 172  French Distich       3
STABS
    Provckes a broil, and stabs you for a jest.  . . . . . O  21  London             229
STAFF
    While yet my steady steps no staff sustains,   . . . . O  10  London              41
    While yet my steddy steps no staff sustains,   . . . . O  10  London           V  41
STAGE
    With warbling eunuchs fill a licens'd stage,   . . . . O  12  London              59
    With warbling eunuchs fill our silenc'd stage,  . . .  O  12  London           V  59
    Hiss'd from the stage, or hooted from the court,  . .  O  15  London             109
    Admires their wond'rous talents for the stage:  . . .  O  16  London             133
    On ev'ry stage the foes of peace attend,   . . . . .  O  33  Vanity Wishes       77
    Superfluous lags the vet'ran on the stage,   . . . . . O  45  Vanity Wishes      308
    And chearless treads the desolated stage,   . . . . .  Y 106  Vanity Wishes    V 308
    And lags superfluous on th' incumbred stage,  . . . .  Y 106  Vanity Wishes    V 308
    First rear'd the Stage, immortal Shakespear rose;  . . O  51  Pro Drury-Lane       2
    Yet still did Virtue deign the Stage to tread,  . . .  O  52  Pro Drury-Lane      33
    And mark the future Periods of the Stage?--  . . . . . O  53  Pro Drury-Lane      40
    The Stage but echoes back the publick Voice.  . . . .  O  53  Pro Drury-Lane      52
    And Truth diffuse her Radiance from the Stage.  . . .  O  53  Pro Drury-Lane      62
    Or right, or wrong, once hooted from the stage;  . . . O  61  Pro Word Wise        2
    Yet dares to venture on the dangerous stage,   . . . . Y  67  Prologue Lethe      11
STAGNANT
    Must dull Suspence corrupt the stagnant mind?  . . . . O  47  Vanity Wishes      344
    Must dull Suspence becalm still the stagnant mind?  .  Y 107  Vanity Wishes    V 344
    That gloomy Slumber of the stagnant Soul;   . . . . .  O 292  Irene               82
    stagnant soul. The gloom of idleness.  . . . . . .  Y 165  Irene            V  82
STAIN
    And stain with blood the Danube or the Rhine;  . . . . O  39  Vanity Wishes      182
    Their Treason throws no Stain upon Irene.   . . . . .  O 324  Irene               18
    To Blood, too mean to stain a Soldier's Sabre.  . . .  O 324  Irene               24
STAIN'D
    No savage more portentous stain'd   . . . . . . . .  O  66  Hor I Ode xxii      13
    No beast more dreadful ever stain'd  . . . . . . .  O  66  Hor I Ode xxii   V  13
```

```
STAIN'D          (CONTINUED)                           PAGE    TITLE           LINE
   No Beast more dreadful ever stain'd  . . . . . . .  O  67  To A. Fuscus        13
   When floods of Nectar stain'd the main, . . . . .  O  71  Hor. Epode II        4
   And stain'd with blood Pelides' vengefull steel. .  Y  18  Tr. Iliad Bk 6     37
STAKE
   And try the Hazard that hast Nought to stake; . . .  O 319  Irene             31
STALK
   And teror and confusion stalk before them  . . . .  Y 115  Irene         V 49E
STALK'D
   And Death exulting stalk'd along the land. . . . .  Y  23  Tr Add. Battle     53
STAMP
   Ambition is the Stamp impress'd by Heav'n  . . . .  O 293  Irene             111
STAND
   In full-blown dignity, see Wolsey stand, . . . . .  O  34  Vanity Wishes      99
   In full blown pow'r see mighty Wolsey stand,  . . .  Y  96  Vanity Wishes  V  99
   In full blown state, see Wolsey stand,  . . . . . .  Y  96  Vanity Wishes  V  99
   Around in beauteous order stand.  . . . . . . . . .  O  73  Hor. Epode II      72
   I stand amaz'd, and ask, if yet I clasp thee.  . .  O 296  Irene             37
   No wit nor honesty could stand . . . . . . . . . .  Y  11  Tr Hor Epode 9     21
   And joy and sorrow stand by turns confest. . . . .  Y  21  Tr. Iliad Bk 6    110
   The steely troops embodied closely stand  . . . . .  Y  24  Tr Add. Battle     78
STANDARD
   The ravish'd standard, and the captive foe, . . . .  O  39  Vanity Wishes     176
   To fix your Standard in Imperial Rome.  . . . . . .  O 309  Irene             31
STANDARDS
   "On Moscow's walls till Gothic standards fly, . . .  O  40  Vanity Wishes     203
STANDING
   Or English honour grew a standing jest. . . . . . .  O  10  London            30
STANDS
   On what foundation stands the warrior's pride, . .  O  40  Vanity Wishes     191
   On what foundation stands the warrior's fame?  . .  Y 101  Vanity Wishes  V 191
   Aspasia stands--  . . . . . . . . . . . . . . . . .  O 314  Irene             11
STAR
   Accus'd the Gods and curs'd each luckless star.  .  Y   6  Virgil Daphnis      6
   Beneath his feet admires each shining star, . . . .  Y   7  Virgil Daphnis     34
STARE
   Till she made the neighbours stare.  . . . . . . .  Y 300  Extemp. Elegy       8
STARR'D
   She's starr'd with pimples o'er, . . . . . . . . .  O 127  To Lyce, Lady      14
STARRY
   Refulgent on his starry throne  . . . . . . . . . .  O  79  Feast St Simon     23
   Ye nymphs whom starry rays invest,  . . . . . . . .  O 126  To Lyce, Lady       1
   To Guide thy passage shall th' Starry Spirits . . .  O 364  Irene          V  26
   Fill all the starry Lamps with double Blaze; . . .  O 322  Irene              8
   Fill all the Starry Lamps with Fav'ring Sky  . . .  O 364  Irene          V  27
      <Radiance>.
STARS
   And wearied angels rest upon their stars spheres .  Y 128  Irene          V  4B
   Thou long'st for Stars that frown on human Kind, .  O 271  Irene              4
   This Night with all her conscious Stars be witness,  O 284  Irene             44
START
   Who start at theft, and blush at perjury?  . . . .  O  13  London            68
   Aghast you start, and scarce with aking sight . . .  O  18  London           186
   Surpriz'd I start, and bless the happy Dream; . . .  O 254  Irene            124
   Start at the Light, and tremble in the Dark;  . . .  O 266  Irene             30
   Perhaps may start at violated Friendship. . . . . .  O 300  Irene             81
STARTED
   We started at the Sound, again enquir'd, . . . . .  O 325  Irene             25
STARTING
   --Scarce repress'd the starting tear;--  . . . . .  O 181  Parody Warton      6
   Absorb'd in Thought; then starting from his Trance,  O 311  Irene              6
STARTS
   The child starts back affrighted at the blaze . . .  Y  20  Tr. Iliad Bk 6    92
STARVES
   And starves exhausted regions in his way; . . . . .  O  42  Vanity Wishes     228
STARVING
   For where can starving merit find a home?  . . . .  O  18  London            191
STATE
   Sucks in the dregs of each corrupted state.  . . .  O  14  London            96
   Or seen a new-made mayor's unwieldy state; . . . .  O  33  Vanity Wishes      58
   Or seen the new-made mayor's unwieldy state;  . . .  Y  94  Vanity Wishes  V  58
   Search every state, and canvass ev'ry pray'r. . . .  O  33  Vanity Wishes      72
   In full blown state, see Wolsey stand, . . . . . .  Y  96  Vanity Wishes  V  99
   To him the church, the state, their pow're resign,  Y  96  Vanity Wishes  V 101
   At length his sov'reign frowns--the train of state  O  34  Vanity Wishes     109
   At once is lost the pride of aweful state,  . . . .  O  35  Vanity Wishes     113
   Now drops at once the pride of aweful state, . . .  O  35  Vanity Wishes  V 113
   In sober state th' imaginary lawn  . . . . . . . .  Y  98  Vanity Wishes  V138B
   The march begins in military state,  . . . . . . .  O  40  Vanity Wishes     205
   Hides from himself his state, and shuns to know, .  O  43  Vanity Wishes     257
   To you alone this happy state remains.  . . . . . .  O  64  Virgil Past.I      16
   Thus fell the Pygmie state, which long had stood .  O  76  Tr Add. Battle     33
   Preserv'd the reliques of the Latian state . . . .  O  78  Festina Lente      18
   And rais'd us from our wretched state, . . . . . .  O  79  Feast St Simon     20
   Thrice ten long years he labour'd for the State; .  O 118  Epitaph Hanmer     14
   When mutual frauds perplex'd the maze of State, . .  O 118  Epitaph Hanmer     24
   Each grace of form, each ornament of state, . . . .  O 141  Tr Rambler 199      7
   Can he restore the State he could not save?  . . .  O 253  Irene            116
   Embroil'd the Turkish State--our Sultan's Father .  O 256  Irene             42
   Flows through each Member of th' embodied State, .  O 256  Irene             58
   No feeble Tyrant of a petty State  . . . . . . . .  O 268  Irene             21

                              317
```

```
STATE          (CONTINUED)                          PAGE    TITLE              LINE
     To paint the Pageantries of guilty State?    . . . . .   O 276 Irene              12
     To State and Pow'r I court thee, not to Ruin:  . . . .   O 279 Irene              80
     I discover by this state & retinue            . . . . .  Y 160 Irene          V   8
     Shake off th' Incumbrances of State a moment,   . . . .  O 289 Irene               7
     Nor left us aught but Flattery and State.      . . . . . O 291 Irene              73
     Shrinks at th' o'erpow'ring Gleams of regal State,  . . O 292 Irene             100
     Shrinks at th' oerpowring blaze of regal State  . . . . O 368 Irene          V  30
     In easy State presides o'er all their Motions,  . . . . O 293 Irene             122
     With gloomy State and agonizing Pomp. . . . . . . .      O 294 Irene             135
     <Ho>w blest our state could every bosom     . . . . .   Y 184 Irene          V  16
     Her lofty mien, and insolence of virtue--my  . . . . .  Y 191 Irene          V  14
         state
     Securely flourish'd the Pygmiean state,      . . . . . .  Y  23 Tr Add. Battle      27
STATES
     Or states mens now, with safer pride content,  . . . .  Y  97 Vanity Wishes   V 123
     And mortgag'd states their grandsires wreaths regret,  . O  39 Vanity Wishes     187
     And mortgag'd states their former wreaths regret,  . . . Y 100 Vanity Wishes   V 187
     And all the Maladies of sinking States.     . . . . . .  O 250 Irene              39
STATESMAN
     Distrest alike, the statesman and the wit,   . . . . . . O  59 Pro Good Nat'd       9
     For us the Statesman labours, Hero fights,   . . . . . . O 247 Irene Epilogue      21
STATESMAN'S
     A Statesman's logick unconvinc'd can hear,   . . . . . . O  13 London              71
     Few know the toiling statesman's fear or care,  . . . .  O  32 Vanity Wishes      47
     Love ends with hope, the sinking statesman's door  . . . O  33 Vanity Wishes      79
     Observe him closely with a Statesman's Eye,  . . . . . . O 255 Irene              10
     Struck with the Wonder of a Statesman's Goodness,  . . . O 274 Irene              45
     Ambitious Cali dreads the Statesman's Arts,  . . . . . . O 300 Irene              74
     Some i'll designing Statesman's base Intrigue!  . . . .  O 326 Irene              36
STATION
     A private Station may discover more;       . . . . . . . O 316 Irene              18
STATUE
     Her statue would have breath'd an added grace,  . . . .  O 189 Seeing Montagu       4
     Deform the beauties of the breathing statue (marble hero Y 177 Irene           V111A
STATUTES
     When statutes glean the refuse of the sword,   . . . .   O  31 Vanity Wishes      31
STAY
     If Genius warm thee, Reader, stay,  . . . . . . . .      O 154 Epita. Hogarth       5
     Comets! come every day--and stay a year.    . . . . . .  O 177 Tr Dist Modena       2
     Leontius stay.      . . . . . . . . . . . .             O 256 Irene              38
     Why did you stay? deserted and betray'd?    . . . . . .  O 317 Irene              34
     While I protract their Stay.  Be swift and faithful.  .  O 319 Irene               4
     Stay--in this dubious Twilight of Conviction,  . . . .   O 321 Irene              43
     Stay but a Moment, and prevailing Truth     . . . . . .  O 321 Irene              46
     Fair Falshood stay.    . . . . . . . . . . .           O 323 Irene               1
     The stormy Sultan rages at our stay.    . . . . . . .    O 329 Irene              12
     Hope not thy threats shall stay   . . . . . . . . .      Y 210 Irene          V  25
     Hector, this heard without a moment's stay,  . . . . .   Y  17 Tr. Iliad Bk 6       1
STEADFAST  SEE STEDFAST
     Strict, on the right he fix'd his steadfast eye,  . . .  O 118 Epitaph Hanmer      29
STEADINESS
     I want alass thy steadiness of Soul    . . . . . . .     O 366 Irene          V  29
STEADY   SEE STEDDY
     While yet my steady steps no staff sustains,  . . . .    O  10 London             41
     Held high the steady scale, but deep'd the sword;  . . . O  22 London            251
     Held high the steady scale, but sheath'd the sword;  . . O  22 London          V 251
     Held high the steady scale, but dropp'd the sword;  . .  O  22 London          V 251
     For such the steady Romans shook the world;  . . . . .   O  39 Vanity Wishes     180
     For these these steady Romans shook the world;  . . . .  Y 100 Vanity Wishes   V 180
     Your passions; guide the reins with steady hand,  . . .  O  77 Festina Lente       4
STEAL
     All that at home no more can beg or steal,   . . . . .   O  15 London            107
     And varied Life steal unperceiv'd away.    . . . . . .   O 279 Irene              91
     Steal unperceiv'd upon her Meditations--   . . . . . .   O 314 Irene              13
     Steal from Abdalla's Eye the Sign to smile.  . . . . .   O 318 Irene               5
     And steal thy Life away. Death's horrid Angel  . . . .   O 327 Irene               9
     And steal your life away.  Death's horrid Angel  . . .   O 368 Irene          V  17
STEALS
     And steals to death from anguish and from shame.  . . .  O  43 Vanity Wishes     254
     Irene steals unheeded from his Tongue,     . . . . . .   O 261 Irene               5
     And softer passion steals upon my Bosom    . . . . . .   O 367 Irene          V  14
STEDDY
     While yet my steddy steps no staff sustains,  . . . .    O  10 London          V  41
STEDFAST
     Wouldst thou to some stedfast Seat,    . . . . . . .     O 144 Tr Boeth. II.4       1
STEEL
     Beneath Pygmean steel what numbers dye!    . . . . . .   O  75 Tr Add. Battle       5
     And Persia felt the force of Grecian steel;  . . . . .   O  76 Tr Add. Battle      38
     None dares with impious steel the grove to rend,  . . .  O 139 Tr Rambler 168       1
     Amidst the Tortures of the burning Steel,    . . . . .   O 272 Irene              15
     And stain'd with blood Pelides' vengefull steel.  . . .  Y  18 Tr. Iliad Bk 6      37
     The wound, and, furious, wave the shining steel.  . . .  Y  26 Tr Add. Battle     133
STEEL'D
     And gainst the pow'r of Venus steel'd my mind.  . . . .  Y  11 Tr Hor Epode 9      30
STEELY
     The steely troops embodied closely stand   . . . . . .   Y  24 Tr Add. Battle      78
STEEP
     Nor down steep cliffs precipitately move   . . . . . .   O  77 Festina Lente       5
     Down the steep hill the roaring torrent pours;  . . . .  O 132 Tr. Rambler 65       2
```

			PAGE	TITLE	LINE
STEEPS					
For why did Wolsey near the steeps of fate,	. . . . .		O 35	Vanity Wishes	125
STEER					
With cautious Secrecy, Leontius steer	. . . . . .		O 284	Irene	50
STELLA					
Bright Stella, form'd for universal Reign,	. . . .		O 96	Hickman Spinet	1
To Stella	. . . .		O 119	To Miss Purse	V T
Why, Stella, was it then decreed,	. . . .		O 120	To Miss Purse	V 11
When Stella strikes the tuneful string	. . . . .		O 120	To Miss Playin	1
Could Stella, sprightly, fair and young,	. . . .		O 121	To Miss Playin	21
Wou'd Stella, sprightly, fair and young,	. . . .		O 121	To Miss Playin	V 21
Stella in Mourning	. . . .		O 122	Stella Mourn.	T
Since Stella still extends her reign,	. . . . . .		O 122	Stella Mourn.	11
The skies, that Stella mourn no more.	. . . . . .		O 122	Stella Mourn.	16
Snatch me, my Stella, to thy arms,	. . . . . .		O 124	Winter's Walk	19
STELLA'S					
Had Stella's gentle touches mov'd the Lyre,	. . . .		O 97	Hickman Spinet	15
And found a Thousand Worlds in Stella's Arms.	. . .		O 97	Hickman Spinet	20
When, lately, Stella's form display'd	. . . . . .		O 122	Stella Mourn.	1
STEM'D					
Stem'd in the Breach the Deluge of Destruction,	. . .		O 295	Irene	28
STEMM'D					
All stemm'd in one sad day the Stygian tyde.	. . . .		Y 18	Tr. Iliad Bk 6	35
STEPS					
While yet my steady steps no staff sustains,	. . . .		O 10	London	41
While yet my steddy steps no staff sustains,	. . . .		O 10	London	V 41
For why did Wolsey by the Steps of fate,	. . . . .		O 35	Vanity Wishes	V 125
Observe your steps; be carefull to command	. . . . .		O 77	Festina Lente	3
The Steps their Saviour trod;	. . . .		O 79	Feast St Simon	15
And turn'd their hasty Steps towards the Garden.	. .		O 269	Irene	39
Guides through the Maze of Life the Steps of Man	. . .		O 346	Irene	V 6
Yet let me watch her dear departing Steps,	. . . . .		O 297	Irene	17
Guide all thy Steps, calm ev'ry stormy Thought,	. . . .		O 303	Irene	21
Close, as we might unseen, we watch'd his Steps;	. . .		O 311	Irene	2
Mock'd our impatient steps, for all was fairy ground.	.		Y 310	Parody of Pope	4
STERN					
Stern Famine guards the solitary coast,	. . . . .		O 41	Vanity Wishes	207
Stern winter, is thy force confest,	. . . . . .		O 123	Winter's Walk	6
Stern winter, in thy force confest,	. . . . . .		O 123	Winter's Walk	V 6
Stern winter now, by spring repress'd,	. . . . . .		O 124	An Ode	1
Till at length stern Pluto cried,	. . . .		O 149	Tr Boet III.12	39
No stern command, no monitory voice	. . . . . .		O 151	The Ant	3
Stern Torture shakes his bloody Scourge before me,	. .		O 266	Irene	15
And stern Composure of despairing Heroes;	. . . . .		O 275	Irene	83
Of stern Sebalias the triumphant Crescent,	. . . .		O 312	Irene	11
Of aspect stern for in his face he wears	. . . . .		Y 24	Tr Add. Battle	82
STILL					
Yet still my calmer thoughts his choice commend,	. . .		O 8	London	3
And life still vig'rous revels in my veins;	. . . . .		O 10	London	42
Still to his int'rest true, where'er he goes,	. . . .		O 16	London	125
Still foe to vice, forsake his Cambrian shade;	. . .		O 23	London	261
Still foe to vice, exert his Cambrian shade;	. . . .		Y 61	London	V 262
Yet still one gen'ral cry the skies assails,	. . . .		O 32	Vanity Wishes	45
Yet still the gen'ral cry the skies assails,	. . . .		O 32	Vanity Wishes	V 45
Still to new heights his restless wishes tow'r,	. . .		O 34	Vanity Wishes	105
New pow'rs are claim'd, new pow'rs are still bestow'd,	.		O 42	Vanity Wishes	233
The still returning tale, and ling'ring jest,	. . .		O 44	Vanity Wishes	275
Still rise the long tale, and ling'ring jest,	. . . .		Y 104	Vanity Wishes	V 275
The watchful guests still hint the last offence,	. .		O 44	Vanity Wishes	279
The treachrous guests still hint the last offence,	. .		Y 104	Vanity Wishes	V 279
But unextinguish'd Avarice still remains,	. . . . .		O 44	Vanity Wishes	285
Still drops some joy from with'ring life away;	. . .		O 45	Vanity Wishes	306
Must dull Suspence becalm still the stagnant mind?	. .		Y 107	Vanity Wishes	V 344
Still raise for good the supplicating voice,	. . . .		O 47	Vanity Wishes	351
Yet still did Virtue deign the Stage to tread,	. . . .		O 52	Pro Drury-Lane	33
But still desires of sordid gain	. . . .		O 73	Hor. Epode II	77
With breasts resolv'd, they follow'd still	. . . . .		O 79	Feast St Simon	16
Unfaded still their former charms they shew,	. . . .		O 84	Epi Dist Moth.	26
Still fierce to threaten, still afraid to fight;	. . .		O 110	To Posterity	10
Still fierce to threaten, still afraid to fight;	. . .		O 110	To Posterity	10
Augustus still survives in Maro's strain,	. . . . .		O 114	On C. Cibber	1
Delighted still to please mankind, or mend,	. . . .		O 118	Epitaph Hanmer	39
Consistent still, though not the same,	. . . . .		O 121	To Miss Playin	34
Since Stella still extends her reign,	. . . . . .		O 122	Stella Mourn.	11
Still wider spreads thy horrid reign,	. . . . . .		O 123	Winter's Walk	7
Still changing with the changeful year,	. . . . .		O 124	Winter's Walk	15
Unblest, still doom'd to wed with misery.	. . . .		O 131	Tr. Rambler 39	1
Delusive hope still points to distant good,	. . . . .		O 133	Tr. Rambler 67	2
Wealth still finds followers, and misfortunes foes.	. .		O 138	Tr Rambler 153	2
Still discord hovers o'er divided thrones.	. . . .		O 140	Tr Rambler 183	2
For still where wishes most abound	. . . . . .		O 144	Tr Boeth. II.2	11
Must bid each wild Desire be still,	. . . . . .		O 146	Tr Boeth III.5	3
Tho' reluctant still refrain,	. . . .		O 150	Tr Boet III.12	45
But still the child squeal'd on.	. . . .		O 157	Par. Hermit I	4
He who still expects deceit,	. . . .		O 176	Tr Metastasi I	5
Yet still he fills affection's eye,	. . . .		O 201	Death Dr Levet	9
Still odious to the Monarch, or the People.	. . . .		O 256	Irene	52
But Greece is still forgot.	. . . .		O 257	Irene	74
His Offers oft repeated, still refus'd,	. . . . .		O 259	Irene	109
Still restless, till I clasp the lovely Maid,	. . . .		O 263	Irene	21

319

```
STILL        (CONTINUED)                              PAGE    TITLE         LINE
        Still full of Amurath!  . . . . . . . . . .  O 264  Irene             20
    Still at Aspasia's Voice a sudden Rapture  . . . O 265  Irene              4
    How blest art thou, still jocund and serene,  .  O 271  Irene              6
    My Heart still beats responsive to the Sultan's;  O 272  Irene             9
    Still fond of Life, groan'd out the dreadful Secret,  O 272  Irene        16
    Still fond of Life reveal'd the dreadfull secret,  .  O 356  Irene     V  33
    Still must we linger in uncertain Hope?  . . .   O 282  Irene              3
    Still languish in our Chains, and dream of Freedom,  . .  O 282  Irene     4
    Born down with Years, still doat upon To-morrow?  . . .  O 283  Irene     20
    Marks for His own still doat upon to Morrow  . . .  O 374  Irene      V  21
    The weary Soldier--Still sees to Morrow  . . .   O 374  Irene          V  30
    Still sees To-morrow drest in Robes of Triumph;  O 283  Irene             29
    Still to the Lover's long-expecting Arms,  . . . O 283  Irene             30
    Still courting his embrace and still eluding  .  Y 155  Irene         V  35
    Still courting his embrace and still eluding  .  Y 155  Irene         V  35
    We still had wander'd on Tartarian Hills.  . . . O 284  Irene             41
    She sighs, she blushes, but she still denies.  . O 287  Irene              8
    Yet should my Soul, still faithful to her Choice,  .  O 289  Irene        13
    Still stretch in vain their longing Arms afar;  . O 292  Irene            91
    Still, still the same--unclouded by Misfortune!  O 294  Irene              3
    Still, still the same--unclouded by Misfortune!  O 294  Irene              3
    Forbear this Triumph--still new Conflicts wait us,  . .  O 298  Irene     25
    But still yet my Soul detests the Bassas  . . .  O 353  Irene          V  22
        treason
    Still, still Distrust sits heavy on my Heart.  . O 301  Irene             95
    Still, still Distrust sits heavy on my Heart.  . O 301  Irene             95
    And still thy Bosom with the Voice of Peace.  .  O 303  Irene             22
    Suspected still?--What Villain's pois'nous Tongue  O 304  Irene           12
    Must Greece, still wretched by her Children's Folly,  . .  O 305  Irene   43
    To still their Murmurs, ere the twentieth Sun  . O 309  Irene             23
    Still Cali lives, and must he live To-morrow?  . O 310  Irene              1
    Whome'er the Hope, still blasted, still renew'd,  O 310  Irene             1
    Whome'er the Hope, still blasted, still renew'd,  O 310  Irene             1
    I love her still, but shall esteem Aspasia:  . . Y 186  Irene          V   5
    Still dost thou flutter in the Jaws of Death?  . O 318  Irene             17
    Still dost thou linger in these fatal bowrs  . . Y 196  Irene         V 18A
    Still labours with imaginary Woe;  . . . . . .   O 320  Irene             22
    Thy sacred Freight shall still the raging Main.  O 322  Irene              6
    The sacred Freight shall still the raging Main.  O 322  Irene          V   6
    The Sultan comes, still gloomy, still enrag'd.   O 330  Irene             26
    The Sultan comes, still gloomy, still enrag'd.   Y 330  Irene             26
    And wish'd--Be still thy Fate to wish in vain.   O 334  Irene             60
    I then (my cheeks still glow with shame) was grown  Y  11  Tr Hor Epode 9  11
    With rage implacable he still persue'd  . . . .  Y  24  Tr Add. Battle    84
STILLNESS
    Like the dread Stillness of condensing Storms. . O 270  Irene             14
STINGING
    Safe from the keen lampoon and stinging jest;  . O  82  Young Author      28
    Safe from the tart lampoon and stinging jest;  . O  82  Young Author   V  28
    Endur'd the stinging lash, and tamely bore the yoke. . .  Y   6  Virgil Daphnis  14
STINGS
    Grief aids disease, remember'd folly stings,  .  O  35  Vanity Wishes    119
STOCK
    Ladies--stock and tend your Hive,  . . . . . .   O 178  Thrale 35 Year    11
STOLE
    I stole unheeded from their ravish'd Eyes,  . .  O 299  Irene             49
    And stole his Life and Mistress from his Sabre?  O 318  Irene             14
STONE
    Whene'er this Stone, now hid beneath the Lake,   O 110  To Posterity       1
    But search the wonders of the dusky stone,  . .  O 141  Tr Rambler 199     5
    Fell down upon the stone;  . . . . . . . . . .   O 157  Par. Hermit I      2
    Fell down upon a stone;  . . . . . . . . . . .   O 157  Par. Hermit I  V   2
    And be the stone with this inscription grac'd:   Y   7  Virgil Daphnis    29
    And pour them on the consecrated stone;  . . .   Y   7  Virgil Daphnis    46
STONES
    To rust on medals, or on stones decay,  . . . .  O  40  Vanity Wishes    190
    Their blood the consecrated stones shall dye:  . O  64  Virgil Past.I     10
STOOD
    On Thames's banks, in silent thought we stood,   O  10  London            21
    Not long they stood, when stooping from their height . .  O  75  Tr Add. Battle   2
    Thus fell the Pygmie state, which long had stood  O  76  Tr Add. Battle   33
    Where the Lyoness stood near,  . . . . . . . .   O 148  Tr Boet III.12     8
    Tantalus astonish'd stood  . . . . . . . . . .   O 149  Tr Boet III.12    37
    And led me to the Shore where Cali stood,  . .   O 254  Irene            127
    In private Conference; beside him stood  . . .   O 275  Irene             79
    Stood torpid in Suspence; but soon Abdalla  . .  O 317  Irene             37
    Soon forth in arms had some bold soldier stood,  Y  23  Tr Add. Battle    40
    Fiercely contending two vast armies stood  . .   Y  23  Tr Add. Battle    56
STOOP
    Stoop from thy Flight, trace back th' entangled Thought,  O 293  Irene   127
    Perhaps I will not stoop to plead my Cause;  . . O 330  Irene             22
STOOPING
    Not long they stood, when stooping from their height . .  O  75  Tr Add. Battle   2
STOOPS
    Stoops from the Blaze like a degenerate Eagle,   O 292  Irene            101
    Stoops at the Blaze like a degenerate Eagle  .   O 368  Irene         V  31
STOP
    Here stop, my soul, thy rapid flight,  . . . .   O 125  An Ode            17
    Life to stop at Thirtyfive,  . . . . . . . . .   O 178  Thrale 35 Year     6
    <t>o stop this raging torrent of destruction . . . . .   Y 117  Irene      V109C
```

```
STOP          (CONTINUED)                              PAGE    TITLE           LINE
     Nor think to say here will I stop  . . . . . . . .    Y 168 Irene          V 132
     He stop unmindfull of observing crowds  . . . . .    Y 187 Irene          V   5
     Dispatch his Guards to stop the flying Traytors,  . . .  O 319 Irene          3
STOP'D
     And stop'd unwilling at her door.  . . . . . .        Y  11 Tr Hor Epode 9     34
STOPP'D
     And stopp'd the heav'nly Voice that call'd on me.  . . . .  O 334 Irene          71
STOPS
     Impeachment stops the speaker's pow'rful breath,  . . .   O  31 Vanity Wishes    19
     Now say, where virtue stops and vice begins?  . . .      O 139 Tr Rambler 173     1
     Sudden he stops, and inward turns his Eyes,  . . . . .    O 311 Irene            5
STOPT
     Silent Wonder stopt the Floods;  . . . . . . . .        O 148 Tr Boet III.12    12
STOR'D
     Why stor'd for Flight? and why prepar'd by Cali?  . . .  O 258 Irene           85
STORE
     With listless eyes the dotard views the store,  . . . .   O  43 Vanity Wishes   263
     New Behns, new Durfeys, yet remain in Store.  . . . .    O  53 Pro Drury-Lane    42
     But swallowing all the mighty Store,  . . . . .          O 144 Tr Boeth. II.2     9
     What Plagues, what Tortures, are in Store for thee,  . .  O 334 Irene            1
STORES
     She gleans the harvest, and she stores the grain.  . . .  O 151 The Ant           8
     She crops the harvest, and she stores the grain.  . . .   O 151 The Ant         V 8
     Pregnant with Stores, that India's Mines might envy,  . .  O 249 Irene           18
     Exhaust the Stores of pious Eloquence,  . . . . .        O 265 Irene            2
STORM
     Tost in one common storm with all the great;  . . . .    O  59 Pro Good Nat'd     8
     When ev'ry Storm in my Domain shall roar,  . . . . .     O 265 Irene           42
     Till ev'ry Storm in my Domain shall roar,  . . . . .     O 354 Irene          V 25
     D<r>ives to (holds o'er) the south or west the  . . . .  Y 136 Irene          V 26
          storm
     --When of late The storm of Heav'ns displeasure thundred  Y 136 Irene          V 27
     When next we meet before we storm the Palace,  . . . .   O 308 Irene           28
STORM'D
     And unresisted Passion storm'd the Breast.  . . . . .    O  51 Pro Drury-Lane     8
STORMING
     We mark'd him storming in Excess of Fury,  . . . . .     O 311 Irene           11
STORMS
     Or storms afflict the ruffled main.  . . . . . . .       O  67 Hor. II Ode IX     4
     <?storms huge> Promontories flie  . . . . . . .          O  76 Tr Add. Battle    22
     In rat'ling storms huge promontories flie  . . . . .     Y  26 Tr Add. Battle  V 140
     Amid the storms of war, with curious eyes  . . . . .     O 130 Tr. Rambler 8     1
     Like the dread Stillness of condensing Storms.  . . .    O 270 Irene           14
     Pour'd Storms of Fire upon our fierce Invaders,  . . .   O 290 Irene           48
     Pourd Storms of fire upon th' approaching Foe  . . . .   O 364 Irene          V  1
     May storms howl gently o'er and learn to spare.  . . .   Y   3 On a Daffodill    8
STORMY
     And terrours of the Stormy Main,  . . . . . . .          O  69 Hor.II Ode 14    14
     Guide all thy Steps, calm ev'ry stormy Thought,  . . .   O 303 Irene           21
     The stormy Sultan rages at our stay.  . . . . . .        O 329 Irene           12
STOUT
     There a stout warriour fainting gasps for breath  . . .  O  76 Tr Add. Battle   16
STRAIN
     Strain out with fault'ring diffidence a lye,  . . . .    O  16 London          130
     Approach, ye minstrels, try the soothing strain,  . . .  O  43 Vanity Wishes   267
     So long renown'd in B<rya>n's deathless strain?  . . .   O 107 Lady F Assizes    2
     Augustus still survives in Maro's strain,  . . . .       O 114 On C. Cibber      1
     Listning forests learnt the Strain,  . . . . . .         O 148 Tr Boet III.12  V  1
     He scorns the meek Address, the suppliant Strain,  . .   O 246 Irene Prologue   31
     Not the Maeonian Bard in lofty strain  . . . . . .       Y  23 Tr Add. Battle   54
STRAINS
     Those names which in immortal strains  . . . . . . .     O  80 Feast St Simon   59
     Such strains as, mingled with the lyre,  . . . . . .     O 188 Epilogue         1
STRAIT
     His money he collected strait,  . . . . . . . .          O  73 Hor. Epode II    75
     'Tis true, the Fellow's handsome, strait and tall;  . .  O 247 Irene Epilogue    7
STRAND
     Or change the rocks of Scotland for the Strand?  . . .   O   9 London          10
     For less than rent the dungeons of the Strand;  . . . .  O  20 London          215
     For less than hires the dungeons of the Strand;  . . .   Y  58 London        V 215
     His fall was destin'd to a barren strand,  . . . . .     O  41 Vanity Wishes   219
     And walk'd into the Strand,  . . . . . . . .             O 158 Par. Hermit II    2
     I walk'd along the Strand,  . . . . . . . .              O 158 Par. Hermit II  V  2
STRANGE
     And, yet more strange! his Veins a Horse shall drain,  .  O 111 To Posterity    25
     All is strange, yet nothing new;  . . . . . . .          O 179 Ridicul Warton    2
     Strange! that this gen'ral Fraud from Day to Day  . . .  O 283 Irene           26
     Such strange Events, such unexpected Chances,  . . . .   O 296 Irene           34
STRANGER
     While Love, a stranger to the blest,  . . . . . .        O  99 Ode Friendship    5
     A turkish Stranger of majestick Mien,  . . . . . .       O 294 Irene            1
     A Stranger to th' Oppressor's savage Joy,  . . . . .     O 329 Irene            6
STRANGER'S
     Where-e'er he turns he meets a stranger's eye,  . . . .  O  35 Vanity Wishes   111
STRANGERS
     Yet strangers in some distant world proclaim  . . . .    Y 120 Irene          V 31A
STRANGLED
     And strangled Freedom perish in the Birth.  . . . . .    O 299 Irene           53
STRATAGEM
     Propitious Hours to Stratagem and Death,  . . . . . .    O 302 Irene            3
```

```
STRATAGEM        (CONTINUED)                                      PAGE    TITLE            LINE
    What Cry? The Stratagem? Did then Abdalla?--   .   .   .   .  O 317  Irene               30
    What cry?  what stratagem?  had then Abdalla-- .   .   .   .  Y 194  Irene           V   30
    This lucky Stratagem shall charm the Sultan,   .   .   .   .  O 319  Irene                5
    Some cruel Stratagem of jealous Beauty!  .   .   .   .   .    O 326  Irene               37
STRATAGEMS
    Abdalla's Rage and Cali's Stratagems.  .   .   .   .   .   .  O 301  Irene               94
STRAY
    Then thro' thy Fields shall scarlet Reptiles stray,   .   .   O 110  To Posterity         7
STRAY'D
    Too far in Sabine woods I stray'd;  .   .   .   .   .   .   .  O  65  Hor I Ode xxii      10
    By Lalage, too far I stray'd,   .   .   .   .   .   .   .   .  O  66  To A. Fuscus        10
STREAM
    Turn'd by his nod the stream of honour flows,  .   .   .   .  O  34  Vanity Wishes      103
    When a river is drain'd by too many channels the stream is   Y 132  Irene           V  41B
        dry.
    Spread by Degrees, and dread th' oppressing Stream;   .   .   O 282  Irene               58
    And stream destructive through his freezing Veins:   .   .   O 308  Irene               31
STREAMERS
    While the breeze whispers and the streamers play.  .   .   . O  82  Young Author         6
STREAMING     SEE DULCET-STREAMING
STREAMS
    From Marlb'rough's eyes the streams of dotage flow,   .   .   O  45  Vanity Wishes      317
    With gentle Hand restrain'd the Streams of Life,  .   .   .   O 252  Irene               97
    The limpid streams with ruefull murmurs flow   .   .   .   .  Y   6  Virgil Daphnis       3
STREET
    Lords of the street, and terrors of the way;   .   .   .   .  O  21  London             231
STREETS
    Roll thro' the streets, and thunder to the skies;  .   .   .  O  18  London             183
    Here life is ventur'd if the streets you roam  .   .   .   .  Y  59  London          V  224
    Thy Streets with Violence of Woe shall sound,  .   .   .   .  O 110  To Posterity         5
    Sacred to Prayer, and wander thro' the Streets;   .   .   .   O 251  Irene               63
    Confus'd about the streets I roam  .   .   .   .   .   .   .   Y  11  Tr Hor Epode 9      33
STRENGTH
    But their lost strength and vigour soon return,   .   .   .   O  76  Tr Add. Battle       8
    The strength of a Bar, and the sweetness of Nard. .   .   .   O 179  Charade!             4
    Exchanges solid Strength for feeble Splendor.  .   .   .   .  O 265  Irene               38
    Improves it's lustre, but impairs its  .   .   .   .   .   .  O 366  Irene           V    4
        Strength.
    Flash out at once, with Strength above Resistance. .   .   .  O 282  Irene               60
    And Strength proportiond to the task of Ruling .   .   .   .  O 369  Irene           V    7
    Who matchless strength and bulk gygantick boasts,  .   .   .  Y  24  Tr Add. Battle      81
STRETCH
    And stretch thy prospects o'er the smiling land,  .   .   .   O  20  London             214
    And stretch thy prospects o'er your fruitfull land,   .   .   Y  58  London          V  214
    Then o'er the World shall Discord stretch her Wings,  .   .   O 110  To Posterity        15
    Still stretch in vain their longing Arms afar; .   .   .   .  O 292  Irene               91
STRETCH'D
    Then leave him stretch'd upon the ling'ring Rack,  .   .   .  O 273  Irene               36
    Stretch'd in the Dust, or tow'ring on his Throne;  .   .   .  O 303  Irene               10
    Had stretch'd the fiery Boaster in the Grave.  .   .   .   .  O 312  Irene               20
STREW'D
    Here with dead mice the marsh was strew'd around;  .   .   .  Y  24  Tr Add. Battle      58
STRICT
    Strict, on the right he fix'd his steadfast eye,  .   .   .   O 118  Epitaph Hanmer      29
STRICTEST
    Those sovereign charms with strictest care employ;   .   .   O  81  Lady Birthday       13
STRIFE
    Remark each anxious toil, each eager strife,   .   .   .   .  O  30  Vanity Wishes        3
    Explore each restless toil, each anxious strife,  .   .   .   Y  92  Vanity Wishes   V    3
    Suspended faction ceas'd from rage and strife, .   .   .   .  O 118  Epitaph Hanmer      17
    How passion's well-accorded strife  .   .   .   .   .   .   . O 121  To Miss Playin      31
    With mental and corporeal strife,  .   .   .   .   .   .   .  O 124  Winter's Walk       18
    Forbears the long-continu'd strife, .   .   .   .   .   .   . O 124  An Ode               2
    From false caresses, causeless strife,  .   .   .   .   .   . O 125  An Ode              25
    Hard was the Strife of Justice and of Love;   .   .   .   .   O 324  Irene               13
STRIKE
    The notes unfelt would strike th' impervious ear,  .   .   .  Y 104  Vanity Wishes   V  269
    Strike thy bosom, sage, and tell,   .   .   .   .   .   .   . O 181  Parody Warton   V    3
    Prospects obscur'd by Distance faintly strike. .   .   .   .  O 261  Irene               19
    To morrow strike--Does then that experienc'd   .   .   .   .  Y 154  Irene           V   19
        wisdom
    Then strike secure, and Heav'n assist the Blow.   .   .   .   O 298  Irene                9
    Thus shall he live to strike th' important Blow,  .   .   .   O 308  Irene               32
STRIKES
    When Stella strikes the tuneful string  .   .   .   .   .   . O 120  To Miss Playin       1
        the Particulam) strikes me with greater horror   .   .   Y 176  Irene             V111C
    Forcefull descending strikes his enemy,  .   .   .   .   .    Y  26  Tr Add. Battle     131
STRING     SEE BOW-STRING
    When old Timotheus struck the vocal String,    .   .   .   .  O  97  Hickman Spinet       9
    When Stella strikes the tuneful string  .   .   .   .   .   . O 120  To Miss Playin       1
    And Wisdom warble from her string.  .   .   .   .   .   .   .  O 121  To Miss Playin      24
    By quiv'ring string, or modulated wind;  .   .   .   .   .    O 192  Tr. Medea II        10
STRIPED
    Striped rainbows round her eyes are seen,  .   .   .   .   .  O 127  To Lyce, Lady       11
STRIPP'D
    Thrice has December stripp'd the tree  .   .   .   .   .   .   Y  11  Tr Hor Epode 9       7
STRIVE
    And strive in vain to laugh at H<erve>y's jest.   .   .   .   O  13  London              74
    And strive in vain to laugh at Clodio's jest.  .   .   .   .  O  13  London          V   74
    Impending death they strive to 'scape in vain  .   .   .   .  O  76  Tr Add. Battle      30
```

```
STRIVE          (CONTINUED)                              PAGE    TITLE          LINE
   The limits fix'd they strive to pass in vain;    . . . .   O  76 Tr Add. Battle    36
   For howe'er we boast and strive,       . . . . . .        O 178 Thrale 35 Year     13
   Nor with too powerfull rivals strive  . . . . . .         Y  11 Tr Hor Epode 9     27
   Wounded and spent, in vain they strive to rise   . . . .  Y  24 Tr Add. Battle     60
STRIVES
   Strives to regain her Empire of the Mind:    . . . . .    O 320 Irene              33
STROKE
   Our trees were blasted by the thunder stroke,    . . . .  O  65 Virgil Past.I      23
   Lest on himself the destin'd stroke descend.     . . . .  O 139 Tr Rambler 168      2
   Burning in vain, delays the Stroke of Death?     . . . .  O 257 Irene              66
   Can Cali dare the Stroke of heav'nly Justice,    . . . .  O 272 Irene               3
   Soon may the final Stroke decide our Fate,   . . . . . .  O 299 Irene              51
   That thus constrain'd we speed the Stroke of Death.  . .  O 327 Irene              30
   And speed the Stroke lest Mercy should o'ertake them. .   O 333 Irene              54
   The birds elude the stroke with cautious care;   . . . .  Y  26 Tr Add. Battle    134
STROKES
   His pow'rful Strokes presiding Truth impress'd,  . . . .  O  51 Pro Drury-Lane      7
STRONG
   Burns from the strong contagion of the gown;     . . . .  O  36 Vanity Wishes     138
   Caught from the strong contagion of the gown;    . . . .  O  36 Vanity Wishes   V 138
   Spreads from the strong contagion of the gown;   . . . .  O  36 Vanity Wishes   V 138
   And strong devotion to the skies aspires,    . . . . .    O  48 Vanity Wishes     358
   When strong devotion fills thy glowing Breast,   . . .    O  48 Vanity Wishes   V 358
   Their Cause was gen'ral, their Supports were strong, . .  O  52 Pro Drury-Lane     25
   The mind of mortals, in perverseness strong, . . . .     O 136 Tr Rambler 132       1
   I too can feel the rapture, fierce and strong;   . . .    O 142 In Baretti Bk.      3
   Down whose current clear and strong, . . . . . . .       O 159 Tr. Rio Verde       2
   When publick Villainy, too strong for Justice,   . . . .  O 250 Irene              40
   Too strong for Love, have hurried him on Death.  . . . .  O 267 Irene              48
   The strong Emotions of my troubled Soul  . . . .         O 275 Irene              87
   And Gratitude's strong Ties restrain my Tongue.  . . . .  O 312 Irene               5
   Whence rise these restless cares? these strong emotions? Y 189 Irene            V   1
   Assist her Efforts with thy strong Persuasion;   . . . .  O 321 Irene              34
   The Tongue, that, forc'd by strong Necessity,    . . . .  O 324 Irene               2
STRONGER
   To stronger Efforts, and maturer Counsels.   . . . . .    O 270 Irene               8
STRONGEST
   The strongest Effort of a female Soul,   . . . . . .      O 278 Irene              62
STROVE
   In vain proud tyrants strove to shake    . . . . . .      O  79 Feast St Simon     13
   Verse and Music vainly strove;   . . . . . . . .         O 149 Tr Boet III.12      16
STRUCK
   Struck with the seat that gave Eliza birth,  . . . . .    O  10 London             23
   When old Timotheus struck the vocal String,  . . . . .    O  97 Hickman Spinet      9
   Struck with the Wonder of a Statesman's Goodness,  . .    O 274 Irene              45
   He struck his tortur'd Breast, and roar'd, Irene:  . . .  O 325 Irene              24
STRUGGLE
   Behold how Lust and Rapine struggle round her.   . . . .  O 252 Irene              82
   Demand a Voice, and struggle into Birth; . . . . . .      O 295 Irene              18
   Let us not struggle with th' eternal Will,   . . . . .    O 320 Irene              16
STRUGGLES
   Or only struggles to be more enslav'd?   . . . . . .      O 281 Irene              41
STRUGGLING
   That struggling pants, and rowls her eye-balls round. .   O  76 Tr Add. Battle     15
   Do they with Pain repress the struggling Shout,  . . .    O 270 Irene              24
   When did contentment with struggling sorrow  . . . .      Y 191 Irene            V  20
      throb?
   Just as the Rack forc'd out his struggling Soul, . . .    O 330 Irene              13
STRUGLE
   Tumultuous passions strugle in her breast    . . . . .    Y  21 Tr. Iliad Bk 6    109
STRUGLING
   Their godlike hero strugling in the skies.   . . . .      Y  26 Tr Add. Battle    129
STRYMON'S
   And Strymon's hollow banks resounded with their groans. . Y  24 Tr Add. Battle     89
STUBBORN
   How rarely reason guides the stubborn choice,    . . . .  O  31 Vanity Wishes      11
STUDENT
   Might well befit the solitary Student,   . . . . . .      O 281 Irene              36
STUDIED
   Themselves they studied, as they felt, they writ, . . .   O  52 Pro Drury-Lane     19
   The studied arts of Luxury:  . . . . . . . . .           O  73 Hor. Epode II       56
STUDIOUS
   Studious to please, and ready to submit, . . . . . .      O  16 London            123
   His studious Patience, and laborious Art,    . . . . .    O  51 Pro Drury-Lane     11
   His country call'd him from the studious shade;  . . .    O 117 Epitaph Hanmer     10
   By wit, by knowledge, studious to be read,   . . . . .    O 141 Tr Rambler 208      3
   Studious to please, yet not asham'd to fail. . . . .      O 246 Irene Prologue     30
STUDY
   Let Study, worn with Virtue's fruitless Lore,    . . . .  O  57 Prologue Comus      9
STUN
   And stun me with the Yellings of Damnation!  . . . . .    O 328 Irene              51
STUPEFACTION
   Snar'd with thy Fears, and maz'd in Stupefaction. . . .   O 318 Irene              18
   Frozen with doubt, and maz'd in stupefaction . . . .      Y 196 Irene            V 18B
STYGIAN
   We all must view the Stygian flood . . . . . .           O  69 Hor.II Ode 14      17
   All stemm'd in one sad day the Stygian tyde. . . . .      Y  18 Tr. Iliad Bk 6     35
SUBDUE
   Wouldst thou subdue th' obdurate Cannibal    . . . . .    O 267 Irene               4
```

		PAGE	TITLE	LINE
SUBDUED				
And though at length subdued, elude thy Vengeance.	. .	O 274	Irene	57
SUBDUES				
And flattery subdues when arms are vain?		O 16	London	122
SUBDUING SEE ALL-SUBDUING				
SUBJECT				
Where common Laws restrain the Prince and Subject,	. .	O 256	Irene	56
The subject World, familiar to Dominion.		O 369	Irene	V 10
And subject Seas roar round their Queen in vain.	. . .	O 309	Irene	29
SUBJECTS				
His foes derision, and his subjects blame, ...		O 43	Vanity Wishes	253
To nobler subjects tune my lyre;		O 78	Feast St Simon	8
Scorn'd by his Subjects, trampled by his Foes;		O 268	Irene	20
SUBLIME				
From one sublime Beginning spring;		O 146	Tr Boeth III.6	2
I rais'd his Thoughts to more sublime Devotion.	. . .	O 274	Irene	46
SUBMISSICN				
With cool submission joins the labouring train,	. . .	O 59	Pro Good Nat'd	3
He ne'er with forc'd Submission waits		O 71	Hor. Epode II	15
Sinks into milkness and softens to submission.		Y 123	Irene	V 99
Fear in her Eye, Submission on her Tongue.		O 259	Irene	120
Vye for my submission, sollicite bondage.		Y 136	Irene	V 27C
SUBMISSIVE				
Submissive and prepar'd for each Event, ...		O 302	Irene	112
SUBMIT				
Studious to please, and ready to submit, ...		O 16	London	123
SUBMITTED				
And rights submitted, left him none to seize.		O 34	Vanity Wishes	108
SUBSIDE				
Art thou too fall'n? ere anger could subside	. . .	O 132	Tr. Rambler 54	1
Shall the whirle, and bid the Rock subside		O 365	Irene	V 4
SUBSIST				
Exiles, the proverb says, subsist on hope.		O 133	Tr. Rambler 67	1
SUBTERRANEOUS				
Like subterraneous tempests with dire eruption burst their caverns		Y 115	Irene	V 49
Why shakes the Ground, when subterraneous Fires	. . .	O 281	Irene	52
SUBTLE				
Revenge and subtle Jealousy shall teach		O 307	Irene	24
SUBTLER				
Others with softer smiles, and subtler art, ...		O 13	London	75
Thy hand that knows the subtler art, ...		O 120	To Miss Purse	5
But, lest I fall by subtler foes, ...		O 126	An Ode	37
The subtler Flames emitted from the Sky, ...		O 282	Irene	59
SUBVERTED				
Did no subverted empire mark his end?		O 41	Vanity Wishes	216
SUCCEED				
At least this Day be calm--If we succeed, ...		O 260	Irene	141
Let nobler Hopes and juster Fears succeed, ...		O 265	Irene	9
Succeed, my Friend, unenvied by Leontius.		O 306	Irene	48
SUCCEEDING				
In angry numbers warn'st succeeding times;		O 23	London	259
In useful satire warn succeeding times;		Y 61	London	V 259
Immortal Patrons of succeeding Days, ...		O 57	Prologue Comus	5
Succeeding years thy early fame destroy;		O 135	Tr Rambler 127	1
The Pride and Terror of succeeding Days, ...		O 268	Irene	12
SUCCEEDS				
The Lust of Gold succeeds the Rage of Conquest, . . .		O 249	Irene	13
SUCCESS				
In Pow'r dependent, in Success deprest.		O 246	Irene Prologue	12
Swoln with Success, secure amidst his native Rocks	. .	O 352	Irene	V 28
And bid Success become the Test of Truth;		O 291	Irene	64
Enrag'd by Wrongs, exulting with Success, ...		O 313	Irene	15
Profuse of Wealth, or bounteous of Success, ...		O 313	Irene	20
Success and Conquest now are empty Sounds, ...		O 333	Irene	44
SUCCESSFUL				
To pour my Prayers for thy successful Reign, ...		O 264	Irene	10
Successful Treasons punish impious Kings.		O 300	Irene	66
Behold him here, in Love, in War successful, ...		O 310	Irene	4
SUCCESSIVE				
The changing year's successive plan		O 231	Tr Horace IV.7	7
SUCCOURS				
And weak Philosophy denies her Succours.		O 252	Irene	92
SUCH				
Let such raise palaces, and manors buy, ...		O 12	London	57
To such, a groaning nation's spoils are giv'n, ...		O 13	London	65
To such, the Plunder of a Land is giv'n, ...		O 13	London	V 65
Scarce can our fields, such crowds at Tyburn die, . . .		O 21	London	242
Well may we fear, such crowds at Tyburn die, ...		Y 60	London	V 242
Such was the scorn that fill'd the sage's mind, . . .		O 33	Vanity Wishes	69
Such bribes the rapid Greek o'er Asia whirl'd, ...		O 39	Vanity Wishes	179
For such the steady Romans shook the world;		O 39	Vanity Wishes	180
For such in distant lands the Britons shine, ...		O 39	Vanity Wishes	181
Such pow'r has praise, that virtue scarce can charm, . .		Y 100	Vanity Wishes	V 183
Such age there is, and who shall wish its end?		O 44	Vanity Wishes	298
Such age there is, and who could wish its end?		O 44	Vanity Wishes	V 298
Such age the is, and who could wish its end?		Y 105	Vanity Wishes	V 298
Such Pleasures quickly would remove		O 72	Hor. Epode II	V 45
Such as the Sun-burnt Sabines were, ...		O 72	Hor. Epode II	49
For such thy beauteous mind, and lovely face, ...		O 107	Lady F Assizes	5
If such on Earth can Bliss bestow, ...		O 146	Tr Boeth III.4	7

```
SUCH          (CONTINUED)                              PAGE    TITLE            LINE
    "Blissful bondage such as mine?  . . . . . . . .    O 185 Anacreon Ode 9      24
    Such strains as, mingled with the lyre,  . . . .    O 188 Epilogue            1
    Before such Foes of more than human Force;  . . .   O 250 Irene              49
    Such had I trusted once as soon as seen,  . . . .   O 255 Irene              17
    Such are the Woes when arbitrary Pow'r,  . . . . .  O 256 Irene              53
    Such heav'nly Beauty form'd for Adoration,  . . .   O 269 Irene              41
    Such Beauty must not shine to vulgar Eyes.  . . .   O 269 Irene              43
    Such slight Defeats but animate the Brave  . . .    O 270 Irene               7
    Such are Love's Joys, the Lenitives of Life,  . .   O 277 Irene              47
    Such ill-tim'd Gravity, such serious Folly,  . . .  O 281 Irene              35
    Such ill-tim'd Gravity, such serious Folly,  . . .  O 281 Irene              35
    With Raptures such as fire the Pagan Crouds,  . .   O 286 Irene               3
    Such Ecstacy of Love! such pure Affection,  . . .   O 295 Irene              15
    Such Ecstacy of Love! such pure Affection,  . . .   O 295 Irene              15
    Such strange Events, such unexpected Chances,  . .  O 296 Irene              34
    Such strange Events, such unexpected Chances,  . .  O 296 Irene              34
    O'erthrow such weak, such accidental Virtue,  . .   O 301 Irene              83
    O'erthrow such weak, such accidental Virtue,  . .   O 301 Irene              83
    Far be such black Ingratitude from Cali,  . . . .   O 306 Irene               4
    And yet such is the condition of human  . . . . .   Y 186 Irene           V   2
      happiness
    Bids Beauty, such as thine, prepare to die. . . .   O 324 Irene               3
    Such Beauty, Sweetness, Love, were cheaply bought,  O 332 Irene              35
    Such Ills are sent for Souls like thine to conquer. O 332 Irene              38
    Such was the Will of Heav'n--A Band of Greeks  . .  O 335 Irene               5
    Sung such a war when in a miry fen  . . . . . . .   Y  23 Tr Add. Battle     55
    Such was the horrour of the dreadfull fight . . .   Y  26 Tr Add. Battle    136
SUCKS
    Sucks in the dregs of each corrupted state. . . .   O  14 London             96
SUDDEN
    There none are swept by sudden fate away,  . . .    O   9 London             11
    And crowd with sudden wealth the rising dome;  . .  O  19 London            203
    Work'd into sudden rage by wintry show'rs,  . . .   O 132 Tr. Rambler 65      1
    Though musick thrills, or sudden sallies seize,  .  O 142 In Baretti Bk.      6
    By sudden blasts, or slow decline,  . . . . . . .   O 200 Death Dr Levet      3
    Think on the sudden Change of human Scenes;  . . .  O 252 Irene              86
    Still at Aspasia's Voice a sudden Rapture  . . . .  O 265 Irene               4
    Some fatal gust of sudden Opposition  . . . . . .   O 374 Irene           V  15
    A sudden Pause th' imperfect Sense suspended,  . .  O 270 Irene              13
    And should he fall unheard, by sudden Justice,  .   O 273 Irene              41
    But why this sudden Warmth?  . . . . . . . . . .    O 281 Irene              48
    If yet this shining Pomp, these sudden Honours,  .  O 289 Irene               1
    If yet these glittring Robes these sudden Splendors O 366 Irene           V  17
    If Dismiss this glittring train these sudden  . .   O 366 Irene           V  17
      Splendors
    A sudden Mist o'ercasts my darken'd Soul,  . . .    O 295 Irene              12
    Sudden he stops, and inward turns his Eyes,  . . .  O 311 Irene               5
    Just as it reach'd my Lips, a sudden Cry  . . . .   O 316 Irene              27
       What Dream of sudden Power  . . . . . . . . .    O 323 Irene               1
    That pour with sudden Violence on Kingdoms,  . . .  O 325 Irene              12
SUFF'RER
    The patient Suff'rer, and the faithful Wife.  . .   O  58 Prologue Comus     32
SUFF'RINGS
    And vent our Suff'rings in clandestine Groans?  .   O 249 Irene               4
SUFFER
    Whate'er perfidious villany can suffer  . . . . .   Y 216 Irene           V  75
SUFFOLK'S
    At length must Suffolk's beauties shine in vain,  . O 107 Lady F Assizes      1
SUGAR
    With cream and sugar soften'd well,  . . . . . .    O 158 Par Hermit III      3
    With cream and sugar temper'd well,  . . . . . .    O 158 Par Hermit III   V  3
SUIT
    Your artful Suit, your Monarch's fierce Denial,  .  O 270 Irene               3
    To hear my suit and give a Queen to Turkey?  . . .  O 372 Irene           V   7
    Let Prudence, ere the Suit be farther urg'd,  . .   O 285 Irene               8
SUITS
    Him no contentious suits in law  . . . . . . . .    O  71 Hor. Epode II      13
    Ill suits us with Guilt the Gaieties of Triumph;  . O 314 Irene              22
SULLEN
    Oh! send them to the sullen mansions dun,  . . .    O 192 Tr. Medea II       13
    Constrains a sullen Smile, and shoots away.  . . .  O 311 Irene               7
    Deaf to the critick, sullen to the friend,  . . .   Y  67 Prologue Lethe      5
SULLY
    And one base action sully all my fame,  . . . . .   O  74 Tr. Iliad Bk 6      6
SULTAN
    And, though refus'd, conceals it from the Sultan. . O 258 Irene              89
    And brought his beauteous Plunder to the Sultan. .  O 258 Irene              96
    The Sultan gaz'd, he wonder'd and he lov'd;  . . .  O 258 Irene              98
    Hold in her Chains the captivated Sultan?  . . . .  O 261 Irene               2
    Why should the Sultan shun the Joys of Beauty,  .   O 261 Irene               7
    Cease, cease thy Censures, for the Sultan comes  .  O 262 Irene              28
    Hail illustrious Sultan  . . . . . . . . . . . .    O 351 Irene           V  23
    Forgive, great Sultan, that intrusive Duty  . . .   O 263 Irene              23
    Receive th' impatient Sultan to thy Arms;  . . .    O 267 Irene              10
    The Sultan from himself derives his Greatness. . .  O 268 Irene              24
    The Sultan comes, impatient for his Love;  . . .    O 272 Irene              12
    Justice demands--But see th' approaching Sultan. .  O 286 Irene              15
    Long be the Sultan bless'd with happy Love!  . . .  O 286 Irene               1
    When soft Security shall prompt the Sultan,  . . .  O 291 Irene              76
    And soft Security shall prompt the Sultan  . . .    O 364 Irene           V   6

                                325
```

```
SULTAN          (CONTINUED)                              PAGE   TITLE           LINE
    It parts you now--The hasty Sultan sign'd  .  .  .  .  .   O 296 Irene              1
    Th' approaching Sultan forc'd me from the Palace;  .  .  . O 299 Irene             47
    Haste, Murza, to the Palace, let the Sultan  .  .  .  .  . O 319 Irene              2
    This lucky Stratagem shall charm the Sultan,  .  .  .  .   O 319 Irene              5
    Fly, Slaves, and call the Sultan to my Rescue.  .  .  .  . O 322 Irene             56
    The Sultan is my Judge.  .  .  .  .  .  .  .  .  .  .  .  . O 323 Irene             12
    This Bay has prov'd my ,fondness for the Sultan;  .  .  .  O 324 Irene             19
       The Sultan knows it,  .  .  .  .  .  .  .  .  .  .  .  . O 324 Irene             20
    Alas! they come, commanded by the Sultan,  .  .  .  .  .   O 325 Irene              8
    Confess your Crime, or lead me to the Sultan,  .  .  .  .  O 326 Irene             41
    The raging Sultan burns till our Return,  .  .  .  .  .  . O 327 Irene             11
    I guess'd her dark Designs, and warn'd the Sultan,  .  .   O 327 Irene             26
    Could we reverse the Sentence of the Sultan,  .  .  .  .   O 328 Irene             38
    Now shalt thou shine the Darling of the Sultan,  .  .  .   O 329 Irene              3
    The stormy Sultan rages at our stay.  .  .  .  .  .  .  .  O 329 Irene             12
    The Sultan comes, still gloomy, still enrag'd.  .  .  .  . O 330 Irene             26
    Thine Orders, mighty Sultan! are perform'd,  .  .  .  .  . O 330 Irene              3
    Forgive, great Sultan! that by Fate prevented,  .  .  .  . O 331 Irene              1
    Great is thy Woe! but think, illustrious Sultan,  .  .  .  O 332 Irene             37
SULTAN'S
    Embroil'd the Turkish State--our Sultan's Father  .  .  .  O 256 Irene             42
    But say, great Bassa, why the Sultan's Anger,  .  .  .     O 257 Irene             65
    Soon as the Sultan's unexpected Fate  .  .  .  .  .  .     O 257 Irene             76
    The Sultan's majesty the warriours rage  .  .  .  .  .     Y 123 Irene         V  98
    The Sultan's majesty the warriours fierceness  .  .  .     Y 123 Irene         V  98
    And teach me to repell the Sultan's Passion.  .  .  .      O 265 Irene              3
    Glide through Irene to the Sultan's Ear.  .  .  .  .  .    O 267 Irene              3
    My Heart still beats responsive to the Sultan's;  .  .  .  O 272 Irene              9
    Aw'd by the Rigour of the Sultan's Justice,  .  .  .  .    O 288 Irene              8
    Perhaps in vain the Sultan's Anger spar'd me,  .  .  .     O 298 Irene             32
    Nor end my Terrors with the Sultan's Death;  .  .  .  .    O 300 Irene             67
    When, summon'd by the Sultan's clam'rous Fury,  .  .  .    O 325 Irene             22
    Should she prevail to gain the Sultan's Presence,  .  .    O 327 Irene             16
    Of her the Sultan's Voice condemn'd to die?  .  .  .  .    O 329 Irene             17
SULTANESS
    Behold our future Sultaness, Abdalla;--  .  .  .  .  .  .  O 267 Irene              1
    And lay the tow'ring Sultaness aside,  .  .  .  .  .  .  . O 289 Irene              8
SULTRY
    Unwholesome Sirius' sultry reign;  .  .  .  .  .  .  .  .  O  69 Hor.II Ode 14      16
SUMMER
    Place me where no soft summer gale  .  .  .  .  .  .  .    O  66 Hor I Ode xxii     17
    Place me where no soft summer Gale  .  .  .  .  .  .  .    O  67 To A. Fuscus       17
    When fruitful summer loads the teeming plain,  .  .  .  .  O 151 The Ant            7
    Then Summer sinks in Autumn's reign,  .  .  .  .  .  .     O 231 Tr Horace IV.7     11
    Fenc'd from the summer breeze, and vernal  .  .  .  .      Y 163 Irene         V  43
       show'r.
    If winter by the fire, if summer in the shade.  .  .  .    Y   7 Virgil Daphnis     48
SUMMER'S
    Spring yield<s> to Summer<'s> sovereign ray,  .  .  .      O 231 Tr Horace IV.7     10
SUMMITS
    Tries the dread summits of Cesarean pow'r,  .  .  .  .     O  42 Vanity Wishes     242
    Their cloudy Summits, and the Sons of Fierceness,  .  .    O 268 Irene             29
    Their snowy summits, and the sons of fierceness  .  .  .   Y 136 Irene         V  29
SUMMON
    Now summon all thy Soul, illustrious Christian!  .  .  .   O 254 Irene              1
SUMMON'D
    Summon'd the singer blythe, and harper gay,  .  .  .  .  . O 192 Tr. Medea II        7
    When, summon'd by the Sultan's clam'rous Fury,  .  .  .  . O 325 Irene             22
SUMMONS
    No summons mock'd by chill delay,  .  .  .  .  .  .  .     O 201 Death Dr Levet     21
    No summons shock'd by chill delay,  .  .  .  .  .  .  .    O 201 Death Dr Levet V  21
    I came obedient to thy friendly Summons,  .  .  .  .  .  . O 253 Irene            105
    Ambitious to prevent the fatal summons  .  .  .  .  .  .   Y 136 Irene         V 27A
    And wait your Summons to report his Conduct.  .  .  .  .   O 310 Irene              7
SUN
    Dark is the sun, and loathsome is the day.  .  .  .  .     O 139 Tr Rambler 171      1
    Where gloom-enamour'd Mischief dreads the Sun,  .  .  .    O 192 Tr. Medea II       15
    When the tenth had set upon our Sorrows,  .  .  .  .  .    O 254 Irene            120
    Live till the Sun forgets to dart his Beams,  .  .  .  .   O 262 Irene              3
    The weary Sun forgets his Revolutions  .  .  .  .  .  .    O 347 Irene         V  30
    You are like the sun the governour of the world  .  .     Y 132 Irene         V  40
    When nought but mine the circling Sun shall  .  .  .  .    O 357 Irene         V  29
       see
    They see the Sun surmount the dark Eclipse,  .  .  .  .    O 287 Irene              5
    Fenc'd from the sun and shelterd from the breeze.  .  .    Y 163 Irene         V  43
    Conducts the Sun, and regulates the Spheres.  .  .  .      O 293 Irene            124
    Rolls on the Sun, and Regulates the Spheres.  .  .  .      O 369 Irene         V  17
    As glittring dewdrops quiver to the sun  .  .  .  .  .     Y 173 Irene         V  19
    At length th' unwilling Sun resigns the World  .  .  .     O 302 Irene              1
    To still their Murmurs, ere the twentieth Sun  .  .  .     O 309 Irene             23
    When the departing sun resigns  .  .  .  .  .  .  .  .  .  Y  38 Lady Leaving        1
SUN-BURNT
    Such as the Sun-burnt Sabines were,  .  .  .  .  .  .  .   O  72 Hor. Epode II      49
SUNG
    Angelick choirs have sung.  .  .  .  .  .  .  .  .  .  .   O  80 Feast St Simon     60
    Sung such a war when in a miry fen  .  .  .  .  .  .  .  . Y  23 Tr Add. Battle      55
SUNK
    But sunk in thoughtless ease, and empty show,  .  .  .     Y  53 London         V 103
    And crowds of godlike Romans sunk to hell.  .  .  .  .     O  77 Festina Lente      16
    Held forth this fatal Scroll, then sunk to nothing.  .  .  O 272 Irene             17
```

		PAGE	TITLE	LINE
SUNK	(CONTINUED)			
Held out this fatal roll--then sunk to Nothing. . . .		O 357	Irene	V 1
Sunk in his Pleasures, confident and gay, ...		O 283	Irene	8
An angry look had sunk him into Hell		O 376	Irene	V 23
An angry look had sunk him into Hell		Y 188	Irene	V 20
Forbear--But thou art sunk beneath Reproach;		O 315	Irene	28
SUNS				
Is not each Realm that smiles with kinder Suns, . . .		O 265	Irene	35
SUNSHINE				
The slave of sunshine and of glocm.		O 124	Winter's Walk	16
SUP				
And sign your will before you sup from home.		O 21	London	225
And make will before you sup from home.		Y 59	London	V 225
SUPERFLUITIES				
With superfluities of joy.		O 191	Tr. Medǝa I	16
SUPERFLUOUS				
Superfluous lags the vet'ran on the stage, ...		O 45	Vanity Wishes	308
And lags superfluous on th' incumbred stage, ...		Y 106	Vanity Wishes	V 308
From grov'ling Business and superfluous Care, . . .		O 246	Irene Prologue	3
'Tis Madness to provoke superfluous Danger, ...		O 318	Irene	21
SUPERIOR				
The guardians yield, by force superior ply'd;		O 47	Vanity Wishes	339
I walk'd superior, through the Blaze of Charms, . . .		O 263	Irene	17
Shine thou distinguish'd by superior Merit, ...		O 264	Irene	29
Thou shin'st, bright Maid, superior to Distress; . . .		O 298	Irene	17
SUPERIOUR				
Let Reason with superiour force controul		O 77	Festina Lente	7
Superiour man descends which		Y 147	Irene	V 39
We oft (notwithstanding this boasted superiour genius		Y 148	Irene	V 49
Superiour Majesty proclaims the Queen, ...		O 288	Irene	2
Superiour Majesty proclaims thee Queen, ...		O 288	Irene	V 2
Those holy Beings, whose superiour Care		O 289	Irene	17
Superiour Man possess'd the Charge of Rule, ...		O 291	Irene	71
Then pleas'd, and conscious of Superiour		O 369	Irene	V 6
Greatness				
While some Archangel of superiour Nature		O 369	Irene	V 13
What can'st thou boast superiour to Demetrius?		O 305	Irene	38
SUPERSTITION				
Now Superstition, Ignorance and Error, ...		O 251	Irene	68
To canonize the Slaves of Superstition, ...		O 309	Irene	34
SUPICION				
Supicion checks the rising transport		Y 186	Irene	V 2
SUPINE				
Now, Tityrus, you, supine and careless laid, ...		O 64	Virgil Past.I	1
SUPINELY				
On some green bank supinely Laid, ...		O 72	Hor. Epode II	30
SUPPLE				
The supple Gaul was born a parasite:		O 16	London	124
Our supple tribes repress their patriot throats, . . .		O 34	Vanity Wishes	95
Warm India's supple Sons should bow, ...		O 146	Tr Boeth III.5	6
SUPPLIANT				
Rules the bold hand, or prompts the suppliant voice; . .		O 31	Vanity Wishes	12
In health, in sickness, thus the suppliant prays; . . .		O 43	Vanity Wishes	256
He scorns the meek Address, the suppliant Strain, . . .		O 246	Irene Prologue	31
And ev'ry Suppliant lift his Eyes to Mecca.		O 264	Irene	32
SUPPLIANTS				
Unnumber'd suppliants croud Preferment's gate, ...		O 33	Vanity Wishes	73
His suppliants scorn him, and his followers fly; . . .		O 35	Vanity Wishes	112
SUPPLICANT				
Condemn'd a needy supplicant to wait, ...		O 41	Vanity Wishes	213
SUPPLICATE				
The bard may supplicate, but cannot bribe.		O 60	Pro Good Nat'd	26
SUPPLICATING				
Still raise for good the supplicating voice, ...		O 47	Vanity Wishes	351
For blessing, raise the supplicating voice, ...		Y 108	Vanity Wishes	V 351
Into his supplicating mothers heart.		O 77	Festina Lente	14
With supplicating tears and pure Devotion		O 364	Irene	V 2
SUPPLIED				
The toil of ev'ry day supplied.		O 201	Death Dr Levet	24
SUPPLIES				
Till fame supplies the universal charm.		O 39	Vanity Wishes	184
Her losses soon the Moon supplies, ...		O 232	Tr Horace IV.7	13
SUPPLY				
With hemp the gallows and the fleet supply.		O 21	London	243
Lest scarce the exhausted should rope supply.		Y 60	London	V 243
Wholsome variety supply.		O 73	Hor. Epode II	62
Can more delicious food supply.		O 73	Hor. Epode II	V 62
SUPPORT				
There prune thy walks, support thy drooping flow'rs, . .		O 20	London	216
There prune thy shades, support the drooping flow'rs, .		Y 58	London	V 216
Whose Ways and Means support the sinking land; . . .		O 21	London	245
Whose Ways and Means support a sinking land;		Y 60	London	V 245
And, fainting, scarce support the liquid weight: . . .		O 74	Tr. Iliad Bk 6	24
Nor couldst thou more support a Life of Sloth		O 264	Irene	19
Support the splendid Miseries of Greatness?		O 268	Irene	18
But how can'st thou support the Woes of Exile? . . .		O 301	Irene	102
My Spirits fail, awhile support me, Vengeance-- . . .		O 334	Irene	72
SUPPORTED				
The Life, which only this Design supported, ...		O 316	Irene	22
SUPPORTS				
Their Cause was gen'ral, their Supports were strong, . .		O 52	Pro Drury-Lane	25

SUPPORTS   (CONTINUED)   PAGE   TITLE   LINE
    Learn here how Heav'n supports the virtuous Mind, . . .   O 246 Irene Prologue   9
    The breast where truth supports the throne of peace. . . Y 193 Irene   V 15
SUPPRESS
    Let Prudence moderate, though not suppress. . . . . .   O 264 Irene   34
    Once more reflect, suppress this infant Folly. . . . .   O 281 Irene   56
SUPREME
    The Myrtle (ensign of supreme command . . . .   O 95 Sprig of Myrtl   3
    Ev'n from the Birth affects supreme Command, ...   O 280 Irene   19
    That reign'st supreme among the pow'rs above, ...   Y 20 Tr. Iliad Bk 6   100
SURE
    Sure the most bitter is a scornful jest; . . . . . .   O 17 London   167
    And sure th' Eternal Master found . . . .   O 201 Death Dr Levet   27
    Sure some kind Sabre in the Heat of Battle, ...   O 252 Irene   93
    Sure, not unconscious of the mighty Blessing, ...   O 256 Irene   59
    Sure all unite to hold her League of Rule . . . . .   O 257 Irene   62
    Sure this is Love which heretofore I conceiv'd . . .   O 349 Irene   V 28
    Sure, chill'd with sixty winter Camps, thy Blood . . .   O 263 Irene   5
    Sure by some wond'rous Sympathy of Souls, ...   O 272 Irene   8
    Sure Heav'n, for Wonders are not wrought in vain, . . .   O 296 Irene   38
    O Happiness! sure thou art all Aspasia's. . . . .   O 310 Irene   14
    Is sure the Smile of unoffended Heav'n. . . . . .   O 314 Irene   9
    Sure 'tis the happy Hour ordain'd above, ...   O 321 Irene   35
    So sure the Fall of Greatness rais'd on Crimes, . . .   O 335 Irene   10
SURELY
    Grown old in courts, thou art not surely one . . . .   O 176 Tr Metastas II   1
SURER
    A surer Passage to his hated Heart. . . . . . .   O 307 Irene   25
SURFACE
    The Surface of the boiling Deep, ...   O 71 Hor. Epode II   12
    Borne on the Surface of the smiling Deep, ...   O 301 Irene   92
SURGE
    Pensive and listning to the beating Surge. . . . . .   O 254 Irene   128
    And where yon Trees wave o'er the foaming Surge . . .   O 304 Irene   2
SURLY
    The rustick grandeur, or the surly grace, ...   O 15 London   102
    Can surly virtue hope to fix a friend? . . . . . .   O 16 London   145
SURMOUNT
    They see the Sun surmount the dark Eclipse, ...   O 287 Irene   5
SURPRISE
    In life's last scene what prodigies surprise, ...   O 45 Vanity Wishes   315
    Part turn their Backs, part seiz'd with wild surprise .   O 76 Tr Add. Battle   28
SURPRISED
    A grizly wolf surprised, and fled. . . . .   O 65 Hor I Ode xxii   12
SURPRIZ'D
    Surpriz'd I start, and bless the happy Dream; . . . .   O 254 Irene   124
SURPRIZE
    Surprize o'erwhelm her, and retard our Flight. . . . .   O 285 Irene   13
SURROUND
    He feels th' unfading wreath surround his head; . . .   O 82 Young Author   22
    And feels the unfading wreath surround his head; . . .   O 82 Young Author   V 22
SURROUNDING
    Behold surrounding kings their pow'r combine, ...   O 40 Vanity Wishes   199
    In vain surrounding kings their pow'rs combine, . . .   Y 101 Vanity Wishes   V 199
SURROUNDS
    The grizly foaming Boar surrounds . . . .   O 72 Hor. Epode II   39
    And twisted toils, surrounds . . . .   O 72 Hor. Epode II   V 40
SURVEY
    The land of heroes and of saints survey; . . . . . .   O 15 London   100
    Survey mankind, from China to Peru; . . . .   O 30 Vanity Wishes   2
    I trace the planets and survey the skies. . . . . .   O 130 Tr. Rambler 8   2
    Attention rise, survey the fair Creation, ...   O 313 Irene   6
SURVEY'D
    Calm conscience then his former life survey'd, ...   O 118 Epitaph Hanmer   41
SURVEY'ST
    Thou, who survey'st these walls with curious eye, . . .   O 117 Epitaph Hanmer   1
SURVEYS
    Surveys the general toil of human kind; . . . . . .   O 59 Pro Good Nat'd   2
    Surveys with new contemplative delight . . . . . .   O 106 Eliza plucking   2
    Surveys his smiling babes, the sons of   Y 122 Irene   V 60
      freedom,
    Surveys the glories of the splendid pile . . . . .   Y 131 Irene   V 36A
    Surveys your Plays with inattentive Glance, ...   O 276 Irene   22
    Surveys your triflings with a careless glance . . . .   O 355 Irene   V 11
    Surveys your actions with a careless glance . . . .   Y 146 Irene   V 22
SURVIV'D
    What has the Wretch that has surviv'd his Country, . .   O 260 Irene   134
SURVIVES
    Augustus still survives in Maro's strain, ...   O 114 On C. Cibber   1
SUSPECTED
    Suspected still?--What Villain's pois'nous Tongue . . .   O 304 Irene   12
SUSPECTS
    But cautious Age suspects the flatt'ring Form, . . .   O 255 Irene   18
SUSPENCE
    Must dull Suspence corrupt the stagnant mind? . . . .   O 47 Vanity Wishes   344
    Must dull Suspence becalm still the stagnant mind? . .   Y 107 Vanity Wishes   V 344
    And give the Tortures of Suspence a Period? . . . .   O 282 Irene   2
    Stood torpid in Suspence; but soon Abdalla . . . . .   O 317 Irene   37
SUSPEND
    Suspend the soft Sollicitudes of Dress; . . . . . .   O 246 Irene Prologue   2
    Suspend the Thought. . . . .   O 252 Irene   79

SUSPEND   (CONTINUED)   PAGE   TITLE   LINE
 Suspend his Sentence--Empire and Irene . . . . . . O 275 Irene 68
 Suspend awhile the Privilege of Pow'r . . . . . . O 289 Irene 5
 Suspend awhile the privilege of powr (and Beauty) . . . O 366 Irene V 21
 Suspend thy Passage to the Seats of Bliss, ... O 308 Irene 9
 Suspend the dreadful Sentence for an Hour? . . . . O 332 Irene 26
SUSPENDED
 And nations on his eye suspended wait; . . . . . . O 40 Vanity Wishes 206
 And hang aloft suspended in the air. . . . . O 76 Tr Add. Battle 7
 Suspended faction ceas'd from rage and strife, ... O 118 Epitaph Hanmer 17
 A sudden Pause th' imperfect Sense suspended, ... O 270 Irene 13
 In these dark Moments of suspended Fate, ... O 313 Irene 1
SUSPICION
 Let artful Flatt'ry now, to lull Suspicion, ... O 267 Irene 2
 The Faith of Mustapha disdains Suspicion; . . . . . . O 273 Irene 30
 Aspasia's Absence will inflame Suspicion; . . . . . . O 296 Irene 5
 That dext'rous Message frees me from Suspicion. . . . O 324 Irene 26
SUSPICIOUS
 Or views his coffers with suspicious eyes, ... O 44 Vanity Wishes 289
 That mark'd my Course, suspicious of my Purpose, . . . O 335 Irene 6
SUSTAIN
 Sustain th' approaching fire's tremendous light; . . . O 18 London 187
 Their foes the shock sustain in Battle skill'd, . . . O 76 Tr Add. Battle 12
 O'erpower'd and faint the Pygmies scarce sustain . . . O 76 Tr Add. Battle 26
 But can thy Friend sustain the glorious Cause, ... O 255 Irene 8
SUSTAIN'D
 Sustain'd the Ballance, but resign'd the Sword; . . . O 22 London V 251
SUSTAINS
 While yet my steady steps no staff sustains, ... O 10 London 41
 While yet my steddy steps no staff sustains, ... O 10 London V 41
 And scarce the lab'ring air sustains the throng . . . Y 25 Tr Add. Battle 95
SWAIN
 In Myrtle groves oft sings the happy swain, ... O 95 Sprig of Myrtl 7
 In Myrtle shades oft sings the happy swain, ... O 95 Sprig of Myrtl V 7
 My Swain is little--true--but be it known, ... O 247 Irene Epilogue 9
 When to the nymphs the swain due homage pays . . . Y   7 Virgil Daphnis V 51
SWAINS
 Ye swains! bestrow the ground with leaves and spread . . Y   7 Virgil Daphnis 26
 The swains shall pay their vows, and thou shalt hear their Y   7 Virgil Daphnis 52
  prayer.
SWALLOWING
 But swallowing all the mighty Store, ... O 144 Tr Boeth. II.2 9
SWAMPY
 There frogs crept croaking o'er the swampy ground. . . Y 24 Tr Add. Battle 59
SWAN
 I pierce the Clouds a tunefull Swan. . . . . O 70 Hor.II Ode XX 12
SWARMS
 Their hungry Swarms the peaceful Vale shall fright . . O 110 To Posterity 9
SWARTHY
 Where Lybia's swarthy offspring burns, ... O 70 Hor.II Ode XX 14
 Whate'er the swarthy Lybian boasts, ... O 73 Hor. Epode II V 57
 And drove the swarthy troops to their own barren sands. . O 78 Festina Lente 20
SWAY
 And sees defenceless realms receive his sway; . . . . O 42 Vanity Wishes 244
 Short sway! fair Austria spreads her mournful charms, . . O 42 Vanity Wishes 245
 Short sway! for Austria spreads her mournful charms, . . Y 103 Vanity Wishes V 245
 And Pantomime, and Song, confirm'd her Sway. . . . . O 52 Pro Drury-Lane 38
 O then, when conquer'd crouds confess thy sway, . . . O 81 Lady Birthday 9
 And yield, reluctant, to despotick Sway. . . . . . . O 96 Hickman Spinet 5
 The Man who pants for ample Sway . . . . O 146 Tr Boeth III.5 1
 Tho' Northern Climes confess thy Sway, ... O 146 Tr Boeth III.5 7
 These when o'er winter's sway, prevail'd the spring . . Y 24 Tr Add. Battle 72
SWAYS
 And sways thy Breast with absolute Dominion, ... O 266 Irene 18
SWEAR
 Can Balbo's eloquence applaud, and swear . . . . . O 17 London 150
 I swear this Eastern Pageantry is Nonsense, ... O 247 Irene Epilogue 13
SWEAT
 To shake in dog-days, in December sweat. . . . . . . O 16 London 143
 Beneath Hyperia's waters shall you sweat, ... O 74 Tr. Iliad Bk 6 23
SWEDISH
 How just his hopes let Swedish Charles decide; . . . . O 40 Vanity Wishes 192
SWEEP
 He sees no boist'rous Tempests sweep . . . . O 71 Hor. Epode II 11
 He sees no Northern Tempests sweep . . . . O 71 Hor. Epode II V 11
 Did roaring Whirlwinds sweep us from the Ramparts: . . O 251 Irene 55
 That sweep away religion arts and freedom . . . . . Y 117 Irene V109D
SWEEPS
 Sweeps o'er the Grove, forsake the lab'ring Bough, . . O 298 Irene 23
 And sweeps th' exulting Conqueror away: . . . . . . O 298 Irene 31
SWEET
 All but the sweet solicitudes of love! . . . . . . O 81 Lady Birthday 6
 How sweet in sleep to pass the careless hours, ... O 135 Tr Rambler 117 1
 "Sweet repast, and soft repose; . . . . O 185 Anacreon Ode 9 30
 The better use of notes, or sweet or shrill, ... O 192 Tr. Medea II 9
 Love, that with sweet Vicissitude relieves . . . . . O 261 Irene 9
 In all the sweet Oblivion of Delight, ... O 269 Irene 13
 In all the sweet forgetfulness of Love . . . . . . O 367 Irene V 26
 In all the sweet forgetfulness of love . . . . . . Y 138 Irene V 13
 And all the sweet varieties of nature . . . . Y 165 Irene V 79

```
SWEETEN                                           PAGE     TITLE           LINE
    Descend, to sweeten Labours once your own.  . . . . .   O 306 Irene            56
SWEETER
    Nor sweeter musick of a virtuous friend,  . . . . . .   O  43 Vanity Wishes    272
SWEETLY
    Tho' when Orpheus sweetly sighing  . . . . . . . .      O 148 Tr Boet III.12  V  5
SWEETNESS
    With fatal sweetness elocution flows,  . . . . . . .    O  31 Vanity Wishes     18
    The strength of a Bar, and the sweetness of Nard. . . . O 179 Charade!           4
    Such Beauty, Sweetness, Love, were cheaply bought,  . . O 332 Irene             35
SWEETS
    To prove the Sweets of Privacy and Friendship,  . . . . O 262 Irene              9
    And taint the sweets of Paradise with envy  . . . . . . Y 184 Irene           V  9
    To tast again the sweets of liberty.  . . . . . . .    Y  19 Tr. Iliad Bk 6    41
SWELL
    And swell with tears the prostituted eye  . . . . .    Y  57 London          V 199
    Grief swell thine Eyes, and Terror chill thy Breast. . . O 110 To Posterity      4
    Your slaughter'd Multitudes that swell the Shore,  . .  O 255 Irene             30
    Swell not thy Soul beyond Advice or Friendship,  . .    O 289 Irene              2
    Swell not your Soul beyond reproof or Counsel  . . .    O 366 Irene           V 18
    Oft shall I swell on our disastrous Friendship  . . .  O 349 Irene           V 11
    Exalt my soul, and swell it into raptures.  . . . . .   Y 189 Irene           V 1F
    Wet the dim eye or swell the throbbing bosom?  . . . .  Y 191 Irene           V 19A
SWELL'D
    How the new Monarch, swell'd with airy Rule,  . . . .   O 306 Irene              1
SWELLING
    Says swelling Crispin, begg'd a cobbler's vote.  . .    O  60 Pro Good Nat'd    22
    The swelling passions to compose,  . . . . . . . . .    O 126 An Ode            39
    On swelling mortals to be proud no more.  . . . . . .   O 135 Tr Rambler 106     2
    But now confirm'd, and swelling with his Conquests,  . . O 257 Irene            70
    And whelms the swelling Architect beneath it.  . . .   O 269 Irene              9
    Like a fell Adder swelling in a Brake.  . . . . . .     O 275 Irene             77
    Why foam the swelling Waves when Tempests rise?  . . .  O 281 Irene             51
    When Heav'n shall bid the swelling Billows rage,  . . . O 300 Irene            60
SWELLINGS
    The swellings of misfortune--  . . . . . . . . .       Y 164 Irene           V 76
SWELLS
    Where Want repines, and Vengeance swells,  . . . . .   O 191 Tr. Medea I       10
    Swells the fair Breast or animates the Glance,  . . . . O 262 Irene            14
    Swells in the Breast, and with resistless Force,  . . . O 280 Irene            20
SWEPT
    There none are swept by sudden fate away,  . . . . .   O   9 London            11
SWIFT
    Swift from pursuing horrors take your way,  . . . . .  O  18 London           188
    Swift o'er the land the dismal rumour flies,  . . . .   O  19 London           196
    And Swift expires a driv'ler and a show.  . . . . . .  O  45 Vanity Wishes    318
    Then, swift as thought, by headlong anger driv'n  . .  O  76 Tr Add. Battle    10
    Swift, let us rush upon the careless Tyrant,  . . . .   O 271 Irene            31
    Did ever Passion make so swift a Progress?  . . . . .  O 281 Irene            55
    While I protract their Stay.  Be swift and faithful. . . O 319 Irene             4
SWIFTER
    Swifter than Icarus Ill flie  . . . . . . . . . .      O  70 Hor.II Ode XX      13
    Swifter than lightning to the fight he flies.  . . . .  Y  21 Tr. Iliad Bk 6   126
SWIFTLY
    Swiftly he sees the imagin'd laurels spread,  . . . .   O  82 Young Author      21
SWIFTNESS
    Arabia's roving Troops, the Sons of Swiftness,  . . . . O 274 Irene            54
SWIM
    Swim darkling down the Current of his fate?  . . . .   O  47 Vanity Wishes    V 346
    And shades of Pygmies swim before their eye.  . . . .   O  77 Tr Add. Battle    48
    The Present, Past, and Future swim before me,  . . . .  O 295 Irene            13
SWOLN
    Swoln with Success, secure amidst his native Rocks  . . O 352 Irene           V 28
SWORD
    Held high the steady scale, but deep'd the sword;  . . . O  22 London          251
    Sustain'd the Ballance, but resign'd the Sword;  . . .  O  22 London         V 251
    Held high the steady scale, but sheath'd the sword;  . . O  22 London        V 251
    Held high the steady scale, but dropp'd the sword;  . . O  22 London         V 251
    For gold his sword the hireling ruffian draws,  . . .   O  31 Vanity Wishes     25
    When statutes glean the refuse of the sword,  . . . .   O  31 Vanity Wishes     31
    His wrathfull sword imbru'd.  . . . . . . . . . .      O  80 Feast St Simon    54
    He bids the Sword destroy, the Flame devour.  . . . .   O  97 Hickman Spinet    14
    Is ripe for Action, and demands the Sword.  . . . . .  O 256 Irene            37
    And lawless Passion, hold the Sword of Justice.  . . .  O 256 Irene            54
    Direct the loaded Cannon, grasp the Sword  . . . . .   O 364 Irene           V 14
    Direct the loaded cannon, grasp the sword  . . . . .   Y 162 Irene           V 41
    The Scale of Justice, and the Sword of Pow'r,  . . . .  O 291 Irene            72
    And Nature's Rights entreat th' asserting Sword.  . . . O 297 Irene             3
    Did not the Cause of Greece restrain my Sword,  . . . . O 299 Irene            41
    Ask to whose Sword the Greeks will trust their Cause,  O 305 Irene            39
    The Rights of Princes let the Sword decide.  . . . . .  O 307 Irene            22
    Shall Monarchs fear to draw the Sword of Justice,  . .  O 312 Irene            21
    The Captive of his Sword. The coward Greeks  . . . . .  O 312 Irene            14
    The Rack expects us, and the Sword pursues.  . . . . .  O 315 Irene             2
    And seize my Sword with disencumber'd Hand.  . . . .   O 316 Irene            29
    Thy Love, Aspasia, calls; restrain thy Sword;  . . . .  O 318 Irene             9
    To court the sword and tempt the glutted rack  . . . .  Y 196 Irene           V 18D
    Once more I dare thy Sword, behold the Prize,  . . . .  O 319 Irene            28
    By that dire sword my sev'n brave brothers dy'd;  . . . Y  18 Tr. Iliad Bk 6   34
    How Turnus by Aeneas' sword expir'd?  . . . . . . .    Y  22 Tr Add. Battle   12
```

```
                                                      PAGE    TITLE           LINE
SWORDS
    Swords, arms and wings are scatter'd o'er the plain   . .   O  76  Tr Add. Battle      18
    The Refuse of our Swords, the Dross of Conquest,      . . .  O 286  Irene                3
    Of slaughter'd Infidels, and Clash of Swords!     .  . . .   O 305  Irene               24
    Whilst beaks and swords engage in bloody fray     .  . .     Y  22  Tr Add. Battle       6
    Fresh foes descending glut their swords with blood.  . .     Y  23  Tr Add. Battle      21
    Temper their swords and point their missive darts.   . .     Y  24  Tr Add. Battle      77
SYCOPHANT
    And scarce a sycophant was fed by pride;    . . . . . .      O  33  Vanity Wishes       56
    And scarce a sycophant could feed on pride;  . . . . . .     Y  94  Vanity Wishes    V  56
SYLVIA
    Why, Sylvia, was it then decreed,   . . . . . . . .          O 120  To Miss Purse       11
SYMPATHETICK
    Vice always found a sympathetick Friend;   . . . . . .       O  52  Pro Drury-Lane      21
SYMPATHISE
    They sympathise with us in every fear  . . . . . . .         Y 134  Irene            V  26
SYMPATHISING
    The sympathising cattle hung their heads   . . . . . .       Y   6  Virgil Daphnis       9
SYMPATHIZ'D
    Shed floods of tears, and sympathiz'd in pain.  . . . .      Y  21  Tr. Iliad Bk 6     129
SYMPATHY
    Sure by some wond'rous Sympathy of Souls,    . . . .         O 272  Irene                8
SYRIAN
    My second, expresses a Syrian perfume;   . . . . . .         O 179  Charade!             2
TABLE
    They first invade your table, then your breast;   . . .      O  17  London             153
TAIL
    They prune the wing and spread the glossy tail  . . . .      O 355  Irene            V  23
    Our little dog has bit his tail  . . . . . . . . .           Y 300  Fanny Burney         4
TAINT
    With slavish tenets taint our poison'd youth,    . . . .     O  12  London              55
    Can sap the principles, or taint the heart;  . . . . . .     O  13  London              76
    But Fear, or Mutiny may taint the Greeks?    . . . . .       O 284  Irene               37
    Nor taint with Care the Privacies of Love.   . . . . . .     O 288  Irene               14
    Then shall these Juices taint Demetrius' Draught,  . . .     O 308  Irene               30
    And taint the sweets of Paradise with envy   . . . . .       Y 184  Irene            V   9
TAINTED
    And gain and grandeur load the tainted gales;   . . . .      O  32  Vanity Wishes       46
    Assails the skies load the tainted gales;    . . . . .       Y  93  Vanity Wishes    V  46
    And gain and greatness load the tainted gales;   . . .       Y  93  Vanity Wishes    V  46
    The Soul once tainted with so foul a Crime,   . . . . .      O 289  Irene               15
    Tainted by Sloth, the Parent of Sedition,    . . . . .       O 309  Irene               20
TAINTS
    Nor taints with death the envenom'd dart,    . . . . .       O  65  Hor I Ode xxii       3
    Nor taints with Death th' envenom'd Dart,    . . . . .       O  66  To A. Fuscus         3
TAKE
    Swift from pursuing horrors take your way,   . . . . .       O  18  London             188
    And Pride and Prudence take her seat in vain.   . . . .      O  46  Vanity Wishes      336
    Conjuring Poet take thy Bride!   . . . . . . . .             O 150  Tr Boet III.12      40
    Bid them come, and take their fill.   . . . . . . .          O 196  Song Congratu.      20
    Come my lads and take your fill.   . . . . . . . .           O 196  Song Congratu.   V  20
    What wild Mistake is this? Take hence with speed   . .       O 325  Irene                4
    But take another to my arms.   . . . . . . . .              Y  11  Tr Hor Epode 9      28
TAKES
    Not one takes warning, by another's end.   . . . . . .       Y  67  Prologue Lethe       6
TALE
    And lisp the tale of Henry's victories;    . . . . . .       O  15  London             120
    The senate's thanks, the gazette's pompous tale,   . . .     O  39  Vanity Wishes      177
    To point a moral, or adorn a tale.   . . . . . . .          O  41  Vanity Wishes      222
    The still returning tale, and ling'ring jest,   . . . .      O  44  Vanity Wishes      275
    Still rise the long tale, and ling'ring jest,   . . . .      Y 104  Vanity Wishes    V 275
    Th' offended burgess hoards his angry tale,   . . . . .      O  60  Pro Good Nat'd      17
    Conceals the moral council in a tale.   . . . . . . .        O 132  Tr. Rambler 65       2
    To you the Tale is told;   . . . . . . . . .                O 150  Tr Boet III.12      55
    And shock the Tyrant with a Tale of Treason.   . . . .       O 255  Irene               29
    Distract my Soul, dispatch thy ling'ring Tale;   . . . .     O 259  Irene              114
    Now, Mustapha, pursue thy Tale of Horror.   . . . .          O 272  Irene                1
    Now Mustapha reveal this Tale of treason    . . . . .        O 369  Irene            V  18
    To shock my Virtue with a Tale of Love.   . . . . .          O 299  Irene               40
    And list'ning to the pleasing Tale of Pow'r,    . . . .      O 303  Irene               30
    The Tale of Women, and the Scorn of Fools?   . . . .         O 305  Irene               29
    Call them--but let them not prolong their Tale,   . . .      O 310  Irene                8
    And tell the horrid Tale with chearful Face;   . . . .       O 329  Irene               11
    And so here begins my tale.   . . .  . . . . .              Y 300  Extemp. Elegy        4
    While many a merry tale, and many a song,    . . . . .       Y 310  Parody of Pope       1
TALENT
    The single talent well employ'd.   . . . . . . .            O 201  Death Dr Levet      28
    His single talent well employ'd.   . . . . . . .            O 201  Death Dr Levet   V  28
TALENTS
    Admires their wond'rous talents for the stage:   . . .       O  16  London             133
TALES
    Or if old womens tales may credit gain,    . . . . . .       O  77  Tr Add. Battle      44
TALK
    Is hazardous but--Talk no more of Hazards    . . . . .       O 365  Irene            V  23
TALKS
    And here a female atheist talks you dead.    . . . . .       O   9  London              18
TALL
    'Tis true, the Fellow's handsome, strait and tall;   . .     O 247  Irene Epilogue       7
TALONS
    Rebellion's vengeful talons seize on Laud.    . . . . .      O  39  Vanity Wishes      168
```

		PAGE	TITLE		LINE
TAME					
	To Robbers furious, and to Lovers tame, ...	O 174	Tr Epitaph Dog		1
TAMELY					
	Endur'd the stinging lash, and tamely bore the yoke. . .	Y 6	Virgil Daphnis		14
TANTALUS					
	Tantalus astonish'd stood	O 149	Tr Boet III.12		37
TAPHON					
	Ton taphon eisoraas ton Olibarioio, Konien	O 171	Epi. Goldsmith		1
	Ton taphon eisoraas ton Oleiberioio, konien	O 171	Epi. Goldsmith	V	1
	Ton taphon eisoraas ton Olibaroio, konien	O 171	Epi. Goldsmith	V	1
TARDY					
	To buried merit raise the tardy bust.	O 38	Vanity Wishes		162
	I bring a tardy Message from Irene.	O 331	Irene		2
TART					
	Safe from the tart lampoon and stinging jest;	O 82	Young Author	V	28
TARTARIAN					
	We still had wander'd on Tartarian Hills.	O 284	Irene		41
TASK					
	This task perform'd, he sought no gainful post, . . .	O 118	Epitaph Hanmer		27
	A task proportion'd to thy mighty mind!	O 136	Tr Rambler 129		2
	"Joyless task without reward:	O 185	Anacreon Ode 9		18
	With wonted Zeal pursue the Task of War, ...	O 264	Irene		30
	With equal zeal persue the task of war	Y 131	Irene	V	30
	And Strength proportiond to the task of Ruling	O 369	Irene	V	1
	Shrinks at the hated Task, for thy Destruction; . . .	O 325	Irene		21
	Shrinks back from the hated task, for thy destruction; .	Y 204	Irene	V	21
TASKS					
	When some proud Grecian dame shall tasks impose, . . .	O 74	Tr. Iliad Bk 6		21
TAST					
	While Hector lives I tast of ev'ry joy	Y 18	Tr. Iliad Bk 6		26
	To tast again the sweets of liberty.	Y 19	Tr. Iliad Bk 6		41
TASTE					
	Your taste in snuff, your judgment in a whore;	O 17	London		149
	His taste in snuff, his judgment in a whore;	Y 55	London	V	149
	Must watch the wild Vicissitudes of Taste;	O 53	Pro Drury-Lane		48
TASTELESS					
	Now pall the tasteless meats, and joyless wines, . . .	O 43	Vanity Wishes		265
	I come from empty Noise, and tasteless Pomp, ...	O 262	Irene		7
	Shall hide me from the tasteless World for ever. . . .	O 333	Irene		48
TASTES					
	And perish ere he tastes the Joys of Conquest.	O 308	Irene		33
TASTFULL					
	Nor crop'd the tastfull herb, nor trac'd the verdant meads	Y 6	Virgil Daphnis		10
TATTER'D					
	The sober trader at a tatter'd cloak, ...	O 17	London		162
TAUGHT					
	Was early taught a Briton's right to prize, ...	O 15	London		119
	The rites that taught us to combine	O 190	Tr. Medea I		3
	His martial Rhet'rick taught the Greeks Resistance; . .	O 263	Irene		26
	Has taught my Slave the Language of Command!	O 323	Irene		2
	Beheld the tragic heroes taught to fear.	Y 67	Prologue Lethe		8
TAUNT					
	And turn the varied taunt a thousand ways.	O 17	London		165
	Dart the quick taunt, and edge the piercing gibe? . . .	O 33	Vanity Wishes		62
	----By taunt and insolence	Y 197	Irene	V	30
TAUNTS					
	Must hear all taunts, and hear without reply.	O 59	Pro Good Nat'd		14
TAX					
	Collect a tax, or farm a lottery, ...	O 12	London		58
	Collect a tax, or form a lottery, ...	O 12	London	V	58
	Nor annual tax was rais'e by annual wars.	Y 94	Vanity Wishes	V	60B
TE					
	Eroon te Bious Birchion, ede Sophon, ...	O 108	Eis Birchion		2
TEA					
	Tea, scandal, ivory teeth, and languid airs;	O 84	Epi Dist Moth.		19
	Another dish of tea.	O 158	Par Hermit III		4
	Thou canst not make the tea so fast	O 159	Par Hermit III		11
TEACH					
	Teach mimick censure her own faults to find, ...	O 81	Lady Birthday		17
	Thy musick teach the nobler art	O 121	To Miss Playin		35
	Teach me, thou venerable bow'r, ...	O 125	An Ode		29
	Bright wisdom teach me Curio's art, ...	O 126	An Ode		38
	O! sooth my Soul, and teach me how to lose thee. . . .	O 253	Irene		103
	Teach me the Grecian arts of soft persuasion	O 349	Irene	V	27
	And teach me to repell the Sultan's Passion.	O 265	Irene		3
	To tune the Tongue, to teach the Eyes to roll, ...	O 278	Irene		64
	Revenge and subtle Jealousy shall teach	O 307	Irene		24
	Will teach a gentler Term.	O 321	Irene		54
	Teach me to range my troopes in just array	Y 22	Tr Add. Battle		5
TEACHES					
	Only teaches how to cheat.	O 176	Tr Metastasi I		6
TEAR					
	To pour at will the counterfeited tear, ...	O 16	London		141
	Now lacerated Friendship claims a tear.	O 45	Vanity Wishes		304
	Vex ev'ry eye, and every bosom tear;	O 84	Epi Dist Moth.		39
	If Merit touch thee, shed a tear, ...	O 154	Epita. Hogarth		6
	--Scarce repress'd the starting tear;--	O 181	Parody Warton		6
	And shed the pitying Tear for lost Irene.	O 292	Irene		97
	An Let fall sometimes a tear for lost Irene	O 349	Irene	V	1
	and drop sometimes a tear for lost Irene	O 349	Irene	V	1

```
TEARS                                                 PAGE   TITLE             LINE
    And swell with tears the prostituted eye  . . . . . .   Y  57  London           V 199
    But you are ever drown'd in tears,  . . . . . . . . .   O  67  Hor. II Ode IX       9
    Restrain your tears and cease your cries,  . . . . .    O  70  Hor.II Ode XX       21
    Mimick your tears, and ridicule your woes;  . . . . .   O  74  Tr. Iliad Bk 6      22
    Tears, at my name, shall drown those beauteous eyes,  . .  O  75  Tr. Iliad Bk 6   27
    Far hence are banish'd vapours, spleen, and tears,  . .  O  84  Epi Dist Moth.     18
    Enough of unavailing Tears, Demetrius,  . . . . . .     O 253  Irene              104
    Or flow dissolving in a Woman's Tears?  . . . . . .     O 255  Irene               25
    In Sighs and Tears, in Transports and Embraces,  . . .  O 269  Irene               15
    In sighs and tears, and transports and embraces,  . . . O 367  Irene            V  27
    Droop at your tears and soften at your smile  . . . .   Y 145  Irene            V   4
    Thus bright in Tears, thus amiable in Ruin,  . . . .    O 276  Irene                7
    With supplicating tears and pure Devotion  . . . . .    O 364  Irene            V   2
    Say, how thou call'dst in Tears upon Demetrius!  . . .  O 295  Irene               26
    Soon might her Tears engage a Lover's Credit;  . . . .  O 327  Irene               17
    But Cries and Tears are vain, compar'd with Patience  . .  O 328  Irene             40
    These Tears, these Pangs, these last Remains of Life,  . O 329  Irene               53
    Could not her Prayers, her Innocence, her Tears,  . . . O 332  Irene               25
    May the morn's earliest tears on thee be shed,  . . . . Y   3  On a Daffodill      11
    To thee I then with tears complain'd  . . . . . . .     Y  11  Tr Hor Epode 9      19
    Her tears in show'rs descending as she spoke.  . . . .  Y  18  Tr. Iliad Bk 6      18
    "Ah! let not tears down that fair count'nance rowl,  . . Y  21  Tr. Iliad Bk 6     113
    Shed floods of tears, and sympathiz'd in pain.  . . . . Y  21  Tr. Iliad Bk 6     129
TEDIOUS
    Bears toilsome Days, and wakes long tedious Nights:  . .  O 247  Irene Epilogue    22
    Break through the Politician's tedious Forms,  . . . .  O 259  Irene              106
    These tedious Narratives of frozen Age  . . . . . .     O 259  Irene              113
    There wear the tedious Hours of Life away,  . . . . .   O 292  Irene               85
    To languish out the tedious hours of life  . . . . .    O 357  Irene            V  14
    Reserv'd to all the Pangs of tedious Death.  . . . . .  O 312  Irene               25
TEEMING
    The teeming mother, anxious for her race,  . . . . .    O  45  Vanity Wishes      319
    With artfull hand the teeming vines,  . . . . . . .     O  71  Hor. Epode II       18
    The teeming Year's whole Product shall devour,  . . . . O 110  To Posterity        11
    When fruitful summer loads the teeming plain,  . . . .  O 151  The Ant              7
TEETH
    Tea, scandal, ivory teeth, and languid airs;  . . . .   O  84  Epi Dist Moth.      19
    Her teeth the night with darkness dyes,  . . . . . .    O 127  To Lyce, Lady       13
TEI
    Tei Kallous dunamei ti telos; Zeus panta dedoken  . . . O 103  Eis Elisses          1
TEIZING
    Bid your teizing doubts depart;  . . . . . . . . .      O 176  Tr Metastasi I       2
TELAMON
    Idomeneus, the godlike Telamon  . . . . . . . . .       Y  19  Tr. Iliad Bk 6      55
TELL
    Let hist'ry tell where rival kings command,  . . . . .  O  31  Vanity Wishes       29
    Historians tell where rival kings command,  . . . . .   Y  93  Vanity Wishes    V  29
    Yet Vane could tell what ills from beauty spring;  . . . O  45  Vanity Wishes      321
    This Night, distinguish'd by your Smile, shall tell,  . .  O  57  Prologue Comus   11
    To tell each Bystander, what none can deny,  . . . . .  O 173  Tr Fr Pantomim       2
    Smite thy bosom, sage, and tell,  . . . . . . . .       O 181  Parody Warton        3
    Strike thy bosom, sage, and tell,  . . . . . . . .      O 181  Parody Warton    V   3
    Tell me, tell me, gentle Dove.  . . . . . . . . .       O 185  Anacreon Ode 9       6
    Tell me, tell me, gentle Dove.  . . . . . . . . .       O 185  Anacreon Ode 9       6
    Tell the woes of wilful waste,  . . . . . . . . .       O 197  Song Congratu.      26
    Tell the spoils of wilful waste,  . . . . . . . . .     O 197  Song Congratu.   V  26
    And tell the Secrets of their conscious Walks;  . . . . O 255  Irene               27
    To tell the Secrets of their conscious Shades  . . . .  O 373  Irene            V  20
    Tell me the Cause, that while thy Name, Demetrius,  . . O 305  Irene               25
    Yet tell.  . . . . . . . . . . . . . .                  O 316  Irene               21
         To tell, or hear, were Waste of Life.  . . . . .   O 316  Irene               21
    Tell how Demetrius shun'd his single Hand,  . . . . .   O 318  Irene               13
    You who tell  . . . . . . . . . . . . .                 Y 209  Irene            V  54
    And tell the horrid Tale with chearful Face;  . . . .   O 329  Irene               11
TELLS
    And Slaves, the Maxim tells, are always Foes.  . . . .  O  46  Vanity Wishes    V330B
    And only credits what Experience tells.  . . . . . .    O 255  Irene               19
TELOS
    Tei Kallous dunamei ti telos; Zeus panta dedoken  . . . O 103  Eis Elisses          1
TEMP'RATE
    But grant, the virtues of a temp'rate prime  . . . . .  O  44  Vanity Wishes      291
    With temp'rate zeal, and wise anxiety;  . . . . . .     O 118  Epitaph Hanmer      30
TEMPER
    Temper their swords and point their missive darts.  . . Y  24  Tr Add. Battle      77
TEMPER'D
    With cream and sugar temper'd well,  . . . . . . .      O 158  Par Hermit III   V   3
TEMPEST
    Loud roars the tempest, high the billows rise,  . . . . O  82  Young Author         8
    The Weight of Years, and totters to the Tempest,  . . . O 250  Irene               45
    Drives on the Tempest of destructive War,  . . . . .    O 268  Irene               26
    Sinks like the sighing of a Tempest spent,  . . . . .   O 275  Irene               92
    Sinks into sighs like the sighing of a Tempest spent  . .  O 367  Irene          V  13
    But when the Tempest with sonorous Wing  . . . . . .    O 298  Irene               22
TEMPESTS
    He sees no boist'rous Tempests sweep  . . . . . . .     O  71  Hor. Epode II       11
    He sees no Northern Tempests sweep  . . . . . . . .     O  71  Hor. Epode II    V  11
    By Eastern Tempests hither tost,  . . . . . . . .       O  73  Hor. Epode II       58
    O'er the sad plains perpetual tempests sigh;  . . . .   O  84  Epi Dist Moth.      32
    There, mid Tempests loudest roars,  . . . . . . .       O 145  Tr Boeth. II.4      17
    Like subterraneous tempests with dire eruption burst their  Y 115  Irene        V  49
```

333

TEMPESTS	(CONTINUED)	PAGE	TITLE	LINE
caverns				
Why foam the swelling Waves when Tempests rise? . . .		O 281	Irene	51
TEMPESTUOUS				
Dear hapless Maid--tempestuous Grief o'erbears		O 252	Irene	77
Dear helpless Maid--tempestuous Grief o'erbears		O 252	Irene	V 77
I felt the Force of his tempestuous Arm, ...		O 307	Irene	19
TEMPLE				
A roving Soldier seiz'd in Sophia's Temple		O 258	Irene	94
In Sophia's Temple!--What Alarm!--Proceed.		O 258	Irene	97
To offer up my vows in the temple built by the Father of Mankind		O 348	Irene	V 1
Implor'd my Leave to visit Mecca's Temple;		O 273	Irene	44
TEMPLES				
Usurp our Temples, and profane our Altars.		O 251	Irene	69
Again her Temples sound with holy Musick:		O 291	Irene	55
Than ruind palaces or flaming temples		Y 177	Irene	V111D
TEMPT				
Nor tempt the snares of wily love.		O 121	To Miss Playin	10
Nor farther tempt the avenging rage of Heaven		Y 168	Irene	V 134
To court the sword and tempt the glutted rack		Y 196	Irene	V 18D
Nor tempt the dangers of this deathfull day		Y 19	Tr. Iliad Bk 6	47
TEMPTATION				
Nor found again the bright Temptation fail?		O 259	Irene	125
TEMPTING				
But thou, should tempting villainy present		O 14	London	85
Lest ropes be wanting in the tempting spring, ...		O 22	London	246
And ropes be wanting in the tempting spring, ...		Y 60	London	V 246
Should tempting Novelty thy cell refrain, ...		O 37	Vanity Wishes	149
Fix not where the tempting Height		O 145	Tr Boeth. II.4	13
TEMPTS				
"Tempts me to be wild again:		O 185	Anacreon Ode 9	22
TEN				
And unrelenting sport ten thousand lives away; . . .		O 83	Epi Dist Moth.	9
Thrice ten long years he labour'd for the State; . . .		O 118	Epitaph Hanmer	14
TEND				
From thee, great God, we spring, to thee we tend, . . .		O 130	Tr. Rambler 7	7
Ladies--stock and tend your Hive, ...		O 178	Thrale 35 Year	11
Here let me tend her with officious Care, ...		O 320	Irene	23
TENDER				
Two tender kids, the hopes of all the flock.		O 64	Virgil Past.I	20
For kind, for tender nymphs the myrtle blooms, ...		O 84	Epi Dist Moth.	14
Cease, lovely thief! my tender limbs to wound, ...		O 106	Eliza plucking	5
The tender infant, meek and mild, ...		O 157	Par. Hermit I	1
Forgive those Fears that shake the tender Frame? . . .		O 266	Irene	25
To tender Friendship, praise him to his Mistress. . . .		O 267	Irene	5
And tender Accents quiver'd on my Lips, ...		O 282	Irene	67
Does not thy Bosom, for I know thee tender, ...		O 329	Irene	5
TENDERNESS				
The Christian's tenderness? or womans weakness		Y 189	Irene	V 1C
TENETS				
With slavish tenets taint our poison'd youth, ...		O 12	London	55
TENTH				
When the tenth Sun had set upon our Sorrows, ...		O 254	Irene	120
TENTS				
Your thin battalions and your empty tents		Y 120	Irene	V 29A
TERM				
Ah! let not Censure term our Fate our Choice, ...		O 53	Pro Drury-Lane	51
Will teach a gentler Term.		O 321	Irene	54
TERMINATE				
Let kind Compulsion terminate the Contest.		O 321	Irene	50
My Hopes, my Wishes, terminate in Life, ...		O 327	Irene	22
TERMS				
Reason with Reason fights on equal Terms, ...		O 287	Irene	9
TEROR				
And teror and confusion stalk before them		Y 115	Irene	V 49E
TERRESTRIAL				
Quaff the full draught of each terrestrial joy		Y 146	Irene	V 20
TERROR SEE TEROR				
Grief swell thine Eyes, and Terror chill thy Breast. . .		O 110	To Posterity	4
Hail, Terror of the Monarchs of the World, ...		O 262	Irene	1
The Pride and Terror of succeeding Days, ...		O 268	Irene	12
And (terror) horrour shudders in their gloomy caverns .		Y 136	Irene	V 31A
This all-subduing hand, this gen'ral terror		Y 136	Irene	V 32
With all the Speed of Terror and of Guilt.		O 275	Irene	86
And plac'd the beamy terror on the ground		Y 20	Tr. Iliad Bk 6	96
TERRORS				
Lords of the street, and terrors of the way;		O 21	London	231
What hopes, what terrors does thy gift create, ...		O 95	Sprig of Myrtl	1
What Fears, what terrors does this gift create, ...		O 95	Sprig of Myrtl	V 1
What Hopes, what Terrors rush upon my Soul!		O 259	Irene	104
Death rises to my View, with all his Terrors;		O 265	Irene	12
Nor end my Terrors with the Sultan's Death;		O 300	Irene	67
And all the terrors of the dreadful main		Y 201	Irene	V 10C
And add new Terrors to the Face of Death.		O 330	Irene	8
TERROURS				
And terrours of the Stormy Main, ...		O 69	Hor.II Ode 14	14
Cast off all idle terrours of hereafter		Y 146	Irene	V 19
TES				
Eis to tes Elisses peri ton Oneiron Ainigma		O 103	Eis Elisses	T

	PAGE	TITLE	LINE
TEST			
And bid Success become the Test of Truth;	O 291	Irene	64
And test thy life in scorn and safety	Y 197	Irene	V 26
TETHER			
Loosen'd from the Minor's tether, ...	O 196	Song Congratu.	5
TEXTURE			
And wove the feeble Texture of her Nerves, ...	O 266	Irene	24
THALES			
When injur'd Thales bids the town farewell, ...	O 8	London	2
While Thales waits the wherry that contains	O 9	London	19
Indignant Thales eyes the neighb'ring town.	O 10	London	34
THAMES'S			
On Thames's banks, in silent thought we stood, ...	O 10	London	21
THAN			
Or like a gibbet better than a wheel;	O 15	London	108
Than when a blockhead's insult points the dart. . . .	O 18	London	169
And raise his treasures higher than before.	O 19	London	205
For less than rent the dungeons of the Strand;	O 20	London	215
For less than hires the dungeons of the Strand; . . .	Y 58	London	V 215
How much more safe the vassal than the lord;	O 31	Vanity Wishes	32
For I shall never think him less than God;	O 64	Virgil Past.I	8
Swifter than Icarus Ill flie	O 70	Hor.II Ode XX	13
More false, more cruel than the seas and wind.	O 82	Young Author	14
More false, more cruel than the seas or wind.	O 82	Young Author	V 14
Not less capricious than a reigning fair, ...	O 95	Sprig of Myrtl	5
Not less capricious than the reigning fair, ...	O 95	Sprig of Myrtl	V 5
Less pleas'd to triumph than to spare.	O 137	Tr Rambler 143	2
Better Years than Thirty five;	O 178	Thrale 35 Year	4
Have a turnip than his father.	O 183	Burlesque Vega	4
Have a turnip than a father.	O 183	Burlesque Vega	V 4
"More than all thou canst not know;	O 186	Anacreon Ode 9	42
Before such Foes of more than human Force;	O 250	Irene	49
Desires more pure, and other Cares than Love.	O 263	Irene	8
Than Amurath--	O 264	Irene	20
Than Amurath, accustom'd to Command, ...	O 264	Irene	21
Than all the Wisdom of the grave Divan.	O 287	Irene	8
Than ruind palaces or flaming temples	Y 177	Irene	V111D
If thou art more than the gay Dream of Fancy, ...	O 310	Irene	12
More than a pleasing Sound without a Meaning, ...	O 310	Irene	13
"Here fairer than his flock the shepherd lyes	Y 7	Virgil Daphnis	30
Far dearer than his own or father's life	Y 18	Tr. Iliad Bk 6	6
Swifter than lightning to the fight he flies.	Y 21	Tr. Iliad Bk 6	126
THANATIO			
Kai Bion, eipen, otan ripses Thanatio Belessi, ...	O 108	Eis Birchion	3
THANK			
Thank Heav'n in daily hymns for my our deliverance . .	Y 166	Irene	V 93
THANKS			
The senate's thanks, the gazette's pompous tale, . . .	O 39	Vanity Wishes	177
Thanks for this kind Relief--with Speed admit him. . .	O 294	Irene	5
Thanks for this kind relief. Conduct him hither . . .	O 370	Irene	V 15
THAT			
217		OMITTED WORD	
THAT'S			
Will she that's false to Heavn, to me be faithfull . .	Y 186	Irene	V 4
THATS			
Or reason with the slave thats saved Demetrius	Y 210	Irene	V 23
TH'			
But hark! th' affrighted crowd's tumultuous cries . . .	O 18	London	182
Sustain th' approaching fire's tremendous light; . . .	O 18	London	187
Fate wings with ev'ry wish th' afflictive dart, . . .	O 31	Vanity Wishes	15
Does envy seize thee? crush th' upbraiding joy, . . .	O 32	Vanity Wishes	39
Th' insidious rival and the gaping heir.	O 32	Vanity Wishes	48
And feed with varied fools th' eternal jest:	O 32	Vanity Wishes	52
And feed with change of new born fools th' eternal jest: . .	Y 94	Vanity Wishes	V 52
Delusive Fortune hears th' incessant call, ...	O 33	Vanity Wishes	75
And detestation rids th' indignant wall.	O 34	Vanity Wishes	90
On weak foundations raise th' enormous weight?	O 35	Vanity Wishes	126
What gave great Villiers to th' assassin's knife, . . .	O 35	Vanity Wishes	129
In sober state th' imaginary lawn	Y 98	Vanity Wishes	V138B
Th' insulted sea with humbler thoughts he gains, . . .	O 42	Vanity Wishes	237
Th' incumber'd oar scarce leaves the dreaded coast . .	O 42	Vanity Wishes	239
No sounds alas would touch th' impervious ear, ...	O 43	Vanity Wishes	269
The notes unfelt would strike th' impervious ear, . . .	Y 104	Vanity Wishes	V 269
And lags superfluous on th' incumbred stage, ...	Y 106	Vanity Wishes	V 308
Perhaps, for who can guess th' Effects of Chance? . . .	O 53	Pro Drury-Lane	45
Th' offended burgess hoards his angry tale, ...	O 60	Pro Good Nat'd	17
The great, 'tis true, can charm th' electing tribe; . .	O 60	Pro Good Nat'd	25
Th' oblivious grave's inviolable shade.	O 62	Pro Word Wise	10
And me to tune at ease th' unequal reeds.	O 64	Virgil Past.I	12
Nor taints with Death th' envenom'd Dart, ...	O 66	To A. Fuscus	3
Nor, Valgius, on th' Armenian shores	O 67	Hor. II Ode IX	5
From th' envious world with scorn I spring, ...	O 70	Hor.II Ode XX	3
Quaff Nectar with th' immortal Gods.	O 70	Hor.II Ode XX	8
And where beneath th' inclement Skie	O 70	Hor.II Ode XX	15
Blest as th' immortal Gods is he	O 71	Hor. Epode II	1
And faintly draw th' inverted Plow.	O 73	Hor. Epode II	70
Rage with disdain, and hope th' approaching war; . . .	O 75	Tr Add. Battle	1
Breathless at length they leave th' unfinish'd war . .	O 76	Tr Add. Battle	6
Th' enormous Gyants smoke upon the Ground.	O 76	Tr Add. Battle	25
And wander sportive o'er th' Elysian plain:	O 77	Tr Add. Battle	43

	PAGE	TITLE		LINE
From bold invaders clear'd th' Italian lands	O 78	Festina Lente		19
Th' Apostles round the world were sent,	O 79	Feast St Simon		25
And scarce can breath th' infected sky,	O 79	Feast St Simon		35
He feels th' unfading wreath surround his head;	O 82	Young Author		22
Receive th' unhappy ghosts of scornful maids.	O 83	Epi Dist Moth.		13
Th' unhappy lovers graves the Myrtle spreads;	O 95	Sprig of Myrtl		10
The Bear enrag'd th' affrighted Moon shall dread;	O 111	To Posterity		17
Henceforth th' inviolable Bloom invade,	O 111	To Posterity		21
Thus early wise, th' endanger'd realm to aid,	O 117	Epitaph Hanmer		9
Th' adoring youth, and envious fair,	O 122	Stella Mourn.		13
This habitant th' aerial regions boast.	O 138	Tr Rambler 161		1
Soon th' aspiring Fabric falls,	O 145	Tr Boeth. II.4		9
Scorning now th' o'erflowing Flood,	O 149	Tr Boet III.12		38
When grasping Bliss th' unsteady mind	O 150	Tr Boet III.12		56
That traced th' essential form of Grace,	O 154	Epita. Hogarth		2
That wav'd th' essential form of Grace,	O 154	Epita. Hogarth	V	2
Who drew th' essential form of Grace;	O 155	Epita. Hogarth	V	2
Here clos'd in Death th' attentive Eyes	O 155	Epita. Hogarth	V	3
May ye th' alternate blessings share	O 189	Epilogue	V	5
And sure th' Eternal Master found	O 201	Death Dr Levet		27
Urg'd by th' imperious Soldier's fierce Command,	O 249	Irene		16
Th' accumulated Wealth of toiling Ages.	O 249	Irene		19
When Avarice corrupts th' emasculated Nation--or	O 347	Irene	V	25
Flows through each Member of th' embodied State,	O 256	Irene		58
Fills all th' astonish'd Empire with Confusion,	O 257	Irene		77
And chang'd th' endearing Smile and am'rous Whisper	O 259	Irene		111
But yet th' Attempt	O 260	Irene		132
Th' inestimable Privilege of Breathing!	O 260	Irene		136
Soon will th' unequal Contest be decided,	O 261	Irene		18
Remote from Tumult, in th' adjoining Palace,	O 263	Irene		1
Think on th' insulting Scorn, the conscious Pangs,	O 266	Irene		19
The future Miseries that wait th' Apostate;	O 266	Irene		20
Th' impetuous Sallies of excessive Virtue,	O 267	Irene		47
Wouldst thou subdue th' obdurate Cannibal	O 267	Irene		4
Receive th' impatient Sultan to thy Arms;	O 267	Irene		10
Distrust th' eternal Fortresses of Nature,	O 268	Irene		31
Th' important Hour had pass'd unheeded by,	O 269	Irene		12
A sudden Pause th' imperfect Sense suspended,	O 270	Irene		13
Th' insidious Bassa fir'd by Disappointment--	O 273	Irene		32
Before th' assembled Troops proclaim his Crimes;	O 273	Irene		35
Th' adoring Soldiers would revenge their Idol.	O 273	Irene		42
Th' eternal Snows that freeze beyond Meotis,	O 274	Irene		59
Let not th' unbounded Greatness of his Mind	O 275	Irene		72
Th' attractive Softness, and th' indearing Smile,	O 277	Irene		51
Th' attractive Softness, and th' indearing Smile,	O 277	Irene		51
Th' enlivening Wit, the penetrating Reason?	O 278	Irene		56
If Greatness please thee, mount th' imperial Seat;	O 279	Irene		84
Where hast thou linger'd while th' encumber'd Hours	O 279	Irene		3
And turn'd th' instructive Page of Human Life,	O 281	Irene		33
Th' unpractis'd Dervise, or sequester'd Faquir.	O 281	Irene		37
Spread by Degrees, and dread th' oppressing Stream;	O 282	Irene		58
Th' appointed Vessel to yon' shaded Bay,	O 284	Irene		51
Or felt th' Impatience of obstructed Love,	O 285	Irene		4
Give me, before th' approaching Hour of Fate,	O 285	Irene		5
Th' unquestion'd Claim of Conquerors, and Kings!	O 286	Irene		9
Can then th' Assassin lift his treach'rous Hand	O 286	Irene		11
Justice demands--But see th' approaching Sultan.	O 286	Irene		15
In my weak Ear th' intoxicating Sounds.	O 288	Irene		6
Not yet inspire th' omniscience of a queen	O 366	Irene	V	19
Shake off th' Incumbrances of State a moment,	O 289	Irene		7
No more I boast th' ambitious Name of Friend,	O 289	Irene		10
Th' Eternal gave it, and that End is Virtue.	O 290	Irene		31
Pourd Storms of fire upon th' approaching Foe	O 364	Irene	V	1
Implor'd th' eternal Power to shield my Country,	O 290	Irene		49
Nor think th' Intention sanctifies the Deed:	O 291	Irene		59
Close like th' eternal Bars of Death upon thee,	O 292	Irene		80
Close like th' eternal Bars of Death upon You	O 357	Irene	V	10
Nor dare to pass th' insuperable Bound.	O 292	Irene		92
Shrinks at th' o'erpow'ring Gleams of regal State,	O 292	Irene		100
Shrinks at th' oerpowring blaze of regal State	O 368	Irene	V	30
Stoop from thy Flight, trace back th' entangled Thought,	O 293	Irene		127
Will not th' Apostate feel the Pangs of Guilt,	O 294	Irene		132
Curst as the Tyrant of th' infernal Realms,	O 294	Irene		134
Dispatch; th' encreasing Danger	O 297	Irene		12
And Nature's Rights entreat th' asserting Sword.	O 297	Irene		3
Destruction flashes from th' insidious Mine,	O 298	Irene		30
And sweeps th' exulting Conqueror away:	O 298	Irene		31
Th' approaching Sultan forc'd me from the Palace;	O 299	Irene		47
Th' Anxieties of Love.	O 300	Irene		55
There shall soft Leisure wing th' excursive Soul,	O 302	Irene		118
At length th' unwilling Sun resigns the World	O 302	Irene		1
Our Bark unseen has reach'd th' appointed Bay,	O 304	Irene		1
While I destroy th' Oppressor of Mankind?	O 305	Irene		37
Nor will I trust th' uncertain Chance of Combat;	O 307	Irene		21
Behold, within th' embow'ring Grove	O 314	Irene		10
Thus shall he live to strike th' important Blow,	O 308	Irene		32
And idolize th' Apostate I contemn.	O 310	Irene		11
Adore the Beauty but despise th' Apostate.	O 350	Irene	V	26
Till conscious of th' incircling Deity,	O 313	Irene		7
See how the Moon through all th' unclouded Sky	O 313	Irene		1

TH'	(CONTINUED)	PAGE	TITLE	LINE
Play'd fearless in th' inviolated Shades.		O 314	Irene	7
Resumes th' imperious Air of haughty Virtue.		O 314	Irene	15
Are these th' unceasing Joys, th' unmingled Pleasures		O 314	Irene	16
Are these th' unceasing Joys, th' unmingled Pleasures		O 314	Irene	16
Is this th' unshaken Confidence in Heav'n?		O 314	Irene	18
Shall throw th' attending Janizaries round thee.		O 319	Irene	34
In vain I listen to th' inviting Call		O 320	Irene	10
Let us not struggle with th' eternal Will,		O 320	Irene	16
Th' expanded hand of lib'ral Heav'n		Y 199	Irene	V 16
To guide thy Passage shall th' aerial Spirits		O 322	Irene	7
To Guide thy passage shall th' Starry Spirits		O 364	Irene	V 26
Th' applauding Sky shall pour forth all its Beams		O 322	Irene	9
Forgive, fair Excellence, th' unwilling Tongue,		O 324	Irene	1
Th' unpitying Ministers of Turkish Justice,		O 325	Irene	9
We ask'd, with tim'rous Tongue, th' Offender's Name,		O 325	Irene	23
Recall th' extorted Doom.--It must be so,		O 326	Irene	40
A Stranger to th' Oppressor's savage Joy,		O 329	Irene	6
The Greek, Demetrius! whom th' expiring Bassa		O 331	Irene	10
Bear off with eager Haste th' unfinish'd Sentence,		O 333	Irene	53
well th' Eternal Mind thus her doom decreed		O 345	Irene	V 34
And in the traytress bad th' apostate bleed		Y 217	Irene	V 12
And mortals trace th' Almighty's path in v<ain>		Y 217	Irene	V 14
By Daphnis' skill th' Armenian tigers broke		Y 6	Virgil Daphnis	13
And sees the motions of th' harmonious sphere;		Y 7	Virgil Daphnis	35
Against th' omnipotence of gold		Y 11	Tr Hor Epode 9	22
Th' atridae there and Tydeus' mighty son,		Y 19	Tr. Iliad Bk 6	54
The fruitfull fields th' industrious people till'd,		Y 23	Tr Add. Battle	28
Not so while long th' undaunted race maintain'd		Y 23	Tr Add. Battle	36
Against th' invading birds their native land:		Y 23	Tr Add. Battle	37
And first a sound invades th' astonish'd ear.		Y 25	Tr Add. Battle	91
Above their heads th' embattled squadrons hung		Y 25	Tr Add. Battle	94
In his fell claws, then into th' air he springs.		Y 26	Tr Add. Battle	126
Then flies aloft; th' astonish'd warriours feel		Y 26	Tr Add. Battle	132
And heard th' ill omen'd catcall's direful cry.		Y 67	Prologue Lethe	10
THE				
	2525		OMITTED WORD	
THEAN				
Kai toios Paphien plexen eroti Thean.		O 172	On Marlborough	2
THEATRE				
Spoken At The Opening Of The Theatre		O 50	Pro Drury-lane	T
Behold this Theatre, and grieve no more.		O 57	Prologue Comus	10
The pompous theatre the tow'ring arch		Y 177	Irene	V 109
THEBAN				
Who has not read the Theban brothers' hate?		Y 22	Tr Add. Battle	14
THEE				
Does envy seize thee? crush th' upbraiding joy,		O 32	Vanity Wishes	39
To thee were solemn toys or empty shew,		O 33	Vanity Wishes	65
And virtue guard thee to the throne of Truth!		O 37	Vanity Wishes	142
Should Reason guide thee with her brightest ray,		O 37	Vanity Wishes	145
Nor think the doom of man revers'd for thee:		O 38	Vanity Wishes	156
By thee wholl citys burn, wholl nations fall!		O 77	Festina Lente	12
By thee Orestes plung'd his vengefull dart		O 77	Festina Lente	13
Hurry'd to death by thee, Flaminius fell,		O 77	Festina Lente	15
In vain for thee the monarch sighs,		O 100	Ode Friendship	19
In vain for thee the tyrant sighs,		O 100	Ode Friendship	V 19
Just Phoebus would devote his plant to thee.		O 106	Eliza plucking	8
Till angels wake thee with a note like thine.		O 113	Epit. Phillips	6
From thee, great God, we spring, to thee we tend,		O 130	Tr. Rambler 7	7
From thee, great God, we spring, to thee we tend,		O 130	Tr. Rambler 7	7
The more I honour thee, the less I love.		O 140	Tr Rambler 188	1
All the World afraid but thee,		O 145	Tr Boeth. II.4	20
All her Charms to thee belong;		O 150	Tr Boet III.12	42
Shall spring to seize thee like an ambush'd foe.		O 152	The Ant	16
If Genius warm thee, Reader, stay,		O 154	Epita. Hogarth	5
If Merit touch thee, shed a tear,		O 154	Epita. Hogarth	6
I Therefore pray thee, Renny dear,		O 158	Par Hermit III	1
I pray thee, gentle Renny dear,		O 158	Par Hermit III	V 1
In its wild ravages distinguish'd thee		Y 115	Irene	V 49B
O! sooth my Soul, and teach me how to lose thee.		O 253	Irene	103
That long to hail thee Chief.		O 254	Irene	137
Awake each Faculty that sleeps within thee,		O 254	Irene	2
And Indias rajas ask their doom from thee		Y 131	Irene	V 32
Not all like thee can brave the Shocks of Fate,		O 266	Irene	34
Courts thee to shake on a dependent Throne;		O 268	Irene	22
These Days of Love and Pleasure charm not thee;		O 271	Irene	2
And arm the Persian Heretick against thee;		O 274	Irene	55
To scatter Happiness and Plenty round thee,		O 278	Irene	69
To State and Pow'r I court thee, not to Ruin:		O 279	Irene	80
For thee, my fair, shall India's spices		Y 150	Irene	V 81
Security shall spread her Shield before thee,		O 279	Irene	82
Pleasure shall spread her downy Pinions o'er thee		O 350	Irene	V 21
And Love infcld thee with his downy Wings.		O 279	Irene	83
For thee shall Forests rise and Rivers flow		O 350	Irene	V 22
And pleasure shall shade thee with her downy pinions		Y 150	Irene	V 83
If Greatness please thee, mount th' imperial Seat;		O 279	Irene	84
If Pleasure charm thee, view this soft Retreat;		O 279	Irene	85
by artists for thee.		O 350	Irene	V 25
To make thee blest each Region shall combine		O 351	Irene	V 26
Who hear thee speak, and not abandon Reason?		O 281	Irene	43

THEE	(CONTINUED)		PAGE	TITLE		LINE
Nor let Demetrius know thee for a Rival.	. . . . . .		O 282	Irene		71
Superiour Majesty proclaims thee Queen,	. . . . .		O 288	Irene	V	2
Long would my Zeal for Mahomet and Thee			O 288	Irene		11
I'll open my breast--clasp thee--forget	. . . . . .		Y 161	Irene	V	13
greatness--						
Close like th' eternal Bars of Death upon thee,	. . .		O 292	Irene		80
Aspasia! do I once again behold thee?	. . . .		O 294	Irene		2
O say, what guardian Pow'r convey'd thee hither.	. . .		O 296	Irene		33
And what protecting angel led thee hither	. . . . .		Y 170	Irene	V	33
I stand amaz'd, and ask, if yet I clasp thee.	. . . . .		O 296	Irene		37
Then--O my Fair, I cannot bid thee goe;	. . . . . .		O 297	Irene		15
Then--O my Fair, I cannot bid thee go;	. . . . . .		O 297	Irene	V	15
Now but reflects those Beams that flow'd from thee.	. .		O 298	Irene		15
And sought this happy Grove in quest of Thee.	. . . .		O 299	Irene		50
anguish of my soul before Thee.	. . . .		Y 189	Irene	V	1
Nor think that Effort lost which rescues thee.	. . . .		O 317	Irene		47
Forbear, Demetrius, 'tis Aspasia calls thee;	. . . .		O 318	Irene		8
Unclasp'd his Iron Gripe to set thee free?	. . . . .		O 318	Irene		16
Fly, Wretch, while yet my Pity grants thee Flight;	. . .		O 319	Irene		23
Alike my Death or thine is gain to thee,	. . . . .		O 319	Irene		32
Shall throw th' attending Janizaries round thee.	. . .		O 319	Irene		34
Depart, Demetrius, lest my Fate involve thee,	. . . .		O 320	Irene		13
Remember, Peace and Anguish are before thee,	. . . .		O 321	Irene		37
Kind Heav'n affords thee, and inviting Mercy	. . . .		O 321	Irene		41
Holds out her Hand to lead thee back to Truth.	. . . .		O 321	Irene		42
Go Happy Bark, thy sacred Freight secures thee	. . . .		O 364	Irene	V	24
But 'tis not mine to judge--I scorn and leave thee.	. .		O 324	Irene		22
But who can hear thee beg without compliance	. . . .		Y 205	Irene	V	33
Already shakes his bloody Sabre o'er thee.	. . . . .		O 327	Irene		10
Does not thy Bosom, for I know thee tender,	. . . .		O 329	Irene		5
Hear! shall I hear thee! did'st thou hear Irene?	. . .		O 333	Irene		56
While she yet beg'd to plead her Cause before thee.	. .		O 334	Irene		67
What Plagues, what Tortures, are in Store for thee,	. .		O 334	Irene		1
May the morn's earliest tears on thee be shed,	. . . .		Y 3	On a Daffodill		11
May throngs of beautous virgins 'round thee crowd,	. .		Y 3	On a Daffodill		13
Cleora's self, fair flower, shall fade like thee,	. . .		Y 4	On a Daffodill		27
To thee I told the causes of my smart,	. . . . . .		Y 11	Tr Hor Epode 9		18
To thee I then with tears complain'd	. . . . . .		Y 11	Tr Hor Epode 9		19
A father, brother, husband, all in thee.	. . . . . .		Y 19	Tr. Iliad Bk 6		45
THEFT						
Who start at theft, and blush at perjury?	. . . . .		O 13	London		68
THEIOS						
Ek Dios estin onar, Theios pot egrapsen Homeros,	. . .		O 103	Eis Elisses		3
THEIR						
Their ambush here relentless ruffians lay,	. . . . . .		O 9	London		15
Explain their country's dear-bought rights away,	. . .		O 11	London		53
Their air, their dress, their politicks import;	. . .		O 15	London		110
Their air, their dress, their politicks import;	. . .		O 15	London		110
Their air, their dress, their politicks import;	. . .		O 15	London		110
No gainful trade their industry can 'scape,	. . . . .		O 15	London		113
And what their Armies lost, their Cringes	. . . . .		O 16	London	V 122
gain?						
And what their Armies lost, their Cringes	. . . . .		O 16	London	V 122
gain?						
Admires their wond'rous talents for the stage:	. . . .		O 16	London		133
Practis'd their master's notions to embrace,	. . . .		O 16	London		136
And as their patron hints the cold or heat,	. . . .		O 16	London		142
Their prudent insults to the poor confine;	. . . . .		O 21	London		233
Hate dogs their flight, and insult mocks their end.	. .		O 33	Vanity Wishes		78
Hate dogs their flight, and insult mocks their end.	. .		O 33	Vanity Wishes		78
Our supple tribes repress their patriot throats,	. . .		O 34	Vanity Wishes		95
Their wish is full to riot and to rail.	. . . . . .		O 34	Vanity Wishes		98
To him the church, the realm, their pow'rs consign,	. .		O 34	Vanity Wishes		101
To him the church, the state, their pow're resign,	. .		Y 96	Vanity Wishes	V 101
What but their wish indulg'd in courts to shine,	. . .		O 36	Vanity Wishes		133
And Sloth's bland Opiates shed their fumes in	. . .		O 37	Vanity Wishes	V 150
vain;						
And mortgag'd states their grandsires wreaths regret,	.		O 39	Vanity Wishes		187
And mortgag'd states their former wreaths regret,	. .		Y 100	Vanity Wishes	V 187
Their grandsires glories debt;	. . . .		Y 100	Vanity Wishes	V 188
Behold surrounding kings their pow'r combine,	. . . .		O 40	Vanity Wishes		199
In vain surrounding kings their pow'rs combine,	. . .		Y 101	Vanity Wishes	V 199
All times their scenes of pompous woes afford,	. . .		O 41	Vanity Wishes		223
And heap their vallies with the gaudy foe;	. . . . .		O 42	Vanity Wishes		236
In vain their gifts the bounteous seasons pour,	. . .		O 43	Vanity Wishes		261
Where then shall Hope and Fear their objects find?	. .		O 47	Vanity Wishes		343
They pleas'd their Age, and did not aim to mend.	. . .		O 52	Pro Drury-Lane		22
Their Cause was gen'ral, their Supports were strong,	. .		O 52	Pro Drury-Lane		25
Their Cause was gen'ral, their Supports were strong,	. .		O 52	Pro Drury-Lane		25
Their Slaves were willing, and their Reign was long;	. .		O 52	Pro Drury-Lane		26
Their Slaves were willing, and their Reign was long;	. .		O 52	Pro Drury-Lane		26
As Tyrants doom their Tools of Guilt to die;	. . .		O 53	Pro Drury-Lane		56
Uncheck'd on both, loud rabbles vent their rage,	. . .		O 59	Pro Good Nat'd		15
Their schemes of spite the poet's foes dismiss,	. . .		O 60	Pro Good Nat'd		19
Their blood the consecrated stones shall dye:	. . . .		O 64	Virgil Past.I		10
Far from their antient fields and humble cots.	. . .		O 64	Virgil Past.I		18
Foretold the coming evil by their dismal croak.	. . .		O 65	Virgil Past.I		25
Their fumes ascending to the Skie;	. . . .		O 69	Hor.II Ode 14		8
Their dugs with milk distended, home!	. . . . . .		O 73	Hor. Epode II		68
Their souls dismiss'd through many a ghastly wound,	. .		O 74	Tr. Iliad Bk 6		18

THEIR (CONTINUED)		PAGE	TITLE		LINE
Not long they stood, when stooping from their height	O	75	Tr Add. Battle		2
Thick from their wounded wings the feathers fly,	O	75	Tr Add. Battle		4
But their lost strength and vigour soon return,	O	76	Tr Add. Battle		8
They clap their wings, and with new fury burn;	O	76	Tr Add. Battle		9
Their foes the shock sustain in Battle skill'd	O	76	Tr Add. Battle		12
Their foes attacks, and wield their arms with pain.	O	76	Tr Add. Battle		27
Their foes attacks, and wield their arms with pain.	O	76	Tr Add. Battle		27
Part turn their Backs, part seiz'd with wild surprise	O	76	Tr Add. Battle		28
For fear retards their flight, the cruell Crane	O	76	Tr Add. Battle		31
Scatters their breathless bodies o'er the plain.	O	76	Tr Add. Battle		32
So by their great decree Assyria fell	O	76	Tr Add. Battle		37
Could cancell their irrevocable Law.	O	76	Tr Add. Battle		40
And shades of Pygmies swim before their eye.	O	77	Tr Add. Battle		48
But move their numrous arms in Musicks sound,	O	77	Tr Add. Battle		51
And drove the swarthy troops to their own barren sands.	O	78	Festina Lente		20
Let them prolong their turgid lays	O	78	Feast St Simon		4
Who to their Lord were ever dear,	O	78	Feast St Simon		10
Their faith, or force them to forsake	O	79	Feast St Simon		14
The Steps their Saviour trod;	O	79	Feast St Simon		15
Their master and their God.	O	79	Feast St Simon		18
Their master and their God.	O	79	Feast St Simon		18
Far from their happy native home	O	79	Feast St Simon		28
To raise them from their fall.	O	79	Feast St Simon		30
And Serpents with their poys'nous breath	O	79	Feast St Simon		41
Whilst you deride their pangs in barb'rous play,	O	83	Epi Dist Moth.		7
No conscious blushes there their cheeks inflame,	O	84	Epi Dist Moth.		24
Unfaded still their former charms they shew,	O	84	Epi Dist Moth.		26
Where e'er they fly their lovers ghosts pursue,	O	84	Epi Dist Moth.		36
Their foul deformities by all descry'd,	O	84	Epi Dist Moth.		40
To ease their pains exert their milder power,	O	84	Epi Dist Moth.		46
Oh, must their ardours cease to glow	O	100	Ode Friendship		25
And Rapine and Pollution mark their Way.	O	110	To Posterity		8
Their hungry Swarms the peaceful Vale shall fright	O	110	To Posterity		9
Kings change their Laws, and Kingdoms change their Kings.	O	110	To Posterity		16
Kings change their Laws, and Kingdoms change their Kings.	O	110	To Posterity		16
Though gold and silk their charms unite,	O	119	To Miss Purse		1
Spread for their prey, the roving coin	O	120	To Miss Purse	V	7
The nymphs, who found their pow'r decline,	O	122	Stella Mourn.		3
In quest of wealth who throw their lives away.	O	132	Tr. Rambler 48		2
Beasts of each kind their fellows spare;	O	138	Tr Rambler 160		1
Leave to the schools their atoms and their void.	O	140	Tr Rambler 180		2
Leave to the schools their atoms and their void.	O	140	Tr Rambler 180		2
From you my labours wait their last reward.	O	141	Tr Rambler 208		2
And deride their utmost Rage.	O	145	Tr Boeth. II.4		22
All from one Source derive their Birth	O	146	Tr Boeth III.6		3
The same their Parent and their King.	O	146	Tr Boeth III.6		4
The same their Parent and their King.	O	146	Tr Boeth III.6		4
Why boast their Birth before his Eyes,	O	147	Tr Boeth III.6		17
And then lament their fall with seeming friendship:	O	176	Tr Metastas II	V	5
Trumpet or lyre--to their harsh bosoms chill,	O	192	Tr. Medea II		11
Joy to see their quarry fly,	O	196	Song Congratu.		14
Bid them come, and take their fill.	O	196	Song Congratu.		20
Scorn their counsel and their pother,	O	197	Song Congratu.		27
Scorn their counsel and their pother,	O	197	Song Congratu.		27
Scorn their Nonsense scorn their pother,	O	197	Song Congratu.	V	27
Scorn their Nonsense scorn their pother,	O	197	Song Congratu.	V	27
His virtues walk'd their narrow round,	O	201	Death Dr Levet		25
The rivers know their banks again,	O	231	Tr Horace IV.7		4
Men will be ever to their Errors blind,	O	247	Irene Epilogue		11
Their Rage, and pall'd their Appetite of Murder;	O	249	Irene		8
Their Rage, and pall'd their Appetite of Murder;	O	249	Irene		8
The groaning Greeks break up their golden Caverns	O	249	Irene		17
That Wealth, too sacred for their Country's Use!	O	250	Irene		20
That Wealth, which granted to their weeping Prince,	O	250	Irene		22
And columns leaning from their central firmness	Y	114	Irene	V	45A
Like subterraneous tempests with dire eruption burst their caverns	Y	115	Irene	V	49
Dominion hovers o'er their conquering banners	Y	115	Irene	V	49D
Conducts their Armies and asserts their Cause.	O	251	Irene		51
Conducts their Armies and asserts their Cause.	O	251	Irene		51
Did unresisted Lightning aid their Cannon,	O	251	Irene		54
His kind Intelligence betray'd their Measures;	O	253	Irene		118
Their Arms prevail'd, though Cali was our Friend.	O	253	Irene		119
And tell the Secrets of their conscious Walks;	O	255	Irene		27
To tell the Secrets of their conscious Shades	O	373	Irene	V	20
And wearied angels rest upon their stars spheres	Y	128	Irene	V	4B
And weary Planets loiter in their Courses.	O	262	Irene		4
Pour forth their Legions, and the roaring Danube	O	264	Irene		17
And Indias rajas ask their doom from thee	Y	131	Irene	V	32
Their cloudy Summits, and the Sons of Fierceness,	O	268	Irene		29
Their snowy summits, and the sons of fierceness	Y	136	Irene	V	29
And (terror) horrour shudders in their gloomy caverns	Y	136	Irene	V	31A
And wish their gloomy Caverns more obscure.	O	268	Irene		32
And turn'd their hasty Steps towards the Garden.	O	269	Irene		39
Does chearless Diffidence oppress their Hearts?	O	270	Irene		22
Or sprightly Hope exalt their kindling Spirits?	O	270	Irene		23
And scatter Discord from their baleful Beams.	O	271	Irene		5
Oft have I rag'd, when their wide-wasting Cannon	O	273	Irene		24

THEIR   (CONTINUED)   PAGE   TITLE   LINE

Th' adoring Soldiers would revenge their Idol. . . . .   O 273   Irene   42
Fierce through the bursting Caverns rend their Way? . .   O 281   Irene   53
Till burning Death shoots through their wither'd Limbs?   O 282   Irene   5
Lead us to Danger, and abash their Victors? . . . . .   O 284   Irene   43
When pale, and anxious for their Years to come, . . .   O 287   Irene   4
And hail unanimous their conqu'ring God. . . . . . .   O 287   Irene   6
Resign their Charge to Baseness and to Ruin. . . . .   O 289   Irene   20
And quit their Charge to Horror and to Ruin. . . . .   O 346   Irene   V 8
Still stretch in vain their longing Arms afar; . . . .   O 292   Irene   91
While vulgar Souls compassionate their Cares, ...   O 293   Irene   115
Gaze at their Height and tremble at their Danger: . . .   O 293   Irene   116
Gaze at their Height and tremble at their Danger: . . .   O 293   Irene   116
In easy State presides o'er all their Motions, ...   O 293   Irene   122
I stole unheeded from their ravish'd Eyes, ...   O 298   Irene   20
Spread wide their kind Arms to Science and to Beauty. .   O 299   Irene   49
Shall dart their am'rous Glances at the Fair, ...   O 353   Irene   V 5
The Greeks disorder'd by their Leader's Absence, . . .   O 304   Irene   35
Ask to whose Sword the Greeks will trust their Cause,   O 304   Irene   10
For ever mourn their Avarice or Factions? . . . . . .   O 305   Irene   39
When Asia's Nations own me for their Lord, ...   O 305   Irene   44
To still their Murmurs, ere the twentieth Sun . . . .   O 306   Irene   5
And subject Seas roar round their Queen in vain. . . .   O 309   Irene   23
And War o'erwhelm them in their Dream of Vice. . . . .   O 309   Irene   29
Call them--but let them not prolong their Tale, . . .   O 309   Irene   37
Aw'd by the Croud, and by their Slaves restrain'd? . .   O 310   Irene   8
Whate'er their Scheme the Bassa's Death defeats it, . .   O 312   Irene   22
While I protract their Stay. Be swift and faithful. .   O 312   Irene   4
Refuse their Office, and uncertain Life . . . . . .   O 319   Irene   4
Their Treason throws no Stain upon Irene. . . . . .   O 320   Irene   21
And spread their Flames resistless o'er the World? . .   O 324   Irene   18
Depress their Spirits, and retard their Speed? . . . .   O 325   Irene   13
Depress their Spirits, and retard their Speed? . . . .   O 325   Irene   15
The fraudful Moments ply their silent Wings, ...   O 325   Irene   15
The treacherous moments ply their silent wings . . .   O 327   Irene   8
And all the withering woods confess their woe . . . .   Y 206   Irene   V 8
The sympathising cattle hung their heads . . . . . .   Y   6   Virgil Daphnis   4
And spread their echoing grief from shore to shore. . .   Y   6   Virgil Daphnis   9
Withdraw their cars and seek the blesst abodes. . . .   Y   6   Virgil Daphnis   12
Rocks send their acclamations to the skie . . . . .   Y   6   Virgil Daphnis   21
The swains shall pay their vows, and thou shalt hear their   Y   7   Virgil Daphnis   40
  prayer.
The swains shall pay their vows, and thou shalt hear their   Y   7   Virgil Daphnis   52
  prayer.
That all the fair their favours sold; . . . .   Y 11   Tr Hor Epode 9   20
Pledge of their love and source of all their joy . . .   Y 18   Tr. Iliad Bk 6   10
Pledge of their love and source of all their joy . . .   Y 18   Tr. Iliad Bk 6   10
Among their flocks the blooming heroes fell . . . .   Y 18   Tr. Iliad Bk 6   36
Where the wild fig trees join their darksom shade . .   Y 19   Tr. Iliad Bk 6   52
Thrice to the wall their dreadfull hosts have led . .   Y 19   Tr. Iliad Bk 6   56
Or their own souls with hopes of vict'ry fir'd." . .   Y 19   Tr. Iliad Bk 6   59
But if by their irrevocable doom . . . .   Y 21   Tr. Iliad Bk 6   117
With dolefull cries their living lord they mourn . .   Y 21   Tr. Iliad Bk 6   130
Their growing fame re'echoes to the skies. . . . .   Y 22   Tr Add. Battle   9
Fresh foes descending glut their swords with blood. . .   Y 23   Tr Add. Battle   21
Scream in the nests and brood their young in peace. . .   Y 23   Tr Add. Battle   35
Against th' invading birds their native land: . . . .   Y 23   Tr Add. Battle   37
Or fix'd the pointed arrows in their hearts. . . . .   Y 23   Tr Add. Battle   43
The Pygmies thus exasp'rated their foes. . . . . . .   Y 23   Tr Add. Battle   51
And dy'd their bulrush-spears in mutual blood. . . . .   Y 24   Tr Add. Battle   57
The injur'd Cranes their murther'd offspring mourn . .   Y 24   Tr Add. Battle   64
Which whet their beaks, for flight their wings prepare, .   Y 24   Tr Add. Battle   70
Which whet their beaks, for flight their wings prepare, .   Y 24   Tr Add. Battle   70
Sharpen their claws, and meditate the war. . . . . .   Y 24   Tr Add. Battle   71
The dark horizon ravish'd their sight. . . . . . .   Y 24   Tr Add. Battle   75
Temper their swords and point their missive darts. . .   Y 24   Tr Add. Battle   77
Temper their swords and point their missive darts. . .   Y 24   Tr Add. Battle   77
Their wings extend themselves across the land. . . .   Y 24   Tr Add. Battle   79
Then rises the brave leader of their hosts . . . . .   Y 24   Tr Add. Battle   80
The feather'd race and thirsted for their blood: . . .   Y 24   Tr Add. Battle   85
Soon as their young began to draw their breath . . . .   Y 24   Tr Add. Battle   86
Soon as their young began to draw their breath . . . .   Y 24   Tr Add. Battle   86
And Strymon's hollow banks resounded with their groans. .   Y 24   Tr Add. Battle   89
But now their cruel enemies draw near . . . .   Y 24   Tr Add. Battle   90
Quickly the Cranes appear before their eyes; . . . .   Y 25   Tr Add. Battle   92
Above their heads th' embattled squadrons hung . . . .   Y 25   Tr Add. Battle   94
The joyfull Cranes triumphant clap their wings; . . .   Y 26   Tr Add. Battle   127
Their godlike hero strugling in the skies. . . . . .   Y 26   Tr Add. Battle   129
Revolving springs their frost repay. . . . .   Y 39   Lady Leaving   10

THEM

They call them Fairies; these now free from care . . .   O 77   Tr Add. Battle   49
Let them prolong their turgid lays . . . .   O 78   Feast St Simon   4
Their faith, or force them to forsake . . . .   O 79   Feast St Simon   14
To raise them from their fall. . . . .   O 79   Feast St Simon   30
Unpitying see them weep, and hear them pray, ...   O 83   Epi Dist Moth.   8
Unpitying see them weep, and hear them pray, ...   O 83   Epi Dist Moth.   8
Nor torturing whalebones pinch them into charms; . . .   O 84   Epi Dist Moth.   23
Around them pleasures wait, and joys for ever new. . .   O 84   Epi Dist Moth.   27
Like them man flourishes, like them decays. . . . .   O 138   Tr Rambler 161   2
Like them man flourishes, like them decays. . . . . .   O 138   Tr Rambler 161   2

THEM	(CONTINUED)		PAGE	TITLE	LINE	
To sink the fatal precipice before them,	. . . . . .		O 176	Tr Metastas II	V	4
Nor call'd them to the gloomy cells	. . . . . .		O 191	Tr. Medea I		9
Oh! send them to the sullen mansions dun,	. . . .		O 192	Tr. Medea II		13
Bid them come, and take their fill.	. . . . . .		O 196	Song Congratu.		20
And teror and confusion stalk before them	. . . .		Y 115	Irene	V	49E
Just as I mark'd them, they forsook the Shore,	. . .		O 269	Irene		38
Ere I could range them on the crowded Deck,	. . . .		O 271	Irene		28
I mark'd them well, and trac'd in either Face	. . .		O 275	Irene		81
Think them a sacred Treasure lent by Heav'n,	. . .		O 302	Irene		6
Till angry Heav'n shall mark them out for Ruin,	. . .		O 309	Irene		36
And War o'erwhelm them in their Dream of Vice.	. . .		O 309	Irene		37
Call them--but let them not prolong their Tale,	. . .		O 310	Irene		8
Call them--but let them not prolong their Tale,	. . .		O 310	Irene		8
Then let me rid them of Irene's Presence:	. . .		O 316	Irene		19
Haste, seize them, guards, be quick--my thoughtless hast			Y 198	Irene	V	34
Bold Slave, I know them both--I know them Traytors.	. .		O 324	Irene		16
Bold Slave, I know them both--I know them Traytors.	. .		O 324	Irene		16
Perfidious!--yes--too well thou know'st them Traytors.	.		O 324	Irene		17
And speed the Stroke lest Mercy should o'ertake them.	.		O 333	Irene		54
And pour them on the consecrated stone;	. . . . .		Y 7	Virgil Daphnis		46
Oft from behind they wounded them with darts	. . .		Y 23	Tr Add. Battle		42
He tore them down and trampled them to death.	. . .		Y 24	Tr Add. Battle		87
He tore them down and trampled them to death.	. . .		Y 24	Tr Add. Battle		87
The fearless Pygmies view them from afar	. . . .		Y 25	Tr Add. Battle		96
THEME						
Forgive my transports on a theme like this,	. . .		O 15	London		97
Aspasia, yet pursue the sacred Theme;	. . . . .		O 265	Irene		1
Alike must fall the poet and his theme.	. . . . .		Y 4	On a Daffodill		28
THEMES						
While I to nobler themes aspire,	. . . . . .		O 78	Feast St Simon		7
THEMSELVES						
Themselves they studied, as they felt, they writ,	. . .		O 52	Pro Drury-Lane		19
No more let coquets to themselves be blind,	. . . .		O 81	Lady Birthday		18
Or lift themselves into the wonted skies.	. . . .		Y 24	Tr Add. Battle		61
Their wings extend themselves across the land.	. . .		Y 24	Tr Add. Battle		79
THEN						
They first invade your table, then your breast;	. . .		O 17	London		153
Then soon your ill-plac'd confidence repay,	. . . .		O 17	London		156
Then thro' the world a wretched vagrant roam,	. . .		O 18	London		190
Fair Justice then, without constraint ador'd,	. . .		O 22	London		250
Then shall thy friend, nor thou refuse his aid,	. . .		O 23	London		260
Then say how hope and fear, desire and hate,	. . .		O 31	Vanity Wishes		5
Then say how fierce desire and raging hate,	. . . .		Y 92	Vanity Wishes	V	5
Then say how hot desire and raging hate,	. . . .		Y 92	Vanity Wishes	V	5
Where then shall Hope and Fear their objects find?	. .		O 47	Vanity Wishes		343
Exhausted Worlds, and then imagin'd new:	. . . .		O 51	Pro Drury-Lane		4
Then Johnson came, instructed from the School,	. . .		O 51	Pro Drury-Lane		9
Then crush'd by Rules, and weaken'd as refin'd,	. . .		O 52	Pro Drury-Lane		29
Then prompt no more the Follies you decry,	. . . .		O 53	Pro Drury-Lane		55
Yet then shall calm reflection bless the night,	. . .		O 62	Pro Word Wise		21
The foaming Boar he then with op'ning hounds	. . .		O 72	Hor. Epode II	V	39
I once admir'd, I'd then despise:	. . . . .		O 73	Hor. Epode II	V	60
Then to the Gods, on solemn days,	. . . . .		O 73	Hor. Epode II		63
She ceas'd; then godlike Hector answer'd kind,--	. .		O 74	Tr. Iliad Bk 6		1
But shall I, then, forsake the unfinish'd war?	. . .		O 74	Tr. Iliad Bk 6		4
Then shall some Argive loud insulting cry,	. . . .		O 74	Tr. Iliad Bk 6		25
Then, swift as thought, by headlong anger driv'n	. . .		O 76	Tr Add. Battle		10
O then, when conquer'd crouds confess thy sway,	. . .		O 81	Lady Birthday		9
Then dances jocund o'er the watery way,	. . . .		O 82	Young Author	V	5
Then melt, ye fair, while crouds around you sigh,	. .		O 84	Epi Dist Moth.		42
O! then the meaning of thy gift impart,	. . . .		O 95	Sprig of Myrtl		11
O! Shall thy flames then cease to glow	. . . .		O 100	Ode Friendship	V	25
Then, O my Country! shalt thou groan distrest,	. . .		O 110	To Posterity		3
Then thro' thy Fields shall scarlet Reptiles stray,	. .		O 110	To Posterity		7
Then o'er the World shall Discord stretch her Wings,	. .		O 110	To Posterity		15
Then, when dark arts obscur'd each fierce debate,	. .		O 118	Epitaph Hanmer		23
Calm conscience then his former life survey'd,	. . .		O 118	Epitaph Hanmer		41
Why, Sylvia, was it then decreed,	. . . . .		O 120	To Miss Purse		11
Why, Stella, was it then decreed,	. . . . .		O 120	To Miss Purse	V	11
Then best enjoy'd, when most improv'd.	. . . .		O 125	An Ode		28
And then lament his fall with seeming friendship:	. .		O 176	Tr Metastas II		5
And then lament their fall with seeming friendship:	. .		O 176	Tr Metastas II	V	5
"Then with luscious plenty gay	. . . . .		O 186	Anacreon Ode 9		35
Then with no throbbing fiery pain,	. . . . .		O 202	Death Dr Levet		33
Then with no throbs of fiery pain,	. . . . .		O 202	Death Dr Levet	V	33
Then Summer sinks in Autumn's reign,	. . . .		O 231	Tr Horace IV.7		11
Then rouzing know the fiery Chief Abdalla,	. . . .		O 254	Irene		125
Then rouzing know the firy Chief Abdallah,	. . . .		O 254	Irene	V	125
Then 'tis decreed. (then death or empire.)	. . . .		Y 130	Irene	V	20
Then 'tis decreed. (then death or empire.)	. . . .		Y 130	Irene	V	20
Then old in honours, and approv'd in faith,	. . .		Y 131	Irene	V	32
Then, Cali, shall the Toils of Battle cease,	. . .		O 265	Irene		44
Then dream of Prayer, and Pilgrimage, and Peace.	. .		O 265	Irene		45
Then dream of (prayer), or (vows) and pilgrimage and peace,	. .		Y 132	Irene	V	45
Then Visions horrid as a Murd'rer's Dreams	. . . .		O 266	Irene		13
Then let us now resolve, nor idly waste	. . . .		O 271	Irene		33
Then let us now resolve, nor idle waste	. . . .		O 271	Irene	V	33
Held forth this fatal Scroll, then sunk to nothing.	. .		O 272	Irene		17
Held out this fatal roll--then sunk to Nothing.	. . .		O 357	Irene	V	1

THEN	(CONTINUED)	PAGE	TITLE	LINE
Then leave him stretch'd upon the ling'ring Rack,	· · ·	O 273	Irene	36
And then leaves the glittering reptile, reasoning insect	· · ·	Y 146	Irene	V 23
And then leaves your actions the busy trifler unregarded	· · ·	O 355	Irene	V 12
Why then has Nature's vain Munificence	· · · · ·	O 276	Irene	24
Why then did Natures vain Munificence	· · · · ·	O 355	Irene	V 13
Whence then those Charms thy Tongue has deign'd to flatter,	· ·	O 277	Irene	26
Why then Those charms your tongue has deign'd to flatter		O 355	Irene	V 15
Then let me once, in honour of our Sex,	· · · · ·	O 277	Irene	49
Then Let me once to right our injur'd Sex	· · · · ·	O 356	Irene	V 16
Must then Ambition's Votaries infringe	· · · · ·	O 280	Irene	15
To morrow strike--Does then that experienc'd wisdom	· · ·	Y 154	Irene	V 19
Can then th' Assassin lift his treach'rous Hand	· · ·	O 286	Irene	11
Then mingle with your slaves without a murmur	· · ·	Y 161	Irene	V 11
Why then did not this warlike Amazon	· · · ·	O 290	Irene	40
Not then with raving Cries I fill'd the City,	· · · ·	O 290	Irene	46
Then Bigotry might send her Slaves to War,	· · · ·	O 291	Irene	63
Then pleas'd, and conscious of Superiour Greatness	· · · · ·	O 369	Irene	V 6
Then--O my Fair, I cannot bid thee goe;	· · · · ·	O 297	Irene	15
Then--O my Fair, I cannot bid thee go;	· · · · ·	O 297	Irene	V 15
Then strike secure, and Heav'n assist the Blow.	· · ·	O 298	Irene	9
Can Abdalla then dissemble,	· · · · · · ·	O 299	Irene	34
Then while he gaz'd upon his yielding Mistress,	· · ·	O 299	Irene	48
Then waste no longer these important Moments	· · ·	O 303	Irene	13
Why has thy Choice then pointed out Leontius,	· · · ·	O 305	Irene	20
Wilt thou then head the Troop upon the Shore,	· · · ·	O 305	Irene	36
Go then, and with united Eloquence	· · · · · ·	O 306	Irene	57
Then shall these Juices taint Demetrius' Draught,	· · ·	O 308	Irene	30
Then shall the Rhodian mourn his sinking Tow'rs,	· · ·	O 309	Irene	26
Then shall Venetia feel the Turkish Pow'r,	· · · ·	O 309	Irene	28
Then seize fair Italy's delightful Coast,	· · · · ·	O 309	Irene	30
Absorb'd in Thought; then starting from his Trance,	· · ·	O 311	Irene	6
Absorb'd by thought; then waking from his dream	· · ·	Y 187	Irene	V 6
Shall then the Greeks, unpunish'd and conceal'd,	· · ·	O 312	Irene	1
Then let me rid them of Irene's Presence:	· · · ·	O 316	Irene	19
What Cry? The Stratagem? Did then Abdalla?--	· · · ·	O 317	Irene	30
What cry? what stratagem? had then Abdalla--	· · · ·	Y 194	Irene	V 30
Then all is past he cried--and darted from us;	· · · ·	O 317	Irene	32
Shall then the Savage live, to boast his Insult,	· · ·	O 318	Irene	12
Has left the slaves behind, nay then there's danger.	· · ·	Y 198	Irene	V 34
Then shall you feel what Language cannot utter,	· · ·	O 326	Irene	43
Is then your Sov'reign's Life so cheaply rated,	· · ·	O 327	Irene	14
Is then conspiracy so slight a crime	· · · · ·	Y 207	Irene	V 14
Then call it not our Cruelty, nor Crime,	· · · · ·	O 327	Irene	28
Then in short Sighs forsook his broken Frame.	· · · ·.	O 331	Irene	16
Then ling'ring with his captive Mistress here.	· · ·	O 331	Irene	9
Was she then guiltless! Has my thoughtless Rage	· · ·	O 332	Irene	18
Then hear, great Mahomet, the Voice of Truth.	· · ·	O 333	Irene	55
Then scorn those flowers to which the Aegyptians bow'd,	· ·	Y 4	On a Daffodil	15
Then we with wine will drown our troubles, laid	· ·	Y 7	Virgil Daphnis	47
I then (my cheeks still glow with shame) was grown	· ·	Y 11	Tr Hor Epode 9	11
Then when repeated bowls unlock'd the heart	· · ·	Y 11	Tr Hor Epode 9	17
To thee I then with tears complain'd	· · · · ·	Y 11	Tr Hor Epode 9	19
Then would I free from torments live	· · · · ·	Y 11	Tr Hor Epode 9	25
Then to the inclement skies expos'd I sat	· · · ·	Y 11	Tr Hor Epode 9	35
Then kist his son and raising to the skies	· · · ·	Y 20	Tr. Iliad Bk 6	97
May then his mother's heart with joys o'erflow	· · ·	Y 20	Tr. Iliad Bk 6	105
Then on his brow the mighty soldier plac'd	· · · ·	Y 21	Tr. Iliad Bk 6	124
Then sought the palace where the menial train	· · ·	Y 21	Tr. Iliad Bk 6	128
Then rises the brave leader of their hosts	· · ·	Y 24	Tr Add. Battle	80
In his fell claws, then into th' air he springs.	· · ·	Y 26	Tr Add. Battle	126
Then flies aloft; th' astonish'd warriours feel	· · ·	Y 26	Tr Add. Battle	132
The rough road then, returning in a round,	· · · · ·	Y 310	Parody of Pope	3
THENCE				
Thence should my Fury drag him down to Tortures;	· · ·	O 274	Irene	64
THEO				
Kupridi, med autou skeptra memele theo.	· · · · · · ·	O 103	Eis Elisses	2
THERE				
There none are swept by sudden fate away,	· · ·	O 9	London	11
There might'st thou find some elegant retreat,	· · ·	O 20	London	212
There prune thy walks, support thy drooping flow'rs,	· ·	O 20	London	216
There prune thy shades, support the drooping flow'rs,	·	Y 58	London	V 216
There ev'ry bush with nature's musick rings,	· ·	O 20	London	220
Only ev'ry bush there artless music sings	· ·	Y 58	London	V 220
There ev'ry breeze bears health upon its wings;	· ·	O 20	London	221
There mark what ills the scholar's life assail,	· · ·	O 38	Vanity Wishes	159
Such age there is, and who shall wish its end?	· · ·	O 44	Vanity Wishes	298
Such age there is, and who could wish its end?	· · ·	Y 44	Vanity Wishes	V 298
But few there are whom hours like these await,	· · ·	O 45	Vanity Wishes	311
There a stout warrior fainting gasps for breath	· · ·	O 76	Tr Add. Battle	16
There trod the Lybian sands,	· · · · ·	O 79	Feast St Simon	39
Nor there confin'd his active Soul;	· · · · ·	O 79	Feast St Simon	43
There begs of heav'n a less distinguish'd lot;	· · ·	O 82	Young Author	29
No pug, nor favourite Cupid there enjoys	· · ·	O 84	Epi Dist Moth.	20
No conscious blushes there their cheeks inflame,	· · ·	O 84	Epi Dist Moth.	24

342

```
THERE          (CONTINUED)                              PAGE   TITLE              LINE
    There, mid Tempests loudest roars,      . . . . . . . .   O 145  Tr Boeth. II.4        17
    And there I met another man    . . . . . . . . . . .      O 158  Par. Hermit II         3
    I there did meet another man   . . . . . . . . . . .      O 158  Par. Hermit II      V  3
    There the Gamester light and jolly    . . . . . . . .     O 196  Song Congratu.      V 15
    There the Lender grave and sly.       . . . . . . . .     O 196  Song Congratu.        16
    There in soft Hints and in ambiguous Phrase,    . . .     O 254  Irene                129
    If there be any Land, as Fame reports,    . . . . .       O 256  Irene                 55
        And there must fall.    . . . . . . . . . . . .       O 260  Irene                132
    There let Aspasia, since my Fair entreats it,   . . .     O 263  Irene                  3
    All there is Hope, and Gaiety, and Courage,   . . . .     O 271  Irene                 26
    There will his boundless Wealth, the Spoil of Asia,  .    O 274  Irene                 50
    There (or might) shall his boundless Wealth the   . .     O 351  Irene               V 13
    There shall he waste thy Frontiers, check thy Conquests,  O 274  Irene                 56
    Claim but the second Place: there mighty Love   . . .     O 280  Irene                 26
    There, with your Soldiers arm'd, and Sails expanded, .    O 284  Irene                 53
    There shalt thou view from far the quiet Cottage,  . .    O 292  Irene                 83
    There wear the tedious Hours of Life away,    . . . .     O 292  Irene                 85
    There shall we find the yet untasted Bliss    . . . .     O 292  Irene                 88
    There when my Thoughts, at interval of Pray'r,  . . .     O 292  Irene                 94
    There shall soft Leisure wing th' excursive Soul,  . .    O 302  Irene                118
    There shall despotick Eloquence resume    . . . . . .     O 302  Irene                120
    There Poetry shall tune her sacred Voice,    . . . . .    O 302  Irene                122
    There I became, nor blush to make it known,   . . . .     O 312  Irene                 13
    There dauntless Truth shall blast the vile Accuser,  .    O 326  Irene                 42
    There had she lull'd me with endearing Falshoods,  . .    O 331  Irene                 18
    Th' atridae there and Tydeus' mighty son,    . . . . .    Y  19  Tr. Iliad Bk 6        54
    There let the web and distaff be your care.   . . . .     Y  21  Tr. Iliad Bk 6       122
    Small bones and mangled bodies scatter'd there  . . .     Y  23  Tr Add. Battle        31
    Had form'd her nest and plac'd her burthen there,  . .    Y  23  Tr Add. Battle        45
    There frogs crept croaking o'er the swampy ground.  .     Y  24  Tr Add. Battle        59
    There she soon became a jilt,   . . . . . . . . . .       Y 300  Extemp. Elegy          9
    But there came a country 'squire    . . . . . . . .       Y 301  Extemp. Elegy         13
THERE'S
    Has left the slaves behind, nay then there's danger. .    Y 198  Irene               V 34
THEREFORE
    I Therefore pray thee, Renny dear,   . . . . . . . .      O 158  Par Hermit III         1
THESE
    Since worth, he cries, in these degen'rate days,   . .    O  10  London                35
    These arts in vain our rugged natives try,   . . . . .    O  16  London               129
    How, when competitors like these contend,    . . . . .    O  16  London               144
    For arts like these preferr'd, admir'd, caress'd,  . .    O  17  London               152
    Yet ev'n these heroes, mischievously gay,    . . . . .    O  21  London               230
    In vain, these dangers past, your doors you close,  . .   O  21  London               236
    Are these thy views? proceed, illustrious youth,   . .    O  37  Vanity Wishes        141
    For these these steady Romans shook the world;  . . .     Y 100  Vanity Wishes       V 180
    For these these steady Romans shook the world;  . . .     Y 100  Vanity Wishes       V 180
    For these in distant lands the Britons shine,   . . .     Y 100  Vanity Wishes       V 181
    But few there are whom hours like these await,  . . .     O  45  Vanity Wishes        311
    These goods for man the laws of heav'n ordain,  . . .     O  48  Vanity Wishes        365
    These goods he grants, who grants the pow'r to gain; .    O  48  Vanity Wishes        366
    With these celestial wisdom calms the mind,   . . . .     O  48  Vanity Wishes        367
    Yet Bards like these aspir'd to lasting Praise,   . .     O  52  Pro Drury-Lane        23
    Leave off, at length, these woman's sighs,    . . . .     O  68  Hor. II Ode IX        17
    Would not these pleasures soon remove    . . . . . . .    O  72  Hor. Epode II         45
    They call them Fairies; these now free from care  . .     O  77  Tr Add. Battle        49
    "While I these transitory blessings scorn,   . . . . .    O  82  Young Author          17
    These dreams were Settle's once and Ogilby's.   . . .     O  82  Young Author          24
    Thou, who survey'st these walls with curious eye,  . .    O 117  Epitaph Hanmer         1
    But on these regions of delight,    . . . . . . . . .     O 121  To Miss Playin        19
    If Truths like these with pleasing Language join;  . .    O 246  Irene Prologue        15
    These all are Trifles, to what we can give.   . . . .     O 247  Irene Epilogue        20
    These Groans were fatal, these Disguises vain:  . . .     O 249  Irene                  6
    These Groans were fatal, these Disguises vain:  . . .     O 249  Irene                  6
    Reserve these Questions for a safer Hour,    . . . . .    O 254  Irene                140
    Sooner these trembling Leaves shall find a Voice,  . .    O 255  Irene                 26
    These tedious Narratives of frozen Age    . . . . . .     O 259  Irene                113
    Yet unacquainted with these soft Emotions    . . . . .    O 263  Irene                 16
    These Years, unconquer'd Mahomet, demand    . . . . .     O 263  Irene                  7
    Well may those Eyes that view these heav'nly Charms, .    O 267  Irene                  6
    Conduct these Queens, Abdalla, to the Palace:   . . .     O 269  Irene                 40
    Attend these queens, Abdallah, to the (palace)  . . .     Y 137  Irene               V 40
    These Days of Love and Pleasure charm not thee;   . .     O 271  Irene                  2
    Too slow these gentle Constellations roll,    . . . .     O 271  Irene                  3
    Molest these private Walks, or Care invade    . . . .     O 272  Irene                 14
    These Hours assign'd to Pleasure and Irene.   . . . .     O 272  Irene                 15
    Are these the Counsels? This the Faith of Cali?   . .     O 272  Irene                 11
    Must I for these renounce the Hope of Heav'n,   . . .     O 276  Irene                 13
    To deck these Bow'rs each Region shall combine,   . .     O 279  Irene                 88
    These Arts I try'd, and to inflame her more,   . . .      O 287  Irene                 14
    If yet this shining Pomp, these sudden Honours,   . .     O 289  Irene                  1
    If yet these glittring Robes these sudden Splendors  .    O 366  Irene               V 17
    If yet these glittring Robes these sudden Splendors  .    O 366  Irene               V 17
    If Dismiss this glittring train these sudden    . . .     O 366  Irene               V 17
        Splendors
    Maxims like these, if generally persued   . . . . . .     O 352  Irene               V  2
    Maxims like these, if once reduc'd to practice  . . .     O 352  Irene               V  2
    Descend to range these Mansions of Misfortune,   . .      O 292  Irene                 95
    Dismiss these needless Fears--a Troop of Greeks   . .     O 301  Irene                 90
    Count not these Hours as Parts of vulgar Time,   . .      O 302  Irene                  5
    Then waste no longer these important Moments   . . .      O 303  Irene                 13
```

THESE   (CONTINUED)

		PAGE	TITLE		LINE
Then shall these Juices taint Demetrius' Draught,	. . .	O 308	Irene		30
Around these fatal Walls, the Tide of War	. . . .	O 312	Irene		8
In these dark Moments of suspended Fate,	. . .	O 313	Irene		1
Whence rise these restless cares? these strong emotions?		Y 189	Irene	V	1
Whence rise these restless cares? these strong emotions?		Y 189	Irene	V	1
These chilling doubts, and agonizing horrours?	. . . .	Y 189	Irene	V	1A
This Calm, these Joys, dear Innocence! are thine,		O 313	Irene		9
Hang Sit these black clouds upon Aspasia's brow?	. . .	Y 191	Irene	V	15
Are these th' unceasing Joys, th' unmingled Pleasures	.	O 314	Irene		16
Still dost thou linger in these fatal bowrs	. . .	Y 196	Irene	V	18A
Are these the rapid Thunderbolts of War,	. . . . .	O 325	Irene		11
What sleepy Charms benumb these active Heroes,	. . .	O 325	Irene		14
These Tears, these Pangs, these last Remains of Life,	.	O 329	Irene		53
These Tears, these Pangs, these last Remains of Life,	.	O 329	Irene		53
These Tears, these Pangs, these last Remains of Life,	.	O 329	Irene		53
If mix'd with these, divine Cleora smile,	. . .	Y 4	On a Daffodill		17
These when o'er winter's sway, prevail'd the spring	. .	Y 24	Tr Add. Battle		72

THESEUS

| Nor can the might of Theseus rend | . . . . | O 232 | Tr Horace IV.7 | | 27 |

THEY

Well may they rise, while I, whose rustick tongue	. . .	O 14	London		79
On Britain's fond credulity they prey.	. . . . . .	O 15	London		112
They sing, they dance, clean shoes, or cure a clap;	. .	O 15	London		114
They sing, they dance, clean shoes, or cure a clap;	. .	O 15	London		114
Well may they venture on the mimick's art,	. . . . .	O 16	London		134
To shake with laughter ere the jest they hear,	. . . .	O 16	London		140
They first invade your table, then your breast;	. . .	O 17	London		153
Flush'd as they are with folly, youth and wine,	. . .	O 21	London		232
Flush'd as they are with youth confused with wine,	. .	Y 59	London	V	232
Afar they mark the flambeau's bright approach,	. . . .	O 21	London		234
And senates heard before they judg'd a cause;	. . .	O 33	Vanity Wishes		60
Evn low built towns where Britain's modish tribe	. . .	Y 94	Vanity Wishes	V	61
They mount, they shine, evaporate, and fall.	. . . .	O 33	Vanity Wishes		76
They mount, they shine, evaporate, and fall.	. . . .	O 33	Vanity Wishes		76
He views, and wonders that they please no more;	. . .	O 43	Vanity Wishes		264
He views, and wonders why they please no more;	. . . .	Y 104	Vanity Wishes	V	264
And mould his passions till they make his will.	. . .	O 44	Vanity Wishes		282
Themselves they studied, as they felt, they writ,	. .	O 52	Pro Drury-Lane		19
Themselves they studied, as they felt, they writ,	. .	O 52	Pro Drury-Lane		19
Themselves they studied, as they felt, they writ,	. .	O 52	Pro Drury-Lane		19
They pleas'd their Age, and did not aim to mend.	. . .	O 52	Pro Drury-Lane		22
They roll, and ever will roll on.	. . . .	O 68	Hor. II Ode 14		4
Not long they stood, when stooping from their height	.	O 75	Tr Add. Battle		2
Breathless at length they leave th' unfinish'd war	. .	O 76	Tr Add. Battle		6
They clap their wings, and with new fury burn;	. . . .	O 76	Tr Add. Battle		9
Impending death they strive to 'scape in vain	. . . .	O 76	Tr Add. Battle		30
The limits fix'd they strive to pass in vain;	. . .	O 76	Tr Add. Battle		36
They call them Fairies; these now free from care	. . .	O 77	Tr Add. Battle		49
With breasts resolv'd, they follow'd still	. . . .	O 79	Feast St Simon		16
Dispersing blessings as they went,	. . . .	O 79	Feast St Simon		26
They, pleas'd, thro' barb'rous nations roam	. . . .	O 79	Feast St Simon		29
Form'd to delight, they use no foreign arms,	. . . .	O 84	Epi Dist Moth.		22
Unfaded still their former charms they shew,	. . . .	O 84	Epi Dist Moth.		26
Where e'er they fly their lovers ghosts pursue,	. . .	O 84	Epi Dist Moth.		36
Inflicting all those ills which once they knew;	. . .	O 84	Epi Dist Moth.		37
For healthful indigence in vain they pray,	. . . .	O 132	Tr. Rambler 48		1
Rivers rested as they ran,	. . . .	O 148	Tr Boet III.12	V	10
Err shall they not, who resolute explore	. . . .	O 192	Tr. Medea II		1
They to the dome where smoke with curling play	. . .	O 192	Tr. Medea II		5
Snatch thy pleasures while they last;	. . . . . .	O 194	On Thrale Hat		2
Snatch your pleasures while they last;	. . . . .	O 194	On Thrale Hat	V	2
For us alone, they Honour's Paths pursue:	. . . .	O 247	Irene Epilogue		16
Inspir'd by us, they Glory's Heights ascend;	. . .	O 247	Irene Epilogue		17
Tho' Wealth, and Pow'r, and Glory they receive,	. . .	O 247	Irene Epilogue		19
Why should they fear?--That Power that kindly spreads		O 250	Irene		31
They put the riches of Cali Bassa on board.	. . .	Y 123	Irene	V	81
Had they prevail'd, I ne'er had known Irene.	. . .	O 263	Irene		27
They sympathise with us in every fear	. . . . .	Y 134	Irene	V	26
They croud my camp with voluntary tribute	. . . .	Y 136	Irene	V	27B
Just as I mark'd them, they forsook the Shore,	. . .	O 269	Irene		38
Do they with Pain repress the struggling Shout,	. . .	O 270	Irene		24
As blasted by my Presence, they withdrew	. . .	O 275	Irene		85
They prune the Wing, and spread the glossy Plumes,	. .	O 277	Irene		36
They prune the wing and spread the glossy tail	. . .	O 355	Irene	V	23
They see the Sun surmount the dark Eclipse,	. . .	O 287	Irene		5
Inform'd they mount the Precipice of Pow'r,	. . . .	O 293	Irene		113
They give the nations laws, and view serene	. . . .	Y 167	Irene	V	117
They cultivate at ease the gentler arts in quiet	. . .	Y 177	Irene	V	117
Willing to delay you here they give you on earth the	. .	Y 184	Irene	V	10
Oft would they find Ingratitude and Treason,	. . . .	O 308	Irene		14
How rarely would they meet in crouded Courts,	. . .	O 308	Irene		16
Alas! they come, commanded by the Sultan,	. . . .	O 325	Irene		8
With dolefull cries their living lord they mourn	. .	Y 21	Tr. Iliad Bk 6		130
Oft from behind they wounded them with darts	. . . .	Y 23	Tr Add. Battle		42
Wounded and spent, in vain they strive to rise	. . .	Y 24	Tr Add. Battle		60

THEY'RE

| Thy pleasures, lasting, as they're great, | . . . . . | O 100 | Ode Friendship | V | 23 |

THICK

| Thick from their wounded wings the feathers fly, | . . . | O 75 | Tr Add. Battle | | 4 |
| Joys insincere! thick clouds invade the skies, | . . . . | O 82 | Young Author | | 7 |

344

	PAGE	TITLE	LINE
THICK (CONTINUED)			
Thick clouds of hostile birds obscure the skies. . . .	Y 25	Tr Add. Battle	93
THICKET			
And heard within the Thicket that conceal'd us, . . .	O 311	Irene	12
THIEF			
One shews the plunder, and one hides the thief. . . .	O 32	Vanity Wishes	44
Cease, lovely thief! my tender limbs to wound, ...	O 106	Eliza plucking	5
THIEVES			
My first, shuts out Thieves from your house or your Room	O 179	Charade!	1
THIN			
Your thin battalions and your empty tents	Y 120	Irene	V 29A
THINE			
And bless thine evening walk and morning toil.	O 20	London	223
Shall Wolsey's wealth, with Wolsey's end be thine? . .	O 35	Vanity Wishes	122
Deign on the passing world to turn thine eyes, ...	O 38	Vanity Wishes	157
Nor shall thine ardours cease to glow	O 100	Ode Friendship	V 25
Grief swell thine Eyes, and Terror chill thy Breast. . .	O 110	To Posterity	4
Till angels wake thee with a note like thine. . . .	O 113	Epit. Phillips	6
If wrought by any hand but thine, ...	O 119	To Miss Purse	4
'tis thine alone to calm the pious breast	O 130	Tr. Rambler 7	5
Thine, Minos, is the main, and thine the land. . . .	O 136	Tr Rambler 129	4
Thine, Minos, is the main, and thine the land. . . .	O 136	Tr Rambler 129	4
Aspasia's thine, and all thy Life is Rapture-- . . .	O 260	Irene	142
Or boasts a happier Soil, already thine?	O 265	Irene	36
Each generous Sentiment is thine, Demetrius, ...	O 267	Irene	38
Empire or Wealth, to Excellence like thine?	O 267	Irene	9
Illustrious Maid, new Wonders fix me thine, ...	O 278	Irene	59
Celestial fair--maid--new wonders fix me thine, . . .	Y 149	Irene	V 59
Will it not charm a Mind like thine exalted, ...	O 278	Irene	67
And ev'n our Prophet's Gardens envy thine:	O 279	Irene	89
And Gennah's happy <to> Gardens envy thine.	O 351	Irene	V 27
A little longer, and she's thine for ever.	O 285	Irene	10
Or tune thine Ear to soothing Adulation, ...	O 289	Irene	4
Affrighted at Impiety like thine, ...	O 289	Irene	19
Now feast thine Eyes, thine Eyes that ne'er hereafter	O 304	Irene	34
Now feast thine Eyes, thine Eyes that ne'er hereafter	O 304	Irene	34
Is not the Fate of Greece and Cali thine?	O 304	Irene	19
Be but my Country free, be thine the Praise;	O 305	Irene	33
Wealth, and Command, and Grandeur shall be thine . . .	O 306	Irene	6
This Calm, these Joys, dear Innocence! are thine, . . .	O 313	Irene	9
Alike my Death or thine is gain to thee, ...	O 319	Irene	32
Be thine, that Wealth can give, or Guilt receive. . .	O 322	Irene	58
Bids Beauty, such as thine, prepare to die.	O 324	Irene	3
The Plot all Cali's, the Detection thine.	O 329	Irene	4
Thine Orders, mighty Sultan! are perform'd, ...	O 330	Irene	3
Well if a Thousand Lives like thine had perish'd; . .	O 332	Irene	34
Such Ills are sent for Souls like thine to conquer. . .	O 332	Irene	38
So much our splendour was encreas'd by thine. . . . ✎	Y 6	Virgil Daphnis	19
THINGS			
What toil in slender things!	O 134	Tr. Rambler 90	1
THINK			
Nor think the doom of man revers'd for thee: . . .	O 38	Vanity Wishes	156
Nor think though learning her last prize bestows, . . .	Y 99	Vanity Wishes	V 165
"Think nothing gain'd, he cries, till nought remain, . .	O 40	Vanity Wishes	202
For I shall never think him less than God;	O 64	Virgil Past.I	8
Ah! think not, in the dang'rous hour, ...	O 121	To Miss Playin	7
Ah! think not, in the dang'rous Bower, ...	O 121	To Miss Playin	V 7
"Think not yet my service hard, ...	O 185	Anacreon Ode 9	17
Nor think our wishes less sincere.	O 188	Epilogue	4
Yet let me think--I see the helpless Maid, ...	O 252	Irene	80
Think on the sudden Change of human Scenes;	O 252	Irene	86
Think on the various Accidents of War;	O 252	Irene	87
Think on the mighty Pow'r of awful Virtue;	O 252	Irene	88
Think on that Providence that guards the Good. . . .	O 252	Irene	89
Think on Revenge and Glory Greece and Love	O 361	Irene	V 5
What! think of Peace while haughty Scanderbeg . . .	O 264	Irene	13
Nor dream of peace, think of rest	Y 130	Irene	V 13
Think on th' insulting Scorn, the conscious Pangs, . .	O 266	Irene	19
Nor think my eyes oerflow with Female	O 357	Irene	V 17
Weakness			
Nor think th' Intention sanctifies the Deed:	O 291	Irene	59
Nor think to say here will I stop	Y 168	Irene	V 132
Nor think thy Cause neglected while I gaze, ...	O 297	Irene	20
Think--but excuse a Woman's needless Caution, . . .	O 298	Irene	5
Think how the sov'reign Arbiter of Kingdoms	O 300	Irene	56
Yet think a Moment, ere you court Destruction, . . .	O 301	Irene	87
Think them a sacred Treasure lent by Heav'n, ...	O 302	Irene	6
Nor think that Effort lost which rescues thee. . . .	O 317	Irene	47
Great is thy Woe! but think, illustrious Sultan, . .	O 332	Irene	37
Think shouldst thou fall how wretched shall we be, . .	Y 19	Tr. Iliad Bk 6	48
THINKS			
Thinks death kind Nature's signal of retreat:	O 48	Vanity Wishes	V 364
Who thinks us Women born to dress and sing	O 247	Irene Epilogue	2
And thinks his fatal Mandates ill obey'd.	O 327	Irene	13
THIRST			
What check restrain your thirst of pow'r and gold? . .	O 13	London	62
With eager thirst, by folly or by fate, ...	O 14	London	95
Resign'd his Thirst of Empire to her Charms, ...	O 97	Hickman Spinet	19
With thirst of knowledge, and with love of truth; . . .	O 117	Epitaph Hanmer	6
Unquench'd the thirst of gain is found;	O 144	Tr Boeth. II.2	12
The Thirst of Empire, and the Love of Glory?	O 278	Irene	58

THIRST   (CONTINUED)   PAGE   TITLE   LINE

	PAGE	TITLE	LINE
THIRST (CONTINUED)			
The thirst of empire and the love of virtue?	Y 149	Irene	V 58
THIRSTED			
The feather'd race and thirsted for their blood:	Y 24	Tr Add. Battle	85
THIRSTS			
No more the glutted Sabre thirsts for Blood,	O 249	Irene	9
THIRSTY			
None fiercer Juba's thirsty land,	O 66	Hor I Ode xxii	15
The lyon's thirsty parent, bore.	O 66	Hor I Ode xxii	V 16
The Lion's thirsty Parent, bore.	O 67	To A. Fuscus	16
Whose blood shall quench some Grecian's thirsty rage,	O 74	Tr. Iliad Bk 6	16
Like thirsty Sailors gazing on the Clouds,	O 282	Irene	5
THIRTY			
Better Years than Thirty five;	O 178	Thrale 35 Year	4
Trifle not at Thirty five:	O 178	Thrale 35 Year	12
Must begin by Thirty five:	O 178	Thrale 35 Year	16
THIRTYFIVE			
We are come to Thirtyfive;	O 178	Thrale 35 Year	2
Life to stop at Thirtyfive,	O 178	Thrale 35 Year	6
O'er the Bounds of Thirtyfive:	O 178	Thrale 35 Year	8
Nature gives at Thirtyfive;	O 178	Thrale 35 Year	10
Life declines from Thirtyfive;	O 178	Thrale 35 Year	14
Must look on Thrale at Thirtyfive.	O 178	Thrale 35 Year	18
THIS			
174			
THITHER		OMITTED WORD	
Thither with eager hast he runs	O 80	Feast St Simon	46
Till thither an huge bird the tumult drew	Y 25	Tr Add. Battle	124
THNETOUS			
Alla tod eis Thnetous Kupris epempseu onar	O 103	Eis Elisses	4
THOMAS			
A Translation Of The Latin Epitaph On Sir Thomas Hanmer	O 117	Epitaph Hanmer	T
THORNY			
And scatters roses in the thorny way	Y 148	Irene	V 43D
Now each parterre with thorny brakes is fill'd	Y 7	Virgil Daphnis	24
THOSE			
In those curs'd walls, devote to vice and gain,	O 10	London	37
Here let those reign, whom pensions can incite	O 11	London	51
Yet ev'n those heroes, mischievously gay,	Y 59	London	V 230
For those who durst not censure, scarce cou'd praise.	O 51	Pro Drury-Lane	14
Those pageant Honours which he scorn'd below:	O 57	Prologue Comus	22
Yet judg'd by those, whose voices ne'er were sold,	O 60	Pro Good Nat'd	27
Those blessings, friend, a deity bestow'd,	O 64	Virgil Past.I	7
Tears, at my name, shall drown those beauteous eyes,	O 75	Tr. Iliad Bk 6	27
Those Saints my numbers grace	O 78	Feast St Simon	9
Those names which in immortal strains	O 80	Feast St Simon	59
Those sovereign charms with strictest care employ;	O 81	Lady Birthday	13
"While I those transitory blessings scorn,	O 82	Young Author	V 17
Those dreams were Settle's once and Ogilby's.	O 82	Young Author	V 24
For those who feel no guilt can know no shame;	O 84	Epi Dist Moth.	25
Inflicting all those ills which once they knew;	O 84	Epi Dist Moth.	37
To weave those nets that catch the heart.	O 120	To Miss Purse	6
But on those regions of delight,	O 121	To Miss Playin	V 19
Thou know'st those arts which blast with envious praise,	O 176	Tr Metastas II	7
And those who wisely wish to wive,	O 178	Thrale 35 Year	17
Soon those nine lives would be past.	O 194	On Thrale Hat	4
From those bright Regions of eternal Day,	O 253	Irene	99
Those pow'rful Tyrants of the Female Breast	O 261	Irene	12
As those that bless the Mansions of the Good.	O 262	Irene	12
For those who could not please by nobler Service.--	O 264	Irene	24
Forgive those Fears that shake the tender Frame?	O 266	Irene	25
Well may those Eyes that view these heav'nly Charms,	O 267	Irene	6
Ah! cease, Irene, cease those flowing Sorrows,	O 276	Irene	3
Whence then those Charms thy Tongue has deign'd to flatter,	O 277	Irene	26
Why then Those charms your tongue has deign'd to flatter	O 355	Irene	V 15
Whence all those Hopes and Fears Despair and Rapture	O 355	Irene	V 18
Those holy Beings, whose superiour Care	O 289	Irene	17
Those holy Beings whose unseen Direction	O 346	Irene	V 5
No more should Greece lament those Prayers rejected.	O 290	Irene	52
Those gloomy walks where Gladness never smiles	Y 165	Irene	V 81
To range those walks of tyranny and lust	Y 165	Irene	V 85
To wander pensive in those gloomy walks	Y 165	Irene	V 85
And in those Bowers of Innocence and Quiet	O 349	Irene	V 7
Now but reflects those Beams that flow'd from thee.	O 298	Irene	15
Those forms of men that play before a beauty	Y 173	Irene	V 18
Those glitt'ring Dew-drops of a vernal Morn,	O 298	Irene	19
--O Demetrius O for a cottage in those happy regions	Y 177	Irene	V 108
O! could the Eyes of Kings, like those of Heav'n,	O 308	Irene	12
Those trembling Limbs--Speak out, thou shiv'ring Traitor.	O 332	Irene	16
What hadst thou lost by slighting those Commands?	O 332	Irene	32
Those Groves, whose Shades embower'd the dear Irene,	O 333	Irene	46
Hew down, ye Guards, those Vassals of Distraction,	O 333	Irene	51
Those Hounds of Blood, that catch the Hint to kill,	O 333	Irene	52
Then scorn those flowers to which the Aegyptians bow'd,	Y 4	On a Daffodill	15

THOSE	(CONTINUED)	PAGE	TITLE	LINE
Those anxious fears that fan'd the flame of Love.		Y 11	Tr Hor Epode 9	24
Withdraws the influence of those eyes,		Y 39	Lady Leaving	7

THOU

		PAGE	TITLE	LINE
But thou, should tempting villainy present		O 14	London	85
Could'st thou resign the park and play content,		O 19	London	210
Could thou resign the park and court content,		Y 58	London	V 210
There might'st thou find some elegant retreat,		O 20	London	212
Thou fly'st for refuge to the wilds of Kent;		O 23	London	257
Then shall thy friend, nor thou refuse his aid,		O 23	London	260
Thou who couldst laugh where want enchain'd caprice,		O 32	Vanity Wishes	53
How wouldst thou shake at Britain's modish tribe,		O 33	Vanity Wishes	61
Speak thou, whose thoughts at humble peace repine,		O 35	Vanity Wishes	121
Or liv'st thou now, with safer pride content,		O 35	Vanity Wishes	123
Rashness! thou spring from whence misfortunes flow!		O 77	Festina Lente	9
Thou to a scene of bloodshed turn'st the Ball,		O 77	Festina Lente	11
Art thou forgotten by the Muse,		O 80	Feast St Simon	50
Thou seem'st at once, bright nymph, a Muse and Grace.		O 107	Lady F Assizes	6
Then, O my Country! shalt thou groan distrest,		O 110	To Posterity	3
Find here that calm thou gav'st so oft before;		O 113	Epit. Phillips	4
Thou, who survey'st these walls with curious eye,		O 117	Epitaph Hanmer	1
And learn his virtues, while thou mourn'st his end.		O 117	Epitaph Hanmer	4
Thou see'st one pleasing form arise,		O 121	To Miss Playin	26
Teach me, thou venerable bow'r,		O 125	An Ode	29
O thou whose pow'r o'er moving worlds presides,		O 129	Tr. Rambler 7	1
Thou joy'st to lose the master in the friend:		O 130	Tr. Rambler 12	4
Art thou too fall'n? ere anger could subside		O 132	Tr. Rambler 54	1
Thou, who began'st a man, wilt end a boy.		O 135	Tr Rambler 127	2
Wouldst thou to some stedfast Seat,		O 144	Tr Boeth. II.4	1
Wouldst thou when fierce Eurus blows		O 144	Tr Boeth. II.4	3
Wouldst thou see the foaming Main,		O 144	Tr Boeth. II.4	5
Thou shalt sit and smile to see		O 145	Tr Boeth. II.4	19
"Go to the Ant thou Sluggard".		O 151	The Ant	V T
That thou wilt give to me,		O 158	Par Hermit III	2
Thou canst not make the tea so fast		O 159	Par Hermit III	11
Grown old in courts, thou art not surely one		O 176	Tr Metastas II	1
Thou know'st those arts which blast with envious praise,		O 176	Tr Metastas II	7
Whence or whither dost thou fly?		O 185	Anacreon Ode 9	2
Whence and whither dost thou fly?		O 185	Anacreon Ode 9	V 2
"More than all thou canst not know;		O 186	Anacreon Ode 9	42
Hadst thou nine lives like a cat,		O 194	On Thrale Hat	3
Where now thou shin'st among thy Fellow-saints,		O 253	Irene	100
Thou that hast long perus'd the Draughts of Nature,		O 255	Irene	11
Thou Thou chilld by sixty winter camps canst gaze on		Y 129	Irene	V 5
Thou Thou chilld by sixty winter camps canst gaze on		Y 129	Irene	V 5
Nor couldst thou more support a Life of Sloth		O 264	Irene	19
Shine thou distinguish'd by superior Merit,		O 264	Irene	29
Thou know'st not yet thy Master's future Greatness,		O 265	Irene	40
When thou art absent		O 265	Irene	11
Wouldst thou subdue th' obdurate Cannibal		O 267	Irene	4
Born to command, as thou to charm Mankind,		O 268	Irene	23
Thou long'st for Stars that frown on human Kind,		O 271	Irene	4
How blest art thou, still jocund and serene,		O 271	Irene	6
Wilt thou dismiss the Savage from the Toils		O 275	Irene	66
Do thou resolve: For see, Irene comes!		O 275	Irene	90
Wilt thou descend, fair Daughter of Perfection,		O 276	Irene	1
Irene rise, thou daughter of perfection--or beauty		Y 145	Irene	V 1
Too high, bright Maid, thou rat'st exterior Grace;		O 277	Irene	30
Where hast thou linger'd while th' encumber'd Hours		O 279	Irene	3
Hast thou grown old amidst the Croud of Courts,		O 281	Irene	32
Know'st thou not yet, when Love invades the Soul,		O 281	Irene	38
Not till this Day thou saw'st this fatal Fair;		O 281	Irene	54
But thou, too old to bear another Cheat,		O 283	Irene	32
What Claim hast thou to plead?		O 286	Irene	8
Dream not of Pow'r thou never can'st attain:		O 291	Irene	69
There shalt thou view from far the quiet Cottage,		O 292	Irene	83
Soon shouldst thou see, how false thy weak Reproach.		O 293	Irene	107
Soon wouldst thou see, how false thy weak Reproach.		O 293	Irene	V 107
Well may'st thou hide in Labyrinths of Sound		O 293	Irene	125
Whoe'er thou art, or whatsoe'er thy Message,		O 294	Irene	4
What Fears, what Griefs, what Dangers hast thou known?		O 295	Irene	22
Say, how thou call'dst in Tears upon Demetrius!		O 295	Irene	26
Thou kind Assistant of my better Angel,		O 298	Irene	10
Thou shin'st, bright Maid, superior to Distress;		O 298	Irene	17
Soon shalt thou scorn, in Safety's Arms repos'd,		O 301	Irene	93
But how can'st thou support the Woes of Exile?		O 301	Irene	102
Can'st thou forget hereditary Splendours,		O 301	Irene	103
Hast thou not search'd my Soul's profoundest Thoughts?		O 304	Irene	18
Wilt thou not head the Troop upon the Shore,		O 305	Irene	36
What can'st thou boast superiour to Demetrius?		O 305	Irene	38
Dar'st thou thus dally with Abdalla's Passion?		O 307	Irene	8
Obtain her and possess, thou know'st thy Rival.		O 307	Irene	17
If thou art more than the gay Dream of Fancy,		O 310	Irene	12
O Happiness! sure thou art all Aspasia's.		O 310	Irene	14
Do thou repay the Gift,		O 313	Irene	18
Thou fountain of existence I pour the		Y 189	Irene	V 1
Forbear--But thou art sunk beneath Reproach;		O 315	Irene	28
Still dost thou flutter in the Jaws of Death?		O 318	Irene	17

THOU   (CONTINUED)   PAGE   TITLE   LINE

	PAGE	TITLE	LINE
Still dost thou linger in these fatal bowrs	Y 196	Irene	V 18A
Well mayst thou call thy Master to the Combat, ...	O 319	Irene	30
Who fearst lest I should gain, or thou	Y 198	Irene	V 32
But soon thou shalt repent: another Moment	O 319	Irene	33
Know'st thou not Cali? know'st thou not Demetrius? . .	O 324	Irene	15
Know'st thou not Cali? know'st thou not Demetrius? . .	O 324	Irene	15
Perfidious!--yes--too well thou know'st them Traytors. . .	O 324	Irene	17
Now shalt thou shine the Darling of the Sultan, . . .	O 329	Irene	3
From his Escape learn thou the Pow'r of Virtue, . . .	O 330	Irene	24
Nor hope his Fortune while thou want'st his Worth. . .	O 330	Irene	25
And thou, the curs'd Accomplice of her Treason, . . .	O 331	Irene	5
Those trembling Limbs--Speak out, thou shiv'ring . . . Traitor.	O 332	Irene	16
What hadst thou lost by slighting those Commands? . . .	O 332	Irene	32
Hear! shall I hear thee! did'st thou hear Irene? . . .	O 333	Irene	56
Had'st thou heard a Moment, ...	O 333	Irene	57
Thou might'st have liv'd, for thou hadst spar'd Irene. . .	O 333	Irene	58
Thou might'st have liv'd, for thou hadst spar'd Irene. . .	O 333	Irene	58
Thou mightst have liv'd, nor had I lost Irene. . . .	Y 214	Irene	V 58
Thou sluggish Idler, dilatory Slave?	O 334	Irene	2
Be thou the favorite of the indulgent sky, ...	Y 3	On a Daffodill	5
And thou impearl'd with dew appear more gay.	Y 3	On a Daffodill	12
And thou shalt flourish by her influence.	Y 4	On a Daffodill	20
Thou shalt with Bacchus equal honours share	Y 7	Virgil Daphnis	51
The swains shall pay their vows, and thou shalt hear their prayer.	Y 7	Virgil Daphnis	52
But dearest Hector while thou liv'st I see	Y 19	Tr. Iliad Bk 6	44
Think shouldst thou fall how wretched shall we be, . .	Y 19	Tr. Iliad Bk 6	48
"Immortal Gods! and thou allmighty Jove	Y 20	Tr. Iliad Bk 6	99

THO'

	PAGE	TITLE	LINE
Tho' grief and fondness in my breast rebel, ...	O 8	London	1
Who scarce forbear, tho' Britain's Court he sing, . . .	O 13	London	69
Tho' confiscation's vulturs hover round.	O 32	Vanity Wishes	36
Tho' confiscation's vulturs clang around.	O 32	Vanity Wishes	V 36
Tho' confiscation's bloodhounds yelp around.	Y 93	Vanity Wishes	V 36
From meaner minds, tho' smaller fines content, ...	O 39	Vanity Wishes	169
What tho' she shine with no Miltonian Fire, ...	O 58	Prologue Comus	27
Tho' Scythia's icy cliff he treads, ...	Y 74	Hor I Ode xxii	V 5
Tho' rapture sings, and beauty shines.	O 125	An Ode	12
Yet, tho' my limbs disease invades, ...	O 125	An Ode	13
For tho' beneath thy haughty Brow	O 146	Tr Boeth III.5	5
Tho' Northern Climes confess thy Sway, ...	O 146	Tr Boeth III.5	7
Tho' when Orpheus made his Moan	O 148	Tr Boet III.12	5
Tho' when Orpheus sweetly sighing	O 148	Tr Boet III.12	V 5
Tho' the Hind approach'd to hear	O 148	Tr Boet III.12	7
Tho' the	O 148	Tr Boet III.12	V 11
Tho' reluctant still refrain, ...	O 150	Tr Boet III.12	45
Tho' now his eightieth year was nigh.	O 202	Death Dr Levet	32
Daring, tho' calm; and vigorous, tho' resign'd. . . .	O 246	Irene Prologue	10
Daring, tho' calm; and vigorous, tho' resign'd. . . .	O 246	Irene Prologue	10
And spare him, Beauties! tho' his Lovers live.	O 246	Irene Prologue	20
Unmov'd tho' Witlings sneer and Rivals rail;	O 246	Irene Prologue	29
Tho' Wealth, and Pow'r, and Glory they receive, . . .	O 247	Irene Epilogue	19
He, tir'd of Slav'ry, tho' the highest Slave, ...	O 253	Irene	113
We come, bright Virgin, tho' relenting Nature	O 325	Irene	20
Tho' no lewd hint the mantling virgin warm.	Y 67	Prologue Lethe	14

THOUGH

	PAGE	TITLE	LINE
Nor think though learning her last prize bestows, . . .	Y 99	Vanity Wishes	V 165
Though dancing mountains witness'd Orpheus near; . . .	O 43	Vanity Wishes	270
Philosophy remain'd, though Nature fled.	O 52	Pro Drury-Lane	34
Here I, though faint myself, must drive my goats, . . .	O 64	Virgil Past.I	17
Though Scythia's icy cliffs he treads, ...	O 65	Hor I Ode xxii	5
Though from no Princes I descend, ...	O 70	Hor.II Ode XX	5
Though fierce Barbarians threatend death	O 79	Feast St Simon	40
Each youth admires, though each admirer dies;	O 83	Epi Dist Moth.	6
Though gold and silk their charms unite, ...	O 119	To Miss Purse	1
Consistent still, though not the same, ...	O 121	To Miss Playin	34
Though favour'd by the pow'rs on high, ...	O 136	Tr Rambler 128	5
But though the numbers for a moment please, ...	O 142	In Baretti Bk.	5
Though musick thrills, or sudden sallies seize, . . .	O 142	In Baretti Bk.	6
Though countless as the Grains of Sand	O 144	Tr Boeth. II.2	1
Though countless as the lamps of night	O 144	Tr Boeth. II.2	3
Their Arms prevail'd, though Cali was our Friend. . . .	O 253	Irene	119
And, though refus'd, conceals it from the Sultan. . . .	O 258	Irene	89
Let Prudence moderate, though not suppress.	O 264	Irene	34
And though built on feeble columns--Its lofty turrets blaze amidst	Y 131	Irene	V 35
Diffuse Irene's Beauty though the World.	O 268	Irene	14
And though at length subdued, elude thy Vengeance. . . .	O 274	Irene	57
to be guilty, though penitent	Y 165	Irene	V 81
Permitted oft, though not inspir'd by Heav'n, ...	O 300	Irene	65
Though Disappointment blast our general Scheme, . . .	O 317	Irene	44
But soon though shalt lament thy daring folly	Y 198	Irene	V 33
Your calmer Though	O 321	Irene	53

THOUGHT

	PAGE	TITLE	LINE
On Thames's banks, in silent thought we stood, ...	O 10	London	21
By plumes is viel'd; see! quick as thought	O 70	Hor.II Ode XX	11
Oh! how my soul abhors so mean a thought.	O 74	Tr. Iliad Bk 6	8
As the sad thought of your impending fate:	O 74	Tr. Iliad Bk 6	20
Then, swift as thought, by headlong anger driv'n . . .	O 76	Tr Add. Battle	10

THOUGHT	(CONTINUED)	PAGE	TITLE		LINE
This thought once form'd, all counsel comes too late,	.	O 82	Young Author		19
What thought of flight, or of defence?		O 121	To Miss Playin		12
Nor only thought the wasted plain, ...		O 123	Winter's Walk	V	5
Suspend the Thought.		O 252	Irene		79
All Thought on her is Madness		O 252	Irene		79
A single Thought now rove, recall it home.		O 255	Irene		7
And mingles unperceiv'd with ev'ry Thought.		O 261	Irene		6
Since Fear predominates in every Thought, ...		O 266	Irene		17
While with incessant Thought laborious Man		O 269	Irene		3
Had not my ready thought remov'd Aspasia		O 367	Irene	V	24
Rose to his Thought, and set his Soul on Fire: . . .		O 270	Irene		11
And, to confirm my Thought, at sight of me, . . .		O 275	Irene		84
At her Approach each ruder Gust of Thought		O 275	Irene		91
Records each Act, each Thought of sov'reign Man, . .		O 276	Irene		21
Records each deed each thought of sovereign Man . .		O 355	Irene	V	10
Do we not share the comprehensive Thought, ...		O 278	Irene		55
Do not we share the comprehensive thought, ...		Y 149	Irene	V	57
I thought, forgive my Fair, the noblest Aim, . . .		O 278	Irene		61
Charm'd with the Thought of blessing human Kind, . .		O 278	Irene		73
If built on settled Thought, this Constancy		O 290	Irene		36
If fix'd on settled thought this Constancy		O 364	Irene	V	8
That sooth the sense, and elevate the thought . . .		Y 165	Irene	V	80
Stoop from thy Flight, trace back th' entangled Thought,		O 293	Irene		127
To noble Thought and gen'rous Emulation, ...		O 298	Irene		14
And thought the petty Dross beneath a Sigh.		O 302	Irene		109
Guide all thy Steps, calm ev'ry stormy Thought, . .		O 303	Irene		21
Absorb'd in Thought; then starting from his Trance, .		O 311	Irene		6
Absorb'd by thought, then waking from his dream . .		Y 187	Irene	V	6
in the whirl of thought		Y 187	Irene	V	6
What more could force attempt or thought contrive . .		Y 194	Irene	V	35
Recoil from Thought, and shudder at myself. . . .		O 322	Irene		12
Far be the Thought--But hear my Protestation. . . .		O 326	Irene		32
Far be the horrid thought--but hear my protestation .		Y 205	Irene	V	32
Now haste to murder, ere returning Thought		O 326	Irene		39
THOUGHTFUL					
How active light, and thoughtful shade, ...		O 121	To Miss Playin		27
THOUGHTLESS					
And lull to servitude a thoughtless age.		O 12	London		60
But lost in thoughtless ease, and empty show, . . .		O 15	London		103
But sunk in thoughtless ease, and empty show, . . .		Y 53	London	V	103
With thoughtless reverence we praise, ...		O 190	Tr. Medea I		2
Permits the blooming maid secure and thoughtless . .		Y 146	Irene	V	18
And gold and flattery--thoughtless mirth--hurry . .		Y 164	Irene	V	72
Glory, the casual Gift of thoughtless Crouds! . . .		O 305	Irene		31
Haste, seize them, guards, be quick--my thoughtless hast		Y 198	Irene	V	34
But let no thoughtless Hint involve Abdalla. . . .		O 329	Irene		15
Was she then guiltless! Has my thoughtless Rage . .		O 332	Irene		18
Rush'd out and seiz'd me, thoughtless and unarm'd, .		O 335	Irene		7
THOUGHTS					
Yet still my calmer thoughts his choice commend, . . .		O 8	London		3
Speak thou, whose thoughts at humble peace repine, . .		O 35	Vanity Wishes		121
Th' insulted sea with humbler thoughts he gains, . .		O 42	Vanity Wishes		237
On life, on morals, be thy thoughts employ'd; . . .		O 140	Tr Rambler 180		1
I rais'd his Thoughts to more sublime Devotion. . .		O 274	Irene		46
And turn thy Thoughts henceforth to Love and Empire. .		O 276	Irene		5
Now pause, great Bassa, from the Thoughts of Blood, .		O 285	Irene		1
There when my Thoughts, at interval of Pray'r, . . .		O 292	Irene		94
And as my thoughts at intervals of Prayer		O 349	Irene	V	9
A thousand Thoughts imperfect and distracted, . . .		O 295	Irene		17
Drive Int'rest, Love, and Vengeance from thy Thoughts, .		O 298	Irene		7
Pure as the Thoughts of infant Innocence?		O 304	Irene		15
Hast thou not search'd my Soul's profoundest Thoughts?		O 304	Irene		18
Yet ere we give our loosen'd Thoughts to Rapture, . .		O 309	Irene		18
The thoughts of happy love, and rescu'd Greece . . .		Y 189	Irene	V	1D
THOUSAND					
In ev'ry face a thousand graces shine, ...		O 16	London		127
And turn the varied taunt a thousand ways.		O 17	London		165
And unrelenting sport ten thousand lives away; . . .		O 83	Epi Dist Moth.		9
And found a Thousand Worlds in Stella's Arms. . . .		O 97	Hickman Spinet		20
Parent of thousand wild desires, ...		O 99	Ode Friendship		6
Mark, when from thousand mingled dyes		O 121	To Miss Playin		25
A thousand horrid Prodigies foretold it.		O 250	Irene		36
And gives a thousand fatal Questions Birth;		O 258	Irene		84
The wily sorc'ress wears a thousand forms, ...		Y 155	Irene	V	26
A thousand Thoughts imperfect and distracted, . . .		O 295	Irene		17
A thousand Questions press upon my Tongue, ...		O 295	Irene		19
At once a Thousand Passions fir'd his Cheek: . . .		O 317	Irene		31
Well if a Thousand Lives like thine had perish'd; . .		O 332	Irene		34
Which gave a thousand pleasures birth.		Y 39	Lady Leaving		8
THOUSANDS					
Has heard unhurt the cries of slaughterd thousands . .		Y 126	Irene	V	145
In that black Day when slaughter'd Thousands fell . .		O 312	Irene		7
Ere he return with Thousands at his Side.		O 320	Irene		9
THRACIA'S					
Too well I know him, since on Thracia's Plains . . .		O 307	Irene		18
THRALE					
Must look on Thrale at Thirtyfive.		O 178	Thrale 35 Year		18
THRALL					
Unless the soul, to vice a thrall, ...		O 129	Tr. Rambler 6		1

THREAT'NING
  And Want hung threat'ning o'er her slow Decay. . . . .   O 58 Prologue Comus   26
  An undistinguish'd Sound of threat'ning Rage. . . . .   O 311 Irene   13
THREAT'NINGS
  Smiles at the Threat'nings of defeated Rage.   . . . .   O 325 Irene   19
THREATEN
  Still fierce to threaten, still afraid to fight;   . . .   O 110 To Posterity   10
THREATEN'D
  Say, how the Tyrant threaten'd, flatter'd, sigh'd,   . .   O 295 Irene   23
  Say, how he threaten'd, flatter'd, sigh'd in vain!   . .   O 295 Irene   24
THREATEND
  Though fierce Barbarians threatend death . . . . . .   O 79 Feast St Simon   40
  He sigh'd, He rag'd, he threatend and he . . . . . .   O 364 Irene   V 20
    flatter'd
  But flatterd threatend, sigh'd and rag'd in vain   . . .   Y 170 Irene   V 24
THREATS
  To Threats of Torture, Death and Violation. . . . . .   O 259 Irene   112
  Forbear thy Threats, proud Prophetess of Ill, ...   O 314 Irene   26
  With idle Threats and fruitless Exclamation, ...   O 327 Irene   7
  With empty threats, and fruitless Exclamation   . . .   O 368 Irene   V 15
  Hope not thy threats shall stay   . . . .   Y 210 Irene   V 25
THREW
  Threw back the glitt'ring Bribe.   . . . .   O 258 Irene   102
THRICE
  Thrice happy Saints--where do I rove? . . . .   O 80 Feast St Simon   55
  Thrice ten long years he labour'd for the State;   . . .   O 118 Epitaph Hanmer   14
  Thrice has December stripp'd the tree . . . .   Y 11 Tr Hor Epode 9   7
  And thrice deform'd the verdant year . . . .   Y 11 Tr Hor Epode 9   8
  Thrice to the wall their dreadfull hosts have led   . .   Y 19 Tr. Iliad Bk 6   56
  And thrice to mount the battlements assay'd . . . .   Y 19 Tr. Iliad Bk 6   57
THRIFT
  Bid the slaves of thrift farewell. . . . .   O 196 Song Congratu.   8
  Bid the Sons of thrift farewell.   . . . .   O 196 Song Congratu.   V 8
THRILLS
  Though musick thrills, or sudden sallies seize,   . . .   O 142 In Baretti Bk.   6
THRISTY
  That pours the dews upon the thristy vales   . . . . .   Y 168 Irene   V135C
THRIVE
  He that ever hopes to thrive . . . .   O 178 Thrale 35 Year   15
THRO
  May balmy spirits thro thy foliage play, ...   Y 3 On a Daffodill   V 10
THROATS
  Our supple tribes repress their patriot throats,   . . .   O 34 Vanity Wishes   95
THROB
  When did contentment with struggling sorrow . . . . .   Y 191 Irene   V 20
    throb?
THROBBING
  And cure the throbbing of an anxious heart; . . . . .   O 95 Sprig of Myrtl   V 12
  Then with no throbbing fiery pain, ...   O 202 Death Dr Levet   33
  Wet the dim eye or swell the throbbing bosom?   . . .   Y 191 Irene   V 19A
THROBBINGS
  And ease the throbbings of an anxious heart;   . . . .   O 95 Sprig of Myrtl   12
THROBS
  Then with no throbs of fiery pain, ...   O 202 Death Dr Levet   V 33
THRONE
  And virtue guard thee to the throne of Truth! . . . .   O 37 Vanity Wishes   142
  Refulgent on his starry throne . . . .   O 79 Feast St Simon   23
  When Hanmer fill'd the chair, and Ann the throne. . . .   O 118 Epitaph Hanmer   22
  And drive discountenanc'd virtue from the throne: . . .   O 176 Tr Metastas II   9
  And chase discountenanc'd virtue from the throne. . . .   O 176 Tr Metastas II   V 9
  The Cloister's Ease, resum'd the tott'ring Throne,   . .   O 256 Irene   44
  My Policy shall raise an easy Throne; . . . .   O 257 Irene   78
  Unshaken be thy Throne as Earth's firm Base, ...   O 262 Irene   2
  Could bear his Son upon the Turkish Throne. . . . . .   O 264 Irene   22
  Courts thee to shake on a dependent Throne; . . . . .   O 268 Irene   22
  Adorn a Throne, and dignify Dominion. . . . .   O 276 Irene   10
  And pushes feeble (thrusts defenseless) virtue from her .   Y 158 Irene   V 13
    throne
  When Cali mounts the Throne Abdalla dies, ...   O 288 Irene   13
  Stretch'd in the Dust, or tow'ring on his Throne; . . .   O 303 Irene   10
  And bid thy visionary Throne farewell. . . . . . .   O 307 Irene   11
  The Breast where Virtue guards the Throne of Peace. . .   O 316 Irene   15
  The breast where truth supports the throne of peace. . .   Y 193 Irene   V 15
  Shook headlong from his throne imperial Jove. . . . .   Y 26 Tr Add. Battle   139
THRONES
  Whether you sit on thrones, or dwell in cots, ...   O 77 Festina Lente   2
  Still discord hovers o'er divided thrones. . . . . .   O 140 Tr Rambler 183   2
THRONG
  With pleasing sound allur'd the rural throng. . . . .   Y 6 Virgil Daphnis   8
  In warring colours shew the warring throng; . . . . .   Y 22 Tr Add. Battle   4
  And scarce the lab'ring air sustains the throng   . . .   Y 25 Tr Add. Battle   95
THRONGS
  May throngs of beauteous virgins 'round thee crowd,   . .   Y 3 On a Daffodill   13
THRO'
  Roll thro' the streets, and thunder to the skies; . . .   O 18 London   183
  Then thro' the world a wretched vagrant roam, ...   O 18 London   190
  Thro' him the rays of regal bounty shine, ...   O 34 Vanity Wishes   102
  Thro' Scythia's icy cliffs he treads, ...   Y 74 Hor I Ode xxii   V 5
  His liquid Wealth thro' barbarous Lands. . . . . . .   O 66 To A. Fuscus   8
  Thro' all the spacious ball; . . . .   O 79 Feast St Simon   27
  They, pleas'd, thro' barb'rous nations roam . . . . .   O 79 Feast St Simon   29

```
                                                      PAGE   TITLE            LINE
THRO'            (CONTINUED)
      Then thro' thy Fields shall scarlet Reptiles stray,   . .   O 110  To Posterity       7
      Here let me thro' the vales pursue   . . . . . .   .   O 125  An Ode             21
      Sacred to Prayer, and wander thro' the Streets;   . . .     O 251  Irene              63
      And balmy spirits thro' thy foliage play,   . . . . .       Y   3  On a Daffodill     10
THROUGH    SEE THRO, THRO'
      Through Freedom's sons no more remonstrance rings,   .      O  34  Vanity Wishes      93
      Through all his veins the fever of renown   . . . .        O  36  Vanity Wishes     137
      Through purple billows and a floating host.   . . . .      O  42  Vanity Wishes     240
      Their souls dismiss'd through many a ghastly wound,   .    O  74  Tr. Iliad Bk 6     18
      O guide me through life's darksome way,   . . . . .        O 100  Ode Friendship     14
      O guide us through life's darksome way,   . . . . .      V O 100  Ode Friendship     14
      His various worth, through varied life attend,   . . .     O 117  Epitaph Hanmer      3
      Nor only through the wasted plain,   . . . . . . .         O 123  Winter's Walk       5
      Well tried through many a varying year,   . . . . .        O 201  Death Dr Levet      5
      Flows through each Member of th' embodied State,   . .     O 256  Irene              58
      Break through the Politician's tedious Forms,   . . .      O 259  Irene             106
      I walk'd superior, through the Blaze of Charms,   .   .    O 263  Irene              17
      Rolls half his Floods unheard through shouting Camps?  .   O 264  Irene              18
      Through half his Course reflects the blaze of       .      O 353  Irene            V  2
        War
      Pours half his Floods unheard through shouting camps  .    O 353  Irene            V 32
      Glide through Irene to the Sultan's Ear.   . . . . .       O 267  Irene               3
      And through the parted Shade disclos'd the Greeks,   .     O 269  Irene              11
      Disperse Rebellion through the Eastern World;   . . .      O 274  Irene              52
      Through shades of peace and flowery labyrinths   . . .     Y 146  Irene            V 21
      Fierce through the bursting Caverns rend their Way?   .    O 281  Irene              53
      Till burning Death shoots through their wither'd Limbs? .  O 282  Irene               6
      Through bowing Slaves, I range the private Rooms,   . .    O 283  Irene              17
      The Soldier lab'ring through a Winter's March,   . . .     O 283  Irene              28
      Guides through the Maze of Life the Steps       . . .      O 346  Irene            V  6
        of Man
      Nor bursting through the ranks in wild distraction        Y 163  Irene            V 47
      To spread Civility through Russian snows   . . . . .      V O 348  Irene            V 21
      To spread Civility through Russia's Forests   . . . .     V O 348  Irene            V 21
      Why shoots this Chilness through thy shaking Nerves?  .    O 295  Irene               6
      And pass'd uninjur'd through the Walks of Death?   . .     O 296  Irene              29
      Through hissing Ages, a proverbial Coward,   . . . .       O 305  Irene              28
      My Name shall echo through the shouting Field;   . . .     O 305  Irene              40
      And stream destructive through his freezing Veins:   .     O 308  Irene              31
      And spread the general Transport through Mankind.   . .    O 308  Irene               5
      Pursue him through his Labyrinths of Treason,   . . .      O 310  Irene               6
      Seize him this Night, and through the private Passage .    O 312  Irene              23
      See how the Moon through all th' unclouded Sky   . . .     O 313  Irene               1
      Persue thy course through boiling eddies,   . . . .       Y 201  Irene            V 10A
      That range lascivious through the lonesome       .         Y   7  Virgil Daphnis   V 50
        roads
      Back through the city trod his former way.   . . . .      Y  17  Tr. Iliad Bk 6      2
THROUGHOUT
      All Men throughout the peopled Earth   . . . . . . .       O 146  Tr Boeth III.6      1
THROW
      In quest of wealth who throw their lives away.   . . .     O 132  Tr. Rambler 48      2
      To mix with nobler Cares, I'll throw aside   . . . .       O 275  Irene              70
      Shall throw th' attending Janizaries round thee.   . .     O 319  Irene              34
      Weak Man with erring Rage may throw the Dart,   . . .      O 335  Irene              14
THROWN
      Thrown beyond the verge of providence   . . . . . .       Y 199  Irene            V 16
THROWS
      Throws his fond Arms about Aspasia's Neck,   . . . .       O 286  Irene               4
      Their Treason throws no Stain upon Irene.   . . . . .      O 324  Irene              18
      When erring Fury throws the random dart   . . . . .        O 345  Irene            V 28
THRUSH
      Betimes the greedy Thrush to kill   . . . . . . . .        O  72  Hor. Epode II      41
THRUSTS
      And pushes feeble (thrusts defenseless) virtue from her .  Y 158  Irene            V 13
        throne
THUND'RING
      Again his thund'ring Voice return'd, Irene.   . . . . .    O 325  Irene              26
THUNDER
      Here falling houses thunder on your head,   . . . .   .    O   9  London             17
      Roll thro' the streets, and thunder to the skies;   . .   O  18  London            183
      Our trees were blasted by the thunder stroke,   . . .     O  65  Virgil Past.I      23
      And can with thunder roar.   . . . . . . . . .            O 127  To Lyce, Lady      16
      Now roll full fraught with Thunder o'er your Head.   .     O 275  Irene              75
THUNDER'D
      At once a hundred Voices thunder'd round me,   . . .       O 271  Irene              29
THUNDERBOLTS
      Are these the rapid Thunderbolts of War, . . . . .   .     O 325  Irene              11
THUNDERS
      He rolls no Thunders o'er the drowsy Pit.   . . . . .      O 246  Irene Prologue     26
THUNDRED
      --When of late The storm of Heav'ns displeasure thundred  Y 136  Irene            V 27
        on you.
THUS
      In health, in sickness, thus the suppliant prays;   . . . O  43  Vanity Wishes     256
      Thus grac'd with humble Virtue's native Charms   . . . .  O  58  Prologue Comus     33
      Thus did the Us'rer Alphius praise,   . . . . . . .       O  73  Hor. Epode II      73
      Thus fell the Pygmie state, which long had stood   . .    O  76  Tr Add. Battle     33
      Thus wak'd to rage by Musick's dreadfull Pow'r,   . . .   O  97  Hickman Spinet     13
      Thus early wise, th' endanger'd realm to aid,   . . .     O 117  Epitaph Hanmer      9
      When charms thus press on ev'ry sense,   . . . . .   .    O 121  To Miss Playin     11
```

THUS   (CONTINUED)

		PAGE	TITLE		LINE
Thus blindly pray'd the fretful fair,		O 122	Stella Mourn.		7
And thus the Mind tormented long		O 145	Tr Boeth III.1		9
Thus I spoke; and speaking sigh'd;		O 181	Parody Warton		5
Thus lightly touch and quickly go.		O 203	Tr. on Skating		4
Thus lightly skim, and haste away.		O 203	Tr. on Skating	V	4
And is it thus Demetrius meets his Friend,		O 249	Irene		1
But thus reserv'd to lure the Wolves of Turkey,		O 250	Irene		24
While thus we mourn the Fortune of Aspasia,		O 253	Irene		107
And bids us thus disguis'd await him here.		O 253	Irene		115
Thus bright in Tears, thus amiable in Ruin,		O 276	Irene		7
Thus bright in Tears, thus amiable in Ruin,		O 276	Irene		7
Thus Life, with loss of Wealth, is well preserv'd,		O 290	Irene		34
Thus meaner Spirits with Amazement mark		O 293	Irene		117
Thus meaner Spirits with amazement see		O 369	Irene	V	11
And thus protected in the gen'ral Ruin,		O 296	Irene		32
That joins us thus, will never part us more.		O 296	Irene		39
Dar'st thou thus dally with Abdalla's Passion?		O 307	Irene		8
Thus shall he live to strike th' important Blow,		O 308	Irene		32
Revive the languid Flow'rs; thus Nature shone		O 314	Irene		3
Thus on deceitful Etna's flow'ry Side,		O 315	Irene		33
Nor thus usurp the Dignity of Virtue.		O 323	Irene		10
That thus you parly with detected Treason?		O 327	Irene		15
That thus constrain'd we speed the Stroke of Death.		O 327	Irene		30
Eternal justice thus her doom decreed		O 345	Irene	V	32
well th' Eternal Mind thus her doom decreed		O 345	Irene	V	34
Thus I t' effect this mighty change design'd		Y 11	Tr Hor Epode 9		29
The Pygmies thus exasp'rated their foes.		Y 23	Tr Add. Battle		51
Cleora thus regretted flies,		Y 39	Lady Leaving		5
O would Cleora thus return,		Y 39	Lady Leaving		11

THY

Turn from the glitt'ring bribe thy scornful eye,		O 14	London		87
And stretch thy prospects o'er the smiling land,		O 20	London		214
And stretch thy prospects o'er your fruitfull land,		Y 58	London	V	214
There prune thy walks, support thy drooping flow'rs,		O 20	London		216
There prune thy walks, support thy drooping flow'rs,		O 20	London		216
There prune thy shades, support the drooping flow'rs,		Y 58	London	V	216
Direct thy rivulets, and twine thy bow'rs;		O 20	London		217
Direct thy rivulets, and twine thy bow'rs;		O 20	London		217
And, while thy grounds a cheap repast afford,		O 20	London		218
And, while thy beds a cheap repast afford,		O 20	London	V	218
On all thy hours security shall smile,		O 20	London		222
And bless thy evening walk and morning toil.		O 20	London	V	223
Then shall thy friend, nor thou refuse his aid,		O 23	London		260
Thy satire point, and animate thy page.		O 23	London		263
Thy satire point, and animate thy page.		O 23	London		263
All aid the farce, and all thy mirth maintain,		O 33	Vanity Wishes		67
How just that scorn ere yet thy voice declare,		O 33	Vanity Wishes		71
Are these thy views? proceed, illustrious youth,		O 37	Vanity Wishes		141
Yet should thy soul indulge the gen'rous heat,		O 37	Vanity Wishes		143
Yet should thy fate indulge the gen'rous heat,		Y 98	Vanity Wishes	V	143
Should tempting Novelty thy cell refrain,		O 37	Vanity Wishes		149
Should no Disease thy torpid veins invade,		O 37	Vanity Wishes		153
Nor should disease thy torpid veins invade,		Y 99	Vanity Wishes	V	153
Nor Melancholy's phantoms haunt thy shade;		O 37	Vanity Wishes		154
Nor Melancholy's spectres haunt thy shade;		Y 99	Vanity Wishes	V	154
When strong devotion fills thy glowing Breast,		O 48	Vanity Wishes		358
Pour forth thy fervours for a healthful mind,		O 48	Vanity Wishes		359
Breathe forth thy fervours for a soul		Y 108	Vanity Wishes	V	359
The floods of rage, and calm thy rufled soul.		O 77	Festina Lente		8
The haughty Persian in thy gore		O 80	Feast St Simon		53
Thy form more lovely, more adorn'd thy mind;		O 80	Lady Birthday		4
Thy form more lovely, more adorn'd thy mind;		O 80	Lady Birthday		4
O then, when conquer'd crouds confess thy sway,		O 81	Lady Birthday		9
What hopes, what terrors does thy gift create,		O 95	Sprig of Myrtl		1
O! then the meaning of thy gift impart,		O 95	Sprig of Myrtl		11
Thy lambent glories only beam		O 100	Ode Friendship		11
Thy milder glories only beam		Y 71	Ode Friendship	V	11
Thy gentle flows of guiltless joys		O 100	Ode Friendship		17
Thy pleasures, permanent as great,		O 100	Ode Friendship		23
Thy pleasures, lasting, as they're great,		O 100	Ode Friendship	V	23
Thy pleasures, charms as great,		Y 71	Ode Friendship	V	23
O! Shall thy flames then cease to glow		O 100	Ode Friendship	V	25
Thy charms at least, fair F<irebrac>e, might inspire		O 107	Lady F Assizes		3
For such thy beauteous mind, and lovely face,		O 107	Lady F Assizes		5
Grief swell thine Eyes, and Terror chill thy Breast,		O 110	To Posterity		4
Thy Streets with Violence of Woe shall sound,		O 110	To Posterity		5
Then thro' thy Fields shall scarlet Reptiles stray,		O 110	To Posterity		7
Illustrious age! how bright thy glories shone,		O 118	Epitaph Hanmer		21
To make thy curious web delight,		O 119	To Miss Purse		2
Thy hand that knows the subtler art,		O 120	To Miss Purse		5
Thy nets may catch, but not confine,		O 120	To Miss Purse		8
Thy nets may snare, but not confine,		O 120	To Miss Purse	V	8
Nor can I hope thy silken chain		O 120	To Miss Purse		9
Thy pictures shall thy conduct frame,		O 121	To Miss Playin		33
Thy pictures shall thy conduct frame,		O 121	To Miss Playin		33
Thy musick teach the nobler art		O 121	To Miss Playin		35
Stern winter, is thy force confest,		O 123	Winter's Walk		6
Stern winter, in thy force confest,		O 123	Winter's Walk	V	6
Still wider spreads thy horrid reign,		O 123	Winter's Walk		7
I feel thy pow'r usurp my breast.		O 123	Winter's Walk		8

THY	(CONTINUED)	PAGE	TITLE	LINE
Unhappy man! behold thy doom,	. . . .	O 124	Winter's Walk	14
Snatch me, my Stella, to thy arms,	. . . .	O 124	Winter's Walk	19
Here stop, my soul, thy rapid flight,	. . . . .	O 125	An Ode	17
We round thy board the cheerful menials see,		O 130	Tr. Rambler 12	5
Succeeding years thy early fame destroy;	. . . . .	O 135	Tr Rambler 127	1
A task proportion'd to thy mighty mind!	. . . . .	O 136	Tr Rambler 129	2
On life, on morals, be thy thoughts employ'd;		O 140	Tr Rambler 180	1
Firm and low thy Mansion found;	. . . . . .	O 145	Tr Boeth. II.4	16
For tho' beneath thy haughty Brow	. . . . .	O 146	Tr Boeth III.5	5
Tho' Northern Climes confess thy Sway,	. . . . .	O 146	Tr Boeth III.5	7
Conquring Poet take thy Bride!	. . . .	O 150	Tr Boet III.12	40
Purchasd by thy powerful Song,	. . . . . .	O 150	Tr Boet III.12	41
Turn on the prudent Ant, thy heedful eyes,	. . . .	O 151	The Ant	1
How long shall sloth usurp thy useless hours,	. . .	O 151	The Ant	9
Dissolve thy vigour, and enchain thy powers?	. . .	O 151	The Ant	10
Dissolve thy vigour, and enchain thy powers?	. . .	O 151	The Ant	10
Unnerve thy vigour, and enchain thy pow'rs;	. . .	O 151	The Ant	V 10
Unnerve thy vigour, and enchain thy pow'rs;	. . .	O 151	The Ant	V 10
While artful shades thy downy couch enclose,	. . .	O 151	The Ant	11
Smite thy bosom, sage, and tell,	. . . . . .	O 181	Parody Warton	3
Strike thy bosom, sage, and tell,	. . . . . .	O 181	Parody Warton	V 3
Scatt'ring, as thy pinions play,	. . . . . .	O 185	Anacreon Ode 9	3
Snatch thy pleasures while they last;	. . . . .	O 194	On Thrale Hat	4
Lavish of thy Grandsire's guineas,	. . . . . .	O 196	Song Congratu.	V 11
Thy praise to merit unrefin'd.	. . . . . .	O 201	Death Dr Levet	12
Thy wealth O city ill-gotten ill-preserv'd	. . . .	Y 113	Irene	V 20
shall				
descend in a proverb among thy enemies		Y 113	Irene	V 21
I felt thy Pains, and trembled for Aspasia.		Y 251	Irene	75
O Providence! extend thy Care to me,	. . . . .	O 252	Irene	90
Where now thou shin'st among thy Fellow-saints,	. .	O 253	Irene	100
I came obedient to thy friendly Summons,	. . .	O 253	Irene	105
And hop'd to share thy Counsels, not thy Sorrows:	. .	O 253	Irene	106
And hop'd to share thy Counsels, not thy Sorrows:	. .	O 253	Irene	106
Now summon all thy Soul, illustrious Christian!		O 254	Irene	1
But can thy Friend sustain the glorious Cause,		O 255	Irene	8
What can reverse thy Doom?	. . . . .	O 257	Irene	73
A Galley mann'd with Greeks, thy charge, Leontius,		O 258	Irene	81
Distract my Soul, dispatch thy ling'ring Tale;		O 259	Irene	114
Aspasia's thine, and all thy Life is Rapture--		O 260	Irene	142
Cease, cease thy Censures, for the Sultan comes	. .	O 262	Irene	28
Unshaken be thy Throne as Earth's firm Base,	. .	O 262	Irene	2
But, Cali, let Irene share thy Prayers;	. .	O 262	Irene	5
Thy Care shall guard this Treasure of my Soul; . . .		O 263	Irene	2
Sure, chill'd with sixty winter Camps, thy Blood	. .	O 263	Irene	5
To pour my Prayers for thy successful Reign,	. . .	O 264	Irene	10
<In> Triumphant at the head of thy new votaries		Y 131	Irene	V 32A
Preach thy dull Politics to vulgar Kings, ...		O 265	Irene	39
Thou know'st not yet thy Master's future Greatness,	. .	O 265	Irene	40
And sways thy Breast with absolute Dominion,	. .	O 266	Irene	18
So shall Timidity assist thy Reason,	. . . .	O 266	Irene	21
And Wisdom into Virtue turn thy Frailty.		O 266	Irene	22
I want alass thy steadiness of Soul	. . . .	O 366	Irene	V 29
Thy awful air, thy dignity of virtue.		Y 134	Irene	V 34
Thy awful air, thy dignity of virtue.		Y 134	Irene	V 34
Thy Soul by Nature great, enlarg'd by Knowledge,	. .	O 266	Irene	35
Well pleas'd to find thy Precepts not forgotten.	. .	O 267	Irene	41
Receive th' impatient Sultan to thy Arms;		O 267	Irene	10
Assembling nations croud thy port.		Y 136	Irene	V 27
What Passions reign among thy Crew, Leontius? . . .		O 270	Irene	21
I see the Gloom that low'rs upon thy Brow, ...		O 271	Irene	1
Now, Mustapha, pursue thy Tale of Horror.		O 272	Irene	1
That clouds thy Brow and labours in thy Bosom . . .		O 369	Irene	V 19
That clouds thy Brow and labours in thy Bosom		O 369	Irene	V 19
There shall he waste thy Frontiers, check thy Conquests,		O 274	Irene	56
There shall he waste thy Frontiers, check thy Conquests,		O 274	Irene	56
And though at length subdued, elude thy Vengeance. . .		O 274	Irene	57
And turn thy Thoughts henceforth to Love and Empire. . .		O 276	Irene	5
Whence then those Charms thy Tongue has deign'd to	. .	O 277	Irene	26
flatter,				
Thy Soul compleats the Triumphs of thy Face.		O 278	Irene	60
Thy Soul compleats the Triumphs of thy Face.		O 278	Irene	60
To see new Cities tow'r at thy Command, ...		O 278	Irene	71
And blasted Kingdoms flourish at thy Smile?		O 278	Irene	72
Unbounded Wealth shall flow beneath thy feet . . .		O 350	Irene	V 23
Aspasia! who can look upon thy Beauties?		O 281	Irene	42
Seize the kind Fair, and press her to thy Bosom. . . .		O 284	Irene	35
If e'er thy Youth has known the Pangs of Absence,	. .	O 285	Irene	3
I go to wait thy Call; this kind Consent		O 285	Irene	15
Disorder sits upon thy Face--retire.		O 286	Irene	17
My Zeal marks Gladness dawning on thy Cheek, . . .		O 286	Irene	2
He 's gone--Here rest, my Soul, thy fainting Wing, . .		O 287	Irene	1
Here recollect thy dissipated Pow'rs.--		O 287	Irene	2
We court thy Gentleness.	. . .	O 288	Irene	9
Swell not thy Soul beyond Advice or Friendship, . .		O 289	Irene	2
To hear the Voice of Truth; dismiss thy Train, . . .		O 289	Irene	6
While I foretell thy Fate; that Office done,--		O 289	Irene	9
But sink among thy Slaves without a Murmur. . . .		O 289	Irene	11
Thy dazzled Soul with all its boasted Greatness, . . .		O 292	Irene	99
Soon shouldst thou see, how false thy weak Reproach. . .		O 293	Irene	107

THY   (CCNTINUED)   PAGE   TITLE   LINE

   Soon wouldst thou see, how false thy weak Reproach. .   .   O 293 Irene   V 107
   Stoop from thy Flight, trace back th' entangled Thought,   O 293 Irene   127
   Whoe'er thou art, or whatsoe'er thy Message, ...   O 294 Irene   4
   Why does the Blood forsake thy lovely Cheek? .   .   .   .   O 295 Irene   5
   Why shoots this Chilness through thy shaking Nerves? .   .   O 295 Irene   6
   Why does thy Soul retire into herself? .   .   .   .   .   O 295 Irene   7
   Recline upon my Breast thy sinking Beauties. .   .   .   .   O 295 Irene   8
   Inform me rather, how thy happy Courage .   .   .   .   .   O 295 Irene   27
   Nor think thy Cause neglected while I gaze, ...   O 297 Irene   20
   Purge well thy Mind from ev'ry private Passion, .   .   .   O 298 Irene   6
   Drive Int'rest, Love, and Vengeance from thy Thoughts, .   O 298 Irene   7
   Fill all thy ardent Breast with Greece and Virtue, .   .   O 298 Irene   8
   My Soul first kindled by thy bright Example, ...   O 298 Irene   13
   Detests thy false Associates black Designs, ...   O 300 Irene   57
   Oh could thy Hand unaided free thy Country, ...   O 300 Irene   63
   Oh could thy Hand unaided free thy Country, ...   O 300 Irene   63
   Each Turkish Boscm burns for thy Destruction, ...   O 300 Irene   73
   Guide all thy Steps, calm ev'ry stormy Thought, .   .   .   O 303 Irene   21
   And still thy Bosom with the Voice of Peace. .   .   .   .   O 303 Irene   22
   Why has thy Choice then pointed out Leontius, ...   O 305 Irene   20
   Tell me the Cause, that while thy Name, Demetrius, .   .   O 305 Irene   25
   Wake from thy Dream of Pow'r to Death and Tortures, .   .   O 307 Irene   10
   And bid thy visionary Throne farewell. .   .   .   .   .   O 307 Irene   11
   Name and enjoy thy Wish-- .   .   .   .   O 307 Irene   12
   Obtain her and possess, thou know'st thy Rival. .   .   .   O 307 Irene   17
   Now joins thy People's, and thy Cali's Prayers, .   .   .   O 308 Irene   8
   Now joins thy People's, and thy Cali's Prayers, .   .   .   O 308 Irene   8
   Suspend thy Passage to the Seats of Bliss, ...   O 308 Irene   9
   Remember Mahomet, and cease thy Labour. .   .   .   .   .   O 310 Irene   3
   O grant thy sacred Influence, pow'rful Virtue! .   .   .   O 313 Irene   5
   Beyond the Mists of Care thy Pinion tow'rs. .   .   .   .   O 313 Irene   8
   Forbear thy Threats, proud Prophetess of Ill, ...   O 314 Irene   26
   Devolve, dear Maid, thy Sorrows on the Wretch, .   .   .   O 316 Irene   16
   Behold thy boasted Honours snatch'd away. .   .   .   .   O 317 Irene   43
   Thy Love, Aspasia, calls; restrain thy Sword; .   .   .   O 318 Irene   9
   Thy Love, Aspasia, calls; restrain thy Sword; .   .   .   O 318 Irene   9
   Snar'd with thy Fears, and maz'd in Stupefaction. .   .   O 318 Irene   18
   Snare'd with thy fears, and senseless of deliverance .   .   Y 196 Irene   V 18
   And drag away thy Life in Scorn and Safety, ...   O 319 Irene   26
   And test thy life in scorn and safety .   .   .   .   .   Y 197 Irene   V 26
   Thy Life, too mean a Prey to lure Abdalla. .   .   .   .   O 319 Irene   27
   Once more I dare thy Sword, behold the Prize, .   .   .   O 319 Irene   28
   Well mayst thou call thy Master to the Combat, .   .   .   O 319 Irene   30
   But soon though shalt lament thy daring folly .   .   .   Y 198 Irene   V 33
   Come haste, and live--Thy Innocence and Truth .   .   .   O 320 Irene   18
   My Soul attends thy Voice, and banish'd Virtue .   .   .   O 320 Irene   32
   Assist her Efforts with thy strong Persuasion; .   .   .   O 321 Irene   34
   Now make thy Choice, while yet the Pow'r of Choice .   .   O 321 Irene   40
   May Penitence attend thy mournful Bed, ...   O 322 Irene   61
   And wing thy latest Pray'r to pitying Heav'n. .   .   .   O 322 Irene   62
   Thy sacred Freight shall still the raging Main. .   .   .   O 322 Irene   6
   Go Happy Bark, thy sacred Freight secures thee .   .   .   O 364 Irene   V 24
   To guide thy Passage shall th' aerial Spirits .   .   .   O 322 Irene   7
   To Guide thy passage shall th' Starry Spirits .   .   .   O 364 Irene   V 26
   Persue thy course through boiling eddies, ...   Y 201 Irene   V 10A
   Thy sacred freight of innocence and truth .   .   .   .   Y 201 Irene   V 10D
   Thy Look, thy Speech, thy Action, all is Wildness-- .   .   O 323 Irene   5
   Thy Look, thy Speech, thy Action, all is Wildness-- .   .   O 323 Irene   5
   Thy Look, thy Speech, thy Action, all is Wildness-- .   .   O 323 Irene   5
   Ask of thy Heart; attend the Voice of Conscience-- .   .   O 323 Irene   7
   That fires thy Cheek, and elevates thy Mien, ...   O 323 Irene   9
   That fires thy Cheek, and elevates thy Mien, ...   O 323 Irene   9
   Whate'er thy Accusation, ...   O 323 Irene   11
       Shrinks at the hated Task, for thy Destruction; .   .   O 325 Irene   21
   Shrinks back from the hated task, for thy destruction; .   Y 204 Irene   V 21
   See the last Witness of thy Guilt and Fear .   .   .   .   O 326 Irene   2
   While unavailing Anger crouds thy Tongue .   .   .   .   .   O 327 Irene   6
   And steal thy Life away. Death's horrid Angel .   .   .   O 327 Irene   9
   Short be thy Pains. .   .   .   .   O 328 Irene   49
   Abdalla, bid thy troubled Breast be calm; .   .   .   .   O 329 Irene   2
   Does not thy Bosom, for I know thee tender, ...   O 329 Irene   5
   Hope not thy threats shall stay .   .   .   .   Y 210 Irene   V 25
   Declare thy Message, and expect thy Doom. .   .   .   .   O 331 Irene   6
   Declare thy Message, and expect thy Doom. .   .   .   .   O 331 Irene   6
   The Queen requested--Wretch, repeat thy Message; .   .   O 331 Irene   V 13
   And if one varied Accent prove thy Falshood, .   .   .   O 332 Irene   14
   Thy Life perhaps--Were but Irene spar'd, ...   O 332 Irene   33
   Great is thy Woe! but think, illustrious Sultan, .   .   O 332 Irene   37
   Rush to the War, display thy dreadful Banners, .   .   .   O 333 Irene   40
   And lead thy Troops victorious round the World. .   .   .   O 333 Irene   41
   And wish'd--Be still thy Fate to wish in vain. .   .   .   O 334 Irene   60
   Torn from the mourning Earth by thy Neglect. .   .   .   O 334 Irene   4
   May no rude blasts thy sacred bloom destroy; .   .   .   Y   3 On a Daffodill   7
   May lambent zephyrs gently wave thy head, ...   Y   3 On a Daffodill   9
   And balmy spirits thro' thy foliage play, ...   Y   3 On a Daffodill   10
   May balmy spirits thro thy foliage play, ...   Y   3 On a Daffodill   V 10
   And view thy charms with no malignant eyes: .   .   .   Y   3 On a Daffodill   14
   Touch'd with thy fate Numidia's lyons roar .   .   .   .   Y   6 Virgil Daphnis   11
   Now, at thy fall incens'd, the rural Gods .   .   .   .   Y   6 Virgil Daphnis   20
   Within the town assemble all thy powers .   .   .   .   Y 19 Tr. Iliad Bk 6   50

```
                                                        PAGE    TITLE            LINE
THYME
      While bees shall feed on thyme, and birds shall haunt the   Y   7 Virgil Daphnis      50
         grove
THYRSIS
      The balmy kiss, for which poor Thyrsis dies;   . . . .   O  84 Epi Dist Moth.     21
      Thyrsis while sings shall the gods . . . . . . . .      Y   7 Virgil Daphnis    V 49
THYSELF
      Bow down and own thyself a Slave.       . . . . . . i   O 146 Tr Boeth III.5     10
      Open to all, true only to thyself, . . . . . . . .     O 176 Tr Metastas II      6
      Now be some Moments Master of thyself,   . . . . . .   O 282 Irene              70
TI
      Tei Kallous dunamei ti telos; Zeus panta dedoken   . . .   O 103 Eis Elisses      1
TIDE   SEE TYDE
      The tide retiring, calls me from the land:   . . . . .   O  22 London           255
      Around these fatal Walls, the Tide of War   . . . . .   O 312 Irene              8
      o'er the tide--providence our guide--   . . . . . . .   Y 199 Irene             V 16A
TIES
      And Gratitude's strong Ties restrain my Tongue.   . . .   O 312 Irene             5
      What Ties to Slaves? what Gratitude to Foes?   . . . .   O 312 Irene             6
TIGERS
      By Daphnis' skill th' Armenian tigers broke   . . . . .   Y   6 Virgil Daphnis     13
TIGRIS
      Where Tigris beats his sounding shore   . . . . . . .   O  80 Feast St Simon     52
TILL
      Who sleeps on brambles till he kills his man;   . . . .   O  21 London           227
      Till conquest unresisted ceas'd to please,   . . . . .   O  34 Vanity Wishes    107
      Till captive Science yields her last retreat;   . . . .   O  37 Vanity Wishes    144
      Till fame supplies the universal charm.   . . . . . .   O  39 Vanity Wishes    184
      "Think nothing gain'd, he cries, till nought remain,   .   O  40 Vanity Wishes    202
      "On Moscow's walls till Gothic standards fly,   . . . .   O  40 Vanity Wishes    203
      Till counted myriads sooth his pride no more;   . . . .   O  42 Vanity Wishes    230
      Fresh praise is try'd till madness fires his mind,   . .   O  42 Vanity Wishes    231
      New praise is try'd till madness fires his mind,   . . .   Y 102 Vanity Wishes   V 231
      Till rude resistance lops the spreading god;   . . . .   O  42 Vanity Wishes    234
      And mould his passions till they make his will.   . . .   O  44 Vanity Wishes    282
      Unlocks his gold, and counts it till he dies.   . . . .   O  44 Vanity Wishes    290
      Till pitying Nature signs the last release,   . . . . .   O  45 Vanity Wishes    309
      Till Shame regain'd the Post that Sense betray'd,   . .   O  52 Pro Drury-Lane    27
      Till Declamation roar'd, while Passion slept.   . . . .   O  52 Pro Drury-Lane    32
      Till Declamation soar'd, whilst Passion slept.   . . . .   O  52 Pro Drury-Lane  V 32
      Till that glad night when all that hate may hiss.   . .   O  60 Pro Good Nat'd    20
      till you to happier climes remove?   . . . . . . . .   O 100 Ode Friendship   V 26
      Till angels wake thee with a note like thine.   . . . .   O 113 Epit. Phillips     6
      Till nature call'd him to the gen'ral doom,   . . . . .   O 118 Epitaph Hanmer    43
      Till at length stern Pluto cried,   . . . . . . . .    O 149 Tr Boet III.12    39
      Till the Realms of Light you gain.   . . . . . . . .   O 150 Tr Boet III.12    46
      Till want, now following fraudulent and slow,   . . . .   O 152 The Ant          15
      Till breathless Fury rested from Destruction   . . . .   O 249 Irene             5
      Live till the tott'ring Earth forsakes its   . . . . .   O 347 Irene            V 29
         Base
      Live till the Sun forgets to dart his Beams,   . . . .   O 262 Irene             3
      Still restless, till I clasp the lovely Maid,   . . . .   O 263 Irene            21
      Till every Nation reverence the Koran,   . . . . . . .   O 264 Irene            31
      Till every Nation reverence our Prophet   . . . . . .   O 354 Irene            V 17
      Till ev'ry Storm in my Domain shall roar,   . . . . .   O 354 Irene            V 25
      Till every Wave shall beat a Turkish Shore.   . . . . .   O 354 Irene            V 26
      --Till every constellation shines for me   . . . . . .   Y 132 Irene            V 45
      Till Affectation, rip'ning to Belief,   . . . . . . .   O 266 Irene            31
      Calmly he heard, till Amurath's Resumption   . . . . .   O 270 Irene            10
      That melt a Heart, impregnable till now,   . . . . . .   O 276 Irene             4
      Not till this Day thou saw'st this fatal Fair;   . . . .   O 281 Irene            54
      Till burning Death shoots through their wither'd Limbs?   .   O 282 Irene             6
      Till interposing Death destroys the Prospect!   . . . .   O 283 Irene            25
      Till interposing Death denys the prospect.   . . . . .   O 374 Irene            V 26
      Till interposing darkness bars the prospect.   . . . .   Y 155 Irene            V 25
      May spare the fatal Bow-string till To-morrow?   . . . .   O 284 Irene            39
      Till in the midst of Arrogance and Fondness,   . . . .   O 299 Irene            46
      Till angry Heav'n shall mark them out for Ruin,   . . .   O 309 Irene            36
      Till conscious of th' incircling Deity,   . . . . . .   O 313 Irene             7
      Till soft Fatigue invite us to repose.   . . . . . . .   O 323 Irene            18
      The raging Sultan burns till our Return,   . . . . . .   O 327 Irene            11
      I heard, and soften'd, till Abdalla brought   . . . . .   O 334 Irene            61
      Detain'd me till Demetrius set me free.   . . . . . .   O 335 Irene             9
      Till thither an huge bird the tumult drew   . . . . . .   Y  25 Tr Add. Battle  124
      Till she made the neighbours stare.   . . . . . . . .   Y 300 Extemp. Elegy     8
      Till purse and carcase both were low.   . . . . . . .   Y 300 Extemp. Elegy    12
TILL'D
      The fruitfull fields th' industrious people till'd,   . .   Y  23 Tr Add. Battle   28
TIM'D  SEE ILL-TIM'D
TIM'ROUS
      Reason! the tim'rous Pilot, that to shun   . . . . . .   O 281 Irene            46
      We ask'd, with tim'rous Tongue, th' Offender's Name,   . .   O 325 Irene            23
TIME
      Time hovers o'er, impatient to destroy,   . . . . . .   O  43 Vanity Wishes    259
      And panting Time toil'd after him in vain:   . . . . .   O  51 Pro Drury-Lane     6
      Time his Hours should never drive   . . . . . . . .    O 178 Thrale 35 Year     7
      Phrase that Time has flung away,   . . . . . . . .    O 179 Ridicul Warton     5
      Adorn'd in Roman time the brightest days,   . . . . .   O 189 Seeing Montagu     2
      Perhaps the flood of time now rolls towards us   . . . .   Y 117 Irene            V 108
      And time hangs his flagging wings   . . . . . . . .    Y 128 Irene            V  4
      O may her Beauties last unchang'd by Time,   . . . . .   O 262 Irene            11
```

TIME (CONTINUED)   PAGE   TITLE   LINE

	PAGE	TITLE	LINE
Is this a Time for Softness or for Sorrow?	O 280	Irene	11
Count not these Hours as Parts of vulgar Time,	O 302	Irene	5
Dispatch, and learn a fitter Time for Pity.	O 328	Irene	44

TIMELY

	PAGE	TITLE	LINE
Yet timely provident, she hastes away	O 151	The Ant	5
And snatch'd her timely from her Country's Fate.	O 252	Irene	9,8

TIMES

	PAGE	TITLE	LINE
In angry numbers warn'st succeeding times;	O 23	London	259
In useful satire warn succeeding times;	Y 61	London	V 259
All times their scenes of pompous woes afford,	O 41	Vanity Wishes	223
Perhaps if Skill could distant Times explore,	O 53	Pro Drury-Lane	41
Shames the mean Pensions of Augustan Times;	O 57	Prologue Comus	4
Wisdom at proper times is well forgot.	O 134	Tr. Rambler 89	1
Times gloomy backward with judicious eyes;	O 192	Tr. Medea II	2

TIMIDITY

	PAGE	TITLE	LINE
So shall Timidity assist thy Reason,	O 266	Irene	21

TIMOTHEUS

	PAGE	TITLE	LINE
When old Timotheus struck the vocal String,	O 97	Hickman Spinet	9

TINSEL

	PAGE	TITLE	LINE
The tinsel glitter, and the specious mein,	O 139	Tr Rambler 168	1

TIR'D

	PAGE	TITLE	LINE
And tir'd like me with follies and with crimes,	O 23	London	258
Tir'd with contempt, she quits the slipp'ry reign,	O 46	Vanity Wishes	335
Tir'd with vain joys, and false alarms,	O 124	Winter's Walk	17
He, tir'd of Slav'ry, tho' the highest Slave,	O 253	Irene	113

TIRE

	PAGE	TITLE	LINE
No dangers fright him, and no labours tire;	O 40	Vanity Wishes	194
"And when feast and frolic tire,	O 186	Anacreon Ode 9	39
To tire the burthen'd rack and gorge destruction	Y 196	Irene	V 18C

TIRES

	PAGE	TITLE	LINE
He tires his Fav'rites with Irene's Praise,	O 261	Irene	3

TIRING

	PAGE	TITLE	LINE
Pope's hallow'd glades, and never tiring views,	O 106	Eliza plucking	3

TIS   SEE 'TIS, IT

	PAGE	TITLE	LINE
Tis cowardise to fear the boasts of folly	Y 197	Irene	V 22

TITLE

	PAGE	TITLE	LINE
And dubious title shakes the madded land,	O 31	Vanity Wishes	30
"For wealth or title, perishable prize;	O 82	Young Author	16
And boast no title but Aspasia's friend	Y 161	Irene	V 14
And fix the fierce Usurper's bloody Title.	O 291	Irene	62
Demetrius justly pleads a double Title,	O 305	Irene	45

TITLED

	PAGE	TITLE	LINE
To pluck a titled Poet's borrow'd wing;	O 13	London	70

TITLES

	PAGE	TITLE	LINE
From dubious titles shakes the madded land,	Y 93	Vanity Wishes	V 30
For what are pompous Titles, proud Alliance,	O 267	Irene	8
Nor Wealth, nor Titles, make Aspasia's Bliss.	O 302	Irene	106

TITYRUS

	PAGE	TITLE	LINE
Now, Tityrus, you, supine and careless laid,	O 64	Virgil Past.I	1

T'

	PAGE	TITLE	LINE
While t' asswage the Pangs of Love	O 149	Tr Boet III.12	15
Thus I t' effect this mighty change design'd	Y 11	Tr Hor Epode 9	29

TO   838   OMITTED WORD

TO-MORROW

	PAGE	TITLE	LINE
Born down with Years, still doat upon To-morrow?	O 283	Irene	20
An useless Life in waiting for To-morrow,	O 283	Irene	23
To gaze with longing Eyes upon To-morrow,	O 283	Irene	24
Still sees To-morrow drest in Robes of Triumph;	O 283	Irene	29
To-morrow brings the visionary Bride.	O 283	Irene	31
May spare the fatal Bow-string till To-morrow?	O 284	Irene	39
I w<ould> have every smile g<enu>ine to<morrow no>	Y 185	Irene	V 3
Still Cali lives, and must he live To-morrow?	O 310	Irene	1
And he'll be hang'd to-morrow.	Y 300	Fanny Burney	5

TO-MORROW'S

	PAGE	TITLE	LINE
And of To-morrow's Action fix the Scene.	O 283	Irene	18
To-morrow's Action? Can that hoary Wisdom	O 283	Irene	19
To-morrow's Dawn shall see the Turkish King	O 303	Irene	9
To-morrow's Dawn shall see the mighty Cali	O 303	Irene	11

TOD

	PAGE	TITLE	LINE
Alla tod eis Thnetous Kupris epempseu onar	O 103	Eis Elisses	4

TOGETHER

	PAGE	TITLE	LINE
You'll leave together with your life,	O 69	Hor.II Ode 14	23
And sister souls together join,	O 100	Ode Friendship	22
And sister minds together join,	Y 71	Ode Friendship	V 22
The mazy dance together trace.	O 231	Tr Horace IV.7	6
No! let us die together.	O 297	Irene	11
Together rise and shoot upon the wing.	Y 24	Tr Add. Battle	73

TOIL

	PAGE	TITLE	LINE
And bless thine evening walk and morning toil.	O 20	London	223
And bless the evening walk and morning toil.	O 20	London	V 223
And bless thy evening walk and morning toil.	O 20	London	V 223
Remark each anxious toil, each eager strife,	O 30	Vanity Wishes	3
Explore each restless toil, each anxious strife,	Y 92	Vanity Wishes	V 3
Walks the wild heath, and sings his toil away.	O 32	Vanity Wishes	38
Toil crush'd conceit, and man was of a piece;	O 32	Vanity Wishes	54
Toil, envy, want, the patron, and the jail.	O 38	Vanity Wishes	160
Toil, envy, want, the Garret, and the jail.	O 38	Vanity Wishes	V 160
Surveys the general toil of human kind;	O 59	Pro Good Nat'd	2
"Toil on, dull croud, in extacy, he cries,	O 82	Young Author	15

TOIL	(CONTINUED)	PAGE	TITLE	LINE

TOIL   (CONTINUED)   PAGE   TITLE   LINE
    Rob without Fear, and fatten without Toil. . . . . .   O 110 To Posterity   14
    What toil in slender things! . . . .   O 134 Tr. Rambler 90   1
    Polish'd with endless toil, my lays . . . . . .   O 139 Tr Rambler 169   1
    As on we toil from day to day, ...   O 200 Death Dr Levet   2
    The toil of ev'ry day supplied. . . . .   O 201 Death Dr Levet   24
    Reward his toils, and he shall toil for you . . . .   Y 146 Irene   V 23A
    Unfit for Toil, and polish'd into Weakness,   O 290 Irene   43
    Rolls with eternal Toil the pond'rous Orbs;   O 293 Irene   120
    Of Happiness, lures on from Toil to Toil, . .   O 310 Irene   2
    Of Happiness, lures on from Toil to Toil, ...   O 310 Irene   2
TOIL'D
    And panting Time toil'd after him in vain: . . . . . O 51 Pro Drury-Lane   6
TOILING
    Few know the toiling statesman's fear or care,   O 32 Vanity Wishes   47
    Th' accumulated Wealth of toiling Ages. . . . . .   O 249 Irene   19
TOILS
    Since unrewarded science toils in vain; . . . . .   O 10 London   38
    Amidst the toils of this returning year, ...   O 59 Pro Good Nat'd   V 4A
    With twisted toils, and op'ning hounds; . . . . .   O 72 Hor. Epode II   40
    And twisted toils, surrounds . . . .   O 72 Hor. Epode II   V 40
    In life's first bloom his publick toils began,   O 117 Epitaph Hanmer   11
    And recollected toils endear'd the shade;.   O 118 Epitaph Hanmer   42
    Then, Cali, shall the Toils of Battle cease,   O 265 Irene   44
    Toils all its languages to flatter me. . . . . .   Y 136 Irene   V 29
    And every language toils to flatter me. . . . . .   Y 136 Irene   V 32B
    Wilt thou dismiss the Savage from the Toils . . .   O 275 Irene   66
    Reward his toils, and he shall toil for you . . . .   Y 146 Irene   V 23A
    And envy the slave that toils whose labour procures her . Y 165 Irene   V 81
        sleep
    Unfit to share this Night's illustrious Toils? . . . O 305 Irene   21
    Resolve to share our Dangers and our Toils, ...   O 320 Irene   29
    No toils shall intercept the nimble deer. . . . . .   Y   7 Virgil Daphnis   39
TOILSOME
    Who lives from toilsome bus'ness free, ...   O 71 Hor. Epode II   2
    Bears toilsome Days, and wakes long tedious Nights: O 247 Irene Epilogue   22
TOIOS
    Toios Ares Brotoloigos eni ptclemoisi memene, . . .   O 172 On Marlborough   1
    Kai toios Paphien plexen eroti Thean. . . . . . .   O 172 On Marlborough   2
TOLD
    To you the Tale is told; . . . .   O 150 Tr Boet III.12   55
    To thee I told the causes of my smart, ...   Y 11 Tr Hor Epode 9   18
TOMB
    Around his tomb let Art and Genius weep, ...   O 39 Vanity Wishes   173
    But left, like Egypt's Kings, a lasting Tomb. . . .   O 51 Pro Drury-Lane   16
    Adorn Philander's head, or grace his tomb.   O 95 Sprig of Myrtl   14
    Pause at this tomb where Hanmer's ashes lie;   O 117 Epitaph Hanmer   2
    Pause on this tomb where Hanmer's ashes lie; . .   O 117 Epitaph Hanmer   V 2
    And virtue's sorrow dignify'd his tomb. . . . . .   O 118 Epitaph Hanmer   44
    Long have I wish'd, before our Prophet's Tomb, . .   O 263 Irene   9
    On his dead body let a tomb be plac'd . . . . .   Y   7 Virgil Daphnis   28
TOMBS
    On names now found alone on books and tombs. . . . . O 134 Tr. Rambler 93   2
TON
    Eis to tes Elisses peri ton Oneiron Ainigma . . .   O 103 Eis Elisses   T
    Ton taphon eisoraas ton Olibarioio, Konien . . . .   O 171 Epi. Goldsmith   1
    Ton taphon eisoraas ton Olibarioio, Konien . . .   O 171 Epi. Goldsmith   1
    Ton taphon eisoraas ton Oleiberioio, konien . . .   O 171 Epi. Goldsmith   V 1
    Ton taphon eisoraas ton Oleiberioio, konien . . .   O 171 Epi. Goldsmith   V 1
    Ton taphon eisoraas ton Oleiberioio, konien . . .   O 171 Epi. Goldsmith   V 1
    Ton taphon eisoraas ton Olibaroio, konien . . . .   O 171 Epi. Goldsmith   V 1
TONGUE
    Well may they rise, while I, whose rustick tongue .   O 14 London   79
    Wit, brav'ry, worth, his lavish tongue bestows;   O 16 London   126
    From ev'ry tongue flows harmony divine.   O 16 London   128
    But everlasting dictates croud his tongue, . . .   O 43 Vanity Wishes   273
    Her tongue like nimble lightning plies, ...   O 127 To Lyce, Lady   15
    Fear in her Eye, Submission on her Tongue, ...   O 259 Irene   120
    Irene steals unheeded from his Tongue, ...   O 261 Irene   5
    His bland Address, and Sorcery of Tongue; . . . .   O 273 Irene   40
    Whence then those Charms thy Tongue has deign'd to .   O 277 Irene   26
        flatter,
    Why then Those charms your tongue has deign'd to . . O 355 Irene   V 15
        flatter
    To tune the Tongue, to teach the Eyes to roll, . .   O 278 Irene   64
    And draw new Virtue from her heav'nly Tongue. . .   O 285 Irene   7
    My tongue with am'rous eloquence displaid . . . .   Y 158 Irene   V 7
    The Dread of instant Death restrains my Tongue?   O 289 Irene   25
    Not idly flutters on a boastful Tongue, ...   O 290 Irene   37
    A thousand Questions press upon my Tongue, ...   O 295 Irene   19
    His Pride and Love by Turns inspir'd his Tongue,   O 299 Irene   43
    Suspected still?--What Villain's pois'nous Tongue .   O 304 Irene   12
    Let every Tongue resound Irene's Praise, ...   O 308 Irene   4
    And Gratitude's strong Ties restrain my Tongue.   O 312 Irene   5
    And Songs of Pleasure warble from the Tongue, . .   O 315 Irene   30
    Forgive, fair Excellence, th' unwilling Tongue, . .   O 324 Irene   1
    The Tongue, that, forc'd by strong Necessity, . . .   O 324 Irene   2
    We ask'd, with tim'rous Tongue, th' Offender's Name, . O 325 Irene   23
    Whence is this Rage? what barb'rous Tongue has wrong'd . O 325 Irene   27
        me?
    While unavailing Anger crouds thy Tongue . . . . . .   O 327 Irene   6

357

```
TONGUE        (CONTINUED)                                    PAGE    TITLE          LINE
     While unavailing passion crouds your tongue  . . . . .  O 368  Irene          V 14
     Perhaps her pois'nous Tongue might blast Abdalla. . . . O 327  Irene            19
     The tongue that forges mandates for destruction  . .    Y 210  Irene          V 25A
TOO
     And pow'r too great to keep, or to resign?  . . . . .   O  36  Vanity Wishes   134
     Whom Pleasure keeps too busy to be wise, . . . . . .    O  46  Vanity Wishes   324
     Approve it only--'tis too late to praise.  . . . . .    O  62  Pro Word Wise    16
     Too far in Sabine woods I stray'd;  . . . . . . . .     O  65  Hor I Ode xxii   10
     By Lalage, too far I stray'd,  . . . . . . . . .        O  66  To A. Fuscus     10
     This thought once form'd, all counsel comes too late,   O  82  Young Author     19
     Too well You know to keep the Slaves You gain. . . . .  O  96  Hickman Spinet    2
     Art thou too fall'n? ere anger could subide . . . .     O 132  Tr. Rambler 54    1
     I too can feel the rapture, fierce and strong; . . . .  O 142  In Baretti Bk.    3
     I too can pour the extemporary song: . . . . . . .      O 142  In Baretti Bk.    4
     That Wealth, too sacred for their Country's Use! . . .  O 250  Irene            20
     That Wealth, too pleasing to be lost for Freedom! . . . O 250  Irene            21
     Lamenting Av'rice now too late discovers . . . . . .    O 250  Irene            26
     When publick Villainy, too strong for Justice, . . . .  O 250  Irene            40
     but if your influence be too wide--your dissipated rays  Y 132  Irene          V 41
     When a river is drain'd by too many channels the stream is  Y 132  Irene       V 41B
         dry.
     Half were too much had Mahomet been Cali. . . . . . .   Y 132  Irene          V 41E
     Too well I know him, his immod'rate Courage, . . . .    O 267  Irene            46
     Too strong for Love, have hurried him on Death. . . .   O 267  Irene            48
     Too slow these gentle Constellations roll, . . . . .    O 271  Irene             3
     Detested Cali too, with artful Wonder, . . . . . . .    O 273  Irene            27
     Too high, bright Maid, thou rat'st exterior Grace; . .  O 277  Irene            30
     Too calm I listen to the flatt'ring Sounds. . . . . .   O 278  Irene            74
     But thou, too old to bear another Cheat, . . . . . .    O 283  Irene            32
     Too fierce, too faithless for Neglect or Trust. . . .   O 288  Irene            14
     Too fierce, too faithless for Neglect or Trust. . . .   O 288  Irene            14
     To rough--Too false too fierce to trust or to neglect   O 374  Irene          V  1
     To rough--Too false too fierce to trust or to neglect   O 374  Irene          V  1
     And wish too late for Innocence and Peace? . . . . .    O 294  Irene           133
     Too much to fear or trust, is equal Weakness. . . . .   O 300  Irene            77
     Too well I know him, since on Thracia's Plains . . . .  O 307  Irene            18
     Nor press too much upon a Lover's Patience. . . . .     O 310  Irene             9
     Thy Life, too mean a Prey to lure Abdalla. . . . . .    O 319  Irene            27
     Perfidious!--yes--too well thou know'st them Traytors.  O 324  Irene            17
     To Blood, too mean to stain a Soldier's Sabre. . . .    O 324  Irene            24
     Perhaps my Zeal too fierce betray'd my Prudence; . . .  O 330  Irene            20
     Nor with too powerfull rivals strive . . . . . . .      Y  11  Tr Hor Epode 9   27
TOOK
     The nurse took up the squealing child, . . . . . .      O 157  Par. Hermit I     3
     Took her from her friends and sire, . . . . . . . .     Y 301  Extemp. Elegy    15
TOOLS
     As Tyrants doom their Tools of Guilt to die; . . . .    O  53  Pro Drury-Lane   56
     Ye Slaves of Cruelty, ye Tools of Rage, . . . . . .     O 332  Irene            22
TORCH
     When pleasure fired her torch at Virtue's flame, . . .  O  62  Pro Word Wise    23
TORCHES
     Dim, scorn'd and impotent, his torches lie. . . . . .   O 133  Tr. Rambler 85    2
TORE
     Tore unresisted from the Giant Hand . . . . . . .       O 312  Irene            10
     Tore, unresisted, from the mighty hand . . . . . .      Y 188  Irene          V 10
     He tore them down and trampled them to death. . . . .   Y  24  Tr Add. Battle   87
TORMENTED
     And thus the Mind tormented long  . . . . . . .         O 145  Tr Boeth III.1    9
TORMENTS
     Torments alike with equal Fire. . . . .                 O  99  Ode Friendship  V  8
     And burning daemons tremble at her torments . . . . .   Y 168  Irene          V135D
     Then would I free from torments live . . . . . .        Y  11  Tr Hor Epode 9   25
TORN
     Torn from the mourning Earth by thy Neglect. . . . .    O 334  Irene             4
TORPID
     Should no Disease thy torpid veins invade, . . . . .    O  37  Vanity Wishes   153
     Nor should disease thy torpid veins invade, . . . .     Y  99  Vanity Wishes  V 153
     The Hand of Art here torpid lies  . . . . . . .         O 154  Epita. Hogarth    1
     The hand of him here torpid lies  . . . . . . .         O 155  Epita. Hogarth V  1
     Stood torpid in Suspence; but soon Abdalla . . . . .    O 317  Irene            37
TORQUATUS
     Not you, Torquatus, boast of Rome, . . . . . . .        O 232  Tr Horace IV.7   21
TORRENT
     Roll darkling down the torrent of his fate? . . . .     O  47  Vanity Wishes   346
     Down cliffs the roaring Torrent pours . . . . . .       O  72  Hor. Epode II    38
     Down the steep hill the roaring torrent pours; . . . .  O 132  Tr. Rambler 65    2
     <t>o stop this raging torrent of destruction . . . .    Y 117  Irene          V109C
     To check this Torrent of imperious Rage, . . . . .      O 327  Irene             5
TORRID
     Or torrid Africk's faithless sands; . . . . . . .       O  65  Hor I Ode xxii  V  6
     Or torrid Afric's faithless Sands, . . . . . . .        O  66  To A. Fuscus      6
     And Afric's torrid Sands in search of Cali. . . . .     O 274  Irene            60
     And Africs torrid shores in search of Cali . . . . .    Y 143  Irene          V 60
TORTUR'D
     His tortur'd Sons shall die before his Face, . . . .    O 111  To Posterity     23
     He struck his tortur'd Breast, and roar'd, Irene: . .   O 325  Irene            24
     The Wretch, whose Guilt declar'd by tortur'd Cali, . .  O 334  Irene            64
     The wretch whose crimes declar'd by tortur'd Cali . .   Y 215  Irene          V 69A
TORTURE
     To Threats of Torture, Death and Violation. . . . . .   O 259  Irene           112
```

```
                                                        PAGE    TITLE           LINE
TORTURE          (CONTINUED)
     Stern Torture shakes his bloody Scourge before me,    .   .   O 266 Irene            15
     Each piercing Torture, every Change of Pain,     .   .   .   .   O 326 Irene            44
TORTURES
     And let the tortures of mistrust     .   .   .   .   .   .   O 100 Ode Friendship      15
     New Tortures for the captive heart.   .   .   .   .   .   O 121 To Miss Playin   V  18
     And weary Cruelty remits her Tortures.   .   .   .   .   .   O 249 Irene            10
     Amidst the Tortures of the burning Steel,   .   .   .   .   O 272 Irene            15
     Thence should my Fury drag him down to Tortures;    .   .   .   O 274 Irene            64
     And give the Tortures of Suspence a Period?   .   .   .   .   O 282 Irene             2
     Wake from thy Dream of Pow'r to Death and Tortures,    .   .   O 307 Irene            10
     I came to heighten Tortures by Reproach,   .   .   .   .   .   O 330 Irene             7
     What Plagues, what Tortures, are in Store for thee,    .   .   O 334 Irene             1
TORTURING
     Nor torturing whalebones pinch them into charms;    .   .   .   O  84 Epi Dist Moth.     23
TOSS
     Will toss us in a morning more?    .   .   .   .   .   .   .   O 232 Tr Horace IV.7      18
TOSS'D
     Toss'd her nose, and shook her rump,    .   .   .   .   .   .   Y 300 Extemp. Elegy       7
TOSSING
     Tossing rave but rave in vain?    .   .   .   .   .   .   .   O 144 Tr Boeth. II.4       6
TOST
     Tost in one common storm with all the great;    .   .   .   O  59 Pro Good Nat'd      8
     By Eastern Tempests hither tost,    .   .   .   .   .   .   .   O  73 Hor. Epode II      58
TOTAL
     Of total Death and careless of Hereafter;   .   .   .   .   O 276 Irene            19
     Secure of total death, and careless of hereafter or gay   .   Y 146 Irene         V  20
TOTT'RING
     The Cloister's Ease, resum'd the tott'ring Throne,    .   .   O 256 Irene            44
     Live till the tott'ring Earth forsakes its   .   .   .   .   O 347 Irene         V  29
          Base
TOTTERS
     The Weight of Years, and totters to the Tempest,    .   .   .   O 250 Irene            45
TOUCH
     No sounds alas would touch th' impervious ear,   .   .   .   O  43 Vanity Wishes     269
     Phillips! whose touch harmonious could remove   .   .   .   O 113 Epit. Phillips      1
     If Merit touch thee, shed a tear,    .   .   .   .   .   .   O 154 Epita. Hogarth      6
     Thus lightly touch and quickly go.   .   .   .   .   .   .   O 203 Tr. on Skating      4
     Force her! profane her with a Touch, and die.    .   .   .   O 296 Irene             8
TOUCH'D
     Touch'd with thy fate Numidia's lyons roar   .   .   .   .   Y   6 Virgil Daphnis     11
     This Hector saw; his soul was touch'd with grief.   .   .   .   Y  21 Tr. Iliad Bk 6    111
TOUCHES
     Had Stella's gentle touches mov'd the Lyre,   .   .   .   .   O  97 Hickman Spinet     15
TOUT
     Tout est cher.     .   .   .   .   .   .   .   .   .   .   O 172 French Distich      4
TOW'R
     And leaves the wealthy traytor in the Tow'r,    .   .   .   O  32 Vanity Wishes      34
     And leaves the bonny Traytor in the Tow'r,   .   .   .   .   O  32 Vanity Wishes   V  34
     Still to new heights his restless wishes tow'r,    .   .   .   O  34 Vanity Wishes     105
     To see new Cities tow'r at thy Command,    .   .   .   .   O 278 Irene            71
     Grasp at Command, and tow'r in quest of Empire;    .   .   .   O 293 Irene           114
TOW'RING
     Ambitious catches at his tow'ring Name:   .   .   .   .   .   O  57 Prologue Comus     20
     With silent Pangs I view the tow'ring Domes,    .   .   .   O 251 Irene            62
     And lay the tow'ring Sultaness aside;   .   .   .   .   .   O 289 Irene             8
     The pompous theatre the tow'ring arch   .   .   .   .   .   Y 177 Irene         V 109
     Stretch'd in the Dust, or tow'ring on his Throne;    .   .   O 303 Irene            10
TOW'RINGS
     To cross the Tow'rings of an equal Soul,   .   .   .   .   .   O 309 Irene            41
TOW'RS
     And tow'rs and triumphs in ideal Greatness;   .   .   .   O 269 Irene             5
     Then shall the Rhodian mourn his sinking Tow'rs,    .   .   .   O 309 Irene            26
     Beyond the Mists of Care thy Pinion tow'rs.    .   .   .   O 313 Irene             8
     And man the walls and fortifie the tow'rs.   .   .   .   .   Y  19 Tr. Iliad Bk 6     51
TOWARDS
     Perhaps the flood of time now rolls towards us   .   .   .   Y 117 Irene         V 108
     And turn'd their hasty Steps towards the Garden.    .   .   .   O 269 Irene            39
TOWN
     When injur'd Thales bids the town farewell,   .   .   .   .   O   8 London             2
     Indignant Thales eyes the neighb'ring town.   .   .   .   .   O  10 London            34
     The sport of boys, and scandall of the town.    .   .   .   Y  11 Tr Hor Epode 9     12
     Alone preserv'd the town from Grecian fire.   .   .   .   .   Y  18 Tr. Iliad Bk 6     14
     Within the town assemble all thy powers   .   .   .   .   .   Y  19 Tr. Iliad Bk 6     50
     Here's a woman of the town,    .   .   .   .   .   .   .   .   Y 300 Extemp. Elegy       1
TOWNS
     Evn low built towns they Britain's modish tribe   .   .   .   Y  94 Vanity Wishes   V  61
TOWRD
     Demetrius towrd--Above the Female pleasures    .   .   .   .   O 371 Irene         V   2
TOYS
     To thee were solemn toys or empty shew,   .   .   .   .   .   O  33 Vanity Wishes      65
     Contemns at length the treachrous toys,   .   .   .   .   .   O 145 Tr Boeth III.1     11
     Far from his Troops, he toys his Hours away.    .   .   .   O 258 Irene            93
     All fading toys, and transitory glories    .   .   .   .   Y 177 Irene         V 110
TRAC'D
     I mark'd them well, and trac'd in either Face   .   .   .   O 275 Irene            81
     Nor crop'd the tastfull herb, nor trac'd the verdant meads   Y   6 Virgil Daphnis     10
TRACE
     Nor hope the British lineaments to trace,   .   .   .   .   O  15 London           101
     For now no more we trace in ev'ry line   .   .   .   .   .   O  34 Vanity Wishes      87
     Or trace his Form on circulating Gold,   .   .   .   .   .   O  58 Prologue Comus     24
```

```
TRACE              (CONTINUED)                                    PAGE    TITLE            LINE
        Mix'd with old Heroes trace the flow'ry meads, . . . .   O  76 Tr Add. Battle       42
        I trace the planets and survey the skies. . . . . .      O 130 Tr. Rambler 8         2
        The mazy dance together trace. . . . . . . . .           O 231 Tr Horace IV.7        6
        Stoop from thy Flight, trace back th' entangled Thought, O 293 Irene               127
        And mortals trace th' Almighty's path in v<ain> . . .    Y 217 Irene           V   14
        And trace the paths of providence in vain. . . . . .     Y 217 Irene           V   15
TRACED
        That traced th' essential form of Grace, . . . . . .     O 154 Epita. Hogarth       2
TRADE
        No gainful trade their industry can 'scape, . . . . .    O  15 London             113
TRADER
        The sober trader at a tatter'd cloak, . . . . . .        O  17 London             162
TRAGEDY
        For Years the Pow'r of Tragedy declin'd; . . . . . .     O  52 Pro Drury-Lane       30
        Irene: A Tragedy. ... . . . . . . . . . . .              O 245 Irene                 T
TRAGIC
        Beheld the tragic heroes taught to fear. . . . . . .     Y  67 Prologue Lethe        8
TRAIN
        And shun the shining train, and golden coach. . . . .    O  21 London             235
        At length his sov'reign frowns--the train of state  . . O  34 Vanity Wishes      109
        With cool submission joins the labouring train, . . .    O  59 Pro Good Nat'd        3
        Ye blooming train, who give despair or joy, . . . . .    O  83 Epi Dist Moth.        1
        Soft Pleasure with her laughing train, . . . . .         O 125 An Ode                6
        Ye glitt'ring Train! whom Lace and Velvet bless, . . .   O 246 Irene Prologue        1
        If Dismiss this glittring train these sudden   . . . .   O 366 Irene           V   17
          Splendors
        To hear the Voice of Truth; dismiss thy Train, . . . .   O 289 Irene                 6
        To hear the voice of truth, dismiss your train . . . .   O 366 Irene           V   22
        Then sought the palace where the menial train . . . .    Y  21 Tr. Iliad Bk 6      128
TRAIT'RESS
        Where 's this fair Trait'ress? Where 's this smiling . . O 330 Irene                 1
          Mischief?
TRAITOR    SEE TRAYTOR
        Each rebel Wish, each traitor Inclination . . . . .      O 287 Irene                11
        Might intercept the Traitor Greek, Demetrius, . . . .    O 331 Irene                 8
        Those trembling Limbs--Speak out, thou shiv'ring . . .   O 332 Irene                16
          Traitor.
TRAITORS
        And bade his new Confederates seize the Traitors. . . .  O 317 Irene                39
TRAMPLE
        The Horse shall trample, or the Plough shall break, . .  O 110 To Posterity          2
TRAMPLED
        Scorn'd by his Subjects, trampled by his Foes; . . . .   O 268 Irene                20
        He tore them down and trampled them to death. . . . .    Y  24 Tr Add. Battle       87
TRAMPLES
        Secure he tramples my declining Fame, . . . . . .        O 257 Irene                71
        Secure he tramples my declining Frame, . . . . . .       O 257 Irene           V   71
TRANCE
        Absorb'd in Thought; then starting from his Trance, . .  O 311 Irene                 6
TRANQUILLITY
        Of Grandeur and Tranquillity combin'd. . . . . . .       O 292 Irene                89
        Tranquillity and Guilt, disjoin'd by Heav'n, . . . .     O 292 Irene                90
TRANSFER
        Perhaps her Malice might transfer the Charge, . . . .    O 327 Irene                18
TRANSFERR'D
        To her transferr'd the Offer of a Crown. . . . . . .     O 259 Irene               124
TRANSFIX'D
        Here lies a fowl transfix'd with many a wound . . . .    O  76 Tr Add. Battle       14
TRANSGRESSION
        Here will I fix the limits of transgression . . . . .    Y 168 Irene           V  133
TRANSIENT
        A transient calm the happy scenes bestow, . . . . .      O  10 London              31
        Yet Greece enjoys no Gleam of transient Hope, . . . .    O 249 Irene                11
        Indulgent nature gives some transient pleasures  . . .   Y 148 Irene           V  43C
TRANSITORY
        "While I these transitory blessings scorn, . . . . .     O  82 Young Author         17
        "While I those transitory blessings scorn, . . . . .     O  82 Young Author    V   17
        All fading toys, and transitory glories . . . . . .      Y 177 Irene           V  110
TRANSLATION
        Translation of Horace. Book I. Ode xxii. . . . . . .     O  65 Hor I Ode xxii        T
        Translation of part of the Dialogue between . . . . .    O  74 Tr. Iliad Bk 6       T
        A Translation Of The Latin Epitaph On Sir Thomas . . .   O 117 Epitaph Hanmer        T
          Hanmer
TRANSMUTED
        For patience sov'reign o'er transmuted ill; . . . . .    O  48 Vanity Wishes      362
TRANSPARENT
        The transparent Fount of Good; . . . . . . . . .         O 147 Tr Boet III.12        2
TRANSPORT
        My fainting Soul with Violence of transport. . . . .     O 371 Irene           V   15
        And spread the general Transport through Mankind. . . .  O 308 Irene                 5
        Supicion checks the rising transport . . . . . . .       Y 186 Irene           V    2
TRANSPORTING
        Are all transporting, all divine. . . . . . . . .        O 100 Ode Friendship       24
TRANSPORTS
        Forgive my transports on a theme like this, . . . . .    O  15 London              97
        With transports kindled, rural ease, . . . . . .         O  73 Hor. Epode II        74
        In Sighs and Tears, in Transports and Embraces, . . .    O 269 Irene                15
        In sighs and tears, and transports and embraces, . . .   O 367 Irene           V   27
TRAPPINGS
        See motley life in modern trappings dress'd, . . . .     O  32 Vanity Wishes       51
```

		PAGE	TITLE		LINE
TRAVELLER					
The needy traveller, serene and gay,	. . . . . .	O 32	Vanity Wishes		37
The needy traveller, secure and gay,	. . . . . .	Y 93	Vanity Wishes	V	37
With bright effulgence The travell\<er\> afar	. . . .	Y 131	Irene	V	36
The traveller persues the flatt'ring wandring splendor	. . . .	Y 155	Irene	V	34
Now, wand'ring o'er the cliffs the traveller	. . . .	Y 23	Tr Add. Battle		30
TRAYTOR					
And leaves the wealthy traytor in the Tow'r,	. . . .	O 32	Vanity Wishes		34
And leaves the bonny Traytor in the Tow'r,	. . . .	O 32	Vanity Wishes	V	34
Betray'd some Traytor lurking near my Bosom.	. . . .	O 273	Irene		23
Disclos'd some Traytor lurking near our Bosoms	. . . .	O 368	Irene	V	3
every traytor inclination each traytor passion	. . . .	Y 158	Irene	V	11
every traytor inclination each traytor passion	. . . .	Y 158	Irene	V	11
Now, Traytor, feel the Fear that chills my Hand.	. . . .	O 318	Irene		20
TRAYTOR'S					
Will not the Patriot share the Traytor's Danger?	. . .	O 300	Irene		62
TRAYTORS					
Dispatch his Guards to stop the flying Traytors,	. . .	O 319	Irene		3
Bold Slave, I know them both--I know them Traytors.	. .	O 324	Irene		16
Perfidious!--yes--too well thou know'st them Traytors.	.	O 324	Irene		17
TRAYTRESS					
And in the traytress bad th' apostate bleed	. . . . .	Y 217	Irene	V	12
TREACH'RCUS					
As treach'rous phantoms in the mist delude,	. . . . .	O 31	Vanity Wishes		9
Improve his heady rage with treach'rous skill,	. . . .	O 44	Vanity Wishes		281
Can then th' Assassin lift his treach'rous Hand	. .	O 286	Irene		11
To find a meaner Fate from treach'rous Friendship--	. .	O 299	Irene		33
And melt her treach'rous Beauties into Ruin.	. . . .	O 315	Irene		37
And melt the treach'rous Beauties into Ruin.	. . . .	O 315	Irene	V	37
TREACHEROUS					
O'er treacherous pleasure's flow'ry ground	. . . . .	O 203	Tr. on Skating	V	3
Beset the treacherous Way with fatal Ambush;	. . . .	O 300	Irene		72
The treacherous moments ply their silent wings	. . . .	Y 206	Irene	V	8
TREACHERY					
Whose Fear, or Rage, or Treachery betray'd us.	. . . .	O 316	Irene		17
TREACHROUS					
The treachrous guests still hint the last offence,	. .	Y 104	Vanity Wishes	V	279
Soon the treachrous Sands retreat,	. . . .	O 145	Tr Boeth. II.4		11
Contemns at length the treachrous toys,	. . . . .	O 145	Tr Boeth III.1		11
TREAD					
To tread the dreary paths without a guide,	. . . . .	O 31	Vanity Wishes		8
Yet still did Virtue deign the Stage to tread,	. . . .	O 52	Pro Drury-Lane		33
And tread in mystick rings the mossie ground.	. . . .	O 77	Tr Add. Battle		52
And tread the living picture in the dust	. . . . .	Y 177	Irene		V111B
TREADS					
And chearless treads the desolated stage,	. . . .	Y 106	Vanity Wishes	V	308
Though Scythia's icy cliffs he treads,	. . . . . .	O 65	Hor I Ode xxii		5
Tho' Scythia's icy cliff he treads,	. . . . . .	Y 74	Hor I Ode xxii	V	5
Thro' Scythia's icy cliffs he treads,	. . . . . .	Y 74	Hor I Ode xxii	V	5
O'er icy Caucusus he treads,	. . . .	O 66	To A. Fuscus		5
TREASON					
And shock the Tyrant with a Tale of Treason.	. . . .	O 255	Irene		29
Now Mustapha reveal this Tale of treason	. . . .	O 369	Irene	V	18
Treason so near us? at the dreadfull name of Treason	. . . .	O 369	Irene	V	20
Treason so near us? at the dreadfull name of Treason	. . . .	O 369	Irene	V	20
Treason so near us? lurking in our Palace	. . . .	O 369	Irene	V	20
Beware of Mustapha, beware of Treason.	. . . .	O 273	Irene		29
But yet, great Emperor, beware of Treason;	. . . .	O 273	Irene		31
Is this the restless Diligence of Treason?	. . . .	O 279	Irene		2
But still yet my Soul detests the Bassas treason	. . . .	O 353	Irene	V	22
Embark'd with Treason on the Seas of Fate,	. . . .	O 300	Irene		59
Oft would they find Ingratitude and Treason,	. . .	O 308	Irene		14
Pursue him through his Labyrinths of Treason,	. . .	O 310	Irene		6
By Treason levell'd with the Dregs of Men.	. . . .	O 311	Irene		17
Proceed, and give a loose to Love and Treason.	. . .	O 316	Irene		20
Their Treason throws no Stain upon Irene.	. . . .	O 324	Irene		18
He knows how near Apostacy to Treason--	. . . .	O 324	Irene		21
That thus you parly with detected Treason?	. . . .	O 327	Irene		15
His Breath prolong'd but to detect her Treason,	. . .	O 331	Irene		15
And thou, the curs'd Accomplice of her Treason,	. . .	O 331	Irene		5
Inflict whatever Treason can deserve,	. . . . .	O 334	Irene		75
TREASON'S					
Has Treason's dire Infection reach'd my Palace?	. . .	O 272	Irene		2
TREASONS					
Successful Treasons punish impious Kings.	. . . .	O 300	Irene		66
By crimes abhord, and treasons not her own	. . . .	Y 217	Irene	V	10A
TREASUR'D					
Deep in my Breast be treasur'd this Resolve,	. . .	O 288	Irene		12
TREASURE					
Thy Care shall guard this Treasure of my Soul;	. . .	O 263	Irene		2
A fancy'd Treasure, and a waking Dream.	. . . .	O 277	Irene		48
Think them a sacred Treasure lent by Heav'n,	. . .	O 302	Irene		6
TREASURES					
And raise his treasures higher than before.	. . . .	O 19	London		205
The dangers gather as the treasures rise.	. . . .	O 31	Vanity Wishes		28
Well pleas'd to search the Treasures of Remembrance,	. .	O 323	Irene		15

```
TREAT                                                        PAGE    TITLE              LINE
        Treat her With all the confidence of artless love  .  .  .   Y 159  Irene             V  17
TREE
        (Cry'd Daphne whisp'ring from the yielding tree;)  .  .  .    O 106  Eliza plucking        6
        Thrice has December stripp'd the tree  .  .  .  .  .  .  .    Y  11  Tr Hor Epode 9        7
TREES
        Our trees were blasted by the thunder stroke,     .  .  .     O  65  Virgil Past.I        23
        Or bends with violent force the trees.          .  .  .  .    O  67  Hor. II Ode IX        8
        Cali, methinks yon waving Trees afford       .  .  .  .  .    O 268  Irene                36
        And where yon Trees wave o'er the foaming Surge  .  .  .      O 304  Irene                 2
        Where the wild fig trees join their darksom shade  .  .  .    Y  19  Tr. Iliad Bk 6       52
TREMBLE
        Start at the Light, and tremble in the Dark;    .  .  .  .    O 266  Irene                30
        Gaze at their Height and tremble at their Danger:  .  .  .    O 293  Irene               116
        And burning daemons tremble at her torments  .  .  .  .  .    Y 168  Irene             V135D
        And Buda fall, and proud Vienna tremble,  .  .  .  .  .  .    O 309  Irene                27
TREMBLED
        I felt thy Pains, and trembled for Aspasia.  .  .  .  .  .    O 251  Irene                75
        I gaz'd, I trembled; but I could not speak:  .  .  .  .  .    O 282  Irene                65
TREMBLES
        And Bacon's mansion trembles o'er his head.  .  .  .  .  .    O  37  Vanity Wishes       140
        Implores our Smiles, and trembles at our Feet:  .  .  .  .    O 277  Irene                40
TREMBLING
        To waft our gallies o'er the trembling earth?  .  .  .  .     Y 115  Irene             V 49H
        Sooner these trembling Leaves shall find a Voice,  .  .  .    O 255  Irene                26
        Sooner the trembling Leaves shall find a Voice,   .  .  .     O 373  Irene             V  19
        Trembling to grant, nor daring to refuse,  .  .  .  .  .  .   O 260  Irene               126
        My trembling nerves--sink at the dreadful scenes of blood    Y 189  Irene             V  1H
            and death
        Of Freedom and of Love: My trembling Joints  .  .  .  .  .    O 320  Irene                11
        Those trembling Limbs--Speak out, thou shiv'ring  .  .  .     O 332  Irene                16
            Traitor.
TREMENDOUS
        Sustain th' approaching fire's tremendous light;  .  .  .     O  18  London              187
TRENT
        For the fair banks of Severn or of Trent;    .  .  .  .  .    O  19  London              211
        The wisest justice on the banks of Trent?   .  .  .  .  .     O  35  Vanity Wishes       124
        The richest Landlord on the banks of Trent?  .  .  .  .  .    O  35  Vanity Wishes     V 124
        The wealthiest landlord on the banks of Trent?  .  .  .  .    Y  97  Vanity Wishes     V 124
TRIBE
        The laureat tribe in servile verse relate,   .  .  .  .  .    O  19  London              198
        The laureat tribe in venal verse relate,    .  .  .  .  .  .  O  19  London            V 198
        How wouldst thou shake at Britain's modish tribe,  .  .  .    O  33  Vanity Wishes        61
        Evn low built towns they Britain's modish tribe  .  .  .      Y  94  Vanity Wishes     V  61
        The great, 'tis true, can charm th' electing tribe;  .  .     O  60  Pro Good Nat'd       25
TRIBES
        Our supple tribes repress their patriot throats,  .  .  .     O  34  Vanity Wishes        95
TRIBUTARY
        This tributary verse receive, my fair,   .  .  .  .  .  .     O  80  Lady Birthday         1
TRIBUTE
        To whom all nations tribute bring.  .  .  .  .  .  .  .  .     O  68  Hor. II Ode IX       20
        They croud my camp with voluntary tribute  .  .  .  .  .      Y 136  Irene             V 27B
TRICKT
        Trickt in Antique Ruff and Bonnet,  .  .  .  .  .  ..  .  .    O 179  Ridicul Warton        7
TRIED    SEE TRY'D
        Well tried through many a varying year,   .  .  .  .  .  .     O 201  Death Dr Levet        5
TRIES
        Tries the dread summits of Cesarean pow'r,  .  .  .  .  .      O  42  Vanity Wishes       242
        Her wings Imagination tries,  .  .  .  .  .  .  .  .  .  .     O 125  An Ode               14
TRIFLE
        Exalt each trifle, ev'ry vice adore,   .  .  .  .  .  .  .     O  17  London              148
        Praise evry trifle, ev'ry vice adore,    .  .  .  .  .  .      Y  55  London            V 148
        Trifle not at Thirty five:  .  .  .  .  .  .  .  .  .  .  .    O 178  Thrale 35 Year       12
        Some petty Passion! some domestick Trifle!   .  .  .  .  .     O 280  Irene                 7
TRIFLER
        And leaves the lovely Trifler unregarded   .  .  .  .  .  .    O 276  Irene                23
        And then leaves your actions the busy trifler  .  .  .  .     O 355  Irene             V  12
            unregarded
TRIFLES
        These all are Trifles, to what we can give.  .  .  .  .  .     O 247  Irene Epilogue       20
        Unmov'd I saw the glitt'ring Trifles perish,  .  .  .  .  .    O 302  Irene               108
TRIFLING
        For trifling sports I quitted grave affairs.  .  .  .  .  .    O 130  Tr. Rambler 10        1
        Unlike the trifling Race of vulgar Beauties,  .  .  .  .  .    O 298  Irene                18
TRIFLINGS
        Surveys your triflings with a careless glance  .  .  .  .     O 355  Irene             V  11
TRIUMPH
        Nor claim the triumph of a letter'd heart;  .  .  .  .  .      O  37  Vanity Wishes       152
        When Learning's Triumph o'er her barb'rous Foes  .  .  .      O  51  Pro Drury-Lane        1
        Less pleas'd to triumph than to spare.   .  .  .  .  .  .      O 137  Tr Rambler 143        2
        In Triumph sits upon our shatter'd Spires,   .  .  .  .  .     O 251  Irene                67
        In triumph sits upon the ruin'd Spires  .  .  .  .  .  .  .    O 351  Irene             V  6
        The dreadful Dissonance of barb'rous Triumph,  .  .  .  .      O 251  Irene                71
        robes of triumph.  .  .  .  .  .  .  .  .  .  .  .  .  .       O 374  Irene             V 31
        Still sees To-morrow drest in Robes of Triumph;  .  .  .      O 283  Irene                29
        The dreadfull dissonance of barbarous triumph  .  .  .  .     Y 169  Irene             V 11
        Forbear this Triumph--still new Conflicts wait us,  .  .      O 298  Irene                25
        Behold him wretched in his double Triumph;  .  .  .  .  .      O 310  Irene                 5
        Ill suits with Guilt the Gaieties of Triumph;  .  .  .  .     O 314  Irene                22
        To grace the Triumph of victorious Virtue;  .  .  .  .  .      O 322  Irene                10
        Robb'd of the Maid, with whom I wish'd to triumph,  .  .      O 333  Irene                42
```

	PAGE	TITLE	LINE
TRIUMPH (CONTINUED)			
Unjustly mortals triumph and complain	Y 217	Irene	V 14
TRIUMPH'D			
Secure, and triumph'd oft' in hostile blood. . . .	O 76	Tr Add. Battle	34
TRIUMPHAL			
The festal blazes, the triumphal show, ...	O 39	Vanity Wishes	175
TRIUMPHANT			
Behold her cross triumphant on the main, ...	O 10	London	27
The Lilies o'er the Vales triumphant spread;	O 111	To Posterity	18
<In> Triumphant at the head of thy new votaries . .	Y 131	Irene	V 32A
Shall guard Aspasia from triumphant Lust.	O 301	Irene	89
Shall soar triumphant on the Wings of Glory, ...	O 305	Irene	26
Of stern Sebalias the triumphant Crescent, ...	O 312	Irene	11
The joyfull Cranes triumphant clap their wings: . . .	Y 26	Tr Add. Battle	127
TRIUMPHS			
And tow'rs and triumphs in ideal Greatness;	O 269	Irene	5
Thy Soul compleats the Triumphs of thy Face.	O 278	Irene	60
Will cloud my Triumphs, and pollute the Day.	O 310	Irene	3
TRIVIAL			
Commits to trivial Chance the Fate of Nations! . . .	O 269	Irene	2
What trivial Accidents determine Fate!	O 367	Irene	V 23
Commits to trivial chance the Work of Fate!	O 374	Irene	V 11
TROD			
The Steps their Saviour trod;	O 79	Feast St Simon	15
There trod the Lybian sands, ...	O 79	Feast St Simon	39
And trod to Bacchus' praise the mystick ground. . .	Y 6	Virgil Daphnis	16
Back through the city trod his former way.	Y 17	Tr. Iliad Bk 6	2
TROJANS			
How would the Trojans brand great Hector's name! . .	O 74	Tr. Iliad Bk 6	5
TROOP			
Dismiss these needless Fears--a Troop of Greeks . . .	O 301	Irene	90
Reclines against the Shore: Our Grecian Troop . . .	O 304	Irene	3
--And loiter'd with his troop remote from Action . .	O 376	Irene	V 15
Wilt thou then head the Troop upon the Shore, ...	O 305	Irene	36
The Queen requested that a chosen Troop	O 331	Irene	7
A chosen Troop--to intercept--Demetrius--	O 331	Irene	12
TROOPES			
Teach me to range my troopes in just array	Y 22	Tr Add. Battle	5
TROOPS			
And drove the swarthy troops to their own barren sands. .	O 78	Festina Lente	20
In vain, when Turkey's troops assail'd our Walls, . .	O 253	Irene	117
Far from his Troops, he toys his Hours away.	O 258	Irene	93
Before th' assembled Troops proclaim his Crimes; . .	O 273	Irene	35
Should we before the Troops proclaim his Crimes . .	O 273	Irene	38
Arabia's roving Troops, the Sons of Swiftness, . . .	O 274	Irene	54
Elude my Vengeance? no--My Troops shall range . . .	O 274	Irene	58
Confirm your Troops; and when the Moon's fair Beam .	O 306	Irene	58
And lead thy Troops victorious round the World. . .	O 333	Irene	41
Or how before Nassau the Gallick troops retir'd? . .	Y 22	Tr Add. Battle	13
The steely troops embodied closely stand	Y 24	Tr Add. Battle	78
TROP			
Trop de frais.	O 172	French Distich	2
TROPHIES			
Augustus' numerous trophies sing;	O 68	Hor. II Ode IX	18
TROUBLE			
From Hector's breast each gloomy trouble flies . . .	Y 18	Tr. Iliad Bk 6	15
TROUBLED			
The strong Emotions of my troubled Soul	O 275	Irene	87
Abdalla, bid thy troubled Breast be calm;	O 329	Irene	2
Restrain your sorrows, calm your troubled soul. . .	Y 21	Tr. Iliad Bk 6	114
TROUBLES			
Then we with wine will drown our troubles, laid . .	Y 7	Virgil Daphnis	47
TROY			
The day will come, in which proud Troy shall yield, .	O 74	Tr. Iliad Bk 6	13
Behold the wife of Hector, guard of Troy!	O 74	Tr. Iliad Bk 6	26
Grant him like me to guard the walls of Troy. . . .	Y 20	Tr. Iliad Bk 6	102
TRUE			
Give to St. David one true Briton more.	O 9	London	8
Still to his int'rest true, where'er he goes, . . .	O 16	London	125
The great, 'tis true, can charm th' electing tribe; .	O 60	Pro Good Nat'd	25
Open to all, true only to thyself, ...	O 176	Tr Metastas II	6
'Tis true, the Fellow's handsome, strait and tall; .	O 247	Irene Epilogue	7
My Swain is little--true--but be it known, ...	O 247	Irene Epilogue	9
My Vows, 'tis true, she hears with less Aversion, . .	O 287	Irene	7
True, she was fair; the Smile of Innocence	O 330	Irene	10
TRUMP			
War sounds the trump, he rushes to the field;	O 40	Vanity Wishes	198
TRUMPET			
Trumpet or lyre--to their harsh bosoms chill, ...	O 192	Tr. Medea II	11
He bids no Trumpet quell the fatal Sound.	O 246	Irene Prologue	24
TRUMPETS			
No trumpets sound, no Soldiers cries, ...	O 71	Hor. Epode II	9
While in my verse the shrilling trumpets sound, . . .	Y 22	Tr Add. Battle	18
TRUST			
The slighted Arts Futurity shall trust, ...	O 57	Prologue Comus	13
My fair, be mindful of the mighty trust, ...	O 81	Lady Birthday	11
And vows to trust the faithless deep no more. . . .	O 82	Young Author	10
"And let the goddess trust her eyes."	O 122	Stella Mourn.	6
In Reason, Nature, Truth he dares to trust:	O 246	Irene Prologue	33
I scorn a Trust unwillingly repos'd;	O 256	Irene	34
The Watchful slumber, and the Crafty trust.	O 283	Irene	13

363

```
TRUST              (CONTINUED)                        PAGE    TITLE            LINE
     Too fierce, too faithless for Neglect or Trust.   . . .   O 288 Irene            14
     To rough--Too false too fierce to trust or to neglect  .  O 374 Irene        V   1
     Too much to fear or trust, is equal Weakness.     .   .   O 300 Irene            77
     Ask to whose Sword the Greeks will trust their Cause,  .  O 305 Irene            39
     Nor will I trust th' uncertain Chance of Combat;  .  . .  O 307 Irene            21
     Nor trust our Passions with her fatal Charms.   . . . .   O 332 Irene            31
TRUSTED
     Such had I trusted once as soon as seen,  . . . . .  .    O 255 Irene            17
TRUSTS
     Trusts without fear, to merit, and to you.   . . . .  .   O  60 Pro Good Nat'd   30
     Trusts without fear, to candour, and to you.  . . .  .    O  60 Pro Good Nat'd V 30
     He who blindly trusts, will find  . . . . . . .          O 176 Tr Metastasi I    3
     Trusts to my Care his Mistress and his Life,  . . .  .    O 283 Irene            10
TRUTH
     And lend a lye the confidence of truth.  . . . . .  .     O  12 London           56
     This mournful truth is ev'ry where confess'd,  . . . .    O  18 London          176
     Wealth heap'd on wealth, nor truth nor safety buys,  .  . O  31 Vanity Wishes    27
     Attentive truth and nature to descry,  . . . . . .  .     O  33 Vanity Wishes    63
     And virtue guard thee to the throne of Truth!  . . .  .   O  37 Vanity Wishes   142
     His pow'rful Strokes presiding Truth impress'd,  . .  .   O  51 Pro Drury-Lane    7
     And Truth diffuse her Radiance from the Stage.  . . .  .  O  53 Pro Drury-Lane   62
     With thirst of knowledge, and with love of truth;  .  .  O 117 Epitaph Hanmer    6
     Might Truth intrude with daring flight,  . . . . . .      O 121 To Miss Playin   20
     More safely truth to urge her claim presumes,  . . .  .  O 134 Tr. Rambler 93    1
     Truth in platonic ornaments bedeck'd,  . . . . . . .     O 134 Tr. Rambler 96    1
     Yet hear, alas! this mournful truth,  . . . . . . .      O 159 Par Hermit III    9
     Yet hear, at last, this mournful truth,  . . . . . .     O 159 Par Hermit III V  9
     In Reason, Nature, Truth he dares to trust:  . . . .  .  O 246 Irene Prologue   33
     Which Love of Greatness, not of Truth, inflames.  . .  . O 262 Irene            27
     To hear the Voice of Truth; dismiss thy Train,  . . .  . O 289 Irene             6
     To hear the voice of truth, dismiss your train  . . .  . O 366 Irene         V  22
     And bid Success become the Test of Truth.  . . . . .  .  O 291 Irene            64
     For daring Truth, and Turbulence of Honour?  . . . .  .  O 299 Irene            37
     The breast where truth supports the throne of peace.  .  Y 193 Irene         V  15
     Come haste, and live--Thy Innocence and Truth  . . .  .  O 320 Irene            18
     Holds out her Hand to lead thee back to Truth.  . . .  . O 321 Irene            42
     Stay but a Moment, and prevailing Truth  . . . . . .  .  O 321 Irene            46
     Thy sacred freight of innocence and truth  . . . . .  .  Y 201 Irene         V 10D
     He knew Irene's Truth.  . . . . . . . . . . . .  .       O 324 Irene            20
     There dauntless Truth shall blast the vile Accuser,  .   O 326 Irene            42
          the voice of truth  . . . . . . . . . . . .  .      Y 210 Irene         V  25
     Then hear, great Mahomet, the Voice of Truth.  . . .  .  O 333 Irene            55
     That useful truth with humour may unite,  . . . . .  .   Y  67 Prologue Lethe   15
TRUTHS
     If Truths like these with pleasing Language join;  . .   O 246 Irene Prologue   15
TRY
     These arts in vain our rugged natives try,  . . . .  .   O  16 London          129
     Approach, ye minstrels, try the soothing strain,  . .  . O  43 Vanity Wishes   267
     The skies are open--let us try the skies:  . . . . .  .  O 136 Tr Rambler 129    5
     And try the Hazard that hast Nought to stake;  . . .  .  O 319 Irene            31
     Not call'd to try the Cause, we hear the Sentence,  .  . O 326 Irene            34
     But let us try to clear our clouded Brows,  . . . . .  . O 329 Irene            10
TRY'D
     Fresh praise is try'd till madness fires his mind,  .  . O  42 Vanity Wishes   231
     New praise is try'd till madness fires his mind,  . .  . Y 102 Vanity Wishes V 231
     To force Applause no modern Arts are try'd.  . . . .  .  O 246 Irene Prologue   22
     These Arts I try'd, and to inflame her more,  . . . .  . O 287 Irene            14
     Well known, long try'd, expect us on the Shore.  . . .  O 301 Irene            91
     Forbear--.i know the long try'd Faith of Cali.  . . .  . O 308 Irene            11
TUMULT
     Remote from Tumult, in th' adjoining Palace,  . . .  .   O 263 Irene             1
     When eer the tumult of unestablish'd Conquest  . . .  .  O 357 Irene         V   6
     Till thither an huge bird the tumult drew  . . . . .  .  Y  25 Tr Add. Battle  124
TUMULTS
     To quit the Tumults of the noisy Camp,  . . . . . .  .   O 264 Irene            11
     That raises tumults in the female bosom seditions  . .   Y 158 Irene         V  12
          (mutinies
     That raises Tumults in the female Breast,  . . . . .  .  O 287 Irene            12
     Freed from the Tumults of unsettled Conquest,  . . .  .  O 291 Irene            77
TUMULTUOUS
     But hark! th' affrighted crowd's tumultuous cries  . .   O  18 London          182
     Tumultuous passions strugle in her breast  . . . . .  .  Y  21 Tr. Iliad Bk 6  109
TUNE
     And me to tune at ease th' unequal reeds.  . . . . .  .  O  64 Virgil Past.I    12
     To nobler subjects tune my lyre;  . . . . . . . .  .     O  78 Feast St Simon    8
     To tune the regulated heart.  . . . . . . . . . .  .     O 121 To Miss Playin   36
     To tune the Tongue, to teach the Eyes to roll,  . . .  . O 278 Irene            64
     Or tune thine Ear to soothing Adulation,  . . . . .  .   O 289 Irene             4
     Or tune your ear to soothing Adulation.  . . . . . .  .  O 366 Irene         V  20
     There Poetry shall tune her sacred Voice,  . . . . .  .  O 302 Irene           122
TUNEFUL
     Diffuse the tuneful lenitives of pain:  . . . . . .  .   O  43 Vanity Wishes   268
     And yield the tuneful lenitives of pain:  . . . . .  .   O  43 Vanity Wishes V 268
     Great George's acts let tuneful Cibber sing;  . . . .   O 114 On C. Cibber      3
     When Stella strikes the tuneful string  . . . . . .  .   O 120 To Miss Playin    1
TUNEFULL
     I pierce the Clouds a tunefull Swan.  . . . . . . .  .   O  70 Hor.II Ode XX    12
TURBULENCE
     For daring Truth, and Turbulence of Honour?  . . . .  .  O 299 Irene            37
```

```
                                                            PAGE    TITLE              LINE
TURGID
    Let them prolong their turgid lays  . . . . . . . .   O  78  Feast St Simon        4
TURK
    Marry a Turk! a haughty, Tyrant King,  . . . . . .   O 247  Irene Epilogue         1
TURKEY
    But thus reserv'd to lure the Wolves of Turkey,    . . .   O 250  Irene            24
    Renounce her Faith, and be the Queen of Turkey;    . . .   O 258  Irene           100
    Prowls like a lyon oer the wealthy Spoils of bleeding .   O 352  Irene          V 29
        Turkey.
    Prowls o'er the wealthy Spoils of bleeding Turkey? . . .   O 264  Irene            15
    To hear my suit and give a Queen to Turkey? . . . . .   O 372  Irene            V  7
    O! did Irene shine the Queen of Turkey,   . . . . . .   O 290  Irene            51
    Have I for this defy'd the Chiefs of Turkey,   . . . .   O 304  Irene            16
    The Pow'r of Turkey waits upon my Call.  . . . . . .   O 319  Irene            24
    The pow'r of Turkey rises at my call  . . . . . .   Y 197  Irene            V 24
TURKEY'S
    In vain, when Turkey's troops assail'd our Walls,   . . .   O 253  Irene           117
    Deliverance is at Hand; for Turkey's Tyrant . . . . .   O 283  Irene             7
    And learn the Rev'rence due to Turkey's Queen.  . . . .   O 322  Irene            55
TURKISH
    Hid in the mean Disguise of Turkish Robes,   . . . . .   O 249  Irene             2
    But now our Turkish Conquerors have quench'd   . . .   O 249  Irene             7
    The Chief, whose Wisdom guides the Turkish Counsels.  . .   O 253  Irene           112
    Embroil'd the Turkish State--our Sultan's Father  . . .   O 256  Irene            42
    The Turkish Pow'rs from Europe shall retreat,  . . .   O 257  Irene            79
    Could bear his Son upon the Turkish Throne.  . . . . .   O 264  Irene            22
    When ev'ry Wave shall beat a Turkish Shore,  . . . . .   O 265  Irene            43
    Till every Wave shall beat a Turkish Shore.  . . . . .   O 354  Irene            V 26
    Comes Mustapha.--Your Turkish Robes conceal you--   . .   O 271  Irene            36
    A turkish Stranger of majestick Mien,  . . . . . .   O 294  Irene             1
    Each Turkish Bosom burns for thy Destruction,  . . .   O 300  Irene            73
    To-morrow's Dawn shall see the Turkish King . . . . .   O 303  Irene             9
    Demand whose Force yon Turkish Heroes dread,   . . .   O 305  Irene            41
    Then shall Venetia feel the Turkish Pow'r,   . . . . .   O 309  Irene            28
    Doom'd me to die with all the Turkish Captains.  . . .   O 313  Irene            16
    For which Aspasia scorn'd the Turkish Crown?  . . . .   O 314  Irene            17
    Th' unpitying Ministers of Turkish Justice.  . . . . .   O 325  Irene             9
TURN
    Turn from the glitt'ring bribe thy scornful eye,   . . .   O  14  London           87
    And turn the varied taunt a thousand ways.   . . . . .   O  17  London          165
    Deign on the passing world to turn thine eyes,   . . .   O  38  Vanity Wishes   157
    Part turn their Backs, part seiz'd with wild surprise .   O  76  Tr Add. Battle   28
    On me you turn the nose.----  . . . . . .   O 140  Tr Rambler 176    1
    Turn on the prudent Ant, thy heedful eyes,   . . . . .   O 151  The Ant           1
    Wheresoe'er I turn my View,  . . . . . . . .   O 179  Ridicul Warton    1
    And Wisdom into Virtue turn thy Frailty.  . . . . . .   O 266  Irene            22
    And turn thy Thoughts henceforth to Love and Empire.  .   O 276  Irene             5
    Nor at the Call of Cali deign'd to turn.   . . . . . .   O 317  Irene            33
TURN'D
    Turn'd by his nod the stream of honour flows,  . . .   O  34  Vanity Wishes   103
    Nor e'er from virtue's paths was turn'd aside,   . . .   O 118  Epitaph Hanmer  V 31
    Orpheus turn'd his eager Sight,  . . . . . . . .   O 150  Tr Boet III.12   50
    And turn'd their hasty Steps towards the Garden.  . . .   O 269  Irene            39
    And turn'd th' instructive Page of Human Life,   . . .   O 281  Irene            33
    Turn'd backwards by the powerful Breath of Heav'n.  . .   O 322  Irene             3
    He turn'd awhile the fortune of the day  . . . . .   Y  25  Tr Add. Battle  123
TURN'ST
    Thou to a scene of bloodshed turn'st the Ball,  . . .   O  77  Festina Lente    11
TURNIP
    Have a turnip than his father.  . . . . . . . .   O 183  Burlesque Vega    4
    Have a turnip than a father.  . . . . . . . .   O 183  Burlesque Vega  V  4
TURNIPS
    If the man who turnips cries,  . . . . . . . .   O 183  Burlesque Vega    1
TURNS    SEE TURN'ST
    Where-e'er he turns he meets a stranger's eye,   . . .   O  35  Vanity Wishes   111
    He turns, with anxious heart and cripled hands,  . . .   O  44  Vanity Wishes   287
    Each Realm where Beauty turns the graceful Shape,  . . .   O 262  Irene            13
    His Pride and Love by Turns inspir'd his Tongue,   . . .   O 299  Irene            43
    Sudden he stops, and inward turns his Eyes,  . . . . .   O 311  Irene             5
    Irradiate and obscure my Breast by Turns:  . . . . . .   O 321  Irene            45
    Heav'n turns its point upon the guilty Heart   . . . .   O 345  Irene            V 29
    And joy and sorrow stand by turns confest.   . . . . .   Y  21  Tr. Iliad Bk 6  110
TURNUS
    How Turnus by Aeneas' sword expir'd?  . . . . . . .   Y  22  Tr Add. Battle   12
TURRETS
    Where ----'s humble turrets rise,  . . . . . . .   O 125  An Ode           16
    And though built on feeble columns--Its lofty turrets  .   Y 131  Irene            V 35
        blaze amidst
TUSCAN
    The mighty Tuscan courts the banish'd Arts  . . . . .   O 302  Irene           116
TUTELARY
    While tutelary Nations guard her Cell.  . . . . . .   O  58  Prologue Comus   36
TWENTIETH
    To still their Murmurs, ere the twentieth Sun  . . .   O 309  Irene            23
TWENTY
    One and Twenty 1810: Improviso on a young heir's coming .   O 196  Song Congratu.  V  T
        of age.
    Long-expected one and twenty  . . . . . . . .   O 196  Song Congratu.    1
TWICE
    Twice since the Morning rose I saw the Bassa,  . . .   O 275  Irene            76
```

TWILIGHT
          PAGE   TITLE   LINE

Entry		PAGE	TITLE	LINE
TWILIGHT				
Stay--in this dubious Twilight of Conviction,	. . . .	O 321	Irene	43
TWINE				
Direct thy rivulets, and twine thy bow'rs;	. . . . .	O 20	London	217
TWINES				
But round the lofty Popular twines	. . . .	O 71	Hor. Epode II	17
TWISTED				
With twisted toils, and op'ning hounds;	. . . . . .	O 72	Hor. Epode II	40
And twisted toils, surrounds	. . . .	O 72	Hor. Epode II	V 40
TWO				
Two tender kids, the hopes of all the flock.	. . . .	O 64	Virgil Past.I	20
Two Men unknown, the Partners of his Bosom;	. . . . .	O 275	Irene	80
Two faithful Captains, Hasan and Caraza,	. . . . . .	O 310	Irene	5
Here have I rais'd four sacred altars, two	. . . . .	Y 7	Virgil Daphnis	43
To great Latona's son, and two to you;	. . . .	Y 7	Virgil Daphnis	44
Two bowls with oyl and milk I'll yearly crown,	. . . .	Y 7	Virgil Daphnis	45
Fiercely contending two vast armies stood	. . . . . .	Y 23	Tr Add. Battle	56
Of two day's long	. . . .	Y 300	Fanny Burney	2
TYBURN				
Scarce can our fields, such crowds at Tyburn die,	. . .	O 21	London	242
Well may we fear, such crowds at Tyburn die,	. . . .	Y 60	London	V 242
TYDE				
All stemm'd in one sad day the Stygian tyde.	. . . .	Y 18	Tr. Iliad Bk 6	35
TYDEUS'				
Th' atridae there and Tydeus' mighty son,	. . . . .	Y 19	Tr. Iliad Bk 6	54
TYRANNICK				
All ye, whose Blood tyrannick Rage effus'd,	. . . . .	O 306	Irene	53
TYRANNIZE				
When vanquish'd Vice shall tyrannize no more.	. . . .	O 321	Irene	36
TYRANNY				
Arthritic tyranny consigns,	. . . .	O 125	An Ode	10
Detested residence of lust and tyranny	. . . . . .	Y 165	Irene	V 79
To range those walks of tyranny and lust	. . . . . .	Y 165	Irene	V 85
The sport of Tyranny, or Lord of Nations.	. . . . .	O 303	Irene	12
TYRANT				
From Persia's tyrant to Bavaria's lord.	. . . . .	O 41	Vanity Wishes	224
We bless the Tyrant, and we hug the Chain.	. . . . .	O 96	Hickman Spinet	8
In vain for thee the tyrant sighs,	. . . . .	O 100	Ode Friendship	V 19
Marry a Turk! a haughty, Tyrant King,	. . . . . .	O 247	Irene Epilogue	1
And shock the Tyrant with a Tale of Treason.	. . . .	O 255	Irene	29
Say, did a Voice from Heav'n restrain the Tyrant?	. .	O 259	Irene	115
No feeble Tyrant of a petty State	. . . . . .	O 268	Irene	21
Swift, let us rush upon the careless Tyrant,	. . . .	O 271	Irene	31
Mean as we are, this Tyrant of the World	. . . . .	O 277	Irene	39
Deliverance is at Hand; for Turkey's Tyrant	. . . .	O 283	Irene	7
the Tyrant leisure --	. . . .	O 357	Irene	V 7
Curst as the Tyrant of th' infernal Realms,	. . . .	O 294	Irene	134
Say, how the Tyrant threaten'd, flatter'd, sigh'd,	. .	O 295	Irene	23
Now, Tyrant, with Satiety of Beauty,	. . . . . .	O 304	Irene	33
bend tyrant adamant--melt harlot	. . . . . .	Y 181	Irene	V 56
Is Greece deliver'd? is the Tyrant fall'n?	. . . .	O 315	Irene	3
Greece is no more, the prosp'rous Tyrant lives,	. . .	O 315	Irene	4
TYRANT'S				
Will he not bend beneath a Tyrant's Frown?	. . . .	O 255	Irene	22
The Tyrant's Death.	. . . .	O 257	Irene	73
See! Mustapha, the Tyrant's Minion, comes;	. . . .	O 260	Irene	143
TYRANTS				
As Tyrants doom their Tools of Guilt to die;	. . . .	O 53	Pro Drury-Lane	56
In vain proud tyrants strove to shake	. . . . . .	O 79	Feast St Simon	13
Those pow'rful Tyrants of the Female Breast	. . . .	O 261	Irene	12
UNACCUSTOM'D				
And unaccustom'd warblings charm the grove (pleasing disson\<ance\>)	.	Y 150	Irene	V 86
UNACQUAINTED				
Yet unacquainted with these soft Emotions	. . . . .	O 263	Irene	16
Lest unacquainted with our bold Attempt,	. . . . . .	O 285	Irene	12
UNACTIVE				
Unactive (unkindled) in the breast--rouse it	. . . .	Y 133	Irene	V 19
UNAFFRIGHTED				
Where unaffrighted by the din of war	. . . .	Y 177	Irene	V 116
UNAIDED				
Oh could thy Hand unaided free thy Country,	. . . . .	O 300	Irene	63
UNANIMATED				
And crush'd the yet unanimated young.	. . . .	Y 23	Tr Add. Battle	49
UNANIMOUS				
And hail unanimous their conqu'ring God.	. . . . . .	O 287	Irene	6
UNAPPEAS'D				
Should Heav'n yet unappeas'd refuse its Aid,	. . . .	O 301	Irene	97
UNARM'D				
Me singing, careless and unarm'd,	. . . . . .	O 65	Hor I Ode xxii	11
Me singing, careless and unarm'd,	. . . .	O 66	To A. Fuscus	11
Rush'd out and seiz'd me, thoughtless and unarm'd,	. .	O 335	Irene	7
UNAVAILING				
Enough of unavailing Tears, Demetrius,	. . . . . .	O 253	Irene	104
While unavailing Anger crouds thy Tongue	. . . . .	O 327	Irene	6
While unavailing passion crouds your tongue	. . . .	O 368	Irene	V 14
Shake off this Weight of unavailing Grief,	. . . .	O 333	Irene	39
UNAW'D				
Sometimes the Wretch unaw'd by Heav'n or Hell,	. . . .	O 300	Irene	78
UNBALLAST				
Now with no weak unballast wing	. . . .	O 70	Hor.II Ode XX	1

		PAGE	TITLE	LINE
UNBLEST				
Unblest, still docm'd to wed with misery.		O 131	Tr. Rambler 39	1
UNBORN				
"Secure of praise from nations yet unborn."		O 82	Young Author	18
"Secure of praise from ages yet unborn."		O 82	Young Author	V 18
UNBORROW'D				
With native Lustre and unborrow'd Greatness,		O 298	Irene	16
UNBOUGHT				
Whose gen'rous Zeal, unbought by flatt'ring Rhimes,		O 57	Prologue Comus	3
With unbought dainties load the board;		O 73	Hor. Epode II	54
UNBOUND				
The parents smil'd, the chief his helm unbound		Y 20	Tr. Iliad Bk 6	95
UNBOUNDED				
Unbounded prospects in his bosom roll,		O 82	Young Author	V 6A
Unbounded Projects lab'ring in his Mind,		O 97	Hickman Spinet	11
Unbounded Masters of the main.		O 189	Epilogue	8
Unbounded Rulers of the main.		O 189	Epilogue	V 8
Let not th' unbounded Greatness of his Mind		O 275	Irene	72
Unbounded Wealth shall flow beneath thy feet		O 350	Irene	V 23
UNBRIB'D				
For who would leave, unbrib'd, Hibernia's land,		O 9	London	9
UNBROKEN				
Unbroken as the sacred Chain of Nature,		O 257	Irene	63
UNCEASING				
Are these th' unceasing Joys, th' unmingled Pleasures		O 314	Irene	16
UNCERTAIN				
Ambiguous emblem of uncertain fate!		O 95	Sprig of Myrtl	2
Still must we linger in uncertain Hope?		O 282	Irene	3
Nor will I trust th' uncertain Chance of Combat;		O 307	Irene	21
Refuse their Office, and uncertain Life		O 320	Irene	21
UNCHA				
Virtue is uncha unvarying as its Authour		O 348	Irene	V 23
UNCHANG'D				
Ennobled, yet unchang'd, if Nature shine:		O 246	Irene Prologue	16
O may her Beauties last unchang'd by Time,		O 262	Irene	11
UNCHECK'D				
Uncheck'd on both, loud rabbles vent their rage,		O 59	Pro Good Nat'd	15
Uncheck'd on both, caprice may vent its rage,		O 59	Pro Good Nat'd	V 15
UNCIVILIZ'D				
That range unciviliz'd from Rock to Rock,		O 268	Irene	30
UNCLAIM'D				
No peaceful desart yet unclaim'd by Spain?		O 18	London	173
UNCLASP'D				
Unclasp'd his Iron Gripe to set thee free?		O 318	Irene	16
UNCLOUDED				
Who set unclouded in the gulphs of fate.		O 45	Vanity Wishes	312
Still, still the same--unclouded by Misfortune!		O 294	Irene	3
See how the Moon through all th' unclouded Sky		O 313	Irene	1
UNCONFIN'D				
Wide-wasting pest! that rages unconfin'd,		O 31	Vanity Wishes	23
Our daring Bard with Spirit unconfin'd,		O 246	Irene Prologue	7
UNCONNECTED				
The raging Madman's unconnected Schemes		O 287	Irene	10
UNCONQUER'D				
Unconquer'd lord of pleasure and of pain;		O 40	Vanity Wishes	196
Unconquer'd bars on earth and sea withstand;		O 136	Tr Rambler 129	3
These Years, unconquer'd Mahomet, demand		O 263	Irene	7
UNCONSCIOUS				
To please by scenes unconscious of offence,		O 62	Pro Word Wise	13
Sure, not unconscious of the mighty Blessing,		O 256	Irene	59
UNCONVINC'D				
A Statesman's logick unconvinc'd can hear,		O 13	London	71
UNCOUNTED				
Unfelt, uncounted, glided by;		O 202	Death Dr Levet	30
UNCOUTH				
Uncouth Words in Disarray:		O 179	Ridicul Warton	6
UNDAUNTED				
At length the undaunted Scythian yields,		O 68	Hor. II Ode IX	22
Not so while long th' undaunted race maintain'd		Y 23	Tr Add. Battle	36
Meantime the Pygmies with undaunted hearts		Y 24	Tr Add. Battle	76
UNDER				
"Under leaves to hide one's head,		O 185	Anacreon Ode 9	27
UNDESIGNING				
This open Friend, this undesigning Hero,		O 299	Irene	38
UNDETECTED				
Should fill the World with Wretches undetected.		O 283	Irene	27
UNDISCOVER'D				
No pathless waste, or undiscover'd shore;		O 18	London	171
UNDISSEMBLED				
For Zeal unguarded, undissembled Hate,		O 299	Irene	36
UNDISTINGUISH'D				
Mix undistinguish'd with the gen'ral Roar.		O 280	Irene	24
An undistinguish'd Sound of threat'ning Rage.		O 311	Irene	13
UNDISTURB'D				
Sleep undisturb'd within this peaceful shrine,		O 113	Epit. Phillips	5
Rest undisturb'd within this humble shrine,		O 113	Epit. Phillips	V 5
UNENCUMBER'D				
Soars unencumber'd with our idle Cares,		O 266	Irene	36
UNENVIED				
Succeed, my Friend, unenvied by Leontius.		O 306	Irene	48

367

```
UNEQUAL                                                      PAGE    TITLE            LINE
      Yet Reason frowns on War's unequal game,    . . . . .  O  39 Vanity Wishes        185
      Yet Reason blush on War's unequal game,     . . . . .  Y 100 Vanity Wishes      V 185
      And me to tune at ease th' unequal reeds.   . . . . .  O  64 Virgil Past.I        12
      For Courage droops unequal to the Combat,   . . . . .  O 252 Irene               91
      Soon will th' unequal Contest be decided,   . . . . .  O 261 Irene               18
      His Air disorder'd, and his Gait unequal,   . . . . .  O 311 Irene                3
UNERRING
      And with unerring shafts distribute fate;   . . . . .  O  83 Epi Dist Moth.       4
      And forming, with unerring art,   . . . . . . .        O 121 To Miss Playin      17
      While Heaven's high Minister whose unerring awfull     . O 355 Irene            V  9
         volume
UNESTABLISH'D
      When eer the tumult of unestablish'd Conquest  . . . . O 357 Irene             V  6
UNEXHAUSTED
      And unexhausted laughter, and edge the piercing gibe . Y  94 Vanity Wishes     V 62
      Where Commerce lavish'd unexhausted Plenty,  . . . . . O 251 Irene               64
      While fair Hungaria's unexhausted Vallies    . . . . . O 264 Irene               16
UNEXPECTED
      With unexpected legions bursts away,    . . . . . . .  O  42 Vanity Wishes       243
      With unexpected legions pow'rs away,    . . . . . . .  Y 103 Vanity Wishes     V 243
      Soon as the Sultan's unexpected Fate    . . . . . . .  O 257 Irene               76
      Meet unexpected Daggers in his Way,     . . . . . . .  O 274 Irene               48
      Did you proclaim this unexpected Conquest?  . . . . .  O 282 Irene               62
      Such strange Events, such unexpected Chances,  . . . . O 296 Irene               34
UNEXPENSIVE
      Why should Cali rebel--unexpensive age  . . . . . . .  Y 120 Irene             V 40
UNEXPERIENCED
      The airy Flights of unexperienced Virtue  . . . . . .  O 347 Irene             V 20
UNEXTINGUISH'D
      But unextinguish'd Avarice still remains,   . . . . .  O  44 Vanity Wishes       285
      While secret Flames, with unextinguish'd Rage,  . . .  O 315 Irene               35
UNFADED
      Unfaded still their former charms they shew,  . . . .  O  84 Epi Dist Moth.      26
UNFADING
      He feels th' unfading wreath surround his head;  . . . O  82 Young Author        22
      And feels the unfading wreath surround his head;  . .  O  82 Young Author      V 22
      Unfading Verdure glads the roving Eye,  . . . . . . .  O 315 Irene               34
UNFEELING
      The Lust of Gold, unfeeling and remorseless!  . . . .  O 249 Irene               14
UNFELT
      The notes unfelt would strike th' impervious ear,  . . Y 104 Vanity Wishes     V 269
      Unfelt, uncounted, glided by;  . . . . . . . . .       O 202 Death Dr Levet      30
UNFETTERD
      Happy whose unfetterd Mind  . . . . . . . . . . .      O 147 Tr Boet III.12       3
UNFINISH'D
      But shall I, then, forsake the unfinish'd war?  . . .  O  74 Tr. Iliad Bk 6       4
      Breathless at length they leave th' unfinish'd war  . . O  76 Tr Add. Battle      6
      Bear off with eager Haste th' unfinish'd Sentence,  . . O 333 Irene              53
UNFIT
      Unfit for Toil, and polish'd into Weakness,  . . . . . O 290 Irene               43
      Unfit to share this Night's illustrious Toils?  . . .  O 305 Irene               21
UNFOLD
      At my Command yon' Iron Gates unfold;  . . . . . . .   O 283 Irene               14
UNFORESEEN
      Foes unforeseen, and Dangers unsuspected.  . . . . .   O 298 Irene               26
UNFORM'D
      Lay pointed at our Batt'ries yet unform'd,  . . . . .  O 273 Irene               25
UNGUARDED
      For Zeal unguarded, undissembled Hate,  . . . . . . .  O 299 Irene               36
UNHAPPY
      Receive th' unhappy ghosts of scornful maids.  . . . . O  83 Epi Dist Moth.      13
      Th' unhappy lovers graves the Myrtle spreads;  . . . . O  95 Sprig of Myrtl      10
      Unhappy man! behold thy doom,   . . . . . . .         O 124 Winter's Walk       14
      Unhappy! whcm to beds of pain  . . . . . .             O 125 An Ode               9
      Unhappy Lot of all that shine in Courts;  . . . . . .  O 256 Irene               50
      Farewell, unhappy Maid, may ev'ry Joy  . . . . . . .   O 322 Irene               57
      Unhappy Fair! Compassion calls upon me  . . . . . .    O 327 Irene                4
      And wept unhappy Pompey's hapless fate?  . . . . . .   Y  22 Tr Add. Battle      15
UNHARMONICUS
      Mine unharmonious verse profanes  . . . . . . . . .    O  80 Feast St Simon      58
UNHEARD
      Rolls half his Floods unheard through shouting Camps? . O 264 Irene              18
      Pours half his Floods unheard through shouting camps . . O 353 Irene           V 32
      And should he fall unheard, by sudden Justice,  . . .  O 273 Irene               41
      Doom'd to her Death unpity'd and unheard,  . . . . .   O 332 Irene               20
UNHEEDED
      Unknown, unheeded, long his Offspring lay,  . . . . .  O  58 Prologue Comus      25
      A floating Atom, Dust that falls unheeded  . . . . .   O 260 Irene              139
      Irene steals unheeded from his Tongue,  . . . . . .    O 261 Irene                5
      Th' important Hour had pass'd unheeded by,  . . . . .  O 269 Irene               12
      To rave unheeded, while the happy Greek,  . . . . . .  O 285 Irene                2
      I stole unheeded from their ravish'd Eyes,  . . . . .  O 299 Irene               49
UNHEEDING
      Inforc'd we love, unheeding recollect.  . . . . . . .  O 134 Tr. Rambler 96       2
UNHURT
      Unhurt by Phoebus fi'ry ray.  . . . . . . . . . .      O  72 Hor. Epode II       36
      Has heard unhurt the cries of slaughterd thousands  . . Y 126 Irene            V 145
UNINJUR'D
      And pass'd uninjur'd through the Walks of Death?  . . . O 296 Irene              29
```

		PAGE	TITLE	LINE
UNITE				
	Though gold and silk their charms unite,	O 119	To Miss Purse	1
	Sure all unite to hold her League of Rule	O 257	Irene	62
	That useful truth with humour may unite,	Y 67	Prologue Lethe	15
UNITED				
	Who hail'd him Speaker, with united voice.	O 118	Epitaph Hanmer	20
	Go then, and with united Eloquence	O 306	Irene	57
UNITES				
	Unites the jarring voices of mankind	Y 136	Irene	V 32A
UNIVERSAL				
	Till fame supplies the universal charm.	O 39	Vanity Wishes	184
	Fill the loud Voice of universal Praise,	O 57	Prologue Comus	16
	Bright Stella, form'd for universal Reign,	O 96	Hickman Spinet	1
	The universal smile of joyfull nature	Y 190	Irene	V 9
UNJUSTLY				
	Hippolytus unjustly slain	O 232	Tr Horace IV.7	25
	Unjustly mortals triumph and complain	Y 217	Irene	V 14
UNKINDLED				
	Unactive (unkindled) in the breast--rouse it	Y 133	Irene	V 19
UNKNOWN				
	Unknown, unheeded, long his Offspring lay,	O 58	Prologue Comus	25
	To distant realms and climes unknown,	O 70	Hor.II Ode XX	18
	While Love, unknown amongst the blest,	O 99	Ode Friendship	V 5
	At Midnight's private Hour a Voice unknown	O 254	Irene	121
	Two Men unknown, the Partners of his Bosom;	O 275	Irene	80
	When Purity, while Fraud was yet unknown,	O 314	Irene	6
UNLAMENTED				
	Live unregarded, unlamented die.	O 14	London	82
UNLESS				
	Unless the soul, to vice a thrall,	O 129	Tr. Rambler 6	1
	Unless the beauteous Fabrick was design'd	O 277	Irene	28
UNLIKE				
	Unlike the ribald, whose licentious jest	O 130	Tr. Rambler 12	1
	Unlike the trifling Race of vulgar Beauties,	O 298	Irene	18
UNLOCK'D				
	Then when repeated bowls unlock'd the heart	Y 11	Tr Hor Epode 9	17
UNLOCKS				
	Unlocks his gold, and counts it till he dies.	O 44	Vanity Wishes	290
UNLOV'D				
	Where wealth unlov'd without a mourner dy'd,	O 33	Vanity Wishes	55
UNMINDFUL				
	And utters Fate, unmindful of Abdalla.	O 306	Irene	3
UNMINDFULL				
	He stop unmindfull of observing crowds	Y 187	Irene	V 5
UNMINGLED				
	Are these th' unceasing Joys, th' unmingled Pleasures	O 314	Irene	16
UNMOV'D				
	Unmov'd tho' Witlings sneer and Rivals rail;	O 246	Irene Prologue	29
	Unmov'd I saw the glitt'ring Trifles perish,	O 302	Irene	108
UNNERV'D				
	Unnerv'd with shrieks the soldier's vig'rous arm	Y 163	Irene	V 48
UNNERVE				
	Unnerve thy vigour, and enchain thy pow'rs;	O 151	The Ant	V 10
UNNUMBER'D				
	Unnumber'd suppliants croud Preferment's gate,	O 33	Vanity Wishes	73
	Unnumber'd maladies his joints invade,	O 44	Vanity Wishes	283
	Unnumber'd maladies each Joint invade,	O 44	Vanity Wishes	V 283
	From Isther's flood unnumber'd flocks arise	Y 24	Tr Add. Battle	69
UNOFFENDED				
	Is sure the Smile of unoffended Heav'n.	O 314	Irene	9
UNPERCEIV'D				
	An age that melts with unperceiv'd decay,	O 44	Vanity Wishes	293
	An age that melts in unperceiv'd decay,	O 44	Vanity Wishes	V 293
	And mingles unperceiv'd with ev'ry Thought.	O 261	Irene	6
	And varied Life steal unperceiv'd away.	O 279	Irene	91
	Oer whom the seasons varied unperceiv'd	Y 163	Irene	V 43
	Steal unperceiv'd upon her Meditations--	O 314	Irene	13
UNPITY'D				
	Doom'd to her Death unpity'd and unheard,	O 332	Irene	20
UNPITYING				
	Unpitying see them weep, and hear them pray,	O 83	Epi Dist Moth.	8
	Unpitying Massacre might waste the World,	O 291	Irene	65
	Th' unpitying Ministers of Turkish Justice,	O 325	Irene	9
UNPOLISH'D				
	My rude unpolish'd song;	O 80	Feast St Simon	57
UNPRACTIS'D				
	Th' unpractis'd Dervise, or sequester'd Faquir.	O 281	Irene	37
UNPRIZ'D				
	Obscure, unpriz'd, and dark, the magnet lies,	O 141	Tr Rambler 199	1
UNPROFITABLE				
	Unprofitable, peaceful, female Virtues!	O 280	Irene	12
UNPUNISH'D				
	Shall then the Greeks, unpunish'd and conceal'd,	O 312	Irene	1
UNPURSU'D				
	Perhaps ev'n now the Lovers unpursu'd	O 322	Irene	4
UNQUENCH'D				
	Unquench'd the thirst of gain is found;	O 144	Tr Boeth. II.2	12
UNQUESTICN'D				
	Th' unquestion'd Claim of Conquerors, and Kings!	O 286	Irene	9
UNQUIET				
	Watch each unquiet Flutter of the Breast,	O 320	Irene	24

		PAGE	TITLE	LINE
UNREAD				
The Laws unread, and flies to his Irene.		O 296	Irene	2
UNREFIN'D				
Thy praise to merit unrefin'd.		O 201	Death Dr Levet	12
UNREGARDED				
Live unregarded, unlamented die.		O 14	London	82
It spreads the wide plain an unregarded ruin.		Y 131	Irene	V 36C
And leaves the lovely Trifler unregarded		O 276	Irene	23
And then leaves your actions the busy trifler unregarded		O 355	Irene	V 12
UNRELENTED				
Inflame with unrelented fires.		Y 71	Ode Friendship	V 8
UNRELENTING				
And unrelenting sport ten thousand lives away;		O 83	Epi Dist Moth.	9
Beneath each Curse of unrelenting Heav'n,		O 292	Irene	86
UNREMITTED				
Year chases year, with unremitted flight,		O 152	The Ant	14
UNREPRESS'D				
Grief and Madness unrepress'd		O 148	Tr Boet III.12	13
UNRESISTED				
Till conquest unresisted ceas'd to please,		O 34	Vanity Wishes	107
And unresisted Passion storm'd the Breast.		O 51	Pro Drury-Lane	8
Did unresisted Lightning aid their Cannon,		O 251	Irene	54
Tore unresisted from the Giant Hand		O 312	Irene	10
Tore, unresisted, from the mighty hand		Y 188	Irene	V 10
The valiant Prince with unresisted force		Y 25	Tr Add. Battle	118
UNRESTRAIN'D				
Frowns unrestrain'd, and dooms me with his Eyes.		O 257	Irene	72
UNREWARDED				
Since unrewarded science toils in vain;		O 10	London	38
Lest unrewarded Mercy lose its Charms.		O 313	Irene	19
UNSEEN				
And leaves, unseen, a dagger in your breast.		O 21	London	241
And plants, unseen, a dagger in your breast.		O 21	London	V 241
Those holy Beings whose unseen Direction		O 346	Irene	V 5
Our Bark unseen has reach'd th' appointed Bay,		O 304	Irene	1
Close, as we might unseen, we watch'd his Steps;		O 311	Irene	2
UNSETTLED				
Young, and unsettled in his Father's Kingdoms,		O 257	Irene	67
Freed from the Tumults of unsettled Conquest,		O 291	Irene	77
UNSHAKEN				
Unshaken be thy Throne as Earth's firm Base,		O 262	Irene	2
This fierce Virago, fearless and unshaken		O 364	Irene	V 13
This fierce virago, fearless and unshaken		Y 162	Irene	V 40
Is this th' unshaken Confidence in Heav'n?		O 314	Irene	18
UNSKILFUL				
From giddy Mahomet's unskilful Hand.		O 256	Irene	46
UNSTEADY				
When grasping Bliss th' unsteady mind		O 150	Tr Boet III.12	56
UNSUCCESSFUL				
When unsuccessful Wars, and civil Factions,		O 256	Irene	41
UNSULLIED				
Unsullied fame, and conscience ever gay.		O 14	London	90
UNSUPPORTED				
But when an earthquake comes weak and unsupported		Y 131	Irene	V 36B
UNSUSPECTED				
And wait Abdalla's unsuspected Visits:		O 260	Irene	145
Foes unforeseen, and Dangers unsuspected.		O 298	Irene	26
UNSUSPECTING				
This Hour I'll beg, with unsuspecting Face,		O 258	Irene	86
UNTAINTED				
Untainted with the Lust of Innovation,		O 257	Irene	61
UNTASTED				
There shall we find the yet untasted Bliss		O 292	Irene	88
UNTO				
When once unto the bottom I		O 159	Par Hermit III	7
UNTOUCH'D				
Untouch'd his cottage, and his slumbers sound,		O 32	Vanity Wishes	35
Untouch'd by fierce Ambition's raging Fires.		O 293	Irene	110
Urg'd me to dash it to the Ground untouch'd,		O 316	Irene	28
UNTRAVELL'D				
Far as Futurity's untravell'd Waste		O 300	Irene	68
UNTWIN'D				
Had not the Breeze untwin'd the meeting Boughs,		O 269	Irene	10
UNUS'D				
Unus'd to Power, and form'd for humbler Scenes,		O 268	Irene	17
UNUSUAL				
Whose early buds unusual glories wear,		Y 3	On a Daffodill	3
UNUTTERABLE				
Unutterable Anguish:		O 328	Irene	49
UNVARYING				
Virtue is uncha unvarying as its Authour		O 348	Irene	V 23
Virtue is fixd unvarying as its Author		O 348	Irene	V 23
UNWHOLESOME				
Unwholesome Sirius' sultry reign;		O 69	Hor.II Ode 14	16
UNWIELDY				
Or seen a new-made mayor's unwieldy state;		O 33	Vanity Wishes	58
Or seen the new-made mayor's unwieldy state;		Y 94	Vanity Wishes	V 58
UNWILLING				
At length th' unwilling Sun resigns the World		O 302	Irene	1
Forgive, fair Excellence, th' unwilling Tongue,		O 324	Irene	1

	PAGE	TITLE	LINE
UNWILLING (CONTINUED)			
And stop'd unwilling at her door.	Y 11	Tr Hor Epode 9	34
UNWILLINGLY			
I scorn a Trust unwillingly repos'd;	O 256	Irene	34
UNWISE			
Shall deem our hoar progenitors unwise.	O 192	Tr. Medea II	4
UNWORTHY			
Claim my divided Soul. This Wretch unworthy	O 275	Irene	69
UP			
And shuts up all the passages of joy:	O 43	Vanity Wishes	260
The nurse took up the squealing child, ...	O 157	Par. Hermit I	3
Have drank the liquor up.	O 159	Par Hermit III	8
The groaning Greeks break up their golden Caverns . .	O 249	Irene	17
To offer up my vows in the temple built by the Father of Mankind	O 348	Irene	V 1
The banefull weeds spring up, and choak the grain. . .	Y 7	Virgil Daphnis	23
UPBRAID			
Upbraid me not with fancy'd Wickedness, ...	O 289	Irene	21
UPBRAIDING			
Does envy seize thee? crush th' upbraiding joy, . .	O 32	Vanity Wishes	39
Hide me, oh hide me from upbraiding Greece, ...	O 316	Irene	12
UPHELD			
In former ages while upheld by fate	Y 23	Tr Add. Battle	26
UPON			
Where Greenwich smiles upon the silver flood: . . .	O 10	London	22
There ev'ry breeze bears health upon its wings; . .	O 20	London	221
And frighted, left upon the field, ...	O 73	Hor. Epode II	66
Th' enormous Gyants smoke upon the Ground.	O 76	Tr Add. Battle	25
Upon the feast of St Simon & St Jude	O 78	Feast St Simon	T
Dr. Johnson upon Friendship	O 99	Ode Friendship	V T
An Epitaph upon the celebrated Claudy Philips, . . .	O 113	Epit. Phillips	V T
To Miss <Carpenter> On her playing upon the Harpsicord .	O 120	To Miss Playin	T
Safe upon the rocky Ground, ...	O 145	Tr Boeth. II.4	15
Fell down upon the stone;	O 157	Par. Hermit I	2
Fell down upon a stone;	O 157	Par. Hermit I	V 2
I put my hat upon my head	O 158	Par. Hermit II	1
As with my hat upon my head	O 158	Par. Hermit II	V 1
And only build upon another's ruin.	O 176	Tr Metastas II	13
"Drop asleep upon his lyre.	O 186	Anacreon Ode 9	40
In Triumph sits upon our shatter'd Spires, ...	O 251	Irene	67
In triumph sits upon the ruin'd Spires	O 351	Irene	V 6
When the tenth Sun had set upon our Sorrows, . . .	O 254	Irene	120
Has Silence press'd her Seal upon his Lips?	O 255	Irene	20
What Hopes, what Terrors rush upon my Soul!	O 259	Irene	104
And seeks the Shades to muse upon Irene;	O 261	Irene	4
And wearied angels rest upon their stars spheres . .	Y 128	Irene	V 4B
And dwell upon the Beauties of Irene.	O 262	Irene	10
And ease my loaded Soul upon her Bosom?	O 263	Irene	22
Could bear his Son upon the Turkish Throne.	O 264	Irene	22
Swift, let us rush upon the careless Tyrant, . . .	O 271	Irene	31
I see the Gloom that low'rs upon thy Brow, ...	O 271	Irene	1
Then leave him stretch'd upon the ling'ring Rack, . .	O 273	Irene	36
Should the fierce North upon his frozen Wings . . .	O 274	Irene	61
And softer passion steals upon my Bosom	O 367	Irene	V 14
Profusely pour'd her Bounties upon Woman?	O 276	Irene	25
Aspasia! who can look upon thy Beauties?	O 281	Irene	42
When will Occasion smile upon our Wishes, ...	O 282	Irene	1
Born down with Years, still doat upon To-morrow? . .	O 283	Irene	20
Marks for His own still doat upon to Morrow	O 374	Irene	V 21
To gaze with longing Eyes upon To-morrow, ...	O 283	Irene	24
Dwells on her Lips, and sighs upon her Breast; . . .	O 286	Irene	5
Disorder sits upon thy Face--retire.	O 286	Irene	17
Detain me here. But Nations call upon me, ...	O 288	Irene	12
Pour'd Storms of Fire upon our fierce Invaders, . .	O 290	Irene	48
Pourd Storms of fire upon th' approaching Foe . . .	O 364	Irene	V 1
Close like th' eternal Bars of Death upon thee, . .	O 292	Irene	80
Close like th' eternal Bars of Death upon You . . .	O 357	Irene	V 10
That pours the dews upon the thristy vales	Y 168	Irene	V135C
Recline upon my Breast thy sinking Beauties:	O 295	Irene	8
A thousand Questions press upon my Tongue, ...	O 295	Irene	19
Say, how thou call'dst in Tears upon Demetrius! . .	O 295	Irene	26
Approving Justice smiles upon your Cause, ...	O 297	Irene	2
Then while he gaz'd upon his yielding Mistress, . .	O 299	Irene	48
To live obscure upon a foreign Coast, ...	O 301	Irene	104
Wilt thou then head the Troop upon the Shore, . . .	O 305	Irene	36
Shall shed his Beams upon the bridal Bed, ...	O 309	Irene	24
Nor press too much upon a Lover's Patience.	O 310	Irene	9
Steal unperceiv'd upon her Meditations--	O 314	Irene	13
Hang Sit these black clouds upon Aspasia's brow? . .	Y 191	Irene	V 15
The Pow'r of Turkey waits upon my Call.	O 319	Irene	24
Will spread resistless Light upon my Soul.	O 321	Irene	47
Their Treason throws no Stain upon Irene.	O 324	Irene	18
Unhappy Fair! Compassion calls upon me	O 327	Irene	4
Let me but live, heap Woes on Woes upon me, ...	O 328	Irene	33
Be charg'd upon my Soul. O, Mercy! Mercy!	O 329	Irene	55
Heav'n turns its point upon the guilty Heart . . .	O 345	Irene	V 29
Together rise and shoot upon the wing.	Y 24	Tr Add. Battle	73
URG'D			
Urg'd headlong on by hatred or by love:	O 77	Festina Lente	6
Urg'd by th' imperious Soldier's fierce Command, . .	O 249	Irene	16
Let Prudence, ere the Suit be farther urg'd, . . .	O 285	Irene	8

URG'D   (CONTINUED)   PAGE   TITLE   LINE
      Urg'd me to dash it to the Ground untouch'd, ...   O 316 Irene   28
      Urg'd us to Speed, and bad us banish Pity, ...   O 332 Irene   30
      Whether urg'd on by seers from heav'n inspir'd   . . . .   Y 19 Tr. Iliad Bk 6   58
URGE
      More safely truth to urge her claim presumes, ...   O 134 Tr. Rambler 93   1
      Fear and Ambition, urge her to Compliance;   . . . .   O 261 Irene   13
      The loudest Cries of Nature urge us forward;   . . . .   O 270 Irene   15
      Forbear--O do not urge me to my Ruin! . . .   .   O 278 Irene   79
      Urge me not on to glittering Guilt, nor pour   . . . .   O 288 Irene   5
      I go, lest Vengeance urge my Hand to Blood, ...   O 324 Irene   23
US
      Quick let us rise, the happy seats explore, ...   O 18 London   174
      And rais'd us from our wretched state, ...   O 79 Feast St Simon   20
      O guide us through life's darksome way, ...   O 100 Ode Friendship   V 14
      What dreary prospects round us rise, ...   O 123 Winter's Walk   2
      The skies are open--let us try the skies: . . . .   O 136 Tr. Rambler 129   5
      That glad us with vicarious light;   . . . .   O 144 Tr Boeth. II.2   4
      The rites that taught us to combine   . . . .   O 190 Tr. Medea I   3
      Will toss us in a morning more? . . . .   O 232 Tr Horace IV.7   18
      Will rouse us in a morning more? . . .   .   O 232 Tr Horace IV.7   V 18
      Who thinks us Women born to dress and sing   . . . .   O 247 Irene Epilogue   2
      But how the Devil should he please us all!   . . . .   O 247 Irene Epilogue   8
      For us alone, they Honour's Paths pursue: . . . .   O 247 Irene Epilogue   16
      Inspir'd by us, they Glory's Heights ascend;   . . . .   O 247 Irene Epilogue   17
      For us the Statesman labours, Hero fights, ...   O 247 Irene Epilogue   21
      Or wake the Dead to warn us of its Fall?   . . . .   O 250 Irene   47
      Pour forth her Dead to warn us of its fall? . . . .   O 365 Irene   V 22
      Did roaring Whirlwinds sweep us from the Ramparts: . .   O 251 Irene   55
      Perhaps the flood of time now rolls towards us   . . . .   Y 117 Irene   V 108
      And bids us thus disguis'd await him here.   . . . .   O 253 Irene   115
      Attends to waft us to Repose and Safety. . . . .   O 258 Irene   82
      They sympathise with us in every fear . . . .   Y 134 Irene   V 26
      Soon would his Art or Valour set us free, ...   O 267 Irene   43
      And bear us far from Servitude and Crimes.   . . . .   O 267 Irene   44
      The loudest Cries of Nature urge us forward;   . . . .   O 270 Irene   15
      Swift, let us rush upon the careless Tyrant, ...   O 271 Irene   31
      Then let us now resolve, nor idly waste . . .   .   O 271 Irene   33
      Then let us now resolve, nor idle waste . . .   .   O 271 Irene   V 33
      Treason so near us? at the dreadfull name of   . . . .   O 369 Irene   V 20
         Treason
      Treason so near us? lurking in our Palace   . . . .   O 369 Irene   V 20
      Deceive--And make us happy by deceiving . . .   .   Y 148 Irene   V 50
      And share the Pleasures of the World . . . .   O 348 Irene   V 20
         between Us
      Pants for the dread Event--But let us reason--   . . . .   O 280 Irene   31
      Lead us to Danger, and abash their Victors? . . . . .   O 284 Irene   43
      Nor left us aught but Flattery and State.   . . . .   O 291 Irene   73
      He comes, perhaps, to separate us forever;   . . . .   O 294 Irene   6
      That joins us thus, will never part us more.   . . . .   O 296 Irene   39
      That joins us thus, will never part us more.   . . . .   O 296 Irene   39
      No! let us die together. . . . .   O 297 Irene   11
      Forbear this Triumph--still new Conflicts wait us, . .   O 298 Irene   25
      Well known, long try'd, expect us on the Shore. . .   O 301 Irene   91
      Now let us wait the last Award of Heav'n, ...   O 302 Irene   113
      Now hover o'er us with propitious Wings, ...   O 306 Irene   51
      now hover oer us and direct our councils . . . .   Y 181 Irene   V 51
      And heard within the Thicket that conceal'd us, . . .   O 311 Irene   12
      Fly, fly, my Love, Destruction rushes on us, ...   O 315 Irene   1
      The Back expects us, and the Sword pursues. . . . .   O 315 Irene   2
      Whose Fear, or Rage, or Treachery betray'd us.   . . . .   O 316 Irene   17
      Then all is past he cried--and darted from us;   . . . .   O 317 Irene   32
      Amazement seiz'd us, and the hoary Bassa . . . .   O 317 Irene   36
      Let us not struggle with th' eternal Will, ...   O 320 Irene   16
      A Galley waits us, and the Winds invite. . . . .   O 321 Irene   52
      Come let us seek new Pleasures in the Palace, ...   O 323 Irene   17
      Till soft Fatigue invite us to repose. . . . .   O 323 Irene   18
      Deem us not deaf to Woe, nor blind to Beauty, ...   O 327 Irene   29
      But let us try to clear our clouded Brows, ...   O 329 Irene   10
      Your fierce Impatience forc'd us from your Presence, . . O 332 Irene   29
      Urg'd us to Speed, and bad us banish Pity, ...   O 332 Irene   30
      Urg'd us to Speed, and bad us banish Pity, ...   O 332 Irene   30
US'RER
      Thus did the Us'rer Alphius praise, ...   O 73 Hor. Epode II   73
USE
      Form'd to delight, they use no foreign arms, ...   O 84 Epi Dist Moth.   22
      Here let me learn the use of life, ...   O 125 An Ode   27
      The better use of notes, or sweet or shrill, ...   O 192 Tr. Medea II   9
      That Wealth, too sacred for their Country's Use! . . .   O 250 Irene   20
      Yet in the Use of Pow'r remember Justice. . . . . .   O 286 Irene   10
      Derives its Value from its Use alone; . . . .   O 290 Irene   29
USEFUL
      In useful satire warn succeeding times;   . . . .   Y 61 London   V 259
      For useful Mirth, and salutary Woe;   . . . .   O 53 Pro Drury-Lane   60
      By harmless merriment, or useful sense.   . . . .   O 62 Pro Word Wise   14
      His useful care was ever nigh, ...   O 201 Death Dr Levet   18
      His useful aid was ever nigh . . . .   O 201 Death Dr Levet   V 18
      That useful truth with humour may unite, ...   Y 67 Prologue Lethe   15
USELESS
      All useless science is an empty boast. . . . .   O 133 Tr. Rambler 83   1
      How long shall sloth usurp thy useless hours, ...   O 151 The Ant   9

		PAGE	TITLE	LINE
USELESS	**(CONTINUED)**			
	An useless Life in waiting for To-morrow, ...	O 283	Irene	23
	Nor rush on useless Wounds with idle Courage.	O 318	Irene	10
	Its useless force the weapon spends in air.	Y 26	Tr Add. Battle	135
USURP				
	I feel thy pow'r usurp my breast.	O 123	Winter's Walk	8
	How long shall sloth usurp thy useless hours, ...	O 151	The Ant	9
	And of his every gift usurp the merit;	O 176	Tr Metastas II	11
	And yet of every gift usurp the merit;	O 176	Tr Metastas II	V 11
	Usurp our Temples, and profane our Altars.	O 251	Irene	69
	Nor thus usurp the Dignity of Virtue.	O 323	Irene	10
USURPER'S				
	And fix the fierce Usurper's bloody Title.	O 291	Irene	62
USURPS				
	In vain proud Man usurps what's Woman's Due;	O 247	Irene Epilogue	15
	Habitual Cowardice usurps the Soul.	O 266	Irene	33
UTMOST				
	And deride their utmost Rage.	O 145	Tr Boeth. II.4	22
UTTER				
	Utter sad groans and lamentable cries.	O 76	Tr Add. Battle	29
	Then shall you feel what Language cannot utter, . . .	O 326	Irene	43
	This forc'd the Cranes to utter dolefull moans, . . .	Y 24	Tr Add. Battle	88
UTTERS				
	And utters Fate, unmindful of Abdalla.	O 306	Irene	3
VACANT				
	Some vain Amusement of a vacant Soul!	O 280	Irene	8
VAGRANT				
	Then thro' the world a wretched vagrant roam, ...	O 18	London	190
VAGRANTS				
	The glitt'ring vagrants shall restrain;	O 120	To Miss Purse	10
VAIN				
	Since unrewarded science toils in vain;	O 10	London	38
	And strive in vain to laugh at Hervey's jest. . . .	O 13	London	74
	And strive in vain to laugh at Clodio's jest. . . .	O 13	London	V 74
	And flattery subdues when arms are vain?	O 16	London	122
	And flattery prevails when arms are vain.	O 16	London	V 122
	These arts in vain our rugged natives try, ...	O 16	London	129
	In vain your mournful narrative disclose, ...	O 19	London	192
	Some fiery fop, with new commission vain, ...	O 21	London	226
	So some fiery fop, with new commission vain, ...	Y 59	London	V 226
	In vain, these dangers past, your doors you close, . .	O 21	London	236
	Whose joys are causeless, or whose griefs are vain. . .	O 33	Vanity Wishes	68
	And Sloth effuse her opiate fumes in vain;	O 37	Vanity Wishes	150
	And Sloth's bland Opiates shed their fumes in vain;	O 37	Vanity Wishes	V 150
	In vain surrounding kings their pow'rs combine, . . .	Y 101	Vanity Wishes	V 199
	Peace courts his hand, but spreads her charms in vain; .	O 40	Vanity Wishes	201
	In vain their gifts the bounteous seasons pour, . . .	O 43	Vanity Wishes	261
	And Pride and Prudence take her seat in vain.	O 46	Vanity Wishes	336
	Which heav'n may hear, nor deem religion vain. . . .	O 47	Vanity Wishes	350
	And panting Time toil'd after him in vain;	O 51	Pro Drury-Lane	6
	That never Briton can in vain excel;	O 57	Prologue Comus	12
	That never Britain can in vain excel;	O 57	Prologue Comus	V 12
	He sees, and pitying sees, vain Wealth bestow . . .	O 57	Prologue Comus	21
	In vain you spend your vows and prayers, ...	O 68	Hor.II Ode 14	3
	In vain we shun the Din of War, ...	O 69	Hor.II Ode 14	13
	In vain with anxious breasts we fear	O 69	Hor.II Ode 14	15
	Impending death they strive to 'scape in vain . . .	O 76	Tr Add. Battle	30
	The limits fix'd they strive to pass in vain; . . .	O 76	Tr Add. Battle	36
	In vain proud tyrants strove to shake	O 79	Feast St Simon	13
	Warn'd by another's fate, vain youth, be wise, . . .	O 82	Young Author	23
	In vain for thee the monarch sighs, ...	O 100	Ode Friendship	19
	In vain for thee the tyrant sighs, ...	O 100	Ode Friendship	V 19
	At length must Suffolk's beauties shine in vain, . . .	O 107	Lady F Assizes	1
	In vain the vary'd work would shine, ...	O 119	To Miss Purse	3
	Deceitful Hope, and vain Desire, ...	O 121	To Miss Playin	13
	Tir'd with vain joys, and false alarms, ...	O 124	Winter's Walk	17
	Whom smiling nature courts in vain, ...	O 125	An Ode	11
	Wild hope, vain fear, alike remov'd, ...	O 125	An Ode	26
	For healthful indigence in vain they pray, ...	O 132	Tr. Rambler 48	1
	At busy hearts in vain love's arrows fly;	O 133	Tr. Rambler 85	1
	Vain man runs headlong, to caprice resign'd;	O 134	Tr Rambler 105	1
	In vain the shining Gifts are sent, ...	O 144	Tr Boeth. II.4	13
	Tossing rave but rave in vain	O 144	Tr Boeth. II.4	6
	"But the liberal grant in vain	O 185	Anacreon Ode 9	21
	Diana calls to life in vain, ...	O 232	Tr Horace IV.7	26
	With Merit needless, and without it vain.	O 246	Irene Prologue	32
	In vain proud Man usurps what's Woman's Due;	O 247	Irene Epilogue	15
	These Groans were fatal, these Disguises vain: . . .	O 249	Irene	6
	Vain expence the parent of necessity the parent of corruption	O 347	Irene	V 26
	Ill-fated Race! So oft besieg'd in vain, ...	O 250	Irene	29
	In vain, when Turkey's troops assail'd our Walls, . . .	O 253	Irene	117
	If chasing past Events with vain Pursuit, ...	O 255	Irene	5
	Burning in vain, delays the Stroke of Death?	O 257	Irene	66
	With vain (fruitless) labour of the daring flight . . .	Y 127	Irene	V 3
	Vain Raptures all--For your inferiour Natures . . .	O 276	Irene	15
	Why then has Nature's vain Munificence	O 276	Irene	24
	Why then did Natures vain Munificence	O 355	Irene	V 13
	Some vain Amusement of a vacant Soul!	O 280	Irene	8
	Because my slighted Passion burns in vain!	O 281	Irene	49

VAIN   (CONTINUED)   PAGE   TITLE   LINE

Entry	Page	Title	Line
What I can grant, you cannot ask in vain—	O 285	Irene	14
And sigh for chearful Poverty in vain;	O 292	Irene	84
Still stretch in vain their longing Arms afar;	O 292	Irene	91
Say, how he threaten'd, flatter'd, sigh'd in vain!	O 295	Irene	24
But flatter'd threatend, sigh'd and rag'd in vain	Y 170	Irene	V 24
Sure Heav'n, for Wonders are not wrought in vain,	O 296	Irene	38
And find our Passions not infus'd in vain.	O 297	Irene	22
Perhaps in vain the Sultan's Anger spar'd me,	O 298	Irene	32
Vain pride & wealth	Y 177	Irene	V 110
And subject Seas roar round their Queen in vain.	O 309	Irene	29
For when was Pow'r beneficent in vain?	O 313	Irene	23
For Non Who was e'er beneficent in vain?	O 377	Irene	V 4
In vain affected Raptures flush the Cheek,	O 315	Irene	29
Return'd with Force that made Resistance vain,	O 317	Irene	38
Infatuate Loiterer, has Fate, in vain,	O 318	Irene	15
Luckless slave Ilfated loiterer has fate in vain	Y 196	Irene	V 15
In vain I listen to th' inviting Call	O 320	Irene	10
In vain I listen to the inviting voice	Y 198	Irene	V 10
Insidious Malice aims her Darts in vain;	O 322	Irene	2
But Cries and Tears are vain, prepare with Patience	O 328	Irene	40
And disappointed Vengeance burns in vain;	O 330	Irene	6
And wish'd—Be still thy Fate to wish in vain.	O 334	Irene	60
And mortals trace th' Almighty's path in v<ain>	Y 217	Irene	V 14
And trace the paths of providence in vain.	Y 217	Irene	V 15
So late admir'd and prais'd, alas! in vain!	Y 4	On a Daffodill	24
In vain the lab'ring hind manures the plain,	Y 6	Virgil Daphnis	22
Your sighs are spent in vain; if fates withstand	Y 21	Tr. Iliad Bk 6	115
In vain, from heaven's black concave, like a cloud,	Y 23	Tr Add. Battle	20
Wounded and spent, in vain they strive to rise	Y 24	Tr Add. Battle	60

VAINLY

Entry	Page	Title	Line
Verse and Music vainly strove;	O 149	Tr Boet III.12	16

VALE

Entry	Page	Title	Line
Some peaceful vale with nature's paintings gay;	O 11	London	46
Perennial roses deck each purple vale,	O 84	Epi Dist Moth.	16
Their hungry Swarms the peaceful Vale shall fright	O 110	To Posterity	9
In a low vale by rocks that pierce the skies	Y 23	Tr Add. Battle	24

VALES

Entry	Page	Title	Line
He scorns the flow'ry vales and verdant fields;	O 81	Young Author	4
The Lilies o'er the Vales triumphant spread;	O 111	To Posterity	18
Here let me thro' the vales pursue	O 125	An Ode	21
That pours the dews upon the thristy vales	Y 168	Irene	V135C

VALGIUS

Entry	Page	Title	Line
Nor, Valgius, on th' Armenian shores	O 67	Hor. II Ode IX	5

VALIANT

Entry	Page	Title	Line
Who hath not heard of Argo's valiant crew?	Y 22	Tr Add. Battle	10
The valiant Prince with unresisted force	Y 25	Tr Add. Battle	118

VALLIES

Entry	Page	Title	Line
And heap their vallies with the gaudy foe;	O 42	Vanity Wishes	236
While fair Hungaria's unexhausted Vallies	O 264	Irene	16
While fair yet Hungaria's inexhausted Vallies	O 352	Irene	V 33

VALOUR

Entry	Page	Title	Line
Soon would his Art or Valour set us free,	O 267	Irene	43

VALUE

Entry	Page	Title	Line
Derives its Value from its Use alone;	O 290	Irene	29

VANE

Entry	Page	Title	Line
Yet Vane could tell what ills from beauty spring;	O 45	Vanity Wishes	321

VANISH

Entry	Page	Title	Line
Dissolve in Air, and vanish into Nothing.	O 265	Irene	8
Fade <glide> from the sight, and Vanish into nothing.	O 358	Irene	V 11

VANITIES

Entry	Page	Title	Line
The glitt'ring Vanities of empty Greatness,	O 265	Irene	6

VANITY

Entry	Page	Title	Line
The Vanity of Human Wishes. ...	O 29	Vanity Wishes	T
Who frown with vanity, who smile with art,	O 46	Vanity Wishes	327

VANQUISH'D

Entry	Page	Title	Line
The vanquish'd hero leaves his broken bands,	O 41	Vanity Wishes	211
When vanquish'd Vice shall tyrannize no more.	O 321	Irene	36

VAPOURS

Entry	Page	Title	Line
Far hence are banish'd vapours, spleen, and tears,	O 84	Epi Dist Moth.	18
And pois'nous vapours, black'ning all the sky,	O 84	Epi Dist Moth.	33

VARIED   SEE VARY'D

Entry	Page	Title	Line
And turn the varied taunt a thousand ways.	O 17	London	165
And feed with varied fools th' eternal jest:	O 32	Vanity Wishes	52
His various worth, through varied life attend,	O 117	Epitaph Hanmer	3
May ye the varied blessings share	O 189	Epilogue	5
The board with varied plenty crown'd	O 191	Tr. Medea I	19
With Purple varied and bedrop'd with Gold,	O 277	Irene	35
And varied Life steal unperceiv'd away.	O 279	Irene	91
Are only varied Modes of endless Being;	O 290	Irene	27
Oer whom the seasons varied unperceiv'd	Y 163	Irene	V 43
And if one varied Accent prove thy Falshood,	O 332	Irene	14

VARIETIES

Entry	Page	Title	Line
Whom Joys with soft varieties invite,	O 46	Vanity Wishes	325
And all the sweet varieties of nature	Y 165	Irene	V 79

VARIETY

Entry	Page	Title	Line
Wholsome variety supply.	O 73	Hor. Epode II	62

VARIOUS

Entry	Page	Title	Line
The various arts of Luxury:	O 73	Hor. Epode II	V 56
(His various plumage sporting in the wind)	O 74	Tr. Iliad Bk 6	2

```
VARIOUS          (CONTINUED)                              PAGE    TITLE            LINE
      His various worth, through varied life attend,  . . . . .   O 117 Epitaph Hanmer      3
      Think on the various Accidents of War;  . . . . . . .       O 252 Irene             87
      And various charms displays to various eyes . . . . .       Y 155 Irene          V  27
      And various charms displays to various eyes . . . . .       Y 155 Irene          V  27
      The various charms displays to various eyes . . . . .       O 374 Irene          V  28
      The various charms displays to various eyes . . . . .       O 374 Irene          V  28
VARNISH
      Ne'er knew to puzzle right, or varnish wrong,  . . . . .    O  14 London             80
VARY'D
      In vain the vary'd work would shine,  . . . . . . .         O 119 To Miss Purse        3
VARYING
      Well tried through many a varying year,  . . . . . .        O 201 Death Dr Levet       5
      The varying Seasons, and revolving Skies,  . . . . .        O 293 Irene            118
VASSAL
      How much more safe the vassal than the lord;  . . . .       O  31 Vanity Wishes       32
VASSALS
      See! while he builds, the gaudy vassals come,  . . . .      O  19 London            202
      From every part, the gaudy vassals come,  . . . . . .       Y  57 London        V  202
      Amidst his gloomy Guards and fiery Vassals . . . . .        O 372 Irene          V  19
      Hew down, ye Guards, those Vassals of Distraction,  . .     O 333 Irene             51
VAST
      His vast Designs, his Plans of boundless Pow'r.  . . .      O 265 Irene             41
      His vast designs, and plans of boundless Empire.  . . .     O 356 Irene          V  29
      Fiercely contending two vast armies stood  . . . . .        Y  23 Tr Add. Battle      56
      Hurling vast mounts against the realms above  . . . .       Y  26 Tr Add. Battle     138
VAULT
      Descend, impetuous, from the vault of Heav'n.  . . . .      O  76 Tr Add. Battle      11
VAULTED
      With cedar vaulted and inlayd with gold  . . . . . .        Y 177 Irene          V111F
VEGETATION
      And vegetation paints the plain.  . . . . . . .             O 125 An Ode              8
      And vegetation plants the plain.  . . . . . . .             O 125 An Ode         V   8
VEIL
      Where clouds condens'd for ever veil  . . . . . .           O  66 Hor I Ode xxii      19
      Where Clouds, condens'd, for ever veil  . . . . . .         O  67 To A. Fuscus        19
      Clouds do not always veil the skies,  . . . . . .           O  67 Hor. II Ode IX       1
      Soon as the Veil of Evening clouds the Sky,  . . . .        O 284 Irene             49
VEILS
      The robes of pleasure and the veils of woe:  . . . . .      O  33 Vanity Wishes       66
VEINS
      And life still vig'rous revels in my veins;  . . . . .      O  10 London             42
      Through all his veins the fever of renown  . . . . .        O  36 Vanity Wishes      137
      Should no Disease thy torpid veins invade,  . . . . .       O  37 Vanity Wishes      153
      Nor should disease thy torpid veins invade,  . . . . .      Y  99 Vanity Wishes  V  153
      And, yet more strange! his Veins a Horse shall drain,  . .  O 111 To Posterity        25
      That froze our Veins, and wither'd all our Powers.  . .     O 251 Irene             57
      Flush in my cheek, and wander in my Veins  . . . . .        O 349 Irene          V  26
      And stream destructive through his freezing Veins:  . .     O 308 Irene             31
      Flush in my cheeks, and sally in veins  . . . . . .         Y 189 Irene          V  1E
VELVET
      Ye glitt'ring Train! whom Lace and Velvet bless,  . . .     O 246 Irene Prologue       1
VENAL
      The laureat tribe in venal verse relate,  . . . . .        O  19 London         V  198
      Despise the dainties of a venal lord:  . . . . . .         O  20 London            219
      The gen'rous scorn of venal pow'r,  . . . . . . .          O 125 An Ode              31
      And quit Inachia's venal charms . . . . . . .              I  11 Tr Hor Epode 9      26
      And quite Inachia's venal charms  . . . . . .              Y  11 Tr Hor Epode 9  V  26
VENERABLE
      Beneath some venerable Shade . . . . . . . .               O  72 Hor. Epode II  V  29
      Most venerable Jude!  . . . . . . . . .                    O  80 Feast St Simon      51
      Teach me, thou venerable bow'r,  . . . . . . .             O 125 An Ode              29
      And weeping, kiss the venerable Ruins:  . . . . . .        O 251 Irene             61
      With venerable Cali's faithful Counsels?  . . . . .        O 272 Irene             10
      Ye venerable ghosts of noble patriots  . . . . . .         Y 181 Irene          V  53
VENERATION
      Beheld with love, with veneration heard.  . . . . . .      O 118 Epitaph Hanmer      26
VENETIA
      Then shall Venetia feel the Turkish Pow'r,  . . . . .      O 309 Irene             28
VENGEANCE
      When vengeance listens to the fool's request.  . . . .     O  31 Vanity Wishes       14
      For English vengeance wars not with the dead.  . . . .     O  61 Pro Word Wise        4
      Where Want repines, and Vengeance swells,  . . . . .       O 191 Tr. Medea I         10
      He murmurs Vengeance at the Name of Cali,  . . . . .       O 256 Irene             48
      Shall feel the Vengeance of an injur'd King.  . . . .      O 273 Irene             33
      And though at length subdued, elude thy Vengeance.  . .    O 274 Irene             57
      Elude my Vengeance? no--My Troops shall range  . . . .     O 274 Irene             58
      When eager Vengeance shows a naked Foe,  . . . . .         O 280 Irene             13
      Drive Int'rest, Love, and Vengeance from thy Thoughts,  .  O 298 Irene              7
      I go, lest Vengeance urge my Hand to Blood,  . . . . .     O 324 Irene             23
      That Vengeance can invent, or Pow'r inflict.  . . . .      O 326 Irene             45
      And disappointed Vengeance burns in vain;  . . . . .       O 330 Irene              6
      My Spirits fail, awhile support me, Vengeance--  . . .     O 334 Irene             72
VENGEFUL
      Rebellion's vengeful talons seize on Laud.  . . . . .      O  39 Vanity Wishes      168
VENGEFULL
      By thee Orestes plung'd his vengefull dart  . . . . .      O  77 Festina Lente       13
      And stain'd with blood Pelides' vengefull steel.  . . .    Y  18 Tr. Iliad Bk 6      37
      Provok'd Diana with a vengefull dart  . . . . . .          Y  19 Tr. Iliad Bk 6      42
VENT
      Uncheck'd on both, loud rabbles vent their rage,  . . .    O  59 Pro Good Nat'd      15
```

VENT	(CONTINUED)	PAGE	TITLE	LINE

VENT   (CONTINUED)   PAGE   TITLE   LINE

| Uncheck'd on both, caprice may vent its rage, | O 59 Pro Good Nat'd | V 15 |
| And vent our Suff'rings in clandestine Groans? | O 249 Irene | 4 |

VENT'ROUS

| Where wav'ring man, betray'd by vent'rous pride, | O 31 Vanity Wishes | 7 |

VENTUR'D

| Here life is ventur'd if the streets you roam | Y 59 London | V 224 |

VENTURE

| Well may they venture on the mimick's art, | O 16 London | 134 |
| Yet dares to venture on the dangerous stage, | Y 67 Prologue Lethe | 11 |

VENUS

Consign'd by Venus to Melissa's hand)	O 95 Sprig of Myrtl	4
"Venus, courted with an ode,	O 185 Anacreon Ode 9	11
"Venus, courted by an ode,	O 185 Anacreon Ode 9	V 11
Venus, the sacred Sisters dispossest,	Y 11 Tr Hor Epode 9	5
And gainst the pow'r of Venus steel'd my mind.	Y 11 Tr Hor Epode 9	30

VERDANT

Some pleasing bank where verdant osiers play,	O 11 London	45
Nor showers immerse the verdant plain;	O 67 Hor. II Ode IX	2
He scorns the flow'ry vales and verdant fields;	O 81 Young Author	4
He scorns the verdant meads and flow'ry fields;	O 81 Young Author	V 4
Beneath the Covert of this verdant Arch	O 275 Irene	78
Nor crop'd the tastfull herb, nor trac'd the verdant meads	Y 6 Virgil Daphnis	10
And thrice deform'd the verdant year	Y 11 Tr Hor Epode 9	8

VERDURE

| Unfading Verdure glads the roving Eye, | O 315 Irene | 34 |
| New verdure ev'ry fading leaf shall fill, | Y 4 On a Daffodill | 19 |

VERGE

| Thrown beyond the verge of providence | Y 199 Irene | V 16 |

VERNAL

The fruit autumnal, and the vernal flow'r,	O 43 Vanity Wishes	262
Fenc'd from the summer breeze, and vernal show'r.	Y 163 Irene	V 43
Those glitt'ring Dew-drops of a vernal Morn,	O 298 Irene	19

VERS'D

| Vers'd in the secret Counsels of the Sky. | O 314 Irene | 27 |

VERSE

The laureat tribe in servile verse relate,	O 19 London	198
The laureat tribe in venal verse relate,	O 19 London	V 198
Shall live for ever in my verse.	O 70 Hor.II Ode XX	24
Mine unharmonious verse profanes	O 80 Feast St Simon	58
This tributary verse receive, my fair,	O 80 Lady Birthday	1
And Spenser's verse prolongs Eliza's reign;	O 114 On C. Cibber	2
Verse and Music vainly strove;	O 149 Tr Boet III.12	16
While in my verse the shrilling trumpets sound,	Y 22 Tr Add. Battle	18

VERSES

| Verses, written at the request of a Gentleman | O 95 Sprig of Myrtl | V T |
| Pettius no more I verses write; | Y 10 Tr Hor Epode 9 | 1 |

VERY

| ... Musician, who died very poor | O 113 Epit. Phillips | V T |
| ... at Bridgnorth, Salop; who died very poor | O 113 Epit. Phillips | V T |

VESSEL

That Vessel, if observ'd, alarms the Court,	O 258 Irene	83
Th' appointed Vessel to yon' shaded Bay,	O 284 Irene	51
I see the distant vessel	Y 201 Irene	V 10

VESTED

| "Vested with a master's right | O 185 Anacreon Ode 9 | 13 |

VET'RAN

| Superfluous lags the vet'ran on the stage, | O 45 Vanity Wishes | 308 |
| The Vet'ran Courtier half reveal'd his Project. | O 254 Irene | 132 |

VEX

| Vex ev'ry eye, and every bosom tear; | O 84 Epi Dist Moth. | 39 |

VEXATION

| Vexation, Fury, Jealousy, Despair, | O 84 Epi Dist Moth. | 38 |

VICARIOUS

| That glad us with vicarious light; | O 144 Tr Boeth. II.2 | 4 |

VICE

Resolved at length, from vice and London far,	O 9 London	5
Who now resolves, from vice and London far,	O 9 London	V 5
In those curs'd walls, devote to vice and gain,	O 10 London	37
Exalt each trifle, ev'ry vice adore,	O 17 London	148
Praise evry trifle, ev'ry vice adore,	Y 55 London	V 148
Still foe to vice, forsake his Cambrian shade;	O 23 London	261
Still foe to vice, exert his Cambrian shade;	Y 61 London	V 262
Vice always found a sympathetick Friend;	O 52 Pro Drury-Lane	21
Unless the soul, to vice a thrall,	O 129 Tr. Rambler 6	1
And proves, by Cato's vice, his claim.	O 138 Tr Rambler 164	2
Now say, where virtue stops and vice begins?	O 139 Tr Rambler 173	1
Save him whose Soul enslav'd to Vice	O 147 Tr Boeth III.6	19
Be Vice and Dulness far away	O 154 Epita. Hogarth	7
All that prey on vice and folly	O 196 Song Congratu.	13
And all that prey in vice or folly	O 196 Song Congratu.	V 13
Vice the harbinger of ruin.	Y 114 Irene	V 39
'Twas Vice that shook our Nerves, 'twas Vice, Leontius	O 251 Irene	56
'Twas Vice that shook our Nerves, 'twas Vice, Leontius	O 251 Irene	56
And know'st the Characters of Vice and Virtue,	O 255 Irene	12
But the sight of friends soul sinking into vice (a soul	Y 177 Irene	V111C
And War o'erwhelm them in their Dream of Vice.	O 309 Irene	37
When daring Vice insults eternal Justice,	O 314 Irene	23
When vanquish'd Vice shall tyrannize no more.	O 321 Irene	36
By vice or passion driv'n	O 345 Irene	V 26

		PAGE	TITLE	LINE

VICISSITUDE
Now fears in dire vicissitude invade, ... O 32 Vanity Wishes   41
New fears in dire vicissitude invade, ... O 32 Vanity Wishes V 41
Love, that with sweet Vicissitude relieves . . . . . O 261 Irene   9
VICISSITUDES
Whom Joys in soft vicissitudes invite, ... Y 107 Vanity Wishes V 325
Must watch the wild Vicissitudes of Taste; . . . . . O 53 Pro Drury-Lane   48
With wild Vicissitudes of Wrong, ... O 145 Tr Boeth III.1   10
VICT'RY
Or their own souls with hopes of vict'ry fir'd." . . . Y 19 Tr. Iliad Bk 6   59
VICTOR
The victor hither brought, a royall slave. . . . . . Y 19 Tr. Iliad Bk 6   39
The victor Cranes the conquer'd realms possess, . . . Y 23 Tr Add. Battle   34
VICTORIES
And lisp the tale of Henry's victories; . . . . . . O 15 London   120
Repeat that prince's victories, ... O 68 Hor. II Ode IX   19
VICTORIOUS
At length our mighty Bard's victorious Lays . . . . . O 57 Prologue Comus   15
With some victorious Heroe's praise . . . . O 78 Feast St Simon   5
Bore me victorious onward, where Demetrius . . . . . O 312 Irene   9
To grace the Triumph of victorious Virtue; . . . . . O 322 Irene   10
And lead thy Troops victorious round the World. . . . O 333 Irene   41
VICTORS
Lead us to Danger, and abash their Victors? . . . . . O 284 Irene   43
VICTORY
And victory hangs doubtfull o'er the field. . . . . . O 76 Tr Add. Battle   13
VIE   SEE VYE
Behold contending nations vie for bondage . . . . . Y 136 Irene   V 26
VIEL'D
By plumes is viel'd; see! quick as thought . . . . . O 70 Hor.II Ode XX   11
VIENNA
And Buda fall, and proud Vienna tremble, ... O 309 Irene   27
VIEW
And call Britannia's glories back to view; . . . . . O 10 London   26
And view each object with another's eye; . . . . . . O 16 London   139
Let observation with extensive view, ... O 30 Vanity Wishes   1
We all must view the Stygian flood . . . . O 69 Hor.II Ode 14   17
And view with cheerful eyes approaching death. . . . O 74 Tr. Iliad Bk 6   10
Sick'ning with fear he longs to view the shore, . . . O 82 Young Author   9
Wheresoe'er I turn my View, ... O 179 Ridicul Warton   1
With silent Pangs I view the tow'ring Domes, ... O 251 Irene   62
Death rises to my View, with all his Terrors; . . . . O 265 Irene   12
Well may those Eyes that view these heav'nly Charms, . O 267 Irene   6
If Pleasure charm thee, view this soft Retreat; . . . O 279 Irene   85
There shalt thou view from far the quiet Cottage, . . O 292 Irene   83
They give the nations laws, and view serene . . . . Y 167 Irene   V 117
And set the glitt'ring Fallacy to view. . . . . . . O 293 Irene   128
And view thy charms with no malignant eyes: . . . . Y 3 On a Daffodill   14
Astonish'd nations view with wild affright . . . . . Y 24 Tr Add. Battle   74
The fearless Pygmies view them from afar . . . . . . Y 25 Tr Add. Battle   96
Who caught the chief, ev'n in his soldiers' view . . . Y 25 Tr Add. Battle 125
VIEW'D
Happy he whose Eyes have view'd . . . . O 147 Tr Boet III.12   1
Fondly view'd his following Bride, ... O 150 Tr Boet III.12   51
VIEWING
Viewing lost and losing died. . . . . O 150 Tr Boet III.12   52
Viewing lost and loving died. . . . . O 150 Tr Boet III.12 V 52
VIEWS
Are these thy views? proceed, illustrious youth, . . . O 37 Vanity Wishes 141
With listless eyes the dotard views the store, . . . O 43 Vanity Wishes 263
He views, and wonders that they please no more; . . . O 43 Vanity Wishes 264
He views, and wonders why they please no more; . . . Y 104 Vanity Wishes V 264
Or views his coffers with suspicious eyes, ... O 44 Vanity Wishes 289
New forms arise, and diff'rent views engage, ... O 45 Vanity Wishes 307
she sees whom diff'rent views engage, ... Y 106 Vanity Wishes V 307
Pope's hallow'd glades, and never tiring views, . . . O 106 Eliza plucking   3
Returns his child; she views his infant charms, . . . Y 20 Tr. Iliad Bk 6 108
Affrighted views; and looking o'er the plain . . . . Y 23 Tr Add. Battle   32
VIG'ROUS
And life still vig'rous revels in my veins; . . . . . O 10 London   42
His vig'rous remedy display'd . . . . O 201 Death Dr Levet   15
Unnerv'd with shrieks the soldier's vig'rous arm . . Y 163 Irene   V 48
VIGILANCE
With cautious Vigilance, at my Command, ... O 310 Irene   4
VIGOROUS
Daring, tho' calm; and vigorous, tho' resign'd. . . . O 246 Irene Prologue   10
VIGOUR
But their lost strength and vigour soon return, . . . O 76 Tr Add. Battle   8
Dissolve thy vigour, and enchain thy powers? . . . . O 151 The Ant   10
Unnerve thy vigour, and enchain thy pow'rs; . . . . . O 151 The Ant   V 10
VILE
There dauntless Truth shall blast the vile Accuser, . . O 326 Irene   42
VILLAIN
Were all our Favours lavish'd on a Villain? . . . . . O 272 Irene   12
To banish Doubt, and brand him for a Villain. . . . . O 273 Irene   21
Said not the Villain in Irene's Chamber . . . . . . O 375 Irene   V 13
VILLAIN'S
London! the needy villain's gen'ral home, ... O 14 London   93
Suspected still?--What Villain's pois'nous Tongue . . O 304 Irene   12
That fawning Villain's forc'd Congratulations . . . . O 310 Irene   2
That hoary Villain's forc'd congratulations . . . . . O 370 Irene   V 22

377

```
                                                         PAGE    TITLE              LINE
VILLAINS
       On fools and villains ne'er descend;    . . . . . . .   O 100 Ode Friendship     18
       Perhaps yourselves the Villains that defame me,  . . .   O 326 Irene             38
VILLAINY
       But thou, should tempting villainy present  . . . . .   O  14 London            85
       When publick Villainy, too strong for Justice,  . . . .  O 250 Irene            40
VILLANY
       Whate'er perfidious villany can suffer   . . . . . .    Y 216 Irene          V  75
VILLIERS
       All Marlb'rough hoarded, or all Villiers spent,   . . .  O  14 London           86
       What gave great Villiers to th' assassin's knife,  . . . O  35 Vanity Wishes   129
VINDICTIVE
       And point vindictive Lightnings at Rebellion,   . . . .  O 300 Irene            61
VINE
       As vines the elms, as grapes adorn the vine,   . . . .   Y   6 Virgil Daphnis   17
VINES
       With artfull hand the teeming vines,  . . . . . . .     O  71 Hor. Epode II     18
       As vines the elms, as grapes adorn the vine,   . . . .   Y   6 Virgil Daphnis   17
VIOLATED
       Oft when the Cries of violated Beauty  . . . . . . .    O 251 Irene            73
       Perhaps may start at violated Friendship.  . . . . . .   O 300 Irene            81
VIOLATION
       To Threats of Torture, Death and Violation.  . . . .    O 259 Irene           112
       And panted on the brink of violation  . . . . . .      Y 124 Irene          V 112
VIOLENCE
       Thy Streets with Violence of Woe shall sound,   . . .    O 110 To Posterity      5
       My fainting Soul with Violence of transport.  . . . .    O 371 Irene          V  15
       Say, how the Hand of Violence was rais'd,  . . . . .    O 295 Irene            25
       Whence is this Violence?  . . . . . . . . .            O 321 Irene            53
       That pour with sudden Violence on Kingdoms,   . . . .    O 325 Irene            12
       Or why should he, whose Violence of Duty  . . . . . .   O 329 Irene            18
       Why should the man whose violence of duty  . . . . .    Y 210 Irene          V  18
VIOLENT
       Or bends with violent force the trees.   . . . . . .    O  67 Hor. II Ode IX     8
VIOLETS
       Where late the lilies mix'd with violets smil'd.  . . .  Y   7 Virgil Daphnis   25
VIRAGO
       This fierce Virago, fearless and unshaken  . . . . .    O 364 Irene          V  13
       This fierce virago, fearless and unshaken  . . . . .    Y 162 Irene          V  40
VIRGIN
       Some virgin Martyr,  . . . . . . . . .                O 252 Irene            95
       A Virgin shining with distinguish'd Charms,  . . . . .   O 258 Irene            95
       We come, bright Virgin, tho' relenting Nature   . . .    O 325 Irene            20
       Tho' no lewd hint the mantling virgin warm.  . . . .    Y  67 Prologue Lethe   14
VIRGIN'S
       Or bribe a virgin's innocence away.  . . . . . . .     O  13 London           78
       But the next blooming virgin's beauteous face  . . . .  Y  12 Tr Hor Epode 9   41
VIRGINS
       But cruel virgins meet severer fates;  . . . . . . .    O  84 Epi Dist Moth.   28
       Adorns my Palace with its brightest Virgins;   . . .    O 263 Irene            15
       I had a hundred Virgins wait around her,  . . . . .     O 287 Irene            16
       May throngs of beauteous virgins 'round thee crowd,  . .  Y   3 On a Daffodill   13
VIRTUE
       Behold rebellious virtue quite o'erthrown,   . . . .     O  13 London           63
       Can surly virtue hope to fix a friend?   . . . . .      O  16 London          145
       How virtue wars with persecuting fate;   . . . . .      O  19 London          199
       And virtue guard thee to the throne of Truth!  . . . .  O  37 Vanity Wishes   142
       This pow'r has praise, that virtue scarce can warm,  . .  O  39 Vanity Wishes   183
       Such pow'r has praise, that virtue scarce can charm,  . . Y 100 Vanity Wishes  V 183
       With distant voice neglected Virtue calls,   . . . .    O  46 Vanity Wishes   333
       And Virtue call'd Oblivion to her Aid.  . . . . . .     O  52 Pro Drury-Lane   28
       Yet still did Virtue deign the Stage to tread,   . . .   O  52 Pro Drury-Lane   33
       Bid scenic Virtue form the rising Age,  . . . . . .     O  53 Pro Drury-Lane   61
       With ardent love of virtue fir'd,  . . . . . . .       O  79 Feast St Simon   38
       What rais'd your Virtue here below,  . . . . . . .     O 100 Ode Friendship  V  27
       In ev'ry act refulgent virtue glow'd.  . . . . . .     O 118 Epitaph Hanmer   16
       As virtue rises in distress,  . . . . . . . . .        O 122 Stella Mourn.    10
       Now say, where virtue stops and vice begins?   . . .    O 139 Tr Rambler 173    1
       And drive discountenanc'd virtue from the throne:  . .   O 176 Tr Metastas II    9
       And chase discountenanc'd virtue from the throne:  . .   O 176 Tr Metastas II V  9
       Or Virtue shall replace on earth.  . . . . . . .       O 232 Tr Horace IV.7   24
       Or Virtue shall restore to earth.  . . . . . . .       O 232 Tr Horace IV.7 V 24
       The airy Flights of unexperienced Virtue  . . . . .     O 347 Irene          V  20
       Think on the mighty Pow'r of awful Virtue;   . . . .    O 252 Irene            88
       Perhaps, enamour'd of resembling Virtue,   . . . . .    O 252 Irene            96
       And know'st the Characters of Vice and Virtue,   . . .   O 255 Irene            12
       Virtue and Liberty engross his Soul,  . . . . . . .    O 255 Irene            32
       For forc'd Compliance, or for zealous Virtue,   . . .    O 256 Irene            51
       Her grateful Sons shine bright with ev'ry Virtue;  . .   O 256 Irene            60
       Did Mahomet reproach or praise her Virtue?  . . . .     O 259 Irene           108
       When weigh'd with Greece, with Virtue, with Aspasia?  . . O 260 Irene           138
       The holy Flame of enterprizing Virtue,  . . . . . .    O 264 Irene            26
       The noble flame of enterprising Virtue  . . . . .      O 371 Irene          V  28
           your feeble fainting virtue  . . . . . . . .        Y 133 Irene          V   9
       Chill my Resolves, and blast my blooming Virtue:  . . .  O 266 Irene            14
       And Wisdom into Virtue turn thy Frailty.  . . . . .     O 266 Irene            22
       Thy awful air, thy dignity of virtue.  . . . . . .     Y 134 Irene          V  34
       Th' impetuous Sallies of excessive Virtue,   . . . .    O 267 Irene            47
       Freed from the harsh severities of virtue  . . . . .    Y 146 Irene          V  23
       The thirst of empire and the love of virtue?   . . .    Y 149 Irene          V  58
       And draw new Virtue from her heav'nly Tongue.  . . . .   O 285 Irene             7
```

```
VIRTUE          (CONTINUED)                              PAGE    TITLE          LINE
     And pushes feeble (thrusts defenseless) virtue from her  .   Y 158  Irene         V  13
        throne
     Guides erring Mortals to the Paths of Virtue,    . . . .    O 289  Irene            18
     Th' Eternal gave it, and that End is Virtue.     . . . .    O 290  Irene            31
     And Virtue cheaply sav'd with loss of Life. . . . . .       O 290  Irene            35
     Virtue is uncha unvarying as its Authour  . . . . . .       O 348  Irene         V  23
     Virtue is fixd unvarying as its Author      . . . . . .     O 348  Irene         V  23
     Angelic Greatness is Angelic Virtue.  . . . . . . .         O 293  Irene           130
     Fill all thy ardent Breast with Greece and Virtue,   . .    O 298  Irene             8
     Calm cf my Cares, and Guardian of my Virtue.    . .         O 298  Irene            12
     To shock my Virtue with a Tale of Love.    . . . . .        O 299  Irene            40
     O'erthrow such weak, such accidental Virtue,    . . .       O 301  Irene            83
     Love be my Wealth, and my Distinction Virtue.   . . . .     O 302  Irene           111
     Glory, the Bribe of avaricious Virtue!   . . . . . .        O 305  Irene            32
     O grant thy sacred Influence, pow'rful Virtue!  . . . .     O 313  Irene             5
     Her lofty mien, and insclence of virtue--my   . . . .       Y 191  Irene         V  14
        state
     Resumes th' imperious Air of haughty Virtue.    . . .       O 314  Irene            15
     Is this the boasted Bliss of conscious Virtue?  . . .       O 314  Irene            19
     Does conscious Virtue shake the fainting knee?  . . .       O 373  Irene         V   8
     The Breast where Virtue guards the Throne of Peace.   .     O 316  Irene            15
     My Soul attends thy Voice, and banish'd Virtue  . . .       O 320  Irene            32
     To grace the Triumph of victorious Virtue;   . . . . .      O 322  Irene            10
     Nor thus usurp the Dignity of Virtue.   . . . . . .         O 323  Irene            10
     From his Escape learn thou the Pow'r of Virtue,   . .       O 330  Irene            24
VIRTUE'S
     In virtue's cause once more exert his rage,   . . . . .     O  23  London          262
     In virtue's cause once more forsake his rage,   . . . .     O  23  London        V 262
     Let Study, worn with Virtue's fruitless Lore,   . . . .     O  57  Prologue Comus    9
     Thus grac'd with humble Virtue's native Charms  . . .       O  58  Prologue Comus   33
     When pleasure fired her torch at Virtue's flame,   . .      O  62  Pro Word Wise    23
     With virtue's sacred ardour glows,   . . . . . . .          O  65  Hor I Ode xxii    2
     With Virtue's sacred Ardour glows,   . . . . . . .          O  66  To A. Fuscus      2
     Nor e'er from virtue's path was lur'd aside,   . . . .      O 118  Epitaph Hanmer   31
     Nor e'er from virtue's paths was turn'd aside,   . . .      O 118  Epitaph Hanmer V 31
     And virtue's sorrow dignify'd his tomb.   . . . . . .       O 118  Epitaph Hanmer   44
     "This is Minerva, cast in Virtue's mould."    . . . . .     O 190  Seeing Montagu    6
VIRTUES
     But grant, the virtues of a temp'rate prime   . . . . .     O  44  Vanity Wishes   291
     When Virtues kindred Virtues meet,   . . . . . . .          O 100  Ode Friendship   21
     When Virtues kindred Virtues meet,   . . . . . . .          O 100  Ode Friendship   21
     What rais'd our Virtues here below,   . . . . . .           O 100  Ode Friendship   27
     And learn his virtues, while thou mourn'st his end.   .     O 117  Epitaph Hanmer    4
     His virtues walk'd their narrow round,   . . . . . .        O 201  Death Dr Levet   25
     Unprofitable, peaceful, female Virtues!   . . . . .         O 280  Irene            12
VIRTUOUS
     Nor sweeter musick of a virtuous friend,   . . . . .        O  43  Vanity Wishes   272
     Learn here how Heav'n supports the virtuous Mind,   . .     O 246  Irene Prologue    9
     Be virtuous Ends pursued by virtuous Means,   . . .         O 291  Irene            58
     Be virtuous Ends pursued by virtuous Means,   . . . .       O 291  Irene            58
     That none are great, or happy, but the Virtuous.   . .      O 294  Irene             8
     But virtuous Passion prompts the great Resolve,   . . .     O 303  Irene            18
VISICNARY
     To-morrow brings the visionary Bride. . . . . . .          O 283  Irene            31
     And bid thy visionary Throne farewell.   . . . . .          O 307  Irene            11
VISIONS
     In pleasing Visions, and assuasive Dreams;   . . . . .      O 253  Irene           102
     In pleasing Visions, and delusive Dreams;   . . . . .       O 253  Irene         V 102
     Then Visions horrid as a Murd'rer's Dreams   . . . . .      O 266  Irene            13
VISIT
     When the revclving seasons shall only visit my dominions    Y 132  Irene         V  44
     Implor'd my Leave to visit Mecca's Temple;   . . . . .      O 273  Irene            44
VISITS
     And visits Britain's hardy Sons . . . . . . . . .          O  80  Feast St Simon   47
     Disarm'd his Rage, and in repeated Visits   . . . . .       O 259  Irene           122
     And wait Abdalla's unsuspected Visits:   . . . . . .        O 260  Irene           145
VITAE
     Frcm Horace.  Integer Vitae, etc.   . . . . . . . .         O  65  Hor I Ode xxii V  T
VITAL
     Death broke at once the vital chain,   . . . . . . .        O 202  Death Dr Levet   35
     And joy to feel the vital Warmth return,   . . . . . .      O 320  Irene            25
VOCAL
     When old Timotheus struck the vocal String,   . . . .       O  97  Hickman Spinet    9
     Love warbles in the vocal groves,   . . . . . . .           O 125  An Ode            7
VOICE
     Rules the bold hand, or prompts the suppliant voice;   . .  O  31  Vanity Wishes    12
     How just that scorn ere yet thy voice declare,   . . .      O  33  Vanity Wishes    71
     Law in his voice, and fortune in his hand:   . . . .        O  34  Vanity Wishes   100
     With distant voice neglected Virtue calls,   . . . .        O  46  Vanity Wishes   333
     Still raise for good the supplicating voice,   . . . .      O  47  Vanity Wishes   351
     For blessing, raise the supplicating voice,   . . . .       Y 108  Vanity Wishes V 351
     The Stage but echoes back the publick Voice.   . . .        O  53  Pro Drury-Lane   52
     Fill the loud Voice of universal Praise,   . . . . .        O  57  Prologue Comus   16
     Her heav'nly voice, and beauteous face.   . . . . .         O  66  Hor I Ode xxii   24
     Her voice and Smiles my Song shall grace.   . . . . .       O  67  To A. Fuscus     24
     Who hail'd him Speaker, with united voice.   . . . .        O 118  Epitaph Hanmer   20
     Once more on wisdom's voice attend.   . . . . . . .         O 125  An Ode           24
     Whose voice created, and whose wisdom guides,   . . .       O 129  Tr. Rambler 7     2
     Insulting chance ne'er call'd with louder voice,   . . .    O 135  Tr Rambler 106    1
     For wisdcm ever echoes nature's voice.   . . . . .          O 138  Tr Rambler 156    1
```

VOICE   (CONTINUED)   PAGE   TITLE   LINE

No stern command, no monitory voice . . . .   O 151 The Ant   3
At Midnight's private Hour a Voice unknown . . .   O 254 Irene   121
Sooner these trembling Leaves shall find a Voice, . . .   O 255 Irene   26
Sooner the trembling Leaves shall find a Voice, . . .   O 373 Irene   V 19
Say, did a Voice from Heav'n restrain the Tyrant? . .   O 259 Irene   115
Still at Aspasia's Voice a sudden Rapture . . . .   O 265 Irene   4
Observe, bright Maid, as his resistless Voice . .   O 268 Irene   25
And yet another Voice, forgive me Greece, . . .   O 270 Irene   18
The pow'rful Voice of Love inflames Demetrius, . . .   O 270 Irene   19
And every Voice was Liberty and Greece. . . . .   O 271 Irene   30
The voice of war no more shall fright . . . . . .   Y 150 Irene   V 82
  Irene
Can Cali's Voice . . . .   O 288 Irene   9
To hear the Voice of Truth; dismiss thy Train, . . .   O 289 Irene   6
To hear the voice of truth, dismiss your train . . .   O 366 Irene   V 22
The Cause that shrinks from Reason's powerful Voice. . . O 293 Irene   126
What well known Voice pronounc'd the grateful Sounds . . O 295 Irene   10
Demand a Voice, and struggle into Birth; . . . .   O 295 Irene   18
There Poetry shall tune her sacred Voice, . . .   O 302 Irene   122
And still thy Bosom with the Voice of Peace. . . .   O 303 Irene   22
With soften'd Voice she dropp'd the faint Refusal, . .   O 303 Irene   31
In vain I listen to the inviting voice . . . .   Y 198 Irene   V 10
My Soul attends thy Voice, and banish'd Virtue . . .   O 320 Irene   32
Ask of thy Heart; attend the Voice of Conscience-- . .   O 323 Irene   7
Again his thund'ring Voice return'd, Irene. . . . .   O 325 Irene   26
Of her the Sultan's Voice condemn'd to die? . . .   O 329 Irene   17
  the voice of truth . . . .   Y 210 Irene   V 25
Then hear, great Mahomet, the Voice of Truth. . . .   O 333 Irene   55
And stopp'd the heav'nly Voice that call'd on me. . . .   O 334 Irene   71
VOICES
Yet judg'd by those, whose voices ne'er were sold, . .   O 60 Pro Good Nat'd   27
Unites the jarring voices of mankind . . . . . .   Y 136 Irene   V 32A
At once a hundred Voices thunder'd round me, ...   O 271 Irene   29
VOID
To dismal realms, and regions void of peace, . . .   O 84 Epi Dist Moth.   30
Were Pope once void of wonted candour found, ...   O 106 Eliza plucking   7
Leave to the schools their atoms and their void. . . .   O 140 Tr Rambler 180   2
"Void of care, and free from dread . . . . . .   O 185 Anacreon Ode 9   33
Nor made a pause, nor left a void; . . . .   O 201 Death Dr Levet   26
Nor made a pause, nor felt a void; . . . .   O 201 Death Dr Levet V 26
VOLUBLE
Obsequious, artful, voluble and gay, ...   O 15 London   111
VOLUME
While Heav'n's high Minister, whose awful Volume . .   O 276 Irene   20
While Heaven's high Minister whose unerring awfull . .   O 355 Irene   V   9
  volume
VOLUNTARY
They croud my camp with voluntary tribute . . . .   Y 136 Irene   V 27B
VOT'RIES
Vot'ries of Fame and Worshippers of Pow'r! . . . .   O 246 Irene Prologue   5
VOTARIES
<In> Triumphant at the head of thy new votaries . .   Y 131 Irene   V 32A
Must then Ambition's Votaries infringe . . . . .   O 280 Irene   15
VOTE
To vote a patriot black, a courtier white; . . .   O 11 London   52
For that blest year when all that vote may rail; . . .   O 60 Pro Good Nat'd   18
Says swelling Crispin, begg'd a cobbler's vote. . . .   O 60 Pro Good Nat'd   22
VOTES
And ask no questions but the price of votes; . . . .   O 34 Vanity Wishes   96
VOW
Long have as oblig'd by vow . . . .   Y 130 Irene   V   9
Attend my prayers propitious, hear my vow, ...   Y   7 Virgil Daphnis   42
VOWS
In vain you spend your vows and prayers, ...   O 68 Hor.II Ode 14   3
And vows to trust the faithless deep no more. . . .   O 82 Young Author   10
"Soft Anacreon's vows I bear, ...   O 185 Anacreon Ode 9   7
"Vows to Myrtale the fair; . . . .   O 185 Anacreon Ode 9   8
To offer up my vows in the temple built by the Father of   O 348 Irene   V   1
  Mankind
Mocks the dull Vows of Solitude and Penance, ...   O 264 Irene   27
Then dream of (prayer), or (vows) and pilgrimage and . . Y 132 Irene   V 45
  peace,
To hear my Vows and give Mankind a Queen? . . . .   O 276 Irene   2
My Vows, 'tis true, she hears with less Aversion, . . .   O 287 Irene   7
Whom neither Vows could fix, nor Favours bind? . . . .   O 330 Irene   2
The swains shall pay their vows, and thou shalt hear their Y   7 Virgil Daphnis   52
  prayer.
VULGAR
See when the vulgar 'scape, despis'd or aw'd, ...   O 39 Vanity Wishes   167
Let vulgar Poets sing, ...   O 78 Feast St Simon   3
Preach thy dull Politics to vulgar Kings, ...   O 265 Irene   39
Such Beauty must not shine to vulgar Eyes. . . . .   O 269 Irene   43
While vulgar Souls compassionate their Cares, ...   O 293 Irene   115
Unlike the trifling Race of vulgar Beauties, ...   O 298 Irene   18
Count not these Hours as Parts of vulgar Time, ...   O 302 Irene   5
VULNERE
Oude lithos, oude Sideron--nostro sequitur de Vulnere .   O 347 Irene   V 23
  sanguis.
VULTURS
Tho' confiscation's vulturs hover round. . . . . . .   O 32 Vanity Wishes   36

```
VULTURS              (CONTINUED)                                  PAGE    TITLE           LINE
     Tho' confiscation's vulters clang around.    . . . . .   O  32 Vanity Wishes     V  36
VYE
     Vye for my submission, sollicite bondage.    . . . . .   Y 136 Irene             V 27C
WAFT
     To waft our gallies o'er the trembling earth?            Y 115 Irene             V 49H
     Attends to waft us to Repose and Safety. . . . . . .     O 258 Irene                82
WAFTS
     That wafts diseases from the sleeping infant.  . . . .   Y 168 Irene             V135B
WAGE
     Let Wit, condemn'd the feeble War to wage  . . . . .     O  57 Prologue Comus        7
WAILINGS
     Shrieks of Affright, and Wailings of Distress. . . . .   O 251 Irene                72
WAIT
     And nations on his eye suspended wait;  . . . . . .      O  40 Vanity Wishes       206
     Condemn'd a needy supplicant to wait, . . . . . . . .    O  41 Vanity Wishes       213
     In whose fair cheeks destructive Cupids wait, . . . .    O  83 Epi Dist Moth.        3
     Around them pleasures wait, and joys for ever new.  . .  O  84 Epi Dist Moth.       27
     From you my labours wait their last reward. . . . . .    O 141 Tr Rambler 208        2
     And wait Abdalla's unsuspected Visits:  . . . . .        O 260 Irene               145
     The future Miseries that wait th' Apostate;  . . . . .   O 266 Irene                20
     I go to wait thy Call; this kind Consent  . . . . .      O 285 Irene                15
     I bad a hundred Virgins wait around her, . . . . . .     O 287 Irene                16
     Forbear this Triumph--still new Conflicts wait us, . .   O 298 Irene                25
     Now let us wait the last Award of Heav'n,   . . . . .    O 302 Irene               113
     To wait remote from Action, and frcm Honour,  . . . .    O 305 Irene                22
     And wait your Summons to report his Conduct.  . . . .    O 310 Irene                 7
     And anxious Angels wait the mighty Birth;   . . . . .    O 313 Irene                 4
WAITED
     Abdalla, while we waited near the Palace,   . . . . .    O 316 Irene                25
WAITING
     And waiting for her weary lord  . . . . . . . .          O  73 Hor. Epode II        53
     An useless Life in waiting for To-morrow,   . . . . .    O 283 Irene                23
WAITS
     While Thales waits the wherry that contains . . . . .    O   9 London               19
     He ne'er with forc'd Submission waits . . . . . . .      O  71 Hor. Epode II        15
     Disaster always waits an early wit.  .' . . . . . .      O 135 Tr Rambler 111         1
     The Pow'r of Turkey waits upon my Call.  . . . . . .     O 319 Irene                24
     A Galley waits us, and the Winds invite.  . . . . . .    O 321 Irene                52
WAK'D
     Thus wak'd to rage by Musick's dreadfull Pow'r,   . .    O  97 Hickman Spinet       13
WAKE
     Some zealous bard to wake the sleeping lyre.  . . . .    O 107 Lady F Assizes        4
     Till angels wake thee with a note like thine. . . . .    O 113 Epit. Phillips        6
     Or wake the Dead to warn us of its Fall? . . . . . .     O 250 Irene                47
     And wake from Ignorance the Western World.  . . . . .    O 302 Irene               123
     Wake from thy Dream of Pow'r to Death and Tortures,  .   O 307 Irene                10
WAKES
     Wakes from his dream, and labours for a joke;   . . . .  O  17 London              163
     Bears toilsome Days, and wakes long tedious Nights:  .   O 247 Irene Epilogue       22
WAKING
     A fancy'd Treasure, and a waking Dream.  . . . . .       O 277 Irene                48
     Absorb'd by thought, then waking from his dream  . . .   Y 187 Irene             V   6
WALK
     And bless thine evening walk and morning toil.  . . . .  O  20 London              223
     And bless the evening walk and morning toil.  . . . .    O  20 London             V 223
     And bless thy evening walk and morning toil.  . . . .    O  20 London             V 223
     The Winter's Walk  . . . . . . . . . .                   O 123 Winter's Walk         T
     And Duty bids me chuse a distant Walk,   . . . . . .     O 288 Irene                13
WALK'D
     And walk'd into the Strand,  . . . . . . . .             O 158 Par. Hermit II        2
     I walk'd along the Strand,  . . . . . . . . . .          O 158 Par. Hermit II    V   2
     His virtues walk'd their narrow round,  . . . . . .      O 201 Death Dr Levet       25
     I walk'd superior, through the Blaze of Charms,  . . .   O 263 Irene                17
WALKS
     There prune thy walks, support thy drooping flow'rs, .   O  20 London              216
     Walks the wild heath, and sings his toil away.  . . .    O  32 Vanity Wishes        38
     And tell the Secrets of their conscious Walks;  . . . .  O 255 Irene                27
     Molest these private Walks, or Care invade  . . . . .    O 272 Irene                14
     Those glcomy walks where Gladness never smiles . . . .   Y 165 Irene             V  81
     To range those walks of tyranny and lust  . . . . .      Y 165 Irene             V  85
     To wander pensive in those gloomy walks  . . . . .       Y 165 Irene             V  85
     And pass'd uninjur'd through the Walks of Death?  . . .  O 296 Irene                29
     Nor dare henceforth to shock Irene's Walks.   . . . .    O 325 Irene                 7
     And saw him skulking in the closest Walks:  . . . . .    O 327 Irene                25
WALL
     From every wall descends the painted face,  . . . . .    Y  95 Vanity Wishes      V  83
     And detestation rids th' indignant wall. . . . . . .     Y  34 Vanity Wishes        90
     And why should odious ruin dawb the wall.  . . . . . .   Y  95 Vanity Wishes      V  90
     And hiss the dauber ruin dawb the wall.  . . . . .       Y  95 Vanity Wishes      V  90
     And rushes joyful to the naked Wall,  . . . . . .        O 298 Irene                29
     The bravest of the Greeks the wall invade.  . . . . .    Y  19 Tr. Iliad Bk 6       53
     Thrice to the wall their dreadfull hosts have led  . .   Y  19 Tr. Iliad Bk 6       56
WALLS
     In those curs'd walls, devote to vice and gain,  . . .   O  10 London               37
     "On Moscow's walls till Gothic standards fly,   . . .    O  40 Vanity Wishes       203
     Thou, who survey'st these walls with curious eye,  . .   O 117 Epitaph Hanmer        1
     When loud Auster shakes her Walls, . . . . . . .         O 145 Tr Boeth. II.4       10
     Did Earthquakes shake our walls? . . . . . . .           O 347 Irene             V   3
     In vain, when Turkey's troops assail'd our Walls,  . .   O 253 Irene               117
     Why, when Destruction rag'd around our Walls,   . . .    O 290 Irene                38
```

WALLS   (CONTINUED)   PAGE   TITLE   LINE
    Around these fatal Walls, the Tide of War   . . . . .   O 312 Irene   8
    And man the walls and fortifie the tow'rs.   . . . . .   Y 19 Tr. Iliad Bk 6   51
    Grant him like me to guard the walls of Troy. . . . .   Y 20 Tr. Iliad Bk 6   102
WAND'RERS
    Observe the feather'd Wand'rers of the Sky, ...   O 277 Irene   34
WAND'RING
    To warn the wand'ring Linnet to the Shade, ...   O 250 Irene   33
    Or wand'ring in the Wilds of future Being, ...   O 255 Irene   6
    Do gay Delusions, wand'ring o'er the Brain, ...   O 277 Irene   44
    The wand'ring Rivulet, and silver Lake, ...   O 280 Irene   23
    Now, wand'ring o'er the cliffs the traveller . . . .   Y 23 Tr Add. Battle   30
WAND'RINGS
    Shall bless our Wand'rings, and propitiate Heav'n. . .   O 320 Irene   19
WANDER
    And wander sportive o'er th' Elysian plain: . . .. . . O 77 Tr Add. Battle   43
    Wealth, Sir John, was made to wander, ... O 196 Song Congratu.   17
    Wealth, my lad, was made to wander, ... O 196 Song Congratu.   V   17
    Let it wander as it will;   . . . . O 196 Song Congratu.   18
    Let it wander if it will;   . . . . O 196 Song Congratu.   V   18
    And wander o'er the Ruins of our Country   . . . . . . O 351 Irene   V   1
    Sacred to Prayer, and wander thro' the Streets;   . . .   O 251 Irene   63
    And croud the fattend fields, the ghosts that wander . . Y 120 Irene   V   31
    Flush in my cheek, and wander in my Veins   . . . . .   O 349 Irene   V   26
    To wander pensive in those gloomy walks   . . . . .   Y 165 Irene   V   85
    Send me to wander on some pathless Shore, ... O 328 Irene   35
WANDER'D
    We still had wander'd on Tartarian Hills.   . . . . .   O 284 Irene   41
WANDRING
    And gay delusions wandring o'er the brain   . . . . .   O 356 Irene   V   11
    The traveller persues the flatt'ring wandring . . . .   Y 155 Irene   V   34
        splendor
WANT
    Thou who couldst laugh where want enchain'd caprice, . . O 32 Vanity Wishes   53
    Toil, envy, want, the patron, and the jail.   . . . . .   O 38 Vanity Wishes   160
    Toil, envy, want, the Garret, and the jail.   . . . . .   O 38 Vanity Wishes   V 160
    He comes, not want and cold his course delay;--   . .   O 41 Vanity Wishes   209
    He comes, nor want nor cold his course delay;------   . . . O 41 Vanity Wishes   V 209
    And Want hung threat'ning o'er her slow Decay. . . .   O 58 Prologue Comus   26
    He feels no want of ill-persuading gold;   . . . . .   O 60 Pro Good Nat'd   28
    If want of skill, or want of care appear, ...   O 62 Pro Word Wise   17
    If want of skill, or want of care appear, ...   O 62 Pro Word Wise   17
    Till want, now following fraudulent and slow, ...   O 152 Irene   15
    Where Want repines, and Vengeance swells, ...   O 191 Tr. Medea I   10
    The guest, without a want, without a wish, ...   O 193 Tr. Medea II   19
    And lonely want retir'd to die.   . . . . O 201 Death Dr Levet   20
    I want alass thy steadiness of Soul   . . . . . . O 366 Irene   V   29
    To Want give Affluence? and to Slav'ry Freedom?   . . .   O 277 Irene   46
    No more should Danger fright, or Want distress . . . .   O 291 Irene   56
    Nor fear the Fair and Learn'd can want Protection. . .   O 302 Irene   115
WANT'ST
    Nor hope his Fortune while thou want'st his Worth. . .   O 330 Irene   25
WANTING
    Lest ropes be wanting in the tempting spring, ...   O 22 London   246
    And ropes be wanting in the tempting spring, ...   Y 60 London   V 246
WANTON
    The Dream of idle Maids and wanton Poets . . . . . .   O 350 Irene   V   1
WANTONS
    Nor sprightly Folly wantons in his Air, ...   O 255 Irene   15
    And laughs and wantons in the Jaws of Death. . . . . .   O 283 Irene   11
WANTS
    Wants ev'n the cheap reward of empty praise; . . . .   O 10 London   36
    The modest wants of ev'ry day   . . . .   O 201 Death Dr Levet   23
WAR
    War sounds the trump, he rushes to the field; . . . .   O 40 Vanity Wishes   198
    And all the sons of ravage croud the war;   . . . . .   O 43 Vanity Wishes   250
    With all the sons of ravage croud the war;   . . . . .   O 43 Vanity Wishes   V 250
    Let Wit, condemn'd the feeble War to wage   . . . . .   O 57 Prologue Comus   7
    In vain we shun the Din of war, ...   O 69 Hor.II Ode 14   13
    But shall I, then, forsake the unfinish'd war? . . . .   O 74 Tr. Iliad Bk 6   4
    Rage with disdain, and hope th' approaching war; . . .   O 75 Tr Add. Battle   1
    Breathless at length they leave th' unfinish'd war . .   O 76 Tr Add. Battle   6
    No more delighted with destructive War, ...   O 97 Hickman Spinet   17
    Or raging factions rush to war, ...   O 126 An Ode   34
    Amid the storms of war, with curious eyes   . . . . .   O 130 Tr. Rambler 8   1
    Of plenteous peace, and prosp'rous war;   . . . . .   O 189 Epilogue   6
    Think on the various Accidents of War;   . . . . .   O 252 Irene   87
    And harrass Greece no more with wasteful War. . . . .   O 257 Irene   80
    Through half his Course reflects the blaze of . . . .   O 353 Irene   V   2
        War
    With wonted Zeal pursue the Task of War, ...   O 264 Irene   30
    With equal zeal persue the task of war   . . . . .   Y 131 Irene   V   30
    Lost in the deluge of impetuous war   . . . . .   Y 136 Irene   V   25
    Drives on the Tempest of destructive War, ...   O 268 Irene   26
    The horrid Images of War and Slaughter   . . . . .   O 268 Irene   34
    And broke the meditated Lines of War. . .   . .   O 273 Irene   26
    And in the (paths) of war and desolation   . . . . .   Y 150 Irene   V   71
    The voice of war no more shall fright . .   . .   Y 150 Irene   V   82
        Irene
    Mix in the War, and shine among the Heroes?   . . . . .   O 290 Irene   41
    Then Bigotry might send her Slaves to War, ...   O 291 Irene   63

382

```
WAR         (CONTINUED)                                        PAGE    TITLE          LINE
     Where unaffrighted by the din of war  . . . . . . . .    Y 177  Irene          V 116
     Intrepid in the flaming Front of War?  . . . . . . . .   O 304  Irene            17
     I rouse to War, and conquer for Irene.  . . . . . . .    O 309  Irene            25
     And War o'erwhelm them in their Dream of Vice.  . . .    O 309  Irene            37
     Behold him here, in Love, in War successful,  . . . .    O 310  Irene             4
     Around these fatal Walls, the Tide of War  . . . . .     O 312  Irene             8
     Are these the rapid Thunderbolts of War,  . . . . . .    O 325  Irene            11
     Rush to the War, display thy dreadful Banners,  . . .    O 333  Irene            40
     To men belongs the dreadfull work of war."  . . . . .   Y  21  Tr. Iliad Bk 6  123
     Sung such a war when in a miry fen  . . . . . . . . .    Y  23  Tr Add. Battle   55
     Sharpen their claws, and meditate the war.  . . . . .   Y  24  Tr Add. Battle   71
     Now bleeds the war afresh, the Crane from high  . . .    Y  26  Tr Add. Battle  130
WAR'S
     Yet Reason frowns on War's unequal game,  . . . . . .    O  39  Vanity Wishes   185
     Yet Reason blush on War's unequal game,  . . . . . .     Y 100  Vanity Wishes  V 185
     And when blest Peace has silenc'd War's Alarms,  . . .   O 247  Irene Epilogue   23
WARBLE
     And Wisdom warble from her string.  . . . . . . . . .    O 121  To Miss Playin   24
     And Songs of Pleasure warble from the Tongue,  . . . .   O 315  Irene            30
WARBLER
     Here ev'ry Warbler of the Sky shall sing;  . . . . .     O 279  Irene            86
WARBLES
     Lamenting warbles out his love,  . . . . . . . . . .     O  72  Hor. Epode II    34
     Love warbles in the vocal groves,  . . . . . . . . .     O 125  An Ode            7
WARBLING
     With warbling eunuchs fill a licens'd stage,  . . . .    O  12  London           59
     With warbling eunuchs fill our silenc'd stage,  . . .    O  12  London         V  59
     O'er all the warbling founts a cooling shade.  . . .     Y   7  Virgil Daphnis   27
WARBLINGS
     And chear the weary passenger with warblings  . . . .    O 355  Irene          V  21
     And unaccustom'd warblings charm the grove  (pleasing    Y 150  Irene          V  86
          disson<ance>
WARLIKE
     Our warlike Prophet loves an active Faith,  . . . . .    O 264  Irene            25
     Our warlike Prophet loves an active zeal  . . . . . .    Y 131  Irene          V  25
     Why then did not this warlike Amazon  . . . . . . . .    O 290  Irene            40
WARM
     This pow'r has praise, that virtue scarce can warm,  . . O  39  Vanity Wishes   183
     Warm with an ardent lover's fondest pray'r.  . . . . .   O  80  Lady Birthday     2
     Warm India's supple Sons should bow,  . . . . . . . .    O 146  Tr Boeth III.5    6
     If Genius warm thee, Reader, stay,  . . . . . . . . .    O 154  Epita. Hogarth    5
     And warm Cayster's flowing banks forsake  . . . . . .    Y  24  Tr Add. Battle   67
     Tho' no lewd hint the mantling virgin warm.  . . . . .   Y  67  Prologue Lethe   14
WARMER
     With warmer Courtship press the yielding Fair,  . . . .  O 287  Irene             9
WARMEST
     Beyond my warmest Hope, or wildest Wishes,  . . . . .    O 296  Irene            35
WARMTH
     With pious Warmth receive our Prophet's Law----  . . .   O 262  Irene            25
     But why this sudden Warmth?  . . . . . . . . . . . .     O 281  Irene            48
     And joy to feel the vital Warmth return,  . . . . . .    O 320  Irene            25
     Perhaps my Warmth exceeded my Commission;  . . . . .     O 330  Irene            21
     Cleora's smiles a genial warmth dispense;  . . . . .     Y   4  On a Daffodill   18
WARN
     In useful satire warn succeeding times;  . . . . . .     Y  61  London         V 259
     To warn the wand'ring Linnet to the Shade,  . . . . .    O 250  Irene            33
     Or wake the Dead to warn us of its Fall?  . . . . . .    O 250  Irene            47
     Pour forth her Dead to warn us of its fall?  . . . . .   O 365  Irene          V  22
WARN'D
     Warn'd by another's fate, vain youth, be wise,  . . . .  O  82  Young Author     23
     I guess'd her dark Designs, and warn'd the Sultan,  . .  O 327  Irene            26
WARN'ST
     In angry numbers warn'st succeeding times;  . . . . .    O  23  London          259
WARNING
     Not one takes warning, by another's end.  . . . . . .    Y  67  Prologue Lethe    6
WARRING
     In warring colours shew the warring throng;  . . . . .   Y  22  Tr Add. Battle    4
     In warring colours shew the warring throng;  . . . . .   Y  22  Tr Add. Battle    4
WARRIOR
     Behold the warrior dwindled to a beau;  . . . . . . .    O  15  London          104
WARRIOR'S
     On what foundation stands the warrior's pride,  . . . .  O  40  Vanity Wishes   191
     On what foundation stands the warrior's fame?  . . . .   Y 101  Vanity Wishes  V 191
     The Warrior's Ardour, and the Patriot's Zeal;  . . . .   O 255  Irene             4
     The Warrior's Labours, and the Monarch's Cares.  . . .   O 261  Irene            10
WARRIOUR
     There a stout warriour fainting gasps for breath  . . .  O  76  Tr Add. Battle   16
     "Why gen'rous warriour will you rashly run  . . . . .    Y  18  Tr. Iliad Bk 6   19
WARRIOUR'S
     Hector shall perish by no warriour's hand.  . . . . .    Y  21  Tr. Iliad Bk 6  116
WARRIOURS
     The Sultan's majesty the warriours rage  . . . . . .     Y 123  Irene          V  98
     The Sultan's majesty the warriours fierceness  . . .     Y 123  Irene          V  98
     Then flies aloft; th' astonish'd warriours feel  . . .   Y  26  Tr Add. Battle  132
WARS
     How virtue wars with persecuting fate;  . . . . . .      O  19  London          199
     Nor annual tax was rais'e by annual wars.  . . . . .     Y  94  Vanity Wishes  V 60B
     For English vengeance wars not with the dead.  . . . .   O  61  Pro Word Wise     4
     When unsuccessful Wars, and civil Factions,  . . . . .   O 256  Irene            41
```

		PAGE	TITLE OMITTED WORD	LINE

WASTE

No pathless waste, or undiscover'd shore;	. . . . .	O 18	London	171
Tell the woes of wilful waste,	. . . .	O 197	Song Congratu.	26
Tell the spoils of wilful waste,	. . . .	O 197	Song Congratu. V	26
Then let us now resolve, nor idly waste	. . . . .	O 271	Irene	33
Then let us now resolve, nor idle waste	. . . .	O 271	Irene V	33
There shall he waste thy Frontiers, check thy Conquests,		O 274	Irene	56
Unpitying Massacre might waste the World,	. . . . .	O 291	Irene	65
Far as Futurity's untravell'd Waste	. . . . .	O 300	Irene	68
Then waste no longer these important Moments	. . .	O 303	Irene	13
To tell, or hear, were Waste of Life.	. . . . .	O 316	Irene	21

WASTED

Where wasted nations raise a single name,	. . . . .	O 39	Vanity Wishes	186
Nor only through the wasted plain,	. . . .	O 123	Winter's Walk	5
Nor only thought the wasted plain,	. . . .	O 123	Winter's Walk V	5
To Bid wasted Regions flourish at her smile	. . . .	O 372	Irene V	8
Insatiate on her wasted Entrails prey,	. . . . .	O 315	Irene	36

WASTEFUL

And harrass Greece no more with wasteful War.	. . . .	O 257	Irene	80

WASTING   SEE WIDE-WASTING

WAT'RY

Jocund he dances o'er the wat'ry way,	. . . .	O 82	Young Author	5

WATCH

Watch the weak hour, and ransack all the heart;	. .	O 17	London	155
And watch the busy scenes of crouded life;	. . . .	O 30	Vanity Wishes	4
Mark the keen glance, and watch the sign to hate.	. . .	O 34	Vanity Wishes	110
Must watch the wild Vicissitudes of Taste;	. . . . .	O 53	Pro Drury-Lane	48
Yet let me watch her dear departing Steps,	. . . .	O 297	Irene	17
Sanguinary joy--Slaves now watch her nod	. . . . .	Y 184	Irene V	9
Shall plume her Charms, and, with attentive Watch,	.	O 318	Irene	4
Shall play the glance, and with attentive watch	. . .	Y 195	Irene V	4
Watch each unquiet Flutter of the Breast,	. . . .	O 320	Irene	24

WATCH'D

Close, as we might unseen, we watch'd his Steps;	. . .	O 311	Irene	2

WATCHFUL

The watchful guests still hint the last offence,	. . .	O 44	Vanity Wishes	279
The Watchful slumber, and the Crafty trust.	. . . . .	O 283	Irene	13

WATCHFULL

Must watchfull providence despatch from Heav'n	. . . .	Y 114	Irene V	46

WATER

Glassy water, glassy water,	. . . .	O 159	Tr. Rio Verde	1
Glassy water, glassy water,	. . . .	O 159	Tr. Rio Verde	1

WATERS

Do the chain'd waters always freeze;	. . . . .	O 67	Hor. II Ode IX	6
Beneath Hyperia's waters shall you sweat,	. . . . .	O 74	Tr. Iliad Bk 6	23
and drink the holy waters the fountain of remission	. . . . .	Y 130	Irene V	11

WATERY

Then dances jocund o'er the watery way,	. . . . . .	O 82	Young Author V	5

WAV'D

That wav'd th' essential form of Grace,	. . . . . .	O 154	Epita. Hogarth V	2

WAV'RING

Where wav'ring man, betray'd by vent'rous pride,	. . .	O 31	Vanity Wishes	7

WAVE

Niphates rolls an humbler wave,	. . . .	O 68	Hor. II Ode IX	21
When ev'ry Wave shall beat a Turkish Shore,	. . . . .	O 265	Irene	43
Till every Wave shall beat a Turkish Shore.	. . . .	O 354	Irene V	26
And where yon Trees wave o'er the foaming Surge	. . .	O 304	Irene	2
May lambent zephyrs gently wave thy head,	. . . . .	Y 3	On a Daffodill	9
The wound, and, furious, wave the shining steel.	. . .	Y 26	Tr Add. Battle	133

WAVES

On Isis banks he waves, from noise withdrawn	. . . .	Y 98	Vanity Wishes	V138A
The waves he lashes, and enchains the wind;	. . . .	O 42	Vanity Wishes	232
Loud roar the billows, high the waves arise,	. . . .	O 82	Young Author V	8
Dashing Waves and shatter'd Shoars,	. . . . . .	O 145	Tr Boeth. II.4	18
Why foam the swelling Waves when Tempests rise?	. . .	O 281	Irene	51
Plays on the quiv'ring Waves, to guide our Flight,	. .	O 306	Irene	59
Bound o'er the sparkling Waves. Go, happy Bark,	. . .	O 322	Irene	5
Dance o'er the Sparkling Waves--Go happy Bark	. . . .	O 364	Irene V	30

WAVING

Cali, methinks yon waving Trees afford	. . . . .	O 268	Irene	36

WAY

Swift from pursuing horrors take your way,	. . . .	O 18	London	188
Lords of the street, and terrors of the way;	. . . .	O 21	London	231
And starves exhausted regions in his way;	. . . . .	O 42	Vanity Wishes	228
Jocund he dances o'er the wat'ry way,	. . . . . .	O 82	Young Author	5
Then dances jocund o'er the watery way,	. . . . . .	O 82	Young Author V	5
O guide me through life's darksome way,	. . . . .	O 100	Ode Friendship	14
O guide us through life's darksome way,	. . . . .	O 100	Ode Friendship V	14
And Rapine and Pollution mark their Way.	. . . . .	O 110	To Posterity	8
Look not on her by the way;	. . . .	O 150	Tr Boet III.12	44
Where is bliss? and which the way?	. . . . .	O 181	Parody Warton	4
What is bliss? and which the way?	. . . . .	O 181	Parody Warton V	4
Liquid fragrance all the way:	. . . . . .	O 185	Anacreon Ode 9	4
And free'd his soul the nearest way.	. . . . .	O 202	Death Dr Levet	36
And forc'd his soul the nearest way.	. . . .	O 202	Death Dr Levet V	36
Rough Winter's blasts to Spring give way,	. . . .	O 231	Tr Horace IV.7	9
Meet unexpected Daggers in his Way,	. . . . . .	O 274	Irene	48
And scatters roses in the thorny way	. . . . . .	Y 148	Irene	V 43D

WAY	(CONTINUED)	PAGE	TITLE	LINE
	And kind Ambition points the Way to Greatness.	O 280	Irene	14
	Fierce through the bursting Caverns rend their Way?	O 281	Irene	53
	But all give way to Rapture and Demetrius.	O 295	Irene	20
	Beset the treacherous Way with fatal Ambush;	O 300	Irene	72
	Back through the city trod his former way.	Y 17	Tr. Iliad Bk 6	2
	Before his face the frighted Cranes gave way.	Y 25	Tr Add. Battle	122
WAYS				
	And turn the varied taunt a thousand ways.	O 17	London	165
	Whose Ways and Means support the sinking land;	O 21	London	245
	Whose Ways and Means support a sinking land;	Y 60	London	V 245
	The Wits of Charles found easier Ways to Fame,	O 52	Pro Drury-Lane	17
WE				
	On Thames's banks, in silent thought we stood,	O 10	London	21
	We kneel, and kiss the consecrated earth;	O 10	London	24
	Well may we fear, such crowds at Tyburn die,	Y 60	London	V 242
	For now no more we trace in ev'ry line	O 34	Vanity Wishes	87
	For we that live to please, must please to live.	O 53	Pro Drury-Lane	54
	From zeal or malice now no more we dread,	O 61	Pro Word Wise	3
	While wretched we about the world must roam,	O 64	Virgil Past.I	3
	Had we not been perverse and careless grown,	O 64	Virgil Past.I	21
	In vain we shun the Din of War,	O 69	Hor.II Ode 14	13
	In vain with anxious breasts we fear	O 69	Hor.II Ode 14	15
	We all must view the Stygian flood	O 69	Hor.II Ode 14	17
	We bid propitious Heav'n prolong your reign,	O 96	Hickman Spinet	7
	We bless the Tyrant, and we hug the Chain.	O 96	Hickman Spinet	8
	We bless the Tyrant, and we hug the Chain.	O 96	Hickman Spinet	8
	Behold my fair, where-e'er we rove,	O 123	Winter's Walk	1
	From thee, great God, we spring, to thee we tend,	O 130	Tr. Rambler 7	7
	From thee, great God, we spring, to thee we tend,	O 130	Tr. Rambler 7	7
	We round thy board the cheerful menials see,	O 130	Tr. Rambler 12	5
	Inforc'd we love, unheeding recollect.	O 134	Tr. Rambler 96	2
	We are come to Thirtyfive;	O 178	Thrale 35 Year	2
	For howe'er we boast and strive,	O 178	Thrale 35 Year	13
	In bed we laugh, in bed we cry,	O 184	Tr. Benserade	1
	In bed we laugh, in bed we cry,	O 184	Tr. Benserade	1
	And born in bed, in bed we die;	O 184	Tr. Benserade	2
	With thoughtless reverence we praise,	O 190	Tr. Medea I	2
	As on we toil from day to day,	O 200	Death Dr Levet	2
	These all are Trifles, to what we can give.	O 247	Irene Epilogue	20
	Did we not see the bars of nature broken?	Y 115	Irene	V 49F
	While thus we mourn the Fortune of Aspasia,	O 253	Irene	107
	To what are we reserv'd?	O 253	Irene	108
	At least this Day be calm--If we succeed,	O 260	Irene	141
	The Weakness we lament, our selves create,	O 266	Irene	26
	We learn to shudder at the rustling Breeze,	O 266	Irene	29
	Well might we fear impending Disappointments.	O 269	Irene	2
	All this we know already from Abdalla.	O 270	Irene	6
	Should we before the Troops proclaim his Crimes	O 273	Irene	38
	Mean as we are, this Tyrant of the World	O 277	Irene	39
	We oft (notwithstanding this boasted superiour genius	Y 148	Irene	V 49
	Do we not share the comprehensive Thought,	O 278	Irene	55
	Do not we share the comprehensive thought,	Y 149	Irene	V 57
	Still must we linger in uncertain Hope?	O 282	Irene	3
	We still had wander'd on Tartarian Hills.	O 284	Irene	41
	Who merits most!--I knew not we were Rivals.	O 284	Irene	46
	We cannot obviate, for we cannot guess.	O 287	Irene	11
	We cannot obviate, for we cannot guess.	O 287	Irene	11
	We court thy Gentleness.	O 288	Irene	9
	There shall we find the yet untasted Bliss	O 292	Irene	88
	If we must part--	O 297	Irene	11
	If we must part--	O 297	Irene	12
	Soon may we meet again, secure and free,	O 303	Irene	23
	O spare the gallant Greek, in him we lose	O 307	Irene	26
	When next we meet before we storm the Palace,	O 308	Irene	28
	When next we meet before we storm the Palace,	O 308	Irene	28
	Yet ere we give our loosen'd Thoughts to Rapture,	O 309	Irene	18
	Close, as we might unseen, we watch'd his Steps;	O 311	Irene	2
	Close, as we might unseen, we watch'd his Steps;	O 311	Irene	2
	With him Abdalla we beheld--	O 311	Irene	8
	We mark'd him storming in Excess of Fury,	O 311	Irene	11
	Abdalla, while we waited near the Palace,	O 316	Irene	25
	We come, bright Virgin, tho' relenting Nature	O 325	Irene	20
	We ask'd, with tim'rous Tongue, th' Offender's Name,	O 325	Irene	23
	We started at the Sound, again enquir'd,	O 325	Irene	25
	Not call'd to try the Cause, we hear the Sentence,	O 326	Irene	34
	we are in danger by this pause	Y 206	Irene	V 11
	That thus constrain'd we speed the Stroke of Death.	O 327	Irene	30
	Could we reverse the Sentence of the Sultan,	O 328	Irene	38
	To meet that Fate we can delay no longer.	O 328	Irene	41
	Then we with wine will drown our troubles, laid	Y 7	Virgil Daphnis	47
	Think shouldst thou fall how wretched shall we be,	Y 19	Tr. Iliad Bk 6	48
	Chear'd the rough road, we wish'd the rough road long,	Y 310	Parody of Pope	2
WEAK				
	Watch the weak hour, and ransack all the heart;	O 17	London	155
	On weak foundations raise th' enormous weight?	O 35	Vanity Wishes	126
	Now with no weak unballast wing	O 70	Hor.II Ode XX	1
	And weak Philosophy denies her Succours.	O 252	Irene	92
	But when an earthquake comes weak and unsupported	Y 131	Irene	V 36B
	So weak is Man, when destin'd to Destruction,	O 283	Irene	12
	In my weak Ear th' intoxicating Sounds.	O 288	Irene	6

WEAK	(CONTINUED)	PAGE	TITLE	LINE

WEAK   (CONTINUED)   PAGE   TITLE   LINE
    Soon shouldst thou see, how false thy weak Reproach. . .   O 293 Irene   107
    Soon wouldst thou see, how false thy weak Reproach.   . .   O 293 Irene   V 107
    O'erthrow such weak, such accidental Virtue, ... O 301 Irene   83
    Let no weak Doubt the gen'rous Hand restrain, ...   O 313 Irene   22
    But my blood freezes and weak nature shudders . . . .   Y 189 Irene   16
    Weak Man with erring Rage may throw the Dart, ...   O 335 Irene   V 16
                                                                                       14
WEAKEN'D
    Then crush'd by Rules, and weaken'd as refin'd, . . .   O 52 Pro Drury-Lane   29
WEAKLY
    And weakly hopes to 'scape the critick's rage. . . . .   Y 67 Prologue Lethe   12
WEAKNESS
    Well might the Weakness of our Empire sink . . . . .   O 250 Irene   48
        Forgive an old Man's Weakness, ...   O 256 Irene   38
    The Weakness we lament, our selves create, ...   O 266 Irene   26
    Each weakness sooth and flatter ev'ry folly. . . . .   Y 134 Irene   V 27
    Unfit for Toil, and polish'd into Weakness, ...   O 290 Irene   43
    Nor think my eyes oerflow with Female . . . .   O 357 Irene   V 17
        Weakness
    Too much to fear or trust, is equal Weakness. . . . .   O 300 Irene   77
    The Christian's tenderness? or womans weakness . . . .   Y 189 Irene   V 1C
WEALH
    The Merchant sees her with wealh, the lover with his . .   O 374 Irene   V 29
        Mistress
    Wealh in her hand, and olive on her brow. . . . . .   O 374 Irene   V 32
WEALTH
    Of dissipated wealth the small remains, ...   O   9 London   20
    Behold our fame, our wealth, our lives your own. . . .   O 13 London   64
    Rais'd from some pleasing dream of wealth and pow'r, . .   O 18 London   184
    Should heaven's just bolts Orgilio's wealth confound, . . O 19 London   194
    And crowd with sudden wealth the rising dome; . . . .   O 19 London   203
    Wealth heap'd on wealth, nor truth nor safety buys, . .   O 31 Vanity Wishes   27
    Wealth heap'd on wealth, nor truth nor safety buys, . .   O 31 Vanity Wishes   27
    Where wealth unlov'd without a mourner dy'd, ...   O 33 Vanity Wishes   55
    Athirst for wealth, and burning to be great; . . . .   O 33 Vanity Wishes   74
    To growing wealth the dedicator flies, ...   O 33 Vanity Wishes   82
    Shall Wolsey's wealth, with Wolsey's end be thine? . .   O 35 Vanity Wishes 122
    He sees, and pitying sees, vain Wealth bestow . . . .   O 57 Prologue Comus   21
    His liquid Wealth o'er barbarous lands. . . . . . .   O 65 Hor I Ode xxii   8
    His liquid Wealth thro' barbarous Lands. . . . . . .   O 66 To A. Fuscus   8
    When ev'n proud wealth and prouder wit obey, ...   O 81 Lady Birthday   10
    "For wealth or title, perishable prize; . . . . . .   O 82 Young Author   16
    From wealth and grandeur easy to descend, ...   O 130 Tr. Rambler 12   3
    In quest of wealth who throw their lives away. . . . .   O 132 Tr. Rambler 48   2
    Wealth still finds followers, and misfortunes foes. . .   O 138 Tr Rambler 153   2
    The lust of wealth can never bear delay. . . . . . .   O 140 Tr Rambler 182   1
    No wealth his life from weary care can save, ...   O 146 Tr Boeth III.3   5
    No care his wealth can carry to the grave. . . . . .   O 146 Tr Boeth III.3   6
    Wealth, Sir John, was made to wander, ...   O 196 Song Congratu.   17
    Wealth, my lad, was made to wander, ...   O 196 Song Congratu. V 17
    Tho' Wealth, and Pow'r, and Glory they receive, . . .   O 247 Irene Epilogue   19
    Th' accumulated Wealth of toiling Ages. . . . . . .   O 249 Irene   19
    That Wealth, too sacred for their Country's Use! . . .   O 250 Irene   20
    Thy wealth O city ill-gotten ill-preserv'd . . . . .   Y 113 Irene   V 20
    That Wealth, too pleasing to be lost for Freedom! . . .   O 250 Irene   21
    That Wealth, which granted to their weeping Prince, . .   O 250 Irene   22
    Empire or Wealth, to Excellence like thine? . . . . .   O 267 Irene   9
    Extends his mighty Schemes of Wealth and Pow'r, . . .   O 269 Irene   4
    With all the allurements of persuasive . . . . . .   Y 142 Irene   V 38
        wealth--gold
    There will his boundless Wealth, the Spoil of Asia, . .   O 274 Irene   50
    There (or might) shall his boundless Wealth the . . .   O 351 Irene   V 13
    Give Wealth to Poverty to Slavery Freedom . . . . .   O 356 Irene   V 13
    Unbounded Wealth shall flow beneath thy feet . . . .   O 350 Irene   V 23
    Thus Life, with loss of Wealth, is well preserv'd, . .   O 290 Irene   34
    His Wealth, his Rank, his Honours he recounted, . . .   O 299 Irene   45
    Nor Wealth, nor Titles, make Aspasia's Bliss. . . . .   O 302 Irene   106
    Vain pride & wealth . . . .   Y 177 Irene   V 110
    Love be my Wealth, and my Distinction Virtue. . . . .   O 302 Irene   111
    Wealth, and Command, and Grandeur shall be thine . . .   O 306 Irene   6
    Profuse of Wealth, or bounteous of Success, ...   O 313 Irene   20
    O Greece! renown'd for Science and for Wealth, ...   O 317 Irene   42
    Be thine, that Wealth can give, or Guilt receive. . . .   O 322 Irene   58
WEALTHIEST
    The wealthiest landlord on the banks of Trent? . . . .   Y 97 Vanity Wishes V 124
WEALTHY
    And leaves the wealthy traytor in the Tow'r, ...   O 32 Vanity Wishes   34
    Prowls like a lyon oer the wealthy Spoils of bleeding .   O 352 Irene   V 29
        Turkey.
    Prowls o'er the wealthy Spoils of bleeding Turkey? . .   O 264 Irene   15
    For you fair Asia spreads her wealthy plains. . . . .   Y 132 Irene   V 41C
WEAPON
    Its useless force the weapon spends in air. . . . . .   Y 26 Tr Add. Battle 135
WEAR
    Wear the gown, and wear the hat, ...   O 194 On Thrale Hat   1
    Wear the gown, and wear the hat, ...   O 194 On Thrale Hat   1
    There wear the tedious Hours of Life away, ...   O 292 Irene   85
    Whose early buds unusual glories wear, ...   Y   3 On a Daffodill   3
WEARIED
    He sees the wearied Oxen bow . . . .   O 73 Hor. Epode II V 69
    And wearied angels rest upon their stars spheres . . .   Y 128 Irene   V 4B

		PAGE	TITLE		LINE
WEARING					
	Wearing out life's evening gray;	O 181	Parody Warton		2
WEARS					
	The wily scrc'ress wears a thousand forms, ...	Y 155	Irene	V	26
	Fierce persecution wears the bleeding world with . . .	Y 164	Irene	V	66
	fraud				
	He wears of late Resentment on his Brow, ...	O 311	Irene		9
	Of aspect stern for in his face he wears	Y 24	Tr Add. Battle		82
WEARY					
	To press the weary minutes flagging wings:	O 44	Vanity Wishes		300
	Loads the lingring minutes weary wings:	Y 105	Vanity Wishes	V	300
	To press the weary minutes hanging wings:	Y 105	Vanity Wishes	V	300
	Prest by the load of life, the weary mind	O 59	Pro Good Nat'd		1
	And waiting for her weary lord	O 73	Hor. Epode II		53
	No wealth his life from weary care can save, ...	O 146	Tr Boeth III.3		5
	Shou'd welcome Sleep relieve the weary Wit, ...	O 246	Irene Prologue		25
	And weary Cruelty remits her Tortures.	O 249	Irene		10
	And weary Murther slumbers o'er the Carnage	O 350	Irene	V	9
	Imagination hangs her weary wings	Y 127	Irene	V	2
	The weary Sun forgets his Revolutions	O 347	Irene	V	30
	And weary Planets loiter in their Courses.	O 262	Irene		4
	And give the weary passenger refreshment.	Y 130	Irene	V	12D
	And chear the weary Passenger with Musick.	O 277	Irene		38
	And chear the weary passenger with warblings	O 355	Irene	V	21
	On weary Mortals sheds the balm of rest	O 356	Irene	V	10
	The weary Soldier--Still sees to Morrow	O 374	Irene	V	30
WEAVE					
	To weave those nets that catch the heart.	O 120	To Miss Purse		6
WEAVES					
	And weaves her bending boughs in pleasing glooms; . . .	O 84	Epi Dist Moth.		15
WEAVING					
	... a Gold and Silk net-work Purse of her own weaving .	O 119	To Miss Purse		T
WEB					
	To make thy curious web delight, ...	O 119	To Miss Purse		2
	To make the curious web delight, ...	O 119	To Miss Purse	V	2
	There let the web and distaff be your care.	Y 21	Tr. Iliad Bk 6		122
WED					
	Unblest, still doom'd to wed with misery.	O 131	Tr. Rambler 39		1
WEEDS					
	The banefull weeds spring up, and choak the grain. . .	Y 7	Virgil Daphnis		23
WEEKLY					
	For growing names the weekly scribbler lies, ...	O 33	Vanity Wishes		81
	To growing names the weekly scribbler lies, ...	Y 95	Vanity Wishes	V	82
	With weekly libels and septennial ale, ...	O 34	Vanity Wishes		97
WEEP					
	Around his tomb let Art and Genius weep, ...	O 39	Vanity Wishes		173
	But hear his death, ye blockheads, hear and weep. . . .	O 39	Vanity Wishes	V	174
	Or weep some falling King.	O 78	Feast St Simon		6
	Unpitying see them weep, and hear them pray, ...	O 83	Epi Dist Moth.		8
WEEPING					
	That Wealth, which granted to their weeping Prince, . .	O 250	Irene		22
	And weeping, kiss the venerable Ruins:	O 251	Irene		61
	A weeping Wife perhaps, or dying Friend, ...	O 280	Irene		9
	Andromache looks back with weeping eyes, ...	Y 21	Tr. Iliad Bk 6		127
	While the sad Pygmies mourn with weeping eyes	Y 26	Tr Add. Battle		128
WEIGH					
	Impartial weigh the Pleasure with the Danger.	O 285	Irene		9
WEIGH'D					
	When weigh'd with Greece, with Virtue, with Aspasia? . .	O 260	Irene		138
WEIGHED					
	Whats Life when weighed with Greece or Aspasia? . . .	O 371	Irene	V	24
WEIGHT					
	On weak foundations raise th' enormous weight?	O 35	Vanity Wishes		126
	And, fainting, scarce support the liquid weight: . . .	O 74	Tr. Iliad Bk 6		24
	The weight of ev'ry rolling sphere, ...	O 79	Feast St Simon		32
	From beneath the cumbrous Weight;	O 145	Tr Boeth. II.4		12
	The Weight of Years, and totters to the Tempest, . . .	O 250	Irene		45
	Shake off this Weight of unavailing Grief, ...	O 333	Irene		39
WEIGHTY					
	In bus'ness dext'rous, weighty in debate, ...	O 118	Epitaph Hanmer		13
	"Weighty charge consign'd to me:	O 185	Anacreon Ode 9		16
	The weighty Charge of Royalty confer;	O 292	Irene		104
WELCOME					
	Shou'd welcome Sleep relieve the weary Wit, ...	O 246	Irene Prologue		25
	How did Aspasia welcome your Address?	O 282	Irene		61
WELL					
	Well may they rise, while I, whose rustick tongue . . .	O 14	London		79
	Well may they venture on the mimick's art, ...	O 16	London		134
	Well may we fear, such crowds at Tyburn die, ...	Y 60	London	V	242
	Too well You know to keep the Slaves You gain.	O 96	Hickman Spinet		2
	Wisdom at proper times is well forgot.	O 134	Tr. Rambler 89		1
	With cream and sugar soften'd well, ...	O 158	Par Hermit III		3
	With cream and sugar temper'd well, ...	O 158	Par Hermit III	V	3
	Well skill'd to sooth a foe with looks of kindness, . .	O 176	Tr Metastas II		3
	Well tried through many a varying year, ...	O 201	Death Dr Levet		5
	The single talent well employ'd.	O 201	Death Dr Levet		28
	His single talent well employ'd.	O 201	Death Dr Levet	V	28
	Well might the Weakness of our Empire sink	O 250	Irene		48
	Exhaust the well of Zemzem.	Y 131	Irene	V	32D
	Well pleas'd to find thy Precepts not forgotten. . . .	O 267	Irene		41
	Too well I know him, his immod'rate Courage, ...	O 267	Irene		46

```
WELL        (CONTINUED)                                   PAGE    TITLE           LINE
     Well may those Eyes that view these heav'nly Charms,  . .   O 267 Irene             6
     Well might we fear impending Disappointments. . . . .      O 269 Irene             2
     I mark'd them well, and trac'd in either Face  . . . .     O 275 Irene            81
     Might well befit the solitary Student,  . . . .  .        O 281 Irene            36
     Well,--'tis decreed--This Night shall fix our Fate. . .   O 284 Irene            48
     Thus Life, with loss of Wealth, is well preserv'd, . .    O 290 Irene            34
     Well may'st thou hide in Labyrinths of Sound  . . .       O 293 Irene           125
     What well known Voice pronounc'd the grateful Sounds . .  O 295 Irene            10
     Purge well thy Mind from ev'ry private Passion,  .  . .   O 298 Irene             6
     Well known, long try'd, expect us on the Shore.  . . .    O 301 Irene            91
     'Tis well--A single Blow compleats our Wishes: . . . .    O 304 Irene             8
     Too well I know him, since on Thracia's Plains . . . .    O 307 Irene            18
     Were now well lost, in hearing how you fail'd. . . . .    O 316 Irene            23
     Well mayst thou call thy Master to the Combat,  . . .     O 319 Irene            30
     Well pleas'd to search the Treasures of Remembrance, . .  O 323 Irene            15
     Perfidious!--yes--too well thou know'st them Traytors. .  O 324 Irene            17
     Has serv'd his Prince so well, demand our Silence?  . .   O 329 Irene            19
     Well if a Thousand Lives like thine had perish'd;  . . .  O 332 Irene            34
     well th' Eternal Mind thus her doom decreed  . . . .  .   O 345 Irene          V 34
WELL-ACCORDED
     How passion's well-accorded strife . . . . . . . . .      O 121 To Miss Playin    31
WELL-FEIGN'D
     With well-feign'd gratitude the pension'd band  . . . .   O  19 London           200
WENT
     Dispersing blessings as they went, . . . . . . . .        O  79 Feast St Simon    26
WENTWORTH
     What murder'd Wentworth, and what exil'd Hyde,  . . . .   O  36 Vanity Wishes    131
WEPT
     And sigh'd and wept at her relentless gate. . . . . .     Y  11 Tr Hor Epode 9    36
     And wept unhappy Pompey's hapless fate? . . . . . .       Y  22 Tr Add. Battle    15
     In which the Pygmie wept his cruelty. . . . . . . .       Y  24 Tr Add. Battle    63
WERE
     No spies were paid, no special juries known,  . . . .     O  22 London           252
     No bribes were paid, no special juries known, . . . .     Y  61 London         V 252
     To thee were solemn toys or empty shew, . . . . . .       O  33 Vanity Wishes     65
     Their Cause was gen'ral, their Supports were strong, . .  O  52 Pro Drury-Lane    25
     Their Slaves were willing, and their Reign was long; . .  O  52 Pro Drury-Lane    26
     Yet judg'd by those, whose voices ne'er were sold, . .    O  60 Pro Good Nat'd    27
     Our trees were blasted by the thunder stroke, . . . .     O  65 Virgil Past.I     23
     Such as the Sun-burnt Sabines were, . . . . . . .         O  72 Hor. Epode II     49
     Who to their Lord were ever dear, . . . . . . . .         O  78 Feast St Simon    10
     Th' Apostles round the world were sent, . . . . .         O  79 Feast St Simon    25
     These dreams were Settle's once and Ogilby's. . . .       O  82 Young Author      24
     Those dreams were Settle's once and Ogilby's. . . .       O  82 Young Author    V 24
     Were Pope once void of wonted candour found,  . . .       O 106 Eliza plucking     7
     His frame was firm, his powers were bright, . . . .       O 202 Death Dr Levet    31
     These Groans were fatal, these Disguises vain: . . .      O 249 Irene              6
     And yet, my Friend, what Miracles were wrought  . . .     O 251 Irene             52
     This were enough, if Cali had been Mahomet  . . . .       Y 132 Irene          V 41D
     Half were too much had Mahomet been Cali. . . . .         Y 132 Irene          V 41E
     Were all our Favours lavish'd on a Villain? . . . .       O 272 Irene             12
     Who merits most!--I knew not we were Rivals. . . . .      O 284 Irene             46
     And wishes Irene were converted by some . . . . . .       Y 186 Irene          V  11
        doctor
     Say, by what Fraud, what Force were you defeated?  . . .  O 315 Irene              6
        To tell, or hear, were Waste of Life. . . . . .        O 316 Irene             21
     Were now well lost, in hearing how you fail'd. . . . ;    O 316 Irene             23
     Thy Life perhaps--were but Irene spar'd, . . . . .        O 332 Irene             33
     Such Beauty, Sweetness, Love, were cheaply bought,  . .   O 332 Irene             35
     And with laborious crouds the plains were fill'd. . .     Y  23 Tr Add. Battle    29
     Till purse and carcase both were low. . . . . . . .       Y 300 Extemp. Elegy     12
WEST
     D<r>ives to (holds o'er) the south or west the  . . . .   Y 136 Irene          V 26
        storm
WESTERN
     All the Western kingdoms  . . . . . . . . . . . .         Y 177 Irene          V 115
     And wake from Ignorance the Western World. . . . . .      O 302 Irene            123
     See! Sol's bright chariot seeks the western main, . . .   Y   4 On a Daffodill    22
WET
     Only dirt, or wet or dry. . . . . . . . . . . .           O 196 Song Congratu.    24
     Wet the dim eye or swell the throbbing bosom? . . . .     Y 191 Irene          V 19A
WHALEBONES
     Nor torturing whalebones pinch them into charms; . . .    O  84 Epi Dist Moth.    23
WHAT
        101
WHAT'S   SEE WHATS                                             OMITTED WORD
     In vain proud Man usurps what's Woman's Due;  . . . .     O 247 Irene Epilogue    15
     Important Hazard! What's that airy Bubble . . . . .       O 260 Irene            137
WHATE'ER
     Secure whate'er he gives, he gives the best. . . . . .    O  48 Vanity Wishes    356
     See! how whate'er remain'd of Man . . . . . . . .         O  70 Hor.II Ode XX     10
     Whate'er the swarthy Lybian boasts, . . . . . . .         O  73 Hor. Epode II   V 57
     Whate'er from India spicy coasts  . . . . . . . .         O  73 Hor. Epode II   V 58
     Whate'er Man's Pride has ravish'd from our Sex. . .       O 291 Irene             75
     Whate'er their Scheme the Bassa's Death defeats it, . .   O 312 Irene              4
        Whate'er thy Accusation, . . . . . . . . . . .         O 323 Irene             11
     Whate'er perfidious villany can suffer  . . . . . .       Y 216 Irene          V 75
WHATEVER
     Whatever course of Life great Jove allots,  . . . . .     O  77 Festina Lente      1
     Inflict whatever Treason can deserve, . . . . . . .       O 334 Irene             75
```

	PAGE	TITLE	LINE
WHATEVER (CONTINUED)			
Whatever Crane confiding in his might	Y 23	Tr Add. Battle	38
WHATS			
Whats Life when weighed with Greece or Aspasia? . . .	O 371	Irene	V 24
WHATSOE'ER			
Whoe'er thou art, or whatsoe'er thy Message, ...	O 294	Irene	4
WHEEL			
Or like a gibbet better than a wheel;	O 15	London	108
And Anguish gnashes on the fatal Wheel.	O 266	Irene	16
WHELMS			
And whelms the swelling Architect beneath it.	O 269	Irene	9
WHEN			
152		OMITTED WORD	
WHENCE			
Rashness! thou spring from whence misfortunes flow! . . .	O 77	Festina Lente	9
Whence or whither dost thou fly?	O 185	Anacreon Ode 9	2
Whence and whither dost thou fly?	O 185	Anacreon Ode 9	V 2
But whence this new sprung Hope?	O 253	Irene	111
Haste to the safe retreat, from whence Demetrius . . .	Y 126	Irene	V 144
Whence then those Charms thy Tongue has deign'd to . . .	O 277	Irene	26
flatter,			
Whence flow the Hopes and Fears, Despair and Rapture, .	O 277	Irene	41
Whence all those Hopes and Fears Despair and	O 355	Irene	V 18
Rapture			
Whence all the Bliss and Agonies of Love?	O 277	Irene	42
Whence all the pleasures, and the pains of love. . . .	Y 148	Irene	V 42
Whence rise these restless cares? these strong emotions? .	Y 189	Irene	V 1
Whence is this Violence?	O 321	Irene	53
Whence is this Rage? what barb'rous Tongue has wrong'd .	O 325	Irene	27
me?			
WHENE'ER			
Whene'er this Stone, now hid beneath the Lake, ...	O 110	To Posterity	1
Whene'er the lab'ring bird with anxious care	Y 23	Tr Add. Battle	44
WHERE			
97		OMITTED WORD	
WHERE-E'ER			
Where-e'er he turns he meets a stranger's eye, ...	O 35	Vanity Wishes	111
Behold my fair, where-e'er we rove, ...	O 123	Winter's Walk	1
WHERE'ER			
Still to his int'rest true, where'er he goes, ...	O 16	London	125
Where'er the battle rages bends his course.	Y 25	Tr Add. Battle	119
WHERESOE'ER			
Wheresoe'er I turn my View, ...	O 179	Ridicul Warton	1
WHEREVER			
Wherever Guilt can fly, Revenge can follow.	O 274	Irene	65
WHERRY			
While Thales waits the wherry that contains	O 9	London	19
WHET			
Which whet their beaks, for flight their wings prepare, . .	Y 24	Tr Add. Battle	70
WHETHER			
Whether you sit on thrones, or dwell in cots, ...	O 77	Festina Lente	2
Whether urg'd on by seers from heav'n inspir'd	Y 19	Tr. Iliad Bk 6	58
WHICH			
Wreaths which at last the dear-bought right convey . .	O 40	Vanity Wishes	189
He left the name, at which the world grew pale, . .	O 41	Vanity Wishes	221
Which heavn may hear	Y 108	Vanity Wishes	V 348
Which heav'n may hear, nor deem religion vain. . . .	O 47	Vanity Wishes	350
For love, which scarce collective man can fill; . . .	O 48	Vanity Wishes	361
Those pageant Honours which he scorn'd below:	O 57	Prologue Comus	22
This night presents a play, which publick rage, . . .	O 61	Pro Word Wise	1
As herbs of which the forrests nigh	O 73	Hor. Epode II	61
As herbs of which the fields nigh	O 73	Hor. Epode II	V 61
The day will come, in which proud Troy shall yield, . .	O 74	Tr. Iliad Bk 6	13
Thus fell the Pygmie state, which long had stood . . .	O 76	Tr Add. Battle	33
Those names which in immortal strains	O 80	Feast St Simon	59
The balmy kiss, for which poor Thyrsis dies;	O 84	Epi Dist Moth.	21
Inflicting all those ills which once they knew; . . .	O 84	Epi Dist Moth.	37
Which gild a lover's lays, ...	O 126	To Lyce, Lady	6
That slowly grows, which must for ever last.	O 142	In Baretti Bk.	8
Which erst in Frost and Freedom lay, ...	O 146	Tr Boeth III.5	8
Thou know'st not those arts which blast with envious praise,	O 176	Tr Metastas II	7
Which aggravate a fault with feign'd excuses, ...	O 176	Tr Metastas II	8
Where is bliss? and which the way?	O 181	Parody Warton	4
What is bliss? and which the way?	O 181	Parody Warton	V 4
"His the letters which you see, ...	O 185	Anacreon Ode 9	15
Had this fair figure which this frame displays, . . .	O 189	Seeing Montagu	1
That Wealth, which granted to their weeping Prince, . .	O 250	Irene	22
Which Cheats interpret, and which Fools regard? . . .	O 250	Irene	43
Which Cheats interpret, and which Fools regard? . . .	O 250	Irene	43
Which lately bless'd my gentle Government, ...	O 257	Irene	75
Which granted, hides my Purpose from the World, . . .	O 258	Irene	88
Which Armies guard, and Citadels inclose?	O 258	Irene	91
Which Love of Greatness, not of Truth, inflames. . . .	O 262	Irene	27
Sure this is Love which heretofore I conceiv'd . . .	O 349	Irene	V 28
Superiour man descends which	Y 147	Irene	V 39
That Hoary Head, that Head which hungry fate	O 374	Irene	V 20
Which squander'd by Neglect, or Fear, or Folly, . . .	O 302	Irene	7
Hypocrisy which I ha<ve> worn is a burthen:	Y 185	Irene	V 2
For which Aspasia scorn'd the Turkish Crown?	O 314	Irene	17
The Life, which only this Design supported, ...	O 316	Irene	22
Nor think that Effort lost which rescues thee.	O 317	Irene	47

```
WHICH           (CONTINUED)                            PAGE   TITLE            LINE
    Against the Head which Innocence secures,  . . . . .   O 322  Irene              1
    Which murder'd Innocence that call'd on me.  . . . .   O 334  Irene             76
    Then scorn those flowers to which the Aegyptians bow'd,  Y   4  On a Daffodill   15
    Which prostrate Memphis own'd her deities.  . . . .   Y   4  On a Daffodill     16
    On dangers which your safety bids you shun,  . . . .  Y  18  Tr. Iliad Bk 6     20
    In which the Pygmie wept his cruelty.  . . . . . .   Y  24  Tr Add. Battle     63
    Which whet their beaks, for flight their wings prepare,  .   Y  24  Tr Add. Battle     70
    Which gave a thousand pleasures birth.  . . . . .   Y  39  Lady Leaving        8
WHILE
    While Thales waits the wherry that contains  . . . . .   O   9  London            19
    While yet my steady steps no staff sustains,  . . . .   O  10  London            41
    While yet my steddy steps no staff sustains,  . . . .   O  10  London          V  41
    Well may they rise, while I, whose rustick tongue  . . .   O  14  London            79
    While all neglect, and most insult your woes.  . . . .   O  19  London           193
    See! while he builds, the gaudy vassals come,  . . . .   O  19  London           202
    And, while thy grounds a cheap repast afford,  . . . .   O  20  London           218
    And, while thy beds a cheap repast afford,  . . . . .   O  20  London         V 218
    While ladies interpose, and slaves debate.  . . . . .   O  41  Vanity Wishes    214
    While growing hopes scarce awe the gath'ring sneer,  . .   O  44  Vanity Wishes    277
    Till Declamation roar'd, while Passion slept.  . . . .   O  52  Pro Drury-Lane    32
    While Crowds aloft the laureat Bust behold,  . . . . .   O  58  Prologue Comus    23
    While Crowds aloft the laureat Dust behold,  . . . . .   O  58  Prologue Comus  V  23
    While tutelary Nations guard her Cell.  . . . . . .   O  58  Prologue Comus    36
    While wretched we about the world must roam,  . . . .   O  64  Virgil Past.I      3
    For while by Chloe's image charm'd,  . . . . . . .   O  65  Hor I Ode xxii     9
    For while in Sabine Forests, charm'd  . . . . . . .   O  66  To A. Fuscus       9
    While I to nobler themes aspire,  . . . . . . . .   O  78  Feast St Simon     7
    While the breeze whispers and the streamers play.  . . .   O  82  Young Author       6
    "While I these transitory blessings scorn,  . . . . .   O  82  Young Author      17
    "While I those transitory blessings scorn,  . . . . .   O  82  Young Author    V  17
    Then melt, ye fair, while crouds around you sigh,  . . .   O  84  Epi Dist Moth.    42
    While Love, a stranger to the blest,  . . . . . . .   O  99  Ode Friendship     5
    While Love, unknown amongst the blest,  . . . . . .   O  99  Ode Friendship  V   5
    While he lies melting in a lewd Embrace;  . . . . . .   O 111  To Posterity      24
    And learn his virtues, while thou mourn'st his end.  . .   O 117  Epitaph Hanmer     4
    But some Zelinda while I sing  . . . . . . . .   O 127  To Lyce, Lady     17
    While t' asswage the Pangs of Love  . . . . . . .   O 149  Tr Boet III.12    15
    While artful shades thy downy couch enclose,  . . . .   O 151  The Ant           11
    Snatch thy pleasures while they last;  . . . . . . .   O 194  On Thrale Hat      2
    Snatch your pleasures while they last;  . . . . . . .   O 194  On Thrale Hat   V   2
    While thus we mourn the Fortune of Aspasia,  . . . . .   O 253  Irene            107
    While Heav'n and Mahomet divide her Fears,  . . . . .   O 260  Irene            127
    What! think of Peace while haughty Scanderbeg  . . . .   O 264  Irene             13
    While fair Hungaria's unexhausted Vallies  . . . . .   O 264  Irene             16
    While fair yet Hungaria's inexhausted Vallies  . . . .   O 352  Irene          V  33
    While with incessant Thought laborious Man  . . . . .   O 269  Irene              3
    Retire with Speed, while I prepare to meet him  . . . .   O 271  Irene             37
    And feel no Sorrow while my Sov'reign smiles.  . . . .   O 272  Irene             11
    While Heav'n's high Minister, whose awful Volume  . .   O 276  Irene             20
    While Heaven's high Minister whose unerring awfull  . .   O 355  Irene          V   9
        volume
    Where hast thou linger'd while th' encumber'd Hours  . .   O 279  Irene              3
    To rave unheeded, while the happy Greek,  . . . . .   O 285  Irene              2
    While I foretell thy Fate; that Office done,--  . . . .   O 289  Irene              9
    But while Demetrius, dear lamented Name!  . . . . .   O 290  Irene             47
    While vulgar Souls compassionate their Cares,  . . . .   O 293  Irene            115
    While some Archangel nearer to Perfection,  . . . . .   O 293  Irene            121
    While some Archangel of superiour Nature  . . . . .   O 369  Irene          V  13
    Nor think thy Cause neglected while I gaze,  . . . . .   O 297  Irene             20
    Then while he gaz'd upon his yielding Mistress,  . . .   O 299  Irene             48
    Tell me the Cause, that while thy Name, Demetrius,  . .   O 305  Irene             25
    While I destroy th' Oppressor of Mankind?  . . . . .   O 305  Irene             37
    While yet the future Fortune of my Country  . . . . .   O 313  Irene              2
    When Purity, while Fraud was yet unknown,  . . . . .   O 314  Irene              6
    While secret Flames, with unextinguish'd Rage,  . . .   O 315  Irene             35
    Abdalla, while we waited near the Palace,  . . . . .   O 316  Irene             25
    Fly, Wretch, while yet my Pity grants thee Flight;  . .   O 319  Irene             23
    While I protract their Stay.  Be swift and faithful.  . .   O 319  Irene              4
    Press not her Flight, while yet her feeble Nerves  . . .   O 320  Irene             20
    Now make thy Choice, while yet the Pow'r of Choice  . .   O 321  Irene             40
    While I not yet familiar to my Crimes,  . . . . . .   O 322  Irene             11
    While unavailing Anger crouds thy Tongue  . . . . .   O 327  Irene              6
    While unavailing passion crouds your tongue  . . . .   O 368  Irene          V  14
    Nor hope his Fortune while thou want'st his Worth.  . .   O 330  Irene             25
    While she yet beg'd to plead her Cause before thee.  . .   O 334  Irene             67
    But while I sing, the nimble moments fly,  . . . . .   Y   4  On a Daffodill    21
    While his sad murder frantick with despair  . . . . .   Y   6  Virgil Daphnis     5
    While boars the rocks, while fish the rivers love,  . .   Y   7  Virgil Daphnis    49
    While boars the rocks, while fish the rivers love,  . .   Y   7  Virgil Daphnis    49
    Thyrsis while sings shall the gods  . . . . . . .   Y   7  Virgil Daphnis  V  49
    While bees shall feed on thyme, and birds shall haunt the   Y   7  Virgil Daphnis    50
        grove
    While Hector lives I tast of ev'ry joy  . . . . .   Y  18  Tr. Iliad Bk 6     26
    But dearest Hector while thou liv'st I see  . . . . .   Y  19  Tr. Iliad Bk 6     44
    While in my verse the shrilling trumpets sound,  . . .   Y  22  Tr Add. Battle     18
    In former ages while upheld by fate  . . . . . .   Y  23  Tr Add. Battle     26
    Not so while long th' undaunted race maintain'd  . . .   Y  23  Tr Add. Battle     36
    While the sad Pygmies mourn with weeping eyes  . . .   Y  26  Tr Add. Battle    128
    While many a merry tale, and many a song,  . . . . .   Y 310  Parody of Pope     1
```

		PAGE	TITLE	LINE	

WHILST
Till Declamation soar'd, whilst Passion slept. . . . . O 52 Pro Drury-Lane V 32
Whilst each Musician of the Grove . . . . O 72 Hor. Epode II 33
Nor whilst she Simons acts persues . . . . O 80 Feast St Simon 49
Whilst you deride their pangs in barb'rous play, . . O 83 Epi Dist Moth. 7
Whilst the bonny Blade carouses, ... O 196 Song Congratu. V 21
Whilst beaks and swords engage in bloody fray . . . . Y 22 Tr Add. Battle 6

WHIRL
in the whirl of thought . . . . Y 187 Irene V 6

WHIRL'D
Such bribes the rapid Greek o'er Asia whirl'd, ... O 39 Vanity Wishes 179

WHIRLE
Shall the whirle, and bid the Rock subside . . . . . O 365 Irene V 4

WHIRLING
Insidious sands, shallows rough rocks and whirling . . Y 201 Irene V 10B
devouring gulphs

WHIRLWINDS
Did roaring Whirlwinds sweep us from the Ramparts: . . O 251 Irene 55

WHISP'RING
(Cry'd Daphne whisp'ring from the yielding tree;) . . . O 106 Eliza plucking 6

WHISPER
And chang'd th' endearing Smile and am'rous Whisper . . O 259 Irene 111
The (coxcombs) whisper and the fopling's song . . . Y 128 Irene V 17
Would shake his wily Head, and closely whisper, . . . O 273 Irene 28

WHISPERS
While the breeze whispers and the streamers play. . . . O 82 Young Author 6

WHITE
To vote a patriot black, a courtier white; . . . . . O 11 London 52

WHITHER
Whence or whither dost thou fly? . . . . O 185 Anacreon Ode 9 2
Whence and whither dost thou fly? . . . . O 185 Anacreon Ode 9 V 2

WHO
Who now resolves, from vice and London far, ... O 9 London V 5
For who would leave, unbrib'd, Hibernia's land, . . . O 9 London 9
Who start at theft, and blush at perjury? . . . . O 13 London 68
Who scarce forbear, tho' Britain's Court he sing, . . . O 13 London 69
Who shares Orgilio's crimes, his fortune shares. . . . O 14 London 84
Mark whom the great caress, who frown on me! . . . . O 14 London 92
Who play from morn to night a borrow'd part; . . . . O 16 London 135
Who dwell on Balbos courtly mien-- . . . . Y 55 London V 150
Who sleeps on brambles till he kills his man; . . . . O 21 London 227
Thou who couldst laugh where want enchain'd caprice, . . O 32 Vanity Wishes 53
Such age there is, and who shall wish its end? . . . O 44 Vanity Wishes 298
Such age there is, and who could wish its end? . . . O 44 Vanity Wishes V 298
Such age the is, and who could wish its end? . . . . Y 105 Vanity Wishes V 298
Who set unclouded in the gulphs of fate. . . . . . O 45 Vanity Wishes 312
Who frown with vanity, who smile with art, ... O 46 Vanity Wishes 327
Who frown with vanity, who smile with art, ... O 46 Vanity Wishes 327
These goods he grants, who grants the pow'r to gain; . . O 48 Vanity Wishes 366
For those who durst not censure, scarce cou'd praise. . O 51 Pro Drury-Lane 14
But who the coming Changes can presage, ... O 52 Pro Drury-Lane 39
Perhaps, for who can guess th' Effects of Chance? . . . O 53 Pro Drury-Lane 45
Ye patriot Crouds, who burn for England's Fame, . . . O 57 Prologue Comus 1
And him who cannot hurt, allow to please; . . . . . O 62 Pro Word Wise 12
This scarce I lead, who left on yonder rock . . . . . O 64 Virgil Past.I 19
Who lives from toilsome bus'ness free, ... O 71 Hor. Epode II 2
Who to their Lord were ever dear, ... O 78 Feast St Simon 10
who was to personate the Ghost of Hermione . . . . O 83 Epi Dist Moth. T
Ye blooming train, who give despair or joy, ... O 83 Epi Dist Moth. 1
For those who feel no guilt can know no shame; . . . O 84 Epi Dist Moth. 25
Who hugs a flatterer for a friend. . . . . O 100 Ode Friendship V 20
... Musician, who died very poor . . . . O 113 Epit. Phillips V T
... at Bridgnorth, Salop; who died very poor . . . O 113 Epit. Phillips V T
Thou, who survey'st these walls with curious eye, . . . O 117 Epitaph Hanmer 1
Who hail'd him Speaker, with united voice. . . . . O 118 Epitaph Hanmer 20
The nymphs, who found their pow'r decline, ... O 122 Stella Mourn. 3
Who shine, by lavish lovers drest, ... O 126 To Lyce, Lady 3
In quest of wealth who throw their lives away. . . . O 132 Tr. Rambler 48 2
Who buys without discretion, buys to sell. . . . . . O 133 Tr. Rambler 82 1
Thou, who began'st a man, wilt end a boy. . . . . O 135 Tr Rambler 127 2
Place may be chang'd; but who can change his mind? . . O 137 Tr Rambler 135 1
The Man who pants for ample Sway . . . . O 146 Tr Boeth III.5 1
Who holds no human Creature mean; . . . . O 147 Tr Boeth III.6 18
Who drew th' essential Form of Grace; . . . . . . O 155 Epita. Hogarth V 2
He who blindly trusts, will find . . . . O 176 Tr Metastasi I 3
He who still expects deceit, ... O 176 Tr Metastasi I 5
Who keeps the rigid rules of ancient honour; . . . . O 176 Tr Metastas II 2
And those who wisely wish to wive, ... O 178 Thrale 35 Year 17
And all who wisely wish to wive, ... O 178 Thrale 35 Year V 17
If the man who turnips cries, ... O 183 Burlesque Vega 1
Err shall they not, who resolute explore . . . . . O 192 Tr. Medea II 1
Who knows if Jove who counts our Score . . . . . . O 232 Tr Horace IV.7 17
Who knows if Jove who counts our Score . . . . . . O 232 Tr Horace IV.7 17
Who thinks us Women born to dress and sing . . . . O 247 Irene Epilogue 2
Besides, he has fifty Wives; and who can bear . . . . O 247 Irene Epilogue 5
For those who could not please by nobler Service.-- . . O 264 Irene 24
Aspasia! who can look upon thy Beauties? . . . . . O 281 Irene 42
Who hear thee speak, and not abandon Reason? . . . . O 281 Irene 43
Who knows, ere this important Morrow rise, ... O 284 Irene 36
Who knows if Mahomet's awaking Anger . . . . . . O 284 Irene 38
Who merits most, Demetrius or Abdalla. . . . . . . O 284 Irene 45

WHO (CONTINUED)   PAGE TITLE LINE

	PAGE	TITLE	LINE
Who merits most!--I knew not we were Rivals.	O 284	Irene	46
For Non Who was e'er beneficent in vain?	O 377	Irene	V 4
Who fearst lest I should gain, or thou	Y 198	Irene	V 32
Who calls for Pardon from a Wretch condemn'd?	O 323	Irene	4
Who charges Guilt on me?	O 323	Irene	6
Who charges Guilt,	O 323	Irene	6
Who charges Guilt! lay by this proud Resentment	O 323	Irene	8
But who can hear thee beg without compliance	Y 205	Irene	V 33
You who tell	Y 209	Irene	V 54
Who? the dead Irene?	O 332	Irene	17
My mother who alone escap'd the grave	Y 19	Tr. Iliad Bk 6	38
Who hath not heard of Argo's valiant crew?	Y 22	Tr Add. Battle	10
Who has not read the Theban brothers' hate?	Y 22	Tr Add. Battle	14
Who to the ground the shatter'd building flung	Y 23	Tr Add. Battle	48
Who matchless strength and bulk gygantick boasts,	Y 24	Tr Add. Battle	81
Who caught the chief, ev'n in his soldiers' view	Y 25	Tr Add. Battle	125

WHO'S

Who's hat was in his hand.	O 158	Par. Hermit II	4

WHOE'ER

Whoe'er thou art, or whatsoe'er thy Message,	O 294	Irene	4

WHOLE

The teeming Year's whole Product shall devour,	O 110	To Posterity	11
To wondring Worlds produc'd the whole,	O 147	Tr Boeth III.6	11
My whole, is a Man in whose converse is shar'd,	O 179	Charade!	3
shall influence whole nations	Y 150	Irene	V 76

WHOLL

By thee wholl citys burn, wholl nations fall!	O 77	Festina Lente	12
By thee wholl citys burn, wholl nations fall!	O 77	Festina Lente	12

WHOLSOME

Wholsome variety supply.	O 73	Hor. Epode II	62

WHOM

But all whom hunger spares, with age decay:	O 9	London	12
Here let those reign, whom pensions can incite	O 11	London	51
Mark whom the great caress, who frown on me!	O 14	London	92
she sees whom diff'rent views engage,	Y 106	Vanity Wishes	V 307
But few there are whom hours like these await,	O 45	Vanity Wishes	311
Whom Pleasure keeps too busy to be wise,	O 46	Vanity Wishes	324
Whom Joys with soft varieties invite,	O 46	Vanity Wishes	325
Whom Joys in soft vicissitudes invite,	Y 107	Vanity Wishes	V 325
The man whom fate has laid, where all must lye.	O 61	Pro Word Wise	6
To whom all nations tribute bring.	O 68	Hor. II Ode IX	20
To whom the church each rolling year	O 78	Feast St Simon	11
to whom a Lady had given a Sprig of Myrtle	O 95	Sprig of Myrtl	V T
Unhappy! whom to beds of pain	O 125	An Ode	9
Whom smiling nature courts in vain,	O 125	An Ode	11
Ye nymphs whom starry rays invest,	O 126	To Lyce, Lady	1
Ye glitt'ring Train! whom Lace and Velvet bless,	O 246	Irene Prologue	1
Oer whom the seasons varied unperceiv'd	Y 163	Irene	V 43
Blest Prince, for whom indulgent Heav'n ordains	O 308	Irene	6
Whom neither Vows could fix, nor Favours bind?	O 330	Irene	2
The Greek, Demetrius! whom th' expiring Bassa	O 331	Irene	10
Robb'd of the Maid, with whom I wish'd to triumph,	O 333	Irene	42

WHOME

Whome no contracted debts molest	O 71	Hor. Epode II	7

WHOME'ER

Whome'er the Hope, still blasted, still renew'd,	O 310	Irene	1

WHORE

Your taste in snuff, your judgment in a whore;	O 17	London	149
His taste in snuff, his judgment in a whore;	Y 55	London	V 149

WHOSE

Well may they rise, while I, whose rustick tongue	O 14	London	79
Whose Ways and Means support the sinking land;	O 21	London	245
Whose Ways and Means support a sinking land;	Y 60	London	V 245
Whose joys are causeless, or whose griefs are vain.	O 33	Vanity Wishes	68
Whose joys are causeless, or whose griefs are vain.	O 33	Vanity Wishes	68
Speak thou, whose thoughts at humble peace repine,	O 35	Vanity Wishes	121
Great souls whose the dear-bought right convey	Y 100	Vanity Wishes	V 189
Whose peaceful day Benevolence endears,	O 44	Vanity Wishes	295
Whose night congratulating Conscience cheers;	O 44	Vanity Wishes	296
Safe in his pow'r, whose eyes discern afar	O 47	Vanity Wishes	353
For love, whose grasp Creation collective man can fill;	Y 108	Vanity Wishes	V 361
Ye Nymphs, whose Bosoms beat at Milton's Name,	O 57	Prologue Comus	2
Whose gen'rous Zeal, unbought by flatt'ring Rhimes,	O 57	Prologue Comus	3
Yet judg'd by those, whose voices ne'er were sold,	O 60	Pro Good Nat'd	27
The man, my friend, whose conscious heart	O 65	Hor I Ode xxii	1
The Man, my Friend, whose conscious Heart	O 66	To A. Fuscus	1
Whose blood shall quench some Grecian's thirsty rage,	O 74	Tr. Iliad Bk 6	16
Whose mortal wounds pour forth a purple flood,	O 76	Tr Add. Battle	20
In whose fair cheeks destructive Cupids wait,	O 83	Epi Dist Moth.	3
Whose snowy breasts, whose animated eyes,	O 83	Epi Dist Moth.	5
Whose snowy breasts, whose animated eyes,	O 83	Epi Dist Moth.	5
Phillips! whose touch harmonious could remove	O 113	Epit. Phillips	1
O thou whose pow'r o'er moving worlds presides,	O 129	Tr. Rambler 7	1
Whose voice created, and whose wisdom guides,	O 129	Tr. Rambler 7	2
Whose voice created, and whose wisdom guides,	O 129	Tr. Rambler 7	2
Unlike the ribald, whose licentious jest	O 130	Tr. Rambler 12	1
Save him whose Soul enslav'd to Vice	O 147	Tr Boeth III.6	19
Happy he whose Eyes have view'd	O 147	Tr Boet III.12	1
Happy whose unfetterd Mind	O 147	Tr Boet III.12	3

```
WHOSE              (CONTINUED)                          PAGE    TITLE              LINE
   To You whose gen'rous Wishes rise . . . . . . . .   O 150  Tr Boet III.12        53
   Down whose current clear and strong,                O 159  Tr. Rio Verde          2
   My whole, is a Man in whose converse is shar'd,     O 179  Charade!               3
   The Chief, whose Wisdom guides the Turkish Counsels. O 253 Irene                112
   Whose quick Impatience seiz'd my doubtful Hand,     O 254  Irene                126
   Whose Soul, perhaps, yet mindful of Aspasia,        O 267  Irene                 39
   While Heav'n's high Minister, whose awful Volume    O 276  Irene                 20
   While Heaven's high Minister whose unerring awfull  O 355  Irene              V   9
      volume
   Those holy Beings, whose superior Care . . . . .    O 289  Irene                 17
   Those holy Beings whose unseen Direction . . . .    O 346  Irene              V   5
   And envy the slave that toils whose labour procures her  Y 165  Irene         V  81
      sleep
   Ask to whose Sword the Greeks will trust their Cause,  O 305  Irene              39
   Demand whose Force yon Turkish Heroes dread, . . .  O 305  Irene                 41
   All ye, whose Blood tyrannick Rage effus'd,         O 306  Irene                 53
   Whose Fear, or Rage, or Treachery betray'd us. . .  O 316  Irene                 17
   Or why should he, whose Violence of Duty . . . . .  O 329  Irene                 18
   Why should the man whose violence of duty . . . .   Y 210  Irene              V  18
   Was this the Maid whose Love I bought with Empire!  O 330  Irene                  9
   Those Groves, whose Shades embower'd the dear Irene, O 333  Irene                 46
   The Wretch, whose Guilt declar'd by tortur'd Cali,  O 334  Irene                 64
   The wretch whose crimes declar'd by tortur'd Cali   Y 215  Irene              V 69A
   Whose early buds unusual glories wear,              Y   3  On a Daffodill         3
   "Whose fame from earth resounded to the skies."     Y   7  Virgil Daphnis        31
   Lyciscus whose soft arms excell . . . . . . . .     Y  12  Tr Hor Epode 9        37
   Or boy, whose snowy neck the flowing ringlets grace. Y 12  Tr Hor Epode 9        42
   Whose sire Eetion in Cilicia reign'd . . . . . .    Y  18  Tr. Iliad Bk 6         7
   Whose direfull rage destroy'd my native land. . . . Y  18  Tr. Iliad Bk 6        29
WHY
   And why should odious ruin dawb the wall. . . . .   Y  95  Vanity Wishes      V  90
   For why did Wolsey near the steeps of fate, . . .   O  35  Vanity Wishes        125
   For why did Wolsey by the Steps of fate, . . . .    O  35  Vanity Wishes      V 125
   Why but to sink beneath misfortune's blow, . . . .  O  35  Vanity Wishes        127
   He views, and wonders why they please no more;      Y 104  Vanity Wishes      V 264
   Why, Sylvia, was it then decreed, . . . . . . .     O 120  To Miss Purse         11
   Why, Stella, was it then decreed, . . . . . . .     O 120  To Miss Purse      V  11
   Why boast their Birth before his Eyes, . . . . .    O 147  Tr Boeth III.6        17
   Why should they fear?--That Power that kindly spreads O 250  Irene                31
   So small a Force? or why should Cali fly? . . . .   O 254  Irene                138
   Why should Cali rebel--unexpensive age . . . .      Y 120  Irene              V  40
   But say, great Bassa, why the Sultan's Anger, . .   O 257  Irene                 65
   Why stor'd for Flight? and why prepar'd by Cali?    O 258  Irene                 85
   Why stor'd for Flight? and why prepar'd by Cali?    O 258  Irene                 85
   Why should the Sultan shun the Joys of Beauty, . .  O 261  Irene                  7
   Why rove I now, when absent from my Fair, . . .     O 263  Irene                 19
   Why all this Glare of splendid Eloquence . . . .    O 276  Irene                 11
   Why then has Nature's vain Munificence . . . . .    O 276  Irene                 24
   Why then did Natures vain Munificence . . . . .     O 355  Irene              V  13
   Why then Those charms your tongue has deign'd to    O 355  Irene              V  15
      flatter
   Why, when the Balm of Sleep descends on Man, . . .  O 277  Irene                 43
   But why this sudden Warmth? . . . . . . . . .       O 281  Irene                 48
   Why roars the Lioness distress'd by Hunger? . . .   O 281  Irene                 50
   Why foam the swelling Waves when Tempests rise?     O 281  Irene                 51
   Why shakes the Ground, when subterraneous Fires     O 281  Irene                 52
   Why, when Destruction rag'd around our Walls,       O 290  Irene                 38
   Why fled this haughty Heroine from the Battle? . .  O 290  Irene                 39
   Why then did not this warlike Amazon . . . . .      O 290  Irene                 40
   Why does the Blood forsake thy lovely Cheek? . .    O 295  Irene                  5
   Why shoots this Chilness through thy shaking Nerves? O 295  Irene                  6
   Why does thy Soul retire into herself? . . . .      O 295  Irene                  7
   Why has thy Choice then pointed out Leontius, . .   O 305  Irene                 20
   Yet! why-- . . . . . . . . . . . . . . . .          O 314  Irene                 10
   Why did you stay? deserted and betray'd? . . . .    O 317  Irene                 34
   Or why should he, whose Violence of Duty . . . .    O 329  Irene                 18
   Why should the man whose violence of duty . . . .   Y 210  Irene              V  18
   "Why gen'rous warriour will you rashly run . . .    Y  18  Tr. Iliad Bk 6        19
WICKED
   That hide in seeming zeal a wicked purpose, . . .   O 176  Tr Metastas II        12
WICKEDNESS
   Upbraid me not with fancy'd Wickedness, . . . .     O 289  Irene                 21
WIDE
   O'er love, o'er fear, extends his wide domain, . .  O  40  Vanity Wishes        195
   O'er love, o'er Force, extends his wide domain,     O  40  Vanity Wishes      V 195
   Spreads wide the hope of plunder and of praise;     O  43  Vanity Wishes        248
   Spreads wide the mighty Moral for Mankind. . . .    O 246  Irene Prologue         8
   Spreads wide the mighty Moral of Mankind. . . .     O 246  Irene Prologue     V   8
   It spreads the wide plain an unregarded ruin. . .   Y 131  Irene              V 36C
   but if your influence be too wide--your dissipated rays  Y 132  Irene          V  41
      will burn no more . . . . . . . . . . .
   Spread wide their kind Arms to Science and to Beauty.  O 353  Irene            V   5
WIDE-WASTING
   Wide-wasting pest! that rages unconfin'd,           O  31  Vanity Wishes         23
   Oft have I rag'd, when their wide-wasting Cannon    O 273  Irene                 24
WIDER
   Still wider spreads thy horrid reign,               O 123  Winter's Walk          7
WIDOW
   A widow I, an helpless orphan he. . . . . . . .     Y  19  Tr. Iliad Bk 6        49
```

WIDOWS

PAGE   TITLE   LINE

The smiling Widows, and protected Orphans. . . . . .   O 291 Irene   57

WIELD

Their foes attacks, and wield their arms with pain. . .   O 76 Tr Add. Battle   27

WIFE

The patient Suff'rer, and the faithful Wife. . . . .   O 58 Prologue Comus   32
Your shady Groves, your pleasing wife, ...   O 69 Hor.II Ode 14   21
A frugal, chast, industrious, Wife, ...   O 72 Hor. Epode II   48
Behold the wife of Hector, guard of Troy! . . . .   O 74 Tr. Iliad Bk 6   26
A weeping Wife perhaps, or dying Friend, ...   O 280 Irene   9
He met Andromache his beauteous wife . . . .   Y 18 Tr. Iliad Bk 6   5
Forgetfull of your wife, forgetfull of your son? . . .   Y 18 Tr. Iliad Bk 6   21

WIFE'S

And for one Man--one Wife's enough in Conscience. . . .   O 247 Irene Epilogue   14

WILD

With ev'ry wild absurdity comply, ...   O 16 London   138
Walks the wild heath, and sings his toil away. . . . .   O 32 Vanity Wishes   38
The fierce Croatian, and the wild Hussar, ...   O 43 Vanity Wishes   249
Must watch the wild Vicissitudes of Taste; . . . . .   O 53 Pro Drury-Lane   48
Part turn their Backs, part seiz'd with wild surprise   O 76 Tr Add. Battle   28
Parent of thousand wild desires, ...   O 99 Ode Friendship   6
Wild hope, vain fear, alike remov'd, ...   O 125 An Ode   26
With wild Vicissitudes of Wrong, ...   O 145 Tr Boeth III.1   10
Must bid each wild Desire be still, ...   O 146 Tr Boeth III.5   3
"Tempts me to be wild again: . . . .   O 185 Anacreon Ode 9   22
Wild as wind, and light as feather . . . .   O 196 Song Congratu.   7
If no wild Draught depart from Reason's Rules, ...   O 246 Irene Prologue   17
And publick Spirit deemd a wild Chimaera . . . . .   O 347 Irene   V   19
In its wild ravages distinguish'd thee . . . . . .   Y 115 Irene   V 49B
Nor bursting through the ranks in wild distraction . .   Y 163 Irene   V   47
Would loose the wild Enthusiast to destroy, ...   O 291 Irene   61
Lost in a wild Perplexity of Joy. . . . .   O 295 Irene   14
Betray'd the wild Emotions of his Mind. . . . . . .   O 311 Irene   4
Cease this wild Roar of savage Exultation; . . . . .   O 318 Irene   6
What wild Mistake is this? Take hence with speed . . .   O 325 Irene   4
Where the wild fig trees join their darksom shade . .   Y 19 Tr. Iliad Bk 6   52
Astonish'd nations view with wild affright . . . .   Y 24 Tr Add. Battle   74

WILDEST

Beyond my warmest Hope, or wildest Wishes, ...   O 296 Irene   35

WILDNESS

Thy Look, thy Speech, thy Action, all is Wildness-- . .   O 323 Irene   5

WILDS

Thou fly'st for refuge to the wilds of Kent; . . . .   O 23 London   257
You fly for refuge to the wilds of Kent: . . . . .   Y 61 London   V 257
Apulia's spacious wilds with gore; . . . .   O 66 Hor I Ode xxii   14
Apulia's spacious Wilds with Gore; . . . .   O 67 To A. Fuscus   14
Or wand'ring in the Wilds of future Being, ...   O 255 Irene   6
Call me to civilize the Russian Wilds, ...   O 292 Irene   105

WILE

Some artful Wile of counterfeited Love! . . . . . .   O 331 Irene   3

WILES

With coy Caresses and with pleasing Wiles . . . . .   O 260 Irene   128

WILFUL

Tell the woes of wilful waste, ...   O 197 Song Congratu.   26
Tell the spoils of wilful waste, ...   O 197 Song Congratu.   V   26

WILL

To pour at will the counterfeited tear, ...   O 16 London   141
And sign your will before you sup from home. . . . .   O 21 London   225
And make will before you sup from home. . . . . .   Y 59 London   V 225
But will not Britain hear the last appeal, ...   O 34 Vanity Wishes   91
And mould his passions till they make his will. . . .   O 44 Vanity Wishes   282
Obedient passions, and a will resign'd; . . . . .   O 48 Vanity Wishes   360
They roll, and ever will roll on. . . . .   O 68 Hor.II Ode 14   4
Will quickly drive away his woe, ...   O 69 Hor.II Ode 14   26
The day will come, in which proud Troy shall yield, . .   O 74 Tr. Iliad Bk 6   13
Obsequious to his heav'nly will . . . .   O 79 Feast St Simon   17
I can't prevent, and will not share. . . . . . .   O 126 An Ode   36
Nor yoke his Reason with his Will: . . . .   O 146 Tr Boeth III.5   4
He who blindly trusts, will find . . . .   O 176 Tr Metastasi I   3
Let it wander as it will; . . . .   O 196 Song Congratu.   18
Let it wander if it will; . . . .   O 196 Song Congratu.   V   18
Will toss us in a morning more? . . . .   O 232 Tr Horace IV.7   18
Will rouse us in a morning more? . . . .   O 232 Tr Horace IV.7   V   18
Men will be ever to their Errors blind, ...   O 247 Irene Epilogue   11
Will he not bend beneath a Tyrant's Frown? . . . . .   O 255 Irene   22
Will he not melt before Ambition's Fire? . . . . .   O 255 Irene   23
Will he not soften in a Friend's Embrace? . . . . .   O 255 Irene   24
Demetrius will not lead me to Dishonour; . . . . .   O 256 Irene   35
But will she yet receive the Faith of Mecca? . . . .   O 261 Irene   11
Soon will th' unequal Contest be decided, ...   O 261 Irene   18
How will the bright Aspasia shine above her! . . . .   O 261 Irene   23
Heav'n will contemn the mercenary Fervour, ...   O 262 Irene   26
At Sight of female Charms will glow no more. . . . .   O 263 Irene   6
will burn no more . . . .   Y 132 Irene   V   41
Will not that Pow'r that form'd the Heart of Woman, . .   O 266 Irene   23
There will his boundless Wealth, the Spoil of Asia, . .   O 274 Irene   50
Will yet Irenes haughty Soul descend . . . . . .   O 372 Irene   V   6
How will the matchless Beauties of Irene, ...   O 276 Irene   6
Will it not charm a Mind like thine exalted, ...   O 278 Irene   67
When will Occasion smile upon our Wishes, ...   O 282 Irene   1
To me my Lover's Fondness will restore, ...   O 291 Irene   74

```
WILL           (CONTINUED)                               PAGE    TITLE           LINE
    Will not th' Apostate feel the Pangs of Guilt,  . . . .   O 294  Irene           132
    Nor think to say here will I stop  . . . . . . . .   Y 168  Irene         V 132
    Here will I fix the limits of transgression  . . . . .   Y 168  Irene         V 133
    That joins us thus, will never part us more.  . . . .   O 296  Irene           39
    Aspasia's Absence will inflame Suspicion;  . . . . .   O 296  Irene           5
    Will not admit a Lover's long Farewell,  . . . . .   O 297  Irene           13
    Will not the Patriot share the Traytor's Danger?  . . .   O 300  Irene           62
    How soon, alas! will Int'rest, Fear, or Envy,  . . . .   O 301  Irene           82
    Will e'er an happier Hour revisit Greece?  . . . . .   O 301  Irene           96
    Nor will his Country's Groans reproach Demetrius.  . .   O 301  Irene           101
    Will now remount the slighted Seat of Empire,  . . . .   O 303  Irene           27
    Ask to whose Sword the Greeks will trust their Cause,  .   O 305  Irene           39
    Nor will I trust th' uncertain Chance of Combat;  . .   O 307  Irene           21
    Will cloud my Triumphs, and pollute the Day.  . . . .   O 310  Irene           3
    Will damp my joys, and cloud the happy days  . . . . .   O 370  Irene         V 23
    Will she that's false to Heavn, to me be faithfull  . .   Y 186  Irene         V 4
    Let us not struggle with th' eternal Will,  . . . .   O 320  Irene           16
    Will spread resistless Light upon my Soul.  . . . . .   O 321  Irene           47
    Will teach a gentler Term.  . . . . . . . .   O 321  Irene           54
    Perhaps I will not stoop to plead my Cause;  . . . .   O 330  Irene           22
    Perhaps I will not bend to plead my cause  . . . . .   Y 210  Irene         V 22
    Such was the Will of Heav'n—A Band of Greeks  . . . .   O 335  Irene           5
    Then we with wine will drown our troubles, laid  . . .   Y   7  Virgil Daphnis    47
    "Why gen'rous warriour will you rashly run  . . . . .   Y  18  Tr. Iliad Bk 6    19
    My death is now decreed my death will come.  . . . .   Y  21  Tr. Iliad Bk 6    118
WILLING
    Their Slaves were willing, and their Reign was long;  . .   O  52  Pro Drury-Lane    26
    Make haste, bright Maid, to rule the willing World;  . .   O 288  Irene           7
    Willing to delay you here they give you on earth the  . .   Y 184  Irene         V 10
WILT
    Thou, who began'st a man, wilt end a boy.  . . . . .   O 135  Tr Rambler 127    2
    That thou wilt give to me,  . . . . . . . .   O 158  Par Hermit III    2
    Wilt thou dismiss the Savage from the Toils  . . . .   O 275  Irene           66
    Wilt thou descend, fair Daughter of Perfection,  . . .   O 276  Irene           1
    Wilt thou then head the Troop upon the Shore,  . . . .   O 305  Irene           36
WILY
    Nor tempt the snares of wily love.  . . . . . . .   O 121  To Miss Playin    10
    Would shake his wily Head, and closely whisper,  . . .   O 273  Irene           28
    The wily sorc'ress wears a thousand forms,  . . . . .   Y 155  Irene         V 26
    I mark'd her wily Messenger afar,  . . . . . . .   O 327  Irene           24
WIND
    The waves he lashes, and enchains the wind;  . . . . .   O  42  Vanity Wishes    232
    (His various plumage sporting in the wind)  . . . . .   O  74  Tr. Iliad Bk 6    2
    More false, more cruel than the seas and wind.  . . . .   O  82  Young Author    14
    More false, more cruel than the seas or wind.  . . . .   O  82  Young Author  V 14
    By quiv'ring string, or modulated wind;  . . . . .   O 192  Tr. Medea II    10
    Wild as wind, and light as feather  . . . . . . .   O 196  Song Congratu.    7
    And listen eager to the rising Wind?  . . . . . . .   O 270  Irene           25
WINDING
    Deep in a winding Creek a Galley lies,  . . . . . .   O 254  Irene           134
WINDS
    Lull'd by the beating winds and dashing show'rs!  . . .   O 135  Tr Rambler 117    2
    Did not our sails receive the wondring winds  . . . .   Y 115  Irene         V 49G
    The fav'ring Winds assist the great Design,  . . . . .   O 304  Irene           6
    A Galley waits us, and the Winds invite.  . . . . . .   O 321  Irene           52
WINE
    Flush'd as they are with folly, youth and wine,  . . .   O  21  London          232
    Flush'd as they are with youth confused with wine,  . .   Y  59  London        V 232
    The wine you kept with so much care  . . . . . . .   O  69  Hor.II Ode 14    27
    And crown the bowl with new-prest wine  . . . . . .   O  72  Hor. Epode II    52
    When fondness melts me, or when wine inflames,  . . . .   O 142  In Baretti Bk.    2
    "Or from wine as courage springs,  . . . . . . .   O 186  Anacreon Ode 9    37
    The joys of music and of wine,  . . . . . . . .   O 190  Tr. Medea I    4
    And aided wine with dulcet-streaming sound.  . . . . .   O 192  Tr. Medea II    8
    Then we with wine will drown our troubles, laid  . . .   Y   7  Virgil Daphnis    47
WINES
    Now pall the tasteless meats, and joyless wines,  . . .   O  43  Vanity Wishes    265
WING
    To pluck a titled Poet's borrow'd wing;  . . . . .   O  13  London          70
    Now with no weak unballast wing  . . . . . . . .   O  70  Hor.II Ode XX    1
    And all the pens of Cupid's wing  . . . . . . . .   O 127  To Lyce, Lady    19
    They prune the Wing, and spread the glossy Plumes,  . .   O 277  Irene           36
    They prune the wing and spread the glossy tail  . . .   O 355  Irene         V 23
    He 's gone—Here rest, my Soul, thy fainting Wing,  . .   O 287  Irene           1
    But when the Tempest with sonorous Wing  . . . . .   O 298  Irene           22
    There shall soft Leisure wing th' excursive Soul,  . .   O 302  Irene           118
    And wing thy latest Pray'r to pitying Heav'n.  . . . .   O 322  Irene           62
    Feather'd battalions, squadrons on the wing  . . . . .   Y  22  Tr Add. Battle    1
    Together rise and shoot upon the wing.  . . . . . .   Y  24  Tr Add. Battle    73
WINGED
    A Winged Messenger, or bid the Grave  . . . . . . .   O 365  Irene         V 21
    Guarded from all but winged enemies  . . . . . . .   Y  23  Tr Add. Battle    25
WINGS
    There ev'ry breeze bears health upon its wings;  . . .   O  20  London          221
    Fate wings with ev'ry wish th' afflictive dart,  . . .   O  31  Vanity Wishes    15
    To press the weary minutes flagging wings:  . . . . .   O  44  Vanity Wishes    300
    Loads the lingring minutes weary wings:  . . . . .   Y 105  Vanity Wishes  V 300
    To press the weary minutes hanging wings:  . . . . .   Y 105  Vanity Wishes  V 300
    Thick from their wounded wings the feathers fly,  . . .   O  75  Tr Add. Battle    4
    They clap their wings, and with new fury burn;  . . . .   O  76  Tr Add. Battle    9
```

395

WINGS (CONTINUED)	PAGE	TITLE	LINE
Swords, arms and wings are scatter'd o'er the plain	O 76	Tr Add. Battle	18
Then o'er the World shall Discord stretch her Wings,	O 110	To Posterity	15
Her wings Imagination tries,	O 125	An Ode	14
"O'er his face extend my wings;	O 186	Anacreon Ode 9	38
Imagination hangs her weary wings	Y 127	Irene	V 2
And time hangs his flagging wings	Y 128	Irene	V 4
Should the fierce North upon his frozen Wings	O 274	Irene	61
Hence from her sable wings returning night	Y 148	Irene	V 43E
And Love infold thee with his downy Wings.	O 279	Irene	83
Shall soar triumphant on the Wings of Glory,	O 305	Irene	26
Now hover o'er us with propitious Wings,	O 306	Irene	51
The fraudful Moments ply their silent Wings,	O 327	Irene	8
The treacherous moments ply their silent wings	Y 206	Irene	V 8
Which whet their beaks, for flight their wings prepare;	Y 24	Tr Add. Battle	70
Their wings extend themselves across the land.	Y 24	Tr Add. Battle	79
The joyfull Cranes triumphant clap their wings:	Y 26	Tr Add. Battle	127
WINTER			
And Winter barricades the realms of Frost;	O 41	Vanity Wishes	208
But when increas'd by Winter shours	O 72	Hor. Epode II	37
Stern winter, is thy force confest,	O 123	Winter's Walk	6
Stern winter, in thy force confest,	O 123	Winter's Walk	V 6
Stern winter now, by spring repress'd,	O 124	An Ode	1
And Winter chils the World again.	O 232	Tr Horace IV.7	12
Sure, chill'd with sixty winter Camps, thy Blood	O 263	Irene	5
Thou Thou chilld by sixty winter camps canst gaze	Y 129	Irene	V 5
If winter by the fire, if summer in the shade.	Y 7	Virgil Daphnis	48
WINTER'S			
The Winter's Walk	O 123	Winter's Walk	T
Rough Winter's blasts to Spring give way,	O 231	Tr Horace IV.7	9
The Soldier lab'ring through a Winter's March,	O 283	Irene	28
These when o'er winter's sway, prevail'd the spring	Y 24	Tr Add. Battle	72
WINTRY			
Work'd into sudden rage by wintry show'rs,	O 132	Tr. Rambler 65	1
Nor feel the inclemencies of wintry air;	Y 3	On a Daffodill	6
WISDOM			
With chearful wisdom and instructive mirth,	O 32	Vanity Wishes	50
With these celestial wisdom calms the mind,	O 48	Vanity Wishes	367
In ev'ry speech persuasive wisdom flow'd,	O 118	Epitaph Hanmer	15
And Wisdom warble from her string.	O 121	To Miss Playin	24
Where wisdom first inform'd my heart.	O 125	An Ode	20
Bright wisdom teach me Curio's art,	O 126	An Ode	38
Whose voice created, and whose wisdom guides,	O 129	Tr. Rambler 7	2
Wisdom at proper times is well forgot.	O 134	Tr. Rambler 89	1
For wisdom ever echoes nature's voice.	O 138	Tr Rambler 156	1
Call to your Aid your Courage, and your Wisdom;	O 252	Irene	85
The Chief, whose Wisdom guides the Turkish Counsels.	O 253	Irene	112
And Wisdom into Virtue turn thy Frailty.	O 266	Irene	22
To-morrow's Action? Can that hoary Wisdom	O 283	Irene	19
To morrow strike--Does then that experienc'd wisdom	Y 154	Irene	V 19
Than all the Wisdom of the grave Divan.	O 287	Irene	8
WISDOM'S			
Once more on wisdom's voice attend.	O 125	An Ode	24
WISE			
And pause awhile from letters, to be wise;	O 38	Vanity Wishes	158
And pause awhile from Learning to be wise;	O 38	Vanity Wishes	V 158
See nations slowly wise, and meanly just,	O 38	Vanity Wishes	161
Fears of the brave, and follies of the wise?	O 45	Vanity Wishes	316
The wise man's follies,	Y 106	Vanity Wishes	V 316
Whom Pleasure keeps too busy to be wise,	O 46	Vanity Wishes	324
Yours is the Charge, ye Fair, ye Wise, ye Brave!	O 58	Prologue Comus	37
Prologue to "A Word to the Wise"	O 61	Pro Word Wise	T
The wise experienc'd Grecian sage	O 68	Hor. II Ode IX	13
Warn'd by another's fate, vain youth, be wise,	O 82	Young Author	23
Thus early wise, th' endanger'd realm to aid,	O 117	Epitaph Hanmer	9
With temp'rate zeal, and wise anxiety;	O 118	Epitaph Hanmer	30
For not the brave, or wise, or great,	O 136	Tr Rambler 128	1
And leave my labours to the learn'd and wise,	O 141	Tr Rambler 208	2
Observe their labours, Sluggard, and be wise.	O 151	The Ant	2
Obscurely wise, and coarsely kind;	O 201	Death Dr Levet	10
Could Omens fright the Resolute and Wise,	O 269	Irene	1
Henceforth be wise, nor hope a second Pardon.	O 323	Irene	3
WISELY			
And those who wisely wish to wive,	O 178	Thrale 35 Year	17
And all who wisely wish to wive,	O 178	Thrale 35 Year	V 17
WISEST			
The wisest justice on the banks of Trent?	O 35	Vanity Wishes	124
WISH			
Fate wings with ev'ry wish th' afflictive dart,	O 31	Vanity Wishes	15
Their wish is full to riot and to rail.	O 34	Vanity Wishes	98
What but their wish indulg'd in courts to shine,	O 36	Vanity Wishes	133
Such age there is, and who shall wish its end?	O 44	Vanity Wishes	298
Such age there is, and who could wish its end?	O 44	Vanity Wishes	V 298
Such age the is, and who could wish its end?	Y 105	Vanity Wishes	V 298
And those who wisely wish to wive,	O 178	Thrale 35 Year	17
And all who wisely wish to wive,	O 178	Thrale 35 Year	V 17
The guest, without a want, without a wish,	O 193	Tr. Medea II	19
And wish their gloomy Caverns more obscure.	O 268	Irene	32
Each rebel Wish, each traitor Inclination	O 287	Irene	11
Shall I not wish to chear afflicted Kings,	O 291	Irene	67

```
WISH          (CONTINUED)                          PAGE    TITLE          LINE
    And wish too late for Innocence and Peace?  . . . . .   O 294  Irene           133
    Name and enjoy thy Wish--  . . . . . . . . . . . . .    O 307  Irene            12
    Nor hope, nor wish, nor live but for Aspasia. . . . .   O 307  Irene            14
    Nor wish for Houries in Irene's Arms. . . . . . . .     O 308  Irene            10
    And wish'd--Be still thy Fate to wish in vain. . . . . O 334  Irene            60
WISH'D
    Nor wish'd for Johnson's Art, or Shakespear's Flame; . .  O  52  Pro Drury-Lane   18
    Nor wish'd to glitter at his country's cost;  . . . . .   O 118  Epitaph Hanmer   28
    Religion calls her from the wish'd Embrace, . . . . .    O 261  Irene            16
    Long have I wish'd, before our Prophet's Tomb, . . . .   O 263  Irene             9
    Robb'd of the Maid, with whom I wish'd to triumph, . .   O 333  Irene            42
    I heard her, pitied her, and wish'd to save her. . . .   O 333  Irene            59
    And wish'd--Be still thy Fate to wish in vain. . . . .   O 334  Irene            60
    And wish'd my rising anger could remove  . . . . . .     Y  11  Tr Hor Epode 9   23
    Chear'd the rough road, we wish'd the rough road long, . Y 310  Parody of Pope    2
WISHES
    The Vanity of Human Wishes. . . . . . . . . . . . . .    O  29  Vanity Wishes     T
    Still to new heights his restless wishes tow'r, . . .    O  34  Vanity Wishes   105
    Must no dislike alarm, no wishes rise,  . . . . . . .    O  47  Vanity Wishes   347
    Enquirer cease alarm, no wishes rise, . . . . . . . .    Y 108  Vanity Wishes  V 347
    Have hopes, and fears, and wishes, just the same; . . . O  59  Pro Good Nat'd   12
    For still where wishes most abound  . . . . . . . . .    O 144  Tr Boeth. II.2   11
    To You whose gen'rous Wishes rise . . . . . . . . . .    O 150  Tr Boet III.12   53
    Nor think our wishes less sincere. . . . . . . . . . .   O 188  Epilogue          4
    Smile on my Wishes, and command the Globe.  . . . . .    O 279  Irene            81
    His glowing Wishes, and his jealous Pangs.  . . . . .    O 280  Irene            28
    When will Occasion smile upon our Wishes, . . . . . .    O 282  Irene             1
    Oppose my Wishes, and--Remember Justice. . . . . . .     O 286  Irene            16
    Beyond my warmest Hope, or wildest Wishes,  . . . . .    O 296  Irene            35
    And granted all his wishes  . . . . . . . . . . . .     Y 179  Irene          V  31
    'Tis well--A single Blow compleats our Wishes:  . . . . O 304  Irene             8
    And wishes Irene were converted by some  . . . . . .     Y 186  Irene          V  11
        doctor
    My Hopes, my Wishes, terminate in Life, . . . . . .     O 327  Irene            22
WIT
    Wit, brav'ry, worth, his lavish tongue bestows; . . . .  O  16  London          126
    Intrigue was Plot, Obscenity was Wit. . . . . . . . .    O  52  Pro Drury-Lane   20
    She saw great Faustus lay the Ghost of Wit: . . . . .    O  52  Pro Drury-Lane   36
    Let Wit, condemn'd the feeble War to wage . . . . . .    O  57  Prologue Comus    7
    Distrest alike, the statesman and the wit, . . . . .     O  59  Pro Good Nat'd    9
    This night our wit, the pert apprentice cries, . . .     O  60  Pro Good Nat'd   23
    To wit, reviving from its author's dust, . . . . . .     O  61  Pro Word Wise     7
    When ev'n proud wealth and prouder wit obey, . . . .     O  81  Lady Birthday    10
    Disaster always waits an early wit.  . . . . . . . .     O 135  Tr Rambler 111    1
    By wit, by knowledge, studious to be read, . . . . .     O 141  Tr Rambler 208    3
    Shou'd welcome Sleep relieve the weary Wit, . . . . .    O 246  Irene Prologue   25
    Th' enlivening Wit, the penetrating Reason? . . . . .    O 278  Irene            56
    The Sparkling Wit the penetrating Reason  . . . . . .    O 356  Irene          V  23
    No wit nor honesty could stand  . . . . . . . . . .     Y  11  Tr Hor Epode 9   21
    Fair source of wit, and love, and mirth, . . . . . .     Y  39  Lady Leaving      6
WITH
    543                                               OMITTED WORD
WITH'RING
    Still drops some joy from with'ring life away; . . . .   O  45  Vanity Wishes   306
WITHDRAW
    Withdraw their cars and seek the blesst abodes.  . . .   Y   6  Virgil Daphnis   21
WITHDRAWN
    On Isis banks he waves, from noise withdrawn  . . . .    Y  98  Vanity Wishes  V138A
WITHDRAWS
    Withdraws the influence of those eyes,  . . . . . .     Y  39  Lady Leaving      7
WITHDREW
    As blasted by my Presence, they withdrew . . . . . .     O 275  Irene            85
    And smiling, conscious of her Charms, withdrew.  . . .   O 282  Irene            69
WITHER'D
    That froze our Veins, and wither'd all our Powers.  .    O 251  Irene            57
    Till burning Death shoots through their wither'd Limbs? . O 282  Irene            6
WITHERING
    And all the withering woods confess their woe . . . .    Y   6  Virgil Daphnis    4
WITHERS
    And every beauty withers at the blast:  . . . . . .     O  84  Epi Dist Moth.   35
WITHIN
    Sleep undisturb'd within this peaceful shrine,  . . . .  O 113  Epit. Phillips    5
    Rest undisturb'd within this humble shrine, . . . . .    O 113  Epit. Phillips  V  5
    Rag'd within the Master's Breast  . . . . . . . . .     O 148  Tr Boet III.12   14
    Awake each Faculty that sleeps within thee, . . . . .    O 254  Irene             2
    And heard within the Thicket that conceal'd us, . . .    O 311  Irene            12
        Behold, within th' embow'ring Grove  . . . . . .    O 314  Irene            10
    And all within is Darkness and Confusion; . . . . .     O 315  Irene            32
    Aspasia now within her Lover's Arms . . . . . . . .     O 325  Irene            17
    Within the town assemble all thy powers . . . . . .     Y  19  Tr. Iliad Bk 6   50
WITHOUT
    And lye without a blush, without a smile; . . . . . .    O  17  London          147
    And lye without a blush, without a smile; . . . . . .    O  17  London          147
    Fair Justice then, without constraint ador'd, . . . .    O  22  London          250
    To tread the dreary paths without a guide, . . . . .     O  31  Vanity Wishes     8
    Where wealth unlov'd without a mourner dy'd, . . . .     O  33  Vanity Wishes    55
    Our anxious Bard, without complaint, may share . . .     O  59  Pro Good Nat'd    5
    Our little Bard, without complaint, may share  . . . .   O  59  Pro Good Nat'd  V  5
    Must hear all taunts, and hear without reply. . . . .    O  59  Pro Good Nat'd   14
    Trusts without fear, to merit, and to you. . . . . .     O  60  Pro Good Nat'd   30
```

WITHOUT   (CONTINUED)   PAGE   TITLE   LINE

	PAGE	TITLE	LINE
Trusts without fear, to candour, and to you.	O 60	Pro Good Nat'd	V 30
I without fun'ral elegies	O 70	Hor.II Ode XX	23
Rob without Fear, and fatten without Toil.	O 110	To Posterity	14
Rob without Fear, and fatten without Toil.	O 110	To Posterity	14
Let pain deserv'd without complaint be borne.	O 131	Tr. Rambler 32	1
Who buys without discretion, buys to sell.	O 133	Tr. Rambler 82	1
For none are rich without content.	O 144	Tr Boeth. II.2	14
"Joyless task without reward:	O 185	Anacreon Ode 9	18
"Fortune's guest, without a home,	O 185	Anacreon Ode 9	26
The guest, without a want, without a wish,	O 193	Tr. Medea II	19
The guest, without a want, without a wish,	O 193	Tr. Medea II	19
The power of art without the show.	O 201	Death Dr Levet	16
With Merit needless, and without it vain.	O 246	Irene Prologue	32
Beheld without Concern, expiring Greece,	O 250	Irene	34
If Happiness can be without Aspasia.	O 253	Irene	110
And reign without a Rival in his Bosom.	O 373	Irene	V 29
For what is Length of Days without Irene?	O 262	Irene	6
Prais'd without Rapture, left without Regret.	O 263	Irene	18
Prais'd without Rapture, left without Regret.	O 263	Irene	18
heav'nly charms without emotion	Y 129	Irene	V 6
But sink among thy Slaves without a Murmur.	O 289	Irene	11
Then mingle with your slaves without a murmur	Y 161	Irene	V 11
On me, should Providence, without a Crime,	O 292	Irene	103
I saw without a sigh the fierce barbarian	Y 176	Irene	V 106
More than a pleasing Sound without a Meaning,	O 310	Irene	13
But who can hear thee beg without compliance	Y 205	Irene	V 33
Hector, this heard without a moment's stay,	Y 17	Tr. Iliad Bk 6	1
Without a boding fear, or anxious sigh,	Y 67	Prologue Lethe	3
WITHSTAND			
Unconquer'd bars on earth and sea withstand;	O 136	Tr Rambler 129	3
Your sighs are spent in vain; if fates withstand	Y 21	Tr. Iliad Bk 6	115
WITLINGS			
Unmov'd tho' Witlings sneer and Rivals rail;	O 246	Irene Prologue	29
WITNESS			
This Night with all her conscious Stars be witness,	O 284	Irene	44
I ask no Witness, but attesting Conscience,	O 305	Irene	34
See the last Witness of thy Guilt and Fear	O 326	Irene	2
WITNESS'D			
Though dancing mountains witness'd Orpheus near;	O 43	Vanity Wishes	270
WITS			
The Wits of Charles found easier Ways to Fame,	O 52	Pro Drury-Lane	17
Intriguing Wits! his artless Plot forgive;	O 246	Irene Prologue	19
Ye Fops be silent! and ye Wits be just!	O 246	Irene Prologue	34
WIVE			
And those who wisely wish to wive,	O 178	Thrale 35 Year	17
And all who wisely wish to wive,	O 178	Thrale 35 Year	V 17
WIVES			
Besides, he has fifty Wives; and who can bear	O 247	Irene Epilogue	5
WOE			
And for a moment lull the sense of woe.	O 10	London	32
The robes of pleasure and the veils of woe:	O 33	Vanity Wishes	66
That life protracted is protracted woe.	O 43	Vanity Wishes	258
For useful Mirth, and salutary Woe;	O 53	Pro Drury-Lane	60
Will quickly drive away his woe,	O 69	Hor.II Ode 14	26
Parent of ills! and source of all our woe!	O 77	Festina Lente	10
Thy Streets with Violence of Woe shall sound,	O 110	To Posterity	5
Of human bliss to human woe.	O 184	Tr. Benserade	4
The horrid pomp of ostentatious woe	Y 168	Irene	V 135
Still labours with imaginary Woe;	O 320	Irene	22
Deem us not deaf to Woe, nor blind to Beauty,	O 327	Irene	29
Great is thy Woe! but think, illustrious Sultan,	O 332	Irene	37
And all the withering woods confess their woe	Y 6	Virgil Daphnis	4
WOES			
While all neglect, and most insult your woes.	O 19	London	193
The glitt'ring eminence exempt from woes;	O 38	Vanity Wishes	V 166
All times their scenes of pompous woes afford,	O 41	Vanity Wishes	223
Mimick your tears, and ridicule your woes;	O 74	Tr. Iliad Bk 6	22
Tell the woes of wilful waste,	O 197	Song Congratu.	26
What e'er our Crimes, our Woes demand Compassion.	O 251	Irene	58
Such are the Woes when arbitrary Pow'r,	O 256	Irene	58
But how can'st thou support the Woes of Exile?	O 301	Irene	102
My Pride shall ne'er protract my Country's Woes;	O 306	Irene	47
Let me but live, heap Woes on Woes upon me,	O 328	Irene	33
Let me but live, heap Woes on Woes upon me,	O 328	Irene	33
Melt at Irene's Fate, and share her Woes?	O 329	Irene	7
WOLF			
A grizly wolf surprised, and fled.	O 65	Hor I Ode xxii	12
A furious wolf approach'd and fled.	O 65	Hor I Ode xxii	V 12
A furious Wolf approach'd, and fled.	O 66	To A. Fuscus	12
WOLSEY			
In full-blown dignity, see Wolsey stand,	O 34	Vanity Wishes	99
In full blown pow'r see mighty Wolsey stand,	Y 96	Vanity Wishes	V 99
In full blown state, see Wolsey stand,	Y 96	Vanity Wishes	V 99
For why did Wolsey near the steeps of fate,	O 35	Vanity Wishes	125
For why did Wolsey by the Steps of fate,	O 35	Vanity Wishes	V 125
WOLSEY'S			
Shall Wolsey's wealth, with Wolsey's end be thine?	O 35	Vanity Wishes	122
Shall Wolsey's wealth, with Wolsey's end be thine?	O 35	Vanity Wishes	122
WOLVES			
Or feasts on Kids the Wolves had kill'd	O 73	Hor. Epode II	65

		PAGE	TITLE	LINE
WOLVES	(CONTINUED)			
But thus reserv'd to lure the Wolves of Turkey,	. . .	O 250	Irene	24
The harmless wolves no more our cattle fear,	. . .	Y 7	Virgil Daphnis	38
WOMAN				
Woman the Source, the Object, and the End.	. . . .	O 247	Irene Epilogue	18
Will not that Pow'r that form'd the Heart of Woman,	.	O 266	Irene	23
Profusely pour'd her Bounties upon Woman?	. . . .	O 276	Irene	25
Made passive Fortitude the Praise of Woman:	. . . .	O 290	Irene	44
Here's a woman of the town,	. . . .	Y 300	Extemp. Elegy	1
WOMAN'S				
Leave off, at length, these woman's sighs,	. . . .	O 68	Hor. II Ode IX	17
Where Woman's not allow'd to speak her Mind;	. . .	O 247	Irene Epilogue	12
In vain proud Man usurps what's Woman's Due;	. . .	O 247	Irene Epilogue	15
Or flow dissolving in a Woman's Tears?	. . .	O 255	Irene	25
But oft conjoins in woman's softer mould/frame	. .	Y 149	Irene V	55
Think--but excuse a Woman's needless Caution,	. .	O 298	Irene	5
Perhaps the Phantoms of a Woman's Fear,	. . . . .	O 300	Irene	71
WOMANS				
The Christian's tenderness? or womans weakness	. . . .	Y 189	Irene V	1C
WOMB				
Lies in the Womb of Providence conceal'd,	. . .	O 313	Irene	3
WOMEN				
Who thinks us Women born to dress and sing	. . . .	O 247	Irene Epilogue	2
The Tale of Women, and the Scorn of Fools?	. . . .	O 305	Irene	29
WOMENS				
Or if old womens tales may credit gain,	. . . . .	O 77	Tr Add. Battle	44
WON				
Where won by bribes, by flatteries implor'd,	. . .	O 18	London	180
By Reason not convinc'd, nor won by Love.	. . . .	O 310	Irene	8
WOND'RING				
And cut with joy the wond'ring Skies.	. . . . . .	O 70	Hor.II Ode XX	4
Bear him aloft above the wond'ring Clouds,	. . .	O 274	Irene	62
WOND'ROUS				
Admires their wond'rous talents for the stage:	. . .	O 16	London	133
Sure by some wond'rous Sympathy of Souls,	. . . .	O 272	Irene	8
WONDER				
Silent Wonder stopt the Floods;	. . . .	O 148	Tr Boet III.12	12
Detested Cali too, with artful Wonder,	. . .	O 273	Irene	27
Struck with the Wonder of a Statesman's Goodness,	. .	O 274	Irene	45
When ev'n as Love was breaking off from Wonder,	. .	O 282	Irene	66
WONDER'D				
The Sultan gaz'd, he wonder'd and he lov'd;	. . . .	O 258	Irene	98
WONDERS				
He views, and wonders that they please no more;	. . .	O 43	Vanity Wishes	264
He views, and wonders why they please no more;	. . .	Y 104	Vanity Wishes V	264
But search the wonders of the dusky stone,	. . . .	O 141	Tr Rambler 199	5
Can brave Leontius call for airy Wonders,	. . .	O 250	Irene	42
Illustrious Maid, new Wonders fix me thine,	. . .	O 278	Irene	59
Celestial fair--maid--new wonders fix me thine,	. .	Y 149	Irene V	59
Sure Heav'n, for Wonders are not wrought in vain,	. .	O 296	Irene	38
WONDRING				
To wondring Worlds produc'd the whole,	. . . .	O 147	Tr Boeth III.6	11
Did not our sails receive the wondring winds	. . .	Y 115	Irene V	49G
Pour forth the Legions and the Wondring Danube	. . . .	O 353	Irene V	1
The Wondring Sky shall shine with Decorations	. . . .	O 364	Irene V	28
WONT				
Nor shall the Lyon, wont of old to reign	. . . . .	O 111	To Posterity	19
WONTED				
Were Pope once void of wonted candour found,	. . .	O 106	Eliza plucking	7
With wonted Zeal pursue the Task of War,	. . . .	O 264	Irene	30
Or lift themselves into the wonted skies.	. . .	Y 24	Tr Add. Battle	61
WOOD				
And the wood rings with Amarillis' name.	. . . . .	O 64	Virgil Past.I	6
WOODCOCK				
The woodcock and the sparrow;	. . . .	Y 300	Fanny Burney	3
WOODS				
Too far in Sabine woods I stray'd;	. . . .	O 65	Hor I Ode xxii	10
Woods to evry Sigh replying,	. . .	O 148	Tr Boet III.12 V	6
Round him danc'd the listning Woods,	. . .	O 148	Tr Boet III.12	11
Round him crowd the listning Woods,	. . .	O 148	Tr Boet III.12 V	11
The fields, and woods, behold, are green,	. . .	O 231	Tr Horace IV.7	2
The fields, and woods, again, are green,	. . . .	O 231	Tr Horace IV.7 V	2
And all the withering woods confess their woe	. .	Y 6	Virgil Daphnis	4
And woods and mountains hail the deity.	. . . . .	Y 7	Virgil Daphnis	41
WORD				
Prologue to "A Word to the Wise"	. . . .	O 61	Pro Word Wise	T
WORDS				
And his last words reproach the faith of kings.	. . .	Y 96	Vanity Wishes V	120
Uncouth Words in Disarray:	. . . .	O 179	Ridicul Warton	6
WORK SEE NET-WORK				
In vain the vary'd work would shine,	. . . . .	O 119	To Miss Purse	3
Once more great nature's work review,	. . .	O 125	An Ode	23
Commits to trivial chance the Work of Fate!	. . . .	O 374	Irene V	11
To men belongs the dreadfull work of war."	. . . .	Y 21	Tr. Iliad Bk 6	123
WORK'D				
Work'd into sudden rage by wintry show'rs,	. . .	O 132	Tr. Rambler 65	1
WORKMANSHIP				
Destroy'd the fairest Workmanship of Heav'n!	. . . .	O 332	Irene	19
WORKS				
My Works shall propagate my fame,	. . . . . .	O 70	Hor.II Ode XX	17
Once more great nature's works renew	. . . .	O 125	An Ode V	23

399

WORKS	(CONTINUED)	PAGE	TITLE	LINE
fasting, pennan<ce> and works of goodness	. . . . .	O 348	Irene	V 15
WORLD				
Then thro' the world a wretched vagrant roam,	. . . . .	O 18	London	190
Deign on the passing world to turn thine eyes,	. . . . .	O 38	Vanity Wishes	157
For such the steady Romans shook the world;	. . . . .	O 39	Vanity Wishes	180
For these these steady Romans shook the world;	. . . . .	Y 100	Vanity Wishes	V 180
He left the name, at which the world grew pale,	. . . .	O 41	Vanity Wishes	221
The queen, the beauty, sets the world in arms;	. . . . .	O 42	Vanity Wishes	246
While wretched we about the world must roam,	. . . .	O 64	Virgil Past.I	3
From th' envious world with scorn I spring,	. . . . . .	O 70	Hor.II Ode XX	3
Not Rome itself that held the world in awe	. . . . .	O 76	Tr Add. Battle	39
Th' Apostles round the world were sent,	. . . . .	O 79	Feast St Simon	25
He pants for room, in one poor World confin'd.	. . . . .	O 97	Hickman Spinet	12
To all the lower world deny'd;	. . . .	O 99	Ode Friendship	4
Then o'er the World shall Discord stretch her Wings,	. .	O 110	To Posterity	15
All the World afraid but thee,	. . . .	O 145	Tr Boeth. II.4	20
And Winter chils the World again.	. . . .	O 232	Tr Horace IV.7	12
And shook the (affrighted) world lab'ring earth licentious conquest		Y 115	Irene	V 49A
Yet strangers in some distant world proclaim	. . . . .	Y 120	Irene	V 31A
Which granted, hides my Purpose from the World,	. . .	O 258	Irene	88
Hail, Terror of the Monarchs of the World,	. . . . .	O 262	Irene	1
You are like the sun the governour of the world	. . . .	Y 132	Irene	V 40
Diffuse Irene's Beauty though the World.	. . . . .	O 268	Irene	14
Shake at my dreaded name and the frighted world	. . . .	Y 136	Irene	V 28
Disperse Rebellion through the Eastern World;	. . . .	O 274	Irene	52
Only to hunt him round the ravag'd World?	. . . . .	O 275	Irene	67
Mean as we are, this Tyrant of the World	. . . . .	O 277	Irene	39
And share the Pleasures of the World	. . . . . .	O 348	Irene	V 20
Should fill the World with Wretches undetected.	. . .	O 283	Irene	27
Make haste, bright Maid, to rule the willing World;	. .	O 288	Irene	7
And fill the bleed<in>g world with desolation	. . . .	O 352	Irene	V 5
Unpitying Massacre might waste the World,	. . . .	O 291	Irene	65
Fierce persecution wears the bleeding world with fraud	. . .	Y 164	Irene	V 66
When social Laws first harmonis'd the World,	. . . .	O 291	Irene	70
the world recovering from its convulsion	. . . . .	Y 164	Irene	V 77
Descend from Heavn, to range the distant World	. . .	O 349	Irene	V 10
The subject World, familiar to Dominion.	. . . . .	O 369	Irene	V 10
A slaughter'd nation, or a shatter'd world.	. . . .	Y 177	Irene	V111E
And wake from Ignorance the Western World.	. . . .	O 302	Irene	123
At length th' unwilling Sun resigns the World	. . . .	O 302	Irene	1
And fill the World with Follies and Impostures,	. . .	O 309	Irene	35
And bid the master Genius rule the World.	. . . .	O 309	Irene	42
And spread their Flames resistless o'er the World?	. .	O 325	Irene	13
And lead thy Troops victorious round the World.	. . .	O 333	Irene	41
Shall hide me from the tasteless World for ever.	. . .	O 333	Irene	48
WORLDS				
Exhausted Worlds, and then imagin'd new:	. . . . .	O 51	Pro Drury-Lane	4
And found a Thousand Worlds in Stella's Arms.	. . . .	O 97	Hickman Spinet	20
O thou whose pow'r o'er moving worlds presides,	. . .	O 129	Tr. Rambler 7	1
To wondring Worlds produc'd the whole,	. . . . .	O 147	Tr Boeth III.6	11
WORN				
Let Study, worn with Virtue's fruitless Lore,	. . . .	O 57	Prologue Comus	9
Hypocrisy which I ha<ve> worn is a burthen:	. . . .	Y 185	Irene	V 2
WORSHIPER				
Pours in the morning worshiper no more;	. . . . . .	O 33	Vanity Wishes	80
Shews pour the morning worshiper no more;	. . . . .	Y 95	Vanity Wishes	V 80
WORSHIPPERS				
Vot'ries of Fame and Worshippers of Pow'r!	. . . .	O 246	Irene Prologue	5
WORTH				
Since worth, he cries, in these degen'rate days,	. . .	O 10	London	35
Wit, brav'ry, worth, his lavish tongue bestows;	. . .	O 16	London	126
Slow Rises Worth, By Poverty Depress'd:	. . . . .	O 18	London	177
Heroic worth, benevolence divine:	. . . . .	O 34	Vanity Wishes	88
And bids afflicted worth retire to peace.	. . . .	O 45	Vanity Wishes	310
His various worth, through varied life attend,	. . .	O 117	Epitaph Hanmer	3
To rural grandeur, and domestick worth;	. . . . .	O 118	Epitaph Hanmer	38
What Worth can merit? or what Faith reward?	. . . .	O 295	Irene	16
Behold a Boaster's Worth. Now snatch, my Fair,	. .	O 320	Irene	7
Nor hope his Fortune while thou want'st his Worth.	. .	O 330	Irene	25
WORTHLESS				
Nor give the generous pain, the worthless joy:	. . . .	O 81	Lady Birthday	14
WORTLEY				
To W<ortley> and to Angels given	. . . .	O 99	Ode Friendship	V 3
WOU'D				
Wou'd Stella, sprightly, fair and young,	. . . . .	O 121	To Miss Playin	V 21
WOULD				
For who would leave, unbrib'd, Hibernia's land,	. . .	O 9	London	9
No sounds alas would touch th' impervious ear,	. . .	O 43	Vanity Wishes	269
The notes unfelt would strike th' impervious ear,	. .	Y 104	Vanity Wishes	V 269
Nor would inexorable Death	. . . .	O 69	Hor.II Ode 14	11
Would not these pleasures soon remove	. . . . .	O 72	Hor. Epode II	45
Such Pleasures quickly would remove	. . . . .	O 72	Hor. Epode II	V 45
So much my Appetite would please	. . . . . .	O 73	Hor. Epode II	60
How would the Trojans brand great Hector's name!	. .	O 74	Tr. Iliad Bk 6	5
Just Phoebus would devote his plant to thee.	. . .	O 106	Eliza plucking	8
In vain the vary'd work would shine,	. . . . .	O 119	To Miss Purse	3
Would ease the hunger of the mind,	. . . . . .	O 144	Tr Boeth. II.2	8
Rapacity would call for more;	. . . .	O 144	Tr Boeth. II.2	10

		PAGE	TITLE	LINE
WOULD	(CONTINUED)			
Would you hope to gain my heart,	. . . .	O 176	Tr Metastasi I	1
Her statue would have breath'd an added grace,	. . . .	O 189	Seeing Montagu	4
And on its basis would have been enroll'd,	. . . . .	O 190	Seeing Montagu	5
Soon those nine lives would be past.	. . . .	O 194	On Thrale Hat	4
What hazards would I shun to clasp for Greece and for	.	Y 125	Irene	V 133
Aspasia				
Soon would his Art or Valour set us free,	. . . . .	O 267	Irene	43
Would shake his wily Head, and closely whisper,	. . .	O 273	Irene	28
Th' adoring Soldiers would revenge their Idol.	. . . .	O 273	Irene	42
Long would my Zeal for Mahomet and Thee	. . . . .	O 288	Irene	11
Would loose the wild Enthusiast to destroy,	. . . . .	O 291	Irene	61
Would break the sacred laws of peace and	. . . . .	O 352	Irene	V 3
order				
Oft would they find Ingratitude and Treason,	. . . .	O 308	Irene	14
How rarely would they meet in crouded Courts,	. . .	O 308	Irene	16
I w<ould> have every smile g<enu>ine to<morrow no>	.	Y 185	Irene	V 3
Then would I free from torments live	. . . . . .	Y 11	Tr Hor Epode 9	25
Some furious soldier would approach that bore	. . .	Y 23	Tr Add. Battle	46
O would Cleora thus return,	. . . .	Y 39	Lady Leaving	11
WOULDST				
How wouldst thou shake at Britain's modish tribe,	. . .	O 33	Vanity Wishes	61
Wouldst thou to some stedfast Seat,	. . . . . .	O 144	Tr Boeth. II.4	1
Wouldst thou when fierce Eurus blows	. . . . . .	O 144	Tr Boeth. II.4	3
Wouldst thou see the foaming Main,	. . . .	O 144	Tr Boeth. II.4	5
Wouldst thou subdue th' obdurate Cannibal	. . . .	O 267	Irene	4
Soon wouldst thou see, how false thy weak Reproach.	. .	O 293	Irene	V 107
WOUND				
Did rival monarchs give the fatal wound?	. . . . .	O 41	Vanity Wishes	217
Their souls dismiss'd through many a ghastly wound,	. .	O 74	Tr. Iliad Bk 6	18
Here lies a fowl transfix'd with many a wound	. . .	O 76	Tr Add. Battle	14
At length deform'd with many a grisly wound	. . . .	O 76	Tr Add. Battle	24
Cease, lovely thief! my tender limbs to wound,	. . .	O 106	Eliza plucking	5
And Murder, all blood-bolter'd, schemes the wound.	. .	O 192	Tr. Medea II	16
The wound, and, furious, wave the shining steel.	. .	Y 26	Tr Add. Battle	133
WOUNDED				
Thick from their wounded wings the feathers fly,	. . .	O 75	Tr Add. Battle	4
Oft from behind they wounded them with darts	. . .	Y 23	Tr Add. Battle	42
Wounded and spent, in vain they strive to rise	. . .	Y 24	Tr Add. Battle	60
WOUNDS				
Fate never wounds more deep the gen'rous heart,	. . .	O 18	London	168
Acquir'd by wounds, and battles bravely fought!	. . .	O 74	Tr. Iliad Bk 6	7
Whose mortal wounds pour forth a purple flood,	. . .	O 76	Tr Add. Battle	20
Nor rush on useless Wounds with idle Courage.	. . .	O 318	Irene	10
WOVE				
And wove the feeble Texture of her Nerves,	. . . . .	O 266	Irene	24
WRATH				
When publick crimes inflame the wrath of heav'n:	. . .	O 13	London	66
Now let him go, pursu'd by silent Wrath,	. . . . .	O 274	Irene	47
The Ministers of Wrath forget Compassion,	. . . . .	O 314	Irene	24
WRATHFULL				
His wrathfull sword imbru'd.	. . . .	O 80	Feast St Simon	54
Soon had the wrathfull faulchion drank his blood.	. .	Y 23	Tr Add. Battle	41
WREATH				
He feels th' unfading wreath surround his head;	. . .	O 82	Young Author	22
And feels the unfading wreath surround his head;	. .	O 82	Young Author	V 22
WREATH'D				
Daphnis with ivy wreath'd the jav'lins round	. . .	Y 6	Virgil Daphnis	15
WREATHS				
And mortgag'd states their grandsires wreaths regret,	.	O 39	Vanity Wishes	187
And mortgag'd states their former wreaths regret,	. .	Y 100	Vanity Wishes	V 187
Wreaths which at last the dear-bought right convey	.	O 40	Vanity Wishes	189
WRETCH				
What has the Wretch that has surviv'd his Country,	.	O 260	Irene	134
Claim my divided Soul. This Wretch unworthy	. . .	O 275	Irene	69
Sometimes the Wretch unaw'd by Heav'n or Hell,	. .	O 300	Irene	78
Devolve, dear Maid, thy Sorrows on the Wretch,	. .	O 316	Irene	16
Fly, Wretch, while yet my Pity grants thee Flight;	.	O 319	Irene	23
Forsake a Wretch abandon'd to Despair,	. . . . .	O 320	Irene	14
Who calls for Pardon from a Wretch condemn'd?	. . .	O 323	Irene	4
The Queen requested--Wretch, repeat the Message;	. .	O 331	Irene	13
The Queen requested--Wretch, repeat thy Message;	. .	O 331	Irene	V 13
The Wretch, whose Guilt declar'd by tortur'd Cali,	.	O 334	Irene	64
The wretch whose crimes declar'd by tortur'd Cali	. .	Y 215	Irene	V 69A
WRETCHED				
Then thro' the world a wretched vagrant roam,	. . .	O 18	London	190
While wretched we about the world must roam,	. . .	O 64	Virgil Past.I	3
And rais'd us from our wretched state,	. . . . .	O 79	Feast St Simon	20
But wretched Man, when once he lies	. . . . . .	O 232	Tr Horace IV.7	14
But he must live to make his Masters wretched?	. .	O 286	Irene	7
Must Greece, still wretched by her Children's Folly,	.	O 305	Irene	43
Behold him wretched in his double Triumph;	. . .	O 310	Irene	5
Ended her wretched life and pierc'd her heart.	. . .	Y 19	Tr. Iliad Bk 6	43
Think shouldst thou fall how wretched shall we be,	.	Y 19	Tr. Iliad Bk 6	48
WRETCHEDNESS				
What care, youre charms from wretchedness shall save	. .	Y 107	Vanity Wishes	V 329
From splendid wretchedness and guilty scepters (grandeur)		Y 166	Irene	V 93
WRETCHES				
Should fill the World with Wretches undetected.	. . .	O 283	Irene	27
WRIT				
Themselves they studied, as they felt, they writ,	. . .	O 52	Pro Drury-Lane	19

401

WRITE
Pettius no more I verses write; . . . . Y 10 Tr Hor Epode 9 1

WRITER
To some retreat the baffled writer flies, ... O 82 Young Author 26

WRITING
Prodigious madness of the writing race! . . . . Y 67 Prologue Lethe 1

WRITTEN
Verses, written at the request of a Gentleman . . . O 95 Sprig of Myrtl V T
   Written By Doctor Freind . . . . O 117 Epitaph Hanmer T

WRONG
Ne'er knew to puzzle right, or varnish wrong, . . O 14 London 80
Perversely grave, or postively wrong. . . . . . O 43 Vanity Wishes 274
Perversely grave, and positively wrong. . . . . Y 104 Vanity Wishes V 274
Or right, or wrong, once hooted from the stage; . . O 61 Pro Word Wise 2
Imbibes with dire docility the wrong. . . . . . O 136 Tr Rambler 132 2
With wild Vicissitudes of Wrong, ... O 145 Tr Boeth III.1 10
Endless Labour to be wrong; . . . . O 179 Ridicul Warton 4

WRONG'D
Whence is this Rage? what barb'rous Tongue has wrong'd . O 325 Irene 27
   me?

WRONGS
My Wrongs, my Fears, my Motives, my Designs:-- . . . . O 256 Irene 40
Enrag'd by Wrongs, exulting with Success, ... O 313 Irene 15

WROUGHT
See! how the mighty Change is wrought! . . . . . O 70 Hor.II Ode XX 9
If wrought by any hand but thine, ... O 119 To Miss Purse 4
And yet, my Friend, what Miracles were wrought . . . O 251 Irene 52
Sure Heav'n, for Wonders are not wrought in vain, . . . O 296 Irene 38

XEINE
Aphrosi me semnen, Xeine, podessi patei . . . . . O 171 Epi. Goldsmith 2

XERXES
Great Xerxes comes to seize the certain prey, ... O 42 Vanity Wishes 227

YE
Some secret cell, ye pow'rs, indulgent give. . . . O 11 London 49
Propose your schemes, ye Senatorian band, ... O 21 London 244
But hear his death, ye blockheads, hear and sleep. . . O 39 Vanity Wishes 174
But hear his death, ye blockheads, hear and weep. . . O 39 Vanity Wishes V 174
Approach, ye minstrels, try the soothing strain, . . . O 43 Vanity Wishes 267
Ye patriot Crouds, who burn for England's Fame, . . . O 46 Vanity Wishes 323
Ye nymphs of rosy lips and radiant eyes, ... O 57 Prologue Comus 1
Ye Nymphs, whose Bosoms beat at Milton's Name, . . . O 57 Prologue Comus 2
Yours is the Charge, ye Fair, ye Wise, ye Brave! . . O 58 Prologue Comus 37
Yours is the Charge, ye Fair, ye Wise, ye Brave! . . O 58 Prologue Comus 37
Yours is the Charge, ye Fair, ye Wise, ye Brave! . . O 58 Prologue Comus 37
Be kind, ye judges, or at least be just: . . . . O 61 Pro Word Wise 8
Ye blooming train, who give despair or joy, . . . O 83 Epi Dist Moth. 1
For you, ye fair, I quit the gloomy plains, ... O 83 Epi Dist Moth. 10
Then melt, ye fair, while crouds around you sigh, . . O 84 Epi Dist Moth. 42
Ye nymphs whom starry rays invest, ... O 126 To Lyce, Lady 1
Be gone ye blockheads, Heraclitus cries, ... O 141 Tr Rambler 208 1
Ye Sons of England, deign to hear, ... O 188 Epilogue 3
Ye Sons of Britain, deign to hear, ... O 188 Epilogue V 3
May ye the varied blessings share . . . . . O 189 Epilogue 5
May ye th' alternate blessings share . . . . . O 189 Epilogue V 5
Ye sons of Melody repair, ... O 191 Tr. Medea I 14
Ye glitt'ring Train! whom Lace and Velvet bless, . . O 246 Irene Prologue 1
Ye Sons of Avarice! a Moment spare: . . . . . O 246 Irene Prologue 4
Ye Fops be silent! and ye Wits be just! . . . . O 246 Irene Prologue 34
Ye Fops be silent! and ye Wits be just! . . . . O 246 Irene Prologue 34
Ye sacred Shades of Patriots and of Martyrs; . . . O 306 Irene 52
Ye holy shades of--martyrs . . . . Y 181 Irene V 52
All ye, whose Blood tyrannick Rage effus'd, ... O 306 Irene 53
Ye venerable ghosts of noble patriots . . . . . Y 181 Irene V 53
Caraza speak--have ye remark'd the Bassa? . . . . O 311 Irene 1
Ye Christian Captives, follow me to Freedom: . . . O 321 Irene 51
Dispatch, ye ling'ring Slaves, or nimbler Hands . . . O 328 Irene 42
Ye Slaves of Cruelty, ye Tools of Rage, ... O 332 Irene 22
Ye Slaves of Cruelty, ye Tools of Rage, ... O 332 Irene 22
Ye blind officious Ministers of Folly, ... O 332 Irene 23
Be just ye Slaves, and, to be just, be cruel, . . . O 333 Irene 51
Hew down, ye Guards, those Vassals of Distraction, . . O 334 Irene 73
Ye swains! bestrow the ground with leaves and spread . . Y 7 Virgil Daphnis 26

YEAR
Year chases year, decay pursues decay, ... O 45 Vanity Wishes 305
Year chases year, decay pursues decay, ... O 45 Vanity Wishes 305
Amidst the toils of this returning year, ... O 59 Pro Good Nat'd V 4A
For that blest year when all that vote may rail; . . O 60 Pro Good Nat'd 18
When rip'ning fruits perfume the year, ... O 72 Hor. Epode II 25
To whom the church each rolling year . . . . . O 78 Feast St Simon 11
Still changing with the changeful year, ... O 124 Winter's Walk 15
Year chases year, with unremitted flight, ... O 152 The Ant 14
Year chases year, with unremitted flight, ... O 152 The Ant 14
Comets! come every day--and stay a year. . . . . O 177 Tr Dist Modena 2
Ling'ring year at last is flown, ... O 196 Song Congratu. 2
Well tried through many a varying year, ... O 201 Death Dr Levet 5
Tho' now his eightieth year was nigh. . . . . . O 202 Death Dr Levet 32
The changing year renews the plain, ... O 231 Tr Horace IV.7 3
Hail lovely flower, first honour of the year! . . . Y 3 On a Daffodill 1
And of a fruitful year fair omens bring. . . . . Y 3 On a Daffodill 4
And of a faithful year fair omens bring. . . . . Y 3 On a Daffodill V 4
And thrice deform'd the verdant year . . . . . Y 11 Tr Hor Epode 9 8

		PAGE	TITLE	LINE

YEAR (CONTINUED)
In half a year of darkness lost. . . . . — Y 38 Lady Leaving — 4
Oft has our bard in this disastrous year, — Y 67 Prologue Lethe — 7

YEAR'S
The teeming Year's whole Product shall devour, — O 110 To Posterity — 11
The changing year's successive plan . . . . — O 231 Tr Horace IV.7 — 7

YEARLY
Two bowls with oyl and milk I'll yearly crown, — Y 7 Virgil Daphnis — 45

YEARS
For Years the Pow'r of Tragedy declin'd; . . . — O 52 Pro Drury-Lane — 30
Alass, dear Friend, the fleeting years . . . — O 68 Hor.II Ode 14 — 1
Thrice ten long years he labour'd for the State; . . — O 118 Epitaph Hanmer — 14
Succeeding years thy early fame destroy; . . . — O 135 Tr Rambler 127 — 1
Long may better Years arrive, ... — O 178 Thrale 35 Year — 3
Oft may better Years arrive, ... — O 178 Thrale 35 Year V 3
Better Years than Thirty five; . . . . . . — O 178 Thrale 35 Year V 4
Years at length are flown, ... — O 196 Song Congratu. V 2
The Weight of Years, and totters to the Tempest, . . — O 250 Irene — 45
These Years, unconquer'd Mahomet, demand . . . — O 263 Irene — 7
Instructed from our infant Years to court . . . — O 266 Irene — 27
Beneath the Load of Business, and of Years. . . . — O 271 Irene — 7
Born down with Years, still doat upon To-morrow? . . — O 283 Irene — 20
When pale, and anxious for their Years to come, . . — O 287 Irene — 4

YELLINGS
And stun me with the Yellings of Damnation! . . . . — O 328 Irene — 51

YELP
Tho' confiscation's bloodhounds yelp around. . . . — Y 93 Vanity Wishes V 36

YES
Perfidious!--yes--too well thou know'st them Traytors. . — O 324 Irene — 17

YET
Yet still my calmer thoughts his choice commend, . . . — O 8 London — 3
While yet my steady steps no staff sustains, . . . — O 10 London — 41
While yet my steddy steps no staff sustains, . . . — O 10 London V 41
No peaceful desart yet unclaim'd by Spain? . . . — O 18 London — 173
Yet ev'n these heroes, mischievously gay, . . . — O 21 London — 230
Yet ev'n those heroes, mischievously gay, . . . — Y 59 London V 230
Yet still one gen'ral cry the skies assails, . . . — O 32 Vanity Wishes — 45
Yet still one gen'ral cry the skies assails, . . . — O 32 Vanity Wishes V 45
How just that scorn ere yet thy voice declare, . . — O 33 Vanity Wishes — 71
Yet should thy soul indulge the gen'rous heat, . . — O 37 Vanity Wishes — 143
Yet should thy fate indulge the gen'rous heat, . . — Y 98 Vanity Wishes V 143
Yet hope not life from grief or danger free, . . — O 37 Vanity Wishes — 155
Yet dream not life from grief or danger free, . . — Y 99 Vanity Wishes V 155
If dreams yet flatter, once again attend, . . . — O 38 Vanity Wishes — 163
If hope yet flatter, once again attend, . . . — Y 99 Vanity Wishes V 163
Yet Reason frowns on War's unequal game, . . . — O 39 Vanity Wishes — 185
Yet Reason blush on War's unequal game, . . . — Y 100 Vanity Wishes V 185
Yet ev'n on this her load Misfortune flings, . . — O 44 Vanity Wishes — 299
Yet Vane could tell what ills from beauty spring; . . — O 45 Vanity Wishes — 321
Enquirer, cease, petitions yet remain, ... — O 47 Vanity Wishes — 349
Yet when the sense of sacred presence fires, . . . — O 48 Vanity Wishes — 357
Yet with the sense of sacred presence prest, . . — O 48 Vanity Wishes V 357
Yet Bards like these aspir'd to lasting Praise, . . — O 52 Pro Drury-Lane — 23
Yet still did Virtue deign the Stage to tread, . . — O 52 Pro Drury-Lane — 33
New Behns, new Durfeys, yet remain in Store. . . — O 53 Pro Drury-Lane — 42
Yet softer Claims the melting Heart engage, . . . — O 58 Prologue Comus — 29
Yet judg'd by those, whose voices ne'er were sold, . . — O 60 Pro Good Nat'd — 27
Yet then shall calm reflection bless the night, . . — O 62 Pro Word Wise — 21
Yet shall I see the blest abodes, ... — O 70 Hor.II Ode XX — 6
Yet, great Maecenas, shall your friend . . . — O 70 Hor.II Ode XX — 7
Yet Hecuba's, nor Priam's hoary age, ... — O 74 Tr. Iliad Bk 6 — 15
"Secure of praise from nations yet unborn." . . — O 82 Young Author — 18
"Secure of praise from ages yet unborn." . . . — O 82 Young Author V 18
The Patriot's fire yet sparkled in the friend. . . — O 118 Epitaph Hanmer — 40
Yet, tho' my limbs disease invades, ... — O 125 An Ode — 13
Yet spite of fair Zelinda's eye, ... — O 127 To Lyce, Lady — 21
E'er yet had happiness compleat; . . . . . — O 136 Tr Rambler 128 — 2
Yet, lay the sonnet for an hour aside, . . . — O 142 In Baretti Bk. — 7
Yet timely provident, she hastes away . . . — O 151 The Ant — 5
But yet the child squeal'd on. . . . . . . — O 157 Par. Hermit I V 4
Yet hear, alas! this mournful truth, ... — O 159 Par Hermit III — 9
Yet hear, at last, this mournful truth, . . . — O 159 Par Hermit III V 9
And yet of every gift usurp the merit; . . . — O 176 Tr Metastasio V 11
Oft in Danger yet alive . . . . — O 178 Thrale 35 Year — 1
All is strange, yet nothing new; . . . . . — O 179 Ridicul Warton — 2
"Think not yet my service hard, ... — O 185 Anacreon Ode 9 — 17
Yet still he fills affection's eye, ... — O 201 Death Dr Levet — 9
Ennobled, yet unchang'd, if Nature shine: . . . — O 246 Irene Prologue — 16
Studious to please, yet not asham'd to fail. . . — O 246 Irene Prologue — 30
And yet, my Friend, what Miracles were wrought . . — O 251 Irene — 52
Yet let me think--I see the helpless Maid . . . — O 252 Irene — 80
Ere yet the Foe found Leisure to be cruel, . . . — O 252 Irene — 94
Yet strangers in some distant world proclaim . . — Y 120 Irene V 31A
But yet th' Attempt . . . . — O 260 Irene — 132
Yet unacquainted with these soft Emotions . . . — O 263 Irene — 16
yet the fierce Albanian lyon . . . . . — Y 130 Irene V 13
While fair yet Hungaria's inexhausted Vallies . . — O 352 Irene V 33
Thou know'st not yet thy Master's future Greatness, . . — O 265 Irene — 40
Aspasia, yet pursue the sacred Theme; . . . — O 265 Irene — 1
If yet one spark of Heav'nly fire remain . . . — Y 133 Irene V 18
Whose Soul, perhaps, yet mindful of Aspasia, . . — O 267 Irene — 39

YET	(CCNTINUED)	PAGE	TITLE		LINE
He yet may live.		O 267	Irene		45
And yet another Voice, forgive me Greece,		O 270	Irene		18
Lay pointed at our Batt'ries yet unform'd,		O 273	Irene		25
But yet, great Emperor, beware of Treason;		O 273	Irene		31
Will yet Irenes haughty Soul descend		O 372	Irene	V	6
Yet can Ambition in Abdalla's Breast		O 280	Irene		25
Yet, on a Day like this, when Expectation		O 280	Irene		30
Know'st thou not yet, when Love invades the Soul,		O 281	Irene		38
Yet in the Use of Pow'r remember Justice.		O 286	Irene		10
Yet in that narrow Space what Dangers rise?--		O 287	Irene		6
If yet this shining Pomp, these sudden Honours,		O 289	Irene		1
If yet these glittring Robes these sudden Splendors		O 366	Irene	V	17
Not yet inspire the Follies of a Queen,		O 289	Irene		3
Not yet inspire th' omniscience of a queen		O 366	Irene	V	19
Yet should my Soul, still faithful to her Choice,		O 289	Irene		13
I am not yet a Queen, or an Apostate.		O 289	Irene		22
(Yet) not with idle cries I fill'd the city		Y 163	Irene	V	46
There shall we find the yet untasted Bliss		O 292	Irene		88
I stand amaz'd, and ask, if yet I clasp thee.		O 296	Irene		37
Yet let me watch her dear departing Steps,		O 297	Irene		17
Yet when your Hand is lifted to destroy,		O 298	Irene		4
But still yet my Soul detests the Bassas treason		O 353	Irene	V	22
Yet think a Mcment, ere you court Destruction,		O 301	Irene		87
Should Heav'n't yet unappeas'd refuse its Aid,		O 301	Irene		97
Yet shall the Conscience of the great Attempt		O 301	Irene		99
if human miseries or affairs yet claim your regard		Y 181	Irene	V	54
Yet ere we give our loosen'd Thoughts to Rapture,		O 309	Irene		18
And yet such is the condition of human happiness		Y 186	Irene	V	2
While yet the future Fortune of my Country		O 313	Irene		2
When Purity, while Fraud was yet unknown,		O 314	Irene		6
Yet! why--		O 314	Irene		10
Yet tell.		O 316	Irene		21
Yet much remains to hope. I shall not call		O 317	Irene		45
Fly, Wretch, while yet my Pity grants thee Flight;		O 319	Irene		23
Press not her Flight, while yet her feeble Nerves		O 320	Irene		20
Now make thy Choice, while yet the Pow'r of Choice		O 321	Irene		40
While I not yet familiar to my Crimes,		O 322	Irene		11
Her piercing Cries yet fill the loaded Air,		O 329	Irene		8
Yet she--fair--so shone first apostate		Y 211	Irene	V	10
Yet ere I quit the Scepter of Dominion,		O 333	Irene		49
While she yet beg'd to plead her Cause before thee.		O 334	Irene		67
And crush'd the yet unanimated young.		Y 23	Tr Add. Battle		49
Ardent of fame, yet fearless of disgrace.		Y 67	Prologue Lethe		2
Yet dares to venture on the dangerous stage,		Y 67	Prologue Lethe		11
YIELD					
No joys to him pacific scepters yield		O 40	Vanity Wishes		197
And yield the tuneful lenitiyes of pain:		O 43	Vanity Wishes	V	268
The guardians yield, by force superior ply'd;		O 47	Vanity Wishes		339
The guardians yield, with force resistless ply'd;		Y 107	Vanity Wishes	V	339
The day will come, in which proud Troy shall yield,		O 74	Tr. Iliad Bk 6		13
And yield, reluctant, to despotick Sway.		O 96	Hickman Spinet		5
To yield to remedies is half the cure.		O 140	Tr Rambler 178		1
Can yield no room to Music's soothing pow'r.		O 193	Tr. Medea II		20
YIELDING					
(Cry'd Daphne whisp'ring from the yielding tree;)		O 106	Eliza plucking		6
With warmer Courtship press the yielding Fair,		O 287	Irene		9
Then while he gaz'd upon his yielding Mistress,		O 299	Irene		48
Her ancient Empire o'er the yielding Heart;		O 302	Irene		121
YIELDS					
To better features yields the frame of gold;		O 34	Vanity Wishes		86
Till captive Science yields her last retreat;		O 37	Vanity Wishes		144
Yields to Renown the Centuries to come.		O 57	Prologue Comus		18
At length the undaunted Scythian yields,		O 68	Hor. II Ode IX		22
Charm'd with the scene the smiling ocean yields,		O 81	Young Author		3
Pleas'd with the scene the smiling ocean yields,		O 81	Young Author	V	3
Spring yield<s> to Summer<'s> sovereign ray,		O 231	Tr Horace IV.7		10
YCKE					
Nor yoke his Reason with his Will:		O 146	Tr Boeth III.5		4
Endur'd the stinging lash, and tamely bore the yoke.		Y 6	Virgil Daphnis		14
YCN					
Cali, methinks yon waving Trees afford		O 268	Irene		36
And where yon Trees wave o'er the foaming Surge		O 304	Irene		2
Demand whose Force yon Turkish Heroes dread,		O 305	Irene		41
YCN'					
At my Command yon' Iron Gates unfold;		O 283	Irene		14
Th' appointed Vessel to yon' shaded Bay,		O 284	Irene		51
YCNDER					
This scarce I lead, who left on yonder rock		O 64	Virgil Past.I		19
YORE					
And scanning right the practices of yore,		O 192	Tr. Medea II		3
YCU					
And here a female atheist talks you dead.		O 9	London		18
Aghast you start, and scarce with aking sight		O 18	London		186
The night you find some elegant retreat,		Y 58	London	V	212
Here life is ventur'd if the streets you roam		Y 59	London	V	224
And sign your will before you sup from home.		O 21	London		225
And make will before you sup from home.		Y 59	London	V	225

YOU   (CONTINUED)

		PAGE	TITLE	LINE
Provckes a broil, and stabs you for a jest.		O 21	London	229
In vain, these dangers past, your doors you close, . .		O 21	London	236
You fly for refuge to the wilds of Kent:		Y 61	London	V 257
Then prompt no more the Follies you decry, ...		O 53	Pro Drury-Lane	55
Trusts without fear, to merit, and to you.		O 60	Pro Good Nat'd	30
Trusts without fear, to candour, and to you.		O 60	Pro Good Nat'd	V 30
Now, Tityrus, you, supine and careless laid, ...		O 64	Virgil Past.I	1
Here at your ease you sing your amorous flame, ...		O 64	Virgil Past.I	5
To you alone this happy state remains.		O 64	Virgil Past.I	16
But you are ever drown'd in tears, ...		O 67	Hor. II Ode IX	9
For Mystes dead you ever mourn;		O 67	Hor. II Ode IX	10
But finds you sad at his return.		O 67	Hor. II Ode IX	12
In vain you spend your vows and prayers, ...		O 68	Hor.II Ode 14	3
You could not gain a Moments breath, ...		O 69	Hor.II Ode 14	9
The wine you kept with so much care		O 69	Hor.II Ode 14	27
Beneath Hyperia's waters shall you sweat, ...		O 74	Tr. Iliad Bk 6	23
Whether you sit on thrones, or dwell in cots, ...		O 77	Festina Lente	2
Whilst you deride their pangs in barb'rous play, . . .		O 83	Epi Dist Moth.	7
For you, ye fair, I quit the gloomy plains, ...		O 83	Epi Dist Moth.	10
Then melt, ye fair, while crouds around you sigh, . .		O 84	Epi Dist Moth.	42
So shall you guiltless reign, and all mankind adore. .		O 84	Epi Dist Moth.	47
Soon must this bough, as you shall fix his doom, . . .		O 95	Sprig of Myrtl	13
Soon shall this sprig, as you shall fix its doom, . .		O 95	Sprig of Myrtl	V 13
Too well You know to keep the Slaves You gain. . . .		O 96	Hickman Spinet	2
Too well You know to keep the Slaves You gain. . . .		O 96	Hickman Spinet	2
till you to happier climes remove?		O 100	Ode Friendship	V 26
On me you turn the nose.----		O 140	Tr Rambler 176	1
From you my labours wait their last reward.		O 141	Tr Rambler 208	2
Till the Realms of Light you gain.		O 150	Tr Boet III.12	46
To You whose gen'rous Wishes rise		O 150	Tr Boet III.12	53
To you the Tale is told;		O 150	Tr Boet III.12	55
Would you hope to gain my heart, ...		O 176	Tr Metastasi I	1
"His the letters which you see, ...		O 185	Anacreon Ode 9	15
"His the letters that you see, ...		O 185	Anacreon Ode 9	V 15
You can hang or drown at last.		O 197	Song Congratu.	28
What with your friend you nobly share		O 232	Tr Horace IV.7	19
At least you rescue from your heir.		O 232	Tr Horace IV.7	20
Not you, Torquatus, boast of Rome, ...		O 232	Tr Horace IV.7	21
You are like the sun the governour of the world . . .		Y 132	Irene	V 40
For you fair Asia spreads her wealthy plains.		Y 132	Irene	V 41C
--When of late The storm of Heav'ns displeasure thundred cn you.		Y 136	Irene	V 27
Comes Mustapha.--Your Turkish Robes conceal you-- . .		O 271	Irene	36
But bids you rove the Paths of Bliss, secure		O 276	Irene	18
Reward his toils, and he shall toil for you		Y 146	Irene	V 23A
For you shall plough the main, and fight the battle .		Y 146	Irene	V 23B
Ordain'd, like you, to flutter and to shine, ...		O 277	Irene	37
Exhausted all her nobler Gifts on you;		O 278	Irene	54
Did you proclaim this unexpected Conquest?		O 282	Irene	62
What I can grant, you cannot ask in vain--		O 285	Irene	14
Close like th' eternal Bars of Death upon You		O 357	Irene	V 10
It parts you now--The hasty Sultan sign'd		O 296	Irene	1
Prudence and Friendship bid me force her from you. . .		O 296	Irene	7
Yet think a Moment, ere you court Destruction, ...		O 301	Irene	87
A sigh, a blush inform'd him You consented		O 366	Irene	V 28
Willing to delay you here they give you on earth the pleasures of		Y 184	Irene	V 10
Willing to delay you here they give you on earth the . .		Y 184	Irene	V 10
Say, by what Fraud, what Force were you defeated? . . .		O 315	Irene	6
Were now well lost, in hearing how you fail'd.		O 316	Irene	23
Why did you stay? deserted and betray'd?		O 317	Irene	34
You may provoke but never can convince		Y 197	Irene	V 31
You perish (for) by your folly not your zeal.		Y 198	Irene	V 32
Quick from my Sight you inauspicious Monsters, ...		O 325	Irene	6
Then shall you feel what Language cannot utter; . . .		O 326	Irene	43
Already brandishes his Sabre o'er You		O 368	Irene	V 18
That thus you parly with detected Treason?		O 327	Irene	15
You who tell		Y 209	Irene	V 54
To great Latona's son, and two to you;		Y 7	Virgil Daphnis	44
"Why gen'rous warriour will you rashly run		Y 18	Tr. Iliad Bk 6	19
On dangers which your safety bids you shun, ...		Y 18	Tr. Iliad Bk 6	20
Soon shall you fall by num'rous hosts opprest		Y 18	Tr. Iliad Bk 6	22

YOU'LL

You'll leave together with your life, ...		O 69	Hor.II Ode 14	23

YCUNG

The young enthusiast quits his ease for fame;		O 36	Vanity Wishes	136
To a Young Lady on her Birth-day		O 80	Lady Birthday	T
The Young Author		O 81	Young Author	T
So the young author panting for a name, ...		O 82	Young Author	11
So the young author panting after fame, ...		O 82	Young Author	V 11
from a young Lady		O 95	Sprig of Myrtl	V T
Could Stella, sprightly, fair and young, ...		O 121	To Miss Playin	21
Wou'd Stella, sprightly, fair and young, ...		O 121	To Miss Playin	V 21
Always young and always pretty, ...		O 175	Tr Easy Phrase	2
Always pretty, always young, ...		O 175	Tr Easy Phrase	3
Always young and always pretty, ...		O 175	Tr Easy Phrase	5
One and Twenty 1810: Improviso on a young heir's coming of age.		O 196	Song Congratu.	V T
Young, and unsettled in his Father's Kingdoms, ...		O 257	Irene	67
That fatal Mistress of the Young, the Lazy, ...		O 283	Irene	21

```
YOUNG            (CONTINUED)                                 PAGE    TITLE          LINE
    Young Man, forbear--The Heat of Youth, no more--    . . .  O 284  Irene            47
    Scream in the nests and brood their young in peace.  . .   Y  23  Tr Add. Battle   35
    And crush'd the yet unanimated young.  . . . . . . .  . .  Y  23  Tr Add. Battle   49
    Soon as their young began to draw their breath  . . . .   Y  24  Tr Add. Battle   86
YOUR
    Here falling houses thunder on your head,  . . . .  . .   O   9  London           17
    Heroes, proceed! what bounds your pride shall hold?  . .  O  13  London           61
    What check restrain your thirst of pow'r and gold?  . .   O  13  London           62
    Behold our fame, our wealth, our lives your own.  . . .   O  13  London           64
    Your taste in snuff, your judgment in a whore;  . . . .   O  17  London          149
    Your taste in snuff, your judgment in a whore;  . . . .   O  17  London          149
    They first invade your table, then your breast;  . . .    O  17  London          153
    They first invade your table, then your breast;  . . .    O  17  London          153
    Explore your secrets with insidious art,  . . . . . .     O  17  London          154
    Then soon your ill-plac'd confidence repay,  . . . . .    O  17  London          156
    Commence your lords, and govern or betray.  . . . . .     O  17  London          157
    Swift from pursuing horrors take your way,  . . . . .     O  18  London          188
    And leave your little All to flames a prey;  . . . . .    O  18  London          189
    In vain your mournful narrative disclose,  . . . . .      O  19  London          192
    While all neglect, and most insult your woes.  . . . .    O  19  London          193
    And stretch thy prospects o'er your fruitfull land,  . .  Y  58  London         V 214
    And sign your will before you sup from home,  . . . .     O  21  London          225
    In vain, these dangers past, your doors you close,  . .   O  21  London          236
    And leaves, unseen, a dagger in your breast.  . . . .     O  21  London          241
    And plants, unseen, a dagger in your breast.  . . . .     O  21  London         V 241
    Propose your schemes, ye Senatorian band,  . . . . .      O  21  London          244
    What care, what rules your heedless charms shall save,    O  46  Vanity Wishes    329
    Each nymph your rival, and each youth your slave?  . . .  O  46  Vanity Wishes    330
    Each nymph your rival, and each youth your slave?  . . .  O  46  Vanity Wishes    330
    Against your fame with fondness hate combines,  . . .     O  46  Vanity Wishes    331
    This Night, distinguish'd by your Smile, shall tell,  . . O  57  Prologue Comus    11
    Play on your pipe beneath this beechen shade;  . . . .    O  64  Virgil Past.I      2
    Here at your ease you sing your amorous flame,  . . . .   O  64  Virgil Past.I      5
    Here at your ease you sing your amorous flame,  . . . .   O  64  Virgil Past.I      5
    No setting Sol can ease your cares,  . . . . . . .        O  67  Hor. II Ode IX    11
    In vain you spend your vows and prayers,  . . . . . .     O  68  Hor.II Ode 14      3
    Your shady Groves, your pleasing wife,  . . . . . .       O  69  Hor.II Ode 14     21
    Your shady Groves, your pleasing wife,  . . . . . .       O  69  Hor.II Ode 14     21
    You'll leave together with your life,  . . . \ . . .      O  69  Hor.II Ode 14     23
    After your death, the lavish heir  . . . . . .           O  69  Hor.II Ode 14     25
    Yet, great Maecenas, shall your friend  . . . . .        O  70  Hor.II Ode XX      7
    Restrain your tears and cease your cries,  . . . . .      O  70  Hor.II Ode XX     21
    Restrain your tears and cease your cries,  . . . . .      O  70  Hor.II Ode XX     21
    As the sad thought of your impending fate:  . . . .      O  74  Tr. Iliad Bk 6    20
    Mimick your tears, and ridicule your woes;  . . . .      O  74  Tr. Iliad Bk 6    22
    Mimick your tears, and ridicule your woes;  . . . .      O  74  Tr. Iliad Bk 6    22
    Observe your steps; be carefull to command  . . . .      O  77  Festina Lente      3
    Your passions; guide the reins with steady hand,  . .    O  77  Festina Lente      4
    Nor let disdain sit low'ring in your eye;  . . . . .      O  84  Epi Dist Moth.    43
    To ease their pains exert your milder power,  . . . .    O  84  Epi Dist Moth.    46
    When in your Eyes resistless Lightnings play,  . . . .   O  96  Hickman Spinet     3
    But when your Musick sooths the raging pain,  . . . .    O  96  Hickman Spinet     6
    We bid propitious Heav'n prolong your reign,  . . . .    O  96  Hickman Spinet     7
    What rais'd your Virtue here below,  . . . . . .         O 100  Ode Friendship   V 27
    Shall aid y<ou>r Happiness above.  . . . . . . .         O 100  Ode Friendship   V 28
    But as your sister of the sky,  . . . . . . . .          O 126  To Lyce, Lady      7
    Bid your teizing doubts depart;  . . . . . . .           O 176  Tr Metastasi I     2
    If at your coming princes disappear,  . . . . . .        O 177  Tr Dist Modena     1
    Ladies--stock and tend your Hive,  . . . . . .           O 178  Thrale 35 Year    11
    My first, shuts out Thieves from your house or your Room O 179  Charade!           1
    My first, shuts out Thieves from your house or your Room O 179  Charade!           1
    And o'er the globe extend your reign,  . . . . . .       O 189  Epilogue           7
    Snatch your pleasures while they last;  . . . . .        O 194  On Thrale Hat    V  2
    Great Sir John, are all your own.  . . . . . .           O 196  Song Congratu.     4
    Great Sir John, are now your own.  . . . . . .           O 196  Song Congratu.   V  4
    Lavish of your Grandsire's guineas,  . . . . . .         O 196  Song Congratu.    11
    Come my lads and take your fill.  . . . . . .            O 196  Song Congratu.   V 20
    What with your friend you nobly share  . . . . .         O 232  Tr Horace IV.7    19
    At least you rescue from your heir.  . . . . . .         O 232  Tr Horace IV.7    20
    When Minos once has fix'd your doom,  . . . . .          O 232  Tr Horace IV.7    22
    Nor bribes your Eyes to prejudice your Heads.  . . .     O 246  Irene Prologue    28
    Nor bribes your Eyes to prejudice your Heads.  . . .     O 246  Irene Prologue    28
    Call to your Aid your Courage, and your Wisdom;  . .     O 252  Irene             85
    Call to your Aid your Courage, and your Wisdom;  . .     O 252  Irene             85
    Call to your Aid your Courage, and your Wisdom;  . . .   O 252  Irene             85
    Your thin battalions and your empty tents  . . . .      Y 120  Irene           V 29A
    Your thin battalions and your empty tents  . . . .      Y 120  Irene           V 29A
    Your slaughter'd Multitudes that swell the Shore,  . .   O 255  Irene             30
    Consult in private, call me when your Scheme  . . . .    O 256  Irene             36
    but if your influence be too wide--your dissipated rays . Y 132  Irene          V 41
    but if your influence be too wide--your dissipated rays . Y 132  Irene          V 41
        your feeble fainting virtue  . . . . . . .           Y 133  Irene           V  9
    Your artful Suit, your Monarch's fierce Denial,  . . .   O 270  Irene              3
    Your artful Suit, your Monarch's fierce Denial,  . . .   O 270  Irene              3
    And your new Charge, that dear, that heavn'ly Maid.--    O 270  Irene              5
    Comes Mustapha.--Your Turkish Robes conceal you--  . .   O 271  Irene             36
    Ransom of Kings, the purchass of your blood  . . .       O 351  Irene           V 14
    Heap'd by your Father's ill-plac'd Bounties on him,  . . O 274  Irene             51
    Now roll full fraught with Thunder o'er your Head.  . .  O 275  Irene             75
    Droop at your tears and soften at your smile  . . . .   Y 145  Irene            V  4
```

```
YOUR          (CCNTINUED)                           PAGE   TITLE          LINE
    Droop at your tears and soften at your smile    . . . .  Y 145  Irene     V   4
    Vain Raptures all--For your inferiour Natures   . . . .  O 276  Irene         15
    Surveys your Plays with inattentive Glance,     . . . .  O 276  Irene         22
    Surveys your triflings with a careless glance   . . . .  O 355  Irene     V  11
    Surveys your actions with a careless glance .   . . . .  Y 146  Irene     V  22
    And then leaves your actions the busy trifler   . . . .  O 355  Irene     V  12
        unregarded
    Why then Those charms your tongue has deign'd to . . .   O 355  Irene     V  15
        flatter
    Important Cares detain'd me from your Counsels.  . . .   O 279  Irene          6
    Hung on your Neck, and hinder'd your Departure.  . . .   O 280  Irene         10
    Hung cn your Neck, and hinder'd your Departure.  . . .   O 280  Irene         10
    How did Aspasia welcome your Address?        . . . .     O 282  Irene         61
    There, with your Soldiers arm'd, and Sails expanded, . . O 284  Irene         53
    Justice demands that I reveal your Crimes;   . . . . .   O 286  Irene         14
    Call to your Aid with boundless Promises     . . . . .   O 287  Irene         10
    Swell not your Soul beyond reproof or Counsel  . . . .   O 366  Irene     V  18
    Or tune your ear to soothing Adulation.      . . . . .   O 366  Irene     V  20
    To hear the voice of truth, dismiss your train  . . . .  O 366  Irene     V  22
    Then mingle with your slaves without a murmur   . . . .  Y 161  Irene     V  11
    Your careless Love betrays your Country's Cause. . . .   O 297  Irene         10
    Your careless Love betrays your Country's Cause. . . .   O 297  Irene         10
    Approving Justice smiles upon your Cause,    . . . . .   O 297  Irene          2
    Yet when your Hand is lifted to destroy,     . . . . .   O 298  Irene          4
    With noisy Falshoods forc'd me from your Arms,  . . . .  O 299  Irene         39
    Return with speed, Leontius, to your Charge;  . . . .    O 304  Irene          9
    Both your religion and your country are      . . . . .   Y 181  Irene     V  52
        ccncern'd
    Both your religion and your country are      . . . . .   Y 181  Irene     V  52
        ccncern'd
    if human miseries or affairs yet claim your    . . . . . Y 181  Irene     V  54
        regard
    Descend, to sweeten Labours once your own.    . . . .    O 306  Irene         56
    Confirm your Troops; and when the Moon's fair Beam  . .  O 306  Irene         58
    To fix your Standard in Imperial Rome.    . . . .        O 309  Irene         31
    And wait your Summons to report his Conduct.   . . . .   O 310  Irene          7
    You perish (for) by your folly not your zeal.   . . . .  Y 198  Irene     V  32
    You perish (for) by your folly not your zeal.   . . . .  Y 198  Irene     V  32
        Your calmer Though . . . . . . . . .                 O 321  Irene         53
    Your Robe of Mourning, and your Dogs of Death.  . . . .  O 325  Irene          5
    Your Robe of Mourning, and your Dogs of Death.  . . . .  O 325  Irene          5
    Confess your Crime, or lead me to the Sultan.   . . . .  O 326  Irene         41
    While unavailing passion crouds your tongue  . . . .     O 368  Irene     V  14
    And steal your life away.  Death's horrid Angel . . . .  O 368  Irene     V  17
    Is then your Sov'reign's Life so cheaply rated,  . . . . O 327  Irene         14
    Is this your ardour for your masters safety  . . . . .   Y 207  Irene     V  14
    Is this your ardour for your masters safety  . . . . .   Y 207  Irene     V  14
    Quick at my Call shall execute your Charge;  . . . . .   O 328  Irene         43
    And may bounteous Heav'n repay the mercy on Your . . .   O 344  Irene     V  27
        Heads
    Frame your Report with circumspective Art,   . . . . .   O 329  Irene         13
    Inflame her Crimes, exalt your own Obedience,   . . . .  O 329  Irene         14
    Your hasty Zeal defrauds the Claim of Justice,  . . . .  O 330  Irene          5
    Could not her Charms repress your Zeal for Murder? . .   O 332  Irene         24
    Your fierce Impatience forc'd us from your Presence, . . O 332  Irene         29
    Your fierce Impatience forc'd us from your Presence, . . O 332  Irene         29
    On dangers which your safety bids you shun,  . . . . .   Y  18  Tr. Iliad Bk 6   20
    Forgetfull of your wife, forgetfull of your son? . . .   Y  18  Tr. Iliad Bk 6   21
    Forgetfull of your wife, forgetfull of your son? . . .   Y  18  Tr. Iliad Bk 6   21
    And Grecian spears shall quiver in your breast.  . . .   Y  18  Tr. Iliad Bk 6   23
    Restrain your sorrows, calm your troubled soul. . . . .  Y  21  Tr. Iliad Bk 6  114
    Restrain your sorrows, calm your troubled soul. . . . .  Y  21  Tr. Iliad Bk 6  114
    Your sighs are spent in vain; if fates withstand  . . .  Y  21  Tr. Iliad Bk 6  115
    Hence to the palace and your maids repair;   . . . . .   Y  21  Tr. Iliad Bk 6  121
    There let the web and distaff be your care.  . . . . .   Y  21  Tr. Iliad Bk 6  122
YOURE
    What care, youre charms from wretchedness shall save . . Y 107  Vanity Wishes  V 329
YCURS
    'Tis yours this Night to bid the Reign commence  . . .   O  53  Pro Drury-Lane   57
    Yours is the Charge, ye Fair, ye Wise, ye Brave!  . . .  O  58  Prologue Comus   37
    'Tis yours to crown Desert--beyond the Grave!   . . . .  O  58  Prologue Comus   38
    Or boasts a happier glebe, is Yours already,   . . . .   O 366  Irene     V  13
    'Tis yours to grant, or to refuse him entrance  . . . .  Y 168  Irene     V   3
YOURSELVES
    Perhaps yourselves the Villains that defame me,  . . .   O 326  Irene         38
YOUTH
    With slavish tenets taint our poison'd youth,   . . . .  O  12  London         55
    Flush'd as they are with folly, youth and wine,  . . .   O  21  London        232
    Flush'd as they are with youth confused with wine,  . .  Y  59  London     V 232
    Farewell!--When youth, and health, and fortune spent, .  O  23  London        256
    Are these thy views? proceed, illustrious youth,  . . .  O  37  Vanity Wishes 141
    Each nymph your rival, and each youth your slave? . . .  O  46  Vanity Wishes 330
    Her Youth laborious, and her blameless Age:  . . . . .   O  58  Prologue Comus   30
    Warn'd by another's fate, vain youth, be wise,   . . .   O  82  Young Author   23
    Each youth admires, though each admirer dies;   . . . .  O  83  Epi Dist Moth.   6
    His force of genius burn'd in early youth,   . . . . .   O 117  Epitaph Hanmer   5
    But shun, rash youth, the gay alcove,    . . . . .       O 121  To Miss Playin   9
    Delighting, as the youth draws nigh,     . . . . .       O 121  To Miss Playin  15
    Th' adoring youth, and envious fair,     . . . . .       O 122  Stella Mourn.   13
        --in all the bloom of honour and of youth   . . .    Y 122  Irene     V  67
```

YOUTH   (CONTINUED)   PAGE   TITLE   LINE
        Restrain the Fervour of impetuous Youth   . . . . .   O 272 Irene   9
        Love is indeed the Privilege of Youth;   . . . .   O 280 Irene   29
        Young Man, forbear--The Heat of Youth, no more-- . . . O 284 Irene   47
        If e'er thy Youth has known the Pangs of Absence, . . . O 285 Irene   3
YOUTHFUL
        This fir'd the youthful King's ambitious Breast,   . . . O 256 Irene   47
ZEAL
        Sign her foes doom, or guard her fav'rites zeal?   . . . O 34 Vanity Wishes   92
        Sign her foes' doom, or guard her patriots zeal,   . . . Y 95 Vanity Wishes   V 92
        Whose gen'rous Zeal, unbought by flatt'ring Rhimes, . . O 57 Prologue Comus   3
        From zeal or malice now no more we dread, ...   O 61 Pro Word Wise   3
        Simon by gen'rous Zeal inspir'd, ...   O 79 Feast St Simon   37
        With temp'rate zeal, and wise anxiety;   . . . . .   O 118 Epitaph Hanmer   30
        That hide in seeming zeal a wicked purpose, ...   O 176 Tr Metastas II   12
        The Warrior's Ardour, and the Patriot's Zeal; . . . .   O 255 Irene   4
        Our warlike Prophet loves an active zeal   . . . . .   Y 131 Irene   V 25
        With wonted Zeal pursue the Task of War, ...   O 264 Irene   30
        With equal zeal persue the task of war   . . . .   Y 131 Irene   V 30
        Cali, this Day with hypocritick Zeal, ...   O 273 Irene   43
        My Zeal marks Gladness dawning on thy Cheek, ...   O 286 Irene   2
        Long would my Zeal for Mahomet and Thee   . . . .   O 288 Irene   11
        For Zeal unguarded, undissembled Hate, ...   O 299 Irene   36
        You perish (for) by your folly not your zeal. . . .   Y 198 Irene   V 32
        Perhaps my Zeal too fierce betray'd my Prudence; . . . O 330 Irene   20
        Your hasty Zeal defrauds the Claim of Justice, ...   O 330 Irene   5
        Could not her Charms repress your Zeal for Murder? . . O 332 Irene   24
ZEALOUS
        Some zealous bard to wake the sleeping lyre. . . . .   O 107 Lady F Assizes   4
        For forc'd Compliance, or for zealous Virtue, ...   O 256 Irene   51
        Should she, for Proselytes are always zealous, ... O 262 Irene   24
ZELINDA
        But some Zelinda while I sing   . . . .   O 127 To Lyce, Lady   17
ZELINDA'S
        Yet spite of fair Zelinda's eye, ...   O 127 To Lyce, Lady   21
ZEMZEM
        Exhaust the well of Zemzem. . . . .   Y 131 Irene   V 32D
ZEPHYRS
        May lambent zephyrs gently wave thy head, ...   Y   3 On a Daffodill   9
ZEUS
        Tei Kallous dunamei ti telos; Zeus panta dedoken . . . O 103 Eis Elisses   1
        Zeus mounos phlogcenti poleis ekperse kerauno, ... O 103 Eis Elisses   5
ZONE
        Place me beneath the burning Zone, ...   O 67 To A. Fuscus   21

2525	160	80	52 (CONT.)	35
THE	NO	LIFE	US	DEMETRIUS
	SHALL		WHOSE	NAME
1524		79		SO
AND	156	STILL	51	THROUGH
	AT		DAY	
1087		77	HAND	34
OF	154	THEE	SEE	
	HE			BEFORE
838		76	49	FRIEND
TO	153	VAIN		IRENE
	NOT		EYES	NATURE
543		74	GREAT	THEM
WITH	152	HIM		THINE
	WHEN		48	THOUGHT
501		73		THUS
IN	.151	CAN	BREAST	WAR
	OUR	SOUL	THOSE	WITHOUT
457				YE
A	148	72	47	
	TH'	WHO		33
454			EV'RY	
HIS	143	71	LIKE	ARMS
	ME	YOU	NEW	AWAY
310				SOON
MY	142	70	46	SULTAN
	NOR	WE	TILL	WHY
280				
HER	139	69	45	32
	YOUR	O'ER		
275			FEAR	HAPPY
FROM	119	67	IT	MIND
	IS	FAIR		WELL
265		WHILE	44	
FOR	107			31
	THOU	66	HAS	
247		ARE	MAN	ART
OR	103	THESE	THERE	BEHOLD
	NOW		WHICH	CARE
222		65		EVER
ON	101	DEATH	43	FIERCE
	WHAT	EACH		GUILT
217			CHARMS	ITS
THAT	99	62	HOPE	STATE
	THEN	HOW	SHE	
216			SHOULD	29
THY	97	61		
	WHERE	HEAV'N	42	ABDALLA
206		THEY		EVERY
BY	96		RAGE	GREECE
	BE	60	WEALTH	OWN
202		FATE	WORLD	SKIES
I	95			
	LOVE	57	41	28
198		POW'R		
THEIR	93	UPON	ONCE	BEAUTY
	YET	WAS		BENEATH
195			40	PRIDE
BUT	92	56		
	AS	MAY	CALI	27
174			VOICE	
THIS	82	55		'TIS
	LET	HERE	39	BRIGHT
165		VIRTUE		CALL
ALL	81	WILL	HEAR	HOUR
	MORE		ONE	INTO
		52	SUCH	NATIONS
		AN		RISE
		IF	38	TONGUE
		SOME		TRUTH
			COULD	
			HEART	26
			MUST	
				BOSOM
			37	FAME
				FATAL
			LONG	HAVE
			TOO	LIVE
				THINK
			36	THOUGH
				WERE
			ASPASIA	WOULD
			DID	
			HAD	25
			O	
			PRAISE	AGE
				BLOOD
				FLY
				FORCE

9 (CONT.)	8 (CONT.)	7 (CONT.)	7 (CONT.)	6 (CONT.)
BROW	CONSCIENCE	BARB'ROUS	WAVES	LOFTY
BURN	CONTENT	BLAST	WEAKNESS	LOW
COUNSELS	CRY	BLISSFUL	WHATE'ER	MELT
CRANES	DESIRE	BLOOM	WIDE	MINGLED
DANGERS	DREADFULL	BLOW	WIPE	MORTALS
DARE	DREW	BLUSH	WINTER	MUSE
DEEP	ELOQUENCE	BRIBE	WOMAN'S	MUSTAPHA
DIRE	FAINTING	BURNING	WOUND	NERVES
DREAMS	FAITHFUL	BUSY	YIELD	NUMBERS
E'ER	FIR'D	CALI'S		OFF
EAGER	FIRES	CAPTIVE		OPEN
EAR	FORTH	CONDEMN'D	6	PETTY
ENVY	GENEROUS	COUNTRY'S		PIOUS
FALSE	GIFT	DARKNESS	ABDALLA'S	PITY
FATHER	GIVES	DECAY	ACTION	PITYING
FLAME	GLOOM	DEGREED	ACTIVE	PLENTY
FORSAKE	GLORY	DISPATCH	AFAR	PLUNDER
FROWN	GROVE	DIVINE	AFFRIGHTED	POET
GAVE	GUILTY	DOMINION	AGES	POVERTY
GLANCE	HAPLESS	DUST	AIRY	POW'RFUL
GODS	HASTY	DWELL	ARISE	PRAYER
GRANDEUR	ILLS	EQUAL	ARMIES	PROCLAIM
HAST	KINGDOMS	FAITHLESS	ARTFUL	PURE
HATE	KNOW'ST	FELT	BAD	PYGMIES
HENCE	KNOWS	FIELD	BEHIND	REGAL
HOARY	LAB'RING	FIERY	BEING	RESTLESS
HOLY	LABOUR	FLATTER	BESTOWS	RESTORE
ILLUSTRIOUS	LANDS	FLOOD	BLEEDING	REVENGE
INVADE	LATE	FOND	BLIND	RISES
LAY	LEAD	FONDNESS	BLOOMING	ROBES
LOOK	LOSE	GAZE	BORE	ROUGH
MAHOMET	LOUD	GUARDS	BREAK	ROVE
MANY	LUST	HAIL	BREEZE	RULE
MERCY	MADE	HEAVEN	CAVERNS	RULES
MOURNFUL	MADNESS	HENCEFORTH	CELL	SABRE
PAINS	MEAN	HOLD	CHAINS	SAFETY
PART	MEN	HUMBLE	CHAMBER	SAVE
POMP	MISTRESS	I'LL	CHANCE	SEATS
PRAY'R	MOMENTS	IMMORTAL	CHARM'D	SECURITY
PRUDENCE	MOST	IMPENDING	CHILD	SEIZ'D
PUBLICK	NATURE'S	IMPERIAL	CHILL	SENTENCE
PURSUE	NYMPHS	INFANT	COAST	SHED
QUICK	ODE	LAW	COMMON	SHOCK
QUIT	OH	MARK'D	CONDUCT	SINKING
RACE	PARENT	MASTER	COURSE	SLAV'RY
RAISE	PAST	MASTER'S	CROWN	SLOTH
RANGE	PAUSE	MIEN	CURS'D	SLOW
REFUSE	PLAINS	MONARCH	DANCE	SOCIAL
REGIONS	POOR	MURDER	DELAY	SOFTER
SAFE	PROVIDENCE	MUSICK	DEMAND	SON
SAW	RAIS'D	MYRTLE	DENY'D	SOV'REIGN
SCENE	REMEMBER	OTHER	DESIGNS	SPARKLING
SEAT	REPOSE	PATHS	DIES	SPENT
SHALT	RETIRE	PERISH	DISMISS	STAND
SHINING	RETURNING	POINT	DRAW	STEEL
SINGLE	REWARD	POMPOUS	DRESS	STORMS
SINK	RIGHT	POURS	DRIVE	STRENGTH
SOULS	RIVAL	PRINCE	EARLY	STRIKE
STELLA	ROCKS	PROPITIOUS	FAREWELL	STRIVE
STERN	ROLLS	FIGHT	FIGHT	SUCCESS
SUPERIOUR	RURAL	RESIGN	FLAMES	SUMMER
TO-MORROW	SAD	ROAM	FLATT'RING	SUSPEND
TORTURES	SAVAGE	ROAR	FLED	SWORDS
TRACE	SCIENCE	RUSH	FLOW'RS	TAINT
TRAIN	SHAME	SANDS	FLOWS	TAKE
VIRTUE'S	SOOTH	SCHEMES	FOLLIES	TASK
WANDER	STROKE	SEARCH	FORMER	TEAR
WISH'D	SWAY	SHAKES	FRIGHT	TEMPESTS
WRETCHED	SWELLING	SLEEP	FULL	THIRST
	TENDER	SNATCH	FURIOUS	THIRTYFIVE
8	TRUE	SPEAK	GHOSTS	THRICE
	TURKEY	SPIRITS	GOD	TIMES
ALONG	TURNS	STATESMAN'S	GREEK	TOWN
ANGER	TWO	STRAIN	GROANS	TREMBLING
ANGRY	UNHAPPY	STRIFE	GUILTLESS	TROOP
APOSTATE	VARIOUS	SUNK	HEAT	TRY
ARDOUR	VEINS	SUPPORT	HISS	TUNE
BATTLE	VIEWS	SWEET	HITHER	UNHEEDED
BEAMS	WASTE	SWELL	HUNG	UNKNOWN
BETTER	WATCH	SWIFT	IMPETUOUS	UP
BLACK	WINE	TERROR	IMPORTANT	URG'D
BLESSINGS	WITHIN	TERRORS	INFLAME	URGE
BLOODY		TOMB	INFLUENCE	USE
BOLD	7	TRIUMPHANT	INSIDIOUS	VENERABLE
BROUGHT		TURN'D	JOIN	VERDANT
BURNS	AMBITIOUS	VERSE	LADY	VIOLENCE
CONFIDENCE	ATTEMPT	VIRTUES	LAMENT	VIRTUOUS
CONFUSION	BANKS	VULGAR	LAVISH	WARM
			LIPS	

4 (CONT.)	4 (CONT.)	3 (CONT.)	3 (CONT.)	3 (CONT.)
MAZE	SKIE	ADORE	COMPASSION	EVENING
MEANER	SLAIN	ADORING	COMPLAIN	EVENT
MEND	SLUMBER	AFFLICTED	COMPLEAT	EVERLASTING
MILLIONS	SMALL	AFFORD	CONCEAL	EXERT
MISCHIEF	SNATCH'D	ALASS	CONFESS'D	EXPANDED
MOCKS	SNOWY	ALREADY	CONFIN'D	EXPIRING
MONARCH'S	SOFTEN	ALTARS	CONFIRM	FABRICK
MOON	SOFTEN'D	ALTERNATE	CONSECRATED	FACTIONS
MORAL	SOLD	AMAZEMENT	CONSPIRE	FADING
MOTHER	SOLDIER'S	AMBITION'S	CONTEMPTUOUS	FAIREST
MOUNT	SOOTHING	AMBUSH	CONTENDING	FANCY'D
MOURNING	SPACIOUS	ANGEL	CONVEY	FEATHER'D
MOVE	SPIRIT	ANIMATE	CORRUPTION	FEED
MURMURS	SPOILS	ANY	COTTAGE	FEELS
MUTUAL	SPRINGS	APPEAR	COUNSEL	FEW
MYSELF	ST	APPOINTED	COUNTERFEITED	FINAL
NECK	STAIN'D	ARTLESS	CRANE	FIVE
NIMBLE	STARRY	ASIA	CREATE	PLATT'RY
NOBLE	STEADY	ASPIRE	CREATION	FLEETING
NOBLES	STORE	AUGHT	CROUDED	FLOCKS
NOD	STORM	AWAIT	CRUSH	FLUSH
NOUGHT	STRAND	AWE	CRUSH'D	FOAMING
NURSE	STRANGE	BAFFLED	DAGGER	FOLLOWING
OBEY	STRATAGEM	BANISH	DAPHNIS	FOOL
OPPRESS'D	STREAM	BANNERS	DARTS	FORETOLD
ORDAIN'D	STRING	BAR	DAWN	FORSAKES
PALACES	STRUCK	BARBAROUS	DE	FORWARD
PANTS	STRUGGLING	BARK	DECIDE	FRIENDLY
PASS	SUBTLER	BEAKS	DECK	FROWNING
PASSAGE	SUCCEEDING	BEAM	DECLAR'D	FROZEN
PATH	SUMMONS	BEAST	DECLINE	FRUITFULL
PATIENCE	SUPERIOR	BEATS	DEED	GAIN'D
PATRIOTS	SUPPLIANT	BEAUTY'S	DEFEATED	GALE
PEOPLE	SURVEY	BEDS	DEITIES	GALES
PERPETUAL	SUSPICION	BEG	DEITY	GALLEY
PERSUES	SUSTAIN	BEGINS	DELIGHTED	GAZ'D
PIETY	TEEMING	BEHOLDS	DELIGHTFUL	GENTLY
PILE	TEMPLE	BEND	DELIVERANCE	GLAD
POINTS	TEMPT	BENEVOLENCE	DELUGE	GLADNESS
POLISH'D	TEMPTING	BEST	DENIES	GLEAM
POUR'D	THEMSELVES	BESTOW	DENY	GLOBE
POWERFUL	THREATS	BESTOW'D	DEPENDENT	GODDESS
PREPAR'D	THROW	BEWARE	DERIDE	GOES
PRESENT	TIR'D	BIRCHION	DESCENDS	GOVERNMENT
PRESERV'D	TO-MORROW'S	BLAND	DESIRES	GRACEFUL
PREVAIL'D	TORTUR'D	BONDAGE	DESOLATION	GRACIOUS
PRIAM'S	TOW'R	BOUGHS	DESPOTICK	GRATEFUL
PRINCES	TOW'RS	BOUNDS	DIFF'RENT	GREATER
PROCEED	TOYS	BOUNTEOUS	DIFFIDENCE	GRIEFS
PROLOGUE	TREAD	BOW	DIGNITY	GROAN
PROLONG	TREMBLE	BOWLS	DISAPPOINTMENT	GUARDIAN
PROSPECTS	TROD	BRANCHES	DISDAINS	GUST
PROTECTED	TYRANNY	BRAVEST	DISGUISE	HADST
QUESTIONS	UNCERTAIN	BREASTS	DISSIPATED	HALLOW'D
QUIET	UNIVERSAL	BRIDE	DISSONANCE	HANG
QUIVER	UNSEEN	BRIGHTEST	DISTRACTION	HANGS
RAPTURES	UNSHAKEN	BRITAIN	DISTRESS'D	HARDY
RAVISH'D	VALE	BRITON	DISTREST	HARMLESS
RAY	VALES	BROTHER	DOOMS	HARRASS
REALM	VEIL	BURST	DOST	HAT
RECORDS	VENAL	BURSTING	DOUBTS	HAZARD
REFLECT	VENUS	BUYS	DOVE	HAZARDS
REPAY	VIRGIN	CANST	DOWNY	HEARS
REQUEST	VIRGINS	CAST	DRANK	HEAVN
RESISTANCE	WARS	CATTLE	DRAUGHT	HECTOR'S
RESOLV'D	WASTED	CAUGHT	DREARY	HELD
RIGHTS	WEALTHY	CAUSELESS	DRESS'D	HEREAFTER
RINGS	WEAR	CAUTION	DRINK	HEROE'S
RIVERS	WEARS	CEAS'D	DRIV'N	HETTY
ROCK	WEEP	CHANGING	DROP	HILL
ROVING	WHOLE	CHARGES	DROPS	HILLS
RUDE	WILY	CHASES	DROWN	HIND
RUSHES	WINDS	CHEAP	DUTY	HIRELING
SABLE	WINTER'S	CHEAPLY	DYING	HOLDS
SAGE	WONDER	CHEAR	EASTERN	HOMAGE
SCHEME	WONDRING	CHECK	EASY	HOPELESS
SEASONS	WORK	CHEERFUL	EIS	HORRORS
SECOND	WORLDS	CITIES	ELIZA	HORSE
SECRETS	WOUNDS	CLAP	ELUDE	HOSTILE
SEEK	WROUGHT	CLAY	EMBATTLED	HOSTS
SEEMING	YIELDING	CLEORA	ENDEARING	HOUSE
SEND		CLIMES	ENEMIES	HOVER
SHATTER'D	3	CLOSELY	ENGLISH	HOWL
SHRINKS		CLOUD	ENJOYS	HURRIED
SILVER	'S	CLOUDED	ENRAG'D	IMAGINARY
SISTER	ACTS	CLOUDY	EPILOGUE	IMPATIENCE
SIT	ADMIR'D	COMBIN'D	ERRING	IMPERFECT
SITS	ADMIRES	COMBINE	ERROR	IMPERIOUS

3 (CONT.)	3 (CONT.)	3 (CONT.)	3 (CONT.)	2 (CONT.)
IMPLOR'D	PALE	SHINES	TITLES	ADAMANT
INCESSANT	PARTS	SHOOTS	TON	ADMIRATION
INCLEMENT	PATRIOT'S	SHORES	TORMENTS	ADMISSION
INDIA'S	PATRONS	SHOU'D	TORPID	ADMIT
INDUSTRICUS	PAYS	SHOUTING	TORRID	ADORN'D
INFORM'D	PENSIVE	SHUNS	TORTURE	AERIAL
INSPIRE	PHOEBUS	SIGHING	TRAITOR	AFFAIRS
INSULTING	PIECE	SIGNAL	TRANSIENT	AFFECTED
INSULTS	PIERCE	SINKS	TRANSLATION	AFFRIGHT
INTERCEPT	PIERCING	SIR	TRANSPORT	AFRAID
JEALCUS	PILGRIMAGE	SIRE	TRANSPORTS	AFRIC'S
JOIN'D	PINIONS	SLAUGHTER	TRAYTORS	AGGRAVATE
JCINS	PLAN	SLEEPING	TREACHEROUS	AGONIES
JOYFULL	PLANETS	SLEEPS	TREACHROUS	AGONIZING
KINDLED	PLANTS	SLIGHT	TREADS	AIDS
KINDNESS	PLOT	SLUMBERS	TREASURE	AIM
KISS	PLUCK	SNARES	TREASURES	ALARM
KNOWLEDGE	POET'S	SOFTNESS	TRIBE	ALIVE
LABYRINTHS	POETS	SOLDIERS	TRIFLE	ALLOW
LADIES	POINTED	SOLITARY	TRIUMPHS	ALLURING
LAKE	POIS'NOUS	SOOTHS	TROUBLED	ALTAR
LAMBENT	POSSESS	SOPHIA'S	TROY	AMAZ'D
LATELY	POST	SOVEREIGN	TRUSTS	AMBIGUOUS
LAUGH	POSTERITY	SPAIN	TUMULTS	ANACREON
LAUGHTER	PRAY	SPAR'D	TUNEFUL	ANACREON'S
LEAGUE	PRETTY	SPARK	TURKEY'S	ANGELIC
LEGIONS	PROCLAIMS	SPEAKING	TYRANT'S	ANNUAL
LETTER'D	PROJECTS	SPEEDY	TYRANTS	ANT
LICENTIOUS	PROPAGATE	SPITE	UNARM'D	ANTIENT
LIGHTNING	PROPHET	SPLENDOUR	UNAVAILING	APOSTACY
LINES	PROPHET'S	SPOIL	UNCLOUDED	APPEAL
LISTNING	PROTRACT	SPOKE	UNCONQUER'D	APPETITE
LCADS	PROVERB	SPOKEN	UNDAUNTED	APPLAUD
LONDON	PROVOKE	SPORTS	UNERRING	APPLAUDING
LOOSE	PROWLS	SPRIGHTLY	UNEXHAUSTED	APULIA'S
LUCKLESS	PRUDENT	SQUADRONS	UNFINISH'D	ARCH
LULL	QUEST	STAGNANT	UNHEARD	ARDOURS
LUSTRE	QUITS	STAIN	UNITE	ARMENIAN
LUXURY	QUIV'RING	STARS	UNNUMBER'D	AROSE
LYBIAN	RAIL	STATES	UNPITYING	ARRAY'D
LYON	RAMPARTS	STEALS	UNREGARDED	ARROWS
MAHOMET'S	RAPINE	STELLA'S	UNTOUCH'D	ARTFULL
MAIDS	RAVE	STOPS	UNWILLING	ASCENDING
MAKES	RAYS	STORES	UTTER	ASHES
MALADIES	REACH'D	STORMY	VASSALS	ASIA'S
MARBLE	READY	STRANGER	VAST	ASSAIL'D
MASTERS	REBEL	STREAMS	VENGEFULL	ASSAILS
MEGCA	REBELLIOUS	STRETCH	VERNAL	ASSIGN'D
MEETS	REGARD	STRETCH'D	VESSEL	ASTYANAX
MELANCHOLY	REGRET	STRIKES	VICISSITUDES	ATOMS
MELTING	REIGNS	STRUGGLE	VIG'ROUS	ATTENDING
MELTS	RELIEF	SUBJECT	VILLAIN	ATTENDS
MENODORUS	REMEMBRANCE	SUBJECTS	VILLAIN'S	ATTENTION
MERITS	REND	SUCCEED	VISITS	ATTRACTIVE
MET	RENEW	SUCCESSFUL	VOICES	AUTHOR'S
MILK	RENEW'D	SUIT	VOTE	AV'RICE
MIMICK	RENOWN	SULLEN	WALK	AVAILS
MINDS	RENOWN'D	SUPERFLUOUS	WALK'D	AVARICIOUS
MINES	REPEAT	SUPPLE	WARN	AWAKING
MINISTERS	REPEATED	SUPPLICATING	WARRIOR'S	BABES
MISS	REPORT	SUPPORTS	WATERS	BALEFUL
MIX	REPRESS	SUPREME	WAYS	BALL
MIX'D	REQUESTED	SUSPENCE	WEIGHTY	BANK
MODEST	RESENTMENT	SWAIN	WEPT	BARDS
MOLEST	RESIGNS	SWARTHY	WESTERN	BATTALIONS
MORN	RETIR'D	SWEEP	WHATEVER	BEACH
MORROW	REV'RENCE	SWEETNESS	WHISPER	BEAT
MORTAL	REVIVE	SWEETS	WILLING	BEATING
MOULD	REVOLVING	SWELLS	WITNESS	BEAUTIOUS
MUSICIAN	ROAD	SWIM	WITS	BECAME
NARROW	ROSES	TAINTED	WOLVES	BEES
NATION'S	SAILS	TASTELESS	WONTED	BEGAN
NECTAR	SAV'D	TAUNT	WORKS	BEGS
NEEDLESS	SAYS	TEA	WOUNDED	BEINGS
NEEDS	SCALE	TEMPLES	WRATH	BENDS
NETS	SCATTER'D	TEND	YON	BESIDES
NEXT	SCORNS	THALES	ZEALOUS	BETRAYS
NOBLEST	SEA	THEATRE		BEWAIL'D
NOISE	SEAS	THEME		BIRD
NOTES	SECURES	THICK	**2**	BIT
NUMIDIA'S	SEEKS	THINKS	'TWAS	BITTER
OBSEQUIOUS	SELL	THIRTY	ABODES	BLEED
OER	SENT	THOUSANDS	ABSENT	BLINDLY
OFFICIOUS	SERENE	THRONG	ACCIDENT	BLOCKHEADS
OFFSPRING	SETS	THROWS	ACCIDENTAL	BLOOMS
OMENS	SEX	THYSELF	ACCIDENTS	BLUSHES
ORPHEUS	SHEPHERD	TIDE	ACCUSTOM'D	BOASTFUL
PAINT	SHEWS	TIRE	ACTIONS	BODIES

BOILING
BOLTS
BONDS
BONNY
BORNE
BORROW'D
BOUGH
BOUGHT
BOUND
BOUNTIES
BOUNTY
BOW'R
BOW'RS
BOWERS
BOWS
BRAKE
BRAND
BREATHING
BRITANNIA'S
BROOD
BROTHERS
BROWS
BUILD
BURIED
BURSTS
BURTHEN
BUS'NESS
BUST
BUY
CAGE
CALMER
CALMLY
CALMS
CAMPS
CANDOUR
CAPRICIOUS
CAPTAINS
CAPTIVES
CARAZA
CARESSES
CARPENTER
CARS
CASSANDER
CASUAL
CATO'S
CELEBRATE
CERTAIN
CHARLES
CHEARFULL
CHEARLESS
CHEAT
CHEATS
CHLOE'S
CHOSEN
CHURCH
CHUSE
CIRCULATING
CLEAR
CLEORA'S
CLIME
COARSELY
COLUMNS
COMMANDS
COMMENCE
COMMERCE
COMMISSION
COMPLAINT
COMPLEATS
COMPREHENSIVE
CONCEALS
CONDENS'D
CONDUCTS
CONFIDENT
CONFINE
CONFOUND
CONFUS'D
CONQU'RING
CONQUER
CONQUEROR
CONQUERORS
CONQUEROUR
CONSENT
CONSIGN'D
CONSORT
CONSPIRACY
CONSTANCY
CONTEMN
CONTEMNS

CONTEST
CONVERTED
CONVICTION
COOL
COSTLY
COTS
COUCH
COULDST
COUNSELLOR
COUNTLESS
COURTED
COURTIER
CREDIT
CREPT
CREW
CRIED
CROSS
CROWN'D
CROWNS
CRY'D
CURRENT
DAGGERS
DAINTIES
DAME
DANGEROUS
DANUBE
DAPHNIS'
DARKLING
DASHING
DAUGHTER
DEAF
DEAR-BOUGHT
DEAREST
DEBT
DECEITFUL
DECEMBER
DEEDS
DECLARE
DEFEATS
DEFENCE
DEFORM'D
DEGENERATE
DEIGN'D
DELIGHTING
DELUDE
DEMETRIUS'
DEPARTING
DEPRESS'D
DERIVES
DESERT
DESERTED
DESIGN
DESIGN'D
DESOLATED
DESPAIRING
DESTROY'D
DETAIN
DETAIN'D
DETECTED
DEVOTE
DEVOUR
DEWS
DEXT'ROUS
DIANA
DICTATES
DIGNIFIES
DIGNIFY'D
DILIGENCE
DIM
DIN
DIOS
DIRECTRESS
DIRECTS
DISARM'D
DISASTROUS
DISCLOS'D
DISCOVER
DISDAIN
DISGRACE
DISGUIS'D
DISH
DISMISS'D
DISORDER'D
DISPERSE
DISPLAID
DISPLAY
DISPLAY'D

DISSOLVE
DIVIDE
DIVIDED
DOAT
DOGS
DOLEFULL
DOMAIN
DOMESTICK
DOOR
DOTAGE
DOUBTFUL
DR
DRAG
DRAMA'S
DRAWS
DREADS
DREGS
DREST
DROOP
DROPP'D
DROSS
DRY
DUTIES
DWELLS
DYES
EASIER
ECHO
ECHOES
ECLIPSE
EFFORT
EFFORTS
EFFULGENCE
EITHER
ELATE
ELMS
EMBLEM
EMBODIED
EMPLOY'D
ENDEARS
ENDS
ENGROSS
ENJOY
ENKINDLED
ENORMOUS
ENQUIRER
ENSLAV'D
ENTERPRIZE
ENTHUSIAST
ENVENOM'D
ENVIES
EPITAPH
ESCAP'D
ESTEEM
EURUS
EVENTS
EVRY
EXCELLENCE
EXEMPT
EXHAUST
EXIL'D
EXILE
EXISTENCE
EXPANDS
EXPECT
EXPECTS
EXPENCE
EXPERIENC'D
EXPERIENCE
EXTENDED
FADE
FADED
FAINTLY
FAIRER
FALL'N
FALLING
FALSHOODS
FAM'D
FAMILIAR
FANCY
FARCE
FARTHER
FASTING
FATES
FAULCHION
FAULT
FAULTS
FAV'RITE
FAVOUR'D

FAWNING
FEARFUL
FEASTS
FED
FELICITY
FEN
FERVOUR
FESTIVE
FIDELITY
FIERCENESS
FIERCER
FIGHTS
FIREBRACE
FIRMNESS
FIRY
FISH
FLAGGING
FLASH
FLATTER'D
FLIE
FLIGHTS
FLOATING
FLOCK
FLOURISH
FLOW'D
FLOWER
FLOWERY
FLUNG
FOLLOWERS
FOPS
FORBIDS
FOREIGN
FORGETFULL
FORGETFULNESS
FORGOTTEN
FORTUNE'S
FOUL
FOUNTAIN
FRAGRANCE
FRAGRANT
FRAUDULENT
FRAY
FREEZE
FREEZES
FREIGHT
FRESH
FROLICK
FRONT
FRUGAL
FRUIT
FRUITFUL
FULL-BLOWN
FUMES
GAINFUL
GAINS
GAPING
GARDEN
GARDENS
GAUDY
GAYETY
GENIAL
GENUINE
GHASTLY
GHOST
GIDDY
GLADES
GLADS
GLANCES
GLASSY
GLEAMS
GLITTER
GLITTERING
GLITTRING
GLORIOUS
GLOWING
GLUTTED
GOODS
GOWN
GRACES
GRAIN
GRANDSIRES
GRATITUDE
GREEN
GREW
GRIPE
GRIZLY
GROV'LING
GUARDED

GUESS
GUESTS
HAIL'D
HAIR
HANMER
HARBINGER
HARES
HARMONIOUS
HARMONY
HARRASS'D
HARSH
HARVEST
HASTEN
HATEFUL
HATRED
HAUNT
HEALTHFUL
HEAP'D
HEAVEN'S
HEAVING
HEIGHTS
HELM
HEREDITARY
HERMIT
HERSELF
HINTS
HISSING
HOAR
HOLLOW
HONESTY
HONOUR'S
HOOTED
HOP'D
HOST
HOUNDS
HOUSES
HUGE
HUNDRED
HUNT
HYDASPES
HYMNS
ICY
IDLY
ILL-PLAC'D
ILL-TIM'D
IMAGIN'D
IMAGINATION
IMBRU'D
IMPARTIAL
IMPLORE
IMPRESS'D
IMPROVE
INACHIA'S
INCENSE
INDIA
INDIGNANT
INEXORABLE
INFLICT
INGRATITUDE
INSATIATE
INSTRUCTED
INSTRUCTIVE
INSULTED
INTERPOSING
INTERVAL
INTRIGUE
INVADERS
INVENT
INVIOLABLE
INVITES
INVITING
INVOLVE
IRON
IRREVOCABLE
ITSELF
JAIL
JARRING
JAWS
JEALOUSY
JOCUND
JOHN
JOHNSON
JOINTS
JOYFUL
JOYLESS
JUDE
JUDG'D
JUDGMENT

JUSTIFIES	MIST	PIT	REPENTANCE	SILK
KAI	MISTAKE	PLATE	REPINE	SILKEN
KEEN	MOCK'D	PLAY'D	REPINES	SIMON
KEEP	MODERN	PLAYING	REPOS'D	SINCERE
KEEPS	MODULATED	PLAYS	REPRESS'D	SINGING
KIDS	MOMENT'S	PLENTEOUS	RESCU'D	SISTERS
KILL	MONSTERS	PLIES	RESCUE	SKILL'D
KINDLING	MONUMENTS	PLOUGH	RESERVE	SLOWLY
KINDLY	MOORISH	PLUCKING	RESOLUTE	SLUGGARD
KINDRED	MOTHER'S	PLUMES	RESOLUTION	SLUMB'RING
KINE	MOTIONS	PLUNDER'D	RESOLVES	SMIL'D
KINGDOM	MCUNTS	PLUTO'S	RESOUNDED	SMOKE
KUPRIS	MOURNFULL	PLY	RESTED	SNEER
LABOUR'D	MOURNS	POLICY	RESTRAIN'D	SNOWS
LAD	MR	POLITICIAN'S	RETARD	SOAR
LALAGE	MULTITUDE	POLLUTE	RETURN'D	SOBER
LAMENTING	MURDER'D	POPE'S	RETURNS	SOLICITUDES
LAMPS	MURZA	PORT	REVEAL	SOMETIMES
LANGUID	MUSIC	POWERFULL	REVELS	SONNET
LATEST	MYRIADS	PRACTIS'D	REVERENCE	SOONER
LAUGHS	MYSTICK	PRAIS'D	REVERSE	SPACE
LAUREAT	NAMELESS	PRAISES	REVIEW	SPARKLED
LAUREL	NATIVES	PRECIPICE	REVIVING	SPECIOUS
LAVISH'D	NAUGHT	PRESCRIBES	RICHES	SPECTRES
LAZY	NECESSITY	PRESIDES	RICHEST	SPEECH
LEADS	NEED	PRESS'D	RIDICULE	SPHERE
LENITIVES	NINE	PREST	RIEN	SPHERES
LEONTARES	NOISY	PREVAIL	RIGID	SPLEEN
LEONTIUS'	NCNSENSE	PREVENT	RIGOUR	SPLENDOR
LETTERS	NOSE	PRICE	RIP'NING	SPREADING
LEVET	NOTE	PRODIGIES	RITES	SPRIG
LEWD	NUM'ROUS	PRODIGY	ROAR'D	SPURN
LIBERAL	O'ERBEARS	PROFANE	ROBE	STANDARD
LILIES	O'ERTHROWN	PROMISES	ROLLING	STANDS
LIMITS	O'ERWHELM	PROMPT	ROMAN	STAR
LINE	CBDURATE	PROSP'ROUS	ROMANS	STARTING
LIV'ST	OBEDIENT	PROTECT	ROSY	STATESMAN
LIVING	OBJECT	PROTECTION	RUFFIAN'S	STATUE
LOITERER	OBLIVION	PROTRACTED	RUIND	STEEP
LCNGING	OBSCUR'D	PROVE	RUMOUR	STINGING
LOOSEN'D	OBSCURELY	PROVOK'D	RUN	STOLE
LORDS	CBSERV'D	PROVOKES	RUNS	STONES
LOSES	OBVIATE	PRUNE	RUSTICK	STOOP
LOSS	ODIOUS	PUG	RUSTLING	STRAINS
LCSSES	OFFENCE	PUNISH	SABINE	STRAIT
LCUDER	OFFER	PURER	SAFER	STRAY'D
LOUDEST	OFFICE	PURITY	SAGE'S	STROVE
LOV'D	ONAR	PURSE	SALLIES	STUDIED
LCVE'S	OPPREST	PURSU'D	SAT	STUPEFACTION
LOVES	ORDAIN	PUT	SATIRE	STYGIAN
LULL'D	ORGILIO'S	QUAFF	SCATTER	SUBLIME
LURES	ORIGINAL	QUEENS	SCATTERS	SUBSIDE
LURKING	ORNAMENTS	QUELL	SCENTS	SUBTERRANEOUS
LUSCIOUS	OTHERS	QUITE	SCEPTER	SUITS
LUXURIOUS	OUDE	QUIVERING	SCEPTERS	SULTANESS
MADMAN'S	OURS	RACKS	SCORNFULL	SUMMITS
MAGNIFICENCE	PAGE	RADIANCE	SCOURGE	SUMMON'D
MAINTAIN'D	PAGEANT	RADIANT	SCYTHIAN	SUNG
MAJESTY	PAINTED	RARELY	SEAL	SUPERSTITION
MALICIOUS	PAINTS	RASH	SECRECY	SUPPLIANTS
MALIGNANT	PARDON	READ	SECURELY	SUPPLIES
MANDATES	PASS'D	REASON'S	SEDITION	SUPPLY
MANN'D	PASSENGER	REASONING	SELF	SUPPRESS
MANSION	PASSING	REBELLION	SENATE'S	SURFACE
MARCH	PASSIVE	RECALL	SEQUESTER'D	SURGE
MARKS	PATHLESS	RECEIVES	SERIOUS	SURLY
MARTIAL	PATRON	RECOLLECT	SERPENTS	SURPRISE
MASSACRE	PAY	REFIN'D	SERVICE	SUSPICIOUS
MAXIM	PEAR	REFLECTS	SERVILE	SUSTAINS
MAZ'D	PENSIONS	REFRAIN	SERVITUDE	SWAINS
MEANING	PERFECTION	REFUGE	SHAFTS	SWEAR
MEANLY	PERFIDIOUS	REFULGENT	SHARES	SWEAT
MEANS	PERFIDY	REBUS'D	SHE'S	SWEEPS
MEEK	PERFORM'D	REGARDS	SHEDS	SWIFTER
MEETING	PERFUME	REINS	SHIELD	T'
MEMELE	PERJURY	REJECTS	SHIN'ST	TAIL
MENIAL	PERPLEXITY	RELAX	SHOARS	TAINTS
MESSENGER	PERSECUTION	RELENTLESS	SHOCKS	TARDY
MESSENGERS	PERSIAN	RELUCTANT	SHOOT	TAST
MIGHT'ST	PERSUASION	REMAIN'D	SHOULDST	TASTE
MILDER	PERSUASIVE	REMONSTRANCE	SHOUT	TAX
MINDFUL	PERSUE	REMORSE	SHOWS	TEETH
MINGLE	PETULANCE	REMOTE	SHRIEKS	TELLS
MINGLES	PHILLIPS	REMOV'D	SHUDDER	TEMP'RATE
MINISTER	PHILOSOPHY	RENOUNCE	SHUDDERS	TEMPESTUOUS
MINOS	PHRASE	RENT	SHUTS	TEN
MISERY	PIERC'D	REPAIR	SICK'NING	TERM
MISFORTUNES	PILOT	REPAST	SILENC'D	TERMINATE

2 (CONT.)

TERROURS
TEST
THANKS
THIEF
THITHER
THORNY
THREAT'NING
THREATEN'D
THREATEND
THROBBING
THRONES
THYRSIS
TIES
TIM'ROUS
TIMELY
TOILING
TOILSOME
TOIOS
TOLD
TOOK
TOOLS
TORE
TOST
TOTAL
TOTT'RING
TOUCH'D
TOWARDS
TRAC'D
TRAGEDY
TRAMPLED
TRANQUILLITY
TRANSITORY
TREASONS
TREE
TREMBLED
TREMBLES
TRENT
TRIBUTE
TRIES
TRIFLES
TRIFLING
TRUMPET
TRUMPETS
TUMULT
TUMULTUOUS
TURRETS
TWENTY
UNACQUAINTED
UNBOUGHT
UNCHANG'D
UNCONFIN'D
UNCONSCIOUS
UNDISTINGUISH'D
UNFADING
UNFELT
UNFIT
UNHURT
UNITED
UNJUSTLY
UNLESS
UNLIKE
UNMOV'D
UNRELENTING
UNREWARDED
UNSETTLED
UNSUSPECTED
UPBRAIDING
USURPS
VALIANT
VALLIES
VANITY
VANQUISH'D
VAPOURS
VARIETIES
VARYING
VENT
VENTURE
VERDURE
VERSES
VERY
VET'RAN
VICISSITUDE
VICTOR
VICTORIES
VIEW'D
VIGOUR
VILLAINS

2 (CONT.)

VILLAINY
VILLIERS
VINES
VIOLATED
VIRAGO
VIRGIN'S
VISIONARY
VISIONS
VISIT
VITAL
VOCAL
VOTARIES
VOW
WAFT
WAITING
WAKES
WAKING
WANTONS
WANTS
WAR'S
WARBLE
WARBLES
WARBLING
WARBLINGS
WARLIKE
WARN'D
WARRING
WARRIOUR
WARRIOURS
WATCHFUL
WATER
WEALH
WEARIED
WEB
WEEKLY
WELCOME
WET
WHAT'S
WHEEL
WHENE'ER
WHERE-E'ER
WHERE'ER
WHETHER
WHOLL
WIDE-WASTING
WINGED
WINTRY
WITHDREW
WITHER'D
WITHSTAND
WOLF
WOLSEY
WOLSEY'S
WOMEN
WON
WOND'RING
WOND'ROUS
WORDS
WORN
WRATHFULL
WREATHS
WRETCHEDNESS
WRITTEN
WRONGS
YEAR'S
YOKE
YON'
ZEUS

1

'MIDST
'ROUND
'SQUIRE
'T
ABANDON
ABANDON'D
ABASH
ABDALLAH
ABDICATED
ABHORD
ABHORS
ABJECT
ABOUND
ABSOLUTE
ABSORB'D
ABSURDITY
ACCENT

1 (CONT.)

ACCENTS
ACCEPT
ACCLAMATIONS
ACCOMPLICE
ACCUMULATED
ACCUS'D
ACCUSATION
ACCUSER
ACHILLES
ACHILLES'
ACQUAINT
ACQUAINTED
ACQUIR'D
ACQUIT
ACRES
ACROSS
ADAMANTINE
ADDED
ADDER
ADDRESS'D
ADDREST
ADDS
ADJOINING
ADMIRER
ADMITTANCE
ADOR'D
ADORATION
ADORNS
ADULATION
ADVANCE
ADVANCES
ADVENT'ROUS
ADVERSE
ADVICE
AEGYPTIANS
AENEAS'
AFFECTATION
AFFECTING
AFFECTION
AFFECTION'S
AFFECTS
AFFLICT
AFFLICTIVE
AFFLUENCE
AFFORDS
AFRESH
AFRICK'S
AGGREGATED
AGHAST
AGONY
AGREE
AIDED
AIMS
AINIGMA
AIRS
AKING
ALBANIAN
ALCOVE
ALE
ALETHEIE
ALFRED'S
ALL-CONSCIOUS
ALL-PITYING
ALL-SUBDUING
ALLA
ALLIANCE
ALLMIGHTY
ALLON
ALLOTS
ALLOW'D
ALLUR'D
ALLUREMENTS
ALLY'D
ALMIGHTY'S
ALPHIUS
AMARILLIS'
AMAZING
AMAZON
AMBROSIAL
AMBUSH'D
AMIABLE
AMID
AMIENS
AMITY
AMONGST
AMOROUS
AMPLE
AMURATH'S

1 (CONT.)

AMUSEMENT
ANCESTORS
ANEW
ANGELICK
ANIMATED
ANIMATES
ANN
ANNOUNC'D
ANNUALL
ANSWER'D
ANTILOCHUS
ANTIQUE
ANXIETIES
ANXIETY
APART
APARTMENTS
APHROSI
APOSTLES
APPEAR'D
APPEAS'D
APPEASE
APPLAUSE
APPLES
APPLY'D
APPRENTICE
APPROBATION
APPROV'D
APPROVE
APPROVING
ARABIA'S
ARBITER
ARBITRARY
ARCHANGEL
ARCHITECT
ARES
ARGIVE
ARGO'S
ARGUE
ARISTIUS
ARM'D
ARMY
AROMATIC
ARRAS
ARRAY
ARRIVE
ARTHRITIC
ARTIFICIAL
ARTISTS
ASCEND
ASEM
ASHAM'D
ASIAN
ASK'D
ASKS
ASLEEP
ASPECT
ASPIR'D
ASPIRATIONS
ASPIRES
ASPIRING
ASSAIL
ASSASSIN
ASSASSIN'S
ASSASSINATION
ASSAY'D
ASSEMBLE
ASSEMBLED
ASSEMBLING
ASSERTING
ASSERTS
ASSISTANT
ASSIZES
ASSOCIATE
ASSOCIATES
ASSUASIVE
ASSUME
ASSWAGE
ASSYRIA
ASTRAY
ATHEIST
ATHIRST
ATLAS
ATOM
ATRIDAE
ATTACK
ATTACKS
ATTAIN
ATTENDANT

1 (CONT.)

ATTESTING
ATTORNEY
ATTRACTED
ATTRACTS
AU
AUCTIONS
AUGUSTAN
AUGUSTUS
AUGUSTUS'
AUKWARD
AUSPICIOUS
AUSTER
AUSTRIA
AUTHORITY
AUTHOUR
AUTOU
AUTUMN
AUTUMN'S
AUTUMNAL
AVENGING
AVERSION
AWAITS
AWAKEN'D
AWARD
AWEFUL
AWKWARD
BACCHUS
BACCHUS'
BACKS
BACKWARD
BACKWARDS
BACON'S
BADE
BALANCE
BALBO'S
BALLANCE
BALM
BANDS
BANE
BANEFUL
BANEFULL
BANQUET
BAR'D
BARBARIAN
BARBARIANS
BARD'S
BARRICADES
BASENESS
BASIS
BASSA'S
BASSAS
BATT'RIES
BATTERS
BATTLEMENTS
BATTLES
BATTRIES
BAUBLES
BAVARIA'S
BAVARIAN
BAYS
BEACONS
BEAMY
BEASTS
BEAU
BEAUTIFUL
BECALM
BECALMS
BECOME
BEDECK'D
BEDROP'D
BEECHEN
BEER
BEFIT
BEG'D
BEGAN'ST
BEGG'D
BEGGAR
BEGGAR'D
BEGGER
BEGGER'D
BEGIN
BEGINNING
BEGUILE
BEHNS
BELESSI
BELIEF
BELIEV'D
BELINDA'S

BELONG	BRIB'D	CENTER	COMETS	CORPOREAL
BELONGS	BRIDAL	CENTRAL	COMFORT	CORRESPONDENCE
BELOV'D	BRIDGNORTH	CENTURIES	COMFORTS	CORRUPT
BENDING	BRIGHTEN'D	CESAREAN	COMMANDED	CORRUPTED
BENEFICENT	BRIGHTENS	CHAIN'D	COMMENC'D	CORRUPTS
BENIGNER	BRIGHTNESS	CHAIR	COMMEND	COST
BENUMB	BRINGS	CHAIROYSA	COMMISSION'D	COTTAGES
BESET	BRINK	CHANCES	COMMITS	COU'D
BESIDE	BRISKER	CHANGEFUL	COMMUNION	COULD'ST
BESIEG'D	BRITISH	CHANGES	COMPANION	COUNCIL
BESIEGERS	BRITON'S	CHANNELS	COMPASSIONATE	COUNCILS
BESTREW'D	BRITONS	CHARACTERS	COMPETENCE	COUNSELL'D
BESTROW	BROCADE	CHARADE	COMPETITORS	COUNSELLS
BETIMES	BROIL	CHARG'D	COMPLAIN'D	COUNT
BETTYS	BROODS	CHARIOT	COMPLAINTS	COUNT'NANCE
BETWEEN	BROTHERS'	CHARIOTS	COMPLETES	COUNTED
BEUTEOUS	BROTOLOIGOS	CHARIS	COMPLY	COURIER
BEWILDER'D	BRYAN'S	CHASING	COMPOSE	COURSES
BEWILDERD	BUBBLE	CHAST	COMPOSURE	COURTIER'S
BIER	BUBBLES	CHATTER'D	COMPULSION	COURTIERS
BIGOT	BUDA	CHEAR'D	COMUS	COURTING
BIGOTRY	BUDS	CHEATED	CONCAVE	COURTLY
BIND	BUILDING	CHECKS	CONCEIT	COURTSHIP
BINDS	BUILDS	CHEER	CONCEIV'D	COVERT
BION	BULK	CHEERS	CONCERN	COXCOMBS
BIOUS	BULLOCKS	CHER	CONCLUDE	COY
BIRTH-DAY	BULLS	CHERRY	CONCORD	CRACKLING
BLACK'NING	BULRUSH-SPEARS	CHILDREN	CONCUR	CRAFTY
BLADE	BULWARKS	CHILDREN'S	CONCUR'D	CRAVE
BLAMELESS	BURDEN	CHILL'D	CONDEMNS	CREAM
BLAZES	BURGESS	CHILLING	CONDENSING	CREATED
BLED	BURN'D	CHILLS	CONDITION	CREATURE
BLEEDS	BURNT	CHILNESS	CONFEDERATES	CREDITORS
BLESST	BURTHEN'D	CHILS	CONFER	CREDITS
BLOCK	BURY	CHIMAERA	CONFERENCE	CREDULITY
BLOCKADE	BUSH	CHIMERAS	CONFIDING	CREEK
BLOCKHEAD'S	BUSIED	CHINA	CONFISCATION'S	CRESCENT
BLOOD-BOLTER'D	BUSTLING	CHOAK	CONFLICTS	CRIMINALS
BLOODHOUNDS	BYSTANDER	CHOIRS	CONFOUNDED	CRINGES
BLOODSHED	CADMUS	CHRIST	CONFUSED	CRIPLED
BLOSSOMS	CAESAR	CHRISTIAN'S	CONGRATULATING	CRISPIN
BLOWS	CAESAR'S	CIBBER	CONGRATULATION	CRITICK
BLUNT	CALAIS	CILICIA	CONGRATULATIONS	CRITICK'S
BLUSH'D	CALL'DST	CIRCLE	CONJECTURE	CRITICKS
BLUSTRING	CAMBRIA'S	CIRCLES	CONJECTURE'S	CROAK
BLYTHE	CAMBRIAN	CIRCLING	CONJOINS	CROAKING
BOAR	CAMILLI	CIRCUMSPECTIVE	CONNUBIAL	CROATIAN
BOARS	CAN'T	CITADELS	CONQUERING	CROP
BOASTER	CANCELL	CITYS	CONQURING	CROP'D
BOASTER'S	CANDIDATE	CIVIL	CONSECRATE	CROPS
BOAT	CANDIDATES	CIVILITY	CONSENTED	CROSS'D
BODING	CANKER'D	CIVILIZE	CONSIGN	CROWD'S
BODLEY'S	CANNIBAL	CLADES	CONSIGNS	CROWDED
BODY	CANONIZE	CLAIM'D	CONSISTENT	CROWS
BOIST'ROUS	CANOPY	CLAM'ROUS	CONSPIRATOR	CRUELL
BOLT	CANT	CLAMOUR	CONSPIRING	CULTIVATE
BON	CANVASS	CLANDESTINE	CONSTELLATION	CUMBROUS
BONES	CAPITULATE	CLANG	CONSTELLATIONS	CUP
BONNET	CAPTIVATE	CLASH	CONSTRAIN'D	CUPID
BOOKS	CAPTIVATED	CLASP'D	CONSTRAINS	CUPID'S
BOON	CAPTIVE'S	CLAUDE	CONSTRAINT	CUPIDS
BOREAS	CARAVANSERAL	CLAUDIUS	CONSULT	CURIO'S
BOROUGH	CARCASE	CLAUDY	CONSUMMATE	CURLING
BOROUGHS	CAREFULL	CLEAN	CONTAGION	CURLS
BORROWD	CARESS	CLEAR'D	CONTAIN	CURSE
BOTTOM	CARESS'D	CLEMENCY	CONTAINS	CURSES
BOUNDED	CARNAGE	CLIFF	CONTEMPLATIVE	CURST
BOW-STRING	CARCUSES	CLIMBS	CONTEMPT	CUT
BOW'D	CARPATHIAN	CLOAK	CONTEND	CUTS
BOWER	CARRY	CLOATH'D	CONTENTIOUS	CYNTHIA
BOWING	CASE	CLODIO'S	CONTENTMENT	CYPRESS
BOWRS	CAT	CLOISTER'S	CONTESTED	DAEDALUS
BOX	CAT-CALLS	CLOS'D	CONTINU'D	DAEMONS
BOYS	CATCALL'S	CLOSEST	CONTRACTED	DAILY
BRAIN	CATCHES	CLOSING	CONTRARIETY	DALLY
BRAKES	CATES	CLOY	CONTRIVANCE	DAMES
BRAMBLE	CATH'RINE	COACH	CONTROUL	DAMN
BRAMBLES	CAUCUSUS	COASTS	CONTROULING	DAMNATION
BRANDISHES	CAUS'D	COAT	CONVENT'S	DAMP
BRASS	CAUSES	COBBLER'S	CONVEY'D	DANAUS'
BRAV'RY	CAUTION'D	COFFERS	CONVINC'D	DANC'D
BRAVELY	CAYSTER'S	COIN	CONVINCE	DANCES
BREACH	CEASES	COLLECT	CONVIVIAL	DANCING
BREAD	CEDAR	COLLECTED	CONVOY	DANG'ROUS
BREAKING	CELEBRATED	COLLECTIVE	CONVULSION	DAPHNE
BREATH'D	CELLS	COLLEGE	COOLING	DAR'D
BREECHES	CEMENT	COMBINES	COQUETS	DAR'ST
BRIAREUS	CENSURES	COMET'S	CORN	DARKEN'D

DARKEST	DESPERATION	DOMINIONS	EMERGING	EXCEEDED
DARKSOM	DESPOTIC	DONE	EMINENCE	EXCEEDING
DARKSOME	DESTROYED	DOORS	EMITTED	EXCEL
DARKVISAG'D	DESTROYS	DOTARD	EMPEROR	EXCELL
DARTED	DETECT	DOTARD'S	EMPIRE'S	EXCELLENT
DASH	DETECTION	DOTH	EMPIRES	EXCESS
DASH'D	DETERMINE	DOUBLE-FORM'D	EMPLOY	EXCESSIVE
DAUBER	DETESTATION	DOUBTFULL	EMPLOYS	EXCHANG'D
DAUGHTER'S	DETESTS	DRAIN	EMULATION	EXCHANGES
DAUGHTERS	DEVIL	DRAIN'D	ENAMOUR'D	EXCISE
DAUNTLESS	DEVOLVE	DRAINS	ENCHAIN	EXCLAMATION
DAVID	DEVOURING	DRAM	ENCHAIN'D	EXCURSIVE
DAWB	DEW	DRAUGHTS	ENCHAINS	EXCUSE
DAWNING	DEW-DROPS	DRIV'LER	ENCHANTING	EXCUSES
DAY'S	DIADEMS	DRIVES	ENCHANTMENT	EXECUTE
DAZZLED	DIALOGUE	DROOPING	ENCIRCLING	EXECUTIONER
DEARER	DID'ST	DROOPS	ENCLOSE	EXIGENCE
DEATH'S	DIFFERENT	DROUSY	ENCOUNTER	EXILES
DEATHFULL	DIFFICULTY	DROVE	ENCREAS'D	EXPECTATION
DEATHLESS	DIGNIFIED	DROWN'D	ENCREASING	EXPELL
DEBARD	DIGNIFY	DROWSY	ENCUMBER'D	EXPELL'D
DEBASED	DIGS	DRUNKARD	ENDANGER'D	EXPIR'D
DEBAUCH'D	DILATORY	DRURY-LANE	ENDEAR'D	EXPIRES
DEBTS	DINNER	DUGS	ENDEARMENTS	EXPLAIN
DECAYS	DIRECTION	DULCET-STREAMING	ENDEAV'RING	EXPOS'D
DECEIT	DIREFUL	DULNESS	ENDED	EXPRESS
DECEIVE	DIREFULL	DULY	ENDUR'D	EXPRESSES
DECEIVING	DIRT	DUMB	ENDURE	EXPREST
DECENT	DISABLED	DUN	ENEMY	EXTACY
DECIDED	DISAGREE	DUNAMEI	ENGLAND	EXTATICK
DECISIONS	DISAPPEAR	DUNGEON'S	ENGLAND'S	EXTEMPORARY
DECK'D	DISAPPOINTED	DUNGEONS	ENI	EXTENSIVE
DECLAMATION	DISAPPOINTMENTS	DURFEYS	ENJOY'D	EXTERIOR
DECLIN'D	DISARRAY	DURST	ENJOYMENT	EXTORTED
DECLINES	DISAST'ROUS	DUSKY	ENLARG'D	EXULTATION
DECLINING	DISASTER	DWINDLED	ENLARGE	EXULTS
DECORATIONS	DISCERN	E'RE	ENLIV'NING	EYE-BALLS
DECOY	DISCERNING	EAGLE	ENLIVENING	FABIUS
DECREE	DISCLOSE	EARLIEST	ENNOBLED	FABLED
DECRY	DISCOUNTENANC'D	EARNEST	ENQUIR'D	FABRIC
DEDICATOR	DISCOVER'D	EARTH'S	ENQUIRES	FACTION
DEDOKEN	DISCOVERS	EARTHLY	ENROB'D	FACTIOUS
DEEMD	DISCRETION	EARTHQUAKE	ENROLL'D	FACULTIES
DEEP'D	DISDAIN'D	EARTHQUAKES	ENSIGN	FACULTY
DEEPEST	DISEASES	ECHOING	ENSNARES	FADES
DEER	DISENCUMBER'D	ECHOIS	ENTANGLED	FAIL'D
DEFACE	DISENTANGLED	ECSTACY	ENTERPRIZING	FAILS
DEFAME	DISGRACD	EDDIES	ENTERTAINMENTS	FAINTS
DEFENCELESS	DISGUISES	EDE	ENTRAILS	FAIRIES
DEFEND	DISHONOUR	EDGE	ENTRANCE	FAIRY
DEFENSELESS	DISJOIN'D	EDWARD	ENTREAT	FAITHFULL
DEFER	DISJOINTED	EER	ENTREATS	FALLACIOUS
DEFORM	DISLIKE	EETION	EPEMPSEU	FALLACY
DEFORMITIES	DISMAY'D	EFFECT	EPIDEMIC	FALSEHOOD
DEFRAUDS	DISORDER	EFFECTS	EPIROT	FALT'RING
DEGEN'RATE	DISPELL	EFFUS'D	EPIRUS	FAMILIES
DEGRADES	DISPELLING	EFFUSE	EPODE	FAMINE
DEGRADING	DISPELLS	EGRAPSEN	EQUALITY	FAN
DEGREES	DISPENSE	EGYPT'S	EQUALLY	FAN'D
DELIBERATION	DISPENSING	EIDEN	EQUIPP'D	FANCIED
DELICIOUS	DISPERS'D	EIGHTIETH	ERASE	FANN'D
DELIGHTS	DISPERSING	EIPEN	ERASMUS	FANS
DELIVER'D	DISPLEASURE	EISORAAS	ERGA	FAQUIR
DELUSIONS	DISPOSE	EK	EROON	FARM
DEMEANOUR	DISPOSSEST	EKPERSE	EROTI	FARMER
DEMOCRITUS	DISSEMBLE	ELDERLY	ERR	FASHION
DENIAL	DISSOLV'D	ELECTING	ERRORS	FAST
DENS	DISSOLVING	ELEGANCE	ERST	FATALL
DENYS	DISTAFF	ELEGANT	ERUPTION	FATHERS
DEPARTURE	DISTANCE	ELEGIES	ESCAPE	FATIGUE
DEPRESS	DISTENDED	ELEGY	ESSAY'D	PATTEN
DEPREST	DISTINCTION	ELEMENTAL	ESSENCE	FATTEND
DEPRIV'D	DISTINCTIONS	ELEMENTS	ESSENTIAL	FAULT'RING
DEPTHS	DISTORTED	ELEVATE	EST	FAUSTUS
DERISION	DISTORTS	ELEVATES	ESTABLISHES	FAVORITE
DERIV'D	DISTRACT	ELISSES	ESTIN	FAVOURING
DERIVATA	DISTRACTED	ELIZA'S	ETC	FAVOURITE
DERIVE	DISTRACTS	ELOCUTION	ETNA'S	FEARFULL
DERVISE	DISTRIBUTE	ELSE	EUNUCHS	FEARFULL'ST
DESART	DIVAN	ELUDED	EUROPE	FEARST
DESARTS	DIVE	ELUDING	EVAPORATE	FEATHER
DESCRY	DOATING	ELYSIAN	EVERDURING	FEATHERS
DESCRY'D	DOCILITY	EMASCULATED	EVIL	FEATURES
DESERTS	DOCTOR	EMBARK'D	EVN	FEEDS
DESERV'D	DOG	EMBOW'RING	EXALTED	FEIGN'D
DESERVE	DOG-DAYS	EMBOWER'D	EXALTS	FELLOW
DESIGNING	DOMES	EMBRACES	EXAMPLE	FELLOW-SAINTS
DESP'RATE	DOMESTIC	EMBROIL'D	EXASP'RATED	FELLOW'S

FELLOWS	FOUR	GLIMPSE	HEAVN'LY	ICARUS
FENC'D	FOWL	GLOOM-ENAMOUR'D	HEAVY	ICE
FERVENT	FOWLS	GLOOMS	HEBRUS	IDEAL
FERVOURS	FRAIL	GLORY'S	HECATOMBS	IDLENESS
FESTAL	FRAILTY	GLOSSY	HECUBA'S	IDLER
FESTINA	FRAIS	GLOW'D	HEEDFUL	IDOL
FETTERS	FRANCE	GLUT	HEEDLESS	IDOLIZE
FEVER	FRANTIC	GLUTTON	HEIGHTEN	IDOLIZES
FI'RY	FRANTICK	GNASHES	HEIGHTEN'D	IDOMENEUS
FICKLE	FRAUDFUL	GOATS	HEIR'S	IGN'RANCE
FICTITIOUS	FRAUDS	GOE	HELAS	ILEX
FIEND	FRAUGHT	GORGE	HELP	ILFATED
FIERCELY	FREE'D	GOTHIC	HEMP	ILIAD
FIFTIETH	FREEDOM'S	GOVERN	HENCEFORWARD	ILION
FIFTY	FREEMEN	GOVERNOUR	HENRY'S	ILL-FATED
FIG	FREES	GRADATIONS	HERACLITUS	ILL-GOTTEN
FIGURE	FREEZING	GRAINS	HERB	ILL-PERSUADING
FINE	FREIND	GRANDSIRE	HERBS	ILL-PRESERV'D
FINES	FRENCH	GRANDSIRE'S	HERDS	ILLPLAC'D
FINGERS	FRET	GRANDSON	HERE'S	IMAGE
FIRD	FRETFUL	GRAPE	HERETICK	IMAGES
FIRE'S	FRIEND'S	GRAPES	HERETOFORE	IMBIBES
FIRED	FRIENDLESS	GRAPHONTA	HERMIONE	IMBITTER
FIRMLY	FRIENDSHIP'S	GRAPSOMENON	HERMIT'S	IMITATED
FIRSTLINGS	FRIGID	GRASP'D	HERO'S	IMMERSE
FIT	FRO'	GRASPING	HEROES'	IMMOD'RATE
FITTER	FROGS	GRASPS	HEROIC	IMMUR'D
FIXD	FROLIC	GRATEFULL	HEROINE	IMPAIRS
FIXED	FRONTIERS	GRATITUDE'S	HERS	IMPART
FLAGITIOUS	FROZE	GRAVE'S	HERSE	IMPEACHMENT
FLAMBEAU'S	FRUITS	GRAVES	HERVEY'S	IMPEARL'D
FLAMINIUS	FRUSTRATE	GRAVITY	HEW	IMPELLED
FLASHES	FRY	GRAY	HIBERNIA'S	IMPELLS
FLATTERER	FULNESS	GRAZE	HICKMAN	IMPERVIOUS
FLATTERIES	FUN'RAL	GRECIAN'S	HIGHER	IMPIETY
FLEECE	FUNERALL	GRECIANS	HIGHEST	IMPLACABLE
FLEET	FURIES	GREEDY	HINDER'D	IMPLORES
FLINGS	FUSCUS	GREENWICH	HIPPOLYTUS	IMPORT
FLOOR	FUTURITY	GRIEVE	HIRES	IMPOSE
FLORENCE	FUTURITY'S	GRIN	HISS'D	IMPOSTURES
FLOURISH'D	GAIETIES	GRIPING	HISSES	IMPOTENT
FLOURISHES	GAIETY	GRISLY	HIST'RY	IMPREGNABLE
FLOURS	GAINST	GROAN'D	HISTORIANS	IMPROV'D
FLOWER-PIECES	GAIT	GROOM	HISTORIES	IMPROVES
FLOWERS	GALILEO'S	GROPES	HISTORIKON	IMPROVING
FLOWN	GALLANT	GROSS	HIVE	IMPROVISO
FLUSH'D	GALLICK	GROUNDLESS	HOARDED	IMPUDENCE
FLUTE	GALLIES	GROUNDS	HOARDS	INATTENTIVE
FLUTTERS	GALLOWS	GROWLS	HOC	INAUSPICIOUS
FLUXIT	GAME	GROWS	HOGARTH'S	INCENS'D
FLY'ST	GAMESOME	GUARDIANS	HOMER'S	INCIRCLING
FOAM	GAMESTER	GUESS'D	HOMEROS	INCITE
FOLIAGE	GARRET	GUINEAS	HONEST	INCLEMENCIES
FOLLOW'D	GARRICK	GULL'D	HONOR	INCLIN'D
FONDEST	GARRISON	GULP	HONOUR'D	INCLINATION
FONDLY	GASPING	GYANTS	HONOURABLE	INCLOSE
FONTE	GASPS	GYGANTICK	HOOTING	INCONSISTENT
FOOD	GATH'RING	HA	HOPE'S	INCONSTANT
FOOL'S	GATHER	HABITANT	HORIZON	INCREAS'D
FOP	GAUL	HABITATION	HORROURS	INCREASE
FOPLING'S	GAURUS	HABITUAL	HOSPITABLE	INCUMBER'D
FOPPERIES	GAV'ST	HAD'ST	HOSTILITIES	INCUMBRANCES
FORBEARS	GAZETTE'S	HAMLET	HOSTILITY	INCUMBRED
FORCEFULL	GAZETTEER	HANDLE	HOUND	INDEARING
FOREBORE	GAZING	HANDSOME	HOURIES	INDEED
FORESHOWN	GEM	HANG'D	HOV'RING	INDIAS
FORESOOK	GENERALLY	HANGING	HOWE'ER	INDIGENCE
FORETELL	GENNAH'S	HANMER'S	HUE	INDIGNATION
FOREVER	GENOA'S	HARBOUR'D	HUG	INDULG'D
FORFEIT	GENTLEMAN	HARBOURS	HUGS	INDULGE
FORGES	GENTLENESS	HARK	HUMANKIND	INDULGENCE
FORGETFUL	GEORGE'S	HARLEY'S	HUMOUR	INDUSTRY
FORGETS	GET	HARLOT	HUNGARIA'S	INESTIMABLE
FORMING	GIANT	HARMONIS'D	HURLING	INFATUATE
FORRESTS	GIBBET	HARPER	HURRIES	INFECTED
FORT	GIBE	HARPSICORD	HURRY	INFECTION
FORTIFIE	GILD	HASAN	HURRY'D	INFERIOUR
FORTIFIES	GIRL'S	HASTES	HURT	INFERNAL
FORTIFY'D	GIVEN	HATES	HUSBAND	INFESST
FORTITUDE	GIVING	HATH	HUSSAR	INFEST
FORTRESS	GLADE	HAZARDOUS	HYDE	INFIDELS
FORTRESSES	GLASS	HE'LL	HYPERBOLIES	INFLICTING
FORTUNES	GLEAN	HEADY	HYPERIA'S	INFOLD
FOUGHT	GLEANS	HEARING	HYPOCRISY	INFORC'D
FOUNDATION	GLEBE	HEATH	HYPOCRITICK	INFORM
FOUNDATIONS	GLIDED	HEAV'N'S	HYPOPLACUS'	INFRINGE
FOUNT	GLIDES	HEAV'NS	I'D	INFUS'D
FOUNTS	GLIMM'RINGS	HEAVE	I'M	INHABITANT

INLAYD
INMOST
INNOCENT
INNOVATICN
INQUIETUDES
INSCRIPTION
INSINCERE
INSTANT
INSTINCT
INSTRUCTION
INSTRUMENT
INSUPERABLE
INT'RESTS
INTEGER
INTELLIGENCE
INTENDED
INTENT
INTENTION
INTERCOURSE
INTERMIX'D
INTERPOSE
INTERPRET
INTIMIDATES
INTOXICATING
INTREATS
INTREPID
INTRIGUING
INTRODUCES
INTRUDE
INTRUSION
INTRUSIVE
INTRUSTS
INVADING
INVASION
INVENTED
INVERTED
INVIOLATED
INVISIBLE
INVOKE
INVOLV'D
INWARD
IRENES
IRRADIATE
IRREPARABLE
ISIS
ISLAND
ISSUED
ISTHER'S
IT'S
ITALIA'S
ITALIAN
ITALY'S
ITINERANT
IVORY
IVY
JANIZARIES
JANIZARY
JAV'LINS
JENNYS
JEWELS
JILT
JOCKY
JOHNSON'S
JCINT
JOKE
JOLLITY
JOLLY
JOY'ST
JOYOUS
JUBA'S
JUDGES
JUDICIOUS
JUICES
JURIES
JUSTER
JUSTLY
JUTTING
KALLOUS
KATES
KEN
KENT
KEPT
KERAUNO
KICK
KILL'D
KILLS
KINDER
KINDLE

KING'S
KISSES
KIST
KITCHENS
KLAIETE
KNEE
KNEEL
KNIFE
KNOWING
KCNIEN
KORAN
KUPRIDI
LABOURD
LABOURING
LACE
LACERATED
LADS
LADY'S
LAGS
LAMB
LAMBKINS
LAMENTABLE
LAMENTED
LAMPOON
LAMERA
LANDLORD
LANGUAGES
LANGUISHING
LARGER
LASCIVIOUS
LASH
LASHES
LATIAN
LATIN
LATONA'S
LAUD
LAUGHING
LAURELS
LAVES
LAVISHES
LAWGIVER
LAWLESS
LAWN
LEADER
LEADER'S
LEAF
LEAFLESS
LEANING
LEAR
LEARNING'S
LEARNT
LEFT-HAND
LEGACY
LEGENDS
LEND
LENDER
LENT
LENTE
IEVELL'D
LIB'RAL
LIBATIONS
LIBELS
LICENCE
LICENS'D
LIFTED
LIGHTLY
LIMPID
LIN'GRING
LINEAMENTS
LINGER'D
LINGRING
LINKS
LINNET
LION
LION'S
LIONESS
LIONS
LIP
LIQUOR
LISP
LIST
LIST'NER
LIST'NING
LISTENS
LISTLESS
LITHOS
LIV'D
LIV'RIED

LIVID
LOATH
LOATHSOME
LOCKS
LODGE
LOGICK
LOITER
LOITER'D
LONELY
LONESOME
LONG-CONTINU'D
LONG-DRAWN
LONG-EXPECTED
LONG-EXPECTING
LONG'ST
LONGS
LOOKING
LOP'D
LOPS
LORE
LOSING
LOTTERY
LOVING
LOW'RING
LOW'RS
LOWER
LUCKY
LUG
LUR'D
LURK
LURKS
LUTE
LUXURIANT
LUXURIES
LYBIA'S
LYCISCUS
LYDIA'S
LYDIAT'S
LYES
LYON'S
LYONESS
LYONS
MAD
MADDED
MADLY
MABCENAS
MAEON'S
MAEONIAN
MAGNET
MAINTAIN
MAINTAINS
MAJESTICK
MAKER'S
MALEVOLENCE
MANGLED
MANLY
MANNERS
MANORS
MANTLING
MANTUAN
MANURES
MANURING
MANY-COLOUR'D
MABEOTIS'
MABKED
MARLB'ROUGH
MARLB'ROUGH'S
MABO'S
MARRY
MARSH
MARTYR
MARTYRS
MASQUERADES
MATTER
MATURER
MAXIMS
MAY'ST
MAYOR'S
MAYST
MAZY
MEANEST
MEANTIME
MEASURE
MEASURES
MEATS
MECCA'S
MED
MEDALS

MEDITATE
MEDITATED
MEDITATES
MEDITATION'S
MEDITATIONS
MEEKNESS
MEIN
MELANCHOLLY
MELANCHOLY'S
MELISSA'S
MELODIOUS
MELODY
MEMBER
MEMENE
MEMPHIS
MENIALS
MENS
MENTAL
MENTION
MEOTIS
MERCENARY
MERCHANDISE
MERCHANT
MERCIES
MERRIMENT
MERRY
METEOR
METHINKS
METHOD
METRON
METROPOLIS
MICE
MID
MIDNIGHT
MIDNIGHT'S
MIDST
MILITARY
MILKNESS
MILTON
MILTON'S
MILTONIAN
MIMICK'S
MIND'S
MINERVA
MINION
MINOR'S
MINSTREL'S
MINSTRELS
MINUTES
MIRACLES
MIRY
MISCHIEVOUSLY
MISERY'S
MISFORTUNE'S
MISLEADS
MISSIVE
MISTRESS'
MISTRUST
MISTS
MISTY
MOAN
MOANS
MOCK
MODEL
MODERATE
MODERATOR
MODES
MODISH
MOLUC
MONASTIC
MONEY
MONGRELS
MONITORY
MONSIEUR
MONTH
MONUMENT
MOON'S
MOOR
MORALS
MORN'S
MORTALITY
MORTGAG'D
MORTGAGE
MORTGAGES
MOSCOW'S
MOSSIE
MOTHERS
MOTION

MOTIVE
MOTIVES
MOTLEY
MOULDRING
MOUNOS
MOUNTAIN
MOUNTAIN'S
MOURN'D
MOURN'ST
MOURNER
MOURNINGS
MOUTON
MOV'D
MOVING
MULTITUDES
MUNIFICENCE
MURD'RER
MURD'RER'S
MURD'RERS
MURM'RING
MURTHER
MURTHER'D
MUSIC'S
MUSICK'S
MUSICKS
MUSING
MUTINY
MYRTALE
MYSTES
N'A
NAIL
NAM'D
NARD
NARRATIVE
NARRATIVES
NASSAU
NATUR'D
NATURES
NAY
NEARER
NEAREST
NEER
NEGLECTS
NEGLIGENCE
NEIGHB'RING
NEIGHBOURS
NEITHER
NEST
NESTS
NET-WORK
NETTLE
NEVER-DYING
NEVER-FADING
NEW-BLOWN
NEW-FOUND
NEW-MADE
NEW-PREST
NIECE
NIGHT'S
NIGHTS
NILUS
NIMBLER
NIPHATES
NOBLY
NODDING
NODS
NOISOME
NON
NORTH
NOSTRO
NOTIONS
NOTWITHSTANDING
NOVELTY
NUMBER
NUMEROUS
NUMROUS
NURSE'S
O'ERBORN
O'ERCAST
O'ERCASTS
O'ERFILL
O'ERFLOWING
O'ERLOOK
O'ERLOOKS
O'ERPOW'RING
O'ERPOWER'D
O'ERSPREAD
O'ERTAKE

O'ERTHROW	PALE-FAC'D	PHLOGOENTI	PRESUMPTUOUS	RAIS'E
O'ERTURNS	PALL	PHUSIKON	PRETENDS	RAISES
O'ERWHELM'D	PALL'D	PHUSIS	PREVAILING	RAISING
O'ERWHELMS	PALLADIUM	PHYSIC	PREVAILS	RAJAS
O'FLOW	PAMPER'D	PICTURE	PREVENTED	RAMBLING
OAK	PAMPHLET	PICTURES	PRIAM	RAN
OAR	PANDER	PIMP	PRIDE'S	RANDOM
OATHS	PANG	PIMPLES	PRIMAEVAL	RANG'D
OBEDIENCE	PANTA	PINCH	PRIME	RANK
OBELISKS	PANTED	PINE	PRINCE'S	RANKS
OBEY'D	PANTOMIME	PINION	PRINCIPLES	RANSACK
OBJECTS	PAPHIEN	PIPE	PRINTS	RANSOM
OBLIG'D	PARAPHRASE	PIRATES	PRISON'S	RAPACITY
OBLIVIOUS	PARASITE	PITIED	PRIVACIES	RAPTUR'D
OBSCENITY	PARENTS	PLAGUES	PRIVACY	RASHLY
OBSCURITY	PARIS	PLANS	PROCLAIM'D	RASHNESS
OBSERVATION	PARK	PLANT	PROCURES	RAT'LING
OBSERVING	PARLY	PLANTED	PRODIGIOUS	RAT'ST
OBSTINATE	PARTED	PLATONIC	PRODUC'D	RATED
OBSTRUCTED	PARTERRE	PLEADS	PRODUCT	RAV'D
OBTAIN	PARTIAL	PLEASURE'S	PROEN	RAVAG'D
OBTAIN'D	PARTICULAM	PLEDGE	PROFANES	RAVAGE
OCCASION	PARTING	PLEIAD'S	PROFOUND	RAVAGES
OCEAN	PARTNERS	PLEXEN	PROFOUNDEST	RAVING
ODOURS	PARTNERSHIP	PLIGHTED	PROFUSE	RE'ECHOES
OERFLOW	PARTY	PLOW	PROFUSELY	READER
OERTHROW	PASSAGES	PLUMAGE	PROGENITORS	REAL
OFFENDED	PASSES	PLUME	PROGRESS	REAR'D
OFFENDER'S	PASSION'S	PLUMP	PROJECT	REASCEND
OFFENDS	PATEI	PLUND'RER	PROLONG'D	REBELLION'S
OFFERS	PATIENT	PLUNG'D	PROLONGS	REBELS
OFTEN	PATRIAM	PLUTO	PROMISCUOUS	RECALS
OGILBY'S	PATRONESS	PLY'D	PROMONTORIES	RECEIVING
OISI	PAULTRY	POCKETS	PRONOUNC'D	RECESSES
OISTA	PAYMENT	PODESSI	PROOF	RECLINE
OLEIBERIOIO	PEACEFULL	POEM	PROPAGATES	RECLINES
OLIBARIOIO	PEASANT	POETRY	PROPER	RECOIL
OLIBAROIC	PEASANTS	POIETEN	PROPHETESS	RECOLLECTED
OLIVE	PECULIAR	POIGNANT	PROPITIATE	RECOMPENCE
OMEN'D	PEERS	POISON'D	PROPORTION'D	RECORD
OMER	PELEUS	POLAR	PROPORTIOND	RECOUNTED
OMMASI	PELIDES'	POLE	PROPOS'D	RECOVERING
OMNIPOTENCE	PENANCE	POLEIS	PROPOSE	RED
OMNISCIENCE	PENETRATING	POLISH	PROSELYTES	REDEEMS
ONE'S	PENITENCE	POLITICKS	PROSPECT	REDUC'D
ONEIRON	PENITENT	POLITICS	PROSPERITY	REEDS
ONWARD	PENS	POLLUTES	PROSTITUTED	REEKING
OP'NING	PENSION	POLLUTION	PROTECTING	REELING
OPENING	PENSION'D	POMPEY'S	PROTESTATION	REFLECTED
OPIATE	PEOPLE'S	POND'ROUS	PROTESTATIONS	REFLECTION
OPIATES	PEOPLED	POPE	PROUDER	REFRESHMENT
OPPOSE	PERENNIAL	POPULACE	PROUDLY	REFUND
OPPOSITICN	PERFECT	POPULAR	PROV'D	REFUSAL
OPPRESS	PERFORM	POPULUMQUE	PROVERBIAL	REGAIN
OPPRESSING	PERI	PORTENTOUS	PROVES	REGAIN'D
OPPRESSION'S	PERIOD	POSSESS'D	PROVIDENT	REGION
OPPRESSOR	PERIODS	POSTIVELY	PROVINCE	REGRETTED
OPPRESSOR'S	PERISH'D	POT	PRUNES	REGULAR
ORANGE	PERISHABLE	POTE	PRY	REGULATE
ORBS	PERJURIES	POTHER	PTOLEMOISI	REGULATED
ORDAINS	PERMANENT	POW'R'S	PUBLIC	REGULATES
ORDER	PERMITS	POWDER'D	PUBLISH'D	REIGN'D
ORDERS	PERMITTED	POYS'NOUS	PULTOWA'S	REIGN'ST
ORESTES	PERPLEX	PRACTICE	PUNISHMENT	REIGNING
ORGILIO	PERPLEX'D	PRACTICES	PURCHASD	REJECT
ORIGIN	PERSECUTING	PRATTLING	PURCHASE	REJECTED
ORNAMENT	PERSIA	PRAY'D	PURCHASS	REKINDLED
ORPHAN	PERSIA'S	PRAY'RS	PURGE	RELATE
ORPHANS	PERSONATE	PRAYS	PURL	RELATION
OSIERS	PERSUADE	PREACH	PURSUED	RELAX'D
OSTENTATIOUS	PERSUE'D	PRECARIOUS	PURSUING	RELEASE
OTAN	PERSUED	PRECEPTS	PURSUIT	RELENTING
OUTDONE	PERT	PRECINCTS	PUSH'D	RELIEVE
OVER	PERU	PRECIPITATELY	PUSHES	RELIEVES
OVERSPREADS	PERUS'D	PRECIPITATES	PUZZLE	RELIGION'S
OWN'D	PERVERSE	PREDOMINATES	PYE	RELIQUES
OWNS	PERVERSELY	PREFERMENT'S	PYGMEAN	REMARK
OXEN	PERVERSENESS	PREFERR'D	PYGMIEAN	REMARK'D
OYL	PEST	PREGNANT	QUARRY	REMEDIES
PACIFIC	PETITIONS	PREJUDICE	QUENCH	REMEDY
PACIFY	PETTIUS	PRELUDE	QUENCH'D	REMEMBER'D
PAGAN	PHARSALIA	PRESAGE	QUITTED	REMITS
PAGEANTRIES	PHASIS	PRESENTING	QUITTING	REMNANT
PAGEANTRY	PHEREI	PRESENTS	QUIVER'D	REMORSELESS
PAID	PHILANDER'S	PRESERVE	RABBLE	REMOUNT
PAINTING	PHILIPS	PRESIDING	RABBLES	RENEWS
PAINTINGS	PHILOSOPHERS	PRESSING	RAIN	RENNY
PALAION	PHILOSOPHIC	PRESUMES	RAINBOWS	REPELL

REPENT
REPLACE
REPLY
REPLY'D
REPLYING
REPORTS
REPRESENTATION
REPROACHFUL
REPROOF
REPTILE
REPTILES
RESCUES
RESEMBLING
RESENTFUL
RESIDENCE
RESOLVED
RESOUND
RESPONSIVE
RESTRAINS
RESTRAINT
RESUM'D
RESUME
RESUMES
RESUMPTION
RETAILS
RETARDS
RETINUE
RETIREMENT
RETIRING
REVEAL'D
REVEALD
REVENGEFUL
REVERS'D
REVISIT
REVOLUTIONS
REWARDS
RHET'RICK
RHIMES
RHINE
RHODIAN
RHONE
RIBALD
RICH
RID
RIDE
RIDS
RIG
RINGLETS
RIOT
RIPE
RIPEN
RIPSES
RIV'LETS
RIVER
RIVULET
RIVULETS
ROARINGS
ROB
ROBB'D
ROBBERS
ROBERT
ROCKY
RCMAN'S
ROOMS
ROPE
ROPES
ROUSES
ROUSING
ROUZING
ROVES
ROWL
ROWLS
ROYALL
ROYALTY
RUBY
RUDENESS
RUDER
RUEFULL
RUFF
RUFFIAN
RUFFIANS
RUFFLED
RUFLED
RUGGED
RUIN'D
RUINOUS
RULERS
RULING

RUMP
RUSH'D
RUSHING
RUSSIA'S
RUSSIAN
RUSSIANS
RUST
SABINES
SADDEN
SADDENS
SAFELY
SAFETY'S
SAID
SAILORS
SALLY
SALOP
SALUTARY
SANCTIFIES
SANCTIFY
SANDY
SANGUINARY
SANGUIS
SAP
SATED
SATIETY
SATURATED
SATURNS
SAVIOUR
SAW'ST
SCAEAN
SCAMANDRIUS
SCANDAL
SCANDALL
SCANDERBEG
SCANNING
SCAP'D
SCARLET
SCARS
SCATT'RING
SCENIC
SCHOLAR'S
SCHOOL
SCHOOLS
SCIENCES
SCIPIOS
SCORE
SCORND
SCORNING
SCOTLAND
SCREAM
SCREAMING
SCREEN
SCRIBBLER
SCROLL
SCYMETAR
SCYTHIA'S
SEA-SAPP'D
SEARCH'D
SEASON'S
SEBALIAS
SEDATE
SEDITIONS
SEDLEY
SEDUC'D
SEDUCING
SEE'ST
SEEDS
SEEM'ST
SEERS
SEJANO
SELECTED
SELF-APPROVING
SELFISH
SELVES
SEMNEN
SENATES
SENATOR
SENATOR'S
SENATORIAN
SENATORS
SENSELESS
SENSES
SENTIMENT
SENTINELS
SEPARATE
SEPARATION
SEPTENNIAL
SEQUITUR

SERAGLIO'S
SERENITY
SERV'D
SERVIA'S
SETTING
SETTLE'S
SETTLED
SEV'N
SEV'NMOUTH'D
SEVERER
SEVERITIES
SEVERITY
SEVERN
SEWER
SHADED
SHADY
SHAKESPEAR
SHAKESPEAR'S
SHAKING
SHALLOWS
SHAMES
SHAPE
SHAR'D
SHARPEN
SHEATH'D
SHEERS
SHELLS
SHELTER
SHELTER'D
SHELTERD
SHEPHERDS
SHEWN
SHIV'RING
SHOCK'D
SHOES
SHOURS
SHOUTS
SHOW'R
SHOWERS
SHRILL
SHRILLING
SHRINE
SHRIVELING
SHRUNK
SHUDD'RING
SHUN'D
SICKENS
SICKNESS
SIDERON
SIEGE
SIGN'D
SIGNS
SIMONS
SIMPLE
SIN
SINGER
SIP
SIRIUS'
SIXTH
SIXTY
SKAITER
SKAITERS
SKEPTRA
SKIFF
SKIM
SKULKING
SKULKS
SLAUGHTERD
SLAVISH
SLEEPY
SLENDER
SLEPT
SLEW
SLIGHTING
SLIGHTLY
SLIPP'RY
SLOTH'S
SLUGGISH
SLY
SMALLER
SMART
SMITE
SMOAK'D
SMOAKING
SMOKING
SNAR'D
SNARE
SNARL

SNARLING
SNEERS
SNIPES
SNOW
SNUFF
SOAR'D
SOARING
SOARS
SOFTEND
SOFTENS
SOIL
SOL
SOL'S
SOLDIERS'
SOLICITATION
SOLID
SOLLICITE
SOLLICITUDES
SOLON
SON'S
SONGS
SONOROUS
SOOTHIN
SOPHON
SORC'RESS
SORCERERS
SORCERY
SORDID
SOU
SOUL'S
SOUNDING
SOUR
SOUTH
SOV'REIGN'S
SPARES
SPARKLES
SPARROW
SPEAKER
SPEAKER'S
SPEARS
SPECIAL
SPECKLED
SPEND
SPENDS
SPENSER'S
SPICES
SPICY
SPIES
SPINET
SPIRES
SPLENDOURS
SPORTING
SPORTIVE
SPRAYS
SPRITELY
SPRUNG
SPURN'D
SPY
SQUANDER'D
SQUEAL'D
SQUEALING
STABS
STAFF
STAKE
STALK
STALK'D
STAMP
STANDARDS
STANDING
STARE
STARR'D
STARTED
STARTS
STARVES
STARVING
STATION
STATUTES
STEADFAST
STEADINESS
STEDDY
STEDFAST
STEEL'D
STEELY
STEEPS
STEER
STEM'D
STEMM'D
STILLNESS

STINGS
STOCK
STOOPING
STOOPS
STOP'D
STOPP'D
STOPT
STOR'D
STORM'D
STORMING
STOUT
STRANGER'S
STRANGERS
STRANGLED
STRATAGEMS
STRAY
STREAMERS
STREET
STREW'D
STRICT
STRICTEST
STRIPED
STRIPP'D
STRIVES
STROKES
STRONGER
STRONGEST
STRUGGLES
STRUGLE
STRUGLING
STRYMON'S
STUBBORN
STUDENT
STUDY
STUN
SUBDUE
SUBDUED
SUBDUES
SUBMISSIVE
SUBMIT
SUBMITTED
SUBSIST
SUBTLE
SUBVERTED
SUCCEEDS
SUCCESSIVE
SUCCOURS
SUCKS
SUFF'RER
SUFF'RINGS
SUFFER
SUFFOLK'S
SUGAR
SULLY
SULTRY
SUMMER'S
SUMMON
SUN-BURNT
SUNS
SUNSHINE
SUP
SUPERFLUITIES
SUPICION
SUPINE
SUPINELY
SUPPLICANT
SUPPLICATE
SUPPLIED
SUPPORTED
SURELY
SURER
SURMOUNT
SURPRISED
SURPRIZ'D
SURPRIZE
SURROUND
SURROUNDING
SURROUNDS
SURVEY'D
SURVEY'ST
SURVIV'D
SURVIVES
SUSPECTED
SUSPECTS
SUSTAIN'D
SWALLOWING
SWAMPY
SWAN

SWARMS
SWAYS
SWEDISH
SWEETEN
SWEETER
SWEETLY
SWELL'D
SWELLINGS
SWEPT
SWIFTLY
SWIFTNESS
SWOLN
SYCOPHANT
SYLVIA
SYMPATHETICK
SYMPATHISE
SYMPATHISING
SYMPATHIZ'D
SYMPATHY
SYRIAN
TABLE
TAKES
TALENT
TALENTS
TALES
TALK
TALKS
TALL
TALONS
TAME
TAMELY
TANTALUS
TAPHON
TART
TARTARIAN
TASKS
TASTES
TASTFULL
TATTER'D
TAUNTS
TE
TEACHES
TEI
TEIZING
TELAMON
TELOS
TEMPER'D
TEMPER'D
TEMPTATION
TEMPTS
TENDERNESS
TENETS
TENTH
TENTS
TERMS
TEROR
TERRESTRIAL
TES
TETHER
TEXTURE
THAMES'S
THANATIO
THANK
THAT'S
THATS
THEAN
THEBAN
THEFT
THEIOS
THEMES
THENCE
THEO
THERE'S
THEREFORE
THESEUS
THEY'RE
THICKET
THIEVES
THIN
THINGS
THIRSTED
THIRSTS
THNETOUS
THOMAS
THOUGHTFUL
THRACIA'S
THRALE
THRALL

THREAT'NINGS
THREATEN
THREW
THRIFT
THRILLS
THRISTY
THRIVE
THROATS
THROBBINGS
THROBS
THRONGS
THROUGHOUT
THROWN
THRUSH
THRUSTS
THUND'RING
THUNDER'D
THUNDERBOLTS
THUNDERS
THUNDRED
THYME
TI
TIGERS
TIGRIS
TILL'D
TIMIDITY
TIMOTHEUS
TINSEL
TIRES
TIRING
TIS
TITLED
TITYRUS
TOD
TOIL'D
TCMBS
TORCH
TORCHES
TORMENTED
TORN
TORQUATUS
TORTURING
TOSS
TOSS'D
TOSSING
TOTTERS
TOUCHES
TOUT
TOW'RINGS
TOWNS
TOWRD
TRACED
TRADE
TRADER
TRAGIC
TRAIT'RESS
TRAITORS
TRAMPLE
TRAMPLES
TRANCE
TRANSFER
TRANSFERR'D
TRANSFIX'D
TRANSGRESSION
TRANSMUTED
TRANSPARENT
TRANSPORTING
TRAPPINGS
TRAYTOR'S
TRAYTRESS
TREACHERY
TREASON'S
TREASUR'D
TREAT
TREMENDOUS
TRIBES
TRIBUTARY
TRICKT
TRIED
TRIFLER
TRIFLINGS
TRIUMPH'D
TRIUMPHAL
TRIVIAL
TROJANS
TROOPES
TROP
TROPHIES

TROUBLE
TROUBLES
TRUMP
TRUSTED
TRUTHS
TUNEFULL
TURBULENCE
TURGID
TURK
TURN'ST
TURNIP
TURNIPS
TURNUS
TUSCAN
TUTELARY
TWENTIETH
TWICE
TWILIGHT
TWINE
TWINES
TWISTED
TYBURN
TYDE
TYDEUS'
TYRANNICK
TYRANNIZE
UNACCUSTOM'D
UNACTIVE
UNAFFRIGHTED
UNAIDED
UNANIMATED
UNANIMOUS
UNAPPEAS'D
UNAW'D
UNBALLAST
UNBLEST
UNBORN
UNBORROW'D
UNBOUND
UNBRIB'D
UNBROKEN
UNCEASING
UNCHA
UNCHECK'D
UNCIVILIZ'D
UNCLAIM'D
UNCLASP'D
UNCONNECTED
UNCONVINC'D
UNCOUNTED
UNCOUTH
UNDER
UNDESIGNING
UNDETECTED
UNDISCOVER'D
UNDISSEMBLED
UNDISTURB'D
UNENCUMBER'D
UNENVIED
UNESTABLISH'D
UNEXPENSIVE
UNEXPERIENCED
UNFADED
UNFEELING
UNFETTERD
UNFOLD
UNFORESEEN
UNFORM'D
UNGUARDED
UNHARMONIOUS
UNHEEDING
UNINJUR'D
UNITES
UNKINDLED
UNLAMENTED
UNLOCK'D
UNLOCKS
UNLOV'D
UNMINDFUL
UNMINDFULL
UNMINGLED
UNNERV'D
UNNERVE
UNOFFENDED
UNPITY'D
UNPOLISH'D
UNPRACTIS'D
UNPRIZ'D

UNPROFITABLE
UNPUNISH'D
UNPURSU'D
UNQUENCH'D
UNQUESTION'D
UNQUIET
UNREAD
UNREFIN'D
UNRELENTED
UNREMITTED
UNREPRESS'D
UNRESTRAIN'D
UNSKILFUL
UNSTEADY
UNSUCCESSFUL
UNSULLIED
UNSUPPORTED
UNSUSPECTING
UNTAINTED
UNTASTED
UNTO
UNTRAVELL'D
UNTWIN'D
UNUS'D
UNUSUAL
UNUTTERABLE
UNVARYING
UNWHOLESOME
UNWIELDY
UNWILLINGLY
UNWISE
UNWORTHY
UPBRAID
UPHELD
US'RER
USURPER'S
UTMOST
UTTERS
VACANT
VAGRANT
VAGRANTS
VAINLY
VALGIUS
VALOUR
VALUE
VANE
VANISH
VANITIES
VARIETY
VARNISH
VARY'D
VASSAL
VAULT
VAULTED
VEGETATION
VEILS
VELVET
VENERATION
VENETIA
VENGEFUL
VENT'ROUS
VENTUR'D
VERGE
VERS'D
VESTED
VEX
VEXATION
VICARIOUS
VICT'RY
VICTORS
VICTORY
VIE
VIEL'D
VIENNA
VIEWING
VIGILANCE
VIGOROUS
VILE
VILLANY
VINDICTIVE
VINE
VIOLATION
VIOLENT
VIOLETS
VITAE
VOLUBLE
VOLUME
VOLUNTARY

VOT'RIES
VOTES
VULNERE
VULTURS
VYE
WAFTS
WAGE
WAILINGS
WAITED
WAK'D
WAND'RERS
WAND'RINGS
WANDER'D
WANDRING
WANT'ST
WANTING
WANTON
WARBLER
WARMER
WARMEST
WARN'ST
WARNING
WARRIOR
WARRIOUR'S
WASTEFUL
WAT'RY
WATCH'D
WATCHFULL
WATERY
WAV'D
WAV'RING
WAVING
WEAKEN'D
WEAKLY
WEALTHIEST
WEAPON
WEARING
WEAVE
WEAVES
WEAVING
WED
WEEDS
WEIGH
WEIGH'D
WELL-ACCORDED
WELL-FEIGN'D
WENT
WENTWORTH
WEST
WHALEBONES
WHATSOE'ER
WHELMS
WHERESOE'ER
WHEREVER
WHERRY
WHET
WHIRL
WHIRL'D
WHIRLE
WHIRLING
WHIRLWINDS
WHISP'RING
WHISPERS
WHITE
WHITHER
WHO'S
WHOE'ER
WHOLSOME
WHOME
WHOME'ER
WHORE
WICKED
WICKEDNESS
WIDER
WIDOW
WIDOWS
WIELD
WIFE'S
WILDEST
WILDNESS
WILE
WILES
WILFUL
WINDING
WINES
WISDOM'S
WISELY
WISEST

WITH'RING
WITHDRAW
WITHDRAWN
WITHDRAWS
WITHERING
WITHERS
WITLINGS
WITNESS'D
WIVE
WIVES
WOMANS
WOMB
WOMENS
WONDER'D
WONT
WOOD
WOODCOCK
WORD
WORK'D
WORKMANSHIP
WORSHIPER
WORSHIPPERS
WORTHLESS
WOU'D
WOVE
WREATH
WREATH'D
WRETCHES
WRIT
WRITE
WRITER
WRITING
WRONG'D
XEINE
XERXES
YEARLY
YELLINGS
YELP
YES
YONDER
YORE
YOU'LL
YCURE
YOURSELVES
YOUTHFUL
ZELINDA
ZELINDA'S
ZEMZEM
ZEPHYRS
ZONE

Concordance to Poems
in Latin

		PAGE	TITLE		LINE
A					
	To a Lady who spoke in Defence of Liberty	O 105	Lady Defence		T
	Vitam a terdecimo sextus mihi finiet annus,	O 215	Tr Greek 9.112		1
	Sunt quibus a lacrymis vix vacat ulla dies.	O 221	Tr Greek 10.84		2
	In Rivum a Mola Stoana Lichfeldiae diffluentem	O 228	Rivum a Stoana		T
	Corusca a radiis Memnonis ora dabant.	Y 28	Aurora Musis		16
AB					
	Ab Jove Maeonides descendere Somnia narrat:	O 103	Elizae Aenigma		3
	Nec miratur opes, celsa speculator ab arce	O 161	Gnothi seauton	V	39
	Summus adesse jubet celsa dominator ab arce;	O 162	Gnothi seauton		45
	Clarus Joannes, reginae affinis, ab alto	O 212	Tr Greek 7.590		1
	Ut tibi laus omni semper ab ore sonet:	O 232	Prayer		8
	Cum caput Hesperiis attolit Phoebus ab undis,	Y 28	Aurora Musis		1
	Fundit ab ore melos,	O 385	Cantico Solom.	D	8
ABDIDIT					
	Pendula secretas abdidit arbor aquas.	O 228	Rivum a Stoana		6
ABDIT					
	Quod mors in cineres solvit, et abdit humo.	O 221	Tr Greek 10.84		4
ABDOMEN					
	Sive abdomen	O 198	Medico Aeger S		7
ABEST					
	Non tenet; esca natat pulchra, sed hamus abest.	O 209	Tr. Greek 5.67		2
	Turbidus imber abest; mittit rosa roscida gemmas,	O 385	Cantico Solom.	D	5
ABIBO					
	Terram adii nudus, de terra nudus abibo.	O 220	Tr Greek 10.58		1
ABIES					
	Surgit amans abies teretis, buxique sequaces	O 91	Messiah		81
ABIT					
	Quot vox missa pedes abit horae parte secunda?	O 229	Epigram IV		1
ABITURUS					
	Cras abiturus	O 199	Medico Aeger S		20
ABJICIT					
	Hic, aurum ut reperit, laqueum abjicit, alter ut aurum	O 213	Tr Greek 9.44		1
ABNUE					
	Magne bonum, omne malum et poscentibus abnue nobis.	O 221	Tr Greek 10.108		2
ABRAMUM					
	Evocat Abramum dein tertia; quarta relinquit	O 226	Septem Aetates		2
ABSIMILIS					
	Praeter Menodotum, nullius absimilis.	O 223	Tr. Gk. 11.213		2
ABSIT					
	Cessat inops rerum, ut torpet, si marmoris absit	O 161	Gnothi seauton		38
ABSQUE					
	Pures absque Timore,	O 109	Post-genitus		17
	Et pingues absque Labore.	O 109	Post-genitus		18
ABSTERGAT					
	Abstergat mundi labem, nec gaudia carnis	O 205	Christianus		2
AC					
	Firmius ac ipsis Mundi stabilita ruinis.	O 92	Messiah	V	119
	Accendit, rerumque modos ac foedera ponit.	O 163	To Dr Lawrence		30
	Spes hominum ac curas cum procul esse jubet.	O 170	Insula Kenneth		16
	Permitte fidens, ac muliebribus,	O 187	Ad T. L. M.D.		18
	Nec sinat semper tremere ac dolere	O 227	A Meditation		3
	Nec sinat semper tremere ac dolore	O 227	A Meditation	V	3
ACADEMIA					
	Quas Natura dedit dotes, Academia promit,	O 85	Adjecere bonae		1
ACCENDAS					
	Corde meo accendas; ardeo totus ego.	O 225	Tr. Gk. 16.209		2
ACCENDAT					
	Et summi accendat pectus amore boni.	O 170	Insula Kenneth	V	16B
ACCENDE					
	Siderea Isaiae, dignos accende furores!	O 88	Messiah		7
ACCENDENT					
	Non litui accendent bellum, non campus ahenis	O 90	Messiah		68
ACCENDIS					
	Sufflato accendis quisquis carbone lucernam,	O 225	Tr. Gk. 16.209		1
ACCENDIT					
	Accendit, rerumque modos ac foedera ponit.	O 163	To Dr Lawrence		30
ACCINCTUS					
	Sic peragam tua jussa libens, accinctus ad omne	O 207	Prayers IV		5
ACCINGAR					
	Restat? an accingar studiis gravioribus audax?	O 162	Gnothi seauton		53
ACCOLA					
	Accola Danubii qualia saevus habet:	O 169	Insula Kenneth		12
ACCRESCUNT					
	Accrescunt tremulis tactu nova robora nervis:	O 90	Messiah		49
	Accrescunt teneris tactu nova robora nervis:	O 90	Messiah	V	49
ACCUMBERE					
	Tu neque dulce putes alienae accumbere mensae,	O 218	Tr Greek 9.573		1
ACER					
	Ille quidem recte, sublimis, doctus, et acer,	O 160	Gnothi seauton		6
	Nec vincis acer, nec pateris pius;	O 187	Ad T. L. M.D.		6
ACHAEMENIDAE					
	Credit, Achaemenidae nuper agellus eram.	O 215	Tr Greek 9.74		2
ACHILLES					
	Alter ut adsit Homerus, adest etenim alter Achilles.	O 218	Tr Greek 9.523		2
ACRI					
	Acri sanguine turgidos	O 164	Recover Eyes		5
ACRIS					
	Nunc minus acris	O 198	Medico Aeger S		5
	Xerxi, tercentum Spartae Mars obstitit acris	O 217	Tr Greek 9.304		3

PAGE   TITLE   LINE

ACTAE
Ipse sui judex, actae bene munera vitae; . . . . O 162 Gnothi seauton 48
ACTUM
Pergit, et imperiis sentit se dulcibus actum. . . . . O 205 Christianus 27
ACUENS
Divitiis acuens aspera corda virum; . . . . O 213 Tr Greek 9.29 2
ACUTIS
Crystallisque latex fractus scintillat acutis, ... O 116 Tr Pope Grotto 4
Hunc oculis Veri Fautrix lustravit acutis, ... O 386 In Birchium D 3
AD
Natus ad optatum perducet coepta parentis. . . . . . O 90 Messiah 72
Ad Urbanum . . . . O 101 Ad Urbanum T
Ad Ricardum Savage, Arm. Humani Generis Amatorem. . . O 102 Ad R. Savage T
Ad foeminam quandam generosam quae libertatis causae . . O 105 Lady Defence T
Ad Lauram parituram Epigramma . . . . O 115 Ad Lauram Epig V T
Lexicon ad finem longo luctamine tandem . . . . . O 160 Gnothi seauton 1
Ad T<homam>. L<aurence>. M<edicum>. D<octissimum>. . . O 186 Ad T.L. M.D. T
Ad Thomam Laurence, Medicum Doctissimum, Cum . . . O 186 Ad T. L. M.D. V T
Peccator, ad latus meum; . . . . O 203 Christ Sinner 2
Sic peragam tua jussa libens, accinctus ad omne . . O 207 Prayers IV 5
Ad Musas Venus haec: Veneri parete, puellae, . . . O 213 Tr Greek 9.39 1
Haec Musae ad Venerem: Sic Marti, diva, mineris; . . . O 213 Tr Greek 9.39 3
Recta ad pauperiem tendit, cui corpora cordi est . . O 222 Tr. Gk. 10.119 1
Ad Divos paribus passibus ire duces; . . . . . . O 225 Tr. Gk. 16.331 4
ADAMANTINA
Vincla coercebunt luctantem adamantina mortem, ... O 90 Messiah 54
ADAUGET
Quingentis quadragenis socialis adauget . . . . . . O 231 Geographia Met 33
ADDAT
Spiritus addat. . . . . O 227 A Meditation 8
ADDE
Veniaeque sancta pacis adde gaudia: . . . . . O 206 Prayers I 8
Undecies centum denos quater adde duosque. . . . . O 229 Epigram IV 2
Russia, myriadas ter denas adde trecentis: . . . . . O 230 Geographia Met 17
ADDI
Vult sibi vicenas millesima myrias addi, ... O 230 Geographia Met 21
Undecimum Camber vult septem millibus addi. . . . . O 231 Geographia Met 36
ADDICAT
Se fidum addicat Christo, mortalia temnens. . . . . . O 205 Christianus 18
ADDIT
Centuriae octavam decadem addit Lucca secundae. . . . O 230 Geographia Met 15
Et quadragenis decades quinque addit Ierne, ... O 231 Geographia Met 32
ADDRESSED
Verses addressed to Dr. Lawrence, composed by Dr. . . . O 162 To Dr Lawrence T
ADES
Fortis, ades, solus tangas venerabile limen. . . . . O 116 Tr Pope Grotto 16
Fortis, ades, tibi sponte patet venerabile limen. . . O 116 Tr Pope Grotto V 16
Facilisque semper confitenti ades reo, ... O 206 Prayers III 2
ADESSE
Summus adesse jubet celsa dominator ab arce; . . . O 162 Gnothi seauton 45
Materiemque rudem, magnaeque parentis adesse . . . . O 163 To Dr Lawrence 21
Hoc statuat, precibus Christus adesse velit: . . . . O 204 Losing Speech 2
Hoc statuant, votis Christus adesse velit: . . . . . O 204 Losing Speech V 2
Sit sacer orbis amor, miseris qui semper adesse . . . O 205 Christianus 7
ADEST
En! Salvator adest; vultus agnoscite caeci . . . . . O 89 Messiah 42
Fidus adest custos, seu nox furat horrida nimbis, . . . O 90 Messiah 62
Fidus adest custos, seu nox furat humida nimbis, . . . O 90 Messiah V 62
Alter ut adsit Homerus, adest etenim alter Achilles. . . O 218 Tr Greek 9.523 2
ADESTE
Huc foedat quos lepra, urit quos febris, adeste! . . . O 88 Messiah 16
ADHUC
Errat adhuc vitreus per prata virentia rivus, ... O 228 Rivum a Stoana 1
ADII
Terram adii nudus, de terra nudus abibo. . . . . . O 220 Tr Greek 10.58 1
ADIRE
Patris Numen adire est. . . . . O 182 Waltoni Piscat 10
ADIT
Quisquis adit lectos elata uxore secundos, ... O 215 Tr Greek 9.133 1
ADJECERE
Adjecere bonae etc. . . . . O 85 Adjecere bonae T
ADJUVAT
Rosae ruborem sic Viola adjuvat . . . . O 102 Ad Urbanum 22
ADMIRANS
Aureaque admirans rutilantis fulgura cristae. . . . . O 91 Messiah 92
ADMONITU
Admonitu, ipsa suas nunciat hora vices. . . . . . . O 170 Insula Kenneth V 18B
ADONI
Unde hic Praxiteles? nudam vidistis, Adoni, ... O 225 Tr. Gk. 16.168 1
ADSCISCIT
Myrias adsciscit sibi nonagesima septem . . . . . . O 229 Geographia Met 4
ADSIT
Adsit, Laura, tibi facilis Lucina dolenti, ... O 115 Ad Lauram Epig 3
Alter ut adsit Homerus, adest etenim alter Achilles. . . O 218 Tr Greek 9.523 2
ADULANTUM
Mater adulantum prolesque, Pecunia, curae, ... O 218 Tr Greek 9.394 1
ADVERSAE
Fortunae malim adversae tolerare procellas, ... O 221 Tr Greek 10.93 1
AEDIFICARE
Multa alere, et multas aedificare domos. . . . . . . O 222 Tr. Gk. 10.119 2

		PAGE	TITLE	LINE
AEGRA				
Sentiet aegra Metus, ...		0 109	Post-genitis	5
Hora perit furtim laetis, mens temporis aegra		0 228	Jactura Tempor	1
AEGRAE				
Menti nec aegrae montibus aviis		0 166	Oda Isle Skye	10
AEGROTAT				
Phoebe fave, aegrotat quae te colit, ulla nec usquam est		0 197	Summ. Lawrence	1
AEGRUM				
Aegrum trahenti spiritum		0 206	Prayers II	8
AEGYPTO				
Myrias Aegypto cessit bis septima pingui.		0 229	Geographia Met	3
AEGYPTUM				
Aegyptum; templo Solomonis quinta superbit;		0 226	Septem Aetates	3
Aegyptum; templo Solomonis quinta supersit;		0 226	Septem Aetates V	3
AEMULI				
Risurus olim nisibus Aemuli;		0 101	Ad Urbanum	14
AENIGMA				
In Elizae Aenigma		0 103	Elizae Aenigma	T
AEQUOR				
Littora deficiens arentia deseret aequor, ...		0 92	Messiah	114
Tutum aliis aequor, me pereunte, fuit.		0 210	Tr Greek 7.282	2
AEQUUM				
Datur nec aequum cuique animum sibi		0 166	Oda Isle Skye	14
AER				
Pascua, qua blandum spirat purissimus aer		0 90	Messiah	58
In sublime rapit, queis terra et pontus et aer		0 163	To Dr Lawrence	32
AERIAEQUE				
Aeriaeque columbae, dantes oscula, jungunt		0 385	Cantico Solom. D	9
AERIS				
Nil opus est aeris sacra de turre sonantis		0 170	Insula Kenneth V 18A
Faelix ante alios nullius debitor aeris;		0 222	Tr Greek 11.50	1
AESTAS				
Una quidem, sic fata volunt, tibi vivitur aestas, . . .		0 171	Tr. Busy Fly	9
AETAS				
Prima parit terras aetas; siccatque secunda;		0 226	Septem Aetates	1
Quid ferat externi velox, quid deterat aetas, ...		0 228	Rivum a Stoana	11
Cum sexagenis, dum plura recluserit aetas, ...		0 230	Geographia Met	19
AETATES				
Septem Aetates		0 226	Septem Aetates	T
AETERNA				
Aeterna tandem liberet clementia, ...		0 206	Prayers III	5
Aeternum Aeterna Luce juvabit opus!		0 393	Tr. of Crashaw D	6
AETERNAE				
Salutis aeternae dator;		0 206	Prayers II	2
AETERNE				
Aeterne rerum conditor, ...		0 206	Prayers II	1
Summe dator vitae, naturae aeterne magister, ...		0 207	Prayers VI	1
AETERNOQUE				
Aeternoque orci dominator vulnere languens		0 90	Messiah	55
AETERNUM				
Aeternum direpta mihi! sed quid moror istis?		0 384	On the Gin-Act D	7
Aeternum Aeterna Luce juvabit opus!		0 393	Tr. of Crashaw D	6
AETHER				
Saxa sonant Deus; ecce Deus! deflectitur aether . . .		0 89	Messiah	36
AETHERA				
Jessaeis surgit, mulcentesque aethera flores		0 88	Messiah	11
Stella mea, observans stellas, Dii me aethera faxint, .		0 212	Tr Greek 7.669	1
AETHEREIS				
Aethereis variata fucis.		0 102	Ad Urbanum	24
Excipit aethereis, Ars omnis plaudit amica, ...		0 161	Gnothi seauton	21
Excipit aethereis, Ars omnis plaudit amico, ...		0 161	Gnothi seauton V	21
AETHERIS				
Aetheris, en! portas sacro fulgore micantes		0 92	Messiah	106
Compagem edificat, coelorum atque aetheris ignes . . .		0 163	To Dr Lawrence	29
AETHRA				
Atque Aethra ambigua pallida luce rubet;		Y 28	Aurora Musis	2
AEVI				
Non operum serie, seriem dum computat aevi, ...		0 162	Gnothi seauton	46
Respice inutiliter lapsi quem poenitet aevi;		0 207	Prayers VI	5
Sufficit hoc votis; flos hic pulcherrimus aevi est, . .		0 215	Tr Greek 9.112	3
Aevi sat novi quam sim brevis; astra tuenti, ...		0 219	Tr Greek 9.577	1
Incrementa aevi non cumulare potes.		0 220	Tr Greek 10.60	4
AEVO				
Eheu! quam longo tecum consumerer aevo!		0 384	On the Gin-Act D	5
AEVUM				
Optavit quicunque senex sibi longius aevum, ...		0 214	Tr Greek 9.55	1
AFFER				
Eloquiumque potens linguis torpentibus affer, ...		0 232	Prayer	7
AFFINIS				
Clarus Joannes, reginae affinis, ab alto		0 212	Tr Greek 7.590	1
AFFIXUS				
Damnatus tenebris, lectoque affixus inerti, ...		0 163	To Dr Lawrence	3
AFFLATU				
Mentibus afflatu terrenas ejice sordes		0 232	Prayer	5
AFRICA				
Myrias, ut menti pateat tota Africa doctae.		0 230	Geographia Met	24
AGAM				
Nec quid agam invenio, meditatus grandia, cogor . . .		0 161	Gnothi seauton	34
Quicquid agam, quocunque ferar, conatibus obstat . . .		0 161	Gnothi seauton	40
Ut tibi quae placeant, omnia promptus agam.		0 207	Prayers V	4

	PAGE	TITLE	LINE
AGAT			
Quot modis mecum, quid agat, requiro, ...	O 168	Oda to Thrale	11
AGE			
Tu quoque securus res age, Nise, tuas.	O 228	Rivum a Stoana	12
Nunc age, certamen nunc ineamus, ait;	O 384	Epigramma	D 2
AGELLI			
Servilem tuti cultum contempsit agelli, ...	O 386	Tr Epi. Madoc	D 3
AGELLUS			
Credit, Achaemenidae nuper agellus eram.	O 215	Tr Greek 9.74	2
AGENDAM			
Concede agendam legibus vitam tuis.	O 206	Prayers I	4
AGENTEM			
. . . filium peregre agentem desiderio nimis	O 186	Ad T. L. M.D.	V T
AGES			
Tecta ineunt; caelebs omnia solus ages;	O 217	Tr Greek 9.359	6
AGGESTAS			
Conspicit aggestas, et se minatur in illis, ...	O 161	Gnothi seauton	43
AGIS			
Sic aliis dives, tu tibi pauper agis.	O 223	Tr. Gk. 11.167	2
AGIT			
Pastor agit pecudes, teneros modo suscipit agnos, . . .	O 90	Messiah	59
Lympha tamen cursus agit indefessa perennis, ...	O 228	Rivum a Stoana	9
AGMEN			
Ante suas agmen Lais habere fores, ...	O 209	Tr. Greek 6.1	2
AGMINA			
Non ultra infestis concurrent agmina signis, ...	O 90	Messiah	66
AGNA			
Per valles sociata lupo lasciviet agna, ...	O 91	Messiah	84
AGNOS			
Pastor agit pecudes, teneros modo suscipit agnos, . . .	O 90	Messiah	59
AGNOSCITE			
En! Salvator adest; vultus agnoscite caeci	O 89	Messiah	42
AGROS			
Harmonia tellus completur lata, per agros	Y 28	Aurora Musis	3
AHENIS			
Non litui accendent bellum, non campus ahenis	O 90	Messiah	68
AIT			
Clam nocte tollit Aulus, et ridens ait;	O 223	Tr. Gk. 11.176	4
Nunc age, certamen nunc ineamus, ait;	O 384	Epigramma	D 2
AJACI			
Hector dat gladium Ajaci, dat balteum et Ajax	O 210	Tr Greek 7.151	1
AJAX			
Hector dat gladium Ajaci, dat balteum et Ajax	O 210	Tr Greek 7.151	1
ALACRES			
Tunc alacres demum surgent, et crastinus ortus	O 393	Tr. of Crashaw	D 5
ALAT			
Ingenium jubeas purior haustus alat.	O 85	Mea nec Falern	6
ALE			
Sic ale, proveniat messis ut ampla boni.	O 207	Prayers VII	4
ALERE			
Multa alere, et multas aedificare domos.	O 222	Tr. Gk. 10.119	2
ALEXANDRI			
Funus Alexandri mentitur fama; fidesque	O 210	Tr Greek 7.239	1
ALIBI			
Latrones, alibi locupletum quaerite tecta, ...	O 219	Tr Greek 9.654	1
ALIENAE			
Tu neque dulce putes alienae accumbere mensae, ...	O 218	Tr Greek 9.573	1
ALIIS			
Tutum aliis aequor, me pereunte, fuit.	O 210	Tr Greek 7.282	2
Nunc huic, nunc aliis cedens, cui farra Menippus . . .	O 215	Tr Greek 9.74	1
Terror inest aliis, moerorque, et siquid habebis . . .	O 222	Tr. Gk. 10.123	5
Sic aliis dives, tu tibi pauper agis.	O 223	Tr. Gk. 11.167	2
ALIMENTA			
Hic, bone vir, sedem, non alimenta, peto.	O 224	Tr. Gk. 11.391	4
ALIMENTACUE			
Nectareos rores, alimentaque mitia coelum	O 88	Messiah	14
ALIOS			
Faelix ante alios nullius debitor aeris;	O 222	Tr Greek 11.50	1
ALIS			
Nuncia sacra Dei, plaudentibus insidet alis.	O 88	Messiah	13
ALIT			
Mortales miseros servat, alit, fovet, ...	O 155	Psalmus 117	6
ALIUS			
Atthide non alius desit Olympus, habet.	O 219	Tr Greek 9.702	2
Et Pari, et Anchisa, non alius, Venerem.	O 225	Tr. Gk. 16.168	2
ALLEVA			
Mentem benignus alleva.	O 206	Prayers II	11
ALMA			
Compositis Pax alma suas, terrasque revisens	O 89	Messiah	23
Ambraciota, vale lux alma, Cleombrotus infit, ...	O 211	Tr Greek 7.471	1
Luce collustret mihi pectus alma, ...	O 227	A Meditation	1
Veris, io! venit alma dies! Philomela canorum	O 385	Cantico Solom.	D 7
Huc, soror alma, veni! pernicibus ocyor Euris	O 385	Cantico Solom.	D 17
Huc, soror alma, veni!	O 385	Cantico Solom.	D 18
ALME			
Alme voco, impatiens noctis metuensque diei.	O 161	Gnothi seauton	31
ALTA			
Nil mortale loquor, coelum mihi carminis alta	O 88	Messiah	2
Secta crepet nimis alta fallax.	O 166	Oda Isle Skye	16
Grandiloquus nimis alta Zeno.	O 166	Oda Isle Skye	V 16
Quam tenet hic, cunctas quae manet, alta quies. . . .	O 211	Tr Greek 7.459	4

```
                                                           PAGE    TITLE            LINE
ALTER
     Me, cane vitato, canis excipit alter; eodem    . . .  O 213  Tr Greek 9.18        1
     Hic, aurum ut reperit, laqueum abjicit, alter ut aurum  .  O 213  Tr Greek 9.44        1
     Alter ut adsit Homerus, adest etenim alter Achilles.  .   O 218  Tr Greek 9.523       2
     Alter ut adsit Homerus, adest etenim alter Achilles.  . .  O 218  Tr Greek 9.523       2
     "Qui scribat meritas, Birchius alter erit."  . . . . .  O 386  In Birchium     D   6
ALTERA
     Altera pars hominum, sanctae rationis alumni,  . . . .  O 163  To Dr Lawrence      19
ALTERI
     Habeo, dedi quod alteri;  . . . . . . . . . . . . . . .  O 165  Tr Doncast Epi       1
ALTIUS
     Altius, en! Lebanon gaudentia culmina tollit,  . . . .  O  89  Messiah             30
ALTO
     Clarus Joannes, reginae affinis, ab alto  . . . . . .  O 212  Tr Greek 7.590       1
ALTRICI
     Haec habet altrici Capra secunda Jovis.  . . . . . . .  O 156  Collari Caprae       2
ALTUM
     Non Fortuna sibi te gratum tollit in altum;  . . . . .  O 218  Tr Greek 9.530       1
ALUMNI
     Altera pars hominum, sanctae rationis alumni,  . . . .  O 163  To Dr Lawrence      19
AMABILE
     Reclusisque oculis infundet amabile lumen,  . . . . .  O  90  Messiah             45
AMANS
     Surgit amans abies teretis, buxique sequaces  . . . .  O  91  Messiah             81
AMARE
     Et colere et leges semper amare tuas. . . . . . . . .  O 208  Prayers VII         10
AMAROR
     Et melli nimio fellis amaror inest.  . . . . . . . . .  O 224  Tr Greek 16.16       2
AMAS
     Summe Deus, qui semper amas quodcunque creasti,  . . .  O 198  Tr. Ash Wed.         1
AMATOREM
     Ad Ricardum Savage, Arm. Humani Generis Amatorem. . . .  O 102  Ad R. Savage         T
AMBIGUA
     Atque Aethra ambigua pallida luce rubet;  . . . . . .  Y  28  Aurora Musis         2
AMBITA
     Perpetui, ambita bis terra, praemia lactis  . . . . .  O 156  Collari Caprae       1
     Perpetua, ambita bis terra, praemia lactis  . . . . .  O 156  Collari Caprae   V   1
AMBITIOSA
     Quid majus mihi spes ambitiosa dabit? . . . . . . . .  O 104  To Eliz Carter       4
AMBO
     Praecones ambo, Nummus utrique Deus.  . . . . . . . .  O 385  The Warehouse    D   2
AMBRACIOTA
     Ambraciota, vale lux alma, Cleombrotus infit,  . . . .  O 211  Tr Greek 7.471       1
AMBROSIIS
     Expleor ambrosiis exhilarorque cibis.  . . . . . . . .  O 219  Tr Greek 9.577       4
AMICA
     Excipit aethereis, Ars omnis plaudit amica,  . . . . .  O 161  Gnothi seauton      21
AMICE
     Amice, majorem querelis,  . . . . . . . . . . . . . .  O 187  Ad T. L. M.D.       19
     Quid tibi, mus, mecum, dixit, amice, tibi?  . . . . .  O 224  Tr. Gk. 11.391       2
AMICO
     Excipit aethereis, Ars omnis plaudit amico,  . . . . .  O 161  Gnothi seauton   V  21
AMICTU
     Sedatas niveo Virtus lucebit amictu.  . . . . . . . .  O  89  Messiah             24
     Pacatas niveo Virtus lucebit amictu.  . . . . . . . .  O  89  Messiah          V  24
AMICUM
     Hostem odit tacite, sed amicum ridet aperte . . . . .  O 197  On Mrs. Thrale       1
AMISSAS
     Amissas modo quaerit oves, revocatque vagantes;  . . .  O  90  Messiah             61
AMITTAT
     Ut florem amittat gratia tota perit  . . . . . . . . .  Y 332  Tr Greek 10.30   V   1
AMOR
     Patrem cujus amor blandior in dies  . . . . . . . . .  O 155  Psalmus 117          5
     Regem cujus amor laetior in dies  . . . . . . . . . .  O 155  Psalmus 117      V   5
     Omnibus unus amor, non est modus unus amoris.  . . . .  O 163  To Dr Lawrence       8
     Quas Amor undarum fingeret esse deas:  . . . . . . . .  O 169  Insula Kenneth      10
     Quas Amor undarum crederet esse deas:  . . . . . . . .  O 169  Insula Kenneth   V  10
     Hic secura quies, hic et honestus amor.  . . . . . . .  O 170  Insula Kenneth      22
     Sit sacer orbis amor, miseris qui semper adesse  . . .  O 205  Christianus          7
     Velle vetet cuiquam non bene sanctus amor.  . . . . .  O 207  Prayers VII          8
     In vos ne missus spicula tendat amor.  . . . . . . . .  O 213  Tr Greek 9.39        2
     Mulcet amor prolis, sopor est sine prole profundus;  .  O 217  Tr Greek 9.360       7
     Divino, sanctus regnet ut intus amor:  . . . . . . . .  O 232  Prayer               6
     Supremis junxit nexibus arctus amor.  . . . . . . . .  O 393  Tr. of Crashaw   D   2
AMORE
     Et summi accendat pectus amore boni.  . . . . . . . .  O 170  Insula Kenneth   V 16B
     Caeco ducit amore,  . . . . . . . . . . . . . . . . .  O 182  Waltoni Piscat      12
     Certa mihi sancto flagret amore fides.  . . . . . . .  O 207  Prayers VII          6
     Quem fundit blando junctus amore dolor;  . . . . . . .  O 212  Tr Greek 7.560       2
AMOREM
     Sola rates struis infidas, et dulcis amorem  . . . . .  O 213  Tr Greek 9.29        3
AMORIS
     Omnibus unus amor, non est modus unus amoris.  . . . .  O 163  To Dr Lawrence       8
AMPHILOCHI
     Mugitum tumulus comprimit Amphilochi.  . . . . . . . .  O 213  Tr Greek 8.137       2
AMPLA
     Sic ale, proveniat messis ut ampla boni.  . . . . . .  O 207  Prayers VII          4
AMPLEXU
     Summus amplexu foveat, beato  . . . . . . . . . . . .  O 227  A Meditation         6
AMPLIUS
     Scire vices ponti facile est, nihil amplius optant  . .  O 163  To Dr Lawrence      15
```

	PAGE	TITLE		LINE
Restat? an accingar studiis gravioribus audax?	O 162	Gnothi seauton		53
. . . Johnson, as he lay confined with an inflamed Eye.	O 162	Ad T. L. M.D.		T
Materies, vastum an late pandatur inane.	O 163	To Dr Lawrence		14
Materia, vastum an late pandatur inane.	O 163	To Dr Lawrence	V	14
The Logical Warehouse: Occasioned by an Auctioneer's	O 385	The Warehouse	D	T
ANAPAESTICAE				
Nugae anapaesticae in lecto lusae. ...	O 198	Medico Aeger	S	T
ANASTASII				
Sanguine Anastasii; cuncta sepulta jacent:	O 212	Tr Greek 7.590		2
ANCHISA				
Et Pari, et Anchisa, non alius, Venerem.	O 225	Tr. Gk. 16.168		2
ANEMONE				
Hic anemone humet, confert narcissus odores	O 209	Tr. Greek 5.74		3
ANGIT				
Lux angit miseros cadens homullos.	O 204	Spes		6
Lux angit, miseros ludens homullos.	O 204	Spes	V	6
ANGLIA				
Centuriae quartae decades quinque Anglia nectit.	O 230	Geographia Met		30
ANGLIACAS				
Angliacas inter pulcherrima Laura puellas,	O 115	Ad Lauram Epig		1
ANGLIAE				
Haec fausta vobis dicimus, Angliae	O 188	Epilogus		2
ANGLICANUM				
(Post Lexicon Anglicanum auctum et emendatum.)	O 160	Gnothi seauton		T
ANGLUS				
Quos laudet vates Graius Romanus et Anglus	O 86	Tr Dryden Milt		1
Quos laudet vates Graecus Romanus et Anglus	O 86	Tr Dryden Milt	V	1
Carmen grande sonans; Anglus utrumque tulit.	O 86	Tr Dryden Milt		4
ANGUSTA				
Res angusta domi, et macrae penuria mentis.	O 161	Gnothi seauton		41
ANIMAE				
Coelestes lambunt animae; ramisque columba,	O 88	Messiah		12
ANIMI				
Hi sunt quos animi generosa insania magni	O 163	To Dr Lawrence		31
Triste nihil passus, animi at de sorte Platonis	O 211	Tr Greek 7.471		3
Pellat et tristes animi tenebras,	O 227	A Meditation		2
ANIMIS				
Exsurge fortis, nunc animis opus,	O 187	Ad T. L. M.D.		14
ANIMO				
Juxta Animo Studiisque felix.	O 101	Ad Urbanum		8
Ingentemque animo seclorum volverat orbem.	O 160	Gnothi seauton		11
Ingentemque animo seclorum volveret orbem.	O 160	Gnothi seauton	V	11
Da veteres noxas animo sic flere novato,	O 198	Tr. Ash Wed.		3
Da veteres culpas animo sic flere novato,	O 198	Tr. Ash Wed.	V	3
Noctes atque dies animo spes laeta recurset,	O 207	Prayers VII		5
In me animo tellus gignit et unda feras,	O 213	Tr Greek 9.18		2
Vive tuo ex animo, vario rumore loquetur	O 214	Tr Greek 9.50		1
ANIMOS				
Forma animos hominum capit, at, si gratia desit,	O 209	Tr. Greek 5.67		1
ANIMOSA				
Sedulitas animosa tendet.	O 101	Ad Urbanum		12
ANIMUM				
Gratum animum laudo; Qui debuit omnia ventis,	O 143	On Lord Anson		1
Datur nec aequum cuique animum sibi	O 166	Oda Isle Skye		14
Paulatim mores, animum, vitamque refingit,	O 205	Christianus		28
ANIMUS				
Congestas animus, laetos aut sumit honores	O 161	Gnothi seauton	V	40
Non Rationis opes Animus, nunc parta recensens,	O 161	Gnothi seauton		42
Non Animus sero nimium dum parta recenset,	O 161	Gnothi seauton	V	42
ANNI				
Volvantur celeres anni! Lux purpuret ortum	O 89	Messiah		25
Anni qua volucris ducitur orbita,	O 155	Psalmus 117		1
ANNIS				
Sexaginta annis non minor unus erit.	O 171	Tr. Busy Fly		12
Me miserum sors omnis habet; florentibus annis	O 215	Tr Greek 9.138		1
Hinc annis palpantur delenda poemata nullis	Y 28	Aurora Musis		11
Hinc annis palpantur delenda poemata palpantur	Y 28	Aurora Musis	V	11
ANNOS				
Impatiens, lenteque fluentes increpat annos.	O 92	Messiah		98
ANNUA				
Menstrua concinnat Sylvanus, & Annua Dona,	O 383	Syl. Urb. Thes	D	1
ANNUE				
Annue, Christe.	O 194	Prayer on Xmas		8
ANNUS				
Tu, quamcunque tibi velox indulserit annus,	O 171	Tr. Busy Fly		5
Vitam a terdecimo sextus mihi finiet annus,	O 215	Tr Greek 9.112		1
ANTE				
Ante Oculos Natos	O 110	Post-genitis		31
Sed timeat semper, caveatque ante omnia, turbae	O 205	Christianus		19
Ante suas agmen Lais habere fores,	O 209	Tr. Greek 6.1		2
Faelix ante alios nullius debitor aeris;	O 222	Tr Greek 11.50		1
ANTIOPE				
Antiope satyrum, Danae aurum, Europa juvencum,	O 214	Tr Greek 9.48		1
ANTIQUA				
Apte antiqua novis miscentur, et utile dulci:	O 383	Syl. Urb. Thes	D	3
ANTRIS				
Non tamen inculti gelidis latuere sub antris,	O 169	Insula Kenneth		11
Nec tamen inculti gelidis latuere sub antris,	O 169	Insula Kenneth	V	11
ANTRUM				
Ingredere! Egeriae sacrum en tibi panditur antrum!	O 116	Tr Pope Grotto		9

		PAGE	TITLE	LINE

ANUS
    Terribili fremitu stridula moeret anus. . . . . . .   O 383 On the Gin-Act   D   2
ANXIETAS
    Anxietas noceat ne tenebrosa mihi. . . . .   O 207 Prayers VII   2
    Quem nulla anxietas, nulla cupido fugit; . . . . . .   O 232 Prayer   2
ACNIDESQUE
    Aonidesque Deae, et mendacis somnia Pindi. . . . . .   O 88 Messiah   5
APERTA
    Tectaque qua fluxit, nunc et aperta fluit. . . . . .   O 228 Rivum a Stoana   10
APERTE
    Hostem odit tacite, sed amicum ridet aperte . . . . .   O 197 On Mrs. Thrale   1
APOLLO
    Tunc vati facilem reprobat Apollo, Sybillae . . . . .   Y 28 Aurora Musis   7
APTAM
    Queis tamen aptam ferre medelam . . . .   O 193 Tr. Medea III   9
APTANS
    Plenum opus effugiens; aptans juga mollia collo . . .   O 205 Christianus   22
APTE
    Apte antiqua novis miscentur, et utile dulci: . . . .   O 383 Syl. Urb. Thes   D   3
APTUM
    Quem decuit majora sequi, majoribus aptum, ...   O 160 Gnothi seauton   7
AQUA
    Nutrit mane, putes esse Heliconis aqua. . . . . . .   Y 28 Aurora Musis   6
AQUARUM
    Quas navis recipit, quantum sit pondus aquarum, . . .   O 229 Epigram III   1
AQUAS
    Nota, Caledonias panditur inter aquas; . . . .   O 169 Insula Kenneth   2
    Clara, Caledonias panditur inter aquas; . . . . . .   O 169 Insula Kenneth   V   2
    Naufragus iratas ille retentat aquas. . . . .   O 215 Tr Greek 9.133   2
    Pendula secretas abdidit arbor aquas. . . . .   O 228 Rivum a Stoana   6
ARABS
    Carpit Arabs, hortis quicquid frondescit eois. . . . .   O 89 Messiah   29
    Pastor Arabs: decies octo sibi Persa requirit. . . . .   O 230 Geographia Met   9
ARAE
    Ecce! cremant genibus tritae regalibus arae. . . . .   O 92 Messiah   103
ARATOR
    Vel Arator vcmere franget, ...   O 109 Post-genitis   4
ARBITER
    Rerum perpetuus temperat Arbiter, ...   O 164 Recover Eyes   2
    Rex summe, solus tu regis arbiter, ...   O 166 Oda Isle Skye   18
ARBOR
    Virgo! virgo parit! felix radicibus arbor . . . . .   O 88 Messiah   10
    Pendula secretas abdidit arbor aquas. . . . .   O 228 Rivum a Stoana   6
ARBOREASQUE
    Arboreasque comas; . . . .   O 385 Cantico Solom.   D   12
ARBORIBUS
    Telluri arboribus ver frondens, sidera coelo, ...   O 214 Tr Greek 9.65   1
ARCA
    Pauper eram, nummis diffluit arca senis; . . . . . .   O 215 Tr Greek 9.138   2
ARCADES
    Quo rege gaudent Arcades, furem boum, ...   O 223 Tr. Gk. 11.176   2
ARCE
    Nec miratur opes, celsa speculator ab arce . . . . .   O 161 Gnothi seauton   V   39
    Summus adesse jubet celsa dominator ab arce; . . . .   O 162 Gnothi seauton   45
ARCHETYPOS
    Proferet archetypos; coelestis gaudia lucis . . . . .   O 92 Messiah   111
ARCHIDICEN
    Videre, Archidicen haec tumulavit humus; . . . . . .   O 226 Tr. Simonides   2
ARCTO
    Sunt qui curriculo timidi versantur in arcto, ...   O 163 To Dr Lawrence   9
ARCTUS
    Supremis junxit nexibus arctus amor. . . . .   O 393 Tr. of Crashaw   D   2
ARDEAT
    Ardeat huic toto sacer ignis pectore, possit . . . .   O 205 Christianus   10
ARDEO
    Corde meo accendas; ardeo totus ego. . . . .   O 225 Tr. Gk. 16.209   2
ARDUA
    Demissumque Deum tellus capit; ardua cedrus, ...   O 89 Messiah   37
    Tantundem est illis, repleat spatia ardua coeli . . .   O 163 To Dr Lawrence   13
    Denique perpetuo contendit in ardua nisu, ...   O 205 Christianus   25
AREA
    Qui duxit sulcos, illi teret area messem, ...   O 90 Messiah   73
ARENAS
    Suave rubere rosis, sitientesque inter arenas . . . .   O 91 Messiah   76
ARENTIA
    Littora deficiens arentia deseret aequor, ...   O 92 Messiah   114
ARGENTEA
    India nascenti, placidaeve argentea noctis . . . . .   O 92 Messiah   109
ARGIVIS
    Clamat et Argivis: Vetuli, ne tangite, vita . . . . .   O 216 Tr Greek 9.163   3
ARGOS
    Non Argos pugilem, non me Messana creavit; . . . . .   O 224 Tr Greek 16.1   1
ARM
    Ad Ricardum Savage, Arm. Humani Generis Amatorem. . .   O 102 Ad R. Savage   T
ARMA
    Quid mirum Maro quod digne canit arma Virumque, . . .   O 85 Mea nec Falern   1
    Materies arti, sua desunt arma labori . . . .   O 161 Gnothi seauton   V   37
    Omnia, dum Macedum gloria et arma premunt. . . . . .   O 216 Tr Greek 9.288   4
    Vincere te potui nuda, quid arma geram? . . . . . .   O 384 Epigramma   D   4
ARMANT
    Nunc armant Veneris lumina tela Jovis. . . . . . .   O 103 Elizae Aenigma   6

435

ARMATAM
    Armatam Pallas Venerem conspexit, et eia . . . . . .   O 384 Epigramma   D   1
ARCMATICAS
    Mittit arcmaticas vallis Saronica nubes, ...   O 89 Messiah   32
ARRIDENS
    Arridens dcmino collacrymansque tuo, ...   O 218 Tr Greek 9.573   4
ARROGAT
    Quis formae modus imperio? Venus arrogat audax . . .   O 103 Elizae Aenigma   1
ARS
    Excipit aethereis, Ars omnis plaudit amica, ...   O 161 Gnothi seauton   21
    Excipit aethereis, Ars omnis plaudit amico, ...   O 161 Gnothi seauton   V 21
ARTE
    Et juvat ingenii vita sine arte rudis. . . . .   O 104 To Eliz Carter   2
    Quam magis exoptes arte valere tua. . . . . .   O 197 Summ. Lawrence   2
    Arte valent isti, mihi robore vivere solo est, ...   O 224 Tr Greek 16.1   3
    Dissimili domus una duos tenet arte tumentes; . . . .   O 385 The Warehouse   D   1
    Arte nova, raraque fide perscripserat ausus . . . . .   O 386 In Birchium   D   1
ARTES
    Omnibus, artes . . . .   O 199 Medico Aeger S   29
ARTI
    Materies arti, sua desunt arma labori . . . . .   O 161 Gnothi seauton   V 37
    Arti ignis lucem tribui, tamen artis et ignis . . . .   O 225 Tr Greek 16.87   1
ARTIFICIS
    Artificis frondent dextrae; palmisque rubeta . . . .   O 91 Messiah   82
    Artificis frondent dextrae; Spinetaque Palmis . . . .   O 91 Messiah   V 82
ARTIS
    Arti ignis lucem tribui, tamen artis et ignis . . . .   O 225 Tr Greek 16.87   1
ARVA
    Sive dies medius morientia torreat arva: . . . . . .   O 90 Messiah   63
    Sive dies medius languentia torreat arva: . . . . . .   O 90 Messiah   V 63
AS
    . . . Johnson, as he lay confined with an inflamed Eye.   O 162 To Dr Lawrence   T
ASCLEPIADES
    Murem Asclepiades sub tecto ut vidit avarus, ...   O 224 Tr. Gk. 11.391   1
ASIAM
    Vicenis quinas, Asiam metata celebrem. . . . . . .   O 230 Geographia Met   22
ASPERA
    Deserti laeta mollescunt aspera voce, ...   O 89 Messiah   34
    Deserta et lata mollescunt aspera voce, ...   O 89 Messiah   V 34
    Aspera, odoratae cedunt mala gramina myrto. . . . . .   O 91 Messiah   83
    Divitiis acuens aspera corda virum; . . . . . .   O 213 Tr Greek 9.29   2
    Rus ornat natura; levat maris aspera lucrum; . . . .   O 217 Tr Greek 9.360   3
ASPICE
    Aspice, diffugiunt ignavae frigora brumae; . . . . .   O 384 Cantico Solom.   D   3
ASPICERE
    Multis ut te oculis sim potis aspicere. . . . . . .   O 212 Tr Greek 7.669   2
ASSIDET
    Assidet huic custos strenua pauperies. . . . . . .   O 219 Tr Greek 9.654   2
ASSURGITQUE
    Assurgitque epicis pagina docta modis. . . . . . .   Y 28 Aurora Musis   10
ASTRA
    Astra mathematicos si modo vera docent. . . . . . .   O 215 Tr Greek 9.112   2
    Aevi sat novi quam sim brevis; astra tuenti, ...   O 219 Tr Greek 9.577   1
AT
    At Seni fluxo sapienter uti . . . .   O 153 In Theatro   15
    At non cavata rupe latescere, ...   O 166 Oda Isle Skye   9
    At nemo feras iras hominum, ...   O 193 Tr. Medea III   6
    Vult Deus, at, qui cuncta dedit tibi, cuncta reposcit. .   O 205 Christianus   24
    Forma animos hominum capit, at, si gratia desit, . . .   O 209 Tr. Greek 5.67   1
    Triste nihil passus, animi at de sorte Platonis . . .   O 211 Tr Greek 7.471   3
    Pulchra est virginitas intacta, at vita periret, . . .   O 218 Tr Greek 9.444   1
    At docet, exemplo, vis sibi quanta, tuo. . . . . . .   O 218 Tr Greek 9.530   2
    At te bonum si noris, et bonis natum, ...   O 224 Tr Greek 13.3   3
    Laevum at utrumque decus, juveni quod praebuit olim . .   O 225 Tr Greek 16.364   3
    At tu quisquis eris, miseri qui cruda poetae . . . .   Y 387 Death Mother   D   1
ATQUE
    Compagem edificat, coelorum atque aetheris ignes . . .   O 163 To Dr Lawrence   29
    Noctes atque dies animo spes laeta recurset, ...   O 207 Prayers VII   5
    Sed Miliae ridens, atque dolens Miliae. . . . . . .   O 218 Tr Greek 9.573   6
    Quam, regum sobolem, nuptam, matrem, atque sororem . .   O 226 Tr. Simonides   3
    Atque Aethra ambigua pallida luce rubet; . . . . .   Y 28 Aurora Musis   2
    "Perge modo, atque tuas olim post funera laudes . . .   O 386 In Birchium   D   5
ATRA
    Tristis et atra quies, et tardae taedia vitae. . . . .   O 161 Gnothi seauton   26
ATRIA
    Atria, pacis opus, surgent, finemque caduci . . . . .   O 90 Messiah   71
    En! formosa tibi porrecta per atria proles . . . . .   O 92 Messiah   96
    En! formosa tibi spatiosa per atria proles . . . . .   O 92 Messiah   V 96
ATTHIDE
    Atthide non alius desit Olympus, habet. . . . . . .   O 219 Tr Greek 9.702   2
ATTOLIT
    Cum caput Hesperiis attolit Phoebus ab undis, ...   Y 28 Aurora Musis   1
ATTOLLET
    Attollet reducis; bellis praetendet olivas . . . . .   O 89 Messiah   22
ATTONITI
    Attoniti dumeta vident inculta coloni . . . .   O 91 Messiah   75
AUCTA
    Proles aucta gravat, rapta orbat, caeca juventae est . .   O 217 Tr Greek 9.359   7
AUCTIONEER'S
    The Logical Warehouse: Occasioned by an Auctioneer's . .   O 385 The Warehouse   D   T

		PAGE	TITLE	LINE
AUCTUM				
(Post Lexicon Anglicanum auctum et emendatum.) · · · · ·		O 160	Gnothi seauton	T
Incultum Studiis, et paucis dotibus auctum · · · · ·		O 161	Gnothi seauton	V 36
AUDACIA				
Puppe gubernatrix sedisti, Audacia, prima, · · · · ·		O 213	Tr Greek 9.29	1
AUDAX				
Quis formae modus imperio? Venus arrogat audax · · · ·		O 103	Elizae Aenigma	1
Restat? an accingar studiis gravioribus audax? · · · ·		O 162	Gnothi seauton	53
Ne stolidae similis leges sibi segreget audax · · · ·		O 205	Christianus	20
De te plebs audax, hic bene et ille male. · · · · ·		O 214	Tr Greek 9.50	2
AUDEBIT				
Nec fremere audebit · · · · · · · · · · · ·		O 109	Post-genitis	27
AUDENT				
Dum statuunt, causisque audent prefigere metam. · · ·		O 163	To Dr Lawrence	36
AUDIIT				
Audiit, irata est ne nova Musa foret. · · · · · · ·		O 214	Tr Greek 9.66	2
AUDITUR				
Auditur Deus! ecce Deus! reboantia circum · · · ·		O 89	Messiah	35
AUFERS				
Si forsan tumulum quo conditur Eumarus aufers, · · · ·		O 210	Tr Greek 7.284	3
AUGENT				
Centuria Ligures augent duo millia quarta. · · · · ·		O 230	Geographia Met	14
AULA				
Illic Leniades humili regnabat in aula, · · · · ·		O 169	Insula Kenneth	7
AULUS				
Clam nocte tollit Aulus, et ridens ait; · · · · ·		O 223	Tr. Gk. 11.176	4
AURE				
Laurenti saltem facili dignarier aure? · · · · ·		O 163	To Dr Lawrence	5
AUREA				
Coelicolae pandunt, torrentisque aurea lucis · · · ·		O 92	Messiah	107
Coelicolae pandunt, crescentis et aurea lucis · · · ·		O 92	Messiah	V 107
Coelicolae pandunt, torrentis aurea lucis · · · ·		O 92	Messiah	V 107
Aurea secla hominum, quorum spectandus ocellis · · · ·		O 213	Tr Greek 9.29	5
AUREAQUE				
Aureaque admirans rutilantis fulgura cristae. · · · ·		O 91	Messiah	92
AUREM				
Aurem faventem precibus O praebe meis; · · · · ·		O 206	Prayers III	3
AURES				
Divinos, surdas sacra vox permulceat aures! · · · · ·		O 89	Messiah	43
AURI				
Auriferasque, auri metuens, scrutare cavernas. · · · ·		O 116	Tr Pope Grotto	8
Quos Gyges cumulos habebat auri; · · · · · · ·		O 215	Tr Greek 9.110	2
AURIFERASQUE				
Auriferasque, auri metuens, scrutare cavernas. · · · ·		O 116	Tr Pope Grotto	8
AURIS				
Harmoniae purgata novos mirabitur auris. · · · ·		O 90	Messiah	48
Vel digiti tractant, oculus vel sentit et auris: · · ·		O 163	To Dr Lawrence	12
Nam vita incertis incerta impellitur auris, · · · ·		O 221	Tr Greek 10.74	3
AURUM				
Solis Ophyraeis crudum tibi montibus aurum · · · ·		O 92	Messiah	104
Hic, aurum ut reperit, laqueum abjicit, alter ut aurum		O 213	Tr Greek 9.44	1
Hic, aurum ut reperit, laqueum abjicit, alter ut aurum		O 213	Tr Greek 9.44	1
Antiope satyrum, Danae aurum, Europa juvencum, · · · ·		O 214	Tr Greek 9.48	1
AUSCULTANS				
Demophilo auscultans nycticorax moritur. · · · · · ·		O 223	Tr. Gk. 11.186	2
AUSIM				
Ut studiis sperem, aut ausim par esse querelis, · · ·		O 160	Gnothi seauton	15
AUSUS				
Qui, mutare vias ausus terraeque marisque, · · · · ·		O 217	Tr Greek 9.304	1
Arte nova, raraque fide perscripserat ausus · · · ·		O 386	In Birchium	D 1
AUT				
Vis boreae gelida, aut rapidi violentia solis. · · · ·		O 89	Messiah	19
Vis boreae gelida, aut nimii violentia solis. · · · ·		O 89	Messiah	V 19
Ut studiis sperem, aut ausim par esse querelis, · · · ·		O 160	Gnothi seauton	15
Congestas animus, laetos aut sumit honores · · · ·		O 161	Gnothi seauton	V 40
Non numerat palmas, aut · · · · · · · · ·		O 162	Gnothi seauton	V 46
Praeteritis fruitur, laetos aut sumit honores · · · ·		O 162	Gnothi seauton	47
Aut, hoc si nimium est, tandem nova lexica poscam? · ·		O 162	Gnothi seauton	54
Voce aut fidibus pellere docuit · · · · · · · ·		O 193	Tr. Medea III	8
Nunquam jugera messibus onusta, aut · · · · · ·		O 215	Tr Greek 9.110	1
Ridere, aut tecum me lacrimare jubet. · · · · · ·		O 216	Tr Greek 9.148	6
Ergo optent homines, aut nunquam in luminis oras · · ·		O 217	Tr Greek 9.359	9
Venisse, aut visa luce repente mori. · · · · · ·		O 217	Tr Greek 9.359	10
Aut periisse; scatet vita benigna bonis. · · · · ·		O 217	Tr Greek 9.360	10
Mulcere, aut pectus triste levare malis. · · · · ·		O 218	Tr Greek 9.375	8
Praetereunt, aut hos praeterit omne bonum. · · · ·		O 220	Tr Greek 10.31	2
Vita omnis scena est ludusque; aut ludere disce · ·		O 221	Tr Greek 10.72	1
Seria seponens, aut mala dura pati. · · · · ·		O 221	Tr Greek 10.72	2
Non opto aut precibus posco ditescere, paucis · · ·		O 222	Tr. Gk. 10.113	1
Cogitat aut loquitur nil vir, nil cogitat uxor, · · ·		O 226	Tr. Greek	1
AUXILIOQUE				
Auxilioque Dei fretus, jam mente serena · · · · ·		O 205	Christianus	26
AVARUS				
Murem Asclepiades sub tecto ut vidit avarus, · · · ·		O 224	Tr. Gk. 11.391	1
AVERTAT				
Ut precibus justas avertat numinis iras · · · · ·		O 170	Insula Kenneth	V 16A
AVES				
Curas mulcentes dulce eruntur aves. · · · · ·		Y 28	Aurora Musis	4
AVIDAE				
Nec probrosa avidae grata sit offa gulae; · · · · ·		O 218	Tr Greek 9.573	2

	PAGE	TITLE		LINE
AVIIS				
Menti nec aegrae montibus aviis	O 166	Oda Isle Skye		10
AVIS				
Leniades magnis nobilitatus avis:	O 169	Insula Kenneth		8
BABYLONA				
Sexta dolet Babylona, et gaudet septima Christo. . . .	O 226	Septem Aetates	V	4
BACCHUS				
Det Bacchus, dederat quale, Lycurge, tibi.	O 218	Tr Greek 9.375		6
BACILLI				
Consuetus fulcro innixus reptare bacilli	O 90	Messiah		50
BALNEA				
Balnea pellem, ...	O 199	Medico Aeger S		19
BALSAMA				
Maturant radii, tibi balsama sudat Idume.	O 92	Messiah		105
BALTEUM				
Hector dat gladium Ajaci, dat balteum et Ajax	O 210	Tr Greek 7.151		1
BANKS				
Versus Collari Caprae Domini Banks inscribendi	O 156	Collari Caprae		T
BANKS'S				
Inscription on the collar of Mr. Banks's Goat	O 156	Collari Caprae	V	T
BARBA				
Hirce, parem nitido te tua barba facit.	O 224	Tr. Gk. 11.430		2
BARBAM				
Qui pascit barbam si crescit mente, Platoni, ...	O 224	Tr. Gk. 11.430		1
BARBARUS				
Barbarus, en! clarum divino lumine templum	O 92	Messiah		100
BEABIT				
Postera sic pastor divinus secla beabit, ...	O 90	Messiah		64
BEANS				
Et me, cuncta beans cui nocuit dies, ...	O 164	Recover Eyes		8
BEATAM				
Ipso fonte bibes, quae circumfusa beatam	O 92	Messiah		112
BEATO				
Summus amplexu foveat, beato	O 227	A Meditation		6
BEATUM				
Me gregi Sanctus socium beatum	O 227	A Meditation		7
BELGA				
Millia Belga novem.	O 231	Geographia Met		34
BELLIS				
Attollet reducis; bellis praetendet olivas	O 89	Messiah		22
BELLUA				
Neque Bellua victa remugit.	O 110	Post-genitis		38
BELLUM				
Non litui accendent bellum, non campus ahenis	O 90	Messiah		68
BENE				
Quam bene ventorum surgere templa jubet!	O 143	On Lord Anson		2
Ipse sui judex, actae bene munera vitae;	O 162	Gnothi seauton		48
Velle vetet cuiquam non bene sanctus amor.	O 207	Prayers VII		8
De te plebs audax, hic bene et ille male.	O 214	Tr Greek 9.50		2
Das bene collatos, quos Roma et Graecia jactat, . . .	O 225	Tr. Gk. 16.331		3
BENIGNA				
Seu fovet mater sobolem benigna, ...	O 168	Oda to Thrale		14
Aut periisse; scatet vita benigna bonis.	O 217	Tr Greek 9.360		10
Hanc statuam ingenio Roma benigna tuo.	O 225	Tr. Gk. 16.331		2
BENIGNE				
Pater benigne, summa semper lenitas, ...	O 206	Prayers I		1
BENIGNI				
Gaudium sacro fluat, et benigni	O 193	Prayer on Xmas		3
BENIGNO				
Me Pater tandem reducem benigno	O 227	A Meditation		5
BENIGNUS				
Mentem benignus alleva.	O 206	Prayers II		11
O Qui benignus crimina ignoscis, pater	O 206	Prayers III		1
BIBES				
Ipso fonte bibes, quae circumfusa beatam	O 92	Messiah		112
BILANCEM				
Justitiaeque manus pretio intemerata bilancem	O 89	Messiah		21
BINAS				
Undecies binas decadas et millia septem	O 230	Geographia Met		6
BIRCHIUM				
In Birchium	O 386	In Birchium	D	T
BIRCHIUS				
Birchius egregios, claraque gesta virum.	O 386	In Birchium	D	2
"Qui scribat meritas, Birchius alter erit."	O 386	In Birchium	D	6
BIS				
Perpetui, ambita bis terra, praemia lactis	O 156	Collari Caprae		1
Perpetua, ambita bis terra, praemia lactis	O 156	Collari Caprae	V	1
Myrias Aegypto cessit bis septima pingui.	O 229	Geographia Met		3
BLANDA				
His blanda certe pax habitat locis:	O 166	Oda Isle Skye		6
Quae nos blanda comes, quae nos perducat eodem, . . .	O 171	Tr. Busy Fly		7
Dum docuit blanda voce natare pater.	O 228	Rivum a Stoana		4
BLANDAM				
Blandam lanifici sociam, sine fine loquacem, ...	O 211	Tr Greek 7.459		3
BLANDIOR				
Patrem cujus amor blandior in dies	O 155	Psalmus 117		5
BLANDO				
Quem fundit blando junctus amore dolor;	O 212	Tr Greek 7.560		2
BLANDUM				
Pascua, qua blandum spirat purissimus aer	O 90	Messiah		58
Stet fides constans, meritoque blandum	O 168	Oda to Thrale		18

		PAGE	TITLE	LINE
BLANDUM	(CONTINUED)			
Fida mercedem, meritoque blandum		O 168	Oda to Thrale	V 18
Mus blandum ridens, respondit, pelle timorem;		O 224	Tr. Gk. 11.391	3
BCNA				
Hic Bona queis opus est venditat, Ille Sonum.		O 385	The Warehouse	D 6
BCNAE				
Adjecere bonae etc.		O 85	Adjecere bonae	T
BCNE				
Hic, bone vir, sedem, non alimenta, peto.		O 224	Tr. Gk. 11.391	4
BCNI				
Et summi accendat pectus amore boni.		O 170	Insula Kenneth	V 16B
Sic ale, proveniat messis ut ampla boni.		O 207	Prayers VII	4
Forte boni, ultrices experiere vices.		O 222	Tr. Gk. 10.123	6
BCNIS				
Dat Menti propriis Musa nitere bonis.		O 85	Adjecere bonae	2
Aut periisse; scatet vita benigna bonis.		O 217	Tr Greek 9.360	10
Hora bonis quasi nunc instet suprema fruaris, ...		O 219	Tr Greek 10.26	1
Plura ut victurus secula, parce bonis:		O 219	Tr Greek 10.26	2
At te bonum si noris, et bonis natum, ...		O 224	Tr Greek 13.3	3
BCNORUM				
Supra Praeco Dei--strepit infra Praeco Bonorum: . . .		O 385	The Warehouse	D 5
BCNUM				
Praetereunt, aut hos praeterit omne bonum.		O 220	Tr Greek 10.31	2
Magne bonum, omne malum et poscentibus abnue nobis. . .		O 221	Tr Greek 10.108	2
At te bonum si noris, et bonis natum, ...		O 224	Tr Greek 13.3	3
BOREAE				
Vis boreae gelida, aut rapidi violentia solis.		O 89	Messiah	19
Vis boreae gelida, aut nimii violentia solis.		O 89	Messiah	V 19
BOTRUS				
Spirat odore botrus.		O 385	Cantico Solom.	D 16
BCUM				
Quo rege gaudent Arcades, furem boum, ...		O 223	Tr. Gk. 11.176	2
BRACHIA				
Hic delusa rudi frustrabar brachia motu, ...		O 228	Rivum a Stoana	3
BREVIS				
Aevi sat novi quam sim brevis; astra tuenti, ...		O 219	Tr Greek 9.577	1
Omnis vita nimis brevis est felicibus, una		O 220	Tr Greek 10.28	1
Vita rosae brevis est; properans si carpere nolis, . .		O 223	Tr Greek 11.53	1
Vitae rosa brevis est; properans si carpere nolis, . .		O 223	Tr Greek 11.53	V 1
BREVIUS				
Tentat iter brevius, magno conamine summam		O 163	To Dr Lawrence	24
BRITANNIS				
Centurias, et tres decadas Europa Britannis.		O 230	Geographia Met	28
BRUMAE				
Aspice, diffugiunt ignavae frigora brumae;		O 384	Cantico Solom.	D 3
BUCCINA				
Buccina disjecit Thebarum moenia, struxit		O 216	Tr Greek 9.250	1
BUXIQUE				
Surgit amans abies teretis, buxique sequaces		O 91	Messiah	81
BY				
Verses addressed to Dr. Lawrence, composed by Dr. . . .		O 162	To Dr Lawrence	T
The Logical Warehouse: Occasioned by an Auctioneer's . .		O 385	The Warehouse	D T
CACHINNIS				
Nec ficto fletu, fictis solvare cachinnis, ...		O 218	Tr Greek 9.573	3
CACHINNO				
Democrite, invisas homines majore cachinno, ...		O 216	Tr Greek 9.148	1
CADAVERA				
Sint Demosthenica ut jurata cadavera voce, ...		O 216	Tr Greek 9.288	5
CADENS				
Lux angit miseros cadens homullos.		O 204	Spes	6
CADENT				
Saxa cadent, solidque liquescent robora montis: . . .		O 92	Messiah	116
CADUCI				
Atria, pacis opus, surgent, finemque caduci		O 90	Messiah	71
CAECA				
Per caeca noctis taedia turbidae, ...		O 187	Ad T. L. M.D.	9
Proles aucta gravat, rapta orbat, caeca juventae est . .		O 217	Tr Greek 9.359	7
Summe Deus, cui caeca patent penetralia cordis; . . .		O 232	Prayer	1
CAECI				
En! Salvator adest; vultus agnoscite caeci		O 89	Messiah	42
CAECO				
Caeco ducit amore, ...		O 182	Waltoni Piscat	12
Spes ludit stolidas, metuque caeco		O 204	Spes	5
CAECUS				
Fert humeris claudum validis per compita caecus, . . .		O 213	Tr Greek 9.13	1
CAELEBS				
Tecta ineunt; caelebs omnia solus ages;		O 217	Tr Greek 9.359	6
Tecta ineunt, caelebs impediere minus;		O 217	Tr Greek 9.360	6
Hunc sequitur caelebs; tertius, orbe, venis.		O 222	Tr Greek 11.50	2
CALCATOS				
Calcatos et Cruciatos		O 110	Post-genitis	32
CALEDONIAS				
Nota, Caledonias panditur inter aquas;		O 169	Insula Kenneth	2
Clara, Caledonias panditur inter aquas;		O 169	Insula Kenneth	V 2
CALENS				
Immatura calens rapitur per saecula vates, ...		O 88	Messiah	8
Ille futura calens rapitur per saecula vates, ...		O 88	Messiah	V 8
CALENTI				
Haud lavit Phido, haud tetigit; mihi febre calenti . .		O 223	Tr. Gk. 11.118	1
CALLIDUS				
Limosum nobis Promus dat callidus haustum, ...		O 85	Mea nec Falern	3

	PAGE	TITLE	LINE
CALLIOPE			
Sit tibi, Calliope, Parnassum, cura, tenenti, ...	O 218	Tr Greek 9.523	1
CALUERUNT			
Coelestis fido caluerunt semina flammae.	O 116	Tr Pope Grotto	14
CALUMNIIS			
Urbane, nullis victe calumniis, ...	O 101	Ad Urbanum	2
CAMBER			
Undecimum Camber vult septem millibus addi.	O 231	Geographia Met	36
CAMOENA			
Quid quod putidulum nostra Camoena sonat?	O 85	Mea nec Falern	2
CAMOENAS			
Participes operae Camoenas.	O 101	Ad Urbanum	16
CAMPUS			
Non litui accendent bellum, non campus ahenis	O 90	Messiah	68
CANE			
Me, cane vitato, canis excipit alter; eodem	O 213	Tr Greek 9.18	1
CANENTEM			
Mnemosyne, ut Sappho mellita voce canentem	O 214	Tr Greek 9.66	1
CANENTI			
Nycticorax cantat lethale, sed ipsa canenti	O 223	Tr. Gk. 11.186	1
CANIS			
Me, cane vitato, canis excipit alter; eodem	O 213	Tr Greek 9.18	1
Sidereus tamen hic territat, ecce, canis!	O 213	Tr Greek 9.18	4
CANIT			
Quid mirum Maro quod digne canit arma Virumque, . . .	O 85	Mea nec Falern	1
CANITIES			
Virtus, canities cauta vigore caret.	O 217	Tr Greek 9.359	8
CANNA			
Canna viret, juncique tremit mutabilis umbra.	O 91	Messiah	79
Canna viret, juncique tremit variabilis umbra.	O 91	Messiah	V 79
CANORIS			
Tene mulceri fidibus canoris?	O 153	In Theatro	5
CANORUM			
Veris, io! venit alma dies! Philomela canorum	O 385	Cantico Solom.	D 7
CANOS			
Quam decet canos male literatos	O 153	In Theatro	3
CANTAT			
Nycticorax cantat lethale, sed ipsa canenti	O 223	Tr. Gk. 11.186	1
CANTICO			
Ex Cantico Solomonis	O 384	Cantico Solom.	D T
CANTORUM			
Tene cantorum modulis stupere?	O 153	In Theatro	6
CANTU			
Hae poterant uvae laeto convivia cantu	O 218	Tr Greek 9.375	7
CANTUM			
Cantum, vitae dulce levamen.	O 193	Tr. Medea III	5
CAPAXQUE			
Subtile ingenium quaero, capaxque mei, ...	O 209	Tr Greek 7.128	2
CAPIT			
Nil majus Natura capit: clarare priores	O 86	Tr Dryden Milt	5
Demissumque Deum tellus capit; ardua cedrus, ...	O 89	Messiah	37
Forma animos hominum capit, at, si gratia desit, . . .	O 209	Tr. Greek 5.67	1
Et senium triplex Nestoris urna capit.	O 215	Tr Greek 9.112	4
CAPRA			
Haec habet altrici Capra secunda Jovis.	O 156	Collari Caprae	2
CAPRAE			
Versus Collari Caprae Domini Banks inscribendi	O 156	Collari Caprae	T
CAPRAES			
Nunc saltu capraes, nunc cursu provocat euros.	O 90	Messiah	V 51
CAPREAS			
Jam saltu capreas, jam cursu provocat euros.	O 90	Messiah	51
CAPTANS			
Captans, nec fastu tumidus, semperque futuro	O 205	Christianus	3
CAPTARE			
Est proprium, et quavis captare indagine verum, . . .	O 163	To Dr Lawrence	7
CAPUT			
Cum caput Hesperiis attolit Phoebus ab undis, ...	Y 28	Aurora Musis	1
CARBONE			
Sufflato accendis quisquis carbone lucernam, ...	O 225	Tr. Gk. 16.209	1
CARENS			
Sit contenta mihi vita dolore carens.	O 222	Tr. Gk. 10.113	2
CARERE			
Teque frui timor est, teque carere dolor.	O 218	Tr Greek 9.394	2
CARET			
Virtus, canities cauta vigore caret.	O 217	Tr Greek 9.359	8
CARMELI			
Et juga Carmeli recreant fragrantia coelum.	O 89	Messiah	33
Culmina Carmeli recreant fragrantia coelum.	O 89	Messiah	V 33
CARMEN			
Carmen grande sonans; Anglus utrumque tulit.	O 86	Tr Dryden Milt	4
CARMINA			
Carmina vis nostri scribant meliora Poetae?	O 85	Mea nec Falern	5
Obstrictasque diu linguas in carmina solvet.	O 90	Messiah	46
Qui veterum modo facta ducum, modo carmina vatum, . . .	O 160	Gnothi seauton	8
CARMINE			
Gentes undique carmine.	O 155	Psalmus 117	4
Sancto dicite carmine.	O 155	Psalmus 117	8
Carmine describit Cellantia Numina digne	Y 28	Aurora Musis	9
CARMINIS			
Nil mortale loquor, coelum mihi carminis alta	O 88	Messiah	2

	PAGE	TITLE		LINE
CARNIS				
Abstergat mundi labem, nec gaudia carnis	O 205	Christianus		2
CARPAT				
Rectius vives, sua quisque carpat	O 153	In Theatro		11
CARPE				
Carpe diem, fugit, heu, non revocanda dies!	O 171	Tr. Busy Fly		6
CARPERE				
Vita rosae brevis est; properans si carpere nolis, . .	O 223	Tr Greek 11.53		1
Vitae rosa brevis est; properans si carpere nolis, . .	O 223	Tr Greek 11.53	V	1
CARPIT				
Carpit Arabs, hortis quicquid frondescit eois.	O 89	Messiah		29
CASA				
Una duas habuit casa cum genitore puellas, ...	O 169	Insula Kenneth		9
Una duas tenuit casa cum genitore puellas, ...	O 169	Insula Kenneth	V	9
Una duas cepit casa cum genitore puellas, ...	O 169	Insula Kenneth	V	9
CASSUS				
Qui jacet hic, servus vixit, nunc, lumine cassus, . . .	O 212	Tr Greek 7.538		1
CATENA				
Scelerum catena me laborantem gravi	O 206	Prayers III		4
CATERNA				
Scelerum caterna me laborantem grave	O 206	Prayers III	V	4
CATERVAS				
Victrix per obstantes catervas	O 101	Ad Urbanum		11
CAUSA				
Interea dubito; tecum me causa nec ulla	O 216	Tr Greek 9.148		5
Verte solum, fient causa timoris opes;	O 217	Tr Greek 9.359		4
Haec postrema tibi sit flendi causa, fluatque . . .	Y 387	Death Mother	D	3
CAUSAE				
. . . causae in sermone patrocinata fuerat.	O 105	Lady Defence	V	T
CAUSARUM				
Causarum series quo moderante fluit, ...	O 207	Prayers VI		2
CAUSAS				
Permissum credit nudas sibi sistere causas, ...	O 163	To Dr Lawrence		20
CAUSIDICI				
Dicite, Causidici, gelido nunc marmore magni	O 213	Tr Greek 8.137		1
CAUSISQUE				
Dum statuunt, causisque audent prefigere metam. . . .	O 163	To Dr Lawrence		36
CAUTA				
Virtus, canities cauta vigore caret.	O 217	Tr Greek 9.359		8
CAVATA				
At non cavata rupe latescere, ...	O 166	Oda Isle Skye		9
CAVE				
Cerbere, te morsu ne petat ille, cave.	O 211	Tr Greek 7.319		2
CAVEATQUE				
Sed timeat semper, caveatque ante omnia, turbae . . .	O 205	Christianus		19
CAVENS				
Divitiis, utrinque cavens, qui tempore parcit, . . .	O 219	Tr Greek 10.26		3
CAVERNAS				
Auriferasque, auri metuens, scrutare cavernas. . . .	O 116	Tr Pope Grotto		8
CECINERUNT				
En! quem turba diu cecinerunt enthea, vates, ...	O 89	Messiah		41
CECROPIDIS				
Cecropidis gravis hic ponor, Martique dicatus, . . .	O 216	Tr Greek 9.288		1
CEDENS				
Nunc huic, nunc aliis cedens, cui farra Menippus . . .	O 215	Tr Greek 9.74		1
CEDERE				
Laeto cedere lumini	O 164	Recover Eyes		3
CEDRUS				
Demissumque Deum tellus capit; ardua cedrus, ...	O 89	Messiah		37
CEDUNT				
Aspera, odoratae cedunt mala gramina myrto.	O 91	Messiah		83
CELAT				
Quem nil vafrities peccantum subdola celat;	O 232	Prayer		3
CELEBREM				
Vicenis quinas, Asiam metata celebrem.	O 230	Geographia Met		22
CELERES				
Volvantur celeres anni! Lux purpuret ortum	O 89	Messiah		25
CELLANTIA				
Carmine describit Cellantia Numina digne	Y 28	Aurora Musis		9
CELSA				
Nec miratur opes, celsa speculator ab arce	O 161	Gnothi seauton	V	39
Summus adesse jubet celsa dominator ab ance;	O 162	Gnothi seauton		45
CENNNETHUS				
Voce ubi Cennethus populos domuisse feroces	O 169	Insula Kenneth		3
CENSUS				
Ingeniumque sui cohibet penuria census.	O 161	Gnothi seauton	V	38
CENTUM				
Undecies centum denos quater adde duosque.	O 229	Epigram IV		2
CENTURIA				
Centuria Ligures augent duo millia quarta.	O 230	Geographia Met		14
CENTURIAE				
Centuriae octavam decadem addit Lucca secundae. . . .	O 230	Geographia Met		15
Centuriae quartae decades quinque Anglia nectit. . .	O 230	Geographia Met		30
CENTURIAS				
Centurias, et tres decadas Europa Britannis.	O 230	Geographia Met		28
Ter sex centurias Hollandia jactat opima	O 231	Geographia Met		35
CENTURIIS				
Cum sex centuriis Judaeo millia septem.	O 229	Geographia Met		2
Cum sex centuriis numerat sex millia Tuscus.	O 230	Geographia Met		13
CEPIT				
Una duas cepit casa cum genitore puellas, ...	O 169	Insula Kenneth	V	9

```
CERBERE
    Cerbere, te morsu ne petat ille, cave.  . . . . . . .     O 211 Tr Greek 7.319       2
CERNERE
    Hoc Veneri speculum; nolo me cernere qualis  . . . . .    O 209 Tr. Greek 6.1        3
    Sum nunc, nec possum cernere qualis eram.   . . . . . .    O 209 Tr. Greek 6.1        4
    Exclamat: Nunc me cernere desinitis.   . . . . . . . .     O 224 Tr. Gk. 11.432       2
CERTA
    Certa mihi sancto flagret amore fides.  . . . . . . .      O 207 Prayers VII          6
    Certa vetet dubitare fides, spes laeta timere,  . . . .    O 207 Prayers VII          7
CERTAM
    Da fidem certam, precibusque fidis  . . . . . . . . .      O 194 Prayer on Xmas       7
CERTAMEN
    Nunc age, certamen nunc ineamus, ait;  . . . . . . .       O 384 Epigramma         D  2
CERTAS
    Particulasque locans, certas certo ordine, pulchram  . .   O 163 To Dr Lawrence      28
    Per certas stabili lege voluta vices,  . . . . . . . .     O 219 Tr Greek 9.577       2
CERTE
    His blanda certe pax habitat locis:  . . . . . . . .      O 166 Oda Isle Skye        6
CERTO
    Particulasque locans, certas certo ordine, pulchram  . .   O 163 To Dr Lawrence      28
CESSARUNT
    Cessarunt; pietas hic quoque cura fuit:  . . . . . . .     O 170 Insula Kenneth      18
CESSAT
    Cessat inops rerum, ut torpet, si marmoris absit  . . .    O 161 Gnothi seauton      38
CESSIT
    Nec male res cessit, subito si funere sponsam,  . . . .    O 222 Tr Greek 11.50       3
    Myrias Aegypto cessit bis septima pingui.  . . . . . .     O 229 Geographia Met       3
CESSURA
    Regiam inundabit, nullis cessura tenebris.  . . . . .      O  92 Messiah            113
CHARUS
    Charus enim cunctis, tanquam, dum vita manebat,  . . .     O 212 Tr Greek 7.560       3
CHERONEAE
    Clara Cheroneae soboles, Plutarche, dicavit  . . . . .     O 225 Tr. Gk. 16.331       1
CHRISTE
    Christe, da tutam trepido quietem,  . . . . . . . . .      O 194 Prayer on Xmas       5
    Christe, spem praesta stabilem timenti;  . . . . . . .     O 194 Prayer on Xmas       6
    Annue, Christe.  . . . . . . . . . . . . . . . . .         O 194 Prayer on Xmas       6
    Da, Christe, poenitentiam,  . . . . . . . . . . . .        O 194 Prayer on Xmas       8
    Veniamque, Christe, da mihi;  . . . . . . . . . . .        O 206 Prayers II           6
    Haec mihi, quo gentes, quo secula, Christe, piasti,  . .   O 208 Prayers VII         11
CHRISTI
    Gratia Christi;  . . . . . . . . . . . . . . . . . .       O 227 A Meditation         4
CHRISTO
    Nunc dies Christo memoranda nato  . . . . . . . . . .      O 193 Prayer on Xmas       1
    Qui cupit in sanctos Christo cogente referri,  . . . .     O 205 Christianus          1
    Se fidum addicat Christo, mortalia temnens.  . . . . .     O 205 Christianus         18
    Ut summa laus sit, summa Christo gloria.  . . . . . .      O 206 Prayers III          6
    Cyrum sexta timet; laetatur septima Christo.  . . . .      O 226 Septem Aetates       4
    Sexta dolet Babylona, et gaudet septima Christo.  . . .    O 226 Septem Aetates    V  4
CHRISTUM
    Per Christum ut veniam sit reperire mihi.  . . . . . .     O 198 Tr. Ash Wed.         4
CHRISTUS
    Hoc statuat, precibus Christus adesse velit:  . . . . .    O 204 Losing Speech        2
    Hoc statuant, votis Christus adesse velit:  . . . . . .    O 204 Losing Speech     V  2
    Mihi dona morte haec impetret Christus sua.  . . . . .     O 206 Prayers I           11
    Solvi, quo Christus cunctis delicta redemit,  . . . .      O 207 Prayers V            5
    Haec nobis Christus promeruisse velit!  . . . . . . .      O 232 Prayer              10
CIBIS
    Exploor ambrosiis exhilarorque cibis.  . . . . . . .      O 219 Tr Greek 9.577        4
CIBOS
    Ut mens utatur corpore, sume cibos.  . . . . . . . .      O 228 Jejunium Cibus        2
CIBUS
    Jejunium et Cibus  . . . . . . . . . . . . . . . .         O 228 Jejunium Cibus       T
CINEREM
    Nil lucri facies; ossa habet et cinerem.  . . . . . .      O 210 Tr Greek 7.284       4
CINERES
    Quod mors in cineres solvit, et abdit humo.  . . . . .     O 221 Tr Greek 10.84       4
CINIS
    Cuncta, cinis cuncta et ludicra, cuncta nihil.  . . .      O 222 Tr. Gk. 10.124       2
CINNAMEIS
    Cinnameis cumulis, Nabathaei munere veris,  . . . . .      O  92 Messiah           V 102
CINNAMEOS
    Cinnameos cumulos, Nabathaei munera veris,  . . . . .      O  92 Messiah            102
CIRCUM
    Auditur Deus! ecce Deus! reboantia circum  . . . . . .     O  89 Messiah             35
    Tolle, Salema, sacros, quam circum gloria pennas  . . .    O  92 Messiah             94
    Omnia percurro trepidus, circum omnia lustro,  . . . .     O 161 Gnothi seauton      32
CIRCUMFUSA
    Ipso fonte bibes, quae circumfusa beatam  . . . . . .      O  92 Messiah            112
CIRCUMSONAT
    Multiplici reducem circumsonat ore magistrum.  . . . .     O 161 Gnothi seauton      23
CITATA
    Hora sic peragit citata cursum;  . . . . . . . . . .       O 204 Spes                 1
CIVIS
    Civis et externus grati; domus hospita nescit  . . . .     O 219 Tr Greek 9.648       1
CLAM
    Clam nocte tollit Aulus, et ridens ait;  . . . . . . .     O 223 Tr. Gk. 11.176       4
CLAMAT
    Clamat et Argivis: Vetuli, ne tangite, vita  . . . . .     O 216 Tr Greek 9.163       3
CLAMO
    Pro nullo; clamo nunc tumulatus idem.  . . . . . . . .     O 209 Tr Greek 7.128       4
```

	PAGE	TITLE		LINE
CLAMOSA				
Nunc clamosa juvant nocturnae gaudia mensae, ...	O 161	Gnothi seauton		29
CLARA				
Clara, Caledonias panditur inter aquas;	O 169	Insula Kenneth	V	2
Patria Sparta mihi est, patria clara virum.	O 224	Tr Greek 16.1		2
Clara Cheroneae soboles, Plutarche, dicavit	O 225	Tr. Gk. 16.331		1
CLARAQUE				
Birchius egregios, claraque gesta virum.	O 386	In Birchium	D	2
CLARARE				
Nil majus Natura capit: clarare priores	O 86	Tr Dryden Milt		5
CLARIS				
Domibus claris exitiales, ...	O 193	Tr. Medea III		7
CLARUM				
Barbarus, en! clarum divino lumine templum	O 92	Messiah		100
CLARUS				
Clarus Joannes, reginae affinis, ab alto	O 212	Tr Greek 7.590		1
CLAUDUM				
Fert humeris claudum validis per compita caecus, . . .	O 213	Tr Greek 9.13		1
CLAUSA				
Ponti profundis clausa recessibus, ...	O 166	Oda Isle Skye		1
CLAUSTRA				
Expectata diu! Naturae claustra refringens	O 89	Messiah		26
CLAUSUS				
Gestiat, et, nullo pietatis limite clausus, ...	O 205	Christianus		8
CLEMENTEM				
Suspiciat tandem clementem in numine patrem.	O 205	Christianus		5
CLEMENTIA				
Aeterna tandem liberet clementia, ...	O 206	Prayers III		5
CLEOMBROTUS				
Ambraciota, vale lux alma, Cleombrotus infit, ...	O 211	Tr Greek 7.471		1
CODICES				
Codices, veri studiosus, inter	O 153	In Theatro		10
COELESTES				
Coelestes lambunt animae; ramisque columba, ...	O 88	Messiah		12
COELESTIA				
Materies; poscunt gravius coelestia plectrum.	O 88	Messiah		3
Materies; poscunt graves coelestia plectrum.	O 88	Messiah	V	3
Induit, et, terris major, coelestia spirat.	O 205	Christianus		30
COELESTIS				
Proferet archetypos; coelestis gaudia lucis	O 92	Messiah		111
Coelestis fido caluerunt semina flammae.	O 116	Tr Pope Grotto		14
COELI				
Copia, Phidiaci foecunda potentia coeli.	O 161	Gnothi seauton		39
Tantundem est illis, repleat spatia ardua coeli . . .	O 163	To Dr Lawrence		13
Gratia Coeli!	O 193	Prayer on Xmas		4
COELICOLAE				
Coelicolae pandunt, torrentisque aurea lucis	O 92	Messiah		107
Coelicolae pandunt, crescentis et aurea lucis	O 92	Messiah	V	107
Coelicolae pandunt, torrentis aurea lucis	O 92	Messiah	V	107
COELICOLUM				
Patrem coelicolum perpetuo colunt	O 155	Psalmus 117		2
Regem coelicolum pepetuo colunt	O 155	Psalmus 117	V	2
COELIQUE				
Dixerat, imperiique vices, coelique meatus, ...	O 160	Gnothi seauton		10
CCELO				
Me, pater omnipotens, de puro respice coelo, ...	O 207	Prayers V		1
Telluri arboribus ver frondens, sidera coelo, ...	O 214	Tr Greek 9.65		1
COELORUM				
Compagem edificat, coelorum atque aetheris ignes . . .	O 163	To Dr Lawrence		29
COELUM				
Nil mortale loquor, coelum mihi carminis alta	O 88	Messiah		2
Nectareos rores, alimentaque mitia coelum	O 88	Messiah		14
Et juga Carmeli recreant fragrantia coelum.	O 89	Messiah		33
Culmina Carmeli recreant fragrantia coelum.	O 89	Messiah	V	33
Nec mirum; restat lepori conscendere coelum, ...	O 213	Tr Greek 9.18		3
CCENAE				
Copia coenae.	O 193	Tr. Medea III		15
COEPTA				
Natus ad optatum perducet coepta parentis.	O 90	Messiah		72
COERCEBUNT				
Vincla coercebunt luctantem adamantina mortem, ...	O 90	Messiah		54
COERULA				
Huc ego delatus placido per coerula cursu	O 169	Insula Kenneth		5
COGENTE				
Qui cupit in sanctos Christo cogente referri, ...	O 205	Christianus		1
COGITAT				
Cogitat aut loquitur nil vir, nil cogitat uxor, . . .	O 226	Tr. Greek		1
Cogitat aut loquitur nil vir, nil cogitat uxor, . . .	O 226	Tr. Greek		1
COGOR				
Nec quid agam invenio, meditatus grandia, cogor . . .	O 161	Gnothi seauton		34
COHIBET				
Ingeniumque sui cohibet penuria census.	O 161	Gnothi seauton	V	38
COHORS				
Importuna cohors, vacuae mala somnia mentis.	O 161	Gnothi seauton		28
COLAM				
Te semper studiis utilibus colam:	O 164	Recover Eyes		12
Te, mente pura, mente tranquilla colam:	O 206	Prayers I		10
COLAT				
O! colat humanum Te foveatque genus!	O 102	Ad R. Savage		2
COLE				
Ingredere O!--Magnam pura cole mente parentem, ...	O 116	Tr Pope Grotto		7

COLE   (CCNTINUED)   PAGE   TITLE   LINE
  Ingredere O!--rerum pura cole mente parentem, ...   O 116 Tr Pope Grotto   V   7
COLENDAS
  Myriadas ter mille homini dat terra colendas.   . . . .   O 230 Geographia Met   20
CCLERE
  Et colere et leges semper amare tuas.   . . . .   O 208 Prayers VII   10
CCLIT
  Phoebe fave, aegrotat quae te colit, ulla nec usquam est O 197 Summ. Lawrence   1
CCLLACRYMANSCUE
  Arridens domino collacrymansque tuo, ...   O 218 Tr Greek 9.573   4
CCLLAR
  Inscription on the collar of Mr. Banks's Goat   . . . .   O 156 Collari Caprae   V   T
CCLLARI
  Versus Collari Caprae Domini Banks inscribendi   . . . . O 156 Collari Caprae   T
COLLATOS
  Das bene collatos, quos Roma et Graecia jactat,   . . .   O 225 Tr. Gk. 16.331   3
COLLO
  Plenum opus effugiens; aptans juga mollia collo   . . .   O 205 Christianus   22
COLLUSTRA
  Summe Pater, puro collustra lumine pectus, ...   O 207 Prayers VII   1
COLLUSTRET
  Luce collustret mihi pectus alma, ...   O 227 A Meditation   1
COLONI
  Attoniti dumeta vident inculta coloni . . . .   O 91 Messiah   75
  Torva ubi rident steriles coloni   . . . .   O 167 Oda to Thrale   3
COLONUS
  Naufragus hic jaceo; contra jacet ecce colonus!   . . .   O 210 Tr Greek 7.265   1
CCLUBRI
  Per ludum pueri injicient, et fessa colubri . . . . .   O 91 Messiah   87
  Serpent per Prata Colubri, ...   O 109 Post-genitis   10
COLUMBA
  Coelestes lambunt animae; ramisque columba, ...   O 88 Messiah   12
COLUMBAE
  Aeriaeque columbae, dantes oscula, jungunt   . . . . .   O 385 Cantico Solom.   D   9
COLUMBAS
  Innocua hic membris permistas membra columbas   . . . .   O 393 Tr. of Crashaw   D   1
COLUNT
  Patrem coelicolum perpetuo colunt   . . . .   O 155 Psalmus 117   2
  Regem coelicolum pepetuo colunt . . . .   O 155 Psalmus 117   V   2
CCMAS
  His redimita comas, mores depone superbos: . . . . .   O 209 Tr. Greek 5.74   5
  Arboreasque comas;   . . . .   O 385 Cantico Solom.   D   12
COMES
  Quae nos blanda comes, quae nos perducat eodem,   . . .   O 171 Tr. Busy Fly   7
  Fida comes mensae, fida comesque tori!   . . . . . .   O 383 On the Gin-Act   D   4
CCMESQUE
  Fida comes mensae, fida comesque tori!   . . . . . .   O 383 On the Gin-Act   D   4
CCMITATA
  Pensilibus fusis, cyatho comitata supremo, ...   O 383 On the Gin-Act   D   1
COMITEM
  Musca, meae comitem, participemque dapis, ...   O 171 Tr. Busy Fly   2
COMMODAT
  Hic oculos socio commodat, ille pedes.   . . . . . .   O 213 Tr Greek 9.13   2
COMPAGEM
  Compagem edificat, coelorum atque aetheris ignes   . . . O 163 To Dr Lawrence   29
COMPITA
  Fert humeris claudum validis per compita caecus,   . . . O 213 Tr Greek 9.13   1
COMPLENT
  Sardiniam cum sexcentis sex millia complent.   . . . .   O 230 Geographia Met   18
COMPLETUR
  Harmonia tellus completur lata, per agros   . . . . .   Y 28 Aurora Musis   3
COMPOSED
  Verses addressed to Dr. Lawrence, composed by Dr.   . . . O 162 To Dr Lawrence   T
CCMPOSITIS
  Compositis Pax alma suas, terrasque revisens   . . . .   O 89 Messiah   23
COMPRIMIT
  Mugitum tumulus comprimit Amphilochi.   . . . .   O 213 Tr Greek 8.137   2
CCMPUTAT
  Non operum serie, seriem dum computat aevi, ...   O 162 Gnothi seauton   46
CONAMINE
  Tentat iter brevius, magno conamine summam   . . . . .   O 163 To Dr Lawrence   24
CONATIBUS
  Quicquid agam, quocunque ferar, conatibus obstat   . . . O 161 Gnothi seauton   40
CONCEDE
  Concede veram poenitentiam, precor, ...   O 206 Prayers I   3
  Concede agendam legibus vitam tuis.   . . . .   O 206 Prayers I   4
CCNCENTUM
  Tollite concentum, Solymaeae tollite nymphae!   . . . .   O 88 Messiah   1
CCNCILIIS
  Conciliis, verique sacros recludere fontes.   . . . . .   O 163 To Dr Lawrence   22
CONCINIT
  Quae lyra. Quam sibi non concinit harmonia!   . . . . .   O 216 Tr Greek 9.250   2
CCNCINNAT
  Menstrua concinnat Sylvanus, & Annua Dona, ...   O 383 Syl. Urb. Thes   D   1
CCNCORS
  Linguarumque omni terra discordia concors   . . . . .   O 161 Gnothi seauton   22
  Linguarumque omni ex terra discordia concors   . . . .   O 161 Gnothi seauton   V   22
CCNCURRENT
  Non ultra infestis concurrent agmina signis, ...   O 90 Messiah   66
CCNDITOR
  Aeterne rerum conditor, ...   O 206 Prayers II   1

	PAGE	TITLE	LINE
CCNDITUR			
Si forsaṇ tumulum quo conditur Eumarus aufers, ...	O 210	Tr Greek 7.284	3
CCNFERT			
Hic anemone humet, confert narcissus odores	O 209	Tr. Greek 5.74	3
CCNFESSUS			
Confessus tantum mente manuque patrem;	O 386	Tr Epi. Madoc	D 2
CCNFINED			
. . . Johnson, as he lay confined with an inflamed Eye.	O 162	To Dr Lawrence	T
CCNFITENTI			
Facilisque semper confitenti ades reo, ...	O 206	Prayers III	2
CCNFUGIS			
Spe non inani confugis, ...	O 203	Christ Sinner	1
CCNFUSA			
Tu secura tamen confusa elementa videbis, ...	O 92	Messiah	117
CCNGESTAS			
Congestas animus, laetos aut sumit honores	O 161	Gnothi seauton	V 40
CCNJUGE			
Paupertas misera est; multae cum conjuge lites	O 217	Tr Greek 9.359	5
Pauperies latitat, cum conjuge gaudia multa	O 217	Tr Greek 9.360	5
CONJUGIUM			
Conjugium, ut pro te des hominem patriae.	O 218	Tr Greek 9.444	4
CONJUNGIT			
Ter tria myriadi conjungit millia quartae, ...	O 230	Geographia Met	29
CONSCENDERE			
Nec mirum; restat lepori conscendere coelum, ...	O 213	Tr Greek 9.18	3
CONSPEXIT			
Armatam Pallas Venerem conspexit, et eia	O 384	Epigramma	D 1
CONSPICIT			
Conspicit aggestas, et se miratur in illis, ...	O 161	Gnothi seauton	43
CCNSTANS			
Stet fides constans, meritoque blandum	O 168	Oda to Thrale	18
CCNSTRICTUS			
Labraque constrictus semesos, jamque terendos	O 218	Tr Greek 9.375	3
CCNSUETA			
Illa triumphatrix Graium consueta procorum	O 209	Tr. Greek 6.1	1
CCNSUETUS			
Consuetus fulcro innixus reptare bacilli	O 90	Messiah	50
Omnia consuetus	O 110	Post-genitis	29
CONSUMERER			
Eheu! quam longo tecum consumerer aevo!	O 384	On the Gin-Act	D 5
CONTEMPSIT			
Servilem tuti cultum contempsit agelli, ...	O 386	Tr Epi. Madoc	D 3
CONTENDIT			
Denique perpetuo contendit in ardua nisu, ...	O 205	Christianus	25
CONTENTA			
Sit contenta mihi vita dolore carens.	O 222	Tr. Gk. 10.113	2
CONTENTI			
Qui sibi sat sapiunt, contenti noscere quantum	O 163	To Dr Lawrence	11
Qui sibi sat sapient, contenti noscere quantum	O 163	To Dr Lawrence	V 11
CCNTEXTAM			
Contextam variis, do, Rhodoclea, tibi:	O 209	Tr. Greek 5.74	2
CCNTRA			
Naufragus hic jaceo; contra jacet ecce colonus! . . .	O 210	Tr Greek 7.265	1
CCNTRAHE			
Nequitiam fugiens, servata contrahe lege	O 218	Tr Greek 9.444	3
CCNTREMET			
In Rabiem tunc contremet Ursa	O 109	Post-genitis	24
CCNVALLES			
Surgite convalles, tumidi subsidite montes!	O 89	Messiah	39
CONVENIT			
Convenit ut natis, inclyta Sparta, tuis.	O 224	Tr Greek 16.1	4
CCNVERSA			
Natio, conversa	O 109	Post-genitis	23
CCNVIVA			
Tangitur haud pedibus tellus; conviva Deorum	O 219	Tr Greek 9.577	3
CONVIVIA			
Qui convivia lautasque dapes	O 193	Tr. Medea III	3
Hae poterant uvae laeto convivia cantu	O 218	Tr Greek 9.375	7
COPIA			
Copia, Phidiaci foecunda potentia coeli.	O 161	Gnothi seauton	39
Copia coenae.	O 193	Tr. Medea III	15
COPORE			
Zosima, quondam solo fuit olim copore serva, ...	Y 320	Tr Gk Epigrams	V 1
CORDA			
Divitiis acuens aspera corda virum;	O 213	Tr Greek 9.29	2
Nunc juvenum terres robore corda senex.	O 225	Tr. Gk. 16.364	2
Vix majore Deus corda furore quatit	Y 28	Aurora Musis	8
CORDE			
Instet, et evellens terroris spicula corde, ...	O 205	Christianus	4
Corde meo accendas; ardeo totus ego.	O 225	Tr. Gk. 16.209	2
CORDI			
Recta ad pauperiem tendit, cui corpora cordi est . . .	O 222	Tr. Gk. 10.119	1
CORDIS			
Summe Deus, cui caeca patent penetralia cordis; . . .	O 232	Prayer	1
COROLLAS			
Nascere, magne puer! Tibi primas, ecce! corollas . . .	O 89	Messiah	27
CORONAM			
Floribus in pratis legi quos ipse, coronam	O 209	Tr. Greek 5.74	1
CORPORA			
Corpora cuncta suis gestit variare figuris, ...	O 163	To Dr Lawrence	27
Recta ad pauperiem tendit, cui corpora cordi est . . .	O 222	Tr. Gk. 10.119	1

CORPORE

		PAGE	TITLE		LINE
Zosima, quae solo fuit olim corpore Serva,		O 114	Tr Gk Epigrams		1
Zosima, quae solo fuit olim corpore serva,		O 212	Tr Gk Epigrams	V	7
Corpore nunc etiam libera facta fuit.		O 114	Tr Gk Epigrams		1
Servus Epictetus, mutilatus corpore vixi		O 114	Tr Gk Epigrams		2
Summe Pater, quodcunque tuum de corpore Numen		O 204	Losing Speech		3
Summe Pater, quodcunque tuae de corpore leges		O 204	Losing Speech		1
Servus, Epictetus, mutilato corpore, vixi,		O 212	Tr Greek 7.676	V	1
Ut mens utatur corpore, sume cibos.		O 228	Jejunium Cibus		1

CORPORI

		PAGE	TITLE		LINE
Succurre praesens corpori,		O 206	Prayers II		9

CORPUS

| Serviat ut menti corpus, jejunia serva; | | O 228 | Jejunium Cibus | | 1 |

CCRRIPE

| Quid salvere jubes me, pessime? Corripe gressus; | | O 211 | Tr Greek 7.318 | | 1 |

CORTINA

| Et cortina novum det revoluta diem! | | O 393 | Tr. of Crashaw | D | 4 |

CORUSCA

| Corusca a radiis Memnonis ora dabant. | | Y 28 | Aurora Musis | | 16 |

CORUSCABIT

| Triste coruscabit radiis; dabit hasta recusa | | O 90 | Messiah | | 69 |

CRAS

| Cras abiturus | | O 199 | Medico Aeger S | | 20 |

CRASTINUS

| Tunc alacres demum surgent, et crastinus ortus | | O 393 | Tr. of Crashaw | D | 5 |

CREASTI

| Summe Deus, qui semper amas quodcunque creasti, | | O 198 | Tr. Ash Wed. | | 1 |

CREAVIT

| Non Argos pugilem, non me Messana creavit; | | O 224 | Tr Greek 16.1 | | 1 |

CREBRIOR

| Heraclite, fluat lacrymarum crebrior imber; | | O 216 | Tr Greek 9.148 | | 3 |

CREDERET

| Quas Amor undarum crederet esse deas: | | O 169 | Insula Kenneth | V | 10 |

CREDIDERIS

| Credideris fletu funera digna tuo, | | Y 387 | Death Mother | D | 2 |

CREDIT

Ima tuas credit permitti, Scaliger, iras.		O 160	Gnothi seauton		13
Permissum credit nudas sibi sistere causas,		O 163	To Dr Lawrence		20
Credit, Achaemenidae nuper agellus eram.		O 215	Tr Greek 9.74		2

CREDO

| His cura credo sedibus exulat; | | O 166 | Oda Isle Skye | | 5 |
| Ditescis, credo, quid restat? quicquid habebis | | O 220 | Tr Greek 10.60 | | 1 |

CREDULIS

| Spondens omnia credulis homullis; | | O 204 | Spes | | 4 |

CREMANT

| Ecce! cremant genibus tritae regalibus arae. | | O 92 | Messiah | | 103 |

CREPARE

| Crepare vaecors, nil sapientiam | | O 186 | Ad T. L. M.D. | | 2 |

CREPET

| Secta crepet nimis alta fallax. | | O 166 | Oda Isle Skye | | 16 |

CRESCENTIA

| Supplicium huic, quoniam crescentia gaudia laesit, | | O 218 | Tr Greek 9.375 | | 5 |

CRESCENTIS

| Coelicolae pandunt, crescentis et aurea lucis | | O 92 | Messiah | V | 107 |

CRESCIT

| Qui pascit barbam si crescit mente, Platoni, | | O 224 | Tr. Gk. 11.430 | | 1 |

CRETAE

| Quovis sanguine cretae | | O 155 | Psalmus 117 | | 3 |

CRETHIDA

| Crethida fabellas dulces garrire peritam | | O 211 | Tr Greek 7.459 | | 1 |

CRIMINA

| O Qui benignus crimina ignoscis, pater | | O 206 | Prayers III | | 1 |
| Quem moestum et timidum crimina dira gravant; | | O 207 | Prayers V | | 2 |

CRIMINE

| Crimine gravatam plurimo mentem leva: | | O 206 | Prayers I | | 2 |
| Multo gravatam crimine | | O 206 | Prayers II | | 10 |

CRISPE

| Quid theatrales tibi, Crispe, pompae? | | O 153 | In Theatro | | 2 |

CRISTAE

| Aureaque admirans rutilantis fulgura cristae. | | O 91 | Messiah | | 92 |

CRUCIATOS

| Calcatos et Cruciatos | | O 110 | Post-genitis | | 32 |

CRUDA

| At tu quisquis eris, miseri qui cruda poetae | | Y 387 | Death Mother | D | 1 |

CRUDOS

| Pectore qui duro, crudos de vite racemos | | O 217 | Tr Greek 9.375 | | 1 |

CRUDUM

| Solis Ophyraeis crudum tibi montibus aurum | | O 92 | Messiah | | 104 |

CRUMENA

| Verte solum, donat plena crumena decus; | | O 217 | Tr Greek 9.360 | | 4 |
| Verte solum, donet plena crumena decus; | | O 217 | Tr Greek 9.360 | V | 4 |

CRYSTALLISQUE

| Crystallisque latex fractus scintillat acutis, | | O 116 | Tr Pope Grotto | | 4 |

CUI

Cui Fronte Sertum in Erudita		O 101	Ad Urbanum		3
Humani studium generis cui pectore fervet,		O 102	Ad R. Savage		1
Et me, cuncta beans cui nocuit dies,		O 164	Recover Eyes		8
Nunc huic, nunc aliis cedens, cui farra Menippus		O 215	Tr Greek 9.74		1
Recta ad pauperiem tendit, cui corpora cordi est		O 222	Tr. Gk. 10.119		1
Summe Deus, cui caeca patent penetralia cordis;		O 232	Prayer		1
Cui pars verbosae, vel datur ima, domus?		O 385	The Warehouse	D	4

		PAGE	TITLE		LINE
CUIQUAM					
	Velle vetet cuiquam non bene sanctus amor.	O 207	Prayers VII		8
CUIQUE					
	Datur nec aequum cuique animum sibi	O 166	Oda Isle Skye		14
	Cuique loco recti paenituisse mali est	O 198	Tr. Ash Wed.	V	2
	Cuique loco recte paenituisse mali est	O 198	Tr. Ash Wed.	V	2
	Cuique esses natus, cuique sodalis, eras.	O 212	Tr Greek 7.560		4
	Cuique esses natus, cuique sodalis, eras.	O 212	Tr Greek 7.560		4
CUJAS					
	Quaerere, quis, cujas, quis pater, unde venis. . . .	O 219	Tr Greek 9.648		2
CUJUS					
	Patrem cujus amor blandior in dies	O 155	Psalmus 117		5
	Regem cujus amor laetior in dies	O 155	Psalmus 117	V	5
CULMINA					
	Altius, en! Lebanon gaudentia culmina tollit, . . .	O 89	Messiah		30
	Culmina Carmeli recreant fragrantia coelum.	O 89	Messiah	V	33
CULPA					
	Ingenio parcas, nec sit mihi culpa rogasse, ...	O 204	Losing Speech		3
	Ingenio parcas, nec sit mihi culpa precari	O 204	Losing Speech	V	3
CULPANDA					
	Non immerito culpanda venit	O 193	Tr. Medea III		1
CULPAS					
	Da veteres culpas animo sic flere novato, ...	O 198	Tr. Ash Wed.	V	3
CULTOR					
	Et pius, et recti cultor: non illa jacere	O 212	Tr Greek 7.590		3
CULTU					
	Quid mihi cum cultu? Probitas inculta nitescit, . .	O 104	To Eliz Carter		1
	Vita ubi nullo decorata cultu	O 167	Oda to Thrale		6
CULTUM					
	Servilem tuti cultum contempsit agelli, ...	O 386	Tr Epi. Madoc	D	3
CULTUQUE					
	Ingreditur, cultuque tuo mansuescere gaudet. . . .	O 92	Messiah		101
CULTUS					
	Ponti inter strepitus sacri non munera cultus . . .	O 170	Insula Kenneth		17
CULULLO					
	Pone metum, rostrum fidens immitte cululo, ...	O 171	Tr. Busy Fly		3
CUM					
	Quid mihi cum cultu? Probitas inculta nitescit, . .	O 104	To Eliz Carter		1
	Cum Lapidem hunc, magni	O 109	Post-genitis		1
	Me, pensi immunis cum jam mihi reddor, inertis . . .	O 161	Gnothi seauton		24
	Nec quaerunt quid, luna, tuo cum fluctibus orbi. . .	O 163	To Dr Lawrence		16
	Sive cum libris novitate pascit	O 168	Oda to Thrale		15
	Sive cum libris novitate pascet	O 168	Oda to Thrale	V	15
	Una duas habuit casa cum genitore puellas, ...	O 169	Insula Kenneth		9
	Una duas tenuit casa cum genitore puellas, ...	O 169	Insula Kenneth	V	9
	Una duas cepit casa cum genitore puellas, ...	O 169	Insula Kenneth	V	9
	Spes hominum ac curas cum procul esse jubet. . . .	O 170	Insula Kenneth		16
	Ad Thomam Laurence, Medicum Doctissimum, Cum . . .	O 186	Ad T. L. M.D.	V	T
	Cum violis; spirant lilia mista rosis.	O 209	Tr. Greek 5.74		4
	Cum procul est, optat, cum venit, quisque senectam	O 214	Tr Greek 9.54		1
	Cum procul est, optat, cum venit, quisque senectam .	O 214	Tr Greek 9.54		1
	Paupertas misera est; multae cum conjuge lites . .	O 217	Tr Greek 9.359		5
	Pauperies latitat, cum conjuge gaudia multa . . .	O 217	Tr Greek 9.360		5
	Cum fugere haud possit fractis Victoria pennis, . .	O 219	Tr Greek 9.647		1
	Cum tacet indoctus, sapientior esse videtur, . . .	O 221	Tr Greek 10.98		1
	Cum sex centuriis Judaeo millia septem.	O 229	Geographia Met		2
	Cum sex centuriis numerat sex millia Tuscus. . . .	O 230	Geographia Met		13
	Sardiniam cum sexcentis sex millia complent. . . .	O 230	Geographia Met		18
	Cum sexagenis, dum plura recluserit aetas, ...	O 230	Geographia Met		19
	Cum caput Hesperiis attolit Phoebus ab undis, . . .	Y 28	Aurora Musis		1
	Quid mirum? cum saxa movet statuasque tacentes . . .	Y 28	Aurora Musis		13
CUMQUE					
	Cumque leone petet tutus praesepe juvencus.	O 91	Messiah		85
CUMULARE					
	Incrementa aevi non cumulare potes.	O 220	Tr Greek 10.60		4
CUMULAS					
	Divitias cumulas, pereuntes negligis horas, ...	O 220	Tr Greek 10.60		3
CUMULIS					
	Cinnameis cumulis, Nabathaei munere veris, ...	O 92	Messiah	V	102
CUMULOS					
	Cinnameos cumulos, Nabathaei munera veris, ...	O 92	Messiah		102
	Versat opum cumulos, et se miratur in illis, . . .	O 161	Gnothi seauton	V	43
	Quos Gyges cumulos habebat auri;	O 215	Tr Greek 9.110		2
CUNCTA					
	Ibunt per cuncta minaces, ...	O 109	Post-genitis		16
	Corpora cuncta suis gestit variare figuris, . . .	O 163	To Dr Lawrence		27
	Et me, cuncta beans cui nocuit dies, ...	O 164	Recover Eyes		8
	Vult Deus, at, qui cuncta dedit tibi, cuncta reposcit.	O 205	Christianus		24
	Vult Deus, at, qui cuncta dedit tibi, cuncta reposcit.	O 205	Christianus		24
	Sanguine Anastasii; cuncta sepulta jacent. . . .	O 212	Tr Greek 7.590		2
	Cuncta, cinis cuncta et ludicra, cuncta nihil. . .	O 222	Tr. Gk. 10.124		2
	Cuncta, cinis cuncta et ludicra, cuncta nihil. . .	O 222	Tr. Gk. 10.124		2
	Cuncta, cinis cuncta et ludicra, cuncta nihil. . .	O 222	Tr. Gk. 10.124		2
	Cur opulentus eges? tua cuncta in foenore ponis. .	O 223	Tr. Gk. 11.167		1
	Sanguine quo gentes, quo secula cuncta piavit, . .	O 232	Prayer		9
CUNCTAS					
	Quam tenet hic, cunctas quae manet, alta quies. . .	O 211	Tr Greek 7.459		4
CUNCTIPARENS					
	Cunctiparens tellus, salve, levis esto pusillo . .	O 211	Tr Greek 7.461		1
CUNCTIS					
	Utile cunctis hoc opus esset;	O 193	Tr. Medea III		10

CUNCTIS	(CONTINUED)	PAGE	TITLE	LINE
Solvi, quo Christus cunctis delicta redemit,	. . . .	O 207	Prayers V	5
Charus enim cunctis, tanquam, dum vita manebat,	. . .	O 212	Tr Greek 7.560	3
CUNCTORUM				
Cunctorum ignoscat vitiis, pietate fruatur.	. . . . .	O 205	Christianus	9
CUPIAT				
Irruptum vitae cupiat servare tenorem;	. . . . . .	O 205	Christianus	13
CUPIDO				
Quem nulla anxietas, nulla cupido fugit;	. . . . . .	O 232	Prayer	2
CUPIT				
Qui cupit in sanctos Christo cogente referri,	. . .	O 205	Christianus	1
Scripta legens, sola vivere mente cupit.	. . . . . .	O 211	Tr Greek 7.471	4
CUR				
Cur opulentus eges? tua cuncta in foenore ponis.	. . .	O 223	Tr. Gk. 11.167	1
CURA				
Te sterili functum cura, vocumque salebris	. . . .	O 161	Gnothi seauton	19
His cura credo sedibus exulat;	. . . . . .	O 166	Oda Isle Skye	5
Cessarunt; pietas hic quoque cura fuit:	. . . .	O 170	Insula Kenneth	18
Cura placere Deo sit prima, sit ultima, sanctae	. . . .	O 205	Christianus	12
Perstrepit omne forum; cura molesta domi est.	. . . .	O 217	Tr Greek 9.359	2
Sit tibi, Calliope, Parnassum, cura, tenenti,	. . . .	O 218	Tr Greek 9.523	1
Nec menti injiciat sordida cura jugum;	. . . . .	O 221	Tr Greek 10.74	2
CURAE				
Omnia, nec curae sunt sua sceptra Jovi.	. . . . . .	O 103	Elizae Aenigma	2
Nascuntur curis curae, vexatque dolorum	. . . . .	O 161	Gnothi seauton	27
Mater adulantum prolesque, Pecunia, curae,	. . . . .	O 218	Tr Greek 9.394	1
CURAQUE				
Pauperieque Irus, curaque prima Deum.	. . . .	O 114	Tr Gk Epigrams	4
Pauperieque Irus, curaque summa Deum.	. . . . . .	O 212	Tr Greek 7.676	2
CURAS				
Et curas felix patrias testabitur orbis.	. . . . . .	O 90	Messiah	65
Seu viri curas pia nupta mulcet,	. . . .	O 168	Oda to Thrale	13
Spes hominum ac curas cum procul esse jubet.	. . . .	O 170	Insula Kenneth	16
Spes hominum et curas gens procul esse velit.	. . . .	O 170	Insula Kenneth V	16
Curas mulcentes dulce eruntur aves.	. . . . .	Y 28	Aurora Musis	4
CURIS				
Nascuntur curis curae, vexatque dolorum	. . . .	O 161	Gnothi seauton	27
Torpesque languescisque curis	. . . .	O 187	Ad T. L. M.D.	11
CURRERE				
Currere formas?	. . . .	O 153	In Theatro	8
CURRICULO				
Sunt qui curriculo timidi versantur in arcto,	. . . .	O 163	To Dr Lawrence	9
CURSU				
Jam saltu capreas, jam cursu provocat euros.	. . . .	O 90	Messiah	51
Nunc saltu capreas, nunc cursu provocat euros.	. . . .	O 90	Messiah V	51
Huc ego delatus placido per coerula cursu.	. . . .	O 169	Insula Kenneth	5
Cursu spiritus	. . . .	O 198	Medico Aeger S	3
CURSUM				
Sic sibi diffisi, lenta experientia cursum	. . . . .	O 163	To Dr Lawrence	17
Hora sic peragit citata cursum;	. . . . . .	O 204	Spes	1
CURSUS				
Per fluctus vitae sic tibi cursus erit.	. . . . .	O 221	Tr Greek 10.74	6
Lympha tamen cursus agit indefessa perennis,	. . . .	O 228	Rivum a Stoana	9
CURVABITUR				
Vomerem, et in falcem rigidus curvabitur ensis.	. . .	O 90	Messiah	70
CUSTOS				
Fidus adest custos, seu nox furat horrida nimbis,	. . .	O 90	Messiah	62
Fidus adest custos, seu nox furat humida nimbis,	. . .	O 90	Messiah V	62
Assidet huic custos strenua pauperies.	. . . . .	O 219	Tr Greek 9.654	2
Hujus palestrae qui vigil custos stetit,	. . . . . .	O 223	Tr. Gk. 11.176	3
CUTIM				
Ille cutim spissam visus hebetare vetabit,	. . . .	O 90	Messiah	44
CYATHO				
Pensilibus fusis, cyatho comitata supremo,	. . . .	O 383	On the Gin-Act D	1
CYCNUM				
Et cycnum fecit Leda petita Jovem.	. . . .	O 214	Tr Greek 9.48	2
CYNTHIA				
Cynthia, tunc latis	. . . . . .	O 109	Post-genitis	25
CYPRIAE				
Haec veniunt Cypriae Somnia missa Deae.	. . . . . .	O 103	Elizae Aenigma	4
CYRUM				
Cyrum sexta timet; laetatur septima Christo.	. . . .	O 226	Septem Aetates	4
Cyrum sexta vocat, laetatur	. . . .	O 226	Septem Aetates V	4
CYTHEREIUS				
Fert humeris, venerabile onus, Cythereius heros	. . .	O 216	Tr Greek 9.163	1
DA				
Christe, da tutam trepido quietem,	. . . .	O 194	Prayer on Xmas	5
Da fidem certam, precibusque fidis	. . . . . .	O 194	Prayer on Xmas	7
Da veteres noxas animo sic flere novato,	. . . . .	O 198	Tr. Ash Wed.	3
Da veteres culpas animo sic flere novato,	. . . . .	O 198	Tr. Ash Wed. V	3
Veniam petenti, sumpe da veniam, pater;	. . . . . .	O 206	Prayers I	7
Da, Christe, poenitentiam,	. . . .	O 206	Prayers II	6
Veniamque, Christe, da mihi;	. . . . . .	O 206	Prayers II	7
Da veniam pacemque mihi, da, mente serena,	. . . .	O 207	Prayers V	3
Da veniam pacemque mihi, da, mente serena,	. . . .	O 207	Prayers V	3
Da, ne sint permissa, pater, mihi praemia frustra,	. .	O 208	Prayers VII	9
Da, ne sint promissa, pater, mihi praemia frustra,	. .	O 208	Prayers VII V	9
Seu prece poscatur, seu non, da Jupiter omne	. . .	O 221	Tr Greek 10.108	1
DABANT				
Queis majus pretium saecula lapsa dabant	. . . . . .	Y 28	Aurora Musis	12
Corusca a radiis Memnonis ora dabant.	. . . .	Y 28	Aurora Musis	16

```
                                                      PAGE    TITLE            LINE
DABIT
   Triste coruscabit radiis; dabit hasta recusa    . . . .   O  90 Messiah          69
   Quid majus mihi spes ambitiosa dabit? . . . . . . . .     O 104 To Eliz Carter    4
DABUNT
   Plus tibi ridendum secula nostra dabunt. . . . . . .      O 216 Tr Greek 9.148     2
DAMNARE
   Quid faciam? tenebrisne pigram damnare senectam  . . .    O 162 Gnothi seauton    52
DAMNATIS
   Damnatis, poenam pro poenis omnibus unam. . . . . .       O 160 Gnothi seauton     5
LAMNATUS
   Damnatus tenebris, lectoque affixus inerti, . . . . .     O 163 To Dr Lawrence     3
DANAE
   Antiope satyrum, Danae aurum, Europa juvencum, . . . .    O 214 Tr Greek 9.48      1
DANTES
   Aeriaeque columbae, dantes oscula, jungunt  . . . .       O 385 Cantico Solom.   D 9
DANUBII
   Accola Danubii qualia saevus habet; . . . . . . .         O 169 Insula Kenneth    12
DAPES
   Qui convivia lautasque dapes . . . . . . . . . .          O 193 Tr. Medea III      3
DAPIS
   Musca, meae comitem, participemque dapis, . . . . .       O 171 Tr. Busy Fly       2
DARE
   In trepidis dare terga rebus. . . . . . . . .             O 186 Ad T. L. M.D.      4
   In dubiis dare terga rebus. . . . . . . . . .             O 186 Ad T. L. M.D.    V 4
DARET
   Scire locum volui quid daret ille novi. . . . . .         O 169 Insula Kenneth     6
   Scire locus volui quid daret iste novi. . . . . .         O 169 Insula Kenneth   V 6
DARIO
   Dario magno non minus ille potest. . . . . . . .          O 212 Tr Greek 7.538     2
DAS
   Das bene collatos, quos Roma et Graecia jactat,  . . .    O 225 Tr. Gk. 16.331     3
DAT
   Limosum nobis Promus dat callidus haustum, . . . . .      O  85 Mea nec Falern     3
   Dat Menti propriis Musa nitere bonis. . . . . . .         O  85 Adjecere bonae     2
   Hector dat gladium Ajaci, dat balteum et Ajax  . . .      O 210 Tr Greek 7.151     1
   Hector dat gladium Ajaci, dat balteum et Ajax  . . .      O 210 Tr Greek 7.151     1
   Dulcia dat natura quidem, mare, sidera, terras, . . .     O 222 Tr. Gk. 10.123     3
   Dat tibi Pythagoram pictor; quod ni ipse tacere  . . .    O 225 Tr. Gk. 16.326     1
   Myriadas ter mille homini dat terra colendas. . . . .     O 230 Geographia Met    20
   Myriadas denas dat, quinque et millia, sexque  . . .      O 230 Geographia Met    27
   Munera luxurians dat pampinus, et generoso . . . . .      O 385 Cantico Solom.   D 13
DATOR
   Salutis aeternae dator; . . . . . . . . .                 O 206 Prayers II         2
   Summe dator vitae, naturae aeterne magister, . . . .      O 207 Prayers VI         1
DATUM
   Non mihi sorte datum; lenti seu sanguinis obsint  . . .   O 160 Gnothi seauton    16
   Tandem dolori plus satis est datum, . . . . . .           O 187 Ad T. L. M.D.     13
DATUR
   Datur nec aequum cuique animum sibi . . . . . .           O 166 Oda Isle Skye     14
   Cui pars verbosae, vel datur ima, domus? . . . . . .      O 385 The Warehouse    D 4
DE
   Nec sibi de gaza praesens quod postulet usus  . . .       O 162 Gnothi seauton    44
   Non sibi de gaza praesens quod postulat usus  . . .       O 162 Gnothi seauton   V 44
   Ode, De Skia Insula . . . . . . . . .                     O 167 Oda to Thrale    V T
   Nil opus est aeris sacra de turre sonantis  . . . . .     O 170 Insula Kenneth   V 18A
   Summe Pater, quodcunque tuum de corpore Numen  . . .      O 204 Losing Speech      1
   Summe Pater, quodcunque tuae de corpore leges  . . .      O 204 Losing Speech    V 1
   Me, pater omnipotens, de puro respice coelo, . . .        O 207 Prayers V          1
   Triste nihil passus, animi at de sorte Platonis  . . .    O 211 Tr Greek 7.471     3
   De te plebs audax, hic bene et ille male. . . . .         O 214 Tr Greek 9.50      2
   Pectore qui duro, crudos de vite racemos . . . . .        O 217 Tr Greek 9.375     1
   Terram adii nudus, de terra nudus abibo. . . . . .        O 220 Tr Greek 10.58     1
DEA
   Et placido tandem haec edidit ore, Dea: . . . . . .       O 386 In Birchium      D 4
DEAE
   Aonidesque Deae, et mendacis somnia Pindi. . . .          O  88 Messiah           5
   Haec veniunt Cypriae Somnia missa Deae. . . . .           O 103 Elizae Aenigma    4
   Neve tibi noceat praenituisse Deae. . . . . . .           O 115 Ad Lauram Epig    4
DEAS
   Quas Amor undarum fingeret esse deas: . . . . .           O 169 Insula Kenneth   10
   Quas Amor undarum crederet esse deas: . . . . .           O 169 Insula Kenneth   V 10
DEBILIS
   Huc nunquam volitat debilis iste puer. . . . . .          O 213 Tr Greek 9.39     4
DEBITA
   Hic, dum debita morti . . . . . . . . .                   O 182 Waltoni Piscat    5
DEBITOR
   Faelix ante alios nullius debitor aeris; . . . . .        O 222 Tr Greek 11.50    1
DEBUIT
   Gratum animum laudo; Qui debuit omnia ventis, . . . .     O 143 On Lord Anson     1
   Qui nil virtuti, sed debuit omnia ventis,  . . . . .      O 143 On Lord Anson   V 1
DEGADAS
   Undecies binas decadas et millia septem  . . . . .        O 230 Geographia Met    6
   Centurias, et tres decadas Europa Britannis. . . .        O 230 Geographia Met   28
DECADEM
   Centuriae octavam decadem addit Lucca secundae.  . . .    O 230 Geographia Met   15
DEGADES
   Centuriae quartae decades quinque Anglia nectit. . . .    O 230 Geographia Met   30
   Et quadragenis decades quinque addit Ierne, . . . . .     O 231 Geographia Met   32
DECEDERE
   Sponte sua demens; nihilum decedere summae  . . . . .     O 205 Christianus      23
```

449

		PAGE	TITLE	LINE
DECET				
Quam decet canos male literatos		O 153	In Theatro	3
DECIDIT				
Saepe tuum in tumulum lacrymarum decidit imber		O 212	Tr Greek 7.560	1
DECIES				
Eheu, quid decies plus mihi sexta dedit!		O 171	Tr. Busy Fly	10
Myriadas decies septem numerare jubebit		O 230	Geographia Met	8
Pastor Arabs: decies octo sibi Persa requirit. . . .		O 230	Geographia Met	9
Myriadas septem decies Europa ducentis		O 230	Geographia Met	25
DECOR				
Quantus ubique Lepos! quantus ubique Decor!		O 383	Syl. Urb. Thes D	2
DECORATA				
Vita ubi nullo decorata cultu		O 167	Oda to Thrale	6
DECUIT				
Quem decuit majora sequi, majoribus aptum, ...		O 160	Gnothi seauton	7
DECUS				
Graeciae et urbs, urbi est ista propago, decus. . . .		O 214	Tr Greek 9.65	2
Verte solum, donat plena crumena decus;		O 217	Tr Greek 9.360	4
Verte solum, donet plena crumena decus;		O 217	Tr Greek 9.360 V	4
Te manet imperii, Roma, perenne decus.		O 219	Tr Greek 9.647	2
Laevum at utrumque decus, juveni quod praebuit olim . .		O 225	Tr. Gk. 16.364	3
DECUSQUE				
O longum, formosa, vale, mihi vita decusque, ...		O 383	On the Gin-Act D	3
DEDERAT				
Det Bacchus, dederat quale, Lycurge, tibi.		O 218	Tr Greek 9.375	6
DEDERE				
Tres tria temporibus secla dedere suis.		O 86	Tr Dryden Milt	2
Quale, sed hostiles quale dedere manus.		O 210	Tr Greek 7.136	2
DEDERIT				
Sive mihi mentem dederit Natura minorem.		O 161	Gnothi seauton	18
DEDI				
Habeo, dedi quod alteri;		O 165	Tr Doncast Epi	1
Habuique, quod dedi mihi;		O 165	Tr Doncast Epi	2
DEDIT				
Virgilio vires Uva Falerna dedit.		O 85	Mea nec Falern	4
Quas Natura dedit dotes, Academia promit, ...		O 85	Adjecere bonae	1
Recte qui fruitur muneribus, dedit.		O 164	Recover Eyes	14
Eheu, quid decies plus mihi sexta dedit!		O 171	Tr. Busy Fly	10
Vult Deus, at, qui cuncta dedit tibi, cuncta reposcit. .		O 205	Christianus	24
DEDOCUISSE				
Dicitur, et vanos dedocuisse deos.		O 169	Insula Kenneth	4
DEERANT				
Mollia non deerant vacuae solatia vitae, ...		O 170	Insula Kenneth	13
DEFENCE				
To a Lady who spoke in Defence of Liberty		O 105	Lady Defence	T
DEFENDITUR				
Dum defenditur imber, ...		O 181	Waltoni Piscat	3
DEFESSO				
Quam grata defesso virentem		O 166	Oda Isle Skye	3
DEFICIENS				
Littora deficiens arentia deseret aequor, ...		O 92	Messiah	114
DEFLECTITUR				
Saxa sonant Deus; ecce Deus! deflectitur aether . . .		O 89	Messiah	36
DEI				
Nuncia sacra Dei, plaudentibus insidet alis.		O 88	Messiah	13
Pollicitis firmata Dei, stabilita ruinis.		O 92	Messiah	119
Auxilioque Dei fretus, jam mente serena		O 205	Christianus	26
Effigiemque Dei, quantum servare licebit, ...		O 205	Christianus	29
Supra Praeco Dei--strepit infra Praeco Bonorum: . . .		O 385	The Warehouse D	5
DEIN				
Evocat Abramum dein tertia; quarta relinquit		O 226	Septem Aetates	2
DELATUS				
Huc ego delatus placido per coerula cursu		O 169	Insula Kenneth	5
DELENDA				
Hinc annis palpantur delenda poemata nullis		Y 28	Aurora Musis	11
Hinc annis palpantur delenda poemata palpantur		Y 28	Aurora Musis V	11
DELICIASQUE				
Deliciasque fugit solitas solitosque labores;		O 162	To Dr Lawrence	2
DELICTA				
Solvi, quo Christus cunctis delicta redemit, ...		O 207	Prayers V	5
DELIRANS				
Et sibi, delirans quanquam et peccator in horas . . .		O 205	Christianus	14
DELUSA				
Hic delusa rudi frustrabar brachia motu, ...		O 228	Rivum a Stoana	3
DEMENS				
Sponte sua demens; nihilum decedere summae		O 205	Christianus	23
DEMENTES				
Horrida dementes		O 109	Post-genitis	19
DEMISSUMQUE				
Demissumque Deum tellus capit; ardua cedrus, ...		O 89	Messiah	37
DEMOCRITE				
Democrite, invisas homines majore cachinno, ...		O 216	Tr Greek 9.148	1
DEMOPHILO				
Demophilo auscultans nycticorax moritur.		O 223	Tr. Gk. 11.186	2
DEMOSTHENICA				
Sint Demosthenica ut jurata cadavera voce, ...		O 216	Tr Greek 9.288	5
DEMUM				
Tunc alacres demum surgent, et crastinus ortus . . .		O 393	Tr. of Crashaw D	5
DENAS				
Russia, myriadas ter denas adde trecentis:		O 230	Geographia Met	17
Myriadas denas dat, quinque et millia, sexque		O 230	Geographia Met	27

	PAGE	TITLE	LINE
DENIQUE			
Quod dicas denique dirum, ...	O 110	Post-genitis	36
Denique perpetuo contendit in ardua nisu, ...	O 205	Christianus	25
DENOS			
Undecies centum denos quater adde duosque.	O 229	Epigram IV	2
DENSA			
Densa fronde salicti	O 181	Waltoni Pisoat	2
DENSAQUE			
Per Trojae flammas, densaque tela, patrem.	O 216	Tr Greek 9.163	2
DENSIS			
Ordinibus surgit densis, vitamque requirit	O 92	Messiah	97
DEO			
Cura placere Deo sit prima, sit ultima, sanctae . . .	O 205	Christianus	12
DEORUM			
Tangitur haud pedibus tellus; conviva Deorum	O 219	Tr Greek 9.577	3
Hermem Deorum nuncium, pennis levem, ...	O 223	Tr. Gk. 11.176	1
Me, rex deorum, tuque, duc, necessitas, ...	O 226	Tr. Cleanthes	1
DEOS			
Dicitur, et vanos dedocuisse deos.	O 169	Insula Kenneth	4
Non poteris, meditans prava, latere Deos.	O 220	Tr Greek 10.27	2
DEPONE			
His redimita comas, mores depone superbos:	O 209	Tr. Greek 5.74	5
DEPOSITURA			
Mox uteri pondus depositura grave, ...	O 115	Ad Lauram Epig	2
DEPROPERAT			
Deproperat tellus, fundit tibi munera, quicquid . . .	O 89	Messiah	28
DES			
Conjugium, ut pro te des hominem patriae.	O 218	Tr Greek 9.444	4
DESCENDERE			
Ab Jove Maeonides descendere Somnia narrat:	O 103	Elizae Aenigma	3
DESCRIBERE			
Sed similem, Plutarche, tuae describere vitam . . .	O 225	Tr. Gk. 16.331	5
DESCRIBIT			
Carmine describit Cellantia Numina digne	Y 28	Aurora Musis	9
DESCRIPSERIS			
His Tempelmanni numeris descripseris orbem.	O 229	Geographia Met	1
DESERET			
Littora deficiens arentia deseret aequor, ...	O 92	Messiah	114
DESERTA			
Deserta et lata mollescunt aspera voce, ...	O 89	Messiah V	34
DESERTI			
Deserti laeta mollescunt aspera voce, ...	O 89	Messiah	34
DESIDERIC			
. . . filium peregre agentem desiderio nimis . . .	O 186	Ad T. L. M.D. V	T
DESIDIAE			
Desidiae sors dura manet, graviorque labore	O 161	Gnothi seauton	25
DESINITIS			
Exclamat: Nunc me cernere desinitis.	O 224	Tr. Gk. 11.432	2
DESINT			
Domino desint.	O 199	Medico Aeger S	30
DESIT			
Forma animos hominum capit, at, si gratia desit, . .	O 209	Tr. Greek 5.67	1
Atthide non alius desit Olympus, habet.	O 219	Tr Greek 9.702	2
DESTITUIT			
Destituit medicina mentis.	O 187	Ad T. L. M.D.	8
DESUNT			
Materies arti, sua desunt arma labori	O 161	Gnothi seauton V	37
Mollia non desunt vacuae solatia vitae, ...	O 170	Insula Kenneth V	13
DET			
Det Bacchus, dederat quale, Lycurge, tibi.	O 218	Tr Greek 9.375	6
Et cortina novum det revoluta diem!	O 393	Tr. of Crashaw D	4
DETERAT			
Quid ferat externi velox, quid deterat aetas, . . .	O 228	Rivum a Stoana	11
DETRUDIT			
Jam teneros fructus detrudit lactea ficus	O 385	Cantico Solom. D	11
DEUM			
Demissumque Deum tellus capit; ardua cedrus, . . .	O 89	Messiah	37
Pauperieque Irus, curaque prima Deum.	O 114	Tr Gk Epigrams	4
Pauperieque Irus, curaque summa Deum.	O 212	Tr Greek 7.676	2
DEUS			
Auditur Deus! ecce Deus! reboantia circum	O 89	Messiah	35
Auditur Deus! ecce Deus! reboantia circum	O 89	Messiah	35
Saxa sonant Deus; ecce Deus! deflectitur aether . .	O 89	Messiah	36
Saxa sonant Deus; ecce Deus! deflectitur aether . .	O 89	Messiah	36
Qua te laude, Deus, qua prece prosequar?	O 164	Recover Eyes	10
Summe Deus, qui semper amas quodcunque creasti, . .	O 198	Tr. Ash Wed.	1
Vult Deus, at, qui cuncta dedit tibi, cuncta reposcit. .	O 205	Christianus	24
Me ducat lux sancta, Deus, lux sancta sequatur; . .	O 207	Prayers IV	3
Summe Deus, cui caeca patent penetralia cordis; . .	O 232	Prayer	1
Vix majore Deus corda furore quatit	Y 28	Aurora Musis	8
Praecones ambo, Nummus utrique Deus.	O 385	The Warehouse D	2
DEXTRAE			
Artificis frondent dextrae; palmisque rubeta . . .	O 91	Messiah	82
Artificis frondent dextrae; Spinetaque Palmis . . .	O 91	Messiah V	82
DIA			
Dia salutares spirant medicamina rami.	O 89	Messiah	17
Tuto eluctatum spatiis Sapientia dia	O 161	Gnothi seauton	20
DICAM			
Dicam; stat virtus non subigenda neci.	O 212	Tr Greek 7.590	4
DICAS			
Quod dicas denique dirum, ...	O 110	Post-genitis	36

DICAS   (CONTINUED)   PAGE   TITLE   LINE
      Ut dicas, spatiis quam latis imperet orbi   . . . . .   O 230 Geographia Met   16
DICAT
      Nec dubitet quem dicat herum, sed, totus in uno,   . . .   O 205 Christianus   17
DICATUS
      Cecropidis gravis hic ponor, Martique dicatus, ...   O 216 Tr Greek 9.288   1
DIGAVIT
      Clara Cheroneae soboles, Plutarche, dicavit . . . . .   O 225 Tr. Gk. 16.331   1
DICIMUS
      Haec fausta vobis dicimus, Angliae . . . .   O 188 Epilogus   2
DICITE
      Sancto dicite carmine.   . . . .   O 155 Psalmus 117   8
      Dicite, Causidici, gelido nunc marmore magni   . . . .   O 213 Tr Greek 8.137   1
DICITUR
      Dicitur, et vanos dedocuisse deos. . . . .   O 169 Insula Kenneth   4
DIEI
      Luna vices revehet; radios pater ipse diei   . . . . .   O 92 Messiah   110
      Alme voco, impatiens noctis metuensque diei.   . . . .   O 161 Gnothi seauton   31
DIEM
      Carpe diem, fugit, heu, non revocanda dies!   . . . . .   O 171 Tr. Busy Fly   6
      Sic diem sequitur dies fugacem! . . . .   O 204 Spes   2
      Si Phoebo, victor nescit obire diem.   . . . . . .   O 210 Tr Greek 7.239   2
      Et cortina novum det revoluta diem! . . . .   O 393 Tr. of Crashaw   D   4
DIES
      Sive dies medius morientia torreat arva: . . . . . .   O 90 Messiah   63
      Sive dies medius languentia torreat arva: . . . . .   O 90 Messiah   V   63
      Patrem cujus amor blandior in dies . . . .   O 155 Psalmus 117   5
      Regem cujus amor laetior in dies   . . . .   O 155 Psalmus 117   V   5
      Et me, cuncta beans cui nocuit dies, ...   O 164 Recover Eyes   8
      Luxerat illa dies, legis gens docta supernae   . . . .   O 170 Insula Kenneth   15
      Fulserat illa dies, legis qua docta supernae   . . . .   O 170 Insula Kenneth   V   15
      Carpe diem, fugit, heu, non revocanda dies!   . . . . .   O 171 Tr. Busy Fly   6
      Nunc dies Christo memoranda nato   . . . .   O 193 Prayer on Xmas   1
      Sic diem sequitur dies fugacem! . . . .   O 204 Spes   2
      Noctes atque dies animo spes laeta recurset, ...   O 207 Prayers VII   5
      Sunt quibus a lacrymis vix vacat ulla dies.   . . . .   O 221 Tr Greek 10.84   2
      Veris, io! venit alma dies! Philomela canorum   . . . .   O 385 Cantico Solom.   D   7
DIFFISI
      Sic sibi diffisi, lenta experientia cursum   . . . . .   O 163 To Dr Lawrence   17
DIFFLUENTEM
      In Rivum a Mola Stoana Lichfeldiae diffluentem . . . .   O 228 Rivum a Stoana   T
DIFFLUIT
      Pauper eram, nummis diffluit arca senis;   . . . . . .   O 215 Tr Greek 9.138   2
DIFFUGIUNT
      Aspice, diffugiunt ignavae frigora brumae;   . . . . .   O 384 Cantico Solom.   D   3
DIGITI
      Vel digiti tractant, oculus vel sentit et auris: . . .   O 163 To Dr Lawrence   12
DIGNA
      Gratia vix restat nomine digna suo.   . . . .   O 220 Tr Greek 10.30   2
      Credideris fletu funera digna tuo, ...   Y 387 Death Mother   D   2
DIGNARIER
      Laurenti saltem facili dignarier aure?   . . . . . .   O 163 To Dr Lawrence   5
DIGNE
      Quid mirum Maro quod digne canit arma Virumque,   . . .   O 85 Mea nec Falern   1
      Carmine describit Cellantia Numina digne   . . . . .   Y 28 Aurora Musis   9
DIGNOS
      Siderea Isaiae, dignos accende furores!   . . . . . .   O 88 Messiah   7
DIGNUS
      Dignus qui multa in lustra senescat, erit.   . . . . .   O 214 Tr Greek 9.55   2
DII
      Stella mea, observans stellas, Dii me aethera faxint,   .   O 212 Tr Greek 7.669   1
DILECTA
      Surge, soror dilecta, mihi lux, gaudia, vita;   . . . .   O 384 Cantico Solom.   D   1
DIMIDIUM
      Dimidium tanti ponderis intret onus.   . . . .   O 229 Epigram III   2
DIODORUS
      Menodotum pinxit Diodorus, et exit imago, ...   O 223 Tr. Gk. 11.213   1
DIRA
      Quem moestum et timidum crimina dira gravant;   . . . .   O 207 Prayers V   2
DIREPTA
      Aeternum direpta mihi! sed quid moror istis?   . . . .   O 384 On the Gin-Act   D   7
DIRO
      Sidera fumabunt, diro labefacta tremore   . . . . . .   O 92 Messiah   115
DIRUM
      Quod dicas denique dirum, ...   O 110 Post-genitis   36
DISCANT
      Thraliae discant resonare nomen . . . .   O 168 Oda to Thrale   19
DISCE
      Vita omnis scena est ludusque; aut ludere disce   . . .   O 221 Tr Greek 10.72   1
DISCEDITE
      Sternite saxa viam, rapidi discedite fluctus!   . . . .   O 89 Messiah   40
DISCESSERIS
      Ut vis, ponte minax, modo tres discesseris ulnas,   . . .   O 210 Tr Greek 7.284   1
DISCIPULUS
      Sacri discipulus libri . . . .   O 164 Recover Eyes   11
      Praestat magistro saepe discipulus suo.   . . . . . .   O 223 Tr. Gk. 11.176   5
DISCORDIA
      Rapiet Discordia Gentes, ...   O 109 Post-genitis   20
      Linguarumque omni terra discordia concors   . . . . .   O 161 Gnothi seauton   22
      Linguarumque omni ex terra discordia concors   . . . .   O 161 Gnothi seauton   V   22

452

```
                                                    PAGE    TITLE              LINE
DISJECIT
     Buccina disjecit Thebarum moenia, struxit   .  .  .  .  .   O 216 Tr Greek 9.250     1
DISPLICEAT
     Displiceat, servet tutum sub pectore rectum:   .   .   .   O 205 Christianus        15
DISSIMILI
     Dissimili domus una duos tenet arte tumentes;   .  .  .  .   O 385 The Warehouse   D  1
DITATUS
     Ditatus magna dote, recondis humo.  .  .  .  .  .  .  .  .   O 222 Tr Greek 11.50     4
DITESCERE
     Non opto aut precibus posco ditescere, paucis   .   ..   ..   O 222 Tr. Gk. 10.113    1
DITESCIS
     Ditescis, credo, quid restat? quicquid habebis  .  ..  ..   O 220 Tr Greek 10.60     1
DITIS
     Et saltu e muro Ditis opaca petit:  .  .  .  .  .  .  .  .   O 211 Tr Greek 7.471     2
DIU
     Expectata diu! Naturae claustra refringens   .   .   .   .   O  89 Messiah          26
     En! quem turba diu cecinerunt enthea, vates,   .   .   .   O  89 Messiah          41
     Obstrictasque diu linguas in carmina solvet.   .   .   .   O  90 Messiah          46
DIURNIS
     Fecerunt rami latebras, tenebrisque diurnis  .  .  .  .  .   O 228 Rivum a Stoana      5
DIVA
     Haec Musae ad Venerem: Sic Marti, diva, mineris;   .   .   O 213 Tr Greek 9.39       3
DIVES
     Sic aliis dives, tu tibi pauper agis.  .  .  .  .  .  .  .   O 223 Tr. Gk. 11.167     2
DIVINAM
     Divinam in sontes iram placavit Jesus;   .   .   .   .   .   O 208 A Meditation       3
DIVINO
     Barbarus, en! clarum divino lumine templum   .   .   .   O  92 Messiah         100
     Divino, sanctus regnet ut intus amor:   .   .   .   .   .   O 232 Prayer            6
DIVINOS
     Divinos, surdas sacra vox permulceat aures!   .  .  .  .  .   O  89 Messiah          43
DIVINUS
     Postera sic pastor divinus secla beabit,  .  .  .  .  .  .   O  90 Messiah          64
DIVITIAS
     Divitias cumulas, pereuntes negligis horas,  .  .  .  .  .   O 220 Tr Greek 10.60     3
DIVITIIS
     Divitiis acuens aspera corda virum;   .   .   .   .   .   .   O 213 Tr Greek 9.29       2
     Divitiis, utrinque cavens, qui tempore parcit,  .  .  .  .   O 219 Tr Greek 10.26      3
     Tempore divitiis utitur, ille sapit.  .  .  .  .  .  .  .   O 219 Tr Greek 10.26      4
DIVOS
     Ad Divos paribus passibus ire duces;   .   .   .   .   .   .   O 225 Tr. Gk. 16.331     4
DIXERAT
     Dixerat, imperiique vices, coelique meatus,  .  .  .  .  .   O 160 Gnothi seauton     10
DIXERE
     Quod nimium est fit ineptum; hinc, ut dixere priores,   .   O 224 Tr Greek 16.16      1
DIXIT
     Quae fausta Romae dixit Horatius,  .  .  .  .  .  .  .  .   O 188 Epilogus            1
     Quid tibi, mus, mecum, dixit, amice, tibi?  .  .  .  .  .   O 224 Tr. Gk. 11.391     2
DO
     Contextam variis, do, Rhodoclea, tibi:   .   .   .   .   .   O 209 Tr. Greek 5.74      2
DOCENT
     Astra mathematicos si modo vera docent.  .  .  .  .  .  .   O 215 Tr Greek 9.112      2
DOCES
     Lucri ulciscendum mox nece sola doces.   .   .   .   .   .   O 213 Tr Greek 9.29       4
DOCET
     Quos soli ducunt sensus, solus docet usus;   .   .   .   O 163 To Dr Lawrence     10
     At docet, exemplo, vis sibi quanta, tuo.  .  .  .  .  .  .   O 218 Tr Greek 9.530      2
     Pallas ubique docet; ridet ubique Venus.  .  .  .  .  .  .   O 383 Syl. Urb. Thes   D  4
DOCTA
     Luxerat illa dies, legis gens docta supernae   .   .   .   O 170 Insula Kenneth     15
     Fulserat illa dies, legis qua docta supernae   .   .   .   O 170 Insula Kenneth  V  15
     Te docta, Laurenti, vetustas  .  .  .  .  .  .  .  .  .   O 187 Ad T. L. M.D.      15
     Assurgitque epicis pagina docta modis.  .  .  .  .  .  .   Y  28 Aurora Musis      10
DOCTAE
     Myrias, ut menti pateat tota Africa doctae.  .  .  .  .  .   O 230 Geographia Met    24
DOCTISSIME
     Quid mecum peragam, quod tu doctissime posses   .   .   .   O 163 To Dr Lawrence      4
DOCTISSIMUM
     Ad T.<homam> L.<aurence> M.<edicum> D.<octissimum>   .   .   O 186 Ad T. L. M.D.       T
     Ad Thomam Laurence, Medicum Doctissimum, Cum   .   .   O 186 Ad T. L. M.D.    V   T
DOCTRINA
     Ingenium, nisi materiem Doctrina ministret,  .  .  .  .  .   O 161 Gnothi seauton     37
     Ingenium, nisi materiem Doctrina ministrat,  .  .  .  .  .   O 161 Gnothi seauton  V  37
DOCTUS
     Ille quidem recte, sublimis, doctus, et acer,  .  .  .  .   O 160 Gnothi seauton      6
DOCUIT
     Voce aut fidibus pellere docuit  .  .  .  .  .  .  .  .  .   O 193 Tr. Medea III       8
     Dum docuit blanda voce natare pater.  .  .  .  .  .  .  .   O 228 Rivum a Stoana      4
DOLENS
     Sed Miliae ridens, atque dolens Miliae.  .  .  .  .  .  .   O 218 Tr Greek 9.573      6
DOLENTI
     Adsit, Laura, tibi facilis Lucina dolenti,  .  .  .  .  .   O 115 Ad Lauram Epig      3
DOLERE
     Nec sinat semper tremere ac dolere  .  .  .  .  .  .  .  .   O 227 A Meditation       3
DOLET
     Sexta dolet Babylona, et gaudet septima Christo.  .  .  .   O 226 Septem Aetates   V  4
DOLISQUE
     Elige iter vitae, ut possis; rixisque dolisque  .  .  .  .   O 217 Tr Greek 9.359      1
DOLOR
     Quem fundit blando junctus amore dolor;   .   .   .   .   O 212 Tr Greek 7.560      2
     Teque frui timor est, teque carere dolor.  .  .  .  .  .  .   O 218 Tr Greek 9.394      2
```

		PAGE	TITLE		LINE

DOLORE
Sit contenta mihi vita dolore carens. . . . . O 222 Tr. Gk. 10.113 2
Nec sinat semper tremere ac dolore . . . . O 227 A Meditation V 3
DOLORI
Tandem dolori plus satis est datum, ... O 187 Ad T. L. M.D. 13
DOLORUM
Nascuntur curis curae, vexatque dolorum . . . . . . O 161 Gnothi seauton 27
DOMI
Res angusta domi, et macrae penuria mentis. . . . . . O 161 Gnothi seauton 41
Perstrepit omne forum; cura molesta domi est. . . . O 217 Tr Greek 9.359 2
Permeat omne forum; vita quieta domi est. . . . O 217 Tr Greek 9.360 2
DOMIBUS
Domibus claris exitiales, ... O 193 Tr. Medea III 7
DOMINABERE
Laetaque Messia semper dominabere rege, ... O 92 Messiah 118
DOMINATOR
Aeternoque orci dominator vulnere languens . . . . . O 90 Messiah 55
Summus adesse jubet celsa dominator ab arce; . . . . O 162 Gnothi seauton 45
DOMINI
Versus Collari Caprae Domini Banks inscribendi . . . . O 156 Collari Caprae T
Quam domini ingentis ferre supercilium. . . . . . O 221 Tr Greek 10.93 2
DOMINO
Domino desint. . . . . O 199 Medico Aeger S 30
Arridens domino collacrymansque tuo, ... O 218 Tr Greek 9.573 4
DOMINUM
Gloria silvarum, dominum inclinata salutet! . . . . . O 89 Messiah 38
DOMOS
Multa alere, et multas aedificare domos. . . . . . O 222 Tr. Gk. 10.119 2
DOMUISSE
Voce ubi Cennethus populos domuisse feroces . . . . . O 169 Insula Kenneth 3
DOMUS
Civis et externus grati; domus hospita nescit . . . . O 219 Tr Greek 9.648 1
Dissimili domus una duos tenet arte tumentes; . . . . O 385 The Warehouse D 1
Cui pars verbosae, vel datur ima, domus? . . . . . . O 385 The Warehouse D 4
DONA
Mihi dona morte haec impetret Christus sua. . . . . . O 206 Prayers I 11
Menstrua concinnat Sylvanus, & Annua Dona, ... O 383 Syl. Urb. Thes D 1
DONAT
Verte solum, donat plena crumena decus; . . . . . . O 217 Tr Greek 9.360 4
DONEC
Hic jaceant; donec Nox transeat horrida nimbis, . . . O 393 Tr. of Crashaw D 3
DONET
Verte solum, donet plena crumena decus; . . . . . . O 217 Tr Greek 9.360 V 4
DOTE
Ditatus magna dote, recondis humo. . . . . O 222 Tr Greek 11.50 4
DOTES
Quas Natura dedit dotes, Academia promit, ... O 85 Adjecere bonae 1
DOTIBUS
Incultum Studiis, et paucis dotibus auctum . . . . . O 161 Gnothi seauton V 36
DR
Verses addressed to Dr. Lawrence, composed by Dr. . . . O 162 To Dr Lawrence T
Verses addressed to Dr. Lawrence, composed by Dr. . . . O 162 To Dr Lawrence T
DRACONIS
Per saxa, ignivomi nuper spelaea draconis, ... O 91 Messiah 78
DUAS
Una duas habuit casa cum genitore puellas, ... O 169 Insula Kenneth 9
Una duas tenuit casa cum genitore puellas, ... O 169 Insula Kenneth V 9
Una duas cepit casa cum genitore puellas, ... O 169 Insula Kenneth V 9
Myriades sibi pulcra duas, duo millia poscit . . . . O 230 Geographia Met 10
DUBIAE
Pectora molli mulcet dubiae . . . . O 193 Tr. Medea III 14
DUBIIS
In dubiis dare terga rebus. . . . . O 186 Ad T. L. M.D. V 4
DUBITARE
Certa vetet dubitare fides, spes laeta timere, ... O 207 Prayers VII 7
DUBITET
Nec dubitet quem dicat herum, sed, totus in uno, . . . O 205 Christianus 17
DUBITO
Interea dubito; tecum me causa nec ulla . . . . . . O 216 Tr Greek 9.148 5
DUC
Me, rex deorum, tuque, duc, necessitas, ... O 226 Tr. Cleanthes 1
DUCAT
Me ducat lux sancta, Deus, lux sancta sequatur; . . . O 207 Prayers IV 3
DUCENTIS
Myriadas septem decies Europa ducentis . . . . . . O 230 Geographia Met 25
DUCES
Ad Divos paribus passibus ire duces; . . . . O 225 Tr. Gk. 16.331 4
DUCIMUS
Molles ducimus horas. . . . . O 181 Waltoni Piscat 4
DUCIT
Caeco ducit amore, ... O 182 Waltoni Piscat 12
DUCITUR
Anni qua volucris ducitur orbita, ... O 155 Psalmus 117 1
DUCUM
Qui veterum modo facta ducum, modo carmina vatum, . . . O 160 Gnothi seauton 8
DUCUNT
Quos soli ducunt sensus, solus docet usus; . . . . . O 163 To Dr Lawrence 10
DULCE
Ut qua dulce strepunt scatebrae, qua laeta virescunt . . O 90 Messiah 57
Ut qua dulce strepent scatebrae, qua laeta virescunt . . O 90 Messiah V 57
Cantum, vitae dulce levamen. . . . . O 193 Tr. Medea III 5

```
                                          PAGE   TITLE               LINE
DULCE          (CONTINUED)
    Dulce papaver.   . . . . . . . . . . .  O 199 Medico Aeger S       14
    Dulce papaper.   . . . . . . . . . . .  O 199 Medico Aeger S    V  14
    Tu neque dulce putes alienae accumbere mensae,  . . .  O 218 Tr Greek 9.573     1
    Curas mulcentes dulce eruntur aves.   . . . . .  Y  28 Aurora Musis        4
    Dulce Venus ridens, lorica nil opus, inquit,   . . . .  O 384 Epigramma       D   3
DULCES
    Crethida fabellas dulces garrire peritam . . . . . .  O 211 Tr Greek 7.459     1
DULCI
    Apte antiqua novis miscentur, et utile dulci:  . . . .  O 383 Syl. Urb. Thes  D   3
DULCIA
    Dulcia dat natura quidem, mare, sidera, terras,   . . .  O 222 Tr. Gk. 10.123     3
DULCIBUS
    Pergit, et imperiis sentit se dulcibus actum.  . . .  O 205 Christianus        27
DULCIS
    Thralia dulcis?  . . . . . . . . . .  O 168 Oda to Thrale       12
    Quorsum dulcis luxuria soni?  . . . . .  O 193 Tr. Medea III       12
    Sola rates struis infidas, et dulcis amorem   . . .  O 213 Tr Greek 9.29       3
DUM
    Non Animus sero nimium dum parta recenset,   . . .  O 161 Gnothi seauton    V  42
    Non operum serie, seriem dum computat aevi, . . . .  O 162 Gnothi seauton      46
    Sanguine dum tumido suffusus flagrat ocellus,   . . .  O 162 To Dr Lawrence      1
    Dum statuunt, causisque audent prefigere metam.  . .  O 163 To Dr Lawrence     36
    Dum defenditur imber,  . . . . . . . . .  O 181 Waltoni Piscat      3
    Hic, dum debita morti  . . . . . . . .  O 182 Waltoni Piscat      5
    Charus enim cunctis, tanquam, dum vita manebat,  . .  O 212 Tr Greek 7.560     3
    Omnia, dum Macedum gloria et arma premunt.  . . . .  O 216 Tr Greek 9.288     4
    Et morbus tegitur, dum premit ora pudor.  . . . .  O 221 Tr Greek 10.98     2
    Dum docuit blanda voce natare pater.  . . . . .  O 228 Rivum a Stoana     4
    Cum sexagenis, dum plura recluserit aetas,   . . . .  O 230 Geographia Met    19
DUMETA
    Attoniti dumeta vident inculta coloni . . . . . .  O  91 Messiah           75
DUO
    Myriades sibi pulcra duas, duo millia poscit  . . . .  O 230 Geographia Met    10
    Centuria Ligures augent duo millia quarta.  . . . .  O 230 Geographia Met    14
DUOS
    Quae potuere duos tertius unus habet. . . . . . .  O  86 Tr Dryden Milt     6
    Dissimili domus una duos tenet arte tumentes;  . . .  O 385 The Warehouse   D   1
DUOSQUE
    Undecies centum denos quater adde duosque.  . . . .  O 229 Epigram IV         2
DURA
    Desidiae sors dura manet, graviorque labore  . . . .  O 161 Gnothi seauton    25
    Heu quam dura preces sprevit, quam surda querelas  . .  O 212 Tr Greek 7.560     5
    Seria seponens, aut mala dura pati.  . . . . . .  O 221 Tr Greek 10.72     2
DURIS
    Nunc veteres duris periere securibus umbrae,   . . . .  O 228 Rivum a Stoana     7
DURO
    Pectore qui duro, crudos de vite racemos . . . . .  O 217 Tr Greek 9.375     1
DUXIT
    Qui duxit sulcos, illi teret area messem,  . . . .  O  90 Messiah           73
    Scaliger ut duxit, tenuis pertaesus opellae,  . . . .  O 160 Gnothi seauton     2
E
    E scopulo numerare fluctus.  . . . . . . .  O 166 Oda Isle Skye      12
    E Waltoni  Piscatore Perfecto excerptum.  . . . . .  O 181 Waltoni Piscat   V   T
    Et saltu e muro Ditis opaca petit:   . . . . . .  O 211 Tr Greek 7.471     2
    E longinquo itidem pontus et orcus erat. . . . . .  O 213 Tr Greek 9.29       6
    Natus eram lacrymans, lacrymans e luce recedo;   . . .  O 221 Tr Greek 10.84     1
ECCE
    Nascere, magne puer! Tibi primas, ecce! oorollas  . .  O  89 Messiah           27
    Auditur Deus! ecce Deus! reboantia circum   . . .  O  89 Messiah           35
    Saxa sonant Deus; ecce Deus! deflectitur aether  . .  O  89 Messiah           36
    Ecce! peregrinis fervent tua limina turbis;  . . . .  O  92 Messiah           99
    Ecce! cremant genibus tritae regalibus arae.  . . . .  O  92 Messiah          103
    Naufragus hic jaceo; contra jacet ecce colonus!  . .  O 210 Tr Greek 7.265     1
    Sidereus tamen hic territat, eoce, canis!  . . .  O 213 Tr Greek 9.18       4
EDIDIT
    Et placido tandem haec edidit ore, Dea:  . . . . .  O 386 In Birchium     D   4
EDIFICAT
    Compagem edificat, coelorum atque aetheris ignes  . .  O 163 To Dr Lawrence     29
EDIT
    Quos pulsata sonos edit lyra pollice, primis  . . .  Y  28 Aurora Musis       15
EFFICIET
    Quid labor efficiet? non nisi nudus ero. . . . . .  O 220 Tr Greek 10.58     2
EFFIGIEMQUE
    Effigiemque Dei, quantum servare licebit,  . . . . .  O 205 Christianus        29
EFFLANT
    Quem efflant quem rem Phoebi naribus ignis equi  . .  Y  28 Aurora Musis    V  14
EFFLAT
    Ignis quem Phoebi naribus efflat equus,  . . . . .  Y  28 Aurora Musis       14
EFFUGIENS
    Plenum opus effugiens; aptans juga mollia collo  . . .  O 205 Christianus        22
EFFUNDET
    Effundet Patria Fletus,  . . . . . . . .  O 109 Post-genitis       6
EGERIAE
    Ingredere! Egeriae sacrum en tibi panditur antrum!  . .  O 116 Tr Pope Grotto     9
EGES
    Cur opulentus eges? tua cuncta in foenore ponis.  . .  O 223 Tr. Gk. 11.167     1
EGO
    Huc ego delatus placido per coerula cursu  . . . .  O 169 Insula Kenneth     5
    Heraclitus ego; indoctae ne laedite linguae,  . . . .  O 209 Tr Greek 7.128     1
    Corde meo accendas; ardeo totus ego.  . . . . .  O 225 Tr. Gk. 16.209     2
```

EGREGIOS
    Birchius egregios, claraque gesta virum. . . . . . .   PAGE TITLE   LINE
                                                O 386 In Birchium   D   2
EHEU
    Eheu, quid decies plus mihi sexta dedit! . . . . .   O 171 Tr. Busy Fly   10
    Eheu! quam longo tecum consumerer aevo! . . . . .   O 384 On the Gin-Act D   5
EIA
    Armatam Pallas Venerem conspexit, et eia . . . . .   O 384 Epigramma   D   1
EJICE
    Mentibus afflatu terrenas ejice sordes . . . . . .   O 232 Prayer   5
ELATA
    Quisquis adit lectos elata uxore secundos, ...   O 215 Tr Greek 9.133   1
ELEGANTE
    Tene per pictas oculo elegante . . . .   O 153 In Theatro   7
ELEMENTA
    Tu secura tamen confusa elementa videbis, ...   O 92 Messiah   117
    Naturae invadens, mundique elementa refingens . . . .   O 163 To Dr Lawrence 25
ELIGAT
    Nec natet, et nunc has partes, nunc eligat illas, . . .   O 205 Christianus   16
ELIGE
    Elige iter vitae, ut possis; rixisque dolisque . . . .   O 217 Tr Greek 9.359   1
    Elige iter vitae, ut mavis; prudentia lausque . . . .   O 217 Tr Greek 9.360   1
ELISA
    Ingenium et mores si pulchra probavit Elisa, ...   O 104 To Eliz Carter   3
ELIZAE
    In Elizae Aenigma . . . .   O 103 Elizae Aenigma   T
ELOQUIUMQUE
    Eloquiumque potens linguis torpentibus affer, ...   O 232 Prayer   7
ELUCTATUM
    Tuto eluctatum spatiis Sapientia dia . . . .   O 161 Gnothi seauton   20
EMENDATUM
    (Post Lexicon Anglicanum auctum et emendatum.) . . . .   O 160 Gnothi seauton   T
EN
    Altius, en! Lebanon gaudentia culmina tollit, ...   O 89 Messiah   30
    En! summo exultant nutantes vertice silvae. . . . .   O 89 Messiah   31
    En! quem turba diu cecinerunt enthea, vates, ...   O 89 Messiah   41
    En! Salvator adest; vultus agnoscite caeci . . . . .   O 89 Messiah   42
    En! formosa tibi porrecta per atria proles . . . . .   O 92 Messiah   96
    En! formosa tibi spatiosa per atria proles . . . . .   O 92 Messiah   V 96
    Barbarus, en! clarum divino lumine templum . . . . .   O 92 Messiah   100
    Aetheris, en! portas sacro fulgore micantes . . . . .   O 92 Messiah   106
    En quoque quod Mirum, ...   O 110 Post-genitis   35
    Ingredere! Egeriae sacrum en tibi panditur antrum! . .   O 116 Tr Pope Grotto   9
    Exiguum en! Priami monumentum; haud ille meretur . . .   O 210 Tr Greek 7.136   1
    En Sexto, Sexti meditatur imago, silente; . . . . .   O 223 Tr. Gk. 11.145   1
ENIM
    Charus enim cunctis, tanquam, dum vita manebat, . . .   O 212 Tr Greek 7.560   3
ENSIS
    Vomerem, et in falcem rigidus curvabitur ensis. . . .   O 90 Messiah   70
ENTHEA
    En! quem turba diu cecinerunt enthea, vates, ...   O 89 Messiah   41
EODEM
    Quae nos blanda comes, quae nos perducat eodem, . . .   O 171 Tr. Busy Fly   7
    Me, cane vitato, canis excipit alter; eodem . . . .   O 213 Tr Greek 9.18   1
EOIS
    Carpit Arabs, hortis quicquid frondescit eois. . . .   O 89 Messiah   29
EPICIS
    Assurgitque epicis pagina docta modis. . . . . . .   Y 28 Aurora Musis   10
EPICTETUS
    Servus Epictetus, mutilatus corpore vixi . . . . .   O 114 Tr Gk Epigrams   3
    Servus, Epictetus, mutilato corpore, vixi, ...   O 212 Tr Greek 7.676   1
EPICURUM
    His sapiens lectis, Epicurum quaerere frustra . . . .   O 222 Tr Greek 11.50   5
EPIGRAMMA
    Ad Lauram parituram Epigramma . . . .   O 115 Ad Lauram Epig   T
    Epigramma . . . .   O 384 Epigramma   D   T
EPILOGUS
    Epilogus . . . .   O 188 Epilogus   T
EPULAE
    Namque, ubi mensas onerant epulae, ...   O 193 Tr. Medea III   11
EQUALES
    Inter equales, sine felle liber, ...   O 153 In Theatro   9
EQUI
    Quem efflant quem rem Phoebi naribus ignis equi . . .   Y 28 Aurora Musis V 14
EQUUS
    Vel Pede Equus tanget, ...   O 109 Post-genitis   3
    Sanguinem Equus sugit, ...   O 110 Post-genitis   37
    Ignis quem Phoebi naribus efflat equus, ...   Y 28 Aurora Musis   14
ERAM
    Sum nunc, nec possum cernere qualis eram. . . . . .   O 209 Tr. Greek 6.1   4
    Credit, Achaemenidae nuper agellus eram. . . . . .   O 215 Tr Greek 9.74   2
    Pauper eram, nummis diffluit arca senis; . . . . .   O 215 Tr Greek 9.138   2
    Natus eram lacrymans, lacrymans e luce recedo; . . .   O 221 Tr Greek 10.84   1
ERAS
    Cuique esses natus, cuique sodalis, eras. . . . . .   O 212 Tr Greek 7.560   4
ERAT
    Jupiter unus erat, qui stravit fulmine gentes; . . .   O 103 Elizae Aenigma   5
    E longinquo itidem pontus et orcus erat. . . . . .   O 213 Tr Greek 9.29   6
ERGO
    Pateris ergo quod populus solet . . . .   O 186 Ad T. L. M.D.   1
    Ergo optent homines, aut nunquam in luminis oras . . .   O 217 Tr Greek 9.359   9

		PAGE	TITLE	LINE

ERIS
Thralia. Quid mavis? tutius hostis eris. . . . . . . O 197 On Mrs. Thrale 2
At tu quisquis eris, miseri qui cruda poetae . . . . Y 387 Death Mother D 1

ERIT
Sexaginta annis non minor unus erit. . . . . O 171 Tr. Busy Fly 12
Dignus qui multa in lustra senescat, erit. . . . . . O 214 Tr Greek 9.55 2
Per fluctus vitae sic tibi cursus erit. . . . . . . O 221 Tr Greek 10.74 6
"Qui scribat meritas, Birchius alter erit." . . . . O 386 In Birchium D 6

ERO
Quid labor efficiet? non nisi nudus ero. . . . . . . O 220 Tr Greek 10.58 2

ERRAT
Errat adhuc vitreus per prata virentia rivus, . . . O 228 Rivum a Stoana 1

ERRORIS
Inter erroris salebrosa longi, ... O 168 Oda to Thrale 9

ERUDITA
Cui Fronte Sertum in Erudita . . . . O 101 Ad Urbanum 3

ERUNTUR
Curas mulcentes dulce eruntur aves. . . . . Y 28 Aurora Musis 4

ESCA
Non tenet; esca natat pulchra, sed hamus abest. . . . O 209 Tr. Greek 5.67 2

ESSE
Liber ut esse velim, suasisti, pulchra Maria: . . . . O 105 Lady Defence 1
Ut studiis sperem, aut ausim par esse querelis, . . . O 160 Gnothi seauton 15
Quas Amor undarum fingeret esse deas: . . . . . . O 169 Insula Kenneth 10
Quas Amor undarum crederet esse deas: . . . . . . O 169 Insula Kenneth V 10
Spes hominum ac curas cum procul esse jubet. . . . . O 170 Insula Kenneth 16
Spes hominum et curas gens procul esse velit. . . . O 170 Insula Kenneth V 16
Cum tacet indoctus, sapientior esse videtur, ... O 221 Tr Greek 10.98 1
Nutrit mane, putes esse Heliconis aqua. . . . . . . Y 28 Aurora Musis 6

ESSES
Cuique esses natus, cuique sodalis, eras. . . . . . O 212 Tr Greek 7.560 4

ESSET
Utile cunctis hoc opus esset; . . . . O 193 Tr. Medea III 10

EST
Aut, hoc si nimium est, tandem nova lexica poscam? . . O 162 Gnothi seauton 54
Est proprium, et quavis captare indagine verum, . . . O 163 To Dr Lawrence 7
Omnibus unus amor, non est modus unus amoris. . . . O 163 To Dr Lawrence 8
Tantundem est illis, repleat spatia ardua coeli . . . O 163 To Dr Lawrence 13
Scire vices ponti facile est, nihil amplius optant . . O 163 To Dr Lawrence 15
Nil opus est aeris sacra de turre sonantis . . . . O 170 Insula Kenneth V 18A
Quo vagor ulterius? quod ubique requiritur hic est; . . O 170 Insula Kenneth 21
Patris Numen adire est. . . . . O 182 Waltoni Piscat 10
Tandem dolori plus satis est datum, ... O 187 Ad T. L. M.D. 13
Phoebe fave, aegrotat quae te colit, ulla nec usquam est O 197 Summ. Lawrence 1
Judice quo scelerum est paenituisse salus, ... O 198 Tr. Ash Wed. 2
Cuique loco recti paenituisse mali est . . . . . . O 198 Tr. Ash Wed. V 2
Cuique loco recte paenituisse mali est . . . . . . O 198 Tr. Ash Wed. V 2
Nunc est pro poena poenituisse reis. . . . . O 208 A Meditation 4
Est mihi quod non te rideo, plena salus. . . . . . O 211 Tr Greek 7.318 2
Et ferus et Timon sub terris; janitor Orci, ... O 211 Tr Greek 7.319 1
Cum procul est, optat, cum venit, quisque senectam . . O 214 Tr Greek 9.54 1
Graeciae et urbs, urbi est ista propago, decus. . . . O 214 Tr Greek 9.65 2
Audiit, irata est ne nova Musa foret. . . . . . . O 214 Tr Greek 9.66 2
Quod vitae satis est, peto, Macrine: . . . . O 215 Tr Greek 9.110 3
Mi, nequid nimis, est nimis probatum. . . . . . . O 215 Tr Greek 9.110 4
Sufficit hoc votis; flos hic pulcherrimus aevi est, . . O 215 Tr Greek 9.112 3
Exiguum est Marti, sed mihi grande lucrum. . . . . . O 216 Tr Greek 9.163 4
Perstrepit omne forum; cura molesta domi est. . . . . O 217 Tr Greek 9.359 2
Paupertas misera est; multae cum conjuge lites . . . O 217 Tr Greek 9.359 5
Proles aucta gravat, rapta orbat, caeca juventae est . . O 217 Tr Greek 9.359 7
Permeat omne forum; vita quieta domi est. . . . . . O 217 Tr Greek 9.360 2
Mulcet amor prolis, sopor est sine prole profundus; . . O 217 Tr Greek 9.360 7
Teque frui timor est, teque carere dolor. . . . . . O 218 Tr Greek 9.394 2
Pulchra est virginitas intacta, at vita periret, . . . O 218 Tr Greek 9.444 1
Omnis vita nimis brevis est felicibus, una . . . . . O 220 Tr Greek 10.28 1
Gratia ter grata est velox, sin forte moretur . . . . O 220 Tr Greek 10.30 1
Nil non mortale est mortalibus; omne quod est hi . . . O 220 Tr Greek 10.31 1
Nil non mortale est mortalibus; omne quod est hi . . . O 220 Tr Greek 10.31 1
Nil non mortale est mortalibus; omne quod est hic . . . O 220 Tr Greek 10.31 V 1
Nil non mortale est mortalibus; omne quod est hic . . . O 220 Tr Greek 10.31 V 1
Vita omnis scena est ludusque; aut ludere disce . . . O 221 Tr Greek 10.72 1
Tale hominum genus est, infirmum, triste, misellum, . . O 221 Tr Greek 10.84 3
Recta ad pauperiem tendit, cui corpora cordi est . . . O 222 Tr. Gk. 10.119 1
Quae sine morte fuga est vitae, quam turba malorum . . O 222 Tr. Gk. 10.123 1
Vita rosae brevis est; properans si carpere nolis, . . O 223 Tr Greek 11.53 1
Vitae rosae brevis est; properans si carpere nolis, . . O 223 Tr Greek 11.53 V 1
Orator statua est, statuaeque orator imago. . . . . . O 223 Tr. Gk. 11.145 2
Patria Sparta mihi est, patria clara virum. . . . . . O 224 Tr Greek 16.1 2
Arte valent isti, mihi robore vivere solo est, ... O 224 Tr Greek 16.1 3
Quod nimium est fit ineptum; hinc, ut dixere priores, . O 224 Tr Greek 16.16 1
Stat: fixum est: nequeunt jam revocare preces. . . . . O 384 On the Gin-Act D 8
Quaeris, Quis prior est fama meritisve; superna . . . O 385 The Warehouse D 3
Hic Bona queis opus est venditat, Ille Sonum. . . . . O 385 The Warehouse D 6

ESTO
Cunctiparens tellus, salve, levis esto pusillo . . . . O 211 Tr Greek 7.461 1

ET
Quos laudet vates Graius Romanus et Anglus . . . . . O 86 Tr Dryden Milt 1
Quos laudet vates Graecus Romanus et Anglus . . . . . O 86 Tr Dryden Milt V 1
Aonidesque Deae, et mendacis somnia Pindi. . . . . . O 88 Messiah 5
Praebeat, et tacite foecundos irriget imbres! . . . . O 88 Messiah 15
Et juga Carmeli recreant fragrantia coelum. . . . . . O 89 Messiah 33

	PAGE	TITLE	LINE
Deserta et lata mollescunt aspera voce,	O 89	Messiah	V 34
Et gremio fotis selectas porrigit herbas,	O 90	Messiah	60
Et curas felix patrias testabitur orbis.	O 90	Messiah	65
Vomerem, et in falcem rigidus curvabitur ensis.	O 90	Messiah	70
Et serae texent vites umbracula proli.	O 90	Messiah	74
Per ludum pueri injicient, et fessa colubri	O 91	Messiah	87
Coelicolae pandunt, crescentis et aurea lucis	O 92	Messiah	V 107
Perpetuo viret et virebit:	O 101	Ad Urbanum	4
Quid et minetur, sollicitus parum,	O 101	Ad Urbanum	6
Et juvat ingenii vita sine arte rudis.	O 104	To Eliz Carter	2
Ingenium et mores si pulchra probavit Elisa,	O 104	To Eliz Carter	3
Vitiantes, et spoliantes;	O 109	Post-genitis	14
Et pingues absque Labore.	O 109	Post-genitis	18
Calcatos et Cruciatos	O 110	Post-genitis	32
Pendet, et incoquitur tectum sine fraude metallum:	O 116	Tr Pope Grotto	6
Splendet, et incoquitur tectum sine fraude metallum:	O 116	Tr Pope Grotto	V 6
(Post Lexicon Anglicanum auctum et emendatum.)	O 160	Gnothi seauton	T
Ille quidem recte, sublimis, doctus, et acer,	O 160	Gnothi seauton	6
Gesserat et quicquid Virtus, Sapientia quicquid	O 160	Gnothi seauton	9
Tristis et atra quies, et tardae taedia vitae.	O 161	Gnothi seauton	26
Tristis et atra quies, et tardae taedia vitae.	O 161	Gnothi seauton	26
Pectus, et ingenium vano se robore jactans.	O 161	Gnothi seauton	36
Incultum Studiis, et paucis dotibus auctum	O 161	Gnothi seauton	V 36
Res angusta domi, et macrae penuria mentis.	O 161	Gnothi seauton	41
Conspicit aggestas, et se miratur in illis,	O 161	Gnothi seauton	43
Versat opum cumulos, et se miratur in illis,	O 161	Gnothi seauton	43
Et rerum volitant rarae per inane figurae.	O 161	Gnothi seauton	V 43
Est proprium, et quavis captare indagine verum,	O 162	Gnothi seauton	51
Vel digiti tractant, oculus vel sentit et auris:	O 163	To Dr Lawrence	7
In sublime rapit, queis terra et pontus et aer	O 163	To Dr Lawrence	12
In sublime rapit, queis terra et pontus et aer	O 163	To Dr Lawrence	32
Et me, cuncta beans cui nocuit dies,	O 163	To Dr Lawrence	32
Luci reddidit et mihi,	O 164	Recover Eyes	8
Dicitur, et vanos dedocuisse deos.	O 164	Recover Eyes	9
Spes hominum et curas gens procul esse velit.	O 169	Insula Kenneth	4
Et summi accendat pectus amore boni.	O 170	Insula Kenneth	V 16
Hic secura quies, hic et honestus amor.	O 170	Insula Kenneth	V 16B
Nam licet, et toto prolue laeta mero.	O 170	Insula Kenneth	22
Permitte fidens, et muliebribus,	O 171	Tr. Busy Fly	4
Opes, triumphos, et subacti	O 187	Ad T. L. M.D.	V 18
Gaudium sacro fluat, et benigni	O 188	Epilogus	3
Instet, et evellens terroris spicula corde,	O 193	Prayer on Xmas	3
Gestiat, et, nullo pietatis limite clausus,	O 205	Christianus	4
Et sibi, delirans quanquam et peccator in horas	O 205	Christianus	8
Et sibi, delirans quanquam et peccator in horas	O 205	Christianus	14
Nec natet, et nunc has partes, nunc eligat illas,	O 205	Christianus	14
Pergit, et imperiis sentit se dulcibus actum.	O 205	Christianus	16
Induit, et, terris major, coelestia spirat.	O 205	Christianus	27
Rege, et tuere, quae nocent pellens procul;	O 205	Christianus	30
Sceleris ut expers omnis, et vacuus metu,	O 206	Prayers I	6
Quem moestum et timidum crimina dira gravant;	O 206	Prayers I	9
Et pro me pretium, tu patiare, pater.	O 207	Prayers V	2
Et colere et leges semper amare tuas.	O 207	Prayers V	6
Et colere et leges semper amare tuas.	O 208	Prayers VII	10
Hector dat gladium Ajaci, dat balteum et Ajax	O 208	Prayers VII	10
Hectori, et exitio munus utrique fuit.	O 210	Tr Greek 7.151	1
Nil lucri facies; ossa habet et cinerem.	O 210	Tr Greek 7.151	2
Et ferus est Timon sub terris; janitor Orci,	O 210	Tr Greek 7.284	4
Et saltu e muro Ditis opaca petit:	O 211	Tr Greek 7.319	1
Et pius, et recti cultor: non illa jacere	O 211	Tr Greek 7.471	2
Et pius, et recti cultor: non illa jacere	O 212	Tr Greek 7.590	3
In me animo tellus gignit et unda feras,	O 212	Tr Greek 7.590	3
Sola rates struis infidas, et dulcis amorem	O 213	Tr Greek 9.18	2
E longinquo itidem pontus et orcus erat.	O 213	Tr Greek 9.29	3
Et cycnum fecit Leda petita Jovem.	O 213	Tr Greek 9.29	6
De te plebs audax, hic bene et ille male.	O 214	Tr Greek 9.48	2
Graeciae et Argivis, urbi est ista propago, decus.	O 214	Tr Greek 9.50	2
Et senium triplex Nestoris urna capit.	O 214	Tr Greek 9.65	2
Clamat et Argivis: Vetuli, ne tangite, vita	O 215	Tr Greek 9.112	4
Spreta jacet Marathon, jacet et Salaminia laurus,	O 216	Tr Greek 9.163	3
Omnia, dum Macedum gloria et arma premunt.	O 216	Tr Greek 9.288	3
Civis et externus grati; domus hospita nescit	O 216	Tr Greek 9.288	4
Quod mors in cineres solvit, et abdit humo.	O 219	Tr Greek 9.648	1
Et morbus tegitur, dum premit ora pudor.	O 221	Tr Greek 10.84	4
Magne bonum, omne malum et poscentibus abnue nobis.	O 221	Tr Greek 10.98	2
Multa alere, et multas aedificare domos.	O 221	Tr Greek 10.108	2
Lunaque quas et sol itque reditque vias.	O 222	Tr. Gk. 10.119	2
Terror inest aliis, moerorque, et siquid habebis	O 222	Tr. Gk. 10.123	4
Cuncta, cinis cuncta et ludicra, cuncta nihil.	O 222	Tr. Gk. 10.123	5
Clam nocte tollit Aulus, et ridens ait;	O 222	Tr. Gk. 10.124	2
Menodotum pinxit Diodorus, et exit imago,	O 223	Tr. Gk. 11.176	4
At te bonum si noris, et bonis natum.	O 223	Tr. Gk. 11.213	1
Tutum hic sedile, et si placet, sopor tutus.	O 224	Tr Greek 13.3	3
Et melli nimio fellis amaror inest.	O 224	Tr Greek 13.3	4
Arti ignis lucem tribui, tamen artis et ignis	O 224	Tr Greek 16.16	2
Et Pari, et Anchisa, non alius, Venerem.	O 225	Tr Greek 16.87	1
Et Pari, et Anchisa, non alius, Venerem.	O 225	Tr. Gk. 16.168	2
Das bene collatos, quos Roma et Graecia jactat,	O 225	Tr. Gk. 16.168	2
Prolem Hippi, et sua qua meliorem secula nullum	O 225	Tr. Gk. 16.331	3
Sexta dolet Babylona, et gaudet septima Christo.	O 226	Tr. Simonides	1
	O 226	Septem Aetates	V 4

		PAGE	TITLE	LINE
ET	(CONTINUED)			
Pellat et tristes animi tenebras,		O 227	A Meditation	2
Tectaque qua fluxit, nunc et aperta fluit.		O 228	Rivum a Stoana	10
Jejunium et Cibus		O 228	Jejunium Cibus	T
Undecies binas decadas et millia septem		O 230	Geographia Met	6
Et quadragenis quoque ter tria millia jungit.		O 230	Geographia Met	26
Myriadas denas dat, quinque et millia, sexque		O 230	Geographia Met	27
Centurias, et tres decadas Europa Britannis.		O 230	Geographia Met	28
Et quadragenis decades quinque addit Ierne,		O 231	Geographia Met	32
Rorem, qui regeles, geniali et gramina succo		Y 28	Aurora Musis	5
Apte antiqua novis miscentur, et utile dulci:		O 383	Syl. Urb. Thes	D 3
Armatam Pallas Venerem conspexit, et eia		O 384	Epigramma	D 1
Munera luxurians dat pampinus, et generoso		O 385	Cantico Solom.	D 13
Et placido tandem haec edidit ore, Dea:		O 386	In Birchium	D 4
Et petiit terras per freta longa novas.		O 386	Tr Epi. Madoc	D 4
Et cortina novum det revoluta diem!		O 393	Tr. of Crashaw	D 4
Tunc alacres demum surgent, et crastinus ortus		O 393	Tr. of Crashaw	D 5
&				
Menstrua concinnat Sylvanus, & Annua Dona,		O 383	Syl. Urb. Thes	D 1
ETC				
Mea nec Falernae Etc.		O 85	Mea nec Falern	T
Adjecere bonae etc.		O 85	Adjecere bonae	T
ETENIM				
Alter ut adsit Homerus, adest etenim alter Achilles.		O 218	Tr Greek 9.523	2
ETIAM				
Corpore nunc etiam libera facta fuit.		O 114	Tr Gk Epigrams	2
EUMARUS				
Si forsan tumulum quo conditur Eumarus aufers,		O 210	Tr Greek 7.284	3
EURIS				
Huc, soror alma, veni! pernicibus ocyor Euris		O 385	Cantico Solom.	D 17
EUROPA				
Antiope satyrum, Danae aurum, Europa juvencum,		O 214	Tr Greek 9.48	1
Myriadas septem decies Europa ducentis		O 230	Geographia Met	25
Centurias, et tres decadas Europa Britannis.		O 230	Geographia Met	28
EUROS				
Jam saltu capreas, jam cursu provocat euros.		O 90	Messiah	51
Nunc saltu capraes, nunc cursu provocat euros.		O 90	Messiah	V 51
EVELLENS				
Instet, et evellens terroris spicula corde,		O 205	Christianus	4
EVENIAT				
Eveniat tantum mitior unda tibi!		O 211	Tr Greek 7.350	2
EVOCAT				
Evocat Abramum dein tertia; quarta relinquit		O 226	Septem Aetates	2
EX				
Linguarumque omni ex terra discordia concors		O 161	Gnothi seauton	V 22
Vive tuo ex animo, vario rumore loquetur		O 214	Tr Greek 9.50	1
Ex Cantico Solomonis		O 384	Cantico Solom.	D T
EXAESTUANTIS				
Exaestuantis pectoris impetum,		O 166	Oda Isle Skye	17
EXCEPTAE				
Exceptae hospitio Musae tribuere libellos		O 216	Tr Greek 9.160	1
EXCERPTUM				
E Waltoni Piscatore Perfecto excerptum.		O 181	Waltoni Piscat	V T
EXCIPIT				
Excipit aethereis, Ars omnis plaudit amica,		O 161	Gnothi seauton	21
Excipit aethereis, Ars omnis plaudit amico,		O 161	Gnothi seauton	V 21
Me, cane vitato, canis excipit alter; eodem		O 213	Tr Greek 9.18	1
EXCLAMAT				
Exclamat: Nunc me cernere desinitis.		O 224	Tr. Gk. 11.432	2
EXEMPLIS				
Fallimur exemplis; temere sibi turba scholarum		O 160	Gnothi seauton	12
EXEMPLO				
At docet, exemplo, vis sibi quanta, tuo.		O 218	Tr Greek 9.530	2
EXERCET				
Imperium qua Turca ferox exercet iniquum.		O 230	Geographia Met	5
EXHALANT				
Suaviter exhalant violaria grata, Sabaeo		O 385	Cantico Solom.	D 15
EXHILARORQUE				
Expleor ambrosiis exhilarorque cibis.		O 219	Tr Greek 9.577	4
EXIGIS				
Qui nec scelestos exigis,		O 206	Prayers II	4
EXIGUUM				
Exiguum en! Priami monumentum; haud ille meretur		O 210	Tr Greek 7.136	1
Exiguum est Marti, sed mihi grande lucrum.		O 216	Tr Greek 9.163	4
EXIT				
Menodotum pinxit Diodorus, et exit imago,		O 223	Tr. Gk. 11.213	1
EXITIALES				
Domibus claris exitiales,		O 193	Tr. Medea III	7
EXITIO				
Hectori, et exitio munus utrique fuit.		O 210	Tr Greek 7.151	2
EXOPTES				
Quam magis exoptes arte valere tua.		O 197	Summ. Lawrence	2
EXOSUS				
Ingemit exosus, scribendaque lexica mandat		O 160	Gnothi seauton	4
EXPECTATA				
Expectata diu! Naturae claustra refringens		O 89	Messiah	26
EXPERIENTIA				
Sic sibi diffisi, lenta experientia cursum		O 163	To Dr Lawrence	17
EXPERIERE				
Forte boni, ultrices experiere vices.		O 222	Tr. Gk. 10.123	6

		PAGE	TITLE		LINE
EXPERS					
Sceleris ut expers omnis, et vacuus metu,	. . . . .	O 206	Prayers I		9
EXPLEOR					
Expleor ambrosiis exhilarorque cibis.		O 219	Tr Greek 9.577		4
EXPLICAT					
Explicat, incinctam radiatae luce tiarae!	. . . . .	O 92	Messiah		95
EXSECUIT					
Venturi exsecuit, vascula prima meri, ...		O 217	Tr Greek 9.375		2
EXSURGE					
Exsurge fortis, nunc animis opus, ...		O 187	Ad T. L. M.D.		14
EXTERNI					
Quid ferat externi velox, quid deterat aetas,	. . . .	O 228	Rivum a Stoana		11
EXTERNUS					
Civis et externus grati; domus hospita nescit	. . . .	O 219	Tr Greek 9.648		1
EXULAT					
His cura credo sedibus exulat;		O 166	Oda Isle Skye		5
EXULTANT					
En! summo exultant nutantes vertice silvae.		O 89	Messiah		31
EYE					
. . . Johnson, as he lay confined with an inflamed Eye.		O 162	To Dr Lawrence		T
FABELLAS					
Crethida fabellas dulces garrire peritam		O 211	Tr Greek 7.459		1
FABRI					
Munera muneribus si retulere fabri.		O 225	Tr Greek 16.87		4
FACE					
Sacri vagantes luminis gressus face		O 206	Prayers I		5
FACIAM					
Quid faciam? tenebrisne pigram damnare senectam	. . .	O 162	Gnothi seauton		52
FACIES					
Nil lucri facies; ossa habet et cinerem.		O 210	Tr Greek 7.284		4
FACILE					
Scire vices ponti facile est, nihil amplius optant	. .	O 163	To Dr Lawrence		15
FACILEM					
Tunc vati facilem reprobat Apollo, Sybillae		Y 28	Aurora Musis		7
FACILI					
Laurenti saltem facili dignarier aure?		O 163	To Dr Lawrence		5
FACILIS					
Adsit, Laura, tibi facilis Lucina dolenti, ...		O 115	Ad Lauram Epig		3
Nunc mihi facilis		O 198	Medico Aeger S		1
FACILISQUE					
Facilisque semper confitenti ades reo, ...		O 206	Prayers III		2
FACIT					
Non vitanda gravem, non toleranda facit?		O 222	Tr. Gk. 10.123		2
Hirce, parem nitido te tua barba facit.		O 224	Tr. Gk. 11.430		2
FACIUNT					
Legitimas faciunt pectora pura preces.		O 170	Insula Kenneth		20
Legitimas faciunt pura labella preces		O 170	Insula Kenneth	V	20
FACTA					
Corpore nunc etiam libera facta fuit.		O 114	Tr Gk Epigrams		2
Qui veterum modo facta ducum, modo carmina vatum,	. . .	O 160	Gnothi seauton		8
Impia facta patrans, homines fortasse latebis,	. . . .	O 220	Tr Greek 10.27		1
FAELIX					
Faelix ante alios nullius debitor aeris;		O 222	Tr Greek 11.50		1
FALCEM					
Vomerem, et in falcem rigidus curvabitur ensis.	. . . .	O 90	Messiah		70
FALERNA					
Virgilio vires Uva Falerna dedit.		O 85	Mea nec Falern		4
FALERNAE					
Mea nec Falernae Etc.		O 85	Mea nec Falern		T
FALLAX					
Secta crepet nimis alta fallax.		O 166	Oda Isle Skye		16
FALLIMUR					
Fallimur exemplis; temere sibi turba scholarum	. . . .	O 160	Gnothi seauton		12
FAMA					
Funus Alexandri mentitur fama; fidesque		O 210	Tr Greek 7.239		1
Quaeris, Quis prior est fama meritisve; superna	. . . .	O 385	The Warehouse	D	3
FAMES					
Seu te saeva fames, levitas sive improba fecit,	. . . .	O 171	Tr. Busy Fly	V	1
FAMULATA					
Gemmaque luxuriae nondum famulata nitenti		O 116	Tr Pope Grotto		5
FARRA					
Nunc huic, nunc aliis cedens, cui farra Menippus	. . . .	O 215	Tr Greek 9.74		1
FASTU					
Captans, nec fastu tumidus, semperque futuro		O 205	Christianus		3
FATA					
Una quidem, sic fata volunt, tibi vivitur aestas,	. . .	O 171	Tr. Busy Fly		9
I, quoniam sic fata vocant: liceat mihi tantum	. . . .	O 384	On the Gin-Act	D	9
FATERI					
Notior ipse mihi fieri, incultumque fateri		O 161	Gnothi seauton		35
Notior ipse mihi fieri, pectusque fateri		O 161	Gnothi seauton	V	35
FATERIS					
Fateris ergo quod populus solet		O 186	Ad T. L. M.D.		1
FATIGATAMQUE					
Novit, fatigatamque nugis		O 102	Ad Urbanum		19
FAUSTA					
Quae fausta Romae dixit Horatius, ...		O 188	Epilogus		1
Haec fausta vobis dicimus, Angliae		O 188	Epilogus		2
FAUSTINE					
Mente senes olim juvenis, Faustine, premebas,	. . . .	O 225	Tr. Gk. 16.364		1
FAUTRIX					
Hunc oculis Veri Fautrix lustravit acutis, ...		O 386	In Birchium	D	3

		PAGE	TITLE		LINE
FAVE					
	Phoebe fave, aegrotat quae te colit, ulla nec usquam est	O 197	Summ. Lawrence		1
FAVENTEM					
	Aurem faventem precibus O praebe meis;	O 206	Prayers III		3
FAXINT					
	Stella mea, observans stellas, Dii me aethera faxint,	O 212	Tr Greek 7.669		1
FEBRE					
	Haud lavit Phido, haud tetigit; mihi febre calenti	O 223	Tr. Gk. 11.118		1
FEBRIS					
	Huc foedat quos lepra, urit quos febris, adeste!	O 88	Messiah		16
FECERUNT					
	Fecerunt nulli sors titulique gravem.	O 226	Tr. Simonides		4
	Fecerunt rami latebras, tenebrisque diurnis	O 228	Rivum a Stoana		5
FECIT					
	Seu te saeva sitis, levitas sive improba fecit,	O 171	Tr. Busy Fly		1
	Seu te saeva fames, levitas sive improba fecit,	O 171	Tr. Busy Fly	V	1
	Et cycnum fecit Leda petita Jovem.	O 214	Tr Greek 9.48		2
FELICI					
	Felici thalamo non, puto, rixa strepit.	O 226	Tr. Greek		2
FELICIBUS					
	Omnis vita nimis brevis est felicibus, una	O 220	Tr Greek 10.28		1
FELICITATIS					
	Felicitatis sedibus	O 206	Prayers II		3
FELIX					
	Virgo! virgo parit! felix radicibus arbor	O 88	Messiah		10
	Et curas felix patrias testabitur orbis.	O 90	Messiah		65
	Juxta Animo Studiisque felix.	O 101	Ad Urbanum		8
FELLE					
	Inter equales, sine felle liber,	O 153	In Theatro		9
FELLIS					
	Et melli nimio fellis amaror inest.	O 224	Tr Greek 16.16		2
FEMINA					
	Quid quod sacrifici versavit femina libros,	O 170	Insula Kenneth		19
FERAR					
	Quicquid agam, quocunque ferar, conatibus obstat	O 161	Gnothi seauton		40
FERAS					
	At nemo feras iras hominum,	O 193	Tr. Medea III		6
	In me animo tellus gignit et unda feras,	O 213	Tr Greek 9.18		2
FERAT					
	Quid ferat externi velox, quid deterat aetas,	O 228	Rivum a Stoana		11
FERET					
	Jam feret ignavus,	O 110	Post-genitis		33
	Quo, lege vestra, vita me feret mea.	O 226	Tr. Cleanthes		2
FEROCES					
	Voce ubi Cennethus populos domuisse feroces	O 169	Insula Kenneth		3
FERORUM					
	Pervagor gentes, hominum ferorum	O 167	Oda to Thrale		5
	Pervagor terras, hominum ferorum	O 167	Oda to Thrale	V	5
FEROX					
	Imperium qua Turca ferox exercet iniquum.	O 230	Geographia Met		5
FERRE					
	Queis tamen aptam ferre medelam	O 193	Tr. Medea III		9
	Quam domini ingentis ferre supercilium.	O 221	Tr Greek 10.93		2
FERT					
	Fert humeris claudum validis per compita caecus,	O 213	Tr Greek 9.13		1
	Fert humeris, venerabile onus, Cythereius heros	O 216	Tr Greek 9.163		1
FERUNTUR					
	Quandoquidem passim nulla ratione feruntur	O 222	Tr. Gk. 10.124		1
FERUS					
	Et ferus est Timon sub terris; janitor Orci,	O 211	Tr Greek 7.319		1
FERVENT					
	Ecce! peregrinis fervent tua limina turbis;	O 92	Messiah		99
FERVET					
	Humani studium generis cui pectore fervet,	O 102	Ad R. Savage		1
FESSA					
	Per ludum pueri injicient, et fessa colubri	O 91	Messiah		87
FESSE					
	Urbane, nullis fesse laboribus,	O 101	Ad Urbanum		1
FESSIS					
	Hic requies fessis; non sacra saevit in umbra	O 89	Messiah		18
	Hic requies fessis; non sacra hac saevit in umbra	O 89	Messiah	V	18
FIAM					
	Fiam scelestus, nec tamen minus sequar.	O 226	Tr. Cleanthes		4
FICTIS					
	Nil movet insolitum, sub legibus omnia fictis	O 163	To Dr Lawrence		35
	Nec ficto fletu, fictis solvare cachinnis,	O 218	Tr Greek 9.573		3
FICTO					
	Nec ficto fletu, fictis solvare cachinnis,	O 218	Tr Greek 9.573		3
FICUS					
	Jam teneros fructus detrudit lactea ficus	O 385	Cantico Solom.	D	11
FIDA					
	Fida mercedem, meritoque blandum	O 168	Oda to Thrale	V	18
	Usque regat gressus gratia fida meos.	O 207	Prayers IV		4
	Fida comes mensae, fida comesque tori!	O 383	On the Gin-Act	D	4
	Fida comes mensae, fida comesque tori!	O 383	On the Gin-Act	D	4
FIDE					
	Arte nova, raraque fide perscripserat ausus	O 386	In Birchium	D	1
FIDEIQUE					
	Sit memor nostri, fideique merces	O 168	Oda to Thrale		17
	Sit memor nostri, fideique solvat	O 168	Oda to Thrale	V	17

```
                                                            PAGE     TITLE              LINE
FIDEM
    Da fidem certam, precibusque fidis  . . . . . . . .     O 194   Prayer on Xmas        7
FIDENS
    Fidens, Superbo frange Silentio;    . . .
    Pone metum, rostrum fidens immitte culullo,  . . . .    O 101   Ad Urbanum           10
    Permitte fidens, ac muliebribus,    . . . . . . .       O 171   Tr. Busy Fly          3
    Permitte fidens, et muliebribus,    . . . . . . .       O 187   Ad T. L. M.D.        18
    Naufragus hic jaceo; fidens tamen utere velis,  . .     O 187   Ad T. L. M.D.     V  18
FIDES                                                       O 210   Tr Greek 7.282        1
    Stet fides constans, meritoque blandum  . . . . .       O 168   Oda to Thrale        18
    Certa mihi sancto flagret amore fides.  . . . . .       O 207   Prayers VII           6
    Certa vetet dubitare fides, spes laeta timere,  . . .   O 207   Prayers VII           7
FIDESQUE
    Funus Alexandri mentitur fama; fidesque  . . . . .      O 210   Tr Greek 7.239        1
FIDIBUS
    Tene mulceri fidibus canoris?   . . . . . . .           O 153   In Theatro            5
    Voce aut fidibus pellere docuit . . . . . . . . .       O 193   Tr. Medea III         8
FIDIS
    Da fidem certam, precibusque fidis  . . . . . . .       O 194   Prayer on Xmas        7
FIDO
    Coelestis fido caluerunt semina flammae.  . . . . .     O 116   Tr Pope Grotto       14
FIDUM
    Se fidum addicat Christo, mortalia temnens.  . . . .    O 205   Christianus          18
FIDUS
    Fidus adest custos, seu nox furat horrida nimbis,  . .  O  90   Messiah              62
    Fidus adest custos, seu nox furat humida nimbis,  . .   O  90   Messiah           V  62
FIELDS    SEE LINCCLN'S
FIENT
    Verte solum, fient causa timoris opes;  . . . . . .     O 217   Tr Greek 9.359        4
FIERI
    Notior ipse mihi fieri, incultumque fateri  . . . .     O 161   Gnothi seauton       35
    Notior ipse mihi fieri, pectusque fateri  . . . . .     O 161   Gnothi seauton    V  35
FIGURAE
    Horruit implexo qua vallis sente, figurae  . . . . .    O  91   Messiah              80
    Et rerum volitant rarae per inane figurae.  . . . .     O 162   Gnothi seauton       51
FIGURIS
    Corpora cuncta suis gestit variare figuris,  . . . .    O 163   To Dr Lawrence       27
FILIA
    Prosequitur lacrymis filia moesta Sami,  . . . . . .    O 211   Tr Greek 7.459        2
FILIUM
    . . filium peregre agentem desiderio nimis  . . . .     O 186   Ad T. L. M.D.     V   T
FINE
    Blandam lanifici sociam, sine fine loquacem,  . . . .   O 211   Tr Greek 7.459        3
FINEM
    Lexicon ad finem longo luctamine tandem  . . . . . .    O 160   Gnothi seauton        1
FINEMQUE
    Atria, pacis opus, surgent, finemque caduci  . . . .    O  90   Messiah              71
FINGERET
    Quas Amor undarum fingeret esse deas;  . . . . . .      O 169   Insula Kenneth       10
FINIET
    Vitam a terdecimo sextus mihi finiet annus,  . . . .    O 215   Tr Greek 9.112        1
FIRMA
    Firma manet virtus; virtuti innitere, tutus  . . . .    O 221   Tr Greek 10.74        5
FIRMATA
    Pollicitis firmata Dei, stabilita ruinis.  . . . . .    O  92   Messiah             119
FIRMIUS
    Firmius ac ipsis Mundi stabilita ruinis.  . . . . . .   O  92   Messiah           V 119
FIT
    Quales sint monades, qua fit inane, sinas.  . . . .     O 222   Tr Greek 11.50        6
    Quod nimium est fit ineptum; hinc, ut dixere priores,  .O 224   Tr Greek 16.16        1
FIXUM
    Stat: fixum est: nequeunt jam revocare preces.  . . .   O 384   On the Gin-Act    D   8
FLAGRAT
    Sanguine dum tumido suffusus flagrat ocellus,  . . .    O 162   To Dr Lawrence        1
FLAGRET
    Certa mihi sancto flagret amore fides.  . . . . . .     O 207   Prayers VII           6
FLAMMA
    Tu mihi, qui flamma movisti pectora sancti  . . . .     O  88   Messiah               6
FLAMMAE
    Coelestis fido caluerunt semina flammae.  . . . . . .   O 116   Tr Pope Grotto       14
FLAMMAS
    Hostiles oculis flammas jaculantia torvis;  . . . .     O  90   Messiah              67
    Per Trojae flammas, densaque tela, patrem.  . . . .     O 216   Tr Greek 9.163        2
FLENDI
    Haec postrema tibi sit flendi causa, fluatque  . . .    Y 387   Death Mother      D   3
FLERE
    Da veteres noxas animo sic flere novato,  . . . . .     O 198   Tr. Ash Wed.          3
    Da veteres culpas animo sic flere novato,  . . . . .    O 198   Tr. Ash Wed.      V   3
FLETU
    Nec ficto fletu, fictis solvare cachinnis,  . . . .     O 218   Tr Greek 9.573        3
    Credideris fletu funera digna tuo,  . . . . . . . .     Y 387   Death Mother      D   2
FLETUS
    Effundet Patria Fletus,   . . . . . . . .               O 109   Post-genitis          6
FLEXUSQUE
    Ille vias vocis pandet, flexusque liquentis  . . . .    O  90   Messiah              47
FLORE
    Quaerenti obveniet mox sine flore rubus.  . . . . .     O 223   Tr Greek 11.53        2
FLOREA
    Florea mansuetae petulantes vincula tigri  . . . . .    O  91   Messiah              86
FLOREBUNT
    Florebunt Lilia Pratis,   . . . . . . . .               O 109   Post-genitis         26
```

		PAGE	TITLE	LINE
FLOREM				
Ut florem amittat gratia tota perit	. . . .	Y 332	Tr Greek 10.30	V 1
FLORENTIBUS				
Me miserum sors omnis habet; florentibus annis	. . . .	O 215	Tr Greek 9.138	1
FLORES				
Jessaeis surgit, mulcentesque aethera flores	. . . .	O 88	Messiah	11
Flores Fructusque vorantes,	. . . .	O 109	Post-genitis	12
FLORIBUS				
Floribus in pratis legi quos ipse, coronam	. . . . .	O 209	Tr. Greek 5.74	1
FLOS				
Sufficit hoc votis; flos hic pulcherrimus aevi est,	. .	O 215	Tr Greek 9.112	3
FLUAT				
Gaudium sacro fluat, et benigni	. . . . . .	O 193	Prayer on Xmas	3
Heraclite, fluat lacrymarum crebrior imber;	. . . .	O 216	Tr Greek 9.148	3
FLUATQUE				
Haec postrema tibi sit flendi causa, fluatque	. . . .	Y 387	Death Mother	D 3
FLUCTIBUS				
Nec quaerunt quid, luna, tuo cum fluctibus orbi.	. . .	O 163	To Dr Lawrence	16
FLUCTU				
Littoraque ut Fluctu,	. . . .	O 109	Post-genitis	7
FLUCTUS				
Sternite saxa viam, rapidi discedite fluctus!	. . .	O 89	Messiah	40
E scopulo numerare fluctus.	. . . .	O 166	Oda Isle Skye	12
In specula numerare fluctus.	. . . .	O 166	Oda Isle Skye	V 12
Te recidunt moderante fluctus.	. . . . . .	O 166	Oda Isle Skye	20
Te resident moderante fluctus.	. . . . . .	O 166	Oda Isle Skye	V 20
Te recedunt moderante fluctus.	. . . . . .	O 166	Oda Isle Skye	V 20
Ingemina fluctus, ingeminaque sonum.	. . . . . .	O 210	Tr Greek 7.284	2
Per fluctus vitae sic tibi cursus erit.	. . . .	O 221	Tr Greek 10.74	6
FLUENTES				
Impatiens, lenteque fluentes increpat annos.	. . . .	O 92	Messiah	98
FLUIT				
Causarum series quo moderante fluit,	. . . .	O 207	Prayers VI	2
Omnesque in partes tracta retracta fluit;	. . . .	O 221	Tr Greek 10.74	4
Tectaque qua fluxit, nunc et aperta fluit.	. . . .	O 228	Rivum a Stoana	10
FLUMINA				
Flumina prorumpunt; non posthac sole rubescet	. . . .	O 92	Messiah	108
FLUXIT				
Tectaque qua fluxit, nunc et aperta fluit.	. . . .	O 228	Rivum a Stoana	10
FLUXO				
At Seni fluxo sapienter uti	. . . .	O 153	In Theatro	15
FOECUNDA				
Nam foecunda rubri	. . . . . . ــ . .	O 109	Post-genitis	9
Copia, Phidiaci foecunda potentia coeli.	. . . .	O 161	Gnothi seauton	39
Millia myriadi septem foecunda secundae	. . . .	O 230	Geographia Met	31
FOECUNDOS				
Praebeat, et tacite foecundos irriget imbres!	. . . .	O 88	Messiah	15
FOEDA				
Foeda latescit.	. . . .	O 167	Oda to Thrale	8
FOEDANTES				
Omnia foedantes,	. . . .	O 109	Post-genitis	13
FOEDAT				
Huc foedat quos lepra, urit quos febris, adeste!	. . .	O 88	Messiah	16
FOEDERA				
Accendit, rerumque modos ac foedera ponit.	. . . . .	O 163	To Dr Lawrence	30
FOEMINAM				
Ad foeminam quandam generosam quae libertatis	. . .	O 105	Lady Defence	V T
FOENORE				
Cur opulentus eges? tua cuncta in foenore ponis.	. .	O 223	Tr. Gk. 11.167	1
FONTE				
Ipso fonte bibes, quae circumfusa beatam	. . . . .	O 92	Messiah	112
Fulsit, in pectus mihi fonte purum	. . . . . .	O 193	Prayer on Xmas	2
FONTES				
Muscosi fontes, silvestria tecta, valete,	. . . .	O 88	Messiah	4
Conciliis, verique sacros recludere fontes.	. . . .	O 163	To Dr Lawrence	22
FORES				
Ante suas agmen Lais habere fores,	. . . . . .	O 209	Tr. Greek 6.1	2
FORET				
Audiit, irata est ne nova Musa foret.	. . . . .	O 214	Tr Greek 9.66	2
FORMA				
Forma animos hominum capit, at, si gratia desit,	. . .	O 209	Tr. Greek 5.67	1
FORMAE				
Quis formae modus imperio? Venus arrogat audax	. . .	O 103	Elizae Aenigma	1
FORMAS				
Currere formas?	. . . .	O 153	In Theatro	8
FORMIS				
Humanae mentis, rerum se pascere formis,	. . . . .	O 163	To Dr Lawrence	6
FORMOSA				
En! formosa tibi porrecta per atria proles	. . . .	O 92	Messiah	96
En! formosa tibi spatiosa per atria proles	. . . .	O 92	Messiah	V 96
O longum, formosa, vale, mihi vita decusque,	. . . .	O 383	On the Gin-Act	D 3
FORNICE				
Marmoreo trepidant qua lentae in fornice guttae,	. . .	O 116	Tr Pope Grotto	3
Marmorea trepidant qua lentae in fornice guttae,	. . .	O 116	Tr Pope Grotto	V 3
FORSAN				
Si forsan tumulum quo conditur Eumarus aufers,	. . . .	O 210	Tr Greek 7.284	3
FORTASSE				
Impia facta patrans, homines fortasse latebis,	. . .	O 220	Tr Greek 10.27	1
FORTE				
Gratia ter grata est velox, sin forte moretur	. . .	O 220	Tr Greek 10.30	1
Forte boni, ultrices experiere vices.	. . . . .	O 222	Tr. Gk. 10.123	6

```
FORTIS                                                  PAGE    TITLE              LINE
     Intende nervos fortis, inanibus  . . .  . . .     O 101 Ad Urbanum            13
     Fortis, ades, solus tangas venerabile limen. . . . O 116 Tr Pope Grotto       16
     Fortis, ades, tibi sponte patet venerabile limen. . . . O 116 Tr Pope Grotto V 16
     Exsurge fortis, nunc animis opus,                 O 187 Ad T. L. M.D.         14
FORTUNA
     Quod nulli proprium versat Fortuna, putabat . . . . . O 215 Tr Greek 9.74      3
     Queis uti poteram quondam Fortuna negavit,  . . . . . O 215 Tr Greek 9.138     3
     Non Fortuna sibi te gratum tollit in altum; . . . . . O 218 Tr Greek 9.530     1
FORTUNAE
     Fortunae malim adversae tolerare procellas, . . . . . O 221 Tr Greek 10.93     1
FORUM
     Perstrepit omne forum; cura molesta domi est. . . . O 217 Tr Greek 9.359       2
     Permeat omne forum; vita quieta domi est.  . . . O 217 Tr Greek 9.360          2
FCTIS
     Et gremio fctis selectas porrigit herbas,  . . . . . O  90 Messiah            60
FCVEAT
     Summus amplexu foveat, beato . . . . . . .        O 227 A Meditation           6
FOVEATQUE
     O! colat humanum Te foveatque genus! . . . . . . . O 102 Ad R. Savage          2
FOVENTE
     Sole fovente, suas. . . . . . . . .               O 385 Cantico Solom.   D  6
FOVET
     Mortales miseros servat, alit, fovet, . . . . .   O 155 Psalmus 117            6
     Seu fovet mater sobolem benigna, . . . . . . . .  O 168 Oda to Thrale         14
FRACTIS
     Cum fugere haud possit fractis Victoria pennis,  . . .  O 219 Tr Greek 9.647    1
FRACTUS
     Crystallisque latex fractus scintillat acutis, . . .  O 116 Tr Pope Grotto     4
FRAGRANTIA
     Et juga Carmeli recreant fragrantia coelum. . . . . O  89 Messiah             33
     Culmina Carmeli recreant fragrantia coelum. . . . . O  89 Messiah         V   33
FRANGE
     Fidens, Superbo frange Silentio; . . . . . . .    O 101 Ad Urbanum            10
FRANGET
     Vel Arator vomere franget, . . . . . . .          O 109 Post-genitis           4
FRAUDE
     Pendet, et incoquitur tectum sine fraude metallum:  . . O 116 Tr Pope Grotto   6
     Splendet, et incoquitur tectum sine fraude metallum: . . O 116 Tr Pope Grotto V 6
FRAUDIS
     "Irrita vanescent priscae vestigia fraudis," . . . . O  89 Messiah            20
FREMENTES
     Prodest vagari, nec frementes . . . . . . . .     O 166 Oda Isle Skye         11
FREMERE
     Nec fremere audebit . . . . . . . . .             O 109 Post-genitis          27
FREMITU
     Terribili fremitu stridula moeret anus. . . . . . O 383 On the Gin-Act  D  2
FRETA
     Et petiit terras per freta longa novas. . . . . . O 386 Tr Epi. Madoc   D  4
FRETUMQUE
     Trajecit montes nauta, fretumque pedes, . . . . . O 217 Tr Greek 9.304        2
FRETUS
     Auxilioque Dei fretus, jam mente serena . . . . . O 205 Christianus           26
FRIGORA
     Frigora, seu nimium longo jacuisse veterno, . . . O 161 Gnothi seauton        17
     Aspice, diffugiunt ignavae frigora brumae; . . . . O 384 Cantico Solom.  D  3
FRIGORE
     Membra viatoris recreabunt frigore linguae. . . . O  91 Messiah              88
FRONDE
     Densa fronde salicti . . . . . . . . .            O 181 Waltoni Piscat         2
FRONDENS
     Telluri arboribus ver frondens, sidera coelo, . . . O 214 Tr Greek 9.65        1
FRONDENT
     Artificis frondent dextrae; palmisque rubeta . . . O  91 Messiah             82
     Artificis frondent dextrae; Spinetaque Palmis . . . O  91 Messiah         V  82
FRONDESCIT
     Carpit Arabs, hortis quicquid frondescit eois. . . . O  89 Messiah            29
FRONTE
     Cui Fronte Sertum in Erudita . . . . . . .        O 101 Ad Urbanum             3
FRONTIS
     Indue reginam, turritae frontis honores . . . . . O  91 Messiah              93
FRUARIS
     Hora bonis quasi nunc instet suprema fruaris, . . . O 219 Tr Greek 10.26       1
FRUATUR
     Cunctorum ignoscat vitiis, pietate fruatur. . . . . . O 205 Christianus        9
FRUCTUS
     Jam teneros fructus detrudit lactea ficus . . . . O 385 Cantico Solom.   D 11
FRUCTUSQUE
     Flores Fructusque vorantes, . . . . . . .         O 109 Post-genitis          12
FRUI
     Teque frui timor est, teque carere dolor. . . . . O 218 Tr Greek 9.394         2
     Omnes si vellent virginitate frui; . . . . . . .  O 218 Tr Greek 9.444         2
FRUITUR
     Praeteritis fruitur, laetos aut sumit honores . . . O 162 Gnothi seauton      47
     Recte qui fruitur muneribus, dedit. . . . . . .   O 164 Recover Eyes          14
FRUSTRA
     Nunc loca sola placent; frustra te, Somne, recumbens . . O 161 Gnothi seauton 30
     Da, ne sint permissa, pater, mihi praemia frustra, . . O 208 Prayers VII       9
     Da, ne sint promissa, pater, mihi praemia frustra, . . O 208 Prayers VII   V   9
     His sapiens lectis, Epicurum quaerere frustra . . . O 222 Tr Greek 11.50       5
```

```
                                                      PAGE     TITLE              LINE
FRUSTRABAR
     Hic delusa rudi frustrabar brachia motu,  . . . . . . .   O 228 Rivum a Stoana      3
FUCIS
     Aethereis variata fucis.  . . . . . . . . . . . .         O 102 Ad Urbanum         24
FUERAT
     . . . causae in sermone patrocinata fuerat.  . . . . .    O 105 Lady Defence     V  T
     Lysigeni, fuerat non gravis ille tibi.  . . . . . .       O 211 Tr Greek 7.461      2
FUERE
     Stabo illis qui sunt, quique fuere, gravis. . . . . .     O 216 Tr Greek 9.288      6
FUGA
     Quae sine morte fuga est vitae, quam turba malorum  . .   O 222 Tr. Gk. 10.123      1
FUGACEM
     Sic diem sequitur dies fugacem!  . . . . . . . . .        O 204 Spes               2
FUGACES
     Horret, ubi vanae species, umbraeque fugaces,  . . . .    O 162 Gnothi seauton     50
FUGERE
     Cum fugere haud possit fractis Victoria pennis,  . . .    O 219 Tr Greek 9.647      1
FUGIENS
     Nequitiam fugiens, servata contrahe lege . . . . . .      O 218 Tr Greek 9.444      3
FUGIT
     Deliciasque fugit solitas solitosque labores;  . . . .    O 162 To Dr Lawrence     2
     Carpe diem, fugit, heu, non revocanda dies!  . . . . .    O 171 Tr. Busy Fly       6
     Quem nulla anxietas, nulla cupido fugit;  . . . . . .     O 232 Prayer             2
FUIT
     Zosima, quae solo fuit olim corpore Serva,  . . . . .     O 114 Tr Gk Epigrams     1
     Zosima, qua solo fuit olim corpore serva,  . . . . .      O 212 Tr Gk Epigrams  V  7
     Zosima, qucndam solo fuit olim copore serva,  . . . .     Y 320 Tr Gk Epigrams  V  1
     Corpore nunc etiam libera facta fuit.  . . . . . .        O 114 Tr Gk Epigrams     2
     Cessarunt; pietas hic quoque cura fuit:  . . . . . .      O 170 Insula Kenneth    18
     Hectori, et exitio munus utrique fuit.  . . . . . .       O 210 Tr Greek 7.151     2
     Tutum aliis aequor, me pereunte, fuit.  . . . . . .       O 210 Tr Greek 7.282     2
FULCRO
     Consuetus fulcro innixus reptare bacilli . . . . . .      O  90 Messiah           50
FULGORE
     Aetheris, en! portas sacro fulgore micantes . . . . .     O  92 Messiah          106
FULGURA
     Aureaque admirans rutilantis fulgura cristae.  . . . .    O  91 Messiah           92
FULMINE
     Jupiter unus erat, qui stravit fulmine gentes;  . . . .   O 103 Elizae Aenigma     5
FULSERAT
     Fulserat illa dies, legis qua docta supernae  . . . .     O 170 Insula Kenneth  V 15
FULSIT
     Fulsit, in pectus mihi fonte purum . . . . . . . .        O 193 Prayer on Xmas     2
FUMABUNT
     Sidera fumabunt, diro labefacta tremore  . . . . . .      O  92 Messiah          115
FUMIS
     Squallet informis, tugurique fumis . . . . . . . .        O 167 Oda to Thrale      7
FUNCTUM
     Te sterili functum cura, vocumque salebris  . . . . .     O 161 Gnothi seauton    19
FUNDAM
     Votaque fundam  . . . . . . . . . . . . . .               O 199 Medico Aeger S    27
FUNDIT
     Deproperat tellus, fundit tibi munera, quicquid  . . .    O  89 Messiah           28
     Quem fundit blando junctus amore dolor;  . . . . . .      O 212 Tr Greek 7.560     2
     Fundit ab ore melos,  . . . . . . . . . . .  .            O 385 Cantico Solom.  D  8
FUNERA
     "Perge modo, atque tuas olim post funera laudes  . . .    O 386 In Birchium     D  5
     Credideris fletu funera digna tuo, . . . . . . . .        Y 387 Death Mother    D  2
FUNERE
     Nec male res cessit, subito si funere sponsam, . . . .    O 222 Tr Greek 11.50     3
FUNUS
     Funus Alexandri mentitur fama; fidesque  . . . . . .      O 210 Tr Greek 7.239     1
FURAT
     Fidus adest custos, seu nox furat horrida nimbis,  . . .  O  90 Messiah           62
     Fidus adest custos, seu nox furat humida nimbis,  . - .   O  90 Messiah        V  62
FUREM
     Quo rege gaudent Arcades, furem boum,  . . . . . . .      O 223 Tr. Gk. 11.176     2
FURES
     Fures absque Timore,  . . . . . . . . . . . .             O 109 Post-genitis      17
FURORE
     Vix majore Deus corda furore quatit  - . . . . . .        Y  28 Aurora Musis       8
FURORES
     Siderea Isaiae, dignos accende furores!  . . . . . .      O  88 Messiah            7
FURTIM
     Hora perit furtim laetis, mens temporis aegra  . . . .    O 228 Jactura Tempor     1
FUSI
     Nunc, per gramina fusi,  . . . . . . . . . . .  .         O 181 Waltoni Piscat     1
FUSIS
     Pensilibus fusis, cyatho comitata supremo,  . . . . .     O 383 On the Gin-Act  D  1
FUTURA
     Ille futura calens rapitur per saecula vates,  . . . .    O  88 Messiah        V   8
FUTURI
     Hic, in se totum longe per opaca futuri  . . . . . .      O 116 Tr Pope Grotto    10
FUTURIS
     Nunc instare futuris,  . . . . . . . . . . . .            O 182 Waltoni Piscat     8
FUTURO
     Captans, nec fastu tumidus, semperque futuro  . . . .     O 205 Christianus        3
GARRIRE
     Crethida fabellas dulces garrire peritam . . . . . .      O 211 Tr Greek 7.459     1
GARRULA
     Garrula mirantur salientis murmura rivi.  . . . . . .     O  91 Messiah           77
```

465

GAUDENT
  Quo rege gaudent Arcades, furem boum, ...   PAGE   TITLE   LINE

	PAGE	TITLE		LINE
GAUDENT				
Quo rege gaudent Arcades, furem boum,	O 223	Tr. Gk. 11.176		2
GAUDENTIA				
Altius, en! Lebanon gaudentia culmina tollit,	O 89	Messiah		30
GAUDET				
Ingreditur, cultuque tuo mansuescere gaudet.	O 92	Messiah		101
Lusibus gaudet puer otiosis,	O 153	In Theatro		13
Sexta dolet Babylona, et gaudet septima Christo.	O 226	Septem Aetates	V	4
Sortitur Pelopis tellus quae nomine gaudet.	O 230	Geographia Met		7
GAUDIA				
Proferet archetypos; coelestis gaudia lucis	O 92	Messiah		111
Gaudia gratus.	O 153	In Theatro		12
Nunc clamosa juvant nocturnae gaudia mensae,	O 161	Gnothi seauton		29
Abstergat mundi labem, nec gaudia carnis	O 205	Christianus		2
Veniaeque sancta pacis adde gaudia:	O 206	Prayers I		8
Pauperies latitat, cum conjuge gaudia multa	O 217	Tr Greek 9.360		5
Supplicium huic, quoniam crescentia gaudia laesit,	O 218	Tr Greek 9.375		5
Surge, soror dilecta, mihi lux, gaudia, vita;	O 384	Cantico Solom.	D	1
GAUDIUM				
Gaudium sacro fluat, et benigni	O 193	Prayer on Xmas		3
GAZA				
Nec sibi de gaza praesens quod postulet usus	O 162	Gnothi seauton		44
Non sibi de gaza praesens quod postulat usus	O 162	Gnothi seauton	V	44
GELIDA				
Vis boreae gelida, aut rapidi violentia solis.	O 89	Messiah		19
Vis boreae gelida, aut nimii violentia solis.	O 89	Messiah	V	19
GELIDAE				
Noctis tristitiam qui gelidae jubet,	O 164	Recover Eyes		4
GELIDIS				
Non tamen inculti gelidis latuere sub antris,	O 169	Insula Kenneth		11
Nec tamen inculti gelidis latuere sub antris,	O 169	Insula Kenneth	V	11
GELIDO				
Dicite, Causidici, gelido nunc marmore magni	O 213	Tr Greek 8.137		1
GEMMAQUE				
Gemmaque luxuriae nondum famulata nitenti	O 116	Tr Pope Grotto		5
GEMMAS				
Turbidus imber abest; mittit rosa roscida gemmas,	O 385	Cantico Solom.	D	5
GENERIS				
Ad Ricardum Savage, Arm. Humani Generis Amatorem.	O 102	Ad R. Savage		T
Humani studium generis cui pectore fervet,	O 102	Ad R. Savage		1
GENEROSA				
Hi sunt quos animi generosa insania magni	O 163	To Dr Lawrence		31
GENEROSAM				
Ad foeminam quandam generosam quae libertatis	O 105	Lady Defence	V	T
GENEROSO				
Munera luxurians dat pampinus, et generoso	O 385	Cantico Solom.	D	13
GENIALE				
Ver geniale venit.	O 384	Cantico Solom.	D	4
GENIALI				
Rorem, qui regeles, geniali et gramina succo	Y 28	Aurora Musis		5
GENIBUS				
Ecce! cremant genibus tritae regalibus arae.	O 92	Messiah		103
GENITIS SEE POST-GENITIS				
GENITORE				
Una duas habuit casa cum genitore puellas,	O 169	Insula Kenneth		9
Una duas tenuit casa cum genitore puellas,	O 169	Insula Kenneth		9
Una duas cepit casa cum genitore puellas,	O 169	Insula Kenneth	V	9
GENS				
Quid moliatur Gens Imitantium,	O 101	Ad Urbanum		5
Gens illa, impatiens per singula quaeque vagandi	O 163	To Dr Lawrence		23
Luxerat illa dies, legis jens docta supernae	O 170	Insula Kenneth		15
Spes hominum et curas gens procul esse velit.	O 170	Insula Kenneth	V	16
GENTES				
Jupiter unus erat, qui stravit fulmine gentes;	O 103	Elizae Aenigma		5
Rapiet Discordia Gentes,	O 109	Post-genitis		20
Gentes undique carmine.	O 155	Psalmus 117		4
Omnes undique Gentes	O 155	Psalmus 117		7
Pervagor gentes, hominum ferorum	O 167	Oda to Thrale		5
Haec mihi, quo gentes, quo secula, Christe, piasti,	O 208	Prayers VII		11
Sanguine quo gentes, quo secula cuncta piavit,	O 232	Prayer		9
GENTI				
Huic quoque, nec genti nec sectae noxius ulli,	O 205	Christianus		6
GENTIS				
Ut tibi, gentis	O 199	Medico Aeger S		24
GENUS				
O! colat humanum Te foveatque genus!	O 102	Ad R. Savage		2
Tale hominum genus est, infirmum, triste, misellum,	O 221	Tr Greek 10.84		3
GEOGRAPHIA				
Geographia Metrica	O 229	Geographia Met		T
GERAM				
Vincere te potui nuda, quid arma geram?	O 384	Epigramma	D	4
GESSERAT				
Gesserat et quicquid Virtus, Sapientia quicquid	O 160	Gnothi seauton		9
GESTA				
Quo tua signantur gesta, Philippe, lapis.	O 216	Tr Greek 9.288		2
Birchius egregios, claraque gesta virum.	O 386	In Birchium	D	2
GESTIAT				
Gestiat, et, nullo pietatis limite clausus,	O 205	Christianus		8
GESTIT				
Corpora cuncta suis gestit variare figuris,	O 163	To Dr Lawrence		27

```
                                                            PAGE    TITLE            LINE
GIGNIT
    In me animo tellus gignit et unda feras,    . . . . . .   O 213 Tr Greek 9.18        2
GLADIUM
    Hector dat gladium Ajaci, dat balteum et Ajax    . . . .  O 210 Tr Greek 7.151       1
GLORIA
    Gloria silvarum, dominum inclinata salutet!  . . . . .    O  89 Messiah             38
    Tolle, Salema, sacros, quam circum gloria pennas   . . .  O  92 Messiah             94
    Ut summa laus sit, summa Christo gloria. . . . . . .      O 206 Prayers III           6
    Omnia, dum Macedum gloria et arma premunt.   . . . . .    O 216 Tr Greek 9.288        4
GOAT
    Inscription on the collar of Mr. Banks's Goat    . . . .  O 156 Collari Caprae      V  T
GRADU
    Lenis inoffenso vitaque morsque gradu.   . . . . . .      Y 387 Death Mother        D  4
GRAECIA
    Das bene collatos, quos Roma et Graecia jactat,   .  . .  O 225 Tr. Gk. 16.331        3
GRAECIAE
    Graeciae et urbs, urbi est ista propago, decus.  . . .    O 214 Tr Greek 9.65         2
GRAECUS
    Quos laudet vates Graecus Romanus et Anglus  . . . . .    O  86 Tr Dryden Milt      V  1
    Sublime ingenium Graecus; Romanus habebat    . . . . .    O  86 Tr Dryden Milt      V  3
GRAIUM
    Illa triumphatrix Graium consueta procorum   . . . . .    O 209 Tr. Greek 6.1         1
GRAIUS
    Quos laudet vates Graius Romanus et Anglus   . . . . .    O  86 Tr Dryden Milt         1
    Sublime ingenium Graius; Romanus habebat . . . . .       O  86 Tr Dryden Milt         3
GRAMINA
    Aspera, odoratae cedunt mala gramina myrto.  . . . . .    O  91 Messiah             83
    Gramina vastantes,  . . . . . . . . . . . . .            O 109 Post-genitis ..      11
    Nunc, per gramina fusi,  . . . . . . . . . . .           O 181 Waltoni Piscat         1
    Rorem, qui regeles, geniali et gramina succo  . . . . .  Y  28 Aurora Musis           5
GRANDE
    Carmen grande sonans; Anglus utrumque tulit.  . . . .    O  86 Tr Dryden Milt         4
    Exiguum est Marti, sed mihi grande lucrum.   . . . . .   O 216 Tr Greek 9.163         4
GRANDIA
    Nec quid agam invenio, meditatus grandia, cogor   . . .  O 161 Gnothi seauton       34
GRANDILOQUUS
    Grandiloquus nimis alta Zeno.  . . . . . . . . .         O 166 Oda Isle Skye       V 16
GRATA
    Quam grata defesso virentem  . . . . . . . . .           O 166 Oda Isle Skye          3
    Nec probrosa avidae grata sit offa gulae;  . . . . . .   O 218 Tr Greek 9.573         2
    Gratia ter grata est velox, sin forte moretur   . . . .  O 220 Tr Greek 10.30         1
    Suaviter exhalant violaria grata, Sabaeo . . . . . .     O 385 Cantico Solom.      D 15
GRATES
    Grates, summe Pater, tuis  . . . . . . . . . . .         O 164 Recover Eyes          13
    Habeam grates;   . . . . . . . . . . . . . .            O 199 Medico Aeger S        26
GRATI
    Civis et externus grati; domus hospita nescit   . . . .  O 219 Tr Greek 9.648         1
GRATIA
    Gratia Coeli!  . . . . . . . . . . . . . .              O 193 Prayer on Xmas         4
    Usque regat gressus gratia fida meos.  . . . . . .      O 207 Prayers IV             4
    Forma animos hominum capit, at, si gratia desit,   . .  O 209 Tr. Greek 5.67         1
    Gratia ter grata est velox, sin forte moretur   . . . . O 220 Tr Greek 10.30         1
    Ut florem amittat gratia tota perit  . . . . . . .      Y 332 Tr Greek 10.30       V  1
    Gratia vix restat nomine digna suo.  . . . . . . .      O 220 Tr Greek 10.30         2
    Gratia nulla hominum mentes tenet, ista Promethei   . . O 225 Tr Greek 16.87         3
    Gratia Christi;  . . . . . . . . . . . . . .            O 227 A Meditation           4
GRATIOR
    Non ulla Musis Pagina gratior,   . . . . . . . . .      O 102 Ad Urbanum            17
GRATUM
    Gratum animum laudo; Qui debuit omnia ventis,   . . . . O 143 On Lord Anson          1
    Non Fortuna sibi te gratum tollit in altum; . . . . .   O 218 Tr Greek 9.530         1
GRATUS
    Gaudia gratus.   . . . . . . . . . . . . . .            O 153 In Theatro            12
GRAVANT
    Quem moestum et timidum crimina dira gravant;   . . . . O 207 Prayers V              2
GRAVAT
    Proles aucta gravat, rapta orbat, caeca juventae est  . O 217 Tr Greek 9.359         7
GRAVATAM
    Crimine gravatam plurimo mentem leva:  . . . . . . .    O 206 Prayers I              2
    Multo gravatam crimine . . . . . . . . . . . .          O 206 Prayers II            10
GRAVE
    Mox uteri pondus depositura grave,   . . . . . . . .    O 115 Ad Lauram Epig         2
    Scelerum caterna me laborantem grave   . . . . . . .    O 206 Prayers III          V  4
GRAVEM
    Non vitanda gravem, non toleranda facit?   . . . . .    O 222 Tr. Gk. 10.123         2
    Fecerunt nulli sors titulique gravem.  . . . . . . .    O 226 Tr. Simonides          4
GRAVES
    Materies; poscunt graves coelestia plectrum. . . . .    O  88 Messiah             V  3
GRAVI
    Scelerum catena me laborantem gravi  . . . . . . .      O 206 Prayers III            4
GRAVIORIBUS
    Restat? an accingar studiis gravioribus audax?  . . .   O 162 Gnothi seauton        53
GRAVIORQUE
    Desidiae sors dura manet, graviorque labore  . . . . .  O 161 Gnothi seauton        25
GRAVIS
    Lysigeni, fuerat non gravis ille tibi.   . . . . .      O 211 Tr Greek 7.461         2
    Cecropidis gravis hic ponor, Martique dicatus,   . . .  O 216 Tr Greek 9.288         1
    Stabo illis qui sunt, quique fuere, gravis.  . . . . .  O 216 Tr Greek 9.288         6
GRAVIUS
    Materies; poscunt gravius coelestia plectrum.   . . . . O  88 Messiah                3
```

	PAGE	TITLE	LINE
GREGI			
Me gregi Sanctus socium beatum . . . '	O 227	A Meditation	7
GREMIO			
Et gremio fotis selectas porrigit herbas, ...	O 90	Messiah	60
GRESSUS			
Sacri vagantes luminis gressus face	O 206	Prayers I	5
Usque regat gressus gratia fida meos.	O 207	Prayers IV	4
Quid salvere jubes me, pessime? Corripe gressus; . . .	O 211	Tr Greek 7.318	1
GROUNDFLCOR			
. . . having the Groundfloor of the Oratory	O 385	The Warehouse	D T
GUBERNATRIX			
Puppe gubernatrix sedisti, Audacia, prima, ...	O 213	Tr Greek 9.29	1
GULAE			
Nec probrosa avidae grata sit offa gulae;	O 218	Tr Greek 9.573	2
GUTTAE			
Marmoreo trepidant qua lentae in fornice guttae, . . .	O 116	Tr Pope Grotto	3
Marmorea trepidant qua lentae in fornice guttae, . . .	O 116	Tr Pope Grotto V	3
GYGES			
Quos Gyges cumulos habebat auri;	O 215	Tr Greek 9.110	2
HABEAM			
Habeam grates;	O 199	Medico Aeger S	26
HABEBAT			
Sublime ingenium Graius; Romanus habebat	O 86	Tr Dryden Milt	3
Sublime ingenium Graecus; Romanus habebat	O 86	Tr Dryden Milt V	3
Quos Gyges cumulos habebat auri;	O 215	Tr Greek 9.110	2
HABEBIS			
Intende jam nervos, habebis	O 101	Ad Urbanum	15
Ditescis, credo, quid restat? quicquid habebis . . .	O 220	Tr Greek 10.60	1
Terror inest aliis, moerorque, et siquid habebis . . .	O 222	Tr. Gk. 10.123	5
HABEO			
Habeo, dedi quod alteri;	O 165	Tr Doncast Epi	1
HABERE			
Ante suas agmen Lais habere fores, ...	O 209	Tr. Greek 6.1	2
HABES			
Permitte summo quicquid habes Patri, ...	O 187	Ad T. L. M.D. V	17
HABET			
Quae potuere duos tertius unus habet.	O 86	Tr Dryden Milt	6
Haec habet altrici Capra secunda Jovis.	O 156	Collari Caprae	2
Accola Danubii qualia saevus habet;	O 169	Insula Kenneth	12
Nil lucri facies; ossa habet et cinerem.	O 210	Tr Greek 7.284	4
Me miserum sors omnis habet; florentibus annis	O 215	Tr Greek 9.138	1
Vita hominum nunc plus quod misereris habet.	O 216	Tr Greek 9.148	4
Atthide non alius desit Olympus, habet.	O 219	Tr Greek 9.702	2
Nox miseris longi temporis instar habet.	O 220	Tr Greek 10.28	2
HABITAT			
His blanda certe pax habitat locis:	O 166	Oda Isle Skye	6
HABUIQUE			
Habuique, quod dedi mihi;	O 165	Tr Doncast Epi	2
HABUISSET			
Pythagoras mallet, vocem habuisset opus.	O 225	Tr. Gk. 16.326	2
HABUIT			
Una duas habuit casa cum genitore puellas, ...	O 169	Insula Kenneth	9
HAC			
Hic requies fessis; non sacra hac saevit in umbra . . .	O 89	Messiah V	18
HAE			
Hae poterant uvae laeto convivia cantu	O 218	Tr Greek 9.375	7
HAEC			
Haec veniunt Cypriae Somnia missa Deae.	O 103	Elizae Aenigma	4
Haec habet altrici Capra secunda Jovis.	O 156	Collari Caprae	2
Haec fausta vobis dicimus, Angliae	O 188	Epilogus	2
Mihi dona morte haec impetret Christus sua.	O 206	Prayers I	11
Haec mihi, quo gentes, quo secula, Christe, piasti, . .	O 208	Prayers VII	11
Haec peritura nitent; tu peritura nites!	O 209	Tr. Greek 5.74	6
Ad Musas Venus haec: Veneri parete, puellae, ...	O 213	Tr Greek 9.39	1
Haec Musae ad Venerem: Sic Marti, diva, mineris; . . .	O 213	Tr Greek 9.39	3
Videre, Archidicen haec tumulavit humus;	O 226	Tr. Simonides	2
Haec nobis Christus promeruisse velit!	O 232	Prayer	10
Et placido tandem haec edidit ore, Dea:	O 386	In Birchium D	4
Haec postrema tibi sit flendi causa, fluatque	Y 387	Death Mother D	3
HAERES			
Inclytus hic haeres magni requiescit Oeni, ...	O 386	Tr Epi. Madoc D	1
HAMUS			
Non tenet; esca natat pulchra, sed hamus abest. . . .	O 209	Tr. Greek 5.67	2
HANC			
Hanc statuam ingenio Rcma benigna tuo.	O 225	Tr. Gk. 16.331	2
HARMONIA			
Quae lyra. Quam sibi non concinit harmonia!	O 216	Tr Greek 9.250	2
Harmonia tellus completur lata, per agros	Y 28	Aurora Musis	3
HARMONIAE			
Harmoniae purgata novos mirabitur auris.	O 90	Messiah	48
HAS			
Nec natet, et nunc has partes, nunc eligat illas, . . .	O 205	Christianus	16
HASTA			
Triste coruscabit radiis; dabit hasta recusa	O 90	Messiah	69
HAUD			
Quanquam haud pugnaces, ...	O 109	Post-genitis	15
Quod poscis, haud unquam tibi	O 203	Christ Sinner	3
Exiguum en! Priami monumentum; haud ille meretur . . .	O 210	Tr Greek 7.136	1
Laetior haud tecum, tecum neque tristior unquam, . . .	O 218	Tr Greek 9.573	5
Tangitur haud pedibus tellus; conviva Deorum	O 219	Tr Greek 9.577	3
Cum fugere haud possit fractis Victoria pennis, . . .	O 219	Tr Greek 9.647	1

		PAGE	TITLE	LINE
HAUD	(CONTINUED)			
Haud lavit Phido, haud tetigit; mihi febre calenti	. .	O 223	Tr. Gk. 11.118	1
Haud lavit Phido, haud tetigit; mihi febre calenti	. .	O 223	Tr. Gk. 11.118	1
Haud mora, surge, soror!		O 384	Cantico Solom.	D 2
HAUSTUM				
Limosum nobis Promus dat callidus haustum,	. . . . .	O 85	Mea nec Falern	3
HAUSTUS				
Ingenium jubeas purior haustus alat.		O 85	Mea nec Falern	6
HAVING				
. . . having the Groundfloor of the Oratory		O 385	The Warehouse	D T
HE				
. . . Johnson, as he lay confined with an inflamed Eye.		O 162	To Dr Lawrence	T
HEBETARE				
Ille cutim spissam visus hebetare vetabit, ...		O 90	Messiah	44
HEBRIDAS				
Insula Kennethi, Inter Hebridas		O 169	Insula Kenneth	V T
HECTOR				
Hector dat gladium Ajaci, dat balteum et Ajax		O 210	Tr Greek 7.151	1
HECTORI				
Hectori, et exitio munus utrique fuit.		O 210	Tr Greek 7.151	2
HELICONIS				
Nutrit mane, putes esse Heliconis aqua.		Y 28	Aurora Musis	6
HENRICUM				
Temporis Henricum rapuit vis vivida mentis;		O 116	Tr Pope Grotto	11
HERACLITE				
Heraclite, fluat lacrymarum crebrior imber;		O 216	Tr Greek 9.148	3
HERACLITUS				
Heraclitus ego; indoctae ne laedite linguae, . . .		O 209	Tr Greek 7.128	1
HERBAS				
Et gremio fotis selectas porrigit herbas, ...		O 90	Messiah	60
HERMEM				
Hermem Deorum nuncium, pennis levem, ...		O 223	Tr. Gk. 11.176	1
HERODOTO				
Herodoto hospitii praemia, quaeque suum.		O 216	Tr Greek 9.160	2
HEROS				
Fert humeris, venerabile onus, Cythereius heros . . .		O 216	Tr Greek 9.163	1
HERUM				
Nec dubitet quem dicat herum, sed, totus in uno, . . .		O 205	Christianus	17
HESPERIIS				
Cum caput Hesperiis attolit Phoebus ab undis, ...		Y 28	Aurora Musis	1
HEU				
Carpe diem, fugit, heu, non revocanda dies!		O 171	Tr. Busy Fly	6
Sollicitus nimis, heu! paternis.		O 187	Ad T. L. M.D.	12
Heu quam dura preces sprevit, quam surda querelas . .		O 212	Tr Greek 7.560	5
HI				
Hi sunt quos animi generosa insania magni		O 163	To Dr Lawrence	31
Nexa patent; hi sunt quos nil mirabile turbat, . . .		O 163	To Dr Lawrence	34
Nil non mortale est mortalibus; omne quod est hi . .		O 220	Tr Greek 10.31	1
HIC				
Hic requies fessis; non sacra saevit in umbra . . .		O 89	Messiah	18
Hic requies fessis; non sacra hac saevit in umbra . .		O 89	Messiah	V 18
Hic, in se totum longe per opaca futuri		O 116	Tr Pope Grotto	10
Hic pia Vindamius traxit suspiria, in ipsa		O 116	Tr Pope Grotto	12
Morte memor patriae; hic Marcmonti pectore prima . .		O 116	Tr Pope Grotto	13
Cessarunt; pietas hic quoque cura fuit:		O 170	Insula Kenneth	18
Quo vagor ulterius? quod ubique requiritur hic est; .		O 170	Insula Kenneth	21
Hic secura quies, hic et honestus amor.		O 170	Insula Kenneth	22
Hic secura quies, hic et honestus amor.		O 170	Insula Kenneth	22
Hic, dum debita morti		O 182	Waltoni Piscat	5
Hic anemone humet, confert narcissus odores		O 209	Tr. Greek 5.74	3
Naufragus hic jaceo; contra jacet ecce colonus! . .		O 210	Tr Greek 7.265	1
Naufragus hic jaceo; fidens tamen utere velis, . . .		O 210	Tr Greek 7.282	1
Quam tenet hic, cunctas quae manet, alta quies. . .		O 211	Tr Greek 7.459	4
Qui jacet hic, servus vixit, nunc, lumine cassus, . .		O 212	Tr Greek 7.538	1
Hic oculos socio commodat, ille pedes.		O 213	Tr Greek 9.13	2
Sidereus tamen hic territat, ecce, canis!		O 213	Tr Greek 9.18	4
Hic, aurum ut reperit, laqueum abjicit, alter ut aurum		O 213	Tr Greek 9.44	1
De te plebs audax, hic bene et ille male.		O 214	Tr Greek 9.50	2
Sufficit hoc votis; flos hic pulcherrimus aevi est, .		O 215	Tr Greek 9.112	3
Cecropidis gravis hic ponor, Martique dicatus, . . .		O 216	Tr Greek 9.288	1
Nil non mortale est mortalibus; omne quod est hic . .		O 220	Tr Greek 10.31	V 1
Hic, bone vir, sedem, non alimenta, peto.		O 224	Tr. Gk. 11.391	4
Poeta, lector, hic quiescit Hipponax, ...		O 224	Tr Greek 13.3	1
Tutum hic sedile, et si placet, sopor tutus. . . .		O 224	Tr Greek 13.3	4
Unde hic Praxiteles? nudam vidistis, Adoni, . . .		O 225	Tr. Gk. 16.168	1
Hic delusa rudi frustrabar brachia motu, ...		O 228	Rivum a Stoana	3
Hic Bona queis opus est venditat, Ille Sonum. . . .		O 385	The Warehouse	D 6
Inclytus hic haeres magni requiescit Oeni, ...		O 386	Tr Epi. Madoc	D 1
Innocua hic membris permistas membra columbas, . . .		O 393	Tr. of Crashaw	D 1
Hic jaceant; donec Nox transeat horrida nimbis, . . .		O 393	Tr. of Crashaw	D 3
HILARARE				
Hilarare suis jussere modis		O 193	Tr. Medea III	4
HINC				
Quod nimium est fit ineptum; hinc, ut dixere priores,		O 224	Tr Greek 16.16	1
Hinc annis palpantur delenda poemata nullis		Y 28	Aurora Musis	11
Hinc annis palpantur delenda poemata palpantur . . .		Y 28	Aurora Musis	V 11
HIPPI				
Prolem Hippi, et sua qua meliorem secula nullum . . .		O 226	Tr. Simonides	1
HIPPONAX				
Poeta, lector, hic quiescit Hipponax, ...		O 224	Tr Greek 13.3	1

469

		PAGE	TITLE		LINE
HIRCE					
Hirce, parem nitido te tua barba facit.		O 224	Tr. Gk. 11.430		2
HIS					
His cura credo sedibus exulat;		O 166	Oda Isle Skye		5
His blanda certe pax habitat locis:		O 166	Oda Isle Skye		6
His redimita comas, mores depone superbos:		O 209	Tr. Greek 5.74		5
His sapiens lectis, Epicurum quaerere frustra		O 222	Tr Greek 11.50		5
His Tempelmanni numeris descripseris orbem.		O 229	Geographia Met		1
HOC					
Aut, hoc si nimium est, tandem nova lexica poscam?		O 162	Gnothi seauton		54
Utile cunctis hoc opus esset;		O 193	Tr. Medea III		10
Hoc quoque superest		O 199	Medico Aeger S		23
Hoc statuat, precibus Christus adesse velit:		O 204	Losing Speech		2
Hoc statuant, votis Christus adesse velit:		O 204	Losing Speech	V	2
Hoc Veneri speculum; nolo me cernere qualis		O 209	Tr. Greek 6.1		3
Nauta, quis hoc jaceat ne percontere sepulchro;		O 211	Tr Greek 7.350		1
Sufficit hoc votis; flos hic pulcherrimus aevi est,		O 215	Tr Greek 9.112		3
Jupiter hoc templum, ut, siquando relinquit Olympum,		O 219	Tr Greek 9.702		1
HOLLANDIA					
Ter sex centurias Hollandia jactat opima		O 231	Geographia Met		35
HOMERUS					
Alter ut adsit Homerus, adest etenim alter Achilles.		O 218	Tr Greek 9.523		2
HOMINEM					
Conjugium, ut pro te des hominem patriae.		O 218	Tr Greek 9.444		4
HOMINES					
Democrite, invisas homines majore cachinno,		O 216	Tr Greek 9.148		1
Ergo optent homines, aut nunquam in luminis oras		O 217	Tr Greek 9.359		9
Impia facta patrans, homines fortasse latebis,		O 220	Tr Greek 10.27		1
HOMINI					
Myriadas ter mille homini dat terra colendas.		O 230	Geographia Met		20
HOMINUM					
Altera pars hominum, sanctae rationis alumni,		O 163	To Dr Lawrence		19
Pervagor gentes, hominum ferorum		O 167	Oda to Thrale		5
Pervagor terras, hominum ferorum		O 167	Oda to Thrale	V	5
Spes hominum ac curas cum procul esse jubet.		O 170	Insula Kenneth		16
Spes hominum et curas gens procul esse velit.		O 170	Insula Kenneth	V	16
Tu, queis laborat sors hominum, mala		O 187	Ad T. L. M.D.		5
Permitte summo res hominum Patri,		O 187	Ad T. L. M.D.		17
At nemo feras iras hominum,		O 193	Tr. Medea III		6
Forma animos hominum capit, at, si gratia desit,		O 209	Tr. Greek 5.67		1
Aurea secla hominum, quorum spectandus ocellis		O 213	Tr Greek 9.29		5
Vita hominum nunc plus quod misereris habet.		O 216	Tr Greek 9.148		4
Tale hominum genus est, infirmum, triste, misellum,		O 221	Tr Greek 10.84		3
Gratia nulla hominum mentes tenet, ista Promethei		O 225	Tr Greek 16.87		3
HOMO					
Unus homo mihi pro sexcentis, turba popelli		O 209	Tr Greek 7.128		3
HOMULLIS					
Spondens omnia credulis homullis;		O 204	Spes		4
HOMULLOS					
Lux angit miseros cadens homullos.		O 204	Spes		6
Lux angit, miseros ludens homullos.		O 204	Spes	V	6
HONESTUS					
Hic secura quies, hic et honestus amor.		O 170	Insula Kenneth		22
HONORES					
Invalidi raptos sceptri plorabit honores.		O 90	Messiah		56
Indue reginam, turritae frontis honores		O 91	Messiah		93
Congesta animus, laetos aut sumit honores		O 161	Gnothi seauton	V	40
Praeteritis fruitur, laetos aut sumit honores		O 162	Gnothi seauton		47
HORA					
Admonitu, ipsa suas nunciat hora vices.		O 170	Insula Kenneth	V	18B
Volvitur hora mihi, volvitur hora tibi!		O 171	Tr. Busy Fly		8
Volvitur hora mihi, volvitur hora tibi!		O 171	Tr. Busy Fly		8
Hora sic peragit citata cursum;		O 204	Spes		1
Mens mea quid quereris? veniet tibi mollior hora,		O 208	A Meditation		1
Hora bonis quasi nunc instet suprema fruaris,		O 219	Tr Greek 10.26		1
Hora perit furtim laetis, mens temporis aegra		O 228	Jactura Tempor		1
Pigritiam incusat, nec minus hora perit.		O 228	Jactura Tempor		2
HORAE					
Quot vox missa pedes abit horae parte secunda?		O 229	Epigram IV		1
HORAS					
Molles ducimus horas.		O 181	Waltoni Piscat		4
Pigrae per horas lucis inutiles,		O 187	Ad T. L. M.D.		10
Et sibi, deliras quanquam et peccator in horas		O 205	Christianus		14
Divitias cumulas, pereuntes negligis horas,		O 220	Tr Greek 10.60		3
HORATIUS					
Quae fausta Romae dixit Horatius,		O 188	Epilogus		1
HORIS					
Insidias meditatur horis.		O 166	Oda Isle Skye		8
HORRET					
Horret, ubi vanae species, umbraeque fugaces,		O 162	Gnothi seauton		50
HORRIDA					
Fidus adest custos, seu nox furat horrida nimbis,		O 90	Messiah		62
Horrida dementes		O 109	Post-genitis		19
Hic jaceant; donec Nox transeat horrida nimbis,		O 393	Tr. of Crashaw	D	3
HORRUIT					
Horruit implexo qua vallis sente, figurae		O 91	Messiah		80
HORTIS					
Carpit Arabs, hortis quicquid frondescit eois.		O 89	Messiah		29
HOS					
Praetereunt, aut hos praeterit omne bonum.		O 220	Tr Greek 10.31		2

		PAGE	TITLE	LINE
HOSPITA				
Civis et externus grati; domus hospita nescit	. . . .	O 219	Tr Greek 9.648	1
HOSPITII				
Herodoto hospitii praemia, quaeque suum.	. . . . . .	O 216	Tr Greek 9.160	2
HOSPITIO				
Exceptae hospitio Musae tribuere libellos	. . . .	O 216	Tr Greek 9.160	1
HOSTEM				
Hostem odit tacite, sed amicum ridet aperte	. . . . .	O 197	On Mrs. Thrale	1
HOSTILES				
Hostiles oculis flammas jaculantia torvis;	. . . .	O 90	Messiah	67
Quale, sed hostiles quale dedere manus.	. . . . .	O 210	Tr Greek 7.136	2
HOSTIS				
Thralia. Quid mavis? tutius hostis eris.	. . . .	O 197	On Mrs. Thrale	2
HUC				
Huc foedat quos lepra, urit quos febris, adeste!	. . .	O 88	Messiah	16
Huc ego delatus placido per coerula cursu	. . .	O 169	Insula Kenneth	5
Huc nunquam volitat debilis iste puer.	. . . .	O 213	Tr Greek 9.39	4
Huc, soror alma, veni! pernicibus ocyor Euris	. .	O 385	Cantico Solom.	D 17
Huc, soror alma, veni!	. . . . . .	O 385	Cantico Solom.	D 18
HUIC				
Huic quoque, nec genti nec sectae noxius ulli,	. . .	O 205	Christianus	6
Ardeat huic toto sacer ignis pectore, possit	. . .	O 205	Christianus	10
Nunc huic, nunc aliis cedens, cui farra Menippus	.	O 215	Tr Greek 9.74	1
Supplicium huic, quoniam crescentia gaudia laesit,	.	O 218	Tr Greek 9.375	5
Assidet huic custos strenua pauperies.	. . . . .	O 219	Tr Greek 9.654	2
HUJUS				
Hujus palestrae qui vigil custos stetit,	. . . . .	O 223	Tr. Gk. 11.176	3
HUMANA				
Humana virtus non sibi sufficit,	. . . . .	O 166	Oda Isle Skye	13
HUMANAE				
Humanae mentis, rerum se pascere formis,	. . . . .	O 163	To Dr Lawrence	6
HUMANI				
Ad Ricardum Savage, Arm. Humani Generis Amatorem.	. . .	O 102	Ad R. Savage	T
Humani studium generis cui pectore fervet,	. . . .	O 102	Ad R. Savage	1
HUMANUM				
O! colat humanum Te foveatque genus!	. . . . . .	O 102	Ad R. Savage	2
HUMERIS				
Fert humeris claudum validis per compita caecus,	. . .	O 213	Tr Greek 9.13	1
Fert humeris, venerabile onus, Cythereius heros	. .	O 216	Tr Greek 9.163	1
HUMET				
Hic anemone humet, confert narcissus odores	. . . .	O 209	Tr. Greek 5.74	3
HUMIDA				
Fidus adest custos, seu nox furat humida nimbis,	. . .	O 90	Messiah	V 62
HUMIDIS				
Obductosque oculos nubibus humidis	. . . . .	O 164	Recover Eyes	6
HUMILI				
Illic Leniades humili regnabat in aula,	. . . . .	O 169	Insula Kenneth	7
HUMO				
Quod mors in cineres solvit, et abdit humo.	. . . .	O 221	Tr Greek 10.84	4
Ditatus magna dote, recondis humo.	. . . . . .	O 222	Tr Greek 11.50	4
HUMUS				
Videre, Archidicen haec tumulavit humus;	. . . . .	O 226	Tr. Simonides	2
HUNC				
Cum Lapidem hunc, magni	. . . . .	O 109	Post-genitis	1
Hunc sequitur caelebs; tertius, orbe, venis.	. . .	O 222	Tr Greek 11.50	2
Hunc oculis Veri Fautrix lustravit acutis,	. . .	O 386	In Birchium	D 3
I				
I, quoniam sic fata vocant: liceat mihi tantum	. . . .	O 384	On the Gin-Act	D 9
IBUNT				
Ibunt per cuncta minaces,	. . . . . .	O 109	Post-genitis	16
IDEM				
Pro nullo; clamo nunc tumulatus idem.	. . .	O 209	Tr Greek 7.128	4
Idem Orcus terrae, sic, pelagoque subest.	. . . .	O 210	Tr Greek 7.265	2
IDUME				
Maturant radii, tibi balsama sudat Idume.	. . . .	O 92	Messiah	105
IERNE				
Et quadragenis decades quinque addit Ierne,	. . . .	O 231	Geographia Met	32
IGNAVAE				
Aspice, diffugiunt ignavae frigora brumae;	. . . .	O 384	Cantico Solom.	D 3
IGNAVUS				
Jam feret ignavus,	. . . . .	O 110	Post-genitis	33
IGNES				
Compagem edificat, coelorum atque aetheris ignes	. . .	O 163	To Dr Lawrence	29
IGNIS				
Ardeat huic toto sacer ignis pectore, possit	. . .	O 205	Christianus	10
Arti ignis lucem tribui, tamen artis et ignis	. .	O 225	Tr Greek 16.87	1
Arti ignis lucem tribui, tamen artis et ignis	. .	O 225	Tr Greek 16.87	1
Ignis quem Phoebi naribus efflat equus,	. . .	Y 28	Aurora Musis	14
Quem efflant quem rem Phoebi naribus ignis equi	.	Y 28	Aurora Musis	V 14
IGNIVOMI				
Per saxa, ignivomi nuper spelaea draconis,	. . .	O 91	Messiah	78
IGNOSCAT				
Cunctorum ignoscat vitiis, pietate fruatur.	. . . .	O 205	Christianus	9
IGNOSCIS				
O Qui benignus crimina ignoscis, pater	. . . .	O 206	Prayers III	1
IGNOTAE				
Inter ignotae strepitus loquelae,	. . . . . .	O 168	Oda to Thrale	10
ILLA				
Gens illa, impatiens per singula quaeque vagandi	. . .	O 163	To Dr Lawrence	23
Luxerat illa dies, legis gens docta supernae	. . .	O 170	Insula Kenneth	15
Fulserat illa dies, legis qua docta supernae	. . .	O 170	Insula Kenneth	V 15

```
ILLA           (CONTINUED)                                    PAGE   TITLE                 LINE
    Illa triumphatrix Graium consueta procorum    . . . . .  O 209  Tr. Greek 6.1           1
    Et pius, et recti cultor: non illa jacere     . . . . .  O 212  Tr Greek 7.590          3
ILLAS
    Nec natet, et nunc has partes, nunc eligat illas,  . . . O 205  Christianus            16
ILLE
    Ille futura calens rapitur per saecula vates,    . . . . O  88  Messiah             V   8
    Ille cutim spissam visus hebetare vetabit,   . . . . . . O  90  Messiah                44
    Ille vias vocis pandet, flexusque liquentis  . . . . . . O  90  Messiah                47
    Ille quidem recte, sublimis, doctus, et acer,   . . . . . O 160  Gnothi seauton         6
    Scire locum volui quid daret ille novi.  . . . . . . .   O 169  Insula Kenneth         6
    Exiguum en! Priami monumentum; haud ille meretur   . . . O 210  Tr Greek 7.136         1
    Cerbere, te morsu ne petat ille, cave.   . . . . . . . . O 211  Tr Greek 7.319         2
    Lysigeni, fuerat non gravis ille tibi.   . . . . . . . . O 211  Tr Greek 7.461         2
    Dario magno non minus ille potest.  . . . . . . . . .    O 212  Tr Greek 7.538         2
    Hic oculos socio commodat, ille pedes.   . . . . . . . . O 213  Tr Greek 9.13          2
    De te plebs audax, hic bene et ille male.   . . . . . .  O 214  Tr Greek 9.50          2
    Ille suum stolidus, nunc putat ille suum.   . . . . . .  O 215  Tr Greek 9.74          4
    Ille suum stolidus, nunc putat ille suum.   . . . . . .  O 215  Tr Greek 9.74          4
    Naufragus iratas ille retentat aquas.  . . . . . . . .   O 215  Tr Greek 9.133         2
    Tempore divitiis utitur, ille sapit.   . . . . . . . . . O 219  Tr Greek 10.26         4
    Hic Bona queis opus est venditat, Ille Sonum.  . . . . . O 385  The Warehouse       D   6
ILLI
    Qui duxit sulcos, illi teret area messem,   . . . . . .  O  90  Messiah               73
ILLIC
    Illic Leniades humili regnabat in aula,   . . . . . . .  O 169  Insula Kenneth         7
ILLIS
    Conspicit aggestas, et se miratur in illis,   . . . . .  O 161  Gnothi seauton        43
    Versat opum cumulos, et se miratur in illis,    . . . .  O 161  Gnothi seauton      V  43
    Tantundem est illis, repleat spatia ardua coeli   . . .  O 163  To Dr Lawrence        13
    Stabo illis qui sunt, quique fuere, gravis.   . . . . .  O 216  Tr Greek 9.288         6
IMA
    Ima tuas credit permitti, Scaliger, iras.   . . . . . .  O 160  Gnothi seauton        13
    Cui pars verbosae, vel datur ima, domus?   . . . . . .   O 385  The Warehouse       D   4
IMAGO
    Saxea Phidiaca spirat imago manu.   . . . . . . . . .    O  85  Adjecere bonae         4
    En Sexto, Sexti meditatur imago, silente;   . . . . . .  O 223  Tr. Gk. 11.145        1
    Orator statua est, statuaeque orator imago.   . . . . .  O 223  Tr. Gk. 11.145        2
    Menodotum pinxit Diodorus, et exit imago,   . . . . . .  O 223  Tr. Gk. 11.213        1
    Nunc ope supplicii vivit imago mei.   . . . . . . . . .  O 225  Tr Greek 16.87        2
IMBER
    Dum defenditur imber,   . . . . . . . . . . . . . .      O 181  Waltoni Piscat         3
    Saepe tuum in tumulum lacrymarum decidit imber   . . .   O 212  Tr Greek 7.560         1
    Heraclite, fluat lacrymarum crebrior imber;   . . . . .  O 216  Tr Greek 9.148         3
    Turbidus imber abest; mittit rosa roscida gemmas,  . .   O 385  Cantico Solom.      D   5
IMBRES
    Praebeat, et tacite foecundos irriget imbres!   . . . .  O  88  Messiah               15
IMBRIBUS
    Strepens procellis, imbribus uvida,   . . . . . . . .    O 166  Oda Isle Skye       V   2
IMITANTIUM
    Quid moliatur Gens Imitantium,   . . . . . . . . . .     O 101  Ad Urbanum            5
IMMATURA
    Immatura calens rapitur per saecula vates,   . . . . .   O  88  Messiah               8
IMMERITO
    Non immerito culpanda venit   . . . . . . . . . . .      O 193  Tr. Medea III         1
IMMISTA
    Immista, sic Iris refulget   . . . . . . . . . . .       O 102  Ad Urbanum           23
IMMITTE
    Pone metum, rostrum fidens immitte cululio,   . . . . .  O 171  Tr. Busy Fly          3
IMMUNIS
    Me, pensi immunis cum jam mihi reddor, inertis   . . .   O 161  Gnothi seauton       24
IMPATIENS
    Impatiens, lenteque fluentes increpat annos.    . . . .  O  92  Messiah              98
    Alme voco, impatiens noctis metuensque diei.   . . . .   O 161  Gnothi seauton       31
    Gens illa, impatiens per singula quaeque vagandi   . .   O 163  To Dr Lawrence       23
IMPEDIERE
    Tecta ineunt, caelebs impediere minus;   . . . . . . .   O 217  Tr Greek 9.360        6
IMPELLITUR
    Nam vita incertis incerta impellitur auris,   . . . . .  O 221  Tr Greek 10.74        3
IMPENDERE
    Ut vitam, poscat si res, impendere vero.   . . . . . .   O 205  Christianus          11
IMPERET
    Ut dicas, spatiis quam latis imperet orbi   . . . . .    O 230  Geographia Met       16
IMPERII
    Te manet imperii, Roma, perenne decus.   . . . . . .     O 219  Tr Greek 9.647        2
IMPERIIQUE
    Dixerat, imperiique vices, coelique meatus,   . . . . .  O 160  Gnothi seauton       10
IMPERIIS
    Pergit, et imperiis sentit se dulcibus actum.   . . . .  O 205  Christianus          27
IMPERIO
    Quis formae modus imperio? Venus arrogat audax   . . .   O 103  Elizae Aenigma        1
    Papa suo regit imperio ter millia quinque.   . . . . .   O 230  Geographia Met       12
IMPERIUM
    Imperium pelagi precantes.   . . . . . . . . . . .       O 188  Epilogus              4
    Imperium qua Turca ferox exercet iniquum.   . . . . .    O 230  Geographia Met        5
IMPETRET
    Mihi dona morte haec impetret Christus sua.   . . . . .  O 206  Prayers I            11
IMPETUM
    Exaestuantis pectoris impetum,   . . . . . . . . . .     O 166  Oda Isle Skye        17
IMPIA
    Impia facta patrans, homines fortasse latebis,   . . . . O 220  Tr Greek 10.27        1
```

```
                                                        PAGE    TITLE              LINE
IMPLEXO
     Horruit implexo qua vallis sente, figurae    . . . . .   0  91 Messiah             80
IMPORTUNA
     Importuna cohors, vacuae mala somnia mentis.    . . . .  0 161 Gnothi seauton       28
IMPROBA
     Seu te saeva sitis, levitas sive improba fecit,    . . . 0 171 Tr. Busy Fly          1
     Seu te saeva fames, levitas sive improba fecit,    . . . 0 171 Tr. Busy Fly     V    1
IN
     Hic requies fessis; non sacra saevit in umbra    . . . . 0  89 Messiah             18
     Hic requies fessis; non sacra hac saevit in umbra  . . . 0  89 Messiah     V       18
     Obstrictasque diu linguas in carmina solvet.   . . . .   0  90 Messiah             46
     Vomerem, et in falcem rigidus curvabitur ensis.    . . . 0  90 Messiah             70
     Cui Fronte Sertum in Erudita . . . . . . . . .          0 101 Ad Urbanum            3
     In Elizae Aenigma  . . . . . . . . . . . . . .          0 103 Elizae Aenigma        T
     To a Lady who spoke in Defence of Liberty  . . .        0 105 Lady Defence          T
     . . . causae in sermone patrocinata fuerat.    . . .    0 105 Lady Defence     V    T
     In Rabiem tunc contremet Ursa  . . . . . . . .          0 109 Post-genitis         24
     Marmoreo trepidant qua lentae in fornice guttae,   . .  0 116 Tr Pope Grotto        3
     Marmorea trepidant qua lentae in fornice guttae,   . .  0 116 Tr Pope Grotto   V    3
     Hic, in se totum longe per opaca futuri    . . . .      0 116 Tr Pope Grotto       10
     Hic pia Vindamius traxit suspiria, in ipsa   . . . .    0 116 Tr Pope Grotto       12
     In Theatro . . . . . . . . . . . . . . . . . .          0 153 In Theatro            T
     Patrem cujus amor blandior in dies . . . . . .          0 155 Psalmus 117           5
     Regem cujus amor laetior in dies   . . . . . . .        0 155 Psalmus 117      V    5
     In lecto. . . . . . . . . . . . . . . . . . . .         0 155 Psalmus 117           9
     In lecto. utrobique Patrem . . . . . . . . . .          0 155 Psalmus 117      V    9
     Conspicit aggestas, et se miratur in illis, . . . .     0 161 Gnothi seauton       43
     Versat opum cumulos, et se miratur in illis,   . . .    0 161 Gnothi seauton   V   43
     Sunt qui curriculo timidi versantur in arcto,  . . .    0 163 To Dr Lawrence        9
     In sublime rapit, queis terra et pontus et aer   . . .  0 163 To Dr Lawrence       32
     In specula numerare fluctus.   . . . . . . . .          0 166 Oda Isle Skye    V   12
     Illic Leniades humili regnabat in aula,    . . . .      0 169 Insula Kenneth        7
     In trepidis dare terga rebus.    . . . . . . . .        0 186 Ad T. L. M.D.         4
     In dubiis dare terga rebus.    . . . . . . . . .        0 186 Ad T. L. M.D.    V    4
     Fulsit, in pectus mihi fonte purum . . . . . .          0 193 Prayer on Xmas        2
     Nugae anapaesticae in lecto lusae. ...                  0 198 Medico Aeger S        T
     Qui cupit in sanctos Christo cogente referri,    . .    0 205 Christianus           1
     Suspiciat tandem clementem in numine patrem.   . .      0 205 Christianus           5
     Et sibi, delirans quanquam et peccator in horas  . .    0 205 Christianus          14
     Nec dubitet quem dicat herum, sed, totus in uno,   . .  0 205 Christianus          17
     Denique perpetuo contendit in ardua nisu,  . . .        0 205 Christianus          25
     In me sparsa manu virtutum semina larga   . . . .       0 207 Prayers VII           3
     In summo ut videas numine laeta patrem;    . . . .      0 208 A Meditation          2
     Divinam in sontes iram placavit Jesus;   . . . .        0 208 A Meditation          3
     Floribus in pratis legi quos ipse, coronam   . . . .    0 209 Tr. Greek 5.74        1
     Saepe tuum in tumulum lacrymarum decidit imber . . .    0 212 Tr Greek 7.560        1
     In me animo tellus gignit et unda feras,   . . . .      0 213 Tr Greek 9.18         2
     In vos ne missus spicula tendat amor.  . . . . .        0 213 Tr Greek 9.39         2
     Dignus qui multa in lustra senescat, erit.   . . .      0 214 Tr Greek 9.55         2
     Ergo optent homines, aut nunquam in luminis oras   . .  0 217 Tr Greek 9.359        9
     Nemo optet nunquam venisse in luminis oras,    . . .    0 217 Tr Greek 9.360        9
     Non Fortuna sibi te gratum tollit in altum;    . . .    0 218 Tr Greek 9.530        1
     In tumulum tecum, morte jubente, trahes?   . . . .      0 220 Tr Greek 10.60        2
     Omnesque in partes tracta retracta fluit;    . . .      0 221 Tr Greek 10.74        4
     Quod mors in cineres solvit, et abdit humo.    . . .    0 221 Tr Greek 10.84        4
     In mentem ut venit nominis, interii.   . . . . .        0 223 Tr. Gk. 11.118        2
     Cur opulentus eges? tua cuncta in foenore ponis.   . .  0 223 Tr. Gk. 11.167        1
     In Rivum a Mola Stoana Lichfeldiae diffluentem   . . .  0 228 Rivum a Stoana        T
     In Locupletissimum ornatissimumque Syl<vani>. Urb<ani>. 0 383 Syl. Urb. Thes.  D    T
     . . . in Lincoln's-Inn-Fields.   . . . . . . . .        0 385 The Warehouse    D    T
     In Birchium  . . . . . . . . . . . . . . . .            0 386 In Birchium      D    T
INANE
     Et rerum volitant rarae per inane figurae.   . . . .    0 162 Gnothi seauton       51
     Materies, vastum an late pandatur inane.   . . . .      0 163 To Dr Lawrence       14
     Materia, vastum an late pandatur inane.    . . . .      0 163 To Dr Lawrence   V   14
     Quales sint monades, qua fit inane, sinas.   . . . .    0 222 Tr Greek 11.50        6
INANI
     Vel spe ludit inani,   . . . . . . . . . . . .          0 182 Waltoni Piscat       13
     Spe non inani confugis,  . . . . . . . . . . .          0 203 Christ Sinner         1
INANIBUS
     Intende nervos fortis, inanibus  . . . . . . .          0 101 Ad Urbanum           13
INCERTA
     Per vitae tenebras rerumque incerta vagantem   . . .    0 207 Prayers IV            1
     Nam vita incertis incerta impellitur auris,    . . . .  0 221 Tr Greek 10.74        3
INCERTIS
     Nam vita incertis incerta impellitur auris,    . . . .  0 221 Tr Greek 10.74        3
INCINCTAM
     Explicat, incinctam radiatae luce tiarae!    . . . .    0  92 Messiah             95
INCLINATA
     Gloria silvarum, dominum inclinata salutet!  . . . .    0  89 Messiah             38
INCLYTA
     Convenit ut patis, inclyta Sparta, tuis.   . . . . .    0 224 Tr Greek 16.1         4
INCLYTUS
     Inclytus hic haeres magni requiescit Oeni,   . . . .    0 386 Tr Epi. Madoc    D    1
INCOLA
     Qui nunc jacet Incola stagni,    . . . . . . . .        0 109 Post-genitis          2
INCOQUITUR
     Pendet, et incoquitur tectum sine fraude metallum:   .  0 116 Tr Pope Grotto        6
     Splendet, et incoquitur tectum sine fraude metallum: .  0 116 Tr Pope Grotto   V    6
INCREMENTA
     Incrementa aevi non cumulare potes.  . . . . . .        0 220 Tr Greek 10.60        4
```

		PAGE	TITLE	LINE
INCREPAT				
Impatiens, lenteque fluentes increpat annos.	O 92	Messiah	98
INCULTA				
Attoniti dumeta vident inculta coloni	O 91	Messiah	75
Quid mihi cum cultu? Probitas inculta nitescit, . . .	O 104	To Eliz Carter	1
INCULTI				
Non tamen inculti gelidis latuere sub antris, ...	O 169	Insula Kenneth	11
Nec tamen inculti gelidis latuere sub antris, ...	O 169	Insula Kenneth	V 11
INCULTUM				
Incultum Studiis, et paucis dotibus auctum	O 161	Gnothi seauton	V 36
INCULTUMQUE				
Notior ipse mihi fieri, incultumque fateri	O 161	Gnothi seauton	35
INCUSAT				
Incusat, semper spe meliora videt.	O 214	Tr Greek 9.54	2
Pigritiam incusat, nec minus hora perit.	O 228	Jactura Tempor	2
INDAGINE				
Est proprium, et quavis captare indagine verum, . . .	O 163	To Dr Lawrence	7
INDEFESSA				
Lympha tamen cursus agit indefessa perennis, . . .	O 228	Rivum a Stoana	9
INDIA				
India nascenti, placidaeve argentea noctis	O 92	Messiah	109
INDIGNATUS				
Vile indignatus studium, nugasque molestas, ...	O 160	Gnothi seauton	3
INDOCTAE				
Heraclitus ego; indoctae ne laedite linguae, . . .	O 209	Tr Greek 7.128	1
INDOCTUS				
Cum tacet indoctus, sapientior esse videtur, . . .	O 221	Tr Greek 10.98	1
INDUE				
Indue reginam, turritae frontis honores	O 91	Messiah	93
INDUIT				
Induit, et, terris major, coelestia spirat.	O 205	Christianus	30
INDULSERIT				
Tu, quamcunque tibi velox indulserit annus, . . .	O 171	Tr. Busy Fly	5
INEAMUS				
Nunc age, certamen nunc ineamus, ait;	O 384	Epigramma	D 2
INEPTUM				
Quod nimium est fit ineptum; hinc, ut dixere priores, .	O 224	Tr Greek 16.16	1
INERTI				
Damnatus tenebris, lectoque affixus inerti, ...	O 163	To Dr Lawrence	3
INERTIS				
Me, pensi immunis cum jam mihi reddor, inertis . . .	O 161	Gnothi seauton	24
INEST				
Terror inest aliis, moerorque, et siquid habebis . . .	O 222	Tr. Gk. 10.123	5
Et melli nimio fellis amaror inest.	O 224	Tr Greek 16.16	2
INEUNT				
Tecta ineunt; caelebs omnia solus ages;	O 217	Tr Greek 9.359	6
Tecta ineunt, caelebs impediere minus;	O 217	Tr Greek 9.360	6
INFANS				
Tractabit palmis infans, motusque trisulcae	O 91	Messiah	90
INFESTIS				
Non ultra infestis concurrent agmina signis, ...	O 90	Messiah	66
INFIDAS				
Sola rates struis infidas, et dulcis amorem	O 213	Tr Greek 9.29	3
INFIRMUM				
Tale hominum genus est, infirmum, triste, misellum, . .	O 221	Tr Greek 10.84	3
INFIT				
Ambraciota, vale lux alma, Cleombrotus infit, ...	O 211	Tr Greek 7.471	1
INFLAMED				
. . . Johnson, as he lay confined with an inflamed Eye.	O 162	To Dr Lawrence	T
INFORMIS				
Squallet informis, tugurique fumis	O 167	Oda to Thrale	7
INFRA				
Supra Praeco Dei--strepit infra Praeco Bonorum: . . .	O 385	The Warehouse	D 5
INFUNDET				
Reclusisque oculis infundet amabile lumen, ...	O 90	Messiah	45
INGEMINA				
Ingemina fluctus, ingeminaque sonum.	O 210	Tr Greek 7.284	2
INGEMINAQUE				
Ingemina fluctus, ingeminaque sonum.	O 210	Tr Greek 7.284	2
INGEMIT				
Ingemit exosus, scribendaque lexica mandat	O 160	Gnothi seauton	4
INGENII				
Et juvat ingenii vita sine arte rudis.	O 104	To Eliz Carter	2
INGENIO				
Ingenio parcas, nec sit mihi culpa rogasse, ...	O 204	Losing Speech	3
Ingenio parcas, nec sit mihi culpa precari	O 204	Losing Speech	V 3
Hanc statuam ingenio Roma benigna tuo.	O 225	Tr. Gk. 16.331	2
INGENIUM				
Ingenium jubeas purior haustus alat.	O 85	Mea nec Falern	6
Sublime ingenium Graius; Romanus habebat . . .	O 86	Tr Dryden Milt	3
Sublime ingenium Graecus; Romanus habebat . . .	O 86	Tr Dryden Milt	V 3
Ingenium et mores si pulchra probavit Elisa, . . .	O 104	To Eliz Carter	3
Pectus, et ingenium vano se robore jactans.	O 161	Gnothi seauton	36
Ingenium, nisi materiem Doctrina ministret, ...	O 161	Gnothi seauton	37
Ingenium, nisi materiem Doctrina ministrat, ...	O 161	Gnothi seauton	V 37
Subtile ingenium quaero, capaxque mei, ...	O 209	Tr Greek 7.128	2
INGENIUMQUE				
Ingeniumque sui cohibet penuria census.	O 161	Gnothi seauton	V 38
INGENTEMQUE				
Ingentemque animo seclorum volverat orbem.	O 160	Gnothi seauton	11
Ingentemque animo seclorum volveret orbem.	O 160	Gnothi seauton	V 11

		PAGE	TITLE		LINE
INGENTIS					
	Quam domini ingentis ferre supercilium.	O 221	Tr Greek 10.93		2
INGREDERE					
	Ingredere O!--Magnam pura cole mente parentem, ...	O 116	Tr Pope Grotto		7
	Ingredere O!--rerum pura cole mente parentem, ...	O 116	Tr Pope Grotto	V	7
	Ingredere! Egeriae sacrum en tibi panditur antrum! . .	O 116	Tr Pope Grotto		9
INGREDITUR					
	Ingreditur, cultuque tuo mansuescere gaudet.	O 92	Messiah		101
INIQUUM					
	Imperium qua Turca ferox exercet iniquum.	O 230	Geographia Met		5
INJICIAT					
	Nec menti injiciat sordida cura jugum;	O 221	Tr Greek 10.74		2
INJICIENT					
	Per ludum pueri injicient, et fessa colubri	O 91	Messiah		87
INN SEE IINCCLN'S					
INNITERE					
	Firma manet virtus; virtuti innitere, tutus	O 221	Tr Greek 10.74		5
INNIXUS					
	Consuetus fulcro innixus reptare bacilli	O 90	Messiah		50
INNOCUA					
	Innocua hic membris permistas membra columbas . . .	O 393	Tr. of Crashaw	D	1
INNOCUOS					
	Ridebit linguae innocuos, squamasque virentes	O 91	Messiah		91
	Ridebit linguae innocuos, squamas viridantes	O 91	Messiah	V	91
INOFFENSO					
	Lenis inoffenso vitaque morsque gradu.	Y 387	Death Mother	D	4
INOPS					
	Cessat inops rerum, ut torpet, si marmoris absit . . .	O 161	Gnothi seauton		38
INQUIT					
	Dulce Venus ridens, lorica nil opus, inquit, ...	O 384	Epigramma	D	3
INSANIA					
	Hi sunt quos animi generosa insania magni	O 163	To Dr Lawrence		31
INSCRIBENDI					
	Versus Ccllari Caprae Domini Banks inscribendi . . .	O 156	Collari Caprae		T
INSCRIPTION					
	Inscription on the collar of Mr. Banks's Goat	O 156	Collari Caprae	V	T
INSIDET					
	Nuncia sacra Dei, plaudentibus insidet alis. . . .	O 88	Messiah		13
INSIDIAS					
	Insidias meditatur horis.	O 166	Oda Isle Skye		8
INSIPIENTIA					
	Proavum vaecors insipientia, ...	O 193	Tr. Medea III		2
INSOLITUM					
	Nil movet insolitum, sub legibus omnia fictis	O 163	To Dr Lawrence		35
INSTAR					
	Nox miseris longi temporis instar habet.	O 220	Tr Greek 10.28		2
INSTARE					
	Nunc instare futuris, ...	O 182	Waltoni Piscat		8
INSTET					
	Instet, et evellens terroris spicula corde, ...	O 205	Christianus		4
	Hora bonis quasi nunc instet suprema fruaris, ...	O 219	Tr Greek 10.26		1
INSULA					
	Ode, De Skia Insula	O 167	Oda to Thrale	V	T
	Insula Sancti Kennethi	O 169	Insula Kenneth		T
	Insula Kennethi, Inter Hebridas	O 169	Insula Kenneth	V	T
INTACTA					
	Pulchra est virginitas intacta, at vita periret, . . .	O 218	Tr Greek 9.444		1
INTEMERATA					
	Justitiaeque manus pretio intemerata bilancem . . .	O 89	Messiah		21
INTENDE					
	Intende nervos fortis, inanibus	O 101	Ad Urbanum		13
	Intende jam nervos, habebis	O 101	Ad Urbanum		15
INTER					
	Suave rubere rosis, sitientesque inter arenas	O 91	Messiah		76
	Angliacas inter pulcherrima Laura puellas, ...	O 115	Ad Lauram Epig		1
	Inter equales, sine vile liber, ...	O 153	In Theatro		9
	Codices, veri studiosus, inter	O 153	In Theatro		10
	Inter erroris salebrosa longi, ...	O 168	Oda to Thrale		9
	Inter ignotae strepitus loquelae, ...	O 168	Oda to Thrale		10
	Insula Kennethi, Inter Hebridas	O 169	Insula Kenneth	V	T
	Nota, Caledonias panditur inter aquas;	O 169	Insula Kenneth		2
	Clara, Caledonias panditur inter aquas;	O 169	Insula Kenneth	V	2
	Ponti inter strepitus sacri non munera cultus	O 170	Insula Kenneth		17
INTEREA					
	Interea dubito; tecum me causa nec ulla	O 216	Tr Greek 9.148		5
INTERII					
	In mentem ut venit nominis, interii.	O 223	Tr. Gk. 11.118		2
INTRET					
	Dimidium tanti ponderis intret onus.	O 229	Epigram III		2
INTUS					
	Divino, sanctus regnet ut intus amor:	O 232	Prayer		6
INUNDABIT					
	Regiam inundabit, nullis cessura tenebris.	O 92	Messiah		113
INUTILES					
	Pigrae per horas lucis inutiles, ...	O 187	Ad T. L. M.D.		10
INUTILITER					
	Respice inutiliter lapsi quem poenitet aevi;	O 207	Prayers VI		5
INVADENS					
	Naturae invadens, mundique elementa refingens . . .	O 163	To Dr Lawrence		25
INVALIDI					
	Invalidi raptos sceptri plorabit honores.	O 90	Messiah		56

```
                                                              PAGE    TITLE               LINE
INVENIO
     Nec quid agam invenio, meditatus grandia, cogor    . . .   O 161 Gnothi seauton        34
INVISAS
     Democrite, invisas homines majore cachinno,  . . . . .     O 216 Tr Greek 9.148         1
IO
     Veris, io! venit alma dies! Philomela canorum   . . .      O 385 Cantico Solom.    D    7
IPSA
     Hic pia Vindamius traxit suspiria, in ipsa  . . . . .      O 116 Tr Pope Grotto        12
     Admonitu, ipsa suas nunciat hora vices.  . . . . . .       O 170 Insula Kenneth    V 18B
     Nycticorax cantat lethale, sed ipsa canenti . . . . .      O 223 Tr. Gk. 11.186         1
IPSE
     Luna vices revehet; radios pater ipse diei  . . . . .      O  92 Messiah             110
     Notior ipse mihi fieri, incultumque fateri  . . . . .      O 161 Gnothi seauton        35
     Notior ipse mihi fieri, pectusque fateri . . . . . .       O 161 Gnothi seauton    V  35
     Ipse sui judex, actae bene munera vitae; . . . . . .       O 162 Gnothi seauton        48
     Floribus in pratis legi quos ipse, coronam  . . . .        O 209 Tr. Greek 5.74         1
     Dat tibi Pythagoram pictor; quod ni ipse tacere  . .       O 225 Tr. Gk. 16.326         1
IPSIS
     Firmius ac ipsis Mundi stabilita ruinis. . . . . . .       O  92 Messiah             V 119
IPSO
     Ipso fonte bibes, quae circumfusa beatam  . . . . . .      O  92 Messiah             112
IRA
     Non ira, non moeror quietis  . . . . . . . . . .           O 166 Oda Isle Skye          7
IRAM
     Divinam in sontes iram placavit Jesus;  . . . . . .        O 208 A Meditation           3
IRAS
     Ima tuas credit permitti, Scaliger, iras. . . . . .        O 160 Gnothi seauton        13
     Ut precibus justas avertat numinis iras  . . . . . .       O 170 Insula Kenneth    V 16A
     At nemo feras iras hominum,  . . . . . . . . . .           O 193 Tr. Medea III          6
IRATA
     Audiit, irata est ne nova Musa foret. . . . . . . .        O 214 Tr Greek 9.66          2
IRATAS
     Naufragus iratas ille retentat aquas. . . . . . . .        O 215 Tr Greek 9.133         2
IRE
     Ad Divos paribus passibus ire duces;  . . . . . . .        O 225 Tr. Gk. 16.331         4
IRIS
     Immista, sic Iris refulget  . . . . . . . . . .            O 102 Ad Urbanum            23
IRRIGET
     Praebeat, et tacite foecundos irriget imbres! . . . .      O  88 Messiah              15
IRRITA
     "Irrita vanescent priscae vestigia fraudis,"  . . . .      O  89 Messiah              20
IRRUPTUM
     Irruptum vitae cupiat servare tenorem;  . . . . . .        O 205 Christianus          13
IRUS
     Pauperieque Irus, curaque prima Deum. . . . . . . . .      O 114 Tr Gk Epigrams        4
     Pauperieque Irus, curaque summa Deum. . . . . . . . .      O 212 Tr Greek 7.676         2
ISAIAE
     Siderea Isaiae, dignos accende furores! . . . . . .        O  88 Messiah               7
ISTA
     Graeciae et urbs, urbi est ista propago, decus. . . .      O 214 Tr Greek 9.65          2
     Gratia nulla hominum mentes tenet, ista Promethei . .      O 225 Tr Greek 16.87         3
ISTE
     Scire locus volui quid daret iste novi. . . . . . .        O 169 Insula Kenneth    V   6
     Huc nunquam volitat debilis iste puer.  . . . . . .        O 213 Tr Greek 9.39          4
ISTI
     Arte valent isti, mihi robore vivere solo est, . . . .     O 224 Tr Greek 16.1          3
ISTIS
     Aeternum direpta mihi! sed quid moror istis? . . . .       O 384 On the Gin-Act    D   7
ITER
     Quisquis iter tendis, vitreas qua lucidus undas  . . .     O 116 Tr Pope Grotto         1
     Tentat iter brevius, magno conamine summam  . . . .        O 163 To Dr Lawrence        24
     Elige iter vitae, ut possis; rixisque dolisque  . . .      O 217 Tr Greek 9.359         1
     Elige iter vitae, ut mavis; prudentia lausque  . . .       O 217 Tr Greek 9.360         1
ITIDEM
     E longinquo itidem pontus et orcus erat. . . . . . .       O 213 Tr Greek 9.29          6
ITQUE
     Itque reditque;  . . . . . . . . . . . . .                 O 198 Medico Aeger S         4
     Lunaque quas et sol itque reditque vias. . . . . .         O 222 Tr. Gk. 10.123         4
JACEANT
     Hic jaceant; donec Nox transeat horrida nimbis,  . . .     O 393 Tr. of Crashaw    D   3
JACEAT
     Nauta, quis hoc jaceat ne percontere sepulchro;  . . .     O 211 Tr Greek 7.350         1
JACENT
     Sub pedibus subjecta jacent; queis ultima primis  . .      O 163 To Dr Lawrence        33
     Sanguine Anastasii; cuncta sepulta jacent:  . . . .        O 212 Tr Greek 7.590         2
JACEO
     Naufragus hic jaceo; contra jacet ecce colonus!  . .       O 210 Tr Greek 7.265         1
     Naufragus hic jaceo; fidens tamen utere velis,  . . .      O 210 Tr Greek 7.282         1
JACERE
     Et pius, et recti cultor: non illa jacere  . . . .         O 212 Tr Greek 7.590         3
JACET
     Qui nunc jacet Incola stagni,  . . . . . . . . .           O 109 Post-genitis          2
     Naufragus hic jaceo; contra jacet ecce colonus!  . . .     O 210 Tr Greek 7.265         1
     Qui jacet hic, servus vixit, nunc, lumine cassus, . . .    O 212 Tr Greek 7.538         1
     Spreta jacet Marathon, jacet et Salaminia laurus, . . .    O 216 Tr Greek 9.288         3
     Spreta jacet Marathon, jacet et Salaminia laurus, . . .    O 216 Tr Greek 9.288         3
JACIT
     Sub pedibus, populo praetereunte, jacit, . . . . . .       O 218 Tr Greek 9.375         4
JACTANS
     Pectus, et ingenium vano se robore jactans. . . . . .      O 161 Gnothi seauton        36
```

		PAGE	TITLE	LINE
JACTAT				
Das bene collatos, quos Roma et Graecia jactat,	. . .	O 225	Tr. Gk. 16.331	3
Ter sex centurias Hollandia jactat opima	. . . . . .	O 231	Geographia Met	35
JACTET				
Parare posse, utcunque jactet	. . . .	O 166	Oda Isle Skye	V 15
JACTURA				
Jactura Temporis	. . . .	O 228	Jactura Tempor	T
JACUISSE				
Frigora, seu nimium longo jacuisse veterno,	. . . . .	O 161	Gnothi seauton	17
JACULANTIA				
Hostiles oculis flammas jaculantia torvis;		O 90	Messiah	67
JAM				
Jam saltu capreas, jam cursu provocat euros.	. . .	O 90	Messiah	51
Jam saltu capreas, jam cursu provocat euros.	. . .	O 90	Messiah	51
Serpentes teneris nil jam lethale minantes	. . . .	O 91	Messiah	89
Serpentes teneris nil jam lethale micantes	. . . .	O 91	Messiah	V 89
Intende jam nervos, habebis	. . . .	O 101	Ad Urbanum	15
Jam feret ignavus,	. . . .	O 110	Post-genitis	33
Me, pensi immunis cum jam mihi reddor, inertis	. . . .	O 161	Gnothi seauton	24
Auxilioque Dei fretus, jam mente serena	. . . .	O 205	Christianus	26
Stat: fixum est: nequeunt jam revocare preces.	. . . .	O 384	On the Gin-Act	D 8
Jam teneros fructus detrudit lactea ficus	. . . . .	O 385	Cantico Solom.	D 11
JAMQUE				
Labraque constrictus semesos, jamque terendos	. . . .	O 218	Tr Greek 9.375	3
JANITOR				
Et ferus est Timon sub terris; janitor Orci,	. . . .	O 211	Tr Greek 7.319	1
JEJUNIA				
Serviat ut menti corpus, jejunia serva;	. . . . . .	O 228	Jejunium Cibus	1
JEJUNIUM				
Jejunium et Cibus	. . . .	O 228	Jejunium Cibus	T
JESSAEIS				
Jessaeis surgit, mulcentesque aethera flores	. . . .	O 88	Messiah	11
JESUS				
Divinam in sontes iram placavit Jesus;	. . . . . .	O 208	A Meditation	3
JOANNES				
Clarus Joannes, reginae affinis, ab alto	. . . . . .	O 212	Tr Greek 7.590	1
JOHNSON				
. . . Johnson, as he lay confined with an inflamed Eye.		O 162	To Dr Lawrence	T
JOVE				
Ab Jove Maeonides descendere Somnia narrat:	. . . . .	O 103	Elizae Aenigma	3
JOVEM				
Et cycnum fecit Leda petita Jovem.	. . . .	O 214	Tr Greek 9.48	2
JOVI				
Omnia, nec curae sunt sua sceptra Jovi.	. . . . . .	O 103	Elizae Aenigma	2
JOVIS				
Nunc armant Veneris lumina tela Jovis.	. . . . . .	O 103	Elizae Aenigma	6
Haec habet altrici Capra secunda Jovis.	. . . . . .	O 156	Collari Caprae	2
JUBEAS				
Ingenium jubeas purior haustus alat.	. . . .	O 85	Mea nec Falern	6
JUBEBIT				
Myriadas decies septem numerare jubebit	. . . . .	O 230	Geographia Met	8
JUBENTE				
In tumulum tecum, morte jubente, trahes?	. . . .	O 220	Tr Greek 10.60	2
JUBES				
Quid salvere jubes me, pessime? Corripe gressus;	. . .	O 211	Tr Greek 7.318	1
JUBET				
Quam bene ventorum surgere templa jubet!	. . . . .	O 143	On Lord Anson	2
Summus adesse jubet celsa dominator ab arce;	. . . .	O 162	Gnothi seauton	45
Noctis tristitiam qui gelidae jubet,	. . . . .	O 164	Recover Eyes	4
Spes hominum ac curas cum procul esse jubet.	. . . .	O 170	Insula Kenneth	16
Ridere, aut tecum me lacrimare jubet.	. . . . .	O 216	Tr Greek 9.148	6
JUDAEO				
Cum sex centuriis Judaeo millia septem.	. . . . . .	O 229	Geographia Met	2
JUDEX				
Ipse sui judex, actae bene munera vitae;	. . . . . .	O 162	Gnothi seauton	48
JUDICE				
Judice quo scelerum est paenituisse salus,	. . . . .	O 198	Tr. Ash Wed.	2
JUGA				
Et juga Carmeli recreant fragrantia coelum.	. . .	O 89	Messiah	33
Plenum opus effugiens; aptans juga mollia collo	. . .	O 205	Christianus	22
JUGERA				
Nunquam jugera messibus onusta, aut	. . . .	O 215	Tr Greek 9.110	1
JUGUM				
Nec menti injiciat sordida cura jugum;	. . . . . .	O 221	Tr Greek 10.74	2
JUNCIQUE				
Canna viret, juncique tremit mutabilis umbra.	. . . .	O 91	Messiah	79
Canna viret, juncique tremit variabilis umbra.	. . . .	O 91	Messiah	V 79
JUNCTUS				
Quem fundit blando junctus amore dolor;	. . . . . .	O 212	Tr Greek 7.560	2
JUNGERE				
Quam quae severis ludicra jungere	. . . . .	O 102	Ad Urbanum	18
JUNGIT				
Se quinquagenis octingentesima jungit	. . . .	O 230	Geographia Met	23
Et quadragenis quoque ter tria millia jungit.	. . . .	O 230	Geographia Met	26
JUNGUNT				
Aeriaeque columbae, dantes oscula, jungunt	. . . .	O 385	Cantico Solom.	D 9
JUNXIT				
Supremis junxit nexibus arctus amor.	. . . .	O 393	Tr. of Crashaw	D 2
JUPITER				
Jupiter unus erat, qui stravit fulmine gentes;	. . .	O 103	Elizae Aenigma	5
Jupiter hoc templum, ut, siquando relinquit Olympum,	. .	O 219	Tr Greek 9.702	1

JUPITER	(CONTINUED)	PAGE	TITLE	LINE
Seu prece poscatur, seu non, da Jupiter omne	. . . .	O 221	Tr Greek 10.108	1
JURATA				
Sint Demosthenica ut jurata cadavera voce,	. . . . .	O 216	Tr Greek 9.288	5
JUSSA				
Sic peragam tua jussa libens, accinctus ad omne	. . .	O 207	Prayers IV	5
JUSSERE				
Hilarare suis jussere modis	O 193	Tr. Medea III	4
JUSTAS				
Ut precibus justas avertat numinis iras	O 170	Insula Kenneth	V 16A
JUSTITIAEQUE				
Justitiaeque manus pretio intemerata bilancem	O 89	Messiah	21
JUSTO				
Tempore justo	O 199	Medico Aeger S	10
JUVABIT				
Aeternum Aeterna Luce juvabit opus!	O 393	Tr. of Crashaw	D 6
JUVANT				
Nunc clamosa juvant nocturnae gaudia mensae, ...	O 161	Gnothi seauton	29
JUVAT				
Et juvat ingenii vita sine arte rudis.	O 104	To Eliz Carter	2
JUVENCUM				
Antiope satyrum, Danae aurum, Europa juvencum, ...	O 214	Tr Greek 9.48	1
JUVENCUS				
Cumque leone petet tutus praesepe juvencus.	O 91	Messiah	85
JUVENEM				
Luxus oblectat Juvenem theatri, ...	O 153	In Theatro	14
JUVENES				
Turba senum, juvenes nunc tribuere seni.	O 225	Tr. Gk. 16.364	4
JUVENI				
Laevum at utrumque decus, juveni quod praebuit olim . .	O 225	Tr. Gk. 16.364	3
JUVENIS				
Praecellit juvenis vi, pietate senex.	O 217	Tr Greek 9.360	8
Mente senes olim juvenis, Faustine, premebas, ...	O 225	Tr. Gk. 16.364	1
JUVENTAE				
Proles aucta gravat, rapta orbat, caeca juventae est . .	O 217	Tr Greek 9.359	7
JUVENTUTEM				
Parca, juventutem non miserata tuam!	O 212	Tr Greek 7.560	6
JUVENUM				
Nunc juvenum terres robore corda senex.	O 225	Tr. Gk. 16.364	2
JUXTA				
Juxta Animo Studiisque felix.	O 101	Ad Urbanum	8
KENNETHI				
Insula Sancti Kennethi	O 169	Insula Kenneth	T
Insula Kennethi, Inter Hebridas	O 169	Insula Kenneth	V T
LABEFACTA				
Sidera fumabunt, diro labefacta tremore	O 92	Messiah	115
LABELLA				
Legitimas faciunt pura labella preces	O 170	Insula Kenneth	V 20
Sint pro legitimis pura labella sacris	O 170	Insula Kenneth	V 20
LABEM				
Abstergat mundi labem, nec gaudia carnis	O 205	Christianus	2
LABOR				
Rura labor lassat; mare mille pericula terrent; . . .	O 217	Tr Greek 9.359	3
Quid labor efficiet? non nisi nudus ero.	O 220	Tr Greek 10.58	2
LABORANTEM				
Scelerum catena me laborantem gravi	O 206	Prayers III	4
Scelerum caterna me laborantem grave	O 206	Prayers III	V 4
LABORAT				
Tu, queis laborat sors hominum, mala	O 187	Ad T. L. M.D.	5
LABORE				
Et pingues absque Labore.	O 109	Post-genitis	18
Desidiae sors dura manet, graviorque labore	O 161	Gnothi seauton	25
LABORES				
Deliciasque fugit solitas solitosque labores;	O 162	To Dr Lawrence	2
Rura labores.	O 167	Oda to Thrale	4
Te medici revocant labores.	O 187	Ad T. L. M.D.	16
LABORI				
Materies arti, sua desunt arma labori	O 161	Gnothi seauton	V 37
LABORIBUS				
Urbane, nullis fesse laboribus, ...	O 101	Ad Urbanum	1
LABRAQUE				
Labraque constrictus semesos, jamque terendos	O 218	Tr Greek 9.375	3
LACHRYMANTES				
Singultans mulcet, lachrymantes terget ocellos. . . .	O 90	Messiah	53
Singultans mulcet, lachrymantes tergit ocellos. . . .	O 90	Messiah	V 53
LACRIMARE				
Ridere, aut tecum me lacrimare jubet.	O 216	Tr Greek 9.148	6
LACRYMANS				
Natus eram lacrymans, lacrymans e luce recedo;	O 221	Tr Greek 10.84	1
Natus eram lacrymans, lacrymans e luce recedo;	O 221	Tr Greek 10.84	1
LACRYMARUM				
Saepe tuum in tumulum lacrymarum decidit imber	O 212	Tr Greek 7.560	1
Heraclite, fluat lacrymarum crebrior imber;	O 216	Tr Greek 9.148	3
LACRYMIS				
Prosequitur lacrymis filia moesta Sami, ...	O 211	Tr Greek 7.459	2
Sunt quibus a lacrymis vix vacat ulla dies.	O 221	Tr Greek 10.84	2
LACTEA				
Jam teneros fructus detrudit lactea ficus	O 385	Cantico Solom.	D 11
LACTIS				
Perpetui, ambita bis terra, praemia lactis	O 156	Collari Caprae	1
Perpetua, ambita bis terra, praemia lactis	O 156	Collari Caprae	V 1

	PAGE	TITLE	LINE
LADY			
To a Lady who spoke in Defence of Liberty	O 105	Lady Defence	T
LAEDITE			
Heraclitus ego; indoctae ne laedite linguae, ...	O 209	Tr Greek 7.128	1
LAESIT			
Supplicium huic, quoniam crescentia gaudia laesit, . .	O 218	Tr Greek 9.375	5
LAETA			
Deserti laeta mollescunt aspera voce, ...	O 89	Messiah	34
Ut qua dulce strepunt scatebrae, qua laeta virescunt . .	O 90	Messiah	57
Ut qua dulce strepent scatebrae, qua laeta virescunt . .	O 90	Messiah	V 57
Nam licet, et toto prolue laeta mero.	O 171	Tr. Busy Fly	4
Noctes atque dies animo spes laeta recurset, ...	O 207	Prayers VII	5
Certa vetet dubitare fides, spes laeta timere, ...	O 207	Prayers VII	7
In summo ut videas numine laeta patrem;	O 208	A Meditation	2
LAETAQUE			
Laetaque Messia semper dominabere rege, ...	O 92	Messiah	118
LAETATUR			
Cyrum sexta timet; laetatur septima Christo.	O 226	Septem Aetates	4
Cyrum sexta vocat, laetatur	O 226	Septem Aetates	V 4
LAETIOR			
Regem cujus amor laetior in dies	O 155	Psalmus 117	V 5
Laetior haud tecum, tecum neque tristior unquam, . . .	O 218	Tr Greek 9.573	5
LAETIS			
Hora perit furtim laetis, mens temporis aegra	O 228	Jactura Tempor	1
LAETITIA			
Sat laetitia, sine subsidiis, ...	O 193	Tr. Medea III	13
LAETO			
Laeto cedere lumini	O 164	Recover Eyes	3
Hae poterant uvae laeto convivia cantu	O 218	Tr Greek 9.375	7
LAETOS			
Congestas animus, laetos aut sumit honores	O 161	Gnothi seauton	V 40
Praeteritis fruitur, laetos aut sumit honores	O 162	Gnothi seauton	47
LAETUS			
Populari Pascua laetus.	O 110	Post-genitis	30
LAEVIA			
Laevia serratis miscens, quadrata rotundis, ...	O 163	To Dr Lawrence	26
LAEVUM			
Laevum at utrumque decus, juveni quod praebuit olim . .	O 225	Tr. Gk. 16.364	3
LAIS			
Ante suas agmen Lais habere fores, ...	O 209	Tr. Greek 6.1	2
LAMBUNT			
Coelestes lambunt animae; ramisque columba, ...	O 88	Messiah	12
LAMPADE			
Pulicibus morsus, restincta lampade, stultus	O 224	Tr. Gk. 11.432	1
LANGUENS			
Aeternoque orci dominator vulnere languens	O 90	Messiah	55
LANGUENTIA			
Sive dies medius languentia torreat arva:	O 90	Messiah	V 63
LANGUESCISQUE			
Torpesque languescisque curis	O 187	Ad T. L. M.D.	11
LANIAT			
Laniat tussis;	O 198	Medico Aeger S	8
LANIFICI			
Blandam lanifici sociam, sine fine loquacem, ...	O 211	Tr Greek 7.459	3
LAPIDEM			
Cum Lapidem hunc, magni	O 109	Post-genitis	1
LAPIS			
Quo tua signantur gesta, Philippe, lapis.	O 216	Tr Greek 9.288	2
LAPSA			
Queis majus pretium saecula lapsa dabant	Y 28	Aurora Musis	12
LAPSI			
Respice inutiliter lapsi quem poenitet aevi;	O 207	Prayers VI	5
LAQUEUM			
Hic, aurum ut reperit, laqueum abjicit, alter ut aurum .	O 213	Tr Greek 9.44	1
Non reperit, nectit quem reperit laqueum.	O 213	Tr Greek 9.44	2
LARGA			
In me sparsa manu virtutum semina larga	O 207	Prayers VII	3
LASCIVIET			
Per valles sociata lupo lasciviet agna, ...	O 91	Messiah	84
LASSAT			
Rura labor lassat; mare mille pericula terrent; . . .	O 217	Tr Greek 9.359	3
LATA			
Deserta et lata mollescunt aspera voce, ...	O 89	Messiah	V 34
Harmonia tellus completur lata, per agros	Y 28	Aurora Musis	3
LATE			
Speluncae late Thamesis praetendit opacae, ...	O 116	Tr Pope Grotto	2
Sed sua regna videns, loca nocte silentia late	O 162	Gnothi seauton	49
Materies, vastum an late pandatur inane.	O 163	To Dr Lawrence	14
Materia, vastum an late pandatur inane.	O 163	To Dr Lawrence	V 14
LATEBIS			
Impia facta patrans, homines fortasse latebis, ...	O 220	Tr Greek 10.27	1
LATEBRAS			
Fecerunt rami latebras, tenebrisque diurnis	O 228	Rivum a Stoana	5
LATERE			
Non poteris, meditans prava, latere Deos.	O 220	Tr Greek 10.27	2
LATESCERE			
At non cavata rupe latescere, ...	O 166	Oda Isle Skye	9
LATESCIT			
Foeda latescit.	O 167	Oda to Thrale	8
LATEX			
Crystallisque latex fractus scintillat acutis, ...	O 116	Tr Pope Grotto	4

	PAGE	TITLE	LINE
LATIS			
Cynthia, tunc latis	O 109	Post-genitis	25
Ut dicas, spatiis quam latis imperet orbi	O 230	Geographia Met	16
LATITAT			
Pauperies latitat, cum conjuge gaudia multa	O 217	Tr Greek 9.360	5
LATRONES			
Latrones, alibi locupletum quaerite tecta, ...	O 219	Tr Greek 9.654	1
LATUERE			
Non tamen inculti gelidis latuere sub antris, ...	O 169	Insula Kenneth	11
Nec tamen inculti gelidis latuere sub antris, ...	O 169	Insula Kenneth V	11
LATUS			
Peccator, ad latus meum;	O 203	Christ Sinner	2
LAUDE			
Qua te laude, Deus, qua prece prosequar?	O 164	Recover Eyes	10
LAUDES			
"Perge modo, atque tuas olim post funera laudes . . .	O 386	In Birchium D	5
LAUDET			
Quos laudet vates Graius Romanus et Anglus	O 86	Tr Dryden Milt	1
Quos laudet vates Graecus Romanus et Anglus	O 86	Tr Dryden Milt V	1
LAUDO			
Gratum animum laudo; Qui debuit omnia ventis, ...	O 143	On Lord Anson	1
LAURA			
Angliacas inter pulcherrima Laura puellas, ...	O 115	Ad Lauram Epig	1
Adsit, Laura, tibi facilis Lucina dolenti, ...	O 115	Ad Lauram Epig	3
LAURAM			
Ad Lauram parituram Epigramma	O 115	Ad Lauram Epig	T
LAURENCE			
Ad T.<homam> L.<aurence> M.<edicum> D.<octissimum> . .	O 186	Ad T. L. M.D.	T
Ad Thomam Laurence, Medicum Doctissimum, Cum	O 186	Ad T. L. M.D. V	T
LAURENTI			
Laurenti saltem facili dignarier aure?	O 163	To Dr Lawrence	5
Te docta, Laurenti, vetustas	O 187	Ad T. L. M.D.	15
LAURUS			
Spreta jacet Marathon, jacet et Salaminia laurus, . . .	O 216	Tr Greek 9.288	3
LAUS			
Ut summa laus sit, summa Christo gloria.	O 206	Prayers III	6
Ut tibi laus omni semper ab ore sonet:	O 232	Prayer	8
LAUSQUE			
Elige iter vitae, ut mavis; prudentia lausque	O 217	Tr Greek 9.360	1
LAUTASQUE			
Qui convivia lautasque dapes	O 193	Tr. Medea III	3
LAVACRA			
Longinquisque oculis nuda lavacra patent.	O 228	Rivum a Stoana	8
LAVI			
Quo toties lavi membra tenella puer;	O 228	Rivum a Stoana	2
LAVIT			
Haud lavit Phido, haud tetigit; mihi febre calenti . .	O 223	Tr. Gk. 11.118	1
LAWRENCE			
Verses addressed to Dr. Lawrence, composed by Dr. . . .	O 162	To Dr Lawrence	T
LAXENT			
Mollia laxent	O 199	Medico Aeger S	18
LAY			
. . . Johnson, as he lay confined with an inflamed Eye.	O 162	To Dr Lawrence	T
LEBANON			
Altius, en! Lebanon gaudentia culmina tollit, ...	O 89	Messiah	30
LECTIS			
His sapiens lectis, Epicurum quaerere frustra	O 222	Tr Greek 11.50	5
LECTO			
In lecto.	O 155	Psalmus 117	9
In lecto. utrobique Patrem	O 155	Psalmus 117 V	9
Nugae anapaesticae in lecto lusae.	O 198	Medico Aeger S	T
LECTOQUE			
Damnatus tenebris, lectoque affixus inerti, ...	O 163	To Dr Lawrence	3
LECTOR			
Poeta, lector, hic quiescit Hipponax, ...	O 224	Tr Greek 13.3	1
LECTOS			
Quisquis adit lectos elata uxore secundos, ...	O 215	Tr Greek 9.133	1
LEDA			
Et cycnum fecit Leda petita Jovem.	O 214	Tr Greek 9.48	2
LEGE			
Nequitiam fugiens, servata contrahe lege	O 218	Tr Greek 9.444	3
Per certas stabili lege voluta vices, ...	O 219	Tr Greek 9.577	2
Quo, lege vestra, vita me feret mea.	O 226	Tr. Cleanthes	2
LEGENS			
Scripta legens, sola vivere mente cupit.	O 211	Tr Greek 7.471	4
LEGES			
Plurima tunc Leges	O 109	Post-genitis	21
Summe Pater, quodcunque tuae de corpore leges	O 204	Losing Speech V	1
Ne stolidae similis leges sibi segreget audax	O 205	Christianus	20
Quas servare velit, leges quas lentus omittat, . . .	O 205	Christianus	21
Et colere et leges semper amare tuas.	O 208	Prayers VII	10
LEGI			
Floribus in pratis legi quos ipse, coronam	O 209	Tr. Greek 5.74	1
LEGIBUS			
Nil movet insolitum, sub legibus omnia fictis	O 163	To Dr Lawrence	35
Concede agendam legibus vitam tuis.	O 206	Prayers I	4
LEGIS			
Luxerat illa dies, legis gens docta supernae	O 170	Insula Kenneth	15
Fulserat illa dies, legis qua docta supernae	O 170	Insula Kenneth V	15
LEGITIMAS			
Legitimas faciunt pectora pura preces.	O 170	Insula Kenneth	20

```
                                                 PAGE   TITLE              LINE
LEGITIMAS        (CONTINUED)
    Legitimas faciunt pura labella preces . . . . . . . .   O 170 Insula Kenneth   V  20
LEGITIMIS
    Sint pro legitimis pectora pura sacris    . . . . . .   O 170 Insula Kenneth   V  20
    Sint pro legitimis pura labella sacris    . . . . . .   O 170 Insula Kenneth   V  20
LENIADES
    Illic Leniades humili regnabat in aula,   . . . . . .   O 169 Insula Kenneth      7
    Leniades magnis nobilitatus avis:   . . . . . . . .     O 169 Insula Kenneth      8
LENIS
    Lenis inoffenso vitaque morsque gradu.   . . . . . .    Y 387 Death Mother     D   4
LENITAS
    Pater benigne, summa semper lenitas,   . . . . . . .    O 206 Prayers I            1
LENTA
    Sic sibi diffisi, lenta experientia cursum  . . . . .   O 163 To Dr Lawrence      17
LENTAE
    Marmoreo trepidant qua lentae in fornice guttae,   . . . O 116 Tr Pope Grotto      3
    Marmorea trepidant qua lentae in fornice guttae,   . . . O 116 Tr Pope Grotto   V  3
LENTEQUE
    Impatiens, lenteque fluentes increpat annos.   . . . .  O  92 Messiah            98
LENTI
    Non mihi sorte datum; lenti seu sanguinis obsint   . . . O 160 Gnothi seauton     16
LENTUS
    Quas servare velit, leges quas lentus omittat,  . . . .  O 205 Christianus        21
LEO
    Leo, sed violare timebit,  . . . . . . . . . . . .      O 109 Post-genitis       28
LECNE
    Cumque leone petet tutus praesepe juvencus.  . . . . .  O  91 Messiah            85
LEPORI
    Nec mirum; restat lepori conscendere coelum,   . . . .  O 213 Tr Greek 9.18       3
LEPOS
    Quantus ubique Lepos! quantus ubique Decor!  . . . . .  O 383 Syl. Urb. Thes   D  2
LEPRA
    Huc foedat quos lepra, urit quos febris, adeste!   . . . O  88 Messiah            16
LETHALE
    Serpentes teneris nil jam lethale minantes   . . . . .  O  91 Messiah            89
    Serpentes teneris nil jam lethale micantes   . . . . .  O  91 Messiah         V  89
    Nycticorax cantat lethale, sed ipsa canenti  . . . . .  O 223 Tr. Gk. 11.186      1
LEVA
    Crimine gravatam plurimo mentem leva:  . . . . . . .    O 206 Prayers I            2
LEVAMEN
    Cantum, vitae dulce levamen. . . . . . . . . . . .      O 193 Tr. Medea III        5
LEVARE
    Mulcere, aut pectus triste levare malis. . . . . . .    O 218 Tr Greek 9.375       8
LEVAT
    Rus ornat natura; levat maris aspera lucrum;   . . . .  O 217 Tr Greek 9.360       3
LEVEM
    Hermem Deorum nuncium, pennis levem,   . . . . . . .    O 223 Tr. Gk. 11.176       1
LEVIS
    Cunctiparens tellus, salve, levis esto pusillo  . . . .  O 211 Tr Greek 7.461      1
LEVITAS
    Seu te saeva sitis, levitas sive improba fecit,   . . . O 171 Tr. Busy Fly         1
    Seu te saeva fames, levitas sive improba fecit,   . . . O 171 Tr. Busy Fly      V  1
LEXICA
    Ingemit exosus, scribendaque lexica mandat   . . . . .  O 160 Gnothi seauton       4
    Aut, hoc si nimium est, tandem nova lexica poscam?   . . O 162 Gnothi seauton      54
LEXICON
    (Post Lexicon Anglicanum auctum et emendatum.)  . . . .  O 160 Gnothi seauton      T
    Lexicon ad finem longo luctamine tandem  . . . . . .    O 160 Gnothi seauton       1
LIBELLOS
    Exceptae hospitio Musae tribuere libellos  . . . . .    O 216 Tr Greek 9.160       1
LIBENS
    Sic peragam tua jussa libens, accinctus ad omne   . . . O 207 Prayers IV           5
LIBENTER
    Sequar libenter; sin reluctari velim, . . . . . . .    O 226 Tr. Cleanthes        3
LIBER
    Liber ut esse velim, suasisti, pulchra Maria:   . . . .  O 105 Lady Defence        1
    Ut maneam liber, pulchra Maria, vale. . . . . . . .    O 105 Lady Defence         2
    Inter equales, sine felle liber,   . . . . . . . .     O 153 In Theatro           9
LIBERA
    Corpore nunc etiam libera facta fuit. . . . . . . .    O 114 Tr Gk Epigrams       2
LIBERET
    Aeterna tandem liberet clementia,  . . . . . . . .     O 206 Prayers III          5
LIBERIORI
    Liberiori  . . . . . . . . . . . . . . . . . .         O 198 Medico Aeger S       2
LIBERTATIS
    Ad foeminam quandam generosam quae libertatis  . . . .  O 105 Lady Defence     V  T
LIBERTY
    To a Lady who spoke in Defence of Liberty  . . . . .    O 105 Lady Defence        T
LIBIDINE
    Vetitaque Libidine pravus. . . . . . . . . . . .       O 110 Post-genitis        34
LIBRI
    Sacri discipulus libri . . . . . . . . . . . . .       O 164 Recover Eyes        11
LIBRIS
    Sive cum libris novitate pascit  . . . . . . . . .     O 168 Oda to Thrale       15
    Sive cum libris novitate pascet  . . . . . . . . .     O 168 Oda to Thrale    V  15
LIBROS
    Sive libros poscant otia, sive lyram. . . . . . . .    O 170 Insula Kenneth      14
    Quid quod sacrifici versavit femina libros,  . . . . .  O 170 Insula Kenneth      19
LICEAT
    I, quoniam sic fata vocant: liceat mihi tantum . . . .  O 384 On the Gin-Act   D  9
```

	PAGE	TITLE		LINE
LICEBIT				
Effigiemque Dei, quantum servare licebit,	O 205	Christianus		29
LICET				
Nam licet, et toto prolue laeta mero.	O 171	Tr. Busy Fly		4
LICHFELDIAE				
In Rivum a Mola Stoana Lichfeldiae diffluentem	O 228	Rivum a Stoana		T
LIGURES				
Centuria Ligures augent duo millia quarta.	O 230	Geographia Met		14
LILIA				
Florebunt Lilia Pratis,	O 109	Post-genitis		26
Cum violis; spirant lilia mista rosis.	O 209	Tr. Greek 5.74		4
LIMEN				
Fortis, ades, solus tangas venerabile limen.	O 116	Tr Pope Grotto		16
Fortis, ades, tibi sponte patet venerabile limen.	O 116	Tr Pope Grotto	V	16
LIMINA				
Ecce! peregrinis fervent tua limina turbis;	O 92	Messiah		99
LIMITE				
Gestiat, et, nullo pietatis limite clausus,	O 205	Christianus		8
LIMOSUM				
Limosum nobis Promus dat callidus haustum,	O 85	Mea nec Falern		3
LINCOLN'S				
. . in Lincoln's-Inn-Fields.	O 385	The Warehouse	D	T
LINGUAE				
Membra viatoris recreabunt frigore linguae.	O 91	Messiah		88
Ridebit linguae innocuos, squamasque virentes	O 91	Messiah		91
Ridebit linguae innocuos, squamas viridantes	O 91	Messiah	V	91
Linguae procacis plumbea Spicula,	O 101	Ad Urbanum		9
Heraclitus ego; indoctae ne laedite linguae,	O 209	Tr Greek 7.128		1
LINGUARUMQUE				
Linguarumque omni terra discordia concors	O 161	Gnothi seauton		22
Linguarumque omni ex terra discordia concors	O 161	Gnothi seauton	V	22
LINGUAS				
Obstrictasque diu linguas in carmina solvet.	O 90	Messiah		46
LINGUIS				
Eloquiumque potens linguis torpentibus affer,	O 232	Prayer		7
LIQUENTIS				
Ille vias vocis pandet, flexusque liquentis	O 90	Messiah		47
LIQUESCENT				
Saxa cadent, solidque liquescent robora montis:	O 92	Messiah		116
LITARE				
Qua solum potero parte, litare tibi.	O 204	Losing Speech	V	4
LITERASQUE				
Prodesse vitae, literasque	O 186	Ad T. L. M.D.		3
LITERATOS				
Quam decet canos male literatos	O 153	In Theatro		3
LITES				
Paupertas misera est; multae cum conjuge lites	O 217	Tr Greek 9.359		5
LITTORA				
Littora deficiens arentia deseret aequor,	O 92	Messiah		114
Littora Sciae.	O 168	Oda to Thrale		20
LITTORAQUE				
Littoraque ut Fluctu,	O 109	Post-genitis		7
LITUI				
Non litui accendent bellum, non campus ahenis	O 90	Messiah		68
LOCA				
Nunc loca sola placent; frustra te, Somne, recumbens	O 161	Gnothi seauton		30
Sed sua regna videns, loca nocte silentia late	O 162	Gnothi seauton		49
LOCANS				
Particulasque locans, certas certo ordine, pulchram	O 163	To Dr Lawrence		28
LOCIS				
His blanda certe pax habitat locis:	O 166	Oda Isle Skye		6
LOCO				
Cuique loco recti paenituisse mali est	O 198	Tr. Ash Wed.	V	2
Cuique loco recte paenituisse mali est	O 198	Tr. Ash Wed.	V	2
LOCUM				
Scire locum volui quid daret ille novi.	O 169	Insula Kenneth		6
LOCUPLETISSIMUM				
In Locupletissimum ornatissimumque Syl<vani>. Urb<ani>.	O 383	Syl. Urb. Thes.	D	T
LOCUPLETUM				
Latrones, alibi locupletum quaerite tecta,	O 219	Tr Greek 9.654		1
LOCUS				
Scire locus volui quid daret iste novi.	O 169	Insula Kenneth	V	6
LOGICAL				
The Logical Warehouse: Occasioned by an Auctioneer's	O 385	The Warehouse	D	T
LONGA				
Et petiit terras per freta longa novas.	O 386	Tr Epi. Madoc	D	4
LONGE				
Hic, in se totum longe per opaca futuri	O 116	Tr Pope Grotto		10
LONGI				
Inter erroris salebrosa longi,	O 168	Oda to Thrale		9
Nox miseris longi temporis instar habet.	O 220	Tr Greek 10.28		2
LONGINQUISQUE				
Longinquisque oculis nuda lavacra patent.	O 228	Rivum a Stoana		8
LONGINQUO				
E longinquo itidem pontus et orcus erat.	O 213	Tr Greek 9.29		6
LONGIUS				
Optarit quicunque senex sibi longius aevum,	O 214	Tr Greek 9.55		1
LONGO				
Lexicon ad finem longo luctamine tandem	O 160	Gnothi seauton		1
Frigora, seu nimium longo jacuisse veterno,	O 161	Gnothi seauton		17
Eheu! quam longo tecum consumerer aevo!	O 384	On the Gin-Act	D	5

	PAGE	TITLE	LINE
LCNGUM			
O longum, formosa, vale, mihi vita decusque, · · · ·	O 383	On the Gin-Act	D 3
LCQUACEM			
Blandam lanifici sociam, sine fine loquacem, · · · ·	O 211	Tr Greek 7.459	3
LOQUELAE			
Inter ignotae strepitus loquelae, · · · · · · ·	O 168	Oda to Thrale	10
LOQUETUR			
Vive tuo ex animo, vario rumore loquetur · · · · · ·	O 214	Tr Greek 9.50	1
LOQUITUR			
Cogitat aut loquitur nil vir, nil cogitat uxor, · · ·	O 226	Tr. Greek	1
LCQUOR			
Nil mortale loquor, coelum mihi carminis alta · · · ·	O 88	Messiah	2
LORICA			
Dulce Venus ridens, lorica nil opus, inquit, · · · ·	O 384	Epigramma	D 3
LUBRICA			
Qua sulcat, reptant tuti per lubrica vitae. · · · · ·	O 163	To Dr Lawrence	18
LUCCA			
Centuriae octavam decadem addit Lucca secundae. · · ·	O 230	Geographia Met	15
LUCE			
Explicat, incinctam radiatae luce tiarae! · · · · ·	O 92	Messiah	95
Venisse, aut visa luce repente mori. · · · · · · ·	O 217	Tr Greek 9.359	10
Natus eram lacrymans, lacrymans e luce recedo; · · · ·	O 221	Tr Greek 10.84	1
Luce collustret mihi pectus alma, · · · · · · · ·	O 227	A Meditation	1
Atque Aethra ambigua pallida luce rubet; · · · · · ·	Y 28	Aurora Musis	2
Aeternum Aeterna Luce juvabit opus! · · · · · · ·	O 393	Tr. of Crashaw	D 6
LUCEBIT			
Sedatas niveo Virtus lucebit amictu. · · · · · · ·	O 89	Messiah	24
Pacatas niveo Virtus lucebit amictu. · · · · · · ·	O 89	Messiah	V 24
LUCEM			
Arti ignis lucem tribui, tamen artis et ignis · · · ·	O 225	Tr Greek 16.87	1
LUCERNAM			
Sufflato accendis quisquis carbone lucernam, · · · · ·	O 225	Tr. Gk. 16.209	1
LUCI			
Luci reddidit et mihi, · · · · · · · · · · · ·	O 164	Recover Eyes	9
LUCIDUS			
Quisquis iter tendis, vitreas qua lucidus undas · · ·	O 116	Tr Pope Grotto	1
LUCINA			
Adsit, Laura, tibi facilis Lucina dolenti, · · · · ·	O 115	Ad Lauram Epig	3
LUCIS			
Coelicolae pandunt, torrentisque aurea lucis · · · · ·	O 92	Messiah	107
Coelicolae pandunt, crescentis et aurea lucis · · · ·	O 92	Messiah	V 107
Coelicolae pandunt, torrentis aurea lucis · · · · ·	O 92	Messiah	V 107
Proferet archetypos; coelestis gaudia lucis · · · · ·	O 92	Messiah	111
Pigrae per horas lucis inutiles, · · · · · · · ·	O 187	Ad T. L. M.D.	10
LUCRI			
Nil lucri facies; ossa habet et cinerem. · · · · · ·	O 210	Tr Greek 7.284	4
Lucri ulciscendum mox nece sola doces. · · · · · ·	O 213	Tr Greek 9.29	4
LUCRUM			
Exiguum est Marti, sed mihi grande lucrum. · · · · ·	O 216	Tr Greek 9.163	4
Rus ornat natura; levat maris aspera lucrum; · · · ·	O 217	Tr Greek 9.360	3
LUCTAMINE			
Lexicon ad finem longo luctamine tandem · · · · · ·	O 160	Gnothi seauton	1
LUCTANTEM			
Vincla coercebunt luctantem adamantina mortem, · · · ·	O 90	Messiah	54
LUCTU			
Resonabunt Oppida Luctu: · · · · · · · · · ·	O 109	Post-genitis	8
LUCTUS			
Luctus mox pariturum. · · · · · · · · · · · ·	O 182	Waltoni Piscat	14
LUDENS			
Lux angit, miseros ludens homullos. · · · · · · ·	O 204	Spes	V 6
LUDERE			
Vita omnis scena est ludusque; aut ludere disce · · ·	O 221	Tr Greek 10.72	1
LUDICRA			
Quam quae severis ludicra jungere · · · · · · · ·	O 102	Ad Urbanum	18
Cuncta, cinis cuncta et ludicra, cuncta nihil. · · · ·	O 222	Tr. Gk. 10.124	2
LUDIT			
Vel spe ludit inani, · · · · · · · · · · · ·	O 182	Waltoni Piscat	13
Spes ludit stolidas, metuque caeco · · · · · · ·	O 204	Spes	5
LUDUM			
Per ludum pueri injicient, et fessa colubri · · · · ·	O 91	Messiah	87
LUDUSQUE			
Vita omnis scena est ludusque; aut ludere disce · · ·	O 221	Tr Greek 10.72	1
LUMEN			
Reclusisque oculis infundet amabile lumen, · · · · ·	O 90	Messiah	45
LUMINA			
Nunc armant Veneris lumina tela Jovis. · · · · · ·	O 103	Elizae Aenigma	6
LUMINE			
Barbarus, en! clarum divino lumine templum · · · · ·	O 92	Messiah	100
Summe Pater, puro collustra lumine pectus, · · · · ·	O 207	Prayers VII	1
Qui jacet hic, servus vixit, nunc, lumine cassus, · · ·	O 212	Tr Greek 7.538	1
LUMINI			
Laeto cedere lumini · · · · · · · · · · · ·	O 164	Recover Eyes	3
LUMINIS			
Sacri vagantes luminis gressus face · · · · · · ·	O 206	Prayers I	5
Ergo optent homines, aut nunquam in luminis oras · · ·	O 217	Tr Greek 9.359	9
Nemo optet nunquam venisse in luminis oras, · · · · ·	O 217	Tr Greek 9.360	9
LUNA			
Luna vices revehet; radios pater ipse diei · · · · ·	O 92	Messiah	110
Nec quaerunt quid, luna, tuo cum fluctibus orbi. · · ·	O 163	To Dr Lawrence	16
LUNAQUE			
Lunaque quas et sol itque reditque vias. · · · · · ·	O 222	Tr. Gk. 10.123	4

	PAGE	TITLE	LINE
LUPO			
Per valles sociata lupo lasciviet agna, ...	O 91	Messiah	84
LUSAE			
Nugae anapaesticae in lecto lusae.	O 198	Medico Aeger S	T
LUSIBUS			
Lusibus gaudet puer ctiosis, ...	O 153	In Theatro	13
LUSTRA			
Dignus qui multa in lustra senescat, erit.	O 214	Tr Greek 9.55	2
LUSTRAVIT			
Hunc oculis Veri Fautrix lustravit acutis, ...	O 386	In Birchium D	3
LUSTRI			
Tertii verso quater orbe lustri, ...	O 153	In Theatro	1
LUSTRO			
Omnia percurro trepidus, circum omnia lustro, . . .	O 161	Gnothi seauton	32
LUX			
Volvantur celeres anni! Lux purpuret ortum	O 89	Messiah	25
Spes novas nova lux parit, secunda	O 204	Spes	3
Lux angit miseros cadens homullos.	O 204	Spes	6
Lux angit, miseros ludens homullos.	O 204	Spes V	6
Me ducat lux sancta, Deus, lux sancta sequatur; . .	O 207	Prayers IV	3
Me ducat lux sancta, Deus, lux sancta sequatur; . .	O 207	Prayers IV	3
Ambraciota, vale lux alma, Cleombrotus infit, . . .	O 211	Tr Greek 7.471	1
Surge, soror dilecta, mihi lux, gaudia, vita; . . .	O 384	Cantico Solom. D	1
LUXERAT			
Luxerat illa dies, legis gens docta supernae . . .	O 170	Insula Kenneth	15
LUXURIA			
Quorsum dulcis luxuria soni?	O 193	Tr. Medea III	12
LUXURIAE			
Gemmaque luxuriae nondum famulata nitenti	O 116	Tr Pope Grotto	5
LUXURIANS			
Munera luxurians dat pampinus, et generoso	O 385	Cantico Solom. D	13
LUXUS			
Luxus oblectat Juvenem theatri, ...	O 153	In Theatro	14
LYCORIDE			
Texente Nymphis serta Lycoride, ...	O 102	Ad Urbanum	21
LYCURGE			
Det Bacchus, dederat quale, Lycurge, tibi.	O 218	Tr Greek 9.375	6
LYMPHA			
Lympha tamen cursus agit indefessa perennis, . . .	O 228	Rivum a Stoana	9
LYRA			
Quae lyra. Quam sibi non concinit harmonia! . . .	O 216	Tr Greek 9.250	2
Quos pulsata sonos edit lyra pollice, primis . . .	Y 28	Aurora Musis	15
LYRAM			
Sive libros poscant otia, sive lyram.	O 170	Insula Kenneth	14
LYSIGENI			
Lysigeni, fuerat non gravis ille tibi.	O 211	Tr Greek 7.461	2
MACEDUM			
Omnia, dum Macedum gloria et arma premunt.	O 216	Tr Greek 9.288	4
MACRAE			
Res angusta domi, et macrae penuria mentis. . . .	O 161	Gnothi seauton	41
MACRINE			
Quod vitae satis est, peto, Macrine:	O 215	Tr Greek 9.110	3
MAEONIDES			
Ab Jove Maeonides descendere Somnia narrat:	O 103	Elizae Aenigma	3
MAGIS			
Quam magis exoptes arte valere tua.	O 197	Summ. Lawrence	2
MAGISTER			
Summe dator vitae, naturae aeterne magister, . . .	O 207	Prayers VI	1
MAGISTRO			
Praestat magistro saepe discipulus suo.	O 223	Tr. Gk. 11.176	5
MAGISTRUM			
Multiplici reducem circumsonat ore magistrum. . . .	O 161	Gnothi seauton	23
MAGNA			
Ditatus magna dote, recondis humo.	O 222	Tr Greek 11.50	4
MAGNAEQUE			
Materiemque rudem, magnaeque parentis adesse . . .	O 163	To Dr Lawrence	21
MAGNAM			
Ingredere O!--Magnam pura cole mente parentem, . . .	O 116	Tr Pope Grotto	7
MAGNE			
Nascere, magne puer! Tibi primas, ecce! corollas . .	O 89	Messiah	27
Recte ut poeniteat, respice, magne parens. . . .	O 207	Prayers VI	6
Magne bonum, omne malum et poscentibus abnue nobis. . .	O 221	Tr Greek 10.108	2
MAGNI			
Cum Lapidem hunc, magni	O 109	Post-genitis	1
Hi sunt quos animi generosa insania magni	O 163	To Dr Lawrence	31
Dicite, Causidici, gelido nunc marmore magni . . .	O 213	Tr Greek 8.137	1
Inclytus hic haeres magni requiescit Oeni, . . .	O 386	Tr Epi. Madoc D	1
MAGNIS			
Leniades magnis nobilitatus avis:	O 169	Insula Kenneth	8
MAGNO			
Tentat iter brevius, magno conamine summam . . .	O 163	To Dr Lawrence	24
Dario magno non minus ille potest.	O 212	Tr Greek 7.538	2
MAJOR			
Induit, et, terris major, coelestia spirat.	O 205	Christianus	30
MAJORA			
Quem decuit majora sequi, majoribus aptum, ...	O 160	Gnothi seauton	7
MAJORE			
Democrite, invisas homines majore cachinno, ...	O 216	Tr Greek 9.148	1
Vix majore Deus corda furore quatit	Y 28	Aurora Musis	8
MAJOREM			
Amice, majorem querelis, ...	O 187	Ad T. L. M.D.	19

		PAGE	TITLE	LINE
MAJORIBUS				
Quem decuit majora sequi, majoribus aptum, ...	O	160	Gnothi seauton	7
MAJUS				
Nil majus Natura capit: clarare priores	O	86	Tr Dryden Milt	5
Quid majus mihi spes ambitiosa dabit?	O	104	To Eliz Carter	4
Queis majus pretium saecula lapsa dabant	Y	28	Aurora Musis	12
MALA				
Aspera, odoratae cedunt mala gramina myrto.	O	91	Messiah	83
Importuna cohors, vacuae mala somnia mentis.	O	161	Gnothi seauton	28
Tu, queis laborat sors hominum, mala	O	187	Ad T. L. M.D.	5
Seria seponens, aut mala dura pati.	O	221	Tr Greek 10.72	2
MALE				
Quam decet canos male literatos	O	153	In Theatro	3
De te plebs audax, hic bene et ille male.	O	214	Tr Greek 9.50	2
Nec male res cessit, subito si funere sponsam, ...	O	222	Tr Greek 11.50	3
MALI				
Cuique loco recti paenituisse mali est	O	198	Tr. Ash Wed.	V 2
Cuique loco recte paenituisse mali est	O	198	Tr. Ash Wed.	V 2
MALIM				
Fortunae malim adversae tolerare procellas, ...	O	221	Tr Greek 10.93	1
MALIS				
Mulcere, aut pectus triste levare malis.	O	218	Tr Greek 9.375	8
MALLET				
Pythagoras mallet, vocem habuisset opus.	O	225	Tr. Gk. 16.326	2
MALORUM				
Quae sine morte fuga est vitae, quam turba malorum . .	O	222	Tr. Gk. 10.123	1
MALUM				
Magne bonum, omne malum et poscentibus abnue nobis. . .	O	221	Tr Greek 10.108	2
MANDAT				
Ingemit exosus, scribendaque lexica mandat	O	160	Gnothi seauton	4
MANDATUM				
Mandatum, vivam sic moriarque tibi.	O	207	Prayers IV	6
MANE				
Nutrit mane, putes esse Heliconis aqua.	Y	28	Aurora Musis	6
MANEAM				
Ut maneam liber, pulchra Maria, vale.	O	105	Lady Defence	2
MANEBAT				
Charus enim cunctis, tanquam, dum vita manebat, . . .	O	212	Tr Greek 7.560	3
MANET				
Desidiae sors dura manet, graviorque labore	O	161	Gnothi seauton	25
Quam tenet hic, cunctas quae manet, alta quies. . . .	O	211	Tr Greek 7.459	4
Te manet imperii, Roma, perenne decus.	O	219	Tr Greek 9.647	2
Firma manet virtus; virtuti innitere, tutus	O	221	Tr Greek 10.74	5
MANSUESCERE				
Ingreditur, cultuque tuo mansuescere gaudet.	O	92	Messiah	101
MANSUETAE				
Florea mansuetae petulantes vincula tigrí	O	91	Messiah	86
MANU				
Saxea Phidiaca spirat imago manu.	O	85	Adjecere bonae	4
In me sparsa manu virtutum semina larga	O	207	Prayers VII	3
MANUQUE				
Confessus tantum mente manuque patrem;	O	386	Tr Epi. Madoc	D 2
MANUS				
Justitiaeque manus pretio intemerata bilancem	O	89	Messiah	21
Quale, sed hostiles quale dedere manus.	O	210	Tr Greek 7.136	2
MARATHON				
Spreta jacet Marathon, jacet et Salaminia laurus, . . .	O	216	Tr Greek 9.288	3
MARCMONTI				
Morte memor patriae; hic Marcmonti pectore prima . . .	O	116	Tr Pope Grotto	13
MARE				
Rura labor lassat; mare mille pericula terrent; . . .	O	217	Tr Greek 9.359	3
Dulcia dat natura quidem, mare, sidera, terras, . . .	O	222	Tr. Gk. 10.123	3
MARIA				
Liber ut esse velim, suasisti, pulchra Maria:	O	105	Lady Defence	1
Ut maneam liber, pulchra Maria, vale.	O	105	Lady Defence	2
MARIS				
Rus ornat natura; levat maris aspera lucrum;	O	217	Tr Greek 9.360	3
MARISQUE				
Qui, mutare vias ausus terraeque marisque, ...	O	217	Tr Greek 9.304	1
MARMOR				
Si sis scelestus, praeteri procul marmor:	O	224	Tr Greek 13.3	2
MARMORA				
Materiam Statuae sic praebet Marmora Tellus, ...	O	85	Adjecere bonae	3
MARMORE				
Dicite, Causidici, gelido nunc marmore magni	O	213	Tr Greek 8.137	1
MARMOREA				
Marmorea trepidant qua lentae in fornice guttae, . . .	O	116	Tr Pope Grotto	V 3
MARMOREO				
Marmoreo trepidant qua lentae in fornice guttae, . . .	O	116	Tr Pope Grotto	3
MARMORIS				
Cessat inops rerum, ut torpet, si marmoris absit . . .	O	161	Gnothi seauton	38
MARO				
Quid mirum Maro quod digne canit arma Virumque, . . .	O	85	Mea nec Falern	1
MARS				
Xerxi, tercentum Spartae Mars obstitit acris	O	217	Tr Greek 9.304	3
MARTI				
Haec Musae ad Venerem: Sic Marti, diva, mineris; . . .	O	213	Tr Greek 9.39	3
Exiguum est Marti, sed mihi grande lucrum.	O	216	Tr Greek 9.163	4
MARTIQUE				
Cecropidis gravis hic ponor, Martique dicatus, ...	O	216	Tr Greek 9.288	1

```
MATER                                                    PAGE    TITLE            LINE
     Seu fovet mater sobolem benigna,      . . . . . . .  O 168 Oda to Thrale        14
     Mater adulantum prolesque, Pecunia, curae,  . . . . .  O 218 Tr Greek 9.394      1
MATERIA
     Materia, vastum an late pandatur inane.    . . . . . . O 163 To Dr Lawrence    V 14
MATERIAM
     Materiam Statuae sic praebet Marmora Tellus,    . . . . O  85 Adjecere bonae      3
MATERIEM
     Ingenium, nisi materiem Doctrina ministret,  . . . .  O 161 Gnothi seauton       37
     Ingenium, nisi materiem Doctrina ministrat,  . . . .  O 161 Gnothi seauton     V 37
MATERIEMQUE
     Materiemque rudem, magnaeque parentis adesse   . . . . O 163 To Dr Lawrence      21
MATERIES
     Materies; poscunt gravius coelestia plectrum.   . . . . O  88 Messiah             3
     Materies; poscunt graves coelestia plectrum.    . . . . O  88 Messiah           V 3
     Materies arti, sua desunt arma labori . . . . . . .  O 161 Gnothi seauton     V 37
     Materies, vastum an late pandatur inane.   . . . . . . O 163 To Dr Lawrence      14
MATHEMATICOS
     Astra mathematicos si modo vera docent.    . . . . . . O 215 Tr Greek 9.112      2
MATREM
     Quam, regum sobolem, nuptam, matrem, atque sororem   . . O 226 Tr. Simonides      3
MATURANT
     Maturant radii, tibi balsama sudat Idume.   . . . . . O  92 Messiah            105
MAVIS
     Thralia. Quid mavis? tutius hostis eris.  . . . . . .  O 197 On Mrs. Thrale      2
     Elige iter vitae, ut mavis; prudentia lausque   . . . . O 217 Tr Greek 9.360      1
ME
     Me, pensi immunis cum jam mihi reddor, inertis  . . . . O 161 Gnothi seauton      24
     Et me, cuncta beans cui nocuit dies,    . . . . . . .  O 164 Recover Eyes        8
     Scelerum catena me laborantem gravi     . . . . . . .  O 206 Prayers III         4
     Scelerum caterna me laborantem grave    . . . . . . .  O 206 Prayers III       V 4
     Numine praesenti me tueare pater!     . . . . . . . .  O 207 Prayers IV          2
     Me ducat lux sancta, Deus, lux sancta sequatur;   . . . O 207 Prayers IV          3
     Me, pater cmnipotens, de puro respice coelo,    . . . . O 207 Prayers V           1
     Et pro me pretium, tu patiare, pater. . . . . . . .   O 207 Prayers V           6
     In me sparsa manu virtutum semina larga   . . . . . .  O 207 Prayers VII         3
     Hoc Veneri speculum; nolo me cernere qualis   . . . . . O 209 Tr. Greek 6.1       3
     Tutum aliis aequor, me pereunte, fuit.  . . . . . . .  O 210 Tr Greek 7.282      2
     Quid salvere jubes me, pessime? Corripe gressus;   . . . O 211 Tr Greek 7.318      1
     Stella mea, observans stellas, Dii me aethera faxint,  . O 212 Tr Greek 7.669      1
     Me, cane vitato, canis excipit alter; eodem   . . . . . O 213 Tr Greek 9.18       1
     In me animo tellus gignit et unda feras,   . . . . . . O 213 Tr Greek 9.18       2
     Me miserum sors omnis habet; florentibus annis  . . . . O 215 Tr Greek 9.138      1
     Interea dubito; tecum me causa nec ulla   . . . . . .  O 216 Tr Greek 9.148      5
     Ridere, aut tecum me lacrimare jubet.  . . . . . . .   O 216 Tr Greek 9.148      6
     Exclamat: Nunc me cernere desinitis.  . . . . . . .   O 224 Tr. Gk. 11.432      2
     Non Argos pugilem, non me Messana creavit;  . . . . .  O 224 Tr Greek 16.1       1
     Me, rex deorum, tuque, duc, necessitas,   . . . . . .  O 226 Tr. Cleanthes       1
     Quo, lege vestra, vita me feret mea.   . . . . . . .   O 226 Tr. Cleanthes       2
     Me Pater tandem reducem benigno   . . . . . . . . .    O 227 A Meditation        5
     Me gregi Sanctus socium beatum    . . . . . . . . .    O 227 A Meditation        7
MEA
     Mea nec Falernae Etc.   . . . . . . . . . . .          O  85 Mea nec Falern      T
     Mens mea quid quereris? veniet tibi mollior hora,  . . . O 208 A Meditation        1
     Stella mea, observans stellas, Dii me aethera faxint,  . O 212 Tr Greek 7.669      1
     Quo, lege vestra, vita me feret mea.   . . . . . . .   O 226 Tr. Cleanthes       2
MEAE
     Musca, meae comitem, participemque dapis,    . . . . . O 171 Tr. Busy Fly        2
MEATUS
     Dixerat, imperiique vices, coelique meatus,   . . . . . O 160 Gnothi seauton      10
MECUM
     Quid mecum peragam, quod tu doctissime posses   . . . . O 163 To Dr Lawrence      4
     Quot modis mecum, quid agat, requiro,  . . . . . . .   O 168 Oda to Thrale       11
     Quid tibi, mus, mecum, dixit, amice, tibi?  . . . . .  O 224 Tr. Gk. 11.391      2
MEDELAM
     Queis tamen aptam ferre medelam   . . . . .. . . . .   O 193 Tr. Medea III       9
MEDICAE
     Medicae Princeps,   . . . . . . . . . . . . . .       O 199 Medico Aeger S      25
MEDICAMINA
     Dia salutares spirant medicamina rami.    . . . . . .  O  89 Messiah            17
MEDICI
     Te medici revocant labores.   . . . . . . . . . .     O 187 Ad T. L. M.D.      16
MEDICINA
     Destituit medicina mentis.    . . . . . . . . . .     O 187 Ad T. L. M.D.       8
MEDICUM
     Ad T<homam>. L<aurence>. M<edicum>. D<octissimum>.   . . O 186 Ad T.L. M.D.        T
     Ad Thcmam Laurence, Medicum Doctissimum, Cum    . . .  O 186 Ad T. L. M.D.     V T
MEDITANS
     Non poteris, meditans prava, latere Deos.   . . . . . O 220 Tr Greek 10.27      2
MEDITATUR
     Insidias meditatur horis.   . . . . . . . . . .       O 166 Oda Isle Skye       8
     En Sexto, Sexti meditatur imago, silente;   . . . . . O 223 Tr. Gk. 11.145      1
MEDITATUS
     Nec quid agam invenio, meditatus grandia, cogor   . . . O 161 Gnothi seauton      34
MEDIUS
     Sive dies medius morientia torreat arva:  . . . . . .  O  90 Messiah            63
     Sive dies medius languentia torreat arva:   . . . . . O  90 Messiah           V 63
MEI
     Subtile ingenium quaero, capaxque mei,  . . . . . . .  O 209 Tr Greek 7.128      2
     Nunc ope supplicii vivit imago mei.    . . . . . . .   O 225 Tr Greek 16.87      2
```

```
                                                      PAGE     TITLE            LINE
MEIS
     Aurem faventem precibus O praebe meis;      . . . . . .   O 206 Prayers III         3
MELIORA
     Carmina vis nostri scribant meliora Poetae? . . . . .    O  85 Mea nec Falern       5
     Incusat, semper spe meliora videt. . . . . . . . .       O 214 Tr Greek 9.54        2
MELIOREM
     Prolem Hippi, et sua qua meliorem secula nullum  . . .   O 226 Tr. Simonides        1
MELIORIS
     Si qua usquam pateat melioris semita vitae, . . . . .    O 161 Gnothi seauton      33
MELLI
     Et melli nimio fellis amaror inest.   . . . . . . .      O 224 Tr Greek 16.16       2
MELLITA
     Mnemosyne, ut Sappho mellita voce canentem  . . . . .    O 214 Tr Greek 9.66        1
MELOS
     Fundit ab ore melos,   . . . . . . . . . .              O 385 Cantico Solom.   D   8
MEMBRA
     Membra viatoris recreabunt frigore linguae. . . . .      O  91 Messiah            88
     Quo toties lavi membra tenella puer;  . . . . .          O 228 Rivum a Stoana       2
     Innocua hic membris permistas membra columbas  . . .     O 393 Tr. of Crashaw  D   1
MEMBRIS
     Innocua hic membris permistas membra columbas  . . . .   O 393 Tr. of Crashaw  D   1
MEMNONIS
     Corusca a radiis Memnonis ora dabant.  . . . . . . .     Y  28 Aurora Musis        16
MEMOR
     Morte memor patriae; hic Marcmonti pectore prima  . . .  O 116 Tr Pope Grotto      13
     Sit memor nostri, fideique merces  . . . . . . .         O 168 Oda to Thrale       17
     Sit memor nostri, fideique solvat  . . . . . . .         O 168 Oda to Thrale   V  17
MEMORANDA
     Nunc dies Christo memoranda nato  . . . . . . . .        O 193 Prayer on Xmas       1
MENDACIS
     Aonidesque Deae, et mendacis somnia Pindi.  . . . . .    O  88 Messiah             5
MENIPPUS
     Nunc huic, nunc aliis cedens, cui farra Menippus  . . .  O 215 Tr Greek 9.74        1
MENODOTUM
     Menodotum pinxit Diodorus, et exit imago,  . . . . .     O 223 Tr. Gk. 11.213       1
     Praeter Menodotum, nullius absimilis.  . . . . . .       O 223 Tr. Gk. 11.213       2
MENS
     Mens mea quid quereris? veniet tibi mollior hora,  . . . O 208 A Meditation         1
     Ut mens utatur corpore, sume cibos.  . . . . . .         O 228 Jejunium Cibus       2
     Hora perit furtim laetis, mens temporis aegra  . . . .   O 228 Jactura Tempor       1
MENSAE
     Nunc clamosa juvant nocturnae gaudia mensae,  . . . .    O 161 Gnothi seauton      29
     Tu neque dulce putes alienae accumbere mensae,  . . .    O 218 Tr Greek 9.573       1
     Fida comes mensae, fida comesque tori!  . . . . .        O 383 On the Gin-Act   D   4
MENSAS
     Namque, ubi mensas onerant epulae,  . . . . . . .        O 193 Tr. Medea III       11
MENSTRUA
     Menstrua concinnat Sylvanus, & Annua Dona,  . . . . .    O 383 Syl. Urb. Thes   D   1
MENTE
     Ingredere O!--Magnam pura cole mente parentem,  . . .    O 116 Tr Pope Grotto       7
     Ingredere O!--rerum pura cole mente parentem,  . . .     O 116 Tr Pope Grotto   V   7
     Auxilioque Dei fretus, jam mente serena  . . . . .       O 205 Christianus        26
     Te, mente pura, mente tranquilla colam:  . . . . .       O 206 Prayers I          10
     Te, mente pura, mente tranquilla colam:  . . . . .       O 206 Prayers I          10
     Da veniam pacemque mihi, da, mente serena,  . . . .      O 207 Prayers V            3
     Scripta legens, sola vivere mente cupit. . .            O 211 Tr Greek 7.471        4
     Qui pascit barbam si crescit mente, Platoni,  . . .      O 224 Tr. Gk. 11.430       1
     Mente senes olim juvenis, Faustine, premebas,  . . .     O 225 Tr. Gk. 16.364       1
     Confessus tantum mente manuque patrem;  . . . . .        O 386 Tr Epi. Madoc    D   2
MENTEM
     Utilibus recreare Mentem. . . . . . . .                 O 102 Ad Urbanum          20
     Sive mihi mentem dederit Natura minorem.  . . . . .      O 161 Gnothi seauton      18
     Sedula mentem;   . . . . . . . . . . .                  O 168 Oda to Thrale       16
     Redde tuis, tibi redde, mentem. . . . . . . .           O 187 Ad T. L. M.D.       20
     Crimine gravatam plurimo mentem leva:  . . . . .         O 206 Prayers I            2
     Mentem benignus alleva.  . . . . . . . .                O 206 Prayers II          11
     In mentem ut venit nominis, interii.  . . . . .          O 223 Tr. Gk. 11.118       2
MENTES
     Gratia nulla hominum mentes tenet, ista Promethei  . . . O 225 Tr Greek 16.87       3
MENTI
     Dat Menti propriis Musa nitere bonis. . . . . . .       O  85 Adjecere bonae        2
     Menti nec aegrae montibus aviis . . . . . . .           O 166 Oda Isle Skye       10
     Nec menti injiciat sordida cura jugum;  . . . . . .      O 221 Tr Greek 10.74       2
     Serviat ut menti corpus, jejunia serva;  . . . . .       O 228 Jejunium Cibus       1
     Myrias, ut menti pateat tota Africa doctae. . . . . .    O 230 Geographia Met      24
MENTIBUS
     Mentibus afflatu terrenas ejice sordes  . . . . . .      O 232 Prayer              5
MENTIS
     Temporis Henricum rapuit vis vivida mentis;  . . . .     O 116 Tr Pope Grotto      11
     Importuna cohors, vacuae mala somnia mentis.  . . .      O 161 Gnothi seauton      28
     Res angusta domi, et macrae penuria mentis.  . . .       O 161 Gnothi seauton      41
     Humanae mentis, rerum se pascere formis,  . . . .        O 163 To Dr Lawrence       6
     Destituit medicina mentis.  . . . . . . .               O 187 Ad T. L. M.D.        8
MENTISQUE
     Mentisque, te tollente, surgunt,  . . . . .             O 166 Oda Isle Skye       19
MENTITUR
     Funus Alexandri mentitur fama; fidesque  . . . . .       O 210 Tr Greek 7.239       1
MEO
     Corde meo accendas; ardeo totus ego.  . . . . . .        O 225 Tr. Gk. 16.209       2
MEOS
     Sanari voluit meos,  . . . . . . . . . . .              O 164 Recover Eyes         7
```

```
MEOS              (CONTINUED)                        PAGE    TITLE              LINE
    Usque regat gressus gratia fida meos. . . . . . .   O 207 Prayers IV            4
MERCEDEM
    Fida mercedem, meritoque blandum    . . . . . . .   O 168 Oda to Thrale    V  18
MERCES
    Sit memor nostri, fideique merces   . . . . . . .   O 168 Oda to Thrale       17
MERETUR
    Exiguum en! Priami monumentum; haud ille meretur  . . .   O 210 Tr Greek 7.136      1
MERI
    Venturi exsecuit, vascula prima meri, . . . . . . .   O 217 Tr Greek 9.375      2
MERITAS
    "Qui scribat meritas, Birchius alter erit." . . . .   O 386 In Birchium     D  6
MERITISVE
    Quaeris, Quis prior est fama meritisve; superna   . . .   O 385 The Warehouse   D  3
MERITOQUE
    Stet fides constans, meritoque blandum    . . . . .   O 168 Oda to Thrale       18
    Fida mercedem, meritoque blandum   . . . . . . .   O 168 Oda to Thrale    V  18
MERO
    Nam licet, et toto prolue laeta mero. . . . . . .   O 171 Tr. Busy Fly         4
    Subrubet uva mero. . . . . . . . . . . . .   O 385 Cantico Solom.   D  14
MESSANA
    Non Argos pugilem, non me Messana creavit;  . . . .   O 224 Tr Greek 16.1      1
MESSEM
    Qui duxit sulcos, illi teret area messem, . . . . .   O  90 Messiah            73
MESSIA
    Messia . . . . . . . . . . . . . . . .   O  88 Messiah             T
    Laetaque Messia semper dominabere rege,   . . . . .   O  92 Messiah           118
MESSIBUS
    Nunquam jugera messibus onusta, aut   . . . . . .   O 215 Tr Greek 9.110      1
MESSIS
    Sic ale, proveniat messis ut ampla boni. . . . . .   O 207 Prayers VII         4
META
    Quem ternet vitae meta propinqua suae,    . . . . .   O 207 Prayers VI          4
METALLUM
    Pendet, et incoquitur tectum sine fraude metallum:  . .   O 116 Tr Pope Grotto      6
    Splendet, et incoquitur tectum sine fraude metallum:  . .   O 116 Tr Pope Grotto   V  6
METAM
    Dum statuunt, causisque audent prefigere metam.   . . .   O 163 To Dr Lawrence      36
METATA
    Vicenis quinas, Asiam metata celebrem.    . . . . .   O 230 Geographia Met       22
METRICA
    Geographia Metrica   . . . . . . . . . . .   O 229 Geographia Met       T
METU
    Sceleris ut expers omnis, et vacuus metu, . . . . .   O 206 Prayers I            9
METUENS
    Auriferasque, auri metuens, scrutare cavernas.    . . .   O 116 Tr Pope Grotto      8
METUENSQUE
    Alme voco, impatiens noctis metuensque diei.    . . .   O 161 Gnothi seauton      31
METUM
    Pone metum, rostrum fidens immitte culullo, . . . .   O 171 Tr. Busy Fly         3
METUQUE
    Spes ludit stolidas, metuque caeco    . . . . . .   O 204 Spes                 5
METUS
    Sentiet aegra Metus, . . . . . . . . . . .   O 109 Post-genitis         5
MEUM
    Peccator, ad latus meum; . . . . . . . . . .   O 203 Christ Sinner        2
MI
    Mi, nequid nimis, est nimis probatum. . . . . . .   O 215 Tr Greek 9.110      4
MICANTES
    Serpentes teneris nil jam lethale micantes  . . . .   O  91 Messiah         V  89
    Aetheris, en! portas sacro fulgore micantes . . . .   O  92 Messiah           106
MIHI
    Nil mortale loquor, coelum mihi carminis alta   . . .   O  88 Messiah             2
    Tu mihi, qui flamma movisti pectora sancti  . . . .   O  88 Messiah             6
    Sic orsus--Qualis rerum mihi nascitur ordo! . . . .   O  88 Messiah             9
    Quid mihi cum cultu? Probitas inculta nitescit,   . . .   O 104 To Eliz Carter      1
    Quid majus mihi spes ambitiosa dabit?   . . . . .   O 104 To Eliz Carter      4
    Non mihi sorte datum; lenti seu sanguinis obsint  . . .   O 160 Gnothi seauton      16
    Sive mihi mentem dederit Natura minorem.    . . . .   O 161 Gnothi seauton      18
    Me, pensi immunis cum jam mihi reddor, inertis  . . .   O 161 Gnothi seauton      24
    Notior ipse mihi fieri, incultumque fateri  . . . .   O 161 Gnothi seauton      35
    Notior ipse mihi fieri, pectusque fateri    . . . .   O 161 Gnothi seauton   V  35
    Luci reddidit et mihi, . . . . . . . . . .   O 164 Recover Eyes         9
    Habuique, quod dedi mihi; . . . . . . . . .   O 165 Tr Doncast Epi       2
    Volvitur hora mihi, volvitur hora tibi!   . . . . .   O 171 Tr. Busy Fly         8
    Eheu, quid decies plus mihi sexta dedit!    . . . .   O 171 Tr. Busy Fly        10
    Fulsit, in pectus mihi fonte purum    . . . . . .   O 193 Prayer on Xmas       2
    Per Christum ut veniam sit reperire mihi. . . . . .   O 198 Tr. Ash Wed.         4
    Nunc mihi facilis    . . . . . . . . . . .   O 198 Medico Aeger S       1
    Ingenio parcas, nec sit mihi culpa rogasse, . . . .   O 204 Losing Speech        3
    Ingenio parcas, nec sit mihi culpa precari  . . . .   O 204 Losing Speech    V  3
    Mihi dona morte haec impetret Christus sua. . . . .   O 206 Prayers I           11
    Veniamque, Christe, da mihi; . . . . . . . . .   O 206 Prayers II           7
    Da veniam pacemque mihi, da, mente serena,  . . . .   O 207 Prayers V            3
    Anxietas noceat ne tenebrosa mihi. . . . . . . .   O 207 Prayers VII          2
    Certa mihi sancto flagret amore fides.    . . . . .   O 207 Prayers VII          6
    Da, ne sint permissa, pater, mihi praemia frustra,  . .   O 208 Prayers VII          9
    Da, ne sint promissa, pater, mihi praemia frustra,  . .   O 208 Prayers VII      V  9
    Haec mihi, quo gentes, quo secula, Christe, piasti, . .   O 208 Prayers VII         11
    Unus homo mihi pro sexcentis, turba popelli . . . .   O 209 Tr Greek 7.128      3
    Est mihi quod non te rideo, plena salus. . . . . .   O 211 Tr Greek 7.318      2
```

MIHI (CONTINUED)	PAGE	TITLE	LINE
Vitam a terdecimo sextus mihi finiet annus,	O 215	Tr Greek 9.112	1
Queis uti nequeo, nunc mihi praebet opes.	O 215	Tr Greek 9.138	4
Exiguum est Marti, sed mihi grande lucrum.	O 216	Tr Greek 9.163	4
Sit contenta mihi vita dolore carens.	O 222	Tr. Gk. 10.113	2
Haud lavit Phido, haud tetigit; mihi febre calenti	O 223	Tr. Gk. 11.118	1
Patria Sparta mihi est, patria clara virum.	O 224	Tr Greek 16.1	2
Arte valent isti, mihi robore vivere solo est,	O 224	Tr Greek 16.1	3
Luce collustret mihi pectus alma,	O 227	A Meditation	1
O longum, formosa, vale, mihi vita decusque,	O 383	On the Gin-Act	D 3
Aeternum direpta mihi! sed quid moror istis?	O 384	On the Gin-Act	D 7
I, quoniam sic fata vocant: liceat mihi tantum	O 384	On the Gin-Act	D 9
Surge, soror dilecta, mihi lux, gaudia, vita;	O 384	Cantico Solom.	D 1
MILIAE			
Sed Miliae ridens, atque dolens Miliae.	O 218	Tr Greek 9.573	6
Sed Miliae ridens, atque dolens Miliae.	O 218	Tr Greek 9.573	6
MILITIBUS			
Militibus; terris sit pelagoque pudor!	O 217	Tr Greek 9.304	4
MILLE			
Te mille succorum potentem	O 187	Ad T. L. M.D.	7
Rura labor lassat; mare mille pericula terrent;	O 217	Tr Greek 9.359	3
Parthenope. Novies vult tellus mille Sicana.	O 230	Geographia Met	11
Myriadas ter mille homini dat terra colendas.	O 230	Geographia Met	20
MILLESIMA			
Vult sibi vicenas millesima myrias addi,	O 230	Geographia Met	21
MILLIA			
Cum sex centuriis Judaeo millia septem.	O 229	Geographia Met	2
Undecies binas decadas et millia septem	O 230	Geographia Met	6
Myriades sibi pulcra duas, duo millia poscit	O 230	Geographia Met	10
Papa suo regit imperio ter millia quinque.	O 230	Geographia Met	12
Cum sex centuriis numerat sex millia Tuscus.	O 230	Geographia Met	13
Centuria Ligures augent duo millia quarta.	O 230	Geographia Met	14
Sardiniam cum sexcentis sex millia complent.	O 230	Geographia Met	18
Et quadragenis quoque ter tria millia jungit.	O 230	Geographia Met	26
Myriadas denas dat, quinque et millia, sexque	O 230	Geographia Met	27
Ter tria myriadi conjungit millia quartae,	O 230	Geographia Met	29
Millia myriadi septem foecunda secundae	O 230	Geographia Met	31
Millia Belga novem.	O 231	Geographia Met	34
MILLIBUS			
Undecimum Camber vult septem millibus addi.	O 231	Geographia Met	36
MINACES			
Ibunt per cuncta minaces,	O 109	Post-genitis	16
MINANTES			
Serpentes teneris nil jam lethale minantes	O 91	Messiah	89
MINAX			
Ut vis, ponte minax, modo tres discesseris ulnas,	O 210	Tr Greek 7.284	1
MINERIS			
Haec Musae ad Venerem: Sic Marti, diva, mineris;	O 213	Tr Greek 9.39	3
MINETUR			
Quid et minetur, sollicitus parum,	O 101	Ad Urbanum	6
MINISTRAT			
Ingenium, nisi materiem Doctrina ministrat,	O 161	Gnothi seauton	V 37
MINISTRET			
Ingenium, nisi materiem Doctrina ministret,	O 161	Gnothi seauton	37
MINOR			
Sexaginta annis non minor unus erit.	O 171	Tr. Busy Fly	12
MINOREM			
Sive mihi mentem dederit Natura minorem.	O 161	Gnothi seauton	18
MINUS			
Nunc minus acris	O 198	Medico Aeger S	5
Dario magno non minus ille potest.	O 212	Tr Greek 7.538	2
Tecta ineunt, caelebs impediere minus;	O 217	Tr Greek 9.360	6
Fiam scelestus, nec tamen minus sequar.	O 226	Tr. Cleanthes	4
Pigritiam incusat, nec minus hora perit.	O 228	Jactura Tempor	2
MIRABILE			
Nexa patent; hi sunt quos nil mirabile turbat,	O 163	To Dr Lawrence	34
MIRABITUR			
Harmoniae purgata novos mirabitur auris.	O 90	Messiah	48
MIRANTUR			
Garrula mirantur salientis murmura rivi.	O 91	Messiah	77
MIRATUR			
Nec miratur opes, celsa speculator ab arce	O 161	Gnothi seauton	V 39
Conspicit aggestas, et se miratur in illis,	O 161	Gnothi seauton	43
Versat opum cumulos, et se miratur in illis,	O 161	Gnothi seauton	V 43
MIRUM			
Quid mirum Maro quod digne canit arma Virumque,	O 85	Mea nec Falern	1
En quoque quod Mirum,	O 110	Post-genitis	35
Nec mirum; restat lepori conscendere coelum,	O 213	Tr Greek 9.18	3
Quid mirum? cum saxa movet statuasque tacentes	Y 28	Aurora Musis	13
MISCENS			
Laevia serratis miscens, quadrata rotundis,	O 163	To Dr Lawrence	26
MISCENTUR			
Apte antiqua novis miscentur, et utile dulci:	O 383	Syl. Urb. Thes	D 3
MISCET			
Saxeas miscet nebulis ruinas,	O 167	Oda to Thrale	2
MISELLUM			
Tale hominum genus est, infirmum, triste, misellum,	O 221	Tr Greek 10.84	3
MISERA			
Paupertas misera est; multae cum conjuge lites	O 217	Tr Greek 9.359	5
MISERATA			
Parca, juventutem non miserata tuam!	O 212	Tr Greek 7.560	6

	PAGE	TITLE		LINE
MISERERIS				
Vita hominum nunc plus quod misereris habet.	O 216	Tr Greek 9.148		4
MISERI				
At tu quisquis eris, miseri qui cruda poetae	Y 387	Death Mother	D	1
MISERIS				
Sit sacer orbis amor, miseris qui semper adesse	O 205	Christianus		7
Nox miseris longi temporis instar habet.	O 220	Tr Greek 10.28		2
MISEROS				
Mortales miseros servat, alit, fovet,	O 155	Psalmus 117		6
Lux angit miseros cadens homullos.	O 204	Spes		6
Lux angit, miseros ludens homullos.	O 204	Spes	V	6
MISERUM				
Me miserum sors omnis habet; florentibus annis	O 215	Tr Greek 9.138		1
MISSA				
Haec veniunt Cypriae Somnia missa Deae.	O 103	Elizae Aenigma		4
Quot vox missa pedes abit horae parte secunda?	O 229	Epigram IV		1
MISSUS				
In vos ne missus spicula tendat amor.	O 213	Tr Greek 9.39		2
MISTA				
Cum violis; spirant lilia mista rosis.	O 209	Tr. Greek 5.74		4
MITIA				
Nectareos rores, alimentaque mitia coelum	O 88	Messiah		14
MITIOR				
Eveniat tantum mitior unda tibi!	O 211	Tr Greek 7.350		2
MITTIT				
Mittit aromaticas vallis Saronica nubes,	O 89	Messiah		32
Turbidus imber abest; mittit rosa roscida gemmas,	O 385	Cantico Solom.	D	5
MNEMOSYNE				
Mnemosyne, ut Sappho mellita voce canentem	O 214	Tr Greek 9.66		1
MODERANTE				
Te recidunt moderante fluctus.	O 166	Oda Isle Skye		20
Te resident moderante fluctus.	O 166	Oda Isle Skye	V	20
Te recedunt moderante fluctus.	O 166	Oda Isle Skye	V	20
Causarum series quo moderante fluit,	O 207	Prayers VI		2
MODIS				
Quot modis mecum, quid agat, requiro,	O 168	Oda to Thrale		11
Hilarare suis jussere modis	O 193	Tr. Medea III		4
Assurgitque epicis pagina docta modis.	Y 28	Aurora Musis		10
MODO				
Pastor agit pecudes, teneros modo suscipit agnos,	O 90	Messiah		59
Amissas modo quaerit oves, revocatque vagantes;	O 90	Messiah		61
Qui veterum modo facta ducum, modo carmina vatum,	O 160	Gnothi seauton		8
Qui veterum modo facta ducum, modo carmina vatum,	O 160	Gnothi seauton		8
Ut modo tentem	O 199	Medico Aeger S		16
Ut vis, ponte minax, modo tres discesseris ulnas,	O 210	Tr Greek 7.284		1
Astra mathematicos si modo vera docent.	O 215	Tr Greek 9.112		2
"Perge modo, atque tuas olim post funera laudes	O 386	In Birchium	D	5
MODOS				
Accendit, rerumque modos ac foedera ponit.	O 163	To Dr Lawrence		30
MODULIS				
Tene cantorum modulis stupere?	O 153	In Theatro		6
MODULUM				
Quisque suum norit modulum; tibi, prime virorum,	O 160	Gnothi seauton		14
MODUS				
Quis formae modus imperio? Venus arrogat audax	O 103	Elizae Aenigma		1
Omnibus unus amor, non est modus unus amoris.	O 163	To Dr Lawrence		8
MOENIA				
Buccina disjecit Thebarum moenia, struxit	O 216	Tr Greek 9.250		1
MOERET				
Terribili fremitu stridula moeret anus.	O 383	On the Gin-Act	D	2
MOEROR				
Non ira, non moeror quietis	O 166	Oda Isle Skye		7
MOERORQUE				
Terror inest aliis, moerorque, et siquid habebis	O 222	Tr. Gk. 10.123		5
MOESTA				
Non planctus, non moesta sonant suspiria, pectus	O 90	Messiah		52
Prosequitur lacrymis filia moesta Sami,	O 211	Tr Greek 7.459		2
MOESTUM				
Quem moestum et timidum crimina dira gravant;	O 207	Prayers V		2
MOLA				
In Rivum a Mola Stoana Lichfeldiae diffluentem	O 228	Rivum a Stoana		T
MOLESTA				
Perstrepit omne forum; cura molesta domi est.	O 217	Tr Greek 9.359		2
MOLESTAS				
Vile indignatus studium, nugasque molestas,	O 160	Gnothi seauton		3
MOLIATUR				
Quid moliatur Gens Imitantium,	O 101	Ad Urbanum		5
MOLLES				
Molles ducimus horas.	O 181	Waltoni Piscat		4
MOLLESCUNT				
Deserti laeta mollescunt aspera voce,	O 89	Messiah		34
Deserta et lata mollescunt aspera voce,	O 89	Messiah	V	34
MOLLI				
Pectora molli mulcet dubiae	O 193	Tr. Medea III		14
MOLLIA				
Mollia non deerant vacuae solatia vitae,	O 170	Insula Kenneth		13
Mollia non desunt vacuae solatia vitae,	O 170	Insula Kenneth	V	13
Mollia laxent	O 199	Medico Aeger S		18
Plenum opus effugiens; aptans juga mollia collo	O 205	Christianus		22
MOLLIOR				
Mens mea quid quereris? veniet tibi mollior hora,	O 208	A Meditation		1

	PAGE	TITLE	LINE
MONADES			
Quales sint monades, qua fit inane, sinas.	O 222	Tr Greek 11.50	6
MONTES			
Surgite convalles, tumidi subsidite montes!	O 89	Messiah	39
Trajecit montes nauta, fretumque pedes,	O 217	Tr Greek 9.304	2
MONTIBUS			
Solis Ophyraeis crudum tibi montibus aurum	O 92	Messiah	104
Menti nec aegrae montibus aviis	O 166	Oda Isle Skye	10
MONTIS			
Saxa cadent, solidque liquescent robora montis:	O 92	Messiah	116
MONUMENTUM			
Exiguum en! Priami monumentum; haud ille meretun	O 210	Tr Greek 7.136	1
MORA			
Haud mora, surge, soror!	O 384	Cantico Solom.	D 2
MORATUR			
Paulum vita moratur,	O 182	Waltoni Piscat	6
MORBIQUE			
Respice quem subigit senium, morbique seniles,	O 207	Prayers VI	3
Respice quem subiget senium, morbique seniles,	O 207	Prayers VI	V 3
MORBUS			
Et morbus tegitur, dum premit ora pudor.	O 221	Tr Greek 10.98	2
MORES			
Ingenium et mores si pulchra probavit Elisa,	O 104	To Eliz Carter	3
Paulatim mores, animum, vitamque refingit,	O 205	Christianus	28
His redimita comas, mores depone superbos:	O 209	Tr. Greek 5.74	5
MORETUR			
Gratia ter grata est velox, sin forte moretur	O 220	Tr Greek 10.30	1
MORI			
Venisse, aut visa luce repente mori.	O 217	Tr Greek 9.359	10
Vivere, te viva, te moriente, mori.	O 384	On the Gin-Act	D 10
MORIARQUE			
Mandatum, vivam sic moriarque tibi.	O 207	Prayers IV	6
MORIENTE			
Vivere, te viva, te moriente, mori.	O 384	On the Gin-Act	D 10
MORIENTIA			
Sive dies medius morientia torreat arva:	O 90	Messiah	63
MORITUR			
Demophilo auscultans nycticorax moritur.	O 223	Tr. Gk. 11.186	2
MOROR			
Aeternum direpta mihi! sed quid moror istis?	O 384	On the Gin-Act	D 7
MORS			
Quod mors in cineres solvit, et abdit humo.	O 221	Tr Greek 10.84	4
MORSQUE			
Lenis inoffenso vitaque morsque gradu.	Y 387	Death Mother	D 4
MORSU			
Cerbere, te morsu ne petat ille, cave.	O 211	Tr Greek 7.319	2
MORSUS			
Pulicibus morsus, restincta lampade, stultus	O 224	Tr. Gk. 11.432	1
MORTALE			
Nil mortale loquor, coelum mihi carminis alta	O 88	Messiah	2
Nil non mortale est mortalibus; omne quod est hi	O 220	Tr Greek 10.31	1
Nil non mortale est mortalibus; omne quod est hic	O 220	Tr Greek 10.31	V 1
MORTALES			
Mortales miseros servat, alit, fovet,	O 155	Psalmus 117	6
MORTALIA			
Se fidum addicat Christo, mortalia temnens.	O 205	Christianus	18
MORTALIBUS			
Nil non mortale est mortalibus; omne quod est hi	O 220	Tr Greek 10.31	1
Nil non mortale est mortalibus; omne quod est hic	O 220	Tr Greek 10.31	V 1
MORTE			
Morte memor patriae; hic Marcmonti pectore prima	O 116	Tr Pope Grotto	13
Mihi dona morte haec impetret Christus sua.	O 206	Prayers I	11
In tumulum tecum, morte jubente, trahes?	O 220	Tr Greek 10.60	2
Quae sine morte fuga est vitae, quam turba malorum	O 222	Tr. Gk. 10.123	1
MORTEM			
Vincla coercebunt luctantem adamantina mortem,	O 90	Messiah	54
MORTI			
Hic, dum debita morti	O 182	Waltoni Piscat	5
MOTU			
Hic delusa rudi frustrabar brachia motu,	O 228	Rivum a Stoana	3
MOTUSQUE			
Tractabit palmis infans, motusque trisulcae	O 91	Messiah	90
MOVET			
Nil movet insolitum, sub legibus omnia fictis	O 163	To Dr Lawrence	35
Quid mirum? cum saxa movet statuasque tacentes	Y 28	Aurora Musis	13
MOVISTI			
Tu mihi, qui flamma movisti pectora sancti	O 88	Messiah	6
MOX			
Mox uteri pondus depositura grave,	O 115	Ad Lauram Epig	2
Luctus mox pariturum.	O 182	Waltoni Piscat	14
Lucri ulciscendum mox nece sola doces.	O 213	Tr Greek 9.29	4
Quaerenti obveniet mox sine flore rubus.	O 223	Tr Greek 11.53	2
MR			
Inscription on the collar of Mr. Banks's Goat	O 156	Collari Caprae	V T
MUGITUM			
Mugitum tumulus comprimit Amphilochi.	O 213	Tr Greek 8.137	2
MULCENTES			
Curas mulcentes dulce eruntur aves.	Y 28	Aurora Musis	4
MULCENTESQUE			
Jessaeis surgit, mulcentesque aethera flores	O 88	Messiah	11

MULCERE

	PAGE	TITLE	LINE
Mulcere, aut pectus triste levare malis.	O 218	Tr Greek 9.375	8

MULCERI

| Tene mulceri fidibus canoris? . . . . | O 153 | In Theatro | 5 |

MULCET

Singultans mulcet, lachrymantes terget ocellos. . . .	O 90	Messiah	53
Singultans mulcet, lachrymantes tergit ocellos. . . .	O 90	Messiah	V 53
Seu viri curas pia nupta mulcet, ...	O 168	Oda to Thrale	13
Pectora molli mulcet dubiae	O 193	Tr. Medea III	14
Mulcet amor prolis, sopor est sine prole profundus; . .	O 217	Tr Greek 9.360	7

MULIEBRIBUS

| Permitte fidens, ac muliebribus, ... | O 187 | Ad T. L. M.D. | 18 |
| Permitte fidens, et muliebribus, ... | O 187 | Ad T. L. M.D. | V 18 |

MULTA

Dignus qui multa in lustra senescat, erit.	O 214	Tr Greek 9.55	2
Pauperies latitat, cum conjuge gaudia multa	O 217	Tr Greek 9.360	5
Multa alere, et multas aedificare domos.	O 222	Tr. Gk. 10.119	2

MULTAE

| Paupertas misera est; multae cum conjuge lites . . . | O 217 | Tr Greek 9.359 | 5 |

MULTAS

| Multa alere, et multas aedificare domos. . . . . . | O 222 | Tr. Gk. 10.119 | 2 |

MULTIPLICI

| Multiplici reducem circumsonat ore magistrum. . . . | O 161 | Gnothi seauton | 23 |

MULTIS

| Multis ut te oculis sim potis aspicere. . . . . . | O 212 | Tr Greek 7.669 | 2 |

MULTO

| Multo gravatam crimine . . . . | O 206 | Prayers II | 10 |

MUNDI

| Firmius ac ipsis Mundi stabilita ruinis. . . . . . | O 92 | Messiah | V 119 |
| Abstergat mundi labem, nec gaudia carnis . . . . . | O 205 | Christianus | 2 |

MUNDIQUE

| Naturae invadens, mundique elementa refingens . . . | O 163 | To Dr Lawrence | 25 |

MUNERA

Deproperat tellus, fundit tibi munera, quicquid . . .	O 89	Messiah	28
Cinnameos cumulos, Nabathaei munera veris, ...	O 92	Messiah	102
Ipse sui judex, actae bene munera vitae;	O 162	Gnothi seauton	48
Ponti inter strepitus sacri non munera cultus . . .	O 170	Insula Kenneth	17
Munera muneribus si retulere fabri.	O 225	Tr Greek 16.87	4
Munera luxurians dat pampinus, et generoso	O 385	Cantico Solom.	D 13

MUNERE

| Cinnameis cumulis, Nabathaei munere veris, ... | O 92 | Messiah | V 102 |

MUNERIBUS

| Recte qui fruitur muneribus, dedit. . . . . . . | O 164 | Recover Eyes | 14 |
| Munera muneribus si retulere fabri. . . . . . . | O 225 | Tr Greek 16.87 | 4 |

MUNUS

| Hectori, et exitio munus utrique fuit. . . . . . . | O 210 | Tr Greek 7.151 | 2 |

MUREM

| Murem Asclepiades sub tecto ut vidit avarus, ... | O 224 | Tr. Gk. 11.391 | 1 |

MURMURA

| Garrula mirantur salientis murmura rivi. . . . . . | O 91 | Messiah | 77 |

MURO

| Et saltu e muro Ditis opaca petit: . . . . | O 211 | Tr Greek 7.471 | 2 |

MUS

| Quid tibi, mus, mecum, dixit, amice, tibi? . . . . . | O 224 | Tr. Gk. 11.391 | 2 |
| Mus blandum ridens, respondit, pelle timorem; . . . | O 224 | Tr. Gk. 11.391 | 3 |

MUSA

| Dat Menti propriis Musa nitere bonis. . . . . . . | O 85 | Adjecere bonae | 2 |
| Audiit, irata est ne nova Musa foret. . . . . . . | O 214 | Tr Greek 9.66 | 2 |

MUSAE

| Haec Musae ad Venerem: Sic Marti, diva, mineris; . . | O 213 | Tr Greek 9.39 | 3 |
| Exceptae hospitio Musae tribuere libellos . . . . | O 216 | Tr Greek 9.160 | 1 |

MUSAS

| Ad Musas Venus haec: Veneri parete, puellae, . . . | O 213 | Tr Greek 9.39 | 1 |

MUSCA

| Musca, meae comitem, participemque dapis, ... | O 171 | Tr. Busy Fly | 2 |

MUSCOSI

| Muscosi fontes, silvestria tecta, valete, ... | O 88 | Messiah | 4 |

MUSIS

| Vacare solis perge Musis, ... | O 101 | Ad Urbanum | 7 |
| Non ulla Musis Pagina gratior, ... | O 102 | Ad Urbanum | 17 |

MUTABILIS

| Canna viret, juncique tremit mutabilis umbra. . . . | O 91 | Messiah | 79 |

MUTABIT

| Mutabit, plurima Reges . . . . | O 109 | Post-genitis | 22 |

MUTARE

| Qui, mutare vias ausus terraeque marisque, ... | O 217 | Tr Greek 9.304 | 1 |

MUTILATO

| Servus, Epictetus, mutilato corpore, vixi, ... | O 212 | Tr Greek 7.676 | 1 |

MUTILATUS

| Servus Epictetus, mutilatus corpore vixi . . . . . | O 114 | Tr Gk Epigrams | 3 |

MYRIADAS

Myriadas decies septem numerare jubebit	O 230	Geographia Met	8
Russia, myriadas ter denas adde trecentis:	O 230	Geographia Met	17
Myriadas ter mille homini dat terra colendas. . . .	O 230	Geographia Met	20
Myriadas septem decies Europa ducentis	O 230	Geographia Met	25
Myriadas denas dat, quinque et millia, sexque . . .	O 230	Geographia Met	27

MYRIADES

| Myriades sibi pulcra duas, duo millia poscit . . . | O 230 | Geographia Met | 10 |

MYRIADI

| Ter tria myriadi conjungit millia quartae, ... | O 230 | Geographia Met | 29 |
| Millia myriadi septem foecunda secundae . . . . . | O 230 | Geographia Met | 31 |

		PAGE	TITLE	LINE
MYRIAS				
Myrias Aegypto cessit bis septima pingui.	• • • •	O 229	Geographia Met	3
Myrias adsciscit sibi nonagesima septem	• • • •	O 229	Geographia Met	4
Vult sibi vicenas millesima myrias addi,	• • •	O 230	Geographia Met	21
Myrias, ut menti pateat tota Africa doctae.	• • • •	O 230	Geographia Met	24
MYRTO				
Aspera, odoratae cedunt mala gramina myrto.	• • • •	O 91	Messiah	83
NABATHAEI				
Cinnameos cumulos, Nabathaei munera veris,	• • •	O 92	Messiah	102
Cinnameis cumulis, Nabathaei munere veris,	• • •	O 92	Messiah	V 102
NAM				
Nam foecunda rubri	• • • • • • •	O 109	Post-genitis	9
Nam licet, et toto prolue laeta mero.	• • •	O 171	Tr. Busy Fly	4
Nam vita incertis incerta impellitur auris,	• • • •	O 221	Tr Greek 10.74	3
NAMQUE				
Namque, ubi mensas onerant epulae,	• • • • • •	O 193	Tr. Medea III	11
NARCISSUS				
Hic anemone humet, confert narcissus odores	• • • •	O 209	Tr. Greek 5.74	3
NARIBUS				
Ignis quem Phoebi naribus efflat equus,	• • •	Y 28	Aurora Musis	14
Quem efflant quem rem Phoebi naribus ignis equi	• • •	Y 28	Aurora Musis	V 14
NARRAT				
Ab Jove Maeonides descendere Somnia narrat:	• • • •	O 103	Elizae Aenigma	3
NASCENTI				
India nascenti, placidaeve argentea noctis	• • • •	O 92	Messiah	109
NASCERE				
Nascere, magne puer! Tibi primas, ecce! corollas	• • •	O 89	Messiah	27
NASCITUR				
Sic orsus--Qualis rerum mihi nascitur ordo!	• • • •	O 88	Messiah	9
NASCUNTUR				
Nascuntur curis curae, vexatque dolorum	• • • •	O 161	Gnothi seauton	27
NATARE				
Dum docuit blanda voce natare pater.	• • • • •	O 228	Rivum a Stoana	4
NATAT				
Non tenet; esca natat pulchra, sed hamus abest.	• • •	O 209	Tr. Greek 5.67	2
NATET				
Nec natet, et nunc has partes, nunc eligat illas,	• • •	O 205	Christianus	16
NATIO				
Natic, ccnversa	• • • • • • • •	O 109	Post-genitis	23
NATIS				
Convenit ut natis, inclyta Sparta, tuis.	• • • • •	O 224	Tr Greek 16.1	4
NATO				
Nunc dies Christo memoranda nato	• • • • • • •	O 193	Prayer on Xmas	1
NATOS				
Ante Oculos Natos	• • • • • • • • •	O 110	Post-genitis	31
NATUM				
At te bonum si noris, et bonis natum,	• • • • • •	O 224	Tr Greek 13.3	3
NATURA				
Quas Natura dedit dotes, Academia promit,	• • • •	O 85	Adjecere bonae	1
Nil majus Natura capit: clarare priores	• • •	O 86	Tr Dryden Milt	5
Sive mihi mentem dederit Natura minorem.	• • •	O 161	Gnothi seauton	18
Rus ornat natura; levat maris aspera lucrum;	• •	O 217	Tr Greek 9.360	3
Dulcia dat natura quidem, mare, sidera, terras,	• • •	O 222	Tr. Gk. 10.123	3
NATURAE				
Expectata diu! Naturae claustra refringens	• • • •	O 89	Messiah	26
Naturae invadens, mundique elementa refringens	• • • •	O 163	To Dr Lawrence	25
Summe dator vitae, naturae aeterne magister,	• • • •	O 207	Prayers VI	1
NATUS				
Natus ad optatum perducet coepta parentis.	• • • •	O 90	Messiah	72
Cuique esses natus, cuique sodalis, eras.	• • • •	O 212	Tr Greek 7.560	4
Natus eram lacrymans, lacrymans e luce recedo;	• • • •	O 221	Tr Greek 10.84	1
NAUFRAGUS				
Naufragus hic jaceo; contra jacet ecce colonus!	• • •	O 210	Tr Greek 7.265	1
Naufragus hic jaceo; fidens tamen utere velis,	• • •	O 210	Tr Greek 7.282	1
Naufragus iratas ille retentat aquas.	• • •	O 215	Tr Greek 9.133	2
NAUTA				
Nauta, quis hoc jaceat ne percontere sepulchro;	• • •	O 211	Tr Greek 7.350	1
Trajecit montes nauta, fretumque pedes,	• • •	O 217	Tr Greek 9.304	2
NAVIS				
Quas navis recipit, quantum sit pondus aquarum,	• • •	O 229	Epigram III	1
NE				
Ne, quae prosunt	• • • • • • • •	O 199	Medico Aeger S	28
Ne stolidae similis leges sibi segreget audax	• • •	O 205	Christianus	20
Anxietas noceat ne tenebrosa mihi.	• • • •	O 207	Prayers VII	2
Da, ne sint permissa, pater, mihi praemia frustra,	• •	O 208	Prayers VII	9
Da, ne sint promissa, pater, mihi praemia frustra,	• •	O 208	Prayers VII	V 9
Heraclitus ego; indoctae ne laedite linguae,	• • •	O 209	Tr Greek 7.128	1
Cerbere, te morsu ne petat ille, cave.	• • •	O 211	Tr Greek 7.319	2
Nauta, quis hoc jaceat ne percontere sepulchro;	• •	O 211	Tr Greek 7.350	1
In vos ne missus spicula tendat amor.	• • • •	O 213	Tr Greek 9.39	2
Audiit, irata est ne nova Musa foret.	• • • •	O 214	Tr Greek 9.66	2
Clamat et Argivis: Vetuli, ne tangite, vita	• • •	O 216	Tr Greek 9.163	3
NEBULIS				
Saxeas miscet nebulis ruinas,	• • • • • • •	O 167	Oda to Thrale	2
NEBULOSA				
Skia sinum nebulosa pandis.	• • • • • • • •	O 166	Oda Isle Skye	4
NEC				
Mea nec Falernae Etc.	• • • • • • • •	O 85	Mea nec Falern	T
Omnia, nec curae sunt sua sceptra Jovi.	• • • •	O 103	Elizae Aenigma	2
Nec fremere audebit	• • • • • • • •	O 109	Post-genitis	27
Nec quid agam invenio, meditatus grandia, cogor	• • •	O 161	Gnothi seauton	34

NEC　　　　　　(CONTINUED)　　　　　　　　　　　　　　　　PAGE　　TITLE　　　　　　　LINE

Nec miratur opes, celsa speculator ab arce . . . . .　O 161 Gnothi seauton　　V　39
Nec sibi de gaza praesens quod postulet usus . . . .　O 162 Gnothi seauton　　　　44
Nec quaerunt quid, luna, tuo cum fluctibus orbi. . .　O 163 To Dr Lawrence　　　16
Menti nec aegrae montibus aviis . . . .　O 166 Oda Isle Skye　　　　10
Prodest vagari, nec frementes . . . .　O 166 Oda Isle Skye　　　　11
Datur nec aequum cuique animum sibi . . . . . .　O 166 Oda Isle Skye　　　　14
Nec tamen inculti gelidis latuere sub antris, . . .　O 169 Insula Kenneth　　V　11
Nec vincis acer, nec pateris pius; . . . .　O 187 Ad T. L. M.D.　　　　6
Nec vincis acer, nec pateris pius; . . . .　O 187 Ad T. L. M.D.　　　　6
Phoebe fave, aegrotat quae te colit, ulla nec usquam est　O 197 Summ. Lawrence　　　1
Ingenio parcas, nec sit mihi culpa rogasse, ...　O 204 Losing Speech　　　　3
Ingenio parcas, nec sit mihi culpa precari . . . .　O 204 Losing Speech　　V　3
Abstergat mundi labem, nec gaudia carnis . . . . .　O 205 Christianus　　　　　2
Captans, nec fastu tumidus, sempergue futuro . . .　O 205 Christianus　　　　　3
Huic quoque, nec genti nec sectae noxius ulli, . .　O 205 Christianus　　　　　6
Huic quoque, nec genti nec sectae noxius ulli, . .　O 205 Christianus　　　　　6
Nec natet, et nunc has partes, nunc eligat illas, .　O 205 Christianus　　　　　16
Nec dubitet quem dicat herum, sed, totus in uno, .　O 205 Christianus　　　　　17
Qui nec scelestos exigis, ...　O 206 Prayers II　　　　　4
Sum nunc, nec possum cernere qualis eram. . . . .　O 209 Tr. Greek 6.1　　　　4
Nec mirum; restat lepori conscendere coelum, . . .　O 213 Tr Greek 9.18　　　　3
Interea dubito; tecum me causa nec ulla . . . . .　O 216 Tr Greek 9.148　　　5
Nec probrosa avidae grata sit offa gulae; . . . .　O 218 Tr Greek 9.573　　　2
Nec ficto fletu, fictis solvare cachinnis, ...　O 218 Tr Greek 9.573　　　3
Prospera sors nec te strepitoso turbine tollat, .　O 221 Tr Greek 10.74　　　1
Nec menti injiciat sordida cura jugum; . . . . . .　O 221 Tr Greek 10.74　　　2
Nec male res cessit, subito si funere sponsam, . .　O 222 Tr Greek 11.50　　　3
Fiam scelestus, nec tamen minus sequar. . . . . .　O 226 Tr. Cleanthes　　　　4
Nec sinat semper tremere ac dolere . . . .　O 227 A Meditation　　　　3
Nec sinat semper tremere ac dolore . . . .　O 227 A Meditation　　V　3
Pigritiam incusat, nec minus hora perit. . . . . .　O 228 Jactura Tempor　　　2
NECE
Lucri ulciscendum mox nece sola doces. . . . . . .　O 213 Tr Greek 9.29　　　　4
NECESSITAS
Me, rex deorum, tuque, duc, necessitas, ...　O 226 Tr. Cleanthes　　　　1
NECI
Dicam; stat virtus non subigenda neci. . . . . . .　O 212 Tr Greek 7.590　　　4
NECTAREOS
Nectareos rores, alimentaque mitia coelum . . . . .　O 88 Messiah　　　　　　　14
NECTIT
Non reperit, nectit quem reperit laqueum. . . . .　O 213 Tr Greek 9.44　　　　2
Centuriae quartae decades quinque Anglia nectit. . . .　O 230 Geographia Met　　30
NEGABITUR
Negabitur solatium. . . . .　O 203 Christ Sinner　　　　4
NEGAVIT
Queis uti poteram quondam Fortuna negavit, ...　O 215 Tr Greek 9.138　　　3
NEGLIGIS
Divitias cumulas, pereuntes negligis horas, ...　O 220 Tr Greek 10.60　　　3
NEMO
At nemo feras iras hominum, ...　O 193 Tr. Medea III　　　　6
Nemo optet nunquam venisse in luminis oras, ...　O 217 Tr Greek 9.360　　　9
NEQUE
Neque Bellua victa remugit. . . . .　O 110 Post-genitis　　　　38
Tu neque dulce putes alienae accumbere mensae, . . .　O 218 Tr Greek 9.573　　　1
Laetior haud tecum, tecum neque tristior unquam, . .　O 218 Tr Greek 9.573　　　5
NEQUEO
Queis uti nequeo, nunc mihi praebet opes. . . . . .　O 215 Tr Greek 9.138　　　4
NEQUEUNT
Stat: fixum est: nequeunt jam revocare preces. . . .　O 384 On the Gin-Act　　D　8
NEQUID
Mi, nequid nimis, est nimis probatum. . . . .　O 215 Tr Greek 9.110　　　4
NEQUITIAM
Nequitiam fugiens, servata contrahe lege . . . . . .　O 218 Tr Greek 9.444　　　3
NERVIS
Accrescunt tremulis tactu nova robora nervis: . . . .　O 90 Messiah　　　　　　　49
Accrescunt teneris tactu nova robora nervis: . . . .　O 90 Messiah　　　　　V　49
NERVOS
Intende nervos fortis, inanibus . . . .　O 101 Ad Urbanum　　　　　13
Intende jam nervos, habebis . . . .　O 101 Ad Urbanum　　　　　15
NESCIT
Si Phoebo, victor nescit obire diem. . . . . . .　O 210 Tr Greek 7.239　　　2
Civis et externus grati; domus hospita nescit . . .　O 219 Tr Greek 9.648　　　1
NESTORIS
Et senium triplex Nestoris urna capit. . . . . . .　O 215 Tr Greek 9.112　　　4
NEVE
Neve tibi noceat praenituisse Deae. . . . .　O 115 Ad Lauram Epig　　　4
NEXA
Nexa patent; hi sunt quos nil mirabile turbat, . . .　O 163 To Dr Lawrence　　　34
NEXIBUS
Supremis junxit nexibus arctus amor. . . . .　O 393 Tr. of Crashaw　　D　2
NI
Dat tibi Pythagoram pictor; quod ni ipse tacere . . .　O 225 Tr. Gk. 16.326　　　1
NIHIL
Scire vices ponti facile est, nihil amplius optant　O 163 To Dr Lawrence　　　15
Triste nihil passus, animi at de sorte Platonis . . .　O 211 Tr Greek 7.471　　　3
Cuncta, cinis cuncta et ludicra, cuncta nihil. . . .　O 222 Tr. Gk. 10.124　　　2
NIHILUM
Sponte sua demens; nihilum decedere summae . . . . .　O 205 Christianus　　　　　23
NIL
Nil majus Natura capit: clarare priores . . . . . .　O 86 Tr Dryden Milt　　　5

```
                                                         PAGE    TITLE              LINE
NIL          (CONTINUED)
    Nil mortale loquor, coelum mihi carminis alta    .  .  .  .  .   O  88 Messiah              2
    Serpentes teneris nil jam lethale minantes   .  .  .  .  .       O  91 Messiah             89
    Serpentes teneris nil jam lethale micantes   .  .  .  .  .       O  91 Messiah          V  89
    Qui nil virtuti, sed debuit omnia ventis,    .  .  .  .  .       O 143 On Lord Anson    V   1
    Nexa patent; hi sunt quos nil mirabile turbat,  .  .  .  .       O 163 To Dr Lawrence      34
    Nil movet insolitum, sub legibus omnia fictis   .  .  .  .       O 163 To Dr Lawrence      35
    Nil opus est aeris sacra de turre sonantis   .  .  .  .  .       O 170 Insula Kenneth   V 18A
    Crepare vaecors, nil sapientiam  .  .  .  .  .  .                 O 186 Ad T. L. M.D.        2
    Nil lucri facies; ossa habet et cinerem.  .  .  .  .             O 210 Tr Greek 7.284       4
    Nil non mortale est mortalibus; omne quod est hi   .  .  .       O 220 Tr Greek 10.31       1
    Nil non mortale est mortalibus; omne quod est hic  .  .  .       O 220 Tr Greek 10.31    V  1
    Cogitat aut loquitur nil vir, nil cogitat uxor,   .  .  .        O 226 Tr. Greek            1
    Cogitat aut loquitur nil vir, nil cogitat uxor,   .  .  .        O 226 Tr. Greek            1
    Quem nil vafrities peccantum subdola celat;  .  .  .  .          O 232 Prayer               3
    Dulce Venus ridens, lorica nil opus, inquit,   .  .  .  .        O 384 Epigramma         D  3
NIMBIS
    Fidus adest custos, seu nox furat horrida nimbis,   .  .  .      O  90 Messiah             62
    Fidus adest custos, seu nox furat humida nimbis,    .  .  .      O  90 Messiah             62
    Hic jaceant; donec Nox transeat horrida nimbis,   .  .  .        O 393 Tr. of Crashaw   D   3
NIMII
    Vis boreae gelida, aut nimii violentia solis.   .  .  .  .       O  89 Messiah          V  19
NIMIO
    Et melli nimio fellis amaror inest.   .  .  .  .  .  .  .        O 224 Tr Greek 16.16       2
NIMIS
    Secta crepet nimis alta fallax.   .  .  .  .  .  .               O 166 Oda Isle Skye       16
    Grandiloquus nimis alta Zeno.   .  .  .  .  .  .  .              O 166 Oda Isle Skye     V  16
    .  .  .  filium peregre agentem desiderio nimis   .  .  .        O 186 Ad T. L. M.D.     V   T
    Sollicitus nimis, heu! paternis.   .  .  .  .  .  .              O 187 Ad T. L. M.D.       12
    Mi, nequid nimis, est nimis probatum.   .  .  .  .              O 215 Tr Greek 9.110       4
    Mi, nequid nimis, est nimis probatum.   .  .  .  .              O 215 Tr Greek 9.110       4
    Omnis vita nimis brevis est felicibus, una   .  .  .  .         O 220 Tr Greek 10.28       1
NIMIUM
    Frigora, seu nimium longo jacuisse veterno,  .  .  .  .  .       O 161 Gnothi seauton       17
    Non Animus sero nimium dum parta recenset,   .  .  .  .  .       O 161 Gnothi seauton    V  42
    Aut, hoc si nimium est, tandem nova lexica poscam?  .  .         O 162 Gnothi seauton       54
    Quod nimium est fit ineptum; hinc, ut dixere priores,  .        O 224 Tr Greek 16.16       1
NISE
    Tu quoque securus res age, Nise, tuas.   .  .  .  .  .           O 228 Rivum a Stoana       12
NISI
    Ingenium, nisi materiem Doctrina ministret,  .  .  .  .          O 161 Gnothi seauton       37
    Ingenium, nisi materiem Doctrina ministrat,  .  .  .  .          O 161 Gnothi seauton    V  37
    Quid labor efficiet? non nisi nudus ero.  .  .  .  .  .          O 220 Tr Greek 10.58       2
NISIBUS
    Risurus olim nisibus Aemuli;  .  .  .  .  .  .  .  .             O 101 Ad Urbanum           14
NISU
    Denique perpetuo contendit in ardua nisu,   .  .  .  .  .        O 205 Christianus          25
NITENT
    Haec peritura nitent; tu peritura nites!  .  .  .  .  .          O 209 Tr. Greek 5.74        6
NITENTI
    Gemmaque luxuriae nondum famulata nitenti   .  .  .  .  .        O 116 Tr Pope Grotto        5
NITERE
    Dat Menti propriis Musa nitere bonis.  .  .  .  .  .  .          O  85 Adjecere bonae        2
NITES
    Haec peritura nitent; tu peritura nites!  .  .  .  .  .          O 209 Tr. Greek 5.74        6
NITESCIT
    Quid mihi cum cultu? Probitas inculta nitescit,   .  .  .        O 104 To Eliz Carter        1
NITIDO
    Hirce, parem nitido te tua barba facit.  .  .  .  .  .  .        O 224 Tr. Gk. 11.430        2
NIVEO
    Sedatas niveo Virtus lucebit amictu.   .  .  .  .  .  .          O  89 Messiah              24
    Pacatas niveo Virtus lucebit amictu.   .  .  .  .  .  .          O  89 Messiah           V  24
NOBILITATUS
    Leniades magnis nobilitatus avis:   .  .  .  .  .  .  .          O 169 Insula Kenneth        8
NOBIS
    Limosum nobis Promus dat callidus haustum,   .  .  .  .          O  85 Mea nec Falern        3
    Magne bonum, omne malum et poscentibus abnue nobis.  .  .        O 221 Tr Greek 10.108       2
    Haec nobis Christus promeruisse velit!  .  .  .  .  .            O 232 Prayer               10
NOCEAT
    Neve tibi noceat praenituisse Deae.   .  .  .  .  .  .           O 115 Ad Lauram Epig         4
    Anxietas noceat ne tenebrosa mihi.   .  .  .  .  .  .  .         O 207 Prayers VII           2
NOCENT
    Rege, et tuere, quae nocent pellens procul;  .  .  .  .  .       O 206 Prayers I             6
NOCTE
    Sed sua regna videns, loca nocte silentia late   .  .  .  .      O 162 Gnothi seauton       49
    Clam nocte tollit Aulus, et ridens ait;  .  .  .  .  .  .        O 223 Tr. Gk. 11.176        4
NOCTES
    Noctes atque dies animo spes laeta recurset,   .  .  .  .        O 207 Prayers VII           5
NOCTIS
    India nascenti, placidaeve argentea noctis   .  .  .  .          O  92 Messiah             109
    Alme voco, impatiens noctis metuensque diei.   .  .  .  .        O 161 Gnothi seauton       31
    Noctis tristitiam qui gelidae jubet,   .  .  .  .  .  .          O 164 Recover Eyes          4
    Per caeca noctis taedia turbidae,   .  .  .  .  .  .  .          O 187 Ad T. L. M.D.         9
NOCTURNAE
    Nunc clamosa juvant nocturnae gaudia mensae,   .  .  .  .        O 161 Gnothi seauton       29
NOCUIT
    Et me, cuncta beans cui nocuit dies,   .  .  .  .  .  .          O 164 Recover Eyes          8
NOLIS
    Vita rosae brevis est; properans si carpere nolis,   .  .        O 223 Tr Greek 11.53        1
    Vitae rosa brevis est; properans si carpere nolis,   .  .        O 223 Tr Greek 11.53     V  1
```

NOLO
    Hoc Veneri speculum; nolo me cernere qualis . . . . .   PAGE   TITLE   LINE
NOMEN

	PAGE	TITLE		LINE
Hoc Veneri speculum; nolo me cernere qualis	O 209	Tr. Greek 6.1		3

NOMEN
Thraliae discant resonare nomen . . . .   O 168 Oda to Thrale   19
NOMINE
Gratia vix restat nomine digna suo. . . . .   O 220 Tr Greek 10.30   2
Sortitur Pelopis tellus quae nomine gaudet. . . . . .   O 230 Geographia Met   7
NOMINIS
In mentem ut venit nominis, interii. . . . . . .   O 223 Tr. Gk. 11.118   2
NON
Hic requies fessis; non sacra saevit in umbra . . .   O 89 Messiah   18
Hic requies fessis; non sacra hac saevit in umbra .   O 89 Messiah   V 18
Non planctus, non moesta sonant suspiria, pectus . .   O 90 Messiah   52
Non planctus, non moesta sonant suspiria, pectus . .   O 90 Messiah   52
Non ultra infestis concurrent agmina signis, . . .   O 90 Messiah   66
Non litui accendent bellum, non campus ahenis . . .   O 90 Messiah   68
Non litui accendent bellum, non campus ahenis . . .   O 90 Messiah   68
Flumina prorumpunt; non posthac sole rubescet . . .   O 92 Messiah   108
Non ulla Musis Pagina deterior, ...   O 102 Ad Urbanum   17
Non mihi sorte datum; lenti seu sanguinis obsint . .   O 160 Gnothi seauton   16
Non Rationis opes Animus, nunc parta recensens, . .   O 161 Gnothi seauton   42
Non Animus sero nimium dum parta recenset, ...   O 161 Gnothi seauton   V 42
Non sibi de gaza praesens quod postulat usus . . .   O 162 Gnothi seauton   V 44
Non operum serie, seriem dum computat aevi, ...   O 162 Gnothi seauton   46
Non numerat palmas, aut . . . .   O 162 Gnothi seauton   V 46
Omnibus unus amor, non est modus unus amoris. . . .   O 163 To Dr Lawrence   8
Non ira, non moeror quietis . . . .   O 166 Oda Isle Skye   7
Non ira, non moeror quietis . . . .   O 166 Oda Isle Skye   7
At non cavata rupe latescere, ...   O 166 Oda Isle Skye   9
Humana virtus non sibi sufficit, ...   O 166 Oda Isle Skye   13
Non tamen inculti gelidis latuere sub antris, . . .   O 169 Insula Kenneth   11
Mollia non deerant vacuae solatia vitae, ...   O 170 Insula Kenneth   13
Mollia non desunt vacuae solatia vitae, ...   O 170 Insula Kenneth   V 13
Ponti inter strepitus sacri non munera cultus . .   O 170 Insula Kenneth   17
Carpe diem, fugit, heu, non revocanda dies! . . .   O 171 Tr. Busy Fly   6
Sexaginta annis non minor unus erit. . . . . .   O 171 Tr. Busy Fly   12
Non immerito culpanda venit . . . .   O 193 Tr. Medea III   1
Spe non inani confugis, ...   O 203 Christ Sinner   1
Velle vetet cuiquam non bene sanctus amor. . . . .   O 207 Prayers VII   8
Non tenet; esca natat pulchra, sed hamus abest. . .   O 209 Tr. Greek 5.67   2
Est mihi quod non te rideo, plena salus. . . . .   O 211 Tr Greek 7.318   2
Lysigeni, fuerat non gravis ille tibi. . . . . .   O 211 Tr Greek 7.461   2
Dario magno non minus ille potest. . . . . . .   O 212 Tr Greek 7.538   2
Parca, juventutem non miserata tuam! . . . . .   O 212 Tr Greek 7.560   6
Et pius, et recti cultor: non illa jacere . . . .   O 212 Tr Greek 7.590   3
Dicam; stat virtus non subigenda neci. . . . .   O 212 Tr Greek 7.590   4
Non reperit, nectit quem reperit laqueum. . . . .   O 213 Tr Greek 9.44   2
Quae lyra. Quam sibi non concinit harmonia! . . .   O 216 Tr Greek 9.250   2
Non Fortuna sibi te gratum tollit in altum; . . .   O 218 Tr Greek 9.530   1
Atthide non alius desit Olympus, habet. . . . .   O 219 Tr Greek 9.702   2
Non poteris, meditans prava, latere Deos. . . . .   O 220 Tr Greek 10.27   2
Nil non mortale est mortalibus; omne quod est hi .   O 220 Tr Greek 10.31   1
Nil non mortale est mortalibus; omne quod est hic .   O 220 Tr Greek 10.31   V 1
Quid labor efficiet? non nisi nudus ero. . . . .   O 220 Tr Greek 10.58   2
Incrementa aevi non cumulare potes. . . . . . .   O 220 Tr Greek 10.60   4
Seu prece poscatur, seu non, da Jupiter omne . . .   O 221 Tr Greek 10.108   1
Non opto aut precibus posco ditescere, paucis . .   O 222 Tr. Gk. 10.113   1
Non vitanda gravem, non toleranda facit? . . . .   O 222 Tr. Gk. 10.123   1
Non vitanda gravem, non toleranda facit? . . . .   O 222 Tr. Gk. 10.123   2
Hic, bone vir, sedem, non alimenta, peto. . . .   O 224 Tr. Gk. 11.391   4
Non Argos pugilem, non me Messana creavit: . . .   O 224 Tr Greek 16.1   1
Non Argos pugilem, non me Messana creavit; . . .   O 224 Tr Greek 16.1   1
Et Pari, et Anchisa, non alius, Venerem. . . . .   O 225 Tr. Gk. 16.168   2
Non poteras, regio non tulit ulla parem. . . . .   O 225 Tr. Gk. 16.331   6
Non poteras, regio non tulit ulla parem. . . . .   O 225 Tr. Gk. 16.331   6
Felici thalamo non, puto, rixa strepit. . . . .   O 226 Tr. Greek   2
NONAGESIMA
Myrias adsciscit sibi nonagesima septem . . . .   O 229 Geographia Met   4
NONDUM
Gemmaque luxuriae nondum famulata nitenti . . . .   O 116 Tr Pope Grotto   5
NORIS
At te bonum si noris, et bonis natum, ...   O 224 Tr Greek 13.3   3
NORIT
Quisque suum norit modulum; tibi, prime virorum, . . .   O 160 Gnothi seauton   14
NOS
Quae nos blanda comes, quae nos perducat eodem, . . .   O 171 Tr. Busy Fly   7
Quae nos blanda comes, quae nos perducat eodem, . . .   O 171 Tr. Busy Fly   7
NOSCERE
Qui sibi sat sapiunt, contenti noscere quantum . . .   O 163 To Dr Lawrence   11
Qui sibi sat sapient, contenti noscere quantum . . .   O 163 To Dr Lawrence   V 11
NOSTRA
Quid quod putidulum nostra Camoena sonat? . . .   O 85 Mea nec Falern   2
Plus tibi ridendum secula nostra dabunt. . . . .   O 216 Tr Greek 9.148   2
NOSTRI
Carmina vis nostri scribant meliora Poetae? . . . .   O 85 Mea nec Falern   5
Sit memor nostri, fideique merces . . . . .   O 168 Oda to Thrale   17
Sit memor nostri, fideique solvat . . . . .   O 168 Oda to Thrale   V 17
NOTA
Nota, Caledonias panditur inter aquas; . . . . . .   O 169 Insula Kenneth   2
NOTIOR
Notior ipse mihi fieri, incultumque fateri . . . . .   O 161 Gnothi seauton   35

		PAGE	TITLE	LINE
NOTIOR	(CONTINUED)			
Notior ipse mihi fieri, pectusque fateri		O 161	Gnothi seauton	V 35
NOVA				
Accrescunt tremulis tactu nova robora nervis:		O 90	Messiah	49
Accrescunt teneris tactu nova robora nervis: . . .		O 90	Messiah	V 49
Aut, hoc si nimium est, tandem nova lexica poscam? . . .		O 162	Gnothi seauton	54
Spes novas nova lux parit, secunda		O 204	Spes	3
Audiit, irata est ne nova Musa foret.		O 214	Tr Greek 9.66	2
Arte nova, raraque fide perscripserat ausus		O 386	In Birchium	D 1
NOVAS				
Spes novas nova lux parit, secunda		O 204	Spes	3
Et petiit terras per freta longa novas.		O 386	Tr Epi. Madoc	D 4
NCVATO				
Da veteres noxas animo sic flere novato, ...		O 198	Tr. Ash Wed.	3
Da veteres culpas animo sic flere novato, ...		O 198	Tr. Ash Wed.	V 3
NOVEM				
Millia Belga novem.		O 231	Geographia Met	34
NOVI				
Scire locum volui quid daret ille novi.		O 169	Insula Kenneth	6
Scire locus volui quid daret iste novi.		O 169	Insula Kenneth	V 6
Aevi sat novi quam sim brevis; astra tuenti, ...		O 219	Tr Greek 9.577	1
NCVIES				
Parthenope. Novies vult tellus mille Sicana.		O 230	Geographia Met	11
NCVIS				
Apte antiqua novis miscentur, et utile dulci:		O 383	Syl. Urb. Thes	D 3
NOVIT				
Novit, fatigatamque nugis		O 102	Ad Urbanum	19
NOVITATE				
Sive cum libris novitate pascit		O 168	Oda to Thrale	15
Sive cum libris novitate pascet		O 168	Oda to Thrale	V 15
NOVOS				
Harmoniae purgata novos mirabitur auris.		O 90	Messiah	48
NCVUM				
Et cortina novum det revoluta diem!		O 393	Tr. of Crashaw	D 4
NCX				
Fidus adest custos, seu nox furat horrida nimbis, . . .		O 90	Messiah	62
Fidus adest custos, seu nox furat humida nimbis, . . .		O 90	Messiah	V 62
Nox miseris longi temporis instar habet.		O 220	Tr Greek 10.28	2
Hic jaceant; donec Nox transeat horrida nimbis, . . .		O 393	Tr. of Crashaw	D 3
NCXAS				
Da veteres noxas animo sic flere novato, ...		O 198	Tr. Ash Wed.	3
NCXIUS				
Huic quoque, nec genti nec sectae noxius ulli, ...		O 205	Christianus	6
NUBES				
Mittit aromaticas vallis Saronica nubes, ...		O 89	Messiah	32
NUBIBUS				
Obductosque oculos nubibus humidis		O 164	Recover Eyes	6
Strepens procellis, uvida nubibus, ...		O 166	Oda Isle Skye	V 2
NUDA				
Permeo terras, ubi nuda rupes		O 167	Oda to Thrale	1
Longinquisque oculis nuda lavacra patent.		O 228	Rivum a Stoana	8
Vincere te potui nuda, quid arma geram?		O 384	Epigramma	D 4
NUDAM				
Unde hic Praxiteles? nudam vidistis, Adoni, ...		O 225	Tr. Gk. 16.168	1
NUDAS				
Permissum credit nudas sibi sistere causas, ...		O 163	To Dr Lawrence	20
NUDUS				
Terram adii nudus, de terra nudus abibo.		O 220	Tr Greek 10.58	1
Terram adii nudus, de terra nudus abibo.		O 220	Tr Greek 10.58	1
Quid labor efficiet? non nisi nudus ero.		O 220	Tr Greek 10.58	2
NUGAE				
Nugae anapaesticae in lecto lusae.		O 198	Medico Aeger S	T
NUGASQUE				
Vile indignatus studium, nugasque molestas, ...		O 160	Gnothi seauton	3
NUGIS				
Novit, fatigatamque nugis		O 102	Ad Urbanum	19
NULLA				
Quandoquidem passim nulla ratione feruntur		O 222	Tr. Gk. 10.124	1
Gratia nulla hominum mentes tenet, ista Promethei . . .		O 225	Tr Greek 16.87	3
Quem nulla anxietas, nulla cupido fugit;		O 232	Prayer	2
Quem nulla anxietas, nulla cupido fugit;		O 232	Prayer	2
NULLI				
Quod nulli proprium versat Fortuna, putabat		O 215	Tr Greek 9.74	3
Fecerunt nulli sors titulique gravem.		O 226	Tr. Simonides	4
NULLIS				
Regiam inundabit, nullis cessura tenebris.		O 92	Messiah	113
Urbane, nullis fesse laboribus, ...		O 101	Ad Urbanum	1
Urbane, nullis victe calumniis, ...		O 101	Ad Urbanum	2
Hinc annis palpantur delenda poemata nullis . . .		Y 28	Aurora Musis	11
NULLIUS				
Faelix ante alios nullius debitor aeris;		O 222	Tr Greek 11.50	1
Praeter Menodotum, nullius absimilis.		O 223	Tr. Gk. 11.213	2
NULLO				
Vita ubi nullo decorata cultu		O 167	Oda to Thrale	6
Gestiat, et, nullo pietatis limite clausus, . . .		O 205	Christianus	8
Pro nullo; clamo nunc tumulatus idem.		O 209	Tr Greek 7.128	4
NULLUM				
Prolem Hippi, et sua qua meliorem secula nullum . . .		O 226	Tr. Simonides	1
NUMEN				
Patris Numen adire est.		O 182	Waltoni Piscat	10
Summe Pater, quodcunque tuum de corpore Numen . . .		O 204	Losing Speech	1

NUMERANTI

	PAGE	TITLE	LINE
Olim, praeteritae numeranti tempora vitae,	O 171	Tr. Busy Fly	11

NUMERARE

E scopulo numerare fluctus.			
In specula numerare fluctus.	O 166	Oda Isle Skye	12
Myriadas decies septem numerare jubebit	O 166	Oda Isle Skye	V 12

NUMERAT

	O 230	Geographia Met	8
Non numerat palmas, aut			
Cum sex centuriis numerat sex millia Tuscus.	O 162	Gnothi seauton	V 46

NUMERIS

	O 230	Geographia Met	13
His Tempelmanni numeris descripseris orbem.	O 229	Geographia Met	1

NUMINA

Carmine describit Cellantia Numina digne	Y 28	Aurora Musis	9

NUMINE

Suspiciat tandem clementem in numine patrem.	O 205	Christianus	5
Numine praesenti me tueare pater!	O 207	Prayers IV	2
In summo ut videas numine laeta patrem;	O 208	A Meditation	2

NUMINIS

Ut precibus justas avertat numinis iras	O 170	Insula Kenneth	V 16A

NUMMIS

Pauper eram, nummis diffluit arca senis;	O 215	Tr Greek 9.138	2

NUMMUS

Praecones ambo, Nummus utrique Deus.	O 385	The Warehouse	D 2

NUNC

Nunc saltu capraes, nunc cursu provocat euros.	O 90	Messiah	V 51
Nunc saltu capraes, nunc cursu provocat euros.	O 90	Messiah	V 51
Nunc armant Veneris lumina tela Jovis.	O 103	Elizae Aenigma	6
Qui nunc jacet Incola stagni,	O 109	Post-genitis	2
Corpore nunc etiam libera facta fuit.	O 114	Tr Gk Epigrams	2
Nunc clamosa juvant nocturnae gaudia mensae,	O 161	Gnothi seauton	29
Nunc loca sola placent; frustra te, Somne, recumbens	O 161	Gnothi seauton	30
Non Rationis opes Animus, nunc parta recensens,	O 161	Gnothi seauton	42
Nunc, per gramina fusi,	O 181	Waltoni Piscat	1
Nunc rescire priora,	O 182	Waltoni Piscat	7
Nunc instare futuris,	O 182	Waltoni Piscat	8
Nunc summi prece sancta	O 182	Waltoni Piscat	9
Exsurge fortis, nunc animis opus,	O 187	Ad T. L. M.D.	14
Nunc dies Christo memoranda nato	O 193	Prayer on Xmas	1
Nunc mihi facilis	O 198	Medico Aeger S	1
Nunc minus acris	O 198	Medico Aeger S	5
Quid nunc superest?	O 199	Medico Aeger S	15
Nec natet, et nunc has partes, nunc eligat illas,	O 205	Christianus	16
Nec natet, et nunc has partes, nunc eligat illas,	O 205	Christianus	16
Nunc est pro poena poenituisse reis.	O 208	A Meditation	4
Sum nunc, nec possum cernere qualis eram.	O 209	Tr. Greek 6.1	4
Pro nullo; clamo nunc tumulatus idem.	O 209	Tr Greek 7.128	4
Qui jacet hic, servus vixit, nunc, lumine cassus,	O 212	Tr Greek 7.538	1
Dicite, Causidici, gelido nunc marmore magni	O 213	Tr Greek 8.137	1
Nunc huic, nunc aliis cedens, cui farra Menippus	O 215	Tr Greek 9.74	1
Nunc huic, nunc aliis cedens, cui farra Menippus	O 215	Tr Greek 9.74	1
Ille suum stolidus, nunc putat ille suum.	O 215	Tr Greek 9.74	4
Queis uti nequeo, nunc mihi praebet opes.'	O 215	Tr Greek 9.138	4
Vita hominum nunc plus quod misereris habet.	O 216	Tr Greek 9.148	4
Hora bonis quasi nunc instet suprema fruaris,	O 219	Tr Greek 10.26	1
Exclamat: Nunc me cernere desinitis.	O 224	Tr. Gk. 11.432	2
Nunc ope supplicii vivit imago mei.	O 225	Tr Greek 16.87	2
Nunc juvenum terres robore corda senex.	O 225	Tr. Gk. 16.364	2
Turba senum, juvenes nunc tribuere seni.	O 225	Tr. Gk. 16.364	4
Nunc veteres duris periere securibus umbrae,	O 228	Rivum a Stoana	7
Tectaque qua fluxit, nunc et aperta fluit.	O 228	Rivum a Stoana	10
Nunc age, certamen nunc ineamus, ait;	O 384	Epigramma	D 2
Nunc age, certamen nunc ineamus, ait;	O 384	Epigramma	D 2

NUNCIA

Nuncia sacra Dei, plaudentibus insidet alis.	O 88	Messiah	13

NUNCIAT

Admonitu, ipsa suas nunciat hora vices.	O 170	Insula Kenneth	V 18B

NUNCIUM

Hermen Deorum nuncium, pennis levem,	O 223	Tr. Gk. 11.176	1

NUNQUAM

Huc nunquam volitat debilis iste puer.	O 213	Tr Greek 9.39	4
Nunquam jugera messibus onusta, aut	O 215	Tr Greek 9.110	1
Ergo optent homines, aut nunquam in luminis oras	O 217	Tr Greek 9.359	9
Nemo optet nunquam venisse in luminis oras,	O 217	Tr Greek 9.360	9

NUPER

Per saxa, ignivomi nuper spelaea draconis,	O 91	Messiah	78
Credit, Achaemenidae nuper agellus eram.	O 215	Tr Greek 9.74	2

NUPTA

Seu viri curas pia nupta mulcet,	O 168	Oda to Thrale	13

NUPTAM

Quam, regum sobolem, nuptam, matrem, atque sororem	O 226	Tr. Simonides	3

NUTANTES

En! summo exultant nutantes vertice silvae.	O 89	Messiah	31

NUTRIT

Nutrit mane, putes esse Heliconis aqua.	Y 28	Aurora Musis	6

NYCTICORAX

Nycticorax cantat lethale, sed ipsa canenti	O 223	Tr. Gk. 11.186	1
Demophilo auscultans nycticorax moritur.	O 223	Tr. Gk. 11.186	2

NYMPHAE

Tollite concentum, Solymaeae tollite nymphae!	O 88	Messiah	1

NYMPHIS

Texente Nymphis serta Lycoride,	O 102	Ad Urbanum	21

O

	PAGE	TITLE	LINE
O! colat humanum Te foveatque genus!	O 102	Ad R. Savage	2
Ingredere O!--Magnam pura cole mente parentem, ...	O 116	Tr Pope Grotto	7
Ingredere O!--rerum pura cole mente parentem, ...	O 116	Tr Pope Grotto V	7
O Qui benignus crimina ignoscis, pater	O 206	Prayers III	1
Aurem faventem precibus O praebe meis;	O 206	Prayers III	3
O longum, formosa, vale, mihi vita decusque, ...	O 383	On the Gin-Act D	3
OBDUCTOSQUE			
Obductosque oculos nubibus humidis	O 164	Recover Eyes	6
OBIRE			
Si Phoebo, victor nescit obire diem.	O 210	Tr Greek 7.239	2
OBLECTAT			
Luxus oblectat Juvenem theatri, ...	O 153	In Theatro	14
OBSERVANS			
Stella mea, observans stellas, Dii me aethera faxint, .	O 212	Tr Greek 7.669	1
OBSINT			
Non mihi sorte datum; lenti seu sanguinis obsint . . .	O 160	Gnothi seauton	16
OBSITA			
Strepens procellis, rupibus obsita, ...	O 166	Oda Isle Skye	2
OBSTANTES			
Victrix per obstantes catervas	O 101	Ad Urbanum	11
OBSTAT			
Quicquid agam, quocunque ferar, conatibus obstat . . .	O 161	Gnothi seauton	40
OBSTITIT			
Xerxi, tercentum Spartae Mars obstitit acris	O 217	Tr Greek 9.304	3
OBSTRICTASQUE			
Obstrictasque diu linguas in carmina solvet.	O 90	Messiah	46
OBVENIET			
Quaerenti obveniet mox sine flore rubus.	O 223	Tr Greek 11.53	2
OCCASIONED			
The Logical Warehouse: Occasioned by an Auctioneer's . .	O 385	The Warehouse D	T
OCELLIS			
Aurea secla hominum, quorum spectandus ocellis	O 213	Tr Greek 9.29	5
OCELLOS			
Singultans mulcet, lachrymantes terget ocellos. . . .	O 90	Messiah	53
Singultans mulcet, lachrymantes tergit ocellos. . . .	O 90	Messiah V	53
OCELLUS			
Sanguine dum tumido suffusus flagrat ocellus, ...	O 162	To Dr Lawrence	1
OCTAVAM			
Centuriae octavam decadem addit Lucca secundae. . . .	O 230	Geographia Met	15
OCTINGENTESIMA			
Se quinquagenis octingentesima jungit	O 230	Geographia Met	23
OCTO			
Pastor Arabs: decies octo sibi Persa requirit. . . .	O 230	Geographia Met	9
OCULIS			
Reclusisque oculis infundet amabile lumen, ...	O 90	Messiah	45
Hostiles oculis flammas jaculantia torvis;	O 90	Messiah	67
Multis ut te oculis sim potis aspicere.	O 212	Tr Greek 7.669	2
Longinquisque oculis nuda lavacra patent.	O 228	Rivum a Stoana	8
Hunc oculis Veri Fautrix lustravit acutis, ...	O 386	In Birchium D	3
OCULO			
Tene per pictas oculo elegante	O 153	In Theatro	7
OCULOS			
Ante Oculos Natos	O 110	Post-genitis	31
Obductosque oculos nubibus humidis	O 164	Recover Eyes	6
Hic oculos socio commodat, ille pedes.	O 213	Tr Greek 9.13	2
OCULUS			
Vel digiti tractant, oculus vel sentit et auris: . . .	O 163	To Dr Lawrence	12
OCYOR			
Huc, soror alma, veni! pernicibus ocyor Euris	O 385	Cantico Solom. D	17
ODA			
Oda	O 166	Oda Isle Skye	T
Oda	O 167	Oda to Thrale	T
ODE			
Ode, De Skia Insula	O 167	Oda to Thrale V	T
ODIT			
Hostem odit tacite, sed amicum ridet aperte	O 197	On Mrs. Thrale	1
ODORATAE			
Aspera, odoratae cedunt mala gramina myrto.	O 91	Messiah	83
ODORE			
Spirat odore botrus.	O 385	Cantico Solom. D	16
ODORES			
Hic anemone humet, confert narcissus odores	O 209	Tr. Greek 5.74	3
OENI			
Inclytus hic haeres magni requiescit Oeni, ...	O 386	Tr Epi. Madoc D	1
OF			
To a Lady who spoke in Defence of Liberty	O 105	Lady Defence	T
Inscription on the collar of Mr. Banks's Goat . . .	O 156	Collari Caprae V	T
. . . having the Groundfloor of the Oratory . . .	O 385	The Warehouse D	T
OFFA			
Nec probrosa avidae grata sit offa gulae;	O 218	Tr Greek 9.573	2
OLIM			
Risurus olim nisibus Aemuli;	O 101	Ad Urbanum	14
Zosima, quae solo fuit olim corpore Serva, ...	O 114	Tr Gk Epigrams	1
Zosima, qua solo fuit olim corpore serva, ...	O 212	Tr Gk Epigrams V	7
Zosima, quondam solo fuit olim copore serva, ...	Y 320	Tr Gk Epigrams V	1
Olim, praeteritae numeranti tempora vitae, ...	O 171	Tr. Busy Fly	11
Mente senes olim juvenis, Faustine, premebas, . . .	O 225	Tr. Gk. 16.364	1
Laevum at utrumque decus, juveni quod praebuit olim . .	O 225	Tr. Gk. 16.364	3
"Perge modo, atque tuas olim post funera laudes . . .	O 386	In Birchium D	5

	PAGE	TITLE	LINE
OLIVAS			
Attollet reducis; bellis praetendet olivas	O 89	Messiah	22
OLYMPUM			
Jupiter hoc templum, ut, siquando relinquit Olympum, . .	O 219	Tr Greek 9.702	1
OLYMPUS			
Atthide non alius desit Olympus, habet.	O 219	Tr Greek 9.702	2
OMITTAT			
Quas servare velit, leges quas lentus omittat, ...	O 205	Christianus	21
OMNE			
Sic peragam tua jussa libens, accinctus ad omne . . .	O 207	Prayers IV	5
Perstrepit omne forum; cura molesta domi est. . . .	O 217	Tr Greek 9.359	2
Permeat omne forum; vita quieta domi est.	O 217	Tr Greek 9.360	2
Nil non mortale est mortalibus; omne quod est hi . . .	O 220	Tr Greek 10.31	1
Nil non mortale est mortalibus; omne quod est hic . . .	O 220	Tr Greek 10.31 V	1
Praetereunt, aut hos praeterit omne bonum.	O 220	Tr Greek 10.31	2
Seu prece poscatur, seu non, da Jupiter omne	O 221	Tr Greek 10.108	1
Magne bonum, omne malum et poscentibus abnue nobis. . .	O 221	Tr Greek 10.108	2
OMNES			
Omnes undique Gentes	O 155	Psalmus 117	7
Omnes si vellent virginitate frui;	O 218	Tr Greek 9.444	2
OMNESQUE			
Omnesque in partes tracta retracta fluit;	O 221	Tr Greek 10.74	4
OMNI			
Linguarumque omni terra discordia concors	O 161	Gnothi seauton	22
Linguarumque omni ex terra discordia concors	O 161	Gnothi seauton V	22
Ut tibi laus omni semper ab ore sonet:	O 232	Prayer	8
OMNIA			
Omnia, nec curae sunt sua sceptra Jovi.	O 103	Elizae Aenigma	2
Omnia foedantes, ...	O 109	Post-genitis	13
Omnia consuetus	O 110	Post-genitis	29
Gratum animum laudo; Qui debuit omnia ventis, ...	O 143	On Lord Anson	1
Qui nil virtuti, sed debuit omnia ventis, ...	O 143	On Lord Anson V	1
Omnia percurro trepidus, circum omnia lustro, ...	O 161	Gnothi seauton	32
Omnia percurro trepidus, circum omnia lustro, ...	O 161	Gnothi seauton	32
Nil movet insolitum, sub legibus omnia fictis	O 163	To Dr Lawrence	35
Spondens omnia credulis homullis;	O 204	Spes	4
Sed timeat semper, caveatque ante omnia, turbae . . .	O 205	Christianus	19
Ut tibi quae placeant, omnia promptus agam.	O 207	Prayers V	4
Omnia, dum Macedum gloria et arma premunt.	O 216	Tr Greek 9.288	4
Tecta ineunt; caelebs omnia solus ages;	O 217	Tr Greek 9.359	6
Omnia qui spectans, omnia ubique regis;	O 232	Prayer	4
Omnia qui spectans, omnia ubique regis;	O 232	Prayer	4
OMNIBUS			
Damnatis, poenam pro poenis omnibus unam.	O 160	Gnothi seauton	5
Omnibus unus amor, non est modus unus amoris.	O 163	To Dr Lawrence	8
Omnibus, artes	O 199	Medico Aeger S	29
OMNIPOTENS			
Me, pater omnipotens, de puro respice coelo, ...	O 207	Prayers V	1
OMNIS			
Excipit aethereis, Ars omnis plaudit amica, ...	O 161	Gnothi seauton	21
Excipit aethereis, Ars omnis plaudit amico, ...	O 161	Gnothi seauton V	21
Sceleris ut expers omnis, et vacuus metu, ...	O 206	Prayers I	9
Me miserum sors omnis habet; florentibus annis . . .	O 215	Tr Greek 9.138	1
Omnis vita nimis brevis est felicibus, una	O 220	Tr Greek 10.28	1
Vita omnis scena est ludusque; aut ludere disce . . .	O 221	Tr Greek 10.72	1
ON			
Inscription on the collar of Mr. Banks's Goat	O 156	Collari Caprae V	T
ONERANT			
Namque, ubi mensas onerant epulae, ...	O 193	Tr. Medea III	11
ONUS			
Fert humeris, venerabile onus, Cythereius heros . . .	O 216	Tr Greek 9.163	1
Dimidium tanti ponderis intret onus.	O 229	Epigram III	2
ONUSTA			
Nunquam jugera messibus onusta, aut	O 215	Tr Greek 9.110	1
OPACA			
Hic, in se totum longe per opaca futuri	O 116	Tr Pope Grotto	10
Et saltu e muro Ditis opaca petit:	O 211	Tr Greek 7.471	2
OPACAE			
Speluncae late Thamesis praetendit opacae, ...	O 116	Tr Pope Grotto	2
OPE			
Nunc ope supplicii vivit imago mei.	O 225	Tr Greek 16.87	2
OPELLAE			
Scaliger ut duxit, tenuis pertaesus opellae, ...	O 160	Gnothi seauton	2
OPERAE			
Participes operae Camoenas.	O 101	Ad Urbanum	16
OPERUM			
Non operum serie, seriem dum computat aevi, ...	O 162	Gnothi seauton	46
OPES			
Temnere opes pretium sceleris, patriamque tueri . . .	O 116	Tr Pope Grotto	15
Nec miratur opes, celsa speculator ab arce	O 161	Gnothi seauton V	39
Non Rationis opes Animus, nunc parta recensens, . . .	O 161	Gnothi seauton	42
Opes, triumphos, et subacti	O 188	Epilogus	3
Queis uti nequeo, nunc mihi praebet opes.	O 215	Tr Greek 9.138	4
Verte solum, fient causa timoris opes;	O 217	Tr Greek 9.359	4
OPHYRAEIS			
Solis Ophyraeis crudum tibi montibus aurum	O 92	Messiah	104
OPIMA			
Ter sex centurias Hollandia jactat opima	O 231	Geographia Met	35
OPPIDA			
Resonabunt Oppida Luctu:	O 109	Post-genitis	8

```
                                                          PAGE    TITLE              LINE
OPTANT
    Scire vices ponti facile est, nihil amplius optant   . .   O 163 To Dr Lawrence    15
OPTARIT
    Optarit quicunque senex sibi longius aevum, . . . . .     O 214 Tr Greek 9.55       1
OPTAT
    Cum procul est, optat, cum venit, quisque senectam   . .   O 214 Tr Greek 9.54       1
OPTATUM
    Natus ad optatum perducet coepta parentis. . . . . .     O  90 Messiah            72
OPTENT
    Ergo optent homines, aut nunquam in luminis oras  . . .   O 217 Tr Greek 9.359      9
OPTET
    Nemo optet nunquam venisse in luminis oras, . . . . .    O 217 Tr Greek 9.360      9
OPTO
    Non opto aut precibus posco ditescere, paucis  . . . .   O 222 Tr. Gk. 10.113      1
OPULENTUS
    Cur opulentus eges? tua cuncta in foenore ponis.  . . .   O 223 Tr. Gk. 11.167      1
OPUM
    Versat opum cumulos, et se miratur in illis,    . . . .   O 161 Gnothi seauton   V 43
OPUS
    Atria, pacis opus, surgent, finemque caduci . . . . .    O  90 Messiah            71
    Nil opus est aeris sacra de turre sonantis  . . . . .    O 170 Insula Kenneth   V 18A
    Exsurge fortis, nunc animis opus, . . . . . . . . .      O 187 Ad T. L. M.D.      14
    Utile cunctis hoc opus esset;  . . . . . . . . . .       O 193 Tr. Medea III      10
    Plenum opus effugiens; aptans juga mollia collo   . .    O 205 Christianus        22
    Pythagoras mallet, vocem habuisset opus. . . . . .       O 225 Tr. Gk. 16.326      2
    Dulce Venus ridens, lorica nil opus, inquit,  . . . .    O 384 Epigramma        D  3
    Hic Bona queis opus est venditat, Ille Sonum. . . . .    O 385 The Warehouse    D  6
    Aeternum Aeterna Luce juvabit opus! . . . . . . .        O 393 Tr. of Crashaw   D  6
ORA
    Et morbus tegitur, dum premit ora pudor. . . . . . .     O 221 Tr Greek 10.98      2
    Corusca a radiis Memnonis ora dabant. . . . . . . .      Y  28 Aurora Musis       16
    Oribus ora suis. . . . . . . . . . . . . . . . .         O 385 Cantico Solom.   D 10
ORAS
    Ergo optent homines, aut nunquam in luminis oras  . . .   O 217 Tr Greek 9.359      9
    Nemo optet nunquam venisse in luminis oras, . . . . .    O 217 Tr Greek 9.360      9
ORATOR
    Orator statua est, statuaeque orator imago. . . . . .    O 223 Tr. Gk. 11.145      2
    Orator statua est, statuaeque orator imago. . . . . .    O 223 Tr. Gk. 11.145      2
ORATORY
    . . . having the Groundfloor of the Oratory  . . . .     O 385 The Warehouse    D  T
ORBAT
    Proles aucta gravat, rapta orbat, caeca juventae est  . .   O 217 Tr Greek 9.359      7
ORBE
    Tertii verso quater orbe lustri,   . . . . . . . .       O 153 In Theatro          1
    Hunc sequitur caelebs; tertius, orbe, venis. . . . .     O 222 Tr Greek 11.50      2
ORBEM
    Ingentemque animo seclorum volverat orbem. . . . . .     O 160 Gnothi seauton     11
    Ingentemque animo seclorum volveret orbem. . . . . .     O 160 Gnothi seauton   V 11
    His Tempelmanni numeris descripseris orbem. . . . . .    O 229 Geographia Met      1
ORBI
    Nec quaerunt quid, luna, tuo cum fluctibus orbi. . . .    O 163 To Dr Lawrence     16
    Ut dicas, spatiis quam latis imperet orbi  . . . . .     O 230 Geographia Met     16
ORBIS
    Et curas felix patrias testabitur orbis. . . . . . .     O  90 Messiah            65
    Sit sacer orbis amor, miseris qui semper adesse   . .    O 205 Christianus         7
ORBITA
    Anni qua volucris ducitur orbita, . . . . . . . . .      O 155 Psalmus 117         1
ORCI
    Aeternoque orci dominator vulnere languens  . . . . .    O  90 Messiah            55
    Et ferus est Timon sub terris; janitor Orci,   . . .     O 211 Tr Greek 7.319      1
ORCUS
    Idem Orcus terrae, sic, pelagoque subest. . . . . .      O 210 Tr Greek 7.265      2
    E longinquo itidem pontus et orcus erat. . . . . . .     O 213 Tr Greek 9.29       6
ORDINE
    Particulasque locans, certas certo ordine, pulchram   . .   O 163 To Dr Lawrence     28
ORDINIBUS
    Ordinibus surgit densis, vitamque requirit  . . . . .    O  92 Messiah            9,7
ORDO
    Sic orsus--Qualis rerum mihi nascitur ordo! . . . . .    O  88 Messiah             9
ORE
    Multiplici reducem circumsonat ore magistrum. . . . .    O 161 Gnothi seauton     23
    Ut tibi laus omni semper ab ore sonet: . . . . . .      O 232 Prayer              8
    Fundit ab ore melos, . . . . . . . . . . . . .          O 385 Cantico Solom.   D  8
    Et placido tandem haec edidit ore, Dea: . . . . . .     O 386 In Birchium      D  4
ORIBUS
    Oribus ora suis. . . . . . . . . . . . . . . . .         O 385 Cantico Solom.   D 10
ORNAT
    Rus ornat natura; levat maris aspera lucrum; . . . .     O 217 Tr Greek 9.360      3
ORNATISSIMUMQUE
    In Locupletissimum ornatissimumque Syl<vani>. Urb<ani>. .   O 383 Syl. Urb. Thes.  D  T
ORSUS
    Sic orsus--Qualis rerum mihi nascitur ordo! . . . . .    O  88 Messiah             9
ORTUM
    Volvantur celeres anni! Lux purpuret ortum . . . . .     O  89 Messiah            25
ORTUS
    Tunc alacres demum surgent, et crastinus ortus . . . .   O 393 Tr. of Crashaw   D  5
OSCULA
    Aeriaeque columbae, dantes oscula, jungunt . . . . .     O 385 Cantico Solom.   D  9
OSSA
    Nil lucri facies; ossa habet et cinerem. . . . . . .     O 210 Tr Greek 7.284      4
```

		PAGE	TITLE		LINE
OTIA					
Sive libros poscant otia, sive lyram.		O 170	Insula Kenneth		14
OTIOSIS					
Lusibus gaudet puer otiosis, ...		O 153	In Theatro		13
OVES					
Amissas modo quaerit oves, revocatque vagantes;	. . .	O 90	Messiah		61
PACATAS					
Pacatas niveo Virtus lucebit amictu.		O 89	Messiah	V	24
PACEMQUE					
Da veniam pacemque mihi, da, mente serena, ...		O 207	Prayers V		3
PACIS					
Atria, pacis opus, surgent, finemque caduci		O 90	Messiah		71
Veniaeque sancta pacis adde gaudia:		O 206	Prayers I		8
PAENITUISSE					
Judice quo scelerum est paenituisse salus, ...		O 198	Tr. Ash Wed.		2
Cuique loco recti paenituisse mali est		O 198	Tr. Ash Wed.	V	2
Cuique loco recte paenituisse mali est		O 198	Tr. Ash Wed.	V	2
PAGINA					
Non ulla Musis Pagina gratior, ...		O 102	Ad Urbanum		17
Assurgitque epicis pagina docta modis.		Y 28	Aurora Musis		10
PALESTRAE					
Hujus palestrae qui vigil custos stetit, ...		O 223	Tr. Gk. 11.176		3
PALLAS					
Pallas ubique docet; ridet ubique Venus.		O 383	Syl. Urb. Thes	D	4
Armatam Pallas Venerem conspexit, et eia		O 384	Epigramma	D	1
PALLIDA					
Atque Aethra ambigua pallida luce rubet;		Y 28	Aurora Musis		2
PALMAS					
Non numerat palmas, aut		O 162	Gnothi seauton	V	46
PALMIS					
Artificis frondent dextrae; Spinetaque Palmis		O 91	Messiah	V	82
Tractabit palmis infans, motusque trisulcae		O 91	Messiah		90
PALMISQUE					
Artificis frondent dextrae; palmisque rubeta		O 91	Messiah		82
PALPANTUR					
Hinc annis palpantur delenda poemata nullis		Y 28	Aurora Musis		11
Hinc annis palpantur delenda poemata palpantur . . .		Y 28	Aurora Musis	V	11
Hinc annis palpantur delenda poemata palpantur . . .		Y 28	Aurora Musis	V	11
PAMPINUS					
Munera luxurians dat pampinus, et generoso		O 385	Cantico Solom.	D	13
PANDATUR					
Materies, vastum an late pandatur inane.		O 163	To Dr Lawrence		14
Materia, vastum an late pandatur inane.		O 163	To Dr Lawrence	V	14
PANDET					
Ille vias vocis pandet, flexusque liquentis		O 90	Messiah		47
PANDIS					
Skia sinum nebulosa pandis.		O 166	Oda Isle Skye		4
PANDITUR					
Ingredere! Egeriae sacrum en tibi panditur antrum! . .		O 116	Tr Pope Grotto		9
Nota, Caledonias panditur inter aquas;		O 169	Insula Kenneth		2
Clara, Caledonias panditur inter aquas;		O 169	Insula Kenneth	V	2
PANDUNT					
Coelicolae pandunt, torrentisque aurea lucis		O 92	Messiah		107
Coelicolae pandunt, crescentis et aurea lucis . . .		O 92	Messiah	V	107
Coelicolae pandunt, torrentis aurea lucis		O 92	Messiah	V	107
PAPA					
Papa suo regit imperio ter millia quinque.		O 230	Geographia Met		12
PAPAPER					
Dulce papaper.		O 199	Medico Aeger S	V	14
PAPAVER					
Dulce papaver.		O 199	Medico Aeger S		14
PAR					
Ut studiis sperem, aut ausim par esse querelis, . . .		O 160	Gnothi seauton		15
PARARE					
Parare posse, ut Stoicorum		O 166	Oda Isle Skye		15
Parare posse, utcunque jactet		O 166	Oda Isle Skye	V	15
PARCA					
Parca, juventutem non miserata tuam!		O 212	Tr Greek 7.560		6
PARCAS					
Ingenio parcas, nec sit mihi culpa rogasse, ...		O 204	Losing Speech		3
Ingenio parcas, nec sit mihi culpa precari		O 204	Losing Speech	V	3
PARCE					
Plura ut victurus secula, parce bonis:		O 219	Tr Greek 10.26		2
PARCIT					
Divitiis, utrinque cavens, qui tempore parcit, . . .		O 219	Tr Greek 10.26		3
PAREM					
Hirce, parem nitido te tua barba facit.		O 224	Tr. Gk. 11.430		2
Non poteras, regio non tulit ulla parem.		O 225	Tr. Gk. 16.331		6
PARENS					
Recte ut poeniteat, respice, magne parens.		O 207	Prayers VI		6
PARENTEM					
Ingredere O!--Magnam pura cole mente parentem, . . .		O 116	Tr Pope Grotto		7
Ingredere O!--rerum pura cole mente parentem, . . .		O 116	Tr Pope Grotto	V	7
PARENTIS					
Natus ad optatum perducet coepta parentis.		O 90	Messiah		72
Materiemque rudem, magnaeque parentis adesse . . .		O 163	To Dr Lawrence		21
PARETE					
Ad Musas Venus haec: Veneri parete, puellae, ...		O 213	Tr Greek 9.39		1
PARI					
Et Pari, et Anchisa, non alius, Venerem.		O 225	Tr. Gk. 16.168		2

502

	PAGE	TITLE	LINE
PARIBUS			
Ad Divos paribus passibus ire duces;	O 225	Tr. Gk. 16.331	4
PARIT			
Virgo! virgo parit! felix radicibus arbor	O 88	Messiah	10
Spes novas nova lux parit, secunda	O 204	Spes	3
Prima parit terras aetas; siccatque secunda;	O 226	Septem Aetates	1
PARITURAM			
Ad Lauram parituram Epigramma	O 115	Ad Lauram Epig	T
PARITURUM			
Luctus mox pariturum.	O 182	Waltoni Piscat	14
PARNASSUM			
Sit tibi, Calliope, Parnassum, cura, tenenti,	O 218	Tr Greek 9.523	1
PARS			
Altera pars hominum, sanctae rationis alumni,	O 163	To Dr Lawrence	19
Cui pars verbosae, vel datur ima, domus?	O 385	The Warehouse	D 4
PARTA			
Non Rationis opes Animus, nunc parta recensens,	O 161	Gnothi seauton	42
Non Animus sero nimium dum parta recenset,	O 161	Gnothi seauton	V 42
PARTE			
Qua solum potero parte, placere tibi.	O 204	Losing Speech	4
Qua solum potero parte, litare tibi.	O 204	Losing Speech	V 4
Quot vox missa pedes abit horae parte secunda?	O 229	Epigram IV	1
PARTES			
Nec natet, et nunc has partes, nunc eligat illas,	O 205	Christianus	16
Omnesque in partes tracta retracta fluit;	O 221	Tr Greek 10.74	4
PARTHENOPE			
Parthenope. Novies vult tellus mille Sicana.	O 230	Geographia Met.	11
PARTICIPEMQUE			
Musca, meae comitem, participemque dapis,	O 171	Tr. Busy Fly	2
PARTICIPES			
Participes operae Camoenas.	O 101	Ad Urbanum	16
PARTICULASQUE			
Particulasque locans, certas certo ordine, pulchram	O 163	To Dr Lawrence	28
PARUM			
Quid et minetur, sollicitus parum,	O 101	Ad Urbanum	6
PARVA			
Parva quidem regio, sed relligione priorum	O 169	Insula Kenneth	1
PASCERE			
Humanae mentis, rerum se pascere formis,	O 163	To Dr Lawrence	6
PASCET			
Sive cum libris novitate pascet	O 168	Oda to Thrale	V 15
PASCIT			
Sive cum libris novitate pascit	O 168	Oda to Thrale	15
Qui pascit barbam si crescit mente, Platoni,	O 224	Tr. Gk. 11.430	1
PASCUA			
Pascua, qua blandum spirat purissimus aer	O 90	Messiah	58
Populari Pascua laetus.	O 110	Post-genitis	30
PASSIBUS			
Ad Divos paribus passibus ire duces;	O 225	Tr. Gk. 16.331	4
PASSIM			
Quandoquidem passim nulla ratione feruntur	O 222	Tr. Gk. 10.124	1
PASSUS			
Triste nihil passus, animi at de sorte Platonis	O 211	Tr Greek 7.471	3
PASTOR			
Pastor agit pecudes, teneros modo suscipit agnos,	O 90	Messiah	59
Postera sic pastor divinus secla beabit,	O 90	Messiah	64
Pastor Arabs: decies octo sibi Persa requirit.	O 230	Geographia Met	9
PATEAT			
Si qua usquam pateat melioris semita vitae,	O 161	Gnothi seauton	33
Myrias, ut menti pateat tota Africa doctae.	O 230	Geographia Met	24
PATENT			
Nexa patent; hi sunt quos nil mirabile turbat,	O 163	To Dr Lawrence	34
Longinquisque oculis nuda lavacra patent.	O 228	Rivum a Stoana	8
Summe Deus, cui caeca patent penetralia cordis;	O 232	Prayer	1
PATER			
Luna vices revehet; radios pater ipse diei	O 92	Messiah	110
Grates, summe Pater, tuis	O 164	Recover Eyes	13
Summe Pater, quodcunque tuum de corpore Numen	O 204	Losing Speech	1
Summe Pater, quodcunque tuae de corpore leges	O 204	Losing Speech	V 1
Pater benigne, summa semper lenitas,	O 206	Prayers I	1
Veniam petenti, summe da veniam, pater;	O 206	Prayers I	7
O Qui benignus crimina ignoscis, pater	O 206	Prayers III	1
Numine praesenti me tueare pater!	O 207	Prayers IV	2
Me, pater omnipotens, de puro respice coelo,	O 207	Prayers V	1
Et pro me pretium, tu patiare, pater.	O 207	Prayers V	6
Summe Pater, puro collustra lumine pectus,	O 207	Prayers VII	1
Da, ne sint permissa, pater, mihi praemia frustra,	O 208	Prayers VII	9
Da, ne sint promissa, pater, mihi praemia frustra,	O 208	Prayers VII	V 9
Quaerere, quis, cujas, quis pater, unde venis.	O 219	Tr Greek 9.648	2
Me Pater tandem reducem benigno	O 227	A Meditation	5
Dum docuit blanda voce natare pater.	O 228	Rivum a Stoana	4
PATERIS			
Nec vincis acer, nec pateris pius;	O 187	Ad T. L. M.D.	6
PATERNIS			
Sollicitus nimis, heu! paternis.	O 187	Ad T. L. M.D.	12
PATET			
Fortis, ades, tibi sponte patet venerabile limen.	O 116	Tr Pope Grotto	V 16
PATI			
Seria seponens, aut mala dura pati.	O 221	Tr Greek 10.72	2
PATIARE			
Et pro me pretium, tu patiare, pater.	O 207	Prayers V	6

```
PATRANS                                                   PAGE   TITLE              LINE
    Impia facta patrans, homines fortasse latebis,  . . . .  O 220  Tr Greek 10.27        1
PATREM
    Patrem coelicolum perpetuo colunt  . . . . . . . .       O 155  Psalmus 117           2
    Patrem cujus amor blandior in dies . . . . . . . .       O 155  Psalmus 117           5
    In lecto. utrobique Patrem  . . . . . . . . .            O 155  Psalmus 117       V   9
    Suspiciat tandem clementem in numine patrem.  . . . .    O 205  Christianus           5
    In summo ut videas numine laeta patrem;  . . . . .       O 208  A Meditation          2
    Per Trojae flammas, densaque tela, patrem.  . . . . .    O 216  Tr Greek 9.163        2
    Confessus tantum mente manuque patrem;  . . . . . . .    O 386  Tr Epi. Madoc     D   2
PATRI
    Permitte summo res hominum Patri,  . . . . . . . . .     O 187  Ad T. L. M.D.        17
    Permitte summo quicquid habes Patri,  . . . . . . .      O 187  Ad T. L. M.D.     V  17
PATRIA
    Effundet Patria Fletus,  . . . . . . . . . .             O 109  Post-genitis          6
    Patria Sparta mihi est, patria clara virum. . . . . .    O 224  Tr Greek 16.1         2
    Patria Sparta mihi est, patria clara virum. . . . . .    O 224  Tr Greek 16.1         2
PATRIAE
    Morte memor patriae; hic Marcmonti pectore prima  . . .  O 116  Tr Pope Grotto       13
    Conjugium, ut pro te des hominem patriae.  . . . . .     O 218  Tr Greek 9.444        4
PATRIAMQUE
    Temnere opes pretium sceleris, patriamque tueri  . .     O 116  Tr Pope Grotto       15
PATRIAS
    Et curas felix patrias testabitur orbis. . . . . . .     O  90  Messiah              65
PATRIS
    Patris Numen adire est.  . . . . . . . . .               O 182  Waltoni Piscat       10
PATROCINATA
    . . . causae in sermone patrocinata fuerat.  . . . .     O 105  Lady Defence      V   T
PAUCIS
    Incultum Studiis, et paucis dotibus auctum  . . . . .    O 161  Gnothi seauton    V  36
    Non opto aut precibus posco ditescere, paucis . . . .    O 222  Tr. Gk. 10.113        1
PAULATIM
    Paulatim mores, animum, vitamque refingit,  . . . . .    O 205  Christianus          28
PAULUM
    Paulum vita moratur,  . . . . . . . . . . .              O 182  Waltoni Piscat        6
PAUPER
    Pauper eram, nummis diffluit arca senis;  . . . . . .    O 215  Tr Greek 9.138        2
    Sic aliis dives, tu tibi pauper agis. . . . . . . .      O 223  Tr. Gk. 11.167        2
PAUPERIEM
    Recta ad pauperiem tendit, cui corpora cordi est  . .    O 222  Tr. Gk. 10.119        1
PAUPERIEQUE
    Pauperieque Irus, curaque prima Deum. . . . . . . .      O 114  Tr Gk Epigrams        4
    Pauperieque Irus, curaque summa Deum. . . . . . . .      O 212  Tr Greek 7.676        2
PAUPERIES
    Pauperies latitat, cum conjuge gaudia multa . . . . .    O 217  Tr Greek 9.360        5
    Assidet huic custos strenua pauperies.  . . . . . .      O 219  Tr Greek 9.654        2
PAUPERTAS
    Paupertas misera est; multae cum conjuge lites  . . .    O 217  Tr Greek 9.359        5
PAX
    Compositis Pax alma suas, terrasque revisens  . . . .    O  89  Messiah              23
    His blanda certe pax habitat locis:  . . . . . . .       O 166  Oda Isle Skye         6
PECCANTI
    Sanguine, peccanti promereare tuo!  . . . . . . . .      O 208  Prayers VII          12
PECCANTUM
    Quem nil vafrities peccantum subdola celat;  . . . .     O 232  Prayer                3
PECCATOR
    Peccator, ad latus meum;  . . . . . . . . .              O 203  Christ Sinner         2
    Et sibi, delirans quanquam et peccator in horas  . .     O 205  Christianus          14
PECTORA
    Tu mihi, qui flamma movisti pectora sancti  . . . . .    O  88  Messiah               6
    Legitimas faciunt pectora pura preces.  . . . . . .      O 170  Insula Kenneth       20
    Sint pro legitimis pectora pura sacris  . . . . . .      O 170  Insula Kenneth    V  20
    Pectora molli mulcet dubiae . . . . . . . . . .          O 193  Tr. Medea III        14
PEGTORE
    Humani studium generis cui pectore fervet,  . . . . .    O 102  Ad R. Savage          1
    Morte memor patriae; hic Marcmonti pectore prima  . . .  O 116  Tr Pope Grotto       13
    Ardeat huic toto sacer ignis pectore, possit  . . . .    O 205  Christianus          10
    Displiceat, servet tutum sub pectore rectum:  . . . .    O 205  Christianus          15
    Pectore qui duro, crudos de vite racemos  . . . . . .    O 217  Tr Greek 9.375        1
PECTORIS
    Exaestuantis pectoris impetum,  . . . . . . . . .        O 166  Oda Isle Skye        17
PECTUS
    Non planctus, non moesta sonant suspiria, pectus  . .    O  90  Messiah              52
    Pectus, et ingenium vano se robore jactans. . . . . .    O 161  Gnothi seauton       36
    Et summi accendat pectus amore boni.  . . . . . . .      O 170  Insula Kenneth    V 16B
    Fulsit, in pectus mihi fonte purum  . . . . . . .        O 193  Prayer on Xmas        2
    Summe Pater, puro collustra lumine pectus,  . . . . .    O 207  Prayers VII           1
    Mulcere, aut pectus triste levare malis. . . . . . .     O 218  Tr Greek 9.375        8
    Luce collustret mihi pectus alma,  . . . . . . .         O 227  A Meditation          1
PECTUSQUE
    Notior ipse mihi fieri, pectusque fateri  . . . . . .    O 161  Gnothi seauton    V  35
PECUDES
    Pastor agit pecudes, teneros modo suscipit agnos,  . .   O  90  Messiah              59
PECUNIA
    Mater adulantum prolesque, Pecunia, curae,  . . . . .    O 218  Tr Greek 9.394        1
PEDE
    Vel Pede Equus tanget,  . . . . . . . . . .              O 109  Post-genitis          3
PEDES
    Hic oculos socio commodat, ille pedes.  . . . . . .      O 213  Tr Greek 9.13         2
    Trajecit montes nauta, fretumque pedes,  . . . . . .     O 217  Tr Greek 9.304        2
    Quot vox missa pedes abit horae parte secunda? . . . .   O 229  Epigram IV            1
```

		PAGE	TITLE	LINE
PEDIBUS				
Sub pedibus subjecta jacent; queis ultima primis	. . .	O 163	To Dr Lawrence	33
Sub pedibus, populo praetereunte, jacit,	. . .	O 218	Tr Greek 9.375	4
Tangitur haud pedibus tellus; conviva Deorum	. . .	O 219	Tr Greek 9.577	3
PELAGI				
Imperium pelagi precantes.	. . . .	O 188	Epilogus	4
PELAGOQUE				
Idem Orcus terrae, sic, pelagoque subest.	. . .	O 210	Tr Greek 7.265	2
Militibus; terris sit pelagoque pudor!	. . .	O 217	Tr Greek 9.304	4
PELLAT				
Pellat et tristes animi tenebras,	. . . . .	O 227	A Meditation	2
PELLE				
Mus blandum ridens, respondit, pelle timorem;	. . .	O 224	Tr. Gk. 11.391	3
PELLEM				
Balnea pellem,	. . . .	O 199	Medico Aeger S	19
PELLENS				
Rege, et tuere, quae nocent pellens procul;	. . .	O 206	Prayers I	6
PELLERE				
Voce aut fidibus pellere docuit	. . . . . .	O 193	Tr. Medea III	8
PELOPIS				
Sortitur Pelopis tellus quae nomine gaudet.	. . .	O 230	Geographia Met	7
PENDET				
Pendet, et incoquitur tectum sine fraude metallum:	. .	O 116	Tr Pope Grotto	6
PENDULA				
Pendula secretas abdidit arbor aquas.	. . . .	O 228	Rivum a Stoana	6
PENETRALIA				
Summe Deus, cui caeca patent penetralia cordis;	. . .	O 232	Prayer	1
PENNAS				
Tolle, Salema, sacros, quam circum gloria pennas	. . .	O 92	Messiah	94
PENNIS				
Cum fugere haud possit fractis Victoria pennis,	. . .	O 219	Tr Greek 9.647	1
Hermem Deorum nuncium, pennis levem,	. . . .	O 223	Tr. Gk. 11.176	1
PENSI				
Me, pensi immunis cum jam mihi reddor, inertis	. . .	O 161	Gnothi seauton	24
PENSILIBUS				
Pensilibus fusis, cyatho comitata supremo,	. . . .	O 383	On the Gin-Act	D 1
PENURIA				
Ingeniumque sui cohibet penuria census.	. . .	O 161	Gnothi seauton	V 38
Res angusta domi, et macrae penuria mentis.	. . .	O 161	Gnothi seauton	41
PEPETUO				
Regem coelicolum pepetuo colunt	. . . .	O 155	Psalmus 117	V 2
PER				
Immatura calens rapitur per saecula vates,	. . .	O 88	Messiah	8
Ille futura calens rapitur per saecula vates,	. . .	O 88	Messiah	V 8
Per saxa, ignivomi nuper spelaea draconis,	. . .	O 91	Messiah	78
Per valles sociata lupo lasciviet agna,	. . .	O 91	Messiah	84
Per ludum pueri injicient, et fessa colubri	. . .	O 91	Messiah	87
En! formosa tibi porrecta per atria proles	. . .	O 92	Messiah	96
En! formosa tibi spatiosa per atria proles	. . .	O 92	Messiah	V 96
Victrix per obstantes catervas	. . . .	O 101	Ad Urbanum	11
Serpent per Prata Colubri,	. . . . .	O 109	Post-genitis	10
Ibunt per cuncta minaces,	. . . . .	O 109	Post-genitis	16
Hic, in se totum longe per opaca futuri	. . .	O 116	Tr Pope Grotto	10
Tene per pictas oculo elegante	. . . .	O 153	In Theatro	7
Et rerum volitant rarae per inane figurae.	. . .	O 162	Gnothi seauton	51
Qua sulcat, reptant tuti per lubrica vitae.	. . .	O 163	To Dr Lawrence	18
Gens illa, impatiens per singula quaeque vagandi.	. . .	O 163	To Dr Lawrence	23
Huc ego delatus placido per coerula cursu	. . .	O 169	Insula Kenneth	5
Nunc, per gramina fusi,	. . . .	O 181	Waltoni Piscat	1
Per caeca noctis taedia turbidae,	. . . .	O 187	Ad T. L. M.D.	9
Pigrae per horas lucis inutiles,	. . . .	O 187	Ad T. L. M.D.	10
Per Christum ut veniam sit reperire mihi.	. . .	O 198	Tr. Ash Wed.	4
Per vitae tenebras rerumque incerta vagantem	. . .	O 207	Prayers IV	1
Fert humeris claudum validis per compita caecus,	. . .	O 213	Tr Greek 9.13	1
Per Trojae flammas, densaque tela, patrem.	. . .	O 216	Tr Greek 9.163	2
Per certis stabili lege voluta vices,	. . .	O 219	Tr Greek 9.577	2
Per fluctus vitae sic tibi cursus erit.	. . .	O 221	Tr Greek 10.74	6
Errat adhuc vitreus per prata virentia rivus,	. . .	O 228	Rivum a Stoana	1
Harmonia tellus completur lata, per agros	. . .	Y 28	Aurora Musis	3
Et petiit terras per freta longa novas.	. . .	O 386	Tr Epi. Madoc	D 4
PERAGAM				
Quid mecum peragam, quod tu doctissime posses	. . .	O 163	To Dr Lawrence	4
Sic peragam tua jussa libens, accinctus ad omne	. . .	O 207	Prayers IV	5
PERAGIT				
Hora sic peragit citata cursum;	. . . . .	O 204	Spes	1
PERCONTERE				
Nauta, quis hoc jaceat ne percontere sepulchro;	. . .	O 211	Tr Greek 7.350	1
PERCURRO				
Omnia percurro trepidus, circum omnia lustro,	. . .	O 161	Gnothi seauton	32
PERDIDI				
Sed quod reliqui, perdidi.	. . . .	O 165	Tr Doncast Epi	3
PERDUCAT				
Quae nos blanda comes, quae nos perducat eodem,	. . .	O 171	Tr. Busy Fly	7
PERDUCET				
Natus ad optatum perducet coepta parentis.	. . .	O 90	Messiah	72
PEREGRE				
. . . filium peregre agentem desiderio nimis	. . .	O 186	Ad T. L. M.D.	V T
PEREGRINIS				
Ecce! peregrinis fervent tua limina turbis;	. . .	O 92	Messiah	99
PERENNE				
Te manet imperii, Roma, perenne decus.	. . . . .	O 219	Tr Greek 9.647	2

	PAGE	TITLE	LINE
PERENNIS			
Lympha tamen cursus agit indefessa perennis, ...	O 228	Rivum a Stoana	9
PEREUNTE			
Tutum aliis aequor, me pereunte, fuit.	O 210	Tr Greek 7.282	2
PEREUNTES			
Divitias cumulas, pereuntes negligis horas, ...	O 220	Tr Greek 10.60	3
PERFECTO			
E Waltoni Piscatore Perfecto excerptum.	O 181	Waltoni Piscat	V T
PERFECTUS			
Waltoni Piscator perfectus	O 181	Waltoni Piscat	T
PERGE			
Vacare solis perge Musis, ...	O 101	Ad Urbanum	7
"Perge modo, atque tuas olim post funera laudes . . .	O 386	In Birchium	D 5
PERGIT			
Pergit, et imperiis sentit se dulcibus actum. . . .	O 205	Christianus	27
PERICULA			
Rura labor lassat; mare mille pericula terrent; . . .	O 217	Tr Greek 9.359	3
PERIERE			
Nunc veteres duris periere securibus umprae, . . .	O 228	Rivum a Stoana	7
PERIISSE			
Aut periisse; scatet vita benigna bonis.	O 217	Tr Greek 9.360	10
PERIRET			
Pulchra est virginitas intacta, at vita periret, . . .	O 218	Tr Greek 9.444	1
PERIT			
Ut florem amittat gratia tota perit	Y 332	Tr Greek 10.30	V 1
Hora perit furtim laetis, mens temporis aegra . . .	O 228	Jactura Tempor	1
Pigritiam incusat, nec minus hora perit.	O 228	Jactura Tempor	2
PERITAM			
Crethida fabellas dulces garrire peritam	O 211	Tr Greek 7.459	1
PERITURA			
Haec peritura nitent; tu peritura nites!	O 209	Tr. Greek 5.74	6
Haec peritura nitent; tu peritura nites!	O 209	Tr. Greek 5.74	6
PERMEAT			
Permeat omne forum; vita quieta domi est.	O 217	Tr Greek 9.360	2
PERMEO			
Permeo terras, ubi nuda rupes	O 167	Oda to Thrale	1
PERMISSA			
Da, ne sint permissa, pater, mihi praemia frustra, . .	O 208	Prayers VII	9
PERMISSUM			
Permissum credit nudas sibi sistere causas, ...	O 163	To Dr Lawrence	20
PERMISTAS			
Innocua hic membris permistas membra columbas . . .	O 393	Tr. of Crashaw	D 1
PERMITTE			
Permitte summo res hominum Patri, ...	O 187	Ad T. L. M.D.	17
Permitte summo quicquid habes Patri, ...	O 187	Ad T. L. M.D.	V 17
Permitte fidens, ac muliebribus, ...	O 187	Ad T. L. M.D.	18
Permitte fidens, et muliebribus, ...	O 187	Ad T. L. M.D.	V 18
PERMITTI			
Ima tuas credit permitti, Scaliger, iras.	O 160	Gnothi seauton	13
PERMULCEAT			
Divinos, surdas sacra vox permulceat aures!	O 89	Messiah	43
PERNICIBUS			
Huc, soror alma, veni! pernicibus ocyor Euris	O 385	Cantico Solom.	D 17
PERPETUA			
Perpetua, ambita bis terra, praemia lactis	O 156	Collari Caprae	V 1
PERPETUI			
Perpetui, ambita bis terra, praemia lactis	O 156	Collari Caprae	1
PERPETUO			
Perpetuo viret et virebit;	O 101	Ad Urbanum	4
Patrem coelicolum perpetuo colunt	O 155	Psalmus 117	2
Denique perpetuo contendit in ardua nisu, ...	O 205	Christianus	25
PERPETUUS			
Rerum perpetuus temperat Arbiter, ...	O 164	Recover Eyes	2
PERSA			
Pastor Arabs: decies octo sibi Persa requirit.	O 230	Geographia Met	9
PERSCRIPSERAT			
Arte nova, raraque fide perscripserat ausus	O 386	In Birchium	D 1
PERSTREPIT			
Perstrepit omne forum; cura molesta domi est.	O 217	Tr Greek 9.359	2
PERTAESUS			
Scaliger ut duxit, tenuis pertaesus opellae, ...	O 160	Gnothi seauton	2
PERVAGOR			
Pervagor gentes, hominum ferorum	O 167	Oda to Thrale	5
Pervagor terras, hominum ferorum	O 167	Oda to Thrale	V 5
PESSIME			
Quid salvere jubes me, pessime? Corripe gressus; . . .	O 211	Tr Greek 7.318	1
PETAT			
Cerbere, te morsu ne petat ille, cave.	O 211	Tr Greek 7.319	2
PETENTI			
Veniam petenti, summe da veniam, pater;	O 206	Prayers I	7
PETET			
Cumque leone petet tutus praesepe juvencus.	O 91	Messiah	85
PETIIT			
Et petiit terras per freta longa novas.	O 386	Tr Epi. Madoc	D 4
PETIT			
Et saltu e muro Ditis opaca petit:	O 211	Tr Greek 7.471	2
PETITA			
Et cycnum fecit Leda petita Jovem.	O 214	Tr Greek 9.48	2
PETO			
Quod vitae satis est, peto, Macrine:	O 215	Tr Greek 9.110	3
Hic, bone vir, sedem, non alimenta, peto.	O 224	Tr. Gk. 11.391	4

	PAGE	TITLE	LINE
PETULANTES			
Florea mansuetae petulantes vincula tigri	O 91	Messiah	86
PHIDIACA			
Saxea Phidiaca spirat imago manu.	O 85	Adjecere bonae	4
PHIDIACI			
Copia, Phidiaci foecunda potentia coeli.	O 161	Gnothi seauton	39
PHIDO			
Haud lavit Phido, haud tetigit; mihi febre calenti . .	O 223	Tr. Gk. 11.118	1
PHILIPPE			
Quo tua signantur gesta, Philippe, lapis.	O 216	Tr Greek 9.288	2
PHILOMELA			
Veris, io! venit alma dies! Philomela canorum	O 385	Cantico Solom. D	7
PHOEBE			
Phoebe fave, aegrotat quae te colit, ulla nec usquam est	O 197	Summ. Lawrence	1
PHOEBI			
Ignis quem Phoebi naribus efflat equus, ...	Y 28	Aurora Musis	14
Quem efflant quem rem Phoebi naribus ignis equi . . .	Y 28	Aurora Musis V	14
PHOEBO			
Si Phoebo, victor nescit obire diem.	O 210	Tr Greek 7.239	2
PHOEBUS			
Cum caput Hesperiis attolit Phoebus ab undis, ...	Y 28	Aurora Musis	1
PIA			
Hic pia Vindamius traxit suspiria, in ipsa	O 116	Tr Pope Grotto	12
Seu viri curas pia nupta mulcet, ...	O 168	Oda to Thrale	13
PIASTI			
Haec mihi, quo gentes, quo secula, Christe, piasti, . .	O 208	Prayers VII	11
PIAVIT			
Sanguine quo gentes, quo secula cuncta piavit, ...	O 232	Prayer	9
PICTAS			
Tene per pictas oculo elegante	O 153	In Theatro	7
PICTOR			
Dat tibi Pythagoram pictor; quod ni ipse tacere . . .	O 225	Tr. Gk. 16.326	1
PIETAS			
Cessarunt; pietas hic quoque cura fuit:	O 170	Insula Kenneth	18
PIETATE			
Cunctorum ignoscat vitiis, pietate fruatur.	O 205	Christianus-	9
Praecellit juvenis vi, pietate senex.	O 217	Tr Greek 9.360	8
PIETATIS			
Gestiat, et, nullo pietatis limite clausus, ...	O 205	Christianus	8
PIGRAE			
Pigrae per horas lucis inutiles, ...	O 187	Ad T. L. M.D.	10
PIGRAM			
Quid faciam? tenebrisne pigram damnare senectam . . .	O 162	Gnothi seauton	52
PIGRITIAM			
Pigritiam incusat, nec minus hora perit.	O 228	Jactura Tempor	2
PINDI			
Aonidesque Deae, et mendacis somnia Pindi.	O 88	Messiah	5
PINGUES			
Et pingues absque Labore.	O 109	Post-genitis	18
PINGUI			
Myrias Aegypto cessit bis septima pingui.	O 229	Geographia Met	3
PINXIT			
Menodotum pinxit Diodorus, et exit imago, ...	O 223	Tr. Gk. 11.213	1
PISCATOR			
Waltoni Piscator perfectus	O 181	Waltoni Piscat	T
PISCATORE			
E Waltoni Piscatore Perfecto excerptum.	O 181	Waltoni Piscat V	T
PIUS			
Nec vincis acer, nec pateris pius;	O 187	Ad T. L. M.D.	6
Et pius, et recti cultor: non illa jacere	O 212	Tr Greek 7.590	3
PLACAVIT			
Divinam in sontes iram placavit Jesus;	O 208	A Meditation	3
PLACEANT			
Ut tibi quae placeant, omnia promptus agam.	O 207	Prayers V	4
PLACENT			
Nunc loca sola placent; frustra te, Somne, recumbens . .	O 161	Gnothi seauton	30
PLACERE			
Qua solum potero parte, placere tibi.	O 204	Losing Speech	4
Cura placere Deo sit prima, sit ultima, sanctae . . .	O 205	Christianus	12
PLACET			
Tutum hic sedile, et si placet, sopor tutus.	O 224	Tr Greek 13.3	4
PLACIDAEVE			
India nascenti, placidaeve argentea noctis	O 92	Messiah	109
PLACIDO			
Huc ego delatus placido per coerula cursu	O 169	Insula Kenneth	5
Et placido tandem haec edidit ore, Dea:	O 386	In Birchium D	4
PLANCTUS			
Non planctus, non moesta sonant suspiria, pectus . . .	O 90	Messiah	52
PLATONI			
Qui pascit barbam si crescit mente, Platoni, ...	O 224	Tr. Gk. 11.430	1
PLATONIS			
Triste nihil passus, animi at de sorte Platonis . . .	O 211	Tr Greek 7.471	3
PLAUDENTIBUS			
Nuncia sacra Dei, plaudentibus insidet alis.	O 88	Messiah	13
PLAUDIT			
Excipit aethereis, Ars omnis plaudit amica, ...	O 161	Gnothi seauton	21
Excipit aethereis, Ars omnis plaudit amico, ...	O 161	Gnothi seauton V	21
PLEBS			
De te plebs audax, hic bene et ille male.	O 214	Tr Greek 9.50	2
PLECTRUM			
Materies; poscunt gravius coelestia plectrum.	O 88	Messiah	3

PLECTRUM   (CONTINUED)   PAGE   TITLE   LINE
    Materies; poscunt graves coelestia plectrum.   . . . .   O 88 Messiah   V   3
PLENA
    Est mihi quod non te rideo, plena salus.   . . . . . .   O 211 Tr Greek 7.318   2
    Verte solum, donat plena crumena decus;   . . . . . .   O 217 Tr Greek 9.360   4
    Verte solum, donet plena crumena decus;   . . . . . .   O 217 Tr Greek 9.360   V   4
PLENUM
    Plenum opus effugiens; aptans juga mollia collo   . . .   O 205 Christianus   22
PLORABIT
    Invalidi raptos sceptri plorabit honores.   . . . . .   O 90 Messiah   56
PIUMBEA
    Linguae procacis plumbea Spicula, ...   O 101 Ad Urbanum   9
PLURA
    Plura ut victurus secula, parce bonis: . . . . . .   O 219 Tr Greek 10.26   2
    Cum sexagenis, dum plura recluserit aetas, ...   O 230 Geographia Met   19
PLURIMA
    Plurima tunc Leges . . . .   O 109 Post-genitis   21
    Mutabit, plurima Reges . . . .   O 109 Post-genitis   22
PLURIMO
    Crimine gravatam plurimo mentem leva: . . . .   O 206 Prayers I   2
PIUS
    Eheu, quid decies plus mihi sexta dedit!   . . . . .   O 171 Tr. Busy Fly   10
    Tandem dolori plus satis est datum, ...   O 187 Ad T. L. M.D.   13
    Plus tibi ridendum secula nostra dabunt. . : . . .   O 216 Tr Greek 9.148   2
    Vita hominum nunc plus quod misereris habet. .   . .   O 216 Tr Greek 9.148   4
PIUTARCHE
    Clara Cheroneae soboles, Plutarche, dicavit   . . . .   O 225 Tr. Gk. 16.331   1
    Sed similem, Plutarche, tuae describere vitam   . . .   O 225 Tr. Gk. 16.331   5
POEMATA
    Hinc annis palpantur delenda poemata nullis   . . . .   Y 28 Aurora Musis   11
    Hinc annis palpantur delenda poemata palpantur   . . .   Y 28 Aurora Musis   V 11
PCENA
    Nunc est pro poena poenituisse reis.   . . . . . .   O 208 A Meditation   4
PCENAM
    Damnatis, poenam pro poenis omnibus unam.   . . . . .   O 160 Gnothi seauton   5
POENIS
    Damnatis, poenam pro poenis omnibus unam.   . . . . .   O 160 Gnothi seauton   5
PCENITEAT
    Recte ut poeniteat, respice, magne parens.   . . . .   O 207 Prayers VI   6
POENITENTIAM
    Concede veram poenitentiam, precor, ...   O 206 Prayers I   3
    Da, Christe, poenitentiam, ...   O 206 Prayers II   6
POENITET
    Quoscumque scelerum poenitet;   . . . . . .   O 206 Prayers II   5
    Respice inutiliter lapsi quem poenitet aevi;   . . .   O 207 Prayers VI   5
POENITUISSE
    Nunc est pro poena poenituisse reis.   . . . .   O 208 A Meditation   4
PCETA
    Poeta, lector, hic quiescit Hipponax, ...   O 224 Tr Greek 13.3   1
POETAE
    Carmina vis nostri scribant meliora Poetae?   . . . .   O 85 Mea nec Falern   5
    At tu quisquis eris, miseri qui cruda poetae   . . . .   Y 387 Death Mother   D   1
PCLLICE
    Quos pulsata sonos edit lyra pollice, primis   . . .   Y 28 Aurora Musis   15
PCLLICITIS
    Pollicitis firmata Dei, stabilita ruinis.   . . . . .   O 92 Messiah   119
ICMPAE
    Quid theatrales tibi, Crispe, pompae? . . . .   O 153 In Theatro   2
PCNDERIS
    Dimidium tanti ponderis intret onus.   . . . .   O 229 Epigram III   2
FCNDUS
    Mox uteri pondus depositura grave, ...   O 115 Ad Lauram Epig   2
    Quas navis recipit, quantum sit pondus aquarum,   . . .   O 229 Epigram III   1
PONE
    Pone metum, rostrum fidens immitte cululio, ...   O 171 Tr. Busy Fly   3
PONIS
    Cur opulentus eges? tua cuncta in foenore ponis.   . . .   O 223 Tr. Gk. 11.167   1
PONIT
    Accendit, rerumque modos ac foedera ponit.   . . . . .   O 163 To Dr Lawrence   30
PCNOR
    Cecropidis gravis hic ponor, Martique dicatus, ...   O 216 Tr Greek 9.288   1
PONTE
    Ut vis, ponte minax, modo tres discesseris ulnas,   . . .   O 210 Tr Greek 7.284   1
PONTI
    Scire vices ponti facile est, nihil amplius optant   . .   O 163 To Dr Lawrence   15
    Ponti profundis clausa recessibus, ...   O 166 Oda Isle Skye   1
    Ponti inter strepitus sacri non munera cultus   . . .   O 170 Insula Kenneth   17
PONTUS
    In sublime rapit, queis terra et pontus et aer   . . . .   O 163 To Dr Lawrence   32
    E longinquo itidem pontus et orcus erat. . . . . . .   O 213 Tr Greek 9.29   6
POPELLI
    Unus homo mihi pro sexcentis, turba popelli   . . . . .   O 209 Tr Greek 7.128   3
POPULARI
    Populari Pascua laetus.   . . . .   O 110 Post-genitis   30
P,CPULO
    Sub pedibus, populo praetereunte, jacit, ...   O 218 Tr Greek 9.375   4
PCPULOS
    Voce ubi Cennethus populos domuisse feroces   . . . .   O 169 Insula Kenneth   3
POPULUS
    Fateris ergo quod populus solet . . . .   O 186 Ad T. L. M.D.   1

		PAGE	TITLE	LINE
PORRECTA				
En! formosa tibi porrecta per atria proles		O 92	Messiah	96
PORRIGIT				
Et gremio fotis selectas porrigit herbas, ...		O 90	Messiah	60
PORTAS				
Aetheris, en! portas sacro fulgore micantes		O 92	Messiah	106
POSCAM				
Aut, hoc si nimium est, tandem nova lexica poscam? . .		O 162	Gnothi seauton	54
POSCANT				
Sive libros poscant otia, sive lyram.		O 170	Insula Kenneth	14
POSCAT				
Ut vitam, poscat si res, impendere vero.		O 205	Christianus	11
POSCATUR				
Seu prece poscatur, seu non, da Jupiter omne		O 221	Tr Greek 10.108	1
POSCENTIBUS				
Magne bonum, omne malum et poscentibus abnue nobis. . .		O 221	Tr Greek 10.108	2
POSCIS				
Quod poscis, haud unquam tibi		O 203	Christ Sinner	3
POSCIT				
Myriades sibi pulcra duas, duo millia poscit		O 230	Geographia Met	10
POSCO				
Non opto aut precibus posco ditescere, paucis		O 222	Tr. Gk. 10.113	1
POSCUNT				
Materies; poscunt gravius coelestia plectrum.		O 88	Messiah	3
Materies; poscunt graves coelestia plectrum.		O 88	Messiah V	3
POSSE				
Parare posse, ut Stoicorum		O 166	Oda Isle Skye	15
Parare posse, utcunque jactet		O 166	Oda Isle Skye V	15
POSSES				
Quid mecum peragam, quod tu doctissime posses		O 163	To Dr Lawrence	4
POSSIS				
Elige iter vitae, ut possis; rixisque dolisque		O 217	Tr Greek 9.359	1
POSSIT				
Ardeat huic toto sacer ignis pectore, possit . . .		O 205	Christianus	10
Cum fugere haud possit fractis Victoria pennis, . . .		O 219	Tr Greek 9.647	1
POSSUM				
Sum nunc, nec possum cernere qualis eram.		O 209	Tr. Greek 6.1	4
POST				
(Post Lexicon Anglicanum auctum et emendatum.) . . .		O 160	Gnothi seauton	T
"Perge modo, atque tuas olim post funera laudes . . .		O 386	In Birchium D	5
POST-GENITIS				
Post-genitis		O 109	Post-genitis	T
POSTERA				
Postera sic pastor divinus secla beabit, ...		O 90	Messiah	64
POSTHAC				
Flumina prorumpunt; non posthac sole rubescet . . .		O 92	Messiah	108
POSTREMA				
Haec postrema tibi sit flendi causa, fluatque . . .		Y 387	Death Mother D	3
POSTULAT				
Non sibi de gaza praesens quod postulat usus		O 162	Gnothi seauton V	44
POSTULET				
Nec sibi de gaza praesens quod postulet usus		O 162	Gnothi seauton	44
POTENS				
Eloquiumque potens linguis torpentibus affer, ...		O 232	Prayer	7
POTENTE				
Potente succo		O 199	Medico Aeger S	13
POTENTEM				
Te mille succorum potentem		O 187	Ad T. L. M.D.	7
POTENTIA				
Copia, Phidiaci foecunda potentia coeli.		O 161	Gnothi seauton	39
POTERAM				
Queis uti poteram quondam Fortuna negavit, ...		O 215	Tr Greek 9.138	3
POTERANT				
Hae poterant uvae laeto convivia cantu		O 218	Tr Greek 9.375	7
POTERAS				
Non poteras, regio non tulit ulla parem.		O 225	Tr. Gk. 16.331	6
POTERIS				
Non poteris, meditans prava, latere Deos.		O 220	Tr Greek 10.27	2
POTERO				
Qua solum potero parte, placere tibi.		O 204	Losing Speech	4
Qua solum potero parte, litare tibi.		O 204	Losing Speech V	4
POTES				
Incrementa aevi non cumulare potes.		O 220	Tr Greek 10.60	4
POTEST				
Dario magno non minus ille potest.		O 212	Tr Greek 7.538	2
POTIS				
Multis ut te oculis sim potis aspicere.		O 212	Tr Greek 7.669	2
POTUERE				
Quae potuere duos tertius unus habet.		O 86	Tr Dryden Milt	6
POTUI				
Vincere te potui nuda, quid arma geram?		O 384	Epigramma D	4
PRAEBE				
Aurem faventem precibus O praebe meis;		O 206	Prayers III	3
PRAEBEAT				
Praebeat, et tacite foecundos irriget imbres!		O 88	Messiah	15
PRAEBET				
Materiam Statuae sic praebet Marmora Tellus, ...		O 85	Adjecere bonae	3
Queis uti nequeo, nunc mihi praebet opes.		O 215	Tr Greek 9.138	4
PRAEBUIT				
Laevum at utrumque decus, juveni quod praebuit olim . .		O 225	Tr. Gk. 16.364	3

	PAGE	TITLE		LINE
PRAECELLIT				
Praecellit juvenis vi, pietate senex.	O 217	Tr Greek 9.360		8
PRAECO				
Supra Praeco Dei--strepit infra Praeco Bonorum:	O 385	The Warehouse	D	5
Supra Praeco Dei--strepit infra Praeco Bonorum:	O 385	The Warehouse	D	5
PRAECONES				
Praecones ambo, Nummus utrique Deus.	O 385	The Warehouse	D	2
PRAEMIA				
Perpetui, ambita bis terra, praemia lactis	O 156	Collari Caprae		1
Perpetua, ambita bis terra, praemia lactis	O 156	Collari Caprae	V	1
Da, ne sint permissa, pater, mihi praemia frustra,	O 208	Prayers VII		9
Da, ne sint promissa, pater, mihi praemia frustra,	O 208	Prayers VII	V	9
Herodoto hospitii praemia, quaeque suum.	O 216	Tr Greek 9.160		2
PRAENITUISSE				
Neve tibi noceat praenituisse Deae.	O 115	Ad Lauram Epig		4
PRAESENS				
Nec sibi de gaza praesens quod postulet usus	O 162	Gnothi seauton		44
Non sibi de gaza praesens quod postulat usus	O 162	Gnothi seauton	V	44
Succurre praesens corpori,	O 206	Prayers II		9
PRAESENTI				
Numine praesenti me tueare pater!	O 207	Prayers IV		2
PRAESEPE				
Cumque leone petet tutus praesepe juvencus.	O 91	Messiah		85
PRAESTA				
Christe, spem praesta stabilem timenti;	O 194	Prayer on Xmas		6
PRAESTAT				
Praestat magistro saepe discipulus suo.	O 223	Tr. Gk. 11.176		5
PRAETENDET				
Attollet reducis; bellis praetendet olivas	O 89	Messiah		22
PRAETENDIT				
Speluncae late Thamesis praetendit opacae,	O 116	Tr Pope Grotto		2
PRAETER				
Praeter Menodotum, nullius absimilis.	O 223	Tr. Gk. 11.213		2
PRAETEREUNT				
Praetereunt, aut hos praeterit omne bonum.	O 220	Tr Greek 10.31		2
PRAETEREUNTE				
Sub pedibus, populo praetereunte, jacit,	O 218	Tr Greek 9.375		4
PRAETERI				
Si sis scelestus, praeteri procul marmor:	O 224	Tr Greek 13.3		2
PRAETERIT				
Praetereunt, aut hos praeterit omne bonum.	O 220	Tr Greek 10.31		2
PRAETERITAE				
Olim, praeteritae numeranti tempora vitae,	O 171	Tr. Busy Fly		11
PRAETERIIIS				
Praeteritis fruitur, laetos aut sumit honores	O 162	Gnothi seauton		47
PRATA				
Serpent per Prata Colubri,	O 109	Post-genitis		10
Errat adhuc vitreus per prata virentia rivus,	O 228	Rivum a Stoana		1
PRATIS				
Florebunt Lilia Pratis,	O 109	Post-genitis		26
Floribus in pratis legi quos ipse, coronam	O 209	Tr. Greek 5.74		1
PRAVA				
Non poteris, meditans prava, latere Deos.	O 220	Tr Greek 10.27		2
PRAVUS				
Vetitaque Libidine pravus.	O 110	Post-genitis		34
PRAXITELES				
Unde hic Praxiteles? nudam vidistis, Adoni,	O 225	Tr. Gk. 16.168		1
PRECANTES				
Imperium pelagi precantes.	O 188	Epilogus		4
PRECARI				
Ingenio parcas, nec sit mihi culpa precari	O 204	Losing Speech	V	3
PRECE				
Qua te laude, Deus, qua prece prosequar?	O 164	Recover Eyes		10
Nunc summi prece sancta	O 182	Waltoni Piscat		9
Seu prece poscatur, seu non, da Jupiter omne	O 221	Tr Greek 10.108		1
PRECES				
Legitimas faciunt pectora pura preces.	O 170	Insula Kenneth		20
Legitimas faciunt pura labella preces	O 170	Insula Kenneth	V	20
Heu quam dura preces sprevit, quam surda querelas	O 212	Tr Greek 7.560		5
Stat: fixum est: nequeunt jam revocare preces.	O 384	On the Gin-Act	D	8
PRECIBUS				
Ut precibus justas avertat numinis iras	O 170	Insula Kenneth	V	16A
Hoc statuat, precibus Christus adesse velit:	O 204	Losing Speech		2
Aurem faventem precibus O praebe meis;	O 206	Prayers III		3
Non opto aut precibus posco ditescere, paucis	O 222	Tr. Gk. 10.113		1
PRECIBUSQUE				
Da fidem certam, precibusque fidis	O 194	Prayer on Xmas		7
PRECOR				
Concede veram poenitentiam, precor,	O 206	Prayers I		3
PREFIGERE				
Dum statuunt, causisque audent prefigere metam.	O 163	To Dr Lawrence		36
PREMEBAS				
Mente senes olim juvenis, Faustine, premebas,	O 225	Tr. Gk. 16.364		1
PREMIT				
Et morbus tegitur, dum premit ora pudor.	O 221	Tr Greek 10.98		2
PREMUNT				
Omnia, dum Macedum gloria et arma premunt.	O 216	Tr Greek 9.288		4
PRETIO				
Justitiaeque manus pretio intemerata bilancem	O 89	Messiah		21
PRETIUM				
Temnere opes pretium sceleris, patriamque tueri	O 116	Tr Pope Grotto		15

```
PRETIUM          (CONTINUED)                                PAGE   TITLE               LINE
    Et pro me pretium, tu patiare, pater. . . . . . . .    O 207  Prayers V              6
    Queis majus pretium saecula lapsa dabant . . . . . .   Y  28  Aurora Musis          12
PRIAMI
    Exiguum en! Priami monumentum; haud ille meretur  . . . O 210  Tr Greek 7.136         1
PRIMA
    Pauperieque Irus, curaque prima Deum. . . . . . . .    O 114  Tr Gk Epigrams         4
    Morte memor patriae; hic Marcmonti pectore prima  . . . O 116  Tr Pope Grotto        13
    Cura placere Deo sit prima, sit ultima, sanctae   . . . O 205  Christianus           12
    Puppe gubernatrix sedisti, Audacia, prima, . . . . .   O 213  Tr Greek 9.29          1
    Venturi exsecuit, vascula prima meri, . . . . . .      O 217  Tr Greek 9.375         2
    Prima parit terras aetas; siccatque secunda;  . . .    O 226  Septem Aetates         1
PRIMAS
    Nascere, magne puer! Tibi primas, ecce! corollas  . . . O  89  Messiah               27
PRIME
    Quisque suum norit modulum; tibi, prime virorum,  . . . O 160  Gnothi seauton        14
PRIMIS
    Sub pedibus subjecta jacent; queis ultima primis  . . . O 163  To Dr Lawrence        33
    Quos pulsata sonos edit lyra pollice, primis  . . . .  Y  28  Aurora Musis          15
PRINCEPS
    Medicae Princeps, . . . . . . . . . . . . .           O 199  Medico Aeger S        25
PRIOR
    Quaeris, Quis prior est fama meritisve; superna   . . . O 385  The Warehouse       D  3
PRIORA
    Nunc rescire priora, . . . . . . . . . . . .          O 182  Waltoni Piscat         7
PRIORES
    Nil majus Natura capit: clarare priores . . . . .     O  86  Tr Dryden Milt         5
    Quod nimium est fit ineptum; hinc, ut dixere priores, .  O 224  Tr Greek 16.16        1
PRIORUM
    Parva quidem regio, sed relligione priorum  . . . .   O 169  Insula Kenneth         1
PRISCAE
    "Irrita vanescent priscae vestigia fraudis," . . . .  O  89  Messiah               20
PRO
    Damnatis, poenam pro poenis omnibus unam. . . . . .   O 160  Gnothi seauton         5
    Sint pro legitimis pectora pura sacris  . . . . . .   O 170  Insula Kenneth      V 20
    Sint pro legitimis pura labella sacris  . . . . . .   O 170  Insula Kenneth      V 20
    Et pro me pretium, tu patiare, pater. . . . . . .     O 207  Prayers V              6
    Nunc est pro poena poenituisse reis. . . . . . . .    O 208  A Meditation           4
    Unus homo mihi pro sexcentis, turba popelli . . . .   O 209  Tr Greek 7.128         3
    Pro nullo; clamo nunc tumulatus idem. . . . . . .     O 209  Tr Greek 7.128         4
    Conjugium, ut pro te des hominem patriae. . . . . .   O 218  Tr Greek 9.444         4
PROAVUM
    Proavum vaecors insipientia, . . . . . . . . . .      O 193  Tr. Medea III          2
PROBATUM
    Mi, nequid nimis, est nimis probatum. . . . . . .     O 215  Tr Greek 9.110         4
PROBAVIT
    Ingenium et mores si pulchra probavit Elisa, . . . .  O 104  To Eliz Carter         3
PROBITAS
    Quid mihi cum cultu? Probitas inculta nitescit, . . . O 104  To Eliz Carter         1
PROBROSA
    Nec probrosa avidae grata sit offa gulae; . . . . .   O 218  Tr Greek 9.573         2
PROCACIS
    Linguae procacis plumbea Spicula, . . . . . . .       O 101  Ad Urbanum             9
PROCELLAS
    Fortunae malim adverse tolerare procellas, . . . .    O 221  Tr Greek 10.93         1
PROCELLIS
    Strepens procellis, rupibus obsita, . . . . . . .     O 166  Oda Isle Skye          2
    Strepens procellis, imbribus uvida, . . . . . . .     O 166  Oda Isle Skye       V  2
    Strepens procellis, uvida nubibus, . . . . . . .      O 166  Oda Isle Skye       V  2
PROCORUM
    Illa triumphatrix Graium consueta procorum  . . . .   O 209  Tr. Greek 6.1          1
PROCUL
    Spes hominum ac curas cum procul esse jubet. . . . .  O 170  Insula Kenneth        16
    Spes hominum et curas gens procul esse velit. . . .   O 170  Insula Kenneth      V 16
    Rege, et tuere, quae nocent pellens procul; . . . .   O 206  Prayers I              6
    Cum procul est, optat, cum venit, quisque senectam . . O 214  Tr Greek 9.54          1
    Si sis scelestus, praeteri procul marmor: . . . . .   O 224  Tr Greek 13.3          2
PRODESSE
    Prodesse vitae, literasque . . . . . . . . . .        O 186  Ad T. L. M.D.          3
PRODEST
    Prodest vagari, nec frementes . . . . . . . . .       O 166  Oda Isle Skye         11
    Tantum prodest  . . . . . . . . . . . . .             O 198  Medico Aeger S         9
    Tantum prodest  . . . . . . . . . . . . .             O 199  Medico Aeger S        12
PROFERET
    Proferet archetypos; coelestis gaudia lucis . . . .   O  92  Messiah              111
PROFUNDIS
    Ponti profundis clausa recessibus, . . . . . . .      O 166  Oda Isle Skye          1
PROFUNDUS
    Mulcet amor prolis, sopor est sine prole profundus; . . O 217  Tr Greek 9.360        7
PROLE
    Mulcet amor prolis, sopor est sine prole profundus; . . O 217  Tr Greek 9.360        7
PROLEM
    Prolem Hippi, et sua qua meliorem secula nullum . . . O 226  Tr. Simonides          1
PROLES
    En! formosa tibi porrecta per atria proles  . . . .   O  92  Messiah               96
    En! formosa tibi spatiosa per atria proles  . . . .   O  92  Messiah             V 96
    Proles aucta gravat, rapta orbat, caeca juventae est . . O 217  Tr Greek 9.359       7
PROLESQUE
    Mater adulantum prolesque, Pecunia, curae, . . . .    O 218  Tr Greek 9.394         1
PROLI
    Et serae texent vites umbracula proli. . . . . . .    O  90  Messiah               74
```

	PAGE	TITLE	LINE
PROLIS			
Mulcet amor prolis, sopor est sine prole profundus; · ·	O 217	Tr Greek 9.360	7
PROLUE			
Nam licet, et toto prolue laeta mero. · · · · · · ·	O 171	Tr. Busy Fly	4
PROMEREARE			
Sanguine, peccanti promereare tuo! · · · · · · · ·	O 208	Prayers VII	12
PROMERUISSE			
Haec nobis Christus promeruisse velit! · · · · ·	O 232	Prayer	10
PROMETHEI			
Gratia nulla hominum mentes tenet, ista Promethei · · ·	O 225	Tr Greek 16.87	3
PROMISSA			
Da, ne sint promissa, pater, mihi praemia frustra, · ·	O 208	Prayers VII	V 9
PROMIT			
Quas Natura dedit dotes, Academia promit, · · · · ·	O 85	Adjecere bonae	1
PROMPTUS			
Ut tibi quae placeant, omnia promptus agam. · · · · ·	O 207	Prayers V	4
PROMUS			
Limosum nobis Promus dat callidus haustum, · · · · ·	O 85	Mea nec Falern	3
PROPAGO			
Graeciae et urbs, urbi est ista propago, decus. · · ·	O 214	Tr Greek 9.65	2
PROPERANS			
Vita rosae brevis est; properans si carpere nolis, · ·	O 223	Tr Greek 11.53	1
Vitae rosa brevis est; properans si carpere nolis, · ·	O 223	Tr Greek 11.53	V 1
PROPINQUA			
Quem terret vitae meta propinqua suae, · · · · ·	O 207	Prayers VI	4
PROPRIIS			
Dat Menti propriis Musa nitere bonis. · · · · · · ·	O 85	Adjecere bonae	2
PROPRIUM			
Est proprium, et quavis captare indagine verum, · · ·	O 163	To Dr Lawrence	7
Quod nulli proprium versat Fortuna, putabat · · · ·	O 215	Tr Greek 9.74	3
PRORUMPUNT			
Flumina prorumpunt; non posthac sole rubescet · · · ·	O 92	Messiah	108
PROSEQUAR			
Qua te laude, Deus, qua prece prosequar? · · · · · ·	O 164	Recover Eyes	10
PROSEQUERETUR			
· · · tristi prosequeretur. · · · · · · · · · ·	O 186	Ad T. L. M.D.	V T
PROSEQUITUR			
Prosequitur lacrymis filia moesta Sami, · · · · ·	O 211	Tr Greek 7.459	2
PROSPERA			
Prospera sors nec te strepitoso turbine tollat, · · ·	O 221	Tr Greek 10.74	1
PROSUNT			
Ne, quae prosunt · · · · · · · · · · · · ·	O 199	Medico Aeger S	28
PROVENIAT			
Sic ale, proveniat messis ut ampla boni. · · · · · ·	O 207	Prayers VII	4
PROVOCAT			
Jam saltu capreas, jam cursu provocat euros. · · · ·	O 90	Messiah	51
Nunc saltu capreas, nunc cursu provocat euros. · · · ·	O 90	Messiah	V 51
PRUDENTIA			
Elige iter vitae, ut mavis; prudentia lausque · · · ·	O 217	Tr Greek 9.360	1
PSALMUS			
Psalmus 117 · · · · · · · · · · · · · ·	O 155	Psalmus 117	T
PUDOR			
Militibus; terris sit pelagoque pudor! · · · · · ·	O 217	Tr Greek 9.304	4
Et morbus tegitur, dum premit ora pudor. · · · · · ·	O 221	Tr Greek 10.98	2
PUELLAE			
Ad Musas Venus haec: Veneri parete, puellae, · · · ·	O 213	Tr Greek 9.39	1
PUELLAS			
Angliacas inter pulcherrima Laura puellas, · · · · ·	O 115	Ad Lauram Epig	1
Una duas habuit casa cum genitore puellas, · · · · ·	O 169	Insula Kenneth	9
Una duas tenuit casa cum genitore puellas, · · · · ·	O 169	Insula Kenneth	V 9
Una duas cepit casa cum genitore puellas, · · · · ·	O 169	Insula Kenneth	V 9
PUER			
Nascere, magne puer! Tibi primas, ecce! corollas · · ·	O 89	Messiah	27
Lusitus gaudet puer otiosis, · · · · · · · · ·	O 153	In Theatro	13
Huc nunquam volitat debilis iste puer. · · · · ·	O 213	Tr Greek 9.39	4
Quo toties lavi membra tenella puer; · · · · · · ·	O 228	Rivum a Stoana	2
PUERI			
Per ludum pueri injicient, et fessa colubri · · · · ·	O 91	Messiah	87
PUGILEM			
Non Argos pugilem, non me Messana creavit; · · · · ·	O 224	Tr Greek 16.1	1
PUGNACES			
Quanquam haud pugnaces, · · · · · · · · · ·	O 109	Post-genitis	15
PULCHERRIMA			
Angliacas inter pulcherrima Laura puellas, · · · · ·	O 115	Ad Lauram Epig	1
PULCHERRIMUS			
Sufficit hoc votis; flos hic pulcherrimus aevi est, · ·	O 215	Tr Greek 9.112	3
PULCHRA			
Ingenium et mores si pulchra probavit Elisa, · · · ·	O 104	To Eliz Carter	3
Liber ut esse velim, suasisti, pulchra Maria: · · · ·	O 105	Lady Defence	1
Ut maneam liber, pulchra Maria, vale. · · · · · ·	O 105	Lady Defence	2
Non tenet; esca natat pulchra, sed hamus abest. · · ·	O 209	Tr. Greek 5.67	2
Pulchra est virginitas intacta, at vita perimet, · ·	O 218	Tr Greek 9.444	1
PULCHRAM			
Particulasque locans, certas certo ordine, pulchram · ·	O 163	To Dr Lawrence	28
PULCRA			
Myriades sibi pulcra duas, duo millia poscit · · · ·	O 230	Geographia Met	10
PULICIBUS			
Pulicibus morsus, restincta lampade, stultus · · · ·	O 224	Tr. Gk. 11.432	1
PULSATA			
Quos pulsata sonos edit lyra pollice, primis · · · ·	Y 28	Aurora Musis	15

		PAGE	TITLE		LINE
PUPPE					
	Puppe gubernatrix sedisti, Audacia, prima, ...	O 213	Tr Greek 9.29		1
PURA					
	Ingredere O!--Magnam pura cole mente parentem, ...	O 116	Tr Pope Grotto		7
	Ingredere O!--rerum pura cole mente parentem, ...	O 116	Tr Pope Grotto	V	7
	Legitimas faciunt pectora pura preces.	O 170	Insula Kenneth		20
	Legitimas faciunt pura labella preces	O 170	Insula Kenneth	V	20
	Sint pro legitimis pectora pura sacris	O 170	Insula Kenneth	V	20
	Sint pro legitimis pura labella sacris	O 170	Insula Kenneth	V	20
	Te, mente pura, mente tranquilla colam:	O 206	Prayers I		10
PURGATA					
	Harmoniae purgata novos mirabitur auris.	O 90	Messiah		48
PURIOR					
	Ingenium jubeas purior haustus alat.	O 85	Mea nec Falern		6
PURISSIMUS					
	Pascua, qua blandum spirat purissimus aer	O 90	Messiah		58
PURO					
	Me, pater omnipotens, de puro respice coelo, ...	O 207	Prayers V		1
	Summe Pater, puro collustra lumine pectus, ...	O 207	Prayers VII		1
PURPURET					
	Volvantur celeres anni! Lux purpuret ortum	O 89	Messiah		25
PURUM					
	Fulsit, in pectus mihi fonte purum	O 193	Prayer on Xmas		2
PUSILLO					
	Cunctiparens tellus, salve, levis esto pusillo	O 211	Tr Greek 7.461		1
PUTABAT					
	Quod nulli proprium versat Fortuna, putabat	O 215	Tr Greek 9.74		3
PUTAT					
	Ille suum stolidus, nunc putat ille suum.	O 215	Tr Greek 9.74		4
PUTES					
	Tu neque dulce putes alienae accumbere mensae, ...	O 218	Tr Greek 9.573		1
	Nutrit mane, putes esse Heliconis aqua.	Y 28	Aurora Musis		6
PUTIDULUM					
	Quid quod putidulum nostra Camoena sonat?	O 85	Mea nec Falern		2
PUTO					
	Felici thalamo non, puto, rixa strepit.	O 226	Tr. Greek		2
PYTHAGORAM					
	Dat tibi Pythagoram pictor; quod ni ipse tacere . . .	O 225	Tr. Gk. 16.326		1
PYTHAGORAS					
	Pythagoras mallet, vocem habuisset opus.	O 225	Tr. Gk. 16.326		2
QUA					
	Ut qua dulce strepunt scatebrae, qua laeta virescunt . .	O 90	Messiah		57
	Ut qua dulce strepunt scatebrae, qua laeta virescunt . .	O 90	Messiah		57
	Ut qua dulce strepent scatebrae, qua laeta virescunt . .	O 90	Messiah	V	57
	Ut qua dulce strepent scatebrae, qua laeta virescunt . .	O 90	Messiah	V	57
	Pascua, qua blandum spirat purissimus aer	O 90	Messiah		58
	Horruit implexo qua vallis sente, figurae	O 91	Messiah		80
	Zosima, qua solo fuit olim corpore serva, ...	O 212	Tr Gk Epigrams	V	7
	Quisquis iter tendis, vitreas qua lucidus undas . . .	O 116	Tr Pope Grotto		1
	Marmoreo trepidant qua lentae in fornice guttae, . . .	O 116	Tr Pope Grotto		3
	Marmorea trepidant qua lentae in fornice guttae, . . .	O 116	Tr Pope Grotto	V	3
	Anni qua volucris ducitur orbita, ...	O 155	Psalmus 117		1
	Si qua usquam pateat melioris semita vitae, ...	O 161	Gnothi seauton		33
	Qua sulcat, reptant tuti per lubrica vitae.	O 163	To Dr Lawrence		18
	Qua te laude, Deus, qua prece prosequar?	O 164	Recover Eyes		10
	Qua te laude, Deus, qua prece prosequar? . . .	O 164	Recover Eyes		10
	Fulserat illa dies, legis qua docta supernae	O 170	Insula Kenneth	V	15
	Qua solum potero parte, placere tibi.	O 204	Losing Speech		4
	Qua solum potero parte, litare tibi.	O 204	Losing Speech	V	4
	Quales sint monades, qua fit inane, sinas. . . .	O 222	Tr Greek 11.50		6
	Prolem Hippi, et sua qua meliorem secula nullum . .	O 226	Tr. Simonides		1
	Tectaque qua fluxit, nunc et aperta fluit.	O 228	Rivum a Stoana		10
	Imperium qua Turca ferox exercet iniquum.	O 230	Geographia Met		5
QUADRAGENIS					
	Et quadragenis quoque ter tria millia jungit. . . .	O 230	Geographia Met		26
	Et quadragenis decades quinque addit Ierne, ...	O 231	Geographia Met		32
	Quingentis quadragenis socialis adauget	O 231	Geographia Met		33
QUADRATA					
	Laevia serratis miscens, quadrata rotundis, ...	O 163	To Dr Lawrence		26
QUAE					
	Quae potuere duos tertius unus habet.	O 86	Tr Dryden Milt		6
	Ipso fonte bibes, quae circumfusa beatam	O 92	Messiah		112
	Quam quae severis ludicra jungere	O 102	Ad Urbanum		18
	Ad foeminam quandam generosam quae libertatis . . .	O 105	Lady Defence	V	T
	Zosima, quae solo fuit olim corpore Serva, ...	O 114	Tr Gk Epigrams		1
	Quae nos blanda comes, quae nos perducat eodem, . .	O 171	Tr. Busy Fly		7
	Quae nos blanda comes, quae nos perducat eodem, . .	O 171	Tr. Busy Fly		7
	Quae fausta Romae dixit Horatius, ...	O 188	Epilogus		1
	Phoebe fave, aegrotat quae te colit, ulla nec usquam est	O 197	Summ. Lawrence		1
	Ne, quae prosunt	O 199	Medico Aeger S		28
	Rege, et tuere, quae nocent pellens procul;	O 206	Prayers I		6
	Ut tibi quae placeant, omnia promptus agam. . . .	O 207	Prayers V		4
	Quam tenet hic, cunctas quae manet, alta quies. . .	O 211	Tr Greek 7.459		4
	Quae lyra. Quam sibi non concinit harmonia! . . .	O 216	Tr Greek 9.250		2
	Quae sine morte fuga est vitae, quam turba malorum	O 222	Tr. Gk. 10.123		1
	Sortitur Pelopis tellus quae nomine gaudet.	O 230	Geographia Met		7
QUAEQUE					
	Gens illa, impatiens per singula quaeque vagandi . . .	O 163	To Dr Lawrence		23
	Herodoto hospitii praemia, quaeque suum.	O 216	Tr Greek 9.160		2
QUAERENTI					
	Quaerenti obveniet mox sine flore rubus.	O 223	Tr Greek 11.53		2

	PAGE	TITLE	LINE
QUAERERE			
Quaerere, quis, cujas, quis pater, unde venis.	O 219	Tr Greek 9.648	2
His sapiens lectis, Epicurum quaerere frustra	O 222	Tr Greek 11.50	5
QUAERIS			
Quaeris, Quis prior est fama meritisve; superna	O 385	The Warehouse D	3
QUAERIT			
Amissas modo quaerit oves, revocatque vagantes;	O 90	Messiah	61
QUAERITE			
Latrones, alibi locupletum quaerite tecta,	O 219	Tr Greek 9.654	1
QUAERITUR			
Quicquid quaeritur ultra,	O 182	Waltoni Piscat	11
QUAERO			
Subtile ingenium quaero, capaxque mei,	O 209	Tr Greek 7.128	2
QUAERUNT			
Nec quaerunt quid, luna, tuo cum fluctibus orbi.	O 163	To Dr Lawrence	16
QUALE			
Quale, sed hostiles quale dedere manus.	O 210	Tr Greek 7.136	2
Quale, sed hostiles quale dedere manus.	O 210	Tr Greek 7.136	2
Det Bacchus, dederat quale, Lycurge, tibi.	O 218	Tr Greek 9.375	6
QUALES			
Quales sint monades, qua fit inane, sinas.	O 222	Tr Greek 11.50	6
QUALIA			
Accola Danubii qualia saevus habet;	O 169	Insula Kenneth	12
QUALIS			
Sic orsus--Qualis rerum mihi nascitur ordo!	O 88	Messiah	9
Hoc Veneri speculum; nolo me cernere qualis	O 209	Tr. Greek 6.1	3
Sum nunc, nec possum cernere qualis eram.	O 209	Tr. Greek 6.1	4
QUAM			
Tolle, Salema, sacros, quam circum gloria pennas	O 92	Messiah	94
Quam quae severis ludicra jungere	O 102	Ad Urbanum	18
Quam bene ventorum surgere templa jubet!	O 143	On Lord Anson	2
Quam decet canos male literatos	O 153	In Theatro	3
Quam grata defesso virentem	O 166	Oda Isle Skye	3
Quam magis exoptes arte valere tua.	O 197	Summ. Lawrence	2
Quam tenet hic, cunctas quae manet, alta quies.	O 211	Tr Greek 7.459	4
Heu quam dura preces sprevit, quam surda querelas	O 212	Tr Greek 7.560	5
Heu quam dura preces sprevit, quam surda querelas	O 212	Tr Greek 7.560	5
Quae lyra. Quam sibi non concinit harmonia!	O 216	Tr Greek 9.250	2
Aevi sat novi quam sim brevis; astra tuenti,	O 219	Tr Greek 9.577	1
Quam domini ingentis ferre supercilium.	O 221	Tr Greek 10.93	2
Quae sine morte fuga est vitae, quam turba malorum	O 222	Tr. Gk. 10.123	1
Quam, regum sobolem, nuptam, matrem, atque sororem	O 226	Tr. Simonides	3
Ut dicas, spatiis quam latis imperet orbi	O 230	Geographia Met	16
Eheu! quam longo tecum consumerer aevo!	O 384	On the Gin-Act D	5
QUAMCUNQUE			
Tu, quamcunque tibi velox indulserit annus,	O 171	Tr. Busy Fly	5
QUANDAM			
Ad foeminam quandam generosam quae libertatis	O 105	Lady Defence V	T
QUANDOQUIDEM			
Quandoquidem passim nulla ratione feruntur	O 222	Tr. Gk. 10.124	1
QUANQUAM			
Quanquam haud pugnaces,	O 109	Post-genitis	15
Et sibi, delirans quanquam et peccator in horas	O 205	Christianus	14
QUANTA			
At docet, exemplo, vis sibi quanta, tuo.	O 218	Tr Greek 9.530	2
QUANTUM			
Qui sibi sat sapiunt, contenti noscere quantum	O 163	To Dr Lawrence	11
Qui sibi sat sapient, contenti noscere quantum	O 163	To Dr Lawrence V	11
Quantum strictam	O 199	Medico Aeger S	17
Effigiemque Dei, quantum servare licebit,	O 205	Christianus	29
Quas navis recipit, quantum sit pondus aquarum,	O 229	Epigram III	1
QUANTUS			
Quantus ubique Lepos! quantus ubique Decor!	O 383	Syl. Urb. Thes D	2
Quantus ubique Lepos! quantus ubique Decor!	O 383	Syl. Urb. Thes D	2
QUARTA			
Evocat Abramum dein tertia; quarta relinquit	O 226	Septem Aetates	2
Centuria Ligures augent duo millia quarta.	O 230	Geographia Met	14
QUARTAE			
Ter tria myriadi conjungit millia quartae,	O 230	Geographia Met	29
Centuriae quartae decades quinque Anglia nectit.	O 230	Geographia Met	30
QUAS			
Quas Natura dedit dotes, Academia promit,	O 85	Adjecere bonae	1
Quas Amor undarum fingeret esse deas:	O 169	Insula Kenneth	10
Quas Amor undarum crederet esse deas:	O 169	Insula Kenneth V	10
Quas servare velit, leges quas lentus omittat,	O 205	Christianus	21
Quas servare velit, leges quas lentus omittat,	O 205	Christianus	21
Lunaque quas et sol itque reditque vias.	O 222	Tr. Gk. 10.123	4
Quas navis recipit, quantum sit pondus aquarum,	O 229	Epigram III	1
QUASI			
Hora bonis quasi nunc instet suprema fruaris,	O 219	Tr Greek 10.26	1
QUATER			
Tertii verso quater orbe lustri,	O 153	In Theatro	1
Undecies centum denos quater adde duosque.	O 229	Epigram IV	2
QUATIT			
Vix majore Deus corda furore quatit	Y 28	Aurora Musis	8
QUAVIS			
Est proprium, et quavis captare indagine verum,	O 163	To Dr Lawrence	7
QUEIS			
In sublime rapit, queis terra et pontus et aer	O 163	To Dr Lawrence	32
Sub pedibus subjecta jacent; queis ultima primis	O 163	To Dr Lawrence	33
Tu, queis laborat sors hominum, mala	O 187	Ad T. L. M.D.	5

```
QUEIS          (CONTINUED)                              PAGE  TITLE              LINE
  Queis tamen aptam ferre medelam  . . . . . . . . .   O 193 Tr. Medea III          9
  Queis uti poteram quondam Fortuna negavit,   . . . . O 215 Tr Greek 9.138         3
  Queis uti nequeo, nunc mihi praebet opes.  . . . . . O 215 Tr Greek 9.138         4
  Queis majus pretium saecula lapsa dabant . . . . . . Y  28 Aurora Musis         12
  Hic Bona queis opus est venditat, Ille Sonum. . . . . O 385 The Warehouse     D   6
QUEM
  En! quem turba diu cecinerunt enthea, vates,  . . . . O  89 Messiah             41
  Quem decuit majora sequi, majoribus aptum,  . . . . . O 160 Gnothi seauton       7
  Nec dubitet quem dicat herum, sed, totus in uno,  . . O 205 Christianus         17
  Quem moestum et timidum crimina dira gravant;  . . . O 207 Prayers V            2
  Respice quem subigit senium, morbique seniles,  . . . O 207 Prayers VI           3
  Respice quem subiget senium, morbique seniles,  . . . O 207 Prayers VI      V    3
  Quem terret vitae meta propinqua suae,  . . . . . . . O 207 Prayers VI           4
  Respice inutiliter lapsi quem poenitet aevi;  . . . . O 207 Prayers V            5
  Quem fundit blando junctus amore dolor;  . . . . . . O 212 Tr Greek 7.560        2
  Non reperit, nectit quem reperit laqueum.  . . . . . O 213 Tr Greek 9.44         2
  Quem nulla anxietas, nulla cupido fugit;  . . . . . . O 232 Prayer               2
  Quem nil vafrities peccantum subdola celat;  . . . . O 232 Prayer               3
  Ignis quem Phoebi naribus efflat equus,  . . . . . . Y  28 Aurora Musis         14
  Quem efflant quem rem Phoebi naribus ignis equi  . . Y  28 Aurora Musis     V  14
  Quem efflant quem rem Phoebi naribus ignis equi  . . Y  28 Aurora Musis     V  14
QUERELAS
  Heu quam dura preces sprevit, quam surda querelas  . . O 212 Tr Greek 7.560       5
QUERELIS
  Ut studiis sperem, aut ausim par esse querelis,  . . . O 160 Gnothi seauton      15
  Amice, majorem querelis,  . . . . . . . . . . . . . . O 187 Ad T. L. M.D.        19
QUERERIS
  Mens mea quid quereris? veniet tibi mollior hora,  . . O 208 A Meditation         1
QUI
  Tu mihi, qui flamma movisti pectora sancti  . . . . . O  88 Messiah              6
  Qui duxit sulcos, illi teret area messem,  . . . . . O  90 Messiah             73
  Jupiter unus erat, qui stravit fulmine gentes;  . . . O 103 Elizae Aenigma       5
  Qui nunc jacet Incola stagni,  . . . . . . . . . . . O 109 Post-genitis         2
  Gratum animum laudo; Qui debuit omnia ventis,  . . . O 143 On Lord Anson        1
  Qui nil virtuti, sed debuit omnia ventis,  . . . . . O 143 On Lord Anson    V    1
  Qui veterum modo facta ducum, modo carmina vatum,  . . O 160 Gnothi seauton      8
  Sunt qui curriculo timidi versantur in arcto,  . . . O 163 To Dr Lawrence       9
  Qui sibi sat sapiunt, contenti noscere quantum  . . . O 163 To Dr Lawrence      11
  Qui sibi sat sapient, contenti noscere quantum  . . . O 163 To Dr Lawrence   V  11
  Vitae qui varias vices  . . . . . . . . . . . . . . . O 164 Recover Eyes         1
  Noctis tristitiam qui gelidae jubet,  . . . . . . . . O 164 Recover Eyes         4
  Recte qui fruitur muneribus, dedit.  . . . . . . . . O 164 Recover Eyes        14
  Qui convivia lautasque dapes  . . . . . . . . . . . . O 193 Tr. Medea III        3
  Summe Deus, qui semper amas quodcunque creasti,  . . O 198 Tr. Ash Wed.         1
  Qui cupit in sanctos Christo cogente referri,  . . . O 205 Christianus          1
  Sit sacer orbis amor, miseris qui semper adesse  . . O 205 Christianus          7
  Vult Deus, at, qui cuncta dedit tibi, cuncta reposcit. O 205 Christianus         24
  Qui nec scelestos exigis,  . . . . . . . . . . . . . O 206 Prayers II           4
  O Qui benignus crimina ignoscis, pater  . . . . . . . O 206 Prayers II          11
  Qui jacet hic, servus vixit, nunc, lumine cassus,  . . O 212 Tr Greek 7.538      1
  Dignus qui multa in lustra senescat, erit.  . . . . . O 214 Tr Greek 9.55        2
  Stabo illis qui sunt, quique fuere, gravis.  . . . . O 216 Tr Greek 9.288       6
  Qui, mutare vias ausus terraeque marisque,  . . . . . O 217 Tr Greek 9.304       1
  Pectore qui duro, crudos de vite racemos .  . . . . . O 217 Tr Greek 9.375       1
  Divitiis, utrinque cavens, qui tempore parcit,  . . . O 219 Tr Greek 10.26       3
  Hujus palestrae qui vigil custos stetit,  . . . . . . O 223 Tr. Gk. 11.176       3
  Qui pascit barbam si crescit mente, Platoni,  . . . . O 224 Tr. Gk. 11.430       1
  Omnia qui spectans, omnia ubique regis;  . . . . . . O 232 Prayer               4
  Rorem, qui regeles, geniali et gramina succo  . . . . Y  28 Aurora Musis         5
  "Qui scribat meritas, Birchius alter erit."  . . . . O 386 In Birchium      D   6
  At tu quisquis eris, miseri qui cruda poetae  . . . . Y 387 Death Mother     D   1
QUIBUS
  Sunt quibus a lacrymis vix vacat ulla dies.  . . . . . O 221 Tr Greek 10.84       2
QUICQUID
  Deproperat tellus, fundit tibi munera, quicquid  . . O  89 Messiah             28
  Carpit Arabs, hortis quicquid frondescit eois.  . . . O  89 Messiah             29
  Gesserat et quicquid Virtus, Sapientia quicquid  . . O 160 Gnothi seauton       9
  Gesserat et quicquid Virtus, Sapientia quicquid  . . O 160 Gnothi seauton       9
  Quicquid agam, quocunque ferar, conatibus obstat  . . O 161 Gnothi seauton      40
  Quicquid quaeritur ultra,  . . . . . . . . . . . . . O 182 Waltoni Piscat      11
  Permitte summo quicquid habes Patri,  . . . . . . . . O 187 Ad T. L. M.D.    V  17
  Ditescis, credo, quid restat? quicquid habebis  . . . O 220 Tr Greek 10.60       1
QUICUNQUE
  Optarit quicunque senex sibi longius aevum,  . . . . O 214 Tr Greek 9.55        1
QUID
  Quid mirum Maro quod digne canit arma Virumque,  . . O  85 Mea nec Falern       1
  Quid quod putidulum nostra Camoena sonat?  . . . . . O  85 Mea nec Falern       2
  Quid moliatur Gens Imitantium,  . . . . . . . . . . . O 101 Ad Urbanum          5
  Quid et minetur, scilicitus parum,  . . . . . . . . . O 101 Ad Urbanum          6
  Quid mihi cum cultu? Probitas inculta nitescit,  . . O 104 To Eliz Carter       1
  Quid majus mihi spes ambitiosa dabit?  . . . . . . . O 104 To Eliz Carter       4
  Quid theatrales tibi, Crispe, pompae?  . . . . . . . O 153 In Theatro           2
  Nec quid agam invenio, meditatus grandia, cogor  . . O 161 Gnothi seauton      34
  Quid faciam? tenebrisne pigram damnare senectam  . . O 162 Gnothi seauton      52
  Quid mecum peragam, quod tu doctissime posses  . . . O 163 To Dr Lawrence       4
  Nec quaerunt quid, luna, tuo cum fluctibus orbi.  . . O 163 To Dr Lawrence      16
  Quot modis mecum, quid agat, requiro,  . . . . . . . O 168 Oda to Thrale       11
  Scire locum volui quid daret ille novi.  . . . . . . O 169 Insula Kenneth       6
  Scire locus volui quid daret iste novi.  . . . . . . O 169 Insula Kenneth   V   6
  Quid quod sacrifici versavit femina libros,  . . . . O 170 Insula Kenneth      19
```

QUID	(CONTINUED)	PAGE	TITLE	LINE
Eheu, quid decies plus mihi sexta dedit!		O 171	Tr. Busy Fly	10
Thralia. Quid mavis? tutius hostis eris.		O 197	On Mrs. Thrale	2
Quid nunc superest?		O 199	Medico Aeger S	15
Mens mea quid quereris? veniet tibi mollior hora, . . .		O 208	A Meditation	1
Quid salvere jubes me, pessime? Corripe gressus; . . .		O 211	Tr Greek 7.318	1
Quid labor efficiet? non nisi nudus ero.		O 220	Tr Greek 10.58	2
Ditescis, credo, quid restat? quicquid habebis . . .		O 220	Tr Greek 10.60	1
Quid tibi, mus, mecum, dixit, amice, tibi?		O 224	Tr. Gk. 11.391	2
Quid ferat externi velox, quid deterat aetas, . . .		O 228	Rivum a Stoana	11
Quid ferat externi velox, quid deterat aetas, . . .		O 228	Rivum a Stoana	11
Quid mirum? cum saxa movet statuasque tacentes		Y 28	Aurora Musis	13
Aeternum direpta mihi! sed quid moror istis? . . .	O 384	On the Gin-Act	D	7
Vincere te potui nuda, quid arma geram?	O 384	Epigramma	D	4
QUIDEM				
Ille quidem recte, sublimis, doctus, et acer, . . .		O 160	Gnothi seauton	6
Parva quidem regio, sed relligione priorum . . .		O 169	Insula Kenneth	1
Una quidem, sic fata volunt, tibi vivitur aestas, . . .		O 171	Tr. Busy Fly	9
Dulcia dat natura quidem, mare, sidera, terras, . . .		O 222	Tr. Gk. 10.123	3
QUIES				
Tristis et atra quies, et tardae taedia vitae.		O 161	Gnothi seauton	26
Hic secura quies, hic et honestus amor.		O 170	Insula Kenneth	22
Quam tenet hic, cunctas quae manet, alta quies. . . .		O 211	Tr Greek 7.459	4
QUIESCIT				
Poeta, lector, hic quiescit Hipponax, ...		O 224	Tr Greek 13.3	1
QUIETA				
Permeat omne forum; vita quieta domi est.		O 217	Tr Greek 9.360	2
QUIETEM				
Christe, da tutam trepido quietem, ...		O 194	Prayer on Xmas	5
QUIETIS				
Non ira, non moeror quietis		O 166	Oda Isle Skye	7
QUINAS				
Vicenis quinas, Asiam metata celebrem.		O 230	Geographia Met	22
QUINGENTIS				
Quingentis quadragenis socialis adauget		O 231	Geographia Met	33
QUINQUAGENIS				
Se quinquagenis octingentesima jungit		O 230	Geographia Met	23
QUINQUE				
Papa suo regit imperio ter millia quinque.		O 230	Geographia Met	12
Myriadas denas dat, quinque et millia, sexque . . .		O 230	Geographia Met	27
Centuriae quartae decades quinque Anglia nectit. . . .		O 230	Geographia Met	30
Et quadragenis decades quinque addit Ierne.		O 231	Geographia Met	32
QUINTA				
Aegyptum; templo Sclomonis quinta superbit;		O 226	Septem Aetates	3
Aegyptum; templo Solomonis quinta supersit;	O 226	Septem Aetates	V	3
QUIQUE				
Stabo illis qui sunt, quique fuere, gravis.		O 216	Tr Greek 9.288	6
QUIS				
Quis formae modus imperio? Venus arrogat audax . . .		O 103	Elizae Aenigma	1
Nauta, quis hoc jaceat ne percontere sepulchro; . . .		O 211	Tr Greek 7.350	1
Quaerere, quis, cujas, quis pater, unde venis. . . .		O 219	Tr Greek 9.648	2
Quaerere, quis, cujas, quis pater, unde venis. . . .		O 219	Tr Greek 9.648	2
Quaeris, Quis prior est fama meritisve; superna . .	O 385	The Warehouse	D	3
QUISQUE				
Rectius vives, sua quisque carpat		O 153	In Theatro	11
Quisque suum norit modulum; tibi, prime virorum, . . .		O 160	Gnothi seauton	14
Cum procul est, optat, cum venit, quisque senectam . .		O 214	Tr Greek 9.54	1
QUISQUIS				
Quisquis iter tendis, vitreas qua lucidus undas . . .		O 116	Tr Pope Grotto	1
Quisquis adit lectos elata uxore secundos, ...		O 215	Tr Greek 9.133	1
Sufflato accendis quisquis carbone lucernam, . . .		O 225	Tr. Gk. 16.209	1
At tu quisquis eris, miseri qui cruda poetae . . .	O 387	Death Mother	D	1
QUO				
Quo vagor ulterius? quod ubique requiritur hic est; . .		O 170	Insula Kenneth	21
Judice quo scelerum est paenituisse salus, ...		O 198	Tr. Ash Wed.	2
Quo revocarit		O 199	Medico Aeger S	21
Solvi, quo Christus cunctis delicta redemit, . . .		O 207	Prayers V	5
Causarum series quo moderante fluit, ...		O 207	Prayers VI	2
Haec mihi, quo gentes, quo secula, Christe, piasti, . .		O 208	Prayers VII	11
Haec mihi, quo gentes, quo secula, Christe, piasti, . .		O 208	Prayers VII	11
Si forsan tumulum quo conditur Eumarus aufers, . . .		O 210	Tr Greek 7.284	3
Quo tua signantur gesta, Philippe, lapis.		O 216	Tr Greek 9.288	2
Quo rege gaudent Arcades, furem boum, ...		O 223	Tr. Gk. 11.176	2
Quo, lege vestra, vita me feret mea.		O 226	Tr. Cleanthes	2
Quo toties lavi membra tenella puer;		O 228	Rivum a Stoana	2
Sanguine quo gentes, quo secula cuncta piavit, . .		O 232	Prayer	9
Sanguine quo gentes, quo secula cuncta piavit, . . .		O 232	Prayer	9
QUOCUNQUE				
Quicquid agam, quocunque ferar, conatibus obstat . . .		O 161	Gnothi seauton	40
QUOD				
Quid mirum Maro quod digne canit arma Virumque, . . .		O 85	Mea nec Falern	1
Quid quod putidulum nostra Camoena sonat?		O 85	Mea nec Falern	2
En quoque quod Mirum, ...		O 110	Post-genitis	35
Quod dicas denique dirum, ...		O 110	Post-genitis	36
Nec sibi de gaza praesens quod postulet usus . . .		O 162	Gnothi seauton	44
Non sibi de gaza praesens quod postulat usus . . .	O 162	Gnothi seauton	V	44
Quid mecum peragam, quod tu doctissime posses . . .		O 163	To Dr Lawrence	4
Habeo, dedi quod alteri;		O 165	Tr Doncast Epi	1
Habuique, quod dedi mihi;		O 165	Tr Doncast Epi	2
Sed quod reliqui, perdidi.		O 165	Tr Doncast Epi	3
Quid quod sacrifici versavit femina libros, ...		O 170	Insula Kenneth	19

516

```
QUOD            (CONTINUED)                                      PAGE    TITLE            LINE
   Quo vagor ulterius? quod ubique requiritur hic est;    . .   O 170 Insula Kenneth      21
   Fateris ergo quod populus solet . . . . . . . .  .      .    O 186 Ad T. L. M.D.        1
   Quod poscis, haud unquam tibi   . . . . . . . .   .          O 203 Christ Sinner        3
   Est mihi quod non te rideo, plena salus.  . . .   . . .      O 211 Tr Greek 7.318       2
   Quod nulli proprium versat Fortuna, putabat . . . .   .      O 215 Tr Greek 9.74        3
   Quod vitae satis est, peto, Macrine:   . . . . . .          O 215 Tr Greek 9.110       3
   Vita hcminum nunc plus quod misereris habet.  .   .   .      O 216 Tr Greek 9.148       4
   Nil non mortale est mortalibus; omne quod est hi    .        O 220 Tr Greek 10.31       1
   Nil non mortale est mortalibus; omne quod est hic   . .      O 220 Tr Greek 10.31    V  1
   Quod mors in cineres solvit, et abdit humo.      .   .  .    O 221 Tr Greek 10.84       4
   Quod nimium est fit ineptum; hinc, ut dixere priores,  .     O 224 Tr Greek 16.16       1
   Dat tibi Pythagoram pictor; quod ni ipse tacere  .   .       O 225 Tr. Gk. 16.326       1
   Laevum at utrumque decus, juveni quod praebuit olim  . .     O 225 Tr. Gk. 16.364       3
QUODCUNQUE
   Summe Deus, qui semper amas quodcunque creasti,   . . .      O 198 Tr. Ash Wed.         1
   Summe Pater, quodcunque tuum de corpore Numen   . . . .      O 204 Losing Speech        1
   Summe Pater, quodcunque tuae de corpore leges   . . . .      O 204 Losing Speech     V  1
QUONDAM
   Zosima, quondam solo fuit olim copore serva,   . . . .       Y 320 Tr Gk Epigrams    V  1
   Queis uti poteram quondam Fortuna negavit, . . . . .         O 215 Tr Greek 9.138       3
QUONIAM
   Supplicium huic, quoniam crescentia gaudia laesit,   . .     O 218 Tr Greek 9.375       5
   I, quoniam sic fata vocant: liceat mihi tantum . . . .       O 384 On the Gin-Act     D 9
QUOQUE
   En quoque quod Mirum,  . . . . . . . . . .  . .              O 110 Post-genitis       35
   Cessarunt; pietas hic quoque cura fuit:  . . . . . .         O 170 Insula Kenneth     18
   Hoc quoque superest . . . . . . . . . .  . .                 O 199 Medico Aeger S     23
   Huic quoque, nec genti nec sectae noxius ulli,  . . . .      O 205 Christianus         6
   Tu quoque securus res age, Nise, tuas.   . . . . .           O 228 Rivum a Stoana     12
   Et quadragenis quoque ter tria millia jungit.  . . . .       O 230 Geographia Met     26
QUORSUM
   Quorsum dulcis luxuria soni? . . . . . . . . .  .            O 193 Tr. Medea III      12
QUORUM
   Aurea secla hominum, quorum spectandus ocellis  . . .   .    O 213 Tr Greek 9.29       5
QUOS
   Quos laudet vates Graius Romanus et Anglus  . . . . . .      O  86 Tr Dryden Milt      1
   Quos laudet vates Graecus Romanus et Anglus  . . . . .       O  86 Tr Dryden Milt   V  1
   Huc foedat quos lepra, urit quos febris, adeste!   . . .     O  88 Messiah           16
   Huc foedat quos lepra, urit quos febris, adeste!   . . .     O  88 Messiah           16
   Quos soli ducunt sensus, solus docet usus;   . . . . .      O 163 To Dr Lawrence     10
   Hi sunt quos animi generosa insania magni   . . . . .       O 163 To Dr Lawrence     31
   Nexa patent; hi sunt quos nil mirabile turbat,  . . . .     O 163 To Dr Lawrence     34
   Floribus in pratis legi quos ipse, coronam   . . . . .      O 209 Tr. Greek 5.74      1
   Quos Gyges cumulos habebat auri;   . . . . . . . .          O 215 Tr Greek 9.110      2
   Das bene collatos, quos Roma et Graecia jactat,  . . . .    O 225 Tr. Gk. 16.331      3
   Quos pulsata sonos edit lyra pollice, primis   . . . . .    Y  28 Aurora Musis       15
QUOSCUMQUE
   Quoscumque scelerum poenitet;   . . . . . . . . .   .        O 206 Prayers II          5
QUOT
   Quot modis mecum, quid agat, requiro, . . . . . . .         O 168 Oda to Thrale      11
   Quot vox missa pedes abit horae parte secunda? . . . .      O 229 Epigram IV          1
QUOVIS
   Quovis sanguine cretae . . . . . . . . . . . . .            O 155 Psalmus 117         3
RABIEM
   In Rabiem tunc contremet Ursa   . . . . . . . .   .         O 109 Post-genitis       24
RACEMOS
   Pectore qui duro, crudos de vite racemos  . . . . . .       O 217 Tr Greek 9.375      1
RADIATAE
   Explicat, incinctam radiatae luce tiarae!   . . . . .       O  92 Messiah           95
RADICIBUS
   Virgo! virgo parit! felix radicibus arbor  . . . . .        O  88 Messiah           10
RADII
   Maturant radii, tibi balsama sudat Idume.   . . . . .       O  92 Messiah          105
RADIIS
   Triste coruscabit radiis; dabit hasta recusa   . . . .      O  90 Messiah           69
   Corusca a radiis Memnonis ora dabant. . . . . . . .         Y  28 Aurora Musis       16
RADIOS
   Luna vices revehet; radios pater ipse diei   . . . . .      O  92 Messiah          110
RAMI
   Dia salutares spirant medicamina rami.   . . . . .          O  89 Messiah           17
   Fecerunt rami latebras, tenebrisque diurnis  . . . . .      O 228 Rivum a Stoana      5
RAMISQUE
   Coelestes lambunt animae; ramisque columba,  . . . . .      O  88 Messiah           12
RAPIDI
   Vis boreae gelida, aut rapidi violentia solis.  . . .       O  89 Messiah           19
   Sternite saxa viam, rapidi discedite fluctus!   . . . .     O  89 Messiah           40
RAPIET
   Rapiet Discordia Gentes,   . . . . . . . . . .              O 109 Post-genitis       20
RAPIT
   In sublime rapit, queis terra et pontus et aer   . . . .    O 163 To Dr Lawrence     32
RAPITUR
   Immatura calens rapitur per saecula vates,   . . . .        O  88 Messiah            8
   Ille futura calens rapitur per saecula vates,   . . . .     O  88 Messiah         V  8
RAPTA
   Proles aucta gravat, rapta orbat, caeca juventae est . .    O 217 Tr Greek 9.359      7
RAPTOS
   Invalidi raptos sceptri plorabit honores.   . . . .         O  90 Messiah           56
RAPUIT
   Temporis Henricum rapuit vis vivida mentis;   . . . .       O 116 Tr Pope Grotto     11
```

517

		PAGE	TITLE		LINE
RARAE					
	Et rerum volitant rarae per inane figurae.	O 162	Gnothi seauton		51
RARAQUE					
	Arte nova, raraque fide perscripserat ausus	O 386	In Birchium	D	1
RATES					
	Sola rates struis infidas, et dulcis amorem	O 213	Tr Greek 9.29		3
RATIONE					
	Quandoquidem passim nulla ratione feruntur	O 222	Tr. Gk. 10.124		1
RATIONIS					
	Non Rationis opes Animus, nunc parta recensens,	O 161	Gnothi seauton		42
	Altera pars hominum, sanctae rationis alumni,	O 163	To Dr Lawrence		19
REBOANTIA					
	Auditur Deus! ecce Deus! reboantia circum	O 89	Messiah		35
REBUS					
	In trepidis dare terga rebus.	O 186	Ad T. L. M.D.		4
	In dubiis dare terga rebus.	O 186	Ad T. L. M.D.	V	4
RECEDO					
	Natus eram lacrymans, lacrymans e luce recedo;	O 221	Tr Greek 10.84		1
RECEDUNT					
	Te recedunt moderante fluctus.	O 166	Oda Isle Skye	V	20
REGENSENS					
	Non Rationis opes Animus, nunc parta recensens,	O 161	Gnothi seauton		42
RECENSET					
	Non Animus sero nimium dum parta recenset,	O 161	Gnothi seauton	V	42
RECESSIBUS					
	Ponti profundis clausa recessibus,	O 166	Oda Isle Skye		1
RECIDUNT					
	Te recidunt moderante fluctus.	O 166	Oda Isle Skye		20
RECIPIT					
	Quas navis recipit, quantum sit pondus aquarum,	O 229	Epigram III		1
REGLUDERE					
	Conciliis, verique sacros recludere fontes.	O 163	To Dr Lawrence		22
RECLUSERIT					
	Cum sexagenis, dum plura recluserit aetas,	O 230	Geographia Met		19
RECLUSISQUE					
	Reclusisque oculis infundet amabile lumen,	O 90	Messiah		45
RECONDIS					
	Ditatus magna dote, recondis humo.	O 222	Tr Greek 11.50		4
REGREABUNT					
	Membra viatoris recreabunt frigore linguae.	O 91	Messiah		88
RECREANT					
	Et juga Carmeli recreant fragrantia coelum.	O 89	Messiah		33
	Culmina Carmeli recreant fragrantia coelum.	O 89	Messiah	V	33
RECREARE					
	Utilibus recreare Mentem.	O 102	Ad Urbanum		20
RECTA					
	Recta ad pauperiem tendit, cui corpora cordi est	O 222	Tr. Gk. 10.119		1
RECTE					
	Ille quidem recte, sublimis, doctus, et acer,	O 160	Gnothi seauton		6
	Recte qui fruitur muneribus, dedit.	O 164	Recover Eyes		14
	Cuique loco recte paenituisse mali est	O 198	Tr. Ash Wed.	V	2
	Recte ut poeniteat, respice, magne parens.	O 207	Prayers VI		6
RECTI					
	Cuique loco recti paenituisse mali est	O 198	Tr. Ash Wed.	V	2
	Et pius, et recti cultor: non illa jacere	O 212	Tr Greek 7.590		3
RECTIUS					
	Rectius vives, sua quisque carpat	O 153	In Theatro		11
RECTUM					
	Displiceat, servet tutum sub pectore rectum:	O 205	Christianus		15
REGUMBENS					
	Nunc loca sola placent; frustra te, Somne, recumbens	O 161	Gnothi seauton		30
RECURSET					
	Noctes atque dies animo spes laeta recurset,	O 207	Prayers VII		5
RECUSA					
	Triste coruscabit radiis; dabit hasta recusa	O 90	Messiah		69
REDDE					
	Redde tuis, tibi redde, mentem.	O 187	Ad T. L. M.D.		20
	Redde tuis, tibi redde, mentem.	O 187	Ad T. L. M.D.		20
REDDIDIT					
	Luci reddidit et mihi,	O 164	Recover Eyes		9
REDDOR					
	Me, pensi immunis cum jam mihi reddor, inertis	O 161	Gnothi seauton		24
REDEMIT					
	Solvi, quo Christus cunctis delicta redemit,	O 207	Prayers V		5
REDIMITA					
	His redimita comas, mores depone superbos:	O 209	Tr. Greek 5.74		5
REDITQUE					
	Itque reditque;	O 198	Medico Aeger S		4
	Lunaque quas et sol itque reditque vias.	O 222	Tr. Gk. 10.123		4
REDUCEM					
	Multiplici reducem circumsonat ore magistrum.	O 161	Gnothi seauton		23
	Me Pater tandem reducem benigno	O 227	A Meditation		5
REDUCIS					
	Attollet reducis; bellis praetendet olivas	O 89	Messiah		22
REFERRI					
	Qui cupit in sanctos Christo cogente referri,	O 205	Christianus		1
REFINGENS					
	Naturae invadens, mundique elementa refingens	O 163	To Dr Lawrence		25
REFINGIT					
	Paulatim mores, animum, vitamque refingit,	O 205	Christianus		28

		PAGE	TITLE	LINE

REFRINGENS
    Expectata diu! Naturae claustra refringens . . . . . O 89 Messiah   26
REFULGET
    Immista, sic Iris refulget . . . . O 102 Ad Urbanum   23
REGALIBUS
    Ecce! cremant genibus tritae regalibus arae. . . . . O 92 Messiah   103
REGAT
    Usque regat gressus gratia fida meos. . . . . O 207 Prayers IV   4
REGE
    Laetaque Messia semper dominabere rege, ... O 92 Messiah   118
    Rege, et tuere, quae nocent pellens procul; . . . . . O 206 Prayers I   6
    Quo rege gaudent Arcades, furem boum, ... O 223 Tr. Gk. 11.176   2
REGELES
    Rorem, qui regeles, geniali et gramina succo   Y 28 Aurora Musis   5
REGEM
    Regem coelicolum pepetuo colunt . . . . . O 155 Psalmus 117 V 2
    Regem cujus amor laetior in dies . . . . . . O 155 Psalmus 117 V 5
REGES
    Mutabit, plurima Reges . . . . O 109 Post-genitis   22
REGIAM
    Regiam inundabit, nullis cessura tenebris. . . . . . O 92 Messiah   113
REGINAE
    Clarus Joannes, reginae affinis, ab alto . . . . . O 212 Tr Greek 7.590   1
REGINAM
    Indue reginam, turritae frontis honores . . . . . O 91 Messiah   93
REGIO
    Parva quidem regio, sed relligione priorum . . . . O 169 Insula Kenneth   1
    Non poteras, regio non tulit ulla parem. . . . . . O 225 Tr. Gk. 16.331   6
REGIS
    Rex summe, solus tu regis arbiter, ... O 166 Oda Isle Skye   18
    Omnia qui spectans, cmnia ubique regis; . . . . . . O 232 Prayer   4
REGIT
    Papa suo regit imperio ter millia quinque. . . . . . O 230 Geographia Met   12
REGNA
    Sed sua regna videns, loca nocte silentia late . . . . O 162 Gnothi seauton   49
REGNABAT
    Illic Leniades humili regnabat in aula, ... O 169 Insula Kenneth   7
REGNET
    Divino, sanctus regnet ut intus amor: . . . . O 232 Prayer   6
REGUM
    Quam, regum sobolem, nuptam, matrem, atque sororem . . O 226 Tr. Simonides   3
REIS
    Nunc est pro poena poenituisse reis. . . . . O 208 A Meditation   4
RELINQUIT
    Jupiter hoc templum, ut, siquando relinquit Olympum, . . O 219 Tr Greek 9.702   1
    Evocat Abramum dein tertia; quarta relinquit . . . . O 226 Septem Aetates   2
RELIQUI
    Sed quod reliqui, perdidi. . . . . O 165 Tr Doncast Epi   3
RELLIGIONE
    Parva quidem regio, sed relligione priorum . . . . . O 169 Insula Kenneth   1
RELUCTARI
    Sequar libenter; sin reluctari velim, ... O 226 Tr. Cleanthes   3
REM
    Quem efflant quem rem Phoebi naribus ignis equi . . . Y 28 Aurora Musis V 14
REMUGIT
    Neque Bellua victa remugit. . . . . O 110 Post-genitis   38
REO
    Facilisque semper confitenti ades reo, ... O 206 Prayers III   2
REPENTE
    Venisse, aut visa luce repente mori. . . . . O 217 Tr Greek 9.359   10
REPERIRE
    Per Christum ut veniam sit reperire mihi. . . . . . O 198 Tr. Ash Wed.   4
REPERIT
    Hic, aurum ut reperit, laqueum abjicit, alter ut aurum . O 213 Tr Greek 9.44   1
    Non reperit, nectit quem reperit laqueum. . . . . . . O 213 Tr Greek 9.44   2
    Non reperit, nectit quem reperit laqueum. . . . . . . O 213 Tr Greek 9.44   2
REPLEAT
    Tantundem est illis, repleat spatia ardua coeli . . . O 163 To Dr Lawrence   13
REPOSCIT
    Vult Deus, at, qui cuncta dedit tibi, cuncta reposcit. . O 205 Christianus   24
REPROBAT
    Tunc vati facilem reprobat Apollo, Sybillae . . . . . Y 28 Aurora Musis   7
REPTANT
    Qua sulcat, reptant tuti per lubrica vitae. . . . . . O 163 To Dr Lawrence   18
REPTARE
    Consuetus fulcro innixus reptare bacilli . . . . . . O 90 Messiah   50
REQUIES
    Hic requies fessis; non sacra saevit in umbra . . . . O 89 Messiah   18
    Hic requies fessis; non sacra hac saevit in umbra . . . O 89 Messiah V 18
REQUIESCIT
    Inclytus hic haeres magni requiescit Oeni, ... O 386 Tr Epi. Madoc D 1
REQUIRIT
    Ordinibus surgit densis, vitamque requirit . . . . . O 92 Messiah   97
    Pastor Axabs: decies octo sibi Persa requirit. . . . . O 230 Geographia Met   9
REQUIRITUR
    Quo vagox ulterius? quod ubique requiritur hic est; . . . O 170 Insula Kenneth   21
REQUIRO
    Quot modis mecum, quid agat, requiro, ... O 168 Oda to Thrale   11
RERUM
    Sic orsus--Qualis rerum mihi nascitur ordo! . . . . . O 88 Messiah   9
    Ingredere O!--rerum pura cole mente parentem, ... O 116 Tr Pope Grotto V 7

RERUM	(CONTINUED)	PAGE	TITLE		LINE
Cessat inops rerum, ut torpet, si marmoris absit		O 161	Gnothi seauton		38
Et rerum volitant rarae per inane figurae.		O 162	Gnothi seauton		51
Humanae mentis, rerum se pascere formis,		O 163	To Dr Lawrence		6
Rerum perpetuus temperat Arbiter,		O 164	Recover Eyes		2
Aeterne rerum conditor,		O 206	Prayers II		1
RERUMQUE					
Accendit, rerumque modos ac foedera ponit.		O 163	To Dr Lawrence		30
Per vitae tenebras rerumque incerta vagantem		O 207	Prayers IV		1
RES					
Res angusta domi, et macrae penuria mentis.		O 161	Gnothi seauton		41
Permitte summo res hominum Patri,		O 187	Ad T. L. M.D.		17
Ut vitam, poscat sibi res, impendere vero.		O 205	Christianus		11
Nec male res cessit, subito si funere sponsam,		O 222	Tr Greek 11.50		3
Tu quoque securus res age, Nise, tuas.		O 228	Rivum a Stoana		12
RESCIRE					
Nunc rescire priora,		O 182	Waltoni Piscat		7
RESIDENT					
Te resident moderante fluctus.		O 166	Oda Isle Skye	V	20
RESONABUNT					
Resonabunt Oppida Luctu:		O 109	Post-genitis		8
RESONARE					
Thraliae discant resonare nomen		O 168	Oda to Thrale		19
RESPICE					
Me, pater omnipotens, de puro respice coelo,		O 207	Prayers V		1
Respice quem subigit senium, morbique seniles,		O 207	Prayers VI		3
Respice quem subiget senium, morbique seniles,		O 207	Prayers VI	V	3
Respice inutiliter lapsi quem poenitet aevi;		O 207	Prayers VI		5
Recte ut poeniteat, respice, magne parens.		O 207	Prayers VI		6
RESPONDIT					
Mus blandum ridens, respondit, pelle timorem;		O 224	Tr. Gk. 11.391		3
RESTAT					
Tempore restat.		O 153	In Theatro		16
Tempora restat.		O 153	In Theatro	V	16
Restat? an accingar studiis gravioribus audax?		O 162	Gnothi seauton		53
Nec mirum; restat lepori conscendere coelum,		O 213	Tr Greek 9.18		3
Gratia vix restat nomine digna suo.		O 220	Tr Greek 10.30		2
Ditescis, credo, quid restat? quicquid habebis		O 220	Tr Greek 10.60		1
RESTINCTA					
Pulicibus morsus, restincta lampade, stultus		O 224	Tr. Gk. 11.432		1
RETENTAT					
Naufragus iratas ille retentat aquas.		O 215	Tr Greek 9.133		2
RETRACTA					
Omnesque in partes tracta retracta fluit;		O 221	Tr Greek 10.74		4
RETULERE					
Munera muneribus si retulere fabri.		O 225	Tr Greek 16.87		4
REVEHET					
Luna vices revehet; radios pater ipse diei		O 92	Messiah		110
REVISENS					
Compositis Pax alma suas, terrasque revisens		O 89	Messiah		23
REVOCANDA					
Carpe diem, fugit, heu, non revocanda dies!		O 171	Tr. Busy Fly		6
REVOCANT					
Te medici revocant labores.		O 187	Ad T. L. M.D.		16
REVOCARE					
Stat: fixum est: nequeunt jam revocare preces.		O 384	On the Gin-Act	D	8
REVOCARIT					
Quo revocarit		O 199	Medico Aeger S		21
REVOCATQUE					
Amissas modo quaerit oves, revocatque vagantes;		O 90	Messiah		61
REVOLUTA					
Et cortina novum det revoluta diem!		O 393	Tr. of Crashaw	D	4
REX					
Rex summe, solus tu regis arbiter,		O 166	Oda Isle Skye		18
Me, rex deorum, tuque, duc, necessitas,		O 226	Tr. Cleanthes		1
RHODOCLEA					
Contextam variis, do, Rhodoclea, tibi:		O 209	Tr. Greek 5.74		2
RICARDUM					
Ad Ricardum Savage, Arm. Humani Generis Amatorem.		O 102	Ad R. Savage		T
RIDEBIT					
Ridebit linguae innocuos, squamasque virentes		O 91	Messiah		91
Ridebit linguae innocuos, squamas viridantes		O 91	Messiah	V	91
RIDENDUM					
Plus tibi ridendum secula nostra dabunt.		O 216	Tr Greek 9.148		2
RIDENS					
Sed Miliae ridens, atque dolens Miliae.		O 218	Tr Greek 9.573		6
Clam nocte tollit Aulus, et ridens ait;		O 223	Tr. Gk. 11.176		4
Mus blandum ridens, respondit, pelle timorem;		O 224	Tr. Gk. 11.391		3
Dulce Venus ridens, lorica nil opus, inquit,		O 384	Epigramma	D	3
RIDENT					
Torva ubi rident steriles coloni		O 167	Oda to Thrale		3
RIDEO					
Est mihi quod non te rideo, plena salus.		O 211	Tr Greek 7.318		2
RIDERE					
Ridere, aut tecum me lacrimare jubet.		O 216	Tr Greek 9.148		6
RIDET					
Hostem odit tacite, sed amicum ridet aperte		O 197	On Mrs. Thrale		1
Pallas ubique docet; ridet ubique Venus.		O 383	Syl. Urb. Thes	D	4
RIGIDUS					
Vomerem, et in falcem rigidus curvabitur ensis.		O 90	Messiah		70

		PAGE	TITLE	LINE
RISURUS				
Risurus olim nisibus Aemuli;		O 101	Ad Urbanum	14
RIVI				
Garrula mirantur salientis murmura rivi.		O 91	Messiah	77
RIVUM				
In Rivum a Mola Stoana Lichfeldiae diffluentem		O 228	Rivum a Stoana	T
RIVUS				
Errat adhuc vitreus per prata virentia rivus, ...		O 228	Rivum a Stoana	1
RIXA				
Felici thalamo non, puto, rixa strepit.		O 226	Tr. Greek	2
RIXISQUE				
Elige iter vitae, ut possis; rixisque dolisque		O 217	Tr Greek 9.359	1
ROBORA				
Accrescunt tremulis tactu nova robora nervis:		O 90	Messiah	49
Accrescunt teneris tactu nova robora nervis:		O 90	Messiah	V 49
Saxa cadent, solidque liquescent robora montis: . . .		O 92	Messiah	116
ROBORE				
Pectus, et ingenium vano se robore jactans.		O 161	Gnothi seauton	36
Arte valent isti, mihi robore vivere solo est, . . .		O 224	Tr Greek 16.1	3
Nunc juvenum terres robore corda senex.		O 225	Tr. Gk. 16.364	2
ROGASSE				
Ingenio parcas, nec sit mihi culpa rogasse, ...		O 204	Losing Speech	3
ROMA				
Te manet imperii, Roma, perenne decus.		O 219	Tr Greek 9.647	2
Hanc statuam ingenio Roma benigna tuo.		O 225	Tr. Gk. 16.331	2
Das bene collatos, quos Roma et Graecia jactat, . . .		O 225	Tr. Gk. 16.331	3
ROMAE				
Quae fausta Romae dixit Horatius, ...		O 188	Epilogus	1
ROMANUS				
Quos laudet vates Graius Romanus et Anglus		O 86	Tr Dryden Milt	1
Quos laudet vates Graecus Romanus et Anglus		O 86	Tr Dryden Milt	V 1
Sublime ingenium Graius; Romanus habebat		O 86	Tr Dryden Milt	3
Sublime ingenium Graecus; Romanus habebat		O 86	Tr Dryden Milt	V 3
ROREM				
Rorem, qui regeles, geniali et gramina succo		Y 28	Aurora Musis	5
RORES				
Nectareos rores, alimentaque mitia coelum		O 88	Messiah	14
ROSA				
Vitae rosa brevis est; properans si carpere nolis, . .		O 223	Tr Greek 11.53	V 1
Turbidus imber abest; mittit rosa roscida gemmas, . . .		O 385	Cantico Solom.	D 5
ROSAE				
Rosae ruborem sic Viola adjuvat		O 102	Ad Urbanum	22
Vita rosae brevis est; properans si carpere nolis, . .		O 223	Tr Greek 11.53	1
ROSCIDA				
Turbidus imber abest; mittit rosa roscida gemmas, . . .		O 385	Cantico Solom.	D 5
ROSIS				
Suave rubere rosis, sitientesque inter arenas		O 91	Messiah	76
Cum violis; spirant lilia mista rosis.		O 209	Tr. Greek 5.74	4
ROSTRUM				
Pone metum, rostrum fidens immitte culullo, ...		O 171	Tr. Busy Fly	3
ROTUNDIS				
Laevia serratis miscens, quadrata rotundis, ...		O 163	To Dr Lawrence	26
RUBERE				
Suave rubere rosis, sitientesque inter arenas		O 91	Messiah	76
RUBESCET				
Flumina prorumpunt; non posthac sole rubescet		O 92	Messiah	108
RUBET				
Atque Aethra ambigua pallida luce rubet;		Y 28	Aurora Musis	2
RUBETA				
Artificis frondent dextrae; palmisque rubeta		O 91	Messiah	82
RUBOREM				
Rosae ruborem sic Viola adjuvat		O 102	Ad Urbanum	22
RUBRI				
Nam foecunda rubri		O 109	Post-genitis	9
RUBUS				
Quaerenti obveniet mox sine flore rubus.		O 223	Tr Greek 11.53	2
RUDEM				
Materiemque rudem, magnaeque parentis adesse		O 163	To Dr Lawrence	21
RUDI				
Hic delusa rudi frustrabar brachia motu, ...		O 228	Rivum a Stoana	3
RUDIS				
Et juvat ingenii vita sine arte rudis.		O 104	To Eliz Carter	2
RUINAS				
Saxeas miscet nebulis ruinas, ...		O 167	Oda to Thrale	2
RUINIS				
Pollicitis firmata Dei, stabilita ruinis.		O 92	Messiah	119
Firmius ac ipsis Mundi stabilita ruinis.		O 92	Messiah	V 119
RUMORE				
Vive tuo ex animo, vario rumore loquetur		O 214	Tr Greek 9.50	1
RUPE				
At non cavata rupe latescere, ...		O 166	Oda Isle Skye	9
RUPES				
Permeo terras, ubi nuda rupes		O 167	Oda to Thrale	1
RUPIBUS				
Strepens procellis, rupibus obsita, ...		O 166	Oda Isle Skye	2
RURA				
Rura labores.		O 167	Oda to Thrale	4
Rura labor lassat; mare mille pericula terrent; . . .		O 217	Tr Greek 9.359	3
RUS				
Rus ornat natura; levat maris aspera lucrum;		O 217	Tr Greek 9.360	3

```
RUSSIA                                                    PAGE    TITLE            LINE
    Russia, myriadas ter denas adde trecentis:   . . . . . .   O 230 Geographia Met     17
RUTILANTIS
    Aureaque admirans rutilantis fulgura cristae.   . . . .   O  91 Messiah            92
SABAEO
    Suaviter exhalant violaria grata, Sabaeo  . . . . . .   O 385 Cantico Solom.   D 15
SACER
    Sit sacer orbis amor, miseris qui semper adesse   . . .   O 205 Christianus         7
    Ardeat huic toto sacer ignis pectore, possit  . . . .   O 205 Christianus        10
SACRA
    Nuncia sacra Dei, plaudentibus insidet alis.  . . . . .   O  88 Messiah            13
    Hic requies fessis; non sacra saevit in umbra  . . . .   O  89 Messiah            18
    Hic requies fessis; non sacra hac saevit in umbra  . . .   O  89 Messiah          V 18
    Divinos, surdas sacra vox permulceat aures!  . . . . .   O  89 Messiah            43
    Nil opus est aeris sacra de turre sonantis  . . . . .   O 170 Insula Kenneth   V 18A
SACRI
    Sacri discipulus libri  . . . . . . .   O 164 Recover Eyes        11
    Ponti inter strepitus sacri non munera cultus  . . . .   O 170 Insula Kenneth     17
    Sacri vagantes luminis gressus face  . . . . . . .   O 206 Prayers I            5
SACRIFICI
    Quid quod sacrifici versavit femina libros,  . . . . .   O 170 Insula Kenneth     19
SACRIS
    Sint pro legitimis pectora pura sacris  . . . . . .   O 170 Insula Kenneth   V 20
    Sint pro legitimis pura labella sacris  . . . . . .   O 170 Insula Kenneth   V 20
SACRO
    Aetheris, en! portas sacro fulgore micantes  . . . . .   O  92 Messiah           106
    Gaudium sacro fluat, et benigni  . . . . . . . .   O 193 Prayer on Xmas       3
SACROS
    Tolle, Salema, sacros, quam circum gloria pennas  . . .   O  92 Messiah            94
    Conciliis, verique sacros recludere fontes. . . . . .   O 163 To Dr Lawrence     22
SACRUM
    Ingredere! Egeriae sacrum en tibi panditur antrum!  . .   O 116 Tr Pope Grotto      9
SAECULA
    Immatura calens rapitur per saecula vates,  . . . . .   O  88 Messiah             8
    Ille futura calens rapitur per saecula vates,  . . . .   O  88 Messiah          V  8
    Queis majus pretium saecula lapsa dabant  . . . . .   Y  28 Aurora Musis       12
SAEPE
    Saepe tuum in tumulum lacrymarum decidit imber  . . . .   O 212 Tr Greek 7.560      1
    Praestat magistro saepe discipulus suo.  . . . . . .   O 223 Tr. Gk. 11.176      5
SAEVA
    Seu te saeva sitis, levitas sive improba fecit,  . . .   O 171 Tr. Busy Fly        1
    Seu te saeva fames, levitas sive improba fecit,  . . .   O 171 Tr. Busy Fly     V  1
SAEVIT
    Hic requies fessis; non sacra saevit in umbra  . . . .   O  89 Messiah            18
    Hic requies fessis; non sacra hac saevit in umbra  . .   O  89 Messiah          V 18
SAEVUS
    Accola Danubii qualia saevus habet;  . . . . . . .   O 169 Insula Kenneth     12
SALAMINIA
    Spreta jacet Marathon, jacet et Salaminia laurus,  . . .   O 216 Tr Greek 9.288      3
SALEBRIS
    Te sterili functum cura, vocumque salebris  . . . . .   O 161 Gnothi seauton     19
SALEBROSA
    Inter erroris salebrosa longi,  . . . . . . . . .   O 168 Oda to Thrale       9
SALEMA
    Tolle, Salema, sacros, quam circum gloria pennas  . . .   O  92 Messiah            94
SALICTI
    Densa fronde salicti  . . . . . . . .   O 181 Waltoni Piscat      2
SALIENTIS
    Garrula mirantur salientis murmura rivi. . . . . . .   O  91 Messiah            77
SALTEM
    Laurenti saltem facili dignarier aure?  . . . . . .   O 163 To Dr Lawrence      5
SALTU
    Jam saltu capreas, jam cursu provocat euros.  . . . . .   O  90 Messiah            51
    Nunc saltu capreas, jam cursu provocat euros.  . . . .   O  90 Messiah          V 51
    Et saltu e muro Ditis opaca petit:  . . . . . . .   O 211 Tr Greek 7.471      2
SALUS
    Judice quo scelerum est paenituisse salus,  . . . . .   O 198 Tr. Ash Wed.        2
    Est mihi quod non te rideo, plena salus. . . . . . .   O 211 Tr Greek 7.318      2
SALUTARES
    Dia salutares spirant medicamina rami.  . . . . . .   O  89 Messiah            17
SALUTET
    Gloria silvarum, dominum inclinata salutet!  . . . . .   O  89 Messiah            38
SALUTIS
    Salutis aeternae dator;  . . . . . . . .   O 206 Prayers II          2
SALVATOR
    En! Salvator adest; vultus agnoscite caeci  . . . . .   O  89 Messiah            42
SALVE
    Cunctiparens tellus, salve, levis esto pusillo  . . . .   O 211 Tr Greek 7.461      1
SALVERE
    Quid salvere jubes me, pessime? Corripe gressus;  . . .   O 211 Tr Greek 7.318      1
SAMI
    Prosequitur lacrymis filia moesta Sami,  . . . . . .   O 211 Tr Greek 7.459      2
SANARI
    Sanari voluit meos,  . . . . . . . . .   O 164 Recover Eyes        7
SANCTA
    Nunc summi prece sancta  . . . . . . . . .   O 182 Waltoni Piscat      9
    Veniaeque sancta pacis adde gaudia:  . . . . . . .   O 206 Prayers I           8
    Me ducat lux sancta, Deus, lux sancta sequatur;  . . .   O 207 Prayers IV          3
    Me ducat lux sancta, Deus, lux sancta sequatur;  . . .   O 207 Prayers IV          3
SANCTAE
    Altera pars hominum, sanctae rationis alumni,  . . . .   O 163 To Dr Lawrence     19
```

```
                                                  PAGE    TITLE              LINE
SANCTAE        (CONTINUED)                        O 205 Christianus           12
    Cura placere Deo sit prima, sit ultima, sanctae     . . .
SANCTI
    Tu mihi, qui flamma movisti pectora sancti   . . . . .   O  88 Messiah                6
    Insula Sancti Kennethi   . . . . . . . . . .             O 169 Insula Kenneth         T
SANCTO
    Sancto dicite carmine. . . . . . . . . .                 O 155 Psalmus 117            8
    Certa mihi sancto flagret amore fides.   . . . . . .     O 207 Prayers VII            6
SANCTOS
    Qui cupit in sanctos Christo cogente referri,    . . . . O 205 Christianus            1
SANCTUS
    Velle vetet cuiquam non bene sanctus amor.   . . . . .   O 207 Prayers VII            8
    Me gregi Sanctus socium beatum   . . . . . . . .         O 227 A Meditation           7
    Divinc, sanctus regnet ut intus amor:    . . . . . .     O 232 Prayer                 6
SANGUINE
    Quovis sanguine cretae   . . . . . . . . .               O 155 Psalmus 117            3
    Sanguine dum tumido suffusus flagrat ocellus,    . . .   O 162 To Dr Lawrence         1
    Acri sanguine turgidos   . . . . . . . . .               O 164 Recover Eyes           5
    Sanguine, peccanti promereare tuo!   . . . . .          O 208 Prayers VII            12
    Sanguine Anastasii; cuncta sepulta jacent:   . . . .    O 212 Tr Greek 7.590          2
    Sanguine quo gentes, quo secula cuncta piavit,   . . . . O 232 Prayer                 9
SANGUINEM
    Sanguinem Equus sugit, . . . . . . . . . . . . .         O 110 Post-genitis          37
SANGUINIS
    Non mihi sorte datum; lenti seu sanguinis obsint   . . . O 160 Gnothi seauton        16
SAPIENS
    His sapiens lectis, Epicurum quaerere frustra    . . . . O 222 Tr Greek 11.50         5
SAPIENT
    Qui sibi sat sapient, contenti noscere quantum   . . . . O 163 To Dr Lawrence   V   11
SAPIENTER
    At Seni fluxo sapienter uti    . . . . . . . . .         O 153 In Theatro            15
SAPIENTIA
    Gesserat et quicquid Virtus, Sapientia quicquid    . . . O 160 Gnothi seauton         9
    Tuto eluctatum spatiis Sapientia dia   . . . . . . .     O 161 Gnothi seauton        20
SAPIENTIAM
    Crepare vaecors, nil sapientiam    . . . . . . . .       O 186 Ad T. L. M.D.          2
SAPIENTICR
    Cum tacet indoctus, sapientior esse videtur,   . . . . . O 221 Tr Greek 10.98         1
SAPIT
    Tempore divitiis utitur, ille sapit.   . . . . . . .     O 219 Tr Greek 10.26         4
SAPIUNT
    Qui sibi sat sapiunt, contenti noscere quantum   . . .   O 163 To Dr Lawrence        11
SAPPHO
    Mnemosyne, ut Sappho mellita voce canentem   . . . .     O 214 Tr Greek 9.66          1
SARDINIAM
    Sardiniam cum sexcentis sex millia complent.   . . . .   O 230 Geographia Met        18
SARONICA
    Mittit aromaticas vallis Saronica nubes, . . . . . . .   O  89 Messiah               32
SAT
    Qui sibi sat sapiunt, contenti noscere quantum   . . .   O 163 To Dr Lawrence        11
    Qui sibi sat sapient, contenti noscere quantum   . . .   O 163 To Dr Lawrence   V   11
    Sat laetitia, sine subsidiis,  . . . . . . . .          O 193 Tr. Medea III         13
    Aevi sat novi quam sim brevis; astra tuenti,   . . . .   O 219 Tr Greek 9.577         1
SATIS
    Tandem dolori plus satis est datum,    . . . . . .       O 187 Ad T. L. M.D.         13
    Quod vitae satis est, peto, Macrine:   . . . . . .       O 215 Tr Greek 9.110         3
SATYRUM
    Antiope satyrum, Danae aurum, Europa juvencum,   . . .   O 214 Tr Greek 9.48          1
SAVAGE
    Ad Ricardum Savage, Arm. Humani Generis Amatorem.  . . . O 102 Ad R. Savage           T
SAXA
    Saxa sonant Deus; ecce Deus! deflectitur aether  . . .   O  89 Messiah               36
    Sternite saxa viam, rapidi discedite fluctus!    . . .   O  89 Messiah               40
    Per saxa, ignivomi nuper spelaea draconis,   . . . .     O  91 Messiah               78
    Saxa cadent, solidque liquescent robora montis:  . . .   O  92 Messiah              116
    Quid mirum? cum saxa movet statuasque tacentes   . . .   Y  28 Aurora Musis          13
SAXEA
    Saxea Phidiaca spirat imago manu.  . . . . . . . .       O  85 Adjecere bonae         4
SAXEAS
    Saxeas miscet nebulis ruinas,  . . . . . . . . .         O 167 Oda to Thrale          2
SCALIGER
    Scaliger ut duxit, tenuis pertaesus opellae,   . . .     O 160 Gnothi seauton         2
    Ima tuas credit permitti, Scaliger, iras.    . . .       O 160 Gnothi seauton        13
SCATEBRAE
    Ut qua dulce strepunt scatebrae, qua laeta virescunt . . O  90 Messiah               57
    Ut qua dulce strepent scatebrae, qua laeta virescunt . . O  90 Messiah          V   57
SCATET
    Aut periisse; scatet vita benigna bonis.   . . . . .     O 217 Tr Greek 9.360        10
SCELERIS
    Temnere opes pretium sceleris, patriamque tueri    . . . O 116 Tr Pope Grotto        15
    Sceleris ut expers omnis, et vacuus metu,    . . . .     O 206 Prayers I              9
SCELERUM
    Judice quo scelerum est paenituisse salus,   . . . .     O 198 Tr. Ash Wed.           2
    Quoscumque scelerum poenitet;  . . . . . . . .          O 206 Prayers II             5
    Scelerum catena me laborantem gravi    . . . . .         O 206 Prayers III            4
    Scelerum caterna me laborantem grave   . . . . . .       O 206 Prayers III      V    4
SCELESTOS
    Qui nec scelestos exigis, . . . . . . . . . .            O 206 Prayers II             4
SCELESTUS
    Si sis scelestus, praeteri procul marmor:    . . . .     O 224 Tr Greek 13.3          2
    Fiam scelestus, nec tamen minus sequar.  . . . . .       O 226 Tr. Cleanthes          4
```

SCENA
    Vita omnis scena est ludusque; aut ludere disce • • •   O 221 Tr Greek 10.72   1

PAGE TITLE   LINE

SCEPTRA
    Omnia, nec curae sunt sua sceptra Jovi. • • • • •   O 103 Elizae Aenigma   2
SCEPTRI
    Invalidi raptos sceptri plorabit honores.   O 90 Messiah   56
SCHOLARUM
    Fallimur exemplis; temere sibi turba scholarum • •   O 160 Gnothi seauton   12
SCIAE
    Littora Sciae. • • • • • •   O 168 Oda to Thrale   20
SCINTILLAT
    Crystallisque latex fractus scintillat acutis, • • • •   O 116 Tr Pope Grotto   4
SCIRE
    Scire vices ponti facile est, nihil amplius optant • •   O 163 To Dr Lawrence   15
    Scire locum volui quid daret ille novi. • • • •   O 169 Insula Kenneth   6
    Scire locus volui quid daret iste novi. • • • • •   O 169 Insula Kenneth V 6
SCOPULO
    E scopulo numerare fluctus. • • • • • •   O 166 Oda Isle Skye   12
SCRIBANT
    Carmina vis nostri scribant meliora Poetae? • • •   O 85 Mea nec Falern   5
SCRIBAT
    "Qui scribat meritas, Birchius alter erit." • •   O 386 In Birchium D 6
SCRIBENDAQUE
    Ingemit exosus, scribendaque lexica mandat • • •   O 160 Gnothi seauton   4
SCRIPTA
    Scripta legens, sola vivere mente cupit. • • • •   O 211 Tr Greek 7.471   4
SCRUTARE
    Auriferasque, auri metuens, scrutare cavernas. • •   O 116 Tr Pope Grotto   8
SE
    Hic, in se totum longe per opaca futuri • • • •   O 116 Tr Pope Grotto   10
    Pectus, et ingenium vano se robore jactans. • •   O 161 Gnothi seauton   36
    Conspicit aggestas, et se miratur in illis, • •   O 161 Gnothi seauton   43
    Versat opum cumulos, et se miratur in illis, • •   O 161 Gnothi seauton V 43
    Humanae mentis, rerum se pascere formis, • •   O 163 To Dr Lawrence   6
    Se fidum addicat Christo, mortalia temnens. • •   O 205 Christianus   18
    Pergit, et imperiis sentit se dulcibus actum. • •   O 205 Christianus   27
    Se quinquagenis octingentesima jungit • • • •   O 230 Geographia Met   23
SECARE
    Secare venam; • • • • • • • •   O 199 Medico Aeger S   11
SECLA
    Tres tria temporibus secla dedere suis. • • •   O 86 Tr Dryden Milt   2
    Postera sic pastor divinus secla beabit, • •   O 90 Messiah   64
    Aurea secla hominum, quorum spectandus ocellis • •   O 213 Tr Greek 9.29   5
SECLORUM
    Ingentemque animo seclorum volverat orbem. • •   O 160 Gnothi seauton   11
    Ingentemque animo seclorum volveret orbem. • •   O 160 Gnothi seauton V 11
SECRETAS
    Pendula secretas abdidit arbor aquas. • • • •   O 228 Rivum a Stoana   6
SECTA
    Secta crepet nimis alta fallax. • • • • •   O 166 Oda Isle Skye   16
SECTAE
    Huic quoque, nec genti nec sectae noxius ulli, • •   O 205 Christianus   6
SECULA
    Haec mihi, quo gentes, quo secula, Christe, piasti, •   O 208 Prayers VII   11
    Plus tibi ridendum secula nostra dabunt. • •   O 216 Tr Greek 9.148   2
    Plura ut victurus secula, parce bonis: • •   O 219 Tr Greek 10.26   2
    Prolem Hippi, et sua qua meliorem secula nullum •   O 226 Tr. Simonides   1
    Sanguine quo gentes, quo secula cuncta piavit, • •   O 232 Prayer   9
SECUNDA
    Haec habet altrici Capra secunda Jovis. • •   O 156 Collari Caprae   2
    Spes novas nova lux parit, secunda • • • •   O 204 Spes   3
    Prima parit terras aetas; siccatque secunda; • •   O 226 Septem Aetates   1
    Quot vox missa pedes abit horae parte secunda? • •   O 229 Epigram IV   1
SECUNDAE
    Centuriae octavam decadem addit Lucca secundae. • •   O 230 Geographia Met   15
    Millia myriadis septem foecunda secundae • • •   O 230 Geographia Met   31
SECUNDOS
    Quisquis adit lectos elata uxore secundos, • • •   O 215 Tr Greek 9.133   1
SECURA
    Tu secura tamen confusa elementa videbis, • • •   O 92 Messiah   117
    Hic secura quies, hic et honestus amor. • • •   O 170 Insula Kenneth   22
SECURIBUS
    Nunc veteres duris periere securibus umbrae, • •   O 228 Rivum a Stoana   7
SECURUS
    Tu quoque securus res age, Nise, tuas. • • •   O 228 Rivum a Stoana   12
SED
    Leo, sed violare timebit, • • • • •   O 109 Post-genitis   28
    Qui nil virtuti, sed debuit omnia ventis, •   O 143 On Lord Anson V 1
    Sed sua regna videns, loca nocte silentia late •   O 162 Gnothi seauton   49
    Sed quod reliqui, perdidi. • • •   O 165 Tr Doncast Epi   3
    Parva quidem regio, sed relligione priorum • •   O 169 Insula Kenneth   1
    Hostem odit tacite, sed amicum ridet aperte • •   O 197 On Mrs. Thrale   1
    Nec dubitet quem dicat herum, sed, totus in uno, • •   O 205 Christianus   17
    Sed timeat semper, caveatque ante omnia, turbae • •   O 205 Christianus   19
    Non tenet; esca natat pulchra, sed hamus abest. • •   O 209 Tr. Greek 5.67   2
    Quale, sed hostiles quale dedere manus. • •   O 210 Tr Greek 7.136   2
    Exiguum est Marti, sed mihi grande lucrum. • •   O 216 Tr Greek 9.163   4
    Sed Miliae ridens, atque dolens Miliae. • •   O 218 Tr Greek 9.573   6
    Nycticorax cantat lethale, sed ipsa canenti • •   O 223 Tr. Gk. 11.186   1
    Sed similem, Plutarche, tuae describere vitam • •   O 225 Tr. Gk. 16.331   5
    Aeternum direpta mihi! sed quid moror istis? • •   O 384 On the Gin-Act D 7

```
                                                         PAGE    TITLE              LINE
SEDATAS
     Sedatas niveo Virtus lucebit amictu.  . . . . . . .  O  89 Messiah               24
SEDEM
     Hic, bone vir, sedem, non alimenta, peto.  . . . .   O 224 Tr. Gk. 11.391         4
SEDIBUS
     His cura credo sedibus exulat;  . . . . . . . . .    O 166 Oda Isle Skye          5
     Felicitatis sedibus . . . . . . . . . . . . . .      O 206 Prayers II             3
SEDILE
     Tutum hic sedile, et si placet, sopor tutus.  . . .  O 224 Tr Greek 13.3          4
SEDISTI
     Puppe gubernatrix sedisti, Audacia, prima,  . . . .  O 213 Tr Greek 9.29          1
SEDULA
     Sedula mentem;  . . . . . . . . . . . . . . . .      O 168 Oda to Thrale         16
SEDULITAS
     Sedulitas animosa tendet. . . . . . . . . . . .      O 101 Ad Urbanum            12
SEGREGET
     Ne stolidae similis leges sibi segreget audax  . . . O 205 Christianus           20
SELECTAS
     Et gremio fotis selectas porrigit herbas,  . . . .   O  90 Messiah               60
SEMESOS
     Labraque constrictus semesos, jamque terendos  . . . O 218 Tr Greek 9.375         3
SEMINA
     Coelestis fido caluerunt semina flammae.  . . . . .  O 116 Tr Pope Grotto        14
     In me sparsa manu virtutum semina larga  . . . . .   O 207 Prayers VII            3
SEMITA
     Si qua usquam pateat melioris semita vitae,  . . . . O 161 Gnothi seauton        33
SEMPER
     Laetaque Messia semper dominabere rege,  . . . . .   O  92 Messiah              118
     Te semper studiis utilibus colam; . . . . . . .      O 164 Recover Eyes          12
     Summe Deus, qui semper amas quodcunque creasti,  . . O 198 Tr. Ash Wed.           1
     Sit sacer orbis amor, miseris qui semper adesse  . . O 205 Christianus            7
     Sed timeat semper, caveatque ante omnia, turbae  . . O 205 Christianus           19
     Pater benigne, summa semper lenitas,  . . . . . .    O 206 Prayers I              1
     Facilisque semper confitenti ades reo,  . . . . .    O 206 Prayers III            2
     Et colere et leges semper amare tuas. . . . . .      O 208 Prayers VII           10
     Incusat, semper spe meliora videt. . . . . . . .     O 214 Tr Greek 9.54          2
     Nec sinat semper tremere ac dolere  . . . . . . .    O 227 A Meditation           3
     Nec sinat semper tremere ac dolore  . . . . . . .    O 227 A Meditation     V     3
     Ut tibi laus omni semper ab ore sonet:  . . . . .    O 232 Prayer                 8
SEMPERQUE
     Captans, nec fastu tumidus, semperque futuro  . . .  O 205 Christianus            3
SENECTAM
     Quid faciam? tenebrisne pigram damnare senectam  . . O 162 Gnothi seauton        52
     Cum procul est, optat, cum venit, quisque senectam   O 214 Tr Greek 9.54          1
SENES
     Mente senes clim juvenis, Faustine, premebas,  . . . O 225 Tr. Gk. 16.364         1
SENESCAT
     Dignus qui multa in lustra senescat, erit. . . . .   O 214 Tr Greek 9.55          2
SENEX
     Optarit quicunque senex sibi longius aevum,  . . . . O 214 Tr Greek 9.55          1
     Praecellit juvenis vi, pietate senex. . . . . . .    O 217 Tr Greek 9.360         8
     Nunc juvenum terres robore corda senex. . . . . .    O 225 Tr. Gk. 16.364         2
SENI
     At Seni fluxo sapienter uti . . . . . . . . . .      O 153 In Theatro            15
     Turba senum, juvenes nunc tribuere seni. . . . . .   O 225 Tr. Gk. 16.364         4
SENILES
     Respice quem subigit senium, morbique seniles,  . .  O 207 Prayers VI             3
     Respice quem subiget senium, morbique seniles,  . .  O 207 Prayers VI       V     3
SENIS
     Pauper eram, nummis diffluit arca senis;  . . . . .  O 215 Tr Greek 9.138         2
SENIUM
     Respice quem subigit senium, morbique seniles,  . .  O 207 Prayers VI             3
     Respice quem subiget senium, morbique seniles,  . .  O 207 Prayers VI       V     3
     Et senium triplex Nestoris urna capit. . . . . .     O 215 Tr Greek 9.112         4
SENSUS
     Quos soli ducunt sensus, solus docet usus;  . . . .  O 163 To Dr Lawrence        10
SENTE
     Horruit implexo qua vallis sente, figurae  . . . .   O  91 Messiah               80
SENTIET
     Sentiet aegra Metus,  . . . . . . . . . . . . .      O 109 Post-genitis           5
SENTIT
     Vel digiti tractant, oculus vel sentit et auris:  .  O 163 To Dr Lawrence        12
     Pergit, et imperiis sentit se dulcibus actum. . . .  O 205 Christianus           27
SENUM
     Turba senum, juvenes nunc tribuere seni. . . . . .   O 225 Tr. Gk. 16.364         4
SEPONENS
     Seria seponens, aut mala dura pati. . . . . . . .    O 221 Tr Greek 10.72         2
SEPTEM
     Septem Aetates  . . . . . . . . . . . . . . . .      O 226 Septem Aetates         T
     Cum sex centuriis Judaeo millia septem. . . . . .    O 229 Geographia Met         2
     Myrias adsciscit sibi nonagesima septem . . . . .    O 229 Geographia Met         4
     Undecies binas decadas et millia septem . . . . .    O 230 Geographia Met         6
     Myriadas decies septem numerare jubebit . . . . .    O 230 Geographia Met         8
     Myriadas septem decies Europa ducentis . . . . .     O 230 Geographia Met        25
     Millia myriadi septem foecunda secundae . . . . .    O 230 Geographia Met        31
     Undecimum Camber vult septem millibus addi. . . . .  O 231 Geographia Met        36
SEPTIMA
     Cyrum sexta timet; laetatur septima Christo. . . . . O 226 Septem Aetates         4
     Sexta dolet Babylona, et gaudet septima Christo. . . O 226 Septem Aetates   V     4
     Myrias Aegypto cessit bis septima pingui. . . . .    O 229 Geographia Met         3
```

	PAGE	TITLE	LINE
SEPULCHRC			
Nauta, quis hoc jaceat ne percontere sepulchro; • • •	O 211	Tr Greek 7.350	1
SEPULTA			
Sanguine Anastasii; cuncta sepulta jacent: • • • •	O 212	Tr Greek 7.590	2
SEQUACES			
Surgit amans abies teretis, buxique sequaces • • • •	O 91	Messiah	81
SEQUAR			
Sequar libenter; sin reluctari velim, • • • • • •	O 226	Tr. Cleanthes	3
Fiam scelestus, nec tamen minus sequar. • • • • • •	O 226	Tr. Cleanthes	4
SEQUATUR			
Me ducat lux sancta, Deus, lux sancta sequatur; • • •	O 207	Prayers IV	3
SEQUI			
Quem decuit majora sequi, majoribus aptum, • • • • •	O 160	Gnothi seauton	7
SEQUITUR			
Sic diem sequitur dies fugacem! • • • • • •	O 204	Spes	2
Hunc sequitur caelebs; tertius, orbe, venis. • • • •	O 222	Tr Greek 11.50	2
SERA			
Sera voluptas. • • • • • • • • • • • • •	O 153	In Theatro	4
SERAE			
Et serae texent vites umbracula proli. • • • • • •	O 90	Messiah	74
SERENA			
Auxilioque Dei fretus, jam mente serena • • • •	O 205	Christianus	26
Da veniam pacemque mihi, da, mente serena, • • • • •	O 207	Prayers V	3
SERIA			
Seria seponens, aut mala dura pati. • • • • • • •	O 221	Tr Greek 10.72	2
SERIE			
Non operum serie, seriem dum computat aevi, • • • • •	O 162	Gnothi seauton	46
SERIEM			
Non operum serie, seriem dum computat aevi, • • • • •	O 162	Gnothi seauton	46
SERIES			
Causarum series quo moderante fluit, • • • • • • •	O 207	Prayers VI	2
SERMCNE			
• • • causae in sermone patrocinata fuerat. • • • •	O 105	Lady Defence	V T
SERO			
Non Animus sero nimium dum parta recenset, • • • • •	O 161	Gnothi seauton	V 42
SERPENT			
Serpent per Prata Colubri, • • • • • • • • •	O 109	Post-genitis	10
SERPENTES			
Serpentes teneris nil jam lethale minantes • • • •	O 91	Messiah	89
Serpentes teneris nil jam lethale micantes • • • •	O 91	Messiah	V 89
SERRATIS			
Laevia serratis miscens, quadrata rotundis, • • • • •	O 163	To Dr Lawrence	26
SERTA			
Texente Nymphis serta Lycoride, • • • • • • • • •	O 102	Ad Urbanum	21
SERTUM			
Cui Fronte Sertum in Erudita • • • • • • • • • •	O 101	Ad Urbanum	3
SERVA			
Zosima, quae solo fuit olim corpore Serva, • • • • •	O 114	Tr Gk Epigrams	1
Zosima, qua solo fuit olim corpore serva, • • • • •	O 212	Tr Gk Epigrams	V 7
Zosima, qucndam solo fuit olim copore serva, • • • •	Y 320	Tr Gk Epigrams	V 1
Serviat ut menti corpus, jejunia serva; • • • • •	O 228	Jejunium Cibus	1
SERVARE			
Irruptum vitae cupiat servare tenorem; • • • • •	O 205	Christianus	13
Quas servare velit, leges quas lentus omittat, • • •	O 205	Christianus	21
Effigiemque Dei, quantum servare licebit, • • • • •	O 205	Christianus	29
SERVAT			
Mortales miseros servat, alit, fovet, • • • • • • •	O 155	Psalmus 117	6
SERVATA			
Nequitiam fugiens, servata contrahe lege • • • • •	O 218	Tr Greek 9.444	3
SERVET			
Displiceat, servet tutum sub pectore rectum: • • • •	O 205	Christianus	15
SERVIAT			
Serviat ut menti corpus, jejunia serva; • • • • •	O 228	Jejunium Cibus	1
SERVILEM			
Servilem tuti cultum contempsit agelli, • • • • •	O 386	Tr Epi. Madoc	D 3
SERVUS			
Servus Epictetus, mutilatus corpore vixi • • •	O 114	Tr Gk Epigrams	3
Qui jacet hic, servus vixit, nunc, lumine cassus, • •	O 212	Tr Greek 7.538	1
Servus, Epictetus, mutilato corpore, vixi, • • • •	O 212	Tr Greek 7.676	1
SEU			
Fidus adest custos, seu nox furat horrida nimbis, • •	O 90	Messiah	62
Fidus adest custos, seu nox furat humida nimbis, • •	O 90	Messiah	V 62
Non mihi sorte datum; lenti seu sanguinis obsint • •	O 160	Gnothi seauton	16
Frigora, seu nimium longo jacuisse veterno, • • • •	O 161	Gnothi seauton	17
Seu viri curas pia nupta mulcet, • • • • • • • •	O 168	Oda to Thrale	13
Seu fovet mater sobolem benigna, • • • • • • •	O 168	Oda to Thrale	14
Seu te saeva sitis, levitas sive improba fecit, • • •	O 171	Tr. Busy Fly	1
Seu te saeva fames, levitas sive improba fecit, • • •	O 171	Tr. Busy Fly	V 1
Seu thoracem • • • • • • • • • • • • •	O 198	Medico Aeger S	6
Seu prece poscatur, seu non, da Jupiter omne • • • •	O 221	Tr Greek 10.108	1
Seu prece poscatur, seu non, da Jupiter omne • • • •	O 221	Tr Greek 10.108	1
SEVERIS			
Quam quae severis ludicra jungere • • • • • • •	O 102	Ad Urbanum	18
SEX			
Cum sex centuriis Judaeo millia septem. • • • • •	O 229	Geographia Met	2
Cum sex centuriis numerat sex millia Tuscus. • • • •	O 230	Geographia Met	13
Cum sex centuriis numerat sex millia Tuscus. • • • •	O 230	Geographia Met	13
Sardiniam cum sexcentis sex millia complent. • • • •	O 230	Geographia Met	18
Ter sex centurias Hollandia jactat opima • • • •	O 231	Geographia Met	35
SEXAGENIS			
Cum sexagenis, dum plura recluserit aetas, • • • • •	O 230	Geographia Met	19

	PAGE	TITLE		LINE
SEXAGINTA				
Sexaginta annis non minor unus erit.	O 171	Tr. Busy Fly		12
SEXCENTIS				
Unus homo mihi pro sexcentis, turba popelli	O 209	Tr Greek 7.128		3
Sardiniam cum sexcentis sex millia complent. . . .	O 230	Geographia Met		18
SEXQUE				
Myriadas denas dat, quinque et millia, sexque . . .	O 230	Geographia Met		27
SEXTA				
Eheu, quid decies plus mihi sexta dedit!	O 171	Tr. Busy Fly		10
Cyrum sexta timet; laetatur septima Christo. . . .	O 226	Septem Aetates		4
Sexta dolet Babylona, et gaudet septima Christo. .	O 226	Septem Aetates	V	4
Cyrum sexta vocat, laetatur	O 226	Septem Aetates	V	4
SEXTI				
En Sexto, Sexti meditatur imago, silente;	O 223	Tr. Gk. 11.145		1
SEXTO				
En Sexto, Sexti meditatur imago, silente;	O 223	Tr. Gk. 11.145		1
SEXTUS				
Vitam a terdecimo sextus mihi finiet annus, ...	O 215	Tr Greek 9.112		1
SI				
Ingenium et mores si pulchra probavit Elisa, . . .	O 104	To Eliz Carter		3
Si qua usquam pateat melioris semita vitae, . . .	O 161	Gnothi seauton		33
Cessat inops rerum, ut torpet, si marmoris absit .	O 161	Gnothi seauton		38
Aut, hoc si nimium est, tandem nova lexica poscam? .	O 162	Gnothi seauton		54
Ut vitam, poscat si res, impendere vero.	O 205	Christianus		11
Forma animos hominum capit, at, si gratia desit, .	O 209	Tr. Greek 5.67		1
Si Phoebo, victor nescit obire diem.	O 210	Tr Greek 7.239		2
Si forsan tumulum quo conditur Eumarus aufers, . .	O 210	Tr Greek 7.284		3
Astra mathematicos si modo vera docent.	O 215	Tr Greek 9.112		2
Omnes si vellent virginitate frui;	O 218	Tr Greek 9.444		2
Nec male res cessit, subito si funere sponsam, . .	O 222	Tr Greek 11.50		3
Vita rosae brevis est; properans si carpere nolis,	O 223	Tr Greek 11.53		1
Vitae rosa brevis est; properans si carpere nolis,	O 223	Tr Greek 11.53	V	1
Qui pascit barbam si crescit mente, Platoni, . . .	O 224	Tr. Gk. 11.430		1
Si sis scelestus, praeteri procul marmor.	O 224	Tr Greek 13.3		2
At te bonum si noris, et bonis natum, ...	O 224	Tr Greek 13.3		3
Tutum hic sedile, et si placet, sopor tutus. . . .	O 224	Tr Greek 13.3		4
Munera muneribus si retulere fabri.	O 225	Tr Greek 16.87		4
SIBI				
Fallimur exemplis; temere sibi turba scholarum . .	O 160	Gnothi seauton		12
Nec sibi de gaza praesens quod postulet usus . . .	O 162	Gnothi seauton		44
Non sibi de gaza praesens quod postulat usus . . .	O 162	Gnothi seauton	V	44
Qui sibi sat sapiunt, contenti noscere quantum . .	O 163	To Dr Lawrence		11
Qui sibi sat sapient, contenti noscere quantum . .	O 163	To Dr Lawrence	V	11
Sic sibi diffisi, lenta experientia cursum . . .	O 163	To Dr Lawrence		17
Permissum credit nudas sibi sistere causas, . . .	O 163	To Dr Lawrence		20
Humana virtus non sibi sufficit, ...	O 166	Oda Isle Skye		13
Datur nec aequum cuique animum sibi	O 166	Oda Isle Skye		14
Et sibi, delirans quanquam et peccator in horas .	O 205	Christianus		14
Ne stolidae similis leges sibi segreget audax . .	O 205	Christianus		20
Optarit quicunque senex sibi longius aevum, . . .	O 214	Tr Greek 9.55		1
Quae lyra. Quam sibi non concinit harmonia! . . .	O 216	Tr Greek 9.250		2
Non Fortuna sibi te gratum tollit in altum; . . .	O 218	Tr Greek 9.530		1
At docet, exemplo, vis sibi quanta, tuo.	O 218	Tr Greek 9.530		2
Myrias adsciscit sibi nonagesima septem	O 229	Geographia Met		4
Pastor Arabs: decies octo sibi Persa requirit. . .	O 230	Geographia Met		9
Myriades sibi pulcra duas, duo millia poscit . . .	O 230	Geographia Met		10
Vult sibi vicenas millesima myrias addi, ...	O 230	Geographia Met		21
SIC				
Materiam Statuae sic praebet Marmora Tellus, . . .	O 85	Adjecere bonae		3
Sic orsus--Qualis rerum mihi nascitur ordo! . . .	O 88	Messiah		9
Postera sic pastor divinus secla beabit, ...	O 90	Messiah		64
Rosae ruborem sic Viola adjuvat	O 102	Ad Urbanum		22
Immista, sic Iris refulget	O 102	Ad Urbanum		23
Sic sibi diffisi, lenta experientia cursum . . .	O 163	To Dr Lawrence		17
Una quidem, sic fata volunt, tibi vivitur aestas,	O 171	Tr. Busy Fly		9
Da veteres noxas animo sic flere novato, ...	O 198	Tr. Ash Wed.		3
Da veteres culpas animo sic flere novato, . . .	O 198	Tr. Ash Wed.	V	3
Hora sic peragit citata cursum;	O 204	Spes		1
Sic diem sequitur dies fugacem!	O 204	Spes		2
Sic peragam tua jussa libens, accinctus ad omne .	O 207	Prayers IV		5
Mandatum, vivam sic moriarque tibi.	O 207	Prayers IV		6
Sic ale, proveniat messis ut ampla boni.	O 207	Prayers VII		4
Idem Orcus terrae, sic, pelagoque subest.	O 210	Tr Greek 7.265		2
Haec Musae ad Venerem: Sic Marti, diva, mineris; .	O 213	Tr Greek 9.39		3
Per fluctus vitae sic tibi cursus erit.	O 221	Tr Greek 10.74		6
Sic aliis dives, tu tibi pauper agis.	O 223	Tr. Gk. 11.167		2
I, quoniam sic fata vocant: liceat mihi tantum . .	O 384	On the Gin-Act	D	9
SICANA				
Parthenope. Novies vult tellus mille Sicana. . . .	O 230	Geographia Met		11
SICCATQUE				
Prima parit terras aetas; siccatque secunda; . . .	O 226	Septem Aetates		1
SIDERA				
Sidera fumabunt, diro labefacta tremore	O 92	Messiah		115
Telluri arboribus ver frondens, sidera coelo, . .	O 214	Tr Greek 9.65		1
Dulcia dat natura quidem, mare, sidera, terras, .	O 222	Tr. Gk. 10.123		3
SIDEREA				
Siderea Isaiae, dignos accende furores!	O 88	Messiah		7
SIDEREUS				
Sidereus tamen hic territat, ecce, canis!	O 213	Tr Greek 9.18		4
SIGNANTUR				
Quo tua signantur gesta, Philippe, lapis.	O 216	Tr Greek 9.288		2

SIGNIS
   Non ultra infestis concurrent agmina signis, ...   O 90 Messiah   66
SILENTE

PAGE   TITLE   LINE

   En Sexto, Sexti meditatur imago, silente; . . . .   O 223 Tr. Gk. 11.145   1
SILENTIA
   Sed sua regna videns, loca nocte silentia late . . . .   O 162 Gnothi seauton   49
SILENTIO
   Fidens, Superbo frange Silentio; . . . .   O 101 Ad Urbanum   10
SILVAE
   En! summo exultant nutantes vertice silvae. . . .   O 89 Messiah   31
SILVARUM
   Gloria silvarum, dominum inclinata salutet! . . . .   O 89 Messiah   38
SILVESTRIA
   Muscosi fontes, silvestria tecta, valete, ...   O 88 Messiah   4
SIM
   Multis ut te oculis sim potis aspicere. . . .   O 212 Tr Greek 7.669   2
   Aevi sat novi quam sim brevis; astra tuenti, . . .   O 219 Tr Greek 9.577   1
SIMILEM
   Sed similem, Plutarche, tuae describere vitam . . .   O 225 Tr. Gk. 16.331   5
SIMILIS
   Ne stolidae similis leges sibi segreget audax . . .   O 205 Christianus   20
SIN
   Gratia ter grata est velox, sin forte moretur . . .   O 220 Tr Greek 10.30   1
   Sequar libenter; sin reluctari velim, ...   O 226 Tr. Cleanthes   3
SINAS
   Quales sint monades, qua fit inane, sinas. . . . .   O 222 Tr Greek 11.50   6
SINAT
   Nec sinat semper tremere ac dolere . . . .   O 227 A Meditation   3
   Nec sinat semper tremere ac dolore . . . .   O 227 A Meditation   V 3
SINE
   Et juvat ingenii vita sine arte rudis. . . .   O 104 To Eliz Carter   2
   Pendet, et incoquitur tectum sine fraude metallum: . .   O 116 Tr Pope Grotto   6
   Splendet, et incoquitur tectum sine fraude metallum: . .   O 116 Tr Pope Grotto   V 6
   Inter equales, sine felle liber, ...   O 153 In Theatro   9
   Sat laetitia, sine subsidiis, ...   O 193 Tr. Medea III   13
   Blandam lanifici sociam, sine fine loquacem, . . .   O 211 Tr Greek 7.459   3
   Mulcet amor prolis, sopor est sine prole profundus; . .   O 217 Tr Greek 9.360   7
   Quae sine morte fuga est vitae, quam turba malorum . .   O 222 Tr. Gk. 10.123   1
   Quaerenti obveniet mox sine flore rubus. . . .   O 223 Tr Greek 11.53   2
SINGULA
   Gens illa, impatiens per singula quaeque vagandi . . .   O 163 To Dr Lawrence   23
SINGULTANS
   Singultans mulcet, lachrymantes terget ocellos. . . .   O 90 Messiah   53
   Singultans mulcet, lachrymantes tergit ocellos. . . .   O 90 Messiah   V 53
SINT
   Sint pro legitimis pectora pura sacris . . . .   O 170 Insula Kenneth   V 20
   Sint pro legitimis pura labella sacris . . . .   O 170 Insula Kenneth   V 20
   Da, ne sint permissa, pater, mihi praemia frustra, . .   O 208 Prayers VII   9
   Da, ne sint promissa, pater, mihi praemia frustra, . .   O 208 Prayers VII   V 9
   Sint Demosthenica ut jurata cadavera voce, . . .   O 216 Tr Greek 9.288   5
   Quales sint monades, qua fit inane, sinas. . . .   O 222 Tr Greek 11.50   6
SINUM
   Skia sinum nebulosa pandis. . . . .   O 166 Oda Isle Skye   4
SIQUANDO
   Jupiter hoc templum, ut, siquando relinquit Olympum, . .   O 219 Tr Greek 9.702   1
SIQUID
   Terror inest aliis, moerorque, et siquid habebis . . .   O 222 Tr. Gk. 10.123   5
SIS
   Si sis scelestus, praeteri procul marmor: . . . . .   O 224 Tr Greek 13.3   2
SISTERE
   Permissum credit nudas sibi sistere causas, ...   O 163 To Dr Lawrence   20
SIT
   Sit memor nostri, fideique merces . . . . . .   O 168 Oda to Thrale   17
   Sit memor nostri, fideique solvat . . . . . .   O 168 Oda to Thrale   V 17
   Per Christum ut veniam sit reperire mihi. . . . .   O 198 Tr. Ash Wed.   4
   Ingenio parcas, nec sit mihi culpa rogasse, . . .   O 204 Losing Speech   3
   Ingenio parcas, nec sit mihi culpa precari . . .   O 204 Losing Speech   V 3
   Sit sacer orbis amor, miseris qui semper adesse . . .   O 205 Christianus   7
   Cura placere Deo sit prima, sit ultima, sanctae . . .   O 205 Christianus   12
   Cura placere Deo sit prima, sit ultima, sanctae . . .   O 205 Christianus   12
   Ut summa laus sit, summa Christo gloria. . . .   O 205 Christianus   12
   Militibus; terris sit pelagoque pudor! . . . .   O 206 Prayers III   6
   Sit tibi, Calliope, Parnassum, cura, tenenti, . . .   O 217 Tr Greek 9.304   4
   Nec probrosa avidae grata sit offa gulae; . . . .   O 218 Tr Greek 9.523   1
   Sit contenta mihi vita dolore carens. . . . .   O 218 Tr Greek 9.573   2
   Quas navis recipit, quantum sit pondus aquarum, . . .   O 222 Tr. Gk. 10.113   2
   Haec postrema tibi sit flendi causa, fluatque . . . .   O 229 Epigram III   1
SITIENTESQUE   Y 387 Death Mother   D 3
   Suave rubere rosis, sitientesque inter arenas . . . .   O 91 Messiah   76
SITIS
   Seu te saeva sitis, levitas sive improba fecit, . . .   O 171 Tr. Busy Fly   1
SIVE
   Sive dies medius morientia torreat arva: . . .   O 90 Messiah   63
   Sive dies medius languentia torreat arva: . . .   O 90 Messiah   V 63
   Sive mihi mentem dederit Natura minorem. . . .   O 161 Gnothi seauton   18
   Sive cum libris novitate pascit . . . .   O 168 Oda to Thrale   15
   Sive cum libris novitate pascet . . . .   O 168 Oda to Thrale   V 15
   Sive libros poscant otia, sive lyram. . . . .   O 170 Insula Kenneth   14
   Sive libros poscant otia, sive lyram. . . . .   O 170 Insula Kenneth   14
   Seu te saeva sitis, levitas sive improba fecit, . . .   O 171 Tr. Busy Fly   1
   Seu te saeva fames, levitas sive improba fecit, . . .   O 171 Tr. Busy Fly   V 1

```
                                                      PAGE    TITLE          LINE
SIVE          (CCNTINUED)                             O 198 Medico Aeger S      7
    Sive abdcmen  . . . . .  .  .  .  .  .  .  .  .
SKIA                                                  O 166 Oda Isle Skye    V  T
    Skia . . . . . . . .  .  .  .  .  .  .  .  .  .   O 166 Oda Isle Skye       4
    Skia sinum nebulosa pandis. . . . . . . . . .     O 167 Oda to Thrale    V  T
    Ode, De Skia Insula  . . . . . . . . .
SOBOLEM                                               O 168 Oda to Thrale      14
    Seu fovet mater sobolem benigna,  . . . . . . .   O 226 Tr. Simonides       3
    Quam, regum sobolem, nuptam, matrem, atque sororem  . .
SOBOLES
    Clara Cheroneae soboles, Plutarche, dicavit . . . . .  O 225 Tr. Gk. 16.331   1
SOCIALIS
    Quingentis quadragenis socialis adauget . . . . . .  O 231 Geographia Met    33
SOCIAM
    Blandam lanifici sociam, sine fine loquacem,      O 211 Tr Greek 7.459      3
SOCIATA
    Per valles sociata lupo lasciviet agna, . . . .   O  91 Messiah            84
SOCIO
    Hic oculos socio commodat, ille pedes.  . . . .   O 213 Tr Greek 9.13       2
SOCIUM
    Me gregi Sanctus socium beatum . . . . . . . .    O 227 A Meditation         7
SODALIS
    Cuique esses natus, cuique sodalis, eras. . . . .  O 212 Tr Greek 7.560      4
SOL
    Lunaque quas et sol itque reditque vias. . . . .  O 222 Tr. Gk. 10.123      4
SOLA
    Nunc loca sola placent; frustra te, Somne, recumbens . .  O 161 Gnothi seauton  30
    Scripta legens, sola vivere mente cupit. . . . . .  O 211 Tr Greek 7.471     4
    Sola rates struis infidas, et dulcis amorem . . . .  O 213 Tr Greek 9.29      3
    Lucri ulciscendum mox nece sola doces. . . . . .  O 213 Tr Greek 9.29      4
SOLATIA
    Mollia non deerant vacuae solatia vitae, . . . . .  O 170 Insula Kenneth    13
    Mollia non desunt vacuae solatia vitae, . . . . .  O 170 Insula Kenneth  V 13
SOLATIUM
    Negabitur solatium. . . . . . . . . . . . .       O 203 Christ Sinner        4
SOLE
    Flumina prorumpunt; non posthac sole rubescet . . .  O  92 Messiah          108
    Sole fovente, suas. . . . . . . . . . . . .       O 385 Cantico Solom.   D  6
SOLET
    Pateris ergo quod populus solet . . . . . . . .   O 186 Ad T. L. M.D.        1
SOLI
    Quos soli ducunt sensus, solus docet usus; . . .   O 163 To Dr Lawrence     10
SOLIDQUE
    Saxa cadent, solidque liquescent robora montis: . . .  O  92 Messiah        116
SOLIS
    Vis boreae gelida, aut rapidi violentia solis. . . . .  O  89 Messiah        19
    Vis boreae gelida, aut nimii violentia solis. . . .  O  89 Messiah       V 19
    Solis Ophyraeis crudum tibi montibus aurum . . . .  O  92 Messiah          104
    Vacare solis perge Musis, . . . . . . . . . .     O 101 Ad Urbanum          7
SOLITAS
    Deliciasque fugit solitas solitosque labores; . . .  O 162 To Dr Lawrence    2
SOLITOSQUE
    Deliciasque fugit solitas solitosque labores; . . .  O 162 To Dr Lawrence    2
SOLLICITUS
    Quid et minetur, sollicitus parum, . . . . . .    O 101 Ad Urbanum          6
    Sollicitus nimis, heu! paternis. . . . . . . .    O 187 Ad T. L. M.D.       12
SOLO
    Zosima, quae solo fuit olim corpore Serva, . . . .  O 114 Tr Gk Epigrams     1
    Zosima, qua solo fuit olim corpore serva, . . . .  O 212 Tr Gk Epigrams   V 7
    Zosima, quondam solo fuit olim copore serva, . . .  Y 320 Tr Gk Epigrams   V 1
    Arte valent isti, mihi robore vivere solo est, . . .  O 224 Tr Greek 16.1    3
SOLOMONIS
    Aegyptum; templo Solomonis quinta superbit; . . . .  O 226 Septem Aetates    3
    Aegyptum; templo Solomonis quinta supersit; . . . .  O 226 Septem Aetates  V 3
    Ex Cantico Solomonis  . . . . . . . . . .         O 384 Cantico Solom.    D  T
SOLUM
    Qua solum potero parte, placere tibi. . . . . .   O 204 Losing Speech        4
    Qua solum potero parte, litare tibi. . . . . .    O 204 Losing Speech      V 4
    Verte solum, fient causa timoris opes; . . . . .  O 217 Tr Greek 9.359      4
    Verte solum, donat plena crumena decus; . . . .   O 217 Tr Greek 9.360      4
    Verte solum, donet plena crumena decus; . . . .   O 217 Tr Greek 9.360    V 4
SOLUS
    Fortis, ades, solus tangas venerabile limen. . . .  O 116 Tr Pope Grotto   16
    Quos soli ducunt sensus, solus docet usus; . . . .  O 163 To Dr Lawrence   10
    Rex summe, solus tu regis arbiter, . . . . . .    O 166 Oda Isle Skye       18
    Tecta ineunt; caelebs omnia solus ages; . . . .   O 217 Tr Greek 9.359      6
SOLVARE
    Nec ficto fletu, fictis solvare cachinnis, . . . .  O 218 Tr Greek 9.573     3
SOLVAT
    Sit memor nostri, fideique solvat . . . . . . .   O 168 Oda to Thrale     V 17
SOLVET
    Obstrictasque diu linguas in carmina solvet. . . .  O  90 Messiah          46
SOLVI
    Solvi, quo Christus cunctis delicta redemit, . . .  O 207 Prayers V          5
SOLVIT
    Quod mors in cineres solvit, et abdit humo. . . . .  O 221 Tr Greek 10.84    4
SOLYMAEAE
    Tollite concentum, Solymaeae tollite nymphae! . . .  O  88 Messiah           1
SOMNE
    Nunc loca sola placent; frustra te, Somne, recumbens . .  O 161 Gnothi seauton  30
```

SCMNIA

	PAGE	TITLE	LINE
Aonidesque Deae, et mendacis somnia Pindi.	O 88	Messiah	5
Ab Jove Maeonides descendere Somnia narrat:	O 103	Elizae Aenigma	3
Haec veniunt Cypriae Somnia missa Deae.	O 103	Elizae Aenigma	4
Importuna cohors, vacuae mala somnia mentis.	O 161	Gnothi seauton	28

SONANS

| Carmen grande sonans; Anglus utrumque tulit. | O 86 | Tr Dryden Milt | 4 |

SONANT

| Saxa sonant Deus; ecce Deus! deflectitur aether | O 89 | Messiah | 36 |
| Non planctus, non moesta sonant suspiria, pectus | O 90 | Messiah | 52 |

SCNANTIS

| Nil opus est aeris sacra de turre sonantis | O 170 | Insula Kenneth | V 18A |

SCNAT

| Quid quod putidulum nostra Camoena sonat? | O 85 | Mea nec Falern | 2 |

SCNET

| Ut tibi laus omni semper ab ore sonet: | O 232 | Prayer | 8 |

SCNI

| Quorsum dulcis luxuria soni? | O 193 | Tr. Medea III | 12 |

SCNOS

| Quos pulsata sonos edit lyra pollice, primis | Y 28 | Aurora Musis | 15 |

SCNTES

| Divinam in sontes iram placavit Jesus; | O 208 | A Meditation | 3 |

SONUM

| Ingemina fluctus, ingeminaque sonum. | O 210 | Tr Greek 7.284 | 2 |
| Hic Bona queis opus est venditat, Ille Sonum. | O 385 | The Warehouse | D 6 |

SOPOR

| Mulcet amor prolis, sopor est sine prole profundus; | O 217 | Tr Greek 9.360 | 7 |
| Tutum hic sedile, et si placet, sopor tutus. | O 224 | Tr Greek 13.3 | 4 |

SORDES

| Mentibus afflatu terrenas ejice sordes | O 232 | Prayer | 5 |

SORDIDA

| Nec menti injiciat sordida cura jugum; | O 221 | Tr Greek 10.74 | 2 |

SOROR

Surge, soror dilecta, mihi lux, gaudia, vita;	O 384	Cantico Solom.	D 1
Haud mora, surge, soror!	O 384	Cantico Solom.	D 2
Huc, soror alma, veni! pernicibus ocyor Euris	O 385	Cantico Solom.	D 17
Huc, soror alma, veni!	O 385	Cantico Solom.	D 18

SOROREM

| Quam, regum sobolem, nuptam, matrem, atque sororem | O 226 | Tr. Simonides | 3 |

SORS

Desidiae sors dura manet, graviorque labore	O 161	Gnothi seauton	25
Tu, queis laborat sors hominum, mala	O 187	Ad T. L. M.D.	5
Me miserum sors omnis habet; florentibus annis	O 215	Tr Greek 9.138	1
Prospera sors nec te strepitoso turbine tollat,	O 221	Tr Greek 10.74	1
Fecerunt nulli sors titulique gravem.	O 226	Tr. Simonides	4

SORTE

| Non mihi sorte datum; lenti seu sanguinis obsint | O 160 | Gnothi seauton | 16 |
| Triste nihil passus, animi at de sorte Platonis | O 211 | Tr Greek 7.471 | 3 |

SORTITUR

| Sortitur Pelopis tellus quae nomine gaudet. | O 230 | Geographia Met | 7 |

SPARSA

| In me sparsa manu virtutum semina larga | O 207 | Prayers VII | 3 |

SPARTA

| Patria Sparta mihi est, patria clara virum. | O 224 | Tr Greek 16.1 | 2 |
| Convenit ut natis, inclyta Sparta, tuis. | O 224 | Tr Greek 16.1 | 4 |

SPARTAE

| Xerxi, tercentum Spartae Mars obstitit acris | O 217 | Tr Greek 9.304 | 3 |

SPATIA

| Tantundem est illis, repleat spatia ardua coeli | O 163 | To Dr Lawrence | 13 |

SPATIIS

| Tuto eluctatum spatiis Sapientia dia | O 161 | Gnothi seauton | 20 |
| Ut dicas, spatiis quam latis imperet orbi | O 230 | Geographia Met | 16 |

SPATIOSA

| En! formosa tibi spatiosa per atria proles | O 92 | Messiah | V 96 |

SPE

Vel spe ludit inani,	O 182	Waltoni Piscat	13
Spe non inani confugis,	O 203	Christ Sinner	1
Incusat, semper spe meliora videt.	O 214	Tr Greek 9.54	2

SPECIES

| Horret, ubi vanae species, umbraeque fugaces, | O 162 | Gnothi seauton | 50 |

SPECTANDUS

| Aurea secla hominum, quorum spectandus ocellis | O 213 | Tr Greek 9.29 | 5 |

SPECTANS

| Omnia qui spectans, omnia ubique regis; | O 232 | Prayer | 4 |

SPECULA

| In specula numerare fluctus. | O 166 | Oda Isle Skye | V 12 |

SPECULATOR

| Nec miratur opes, celsa speculator ab arce | O 161 | Gnothi seauton | V 39 |

SPECULUM

| Hoc Veneri speculum; nolo me cernere qualis | O 209 | Tr. Greek 6.1 | 3 |

SPELAEA

| Per saxa, ignivomi nuper spelaea draconis, | O 91 | Messiah | 78 |

SPELUNCAE

| Speluncae late Thamesis praetendit opacae, | O 116 | Tr Pope Grotto | 2 |

SPEM

| Christe, spem praesta stabilem timenti; | O 194 | Prayer on Xmas | 6 |

SPEREM

| Ut studiis sperem, aut ausim par esse querelis, | O 160 | Gnothi seauton | 15 |

SPES

| Quid majus mihi spes ambitiosa dabit? | O 104 | To Eliz Carter | 4 |
| Spes hominum ac curas cum procul esse jubet. | O 170 | Insula Kenneth | 16 |

SPES	(CONTINUED)	PAGE	TITLE	LINE
Spes hominum et curas gens procul esse velit.		O 170	Insula Kenneth	V 16
Spes		O 204	Spes	T
Spes novas nova lux parit, secunda		O 204	Spes	3
Spes ludit stolidas, metuque caeco		O 204	Spes	5
Noctes atque dies animo spes laeta recurset, ...		O 207	Prayers VII	5
Certa vetet dubitare fides, spes laeta timere, ...		O 207	Prayers VII	7
SPICULA				
Linguae procacis plumbea Spicula, ...		O 101	Ad Urbanum	9
Instet, et evellens terroris spicula corde, ...		O 205	Christianus	4
In vos ne missus spicula tendat amor.		O 213	Tr Greek 9.39	2
SPINETAQUE				
Artificis frondent dextrae; Spinetaque Palmis		O 91	Messiah	V 82
SPIRANT				
Dia salutares spirant medicamina rami.		O 89	Messiah	17
Cum violis; spirant lilia mista rosis.		O 209	Tr. Greek 5.74	4
SPIRAT				
Saxea Phidiaca spirat imago manu.		O 85	Adjecere bonae	4
Pascua, qua blandum spirat purissimus aer		O 90	Messiah	58
Induit, et, terris major, coelestia spirat.		O 205	Christianus	30
Spirat odore botrus.		O 385	Cantico Solom.	D 16
SPIRITUM				
Aegrum trahenti spiritum		O 206	Prayers II	8
SPIRITUS				
Cursu spiritus		O 198	Medico Aeger S	3
Spiritus addat.		O 227	A Meditation	8
SPISSAM				
Ille cutim spissam visus hebetare vetabit, ...		O 90	Messiah	44
SPLENDET				
Splendet, et incoquitur tectum sine fraude metallum: . .		O 116	Tr Pope Grotto	V 6
SPOKE				
To a Lady who spoke in Defence of Liberty		O 105	Lady Defence	T
SPOLIANTES				
Vitiantes, et spoliantes;		O 109	Post-genitis	14
SPONDENS				
Spondens omnia credulis homullis;		O 204	Spes	4
SPONSAM				
Nec male res cessit, subito si funere sponsam, ...		O 222	Tr Greek 11.50	3
SPONTE				
Fortis, ades, tibi sponte patet venerabile limen. . . .		O 116	Tr Pope Grotto	V 16
Sponte sua demens; nihilum decedere summae		O 205	Christianus	23
SPRETA				
Spreta jacet Marathon, jacet et Salaminia laurus, . . .		O 216	Tr Greek 9.288	3
SPREVIT				
Heu quam dura preces sprevit, quam surda querelas . . .		O 212	Tr Greek 7.560	5
SQUALLET				
Squallet informis, tugurique fumis		O 167	Oda to Thrale	7
SQUAMAS				
Ridebit linguae innocuos, squamas viridantes		O 91	Messiah	V 91
SQUAMASQUE				
Ridebit linguae innocuos, squamasque virentes		O 91	Messiah	91
STABILEM				
Christe, spem praesta stabilem timenti;		O 194	Prayer on Xmas	6
STABILI				
Per certas stabili lege voluta vices, ...		O 219	Tr Greek 9.577	2
STABILITA				
Pollicitis firmata Dei, stabilita ruinis.		O 92	Messiah	119
Firmius ac ipsis Mundi stabilita ruinis.		O 92	Messiah	V 119
STABO				
Stabo illis qui sunt, quique fuere, gravis.		O 216	Tr Greek 9.288	6
STAGNI				
Qui nunc jacet Incola stagni, ...		O 109	Post-genitis	2
STAT				
Dicam; stat virtus non subigenda neci.		O 212	Tr Greek 7.590	4
Stat: fixum est: nequeunt jam revocare preces.		O 384	On the Gin-Act	D 8
STATUA				
Orator statua est, statuaeque orator imago.		O 223	Tr. Gk. 11.145	2
STATUAE				
Materiam Statuae sic praebet Marmora Tellus, ...		O 85	Adjecere bonae	3
STATUAEQUE				
Orator statua est, statuaeque orator imago.		O 223	Tr. Gk. 11.145	2
STATUAM				
Hanc statuam ingenio Roma benigna tuo.		O 225	Tr. Gk. 16.331	2
STATUANT				
Hoc statuant, votis Christus adesse velit:		O 204	Losing Speech	V 2
STATUASQUE				
Quid mirum? cum saxa movet statuasque tacentes . . .		Y 28	Aurora Musis	13
STATUAT				
Hoc statuat, precibus Christus adesse velit:		O 204	Losing Speech	2
STATUUNT				
Dum statuunt, causisque audent prefigere metam. . . .		O 163	To Dr Lawrence	36
STELLA				
Stella mea, observans stellas, Dii me aethera faxint, .		O 212	Tr Greek 7.669	1
STELLAS				
Stella mea, observans stellas, Dii me aethera faxint, .		O 212	Tr Greek 7.669	1
STERILES				
Torva ubi rident steriles coloni		O 167	Oda to Thrale	3
STERILI				
Te sterili functum cura, vocumque salebris		O 161	Gnothi seauton	19
STERNITE				
Sternite saxa viam, rapidi discedite fluctus!		O 89	Messiah	40

```
STET                                              PAGE   TITLE            LINE
    Stet fides constans, meritoque blandum  . . . . . .  O 168 Oda to Thrale        18
STETIT
    Hujus palestrae qui vigil custos stetit, . . . . . .  O 223 Tr. Gk. 11.176       3
STOANA
    In Rivum a Mola Stoana Lichfeldiae diffluentem  . . . .  O 228 Rivum a Stoana      T
STOICORUM
    Parare posse, ut Stoicorum  . . . . . . . . .  O 166 Oda Isle Skye       15
STOLIDAE
    Ne stolidae similis leges sibi segreget audax  . .  . . . .  O 205 Christianus       20
STOLIDAS
    Spes ludit stolidas, metuque caeco . . . . . . . .  O 204 Spes             5
STOLIDUS
    Ille suum stolidus, nunc putat ille suum.  . . . . .  O 215 Tr Greek 9.74        4
STRAVIT
    Jupiter unus erat, qui stravit fulmine gentes;  . . . .  O 103 Elizae Aenigma      5
STRENUA
    Assidet huic custos strenua pauperies.  . . . . . .  O 219 Tr Greek 9.654        2
STREPENS
    Strepens procellis, rupibus obsita,  . . . . . . .  O 166 Oda Isle Skye        2
    Strepens procellis, imbribus uvida,  . . . . . . . .  O 166 Oda Isle Skye   V   2
    Strepens procellis, uvida nubibus, . . . . . . . . .  O 166 Oda Isle Skye   V   2
STREPENT
    Ut qua dulce strepent scatebrae, qua laeta virescunt  . .  O  90 Messiah       V  57
STREPIT
    Felici thalamo non, puto, rixa strepit. . . . . . .  O 226 Tr. Greek           2
    Supra Praeco Dei--strepit infra Praeco Bonorum:  . . .  O 385 The Warehouse   D   5
STREPITOSO
    Prospera sors nec te strepitoso turbine tollat,  . . .  O 221 Tr Greek 10.74       1
STREPITUS
    Inter ignotae strepitus loquelae,  . . . . . . . .  O 168 Oda to Thrale       10
    Ponti inter strepitus sacri non munera cultus  . . . .  O 170 Insula Kenneth      17
STREPUNT
    Ut qua dulce strepunt scatebrae, qua laeta virescunt  . .  O  90 Messiah           57
STRICTAM
    Quantum strictam . . . . . . . . . . . . .  O 199 Medico Aeger S       17
STRIDULA
    Terribili fremitu stridula moeret anus. . . . . . .  O 383 On the Gin-Act   D   2
STRUIS
    Sola rates struis infidas, et dulcis amorem . . . . .  O 213 Tr Greek 9.29        3
STRUXIT
    Buccina disjecit Thebarum moenia, struxit  . . . . .  O 216 Tr Greek 9.250       1
STUDIIS
    Ut studiis sperem, aut ausim par esse querelis,  . . .  O 160 Gnothi seauton      15
    Incultum Studiis, et paucis dotibus auctum  . . . .  O 161 Gnothi seauton   V  36
    Restat? an accingar studiis gravioribus audax?  . . . .  O 162 Gnothi seauton      53
    Te semper studiis utilibus colam:  . . . . . . .  O 164 Recover Eyes        12
STUDIISQUE
    Juxta Animo Studiisque felix.  . . . . . . . .  O 101 Ad Urbanum           8
STUDIOSUS
    Codices, veri studiosus, inter  . . . . . . . .  O 153 In Theatro          10
STUDIUM
    Humani studium generis cui pectore fervet,  . . . . .  O 102 Ad R. Savage         1
    Vile indignatus studium, nugasque molestas,  . . . . .  O 160 Gnothi seauton       3
STULTUS
    Pulicibus morsus, restincta lampade, stultus  . . . .  O 224 Tr. Gk. 11.432       1
STUPERE
    Tene cantorum modulis stupere?  . . . . . . . .  O 153 In Theatro           6
SUA
    Omnia, nec curae sunt sua sceptra Jovi. . . . . .  O 103 Elizae Aenigma       2
    Rectius vives, sua quisque carpat . . . . . . .  O 153 In Theatro          11
    Materies arti, sua desunt arma labori . . . . . .  O 161 Gnothi seauton   V  37
    Sed sua regna videns, loca nocte silentia late  . . .  O 162 Gnothi seauton      49
    Sponte sua demens; nihilum decedere summae  . . . .  O 205 Christianus         23
    Mihi dona morte haec impetret Christus sua. . . . . .  O 206 Prayers I          11
    Prolem Hippi, et sua qua meliorem secula nullum  . . .  O 226 Tr. Simonides        1
SUAE
    Quem terret vitae meta propinqua suae,  . . . . . .  O 207 Prayers VI           4
SUAS
    Compositis Pax alma suas, terrasque revisens  . . . .  O  89 Messiah            23
    Admonitu, ipsa suas nunciat hora vices. . . . . . .  O 170 Insula Kenneth   V 18B
    Ante suas agmen Lais habere fores, . . . . . . . .  O 209 Tr. Greek 6.1        2
    Sole fovente, suas. . . . . . . . . . . . .  O 385 Cantico Solom.   D   6
SUASISTI
    Liber ut esse velim, suasisti, pulchra Maria:  . . . .  O 105 Lady Defence         1
SUAVE
    Suave rubere rosis, sitientesque inter arenas  . . . .  O  91 Messiah            76
SUAVIS
    Thralia suavis. . . . . . . . . . . . . .  O 199 Medico Aeger S       22
SUAVITER
    Suaviter exhalant violaria grata, Sabaeo . . . . . .  O 385 Cantico Solom.   D  15
SUB
    Sub pedibus subjecta jacent; queis ultima primis  . . .  O 163 To Dr Lawrence      33
    Nil movet insolitum, sub legibus omnia fictis  . . . .  O 163 To Dr Lawrence      35
    Non tamen inculti gelidis latuere sub antris,  . . . .  O 169 Insula Kenneth      11
    Nec tamen inculti gelidis latuere sub antris,  . . . .  O 169 Insula Kenneth   V  11
    Displiceat, servet tutum sub pectore rectum:  . . . .  O 205 Christianus         15
    Et ferus est Timon sub terris; janitor Orci  . . . .  O 211 Tr Greek 7.319       1
    Sub pedibus, populo praetereunte, jacit,  . . . . .  O 218 Tr Greek 9.375       4
    Murem Asclepiades sub tecto ut vidit avarus,  . . . .  O 224 Tr. Gk. 11.391       1
```

	PAGE	TITLE	LINE
SUBACTI			
Opes, triumphos, et subacti	O 188	Epilogus	3
SUBDOLA			
Quem nil vafrities peccantum subdola celat;	O 232	Prayer	3
SUBEST			
Idem Orcus terrae, sic, pelagoque subest..	O 210	Tr Greek 7.265	2
SUBIGENDA			
Dicam; stat virtus non subigenda neci.	O 212	Tr Greek 7.590	4
SUBIGET			
Respice quem subiget senium, morbique seniles,	O 207	Prayers VI	V 3
SUBIGIT			
Respice quem subigit senium, morbique seniles, ...	O 207	Prayers VI	3
SUBITO			
Nec male res cessit, subito si funere sponsam, ...	O 222	Tr Greek 11.50	3
SUBJECTA			
Sub pedibus subjecta jacent; queis ultima primis . . .	O 163	To Dr Lawrence	33
SUBLIME			
Sublime ingenium Graius; Romanus habebat	O 86	Tr Dryden Milt	3
Sublime ingenium Graecus; Romanus habebat	O 86	Tr Dryden Milt	V 3
In sublime rapit, queis terra et pontus et aer	O 163	To Dr Lawrence	32
SUBLIMIS			
Ille quidem recte, sublimis, doctus, et acer, ...	O 160	Gnothi seauton	6
SUBRUBET			
Subrubet uva mero.	O 385	Cantico Solom.	D 14
SUBSIDIIS			
Sat laetitia, sine subsidiis, ...	O 193	Tr. Medea III	13
SUBSIDITE			
Surgite convalles, tumidi subsidite montes!	O 89	Messiah	39
SUBTILE			
Subtile ingenium quaero, capaxque mei, ...	O 209	Tr Greek 7.128	2
SUCCO			
Potente succo	O 199	Medico Aeger S	13
Rorem, qui regeles, geniali et gramina succo	Y 28	Aurora Musis	5
SUCCORUM			
Te mille succorum potentem	O 187	Ad T. L. M.D.	7
SUCCURRE			
Succurre praesens corpori, ...	O 206	Prayers II	9
SUDAT			
Maturant radii, tibi balsama sudat Idume.	O 92	Messiah	105
SUFFICIT			
Humana virtus non sibi sufficit, ...	O 166	Oda Isle Skye	13
Sufficit hoc votis; flos hic pulcherrimus aevi est, . .	O 215	Tr Greek 9.112	3
SUFFLATO			
Sufflato accendis quisquis carbone lucernam, ...	O 225	Tr. Gk. 16.209	1
SUFFUSUS			
Sanguine dum tumido suffusus flagrat ocellus, ...	O 162	To Dr Lawrence	1
SUGIT			
Sanguinem Equus sugit, ...	O 110	Post-genitis	37
SUI			
Ingeniumque sui cohibet penuria census.	O 161	Gnothi seauton	V 38
Ipse sui judex, actae bene munera vitae;	O 162	Gnothi seauton	48
SUIS			
Tres tria temporibus secla dedere suis.	O 86	Tr Dryden Milt	2
Corpora cuncta suis gestit variare figuris, ...	O 163	To Dr Lawrence	27
Hilarare suis jussere modis	O 193	Tr. Medea III	4
Oribus ora suis.	O 385	Cantico Solom.	D 10
SULCAT			
Qua sulcat, reptant tuti per lubrica vitae.	O 163	To Dr Lawrence	18
SULCOS			
Qui duxit sulcos, illi teret area messem, ...	O 90	Messiah	73
SUM			
Sum nunc, nec possum cernere qualis eram.	O 209	Tr. Greek 6.1	4
SUME			
Ut mens utatur corpore, sume cibos.	O 228	Jejunium Cibus	2
SUMIT			
Congestas animus, laetos aut sumit honores	O 161	Gnothi seauton	V 40
Praeteritis fruitur, laetos aut sumit honores	O 162	Gnothi seauton	47
SUMMA			
Pater benigne, summa semper lenitas, ...	O 206	Prayers I	1
Ut summa laus sit, summa Christo gloria.	O 206	Prayers III	6
Ut summa laus sit, summa Christo gloria.	O 206	Prayers III	6
Pauperieque Irus, curaque summa Deum.	O 212	Tr Greek 7.676	2
SUMMAE			
Sponte sua demens; nihilum decedere summae	O 205	Christianus	23
SUMMAM			
Tentat iter brevius, magno conamine summam	O 163	To Dr Lawrence	24
SUMME			
Grates, summe Pater, tuis	O 164	Recover Eyes	13
Rex summe, solus tu regis arbiter, ...	O 166	Oda Isle Skye	18
Summe Deus, qui semper amas quodcunque creasti, . . .	O 198	Tr. Ash Wed.	1
Summe Pater, quodcunque tuum de corpore Numen	O 204	Losing Speech	1
Summe Pater, quodcunque tuae de corpore leges	O 204	Losing Speech	V 1
Veniam petenti, summe da veniam, pater;	O 206	Prayers I	7
Summe dator vitae, naturae aeterne magister, ...	O 207	Prayers VI	1
Summe Pater, puro collustra lumine pectus, ...	O 207	Prayers VII	1
Summe Deus, cui caeca patent penetralia cordis; . . .	O 232	Prayer	1
SUMMI			
Et summi accendat pectus amore boni.	O 170	Insula Kenneth	V 16B
Nunc summi prece sancta	O 182	Waltoni Piscat	9
SUMMO			
En! summo exultant nutantes vertice silvae.	O 89	Messiah	31

	PAGE	TITLE		LINE
SUMMO (CONTINUED)				
Permitte summo res hominum Patri, ...	O 187	Ad T. L. M.D.		17
Permitte summo quicquid habes Patri, ...	O 187	Ad T. L. M.D.	V	17
In summo ut videas numine laeta patrem;	O 208	A Meditation		2
SUMMUS				
Summus adesse jubet celsa dominator ab arce;	O 162	Gnothi seauton		45
Summus amplexu foveat, beato	O 227	A Meditation		6
SUNT				
Omnia, nec curae sunt sua sceptra Jovi.	O 103	Elizae Aenigma		2
Sunt qui curricule timidi versantur in arcto, ...	O 163	To Dr Lawrence		9
Hi sunt quos animi generosa insania magni	O 163	To Dr Lawrence		31
Nexa patent; hi sunt quos nil mirabile turbat, ...	O 163	To Dr Lawrence		34
Stabo illis qui sunt, quique fuere, gravis.	O 216	Tr Greek 9.288		6
Sunt quibus a lacrymis vix vacat ulla dies.	O 221	Tr Greek 10.84		2
SUO				
Gratia vix restat nomine digna suo.	O 220	Tr Greek 10.30		2
Praestat magistro saepe discipulus suo.	O 223	Tr. Gk. 11.176		5
Papa suo regit imperio ter millia quinque.	O 230	Geographia Met		12
SUPERBIT				
Aegyptum; templo Solomonis quinta superbit;	O 226	Septem Aetates		3
SUPERBO				
Fidens, Superbo frange Silentio;	O 101	Ad Urbanum		10
SUPERBOS				
His redimita comas, mores depone superbos:	O 209	Tr. Greek 5.74		5
SUPERCILIUM				
Quam domini ingentis ferre supercilium.	O 221	Tr Greek 10.93		2
SUPEREST				
Quid nunc superest?	O 199	Medico Aeger S		15
Hoc quoque superest	O 199	Medico Aeger S		23
SUPERNA				
Quaeris, Quis prior est fama meritisve; superna . . .	O 385	The Warehouse	D	3
SUPERNAE				
Luxerat illa dies, legis gens docta supernae	O 170	Insula Kenneth		15
Fulserat illa dies, legis qua docta supernae	O 170	Insula Kenneth	V	15
SUPERSIT				
Aegyptum; templo Solomonis quinta supersit;	O 226	Septem Aetates	V	3
SUPPLICII				
Nunc ope supplicii vivit imago mei.	O 225	Tr Greek 16.87		2
SUPPLICIUM				
Supplicium huic, quoniam crescentia gaudia laesit, . .	O 218	Tr Greek 9.375		5
SUPRA				
Supra Praeco Dei--strepit infra Praeco Bonorum: . . .	O 385	The Warehouse	D	5
SUPREMA				
Hora bonis quasi nunc instet suprema fruaris, ...	O 219	Tr Greek 10.26		1
SUPREMIS				
Supremis junxit nexibus arctus amor.	O 393	Tr. of Crashaw	D	2
SUPREMO				
Pensilibus fusis, cyatho comitata supremo, ...	O 383	On the Gin-Act	D	1
SURDA				
Heu quam dura preces sprevit, quam surda querelas . . .	O 212	Tr Greek 7.560		5
SURDAS				
Divinos, surdas sacra vox permulceat aures!	O 89	Messiah		43
SURGE				
Surge, soror dilecta, mihi lux, gaudia, vita;	O 384	Cantico Solom.	D	1
Haud mora, surge, soror!	O 384	Cantico Solom.	D	2
SURGENT				
Atria, pacis opus, surgent, finemque caduci	O 90	Messiah		71
Tunc alacres demum surgent, et crastinus ortus . . .	O 393	Tr. of Crashaw	D	5
SURGERE				
Quam bene ventorum surgere templa jubet!	O 143	On Lord Anson		2
SURGIT				
Jessaeis surgit, mulcentesque aethera flores	O 88	Messiah		11
Surgit amans abies teretis, buxique sequaces	O 91	Messiah		81
Ordinibus surgit densis, vitamque requirit	O 92	Messiah		97
SURGITE				
Surgite convalles, tumidi subsidite montes!	O 89	Messiah		39
SURGUNT				
Mentisque, te tollente, surgunt, ...	O 166	Oda Isle Skye		19
SUSCIPIT				
Pastor agit pecudes, teneros modo suscipit agnos, . . .	O 90	Messiah		59
SUSPICIAT				
Suspiciat tandem clementem in numine patrem.	O 205	Christianus		5
SUSPIRIA				
Non planctus, non moesta sonant suspiria, pectus . . .	O 90	Messiah		52
Hic pia Vindamius traxit suspiria, in ipsa	O 116	Tr Pope Grotto		12
SUUM				
Quisque suum norit modulum; tibi, prime virorum, . . .	O 160	Gnothi seauton		14
Ille suum stolidus, nunc putat ille suum.	O 215	Tr Greek 9.74		4
Ille suum stolidus, nunc putat ille suum.	O 215	Tr Greek 9.74		4
Herodoto hospitii praemia, quaeque suum.	O 216	Tr Greek 9.160		2
SYBILLAE				
Tunc vati facilem reprobat Apollo, Sybillae	Y 28	Aurora Musis		7
SYLVANI				
In Locupletissimum ornatissimumque Syl<vani>. Urb<ani>. .	O 383	Syl. Urb. Thes.	D	T
SYLVANUS				
Menstrua concinnat Sylvanus, & Annua Dona, ...	O 383	Syl. Urb. Thes	D	1
TACENTES				
Quid mirum? cum saxa movet statuasque tacentes	Y 28	Aurora Musis		13
TACERE				
Dat tibi Pythagoram pictor; quod ni ipse tacere . . .	O 225	Tr. Gk. 16.326		1

```
                                                         PAGE   TITLE              LINE
TACET
   Cum tacet indoctus, sapientior esse videtur,    . . . .   O 221 Tr Greek 10.98        1
TACITE
   Praebeat, et tacite foecundos irriget imbres!    . . . .   O  88 Messiah            15
   Hostem odit tacite, sed amicum ridet aperte . . . . .     O 197 On Mrs. Thrale       1
TACTU
   Accrescunt tremulis tactu nova robora nervis:    . . . .   O  90 Messiah            49
   Accrescunt teneris tactu nova robora nervis:    . . . .   O  90 Messiah          V  49
TAEDIA
   Tristis et atra quies, et tardae taedia vitae. . . . . .   O 161 Gnothi seauton      26
   Per caeca noctis taedia turbidae,    . . . . . .          O 187 Ad T. L. M.D.         9
TALE
   Tale hominum genus est, infirmum, triste, misellum,  . .   O 221 Tr Greek 10.84       3
TAMEN
   Tu secura tamen confusa elementa videbis,    . . . . .    O  92 Messiah           117
   Non tamen inculti gelidis latuere sub antris,   . . . .   O 169 Insula Kenneth      11
   Nec tamen inculti gelidis latuere sub antris,   . . . .   O 169 Insula Kenneth   V  11
   Queis tamen aptam ferre medelam . . . . . .              O 193 Tr. Medea III        9
   Naufragus hic jaceo; fidens tamen utere velis,   . . . .  O 210 Tr Greek 7.282       1
   Sidereus tamen hic territat, ecce, canis!    . . . . .    O 213 Tr Greek 9.18        4
   Arti ignis lucem tribui, tamen artis et ignis   . . . .   O 225 Tr Greek 16.87       1
   Fiam scelestus, nec tamen minus sequar. . . . . . .       O 226 Tr. Cleanthes        4
   Lympha tamen cursus agit indefessa perennis,    . . . .   O 228 Rivum a Stoana       9
TANDEM
   Lexicon ad finem longo luctamine tandem . . . . . .       O 160 Gnothi seauton       1
   Aut, hoc si nimium est, tandem nova lexica poscam?   . .   O 162 Gnothi seauton      54
   Tandem dolori plus satis est datum,    . . . . . .        O 187 Ad T. L. M.D.        13
   Suspiciat tandem clementem in numine patrem.    . . . .   O 205 Christianus          5
   Aeterna tandem liberet clementia,    . . . . . . .        O 206 Prayers III           5
   Me Pater tandem reducem benigno . . . . . . .            O 227 A Meditation          5
   Et placido tandem haec edidit ore, Dea:   . . . . . .     O 386 In Birchium      D   4
TANGAS
   Fortis, ades, solus tangas venerabile limen.    . . . .   O 116 Tr Pope Grotto      16
TANGET
   Vel Pede Equus tanget,  . . . . . . . . . . .            O 109 Post-genitis          3
TANGITE
   Clamat et Argivis: Vetuli, ne tangite, vita . . . . .     O 216 Tr Greek 9.163       3
TANGITUR
   Tangitur haud pedibus tellus; conviva Deorum    . . . .   O 219 Tr Greek 9.577       3
TANQUAM
   Charus enim cunctis, tanquam, dum vita manebat,   . . .   O 212 Tr Greek 7.560       3
TANTI
   Dimidium tanti ponderis intret onus. . . . . . . .        O 229 Epigram III          2
TANTUM
   Tantum prodest  . . . . . . . . . . . . .               O 198 Medico Aeger S        9
   Tantum prodest . . . . . . . . . . . .                  O 199 Medico Aeger S       12
   Eveniat tantum mitior unda tibi! . . . . . . .           O 211 Tr Greek 7.350        2
   I, quoniam sic fata vocant: liceat mihi tantum . . . .    O 384 On the Gin-Act   D   9
   Confessus tantum mente manuque patrem;   . . . . . .      O 386 Tr Epi. Madoc    D   2
TANTUNDEM
   Tantundem est illis, repleat spatia ardua coeli   . . .   O 163 To Dr Lawrence      13
TARDAE
   Tristis et atra quies, et tardae taedia vitae. . . . . .   O 161 Gnothi seauton      26
TE
   O! colat humanum Te foveatque genus!  . . . . . . .       O 102 Ad R. Savage         2
   Te sterili functum cura, vocumque salebris   . . . . .    O 161 Gnothi seauton      19
   Nunc loca sola placent; frustra te, Somne, recumbens . .   O 161 Gnothi seauton      30
   Qua te laude, Deus, qua prece prosequar?    . . . . .     O 164 Recover Eyes        10
   Te semper studiis utilibus colam:   . . . . . . .         O 164 Recover Eyes        12
   Mentisque, te tollente, surgunt, . . . . . . . .          O 166 Oda Isle Skye       19
   Te recidunt moderante fluctus. . . . . . . . . .          O 166 Oda Isle Skye       20
   Te resident moderante fluctus. . . . . . . . . .          O 166 Oda Isle Skye    V  20
   Te recedunt moderante fluctus. . . . . . . . . .          O 166 Oda Isle Skye    V  20
   Seu te saeva sitis, levitas sive improba fecit,   . . .   O 171 Tr. Busy Fly         1
   Seu te saeva fames, levitas sive improba fecit,   . . .   O 171 Tr. Busy Fly     V   1
   Te mille succorum potentem  . . . . . . . . .            O 187 Ad T. L. M.D.         7
   Te docta, Laurenti, vetustas   . . . . . . . .           O 187 Ad T. L. M.D.        15
   Te medici revocant labores.   . . . . . . . .            O 187 Ad T. L. M.D.        16
   Phoebe fave, aegrotat quae te colit, ulla nec usquam est   O 197 Summ. Lawrence      1
   Te, mente pura, mente tranquilla colam:   . . . . . .     O 206 Prayers I           10
   Est mihi quod non te rideo, plena salus. . . . . . .      O 211 Tr Greek 7.318       2
   Cerbere, te morsu ne petat ille, cave.   . . . . . .      O 211 Tr Greek 7.319       2
   Multis ut te oculis sim potis aspicere.   . . . . . .     O 212 Tr Greek 7.669       2
   De te plebs audax, hic bene et ille male.   . . . . .     O 214 Tr Greek 9.50        2
   Conjugium, ut pro te des hominem patriae.    . . . . .    O 218 Tr Greek 9.444       4
   Non Fortuna sibi te gratum tollit in altum;    . . . .    O 218 Tr Greek 9.530       1
   Te manet imperii, Roma, perenne decus. . . . . . .        O 219 Tr Greek 9.647       2
   Prospera sors nec te strepitoso turbine tollat,   . . .   O 221 Tr Greek 10.74       1
   Hirce, parem nitido te tua barba facit.   . . . . . .     O 224 Tr. Gk. 11.430       2
   At te bonum si noris, et bonis natum,   . . . . . .       O 224 Tr Greek 13.3        3
   Vivere, te viva, te moriente, mori.   . . . . . . .       O 384 On the Gin-Act   D  10
   Vivere, te viva, te moriente, mori.   . . . . . . .       O 384 On the Gin-Act   D  10
   Vincere te potui nuda, quid arma geram?    . . . . . .    O 384 Epigramma        D   4
TECTA
   Muscosi fontes, silvestria tecta, valete,   . . . . .     O  88 Messiah             4
   Tecta ineunt; caelebs omnia solus ages;   . . . . . .     O 217 Tr Greek 9.359       6
   Tecta ineunt, caelebs impediere minus;   . . . . . .      O 217 Tr Greek 9.360       6
   Latrones, alibi locupletum quaerite tecta,   . . . . .    O 219 Tr Greek 9.654       1
TECTAQUE
   Tectaque qua fluxit, nunc et aperta fluit.   . . . . .    O 228 Rivum a Stoana      10
```

```
TECTO                                                           PAGE   TITLE           LINE
     Murem Asclepiades sub tecto ut vidit avarus,    . . . .   O 224  Tr. Gk. 11.391     1
TECTUM
     Pendet, et incoquitur tectum sine fraude metallum:   . .  O 116  Tr Pope Grotto     6
     Splendet, et incoquitur tectum sine fraude metallum: . .  O 116  Tr Pope Grotto  V  6
TECUM
     Interea dubito; tecum me causa nec ulla   . . . . . .     O 216  Tr Greek 9.148     5
     Ridere, aut tecum me lacrimare jubet.    . . . . . .      O 216  Tr Greek 9.148     6
     Laetior haud tecum, tecum neque tristior unquam,    . .   O 218  Tr Greek 9.573     5
     Laetior haud tecum, tecum neque tristior unquam,    . .   O 218  Tr Greek 9.573     5
     In tumulum tecum, morte jubente, trahes?    . . . . .     O 220  Tr Greek 10.60     2
     Eheu! quam longo tecum consumerer aevo!   . . . . . .     O 384  On the Gin-Act   D 5
TEGITUR
     Et morbus tegitur, dum premit ora pudor.    . . . . . .   O 221  Tr Greek 10.98     2
TELA
     Nunc armant Veneris lumina tela Jovis.   . . . . . .      O 103  Elizae Aenigma     6
     Per Trojae flammas, densaque tela, patrem.   . . . . .    O 216  Tr Greek 9.163     2
TELLURI
     Telluri arboribus ver frondens, sidera coelo,   . . . .  O 214  Tr Greek 9.65      1
TELLUS
     Materiam Statuae sic praebet Marmora Tellus,    . . . .   O  85  Adjecere bonae     3
     Deproperat tellus, fundit tibi munera, quicquid    . .    O  89  Messiah           28
     Demissumque Deum tellus capit; ardua cedrus,    . . . .   O  89  Messiah           37
     Cunctiparens tellus, salve, levis esto pusillo  . . . .   O 211  Tr Greek 7.461     1
     In me animo tellus gignit et unda feras,    . . . . . .   O 213  Tr Greek 9.18      2
     Tangitur haud pedibus tellus; conviva Deorum    . . . .   O 219  Tr Greek 9.577     3
     Sortitur Pelopis tellus quae nomine gaudet.   . . . . .   O 230  Geographia Met     7
     Parthenope.   Novies vult tellus mille Sicana.   . . .    O 230  Geographia Met    11
     Harmonia tellus completur lata, per agros   . . . . .     Y  28  Aurora Musis       3
TEMERE
     Fallimur exemplis; temere sibi turba scholarum  . . . .   O 160  Gnothi seauton    12
TEMNENS
     Se fidum addicat Christo, mortalia temnens.   . . . . .   O 205  Christianus       18
TEMNERE
     Temnere opes pretium sceleris, patriamque tueri   . . .   O 116  Tr Pope Grotto    15
TEMPELMANNI
     His Tempelmanni numeris descripseris orbem.   . . . . .   O 229  Geographia Met     1
TEMPERAT
     Rerum perpetuus temperat Arbiter,    . . . . . . . .      O 164  Recover Eyes       2
TEMPLA
     Quam bene ventorum surgere templa jubet!    . . . . . .   O 143  On Lord Anson      2
TEMPLO
     Aegyptum; templo Solomonis quinta superbit;    . . . .    O 226  Septem Aetates     3
     Aegyptum; templo Solomonis quinta supersit;    . . . .    O 226  Septem Aetates  V  3
TEMPLUM
     Barbarus, en! clarum divino lumine templum   . . . . .    O  92  Messiah          100
     Jupiter hoc templum, ut, siquando relinquit Olympum,  . . O 219  Tr Greek 9.702     1
TEMPORA
     Tempora restat.   . . . . . . . . . . . . . .            O 153  In Theatro      V 16
     Olim, praeteritae numeranti tempora vitae,   . . . . .    O 171  Tr. Busy Fly      11
TEMPORE
     Tempore restat.   . . . . . . . . . . . . . .            O 153  In Theatro        16
     Tempore justo   . . . . . . . . . . . . . . .            O 199  Medico Aeger S    10
     Divitiis, utrinque cavens, qui tempore parcit,   . . . . O 219  Tr Greek 10.26     3
     Tempore divitiis utitur, ille sapit.    . . . . . . . .  O 219  Tr Greek 10.26     4
TEMPORIBUS
     Tres tria temporibus secla dedere suis.    . . . . . .   O  86  Tr Dryden Milt     2
TEMPORIS
     Temporis Henricum rapuit vis vivida mentis;    . . . . . O 116  Tr Pope Grotto    11
     Nox miseris longi temporis instar habet.   . . . . . .   O 220  Tr Greek 10.28     2
     Jactura Temporis   . . . . . . . . . . . . . .           O 228  Jactura Tempor     T
     Hora perit furtim laetis, mens temporis aegra   . . . .  O 228  Jactura Tempor     1
TENDAT
     In vos ne missus spicula tendat amor.    . . . . . . .   O 213  Tr Greek 9.39      2
TENDET
     Sedulitas animosa tendet.    . . . . . . . . . . .       O 101  Ad Urbanum        12
TENDIS
     Quisquis iter tendis, vitreas qua lucidus undas   . . .  O 116  Tr Pope Grotto     1
TENDIT
     Recta ad pauperiem tendit, cui corpora cordi est   . . . O 222  Tr. Gk. 10.119     1
TENE
     Tene mulceri fidibus canoris?    . . . . . . . . .       O 153  In Theatro         5
     Tene cantorum modulis stupere?   . . . . . . . . .       O 153  In Theatro         6
     Tene per pictas oculo elegante   . . . . . . . . .       O 153  In Theatro         7
TENEBRAS
     Per vitae tenebras rerumque incerta vagantem   . . . .   O 207  Prayers IV         1
     Pellat et tristes animi tenebras,    . . . . . . . .     O 227  A Meditation       2
TENEBRIS
     Regiam inundabit, nullis cessura tenebris.   . . . . .   O  92  Messiah          113
     Damnatus tenebris, lectoque affixus inerti,   . . . . .  O 163  To Dr Lawrence     3
TENEBRISNE
     Quid faciam? tenebrisne pigram damnare senectam   . . .  O 162  Gnothi seauton    52
TENEBRISQUE
     Fecerunt rami latebras, tenebrisque diurnis   . . . . .  O 228  Rivum a Stoana     5
TENEBROSA
     Anxietas noceat ne tenebrosa mihi.   . . . . . . . .     O 207  Prayers VII        2
TENELLA
     Quo toties lavi membra tenella puer;    . . . . . . .    O 228  Rivum a Stoana     2
TENENTI
     Sit tibi, Calliope, Parnassum, cura, tenenti,    . . . . O 218  Tr Greek 9.523     1
```

```
TENERIS                                                        PAGE    TITLE            LINE
    Accrescunt teneris tactu nova robora nervis:    . . . .    O  90  Messiah        V  49
    Serpentes teneris nil jam lethale minantes    . . . . .    O  91  Messiah           89
    Serpentes teneris nil jam lethale micantes    . . . . .    O  91  Messiah        V  89
TENEROS
    Pastor agit pecudes, teneros modo suscipit agnos,  . . .   O  90  Messiah           59
    Jam teneros fructus detrudit lactea ficus    . . . . .     O 385  Cantico Solom.  D  11
TENET
    Non tenet; esca natat pulchra, sed hamus abest.    . . .   O 209  Tr. Greek 5.67     2
    Quam tenet hic, cunctas quae manet, alta quies.    . . .   O 211  Tr Greek 7.459     4
    Gratia nulla hominum mentes tenet, ista Promethei  . . .   O 225  Tr Greek 16.87     3
    Dissimili domus una duos tenet arte tumentes;    . . . .   O 385  The Warehouse   D   1
TENOREM
    Irruptum vitae cupiat servare tenorem;    . . . . . .      O 205  Christianus       13
TENTAT
    Tentat iter brevius, magno conamine summam    . . . . .    O 163  To Dr Lawrence    24
TENTEM
    Ut modo tentem    . . . . . . . . .                        O 199  Medico Aeger S    16
TENUIS
    Scaliger ut duxit, tenuis pertaesus opellae,    . . . .    O 160  Gnothi seauton     2
TENUIT
    Una duas tenuit casa cum genitore puellas,    . . . . .    O 169  Insula Kenneth  V   9
TEQUE
    Teque frui timor est, teque carere dolor.    . . . . .     O 218  Tr Greek 9.394     2
    Teque frui timor est, teque carere dolor.    . . . . .     O 218  Tr Greek 9.394     2
TER
    Gratia ter grata est velox, sin forte moretur   . . . .    O 220  Tr Greek 10.30     1
    Papa suo regit imperio ter millia quinque.    . . . . .    O 230  Geographia Met    12
    Russia, myriadas ter denas adde trecentis:    . . . . .    O 230  Geographia Met    17
    Myriadas ter mille homini dat terra colendas.   . . . .    O 230  Geographia Met    20
    Et quadragenis quoque ter tria millia jungit.   . . . .    O 230  Geographia Met    26
    Ter tria myriadi conjungit millia quartae,    . . . . .    O 230  Geographia Met    29
    Ter sex centurias Hollandia jactat opima   . . . . . .     O 231  Geographia Met    35
TERCENTUM
    Xerxi, tercentum Spartae Mars obstitit acris   . . . . .   O 217  Tr Greek 9.304     3
TERDECIMO
    Vitam a terdecimo sextus mihi finiet annus,   . . . . .    O 215  Tr Greek 9.112     1
TERENDOS
    Labraque constrictus semesos, jamque terendos   . . . .    O 218  Tr Greek 9.375     3
TERET
    Qui duxit sulcos, illi teret area messem,    . . . . .     O  90  Messiah           73
TERETIS
    Surgit amans abies teretis, buxique sequaces    . . . .    O  91  Messiah           81
TERGA
    In trepidis dare terga rebus.    . . . . . . . .           O 186  Ad T. L. M.D.      4
    In dubiis dare terga rebus.    . . . . . . . .             O 186  Ad T. L. M.D.   V   4
TERGET
    Singultans mulcet, lachrymantes terget ocellos.    . . .   O  90  Messiah           53
TERGIT
    Singultans mulcet, lachrymantes tergit ocellos.    . , .   O  90  Messiah        V  53
TERRA
    Perpetui, ambita bis terra, praemia lactis   . . . . .     O 156  Collari Caprae     1
    Perpetua, ambita bis terra, praemia lactis   . . . . .     O 156  Collari Caprae  V   1
    Linguarumque omni terra discordia concors   . . . . .      O 161  Gnothi seauton    22
    Linguarumque omni ex terra discordia concors   . . . .     O 161  Gnothi seauton  V  22
    In sublime rapit, queis terra et pontus et aer   . . .     O 163  To Dr Lawrence    32
    Terram adii nudus, de terra nudus abibo.    . . . . .      O 220  Tr Greek 10.58     1
    Myriadas ter mille homini dat terra colendas.   . . . .    O 230  Geographia Met    20
TERRAE
    Idem Orcus terrae, sic, pelagoque subest.    . . . . .     O 210  Tr Greek 7.265     2
TERRAEQUE
    Qui, mutare vias ausus terraeque marisque,    . . . . .    O 217  Tr Greek 9.304     1
TERRAM
    Terram adii nudus, de terra nudus abibo.    . . . . . .    O 220  Tr Greek 10.58     1
TERRAS
    Permeo terras, ubi nuda rupes    . . . . . . . .           O 167  Oda to Thrale      1
    Pervagor terras, hominum ferorum    . . . . . . .          O 167  Oda to Thrale   V   5
    Dulcia dat natura quidem, mare, sidera, terras,    . . .   O 222  Tr. Gk. 10.123     3
    Prima parit terras aetas; siccatque secunda;   . . . .     O 226  Septem Aetates     1
    Et petiit terras per freta longa novas.    . . . . .       O 386  Tr Epi. Madoc   D   4
TERRASQUE
    Compositis Pax alma suas, terrasque revisens   . . . .     O  89  Messiah           23
TERRENAS
    Mentibus afflatu terrenas ejice sordes   . . . . . .       O 232  Prayer             5
TERRENT
    Rura labor lassat; mare mille pericula terrent;   . . .    O 217  Tr Greek 9.359     3
TERRES
    Nunc juvenum terres robore corda senex.    . . . . .       O 225  Tr. Gk. 16.364     2
TERRET
    Quem terret vitae meta propinqua suae,    . . . . .        O 207  Prayers VI         4
TERRIBILI
    Terribili fremitu stridula moeret anus.    . . . . .       O 383  On the Gin-Act  D   2
TERRIS
    Induit, et, terris major, coelestia spirat. . . . . .      O 205  Christianus       30
    Et ferus est Timon sub terris; janitor Orci,   . . . .     O 211  Tr Greek 7.319     1
    Militibus; terris sit pelagoque pudor!   . . . . . .       O 217  Tr Greek 9.304     4
TERRITAT
    Sidereus tamen hic territat, ecce, canis!   . . . . .      O 213  Tr Greek 9.18      4
TERROR
    Terror inest aliis, moerorque, et siquid habebis   . . .   O 222  Tr. Gk. 10.123     5
```

```
TERRORIS                                                  PAGE    TITLE              LINE
    Instet, et evellens terroris spicula corde, . . . . .  O 205 Christianus            4
TERTIA
    Evocat Abramum dein tertia; quarta relinquit   . . .   O 226 Septem Aetates         2
TERTII
    Tertii verso quater orbe lustri, . . . . . . . .       O 153 In Theatro             1
TERTIUS
    Quae potuere duos tertius unus habet. . . . . . .      O  86 Tr Dryden Milt         6
    Hunc sequitur caelebs; tertius, orbe, venis.   . . .   O 222 Tr Greek 11.50         2
TESTABITUR
    Et curas felix patrias testabitur orbis. . . . . .     O  90 Messiah              65
TETIGIT
    Haud lavit Phido, haud tetigit; mihi febre calenti  .  . O 223 Tr. Gk. 11.118       1
TEXENT
    Et serae texent vites umbracula proli.  . . . . . .    O  90 Messiah              74
TEXENTE
    Texente Nymphis serta Lycoride, . . . . . . . . .      O 102 Ad Urbanum           21
THALAMO
    Felici thalamo non, puto, rixa strepit.  . . . . . .   O 226 Tr. Greek             2
THAMESIS
    Speluncae late Thamesis praetendit opacae,  . . . .    O 116 Tr Pope Grotto        2
THE
    Inscription on the collar of Mr. Banks's Goat   . . .  O 156 Collari Caprae    V   T
    The Logical Warehouse: Occasioned by an Auctioneer's . O 385 The Warehouse     D   T
    . . . having the Groundfloor of the Oratory  . . .     O 385 The Warehouse     D   T
    . . . having the groundfloor of the oratory  . . .     O 385 The Warehouse     D   T
THEATRALES
    Quid theatrales tibi, Crispe, pompae? . . . . . . .    O 153 In Theatro             2
THEATRI
    Luxus oblectat Juvenem theatri, . . . . . . . . .      O 153 In Theatro            14
THEATRO
    In Theatro . . . . . . . . . . . . . . . . . .         O 153 In Theatro             T
THEBARUM
    Buccina disjecit Thebarum moenia, struxit  . . . .     O 216 Tr Greek 9.250         1
THESAURUM
    . . .      Thesaurum  . . . . . . . . . . . .          O 383 Syl. Urb. Thes.  D   T
THOMAM
    Ad T<homam>. L<aurence>. M<edicum>. D<octissimum>.  .  O 186 Ad T.L. M.D.           T
    Ad Thomam Laurence, Medicum Doctissimum, Cum  . . .    O 186 Ad T. L. M.D.    V   T
THORACEM
    Seu thoracem . . . . . . . . . . . . . . . . .         O 198 Medico Aeger S         6
THRALIA
    Thralia dulcis? . . . . . . . . . . . . . . .          O 168 Oda to Thrale        12
    Thralia. Quid mavis? tutius hostis eris. . . . . .     O 197 On Mrs. Thrale         2
    Thralia suavis. . . . . . . . . . . . . . . .          O 199 Medico Aeger S       22
THRALIAE
    Thraliae discant resonare nomen  . . . . . . . .       O 168 Oda to Thrale        19
TIARAE
    Explicat, incinctam radiatae luce tiarae!  . . . .     O  92 Messiah              95
TIBI
    Nascere, magne puer! Tibi primas, ecce! corollas  . .  O  89 Messiah              27
    Deproperat tellus, fundit tibi munera, quicquid  . .   O  89 Messiah              28
    En! formosa tibi porrecta per atria proles  . . .      O  92 Messiah             9,6
    En! formosa tibi spatiosa per atria proles  . . .      O  92 Messiah        V    9,6
    Solis Ophyraeis crudum tibi montibus aurum  . . .      O  92 Messiah             104
    Maturant radii, tibi balsama sudat Idume.  . . . .     O  92 Messiah             105
    Adsit, Laura, tibi facilis Lucina dolenti, . . . .     O 115 Ad Lauram Epig         3
    Neve tibi noceat praenituisse Deae. . . . . . . .      O 115 Ad Lauram Epig         4
    Ingredere! Egeriae sacrum en tibi panditur antrum!  .  O 116 Tr Pope Grotto        9
    Fortis, ades, tibi sponte patet venerabile limen. . .  O 116 Tr Pope Grotto   V   16
    Quid theatrales tibi, Crispe, pompae? . . . . . . .    O 153 In Theatro             2
    Quisque suum norit modulum; tibi, prime virorum, . .   O 160 Gnothi seauton        14
    Tu, quamcunque tibi velox indulserit annus, . . . .    O 171 Tr. Busy Fly          5
    Volvitur hora mihi, volvitur hora tibi! . . . . .      O 171 Tr. Busy Fly          8
    Una quidem, sic fata volunt, tibi vivitur aestas,  . . O 171 Tr. Busy Fly          9
    Redde tuis, tibi redde, mentem. . . . . . . . .        O 187 Ad T. L. M.D.        20
    Ut tibi, gentis  . . . . . . . . . . . . . . .         O 199 Medico Aeger S       24
    Quod poscis, haud unquam tibi  . . . . . . . .         O 203 Christ Sinner         3
    Qua solum potero parte, placere tibi. . . . . . .      O 204 Losing Speech         4
    Qua solum potero parte, litare tibi. . . . . . . .     O 204 Losing Speech    V   4
    Vult Deus, at, qui cuncta dedit tibi, cuncta reposcit. . O 205 Christianus        24
    Mandatum, vivam sic moriarque tibi. . . . . . .        O 207 Prayers IV            6
    Ut tibi quae placeant, omnia promptus agam. . . . . .  O 207 Prayers V             4
    Mens mea quid quereris? veniet tibi mollior hora, . .  O 208 A Meditation          1
    Contextam variis, do, Rhodoclea, tibi: . . . . . .     O 209 Tr. Greek 5.74        2
    Eveniat tantum mitior unda tibi! . . . . . . . .       O 211 Tr Greek 7.350        2
    Lysigeni, fuerat non gravis ille tibi. . . . . . .     O 211 Tr Greek 7.461        2
    Plus tibi ridendum secula nostra dabunt. . . . . .     O 216 Tr Greek 9.148        2
    Det Bacchus, dederat quale, Lycurge, tibi. . . . .     O 218 Tr Greek 9.375        6
    Sit tibi, Calliope, Parnassum, cura, tenenti, . . . .  O 218 Tr Greek 9.523        1
    Per fluctus vitae sic tibi cursus erit. . . . . .      O 221 Tr Greek 10.74        6
    Sic aliis dives, tu tibi pauper agis. . . . . . .      O 223 Tr. Gk. 11.167        2
    Quid tibi, mus, mecum, dixit, amice, tibi? . . . .     O 224 Tr. Gk. 11.391        2
    Quid tibi, mus, mecum, dixit, amice, tibi? . . . .     O 224 Tr. Gk. 11.391        2
    Dat tibi Pythagoram pictor; quod ni ipse tacere   . .  O 225 Tr. Gk. 16.326        1
    Ut tibi laus omni semper ab ore sonet: . . . . .       O 232 Prayer                8
    Haec postrema tibi sit flendi causa, fluatque  . . .   Y 387 Death Mother     D   3
TIGRI
    Florea mansuetae petulantes vincula tigri  . . . . .   O  91 Messiah              86
TIMEAT
    Sed timeat semper, caveatque ante omnia, turbae   . .  O 205 Christianus          19
```

		PAGE	TITLE	LINE
TIMEBIT				
Leo, sed violare timebit, ...		O 109	Post-genitis	28
TIMENTI				
Christe, spem praesta stabilem timenti;		O 194	Prayer on Xmas	6
TIMERE				
Certa vetet dubitare fides, spes laeta timere, ...		O 207	Prayers VII	7
TIMET				
Cyrum sexta timet; laetatur septima Christo.		O 226	Septem Aetates	4
TIMIDI				
Sunt qui curriculo timidi versantur in arcto, ...		O 163	To Dr Lawrence	9
TIMIDUM				
Quem moestum et timidum crimina dira gravant;		O 207	Prayers V	2
TIMON				
Et ferus est Timon sub terris; janitor Orci,		O 211	Tr Greek 7.319	1
TIMOR				
Teque frui timor est, teque carere dolor.		O 218	Tr Greek 9.394	2
TIMORE				
Fures absque Timore, ...		O 109	Post-genitis	17
TIMOREM				
Mus blandum ridens, respondit, pelle timorem;		O 224	Tr. Gk. 11.391	3
TIMORIS				
Verte solum, fient causa timoris opes;		O 217	Tr Greek 9.359	4
TITULIQUE				
Fecerunt nulli sors titulique gravem.		O 226	Tr. Simonides	4
TO				
To a lady who spoke in Defence of Liberty		O 105	Lady Defence	T
Verses addressed to Dr. Lawrence, composed by Dr. . . .		O 162	To Dr Lawrence	T
TOLERANDA				
Non vitanda gravem, non toleranda facit?		O 222	Tr. Gk. 10.123	2
TOLERARE				
Fortunae malim adversae tolerare procellas, ...		O 221	Tr Greek 10.93	1
TOLLAT				
Prospera sors nec te strepitoso turbine tollat, ...		O 221	Tr Greek 10.74	1
TOLLE				
Tolle, Salema, sacros, quam circum gloria pennas . . .		O 92	Messiah	94
TOLLENTE				
Mentisque, te tollente, surgunt, ...		O 166	Oda Isle Skye	19
TOLLIT				
Altius, en! Lebanon gaudentia culmina tollit, . . .		O 89	Messiah	30
Non Fortuna sibi te gratum tollit in altum;		O 218	Tr Greek 9.530	1
Clam nocte tollit Aulus, et ridens ait;		O 223	Tr. Gk. 11.176	4
TOLLITE				
Tollite concentum, Solymaeae tollite nymphae!		O 88	Messiah	1
Tollite concentum, Solymaeae tollite nymphae!		O 88	Messiah	1
TORI				
Fida comes mensae, fida comesque tori!		O 383	On the Gin-Act D	4
TORPENTIBUS				
Eloquiumque potens linguis torpentibus affer, ...		O 232	Prayer	7
TORPESQUE				
Torpesque languescisque curis		O 187	Ad T. L. M.D.	11
TORPET				
Cessat inops rerum, ut torpet, si marmoris absit . . .		O 161	Gnothi seauton	38
TORREAT				
Sive dies medius morientia torreat arva:		O 90	Messiah	63
Sive dies medius languentia torreat arva:		O 90	Messiah V	63
TORRENTIS				
Coelicolae pandunt, torrentis aurea lucis		O 92	Messiah V	107
TORRENTISQUE				
Coelicolae pandunt, torrentisque aurea lucis		O 92	Messiah	107
TORVA				
Torva ubi rident steriles coloni		O 167	Oda to Thrale	3
TORVIS				
Hostiles oculis flammas jaculantia torvis;		O 90	Messiah	67
TOTA				
Ut florem amittat gratia tota perit		Y 332	Tr Greek 10.30 V	1
Myrias, ut menti pateat tota Africa doctae.		O 230	Geographia Met	24
TOTIES				
Quo toties lavi membra tenella puer;		O 228	Rivum a Stoana	2
TOTO				
Nam licet, et toto prolue laeta mero.		O 171	Tr. Busy Fly	4
Ardeat huic toto sacer ignis pectore, possit		O 205	Christianus	10
TOTUM				
Hic, in se totum longe per opaca futuri		O 116	Tr Pope Grotto	10
TOTUS				
Nec dubitet quem dicat herum, sed, totus in uno, . . .		O 205	Christianus	17
Corde meo accendas; ardeo totus ego.		O 225	Tr. Gk. 16.209	2
TRACTA				
Omnesque in partes tracta retracta fluit;		O 221	Tr Greek 10.74	4
TRACTABIT				
Tractabit palmis infans, motusque trisulcae		O 91	Messiah	90
TRACTANT				
Vel digiti tractant, oculus vel sentit et auris: . . .		O 163	To Dr Lawrence	12
TRAHENTI				
Aegrum trahenti spiritum		O 206	Prayers II	8
TRAHES				
In tumulum tecum, morte jubente, trahes?		O 220	Tr Greek 10.60	2
TRAJECIT				
Trajecit montes nauta, fretumque pedes, ...		O 217	Tr Greek 9.304	2
TRANQUILLA				
Te, mente pura, mente tranquilla colam:		O 206	Prayers I	10

```
                                                          PAGE   TITLE              LINE
TRANSEAT
    Hic jaceant; donec Nox transeat horrida nimbis,   . . .   O 393 Tr. of Crashaw   D   3
TRAXIT
    Hic pia Vindamius traxit suspiria, in ipsa   . . . . .    O 116 Tr Pope Grotto       12
TRECENTIS
    Russia, myriadas ter denas adde trecentis:   . . . . .    O 230 Geographia Met       17
TREMERE
    Nec sinat semper tremere ac dolere . . . . . . . .        O 227 A Meditation          3
    Nec sinat semper tremere ac dolore . . . . . . . .        O 227 A Meditation     V    3
TREMIT
    Canna viret, juncique tremit mutabilis umbra.  . . . .    O  91 Messiah              79
    Canna viret, juncique tremit variabilis umbra. . . . .    O  91 Messiah         V   79
TREMORE
    Sidera fumabunt, diro labefacta tremore  . . . . . .      O  92 Messiah             115
TREMULIS
    Accrescunt tremulis tactu nova robora nervis:  . . . .    O  90 Messiah              49
TREPIDANT
    Marmoreo trepidant qua lentae in fornice guttae,   . . .  O 116 Tr Pope Grotto        3
    Marmorea trepidant qua lentae in fornice guttae,   . . .  O 116 Tr Pope Grotto   V    3
TREPIDIS
    In trepidis dare terga rebus.  . . . . . . . .           O 186 Ad T. L. M.D.         4
TREPIDO
    Christe, da tutam trepido quietem, . . . . . . . .       O 194 Prayer on Xmas        5
TREPIDUS
    Omnia percurro trepidus, circum omnia lustro,  . . . .    O 161 Gnothi seauton       32
TRES
    Tres tria temporibus secla dedere suis.  . . . . .       O  86 Tr Dryden Milt        2
    Ut vis, ponte minax, modo tres discesseris ulnas,  . . .  O 210 Tr Greek 7.284        1
    Centurias, et tres decadas Europa Britannis.   . . . .    O 230 Geographia Met       28
TRIA
    Tres tria temporibus secla dedere suis.  . . . . .       O  86 Tr Dryden Milt        2
    Et quadragenis quoque ter tria millia jungit.  . . . .    O 230 Geographia Met       26
    Ter tria myriadi conjungit millia quartae, . . . . .     O 230 Geographia Met       29
TRIBUERE
    Exceptae hospitio Musae tribuere libellos  . . . . .     O 216 Tr Greek 9.160        1
    Turba senum, juvenes nunc tribuere seni. . . . . . .     O 225 Tr. Gk. 16.364        4
TRIBUI
    Arti ignis lucem tribui, tamen artis et ignis  . . . .    O 225 Tr Greek 16.87        1
TRIPLEX
    Et senium triplex Nestoris urna capit.   . . . . . .     O 215 Tr Greek 9.112        4
TRISTE
    Triste coruscabit radiis; dabit hasta recusa   . . . .    O  90 Messiah              69
    Triste nihil passus, animi at de sorte Platonis  . . .    O 211 Tr Greek 7.471        3
    Mulcere, aut pectus triste levare malis. . . . . . .     O 218 Tr Greek 9.375        8
    Tale hominum genus est, infirmum, triste, misellum,  . .  O 221 Tr Greek 10.84        3
TRISTES
    Pellat et tristes animi tenebras,  . . . . . . . .       O 227 A Meditation          2
TRISTI
    . . . tristi prosequeretur.   . . . . . . . . .          O 186 Ad T. L. M.D.    V    T
TRISTIOR
    Laetior haud tecum, tecum neque tristior unquam,   . . .  O 218 Tr Greek 9.573        5
TRISTIS
    Tristis et atra quies, et tardae taedia vitae. . . . .    O 161 Gnothi seauton       26
TRISTITIAM
    Noctis tristitiam qui gelidae jubet, . . . . . . .       O 164 Recover Eyes          4
TRISULCAE
    Tractabit palmis infans, motusque trisulcae  . . . .     O  91 Messiah              90
TRITAE
    Ecce! cremant genibus tritae regalibus arae.   . . .     O  92 Messiah             103
TRIUMPHATRIX
    Illa triumphatrix Graium consueta procorum   . . . .     O 209 Tr. Greek 6.1         1
TRIUMPHOS
    Opes, triumphos, et subacti  . . . . . . . . . .         O 188 Epilogus              3
TROJAE
    Per Trojae flammas, densaque tela, patrem. . . . .       O 216 Tr Greek 9.163        2
TU
    Tu mihi, qui flamma movisti pectora sancti   . . . .     O  88 Messiah               6
    Tu secura tamen confusa elementa videbis,  . . . . .     O  92 Messiah             117
    Quid mecum peragam, quod tu doctissime posses  . . . .    O 163 To Dr Lawrence        4
    Rex summe, solus tu regis arbiter, . . . . . . . .       O 166 Oda Isle Skye        18
    Tu, quamcunque tibi velox indulserit annus,  . . . .     O 171 Tr. Busy Fly          5
    Tu, queis laborat sors hominum, mala . . . . . .        O 187 Ad T. L. M.D.         5
    Et pro me pretium, tu patiare, pater.  . . . . . .       O 207 Prayers V             6
    Haec peritura nitent; tu peritura nites! . . . . .       O 209 Tr. Greek 5.74        6
    Tu neque dulce putes alienae accumbere mensae, . . . .    O 218 Tr Greek 9.573        1
    Sic aliis dives, tu tibi pauper agis.  . . . . . .       O 223 Tr. Gk. 11.167        2
    Tu quoque securus res age, Nise, tuas. . . . . . .       O 228 Rivum a Stoana       12
    At tu quisquis eris, miseri qui cruda poetae   . . . .    Y 387 Death Mother    D    1
TUA
    Ecce! peregrinis fervent tua limina turbis; . . . .       O  92 Messiah              99
    Quam magis exoptes arte valere tua.  . . . . . .        O 197 Summ. Lawrence        2
    Sic peragam tua jussa libens, accinctus ad omne  . .      O 207 Prayers IV            5
    Quo tua signantur gesta, Philippe, lapis.. . . . .       O 216 Tr Greek 9.288        2
    Cur opulentus eges? tua cuncta in foenore ponis.   . .    O 223 Tr. Gk. 11.167        1
    Hirce, parem nitido te tua barba facit.  . . . . .       O 224 Tr. Gk. 11.430        2
TUAE
    Summe Pater, quodcunque tuae de corpore leges  . . .     O 204 Losing Speech    V    1
    Sed similem, Plutarche, tuae describere vitam  . . .     O 225 Tr. Gk. 16.331        5
TUAM
    Parca, juventutem non miserata tuam! . . . . . . .       O 212 Tr Greek 7.560        6
```

	PAGE	TITLE	LINE
TUAS			
Ima tuas credit permitti, Scaliger, iras.	O 160	Gnothi seauton	13
Et colere et leges semper amare tuas.	O 208	Prayers VII	10
Tu quoque securus res age, Nise, tuas.	O 228	Rivum a Stoana	12
"Perge modo, atque tuas olim post funera laudes	O 386	In Birchium	D 5
TUEARE			
Numine praesenti me tueare pater!	O 207	Prayers IV	2
TUENTI			
Aevi sat novi quam sim brevis; astra tuenti,	O 219	Tr Greek 9.577	1
TUERE			
Rege, et tuere, quae nocent pellens procul;	O 206	Prayers I	6
TUERI			
Temnere opes pretium sceleris, patriamque tueri	O 116	Tr Pope Grotto	15
TUGURIQUE			
Squallet informis, tugurique fumis	O 167	Oda to Thrale	7
TUIS			
Grates, summe Pater, tuis	O 164	Recover Eyes	13
Redde tuis, tibi redde, mentem.	O 187	Ad T. L. M.D.	20
Concede agendam legibus vitam tuis.	O 206	Prayers I	4
Convenit ut natis, inclyta Sparta, tuis.	O 224	Tr Greek 16.1	4
TULIT			
Carmen grande sonans; Anglus utrumque tulit.	O 86	Tr Dryden Milt	4
Non poteras, regio non tulit ulla parem.	O 225	Tr. Gk. 16.331	6
TUMENTES			
Dissimili domus una duos tenet arte tumentes;	O 385	The Warehouse	D 1
TUMIDI			
Surgite convalles, tumidi subsidite montes!	O 89	Messiah	39
TUMIDO			
Sanguine dum tumido suffusus flagrat ocellus,	O 162	To Dr Lawrence	1
TUMIDUS			
Captans, nec fastu tumidus, semperque futuro	O 205	Christianus	3
TUMULATUS			
Pro nullo; clamo nunc tumulatus idem.	O 209	Tr Greek 7.128	4
TUMULAVIT			
Videre, Archidicen haec tumulavit humus;	O 226	Tr. Simonides	2
TUMULUM			
Si forsan tumulum quo conditur Eumarus aufers,	O 210	Tr Greek 7.284	3
Saepe tuum in tumulum lacrymarum decidit imber	O 212	Tr Greek 7.560	1
In tumulum tecum, morte jubente, trahes?	O 220	Tr Greek 10.60	2
TUMULUS			
Mugitum tumulus comprimit Amphilochi.	O 213	Tr Greek 8.137	2
TUNC			
Plurima tunc Leges	O 109	Post-genitis	21
In Rabiem tunc contremet Ursa	O 109	Post-genitis	24
Cynthia, tunc latis	O 109	Post-genitis	25
Tunc vati facilem reprobat Apollo, Sybillae	Y 28	Aurora Musis	7
Tunc alacres demum surgent, et crastinus ortus	O 393	Tr. of Crashaw	D 5
TUO			
Ingreditur, cultuque tuo mansuescere gaudet.	O 92	Messiah	101
Nec quaerunt quid, luna, tuo cum fluctibus orbi.	O 163	To Dr Lawrence	16
Sanguine, peccanti promereare tuo!	O 208	Prayers VII	12
Vive tuo ex animo, vario rumore loquetur	O 214	Tr Greek 9.50	1
At docet, exemplo, vis sibi quanta, tuo.	O 218	Tr Greek 9.530	2
Arridens dcmino collacrymansque tuo,	O 218	Tr Greek 9.573	4
Hanc statuam ingenio Roma benigna tuo.	O 225	Tr. Gk. 16.331	2
Credideris fletu funera digna tuo,	Y 387	Death Mother	D 2
TUQUE			
Me, rex deorum, tuque, duc, necessitas,	O 226	Tr. Cleanthes	1
TURBA			
En! quem turba diu cecinerunt enthea, vates,	O 89	Messiah	41
Fallimur exemplis; temere sibi turba scholarum	O 160	Gnothi seauton	12
Unus homo mihi pro sexcentis, turba popelli	O 209	Tr Greek 7.128	3
Quae sine morte fuga est vitae, quam turba malorum	O 222	Tr. Gk. 10.123	1
Turba senum, juvenes nunc tribuere seni.	O 225	Tr. Gk. 16.364	4
TURBAE			
Sed timeat semper, caveatque ante omnia, turbae	O 205	Christianus	19
TURBAT			
Nexa patent; hi sunt quos nil mirabile turbat,	O 163	To Dr Lawrence	34
TURBIDAE			
Per caeca noctis taedia turbidae,	O 187	Ad T. L. M.D.	9
TURBIDUS			
Turbidus imber abest; mittit rosa roscida gemmas,	O 385	Cantico Solom.	D 5
TURBINE			
Prospera sors nec te strepitoso turbine tollat,	O 221	Tr Greek 10.74	1
TURBIS			
Ecce! peregrinis fervent tua limina turbis;	O 92	Messiah	99
TURCA			
Imperium qua Turca ferox exercet iniquum.	O 230	Geographia Met	5
TURGIDOS			
Acri sanguine turgidos	O 164	Recover Eyes	5
TURRE			
Nil opus est aeris sacra de turre sonantis	O 170	Insula Kenneth	V 18A
TURRITAE			
Indue reginam, turritae frontis honores	O 91	Messiah	93
TUSCUS			
Cum sex centuriis numerat sex millia Tuscus.	O 230	Geographia Met	13
TUSSIS			
Laniat tussis;	O 198	Medico Aeger S	8
TUTAM			
Christe, da tutam trepido quietem,	O 194	Prayer on Xmas	5

```
TUTI                                                         PAGE   TITLE               LINE
     Qua sulcat, reptant tuti per lubrica vitae.  . . . . .  O 163  To Dr Lawrence        18
     Servilem tuti cultum contempsit agelli,  . . . . . .    O 386  Tr Epi. Madoc      D   3
TUTIUS
     Thralia. Quid mavis? tutius hostis eris.  . . . . . .    O 197  On Mrs. Thrale         2
TUTO
     Tuto eluctatum spatiis Sapientia dia  . . . . . . .      O 161  Gnothi seauton        20
TUTUM
     Displiceat, servet tutum sub pectore rectum:            O 205  Christianus           15
     Tutum aliis aequor, me pereunte, fuit.  . . . . .        O 210  Tr Greek 7.282         2
     Tutum hic sedile, et si placet, sopor tutus.  . . .      O 224  Tr Greek 13.3          4
TUTUS
     Cumque leone petet tutus praesepe juvencus.  . . . . .   O  91  Messiah               85
     Firma manet virtus; virtuti innitere, tutus  . . . .    O 221  Tr Greek 10.74         5
     Tutum hic sedile, et si placet, sopor tutus.  . . .      O 224  Tr Greek 13.3          4
TUUM
     Summe Pater, quodcunque tuum de corpore Numen  . . . .   O 204  Losing Speech          1
     Saepe tuum in tumulum lacrymarum decidit imber  . . .    O 212  Tr Greek 7.560         1
UBI
     Horret, ubi vanae species, umbraeque fugaces,           O 162  Gnothi seauton        50
     Permeo terras, ubi nuda rupes  . . . . . . . .           O 167  Oda to Thrale          1
     Torva ubi rident steriles coloni  . . . . . . .          O 167  Oda to Thrale          3
     Vita ubi nullo decorata cultu  . . . . . . . .           O 167  Oda to Thrale          6
     Voce ubi Cennnethus populos domuisse feroces  . . .      O 169  Insula Kenneth         3
     Namque, ubi mensas onerant epulae,  . . . . . . .        O 193  Tr. Medea III         11
UBIQUE
     Quo vagor ulterius? quod ubique requiritur hic est;  .   O 170  Insula Kenneth        21
     Omnia qui spectans, omnia ubique regis;  . . . . . .     O 232  Prayer                 4
     Quantus ubique Lepos! quantus ubique Decor!  . . . .     O 383  Syl. Urb. Thes     D   2
     Quantus ubique Lepos! quantus ubique Decor!  . . . .     O 383  Syl. Urb. Thes     D   2
     Pallas ubique docet; ridet ubique Venus.  . . . . . .    O 383  Syl. Urb. Thes     D   4
     Pallas ubique docet; ridet ubique Venus.  . . . . . .    O 383  Syl. Urb. Thes     D   4
ULCISCENDUM
     Lucri ulciscendum mox nece sola doces.  . . . . . .      O 213  Tr Greek 9.29          4
ULLA
     Non ulla Musis Pagina gratior,  . . . . . . . .          O 102  Ad Urbanum            17
     Phoebe fave, aegrotat quae te colit, ulla nec usquam est O 197  Summ. Lawrence         1
     Interea dubito; tecum me causa nec ulla  . . . . .       O 216  Tr Greek 9.148         5
     Sunt quibus a lacrymis vix vacat ulla dies.  . . . .     O 221  Tr Greek 10.84         2
     Non poteras, regio non tulit ulla parem.  . . . . . .    O 225  Tr. Gk. 16.331         6
ULLI
     Huic quoque, nec genti nec sectae noxius ulli,  . . . .  O 205  Christianus            6
ULNAS
     Ut vis, ponte minax, modo tres discesseris ulnas,  . .   O 210  Tr Greek 7.284         1
ULTERIUS
     Quo vagor ulterius? quod ubique requiritur hic est;  .   O 170  Insula Kenneth        21
ULTIMA
     Sub pedibus subjecta jacent; queis ultima primis  . .    O 163  To Dr Lawrence        33
     Cura placere Deo sit prima, sit ultima, sanctae  . .     O 205  Christianus           12
ULTRA
     Non ultra infestis concurrent agmina signis,  . . . .    O  90  Messiah               66
     Quicquid quaeritur ultra,  . . . . . . . . . . .         O 182  Waltoni Piscat        11
ULTRICES
     Forte boni, ultrices experiere vices.  . . . . . . .     O 222  Tr. Gk. 10.123         6
UMBRA
     Hic requies fessis; non sacra saevit in umbra  . . . .   O  89  Messiah               18
     Hic requies fessis; non sacra hac saevit in umbra  . .   O  89  Messiah            V  18
     Canna viret, juncique tremit mutabilis umbra.  . . . .   O  91  Messiah               79
     Canna viret, juncique tremit variabilis umbra.  . . .    O  91  Messiah            V  79
UMBRACULA
     Et serae texent vites umbracula proli.  . . . . . .      O  90  Messiah               74
UMBRAE
     Nunc veteres duris periere securibus umbrae,  . . . .    O 228  Rivum a Stoana         7
UMBRAEQUE
     Horret, ubi vanae species, umbraeque fugaces,  . . . .   O 162  Gnothi seauton        50
UNA
     Una duas habuit casa cum genitore puellas,  . . . . .    O 169  Insula Kenneth         9
     Una duas tenuit casa cum genitore puellas,  . . . . .    O 169  Insula Kenneth         9
     Una duas cepit casa cum genitore puellas,  . . . . .     O 169  Insula Kenneth     V   9
     Una quidem, sic fata volunt, tibi vivitur aestas,  . .   O 171  Tr. Busy Fly           9
     Omnis vita nimis brevis est felicibus, una  . . . .      O 220  Tr Greek 10.28         1
     Dissimili domus una duos tenet arte tumentes;  . . . .   O 385  The Warehouse      D   1
UNAM
     Damnatis, poenam pro poenis omnibus unam.  . . . . . .   O 160  Gnothi seauton         5
UNDA
     Eveniat tantum mitior unda tibi!  . . . . . . .          O 211  Tr Greek 7.350         2
     In me animo tellus gignit et unda feras,  . . . . .      O 213  Tr Greek 9.18          2
UNDARUM
     Quas Amor undarum fingeret esse deas:  . . . . . .       O 169  Insula Kenneth        10
     Quas Amor undarum crederet esse deas:  . . . . . .       O 169  Insula Kenneth     V  10
UNDAS
     Quisquis iter tendis, vitreas qua lucidus undas  . . .   O 116  Tr Pope Grotto         1
UNDE
     Quaerere, quis, cujas, quis pater, unde venis.  . . . .  O 219  Tr Greek 9.648         2
     Unde hic Praxiteles? nudam vidistis, Adoni,  . . . . .   O 225  Tr. Gk. 16.168         1
UNDECIES
     Undecies centum denos quater adde duosque.  . . . . .    O 229  Epigram IV             2
     Undecies binas decadas et millia septem  . . . . .       O 230  Geographia Met         6
UNDECIMUM
     Undecimum Camber vult septem millibus addi.  . . . . .   O 231  Geographia Met        36
```

	PAGE	TITLE	LINE
UNDIQUE			
Gentes undique carmine.	O 155	Psalmus 117	4
Omnes undique Gentes	O 155	Psalmus 117	7
UNDIS			
Cum caput Hesperiis attolit Phoebus ab undis, ...	Y 28	Aurora Musis	1
UNO			
Nec dubitet quem dicat herum, sed, totus in uno, . . .	O 205	Christianus	17
UNQUAM			
Quod poscis, haud unquam tibi	O 203	Christ Sinner	3
Laetior haud tecum, tecum neque tristior unquam, . . .	O 218	Tr Greek 9.573	5
UNUS			
Quae potuere duos tertius unus habet.	O 86	Tr Dryden Milt	6
Jupiter unus erat, qui stravit fulmine gentes;	O 103	Elizae Aenigma	5
Omnibus unus amor, non est modus unus amoris. . . .	O 163	To Dr Lawrence	8
Omnibus unus amor, non est modus unus amoris. . . .	O 163	To Dr Lawrence	8
Sexaginta annis non minor unus erit.	O 171	Tr. Busy Fly	12
Unus homo mihi pro sexcentis, turba popelli	O 209	Tr Greek 7.128	3
URBANE			
Urbane, nullis fesse laboribus, ...	O 101	Ad Urbanum	1
Urbane, nullis victe calumniis, ...	O 101	Ad Urbanum	2
URBANI			
In Locupletissimum ornatissimumque Syl<vani>. Urb<ani>. .	O 383	Syl. Urb. Thes. D	T
URBANUM			
Ad Urbanum	O 101	Ad Urbanum	T
URBI			
Graeciae et urbs, urbi est ista propago, decus. . . .	O 214	Tr Greek 9.65	2
URBS			
Graeciae et urbs, urbi est ista propago, decus. . . .	O 214	Tr Greek 9.65	2
URIT			
Huc foedat quos lepra, urit quos febris, adeste! . . .	O 88	Messiah	16
URNA			
Et senium triplex Nestoris urna capit.	O 215	Tr Greek 9.112	4
URSA			
In Rabiem tunc contremet Ursa	O 109	Post-genitis	24
USQUAM			
Si qua usquam pateat melioris semita vitae, ...	O 161	Gnothi seauton	33
Phoebe fave, aegrotat quae te colit, ulla nec usquam est	O 197	Summ. Lawrence	1
USQUE			
Usque regat gressus gratia fida meos.	O 207	Prayers IV	4
USUS			
Nec sibi de gaza praesens quod postulet usus . . .	O 162	Gnothi seauton	44
Non sibi de gaza praesens quod postulat usus . . .	O 162	Gnothi seauton V	44
Quos soli ducunt sensus, solus docet usus;	O 163	To Dr Lawrence	10
UT			
Ut qua dulce strepunt scatebrae, qua laeta virescunt . .	O 90	Messiah	57
Ut qua dulce strepent scatebrae, qua laeta virescunt . .	O 90	Messiah V	57
Liber ut esse velim, suasisti, pulchra Maria: . . .	O 105	Lady Defence	1
Ut maneam liber, pulchra Maria, vale.	O 105	Lady Defence	2
Littoraque ut Fluctu, ...	O 109	Post-genitis	7
Scaliger ut duxit, tenuis pertaesus opellae, . . .	O 160	Gnothi seauton	2
Ut studiis sperem, aut ausim par esse querelis, . . .	O 160	Gnothi seauton	15
Cessat inops rerum, ut torpet, si marmoris absit . .	O 161	Gnothi seauton	38
Parare posse, ut Stoicorum	O 166	Oda Isle Skye	15
Ut precibus justas avertat numinis iras	O 170	Insula Kenneth V	16A
Per Christum ut veniam sit reperire mihi.	O 198	Tr. Ash Wed.	4
Ut modo tentem	O 199	Medico Aeger S	16
Ut tibi, gentis	O 199	Medico Aeger S	24
Ut vitam, poscat si res, impendere vero.	O 205	Christianus	11
Sceleris ut expers omnis, et vacuus metu, ...	O 206	Prayers I	9
Ut summa laus sit, summa Christo gloria.	O 206	Prayers III	6
Ut tibi quae placeant, omnia promptus agam.	O 207	Prayers V	4
Recte ut poeniteat, respice, magne parens.	O 207	Prayers VI	6
Sic ale, proveniat messis ut ampla boni.	O 207	Prayers VII	4
In summo ut videas numine laeta patrem;	O 208	A Meditation	2
Ut vis, ponte minax, modo tres discesseris ulnas, . . .	O 210	Tr Greek 7.284	1
Multis ut te oculis sim potis aspicere.	O 212	Tr Greek 7.669	2
Hic, aurum ut reperit, laqueum abjicit, alter ut aurum .	O 213	Tr Greek 9.44	1
Hic, aurum ut reperit, laqueum abjicit, alter ut aurum .	O 213	Tr Greek 9.44	1
Mnemosyne, ut Sappho mellita voce canentem	O 214	Tr Greek 9.66	1
Sint Demosthenica ut jurata cadavera voce, ...	O 216	Tr Greek 9.288	5
Elige iter vitae, ut possis; rixisque dolisque . . .	O 217	Tr Greek 9.359	1
Elige iter vitae, ut mavis; prudentia lausque . . .	O 217	Tr Greek 9.360	1
Conjugium, ut pro te des hominem patriae.	O 218	Tr Greek 9.444	4
Alter ut adsit Homerus, adest etenim alter Achilles. .	O 218	Tr Greek 9.523	2
Jupiter hoc templum, ut, siquando relinquit Olympum, . .	O 219	Tr Greek 9.702	1
Plura ut victurus secula, parce bonis:	O 219	Tr Greek 10.26	2
Ut florem amittat gratia tota perit	Y 332	Tr Greek 10.30 V	1
In mentem ut venit nominis, interii.	O 223	Tr. Gk. 11.118	2
Murem Asclepiades sub tecto ut vidit avarus, ...	O 224	Tr. Gk. 11.391	1
Convenit ut natis, inclyta Sparta, tuis.	O 224	Tr Greek 16.1	4
Quod nimium est fit ineptum; hinc, ut dixere priores, .	O 224	Tr Greek 16.16	1
Serviat ut menti corpus, jejunia serva;	O 228	Jejunium Cibus	1
Ut mens utatur corpore, sume cibos.	O 228	Jejunium Cibus	2
Ut dicas, spatiis quam latis imperet orbi	O 230	Geographia Met	16
Myrias, ut menti pateat tota Africa doctae.	O 230	Geographia Met	24
Divino, sanctus regnet ut intus amor:	O 232	Prayer	6
Ut tibi laus omni semper ab ore sonet:	O 232	Prayer	8
UTATUR			
Ut mens utatur corpore, sume cibos.	O 228	Jejunium Cibus	2
UTCUNQUE			
Parare posse, utcunque jactet	O 166	Oda Isle Skye V	15

PAGE TITLE LINE

UTERE
  Naufragus hic jaceo; fidens tamen utere velis, ... O 210 Tr Greek 7.282 1
UTERI
  Mox uteri pondus depositura grave, ... O 115 Ad Lauram Epig 2
UTI
  At Seni fluxo sapienter uti . . . . O 153 In Theatro 15
  Queis uti poteram quondam Fortuna negavit, ... O 215 Tr Greek 9.138 3
  Queis uti nequeo, nunc mihi praebet opes. . . . . . . O 215 Tr Greek 9.138 4
UTILE
  Utile cunctis hoc opus esset; . . . . O 193 Tr. Medea III 10
  Apte antiqua novis miscentur, et utile dulci: . . . . O 383 Syl. Urb. Thes D 3
UTILIBUS
  Utilibus recreare Mentem. . . . . O 102 Ad Urbanum 20
  Te semper studiis utilibus colam: . . . . O 164 Recover Eyes 12
UTITUR
  Tempore divitiis utitur, ille sapit. . . . . O 219 Tr Greek 10.26 4
UTRINQUE
  Divitiis, utrinque cavens, qui tempore parcit, . . . O 219 Tr Greek 10.26 3
UTRIQUE
  Hectori, et exitio munus utrique fuit. . . . . . . O 210 Tr Greek 7.151 2
  Praecones ambo, Nummus utrique Deus. . . . . O 385 The Warehouse D 2
UTROBIQUE
  In lecto. utrobique Patrem . . . . O 155 Psalmus 117 V 9
UTRUMQUE
  Carmen grande sonans; Anglus utrumque tulit. . . . . O 86 Tr Dryden Milt 4
  Laevum at utrumque decus, juveni quod praebuit olim . . O 225 Tr. Gk. 16.364 3
UVA
  Virgilio vires Uva Falerna dedit. . . . . O 85 Mea nec Falern 4
  Subrubet uva mero. . . . . O 385 Cantico Solom. D 14
UVAE
  Hae poterant uvae laeto convivia cantu . . . . O 218 Tr Greek 9.375 7
UVIDA
  Strepens procellis, imbribus uvida, ... O 166 Oda Isle Skye V 2
  Strepens procellis, uvida nubibus, ... O 166 Oda Isle Skye V 2
UXOR
  Cogitat aut loquitur nil vir, nil cogitat uxor, . . . O 226 Tr. Greek 1
UXORE
  Quisquis adit lectos elata uxore secundos, ... O 215 Tr Greek 9.133 1
VACARE
  Vacare solis perge Musis, ... O 101 Ad Urbanum 7
VACAT
  Sunt quibus a lacrymis vix vacat ulla dies. . . . . . O 221 Tr Greek 10.84 2
VACUAE
  Importuna cohors, vacuae mala somnia mentis. . . . . O 161 Gnothi seauton 28
  Mollia non deerant vacuae solatia vitae, ... O 170 Insula Kenneth 13
  Mollia non desunt vacuae solatia vitae, ... O 170 Insula Kenneth V 13
VACUUS
  Sceleris ut expers omnis, et vacuus metu, ... O 206 Prayers I 9
VAECORS
  Crepare vaecors, nil sapientiam . . . . O 186 Ad T. L. M.D. 2
  Proavum vaecors insipientia, ... O 193 Tr. Medea III 2
VAFRITIES
  Quem nil vafrities peccantum subdola celat; . . . . O 232 Prayer 3
VAGANDI
  Gens illa, impatiens per singula quaeque vagandi . . . O 163 To Dr Lawrence 23
VAGANTEM
  Per vitae tenebras rerumque incerta vagantem . . . . O 207 Prayers IV 1
VAGANTES
  Amissas modo quaerit oves, revocatque vagantes; . . . O 90 Messiah 61
  Sacri vagantes luminis gressus face . . . . O 206 Prayers I 5
VAGARI
  Prodest vagari, nec frementes . . . . O 166 Oda Isle Skye 11
VAGOR
  Quo vagor ulterius? quod ubique requiritur hic est; . . O 170 Insula Kenneth 21
VALE
  Ut maneam liber, pulchra Maria, vale. . . . . . . O 105 Lady Defence 2
  Ambraciota, vale lux alma, Cleombrotus infit, ... O 211 Tr Greek 7.471 1
  O longum, formosa, vale, mihi vita decusque, ... O 383 On the Gin-Act D 3
VALENT
  Arte valent isti, mihi robore vivere solo est, ... O 224 Tr Greek 16.1 3
VALEQUE
  Vive valeque. . . . . O 199 Medico Aeger S 31
VALERE
  Quam magis exoptes arte valere tua. . . . . O 197 Summ. Lawrence 2
VALETE
  Muscosi fontes, silvestria tecta, valete, ... O 88 Messiah 4
VALIDIS
  Fert humeris claudum validis per compita caecus, . . . O 213 Tr Greek 9.13 1
VALLES
  Per valles sociata lupo lasciviet agna, ... O 91 Messiah 84
VALLIS
  Mittit aromaticas vallis Saronica nubes, ... O 89 Messiah 32
  Horruit implexo qua vallis sente, figurae . . . . . O 91 Messiah 80
VANAE
  Horret, ubi vanae species, umbraeque fugaces, ... O 162 Gnothi seauton 50
VANESCENT
  "Irrita vanescent priscae vestigia fraudis," . . . . O 89 Messiah 20
VANO
  Pectus, et ingenium vano se robore jactans. . . . . O 161 Gnothi seauton 36
VANOS
  Dicitur, et vanos dedocuisse deos. . . . . O 169 Insula Kenneth 4

		PAGE	TITLE		LINE
VARIABILIS					
	Canna viret, juncique tremit variabilis umbra.	O 91	Messiah	V	79
VARIARE					
	Corpora cuncta suis gestit variare figuris, ...	O 163	To Dr Lawrence		27
VARIAS					
	Vitae qui varias vices	O 164	Recover Eyes		1
VARIATA					
	Aethereis variata fucis.	O 102	Ad Urbanum		24
VARIIS					
	Contextam variis, do, Rhodoclea, tibi:	O 209	Tr. Greek 5.74		2
VARIO					
	Vive tuo ex animo, vario rumore loquetur	O 214	Tr Greek 9.50		1
VASCULA					
	Venturi exsecuit, vascula prima meri, ...	O 217	Tr Greek 9.375		2
VASTANTES					
	Gramina vastantes, ...	O 109	Post-genitis		11
VASTUM					
	Materies, vastum an late pandatur inane.	O 163	To Dr Lawrence		14
	Materia, vastum an late pandatur inane.	O 163	To Dr Lawrence	V	14
VATES					
	Quos laudet vates Graius Romanus et Anglus	O 86	Tr Dryden Milt		1
	Quos laudet vates Graecus Romanus et Anglus	O 86	Tr Dryden Milt	V	1
	Immatura calens rapitur per saecula vates, ...	O 88	Messiah		8
	Ille futura calens rapitur per saecula vates, ...	O 88	Messiah	V	8
	En! quem turba diu cecinerunt enthea, vates, ...	O 89	Messiah		41
VATI					
	Tunc vati facilem reprobat Apollo, Sybillae	Y 28	Aurora Musis		7
VATUM					
	Qui veterum modo facta ducum, modo carmina vatum, . . .	O 160	Gnothi seauton		8
VEL					
	Vel Pede Equus tanget, ...	O 109	Post-genitis		3
	Vel Arator vomere franget, ...	O 109	Post-genitis		4
	Vel digiti tractant, oculus vel sentit et auris: . . .	O 163	To Dr Lawrence		12
	Vel digiti tractant, oculus vel sentit et auris: . . .	O 163	To Dr Lawrence		12
	Vel spe ludit inani, ...	O 182	Waltoni Piscat		13
	Cui pars verbosae, vel datur ima, domus?	O 385	The Warehouse	D	4
VELIM					
	Liber ut esse velim, suasisti, pulchra Maria:	O 105	Lady Defence		1
	Sequar libenter; sin reluctari velim, ...	O 226	Tr. Cleanthes		3
VELIS					
	Naufragus hic jaceo; fidens tamen utere velis, ...	O 210	Tr Greek 7.282		1
VELIT					
	Spes hominum et curas gens procul esse velit.	O 170	Insula Kenneth	V	16
	Hoc statuat, precibus Christus adesse velit:	O 204	Losing Speech		2
	Hoc statuant, votis Christus adesse velit:	O 204	Losing Speech	V	2
	Quas servare velit, leges quas lentus omittat, ...	O 205	Christianus		21
	Haec nobis Christus promeruisse velit!	O 232	Prayer		10
VELLE					
	Velle vetet cuiquam non bene sanctus amor.	O 207	Prayers VII		8
VELLENT					
	Omnes si vellent virginitate frui;	O 218	Tr Greek 9.444		2
VELOX					
	Tu, quamcunque tibi velox indulserit annus, ...	O 171	Tr. Busy Fly		5
	Gratia ter grata est velox, sin forte moretur	O 220	Tr Greek 10.30		1
	Quid ferat externi velox, quid deterat aetas, ...	O 228	Rivum a Stoana		11
VENAM					
	Secare venam;	O 199	Medico Aeger S		11
VENDITAT					
	Hic Bona queis opus est venditat, Ille Sonum.	O 385	The Warehouse	D	6
VENERABILE					
	Fortis, ades, solus tangas venerabile limen. . . .	O 116	Tr Pope Grotto		16
	Fortis, ades, tibi sponte patet venerabile limen. . .	O 116	Tr Pope Grotto	V	16
	Fert humeris, venerabile onus, Cythereius heros . . .	O 216	Tr Greek 9.163		1
VENEREM					
	Haec Musae ad Venerem: Sic Marti, diva, mineris; . . .	O 213	Tr Greek 9.39		3
	Et Pari, et Anchisa, non alius, Venerem.	O 225	Tr. Gk. 16.168		2
	Armatam Pallas Venerem conspexit, et eia	O 384	Epigramma	D	1
VENERI					
	Hoc Veneri speculum; nolo me cernere qualis	O 209	Tr. Greek 6.1		3
	Ad Musas Venus haec: Veneri parete, puellae, ...	O 213	Tr Greek 9.39		1
VENERIS					
	Nunc armant Veneris lumina tela Jovis.	O 103	Elizae Aenigma		6
VENI					
	Huc, soror alma, veni! pernicibus ocyor Euris . . .	O 385	Cantico Solom.	D	17
	Huc, soror alma, veni!	O 385	Cantico Solom.	D	18
VENIAEQUE					
	Veniaeque sancta pacis adde gaudia:	O 206	Prayers I		8
VENIAM					
	Per Christum ut veniam sit reperire mihi.	O 198	Tr. Ash Wed.		4
	Veniam petenti, summe da veniam, pater;	O 206	Prayers I		7
	Veniam petenti, summe da veniam, pater;	O 206	Prayers I		7
	Da veniam pacemque mihi, da, mente serena, ...	O 207	Prayers V		3
VENIAMQUE					
	Veniamque, Christe, da mihi;	O 206	Prayers II		7
VENIET					
	Mens mea quid quereris? veniet tibi mollior hora, . . .	O 208	A Meditation		1
VENIS					
	Quaerere, quis, cujas, quis pater, unde venis. . . .	O 219	Tr Greek 9.648		2
	Hunc sequitur caelebs; tertius, orbe, venis. . . .	O 222	Tr Greek 11.50		2
VENISSE					
	Venisse, aut visa luce repente mori.	O 217	Tr Greek 9.359		10

VENISSE   (CONTINUED)   PAGE   TITLE   LINE
    Nemo optet nunquam venisse in luminis oras, ...   O 217 Tr Greek 9.360   9
VENIT
    Non immerito culpanda venit . . . .   O 193 Tr. Medea III   1
    Cum procul est, optat, cum venit, quisque senectam . .   O 214 Tr Greek 9.54   1
    In mentem ut venit nominis, interii. . . . .   O 223 Tr. Gk. 11.118   2
    Ver geniale venit. . . . .   O 384 Cantico Solom.   D   4
    Veris, io! venit alma dies! Philomela canorum . . . .   O 385 Cantico Solom.   D   7
VENIUNT
    Haec veniunt Cypriae Somnia missa Deae. . . . . . .   O 103 Elizae Aenigma   4
VENTIS
    Gratum animum laudo; Qui debuit omnia ventis, . . .   O 143 On Lord Anson   1
    Qui nil virtuti, sed debuit omnia ventis, ...   O 143 On Lord Anson   V   1
VENTORUM
    Quam bene ventorum surgere templa jubet! . . . . . .   O 143 On Lord Anson   2
VENTURI
    Venturi exsecuit, vascula prima meri, ...   O 217 Tr Greek 9.375   2
VENUS
    Quis formae modus imperio? Venus arrogat audax . . .   O 103 Elizae Aenigma   1
    Ad Musas Venus haec: Veneri parete, puellae, ...   O 213 Tr Greek 9.39   1
    Pallas ubique docet; ridet ubique Venus. . . . . . .   O 383 Syl. Urb. Thes   D   4
    Dulce Venus ridens, lorica nil opus, inquit, ...   O 384 Epigramma   D   3
VER
    Telluri arboribus ver frondens, sidera coelo, ...   O 214 Tr Greek 9.65   1
    Ver geniale venit. . . . .   O 384 Cantico Solom.   D   4
VERA
    Astra mathematicos si modo vera docent. . . . . . .   O 215 Tr Greek 9.112   2
VERAM
    Concede veram poenitentiam, precor, ...   O 206 Prayers I   3
VERBOSAE
    Cui pars verbosae, vel datur ima, domus? . . . . . .   O 385 The Warehouse   D   4
VERI
    Codices, veri studiosus, inter . . . .   O 153 In Theatro   10
    Hunc oculis Veri Fautrix lustravit acutis, ...   O 386 In Birchium   D   3
VERIQUE
    Conciliis, verique sacros recludere fontes. . . . .   O 163 To Dr Lawrence   22
VERIS
    Cinnameos cumulos, Nabathaei munera veris, ...   O 92 Messiah   102
    Cinnameis cumulis, Nabathaei munere veris, ...   O 92 Messiah   V 102
    Veris, io! venit alma dies! Philomela canorum . . .   O 385 Cantico Solom.   D   7
VERO
    Ut vitam, poscat si res, impendere vero. . . . . . .   O 205 Christianus   11
VERSANTUR
    Sunt qui curriculo timidi versantur in arcto, . . .   O 163 To Dr Lawrence   9
VERSAT
    Versat opum cumulos, et se miratur in illis, ...   O 161 Gnothi seauton   V 43
    Quod nulli proprium versat Fortuna, putabat . . . .   O 215 Tr Greek 9.74   3
VERSAVIT
    Quid quod sacrifici versavit femina libros, ...   O 170 Insula Kenneth   19
VERSES
    Verses addressed to Dr. Lawrence, composed by Dr. . .   O 162 To Dr Lawrence   T
VERSO
    Tertii verso quater orbe lustri, ...   O 153 In Theatro   1
VERSUS
    Versus Collari Caprae Domini Banks inscribendi . . . .   O 156 Collari Caprae   T
VERTE
    Verte solum, fient causa timoris opes; . . . . . .   O 217 Tr Greek 9.359   4
    Verte solum, donat plena crumena decus; . . . . . .   O 217 Tr Greek 9.360   4
    Verte solum, donet plena crumena decus; . . . . . .   O 217 Tr Greek 9.360   V   4
VERTICE
    En! summo exultant nutantes vertice silvae. . . . . .   O 89 Messiah   31
VERUM
    Est proprium, et quavis captare indagine verum, . . .   O 163 To Dr Lawrence   7
VESTIGIA
    "Irrita vanescent priscae vestigia fraudis," . . . .   O 89 Messiah   20
VESTRA
    Quo, lege vestra, vita me feret mea. . . . .   O 226 Tr. Cleanthes   2
VETABIT
    Ille cutim spissam visus hebetare vetabit, ...   O 90 Messiah   44
VETERES
    Da veteres noxas animo sic flere novato, ...   O 198 Tr. Ash Wed.   3
    Da veteres culpas animo sic flere novato, ...   O 198 Tr. Ash Wed.   V   3
    Nunc veteres duris periere securibus umbrae, . . .   O 228 Rivum a Stoana   7
VETERNO
    Frigora, seu nimius longo jacuisse veterno, ...   O 161 Gnothi seauton   17
VETERUM
    Qui veterum modo facta ducum, modo carmina vatum, . .   O 160 Gnothi seauton   8
VETET
    Certa vetet dubitare fides, spes laeta timere, . . .   O 207 Prayers VII   7
    Velle vetet cuiquam non bene sanctus amor. . . . . .   O 207 Prayers VII   8
VETITAQUE
    Vetitaque Libidine pravus. . . . .   O 110 Post-genitis   34
VETULI
    Clamat et Argivis: Vetuli, ne tangite, vita . . . .   O 216 Tr Greek 9.163   3
VETUSTAS
    Te docta, Laurenti, vetustas . . . .   O 187 Ad T. L. M.D.   15
VEXATQUE
    Nascuntur curis curae, vexatque dolorum . . . . .   O 161 Gnothi seauton   27
VIAM
    Sternite saxa viam, rapidi discedite fluctus! . . . .   O 89 Messiah   40

VIAS	PAGE	TITLE	LINE
Ille vias vocis pandet, flexusque liquentis	O 90	Messiah	47
Qui, mutare vias ausus terraeque marisque, ...	O 217	Tr Greek 9.304	1
Lunaque quas et sol itque reditque vias.	O 222	Tr. Gk. 10.123	4
VIATORIS			
Membra viatoris recreabunt frigore linguae.	O 91	Messiah	88
VICENAS			
Vult sibi vicenas millesima myrias addi, ...	O 230	Geographia Met	21
VICENIS			
Vicenis quinas, Asiam metata celebrem.	O 230	Geographia Met	22
VICES			
Luna vices revehet; radios pater ipse diei	O 92	Messiah	110
Dixerat, imperiique vices, coelique meatus, ...	O 160	Gnothi seauton	10
Scire vices ponti facile est, nihil amplius optant . .	O 163	To Dr Lawrence	15
Vitae qui varias vices	O 164	Recover Eyes	1
Admonitu, ipsa suas nunciat hora vices.	O 170	Insula Kenneth	V 18B
Per certas stabili lege voluta vices, ...	O 219	Tr Greek 9.577	2
Forte boni, ultrices experiere vices.	O 222	Tr. Gk. 10.123	6
VICTA			
Neque Bellua victa remugit.	O 110	Post-genitis	38
VICTE			
Urbane, nullis victe calumniis, ...	O 101	Ad Urbanum	2
VICTOR			
Si Phoeba, victor nescit obire diem.	O 210	Tr Greek 7.239	2
VICTORIA			
Cum fugere haud possit fractis Victoria pennis, . . .	O 219	Tr Greek 9.647	1
VICTRIX			
Victrix per obstantes catervas	O 101	Ad Urbanum	11
VICTURUS			
Plura ut victurus secula, parce bonis:	O 219	Tr Greek 10.26	2
VIDEAS			
In summo ut videas numine laeta patrem;	O 208	A Meditation	2
VIDEBIS			
Tu secura tamen confusa elementa videbis, ...	O 92	Messiah	117
VIDENS			
Sed sua regna videns, loca nocte silentia late . . .	O 162	Gnothi seauton	49
VIDENT			
Attoniti dumeta vident inculta coloni	O 91	Messiah	75
VIDERE			
Videre, Archidicen haec tumulavit humus;	O 226	Tr. Simonides	2
VIDET			
Incusat, semper spe meliora videt.	O 214	Tr Greek 9.54	2
VIDETUR			
Cum tacet indoctus, sapientior esse videtur, ...	O 221	Tr Greek 10.98	1
VIDISTIS			
Unde hic Praxiteles? nudam vidistis, Adoni, ...	O 225	Tr. Gk. 16.168	1
VIDIT			
Murem Asclepiades sub tecto ut vidit avarus, ...	O 224	Tr. Gk. 11.391	1
VIGIL			
Hujus palestrae qui vigil custos stetit, ...	O 223	Tr. Gk. 11.176	3
VIGORE			
Virtus, canities cauta vigore caret.	O 217	Tr Greek 9.359	8
VILE			
Vile indignatus studium, nugasque molestas, ...	O 160	Gnothi seauton	3
VINCERE			
Vincere te potui nuda, quid arma geram?	O 384	Epigramma	D 4
VINCIS			
Nec vincis acer, nec pateris pius;	O 187	Ad T. L. M.D.	6
VINCLA			
Vincla coercebunt luctantem adamantina mortem, ...	O 90	Messiah	54
VINCULA			
Florea mansuetae petulantes vincula tigri	O 91	Messiah	86
VINDAMIUS			
Hic pia Vindamius traxit suspiria, in ipsa	O 116	Tr Pope Grotto	12
VIOLA			
Rosae ruborem sic Viola adjuvat	O 102	Ad Urbanum	22
VIOLARE			
Leo, sed violare timebit, ...	O 109	Post-genitis	28
VIOLARIA			
Suaviter exhalant violaria grata, Sabaeo	O 385	Cantico Solom.	D 15
VIOLENTIA			
Vis boreae gelida, aut rapidi violentia solis.	O 89	Messiah	19
Vis boreae gelida, aut nimii violentia solis.	O 89	Messiah	V 19
VIOLIS			
Cum violis; spirant lilia mista rosis.	O 209	Tr. Greek 5.74	4
VIR			
Hic, bone vir, sedem, non alimenta, peto.	O 224	Tr. Gk. 11.391	4
Cogitat aut loquitur nil vir, nil cogitat uxor, . . .	O 226	Tr. Greek	1
VIREBIT			
Perpetuo viret et virebit;	O 101	Ad Urbanum	4
VIRENTEM			
Quam grata defesso virentem	O 166	Oda Isle Skye	3
VIRENTES			
Ridebit linguae innocuos, squamasque virentes	O 91	Messiah	91
VIRENTIA			
Errat adhuc vitreus per prata virentia rivus, ...	O 228	Rivum a Stoana	1
VIRES			
Virgilio vires Uva Falerna dedit.	O 85	Mea nec Falern	4
VIRESCUNT			
Ut qua dulce strepunt scatebrae, qua laeta virescunt . .	O 90	Messiah	57
Ut qua dulce strepent scatebrae, qua laeta virescunt . .	O 90	Messiah	V 57

```
VIRET                                                      PAGE   TITLE             LINE
   Canna viret, juncique tremit mutabilis umbra.  . . . . .  O  91 Messiah            79
   Canna viret, juncique tremit variabilis umbra. . . . . .  O  91 Messiah         V  79
   Perpetuo viret et virebit;                     . . . . .  O 101 Ad Urbanum          4
VIRGILIO
   Virgilio vires Uva Falerna dedit.      . . . . . . . . .  O  85 Mea nec Falern      4
VIRGINITAS
   Pulchra est virginitas intacta, at vita periret,  . . .  O 218 Tr Greek 9.444      1
VIRGINITATE
   Omnes si vellent virginitate frui; . . . . . . . . .      O 218 Tr Greek 9.444      2
VIRGO
   Virgo! virgo parit! felix radicibus arbor      . . . . .  O  88 Messiah            10
   Virgo! virgo parit! felix radicibus arbor      . . . . .  O  88 Messiah            10
VIRI
   Seu viri curas pia nupta mulcet,    . . . . . . . . .     O 168 Oda to Thrale      13
VIRIDANTES
   Ridebit linguae innocuos, squamas viridantes   . . . .    O  91 Messiah         V  91
VIRORUM
   Quisque suum norit modulum; tibi, prime virorum, . . .    O 160 Gnothi seauton     14
VIRTUS
   Sedatas niveo Virtus lucebit amictu.   . . . . . . . .    O  89 Messiah            24
   Pacatas niveo Virtus lucebit amictu.   . . . . . . . .    O  89 Messiah         V  24
   Gesserat et quicquid Virtus, Sapientia quicquid  . . .    O 160 Gnothi seauton      9
   Humana virtus non sibi sufficit,    . . . . . . . . .     O 166 Oda Isle Skye      13
   Dicam; stat virtus non subigenda neci. . . . . . . .      O 212 Tr Greek 7.590      4
   Virtus, canities cauta vigore caret.   . . . . . . . .    O 217 Tr Greek 9.359      8
   Firma manet virtus; virtuti innitere, tutus  . . . . .    O 221 Tr Greek 10.74      5
VIRTUTI
   Qui nil virtuti, sed debuit omnia ventis,    . . . . .    O 143 On Lord Anson    V  1
   Firma manet virtus; virtuti innitere, tutus  . . . . .    O 221 Tr Greek 10.74      5
VIRTUTUM
   In me sparsa manu virtutum semina larga  . . . . . . .    O 207 Prayers VII         3
VIRUM
   Divitiis acuens aspera corda virum;    . . . . . . .      O 213 Tr Greek 9.29       2
   Patria Sparta mihi est, patria clara virum.  . . . . .    O 224 Tr Greek 16.1       2
   Birchius egregios, claraque gesta virum. . . . . . .      O 386 In Birchium       D  2
VIRUMQUE
   Quid mirum Maro quod digne canit arma Virumque,  . . .    O  85 Mea nec Falern      1
VIS
   Carmina vis nostri scribant meliora Poetae? . . . . . .   O  85 Mea nec Falern      5
   Vis boreae gelida, aut rapidi violentia solis. . . . .    O  89 Messiah            19
   Vis boreae gelida, aut nimii violentia solis.  . . . .    O  89 Messiah         V  19
   Temporis Henricum rapuit vis vivida mentis;    . . . .    O 116 Tr Pope Grotto     11
   Ut vis, ponte minax, modo tres discesseris ulnas, . . .   O 210 Tr Greek 7.284      1
   At docet, exemplo, vis sibi quanta, tuo. . . . . . .      O 218 Tr Greek 9.530      1
VISA
   Venisse, aut visa luce repente mori.   . . . . . . .      O 217 Tr Greek 9.359     10
VISUS
   Ille cutim spissam visus hebetare vetabit,   . . . . .    O  90 Messiah            44
VITA
   Et juvat ingenii vita sine arte rudis.   . . . . . .      O 104 To Eliz Carter      2
   Vita ubi nullo decorata cultu   . . . . . . . . . .       O 167 Oda to Thrale       6
   Paulum vita moratur,    . . . . . . . . . . . .           O 182 Waltoni Piscat      6
   Charus enim cunctis, tanquam, dum vita manebat,  . . .    O 212 Tr Greek 7.560      3
   Vita hominum nunc plus quod misereris habet.   . . . .    O 216 Tr Greek 9.148      4
   Clamat et Argivis: Vetuli, ne tangite, vita  . . . .      O 216 Tr Greek 9.163      3
   Permeat cmne forum; vita quieta domi est.    . . . .      O 217 Tr Greek 9.360      2
   Aut periisse; scatet vita benigna bonis.   . . . . .      O 217 Tr Greek 9.360     10
   Pulchra est virginitas intacta, at vita periret,  . .     O 218 Tr Greek 9.444      1
   Omnis vita nimis brevis est felicibus, una   . . . .      O 220 Tr Greek 10.28      1
   Vita omnis scena est ludusque; aut ludere disce  . .      O 221 Tr Greek 10.72      1
   Nam vita incertis incerta impellitur auris,  . . . .      O 221 Tr Greek 10.74      3
   Sit contenta mihi vita dolore carens.    . . . . . .      O 222 Tr. Gk. 10.113      2
   Vita rosae brevis est; properans si carpere nolis,  .     O 223 Tr Greek 11.53      1
   Quo, lege vestra, vita me feret mea.   . . . . . .        O 226 Tr. Cleanthes       2
   O longum, formosa, vale, mihi vita decusque,   . . . .    O 383 On the Gin-Act    D  3
   Surge, soror dilecta, mihi lux, gaudia, vita;  . . . .    O 384 Cantico Solom.    D  1
VITAE
   Tristis et atra quies, et tardae taedia vitae.   . . .    O 161 Gnothi seauton     26
   Si qua usquam pateat melioris semita vitae,  . . . .      O 161 Gnothi seauton     33
   Ipse sui judex, actae bene munera vitae;   . . . . .      O 162 Gnothi seauton     48
   Qua sulcat, reptant tuti per lubrica vitae.  . . . .      O 163 To Dr Lawrence     18
   Vitae qui varias vices   . . . . . . . . . . .            O 164 Recover Eyes        1
   Mollia non deerant vacuae solatia vitae,   . . . . .      O 170 Insula Kenneth     13
   Mollia non desunt vacuae solatia vitae,    . . . . .      O 170 Insula Kenneth   V 13
   Olim, praeteritae numeranti tempora vitae,   . . . .      O 171 Tr. Busy Fly       11
   Prodesse vitae, literasque   . . . . . . . . . .          O 186 Ad T. L. M.D.       3
   Cantum, vitae dulce levamen.   . . . . . . . . .          O 193 Tr. Medea III       5
   Irruptum vitae cupiat servare tenorem;   . . . . . .      O 205 Christianus        13
   Per vitae tenebras rerumque incerta vagantem   . . .      O 207 Prayers IV          1
   Summe dator vitae, naturae aeterne magister,   . . . .    O 207 Prayers VI          1
   Quem terret vitae meta propinqua suae,   . . . . .        O 207 Prayers VI          4
   Quod vitae satis est, peto, Macrine:   . . . . . . .      O 215 Tr Greek 9.110      3
   Elige iter vitae, ut possis; rixisque dolisque . . .      O 217 Tr Greek 9.359      1
   Elige iter vitae, ut mavis; prudentia lausque  . . .      O 217 Tr Greek 9.360      1
   Per fluctus vitae sic tibi cursus erit.  . . . . . .      O 221 Tr Greek 10.74      6
   Quae sine morte fuga est vitae, quam turba malorum        O 222 Tr. Gk. 10.123      1
   Vitae rosa brevis est; properans si carpere nolis,  .     O 223 Tr Greek 11.53   V  1
VITAM
   Ut vitam, poscat si res, impendere vero. . . . . . .      O 205 Christianus        11
   Concede agendam legibus vitam tuis.  . . . . . . . .      O 206 Prayers I           4
```

VITAM	(CONTINUED)	PAGE	TITLE		LINE
Vitam a terdecimo sextus mihi finiet annus, ...		O 215	Tr Greek 9.112		1
Sed similem, Plutarche, tuae describere vitam		O 225	Tr. Gk. 16.331		5
VITAMQUE					
Ordinibus surgit densis, vitamque requirit		O 92	Messiah		97
Paulatim mores, animum, vitamque refingit, ...		O 205	Christianus		28
VITANDA					
Non vitanda gravem, non toleranda facit?		O 222	Tr. Gk. 10.123		2
VITAQUE					
Lenis inoffenso vitaque morsque gradu.		Y 387	Death Mother	D	4
VITATO					
Me, cane vitato, canis excipit alter; eodem		O 213	Tr Greek 9.18		1
VITE					
Pectore qui duro, crudos de vite racemos		O 217	Tr Greek 9.375		1
VITES					
Et serae texent vites umbracula proli.		O 90	Messiah		74
VITIANTES					
Vitiantes, et spoliantes;		O 109	Post-genitis		14
VITIIS					
Cunctorum ignoscat vitiis, pietate fruatur.		O 205	Christianus		9
VITREAS					
Quisquis iter tendis, vitreas qua lucidus undas		O 116	Tr Pope Grotto		1
VITREUS					
Errat adhuc vitreus per prata virentia rivus, ...		O 228	Rivum a Stoana		1
VIVA					
Vivere, te viva, te moriente, mori.		O 384	On the Gin-Act	D	10
VIVAM					
Mandatum, vivam sic moriarque tibi.		O 207	Prayers IV		6
VIVE					
Vive valeque.		O 199	Medico Aeger S		31
Vive tuo ex animo, vario rumore loquetur		O 214	Tr Greek 9.50		1
VIVERE					
Scripta legens, sola vivere mente cupit.		O 211	Tr Greek 7.471		4
Arte valent isti, mihi robore vivere solo est, ...		O 224	Tr Greek 16.1		3
Vivere, te viva, te moriente, mori.		O 384	On the Gin-Act	D	10
VIVES					
Rectius vives, sua quisque carpat		O 153	In Theatro		11
VIVIDA					
Temporis Henricum rapuit vis vivida mentis;		O 116	Tr Pope Grotto		11
VIVIT					
Nunc ope supplicii vivit imago mei.		O 225	Tr Greek 16.87		2
VIVITUR					
Una quidem, sic fata volunt, tibi vivitur aestas, . . .		O 171	Tr. Busy Fly		9
VIX					
Gratia vix restat nomine digna suo.		O 220	Tr Greek 10.30		2
Sunt quibus a lacrymis vix vacat ulla dies.		O 221	Tr Greek 10.84		2
Vix majore Deus corda furore quatit		Y 28	Aurora Musis		8
VIXI					
Servus Epictetus, mutilatus corpore vixi		O 114	Tr Gk Epigrams		3
Servus, Epictetus, mutilato corpore, vixi, ...		O 212	Tr Greek 7.676		1
VIXIT					
Qui jacet hic, servus vixit, nunc, lumine cassus, . . .		O 212	Tr Greek 7.538		1
VOBIS					
Haec fausta vobis dicimus, Angliae		O 188	Epilogus		2
VOCANT					
I, quoniam sic fata vocant: liceat mihi tantum		O 384	On the Gin-Act	D	9
VOCAT					
Cyrum sexta vocat, laetatur		O 226	Septem Aetates	V	4
VOCE					
Deserti laeta mollescunt aspera voce, ...		O 89	Messiah		34
Deserta et lata mollescunt aspera voce, ...		O 89	Messiah	V	34
Voce ubi Cennethus populos domuisse feroces		O 169	Insula Kenneth		3
Voce aut fidibus pellere docuit		O 193	Tr. Medea III		8
Mnemosyne, ut Sappho mellita voce canentem		O 214	Tr Greek 9.66		1
Sint Demosthenica ut jurata cadavera voce, ...		O 216	Tr Greek 9.288		5
Dum docuit blanda voce natare pater.		O 228	Rivum a Stoana		4
VOCEM					
Pythagoras mallet, vocem habuisset opus.		O 225	Tr. Gk. 16.326		2
VOCIS					
Ille vias vocis pandet, flexusque liquentis		O 90	Messiah		47
VOCO					
Alme voco, impatiens noctis metuensque diei.		O 161	Gnothi seauton		31
VOCUMQUE					
Te sterili functum cura, vocumque salebris		O 161	Gnothi seauton		19
VOLITANT					
Et rerum volitant rarae per inane figurae.		O 162	Gnothi seauton		51
VOLITAT					
Huc nunquam volitat debilis iste puer.		O 213	Tr Greek 9.39		4
VOLUCRIS					
Anni qua volucris ducitur orbita, ...		O 155	Psalmus 117		1
VOLUI					
Scire locum volui quid daret ille novi.		O 169	Insula Kenneth		6
Scire locus volui quid daret iste novi.		O 169	Insula Kenneth	V	6
VOLUIT					
Sanari voluit meos, ...		O 164	Recover Eyes		7
VOLUNT					
Una quidem, sic fata volunt, tibi vivitur aestas, . . .		O 171	Tr. Busy Fly		9
VOLUPTAS					
Sera voluptas.		O 153	In Theatro		4
VCLUTA					
Per certas stabili lege voluta vices, ...		O 219	Tr Greek 9.577		2

```
VCLVANTUR                                                    PAGE    TITLE           LINE
    Volvantur celeres anni! Lux purpuret ortum     . . . . .  O  89 Messiah            25
VCLVERAT
    Ingentemque animo seclorum volverat orbem.     . . . . .  O 160 Gnothi seauton     11
VCLVERET
    Ingentemque animo seclorum volveret orbem.     . . . . .  O 160 Gnothi seauton   V 11
VCLVITUR
    Volvitur hora mihi, volvitur hora tibi!     . . . . . .   O 171 Tr. Busy Fly        8
    Volvitur hora mihi, volvitur hora tibi!     . . . . . .   O 171 Tr. Busy Fly        8
VOMERE
    Vel Arator vomere franget,     . . . . . . . . . . .      O 109 Post-genitis        4
VCMEREM
    Vomerem, et in falcem rigidus curvabitur ensis.     . . . O  90 Messiah            70
VORANTES
    Flores Fructusque vorantes,     . . . . . . . . . .       O 109 Post-genitis       12
VOS
    In vos ne missus spicula tendat amor. . . . . . . . .     O 213 Tr Greek 9.39       2
VOTAQUE
    Votaque fundam     . . . . . . . . . .                    O 199 Medico Aeger S     27
VOTIS
    Hoc statuant, votis Christus adesse velit:     . . . . .  O 204 Losing Speech    V  2
    Sufficit hoc votis; flos hic pulcherrimus aevi est,   . . O 215 Tr Greek 9.112      3
VCX
    Divinos, surdas sacra vox permulceat aures!     . . . . . O  69 Messiah            43
    Quot vox missa pedes abit horae parte secunda? . . . .    O 229 Epigram IV          1
VULNERE
    Aeternoque orci dominator vulnere languens     . . . . .  O  90 Messiah            55
VULT
    Vult Deus, at, qui cuncta dedit tibi, cuncta reposcit.  . O 205 Christianus        24
    Parthenope. Novies vult tellus mille Sicana.    . . . .   O 230 Geographia Met     11
    Vult sibi vicenas millesima myrias addi,  . . . . . . .   O 230 Geographia Met     21
    Undecimum Camber vult septem millibus addi. . . . . . .   O 231 Geographia Met     36
VULTUS
    En! Salvator adest; vultus agnoscite caeci     . . . . .  O  89 Messiah            42
WALTONI
    Waltoni Piscator perfectus     . . . . . . . . .         O 181 Waltoni Piscat       T
    E Waltoni  Piscatore Perfecto excerptum. . . . . . . .   O 181 Waltoni Piscat   V   T
WAREHOUSE
    The Logical Warehouse: Occasioned by an Auctioneer's  . . O 385 The Warehouse    D   T
WHO
    To a Lady who spoke in Defence of Liberty     . . . . .   O 105 Lady Defence         T
WITH
    . . . Johnson, as he lay confined with an inflamed Eye.   O 162 To Dr Lawrence       T
XERXI
    Xerxi, tercentum Spartae Mars obstitit acris     . . . .  O 217 Tr Greek 9.304       3
ZENO
    Grandiloquus nimis alta Zeno.     . . . . . . . . .       O 166 Oda Isle Skye    V  16
ZOSIMA
    Zosima, quae solo fuit olim corpore Serva,     . . . . .  O 114 Tr Gk Epigrams       1
    Zosima, qua solo fuit olim corpore serva,     . . . . .   O 212 Tr Gk Epigrams   V   7
    Zosima, quondam solo fuit olim copore serva,    . . . .   Y 320 Tr Gk Epigrams   V   1
```

Column — 107

ET

51

NON

47

IN

45

EST

42

UT

38

MIHI
NUNC

35

TIBI

33

NEC

30

HIC
QUI

27

QUID

26

PER
TE

23

ME

22

QUOD

21

CUM

19

VITAE

18

AUT
QUA
SIC

17

SI
SIBI
VITA

16

ILLE
QUAE
QUAM

15

SED

14

NIL
OMNIA
PATER

Column — 14 (CONT.)

QUEM
QUO

13

AD
SIT

12

HAEC
MILLIA
TU

11

AT
CUNCTA
DEUS
DUM
EN
HOMINUM
SEMPER

10

AMOR
DA
DIES
NE
QUOS

9

DAT
DE
HAUD
INTER
JAM
MENTE
OPUS
SEU
TELLUS

8

GAUDIA
HABET
HOC
HORA
MODO
PRO
QUEIS
QUICQUID
SEPTEM
SINE
SUMME
TAMEN
TUO

7

AB
CUI
CURA
ECCE
GENTES
GRATIA
LUX
MENTEM
NIMIS
OMNE
PATREM
PECTUS
RERUM
SE
SIVE
SPES
SUA
SUB
TANDEM
TER
VICES

6

ALMA
ANIMO

Column — 6 (CONT.)

ATQUE
CHRISTE
CORPORE
DULCE
ESSE
INGENIUM
LAETA
LUCE
MUNERA
OLIM
OPES
PRIMA
QUAS
QUOQUE
SANGUINE
SUNT
TECUM
TUA
UBI
UBIQUE
UNUS
VEL
VIRTUS
VOCE

5

A
AC
AEVI
ALTER
ARTE
BENE
BONIS
CHRISTO
DEDIT
DEI
E
FLUCTUS
FUIT
HIS
HUC
HUIC
IMAGO
IPSE
JACET
JUBET
LEGES
MENTI
MENTIS
MINUS
MYRIADAS
NATURA
NOVA
O
OCULIS
OMNIS
PECTORE
PULCHRA
QUIS
RES
RESTAT
SAXA
SECULA
SEX
SINT
SORS
TANTUM
TERRA
TERRAS
TUNC
TURBA
ULLA
VENIT
VIS

4

ADESSE
ALIIS
ALTA
AMORE
AN
ANTE
ARMA
ASPERA
AUDAX
AURUM

Column — 4 (CONT.)

CAPIT
CHRISTUS
COELUM
CUIQUE
CURAS
DECIES
DECUS
DIEM
ERAM
ERIT
FIDA
FIDENS
GAUDET
GENS
GLORIA
GRAMINA
GRATA
HONORES
HORAS
IGNIS
ILLA
IMBER
ITER
LINGUAE
MAGNI
MALA
MANET
MEA
MILLE
MIRUM
MORTE
MOX
MULCET
MYRIAS
NIMIUM
NOCTIS
NULLA
NULLIS
NUNQUAM
ORE
PLUS
PRECIBUS
PROCUL
PUER
QUANTUM
QUIDEM
QUINQUE
QUISQUIS
RECTE
RESPICE
RIDENS
SACRA
SANCTA
SECUNDA
SOLA
SOLUS
SOMNIA
SOROR
SPIRAT
STUDIIS
SUAS
SUIS
SUMMA
SUUM
TECTA
TEMPORE
TEMPORIS
TENET
THE
TRISTE
TUAS
TUIS
UNA
VELIT
VENIAM
VENUS
VITAM
VULT

3

ADDE
ADEST
AETAS
AGAM
ANIMI
ANIMUM
ANNIS

Column — 3 (CONT.)

AQUAS
ARDUA
AURIS
BENIGNA
BLANDA
BLANDUM
BONI
BONUM
BREVIS
CAECA
CAELEBS
CARMINA
CARMINE
CAUSA
CERNERE
CIRCUM
CLARA
COELI
CORDA
CREDIT
CUMULOS
CUNCTIS
CURAE
CURSU
CUSTOS
DEAE
DEORUM
DEUM
DIU
DIVITIIS
DOCET
DOCTA
DOMI
DOMUS
DULCIS
DURA
EGO
EQUUS
EUROPA
EX
FACTA
FELIX
FIDES
FLUIT
FOECUNDA
FORTIS
FORTUNA
FRUSTRA
FUGIT
FUNDIT
GRAVIS
GRESSUS
HABEBIS
HEU
HI
HOMINES
HORRIDA
HUNC
ILLIS
IMPATIENS
INANE
IPSA
IRAS
JUPITER
LABORES
LATE
LEGE
LIBER
LONGO
LUCIS
LUMINE
LUMINIS
MAGNE
MAJUS
MALE
MATERIES
MECUM
MEMBRA
MENS
MENSAE
MODIS
MOLLIA
MORES
MULTA
NAM
NATURAE
NATUS
NAUFRAGUS

3 (CCNT.)	2 (CONT.)	2 (CONT.)	2 (CONT.)	2 (CONT.)
NEQUE	AERIS	DISCIPULUS	INSTET	NEMO
NIHIL	AETERNA	DISCORDIA	INSULA	NERVOS
NOBIS	AETERNE	DIVINO	INTENDE	NESCIT
NOX	AETERNUM	DIXIT	IRUS	NIMBIS
NUDA	AETHERA	DOCUIT	ISTA	NISI
NUDUS	AETHEREIS	DOLOR	ISTE	NOCEAT
NULLO	AETEERIS	DOLORE	ITQUE	NOCTE
NUMINE	AGE	DOMINATOR	JACENT	NOMINE
OCULOS	AGIT	DOMINI	JACEO	NOS
OF	AIT	DOMINO	JACTAT	NOSTRA
OMNIBUS	ALIUS	DONA	JOVIS	NOSTRI
ORA	AMICE	DR	JUGA	NOVAS
PALPANTUR	ANGLUS	DUAS	JUNGIT	NOVI
PARIT	ANIMUS	DUO	JUVENIS	NUBIBUS
PASTOR	ANNI	DUOS	LABELLA	NULLI
PATENT	ANNUS	DUXIT	LABOR	NULLIUS
PATRIA	ANXIETAS	EHEU	LABORE	NUMEN
PECTORA	ARABS	ELEMENTA	LACRYMANS	NUMERARE
PEDES	ARBITER	ELIGE	LACRYMARUM	NUMERAT
PEDIBUS	ARBOR	EODEM	LACRYMIS	NUPER
PERIT	ARCE	EPICTETUS	LAETIOR	NYCTICORAX
PERPETUO	ARTI	EPIGRAMMA	LAETO	ODA
PONTI	ASTRA	ERAT	LAETOS	OMNES
PRAEMIA	ATRIA	ERGO	LAQUEUM	OMNI
PRECE	AUCTUM	ERIS	LATA	ONUS
PRECES	AUREA	ETC	LATIS	OPACA
PRETIUM	AURI	EXCIPIT	LAURA	ORAS
PRODEST	AUSUS	EXIGUUM	LAURENTI	ORATOR
PURA	BENIGNUS	FACILIS	LAUS	ORBE
QUADRAGENIS	BIRCHIUS	FACIT	LECTO	ORBEM
QUALE	BIS	FAMA	LEGIBUS	ORBI
QUALIS	BY	FATA	LEGITIMIS	ORBIS
QUIES	CAECO	FAUSTA	LENIADES	ORCI
QUISQUE	CANIS	FEGERUNT	LETHALE	ORCUS
REGE	CELSA	FEGIT	LEXICA	PACIS
REPERIT	CENTURIAE	FEBAS	LEXICON	PAENITUISSE
RCBORE	CENTURIAS	FERET	LIBROS	PAGINA
RCMA	CENTURIIS	FERRE	LILIA	PALLAS
SACRI	CERTA	FERT	LITTORA	PALMIS
SANCTUS	CERTAS	FICTIS	LOCA	PANDITUR
SAT	CESSIT	FIDIBUS	LONGI	PAREM
SCELERUM	COELESTIA	FIGURAE	LUCRI	PARENTIS
SECLA	COELESTIS	FIT	LUCRUM	PARS
SENEX	COELO	FLAMMAS	LUDICRA	PARTE
SERVARE	COGITAT	FLETU	LUDIT	PARTES
SERVUS	COLAM	FLORES	LUNA	PASCIT
SIDERA	COLONI	FLUAT	LYRA	PASCUA
SKIA	COLUBRI	FONTE	MAGNO	PATEAT
SOLIS	CCMAS	FONTES	MAJORE	PATRIAE
SOLUM	COMES	FORMOSA	MANU	PAUCIS
SPE	CONCEDE	FORTE	MANUS	PAUPER
SPICULA	CONJUGE	FORUM	MARE	PAUPERIEQUE
SUMMO	CONSUETUS	FOVET	MARIA	PAUPERIES
SUO	CONVIVIA	FRIGORA	MARTI	PAX
SURGIT	COPIA	FRUI	MATER	PECCATOR
TENE	CORDE	FRUITUR	MAVIS	PELAGOQUE
TERRIS	CORPORA	FUERAT	MEDITATUR	PENNIS
THRALIA	CREDO	FUNERA	MEI	PENURIA
TOLLIT	CRIMINA	GENERIS	MELIORA	PERAGAM
TRES	CRIMINE	GENUS	MEMOR	PERGE
TRIA	CULMINA	GESTA	MENODOTUM	PERITURA
TUMULUM	CULTU	GRAECUS	MEOS	PERMITTE
TUTUM	CUPIT	GRAIUS	MERO	PETO
TUTUS	CURAQUE	GRANDE	MESSIA	PIA
UTI	CURIS	GRATES	MICANTES	PIETATE
VALE	CURSUM	GRATUM	MILIAE	PIUS
VATES	CURSUS	GRAVATAM	MIRATUR	PLACERE
VELOX	DABANT	GRAVE	MISERIS	PLACIDO
VENEREM	DABIT	GRAVEM	MISEROS	PLENA
VIAS	DATOR	HABEBAT	MISSA	PLURA
VIRUM	DATUM	HARMONIA	MITTIT	PLURIMA
VIVERE	DATUR	HINC	MODERANTE	PLUTARCHE
VIX	DECADAS	HOSTILES	MODUS	POENITENTIAM
	DECADES	HUMANI	MOESTA	POENITET
	DEDERE	HUMERIS	MONTES	POETAE
	DEDI	HUMO	MONTIBUS	PONDUS
2	DENAS	IDEM	MORI	PONTUS
ABEST	DENIQUE	IMA	MORTALE	POSSIT
ABSQUE	DEOS	IMPERIO	MOVET	POST
ACER	DESIT	IMPERIUM	MUNDI	PRAEBET
ACRIS	DESUNT	INANI	MUNERIBUS	PRAECO
ACUTIS	DET	INCERTA	MUS	PRAESENS
ADDI	DIA	INCULTA	MUSA	PRATA
ADDIT	DICAS	INCUSAT	MUSAE	PRATIS
ADES	DICITE	INEST	MUSIS	PRIMIS
ADSIT	DIEI	INEUNT	MYRIADI	PRIORES
AEGRA	DIGNA	INGENIO	NAUTA	PROLES
AEQUOR	DIGNE	INGREDERE	NECTIT	PROPRIUM
AER				

553

BREVIUS	CERBERE	CONCINNAT	CURRERE	DICIMUS
BRITANNIS	CERTAM	CONCORS	CURRICULO	DICITUR
BRUMAE	CERTAMEN	CONCURRENT	CURVABITUR	DIFFISI
BUCCINA	CERTE	CONDITOR	CUTIM	DIFFLUENTEM
BUXIQUE	CERTO	CONDITUR	CYATHO	DIFFLUIT
CACHINNIS	CESSARUNT	CONFERT	CYCNUM	DIFFUGIUNT
CACHINNO	CESSAT	CONFESSUS	CYNTHIA	DIGITI
CADAVERA	CESSURA	CONFINED	CYPRIAE	DIGNARIER
CADENS	CHABUS	CONFITENTI	CYRUM	DIGNOS
CADENT	CHERONEAE	CONFUGIS	CYTHEREIUS	DIGNUS
CADUCI	CHRISTI	CONGESTAS	DABUNT	DII
CAECI	CHRISTUM	CONJUGIUM	DAMNARE	DILECTA
CAECUS	CIBIS	CONJUNGIT	DAMNATIS	DIMIDIUM
CALCATOS	CIBOS	CONSCENDERE	DAMNATUS	DIODORUS
CALEDONIAS	CIBUS	CONSPEXIT	DANAE	DIRA
CALENS	CINEREM	CONSPICIT	DANTES	DIREPTA
CALENTI	CINERES	CONSTANS	DANUBII	DIRO
CALLIDUS	CINIS	CONSTRICTUS	DAPES	DIRUM
CALLIOPE	CINNAMEIS	CONSUETA	DAPIS	DISCANT
CALUERUNT	CINNAMEOS	CONSUMERER	DARE	DISCE
CALUMNIIS	CIRCUMFUSA	CONTEMPSIT	DARET	DISCEDITE
CAMBER	CIRCUMSONAT	CONTENDIT	DARIO	DISCESSERIS
CAMOENA	CITATA	CONTENTA	DAS	DISJECIT
CAMOENAS	CIVIS	CONTENTI	DEA	DISPLICEAT
CAMPUS	CLAM	CONTEXTAM	DEAS	DISSIMILI
CANE	CLAMAT	CONTRA	DEBILIS	DITATUS
CANENTEM	CLAMO	CONTRAHE	DEBITA	DITESCERE
CANENTI	CLAMOSA	CONTREMET	DEBITOR	DITESCIS
CANIT	CLARAQUE	CONVALLES	DEBUIT	DITIS
CANITIES	CLARARE	CONVENIT	DECADEM	DIURNIS
CANNA	CLARIS	CONVERSA	DECEDERE	DIVA
CANORIS	CLARUM	CONVIVA	DECET	DIVES
CANORUM	CLARUS	CORDI	DECIDIT	DIVINAM
CANOS	CLAUDUM	CORDIS	DECOR	DIVINOS
CANTAT	CLAUSA	COROLLAS	DECORATA	DIVINUS
CANTICO	CLAUSTRA	CORONAM	DECUIT	DIVITIAS
CANTORUM	CLAUSUS	CORPORI	DECUSQUE	DIVOS
CANTU	CLEMENTEM	CORPUS	DEDERAT	DIXERAT
CANTUM	CLEMENTIA	CORRIPE	DEDERIT	DIXERE
CAPAXQUE	CLEOMBROTUS	CORTINA	DEDOCUISSE	DO
CAPRA	CODICES	CORUSCA	DEERANT	DOCENT
CAPRAE	COELESTES	CORUSCABIT	DEFENCE	DOCES
CAPREAS	COELICOLAE	CRAS	DEFENDITUR	DOCTAE
CAPTANS	COELICOLUM	CRASTINUS	DEFESSO	DOCTISSIME
CAPTARE	COELIQUE	CREASTI	DEFICIENS	DOCTISSIMUM
CAPUT	COELORUM	CREAVIT	DEFLECTITUR	DOCTRINA
CARBONE	COENAE	CREBRIOR	DEIN	DOCTUS
CARENS	COEPTA	CREDERET	DELATUS	DOLENS
CARERE	COERCEBUNT	CREDIDERIS	DELENDA	DOLENTI
CARET	COERULA	CREDULIS	DELICIASQUE	DOLERE
CARMELI	COGENTE	CREMANT	DELICTA	DOLET
CARMEN	COGOR	CREPARE	DELIRANS	DOLISQUE
CARMINIS	COHIBET	CREPET	DELUSA	DOLORI
CARNIS	COHORS	CRESCENTIA	DEMENS	DOLORUM
CARPAT	COLAT	CRESCENTIS	DEMENTES	DOMIBUS
CARPE	COLE	CRESCIT	DEMISSUMQUE	DOMINABERE
CARPERE	COLENDAS	CRETAE	DEMOCRITE	DOMINUM
CARPIT	COLERE	CRETHIDA	DEMOPHILO	DOMOS
CASA	COLIT	CRISPE	DEMOSTHENICA	DOMUISSE
CASSUS	COLLACRYMANSQUE	CRISTAE	DEMUM	DONAT
CATENA	CCLLAR	CRUCIATOS	DENOS	DONEC
CATERVAS	CCLLARI	CRUDA	DENSA	DONET
CAUSAE	COLLATOS	CRUDOS	DENSAQUE	DOTE
CAUSARUM	CCLLO	CRUDUM	DENSIS	DOTES
CAUSAS	COLLUSTRA	CRUMENA	DEO	DOTIBUS
CAUSIDICI	COLLUSTRET	CRYSTALLISQUE	DEPONE	DRACONIS
CAUSISQUE	COLONUS	CUIQUAM	DEPOSITURA	DUBIAE
CAUTA	COLUMBA	CUJAS	DEPROPERAT	DUBIIS
CAVATA	COLUMBAE	CUJUS	DES	DUBITARE
CAVE	COLUMBAS	CULPA	DESCENDERE	DUBITET
CAVEATQUE	COLUNT	CULPANDA	DESCRIBERE	DUBITO
CAVENS	CCMESQUE	CULPAS	DESCRIBIT	DUC
CAVERNAS	CCMITATA	CULTOR	DESCRIPSERIS	DUCAT
CECINERUNT	COMITEM	CULTUM	DESERET	DUCENTIS
CECROPIDIS	CCMMODAT	CULTUQUE	DESERTA	DUCES
CEDENS	CCMPAGEM	CULTUS	DESERTI	DUCIMUS
CEDERE	COMPITA	CULULLO	DESIDERIO	DUCIT
CEDRUS	COMPLENT	CUMQUE	DESIDIAE	DUCITUR
CEDUNT	COMPLETUR	CUMULARE	DESINITIS	DUCUM
CELAT	COMPOSED	CUMULAS	DESINT	DUCUNT
CELEBREM	COMPOSITIS	CUMULIS	DESTITUIT	DULCES
CELERES	COMPRIMIT	CUNCTAS	DETERAT	DULCI
CELLANTIA	COMPUTAT	CUNCTIPARENS	DETRUDIT	DULCIA
CENNETHUS	CONAMINE	CUNCTORUM	DEXTRAE	DULCIBUS
CENSUS	CONATIBUS	CUPIAT	DICAM	DUMETA
CENTUM	CONCENTUM	CUPIDO	DICAT	DUOSQUE
CENTURIA	CONCILIIS	CUR	DICATUS	DURIS
CEPIT	CONCINIT		DICAVIT	DURO

1 (CONT.)	1 (CONT.)	1 (CONT.)	1 (CONT.)	1 (CONT.)
EDIDIT	FALCEM	FOEDERA	GENIALE	HORTIS
EDIFICAT	FALERNA	FOEMINAM	GENIALI	HOS
EDIT	FALERNAE	FOENORE	GENIBUS	HOSPITA
EFFICIET	FALLAX	FORES	GENITORE	HOSPITII
EFFIGIEMQUE	FALLIMUR	FORET	GENTI	HOSPITIO
EFFLAT	FAMES	FORMA	GENTIS	HOSTEM
EFFUGIENS	FAMULATA	FORMAE	GEOGRAPHIA	HOSTIS
EFFUNDET	FARRA	FORMAS	GERAM	HUJUS
EGERIAE	FASTU	FORMIS	GESSERAT	HUMANA
EGES	FATERI	FORNICE	GESTIAT	HUMANAE
EGREGIOS	FATERIS	FORSAN	GESTIT	HUMANUM
EIA	FATIGATAMQUE	FORTASSE	GIGNIT	HUMET
EJICE	FAUSTINE	FORTUNAE	GLADIUM	HUMIDA
ELATA	FAUTRIX	POTIS	GOAT	HUMIDIS
ELEGANTE	FAVE	FOVEAT	GRADU	HUMILI
ELIGAT	FAVENTEM	FOVEATQUE	GRAECIA	HUMUS
ELISA	FAXINT	FOVENTE	GRAECIAE	I
ELIZAE	FEBRE	FRACTIS	GRAIUM	IBUNT
ELOQUIUMQUE	FEBRIS	FRACTUS	GRANDIA	IDUME
ELUCTATUM	FELICI	FRAGRANTIA	GRANDILOQUUS	IERNE
EMENDATUM	FELICIBUS	FRANGE	GRATI	IGNAVAE
ENIM	FELICITATIS	FRANGET	GRATIOR	IGNAVUS
ENSIS	FELLE	FRAUDE	GRATUS	IGNES
ENTHEA	FELLIS	FRAUDIS	GRAVANT	IGNIVOMI
EOIS	FEMINA	FREMENTES	GRAVAT	IGNOSCAT
EPICIS	FERAR	FREMERE	GRAVES	IGNOSCIS
EPICURUM	FERAT	FREMITU	GRAVI	IGNOTAE
EPILOGUS	FEROCES	FRETA	GRAVIORIBUS	ILLAS
EPULAE	FERORUM	FRETUMQUE	GRAVIORQUE	ILLI
EQUALES	FERGX	FRETUS	GRAVIUS	ILLIC
EQUI	FERUNTUR	FRIGORE	GREGI	IMBRES
ERAS	FERUS	FRONDE	GREMIO	IMBRIBUS
ERO	FERVENT	FRONDENS	GROUNDFLOOR	IMITANTIUM
ERRAT	FERVET	FRONDENT	GUBERNATRIX	IMMATURA
ERRORIS	FESSA	FRONDESCIT	GULAE	IMMERITO
ERUDITA	FESSE	FRONTE	GUTTAE	IMMISTA
ERUNTUR	FESSIS	FRONTIS	GYGES	IMMITTE
ESCA	FIAM	FRUARIS	HABEAM	IMMUNIS
ESSES	FICTO	FRUATUR	HABEO	IMPEDIERE
ESSET	FICUS	FRUCTUS	HABERE	IMPELLITUR
ESTO	FIDE	FRUCTUSQUE	HABES	IMPENDERE
ETENIM	FIDEIQUE	FRUSTRABAR	HABITAT	IMPERET
ETIAM	FIDEM	FUCIS	HABUIQUE	IMPERII
EUMARUS	FIDESQUE	FUERE	HABUISSET	IMPERIIQUE
EURIS	FIDIS	FUGA	HABUIT	IMPERIIS
EUROS	FIDO	FUGACEM	HAC	IMPETRET
EVELLENS	FIDUM	FUGACES	HAE	IMPETUM
EVENIAT	FIDUS	FUGERE	HAERES	IMPIA
EVOCAT	FIENT	FUGIENS	HAMUS	IMPLEXO
EXAESTUANTIS	FIERI	FULCRO	HANC	IMPORTUNA
EXCEPTAE	FIGURIS	FULGORE	HARMONIAE	IMPROBA
EXCERPTUM	FILIA	FULGURA	HAS	INANIBUS
EXCLAMAT	FILIUM	FULMINE	HASTA	INCERTIS
EXEMPLIS	FINE	FULSERAT	HAUSTUM	INCINCTAM
EXEMPLO	FINEM	FULSIT	HAUSTUS	INCLINATA
EXERCET	FINEMQUE	FUMABUNT	HAVING	INCLYTA
EXHALANT	FINGERET	FUMIS	HE	INCLYTUS
EXHILARORQUE	FINIET	FUNCTUM	HEBETARE	INCOLA
EXIGIS	FIRMA	FUNDAM	HEBRIDAS	INCOQUITUR
EXIT	FIRMATA	FUNERE	HECTOR	INCREMENTA
EXITIALES	FIRMIUS	FUNUS	HECTORI	INCREPAT
EXITIO	FIXUM	FUBAT	HELICONIS	INCULTI
EXOPTES	FLAGRAT	FUREM	HENRICUM	INCULTUM
EXOSUS	FLAGRET	FURES	HERACLITE	INCULTUMQUE
EXPECTATA	FLAMMA	FURORE	HERACLITUS	INDAGINE
EXPERIENTIA	FLAMMAE	FURORES	HERBAS	INDEFESSA
EXPERIERE	FLENDI	FURTIM	HERMEM	INDIA
EXPERS	FLERE	FUSI	HERODOTO	INDIGNATUS
EXPLEOR	FLETUS	FUSIS	HEROS	INDOCTAE
EXPLICAT	FLEXUSQUE	FUTURA	HERUM	INDOCTUS
EXSECUIT	FLOBE	FUTURI	HESPERIIS	INDUE
EXSURGE	FLOREA	FUTURIS	HILARARE	INDUIT
EXTERNI	FLOREBUNT	FUTURO	HIPPI	INDULSERIT
EXTERNUS	FLOREM	GARRIRE	HIPPONAX	INEAMUS
EXULAT	FLORENTIBUS	GARRULA	HIRCE	INEPTUM
EXULTANT	FLORIBUS	GAUDENT	HOLLANDIA	INERTI
EYE	FLOS	GAUDENTIA	HOMERUS	INERTIS
FABELLAS	FLUATQUE	GAUDIUM	HOMINEM	INFANS
FABRI	FLUCTIBUS	GAZA	HOMINI	INFESTIS
FACE	FLUCTU	GELIDA	HOMO	INFIDAS
FACIAM	FLUENTES	GELIDAE	HOMULLIS	INFIRMUM
FACIES	FLUMINA	GELIDIS	HOMULLOS	INFIT
FACILE	FLUXIT	GELIDO	HONESTUS	INFLAMED
FACILEM	FLUXO	GEMMAQUE	HORAE	INFORMIS
FACILI	FOECUNDOS	GEMMAS	HORATIUS	INFRA
FACILISQUE	FOEDA	GENEROSA	HORIS	INFUNDET
FACIUNT	FOEDANTES	GENEROSAM	HORRET	INGEMINA
FAELIX	FOEDAT	GENEROSO	HORRUIT	INGEMINAQUE

INGEMIT	JURATA	LEGIS	LUDUSQUE	MELOS
INGENII	JUSSA	LEGITIMAS	LUMEN	MEMBRIS
INGENIUMCQUE	JUSSERE	LENIS	LUMINA	MEMNONIS
INGENTEMQUE	JUSTAS	LENITAS	LUMINI	MEMORANDA
INGENTIS	JUSTITIAEQUE	LENTA	LUNAQUE	MENDACIS
INGREDITUR	JUSTO	LENTAE	LUPO	MENIPPUS
INIQUUM	JUVABIT	LENTEQUE	LUSAE	MENSAS
INJICIAT	JUVANT	LENTI	LUSIBUS	MENSTRUA
INJICIENT	JUVAT	LENTUS	LUSTRA	MENTES
INNITERE	JUVENCUM	LEO	LUSTRAVIT	MENTIBUS
INNIXUS	JUVENCUS	LEONE	LUSTRI	MENTISQUE
INNOCUA	JUVENEM	LEPORI	LUSTRO	MENTITUR
INNOCUOS	JUVENES	LEPOS	LUXERAT	MEO
INOFFENSO	JUVENI	LEPRA	LUXURIA	MERCEDEM
INOPS	JUVENTAE	LEVA	LUXURIAE	MERCES
INQUIT	JUVENTUTEM	LEVAMEN	LUXURIANS	MERETUR
INSANIA	JUVENUM	LEVARE	LUXUS	MERI
INSCRIBENDI	JUXTA	LEVAT	LYCORIDE	MERITAS
INSCRIPTION	KENNETHI	LEVEM	LYCURGE	MERITISVE
INSIDET	LABEFACTA	LEVIS	LYMPHA	MERITOQUE
INSIDIAS	LABEM	LEVITAS	LYRAM	MESSANA
INSIPIENTIA	LABORANTEM	LIBELLOS	LYSIGENI	MESSEM
INSOLITUM	LABORAT	LIBENS	MACEDUM	MESSIBUS
INSTAR	LABORI	LIBENTER	MACRAE	MESSIS
INSTARE	LABORIBUS	LIBERA	MACRINE	META
INTACTA	LABRAQUE	LIBERET	MAEONIDES	METALLUM
INTEMERATA	LACHRYMANTES	LIBERIORI	MAGIS	METAM
INTEREA	LACRIMARE	LIBERTATIS	MAGISTER	METATA
INTERII	LACTEA	LIBERTY	MAGISTRO	METRICA
INTRET	LACTIS	LIBIDINE	MAGISTRUM	METU
INTUS	LADY	LIBRI	MAGNA	METUENS
INUNDABIT	LAEDITE	LIBRIS	MAGNAEQUE	METUENSQUE
INUTILES	LAESIT	LICEAT	MAGNAM	METUM
INUTILITER	LAETAQUE	LICEBIT	MAGNIS	METUQUE
INVADENS	LAETATUR	LICET	MAJOR	METUS
INVALIDI	LAETIS	LICHFELDIAE	MAJORA	MEUM
INVENIO	LAETITIA	LIGURES	MAJOREM	MI
INVISAS	LAETUS	LIMEN	MAJORIBUS	MILITIBUS
IO	LAEVIA	LIMINA	MALI	MILLESIMA
IPSIS	LAEVUM	LIMITE	MALIM	MILLIBUS
IPSO	LAIS	LIMOSUM	MALIS	MINACES
IRA	LAMBUNT	LINCOLN'S	MALLET	MINANTES
IRAM	LAMPADE	LINGUARUMQUE	MALORUM	MINAX
IRATA	LANGUENS	LINGUAS	MALUM	MINERIS
IRATAS	LANGUENTIA	LINGUIS	MANDAT	MINETUR
IRE	LANGUESCISQUE	LIQUENTIS	MANDATUM	MINISTRAT
IRIS	LANIAT	LIQUESCENT	MANE	MINISTRET
IRRIGET	LANIFICI	LITARE	MANEAM	MINOR
IRRITA	LAPIDEM	LITERASQUE	MANEBAT	MINOREM
IRRUPTUM	LAPIS	LITERATOS	MANSUESCERE	MIRABILE
ISAIAE	LAPSA	LITES	MANSUETAE	MIRABITUR
ISTI	LAPSI	LITTORAQUE	MANUQUE	MIRANTUR
ISTIS	LARGA	LITUI	MARATHON	MISCENS
ITIDEM	LASCIVIET	LOCANS	MARCMONTI	MISCENTUR
JACEANT	LASSAT	LOCIS	MARIS	MISCET
JACEAT	LATEBIS	LOCO	MARISQUE	MISELLUM
JACERE	LATEBRAS	LOCUM	MARMOR	MISERA
JACIT	LATERE	LOCUPLETISSIMUM	MARMORA	MISERATA
JACTANS	LATESCERE	LOCUPLETUM	MARMORE	MISERERIS
JACTET	LATESCIT	LOCUS	MARMOREA	MISERI
JACTURA	LATEX	LOGICAL	MARMOREO	MISERUM
JACUISSE	LATITAT	LONGA	MARMORIS	MISSUS
JACULANTIA	LATRONES	LONGE	MARO	MISTA
JAMQUE	LATUERE	LONGINQUISQUE	MARS	MITIA
JANITOR	LATUS	LONGINQUO	MARTIQUE	MITIOR
JEJUNIA	LAUDE	LONGIUS	MATERIA	MNEMOSYNE
JEJUNIUM	LAUDES	LONGUM	MATERIAM	MODOS
JESSAEIS	LAUDET	LOQUACEM	MATERIEM	MODULIS
JESUS	LAUDO	LOQUELAE	MATERIEMQUE	MODULUM
JOANNES	LAURAM	LOQUETUR	MATHEMATICOS	MOENIA
JOHNSON	LAURENCE	LOQUITUR	MATREM	MOERET
JOVE	LAURUS	LOQUOR	MATURANT	MOEROR
JOVEM	LAUSQUE	LORICA	MEAE	MOERORQUE
JOVI	LAUTASQUE	LUBRICA	MEATUS	MOESTUM
JUBEAS	LAVACRA	LUCCA	MEDELAM	MOLA
JUBEBIT	LAVI	LUCEBIT	MEDICAE	MOLESTA
JUBENTE	LAVIT	LUCEM	MEDICAMINA	MOLESTAS
JUBES	LAWRENCE	LUCERNAM	MEDICI	MOLIATUR
JUDAEO	LAXENT	LUCI	MEDICINA	MOLLES
JUDEX	LAY	LUCIDUS	MEDICUM	MOLLESCUNT
JUDICE	LEBANON	LUCINA	MEDITANS	MOLLI
JUGERA	LECTIS	LUCTAMINE	MEDITATUS	MOLLIOR
JUGUM	LECTOQUE	LUCTANTEM	MEDIUS	MONADES
JUNCIQUE	LECTOR	LUCTU	MEIS	MONTIS
JUNCTUS	LECTOS	LUCTUS	MELIOREM	MONUMENTUM
JUNGERE	LEDA	LUDENS	MELIORIS	MORA
JUNGUNT	LEGENS	LUDERE	MELLI	MORATUR
JUNXIT	LEGI	LUDUM	MELLITA	MORBIQUE

MORBUS	NISIBUS	OMITTAT	PATRIAS	PIGRAM
MORETUR	NISU	OMNESQUE	PATRIS	PIGRITIAM
MORIARQUE	NITENT	OMNIPOTENS	PATROCINATA	PINDI
MORIENTE	NITENTI	ON	PAULATIM	PINGUES
MORIENTIA	NITERE	ONERANT	PAULUM	PINGUI
MORITUR	NITES	ONUSTA	PAUPERIEM	PINXIT
MOROR	NITESCIT	OPACAE	PAUPERTAS	PISCATOR
MORS	NITIDO	OPE	PECCANTI	PISCATORE
MORSQUE	NIVEO	OPELLAE	PECCANTUM	PLACAVIT
MORSU	NOBILITATUS	OPERAE	PECTORIS	PLACEANT
MORSUS	NOCENT	OPERUM	PECTUSQUE	PLACENT
MORTALES	NOCTES	OPHYRAEIS	PECUDES	PLACET
MORTALIA	NOCTURNAE	OPIMA	PECUNIA	PLACIDAEVE
MORTALIBUS	NOCUIT	OPPIDA	PEDE	PLANCTUS
MORTEM	NOLIS	OPTANT	PELAGI	PLATONI
MORTI	NCLC	OPTARIT	PELLAT	PLATONIS
MOTU	NOMEN	OPTAT	PELLE	PLAUDENTIBUS
MOTUSQUE	NOMINIS	OPTATUM	PELLEM	PLAUDIT
MOVISTI	NONAGESIMA	OPTENT	PELLENS	PLEBS
MR	NONDUM	OPTET	PELLERE	PLECTRUM
MUGITUM	NORIS	OPTO	PELOPIS	PLENUM
MULCENTES	NORIT	OPULENTUS	PENDET	PLORABIT
MULCENTESQUE	NOSCERE	OPUM	PENDULA	PLUMBEA
MULCERE	NOTA	ORATORY	PENETRALIA	PLURIMO
MULCERI	NOTIOR	ORBAT	PENNAS	POEMATA
MULIEBRIBUS	NOVATO	ORBITA	PENSI	POENA
MULTAE	NOVEM	ORDINE	PENSILIBUS	POENAM
MULTAS	NOVIES	ORDINIBUS	PEPETUO	POENIS
MULTIPLICI	NOVIS	ORDO	PERAGIT	POENITEAT
MULTIS	NOVIT	ORIBUS	PERCONTERE	POENITUISSE
MULTO	NOVITATE	ORNAT	PERCURRO	POETA
MUNDIQUE	NOVOS	ORNATISSIMUMQUE	PERDIDI	POLLICE
MUNERE	NOVUM	ORSUS	PERDUCAT	POLLICITIS
MUNUS	NOXAS	ORTUM	PERDUCET	POMPAE
MUREM	NOXIUS	ORTUS	PEREGRE	PONDERIS
MURMURA	NUBES	OSCULA	PEREGRINIS	PONE
MURO	NUDAM	OSSA	PERENNE	PONIS
MUSAS	NUDAS	OTIA	PERENNIS	PONIT
MUSCA	NUGAE	OTIOSIS	PEREUNTE	PONOR
MUSCOSI	NUGASQUE	OVES	PEREUNTES	PONTE
MUTABILIS	NUGIS	PACATAS	PERFECTO	POPELLI
MUTABIT	NULLUM	PACEMQUE	PERFECTUS	POPULARI
MUTARE	NUMERANTI	PALESTRAE	PERGIT	POPULO
MUTILATO	NUMERIS	PALLIDA	PERICULA	POPULOS
MUTILATUS	NUMINA	PALMAS	PERIERE	POPULUS
MYRIADES	NUMINIS	PALMISQUE	PERIISSE	PORRECTA
MYRTO	NUMMIS	PAMPINUS	PERIRET	PORRIGIT
NABATHAEI	NUMMUS	PANDATUR	PERITAM	PORTAS
NAMQUE	NUNCIA	PANDET	PERMEAT	POSCAM
NARCISSUS	NUNCIAT	PANDIS	PERMEO	POSCANT
NARIBUS	NUNCIUM	PANDUNT	PERMISSA	POSCAT
NARRAT	NUPTA	PAPA	PERMISSUM	POSCATUR
NASCENTI	NUPTAM	PAPAPER	PERMISTAS	POSCENTIBUS
NASCERE	NUTANTES	PAPAVER	PERMITTI	POSCIS
NASCITUR	NUTRIT	PAR	PERMULCEAT	POSCIT
NASCUNTUR	NYMPHAE	PARARE	PERNICIBUS	POSCO
NATARE	NYMPHIS	PARCA	PERPETUA	POSCUNT
NATAT	OBDUCTOSQUE	PARCAS	PERPETUI	POSSE
NATET	OBIRE	PARCE	PERPETUUS	POSSES
NATIO	OBLECTAT	PARCIT	PERSA	POSSIS
NATIS	OBSERVANS	PARENS	PERSCRIPSERAT	POSSUM
NATO	OBSINT	PARENTEM	PERSTREPIT	POST-GENITIS
NATOS	OBSITA	PARETE	PERTAESUS	POSTERA
NATUM	OBSTANTES	PARI	PERVAGOR	POSTHAC
NAVIS	OBSTAT	PARIBUS	PESSIME	POSTREMA
NEBULIS	OBSTITIT	PARITURAM	PETAT	POSTULAT
NEBULOSA	OBSTRICTASQUE	PARITURUM	PETENTI	POSTULET
NECE	OBVENIET	PARNASSUM	PETET	POTENS
NECESSITAS	OCCASIONED	PARTA	PETIIT	POTENTE
NECI	OCELLIS	PARTHENOPE	PETIT	POTENTEM
NECTAREOS	OCELLOS	PARTICIPEMQUE	PETITA	POTENTIA
NEGABITUR	OCELLUS	PARTICIPES	PETULANTES	POTERAM
NEGAVIT	OCTAVAM	PARTICULASQUE	PHIDIACA	POTERANT
NEGLIGIS	OCTINGENTESIMA	PARUM	PHIDIACI	POTERAS
NEQUEO	OCTO	PARVA	PHIDO	POTERO
NEQUEUNT	OCULO	PASCERE	PHILIPPE	POTES
NEQUID	OCULUS	PASCET	PHILOMELA	POTEST
NEQUITIAM	OCYOR	PASSIBUS	PHOEBE	POTIS
NERVIS	ODE	PASSIM	PHOEBI	POTUERE
NESTORIS	ODIT	PASSUS	PHOEBO	POTUI
NEVE	ODORATAE	PATERIS	PHOEBUS	PRAEBE
NEXA	ODORE	PATERNIS	PIASTI	PRAEBEAT
NEXIBUS	ODORES	PATET	PIAVIT	PRAEBUIT
NI	OENI	PATI	PICTAS	PRAECELLIT
NIHILUM	OFFA	PATIARE	PICTOR	PRAECONES
NIMII	OLIVAS	PATRANS	PIETAS	PRAENITUISSE
NIMIO	OLYMPUM	PATRI	PIETATIS	PRAESENTI
NISE	OLYMPUS	PATRIAMQUE	PIGRAE	

PRAESEPE	PUSILLO	REFINGIT	RUSSIA	SERA
PRAESTA	PUTABAT	REFRINGENS	RUTILANTIS	SERAE
PRAESTAT	PUTAT	REFULGET	SABAEO	SERIA
PRAETENDET	PUTIDULUM	REGALIBUS	SACRIFICI	SERIE
PRAETENDIT	PUTO	REGAT	SACRUM	SERIEM
PRAETER	PYTHAGORAM	REGELES	SAEVA	SERIES
PRAETEREUNT	PYTHAGORAS	REGES	SAEVIT	SERMONE
PRAETEREUNTE	QUADRATA	REGIAM	SAEVUS	SERO
PRAETERI	CUAERENTI	REGINAE	SALAMINIA	SERPENT
PRAETERII	QUAERIS	REGINAM	SALEBRIS	SERPENTES
PRAETERITAE	CUAERIT	REGIT	SALEBROSA	SERRATIS
PRAETERITIIS	QUAERITE	REGNA	SALEMA	SERTA
PRAVA	CUAERITUR	REGNABAT	SALICTI	SERTUM
PRAVUS	QUAERO	REGNET	SALIENTIS	SERVAT
PRAXITELES	CUAERUNT	REGUM	SALTEM	SERVATA
PRECANTES	QUALES	REIS	SALUTARES	SERVET
PRECARI	QUALIA	RELIQUI	SALUTET	SERVIAT
PRECIBUSQUE	QUAMCUNQUE	RELLIGIONE	SALUTIS	SERVILEM
PRECOR	QUANDAM	RELUCTARI	SALVATOR	SEVERIS
PREFIGERE	QUANDOQUIDEM	REM	SALVE	SEXAGENIS
PREMEBAS	QUANTA	REMUGIT	SALVERE	SEXAGINTA
PREMIT	QUASI	REO	SAMI	SEXQUE
PREMUNT	QUATIT	REPENTE	SANARI	SEXTI
PRETIO	QUAVIS	REPERIRE	SANCTOS	SEXTO
PRIAMI	QUERELAS	REPLEAT	SANGUINEM	SEXTUS
PRIMAS	QUERERIS	REPOSCIT	SANGUINIS	SICANA
PRIME	QUIBUS	REPROBAT	SAPIENS	SICCATQUE
PRINCEPS	QUICUNQUE	REPTANT	SAPIENT	SIDEREA
PRIOR	QUIESCIT	REPTARE	SAPIENTER	SIDEREUS
PRIORA	QUIETA	REQUIES	SAPIENTIAM	SIGNANTUR
PRIORUM	QUIETEM	REQUIESCIT	SAPIENTIOR	SIGNIS
PRISCAE	QUIETIS	REQUIRITUR	SAPIT	SILENTE
PROAVUM	QUINAS	REQUIRO	SAPIUNT	SILENTIA
PROBATUM	QUINGENTIS	RESCIRE	SAPPHO	SILENTIO
PROBAVIT	CUINQUAGENIS	RESIDENT	SARDINIAM	SILVAE
PROBITAS	QUINTA	RESONABUNT	SARONICA	SILVARUM
PROBROSA	QUIQUE	RESONARE	SATYRUM	SILVESTRIA
PROCACIS	QUOCUNQUE	RESPONDIT	SAVAGE	SIMILEM
PROCELLAS	QUOESUM	RESTINCTA	SAXEA	SIMILIS
PROCELLIS	QUORUM	RETENTAT	SAXEAS	SINAS
PROCORUM	CUOSCUMQUE	RETRACTA	SCATEBRAE	SINAT
PRODESSE	QUOVIS	RETULERE	SCATET	SINGULA
PROFERET	RABIEM	REVEHET	SCELESTOS	SINGULTANS
PROFUNDIS	RACEMOS	REVISENS	SCENA	SINUM
PROFUNDUS	RADIATAE	REVOCANDA	SCEPTRA	SIQUANDO
PROLE	RADICIBUS	REVOCANT	SCEPTRI	SIQUID
PROLEM	RADII	REVOCARE	SCHOLARUM	SIS
PROLESQUE	RADIOS	REVOCARIT	SCIAE	SISTERE
PROLI	RAMISQUE	REVOCATQUE	SCINTILLAT	SITIENTESQUE
PROLIS	RAPIET	REVOLUTA	SCOPULO	SITIS
PROLUE	RAPIT	RHODOCLEA	SCRIBANT	SOBOLES
PROMEREARE	RAPITUR	RICARDUM	SCRIBAT	SOCIALIS
PROMERUISSE	RAPTA	RIDEBIT	SCRIBENDAQUE	SOCIAM
PROMETHEI	RAPTOS	RIDENDUM	SCRIPTA	SOCIATA
PROMISSA	RAPUIT	RIDENT	SCRUTARE	SOCIO
PROMIT	RARAE	RIDEO	SECARE	SOCIUM
PROMPTUS	RARAQUE	RIDERE	SECLORUM	SODALIS
PROMUS	RATES	RIGIDUS	SECRETAS	SOL
PROPAGO	RATIONE	RISURUS	SECTA	SOLATIA
PROPERANS	REBCANTIA	RIVI	SECTAE	SOLATIUM
PROPINQUA	REBUS	RIVUM	SECUNDOS	SOLET
PROPRIIS	RECEDO	RIVUS	SECURIBUS	SOLI
PRORUMPUNT	RECEDUNT	RIXA	SECURUS	SOLIDQUE
PROSEQUAR	RECENSENS	RIXISQUE	SEDATAS	SOLITAS
PROSEQUERETUR	RECENSET	ROGASSE	SEDEM	SOLITOSQUE
PROSEQUITUR	RECESSIBUS	ROMAE	SEDILE	SOLVARE
PROSPERA	RECIDUNT	ROREM	SEDISTI	SOLVAT
PROSUNT	RECIPIT	RORES	SEDULA	SOLVET
PROVENIAT	RECLUDERE	ROSCIDA	SEDULITAS	SOLVI
PROVOCAT	RECLUSERIT	ROSTRUM	SEGREGET	SOLVIT
PRUDENTIA	RECLUSISQUE	ROTUNDIS	SELECTAS	SOLYMAEAE
PSALMUS	RECONDIS	RUBERE	SEMESOS	SOMNE
PUELLAE	RECREABUNT	RUBESCET	SEMITA	SONANS
PUERI	RECREANT	RUBET	SEMPERQUE	SONANTIS
PUGILEM	RECREARE	RUBETA	SENES	SONAT
PUGNACES	RECTA	RUBOREM	SENESCAT	SONET
PULCHERRIMA	RECTIUS	RUBRI	SENILES	SONI
PULCHERRIMUS	RECTUM	RUBUS	SENIS	SONOS
PULCHRAM	RECUMBENS	RUDEM	SENSUS	SONTES
PULCRA	RECURSET	RUDI	SENTE	SORDES
PULICIBUS	RECUSA	RUDIS	SENTIET	SORDIDA
PULSATA	REDDIDIT	RUINAS	SENUM	SOROREM
PUPPE	REDDOR	RUINIS	SEPONENS	SORTITUR
PURGATA	REDEMIT	RUMORE	SEPULCHRO	SPARSA
PURIOR	REDIMITA	RUPE	SEPULTA	SPARTAE
PURISSIMUS	REDUCIS	RUPES	SEQUACES	SPATIA
PURPURET	REFERRI	RUPIBUS	SEQUATUR	SPATIOSA
PURUM	REFINGENS	RUS	SEQUI	SPECIES

SPECTANDUS	SUME	TESTABITUR	TUQUE	VENTORUM
SPECTANS	SUMMAE	TETIGIT	TURBAE	VENTURI
SPECULA	SUMMAM	TEXENT	TURBAT	VERA
SPECULATOR	SUPERBIT	TEXENTE	TURBIDAE	VERAM
SPECULUM	SUPERBO	THALAMO	TURBIDUS	VERBOSAE
SPELAEA	SUPERBOS	THAMESIS	TURBINE	VERIQUE
SPELUNCAE	SUPERCILIUM	THEATRALES	TURBIS	VERO
SPEM	SUPERNA	THEATRI	TURCA	VERSANTUR
SPEREM	SUPERNAE	THEATRO	TURGIDOS	VERSAVIT
SPINETAQUE	SUPERSIT	THEBARUM	TURRE	VERSES
SPIRITUM	SUPPLICII	THESAURUM	TURRITAE	VERSO
SPISSAM	SUPPLICIUM	THOMAM	TUSCUS	VERSUS
SPLENDET	SUPRA	THORACEM	TUSSIS	VERTICE
SPOKE	SUPREMA	THRALIAE	TUTAM	VERUM
SPOLIANTES	SUPREMIS	TIARAE	TUTIUS	VESTIGIA
SPONDENS	SUPREMO	TIGRI	TUTO	VESTRA
SPONSAM	SURDA	TIMEAT	ULCISCENDUM	VETABIT
SPRETA	SURDAS	TIMEBIT	ULLI	VETERNO
SPREVIT	SURGERE	TIMENTI	ULNAS	VETERUM
SQUALLET	SURGITE	TIMERE	ULTERIUS	VETITAQUE
SQUAMAS	SURGUNT	TIMET	ULTRICES	VETULI
SQUAMASQUE	SUSCIPIT	TIMIDI	UMBRACULA	VETUSTAS
STABILEM	SUSPICIAT	TIMIDUM	UMBRAE	VEXATQUE
STABILI	SYBILLAE	TIMON	UMBRAEQUE	VIAM
STABILITA	SYLVANI	TIMOR	UNAM	VIATORIS
STABO	SYLVANUS	TIMORE	UNDARUM	VICENAS
STAGNI	TACENTES	TIMOREM	UNDAS	VICENIS
STATUA	TACERE	TIMORIS	UNDECIMUM	VICTA
STATUAE	TACET	TITULIQUE	UNDIS	VICTE
STATUAEQUE	TACTU	TOLERANDA	UNO	VICTOR
STATUAM	TALE	TOLERARE	URBANI	VICTORIA
STATUANT	TANGAS	TOLLAT	URBANUM	VICTRIX
STATUASQUE	TANGET	TOLLE	URBI	VICTURUS
STATUAT	TANGITE	TOLLENTE	URBS	VIDEAS
STATUUNT	TANGITUR	TORI	URIT	VIDEBIS
STELLA	TANCUAM	TORPENTIBUS	URNA	VIDENS
STELLAS	TANTI	TORPESQUE	URSA	VIDENT
STERILES	TANTUNDEM	TORPET	USQUE	VIDERE
STERILI	TARDAE	TORREAT	UTATUR	VIDET
STERNITE	TECTAQUE	TORRENTIS	UTCUNQUE	VIDETUR
STET	TECTO	TORRENTISQUE	UTERE	VIDISTIS
STETIT	TECTUM	TORVA	UTERI	VIDIT
STOANA	TEGITUR	TORVIS	UTITUR	VIGIL
STOICORUM	TELLURI	TOTIES	UTRINQUE	VIGORE
STOLIDAE	TEMERE	TOTUM	UTROBIQUE	VILE
STOLIDAS	TEMNENS	TRACTA	UVAE	VINCERE
STOLIDUS	TEMNERE	TRACTABIT	UXOR	VINCIS
STRAVIT	TEMPELMANNI	TRACTANT	UXORE	VINCLA
STRENUA	TEMPERAT	TRAHENTI	VACARE	VINCULA
STREPENS	TEMPLA	TRAHES	VACAT	VINDAMIUS
STREPENT	TEMPLO	TRAJECIT	VACUUS	VIOLA
STREPITOSO	TEMPORIBUS	TRANQUILLA	VAFRITIES	VIOLARE
STREPUNT	TENDAT	TRANSEAT	VAGANDI	VIOLARIA
STRICTAM	TENDET	TRAXIT	VAGANTEM	VIOLENTIA
STRIDULA	TENDIS	TRECENTIS	VAGARI	VIOLIS
STRUIS	TENDIT	TREMERE	VAGOR	VIREBIT
STRUXIT	TENEBRISNE	TREMIT	VALENT	VIRENTEM
STUDIISQUE	TENEBRISQUE	TREMORE	VALEQUE	VIRENTES
STUDIOSUS	TENEBROSA	TREMULIS	VALERE	VIRENTIA
STULTUS	TENELLA	TREPIDANT	VALETE	VIRES
STUPERE	TENENTI	TREPIDIS	VALIDIS	VIRESCUNT
SUAE	TENOREM	TREPIDO	VALLES	VIRGILIO
SUASISTI	TENTAT	TREPIDUS	VANAE	VIRGINITAS
SUAVE	TENTEM	TRIBUI	VANESCENT	VIRGINITATE
SUAVIS	TENUIS	TRIPLEX	VANO	VIRI
SUAVITER	TENUIT	TRISTES	VANOS	VIRIDANTES
SUBACTI	TERCENTUM	TRISTI	VARIABILIS	VIRORUM
SUBDOLA	TERDECIMO	TRISTIOR	VARIARE	VIRTUTUM
SUBEST	TERENDOS	TRISTIS	VARIAS	VIRUMQUE
SUBIGENDA	TERET	TRISTITIAM	VARIATA	VISA
SUBIGET	TERETIS	TRISULCAE	VARIIS	VISUS
SUBIGIT	TERGA	TRITAE	VARIO	VITANDA
SUBITO	TERGET	TRIUMPHATRIX	VASCULA	VITAQUE
SUBJECTA	TERGIT	TRIUMPHOS	VASTANTES	VITATO
SUBLIMIS	TERRAE	TROJAE	VASTUM	VITE
SUBRUBET	TERRAEQUE	TUAM	VATI	VITES
SUBSIDIIS	TERRAM	TUEARE	VATUM	VITIANTES
SUBSIDITE	TERRASQUE	TUENTI	VELIS	VITIIS
SUBTILE	TERRENAS	TUERE	VELLE	VITREAS
SUCCORUM	TERRENT	TUERI	VELLENT	VITREUS
SUCCURRE	TERRES	TUGURIQUE	VENAM	VIVA
SUDAT	TERRET	TUMENTES	VENDITAT	VIVAM
SUFFLATO	TERRIBILI	TUMIDI	VENERIS	VIVES
SUFFUSUS	TERRITAT	TUMIDO	VENIAEQUE	VIVIDA
SUGIT	TERROR	TUMIDUS	VENIAMQUE	VIVIT
SULCAT	TERRORIS	TUMULATUS	VENIET	VIVITUR
SULCOS	TERTIA	TUMULAVIT	VENIUNT	VIXIT
SUM	TERTII	TUMULUS	VENTIS	VOBIS

```
VOCANT
VOCAT
VOCEM
VOCIS
VOCO
VOCUMQUE
VOLITANT
VOLITAT
VCLUCRIS
VOLUI
VCLUIT
VOLUNT
VOLUPTAS
VOLUTA
VOLVANTUR
VOLVERAT
VOLVERET
VOMERE
VOMEREM
VORANTES
VOS
VOTAQUE
VULNERE
VULTUS
WALTONI
WAREHOUSE
WHO
WITH
XERXI
ZENO
ZOSIMA
```

Concordance to Poems
of Doubtful Attribution

A   PAGE   TITLE   LINE
     10   OMITTED WORD

ACTING
    Content with thinking right, and acting well, ...   O 392 The Happy Life   14
AID
    Which demands the toilet's aid, ...   O 389 Natural Beauty   23
AIM
    Contented live, and aim not to be great; . . . . . .   O 392 The Happy Life   2
AIR
    If her easy air express . . . .   O 389 Natural Beauty   5
    Stella's eyes, and air, and face . . . .   O 389 Natural Beauty   7
ALL
    Not all their charms, tho' all unite, ...   O 388 A Song   5
    Not all their charms, tho' all unite, ...   O 388 A Song   5
    Not all the gems on India's shore, ...   O 388 A Song   7
    Not all Peru's unbounded store, ...   O 388 A Song   8
    Not all the power, nor all the fame . . . . . .   O 388 A Song   9
    Not all the power, nor all the fame . . . . . .   O 388 A Song   9
    In lovely Stella all combine, ...   O 388 A Song   17
    All the silent hours employ; . . . .   O 390 An Evening Ode   V   18
    Lovers all but Love disdain. . . . .   O 390 An Evening Ode   22
    Love possesses all the breast. . . . .   O 390 An Evening Ode   V   22
    Which not all India's treasure buys! . . . . . .   O 391 Vanity Wealth   6
    No--all that 's worth a wish, a thought, ...   O 391 Vanity Wealth   11
    Ere Youth and all its joys are fled; . . . . . .   O 391 Vanity Wealth   22
ALLURE
    Yet nature's charms allure my eyes, ...   O 388 A Song   13
ALONE
    Which alone can please by chance, ...   O 389 Natural Beauty   20
    I those charms alone can prize, ...   O 389 Natural Beauty   25
AMBITION
    And see the turrets of ambition sink; . . . . . .   O 392 The Happy Life   16
AN
     4   OMITTED WORD
AND
     32   OMITTED WORD
APPEAR
    Still her charms appear the same. . . . .   O 389 Natural Beauty   14
APPROV'D
    The soft lamented, and the brave approv'd. . . . .   O 387 On Lord Lovat   6
APPROVE
    Nor knowledge, which the learn'd approve, ...   O 388 A Song   11
    Still we love, and still approve. . . . .   O 389 Natural Beauty   18
ARE
     4   OMITTED WORD
ARMOUR
    Venus in armour Pallas chanc'd to view, ...   O 384 Englished   1
ARMS
    Naked I conquer'd you, what need of arms? . . . . .   O 384 Englished   4
AROUND
    Sheds around a lambent light; . . . .   O 390 An Evening Ode   V   14
ART
    And, lovely Stella! thou art mine. . . . .   O 388 A Song   18
    Beauty, which depends on art, ...   O 389 Natural Beauty   21
AT
     2   OMITTED WORD
AUTHORS
    Who with wise authors pass the instructive day, . . .   O 392 The Happy Life   7
AV'RICE
    With Av'rice painful vigils keep. . . . .   O 391 Vanity Wealth   2
AWAY
    And wonder how the moments stole away; . . . . .   O 392 The Happy Life   8
BALM
    Come, taste with me the balm of life, ...   O 391 Vanity Wealth   23
BALMERINO
    The brave, Balmerino, were on thy side; . . . . .   O 387 On Lord Lovat   2
BE
    In life, can Love be bought with gold? . . . . .   O 391 Vanity Wealth   9
    Are Friendship's pleasures to be sold? . . . . . .   O 391 Vanity Wealth   10
    And be, by blessing Beauty, blest. . . . .   O 391 Vanity Wealth   20
    And scorn, oh! let that scorn be thine! . . . . .   O 392 Vanity Wealth   27
    Contented live, and aim not to be great; . . . . .   O 392 The Happy Life   2
BEAM
    Silver'd o'er with Cynthia's beam. . . . .   O 390 An Evening Ode   6
BEAT
    Breasts that beat, and cheeks that glow. . . . . .   O 390 An Evening Ode   16
BEAUTY
    The Natural Beauty To Stella . . . .   O 389 Natural Beauty   T
    Beauty, which depends on art, ...   O 389 Natural Beauty   21
    And be, by blessing Beauty, blest. . . . .   O 391 Vanity Wealth   20
BEDECK
    Brilliant drops bedeck the mead, ...   O 390 An Evening Ode   3
BEHELD
    Beheld his death so decently unmov'd, ...   O 387 On Lord Lovat   5
BEHOLD
    Behold its weary cares, its noisy strife; . . . .   O 392 The Happy Life   12
BEST
    Silence, best, and conscious shades . . . . . .   O 390 An Evening Ode   19
    Silence, best, and dusky shades . . . .   O 390 An Evening Ode   V   19
BEYOND
    Who not retir'd beyond the sight of life, ...   O 392 The Happy Life   11

BIND
    Cease, then, on trash thy hopes to bind, ... O 391 Vanity Wealth   13
BLAMELESS
    And mingle blameless with their native dust. . . . . O 393 The Happy Life   20
BLESS
    And bless the lib'ral hand of bounteous Heaven; . . . O 392 The Happy Life   6
BLESSING
    And be, by blessing Beauty, blest. . . . . O 391 Vanity Wealth   20
BLEST
    And be, by blessing Beauty, blest. . . . . O 391 Vanity Wealth   20
BOAST
    I boast whate'er for man was meant. . . . . . . O 392 Vanity Wealth   25
BOSCM
    Can touch my boscm with delight. . . . . O 388 A Song   6
BCUGHT
    In life, can Love be bought with gold? . . . . . O 391 Vanity Wealth   9
BCUNTEOUS
    And bless the lib'ral hand of bounteous Heaven; . . . O 392 The Happy Life   6
BCWL
    Where Mirth and Temp'rance mix the bowl. . . . . . O 391 Vanity Wealth   18
BRAVE
    The brave, Balmerino, were on thy side; . . . . . O 387 On Lord Lovat   2
    The soft lamented, and the brave approv'd. . . . . O 387 On Lord Lovat   6
    The brave regret not, for he was not brave; . . . . O 387 On Lord Lovat   13
    The brave regret not, for he was not brave; . . . . O 387 On Lord Lovat   13
BREAST
    Love possesses all the breast. . . . . O 390 An Evening Ode V 22
    To virtuous Love resign thy breast, ... O 391 Vanity Wealth   19
BREASTS
    Breasts that beat, and cheeks that glow. . . . . . O 390 An Evening Ode   16
BREATH'D
    Still endless sighs are breath'd for more. . . . . O 391 Vanity Wealth   4
BREATHE
    Breathe out the vital flame in humble trust, . . . O 393 The Happy Life   19
BREEZES
    Cooling breezes shake the reed; . . . . O 390 An Evening Ode   4
BRILLIANT
    Brilliant drops bedeck the mead, ... O 390 An Evening Ode   3
BRINGS
    Sheds the grateful gifts she brings; . . . . O 390 An Evening Ode   2
BRINK
    Mark rashness sporting on perdition's brink, ... O 392 The Happy Life   15
BROCADE
    Pendant gems and rich brocade; . . . . O 389 Natural Beauty   10
    Pendant gems, and rich brocade! . . . . O 389 Natural Beauty   24
BROODING
    No more thus brooding o'er yon heap, ... O 391 Vanity Wealth   1
BURNING
    Phoebus drives his burning car, ... O 390 An Evening Ode   11
BUT
        5   OMITTED WORD
BUYS
    Which not all India's treasure buys! . . . . O 391 Vanity Wealth   6
BY
        6   OMITTED WORD
CALM
    Who gently taught by calm experience find . . . . . O 392 The Happy Life   9
CAN
    Can touch my bosom with delight. . . . . O 388 A Song   6
    To form one wish my soul can move. . . . . O 388 A Song   12
    Which alone can please by chance, ... O 389 Natural Beauty   20
    I those charms alone can prize, ... O 389 Natural Beauty   25
    E'er can make or more or less. . . . . O 389 Natural Beauty   28
    Can gold remove the mortal hour? . . . . O 391 Vanity Wealth   8
    In life, can Love be bought with gold? . . . . . . O 391 Vanity Wealth   9
CAR
    Phoebus drives his burning car, ... O 390 An Evening Ode   11
CARE
    Whose life not sunk in sloth is free from care, . . . O 392 The Happy Life   3
CARES
    Behold its weary cares, its noisy strife; . . . . . O 392 The Happy Life   12
CASUAL
    Vain the casual transient glance, ... O 389 Natural Beauty   19
GATCH
    O! quit the shadow, catch the prize, ... O 391 Vanity Wealth   5
ÇAUSE
    No whig compassions, for he left the cause; . . . . O 387 On Lord Lovat   12
CEASE
    Cease, then, on trash thy hopes to bind, ... O 391 Vanity Wealth   13
CELL
    And safe in virtue's philosophick cell, ... O 392 The Happy Life   13
CHANC'D
    Venus in armour Pallas chanc'd to view, ... O 384 Englished   1
CHANCE
    Which alone can please by chance, ... O 389 Natural Beauty   20
CHANGE
    Nor tost by change, nor stagnant in despair; . . . . O 392 The Happy Life   4
CHANGING
    Changing with the changing heart, ... O 389 Natural Beauty   22
    Changing with the changing heart, ... O 389 Natural Beauty   22

		PAGE	TITLE	LINE
CHARM				
	Charm with undiminish'd grace.	O 389	Natural Beauty	8
CHARMS				
	Love's queen reply'd, and smil'd a world of charms,	O 384	Englished	3
	Not all their charms, tho' all unite,	O 388	A Song	5
	Yet nature's charms allure my eyes,	O 388	A Song	13
	Nor seek I nature's charms in vain:	O 388	A Song	16
	Still her charms appear the same.	O 389	Natural Beauty	14
	I those charms alone can prize,	O 389	Natural Beauty	25
CHEARFULLY				
	Who chearfully receive each mercy given,	O 392	The Happy Life	5
CHEEKS				
	Breasts that beat, and cheeks that glow.	O 390	An Evening Ode	16
CHEQUER'D				
	Near, the chequer'd, lonely grove	O 390	An Evening Ode	7
CHILD				
	No child laments the tyrant of his son;	O 387	On Lord Lovat	10
CHINTZ				
	If her chintz, with less expence,	O 389	Natural Beauty	11
CIRCUMSTANCE				
	Which nor circumstance, nor dress	O 389	Natural Beauty	27
CLAIM				
	That heroes, kings, or poets claim,	O 388	A Song	10
CLAY				
	Mere things of clay, that dig the mine.	O 392	Vanity Wealth	28
COMBINE				
	In lovely Stella all combine,	O 388	A Song	17
COME				
	Come, taste with me the balm of life,	O 391	Vanity Wealth	23
COMPASSIONS				
	No whig compassions, for he left the cause;	O 387	On Lord Lovat	12
CONQUER'D				
	Naked I conquer'd you, what need of arms?	O 384	Englished	4
CONSCIOUS				
	Conscious worth, or soft distress,	O 389	Natural Beauty	6
	Still she lights the conscious flame,	O 389	Natural Beauty	V 13
	Silence, best, and conscious shades	O 390	An Evening Ode	19
CONSTANT				
	Still she lights the constant flame,	O 389	Natural Beauty	13
	Which from constant nature rise,	O 389	Natural Beauty	26
CONTENT				
	In health, and Stella, and content:	O 392	Vanity Wealth	26
	Content with thinking right, and acting well,	O 392	The Happy Life	14
CONTENTED				
	Contented live, and aim not to be great;	O 392	The Happy Life	2
COOLING				
	Cooling breezes shake the reed;	O 390	An Evening Ode	4
CRIMES				
	Radcliffe, unhappy in his crimes of youth,	O 387	On Lord Lovat	3
CRYSTAL				
	The murmurs of the crystal rill,	O 388	A Song	3
CURL				
	Shake the reed, and curl the stream,	O 390	An Evening Ode	5
CYNTHIA'S				
	Silver'd o'er with Cynthia's beam.	O 390	An Evening Ode	6
DAR'D				
	And dar'd her much th' old quarrel to renew;	O 384	Englished	2
DAY				
	Who with wise authors pass the instructive day,	O 392	The Happy Life	7
DE				
	To proton Moros, to de deuteron eilen Erasmos,	O 394	Epigram More	1
	To proton Moros, to de deuteron eren eilen Erasmos	Y 389	Epigram More	V 1
DEATH				
	Beheld his death so decently unmov'd,	O 387	On Lord Lovat	5
DECAY				
	In peace decay, with resignation die;	O 393	The Happy Life	18
DECENTLY				
	Beheld his death so decently unmov'd,	O 387	On Lord Lovat	5
DELIA				
	An Evening Ode to Delia	O 390	An Evening Ode	V T
DELIGHT				
	Can touch my bosom with delight.	O 388	A Song	6
DEMANDS				
	Which demands the toilet's aid,	O 389	Natural Beauty	23
DEPENDS				
	Beauty, which depends on art,	O 389	Natural Beauty	21
DESPAIR				
	Nor tost by change, nor stagnant in despair;	O 392	The Happy Life	4
DEUTERON				
	To proton Moros, to de deuteron eilen Erasmos,	O 394	Epigram More	1
	To proton Moros, to de deuteron eren eilen Erasmos	Y 389	Epigram More	V 1
DEWY				
	Lightly o'er the dewy way;	O 390	An Evening Ode	10
DIE				
	In peace decay, with resignation die;	O 393	The Happy Life	18
DIG				
	Mere things of clay, that dig the mine.	O 392	Vanity Wealth	28
DISDAIN				
	Lovers all but Love disdain.	O 390	An Evening Ode	22
DISPLAY'D				
	If on her we see display'd	O 389	Natural Beauty	9

```
                                                       PAGE    TITLE              LINE
DISSOLVE
     Of life without a pang dissolve the tie,  . . . . . . .   O 393 The Happy Life        17
DISTRESS
     Conscious worth, or soft distress, . . . . . . . .   O 389 Natural Beauty         6
DONE
     No fair forgets the ruin he has done;  . . . . . .   O 387 On Lord Lovat          9
DRESS
     Which nor circumstance, nor dress  . . . . . . . .   O 389 Natural Beauty        27
DRIVES
     Phoebus drives his burning car,  . . . . . . . . .   O 390 An Evening Ode        11
DROPS
     Brilliant drops bedeck the mead,  . . . . . . . .    O 390 An Evening Ode         3
DUSKY
     Silence, best, and dusky shades . . . . . . . .      O 390 An Evening Ode     V  19
DUST
     And mingle blameless with their native dust.  . . . .   O 393 The Happy Life        20
DY'D
     Pity'd by gentle minds Kilmarnock dy'd;  . . . . .   O 387 On Lord Lovat          1
E'ER
     E'er can make or more or less.  . . . . . . . .      O 389 Natural Beauty        28
EACH
     Who chearfully receive each mercy given,  . . . . .   O 392 The Happy Life         5
EARTH
     Fix'd on earth, or glancing round,  . . . . . . .    O 389 Natural Beauty         2
EASY
     If her easy air express  . . . . . . . . .          O 389 Natural Beauty         5
     Flows in easy negligence,  . . . . . . . . .        O 389 Natural Beauty        12
ECHEI
     To triton ek Mouson stemma Mikyllos echei.  . . . . . .   O 394 Epigram More         2
EILEN
     To proton Moros, to de deuteron eilen Erasmos, . . . .   O 394 Epigram More         1
     To proton Moros, to de deuteron eren eilen Erasmos  . .   Y 389 Epigram More     V  1
EK
     To triton ek Mouson stemma Mikyllos echei.  . . . . .    O 394 Epigram More         2
EMPLOY
     Ev'ning's silent hours employ;  . . . . . . . .      O 390 An Evening Ode        18
     All the silent hours employ;  . . . . . . . . .      O 390 An Evening Ode     V  18
END
     But Lovat's end indiff'rently we view,  . . . . . .   O 387 On Lord Lovat          7
ENDLESS
     Still endless sighs are breath'd for more.  . . . . .   O 391 Vanity Wealth          4
ENGAGE
     Let nobler views engage thy mind. . . . . . . .      O 391 Vanity Wealth         14
ENGLISHED
     Englished  . . . . . . . . . . . .                  O 384 Englished           D  T
EQUAL
     No riches equal to a well form'd mind;  . . . . . .   O 392 The Happy Life        10
ERASMOS
     To proton Moros, to de deuteron eilen Erasmos, . . . .   O 394 Epigram More         1
     To proton Moros, to de deuteron eren eilen Erasmos  . .   Y 389 Epigram More     V  1
ERE
     Ere Youth and all its joys are fled;  . . . . . .    O 391 Vanity Wealth         22
EREN
     To proton Moros, to de deuteron eren eilen Erasmos  . .   Y 389 Epigram More     V  1
EV'NING
     Ev'ning now, from purple wings,  . . . . . . . .     O 390 An Evening Ode         1
EV'NING'S
     Ev'ning's silent hours employ;  . . . . . . . .      O 390 An Evening Ode        18
EVENING
     An Evening Ode To Stella  . . . . . . . . .          O 390 An Evening Ode         T
     An Evening Ode to Delia  . . . . . . . . .           O 390 An Evening Ode     V  T
EXECUTION
     On Lord Lovat's Execution  . . . . . . . . .         O 387 On Lord Lovat          T
EXPENCE
     If her chintz, with less expence,  . . . . . . . .   O 389 Natural Beauty        11
EXPERIENCE
     Who gently taught by calm experience find  . . . . .   O 392 The Happy Life         9
EXPRESS
     If her easy air express  . . . . . . . . . .        O 389 Natural Beauty         5
EYES
     Yet nature's charms allure my eyes,  . . . . . .     O 388 A Song               13
     Whether Stella's eyes are found  . . . . . . . .     O 389 Natural Beauty         1
     Stella's eyes, and air, and face  . . . . . . .      O 389 Natural Beauty         7
FACE
     If her face with pleasure glow,  . . . . . . . .     O 389 Natural Beauty         3
     Stella's eyes, and air, and face  . . . . . . .      O 389 Natural Beauty         7
FAIR
     No fair forgets the ruin he has done;  . . . . . .   O 387 On Lord Lovat          9
     Fair Virtue gives, unbrib'd, unbought.  . . . . .    O 391 Vanity Wealth         12
FAME
     Not all the power, nor all the fame  . . . . . .     O 388 A Song                9
     And knowledge, wealth and fame I prize;  . . . . .   O 388 A Song               14
     Fame, wealth and knowledge I obtain,  . . . . . .    O 388 A Song               15
FAR
     Hence, my lovely Stella, far;  . . . . . . . .       O 390 An Evening Ode        12
FATE
     ----But Lovat's fate indiff'rently we view,  . . . .   O 387 On Lord Lovat      V  7
FEAST
     Thus taste the feast by Nature spread,  . . . . .    O 391 Vanity Wealth         21
FIND
     Who gently taught by calm experience find  . . . . .   O 392 The Happy Life         9
```

```
                                                    PAGE    TITLE           LINE
FIX'D
    Fix'd on earth, or glancing round,  . . . . . . .   O 389 Natural Beauty     2
FLAME
    Still she lights the constant flame,  . . . . . .   O 389 Natural Beauty    13
    Still she lights the conscious flame,  . . . . .    O 389 Natural Beauty  V 13
    Breathe out the vital flame in humble trust,  . . . O 393 The Happy Life    19
FLED
    Ere Youth and all its joys are fled;  . . . . . .   O 391 Vanity Wealth     22
FLOW'RY
    The fragrance of the flow'ry vales,  . . . . . . .  O 388 A Song             2
FLOWS
    Flows in easy negligence,  . . . . . . . . . .      O 389 Natural Beauty    12
FCR
         5                                              OMITTED WORD
FORGETS
    No fair forgets the ruin he has done;  . . . . . .  O 387 On Lord Lovat      9
FORM
    To form one wish my soul can move.  . . . . . . .   O 388 A Song            12
FORM'D
    No riches equal to a well form'd mind;  . . . . .   O 392 The Happy Life    10
FCUND
    Whether Stella's eyes are found  . . . . . . . .    O 389 Natural Beauty     1
FRAGRANCE
    The fragrance of the flow'ry vales,  . . . . . .    O 388 A Song             2
FREE
    Whose life not sunk in sloth is free from care,  . . O 392 The Happy Life    3
FRIEND
    The Vanity of Wealth An Ode To a Friend  . . . . .  O 391 Vanity Wealth      T
FRIENDSHIP'S
    Are Friendship's pleasures to be sold?  . . . . .   O 391 Vanity Wealth     10
FROM
         4                                              OMITTED WORD
GALES
    Not the soft sighs of vernal gales,  . . . . . . .  O 388 A Song             1
GEMS
    Not all the gems on India's shore,  . . . . . . .   O 388 A Song             7
    Pendant gems and rich brocade;  . . . . . . . .     O 389 Natural Beauty    10
    Pendant gems, and rich brocade!  . . . . . . . .    O 389 Natural Beauty    24
GENTLE
    Pity'd by gentle minds Kilmarnock dy'd;  . . . . .  O 387 On Lord Lovat      1
GENTLY
    Who gently taught by calm experience find  . . . .  O 392 The Happy Life     9
GIFTS
    Sheds the grateful gifts she brings;  . . . . . .   O 390 An Evening Ode     2
GIVE
    Other pleasures give them pain,  . . . . . . . .    O 390 An Evening Ode    21
GIVEN
    Who chearfully receive each mercy given,  . . . .   O 392 The Happy Life     5
GIVES
    Fair Virtue gives, unbrib'd, unbought.  . . . . .   O 391 Vanity Wealth     12
GLANCE
    Vain the casual transient glance,  . . . . . . .    O 389 Natural Beauty    19
GLANCING
    Fix'd on earth, or glancing round,  . . . . . . .   O 389 Natural Beauty     2
GLOW
    If her face with pleasure glow,  . . . . . . . .    O 389 Natural Beauty     3
    Breasts that beat, and cheeks that glow.  . . . .   O 390 An Evening Ode    16
GOLD
    To purchase heav'n, has gold the pow'r?  . . . .    O 391 Vanity Wealth      7
    Can gold remove the mortal hour?  . . . . . . .     O 391 Vanity Wealth      8
    In life, can Love be bought with gold?  . . . . .   O 391 Vanity Wealth      9
GRACE
    Charm with undiminish'd grace.  . . . . . . . .     O 389 Natural Beauty     8
GRATEFUL
    Sheds the grateful gifts she brings;  . . . . . .   O 390 An Evening Ode     2
GREAT
    Contented live, and aim not to be great;  . . . .   O 392 The Happy Life     2
GROVE
    The vocal grove, the verdant hill;  . . . . . . .   O 388 A Song             4
    Near, the chequer'd, lonely grove  . . . . . . .    O 390 An Evening Ode     7
HAND
    And bless the lib'ral hand of bounteous Heaven;  . . O 392 The Happy Life    6
HAPPY
    The Happy Life  . . . . . . . . . . . . .           O 392 The Happy Life     T
    Thrice happy they, who in an humble state  . . . .  O 392 The Happy Life     1
HAS
    No fair forgets the ruin he has done;  . . . . . .  O 387 On Lord Lovat      9
    To purchase heav'n, has gold the pow'r?  . . . .    O 391 Vanity Wealth      7
HE
         5                                              OMITTED WORD
HEALTH
    In health, and Stella, and content:  . . . . . .    O 392 Vanity Wealth     26
HEAP
    No more thus brooding o'er yon heap,  . . . . . .   O 391 Vanity Wealth      1
HEARS
    Hears, and keeps thy secrets, Love.--  . . . . .    O 390 An Evening Ode     8
HEART
    Changing with the changing heart,  . . . . . . .    O 389 Natural Beauty    22
HEARTS
    Please the hearts that Love invades;  . . . . . .   O 390 An Evening Ode    20
```

		PAGE	TITLE	LINE
HEAV'N				
	To purchase heav'n, has gold the pow'r?	O 391	Vanity Wealth	7
HEAVEN				
	And bless the lib'ral hand of bounteous Heaven; . . .	O 392	The Happy Life	6
HENCE				
	Hence, my lovely Stella, far;	O 390	An Evening Ode	12
HER				
	6		OMITTED WORD	
HEROES				
	That heroes, kings, or poets claim, ...	O 388	A Song	10
HILL				
	The vocal grove, the verdant hill;	O 388	A Song	4
HIM				
	1		OMITTED WORD	
HIS				
	5		OMITTED WORD	
HONEST				
	The honest mourn not, knowing him a knave.	O 387	On Lord Lovat	14
HOPES				
	Cease, then, on trash thy hopes to bind, ...	O 391	Vanity Wealth	13
HOUR				
	Can gold remove the mortal hour?	O 391	Vanity Wealth	8
HOURS				
	Ev'ning's silent hours employ;	O 390	An Evening Ode	18
	All the silent hours employ;	O 390	An Evening Ode	V 18
	In social hours indulge thy soul, ...	O 391	Vanity Wealth	17
HOW				
	And wonder how the moments stole away;	O 392	The Happy Life	8
HUMBLE				
	Thrice happy they, who in an humble state	O 392	The Happy Life	1
	Breathe out the vital flame in humble trust, ...	O 393	The Happy Life	19
I				
	Naked I conquer'd you, what need of arms?	O 384	Englished	4
	And knowledge, wealth and fame I prize;	O 388	A Song	14
	Fame, wealth and knowledge I obtain, ...	O 388	A Song	15
	Nor seek I nature's charms in vain:	O 388	A Song	16
	I those charms alone can prize, ...	O 389	Natural Beauty	25
	I boast whate'er for man was meant.	O 392	Vanity Wealth	25
IF				
	If her face with pleasure glow, ...	O 389	Natural Beauty	3
	If she sigh at others woe, ...	O 389	Natural Beauty	4
	If her easy air express	O 389	Natural Beauty	5
	If on her we see display'd	O 389	Natural Beauty	9
	If her chintz, with less expence, ...	O 389	Natural Beauty	11
	If she strikes the vocal strings, ...	O 389	Natural Beauty	15
	If she 's silent, speaks, or sings, ...	O 389	Natural Beauty	16
	If she sit, or if she move, ...	O 389	Natural Beauty	17
	If she sit, or if she move, ...	O 389	Natural Beauty	17
IN				
	18		OMITTED WORD	
INDIA'S				
	Not all the gems on India's shore, ...	O 388	A Song	7
	Which not all India's treasure buys!	O 391	Vanity Wealth	6
INDIFF'RENTLY				
	But Lovat's end indiff'rently we view, ...	O 387	On Lord Lovat	7
	----But Lovat's fate indiff'rently we view, ...	O 387	On Lord Lovat	V 7
INDULGE				
	In social hours indulge thy soul, ...	O 391	Vanity Wealth	17
INSTRUCTIVE				
	Who with wise authors pass the instructive day, . . .	O 392	The Happy Life	7
INVADES				
	Please the hearts that Love invades;	O 390	An Evening Ode	20
'S				
	If she 's silent, speaks, or sings, ...	O 389	Natural Beauty	16
	No--all that 's worth a wish, a thought, ...	O 391	Vanity Wealth	11
IS				
	1		OMITTED WORD	
ITS				
	Ere Youth and all its joys are fled;	O 391	Vanity Wealth	22
	Behold its weary cares, its noisy strife;	O 392	The Happy Life	12
	Behold its weary cares, its noisy strife;	O 392	The Happy Life	12
JOY				
	Let us now, in whisper'd joy, ...	O 390	An Evening Ode	17
	Let us there, in whisper'd joy, ...	O 390	An Evening Ode	V 17
JOYS				
	Ere Youth and all its joys are fled;	O 391	Vanity Wealth	22
JUST				
	Light that serves but just to show	O 390	An Evening Ode	15
	Light that seems but just to show	O 390	An Evening Ode	V 15
KEEP				
	With Av'rice painful vigils keep.	O 391	Vanity Wealth	2
KEEPS				
	Hears, and keeps thy secrets, Love.--	O 390	An Evening Ode	8
KILMARNOCK				
	Pity'd by gentle minds Kilmarnock dy'd;	O 387	On Lord Lovat	1
KING				
	True to no king, to no religion true:	O 387	On Lord Lovat	8
KINGS				
	That heroes, kings, or poets claim, ...	O 388	A Song	10
KNAVE				
	The honest mourn not, knowing him a knave.	O 387	On Lord Lovat	14

		PAGE	TITLE	LINE
KNOWING				
The honest mourn not, knowing him a knave.		O 387	On Lord Lovat	14
KNOWLEDGE				
Nor knowledge, which the learn'd approve, ...		O 388	A Song	11
And knowledge, wealth and fame I prize;		O 388	A Song	14
Fame, wealth and knowledge I obtain, ...		O 388	A Song	15
LAMBENT				
Round us pours a lambent light;		O 390	An Evening Ode	14
Sheds around a lambent light;		O 390	An Evening Ode V	14
LAMENTED				
The soft lamented, and the brave approv'd.		O 387	On Lord Lovat	6
LAMENTS				
No child laments the tyrant of his son;		O 387	On Lord Lovat	10
LAY				
Or learn the Muse's moral lay;		O 391	Vanity Wealth	16
LEARN				
Or learn the Muse's moral lay;		O 391	Vanity Wealth	16
LEARN'D				
Nor knowledge, which the learn'd approve, ...		O 388	A Song	11
LEFT				
No whig compassions, for he left the cause;		O 387	On Lord Lovat	12
LESS				
If her chintz, with less expence, ...		O 389	Natural Beauty	11
E'er can make or more or less.		O 389	Natural Beauty	28
LET				
Stella! thither let us stray, ...		O 390	An Evening Ode	9
Let us now, in whisper'd joy, ...		O 390	An Evening Ode	17
Let us there, in whisper'd joy, ...		O 390	An Evening Ode V	17
Let nobler views engage thy mind.		O 391	Vanity Wealth	14
And scorn, oh! let that scorn be thine!		O 392	Vanity Wealth	27
LIB'RAL				
And bless the lib'ral hand of bounteous Heaven; . . .		O 392	The Happy Life	6
LIFE				
In life, can Love be bought with gold?		O 391	Vanity Wealth	9
Come, taste with me the balm of life, ...		O 391	Vanity Wealth	23
The Happy Life		O 392	The Happy Life	T
Whose life not sunk in sloth is free from care, . . .		O 392	The Happy Life	3
Who not retir'd beyond the sight of life, ...		O 392	The Happy Life	11
Of life without a pang dissolve the tie, ...		O 393	The Happy Life	17
LIGHT				
Round us pours a lambent light;		O 390	An Evening Ode	14
Sheds around a lambent light;		O 390	An Evening Ode V	14
Light that serves but just to show		O 390	An Evening Ode	15
Light that seems but just to show		O 390	An Evening Ode V	15
LIGHTLY				
Lightly o'er the dewy way;		O 390	An Evening Ode	10
LIGHTS				
Still she lights the constant flame, ...		O 389	Natural Beauty	13
Still she lights the conscious flame, ...		O 389	Natural Beauty V	13
LIVE				
Contented live, and aim not to be great;		O 392	The Happy Life	2
LONELY				
Near, the chequer'd, lonely grove		O 390	An Evening Ode	7
LORD				
On Lord Lovat's Execution		O 387	On Lord Lovat	T
LOVAT'S				
On Lord Lovat's Execution		O 387	On Lord Lovat	T
But Lovat's end indiff'rently we view, ...		O 387	On Lord Lovat	7
----But Lovat's fate indiff'rently we view, ...		O 387	On Lord Lovat V	7
LOVE				
Still we love, and still approve.		O 389	Natural Beauty	18
Hears, and keeps thy secrets, Love.--		O 390	An Evening Ode	8
Please the hearts that Love invades;		O 390	An Evening Ode	20
Lovers all but Love disdain.		O 390	An Evening Ode	22
Love possesses all the breast.		O 390	An Evening Ode V	22
In life, can Love be bought with gold?		O 391	Vanity Wealth	9
To virtuous Love resign thy breast, ...		O 391	Vanity Wealth	19
LOVE'S				
Love's queen reply'd, and smil'd a world of charms, . .		O 384	Englished	3
LOVELY				
In lovely Stella all combine, ...		O 388	A Song	17
And, lovely Stella! thou art mine.		O 388	A Song	18
Hence, my lovely Stella, far;		O 390	An Evening Ode	12
LOVERS				
Lovers all but Love disdain.		O 390	An Evening Ode	22
MAKE				
E'er can make or more or less.		O 389	Natural Beauty	28
MAN				
I boast whate'er for man was meant.		O 392	Vanity Wealth	25
MARK				
Mark rashness sporting on perdition's brink, ...		O 392	The Happy Life	15
ME				
Come, taste with me the balm of life, ...		O 391	Vanity Wealth	23
MEAD				
Brilliant drops bedeck the mead, ...		O 390	An Evening Ode	3
MEANT				
I boast whate'er for man was meant.		O 392	Vanity Wealth	25
MERCY				
Who chearfully receive each mercy given, ...		O 392	The Happy Life	5
MERE				
Mere things of clay, that dig the mine.		O 392	Vanity Wealth	28

MIKYLLOS

		PAGE	TITLE	LINE
To triton ek Mouson stemma Mikyllos echei.	. . . . .	O 394	Epigram More	2

MIND

| Let nobler views engage thy mind. . . | . . . . . . | O 391 | Vanity Wealth | 14 |
| No riches equal to a well form'd mind; | . . . . . . | O 392 | The Happy Life | 10 |

MINDS

| Pity'd by gentle minds Kilmarnock dy'd; | . . . . . . | O 387 | On Lord Lovat | 1 |

MINE

| And, lovely Stella! thou art mine. . . | . . . . . | O 388 | A Song | 18 |
| Mere things of clay, that dig the mine. | . . . . . | O 392 | Vanity Wealth | 28 |

MINGLE

| And mingle blameless with their native dust. | . . . . | O 393 | The Happy Life | 20 |

MIRTH

| Where Mirth and Temp'rance mix the bowl. | . . . . . . | O 391 | Vanity Wealth | 18 |

MISTOOK

| Steady in what he still mistook for truth, | . . . . . | O 387 | On Lord Lovat | 4 |

MIX

| Where Mirth and Temp'rance mix the bowl. | . . . . . . | O 391 | Vanity Wealth | 18 |

MOMENTS

| And wonder how the moments stole away; | . . . . . . | O 392 | The Happy Life | 8 |

MORAL

| Or learn the Muse's moral lay; | . . . . | O 391 | Vanity Wealth | 16 |

MORE

E'er can make or more or less.	. . . . . .	O 389	Natural Beauty	28
No more thus brooding o'er yon heap,	. . . . . .	O 391	Vanity Wealth	1
Still endless sighs are breath'd for more.	. . . . .	O 391	Vanity Wealth	4

MOROS

| To proton Moros, to de deuteron eilen Erasmós, | . . . . | O 394 | Epigram More | 1 |
| To proton Moros, to de deuteron eren eilen Erasmos | . . | Y 389 | Epigram More | V 1 |

MORTAL

| Can gold remove the mortal hour? | . . . . | O 391 | Vanity Wealth | 8 |

MOURN

| The honest mourn not, knowing him a knave. | . . . . . . | O 387 | On Lord Lovat | 14 |

MOUSON

| To triton ek Mouson stemma Mikyllos echei. | . . . . . | O 394 | Epigram More | 2 |

MOVE

| To form one wish my soul can move. | . . . . | O 388 | A Song | 12 |
| If she sit, or if she move, | . . . . | O 389 | Natural Beauty | 17 |

MUCH

| And dar'd her much th' old quarrel to renew; | . . . . | O 384 | Englished | 2 |

MURMURS

| The murmurs of the crystal rill, | . . . . | O 388 | A Song | 3 |

MUSE'S

| Or learn the Muse's moral lay; | . . . . | O 391 | Vanity Wealth | 16 |

MY

Can touch my bosom with delight.	. . . .	O 388	A Song	6
To form one wish my soul can move.	. . . .	O 388	A Song	12
Yet nature's charms allure my eyes,	. . . . . .	O 388	A Song	13
Hence, my lovely Stella, far;	. . . .	O 390	An Evening Ode	12

NAKED

| Naked I conquer'd you, what need of arms? | . . . . . | O 384 | Englished | 4 |

NATIVE

| And mingle blameless with their native dust. | . . . . | O 393 | The Happy Life | 20 |

NATURAL

| The Natural Beauty To Stella . . . . | O 389 | Natural Beauty | T |

NATURE

| Which from constant nature rise, | . . . . . . | O 389 | Natural Beauty | 26 |
| Thus taste the feast by Nature spread, | . . . . . . | O 391 | Vanity Wealth | 21 |

NATURE'S

| Yet nature's charms allure my eyes, | . . . . . . | O 388 | A Song | 13 |
| Nor seek I nature's charms in vain: | . . . . . . | O 388 | A Song | 16 |

NEAR

| Near, the chequer'd, lonely grove | . . . . | O 390 | An Evening Ode | 7 |

NEED

| Naked I conquer'd you, what need of arms? | . . . . . | O 384 | Englished | 4 |

NEGLIGENCE

| Flows in easy negligence, ... | O 389 | Natural Beauty | 12 |

NIGHT

| In his stead, the Queen of Night | . . . . | O 390 | An Evening Ode | 13 |

NO

9

NOBLER   OMITTED WORD

| Let nobler views engage thy mind. | . . . . | O 391 | Vanity Wealth | 14 |

NOISY

| Behold its weary cares, its noisy strife; | . . . . . | O 392 | The Happy Life | 12 |

NOR

Not all the power, nor all the fame	. . . . .	O 388	A Song	9
Nor knowledge, which the learn'd approve,	. . . . .	O 388	A Song	11
Nor seek I nature's charms in vain:	. . . . .	O 388	A Song	16
Which nor circumstance, nor dress	. . . . . .	O 389	Natural Beauty	27
Which nor circumstance, nor dress	. . . . . .	O 389	Natural Beauty	27
Nor tost by change, nor stagnant in despair;	. . . .	O 392	The Happy Life	4
Nor tost by change, nor stagnant in despair;	. . . .	O 392	The Happy Life	4

NOT

12

NOW   OMITTED WORD

2

O   OMITTED WORD

| O! quit the shadow, catch the prize, | . . . . | O 391 | Vanity Wealth | 5 |

O'ER

| Silver'd o'er with Cynthia's beam. | . . . . | O 390 | An Evening Ode | 6 |

```
O'ER            (CONTINUED)                        PAGE    TITLE              LINE
    Lightly o'er the dewy way;  . . . . . . . . .   O 390  An Evening Ode       10
    No more thus brooding o'er yon heap,  . . . . . O 391  Vanity Wealth         1
OBTAIN
    Fame, wealth and knowledge I obtain,  . . . . . O 388  A Song               15
ODE
    An Evening Ode To Stella  . . . . . . . . . .   O 390  An Evening Ode        T
    An Evening Ode to Delia   . . . . . . . . . .   O 390  An Evening Ode    V   T
    The Vanity of Wealth An Ode To a Friend  . . .  O 391  Vanity Wealth         T
OF
            15                                              OMITTED WORD
OH
    And scorn, oh! let that scorn be thine!  . . . .  O 392  Vanity Wealth      27
OLD
    And dar'd her much th' old quarrel to renew;  . . . .  O 384  Englished       2
CN
            8                                               OMITTED WORD
ONE
    To form one wish my soul can move.  . . . . . . .  O 388  A Song            12
OR
            8                                               OMITTED WORD
OTHER
    Other pleasures give them pain,  . . . . . . . .  O 390  An Evening Ode     21
    Other passions then at rest,  . . . . . . . . .   O 390  An Evening Ode  V  21
OTHERS
    If she sigh at others woe,  . . . . . . . . . .   O 389  Natural Beauty      4
OUT
    Breathe out the vital flame in humble trust,  . . . .  O 393  The Happy Life  19
PAIN
    Other pleasures give them pain,  . . . . . . . .  O 390  An Evening Ode     21
PAINFUL
    With Av'rice painful vigils keep.  . . . . . . .  O 391  Vanity Wealth       2
PALLAS
    Venus in armour Pallas chanc'd to view,  . . . .  O 384  Englished           1
PANG
    Of life without a pang dissolve the tie,  . . . . . O 393  The Happy Life   17
PASS
    Who with wise authors pass the instructive day,  . . .  O 392  The Happy Life  7
PASSIONS
    Other passions then at rest,  . . . . . . . . .   O 390  An Evening Ode  V  21
PEACE
    In peace decay, with resignation die;  . . . . . .  O 393  The Happy Life   18
PENDANT
    Pendant gems and rich brocade;  . . . . . . . .   O 389  Natural Beauty     10
    Pendant gems, and rich brocade!  . . . . . . . .  O 389  Natural Beauty     24
PERDITION'S
    Mark rashness sporting on perdition's brink,  . . .  O 392  The Happy Life   15
PERU'S
    Not all Peru's unbounded store,  . . . . . . . .  O 388  A Song              8
PHILOSOPHICK
    And safe in virtue's philosophick cell,  . . . . .  O 392  The Happy Life   13
PHOEBUS
    Phoebus drives his burning car,  . . . . . . . .  O 390  An Evening Ode     11
PITIES
    No tory pities, thinking what he was;  . . . . . .  O 387  On Lord Lovat    11
PITY'D
    Pity'd by gentle minds Kilmarnock dy'd;  . . . . .  O 387  On Lord Lovat     1
PLEASE
    Which alone can please by chance,  . . . . . . .  O 389  Natural Beauty     20
    Please the hearts that Love invades;  . . . . . .  O 390  An Evening Ode     20
PLEASURE
    If her face with pleasure glow,  . . . . . . . .  O 389  Natural Beauty      3
PLEASURES
    Other pleasures give them pain,  . . . . . . . .  O 390  An Evening Ode     21
    Are Friendship's pleasures to be sold?  . . . . .  O 391  Vanity Wealth     10
POETS
    That heroes, kings, or poets claim,  . . . . . .  O 388  A Song             10
POMP
    Secure from pomp, and wealth, and strife.  . . . .  O 391  Vanity Wealth    24
POSSESSES
    Love possesses all the breast.  . . . . . . . .   O 390  An Evening Ode  V  22
POURS
    Round us pours a lambent light;  . . . . . . . .  O 390  An Evening Ode     14
POW'R
    To purchase heav'n, has gold the pow'r?  . . . . .  O 391  Vanity Wealth     7
POWER
    Not all the power, nor all the fame  . . . . . .  O 388  A Song              9
PRESENT
    Still unenjoy'd the present store,  . . . . . . .  O 391  Vanity Wealth       3
PRIZE
    And knowledge, wealth and fame I prize;  . . . . .  O 388  A Song           14
    I those charms alone can prize,  . . . . . . . .  O 389  Natural Beauty     25
    O! quit the shadow, catch the prize,  . . . . . .  O 391  Vanity Wealth      5
PROTON
    To proton Moros, to de deuteron eilen Erasmos,  . . . .  O 394  Epigram More  1
    To proton Moros, to de deuteron eren eilen Erasmos  . .  Y 389  Epigram More  V  1
PURCHASE
    To purchase heav'n, has gold the pow'r?  . . . . .  O 391  Vanity Wealth     7
PURPLE
    Ev'ning now, from purple wings,  . . . . . . . .  O 390  An Evening Ode      1
```

```
                                                                        PAGE   TITLE             LINE
QUARREL
      And dar'd her much th' old quarrel to renew;     . . . .     O 384 Englished               2
QUEEN
      Love's queen reply'd, and smil'd a world of charms,    . .   O 384 Englished               3
      In his stead, the Queen of Night      . . . . . . . . .      O 390 An Evening Ode          13
QUIT
      O! quit the shadow, catch the prize,    . . . . . . . .      O 391 Vanity Wealth           5
RADCLIFFE
      Radcliffe, unhappy in his crimes of youth,    . . . . .      O 387 On Lord Lovat           3
RASHNESS
      Mark rashness sporting on perdition's brink,    . . . .      O 392 The Happy Life          15
RECEIVE
      Who chearfully receive each mercy given,  . . . . . .        O 392 The Happy Life          5
REED
      Cooling breezes shake the reed;  . . . . . . . . . .         O 390 An Evening Ode          4
      Shake the reed, and curl the stream,    . . . . . . .        O 390 An Evening Ode          5
REGRET
      The brave regret not, for he was not brave;  . . . . .       O 387 On Lord Lovat           13
RELIGION
      True to no king, to no religion true:  . . . . . . .         O 387 On Lord Lovat           8
REMOVE
      Can gold remove the mortal hour?    . . . . . . . .          O 391 Vanity Wealth           8
RENEW
      And dar'd her much th' old quarrel to renew;    . . . .      O 384 Englished               2
REPLY'D
      Love's queen reply'd, and smil'd a world of charms,    . .   O 384 Englished               3
RESIGN
      To virtuous Love resign thy breast,     . . . . . . .        O 391 Vanity Wealth           19
RESIGNATION
      In peace decay, with resignation die;  . . . . . . .         O 393 The Happy Life          18
REST
      Other passions then at rest,  . . . . . . . . . .           O 390 An Evening Ode        V  21
RETIR'D
      Who not retir'd beyond the sight of life,   . . . . .        O 392 The Happy Life          11
RICH
      Pendant gems and rich brocade;  . . . . . . . . .           O 389 Natural Beauty          10
      Pendant gems, and rich brocade!  . . . . . . . .            O 389 Natural Beauty          24
RICHES
      No riches equal to a well form'd mind;   . . . . . .         O 392 The Happy Life          10
RIGHT
      Content with thinking right, and acting well,   . . . .      O 392 The Happy Life          14
RILL
      The murmurs of the crystal rill,    . . . . . . . .          O 388 A Song                  3
RISE
      Which from constant nature rise,    . . . . . . . .          O 389 Natural Beauty          26
ROUND
      Fix'd on earth, or glancing round,  . . . . . . . .          O 389 Natural Beauty          2
      Round us pours a lambent light;  . . . . . . . . .           O 390 An Evening Ode          14
RUIN
      No fair forgets the ruin he has done;  . . . . . . .         O 387 On Lord Lovat           9
SAFE
      And safe in virtue's philosophick cell,    . . . . . .       O 392 The Happy Life          13
SAME
      Still her charms appear the same.   . . . . . . . .          O 389 Natural Beauty          14
SCIENCE
      With Science tread the wond'rous way,   . . . . . . .        O 391 Vanity Wealth           15
SCORN
      And scorn, oh! let that scorn be thine!    . . . . . .       O 392 Vanity Wealth           27
      And scorn, oh! let that scorn be thine!    . . . . . .       O 392 Vanity Wealth           27
SECRETS
      Hears, and keeps thy secrets, Love.--    . . . . . .         O 390 An Evening Ode          8
SECURE
      Secure from pomp, and wealth, and strife.   . . . . .        O 391 Vanity Wealth           24
SEE
      If on her we see display'd    . . . . . . . . . .            O 389 Natural Beauty          9
      And see the turrets of ambition sink;  . . . . . . .         O 392 The Happy Life          16
SEEK
      Nor seek I nature's charms in vain:    . . . . . . .         O 388 A Song                  16
SEEMS
      Light that seems but just to show    . . . . . . . .         O 390 An Evening Ode       V  15
SERVES
      Light that serves but just to show   . . . . . . . .         O 390 An Evening Ode          15
SHADES
      Silence, best, and conscious shades    . . . . . . .         O 390 An Evening Ode          19
      Silence, best, and dusky shades  . . . . . . . .            O 390 An Evening Ode       V  19
SHADOW
      O! quit the shadow, catch the prize,    . . . . . . .        O 391 Vanity Wealth           5
SHAKE
      Cooling breezes shake the reed;  . . . . . . . . .           O 390 An Evening Ode          4
      Shake the reed, and curl the stream,    . . . . . .          O 390 An Evening Ode          5
SHE
      If she sigh at others woe,    . . . . . . . . . .            O 389 Natural Beauty          4
      Still she lights the constant flame,    . . . . . . .        O 389 Natural Beauty          13
      Still she lights the conscious flame,   . . . . . . .        O 389 Natural Beauty       V  13
      If she strikes the vocal strings,   . . . . . . . .          O 389 Natural Beauty          15
      If she 's silent, speaks, or sings,    . . . . . . .         O 389 Natural Beauty          16
      If she sit, or if she move,   . . . . . . . . .             O 389 Natural Beauty          17
      If she sit, or if she move,   . . . . . . . . .             O 389 Natural Beauty          17
      Sheds the grateful gifts she brings;   . . . . . . .         O 390 An Evening Ode          2
SHEDS
      Sheds the grateful gifts she brings;   . . . . . . .         O 390 An Evening Ode          2
```

		PAGE	TITLE	LINE
SHEDS	(CONTINUED)			
	Sheds around a lambent light;	O 390	An Evening Ode	V 14
SHORE				
	Not all the gems on India's shore, ...	O 388	A Song	7
SHOW				
	Light that serves but just to show	O 390	An Evening Ode	15
	Light that seems but just to show	O 390	An Evening Ode	V 15
SIDE				
	The brave, Balmerino, were on thy side;	O 387	On Lord Lovat	2
SIGH				
	If she sigh at others woe, ...	O 389	Natural Beauty	4
SIGHS				
	Not the soft sighs of vernal gales, ...	O 388	A Song	1
	Still endless sighs are breath'd for more.	O 391	Vanity Wealth	4
SIGHT				
	Who not retir'd beyond the sight of life, ...	O 392	The Happy Life	11
SILENCE				
	Silence, best, and conscious shades	O 390	An Evening Ode	19
	Silence, best, and dusky shades	O 390	An Evening Ode	V 19
SILENT				
	If she 's silent, speaks, or sings, ...	O 389	Natural Beauty	16
	Ev'ning's silent hours employ;	O 390	An Evening Ode	18
	All the silent hours employ;	O 390	An Evening Ode	V 18
SILVER'D				
	Silver'd o'er with Cynthia's beam.	O 390	An Evening Ode	6
SINGS				
	If she 's silent, speaks, or sings, ...	O 389	Natural Beauty	16
SINK				
	And see the turrets of ambition sink;	O 392	The Happy Life	16
SIT				
	If she sit, or if she move, ...	O 389	Natural Beauty	17
SLOTH				
	Whose life not sunk in sloth is free from care, . . .	O 392	The Happy Life	3
SMIL'D				
	Love's queen reply'd, and smil'd a world of charms, . .	O 384	Englished	3
SO				
	Beheld his death so decently unmov'd, ...	O 387	On Lord Lovat	5
SOCIAL				
	In social hours indulge thy soul, ...	O 391	Vanity Wealth	17
SOFT				
	The soft lamented, and the brave approv'd.	O 387	On Lord Lovat	6
	Not the soft sighs of vernal gales, ...	O 388	A Song	1
	Conscious worth, or soft distress, ...	O 389	Natural Beauty	6
SOLD				
	Are Friendship's pleasures to be sold?	O 391	Vanity Wealth	10
SON				
	No child laments the tyrant of his son;	O 387	On Lord Lovat	10
SONG				
	A Song	O 388	A Song	T
SOUL				
	To form one wish my soul can move.	O 388	A Song	12
	In social hours indulge thy soul, ...	O 391	Vanity Wealth	17
SPEAKS				
	If she 's silent, speaks, or sings, ...	O 389	Natural Beauty	16
SPORTING				
	Mark rashness sporting on perdition's brink, ...	O 392	The Happy Life	15
SPREAD				
	Thus taste the feast by Nature spread, ...	O 391	Vanity Wealth	21
STAGNANT				
	Nor tost by change, nor stagnant in despair;	O 392	The Happy Life	4
STATE				
	Thrice happy they, who in an humble state	O 392	The Happy Life	1
STEAD				
	In his stead, the Queen of Night	O 390	An Evening Ode	13
STEADY				
	Steady in what he still mistook for truth, ...	O 387	On Lord Lovat	4
STELLA				
	In lovely Stella all combine, ...	O 388	A Song	17
	And, lovely Stella! thou art mine.	O 388	A Song	18
	The Natural Beauty To Stella	O 389	Natural Beauty	T
	An Evening Ode To Stella	O 390	An Evening Ode	T
	Stella! thither let us stray, ...	O 390	An Evening Ode	9
	Hence, my lovely Stella, far;	O 390	An Evening Ode	12
	In health, and Stella, and content:	O 392	Vanity Wealth	26
STELLA'S				
	Whether Stella's eyes are found	O 389	Natural Beauty	1
	Stella's eyes, and air, and face	O 389	Natural Beauty	7
STEMMA				
	To triton ek Mouson stemma Mikyllos echei.	O 394	Epigram More	2
STILL				
	Steady in what he still mistook for truth, ...	O 387	On Lord Lovat	4
	Still she lights the constant flame, ...	O 389	Natural Beauty	13
	Still she lights the conscious flame, ...	O 389	Natural Beauty	V 13
	Still her charms appear the same.	O 389	Natural Beauty	14
	Still we love, and still approve.	O 389	Natural Beauty	18
	Still we love, and still approve.	O 389	Natural Beauty	18
	Still unenjoy'd the present store, ...	O 391	Vanity Wealth	3
	Still endless sighs are breath'd for more.	O 391	Vanity Wealth	4
STOLE				
	And wonder how the moments stole away;	O 392	The Happy Life	8

STORE
    Not all Peru's unbounded store, ...   O 388 A Song   8
    Still unenjoy'd the present store, ...   O 391 Vanity Wealth   3
STRAY
    Stella! thither let us stray, ...   O 390 An Evening Ode 9
STREAM
    Shake the reed, and curl the stream, ...   O 390 An Evening Ode 5
STRIFE
    Secure from pomp, and wealth, and strife. . . . . .   O 391 Vanity Wealth 24
    Behold its weary cares, its noisy strife; . . . . .   O 392 The Happy Life 12
STRIKES
    If she strikes the vocal strings, ...   O 389 Natural Beauty 15
STRINGS
    If she strikes the vocal strings, ...   O 389 Natural Beauty 15
SUNK
    Whose life not sunk in sloth is free from care, . . .   O 392 The Happy Life 3
TASTE
    Thus taste the feast by Nature spread, ...   O 391 Vanity Wealth 21
    Come, taste with me the balm of life, ...   O 391 Vanity Wealth 23
TAUGHT
    Who gently taught by calm experience find . . . . .   O 392 The Happy Life 9
TEMP'RANCE
    Where Mirth and Temp'rance mix the bowl. . . . . . .   O 391 Vanity Wealth 18
THAT
        9   OMITTED WORD
TH'
    And dar'd her much th' old quarrel to renew; . . . .   O 384 Englished   2
THE
        58   OMITTED WORD
THEIR
    Not all their charms, tho' all unite, ...   O 388 A Song   5
    And mingle blameless with their native dust. . . . .   O 393 The Happy Life 20
THEM
    Other pleasures give them pain, ...   O 390 An Evening Ode 21
THEN
    Other passions then at rest, ...   O 390 An Evening Ode V 21
    Cease, then, on trash thy hopes to bind, ...   O 391 Vanity Wealth 13
THERE
    Let us there, in whisper'd joy, ...   O 390 An Evening Ode V 17
THEY
    Thrice happy they, who in an humble state . . . . .   O 392 The Happy Life 1
THINE
    And scorn, oh! let that scorn be thine! . . . . . .   O 392 Vanity Wealth 27
THINGS
    Mere things of clay, that dig the mine. . . . . . .   O 392 Vanity Wealth 28
THINKING
    No tory pities, thinking what he was; . . . . .   O 387 On Lord Lovat 11
    Content with thinking right, and acting well, ...   O 392 The Happy Life 14
THITHER
    Stella! thither let us stray, ...   O 390 An Evening Ode 9
THO'
    Not all their charms, tho' all unite, ...   O 388 A Song   5
THOSE
    I those charms alone can prize, ...   O 389 Natural Beauty 25
THOU
    And, lovely Stella! thou art mine. . . . .   O 388 A Song   18
THOUGHT
    No--all that 's worth a wish, a thought, ...   O 391 Vanity Wealth 11
THRICE
    Thrice happy they, who in an humble state . . . . .   O 392 The Happy Life 1
THUS
    No more thus brooding o'er yon heap, ...   O 391 Vanity Wealth 1
    Thus taste the feast by Nature spread, ...   O 391 Vanity Wealth 21
THY
    The brave, Balmerino, were on thy side; . . . . . .   O 387 On Lord Lovat 2
    Hears, and keeps thy secrets, Love.-- . . . . . .   O 390 An Evening Ode 8
    Cease, then, on trash thy hopes to bind, ...   O 391 Vanity Wealth 13
    Let nobler views engage thy mind. . . . .   O 391 Vanity Wealth 14
    In social hours indulge thy soul, ...   O 391 Vanity Wealth 17
    To virtuous Love resign thy breast, ...   O 391 Vanity Wealth 19
TIE
    Of life without a pang dissolve the tie, ...   O 393 The Happy Life 17
TO
        22   OMITTED WORD
TOILET'S
    Which demands the toilet's aid, ...   O 389 Natural Beauty 23
TORY
    No tory pities, thinking what he was; . . . .   O 387 On Lord Lovat 11
TOST
    Nor tost by change, nor stagnant in despair; . . . .   O 392 The Happy Life 4
TOUCH
    Can touch my bosom with delight. . . . . . .   O 388 A Song   6
TRANSIENT
    Vain the casual transient glance, ...   O 389 Natural Beauty 19
TRASH
    Cease, then, on trash thy hopes to bind, ...   O 391 Vanity Wealth 13
TREAD
    With Science tread the wond'rous way, ...   O 391 Vanity Wealth 15
TREASURE
    Which not all India's treasure buys! . . . . . .   O 391 Vanity Wealth 6

	PAGE	TITLE	LINE
TRITON			
To triton ek Mouson stemma Mikyllos echei.	O 394	Epigram More	2
TRUE			
True to no king, to no religion true:	O 387	On Lord Lovat	8
True to no king, to no religion true:	O 387	On Lord Lovat	8
TRUST			
Breathe out the vital flame in humble trust, ...	O 393	The Happy Life	19
TRUTH			
Steady in what he still mistook for truth, ...	O 387	On Lord Lovat	4
TURRETS			
And see the turrets of ambition sink;	O 392	The Happy Life	16
TYRANT			
No child laments the tyrant of his son;	O 387	On Lord Lovat	10
UNBOUGHT			
Fair Virtue gives, unbrib'd, unbought.	O 391	Vanity Wealth	12
UNBOUNDED			
Not all Peru's unbounded store, ...	O 388	A Song	8
UNBRIB'D			
Fair Virtue gives, unbrib'd, unbought.	O 391	Vanity Wealth	12
UNDIMINISH'D			
Charm with undiminish'd grace.	O 389	Natural Beauty	8
UNENJOY'D			
Still unenjoy'd the present store, ...	O 391	Vanity Wealth	3
UNHAPPY			
Radcliffe, unhappy in his crimes of youth, ...	O 387	On Lord Lovat	3
UNITE			
Not all their charms, tho' all unite, ...	O 388	A Song	5
UNMOV'D			
Beheld his death so decently unmov'd, ...	O 387	On Lord Lovat	5
US			
Stella! thither let us stray, ...	O 390	An Evening Ode	9
Round us pours a lambent light;	O 390	An Evening Ode	14
Let us now, in whisper'd joy, ...	O 390	An Evening Ode	17
Let us there, in whisper'd joy, ...	O 390	An Evening Ode	V 17
VAIN			
Nor seek I nature's charms in vain:	O 388	A Song	16
Vain the casual transient glance, ...	O 389	Natural Beauty	19
VALES			
The fragrance of the flow'ry vales, ...	O 388	A Song	2
VANITY			
The Vanity of Wealth An Ode To a Friend	O 391	Vanity Wealth	T
VENUS			
Venus in armour Pallas chanc'd to view, ...	O 384	Englished	1
VERDANT			
The vocal grove, the verdant hill;	O 388	A Song	4
VERNAL			
Not the soft sighs of vernal gales, ...	O 388	A Song	1
VIEW			
Venus in armour Pallas chanc'd to view, ...	O 384	Englished	1
But Lovat's end indiff'rently we view, ...	O 387	On Lord Lovat	7
----But Lovat's fate indiff'rently we view, ...	O 387	On Lord Lovat	V 7
VIEWS			
Let nobler views engage thy mind.	O 391	Vanity Wealth	14
VIGILS			
With Av'rice painful vigils keep.	O 391	Vanity Wealth	2
VIRTUE			
Fair Virtue gives, unbrib'd, unbought.	O 391	Vanity Wealth	12
VIRTUE'S			
And safe in virtue's philosophick cell, ...	O 392	The Happy Life	13
VIRTUOUS			
To virtuous Love resign thy breast, ...	O 391	Vanity Wealth	19
VITAL			
Breathe out the vital flame in humble trust, ...	O 393	The Happy Life	19
VOCAL			
The vocal grove, the verdant hill;	O 388	A Song	4
If she strikes the vocal strings, ...	O 389	Natural Beauty	15
WAS 3		OMITTED WORD	
WAY			
Lightly o'er the dewy way;	O 390	An Evening Ode	10
With Science tread the wond'rous way, ...	O 391	Vanity Wealth	15
WE			
But Lovat's end indiff'rently we view, ...	O 387	On Lord Lovat	7
----But Lovat's fate indiff'rently we view, ...	O 387	On Lord Lovat	V 7
If on her we see display'd	O 389	Natural Beauty	9
Still we love, and still approve.	O 389	Natural Beauty	18
WEALTH			
And knowledge, wealth and fame I prize;	O 388	A Song	14
Fame, wealth and knowledge I obtain, ...	O 388	A Song	15
The Vanity of Wealth An Ode To a Friend	O 391	Vanity Wealth	T
Secure from pomp, and wealth, and strife.	O 391	Vanity Wealth	24
WEARY			
Behold its weary cares, its noisy strife;	O 392	The Happy Life	12
WELL			
No riches equal to a well form'd mind;	O 392	The Happy Life	10
Content with thinking right, and acting well, ...	O 392	The Happy Life	14
WERE			
The brave, Balmerino, were on thy side;	O 387	On Lord Lovat	2
WHAT 3		OMITTED WORD	

WHATE'ER
    I boast whate'er for man was meant. . . . . O 392 Vanity Wealth 25
WHERE
         1   OMITTED WORD
WHETHER
    Whether Stella's eyes are found . . . . O 389 Natural Beauty 1
WHICH
    Nor knowledge, which the learn'd approve, ... O 388 A Song 11
    Which alone can please by chance, ... O 389 Natural Beauty 20
    Beauty, which depends on art, ... O 389 Natural Beauty 21
    Which demands the toilet's aid, ... O 389 Natural Beauty 23
    Which from constant nature rise, ... O 389 Natural Beauty 26
    Which nor circumstance, nor dress . . . . O 389 Natural Beauty 27
    Which not all India's treasure buys! . . . . O 391 Vanity Wealth 6
WHIG
    No whig compassions, for he left the cause; . . . . . O 387 On Lord Lovat 12
WHISPER'D
    Let us now, in whisper'd joy, ... O 390 An Evening Ode 17
    Let us there, in whisper'd joy, ... O 390 An Evening Ode V 17
WHO
    Thrice happy they, who in an humble state . . . . . O 392 The Happy Life 1
    Who chearfully receive each mercy given, ... O 392 The Happy Life 5
    Who with wise authors pass the instructive day, . . . O 392 The Happy Life 7
    Who gently taught by calm experience find . . . . . O 392 The Happy Life 9
    Who not retir'd beyond the sight of life, ... O 392 The Happy Life 11
WHOSE
    Whose life not sunk in sloth is free from care, . . . O 392 The Happy Life 3
WINGS
    Ev'ning now, from purple wings, ... O 390 An Evening Ode 1
WISE
    Who with wise authors pass the instructive day, . . . O 392 The Happy Life 7
WISH
    To form one wish my soul can move. . . . . O 388 A Song 12
    No--all that 's worth a wish, a thought, ... O 391 Vanity Wealth 11
WITH
        14   OMITTED WORD
WITHOUT
    Of life without a pang dissolve the tie, ... O 393 The Happy Life 17
WOE
    If she sigh at others woe, ... O 389 Natural Beauty 4
WOND'ROUS
    With Science tread the wond'rous way, ... O 391 Vanity Wealth 15
WONDER
    And wonder how the moments stole away; . . . . . . O 392 The Happy Life 8
WORLD
    Love's queen reply'd, and smil'd a world of charms, . . O 384 Englished 3
WORTH
    Conscious worth, or soft distress, ... O 389 Natural Beauty 6
    No--all that 's worth a wish, a thought, ... O 391 Vanity Wealth 11
YET
    Yet nature's charms allure my eyes, ... O 388 A Song 13
YON
    No more thus brooding o'er yon heap, ... O 391 Vanity Wealth 1
YOU
    Naked I conquer'd you, what need of arms? . . . . . O 384 Englished 4
YOUTH
    Radcliffe, unhappy in his crimes of youth, ... O 387 On Lord Lovat 3
    Ere Youth and all its joys are fled; . . . . O 391 Vanity Wealth 22

58

THE

32

AND

22

TO

18

IN

15

OF

14

WITH

12

ALL
NOT

10

A

9

IF
NO
THAT

8

ON
OR

7

CAN
NOR
SHE
STELLA
STILL
WHICH

6

BY
CHARMS
HER
I
LIFE
LOVE
THY

5

BE
BUT
FOR
HE
HIS
WHO

4

AN
ARE
BRAVE
FROM
LET
MY
WEALTH

3

BEAUTY
CONSCIOUS
EYES
FAME
GEMS
GOLD

ITS
KNOWLEDGE
LOVELY
MORE
O'ER
PRIZE
SOFT
US
WAS
WE
WHAT

2

'S
AIR
ALONE
APPROVE
ART
AT
BREAST
BROCADE
CHANGING
CONSTANT
CONTENT
EASY
FACE
FAIR
FLAME
GLOW
GROVE
HAPPY
HAS
HOURS
HUMBLE
INDIA'S
LESS
LIGHT
LOVAT'S
MIND
MINE
MOVE
NATURE
NATURE'S
NOW
ODE
PENDANT
PLEASE
PLEASURES
QUEEN
REED
RICH
ROUND
SCORN
SEE
SHAKE
SHEDS
SIGHS
SILENT
SOUL
STELLA'S
STORE
STRIFE
TASTE
THEIR
THEN
THINKING
THUS
TRUE
VAIN
VIEW
VOCAL
WAY
WELL
WISH
WORTH
YOUTH

1

ACTING
AID
AIM
ALLURE
AMBITION
APPEAR
APPROV'D
ARMOUR

ARMS
AROUND
AUTHORS
AV'RICE
AWAY
BALM
BALMERINO
BEAM
BEAT
BEDECK
BEHELD
BEHOLD
BEST
BEYOND
BIND
BLAMELESS
BLESS
BLESSING
BLEST
BOAST
BOSOM
BOUGHT
BOUNTEOUS
BOWL
BREASTS
BREATH'D
BREATHE
BREEZES
BRILLIANT
BRINGS
BRINK
BROODING
BURNING
BUYS
CALM
CAR
CARE
CARES
CASUAL
CATCH
CAUSE
CEASE
CELL
CHANC'D
CHANCE
CHANGE
CHARM
CHEARFULLY
CHEEKS
CHEQUER'D
CHILD
CHINTZ
CIRCUMSTANCE
CLAIM
CLAY
COMBINE
COME
COMPASSIONS
CONQUER'D
CONTENTED
COOLING
CRIMES
CRYSTAL
CURL
CYNTHIA'S
DAR'D
DAY
DE
DEATH
DECAY
DECENTLY
DELIA
DELIGHT
DEMANDS
DEPENDS
DESPAIR
DEUTERON
DEWY
DIE
DIG
DISDAIN
DISPLAY'D
DISSOLVE
DISTRESS
DONE
DRESS
DRIVES
DROPS

DUSKY
DUST
DY'D
E'ER
EACH
EARTH
ECHEI
EILEN
EK
EMPLOY
END
ENDLESS
ENGAGE
ENGLISHED
EQUAL
ERASMOS
ERE
EREN
EV'NING
EV'NING'S
EVENING
EXECUTION
EXPENCE
EXPERIENCE
EXPRESS
FAR
FATE
FEAST
FIND
FIX'D
FLED
FLOW'RY
FLOWS
FORGETS
FORM
FORM'D
FOUND
FRAGRANCE
FREE
FRIEND
FRIENDSHIP'S
GALES
GENTLE
GENTLY
GIFTS
GIVE
GIVEN
GIVES
GLANCE
GLANCING
GRACE
GRATEFUL
GREAT
HAND
HEALTH
HEAP
HEARS
HEART
HEARTS
HEAV'N
HEAVEN
HENCE
HEROES
HILL
HIM
HONEST
HOPES
HOUR
HOW
INDIFF'RENTLY
INDULGE
INSTRUCTIVE
INVADES
IS
JOY
JOYS
JUST
KEEP
KEEPS
KILMARNOCK
KING
KINGS
KNAVE
KNOWING
LAMBENT
LAMENTED
LAMENTS
LAY

LEARN
LEARN'D
LEFT
LIB'RAL
LIGHTLY
LIGHTS
LIVE
LONELY
LORD
LOVE'S
LOVERS
MAKE
MAN
MARK
ME
MEAD
MEANT
MERCY
MERE
MIKYLLOS
MINDS
MINGLE
MIRTH
MISTOOK
MIX
MOMENTS
MORAL
MOROS
MORTAL
MOURN
MOUSON
MUCH
MURMURS
MUSE'S
NAKED
NATIVE
NATURAL
NEAR
NEED
NEGLIGENCE
NIGHT
NOBLER
NOISY
O
OBTAIN
OH
OLD
ONE
OTHER
OTHERS
OUT
PAIN
PAINFUL
PALLAS
PANG
PASS
PASSIONS
PEACE
PERDITION'S
PERU'S
PHILOSOPHICK
PHOEBUS
PITIES
PITY'D
PLEASURE
POETS
POMP
POSSESSES
POURS
POW'R
POWER
PRESENT
PROTON
PURCHASE
PURPLE
QUARREL
QUIT
RADCLIFFE
RASHNESS
RECEIVE
REGRET
RELIGION
REMOVE
RENEW
REPLY'D
RESIGN
RESIGNATION
REST

RETIR'D   VIEWS
RICHES   VIGILS
RIGHT   VIRTUE
RILL   VIRTUE'S
RISE   VIRTUOUS
RUIN   VITAL
SAFE   WEARY
SAME   WERE
SCIENCE   WHATE'ER
SECRETS   WHERE
SECURE   WHETHER
SEEK   WHIG
SEEMS   WHISPER'D
SERVES   WHOSE
SHADES   WINGS
SHADOW   WISE
SHORE   WITHOUT
SHOW   WOE
SIDE   WOND'ROUS
SIGH   WONDER
SIGHT   WORLD
SILENCE   YET
SILVER'D   YON
SINGS   YOU
SINK
SIT
SLOTH
SMIL'D
SO
SOCIAL
SOLD
SON
SONG
SPEAKS
SPORTING
SPREAD
STAGNANT
STATE
STEAD
STEADY
STEMMA
STOLE
STRAY
STREAM
STRIKES
STRINGS
SUNK
TAUGHT
TEMP'RANCE
TH'
THEM
THERE
THEY
THINE
THINGS
THITHER
THO'
THOSE
THOU
THOUGHT
THRICE
TIE
TOILET'S
TORY
TOST
TOUCH
TRANSIENT
TRASH
TREAD
TREASURE
TRITON
TRUST
TRUTH
TURRETS
TYRANT
UNBOUGHT
UNBOUNDED
UNBRIB'D
UNDIMINISH'D
UNENJOY'D
UNHAPPY
UNITE
UNMOV'D
VALES
VANITY
VENUS
VERDANT
VERNAL